ZONDERVAN

# TNIV
## COMPACT
## CONCORDANCE

TODAY'S NEW INTERNATIONAL VERSION

# ZONDERVAN

# TNIV
## COMPACT
## CONCORDANCE

## JOHN R. KOHLENBERGER III
### EDITOR

## SARAH N. KOHLENBERGER
### ASSISTANT EDITOR

ZONDERVAN.com/
AUTHOR**TRACKER**
*follow your favorite authors*

The *Zondervan TNIV Compact Concordance*
Copyright © 2008 by John R. Kohlenberger III

Requests for information should be addressed to:

Zondervan, *Grand Rapids, Michigan 49530*

ISBN-13: 978-0-310-26503-0
ISBN-10: 0-310-26503-7

*Printed in the United States of America*

08 09 10 11 12 13 14 15 16 • 20 19 18 17 16 15 14 13 12 11 10 9 8 7 6 5 4 3 2 1

# Dedication

To Peter Furler
with great respect and admiration

Sing to the LORD a new song;
    sing to the LORD, all the earth.
Sing to the LORD, praise his name;
    proclaim his salvation day after day.
Declare his glory among the nations,
    his marvelous deeds among all peoples.

Psalm 96:1–3 (TNIV)

# Contents

# Acknowledgments

Small though the *Zondervan TNIV Compact Concordance* may be, it is the product of the energies of many individuals in addition to the editor whose name is on the cover.

I must start with grateful thanks to God for allowing me the time and clarity to produce this book during my battle with advanced prostate cancer. My wife Carolyn and our children, Sarah and Josh, have been so precious and dear these past five years. I have drawn endless strength and support from my family, my *mishpachah,* at Cascade View Covenant Church.

Stan Gundry, Senior Vice-President and Editor-in-Chief, and Bruce Ryskamp, President and CEO Pro Tem, have been great friends and encouragement throughout the process. Verlyn Verbrugge, Senior editor at large, and proofreader Dawn Anderson made many helpful suggestions and caught many mistakes and inconsistencies.

Sarah Kohlenberger was invaluable as assistant editor. Jess Gross did an excellent job assisting with the typesetting. Brent Knopf created valuable programming to help us convert *The NIV Compact Concordance* into this TNIV edition.

# Introduction:
# How to Use This Book

A concordance is an index to a book. It is usually arranged in alphabetical order and shows the location of key words in the book. In addition, it often supplies several words of the context in which each word is found.

The *Zondervan TNIV Compact Concordance* (*ZTNIVCC*) is the first concordance to Today's New International Version (TNIV) published independently of TNIV Bibles. The first concordance to the TNIV appeared in the first edition of the New Testament (NT) in 2002. This NT-only concordance had 2,104 word entries and 6,400 Scripture references. Included in some editions of the complete TNIV Bible in 2005 was the shorter TNIV Bible concordance with 2,464 word entries and more than 11,000 Scripture references. The longer TNIV Bible concordance was introduced in *The TNIV Study Bible* in 2006, with 4,787 word entries and nearly 35,000 Scripture references.

The *ZTNIVCC* is based on the best-selling *NIV Compact Concordance* (1993), itself an abridgment of the award-winning *Strongest NIV Exhaustive Concordance* (1990). All 363,965 occurrences of the 14,452 NIV words, numerals, and compound proper names from the main concordance of the *Exhaustive* were scanned to select those most significant for general biblical knowledge, theology, and spiritual development. More than half of the vocabulary of the TNIV and 70,000 biblical references are represented in this contribution to the TNIV reference library.

## FEATURES OF THE ZONDERVAN TNIV COMPACT CONCORDANCE
The *ZTNIVCC* has four major features: (1) concordance entries, (2) key phrase indexes, (3) capsule biographies, and (4) KJV "See" references.

### Concordance Entries
The *ZTNIVCC* indexes 7,531 of the 14,404 words in the TNIV from Aaron to Zuzites to 675,000. The 56,671 context lines represent 57,767 occurrences of these words. Below is a typical entry from the *ZTNIVCC*:

### AVENGES* [VENGEANCE]
| | | |
|---|---|---|
| 2Sa | 22:48 | He is the God who **a** me, who puts |
| Ps | 9:12 | For he who **a** blood remembers; |
| | 18:47 | He is the God who **a** me, |
| | 94: 1 | The LORD is a God who **a**. O God who **a**, |

Entries are arranged in alphabetical order. Numerals follow the letter Z. Entries index words exactly as they are spelled in the TNIV. The asterisk (*) marks entries that index every occurrence of the word in the TNIV; 2,396 entries are exhaustive, including frequently-occurring words like "faith," "grace," and "love."

Related words, if any, follow in brackets []. Rather than listing all related words after each indexed word, the editor chose one indexed word to act as the "group heading." All related words are listed after the group heading, and each of the related word headings points back to the group heading. By looking up the related word, you can study additional texts containing other forms of the word and other members of the word's cognate "family." For example, VENGEANCE lists six additional terms you can study within the *ZTNIVCC* to get a fuller biblical picture of revenge, both human and divine.

There are two entries for LORD and LORD'S. The proper name of God, "Yahweh," is represented in the TNIV as LORD in small capital letters. The title "Lord" is capitalized when referring to God and in lower case when referring to a human being or false god. "Lord" and "lord" are indexed in the *ZTNIVCC* under the heading LORD and "Lord's" under the heading LORD'S. "LORD" is indexed under the heading †LORD and "LORD's" under the heading †LORD'S.

Contexts are organized in biblical order. A key to the abbreviations of the books of the Bible follows the introduction on page xii. Only the first appearance of a book's abbreviation is listed, as in the case of Ps (Psalms) in the example on page ix. The purpose of context lines in a concordance is simply to help the reader recognize or locate a specific verse in the Bible. For word study—or any kind of Bible study—the context offered by a concordance is rarely enough to go on. Nevertheless, sometimes a short sentence or a whole verse fits on one line, as in the case of John 11:35, "Jesus wept."

*Taken by themselves, context lines can and do misrepresent the teaching of Scripture by taking statements out of the larger context.* "There is no God" is a context taken straight from Psalm 14:1. Of course the Bible does not teach this; it is what "Fools say in their hearts"! Similarly, a context for Leviticus 24:16 might read, "the LORD is to be put to death" while the text actually says, "anyone who blasphemes the name of the LORD is to be put to death."

Great care has been taken by the editor, programmer, and proofreaders of the *ZTNIVCC* to create contexts that are informative and accurate. But the reader should always check word contexts by looking them up in the TNIV itself. "The Wicked Bible," a KJV edition of 1631, accidentally omitted the word "not" from the seventh commandment, for which the printers were fined 300 pounds sterling! Though there are no longer such fines for misleading contexts, the editor and publisher are still deeply concerned that the *ZTNIVCC* be used discerningly.

As noted in "A Word to the Reader," the translators' preface to the TNIV:

> Mark 16:9–20 and John 7:53—8:11, although long accorded virtually equal status with the rest of the Gospels in which they stand, have a very questionable—and confused—standing in the textual history of the New Testament . . . A different typeface has now been chosen for these passages to indicate even more clearly their uncertain status.

Contexts to these verses in Mark and John are in italics, reflecting the formatting of the TNIV.

## Key Phrase Indexes
Following the entries for 194 highly frequent words are 252 key phrase indexes:

**FEAR**
...

**FEAR OF THE †LORD** 2Ch 17:10; 19:7, 9; Ps 19:9; 34:11; 111:10; Pr 1:7; 2:5; 9:10; 10:27; 14:27; 15:16, 33; 16:6; 19:23; 22:4; 23:17; Isa 11:2, 3; 33:6

**†LORD**
...

**FEAR OF THE †LORD** See FEAR

These list biblical references to all occurrences of significant phrases—11,889 total references—but without contexts. Thus even in this compact concordance, you can find every reference for such phrases as the FEAR OF THE LORD, HOLY SPIRIT, SON OF GOD and SON OF MAN. Phrases are indexed at only one location; other words in the phrase are cross-referenced to the index. In the example above, FEAR OF THE †LORD is indexed under FEAR with a cross-reference at †LORD.

## Capsule Biographies

Capsule biographies give significant information on 296 prominent individuals:

### DEBORAH

1. Female prophet and judge who led Israel to victory over Canaanites (Jdg 4–5).
2. Rebekah's nurse (Ge 35:8).

It is easier to represent and to locate key events in an individual's life in such an entry, rather than by using context lines, especially in the entry on Jesus. As in the example above, different individuals of the same name are distinguished by separately numbered biographies. These entries index 1,979 biblical texts.

## KJV "See" References

The King James, or Authorized, Version has been the dominant English Bible translation from the early seventeenth century to the latter half of the twentieth century. Because of this, the KJV has had profound impact on the language of both the church and English-speaking society. To help users familiar with KJV vocabulary find the proper TNIV terms, 80 KJV words appear in 61 KJV "See" references, pointing to 112 TNIV words and phrase. These include such headings as:

### COMFORTER (KJV: of the Holy Spirit) See also ADVOCATE

### [HOLY] GHOST (KJV) See [HOLY] SPIRIT

Note that multiple-word "See" references, such as HOLY SPIRIT, do *not* refer to a multiple-word heading. Rather, they direct the user to look for that *combination* of words under the heading for *any* of the words in the multiple-word reference. The KJV "ghost" is usually translated in the TNIV as "spirit," and the phrase "Holy Ghost" is always translated "Holy Spirit" in the TNIV. In the case of this phrase, "Holy Spirit" is indexed exhaustively in the entry HOLY. But this is not the case for all multiple-word references.

## Special NIV References

The TNIV is about 95% indentical to the NIV, but there are some noticeable differences in vocabulary that could affect users of the the *ZTNIVCC*. Some proper and place names are spelled differently. For example, the NIV "Abimelech" is "Abimelek" in the TNIV. These words alphabetize similarly, but where spelling changes location of a proper name, it is cross referenced. This occurs in the case of NIV "Korazin," which references the TNIV entry "Chorazin."

Two words common to English Bible translations are not used in the TNIV: "saints" and "*Selah*." As explained in "A Word to the Reader":

> Concerning "saints," current usage (as reflected in major dictionaries of the English language) burdens it with meanings that lie outside the sense of the original-language words. The main Old Testament term that has traditionally been rendered "saints" refers to those who are faithful to God. The New Testament term primarily designates those who have become followers of the Christian Way as people consecrated to God and thus belonging to the Lord in a special sense. . . .

> Although *Selah*, used mainly in the Psalms, is probably a musical term, its meaning is uncertain. Since it may interrupt reading and distract the reader, this word has not been kept in the English text, but every occurrence has been signaled by a footnote.

Because the editor believes users want to know where "saints" was used in the NIV and how these texts are translated in the TNIV, a complete list of TNIV translations and NIV references occurs in the entry SAINTS. Similarly, all NIV references to "*Selah*" are listed in the entry SELAH.

# Abbreviations and Symbols

**Other Abbreviations and Symbols**

\* ... following entry heading
= exhaustive entry

†LORD ............ LORD

†LORD'S ........ LORD's

KJV ... King James Version

NIV ..... New International Version

T ............. Psalm title

TNIV ....... Today's New International Version

# ZONDERVAN

# TNIV
# COMPACT
# CONCORDANCE

# A

# AARON

Genealogy of (Ex 6:16–20; Jos 21:4, 10; 1Ch 6:3–15).

Priesthood of (Ex 28:1; Nu 17; Heb 5:1–4; 7), garments (Ex 28; 39), consecration (Ex 29), ordination (Lev 8).

Spokesman for Moses (Ex 4:14–16, 27–31; 7:1–2). Supported Moses' hands in battle (Ex 17:8–13). Built golden calf (Ex 32; Dt 9:20). Talked against Moses (Nu 12). Priesthood opposed (Nu 16); staff budded (Nu 17). Forbidden to enter land (Nu 20:1–12). Death (Nu 20:22–29; 33:38–39).

## AARON AND HIS SONS  See SONS

## SON OF AARON  See SON

## SONS OF AARON  See SONS

## AARON'S SONS  See SONS

## ABADDON*

Rev  9:11  whose name in Hebrew is **A**

## ABANDON  [ABANDONED]

Dt     4:31  he will not **a** or destroy you
Jos  10: 6  "Do not **a** your servants.
1Ki   6:13  and will not **a** my people Israel."
2Ch 12: 5  I now **a** you to Shishak.' "
Ne     9:19  compassion you did not **a** them
         9:31  not put an end to them or **a** them,
Ps    16:10  because you will not **a** me
       138: 8  do not **a** the works of your hands.
Jer   12: 7  forsake my house, **a** my inheritance;
Ac     2:27  because you will not **a** me
1Ti    4: 1  in later times some will **a** the faith

## ABANDONED  [ABANDON]

Ge    24:27  who has not **a** his kindness
Dt    29:25  because this people **a** the covenant
       32:15  He **a** the God who made him
Jdg    6:13  now the LORD has **a** us and given
1Ki   18:18  You have **a** the LORD's
Isa   54: 7  "For a brief moment I **a** you,
Ac     2:31  that he was not **a** to the realm
Ro     1:27  also **a** natural relations with women
2Co    4: 9  persecuted, but not **a**;

## ABBA*

Mk  14:36  "**A**, Father," he said,
Ro    8:15  And by him we cry, "**A**, Father."
Gal   4: 6  the Spirit who calls out, "**A**, Father."

## ABDON

A judge of Israel (Jdg 12:13–15).

## ABEDNEGO

Deported to Babylon with Daniel (Da 1:1–6). Name changed from Azariah (Da 1:7). Refused defilement by food (Da 1:8–20). Refused idol worship (Da 3:1–12); saved from furnace (Da 3:13–30).

## ABEL

Second son of Adam (Ge 4:2). Offered proper sacrifice (Ge 4:4; Heb 11:4). Murdered by Cain (Ge 4:8; Mt 23:35; Lk 11:51; 1Jn 3:12).

## ABHOR*

Lev  26:11  among you, and I will not **a** you.
       26:15  reject my decrees and **a** my laws
       26:30  of your idols, and I will **a** you.
       26:44  or **a** them so as to destroy them
Ps    26: 5  I **a** the assembly of evildoers
       139:21  **a** those who are in rebellion against
Am     6: 8  "I **a** the pride of Jacob and detest
Ro     2:22  You who **a** idols, do you rob

## ABIATHAR

High priest in days of Saul and David (1Sa 22; 2Sa 15; 1Ki 1–2; Mk 2:26). Escaped Saul's slaughter of priests (1Sa 22:18–23). Supported David in Absalom's revolt (2Sa 15:24–29). Supported Adonijah (1Ki 1:7–42); deposed by Solomon (1Ki 2:22–35; cf. 1Sa 2:31–35).

## ABIB  See AVIV

## ABIGAIL

1. Sister of David (1Ch 2:16–17).
2. Wife of Nabal (1Sa 25:30); pled for his life with David (1Sa 25:14–35). Became David's wife after Nabal's death (1Sa 25:36–42); bore him Kileab (2Sa 3:3) also known as Daniel (1Ch 3:1).

## ABIHU

Son of Aaron (Ex 6:23; 24:1, 9); killed for offering unauthorized fire (Lev 10; Nu 3:2–4; 1Ch 24:1–2).

## ABIJAH

1. Second son of Samuel (1Ch 6:28); a corrupt judge (1Sa 8:1–5).
2. An Aaronic priest (1Ch 24:10; Lk 1:5).
3. Son of Jeroboam I of Israel; died as prophesied by Ahijah (1Ki 14:1–18).
4. Son of Rehoboam; king of Judah who fought Jeroboam I attempting to reunite the kingdom (1Ki 14:31—15:8; 2Ch 12:16–14:1; Mt 1:7).

## ABILITY*  [ABLE]

Ge    47: 6  of any among them with special **a**,
Ex    31: 6  given **a** to all the skilled workers
       35:34  tribe of Dan, the **a** to teach others.
       36: 1  **a** to know how to carry out all
       36: 2  to whom the LORD had given **a**
Dt     8:18  for it is he who gives you the **a**
Ezr    2:69  According to their **a** they gave
Ecc    5:19  and the **a** to enjoy them,
       6: 2  does not grant the **a** to enjoy
Da     5:12  and also the **a** to interpret dreams,
Mt    25:15  one bag, each according to his **a**.
Ac     8:19  this **a** so that everyone on whom I
2Co    1: 8  far beyond our **a** to endure,
       8: 3  were able, and even beyond their **a**.

## ABIMELEK

1. King of Gerar who took Abraham's wife Sarah,

believing her to be his sister (Ge 20). Later made a covenant with Abraham (Ge 21:22–33).

2. King of Gerar who took Isaac's wife Rebekah, believing her to be his sister (Ge 26:1–11). Later made a covenant with Isaac (Ge 26:12–31).

3. Son of Gideon (Jdg 8:31). Attempted to make himself king (Jdg 9).

## ABIRAM

Sided with Dathan in rebellion against Moses and Aaron (Nu 16; 26:9; Dt 11:6).

## ABISHAG

Shunammite virgin; attendant of David in his old age (1Ki 1:1–15; 2:17–22).

## ABISHAI

Son of Zeruiah, David's sister (1Sa 26:6; 1Ch 2:16). One of David's chief warriors (1Ch 11:15–21): against Edom (1Ch 18:12–13), Ammon (2Sa 10), Absalom (2Sa 18), Sheba (2Sa 20). Wanted to kill Saul (1Sa 26), killed Abner (2Sa 2:18–27; 3:22–39), wanted to kill Shimei (2Sa 16:5–13; 19:16–23).

## ABLAZE

| Dt | 5:23 | while the mountain was a with fire, |
| Da | 7: 9 | with fire, and its wheels were all a. |
| Rev | 8: 8 | all a, was thrown into the sea. |

## ABLE [ABILITY, DISABLED, ENABLE, ENABLED, ENABLES, ENABLING]

| Ge | 13: 6 | that they were not a to stay together. |
| Lev | 26:37 | So you will not be a to stand before |
| Nu | 14:16 | 'The LORD was not a to bring |
| Jos | 24:19 | people, "You are not a to serve |
| 1Sa | 17:33 | "You are not a to go out against |
| 1Ki | 3: 9 | who is a to govern this great people |
| 1Ch | 29:14 | that we should be a to give as |
| 2Ch | 2: 6 | who is a to build a temple for him, |
| Job | 41:10 | Who then is a to stand against me? |
| Pr | 17:16 | when they are not a to understand it? |
| Eze | 7:19 | gold will not be a to deliver them |
| Da | 2:26 | "Are you a to tell me what I saw |
| | 3:17 | the God we serve is a to deliver us, |
| | 4:37 | walk in pride he is a to humble. |
| Hos | 5:13 | But he is not a to cure you, not a |
| Mt | 9:28 | you believe that I am a to do this?" |
| | 26:61 | 'I am a to destroy the temple of God |
| Lk | 13:24 | will try to enter and will not be a to. |
| | 14:30 | to build and wasn't a to finish.' |
| | 21:15 | your adversaries will be a to resist |
| | 21:36 | pray that you may be a to escape all |
| | 21:36 | you may be a to stand before |
| Ac | 5:39 | you will not be a to stop these men; |
| | 11:29 | The disciples, as each one was a, |
| | 15:10 | we nor our ancestors have been a |
| | 22:13 | very moment I was a to see him. |
| Ro | 8:39 | will be a to separate us |
| | 11:23 | for God is a to graft them in again. |
| | 14: 4 | the Lord is a to make them stand. |
| | 16:25 | to him who is a to establish you |
| 2Co | 8: 3 | they gave as much as they were a, |
| | 9: 8 | God is a to bless you abundantly, |
| Eph | 3: 4 | you will be a to understand my |
| | 3:20 | to him who is a to do immeasurably |

| Eph | 6:13 | you may be a to stand your ground, |
| 1Ti | 3: 2 | respectable, hospitable, a to teach, |
| 2Ti | 1:12 | that he is a to guard what I have |
| | 2:24 | be kind to everyone, a to teach, |
| | 3: 7 | never a to come to a knowledge |
| | 3:15 | which are a to make you wise |
| Heb | 2:18 | he is a to help those who are being |
| | 3:19 | we see that they were not a to enter, |
| | 5: 2 | He is a to deal gently with those |
| | 7:25 | Therefore he is a to save completely |
| | 9: 9 | sacrifices being offered were not a |
| Jas | 3: 2 | a to keep their whole body in check. |
| | 4:12 | Judge, the one who is a to save |
| 2Pe | 1:15 | my departure you will always be a |
| Jude | 1:24 | To him who is a to keep you |
| Rev | 5: 5 | He is a to open the scroll and its |

## ABNER

Cousin of Saul and commander of his army (1Sa 14:50; 17:55–57; 26). Made Ish-Bosheth king after Saul (2Sa 2:8–10), but later defected to David (2Sa 3:6–21). Killed Asahel (2Sa 2:18–32), for which he was killed by Joab and Abishai (2Sa 3:22–39).

## ABODE*

| Job | 38:19 | "What is the way to the a of light? |
| Isa | 33:20 | a peaceful a, a tent that will not be |

## ABOLISH* [ABOLISHED]

| Da | 11:31 | and will a the daily sacrifice. |
| Hos | 2:18 | and battle I will a from the land, |
| Mt | 5:17 | think that I have come to a the Law |
| | 5:17 | I have not come to a them |

## ABOLISHED* [ABOLISH]

| Da | 12:11 | the time that the daily sacrifice is a |
| Gal | 5:11 | the offense of the cross has been a. |

## ABOMINATION* [ABOMINATIONS]

| Da | 9:27 | set up an a that causes desolation, |
| | 11:31 | set up the a that causes desolation. |
| | 12:11 | the a that causes desolation is set |
| Mt | 24:15 | in the holy place 'the a that causes |
| Mk | 13:14 | "When you see 'the a that causes |

## ABOMINATIONS* [ABOMINATION]

| Pr | 26:25 | them, for seven a fill their hearts. |
| Isa | 66: 3 | ways, and they delight in their a; |
| Rev | 17: 5 | AND OF THE A OF THE EARTH. |

## ABOUND [ABOUNDING, ABOUNDS]

| Ps | 72: 7 | and prosperity a till the moon is no |
| | 72:16 | May grain a throughout the land; |
| 2Co | 9: 8 | you will a in every good work. |
| Php | 1: 9 | that your love may a more and more |

## ABOUNDING* [ABOUND]

| Ex | 34: 6 | to anger, a in love and faithfulness, |
| Nu | 14:18 | a in love and forgiving sin |
| Dt | 33:23 | "Naphtali is a with the favor |
| Ne | 9:17 | slow to anger and a in love. |

Ps    86: 5   **a** in love to all who call to you.
      86:15   to anger, **a** in love and faithfulness.
     103: 8   gracious, slow to anger, **a** in love.
Pr     8:24   there were no springs **a** with water;
Joel   2:13   slow to anger and **a** in love, and he
Jnh    4: 2   slow to anger and **a** in love, a God

## ABOUNDS* [ABOUND]

Hab   1: 3   there is strife, and conflict **a**.
2Co   1: 5   also our comfort **a** through Christ.

## ABOVE

Ge     3:14   "Cursed are you **a** all livestock
      28:13   There **a** it stood the LORD, and he
Lev   26:19   and make the sky **a** you like iron
Dt     4:39   that the LORD is God in heaven **a**
Ps     8: 1   have set your glory **a** the heavens.
      18:48   You exalted me **a** my foes;
      57: 5   Be exalted, O God, **a** the heavens;
      68:33   to him who rides the ancient skies **a**,
      95: 3   great God, the great King **a** all gods.
     103:11   high as the heavens are **a** the earth,
Da    11:36   and magnify himself **a** every god
Mt    10:24   "Students are not **a** their teacher, nor
               servants **a** their master.
Jn     3:31   The one who comes from **a** is **a** all;
       3:31   who comes from heaven is **a** all.
       8:23   "You are from below; I am from **a**.
Ro    12:10   Honor one another **a** yourselves.
Php    2: 9   him the name that is **a** every name,
Col    3: 2   Set your minds on things **a**,
1Ti    3: 2   the overseer is to be **a** reproach,
Jas    1:17   good and perfect gift is from **a**,
1Pe    4: 8   **A** all, love each other deeply,

## ABRAHAM [ABRAM]

   Abram, son of Terah (Ge 11:26–27), husband of Sarah (Ge 11:29).
   Covenant relation with the LORD (Ge 12:1–3; 13:14–17; 15; 17; 22:15–18; Ex 2:24; Ne 9:8; Ps 105; Mic 7:20; Lk 1:68–75; Ro 4; Heb 6:13–15).
   Called from Ur, via Haran, to Canaan (Ge 12:1; Ac 7:2–4; Heb 11:8–10). Moved to Egypt, nearly lost Sarah to Pharoah (Ge 12:10–20). Divided the land with Lot; settled in Hebron (Ge 13). Saved Lot from four kings (Ge 14:1–16); blessed by Melchizedek (Ge 14:17–20; Heb 7:1–20). Declared righteous by faith (Ge 15:6; Ro 4:3; Gal 3:6–9). Fathered Ishmael by Hagar (Ge 16).
   Name changed from Abram (Ge 17:5; Ne 9:7). Circumcised (Ge 17; Ro 4:9–12). Entertained three visitors (Ge 18); promised a son by Sarah (Ge 18:9–15; 17:16). Questioned destruction of Sodom and Gomorrah (Ge 18:16 33). Moved to Gerar; nearly lost Sarah to Abimelek (Ge 20). Fathered Isaac by Sarah (Ge 21:1–7; Ac 7:8; Heb 11:11–12); sent away Hagar and Ishmael (Ge 21:8–21; Gal 4:22–30). Covenant with Abimelek (Ge 21:22–32). Tested by offering Isaac (Ge 22; Heb 11:17–19; Jas 2:21–24). Sarah died; bought field of Ephron for burial (Ge 23). Secured wife for Isaac (Ge 24). Fathered children by Keturah (Ge 25:1–6; 1Ch 1:32–33). Death (Ge 25:7–11).
   Called servant of God (Ge 26:24), friend of God (2Ch 20:7; Isa 41:8; Jas 2:23), prophet (Ge 20:7), father of Israel (Ex 3:15; Isa 51:2; Mt 3:9; Jn 8:39–58).

**FATHER ABRAHAM**   See FATHER

**GOD OF ABRAHAM**   See GOD

## ABRAM [ABRAHAM]

Ge    17: 5   No longer will you be called **A**;

## ABSALOM

   Son of David by Maacah (2Sa 3:3; 1Ch 3:2). Killed Amnon for rape of his sister Tamar; banished by David (2Sa 13). Returned to Jerusalem; received by David (2Sa 14). Rebelled against David (2Sa 15–17). Killed (2Sa 18).

## ABSENT

Col    2: 5   For though I am **a** from you

## ABSOLUTE*

1Ti    5: 2   women as sisters, with **a** purity.

## ABSTAIN* [ABSTAINED]

Ex    19:15   **A** from sexual relations."
Nu     6: 3   they must **a** from wine and other
Ac    15:20   telling them to **a** from food polluted
      15:29   You are to **a** from food sacrificed
      21:25   they should **a** from food sacrificed
Ro    14: 6   those who **a** do so to the Lord
1Ti    4: 3   order them to **a** from certain foods,
1Pe    2:11   and exiles, to **a** from sinful desires,

## ABSTAINED* [ABSTAIN]

Ex    31:17   on the seventh day he **a** from work

## ABUNDANCE [ABUNDANT]

Ge    41:29   great **a** are coming throughout
Job   36:31   the nations and provides food in **a**.
Ps    36: 8   They feast on the **a** of your house;
      66:12   but you brought us to a place of **a**.
Ecc    5:12   but the **a** of the rich permits them no
Isa   66:11   and delight in her overflowing **a**."
Jer    2:22   and use an **a** of cleansing powder,
Mt    13:12   given more, and they will have an **a**.
      25:29   given more, and they will have an **a**.
Lk    12:15   not consist in an **a** of possessions."
1Pe    1: 2   Grace and peace be yours in **a**.
2Pe    1: 2   yours in **a** through the knowledge
Jude   1: 2   peace and love be yours in **a**.

## ABUNDANT [ABUNDANCE, ABUNDANTLY]

Dt    28:11   will grant you **a** prosperity—
      32: 2   grass, like **a** rain on tender plants.
Job   36:28   **a** showers fall on the human race.
Ps    68: 9   You gave **a** showers, O God;
      78:15   gave them water as **a** as the seas;
     132:15   I will bless her with **a** provisions;
     145: 7   They celebrate your **a** goodness
Pr    12:11   work their land will have **a** food,
      28:19   work their land will have **a** food,
Jer   33: 9   will tremble at the **a** prosperity
Eze   17: 5   planted it like a willow by **a** water,
      31: 7   for its roots went down to **a** waters.
Joel   2:23   He sends you **a** showers,
Ro     5:17   who receive God's **a** provision

## ABUNDANTLY [ABUNDANT]
Jos 17:14 and the LORD has blessed us **a**."
1Ti 1:14 our Lord was poured out on me **a**,

## ABUSE [ABUSIVE]
Pr 9: 7 rebukes the wicked incurs **a**.
1Pe 4: 4 wild living, and they heap **a** on you.
2Pe 2:10 not afraid to heap **a** on celestial beings;
2Pe 2:11 do not heap **a** on such beings
Jude 1: 8 and heap **a** on celestial beings.

## ABUSIVE* [ABUSE]
Ac 18: 6 they opposed Paul and became **a**,
2Ti 3: 2 proud, **a**, disobedient to their

## ABYSS*
Lk 8:31 not to order them to go into the **A**.
Rev 9: 1 given the key to the shaft of the **A**.
    9: 2 When he opened the **A**, smoke rose
    9: 2 darkened by the smoke from the **A**.
    9:11 king over them the angel of the **A**,
    11: 7 up from the **A** will attack them,
    17: 8 will come up out of the **A** and go
    20: 1 having the key to the **A** and holding
    20: 3 He threw him into the **A**, and locked

## ACACIA
Ex 25:10 them make an ark of **a** wood—
    25:23 "Make a table of **a** wood—
    26:15 "Make upright frames of **a** wood
    27: 1 "Build an altar of **a** wood,

## ACCENT*
Mt 26:73 your **a** gives you away."

## ACCEPT [ACCEPTABLE,
    ACCEPTANCE, ACCEPTED,
    ACCEPTS]
Ge 14:23 that I will **a** nothing belonging
Ex 23: 8 "Do not **a** a bribe, for a bribe blinds
Lev 26:23 things you do not **a** my correction
Dt 16:19 Do not **a** a bribe, for a bribe blinds
2Sa 24:23 the LORD your God **a** you."
Job 2:10 Shall we **a** good from God, and not
    42: 8 and I will **a** his prayer and not deal
Ps 119:108 **A**, LORD, the willing praise of my
Pr 4:10 my son, **a** what I say, and the years
    10: 8 The wise in heart **a** commands,
    19:20 Listen to advice and **a** discipline,
Eze 43:27 Then I will **a** you,
Zep 3: 7 you will fear me and **a** correction!'
Mal 1:10 "and I will **a** no offering from your
Mt 11:14 And if you are willing to **a** it, he is
    19:11 "Not everyone can **a** this word,
Jn 3:11 you people do not **a** our testimony.
    5:41 "I do not **a** glory from human
    14:17 The world cannot **a** him, because it
Ac 22:18 here will not **a** your testimony
Ro 14: 1 **A** those whose faith is weak,
    15: 7 **A** one another, then, just as Christ
1Co 2:14 the Spirit does not **a** the things
Jas 1:21 humbly **a** the word planted in you,
1Jn 5: 9 We **a** human testimony, but God's

## ACCEPTABLE [ACCEPT]
Pr 21: 3 just is more **a** to the LORD than
Isa 58: 5 call a fast, a day **a** to the LORD?
Php 4:18 a fragrant offering, an **a** sacrifice,
1Pe 2: 5 offering spiritual sacrifices **a** to God

## ACCEPTANCE* [ACCEPT]
Ro 11:15 what will their **a** be but life
1Ti 1:15 saying that deserves full **a**:
    4: 9 saying that deserves full **a**.

## ACCEPTED [ACCEPT]
Ge 4: 7 do what is right, will you not be **a**?
Lev 1: 4 it will be **a** on your behalf to make
    7:18 the one who offered it will not be **a**.
1Sa 8: 3 after dishonest gain and **a** bribes
Job 42: 9 and the LORD **a** Job's prayer.
Lk 4:24 "prophets are not **a** in their
Ac 2:41 Those who **a** his message were
Ro 10:16 all the Israelites **a** the good news.
    15: 7 then, just as Christ **a** you, in order
2Co 11: 4 different gospel from the one you **a**,
Gal 1: 9 you a gospel other than what you **a**,
1Th 2:13 us, you **a** it not as a human word,

## ACCEPTS [ACCEPT]
Dt 27:25 "Cursed is anyone who **a** a bribe
Ps 6: 9 the LORD **a** my prayer.
Zep 3: 2 obeys no one, she **a** no correction.
Jn 3:32 heard, but no one **a** his testimony.
    13:20 whoever **a** anyone I send **a** me;
    13:20 whoever **a** me **a** the one who sent
Jas 1:27 that God our Father **a** as pure

## ACCESS*
Est 1:14 Media who had special **a** to the king
Ro 5: 2 through whom we have gained **a**
Eph 2:18 through him we both have **a**

## ACCLAIM*
Ps 89:15 those who have learned to **a** you,
Isa 24:14 from the west they **a** the LORD's

## ACCOMPANIED [ACCOMPANY]
1Co 10: 4 from the spiritual rock that **a** them,
Jas 2:17 itself, if it is not **a** by action, is dead.

## ACCOMPANIES* [ACCOMPANY]
Isa 40:10 him, and his recompense **a** him.
    62:11 and his recompense **a** him.' "
2Co 9:13 obedience that **a** your confession

## ACCOMPANY [ACCOMPANIED,
    ACCOMPANIES]
Dt 28: 2 **a** you if you obey the LORD your
Ecc 8:15 joy will **a** them in their toil all
Mk 16:17 *these signs will **a** those who believe:*

## ACCOMPLICES*
Pr 29:24 The **a** of thieves are their own

## ACCOMPLISH [ACCOMPLISHED]
Dt 9: 5 to **a** what he swore to your fathers,
2Ki 19:31 of the LORD Almighty will **a** this.

Ecc　2: 2　And what does pleasure **a**?"
Isa　9: 7　of the LORD Almighty will **a** this.
　　44:28　shepherd and will **a** all that I please;
　　55:11　but will **a** what I desire and achieve

## ACCOMPLISHED [ACCOMPLISH]

Isa　26:12　all that we have **a** you have done
Mt　5:18　from the Law until everything is **a**.
Eph　3:11　that he **a** in Christ Jesus our Lord.
Rev　10: 7　the mystery of God will be **a**, just as

## ACCORD [ACCORDANCE, ACCORDING]

Nu　24:13　could not do anything of my own **a**,
Jn　10:18　me, but I lay it down of my own **a**.

## ACCORDANCE [ACCORD]

Nu　14:19　In **a** with your great love,
2Ki　14:25　in **a** with the word of the LORD,
　　23:25　in **a** with all the Law of Moses.
Ps 119:149　Hear my voice in **a** with your love;
Eze　35:11　I will treat you in **a** with the anger
Ac　24:14　everything that is in **a** with the Law
Ro　8: 5　those who live in **a** with the Spirit
Ro　12: 6　prophesy in **a** with your faith;
Eph　1: 5　in **a** with his pleasure and will—
2Th　2: 9　of the lawless one will be in **a**
Heb 10: 8　they were offered in **a** with the law.

## ACCORDING [ACCORD]

Ge　1:11　seed in it, **a** to their various kinds."
Ex　26:30　the tabernacle **a** to the plan shown
Dt　26:13　the widow, **a** to all you commanded.
2Ch　6:30　deal with everyone **a** to all they do,
Ps　18:24　The LORD has rewarded me **a** to my
　　　　righteousness, **a** to the cleanness of my
　　　　hands
　　119: 9　By living **a** to your word.
Pr　12: 8　People are praised **a** to their
Hos 12: 2　he will punish Jacob **a** to his ways and
　　　　repay him **a** to his deeds.
Mt　9:29　"**A** to your faith let it be done
Jn　19: 7　a law, and **a** to that law he must die,
Ro　8: 4　who do not live **a** to the sinful nature
　　　　but **a** to the Spirit.
Gal　3:29　seed, and heirs **a** to the promise.
2Ti　2: 5　except by competing **a** to the rules.
1Jn　5:14　that if we ask anything **a** to his will,
Rev 20:12　The dead were judged **a** to what

## ACCOUNT [ACCOUNTABLE, ACCOUNTING]

Ge　2: 4　This is the **a** of the heavens
　　5: 1　This is the written **a** of Adam's
　　6: 9　This is the **a** of Noah and his
　　10: 1　This is the **a** of Shem,
　　11:10　This is the **a** of Shem's family line.
　　11:27　This is the **a** of Terah's family line.
　　25:12　This is the **a** of the family line
　　25:19　This is the **a** of the family line
　　36: 1　This is the **a** of the family line
　　36: 9　This is the **a** of the family line
　　37: 2　This is the **a** of Jacob's family line.
Dt　18:19　call to **a** anyone who does not listen
Jos　22:23　the LORD himself call us to **a**.

Mt　12:36　will have to give **a** on the day
　　26:31　night you will all fall away on **a**
Lk　16: 2　Give an **a** of your management,
Ro　14:12　we will all give an **a** of ourselves
Heb　4:13　of him to whom we must give **a**.
1Jn　2:12　your sins have been forgiven on **a**

## ACCOUNTABLE* [ACCOUNT]

Eze　3:18　I will hold you **a** for their blood.
　　3:20　I will hold you **a** for their blood.
　　33: 6　I will hold the watchman **a** for their
　　33: 8　I will hold you **a** for their blood.
　　34:10　and will hold them **a** for my flock.
Da　6: 2　The satraps were made **a** to them so
Jnh　1:14　Do not hold us **a** for killing
Ro　3:19　and the whole world held **a** to God.

## ACCOUNTING [ACCOUNT]

Ge　9: 5　lifeblood I will surely demand an **a**.
　　　　I will demand an **a** from every
　　9: 5　I will demand an **a** for the life

## ACCREDITED* [CREDIT]

Ac　2:22　of Nazareth was a man **a** by God

## ACCUMULATE* [ACCUMULATED]

Dt　17.17　He must not **a** large amounts

## ACCUMULATED [ACCUMULATE]

2Ch　1:14　Solomon **a** chariots and horses;

## ACCURATE [ACCURATELY]

Dt　25:15　You must have **a** and honest
Pr　11: 1　but **a** weights find favor with him.
Eze　45:10　You are to use **a** scales, an **a** ephah and
　　　　an **a** bath.

## ACCURATELY* [ACCURATE]

Ac　18:25　fervor and taught about Jesus **a**,

## ACCURSED [CURSE]

2Pe　2:14　are experts in greed—an **a** brood!

## ACCUSATION [ACCUSE]

Mic　6: 2　you mountains, the LORD's **a**;
Col　1:22　without blemish and free from **a**—
1Ti　5:19　not entertain an **a** against an elder

## ACCUSATIONS [ACCUSE]

Ac　26: 2　against all the accusations of the Jews,

## ACCUSE [ACCUSATION, ACCUSATIONS, ACCUSED, ACCUSER, ACCUSERS, ACCUSES, ACCUSING]

Ps 103: 9　He will not always **a**, nor will he
Pr　3:30　Do not **a** anyone for no reason—
Zec　3: 1　standing at his right side to **a** him.
Mt　12:10　Looking for a reason to **a** Jesus,
Lk　3:14　money and don't **a** people falsely—
1Pe　2:12　though they **a** you of doing wrong,

## ACCUSED [ACCUSE]
Mk 15: 3 The chief priests **a** him of many
Ac 22:30 exactly why Paul was being **a**

## ACCUSER [ACCUSE]
Job 31:35 let my **a** put his indictment
Ps 109: 6 let an **a** stand at his right hand.
Jn 5:45 Your **a** is Moses, on whom your
Rev 12:10 For the **a** of our brothers and sisters,

## ACCUSERS [ACCUSE]
Ps 109:20 be the LORD's payment to my **a**,
Isa 50: 8 Who are my **a**? Let them confront

## ACCUSES* [ACCUSE]
Job 40: 2 Let him who **a** God answer him!"
Isa 54:17 will refute every tongue that **a** you.
Rev 12:10 who **a** them before our God day

## ACCUSING [ACCUSE]
Ps 31:20 in your dwelling from **a** tongues.
Ro 2:15 and their thoughts now **a**, now even

## ACHAN*
Sin at Jericho caused defeat at Ai; stoned (Jos 7; 22:20; 1Ch 2:7).

## ACHE*
Pr 14:13 Even in laughter the heart may **a**,

## ACHIEVE [ACHIEVED, ACHIEVEMENT]
Job 5:12 so that their hands **a** no success.
Ps 45: 4 your right hand **a** awesome deeds.
Isa 55:11 **a** the purpose for which I sent it.

## ACHIEVED [ACHIEVE]
Isa 63: 5 my own arm **a** salvation for me,

## ACHIEVEMENT* [ACHIEVE]
Ecc 4: 4 all **a** spring from one person's envy

## ACHISH
King of Gath before whom David feigned insanity (1Sa 21:10–15). Later "ally" of David (2Sa 27–29).

## ACHOR
Jos 7:26 called the Valley of **A** ever since.
Hos 2:15 will make the Valley of **A** a door

## ACKNOWLEDGE
[ACKNOWLEDGED, ACKNOWLEDGES, ACKNOWLEDGMENT]
1Ch 28: 9 Solomon, **a** the God of your father,
Ps 79: 6 on the nations that do not **a** you,
Ps 91:14 for they **a** my name.
Isa 59:12 with us, and we **a** our iniquities:
Jer 3:13 Only **a** your guilt—
9: 3 they do not **a** me,"
Da 4:25 you until you **a** that the Most High

Hos 6: 3 Let us **a** the LORD; let us press on to **a** him.
Mt 10:32 also **a** before my Father in heaven.
Lk 12: 8 will also **a** before the angels of God.
Jn 12:42 would not openly **a** their faith
Php 2:11 every tongue **a** that Jesus Christ is Lord,
1Th 5:12 to **a** those who work hard
Heb 3: 1 we **a** as our apostle and high priest.
1Jn 4: 3 spirit that does not **a** Jesus is not
2Jn 1: 7 who do not **a** Jesus Christ as

## ACKNOWLEDGED
[ACKNOWLEDGE]
Lk 7:29 words, **a** that God's way was right,

## ACKNOWLEDGES*
[ACKNOWLEDGE]
Mt 10:32 "Whoever publicly **a** me I will
Lk 12: 8 whoever publicly **a** me, the Son
1Jn 2:23 whoever **a** the Son has the Father
4: 2 Every spirit that **a** that Jesus Christ
4:15 If anyone **a** that Jesus is the Son

## ACKNOWLEDGMENT*
[ACKNOWLEDGE]
Hos 4: 1 no love, no **a** of God in the land.
6: 6 **a** of God rather than burnt offerings.

## ACQUIRED [ACQUIRES]
Ge 12:16 sake, and Abram **a** sheep and cattle,
Ru 4:10 I have also **a** Ruth the Moabite,
Jer 48:36 The wealth they **a** is gone.

## ACQUIRES* [ACQUIRED]
Pr 18:15 heart of the discerning **a** knowledge,

## ACQUIT [ACQUITTED, ACQUITTING]
Ex 23: 7 to death, for I will not **a** the guilty.

## ACQUITTED* [ACQUIT]
Mt 12:37 For by your words you will be **a**,

## ACQUITTING* [ACQUIT]
Dt 25: 1 **a** the innocent and condemning
Pr 17:15 **A** the guilty and condemning

## ACT [ACTED, ACTION, ACTIONS, ACTIVE, ACTIVITY, ACTS]
Nu 23:19 Does he speak and then not **a**?
1Ki 2: 2 "So be strong, **a** like a man,
8:32 then hear from heaven and **a**.
8:39 Forgive and **a**; deal with everyone
Ps 106: 3 Blessed are those who **a** justly,
119:126 It is time for you to **a**, LORD;
Isa 43:13 When I **a**, who can reverse it?"
52:13 See, my servant will **a** wisely;
Jn 8: 4 *woman was caught in the **a** of adultery.*

## ACTED [ACT]
Ac 3:17 I know that you **a** in ignorance,
1Ti 1:13 I was shown mercy because I **a**

## ACTION [ACT]
2Co 9: 2 has stirred most of them to a.
Jas 2:17 if it is not accompanied by a,

## ACTIONS [ACT]
Pr 20:11 small children are known by their a,
Mt 11:19 wisdom is proved right by her a."
Gal 6: 4 Each of you should test your own a.
Tit 1:16 God, but by their a they deny him.

## ACTIVE* [ACT]
Heb 4:12 For the word of God is alive and a.

## ACTIVITY [ACT]
Ecc 3: 1 for every a under the heavens:
3:17 for there will be a time for every a,

## ACTS [ACT]
Ex 7: 4 mighty a of judgment I will bring
1Ch 16: 9 tell of all his wonderful a.
Ps 71:16 come and proclaim your mighty a,
71:24 tell of your righteous a all day long,
105: 2 tell of all his wonderful a.
106: 2 Who can proclaim the mighty a
145: 4 they tell of your mighty a.
145:12 people may know of your mighty a
150: 2 Praise him for his a of power;
Pr 12:10 but the kindest a of the wicked are
Isa 64: 6 all our righteous a are like filthy
Mt 6: 1 not to do your 'a of righteousness'
Ro 1:27 Men committed shameful a
Gal 5:19 The a of the sinful nature are
Rev 15: 4 you, for your righteous a have been
19: 8 the righteous a of God's people.)

## ADAM
1. First man (Ge 1:26—2:25; Ro 5:14; 1Ti 2:13). Sin of (Ge 3; Hos 6:7; Ro 5:12–21). Children of (Ge 4:15:5). Death of (Ge 5:5; Ro 5:12–21; 1Co 15:22).
2. Town (Jos 3:16).

## ADAR
Month in which temple was rebuilt (Ezr 6:15); celebration of Purim (Est 3:7; 9:1–21).

## ADD [ADDED, ADDS]
Dt 4: 2 Do not a to what I command you
12:32 do not a to it or take away from it.
Pr 1: 5 wise listen and a to their learning,
9: 9 and they will a to their learning.
30: 6 Do not a to his words, or he will
Mt 6:27 you by worrying a a single hour
Lk 12:25 you by worrying can a a single hour
2Pe 1: 5 make every effort to a to your faith
Rev 22:18 them, God will a to you the plagues

## ADDED [ADD]
Pr 9:11 and years will be a to your life.
Ecc 3:14 nothing can be a to it and nothing
Ac 2:47 the Lord a to their number daily
5:14 Lord and were a to their number.
Gal 3:19 It was a because of transgressions

## ADDICTED*
Tit 2: 3 to be slanderers or a to much wine,

## ADDS [ADD]
Pr 10:27 fear of the LORD a length to life,

## ADMAH
Dt 29:23 and Gomorrah, A and Zeboyim,
Hos 11: 8 How can I treat you like A?

## ADMINISTER [ADMINISTRATION]
1Ki 3:28 had wisdom from God to a justice.
Zec 7: 9 'A true justice;
2Co 8:19 which we a in order to honor

## ADMINISTRATION* [ADMINISTER]
Eph 3: 2 heard about the a of God's grace
3: 9 to everyone the a of this mystery,

## ADMIRABLE*
Php 4: 8 whatever is lovely, whatever is a—

## ADMIT
Job 27: 5 I will never a you are in the right;

## ADMONISH* [ADMONISHING]
Col 3:16 and a one another with all wisdom
1Th 5:12 for you in the Lord and who a you.

## ADMONISHING* [ADMONISH]
Col 1:28 a and teaching everyone with all

## ADONIJAH
1. Son of David by Haggith (2Sa 3:4; 1Ch 3:2). Attempted to be king after David; killed by Solomon's order (1Ki 1–2).
2. Levite; teacher of the Law (2Ch 17:8).

## ADOPTED* [ADOPTION]
Est 2:15 (the young woman Mordecai had a,
Ps 106:35 the nations and a their customs.

## ADOPTION* [ADOPTED]
Ro 8:15 brought about your a to sonship.
8:23 as we wait eagerly for our a,
9: 4 Theirs is the a; theirs the divine
Gal 4: 5 we might receive a to sonship.
Eph 1: 5 he predestined us for a

## ADORE*
SS 1: 4 How right they are to a you!

## ADORN [ADORNED, ADORNMENT, ADORNS]
Pr 1: 9 head and a chain to a your neck.
Isa 60: 7 and I will a my glorious temple.
Jer 4:30 You a yourself in vain.
1Pe 3: 5 hope in God used to a themselves.

## ADORNED [ADORN]
Eze 16:11 I a you with jewelry: I put bracelets

## ADORNMENT* [ADORN]

1Pe  3: 3  should not come from outward a,

## ADORNS* [ADORN]

Ps  93: 5  holiness a your house for endless
Pr  15: 2  The tongue of the wise a knowledge,
Isa  61:10  as a bridegroom a his head like
     61:10  as a bride a herself with her jewels.

## ADULLAM

1Sa  22: 1  Gath and escaped to the cave of A.
1Ch  11:15  David to the rock at the cave of A,

## ADULTERER* [ADULTERY]

Lev  20:10  both the a and the adulteress are
Job  24:15  The eye of the a watches for dusk;
Heb  13: 4  for God will judge the a and all

## ADULTERERS [ADULTERY]

Jer  23:10  The land is full of a;
Hos  7: 4  They are all a, burning like an oven
Mal  3: 5  against sorcerers, a and perjurers,
1Co  6: 9  nor idolaters nor a nor male

## ADULTERESS [ADULTERY]

Hos  3: 1  she is loved by another and is an a.
Mt  5:32  causes her to become an a,

## ADULTERIES [ADULTERY]

Jer  3: 8  sent her away because of all her a.
Rev  14: 8  the maddening wine of her a."
     19: 2  who corrupted the earth by her a.

## ADULTEROUS [ADULTERY]

Pr  2:16  save you also from the a woman,
    5: 3  For the lips of the a woman drip honey,
    23:27  for an a woman is a deep pit
Eze  6: 9  have been grieved by their a hearts,
Hos  1: 2  for like an a wife this land is guilty
Mt  16: 4  and a generation looks for a sign,
Mk  8:38  and my words in this a and sinful
Jas  4: 4  You a people, don't you know

## ADULTERY [ADULTERER, ADULTERERS, ADULTERESS, ADULTERIES, ADULTEROUS]

Ex  20:14  "You shall not commit a.
Dt  5:18  "You shall not commit a.
Ps  51: T  *David had committed a with Bathsheba.*
Pr  6:32  a man who commits a has no sense;
Eze  23:37  for they have committed a
     23:37  They committed a with their idols;
Mt  5:27  was said, 'You shall not commit a.'
    5:28  lustfully has already committed a.
    5:32  the divorced woman commits a.
    15:19  murder, a, sexual immorality, theft,
    19: 9  another woman commits a."
    19:18  you shall not commit a, you shall
Mk  10:11  woman commits a against her.
    10:12  another man, she commits a."
    10:19  you shall not commit a, you shall
Lk  16:18  marries another woman commits a,

Lk  16:18  a divorced woman commits a.
    18:20  'You shall not commit a, you shall
Jn  8: 3  *brought in a woman caught in a.*
Ro  2:22  that people should not commit a, do you commit a?
Jas  2:11  "You shall not commit a,"
    2:11  If you do not commit a but do
Rev  18: 3  of the earth committed a with her,

## ADULTS*

1Co  14:20  be infants, but in your thinking be a.

## ADVANCE [ADVANCED]

2Sa  22:30  your help I can a against a troop;
Ps  27: 2  When the wicked a against me
Ro  9:23  whom he prepared in a for glory—
Gal  3: 8  and announced the gospel in a
Eph  2:10  which God prepared in a for us
Php  1:12  has actually served to a the gospel.

## ADVANCED [ADVANCE]

Job  32: 7  a years should teach wisdom.'

## ADVANTAGE

Ex  22:22  "Do not take a of a widow
Lev  25:14  them, do not take a of each other.
Dt  24:14  Do not take a of a hired worker who
Ecc  6: 8  What a have the wise over fools?
    7:12  but the a of knowledge is this:
Ro  3: 1  What a, then, is there in being
2Co  11:20  exploit you or take a of you or push
1Th  4: 6  should wrong or take a of a brother
Jude  1:16  and flatter others for their own a.

## ADVERSARIES [ADVERSARY]

Dt  32:41  I will take vengeance on my a
Ps  44: 7  enemies, you put our a to shame.
    56: 2  My a pursue me all day long;

## ADVERSARY [ADVERSARIES, ADVERSITY]

Mt  5:25  with your a who is taking you
    5:25  or your a may hand you over
Lk  18: 3  'Grant me justice against my a.'

## ADVERSITY* [ADVERSARY]

Pr  17:17  and a brother is born for a time of a.
Isa  30:20  the Lord gives you the bread of a

## ADVICE [ADVISERS]

Nu  31:16  the ones who followed Balaam's a
2Sa  20:22  to all the people with her wise a,
2Ch  10:13  Rejecting the a of the elders,
    10:14  he followed the a of the young men
Pr  1:25  since you disregard all my a and do
    12: 5  but the a of the wicked is deceitful.
    12:15  to them, but the wise listen to a.
    19:20  Listen to a and accept discipline,
    20:18  Plans are established by seeking a;
    27: 9  of a friend springs from their heartfelt a.

## ADVISERS [ADVICE]

Pr  11:14  but victory is won through many a.
    15:22  but with many a they succeed.

Pr   24: 6  and victory is won through many **a**.

## ADVOCATE*
Job  16:19  is in heaven; my **a** is on high.
Jn   14:16  he will give you another **a** to help
     14:26  the **A**, the Holy Spirit, whom the Father
     15:26  "When the **A** comes, whom I will send
     16: 7  the **A** will not come to you; but if I go,
1Jn   2: 1  an **a** with the Father—Jesus Christ,

## AENEAS*
Paralytic healed by Peter (Ac 9:33–34).

## AFFAIRS
Ps  112: 5  who conduct their **a** with justice.
Pr   31:27  She watches over the **a** of her
1Co   7:32  is concerned about the Lord's **a**—
      7:33  about the **a** of this world—

## AFFECTION
Dt   10:15  Yet the LORD set his **a** on your
2Co   6:12  We are not withholding our **a**
2Pe   1: 7  mutual **a**; and to mutual **a**, love.

## AFFLICTED  [AFFLICTION]
Jos  24: 5  and I **a** the Egyptians by what I did
Ru    1:21  The LORD has **a** me;
Job   2: 7  **a** Job with painful sores
     36: 6  alive but gives the **a** their rights.
Ps    9:12  he does not ignore the cries of the **a**.
      9:18  the hope of the **a** will never perish.
     34: 2  let the **a** hear and rejoice.
     73:14  All day long I have been **a**,
    119:67  Before I was **a** I went astray,
    119:71  me to be **a** so that I might learn your
    119:75  that in faithfulness you have **a** me.
Isa  49:13  will have compassion on his **a** ones.
     53: 4  by God, stricken by him, and **a**.
     53: 7  He was oppressed and **a**, yet he did
Na    1:12  Although I have **a** you, Judah, I will

## AFFLICTION  [AFFLICTED, AFFLICTIONS]
Dt   16: 3  the bread of **a**, because you left
Ps  107:41  he lifted the needy out of their **a**
Isa  30:20  of adversity and the water of **a**,
     48:10  have tested you in the furnace of **a**.
La    1: 9  on my **a**, for the enemy has
      3:33  For he does not willingly bring **a**
Ro   12:12  hope, patient in **a**, faithful in prayer.

## AFFLICTIONS  [AFFLICTION]
Lev  26:21  I will multiply your **a** seven times
Col   1:24  still lacking in regard to Christ's **a**,
Rev   2: 9  I know your **a** and your poverty—

## AFRAID  [FEAR]
Ge    3:10  and I was **a** because I was naked;
     26:24  Do not be **a**, for I am with you;
     50:19  Joseph said to them, "Don't be **a**.
Ex    2:14  Then Moses was **a** and thought,
      3: 6  because he was **a** to look at God.
     34:30  and they were **a** to come near him.
Lev  26: 6  down and no one will make you **a**.
Dt    1:21  Do not be **a**; do not be

Dt    1:29  not be terrified; do not be **a** of them.
      2: 4  They will be **a** of you, but be very
     20: 3  Do not be fainthearted or **a**;
Jos  10:25  Joshua said to them, "Do not be **a**;
Ru    3:11  And now, my daughter, don't be **a**.
1Sa  15:24  I was **a** of the men and so I gave
     18:12  Saul was **a** of David,
1Ki  19: 3  Elijah was **a** and ran for his life.
2Ki  25:24  "Do not be **a** of the Babylonian
1Ch  13:12  David was **a** of God that day
Ne    2: 2  I was very much **a**,
Ps   27: 1  of my life—of whom shall I be **a**?
     56: 3  When I am **a**, I put my trust in you.
     56: 4  in God I trust and am not **a**.
Pr    3:24  you lie down, you will not be **a**;
Isa  12: 2  I will trust and not be **a**.
     44: 8  Do not tremble, do not be **a**.
Jer   1: 8  Do not be **a** of them, for I am
     30:10  " 'So do not be **a**, Jacob my servant;
Eze  39:26  land with no one to make them **a**.
Da    4: 5  I had a dream that made me **a**.
Mt    8:26  of little faith, why are you so **a**?"
     10:28  Do not be **a** of those who kill
     10:28  be **a** of the One who can destroy
     10:31  So don't be **a**; you are worth more
Mk    5:36  said, Jesus told him, "Don't be **a**;
Lk    9:34  and they were **a** as they entered
     12:32  "Do not be **a**, little flock, for your
Jn   14:27  hearts be troubled and do not be **a**.
Ac   27:24  and said, 'Do not be **a**, Paul.
Heb  13: 6  Lord is my helper; I will not be **a**.
2Pe   2:10  they are not **a** to heap abuse
Rev   2:10  Do not be **a** of what you are

## AGABUS*
A Christian prophet (Ac 11:28; 21:10).

## AGAG  [AGAGITE]
King of Amalekites not killed by Saul (1Sa 15).

## AGAGITE  [AGAG]
Est   8: 3  end to the evil plan of Haman the **A**,

## AGAIN
Mk    8:31  be killed and after three days rise **a**.
Jn    2:19  and I will raise it **a** in three days."
      3: 7  at my saying, 'You must be born **a**.'
Heb   6: 6  crucifying the Son of God all over **a**
Rev   7:16  'Never **a** will they hunger; never **a**

## AGE  [AGE-OLD, AGED, AGES]
Mt   13:39  The harvest is the end of the **a**,
Lk   18:30  many times as much in this **a**, and in
              the **a** to come eternal life."
Tit   2:12  and godly lives in this present **a**,

## AGE-OLD  [AGE, OLD]
Hab   3: 6  and the **a** hills collapsed—

## AGED  [AGE]
Job  12:12  Is not wisdom found among the **a**?
Pr   17: 6  children are a crown to the **a**,
Pr   30:17  that scorns an **a** mother,

## AGES [AGE]

Pr   8:23  I was formed long **a** ago,
Ro  16:25  the mystery hidden for long **a** past,
Eph  2: 7  in the coming **a** he might show
       3: 9  for **a** past was kept hidden in God,
Col   1:26  that has been kept hidden for **a**
Heb  9:26  the culmination of the **a** to do away

## AGO

Ps  74: 2  the people you purchased long **a**,
    74:12  But God is my King from long **a**;
Jude  1: 4  condemnation was written about long **a**

## AGONY

Jer   4:19  Oh, the **a** of my heart!
Lk  16:24  because I am in **a** in this fire.'
Ac   2:24  freeing him from the **a** of death,
Rev 16:10  People gnawed their tongues in **a**

## AGREE [AGREEMENT, AGREES, DISAGREEMENT]

Mt  18:19  earth **a** about anything you ask for,
Mk  14:59  even then their testimony did not **a**.
Ro   7:16  want to do, I **a** that the law is good.

## AGREEMENT [AGREE]

Da  11:23  After coming to an **a** with him,
2Co  6:16  What **a** is there between the temple
1Jn  5: 8  and the three are in **a**.

## AGREES* [AGREE]

Ac   7:42  This **a** with what is written
1Co  4:17  Jesus, which **a** with what I teach

## AGRIPPA*

Descendant of Herod; king before whom Paul pled his case in Caesarea (Ac 25:13—26:32).

## AHAB

1. Son of Omri; king of Israel (1Ki 16:28—22:40), husband of Jezebel (1Ki 16:31). Promoted Baal worship (1Ki 16:31–33); opposed by Elijah (1Ki 17:1; 18; 21), a prophet (1Ki 20:35–43), Micaiah (1Ki 22:1–28). Defeated Ben-Hadad (1Ki 20). Killed for failing to kill Ben-Hadad and for murder of Naboth (1Ki 20:35–21:40).
2. A false prophet (Jer 29:21–22).

## AHASUERUS See XERXES

## AHAZ

Son of Jotham; king of Judah, (2Ki 16; 2Ch 28; Mt 1:9). Idolatry of (2Ki 16:3–4, 10–18; 2Ch 28:1–4, 22–25). Defeated by Aram and Israel (2Ki 16:5–6; 2Ch 28:5–15). Sought help from Assyria rather than the LORD (2Ki 16:7–9; 2Ch 28:16–21; Isa 7).

## AHAZIAH

1. Son of Ahab; king of Israel (1Ki 22:51–2Ki 1:18; 2Ch 20:35–37). Made an unsuccessful alliance with Jehoshaphat (2Ch 20:35–37). Died for seeking Baal rather than the LORD (2Ki 1).
2. Son of Jehoram; king of Judah (2Ki 8:25–29; 9:14–29), also called Jehoahaz (2Ch 21:17—22:9;

25:23). Killed by Jehu while visiting Joram (2Ki 9:14–29; 2Ch 22:1–9).

## AHEAD [HEAD]

1Co 11:21  of you go **a** with your own private
Php  3:13  and straining toward what is **a**,
1Ti  5:24  the place of judgment **a** of them;
Heb 11:26  because he was looking **a** to his
2Jn  1: 9  Anyone who runs **a** and does not

## AHIJAH

1. Priest during Sauls reign (1Sa 14:3,18).
2. Prophet of Shiloh (1Ki 11:29–39; 14:1–18).

## AHIKAM

Father of Gedaliah (2Ki 25:22), protector of Jeremiah (Jer 26:24).

## AHIMAAZ

1. Father-in-law of Saul (1Sa 14:50).
2. Son of Zadok, the high priest, loyal to David (2Sa 15:27,36; 17:17–20; 18:19–33).

## AHIMELEK

1. Priest who helped David in his flight from Saul (1Sa 21–22).
2. One of David's warriors (1Sa 26:6).

## AHINOAM

1. Wife of Saul (1Sa 14:50).
2. Wife of David (1Sa 25:43; 30:5; 1Ch 3:1).

## AHITHOPHEL

One of David's counselors who sided with Absalom (2Sa 15:12, 31–37; 1Ch 27:33–34); committed suicide when his advice was ignored (2Sa 16:15—17:23).

## AI

Jos  7: 4  they were routed by the men of **A**,
     8:26  he had destroyed all who lived in **A**.

## AID

Ge 50:25  "God will surely come to your **a**,
Ex 13:19  "God will surely come to your **a**,
Ru  1: 6  had come to the **a** of his people
Isa 38:14  Lord, come to my **a**!"
Php  4:16  you sent me **a** more than once

## AIM* [AIMLESSLY]

Ps 21:12  turn their backs when you **a** at them
   64: 3  **a** cruel words like deadly arrows.
Ac 20:24  my only **a** is to finish the race
1Co  7:34  Her **a** is to be devoted to the Lord

## AIMLESSLY* [AIM]

Pr  5: 6  her paths wander **a**,
1Co  9:26  do not run like someone running **a**;

## AIR [MIDAIR]

1Co  9:26  not fight like a boxer beating the **a**.
   14: 9  You will just be speaking into the **a**.
Eph  2: 2  of the ruler of the kingdom of the **a**,
1Th  4:17  the clouds to meet the Lord in the **a**.

Rev 16:17  poured out his bowl into the **a**,

## AKELDAMA* [BLOOD, FIELD]
Ac  1:19  called that field in their language **A**,

## ALABASTER*
Mt 26: 7  him with an **a** jar of very expensive
Mk 14: 3  a woman came with an **a** jar of very
Lk  7:37  so she came there with an **a** jar

## ALARM [ALARMED]
Joel 2: 1  sound the **a** on my holy hill.
2Co 7:11  indignation, what **a**, what longing,

## ALARMED [ALARM]
Mk 13: 7  and rumors of wars, do not be **a**.
Ac 22:29  The commander himself was **a**
2Th 2: 2  or **a** by the teaching allegedly

## ALERT*
Jos  8: 4  far from it. All of you be on the **a**.
Ps 17:11  me, with eyes **a**, to throw me
Isa 21: 7  on camels, let him be **a**, fully **a**."
Mk 13:33  Be **a**! You do not know
Eph 6:18  be **a** and always keep on praying
1Pe 1:13  with minds that are **a** and fully sober,
     4: 7  Therefore be **a** and of sober mind.
     5: 8  Be **a** and of sober mind.

## ALEXANDER
Ac 19:33  in the crowd pushed **A** to the front,
1Ti 1:20  Among them are Hymenaeus and **A**,
2Ti 4:14  **A** the metalworker did me a great

## ALIEN* [ALIENATED]
Isa 28:21  perform his task, his **a** task.

## ALIENATED* [ALIEN]
Job 19:13  "He has **a** my family from me;
Gal  5: 4  by the law have been **a** from Christ;
Col  1:21  Once you were **a** from God

## ALIVE [LIVE]
Ge  7: 3  their various kinds **a** throughout
Dt  6:24  might always prosper and be kept **a**,
1Sa 2: 6  LORD brings death and makes **a**;
Pr  1:12  let's swallow them **a**, like the grave,
Lk 24:23  vision of angels, who said he was **a**.
Ac  1: 3  convincing proofs that he was **a**.
Ro  6:11  to sin but **a** to God in Christ Jesus.
     7: 9  Once I was **a** apart from the law;
1Co 15:22  die, so in Christ all will be made **a**.
Col  2:13  nature, God made you **a** with Christ.
1Th 4:17  we who are still **a** and are left will
Heb 4:12  For the word of God is **a** and active.
Rev 1:18  now look, I am **a** for ever and ever!

## ALL ISRAEL See ISRAEL

## ALL ... HEART See HEART

## ALL PEOPLE See PEOPLE

## ALL PEOPLES See PEOPLES

## ALL THE PEOPLE See PEOPLE

## ALL THE PEOPLES See PEOPLES

## ALLEGIANCE
Ro  6:17  teaching that has now claimed your **a**.

## ALLELUIA See HALLELUJAH

## ALLIANCE [ALLY]
1Ki 3: 1  Solomon made an **a** with Pharaoh
Isa 30: 1  forming an **a**, but not by my Spirit,

## ALLOTMENT [ALLOTS, ALLOTTED]
Dt 14:29  so that the Levites (who have no **a**
Eze 48:13  the Levites will have an **a** 25,000

## ALLOTS [ALLOTMENT]
Job 27:13  "Here is the fate God **a**

## ALLOTTED [ALLOTMENT]
Nu 34: 2  will be **a** to you as an inheritance is
Da 12:13  rise to receive your **a** inheritance."

## ALLOW [ALLOWED]
Ps 132: 4  I will **a** no sleep to my eyes
Pr  6: 4  **A** no sleep to your eyes, no slumber
Lk  4:41  and would not **a** them to speak,
Ac 16: 7  Spirit of Jesus would not **a** them to.

## ALLOWED [ALLOW]
Ac 28:16  Paul was **a** to live by himself,
1Co 14:34  They are not **a** to speak, but must be
Rev 9: 5  They were not **a** to kill them
Rev 16: 8  sun was **a** to scorch people with fire.

## ALLY [ALLIANCE]
Isa 48:14  The LORD's chosen **a** will carry

## ALMIGHTY [MIGHT]
Ge 17: 1  to him and said, "I am God **A**;
Ex  6: 3  to Isaac and to Jacob as God **A**,
Nu 24: 4  who sees a vision from the **A**,
Ru  1:20  because the **A** has made my life
2Sa 7:26  'The LORD **A** is God over Israel!'
Job 6: 4  The arrows of the **A** are in me,
     11: 7  Can you probe the limits of the **A**?
     21:15  Who is the **A**, that we should serve
     33: 4  the breath of the **A** gives me life.
Ps 84: 3  LORD **A**, my King and my God.
     89: 8  Who is like you, LORD God **A**?
     91: 1  will rest in the shadow of the **A**.
Isa  6: 3  "Holy, holy, holy is the LORD **A**;
     47: 4  the LORD **A** is his name—
     48: 2  the LORD **A** is his name:
     51:15  the LORD **A** is his name.
     54: 5  the LORD **A** is his name—
Jer 11:17  The LORD **A**, who planted you,
Am  5:14  the LORD God **A** will be with you,
     5:15  the LORD God **A** will have mercy
Zec  8:22  to Jerusalem to seek the LORD **A**
Mal  3:10  says the LORD **A**, "and see if I
Rev 4: 8  holy is the Lord God **A**,' who was,
     19: 6  For our Lord God **A** reigns.

## †LORD GOD ALMIGHTY See GOD

## †LORD ALMIGHTY See †LORD

## †LORD ALMIGHTY SAYS See †LORD

## ALOFT*
Dt 32:11 catch them and carries them **a**.

## ALONE [LONELY]
| | | |
|---|---|---|
| Ge | 2:18 | "It is not good for the man to be **a**. |
| Ex | 18:18 | you cannot handle it **a**. |
| Dt | 8: 3 | that people do not live on bread **a** |
| Ne | 9: 6 | You **a** are the LORD. |
| Ps | 76: 7 | It is you **a** who are to be feared. |
| | 148:13 | LORD, for his name **a** is exalted; |
| Mt | 4: 4 | 'People do not live on bread **a**, |
| Mk | 2: 7 | Who can forgive sins but God **a**?" |
| | 10:18 | "No one is good—except God **a**. |
| Jas | 2:24 | by what they do and not by faith **a**. |
| Rev | 15: 4 | For you **a** are holy. All nations will |

## ALPHA*
| | | |
|---|---|---|
| Rev | 1: 8 | "I am the **A** and the Omega," |
| | 21: 6 | I am the **A** and the Omega, |
| | 22:13 | I am the **A** and the Omega, the First |

## ALREADY [READY]
| | | |
|---|---|---|
| Php | 3:12 | Not that I have **a** obtained all this, or |
| | | have **a** arrived at my goal, |
| 2Th | 2: 2 | that the day of the Lord has **a** come. |
| | 2: 7 | power of lawlessness is **a** at work; |
| 2Ti | 2:18 | the resurrection has **a** taken place, |
| 1Jn | 2: 8 | and the true light is **a** shining. |

## ALTAR [ALTARS]
| | | |
|---|---|---|
| Ge | 8:20 | Noah built an **a** to the LORD and, |
| | 12: 7 | So he built an **a** there |
| | 13:18 | There he built an **a** to the LORD. |
| | 22: 9 | Abraham built an **a** there |
| | 22: 9 | his son Isaac and laid him on the **a**, |
| | 26:25 | Isaac built an **a** there and called |
| | 33:20 | There he set up an **a** and called it El |
| | 35: 1 | and build an **a** there to God, |
| Ex | 17:15 | Moses built an **a** and called it |
| | 20:24 | " 'Make an **a** of earth for me |
| | 27: 1 | "Build an **a** of acacia wood, |
| | 30: 1 | "Make an **a** of acacia wood |
| | 37:25 | They made the **a** of incense |
| Dt | 27: 5 | Build there an **a** to the LORD your God, |
| | | an **a** of stones. |
| Jos | 8:30 | on Mount Ebal an **a** to the LORD, |
| | 22:10 | Manasseh built an imposing **a** there |
| Jdg | 6:24 | So Gideon built an **a** to the LORD |
| | 21: 4 | the next day the people built an **a** |
| 1Sa | 7:17 | he built an **a** there to the LORD. |
| | 14:35 | Then Saul built an **a** to the LORD; |
| 2Sa | 24:25 | David built an **a** to the LORD |
| 1Ki | 12:33 | sacrifices on the **a** he had built |
| | 12:33 | went up to the **a** to make offerings. |
| | 13: 2 | cried out against the **a** by the word of |
| | | the LORD: "**A**, **a**! |
| | 16:32 | He set up an **a** for Baal |
| | 18:30 | he repaired the **a** of the LORD, |
| 2Ki | 16:10 | He saw an **a** in Damascus and sent to |
| | | Uriah the priest a sketch of the **a**, |
| 1Ch | 21:26 | David built an **a** to the LORD |
| | 21:26 | heaven on the **a** of burnt offering. |

| | | |
|---|---|---|
| 2Ch | 4: 1 | made a bronze **a** twenty cubits long, |
| | 4:19 | the golden **a**; the tables |
| | 15: 8 | He repaired the **a** of the LORD |
| | 32:12 | 'You must worship before one **a** |
| | 33:16 | he restored the **a** of the LORD |
| Ezr | 3: 2 | began to build the **a** of the God |
| Isa | 6: 6 | he had taken with tongs from the **a**. |
| La | 2: 7 | The Lord has rejected his **a** |
| Eze | 40:47 | the **a** was in front of the temple. |
| Am | 9: 1 | I saw the Lord standing by the **a**, |
| Mal | 1: 7 | "By offering defiled food on my **a**. |
| Mt | 5:24 | your gift there in front of the **a**. |
| | 23:18 | 'If anyone swears by the **a**, it means |
| | 23:18 | by the gift on the **a** is bound |
| Ac | 17:23 | worship, I even found an **a** with this |
| 1Co | 10:18 | the sacrifices participate in the **a**? |
| Heb | 13:10 | We have an **a** from which those |
| Jas | 2:21 | he offered his son Isaac on the **a**? |
| Rev | 6: 9 | I saw under the **a** the souls of those |

## ALTARS [ALTAR]
| | | |
|---|---|---|
| Ex | 34:13 | Break down their **a**, smash their |
| Nu | 23: 1 | said, "Build me seven **a** here, |
| 2Ch | 33: 3 | he also erected **a** to the Baals |
| | 34: 4 | Under his direction the **a** |
| | 34: 4 | cut to pieces the incense **a** that were |

## ALTER* [ALTERED]
Ps 89:34 or **a** what my lips have uttered.

## ALTERED* [ALTER]
Da 6: 8 it in writing so that it cannot be **a**—

## ALWAYS
| | | |
|---|---|---|
| Dt | 12:28 | so that it may **a** go well with you |
| | 15:11 | There will **a** be poor people |
| 1Ch | 16:11 | and his strength; seek his face **a**. |
| Ps | 16: 8 | I keep my eyes **a** on the LORD. |
| | 51: 3 | and my sin is **a** before me. |
| | 119:44 | I will **a** obey your law, for ever |
| | 119:98 | Your commands are **a** with me |
| Pr | 6:21 | Bind them **a** on your heart; |
| | 28:14 | are those who **a** tremble before |
| Jer | 12: 1 | You are **a** righteous, LORD, |
| Hos | 12: 6 | justice, and wait for your God **a**. |
| Mt | 26:11 | The poor you will **a** have with you, but |
| | | you will not **a** have me. |
| | 28:20 | And surely I am with you **a**, |
| Jn | 5:17 | "My Father is **a** at his work to this |
| Ac | 2:25 | " 'I saw the Lord **a** before me. |
| | 7:51 | You **a** resist the Holy Spirit! |
| 1Co | 13: 7 | It **a** protects, **a** trusts, **a** hopes, |
| Eph | 5:20 | **a** giving thanks to God the Father |
| Php | 4: 4 | Rejoice in the Lord **a**. I will say it |
| Phm | 1: 4 | I **a** thank my God as I remember |
| Heb | 7:25 | because he **a** lives to intercede |
| 1Pe | 3:15 | **A** be prepared to give an answer |

## AMALEK [AMALEKITES]
Ex 17:14 the name of **A** from under heaven."

## AMALEKITES [AMALEK]
| | | |
|---|---|---|
| Ex | 17: 8 | The **A** came and attacked |
| Dt | 25:17 | Remember what the **A** did to you |
| 1Sa | 15: 3 | attack the **A** and totally destroy all |

1Sa 15: 8 He took Agag king of the **A** alive,

## AMASA

Nephew of David (1Ch 2:17). Commander of Absalom's forces (2Sa 17:24–27). Returned to David (2Sa 19:13). Killed by Joab (2Sa 20:4–13).

## AMASSES*

Pr 28: 8 profit from the poor **a** it for another,

## AMAZED [AMAZEMENT]

Mk 1:22 The people were **a** at his teaching,
6: 6 He was **a** at their lack of faith.
10:24 The disciples were **a** at his words.
Jn 7:21 and you are all **a**.
Ac 2: 7 Utterly **a**, they asked:
13:12 for he was **a** at the teaching

## AMAZEMENT [AMAZED, AMAZING]

Lk 24:41 not believe it because of joy and **a**,

## AMAZIAH

1. Son of Joash; king of Judah (2Ki 14; 2Ch 25). Defeated Edom (2Ki 14:7; 2Ch 25:5–13); defeated by Israel for worshiping Edom's gods (2Ki 14:8–14; 2Ch 25:14–24).
2. Idolatrous priest who opposed Amos (Am 7:10–17).

## AMAZING* [AMAZEMENT]

Jos 3: 5 the Lord will do **a** things among
Jdg 13:19 the Lord did an **a** thing while
Pr 30:18 three things that are too **a** for me,

## AMBASSADOR* [AMBASSADORS]

Eph 6:20 for which I am an **a** in chains.

## AMBASSADORS [AMBASSADOR]

2Co 5:20 We are therefore Christ's **a**,

## AMBITION*

Ro 15:20 It has always been my **a** to preach
Gal 5:20 fits of rage, selfish **a**, dissensions,
Php 1:17 preach Christ out of selfish **a**,
2: 3 Do nothing out of selfish **a** or vain
1Th 4:11 to make it your **a** to lead a quiet life:
Jas 3:14 envy and selfish **a** in your hearts,
3:16 where you have envy and selfish **a**,

## AMBUSH

Hos 6: 9 As marauders lie in **a** for a victim,
Ac 23:21 of them are waiting in **a** for him.
25: 3 they were preparing an **a** to kill him

## AMEN

Dt 27:15 Then all the people shall say, "**A**!"
1Co 14:16 say "**A**" to your thanksgiving,
2Co 1:20 so through him the "**A**" is spoken
Rev 3:14 These are the words of the **A**,
22:20 says, "Yes, I am coming soon." **A**.

## AMENDS*

Job 20:10 His children must make **a** to the poor;
Pr 14: 9 Fools mock at making **a** for sin,

## AMMONITES

Ge 19:38 he is the father of the **A** of today.
Dt 2:19 When you come to the **A**, do not
2:19 of any land belonging to the **A**.
Jdg 11: 4 the **A** were fighting against Israel,
1Ki 11: 5 Molek the detestable god of the **A**.
Jer 49: 6 I will restore the fortunes of the **A**,"
Eze 25:10 Moab along with the **A** to the people
25:10 that the **A** will not be remembered
Zep 2: 9 like Sodom, the **A** like Gomorrah—

## AMNON

Firstborn of David (2Sa 3:2; 1Ch 3:1). Killed by Absalom for raping his sister Tamar (2Sa 13).

## AMON

1. Son of Manasseh; king of Judah (2Ki 21:18–26; 1Ch 3:14; 2Ch 33:21–25).
2. Ruler of Samaria under Ahab (1Ki 22:26; 2Ch 18:25).

## AMORITES

Ge 15:16 of the **A** has not yet reached its full
Nu 21:31 So Israel settled in the land of the **A**.
Jdg 6:10 do not worship the gods of the **A**,
Am 2: 9 "Yet I destroyed the **A** before them,

## AMOS

1. Prophet from Tekoa (Am 1:1; 7:10–17).
2. Ancestor of Jesus (Lk 3:25).

## ANAK [ANAKITES]

Nu 13:28 even saw descendants of **A** there.
Jos 15:13 (Arba was the ancestor of **A**.)

## ANAKITES [ANAK]

Dt 1:28 We even saw the **A** there.' "
2:10 and numerous, and as tall as the **A**.
9: 2 The people are strong and tall—**A**!
9: 2 "Who can stand up against the **A**?"
Jos 11:22 No **A** were left in Israelite territory;

## ANANIAS

1. Husband of Sapphira; died for lying to God (Ac 5:1–11).
2. Disciple who baptized Saul (Ac 9:10–19).
3. High priest at Paul's arrest (Ac 22:30—24:1).

## ANATHEMA See CURSE, CURSED

## ANCESTORS [ANCESTRY]

Ex 13: 5 land he swore to your **a** to give you,
Dt 4:31 forget the covenant with your **a**,
5: 3 not with our **a** that the Lord made
10:15 Lord set his affection on your **a** and
30: 9 just as he delighted in your **a**,
32:17 gods your **a** did not fear.
Jos 24:14 Throw away the gods your **a** worshiped
1Ki 8:57 as he was with our **a**;
19: 4 I am no better than my **a**."

Ezr   5:12  our **a** angered the God of heaven,
     10:11  the God of your **a**,
Ne    9: 9  saw the suffering of our **a** in Egypt;
Ps   22: 4  In you our **a** put their trust;
Jer   7: 7  land I gave your **a** for ever and ever.
Am    2: 4  gods, the gods their **a** followed,
Zec   1: 4  Do not be like your **a**,
Lk   11:47  and it was your **a** who killed them.
Jn    4:20  Our **a** worshiped on this mountain,
      6:58  Your **a** ate manna and died,
Heb   1: 1  the past God spoke to our **a** through
      8: 9  covenant I made with their **a** when I
1Pe   1:18  life handed down to you from your **a**,
2Pe   3: 4  Ever since our **a** died,

## GOD OF ... ANCESTORS See GOD

## ANCESTRY [ANCESTORS]
Ro    9: 5  them is traced the human **a**

## ANCHOR
Heb   6:19  We have this hope as an **a**

## ANCIENT
Ps   68:33  to him who rides the **a** skies above,
    119:52  LORD, your **a** laws, and I find
Pr   22:28  not move an **a** boundary stone set
Isa  43:13  Yes, and from **a** days I am he.
     44: 7  since I established my **a** people,
Da    7: 9  and the **A** of Days took his seat.
      7:13  He approached the **A** of Days
      7:22  until the **A** of Days came
Rev  12: 9  that **a** serpent called the devil,
     20: 2  that **a** serpent, who is the devil,

## ANDREW*
Apostle; brother of Simon Peter (Mt 4:18; 10:2;
Mk 1:16–18, 29; 3:18; 13:3; Lk 6:14; Jn 1:35–44;
6:8–9; 12:22; Ac 1:13).

## ANGEL [ANGELIC, ANGELS, ARCHANGEL]
Ge   16: 7  The **a** of the LORD found Hagar
     21:17  the **a** of God called to Hagar
     22:11  the **a** of the LORD called
     24: 7  he will send his **a** before you so
     31:11  The **a** of God said to me
     48:16  the **A** who has delivered me from all
Ex    3: 2  There the **a** of the LORD appeared
     14:19  Then the **a** of God, who had been
     23:20  I am sending an **a** ahead of you
     32:34  of, and my **a** will go before you.
     33: 2  I will send an **a** before you
Nu   20:16  and sent an **a** and brought us
     22:22  and the **a** of the LORD stood
Jdg   2: 1  The **a** of the LORD went
      6:12  When the **a** of the LORD appeared
      6:22  that it was the **a** of the LORD,
      6:22  I have seen the **a** of the LORD
     13: 3  The **a** of the LORD appeared
1Sa  29: 9  pleasing in my eyes as an **a** of God;
2Sa  14:17  my lord the king is like an **a** of God
     19:27  My lord the king is like an **a**
     24:16  When the **a** stretched out his hand
     24:16  the **a** who was afflicting the people,
     24:16  The **a** of the LORD was

1Ki  13:18  an **a** said to me by the word
     19: 7  The **a** of the LORD came back
2Ki   1: 3  the **a** of the LORD said to Elijah
     19:35  That night the **a** of the LORD went
Job  33:23  Yet if there is an an **a** at their side,
Ps   34: 7  The **a** of the LORD encamps
Da    3:28  who has sent his **a** and rescued his
      6:22  My God sent his **a**, and he shut
Hos  12: 4  He struggled with the **a**
Zec   1:11  to the **a** of the LORD who was
      3: 1  the high priest standing before the **a**
Mt    1:20  an **a** of the Lord appeared to him
      2:13  an **a** of the Lord appeared to Joseph
     28: 2  for an **a** of the Lord came down
Lk    1:11  an **a** of the Lord appeared to him,
      1:26  God sent the **a** Gabriel to Nazareth,
      2: 9  An **a** of the Lord appeared to them,
     22:43  An **a** from heaven appeared to him
Jn   12:29  others said an **a** had spoken to him.
Ac    5:19  during the night an **a** of the Lord
      6:15  his face was like the face of an **a**.
      7:30  an **a** appeared to Moses
      8:26  Now an **a** of the Lord said to Philip,
     10: 3  He distinctly saw an **a** of God,
     12: 7  Suddenly an **a** of the Lord appeared
     27:23  Last night an **a** of the God whose I
1Co  10:10  and were killed by the destroying **a**.
2Co  11:14  Satan himself masquerades as an **a**
Gal   1: 8  or an **a** from heaven should preach
      4:14  me as if I were an **a** of God, as if I
Rev   1: 1  by sending his **a** to his servant John,
      2: 1  "To the **a** of the church in Ephesus
      5: 2  I saw a mighty **a** proclaiming
      7: 2  I saw another **a** coming
      8: 3  Another **a**, who had a golden
      9:11  They had as king over them the **a**
     14: 6  I saw another **a** flying in midair,
     16: 2  The first **a** went and poured out his
     17: 3  the **a** carried me away in the Spirit
     19:17  And I saw an **a** standing in the sun,

## ANGEL OF GOD Ge 21:17; 31:11; Ex 14:19;
Jdg 6:20; 13:6, 9; 1Sa 29:9; 2Sa 14:17, 20;
19:27; Ac 10:3; Gal 4:14

## ANGEL OF THE LORD Mt 1:20, 24; 2:13,
19; 28:2; Lk 1:11; 2:9; Ac 5:19; 8:26; 12:7, 23

## ANGEL OF THE †LORD Ge 16:7, 9, 11;
22:11, 15; Ex 3:2; Nu 22:22, 23, 24, 25, 26, 27,
31, 32, 34, 35; Jdg 2:1, 4; 5:23; 6:11, 12, 21, 21,
22, 22; 13:3, 13, 15, 16, 16, 17, 20, 21, 21; 2Sa
24:16; 1Ki 19:7; 2Ki 1:3, 15; 19:35; 1Ch 21:12,
15, 16, 18, 30; Ps 34:7; 35:5, 6; Isa 37:36; Zec
1:11, 12; 3:1, 5, 6; 12:8

## ANGELIC* [ANGEL]
1Co 13: 1  If I speak in human or **a** tongues,

## ANGELS [ANGEL]
Ge   19: 1  The two **a** arrived at Sodom
     28:12  and the **a** of God were ascending
     32: 1  his way, and the **a** of God met him.
Job   1: 6  One day the **a** came to present
Ps   78:25  Human beings ate the bread of **a**;
     91:11  will command his **a** concerning you
    103:20  you his **a**, you mighty ones who do

| Mt | 4: 6 | will command his **a** concerning you, |
|---|---|---|
| | 13:39 | of the age, and the harvesters are **a**. |
| | 18:10 | that their **a** in heaven always see |
| | 25:41 | fire prepared for the devil and his **a**. |
| Mk | 8:38 | his Father's glory with the holy **a**." |
| | 12:25 | they will be like the **a** in heaven. |
| | 13:32 | knows, not even the **a** in heaven, |
| Lk | 2:15 | When the **a** had left them and gone |
| | 4:10 | will command his **a** concerning you |
| | 12: 9 | me will be disowned before the **a** |
| | 16.22 | and the **a** carried him to Abraham's |
| | 20:36 | for they are like the **a**. |
| Jn | 1:51 | and the **a** of God ascending |
| Ac | 7:53 | the law that was given through **a** |
| | 23: 8 | that there are neither **a** nor spirits, |
| Ro | 8:38 | death nor life, neither **a** nor demons, |
| 1Co | 4: 9 | to **a** as well as to human beings. |
| | 6: 3 | you not know that we will judge **a**? |
| | 11:10 | her own head, because of the **a**. |
| Gal | 3:19 | The law was given through the **a** |
| Col | 2:18 | and the worship of **a** disqualify you. |
| 2Th | 1: 7 | in blazing fire with his powerful **a**. |
| 1Ti | 3:16 | was seen by **a**, was preached among |
| | 5:21 | and Christ Jesus and the elect **a**, |
| Heb | 1: 4 | the **a** as the name he has inherited is |
| | 1: 6 | "Let all God's **a** worship him." |
| | 1: 7 | In speaking of the **a** he says, "He makes |
| | | his **a** spirits, |
| | 1:14 | Are not all **a** ministering spirits sent |
| | 2: 2 | spoken through **a** was binding, |
| | 2: 7 | made them a little lower than the **a**; |
| | 2: 9 | who was made lower than the **a** |
| | 12:22 | thousands of **a** in joyful assembly, |
| | 13: 2 | hospitality to **a** without knowing it. |
| 1Pe | 1:12 | Even a long to look into these |
| | 3:22 | with **a**, authorities and powers |
| 2Pe | 2: 4 | if God did not spare **a** when they |
| Jude | 1: 6 | And the **a** who did not keep their |
| Rev | 1:20 | The seven stars are the **a** |
| | 3: 5 | names before my Father and his **a**. |
| | 5:11 | and heard the voice of many **a**, |
| | 7: 1 | this I saw four **a** standing at the four |
| | 8: 2 | I saw the seven **a** who stand before |
| | 9:14 | "Release the four **a** who are bound |
| | 12: 7 | and his **a** fought against the dragon, |
| | 12: 7 | and the dragon and his **a** fought back. |
| | 15: 1 | seven **a** with the seven last |
| | 21:12 | and with twelve **a** at the gates. |

## ANGER [ANGERED, ANGRY]

| Ex | 4:14 | Then the LORD's **a** burned against |
|---|---|---|
| | 15: 7 | You unleashed your burning **a**; |
| | 22:24 | My **a** will be aroused, and I will kill |
| | 32:10 | so that my **a** may burn against them |
| | 32:11 | "why should your **a** burn against |
| | 32:12 | Turn from your fierce **a**; |
| | 32:19 | his **a** burned and he threw |
| | 34: 6 | slow to **a**, abounding in love |
| Lev | 26:28 | in my **a** I will be hostile toward you, |
| Nu | 11: 1 | he heard them his **a** was aroused. |
| | 11:33 | the **a** of the LORD burned against |
| | 12: 9 | The **a** of the LORD burned against |
| | 14:18 | 'The LORD is slow to **a**, |
| | 25:11 | has turned my **a** away |
| | 32:10 | The LORD's **a** was aroused |
| Dt | 6:15 | God and his **a** will burn against you, |
| | 9:19 | I feared the **a** and wrath |

| Dt | 29:28 | In furious **a** and in great wrath |
|---|---|---|
| Jos | 7: 1 | So the LORD's **a** burned against |
| | 7:26 | LORD turned from his fierce **a**. |
| Jdg | 2:12 | They aroused the LORD's **a** |
| | 14:19 | Burning with **a**, he returned to his |
| 1Sa | 20:30 | Saul's **a** flared up at Jonathan |
| 2Sa | 12: 5 | burned with **a** against the man |
| 1Ki | 16:13 | they aroused the **a** of the LORD, |
| 2Ki | 22:13 | Great is the LORD's **a** that burns |
| | 24:20 | of the LORD's **a** that all this |
| Ne | 9:17 | slow to **a** and abounding in love. |
| Ps | 30: 5 | For his **a** lasts only a moment, |
| | 37: 8 | Refrain from **a** and turn from wrath; |
| | 78:38 | Time after time he restrained his **a** |
| | 86:15 | slow to **a**, abounding in love |
| | 90: 7 | We are consumed by your **a** |
| | 103: 8 | slow to **a**, abounding in love. |
| | 103: 9 | nor will he harbor his **a** forever; |
| | 145: 8 | slow to **a** and rich in love. |
| Pr | 15: 1 | wrath, but a harsh word stirs up **a**. |
| | 29: 8 | up a city, but the wise turn away **a**. |
| | 30:33 | so stirring up **a** produces strife." |
| Ecc | 7: 9 | for **a** resides in the lap of fools. |
| Isa | 63: 6 | I trampled the nations in my **a**; |
| Da | 9:16 | turn away your **a** and your wrath |
| Joel | 2:13 | slow to **a** and abounding in love, |
| Jnh | 3: 9 | from his fierce **a** so that we will not |
| | 4: 2 | slow to **a** and abounding in love, |
| Na | 1: 3 | The LORD is slow to **a** but great |
| Mk | 3: 5 | He looked around at them in **a** and, |
| 2Co | 12:20 | jealousy, outbursts of **a**, factions, |
| Eph | 4:26 | "In your **a** do not sin": Do not let |
| Col | 3: 8 | **a**, rage, malice, slander, and filthy |
| Jas | 1:20 | because our **a** does not produce |

## ANGER OF THE †LORD Nu 11:33; 12:9;
Dt 9:7; Jdg 3:8; 2Sa 24:1; 1Ki 15:30; 16:13, 26, 33; 22:53; 2Ch 25:15; 28:25; 29:8; Jer 4:8; 23:20; 25:37; 30:24; 51:45

## ANGERED [ANGER]

| Ezr | 5:12 | because our ancestors **a** the God |
|---|---|---|
| Ps | 78:58 | They **a** him with their high places; |
| Pr | 22:24 | with those who are easily **a**, |
| 1Co | 13: 5 | it is not easily **a**, it keeps no record |

## ANGRY [ANGER]

| Ge | 4: 5 | So Cain was very **a**, and his face |
|---|---|---|
| Dt | 4:21 | The LORD was **a** with me because |
| Jdg | 18:25 | of the men may get **a** and attack you, |
| Ps | 2:12 | or he will be **a** and you and your |
| | 95:10 | For forty years I was **a** |
| Pr | 29:22 | An **a** person stirs up dissension, |
| Isa | 34: 2 | The LORD is **a** with all nations; |
| Jer | 3:12 | the LORD, 'I will not be **a** forever. |
| Jnh | 4: 1 | very wrong, and he became **a** |
| | 4: 4 | "Is it right for you to be **a**?" |
| Mic | 7:18 | You do not stay **a** forever |
| Mt | 5:22 | that anyone who is **a** with a brother |
| Lk | 15:28 | "The older brother became **a** |
| Jn | 7:23 | why are you **a** with me for healing |
| Heb | 3:17 | whom was he **a** for forty years? |
| Jas | 1:19 | to speak and slow to become **a**, |
| Rev | 11:18 | The nations were **a**, and your wrath |

## ANGUISH

| | | |
|---|---|---|
| 1Sa | 1:10 | In her deep **a** Hannah prayed |
| Ps | 6: 3 | My soul is in deep **a**. |
| Pr | 31: 6 | wine for those who are in **a**! |
| Jer | 4:19 | Oh, my **a**, my **a**! I writhe in pain. |
| La | 1: 4 | women grieve, and she is in bitter **a**. |
| Zep | 1:15 | a day of distress and **a**, a day |
| Lk | 21:25 | nations will be in **a** and perplexity |
| | 22:44 | And being in **a**, he prayed more |
| Jn | 16:21 | is born she forgets the **a** because |
| Ro | 9: 2 | sorrow and unceasing **a** in my heart. |

## ANIMAL [ANIMALS]

| | | |
|---|---|---|
| Lev | 20:15 | man has sexual relations with an **a**, |
| | 20:15 | and you must kill the **a**. |
| Dt | 14: 6 | You may eat any **a** that has |
| Ps | 50:10 | for every **a** of the forest is mine, |
| Da | 8: 4 | No **a** could stand against it, |

## ANIMALS [ANIMAL]

| | | |
|---|---|---|
| Ge | 1:24 | and wild **a**, each according to its |
| | 7:16 | The **a** going in were male |
| | 2:19 | formed out of the ground all the wild **a** |
| Lev | 11:46 | are the regulations concerning **a**, |
| Dt | 14: 4 | These are the **a** you may eat: |
| Job | 12: 7 | "But ask the **a**, and they will teach |
| Ps | 36: 6 | You, LORD, preserve both people and **a**. |
| Ecc | 3:19 | human beings is like that of the **a**; |
| | 3:19 | humans have no advantage over **a**. |
| Isa | 43:20 | The wild **a** honor me, the jackals |
| Eze | 34:28 | nor will wild **a** devour them. |
| Jnh | 3: 8 | people and **a** be covered with sackcloth. |
| Hab | 2:17 | destruction of **a** will terrify you. |
| Mal | 1: 8 | you offer blind **a** for sacrifice, |
| | 1: 8 | you sacrifice lame or diseased **a**, |
| Mk | 1:13 | He was with the wild **a**, and angels |
| Ac | 11: 6 | and saw four-footed **a** of the earth, |
| | 15:20 | from the meat of strangled **a** |
| 2Pe | 2:12 | like unreasoning **a**, |

## ANNA*

Female prophet who spoke about the child Jesus (Lk 2:36–38).

## ANNALS

**BOOK OF THE ANNALS** 1Ki 11:41; 14:19, 29; 15:7, 23, 31; 16:5, 14, 20, 27; 22:39, 45; 2Ki 1:18; 8:23; 10:34; 12:19; 13:8, 12; 14:15, 18, 28; 15:6, 11, 15, 21, 26, 31, 36; 16:19; 20:20; 21:17, 25; 23:28; 24:5; 1Ch 27:24; Ne 12:23; Est 2:23; 10:2

## ANNAS

High priest A.D. 6–15 (Lk 3:2; Jn 18:13,24; Ac 4:6).

## ANNIHILATE

| | | |
|---|---|---|
| Dt | 9: 3 | drive them out and **a** them quickly, |
| Est | 3:13 | to destroy, kill and **a** all the Jews— |
| | 8:11 | **a** the armed men of any nationality |
| Da | 11:44 | a great rage to destroy and **a** many. |

## ANNOUNCE [ANNOUNCED]

| | | |
|---|---|---|
| Mt | 6: 2 | the needy, do not **a** it with trumpets, |

## ANNOUNCED [ANNOUNCE]

| | | |
|---|---|---|
| Ps | 68:11 | The Lord **a** the word, and great was |
| Isa | 48: 5 | before they happened I **a** them |
| Gal | 3: 8 | faith, and **a** the gospel in advance |
| Heb | 2: 3 | which was first **a** by the Lord, |
| Rev | 10: 7 | just as he **a** to his servants |

## ANNOYANCE*

| | | |
|---|---|---|
| Pr | 12:16 | Fools show their **a** at once, |

## ANNUAL*

| | | |
|---|---|---|
| Ex | 30:10 | This **a** atonement must be made |
| Jdg | 21:19 | there is the **a** festival of the LORD |
| 1Sa | 1:21 | offer the **a** sacrifice to the LORD |
| | 2:19 | her husband to offer the **a** sacrifice. |
| | 20: 6 | because an **a** sacrifice is being made |
| 2Ch | 8:13 | Moons and the three **a** festivals— |
| Heb | 10: 3 | those sacrifices are an **a** reminder |

## ANOINT [ANOINTED, ANOINTING]

| | | |
|---|---|---|
| Ex | 30:26 | Then use it to **a** the tent of meeting, |
| | 30:30 | "**A** Aaron and his sons |
| Jdg | 9:15 | really want to **a** me king over you, |
| 1Sa | 9:16 | **A** him ruler over my people Israel; |
| | 15: 1 | to **a** you king over his people Israel; |
| 1Ki | 1:34 | Nathan the prophet **a** him king over |
| | 19:16 | **a** Jehu son of Nimshi king over Israel, |
| | | and **a** Elisha |
| 2Ki | 9: 3 | I **a** you king over Israel.' |
| Ps | 23: 5 | You **a** my head with oil; |
| Ecc | 9: 8 | and always **a** your head with oil. |
| Da | 9:24 | and to **a** the Most Holy Place. |
| Mk | 16: 1 | that they might go to **a** Jesus' body. |
| Jas | 5:14 | **a** them with oil in the name |

## ANOINTED [ANOINT]

| | | |
|---|---|---|
| Ge | 31:13 | where you **a** a pillar and where you |
| Lev | 7:36 | On the day they were **a**, the LORD |
| 1Sa | 2:10 | king and exalt the horn of his **a**." |
| | 10: 1 | not the LORD **a** you ruler over his |
| | 16:13 | oil and **a** him in the presence of his |
| | 24: 6 | the LORD's **a**, or lay my hand on him; |
| | 24: 6 | for he is the **a** of the LORD." |
| 2Sa | 1:14 | hand to destroy the LORD's **a**?" |
| | 2: 4 | there they **a** David king over |
| | 5: 3 | and they **a** David king over Israel. |
| | 19:21 | He cursed the LORD's **a**." |
| 1Ki | 1:39 | from the sacred tent and **a** Solomon. |
| 1Ch | 16:22 | "Do not touch my **a** ones; |
| 2Ch | 6:42 | God, do not reject your **a** one. |
| Ps | 2: 2 | the LORD and against his **a**, |
| | 105:15 | "Do not touch my **a** ones; |
| Isa | 61: 1 | because the LORD has **a** me |
| Da | 9:26 | the **A** One will be put to death |
| Hab | 3:13 | your people, to save your **a** one. |
| Zec | 4:14 | "These are the two who are **a** |
| Lk | 4:18 | because he has **a** me to proclaim |
| Ac | 4:26 | the Lord and against his **a** one.' |
| | 10:38 | how God **a** Jesus of Nazareth |
| 2Co | 1:21 | you stand firm in Christ. He **a** us, |

## ANOINTED ONE 1Sa 2:35; 2Ch 6:42; Ps 28:8; 84:9; 89:38, 51; 132:10, 17; Da 9:25, 26; Hab 3:13; Ac 4:26

## ANOINTING [ANOINT]

| | | |
|---|---|---|
| Ex | 30:25 | Make these into a sacred **a** oil, |
| | 30:25 | It will be the sacred **a** oil. |
| Lev | 8:12 | He poured some of the **a** oil |
| 1Ch | 29:22 | **a** him before the LORD to be ruler |
| Ps | 45: 7 | your companions by **a** you |
| Heb | 1: 9 | your companions by **a** you |
| 1Jn | 2:20 | you have an **a** from the Holy One, |
| | 2:27 | the **a** you received from him |
| | 2:27 | as his **a** teaches you about all things and as that **a** is real, |

## ANOINTING OIL See OIL

## ANOTHER

| | | |
|---|---|---|
| Lev | 19:11 | " 'Do not deceive one **a**. |
| Pr | 27:17 | iron, so one person sharpens **a**. |
| Ecc | 4: 4 | spring from one person's envy of **a**. |
| Isa | 48:11 | I will not yield my glory to **a**. |
| Lk | 19:44 | They will not leave one stone on **a**, |
| Jn | 13:34 | command I give you: Love one **a**. |
| | 13:34 | loved you, so you must love one **a**. |
| Ro | 12:10 | Be devoted to one **a** in love. Honor one **a** above yourselves. |
| 1Co | 16:20 | Greet one **a** with a holy kiss. |
| Col | 3:16 | admonish one **a** with all wisdom |
| 1Th | 4:18 | encourage one **a** with these words. |
| Heb | 3:13 | But encourage one **a** daily, as long |
| | 13: 1 | Keep on loving one **a** as brothers |
| 1Pe | 3: 8 | love one **a**, |
| 1Jn | 3:16 | lay down our lives for one **a**. |
| | 3:23 | to love one **a** as he commanded us. |
| | 4:21 | God must also love one **a**. |

## ONE ANOTHER See ONE

## ANSWER [ANSWERED, ANSWERS]

| | | |
|---|---|---|
| 1Ki | 18:26 | "Baal, **a** us!" they shouted. |
| | 18:37 | **A** me, LORD, **a** me, so these |
| Job | 30:20 | out to you, God, but you do not **a**; |
| | 40: 2 | Let him who accuses God **a** him!" |
| Ps | 38:15 | you will **a**, Lord my God. |
| Pr | 15: 1 | A gentle **a** turns away wrath, |
| | 16: 1 | LORD comes the proper **a** of the tongue. |
| | 18:13 | To **a** before listening— |
| | 24:26 | An honest **a** is like a kiss |
| | 26: 5 | **A** fools according to their folly, |
| Ecc | 10:19 | and money is the **a** for everything. |
| Lk | 23: 9 | questions, but Jesus gave him no **a**. |
| 1Pe | 3:15 | give an **a** to everyone who asks you |

## ANSWERED [ANSWER]

| | | |
|---|---|---|
| Ge | 25:21 | The LORD **a** his prayer, and his |
| 1Ch | 21:26 | the LORD **a** him with fire |
| Ps | 118:21 | will give you thanks, for you **a** me; |

## ANSWERS [ANSWER]

| | | |
|---|---|---|
| 1Ki | 18:24 | The god who **a** by fire—he is God." |

## ANT* [ANTS]

| | | |
|---|---|---|
| Pr | 6: 6 | Go to the **a**, you sluggard; |

## ANTICHRIST* [ANTICHRISTS]

| | | |
|---|---|---|
| 1Jn | 2:18 | you have heard that the **a** is coming, |
| | 2:22 | Such a person is the **a**— |
| | 4: 3 | This is the spirit of the **a**, which you |

| | | |
|---|---|---|
| 2Jn | 1: 7 | person is the deceiver and the **a**. |

## ANTICHRISTS* [ANTICHRIST]

| | | |
|---|---|---|
| 1Jn | 2:18 | even now many **a** have come. |

## ANTIOCH

| | | |
|---|---|---|
| Ac | 11:26 | he found him, he brought him to **A**. |
| | 11:26 | were called Christians first at **A**. |
| | 13: 1 | the church at **A** there were prophets |
| Gal | 2:11 | When Cephas came to **A**, I opposed |

## ANTIPAS* [HEROD]

| | | |
|---|---|---|
| Rev | 2:13 | in me, not even in the days of **A**, |

## ANTS* [ANT]

| | | |
|---|---|---|
| Pr | 30:25 | **A** are creatures of little strength, |

## ANXIETIES* [ANXIOUS]

| | | |
|---|---|---|
| Lk | 21:34 | drunkenness and the **a** of life, |

## ANXIETY [ANXIOUS]

| | | |
|---|---|---|
| Pr | 12:25 | **A** weighs down the heart, |
| Ecc | 11:10 | banish **a** from your heart and cast |
| 1Pe | 5: 7 | Cast all your **a** on him because he |

## ANXIOUS [ANXIETIES, ANXIETY]

| | | |
|---|---|---|
| Php | 4: 6 | Do not be **a** about anything, |

## ANYTHING

| | | |
|---|---|---|
| Ge | 18:14 | Is **a** too hard for the LORD? |
| Pr | 14:15 | The simple believe **a**, |
| Jer | 32:27 | Is **a** too hard for me? |
| Mk | 2:12 | "We have never seen **a** like this!" |
| 1Jn | 2:15 | not love the world or **a** in the world. |
| | 3:22 | and receive from him **a** we ask, |

## APART [PART]

| | | |
|---|---|---|
| Lev | 20:26 | I have set you **a** from the nations |
| Isa | 45:21 | And there is no God **a** from me, |
| Jn | 15: 5 | **a** from me you can do nothing. |
| Ro | 1: 1 | and set **a** for the gospel of God— |
| | 3:21 | But now **a** from the law |
| Gal | 1:15 | who set me **a** from birth and called |

## APOLLOS

Christian from Alexandria, learned in the Scriptures; instructed by Aquila and Priscilla (Ac 18:24–28). Ministered at Corinth (Ac 19:1; 1Co 1:12; 3; Tit 3:13).

## APOLLYON*

| | | |
|---|---|---|
| Rev | 9:11 | Abaddon and in Greek is **A** (that is, |

## APOSTLE [APOSTLES, APOSTLES', APOSTLESHIP, SUPER-APOSTLES]

| | | |
|---|---|---|
| Ro | 1: 1 | called to be an **a** and set apart |
| | 11:13 | Inasmuch as I am the **a** |
| 1Co | 1: 1 | called to be an **a** of Christ Jesus |
| | 9: 1 | Am I not an **a**? Have I not seen |
| | 15: 9 | not even deserve to be called an **a**, |
| 2Co | 12:12 | among you the marks of a true **a**, |
| Gal | 2: 8 | at work in Peter as an **a** to the Jews, |
| | 2: 8 | work in me as an **a** to the Gentiles. |

1Ti 1: 1 Paul, an **a** of Christ Jesus
2: 7 I was appointed a herald and an **a**—
2Ti 1:11 a herald and an **a** and a teacher.
Heb 3: 1 whom we acknowledge as our **a**
1Pe 1: 1 Peter, an **a** of Jesus Christ,

## APOSTLES [APOSTLE]

See also Andrew, Bartholomew, James, John, Judas, Matthew, Matthias, Nathanael, Paul, Peter, Philip, Simon, Thaddaeus, Thomas.
Mt 10: 2 are the names of the twelve **a**:
Lk 6:13 them, whom he also designated **a**:
11:49 'I will send them prophets and **a**,
Ac 1:26 so he was added to the eleven **a**.
2:43 and signs performed by the **a**.
5:18 They arrested the **a** and put them
8: 1 and all except the **a** were scattered
14:14 when the **a** Barnabas and Paul heard
Ro 16: 7 They are outstanding among the **a**,
1Co 12:28 placed in the church first of all **a**,
15: 9 For I am the least of the **a** and do
2Co 11:13 For such persons are false **a**,
11:13 masquerading as **a** of Christ.
Eph 2:20 built on the foundation of the **a**
4:11 So Christ himself gave the **a**,
Rev 2: 2 have tested those who claim to be **a**
21:14 names of the twelve **a** of the Lamb.

## APOSTLES' [APOSTLE]

Ac 2:42 themselves to the **a'** teaching
4:35 and put it at the **a'** feet, and it was
8:18 at the laying on of the **a'** hands,

## APOSTLESHIP* [APOSTLE]

Ro 1: 5 and **a** to call all the Gentiles to faith
1Co 9: 2 you are the seal of my **a** in the Lord.

## APPALLED

Isa 52:14 Just as there were many who were **a**
Da 8:27 I was **a** by the vision; it was beyond

## APPEAL

Ac 25:11 me over to them. I **a** to Caesar!"
2Co 5:20 God were making his **a** through us.
Phm 1: 9 yet I prefer to **a** to you on the basis
1Pe 5: 1 I **a** as a fellow elder and a witness

## APPEAR [APPEARANCE, APPEARANCES, APPEARED, APPEARING, APPEARS]

Ge 1: 9 to one place, and let dry ground **a**."
Ex 23:15 is to **a** before me empty-handed.
Lev 16: 2 For I will **a** in the cloud over
Mt 24:30 of the Son of Man will **a** in the sky,
Mk 13:22 false prophets will **a** and perform
Lk 19:11 of God was going to **a** at once.
2Co 5:10 we must all **a** before the judgment
Col 3: 4 you also will **a** with him in glory.
Heb 9:24 now to **a** for us in God's presence.
9:28 and he will **a** a second time,

## APPEARANCE [APPEAR]

1Sa 16: 7 "Do not consider his **a** or his
16: 7 People look at the outward **a**,
2Sa 14:25 for his handsome **a** as Absalom.

Isa 52:14 his **a** was so disfigured beyond
53: 2 in his **a** that we should desire him.
Eze 1:28 Like the **a** of a rainbow
1:28 This was the **a** of the likeness
Mt 28: 3 His **a** was like lightning, and his
Php 2: 8 being found in **a** as a human being,
Rev 4: 3 had the **a** of jasper and ruby.

## APPEARANCES* [APPEAR]

Jn 7:24 Stop judging by mere **a**, but instead
2Co 10: 7 You are judging by **a**.

## APPEARED [APPEAR]

Ge 12: 7 The LORD **a** to Abram and said,
12: 7 to the LORD, who had **a** to him.
26: 2 The LORD **a** to Isaac and said,
35: 9 God **a** to him again and blessed
Ex 3: 2 the angel of the LORD **a** to him
Nu 14:10 the glory of the LORD **a** at the tent
Jdg 6:12 angel of the LORD **a** to Gideon,
13: 3 The angel of the LORD **a** to her
1Ki 3: 5 Gibeon the LORD **a** to Solomon
Mt 1:20 an angel of the Lord **a** to him
Mk 1: 4 John the Baptist **a** in the wilderness,
9: 4 And there **a** before them Elijah
Lk 2: 9 An angel of the Lord **a** to them,
24:34 Lord has risen and has **a** to Simon."
Jn 21:14 This was now the third time Jesus **a**
Ac 1: 3 He **a** to them over a period of forty
12: 7 Suddenly an angel of the Lord **a**
1Co 15: 5 and that he **a** to Cephas,
Tit 2:11 of God has **a** that offers salvation
Heb 9:26 But he has **a** once for all
1Jn 3: 8 The reason the Son of God **a** was

## APPEARING [APPEAR]

1Ti 6:14 blame until the **a** of our Lord Jesus
2Ti 1:10 now been revealed through the **a**
4: 8 to all who have longed for his **a**.
Tit 2:13 the **a** of the glory of our great God

## APPEARS [APPEAR]

Pr 14:12 a way that **a** to be right,
16:25 There is a way that **a** to be right,
SS 6:10 Who is this that **a** like the dawn,
Mal 3: 2 Who can stand when he **a**?
Col 3: 4 who is your life, **a**, then you
Jas 4:14 You are a mist that **a** for a little
1Pe 5: 4 And when the Chief Shepherd **a**,
1Jn 2:28 that when he **a** we may be confident
3: 2 But we know that when Christ **a**,

## APPETITE

Pr 13: 2 the unfaithful have an **a** for violence.
16:26 The **a** of laborers works for them;
Ecc 6: 7 mouth, yet the **a** is never satisfied.
Jer 50:19 their **a** will be satisfied on the hills

## APPLE [APPLES]

Dt 32:10 he guarded him as the **a** of his eye,
Ps 17: 8 Keep me as the **a** of your eye;
Zec 2: 8 whoever touches you touches the **a**

## APPLES* [APPLE]

Pr 25:11 Like **a** of gold in settings of silver is

SS    2: 5   refresh me with **a**, for I am faint
       7: 8   the fragrance of your breath like **a**,

## APPLICATION* [APPLY]
Heb 11:28   kept the Passover and the **a** of blood,

## APPLIED [APPLY]
Ecc   1:13   I **a** my mind to study
       1:17   I **a** myself to the understanding
1Co   4: 6   I have **a** these things to myself

## APPLY [APPLICATION, APPLIED, APPLYING]
Pr    22:17   **a** your heart to what I teach,
       23:12   A your heart to instruction and your

## APPLYING [APPLY]
Pr     2: 2   and **a** your heart to understanding—

## APPOINT [APPOINTED]
Nu    3:10   A Aaron and his sons to serve as
Dt    17:15   to **a** over you the king the LORD
1Sa    8: 5   now **a** a king to lead us, such as all
Ps    61: 7   **a** your love and faithfulness
1Th    5: 9   For God did not **a** us to suffer wrath
Tit    1: 5   and **a** elders in every town, as I
Rev   11: 3   I will **a** my two witnesses,

## APPOINTED [APPOINT]
Lev   23: 2   'These are my **a** festivals, the **a**
Dt     1:15   **a** them to have authority over you—
1Ki    1:35   I have **a** him ruler over Israel
Ezr    1: 2   he has **a** me to build a temple
Da    11:27   an end will still come at the **a** time.
Mic    6: 9   the rod and the One who **a** it.
Hab    2: 3   For the revelation awaits an **a** time;
Mk     3:16   These are the twelve he **a**:
Lk     1:20   will come true at their **a** time."
       10: 1   this the Lord **a** seventy-two others
Jn    15:16   you and **a** you so that you might go
Ac    15: 2   So Paul and Barnabas were **a**,
Ro     9: 9   "At the **a** time I will return,
Heb    1: 2   Son, whom he **a** heir of all things,

## APPOINTED FESTIVALS Lev 23:2, 2, 4, 37,
44; Nu 10:10; 29:39; 1Ch 23:31; 2Ch 2:4; 31:3;
Ezr 3:5; Ne 10:33; Isa 1:14; La 1:4; 2:6; Eze
36:38; 44:24; 45:17; 46:9, 11; Hos 2:11; 9:5;
12:9; Zep 3:18

## APPOINTED TIME Ge 18:14; Ex 13:10;
23:15; 34:18; Nu 9:2, 3, 7, 13; 28:2; Ps 75:2;
102:13; Jer 33:20; Da 8:19; 11:27, 29, 35; Hab
2:3; Mt 8:29; 26:16; Lk 1:20; Ro 9:9; 1Co 4:5

## APPROACH [APPROACHING]
Ex    24: 2   but Moses alone is to **a** the LORD;
Eph    3:12   in him we may **a** God with freedom
Heb    4:16   then **a** God's throne of grace

## APPROACHING [APPROACH]
Heb 10:25   all the more as you see the Day **a**.
1Jn    5:14   is the confidence we have in **a** God:

## APPROPRIATE*
Ge    49:28   giving each the blessing **a** to him.
Ecc    5:18   it is **a** for people to eat, to drink
1Ti    2:10   deeds, **a** for women who profess
Tit    2: 1   teach what is **a** to sound doctrine.

## APPROVAL [APPROVE]
Jdg   18: 6   Your journey has the LORD's **a**."
Jn     6:27   the Father has placed his seal of **a**."
Ro    14:18   pleasing to God and receives human **a**.
1Co  11:19   to show which of you have God's **a**.
Gal    1:10   Am I now trying to win human **a**, or
               God's **a**?

## APPROVE [APPROVAL, APPROVED]
Ro     1:32   also **a** of those who practice them.
       2:18   **a** of what is superior because you
       12: 2   to test and **a** what God's will is—
       14:22   condemn themselves by what they **a**.

## APPROVED* [APPROVE]
Ecc    9: 7   God has already **a** what you do.
Ac     8: 1   And Saul **a** of their killing him.
2Co  10:18   commend themselves who are **a**,
1Th    2: 4   we speak as those **a** by God to be
2Ti    2:15   to present yourself to God as one **a**,

## APT*
Pr    15:23   finds joy in giving an **a** reply—

## AQUILA*
Husband of Priscilla; co-worker with Paul, instructor of Apollos (Ac 18; Ro 16:3; 1Co 16:19; 2Ti 4:19).

## ARABAH
Dt     4:49   included all the **A** east of the Jordan,
Zec   14:10   Jerusalem, will become like the **A**.

## ARABIA [ARABS]
Isa   21:13   A prophecy concerning **A**:
       21:13   who camp in the thickets of **A**,
Gal    1:17   before I was, but I went into **A**.
       4:25   Hagar stands for Mount Sinai in **A**

## ARABS [ARABIA]
Ne     4: 7   the **A**, the Ammonites
Ac     2:11   Cretans and **A**—we hear them

## ARAM [ARAMAIC, ARAMEAN, PADDAN ARAM]
Jdg   10: 6   and the gods of **A**, the gods
2Ki   13: 3   under the power of Hazael king of **A**
2Ch   16: 7   you relied on the king of **A** and not
       16: 7   the king of **A** has escaped from your

## ARAMAIC [ARAM]
2Ki   18:26   "Please speak to your servants in **A**,
Ezr    4: 7   The letter was written in **A** script and in
               the **A** language.
Jn    19:20   and the sign was written in **A**,
Ac    21:40   were all silent, he said to them in **A**:
       26:14   I heard a voice saying to me in **A**,

## ARAMEAN [ARAM]

Ge  31:20  Jacob deceived Laban the A by not
Dt  26: 5  "My father was a wandering A,

## ARARAT

Ge   8: 4  came to rest on the mountains of A.

## ARAUNAH

2Sa 24:16  the threshing floor of A the Jebusite.
1Ch 21:25  So David paid A six hundred
2Ch  3: 1  the threshing floor of A the Jebusite,

## ARBITER* [ARBITRATE]

Lk  12:14  me a judge or an a between you?"

## ARBITRATE* [ARBITER]

Job  9:33  were someone to a between us,

## ARCHANGEL* [ANGEL]

1Th  4:16  with the voice of the a
Jude  1: 9  But even the a Michael, when he

## ARCHELAUS*

Mt   2:22  he heard that A was reigning

## ARCHER [ARCHERS]

Ge  21:20  lived in the desert and became an a.
Pr  26:10  Like an a who wounds at random is

## ARCHERS [ARCHER]

Ge  49:23  With bitterness a attacked him;
Job 16:13  his a surround me. Without pity,
Jer  50:29  "Summon a against Babylon,

## ARCHIPPUS*

Co-worker of Paul (Col 4:17; Phm 2).

## ARCHITECT*

Heb 11:10  whose a and builder is God.

## ARENA*

1Co  4: 9  those condemned to die in the a.

## AREOPAGUS*

Ac  17:19  brought him to a meeting of the A,
     17:22  stood up in the meeting of the A
     17:34  a member of the A, also a woman

## ARGUE [ARGUING, ARGUMENT, ARGUMENTS]

Job 13: 3  and to a my case with God.
    13: 8  Will you a the case for God?
Isa 43:26  for me, let us a the matter together;
Ac   6: 9  who began to a with Stephen.

## ARGUING [ARGUE]

Ac  19: 8  a persuasively about the kingdom
Php  2:14  everything without grumbling or a,

## ARGUMENT [ARGUE]

Lk   9:46  An a started among the disciples as
Heb  6:16  what is said and puts an end to all a.

## ARGUMENTS [ARGUE]

Isa 41:21  "Set forth your a," says Jacob's
2Co 10: 5  We demolish a and every
Col  2: 4  deceive you by fine-sounding a.
2Ti  2:23  to do with foolish and stupid a,
Tit  3: 9  and genealogies and a and quarrels

## ARIMATHEA

Jn  19:38  Joseph of A asked Pilate

## ARISE [RISE]

2Ch  6:41  "Now a, LORD God, and come
Pr  31:28  Her children a and call her blessed;
SS   2:10  beloved spoke and said to me, "A,
Isa 60: 1  "A, shine, for your light has come,
Da  11: 3  Then a mighty king will a,

## ARISTARCHUS*

Companion of Paul (Ac 19:29; 20:4; 27:2; Col 4:10; Phm 1:24).

## ARK

Ge   6:14  So make yourself an a of cypress
Ex  25:10  "Have them make an a of acacia wood
    25:16  Then put in the a the tablets
    37: 1  Bezalel made the a of acacia wood—
Nu  10:35  Whenever the a set out, Moses said,
Dt  10: 2  Then you are to put them in the a."
    10: 5  put the tablets in the a I had made,
Jos  3: 3  you see the a of the covenant
1Sa  4:11  The a of God was captured,
     6: 3  "If you return the a of the god
     7: 2  The a remained at Kiriath Jearim
2Sa  6:17  They brought the a of the LORD
1Ki  8: 9  in the a except the two stone tablets
1Ch 13: 9  reached out his hand to steady the a,
2Ch 35: 3  "Put the sacred a in the temple
Lk  17:27  up to the day Noah entered the a.
Heb  9: 4  the gold-covered a of the covenant.
     9: 4  This a contained the gold jar
    11: 7  in holy fear built an a to save his
Rev 11:19  within his temple was seen the a

**ARK OF GOD** 1Sa 3:3; 4:11, 13, 17, 18, 19, 21, 22; 5:1, 10, 10; 14:18; 2Sa 6:2, 3, 4, 6, 7, 12, 12; 7:2; 15:24, 25, 29; 1Ch 13:5, 6, 7, 12, 14; 15:1, 2, 15, 24; 16:1; 2Ch 1:4

**ARK OF THE COVENANT** Ex 25:22; 26:33, 34; 27:21; 30:6, 26, 36; 31:7; 39:35; 40:3, 5, 21; Lev 24:3; Nu 4:5; 7:89; 10:33; 17:4, 10; Dt 10:8; 31:9, 25, 26; Jos 3:3, 6, 8, 11, 14, 17; 4:7, 9, 16, 18; 6:6; 8:33; Jdg 20:27; 1Sa 4:4, 4; 2Sa 15:24; 1Ki 6:19; 1Ch 15:25, 26, 28, 29; 16:6, 37; 17:1; 22:19; 28:2, 18; Jer 3:16; Heb 9:4

**ARK OF THE †LORD** Jos 3:13; 4:5, 11; 6:7, 11, 12, 13, 13; 7:6; 1Sa 4:6; 5:3, 4; 6:1, 2, 8, 11, 15, 18, 19, 21; 7:1, 1; 2Sa 6:9, 10, 11, 13, 15, 16, 17; 1Ki 8:4; 1Ch 15:2, 3, 12, 14; 16:4; 2Ch 8:11

## ARM [ARMED, ARMIES, ARMOR, ARMOR-BEARER, ARMS, ARMY]

Ex   6: 6  redeem you with an outstretched a
Nu  11:23  "Is the LORD's a too short?

| | | |
|---|---|---|
| Dt | 4:34 | mighty hand and an outstretched **a**, |
| | 7:19 | the mighty hand and outstretched **a**, |
| 1Ki | 8:42 | hand and your outstretched **a**— |
| 2Ch | 32: 8 | With him is only the **a** of flesh, |
| Job | 40: 9 | Do you have an **a** like God's, |
| Ps | 44: 3 | nor did their **a** bring them victory; |
| | 44: 3 | your **a**, and the light of your face, |
| | 98: 1 | his holy **a** have worked salvation |
| SS | 8: 3 | His left **a** is under my head and his |
| | | right **a** embraces me |
| Isa | 40:10 | with power, and his **a** rules for him. |
| Jer | 27: 5 | and outstretched **a** I made the earth |
| 1Pe | 4: 1 | **a** yourselves also with the same |

## ARMAGEDDON*

Rev 16:16  the place that in Hebrew is called **A**.

## ARMED [ARM]

2Sa 22:40  You **a** me with strength for battle;
Mk 14:43  him was a crowd **a** with swords

## ARMIES [ARM]

| | | |
|---|---|---|
| 1Sa | 17:10 | "This day I defy the **a** of Israel! |
| | 17:36 | because he has defied the **a** |
| Lk | 21:20 | Jerusalem being surrounded by **a**, |
| Rev | 19:14 | The **a** of heaven were following |

## ARMOR [ARM]

| | | |
|---|---|---|
| 1Ki | 20:11 | his **a** should not boast like one who |
| | 22:34 | the breastplate and the scale **a**. |
| 1Ch | 10:10 | They put his **a** in the temple of their |
| Ps | 35: 2 | Take up shield and **a**; |
| Jer | 46: 4 | Polish your spears, put on your **a**! |
| Ro | 13:12 | darkness and put on the **a** of light. |
| Eph | 6:11 | Put on the full **a** of God, so that you |
| | 6:13 | Therefore put on the full **a** of God, |

## ARMOR-BEARER [ARM]

| | | |
|---|---|---|
| 1Sa | 14: 6 | Jonathan said to his young **a**, |
| | 31: 4 | Saul said to his **a**, "Draw your sword |
| | 31: 4 | But his **a** was terrified and would |

## ARMS [ARM]

| | | |
|---|---|---|
| Ge | 16: 5 | I put my servant in your **a**, and now |
| Dt | 33:27 | underneath are the everlasting **a**. |
| Jdg | 16:12 | he snapped the ropes off his **a** as |
| Ps | 18:32 | It is God who **a** me with strength |
| Pr | 31:17 | her **a** are strong for her tasks. |
| | 31:20 | She opens her **a** to the poor |
| SS | 5:14 | His **a** are rods of gold set |
| Isa | 40:11 | He gathers the lambs in his **a** |
| Mk | 10:16 | And he took the children in his **a**, |
| Heb | 12:12 | strengthen your feeble **a** and weak |

## ARMY [ARM]

| | | |
|---|---|---|
| Ex | 14:17 | glory through Pharaoh and all his **a**, |
| Jos | 5:14 | of the **a** of the LORD I have now |
| Ps | 33:16 | king is saved by the size of his **a**; |
| Eze | 37:10 | and stood up on their feet—a vast **a**. |
| Joel | 2: 2 | a large and mighty **a** comes, such as |
| | 2: 5 | like a mighty **a** drawn up for battle. |
| | 2:25 | my great **a** that I sent among you. |
| Rev | 19:19 | the rider on the horse and his **a**. |

## ARNON

Nu 21:13  there and camped alongside the **A**,
   21:13  The **A** is the border of Moab,
Jer 48:20  by the **A** that Moab is destroyed.

## AROMA

| | | |
|---|---|---|
| Ge | 8:21 | The LORD smelled the pleasing **a** |
| Ex | 29:18 | a pleasing **a**, a food offering |
| Lev | 1: 9 | an **a** pleasing to the LORD. |
| Nu | 15: 3 | as an **a** pleasing to the LORD— |
| 2Co | 2:14 | spread the **a** of the knowledge of him |
| | 2:15 | God the pleasing **a** of Christ among |
| | 2:16 | we are an **a** that brings death; |

## AROMA PLEASING  See PLEASING

## PLEASING AROMA  See PLEASING

## AROUND

| | | |
|---|---|---|
| Jos | 6: 4 | day, march **a** the city seven times, |
| Ezr | 3: 3 | their fear of the peoples **a** them, |
| | 9: 2 | holy race with the peoples **a** them. |
| Ps | 3: 3 | are a shield **a** me, my glory, the one |
| | 48:12 | Walk about Zion, go **a** her, |
| Zec | 2: 5 | I myself will be a wall of fire **a** it,' |
| Lk | 2: 9 | the glory of the Lord shone **a** them, |
| 1Pe | 5: 8 | the devil prowls **a** like a roaring lion |

## AROUSE [ROUSE]

| | | |
|---|---|---|
| Dt | 31:29 | sight of the LORD and **a** his anger |
| 1Ki | 16:33 | to **a** the anger of the LORD, |
| SS | 2: 7 | Do not **a** or awaken love until it so |
| Jer | 25: 6 | do not **a** my anger |
| Eze | 8:17 | violence and continually **a** my anger? |
| Ro | 11:14 | I may somehow **a** my own people |
| 1Co | 10:22 | we trying to **a** the Lord's jealousy? |

## AROUSED [ROUSE]

| | | |
|---|---|---|
| Ex | 22:24 | My anger will be **a**, and I will kill |
| Nu | 11: 1 | he heard them his anger was **a**. |
| Dt | 9: 7 | never forget how you **a** the anger |
| Jdg | 2:12 | They **a** the LORD's anger |
| 2Ki | 17:11 | wicked things that **a** the LORD's anger. |
| Ps | 78:58 | they **a** his jealousy with their idols. |
| Jer | 8:19 | "Why have they **a** my anger |
| Hos | 11: 8 | all my compassion is **a**. |
| Ro | 7: 5 | the sinful passions **a** by the law |

## ARRAYED*

Ps 110: 3  **A** in holy splendor, your young men
Isa 61:10  **a** me in a robe of his righteousness,

## ARREST [ARRESTED]

Mt 10:19  But when they **a** you, do not worry
Mk 14: 1  looking for some sly way to **a** Jesus

## ARRESTED [ARREST]

| | | |
|---|---|---|
| Mt | 14: 3 | Now Herod had **a** John and bound |
| | 26:50 | forward, seized Jesus and **a** him. |
| Ac | 5:18 | They **a** the apostles and put them |
| | 12: 1 | King Herod **a** some who belonged |
| | 28:17 | I was **a** in Jerusalem and handed |

## ARROGANCE [ARROGANT, ARROGANTLY]

1Sa 2: 3 or let your mouth speak such **a**,
15:23 and **a** like the evil of idolatry.
Pr 8:13 I hate pride and **a**, evil behavior
Jer 48:29 her pride and **a** and the haughtiness
Hos 7:10 Israel's **a** testifies against him,
Mk 7:22 lewdness, envy, slander, **a** and folly.
2Co 12:20 slander, gossip, **a** and disorder.

## ARROGANT [ARROGANCE]

Ne 9:16 became **a** and stiff-necked, and did
Ps 5: 5 The **a** cannot stand in your
73: 3 For I envied the **a** when I saw
119:78 May the **a** be put to shame
Pr 21:24 The proud and **a**—
Hab 2: 5 he is **a** and never at rest.
Mal 3:15 But now we call the **a** blessed.
Ro 1:30 God-haters, insolent, **a** and boastful;
11:20 Do not be **a**, but tremble.
1Co 4:18 Some of you have become **a**, as if I
1Ti 6:17 this present world not to be **a** nor
2Pe 2:10 Bold and **a**, they are not afraid

## ARROGANTLY [ARROGANCE]

Mal 3:13 "You have spoken **a** against me,"

## ARROW [ARROWS]

1Sa 20:36 boy ran, he shot an **a** beyond him.
Ps 91: 5 of night, nor the **a** that flies by day,
Pr 25:18 or a sharp **a** is one who gives false
Jer 9: 8 Their tongue is a deadly **a**;

## ARROWS [ARROW]

Dt 32:42 I will make my **a** drunk with blood,
2Ki 13:15 "Get a bow and some **a**," and he
Job 6: 4 The **a** of the Almighty are in me,
Ps 38: 2 Your **a** have pierced me, and your
64: 3 and aim cruel words like deadly **a**.
64: 7 But God will shoot them with his **a**;
127: 4 Like **a** in the hands of a warrior are
Pr 26:18 Like a maniac shooting flaming **a**
La 3:13 He pierced my heart with **a** from his
Eph 6:16 you can extinguish all the flaming **a**

## ARTAXERXES

King of Persia; allowed rebuilding of temple under Ezra (Ezr 4; 7), and of walls of Jerusalem under his cupbearer Nehemiah (Ne 2; 5:14; 13:6).

## ARTEMIS

Ac 19:27 of the great goddess **A** will be

## ARTS

Ex 7:11 the same things by their secret **a**:
8:18 to produce gnats by their secret **a**,
Rev 21: 8 those who practice magic **a**,
22:15 those who practice magic **a**,

## ASA

King of Judah (1Ki 15:8–24; 1Ch 3:10; 2Ch 14–16). Godly reformer (2Ch 15); in later years defeated Israel with help of Aram, not the LORD (1Ki 15:16–22; 2Ch 16).

## ASAHEL

1. Nephew of David, one of his warriors (2Sa 23:24; 1Ch 2:16; 11:26; 27:7). Killed by Abner (2Sa 2); avenged by Joab (2Sa 3:22–39).
2. Levite; teacher (2Ch 17:8).

## ASAPH

1. Recorder to Hezekiah (2Ki 18:18, 37; Isa 36:3, 22).
2. Levitical musician (1Ch 6:39; 15:17–19; 16:4–7, 37). Sons of (1Ch 25; 2Ch 5:12; 20:14; 29:13; 35:15; Ezr 2:41; 3:10; Ne 7:44; 11:17; 12:27–47). Psalms of (2Ch 29:30; Ps 50; 73–83).

## ASCEND* [ASCENDED, ASCENDING, ASCENTS]

Dt 30:12 "Who will **a** into heaven to get it
Ps 24: 3 Who may **a** the mountain
Isa 14:13 in your heart, "I will **a** to heaven;
14:14 I will **a** above the tops of the clouds;
Jn 6:62 of Man **a** to where he was before!
Ac 2:34 For David did not **a** to heaven,
Ro 10: 6 heart, 'Who will **a** into heaven?' "

## ASCENDED [ASCEND]

Ps 47: 5 God has **a** amid shouts of joy,
68:18 When you **a** on high, you took
Isa 37:24 many chariots I have **a** the heights
Eph 4: 8 "When he **a** on high, he took many
Heb 4:14 a great high priest who has **a** into heaven,

## ASCENDING* [ASCEND]

Ge 28:12 and the angels of God were **a**
Eze 41: 7 the temple was built in a stages,
Jn 1:51 the angels of God **a** and descending
20:17 'I am **a** to my Father and your Father,

## ASCENTS* [ASCEND]

Songs of ascents (Ps 120–134).

## ASCRIBE*

1Ch 16:28 **A** to the LORD, all you families
16:28 **a** to the LORD glory and strength.
16:29 **A** to the LORD the glory due his
Job 36: 3 I will **a** justice to my Maker.
Ps 29: 1 **A** to the LORD, you heavenly beings, **a** to the LORD glory
29: 2 **A** to the LORD the glory due his
96: 7 **A** to the LORD, all you families
96: 7 **a** to the LORD glory and strength.
96: 8 **A** to the LORD the glory due his

## ASH [ASHES]

1Sa 2: 8 and lifts the needy from the **a** heap;
La 4: 5 in purple now lie on **a** heaps.

## ASHAMED [SHAME]

Isa 29:22 "No longer will Jacob be **a**;
Jer 48:13 Then Moab will be **a** of Chemosh,
48:13 of Israel was **a** when they trusted
Eze 43:10 that they may be **a** of their sins.
Mk 8:38 If any of you are **a** of me and my
8:38 the Son of Man will be **a** of you

Ro    1:16  I am not **a** of the gospel, because it
      6:21  from the things you are now **a** of?
Php   1:20  and hope that I will in no way be **a**,
2Ti   1: 8  So do not be **a** of the testimony
      2:15  a worker who does not need to be **a**
Tit   2: 8  you may be **a** because they have
Heb   2:11  So Jesus is not **a** to call them
      11:16  Therefore God is not **a** to be called

## ASHDOD

Jos   13: 3  the five Philistine rulers in Gaza, **A**,
1Sa   5: 1  they took it from Ebenezer to **A**.
Ne    13:23  who had married women from **A**,

## ASHER

Son of Jacob by Zilpah (Ge 30:13; 35:26; 46:17;
Ex 1:4; 1Ch 2:2). Tribe of blessed (Ge 49:20; Dt
33:24–25), numbered (Nu 1:40–41; 26:44–47), allotted land (Jos 10:24–31; Eze 48:2), failed to fully possess (Jdg 1:31–32), failed to support Deborah (Jdg
5:17), supported Gideon (Jdg 6:35; 7:23) and David
(1Ch 12:36), 12,000 from (Rev 7:6).

## ASHERAH  [ASHERAHS]

Ex    34:13  stones and cut down their **A** poles.
Jdg   6:25  and cut down the **A** pole beside it.
1Ki   14:15  LORD's anger by making **A** poles.
      18.19  and the four hundred prophets of **A**,
2Ch   34: 4  smashed the **A** poles and the idols.

## ASHERAHS*  [ASHERAH]

Jdg   3: 7  God and served the Baals and the **A**.

## ASHES  [ASH]

Ge    18:27  though I am nothing but dust and **a**,
Est   4: 1  put on sackcloth and **a**, and went
Job   42: 6  myself and repent in dust and **a**."
Ps    102: 9  For I eat **a** as my food and mingle
Isa   61: 3  them a crown of beauty instead of **a**,
Mt    11:21  long ago in sackcloth and **a**.

## ASHKELON

Jdg   1:18  also took Gaza, **A** and Ekron—
2Sa   1:20  proclaim it not in the streets of **A**,

## ASHTORETH  [ASHTORETHS]

1Ki   11: 5  He followed **A** the goddess

## ASHTORETHS  [ASHTORETH]

Jdg   2:13  him and served Baal and the **A**.
1Sa   7: 4  put away their Baals and **A**,

## ASIA

Ac    2: 9  and Cappadocia, Pontus and **A**,
      16: 6  the word in the province of **A**.
Rev   1: 4  seven churches in the province of **A**:

## ASK  [ASKED, ASKS]

Ex    12:26  And when your children **a** you,
Dt    32: 7  **A** your father and he will tell you,
Ps    27: 4  One thing I **a** from the LORD,
Pr    30: 7  "Two things I **a** of you, LORD;
Isa   7:11  "**A** the LORD your God for a sign,
      65: 1  to those who did not **a** for me;

Mal   1: 2  "But you **a**, 'How have you loved
Mt    6: 8  what you need before you **a** him.
      7: 7  "**A** and it will be given to you;
Mk    11:24  you, whatever you **a** for in prayer,
Lk    11:13  Holy Spirit to those who **a** him!"
Jn    14:14  You may **a** me for anything in my
Eph   3:20  do immeasurably more than all we **a**
Jas   4: 3  When you **a**, you do not receive,
      4: 3  because you **a** with wrong motives,
1Jn   3:22  receive from him anything we **a**,

## ASKED  [ASK]

Ps    106:15  So he gave them what they **a** for,
Lk    22:31  Satan has **a** to sift all of you as
Jn    16:24  Until now you have not **a**

## ASKS  [ASK]

Lk    6:30  Give to everyone who **a** you,
      11:10  For everyone who **a** receives;
      11:29  It **a** for a sign, but none will be

## ASLEEP  [SLEEP]

Mk    5:39  The child is not dead but **a**."
      14:37  he said to Peter, "are you **a**?
Jn    11:11  "Our friend Lazarus has fallen **a**;
1Co   15:18  who have fallen **a** in Christ are lost.

## ASPIRES*

1Ti   3: 1  Whoever **a** to be an overseer

## ASSASSINATE  [ASSASSINATED]

Est   6: 2  had conspired to **a** King Xerxes.

## ASSASSINATED  [ASSASSINATE]

2Ki   21:23  him and **a** the king in his palace.
      25:25  came with ten men and **a** Gedaliah

## ASSEMBLE  [ASSEMBLED, ASSEMBLY]

Ps    102:22  and the kingdoms **a** to worship
Zep   3: 8  I have decided to **a** the nations,

## ASSEMBLED  [ASSEMBLE]

Ne    8: 1  all the people **a** with one accord
Est   9:16  also **a** to protect themselves and get
1Co   5: 4  So when you are **a** and I am

## ASSEMBLY  [ASSEMBLE]

Nu    14:10  the whole **a** talked about stoning
      16:21  from this **a** so I can put an end
Dt    23: 1  or cutting may enter the **a**
2Ch   29:28  The whole **a** bowed in worship,
Ps    1: 5  nor sinners in the **a** of the righteous.
      22:22  in the **a** I will praise you.
      35:18  I will give you thanks in the great **a**;
      82: 1  God presides in the great **a**;
      149: 1  praise in the **a** of his faithful people.
Joel  1:14  Declare a holy fast; call a sacred **a**.
Heb   2:12  in the **a** I will sing your praises."
      12:22  thousands of angels in joyful **a**,

## ASSERTED

1Th   2: 6  we could have **a** our prerogatives.

# ASSIGNED

1Ki  7:14  and did all the work **a** to him.
Ps  16: 5  you have **a** me my portion and my
Isa  53: 9  He was **a** a grave with the wicked,
Mk  13:34  each with an **a** task, and tells
1Co  3: 5  as the Lord has **a** to each his task.
     7:17  whatever situation the Lord has **a**
2Co 10:13  of service God himself has **a** to us,

# ASSIST

Nu  8:26  They may **a** their brothers
Ro  15:24  have you **a** me on my journey there,

# ASSOCIATE

Jos  23: 7  Do not **a** with these nations
Ps  26: 4  nor do I **a** with hypocrites.
Pr  22:24  do not **a** with those who are easily
Jn  4: 9  Jews do not **a** with Samaritans.)
Ac  10:28  our law for a Jew to **a** with Gentiles
Ro  12:16  be willing to **a** with people of low
1Co  5: 9  in my letter not to **a** with sexually
     5:11  you must not **a** with any who claim
2Th  3:14  Do not **a** with them, in order

# ASSURANCE  [ASSURED]

Job  24:22  established, they have no **a** of life.
1Ti  3:13  great **a** in their faith in Christ Jesus.
Heb 10:22  a sincere heart in full **a** of faith,

# ASSURED  [ASSURANCE]

Jos  2:14  the men **a** her. "If you don't tell
Col  4:12  the will of God, mature and fully **a**.

# ASSYRIA  [ASSYRIANS]

Ge  10:11  From that land he went to **A**,
2Ki  15:29  Tiglath-Pileser king of **A** came
     15:29  and deported the people to **A**.
     18:11  The king of **A** deported Israel to **A**
     19:10  into the hands of the king of **A**.'
Isa  30:31  voice of the LORD will shatter **A**;
Jer  50:18  his land as I punished the king of **A**.
Hos 14: 3  **A** cannot save us; we will not mount

## KING OF ASSYRIA  See KING

# ASSYRIANS  [ASSYRIA]

Isa  10:24  do not be afraid of the **A**, who beat
Eze  23: 5  she lusted after her lovers, the **A**—

# ASTONISHED

Mt  22:33  they were **a** at his teaching.
Ac  4:13  they were **a** and they took note

# ASTRAY  [STRAY]

Nu  5:12  'If a man's wife goes **a** and is
Dt  17:17  wives, or his heart will be led **a**.
1Ki  11: 3  and his wives led him **a**.
2Ki  21: 9  Manasseh led them **a**, so that they
Ps  58: 3  Even from birth the wicked go **a**;
    119:67  Before I was afflicted I went **a**,
Pr  7:21  persuasive words she led him **a**;
    10:17  ignores correction leads others **a**.
    20: 1  whoever is led **a** by them is not
Isa  53: 6  have gone **a**, each of us has turned
Jer  50: 6  their shepherds have led them **a**

Am  2: 4  because they have been led **a**
Gal  2:13  hypocrisy even Barnabas was led **a**.
1Pe  2:25  For "you were like sheep going **a**,"
1Jn  3: 7  do not let anyone lead you **a**.
Rev  12: 9  Satan, who leads the whole world **a**.

# ASTROLOGERS

Isa  47:13  Let your **a** come forward,
Da  2: 2  **a** to tell him what he had dreamed.

# ATE  [EAT]

Ge  3: 6  wisdom, she took some and **a** it.
    3: 6  who was with her, and he **a** it.
    3:13  serpent deceived me, and I **a**."
    27:25  Jacob brought it to him and he **a**;
Ex  16:35  The Israelites **a** manna forty years,
    16:35  they **a** manna until they reached
Nu  25: 2  The people **a** the sacrificial meal
Ru  2:14  She **a** all she wanted and had some
2Sa  9:11  So Mephibosheth **a** at David's table
2Ki  6:29  So we cooked my son and **a** him.
Ezr  10: 6  he **a** no food and drank no water,
Ps  78:25  Human beings **a** the bread
Jer  15:16  When your words came, I **a** them;
Eze  3: 3  So I **a** it, and it tasted as sweet as
Mt  14:20  They all **a** and were satisfied,
    15:37  They all **a** and were satisfied,
Mk  6:42  They all **a** and were satisfied,
Lk  9:17  They all **a** and were satisfied,
Jn  6:58  Your ancestors **a** manna and died,
1Co 10: 3  They all **a** the same spiritual food
Rev  10:10  from the angel's hand and **a** it.

# ATHALIAH

Granddaughter of Omri; wife of Jehoram and mother of Ahaziah; encouraged their evil ways (2Ki 8:18, 27; 2Ch 22:2). At death of Ahaziah she made herself queen, killing all his sons but Joash (2Ki 11:1–3; 2Ch 22:10–12); killed six years later when Joash revealed (2Ki 11:4–16; 2Ch 23:1–15).

# ATHENS

Ac  17:16  Paul was waiting for them in **A**,

# ATHLETE*

2Ti  2: 5  competes as an **a** does not receive

# ATONE*  [ATONEMENT]

Ex  30:15  to the LORD to **a** for your lives.
2Ch 29:24  for a sin offering to **a** for all Israel,
Da  9:24  an end to sin, to **a** for wickedness,

# ATONED*  [ATONEMENT]

Dt  21: 8  And the bloodshed will be **a** for.
1Sa  3:14  of Eli's house will never be **a**
Pr  16: 6  love and faithfulness sin is **a** for;
Isa  6: 7  is taken away and your sin **a** for."
    22:14  day this sin will not be **a** for,"
    27: 9  will Jacob's guilt be **a** for, and this

# ATONEMENT  [ATONE, ATONED]

Ex  25:17  "Make an **a** cover of pure gold—
    29:36  day as a sin offering to make **a**.
    29:36  Purify the altar by making **a** for it,
    30:10  Once a year Aaron shall make **a**

Ex   30:10  This annual **a** must be made
     32:30  perhaps I can make **a** for your sin."
Lev  17:11  you to make **a** for yourselves
     17:11  blood that makes **a** for one's life.
     23:27  this seventh month is the Day of **A**.
Nu   25:13  God and made **a** for the Israelites."
1Ch   6:49  Holy Place, making **a** for Israel,
Ro    3:25  presented Christ as a sacrifice of **a**,
Heb   2:17  that he might make **a** for the sins

## ATTACK [ATTACKED, ATTACKS]

1Sa  17:48  Philistine moved closer to **a** him,
     24: 7  and did not allow them to **a** Saul.
Ps  109: 3  they **a** me without cause.
Isa  54:15  If anyone does **a** you, it will not be
Ac   18:10  no one is going to **a** and harm you,
2Ti   4:18  will rescue me from every evil **a**,
Rev  11: 7  up from the Abyss will **a** them,

## ATTACKED [ATTACK]

Ge    4: 8  Cain **a** his brother Abel and killed
Ex   17: 8  and **a** the Israelites at Rephidim.
Est   8: 7  Jew, "Because Haman **a** the Jews,

## ATTACKS [ATTACK]

Ex   21:15  "Anyone who **a** their father
Lk   11:22  But when someone stronger **a**
Jn   10:12  Then the wolf **a** the flock

## ATTAIN* [ATTAINED, ATTAINING]

Ps  139: 6  for me, too lofty for me to **a**.
Pr    2:19  to her return or **a** the paths of life.
     11:19  Truly the righteous **a** life,

## ATTAINED* [ATTAIN]

Pr   16:31  it is **a** in the way of righteousness.
     30: 3  **a** to the knowledge of the Holy One.
Ro    9:31  righteousness, have not **a** their goal.
Php   3:16  live up to what we have already **a**.
Heb   7:11  could have been **a** through

## ATTAINING* [ATTAIN]

Eph   4:13  mature, **a** to the whole measure
Php   3:11  **a** to the resurrection from the dead.

## ATTENDANTS [ATTENDED]

Ge   24:61  Then Rebekah and her **a** got ready
Est   2: 9  He assigned to her seven female **a**

## ATTENDED [ATTENDANTS]

Da    7:10  Thousands upon thousands **a** him;
Mt    4:11  him, and angels came and **a** him.
Mk    1:13  the wild animals, and angels **a** him.

## ATTENTION [ATTENTIVE]

Ex    4: 8  you or pay **a** to the first sign,
     15:26  if you pay **a** to his commands
     16:20  some of them paid no **a** to Moses;
Dt   28:13  If you pay **a** to the commands
1Ki  18:29  no one answered, no one paid **a**.
Ne    8:13  the teacher to give **a** to the words
Pr    4: 1  pay **a** and gain understanding.
      4:20  My son, pay **a** to what I say;
      5: 1  My son, pay **a** to my wisdom,
     17: 4  a liar pays **a** to a destructive tongue.

Pr   22:17  Pay **a** and turn your ear
Ecc   7:21  Do not pay **a** to every word people
Isa  42:20  many things, but have paid no **a**;
Jer  44: 5  But they did not listen or pay **a**;
Tit   1:14  and will pay no **a** to Jewish myths
Heb   2: 1  We must pay the most careful **a**,
Jas   2: 3  If you show special **a** to the one
2Pe   1:19  and you will do well to pay **a** to it,
3Jn   1:10  I will call **a** to what he is doing,

## ATTENTIVE [ATTENTION]

2Ch   6:40  your ears **a** to the prayers offered
Ne    1:11  let your ear be **a** to the prayer of this
1Pe   3:12  and his ears are **a** to their prayer,

## ATTITUDE [ATTITUDES]

Ge   31: 2  Laban's **a** toward him was not what
1Ki  11:11  "Since this is your **a** and you have
Ezr   6:22  joy by changing the **a** of the king
Da    3:19  and his **a** toward them changed.
Eph   4:23  made new in the **a** of your minds;
Php   2: 5  have the same **a** of mind Christ
1Pe   4: 1  yourselves also with the same **a**,

## ATTITUDES* [ATTITUDE]

Heb   4:12  the thoughts and **a** of the heart.

## ATTRACT* [ATTRACTED, ATTRACTIVE]

Isa  53: 2  no beauty or majesty to **a** us to him,

## ATTRACTED [ATTRACT]

Est   2:17  Now the king was **a** to Esther more

## ATTRACTIVE [ATTRACT]

Tit   2:10  teaching about God our Savior **a**.

## AUDACITY*

Lk   11: 8  because of your shameless **a**

## AUDIENCE

2Ch   9:23  of the earth sought **a** with Solomon
Pr   29:26  Many seek an **a** with a ruler, but it

## AUGUSTUS*

Lk    2: 1  those days Caesar **A** issued a decree

## AUTHOR*

Ac    3:15  You killed the **a** of life, but God

## AUTHORITIES* [AUTHORITY]

Lk   12:11  rulers and **a**, do not worry
Jn    7:26  Have the **a** really concluded that he
Ac   16:19  into the marketplace to face the **a**.
Ro   13: 1  be subject to the governing **a**,
     13: 1  The **a** that exist have been
     13: 1  it is necessary to submit to the **a**,
     13: 6  for the **a** are God's servants,
Eph   3:10  rulers and **a** in the heavenly realms,
      6:12  against the **a**, against the powers
Col   1:16  thrones or powers or rulers or **a**;
      2:15  having disarmed the powers and **a**,
Tit   3: 1  people to be subject to rulers and **a**,
1Pe   3:22  **a** and powers in submission to him.

## AUTHORITY [AUTHORITIES]

| | | |
|---|---|---|
| Jer | 5:31 | the priests rule by their own **a**, |
| Da | 7: 6 | heads, and it was given **a** to rule. |
| Mt | 7:29 | because he taught as one who had **a**, |
| | 9: 6 | the Son of Man has **a** on earth |
| | 28:18 | "All **a** in heaven and on earth has |
| Mk | 1:27 | A new teaching—and with **a**! |
| | 10:42 | high officials exercise **a** over them. |
| | 11:28 | what **a** are you doing these things?" |
| | 11:28 | "And who gave you **a** to do this?" |
| Lk | 4:32 | teaching, because his words had **a**. |
| | 5:24 | the Son of Man has **a** on earth |
| | 7: 8 | For I myself am a man under **a**, |
| Jn | 10:18 | I have **a** to lay it down and **a** to take |
| Ac | 1: 7 | the Father has set by his own **a**. |
| Ro | 7: 1 | the law has **a** over someone only as |
| | 13: 1 | for there is no **a** except |
| | 13: 2 | rebels against the **a** is rebelling |
| 1Co | 7: 4 | wife does not have **a** over her own body |
| | 7: 4 | husband does not have **a** over his own |
| | 11:10 | ought to have **a** over her own head, |
| | 15:24 | all dominion, **a** and power. |
| 2Co | 10: 8 | freely about the **a** the Lord gave us |
| Col | 2:10 | is the head over every power and **a**. |
| 1Ti | 2: 2 | for kings and all those in **a**, that we |
| | 2:12 | to teach or to assume **a** over a man; |
| Tit | 2:15 | Encourage and rebuke with all **a**. |
| Heb | 13:17 | your leaders and submit to their **a**, |
| 1Pe | 2:13 | the Lord's sake to every human **a**: |
| | 2:13 | to the emperor, as the supreme **a**, |
| 2Pe | 2:10 | of the sinful nature and despise **a**. |
| Jude | 1: 6 | did not keep their positions of **a** |
| Rev | 2:27 | just as I have received **a** from my |
| | 12:10 | our God, and the **a** of his Messiah. |
| | 13: 4 | the dragon because he had given **a** |

## AUTUMN*

| | | |
|---|---|---|
| Dt | 11:14 | its season, both **a** and spring rains, |
| Ps | 84: 6 | the **a** rains also cover it with pools. |
| Jer | 5:24 | who gives **a** and spring rains |
| Joel | 2:23 | for he has given you the **a** rains |
| | 2:23 | both **a** and spring rains, |
| Jas | 5: 7 | crop, patiently waiting for the **a** |
| Jude | 1:12 | **a** trees, without fruit and uprooted— |

## AVENGE [VENGEANCE]

| | | |
|---|---|---|
| Lev | 26:25 | on you to **a** the breaking |
| Dt | 32:35 | It is mine to **a**; I will repay. |
| | 32:43 | people, for he will **a** the blood of his |
| 1Sa | 24:12 | may the LORD **a** the wrongs you |
| 2Ki | 9: 7 | I will **a** the blood of my servants |
| Est | 8:13 | on that day to **a** themselves on their |
| Ps | 79:10 | that you **a** the outpoured blood |
| Pr | 20:22 | Wait for the LORD, and he will **a** you. |
| Jer | 5: 9 | "Should I not **a** myself on such |
| Ro | 12:19 | "It is mine to **a**; I will repay," |
| Heb | 10:30 | him who said, "It is mine to **a**; |
| Rev | 6:10 | of the earth and **a** our blood?" |

## AVENGED [VENGEANCE]

| | | |
|---|---|---|
| Ge | 4:24 | If Cain is **a** seven times, |
| Eze | 5:13 | them will subside, and I will be **a**. |
| Rev | 19: 2 | He has **a** on her the blood of his |

## AVENGER [VENGEANCE]

| | | |
|---|---|---|
| Nu | 35:12 | will be places of refuge from the **a**, |
| Jos | 20: 3 | find protection from the **a** of blood. |
| Ps | 8: 2 | to silence the foe and the **a**. |

## AVENGES* [VENGEANCE]

| | | |
|---|---|---|
| 2Sa | 22:48 | He is the God who **a** me, who puts |
| Ps | 9:12 | For he who **a** blood remembers; |
| | 18:47 | He is the God who **a** me, |
| | 94: 1 | The LORD is a God who **a**. O God |
| | | who **a**, |

## AVENGING* [VENGEANCE]

| | | |
|---|---|---|
| 1Sa | 25:26 | and from **a** yourself with your own |
| | 25:33 | from **a** myself with my own hands. |
| Na | 1: 2 | The LORD is a jealous and **a** God; |

## AVIV*

The month of the Exodus and Passover (Ex 13:4; 23:15; 34:18; Dt 16:1).

## AVOID [AVOIDED, AVOIDS]

| | | |
|---|---|---|
| Pr | 4:15 | **A** it, do not travel on it; turn from it |
| | 15:12 | so they **a** the wise. |
| | 20: 3 | It is to one's honor to **a** strife, |
| | 20:19 | so a anyone who talks too much. |
| Ecc | 7:18 | fears God will **a** all [extremes]. |
| Ac | 15:29 | You will do well to **a** these things. |
| Gal | 6:12 | they do this is to **a** being persecuted |
| 1Th | 4: 3 | you should **a** sexual immorality; |
| 2Ti | 2:16 | **A** godless chatter, because those |
| Tit | 3: 9 | But **a** foolish controversies |

## AVOIDED* [AVOID]

| | | |
|---|---|---|
| Pr | 16: 6 | the fear of the LORD evil is **a**. |

## AVOIDS* [AVOID]

| | | |
|---|---|---|
| Pr | 16:17 | The highway of the upright **a** evil; |

## AWAIT [WAIT]

| | | |
|---|---|---|
| Jer | 48:43 | Terror and pit and snare **a** you, |
| Gal | 5: 5 | faith we eagerly **a** through the Spirit |
| Php | 3:20 | we eagerly **a** a Savior from there, |

## AWAITS [WAIT]

| | | |
|---|---|---|
| Ps | 65: 1 | Praise **a** you, our God, in Zion; |
| Pr | 15:10 | Stern discipline **a** those who leave |
| | 28:22 | are unaware that poverty **a** them. |
| Ecc | 3:19 | the same fate **a** them both: |
| Ob | 1: 5 | oh, what a disaster **a** you!— |
| Hab | 2: 3 | the revelation **a** an appointed time; |

## AWAKE [WAKE]

| | | |
|---|---|---|
| Ps | 35:23 | **A**, and rise to my defense! |
| | 57: 8 | **A**, my soul! **A**, harp and lyre! |
| Pr | 6:22 | when you **a**, they will speak to you. |
| | 20:13 | stay **a** and you will have food |
| Isa | 51: 9 | **A**, **a**, arm of the LORD, |
| | 51: 9 | **A**, as in days gone by, |
| | 52: 1 | **A**, **a**, Zion, clothe yourself |
| Da | 12: 2 | sleep in the dust of the earth will **a**: |
| 1Th | 5: 6 | let us be **a** and sober. |
| | 5:10 | so that, whether we are **a** or asleep, |
| Rev | 16:15 | Blessed are those who stay **a** |

## AWAKEN [WAKE]
Ps 108: 2 harp and lyre! I will a the dawn.
SS     8: 4 arouse or a love until it so desires.

## AWARD*
2Ti   4: 8 Judge, will a to me on that day—

## AWARE
Ex  34:29 he was not a that his face was
Nu  15:24 without the community being a
Mt  24:50 him and at an hour he is not a of.
Lk  12:46 him and at an hour he is not a of.
Gal   4:21 are you not a of what the law says?

## AWAY
Ge    5:24 no more, because God took him a.
       30:23 "God has taken a my disgrace."
       31:49 me when we are a from each other.
Dt     9:12 They have turned a quickly
2Sa 12:13 "The LORD has taken a your sin.
Ezr 10:19 hands in pledge to put a their wives,
Job   1:21 gave and the LORD has taken a;
Ps   51: 2 Wash a all my iniquity and cleanse
      148: 6 a decree that will never pass a.
Pr   14: 7 Stay a from the foolish, for you will
       15: 1 A gentle answer turns a wrath,
Ecc   3: 6 time to keep and a time to throw a,
SS    8:14 Come a, my beloved, and be like
Eze 11:15 'They are far a from the LORD;
Jnh   1: 3 But Jonah ran a from the LORD
Na    1:12 they will be destroyed and pass a.
Zep   1: 2 "I will sweep a everything
       3:15 has taken a your punishment, he has
Mk    4:17 of the word, they quickly fall a.
       13:31 Heaven and earth will pass a,
       13:31 but my words will never pass a.
Lk   24: 2 They found the stone rolled a
Jn    1:29 who takes a the sin of the world!
       6:37 comes to me I will never drive a.
       14:28 'I am going a and I am coming back
1Co   7:31 in its present form is passing a.
2Co   3:16 turns to the Lord, the veil is taken a.
1Jn   2:17 The world and its desires pass a,
Rev   7:17 God will wipe a every tear

## AWE* [AWESOME, OVERAWED]
Jos   4:14 stood in a of him all the days
       4:14 as they had stood in a of Moses.
1Sa 12:18 So all the people stood in a
1Ki   3:28 they held the king in a, because they
Job 25: 2 "Dominion and a belong to God;
Ps   65: 8 filled with a at your wonders;
      119:120 I stand in a of your laws.
Isa  29:23 will stand in a of the God of Israel.
Jer   2:19 your God and have no a of me,"
       33: 9 they will be in a and will tremble
Hab   3: 2 I stand in a of your deeds, LORD.
Mal   2: 5 me and stood in a of my name.
Mt    9: 8 saw this, they were filled with a;
Lk    1:65 The neighbors were all filled with a,
       5:26 They were filled with a and said,
       7:16 They were all filled with a
Ac    2:43 Everyone was filled with a
Heb 12:28 acceptably with reverence and a,

## AWESOME* [AWE]
Ge  28:17 and said, "How a is this place!
Ex  15:11 majestic in holiness, a in glory,
       34:10 among will see how a is the work
Dt    4:34 or by great and a deeds, like all
       7:21 is among you, is a great and a God.
      10:17 God, mighty and a, who shows no
      10:21 a wonders you saw with your own
      28:58 revere this glorious and a name—
      34:12 or performed the a deeds that Moses
Jdg  13: 6 looked like an angel of God, very a.
2Sa   7:23 a wonders by driving out nations
1Ch 17:21 a wonders by driving out nations
Ne    1: 5 the great and a God, who keeps his
       4:14 who is great and a, and fight
       9:32 God, mighty and a, who keeps his
Job 10:16 again display your a power against
       37:22 God comes in a majesty.
Ps   45: 4 let your right hand achieve a deeds.
       47: 2 For the LORD Most High is a,
       65: 5 You answer us with a and righteous
       66: 3 to God, "How a are your deeds!
       66: 5 done, his a deeds for humankind!
       68:35 You, God, are a in your sanctuary;
       89: 7 he is more a than all who surround
       99: 3 them praise your great and a name—
      106:22 of Ham and a deeds by the Red Sea.
      111: 9 holy and a is his name.
      145: 6 tell of the power of your a works—
Isa  64: 3 you did a things that we did not
Eze   1:18 Their rims were high and a, and all
       1:22 a vault, sparkling like crystal, and a.
Da    2:31 dazzling statue, a in appearance.
       9: 4 the great and a God, who keeps his
Zep   2:11 The LORD will be a to them

## AWFUL
Jdg  20: 3 us how this a thing happened."
Ne    9:18 they committed a blasphemies.
Jer  30: 7 How a that day will be!

## AWL*
Ex   21: 6 and pierce his ear with an a.
Dt   15:17 take an a and push it through his ear

## AWOKE [WAKE]
Ge    9:24 When Noah a from his wine
       28:16 When Jacob a from his sleep,
Jdg  16:20 He a from his sleep and thought,
1Ki   3:15 Then Solomon a—and he realized it
Ps   78:65 Then the Lord a as from sleep,

## AX [AXHEAD]
Ecc 10:10 If the a is dull and its edge
Isa  10:15 Does the a raise itself above the one
Mt    3:10 The a is already at the root

## AXHEAD* [AX]
2Ki   6: 5 a tree, the iron a fell into the water.

## AZARIAH
   1. King of Judah; see Uzziah (2Ki 15:1–7).
   2. Prophet (2Ch 15:1–8).
   3. Opponent of Jeremiah (Jer 43:2).
   4. Jewish exile; see Abednego (Da 1:6–19).

# B

## BAAL [BAAL-BERITH, BAAL-ZEBUB, BAALS]
Nu 25: 3 yoked themselves to the **B** of Peor.
Jdg 2:13 and served **B** and the Ashtoreths.
6:31 If **B** really is a god, he can defend
1Ki 16:32 an altar for **B** in the temple of **B**
18:25 Elijah said to the prophets of **B**,
19:18 knees have not bowed down to **B**
2Ki 3: 2 the sacred stone of **B** that his father
10:28 So Jehu destroyed **B** worship
2Ch 23:17 the people went to the temple of **B**
23:17 killed Mattan the priest of **B** in front
Jer 19: 5 They have built the high places of **B**
19: 5 in the fire as offerings to **B**—
Hos 13: 1 he became guilty of **B** worship
Ro 11: 4 have not bowed the knee to **B**."

## BAAL-BERITH [BAAL]
Jdg 8:33 They set up **B** as their god

## BAAL-ZEBUB [BAAL, BEELZEBUL]
2Ki 1: 2 "Go and consult **B**, the god

## BAALS [BAAL]
Jdg 3: 7 and served the **B** and the Asherahs.
10:10 our God and serving the **B**."
1Sa 7: 4 So the Israelites put away their **B**
2Ch 17: 3 He did not consult the **B**
34: 4 the altars of the **B** were torn down;

## BAASHA
King of Israel (1Ki 15:16—16:7; 2Ch 16:1–6).

## BABBLER* [BABBLING]
Ac 17:18 "What is this **b** trying to say?"

## BABBLING* [BABBLER]
Mt 6: 7 do not keep on **b** like pagans,

## BABEL* [BABYLON]
Ge 11: 9 That is why it was called **B**—

## BABIES* [BABY]
Ge 25:22 The **b** jostled each other within her,
Ex 2: 6 "This is one of the Hebrew **b**,"
Lk 18:15 bringing **b** to Jesus for him to place
Ac 7:19 their newborn **b** so that they would
1Pe 2: 2 Like newborn **b**, crave pure spiritual

## BABY [BABIES, BABY'S]
Ex 2: 6 She opened it and saw the **b**.
2: 9 "Take this **b** and nurse him for me,
2: 9 So the woman took the **b** and nursed
1Ki 3:26 my lord, give her the living **b**!
Isa 49:15 "Can a mother forget the **b** at her
Lk 1:41 greeting, the **b** leaped in her womb.
1:44 the **b** in my womb leaped for joy.
1:57 time for Elizabeth to have her **b**,
2: 6 the time came for the **b** to be born,

Lk 2:12 You will find a **b** wrapped in cloths
2:16 and the **b**, who was lying
Jn 16:21 her **b** is born she forgets the anguish

## BABY'S* [BABY]
Ex 2: 8 the girl went and got the **b** mother.

## BABYLON [BABEL, BABYLONIANS]
Ge 10:10 first centers of his kingdom were **B**,
1Ch 9: 1 were taken captive to **B** because
2Ch 36:18 He carried to **B** all the articles
36:20 carried into exile to **B** the remnant,
Ps 137: 1 By the rivers of **B** we sat and wept
Isa 14: 4 up this taunt against the king of **B**:
21: 9 '**B** has fallen, has fallen!
Jer 29:10 seventy years are completed for **B**,
51:34 king of **B** has devoured us, he has
51:37 **B** will be a heap of ruins, a haunt
Da 4:30 not this the great **B** I have built as
1Pe 5:13 She who is in **B**, chosen together
Rev 14: 8 Fallen is **B** the Great,' which made
17: 5 written on her forehead: MYSTERY **B**
18: 2 " 'Fallen! Fallen is **B** the Great!'

## KING OF BABYLON See KING

## BABYLONIANS [BABYLON]
Jer 32: 5 If you fight against the **B**, you will
38: 2 goes over to the **B** will live.
Da 1: 4 the language and literature of the **B**.
Hab 1: 6 I am raising up the **B**, that ruthless

## BACK [BACKS, BACKSLIDING, BACKSLIDINGS]
Ge 3:24 a flaming sword flashing **b** and forth
19:26 But Lot's wife looked **b**, and she
Ex 22: 7 thief, if caught, must pay **b** double.
Ru 1:15 "your sister-in-law is going **b** to her
1:15 and her gods. Go **b** with her."
2: 6 "She is the Moabite who came **b**
1Sa 25:21 He has paid me **b** evil for good.
2Ki 20:11 made the shadow go **b** the ten steps
Ps 31:23 him, but the proud he pays **b** in full.
51:13 ways, and sinners will turn **b** to you.
90: 3 You turn people **b** to dust, saying,
SS 6:13 Come **b**, come **b**, O Shulammite!
come **b**, come **b**,
Isa 38:17 have put all my sins behind your **b**.
Jer 29:14 will bring you **b** from captivity.
29:14 will bring you **b** to the place
La 3:64 Pay them **b** what they deserve,
Mt 28: 2 rolled **b** the stone and sat on it.
Ro 9:20 human being, to talk **b** to God?
Gal 4: 9 that you are turning **b** to those weak
Eph 4:14 tossed **b** and forth by the waves,
1Th 5:15 nobody pays **b** wrong for wrong,
Heb 6: 6 away, to be brought **b** to repentance.
10:39 we are not of those who shrink **b**

## BACKBITING See SLANDER

## BACKS [BACK]
Ex 23:27 make all your enemies turn their **b**
Ne 9:29 Stubbornly they turned their **b**
Pr 19:29 and beatings for the **b** of fools.

Isa  59:13  LORD, turning our **b** on our God,
2Pe   2:21  turn their **b** on the sacred command

## BACKSLIDERS, -ING  See also
FAITHLESS, STUBBORN,
UNFAITHFUL, WAYWARDNESS

## BACKSLIDING* [BACK]
Jer   2:19  your **b** will rebuke you.
       3:22  I will cure you of **b**."
      14: 7  For our **b** is great; we have sinned
      15: 6  "You keep on **b**. So I will lay hands
Eze  37:23  save them from all their sinful **b**,

## BACKSLIDINGS* [BACK]
Jer   5: 6  rebellion is great and their **b** many.

## BAD
Ge   37: 2  he brought their father a **b** report
Ex    7:21  and the river smelled so **b**
Nu   13:32  among the Israelites a **b** report
Ecc   7:14  but when times are **b**, consider:
Isa   5: 2  grapes, but it yielded only **b** fruit.
Jer  24: 2  **b** figs, so **b** they could not be eaten.
Mt    7:17  good fruit, but a **b** tree bears **b** fruit.
     12:33  make a tree **b** and its fruit will be **b**,

## BADGERS  See SEA COWS

## BAG
Mic   6:11  scales, with a **b** of false weights?
Mt   25:15  and to another one **b**,
Lk   10: 4  Do not take a purse or **b** or sandals;
Jn   12: 6  as keeper of the money **b**, he used

## BAKED [BAKER]
Ex   12:39  they **b** loaves of unleavened bread.
Lev   6:17  It must not be **b** with yeast;
Da    2:33  partly of iron and partly of **b** clay.

## BAKER [BAKED]
Ge   40: 1  the **b** of the king of Egypt offended

## BALAAM
   Prophet who attempted to curse Israel (Nu 22–24;
Dt 23:4–5; 2Pe 2:15; Jude 11; Rev 2:14). Killed in Is-
rael's vengeance on Midianites (Nu 31:8; Jos 13:22).

## BALAK
   Moabite king who hired Balaam to curse Israel (Nu
22–24; Jos 24:9).

## BALANCE
Ps   62: 9  If weighed on a **b**, they are nothing;
Isa  40:12  on the scales and the hills in a **b**?

## BALD [BALDY]
Isa   3:17  LORD will make their scalps **b**."
Mic   1:16  make yourself as **b** as the vulture,

## BALDY [BALD]
2Ki   2:23  "Get out of here, **b**!" they said.

## BALM
Jer   8:22  Is there no **b** in Gilead? Is there no

## BAN*
1Ch   2: 7  by violating the **b** on taking devoted

## BAND
Ps    2: 2  rulers **b** together against the LORD
Ac    4:26  the rulers **b** together against the Lord

## BANDAGED*
Isa   1: 6  not cleansed or **b** or soothed
Lk   10:34  He went to him and **b** his wounds,

## BANDIT* [BANDITS]
Pr   23:28  Like a **b** she lies in wait,

## BANDITS* [BANDIT]
Ezr   8:31  from enemies and **b** along the way.
Hos   7: 1  into houses, **b** rob in the streets;
2Co  11:26  in danger from **b**, in danger

## BANISH [BANISHED]
Ecc  11:10  **b** anxiety from your heart and cast
Jer  25:10  I will **b** from them the sounds of joy
Zec  13: 2  I will **b** the names of the idols

## BANISHED [BANISH]
Ge    3:23  So the LORD God **b** him
Dt   30: 4  you have been **b** to the most distant
Jnh   2: 4  said, 'I have been **b** from your sight;

## BANK [BANKS]
Ge   41:17  I was standing on the **b** of the Nile,
Ex    2: 3  put it among the reeds along the **b**
      7:15  Wait on the **b** of the Nile to meet
2Ki   2:13  and stood on the **b** of the Jordan.
Mk    5:13  rushed down the steep **b**

## BANKS [BANK]
Eze  47:12  will grow on both **b** of the river.

## BANNER
Ex   17:15  and called it The LORD is my **B**.
SS    2: 4  hall, and let his **b** over me be love.
Isa  11:10  of Jesse will stand as a **b**

## BANQUET [BANQUETS]
1Sa  25:36  in the house holding a **b** like
Est   1: 3  of his reign he gave a **b** for all his
      6:14  away to the **b** Esther had prepared.
      7: 1  Haman went to Queen Esther's **b**,
SS    2: 4  Let him lead me to the **b** hall,
Isa  25: 6  for all peoples, a **b** of aged wine—
Da    5: 1  King Belshazzar gave a great **b**
Mt   22: 4  Come to the wedding **b**.'
Lk   14:13  But when you give a **b**,

## BANQUETS [BANQUET]
Mk   12:39  and the places of honor at **b**.

## BAPTISM* [BAPTIZE]
Mt   21:25  John's **b**—where did it come from?

Mk   1: 4  preaching a **b** of repentance
       10:38  with the **b** I am baptized with?"
       10:39  with the **b** I am baptized with,
       11:30  John's **b**—was it from heaven,
Lk    3: 3  preaching a **b** of repentance
       12:50  But I have a **b** to undergo, and what
       20: 4  John's **b**—was it from heaven,
Ac   1:22  beginning from John's **b** to the time
       10:37  after the **b** that John preached—
       13:24  and **b** to all the people of Israel.
       18:25  though he knew only the **b** of John.
       19: 3  "Then what **b** did you receive?"
       19: 3  "John's **b**," they replied.
       19: 4  "John's **b** was a **b** of repentance.
Ro    6: 4  with him through **b** into death
Eph  4: 5  one Lord, one faith, one **b**;
Col  2:12  having been buried with him in **b**,
1Pe  3:21  this water symbolizes **b** that now

## BAPTIST [BAPTIZE]
Mt    3: 1  In those days John the **B** came,
       11:11  anyone greater than John the **B**;
       14: 8  on a platter the head of John the **B**."
       16:14  replied, "Some say John the **B**;

## BAPTIZE* [BAPTISM, BAPTIST,
## BAPTIZED, BAPTIZING]
Mt    3:11  "I **b** you with water for repentance.
       3:11  He will **b** you with the Holy Spirit
Mk   1: 8  I **b** you with water, but he will **b** you
Lk   3:16  them all, "I **b** you with water.
       3:16  He will **b** you with the Holy Spirit
Jn    1:25  do you **b** if you are not the Messiah,
       1:26  "I **b** with water," John replied,
       1:33  the one who sent me to **b** with water
       1:33  remain is the one who will **b**
1Co  1:14  that I did not **b** any of you except
       1:17  For Christ did not send me to **b**,

## BAPTIZED* [BAPTIZE]
Mt    3: 6  they were **b** by him in the Jordan
       3:13  to the Jordan to be **b** by John.
       3:14  "I need to be **b** by you, and do you
       3:16  As soon as Jesus was **b**, he went
Mk   1: 5  they were **b** by him in the Jordan
       1: 9  and was **b** by John in the Jordan.
       10:38  be **b** with the baptism I am **b** with?"
       10:39  be **b** with the baptism I am **b** with,
       16:16  *Whoever believes and is **b** will be saved,*
Lk    3: 7  crowds coming out to be **b** by him,
       3:12  Even tax collectors came to be **b**.
       3:21  were being **b**, Jesus was **b** too.
       7:29  because they had been **b** by John.
       7:30  because they had not been **b**
Jn    3:22  spent some time with them, and **b**.
       3:23  people were coming and being **b**.
       4: 2  in fact it was not Jesus who **b**,
Ac    1: 5  For John **b** with water,
       1: 5  in a few days you will be **b**
       2:38  "Repent and be **b**, every one
       2:41  who accepted his message were **b**,
       8:12  they were **b**, both men and women.
       8:13  Simon himself believed and was **b**.
       8:16  they had simply been **b**
       8:36  stand in the way of my being **b**?"
       8:38  into the water and Philip **b** him.

Ac    9:18  He got up and was **b**,
       10:47  the way of their being **b** with water.
       10:48  ordered that they be **b** in the name
       11:16  'John **b** with water,
       11:16  you will be **b** with the Holy Spirit.'
       16:15  members of her household were **b**,
       16:33  he and all his household were **b**.
       18: 8  heard Paul believed and were **b**.
       19: 5  they were **b** into the name
       22:16  up, be **b** and wash your sins away,
Ro    6: 3  who were **b** into Christ Jesus were **b**
              into his death?
1Co  1:13  Were you **b** into the name of Paul?
       1:15  say that you were **b** into my name.
       1:16  I also **b** the household of Stephanas;
       1:16  don't remember if I **b** anyone else.)
       10: 2  They were all **b** into Moses
       12:13  we were all **b** by one Spirit so as
       15:29  what will those do who are **b**
       15:29  why are people **b** for them?
Gal  3:27  of you who were **b** into Christ have

## BAPTIZING* [BAPTIZE]
Mt    3: 7  coming to where he was **b**, he said
       28:19  **b** them in the name of the Father
Jn    1:28  of the Jordan, where John was **b**.
       1:31  the reason I came **b** with water was
       3:23  also was **b** at Aenon near Salim,
       3:26  he is **b**, and everyone is going
       4: 1  and **b** more disciples than John—
       10:40  the place where John had been **b**

## BAR [BARRED]
Jdg 16: 3  posts, and tore them loose, **b** and all.

## BAR-JESUS*
Ac  13: 6  sorcerer and false prophet named **B**,

## BARABBAS*
Prisoner released by Pilate instead of Jesus (Mt 27:16–26; Mk 15:7–15; Lk 23:18–19; Jn 18:40).

## BARAK*
Judge who fought with Deborah against Canaanites (Jdg 4–5; 1Sa 12:11; Heb 11:32).

## BARBARIAN*
Col  3:11  circumcised or uncircumcised, **b**,

## BARBARIANS  See FOREIGNER(S)

## BARBS*
Nu 33:55  remain will become **b** in your eyes

## BARE [BAREFOOT, BARREN]
Jdg 14: 6  his **b** hands as he might have torn
Isa 52:10  The LORD will lay **b** his holy arm
1Co 14:25  the secrets of their hearts are laid **b**.
Heb  4:13  and laid **b** before the eyes of him
2Pe  3:10  everything done in it will be laid **b**.

## BAREFOOT [BARE, FOOT]
Isa 20: 3  gone stripped and **b** for three years,
Mic  1: 8  I will go about **b** and naked.

## BARGAIN
Isa  36: 8  now, make a **b** with my master,

## BARK
Ge  30:37  stripes on them by peeling the **b**
Ex  11: 7  among the Israelites not a dog will **b**

## BARLEY
Ru   1:22  in Bethlehem as the **b** harvest was
2Ki  7: 1  two seahs of **b** for a shekel
Jn   6: 9  is a boy with five small **b** loaves
Rev  6: 6  six pounds of **b** for a day's wages,

## BARN [BARNS]
Hag  2:19  Is there yet any seed left in the **b**?
Lk   3:17  and to gather the wheat into his **b**,

## BARNABAS [JOSEPH]
Disciple, originally Joseph (Ac 4:36), prophet (Ac 13:1), apostle (Ac 14:14). Brought Paul to apostles (Ac 9:27), Antioch (Ac 11:22–29; Gal 2:1–13), on the first missionary journey (Ac 13–14). Together at Jerusalem Council, they separated over John Mark (Ac 15). Later co-workers (1Co 9:6; Col 4:10).

## BARNS* [BARN]
Dt   28: 8  will send a blessing on your **b**
Ps  144:13  Our **b** will be filled with every kind
Pr   3:10  your **b** will be filled to overflowing,
Mt   6:26  not sow or reap or store away in **b**,
Lk  12:18  I will tear down my **b** and build

## BARRED [BAR]
Jos  6: 1  gates of Jericho were securely **b**
Pr  18:19  disputes are like the **b** gates
Jnh  2: 6  the earth beneath **b** me in forever.

## BARREN [BARE]
Ex  23:26  will miscarry or be **b** in your land.
1Sa  2: 5  She who was **b** has borne seven
Isa 54: 1  "Sing, **b** woman, you who never
Gal  4:27  "Be glad, **b** woman, you who never

## BARRIER*
Jer  5:22  sea, an everlasting **b** it cannot cross.
Eph  2:14  the two one and has destroyed the **b**,

## BARSABBAS*
Ac   1:23  Joseph called **B** (also known as
    15:22  They chose Judas (called **B**)

## BARTER*
Job  6:27  fatherless and **b** away your friend.
    41: 6  Will traders **b** for it?
La   1:11  they **b** their treasures for food

## BARTHOLOMEW*
Apostle (Mt 10:3; Mk 3:18; Lk 6:14; Ac 1:13). Possibly also called Nathanael (Jn 1:45–49; 21:2).

## BARTIMAEUS*
Blind man healed by Jesus (Mk 10:46–52).

## BARUCH
Jeremiah's secretary (Jer 32:12–16; 36; 43:1–6; 45:1–2).

## BARZILLAI
1. Gileadite who aided David during Absalom's revolt (2Sa 17:27; 19:31–39).
2. Son-in-law of 1. (Ezr 2:61; Ne 7:63).

## BASE [BASING, BASIS]
Ex  29:12  out the rest of it at the **b** of the altar.
Job 30: 8  A **b** and nameless brood, they were

## BASHAN
Nu  21:33  went up along the road toward **B**,
    21:33  Og king of **B** and his whole army
Jos 13:30  Mahanaim and including all of **B**,
    13:30  the entire realm of Og king of **B**—
    13:30  all the settlements of Jair in **B**,
    22: 7  Moses had given land in **B**,
Ps  22:12  strong bulls of **B** encircle me.
Am   4: 1  you cows of **B** on Mount Samaria,

## BASIN
Ex  30:18  "Make a bronze **b**, with its bronze
1Ki  7:30  and each had a **b** resting on four
Jn  13: 5  he poured water into a **b** and began

## BASING [BASE]
Isa 36: 4  what are you **b** this confidence

## BASIS [BASE]
Da   6: 5  said, "We will never find any **b**
Jn  18:38  "I find no **b** for a charge against
Phm  1: 9  to appeal to you on the **b** of love.

## BASKET [BASKETFULS, BASKETS]
Ex   2: 3  she got a papyrus **b** for him
Dt  28: 5  Your **b** and your kneading trough
Isa 40:12  has held the dust of the earth in a **b**,
Am   8: 1  a **b** of ripe fruit.
Zec  5: 6  He replied, "It is a **b**."
Ac   9:25  him in a **b** through an opening
2Co 11:33  I was lowered in a **b** from a window

## BASKETFULS [BASKET]
Mt  14:20  picked up twelve **b** of broken pieces
    15:37  picked up seven **b** of broken pieces
    16: 9  and how many **b** you gathered?

## BASKETS [BASKET]
Mt  13:48  and collected the good fish in **b**,

## BATCH*
Ro  11:16  is holy, then the whole **b** is holy;
1Co  5: 6  a little yeast leavens the whole **b**
    5: 7  you may be a new unleavened **b**—
Gal  5: 9  yeast works through the whole **b**

## BATH [BATHE]
Eze 45:10  accurate ephah and an accurate **b**.
Jn  13:10  "Those who have had a **b** need only

## BATHE [BATH, BATHED, BATHING]
Ex    2: 5  went down to the Nile to **b**, and her
Dt  33:24  and let him **b** his feet in oil.

## BATHED [BATHE]
Isa 34: 6  sword of the LORD is **b** in blood,
Eze 16: 9  " 'I **b** you with water and washed

## BATHING [BATHE]
2Sa 11: 2  From the roof he saw a woman **b**.

## BATHSHEBA
Wife of Uriah who committed adultery with and became wife of David (2Sa 11; Ps 51), mother of Solomon (2Sa 12:24; 1Ki 1–2; 1Ch 3:5).

## BATTLE [BATTLEMENTS, BATTLES]
Ex  13:18  went up out of Egypt ready for **b**.
Jos    4:13  **b** crossed over before the LORD
1Sa 17:47  for the **b** is the LORD's, and he
2Sa    1:25  "How the mighty have fallen in **b**!
       22:35  He trains my hands for **b**;
1Ki 22:30  "I will enter the battle in disguise,
       22:30  disguised himself and went into **b**.
2Ch 20:15  For the **b** is not yours, but God's.
Ps   24: 8  mighty, the LORD mighty in **b**.
Ecc   9:11  to the swift or the **b** to the strong,
Isa  31: 4  come down to do **b** on Mount Zion
Eze 13: 5  it will stand firm in the **b** on the day
Hos   1: 7  bow, sword or **b**, or by horses
        2:18  and **b** I will abolish from the land,
Ob    1: 1  "Rise, let us go against her for **b**"—
Jas   4: 1  from your desires that **b** within you?
Rev 16:14  them for the **b** on the great day
       20: 8  and to gather them for **b**.

## BATTLEMENTS* [BATTLE]
Isa 54:12  I will make your **b** of rubies,

## BATTLES* [BATTLE]
1Sa   8:20  to go out before us and fight our **b**."
       18:17  and fight the **b** of the LORD."
       25:28  because you fight the LORD's **b**,
2Ch 32: 8  God to help us and to fight our **b**."

## BEAM* [BEAMS]
Ezr   6:11  a **b** is to be pulled from their house

## BEAMS [BEAM]
1Ki   6: 9  roofing it with **b** and cedar planks.
Ne    3: 3  They laid its **b** and put its doors
Jer  22: 7  they will cut up your fine cedar **b**
Zep   2:14  the **b** of cedar will be exposed.

## BEAR [BEARABLE, BEARING, BEARS, BIRTH, BIRTHRIGHT, BORE, BORN, BORNE, CHILDBEARING, CHILDBIRTH, FIRSTBORN, NATIVE-BORN, NEWBORN, REBIRTH]
Ge    4:13  punishment is more than I can **b**.
       17:19  your wife Sarah will **b** you a son,
Ex  28:12  Aaron is to **b** the names on his
1Sa 17:36  has killed both the lion and the **b**;

Job   9: 9  He is the Maker of the **B** and Orion,
Ps   38: 4  me like a burden too heavy to **b**.
       92:14  They will still **b** fruit in old age,
Pr   17:12  meet a **b** robbed of her cubs than
Isa  11: 1  from his roots a Branch will **b** fruit.
       11: 7  The cow will feed with the **b**,
       53:11  many, and he will **b** their iniquities.
Jer  14: 9  us, LORD, and we **b** your name;
Eze 14:10  They will **b** their guilt—
Da    7: 5  second beast, which looked like a **b**.
Am    5:19  fled from a lion only to meet a **b**,
Mt    7:18  A good tree cannot **b** bad fruit,
       7:18  and a bad tree cannot **b** good fruit.
Lk    1:13  wife Elizabeth will **b** you a son,
        1:42  and blessed is the child you will **b**!
       21:13  you will **b** testimony to me.
Jn   15: 2  branch that does **b** fruit he prunes so
       15: 8  that you **b** much fruit,
       15:16  so that you might go and **b** fruit—
Ro    7: 4  order that we might **b** fruit for God.
       15: 1  We who are strong ought to **b**
1Co 10:13  be tempted beyond what you can **b**.
       15:49  man, so shall we **b** the image
Gal   6:17  for I **b** on my body the marks
Col   3:13  **B** with each other and forgive one
1Pe   2:19  commendable if you **b** up under the
        4:16  but praise God that you **b** that name.
Rev 13: 2  but had feet like those of a **b**

## BEARABLE [BEAR]
Mt  10:15  it will be more **b** for Sodom

## BEARD
Lev 19:27  head or clip off the edges of your **b**.
Isa  50: 6  to those who pulled out my **b**;
Jer  48:37  head is shaved and every **b** cut off;

## BEARING [BEAR]
Ge    1:12  plants **b** seed according to their
        1:12  kinds and trees **b** fruit with seed in it
Nu  13:23  cut off a branch **b** a single cluster
Pr   30:29  stride, four that move with stately **b**:
Joel   2:22  The trees are **b** their fruit;
Ro    2:15  their consciences also **b** witness,
Eph   4: 2  patient, **b** with one another in love.
Col    1: 6  the gospel is **b** fruit and growing
        1:10  **b** fruit in every good work,
Heb 13:13  the camp, **b** the disgrace he bore.
Rev 22: 2  tree of life, **b** twelve crops of fruit,

## BEARS [BEAR]
Ge  49:21  a doe set free that **b** beautiful fawns.
1Ki   8:43  this house I have built **b** your Name.
2Ki   2:24  Then two **b** came out of the woods
Ps   68:19  Savior, who daily **b** our burdens.
Jer   7:11  which **b** my Name, become a den
Da    9:18  of the city that **b** your Name.
Gal   4:24  and **b** children who are to be slaves:

## BEAST [BEASTS]
Isa  35: 9  will be there, nor any ravenous **b**;
Da    7: 6  and there before me was another **b**,
        7: 6  This **b** had four heads, and it was
Rev 11: 7  the **b** that comes up from the Abyss
       13: 1  I saw a **b** coming out of the sea.
       13: 2  The **b** I saw resembled a leopard,

Rev 13: 2  The dragon gave the **b** his power
13:11  Then I saw another **b**,
13:18  calculate the number of the **b**, for it
16: 2  people who had the mark of the **b**
17: 3  on a scarlet **b** that was covered
19:20  But the **b** was captured,
19:20  who had received the mark of the **b**
20: 4  They had not worshiped the **b** or his

## BEASTS [BEAST]
Lev 26: 6  I will remove wild **b** from the land,
Jer 12: 9  Go and gather all the wild **b**;
Eze 5:17  send famine and wild **b** against you,
Da 7: 3  Four great **b**, each different
1Co 15:32  If I fought wild **b** in Ephesus
Rev 6: 8  and by the wild **b** of the earth.

## BEAT [BEATEN, BEATING, BEATINGS, BEATS]
Dt 24:20  When you **b** the olives from your
Ne 13:25  I **b** some of them and pulled
Ps 78:66  He **b** back his enemies; he put them
Pr 23:35  They **b** me, but I don't feel it!
SS 5: 7  They **b** me, they bruised me;
Isa 2: 4  They will **b** their swords
Joel 3:10  **B** your plowshares into swords
Mic 4: 3  They will **b** their swords
Mt 7:25  blew and **b** against that house;
Ac 22:19  and **b** those who believe in you.

## BEATEN [BEAT]
Ex 5:16  Your servants are being **b**,
Nu 22:32  him, "Why have you **b** your donkey
Jer 20: 2  he had Jeremiah the prophet **b**
Lk 12:48  deserving punishment will be **b**
Ac 16:22  them to be stripped and **b** with rods.
2Co 6: 9  yet we live on; **b**, and yet not killed;
11:25  Three times I was **b** with rods,

## BEATING [BEAT]
Ex 2:11  He saw an Egyptian **b** a Hebrew,
1Co 9:26  I do not fight like a boxer **b** the air.
1Pe 2:20  if you receive a **b** for doing wrong

## BEATINGS [BEAT]
Pr 19:29  and **b** for the backs of fools.

## BEATS* [BEAT]
Ex 21:20  "Anyone who **b** their male

## BEAUTIFUL* [BEAUTY]
Ge 6: 2  saw that these daughters were **b**,
12:11  "I know what a **b** woman you are.
12:14  saw that Sarai was a very **b** woman.
24:16  The girl was very **b**, a virgin;
26: 7  of Rebekah, because she is **b**."
29:17  had a lovely figure and was **b**.
49:21  is a doe set free that bears **b** fawns.
Nu 24: 5  "How **b** are your tents, Jacob,
Dt 21:11  among the captives a **b** woman
Jos 7:21  I saw in the plunder a **b** robe
1Sa 25: 3  was an intelligent and **b** woman,
2Sa 11: 2  The woman was very **b**,
13: 1  the **b** sister of Absalom son
14:27  Tamar, and she became a **b** woman.

1Ki 1: 3  throughout Israel for a **b** girl
1: 4  The girl was very **b**; she took care
Est 2: 2  search be made for **b** young virgins
2: 3  bring all these **b** young women
2: 7  had a lovely figure and was **b**.
Job 42:15  there found women as **b** as Job's
Ps 48: 2  **B** in its loftiness, the joy
Pr 11:22  snout is a **b** woman who shows no
24: 4  are filled with rare and **b** treasures.
Ecc 3:11  He has made everything **b** in its
SS 1. 8  you do not know, most **b** of women,
1:10  Your cheeks are **b** with earrings,
1:15  How **b** you are, my darling!
1:15  Oh, how **b**! Your eyes are doves.
2:10  my darling, my **b** one,
2:13  my **b** one, come with me."
4: 1  How **b** you are, my darling!
4: 1  Oh, how **b**! Your eyes behind your
4: 7  All **b** you are, my darling;
5: 9  than others, most **b** of women?
6: 1  beloved gone, most **b** of women?
6: 4  You are as **b** as Tirzah, my darling,
7: 1  How **b** your sandaled feet,
7: 6  How **b** you are and how pleasing,
Isa 4: 2  the Branch of the LORD will be **b**
28: 5  a **b** wreath for the remnant of his
52: 7  How **b** on the mountains are the feet
Jer 3:19  land, the most **b** inheritance of any
6. 2  Daughter Zion, so **b** and delicate.
11:16  olive tree with fruit **b** in form.
46:20  "Egypt is a **b** heifer, but a gadfly is
Eze 7:20  They took pride in their **b** jewelry
16:12  ears and a **b** crown on your head.
16:13  You became very **b** and rose to be
20: 6  and honey, the most **b** of all lands.
20:15  and honey, the most **b** of all lands—
23:42  sister and **b** crowns on their heads.
27:24  they traded with you **b** garments,
31: 3  with **b** branches overshadowing
31: 9  I made it **b** with abundant branches,
33:32  who sings love songs with a **b** voice
Da 4:12  Its leaves were **b**, its fruit abundant,
4:21  with **b** leaves and abundant fruit,
8: 9  to the east and toward the **B** Land.
11:16  will establish himself in the **B** Land
11:41  He will also invade the **B** Land.
11:45  the seas at the **b** holy mountain.
Zec 9:17  How attractive and **b** they will be!
Mt 23:27  which look **b** on the outside
26:10  She has done a **b** thing to me.
Mk 14: 6  She has done a **b** thing to me.
Lk 21: 5  temple was adorned with **b** stones
Ac 3: 2  carried to the temple gate called **B**,
3:10  begging at the temple gate called **B**,
Ro 10:15  "How **b** are the feet of those who

## BEAUTIFULLY* [BEAUTY]
Rev 21: 2  prepared as a bride **b** dressed for her

## BEAUTY* [BEAUTIFUL, BEAUTIFULLY]
Est 1:11  order to display her **b** to the people
2: 3  let **b** treatments be given to them.
2: 9  provided her with her **b** treatments
2:12  months of **b** treatments prescribed
Ps 27: 4  to gaze on the **b** of the LORD

| | | |
|---|---|---|
| Ps | 45:11 | the king be enthralled by your **b**; |
| | 50: 2 | Zion, perfect in **b**, God shines forth. |
| Pr | 6:25 | Do not lust in your heart after her **b** |
| | 31:30 | is deceptive, and **b** is fleeting; |
| Isa | 3:24 | instead of **b**, branding. |
| | 28: 1 | his glorious **b**, set on the head |
| | 28: 4 | his glorious **b**, set on the head |
| | 33:17 | Your eyes will see the king in his **b** |
| | 53: 2 | He had no **b** or majesty to attract us |
| | 61: 3 | them a crown of **b** instead of ashes, |
| La | 2:15 | that was called the perfection of **b**, |
| Eze | 16:14 | the nations on account of your **b**, |
| | 16:14 | had given you made your **b** perfect, |
| | 16:15 | you trusted in your **b** and used your |
| | 16:15 | passed by and your **b** became his. |
| | 16:16 | to him, and he possessed your **b**. |
| | 16:25 | lofty shrines and degraded your **b**, |
| | 27: 3 | say, Tyre, "I am perfect in **b**." |
| | 27: 4 | your builders brought your **b** |
| | 27:11 | they brought your **b** to perfection. |
| | 28: 7 | draw their swords against your **b** |
| | 28:12 | full of wisdom and perfect in **b**. |
| | 28:17 | became proud on account of your **b**, |
| | 31: 7 | It was majestic in **b**, with its |
| | 31: 8 | the garden of God could match its **b**. |
| Jas | 1:11 | blossom falls and its **b** is destroyed. |
| 1Pe | 3: 3 | Your **b** should not come |
| | 3: 4 | the unfading **b** of a gentle and quiet |

## BECAME [BECOME]

| | | |
|---|---|---|
| Ge | 2: 7 | of life, and the man **b** a living being. |
| Ex | 7:10 | and his officials, and it **b** a snake. |
| | 15:25 | the water, and the water **b** sweet. |
| Lev | 18:27 | before you, and the land **b** defiled. |
| Jdg | 8:27 | and it **b** a snare to Gideon and his |
| 2Ki | 17:15 | idols and themselves **b** worthless. |
| 1Ch | 11: 9 | And David **b** more and more |
| 2Ch | 17:12 | Jehoshaphat **b** more and more |
| | 26:16 | But after Uzziah **b** powerful, |
| Jn | 1:14 | The Word **b** flesh and made his |
| 1Co | 9:20 | To the Jews I **b** like a Jew, to win |
| | 9:20 | under the law I **b** like one under |
| 2Co | 8: 9 | yet for your sake he **b** poor, |

## BECOME [BECAME]

| | | |
|---|---|---|
| Ge | 2:24 | his wife, and they will **b** one flesh. |
| | 9:15 | again will the waters **b** a flood |
| Dt | 8:14 | your heart will **b** proud and you will |
| Jdg | 16: 7 | I'll **b** as weak as any other man." |
| Ps | 2: 7 | today I have **b** your father. |
| Pr | 13:20 | Walk with the wise and **b** wise, |
| Lk | 4: 3 | of God, tell this stone to **b** bread." |
| Jn | 1:12 | he gave the right to **b** children |
| | 3:30 | He must **b** greater; I must **b** less." |
| Ac | 4:11 | which has **b** the cornerstone.' |
| Rev | 11:15 | the world has **b** the kingdom of our |

## BED [BEDS, SICKBED]

| | | |
|---|---|---|
| Ge | 39: 7 | and said, "Come to **b** with me!" |
| | 48: 2 | his strength and sat up on the **b**. |
| 2Sa | 13:11 | her and said, "Come to **b** with me, |
| 1Ki | 1:47 | the king bowed in worship on his **b** |
| Ps | 41: 3 | restores them from their **b** of illness. |
| Pr | 26:14 | hinges, so a sluggard turns on the **b**. |
| SS | 1:16 | And our **b** is verdant. |
| Isa | 28:20 | The **b** is too short to stretch out on, |

| | | |
|---|---|---|
| Mt | 8:14 | Peter's mother-in-law lying in **b** |
| Lk | 11: 7 | and my children and I are in **b**. |
| | 17:34 | night two people will be in one **b**; |
| Heb | 13: 4 | and the marriage **b** kept pure, |
| Rev | 2:22 | I will cast her on a **b** of suffering, |

## BEDS [BED]

| | | |
|---|---|---|
| Ps | 36: 4 | Even on their **b** they plot evil; |
| Mic | 2: 1 | to those who plot evil on their **b**! |
| Ac | 5:15 | laid them on **b** and mats so |

## BEELZEBUL* [BAAL-ZEBUB]

| | | |
|---|---|---|
| Mt | 10:25 | head of the house has been called **B**, |
| | 12:24 | only by **B**, the prince of demons, |
| | 12:27 | if I drive out demons by **B**, |
| Mk | 3:22 | "He is possessed by **B**! |
| Lk | 11:15 | "By **B**, the prince of demons, |
| | 11:18 | I drive out demons by **B**. |
| | 11:19 | Now if I drive out demons by **B**, |

## BEER

| | | |
|---|---|---|
| 1Sa | 1:15 | I have not been drinking wine or **b**; |
| Pr | 20: 1 | Wine is a mocker and **b** a brawler; |
| | 31: 4 | drink wine, not for rulers to crave **b**, |
| | 31: 6 | Let **b** be for those who are |
| Isa | 24: 9 | the **b** is bitter to its drinkers. |
| | 28: 7 | stagger from wine and reel from **b**: |
| | 28: 7 | and prophets stagger from **b** and are |
| | 29: 9 | from wine, stagger, but not from **b**. |
| | 56:12 | Let us drink our fill of **b**! |
| Mic | 2:11 | for you plenty of wine and **b**,' |

## BEERSHEBA

| | | |
|---|---|---|
| Ge | 21:14 | and wandered in the Desert of **B**. |
| | 21:33 | planted a tamarisk tree in **B**, |
| | 22:19 | for **B**. And Abraham stayed in **B**. |
| | 46: 1 | and when he reached **B**, he offered |
| Jdg | 20: 1 | all the Israelites from Dan to **B** |
| 1Sa | 3:20 | Dan to **B** recognized that Samuel |
| 2Sa | 3:10 | Israel and Judah from Dan to **B**." |
| | 17:11 | Let all Israel, from Dan to **B** |
| | 24: 2 | the tribes of Israel from Dan to **B** |
| | 24:15 | of the people from Dan to **B** died. |
| 1Ki | 4:25 | from Dan to **B**, lived in safety, |
| 1Ch | 21: 2 | count the Israelites from **B** to Dan. |
| 2Ch | 30: 5 | throughout Israel, from **B** to Dan, |
| Am | 8:14 | 'As surely as the god of **B** lives'— |

## BEES*

| | | |
|---|---|---|
| Dt | 1:44 | they chased you like a swarm of **b** |
| Jdg | 14: 8 | in it he saw a swarm of **b** and some |
| Ps | 118:12 | They swarmed around me like **b**, |
| Isa | 7:18 | and for **b** from the land of Assyria. |

## BEFORE [BEFOREHAND]

| | | |
|---|---|---|
| Ge | 10: 9 | was a mighty hunter **b** the LORD. |
| | 18:22 | remained standing **b** the LORD. |
| | 24:15 | **B** he had finished praying, |
| | 27: 4 | may give you my blessing **b** I die." |
| Ex | 4:21 | that you perform **b** Pharaoh all |
| | 9:11 | could not stand **b** Moses because |
| | 20: 3 | shall have no other gods **b** me. |
| | 32: 1 | make us gods who will go **b** us. |
| | 33: 2 | I will send an angel **b** you and drive |
| Lev | 10: 2 | them, and they died **b** the LORD. |

Nu   17: 7  placed the staffs **b** the LORD
Dt    7:22  will drive out those nations **b** you,
      11:26  I am setting **b** you today a blessing
      30:15  I set **b** you today life and prosperity,
1Sa   4: 7  Nothing like this has happened **b**.
Ps  139: 4  **B** a word is on my tongue you,
Pr   16:18  Pride goes **b** destruction, a haughty
            spirit **b** a fall.
      18:12  **B** a downfall the heart is haughty,
      18:12  but humility comes **b** honor.
      18:13  To answer **b** listening—that is folly
Isa  43:10  **B** me no god was formed, nor will
      48: 5  **b** they happened I announced them
      65:24  **B** they call I will answer;
Mt    6: 8  what you need **b** you ask him.
      11:10  who will prepare your way **b** you.'
      24:38  For in the days **b** the flood,
Lk   22:34  Peter, **b** the rooster crows today,
Jn    8:58  answered, "**b** Abraham was born,
      13:19  "I am telling you now **b** it happens,
      17: 5  I had with you **b** the world began.
Col   1:17  He is **b** all things, and in him all
1Ti   5:20  sinning you are to reprove **b** everyone,
Tit   1: 2  promised **b** the beginning of time,
1Pe   1:20  He was chosen **b** the creation

## BEFOREHAND  [BEFORE]

Mk   13:11  do not worry **b** about what to say
Ac    4:28  will had decided **b** should happen.
Ro    1: 2  gospel he promised **b** through his

## BEG  [BEGGAR, BEGGED, BEGGING]

La    4: 4  the children **b** for bread, but no one
Lk   16: 3  to dig, and I'm ashamed to **b**—
Ac    3: 2  where he was put every day to **b**

## BEGGAR  [BEG]

Lk   16:20  gate was laid a **b** named Lazarus,

## BEGGED  [BEG]

Mt    8:31  The demons **b** Jesus, "If you drive
Mk    6:56  They **b** him to let them touch even

## BEGGING  [BEG]

Ps   37:25  forsaken or their children **b** bread.
Ac   16: 9  of Macedonia standing and **b** him,

## BEGINNING

Ge    1: 1  In the **b** God created the heavens
Ps  102:25  In the **b** you laid the foundations
     111:10  of the LORD is the **b** of wisdom;
Pr    1: 7  the LORD is the **b** of knowledge,
      4: 7  The **b** of wisdom is this:
      9:10  of the LORD is the **b** of wisdom,
Ecc   3:11  fathom what God has done from **b**
      7: 8  end of a matter is better than its **b**,
Isa  40:21  Has it not been told you from the **b**?
      46:10  I make known the end from the **b**,
Da   12: 1  from the **b** of nations until then.
Mt   19: 8  But it was not this way from the **b**.
      24: 8  All these are the **b** of birth pains.
      24:21  from the **b** of the world until now—
Mk    1: 1  The **b** of the good news about Jesus
Lk    1: 3  investigated everything from the **b**,
Jn    1: 1  In the **b** was the Word,

Jn    8:44  He was a murderer from the **b**,
      15:27  you have been with me from the **b**.
Ac    1:22  **b** from John's baptism to the time
Gal   3: 3  After **b** with the Spirit, are you now
Heb   7: 3  without **b** of days or end of life,
2Pe   2:20  at the end than they were at the **b**.
1Jn   1: 1  That which was from the **b**,
      3: 8  devil has been sinning from the **b**.
2Jn   1: 6  As you have heard from the **b**,
Rev  21: 6  and the Omega, the **B** and the End.
      22:13  and the Last, the **B** and the End.

## BEGRUDGING*

Pr   23: 6  Do not eat the food of a **b** host,

## BEHALF

Ge   25:21  to the LORD on **b** of his wife,
Lev  22:19  that it may be accepted on your **b**.
      22:20  it will not be accepted on your **b**.
1Sa  14: 6  the LORD will act in our **b**.
2Sa  24:25  LORD answered his prayer in **b**
Jn    8:14  "Even if I testify on my own **b**,
      16:26  that I will ask the Father on your **b**.

## BEHAVE  [BEHAVIOR]

Ro   13:13  Let us **b** decently, as in the daytime,

## BEHAVIOR  [BEHAVE]

Pr    1: 3  for receiving instruction in prudent **b**,
Col   1:21  your minds because of your evil **b**.
1Pe   3: 1  words by the **b** of their wives,
      3:16  maliciously against your good **b**

## BEHEADED

Lk    9: 9  But Herod said, "I **b** John.
Rev  20: 4  of those who had been **b** because

## BEHEMOTH*

Job  40:15  "Look at the **b**, which I made along

## BEHIND

Mt   16:23  turned and said to Peter, "Get **b** me,
Mk   14:52  fled naked, leaving his garment **b**.
Lk    2:43  the boy Jesus stayed **b** in Jerusalem,
1Co  13:11  I put the ways of childhood **b** me.
Php   3:13  Forgetting what is **b** and straining
1Ti   5:24  the sins of others trail **b** them.

## BEHOLD*

Nu   24:17  but not now; I **b** him, but not near.

## BEING  [BEINGS]

Ge    2: 7  life, and the man became a living **b**.
2Sa   7:19  this decree, Sovereign LORD, is for a
            human **b**!
Job  10:19  If only I had never come into **b**,
Ps  103: 1  all my inmost **b**, praise his holy
     130: 5  for the LORD, my whole **b** waits,
     139:13  For you created my inmost **b**;
Pr   23:16  my inmost **b** will rejoice when your
1Co  15:45  first Adam became a living **b**";
Eph   3:16  through his Spirit in your inner **b**,
Php   2: 6  Who, **b** in very nature God, did not
2Pe   3: 5  the heavens came into **b** and the earth
Rev   4:11  were created and have their **b**."

## BEINGS [BEING]

| | | |
|---|---|---|
| 2Sa | 7:14 | punish him with a rod wielded by human **b**, |
| Ps | 8: 5 | a little lower than the heavenly **b** |
| | 78:25 | Human **b** ate the bread of angels; |
| | 89: 6 | the LORD among the heavenly **b**? |
| | 146: 3 | in human **b**, who cannot save. |
| Ac | 5: 4 | not lied just to human **b** but to God." |
| | 5:29 | obey God rather than human **b**! |
| Ro | 1:18 | godlessness and wickedness of human **b** |
| 1Co | 3: 3 | not acting like mere human **b**? |
| 1Ti | 2: 5 | one mediator between God and human **b**, |
| 2Pe | 2:10 | afraid to heap abuse on celestial **b**; |
| | 2:11 | on such **b** when bringing judgment |
| Jude | 1: 8 | and heap abuse on celestial **b**. |
| Rev | 18:13 | and human **b** sold as slaves. |

## BEL

Isa   46: 1   **B** bows down, Nebo stoops low;

## BELIAL*

2Co   6:15   is there between Christ and **B**?

## BELIEVE [BELIEVED, BELIEVER, BELIEVERS, BELIEVES, BELIEVING]

| | | |
|---|---|---|
| Ex | 4: 1 | "What if they do not **b** me or listen |
| | 4: 5 | so that they may **b** that the LORD, |
| Nu | 14:11 | How long will they refuse to **b** |
| 1Ki | 10: 7 | I did not **b** these things until I came |
| 2Ch | 32:15 | Do not **b** him, for no god of any |
| Ps | 78:32 | spite of his wonders, they did not **b**. |
| Pr | 14:15 | The simple **b** anything, |
| Isa | 43:10 | so that you may know and **b** me |
| Hab | 1: 5 | in your days that you would not **b**, |
| Mt | 9:28 | "Do you **b** that I am able to do |
| | 18: 6 | those who **b** in me— |
| | 21:22 | If you **b**, you will receive whatever |
| | 24:23 | or, 'There he is!' do not **b** it. |
| | 27:42 | the cross, and we will **b** in him. |
| Mk | 1:15 | Repent and **b** the good news!" |
| | 5:36 | told him, "Don't be afraid; just **b**." |
| | 9:24 | the boy's father exclaimed, "I do **b**; |
| | 9:42 | those who **b** in me— |
| | 11:23 | but **b** that what you say will happen, |
| | 11:24 | prayer, **b** that you have received it, |
| | 15:32 | the cross, that we may see and **b**." |
| | 16:16 | *does not **b** will be condemned.* |
| | 16:17 | *signs will accompany those who **b**:* |
| Lk | 8:12 | so that they may not **b** and be saved. |
| | 8:13 | They **b** for a while, but in the time |
| | 8:50 | just **b**, and she will be healed." |
| | 22:67 | "If I tell you, you will not **b** me, |
| | 24:11 | But they did not **b** the women, |
| | 24:25 | how slow to **b** all that the prophets |
| Jn | 1: 7 | so that through him all might **b**. |
| | 3:12 | of earthly things and you do not **b**; |
| | 3:12 | will you **b** if I speak of heavenly |
| | 3:18 | does not **b** stands condemned |
| | 4:21 | Jesus replied, "**b** me, a time is |
| | 4:42 | "We no longer **b** just because |
| | 5:38 | for you do not **b** the one he sent. |
| | 5:47 | since you do not **b** what he wrote, |
| | 5:47 | are you going to **b** what I say?" |
| | 6:29 | to **b** in the one he has sent." |

| | | |
|---|---|---|
| Jn | 6:69 | We have come to **b** and to know |
| | 7: 5 | even his own brothers did not **b** |
| | 8:24 | if you do not **b** that I am he, |
| | 9:35 | "Do you **b** in the Son of Man?" |
| | 9:38 | "Lord, I **b**," and he worshiped him. |
| | 10:26 | you do not **b** because you are not |
| | 10:37 | Do not **b** me unless I do the works |
| | 10:38 | even though you do not **b** me, |
| | 11:27 | him, "I **b** that you are the Messiah, |
| | 11:40 | "Did I not tell you that if you **b**, |
| | 12:37 | they still would not **b** in him. |
| | 12:39 | For this reason they could not **b**, |
| | 12:44 | "Those who **b** in me do not **b** in me |
| | 13:19 | it does happen you will **b** that I am |
| | 14:10 | Don't you **b** that I am in the Father, |
| | 14:11 | **B** me when I say that I am |
| | 14:11 | or at least **b** on the evidence |
| | 14:29 | that when it does happen you will **b**. |
| | 16:30 | This makes us **b** that you came |
| | 16:31 | "Do you now **b**?" Jesus replied. |
| | 17:20 | those who will **b** in me through their |
| | 19:35 | he testifies so that you also may **b**. |
| | 20:27 | into my side. Stop doubting and **b**." |
| | 20:31 | you may **b** that Jesus is the Messiah, |
| Ac | 13:41 | your days that you would never **b**, |
| | 15: 7 | the message of the gospel and **b**. |
| | 16:31 | They replied, "**B** in the Lord Jesus, |
| | 19: 4 | He told the people to **b** in the one |
| | 22:19 | and beat those who **b** in you. |
| | 24:14 | I **b** everything that is in accordance |
| | 26:27 | Agrippa, do you **b** the prophets? |
| | 28:24 | he said, but others would not **b**. |
| Ro | 3:22 | faith in Jesus Christ to all who **b**. |
| | 4:11 | he is the father of all who **b** |
| | 6: 8 | we **b** that we will also live with him. |
| | 10:10 | For it is with your heart that you **b** |
| | 10:14 | how can they **b** in the one of whom |
| 1Co | 1:21 | was preached to save those who **b**. |
| 2Co | 4:13 | faith, we also **b** and therefore speak, |
| Gal | 3:22 | might be given to those who **b**. |
| Eph | 1:19 | great power for us who **b**. |
| Php | 1:29 | of Christ not only to **b** on him, |
| 1Th | 2:13 | is indeed at work in you who **b**. |
| | 4:14 | We **b** that Jesus died and rose again, |
| | 4:14 | so we **b** that God will bring |
| 2Th | 2:11 | delusion so that they will **b** the lie |
| 1Ti | 1:16 | for those who would **b** in him |
| | 4: 3 | with thanksgiving by those who **b** |
| | 4:10 | and especially of those who **b**. |
| Tit | 1: 6 | a man whose children **b** and are not |
| Heb | 10:39 | but of those who **b** and are saved. |
| | 11: 6 | comes to him must **b** that he exists |
| Jas | 1: 6 | you ask, you must **b** and not doubt, |
| | 2:19 | You **b** that there is one God. Good! |
| | 2:19 | Even the demons **b** that— |
| 1Pe | 1: 8 | you **b** in him and are filled |
| | 2: 7 | Now to you who **b**, this stone is |
| | 2: 7 | But to those who do not **b**, |
| | 3: 1 | if any of them do not **b** the word, |
| 1Jn | 3:23 | to **b** in the name of his Son, |
| | 4: 1 | Dear friends, do not **b** every spirit, |
| | 5:13 | things to you who **b** in the name |
| Jude | 1: 5 | later destroyed those who did not **b**. |

## BELIEVED [BELIEVE]

| | | |
|---|---|---|
| Ge | 15: 6 | Abram **b** the LORD, and he |
| Ex | 4:31 | and they **b**. And when they heard |

Ps 106:12 Then they **b** his promises and sang
Isa 53: 1 Who has **b** our message
Jnh 3: 5 The Ninevites **b** God.
Lk 1:45 Blessed is she who has **b**
Jn 1:12 to those who **b** in his name, he gave
2:22 Then they **b** the scripture
3:18 already because they have not **b**
4:53 So he and his whole household **b**.
5:46 If you **b** Moses, you would believe
7:39 whom those who **b** in him were
7:48 rulers or of the Pharisees **b** in him?
8:31 To the Jews who had **b** him,
10:42 And in that place many **b** in Jesus.
12:38 who has **b** our message
17: 8 you, and they **b** that you sent me.
20: 8 also went inside. He saw and **b**.
20:29 you have seen me, you have **b**;
20:29 who have not seen and yet have **b**."
Ac 4: 4 But many who heard the message **b**;
4: 4 the number of men who **b** grew
5:14 more men and women **b** in the Lord
8:12 they **b** Philip as he proclaimed
9:42 and many people **b** in the Lord.
11:17 them the same gift he gave us who **b**
13:12 he **b**, for he was amazed
13:48 were appointed for eternal life **b**.
14: 1 great number of Jews and Greeks **b**.
17:12 Many of them **b**, as did
18: 8 his entire household **b** in the Lord;
18: 8 of the Corinthians who heard Paul **b**
19: 2 the Holy Spirit when you **b**?"
21:20 many thousands of Jews have **b**,
Ro 4: 3 "Abraham **b** God, and it was
10:14 call on the one they have not **b** in?
10:16 "Lord, who has **b** our message?"
1Co 15: 2 Otherwise, you have **b** in vain.
Gal 3: 6 So also Abraham "**b** God, and it
Eph 1:13 When you **b**, you were marked
2Th 1:10 at among all those who have **b**.
1:10 because you **b** our testimony to you.
2.12 condemned who have not **b** the truth
1Ti 3:16 the nations, was **b** on in the world,
2Ti 1:12 because I know whom I have **b**,
Heb 4: 3 Now we who have **b** enter that rest,
Jas 2:23 that says, "Abraham **b** God, and it
1Jn 5:10 they have not **b** the testimony God

## BELIEVER [BELIEVE]

1Ki 18: 3 (Obadiah was a devout **b**
Ac 16: 1 a **b** but whose father was a Greek.
16:15 you consider me a **b** in the Lord,"
1Co 7:12 brother has a wife who is not a **b**
7:13 has a husband who is not a **b** and he
2Co 6:15 what does a **b** have in common
1Ti 5:16 any woman who is a **b** has widows

## BELIEVERS [BELIEVE]

Jn 4:41 of his words many more became **b**.
Ac 1:15 up among the **b** (a group numbering
2:44 All the **b** were together and had
4:32 All the **b** were one in heart
5:12 all the **b** used to meet together
9:41 Then he called for the **b**,
10:45 The circumcised **b** who had come
11: 2 the circumcised **b** criticized him
15: 2 along with some other **b**, to go

Ac 15: 5 some of the **b** who belonged
15:23 To the Gentile **b** in Antioch,
15:32 encourage and strengthen the **b**.
21:25 As for the Gentile **b**, we have
1Co 6: 5 to judge a dispute between **b**?
14:22 a sign, not for **b** but for unbelievers;
14:22 is not for unbelievers but for **b**.
2Co 11:26 in danger from false **b**.
Gal 2: 4 because some false **b** had infiltrated
6:10 those who belong to the family of **b**.
1Th 1: 7 a model to all the **b** in Macedonia
1Ti 4:12 set an example for the **b** in speech,
6: 2 just because they are fellow **b**.
6: 2 masters are dear to them as fellow **b**
Jas 2: 1 **b** in our glorious Lord Jesus Christ
1Pe 2:17 love your fellow **b**, fear God,
3Jn 1:10 he refuses to welcome other **b**.

## BELIEVES* [BELIEVE]

Mk 9:23 is possible for one who **b**."
16:16 *Whoever **b** and is baptized will be saved*
Jn 3:15 everyone who **b** may have eternal
3:16 whoever **b** in him shall not perish
3:18 Whoever **b** in him is not
3:36 Whoever **b** in the Son has eternal
5:24 **b** him who sent me has eternal life
6:35 and whoever **b** in me will never be
6:40 and **b** in him shall have eternal life,
6:47 tell you, whoever **b** has eternal life.
7:38 Whoever **b** in me, as Scripture has
11:25 Anyone who **b** in me will live,
12:46 that no one who **b** in me should stay
Ac 10:43 that everyone who **b** in him receives
13:39 him everyone who **b** is set free
Ro 1:16 brings salvation to everyone who **b**:
9:33 one who **b** in him will never
10: 4 righteousness for everyone who **b**.
10·11 **b** in him will never be put to shame."
1Jn 5: 1 Everyone who **b** that Jesus is
5: 5 Only the one who **b** that Jesus is
5:10 Whoever **b** in the Son of God

## BELIEVING* [BELIEVE]

Jn 11:26 lives by **b** in me will never die.
20:31 by **b** you may have life in his name.
Ac 9:26 not **b** that he really was a disciple.
1Co 7:14 sanctified through her **b** husband.
9: 5 have the right to take a **b** wife along
Gal 3: 2 the law, or by **b** what you heard?
3: 5 or by your **b** what you heard?
1Ti 6: 2 Those who have **b** masters should

## BELLIES* [BELLY]

Job 15: 2 fill their **b** with the hot east wind?
Ps 17:14 stored up for the wicked fill their **b**;

## BELLY [BELLIES]

Ge 3:14 You will crawl on your **b** and you
Jdg 3:21 and plunged it into the king's **b**.
2Sa 20:10 and Joab plunged it into his **b**,
Da 2:32 of silver, its **b** and thighs of bronze,
Mt 12:40 three nights in the **b** of a huge fish,

## BELONG [BELONGED, BELONGING, BELONGINGS, BELONGS]

Ge  40: 8  "Do not interpretations **b** to God?
Ex  13:12  of your livestock **b** to the LORD.
Lev 25:55  for the Israelites **b** to me as servants.
Dt  10:14  LORD your God **b** the heavens,
    29:29  The secret things **b** to the LORD
    29:29  but the things revealed **b** to us
Job 12:13  "To God **b** wisdom and power;
    12:16  To him **b** strength and insight;
    25: 2  "Dominion and awe **b** to God;
Ps  47: 9  for the kings of the earth **b** to God;
    95: 4  and the mountain peaks **b** to him.
   115:16  The highest heavens **b**
Pr  16: 1  To human beings **b** the plans
SS   7:10  I **b** to my beloved, and his desire is
Isa 44: 5  Some will say, 'I **b** to the LORD';
Jer  5:10  for these people do not **b**
Jn   8:44  You **b** to your father, the devil,
     8:47  hear is that you do not **b** to God."
    15:19  As it is, you do not **b** to the world,
Ro   1: 6  those Gentiles who are called to **b**
     7: 4  that you might **b** to another, to him
     8: 9  of Christ, they do not **b** to Christ.
    14: 8  we live or die, we **b** to the Lord.
1Co  7:39  wishes, but he must **b** to the Lord.
     9:19  Though I am free and **b** to no one,
    12:15  not a hand, I do not **b** to the body,"
    15:23  when he comes, those who **b** to him.
2Co 10: 7  that we **b** to Christ just as much
Gal  3:29  If you **b** to Christ, then you are
     5:24  Those who **b** to Christ Jesus have
     6:10  to those who **b** to the family
1Th  5: 5  We do not **b** to the night
     5: 8  But since we **b** to the day, let us be
1Jn  2:19  us, but they did not really **b** to us.
     3:19  how we know that we **b** to the truth

## BELONGED [BELONG]

Jn  15:19  If you **b** to the world, it would love
Ac   9: 2  if he found any there who **b**
    12: 1  King Herod arrested some who **b**
1Jn  2:19  For if they had **b** to us, they would
     2:19  showed that none of them **b** to us.
     3:12  who **b** to the evil one and murdered

## BELONGING [BELONG]

Ge  14:23  that I will accept nothing **b** to you,
Nu  16:26  Do not touch anything **b** to them,
Ru   2: 3  herself working in a field **b** to Boaz,

## BELONGINGS [BELONG]

Jer 46:19  Pack your **b** for exile, you who live
Eze 12: 4  bring out your **b** packed for exile.

## BELONGS [BELONG]

Ex  34:19  offspring of every womb **b** to me,
Lev 27:30  from the trees, **b** to the LORD;
Dt   1:17  of anyone, for judgment **b** to God.
Job 41:11  Everything under heaven **b** to me.
Ps  22:28  for dominion **b** to the LORD
    89:18  Indeed, our shield **b** to the LORD,
   111:10  To him **b** eternal praise.
Jer 46:10  But that day **b** to the Lord,

Eze 18: 4  For everyone **b** to me, the parent as
Mt  19:14  of heaven **b** to such as these."
Jn   8:47  Whoever **b** to God hears what God
    16:15  All that **b** to the Father is mine.
Ro  12: 5  and each member **b** to all the others.
Col  3: 5  whatever **b** to your earthly nature:
Rev  7:10  "Salvation **b** to our God, who sits

## BELOVED* [LOVE]

Dt  33:12  "Let the **b** of the LORD rest
SS   1:13  My **b** is to me a sachet of myrrh
     1:14  My **b** is to me a cluster of henna
     1:16  How handsome you are, my **b**!
     2: 3  forest is my **b** among the young men.
     2: 8  Listen! My **b**! Look! Here he comes,
     2: 9  My **b** is like a gazelle or a young stag.
     2:10  My **b** spoke and said to me,
     2:16  My **b** is mine and I am his;
     2:17  my **b**, and be like a gazelle
     4:16  Let my **b** come into his garden
     5: 2  Listen! My **b** is knocking:
     5: 4  **b** thrust his hand through the
     5: 5  I arose to open for my **b**,
     5: 6  opened for my **b**, but my **b** had left;
     5: 8  if you find my **b**,
     5: 9  How is your **b** better than others,
     5: 9  How is your **b** better than others,
     5:10  My **b** is radiant and ruddy,
     5:16  This is my **b**, this is my friend,
     6: 1  Where has your **b** gone, most beautiful
     6: 1  Which way did your **b** turn,
     6: 2  My **b** has gone down to his garden,
     6: 3  my **b** is mine; he browses among the
     7: 9  wine go straight to my **b**, flowing gently
     7:10  belong to my **b**, and his desire is for me.
     7:11  my **b**, let us go to the countryside,
     7:13  stored up for you, my **b**.
     8: 5  the wilderness leaning on her **b**?
     8:14  Come away, my **b**, and be like a gazelle
Jer 11:15  "What is my **b** doing in my temple

## BELOVED'S* [LOVE]

SS   6: 3  I am my **b** and my beloved is mine;

## BELOW

Dt   4:39  in heaven above and on the earth **b**.
Isa 37:31  the house of Judah will take root **b**
Jn   8:23  But he continued, "You are from **b**;
Ac   2:19  above and signs on the earth **b**,

## BELSHAZZAR

King of Babylon in days of Daniel (Da 5).

## BELT

Ex  12:11  with your cloak tucked into your **b**,
1Sa 18: 4  even his sword, his bow and his **b**.
1Ki 18:46  tucking his cloak into his **b**, he ran
2Ki  1: 8  had a leather **b** around his waist."
     4:29  "Tuck your cloak into your **b**,
     9: 1  "Tuck your cloak into your **b**,
Isa 11: 5  Righteousness will be his **b**
Jer 13: 1  buy a linen **b** and put it around your
Da  10: 5  with a **b** of fine gold from Uphaz
Mk   1: 6  with a leather **b** around his waist,
Eph  6:14  the **b** of truth buckled around your

## BELTESHAZZAR [DANIEL]
Da  1: 7  to Daniel, the name **B**;

## BEN HINNOM
2Ki 23:10  Topheth, which was in the Valley of **B**,
Jer  7:31  in the Valley of **B** to burn their sons

## BEN-HADAD [HADAD]
   1. King of Syria in time of Asa (1Ki 15:18–20; 2Ch 16:2–4).
   2. King of Syria in time of Ahab (1Ki 20; 2Ki 5–7; 8:7–15).
   3. King of Syria in time of Jehoahaz (2Ki 13:3, 24–25; Am 1:4).

## BEN-ONI* [BENJAMIN]
Ge 35:18  she named her son **B**.

## BENAIAH
   A commander of Davids army (2Sa 8:18; 20:23; 23:20–30); loyal to Solomon (1Ki 1:8—2:46; 4:4).

## BEND [BENT]
2Sa 22:35  my arms can **b** a bow of bronze.
Zec  9:13  I will **b** Judah as I **b** my bow and fill

## BENEFICIAL* [BENEFIT]
1Co  6:12  but not everything is **b**.
     10:23  but not everything is **b**.

## BENEFIT [BENEFICIAL, BENEFITS]
Job 22: 2  **b** to God? Can even the wise **b** him?
Pr  11:17  Those who are kind **b** themselves,
Isa 38:17  my **b** that I suffered such anguish.
Jn  11:42  the **b** of the people standing here,
Ro   6:22  the **b** you reap leads to holiness,
2Co  1:15  you first so that you might **b** twice.
     4:15  All this is for your **b**,
Phm  1:20  that I may have some **b** from you

## BENEFITS* [BENEFIT]
Dt  18: 8  He is to share equally in their **b**,
Ps 103: 2  my soul, and forget not all his **b**—
Ecc  7:11  thing and **b** those who see the sun.
Jn   4:38  and you have reaped the **b** of their

## BENJAMIN [BEN-ONI]
   Twelfth son of Jacob by Rachel (Ge 35:16–24; 46:19–21; 1Ch 2:2). Jacob refused to send him to Egypt, but relented (Ge 42–45). Tribe of blessed (Ge 49:27; Dt 33:12), numbered (Nu 1:37; 26:41), allotted land (Jos 18:11–28; Eze 48:23), failed to fully possess (Jdg 1:21), ncarly obliterated (Jdg 20–21), sided with Ish-Bosheth (2Sa 2), but turned to David (1Ch 12:2, 29). 12,000 from (Rev 7:8).

## BENT [BEND]
1Sa 24: 9  say, 'David is **b** on harming you'?
Ps  44:16  of the enemy, who is **b** on revenge.
    69:23  see, and their backs be **b** forever.
Isa 32: 6  their hearts are **b** on evil:
Hos 11: 4  cheek, and I **b** down to feed them.
Lk  13:11  She was **b** over and could not
Jn  20: 5  He **b** over and looked in at the strips

Ro  11:10  see, and their backs be **b** forever."
Rev  6: 2  out as a conqueror **b** on conquest.

## BERAKAH
2Ch 20:26  called the Valley of **B** to this day.

## BEREA [BEREAN]
Ac  17:10  sent Paul and Silas away to **B**.

## BEREAN* [BEREA]
Ac  17:11  **B** Jews were of more noble character

## BEREAVE* [BEREAVED, BEREAVEMENT, BEREAVES]
Hos  9:12  children, I will **b** them of every one.

## BEREAVED* [BEREAVE]
Ge  43:14  As for me, if I am **b**, I am **b**."
Ps  35:12  and leave me like one **b**.
Isa 49:21  I was **b** and barren; I was exiled

## BEREAVEMENT* [BEREAVE]
Isa 49:20  born during your **b** will yet say
Jer 15: 7  I will bring **b** and destruction on my

## BEREAVES* [BEREAVE]
La   1:20  Outside, the sword **b**; inside, there is

## BESIDES
Dt  32:39  There is no god **b** me. I put to death
1Sa  2: 2  there is no one **b** you; there is no
2Sa 22:32  For who is God **b** the LORD?
Ps  18:31  For who is God **b** the LORD?
    73:25  earth has nothing I desire **b** you.
Isa 47: 8  'I am, and there is none **b** me.
    64: 4  no eye has seen any God **b** you,
Zep  2:15  And there is none **b** me."

## BESIEGED [SIEGE]
La   3: 5  He has **b** me and surrounded me
Da   1: 1  Babylon came to Jerusalem and **b** it.
Zec 12: 2  Judah will be **b** as well as

## BEST [GOOD]
Ge  45:18  I will give you the **b** of the land
    47: 6  your brothers in the **b** part
Ex  15: 4  The **b** of Pharaoh's officers are
Nu  18:29  as the LORD's portion the **b**
Dt  33:16  with the **b** gifts of the earth and its
Ps  90:10  the **b** of them are but trouble
SS   7: 9  and your mouth like the **b** wine.
Isa  1:19  you will eat the **b** from the land;
    48:17  who teaches you what is **b** for you,
Eze 44:30  The **b** of all the firstfruits and of all
Mic  7: 4  The **b** of them is like a brier,
Jn   2:10  but you have saved the **b** till now."
Php  1:10  you may be able to discern what is **b**
2Ti  2:15  Do your **b** to present yourself

## BESTOW* [BESTOWED, BESTOWER, BESTOWING, BESTOWS]
Ps  31:19  which you **b** in the sight of all
Isa 45: 4  name and **b** on you a title of honor,

Isa 61: 3 to **b** on them a crown of beauty
62: 2 that the mouth of the LORD will **b**.
Jer 23: 2 I will **b** punishment on you

## BESTOWED [BESTOW]
1Ch 29:25 **b** on him royal splendor such as no

## BESTOWER* [BESTOW]
Isa 23: 8 this against Tyre, the **b** of crowns,

## BESTOWING* [BESTOW]
Pr 8:21 **b** a rich inheritance on those who

## BESTOWS* [BESTOW]
Job 5:10 He **b** rain on the earth;
Ps 84:11 the LORD **b** favor and honor;
133: 3 For there the LORD **b** his blessing,

## BETH AVEN
Hos 4:15 Gilgal; do not go up to **B**.
10: 5 fear for the calf-idol of **B**.

## BETH SHAN
Jdg 1:27 did not drive out the people of **B**
1Sa 31:10 his body to the wall of **B**.

## BETH SHEMESH
1Sa 6:14 came to the field of Joshua of **B**,

## BETHANY
Mt 26: 6 While Jesus was in **B** in the home
Mk 11:12 next day as they were leaving **B**,
Jn 1:28 This all happened at **B** on the other

## BETHEL [EL BETHEL, LUZ]
Ge 12: 8 he went on toward the hills east of **B**
12: 8 with **B** on the west and Ai
28:19 He called that place **B**,
31:13 I am the God of **B**, where you
35: 8 was buried under the oak below **B**.
Jos 8: 9 and lay in wait between **B** and Ai,
Jdg 20:18 The Israelites went up to **B**
1Sa 7:16 went on a circuit from **B** to Gilgal
1Ki 12:29 One he set up in **B**, and the other
13:11 a certain old prophet living in **B**,
2Ki 2: 2 the LORD has sent me to **B**."
2: 2 So they went down to **B**.
10:29 worship of the golden calves at **B**
23:15 Even the altar at **B**, the high place
Am 4: 4 "Go to **B** and sin; go to Gilgal
7:10 the priest of **B** sent a message

## BETHESDA*
Jn 5: 2 which in Aramaic is called **B**

## BETHLEHEM [EPHRATH]
Ge 35:19 on the way to Ephrath (that is, **B**).
Ru 1: 1 So a man from **B** in Judah,
1:19 went on until they came to **B**.
1:19 When they arrived in **B**, the whole
4:11 in Ephrathah and be famous in **B**.
1Sa 16: 1 I am sending you to Jesse of **B**.
2Sa 23:15 from the well near the gate of **B**!"
Mic 5: 2 "But you, **B** Ephrathah, though you

Mt 2: 1 After Jesus was born in **B** in Judea,
2: 6 " 'But you, **B**, in the land
2:16 gave orders to kill all the boys in **B**
Lk 2:15 "Let's go to **B** and see this thing
Jn 7:42 David's descendants and from **B**,

## BETHPHAGE
Mt 21: 1 came to **B** on the Mount of Olives,

## BETHSAIDA
Mt 11:21 Woe to you, **B**! If the miracles
Jn 12:21 Philip, who was from **B** in Galilee,

## BETRAY [BETRAYED, BETRAYER, BETRAYING, BETRAYS]
Ps 89:33 nor will I ever **b** my faithfulness.
Pr 11:13 Gossips **b** a confidence,
16:10 and his mouth does not **b** justice.
25: 9 do not **b** another's confidence,
Isa 24:16 The treacherous **b**!
24:16 With treachery the treacherous **b**!"
Mt 10:21 "Brother will **b** brother to death,
24:10 faith and will **b** and hate each other,
26:21 I tell you, one of you will **b** me."
Jn 13:11 he knew who was going to **b** him,

## BETRAYED [BETRAY]
La 1: 2 All her friends have **b** her;
Mt 27: 4 said, "for I have **b** innocent blood."
Lk 21:16 You will be **b** even by parents,
Jn 18: 2 Now Judas, who **b** him,

## BETRAYER [BETRAY]
Mk 14:42 Let us go! Here comes my **b**!"

## BETRAYING [BETRAY]
Lk 22:48 are you **b** the Son of Man

## BETRAYS [BETRAY]
Pr 20:19 A gossip **b** a confidence;
Hab 2: 5 indeed, wine **b** him; he is arrogant
Mk 14:21 to that man who **b** the Son of Man!

## BETROTH
Hos 2:19 I will **b** you to me forever; I will **b**

## BETTER [GOOD]
Nu 11:18 We were **b** off in Egypt!"
1Sa 15:22 To obey is **b** than sacrifice,
15:22 and to heed is **b** than the fat of rams.
Ps 37:16 **B** the little that the righteous have
63: 3 Because your love is **b** than life,
118: 8 It is **b** to take refuge in the LORD
Pr 8:19 My fruit is **b** than fine gold;
12: 9 **B** to be a nobody and yet have
15:16 **B** a little with the fear
15:17 **B** a small serving of vegetables
16: 8 **B** a little with righteousness than
16:16 How much **b** to get wisdom than
16:19 **B** to be lowly in spirit along
16:32 **B** a patient person than a warrior,
17: 1 **B** a dry crust with peace and quiet
17:12 **B** to meet a bear robbed of her cubs
19: 1 **B** the poor whose walk is blameless

Pr  19:22  **b** to be poor than a liar.
    21: 9  **B** to live on a corner of the roof than
    21:19  **B** to live in a desert than
    22: 1  to be esteemed is **b** than silver
    27: 5  **B** is open rebuke than hidden love.
    28: 6  **B** the poor whose walk is blameless
Ecc  2:13  I saw that wisdom is **b** than folly,
     2:13  just as light is **b** than darkness.
     2:24  People can do nothing **b** than to eat
     3:12  there is nothing **b** for people than
     3:22  there is nothing **b** for people than
     4: 3  **b** than both is the one who has not
     4: 6  **B** one handful with tranquillity than
     4: 9  Two are **b** than one, because they
     4:13  **B** a poor but wise youth than an old
     5: 5  It is **b** not to make a vow than
     6: 3  that a stillborn child is **b** off than he.
     6: 9  **B** what the eye sees than the roving
     7: 1  good name is **b** than fine perfume,
     7: 1  the day of death **b** than the day
     7: 2  It is **b** to go to a house of mourning
     7: 3  Frustration is **b** than laughter,
     7: 5  It is **b** to heed the rebuke of a wise
     7: 8  of a matter is **b** than its beginning,
     7: 8  and patience is **b** than pride.
     8:12  that it will go **b** with those who fear
     8:15  life, because there is nothing **b**
     9: 4  even a live dog is **b** off than a dead
     9:16  said, "Wisdom is **b** than strength."
     9:18  Wisdom is **b** than weapons of war,
SS   5: 9  How is your beloved **b** than others,
Jnh  4: 3  life, for it is **b** for me to die than
Mt   5:29  It is **b** for you to lose one part
     18: 6  it would be **b** for them if a large
     26:24  It would be **b** for him if he had not
Lk   5:39  new, for you say, 'The old is **b**.' "
     10:42  Mary has chosen what is **b**, and it
1Co  7: 9  for it is **b** to marry than to burn
Eph  1:17  so that you may know him **b**.
Heb  6: 9  we are convinced of **b** things
     7:19  and a **b** hope is introduced,
     7:22  the guarantor of a **b** covenant.
     8: 6  is established on **b** promises.
     9:23  with **b** sacrifices than these.
     10:34  you knew that you yourselves had **b**
     11: 4  brought God a **b** offering than Cain
     11:16  they were longing for a **b** country—
     11:35  might gain an even **b** resurrection.
     11:40  God had planned something **b** for us
     12:24  that speaks a **b** word than the blood
1Pe  3:17  It is **b**, if it is God's will, to suffer
2Pe  2:21  It would have been **b** for them not

## BETWEEN
Ge   3:15  And I will put enmity **b** you
     3:15  and **b** your offspring and hers;
     16: 5  May the LORD judge **b** you
     31:44  I, and let it serve as a witness **b** us."
Lev  10:10  that you can distinguish **b** the holy
     10:10  **b** the unclean and the clean,
1Sa  4: 4  who is enthroned **b** the cherubim.
Ro   10:12  For there is no difference **b** Jew
1Ti  2: 5  and one mediator **b** God and human

## BEULAH*
Isa  62: 4  called Hephzibah, and your land **B**;

## BEWARE*
2Ki  6: 9  "**B** of passing that place,
Job  36:21  **B** of turning to evil, which you seem
Isa  22:17  "**B**, the LORD is about to take
Jer  7:32  So **b**, the days are coming,
     9: 4  "**B** of your friends; do not trust any
     19: 6  So **b**, the days are coming,
Lk   20:46  "**B** of the teachers of the law.

## BEWITCHED* [WITCHCRAFT]
Gal  3: 1  Who has **b** you? Before your very

## BEYOND
Dt   30:11  too difficult for you or **b** your reach.
Jos  24: 2  lived **b** the Euphrates River
Jdg  13:18  It is **b** understanding."
Job  36:26  great is God—**b** our understanding!
     37:23  The Almighty is **b** our reach
Ecc  7:23  to be wise"—but this was **b** me.
Jer  17: 9  above all things and **b** cure.
     30:12  is incurable, your injury **b** healing.
Ro   11:11  stumble so as to fall **b** recovery?
1Co  4: 6  "Do not go **b** what is written."
     10:13  let you be tempted **b** what you can
2Co  1: 8  pressure, far **b** our ability to endure,
     10:16  the gospel in the regions **b** you.

## BEZALEL
Judahite craftsman in charge of building the tabernacle (Ex 31:1–11; 35:30—39:31).

## BIDDING*
Ps   103:20  you mighty ones who do his **b**,
     148: 8  clouds, stormy winds that do his **b**,

## BIER
Lk   7:14  touched the **b** they were carrying him
                 on,

## BILDAD
One of Job's friends (Job 2:11; 8; 18; 25).

## BILHAH
Servant of Rachel, mother of Jacob's sons Dan and
Naphtali (Ge 30:1–7; 35:25; 46:23–25).

## BIND [BINDING, BINDS, BOUND]
Dt   6: 8  and **b** them on your foreheads.
Ne   10:29  and **b** themselves with a curse
Pr   3: 3  **b** them around your neck,
     6:21  **B** them always on your heart;
     7: 3  **B** them on your fingers;
Isa  8:16  **B** up this testimony of warning
     56: 6  foreigners who **b** themselves
     61: 1  He has sent me to **b**
Eze  34:16  I will **b** up the injured
Mt   16:19  whatever you **b** on earth will be
     18:18  whatever you **b** on earth will be

## BINDING [BIND]
Heb  2: 2  spoken through angels was **b**,

## BINDS [BIND]
Job  5:18  For he wounds, but he also **b** up;

Isa  30:26  when the LORD **b** up the bruises
Col   3:14  which **b** them all together in perfect

## BIRD [BIRDS]
Ge    1:21  and every winged **b** according to its
      6:20  Two of every kind of **b**, of every
Dt   14:11  You may eat any clean **b**.
Ps   50:11  I know every **b** in the mountains,
Pr    6: 5  hunter, like a **b** from the snare
      7:23  liver, like a **b** darting into a snare,
     27: 8  Like a **b** that flees its nest is anyone
Ecc  10:20  because a **b** in the sky may carry
     10:20  a **b** on the wing may report what
Isa  46:11  From the east I summon a **b** of prey;

## BIRDS [BIRD]
Jer   7:33  people will become food for the **b**
Da    4:12  and the **b** lived in its branches;
Hos  11:11  They will come trembling like **b**
Mt    6:26  Look at the **b** of the air; they do not
      8:20  have holes and **b** have nests,
     13: 4  path, and the **b** came and ate it up.
Mk    4:32  the **b** can perch in its shade."
Rev  19:21  all the **b** gorged themselves on their

## BIRTH [BEAR]
Ge    3:16  pain you will give **b** to children.
Lev  12: 7  for the woman who gives **b** to a boy
Dt   32:18  you forgot the God who gave you **b**.
1Sa   2:21  she gave **b** to three sons and two
Job   3: 1  mouth and cursed the day of his **b**.
Ps   51: 5  Surely I was sinful at **b**,
     58: 3  Even from **b** the wicked go astray;
     71: 6  From **b** I have relied on you;
Pr    8:24  I was given **b**, when there were no
Ecc   7: 1  of death better than the day of **b**.
Isa   7:14  will conceive and give **b** to a son,
      8: 3  she conceived and gave **b** to a son.
     26:18  in pain, but we gave **b** to wind.
Jer   2:27  and to stone, 'You gave me **b**.'
Mt    1:18  This is how the **b** of Jesus
      1:21  She will give **b** to a son, and you are
     24: 8  these are the beginning of **b** pains.
Lk    1:57  have her baby, she gave **b** to a son.
Jn    3: 6  Flesh gives **b** to flesh, but the Spirit
            gives **b** to spirit.
      9: 1  along, he saw a man blind from **b**.
Gal   1:15  who set me apart from **b** and called
Jas   1:15  has conceived, it gives **b** to sin;
      1:15  it is full-grown, gives **b** to death.
1Pe   1: 3  great mercy he has given us new **b**
Rev  12: 5  She gave **b** to a son, a male child,

## BIRTHRIGHT [BEAR]
Ge   25:34  up and left. So Esau despised his **b**.

## BIT [BITE, BITS]
Nu   21: 6  they **b** the people and many
2Ki  19:28  your nose and my **b** in your mouth,

## BITE [BIT, BITES, BITTEN]
Am    5:19  the wall only to have a snake **b** him.

## BITES [BITE]
Pr   23:32  In the end it **b** like a snake

## BITS [BIT]
Jas   3: 3  When we put **b** into the mouths

## BITTEN [BITE]
Nu   21: 8  anyone who is **b** can look at it

## BITTER [BITTERLY, BITTERNESS, EMBITTER]
Ex    1:14  They made their lives **b** with harsh
     12: 8  along with **b** herbs, and bread made
Nu    5:19  may this **b** water that brings a curse
Ru    1:20  Almighty has made my life very **b**.
Pr    5: 4  but in the end she is **b** as gall,
     27: 7  hungry even what is **b** tastes sweet.
Rev   8:11  A third of the waters turned **b**,
      8:11  from the waters that had become **b**.

## BITTERLY [BITTER]
1Sa   1:10  prayed to the LORD, weeping **b**.

## BITTERNESS [BITTER]
Pr   14:10  Each heart knows its own **b**, and no
     17:25  and **b** to the mother who bore them.
Ro    3:14  mouths are full of cursing and **b**."
Eph   4:31  Get rid of all **b**, rage and anger,

## BLACK
Zec   6: 6  the **b** horses is going toward
Mt    5:36  make even one hair white or **b**.
Rev   6: 5  and there before me was a **b** horse!
      6:12  The sun turned **b** like sackcloth

## BLAME [BLAMELESS, BLAMELESSLY]
Ro    9:19  "Then why does God still **b** us?
1Ti   5: 7  so that no one may be open to **b**.
      6:14  or **b** until the appearing of our Lord

## BLAMELESS* [BLAME]
Ge    6: 9  **b** among the people of his time,
     17: 1  walk before me faithfully and be **b**.
Dt   18:13  You must be **b** before the LORD
2Sa  22:24  I have been **b** before him and have
     22:26  to the **b** you show yourself **b**,
Job   1: 1  This man was **b** and upright;
      1: 8  he is **b** and upright, a man who fears
      2: 3  he is **b** and upright, a man who fears
      4: 6  and your **b** ways your hope?
      8:20  "Surely God does not reject the **b**
      9:20  if I were **b**, it would pronounce me
      9:21  "Although I am **b**, I have no
      9:22  say, 'He destroys both the **b**
     12: 4  though righteous and **b**!
     22: 3  would he gain if your ways were **b**?
     31: 6  and he will know that I am **b**—
Ps   15: 2  Those whose walk is **b**, who do
     18:23  I have been **b** before him and have
     18:25  to the **b** you show yourself **b**,
     19:13  Then I will be **b**, innocent of great
     26: 1  me, LORD, for I have led a **b** life;
     26:11  I lead a **b** life; redeem me and be
     37:18  The **b** spend their days under
     37:37  Consider the **b**, observe the upright;
     50:23  to the **b** I will show my salvation."
     84:11  from those whose walk is **b**.

Ps 101: 2 I will be careful to lead a **b** life—
101: 2 affairs of my house with a **b** heart.
101: 6 those whose walk is **b** will minister
119: 1 Blessed are those whose ways are **b**,
119:80 my heart be **b** toward your decrees,
Pr   2: 7 is a shield to those whose walk is **b**,
2:21 the land, and the **b** will remain in it;
11: 5 of the **b** makes their paths straight,
11:20 delights in those whose ways are **b**.
19: 1 the poor whose walk is **b** than a fool
20: 7 The righteous lead **b** lives;
28: 6 poor whose walk is **b** than the rich
28:10 trap, but the **b** will receive a good
28:18 whose walk is **b** are kept safe,
Eze 28:15 You were **b** in your ways
1Co 1: 8 so that you will be **b** on the day
Eph 1: 4 world to be holy and **b** in his sight.
5:27 any other blemish, but holy and **b**.
Php 1:10 be pure and **b** for the day of Christ,
2:15 so that you may become **b** and pure,
1Th 2:10 and **b** we were among you who
3:13 your hearts so that you will be **b**
5:23 body be kept **b** at the coming of our
Tit  1: 6 An elder must be **b**, faithful to his
1: 7 God's household, he must be **b**—
Heb 7:26 one who is holy, **b**, pure, set apart
2Pe 3:14 spotless, **b** and at peace with him.
Rev 14: 5 found in their mouths; they are **b**.

## BLAMELESSLY* [BLAME]

Lk  1: 6 Lord's commands and decrees **b**.

## BLASPHEME* [BLASPHEMED, BLASPHEMER, BLASPHEMES, BLASPHEMIES, BLASPHEMING, BLASPHEMOUS, BLASPHEMY]

Ex 22:28 "Do not **b** God or curse the ruler
Lev 24:16 **b** the Name are to be put to death.
Ac 26:11 and I tried to force them to **b**.
1Ti 1:20 over to Satan to be taught not to **b**.
2Pe 2:12 these people **b** in matters they do
Rev 13: 6 It opened its mouth to **b** God,

## BLASPHEMED* [BLASPHEME]

Lev 24:11 of the Israelite woman **b** the Name
1Sa 3:13 his sons **b** God, and he failed
2Ki 19: 6 of the king of Assyria have **b** me.
19:22 Who is it you have ridiculed and **b**?
Isa 37: 6 of the king of Assyria have **b** me.
37:23 Who is it you have ridiculed and **b**?
52: 5 day long my name is constantly **b**.
Eze 20:27 also your ancestors **b** me by being
Ac 19:37 robbed temples nor **b** our goddess.
Ro 2:24 "God's name is **b** among

## BLASPHEMER* [BLASPHEME]

Lev 24:14 "Take the **b** outside the camp.
24:23 they took the **b** outside the camp
1Ti 1:13 Even though I was once a **b**

## BLASPHEMES* [BLASPHEME]

Lev 24:16 anyone who **b** the name
Nu 15:30 **b** the LORD and must be cut off
Mk 3:29 whoever **b** against the Holy Spirit
Lk 12:10 but anyone who **b** against the Holy

## BLASPHEMIES* [BLASPHEME]

Ne  9:18 or when they committed awful **b**.
9:26 they committed awful **b**.
Mk 3:28 all their sins and all the **b** they utter.
Rev 13: 5 a mouth to utter proud words and **b**

## BLASPHEMING* [BLASPHEME]

Mt  9: 3 to themselves, "This fellow is **b**!"
Mk 2: 7 He's **b**! Who can forgive sins
Jas 2: 7 who are **b** the noble name

## BLASPHEMOUS* [BLASPHEME]

Ac  6:11 "We have heard Stephen speak **b** words
Rev 13: 1 horns, and on each head a **b** name.
17: 3 beast that was covered with **b** names

## BLASPHEMY* [BLASPHEME]

Mt 12:31 will be forgiven every sin and **b**.
12:31 But **b** against the Spirit will not be
26:65 clothes and said, "He has spoken **b**!
26:65 Look, now you have heard the **b**.
Mk 14:64 "You have heard the **b**.
Lk 5:21 "Who is this fellow who speaks **b**?
Jn 10:33 replied, "but for **b**, because you,
10:36 you accuse me of **b** because I said,

## BLAST* [BLASTS]

Ex 15: 8 By the **b** of your nostrils the waters
19:13 sounds a long **b** may they approach
19:16 and a very loud trumpet **b**.
Nu 10: 5 When a trumpet **b** is sounded,
10: 6 At the sounding of a second **b**,
10: 6 The **b** will be the signal for setting
10: 9 you, sound a **b** on the trumpets.
Jos 6: 5 you hear them sound a long **b**
6:16 the priests sounded the trumpet **b**,
2Sa 22:16 at the **b** of breath from his nostrils.
Job 4: 9 the **b** of his anger they are no more.
39:25 At the **b** of the trumpet it snorts,
Ps 18:15 at the **b** of breath from your nostrils.
98: 6 and the **b** of the ram's horn—
147:17 Who can withstand his icy **b**?
Isa 27: 8 with his fierce **b** he drives her out,
Eze 22:20 furnace to be melted with a fiery **b**,
Am 2: 2 war cries and the **b** of the trumpet.
Heb 12:19 to a trumpet **b** or to such a voice

## BLASTS* [BLAST]

Lev 23:24 commemorated with trumpet **b**.
Rev 8:13 because of the trumpet **b** about to be

## BLAZED [BLAZING]

Dt 4:11 of the mountain while it **b** with fire
2Sa 22: 9 his mouth, burning coals **b** out of it.
Jnh 4: 8 the sun **b** on Jonah's head so that he

## BLAZING [BLAZED]

Ge 15:17 firepot with a **b** torch appeared
SS 8: 6 It burns like a **b** fire, like a mighty
Isa 62: 1 dawn, her salvation like a **b** torch.
Eze 20:47 The **b** flame will not be quenched,
Da 3: 6 be thrown into a **b** furnace."
7:11 destroyed and thrown into the **b** fire.
Mt 13:50 and throw them into the **b** furnace,
2Th 1: 7 heaven in **b** fire with his powerful

Rev  1:14  snow, and his eyes were like **b** fire.
    8:10  and a great star, **b** like a torch,
   19:12  His eyes are like **b** fire, and on his

## BLEATING*

1Sa 15:14  then is this **b** of sheep in my ears?

## BLEEDING [BLOOD]

Lev 12: 4  days to be purified from her **b**.
Lk   8:43  was there who had been subject to **b**

## BLEMISH* [BLEMISHED, BLEMISHES]

Lev 22:21  without defect or **b** to be acceptable.
Nu  19: 2  you a red heifer without defect or **b**
2Sa 14:25  of his foot there was no **b** in him.
Eph  5:27  stain or wrinkle or any other **b**,
Col  1:22  in his sight, without **b** and free
1Pe  1:19  Christ, a lamb without **b** or defect.

## BLEMISHED* [BLEMISH]

Mal  1:14  sacrifices a **b** animal to the Lord.

## BLEMISHES* [BLEMISH]

2Pe  2:13  They are blots and **b**,
Jude  1:12  These people are **b** at your love

## BLESS [BLESSED, BLESSES, BLESSING, BLESSINGS]

Ge  12: 3  I will **b** those who **b** you,
   17:16  I will **b** her and will surely give you
   22:17  I will surely **b** you and make your
   26: 3  I will be with you and will **b** you.
   26:24  I will **b** you and will increase
   27:29  and those who **b** you be blessed."
   27:34  cry and said to his father, "**B** me—
   28: 3  May God Almighty **b** you and make
   32:26  not let you go unless you **b** me."
   48: 9  them to me so I may **b** them."
Ex  12:32  have said, and go. And also **b** me."
   20:24  I will come to you and **b** you.
Nu   6:24  " ' "The LORD **b** you and keep you;
   22: 6  know that whoever you **b** is blessed,
   23:20  I have received a command to **b**;
Dt   1:11  times and **b** you as he has promised!
   7:13  He will love you and **b** you
   7:13  He will **b** the fruit of your womb,
  14:29  the LORD your God may **b** you
  15: 4  inheritance, he will richly **b** you,
  16:15  the LORD your God will **b** you
  23:20  the LORD your God may **b** you
  24:19  the LORD your God may **b** you
  26:15  and **b** your people Israel
  27:12  on Mount Gerizim to **b** the people:
  33:11  **B** all his skills, LORD, and be
Jos   8:33  he gave instructions to **b** the people
Jdg 17: 2  "The LORD **b** you, my son!"
Ru   2: 4  "The LORD **b** you!"
   3:10  "The LORD **b** you,
1Sa  2:20  Eli would **b** Elkanah and his wife,
2Sa  2: 5  "The LORD **b** you for showing
   21: 3  so that you will **b** the LORD's
1Ch  4:10  that you would **b** me and enlarge
Ps   5:12  LORD, you **b** the righteous;
   28: 9  your people and **b** your inheritance;

Ps  67: 1  May God be gracious to us and **b** us
   72:15  pray for him and **b** him all day long.
  109:28  While they curse, may you **b**;
  115:12  remembers us and will **b** us:
  115:12  He will **b** the house of Israel, he will **b**
      the house of Aaron,
  118:26  the house of the LORD we **b** you.
Pr  30:11  fathers and do not **b** their mothers;
Isa 19:25  The LORD Almighty will **b** them,
Jer 31:23  'The LORD **b** you, you prosperous
Hag  2:19  this day on I will **b** you.' "
Zec  4: 7  to shouts of 'God **b** it! God **b** it!' "
Lk   6:28  **b** those who curse you,
Ro  12:14  **B** those who persecute you;
1Co  4:12  When we are cursed, we **b**;
2Co  9: 8  And God is able to **b** you abundantly,
Heb  6:14  "I will surely **b** you and give you

## BLESSED [BLESS]

Ge   1:22  God **b** them and said, "Be fruitful
   2: 3  Then God **b** the seventh day
   9: 1  Then God **b** Noah and his sons,
  14:19  and he **b** Abram, saying, "**B** be
  22:18  all nations on earth will be **b**,
  28:14  on earth will be **b** through you
  39: 5  the LORD **b** the household
  47: 7  After Jacob **b** Pharaoh,
Ex  20:11  Therefore the LORD **b** the Sabbath
  39:43  So Moses **b** them.
Lev  9:22  toward the people and **b** them.
Nu  24: 9  "May those who bless you be **b**
Dt  12: 7  the LORD your God has **b** you.
  28: 3  You will be **b** in the city and **b**
Jos  22: 6  Then Joshua **b** them and sent them
Jdg  5:24  "Most **b** of women be Jael, the wife
   5:24  most **b** of tent-dwelling women.
  13:24  He grew and the LORD **b** him,
1Ch 17:27  LORD, have **b** it, and it will be **b**
Ne   9: 5  "**B** be your glorious name, and may
Job  5:17  "**B** are those whom God corrects;
Ps   1: 1  **B** are those who do not walk in step
   2:12  **B** are all who take refuge in him.
  32: 1  **B** are those whose transgressions
  33:12  **B** is the nation whose God is
  40: 4  **B** are those who make the LORD
  41: 1  **B** are those who have regard
  84: 5  **B** are those whose strength is
  89:15  **B** are those who have learned
  94:12  **B** are those you discipline, LORD,
  106: 3  **B** are those who act justly,
  112: 1  **B** are those who fear the LORD,
  118:26  **B** is he who comes in the name
  119: 1  **B** are those whose ways are
  119: 2  **B** are those who keep his statutes
  127: 5  **B** is the man whose quiver is full
  128: 1  **B** are all who fear the LORD,
  144:15  **B** is the people of whom this is true;
  144:15  **b** is the people whose God is
Pr   3:13  **B** are those who find wisdom,
   8:34  **B** are those who listen to me,
  22: 9  The generous will themselves be **b**,
  28:20  A faithful person will be richly **b**,
  29:18  but **b** are those who heed wisdom's
  31:28  Her children arise and call her **b**;
SS   6: 9  women saw her and called her **b**;
Isa 30:18  **B** are all who wait for him!
Mal  3:12  all the nations will call you **b**,

Mal  3:15  But now we call the arrogant **b**.
Mt   5: 3  "**B** are the poor in spirit, for theirs
     5: 4  **B** are those who mourn, for they
     5: 5  **B** are the meek, for they will inherit
     5: 6  **B** are those who hunger and thirst
     5: 7  **B** are the merciful, for they will be
     5: 8  **B** are the pure in heart, for they will
     5: 9  **B** are the peacemakers, for they will
     5:10  **B** are those who are persecuted
     5:11  "**B** are you when people insult you,
    11: 6  **B** is anyone who does not stumble
Mk  11: 9  "**B** is he who comes in the name
Lk   1:42  "**B** are you among women, and **b** is
     1:48  on all generations will call me **b**,
     6:20  "**B** are you who are poor, for yours
     6:21  **B** are you who hunger now, for you
     6:21  **B** are you who weep now, for you
     6:22  **B** are you when people hate you,
Jn  12:13  "**B** is he who comes in the name
    12:13  "**B** is the king of Israel!"
    13:17  things, you will be **b** if you do them.
Ac  20:35  'It is more **b** to give than
Ro   4: 7  "**B** are those whose transgressions
Gal  3: 8  nations will be **b** through you."
Eph  1: 3  who has **b** us in the heavenly realms
1Ti  6:15  God, the **b** and only Ruler, the King
Tit  2:13  while we wait for the **b** hope—
Heb  7: 7  without doubt the lesser is **b**
Jas  1:12  **B** are those who persevere under
     5:11  we count as **b** those who have
1Pe  3:14  suffer for what is right, you are **b**.
Rev  1: 3  **B** is the one who reads aloud
     1: 3  and **b** are those who hear it and take
    14:13  **B** are the dead who die in the Lord
    16:15  **B** are those who stay awake
    19: 9  '**B** are those who are invited
    20: 6  **B** and holy are those who have part
    22: 7  **B** are those who keep the words
    22:14  "**B** are those who wash their robes,

## BLESSES [BLESS]

Ps  29:11  the Lord **b** his people with peace.
Ro  10:12  all and richly **b** all who call on him,

## BLESSING [BLESS]

Ge  12: 2  name great, and you will be a **b**.
    27: 4  I may give you my **b** before I die."
    48:20  name will Israel pronounce this **b**:
    49:28  giving each the **b** appropriate
Dt  11:26  I am setting before you today a **b**
    23: 5  but turned the curse into a **b** for you,
    33: 1  This is the **b** that Moses the man
Ne  13: 2  however, turned the curse into a **b**.)
Pr  10:22  The **b** of the Lord brings wealth,
Eze 34:26  the places surrounding my hill a **b**.
    34:26  there will be showers of **b**.
Joel 2:14  and relent and leave behind a **b**—
Zec  8:13  I will save you, and you will be a **b**.
Mal  3:10  out so much **b** that there will not be
Lk  24:51  While he was **b** them, he left them
Ro  15:29  the full measure of the **b** of Christ.
Gal  3:14  in order that the **b** given to Abraham
Heb 12:17  when he wanted to inherit this **b**,
    12:17  Even though he sought the **b**
1Pe  3: 9  repay evil with **b**, because to this
     3: 9  called so that you may inherit a **b**.

## BLESSINGS [BLESS]

Ge  49:26  father's **b** are greater than the **b**
Dt  11:29  proclaim on Mount Gerizim the **b**,
Jos  8:34  of the law—the **b** and the curses—
1Ch 23:13  to pronounce **b** in his name forever.
Pr  10: 6  **B** crown the head of the righteous,
Mal  2: 2  on you, and I will curse your **b**.
Ac  13:34  holy and sure **b** promised to David.'
Ro  15:27  have shared in the Jews' spiritual **b**,
    15:27  to share with them their material **b**.

## BLEW [BLOW]

Ex  15:10  But you **b** with your breath,
Jos  6: 9  of the priests who **b** the trumpets,
Hag  1: 9  What you brought home, I **b** away.
Mt   7:25  the winds **b** and beat against

## BLIND [BLINDED, BLINDNESS, BLINDS]

Ex   4:11  gives them sight or makes them **b**?
Dt  27:18  is anyone who leads the **b** astray
2Sa  5: 8  and **b**' who are David's enemies."
     5: 8  "The '**b** and lame' will not enter
Job 29:15  I was eyes to the **b** and feet
Ps 146: 8  the Lord gives sight to the **b**,
Isa 42:19  Who is **b** but my servant, and deaf
    42:19  **b** like the servant of the Lord?
    56:10  Israel's watchmen are **b**, they all
Mt   9:27  there, two **b** men followed him,
    11: 5  The **b** receive sight, the lame walk,
    15:14  Leave them; they are **b** guides.
    15:14  If the **b** lead the **b**, both will fall
    23:16  "Woe to you, **b** guides! You say,
Mk  10:46  were leaving the city, a **b** man,
Lk   6:39  "Can the **b** lead the **b**?
Jn   9: 1  along, he saw a man **b** from birth.
     9:25  I do know. I was **b** but now I see!"
Ac   9: 9  For three days he was **b**, and did not
Ro   2:19  that you are a guide for the **b**, a light
2Pe  1: 9  you are nearsighted and **b**, and you
Rev  3:17  wretched, pitiful, poor, **b** and naked.

## BLINDED* [BLIND]

Zec 11:17  withered, his right eye totally **b**!"
Jn  12:40  "He has **b** their eyes and hardened
Ac  22:11  the brilliance of the light had **b** me.
2Co  4: 4  god of this age has **b** the minds
1Jn  2:11  because the darkness has **b** them.

## BLINDFOLDED

Mk  14:65  they **b** him, struck him with their

## BLINDNESS [BLIND]

Ge  19:11  with **b** so that they could not find
2Ki  6:18  So he struck them with **b**, as Elisha

## BLINDS [BLIND]

Dt  16:19  for a bribe **b** the eyes of the wise

## BLOCK

Isa 44:19  Shall I bow down to a **b** of wood?"
Eze  4: 1  son of man, take a **b** of clay,
    14: 7  a wicked stumbling **b** before their
Mt  16:23  You are a stumbling **b** to me;

Ro  11: 9  a stumbling **b** and a retribution
    14:13  mind not to put any stumbling **b**
1Co  1:23  a stumbling **b** to Jews
2Co  6: 3  We put no stumbling **b** in anyone's

# BLOOD [AKELDAMA, BLEEDING, BLOODSHED, BLOODSHOT, BLOODTHIRSTY, LIFEBLOOD]

Ge   4:10  Your brother's **b** cries out to me
     9: 6  "Whoever sheds human **b**,
     9: 6  human beings shall their **b** be shed;
Ex   4:25  "Surely you are a bridegroom of **b**
     7:17  Nile, and it will be changed into **b**.
    12:13  The **b** will be a sign for you
    12:13  and when I see the **b**, I will pass
    24: 8  Moses then took the **b**, sprinkled it
    24: 8  "This is the **b** of the covenant,
Lev  7:27  Anyone who eats **b** must be cut off
    16:15  and take its **b** behind the curtain
    16:15  with it as he did with the bull's **b**:
    17:11  For the life of a creature is in the **b**,
    17:11  it is the **b** that makes atonement
    17:14  the life of every creature is its **b**.
Dt  12:23  not eat the **b**, because the **b** is the life,
Ps  50:13  of bulls or drink the **b** of goats?
    59: 2  save me from those who are after my **b**.
    72:14  for precious is their **b** in his sight.
   106:38  They shed innocent **b**, the **b** of their
Pr   6:17  tongue, hands that shed innocent **b**,
Isa  1:11  I have no pleasure in the **b** of bulls
     9: 5  garment rolled in **b** will be destined
    34: 6  sword of the LORD is bathed in **b**,
    34: 6  the **b** of lambs and goats.
Eze  3:18  hold you accountable for their **b**.
Joel 2:31  the moon to **b** before the coming
     3:21  leave their innocent **b** unpunished?
Na   3: 1  Woe to the city of **b**, full of lies,
Hab  2: 8  For you have shed human **b**;
Mt  23:30  in shedding the **b** of the prophets.'
    26:28  This is my **b** of the covenant,
    27: 6  the treasury, since it is **b** money."
    27: 8  why it has been called the Field of **B**
    27:24  "I am innocent of this man's **b**,"
Mk  14:24  "This is my **b** of the covenant,
Lk  22:44  his sweat was like drops of **b** falling
Jn   6:53  of the Son of Man and drink his **b**,
    19:34  bringing a sudden flow of **b**
Ac   2:20  the moon to **b** before the coming
    15:20  of strangled animals and from **b**.
    20:26  I am innocent of the **b** of everyone.
Ro   3:25  through the shedding of his **b**—
     5: 9  we have now been justified by his **b**,
1Co 11:25  cup is the new covenant in my **b**;
Eph  1: 7  we have redemption through his **b**,
     2:13  brought near by the **b** of Christ.
     6:12  struggle is not against flesh and **b**,
Col  1:20  by making peace through his **b**,
Heb  9: 7  year, and never without **b**, which he
     9:12  not enter by means of the **b** of goats
     9:12  Place once for all by his own **b**,
     9:20  said, "This is the **b** of the covenant,
     9:22  everything be cleansed with **b**,
     9:22  of **b** there is no forgiveness.
    12:24  the sprinkled **b** that speaks a better word
           than the **b** of Abel.
1Pe  1:19  but with the precious **b** of Christ,

1Jn  1: 7  another, and the **b** of Jesus, his Son,
     5: 6  by water only, but by water and **b**.
Rev  1: 5  has freed us from our sins by his **b**,
     5: 9  with your **b** you purchased for God
     6:10  of the earth and avenge our **b**?"
     6:12  hair, the whole moon turned **b** red,
     7:14  them white in the **b** of the Lamb.
     8: 8  A third of the sea turned into **b**,
    12:11  over him by the **b** of the Lamb
    19:13  He is dressed in a robe dipped in **b**,

## FLESH AND BLOOD See FLESH

## BLOODGUILT* [GUILT]
Ps  51:14  Deliver me from **b**, O God, you who

## BLOODSHED [BLOOD]
Nu  35:33  **B** pollutes the land, and atonement
Isa  5: 7  he looked for justice, but saw **b**;
Jer 48:10  who keep their swords from **b**!
Eze 35: 6  Since you did not hate **b**, **b** will
Hab  2:12  to him who builds a city with **b**

## BLOODSHOT* [BLOOD]
Pr  23:29  Who has **b** eyes?

## BLOODTHIRSTY* [BLOOD]
Ps   5: 6  The **b** and deceitful you, LORD,
    26: 9  my life with those who are **b**,
    55:23  the **b** and deceitful will not live
   139:19  Away from me, you who are **b**!
Pr  29:10  The **b** hate people of integrity

## BLOOM
SS   2:15  our vineyards that are in **b**.
Isa 35: 2  it will burst into **b**; it will rejoice

## BLOSSOM
Isa 35: 1  the wilderness will rejoice and **b**.
Hos 14: 5  dew to Israel; he will **b** like a lily.

## BLOT [BLOTS, BLOTTED]
Ex  17:14  because I will completely **b**
    32:32  then **b** me out of the book you have
Dt   9:14  **b** out their name from under heaven.
Ne   4: 5  or **b** out their sins from your sight,
Ps  51: 1  to your great compassion **b** out my
Jer 18:23  or **b** out their sins from your sight.
Rev  3: 5  I will never **b** out their names

## BLOTS [BLOT]
Isa 43:25  "I, even I, am he who **b** out your

## BLOTTED [BLOT]
Dt  25: 6  so that his name will not be **b**

## BLOW [BLEW, BLOWN, BLOWS]
Jer 14:17  a grievous wound, a crushing **b**.
Eze 33: 6  does not **b** the trumpet to warn
Joel 2: 1  **B** the trumpet in Zion;

## BLOWN [BLOW]
Eph  4:14  and **b** here and there by every wind
Jas  1: 6  of the sea, **b** and tossed by the wind.

Jude  1:12  without rain, **b** along by the wind;

## BLOWS [BLOW]
Pr    6:33  **B** and disgrace are his lot, and his
      20:30  **B** and wounds cleanse away evil,
Isa  40: 7  the breath of the LORD **b** on them.
Jn    3: 8  The wind **b** wherever it pleases.

## BLUE
Ex  24:10  lapis lazuli, as **b** blue as the sky.
      26:31  "Make a curtain of **b**,
      28:31  of the ephod entirely of **b** cloth,
Rev  9:17  red, dark **b**, and yellow as sulfur.

## BLUSH*
Jer    3: 3  you refuse to **b** with shame.
        6:15  they do not even know how to **b**.
        8:12  they do not even know how to **b**.

## BOANERGES*
Mk    3:17  John (to them he gave the name **B**,

## BOARDS
Ex  27: 8  Make the altar hollow, out of **b**.
1Ki   6:15  lined its interior walls with cedar **b**,

## BOAST [BOASTED, BOASTERS, BOASTFUL, BOASTING, BOASTS]
1Ki  20:11  his armor should not **b** like one who
Ps  44: 8  In God we make our **b** all day long,
      52: 1  Why do you **b** of evil, you mighty
      52: 1  Why do you **b** all day long,
      75: 4  To the arrogant I say, '**B** no more,'
      97: 7  put to shame, those who **b** in idols—
Pr  27: 1  Do not **b** about tomorrow, for you
Isa  45:25  LORD and will make their **b** in him.
Jer    9:23  "Let not the wise **b** of their wisdom
        9:23  or the strong **b** of their strength
        9:23  or the rich **b** of their riches,
        9:24  but let those who **b b** about this:
Ro    2:17  rely on the law and **b** in God;
Ro    2:23  You who **b** in the law,
Ro    5: 2  we **b** in the hope of the glory
1Co   1:31  "Let those who **b** in the Lord."
      13: 4  envy, it does not **b**, it is not proud.
2Co 10: 8  So even if I **b** somewhat freely
      10:17  "Let those who **b b** in the Lord."
      11:30  If I must **b**, I will **b** of the things
Gal   6:14  May I never **b** except in the cross
Eph   2: 9  not by works, so that no one can **b**.
Php   2:16  then I will be able to **b** on the day
        3: 3  who **b** in Christ Jesus,s
Jas    3:14  do not **b** about it or deny the truth.
        4:16  you **b** in your arrogant schemes.

## BOASTED [BOAST]
Est    5:11  Haman **b** to them about his vast
Ac    8: 9  He **b** that he was someone great,

## BOASTERS* [BOAST]
Jer  48:45  of Moab, the skulls of the noisy **b**.

## BOASTFUL* [BOAST]
Ps  12: 3  flattering lips and every **b** tongue—

Da    7:11  the **b** words the horn was speaking.
Ro    1:30  insolent, arrogant and **b**;
2Ti    3: 2  lovers of money, **b**, proud, abusive,
2Pe   2:18  For they mouth empty, **b** words and,

## BOASTING [BOAST]
Php   1:26  your **b** in Christ Jesus will abound
1Co   5: 6  Your **b** is not good. Don't you know
2Co 10:13  will confine our **b** to the sphere
Jas    4:16  All such **b** is evil.
1Jn    2:16  and their **b** about what they have  .

## BOASTS [BOAST]
Pr  20:14  goes off and **b** about the purchase.
Rev  18: 7  In her heart she **b**, 'I sit enthroned

## BOAT [BOATS]
Mt    4:21  in a **b** with their father Zebedee,
        8:23  he got into the **b** and his disciples
      13: 2  around him that he got into a **b**
      14:13  he withdrew by **b** privately
      14:29  Then Peter got down out of the **b**,
Jn    21: 6  your net on the right side of the **b**

## BOATS [BOAT]
Lk    5: 7  filled both **b** so full that they began

## BOAZ
Wealthy Bethlehemite who showed favor to Ruth (Ru 2), married her (Ru 4). Ancestor of David (Ru 4:18–22; 1Ch 2:12–15), Jesus (Mt 1:5–16; Lk 3:23–32).

## BODIES [BODY]
Lev  19:28  " 'Do not cut your **b** for the dead
Nu  14:29  In this wilderness your **b** will fall—
1Ch 10:12  men went and took the **b** of Saul
Isa  26:19  will live, LORD; their **b** will rise—
Da    3:27  that the fire had not harmed their **b**,
Lk    21:26  for the heavenly **b** will be shaken.
Ro    1:24  of their **b** with one another.
      12: 1  to offer your **b** as a living sacrifice,
1Co   6:15  not know that your **b** are members
        6:18  sin against their own **b**.
        6:19  your **b** are temples of the Holy Spirit,
        6:20  honor God with your **b**.
Eph   5:28  to love their wives as their own **b**.
Php   3:21  will transform our lowly **b** so
Heb 10:22  and having our **b** washed with pure
Jude  1: 8  ungodly people pollute their own **b**,

## BODILY [BODY]
Col    2: 9  fullness of the Deity lives in **b** form,

## BODY [BODIES, BODILY, EMBODIMENT]
Ge  15: 4  from your own **b** will be your heir."
2Sa   7:12  who will come from your own **b**,
Ps  139:16  your eyes saw my unformed **b**.
Pr  14:30  A heart at peace gives life to the **b**,
Ecc  12:12  end, and much study wearies the **b**.
Zec  13: 6  'What are these wounds on your **b**?'
Mal   2:15  You belong to him in **b** and spirit.
Mt  10:28  not be afraid of those who kill the **b**
      10:28  can destroy both soul and **b** in hell.

Mt 26:26 "Take and eat; this is my **b**."
27:58 he asked for Jesus' **b**, and Pilate
Mk 14:22 saying, "Take it; this is my **b**."
Lk 11:34 Your eye is the lamp of your **b**.
11:34 your whole **b** also is full of light.
11:34 your **b** also is full of darkness.
12: 4 not be afraid of those who kill the **b**
22:19 "This is my **b** given for you;
Jn 13:10 their whole **b** is clean.
Ac 2:31 of the dead, nor did his **b** see decay.
Ro 8:10 even though your **b** is subject
12: 4 us has one **b** with many members,
1Co 6:13 The **b**, however, is not meant
6:13 for the Lord, and the Lord for the **b**.
7: 4 not have authority over her own **b**
7: 4 not have authority over his own **b**
9:27 I strike a blow to my **b** and make it
11:24 "This is my **b**, which is for you;
12:12 Just as a **b**, though one, has many parts,
but all its many parts form one **b**,
12:13 by one Spirit so as to form one **b**—
12:24 God has put the **b** together,
15:44 a natural **b**, it is raised a spiritual **b**.
2Co 5: 8 would prefer to be away from the **b**
Gal 6:17 I bear on my **b** the marks of Jesus.
Eph 1:23 which is his **b**, the fullness of him
4:25 for we are all members of one **b**.
5:30 for we are members of his **b**.
Php 1:20 Christ will be exalted in my **b**,
Col 1:24 for the sake of his **b**, which is
1Th 4: 4 learn to control your own **b** in a way
Heb 10: 5 desire, but a **b** you prepared for me;
Jas 2:26 As the **b** without the spirit is dead,
1Pe 2:24 bore our sins" in his **b** on the cross,
Jude 1: 9 with the devil about the **b** of Moses,

## BOILS
Ex 9: 9 festering **b** will break out on people
Dt 28:27 will afflict you with the **b** of Egypt

## BOLD [BOLDLY, BOLDNESS, EMBOLDENED]
Pr 21:29 The wicked put up a **b** front,
28: 1 but the righteous are as **b** as a lion.
2Co 3:12 we have such a hope, we are very **b**.
10: 1 but "**b**" toward you when away!
Phm 1: 8 although in Christ I could be **b**

## BOLDLY [BOLD]
Ex 14: 8 Israelites, who were marching out **b**.
Ac 4:31 Spirit and spoke the word of God **b**.
9:28 speaking **b** in the name of the Lord.
14: 3 time there, speaking **b** for the Lord,

## BOLDNESS* [BOLD]
Ac 4:29 to speak your word with great **b**.
28:31 with all **b** and without hindrance!

## BOLTS
Job 38:35 Do you send the lightning **b** on their
Ps 18:14 great **b** of lightning he routed them.

## BONDAGE
Ezr 9: 9 God has not forsaken us in our **b**.
Ro 8:21 will be liberated from its **b** to decay

## BONE [BONES]
Ge 2:23 "This is now **b** of my bones
Pr 25:15 and a gentle tongue can break a **b**.
Eze 37: 7 and the bones came together, **b** to **b**.

## BONES [BONE]
Ge 50:25 you must carry my **b** up from this
Ex 12:46 Do not break any of the **b**.
Jos 24:32 And Joseph's **b**, which the Israelites
2Ki 13:21 When the body touched Elisha's **b**,
Ps 22:14 water, and all my **b** are out of joint.
22:17 All my **b** are on display;
34:20 he protects all their **b**, not one
Pr 14:30 life to the body, but envy rots the **b**.
15:30 and good news gives health to the **b**.
Jer 20: 9 like a fire, a fire shut up in my **b**.
Eze 37: 4 me, "Prophesy to these **b** and say
37: 4 them, 'Dry **b**, hear the word
Mt 23:27 inside are full of the **b** of the dead
Jn 19:36 "Not one of his **b** will be broken,"
Heb 11:22 concerning the burial of his **b**.

## BOOK [BOOKS]
Ex 24: 7 Then he took the **B** of the Covenant
32:33 against me I will blot out of my **b**.
Dt 31:24 finished writing in a **b** the words
Jos 1: 8 Keep this **B** of the Law always
23: 6 that is written in the **B** of the Law
2Ki 22: 8 "I have found the **B** of the Law
2Ch 34:15 "I have found the **B** of the Law
Ne 8: 8 They read from the **B** of the Law
Ps 69:28 they be blotted out of the **b** of life
Da 12: 1 name is found written in the **b**—
Jn 20:30 which are not recorded in this **b**.
Ac 1: 1 In my former **b**, Theophilus, I wrote
8:28 in his chariot reading the **B** of Isaiah
Php 4: 3 whose names are in the **b** of life.
Rev 3: 5 out their names from the **b** of life,
13: 8 been written in the Lamb's **b** of life,
17: 8 have not been written in the **b** of life
20:12 **b** was opened, which is the **b** of life,
20:15 written in the **b** of life were thrown
21:27 are written in the Lamb's **b** of life.

## BOOK OF THE LAW See LAW

## BOOK OF THE ANNALS See ANNALS

## WRITTEN IN THE BOOK See WRITTEN

## BOOKS* [BOOK]
Ecc 12:12 Of making many **b** there is no end,
Da 7:10 was seated, and the **b** were opened.
Jn 21:25 for the **b** that would be written.
Rev 20:12 the throne, and **b** were opened.
20:12 they had done as recorded in the **b**.

## BOOTH
Lk 5:27 the name of Levi sitting at his tax **b**.

## BORDER [BORDERS]
2Ch 9:26 Philistines, as far as the **b** of Egypt.
Ps 78:54 them to the **b** of his holy land,

## BORDERS [BORDER]
Ex 23:31 "I will establish your **b**

Mal 1: 5 even beyond the **b** of Israel!'

## BORE [BEAR]
Dt 32:18 deserted the Rock, who **b** you;
Isa 53: 4 took up our pain and **b** our suffering,
    53:12 For he **b** the sin of many, and made
Mt 8:17 our infirmities and **b** our diseases."
Ro 7: 5 in us, so that we **b** fruit for death.
Heb 13:13 the camp, bearing the disgrace he **b**.
1Pe 2:24 "He himself **b** our sins" in his body
Rev 17: 6 of those who **b** testimony to Jesus.

## BORN [BEAR]
Ge 17:17 himself, "Will a son be **b** to a man
Job 14: 1 "Mortals, **b** of woman, are of few
Ps 90: 2 Before the mountains were **b** or you
Pr 17:17 and a brother is **b** for a time
Ecc 3: 2 a time to be **b** and a time to die,
Isa 9: 6 For to us a child is **b**, to us a son is
    66: 8 Can a country be **b** in a day
Jer 1: 5 before you were **b** I set you apart;
Mt 2: 1 After Jesus was **b** in Bethlehem
Lk 1:35 one to be **b** will be called the Son
    2:11 of David a Savior has been **b** to you;
    7:28 among those **b** of women there is no
Jn 1:13 children **b** not of natural descent,
    1:13 or a husband's will, but **b** of God.
    3: 3 of God without being **b** again."
    3: 5 of God without being **b** of water
    3: 7 my saying, 'You must be **b** again.'
    3: 8 it is with everyone **b** of the Spirit."
    8:58 "before Abraham was **b**, I am!"
1Co 15: 8 to me also, as to one abnormally **b**.
Gal 4: 4 God sent his Son, **b** of a woman,
1Pe 1:23 For you have been **b** again,
1Jn 3: 9 Those who are **b** of God will not
    3: 9 because they have been **b** of God.
    4: 7 Everyone who loves has been **b**
    5: 1 Jesus is the Messiah is **b** of God,
    5: 4 everyone **b** of God overcomes
    5:18 the One who was **b** of God keeps
Rev 12: 4 her child the moment he was **b**.

## BORNE [BEAR]
Hos 5:15 until they have **b** their guilt

## BORROW [BORROWER]
Dt 15: 6 many nations but will **b** from none.
Ps 37:21 The wicked **b** and do not repay,
Mt 5:42 the one who wants to **b** from you.

## BORROWER* [BORROW]
Ex 22:15 animal, the **b** will not have to pay.
Pr 22: 7 and the **b** is slave to the lender.
Isa 24: 2 as for buyer, for **b** as for lender,

## BOTHER [BOTHERING]
Lk 8:49 "Don't **b** the teacher anymore."
    11: 7 one inside answers, 'Don't **b** me.

## BOTHERING [BOTHER]
Lk 18: 5 yet because this widow keeps **b** me,

## BOTTLE*
1Sa 10: 1 Samuel took a **b** of olive oil and poured

## BOTTOM
Am 9: 3 from my eyes at the **b** of the sea,
Mk 15:38 was torn in two from top to **b**.

## BOUGHS
Ps 118:27 With **b** in hand, join in the festal
Eze 31: 6 the birds of the sky nested in its **b**,

## BOUGHT [BUY]
Ge 25:10 the field Abraham had **b**
Ex 15:16 until the people you **b** pass by.
2Sa 24:24 So David **b** the threshing floor
Ne 5: 8 we have **b** back our fellow Jews
Job 28:15 It cannot be **b** with the finest gold,
Mt 13:46 and sold everything he had and **b** it.
Ac 1:18 for his wickedness, Judas **b** a field;
    20:28 which he **b** with his own blood.
1Co 6:20 you were **b** at a price.
    7:23 You were **b** at a price;
2Pe 2: 1 the sovereign Lord who **b** them—

## BOUND [BIND]
Ge 22: 9 He **b** his son Isaac and laid him
Pr 22:15 Folly is **b** up in the heart of a child,
Jer 39: 7 **b** him with bronze shackles to take
    40: 1 He had found Jeremiah **b** in chains
Mt 16:19 bind on earth will be **b** in heaven,
    18:18 bind on earth will be **b** in heaven,
Lk 13:16 whom Satan has kept **b** for eighteen
    13:16 the Sabbath day from what **b** her?"
Ro 7: 2 by law a married woman is **b** to her
1Co 7:15 sister is not **b** in such circumstances;
    7:39 A woman is **b** to her husband as
Jude 1: 6 **b** with everlasting chains
Rev 9:14 "Release the four angels who are **b**
    20: 2 and **b** him for a thousand years.

## BOUNDARIES [BOUNDARY]
Ps 74:17 It was you who set all the **b**
Ac 17:26 and the **b** of their lands.

## BOUNDARY [BOUNDARIES, BOUNDLESS, BOUNDS]
Nu 34: 3 Your southern **b** will start in the east
Dt 19:14 move your neighbor's **b** stone set
Job 24: 2 There are those who move **b** stones;
Ps 16: 6 The **b** lines have fallen for me
    104: 9 You set a **b** they cannot cross;
Pr 15:25 sets the widow's **b** stones in place.
    22:28 Do not move an ancient **b** stone set
Eze 47:15 "This is to be the **b** of the land:
Hos 5:10 are like those who move **b** stones.

## BOUNDLESS [BOUNDARY]
Ps 119:96 but your commands are **b**.
Eph 3: 8 the **b** riches of Christ,

## BOUNDS* [BOUNDARY]
Hos 4: 2 they break all **b**, and bloodshed
2Co 7: 4 all our troubles my joy knows no **b**.

## BOUNTY*
Ge 49:26 than the **b** of the age-old hills.
Dt 28:12 the storehouse of his **b**, to send rain

1Ki 10:13 he had given her out of his royal **b**.
Ps 65:11 You crown the year with your **b**,
68:10 settled in it, and from your **b**, God,
Jer 31:12 will rejoice in the **b** of the LORD—
31:14 people will be filled with my **b**,"

## BOYS
2Ki 2:24 and mauled forty-two of the **b**.

## BOW [BOWED, BOWS]
Ge 27:29 you and peoples **b** down to you.
Dt 5: 9 You shall not **b** down to them
Jos 23: 7 not serve them or **b** down to them.
2Sa 1:18 this lament of the **b** (it is written
22:35 my arms can bend a **b** of bronze.
1Ki 22:34 But someone drew his **b** at random
Ps 5: 7 in reverence I **b** down toward your
44: 6 I put no trust in my **b**, my sword
95: 6 Come, let us **b** down in worship,
138: 2 I will **b** down toward your holy
Isa 44:19 Shall I **b** down to a block
45:23 Before me every knee will **b**;
Mt 4: 9 "if you will **b** down and worship
Ro 14:11 Lord, 'every knee will **b** before me;
Php 2:10 name of Jesus every knee should **b**,
Rev 6: 2 Its rider held a **b**, and he was given

## BOWED [BOW]
Ge 18: 2 meet them and **b** low to the ground.
37: 7 around mine and **b** down to it."
42: 6 they **b** down to him with their faces
Ex 34: 8 Moses **b** to the ground at once
2Ch 33: 3 He **b** down to all the starry hosts
Ps 35:14 I **b** my head in grief as though
38: 6 I am **b** down and brought very low;
145:14 fall and lifts up all who are **b** down.
146: 8 lifts up those who are **b** down,
Mt 2:11 and they **b** down and worshiped
Jn 19:30 he **b** his head and gave up his spirit.

## BOWELS
2Ch 21:15 **b**, until the disease causes your **b**

## BOWL [BOWLS]
Mk 4:21 bring in a lamp to put it under a **b**
Rev 16: 2 and poured out his **b** on the land,

## BOWLS [BOWL]
Rev 5: 8 they were holding golden **b** full
16: 1 pour out the seven **b** of God's wrath

## BOWS [BOW]
Ps 66: 4 All the earth **b** down to you;
Isa 44:15 he makes an idol and **b** down to it.
46: 1 Bel **b** down, Nebo stoops low;

## BOY [BOY'S, BOYS]
Ge 21:17 God has heard the **b** crying as he
22:12 "Do not lay a hand on the **b**,"
Lev 12: 3 On the eighth day the **b** is to be
Jdg 13: 5 by a razor because the **b** is to be
1Sa 2:11 the **b** ministered before the LORD
3: 8 that the LORD was calling the **b**.
Isa 7:16 for before the **b** knows enough
8: 4 Before the **b** knows how to say 'My

Mt 17:18 and it came out of the **b**, and he was
Lk 2:43 home, the **b** Jesus stayed behind

## BOY'S [BOY]
1Ki 17:22 and the **b** life returned to him,
2Ki 4:34 out on him, the **b** body grew warm.

## BOYS [BOY]
Ge 25:24 there were twin **b** in her womb.
38:27 there were twin **b** in her womb.
Ex 1:18 Why have you let the **b** live?"
Mt 2:16 orders to kill all the **b** in Bethlehem

## BRACE*
Na 2: 1 watch the road, **b** yourselves,

## BRACELETS
Ge 24:22 two gold **b** weighing ten shekels.
Eze 16:11 I put **b** on your arms and a necklace

## BRAG*
Am 4: 5 **b** about your freewill offerings—

## BRAIDS
Jdg 16:13 you weave the seven **b** of my head
16:13 Delilah took the seven **b** of his head,

## BRANCH [BRANCHES]
Nu 13:23 they cut off a **b** bearing a single
Isa 4: 2 that day the **B** of the LORD will be
11: 1 from his roots a **B** will bear fruit.
14:19 out of your tomb like a rejected **b**;
Jer 23: 5 raise up for David a righteous **B**,
33:15 I will make a righteous **B** sprout
Zec 3: 8 going to bring my servant, the **B**.
6:12 is the man whose name is the **B**,
6:12 and he will **b** out from his place
Jn 15: 2 He cuts off every **b** in me that bears
15: 2 while every **b** that does bear fruit he
15: 4 No **b** can bear fruit by itself;

## BRANCHES [BRANCH]
Ge 30:38 he placed the peeled **b** in all
Ex 25:32 Six **b** are to extend from the sides
Dt 24:20 do not go over the **b** a second time.
Eze 17: 6 Its **b** turned toward him, but its roots
17: 6 and produced **b** and put out leafy
Zec 4:12 are these two olive **b** beside the two
Lk 13:19 tree, and the birds perched in its **b**."
Jn 12:13 They took palm **b** and went
15: 5 "I am the vine; you are the **b**.
Ro 11:21 if God did not spare the natural **b**,
Rev 7: 9 were holding palm **b** in their hands.

## BRAVE [BRAVEST]
2Sa 2: 7 then, be strong and **b**, for Saul your
13:28 you this order? Be strong and **b**."
1Ch 12: 8 They were **b** warriors,

## BRAVEST* [BRAVE]
2Sa 17:10 Then even the **b** soldier,
Am 2:16 Even the **b** warriors will flee naked

## BRAWLER*
Pr    20: 1  Wine is a mocker and beer a **b**;

## BRAZEN*
Pr     7:13  him and with a **b** face she said:
Jer    3: 3  Yet you have the **b** look
Eze  16:30  things, acting like a **b** prostitute!

## BREACH [BREAK]
Ps  106:23  stood in the **b** before him to keep his

## BREACHING [BREAK]
Pr    17:14  Starting a quarrel is like **b** a dam;

## BREAD
Ex    12: 8  herbs, and **b** made without yeast.
      12:17  the Festival of Unleavened **B**,
      16: 4  "I will rain down **b** from heaven
      23:15  the Festival of Unleavened **B**;
      23:15  for seven days eat **b** made without
      25:30  Put the **b** of the Presence on this
Dt     8: 3  that people do not live on **b** alone
      16: 3  Do not eat it with **b** made
      16: 3  eat unleavened **b**, the **b** of affliction,
1Ki  17: 6  The ravens brought him **b** and meat
      22:27  give him nothing but **b** and water
2Ch   4:19  on which was the **b** of the Presence;
Ne     9:15  their hunger you gave them **b**
Ps    37:25  forsaken or their children begging **b**.
      41: 9  one who shared my **b**, has lifted
      78:25  Human beings ate the **b** of angels;
Pr    30: 8  riches, but give me only my daily **b**.
Isa   55: 2  Why spend money on what is not **b**,
Mt     4: 3  God, tell these stones to become **b**."
       4: 4  'People do not live on **b** alone,
       6:11  Give us today our daily **b**.
      15:33  "Where could we get enough **b**
      16: 5  lake, the disciples forgot to take **b**.
      26:26  Jesus took **b**, and when he had given
Lk    11: 3  Give us each day our daily **b**.
      22:19  And he took **b**, gave thanks
      24:35  by them when he broke the **b**.
Jn     6:33  For the **b** of God is the **b** that comes
       6:35  Jesus declared, "I am the **b** of life.
       6:41  "I am the **b** that came down
       6:48  I am the **b** of life.
       6:51  I am the living **b** that came down
       6:51  eats of this **b** will live forever.
       6:51  This **b** is my flesh, which I will give
      13:27  As soon as Judas took the **b**,
      21:13  took the **b** and gave it to them,
Ac     2:42  to the breaking of **b** and to prayer.
1Co  10:16  And is not the **b** that we break
      11:23  the night he was betrayed, took **b**,
      11:26  For whenever you eat this **b**
2Th    3:12  settle down and earn the **b** they eat.

## THE FESTIVAL OF UNLEAVENED
   **BREAD** See FESTIVAL

## BREAK [BREACH, BREACHING,
   BREAKERS, BREAKING, BREAKS,
   BROKE, BROKEN, BROKENNESS,
   LAWBREAKER, LAWBREAKERS]
Ex   12:46  Do not **b** any of the bones.

Nu    30: 2  he must not **b** his word but must do
Jos  22:16  'How could you **b** faith
Jdg    2: 1  'I will never **b** my covenant
Ps     2: 9  will **b** them with a rod of iron;
Pr    25:15  and a gentle tongue can **b** a bone.
Isa   42: 3  A bruised reed he will not **b**,
Mt    12:20  A bruised reed he will not **b**,
      15: 3  why do you **b** the command of God
Jn    19:33  dead, they did not **b** his legs.
Ac    20: 7  week we came together to **b** bread.
Ro     2:25  law, but if you **b** the law, you have
1Co  10:16  the bread that we **b** a participation
Rev    5: 2  "Who is worthy to **b** the seals

## BREAKERS* [BREAK]
Ps    42: 7  waves and **b** have swept over me.
      93: 4  mightier than the **b** of the sea—
Jnh    2: 3  all your waves and **b** swept over me.

## BREAKING [BREAK]
Ex    32:19  **b** them to pieces at the foot
Lev  26:44  **b** my covenant with them. I am
Dt    31:20  rejecting me and **b** my covenant.
Jos    9:20  fall on us for **b** the oath we swore
Eze  16:59  despised my oath by **b** the covenant.
      17:18  despised the oath by **b** the covenant.
Zec  11:14  **b** the family bond between Judah
Ac     2:42  to the **b** of bread and to prayer.
Ro     2:23  do you dishonor God by **b** the law?
Jas    2:10  just one point is guilty of **b** all of it.

## BREAKS [BREAK]
Ex     1:10  if war **b** out, will join our enemies.
Ps    29: 5  voice of the LORD **b** the cedars;
      76:12  He **b** the spirit of rulers; he is feared
Jer   23:29  "and like a hammer that **b** a rock
Da     2:40  for iron **b** and smashes everything—
1Jn    3: 4  Everyone who sins **b** the law;

## BREAST [BREASTPIECE,
   BREASTPLATE, BREASTPLATES,
   BREASTS]
Ps    22: 9  me feel secure on my mother's **b**.
Eze  21:12  Therefore beat your **b**.
Lk    18:13  but beat his **b** and said, 'God,

## BREASTPIECE [BREAST]
Ex    28:15  "Fashion a **b** for making decisions—
      28:30  Urim and the Thummim in the **b**,

## BREASTPLATE [BREAST]
Isa   59:17  He put on righteousness as his **b**,
Eph    6:14  with the **b** of righteousness in place,
1Th    5: 8  putting on faith and love as a **b**,

## BREASTPLATES [BREAST]
Rev    9: 9  They had **b** like **b** of iron,

## BREASTS [BREAST]
Pr     5:19  may her **b** satisfy you always,
SS     4: 5  Your **b** are like two fawns, like twin
La     4: 3  Even jackals offer their **b** to nurse
Na     2: 7  moan like doves and beat on their **b**.

## BREATH [BREATHED, BREATHING, GOD-BREATHED]

Ge   1:30  everything that has the **b** of life
      2: 7  into his nostrils the **b** of life,
      6:17  every creature that has the **b** of life
Ex  15:10  But you blew with your **b**,
2Sa 22:16  at the blast of **b** from his nostrils.
Job  27: 3  me, the **b** of God in my nostrils,
Ps   39: 5  Everyone is but a **b**, even those who
   150: 6  that has **b** praise the LORD.
Ecc  3:19  All have the same **b**;
La    4:20  our very life, was caught in their
Eze 37: 8  them, but there was no **b** in them.
Ac  17:25  he himself gives everyone life and **b**
Rev 11:11  a half days the **b** of life from God
   13:15  given power to give **b** to the image

## BREATHED [BREATH]

Ge   2: 7  **b** into his nostrils the breath of life,
Mk 15:37  With a loud cry, Jesus **b** his last.
Jn  20:22  with that he **b** on them and said,

## BREATHING [BREATH]

Ac   9: 1  Saul was still **b** out murderous

## BRIBE [BRIBED, BRIBERY, BRIBES]

Ex  23: 8  "Do not accept a **b**, for a **b** blinds
Dt  16:19  Do not accept a **b**, for a **b** blinds
  27:25  "Cursed is anyone who accepts a **b**
1Sa 12: 3  whose hand have I accepted a **b**
Pr   6:35  he will refuse a **b**, however great it
Ecc  7: 7  fools, and a **b** corrupts the heart.
Isa  5:23  who acquit the guilty for a **b**,
Mic  3:11  Her leaders judge for a **b**, her priests
Ac  24:26  that Paul would offer him a **b**, so he

## BRIBED* [BRIBE]

Ezr  4: 5  They **b** officials to work against them

## BRIBERY* [BRIBE]

2Ch 19: 7  is no injustice or partiality or **b**."

## BRIBES [BRIBE]

Dt  10:17  no partiality and accepts no **b**.
1Sa  8: 3  accepted **b** and perverted justice.

## BRICK [BRICKS]

Ge  11: 3  They used **b** instead of stone,
Ex   1:14  lives bitter with harsh labor in **b**

## BRICKS [BRICK]

Ge  11: 3  "Come, let's make **b** and bake them

## BRIDE [BRIDE-PRICE]

Ge  34:12  Make the price for the **b** and the gift
1Sa 18:25  for the **b** than a hundred Philistine
Ps  45: 9  at your right hand is the royal **b**
SS   4: 8  my **b**, come with me from Lebanon.
Isa 49:18  you will put them on, like a **b**.
  62: 5  as a bridegroom rejoices over his **b**,
Jer  2:32  a **b** her wedding ornaments?
Jn   3:29  The **b** belongs to the bridegroom.
Rev 19: 7  and his **b** has made herself ready.
  21: 2  prepared as a **b** beautifully dressed

Rev 21: 9  I will show you the **b**, the wife
  22:17  The Spirit and the **b** say, "Come!"

## BRIDE-PRICE* [BRIDE]

Ex  22:16  he must pay the **b**, and she shall be
  22:17  he must still pay the **b** for virgins.

## BRIDEGROOM

Ex   4:25  "Surely you are a **b** of blood
Ps  19: 5  which is like a **b** coming out of his
Jer  25:10  the voices of bride and **b**, the sound
Mt  25: 1  lamps and went out to meet the **b**.
  25: 5  The **b** was a long time in coming,
Mk  2:20  will come when the **b** will be taken
Rev 18:23  The voice of **b** and bride will never

## BRIDLE

Pr  26: 3  a **b** for the donkey, and a rod

## BRIEF*

Ezr  9: 8  for a **b** moment, the LORD our
Job 20: 5  that the mirth of the wicked is **b**,
Isa 54: 7  "For a **b** moment I abandoned you,

## BRIER* [BRIERS]

Mic  7: 4  The best of them is like a **b**,

## BRIERS [BRIER]

Isa 55:13  instead of **b** the myrtle will grow.
Lk  6:44  from thornbushes, or grapes from **b**.

## BRIGHT [BRIGHTENS, BRIGHTER, BRIGHTNESS]

SS   6:10  dawn, fair as the moon, **b** as the sun,
Lk  9:29  his clothes became as **b** as a flash
Ac  22: 6  suddenly a **b** light from heaven
Rev 19: 8  Fine linen, **b** and clean, was given
  22:16  of David, and the **b** Morning Star."

## BRIGHTENS* [BRIGHT]

Pr  16:15  When a king's face **b**, it means life;
Ecc  8: 1  Wisdom **b** the face and changes its

## BRIGHTER [BRIGHT]

Pr   4:18  shining ever **b** till the full light
Ac  26:13  a light from heaven, **b** than the sun,

## BRIGHTNESS* [BRIGHT]

2Sa 22:13  Out of the **b** of his presence bolts
  23: 4  like the **b** after rain that brings grass
Ps  18:12  Out of the **b** of his presence clouds
Isa 59: 9  for **b**, but we walk in deep shadows.
  60: 3  and kings to the **b** of your dawn.
  60:19  nor will the **b** of the moon shine
Da  12: 3  who are wise will shine like the **b**
Am  5:20  pitch-dark, without a ray of **b**?

## BRILLIANCE* [BRILLIANT]

Ac  22:11  because the **b** of the light had
Rev  1:16  was like the sun shining in all its **b**.
  21:11  its **b** was like that of a very precious

## BRILLIANT* [BRILLIANCE]
Ecc   9:11  or wealth to the **b** or favor
Eze   1: 4  lightning and surrounded by **b** light.
      1:27  and **b** light surrounded him.

## BRIM*
Pr    3:10  and your vats will **b** over with new
Jn    2: 7  so they filled them to the **b**.

## BRIMSTONE  See SULFUR

## BRING  [BRINGING, BRINGS, BROUGHT]
Ge    6:17  I am going to **b** floodwaters
      6:19  You are to **b** into the ark two of all
     28:15  and I will **b** you back to this land.
Ex    3: 8  to **b** them up out of that land
      6:26  "**B** the Israelites out of Egypt
     18:22  have them **b** every difficult case
     25: 2  the Israelites to **b** me an offering.
     32:12  do not **b** disaster on your people.
Nu   20: 5  Why did you **b** us up out of Egypt
Dt   24: 4  Do not **b** sin upon the land
     26:10  now I **b** the firstfruits of the soil
1Ki  21:21  'I am going to **b** disaster on you,
2Ki  22:16  I am going to **b** disaster on this
Pr    3: 8  This will **b** health to your body
     10: 4  but diligent hands **b** wealth.
     11:17  the cruel **b** ruin on themselves.
     15:20  Wise children **b** joy to their father,
     18: 6  The lips of fools **b** them strife,
     29:11  but the wise **b** calm in the end.
Isa  40: 9  You who **b** good news to Zion,
     40: 9  You who **b** good news to Jerusalem,
     52: 7  the feet of those who **b** good news,
     52: 7  proclaim peace, who **b** good tidings,
     54: 7  deep compassion I will **b** you back.
Jer  24: 6  and I will **b** them back to this land.
Eze   5:17  and I will **b** the sword against you.
Da    9:24  to **b** in everlasting righteousness,
Hos   4: 1  a charge to **b** against you who live
Lk    6:45  Good people **b** good things
     12:51  Do you think I came to **b** peace
Jn   10:16  this sheep pen. I must **b** them also.
Ro   10:15  feet of those who **b** good news!'"
1Co   8: 8  But food does not **b** us near to God;
2Jn   1:10  to you and does not **b** this teaching,
Rev  15: 4  Lord, and **b** glory to your name?

## BRINGING  [BRING]
Ex   36: 5  "The people are **b** more than
Isa   1:13  Stop **b** meaningless offerings!
Mt   27:13  testimony they are **b** against you?"
Lk   18:15  **b** babies to Jesus for him to place
Heb   2:10  In **b** many sons and daughters

## BRINGS  [BRING]
Dt    6:10  the LORD your God **b** you
1Sa   2: 6  "The LORD **b** death and makes
      2: 6  he **b** down to the grave and raises
Pr   12:18  but the tongue of the wise **b** healing.
Ro    4:15  because the law **b** wrath.
2Co   7:10  Godly sorrow **b** repentance
      7:10  regret, but worldly sorrow **b** death.
Heb   1: 6  when God **b** his firstborn

## BRITTLE*
Da    2:42  will be partly strong and partly **b**.

## BROAD
2Sa  12:11  sleep with your wives in **b** daylight.
Isa  33:21  It will be like a place of **b** rivers
Mt    7:13  gate and **b** is the road that leads
2Pe   2:13  pleasure is to carouse in **b** daylight.

## BROKE  [BREAK]
Ex    9:10  and festering boils **b** out on people
     34: 1  on the first tablets, which you **b**.
2Ch  34: 4  These he **b** to pieces and scattered
     36:19  and **b** down the wall of Jerusalem;
Jer  31:32  Egypt, because they **b** my covenant,
Eze  44: 7  and blood, and you **b** my covenant.
Zec  11:10  took my staff called Favor and **b** it,
Mt   26:26  he **b** it and gave it to his disciples,
     27:52  and the tombs **b** open. The bodies
Mk   14:22  he **b** it and gave it to his disciples,
Ac    2:46  They **b** bread in their homes and ate
     20:11  he went upstairs again and **b** bread
1Co  11:24  had given thanks, he **b** it and said,
Rev  16: 2  festering sores **b** out on the people

## BROKEN  [BREAK]
1Sa   2:10  who oppose the LORD will be **b**.
      4:18  His neck was **b** and he died, for he
      5: 4  hands had been **b** off and were lying
Ne    1: 3  The wall of Jerusalem is **b** down,
Ps   34:20  bones, not one of them will be **b**.
     51:17  My sacrifice, O God, is a **b** spirit;
     51:17  a **b** and contrite heart you, God,
Ecc   4:12  of three strands is not quickly **b**.
     12: 6  is severed, and the golden bowl is **b**;
     12: 6  spring, and the wheel **b** at the well,
Jer   2:13  **b** cisterns that cannot hold water.
Da    8: 8  its power the large horn was **b** off,
Hos   6: 7  at Adam, they have **b** the covenant;
Lk   20:18  on that stone will be **b** to pieces,
Jn    7:23  that the law of Moses may not be **b**,
     10:35  and Scripture cannot be **b**—
     19:36  "Not one of his bones will be **b**,"
Ro   11:20  they were **b** off because of unbelief,

## BROKENHEARTED* [HEART]
Ps   34:18  The LORD is close to the **b**
    109:16  the poor and the needy and the **b**.
    147: 3  He heals the **b** and binds up their
Isa  61: 1  He has sent me to bind up the **b**,

## BROKENNESS* [BREAK]
Isa  65:14  of heart and wail in **b** of spirit.

## BRONZE
Ge    4:22  forged all kinds of tools out of **b**
Ex   27: 2  piece, and overlay the altar with **b**.
     30:18  "Make a **b** basin, with its **b** stand,
Lev  26:19  and the ground beneath you like **b**.
Nu   21: 9  So Moses made a **b** snake and put it
Dt   28:23  The sky over your head will be **b**,
1Ki   7:15  cast two **b** pillars, each eighteen
      7:27  also made ten movable stands of **b**;
2Ki  16:14  As for the **b** altar that stood before
     25:13  Babylonians broke up the **b** pillars,

2Ki 25:13 the **b** Sea that were at the temple
    25:13 and they carried the **b** to Babylon.
Ps 18:34 my arms can bend a bow of **b**.
Isa 48: 4 were iron, your forehead was **b**.
Da 2:32 of silver, its belly and thighs of **b**,
    10: 6 legs like the gleam of burnished **b**.
Zec 6: 1 mountains of **b**.
Rev 1:15 His feet were like **b** glowing
    2:18 and whose feet are like burnished **b**.

## BROOD

Nu 32:14 "And here you are, a **b** of sinners,
Job 30: 8 A base and nameless **b**, they were
Isa 57: 4 Are you not a **b** of rebels,
Lk 3: 7 baptized by him, "You **b** of vipers!
2Pe 2:14 are experts in greed—an accursed **b**!

## BROOK

1Ki 17: 4 You will drink from the **b**, and I
Ps 110: 7 will drink from a **b** along the way,

## BROOM

1Ki 19: 4 He came to a **b** bush, sat down

## BROTHER [BROTHER'S, BROTHER-IN-LAW, BROTHERHOOD, BROTHERS]

Ge 4: 8 Cain attacked his **b** Abel and killed
    20:13 say of me, "He is my **b**." ' "
    27:41 then I will kill my **b** Jacob."
    42:20 you must bring your youngest **b**
    43:30 Deeply moved at the sight of his **b**,
    45: 4 "I am your **b** Joseph, the one you
Ex 7: 1 your **b** Aaron will be your prophet.
Dt 25: 5 Her husband's **b** shall take her
2Sa 13:12 "No, my **b**!" she said to him.
Pr 17:17 a **b** is born for a time of adversity.
    18:24 a friend who sticks closer than a **b**.
SS 8: 1 If only you were to me like a **b**,
Isa 19: 2 **b** will fight against **b**,
Ob 1:10 the violence against your **b** Jacob,
Mt 5:22 that anyone who is angry with a **b**
    5:22 anyone who says to a **b** or sister,
    10:21 "**B** will betray **b** to death,
    18:15 "If a **b** or sister sins, go and point
Mk 3:35 Whoever does God's will is my **b**
Lk 15:28 "The older **b** became angry
    17: 3 "If a **b** or sister sins against you,
Ro 14:13 obstacle in the way of a **b** or sister.
    14:15 If your **b** or sister is distressed
    14:15 not by your eating destroy your **b**
    14:21 anything else that will cause your **b**
1Co 6: 6 one **b** goes to law against another—
    7:15 The **b** or sister is not bound
    8:13 if what I eat causes my **b** or sister
Phm 1:16 but better than a slave, as a dear **b**.
    1:16 a fellow man and as a **b** in the Lord.
Jas 2:15 Suppose a **b** or sister is without
    4:11 Anyone who speaks against a **b**
1Jn 3:17 and sees a **b** or sister in need but has
    4:20 If we say we love God yet hate a **b**
    5:16 If you see any **b** or sister commit

## BROTHER OR SISTER Nu 6:7; Mt 5:22, 22,
23; 18:15, 35; Lk 17:3; Ro 14:10, 10; 14:13, 15,

15, 21; 1Co 7:15; 8:11, 13; 1Th 4:6; Jas 2:15;
4:11; 1Jn 3:17; 4:20; 5:16

## BROTHER'S [BROTHER]

Ge 4: 9 "Am I my **b** keeper?"
Dt 25: 7 does not want to marry his **b** wife,
    25: 7 to carry on his **b** name in Israel.
Mk 6:18 for you to have your **b** wife."

## BROTHER-IN-LAW [BROTHER]

Ge 38: 8 your duty to her as a **b** to raise
Dt 25: 5 her and fulfill the duty of a **b** to her.

## BROTHERHOOD* [BROTHER]

Am 1: 9 to Edom, disregarding a treaty of **b**,

## BROTHERS [BROTHER]

Ge 9:25 of slaves will he be to his **b**."
    27:29 Be lord over your **b**, and may
    37:11 His **b** were jealous of him, but his
Jdg 9: 5 one stone murdered his seventy **b**,
2Ch 21:13 have also murdered your own **b**,
Hos 2: 1 "Say of your **b**, 'My people,'
Mt 12:49 "Here are my mother and my **b**.
    19:29 everyone who has left houses or **b**
    25:40 did for one of the least of these **b**
Mk 3:33 "Who are my mother and my **b**?"
    12:20 Now there were seven **b**.
Lk 21:16 will be betrayed even by parents, **b**,
    22:32 turned back, strengthen your **b**."
Jn 7: 5 For even his own **b** did not believe
Ro 8:29 be the firstborn among many **b**
Eph 6:23 Peace to the **b** and sisters, and love
Col 1: 2 the faithful **b** and sisters in Christ:
1Th 4:10 you do love all the **b** and sisters
2Th 3: 6 we command you, **b** and sisters,
1Ti 5: 1 Treat younger men as **b**,
Heb 2:11 Jesus is not ashamed to call them **b**
    2:17 reason he had to be made like his **b**
    13: 1 Keep on loving one another as **b**
1Jn 3:10 are those who do not love their **b**
Rev 12:10 the accuser of our **b** and sisters,

## BROTHERS AND SISTERS Jos 2:13; 6:23;
Job 42:11; Mt 25:40; Lk 14:26; Ac 1:16; 2:29;
3:17; 6:3; 12:17; 13:26, 38; Ro 1:13; 7:1, 4; 8:12,
29; 10:1; 11:25; 12:1; 15:14, 30; 16:14, 17; 1Co
1:10, 11, 26; 2:1; 3:1; 4:6; 6:8; 7:24, 29; 10:1;
11:33; 12:1; 14:6, 20, 26, 39; 15:1, 6, 50, 58;
16:15, 20; 2Co 1:8; 8:1; 11:9; 13:11; Gal 1:2, 11;
3:15; 4:12, 28, 31; 5:11, 13; 6:1, 18; Eph 6:23;
Php 1:12, 14; 3:1, 13, 17; 4:1, 8, 21; Col 1:2;
4:15; 1Th 1:4; 2:1, 9, 14, 17; 3:7; 4:1, 10, 13;
5:1, 4, 12, 14, 25, 27; 2Th 1:3; 2:1, 13, 15; 3:1, 6,
13; 1Ti 4:6; 2Ti 4:21; Heb 2:11, 12, 17; 3:1, 12;
10:19; 13:1, 22; Jas 1:2, 16, 19; 2:1, 5, 14; 3:1,
10, 12; 4:11; 5:7, 9, 10, 12, 19; 2Pe 1:10; 1Jn
3:10, 13; 3Jn 1:5; Rev 6:11; 12:10; 19:10

## BROUGHT [BRING]

Ge 2:19 He **b** them to the man to see what he
    2:22 of the man, and he **b** her to the man.
    15: 7 LORD, who **b** you out of Ur
    21: 6 Sarah said, "God has **b** me laughter,
Ex 13: 9 For the LORD **b** you out of Egypt

| | | |
|---|---|---|
| Ex | 18:26 | The difficult cases they **b** to Moses, |
| | 32: 1 | for this fellow Moses who **b** us |
| Nu | 11:11 | "Why have you **b** this trouble |
| | 21: 5 | said, "Why have you **b** us |
| Dt | 8:15 | He **b** you water out of hard rock. |
| Jdg | 2: 1 | "I **b** you up out of Egypt and led |
| 1Ch | 11:14 | the LORD **b** about a great victory. |
| Ne | 9:15 | in their thirst you **b** them water |
| Ps | 18:19 | He **b** me out into a spacious place; |
| | 30: 3 | **b** me up from the realm of the dead; |
| Pr | 8:22 | "The LORD **b** me forth as the first |
| La | 1: 5 | The LORD has **b** her grief because |
| Eze | 11: 1 | **b** me to the gate of the house |
| | 37: 1 | and he **b** me out by the Spirit |
| Da | 5:13 | So Daniel was **b** before the king, |
| | 5:13 | the exiles my father the king **b** |
| Jnh | 2: 6 | my God, **b** my life up from the pit. |
| Mk | 6:28 | and **b** back his head on a platter. |
| | 8:22 | and some people **b** a blind man |
| | 12:16 | They **b** the coin, and he asked them, |
| | 15:22 | They **b** Jesus to the place called |
| Ro | 5:20 | The law was **b** in so that |
| | 6:13 | God as those who have been **b** |
| 2Co | 3: 7 | Now if the ministry that **b** death, |
| Eph | 2:13 | were far away have been **b** near |
| Col | 2:10 | in Christ you have been **b** to fullness. |
| 1Ti | 6: 7 | For we **b** nothing into the world, |
| Heb | 6: 6 | away, to be **b** back to repentance. |
| | 11: 4 | By faith Abel **b** God a better offering |

## BROW

| | | |
|---|---|---|
| Ge | 3:19 | your **b** you will eat your food until |

## BROWN*

| | | |
|---|---|---|
| Zec | 1: 8 | him were red, **b** and white horses. |

## BRUISE* [BRUISED, BRUISES]

| | | |
|---|---|---|
| Ex | 21:25 | wound for wound, **b** for **b**. |

## BRUISED [BRUISE]

| | | |
|---|---|---|
| Isa | 42: 3 | A **b** reed he will not break, |
| Mt | 12:20 | A **b** reed he will not break, |

## BRUISES* [BRUISE]

| | | |
|---|---|---|
| Pr | 23:29 | Who has needless **b**? |
| Isa | 30:26 | LORD binds up the **b** of his people |

## BRUTAL* [BRUTE]

| | | |
|---|---|---|
| Eze | 21:31 | deliver you into the hands of **b** men, |
| 2Ti | 3: 3 | without self-control, **b**, not lovers |

## BRUTE* [BRUTAL, BRUTES]

| | | |
|---|---|---|
| Ps | 73:22 | I was a **b** beast before you. |
| Pr | 30: 2 | I am only a **b**, not a man; |

## BRUTES* [BRUTE]

| | | |
|---|---|---|
| Tit | 1:12 | always liars, evil **b**, lazy gluttons." |

## BUBBLING*

| | | |
|---|---|---|
| Isa | 35: 7 | a pool, the thirsty ground **b** springs. |

## BUCKET*

| | | |
|---|---|---|
| Isa | 40:15 | the nations are like a drop in a **b**; |

## BUCKLED*

| | | |
|---|---|---|
| Eph | 6:14 | belt of truth **b** around your waist, |

## BUD [BUDDED]

| | | |
|---|---|---|
| Isa | 27: 6 | Israel will **b** and blossom and fill all |
| Hab | 3:17 | Though the fig tree does not **b** |

## BUDDED [BUD]

| | | |
|---|---|---|
| Nu | 17: 8 | had not only sprouted but had **b**, |
| Eze | 7:10 | forth, the rod has **b**, arrogance has |
| Heb | 9: 4 | Aaron's staff that had **b**, |

## BUILD [BUILDER, BUILDERS, BUILDING, BUILDINGS, BUILDS, BUILT, REBUILD, REBUILT]

| | | |
|---|---|---|
| Ge | 6:15 | This is how you are to **b** it: |
| | 11: 4 | "Come, let us **b** ourselves a city, |
| Ex | 27: 1 | "**B** an altar of acacia wood, |
| Nu | 23: 1 | said, "**B** me seven altars here, |
| Dt | 6:10 | flourishing cities you did not **b**, |
| 2Sa | 7: 5 | Are you the one to **b** me a house |
| 1Ki | 6: 1 | he began to **b** the temple |
| Ezr | 1: 3 | and **b** the temple of the LORD, |
| Ps | 51:18 | Zion, to **b** up the walls of Jerusalem. |
| Ecc | 3: 3 | a time to tear down and a time to **b**, |
| Isa | 57:14 | "**B** up, **b** up, prepare the road! |
| | 62:10 | **B** up, **b** up the highway! |
| Mic | 3:10 | who **b** Zion with bloodshed, |
| Zep | 1:13 | Though they **b** houses, they will not |
| Hag | 1: 8 | bring down timber and **b** the house, |
| Mt | 16:18 | and on this rock I will **b** my church, |
| | 23:29 | You **b** tombs for the prophets |
| | 27:40 | the temple and **b** it in three days, |
| Jn | 2:20 | forty-six years to **b** this temple, |
| Ac | 20:32 | which can **b** you up and give you |
| Ro | 15: 2 | for their good, to **b** them up. |
| 1Co | 3:10 | each one should **b** with care. |
| | 14:12 | excel in those that **b** up the church. |
| 1Th | 5:11 | one another and **b** each other up, |

## BUILDER* [BUILD]

| | | |
|---|---|---|
| Isa | 62: 5 | so will your **B** marry you; |
| 1Co | 3:10 | I laid a foundation as a wise **b**, |
| | 3:14 | the **b** will receive a reward. |
| | 3:15 | the **b** will suffer loss but yet |
| Heb | 3: 3 | just as the **b** of a house has greater |
| | 3: 4 | but God is the **b** of everything. |
| | 11:10 | whose architect and **b** is God. |

## BUILDERS [BUILD]

| | | |
|---|---|---|
| Ps | 118:22 | The stone the **b** rejected has become |
| | 127: 1 | builds the house, the **b** labor in vain. |
| Mt | 21:42 | " 'The stone the **b** rejected has |
| Mk | 12:10 | " 'The stone the **b** rejected has |
| Lk | 20:17 | " 'The stone the **b** rejected has |
| Ac | 4:11 | is " 'the stone you **b** rejected, |
| 1Pe | 2: 7 | "The stone the **b** rejected has |

## BUILDING [BUILD]

| | | |
|---|---|---|
| Ge | 11: 5 | the city and the tower they were **b**. |
| 1Ki | 9: 1 | Solomon had finished **b** the temple |
| 2Ki | 25: 9 | Every important **b** he burned down. |
| Ezr | 4: 1 | the exiles were **b** a temple |
| Ne | 4:17 | who were **b** the wall. |

Mic  7:11  The day for **b** your walls will come,
Lk  6:48  They are like a man **b** a house,
Ro  15:20  I would not be **b** on someone else's
1Co  3: 9  you are God's field, God's **b**.
2Co  5: 1  is destroyed, we have a **b** from God,
10: 8  authority the Lord gave us for **b** you
13:10  the Lord gave me for **b** you up,
Eph  2:21  him the whole **b** is joined together
4:29  only what is helpful for **b** others
Jude  1:20  by **b** yourselves up in your most

## BUILDINGS [BUILD]

Mk  13: 1  What magnificent **b**!"

## BUILDS [BUILD]

Ps  127: 1  Unless the LORD **b** the house,
147: 2  The LORD **b** up Jerusalem;
Pr  14: 1  The wise woman **b** her house,
Jer  22:13  "Woe to him who **b** his palace
Hab  2: 9  "Woe to him who **b** his house
2:12  "Woe to him who **b** a city
1Co  3:12  If anyone **b** on this foundation using
8: 1  puffs up while love **b** up.
Eph  4:16  grows and **b** itself up in love,

## BUILT [BUILD]

Ge  8:20  Noah **b** an altar to the LORD and,
12: 7  So he **b** an altar there
22: 9  about, Abraham **b** an altar there
26:25  Isaac **b** an altar there and called
35: 7  There he **b** an altar, and he called
Ex  17:15  Moses **b** an altar and called it
24: 4  **b** an altar at the foot of the mountain
32: 5  he **b** an altar in front of the calf
Jos  8:30  Joshua **b** on Mount Ebal an altar
22:11  heard that they had **b** the altar
Jdg  6:24  So Gideon **b** an altar to the LORD
1Sa  7:17  he **b** an altar there to the LORD.
14:35  Then Saul **b** an altar to the LORD;
2Sa  24:25  David **b** an altar to the LORD
1Ki  6:14  So Solomon **b** the temple
12:31  Jeroboam **b** shrines on high places
2Ki  23:12  the altars Manasseh had **b** in the two
Ezr  3: 3  they **b** the altar on its foundation
Ps  122: 3  Jerusalem is **b** like a city that is
Pr  9: 1  Wisdom has **b** her house;
24: 3  By wisdom a house is **b**,
Hos  10: 1  his fruit increased, he **b** more altars;
Zec  8: 9  strong so that the temple may be **b**.'
Mt  7:24  is like a wise man who **b** his house
Lk  6:49  are like a man who **b** a house
Ac  17:24  does not live in temples **b** by hands.
1Co  3:14  If what has been **b** survives,
14:26  done so that the church may be **b** up.
2Co  5: 1  in heaven, not **b** by human hands.
Eph  2:20  **b** on the foundation of the apostles
4:12  that the body of Christ may be **b**
Col  2: 7  rooted and **b** up in him,
Heb  11: 7  in holy fear **b** an ark to save his
1Pe  2: 5  are being **b** into a spiritual house
3:20  of Noah while the ark was being **b**.

## BULL [BULLS]

Ex  21:28  "If a **b** gores a man or a woman
21:28  death, the **b** is to be stoned to death,
21:28  of the **b** will not be held responsible.

Lev  1: 5  to slaughter the young **b** before
4: 3  LORD a young **b** without defect as
16: 6  offer the **b** for his own sin offering
Ps  50: 9  I have no need of a **b** from your stall
106:20  glorious God for an image of a **b**,
Isa  66: 3  whoever sacrifices a **b** is like one

## BULLS [BULL]

Ex  24: 5  sacrificed young **b** as fellowship
Nu  23: 1  prepare seven **b** and seven rams
29:13  a burnt offering of thirteen young **b**,
1Ki  7:25  The Sea stood on twelve **b**,
1Ch  29:21  a thousand **b**, a thousand rams
Ezr  6:17  of God they offered a hundred **b**,
Ps  22:12  Many **b** surround me; strong **b**
50:13  Do I eat the flesh of **b** or drink
Jer  52:20  and the twelve bronze **b** under it,
Heb  10: 4  It is impossible for the blood of **b**

## BURDEN [BURDENED, BURDENS, BURDENSOME]

Nu  11:14  the **b** is too heavy for me.
Ps  38: 4  overwhelmed me like a **b** too heavy
Ecc  1:13  What a heavy **b** God has laid
3:10  I have seen the **b** God has laid
Isa  1:14  They have become a **b** to me;
10:27  that day their **b** will be lifted
Mal  1:13  And you say, 'What a **b**!'
Mt  11:30  my yoke is easy and my **b** is light."
Ac  15:28  and to us not to **b** you with anything
2Co  11: 9  something, I was not a **b** to anyone,
11: 9  kept myself from being a **b** to you
12:14  and I will not be a **b** to you,
2Th  3: 8  so that we would not be a **b** to any
Heb  13:17  joy, not a **b**, for that would be of no
Rev  2:24  'I will not impose any other **b**

## BURDENED* [BURDEN]

Isa  43:23  I have not **b** you with grain
43:24  But you have **b** me with your sins
Mic  6: 3  How have I **b** you? Answer me.
Mt  11:28  all you who are weary and **b**, and I
2Co  5: 4  we groan and are **b**, because we do
Gal  5: 1  do not let yourselves be **b** again
1Ti  5:16  not let the church be **b** with them,

## BURDENS [BURDEN]

Ps  68:19  our Savior, who daily bears our **b**.
Lk  11:46  down with **b** they can hardly carry,
Gal  6: 2  Carry each other's **b**, and in this

## BURDENSOME* [BURDEN]

Isa  46: 1  images that are carried about are **b**,
1Jn  5: 3  And his commands are not **b**,

## BURIAL [BURY]

Ge  23: 4  for a **b** site here so I can bury my
49:30  the field as a **b** place from Ephron
Mt  26:12  body, she did it to prepare me for **b**.
27: 7  to buy the potter's field as a **b** place

## BURIED [BURY]

Ge  15:15  in peace and be **b** at a good old age.
Ru  1:17  die I will die, and there I will be **b**.
Ecc  8:10  Then too, I saw the wicked **b**—

Ro    6: 4  We were therefore **b** with him
1Co 15: 4  that he was **b**, that he was raised
Col   2:12  having been **b** with him in baptism,

## BURN [BURNED, BURNING, BURNT]

Ex    3: 2  the bush was on fire it did not **b** up.
     21:25  **b** for **b**, wound for wound,
Dt    6:15  and his anger will **b** against you,
      7· 5  poles and **b** their idols in the fire.
    29:20  wrath and zeal will **b** against them.
Ps   79: 5  long will your jealousy **b** like fire?
   89:46  long will your wrath **b** like fire?
Jer   7:31  of Ben Hinnom to **b** their sons
Lk    3:17  barn, but he will **b** up the chaff
1Co  7: 9  to marry than to **b** with passion.
2Co 11:29  into sin, and I do not inwardly **b**?

## BURNED [BURN]

Ex   4:14  the LORD's anger **b** against Moses
   32:19  his anger **b** and he threw the tablets
Nu  11: 3  the LORD had **b** among them.
Pr   6:27  his lap without his clothes being **b**?
Jer 36:23  until the entire scroll was **b**
1Co  3:15  If it is **b** up, the builder will suffer
Heb  6: 8  In the end it will be **b**.
Rev  8: 7  A third of the earth was **b** up, a third

## BURNING [BURN]

Ex  27:20  so that the lamps may be kept **b**.
Lev  6: 9  the fire must be kept **b** on the altar.
Ps  18:28  You, LORD, keep my lamp **b**;
  118:12  consumed as quickly as **b** thorns;
Pr  25:22  you will heap **b** coals on his head,
Am  4:11  You were like a **b** stick snatched
Zec  3: 2  Is not this man a **b** stick snatched
Ac   7:30  the flames of a **b** bush in the desert
Ro  12:20  you will heap **b** coals on his head."
Rev 19:20  alive into the fiery lake of **b** sulfur.
  20:10  was thrown into the lake of **b** sulfur,
  21: 8  to the fiery lake of **b** sulfur.

## BURNISHED*

1Ki  7:45  of the LORD were of **b** bronze.
Eze  1: 7  of a calf and gleamed like **b** bronze.
Da  10: 6  and legs like the gleam of **b** bronze,
Rev  2:18  and whose feet are like **b** bronze.

## BURNT [BURN]

Ge   8:20  birds, he sacrificed **b** offerings on it.
  22: 2  Sacrifice him there as a **b** offering
Ex  10:25  **b** offerings to present to the LORD
  18:12  brought a **b** offering and other
  40: 6  "Place the altar of **b** offering
Lev  1: 3  the offering is a **b** offering
  6: 9  the regulations for the **b** offering:
  6: 9  The **b** offering is to remain
Jos  8:31  offered to the LORD **b** offerings
  22:26  but not for **b** offerings or sacrifices.'
Jdg  6:26  the second bull as a **b** offering."
  13:16  But if you prepare a **b** offering,
1Ki  3: 4  offered a thousand **b** offerings
  9:25  year Solomon sacrificed **b** offerings
  10: 5  and the **b** offerings he made
Ezr  3: 2  Israel to sacrifice **b** offerings on it,

Ezr  8:35  captivity sacrificed **b** offerings
  8:35  All this was a **b** offering
Job  1: 5  he would sacrifice a **b** offering
Ps  51:16  do not take pleasure in **b** offerings.
Isa  1:11  more than enough of **b** offerings,
  40:16  its animals enough for **b** offerings.
Eze 43:18  for sacrificing **b** offerings
Hos  6: 6  of God rather than **b** offerings.
Mic  6: 6  I come before him with **b** offerings,
Mk 12:33  more important than all **b** offerings
Heb 10: 6  with **b** offerings and sin offerings

## BURNT OFFERING Ge 22:2, 3, 6, 7, 8, 13;
Ex 18:12; 29:18, 25, 42; 30:9, 28; 31:9; 35:16;
38:1; 40:6, 10, 29; Lev 1:3, 4, 6, 9, 10, 13, 14,
17; 3:5; 4:7, 10, 18, 24, 25, 29, 30, 33, 34; 5:7,
10; 6:9, 9, 10, 12, 25; 7:2, 8, 37; 8:18, 21, 28;
9:2, 3, 7, 12, 13, 14, 16, 17, 22, 24; 10:19; 12:6,
8; 14:13, 19, 22, 31; 15:15, 30; 16:3, 5, 24, 24;
17:8; 22:18; 23:12, 18; Nu 6:11, 14, 16; 7:15, 21,
27, 33, 39, 45, 51, 57, 63, 69, 75, 81, 87; 8:12;
15:5, 8, 24; 28:3, 6, 10, 10, 11, 13, 14, 15, 19, 23,
24, 27, 31; 29:2, 8, 11, 13, 16, 19, 22, 25, 28, 31,
34, 36, 38; Dt 13:16; Jdg 6:26; 11:31; 13:16, 23;
1Sa 6:14; 7:9, 10; 13:9, 9, 12; 2Sa 24:22; 2Ki
10:25; 16:13, 15, 15, 15; 1Ch 6:49; 16:40; 21:24,
26, 29; 22:1; 2Ch 7:1; 29:18, 24, 27, 28; Ezr
8:35; Job 1:5; 42:8; Eze 43:24; 45:23; 46:2, 4,
12, 12, 13, 15

## BURNT OFFERINGS Ge 8:20; Ex 10:25;
20:24; 24:5; 32:6; 40:29; Lev 23:37; Nu 10:10;
15:3; 29:6, 39; Dt 12:6, 11, 13, 27; 27:6; 33:10;
Jos 8:31; 22:23, 26, 27, 28, 29; Jdg 20:26; 21:4;
1Sa 6:15; 10:8; 15:22; 2Sa 6:17, 18; 24:24, 25;
1Ki 3:4, 15; 8:64, 64; 9:25; 10:5; 2Ki 5:17;
10:24; 16:15; 1Ch 16:1, 2, 40; 21:23, 26; 23:31;
29:21; 2Ch 1:6; 2:4; 4:6; 7:7, 7; 8:12; 9:4; 13:11;
23:18; 24:14, 14; 29:7, 31, 32, 32, 34, 35, 35;
30:15; 31:2, 3, 3; 35:12, 14, 16; Ezr 3:2, 3, 4, 5,
6; 6:9; 8:35; Ne 10:33; Ps 20:3; 40:6; 50:8;
51:16, 19; 66:13; Isa 1:11; 40:16; 43:23; 56:7;
Jer 6:20; 7:21, 22; 14:12; 17:26; 33:18; Eze
40:38, 39, 42, 42; 43:18, 27; 44:11; 45:15, 17,
17, 25; Hos 6:6; Am 5:22; Mic 6:6; Mk 12:33;
Heb 10:6, 8

## BURST

Ge   7:11  the springs of the great deep **b** forth,
Job 32:19  wine, like new wineskins ready to **b**.
Ps  60: 1  rejected us, God, and **b** upon us;
  98: 4  **b** into jubilant song with music;
Isa  35: 2  it will **b** into bloom; it will rejoice
  44:23  **B** into song, you mountains,
  49:13  **b** into song, you mountains!
  52: 9  **B** into songs of joy together,
  54: 1  **b** into song, shout for joy, you who
  55:12  hills will **b** into song before you,
Jer 23:19  the storm of the LORD will **b**
Eze  7:10  Doom has **b** forth, the rod has
Lk   5:37  do, the new wine will **b** the skins;
Ac   1:18  his body **b** open and all his

## BURY [BURIAL, BURIED]

Ge  23: 4  site here so I can **b** my dead."
  47:29  Do not **b** me in Egypt,

Ge 50: 7 So Joseph went up to **b** his father.
Pr 19:24 Sluggards **b** their hands in the dish
Mt 8:22 and let the dead **b** their own dead."
Lk 9:60 "Let the dead **b** their own dead,

## BUSH

Ex 3: 2 in flames of fire from within a **b**.
 3: 2 though the **b** was on fire it did not
Dt 33:16 of him who dwelt in the burning **b**.
Mk 12:26 in the account of the burning **b**,
Lk 20:37 But in the account of the burning **b**,
Ac 7:35 angel who appeared to him in the **b**.

## BUSINESS

Ecc 4: 8 too is meaningless—a miserable **b**!
Da 8:27 got up and went about the king's **b**.
Ac 19:24 in no little **b** for the skilled workers
1Co 5:12 What **b** is it of mine to judge those
1Th 4:11 You should mind your own **b**
Jas 1:11 even while they go about their **b**.
 4:13 there, carry on **b** and make money."

## BUSY [BUSYBODIES]*

1Ki 18:27 is deep in thought, or **b**, or traveling.
 20:40 While your servant was **b** here
Hag 1: 9 each of you is **b** with his own house.
2Th 3:11 They are not **b**; they are busybodies.
Tit 2: 5 pure, to be **b** at home, to be kind,

## BUSYBODIES [BUSY]*

2Th 3:11 They are not busy; they are **b**.
1Ti 5:13 idlers, but also **b** who talk nonsense,

## BUY [BOUGHT, BUYS]

Ge 41:57 to Egypt to **b** grain from Joseph,
Ex 21: 2 "If you **b** a Hebrew servant, he is
Dt 28:68 slaves, but no one will **b** you.
Ru 4: 5 the day you **b** the land from Naomi,
2Sa 24:21 "To **b** your threshing floor,"
Pr 23:23 **B** the truth and do not sell it—
Isa 55: 1 have no money, come, **b** and eat!
 55: 1 **b** wine and milk without money
Jer 32: 7 and say, '**B** my field at Anathoth,
 32: 7 it is your right and duty to **b** it.'
Mt 27: 7 **b** the potter's field as a burial place
Rev 3:18 I counsel you to **b** from me gold
 13:17 so that they could not **b** or sell

## BUYS* [BUY]

Lev 22:11 But if a priest **b** a slave with money,
Pr 31:16 She considers a field and **b** it;
Rev 18:11 her because no one **b** their cargoes

## BYWORD [WORD]

1Ki 9: 7 become a **b** and an object of ridicule
Job 17: 6 "God has made me a **b** to everyone,
Ps 44:14 made us a **b** among the nations;
Eze 23:10 She became a **b** among women,
Joel 2:17 of scorn, a **b** among the nations.

# C

## CAESAR

Mt 22:21 "Give back to **C** what is Caesar's,
Lk 2: 1 In those days **C** Augustus issued
 3: 1 year of the reign of Tiberius **C**—
Jn 19:12 this man go, you are no friend of **C**.
 19:12 claims to be a king opposes **C**."
Ac 25:11 me over to them. I appeal to **C**!"
 26:32 free if he had not appealed to **C**."

## CAESAREA

Mt 16:13 came to the region of **C** Philippi,
Ac 10: 1 At **C** there was a man named
 12:19 Herod went from Judea to **C**
 25: 4 "Paul is being held at **C**, and I

## CAIAPHAS*

High priest at trial of Jesus (Mt 26:3, 57; Lk 3:2; Jn 11:49; 18:13–28); at trial of disciples (Ac 4:6).

## CAIN*

Firstborn of Adam (Ge 4:1), murdered brother Abel (Ge 4:1–25; Heb 11:4; 1Jn 3:12; Jude 11).

## CAKES

Jer 7:18 and make **c** to offer to the Queen
 44:19 we were making **c** impressed
Hos 3: 1 gods and love the sacred raisin **c**."

## CALAMITIES [CALAMITY]

Dt 31:17 Many disasters and **c** will come
 31:21 many disasters and **c** come on them,
 32:23 "I will heap **c** on them and spend
1Sa 10:19 you out of all your disasters and **c**.
La 3:38 mouth of the Most High that both **c**

## CALAMITY [CALAMITIES]

Ne 13:18 that our God brought all this **c** on us
Pr 21:23 tongues keep themselves from **c**.
 22: 8 who sow injustice reap **c**,
 24:16 the wicked stumble when **c** strikes.
Eze 7:26 **C** upon **c** will come, and rumor
Joel 2:13 love, and he relents from sending **c**.
Jnh 4: 2 a God who relents from sending **c**.

## CALCULATE*

Rev 13:18 who have insight **c** the number

## CALEB

Judahite who spied out Canaan (Nu 13:6); allowed to enter land because of faith (Nu 13:30—14:38; Dt 1:36). Given Hebron (Jos 14:6—15:19).

## CALF [CALF-IDOL, CALVES]

Ex 32: 4 into an idol cast in the shape of a **c**,
Dt 9:16 an idol cast in the shape of a **c**.
Pr 15:17 love than a fattened **c** with hatred.
Isa 11: 6 the **c** and the lion and the yearling
Jer 31:18 disciplined me like an unruly **c**,
Lk 15:23 Bring the fattened **c** and kill it.

Ac    7:41   they made an idol in the form of a **c**.

## CALF-IDOL [CALF, IDOL]

Hos   8: 5   Samaria, throw out your **c**!

## CALL [CALLED, CALLING, CALLS, SO-CALLED]

Ge    4:26   time people began to **c** on the name
    30:13   The women will **c** me happy."
Ex    3:15   **c** me from generation to generation.
Dt    4:26   I **c** the heavens and the earth as
Ru    1:20   "Don't **c** me Naomi," she told
    1:20   "**C** me Mara, because the Almighty
1Ki  18:24   you **c** on the name of your god,
    18:24   I will **c** on the name of the LORD.
1Ch  16: 8   to the LORD, **c** on his name;
Ps    4: 1   Answer me when I **c** to you,
    10:13   "He won't **c** us to account"?
    50:15   and **c** on me in the day of trouble;
    61: 2   the ends of the earth I **c** to you, I **c**
    86: 3   me, Lord, for I **c** to you all day long.
    105: 1   to the LORD, **c** on his name;
    116:13   and **c** on the name of the LORD.
    145:18   all who **c** on him, to all who **c**
Pr    1:28   "Then they will **c** to me but I will
    8: 1   Does not wisdom **c** out?
    31:28   Her children arise and **c** her blessed;
Ecc   3:15   and God will **c** the past to account.
Isa   5:20   Woe to those who **c** evil good
    7:14   to a son, and will **c** him Immanuel.
    12: 4   to the LORD, **c** on his name;
    55: 6   **c** on him while he is near.
    65:24   Before they **c** I will answer;
Jer   33: 3   'C to me and I will answer you
La    3:21   Yet this I **c** to mind and therefore I
Hos   1: 4   said to Hosea, "C him Jezreel,
    2:16   "you will **c** me 'my husband';
    2:16   will no longer **c** me 'my master.'
Jnh   1: 6   Get up and **c** on your god!
    3: 8   Let everyone **c** urgently on God.
Zep   3: 9   all of them may **c** on the name
Zec   13: 9   They will **c** on my name and I will
Mal   3:12   all the nations will **c** you blessed,
Mt    1:23   they will **c** him Immanuel."
    9:13   I have not come to **c** the righteous,
Mk   10:18   "Why do you **c** me good?"
Lk    1:31   and you are to **c** him Jesus.
    6:46   "Why do you **c** me, 'Lord, Lord,'
Jn    13:13   "You **c** me 'Teacher' and 'Lord,'
    15:15   I no longer **c** you servants,
Ac    2:39   all whom the Lord our God will **c**."
    9:14   to arrest all who **c** on your name."
    10:15   "Do not **c** anything impure
Ro    10:12   and richly blesses all who **c** on him,
    11:29   gifts and his **c** are irrevocable.
1Co   1: 2   all those everywhere who **c**
1Th   4: 7   For God did not **c** us to be impure,
2Ti   2:22   along with those who **c** on the Lord
Heb   2:11   is not ashamed to **c** them brothers
Jas   5:14   Let them **c** the elders of the church

## CALLED [CALL]

Ge    1: 5   God **c** the light "day,"
    1: 5   and the darkness he **c** "night."
    1: 8   God **c** the vault "sky."
    1:10   God **c** the dry ground "land,"

Ge    1:10   the gathered waters he **c** "seas."
    2:19   and whatever the man **c** each living
    2:23   she shall be **c** 'woman,' for she was
    5: 2   he **c** them "human beings."
    12: 8   and **c** on the name of the LORD.
    17: 5   No longer will you be **c** Abram;
    21:33   and there he **c** on the name
    26:25   and **c** on the name of the LORD.
Ex    3: 4   God **c** to him from within the bush,
    16:31   people of Israel **c** the bread manna.
    19: 3   and the LORD **c** to him
1Sa   3: 4   Then the LORD **c** Samuel.
2Ch   7:14   my people, who are **c** by my name,
Ne    13:25   them and **c** curses down on them.
Ps    34: 6   This poor man **c**, and the LORD
    116: 4   I **c** on the name of the LORD:
SS    6: 9   women saw her and **c** her blessed;
Isa   9: 6   he will be **c** Wonderful Counselor,
    49: 1   Before I was born the LORD **c** me;
    56: 7   for my house will be **c** a house
La    3:55   I **c** on your name, LORD,
Hos   11: 1   him, and out of Egypt I **c** my son.
Mt    1:16   of Jesus who is **c** the Messiah.
    2:15   "Out of Egypt I **c** my son."
    5: 9   for they will be **c** children of God.
    21:13   " 'My house will be **c** a house
    23: 8   "But you are not to be **c** 'Rabbi,'
Lk    1:32   will be **c** the Son of the Most High.
    1:35   to be born will be **c** the Son of God.
    1:76   will be **c** a prophet of the Most
    23:46   Jesus **c** out with a loud voice,
Jn    10:35   If he **c** them 'gods,' to whom
    15:15   Instead, I have **c** you friends,
Ro    1: 1   **c** to be an apostle and set apart
    1: 6   are among those Gentiles who are **c**
    1: 7   by God and **c** to be his holy people:
    8:28   who have been **c** according to his
    8:30   he also **c**; those he **c**,
1Co   1: 1   **c** to be an apostle of Christ Jesus
    1: 2   Jesus and **c** to be his holy people,
    1: 9   who has **c** you into fellowship
    1:24   but to those whom God has **c**,
    1:26   of what you were when you were **c**.
    7:15   God has **c** us to live in peace.
    7:17   to you, just as God has **c** you.
Gal   1: 6   quickly deserting the one who **c** you
    1:15   from birth and **c** me by his grace,
    5:13   and sisters, were **c** to be free.
Eph   1:18   the hope to which he has **c** you,
    4: 4   **c** to one hope when you were **c**;
Php   3:14   which God has **c** me heavenward
Col   3:15   of one body you were **c** to peace.
2Th   2:14   He **c** you to this through our gospel,
1Ti   6:12   you were **c** when you made your
2Ti   1: 9   has saved us and **c** us to a holy life—
Heb   9:15   that those who are **c** may receive
    11:16   is not ashamed to be **c** their God,
Jas   2:23   and he was **c** God's friend.
1Pe   1:15   But just as he who **c** you is holy,
    2: 9   the praises of him who **c** you
    3: 9   to this you were **c** so that you may
    5:10   who **c** you to his eternal glory
2Pe   1: 3   of him who **c** us by his own glory
1Jn   3: 1   we should be **c** children of God!
Jude   1: 1   To those who have been **c**, who are
Rev   12: 9   that ancient serpent **c** the devil,
    16:16   that in Hebrew is **c** Armageddon.

Rev 17:14 and with him will be his **c**,
    19:11 whose rider is **c** Faithful and True.

## CALLING [CALL]

1Sa   3: 8 that the LORD was **c** the boy.
Isa   6: 3 And they were **c** to one another:
    40: 3 A voice of one **c**:
    41: 2 east, **c** him in righteousness to his
Mt   3: 3 "A voice of one **c** in the wilderness,
Mk   1: 3 "a voice of one **c** in the wilderness,
    10:49 On your feet! He's **c** you."
Lk   3: 4 "A voice of one **c** in the wilderness,
Jn   1:23 the voice of one **c** in the wilderness,
Ac  22:16 your sins away, **c** on his name.'
Eph  4: 1 worthy of the **c** you have received.
2Th  1:11 God may make you worthy of his **c**,
Heb  3: 1 who share in the heavenly **c**,
2Pe  1:10 make every effort to confirm your **c**

## CALLOUS* [CALLOUSED]

Ps  17:10 They close up their **c** hearts,
   73: 7 From their **c** hearts comes iniquity;
  119:70 Their hearts are **c** and unfeeling,

## CALLOUSED* [CALLOUS]

Isa  6:10 Make the heart of this people **c**;
Mt  13:15 this people's heart has become **c**;
Ac  28:27 this people's heart has become **c**;

## CALLS [CALL]

Ps  147: 4 the stars and **c** them each by name.
Pr   1:20 Out in the open wisdom **c** aloud,
Isa  40:26 by one, and **c** them each by name.
Hos  7: 7 fall, and none of them **c** on me.
Joel  2:32 everyone who **c** on the name
    2:32 the survivors whom the LORD **c**.
Mt  22:43 by the Spirit, **c** him 'Lord'?
Jn  10: 3 He **c** his own sheep by name
Ac  2:21 everyone who **c** on the name
Ro  9:12 not by works but by him who **c**—
  10:13 "Everyone who **c** on the name
1Th  2:12 who **c** you into his kingdom
   5:24 The one who **c** you is faithful,
Rev  2:20 Jezebel, who **c** herself a prophet.
  13:10 This **c** for patient endurance
  13:18 This **c** for wisdom. Let those who
  14:12 This **c** for patient endurance
  17: 9 "This **c** for a mind with wisdom.

## CALM [CALMED]

Ps  107:30 They were glad when it grew **c**,
Pr  15:18 but those who are patient **c** a quarrel.
  29:11 but the wise bring **c** in the end.
Isa  7: 4 careful, keep **c** and don't be afraid.
Eze 16:42 I will be **c** and no longer angry.
Jnh  1:11 to make the sea **c** down for us?"
Mk  4:39 died down and it was completely **c**.

## CALMED* [CALM]

Ne  8:11 The Levites **c** all the people,
Ps 131: 2 But I have **c** myself

## CALVARY See SKULL

## CALVES [CALF]

2Ki 10:29 worship of the golden **c** at Bethel
Mal  4: 2 go out and frolic like well-fed **c**.
Heb  9:12 means of the blood of goats and **c**;

## CAME [COME]

Ge  7: 6 when the floodwaters **c** on the earth.
  11: 5 the LORD **c** down to see the city
Ex  13: 3 this day, the day you **c** out of Egypt,
  34: 5 the LORD **c** down in the cloud
Lev  9:24 Fire **c** out from the presence
Nu  12: 5 the LORD **c** down in a pillar
  24: 2 by tribe, the Spirit of God **c** on him
Jdg  3:10 The Spirit of the LORD **c** on him,
   6:34 Spirit of the LORD **c** on Gideon,
  11:29 Spirit of the LORD **c** on Jephthah.
  14: 6 The Spirit of the LORD **c** on him
  14:19 the Spirit of the LORD **c** on him
  15:14 Lehi, the Philistines **c** toward him
  15:14 The Spirit of the LORD **c** on him
1Sa 10:10 the Spirit of God **c** on him in power,
  11: 6 the Spirit of God **c** on him in power,
  16:13 the Spirit of the LORD **c** on David
  16:23 the spirit from God **c** on Saul,
  18:10 an evil spirit from God **c** forcefully
  19: 9 the LORD **c** on Saul as he was
  19:20 the Spirit of God **c** on Saul's men,
  19:23 But the Spirit of God **c** even on him,
  19:23 walked along prophesying until he **c**
1Ch 12:18 Then the Spirit **c** on Amasai,
2Ch 15: 1 The Spirit of God **c** on Azariah son
  20:14 of the LORD **c** on Jahaziel son
  24:20 the Spirit of God **c** on Zechariah son
Eze  2: 2 the Spirit **c** into me and raised me
   3:24 Then the Spirit **c** into me and raised
  11: 5 the Spirit of the LORD **c** on me,
Ac  10:44 the Holy Spirit **c** on all who heard
  11:15 the Holy Spirit **c** on them as he had
  19: 6 on them, the Holy Spirit **c** on them,

## WORD OF THE †LORD CAME See
WORD

## CAMEL [CAMEL'S]

Lev 11: 4 The **c**, though it chews the cud,
Mt  19:24 easier for a **c** to go through the eye
  23:24 strain out a gnat but swallow a **c**.
Mk  10:25 easier for a **c** to go through the eye
Lk  18:25 easier for a **c** to go through the eye

## CAMEL'S [CAMEL]

Mk  1: 6 John wore clothing made of **c** hair,

## CAMP [CAMPED, ENCAMP, ENCAMPED, ENCAMPS]

Ge  32: 2 he said, "This is the **c** of God!"
Ex  16:13 quail came and covered the **c**,
  16:13 was a layer of dew around the **c**.
  33: 7 it outside the **c** some distance away,
  33: 7 to the tent of meeting outside the **c**.
Nu  11:26 and Medad, had remained in the **c**.
  11:26 and they prophesied in the **c**.
Dt  23:14 about in your **c** to protect you

Dt   23:14  Your **c** must be holy, so that he will
1Sa    4: 7  "A god has come into the **c**,"
      26: 5  Saul was lying inside the **c**,
Heb  13:13  go to him outside the **c**,

**OUTSIDE THE CAMP** Ex 29:14; 33:7, 7;
    Lev 4:12, 21; 6:11; 8:17; 9:11; 10:4, 5; 13:46;
    14:3; 16:27; 24:14, 23; Nu 5:3, 4; 12:14, 15;
    15:35, 36; 19:3, 9; 31:13, 19; Dt 23:10, 12; Jos
    6:23; Heb 13:11, 13

## CAMPED [CAMP]

Ex   19: 2  Israel **c** there in the desert in front
Nu   33:49  of Moab they **c** along the Jordan
Jos   3: 1  where they **c** before crossing over.

## CAN [CAN'T, CANNOT]

Ge    4:13  punishment is more than I **c** bear.
      15: 5  if indeed you **c** count them."
      19: 5  out to us so that we **c** have sex
     41:15  a dream, and no one **c** interpret it.
     41:15  hear a dream you **c** interpret it."
Nu   23: 8  How **c** I curse those whom God has
      23: 8  How **c** I denounce those whom
Dt   32:39  no one **c** deliver out of my hand.
Job  25: 4  **c** a mortal be righteous before God?
      25: 4  How **c** one born of woman be pure?
      40: 4  how **c** I reply to you?
Ps   49: 7  No one **c** redeem the life of another
      56: 4  What **c** mere mortals do to me?
     139: 7  Where **c** I go from your Spirit?
     139: 7  Where **c** I flee from your presence?
Pr   20: 6  but a faithful person who **c** find?
     31:10  wife of noble character who **c** find?
Ecc   2:24  People **c** do nothing better than
      7:13  Who **c** straighten what he has made
Isa  22:22  what he opens no one **c** shut,
     22:22  and what he shuts no one **c** open.
      64: 5  How then **c** we be saved?
Jer  33:20  'If you **c** break my covenant
Eze  37: 3  "Son of man, **c** these bones live?"
Da    2: 9  I will know that you **c** interpret it
Hos  11: 8  "How **c** I give you up, Ephraim?
      11: 8  How **c** I hand you over, Israel?
      11: 8  How **c** I treat you like Admah?
      11: 8  How **c** I make you like Zeboyim?
Joel  2:11  it is dreadful. Who **c** endure it?
Mt    6:24  "No one **c** serve two masters.
Mk    2: 7  Who **c** forgive sins but God alone?"
Lk    3: 8  these stones God **c** raise up children
     18:26  this asked, "Who then **c** be saved?"
Jn    3: 4  "How **c** anyone be born when they
      6:44  "No one **c** come to me unless
      15: 5  apart from me you **c** do nothing.
Ro    8:31  God is for us, who **c** be against us?
     10:14  **c** they call on the one they have not
     10:14  how **c** they believe in the one
     10:14  how **c** they hear without someone
1Co  13: 2  prophecy and **c** fathom all mysteries
      13: 2  have a faith that **c** move mountains,
Php   4:13  I **c** do all this through him who
Heb  13: 6  What **c** human beings do to me?"
Jas   2:14  **C** such faith save them?
      3: 8  but no one **c** tame the tongue. It is
1Jn   4: 2  is how you **c** recognize the Spirit
Rev   3: 7  What he opens no one **c** shut,
      3: 7  and what he shuts no one **c** open.

Rev  13: 4  Who **c** make war against it?"

## CAN'T [CAN]

Mt   27:42  they said, "but he **c** save himself!
Jn   13:37  "Lord, why **c** I follow you now?

## CANA

Jn    2: 1  third day a wedding took place at **C**

## CANAAN [CANAANITE,
    CANAANITES]

Ge    9:25  he said, "Cursed be **C**!
     13:12  Abram lived in the land of **C**,
      42: 5  famine was in the land of **C** also.
Ex    6: 4  them to give them the land of **C**,
Lev  14:34  "When you enter the land of **C**,
     25:38  of Egypt to give you the land of **C**
Nu   13: 2  some men to explore the land of **C**,
     33:51  'When you cross the Jordan into **C**,
Dt   32:49  and view **C**, the land I am giving
Jdg   4: 2  into the hands of Jabin king of **C**,
1Ch  16:18  **C** as the portion you will inherit."
Ps  106:38  they sacrificed to the idols of **C**,
Zep   2: 5  of the LORD is against you, **C**,
Ac   13:19  he overthrew seven nations in **C**,

## CANAANITE [CANAAN]

Ge   10:18  Later the **C** clans scattered
      28: 1  "Do not marry a **C** woman.
Jos   5: 1  all the **C** kings along the coast heard
Jdg   1:32  lived among the **C** inhabitants
Zec  14:21  day there will no longer be a **C**
Mt   15:22  A **C** woman from that vicinity came

## CANAANITES [CANAAN]

Ge   12: 6  At that time the **C** were in the land.
Ex   33: 2  before you and drive out the **C**,
Jdg   1: 1  go up first to fight against the **C**?"
      3: 5  The Israelites lived among the **C**,

## CANCEL [CANCELED, CANCELING]

Dt   15: 1  every seven years you must **c** debts.
Ne   10:31  the land and will **c** all debts.

## CANCELED [CANCEL]

Mt   18:27  on him, **c** the debt and let him go.
Col   2:14  having **c** the charge of our legal

## CANCELING [CANCEL]

Dt   15: 2  for **c** debts has been proclaimed.
     31:10  in the year for **c** debts,

## CANNOT [CAN]

Ex   19:23  "The people **c** come up Mount
     33:20  he said, "you **c** see my face, for no
Nu   11:14  I **c** carry all these people by myself;
2Sa   5: 6  thought, "David **c** get in here."
1Ki   8:27  the highest heaven, **c** contain you.
Job  12:14  What he tears down **c** be rebuilt;
     12:14  those he imprisons **c** be released.
Ps    5: 5  The arrogant **c** stand in your
     115: 5  mouths, but **c** speak, eyes, but **c** see.
Ecc   1:15  What is crooked **c** be straightened;
      1:15  what is lacking **c** be counted.

SS    8: 7  Many waters c quench love; rivers c
Isa  45:20  wood, who pray to gods that c save.
Da    6: 8  it in writing so that it c be altered—
      6: 8  and Persians, which c be repealed."
Mt    5:14  A city on a hill c be hidden.
     16: 3  but you c interpret the signs
Mk    3:24  against itself, that kingdom c stand.
Lk   16:13  You c serve both God and money."
Ro    8: 8  by the sinful nature c please God.
Jas   1:13  For God c be tempted by evil,
1Jn   5:18  safe, and the evil one c harm them.

## CANOPY*

2Sa  22:12  made darkness his c around him—
2Ki  16:18  He took away the Sabbath c
Ps   18:11  his covering, his c around him—
Isa   4: 5  everything the glory will be a c.
     40:22  stretches out the heavens like a c,
Jer  43:10  he will spread his royal c

## CAPERNAUM

Mt    4:13  he went and lived in C, which was
     11:23  And you, C, will you be lifted
Jn    6:59  teaching in the synagogue in C.

## CAPITAL

Dt   21:22  anyone guilty of a c offense is put

## CAPSTONE* [STONE; see also CORNERSTONE]

Zec   4: 7  he will bring out the c to shouts
      4:10  chosen c in the hand of Zerubbabel?"

## CAPTAIN

2Ki   1: 9  sent to Elijah a c with his company
      1: 9  The c went up to Elijah, who was
Jnh   1: 6  The c went to him and said,
Rev  18:17  "Every sea c, and all who travel

## CAPTIVATE* [CAPTURE]

Pr    6:25  or let her c you with her eyes.

## CAPTIVE [CAPTURE]

Ge   14:14  that his relative had been taken c,
Ps   69:33  and does not despise his c people.
SS    7: 5  the king is held c by its tresses.
Isa  52: 2  your neck, Daughter Zion, now a c.
Jer  13:17  the LORD's flock will be taken c.
Eze  21:24  have done this, you will be taken c.
Ac    8:23  are full of bitterness and c to sin."
2Co  10: 5  we take c every thought to make it
Col   2: 8  no one takes you c through hollow
2Ti   2:26  who has taken them c to do his will.

## CAPTIVES [CAPTURE]

Ps   68:18  ascended on high, you took many c;
Isa  14: 2  They will make c of their captors
     61: 1  to proclaim freedom for the c
Eph   4: 8  he took many c and gave gifts to his

## CAPTIVITY [CAPTURE]

Dt   28:41  them, because they will go into c.
2Ki  25:21  So Judah went into c,
Ps  144:14  no going into c, no cry of distress

Jer  15: 2  those for c, to c.'
     30: 3  Judah back from c and restore them
     52:27  So Judah went into c,
Eze  29:14  I will bring them back from c
Rev  13:10  "If anyone is to go into c, into c

## CAPTORS [CAPTURE]

1Ki   8:47  land of their c and say,
      8:50  cause their c to show them mercy;
Ps  137: 3  for there our c asked us for songs,

## CAPTURE [CAPTIVATE, CAPTIVE, CAPTIVES, CAPTIVITY, CAPTORS, CAPTURED]

1Sa   4:21  because of the c of the ark of God
     19:14  When Saul sent the men to c David,
     23:26  in on David and his men to c them,
Mt   26:55  out with swords and clubs to c me?

## CAPTURED [CAPTURE]

1Sa   4:11  The ark of God was c, and Eli's two
2Sa   5: 7  David c the fortress of Zion—
2Ki  17: 6  the king of Assyria c Samaria
Rev  19:20  But the beast was c, and with him

## CARAVAN

2Ch   9: 1  Arriving with a very great c—

## CARCASS [CARCASSES]

Jdg  14: 9  taken the honey from the lion's c.
Mt   24:28  Wherever there is a c,

## CARCASSES [CARCASS]

Dt   28:26  Your c will be food for all the birds
1Sa  17:46  This very day I will give the c
Jer   7:33  the c of this people will become

## CARE [CARED, CAREFREE, CAREFUL, CAREFULLY, CARELESSLY, CARES, CARING]

Ge    2:15  of Eden to work it and take c of it.
Nu    3:25  for the c of the tabernacle and tent,
Dt    7:11  take c to follow the commands,
1Ki   1: 2  to serve the king and take c of him.
Ps    8: 4  human beings that you c for them?
     65: 9  You c for the land and water it;
     95: 7  of his pasture, the flock under his c.
    144: 3  human beings that you c for them,
Pr   12:10  The righteous c for the needs
     29: 7  The righteous c about justice
Jer  15:15  remember me and c for me.
Eze  34: 2  of Israel who only take c
     34: 2  Should not shepherds take c
Zec  10: 3  the LORD Almighty will c for his
Mk    5:26  had suffered a great deal under the c
Lk   10:34  him to an inn and took c of him.
     18: 4  fear God or c what people think,
Jn   21:16  Jesus said, "Take c of my sheep."
1Co   3:10  But each one should build with c.
      4: 3  I c very little if I am judged by you
Eph   5:29  they feed and c for them,
1Ti   3: 5  family, how can he take c of God's
      6:20  what has been entrusted to your c.
Heb   2: 6  human beings that you c for them?

1Pe    5: 2   of God's flock that is under your **c**,
Rev  12: 6   where she might be taken **c**

## CARED [CARE]
Hos 12:13   Egypt, by a prophet he **c** for him.
Mk  15:41   followed him and **c** for his needs.

## CAREFREE* [CARE]
Eze 23:42   noise of a **c** crowd was around her;

## CAREFUL* [CARE]
Ge   31:24   "Be **c** not to say anything to Jacob,
        31:29   'Be **c** not to say anything to Jacob,
Ex   19:12   'Be **c** that you do not approach
        23:13   "Be **c** to do everything I have said
        34:12   Be **c** not to make a treaty with those
        34:15   "Be **c** not to make a treaty
Lev 18: 4   laws and be **c** to follow my decrees.
        25:18   decrees and be **c** to obey my laws,
        26: 3   and are **c** to obey my commands,
Dt     2: 4   will be afraid of you, but be very **c**.
          4: 9   Only be **c**, and watch yourselves
        4:23   Be **c** not to forget the covenant
        5:32   So be **c** to do what the LORD your
          6: 3   be **c** to obey so that it may go well
        6:12   be **c** that you do not forget
        6:25   we are **c** to obey all this law before
        7:12   these laws and are **c** to follow them,
          8: 1   Be **c** to follow every command I am
        8:11   Be **c** that you do not forget
      11:16   Be **c**, or you will be enticed to turn
        12: 1   laws you must be **c** to follow
        12:13   Be **c** not to sacrifice your burnt
        12:19   Be **c** not to neglect the Levites as
        12:28   Be **c** to obey all these regulations I
        12:30   be **c** not to be ensnared by inquiring
        15: 5   are **c** to follow all these commands I
        15: 9   Be **c** not to harbor this wicked
        17:10   Be **c** to do everything they instruct
        24: 8   be very **c** to do exactly as
Jos    1: 7   Be **c** to obey all the law my servant
          1: 8   that you may be **c** to do everything
        22: 5   be very **c** to keep the commandment
        23: 6   be **c** to obey all that is written
        23:11   So be very **c** to love the LORD
1Ki    8:25   if only your descendants are **c** in all
2Ki 10:31   Yet Jehu was not **c** to keep the law
        17:37   You must always be **c** to keep
        21: 8   only they will be **c** to do everything
1Ch 22:13   if you are **c** to observe the decrees
        28: 8   Be **c** to follow all the commands
2Ch  6:16   if only your descendants are **c** in all
        33: 8   only they will be **c** to do everything
Ezr    4:22   Be **c** not to neglect this matter.
Job 36:18   Be **c** that no one entices you
Ps   45:10   Listen, daughter, and pay **c** attention:
      101: 2   I will be **c** to lead a blameless life—
Pr     4:26   Give **c** thought to the paths for your
        13:24   but those who love them are **c**
        21:28   but a **c** listener will testify
        27:23   give **c** attention to your herds;
Isa    7: 4   him, 'Be **c**, keep calm and don't be
Jer  17:21   Be **c** not to carry a load
        17:24   But if you are **c** to obey me,
        22: 4   For if you are **c** to carry out these
Eze  11:20   decrees and be **c** to keep my laws.

Eze 18:19   has been **c** to keep all my decrees,
        20:19   decrees and be **c** to keep my laws.
        20:21   they were not **c** to keep my laws,
        36:27   decrees and be **c** to keep my laws.
        37:24   laws and be **c** to keep my decrees.
Mic    7: 5   in your embrace be **c** of your words.
Hag    1: 5   "Give **c** thought to your ways.
          1: 7   "Give **c** thought to your ways.
        2:15   " 'Now give **c** thought to this
        2:18   give **c** thought to the day
        2:18   temple was laid. Give **c** thought:
Mt     2: 8   and make a **c** search for the child.
          6: 1   "Be **c** not to do your 'acts
        16: 6   "Be **c**," Jesus said to them.
        23: 3   you must be **c** to do everything
Mk     8:15   "Be **c**," Jesus warned them.
Lk   21:34   "Be **c**, or your hearts will be
Ro   12:17   Be **c** to do what is right in the eyes
1Co    8: 9   Be **c**, however, that the exercise
        10:12   firm, be **c** that you don't fall!
Eph    5:15   Be very **c**, then, how you live—
2Ti    4: 2   great patience and **c** instruction.
Tit    3: 8   God may be **c** to devote themselves
Heb    2: 1   We must pay the most **c** attention,
          4: 1   let us be **c** that none of you be found

## CAREFULLY [CARE]
Ex   15:26   "If you listen **c** to the LORD your
Dt   28:58   If you do not **c** follow all the words
Pr   12:26   The righteous choose their friends **c**,
Da   10:11   consider **c** the words I am

## CARELESSLY* [CARE]
Lev    5: 4   any matter one might **c** swear about—

## CARES* [CARE]
Dt   11:12   a land the LORD your God **c** for;
Job 39:16   she **c** not that her labor was in vain,
Ps   55:22   Cast your **c** on the LORD and he
      142: 4   no one **c** for my life.
Ecc    5: 3   comes when there are many **c**,
Jer  12:11   because there is no one who **c**.
        30:17   outcast, Zion for whom no one **c**.'
Na     1: 7   He **c** for those who trust in him,
Jn   10:13   hand and **c** nothing for the sheep.
1Th    2: 7   a nursing mother **c** for her children,
1Pe    5: 7   on him because he **c** for you.

## CARGO
Eze  27:25   with heavy **c** as you sail the sea.
Jnh    1: 5   And they threw the **c** into the sea
Ac   27:18   began to throw the **c** overboard.

## CARING* [CARE]
1Ti    5: 4   practice by **c** for their own family

## CARMEL
1Sa  25: 5   "Go up to Nabal at **C** and greet him
1Ki  18:20   the prophets on Mount **C**.

## CARNAL, CARNALLY See
MATERIAL, SINFUL, SINFUL
NATURE, UNSPIRITUAL, WORLDLY

## CARNELIAN
Ex    28:17  first row shall be c, chrysolite

## CAROUSE* [CAROUSING]
2Pe    2:13  of pleasure is to c in broad daylight.

## CAROUSING* [CAROUSE]
Ro    13:13  not in c and drunkenness,
1Pe     4: 3  orgies, c and detestable idolatry.

## CARPENTER* [CARPENTER'S, CARPENTERS]
Isa   44:13  The c measures with a line
Mk     6: 3  Isn't this the c? Isn't this Mary's

## CARPENTER'S* [CARPENTER]
Mt    13:55  "Isn't this the c son?

## CARPENTERS [CARPENTER]
1Ch   14: 1  and c to build a palace for him.
2Ch   24:12  c to restore the LORD's temple,
Ezr    3: 7  gave money to the masons and c,

## CARRIED [CARRY]
Ge    14:12  also c off Abram's nephew Lot
       40:15  I was forcibly c off from the land
Ex    19: 4  and how I c you on eagles' wings
Dt     1:31  how the LORD your God c you,
       31: 9  who c the ark of the covenant
       33:21  he c out the LORD's righteous
Jos    3:15  as the priests who c the ark reached
1Sa    5: 2  they c the ark into Dagon's temple
      17:34  and c off a sheep from the flock,
2Ki   24:14  He c all Jerusalem into exile:
Ezr    6:12  Let it be c out with diligence.
Est    2: 6  who had been c into exile
Ecc    8:11  for a crime is not quickly c out,
Isa   63: 9  up and c them all the days of old.
Jer   52:28  the people Nebuchadnezzar c
Jn    20:15  if you have c him away, tell me
Heb   13: 9  Do not be c away by all kinds
2Pe    1:21  God as they were c along
       3:17  you may not be c away by the error
Rev   17: 3  the angel c me away in the Spirit
       21:10  And he c me away in the Spirit

## CARRIES [CARRY]
Nu    11:12  as a nurse c an infant, to the land
Dt     1:31  as a father c his son, all the way you
       32:11  to catch them and c them aloft.
Isa   40:11  arms and c them close to his heart;
       44:26  who c out the words of his servants

## CARRY [CARRIED, CARRIES, CARRYING]
Ge    47:30  c me out of Egypt and bury me
       50:25  you must c my bones up from this
Ex    13:19  you must c my bones up with you
Lev   16:22  The goat will c on itself all their

Lev   26:15  and fail to c out all my commands
Dt    10: 8  of Levi to c the ark of the covenant
1Ch   15: 2  the Levites may c the ark of God,
       15: 2  the LORD chose them to c the ark
Isa   45:20  Ignorant are those who c about idols
       46: 4  I have made you and I will c you;
Jer   51:12  The LORD will c out his purpose,
Hos   11: 9  I will not c out my fierce anger,
Mt     3:11  whose sandals I am not worthy to c.
       27:32  and they forced him to c the cross.
Lk    14:27  whoever does not c their cross
2Co    4:10  We always c around in our body
Gal    6: 2  C each other's burdens, and in this
       6: 5  each of you should c your own load.

## CARRYING [CARRY]
Lk     5:18  Some men came c a paralyzed man
      22:10  a man c a jar of water will meet
Jn    19:17  C his own cross, he went
1Jn    5: 2  God and c out his commands.

## CART
1Sa    6: 7  get a new c ready, with two cows
       6: 7  Hitch the cows to the c, but take
1Ch   13: 7  from Abinadab's house on a new c,

## CARVED
Nu    33:52  Destroy all their c images and their
1Ki    6:32  olive-wood doors he c cherubim,
Ps    74: 6  They smashed all the c paneling
     144:12  our daughters will be like pillars c
Eze   41:18  were c cherubim and palm trees.
Hab    2:18  value is an idol that someone has c?

## CASE [CASES]
Ex    18:22  have them bring every difficult c
Jos   20: 4  state their c before the elders
2Sa   15: 4  a complaint or c could come to me
1Ki   15: 5  except in the c of Uriah the Hittite.
2Ki    8: 6  he assigned an official to her c
Job   13: 8  Will you argue the c for God?
Pr    22:23  for the LORD will take up their c
       23:11  he will take up their c against you.
Isa    1:17  fatherless, plead the c of the widow.
       41:21  "Present your c," says the LORD.
Jer   12: 1  when I bring a c before you.
La     3:58  You, Lord, took up my c;
Mic    7: 9  I plead my c before the mountains;
Ac    23:35  said, "I will hear your c when your
       25:14  Festus discussed Paul's c

## CASES [CASE]
Ex    18:26  The difficult c they brought
1Co    6: 2  not competent to judge trivial c?

## CAST [CASTING, CASTS, DOWNCAST]
Ex    32: 4  made it into an idol c in the shape
Lev   16: 8  He is to c lots for the two goats—
Jos   18: 8  I will c lots for you here at Shiloh
1Ki    7:15  He c two bronze pillars,
Est    3: 7  is, the lot) was c in the presence
       9:24  them and had c the *pur* (that is,
Ps    22:18  them and c lots for my garment.
       55:22  C your cares on the LORD and he

| | | |
|---|---|---|
| Ps | 71: 9 | Do not c me away when I am old; |
| Pr | 16:33 | The lot is c into the lap, but its |
| Isa | 14:12 | You have been c down to the earth, |
| La | 3:31 | For people are not c off by the Lord |
| Joel | 3: 3 | They c lots for my people |
| Ob | 1:11 | his gates and c lots for Jerusalem, |
| Jnh | 1: 7 | let us c lots to find out who is |
| | 1: 7 | They c lots and the lot fell on Jonah. |
| Jn | 19:24 | them and c lots for my garment." |
| Ac | 1:26 | Then they c lots, and the lot fell |
| 1Pc | 5: 7 | C all your anxiety on him because |

## CASTING* [CAST]

| | | |
|---|---|---|
| 1Ch | 24: 5 | 24:5 divided them impartially by c lots, |
| Pr | 18:18 | C the lot settles disputes and keeps |
| Eze | 26: 3 | you, like the sea c up its waves. |
| Mt | 4:18 | They were c a net into the lake, |
| | 27:35 | they divided up his clothes by c lots. |
| Mk | 1:16 | his brother Andrew c a net |
| Lk | 23:34 | they divided up his clothes by c lots. |

## CASTS [CAST]

| | | |
|---|---|---|
| Dt | 18:11 | or c spells, or who is a medium |
| Isa | 40:19 | a metal worker c it, and a goldsmith |
| | 44:10 | Who shapes a god and c an idol, |

## CATASTROPHE*

| | | |
|---|---|---|
| Ge | 19:29 | the c that overthrew the cities where |
| Isa | 47:11 | a c you cannot foresee will suddenly |

## CATCH [CATCHES, CAUGHT]

| | | |
|---|---|---|
| Mt | 17:27 | Take the first fish you c; |
| Lk | 5: 4 | and let down the nets for a c." |
| | 11:54 | waiting to c him in something he |
| | 20:20 | They hoped to c Jesus in something |

## CATCHES [CATCH]

| | | |
|---|---|---|
| Job | 5:13 | He c the wise in their craftiness, |
| 1Co | 3:19 | "He c the wise in their craftiness"; |

## CATTLE

| | | |
|---|---|---|
| Ge | 12:16 | and Abram acquired sheep and c, |
| 1Sa | 15:14 | What is this lowing of c that I |
| 2Sa | 12: 2 | a very large number of sheep and c, |
| Ps | 50:10 | mine, and the c on a thousand hills. |
| | 104:14 | He makes grass grow for the c, |
| Hab | 3:17 | in the pen and no c in the stalls, |
| Jn | 2:14 | courts he found people selling c, |

## CAUGHT [CATCH]

| | | |
|---|---|---|
| Ge | 22:13 | in a thicket he saw a ram c by its |
| | 39:12 | She c him by his cloak and said, |
| Ex | 22: 7 | the thief, if c, must pay back double. |
| Dt | 24: 7 | If someone is c kidnapping another |
| 2Sa | 18: 9 | Absalom's hair got c in the tree. |
| Lk | 5: 5 | all night and haven't c anything. |
| Jn | 8: 4 | *this woman was c in the act of adultery.* |
| 2Co | 12: 2 | Christ who fourteen years ago was c |
| Gal | 6: 1 | if someone is c in a sin, you who |
| 1Th | 4:17 | are left will be c up together |

## CAUSE [CAUSED, CAUSES]

| | | |
|---|---|---|
| Ex | 23:33 | or they will c you to sin against me, |
| Dt | 10:18 | He defends the c of the fatherless |
| Jdg | 6:31 | "Are you going to plead Baal's c? |

| | | |
|---|---|---|
| Ps | 7:16 | The trouble they c recoils on them; |
| | 9: 4 | you have upheld my right and my c, |
| | 25: 3 | those who are treacherous without c. |
| | 82: 3 | uphold the c of the poor |
| | 109: 3 | they attack me without c. |
| | 119:86 | for I am being persecuted without c. |
| | 119:154 | Defend my c and redeem me; |
| Pr | 24:28 | against your neighbor without c— |
| Ecc | 8: 3 | Do not stand up for a bad c, for he |
| Isa | 1:23 | They do not defend the c |
| Jer | 5.28 | defend the just c of the poor. |
| | 51:36 | I will defend your c and avenge |
| La | 3:59 | wrong done to me. Uphold my c! |
| Mt | 18: 7 | the things that c people to stumble! |
| Lk | 17: 2 | for you to c one of these little ones |
| Ro | 14:21 | else that will c your brother or sister |
| | 16:17 | watch out for those who c divisions |
| 1Co | 8:13 | so that I will not c them to fall. |
| | 10:32 | Do not c anyone to stumble, |
| Rev | 13:15 | and c all who refused to worship |

## CAUSED [CAUSE]

| | | |
|---|---|---|
| 1Ki | 14:16 | and has c Israel to commit." |
| 2Ki | 23:15 | of Nebat, who had c Israel to sin— |

## CAUSES [CAUSE]

| | | |
|---|---|---|
| Isa | 8:14 | he will be a stone that c people |
| Mt | 5:29 | If your right eye c you to stumble, |
| | 5:30 | if your right hand c you to stumble, |
| | 5:32 | c her to become an adulteress, |
| | 18: 6 | "If anyone c one of these little |
| | 18: 8 | hand or your foot c you to stumble, |
| Ro | 14:20 | eat anything that c someone else |
| 1Co | 8:13 | if what I eat c my brother or sister |
| Jas | 4: 1 | What c fights and quarrels among |
| 1Pe | 2: 8 | "A stone that c people to stumble |

## CAVE [CAVERNS, CAVES]

| | | |
|---|---|---|
| Ge | 19:30 | and his two daughters lived in a c. |
| | 23: 9 | so he will sell me the c |
| | 25: 9 | in the c of Machpelah near Mamre, |
| | 49:29 | my fathers in the c in the field |
| Jos | 10:16 | and hidden in the c at Makkedah. |
| 1Sa | 22: 1 | and escaped to the c of Adullam. |
| | 24: 3 | a c was there, and Saul went |
| | 24: 3 | and his men were far back in the c. |
| 1Ki | 19: 9 | There he went into a c and spent |
| Ps | 57: T | *he had fled from Saul into the c.* |
| | 142: T | *of David. When he was in the c.* |

## CAVERNS* [CAVE]

| | | |
|---|---|---|
| Isa | 2:21 | They will flee to c in the rocks |

## CAVES [CAVE]

| | | |
|---|---|---|
| 1Ki | 18: 4 | prophets and hidden them in two c, |
| Isa | 2:19 | People will flee to c in the rocks |
| Heb | 11:38 | and in c and holes in the ground. |
| Rev | 6:15 | hid in c and among the rocks |

## CEASE

| | | |
|---|---|---|
| Ge | 8:22 | winter, day and night will never c." |
| Ne | 9:19 | of cloud did not c to guide them |
| Ps | 46: 9 | He makes wars c to the ends |
| 1Co | 13: 8 | there are prophecies, they will c; |

## CEDAR [CEDARS]

2Sa 7: 2 living in a house of c, while the ark
1Ki 5:10 Solomon supplied with all the c
2Ch 25:18 sent a message to a c in Lebanon,
Ezr 3: 7 that they would bring c logs by sea
Job 40:17 Its tail sways like a c; the sinews
Ps 92:12 they will grow like a c of Lebanon;
SS 8: 9 we will enclose her with panels of c.
Eze 31: 3 Assyria, once a c in Lebanon,
Hos 14: 5 Like a c of Lebanon he will send

## CEDARS [CEDAR]

Nu 24: 6 LORD, like c beside the waters.
Ps 29: 5 voice of the LORD breaks the c;
29: 5 breaks in pieces the c of Lebanon.

## CELEBRATE* [CELEBRATED, CELEBRATING, CELEBRATION, CELEBRATIONS]

Ex 10: 9 because we are to c a festival
12:14 to come you shall c it as a festival
12:17 "C the Festival of Unleavened
12:17 C this day as a lasting ordinance
12:47 community of Israel must c it.
12:48 c the LORD's Passover must have
23:14 times a year you are to c a festival
23:15 "C the Festival of Unleavened
23:16 "C the Festival of Harvest
23:16 "C the Festival of Ingathering
34:18 "C the Festival of Unleavened
34:22 "C the Festival of Weeks
Lev 23:39 c the festival to the LORD
23:41 C this as a festival to the LORD
23:41 c it in the seventh month.
Nu 9: 2 "Have the Israelites c the Passover
9: 3 C it at the appointed time,
9: 4 told the Israelites to c the Passover,
9: 6 of them could not c the Passover
9:10 are still to c the LORD's Passover,
Nu 9:12 When they c the Passover,
9:13 on a journey fails to c the Passover,
9:14 also to c the LORD's Passover
29:12 C a festival to the LORD for seven
Dt 16: 1 c the Passover of the LORD your
16:10 Then c the Festival of Weeks
16:13 C the Festival of Tabernacles
16:15 For seven days c the festival
Jdg 16:23 to Dagon their god and to c, saying,
2Sa 6:21 I will c before the LORD.
2Ki 23:21 "C the Passover to the LORD
2Ch 30: 1 and c the Passover to the LORD,
30: 2 Jerusalem decided to c the Passover
30: 3 They had not been able to c it
30: 5 and c the Passover to the LORD,
30:13 in Jerusalem to c the Festival
30:23 to c the festival seven more days;
Ne 8:12 of food and to c with great joy,
12:27 to c joyfully the dedication
Est 9:21 have them c annually the fourteenth
Ps 2:11 and c his rule with trembling.
145: 7 They c your abundant goodness
Isa 30:29 as on the night you c a holy festival;
Hos 5: 7 When they c their New Moon feasts,
Na 1:15 C your festivals, Judah, and fulfill
Zec 14:16 and to c the Festival of Tabernacles.

Zec 14:18 up to c the Festival of Tabernacles.
14:19 up to c the Festival of Tabernacles.
Mt 26:18 I am going to c the Passover
Lk 15:23 and kill it. Let's have a feast and c.
15:24 and is found.' So they began to c.
15:29 me even a young goat so I could c
15:32 But we had to c and be glad,
Rev 11:10 will c by sending each other gifts,

## CELEBRATED [CELEBRATE]

Jos 5:10 the Israelites c the Passover.
1Ki 8:65 They c it before the LORD our
2Ki 23:23 this Passover was c to the LORD
2Ch 30: 5 It had not been c in large numbers
35: 1 Josiah c the Passover to the LORD
Ezr 3: 4 they c the Festival of Tabernacles
6:19 month, the exiles c the Passover.
Ne 8:17 the Israelites had not c it like this.
Est 9:28 never cease to be c by the Jews,

## CELEBRATING [CELEBRATE]

1Ch 15:29 she saw King David dancing and c,
Est 8:17 the Jews, with feasting and c.

## CELEBRATION [CELEBRATE]

Est 9:22 and their mourning into a day of c.
Col 2:16 a New Moon c or a Sabbath day.

## CELEBRATIONS* [CELEBRATE]

Hos 2:11 I will stop all her c:

## CELESTIAL*

2Pe 2:10 afraid to heap abuse on c beings;
Jude 1: 8 and heap abuse on c beings.

## CELL*

Jer 37:16 put into a vaulted c in a dungeon,
Ac 12: 7 appeared and a light shone in the c.
16:24 he put them in the inner c

## CENSER [CENSERS]

Lev 16:12 is to take a c full of burning coals
Nu 16:18 So each one took his c, put burning
2Ch 26:19 who had a c in his hand ready
Eze 8:11 Each had a c in his hand,
Rev 8: 3 who had a golden c, came and stood

## CENSERS [CENSER]

Lev 10: 1 sons Nadab and Abihu took their c,
Nu 16:38 the c of the men who sinned
16:38 Hammer the c into sheets to overlay

## CENSUS

Ex 30:12 "When you take a c of the Israelites
Nu 1: 2 "Take a c of the whole Israelite
26: 2 "Take a c of the whole Israelite
2Sa 24: 1 "Go and take a c of Israel
1Ch 21: 1 incited David to take a c of Israel.
Lk 2: 1 a decree that a c should be taken

## CENTER

Eze 48: 8 the sanctuary will be in the c of it.
48:15 The city will be in the c of it
Rev 4: 6 In the c, around the throne,

Rev  5: 6  standing in the **c** before the throne,
     7:17  the **c** before the throne will be their

# CENTURION

Mt   8: 5  Capernaum, a **c** came to him,
    27:54  When the **c** and those with him who
Mk  15:39  And when the **c**, who stood there
Lk   7: 3  The **c** heard of Jesus and sent some
    23:47  The **c**, seeing what had happened,
Ac  10: 1  a **c** in what was known as the Italian
    22:25  Paul said to the **c** standing there,
    27: 1  handed over to a **c** named Julius,

# CEPHAS [PETER]

Jn   1:42  You will be called **C**" (which,
1Co  1:12  another, "I follow **C**";
     3:22  Paul or Apollos or **C** or the world
     9: 5  and the Lord's brothers and **C**?
Gal  2:11  When **C** came to Antioch, I opposed

# CEREMONIAL* [CEREMONY]

Lev 14: 2  at the time of their **c** cleansing,
    15:13  off seven days for his **c** cleansing;
Mk   7: 3  they give their hands a **c** washing,
Jn   2: 6  used by the Jews for **c** washing,
     3:25  Jew over the matter of **c** washing.
    11:55  for their **c** cleansing before
    18:28  to avoid **c** uncleanness they did not
Heb  9:10  and drink and various **c** washings—
    13: 9  not by the eating of **c** foods,

# CEREMONIALLY* [CEREMONY]

Lev  4:12  outside the camp to a place **c** clean,
     5: 2  touches anything **c** unclean—
     6:11  the camp to a place that is **c** clean.
     7:19  touches anything **c** unclean must not
     7:19  meat, anyone **c** clean may eat it.
    10:14  Eat them in a **c** clean place;
    11: 4  it is **c** unclean for you.
    12: 2  to a son will be **c** unclean for seven
    12: 7  she will be **c** clean from her flow
    13: 3  he shall pronounce them **c** unclean.
    14: 8  then they will be **c** clean.
    15:28  and after that she will be **c** clean.
    15:33  with a woman who is **c** unclean.
    17:15  they will be **c** unclean till evening;
    21: 1  must not make himself **c** unclean
    22: 3  of your descendants is **c** unclean
    27:11  they vowed is a **c** unclean animal—
Nu   5: 2  who is **c** unclean because of a dead
     6: 7  not make themselves **c** unclean
     8: 6  Israelites and make them **c** clean.
     9: 6  day because they were **c** unclean
     9:13  if anyone who is **c** clean and not
    18:11  household who is **c** clean may eat it.
    18:13  household who is **c** clean may eat it.
    19: 7  but he will be **c** unclean till evening.
    19: 9  in a **c** clean place outside the camp.
    19:18  a man who is **c** clean is to take some
Dt  12:15  Both the **c** unclean and the clean
    12:22  Both the **c** unclean and the clean
    14: 7  they are **c** unclean for you.
    15:22  Both the **c** unclean and the clean
1Sa 20:26  to David to make him **c** unclean—
2Ch 13:11  set out the bread on the **c** clean table
    30:17  for all those who were not **c** clean

Ezr  6:20  themselves and were all **c** clean.
Ne  12:30  Levites had purified themselves **c**,
Isa 66:20  of the LORD in **c** clean vessels.
Eze 22:10  period, when they are **c** unclean.
Ac  24:18  I was **c** clean when they found me
Heb  9:13  on those who are **c** unclean sanctify

# CEREMONIES* [CEREMONY]

Heb  9:21  and everything used in its **c**.

# CEREMONY* [CEREMONIAL, CEREMONIALLY, CEREMONIES]

Ge  50:11  Egyptians are holding a solemn **c**
Ex  12:25  you as he promised, observe this **c**.
    12:26  'What does this **c** mean to you?'
    13: 5  are to observe this **c** in this month:

# CERTAIN [CERTAINTY]

Heb 11: 1  and **c** of what we do not see.

# CERTAINTY* [CERTAIN]

Lk   1: 4  you may know the **c** of the things
Jn  17: 8  They knew with **c** that I came

# CERTIFICATE* [CERTIFIED]

Dt  24: 1  her, and he writes her a **c** of divorce,
    24: 3  her and writes her a **c** of divorce,
Isa 50: 1  "Where is your mother's **c**
Jer  3: 8  I gave faithless Israel her **c**
Mt   5:31  divorces his wife must give her a **c**
    19: 7  a man give his wife a **c** of divorce
Mk  10: 4  a man to write a **c** of divorce

# CERTIFIED* [CERTIFICATE]

Jn   3:33  person who has accepted it has **c**

# CHAFF

Ps   1: 4  They are like **c** that the wind blows
    35: 5  May they be like **c** before the wind,
Isa 33:11  You conceive **c**, you give birth
Da   2:35  became like **c** on a threshing floor
Hos 13: 3  like **c** swirling from a threshing
Zep  2: 2  that day passes like windblown **c**,
Mt   3:12  up the **c** with unquenchable fire."

# CHAIN [CHAINED, CHAINS]

Ge  41:42  and put a gold **c** around his neck.
Pr   1: 9  head and a **c** to adorn your neck.
Da   5: 7  and have a gold **c** placed around his
Mk   5: 3  him anymore, not even with a **c**.
Ac  28:20  Israel that I am bound with this **c**."
Rev 20: 1  and holding in his hand a great **c**.

# CHAINED [CHAIN]

Mk   5: 4  For he had often been **c** hand
2Ti  2: 9  the point of being **c** like a criminal.
     2: 9  But God's word is not **c**.

# CHAINS [CHAIN]

Ex  28:14  and two braided **c** of pure gold,
    28:14  rope, and attach the **c** to the settings.
Ps   2: 3  "Let us break their **c** and throw off
Ecc  7:26  is a trap and whose hands are **c**.
La   3: 7  he has weighed me down with **c**.

Mk 5: 4 but he tore the c apart and broke
Ac 12: 7 and the c fell off Peter's wrists.
16:26 open, and everyone's c came loose.
Eph 6:20 for which I am an ambassador in c.
Php 1: 7 whether I am in c or defending
Col 4:18 Remember my c. Grace be
2Ti 1:16 me and was not ashamed of my c.
Phm 1:10 became my son while I was in c.
Heb 11:36 and even c and imprisonment.
Jude 1: 6 with everlasting c for judgment

## CHAIR
1Sa 4:18 Eli fell backward off his c

## CHALDEA [CHALDEAN, CHALDEANS]
Eze 23:16 and sent messengers to them in C.

## CHALDEAN* [CHALDEA]
Ezr 5:12 the hands of Nebuchadnezzar the C,

## CHALDEANS [CHALDEA]
Ge 11:31 from Ur of the C to go to Canaan.
Ne 9: 7 brought him out of Ur of the C

## CHALLENGE [CHALLENGED]
Jer 49:19 Who is like me and who can c me?

## CHALLENGED [CHALLENGE]
Jn 8:13 The Pharisees c him, "Here you
18:26 whose ear Peter had cut off, c him,

## CHAMBER [CHAMBERS]
Job 37: 9 The tempest comes out from its c,

## CHAMBERS [CHAMBER]
Ps 104:13 the mountains from his upper c;
SS 1: 4 Let the king bring me into his c.

## CHAMPION* [CHAMPIONS]
1Sa 17: 4 A c named Goliath, who was
17:23 Goliath, the Philistine c from Gath,
Ps 19: 5 like a c rejoicing to run his course.
Isa 42:13 The LORD will march out like a c,

## CHAMPIONS* [CHAMPION]
Isa 5:22 wine and c at mixing drinks,

## CHANCE
1Sa 6: 9 us but that it happened to us by c."
Ecc 9:11 but time and c happen to them all.

## CHANGE [CHANGED, CHANGERS]
Nu 23:19 being, that he should c his mind.
1Sa 15:29 of Israel does not lie or c his mind;
15:29 being, that he should c his mind."
1Ki 8:47 if they have a c of heart in the land
Ps 110: 4 has sworn and will not c his mind:
Jer 7: 5 If you really c your ways and your
13:23 Can an Ethiopian c his skin
Eze 1:17 wheels did not c direction
Mal 3: 6 "I the LORD do not c. So you,
Mt 18: 3 unless you c and become like little

Heb 7:21 has sworn and will not c his mind:
Jas 1:17 lights, who does not c like shifting

## CHANGED [CHANGE]
1Sa 10: 9 to leave Samuel, God c Saul's heart,
Jer 2:11 Has a nation ever c its gods?
Da 3:19 and his attitude toward them c.
6:15 edict that the king issues can be c."
Hos 11: 8 My heart is c within me;
Lk 9:29 the appearance of his face c, and his
1Co 15:51 not all sleep, but we will all be c—
Heb 1:12 like a garment they will be c.
7:12 the priesthood is c, the law must be c

## CHANGERS* [CHANGE]
Mt 21:12 overturned the tables of the money c
Mk 11:15 overturned the tables of the money c
Jn 2:15 scattered the coins of the money c

## CHARACTER*
Ru 3:11 that you are a woman of noble c.
Pr 12: 4 of noble c is her husband's crown,
31:10 A wife of noble c who can find?
Ac 17:11 were of more noble c than those
Ro 5: 4 perseverance, c; and c, hope.
1Co 15:33 "Bad company corrupts good c."

## CHARGE [CHARGED, CHARGES, CHARGING]
Ge 39: 4 Potiphar put him in c of his
39:22 So the warden put Joseph in c of all
41:40 You shall be in c of my palace,
Nu 4:16 is to have c of the oil for the light,
4:16 is to be in c of the entire tabernacle
Dt 23:19 Do not c an Israelite interest,
Job 34:13 Who put him in c of the whole
Ps 69:27 C them with crime upon crime;
SS 5: 8 Daughters of Jerusalem, I c you—
Hos 12: 2 The LORD has a c to bring against
Mt 24:47 you, he will put him in c of all his
Jn 13:29 Since Judas had c of the money,
18:38 "I find no basis for a c against him.
Ro 8:33 will bring any c against those whom
1Co 9:18 the gospel I may offer it free of c,
2Co 11: 7 the gospel of God to you free of c?
Gal 3:24 law was put in c of us until Christ came
Col 2:14 canceled the c of our legal indebtedness,
2Ti 4: 1 and his kingdom, I give you this c:
Phm 1:18 or owes you anything, c it to me.
Rev 14:18 another angel, who had c of the fire,
16: 5 I heard the angel in c of the waters

## CHARGED [CHARGE]
Ro 5:13 but sin is not c against anyone's

## CHARGES [CHARGE]
Job 4:18 if he c his angels with error,
Ps 50: 8 I bring no c against you
Isa 50: 8 Who then will bring c against me?
Jer 25:31 the LORD will bring c against
Lk 23:14 no basis for your c against him.
Ac 24: 1 they brought their c against Paul

## CHARGING [CHARGE]
Job 1:22 this, Job did not sin by c God

## CHARIOT [CHARIOTS]
| | | |
|---|---|---|
| Ge | 41:43 | in a **c** as his second-in-command, |
| 1Ki | 22:34 | The king told his **c** driver, |
| 2Ki | 2:11 | suddenly a **c** of fire and horses |
| 2Ch | 1:17 | They imported a **c** from Egypt |
| Ps | 104: 3 | He makes the clouds his **c** and rides |
| Zec | 6: 2 | The first **c** had red horses, |
| Ac | 8:28 | was sitting in his **c** reading the Book |

## CHARIOTS [CHARIOT]
| | | |
|---|---|---|
| Ex | 14. 7 | He took six hundred of the best **c**, |
| | 14: 7 | along with all the other **c** of Egypt, |
| | 15:19 | **c** and horsemen went into the sea, |
| Jos | 11: 4 | a large number of horses and **c**— |
| | 17:18 | though the Canaanites have **c** fitted |
| Jdg | 4: 3 | he had nine hundred **c** fitted |
| 2Sa | 8: 4 | David captured a thousand of his **c**, |
| 2Ki | 6:17 | and **c** of fire all around Elisha. |
| 2Ch | 1:14 | Solomon accumulated **c** and horses; |
| | 1:14 | he had fourteen hundred **c** |
| Ps | 20: 7 | Some trust in **c** and some in horses, |
| | 68:17 | The **c** of God are tens of thousands |
| Na | 2: 3 | The metal on the **c** flashes |
| Hag | 2:22 | I will overthrow **c** and their drivers; |
| Rev | 9: 9 | horses and **c** rushing into battle. |

## CHARM* [CHARMING, CHARMS]
| | | |
|---|---|---|
| Pr | 17: 8 | A bribe is seen as a **c** by those who |
| | 31:30 | **C** is deceptive, and beauty is |

## CHARMING* [CHARM]
| | | |
|---|---|---|
| Pr | 26:25 | Though their speech is **c**, do not |
| SS | 1:16 | Oh, how **c**! And our bed is verdant. |

## CHARMS* [CHARM]
| | | |
|---|---|---|
| Isa | 3:20 | sashes, the perfume bottles and **c**, |
| Eze | 13:18 | the women who sew magic **c** on all |
| | 13:20 | I am against your magic **c** |

## CHASE [CHASED, CHASING]
| | | |
|---|---|---|
| Lev | 26: 8 | Five of you will **c** a hundred, |
| | 26: 8 | hundred of you will **c** ten thousand, |
| Dt | 32:30 | How could one man **c** a thousand, |
| Pr | 12:11 | but those who **c** fantasies have no sense. |
| | 28:19 | those who **c** fantasies will have their fill |
| Hos | 2: 7 | She will **c** after her lovers but not |

## CHASED [CHASE]
| | | |
|---|---|---|
| Dt | 1:44 | they **c** you like a swarm of bees |
| Jos | 7: 5 | They **c** the Israelites from the city |

## CHASING [CHASE]
| | | |
|---|---|---|
| Ecc | 1:14 | are meaningless, a **c** after the wind. |

## CHASM*
| | | |
|---|---|---|
| Lk | 16:26 | you a great **c** has been set in place, |

## CHASTENED*
| | | |
|---|---|---|
| Job | 33:19 | they may be **c** on a bed of pain |
| Ps | 118:18 | The LORD has **c** me severely, |

## CHATTER* [CHATTERING]
| | | |
|---|---|---|
| 1Ti | 6:20 | Turn away from godless **c** |
| 2Ti | 2:16 | Avoid godless **c**, because those who |

## CHATTERING* [CHATTER]
| | | |
|---|---|---|
| Pr | 10: 8 | but a **c** fool comes to ruin. |
| | 10:10 | grief, and a **c** fool comes to ruin. |

## CHEAPER*
| | | |
|---|---|---|
| Jn | 2:10 | the **c** wine after the guests have had |

## CHEAT* [CHEATED, CHEATING]
| | | |
|---|---|---|
| Lev | 6: 2 | or if they **c** a neighbor, |
| Mal | 1:14 | "Cursed is the **c** who has |
| 1Co | 6: 8 | you yourselves **c** and do wrong, |

## CHEATED* [CHEAT]
| | | |
|---|---|---|
| Ge | 31: 7 | yet your father has **c** me |
| 1Sa | 12: 3 | Whom have I **c**? Whom have I |
| | 12: 4 | "You have not **c** or oppressed us," |
| Lk | 19: 8 | if I have **c** anybody out of anything, |
| 1Co | 6: 7 | Why not rather be **c**? |

## CHEATING* [CHEAT]
| | | |
|---|---|---|
| Am | 8: 5 | price and **c** with dishonest scales, |

## CHEEK* [CHEEKS]
| | | |
|---|---|---|
| Job | 16:10 | they strike my **c** in scorn and unite |
| Hos | 11: 4 | to the **c**, and I bent down to feed |
| Mic | 5: 1 | Israel's ruler on the **c** with a rod. |
| Mt | 5:39 | right **c**, turn to them the other **c** also. |
| Lk | 6:29 | If someone slaps you on one **c**, |

## CHEEKS* [CHEEK]
| | | |
|---|---|---|
| SS | 1:10 | Your **c** are beautiful with earrings, |
| | 5:13 | His **c** are like beds of spice yielding |
| Isa | 50: 6 | my **c** to those who pulled out my |
| La | 1: 2 | weeps at night, tears are on her **c**. |
| | 3:30 | Let them offer their **c** to one who |

## CHEER* [CHEERFUL, CHEERFULLY, CHEERING, CHEERS]
| | | |
|---|---|---|
| 1Ki | 21: 7 | Get up and eat! **C** up. I'll get you |
| Mk | 10:49 | they called to the blind man, "**C** up! |

## CHEERFUL* [CHEER]
| | | |
|---|---|---|
| Pr | 15:13 | A happy heart makes the face **c**, |
| | 15:15 | but the **c** heart has a continual feast. |
| | 17:22 | A **c** heart is good medicine, |
| 2Co | 9: 7 | compulsion, for God loves a **c** giver. |

## CHEERFULLY* [CHEER]
| | | |
|---|---|---|
| Ro | 12: 8 | if it is to show mercy, do it **c**. |

## CHEERING* [CHEER]
| | | |
|---|---|---|
| 1Ki | 1:45 | From there they have gone up **c**, |
| 2Ch | 23:12 | the people running and **c** the king, |
| Ecc | 2: 3 | I tried **c** myself with wine, |

## CHEERS* [CHEER]
| | | |
|---|---|---|
| Jdg | 9:13 | wine, which **c** both gods and human |
| Pr | 12:25 | the heart, but a kind word **c** it up. |

## CHEMOSH
| | | |
|---|---|---|
| Nu | 21:29 | You are destroyed, people of **C**! |
| 1Ki | 11: 7 | high place for **C** the detestable god |
| 2Ki | 23:13 | for **C** the vile god of Moab, |

Jer 48: 7 and **C** will go into exile,

## CHERISH* [CHERISHED]
Ps 83: 3 they plot against those you **c**.
Pr 4: 8 **C** her, and she will exalt you;
19: 8 who **c** understanding will soon prosper.

## CHERISHED* [CHERISH]
Ps 66:18 If I had **c** sin in my heart, the Lord
Pr 4: 3 still tender, and **c** by my mother.
Hos 9:16 I will slay their **c** offspring."

## CHERUB [CHERUBIM]
Ex 25:19 Make one **c** on one end
25:19 end and the second **c** on the other;
1Ki 6:26 The height of each **c** was ten cubits.
2Ch 3:11 of the first **c** was five cubits long
3:11 touched the wing of the other **c**.
Eze 10:14 One face was that of a **c**, the second
28:14 You were anointed as a guardian **c**,
41:18 Each **c** had two faces:

## CHERUBIM [CHERUB]
Ge 3:24 east side of the Garden of Eden **c**
Ex 25:18 make two **c** out of hammered gold
26: 1 with **c** worked into them by skilled
Nu 7:89 from between the two **c**
1Sa 4: 4 who is enthroned between the **c**.
2Sa 6: 2 who is enthroned between the **c**
22:11 He mounted the **c** and flew;
1Ki 6:23 inner sanctuary he made a pair of **c**
2Ki 19:15 enthroned between the **c**, you alone
1Ch 13: 6 who is enthroned between the **c**—
2Ch 3: 7 gold, and he carved **c** on the walls.
Ps 18:10 He mounted the **c** and flew;
80: 1 who sit enthroned between the **c**,
99: 1 he sits enthroned between the **c**,
Isa 37:16 enthroned between the **c**, you alone
Eze 9: 3 of Israel went up from above the **c**,
10: 1 that was over the heads of the **c**.
41:18 were carved **c** and palm trees.
41:18 Palm trees alternated with **c**.
Heb 9: 5 the ark were the **c** of the Glory,

## CHEST [CHESTS]
2Ki 12: 9 Jehoiada the priest took a **c**
12: 9 entrance put into the **c** all the money
Da 2:32 pure gold, its **c** and arms of silver,
Rev 1:13 and with a golden sash around his **c**.

## CHESTS* [CHEST]
Rev 15: 6 wore golden sashes around their **c**.

## CHEW [CHEWS]
Lev 11: 4 are some that only **c** the cud or only
Dt 14: 7 of those that **c** the cud or that have
14: 7 Although they **c** the cud, they do not

## CHEWS [CHEW]
Lev 11: 3 a divided hoof and that **c** the cud.

## CHICKS*
Mt 23:37 a hen gathers her **c** under her wings,
Lk 13:34 a hen gathers her **c** under her wings,

## CHIEF [CHIEFS]
2Sa 23:13 of the thirty **c** warriors came down
Ezr 7: 5 the son of Aaron the **c** priest—
Da 10:13 one of the **c** princes, came to help
Mt 20:18 be delivered over to the **c** priests
27: 6 The **c** priests picked up the coins
Mk 15: 3 The **c** priests accused him of many
Eph 2:20 Jesus himself as the **c** cornerstone.
1Pe 5: 4 And when the **C** Shepherd appears,

## CHIEF PRIEST 2Ki 25:18; 2Ch 19:11; 24:6, 11; 26:20; 31:10; Ezr 7:5; Jer 52:24; Ac 19:14

## CHIEF PRIESTS Mt 2:4; 16:21; 20:18; 21:15, 23, 45; 26:3, 14, 47, 59; 27:1, 3, 6, 12, 20, 41, 62; 28:11, 12; Mk 8:31; 10:33; 11:18, 27; 12:12; 14:1, 10, 43, 53, 55; 15:1, 3, 10, 11, 31; Lk 9:22; 19:47; 20:1, 19; 22:2, 4, 52, 66; 23:4, 10, 13; 24:20; Jn 7:32, 45; 11:47, 57; 12:10; 18:3, 35; 19:6, 15, 21; Ac 4:23; 5:24; 9:14, 21; 22:30; 23:14; 25:2, 15; 26:10, 12

## CHIEFS [CHIEF]
1Ch 11:10 These were the **c** of David's mighty

## CHILD [CHILDHOOD, CHILDLESS, CHILDREN, CHILDREN'S, GRANDCHILDREN]
Ge 4:25 "God has granted me another **c**
17:17 Will Sarah bear a **c** at the age
Ex 2: 2 When she saw that he was a fine **c**,
Jdg 11:34 She was an only **c**. Except for her
Ru 4:16 Then Naomi took the **c** in her arms
1Sa 1:27 I prayed for this **c**, and the LORD
2Sa 12:16 David pleaded with God for the **c**.
1Ki 3: 7 I am only a little **c** and do not know
2Ch 22:11 she hid the **c** from Athaliah so she
Job 3:16 in the ground like a stillborn **c**,
Ps 131: 2 I am like a weaned **c** with its
131: 2 like a weaned **c** I am content.
Pr 22:15 Folly is bound up in the heart of a **c**,
Ecc 6: 3 a stillborn **c** is better off than he.
Eze 18:20 **c** will not share the guilt of the parent,
Isa 9: 6 For to us a **c** is born, to us a son is
11: 6 and a little **c** will lead them.
54: 1 woman, you who never bore a **c**;
66:13 As a mother comforts her **c**, so will
Hos 11: 1 "When Israel was a **c**, I loved him,
Zec 12:10 for him as one mourns for an only **c**,
Mt 2:11 they saw the **c** with his mother
18: 2 He called a little **c**, whom he placed
Mk 5:39 The **c** is not dead but asleep."
10:15 of God like a little **c** will never enter
Lk 1:42 and blessed is the **c** you will bear!
1:80 And the **c** grew and became strong
Ac 13:10 "You are a **c** of the devil
1Co 13:11 When I was a **c**, I talked like a **c**,
13:11 thought like a **c**, I reasoned like a **c**.
Heb 11:23 they saw he was no ordinary **c**,
12: 6 chastens everyone he accepts as his **c**."
1Jn 5: 1 loves the father loves his **c** as well.
Rev 12: 4 it might devour her **c** the moment he

## CHILDBEARING* [BEAR]
Ge 3:16 make your pains in **c** very severe;
18:11 old, and Sarah was past the age of **c**.

1Ti  2:15 women will be saved through c—
Heb 11:11 Sarah, who was past c age,

## CHILDBIRTH [BEAR]
Ro   8:22 as in the pains of c right
Gal  4:19 the pains of c until Christ is formed

## CHILDHOOD [CHILD]
Ge   8:21 of the human heart is evil from c.
1Co 13:11 I put the ways of c behind me.

## CHILDLESS [CHILD]
Ge  11:30 Now Sarai was c because
    15: 2 can you give me since I remain c
    25:21 because she was c.
    29:31 but Rachel remained c.
1Sa 15:33 your sword has made women c,
    15:33 your mother be c among women."
Ps 113: 9 He settles the c woman in her home
Lk   1: 7 c because Elizabeth was not able
    23:29 'Blessed are the c women,

## CHILDREN [CHILD]
Ge   3:16 with pain you will give birth to c.
    21: 7 Abraham that Sarah would nurse c?
Ex  20: 5 punishing the c for the sin
Lev 20: 3 for by sacrificing his c to Molek,
Dt   4: 9 Teach them to your c and to their c
     6: 7 Impress them on your c.
     6:20 In the future, when your c ask you,
    11:19 Teach them to your c,
    14: 1 You are the c of the Lord your
    24:16 are not to be put to death for their c,
    24:16 nor c put to death for their parents;
    29:29 belong to us and to our c forever,
    30:19 life, so that you and your c may live
    32:46 you may command your c to obey
Jos  4: 6 when your c ask you, 'What do
1Sa  2: 5 who was barren has borne seven c,
Ezr 10:44 some of them had c by these wives.
Ne  13:24 Half of their c spoke the language
Job  1: 5 "Perhaps my c have sinned
Ps   8: 2 Through the praise of c and infants
    37:25 forsaken or their c begging bread.
    78: 5 our ancestors to teach their c,
   103:13 As a father has compassion on his c,
   112: 2 Their c will be mighty in the land;
   127: 3 C are a heritage from the Lord,
Pr  10: 1 Wise c bring joy to their father,
    13:24 who spare the rod hate their c,
Pr  14:26 and for their c it will be a refuge.
    17: 6 Children's c are a crown
    17: 6 and parents are the pride of their c.
    20: 7 blessed are their c after them.
    20:11 small c are known by their actions,
    22: 6 Start c off on the way they should go,
    23:13 Do not withhold discipline from c;
    29:15 but c left to themselves disgrace their
    29:17 Discipline your c, and they will
    31:28 Her c arise and call her blessed;
Isa  1: 4 of evildoers, c given to corruption!
    49:25 with you, and your c I will save.
    54:13 All your c will be taught by the Lord,
Jer  4:22 They are senseless c; they have no
    31:15 Rachel weeping for her c
La   4: 4 the c beg for bread, but no one gives

Eze  5:10 their c, and c will eat their parents.
    23:37 they even sacrificed their c,
Hos  1:10 be called 'c of the living God.'
     2: 4 c, because they are the c of adultery.
Joel 1: 3 c, and let your c tell it to their c,
     1: 3 and their c to the next generation.
Zec 10: 7 Their c will see it and be joyful;
Mal  4: 6 the hearts of the parents to their c,
     4: 6 the hearts of the c to their parents;
Mt   2:18 Rachel weeping for her c
     3: 9 these stones God can raise up c
     5: 9 they will be called c of God.
     7:11 how to give good gifts to your c,
    11:25 and revealed them to little c.
    18: 3 you change and become like little c,
    19:14 said, "Let the little c come to me,
    21:16 you hear what these c are saying?"
    21:16 " 'From the lips of c and infants
Mk   9:37 these little c in my name welcomes
    10:14 them, "Let the little c come to me,
    10:16 And he took the c in his arms,
    10:30 sisters, mothers, c and fields—
    13:12 C will rebel against their parents
Lk   6:35 and you will be c of the Most High,
    10:21 and revealed them to little c.
    18:16 But Jesus called the c to him
    18:16 said, "Let the little c come to me,
Jn   1:12 gave the right to become c of God—
     8.39 "If you were Abraham's c,"
    12:36 so that you may become c of light."
Ac   2:39 your c and for all who are far off—
Ro   8:14 Spirit of God are the c of God.
     8:16 with our spirit that we are God's c.
     9: 8 is not the natural c who are God's c,
     9: 8 it is the c of the promise who are
     9:26 called 'c of the living God.' "
1Co 14:20 and sisters, stop thinking like c.
2Co 12:14 all, c should not have to save
    12:14 their parents, but parents for their c.
Gal  3: 7 that those who have faith are c
     3:26 you are all c of God through faith,
     4: 7 no longer slaves, but God's c;
     4:24 and bears c who are to be slaves:
Eph  5: 8 light in the Lord. Live as c of light
     6: 1 C, obey your parents in the Lord,
     6: 4 Fathers, do not exasperate your c;
Php  2:15 "c of God without fault in a warped
Col  3:20 C, obey your parents in everything,
     3:21 do not embitter your c, or they will
1Th  2: 7 we were like young c among you.
     2: 7 as a nursing mother cares for her c,
     5: 5 are all c of the light and c of the day.
1Ti  3: 4 well and see that his c obey him,
     3:12 wife and must manage his c and his
     5:10 such as bringing up c,
     5:14 to have c, to manage their homes
Tit  1: 6 a man whose c believe and are not
     2: 4 to love their husbands and c,
Heb  2:13 am I, and the c God has given me."
    12: 7 God is treating you as his c.
    12: 8 you are not legitimate c at all.
1Pe  1:14 As obedient c, do not conform
1Jn  3: 1 that we should be called c of God!
     3:10 This is how we know who the c
     3:10 are and who the c of the devil are:
     3:10 not do what is right are not God's c;
     5:19 We know that we are c of God,

2Jn   1: 1  lady chosen by God and to her **c**,
3Jn   1: 4  to hear that my **c** are walking
Rev 21: 7  their God and they will be my **c**.

## CHILDREN'S [CHILD]
Pr    13:22  an inheritance for their **c** children,
      17: 6  **C** children are a crown to the aged,
Jer   31:29  and the **c** teeth are set on edge.'
Eze   18: 2  and the **c** teeth are set on edge'?
Mt    15:26  "It is not right to take the **c** bread

## CHISEL [CHISELED]
Ex    34: 1  "**C** out two stone tablets like

## CHISELED [CHISEL]
Dt    10: 3  **c** out two stone tablets like the first

## CHOICE [CHOICEST, CHOOSE, CHOOSES, CHOSE, CHOSEN]
1Ch  21:11  the LORD says: 'Take your **c**:
Pr     8:10  knowledge rather than **c** gold,
      10:20  tongue of the righteous is **c** silver,
      18: 8  words of a gossip are like **c** morsels;
SS     4:13  of pomegranates with **c** fruits,
       4:16  into his garden and taste its **c** fruits.
Jer    2:21  I had planted you like a **c** vine
Da     1:16  So the guard took away their **c** food
      10: 3  I ate no **c** food; no meat or wine
Ro     8:20  not by its own **c**, but by the will

## CHOICEST [CHOICE]
Dt    33:15  with the **c** gifts of the ancient
Isa    5: 2  and planted it with the **c** vines.
      16: 8  have trampled down the **c** vines,

## CHOIR* [CHOIRS]
Ne    12:38  The second **c** proceeded

## CHOIRS [CHOIR]
1Ch  15:27  in charge of the singing of the **c**.
Ne    12:31  assigned two large **c** to give thanks.

## CHOKE [CHOKED]
Mt    18:28  He grabbed him and began to **c** him.

## CHOKED* [CHOKE]
Mt    13: 7  which grew up and **c** the plants.
Mk     4: 7  which grew up and **c** the plants,
Lk     8: 7  grew up with it and **c** the plants.
       8:14  go on their way they are **c** by life's

## CHOOSE [CHOICE]
Nu    14: 4  "We should **c** a leader and go back
      17: 5  belonging to the man I **c** will sprout,
Dt    12:14  the place the LORD will **c** in one
      30:19  Now **c** life, so that you and your
Jos   24:15  **c** for yourselves this day whom you
2Ki   18:32  **C** life and not death!
Ps    65: 4  Blessed are those you **c** and bring
Pr     1:29  and did not to fear the LORD.
       3:31  the violent or **c** any of their ways.
       8:10  **C** my instruction instead of silver,
Isa    7:15  to reject the wrong and **c** the right,
      14: 1  once again he will **c** Israel and will

Zec    2:12  land and will again **c** Jerusalem.
Jn    15:16  You did not **c** me, but I chose you
Ac     1:21  Therefore it is necessary to **c** one
       6: 3  **c** seven men from among you who
      15:14  to **c** a people for his name
2Co   12: 6  Even if I should **c** to boast, I would
Php    1:22  Yet what shall I **c**? I do not know!
1Pe    4: 3  the past doing what pagans **c** to do—

## CHOOSES [CHOICE]
Nu    16: 7  The man the LORD **c** will be
Ps    68:16  the mountain where God **c** to reign,
Mt    11:27  to whom the Son **c** to reveal him.
Lk    10:22  to whom the Son **c** to reveal him."
Jn     7:17  Anyone who **c** to do the will of God
Jas    4: 4  Anyone who **c** to be a friend

## CHORAZIN*
Mt    11:21  "Woe to you, **C**! Woe to you,
Lk    10:13  "Woe to you, **C**! Woe to you,

## CHOSE [CHOICE]
Ge    13:11  So Lot **c** for himself the whole plain
Dt     4:37  and **c** their descendants after them,
      10:15  and he **c** you, their descendants,
Jdg    5: 8  God **c** new leaders when war came
1Sa    2:28  I **c** your ancestor out of all the tribes
      17:40  hand, **c** five smooth stones
Ne     9: 7  who **c** Abram and brought him
Ps    33:12  the people he **c** for his inheritance.
      78:70  He **c** David his servant and took
Isa   65:12  sight and **c** what displeases me."
Eze   20: 5  On the day I **c** Israel, I swore
Lk     6:13  to him and **c** twelve of them,
Jn    15:16  but I **c** you and appointed you so
Ac     6: 5  They **c** Stephen, a man full of faith
      15:22  They **c** Judas (called Barsabbas)
      15:40  but Paul **c** Silas and left,
1Co    1:27  But God **c** the foolish things
       1:27  God **c** the weak things of the world
Eph    1: 4  For he **c** us in him before
2Th    2:13  because God **c** you as firstfruits
Heb   11:25  He **c** to be mistreated along
Jas    1:18  He **c** to give us birth through

## CHOSEN [CHOICE]
Ge    18:19  For I have **c** him, so that he will
Ex    31: 2  "See, I have **c** Bezalel son of Uri,
Lev   16:10  the goat by lot as the scapegoat
Dt     7: 6  The LORD your God has **c** you
Jdg   10:14  and cry out to the gods you have **c**.
1Sa    8:18  for relief from the king you have **c**,
      16: 1  I have **c** one of his sons to be king."
1Ki    8:44  LORD toward the city you have **c**
Ne     1: 9  the place I have **c** as a dwelling
Ps    89: 3  made a covenant with my **c** one,
      105: 6  descendants of Abraham, his **c** ones,
      119:30  I have **c** the way of faithfulness;
Isa   41: 1  whom I have **c**, you descendants
Am     3: 2  "You only have I **c** of all
Hag    2:23  ring, for I have **c** you,'
Zec    2: 2  who has **c** Jerusalem, rebuke you!
Mt    12:18  "Here is my servant whom I have **c**,
      22:14  many are invited, but few are **c**."
Mk    13:20  whom he has **c**, he has shortened
Lk     9:35  "This is my Son, whom I have **c**;

| | | |
|---|---|---|
| Lk | 10:42 | Mary has **c** what is better, and it |
| | 23:35 | if he is God's Messiah, the **C** One." |
| Jn | 1:34 | I testify that this is God's **C** One." |
| | 6:70 | "Have I not **c** you, the Twelve? |
| | 15:19 | but I have **c** you out of the world. |
| Ac | 9:15 | This man is my **c** instrument |
| Ro | 8:33 | against those whom God has **c**? |
| | 11: 5 | the present time there is a remnant **c** |
| Eph | 1:11 | In him we were also **c**, having been |
| Col | 3:12 | as God's **c** people, holy and dearly |
| 1Th | 1: 4 | loved by God, that he has **c** you, |
| Jas | 2: 5 | Has not God **c** those who are poor |
| 1Pe | 1:20 | He was **c** before the creation |
| | 2: 4 | by human beings but **c** by God |
| | 2: 9 | But you are a **c** people, a royal |
| 2Jn | 1: 1 | To the lady **c** by God and to her |
| Rev | 17:14 | his called, **c** and faithful followers." |

# CHRIST [CHRIST'S, CHRISTIAN, CHRISTIANS, MESSIAH, MESSIAHS]

| | | |
|---|---|---|
| Jn | 1:17 | and truth came through Jesus **C**. |
| | 1:41 | found the Messiah" (that is, the **C**). |
| | 4:25 | Messiah" (called **C**) "is coming. |
| Ac | 3: 6 | In the name of Jesus **C** of Nazareth, |
| | 4:10 | by the name of Jesus **C** of Nazareth, |
| | 9:34 | said to him, "Jesus **C** heals you. |
| Ro | 1: 4 | from the dead: Jesus **C** our Lord. |
| | 3:22 | faith in Jesus **C** to all who believe. |
| | 5: 1 | with God through our Lord Jesus **C**, |
| | 5: 6 | powerless, **C** died for the ungodly. |
| | 5: 8 | we were still sinners, **C** died for us. |
| | 5:11 | in God through our Lord Jesus **C**, |
| | 5:17 | life through the one man, Jesus **C**! |
| | 6: 4 | just as **C** was raised from the dead |
| | 6:23 | is eternal life in **C** Jesus our Lord. |
| | 7: 4 | to the law through the body of **C**, |
| | 8: 1 | for those who are in **C** Jesus, |
| | 8: 9 | Spirit of **C**, they do not belong to **C**. |
| | 8:17 | heirs of God and co-heirs with **C**, |
| | 8:35 | separate us from the love of **C**? |
| | 10: 4 | **C** is the culmination of the law so |
| | 12: 5 | so in **C** we, though many, form one |
| | 13:14 | yourselves with the Lord Jesus **C**, |
| | 14: 9 | **C** died and returned to life so that he |
| | 15: 3 | even **C** did not please himself but, |
| | 15: 5 | toward each other that **C** Jesus had, |
| | 15: 7 | then, just as **C** accepted you, |
| | 16:18 | people are not serving our Lord **C**, |
| 1Co | 1: 2 | to those sanctified in **C** Jesus |
| | 1: 2 | on the name of our Lord Jesus **C**— |
| | 1: 7 | for our Lord Jesus **C** to be revealed. |
| | 1:13 | Is **C** divided? Was Paul crucified |
| | 1:17 | For **C** did not send me to baptize, |
| | 1:17 | lest the cross of **C** be emptied of its |
| | 1:23 | but we preach **C** crucified: |
| | 1:30 | of him that you are in **C** Jesus, |
| | 2: 2 | while I was with you except Jesus **C** |
| | 2:16 | But we have the mind of **C**. |
| | 3:11 | one already laid, which is Jesus **C**. |
| | 5: 7 | For **C**, our Passover lamb, has been |
| | 6:15 | bodies are members of **C** himself? |
| | 6:15 | take the members of **C** and unite |
| | 8: 6 | Jesus **C**, through whom all things |
| | 8:12 | weak conscience, you sin against **C**. |
| | 10: 4 | them, and that rock was **C**. |
| | 10: 9 | We should not test **C**, |

| | | |
|---|---|---|
| | 11: 1 | as I follow the example of **C**. |
| | 11: 3 | that the head of every man is **C**, |
| | 11: 3 | is man, and the head of **C** is God. |
| | 12:27 | Now you are the body of **C**, |
| | 15: 3 | that **C** died for our sins according |
| | 15:14 | And if **C** has not been raised, |
| | 15:22 | die, so in **C** all will be made alive. |
| | 15:57 | victory through our Lord Jesus **C**. |
| 2Co | 1: 5 | abundantly in the sufferings of **C**, |
| | 1: 5 | our comfort abounds through **C**. |
| | 3: 3 | show that you are a letter from **C**, |
| | 3:14 | because only in **C** is it taken away. |
| | 4: 4 | gospel that displays the glory of **C**, |
| | 4: 5 | but Jesus **C** as Lord, and ourselves |
| | 4: 6 | glory displayed in the face of **C**. |
| | 5:10 | before the judgment seat of **C**, |
| | 5:17 | if anyone is in **C**, the new creation |
| | 6:15 | What harmony is there between **C** |
| | 10: 1 | the meekness and gentleness of **C**, |
| | 11: 2 | to **C**, so that I might present you as |
| | 11:13 | masquerading as apostles of **C**. |
| Gal | 1: 7 | are trying to pervert the gospel of **C**. |
| | 2: 4 | on the freedom we have in **C** Jesus |
| | 2:16 | the law, but by faith in Jesus **C**. |
| | 2:16 | have put our faith in **C** Jesus that we |
| | 2:16 | we may be justified by faith in **C** |
| | 2:17 | if, in seeking to be justified in **C**, |
| | 2:17 | that mean that **C** promotes sin? |
| | 2:20 | I have been crucified with **C** |
| | 2:20 | I no longer live, but **C** lives in me. |
| | 2:21 | the law, **C** died for nothing!" |
| | 3:13 | **C** redeemed us from the curse |
| | 3:16 | meaning one person, who is **C**. |
| | 3:26 | So in **C** Jesus you are all children |
| | 4:19 | pains of childbirth until **C** is formed |
| | 5: 1 | is for freedom that **C** has set us free. |
| | 5: 4 | the law have been alienated from **C**; |
| | 5:24 | to **C** Jesus have crucified the sinful |
| | 6:14 | in the cross of our Lord Jesus **C**, |
| Eph | 1: 3 | God and Father of our Lord Jesus **C**, |
| | 1: 3 | with every spiritual blessing in **C**. |
| | 1:10 | in heaven and on earth under **C**. |
| | 1:20 | when he raised **C** from the dead |
| | 2: 5 | made us alive with **C** even when we |
| | 2:10 | created in **C** Jesus to do good |
| | 2:12 | that time you were separate from **C**, |
| | 2:20 | with **C** Jesus himself as the chief |
| | 3: 8 | Gentiles the boundless riches of **C**, |
| | 3:17 | so that **C** may dwell in your hearts |
| | 4: 7 | has been given as **C** apportioned it. |
| | 4:13 | whole measure of the fullness of **C**. |
| | 4:15 | into him who is the head, that is, **C**. |
| | 4:32 | other, just as in **C** God forgave you. |
| | 5: 2 | just as **C** loved us and gave himself |
| | 5:21 | one another out of reverence for **C**. |
| | 5:23 | the head of the wife as **C** is the head |
| | 5:25 | just as **C** loved the church and gave |
| Php | 1: 6 | completion until the day of **C** Jesus. |
| | 1:18 | false motives or true, **C** is preached. |
| | 1:21 | to me, to live is **C** and to die is gain. |
| | 1:23 | I desire to depart and be with **C**, |
| | 1:27 | a manner worthy of the gospel of **C**. |
| | 1:29 | on behalf of **C** not only to believe |
| | 2: 5 | same attitude of mind **C** Jesus had: |
| | 2:11 | acknowledge that Jesus **C** is Lord, |
| | 3: 7 | now consider loss for the sake of **C**. |
| | 3:10 | I want to know **C**—yes, to know |

| | | |
|---|---|---|
| Php | 3:18 | live as enemies of the cross of **C**. |
| | 4:19 | to the riches of his glory in **C** Jesus. |
| Col | 1: 4 | have heard of your faith in **C** Jesus |
| | 1:27 | which is **C** in you, the hope |
| | 1:28 | present everyone fully mature in **C**. |
| | 2: 2 | the mystery of God, namely, **C**, |
| | 2: 6 | as you received **C** Jesus as Lord, |
| | 2: 9 | For in **C** all the fullness of the Deity |
| | 2:13 | nature, God made you alive with **C**. |
| | 2:17 | the reality, however, is found in **C**. |
| | 3: 1 | you have been raised with **C**, |
| | 3: 1 | where **C** is seated at the right hand |
| | 3: 3 | your life is now hidden with **C** |
| | 3:15 | Let the peace of **C** rule in your |
| | 3:16 | of **C** dwell among you richly as you |
| 1Th | 4:16 | and the dead in **C** will rise first. |
| | 5: 9 | salvation through our Lord Jesus **C**. |
| | 5:18 | this is God's will for you in **C** Jesus. |
| 2Th | 2: 1 | the coming of our Lord Jesus **C** |
| | 2:14 | in the glory of our Lord Jesus **C**. |
| 1Ti | 1:12 | I thank **C** Jesus our Lord, who has |
| | 1:15 | **C** Jesus came into the world to save |
| | 1:16 | **C** Jesus might display his immense |
| | 2: 5 | God and human beings, **C** Jesus, |
| | 4: 6 | will be a good minister of **C** Jesus, |
| | 6:14 | the appearing of our Lord Jesus **C**, |
| 2Ti | 1: 9 | us in **C** Jesus before the beginning |
| | 1:10 | appearing of our Savior, **C** Jesus, |
| | 2: 1 | in the grace that is in **C** Jesus. |
| | 2: 3 | like a good soldier of **C** Jesus. |
| | 2: 8 | Remember Jesus **C**, |
| | 2:10 | the salvation that is in **C** Jesus, |
| | 3:12 | life in **C** Jesus will be persecuted, |
| | 3:15 | salvation through faith in **C** Jesus. |
| | 4: 1 | the presence of God and of **C** Jesus, |
| Tit | 2:13 | our great God and Savior, Jesus **C**, |
| Phm | 1: 6 | thing we share for the sake of **C**. |
| | 1:20 | in the Lord; refresh my heart in **C**. |
| Heb | 3: 6 | **C** is faithful as the Son over God's |
| | 3:14 | We have come to share in **C**, |
| | 5: 5 | **C** did not take on himself the glory |
| | 6: 1 | the elementary teachings about **C** |
| | 9:11 | when **C** came as high priest |
| | 9:15 | For this reason **C** is the mediator |
| | 9:24 | **C** did not enter a sanctuary made |
| | 9:26 | Otherwise **C** would have had |
| | 9:28 | so **C** was sacrificed once to take |
| | 10:10 | of the body of Jesus **C** once for all. |
| | 11:26 | for the sake of **C** as of greater value |
| | 13: 8 | Jesus **C** is the same yesterday |
| 1Pe | 1: 2 | Spirit, to be obedient to Jesus **C** |
| | 1: 3 | and Father of our Lord Jesus **C**! |
| | 1: 3 | of Jesus **C** from the dead, |
| | 1:11 | the Spirit of **C** in them was pointing |
| | 1:11 | he predicted the sufferings of **C** |
| | 1:19 | but with the precious blood of **C**, |
| | 2:21 | called, because **C** suffered for you, |
| | 3:15 | But in your hearts revere **C** as Lord. |
| | 3:18 | For **C** also suffered once for sins, |
| | 3:21 | you by the resurrection of Jesus **C**, |
| | 4: 1 | since **C** suffered in his body, |
| | 4:13 | participate in the sufferings of **C**, |
| | 4:14 | insulted because of the name of **C**, |
| 2Pe | 1: 1 | a servant and apostle of Jesus **C**, |
| | 1: 1 | Savior Jesus **C** have received a faith |
| | 1:16 | of our Lord Jesus **C** in power, |
| | 3:18 | of our Lord and Savior Jesus **C**. |

| | | |
|---|---|---|
| 1Jn | 2: 1 | Jesus **C**, the Righteous One. |
| | 3:16 | Jesus **C** laid down his life for us. |
| | 3:23 | Jesus **C**, and to love one another as |
| | 4: 2 | that Jesus **C** has come in the flesh is |
| | 5: 6 | came by water and blood—Jesus **C**. |
| | 5:20 | is true by being in his Son Jesus **C**. |
| 2Jn | 1: 7 | not acknowledge Jesus **C** as coming |
| | 1: 9 | teaching of **C** does not have God; |
| Jude | 1: 1 | a servant of Jesus **C** and a brother |
| | 1: 1 | the Father and kept for Jesus **C**: |
| | 1: 4 | deny Jesus **C** our only Sovereign |
| | 1:17 | of our Lord Jesus **C** foretold. |
| Rev | 1: 1 | The revelation from Jesus **C**, |
| | 1: 5 | and from Jesus **C**, who is |
| | 20: 4 | reigned with **C** a thousand years. |
| | 20: 6 | of **C** and will reign with him |

## CHRIST JESUS See JESUS

## JESUS CHRIST See JESUS

## LORD JESUS CHRIST See JESUS

## CHRIST'S* [CHRIST]

| | | |
|---|---|---|
| 1Co | 7:22 | were free when called are **C** slaves. |
| | 9:21 | God's law but am under **C** law), |
| 2Co | 2:14 | leads us as captives in **C** triumphal |
| | | procession |
| | 5:14 | For **C** love compels us, because we |
| | 5:20 | We are therefore **C** ambassadors, |
| | 5:20 | We implore you on **C** behalf: |
| | 12: 9 | so that **C** power may rest on me. |
| | 12:10 | for **C** sake, I delight in weaknesses, |
| Col | 1:22 | by **C** physical body through death |
| | 1:24 | lacking in regard to **C** afflictions, |
| 2Th | 3: 5 | into God's love and **C** perseverance. |
| 1Pe | 5: 1 | a witness of **C** sufferings who |

## CHRISTIAN* [CHRIST]

| | | |
|---|---|---|
| Ac | 26:28 | you can persuade me to be a **C**?" |
| 1Pe | 4:16 | if you suffer as a **C**, do not be |

## CHRISTIANS* [CHRIST]

| | | |
|---|---|---|
| Ac | 11:26 | The disciples were called **C** first |

## CHRONICLES*

| | | |
|---|---|---|
| Est | 6: 1 | so he ordered the book of the **c**, |

## CHURCH [CHURCHES]

| | | |
|---|---|---|
| Mt | 16:18 | and on this rock I will build my **c**, |
| | 18:17 | still refuse to listen, tell it to the **c**; |
| | 18:17 | if they refuse to listen even to the **c**, |
| Ac | 5:11 | Great fear seized the whole **c** and all |
| | 8: 1 | broke out against the **c** in Jerusalem, |
| | 8: 3 | But Saul began to destroy the **c**. |
| | 12: 1 | some who belonged to the **c**, |
| | 14:23 | elders for them in each **c** and, |
| | 15: 4 | they were welcomed by the **c** |
| | 20:28 | Be shepherds of the **c** of God, |
| Ro | 16: 5 | also the **c** that meets at their house. |
| 1Co | 4:17 | what I teach everywhere in every **c**. |
| | 5:12 | mine to judge those outside the **c**? |
| | 6: 4 | way of life is scorned in the **c**? |
| | 10:32 | Jews, Greeks or the **c** of God— |
| | 11:18 | that when you come together as a **c**, |
| | 12:28 | God has placed in the **c** first of all |
| | 14: 4 | but those who prophesy edify the **c**. |

1Co 14:12 to excel in those that build up the **c**.
14:26 done so that the **c** may be built up.
14:35 for a woman to speak in the **c**.
15: 9 because I persecuted the **c** of God.
Gal 1:13 how intensely I persecuted the **c**
Eph 1:22 to be head over everything for the **c**,
3:10 through the **c**, the manifold wisdom
5:23 wife as Christ is the head of the **c**,
5:25 just as Christ loved the **c** and gave
Php 3: 6 as for zeal, persecuting the **c**;
Col 1:18 he is the head of the body, the **c**;
1:24 the sake of his body, which is the **c**.
1Ti 3: 5 how can he take care of God's **c**?)
5:16 not let the **c** be burdened with them,
5:16 the **c** can help those widows who
Heb 12:23 to the **c** of the firstborn,
Jas 5:14 the elders of the **c** to pray over them
3Jn 1: 9 I wrote to the **c**, but Diotrephes,

## CHURCHES [CHURCH]
Ac 15:41 and Cilicia, strengthening the **c**.
16: 5 So the **c** were strengthened
1Co 7:17 is the rule I lay down in all the **c**.
11:16 nor do the **c** of God.
14:34 should remain silent in the **c**.
2Co 11: 8 I robbed other **c** by receiving
1Th 2:14 imitators of God's **c** in Judea,
2:14 the same things those **c** suffered
2Th 1: 4 among God's **c** we boast about your
Rev 1: 4 To the seven **c** in the province
1:20 stars are the angels of the seven **c**,
1:20 seven lampstands are the seven **c**.
2: 7 hear what the Spirit says to the **c**.
22:16 to give you this testimony for the **c**.

## CHURNING
Pr 30:33 For as **c** cream produces butter,
Da 7: 2 winds of heaven **c** up the great sea.

## CILICIA
Ac 21:39 from Tarsus in **C**, a citizen of no

## CIRCLE [CIRCLED, CIRCLING, CIRCUIT, CIRCULAR, ENCIRCLE, ENCIRCLED]
Isa 40:22 enthroned above the **c** of the earth,
Mk 3:34 at those seated in a **c** around him

## CIRCLED* [CIRCLE]
Jos 6:15 that day they **c** the city seven times.

## CIRCLING* [CIRCLE]
Jos 6:11 carried around the city, **c** it once.

## CIRCUIT* [CIRCLE]
1Sa 7:16 year he went on a **c** from Bethel
Ps 19: 6 and makes its **c** to the other;

## CIRCULAR [CIRCLE]
2Ch 4: 2 the Sea of cast metal, **c** in shape,

## CIRCULATED*
Mt 28:15 has been widely **c** among the Jews

## CIRCUMCISE* [CIRCUMCISED, CIRCUMCISION]
Dt 10:16 **C** your hearts, therefore, and do not
30: 6 LORD your God will **c** your hearts
Jos 5: 2 knives and **c** the Israelites again."
Jer 4: 4 **C** yourselves to the LORD, **c** your
Lk 1:59 eighth day they came to **c** the child,
2:21 when it was time to **c** the child,
Jn 7:22 you **c** a boy on the Sabbath.
Ac 21:21 telling them not to **c** their children

## CIRCUMCISED [CIRCUMCISE]
Ge 17:10 Every male among you shall be **c**.
17:26 his son Ishmael were both **c**
21: 4 was eight days old, Abraham **c** him,
Lev 12: 3 On the eighth day the boy is to be **c**.
Jos 5: 3 **c** the Israelites at Gibeath Haaraloth.
Ac 10:45 The **c** believers who had come
11: 2 the **c** believers criticized him
15: 1 "Unless you are **c**,
16: 3 so he **c** him because of the Jews
Ro 2:26 those who are not **c** keep the law's
2:26 be regarded as though they were **c**?
4: 9 Is this blessedness only for the **c**,
1Co 7:18 Was a man already **c** when he was
7:18 he was called? He should not be **c**.
Gal 5: 2 you that if you let yourselves be **c**,
6:13 even those who are **c** keep the law,
6:13 you to be **c** that they may boast
Col 2:11 **c** with a circumcision not performed
2:11 put off when you were **c** by Christ,
3:11 Gentile or Jew, **c** or uncircumcised,

## CIRCUMCISION [CIRCUMCISE]
Ro 2:25 **C** has value if you observe the law,
2:29 and **c** is **c** of the heart, by the Spirit,
1Co 7:19 **C** is nothing and uncircumcision is
Gal 2:12 those who belonged to the **c** group.
5: 6 Jesus neither **c** nor uncircumcision
Php 3: 3 For it is we who are the **c**, we who
Col 2:11 circumcised with a **c** not performed
Tit 1:10 especially those of the **c** group.

## CIRCUMSTANCES
1Co 7:15 or sister is not bound in such **c**;
Php 4:11 to be content whatever the **c**.
1Th 5:18 give thanks in all **c**; for this is God's
Jas 1: 9 Believers in humble **c** ought to take

## CISTERN [CISTERNS]
Ge 37:22 Throw him into this **c** here
2Ki 18:31 and drink water from your own **c**,
Pr 5:15 Drink water from your own **c**,
Jer 38: 6 and put him into the **c** of Malkijah,
38: 6 Jeremiah by ropes into the **c**;

## CISTERNS [CISTERN]
Ge 37:20 and throw him into one of these **c**
Jer 2:13 living water, and have dug their own **c**,
broken **c** that cannot hold water.

## CITADEL [CITADELS]
2Sa 12:26 and captured the royal **c**.
Ne 1: 1 year, while I was in the **c** of Susa,

## CITADELS* [CITADEL]

| | | |
|---|---|---|
| Ps | 48: 3 | God is in her c; he has shown |
| | 48:13 | view her c, that you may tell |
| | 122: 7 | walls and security within your c." |
| Isa | 34:13 | Thorns will overrun her c, |

## CITIES [CITY]

| | | |
|---|---|---|
| Ge | 13:12 | while Lot lived among the c |
| | 19:25 | Thus he overthrew those c |
| | 19:25 | destroying all those living in the c— |
| | 24:60 | offspring possess the c of their enemies. |
| Nu | 13:28 | and the c are fortified and very |
| | 21: 2 | we will totally destroy their c." |
| | 35:11 | some towns to be your c of refuge, |
| Dt | 6:10 | flourishing c you did not build, |
| Jos | 24:13 | did not toil and c you did not build; |
| Ps | 69:35 | Zion and rebuild the c of Judah. |
| Isa | 64:10 | Your sacred c have become |
| Jer | 4:16 | raising a war cry against the c |
| Lk | 19:17 | small matter, take charge of ten c.' |
| | 19:19 | 'You take charge of five c.' |
| 2Pe | 2: 6 | if he condemned the c of Sodom |
| Rev | 16:19 | and the c of the nations collapsed. |

## CITIZEN [CITIZENS, CITIZENSHIP]

| | | |
|---|---|---|
| Ac | 21:39 | in Cilicia, a c of no ordinary city. |
| | 22:25 | to flog a Roman c who hasn't even |

## CITIZENS [CITIZEN]

| | | |
|---|---|---|
| Ac | 16:38 | that Paul and Silas were Roman c, |
| Eph | 2:19 | but fellow c with God's people |
| 1Th | 2:14 | You suffered from your fellow c |

## CITIZENSHIP* [CITIZEN]

| | | |
|---|---|---|
| Ac | 22:28 | to pay a lot of money for my c." |
| Eph | 2:12 | excluded from c in Israel |
| Php | 3:20 | But our c is in heaven. |

## CITY [CITIES]

| | | |
|---|---|---|
| Ge | 4:17 | Cain was then building a c, and he |
| | 11: 4 | let us build ourselves a c, |
| | 18:24 | are fifty righteous people in the c? |
| | 19:14 | LORD is about to destroy the c!" |
| Dt | 28: 3 | You will be blessed in the c |
| | 28:16 | You will be cursed in the c |
| Jos | 6:16 | the LORD has given you the c! |
| | 18:28 | Haeleph, the Jebusite c (that is, |
| Jdg | 16: 3 | took hold of the doors of the c gate, |
| 2Sa | 5: 9 | fortress and called it the C of David. |
| 1Ki | 8:44 | the LORD toward the c you have |
| 1Ch | 11: 7 | and so it was called the C of David. |
| Ne | 11: 1 | the holy c, while the remaining nine |
| Ps | 46: 4 | river whose streams make glad the c |
| | 48: 1 | praise, in the c of our God, his holy |
| | 122: 3 | Jerusalem is built like a c that is |
| | 127: 1 | the LORD watches over the c, |
| Pr | 8: 3 | beside the gate leading into the c, |
| | 11:10 | the righteous prosper, the c rejoices; |
| | 31:23 | husband is respected at the c gate, |
| | 31:31 | works bring her praise at the c gate. |
| Isa | 1:21 | See how the faithful c has become |
| | 1:26 | Afterward you will be called the C |
| | 1:26 | of Righteousness, the Faithful C." |
| Jer | 34: 2 | to give this c into the hands |
| | 34:22 | and I will bring them back to this c. |

| | | |
|---|---|---|
| La | 1: 1 | How deserted lies the c, once so full |
| Eze | 4: 1 | and draw the c of Jerusalem on it. |
| | 11: 3 | This c is a pot, and we are the meat |
| Da | 9:24 | your holy c to finish transgression, |
| Jnh | 1: 2 | "Go to the great c Nineveh |
| | 4:11 | concern for the great c Nineveh, |
| Hab | 2:12 | him who builds a c with bloodshed |
| Zep | 2:15 | This is the c of revelry that lived |
| Zec | 14: 2 | the c will be captured, the houses |
| | 14: 2 | Half of the c will go into exile, |
| | 14: 2 | people will not be taken from the c. |
| Mt | 4: 5 | the devil took him to the holy c |
| | 5:14 | A c on a hill cannot be hidden. |
| Ac | 18:10 | I have many people in this c." |
| Heb | 11:10 | forward to the c with foundations, |
| | 12:22 | Zion, to the c of the living God, |
| | 13:14 | here we do not have an enduring c, |
| | 13:14 | we are looking for the c that is |
| Rev | 2:13 | who was put to death in your c— |
| | 3:12 | and the name of the c of my God, |
| | 11: 2 | trample on the holy c for 42 months. |
| | 16:19 | The great c split into three parts, |
| | 17:18 | The woman you saw is the great c |
| | 18:10 | great c, you mighty c of Babylon! |
| | 20: 9 | of God's people, the c he loves. |
| | 21: 2 | I saw the Holy C, the new |
| | 22: 3 | and of the Lamb will be in the c, |

## CITY OF DAVID
2Sa 5:7, 9; 6:10, 12, 16; 1Ki 2:10; 3:1; 8:1; 9:24; 11:27, 43; 14:31; 15:8; 22:50; 2Ki 8:24; 9:28; 12:21; 14:20; 15:7, 38; 16:20; 1Ch 11:5, 7; 13:13; 15:1, 29; 2Ch 5:2; 8:11; 9:31; 12:16; 14:1; 16:14; 21:1, 20; 24:16, 25; 27:9; 32:5, 30; 33:14; Ne 3:15; 12:37; Isa 22:9

## HOLY CITY  See HOLY

## CIVILIAN*

| | | |
|---|---|---|
| 2Ti | 2: 4 | a soldier gets involved in c affairs; |

## CLAIM [CLAIMED, CLAIMING, CLAIMS, RECLAIM]

| | | |
|---|---|---|
| Job | 41:11 | Who has a c against me that I must |
| Pr | 25: 6 | and do not c a place among his great |
| Jn | 9:41 | but now that you c you can see, |
| | 10:33 | you, a mere man, c to be God." |
| Tit | 1:16 | They c to know God, but by their |
| Jas | 2:14 | if people c to have faith |
| 1Jn | 1: 6 | If we c to have fellowship with him |
| | 1: 8 | If we c to be without sin, |
| | 1:10 | If we c we have not sinned, |
| | 2: 9 | Those who c to be in the light |
| Rev | 2: 2 | you have tested those who c to be |
| | 3: 9 | who c to be Jews though they are |

## CLAIMED [CLAIM]

| | | |
|---|---|---|
| Jn | 19: 7 | because he c to be the Son of God." |
| | 19:21 | but that this man c to be king |
| Ro | 1:22 | Although they c to be wise, |

## CLAIMING [CLAIM]

| | | |
|---|---|---|
| Mk | 13: 6 | Many will come in my name, c, |

## CLAIMS [CLAIM]

| | | |
|---|---|---|
| 1Jn | 2: 6 | Whoever c to live in him must live |

## CLAN [CLANS]
Ge 24:40 a wife for my son from my own c
Lev 25:10 family property and to your own c.
25:49 relative in their c may redeem them.
Nu 27: 4 from his c because he had no son?
1Sa 18:18 what is my family or my c in Israel,

## CLANGING*
1Co 13: 1 a resounding gong or a c cymbal.

## CLANS [CLAN]
Nu 1: 2 Israelite community by their c
Jos 14: 1 of the tribal c of Israel allotted
Mic 5: 2 though you are small among the c

## CLAP* [CLAPPED, CLAPS]
Job 21: 5 c your hand over your mouth.
Ps 47: 1 C your hands, all you nations;
98: 8 Let the rivers c their hands,
Pr 30:32 evil, c your hand over your mouth!
Isa 55:12 trees of the field will c their hands.
La 2:15 All who pass your way c their hands
Na 3:19 about you c their hands at your fall,

## CLAPPED* [CLAP]
2Ki 11:12 and the people c their hands
Eze 25: 6 Because you have c your hands

## CLAPS* [CLAP]
Job 27:23 It c its hands in derision and hisses
34:37 scornfully he c his hands among us

## CLASPED* [CLASPS]
Mt 28: 9 him, c his feet and worshiped him.

## CLASPS [CLASPED]
Ex 26: 6 make fifty gold c and use them

## CLASSIFY*
2Co 10:12 We do not dare to c or compare

## CLAUDIUS*
Ac 11:28 happened during the reign of C.)
18: 2 because C had ordered all Jews
23:26 C Lysias, To His Excellency,

## CLAWS*
Da 4:33 and his nails like the c of a bird.
7:19 with its iron teeth and bronze c—

## CLAY
Job 10: 9 that you molded me like c.
33: 6 in God's sight; I too am a piece of c.
Isa 29:16 potter were thought to be like the c!
41:25 as if he were a potter treading the c.
45: 9 Does the c say to the potter,
64: 8 We are the c, you are the potter;
Jer 18: 6 "Like c in the hand of the potter,
19: 1 "Go and buy a c jar from a potter.
La 4: 2 are now considered as pots of c,
Eze 4: 1 take a block of c, put it in front
Da 2:33 partly of iron and partly of baked c.
Ro 9:21 the same lump of c some pottery
2Co 4: 7 this treasure in jars of c to show

2Ti 2:20 and silver, but also of wood and c;

## CLEAN [CLEANNESS, CLEANSE, CLEANSED, CLEANSING]
Ge 7: 2 pairs of every kind of c animal,
Lev 4:12 the camp to a place ceremonially c,
10:10 between the unclean and the c,
16:30 you will be c from all your sins.
Dt 14:11 You may eat any c bird.
Ps 24: 4 Those who have c hands and a pure
51: 7 me with hyssop, and I will be c;
Pr 20: 9 I am c and without sin"?
Ecc 9: 2 and the bad, the c and the unclean,
Eze 36:25 c water on you, and you will be c;
Zec 3: 5 I said, "Put a c turban on his head."
3: 5 So they put a c turban on his head
Mt 8: 2 are willing, you can make me c."
12:44 swept c and put in order.
23:25 You c the outside of the cup
27:59 body, wrapped it in a c linen cloth,
Mk 7:19 this, Jesus declared all foods c.)
Jn 13:10 their whole body is c.
13:10 And you are c, though not every one
15: 3 You are already c because
Ac 10:15 impure that God has made c."
Ro 14:20 All food is c, but it is wrong
Rev 15: 6 They were dressed in c,
19: 8 linen, bright and c, was given her
19:14 dressed in fine linen, white and c.

## CLEANNESS [CLEAN]
2Sa 22:25 according to my c in his sight.
Ps 18:20 the c of my hands he has rewarded

## CLEANSE [CLEAN]
Ps 51: 2 my iniquity and c me from my sin.
51: 7 C me with hyssop, and I will be
Pr 20:30 Blows and wounds c away evil,
Zec 13: 1 to c them from sin and impurity.
Mt 10: 8 the dead, c those who have leprosy,
2Ti 2:21 Those who c themselves from the latter
Heb 9:14 c our consciences from acts
10:22 having our hearts sprinkled to c us

## CLEANSED [CLEAN]
Jos 22:17 very day we have not c ourselves
2Ki 5:10 will be restored and you will be c."
Pr 30:12 eyes and yet are not c of their filth;
Isa 1: 6 not c or bandaged or soothed
Mt 8: 3 Immediately he was c of his leprosy.
11: 5 those who have leprosy are c,
Lk 4:27 prophet, yet not one of them was c—
17:14 And as they went, they were c.
Heb 9:22 nearly everything be c with blood,
10: 2 worshipers would have been c once
2Pe 1: 9 that you have been c from your past

## CLEANSING [CLEAN]
Mk 1:44 that Moses commanded for your c,
Eph 5:26 c her by the washing with water

## CLEAR [CLEARED, CLEARLY]
Lev 24: 2 to bring you c oil of pressed olives
Ne 8: 8 making it c and giving the meaning
Mt 3:12 and he will c his threshing floor,

1Co 4: 4 My conscience is c, but that does
1Ti 3: 9 of the faith with a c conscience.
2Ti 1: 3 with a c conscience, as night
Heb 13:18 are sure that we have a c conscience
1Pe 3:16 keeping a c conscience,
Rev 4: 6 like a sea of glass, c as crystal.
21:11 jewel, like a jasper, c as crystal.
22: 1 of the water of life, as c as crystal,

## CLEARED [CLEAR]

Ps 80: 9 You c the ground for it, and it took
Isa 5: 2 He dug it up and c it of stones

## CLEARLY [CLEAR]

Mk 8:25 restored, and he saw everything c.
Lk 6:42 you will see c to remove the speck
Ro 1:20 have been c seen, being understood

## CLEFT* [CLEFTS]

Ex 33:22 I will put you in a c in the rock

## CLEFTS [CLEFT]

SS 2:14 My dove in the c of the rock,
Ob 1: 3 you who live in the c of the rocks

## CLEVER*

Isa 3: 3 skilled worker and c enchanter.
5:21 own eyes and c in their own sight.

## CLIMAX*

Eze 21:25 of punishment has reached its c,
21:29 of punishment has reached its c.
35: 5 time their punishment reached its c,

## CLIMB [CLIMBED]

1Sa 14:10 we will c up, because that will be
SS 7: 8 I said, "I will c the palm tree;
Am 9: 2 Though they c up to the heavens

## CLIMBED [CLIMB]

Lk 19: 4 c a sycamore-fig tree to see him,

## CLING [CLUNG]

Ps 31: 6 I hate those who c to worthless
63: 8 I c to you;
137: 6 May my tongue c to the roof of my
Jnh 2: 8 "Those who c to worthless idols
Ro 12: 9 Hate what is evil; c to what is good.

## CLOAK [CLOAKS]

Ge 39:12 She caught him by his c and said,
39:12 But he left his c in her hand and ran
Ex 4: 6 "Put your hand inside your c."
4: 6 So Moses put his hand into his c,
12:11 with your c tucked into your belt,
22:26 take your neighbor's c as a pledge,
Dt 22:12 the four corners of the c you wear.
1Ki 11:30 hold of the new c he was wearing
18:46 and, tucking his c into his belt,
2Ki 2: 8 Elijah took his c, rolled it
2:13 He picked up the c that had fallen
4:29 "Tuck your c into your belt,
9: 1 to him, "Tuck your c into your belt,
Mk 13:16 in the field go back to get their c.

Lk 8:44 him and touched the edge of his c,

## CLOAKS [CLOAK]

Mk 11: 8 Many people spread their c

## CLOSE [CLOSED, CLOSER, ENCLOSE, ENCLOSED]

1Sa 18: 9 Saul kept a c eye on David.
2Ki 11: 8 Stay c to the king wherever he
Ps 34:18 The LORD is c
41: 9 Even my c friend, someone I
55:13 myself, my companion, my c friend,
148:14 of Israel, the people c to his heart.
Pr 16:28 and gossips separate c friends.
28:27 those who c their eyes to them receive
Isa 40:11 arms and carries them c to his heart;
Jer 30:21 him near and he will come c to me—
30:21 will devote himself to be c to me?'
Da 12: 4 c up and seal the words of the scroll
Joel 2: 1 LORD is coming. It is c at hand—
Zec 13: 7 against the man who is c to me!"
Mt 6: 6 c the door and pray to your Father,
Rev 6: 8 Hades was following c behind him.

## CLOSED [CLOSE]

Ge 2:21 and then c up the place with flesh.
1Sa 1: 5 and the LORD had c her womb.
Jer 6:10 Their ears are c so they cannot hear.
Da 12: 9 because the words are c
Mt 13:15 ears, and they have c their eyes.
Ac 28:27 ears, and they have c their eyes.

## CLOSER [CLOSE]

Ex 3: 5 "Do not come any c," God said.
Pr 18:24 a friend who sticks c than a brother.

## CLOTH [CLOTHS]

Ex 28:31 robe of the ephod entirely of blue c,
Dt 22:17 shall display the c before the elders
2Ki 8:15 But the next day he took a thick c,
Mt 9:16 of unshrunk c on an old garment,
27:59 body, wrapped it in a clean linen c,

## CLOTHE [CLOTHED, CLOTHES, CLOTHING]

Ps 45: 3 c yourself with splendor
132:16 I will c her priests with salvation,
132:18 I will c his enemies with shame,
Isa 52: 1 Zion, c yourself with strength!
Mal 2:16 people c themselves with injustice,"
Mt 25:43 clothes and you did not c me, I was
Lk 12:28 fire, how much more will he c you—
Ro 13:14 c yourselves with the Lord Jesus
1Co 15:53 the perishable must c itself
Col 3:12 c yourselves with compassion,
1Pe 5: 5 c yourselves with humility toward

## CLOTHED [CLOTHE]

Ge 3:21 for Adam and his wife and c them.
2Ch 6:41 LORD God, be c with salvation,
Ps 30:11 my sackcloth and c me with joy,
104: 1 you are c with splendor
Pr 31:22 she is c in fine linen and purple.
31:25 She is c with strength and dignity;
Isa 61:10 For he has c me with garments

Zec  3:  5  clean turban on his head and c him,
Mt  25:36  I needed clothes and you c me,
Lk  24:49  the city until you have been c
Jn  19:  2  They c him in a purple robe
2Co  5:  2  to be c with our heavenly dwelling,
Gal  3:27  into Christ have c yourselves
Rev  12:  1  a woman c with the sun,

## CLOTHES [CLOTHE]

Dt   8:  4  Your c did not wear out and your
    29:  5  wilderness, your c did not wear out,
Ps  22:18  They divide my c among them
Pr   6:27  his lap without his c being burned?
Jer  52:33  So Jehoiachin put aside his prison c
Hag  1:  6  You put on c, but are not warm.
Zec  3:  3  filthy c as he stood before the angel.
Mt   6:25  the body more important than c?
    6:28  "And why do you worry about c?
  17:  2  his c became as white as the light.
  22:12  you get in here without wedding c?'
  25:36  I needed c and you clothed me,
  27:35  they divided up his c by casting lots.
Jn  11:44  "Take off the grave c and let him
Ac  10:30  a man in shining c stood before me
1Ti  2:  9  or gold or pearls or expensive c,
Jas  2:  2  wearing a gold ring and fine c,
   2:  2  a poor person in filthy old c
1Pe  3:  3  wearing of gold jewelry and fine c.
Rev 16:15  who stay awake and keep their c on,

## CLOTHING [CLOTHE]

Ex   3:22  articles of silver and gold and for c,
  12:35  articles of silver and gold and for c.
Dt  22:  5  A woman must not wear men's c,
  22:  5  nor a man wear women's c,
Job  29:14  I put on righteousness as my c;
Ps 102:26  Like c you will change them
Da   7:  9  His c was as white as snow;
Mt   7:15  They come to you in sheep's c,
Mk  1:  6  John wore c made of camel's hair,
1Ti  6:  8  But if we have food and c, we will
Jude 1:23  hating even the c stained

## CLOTHS* [CLOTH]

Eze 16:  4  rubbed with salt or wrapped in c.
Lk   2:  7  She wrapped him in c and placed
   2:12  You will find a baby wrapped in c

## CLOUD [CLOUDS, THUNDERCLOUD]

Ex  13:21  them in a pillar of c to guide them
  19:  9  going to come to you in a dense c,
  24:18  Moses entered the c as he went
  40:34  the c covered the tent of meeting,
Nu  9:15  law, was set up, the c covered it.
   9:15  evening till morning the c
1Ki  8:10  Place, the c filled the temple
  18:44  "A c as small as a man's hand is
Ne  9:19  day the pillar of c did not cease
Ps 105:39  He spread out a c as a covering,
Pr  16:15  his favor is like a rain c in spring.
Isa  19:  1  the LORD rides on a swift c and is
Eze  1:  4  an immense c with flashing
Mk  9:  7  Then a c appeared and covered
  9:  7  them, and a voice came from the c:
Lk  21:27  of Man coming in a c with power

Ac   1:  9  and a c hid him from their sight.
1Co 10:  2  all baptized into Moses in the c
Heb 12:  1  by such a great c of witnesses, let us
Rev 10:  1  He was robed in a c, with a rainbow
  11:12  And they went up to heaven in a c,
  14:14  and there before me was a white c,
  14:14  seated on the c was one like a son

## CLOUDS [CLOUD]

Ge   9:13  I have set my rainbow in the c,
Dt  33:26  you and on the c in his majesty.
1Ki 18:45  the sky grew black with c, the wind
Ps  68:  4  name, extol him who rides on the c;
  104:  3  He makes the c his chariot and rides
Pr   8:28  when he established the c
  25:14  Like c and wind without rain is one
Isa  14:14  will ascend above the tops of the c;
Eze  1:28  of a rainbow in the c on a rainy day,
Da   7:13  man, coming with the c of heaven.
Joel  2:  2  gloom, a day of c and blackness.
Na   1:  3  storm, and c are the dust of his feet.
Zep  1:15  gloom, a day of c and blackness—
Mt  24:30  of Man coming on the c of heaven,
  26:64  and coming on the c of heaven."
1Th  4:17  them in the c to meet the Lord
Jude 1:12  They are c without rain,
Rev  1:  7  he is coming with the c,"

## CLUB [CLUBS]

Pr  25:18  Like a c or a sword or a sharp arrow
Isa  10:  5  in whose hand is the c of my wrath!
Jer  51:20  "You are my war c, my weapon

## CLUBS [CLUB]

Mk  14:43  a crowd armed with swords and c,

## CLUNG* [CLING]

Ru   1:14  good-by, but Ruth c to her.
2Ki  3:  3  Nevertheless he c to the sins
La   1:  9  Her filthiness c to her skirts;

## CLUSTER

Nu  13:23  cut off a branch bearing a single c

## CO-HEIRS* [INHERIT]

Ro   8:17  heirs of God and c with Christ,

## CO-WORKERS* [WORK]

Ro  16:  3  and Aquila, my c in Christ Jesus.
1Co  3:  9  we are God's c; you are God's field,
2Co  6:  1  As God's c we urge you not to receive
Php  4:  3  Clement and the rest of my c,
Col  4:11  Jews among my c for the kingdom

## COAL* [COALS]

2Sa 14:  7  out the only burning c I have left,
Isa  6:  6  flew to me with a live c in his hand,

## COALS [COAL]

Nu  16:37  scatter the c some distance away,
Ps  11:  6  On the wicked he will rain fiery c
  18:  8  mouth, burning c blazed out of it.
Pr   6:28  walk on hot c without his feet being
  25:22  you will heap burning c on his head,
Eze  1:13  living creatures was like burning c

Eze 10: 2 burning **c** from among the cherubim
Ro 12:20 this, you will heap burning **c** on his

## COARSE*
Eph  5: 4 foolish talk or **c** joking, which are

## COAST
Nu 34: 6 western boundary will be the **c**

## COAT [COATED]
Ge  6:14 rooms in it and **c** it with pitch inside
Dt 27: 4 you today, and **c** them with plaster.
1Sa 17: 5 wore a **c** of scale armor of bronze
Mt  5:40 hand over your **c** as well.

## COAT OF MANY COLOURS
(KJV) See [RICHLY
ORNAMENTED] ROBE

## COATED* [COAT]
Ex  2: 3 basket for him and **c** it with tar

## COBRA*
Ps 58: 4 that of a **c** that has stopped its ears,
91:13 You will tread on the lion and the **c**;
Isa 11: 8 will play near the hole of the **c**;

## CODE*
Ro  2:27 even though you have the written **c**
2:29 by the Spirit, not by the written **c**.
7: 6 not in the old way of the written **c**.

## COFFIN*
Ge 50:26 him, he was placed in a **c** in Egypt.

## COILED* [COILING]
2Sa 22: 6 The cords of the grave **c** around me;
Ps 18: 5 The cords of the grave **c** around me;

## COILING* [COILED]
Isa 27: 1 serpent, Leviathan the **c** serpent;

## COIN* [COINS]
Mt 17:27 and you will find a four-drachma **c**.
22:19 Show me the **c** used for paying
Mk 12:16 They brought the **c**, and he asked
Lk 15: 9 I have found my lost **c**.'

## COINS [COIN]
Mt 18:28 servants who owed him a hundred
silver **c**.
Lk 15: 8 suppose a woman has ten silver **c**
Jn  2:15 he scattered the **c** of the money

## COLD
Ge  8:22 seedtime and harvest, **c** and heat,
Pr 25:25 Like **c** water to a weary soul is good
Zec 14: 6 no sunlight, no **c**, frosty darkness.
Mt 10:42 anyone gives even a cup of **c** water
24:12 the love of most will grow **c**,
Rev  3:16 neither hot nor **c**—I am about to spit

## COLLAPSE [COLLAPSED]
Jos  6: 5 the wall of the city will **c**
Mt 15:32 hungry, or they may **c** on the way."

## COLLAPSED [COLLAPSE]
Rev 11:13 earthquake and a tenth of the city **c**.
16:19 parts, and the cities of the nations **c**.

## COLLECT [COLLECTED,
COLLECTION, COLLECTOR,
COLLECTORS]
Ne 10:37 it is the Levites who **c** the tithes
Mk 12: 2 to the tenants to **c** from them some

## COLLECTED [COLLECT]
Mt 13:48 down and **c** the good fish in baskets,
Heb  7: 6 yet he **c** a tenth from Abraham

## COLLECTION* [COLLECT]
Isa 57:13 help, let your **c** of idols save you!
1Co 16: 1 about the **c** for the Lord's people:

## COLLECTOR [COLLECT]
Da 11:20 out a tax **c** to maintain the royal
Mt 10: 3 Thomas and Matthew the tax **c**;
Lk  5:27 and saw a tax **c** by the name of Levi
18:10 one a Pharisee and the other a tax **c**.
19: 2 he was a chief tax **c** and was

## TAX COLLECTOR See TAX

## COLLECTORS [COLLECT]
Mt  5:46 Are not even the tax **c** doing that?
9:10 many tax **c** and sinners came
11:19 a friend of tax **c** and sinners.'
17:24 the **c** of the two-drachma temple tax
21:32 but the tax **c** and the prostitutes did.

## TAX COLLECTORS See TAX

## COLONNADE*
1Ki  7: 6 He made a **c** fifty cubits long
Jn 10:23 courts walking in Solomon's **C**.
Ac  3:11 in the place called Solomon's **C**.
5:12 to meet together in Solomon's **C**.

## COLONY*
Ac 16:12 a Roman **c** and the leading city

## COLT
Ge 49:11 a vine, his **c** to the choicest branch;
Zec  9: 9 donkey, on a **c**, the foal of a donkey.
Mt 21: 5 a donkey, and on a **c**, the foal
Jn 12:15 is coming, seated on a donkey's **c**."

## COMB*
Pr 24:13 honey from the **c** is sweet to your
27: 7 is full loathes honey from the **c**,

## COME [CAME, COMES, COMING]
Ge  8:16 "**C** out of the ark, you and your
15:16 your descendants will **c** back here,
38:16 by the roadside and said, "**C** now,
39: 7 and said, "**C** to bed with me!"

Ge 50:24 But God will surely c to your aid
Ex   3: 5 "Do not c any closer," God said.
    19:11 that day the LORD will c down
    24: 1 to Moses, "C up to the LORD,
Nu  24:17 A star will c out of Jacob;
Dt  28: 2 All these blessings will c on you
    28:45 All these curses will c on you.
Jos 23:15 has promised you have c to you,
Ru   1: 6 that the LORD had c to the aid
1Sa  4: 7 "A god has c into the camp,"
2Sa  7:12 who will c from your own body,
Ps  14: 7 salvation for Israel would c
    17: 2 Let my vindication c from you;
    24: 7 that the King of glory may c in.
    31: 2 ear to me, c quickly to my rescue;
    40:13 c quickly, LORD, to help me.
    88: 2 May my prayer c before you;
    90:10 Our days may c to seventy years,
    91:10 no disaster will c near your tent.
   119:41 May your unfailing love c to me,
   121: 1 where does my help c from?
   132: 8 and c to your resting place,
   144: 5 your heavens, LORD, and c down;
Pr   2: 6 from his mouth c knowledge
     9: 4 "Let all who are simple c to my
    10:28 hopes of the wicked c to nothing.
    24:34 poverty will c on you like a thief
Ecc  1: 4 Generations c and generations go,
     9:12 one knows when their hour will c:
    11: 8 Everything to c is meaningless.
SS   2:13 Arise, c, my darling;
     2:13 my beautiful one, c with me."
Isa  1:18 "C now, let us reason together,"
    37:32 out of Jerusalem will c a remnant,
    41:22 Or declare to us the things to c,
    59:20 "The Redeemer will c to Zion,
Jer 51:45 "C out of her, my people!
Eze  7: 6 The end has c! The end has c!
    36: 8 Israel, for they will soon c home.
    37: 5 enter you, and you will c to life.
Hos  1:11 people of Israel will c together;
     3: 5 They will c trembling
Hab  2: 3 it will certainly c and will not delay.
Mal  3: 5 "So I will c to put you on trial.
Mt   2: 2 it rose and have c to worship him."
     4:19 "C, follow me," Jesus said, "and I
     6:10 your kingdom c, your will be done,
    10:34 suppose that I have c to bring peace
    10:34 I did not c to bring peace,
    12:28 the kingdom of God has c upon you.
    15:19 For out of the heart c evil thoughts,
    17:12 Elijah has already c, and they did
    18:20 two or three c together in my name,
    19:14 "Let the little children c to me,
    20:28 Son of Man did not c to be served,
    24: 5 For many will c in my name,
    27:40 C down from the cross, if you are
Jn   2: 4 "My hour has not yet c."
     6:37 whom the Father gives me will c
    12:23 "The hour has c for the Son of Man
    14: 3 I will c back and take you to be
Ac   1:11 will c back in the same way you
1Co 16:22 let that person be cursed! C, Lord!
Gal  4: 4 But when the set time had fully c,
2Th  2: 2 the day of the Lord has already c.
Heb 10: 9 I am, I have c to do your will."
    12:22 But you have c to Mount Zion,

Heb 12:22 You have c to thousands
Jas  4: 8 C near to God and he will c near
1Pe  2: 4 As you c to him, the living Stone—
2Pe  3: 9 but everyone to c to repentance.
1Jn  2:18 even now many antichrists have c.
     4: 2 that Jesus Christ has c in the flesh is
Rev  1: 4 and who is to c, and from the seven
     4: 8 who was, and is, and is to c."
    22:17 The Spirit and the bride say, "C!"
    22:17 And let those who hear say, "C!"
    22:17 Let those who are thirsty c;
    22:20 Amen. C, Lord Jesus.

## DAYS TO COME See DAYS

## COMES [COME]

1Ch 16:33 LORD, for he c to judge the earth.
    29:14 Everything c from you,
    29:14 and we have given you only what c
Ps   3: 8 From the LORD c deliverance.
    96:13 for he c, he c to judge the earth.
   118:26 Blessed is he who c in the name
   121: 2 My help c from the LORD,
Pr  10: 8 but a chattering fool c to ruin.
    11: 2 When pride c, then c disgrace,
    11: 2 but with humility c wisdom.
    11:27 but evil c to those who search for it.
    15:33 and humility c before honor.
Ecc  5:15 Everyone c naked from their
     5:15 and as everyone c, so they depart.
Isa 40:10 See, the Sovereign LORD c
Eze  7:10 " 'See, the day! See, it c!
Jnh  2: 9 'Salvation c from the LORD.' "
Zec 14: 7 When evening c, there will be light.
Mt  12:43 "When an evil spirit c
    21: 5 'See, your king c to you,
Mk  11: 9 "Blessed is he who c in the name
Lk  18: 8 when the Son of Man c, will he find
Jn   3:31 The one who c from above is
     3:31 The one who c from heaven is
     6:33 God is the bread that c down
    10:10 The thief c only to steal and kill
    14: 6 No one c to the Father except
    15:26 "When the Advocate c, whom I
    16:13 the Spirit of truth, c, he will guide
Ac   1: 8 when the Holy Spirit c on you;
Ro   4:13 through the righteousness that c
1Co 11:12 But everything c from God.
2Co  3: 5 but our competence c from God.
Php  3: 9 of my own that c from the law,
     3: 9 the righteousness that c from God
1Jn  2:21 and because no lie c from the truth.
     4: 7 one another, for love c from God.
2Jn  1:10 If anyone c to you and does not
Rev 11: 5 them, fire c from their mouths
    11: 7 the beast that c up from the Abyss

## COMFORT* [COMFORTED, COMFORTER, COMFORTERS, COMFORTING, COMFORTS]

Ge   5:29 said, "He will c us in the labor
    37:35 sons and daughters came to c him,
1Ch  7:22 and his relatives came to c him.
Job  2:11 and sympathize with him and c him.
     7:13 When I think my bed will c me
    16: 5 c from my lips would bring you

Job 36:16 to the **c** of your table laden
Ps 23: 4 your rod and your staff, they **c** me.
71:21 my honor and **c** me once more.
119:50 My **c** in my suffering is this:
119:52 ancient laws, and I find **c** in them.
119:76 May your unfailing love be my **c**,
119:82 I say, "When will you **c** me?"
Isa 40: 1 **C**, **c** my people, says your God.
51: 3 The Lord will surely **c** Zion
51:19 come upon you—who can **c** you?—
57:18 guide them and restore **c** to them,
61: 2 of our God, to **c** all who mourn,
66:13 comforts her child, so will I **c** you;
Jer 16: 7 offer food to **c** those who mourn
31:13 I will give them **c** and joy instead
La 1: 2 all her lovers there is none to **c** her.
1: 9 there was none to **c** her.
1:16 No one is near to **c** me, no one
1:17 hands, but there is no one to **c** her.
1:21 but there is no one to **c** me.
2:13 that I may **c** you, Virgin Daughter
Eze 16:54 all you have done in giving them **c**.
Na 3: 7 Where can I find anyone to **c** you?"
Zec 1:17 the Lord will again **c** Zion
10: 2 that are false, they give **c** in vain.
Lk 6:24 you have already received your **c**.
Jn 11:19 Mary to **c** them in the loss of their
1Co 14: 3 encouragement and **c**.
2Co 1: 3 of compassion and the God of all **c**,
1: 4 so that we can **c** those in any trouble
1: 4 with the **c** we ourselves receive
1: 5 also our **c** abounds through Christ.
1: 6 it is for your **c** and salvation;
1: 6 it is for your **c**, which produces
1: 7 so also you share in our **c**.
2: 7 you ought to forgive and **c** him,
7: 7 but also by the **c** you had given him.
Php 2: 1 Christ, if any **c** from his love, if any
Col 4:11 and they have proved a **c** to me.

## COMFORTED* [COMFORT]

Ge 24:67 Isaac was **c** after his mother's death.
37:35 comfort him, but he refused to be **c**.
2Sa 12:24 Then David **c** his wife Bathsheba,
Job 42:11 They **c** and consoled him over all
Ps 77: 2 hands, and I would not be **c**.
86:17 Lord, have helped me and **c** me.
Isa 12: 1 has turned away and you have **c** me.
52: 9 for the Lord has **c** his people,
54:11 lashed by storms and not **c**, I will
66:13 and you will be **c** over Jerusalem."
Jer 31:15 for her children and refusing to be **c**,
Mt 2:18 for her children and refusing to be **c**.
5: 4 those who mourn, for they will be **c**.
Lk 16:25 but now he is **c** here and you are
Ac 20:12 man home alive and were greatly **c**.
2Co 1: 6 if we are **c**, it is for your comfort,
7: 6 **c** us by the coming of Titus,

## COMFORTER* [COMFORT]

Ecc 4: 1 and they have no **c**; power was
4: 1 and they have no **c**.
Jer 8:18 You who are my **C** in sorrow,

## COMFORTER (KJV: of the Holy Spirit) See also ADVOCATE

## COMFORTERS* [COMFORT]

Job 16: 2 you are miserable **c**, all of you!
Ps 69:20 was none, for **c**, but I found none.

## COMFORTING* [COMFORT]

Isa 66:11 and be satisfied at her **c** breasts;
Zec 1:13 and **c** words to the angel who talked
Jn 11:31 been with Mary in the house, **c** her,
1Th 2:12 **c** and urging you to live lives

## COMFORTS* [COMFORT]

Job 29:25 I was like one who **c** mourners.
Isa 49:13 For the Lord **c** his people
51:12 "I, even I, am he who **c** you.
66:13 As a mother **c** her child, so will I
2Co 1: 4 who **c** us in all our troubles,
7: 6 But God, who **c** the downcast,

## COMING [COME]

Ex 32: 1 Moses was so long in **c** down
Ecc 10:14 No one knows what is **c**—
Isa 13: 9 See, the day of the Lord is **c**—
Jer 7:32 the days are **c**, declares the Lord,
Eze 43: 2 of the God of Israel **c** from the east.
Da 7:13 of man, **c** with the clouds of heaven.
Joel 2: 1 for the day of the Lord is **c**.
Mic 1: 3 The Lord is **c** from his dwelling
Zep 1:14 near and **c** quickly.
Mk 13:26 will see the Son of Man **c** in clouds
1Th 1:10 who rescues us from the **c** wrath.
2Th 2: 1 Concerning the **c** of our Lord Jesus
Heb 10:37 he who is **c** will come and will not
Jas 5: 8 firm, because the Lord's **c** is near.
2Pe 1:16 about the **c** of our Lord Jesus Christ
3: 4 "Where is this '**c**' he promised?
Jude 1:14 the Lord is **c** with thousands
Rev 1: 7 "Look, he is **c** with the clouds,"
3:11 I am **c** soon. Hold on to what you
13: 1 And I saw a beast **c** out of the sea.
19:15 **C** out of his mouth is a sharp sword
21: 2 **c** down out of heaven from God,
21:10 **c** down out of heaven from God.
22: 7 "Look, I am **c** soon!

## DAYS ARE COMING See DAYS

## COMMAND [COMMANDED, COMMANDER, COMMANDING, COMMANDMENT, COMMANDMENTS, COMMANDS]

Ex 7: 2 You are to say everything I **c** you,
34:11 Obey what I **c** you today.
Nu 14:41 are you disobeying the Lord's **c**?
24:13 to go beyond the **c** of the Lord—
Dt 4: 2 Do not add to what I **c** you and do
8: 1 to follow every **c** I am giving you
12:32 See that you do all I **c** you;
15:11 Therefore I **c** you to be openhanded
30:16 For I **c** you today to love
32:46 so that you may **c** your children
1Sa 13:14 you have not kept the Lord's **c**."

1Ki 11:10 did not keep the LORD's **c**.
Ps 91:11 he will **c** his angels concerning you
148: 5 for at his **c** they were created,
Pr 6:23 For this **c** is a lamp,
8:29 the waters would not overstep his **c**,
13:13 whoever respects a **c** is rewarded.
Ecc 8: 2 Obey the king's **c**, I say,
Jer 1: 7 you to and say whatever I **c** you.
1:17 and say to them whatever I **c** you.
7:23 but I gave them this **c**:
7:23 Walk in obedience to all I **c** you,
11: 4 me and do everything I **c** you,
26: 2 Tell them everything I **c** you;
La 1:18 yet I rebelled against his **c**.
Joel 2:11 mighty is the army that obeys his **c**.
Mt 4: 6 " 'He will **c** his angels concerning
15: 3 why do you break the **c** of God
Lk 4:10 " 'He will **c** his angels concerning
Jn 10:18 This **c** I received from my Father."
12:50 I know that his **c** leads to eternal
13:34 "A new **c** I give you:
15:12 My **c** is this: Love each other as I
15:14 are my friends if you do what I **c**.
15:17 This is my **c**: Love each other.
Ro 13: 9 are summed up in this one **c**:
1Co 14:37 I am writing to you is the Lord's **c**.
Gal 5:14 is fulfilled in keeping this one **c**:
1Ti 1: 5 The goal of this **c** is love,
1:18 giving you this **c** in keeping
6:14 to keep this **c** without spot or blame
6:17 **C** those who are rich in this present
Heb 9:19 Moses had proclaimed every **c** of the
11: 3 the universe was formed at God's **c**,
2Pe 2:21 on the sacred **c** that was passed
3: 2 and the **c** given by our Lord
1Jn 2: 7 I am not writing you a new **c**
2: 7 This old **c** is the message you have
3:23 And this is his **c**: to believe
4:21 And he has given us this **c**:
2Jn 1: 6 his **c** is that you walk in love.
Rev 3:10 Since you have kept my **c** to endure

## COMMANDED [COMMAND]

Ge 2:16 And the LORD God **c** the man,
3:11 from the tree that I **c** you not to eat
7: 5 Noah did all that the LORD **c** him.
50:12 Jacob's sons did as he had **c** them:
Ex 7: 6 did just as the LORD **c** them.
19: 7 all the words the LORD had **c** him
Dt 4: 5 laws as the LORD my God **c** me,
6:24 The LORD **c** us to obey all these
18:20 in my name anything I have not **c**,
Jos 1: 9 Have I not **c** you? Be strong
1:16 "Whatever you have **c** us we will
2Sa 5:25 So David did as the LORD **c** him,
2Ki 17:13 entire Law that I **c** your ancestors
21: 8 be careful to do everything I **c** them
2Ch 33: 8 do everything I **c** them concerning
Ps 33: 9 came to be; he **c**, and it stood firm.
78: 5 which he **c** our ancestors to teach
Isa 13: 3 I have **c** my holy ones;
Am 2:12 and **c** the prophets not to prophesy.
Jnh 2:10 And the LORD **c** the fish, and it
Mt 28:20 to obey everything I have **c** you.
Lk 8:29 For Jesus had **c** the evil spirit
Jn 12:49 the Father who sent me **c** me to say
14:31 exactly what my Father has **c** me.

Ac 10:42 He **c** us to preach to the people
1Co 9:14 way, the Lord has **c** that those who
1Jn 3:23 and to love one another as he **c** us.
2Jn 1: 4 in the truth, just as the Father **c** us.

## AS THE †LORD ... COMMANDED See
†LORD

## COMMANDER [COMMAND]

Jos 5:15 The **c** of the LORD's army replied,
2Ki 18:17 king of Assyria sent his supreme **c**,
18:17 and his field **c** with a large army,
Da 8:11 great as the **c** of the army

## COMMANDING [COMMAND]

Dt 30:11 Now what I am **c** you today is not
2Ti 2: 4 they try to please their **c** officer.

## COMMANDMENT* [COMMAND]

Jos 22: 5 be very careful to keep the **c**
Mt 22:36 which is the greatest **c** in the Law?"
22:38 This is the first and greatest **c**.
Mk 12:31 There is no **c** greater than these."
Lk 23:56 the Sabbath in obedience to the **c**.
Ro 7: 8 the opportunity afforded by the **c**,
7: 9 but when the **c** came, sin sprang
7:10 that the very **c** that was intended
7:11 the opportunity afforded by the **c**,
7:11 and through the **c** put me to death.
7:12 and the **c** is holy,
7:13 that through the **c** sin might become
Eph 6: 2 which is the first **c** with a promise—

## COMMANDMENTS* [COMMAND]

Ex 20: 6 those who love me and keep my **c**.
24:12 **c** I have written for their instruction."
34:28 words of the covenant—the Ten **C**.
Dt 4:13 the Ten **C**, which he commanded
5:10 those who love me and keep my **c**.
5:22 These are the **c** the LORD
6: 6 These **c** that I give you today are
7: 9 of those who love him and keep his **c**.
9:10 On them were all the **c** the LORD
10: 4 the Ten **C** he had proclaimed to you
Ne 1: 5 those who love him and keep his **c**,
Ecc 12:13 Fear God and keep his **c**, for this is
Da 9: 4 who love him and keep his **c**,
Mt 19:17 you want to enter life, keep the **c**."
22:40 the Prophets hang on these two **c**."
Mk 10:19 You know the **c**: 'You shall not
12:28 "Of all the **c**, which is the most
Lk 18:20 You know the **c**: 'You shall not
Ro 13: 9 The **c**, "You shall not commit

## COMMANDS [COMMAND]

Ge 26: 5 keeping my **c**, my decrees and my
Ex 25:22 give you all my **c** for the Israelites.
34:32 gave them all the **c** the LORD had
Lev 4: 2 in any of the LORD's **c**—
22:31 "Keep my **c** and follow them.
26: 3 and are careful to obey my **c**,
26:15 and fail to carry out all my **c** and so
Nu 15:39 so you will remember all the **c**
Dt 5:29 fear me and keep all my **c** always,
7:11 take care to follow the **c**,
11: 1 decrees, his laws and his **c** always.

Dt 11:28 if you disobey the c of the LORD
    28: 1 carefully follow all his c I give you
    30:10 and keep his c and decrees that are
Jos 22: 5 to keep his c, to hold fast to him
Jdg 3: 4 they would obey the LORD's c,
1Sa 12:14 him and do not rebel against his c,
1Ki 2: 3 and keep his decrees and c, his laws
    8:58 in obedience to him and keep the c,
    8:61 live by his decrees and obey his c,
1Ch 28: 7 is unswerving in carrying out my c
    29:19 devotion to keep your c,
2Ch 31:21 in obedience to the law and the c,
Ezr 9:10 For we have forsaken the c
Ps 19: 8 The c of the LORD are radiant,
    78: 7 his deeds but would keep his c.
    112: 1 who find great delight in his c.
    119:10 do not let me stray from your c.
    119:32 I run in the path of your c, for you
    119:35 Direct me in the path of your c,
    119:47 in your c because I love them.
    119:48 I reach out for your c, which I love,
    119:73 me understanding to learn your c.
    119:86 All your c are trustworthy;
    119:96 a limit, but your c are boundless.
    119:98 Your c are always with me
    119:115 that I may keep the c of my God!
    119:127 I love your c more than gold,
    119:131 mouth and pant, longing for your c.
    119:143 me, but your c give me delight.
    119:151 LORD, and all your c are true.
    119:172 word, for all your c are righteous.
    119:176 for I have not forgotten your c.
Pr 2: 1 words and store up my c within you,
    3: 1 but keep my c in your heart,
    7: 2 Keep my c and you will live;
    10: 8 The wise in heart accept c,
Isa 48:18 only you had paid attention to my c,
Jer 7:22 I did not just give them c
Mt 5:19 sets aside one of the least of these c
    5:19 teaches these c will be called great
Mk 7: 9 way of setting aside the c of God
Lk 1: 6 observing all the Lord's c and decrees
Jn 14:15 "If you love me, keep my c.
    14:21 Whoever has my c and keeps them
    15:10 If you keep my c, you will remain
    15:10 just as I have kept my Father's c
Ac 17:30 now he c all people everywhere
1Co 7:19 Keeping God's c is what counts.
Eph 2:15 in his flesh the law with its c
Col 2:22 are based on merely human c
1Jn 2: 3 come to know him if we keep his c.
    2: 4 but do not do what he c are liars,
    3:22 because we keep his c and do what
    3:24 Those who keep his c live in him,
    5: 2 loving God and carrying out his c.
    5: 3 his c. And his c are not burdensome.
2Jn 1: 6 that we walk in obedience to his c.
Rev 12:17 those who keep God's c and hold fast
    14:12 people of God who keep his c and

## COMMANDS OF THE †LORD Lev 4:22;
Nu 15:39; Dt 4:2; 6:17; 8:6; 11:27, 28; 28:9, 13;
2Ki 17:16, 19; 1Ch 28:8; Ps 19:8

## COMMEMORATE
Ex 12:14 "This is a day you are to c;

## COMMEND* [COMMENDABLE, COMMENDED, COMMENDS]
Ecc 8:15 So I c the enjoyment of life,
Ro 16: 1 I c to you our sister Phoebe,
2Co 3: 1 we beginning to c ourselves again?
    4: 2 the truth plainly we c ourselves
    5:12 We are not trying to c ourselves
    6: 4 God we c ourselves in every way:
    10:12 with some who c themselves.
2Co 10:18 who c themselves who are approved,
1Pe 2:14 wrong and to c those who do right.

## COMMENDABLE* [COMMEND]
1Pe 2:19 For it is c if you bear up under
    2:20 you endure it, this is c before God.

## COMMENDED* [COMMEND]
Ne 11: 2 The people c all who volunteered
Job 29:11 of me, and those who saw me c me,
Lk 16: 8 "The master c the dishonest
Ac 15:40 c by the believers to the grace
Ro 13: 3 do what is right and you will be c.
2Co 12:11 I ought to have been c by you,
Heb 11: 2 This is what the ancients were c for.
    11: 4 By faith he was c as righteous,
    11: 5 he was c as one who pleased God.
    11:39 These were all c for their faith,

## COMMENDS* [COMMEND]
Ps 145: 4 One generation c your works
2Co 10:18 but those whom the Lord c.

## COMMISSION
Dt 3:28 But c Joshua, and encourage
Col 1:25 its servant by the c God gave me

## COMMIT [COMMITS, COMMITTED]
Ex 20:14 "You shall not c adultery.
Dt 5:18 "You shall not c adultery.
1Sa 7: 3 and c yourselves to the LORD
1Ki 14:16 and has caused Israel to c.
2Ki 21:16 sin that he had caused Judah to c,
Ps 31: 5 Into your hands I c my spirit;
    37: 5 C your way to the LORD;
Pr 16: 3 C to the LORD whatever you do,
Mt 5:27 was said, 'You shall not c adultery.'
    19:18 you shall not c adultery, you shall
Mk 10:19 you shall not c adultery, you shall
Lk 18:20 'You shall not c adultery, you shall
    23:46 into your hands I c my spirit."
Ac 20:32 "Now I c you to God
Ro 2:22 not c adultery, do you c adultery?
    13: 9 "You shall not c adultery,"
1Co 10: 8 We should not c sexual immorality,
Jas 2:11 "You shall not c adultery,"
    2:11 If you do not c adultery but do c
1Pe 4:19 to God's will should c themselves
1Jn 5:16 or sister c a sin that does not lead
Rev 2:22 I will make those who c adultery

## COMMITS [COMMIT]
Lev 20:10 a man c adultery with another man's
Pr 6:32 a man who c adultery has no sense;
    29:22 a hot-tempered person c many sins.
Ecc 8:12 a wicked person who c a hundred

Eze 18:14 who sees all the sins his father **c**,
     22:11 you one man **c** a detestable offense
Mt   5:32 the divorced woman **c** adultery."
     19: 9 marries another woman **c** adultery."
Mk 10:11 another woman **c** adultery against
     10:12 another man, she **c** adultery."
Lk 16:18 marries another woman **c** adultery,
     16:18 a divorced woman **c** adultery.

## COMMITTED [COMMIT]

Ge 50:17 the wrongs they **c** in treating you so
Ex 32:30 the people, "You have **c** a great sin.
Nu   5: 7 must confess the sin they have **c**.
Jdg 20: 6 because they **c** this lewd
1Ki  8:61 may your hearts be fully **c**
     15:14 Asa's heart was fully **c**
2Ch 16: 9 those whose hearts are fully **c**
Jer   2:13 "My people have **c** two sins:
     3: 9 the land and **c** adultery with stone
Eze 18:24 of the sins they have **c**, they will die.
Mt   5:28 lustfully has already **c** adultery
     11:27 "All things have been **c** to me
     27:23 What crime has he **c**?" asked Pilate.
Lk 10:22 "All things have been **c** to me
Ac 14:23 and fasting, **c** them to the Lord,
Ro   1:27 Men **c** shameful acts with other
     3:25 the sins **c** beforehand unpunished—
1Co  9:17 I am simply discharging the trust **c**
2Co  5:19 And he has **c** to us the message
1Pe  2:22 "He **c** no sin, and no deceit was
Rev 17: 2 her the kings of the earth **c** adultery,
     18: 3 of the earth **c** adultery with her,

## COMMON

Ge 11: 1 had one language and a **c** speech.
Lev 10:10 between the holy and the **c**,
Pr 22: 2 Rich and poor have this in **c**:
     29:13 and the oppressor have this in **c**:
Ecc  9: 2 All share a **c** destiny—
Eze 22:26 between the holy and the **c**;
Ac   2:44 together and had everything in **c**.
1Co 10:13 has overtaken you except what is **c**
     12: 7 of the Spirit is given for the **c** good.
2Co  6:14 and wickedness have in **c**?
     6:15 what does a believer have in **c**

## COMMUNION See FELLOWSHIP, PARTICIPATION

## COMMUNITY

Ge 28: 3 your numbers until you become a **c**
     35:11 a **c** of nations will come from you,
     48: 4 I will make you a **c** of peoples, and I
Ex   2: 2 desert the whole **c** grumbled against
Lev  4:13 " 'If the whole Israelite **c** sins
     4:13 even though the **c** is unaware
Nu 14:27 will this wicked **c** grumble against
Pr   6:19 stirs up dissension in the **c**.

## COMPANION [COMPANIONS]

1Ki 20:35 of the prophets said to his **c**,
Job 30:29 a brother of jackals, a **c** of owls.
Ps 55:13 like myself, my **c**, my close friend,
     55:20 My **c** attacks his friends;
Pr 13:20 wise, for a **c** of fools suffers harm.

Pr 29: 3 but a **c** of prostitutes squanders his
Rev  1: 9 your brother and **c** in the suffering

## COMPANIONS [COMPANION]

Ps 38:11 **c** avoid me because of my wounds;
     45: 7 you above your **c** by anointing you
Pr 28: 7 **c** of gluttons disgrace their parents.
Heb  1: 9 you above your **c** by anointing you

## COMPANY

2Ki  2: 7 men from the **c** of the prophets went
     4:38 While the **c** of the prophets was
     4:38 pot and cook some stew for this **c**."
Ps 14: 5 is present in the **c** of the righteous.
Pr 21:16 comes to rest in the **c** of the dead.
     24: 1 the wicked, do not desire their **c**;
Jer 15:17 I never sat in the **c** of revelers,
Lk   2:13 Suddenly a great **c** of the heavenly
1Co 15:33 "Bad **c** corrupts good character."

## COMPARE* [COMPARED, COMPARING, COMPARISON]

Job 28:17 Neither gold nor crystal can **c**
     28:19 The topaz of Cush cannot **c** with it;
     39:13 though they cannot **c** with the wings
Ps 40: 5 None can **c** with you;
     86: 8 no deeds can **c** with yours.
     89: 6 skies above can **c** with the LORD?
Pr   3:15 nothing you desire can **c** with her.
     8:11 nothing you desire can **c** with her.
Isa 40:18 With whom, then, will you **c** God?
     40:25 "To whom will you **c** me?
     46: 5 "With whom will you **c** me
La   2:13 With what can I **c** you,
Eze 31: 8 nor could the plane trees **c** with its
Da   1:13 **c** our appearance
Mt 11:16 "To what can I **c** this generation?
Lk   7:31 what, then, can I **c** the people of this
     13:18 of God like? What shall I **c** it to?
     13:20 "What shall I **c** the kingdom of God
2Co 10:12 or **c** ourselves with some who
     10:12 and **c** themselves with themselves,

## COMPARED* [COMPARE]

Jdg  8: 2 "What have I accomplished **c**
     8: 3 What was I able to do **c** to you?"
Isa 46: 5 will you liken me that we may be **c**?
Eze 31: 2 " 'Who can be **c** with you
     31:18 the trees of Eden can be **c** with you
Ro   5:16 Nor can the gift of God be **c** with

## COMPARING* [COMPARE]

Ro   8:18 present sufferings are not worth **c**
2Co  8: 8 of your love by **c** it
Gal  6: 4 without **c** yourself to somebody

## COMPARISON* [COMPARE]

2Co  3:10 was glorious has no glory now in **c**

## COMPASSION* [COMPASSIONATE, COMPASSIONS]

Ex 33:19 I will have **c** on whom I will have **c**.
Dt 13:17 show you mercy, have **c** on you,
     28:54 man among you will have no **c**
     30: 3 your fortunes and have **c** on you

2Ki 13:23 had c and showed concern for them
2Ch 30: 9 your children will be shown c
Ne  9:19 of your great c you did not abandon
     9:27 and in your great c you gave them
     9:28 in your c you delivered them time
Ps  51: 1 to your great c blot out my
    77: 9 Has he in anger withheld his c?"
    90:13 will it be? Have c on your servants.
   102:13 You will arise and have c on Zion,
   103: 4 pit and crowns you with love and c,
   103:13 As a father has c on his children,
   103:13 so the LORD has c on those who
   116: 5 our God is full of c.
   119:77 Let your c come to me that I may
  119:156 Your c, LORD, is great;
   145: 9 he has c on all he has made.
Isa 13:18 infants, nor will they look with c
    14: 1 The LORD will have c on Jacob;
    27:11 so their Maker has no c on them,
    30:18 he will rise up to show you c.
    49:10 He who has c on them will guide
    49:13 will have c on his afflicted ones.
    49:15 and have no c on the child she has
    51: 3 and will look with c on all her ruins;
    54: 7 with deep c I will bring you back.
    54: 8 everlasting kindness I will have c
    54:10 says the LORD, who has c on you.
    60:10 you, in favor I will show you c.
    63: 7 Israel, according to his c and many
    63:15 and c are withheld from us.
Jer 12:15 I will again have c and will bring
    13:14 or c to keep me from destroying
    21: 7 show them no mercy or pity or c.'
    30:18 tents and have c on his dwellings;
    31:20 I have great c for him,"
    33:26 fortunes and have c on them.' "
    42:12 you c so that he will have c on you
La   3:32 grief, he will show c, so great is his
Eze  9: 5 and kill, without showing pity or c.
    16: 5 or had c enough to do any of these
    39:25 and will have c on all the people
Da   1: 9 to show favor and c to Daniel,
Hos  2:19 and justice, in love and c.
    11: 8 all my c is aroused.
    13:14 "I will have no c,
    14: 3 for in you the fatherless find c."
Jnh  3: 9 with c turn from his fierce anger so
Mic  7:19 You will again have c on us;
Zec  7: 9 show mercy and c to one another.
    10: 6 I will restore them because I have c
Mal  3:17 just as a father has c and spares his
Mt   9:36 saw the crowds, he had c on them,
    14:14 he had c on them and healed their
    15:32 and said, "I have c for these people;
    20:34 Jesus had c on them and touched
Mk   6:34 a large crowd, he had c on them,
     8: 2 "I have c for these people;
Lk  15:20 him and was filled with c for him;
Ro   9:15 I will have c on whom I have c."
2Co  1: 3 the Father of c and the God of all
Php  2: 1 the Spirit, if any tenderness and c,
Col  3:12 clothe yourselves with c, kindness,
Jas  5:11 The Lord is full of c and mercy.

## COMPASSIONATE* [COMPASSION]
Ex  22:27 out to me, I will hear, for I am c.
    34: 6 LORD, the c and gracious God,
2Ch 30: 9 LORD your God is gracious and c.
Ne   9:17 gracious and c, slow to anger
Ps  86:15 you, Lord, are a c and gracious God,
   103: 8 The LORD is c and gracious,
   111: 4 the LORD is gracious and c.
   112: 4 for those who are gracious and c
   145: 8 The LORD is gracious and c,
La   4:10 their own hands c women have
Joel 2:13 for he is gracious and c,
Jnh  4: 2 that you are a gracious and c God,
Eph  4:32 Be kind and c to one another,
1Pe  3: 8 love one another, be c and humble.

## COMPASSIONS* [COMPASSION]
La   3:22 not consumed, for his c never fail.

## COMPEL [COMPELLED, COMPELS, COMPULSION]
Lk  14:23 country lanes and c them to come

## COMPELLED [COMPEL]
Ac  20:22 "And now, c by the Spirit, I am
1Co  9:16 cannot boast, since I am c to preach.

## COMPELS* [COMPEL]
Ex   3:19 you go unless a mighty hand c him.
Job 32:18 and the spirit within me c me;
2Co  5:14 For Christ's love c us, because we

## COMPETENCE* [COMPETENT]
2Co  3: 5 but our c comes from God.

## COMPETENT* [COMPETENCE]
Ro  15:14 and c to instruct one another.
1Co  6: 2 are you not c to judge trivial cases?
2Co  3: 5 Not that we are c in ourselves
     3: 6 He has made us c as ministers

## COMPETES*
1Co  9:25 Everyone who c in the games goes
2Ti  2: 5 anyone who c as an athlete does not

## COMPILED*
Pr  25: 1 c by the men of Hezekiah king of Judah

## COMPLACENCY* [COMPLACENT]
Pr   1:32 and the c of fools will destroy them;
Eze 30: 9 ships to frighten Cush out of her c.

## COMPLACENT* [COMPLACENCY]
Isa 32: 9 You women who are so c,
    32:11 Tremble, you c women;
Am   6: 1 Woe to you who are c in Zion,
Zep  1:12 lamps and punish those who are c,

## COMPLAIN [COMPLAINED, COMPLAINT, COMPLAINTS]
Job  7:11 I will c in the bitterness of my soul.
Isa 29:24 those who c will accept

Isa 40:27  Why do you **c**, Jacob? Why do you
La  3:39  Why should the living **c**

## COMPLAINED [COMPLAIN]
Nu 11: 1  Now the people **c** about their

## COMPLAINT [COMPLAIN]
Job 10: 1  I will give free rein to my **c**
Ps  64: 1  Hear me, my God, as I voice my **c**;
    142: 2  I pour out before him my **c**;
Hab  2: 1  what answer I am to give to this **c**.

## COMPLAINTS* [COMPLAIN]
Nu 14:27  I have heard the **c** of these
Pr 23:29  Who has **c**? Who has needless

## COMPLETE [COMPLETED, COMPLETELY, COMPLETENESS, COMPLETION]
Dt  16:15  your hands, and your joy will be **c**.
2Ki 12:15  because they acted with **c** honesty.
Jn   3:29  That joy is mine, and it is now **c**.
    15:11  in you and that your joy may be **c**.
    16:24  will receive, and your joy will be **c**.
    17:23  that they may be brought to **c** unity.
Ac  20:24  **c** the task the Lord Jesus has given
2Co  7:16  I am glad I can have **c** confidence
    10: 6  once your obedience is **c**.
Php  2: 2  then make my joy **c** by being
Col  4:17  you **c** the work you have received
Jas  1: 4  so that you may be mature and **c**,
     2:22  his faith was made **c** by what he did.
1Jn  1: 4  We write this to make our joy **c**.
     2: 5  for God is truly made **c** in them.
     4:12  in us and his love is made **c** in us.
     4:17  is how love is made **c** among us so
2Jn  1:12  to face, so that our joy may be **c**.

## COMPLETED [COMPLETE]
Ge   2: 1  and the earth were **c** in all their vast
Ex  39:32  the tent of meeting, was **c**.
1Ki  6:14  Solomon built the temple and **c** it.
2Ch 36:21  until the seventy years were **c**
Ezr  6:15  The temple was **c** on the third day
Ne   6:15  So the wall was **c**
Isa 40:   her that her hard service has been **c**,
Jer 29:10  seventy years are **c** for Babylon,
Da  11:36  until the time of wrath is **c**, for what
    12: 7  broken, all these things will be **c**."
Lk  12:50  constraint I am under until it is **c**!
Rev 15: 1  because with them God's wrath is **c**.

## COMPLETELY [COMPLETE]
Ex  11: 1  he does, he will drive you out **c**.
Nu  21: 3  They **c** destroyed them and their
Jos 17:13  labor but did not drive them out **c**.
Jdg  1:28  labor but never drove them out **c**.
1Sa 15: 9  they were unwilling to destroy **c**,
Ps  37:28  Wrongdoers will be **c** destroyed;
Jer 14:19  Have you rejected Judah **c**?
    30:11  'Though I **c** destroy all the nations
    30:11  scatter you, I will not **c** destroy you.
Mk   3: 5  it out, and his hand was **c** restored.
     4:39  wind died down and it was **c** calm.
Ac   3:16  through him that has **c** healed him,

2Pe  1:19  message as something **c** reliable,

## COMPLETENESS* [COMPLETE]
1Co 13:10  but when **c** comes,

## COMPLETION [COMPLETE]
Php  1: 6  on to **c** until the day of Christ Jesus.

## COMPLIMENTS*
Pr  23: 8  eaten and will have wasted your **c**.

## COMPREHEND* [COMPREHENDED, COMPREHENDS]
Ecc  8:17  No one can **c** what goes on under
     8:17  they know, they cannot really **c** it.

## COMPREHENDED* [COMPREHEND]
Job 38:18  Have you **c** the vast expanses

## COMPREHENDS* [COMPREHEND]
Job 28:13  No mortal **c** its worth; it cannot be

## COMPULSION* [COMPEL]
1Co  7:37  who is under no **c** but has control
2Co  9: 7  not reluctantly or under **c**, for God

## CONCEAL [CONCEALED, CONCEALS]
Ps  40:10  I do not **c** your love and your
Pr  25: 2  It is the glory of God to **c** a matter;
    28:13  Those who **c** their sins do not prosper,
Isa 26:21  the earth will **c** its slain no longer.

## CONCEALED [CONCEAL]
Isa 49: 2  arrow and **c** me in his quiver.
Jer 16:17  me, nor is their sin **c** from my eyes.
Mt  10:26  There is nothing **c** that will not be
Mk   4:22  whatever is **c** is meant to be brought
Lk   8:17  nothing **c** that will not be known
    12: 2  There is nothing **c** that will not be

## CONCEALS* [CONCEAL]
Pr  10:11  the mouth of the wicked **c** violence.
    10:18  Whoever **c** hatred with lying lips

## CONCEIT* [CONCEITED, CONCEITS]
Isa 16: 6  her overweening pride and **c**,
Jer 48:29  her overweening pride and **c**,
Php  2: 3  out of selfish ambition or vain **c**.

## CONCEITED* [CONCEIT]
1Sa 17:28  I know how **c** you are and how
2Co 12: 7  order to keep me from becoming **c**,
Gal  5:26  Let us not become **c**,
1Ti  3: 6  he may become **c** and fall under
     6: 4  they are **c** and understand nothing.
2Ti  3: 4  rash, **c**, lovers of pleasure rather

## CONCEITS* [CONCEIT]
Ps 73: 7 the evil c of their minds know no

## CONCEIVE [CONCEIVED, CONCEIVING]
Ge 29:31 he enabled her to c,
30:22 to her and enabled her to c.
Nu 11:12 Did I c all these people? Did I give
Job 15:35 They c trouble and give birth
Ps 7:14 Those who are pregnant with evil c trouble
Isa 33:11 You c chaff, you give birth to straw;

## CONCEIVED [CONCEIVE]
Ps 51: 5 from the time my mother c me.
Isa 8: 3 and she c and gave birth to a son.
Mt 1:20 because what is c in her is
1Co 2: 9 and what no human mind has c—
Jas 1:15 after desire has c, it gives birth

## CONCEIVING* [CONCEIVE]
Ge 20:18 c because of Abraham's wife Sarah.

## CONCERN* [CONCERNED]
Ge 39: 6 he did not c himself with anything
39: 8 "my master does not c himself
1Sa 23:21 LORD bless you for your c for me.
2Ki 13:23 showed c for them because of his
Job 9:21 blameless, I have no c for myself;
19: 4 my error remains my c alone.
Ps 131: 1 I do not c myself with great matters
Pr 29: 7 but the wicked have no such c.
Eze 36:21 I had c for my holy name,
Jnh 4:11 not have c for the great city Nineveh,
Ac 18:17 and Gallio showed no c whatever.
1Co 7:32 I would like you to be free from c.
12:25 that its parts should have equal c
2Co 7: 7 deep sorrow, your ardent c for me,
7:11 what c, what readiness to see justice
8:16 of Titus the same c I have for you.
11:28 of my c for all the churches.
Php 2:20 show genuine c for your welfare.
4:10 at last you renewed your c for me.

## CONCERNED [CONCERN]
Ex 2:25 the Israelites and was c about them.
3: 7 and I am c about their suffering.
4:31 that the LORD was c about them
Ps 142: 4 at my right hand; no one is c for me.
Eze 36: 9 I am c for you and will look on you
Jnh 4:10 "You have been c about this gourd,
1Co 7:32 An unmarried man is c
9: 9 Is it about oxen that God is c?
Php 4:10 Indeed, you were c, but you had no

## CONCESSION*
1Co 7: 6 I say this as a c, not as a command.

## CONCUBINE [CONCUBINES]
Ge 35:22 and slept with his father's c Bilhah,
Jdg 19: 9 the man, with his c and his servant,
2Sa 3: 7 had had a c named Rizpah daughter
3: 7 did you sleep with my father's c?"

## CONCUBINES [CONCUBINE]
Ge 25: 6 he gave gifts to the sons of his c
2Sa 5:13 David took more c and wives
1Ki 11: 3 of royal birth and three hundred c,
Da 5: 3 wives and his c drank from them.

## CONDEMN* [CONDEMNATION, CONDEMNED, CONDEMNING, CONDEMNS, SELF-CONDEMNED]
Job 9:20 innocent, my mouth would c me;
34:17 Will you c the just and mighty One?
34:29 if he remains silent, who can c him?
40: 8 Would you c me to justify yourself?
Ps 94:21 and c the innocent to death.
109: 7 guilty, and may his prayers c him.
109:31 lives from those who would c them.
Isa 50: 9 Who will c me? They will all wear
Mt 12:41 with this generation and c it;
12:42 with this generation and c it;
20:18 of the law. They will c him to death
Mk 10:33 They will c him to death and will
Lk 6:37 Do not c, and you will not be
11:31 of this generation and c them,
11:32 with this generation and c it,
Jn 3:17 Son into the world to c the world,
7:51 "Does our law c a man without first
8:11 "Then neither do I c you,"
12:48 words I have spoken will c them
Ro 2:27 yet obeys the law will c you who,
8:34 Who then can c? No one.
14:22 are those who do not c themselves
2Co 7: 3 I do not say this to c you;
1Jn 3:20 If our hearts c us, we know that God
3:21 if our hearts do not c us, we have
Jude 1: 9 dare to c him for slander but said,

## CONDEMNATION* [CONDEMN]
Eze 33:12 former wickedness will not bring c.
Ro 3: 8 good may result"? Their c is just!
5:16 followed one sin and brought c,
5:18 just as one trespass resulted in c
8: 1 there is now no c for those who are
2Co 3: 9 ministry that brought c was glorious,
2Pe 2: 3 Their c has long been hanging over
Jude 1: 4 individuals whose c was written

## CONDEMNED* [CONDEMN]
Dt 13:17 of those c things shall be found
Job 32: 3 to refute Job, and yet had c him.
Ps 34:21 the foes of the righteous will be c.
34:22 who takes refuge in him will be c.
37:33 let them be c when brought to trial.
79:11 your strong arm preserve those c
102:20 and release those c to death."
Mt 12: 7 you would not have c the innocent.
12:37 and by your words you will be c."
23:33 How will you escape being c
27: 3 saw that Jesus was c, he was seized
Mk 14:64 They all c him as worthy of death.
16:16 but whoever does not believe will be c.
Lk 6:37 not condemn, and you will not be c.
Jn 3:18 Whoever believes in him is not c,
3:18 not believe stands c already because
5:29 done what is evil will rise to be c.
8:10 where are they? Has no one c you?"

Jn    16:11  prince of this world now stands **c**.
Ac    25:15  against him and asked that he be **c**.
Ro     3: 7  glory, why am I still **c** as a sinner?"
       8: 3  And so he **c** sin in human flesh,
      14:23  those who have doubts are **c** if they
1Co    4: 9  like those **c** to die in the arena.
      11:32  that we will not be finally **c**
Gal    2:11  because he stood **c**.
Col    2:14  which stood against us and **c** us;
2Th    2:12  all will be **c** who have not believed
Tit    2: 8  of speech that cannot be **c**,
Heb   11: 7  By his faith he **c** the world
Jas    5: 6  You have **c** and murdered
       5:12  Otherwise you will be **c**.
2Pe    2: 6  if he **c** the cities of Sodom
Rev   19: 2  He has **c** the great prostitute who

## CONDEMNING* [CONDEMN]

Dt    25: 1  the innocent and **c** the guilty.
1Ki    8:32  **c** the guilty by bringing down
2Ch    6:23  **c** the guilty and bringing down
Pr    17:15  the guilty and **c** the innocent—
Ac    13:27  yet in **c** him they fulfilled the words
Ro     2: 1  you are **c** yourself, because you who

## CONDEMNS* [CONDEMN]

Job   15: 6  Your own mouth **c** you, not mine;
Pr    12: 2  but he **c** those who devise wicked
      14:34  but sin **c** any people.

## CONDITION

Mt    12:45  the final **c** of that person is worse

## CONDUCT [CONDUCTED, SAFE-
CONDUCT]

Job   34:11  on them what their **c** deserves.
Ps   112: 5  who **c** their affairs with justice.
Pr    20:11  so is their **c** really pure and upright?
      21: 8  but the **c** of the innocent is upright.
Ecc    6: 8  how to **c** themselves before others?
Jer    4:18  "Your own **c** and actions have
       6:15  they ashamed of their detestable **c**?
      17:10  everyone according to their **c**,
Eze    7: 3  I will judge you according to your **c**
1Ti    3:15  how people ought to **c** themselves
       4:12  in **c**, in love, in faith and in purity.

## CONDUCTED* [CONDUCT]

2Co    1:12  we have **c** ourselves in the world,

## CONFESS* [CONFESSED,
CONFESSES, CONFESSING,
CONFESSION]

Lev    5: 5  they must **c** in what way they have
      16:21  goat and **c** over it all the wickedness
      26:40  if they will **c** their sins and the sins
Nu     5: 7  must **c** the sin they have committed
Ne     1: 6  I **c** the sins we Israelites,
Ps    32: 5  "I will **c** my transgressions
      38:18  I **c** my iniquity; I am troubled by my
Pr    28:13  who **c** and renounce them find mercy.
Jn     1:20  He did not fail to **c**, but confessed
Ro    14:11  every tongue will **c** to God.' "
Jas    5:16  Therefore **c** your sins to each other
1Jn    1: 9  If we **c** our sins, he is faithful

## CONFESSED* [CONFESS]

1Sa    7: 6  day they fasted and there they **c**,
Ne     9: 2  stood in their places and **c** their sins
Da     9: 4  to the LORD my God and **c**:
Jn     1:20  confess, but **c** freely, "I am not
Ac    19:18  and openly **c** what they had done.

## CONFESSES* [CONFESS]

2Ti    2:19  "Everyone who **c** the name

## CONFESSING* [CONFESS]

Ezr   10: 1  While Ezra was praying and **c**,
Da     9:20  **c** my sin and the sin of my people
Mt     3: 6  **C** their sins, they were baptized
Mk     1: 5  **C** their sins, they were baptized

## CONFESSION* [CONFESS]

Ne     9: 3  and spent another quarter in **c**
2Co    9:13  accompanies your **c** of the gospel
1Ti    6:12  when you made your good **c**
       6:13  Pontius Pilate made the good **c**,

## CONFIDE* [CONFIDES]

Jdg   16:15  love you,' when you won't **c** in me?

## CONFIDENCE* [CONFIDENT]

Jdg    9:26  and its citizens put their **c** in him.
2Ki   18:19  what are you basing this **c** of yours?
2Ch   32: 8  And the people gained **c** from what
      32:10  On what are you basing your **c**,
Job    4: 6  Should not your piety be your **c**
Ps    71: 5  LORD, my **c** since my youth.
Pr     3:32  but takes the upright into his **c**.
      11:13  Gossips betray a **c**,
      20:19  A gossip betrays a **c**;
      25: 9  to court, do not betray another's **c**,
      31:11  Her husband has full **c** in her
Isa   32:17  will be quietness and **c** forever.
      36: 4  what are you basing this **c** of yours?
Jer   17: 7  in the LORD, whose **c** is in him.
      49:31  ease, which lives in **c**,"
Eze   29:16  will no longer be a source of **c**
Mic    7: 5  put no **c** in a friend.
2Co    2: 3  I had **c** in all of you, that you would
       3: 4  Such **c** we have through Christ
       7:16  I am glad I can have complete **c**
       8:22  so because of his great **c** in you.
Eph    3:12  approach God with freedom and **c**.
Php    3: 3  and who put no **c** in the flesh—
       3: 4  I myself have reasons for such **c**.
       3: 4  have reasons to put **c** in the flesh,
2Th    3: 4  We have **c** in the Lord that you are
Heb    3: 6  if indeed we hold firmly to our **c**
       4:16  God's throne of grace with **c**,
      10:19  since we have **c** to enter the Most
      10:35  So do not throw away your **c**;
      13: 6  So we say with **c**, "The Lord is my
      13:17  Have **c** in your leaders and submit
1Jn    3:21  condemn us, we have **c** before God
       4:17  us so that we will have **c** on the day
       5:14  This is the **c** we have

## CONFIDENT* [CONFIDENCE]

Job    6:20  distressed, because they had been **c**;
Ps    27: 3  against me, even then I will be **c**.

Ps 27:13 I remain c of this: I will see
Lk 18: 9 To some who were c of their own
2Co 1:15 Because I was c of this, I wanted
5: 6 Therefore we are always c
5: 8 We are c, I say, and would prefer
9: 4 be ashamed of having been so c.
10: 7 If anyone is c that they belong
Gal 5:10 I am c in the Lord that you will take
Php 1: 6 being c of this, that he who began
1:14 have become c in the Lord
2:24 I am c in the Lord that I myself
Phm 1:21 C of your obedience, I write to you,
1Jn 2:28 that when he appears we may be c

## CONFIDES* [CONFIDE]
Ps 25:14 The LORD c in those who fear

## CONFINED
Ge 40: 3 same prison where Joseph was c.
Ps 88: 8 I am c and cannot escape;
Jer 32: 2 Jeremiah the prophet was c
33: 1 While Jeremiah was still c
39:15 While Jeremiah had been c

## CONFIRM [CONFIRMED, CONFIRMING]
Ge 26: 3 will c the oath I swore to your father
Dt 29:13 to c you this day as his people,
Da 9:27 He will c a covenant with many
2Pe 1:10 to c your calling and election.

## CONFIRMED [CONFIRM]
Dt 4:31 which he c to them by oath.
Ps 105:10 He c it to Jacob as a decree, to Israel
Ac 14: 3 who c the message of his grace
Ro 15: 8 made to the patriarchs might be c
Heb 2: 3 was c to us by those who heard him.

## CONFIRMING* [CONFIRM]
2Ki 23: 3 thus c the words of the covenant
1Co 1: 6 thus c our testimony about Christ
Php 1: 7 or defending and c the gospel,

## CONFLICT
Gal 5:17 They are in c with each other,
Heb 10:32 in a great c full of suffering.

## CONFORM* [CONFORMED, CONFORMITY, CONFORMS]
Ro 12: 2 Do not c to the pattern of this world,
1Pe 1:14 do not c to the evil desires you had

## CONFORMED* [CONFORM]
Eze 5: 7 You have not even c
11:12 but have c to the standards
Ac 26: 5 I c to the strictest sect of
Ro 8:29 predestined to be c to the image

## CONFORMITY* [CONFORM]
Eph 1:11 out everything in c with the purpose

## CONFORMS* [CONFORM]
1Ti 1:11 that c to the gospel concerning

## CONFRONT [CONFRONTED, CONFRONTS]
Ex 9:13 morning, c Pharaoh and say to him,
Job 9:32 that we might c each other in court.
Ps 17:13 LORD, c them, bring them down;
Eze 22: 2 Then c her with all her detestable

## CONFRONTED [CONFRONT]
2Sa 22: 6 the snares of death c me.
Ps 18:18 They c me in the day of my disaster,

## CONFRONTS* [CONFRONT]
Job 31:14 what will I do when God c me?

## CONFUSE* [CONFUSION]
Ge 11: 7 and c their language so they will not
Ps 55: 9 Lord, c the wicked, confound their

## CONFUSION [CONFUSE]
Ex 14:24 Egyptian army and threw it into c.
23:27 into c every nation you encounter.
Dt 7:23 into great c until they are destroyed.
28:28 madness, blindness and c of mind.
Jos 10:10 threw them into c before Israel,
1Sa 14:20 They found the Philistines in total c,
Ps 70: 2 seek my life be put to shame and c;
Jer 51:34 us, he has thrown us into c, he has
Mic 7: 4 Now is the time of their c.
Gal 5:10 is throwing you into c will have

## CONGREGATION* [CONGREGATIONS]
Ps 26:12 in the great c I will praise
68:26 Praise God in the great c;
Ac 13:43 When the c was dismissed,

## CONGREGATIONS* [CONGREGATION]
1Co 14:33 as in all the c of the Lord's people.

## CONNECTION
Col 2:19 They have lost c with the head,

## CONQUER [CONQUERED, CONQUEROR, CONQUERORS]
Rev 13: 7 against God's people and to c them.

## CONQUERED [CONQUER]
Jos 10:42 and their lands Joshua c in one
Heb 11:33 who through faith c kingdoms,

## CONQUEROR* [CONQUER]
Mic 1:15 I will bring a c against you who live
Rev 6: 2 he rode out as a c bent on conquest.

## CONQUERORS* [CONQUER]
Ro 8:37 are more than c through him who

## CONSCIENCE* [CONSCIENCE-STRICKEN, CONSCIENCES, CONSCIENTIOUS]
Ge 20: 5 I have done this with a clear c

Ge 20: 6 I know you did this with a clear **c**,
1Sa 25:31 have on his **c** the staggering burden
Job 27: 6 my **c** will not reproach me as long
Ac 23: 1 to God in all good **c** to this day."
24:16 to keep my **c** clear before God
Ro 9: 1 my **c** confirms it through the Holy
13: 5 but also as a matter of **c**.
1Co 4: 4 My **c** is clear, but that does not
8: 7 a god, and since their **c** is weak, it is
8:10 if anyone with a weak **c** sees you,
8:12 in this way and wound their weak **c**,
10:25 without raising questions of **c**,
10:27 you without raising questions of **c**.
10:28 told you and for the sake of **c**.
10:29 am referring to the other person's **c**,
10:29 being judged by another's **c**?
2Co 1:12 Our **c** testifies that we have
4: 2 to everyone's **c** in the sight of God.
5:11 and I hope it is also plain to your **c**.
1Ti 1: 5 and a good **c** and a sincere faith.
1:19 holding on to faith and a good **c**,
3: 9 truths of the faith with a clear **c**.
2Ti 1: 3 with a clear **c**, as night and day I
Heb 9: 9 able to clear the **c** of the worshiper.
10:22 to cleanse us from a guilty **c**
13:18 We are sure that we have a clear **c**
1Pe 3:16 keeping a clear **c**, so that those who
3:21 the pledge of a clear **c** toward God.

## CONSCIENCE-STRICKEN*
[CONSCIENCE]
1Sa 24: 5 David was **c** for having cut off
2Sa 24:10 David was **c** after he had counted

## CONSCIENCES* [CONSCIENCE]
Ro 2:15 hearts, their **c** also bearing witness,
1Ti 4: 2 whose **c** have been seared as
Tit 1:15 their minds and **c** are corrupted.
Heb 9:14 cleanse our **c** from acts that lead

## CONSCIENTIOUS* [CONSCIENCE]
2Ch 29:34 for the Levites had been more **c**

## CONSCIOUS*
Ro 3:20 through the law we become **c** of our
1Pe 2:19 unjust suffering because you are **c**

## CONSECRATE [CONSECRATED]
Ex 13: 2 "**C** to me every firstborn male.
19:10 "Go to the people and **c** them today
28:41 **C** them so they may serve me as
40: 9 **c** it and all its furnishings, and it
Lev 20: 7 " '**C** yourselves and be holy,
25:10 **C** the fiftieth year and proclaim
Jos 7:13 "Go, **c** the people. Tell them,
1Ch 15:12 fellow Levites are to **c** yourselves
2Ch 29: 5 **C** yourselves now and **c** the temple

## CONSECRATED [CONSECRATE]
Ex 29:43 and the place will be **c** by my glory.
Lev 8:30 So he **c** Aaron and his garments
Nu 15:40 and will be **c** to your God.
1Sa 21: 4 there is some **c** bread here—
2Ch 7:16 **c** this temple so that my Name may
Ps 50: 5 "Gather to me this **c** people,

Mk 2:26 house of God and ate the **c** bread,
Lk 2:23 male is to be **c** to the Lord"),
1Ti 4: 5 because it is **c** by the word of God

## CONSENT
1Co 7: 5 other except perhaps by mutual **c**
Phm 1:14 want to do anything without your **c**,

## CONSEQUENCES
Eze 16:58 You will bear the **c** of your

## CONSIDER [CONSIDERATE, CONSIDERED, CONSIDERS]
Dt 17:20 not **c** himself better than his fellow
1Sa 12:24 **c** what great things he has done
16: 7 "Do not **c** his appearance or his
2Ch 19: 6 them, "**C** carefully what you do,
Job 37:14 stop and **c** God's wonders.
Ps 5: 1 to my words, Lord, **c** my lament.
8: 3 When I **c** your heavens, the work
50:22 "**C** this, you who forget God, or I
77:12 I will **c** all your works and meditate
143: 5 and **c** what your hands have done.
Pr 6: 6 **c** its ways and be wise!
20:25 and only later to **c** one's vows.
Ecc 2:12 I turned my thoughts to **c** wisdom,
7:13 **C** what God has done:
Isa 47: 7 you did not **c** these things or reflect
Jer 2:31 **c** the word of the Lord.
La 1:11 Lord, and **c**, for I am despised."
Mk 4:24 "**C** carefully what you hear,"
Lk 12:24 **C** the ravens: They do not sow
12:27 "**C** how the wild flowers grow.
Ac 20:24 I **c** my life worth nothing to me;
Ro 11:22 **C** therefore the kindness
14: 5 Some **c** one day more sacred than
Php 2: 6 God, did not **c** equality with God
3: 8 I **c** everything a loss because
3: 8 I **c** them garbage, that I may gain
Heb 10:24 And let us **c** how we may spur one
12: 3 **C** him who endured such opposition
Jas 1: 2 **C** it pure joy, my brothers
1:26 Those who **c** themselves religious

## CONSIDERATE* [CONSIDER]
Tit 3: 2 to be peaceable and **c**, and always
Jas 3:17 then peace-loving, **c**, submissive,
1Pe 2:18 only to those who are good and **c**,
3: 7 the same way be **c** as you live

## CONSIDERED [CONSIDER]
1Ki 16:31 He not only **c** it trivial to commit
Job 1: 8 "Have you **c** my servant Job?
2: 3 "Have you **c** my servant Job?
34: 6 Although I am right, I am **c** a liar;
Ps 44:22 we are **c** as sheep to be slaughtered.
Isa 53: 4 yet we **c** him punished by God,
Hos 9: 7 the prophet is **c** a fool, anyone who
Mt 14: 5 because they **c** him a prophet.
Ro 8:36 all day long; we are **c** as sheep to be
1Ti 1:12 that he **c** me trustworthy,
Heb 11:11 children because she **c** him faithful
Jas 2:21 not our father Abraham **c** righteous
2:25 Rahab the prostitute **c** righteous

## CONSIDERS [CONSIDER]
Pr   31:16  She c a field and buys it; out of her

## CONSIST [CONSISTS]
Lk   12:15  life does not c in an abundance

## CONSISTS [CONSIST]
Eph   5: 9  fruit of the light c in all goodness,

## CONSOLATION* [CONSOLE]
Job   6:10  Then I would still have this c—
      21: 2  let this be the c you give me.
Ps   94:19  within me, your c brought me joy.
Lk    2:25  He was waiting for the c of Israel,

## CONSOLATIONS* [CONSOLE]
Job  15:11  Are God's c not enough for you,

## CONSOLE* [CONSOLATION, CONSOLATIONS]
Job  21:34  "So how can you c me with your
Isa  22: 4  not try to c me over the destruction
     51:19  famine and sword—who can c you?
Jer  16: 7  anyone give them a drink to c them.

## CONSORT*
Hos   4:14  because the men themselves c

## CONSPIRACY [CONSPIRE]
Ps   64: 2  Hide me from the c of the wicked,
Isa   8:12  c everything this people calls a c;

## CONSPIRE [CONSPIRACY]
Ps    2: 1  Why do the nations c
     59: 3  Powerful people c against me for no
Mic   7: 3  they all c together.
Ac    4:27  to c against your holy servant Jesus,

## CONSTANT [CONSTANTLY]
Dt   28:66  You will live in c suspense,
Pr   19:13  wife is like the c dripping of a leaky
Ac   27:33  "you have been in c suspense
Heb   5:14  by c use have trained themselves

## CONSTANTLY [CONSTANT]
Pr    8:30  Then I was c at his side.
Ac    1:14  all joined together c in prayer,

## CONSTRAINT*
Lk   12:50  c I am under until it is completed!

## CONSTRUCTIVE*
1Co  10:23  but not everything is c.

## CONSULT [CONSULTED, CONSULTS]
1Sa  28: 8  "C a spirit for me," he said,
2Ki   1: 2  "Go and c Baal-Zebub, the god
      8: 8  C the LORD through him;
2Ch  17: 3  He did not c the Baals
     25:15  "Why do you c this people's gods,
Isa   8:19  someone tells you to c mediums

Isa   8:19  Why c the dead on behalf
     40:14  Whom did the LORD c
Eze  21:21  lots with arrows, he will c his idols,
Hos   4:12  My people c a wooden idol and are
Gal   1:16  was not to c any human being.

## CONSULTED [CONSULT]
1Ch  10:13  and even c a medium for guidance,

## CONSULTS* [CONSULT]
Dt   18:11  or spiritist or who c the dead.
Eze  14:10  be as guilty as the one who c him.

## CONSUME [CONSUMED, CONSUMES, CONSUMING]
Dt    5:25  This great fire will c us, and we will
Ps   21: 9  his wrath, and his fire will c them.
     59:13  c them in wrath, c them till they are
Isa  26:11  reserved for your enemies c them.
Jer  17:27  that will c her fortresses.' "
Eze  15: 7  of the fire, the fire will yet c them.
Jn    2:17  "Zeal for your house will c me."
Heb  10:27  raging fire that will c the enemies

## CONSUMED [CONSUME]
Lev  10: 2  presence of the LORD and c them,
Nu   11: 1  c some of the outskirts of the camp.
     16:35  c the 250 men who were offering
2Ki   1:10  fell from heaven and c the captain
2Ch   7: 1  heaven and c the burnt offering
Ps   37:20  be c, they will go up in smoke.
     90: 7  We are c by your anger and terrified
Ecc  10:12  but fools are c by their own lips.
La    3:22  LORD's great love we are not c,
Zep   3: 8  The whole world will be c
Zec   9: 4  on the sea, and she will be c by fire.
Rev  18: 8  She will be c by fire, for mighty is

## CONSUMES [CONSUME]
Ps   69: 9  for zeal for your house c me,

## CONSUMING [CONSUME]
Ex   24:17  the LORD looked like a c fire
Dt    4:24  For the LORD your God is a c fire,
2Sa  22: 9  c fire came from his mouth,
Heb  12:29  for our "God is a c fire."

## CONTAIN* [CONTAINED, CONTAINS]
1Ki   8:27  the highest heaven, cannot c you.
2Ch   2: 6  the highest heavens, cannot c him?
      6:18  the highest heavens, cannot c you.
Ecc   8: 8  one has power over the wind to c it,
2Pe   3:16  His letters c some things that are

## CONTAINED* [CONTAIN]
Ac   10:12  It c all kinds of four-footed animals,
Heb   9: 4  This ark c the gold jar of manna,

## CONTAINS [CONTAIN]
Pr   15: 6  of the righteous c great treasure,

## CONTAMINATES*
2Co   7: 1  from everything that c body

## CONTEMPLATE*
2Co  3:18  unveiled faces c the Lord's glory,

## CONTEMPT [CONTEMPTIBLE]
Nu  14:11  will these people treat me with c?
Dt  17:12  Anyone who shows c for the judge
1Sa  2:17  the LORD's offering with c.
    25:39  Nabal for treating me with c.
Ps  123: 3  us, for we have endured no end of c.
Pr  14:31  oppresses the poor shows c for their
    17: 5  Whoever mocks the poor shows c
    18: 3  so does c, and with shame comes
Da  12: 2  others to shame and everlasting c.
Mal  1: 6  "It is you priests who show c
     1: 6  'How have we shown c for your
Ro   2: 4  do you show c for the riches of his
    14: 3  must not treat with c the one who does
Gal  4:14  you did not treat me with c or scorn.
1Th  5:20  Do not treat prophecies with c

## CONTEMPTIBLE [CONTEMPT]
Pr  30:23  a c woman who gets married,

## CONTEND [CONTENDED,
CONTENDING, CONTENDS,
CONTENTIOUS]
Ge   6: 3  "My Spirit will not c with human
Jdg  6:32  saying, "Let Baal c with him,"
Ps  35: 1  C, LORD, with those who c
Isa  49:25  I will c with those who c with you,
Jude  1: 3  urge you to c for the faith

## CONTENDED* [CONTEND]
Dt  33: 8  you c with him at the waters
Php  4: 3  help these women since they have c

## CONTENDING* [CONTEND]
Col  2: 1  know how hard I am c for you

## CONTENDS* [CONTEND]
Job 40: 2  "Will the one who c
Jer  15:10  whom the whole land strives and c!

## CONTENT* [CONTENTMENT]
Ge  25:27  Jacob was c to stay at home
Jos  7: 7  If only we had been c to stay
Ps  131: 2  like a weaned child I am c.
Pr  13:25  The righteous eat to their hearts' c,
    19:23  then one rests c,
Ecc  4: 8  toil, yet his eyes were not c with his
Lk   3:14  be c with your pay."
Php  4:11  to be c whatever the circumstances.
     4:12  learned the secret of being c in any
1Ti  6: 8  and clothing, we will be c with that.
Heb 13: 5  and be c with what you have,

## CONTENTIOUS* [CONTEND]
1Co 11:16  If anyone wants to be c about this,

## CONTENTMENT* [CONTENT]
Job 36:11  in prosperity and their years in c.
SS   8:10  in his eyes like one bringing c.
1Ti  6: 6  But godliness with c is great gain.

## CONTINUAL [CONTINUE]
Pr  15:15  but the cheerful heart has a c feast.

## CONTINUALLY [CONTINUE]
Lev 24: 2  the lamps may be kept burning c.
Nu   4: 7  the bread that is c there is to remain
Isa  27: 3  LORD, watch over it; I water it c.
Lk  24:53  And they stayed c at the temple,
1Th  5:17  pray c,
Heb 13:15  let us c offer to God a sacrifice

## CONTINUE [CONTINUAL,
CONTINUALLY, CONTINUED,
CONTINUES, CONTINUING]
1Ch 17:27  that it may c forever in your sight;
2Ch  6:14  your servants who c wholeheartedly
Ps  36:10  C your love to those who know you,
    89:36  that his line will c forever and his
Jer  3: 5  Will your wrath c forever?'
Ac  13:43  urged them to c in the grace of God.
Ro  11:22  provided that you c in his kindness.
2Co  1:10  our hope that he will c to deliver us,
Gal  3:10  "Cursed is everyone who does not c
Php  2:12  c to work out your salvation
Col  1:23  if you c in your faith,
     2: 6  as Lord, c to live your lives in him,
1Ti  2:15  if they c in faith, love and holiness
2Ti  3:14  c in what you have learned and have
1Jn  2:28  dear children, c in him,
     3: 9  are born of God will not c to sin,
     5:18  born of God does not c to sin;
2Jn  1: 9  does not c in the teaching of Christ
Rev 22:11  Let those who do wrong c to do
    22:11  let those who are vile c to be vile;
    22:11  let those who do right c to do right;
    22:11  and let those who are holy c to be

## CONTINUED [CONTINUE]
Jdg  1:29  the Canaanites c to live there among
Ps  78:17  But they c to sin against him,
Isa  64: 5  But when we c to sin against them,
Ac  14: 7  where they c to preach the gospel.

## CONTINUES [CONTINUE]
Ps  100: 5  his faithfulness c through all
    119:90  Your faithfulness c through all
2Co 10:15  hope is that, as your faith c to grow,
1Jn  3: 6  No one who c to sin has either seen

## CONTINUING [CONTINUE]
Ro  13: 8  except the c debt to love one

## CONTRARY
Lev 10: 1  the LORD, c to his command.
2Ch 30:18  the Passover, c to what was written.
Ac  18:13  worship God in ways c to the law."
Ro  11:24  and c to nature were grafted
Gal  5:17  the sinful nature desires what is c
     5:17  and the Spirit what is c to the sinful

## CONTRIBUTION
[CONTRIBUTIONS]
Ro  15:26  to make a c for the poor among

## CONTRIBUTIONS
[CONTRIBUTION]

2Ch 24:10 all the people brought their c gladly,
31:12 they faithfully brought in the c,

## CONTRITE*

Ps 51:17 a broken and c heart you, God,
Isa 57:15 with those who are c and lowly
57:15 and to revive the heart of the c.
66: 2 who are humble and c in spirit,

## CONTROL [CONTROLLED, CONTROLS, SELF-CONTROL, SELF-CONTROLLED]

Ex 32:25 that Aaron had let them get out of c
Jos 18: 1 country was brought under their c,
Ecc 2:19 Yet they will have c over all the toil
Ro 6:20 free from the c of righteousness.
1Co 7: 9 But if they cannot c themselves,
7:37 but has c over his own will,
1Th 4: 4 should learn to c your own body
1Jn 5:19 the whole world is under the c
Rev 16: 9 God, who had c over these plagues,

## CONTROLLED [CONTROL]

Ps 32: 9 understanding but must be c by bit
Ro 7: 5 we were c by our sinful nature,
8: 6 The mind c by the sinful nature is
8: 6 but the mind c by the Spirit is life

## CONTROLS* [CONTROL]

Job 37:15 Do you know how God c the clouds

## CONTROVERSIAL*
[CONTROVERSIES]

1Ti 1: 4 Such things promote c speculations

## CONTROVERSIES*
[CONTROVERSIAL]

Ac 26: 3 with all the Jewish customs and c.
1Ti 6: 4 They have an unhealthy interest in c
Tit 3: 9 But avoid foolish c and genealogies

## CONVERSATION

Col 4: 6 Let your c be always full of grace,

## CONVERT* [CONVERTED, CONVERTS]

Mt 23:15 over land and sea to win a single c,
23:15 make that c twice as much a child
Ac 6: 5 from Antioch, a c to Judaism.
Ro 16: 5 who was the first c to Christ
1Ti 3: 6 He must not be a recent c, or he

## CONVERTED* [CONVERT]

Ac 15: 3 told how the Gentiles had been c.

## CONVERTS* [CONVERT]

Ac 2:11 (both Jews and c to Judaism);
13:43 devout c to Judaism followed Paul
1Co 16:15 of Stephanas were the first c

## CONVICT* [CONVICTED, CONVICTION]

Dt 19:15 is not enough to c anyone accused
2Sa 14:13 does he not c himself, for the king
Pr 24:25 go well with those who c the guilty,
Jude 1:15 and to c all the ungodly of all

## CONVICTED* [CONVICT]

1Co 14:24 they are c of sin and are brought
Jas 2: 9 and are c by the law as lawbreakers.

## CONVICTION* [CONVICT]

Heb 3:14 till the end our original c.
1Th 1: 5 with the Holy Spirit and deep c.

## CONVINCED* [CONVINCING]

Ge 45:28 And Israel said, "I'm c!
Lk 16:31 they will not be c even if someone
Ac 19:26 hear how this fellow Paul has c
26: 9 "I too was c that I ought to do all
26:26 I am c that none of this has escaped
28:24 Some were c by what he said,
Ro 2:19 if you are c that you are a guide
8:38 I am c that neither death nor life,
14: 5 Everyone should be fully c in their
14:14 I am c, being fully persuaded
15:14 I myself am c, my brothers
2Co 5:14 because we are c that one died
Php 1:25 C of this, I know that I will remain,
2Ti 1:12 am c that he is able to guard what I
3:14 have learned and have become c of,
Heb 6: 9 we are c of better things in your case

## CONVINCING* [CONVINCED]

Ac 1: 3 and gave many c proofs that he was

## CONVULSION*

Mk 9:20 immediately threw the boy into a c.
Lk 9:42 threw him to the ground in a c.

## COOK [COOKED]

Ex 23:19 "Do not c a young goat in its
Eze 24:10 C the meat well,

## COOKED [COOK]

2Ki 6:29 So we c my son and ate him.
La 4:10 women have c their own children,

## COOL*

Ge 3: 8 in the garden in the c of the day,
Jer 18:14 Do its c waters from distant sources
Lk 16:24 his finger in water and c my tongue,

## COPIED* [COPY]

Jos 8:32 Joshua c on stones the law
Eze 16:47 and c their detestable practices,

## COPIES [COPY]

Heb 9:23 for the c of the heavenly things

## COPPER

Mt 10: 9 or c to take with you in your belts—
Mk 12:42 and put in two very small c coins,

## COPY [COPIED, COPIES]
Dt    17:18  himself on a scroll a **c** of this law,
2Ki   11:12  him with a **c** of the covenant
Heb    8: 5  They serve at a sanctuary that is a **c**
       9:24  that was only a **c** of the true one;

## CORBAN*
Mk     7:11  their father or mother is **C** (that is,

## CORD [CORDS]
Ge    38:18  "Your seal and its **c**, and the staff
Nu    15:38  with a blue **c** on each tassel.
Jos    2:18  you have tied this scarlet **c**
Ecc    4:12  A **c** of three strands is not quickly

## CORDS [CORD]
2Sa   22: 6  The **c** of the grave coiled around
Job    4:21  Are not the **c** of their tent pulled up,
Ps   129: 4  me free from the **c** of the wicked."
Pr     5:22  the **c** of their sins hold them fast.
Isa   54: 2  lengthen your **c**, strengthen your
Hos   11: 4  I led them with **c** of human
Jn     2:15  So he made a whip out of **c**,

## CORINTH [CORINTHIANS]
Ac    18: 1  this, Paul left Athens and went to **C.**
1Co    1: 2  To the church of God in **C**, to those
2Co    1: 1  To the church of God in **C**,

## CORINTHIANS* [CORINTH]
Ac    18: 8  of the **C** who heard Paul believed
2Co    6:11  We have spoken freely to you, **C**,

## CORN [EARS OF] See GRAIN
[HEADS OF], KERNEL

## CORNELIUS*
Roman to whom Peter preached; first Gentile Christian (Ac 10).

## CORNER [CORNERS, CORNERSTONE]
Ru     3: 9  "Spread the **c** of your garment over
1Sa   24: 4  and cut off a **c** of Saul's robe.
Pr     7:12  in the squares, at every **c** she lurks.)
      21: 9  on a **c** of the roof than share a house
Eze    5: 8  I spread the **c** of my garment over
Ac    26:26  because it was not done in a **c**.

## CORNERS [CORNER]
Dt    22:12  on the four **c** of the cloak you wear.
Isa   41: 9  from its farthest **c** I called you.
Eze    7: 2  come upon the four **c** of the land!
Mt     6: 5  on the street **c** to be seen by others.
      22: 9  Go to the street **c** and invite
Ac    10:11  being let down to earth by its four **c**.
Rev    7: 1  standing at the four **c** of the earth,
      20: 8  nations in the four **c** of the earth—

## CORNERSTONE* [CORNER, STONE; see also CAPSTONE]
Job   38: 6  its footings set, or who laid its **c**—
Ps   118:22  builders rejected has become the **c**;

Isa   28:16  a precious **c** for a sure foundation;
Jer   51:26  rock will be taken from you for a **c**,
Zec   10: 4  From Judah will come the **c**,
Mt    21:42  the builders rejected has become the **c**;
Mk    12:10  the builders rejected has become the **c**;
Lk    20:17  the builders rejected has become the **c**'?
Ac     4:11  which has become the **c**.'
Eph    2:20  Christ Jesus himself as the chief **c**.
1Pe    2: 6  a chosen and precious **c**, and the one
       2: 7  builders rejected has become the **c**,"

## CORRECT* [CORRECTED, CORRECTING, CORRECTION, CORRECTLY, CORRECTS]
Job    6:26  Do you mean to **c** what I say,
      40: 2  contends with the Almighty **c** him?
2Ti    4: 2  **c**, rebuke and encourage—

## CORRECTED* [CORRECT]
Pr    29:19  Servants cannot be **c** by mere

## CORRECTING* [CORRECT]
2Ti    3:16  **c** and training in righteousness,

## CORRECTION* [CORRECT]
Lev   26:23  these things you do not accept my **c**
Job   36:10  He makes them listen to **c**
Pr     5:12  How my heart spurned **c**!
       6:23  **c** and instruction are the way to life,
      10:17  but whoever ignores **c** leads others
      12: 1  but whoever hates **c** is stupid.
      13:18  but whoever heeds **c** is honored.
      15: 5  whoever heeds **c** shows prudence.
      15:10  those who hate **c** will die.
      15:12  Mockers resent **c**, so they avoid
      15:31  heeds life-giving **c** will be at home
      15:32  who heed **c** gain understanding.
Jer    2:30  they did not respond to **c**.
       5: 3  crushed them, but they refused **c**.
       7:28  LORD its God or responded to **c**.
Zep    3: 2  She obeys no one, she accepts no **c**.
       3: 7  you will fear me and accept **c**!'

## CORRECTLY* [CORRECT]
Jdg   12: 6  he could not pronounce the word **c**,
Jer    1:12  to me, "You have seen **c**, for I am
Lk     7:43  "You have judged **c**," Jesus said.
      10:28  "You have answered **c**,"
Jn     7:24  appearances, but instead judge **c**."
2Ti    2:15  who **c** handles the word of truth.

## CORRECTS* [CORRECT]
Job    5:17  "Blessed are those whom God **c**;
Pr     9: 7  Whoever **c** a mocker invites insults;

## CORRODED*
Jas    5: 3  Your gold and silver are **c**.

## CORRUPT [CORRUPTED, CORRUPTION, CORRUPTS]
Ge     6:11  Now the earth was **c** in God's sight
Ex    32: 7  up out of Egypt, have become **c**.
Dt     4:16  so that you do not become **c**
Jdg    2:19  to ways even more **c** than those

Ps 14: 1 They are c, their deeds are vile;
53: 3 has turned away, all have become c;
Pr 4:24 keep c talk far from your lips.
6:12 who go about with c mouths,
19:28 A c witness mocks at justice,
Da 6: 4 and neither c nor negligent.
Ac 2:40 yourselves from this c generation."

## CORRUPTED [CORRUPT]
Eze 28:17 you c your wisdom because of your
2Co 7: 2 wronged no one, we have c no one,
Tit 1:15 but to those who are c and do not
1:15 their minds and consciences are c.
Jude 1:23 even the clothing stained by c flesh.
Rev 19: 2 the great prostitute who c the earth

## CORRUPTION [CORRUPT]
Ezr 9:11 land polluted by the c of its peoples.
Da 6: 4 They could find no c in him,
2Pe 1: 4 having escaped the c in the world
2:20 they have escaped the c of the world

## CORRUPTS* [CORRUPT]
Ecc 7: 7 into fools, and a bribe c the heart.
1Co 15:33 "Bad company c good character."
Jas 3: 6 It c the whole person, sets the whole

## COST [COSTLY, COSTS]
Nu 16:38 who sinned at the c of their lives.
Jos 6:26 the c of his firstborn son he will lay
6:26 at the c of his youngest he will set
2Sa 24:24 burnt offerings that c me nothing."
1Ki 16:34 at the c of his firstborn son Abiram,
16:34 at the c of his youngest son Segub,
Pr 4: 7 Though it c all you have,
7:23 little knowing it will c him his life.
Isa 55: 1 milk without money and without c.
Lk 14:28 and estimate the c to see if you have
Rev 21: 6 thirsty I will give water without c

## COSTLY [COST]
Ps 49: 8 the ransom for a life is c,
1Co 3:12 using gold, silver, c stones, wood,
Rev 18:12 every kind made of ivory, c wood,

## COSTS [COST]
Pr 6:31 though it c him all the wealth of his

## COULD
Ge 13:16 so that if anyone c count the dust,
13:16 then your offspring c be counted.
Ex 40:35 Moses c not enter the tent
Nu 22:18 I c not do anything great or small
2Ch 7: 2 The priests c not enter the temple
25:15 which c not save their own people
Eze 14:14 they c save only themselves by their
Mt 22:46 No one c say a word in reply,
Mk 6: 5 He c not do any miracles there,
Jn 12:39 For this reason they c not believe,
Rev 15: 8 no one c enter the temple until

## COUNCIL [COUNCILS]
Job 15: 8 Do you listen in on God's c?
Ps 89: 7 the c of the holy ones God is greatly
107:32 and praise him in the c of the elders.

Mk 15:43 a prominent member of the C,
Jn 3: 1 a member of the Jewish ruling c.
Ac 17:33 At that, Paul left the C.

## COUNCILS [COUNCIL]
Mk 13: 9 will be handed over to the local c

## COUNSEL [COUNSELOR, COUNSELORS, COUNSELS]
2Ch 18: 4 "First seek the c of the LORD."
25:16 this and have not listened to my c."
Job 12:13 c and understanding are his.
Ps 73:24 You guide me with your c,
Pr 8:14 C and sound judgment are mine;
15:22 Plans fail for lack of c,
Isa 11: 2 the Spirit of c and of might,
1Ti 5:14 So I c younger widows to marry,
Rev 3:18 I c you to buy from me gold refined

## COUNSELOR [COUNSEL]
Isa 9: 6 And he will be called Wonderful C,
40:13 or instruct the LORD as his c?
Ro 11:34 Or who has been his c?"

## COUNSELORS [COUNSEL]
Ps 119:24 are my delight; they are my c.

## COUNSELS* [COUNSEL]
Ps 16: 7 I will praise the LORD, who c me;

## COUNT [COUNTED, COUNTING, COUNTLESS, COUNTS]
Ge 13:16 so that if anyone could c the dust,
15: 5 up at the heavens and c the stars—
15: 5 if indeed you can c them."
16:10 they will be too numerous to c."
Nu 1: 3 You and Aaron are to c according to
23:10 Who can c the dust of Jacob
31:26 community are to c all the women
Job 38:37 has the wisdom to c the clouds?
Ps 32: 2 the LORD does not c against them
48:12 Zion, go around her, c her towers,
139:18 Were I to c them, they would
Eze 33:12 former righteousness will c for nothing.
Ro 4: 8 Lord will never c against them."
6:11 c yourselves dead to sin but alive
Rev 7: 9 great multitude that no one could c,

## COUNTED [COUNT]
Ge 13:16 dust, then your offspring could be c.
Nu 1:19 so he c them in the Desert of Sinai:
2Sa 24:10 after he had c the fighting men,
Hos 1:10 which cannot be measured or c.
Mt 26:15 So they c out for him thirty pieces
Ac 5:41 because they had been c worthy
2Th 1: 5 as a result you will be c worthy

## COUNTERFEIT*
1Jn 2:27 and as that anointing is real, not c—

## COUNTING [COUNT]
2Co 5:19 not c people's sins against them.

## COUNTLESS [COUNT]

Nu  10:36  to the **c** thousands of Israel."
Heb 11:12  and as **c** as the sand on the seashore.

## COUNTRIES [COUNTRY]

Dt  29:16  how we passed through the **c**
Isa 36:20  the gods of these **c** have been able
Eze 11:16  and scattered them among the **c**,
    11:16  in the **c** where they have gone.'
    20:34  you from the **c** where you have been
Da   9: 7  in all the **c** where you have scattered
Zec  8: 7  my people from the **c** of the east

## COUNTRY [COUNTRIES]

Ge  12: 1  "Go from your **c**, your people
    15:13  will be strangers in a **c** not their own
Ex   1:10  fight against us and leave the **c**."
     6:11  to let the Israelites go out of his **c**."
Dt  28: 3  in the city and blessed in the **c**.
    28:16  in the city and cursed in the **c**.
Jos  9: 6  "We have come from a distant **c**;
    11:16  the hill **c**, all the Negev, the whole
Pr  28: 2  When a **c** is rebellious, it has many
    29: 4  By justice a king gives a **c** stability,
Isa 66: 8  Can a **c** be born in a day or a nation
Jer 17: 3  because of sin throughout your **c**.
Lk  15:13  had, set off for a distant **c** and there
Jn   4:44  have no honor in their own **c**.)
2Co 11:26  in danger in the **c**, in danger at sea;
Heb 11:14  are looking for a **c** of their own.

## HILL COUNTRY See HILL

## COUNTS [COUNT]

Jn   6:63  the flesh **c** for nothing.
1Co  7:19  God's commands is what **c**.
Gal  5: 6  **c** is faith expressing itself through

## COURAGE* [COURAGEOUS]

Jos  2:11  everyone's **c** failed because of you,
     5: 1  they no longer had the **c** to face
2Sa  4: 1  he lost **c**, and all Israel became
     7:27  So your servant has found **c** to pray
1Ch 17:25  So your servant has found **c** to pray
2Ch 15: 8  son of Oded the prophet, he took **c**.
    19:11  Act with **c**, and may the LORD be
Ezr  7:28  I took **c** and gathered leaders
    10: 4  support you, so take **c** and do it."
Ps 107:26  in their peril their **c** melted away.
Eze 22:14  Will your **c** endure or your hands be
Da  11:25  and **c** against the king of the South.
Mt  14:27  immediately said to them: "Take **c**!
Mk   6:50  he spoke to them and said, "Take **c**!
Ac   4:13  When they saw the **c** of Peter
    23:11  stood near Paul and said, "Take **c**!
    27:22  now I urge you to keep up your **c**,
    27:25  So keep up your **c**, men, for I have
Php  1:20  will have sufficient **c** so that now as

## COURAGEOUS* [COURAGE]

Dt  31: 6  Be strong and **c**. Do not be afraid
    31: 7  "Be strong and **c**, for you must go
    31:23  "Be strong and **c**, for you will bring
Jos  1: 6  Be strong and **c**, because you will
     1: 7  "Be strong and very **c**. Be careful

Jos  1: 9  Be strong and **c**. Do not be afraid;
     1:18  put to death. Only be strong and **c**!"
    10:25  Be strong and **c**. This is what
1Ch 22:13  Be strong and **c**. Do not be afraid
    28:20  "Be strong and **c**, and do the work.
2Ch 26:17  eighty other **c** priests of the LORD
    32: 7  "Be strong and **c**. Do not be afraid
1Co 16:13  firm in the faith; be **c**; be strong.

## COURSE

Ps  19: 5  a champion rejoicing to run his **c**.
Pr   2: 8  for he guards the **c** of the just
    15:21  understanding keep a straight **c**.
    16: 9  hearts human beings plan their **c**,
    17:23  in secret to pervert the **c** of justice.
Ecc  1: 6  it goes, ever returning on its **c**.
Jas  3: 6  sets the whole **c** of one's life on fire,

## COURT [COURTS, COURTYARD]

Dt  25: 1  they are to take it to **c**
Jdg  4: 5  She held **c** under the Palm
Job  9:32  we might confront each other in **c**.
Pr  22:22  and do not crush the needy in **c**,
    25: 8  do not bring hastily to **c**, for what
    25: 9  If you take your neighbor to **c**,
    29: 9  a wise person goes to **c** with a fool,
Isa  3:13  The LORD takes his place in **c**;
Mt   5:25  adversary who is taking you to **c**.
Ac  25:10  am now standing before Caesar's **c**,
1Co  4: 3  judged by you or by any human **c**;
Jas  2: 6  ones who are dragging you into **c**?

## COURTS [COURT]

Dt  17: 8  If cases come before your **c** that are
1Ch 28: 6  who will build my house and my **c**,
Ps  65: 4  and bring near to live in your **c**!
    84:10  in your **c** than a thousand elsewhere;
   100: 4  thanksgiving and his **c** with praise;
Isa  1:12  this of you, this trampling of my **c**?
Am   5:15  maintain justice in the **c**.
Zec  8:16  true and sound judgment in your **c**;
Lk   2:46  days they found him in the temple **c**,
    20: 1  teaching the people in the temple **c**
    22:53  day I was with you in the temple **c**,
Jn   2:14  the temple **c** he found people selling
Ac   5:42  in the temple **c** and from house

## COURTYARD [COURT]

Ex  27: 9  "Make a **c** for the tabernacle.
1Ki  7: 9  from the outside to the great **c**
Mk  14:66  While Peter was below in the **c**,

## COUSIN

Lev 25:49  or a **c** or any blood relative in their
Est  2: 7  Mordecai had a **c** named Hadassah,
Col  4:10  as does Mark, the **c** of Barnabas.

## COVENANT [COVENANTS]

Ge   6:18  But I will establish my **c** with you,
     9: 9  "I now establish my **c** with you
    15:18  that day the LORD made a **c**
    17: 2  I will make my **c** between me
    31:44  now, let's make a **c**, you and I,
Ex   2:24  he remembered his **c** with Abraham,
     6: 5  and I have remembered my **c**.

Ex   19: 5  if you obey me fully and keep my c,
     24: 7  he took the Book of the C and read
     34:28  on the tablets the words of the c—
Lev  26: 9  and I will keep my c with you.
Dt    4:13  He declared to you his c, the Ten
     29: 1  of the c the LORD commanded
     29: 1  addition to the c he had made
Jos   3: 6  "Take up the ark of the c and pass
Jdg   2: 1  'I will never break my c with you,
1Sa  20:16  So Jonathan made a c
     23:18  them made a c before the LORD.
1Ki   8: 1  ark of the LORD's c from Zion,
      8:21  which is the c of the LORD that he
      8:23  you who keep your c of love
2Ki  23: 2  all the words of the Book of the C,
1Ch  16:15  He remembers his c forever,
2Ch  34:30  all the words of the Book of the C,
Ne    1: 5  who keeps his c of love with those
Job  31: 1  "I made a c with my eyes not
Ps   78:37  him, they were not faithful to his c.
    105: 8  He remembers his c forever,
    132:12  If your sons keep my c
Pr    2:17  ignored the c she made before God.
Isa  42: 6  make you to be a c for the people
     42:19  blind like the one in c with me,
     61: 8  make an everlasting c with them.
Jer  11: 2  "Listen to the terms of this c
     31:31  I will make a new c with the house
     32:40  I will make an everlasting c
Eze  16:60  Yet I will remember the c I made
     16:60  I will establish an everlasting c
     37:26  I will make a c of peace with them;
     37:26  it will be an everlasting c.
Da    9:27  He will confirm a c with many
     11:28  heart will be set against the holy c.
Hos   6: 7  As at Adam, they have broken the c;
Mal   2:14  partner, the wife of your marriage c.
      3: 1  the messenger of the c, whom you
Mt   26:28  This is my blood of the c, which is
Mk   14:24  "This is my blood of the c, which is
Lk   22:20  "This cup is the new c in my blood,
Ro   11:27  this is my c with them when I take
1Co  11:25  "This cup is the new c in my blood;
2Co   3: 6  competent as ministers of a new c—
Gal   3:17  aside the c previously established
      4:24  One c is from Mount Sinai
Heb   7:22  become the guarantor of a better c.
      8: 8  I will make a new c with the house
      9:15  Christ is the mediator of a new c,
      9:15  the sins committed under the first c.
     12:24  to Jesus the mediator of a new c,
Rev  11:19  his temple was seen the ark of his c.

## ARK OF THE COVENANT  See ARK

## COVENANT OF THE †LORD  Nu 10:33;
Dt 4:23; 10:8; 29:25; 31:9, 25, 26; Jos 3:3, 17;
4:7, 18; 6:6; 7:15; 8:33; 23:16; 1Sa 4:4; 1Ki
6:19; 8:21; 1Ch 15:25, 26, 28, 29; 16:37; 17:1;
22:19; 28:2, 18; 2Ch 6:11; Jer 3:16; 22:9

## EVERLASTING COVENANT  See
EVERLASTING

## COVENANTS*  [COVENANT]
Ro    9: 4  the c, the receiving of the law,
Gal   4:24  for the women represent two c.

Eph   2:12  foreigners to the c of the promise,

## COVER  [COVER-UP, COVERED, COVERING, COVERINGS, COVERS, GOLD-COVERED]
Ex   25:17  "Make an atonement c of pure
     25:21  Place the c on top of the ark and put
     33:22  and c you with my hand until I have
Lev  16: 2  front of the atonement c on the ark,
     16: 2  in the cloud over the atonement c.
Nu    4: 6  Then they are to c the curtain
Ne    4: 5  Do not c up their guilt or blot
Ps    5: 5  to you and did not c up my iniquity.
     91: 4  He will c you with his feathers,
Jer  51:42  its roaring waves will c her.
Eze  13:10  is built, they c it with whitewash,
Hos  10: 8  will grow up and c their altars.
     10: 8  will say to the mountains, "C us!"
Hab   2:14  the LORD as the waters c the sea.
Lk   23:30  and to the hills, "C us!" '
1Co  11: 6  For if a woman does not c her head,
     11: 6  shaved, then she should c her head.
     11: 7  A man ought not to c his head,
Jas   5:20  death and c over a multitude of sins.

## COVER-UP*  [COVER]
1Pe   2:16  do not use your freedom as a c

## COVERED  [COVER]
Ge    7:20  c the mountains to a depth of more
     38:14  c herself with a veil to disguise
Ex   10:22  total darkness c all Egypt for three
     14:28  flowed back and c the chariots
     16:13  evening quail came and c the camp,
     19:18  Mount Sinai was c with smoke,
     24:15  up on the mountain, the cloud c it,
     40:34  the cloud c the tent of meeting,
Nu    9:15  law, was set up, the cloud c it.
Jdg   6:39  and let the ground be c with dew."
Ps   32: 1  are forgiven, whose sins are c.
     85: 2  of your people and c all their sins.
Isa   6: 2  With two wings they c their faces,
      6: 2  with two they c their feet,
     51:16  c you with the shadow of my hand—
Da    9: 7  but this day we are c with shame—
Ob    1:10  Jacob, you will be c with shame;
Jnh   3: 8  and animals be c with sackcloth.
Mk    9: 7  a cloud appeared and c them,
Ro    4: 7  are forgiven, whose sins are c.
1Co  11: 4  with his head c dishonors his head.
Rev   4: 6  and they were c with eyes, in front
     17: 3  that was c with blasphemous names

## COVERING  [COVER]
Ex   35:11  the tabernacle with its tent and its c,
1Co  11:15  For long hair is given to her as a c.

## COVERINGS  [COVER]
Ge    3: 7  together and made c for themselves.
Pr   31:22  She makes c for her bed;

## COVERS  [COVER]
Ex   22:15  money paid for the hire c the loss.
Pr   10:12  but love c over all wrongs.
     17: 9  would foster love c over an offense,

Isa   25: 7  peoples, the sheet that c all nations;
2Co    3:15  Moses is read, a veil c their hearts.
1Pe    4: 8  because love c over a multitude

## COVET* [COVETED, COVETING]
Ex    20:17  not c your neighbor's house.
      20:17  not c your neighbor's wife,
      34:24  no one will c your land when you
Dt     5:21  "You shall not c your neighbor's
       7:25  Do not c the silver and gold
Mic    2: 2  They c fields and seize them,
Ro     7: 7  had not said, "You shall not c."
      13: 9  "You shall not c," and whatever
Jas    4: 2  You c but you cannot get what you

## COVETED* [COVET]
Jos    7:21  shekels, I c them and took them.
Ac    20:33  I have not c anyone's silver or gold

## COVETING* [COVET]
Ro     7: 7  not have known what c really was
       7: 8  produced in me every kind of c.

## COW [COWS]
Isa   11: 7  The c will feed with the bear,

## COWARDLY* [COWER]
Rev   21: 8  But the c, the unbelieving, the vile,

## COWER [COWARDLY]
Dt    33:29  Your enemies will c before you,

## COWS [COW]
Ge    41: 2  of the river there came up seven c,
1Sa    6: 7  with two c that have calved
       6: 7  Hitch the c to the cart, but take their
Job   21:10  their c calve and do not miscarry.
Am     4: 1  you c of Bashan on Mount Samaria,

## CRAFT* [CRAFTINESS, CRAFTS, CRAFTSMAN, CRAFTSMEN, CRAFTY]
1Ch   28:21  person skilled in any c will help you

## CRAFTINESS* [CRAFT]
Job    5:13  He catches the wise in their c,
1Co    3:19  "He catches the wise in their c";
Eph    4:14  and c of people in their deceitful

## CRAFTS* [CRAFT]
Ex    31: 5  to engage in all kinds of c.
      35:33  to engage in all kinds of artistic c.

## CRAFTSMAN* [CRAFT]
Ex    39: 8  breastpiece—the work of a skilled c.

## CRAFTSMEN [CRAFT]
Zec    1:20  the LORD showed me four c.

## CRAFTY* [CRAFT]
Ge     3: 1  the serpent was more c than any
1Sa   23:22  They tell me he is very c.
Job    5:12  He thwarts the plans of the c,

Job   15: 5  you adopt the tongue of the c.
Pr     7:10  like a prostitute and with c intent.
2Co   12:16  Yet, c fellow that I am, I caught you

## CRAG [CRAGS]
Ps    78:16  he brought streams out of a rocky c

## CRAGS [CRAG]
1Sa   24: 2  and his men near the C of the Wild

## CRASH*
Zep    1:10  Quarter, and a loud c from the hills.
Mt     7:27  house, and it fell with a great c."

## CRAVE* [CRAVED, CRAVING, CRAVINGS]
Nu    11: 4  with them began to c other food,
Dt    12:20  you, and you c meat and say,
Pr    21:10  The wicked c evil;
      21:26  All day long they c for more,
      23: 3  Do not c his delicacies, for that food
      23: 6  host, do not c his delicacies;
      31: 4  drink wine, not for rulers to c beer,
Mic    7: 1  to eat, none of the early figs that I c.
1Pe    2: 2  babies, c pure spiritual milk,

## CRAVED* [CRAVE]
Nu    11:34  the people who had c other food.
Ps    78:18  test by demanding the food they c.
      78:29  he had given them what they c.
      78:30  they had turned from what they c,

## CRAVING* [CRAVE]
Job   20:20  he will have no respite from his c;
Ps   106:14  In the desert they gave in to their c;
Pr    10: 3  but he thwarts the c of the wicked.
      21:25  The c of sluggards will be the death
Jer    2:24  desert, sniffing the wind in her c—

## CRAVINGS* [CRAVE]
Ps    10: 3  boast about the c of their hearts;
Eph    2: 3  gratifying the c of our sinful nature
1Jn    2:16  the c of sinful people, the lust

## CRAWL*
Ge     3:14  You will c on your belly and you
Mic    7:17  like creatures that c on the ground.

## CREAM
Pr    30:33  For as churning c produces butter,

## CREATE* [CREATED, CREATES, CREATING, CREATION, CREATIONS, CREATOR]
Ps    51:10  C in me a pure heart, O God,
Isa    4: 5  the LORD will c over all of Mount
      45: 7  I form the light and c darkness,
      45: 7  I bring prosperity and c disaster;
      45:18  he did not c it to be empty,
      65:17  I will c new heavens and a new
      65:18  and rejoice forever in what I will c,
      65:18  for I will c Jerusalem to be a delight
Jer   31:22  The LORD will c a new thing

Mal  2:10  Did not one God c us? Why do we
Eph  2:15  His purpose was to c in himself one

## CREATED* [CREATE]
Ge   1: 1  In the beginning God c the heavens
     1:21  So God c the great creatures
     1:27  So God c human beings in his own
     1:27  c them; male and female he c them.
     2: 4  and the earth when they were c,
     5: 1  When God c human beings,
     5: 2  He c them male and female
     5: 2  And when they were c, he called
     6: 7  the earth the human race I have c—
Dt   4:32  the day God c human beings
Ps  89:12  You c the north and the south;
    89:47  futility you have c all humanity!
   102:18  a people not yet c may praise
   104:30  they are c, and you renew the face
   139:13  For you c my inmost being;
   148: 5  for at his command they were c,
Ecc  7:29  God c humankind upright, but
Isa 40:26  to the heavens: Who c all these?
    41:20  that the Holy One of Israel has c it.
    42: 5  he who c the heavens and stretched
    43: 1  he who c you, Jacob, he who
    43: 7  my name, whom I c for my glory,
    45: 8  I, the LORD, have c it.
    45:12  the earth and c human beings on it.
    45:18  he who c the heavens, he is God;
    48: 7  They are c now, and not long ago;
    54:16  it is I who c the blacksmith who
    54:16  it is I who have c the destroyer
    57:16  the very people I have c.
Eze 21:30  In the place where you were c,
    28:13  day you were c they were prepared.
    28:15  day you were c till wickedness was
Mk  13:19  when God c the world, until now—
Ro   1:25  and served c things rather than
1Co 11: 9  neither was man c for woman,
Eph  2:10  c in Christ Jesus to do good works,
     3: 9  hidden in God, who c all things.
     4:24  the new self, c to be like God in true
Col  1:16  For in him all things were c:
     1:16  all things have been c through him
1Ti  4: 3  which God c to be received
     4: 4  For everything God c is good,
Heb 12:27  that is, c things—so that what
Jas  1:18  be a kind of firstfruits of all he c.
Rev  4:11  for you c all things, and by your
     4:11  by your will they were c and have
    10: 6  who c the heavens and all that is

## CREATES* [CREATE]
Am   4:13  the mountains, who c the wind,

## CREATING* [CREATE]
Ge   2: 3  all the work of c that he had done.
Isa 57:19  c praise on the lips of the mourners

## CREATION* [CREATE]
Ps  96:13  Let all c rejoice before the LORD,
Mt  13:35  I will utter things hidden since the c
    25:34  for you since the c of the world.
Mk  10: 6  of c God 'made them male
    16:15  and preach the gospel to all c.
Jn  17:24  because you loved me before the c

Ro   1:20  For since the c of the world God's
     8:19  The c waits in eager expectation
     8:20  For the c was subjected
     8:21  that the c itself will be liberated
     8:22  the whole c has been groaning as
     8:39  nor anything else in all c, will be
2Co  5:17  is in Christ, the new c has come:
Gal  6:15  what counts is the new c.
Eph  1: 4  us in him before the c of the world
Col  1:15  God, the firstborn over all c.
Heb  4: 3  work has been finished since the c
     4:13  Nothing in all c is hidden
     9:11  that is to say, is not a part of this c.
     9:26  suffer many times since the c
1Pe  1:20  He was chosen before the c
2Pe  3: 4  as it has since the beginning of c."
Rev  3:14  true witness, the ruler of God's c.
    13: 8  was slain from the c of the world.
    17: 8  the c of the world will be astonished

## CREATIONS* [CREATE]
Hab  2:18  who make them trust in their own c;

## CREATOR* [CREATE]
Ge  14:19  Most High, C of heaven and earth.
    14:22  Most High, C of heaven and earth,
Dt  32: 6  your C, who made you and formed
Ecc 12: 1  Remember your C in the days
Isa 27:11  and their C shows them no favor.
    40:28  God, the C of the ends of the earth.
    43:15  Holy One, Israel's C, your King."
Mt  19: 4  at the beginning the C 'made them
Ro   1:25  created things rather than the C—
Col  3:10  in knowledge in the image of its C.
1Pe  4:19  themselves to their faithful C

## CREATURE [CREATURES]
Ge   1:28  over every living c that moves
     7: 4  earth every living c I have made."
Lev 11:42  You are not to eat any c that moves
    17:11  For the life of a c is in the blood,
    17:14  the life of every c is its blood.
    17:14  must not eat the blood of any c,
Job 12:10  In his hand is the life of every c
Ps 136:25  He gives food to every c.
Eze  1:15  on the ground beside each c with its
Rev  4: 7  The first living c was like a lion,
     5:13  Then I heard every c in heaven

## CREATURES [CREATURE]
Ge   1:20  "Let the water teem with living c,
     1:24  the land produce living c according
     1:24  c that move along the ground,
     6:19  bring into the ark two of all living c,
     8:21  again will I destroy all living c, as I
     9:16  and all living c of every kind
Ps 104:24  the earth is full of your c.
Pr  30:25  Ants are c of little strength, yet they
Eze  1: 5  was what looked like four living c.
    10:15  These were the living c I had seen
    47: 9  living c will live wherever the river
Rev  4: 6  were four living c, and they were
     5: 6  encircled by the four living c
     8: 9  third of the living c in the sea died,
    19: 4  and the four living c fell down

## CREDIT [ACCREDITED, CREDITED, CREDITOR, CREDITORS, CREDITS]
Lk    6:33  good to you, what c is that to you?
Ro    4:24  to whom God will c righteousness—
1Pe   2:20  it to your c if you receive a beating

## CREDITED [CREDIT]
Ge   15: 6  and he c it to him as righteousness.
Ps  106:31  This was c to him as righteousness
Eze  18:20  of the righteous will be c to them,
Ro    4: 3  it was c to him as righteousness.”
       4: 4  their wages are not c to them as
Gal   3: 6  it was c to him as righteousness.”
Php   4:17  is that more be c to your account.
Jas   2:23  it was c to him as righteousness,”

## CREDITOR [CREDIT]
Dt   15: 2  Every c shall cancel any loan they
Ps  109:11  May a c seize all he has;

## CREDITORS* [CREDIT]
Isa  50: 1  Or to which of my c did I sell you?
Hab   2: 7  Will not your c suddenly arise?

## CREDITS* [CREDIT]
Ro    4: 6  to whom God c righteousness apart

## CRETANS* [CRETE]
Ac    2:11  converts to Judaism); C and Arabs—
Tit   1:12  “C are always liars, evil brutes,

## CRETE [CRETANS]
Ac   27:12  This was a harbor in C, facing both
Tit   1: 5  The reason I left you in C was

## CRIED [CRY]
Ex    2:23  groaned in their slavery and c out,
      14:10  terrified and c out to the LORD.
Nu   20:16  but when we c out to the LORD,
Jos  24: 7  But they c to the LORD for help,
Jdg   3: 9  But when they c out to the LORD,
      4: 3  they c to the LORD for help.
      6: 6  the Israelites that they c
     10:12  you and you c to me for help, did I
1Sa   7: 9  He c out to the LORD on Israel’s
     12: 8  they c to the LORD for help,
     28:12  she c out at the top of her voice
Job  29:12  because I rescued the poor who c
Ps   18: 6  I c to my God for help.
      22: 5  They c to you and were saved;
     107:13  Then they c to the LORD in their
Jnh   1: 5  and each c out to his own god.
      1:14  Then they c out to the LORD,
Mt   14:30  beginning to sink, c out, “Lord,
     27:46  three in the afternoon Jesus c
Rev  19: 4  And they c: “Amen, Hallelujah!”

## CRIES [CRY]
Ge    4:10  Your brother’s blood c out to me
Pr    8: 3  the city, at the entrance, she c aloud:

## CRIME [CRIMES, CRIMINAL, CRIMINALS]
1Sa  20: 1  What is my c? How have I wronged

Ps   69:27  Charge them with c upon c;
Mk   15:14  “Why? What c has he committed?”
Ac   28:18  not guilty of any c deserving death.

## CRIMES [CRIME]
Rev  18: 5  and God has remembered her c.

## CRIMINAL* [CRIME]
Lk   23:40  But the other c rebuked him.
Jn   18:30  “If he were not a c,” they replied,
2Ti   2: 9  the point of being chained like a c.
1Pe   4:15  or thief or any other kind of c,

## CRIMINALS [CRIME]
Lk   23:32  both c, were also led out with him

## CRIMSON
Isa   1:18  though they are red as c, they shall
     63: 1  with his garments stained c?

## CRIPPLED
Mt   15:30  the c, the mute and many others,
Mk    9:45  to enter life c than to have two feet
Lk   14:13  invite the poor, the c, the lame,

## CRISIS*
1Co   7:26  Because of the present c, I think

## CRITICISM*
2Co   8:20  want to avoid any c of the way we

## CROOKED*
Dt   32: 5  they are a warped and c generation.
Ps  125: 5  to c ways the LORD will banish
Pr    2:15  whose paths are c and who are
      8: 8  none of them is c or perverse.
     10: 9  whoever takes c paths will be found
Ecc   1:15  What is c cannot be straightened;
      7:13  can straighten what he has made c?
Isa  59: 8  They have turned them into c roads;
La    3: 9  he has made my paths c.
Lk    3: 5  The c roads shall become straight,
Php   2:15  fault in a warped and c generation.”

## CROP [CROPS]
Isa   5: 2  he looked for a c of good grapes,
Mt   13: 8  good soil, where it produced a c—
     21:41  his share of the c at harvest time.”
Jn    4:36  even now they harvest the c

## CROPS [CROP]
Ge    4:12  it will no longer yield its c for you.
Pr    3: 9  with the firstfruits of all your c;
     10: 5  He who gathers c in summer is
     28: 3  like a driving rain that leaves no c.
Eze  34:29  for them a land renowned for its c,
     36:30  of the trees and the c of the field,
Zec   8:12  the ground will produce its c,
2Ti   2: 6  the first to receive a share of the c.
Rev  22: 2  tree of life, bearing twelve c of fruit,

## CROSS [CROSSED, CROSSES, CROSSING, CROSSROADS]
Dt    4:21  swore that I would not c the Jordan

| | | |
|---|---|---|
| Dt | 12:10 | But you will c the Jordan and settle |
| | 30:13 | "Who will c the sea to get it |
| | 31: 3 | your God himself will c over ahead |
| | 31: 3 | also will c over ahead of you, |
| Jos | 3:14 | people broke camp to c the Jordan, |
| Ps | 104: 9 | You set a boundary they cannot c; |
| Jer | 5:22 | an everlasting barrier it cannot c. |
| | 5:22 | they may roar, but they cannot c it. |
| Mt | 10:38 | Whoever does not take up their c |
| | 16:24 | and take up their c and follow me. |
| Mk | 15:21 | and they forced him to carry the c. |
| | 15:30 | come down from the c and save |
| Jn | 19:17 | Carrying his own c, he went |
| | 19:25 | Near the c of Jesus stood his |
| Ac | 2:23 | him to death by nailing him to the c. |
| | 5:30 | you killed by hanging him on a c. |
| 1Co | 1:17 | lest the c of Christ be emptied of its |
| | 1:18 | the message of the c is foolishness |
| Gal | 5:11 | offense of the c has been abolished. |
| | 6:12 | being persecuted for the c of Christ. |
| | 6:14 | in the c of our Lord Jesus Christ, |
| Eph | 2:16 | both of them to God through the c, |
| Php | 2: 8 | even death on a c! |
| | 3:18 | live as enemies of the c of Christ. |
| Col | 1:20 | through his blood, shed on the c. |
| | 2:14 | has taken it away, nailing it to the c. |
| | 2:15 | triumphing over them by the c. |
| Heb | 12: 2 | joy set before him he endured the c, |
| 1Pe | 2:24 | bore our sins" in his body on the c, |

## CROSSED [CROSS]

| | | |
|---|---|---|
| Jos | 4: 7 | When it c the Jordan, the waters |
| 2Ki | 2: 8 | and the two of them c over on dry |
| Jn | 5:24 | but has c over from death to life. |

## CROSSES [CROSS]

| | | |
|---|---|---|
| Jn | 19:31 | left on the c during the Sabbath, |

## CROSSING [CROSS]

| | | |
|---|---|---|
| Ge | 48:14 | and c his arms, he put his left hand |
| Dt | 4:14 | the land that you are c the Jordan |

## CROSSROADS* [CROSS, ROAD]

| | | |
|---|---|---|
| Jer | 6:16 | "Stand at the c and look; |
| Ob | 1:14 | at the c to cut down their fugitives, |

## CROUCHING

| | | |
|---|---|---|
| Ge | 4: 7 | what is right, sin is c at your door; |

## CROW [CROWED, CROWS]

| | | |
|---|---|---|
| Jn | 18:27 | at that moment a rooster began to c. |

## CROWD [CROWDING, CROWDS]

| | | |
|---|---|---|
| Ex | 23: 2 | "Do not follow the c in doing |
| | 23: 2 | pervert justice by siding with the c, |
| Eze | 7:12 | for my wrath is on the whole c. |
| Mt | 21: 8 | A very large c spread their cloaks |
| Lk | 9:13 | we go and buy food for all this c." |
| Jn | 7:31 | many in the c put their faith in him. |

## CROWDING [CROWD]

| | | |
|---|---|---|
| Mk | 3: 9 | him, to keep the people from c him. |
| | 5:31 | see the people c against you," |

## CROWDS [CROWD]

| | | |
|---|---|---|
| Mt | 9:36 | When he saw the c, he had |
| Ac | 8: 6 | When the c heard Philip and saw |
| | 17:13 | agitating the c and stirring them up. |

## CROWED [CROW]

| | | |
|---|---|---|
| Mt | 26:74 | Immediately a rooster c. |

## CROWN [CROWNED, CROWNS]

| | | |
|---|---|---|
| Job | 19: 9 | and removed the c from my head. |
| | 31:36 | shoulder, I would put it on like a c. |
| Pr | 4: 9 | and present you with a glorious c." |
| | 10: 6 | Blessings c the head |
| | 12: 4 | noble character is her husband's c, |
| | 14:24 | The wealth of the wise is their c, |
| | 16:31 | Gray hair is a c of splendor; |
| | 17: 6 | Children's children are a c |
| | 27:24 | a c is not secure for all generations. |
| Isa | 35:10 | everlasting joy will c their heads. |
| | 51:11 | everlasting joy will c their heads. |
| | 61: 3 | on them a c of beauty instead |
| | 62: 3 | You will be a c of splendor |
| La | 5:16 | The c has fallen from our head. |
| Eze | 16:12 | ears and a beautiful c on your head. |
| Zec | 9:16 | sparkle in his land like jewels in a c. |
| Mt | 27:29 | then twisted together a c of thorns |
| Mk | 15:17 | then twisted together a c of thorns |
| Jn | 19: 2 | The soldiers twisted together a c |
| | 19: 5 | came out wearing the c of thorns |
| 1Co | 9:25 | do it to get a c that will not last, |
| | 9:25 | do it to get a c that will last forever. |
| Php | 4: 1 | my joy and c, stand firm in the Lord |
| 1Th | 2:19 | the c in which we will glory |
| 2Ti | 2: 5 | not receive the victor's c except |
| | 4: 8 | store for me the c of righteousness, |
| Jas | 1:12 | they will receive the c of life |
| 1Pe | 5: 4 | you will receive the c of glory |
| Rev | 2:10 | will give you life as your victor's c. |
| | 3:11 | so that no one will take your c. |
| | 6: 2 | and he was given a c, and he rode |
| | 12: 1 | and a c of twelve stars on her head. |
| | 14:14 | of man with a c of gold on his head |

## CROWNED* [CROWN]

| | | |
|---|---|---|
| Ps | 8: 5 | beings and c them with glory |
| Pr | 14:18 | the prudent are c with knowledge. |
| SS | 3:11 | which his mother c him on the day |
| Heb | 2: 7 | you c them with glory and honor |
| | 2: 9 | now c with glory and honor because |

## CROWNS [CROWN]

| | | |
|---|---|---|
| Ps | 103: 4 | life from the pit and c you with love |
| | 149: 4 | he c the humble with victory. |
| Isa | 23: 8 | the bestower of c, whose merchants |
| Jer | 13:18 | for your glorious c will fall |
| Rev | 4: 4 | and had c of gold on their heads. |
| | 4:10 | They lay their c before the throne |
| | 9: 7 | heads they wore something like c |
| | 12: 3 | ten horns and seven c on its heads. |
| | 13: 1 | with ten c on its horns, and on each |
| | 19:12 | fire, and on his head are many c. |

## CROWS [CROW]

| | | |
|---|---|---|
| Mt | 26:34 | night, before the rooster c, you will |

## CRUCIFIED* [CRUCIFY]
| | | |
|---|---|---|
| Mt | 20:19 | to be mocked and flogged and c. |
| | 26: 2 | Man will be handed over to be c." |
| | 27:26 | and handed him over to be c. |
| | 27:35 | When they had c him, they divided |
| | 27:38 | Two rebels were c with him, |
| | 27:44 | the same way the rebels who were c |
| | 28: 5 | are looking for Jesus, who was c. |
| Mk | 15:15 | and handed him over to be c. |
| | 15:24 | And they c him. Dividing up his |
| | 15:25 | in the morning when they c him. |
| | 15:27 | They c two rebels with him, |
| | 15:32 | Those c with him also heaped |
| | 16: 6 | for Jesus the Nazarene, who was c. |
| Lk | 23:23 | insistently demanded that he be c, |
| | 23:33 | called the Skull, they c him there, |
| | 24: 7 | be c and on the third day be raised |
| | 24:20 | sentenced to death, and they c him; |
| Jn | 19:16 | handed him over to them to be c. |
| | 19:18 | Here they c him, and with him two |
| | 19:20 | where Jesus was c was near the city, |
| | 19:23 | When the soldiers c Jesus, they took |
| | 19:32 | the first man who had been c |
| | 19:41 | At the place where Jesus was c, |
| Ac | 2:36 | Jesus, whom you c, both Lord |
| | 4:10 | whom you c but whom God raised |
| Ro | 6: 6 | that our old self was c with him so |
| 1Co | 1:13 | Was Paul c for you? |
| | 1:23 | but we preach Christ c: |
| | 2: 2 | you except Jesus Christ and him c. |
| | 2: 8 | they would not have c the Lord |
| 2Co | 13: 4 | to be sure, he was c in weakness, |
| Gal | 2:20 | I have been c with Christ and I no |
| | 3: 1 | Christ was clearly portrayed as c. |
| | 5:24 | Christ Jesus have c the sinful nature |
| | 6:14 | which the world has been c to me, |
| Rev | 11: 8 | Egypt, where also their Lord was c. |

## CRUCIFY* [CRUCIFIED, CRUCIFYING]
| | | |
|---|---|---|
| Mt | 23:34 | Some of them you will kill and c; |
| | 27:22 | They all answered, "C him!" |
| | 27:23 | shouted all the louder, "C him!" |
| | 27:31 | Then they led him away to c him. |
| Mk | 15:13 | "C him!" they shouted. |
| | 15:14 | shouted all the louder, "C him!" |
| | 15:20 | Then they led him out to c him. |
| Lk | 23:21 | shouting, "C him! C him!" |
| Jn | 19: 6 | they shouted, "C! C!" |
| | 19: 6 | "You take him and c him. |
| | 19:10 | either to free you or to c you?" |
| | 19:15 | Take him away! C him!" |
| | 19:15 | "Shall I c your king?" |

## CRUCIFYING* [CRUCIFY]
| | | |
|---|---|---|
| Heb | 6: 6 | their loss they are c the Son of God |

## CRUEL [CRUELTY]
| | | |
|---|---|---|
| Dt | 28:33 | but c oppression all your days. |
| Pr | 11:17 | but the c bring ruin on themselves. |
| | 12:10 | the kindest acts of the wicked are c. |
| | 27: 4 | Anger is c and fury overwhelming, |
| Isa | 13: 9 | a c day, with wrath and fierce |

## CRUELTY* [CRUEL]
| | | |
|---|---|---|
| Na | 3:19 | for who has not felt your endless c? |

## CRUMBS*
| | | |
|---|---|---|
| Mt | 15:27 | "Even the dogs eat the c that fall |
| Mk | 7:28 | the table eat the children's c." |

## CRUSH [CRUSHED]
| | | |
|---|---|---|
| Ge | 3:15 | he will c your head, and you will |
| Nu | 24:17 | He will c the foreheads of Moab, |
| Ps | 68:21 | Surely God will c the heads of his |
| Isa | 53:10 | it was the LORD's will to c him |
| Da | 2:40 | so it will c and break all the others. |
| Ro | 16:20 | peace will soon c Satan under your |

## CRUSHED [CRUSH]
| | | |
|---|---|---|
| Ps | 34:18 | and saves those who are c in spirit. |
| | 51: 8 | let the bones you have c rejoice. |
| Pr | 17:22 | but a c spirit dries up the bones. |
| | 18:14 | but a c spirit who can bear? |
| Isa | 53: 5 | he was c for our iniquities; |
| Jer | 8:21 | Since my people are c, I am c; |
| Eze | 36: 3 | ravaged and c you from every side |
| Da | 7: 7 | it c and devoured its victims |
| Mt | 21:44 | anyone on whom it falls will be c." |
| 2Co | 4: 8 | pressed on every side, but not c; |

## CRY [CRIED, CRIES, CRYING]
| | | |
|---|---|---|
| Ex | 2:23 | and their c for help because of their |
| | 3: 9 | And now the c of the Israelites has |
| Nu | 20:16 | he heard our c and sent an angel |
| Jdg | 10:14 | c out to the gods you have chosen. |
| 1Sa | 9:16 | people, for their c has reached me." |
| 1Ki | 17:22 | The LORD heard Elijah's c, |
| Ps | 5: 2 | Hear my c for help, my King |
| | 6: 9 | The LORD has heard my c |
| | 29: 9 | And in his temple all c, "Glory!" |
| | 34:15 | and his ears are attentive to their c. |
| | 40: 1 | he turned to me and heard my c. |
| | 130: 1 | Out of the depths I c to you, |
| Pr | 2: 3 | and c aloud for understanding, |
| | 21:13 | to the c of the poor will also c |
| Isa | 3: 7 | But in that day he will c out, |
| Jer | 4:31 | I hear a c as of a woman in labor, |
| | 4:31 | the c of Daughter Zion gasping |
| | 14:12 | they fast, I will not listen to their c; |
| La | 2:18 | The hearts of the people c |
| Hos | 7:14 | They do not c out to me from their |
| Hab | 2:11 | The stones of the wall will c out, |
| Lk | 19:40 | keep quiet, the stones will c out." |
| Ro | 8:15 | And by him we c, "Abba, Father." |
| Rev | 18:10 | they will stand far off and c: |

## CRYING [CRY]
| | | |
|---|---|---|
| Ge | 21:17 | God heard the boy c, and the angel |
| | 21:17 | has heard the boy c as he lies there. |
| Jn | 20:11 | Mary stood outside the tomb c. |
| Rev | 21: 4 | death' or mourning or c or pain, |

## CRYSTAL*
| | | |
|---|---|---|
| Job | 28:17 | Neither gold nor c can compare |
| Eze | 1:22 | sparkling like c, and awesome. |
| Rev | 4: 6 | looked like a sea of glass, clear as c. |
| | 21:11 | jewel, like a jasper, clear as c. |
| | 22: 1 | life, as clear as c, |

## CUBITS

Ge   6:15  three hundred **c** long, fifty **c** wide and
            thirty **c** high.
1Sa 17: 4  His height was six **c** and a span.

## CUBS

2Sa 17: 8  as a wild bear robbed of her **c**.
Pr   17:12  bear robbed of her **c** than a fool bent
Hos 13: 8  Like a bear robbed of her **c**, I will

## CUD

Lev 11: 3  a divided hoof and that chews the **c**.
Dt   14: 6  a divided hoof and that chews the **c**.

## CULMINATION*

Ro   10: 4  Christ is the **c** of the law
1Co 10:11  the **c** of the ages has come.
Heb  9:26  once for all at the **c** of the ages

## CULTIVATE* [CULTIVATED]

Dt   28:39  You will plant vineyards and **c** them
Ps 104:14  cattle, and plants for people to **c**—

## CULTIVATED [CULTIVATE]

Ro   11:24  were grafted into a **c** olive tree,

## CUNNING*

Ps   64: 6  the human mind and heart are **c**.
      83: 3  **c** they conspire against your people;
2Co 11: 3  was deceived by the serpent's **c**,
Eph  4:14  by the **c** and craftiness of people

## CUP [CUPS]

Ge   40:11  Pharaoh's **c** was in my hand, and I
      40:11  **c** and put the **c** in his hand."
      44: 2  Then put my **c**, the silver one,
2Sa 12: 3  drank from his **c** and even slept
1Ki  7:26  and its rim was like the rim of a **c**,
Ps   23: 5  my head with oil; my **c** overflows.
      75: 8  of the LORD is a **c** full of foaming
Pr   23:31  when it sparkles in the **c**, when it
Isa  51:22  of your hand the **c** that made you
      51:22  from that **c**, the goblet of my wrath,
Jer  25:15  my hand this **c** filled with the wine
Eze  23:31  so I will put her **c** into your hand.
Mt   10:42  anyone gives even a **c** of cold water
      20:22  "Can you drink the **c** I am going
      23:25  You clean the outside of the **c**
      23:26  First clean the inside of the **c**
      26:27  Then he took the **c**, and when he
      26:39  may this **c** be taken from me.
Mk   9:41  anyone who gives you a **c** of water
      10:38  "Can you drink the **c** I drink or be
      14:23  Then he took the **c**, and when he
      14:36  Take this **c** from me.
Lk   11:39  Pharisees clean the outside of the **c**
      22:17  After taking the **c**, he gave thanks
      22:20  way, after the supper he took the **c**,
      22:20  "This **c** is the new covenant in my
      22:42  you are willing, take this **c** from me;
Jn   18:11  Shall I not drink the **c** the Father has
1Co  10:21  You cannot drink the **c** of the Lord
      10:21  of the Lord and the **c** of demons too;
      11:25  after supper he took the **c**, saying,
      11:25  "This **c** is the new covenant in my

1Co 11:27  or drinks the **c** of the Lord
Rev 14:10  full strength into the **c** of his wrath.
      16:19  gave her the **c** filled with the wine
      17: 4  She held a golden **c** in her hand,
      18: 6  a double portion from her own **c**.

## CUPBEARER

Ge   40: 1  the **c** and the baker of the king
      41: 9  Then the chief **c** said to Pharaoh,
Ne   1:11  of this man." I was **c** to the king.

## CUPS [CUP]

Ex   25:33  Three **c** shaped like almond flowers
Mk   7: 4  such as the washing of **c**,

## CURDS

Ge   18: 8  He then brought some **c** and milk
Dt   32:14  with **c** and milk from herd and flock
Isa  7:15  He will be eating **c** and honey
Eze  34: 3  You eat the **c**, clothe yourselves

## CURE [CURED]

2Ki  5: 3  He would **c** him of his leprosy."
Jer  17: 9  above all things and beyond **c**.
      30:15  wound, your pain that has no **c**?
Hos  5:13  But he is not able to **c** you, not able
Lk   9: 1  out all demons and to **c** diseases,

## CURED [CURE]

Lk   6:18  troubled by evil spirits were **c**,
Jn   5: 9  At once the man was **c**;
Ac   19:12  their illnesses were **c** and the evil
      28: 9  sick on the island came and were **c**.

## CURRENTS*

Jnh  2: 3  seas, and the **c** swirled about me;

## CURSE [ACCURSED, CURSED, CURSES, CURSING]

Ge   4:11  Now you are under a **c** and driven
      8:21  again will I **c** the ground because
      12: 3  and whoever curses you I will **c**;
      27:13  him, "My son, let the **c** fall on me.
Ex   22:28  God or the ruler of your people.
Lev  22:28  " 'Do not **c** the deaf or put
      24:11  blasphemed the Name with a **c**;
Nu   5:18  holds the bitter water that brings a **c**.
      22: 6  come and put a **c** on these people,
      22: 6  and whoever you **c** is cursed."
      22:12  You must not put a **c** on those
Dt   11:26  you today a blessing and a **c**—
      11:28  the **c** if you disobey the commands
      21:23  is hung on a pole is under God's **c**.
      23: 5  turned the **c** into a blessing for you,
Jos  9:23  You are now under a **c**:
      24: 9  son of Beor to put a **c** on you.
2Sa 16: 9  should this dead dog **c** my lord
2Ki 10:24  and called down a **c** on them
Ne   10:29  and bind themselves with a **c**
      13: 2  Balaam to call a **c** down on them.
      13: 2  turned the **c** into a blessing.)
Job  1:11  he will surely **c** you to your face."
      2: 5  he will surely **c** you to your face."
      2: 9  **C** God and die!"
Ps   62: 4  they bless, but in their hearts they **c**.

| | | |
|---|---|---|
| Ps | 109:28 | While they **c**, may you bless; |
| Pr | 3:33 | The LORD's **c** is on the house |
| | 20:20 | If you **c** your father or mother, |
| | 30:11 | "There are those who **c** their fathers |
| Isa | 24: 6 | Therefore a **c** consumes the earth; |
| Jer | 24: 9 | a **c** and an object of ridicule, |
| | 42:18 | a **c** and an object of reproach; |
| | 44:12 | a curse and an object of reproach. |
| La | 3:65 | hearts, and may your **c** be on them! |
| Mal | 2: 2 | Almighty, "I will send a **c** on you, |
| | 2: 2 | and I will **c** your blessings. |
| Lk | 6:28 | bless those who **c** you, |
| Jn | 7:49 | of the law—there is a **c** on them." |
| Ro | 12:14 | bless and do not **c**. |
| Gal | 1: 8 | let that person be under God's **c**! |
| | 1: 9 | let that person be under God's **c**! |
| | 3:10 | on observing the law are under a **c**, |
| | 3:13 | **c** of the law by becoming a **c** for us, |
| Jas | 3: 9 | and with it we **c** human beings, |
| Rev | 22: 3 | No longer will there be any **c**. |

## CURSED [CURSE]

| | | |
|---|---|---|
| Ge | 3:14 | "**C** are you above all livestock |
| | 3:17 | "**C** is the ground because of you; |
| | 9:25 | he said, "**C** be Canaan! |
| | 27:29 | May those who curse you be **c** |
| Lev | 20: 9 | Because they have **c** their father |
| Nu | 22: 6 | and whoever you curse is **c**." |
| | 23. 8 | I curse those whom God has not **c**? |
| Dt | 27:15 | "**C** is anyone who makes an idol— |
| | 27:16 | "**C** is anyone who dishonors their |
| | 27:17 | "**C** is anyone who moves their |
| | 27:18 | "**C** is anyone who leads the blind |
| | 27:19 | "**C** is anyone who withholds justice |
| | 27:20 | "**C** is anyone who sleeps with his |
| | 27:21 | "**C** is anyone who has sexual |
| | 27:22 | "**C** is anyone who sleeps with his |
| | 27:23 | "**C** is anyone who sleeps with his |
| | 27:24 | "**C** is anyone who kills their |
| | 27:25 | "**C** is anyone who accepts a bribe |
| | 27:26 | "**C** is anyone who does not uphold |
| | 28:16 | You will be **c** in the city and **c** |
| Jos | 6:26 | "**C** before the LORD is anyone |
| 1Sa | 17:43 | the Philistine **c** David by his gods. |
| 2Sa | 16: 7 | As he **c**, Shimei said, "Get out, |
| | 19:21 | He **c** the LORD's anointed." |
| 2Ki | 9:34 | "Take care of that **c** woman," |
| Job | 1: 5 | sinned and **c** God in their hearts." |
| | 3: 1 | his mouth and **c** the day of his birth. |
| Pr | 24:24 | will be **c** by peoples and denounced |
| Jer | 17: 5 | "**C** are those who trust in mortals, |
| Mal | 1:14 | "**C** is the cheat who has |
| Mk | 11:21 | The fig tree you **c** has withered!" |
| Ro | 9: 3 | I could wish that I myself were **c** |
| 1Co | 4:12 | When we are **c**, we bless; |
| | 12: 3 | "Jesus be **c**," and no one can say, |
| | 16:22 | let that person be **c**! Come, Lord! |
| Gal | 3:10 | "**C** is everyone who does not |
| | 3:13 | "**C** is everyone who is hung |
| Heb | 6: 8 | and is in danger of being **c**. |
| Rev | 16: 9 | heat and they **c** the name of God, |
| | 16:11 | and **c** the God of heaven because |
| | 16:21 | they **c** God on account of the plague |

## CURSES [CURSE]

| | | |
|---|---|---|
| Ge | 12: 3 | you, and whoever **c** you I will curse; |

| | | |
|---|---|---|
| Ex | 21:17 | "Anyone who **c** their father |
| Lev | 20: 9 | " 'Anyone who **c** their father |
| | 24:15 | 'Anyone who **c** their God will be |
| Nu | 5:23 | priest is to write these **c** on a scroll |
| Dt | 11:29 | blessings, and on Mount Ebal the **c**. |
| | 27:13 | on Mount Ebal to pronounce **c**: |
| | 28:15 | all these **c** will come on you |
| Jos | 8:34 | the blessings and the **c**—just as it is |
| 2Ch | 34:24 | all the **c** written in the book that has |
| Ne | 13:25 | them and called **c** down on them |
| Pr | 28:27 | their eyes to them receive many **c**. |
| Mt | 15: 4 | and 'Anyone who **c** their father |
| Mk | 14:71 | He began to call down **c**, and he |

## CURSING [CURSE]

| | | |
|---|---|---|
| 2Sa | 16:10 | If he is **c** because the LORD said |
| Ps | 109:18 | He wore **c** as his garment; |
| Hos | 4: 2 | There is only **c**, lying and murder, |
| Ro | 3:14 | "Their mouths are full of **c** |
| Jas | 3:10 | the same mouth come praise and **c**. |

## CURTAIN [CURTAINS]

| | | |
|---|---|---|
| Ex | 26:31 | "Make a **c** of blue, |
| | 26:36 | to the tent make a **c** of blue, |
| Mt | 27:51 | that moment the **c** of the temple was |
| Mk | 15:38 | The **c** of the temple was torn in two |
| Lk | 23:45 | the **c** of the temple was torn in two. |
| Heb | 6:19 | the inner sanctuary behind the **c**, |
| | 9: 3 | Behind the second **c** was a room |
| | 10:20 | way opened for us through the **c**, |

## CURTAINS [CURTAIN]

| | | |
|---|---|---|
| Ex | 26: 1 | with ten **c** of finely twisted linen |
| Nu | 3:26 | the **c** of the courtyard, the curtain |

## CUSH [CUSHITE]

| | | |
|---|---|---|
| Ge | 2:13 | winds through the entire land of C. |
| | 10: 6 | **C**, Egypt, Put and Canaan. |
| Ps | 7: T | *sang to the LORD concerning C,* |
| Isa | 20: 3 | and portent against Egypt and C, |

## CUSHITE [CUSH]

| | | |
|---|---|---|
| Nu | 12: 1 | his **C** wife, for he had married a C. |
| 2Sa | 18:21 | Then Joab said to a **C**, "Go, |
| | 18:21 | The **C** bowed down before Joab |
| Jer | 38: 7 | a **C**, an official in the royal palace, |

## CUSTODY

| | | |
|---|---|---|
| Gal | 3:23 | held in **c** under the law, |

## CUSTOM [CUSTOMS]

| | | |
|---|---|---|
| Job | 1: 5 | This was Job's regular **c**. |
| Mk | 10: 1 | and as was his **c**, he taught them. |
| | 15: 6 | Now it was the **c** at the festival |
| Lk | 4:16 | into the synagogue, as was his **c**. |
| Ac | 15: 1 | according to the **c** taught by Moses, |
| | 17: 2 | As was his **c**, Paul went |

## CUSTOMS [CUSTOM]

| | | |
|---|---|---|
| Lev | 18:30 | the detestable **c** that were practiced |
| | 20:23 | to the **c** of the nations I am going |
| Ps | 106:35 | with the nations and adopted their **c**. |
| Jn | 19:40 | in accordance with Jewish burial **c**. |
| Gal | 2:14 | force Gentiles to follow Jewish **c**? |

## CUT [CUTS, CUTTING]

Ge 15:10 him, **c** them in two and arranged
15:10 birds, however, he did not **c** in half.
17:14 flesh, will be **c** off from his people;
Ex 34:13 and **c** down their Asherah poles.
Lev 19:27 " 'Do not **c** the hair at the sides
19:28 " 'Do not **c** your bodies
21: 5 of their beards or **c** their bodies.
Dt 20:20 you may **c** down trees that you
Jos 4: 7 the Jordan was **c** off before the ark
4: 7 the waters of the Jordan were **c** off.
Jdg 21: 6 "Today one tribe is **c** off
1Sa 17:51 he **c** off his head with the sword.
24: 4 and **c** off a corner of Saul's robe.
2Sa 14:26 Whenever he **c** the hair of his head—
14:26 to **c** his hair once a year because it
1Ki 3:25 "**C** the living child in two and give
2Ch 15:16 Asa **c** it down, broke it
31: 1 and **c** down the Asherah poles.
34: 7 and **c** to pieces all the incense altars
Ps 31:22 said, "I am **c** off from your sight!"
118:10 name of the LORD I **c** them down.
Pr 2:22 the wicked will be **c** off
23:18 you, and your hope will not be **c** off.
Isa 9:14 So the LORD will **c** off from Israel
51: 1 to the rock from which you were **c**
53: 8 For he was **c** off from the land
Jer 34:18 I will treat like the calf they **c** in two
Eze 37:11 and our hope is gone; we are **c** off.'
Da 2:45 of the vision of the rock **c**
Mt 3:10 produce good fruit will be **c** down
24:22 "If those days had not been **c** short,
Mk 9:43 hand causes you to stumble, **c** it off.
15:46 placed it in a tomb **c** out of rock.
Jn 18:26 the man whose ear Peter had **c** off,
Ac 2:37 they were **c** to the heart and said
Ro 11:22 Otherwise, you also will be **c** off.
1Co 11: 6 might as well have her hair **c** off;

**MUST BE CUT OFF** See MUST

## CUTS [CUT]

Jn 15: 2 He **c** off every branch in me

## CUTTING [CUT]

Pr 26: 6 of a fool is like **c** off one's feet
Jn 18:10 priest's servant, **c** off his right ear.

## CYMBAL* [CYMBALS]

1Co 13: 1 a resounding gong or a clanging **c**.

## CYMBALS [CYMBAL]

2Sa 6: 5 lyres, timbrels, sistrums and **c**.
1Ch 15:16 lyres, harps and **c**.
2Ch 5:12 dressed in fine linen and playing **c**,
29:25 in the temple of the LORD with **c**,
Ezr 3:10 Levites (the sons of Asaph) with **c**,
Ne 12:27 and with the music of **c**,
Ps 150: 5 of **c**, praise him with resounding **c**.

## CYPRESS

Ge 6:14 So make yourself an ark of **c** wood;

## CYPRUS

Ac 4:36 a Levite from **C**, whom the apostles

Ac 13: 4 Seleucia and sailed from there to **C**.

## CYRENE

Lk 23:26 they seized Simon from **C**, who was

## CYRUS

Persian king who allowed exiles to return (2Ch 36:22—Ezr 1:8), to rebuild temple (Ezr 5:13—6:14), as appointed by the LORD (Isa 44:28—45:13).

---

# D

## DAGON [DAGON'S]

Jdg 16:23 offer a great sacrifice to **D** their god
1Ch 10:10 hung up his head in the temple of **D**.

## DAGON'S [DAGON]

1Sa 5: 2 they carried the ark into **D** temple

## DAILY [DAY]

1Ki 4:22 Solomon's **d** provisions were thirty
2Ch 8:13 according to the **d** requirement
Job 23:12 of his mouth more than my **d** bread.
Ps 68:19 Savior, who **d** bears our burdens.
Pr 30: 8 but give me only my **d** bread.
Da 8:13 vision concerning the **d** sacrifice,
11:31 and will abolish the **d** sacrifice,
Mt 6:11 Give us today our **d** bread.
Lk 9:23 take up their cross **d** and follow me.
11: 3 Give us each day our **d** bread.
Jas 2:15 sister is without clothes and **d** food.

## DAMASCUS

2Ki 8: 7 Elisha went to **D**, and Ben-Hadad
16:10 Then King Ahaz went to **D** to meet
16:10 He saw an altar in **D** and sent
Isa 7: 8 **D**, and the head of **D** is only Rezin.
17: 1 A prophecy concerning **D**: "See,
Jer 49:23 Concerning **D**: "Hamath and Arpad
Am 1: 3 "For three sins of **D**, even for four,
Ac 9: 3 As he neared **D** on his journey,
22: 6 "About noon as I came near **D**,
Gal 1:17 Later I returned to **D**.

## DAN

1. Son of Jacob by Bilhah (Ge 30:4–6; 35:25; 46:23). Tribe of blessed (Ge 49:16–17; Dt 33:22), numbered (Nu 1:39; 26:43), allotted land (Jos 19:40–48; Eze 48:1), failed to fully possess (Jdg 1:34–35), failed to support Deborah (Jdg 5:17), possessed Laish/Dan (Jdg 18).
2. Northernmost city in Israel (Ge 14:14; Jdg 18; 20:1).

## DANCE [DANCED, DANCES, DANCING]

Ecc 3: 4 a time to mourn and a time to **d**,
Jer 31: 4 and go out to **d** with the joyful.
31:13 young women will **d** and be glad,
Lk 7:32 the pipe for you, and you did not **d**;

## DANCED* [DANCE]

1Sa 18: 7 As they **d**, they sang:
1Ki 18:26 they **d** around the altar they had
Mt 14: 6 the daughter of Herodias **d** for them
Mk 6:22 daughter of Herodias came in and **d**,

## DANCES* [DANCE]

1Sa 21:11 he the one they sing about in their **d**:
   29: 5 the David they sang about in their **d**:

## DANCING [DANCE]

Ex 15:20 followed her, with timbrels and **d**.
   32:19 the camp and saw the calf and the **d**,
Jdg 11:34 daughter, **d** to the sound of timbrels!
   21:23 While the young women were **d**,
2Sa 6:14 David was **d** before the LORD
   6:16 leaping and **d** before the LORD,
1Ch 15:29 when she saw King David **d**
Ps 30:11 You turned my wailing into **d**;
   149: 3 Let them praise his name with **d**
La 5:15 our **d** has turned to mourning.

## DANGER

Pr 22: 3 The prudent see **d** and take refuge,
   27:12 The prudent see **d** and take refuge,
Mt 5:22 will be in **d** of the fire of hell.
Ac 19:40 is, we are in **d** of being charged
Ro 8:35 famine or nakedness or **d** or sword?
2Co 11:26 in **d** from my own people, in **d** from
         Gentiles;
   11:26 and in **d** from false believers.
Heb 6: 8 and is in **d** of being cursed.

## DANIEL

1. Hebrew exile to Babylon, name changed to Bel-
teshazzar (Da 1:6–7). Refused to eat unclean food
(Da 1:8–21). Interpreted Nebuchadnezzar's dreams
(Da 2; 4), writing on the wall (Da 5). Thrown into
lion's den (Da 6). Visions of (Da 7–12).
   2. Son of David (1Ch 3:1).

## DARE [DARED]

Jn 9:34 sin at birth; how **d** you lecture us!"
Ac 7:32 with fear and did not **d** to look.
Ro 5: 7 person someone might possibly **d**

## DARED [DARE]

Mk 12:34 then on no one **d** ask him any more
Jn 21:12 None of the disciples **d** ask him,

## DARIUS

1. King of Persia (Ezr 4:5), allowed rebuilding of
temple (Ezr 5–6).
   2. Mede who conquered Babylon (Da 5:31).

## DARK [DARKENED, DARKENS,
   DARKEST, DARKNESS]

2Sa 22:10 **d** clouds were under his feet.
2Ch 6: 1 that he would dwell in a **d** cloud;
Ps 35: 6 may their path be **d** and slippery,
   139:12 even the darkness will not be **d**
Pr 2:13 the straight paths to walk in **d** ways,
SS 1: 5 **D** am I, yet lovely,
   1: 5 Jerusalem, **d** like the tents of Kedar,

Isa 50:10 Let those who walk in the **d**,
Jer 4:28 and the heavens above grow **d**,
Lk 12: 3 you have said in the **d** will be heard
Jn 12:35 in the **d** do not know where they are
Ro 2:19 a light for those who are in the **d**,
Eph 6:12 against the powers of this **d** world
2Pe 1:19 it, as to a light shining in a **d** place,
Rev 8:12 so that a third of them turned **d**.

## DARKENED [DARK]

SS 1: 6 am dark, because I am **d** by the sun.
Joel 2:10 the sun and moon are **d**,
Mt 24:29 of those days " 'the sun will be **d**,
Ro 1:21 and their foolish hearts were **d**.
Eph 4:18 They are **d** in their understanding
Rev 9: 2 sky were **d** by the smoke

## DARKENS* [DARK]

Am 5: 8 into dawn and **d** day into night,

## DARKEST* [DARK]

Ps 23: 4 though I walk through the **d** valley,
   88 6 lowest pit, in the **d** depths.

## DARKNESS [DARK]

Ge 1: 2 **d** was over the surface of the deep,
   1: 4 he separated the light from the **d**.
   15:12 thick and dreadful **d** came over him.
Ex 10:22 total **d** covered all Egypt for three
   14:20 the night the cloud brought **d**
   20:21 approached the thick **d** where God
Dt 5:23 you heard the voice out of the **d**,
Jos 24: 7 and he put **d** between you
2Sa 22:29 the LORD turns my **d** into light.
Job 12:22 of **d** and brings utter **d** into the light.
Ps 18:11 He made **d** his covering, his canopy
   91: 6 the pestilence that stalks in the **d**,
   97: 2 Clouds and thick **d** surround him;
   107:10 Some sat in **d**, in utter **d**,
   112: 4 Even in **d** light dawns
   139:12 even the **d** will not be dark to you;
   139:12 like the day, for **d** is as light to you.
Pr 4:19 way of the wicked is like deep **d**;
Ecc 2:13 folly, just as light is better than **d**.
   5:17 All their days they eat in **d**,
Isa 5:20 who put **d** for light and light for **d**,
   9: 2 walking in **d** have seen a great light;
   9: 2 land of deep **d** a light has dawned.
   42:16 I will turn the **d** into light before
   45: 7 I form the light and create **d**, I bring
   58:10 then your light will rise in the **d**,
   61: 1 and release from **d** for the prisoners,
Jer 13:16 your God before he brings the **d**,
   13:16 he will turn it to utter **d** and change
Joel 2:31 The sun will be turned to **d**
Am 5:20 not the day of the LORD be **d**,
Na 1: 8 he will pursue his foes into **d**.
Zep 1:15 and ruin, a day of **d** and gloom,
Mt 4:16 living in **d** have seen a great light;
   6:23 within you is **d**, how great is that **d**!
   22:13 into the **d**, where there will be
Lk 11:34 your body also is full of **d**.
   23:44 **d** came over the whole land until
Jn 1: 5 The light shines in the **d**, and the **d**
   3:19 but people loved **d** instead of light
   8:12 follows me will never walk in **d**,

Ac   2:20   The sun will be turned to **d**
Ro   13:12  So let us put aside the deeds of **d**
2Co  4: 6   "Let light shine out of **d**," made his
      6:14  fellowship can light have with **d**?
Eph  5: 8   For you were once **d**, but now you
      5:11  to do with the fruitless deeds of **d**,
Col  1:13   rescued us from the dominion of **d**
1Th  5: 5   not belong to the night or to the **d**.
1Pe  2: 9   out of **d** into his wonderful light.
2Pe  2: 4   putting them in chains of **d**
      2:17  Blackest **d** is reserved for them.
1Jn  1: 5   in him there is no **d** at all.
      2: 8   because the **d** is passing and the true
      2: 9   a fellow believer are still in the **d**.
Jude 1: 6   these he has kept in **d**,
      1:13  whom blackest **d** has been reserved
Rev  16:10  and its kingdom was plunged into **d**.

# DARLING
SS   1:15   How beautiful you are, my **d**!
      2:10  me, "Arise, my **d**, my beautiful one,
      5: 2   me, my sister, my **d**, my dove,

# DASH [DASHED]
2Ki  8:12   **d** their little children to the ground,
Ps   2: 9   you will **d** them to pieces like
Lk   19:44  They will **d** you to the ground,
Rev  2:27   will **d** them to pieces like pottery'—

# DASHED [DASH]
Hos  10:14  when mothers were **d** to the ground
Na   3:10   Her infants were **d** to pieces

# DATES*
2Sa  6:19   a cake of **d** and a cake of raisins
1Ch  16: 3  a cake of **d** and a cake of raisins
Ac   1: 7   or **d** the Father has set by his own
1Th  5: 1   **d** we do not need to write to you,

# DATHAN*
Involved in Korah's rebellion against Moses and Aaron (Nu 16:1–27; 26:9; Dt 11:6; Ps 106:17).

# DAUGHTER [DAUGHTER-IN-LAW, DAUGHTERS, DAUGHTERS-IN-LAW]
Ge   19:31  One day the older **d** said
      24:24  him, "I am the **d** of Bethuel, the son
      29:10  When Jacob saw Rachel **d** of Laban,
      34: 3  was drawn to Dinah **d** of Jacob;
      38: 2  There Judah met the **d**
Ex   2: 5   Pharaoh's **d** went down to the Nile
      21: 7  "If a man sells his **d** as a servant,
Lev  12: 5   If she gives birth to a **d**, for two
Nu   27: 8  no son, give his inheritance to his **d**.
Jdg  11:34  come out to meet him but his **d**,
      11:34  for her he had neither son nor **d**.
Ru   2: 2   said to her, "Go ahead, my **d**."
      3:10  bless you, my **d**," he replied.
1Sa  18:20  Now Saul's **d** Michal was in love
2Sa  6:16   Michal **d** of Saul watched
1Ki  11: 1  women besides Pharaoh's **d**—
Est  2: 7   had taken her as his own **d** when her
Ps   9:14   your praises in the gates of **D** Zion,
      137: 8 **D** Babylon, doomed to destruction,

Isa  47: 1  sit in the dust, Virgin **D** Babylon;
      52: 2  the chains on your neck, **D** Zion,
      62:11  "Say to **D** Zion, 'See, your Savior
Jer  6: 2   I will destroy **D** Zion, so beautiful
      46:11  and get balm, Virgin **D** Egypt.
Eze  16:45  You are a true **d** of your mother,
Mic  7: 6   a **d** rises up against her mother,
Zep  3:14   Sing, **D** Zion; shout aloud, Israel!
      3:14  with all your heart, **D** Jerusalem!
Zec  9: 9   Rejoice greatly, **D** Zion! Shout,
Mt   14: 6  Herod's birthday the **d** of Herodias
      15:28  her **d** was healed from that very
Mk   5:35   "Your **d** is dead," they said.
      7:29  the demon has left your **d**."
Lk   12:53  mother against **d** and **d** against

# DAUGHTER JERUSALEM
2Ki 19:21; Isa 37:22; La 2:13, 15; Mic 4:8; Zep 3:14; Zec 9:9

# DAUGHTER ZION
2Ki 19:21; Ps 9:14; Isa 1:8; 10:32; 16:1; 37:22; 52:2; 62:11; Jer 4:31; 6:2, 23; La 1:6; 2:1, 4, 8, 10, 13, 18; 4:22; Mic 1:13; 4:8, 10, 13; Zep 3:14; Zec 2:10; 9:9; Mt 21:5; Jn 12:15

# DAUGHTER-IN-LAW [DAUGHTER]
Ge   11:31  and his **d** Sarai, the wife of his son
      38:16  Not realizing that she was his **d**,
Lev  20:12  man has sexual relations with his **d**,
Ru   1:22   her **d**, arriving in Bethlehem as
1Ch  2: 4   Judah's **d** Tamar bore Perez
Mic  7: 6   a **d** against her mother-in-law—
Mt   10:35  a **d** against her mother-in-law—

# DAUGHTERS [DAUGHTER]
Ge   6: 2   saw that these **d** were beautiful,
      6: 4   went to the **d** of the human beings
      19:36  So both of Lot's **d** became pregnant
      29:16  Now Laban had two **d**; the name
Ex   2:16   Now a priest of Midian had seven **d**,
Nu   27: 1  The **d** of Zelophehad son of Hepher,
      27: 1  The names of the **d** were Mahlah,
      36:10  So Zelophehad's **d** did as
Dt   7: 3   Do not give your **d** to their sons
      7: 3   sons or take their **d** for your sons,
      12:31  and **d** in the fire as sacrifices to their
Ezr  9:12   do not give your **d** in marriage
      9:12   sons or take their **d** for your sons.
Job  42:15  women as beautiful as Job's **d**,
Ps   144:12 our **d** will be like pillars carved
Pr   30:15  "The leech has two **d**. 'Give!'
SS   1: 5   yet lovely, **d** of Jerusalem, dark like
Eze  23: 2  two women, **d** of the same mother.
Joel 2:28   Your sons and **d** will prophesy,
Lk   23:28  and said to them, "**D** of Jerusalem,
Ac   2:17   Your sons and **d** will prophesy,
      21: 9  four unmarried **d** who prophesied.
2Co  6:18   and you will be my sons and **d**,
1Pe  3: 6   You are her **d** if you do what is right

# DAUGHTERS OF JERUSALEM
SS 1:5; 2:7; 3:5, 10; 5:8, 16; 8:4; Lk 23:28

# DAUGHTERS-IN-LAW [DAUGHTER]
Ru   1: 8   Then Naomi said to her two **d**,

# DAVID

Son of Jesse (Ru 4:17–22; 1Ch 2:13–15), ancestor of Jesus (Mt 1:1–17; Lk 3:31). Wives and children (1Sa 18; 25:39–44; 2Sa 3:2–5; 5:13–16; 11:27; 1Ch 3:1–9).

Anointed king by Samuel (1Sa 16:1–13). Musician to Saul (1Sa 16:14–23; 18:10). Killed Goliath (1Sa 17). Relation with Jonathan (1Sa 18:1–4; 19–20; 23:16–18; 2Sa 1). Disfavor of Saul (1Sa 18:6—23:29). Spared Saul's life (1Sa 24; 26). Among Philistines (1Sa 21:10–14; 27–30). Lament for Saul and Jonathan (2Sa 1).

Anointed king of Judah (2Sa 2:1–11). Conflict with house of Saul (2Sa 2–4). Anointed king of Israel (2Sa 5:1–4; 1Ch 11:1–3). Conquered Jerusalem (2Sa 5:6–10; 1Ch 11;4–9). Brought ark to Jerusalem (2Sa 6; 1Ch 13; 15–16). The LORD promised eternal dynasty (2Sa 7; 1Ch 17; Ps 132). Showed kindness to Mephibosheth (2Sa 9). Adultery with Bathsheba, murder of Uriah (2Sa 11–12). Son Amnon raped daughter Tamar; killed by Absalom (2Sa 13). Absalom's revolt (2Sa 14–17); death (2Sa 18). Sheba's revolt (2Sa 20). Victories: Philistines (2Sa 5:17–25; 21:15–22; 1Ch 14:8–17; 20:4–8), Ammonites (2Sa 10; 1Ch 19), various (2Sa 8; 1Ch 18). Mighty men (2Sa 23:8–39; 1Ch 11–12). Punished for numbering army (2Sa 24; 1Ch 21). Appointed Solomon king (1Ki 1:28—2:9). Prepared for building of temple (1Ch 22–29). Last words (2Sa 23:1–7) Death (1Ki 2:10–12; 1Ch 29:28).

Psalmist (Mt 22:43–45), musician (Am 6:5), prophet (2Sa 23:2–7; Ac 1:16; 2:30).

Psalms of: 2 (Ac 4:25), 3–32, 34–41, 51–65, 68–70, 86, 95 (Heb 4:7), 101, 103, 108–110, 122, 124, 131, 133, 138–145.

## CITY OF DAVID See CITY

## HOUSE OF DAVID See HOUSE

## SON OF DAVID See SON

# DAWN [DAWNED, DAWNS]

Job 38:12 morning, or shown the **d** its place,
Ps  37: 6 righteous reward shine like the **d**,
    57: 8 harp and lyre! I will awaken the **d**.
   139: 9 If I rise on the wings of the **d**, if I
SS   6:10 Who is this that appears like the **d**,
Isa 14:12 heaven, morning star, son of the **d**!
    62: 1 her vindication shines out like the **d**,
Am   4:13 to mortals, who turns **d** to darkness,
Mt  28: 1 at **d** on the first day of the week,

# DAWNED [DAWN]

Isa  9: 2 land of deep darkness a light has **d**.
Mt   4:16 the shadow of death a light has **d**."

# DAWNS* [DAWN]

Ps  65: 8 where morning **d**, where evening
   112: 4 in darkness light **d** for the upright,
Hos 10:15 When that day **d**, the king of Israel
2Pe  1:19 until the day **d** and the morning star

# DAY [DAILY, DAY'S, DAYBREAK, DAYLIGHT, DAYS, MIDDAY]

Ge   1: 5 God called the light "**d**,"

Ge   1: 5 and there was morning—the first **d**.
     1: 8 there was morning—the second **d**.
     1:13 and there was morning—the third **d**.
     1:19 and there was morning—the fourth **d**.
     1:23 and there was morning—the fifth **d**.
     1:31 and there was morning—the sixth **d**.
     2: 2 the seventh **d** God had finished
     2: 2 so on the seventh **d** he rested
     8:22 **d** and night will never cease."
Ex  12:17 on this very **d** that I brought your
    12:17 Celebrate this **d** as a lasting
    13:21 By **d** the LORD went ahead
    13:21 so that they could travel by **d**
    16:30 the people rested on the seventh **d**.
    20: 8 "Remember the Sabbath **d**
    40: 2 on the first **d** of the first month.
Lev 12: 3 On the eighth **d** the boy is to be
    16:30 on this **d** atonement will be made
    23:28 **d**, because it is the **D** of Atonement,
Nu  14:14 before them in a pillar of cloud by **d**
Dt   1:33 in fire by night and in a cloud by **d**,
    24:15 their wages each **d** before sunset,
    30:19 This **d** I call the heavens
    34: 6 this **d** no one knows where his grave
Jos  1: 8 meditate on it **d** and night,
    10:14 has never been a **d** like it before
    10:14 a **d** when the LORD listened
2Ki  7: 9 This is a **d** of good news and we are
    25:30 **D** by **d** the king gave Jehoiachin
1Ch 16:23 proclaim his salvation **d** after **d**.
Ne   8:10 This **d** is holy to our Lord.
     8:18 **D** after **d**, from the first **d** to the last,
Ps   1: 2 and meditate on his law **d** and night.
    19: 2 **D** after **d** they pour forth speech;
    37:13 for he knows his **d** is coming.
    50:15 and call on me in the **d** of trouble;
    84:10 Better is one **d** in your courts than
    96: 2 proclaim his salvation **d** after **d**.
   118:24 The LORD has done it this very **d**;
   119:97 I meditate on it all **d** long.
   119:164 Seven times a **d** I praise you
Pr  11: 4 is worthless in the **d** of wrath,
    27: 1 do not know what a **d** may bring.
Ecc  7: 1 the **d** of death better than the **d**
Isa  2:12 The LORD Almighty has a **d**
    13: 9 the **d** of the LORD is coming—
    13: 9 a cruel **d**, with wrath and fierce
    49: 8 in the **d** of salvation I will help you;
    60:19 sun will no more be your light by **d**,
    66: 8 Can a country be born in a **d**
Jer 17:22 but keep the Sabbath **d** holy, as I
    30: 7 How awful that **d** will be!
    46:10 But that **d** belongs to the Lord,
    46:10 a **d** of vengeance, for vengeance
    50:31 "for your **d** has come, the time
Eze  4: 6 you 40 days, a **d** for each year.
     7: 7 The time has come! The **d** is near!
    30: 2 and say, "Alas for that **d**!"
Da   6:13 He still prays three times a **d**."
Joel 1:15 Alas for that **d**! For the **d**
     2:31 great and dreadful **d** of the LORD.
Am   5:18 "On the **d** I punish Israel for their
     5:20 Will not the **d** of the LORD be
Ob   1:15 "The **d** of the LORD is near for all
Mic  7: 4 The **d** of your watchmen has come,
     7: 4 has come, the **d** God visits you.
Hab  3:16 wait patiently for the **d** of calamity

Zep  1:14  The great **d** of the Lord is near—
     1:14  cry on the **d** of the Lord is bitter;
     3: 5  and every new **d** he does not fail,
Zec  2:11  be joined with the Lord in that **d**
     14: 1  A **d** of the Lord is coming,
     14: 7  It will be a unique **d**—a **d** known
Mal  3: 2  But who can endure the **d** of his
     4: 5  dreadful **d** of the Lord comes.
Mt  10:15  on the **d** of judgment than
    12:36  give account on the **d** of judgment
    20:19  On the third **d** he will be raised
    24:38  up to the **d** Noah entered the ark;
    25:13  because you do not know the **d**
    28: 1  at dawn on the first **d** of the week,
Lk   1:59  On the eighth **d** they came
     2:21  On the eighth **d**, when it was time
    11: 3  Give us each **d** our daily bread.
    17:24  in his **d** will be like the lightning,
    24:46  rise from the dead on the third **d**,
Jn   6:40  I will raise them up at the last **d**."
Ac   2: 1  When the **d** of Pentecost came,
     2:20  the great and glorious **d** of the Lord.
     2:46  Every **d** they continued to meet
     5:42  **D** after **d**, in the temple courts
    17:11  examined the Scriptures every **d**
    17:31  he has set a **d** when he will judge
Ro   2: 5  yourself for the **d** of God's wrath,
    14: 5  Some consider one **d** more sacred
1Co  5: 5  may be saved on the **d** of the Lord.
    15: 4  on the third **d** according
    15:31  I face death every **d**—yes, just as
2Co  4:16  inwardly we are being renewed **d**
     4:16  we are being renewed **d** by **d**.
     6: 2  in the **d** of salvation I helped you."
     6: 2  favor, now is the **d** of salvation.
    11:25  a night and a **d** in the open sea,
Eph  4:30  were sealed for the **d** of redemption.
     6:13  so that when the **d** of evil comes,
Php  1: 6  to completion until the **d** of Christ
1Th  5: 2  the **d** of the Lord will come like
     5: 8  But since we belong to the **d**, let us
2Th  2: 2  the **d** of the Lord has already come.
Heb  7:27  not need to offer sacrifices **d** after **d**,
2Pe  3: 8  With the Lord a **d** is like a thousand
     3: 8  and a thousand years are like a **d**.
     3:10  the **d** of the Lord will come like
1Jn  4:17  confidence on the **d** of judgment:
Jude 1: 6  chains for judgment on the great **D**.
Rev  1:10  On the Lord's **D** I was in the Spirit,
     6:17  the great **d** of their wrath has come,
     8:12  A third of the **d** was without light,
    16:14  on the great **d** of God Almighty.
    20:10  They will be tormented **d** and night
    21:25  On no **d** will its gates ever be shut,

**DAY OF THE LORD**  Ac 2:20; 1Co 5:5; 2Co
   1:14; 1Th 5:2; 2Th 2:2; 2Pe 3:10

**DAY OF THE †LORD**  Isa 13:6, 9; Eze 13:5;
   30:3; Joel 1:15; 2:1, 11, 31; 3:14; Am 5:18, 18,
   20; Ob 1:15; Zep 1:7, 14, 14; Zec 14:1; Mal 4:5

**THIRD DAY**  Ge 1:13; 22:4; 31:22; 40:20;
   42:18; Ex 19:11, 15, 16; Lev 7:17, 18; 19:6, 7;
   Nu 7:24; 19:12; 29:20; Jos 9:17; Jdg 20:30; 1Sa
   30:1; 2Sa 1:2; 1Ki 3:18; 2Ki 20:5, 8; Ezr 6:15;
   Est 5:1; Hos 6:2; Mt 16:21; 17:23; 20:19; 27:64;

Lk 9:22; 13:32; 18:33; 24:7, 21, 46; Jn 2:1; Ac
   10:40; 27:19; 1Co 15:4

## DAY'S  [DAY]

1Ki 19: 4  while he himself went a **d** journey
Ac   1:12  a Sabbath **d** walk from the city.

## DAYBREAK  [DAY]

Ge  32:24  and a man wrestled with him till **d**.
Ex  14:27  at **d** the sea went back to its place.
Lk   4:42  At **d**, Jesus went out to a solitary
    22:66  At **d** the council of the elders
Ac   5:21  At **d** they entered the temple courts,

## DAYLIGHT  [DAY, LIGHT]

2Sa 12:12  in broad **d** before all Israel.' "
Mt  10:27  I tell you in the dark, speak in the **d**;
Lk  12: 3  in the dark will be heard in the **d**,
2Pe  2:13  of pleasure is to carouse in broad **d**.

## DAYS  [DAY]

Ge   1:14  serve as signs to mark seasons and **d**
     3:14  you will eat dust all the **d** of your
     3:17  will eat of it all the **d** of your life.
     7: 4  Seven **d** from now I will send rain
     7: 4  send rain on the earth for forty **d**
Ex  24:18  he stayed on the mountain forty **d**
    34:28  was there with the Lord forty **d**
Nu  13:25  At the end of forty **d** they returned
    14:34  the forty **d** you explored the land—
Dt  17:19  he is to read it all the **d** of his life so
    32: 7  Remember the **d** of old;
Jdg 17: 6  In those **d** Israel had no king;
    18: 1  In those **d** Israel had no king.
    18: 1  in those **d** the tribe of the Danites
    21:25  In those **d** Israel had no king;
1Sa 17:16  forty **d** the Philistine came forward
1Ki 19: 8  he traveled forty **d** and forty nights
Ps  21: 4  length of **d**, for ever and ever.
    23: 6  love will follow me all the **d** of my
    34:12  life and desires to see many good **d**,
    39: 5  You have made my **d** a mere
    90:10  Our **d** may come to seventy years,
    90:12  Teach us to number our **d**, that we
   103:15  for mortals, their **d** are like grass,
   128: 5  of Jerusalem all the **d** of your life.
Pr   9:11  For through wisdom your **d** will be
    31:12  good, not harm, all the **d** of her life.
Ecc  9: 9  all the **d** of this meaningless life
    12: 1  your Creator in the **d** of your youth,
    12: 1  before the **d** of trouble come
Isa 43:13  Yes, and ancient **d** I am he.
    53:10  see his offspring and prolong his **d**,
Da   7: 9  and the Ancient of **D** took his seat.
     7:13  He approached the Ancient of **D**
     7:22  until the Ancient of **D** came
    12:11  is set up, there will be 1,290 **d**.
    12:12  and reaches the end of the 1,335 **d**.
Hos  3: 5  and to his blessings in the last **d**.
Joel 2:29  I will pour out my Spirit in those **d**.
Mt   4: 2  After fasting forty **d** and forty
Mk   1:13  he was in the wilderness forty **d**,
    10:34  Three **d** later he will rise."
Lk   4: 2  where for forty **d** he was tempted
     4: 2  He ate nothing during those **d**,
    19:43  The **d** will come on you when your

| Ac | 1: 3 | to them over a period of forty **d** |
| | 2:17 | " 'In the last **d**, God says, I will |
| Gal | 4:10 | You are observing special **d** |
| Eph | 5:16 | opportunity, because the **d** are evil. |
| 2Ti | 3: 1 | will be terrible times in the last **d**. |
| Heb | 1: 2 | in these last **d** he has spoken to us |
| 2Pe | 3: 3 | that in the last **d** scoffers will come, |
| Rev | 11: 3 | and they will prophesy for 1,260 **d**, |
| | 11:11 | a half **d** the breath of life from God |
| | 12: 6 | might be taken care of for 1,260 **d**. |

## DAYS ARE COMING Jer 7:32; 9:25; 16:14;
19:6; 23:5, 7; 30:3; 31:27, 31, 38; 33:14; 48:12;
49:2; 51:52; Am 8:11; 9:13; Heb 8:8

## DAYS TO COME Ge 49:1; Ex 13:14; Nu
24:14; Dt 31:29; Pr 31:25; Isa 27:6; 30:8; Jer
23:20; 30:24; 48:47; 49:39; Eze 38:16; Da 2:28

## FORTY DAYS See FORTY

## DAYSPRING (KJV) See DAWN, [RISING] SUN

## DAZZLING*

| Da | 2:31 | an enormous, **d** statue, |
| Mk | 9: 3 | His clothes became **d** white, |

## DEACON* [DEACONS]

| 1Ti | 3:12 | A **d** must be faithful to his wife |

## DEACONS* [DEACON]

| Ro | 16: 1 | sister Phoebe, a **d** of the church |
| Php | 1: 1 | together with the overseers and **d**: |
| 1Ti | 3: 8 | way, **d** are to be worthy of respect, |
| | 3:10 | against them, let them serve as **d**. |

## DEAD [DIE]

| Ex | 12:30 | was not a house without someone **d**. |
| Lev | 17:15 | who eats anything found **d** or torn |
| | 19:28 | not cut your bodies for the **d** or put |
| Nu | 16:48 | stood between the living and the **d**, |
| Dt | 18:11 | or spiritist or who consults the **d**. |
| Ru | 4: 5 | the Moabite, the **d** man's widow, |
| | 4: 5 | name of the **d** with his property." |
| 1Ch | 10: 1 | and many fell **d** on Mount Gilboa. |
| Ps | 6: 5 | Among the **d** no one proclaims your |
| | 115:17 | It is not the **d** who praise |
| Pr | 2:18 | and her paths to the spirits of the **d**. |
| Ecc | 9: 4 | a live dog is better off than a **d** lion! |
| Isa | 8:19 | Why consult the **d** on behalf |
| Mt | 8:22 | me, and let the **d** bury their own **d**." |
| | 9:24 | The girl is not **d** but asleep." |
| | 10: 8 | raise the **d**, cleanse those who have |
| | 11: 5 | the deaf hear, the **d** are raised, |
| | 14: 2 | he has risen from the **d**! |
| | 23:27 | full of the bones of the **d** |
| | 28: 7 | 'He has risen from the **d** and is |
| Mk | 12:27 | He is not the God of the **d**, |
| Lk | 15:24 | For this son of mine was **d** and is |
| | 20:37 | even Moses showed that the **d** rise, |
| | 24: 5 | look for the living among the **d**? |
| | 24:46 | and rise from the **d** on the third day, |
| Jn | 5:21 | For just as the Father raises the **d** |
| | 11:44 | The **d** man came out, his hands |
| | 20: 9 | that Jesus had to rise from the **d**.) |

| Jn | 21:14 | after he was raised from the **d**. |
| Ac | 2:24 | But God raised him from the **d**, |
| Ro | 6:11 | count yourselves **d** to sin but alive |
| 1Co | 15:12 | Christ has been raised from the **d**, |
| | 15:12 | there is no resurrection of the **d**? |
| | 15:29 | those do who are baptized for the **d**? |
| | 15:29 | If the **d** are not raised at all, why are |
| 2Co | 4:14 | the Lord Jesus from the **d** will |
| Eph | 2: 1 | you were **d** in your transgressions |
| | 5:14 | rise from the **d**, and Christ will |
| Php | 3:11 | to the resurrection from the **d** |
| Col | 2:13 | When you were **d** in your sins |
| 1Th | 4:16 | and the **d** in Christ will rise first. |
| 2Ti | 4: 1 | who will judge the living and the **d**, |
| Heb | 11:19 | that God could even raise the **d**, |
| Jas | 2:26 | is **d**, so faith without deeds is **d**. |
| 1Pe | 4: 5 | ready to judge the living and the **d**. |
| Rev | 1: 5 | the firstborn from the **d**, |
| | 1:18 | I was **d**, and now look, I am alive |
| | 11:18 | time has come for judging the **d**, |
| | 14:13 | Blessed are the **d** who die |
| | 20:12 | And I saw the **d**, great and small, |
| | 20:12 | The **d** were judged according |

## DEAF

| Ex | 4:11 | Who makes them **d** or mute? |
| Lev | 19:14 | " 'Do not curse the **d** or put |
| Pr | 28: 9 | If anyone turns a **d** ear to my |
| Isa | 29:18 | that day the **d** will hear the words |
| | 35: 5 | and the ears of the **d** unstopped. |
| | 42:19 | and **d** like the messenger I send? |
| Lk | 7:22 | leprosy are cleansed, the **d** hear, |

## DEAL [DEALING, DEALT]

| Ex | 8:22 | day I will **d** differently with the land |
| 2Ch | 6:30 | and **d** with everyone according to all |
| Heb | 5: 2 | He is able to **d** gently with those |

## DEALING [DEAL]

| 2Co | 13 3 | not weak in **d** with you, |

## DEALT [DEAL]

| Ps | 18:20 | The LORD has **d** with me |
| 1Th | 2:11 | you know that we **d** with each |

## DEAR* [DEARER, DEARLY]

| 2Sa | 1:26 | you were very **d** to me. |
| Ps | 102:14 | her stones are **d** to your servants; |
| Jer | 31:20 | Is not Ephraim my **d** son, the child |
| Ac | 15:25 | to you with our **d** friends Barnabas |
| Ro | 12:19 | not take revenge, my **d** friends, |
| | 16: 5 | Greet my **d** friend Epenetus, |
| | 16: 8 | my **d** friend in the Lord. |
| | 16: 9 | in Christ, and my **d** friend Stachys. |
| | 16:12 | Greet my **d** friend Persis, |
| 1Co | 4:14 | but to warn you as my **d** children. |
| | 10:14 | Therefore, my **d** friends, |
| | 15:58 | my **d** brothers and sisters, |
| 2Co | 7: 1 | we have these promises, **d** friends, |
| | 12:19 | and everything we do, **d** friends, |
| Gal | 4:19 | My **d** children, for whom I am again |
| Eph | 6:21 | the **d** brother and faithful servant |
| Php | 2:12 | Therefore, my **d** friends, as you |
| | 4: 1 | in the Lord in this way, **d** friends! |
| Col | 1: 7 | Epaphras, our **d** fellow servant, |
| | 4: 7 | He is a **d** brother, a faithful minister |

| | | |
|---|---|---|
| Col | 4: 9 | our faithful and **d** brother, who is |
| | 4:14 | Our **d** friend Luke, the doctor, |
| 1Th | 4:10 | we urge you, **d** friends, to do so |
| 1Ti | 6: 2 | better because their masters are **d** |
| 2Ti | 1: 2 | To Timothy, my **d** son: |
| Phm | 1: 1 | To Philemon our **d** friend |
| | 1:16 | better than a slave, as a **d** brother. |
| | 1:16 | He is very **d** to me but even dearer |
| Heb | 6: 9 | though we speak like this, **d** friends, |
| Jas | 1:16 | deceived, my **d** brothers and sisters. |
| | 1:19 | My **d** brothers and sisters, take note |
| | 2: 5 | Listen, my **d** brothers and sisters: |
| 1Pe | 2:11 | **D** friends, I urge you, as foreigners |
| | 4:12 | **D** friends, do not be surprised |
| 2Pe | 3: 1 | **D** friends, this is now my second |
| | 3: 8 | not forget this one thing, **d** friends: |
| | 3:14 | So then, **d** friends, since you are |
| | 3:15 | just as our **d** brother Paul also wrote |
| | 3:17 | Therefore, **d** friends, since you have |
| 1Jn | 2: 1 | My **d** children, I write this to you so |
| | 2: 7 | **D** friends, I am not writing you |
| | 2:12 | I am writing to you, **d** children, |
| | 2:14 | I write to you, **d** children, |
| | 2:18 | **D** children, this is the last hour; |
| | 2:28 | And now, **d** children, |
| | 3: 2 | **D** friends, now we are children |
| | 3: 7 | **D** children, do not let anyone lead |
| | 3:18 | **D** children, let us not love |
| | 3:21 | **D** friends, if our hearts do not |
| | 4: 1 | **D** friends, do not believe every |
| | 4: 4 | You, **d** children, are from God |
| | 4: 7 | **D** friends, let us love one another, |
| | 4:11 | **D** friends, since God so loved us, |
| | 5:21 | **D** children, keep yourselves |
| 2Jn | 1: 5 | And now, **d** lady, I am not writing |
| 3Jn | 1: 1 | To my **d** friend Gaius, whom I love |
| | 1: 2 | **D** friend, I pray that you may enjoy |
| | 1: 5 | **D** friend, you are faithful in what |
| | 1:11 | **D** friend, do not imitate what is evil |
| Jude | 1: 3 | **D** friends, although I was very eager |
| | 1:17 | But, **d** friends, remember what |
| | 1:20 | But you, **d** friends, by building |

## DEARER* [DEAR]
Phm  1:16  is very dear to me but even **d** to you,

## DEARLY* [DEAR]

| | | |
|---|---|---|
| Hos | 4:18 | their rulers **d** love shameful ways. |
| Eph | 5: 1 | therefore, as **d** loved children |
| Col | 3:12 | holy and **d** loved, clothe yourselves |

## DEATH [DIE]

| | | |
|---|---|---|
| Ex | 21:12 | a fatal blow is to be put to **d**. |
| | 21:15 | father or mother is to be put to **d**. |
| | 21:16 | kidnaps someone is to be put to **d**, |
| | 21:17 | father or mother is to be put to **d**. |
| | 22:19 | with an animal is to be put to **d**. |
| | 23: 7 | an innocent or honest person to **d**, |
| | 31:14 | who desecrates it is to be put to **d**; |
| | 31:15 | on the Sabbath day is to be put to **d**. |
| Nu | 35:16 | the murderer is to be put to **d** |
| Dt | 13: 5 | or dreamer must be put to **d** |
| | 17: 6 | witnesses a person is to be put to **d**, |
| | 17: 6 | is to be put to **d** on the testimony |
| | 30:19 | that I have set before you life and **d**, |
| | 32:39 | I put to **d** and I bring to life, I have |

| | | |
|---|---|---|
| Ru | 1:17 | if even **d** separates you and me." |
| 2Ki | 4:40 | of God, there is **d** in the pot!" |
| | 19:35 | put to **d** a hundred and eighty-five |
| 2Ch | 23:15 | grounds, and there they put her to **d**. |
| | 25: 4 | he did not put their children to **d**, |
| | 25: 4 | "Parents shall not be put to **d** |
| | 25: 4 | nor children be put to **d** for their |
| Job | 26: 6 | **D** is naked before God; |
| Ps | 18: 4 | The cords of **d** entangled me; |
| | 44:22 | for your sake we face **d** all day long; |
| | 89:48 | Who can live and not see **d**, or who |
| | 116:15 | the LORD is the **d** of those faithful |
| Pr | 5: 5 | Her feet go down to **d**; |
| | 8:36 | all who hate me love **d**." |
| | 10: 2 | but righteousness delivers from **d**. |
| | 11:19 | those who pursue evil go to their **d**. |
| | 14:12 | be right, but in the end it leads to **d**. |
| | 15:11 | **D** and Destruction lie open before |
| | 16:25 | be right, but in the end it leads to **d**. |
| | 18:21 | tongue has the power of life and **d**, |
| | 19:18 | do not be a willing party to their **d**. |
| | 21:25 | of sluggards will be the **d** of them, |
| | 23:14 | with the rod and save them from **d**. |
| | 27:20 | **D** and Destruction are never |
| Ecc | 7: 2 | for **d** is the destiny of everyone; |
| SS | 8: 6 | for love is as strong as **d**, |
| Isa | 25: 8 | he will swallow up **d** forever. |
| | 53:12 | he poured out his life unto **d**, |
| Jer | 15: 2 | " 'Those destined for **d**, to **d**; |
| | 26:16 | man should not be sentenced to **d**! |
| Eze | 18:23 | any pleasure in the **d** of the wicked? |
| | 18:32 | take no pleasure in the **d** of anyone, |
| | 33:11 | no pleasure in the **d** of the wicked, |
| Hos | 13:14 | **d**. Where, O **d**, are your plagues? |
| Mt | 10:21 | "Brother will betray brother to **d**, |
| | 10:21 | their parents and have them put to **d**. |
| | 16:18 | the gates of **d** will not overcome it. |
| | 16:28 | here will not taste **d** before they see |
| | 26:66 | "He is worthy of **d**," |
| Jn | 5:24 | but has crossed over from **d** to life. |
| | 8:51 | obeys my word will never see **d**." |
| Ac | 2:24 | **d**, because it was impossible for **d** |
| Ro | 4:25 | He was delivered over to **d** for our |
| | 5:12 | and **d** through sin, and in this way **d** |
| | 6: 3 | Jesus were baptized into his **d**? |
| | 6:23 | For the wages of sin is **d**, |
| | 7:24 | will rescue me from this body of **d**? |
| | 8:13 | the Spirit you put to **d** the misdeeds |
| | 8:36 | your sake we face **d** all day long; |
| 1Co | 15:21 | For since **d** came through a human |
| | 15:26 | The last enemy to be destroyed is **d**. |
| | 15:31 | I face **d** every day—yes, |
| | 15:55 | "Where, O **d**, is your victory? |
| | 15:55 | Where, O **d**, is your sting?" |
| 2Co | 4:10 | around in our body the **d** of Jesus, |
| Php | 2: 8 | obedient to **d**—even **d** on a cross! |
| 2Ti | 1:10 | Jesus, who has destroyed **d** and has |
| Heb | 2:14 | by his **d** he might break the power |
| | 2:14 | of him who holds the power of **d**— |
| Jas | 5:20 | way of error will save them from **d** |
| 1Pe | 3:18 | He was put to **d** in the body |
| 1Jn | 3:14 | that we have passed from **d** to life, |
| | 3:14 | who does not love remains in **d**. |
| | 5:16 | commit a sin that does not lead to **d**, |
| | 5:16 | **d**. There is a sin that leads to **d**. |
| Rev | 1:18 | And I hold the keys of **d** and Hades. |
| | 2:11 | not be hurt at all by the second **d**. |

Rev 6: 8 Its rider was named **D**, and Hades
9: 6 those days people will seek **d**
9: 6 long to die, but **d** will elude them.
20: 6 The second **d** has no power over
20:14 Then **d** and Hades were thrown
20:14 The lake of fire is the second **d**.
21: 4 There will be no more **d'**
21: 8 This is the second **d**."

## PUT ... TO DEATH See PUT

## DEBATE* [DEBATED, DEBATING]
Ac  15: 2 into sharp dispute and **d** with them.
17:18 philosophers began to **d** with him.
18:28 refuted the Jews in public **d**,

## DEBATED* [DEBATE]
Ac   9:29 and **d** with the Hellenistic Jews,

## DEBATING* [DEBATE]
Mk 12:28 of the law came and heard them **d**.

## DEBAUCHERY*
Ro  13:13 not in sexual immorality and **d**,
2Co 12:21 and **d** in which they have indulged.
Gal  5:19 sexual immorality, impurity and **d**;
Eph  5:18 get drunk on wine, which leads to **d**.
1Pe  4: 3 living in **d**, lust, drunkenness,

## DEBIR
Jos  12:13 the king of **D** one the king of Geder
Jdg   1:11 **D** (formerly called Kiriath Sepher).

## DEBORAH
1. Female prophet and judge who led Israel to victory over Canaanites (Jdg 4–5).
2. Rebekah's nurse (Ge 35:8).

## DEBT* [DEBTOR, DEBTORS, DEBTS]
Dt   15: 3 you must cancel any **d** one of your
24: 6 as security for a **d**,
1Sa 22: 2 or in **d** or discontented gathered
Job 24: 9 infant of the poor is seized for a **d**.
Mt  18:25 that he had be sold to repay the **d**.
18:27 him, canceled the **d** and let him go.
18:30 into prison until he could pay the **d**.
18:32 said, 'I canceled all that **d** of yours
Lk   7:43 who had the bigger **d** forgiven."
Ro  13: 8 Let no **d** remain outstanding,
13: 8 except the continuing **d** to love one

## DEBTOR* [DEBT]
Isa  24: 2 as for lender, for **d** as for creditor.

## DEBTORS* [DEBT]
Mt   6:12 as we also have forgiven our **d**.
Lk  16: 5 called in each one of his master's **d**.

## DEBTS* [DEBT]
Dt   15: 1 seven years you must cancel **d**.
15: 2 canceling **d** has been proclaimed.
15: 9 the year for canceling **d**, is near,"
31:10 in the year for canceling **d**,
2Ki  4: 7 "Go, sell the oil and pay your **d**.
Ne  10:31 the land and will cancel all **d**.

Pr   22:26 in pledge or puts up security for **d**;
Mt   6:12 And forgive us our **d**, as we
Lk   7:42 back, so he forgave the **d** of both.

## DECAPOLIS*
Mt   4:25 from Galilee, the **D**, Jerusalem,
Mk   5:20 tell in the **D** how much Jesus had done
7:31 of Galilee and into the region of the **D**.

## DECAY*
Ps  16:10 will you let your faithful one see **d**.
49: 9 should live on forever and not see **d**.
49:14 Their forms will **d** in the grave,
Ps  55:23 down the wicked into the pit of **d**;
Pr   12: 4 but a disgraceful wife is like **d** in his
Isa   5:24 so their roots will **d** and their
Hab  3:16 **d** crept into my bones, and my legs
Ac   2:27 you will not let your holy one see **d**.
2:31 of the dead, nor did his body see **d**.
13:34 so that he will never be subject to **d**.
13:35 will not let your holy one see **d**.'
13:37 raised from the dead did not see **d**.
Ro   8:21 be liberated from its bondage to **d**

## DECEIT [DECEIVE]
Job 15:35 their womb fashions **d**."
Ps  32: 2 them and in whose spirit is no **d**.
50.19 for evil and harness your tongue to **d**
101: 7 No one who practices **d** will dwell
Pr   26:24 but in their hearts they harbor **d**.
Isa  53: 9 nor was any **d** in his mouth.
Jer   5:27 of birds, their houses are full of **d**;
Da   8:25 He will cause **d** to prosper, and he
Mk   7:22 greed, malice, **d**, lewdness, envy,
Jn    1:47 Israelite in whom there is no **d**."
Ac  13:10 You are full of all kinds of **d**
Ro   1:29 envy, murder, strife, **d** and malice.
3:13 their tongues practice **d**."
1Pe  2: 1 yourselves of all malice and all **d**,
2:22 and no **d** was found in his mouth."

## DECEITFUL [DECEIVE]
Ps  17: 1 it does not rise from **d** lips.
26: 4 I do not sit with the **d**, nor do I
43: 1 Rescue me from those who are **d** and
55:23 and will not live out half their days.
119:29 Keep me from **d** ways;
Pr   12: 5 but the advice of the wicked is **d**.
14:25 saves lives, but a false witness is **d**.
Jer  17: 9 The heart is **d** above all things
Hos 10: 2 Their heart is **d**, and now they must
2Co 11:13 are false apostles, **d** workers,
Eph  4:14 of people in their **d** scheming.
4:22 is being corrupted by its **d** desires;
1Pe  3:10 evil and your lips from **d** speech.
Rev 21:27 who does what is shameful or **d**,

## DECEITFULLY [DECEIVE]
Zec 10: 2 The idols speak **d**, diviners see

## DECEITFULNESS* [DECEIVE]
Mt  13:22 and the **d** of wealth choke the word,
Mk   4:19 the **d** of wealth and the desires
Heb  3:13 of you may be hardened by sin's **d**.

## DECEIVE [DECEIT, DECEITFUL, DECEITFULLY, DECEITFULNESS, DECEIVED, DECEIVER, DECEIVERS, DECEIVES, DECEIVING, DECEPTION, DECEPTIVE]

Lev 19:11 " 'Do not **d** one another.
Jos 9:22 said, "Why did you **d** us by saying,
1Sa 19:17 "Why did you **d** me like this
Job 13: 9 Could you **d** him as you might **d**
Pr 14: 5 An honest witness does not **d**,
Jer 29: 8 and diviners among you **d** you.
37: 9 Do not **d** yourselves, thinking,
Zec 13: 4 garment of hair in order to **d**.
Mt 24: 5 am the Messiah,' and will **d** many.
24:11 will appear and **d** many people.
24:24 great signs and wonders to **d**,
Mk 13: 6 'I am he,' and will **d** many.
13:22 and perform signs and wonders to **d**,
Ro 16:18 flattery they **d** the minds of naive
1Co 3:18 Do not **d** yourselves. If any of you
Gal 6: 3 you are nothing, you **d** yourselves.
Eph 5: 6 Let no one **d** you with empty words,
Col 2: 4 no one may **d** you by fine-sounding
2Th 2: 3 Don't let anyone **d** you in any way,
Jas 1:22 to the word, and so **d** yourselves.
1:26 tight rein on their tongues **d** themselves,
1Jn 1: 8 we **d** ourselves and the truth is not
Rev 20: 8 to **d** the nations in the four corners

## DECEIVED [DECEIVE]

Ge 3:13 said, "The serpent **d** me, and I ate."
31:20 Jacob **d** Laban the Aramean by not
Jer 20: 7 You **d** me, LORD, and I was **d**;
Hos 7:11 like a dove, easily **d** and senseless—
Ob 1: 3 The pride of your heart has **d** you,
Lk 21: 8 "Watch out that you are not **d**.
Jn 7:47 "You mean he has **d** you also?"
Ro 7:11 by the commandment, **d** me,
1Co 6: 9 Do not be **d**: Neither the sexually
2Co 11: 3 just as Eve was **d** by the serpent's
Gal 6: 7 Do not be **d**: God cannot be
1Ti 2:14 **d**; it was the woman who was **d**
2Ti 3:13 to worse, deceiving and being **d**.
Tit 3: 3 **d** and enslaved by all kinds
Jas 1:16 Don't be **d**, my dear brothers
Rev 13:14 it **d** the inhabitants of the earth.
20:10 And the devil, who **d** them,

## DECEIVER* [DECEIVE]

Job 12:16 both deceived and **d** are his.
Jer 9: 4 For every one of them is a **d**,
Mt 27:63 while he was still alive that **d** said,
2Jn 1: 7 Any such person is the **d**

## DECEIVERS* [DECEIVE]

Job 11:11 Surely he recognizes **d**; and when
Ps 49: 5 when wicked **d** surround me—
Mic 2:11 If liars and **d** come and say,
2Jn 1: 7 Many **d**, who do not acknowledge

## DECEIVES* [DECEIVE]

Pr 26:19 is one who **d** a neighbor and says,
Jer 9: 5 Friend **d** friend, and no one speaks
Mt 24: 4 "Watch out that no one **d** you.

Mk 13: 5 "Watch out that no one **d** you.
Jn 7:12 replied, "No, he **d** the people."
2Th 2:10 that wickedness **d** those who are

## DECEIVING* [DECEIVE]

Lev 6: 2 the LORD by **d** a neighbor
1Ti 4: 1 the faith and follow **d** spirits
2Ti 3:13 bad to worse, **d** and being deceived.
Rev 20: 3 from **d** the nations anymore until

## DECENCY* [DECENTLY]

1Ti 2: 9 modestly, with **d** and propriety,

## DECENTLY* [DECENCY]

Ro 13:13 Let us behave **d**, as in the daytime,

## DECEPTION* [DECEIVE]

Ps 12: 2 lips but harbor **d** in their hearts.
Pr 14: 8 ways, but the folly of fools is **d**.
26:26 malice may be concealed by **d**,
Jer 3:23 on the hills and mountains is a **d**;
9: 6 You live in the midst of **d**;
Hos 10:13 evil, you have eaten the fruit of **d**.
Mt 27:64 This last **d** will be worse than
2Co 4: 2 we do not use **d**, nor do we distort
Tit 1:10 full of meaningless talk and **d**,

## DECEPTIVE* [DECEIVE]

Pr 11:18 The wicked earn **d** wages, but those
23: 3 his delicacies, for that food is **d**.
31:30 Charm is **d**, and beauty is fleeting;
Jer 7: 4 Do not trust in **d** words and say,
7: 8 you are trusting in **d** words that are
15:18 You are to me like a **d** brook,
Mic 1:14 of Akzib will prove **d** to the kings
Col 2: 8 through hollow and **d** philosophy,

## DECIDE [DECIDED, DECISION, DECISIONS]

Ex 18:16 me, and I **d** between the parties
1Sa 24:15 be our judge and **d** between us.
Isa 11: 3 or **d** by what he hears with his ears;
Eze 44:24 and **d** it according to my ordinances.
Jn 19:24 "Let's **d** by lot who will get it."
Ac 24:22 he said, "I will **d** your case."

## DECIDED [DECIDE]

Ge 41:32 that the matter has been firmly **d**
Jdg 4: 5 up to her to have their disputes **d**
Jer 4:28 I have **d** and will not turn back."
Mt 27: 7 So they **d** to use the money to buy
Ac 4:28 and will had **d** beforehand should
2Co 9: 7 you should give what you have **d**

## DECISION [DECIDE]

Ex 28:29 **d** as a continuing memorial before
Pr 16:33 but its every **d** is from the LORD.
Joel 3:14 multitudes in the valley of **d**.
3:14 LORD is near in the valley of **d**.
Mk 15: 1 the whole Sanhedrin, reached a **d**.
Jn 1:13 nor of human **d** or a husband's will,

## DECISIONS [DECIDE]

Ex 28:15 a breastpiece for making **d**—

Nu  27:21  priest, who will obtain **d** for him
Isa  28: 7  they stumble when rendering **d**.
Jn   8:16  But if I do judge, my **d** are true,

## DECLARE [DECLARED, DECLARING]

Ex  22: 9  whom the judges **d** guilty must pay
Dt   5: 1  and laws I **d** in your hearing today.
1Ch 16:24  **D** his glory among the nations,
Ps   5:10  **D** them guilty, O God!
    19: 1  The heavens **d** the glory of God;
    40: 5  deeds, they would be too many to **d**.
    96: 3  **D** his glory among the nations,
Isa  42: 9  taken place, and new things I **d**;
Joel 1:14  **D** a holy fast; call a sacred
Ro  10: 9  you **d** with your mouth, "Jesus is Lord,"
Heb  2:12  "I will **d** your name to my brothers

## DECLARED [DECLARE]

Dt   4:13  He **d** to you his covenant, the Ten
    26:17  You have **d** this day
1Ki  8:53  just as you **d** through your servant
Mk   7:19  saying this, Jesus **d** all foods clean.)
Ro   2:13  the law who will be **d** righteous.
     3:20  Therefore no one will be **d** righteous
Heb  3:11  So I **d** on oath in my anger,

## DECLARES THE †LORD See †LORD

## DECLARES THE SOVEREIGN †LORD
See †LORD

## DECLARING* [DECLARE]

Ps  22:31  **d** to a people yet unborn:
    71: 8  praise, **d** your splendor all day long.
Jer 50:28  Babylon **d** in Zion how the LORD
Ac   2:11  we hear them **d** the wonders of God

## DECREE [DECREED, DECREES]

1Ch 16:17  He confirmed it to Jacob as a **d**,
Ezr  5:13  King Cyrus issued a **d** to rebuild
Est  3: 9  let a **d** be issued to destroy them,
     8: 8  Now write another **d** in the king's
Ps   2: 7  I will proclaim the LORD's **d**:
     7: 6  Awake, my God; **d** justice.
    81: 4  this is a **d** for Israel, an ordinance
   148: 6  he issued a **d** that will never pass
Jer 51:12  his **d** against the people of Babylon.
Da   2:13  So the **d** was issued to put the wise
     4:24  and this is the **d** the Most High has
     6: 7  enforce the **d** that anyone who prays
     6: 8  Majesty, issue the **d** and put it in writing
Lk   2: 1  days Caesar Augustus issued a **d**
Ro   1:32  they know God's righteous **d**

## DECREED [DECREE]

1Ki 22:23  The LORD has **d** disaster
2Ki  8: 1  because the LORD has **d** a famine
Est  9:31  and Queen Esther had **d** for them,
Ps  78: 5  He **d** statutes for Jacob
Pr  31: 5  forget what has been **d**,
Isa 10:22  Destruction has been **d**,
Jer 13:25  lot, the portion I have **d** for you,"
    40: 2  LORD your God **d** this disaster
La   3:37  it happen if the Lord has not **d** it?
Da   9:24  "Seventy 'sevens' are **d** for your
Lk  22:22  Son of Man will go as it has been **d**.

## DECREES [DECREE]

Ge  26: 5  my **d** and my instructions."
Ex  15:26  to his commands and keep all his **d**,
    18:20  Teach them his **d** and instructions,
Lev 10:11  Israelites all the **d** the LORD has
    18: 4  laws and be careful to follow my **d**.
    18:26  you must keep my **d** and my laws.
    26: 3  " 'If you follow my **d** and are
    26:15  and if you reject my **d** and abhor my
Dt   4: 5  I have taught you **d** and laws as
Jos 24:25  Shechem he reaffirmed for them **d**
1Ki  6:12  if you follow my **d**, observe my
1Ki 11:33  nor kept my **d** and laws as David,
Ps 119:12  to you, LORD; teach me your **d**.
   119:16  I delight in your **d**; I will not neglect
   119:48  love, that I may meditate on your **d**.
   119:112  on keeping your **d** to the very end.
Pr   8:15  rulers issue **d** that are just;
Isa 10: 1  to those who issue oppressive **d**,
Jer 31:35  who **d** the moon and stars to shine
Eze  5: 6  laws and **d** more than the nations
     5: 6  my laws and has not followed my **d**.
Zec  1: 6  But did not my words and my **d**,
Mal  4: 4  the **d** and laws I gave him at Horeb
Ac  17: 7  They are all defying Caesar's **d**,

## DEDICATE [DEDICATED, DEDICATION, REDEDICATE]

Lev 27: 2  makes a special vow to **d** a person
Pr  20:25  It is a trap to **d** something rashly

## DEDICATED [DEDICATE]

Lev 21:12  it, because he has been **d**
Nu  18: 6  **d** to the LORD to do the work
Jdg 13: 5  **d** to God from the womb.
2Sa  8:11  King David **d** these articles
1Ki  7:51  the things his father David had **d**—
     8:63  all the Israelites **d** the temple
2Ch 29:31  "You have now **d** yourselves
Ne   3: 1  They **d** it and set its doors in place,
     3: 1  which they **d**, and as far as
Lk  21: 5  stones **d** and with gifts **d** to God.

## DEDICATION [DEDICATE]

Nu   6: 2  a vow of **d** to the LORD
     6: 9  the hair that symbolizes their **d**,
     6:19  off the hair that symbolizes their **d**,
2Ch  7: 9  they had celebrated the **d** of the altar
Ezr  6:16  celebrated the **d** of the house of God
Ne  12:27  At the **d** of the wall of Jerusalem,
    12:27  celebrate joyfully the **d** with songs
Ps  30: T  *For the **d** of the temple.*
Da   3: 2  to the **d** of the image he had set up.
Jn  10:22  came the Festival of **D** at Jerusalem.
1Ti  5:11  sensual desires overcome their **d**

## DEED [DEEDS]

Ecc  3:17  activity, a time to judge every **d**."
    12:14  For God will bring every **d**
Jer 32:10  I signed and sealed the **d**, had it
Lk  24:19  powerful in word and **d** before God
Col  3:17  whether in word or **d**, do it all
2Th  2:17  strengthen you in every good **d**

## DEEDS [DEED]

| | | |
|---|---|---|
| Dt | 3:24 | or on earth who can do the **d** |
| | 4:34 | or by great and awesome **d**, like all |
| | 34:12 | or performed the awesome **d** |
| 1Sa | 2: 3 | knows, and by him **d** are weighed. |
| | 24:13 | 'From evildoers come evil **d**,' so my |
| 1Ch | 16:24 | his marvelous **d** among all peoples. |
| Ezr | 9:13 | to us is a result of our evil **d** and our |
| Job | 34:25 | Because he takes note of their **d**, |
| Ps | 26: 7 | and telling of all your wonderful **d**. |
| | 28: 4 | Repay them for their **d** and for their |
| | 45: 4 | your right hand achieve awesome **d**. |
| | 65: 5 | us with awesome and righteous **d**, |
| | 66: 3 | to God, "How awesome are your **d**! |
| | 71:17 | this day I declare your marvelous **d**. |
| | 72:18 | Israel, who alone does marvelous **d**. |
| | 73:28 | I will tell of all your **d**. |
| | 75: 1 | people tell of your wonderful **d**. |
| | 77:11 | I will remember the **d** |
| | 77:12 | and meditate on all your mighty **d**." |
| | 78: 4 | next generation the praiseworthy **d** |
| | 78: 7 | would not forget his **d** but would |
| | 86: 8 | no **d** can compare with yours. |
| | 86:10 | you are great and do marvelous **d**; |
| | 88:12 | or your righteous **d** in the land |
| | 90:16 | May your **d** be shown to your |
| | 92: 4 | For you make me glad by your **d**, |
| | 96: 3 | his marvelous **d** among all peoples. |
| | 107: 8 | and his wonderful **d** for humankind, |
| | 107:15 | and his wonderful **d** for humankind, |
| | 107:21 | and his wonderful **d** for humankind, |
| | 107:24 | his wonderful **d** in the deep. |
| | 107:31 | and his wonderful **d** for humankind. |
| | 111: 3 | Glorious and majestic are his **d**, |
| | 141: 4 | I take part in wicked **d** along |
| | 145: 6 | and I will proclaim your great **d**. |
| Pr | 5:22 | The evil **d** of the wicked ensnare |
| Isa | 1:16 | Take your evil **d** out of my sight! |
| Jer | 32:19 | purposes and mighty are your **d**. |
| | 32:19 | their conduct and their **d** deserve. |
| Eze | 22:28 | Her prophets whitewash these **d** |
| Hos | 5: 4 | "Their **d** do not permit them |
| Ob | 1:15 | your **d** will return upon your own |
| Hab | 3: 2 | I stand in awe of your **d**, LORD. |
| Mt | 5:16 | that they may see your good **d** |
| Lk | 1:51 | He has performed mighty **d** with his |
| | 23:41 | we are getting what our **d** deserve. |
| Jn | 3:19 | of light because their **d** were evil. |
| Ac | 26:20 | their repentance by their **d**. |
| 1Ti | 2:10 | but with good **d**, |
| | 5:10 | and is well known for her good **d**, |
| | 5:10 | herself to all kinds of good **d**. |
| | 6:18 | good, to be rich in good **d**, and to be |
| Heb | 10:24 | another on toward love and good **d**, |
| Jas | 2:14 | claim to have faith but have no **d**? |
| | 2:18 | say, "You have faith; I have **d**." |
| | 2:18 | Show me your faith without **d**, and I |
| | 2:26 | is dead, so faith without **d** is dead. |
| 1Pe | 2:12 | they may see your good **d** |
| Rev | 2: 2 | I know your **d**, your hard work |
| | 2:19 | I know your **d**, your love and faith, |
| | 2:23 | each of you according to your **d**. |
| | 3: 1 | I know your **d**; you have |
| | 3: 2 | I have found your **d** unfinished |
| | 3: 8 | I know your **d**. See, I have placed |
| | 3:15 | I know your **d**, that you are neither |
| | 14:13 | labor, for their **d** will follow them." |

| | | |
|---|---|---|
| Rev | 15: 3 | "Great and marvelous are your **d**, |

## DEEP [DEPTH, DEPTHS]

| | | |
|---|---|---|
| Ge | 1: 2 | was over the surface of the **d**, |
| | 2:21 | caused the man to fall into a **d** sleep; |
| | 7:11 | the springs of the great **d** burst forth, |
| | 15:12 | Abram fell into a **d** sleep, |
| Ex | 15: 5 | The **d** waters have covered them; |
| 1Sa | 26:12 | LORD had put them into a **d** sleep. |
| 2Sa | 22:17 | he drew me out of **d** waters. |
| Job | 34:22 | There is no **d** shadow, no utter darkness, |
| Ps | 36: 6 | your justice like the great **d**. |
| | 42: 7 | **D** calls to **d** in the roar of your |
| Pr | 4:19 | of the wicked is like **d** darkness; |
| | 9:18 | guests are **d** in the realm of the dead. |
| | 22:14 | of an adulterous woman is a **d** pit; |
| | 25: 3 | heavens are high and the earth is **d**, |
| Isa | 29:10 | has brought over you a **d** sleep: |
| La | 2:13 | Your wound is as **d** as the sea. |
| Eze | 23:32 | your sister's cup, a cup large and **d**; |
| Da | 2:22 | He reveals **d** and hidden things; |
| | 8:18 | I was in a **d** sleep, with my face |
| | 10: 9 | I fell into a **d** sleep, my face |
| Jnh | 1: 5 | he lay down and fell into a **d** sleep. |
| | 2: 3 | You hurled me into the **d**, |
| Lk | 5: 4 | "Put out into **d** water, and let down |
| Ac | 20: 9 | sinking into a **d** sleep as Paul talked |
| 1Co | 2:10 | all things, even the **d** things of God. |
| 1Ti | 3: 9 | They must keep hold of the **d** truths |
| Rev | 2:24 | learned Satan's so-called **d** secrets, |

## DEER

| | | |
|---|---|---|
| Ps | 42: 1 | As the **d** pants for streams of water, |
| Pr | 5:19 | A loving doe, a graceful **d**— |
| Hab | 3:19 | makes my feet like the feet of a **d**, |

## DEFAMED*

| | | |
|---|---|---|
| Isa | 48:11 | How can I let myself be **d**? |

## DEFEAT [DEFEATED]

| | | |
|---|---|---|
| Jdg | 2:15 | was against them to **d** them, just as |
| 1Sa | 4: 3 | "Why did the LORD bring **d** on us |
| Ps | 92:11 | My eyes have seen the **d** of my |

## DEFEATED [DEFEAT]

| | | |
|---|---|---|
| Nu | 14:42 | You will be **d** by your enemies, |
| Jos | 12: 1 | the land whom the Israelites had **d** |
| 1Co | 6: 7 | have been completely **d** already. |

## DEFECT

| | | |
|---|---|---|
| Lev | 22:20 | Do not bring anything with a **d**, |
| 1Pe | 1:19 | Christ, a lamb without blemish or **d**. |

## DEFEND [DEFENDED, DEFENDER, DEFENDING, DEFENDS, DEFENSE]

| | | |
|---|---|---|
| Jdg | 6:31 | he can **d** himself when someone |
| Job | 13:15 | I will surely **d** my ways to his face. |
| Ps | 72: 4 | May he **d** the afflicted among |
| | 74:22 | Rise up, O God, and **d** your cause; |
| | 82: 2 | "How long will you **d** the unjust |
| | 119:154 | **D** my cause and redeem me; |
| Pr | 31: 9 | **d** the rights of the poor and needy. |
| Isa | 1:17 | **D** the cause of the fatherless, |
| | 1:23 | They do not **d** the cause |
| Jer | 5:28 | they do not **d** the just cause |

Jer 51:36 I will **d** your cause and avenge you;
Lk 12:11 about how you will **d** yourselves
21:14 how you will **d** yourselves.

## DEFENDED [DEFEND]
Jer 22:16 He **d** the cause of the poor

## DEFENDER [DEFEND]
Ex 22: 2 the **d** is not guilty of bloodshed;
Ps 68: 5 to the fatherless, a **d** of widows,
Pr 23:11 for their **D** is strong; he will take
Isa 19:20 he will send them a savior and **d**,

## DEFENDING [DEFEND]
Ps 10:18 **d** the fatherless and the oppressed,
Ro 2:15 now accusing, now even **d** them.)
Php 1: 7 and, whether I am in chains or **d**

## DEFENDS* [DEFEND]
Dt 10:18 He **d** the cause of the fatherless
33: 7 With his own hands he **d** his cause.
Isa 51:22 says, your God, who **d** his people:

## DEFENSE [DEFEND]
Ex 15: 2 LORD is my strength and my **d**;
Job 31:35 I sign now my **d**—let the Almighty
Ps 35:23 Awake, and rise to my **d**!
Isa 12: 2 the LORD, is my strength and my **d**;
Ac 22: 1 and fathers, listen now to my **d**."
25: 8 Then Paul made his **d**: "I have done
26: 1 with his hand and began his **d**:
Php 1:16 I am put here for the **d** of the gospel.

## DEFERRED*
Pr 13:12 Hope **d** makes the heart sick,

## DEFIANT* [DEFY]
Pr 7:11 (She is unruly and **d**,
Jude 1:15 **d** words ungodly sinners have spoken

## DEFIED [DEFY]
1Sa 17:36 because he has **d** the armies
1Ki 13:26 is the man of God who **d** the word
Jer 48:26 drunk, for she has **d** the LORD.
Da 3:28 in him and **d** the king's command

## DEFILE [DEFILED, DEFILES]
Ex 20:25 for you will **d** it if you use a tool
Lev 11:43 Do not **d** yourselves by any of these
18:28 And if you **d** the land, it will vomit
Eze 20: 7 do not **d** yourselves with the idols
Da 1: 8 But Daniel resolved not to **d** himself
Mk 7:18 enters you from the outside can **d** you?
Rev 14: 4 are those who did not **d** themselves

## DEFILED [DEFILE]
Ge 34: 5 that his daughter Dinah had been **d**,
Lev 18:25 Even the land was **d**; so I punished
Jos 22:19 If the land you possess is **d**,
Isa 24: 5 The earth is **d** by its people;
Jer 16:18 because they have **d** my land
Mal 1: 7 "By offering **d** food on my altar.
1: 7 you ask, 'How have we **d** you?'

## DEFILES [DEFILE]
Mt 15:11 that is what **d** you."
Mk 7:15 comes out of you that **d** you."

## DEFRAUD [FRAUD]
Lev 19:13 " 'Do not **d** your neighbors or rob
Mk 10:19 you shall not **d**, honor your father

## DEFY [DEFIANT, DEFIED]
1Sa 17:10 "This day I **d** the armies of Israel!

## DEITY*
Col 2: 9 Christ all the fullness of the **D** lives

## DELAY [DELAYED]
Ps 40:17 you are my God, do not **d**.
Ecc 5: 4 a vow to God, do not **d** to fulfill it.
Isa 48: 9 my own name's sake I **d** my wrath;
Da 9:19 do not **d**, because your city and your
Hab 2: 3 it will certainly come and will not **d**.
Heb 10:37 coming will come and will not **d**."
Rev 10: 6 and said, "There will be no more **d**!

## DELAYED [DELAY]
Jos 10:13 and **d** going down about a full day.
Isa 46:13 and my salvation will not be **d**.

## DELIBERATE*
Ac 2:23 handed over to you by God's **d** plan

## DELICACIES* [DELICACY]
Ge 49:20 he will provide **d** fit for a king.
Ps 141: 4 do not let me eat of their **d**.
Pr 23: 3 Do not crave his **d**, for that food is
23: 6 begrudging host, do not crave his **d**;
Jer 51:34 us and filled his stomach with our **d**,
La 4: 5 Those who once ate **d** are destitute

## DELICACY* [DELICACIES]
SS 7:13 and at our door is every **d**, both new

## DELICIOUS*
Pr 9:17 food eaten in secret is **d**!"

## DELIGHT* [DELIGHTED, DELIGHTFUL, DELIGHTING, DELIGHTS]
Lev 26:31 and I will take no **d** in the pleasing
Dt 30: 9 The LORD will again **d** in you
1Sa 2: 1 enemies, for I **d** in your deliverance
15:22 "Does the LORD **d** in burnt
Ne 1:11 of your servants who **d** in revering
Job 22:26 then you will find **d** in the Almighty
27:10 Will they find **d** in the Almighty?
Ps 1: 2 but who **d** in the law of the LORD
16: 3 noble people in whom is all my **d**."
35: 9 the LORD and **d** in his salvation.
35:27 May those who **d** in my vindication
37: 4 Take **d** in the LORD and he will
37:23 steps of those who **d** in him;
43: 4 of God, to God, my joy and my **d**.
51:16 You do not **d** in sacrifice, or I would
51:19 you will **d** in the sacrifices

Ps  62: 4  my lofty place; they take **d** in lies.
68:30  Scatter the nations who **d** in war.
111: 2  are pondered by all who **d** in them.
112: 1  who find great **d** in his commands.
119:16  I **d** in your decrees; I will not
119:24  Your statutes are my **d**; they are my
119:35  your commands, for there I find **d**.
119:47  for I **d** in your commands because I
119:70  and unfeeling, but I **d** in your law.
119:77  I may live, for your law is my **d**.
119:92  If your law had not been my **d**,
119:143  me, but your commands give me **d**.
119:174  LORD, and your law gives me **d**.
147:10  nor his **d** in the power of human
149: 4  the LORD takes **d** in his people;
Pr  1:22  How long will mockers **d**
2:14  who **d** in doing wrong and rejoice
8:30  I was filled with **d** day after day,
10:23  who have understanding **d** in wisdom.
18: 2  but **d** in airing their own opinions.
23:26  and let your eyes **d** in my ways,
Ecc  2:10  My heart took **d** in all my labor,
SS  1: 4  We rejoice and **d** in you;
2: 3  I **d** to sit in his shade, and his fruit is
Isa  11: 3  he will **d** in the fear of the LORD.
13:17  for silver and have no **d** in gold.
32:14  wasteland forever, the **d** of donkeys,
42: 1  my chosen one in whom I **d**;
55: 2  and you will **d** in the richest of fare.
58:13  if you call the Sabbath a **d**
61:10  I **d** greatly in the LORD;
62: 4  for the LORD will take **d** in you,
65:18  for I will create Jerusalem to be a **d**
65:19  Jerusalem and take **d** in my people;
66: 3  and they **d** in their abominations;
66:11  **d** in her overflowing abundance."
Jer  9:24  earth, for in these I **d**,"
15:16  they were my joy and my heart's **d**,
31:20  my dear son, the child in whom I **d**?
49:25  abandoned, the town in which I **d**?
Eze  24:16  away from you the **d** of your eyes,
24:21  you take pride, the **d** of your eyes,
24:25  joy and glory, the **d** of their eyes,
Hos  7: 3  "They **d** the king with their
Mic  1:16  for the children in whom you **d**;
7:18  angry forever but **d** to show mercy.
Zep  3:17  He will take great **d** in you;
Mt  12:18  chosen, the one I love, in whom I **d**;
Mk  12:37  large crowd listened to him with **d**.
Lk  1:14  He will be a joy and **d** to you,
Ro  7:22  in my inner being I **d** in God's law;
1Co 13: 6  Love does not **d** in evil but rejoices
2Co 12:10  for Christ's sake, I **d** in weaknesses,
Col  2: 5  and **d** to see how disciplined you are

## DELIGHTED [DELIGHT]

Ex  18: 9  Jethro was **d** to hear about all
Dt  30: 9  just as he **d** in your ancestors,
2Sa 22:20  he rescued me because he **d** in me.
2Ch  9: 8  who has **d** in you and placed you
Est  5:14  This suggestion **d** Haman,
Isa  5: 7  of Judah are the vines he **d** in.
Lk  13:17  but the people were **d** with all
22: 5  They were **d** and agreed to give him
2Th  2:12  the truth but have **d** in wickedness.

## DELIGHTFUL* [DELIGHT]

Ps  16: 6  surely I have a **d** inheritance.
SS  1: 2  for your love is more **d** than wine.
4:10  How **d** is your love, my sister,
Mal  3:12  for yours will be a **d** land,"

## DELIGHTING* [DELIGHT]

Pr  8:31  whole world and **d** in humankind.

## DELIGHTS [DELIGHT]

Est  6: 6  for the man the king **d** to honor?"
Ps  22: 8  deliver him, since he **d** in him."
35:27  who **d** in the well-being of his
36: 8  them drink from your river of **d**.
147:11  the LORD **d** in those who fear
Pr  3:12  he loves, as a father the son he **d** in.
11:20  but he **d** in those whose ways are
12:22  he **d** in people who are trustworthy.
14:35  A king **d** in a wise servant,
29:17  they will bring you the **d** you desire.
SS  7: 6  how pleasing, my love, with your **d**!
Col  2:18  Do not let anyone who **d** in false

## DELILAH

Philistine woman who betrayed Samson (Jdg 16:4–22).

## DELIVER [DELIVERANCE, DELIVERED, DELIVERER, DELIVERS]

Nu  21: 2  "If you will **d** these people into our
Dt  7:23  LORD your God will **d** them over
32:39  and no one can **d** out of my hand.
Jos  8:18  for into your hand I will **d** the city."
2Ch 32:14  can your god **d** you from my hand?
Ps  6: 4  Turn, LORD, and **d** me;
22: 8  Let him **d** him, since he delights
50:15  I will **d** you, and you will honor
51:14  **D** me from bloodguilt, O God,
72:12  For he will **d** the needy who cry out,
109:21  of the goodness of your love, **d** me.
Isa  50: 2  Was my arm too short to **d** you?
Eze  7:19  gold will not be able to **d** them
Da  3:17  able to **d** us, then he will **d** us
Hos 13:14  will **d** them from the power of the grave;
Mt  6:13  but **d** us from the evil one.'
2Co  1:10  deadly peril, and he will **d** us again.
1:10  hope that he will continue to **d** us,

## DELIVERANCE [DELIVER]

Ge  45: 7  and to save your lives by a great **d**.
Ex  14:13  you will see the **d** the LORD will
1Sa  2: 1  my enemies, for I delight in your **d**.
Est  4:14  and **d** for the Jews will arise
Ps  3: 8  From the LORD comes **d**.
32: 7  and surround me with songs of **d**.
33:17  A horse is a vain hope for **d**;
78:22  not believe in God or trust in his **d**.
Isa  45:24  'In the LORD alone are **d**
Ob  1:17  But on Mount Zion will be **d**;
Php  1:19  to me will turn out for my **d**.

## DELIVERED [DELIVER]

Ge  48:16  the Angel who has **d** me from all
Jos  6: 2  I have **d** Jericho into your hands,

Jdg 16:23 "Our god has **d** Samson,
Job 33:28 God has **d** us from going down
Ps  34: 4 he **d** me from all my fears.
    60: 5 hand, that those you love may be **d**.
    107: 6 and he **d** them from their distress.
    116: 8 LORD, have **d** me from death,
Isa  1:27 Zion will be **d** with justice,
Da   7:25 holy people will be **d** into his hands
    12: 1 written in the book—will be **d**.
Ro   4:25 He was **d** over to death for our sins
2Th  3: 2 pray that we may be **d** from wicked

## DELIVERER* [DELIVER]

Jdg  3: 9 he raised up for them a **d**,
     3:15 the LORD, and he gave them a **d**—
2Sa 22: 2 is my rock, my fortress and my **d**;
2Ki 13: 5 The LORD provided a **d** for Israel,
Ps  18: 2 is my rock, my fortress and my **d**;
    40:17 You are my help and my **d**;
    70: 5 You are my help and my **d**;
    140: 7 my strong **d**, you shield my head
    144: 2 my stronghold and my **d**, my shield,
Ac   7:35 be their ruler and **d** by God himself,
Ro  11:26 "The **d** will come from Zion;

## DELIVERS [DELIVER]

Ps  34:17 he **d** them from all their troubles.
    34:19 the LORD **d** them from them all;
    37:40 The LORD helps them and **d** them;
    37:40 he **d** them from the wicked
Pr  10: 2 but righteousness **d** from death.

## DELUDED* [DELUSION]

Pr  28:11 discerning sees how **d** they are.
Isa 44:20 on ashes, a **d** heart misleads them;
Rev 19:20 these signs he had **d** those who had

## DELUSION* [DELUDED, DELUSIONS]

2Th  2:11 God sends them a powerful **d** so

## DELUSIONS* [DELUSION]

Ps   4: 2 How long will you love **d** and seek
Ps 119:118 for their **d** come to nothing.
Jer 14:14 and the **d** of their own minds.
    23:26 who prophesy the **d** of their own

## DEMAND [DEMANDED]

Ge   9: 5 I will surely **d** an accounting.
Lk   6:30 belongs to you, do not **d** it back.
1Co  1:22 Jews **d** signs and Greeks look

## DEMANDED [DEMAND]

Lk  12:20 This very night your life will be **d**
    12:48 been given much, much will be **d**;

## DEMAS*

Associate of Paul (Col 4:14; 2Ti 4:10; Phm 24).

## DEMETRIUS

Ac  19:24 A silversmith named **D**, who made
3Jn  1:12 **D** is well spoken of by everyone—

## DEMOLISH [DEMOLISHED]

Nu  33:52 idols, and **d** all their high places.
Hos 10: 2 The LORD will **d** their altars
2Co 10: 4 have divine power to **d** strongholds.

## DEMOLISHED [DEMOLISH]

Jdg  6:28 there was Baal's altar, **d**,
2Ch 33: 3 places his father Hezekiah had **d**;

## DEMON* [DEMON-POSSESSED, DEMONIC, DEMONS]

Mt   9:33 And when the **d** was driven out,
    11:18 drinking, and they say, 'He has a **d**.'
    17:18 Jesus rebuked the **d**, and it came
Mk   7:26 She begged Jesus to drive the **d**
     7:29 the **d** has left your daughter."
     7:30 lying on the bed, and the **d** gone.
Lk   4:33 there was a man possessed by a **d**,
     4:35 the **d** threw the man down before
     7:33 wine, and you say, 'He has a **d**.'
     8:29 driven by the **d** into solitary places.
     9:42 the **d** threw him to the ground
    11:14 was driving out a **d** that was mute.
    11:14 When the **d** left, the man who had
Jn   8:49 "I am not possessed by a **d**,"
    10:21 possessed by a **d**. Can a **d** open the eyes

## DEMON-POSSESSED* [DEMON, POSSESS]

Mt   4:24 pain, the **d**, those having seizures,
     8:16 many who were **d** were brought
     8:28 two **d** men coming from the tombs
     8:33 what had happened to the **d** men.
     9:32 a man who was **d** and could not talk
    12:22 they brought him a **d** man who was
    15:22 daughter is **d** and suffering terribly."
Mk   1:32 brought to Jesus all the sick and **d**
     5:16 what had happened to the **d** man—
     5:18 the man who had been **d** begged
Lk   8:27 he was met by a **d** man
     8:36 the people how the **d** man had been
Jn   7:20 "You are **d**," the crowd answered.
     8:48 that you are a Samaritan and **d**?"
     8:52 "Now we know that you are **d**!
    10:20 them said, "He is **d** and raving mad.
Ac  19:13 Lord Jesus over those who were **d**.

## DEMONIC* [DEMON]

Jas  3:15 but is earthly, unspiritual, **d**.
Rev 16:14 They are **d** spirits that perform signs,

## DEMONS* [DEMON]

Dt  32:17 They sacrificed to **d**, which are not
Ps 106:37 their sons and their daughters to **d**.
Mt   7:22 and in your name drive out **d**
     8:31 The **d** begged Jesus, "If you drive
     9:34 the prince of **d** that he drives out **d**."
    10: 8 those who have leprosy, drive out **d**.
    12:24 the prince of **d**, that this fellow drives
          out **d**."
    12:27 And if I drive out **d** by Beelzebul,
    12:28 the Spirit of God that I drive out **d**,
Mk   1:34 He also drove out many **d**, but he
     1:34 not let the **d** speak because they
     1:39 their synagogues and driving out **d**.

Mk   3:15  and to have authority to drive out **d**.
       3:22  the prince of **d** he is driving out **d**."
       5:12  The **d** begged Jesus, "Send us
       5:15  been possessed by the legion of **d**,
       6:13  They drove out many **d**
       9:38  "we saw someone driving out **d**
   16: 9  *out of whom he had driven seven **d**.*
   16:17  *In my name they will drive out **d**;*
Lk   4:41  **d** came out of many people,
     8: 2  from whom seven **d** had come out;
     8:30  because many **d** had gone into him.
     8:32  The **d** begged Jesus to let them go
     8:33  When the **d** came out of the man,
     8:35  man from whom the **d** had gone out,
     8:38  The man from whom the **d** had gone
     9: 1  authority to drive out all **d**
     9:49  "we saw someone driving out **d**
   10:17  even the **d** submit to us in your
   11:15  the prince of **d**, he is driving out **d**."
   11:18  that I drive out **d** by Beelzebul.
   11:19  Now if I drive out **d** by Beelzebul,
   11:20  if I drive out **d** by the finger of God,
   13:32  'I will keep on driving out **d**
Ro   8:38  life, neither angels nor **d**,
1Co 10:20  sacrifices of pagans are offered to **d**,
   10:20  want you to be participants with **d**.
   10:21  of the Lord and the cup of **d** too;
   10:21  the Lord's table and the table of **d**.
1Ti   4: 1  spirits and things taught by **d**.
Jas   2:19  Good! Even the **d** believe that—
Rev  9:20  they did not stop worshiping **d**,
   18: 2  She has become a dwelling for **d**

## DEMONSTRATE*
[DEMONSTRATES,
DEMONSTRATION]

Ac  26:20  turn to God and **d** their repentance
Ro   3:25  He did this to **d** his justice,
     3:26  he did it to **d** his justice

## DEMONSTRATES*
[DEMONSTRATE]

Ro   5: 8  God **d** his own love for us in this:

## DEMONSTRATION*
[DEMONSTRATE]

1Co  2: 4  but with a **d** of the Spirit's power,

## DEN

Jer   7:11  become a **d** of robbers to you?
Da   6: 7  shall be thrown into the lions' **d**.
Na   2:11  Where now is the lions' **d**, the place
Mt  21:13  but you are making it 'a **d**
Mk  11:17  But you have made it 'a **d**
Lk  19:46  but you have made it 'a **d**

## DENARII* [DENARIUS]

Lk   7:41  One owed him five hundred **d**,
   10:35  he took out two **d** and gave them

## DENARIUS [DENARII]

Mt  20: 2  agreed to pay them a **d** for the day
Mk  12:15  "Bring me a **d** and let me look
Lk  20:24  "Show me a **d**. Whose image

## DENIED [DENY]

Ecc  2:10  I **d** myself nothing my eyes desired;
Mt  26:70  But he **d** it before them all.
Jn  18:25  He **d** it, saying, "I am not."
1Ti   5: 8  has **d** the faith and is worse than
Rev  3: 8  my word and have not **d** my name.

## DENIES [DENY]

1Jn  2:22  It is whoever **d** that Jesus is
     2:23  No one who **d** the Son has

## DENOUNCE [DENOUNCED]

Nu  23: 7  'curse Jacob for me; come, **d** Israel.'

## DENOUNCED [DENOUNCE]

Nu  23: 8  those whom the LORD has not **d**?

## DENY [DENIED, DENIES, DENYING, SELF-DENIAL]

Ex  23: 6  "Do not **d** justice to your poor
Lev 16:29  month you must **d** yourselves
   23:27  a sacred assembly and **d** yourselves,
Job  27: 5  till I die, I will not **d** my integrity.
Isa   5:23  a bribe, but **d** justice to the innocent.
La   3:35  **d** people their rights before the Most
Am   2: 7  and **d** justice to the oppressed.
Mt  16:24  to be my disciple must **d** themselves
Mk   8:34  to be my disciple must **d** themselves
Lk   9:23  to be my disciple must **d** themselves
   22:34  you will **d** three times that you
Ac   4:16  a notable sign, and we cannot **d** it.
Tit   1:16  but by their actions they **d** him.
Jas   3:14  do not boast about it or **d** the truth.
Jude 1: 4  **d** Jesus Christ our only Sovereign

## DENYING* [DENY]

Eze 22:29  the foreigner, **d** them justice.
2Ti   3: 5  a form of godliness but **d** its power.
2Pe  2: 1  even **d** the sovereign Lord who
1Jn  2:22  the antichrist—**d** the Father

## DEPART [DEPARTED, DEPARTS, DEPARTURE]

Ge  49:10  The scepter will not **d** from Judah,
2Sa 12:10  the sword will never **d** from your
Job  1:21  mother's womb, and naked I will **d**.
Ecc  5:15  as everyone comes, so they **d**.
Isa 52:11  **D, d**, go out from there!
Mt  25:41  say to those on his left, '**D** from me,
Php  1:23  I desire to **d** and be with Christ,

## DEPARTED [DEPART]

1Sa  4:21  "The Glory has **d** from Israel"—
   16:14  of the LORD had **d** from Saul,
   28:15  God has **d** from me.
Ps 119:102  I have not **d** from your laws, for you
La   1: 6  All the splendor has **d**
Eze 10:18  glory of the LORD **d** from over
2Ti  2:18  who have **d** from the truth.

## DEPARTS* [DEPART]

Ps 146: 4  When their spirit **d**, they return
Ecc  6: 4  without meaning, it **d** in darkness,

# DEPARTURE [DEPART]
Lk   9:31   They spoke about his **d**, which he
2Ti   4: 6   and the time for my **d** is near.
2Pe   1:15   after my **d** you will always be able

# DEPEND [DEPENDED, DEPENDING, DEPENDS]
Ps   62: 7   salvation and my honor **d** on God;
Jer   17: 5   who **d** on flesh for their strength
     49:11   Your widows too can **d** on me.' "
Ro    9:16   **d** on human desire or effort,

# DEPENDED [DEPEND]
Hos 10:13   Because you have **d** on your own

# DEPENDING [DEPEND]
2Ki 18:20   On whom are you **d**, that you rebel

# DEPENDS* [DEPEND]
Ro   12:18   as far as it **d** on you,
Gal   3:18   For if the inheritance **d** on the law,
      3:18   then it no longer **d** on the promise;
Col   2: 8   which **d** on human tradition

# DEPORTED
2Ki 15:29   and **d** the people to Assyria.
     24:16   also **d** to Babylon the entire force

# DEPOSES*
Da    2:21   he **d** kings and raises up others.

# DEPOSIT [DEPOSITED]
Mt   25:27   you should have put my money on **d**
Lk   19:23   then didn't you put my money on **d**,
2Co   1:22   put his Spirit in our hearts as a **d**,
       5: 5   who has given us the Spirit as a **d**,
Eph   1:14   who is a **d** guaranteeing our
2Ti   1:14   Guard the good **d** that was entrusted

# DEPOSITED* [DEPOSIT]
1Sa 10:25   a scroll and **d** it before the LORD.
Ezr   6: 5   they are to be **d** in the house of God.

# DEPRAVED* [DEPRAVITY]
Eze 16:47   you soon became more **d** than they.
     23:11   she was more **d** than her sister.
Ro    1:28   so God gave them over to a **d** mind,
2Ti   3: 8   They are men of **d** minds, who,
2Pe   2: 2   Many will follow their **d** conduct
       2: 7   by the **d** conduct of the lawless

# DEPRAVITY* [DEPRAVED]
Ps   12: 8   **d** is honored by the human race.
Ro    1:29   of wickedness, evil, greed and **d**.
2Pe   2:19   they themselves are slaves of **d**—

# DEPRIVE [DEPRIVED]
Dt   24:17   Do not **d** the foreigner
Pr   18: 5   and so **d** the innocent of justice.
     31: 5   **d** all the oppressed of their rights.
Isa  10: 2   to **d** the poor of their rights
     29:21   with false testimony **d** the innocent
La    3:36   to **d** them of justice—would not

Am    5:12   **d** the poor of justice in the courts.
Mal   3: 5   and **d** the foreigners among you
1Co   7: 5   Do not **d** each other except perhaps

# DEPRIVED [DEPRIVE]
Jer   5:25   your sins have **d** you of good.

# DEPTH [DEEP]
Ro    8:39   neither height nor **d**, nor anything
     11:33   the **d** of the riches of the wisdom
Php   1: 9   more in knowledge and **d** of insight,

# DEPTHS [DEEP]
Ex   15: 5   they sank to the **d** like a stone.
Ps   69: 2   I sink in the miry **d**, where there is
    130: 1   Out of the **d** I cry to you, LORD;
Mt   18: 6   were drowned in the **d** of the sea.

# DERIDE* [DERISION]
Pr   11:12   have no sense **d** their neighbors,

# DERISION [DERIDE]
Eze 23:32   it will bring scorn and **d**, for it holds
Mic   6:16   over to ruin and your people to **d**;

# DERIVES*
Eph   3:15   in heaven and on earth **d** its name.

# DESCEND [DESCENDANT, DESCENDANTS, DESCENDED, DESCENDING, DESCENT]
Dt   32: 2   like rain and my words **d** like dew,
Ro   10: 7   "or 'Who will **d** into the deep?' "

# DESCENDANT [DESCEND]
Ro    1: 3   to his earthly life was a **d** of David,

# DESCENDANTS [DESCEND]
Ge    9: 9   with you and with your **d** after you
     15:18   "To your **d** I give this land,
Ex   12:24   ordinance for you and your **d**.
     28:43   ordinance for Aaron and his **d**.
Dt    4:37   and chose their **d** after them,
2Sa 22:51   to David and his **d** forever."
Ps  132:11   "One of your own **d** I will place
Jer  31:17   So there is hope for your **d**,"
Jn    7:42   Messiah will come from David's **d**
Ac    2:30   place one of his **d** on his throne.
       8:33   Who can speak of his **d**? For his life

# DESCENDED [DESCEND]
Ex   19:18   because the LORD **d** on it in fire.
Lk    3:22   the Holy Spirit **d** on him in bodily
Eph   4: 9   except that he also **d** to the lower,
2Ti   2: 8   raised from the dead, **d** from David.
Heb   7:14   is clear that our Lord **d** from Judah,

# DESCENDING [DESCEND]
Ge   28:12   of God were ascending and **d** on it.
Mt    3:16   saw the Spirit of God **d** like a dove
Mk    1:10   and the Spirit **d** on him like a dove.
Jn    1:51   and **d** on' the Son of Man.'"

## DESCENT [DESCEND]
Jn 1:13 children born not of natural **d**,

## DESECRATE [DESECRATED, DESECRATING]
Eze 7:22 robbers will **d** the place I treasure.
Mt 12: 5 duty in the temple **d** the Sabbath
Ac 24: 6 and even tried to **d** the temple;

## DESECRATED [DESECRATE]
Mal 2:11 Judah has **d** the sanctuary

## DESECRATING* [DESECRATE]
Ne 13:17 you are doing—**d** the Sabbath day?
 13:18 against Israel by **d** the Sabbath."
Isa 56: 2 who keep the Sabbath without **d** it,
 56: 6 who keep the Sabbath without **d** it
Eze 44: 7 **d** my temple while you offered me

## DESERT [DESERTED, DESERTING, DESERTS]
Pr 19: 4 the closest friends of the poor **d** them.
 21:19 live in a **d** than with a quarrelsome
Isa 32:15 and the **d** becomes a fertile field,
 35: 6 the wilderness and streams in the **d**.
 40: 3 make straight in the **d** a highway

## DESERTED [DESERT]
Dt 32:18 You **d** the Rock, who bore you;
Isa 62: 4 No longer will they call you **D**,
La 1: 1 How **d** lies the city, once so full
Mt 26:56 all the disciples **d** him and fled.
2Ti 4:10 this world, has **d** me and has gone

## DESERTING [DESERT]
Gal 1: 6 you are so quickly **d** the one who

## DESERTS [DESERT]
Zec 11:17 shepherd, who **d** the flock!

## DESERVE* [DESERVED, DESERVES, DESERVING]
Ge 40:15 I have done nothing to **d** being put
Lev 26:21 seven times over, as your sins **d**.
Jdg 20:10 it can give them what they **d** for this
1Ki 2:26 You **d** to die, but I will not put you
Ps 28: 4 and bring back on them what they **d**.
 94: 2 pay back to the proud what they **d**.
 103:10 he does not treat us as our sins **d**
Ecc 8:14 who get what the wicked **d**,
 8:14 who get what the righteous **d**.
Isa 66: 6 repaying his enemies all they **d**.
Jer 14:16 out on them the calamity they **d**.
 17:10 according to what their deeds **d**."
 21:14 I will punish you as your deeds **d**,
 32:19 their conduct and as their deeds **d**.
 49:12 those who do not **d** to drink the cup
La 3:64 Pay them back what they **d**,
Eze 16:59 I will deal with you as you **d**,
Zec 1: 6 to us what our ways and practices **d**,
Mt 8: 8 I do not **d** to have you come under
 22: 8 those I invited did not **d** to come.
Lk 7: 6 I do not **d** to have you come under
 10: 7 for workers **d** their wages.

## DESERVED* [DESERVE]
2Sa 19:28 grandfather's descendants **d** nothing
Ezr 9:13 punished us less than our sins **d**
Job 33:27 right, but we did not get what we **d**.
Ac 23:29 no charge against him that **d** death

## DESERVES* [DESERVE]
Nu 35:31 the life of a murderer, who **d** to die.
Dt 25: 2 the one who is guilty **d** to be beaten,
 25: 2 the number of lashes the crime **d**,
Jdg 9:16 Have you treated him as he **d**?
Job 34:11 on them what their conduct **d**.
Jer 51: 6 he will repay her what she **d**.
Lk 7: 4 "This man **d** to have you do this,
Ac 26:31 is not doing anything that **d** death
1Ti 1:15 saying that **d** full acceptance:
 4: 9 saying that **d** full acceptance.

## DESERVING [DESERVE]
Mt 10:13 If the home is **d**, let your peace rest
Ac 28:18 was not guilty of any crime **d** death.
Eph 2: 3 we were by nature **d** of wrath.

## DESIGNATE [DESIGNATED]
Ex 21:13 they are to flee to a place I will **d**.
Jos 20: 2 "Tell the Israelites to **d** the cities

## DESIGNATED [DESIGNATE]
Lk 6:13 of them, whom he also **d** apostles:
Heb 5:10 was **d** by God to be high priest

## DESIRABLE* [DESIRE]
Ge 3: 6 and also **d** for gaining wisdom,
Pr 22: 1 name is more **d** than great riches;

## DESIRE* [DESIRABLE, DESIRED, DESIRES]
Ge 3:16 Your **d** will be for your husband,
Dt 5:21 You shall not set your **d** on your
1Sa 9:20 to whom is all the **d** of Israel turned,
2Sa 19:38 anything you **d** from me I will do
 23: 5 salvation and grant me my every **d**.
2Ki 9:15 "If you **d** to make me king,
1Ch 28: 9 understands every **d** and every thought.
2Ch 1:11 "Since this is your heart's **d**
 9: 8 and his **d** to uphold them forever,
Job 13: 3 But I **d** to speak to the Almighty
 21:14 We have no **d** to know your ways.
Ps 10:17 LORD, hear the **d** of the afflicted;
 20: 4 May he give you the **d** of your heart
 21: 2 You have granted him his heart's **d**
 27:12 turn me over to the **d** of my foes,
 40: 6 and offering you did not **d**—
 40: 8 I **d** to do your will, my God;
 40:14 may all who **d** my ruin be turned

Ps    41: 2  give them over to the **d** of their foes.
      70: 2  may all who **d** my ruin be turned
      73:25  earth has nothing I **d** besides you.
Pr     3:15  nothing you **d** can compare
       8:11  and nothing you **d** can compare
      10:24  what the righteous **d** will be
      11:23  The **d** of the righteous ends only
      12:12  The wicked **d** the plunder
      19: 2  **D** without knowledge is not good—
      24: 1  the wicked, do not **d** their company;
      29:17  they will bring you the delights you **d**.
Ecc    6: 2  they lack nothing their hearts **d**,
      12: 5  along and **d** no longer is stirred.
SS     6:12  it, my **d** set me among the royal
       7:10  to my beloved, and his **d** is for me.
Isa   26: 8  and renown are the **d** of our hearts.
      53: 2  appearance that we should **d** him.
      55:11  but will accomplish what I **d**
Eze   24:25  their heart's **d**, and their sons
Hos    6: 6  For I **d** mercy, not sacrifice,
Mic    7: 3  the powerful dictate what they **d**—
Mal    3: 1  covenant, whom you **d**, will come,"
Mt     9:13  'I **d** mercy, not sacrifice.'
      12: 7  what these words mean, 'I **d** mercy,
Ro     7:18  For I have the **d** to do what is good,
       9:16  depend on human **d** or effort,
      10: 1  my heart's **d** and prayer to God
1Co   12:31  Now eagerly the greater gifts.
      14: 1  of love and eagerly **d** spiritual gifts,
2Co    8:10  give but also to have the **d** to do so.
       8:13  Our **d** is not that others might be
Php    1:23  I **d** to depart and be with Christ,
       4:17  Not that I **d** your gifts; what I **d** is
2Th    1:11  fruition your every **d** for goodness
Heb   10: 5  and offering you did not **d**,
      10: 8  and sin offerings you did not **d**,
      13:18  **d** to live honorably in every way.
Jas    1:14  dragged away by your own evil **d**
       1:15  after **d** has conceived, it gives birth
       4: 2  You **d** but do not have, so you kill.
2Pe    2:10  of those who follow the corrupt **d**

# DESIRED [DESIRE]
1Ki    9: 1  and had achieved all he had **d** to do,
Ps    51: 6  you **d** faithfulness even in the womb;
Ecc    2:10  I denied myself nothing my eyes **d**;
Da    11:37  or for the one **d** by women, nor will
Hag    2: 7  what is **d** by all nations will come,
Lk    22:15  them, "I have eagerly **d** to eat this

# DESIRES* [DESIRE]
Ge     4: 7  it **d** to have you, but you must rule
      41:16  will give Pharaoh the answer he **d**."
2Sa    3:21  rule over all that your heart **d**."
      14:14  But that is not what God **d**;
1Ki   11:37  will rule over all that your heart **d**;
1Ch   29:18  keep these **d** and thoughts
Job   17:11  Yet the **d** of my heart
      31:16  "If I have denied the **d** of the poor
Ps    34:12  life and **d** to see many good days,
      37: 4  he will give you the **d** of your heart.
     103: 5  who satisfies your **d** with good
     140: 8  Do not grant the wicked their **d**,
     145:16  satisfy the **d** of every living thing.
     145:19  He fulfills the **d** of those who fear
Pr    11: 6  the unfaithful are trapped by evil **d**.

Pr    13: 4  but the **d** of the diligent are fully
      19:22  What a person **d** is unfailing love;
SS     2: 7  arouse or awaken love until it so **d**.
       3: 5  arouse or awaken love until it so **d**.
       8: 4  arouse or awaken love until it so **d**.
Hab    2: 4  is puffed up; his **d** are not upright—
Mk     4:19  and the **d** for other things come
Jn     8:44  want to carry out your father's **d**.
Ro     1:24  over in the sinful **d** of their hearts
       6:12  body so that you obey its evil **d**.
       8: 5  minds set on what that nature **d**;
       8: 5  their minds set on what the Spirit **d**.
      13:14  to gratify the **d** of the sinful nature.
Gal    5:16  and you will not gratify the **d**
       5:17  the sinful nature **d** what is contrary
       5:24  sinful nature with its passions and **d**.
Eph    2: 3  and following its **d** and thoughts.
       4:22  is being corrupted by its deceitful **d**;
Col    3: 5  lust, evil **d** and greed, which is
1Ti    3: 1  to be an overseer **d** a noble task.
       5:11  when their sensual **d** overcome their
       6: 9  harmful **d** that plunge people
2Ti    2:22  Flee the evil **d** of youth and pursue
       3: 6  are swayed by all kinds of evil **d**,
       4: 3  to suit their own **d**, they will gather
Jas    1:20  the righteousness that God **d**.
       4: 1  from your **d** that battle within you?
1Pe    1:14  do not conform to the evil **d** you had
       2:11  to abstain from sinful **d**, which war
       4: 2  their earthly lives for evil human **d**,
2Pe    1: 4  in the world caused by evil **d**.
       2:18  the lustful **d** of sinful human nature,
       3: 3  and following their own evil **d**.
1Jn    2:17  The world and its **d** pass away,
Jude   1:16  they follow their own evil **d**;
       1:18  will follow their own ungodly **d**."

# DESOLATE [DESOLATION]
Lev   26:34  years all the time that it lies **d**
Isa    1: 7  Your country is **d**, your cities
      54: 1  the children of the **d** woman than
Jer   50:23  How **d** is Babylon among
Da     9:17  look with favor on your **d** sanctuary.
Lk    13:35  Look, your house is left to you **d**.
Gal    4:27  the children of the **d** woman than

# DESOLATION [DESOLATE]
2Ch   36:21  all the time of its **d** it rested,
Da     9:27  set up an abomination that causes **d**,
      11:31  up the abomination that causes **d**.
      12:11  abomination that causes **d** is set up,
Mt    24:15  'the abomination that causes **d**,'
Mk    13:14  causes **d**' standing where it does not
Lk    21:20  you will know that its **d** is near.

# DESPAIR [DESPAIRED, DESPAIRING]
Isa   61: 3  of praise instead of a spirit of **d**.
2Co    4: 8  perplexed, but not in **d**;

# DESPAIRED* [DESPAIR]
2Co    1: 8  to endure, so that we **d** of life itself.

# DESPAIRING* [DESPAIR]
Dt    28:65  weary with longing, and a **d** heart.
Jer   14: 3  dismayed and **d**, they cover their heads.

## DESPERATE*

| | | |
|---|---|---|
| 2Sa | 12:18 | He may do something **d**." |
| Job | 6:26 | treat my **d** words as wind? |
| Ps | 60: 3 | have shown your people **d** times; |
| | 79: 8 | to meet us, for we are in **d** need. |
| | 142: 6 | Listen to my cry, for I am in **d** need; |

## DESPISE [DESPISED, DESPISES]

| | | |
|---|---|---|
| Ge | 16: 4 | she began to **d** her mistress. |
| Dt | 23: 7 | Do not **d** an Edomite, |
| | 23: 7 | Do not **d** an Egyptian, |
| 2Sa | 12: 9 | Why did you **d** the word |
| Job | 5:17 | so do not **d** the discipline |
| | 42: 6 | Therefore I **d** myself and repent |
| Ps | 51:17 | contrite heart you, God, will not **d**. |
| | 102:17 | he will not **d** their plea. |
| Pr | 1: 7 | but fools **d** wisdom and instruction. |
| | 3:11 | do not **d** the LORD's discipline, |
| | 6:30 | People do not **d** a thief if he steals |
| | 14:21 | It is a sin to **d** one's neighbor, |
| | 15:20 | but foolish children **d** their mother. |
| | 15:32 | Those who disregard discipline **d** themselves, |
| | 23:22 | do not **d** your mother when she is |
| Jer | 14:21 | the sake of your name do not **d** us; |
| Mic | 3: 9 | who **d** justice and distort all that is |
| Zec | 4:10 | "Who dares **d** the day of small things, |
| Mt | 6:24 | devoted to the one and **d** the other. |
| | 18:10 | do not **d** one of these little ones. |
| Lk | 16:13 | devoted to the one and **d** the other. |
| 1Co | 11:22 | Or do you **d** the church of God |
| Tit | 2:15 | Do not let anyone **d** you. |
| 2Pe | 2:10 | of the sinful nature and **d** authority. |

## DESPISED [DESPISE]

| | | |
|---|---|---|
| Ge | 25:34 | up and left. So Esau **d** his birthright. |
| 1Sa | 17:42 | health and handsome, and he **d** him. |
| 2Sa | 6:16 | the LORD, she **d** him in her heart. |
| Ps | 22: 6 | by everyone, **d** by the people. |
| Pr | 12: 8 | and those with warped minds are **d**. |
| Ecc | 9:16 | But the poor man's wisdom is **d**, |
| Isa | 53: 3 | He was **d** and rejected by others, |
| | 53: 3 | people hide their faces he was **d**, |
| 1Co | 1:28 | of this world and the **d** things— |

## DESPISES [DESPISE]

| | | |
|---|---|---|
| Job | 36: 5 | "God is mighty, but **d** no one; |

## DESTINE* [DESTINED, DESTINY, PREDESTINED]

| | | |
|---|---|---|
| Isa | 65:12 | I will **d** you for the sword, and all |

## DESTINED [DESTINE]

| | | |
|---|---|---|
| Ps | 49:14 | They are like sheep and are **d** to die; |
| Jer | 43:11 | bringing death to those **d** for death, |
| | 43:11 | captivity to those **d** for captivity, |
| Lk | 2:34 | "This child is **d** to cause the falling |
| 1Co | 2: 7 | that God **d** for our glory before time |
| Col | 2:22 | things that are all **d** to perish |
| 1Th | 3: 3 | quite well that we are **d** for them. |
| Heb | 9:27 | Just as people are **d** to die once, |
| 1Pe | 2: 8 | which is also what they were **d** for. |

## DESTINY* [DESTINE]

| | | |
|---|---|---|
| Job | 8:13 | Such is the **d** of all who forget God; |

| | | |
|---|---|---|
| Ps | 73:17 | then I understood their final **d**. |
| Ecc | 7: 2 | for death is the **d** of everyone; |
| | 9: 2 | All share a common **d**— |
| | 9: 3 | The same **d** overtakes all. |
| Isa | 65:11 | and fill bowls of mixed wine for **D**, |
| Php | 3:19 | Their **d** is destruction, their god is |

## DESTITUTE

| | | |
|---|---|---|
| Ps | 102:17 | will respond to the prayer of the **d**; |
| Pr | 31: 8 | for the rights of all who are **d**. |
| Heb | 11:37 | in sheepskins and goatskins, **d**, |

## DESTROY [DESTROYED, DESTROYER, DESTROYING, DESTROYS, DESTRUCTION, DESTRUCTIVE]

| | | |
|---|---|---|
| Ge | 6:13 | I am surely going to **d** both them |
| | 9:11 | will there be a flood to **d** the earth." |
| | 18:28 | Will you **d** the whole city for lack |
| | 18:28 | there," he said, "I will not **d** it." |
| Ex | 33: 3 | and I might **d** you on the way." |
| Dt | 6:15 | he will **d** you from the face |
| | 7: 2 | them, then you must **d** them totally. |
| 1Sa | 15: 9 | were unwilling to **d** completely, |
| 1Ch | 21:15 | God sent an angel to **d** Jerusalem. |
| Est | 3: 6 | a way to **d** all Mordecai's people, |
| Ps | 94:23 | and **d** them for their wickedness; |
| | 94:23 | the LORD our God will **d** them. |
| Pr | 1:32 | complacency of fools will **d** them; |
| | 11: 9 | the godless **d** their neighbors, |
| Isa | 65: 8 | grapes and people say, 'Don't **d** it, |
| | 65: 8 | of my servants; I will not **d** them all. |
| Jer | 4:27 | though I will not **d** it completely. |
| Mt | 10:28 | of the One who can **d** both soul |
| Mk | 14:58 | say, 'I will **d** this temple made |
| Lk | 4:34 | Have you come to **d** us? |
| Jn | 10:10 | comes only to steal and kill and **d**; |
| Ac | 8: 3 | But Saul began to **d** the church. |
| Gal | 1:13 | the church of God and tried to **d** it. |
| Rev | 11:18 | destroying those who **d** the earth." |

## DESTROYED [DESTROY]

| | | |
|---|---|---|
| Ge | 9:11 | again will all life be **d** by the waters |
| | 19:29 | So when God **d** the cities |
| Dt | 8:19 | you today that you will surely be **d**. |
| Jos | 24: 8 | I **d** them from before you, and you |
| 2Ki | 10:28 | So Jehu **d** Baal worship in Israel. |
| Est | 7: 4 | my people have been sold to be **d**, |
| Job | 19:26 | And after my skin has been **d**, |
| Ps | 1: 6 | way of the wicked will be **d**. |
| | 37: 9 | For those who are evil will be **d**, |
| | 37:38 | But all sinners will be **d**; |
| Pr | 6:15 | they will suddenly be **d**— |
| | 11: 3 | but the unfaithful are **d** by their |
| | 29: 1 | many rebukes will suddenly be **d**— |
| Da | 2:44 | up a kingdom that will never be **d**, |
| | 6:26 | his kingdom will not be **d**, |
| | 7:11 | and its body **d** and thrown |
| Hos | 4: 6 | my people are **d** from lack |
| Lk | 17:27 | Then the flood came and **d** them all. |
| 1Co | 8:11 | Christ died, is **d** by your knowledge. |
| | 15:24 | Father after he has **d** all dominion, |
| | 15:26 | The last enemy to be **d** is death. |
| 2Co | 4: 9 | struck down, but not **d**. |
| | 5: 1 | if the earthly tent we live in is **d**, |

Gal   5:15   out or you will be **d** by each other.
Eph   2:14   the two one and has **d** the barrier,
2Ti   1:10   who has **d** death and has brought
Heb 10:39   of those who shrink back and are **d**,
2Pe   2:12   born only to be caught and **d**,
        3:10   the elements will be **d** by fire,
Jude  1: 5   later **d** those who did not believe.

## DESTROYER [DESTROY]

Ex   12:23   and he will not permit the **d** to enter
Jer   6:26   for suddenly the **d** will come
Heb 11:28   that the **d** of the firstborn would not

## DESTROYING [DESTROY]

Ps 106:23   him to keep his wrath from **d** them.
Jer  23: 1   "Woe to the shepherds who are **d**
1Co 10:10   and were killed by the **d** angel.
Rev 11:18   for **d** those who destroy the earth."

## DESTROYS [DESTROY]

Pr   6:32   whoever does so **d** himself.
      18: 9   is a close relative of one who **d**.
      28:24   wrong," is partner to one who **d**.
Ecc   9:18   of war, but one sinner **d** much good.
Lk   12:33   no thief comes near and no moth **d**.
1Co   3:17   If anyone **d** God's temple, God will

## DESTRUCTION [DESTROY]

Nu   32:15   you will be the cause of their **d**."
Dt    7:10   him he will repay to their face by **d**;
Pr   16:18   Pride goes before **d**, a haughty spirit
      17:19   builds a high gate invites **d**.
      24:22   for those two will send sudden **d**
      27:20   Death and **D** are never satisfied,
Isa  10:22   **D** has been decreed,
Hos 13:14   Where, O grave, is your **d**?
Hab   2:17   your **d** of animals will terrify you.
Mt    7:13   and broad is the road that leads to **d**,
Lk    6:49   collapsed and its **d** was complete."
Jn   17:12   lost except the one doomed to **d** so
Ro    9:22   of his wrath—prepared for **d**?
1Co   5: 5   hand this man over to Satan for the **d**
Gal   6: 8   nature, from that nature will reap **d**;
Php   3:19   Their destiny is **d**, their god is their
1Th   5: 3   **d** will come on them suddenly,
2Th   1: 9   will be punished with everlasting **d**
        2: 3   is revealed, the man doomed to **d**.
1Ti   6: 9   that plunge people into ruin and **d**.
2Pe   2: 1   bringing swift **d** on themselves.
        2: 3   and their **d** has not been sleeping.
        3: 7   of judgment and **d** of the ungodly.
        3:12   bring about the **d** of the heavens
        3:16   the other Scriptures, to their own **d**.
Rev 17: 8   up out of the Abyss and go to its **d**.
      17:11   to the seven and is going to his **d**.

## DESTRUCTIVE [DESTROY]

Ex   12:13   No **d** plague will touch you when I
Pr   17: 4   liar pays attention to a **d** tongue.
2Pe   2: 1   will secretly introduce **d** heresies,

## DETERMINED [DETERMINES]

Jdg   1:27   for the Canaanites were **d** to live
        1:35   the Amorites were **d** also to hold
Ru    1:18   realized that Ruth was **d** to go

2Sa  17:14   the LORD had **d** to frustrate
Job  14: 5   The days of mortals are **d**;
Isa  14:26   This is the plan **d** for the whole
Da   11:36   for what has been **d** must take place.
1Co 15:38   But God gives it a body as he has **d**,

## DETERMINES* [DETERMINED]

Ps 147: 4   He **d** the number of the stars
1Co 12:11   them to each one, just as he **d**.

## DETEST [DETESTABLE, DETESTED, DETESTS]

Dt    7:26   Regard it as vile and utterly **d** it,
Job  19:19   All my intimate friends **d** me;
Ps    5: 6   bloodthirsty and deceitful you, LORD, **d**.
    119:163   and **d** falsehood but I love your law.
Pr    8: 7   is true, for my lips **d** wickedness.
      13:19   soul, but fools **d** turning from evil.
      16:12   Kings **d** wrongdoing, for a throne is
      24: 9   folly are sin, and people **d** a mocker.
      29:27   The righteous **d** the dishonest;
      29:27   the wicked **d** the upright.
Am    5:10   and **d** the one who tells the truth.
        6: 8   pride of Jacob and **d** his fortresses;

## DETESTABLE [DETEST]

Ge   46:34   for all shepherds are **d**
Dt   18: 9   to imitate the **d** ways of the nations
Pr    6:16   hates, seven that are **d** to him:
      21:27   The sacrifice of the wicked is **d**—
      28: 9   instruction, even their prayers are **d**.
Isa   1:13   Your incense is **d** to me.
      41:24   those who choose you are **d**.
      44:19   Shall I make a **d** thing from what is
Jer  44: 4   'Do not do this **d** thing that I hate!'
Eze   5: 9   Because of all your **d** idols, I will do
        8:13   doing things that are even more **d**."
Mal   2:11   A **d** thing has been committed
Lk   16:15   What people value highly is **d**
Tit   1:16   They are **d**, disobedient and unfit
1Pe   4: 3   orgies, carousing and **d** idolatry.
Rev 18: 2   for every unclean and **d** animal.

## DETESTED* [DETEST]

Zec 11: 8   The flock **d** me, and I grew weary

## DETESTS* [DETEST]

Dt   22: 5   the LORD your God **d** anyone who
      23:18   the LORD your God **d** them both.
      25:16   the LORD your God **d** anyone who
Pr    3:32   For the LORD **d** the perverse
Pr   11: 1   The LORD **d** dishonest scales,
      11:20   The LORD **d** those whose hearts
      12:22   The LORD **d** lying lips, but he
      15: 8   The LORD **d** the sacrifice
      15: 9   The LORD **d** the way
      15:26   The LORD **d** the thoughts
      16: 5   The LORD **d** all the proud
      17:15   the LORD **d** them both.
      20:10   the LORD **d** them both.
      20:23   The LORD **d** differing weights,

## DEVIATE*

2Ch   8:15   They did not **d** from the king's

## DEVICES [DEVISE]
Ps 81:12 hearts to follow their own **d**.

## DEVIL* [DEVIL'S]
| | | |
|---|---|---|
| Mt | 4: 1 | wilderness to be tempted by the **d**. |
| | 4: 5 | Then the **d** took him to the holy city |
| | 4: 8 | Again, the **d** took him to a very high |
| | 4:11 | Then the **d** left him, and angels |
| | 13:39 | the enemy who sows them is the **d**. |
| | 25:41 | the eternal fire prepared for the **d** |
| Lk | 4: 2 | forty days he was tempted by the **d**. |
| | 4: 3 | The **d** said to him, "If you are |
| | 4: 5 | The **d** led him up to a high place |
| | 4: 9 | The **d** led him to Jerusalem and had |
| | 4:13 | the **d** had finished all this tempting, |
| | 8:12 | then the **d** comes and takes away |
| Jn | 6:70 | Yet one of you is a **d**!" |
| | 8:44 | the **d**, and you want to carry |
| | 13: 2 | the **d** had already prompted Judas, |
| Ac | 10:38 | who were under the power of the **d**, |
| | 13:10 | "You are a child of the **d** |
| Eph | 4:27 | and do not give the **d** a foothold. |
| 1Ti | 3: 6 | under the same judgment as the **d**. |
| 2Ti | 2:26 | and escape from the trap of the **d**, |
| Heb | 2:14 | the power of death—that is, the **d**— |
| Jas | 4: 7 | Resist the **d**, and he will flee |
| 1Pe | 5: 8 | Your enemy the **d** prowls around |
| 1Jn | 3: 8 | who does what is sinful is of the **d**, |
| | 3: 8 | because the **d** has been sinning |
| | 3:10 | and who the children of the **d** are: |
| Jude | 1: 9 | disputing with the **d** about the body |
| Rev | 2:10 | the **d** will put some of you in prison |
| | 12: 9 | that ancient serpent called the **d**, |
| | 12:12 | sea, because the **d** has gone down |
| | 20: 2 | serpent, who is the **d**, or Satan, |
| | 20:10 | And the **d**, who deceived them, |

## DEVIL'S* [DEVIL]
| | | |
|---|---|---|
| Eph | 6:11 | your stand against the **d** schemes. |
| 1Ti | 3: 7 | fall into disgrace and into the **d** trap. |
| 1Jn | 3: 8 | appeared was to destroy the **d** work. |

## DEVILS (KJV) See DEMONS, GOAT [IDOLS]

## DEVIOUS* [DEVISE]
| | | |
|---|---|---|
| 2Sa | 22:27 | to the **d** you show yourself shrewd. |
| Ps | 18:26 | to the **d** you show yourself shrewd. |
| Pr | 2:15 | and who are **d** in their ways. |
| | 14: 2 | those who despise him are **d** in their |
| | 21: 8 | The way of the guilty is **d**, |

## DEVISE [DEVICES, DEVIOUS, DEVISED, DEVISES]
| | | |
|---|---|---|
| Pr | 12: 2 | condemns those who **d** wicked schemes. |
| Pr | 14:17 | those who **d** evil schemes are hated. |
| Isa | 8:10 | **D** your strategy, but it will be |

## DEVISED [DEVISE]
| | | |
|---|---|---|
| Est | 8: 5 | **d** and wrote to destroy the Jews |
| Mt | 28:12 | met with the elders and **d** a plan, |
| 2Pe | 1:16 | did not follow cleverly **d** stories |

## DEVISES [DEVISE]
| | | |
|---|---|---|
| Pr | 6:18 | a heart that **d** wicked schemes, |
| Na | 1:11 | against the LORD and **d** wicked plans. |

## DEVOTE* [DEVOTED, DEVOTING, DEVOTION, DEVOUT]
| | | |
|---|---|---|
| 1Ch | 22:19 | Now **d** your heart and soul |
| 2Ch | 31: 4 | Levites so they could **d** themselves |
| Job | 11:13 | "Yet if you **d** your heart to him |
| Jer | 30:21 | who is he who will **d** himself to be |
| Mic | 4:13 | You will **d** their ill-gotten gains |
| 1Co | 7: 5 | that you may **d** yourselves to prayer. |
| Col | 4: 2 | **D** yourselves to prayer, |
| 1Ti | 1: 4 | or to **d** themselves to myths |
| | 4:13 | **d** yourself to the public reading |
| Tit | 3: 8 | God may be careful to **d** themselves |
| | 3:14 | people must learn to **d** themselves |

## DEVOTED [DEVOTE]
| | | |
|---|---|---|
| Jos | 6:18 | But keep away from the **d** things, |
| | 7: 1 | unfaithful in regard to the **d** things; |
| 1Ki | 11: 4 | and his heart was not fully **d** |
| 2Ch | 17: 6 | His heart was **d** to the ways |
| Ezr | 7:10 | For Ezra had **d** himself to the study |
| Ne | 5:16 | I **d** myself to the work on this wall. |
| Eze | 20:16 | For their hearts were **d** to their idols. |
| Mt | 6:24 | or you will be **d** to the one |
| Mk | 7:11 | is Corban (that is, **d** to God)— |
| Ac | 2:42 | They **d** themselves to the apostles' |
| | 18: 5 | Paul **d** himself exclusively |
| Ro | 12:10 | Be **d** to one another in love. |
| 1Co | 7:34 | Her aim is to be **d** to the Lord |
| | 16:15 | and they have **d** themselves |
| 2Co | 7:12 | for yourselves how **d** to us you are. |

## DEVOTING* [DEVOTE]
1Ti 5:10 **d** herself to all kinds of good deeds.

## DEVOTION* [DEVOTE]
| | | |
|---|---|---|
| 2Ki | 20: 3 | with wholehearted **d** and have done |
| 1Ch | 28: 9 | serve him with wholehearted **d** |
| | 29: 3 | in my **d** to the temple of my God I |
| | 29:19 | son Solomon the wholehearted **d** |
| 2Ch | 32:32 | his acts of **d** are written in the vision |
| | 35:26 | and his acts of **d** in accordance |
| Job | 15: 4 | piety and hinder **d** to God. |
| Isa | 38: 3 | with wholehearted **d** and have done |
| Jer | 2: 2 | " 'I remember the **d** of your |
| 1Co | 7:35 | way in undivided **d** to the Lord. |
| 2Co | 11: 3 | your sincere and pure **d** to Christ. |

## DEVOUR [DEVOURED, DEVOURING, DEVOURS]
| | | |
|---|---|---|
| Lev | 26:38 | the land of your enemies will **d** you. |
| Dt | 28:38 | little, because locusts will **d** it. |
| 2Sa | 2:26 | to Joab, "Must the sword **d** forever? |
| 1Ki | 21:23 | 'Dogs will **d** Jezebel by the wall |
| 2Ki | 9:36 | Jezreel dogs will **d** Jezebel's flesh. |
| Jer | 5:17 | They will **d** your harvests and food, |
| | | **d** your sons |
| | 46:10 | The sword will **d** till it is satisfied, |
| Mk | 12:40 | They **d** widows' houses |
| 1Pe | 5: 8 | lion looking for someone to **d**. |

## DEVOURED [DEVOUR]

Isa   1:20   rebel, you will be **d** by the sword."
Jer 30:16   all who devour you will be **d**;
Rev 20: 9   down from heaven and **d** them.

## DEVOURING [DEVOUR]

Mal   3:11   prevent pests from **d** your crops,
Gal   5:15   you keep on biting and **d** each other,

## DEVOURS [DEVOUR]

2Sa 11:25   the sword **d** one as well as another.
Ps   50: 3   a fire **d** before him, and around him
Rev 11: 5   their mouths and **d** their enemies.

## DEVOUT* [DEVOTE]

1Ki 18: 3   (Obadiah was a **d** believer
Isa 57: 1   the **d** are taken away, and no one
Lk   2:25   Simeon, who was righteous and **d**.
Ac   10: 2   He and all his family were **d**
     10: 7   and a **d** soldier who was one of his
     13:43   **d** converts to Judaism followed Paul
     22:12   He was a **d** observer of the law

## DEW

Ge 27:28   May God give you of heaven's **d**
Ex 16:13   was a layer of **d** around the camp.
Dt 32: 2   rain and my words descend like **d**,
Jdg   6:37   If there is **d** only on the fleece
Job 38:28   Who fathers the drops of **d**?
Pr 19:12   but his favor is like **d** on the grass.
Hos   6: 4   like the early **d** that disappears.
     14: 5   I will be like the **d** to Israel;
Hag   1:10   the heavens have withheld their **d**

## DIADEM*

Isa 62: 3   a royal **d** in the hand of your God.

## DIANA See ARTEMIS

## DICTATED

Jer 36: 4   while Jeremiah **d** all the words
     45: 1   the words Jeremiah the prophet **d**

## DIDYMUS* [THOMAS]

Alternate name of the disciple Thomas (Jn 11:16; 20:24; 21:2).

## DIE [DEAD, DEATH, DIED, DIES, DYING]

Ge   2:17   you eat of it you will certainly **d**."
     3: 3   must not touch it, or you will **d**.' "
     3: 4   "You will not certainly **d**,"
Ex 11: 5   Every firstborn son in Egypt will **d**,
     14:11   you brought us to the desert to **d**'?
Nu 23:10   Let me **d** the death of the righteous,
Dt 24:16   each of you will **d** for your own sin.
Ru   1:17   Where you **d** I will **d**, and there I
2Ki 14: 6   of you will **d** for your own sin."
Job   2: 9   Curse God and **d**!"
Ps 37: 2   green plants they will soon **d** away.
    118:17   I will not **d** but live, and will
Pr   5:23   For lack of discipline they will **d**,
     10:21   many, but fools **d** for lack of sense.
     11: 7   Hopes placed in mortals **d** with them;

Pr 15:10   those who hate correction will **d**.
     23:13   them with the rod, they will not **d**.
Ecc   2:16   Like the fool, the wise too must **d**!
     3: 2   a time to be born and a time to **d**,
Isa 22:13   you say, "for tomorrow we **d**!"
     66:24   their worm will not **d**, nor will their
Jer 31:30   everyone will **d** for their own sin;
Eze   3:18   those wicked people will **d** for their
     18: 4   one who sins is the one who will **d**.
     18:31   Why will you **d**, house of Israel?
     33: 8   those wicked people will **d** for their
Jnh   4: 8   He wanted to **d**, and said, "It would
     4: 8   be better for me to **d** than to live."
Hab   1:12   my Holy One, you will never **d**.
Mt 26:35   "Even if I have to **d** with you, I will
     26:52   all who draw the sword will **d**
Mk   9:48   where " 'their worm does not **d**,
Jn   6:50   which people may eat and not **d**.
     8:21   for me, and you will **d** in your sin.
     11:25   in me will live, even though they **d**;
     11:26   by believing in me will never **d**.
     21:23   that this disciple would not **d**.
Ro   5: 7   Very rarely will anyone **d**
     14: 7   we do not **d** to ourselves alone.
     14: 8   and if we **d**, we **d** to the Lord.
1Co 15:22   For as in Adam all **d**, so in Christ all
     15:32   eat and drink, for tomorrow we **d**."
Php   1:21   me, to live is Christ and to **d** is gain.
Heb   9:27   as people are destined to **d** once,
1Pe   2:24   so that we might **d** to sins and live
Rev   9: 6   they will long to **d**, but death will
     14:13   Blessed are the dead who **d**

## MUST DIE See MUST

## DIED [DIE]

Lev 10: 2   and they **d** before the LORD.
Nu   3: 4   however, **d** before the LORD
     14: 2   them, "If only we had **d** in Egypt!
     16:49   14,700 people **d** from the plague,
Jdg 16:30   more when he **d** than while he lived.
2Sa 24:15   people from Dan to Beersheba **d**.
1Ki   3:19   this woman's son **d** because she lay
1Ch 10:13   Saul **d** because he was unfaithful
Mk 15:39   saw how he **d**, he said,
Lk 16:22   "The time came when the beggar **d**
     16:22   The rich man also **d** and was buried.
Jn   6:58   Your ancestors ate manna and **d**,
Ro   5: 6   powerless, Christ **d** for the ungodly.
     5: 8   were still sinners, Christ **d** for us.
     6: 2   We are those who have **d** to sin;
     6: 8   Now if we **d** with Christ, we believe
     6:10   The death he **d**, he **d** to sin once
     14: 9   Christ **d** and returned to life so
1Co   8:11   for whom Christ **d**, is destroyed
     15: 3   that Christ **d** for our sins according
2Co   5:14   one **d** for all, and therefore all **d**.
     5:15   And he **d** for all, that those who live
     5:15   but for him who **d** for them and was
Gal   2:19   through the law I **d** to the law so
Col   2:20   Since you **d** with Christ
     3: 3   For you **d**, and your life is now
1Th   4:14   We believe that Jesus **d** and rose
     5:10   He **d** for us so that, whether we are
2Ti   2:11   If we **d** with him, we will also live
Heb   9:15   now that he has **d** as a ransom to set
     11:13   still living by faith when they **d**.

Rev 2: 8 Last, who **d** and came to life again.
    8: 9 of the living creatures in the sea **d**,
    8:11 many people **d** from the waters
    16: 3 and every living thing in the sea **d**.

## DIES [DIE]

Job 14:14 If someone **d**, will they live again?
Ecc  3:19 As one **d**, so **d** the other.
Jn  12:24 of wheat falls to the ground and **d**,
    12:24 But if it **d**, it produces many seeds.
Ro   7: 2 but if her husband **d**, she is released
1Co  7:39 But if her husband **d**, she is free
    15:36 does not come to life unless it **d**.

## DIFFERENCE* [DIFFERENT]

2Sa 19:35 Can I tell the **d** between what is
2Ch 12: 8 may learn the **d** between serving me
Eze 22:26 there is no **d** between the unclean
    44:23 my people the **d** between the holy
Ro   3:22 There is no **d** between Jew
    10:12 For there is no **d** between Jew
Gal  2: 6 whatever they were makes no **d**

## DIFFERENCES* [DIFFERENT]

1Co 11:19 doubt there have to be **d** among you

## DIFFERENT* [DIFFERENCE, DIFFERENCES, DIFFERENTLY, DIFFERING, DIFFERS]

Lev 19:19 " 'Do not mate **d** kinds
Nu  14:24 my servant Caleb has a **d** spirit
1Sa 10: 6 you will be changed into a **d** person.
Est  1: 7 of gold, each one **d** from the other,
     3: 8 Their customs are **d** from those
Da   7: 3 great beasts, each **d** from the others,
     7: 7 It was **d** from all the former beasts,
     7:19 which was **d** from all the others
     7:23 It will be **d** from all the other
     7:24 will arise, **d** from the earlier ones;
    11:29 this time the outcome will be **d**
Eze 15: 2 how is the wood of a vine **d**
Mk  16:12 *Jesus appeared in a **d** form to two*
Ro  12: 6 We have **d** gifts,
1Co  4: 7 who makes you **d** from anyone else?
    12: 4 There are **d** kinds of gifts,
    12: 5 There are **d** kinds of service,
    12: 6 There are **d** kinds of working,
    12:10 to another speaking in **d** kinds
    12:28 guidance, and of **d** kinds of tongues.
2Co 11: 4 you receive a **d** spirit from the Spirit
    11: 4 or a **d** gospel from the one you
Gal  1: 6 and are turning to a **d** gospel—
     4: 1 as heirs are underage they are no **d**
Heb  7:13 things are said belonged to a **d** tribe,
Jas  2:25 and sent them off in a **d** direction?

## DIFFERENTLY* [DIFFERENT]

Ex   8:22 that day I will deal **d** with the land
Php  3:15 And if on some point you think **d**,

## DIFFERING* [DIFFERENT]

Dt  25:13 Do not have two **d** weights in your
    25:14 Do not have two **d** measures in your
Pr  20:10 **D** weights and **d** measures—
    20:23 The LORD detests **d** weights,

## DIFFERS* [DIFFERENT]

1Co 15:41 and star **d** from star in splendor.

## DIFFICULT [DIFFICULTIES]

Ge  47: 9 My years have been few and **d**,
Ex  18:22 but have them bring every **d** case
Dt  30:11 commanding you today is not too **d**
2Ki  2:10 "You have asked a **d** thing,"
Da   2:11 What the king asks is too **d**.
     4: 9 and no mystery is too **d** for you.
Ac  15:19 that we should not make it **d**

## DIFFICULTIES* [DIFFICULT]

2Co 12:10 in hardships, in persecutions, in **d**.

## DIG [DIGS, DUG]

Dt   6:11 wells you did not **d**, and vineyards
Eze  8: 8 "Son of man, now **d** into the wall."
Am   9: 2 Though they **d** down to the depths

## DIGNITY

Ex  28: 2 your brother Aaron to give him **d**
Pr  31:25 She is clothed with strength and **d**;

## DIGS [DIG]

Pr  26:27 If anyone **d** a pit, they themselves

## DILIGENCE [DILIGENT]

Ezr  5: 8 The work is being carried on with **d**
Heb  6:11 to show this same **d** to the very end,

## DILIGENT* [DILIGENCE, DILIGENTLY]

2Ch 24:13 men in charge of the work were **d**,
Pr  10: 4 poverty, but **d** hands bring wealth.
    12:24 **D** hands will rule, but laziness ends
    12:27 the **d** feed on the riches of the hunt.
    13: 4 desires of the **d** are fully satisfied.
    21: 5 The plans of the **d** lead to profit as
1Ti  4:15 Be **d** in these matters;

## DILIGENTLY* [DILIGENT]

Zec  6:15 you **d** obey the LORD your God."
Jn   5:39 study the Scriptures **d** because you
Ro  12: 8 if it is to lead, do it **d**; if it is to show

## DINAH*

Only daughter of Jacob, by Leah (Ge 30:21; 46:15). Raped by Shechem; avenged by Simeon and Levi (Ge 34).

## DINE [DINNER]

Pr  23: 1 When you sit to **d** with a ruler,

## DINNER [DINE]

Mk   2:15 While Jesus was having **d** at Levi's
Lk  14:12 "When you give a luncheon or **d**,

## DIOTREPHES*

3Jn  1: 9 church, but **D**, who loves to be first,

## DIP [DIPPED, DIPPING, DIPS]

Ps  58:10 when they **d** their feet in the blood

## DIPPED [DIP]
2Ki  5:14  **d** himself in the Jordan seven times,
Mt  26:23  "The one who has **d** his hand
Rev 19:13  He is dressed in a robe **d** in blood,

## DIPPING* [DIP]
Jn   13:26  Then, **d** the piece of bread, he gave

## DIPS* [DIP]
Mk  14:20  "one who **d** bread into the bowl

## DIRECT [DIRECTED, DIRECTIVES, DIRECTS]
Ge  18:19  so that he will **d** his children and his
Ps  119:35  **D** me in the path of your
     119:133  **D** my footsteps according to your
Jer  10:23  it is not for them to **d** their steps.
2Th  3: 5  May the Lord **d** your hearts
1Ti  5:17  The elders who **d** the affairs

## DIRECTED [DIRECT]
Ge  24:51  master's son, as the LORD has **d**."
Nu  16:40  as the LORD **d** him through
Dt   2: 1  Red Sea, as the LORD had **d** me.
      6: 1  laws the LORD your God **d** me
Jos  11: 9  did to them as the LORD had **d**:
Pr  20:24  A person's steps are **d**
Jer  13: 2  as the LORD **d**, and put it around
Mt  26:19  disciples did as Jesus had **d** them
Ac   7:44  It had been made as God **d** Moses,
Tit   1: 5  elders in every town, as I **d** you.

## DIRECTIVES* [DIRECT]
1Co 11:17  In the following **d** I have no praise

## FOR THE DIRECTOR OF MUSIC See
    MUSIC

## DIRECTS* [DIRECT]
Jdg  20: 9  We'll go up against it as the lot **d**.
Ps  42: 8  By day the LORD **d** his love,
Isa  48:17  who **d** you in the way you should

## DIRGE*
Mt  11:17  we sang a **d**, and you did not
Lk   7:32  we sang a **d**, and you did not cry.'

## DISABLED* [ABLE]
2Sa  4: 4  he fell and became **d**.
Jn   5: 3  a great number of **d** people used
Heb 12:13  so that the lame may not be **d**,

## DISAGREEMENT* [AGREE]
Ac  15:39  They had such a sharp **d** that they

## DISAPPEAR [DISAPPEARED, DISAPPEARS]
Nu  27: 4  Why should our father's name **d**
Ru   4:10  his name will not **d** from among his
Mt   5:18  until heaven and earth **d**,
      5:18  by any means **d** from the Law until
Lk  16:17  earth to **d** than for the least stroke
Heb  8:13  is obsolete and outdated will soon **d**.
2Pe  3:10  The heavens will **d** with a roar;

## DISAPPEARED* [DISAPPEAR]
Jdg  6:21  And the angel of the LORD **d**.
1Ki  20:40  busy here and there, the man **d**."
Lk  24:31  him, and he **d** from their sight.

## DISAPPEARS [DISAPPEAR]
Hos 13: 3  like the early dew that **d**, like chaff
1Co 13:10  comes, what is in part **d**.

## DISAPPOINTED
Ps  22: 5  in you they trusted and were not **d**.
Isa  49:23  who hope in me will not be **d**."

## DISAPPROVE*
Pr  24:18  the LORD will see and **d** and turn

## DISARMED* [DISARMS]
Col   2:15  And having **d** the powers

## DISARMS* [DISARMED]
Job 12:21  on nobles and **d** the mighty.

## DISASTER [DISASTERS]
Ex  32:12  and do not bring **d** on your people.
Dt  32:35  their day of **d** is near and their doom
Jos  24:20  he will turn and bring **d** on you
2Ch  7:22  that is why he brought all this **d**
Est   8: 6  how can I bear to see **d** fall on my
Ps  57: 1  of your wings until the **d** has passed.
Pr   1:26  turn will laugh when **d** strikes you;
      3:25  Have no fear of sudden **d**
      6:15  Therefore **d** will overtake them
     16: 4  even the wicked for a day of **d**.
     17: 5  whoever gloats over **d** will not go
     27:10  house when **d** strikes you—
Isa   3: 9  They have brought **d**
     45: 7  I bring prosperity and create **d**;
Jer   4:20  **D** follows **d**; the whole land lies
     17:17  you are my refuge in the day of **d**.
     18: 8  not inflict on it the **d** I had planned.
Eze   7: 5  the Sovereign LORD says: " '**D**!
      7: 5  Unheard-of **d**! See, it comes!
Ob   1:13  of my people in the day of their **d**,
      1:13  their calamity in the day of their **d**,
      1:13  their wealth in the day of their **d**.

## DISASTERS [DISASTER]
Dt  31:17  Many **d** and calamities will come
     31:17  ask, 'Have not these **d** come on us

## DISCERN* [DISCERNED, DISCERNING, DISCERNMENT]
Dt  32:29  this and **d** what their end will be!
Job  6:30  Can my mouth not **d** malice?
     34: 4  Let us **d** for ourselves what is right;
Ps  19:12  But who can **d** their own errors?
     139: 3  You **d** my going out and my lying
Php  1:10  you may be able to **d** what is best

## DISCERNED* [DISCERN]
1Co  2:14  because they are **d** only through

## DISCERNING* [DISCERN]
Ge  41:33  now let Pharaoh look for a **d**

Ge 41:39 there is no one so **d** and wise as you.
2Sa 14:17 is like an angel of God in **d** good
1Ki 3: 9 So give your servant a **d** heart
     3:12 I will give you a wise and **d** heart,
Pr 1: 5 and let the **d** get guidance—
     8: 9 To the **d** all of them are right;
    10:13 is found on the lips of the **d**,
    14: 6 knowledge comes easily to the **d**.
    14:33 reposes in the heart of the **d**
    15:14 The **d** heart seeks knowledge,
    16:21 The wise in heart are called **d**,
    17:10 A rebuke impresses a **d** person
    17:24 A **d** person keeps wisdom in view,
    17:28 and **d** if they hold their tongues.
    18:15 heart of the **d** acquires knowledge,
    19:25 rebuke the **d**, and they will gain
    28: 7 who heed instruction are **d** children,
    28:11 and **d** sees how deluded they are.
Da 2:21 to the wise and knowledge to the **d**.
Hos 14: 9 Who is **d**? Let them understand.
1Co 11:29 without **d** the body of Christ
    11:31 more **d** with regard to ourselves,

## DISCERNMENT* [DISCERN]
Dt 32:28 without sense, there is no **d** in them.
1Ki 3:11 but for **d** in administering justice,
2Ch 2:12 endowed with intelligence and **d**,
Job 12:20 and takes away the **d** of elders.
Ps 119:125 give me **d** that I may understand
Pr 28: 2 a ruler with **d** and knowledge

## DISCHARGE [DISCHARGED, DISCHARGING]
Lev 15: 2 bodily **d**, such a **d** is unclean.
2Ti 4: 5 **d** all the duties of your ministry.

## DISCHARGED* [DISCHARGE]
Jdg 3:22 the blade, and his bowels **d**.
Ecc 8: 8 As no one is **d** in time of war,

## DISCHARGING* [DISCHARGE]
1Co 9:17 I am simply **d** the trust committed

## DISCIPLE [DISCIPLES, DISCIPLES']
Am 7:14 nor the **d** of a prophet,
Mt 10:42 little ones who is known to be my **d**,
Lk 14:26 such a person cannot be my **d**.
    14:27 and follow me cannot be my **d**.
Jn 9:28 and said, "You are this fellow's **d**!
    13:23 of them, the **d** whom Jesus loved,
    18:15 and another **d** were following Jesus.
    19:26 and the **d** whom he loved standing
    19:38 Now Joseph was a **d** of Jesus,
    20: 2 to Simon Peter and the other **d**,
    21: 7 the **d** whom Jesus loved said
    21:20 that the **d** whom Jesus loved was
Ac 9:10 there was a **d** named Ananias.
    16: 1 where a **d** named Timothy lived,

## DISCIPLES [DISCIPLE]
Mt 9:10 came and ate with him and his **d**.
    10: 1 Jesus called his twelve **d** to him
    26:56 Then all the **d** deserted him
    28:19 go and make **d** of all nations,
Mk 3: 7 withdrew with his **d** to the lake,

Mk 6:29 John's **d** came and took his body
    7: 5 "Why don't your **d** live according
Lk 6:13 he called his **d** to him and chose
    9:46 An argument started among the **d** as
    11: 1 to pray, just as John taught his **d**."
Lk 14:33 you have cannot be my **d**.
Jn 2:11 and his **d** put their faith in him.
    6:66 this time many of his **d** turned back
    8:31 to my teaching, you are really my **d**.
    12:16 At first his **d** did not understand all
    13:35 will know that you are my **d**, if you
    15: 8 showing yourselves to be my **d**.
    20:20 The **d** were overjoyed when they
Ac 6: 1 the number of **d** was increasing,
    11:26 The **d** were called Christians first
    14:22 strengthening the **d** and encouraging
    18:23 and Phrygia, strengthening all the **d**.

## DISCIPLES'* [DISCIPLE]
Jn 13: 5 basin and began to wash his **d'** feet,

## DISCIPLINE* [DISCIPLINED, DISCIPLINES, SELF-DISCIPLINE]
Dt 4:36 made you hear his voice to **d** you.
    11: 2 experienced the **d** of the LORD
    21:18 not listen to them when they **d** him,
Job 5:17 so do not despise the **d**
Ps 6: 1 in your anger or **d** me in your wrath.
    38: 1 in your anger or **d** me in your wrath.
    39:11 rebuke and **d** people for their sins,
    94:12 Blessed are those you **d**, LORD,
Pr 3:11 do not despise the LORD's **d**,
    5:12 You will say, "How I hated **d**!
    5:23 For lack of **d** they will die,
    10:17 Whoever heeds **d** shows the way
    12: 1 Whoever loves **d** loves knowledge,
    13:18 Whoever disregards **d** comes
    13:24 love them are careful to **d** them.
    15: 5 A fool spurns a parent's **d**,
    15:10 Stern **d** awaits those who leave
    15:32 who disregard **d** despise themselves,
    19:18 **D** your children, for in that there is
    19:20 Listen to advice and accept **d**,
    22:15 the rod of **d** will drive it far away.
    23:13 Do not withhold **d** from children;
    29:17 **D** your children, and they will give
Jer 10:24 **D** me, LORD, but only in due measure
    17:23 would not listen or respond to **d**.
    30:11 I will **d** you but only in due
    32:33 would not listen or respond to **d**.
    46:28 I will **d** you but only in due
Hos 5: 2 I will **d** all of them.
1Co 4:21 come to you with a rod of **d**,
Heb 12: 5 do not make light of the Lord's **d**,
    12: 7 Endure hardship as **d**;
    12: 8 and everyone undergoes **d**—
    12:11 No **d** seems pleasant at the time,
Rev 3:19 Those whom I love I rebuke and **d**.

## DISCIPLINED* [DISCIPLINE]
Isa 26:16 when you **d** them, they could barely
Jer 31:18 'You **d** me like an unruly calf, and I have been **d**.
1Co 11:32 we are being **d** so that we will not
Col 2: 5 delight to see how **d** you are
Tit 1: 8 self-controlled, upright, holy and **d**.

Heb 12: 7 For what children are not **d** by their
    12: 8 If you are not **d**—
    12: 9 we have all had parents who **d** us
    12:10 Our parents **d** us for a little while as

## DISCIPLINES* [DISCIPLINE]
Dt   8: 5 your heart that as a man **d** his son,
     8: 5 so the LORD your God **d** you.
Ps  94:10 Does he who **d** nations not punish?
Pr   3:12 because the LORD **d** those he
Heb 12: 6 because the Lord **d** those he loves,
    12:10 but God **d** us for our good, that we

## DISCLOSED
Mk   4:22 whatever is hidden is meant to be **d**,
Lk   12: 2 nothing concealed that will not be **d**,
Col  1:26 but is now **d** to the Lord's people.
Heb  9: 8 had not yet been **d** as long as

## DISCORD*
Est  1:18 will be no end of disrespect and **d**.
Gal  5:20 hatred, **d**, jealousy, fits of rage,

## DISCOURAGE* [DISCOURAGED, DISCOURAGEMENT]
Nu  32: 7 Why do you **d** the Israelites
Ezr  4: 4 set out to **d** the people of Judah

## DISCOURAGED* [DISCOURAGE]
Nu  32: 9 they **d** the Israelites from entering
Dt   1:21 Do not be afraid; do not be **d**."
    31: 8 Do not be afraid; do not be **d**."
Jos  1: 9 do not be **d**, for the LORD your
     8: 1 "Do not be afraid; do not be **d**.
    10:25 "Do not be afraid; do not be **d**.
1Ch 22:13 Do not be afraid or **d**.
    28:20 Do not be afraid or **d**,
2Ch 20:15 or **d** because of this vast army.
    20:17 Do not be afraid; do not be **d**.
    32: 7 or **d** because of the king of Assyria
Job  4: 5 trouble comes to you, and you are **d**;
Isa 42: 4 or be **d** till he establishes justice
Eph  3:13 not to be **d** because of my sufferings
Col  3:21 children, or they will become **d**.

## DISCOURAGEMENT* [DISCOURAGE]
Ex   6: 9 not listen to him because of their **d**

## DISCOVER [DISCOVERED]
Ecc  7:14 you cannot **d** anything about your
     8:17 it out, but no one can **d** its meaning.

## DISCOVERED [DISCOVER]
Jdg 16: 9 the secret of his strength was not **d**.
2Ki 23:24 that Hilkiah the priest had **d**
Ecc  7:27 the Teacher, "this is what I have **d**:

## DISCREDIT* [DISCREDITED]
Ne   6:13 would give me a bad name to **d** me.
Job 40: 8 "Would you **d** my justice?

## DISCREDITED* [DISCREDIT]
Ac  19:27 the great goddess Artemis will be **d**;

2Co  6: 3 so that our ministry will not be **d**.

## DISCREETLY* [DISCRETION]
Pr  26:16 than seven people who answer **d**.

## DISCRETION* [DISCREETLY]
1Ch 22:12 May the LORD give you **d**
Pr   1: 4 knowledge and **d** to the young—
     2:11 **D** will protect you,
     3:21 preserve sound judgment and **d**;
     5: 2 that you may maintain **d** and your
     8:12 I possess knowledge and **d**.
    11:22 a beautiful woman who shows no **d**.

## DISCRIMINATE* [DISCRIMINATED]
Ac  15: 9 He did not **d** between us and them,

## DISCRIMINATED* [DISCRIMINATE]
Jas  2: 4 have you not **d** among yourselves

## DISCUSSED [DISCUSSION]
Mk   8:16 They **d** this with one another
    11:31 They **d** it among themselves

## DISCUSSING [DISCUSSION]
Lk  24:17 "What are you **d** together as you

## DISCUSSION [DISCUSSED, DISCUSSING]
Mk   8:17 Aware of their **d**, Jesus asked them:

## DISEASE [DISEASED, DISEASES]
Dt   7:15 will keep you free from every **d**.
    28:22 will strike you with wasting **d**,
1Ki  8:37 whatever disaster or **d** may come,
Ps 106:15 but sent a wasting **d** among them.
Mt   4:23 healing every **d** and sickness among
     9:35 and healing every **d** and sickness.
    10: 1 and to heal every **d** and sickness.

## DISEASED [DISEASE]
Mal  1: 8 you sacrifice lame or **d** animals,

## DISEASES [DISEASE]
Dt   7:15 on you the horrible **d** you knew
    28:21 with **d** until he has destroyed you
Ps 103: 3 all your sins and heals all your **d**,
Mt   8:17 up our infirmities and bore our **d**."
Mk   3:10 those with **d** were pushing forward
Lk   9: 1 drive out all demons and to cure **d**,

## DISFIGURE* [DISFIGURED]
Mt   6:16 for they **d** their faces to show others

## DISFIGURED* [DISFIGURE]
Lev 21:18 is blind or lame, **d** or deformed;
Isa 52:14 his appearance was so **d** beyond

## DISGRACE [DISGRACED, DISGRACEFUL, DISGRACES]
Ge  30:23 said, "God has taken away my **d**."
1Sa 17:26 and removes this **d** from Israel?
Ps  44:15 I live in **d** all day long, and my face

Ps  52: 1  you who are a **d** in the eyes of God?
    74:21  Do not let the oppressed retreat in **d**;
Pr   6:33  Blows and **d** are his lot, and his
    11: 2  then comes **d**, but with humility
    19:26  is a child who brings shame and **d**.
    28: 7  companions of gluttons **d** their parents.
    29:15  left to themselves **d** their mother.
Isa  4: 1  by your name. Take away our **d**!"
Eze 16:52  Bear your **d**, for you have furnished
    16:52  be ashamed and bear your **d**, for you
    36:30  will no longer suffer **d** among
Mt   1:19  not want to expose her to public **d**,
Lk   1:25  and taken away my **d** among
Ac   5:41  worthy of suffering **d** for the Name.
1Co 11: 6  if it is a **d** for a woman to have her
    11:14  a man has long hair, it is a **d** to him,
1Ti  3: 7  so that he will not fall into **d**
Heb  6: 6  and subjecting him to public **d**.
    11:26  He regarded **d** for the sake of Christ
    13:13  the camp, bearing the **d** he bore.

## DISGRACED [DISGRACE]
2Sa 13:22  because he had **d** his sister Tamar.
Ezr  9: 6  "I am too ashamed and **d**, my God,
Isa 45:17  you will never be put to shame or **d**,
Jer  2:26  "As a thief is **d** when he is caught,
    2:26  so the house of Israel is **d**—

## DISGRACEFUL *[DISGRACE]
Pr  10: 5  sleeps during harvest is a **d** son.
    12: 4  a **d** wife is like decay in his bones.
    17: 2  servant will rule over a **d** son
Hos  4: 7  their glorious God for something **d**.
1Co 14:35  for it is **d** for a woman to speak

## DISGRACES* [DISGRACE]
Lev 21: 9  a prostitute, she **d** her father;

## DISGUISE [DISGUISED]
Ge  38:14  herself with a veil to **d** herself,
2Ch 18:29  "I will enter the battle in **d**, but you
Pr  26:24  Enemies **d** themselves with their lips,

## DISGUISED [DISGUISE]
2Ch 35:22  **d** himself to engage him in battle.

## DISH [DISHES]
Pr  19:24  Sluggards bury their hands in the **d**
Mt  23:25  clean the outside of the cup and **d**,

## DISHEARTENED [HEART]
1Th  5:14  encourage the **d**, help the weak,

## DISHES [DISH]
Ex  25:29  make its plates and **d** of pure gold,
Ezr  1: 9  gold **d** 30 silver **d** 1,000 silver pans

## DISHONEST*
Ex  18:21  trustworthy men who hate **d** gain—
Lev 19:35  " 'Do not use **d** standards
1Sa  8: 3  They turned aside after **d** gain
Pr  11: 1  The LORD detests **d** scales,
    13:11  **D** money dwindles away,
    20:23  and **d** scales do not please him.
    29:27  The righteous detest the **d**;

Jer 22:17  your heart are set only on **d** gain,
Eze 28:18  **d** trade you have desecrated your
Hos 12: 7  The merchants use **d** scales;
Am   8: 5  the price and cheating with **d** scales,
Mic  6:11  Shall I acquit a person with **d** scales,
Lk  16: 8  commended the **d** manager because
    16:10  whoever is **d** with very little will also
            be **d** with much.
1Ti  3: 8  much wine, and not pursuing **d** gain.
Tit  1: 7  not violent, not pursuing **d** gain.
    1:11  and that for the sake of **d** gain.
1Pe  5: 2  not pursuing **d** gain,

## DISHONOR* [DISHONORED, DISHONORS]
Lev 18: 7  " 'Do not **d** your father by having
    18: 8  that would **d** your father.
    18:10  that would **d** you.
    18:14  " 'Do not **d** your father's brother
    18:16  that would **d** your brother.
    20:19  for that would **d** a close relative;
Dt  22:30  he must not **d** his father's bed.
Pr  30: 9  steal, and so **d** the name of my God.
Jer 14:21  do not **d** your glorious throne.
    20:11  their **d** will never be forgotten.
La   2: 2  its princes down to the ground in **d**.
Eze 22:10  are those who **d** their father's bed;
Jn   8:49  I honor my Father and you **d** me.
Ro   2:23  do you **d** God by breaking the law?
1Co 13: 5  It does not **d** others,
    15:43  it is sown in **d**, it is raised in glory;
2Co  6: 8  through glory and **d**, bad report

## DISHONORED* [DISHONOR]
Lev 20:11  his father's wife, he has **d** his father.
    20:17  He has **d** his sister and will be held
    20:20  with his aunt, he has **d** his uncle.
    20:21  act of impurity; he has **d** his brother.
Dt  21:14  her as a slave, since you have **d** her.
Ezr  4:14  not proper for us to see the king **d**,
1Co  4:10  You are honored, we are **d**!
Jas  2: 6  you have **d** the poor.

## DISHONORS* [DISHONOR]
Dt  27:16  is anyone who **d** their father
    27:20  wife, for he **d** his father's bed."
Job 20: 3  I hear a rebuke that **d** me, and my
Mic  7: 6  For a son **d** his father, a daughter
1Co 11: 4  with his head covered **d** his head.
    11: 5  her head uncovered **d** her head—

## DISILLUSIONMENT*
Ps   7:14  conceive trouble and give birth to **d**.

## DISMAYED
1Sa 17:11  and all the Israelites were **d**
Isa 41:10  do not be **d**, for I am your God.

## DISOBEDIENCE* [DISOBEY]
Jos 22:22  in rebellion or **d** to the LORD,
Jer 43: 7  So they entered Egypt in **d**
Ro   5:19  just as through the **d** of the one man
    11:30  received mercy as a result of their **d**,
    11:32  has bound everyone over to **d** so
2Co 10: 6  be ready to punish every act of **d**,

Heb 2: 2 and **d** received its just punishment,
    4: 6 did not go in because of their **d**,
    4:11 by following their example of **d**.

## DISOBEDIENT* [DISOBEY]

Ne   9:26 they were **d** and rebelled against
Lk   1:17 and the **d** to the wisdom
Ac  26:19 I was not **d** to the vision
Ro  10:21 long I have held out my hands to a **d**
    11:30 were at one time **d** to God have now
    11:31 so they too have now become **d**
Eph  2: 2 is now at work in those who are **d**.
     5: 6 wrath comes on those who are **d**.
     5:12 to mention what the **d** do in secret.
2Ti  3: 2 proud, abusive, **d** to their parents,
Tit  1: 6 to the charge of being wild and **d**.
     1:16 **d** and unfit for doing anything good.
     3: 3 At one time we too were foolish, **d**,
Heb 11:31 not killed with those who were **d**.
1Pe  3:20 to those who were **d** long ago

## DISOBEY* [DISOBEDIENCE, DISOBEDIENT, DISOBEYED, DISOBEYING, DISOBEYS]

Dt  11:28 the curse if you **d** the commands
2Ch 24:20 'Why do you **d** the LORD's
Est  3: 3 "Why do you **d** the king's
Jer 42:13 and so **d** the LORD your God,
Ro   1:30 of doing evil; they **d** their parents;
1Pe  2: 8 because they **d** the message—

## DISOBEYED* [DISOBEY]

Nu  14:22 in the wilderness but who **d** me
    27:14 Zin, both of you **d** my command
Jdg  2: 2 Yet you have **d** me. Why have you
Ne   9:29 arrogant and **d** your commands.
Isa 24: 5 they have **d** the laws,
Jer 43: 4 and all the people **d** the LORD's
Lk  15:29 for you and never **d** your orders.
Heb  3:18 enter his rest if not to those who **d**?

## DISOBEYING* [DISOBEY]

Nu  14:41 said, "Why are you **d** the LORD's

## DISOBEYS* [DISOBEY]

Eze 33:12 'If someone who is righteous **d**,

## DISORDER*

Job 10:22 of utter darkness and **d**, where even
1Co 14:33 For God is not a God of **d**
2Co 12:20 slander, gossip, arrogance and **d**.
Jas  3:16 there you find **d** and every evil

## DISOWN [DISOWNED, DISOWNS]

Pr  30: 9 I may have too much and **d** you
Mt  10:33 me I will **d** before my Father
    26:35 to die with you, I will never **d** you."
Mk  14:30 twice you yourself will **d** me three
2Ti  2:12 If we **d** him, he will also **d** us;

## DISOWNED [DISOWN]

Lk  12: 9 me will be **d** before the angels
Ac   3:13 and you **d** him before Pilate,
     3:14 You **d** the Holy and Righteous One

## DISOWNS [DISOWN]

Lk  12: 9 But whoever publicly **d** me will be

## DISPERSE [DISPERSES]

Eze 12:15 when I **d** them among the nations

## DISPERSES* [DISPERSE]

Dt  30: 1 LORD your God **d** you among
Job 12:23 he enlarges nations, and **d** them.

## DISPLACES*

Pr  30:23 and a servant who **d** her mistress.

## DISPLAY [DISPLAYED, DISPLAYS]

Ps  19: 2 night after night they **d** knowledge.
    22:17 All my bones are on **d**;
Pr  14:29 but the quick-tempered **d** folly.
Isa 49: 3 in whom I will **d** my splendor."
Eze 28:22 among you I will **d** my glory.
    39:21 "I will **d** my glory among
Ro   9:17 that I might **d** my power in you
1Co  4: 9 God has put us apostles on **d**
1Ti  1:16 Christ Jesus might **d** his immense

## DISPLAYED [DISPLAY]

Ex  14:31 power the LORD **d** against
Jn   9: 3 the works of God might be **d** in him.

## DISPLAYS* [DISPLAY]

Ps   7:11 a God who **d** his wrath every day.
Isa 44:23 Jacob, he **d** his glory in Israel.
2Co  4: 4 that **d** the glory of Christ,
2Th  2: 9 sorts of **d** of power through signs

## DISPLEASE [DISPLEASED]

Nu  11:11 What have I done to **d** you that you
1Th  2:15 They **d** God and are hostile

## DISPLEASED [DISPLEASE]

2Sa 11:27 thing David had done **d** the LORD.
Isa 59:15 and was **d** that there was no justice.

## DISPOSAL

Ro   9:21 and some for **d** of refuse?

## DISPUTABLE* [DISPUTE]

Ro  14: 1 without quarreling over **d** matters.

## DISPUTE [DISPUTABLE, DISPUTES, DISPUTING]

Job  9: 3 Though they wished to **d** with him,
Pr  17:14 the matter before a **d** breaks out.
Lk  22:24 A **d** also arose among them as
Ac  15: 2 Barnabas into sharp **d** and debate
1Co  6: 1 If any of you has a **d** with another,

## DISPUTES [DISPUTE]

Pr  18:18 Casting the lot settles **d** and keeps
Isa  2: 4 and will settle **d** for many peoples.
1Co  6: 4 if you have **d** about such matters,

## DISPUTING* [DISPUTE]

1Ti  2: 8 up holy hands without anger or **d**.

Jude 1: 9 when he was **d** with the devil

## DISQUALIFIED* [DISQUALIFY]
1Co 9:27 I myself will not be **d** for the prize.

## DISQUALIFY* [DISQUALIFIED]
Col 2:18 and the worship of angels **d** you.

## DISREGARD* [DISREGARDED, DISREGARDS]
Pr 1:25 since you **d** all my advice
8:33 be wise; do not disregard it.
15:32 who **d** discipline despise themselves,

## DISREGARDED* [DISREGARD]
Isa 40:27 my cause is **d** by my God"?

## DISREGARDS* [DISREGARD]
Pr 13:18 Whoever **d** discipline comes to poverty

## DISREPUTE*
2Pe 2: 2 will bring the way of truth into **d**.

## DISRUPTING*
Tit 1:11 because they are **d** whole households

## DISSENSION* [DISSENSIONS]
Pr 6:14 they always stir up **d**.
6:19 and a person who stirs up **d**
10:12 Hatred stirs up **d**, but love covers
15:18 The hot-tempered stir up **d**,
16:28 The perverse stir up **d**, and gossips
28:25 The greedy stir up **d**, but those who
29:22 An angry person stirs up **d**,
Ro 13:13 debauchery, not in **d** and jealousy.

## DISSENSIONS* [DISSENSION]
Gal 5:20 of rage, selfish ambition, **d**,

## DISSIPATION*
Lk 21:34 hearts will be weighed down with **d**,

## DISSOLVED*
Isa 34: 4 All the stars in the sky will be **d**

## DISTANCE [DISTANT]
Ex 2: 4 at a **d** to see what would happen
33: 7 it outside the camp some **d** away,
Dt 32:52 you will see the land only from a **d**;
Mk 14:54 Peter followed him at a **d**,
15:40 women watching from a **d**.
Heb 11:13 them and welcomed them from a **d**,

## DISTANT [DISTANCE]
Jos 9: 6 "We have come from a **d** country;
Isa 49: 1 hear this, you **d** nations:
66:19 to the **d** islands that have not heard
Jer 5:15 am bringing a **d** nation against you—
Zep 2:11 **D** nations will bow down to him,

## DISTINCTION
Ex 8:23 I will make a **d** between my people

## DISTINGUISH [DISTINGUISHING]
Lev 10:10 so that you can **d** between the holy
1Ki 3: 9 and to **d** between right and wrong.
Heb 5:14 have trained themselves to **d** good

## DISTINGUISHING [DISTINGUISH]
1Co 12:10 to another **d** between spirits,

## DISTORT*
Jer 23:36 So you **d** the words of the living
Mic 3: 9 despise justice and **d** all that is right;
Ac 20:30 **d** the truth in order to draw away
2Co 4: 2 nor do we **d** the word of God.
2Pe 3:16 ignorant and unstable people **d**,

## DISTRACTED*
Lk 10:40 Martha was **d** by all the preparations

## DISTRESS [DISTRESSED, DISTRESSES]
Jdg 2:15 They were in great **d**.
2Sa 22: 7 "In my **d** I called to the LORD;
2Ch 15: 4 in their **d** they turned to the LORD,
Ne 9:37 as they please. We are in great **d**.
Est 4: 4 about Mordecai, she was in great **d**.
Ps 18: 6 In my **d** I called to the LORD;
77: 2 When I was in **d**, I sought the Lord;
81: 7 In your **d** you called and I rescued
86: 7 When I am in **d**, I call to you,
107: 6 and he delivered them from their **d**.
116: 3 I was overcome by **d** and sorrow.
120: 1 I call on the LORD in my **d**,
Jnh 2: 2 "In my **d** I called to the LORD,
Mt 24:21 For then there will be great **d**,
Jas 1:27 and widows in their **d** and to keep

## DISTRESSED [DISTRESS]
Isa 63: 9 In all their distress he too was **d**,
Mk 14:33 and he began to be deeply **d**
Ro 14:15 sister is **d** because of what you eat,

## DISTRESSES* [DISTRESS]
2Co 6: 4 in troubles, hardships and **d**;

## DISTRIBUTE [DISTRIBUTED, DISTRIBUTION]
Nu 33:54 **D** the land by lot, according to your
Eze 47:21 are to **d** this land among yourselves

## DISTRIBUTED [DISTRIBUTE]
Jos 18:10 there he **d** the land to the Israelites
Heb 2: 4 of the Holy Spirit **d** according to his

## DISTRIBUTION* [DISTRIBUTE]
Ac 6: 1 overlooked in the daily **d** of food.

## DISTURBANCE* [DISTURBED]
Ac 19:23 time there arose a great **d**
24:18 me, nor was I involved in any **d**.

## DISTURBED [DISTURBANCE]
1Sa 28:15 "Why have you **d** me by bringing
Ps 42: 5 Why so **d** within me?

Da    7:15  that passed through my mind **d** me.
Ac    4: 2  They were greatly **d** because
     15:24  without our authorization and **d** you,

## DIVIDE [DIVIDED, DIVIDING, DIVISION, DIVISIONS, DIVISIVE]

Ex   14:16  hand over the sea to **d** the water so
Ps   22:18  They **d** my clothes among them
Isa  53:12  he will **d** the spoils with the strong,
Lk   12:13  tell my brother to **d** the inheritance
Jude  1:19  These are the people who **d** you,

## DIVIDED [DIVIDE]

Ex   14:21  it into dry land. The waters were **d**,
Lev  11: 3  eat any animal that has a **d** hoof
Jos  14: 5  So the Israelites **d** the land, just as
2Ki   2: 8  The water **d** to the right
Ne    9:11  You **d** the sea before them,
Isa  63:12  hand, who **d** the waters before them,
Da    5:28  Your kingdom is **d** and given
Mt   12:25  "Every kingdom **d** against itself
     12:25  or household **d** against itself will not
Lk   11:18  If Satan is **d** against himself,
     23:34  they **d** up his clothes by casting lots.
1Co   1:13  Is Christ **d**? Was Paul crucified

## DIVIDING [DIVIDE]

Jos  19:51  And so they finished **d** the land.
Jn   19:23  his clothes, **d** them into four shares,
Eph   2:14  the barrier, the **d** wall of hostility,
Heb   4:12  it penetrates even to **d** soul

## DIVINATION [DIVINATIONS, DIVINE, DIVINER, DIVINERS]

Ge   44: 5  drinks from and also uses for **d**?
Lev  19:26  " 'Do not practice **d** or seek
Nu   23:23  There is no **d** against Jacob, no evil
Dt   18:10  the fire, who practices **d** or sorcery,
1Sa  15:23  For rebellion is like the sin of **d**,
Eze  13:23  see false visions or practice **d**.

## DIVINATIONS [DIVINATION]

Jer  14:14  prophesying to you false visions, **d**,
Eze  13: 6  visions are false and their **d** a lie.

## DIVINE [DIVINATION]

Isa  35: 4  with **d** retribution he will come
Ro    1:20  his eternal power and **d** nature—
      9: 4  theirs the **d** glory, the covenants,
2Co  10: 4  they have **d** power to demolish
2Pe   1: 3  His **d** power has given us everything

## DIVINER* [DIVINATION]

Isa   3: 2  the prophet, the **d** and the elder,
Da    2:27  or **d** can explain to the king

## DIVINERS [DIVINATION]

Isa  44:25  false prophets and makes fools of **d**,
Jer  29: 8  and **d** among you deceive you.
Zec  10: 2  deceitfully, **d** see visions that lie;

## DIVISION [DIVIDE]

Lk   12:51  peace on earth? No, I tell you, but **d**.
1Co  12:25  there should be no **d** in the body,

## DIVISIONS [DIVIDE]

Ex   12:41  day, all the LORD's **d** left Egypt.
Nu    1: 3  according to their **d** all the men
1Ch  23: 6  David separated the Levites into **d**
Ro   16:17  to watch out for those who cause **d**
1Co   1:10  and that there be no **d** among you,
     11:18  as a church, there are **d** among you,

## DIVISIVE* [DIVIDE]

Tit   3:10  Warn **d** people once, and then warn

## DIVORCE* [DIVORCED, DIVORCES]

Dt   22:19  he must not **d** her as long as he
     22:29  He can never **d** her as long as he
     24: 1  and he writes her a certificate of **d**,
     24: 3  her and writes her a certificate of **d**,
Isa  50: 1  is your mother's certificate of **d**
Jer   3: 8  faithless Israel her certificate of **d**
Mal   2:16  "I hate **d**," says the LORD God
Mt    1:19  he had in mind to **d** her quietly.
      5:31  must give her a certificate of **d**.'
     19: 3  for a man to **d** his wife for any
     19: 7  a man give his wife a certificate of **d**
     19: 8  to **d** your wives because your hearts
Mk   10: 2  it lawful for a man to **d** his wife?"
     10: 4  a man to write a certificate of **d**
1Co   7:11  And a husband must not **d** his wife.
      7:12  to live with him, he must not **d** her.
      7:13  to live with her, she must not **d** him.

## DIVORCED* [DIVORCE]

Lev  21: 7  or **d** from their husbands,
     21:14  not marry a widow, a **d** woman,
     22:13  daughter becomes a widow or is **d**,
Nu   30: 9  or **d** woman will be binding on her.
Dt   24: 4  then her first husband, who **d** her,
1Ch   8: 8  after he had **d** his wives Hushim
Eze  44:22  not marry widows or **d** women;
Mt    5:32  who marries the **d** woman commits
Lk   16:18  who marries a **d** woman commits

## DIVORCES* [DIVORCE]

Jer   3: 1  "If a man **d** his wife and she leaves
Mt    5:31  'Anyone who **d** his wife must give
      5:32  tell you that anyone who **d** his wife,
     19: 9  tell you that anyone who **d** his wife,
Mk   10:11  "Anyone who **d** his wife
     10:12  if she **d** her husband and marries
Lk   16:18  "Anyone who **d** his wife

## DO [DOES, DOING, DONE]

Ge    4: 7  But if you **d** not **d** what is right,
     18:25  be it from you to **d** such a thing—
     18:25  the Judge of all the earth **d** right?"
Ex   19: 8  "We will **d** everything the LORD
     20:10  On it you shall not **d** any work,
Lev  18: 3  You must not **d** as they **d** in Egypt,
Nu    9:11  but they are to **d** it on the fourteenth day
Jos   1: 8  be careful to **d** everything written
2Ki  17:15  ordered them, "**D** not **d** as they **d**."
Ps   37: 3  Trust in the LORD and **d** good;
    143:10  Teach me to **d** your will, for you are
Pr    4:23  for everything you **d** flows from it.
     16: 3  to the LORD whatever you **d**,
     31:29  "Many women **d** noble things,

Ecc  2:24  People can **d** nothing better than
Jer  22:  3  **D** what is just and right.
     22:  3  **D** no wrong or violence
Eze  16:30  when you **d** all these things,
Mt  23:  3  But **d** not **d** what they **d**, for they **d**
Mk  3:  4  to **d** good or to **d** evil, to save life
      6:  5  He could not **d** any miracles there,
Lk   6:31  **D** to others as you would have them **d**
Jn   6:28  "What must we **d** to **d** the works
      7:17  Anyone who chooses to **d** the will
Ac  16:30  "Sirs, what must I **d** to be saved?"
   22:10  " 'What shall I **d**, Lord?' I asked.
Ro   7:15  to **d** I **d** not **d**, but what I hate I **d**.
Gal   6:10  let us **d** good to all people,
Eph  3:20  to **d** immeasurably more than all we
Col  3:17  And whatever you **d**,
     3:17  deed, **d** it all in the name of the Lord
Heb  6:  9  things that have to **d** with salvation.
Jas  1:25  they will be blessed in what they **d**.
1Pe  3:11  Turn from evil and **d** good;

## DO NOT FEAR See FEAR

## DOCTOR

Mt  9:12  "It is not the healthy who need a **d**,
Col  4:14  the **d**, and Demas send greetings.

## DOCTRINE* [DOCTRINES]

1Ti  1:10  else is contrary to the sound **d**
     4:16  Watch your life and **d** closely.
2Ti  4:  3  people will not put up with sound **d**.
Tit  1:  9  he can encourage others by sound **d**
    2:  1  what is appropriate to sound **d**.

## DOCTRINES* [DOCTRINE]

1Ti  1:  3  not to teach false **d** any longer

## DOE

Ge  49:21  "Naphtali is a **d** set free that bears
Pr   5:19  A loving **d**, a graceful deer—

## DOEG*

    Edomite; Saul's head shepherd; murdered 85 priests at Nob (1Sa 21:7; 22:6–23; Ps 52).

## DOES [DO]

Dt  32:  4  A faithful God who **d** no wrong,
Ps  15:  5  Whoever **d** these things will never
  135:  6  The Lord **d** whatever pleases
  145:13  he promises and faithful in all he **d**.
Ecc  3:14  that everything God **d** will endure
Da  9:14  God is righteous in everything he **d**;
Zep  3:  5  and every new day he **d** not fail,
Mk  3:35  Whoever **d** God's will is my brother
Jn  5:19  the Father **d** the Son also **d**.
Ro  10:  5  "Whoever **d** these things will live
Gal  3:12  "Whoever **d** these things will live

## DOG [DOGS]

Jdg  7:  5  their tongues like a **d** from those
1Sa 17:43  "Am I a **d**, that you come at me
Pr  26:11  As a **d** returns to its vomit, so fools
Ecc  9:  4  even a live **d** is better off than
2Pe  2:22  "A **d** returns to its vomit," and,

## DOGS [DOG]

1Ki 21:19  In the place where **d** licked
2Ki  9:10  **d** will devour her on the plot
Ps  22:16  **D** surround me, a pack of villains
Isa  56:11  They are **d** with mighty appetites;
Mt  7:  6  "Do not give **d** what is sacred;
  15:26  bread and toss it to the **d**."
Php  3:  2  Watch out for those **d**,
Rev 22:15  Outside are the **d**, those who

## DOING [DO]

Mk 11:28  authority are you **d** these things?"
1Pe  3:17  to suffer for **d** good than for **d** evil.

## DOMINION

Job 25:  2  "**D** and awe belong to God;
Ps  22:28  for **d** belongs to the Lord and he
Da   4:  3  his **d** endures from generation
1Co 15:24  Father after he has destroyed all **d**,
Eph  1:21  power and **d**, and every name
Col  1:13  rescued us from the **d** of darkness

## DONE [DO]

Ge  3:13  "What is this you have **d**?"
   4:10  Lord said, "What have you **d**?
Ex  18:  9  the good things the Lord had **d**
Est  6:  6  "What should be **d** for the man
Ps  46:  8  and see what the Lord has **d**,
   66:  5  and see what God has **d**,
   71:19  skies, you who have **d** great things.
   98:  1  song, for he has **d** marvelous things;
  105:  5  Remember the wonders he has **d**,
  118:24  The Lord has **d** it this very day;
Pr  19:17  reward them for what they have **d**.
  24:12  according to what they have **d**?
  31:31  Honor her for all that her hands have **d**,
Ecc  1:  9  what has been **d** will be **d** again;
   8:17  then I saw all that God has **d**.
Isa  25:  1  you have **d** wonderful things,
Jer  50:29  for her deeds; do to her as she has **d**.
Eze 11:21  their own heads what they have **d**,
Joel  2:21  the Lord has **d** great things!
Ob  1:15  As you have **d**, it will be **d** to you;
Mic  6:  3  "My people, what have I **d** to you?
Mt  6:10  your will be **d**, on earth as it is
  26:42  I drink it, may your will be **d**."
Lk  19:17  " 'Well **d**, my good servant!'
Jn  15:  7  and it will be **d** for you.
Ac  19:18  openly confessed what they had **d**.
Rev 16:17  from the throne, saying, "It is **d**!"
  18:  6  her back double for what she has **d**.
  20:12  what they had **d** as recorded
  21:  6  He said to me: "It is **d**. I am

## DONKEY [DONKEY'S]

Nu  22:30  The **d** said to Balaam, "Am I not your own **d**,
Zec  9:  9  on a **d**, on a colt, the foal of a **d**.
Mt  21:  5  **d**, and on a colt, the foal of a **d**.' "
2Pe  2:16  rebuked for his wrongdoing by a **d**—

## DONKEY'S [DONKEY]

Nu  22:28  the Lord opened the **d** mouth,
Jdg 15:16  With a **d** jawbone I have killed

## DOOMED
Ps 137: 8 Daughter Babylon, **d** to destruction,
Jn  17:12 None has been lost except the one **d**
2Th  2: 3 revealed, the man **d** to destruction.

## DOOR [DOORFRAME, DOORFRAMES, DOORKEEPER, DOORPOST, DOORS, DOORWAY]
Ge   4: 7 is right, sin is crouching at your **d**;
    19: 9 moved forward to break down the **d**.
Dt  15:17 it through his ear lobe into the **d**,
Jdg 19:22 Pounding on the **d**, they shouted
Job 31:32 for my **d** was always open
Ps 141: 3 keep watch over the **d** of my lips.
Pr   5: 8 do not go near the **d** of her house,
    9:14 She sits at the **d** of her house,
   26:14 As a **d** turns on its hinges,
Mt   6: 6 close the **d** and pray to your Father,
    7: 7 and the **d** will be opened to you.
Lk  13:24 effort to enter through the narrow **d**,
Ac  12:14 and exclaimed, "Peter is at the **d**!"
   14:27 how he had opened a **d** of faith
1Co 16: 9 because a great **d** for effective work
2Co 2:12 that the Lord had opened a **d** for me,
Col  4: 3 God may open a **d** for our message,
Jas  5: 9 The Judge is standing at the **d**!
Rev  3: 8 I have placed before you an open **d**
   3:20 I stand at the **d** and knock.
   3:20 hears my voice and opens the **d**,
   4: 1 before me was a **d** standing open

## DOORFRAME [DOOR, FRAME]
Ex  12:23 sides of the **d** and will pass over

## DOORFRAMES [DOOR, FRAME]
Dt   6: 9 Write them on the **d** of your houses

## DOORKEEPER [DOOR, KEEP]
Ps  84:10 I would rather be a **d** in the house

## DOORPOST [DOOR, POSTS]
Ex  21: 6 the **d** and pierce his ear with an awl.

## DOORS [DOOR]
1Ki  6:31 to the inner sanctuary he made **d**
Ne   3: 1 dedicated it and set its **d** in place,
Ps  24: 7 you ancient **d**, that the King of glory
Mal  1:10 one of you would shut the temple **d**,
Jn  20:26 Though the **d** were locked,
Ac   5:19 of the Lord opened the **d** of the jail
   16:26 At once all the prison **d** flew open,

## DOORWAY [DOOR, WAY]
Ex  12:23 doorframe and will pass over that **d**,

## DORCAS* [TABITHA]
    Disciple, also known as Tabitha, whom Peter raised from the dead (Ac 9:36–43).

## DOUBLE [DOUBLE-EDGED, DOUBLE-MINDED]
Ex  22: 7 the thief, if caught, must pay back **d**.
1Sa  1: 5 he gave a **d** portion because he

2Ki  2: 9 "Let me inherit a **d** portion of your
Isa 40: 2 the LORD's hand **d** for all her sins.
   61: 7 shame you will receive a **d** portion,
   61: 7 so you will inherit a **d** portion
Hos 10:10 to put them in bonds for their **d** sin.
1Ti  5:17 church well are worthy of **d** honor,
Rev 18: 6 pay her back **d** for what she has

## DOUBLE-EDGED* [DOUBLE, EDGE]
Jdg  3:16 Now Ehud had made a **d** sword
Ps 149: 6 and a **d** sword in their hands,
Pr   5: 4 is bitter as gall, sharp as a **d** sword.
Heb  4:12 Sharper than any **d** sword,
Rev  1:16 of his mouth was a sharp, **d** sword.
   2:12 of him who has the sharp, **d** sword.

## DOUBLE-MINDED* [DOUBLE, MIND]
Ps 119:113 I hate **d** people, but I love your law.
Jas  1: 8 they are **d** and unstable in all they
    4: 8 and purify your hearts, you **d**.

## DOUBT [DOUBTED, DOUBTING, DOUBTS]
Mt  14:31 faith," he said, "why did you **d**?"
   21:21 if you have faith and do not **d**,
Mk  11:23 sea,' and do not **d** in your heart
Jas  1: 6 you must believe and not **d**,
Jude 1:22 Be merciful to those who **d**;

## DOUBTED* [DOUBT]
Mt  28:17 they worshiped him; but some **d**.

## DOUBTING* [DOUBT]
Jn  20:27 it into my side. Stop **d** and believe."

## DOUBTS* [DOUBT]
Lk  24:38 and why do **d** rise in your minds?
Ro  14:23 those who have **d** are condemned
Jas  1: 6 because the one who **d** is like

## DOUGH
Ex  12:39 With the **d** the Israelites had brought
   12:39 The **d** was without yeast because
Lk  13:21 until it worked all through the **d**."
1Co  5: 6 yeast leavens the whole batch of **d**?
Gal  5: 9 through the whole batch of **d**."

## DOVE [DOVES]
Ge   8: 8 he sent out a **d** to see if the water
Ps  55: 6 "Oh, that I had the wings of a **d**!
SS   5: 2 my darling, my **d**, my flawless one.
Hos  7:11 "Ephraim is like a **d**,
Mk   1:10 Spirit descending on him like a **d**.

## DOVES [DOVE]
Lev 12: 8 she is to bring two **d** or two young
SS   4: 1 Your eyes behind your veil are **d**.
Isa 59:11 we moan mournfully like **d**.
Eze  7:16 Like **d** of the valleys, they will all
Mt  10:16 as snakes and as innocent as **d**.
   21:12 and the benches of those selling **d**.
Lk   2:24 "a pair of **d** or two young pigeons."

## DOWN [DOWNCAST, DOWNFALL]

Ge   11: 5  the LORD came **d** to see the city
     18:21  that I will go **d** and see if what they
     46: 3  "Do not be afraid to go **d** to Egypt,
Ex    3: 8  So I have come **d** to rescue them
     19:11  that day the LORD will come **d**
     34: 5  the LORD came **d** in the cloud
Nu   11:25  the LORD came **d** in the cloud
2Sa 22:10  He parted the heavens and came **d**;
Ne    1: 3  The wall of Jerusalem is broken **d**,
      9:13  "You came **d** on Mount Sinai;
Ps   18:16  He reached **d** from on high and took
     23: 2  He makes me lie **d** in green
    113: 6  who stoops **d** to look on the heavens
Pr    5: 5  Her feet go **d** to death;
Ecc   3: 3  a time to tear **d** and a time to build,
Da    8:10  some of the starry host **d** to the earth
Mt    7:25  The rain came **d**, the streams rose,
Mk    6:40  So they sat **d** in groups of hundreds
     15:30  come **d** from the cross and save
Lk    4: 9  said, "throw yourself **d** from here.
Jn    6:41  bread that came **d** from heaven."
     10:11  The good shepherd lays **d** his life
Heb   1: 3  sins, he sat **d** at the right hand
      8: 1  who sat **d** at the right hand
     10:12  he sat **d** at the right hand of God,
     12: 2  sat **d** at the right hand of the throne
1Jn   3:16  Jesus Christ laid **d** his life for us.
      3:16  we ought to lay **d** our lives for one
Rev   3:12  which is coming **d** out of heaven
     12: 9  The great dragon was hurled **d**—
     21: 2  coming **d** out of heaven from God,
     21:10  coming **d** out of heaven from God.

## DOWNCAST [DOWN, CAST]

1Sa   1:18  and her face was no longer **d**.
Ps   42: 5  Why, my soul, are you **d**?
La    3:20  them, and my soul is **d** within me.
Lk   24:17  They stood still, their faces **d**.
2Co   7: 6  who comforts the **d**, comforted us

## DOWNFALL [DOWN, FALL]

2Ch 28:23  But they were his **d** and the **d** of all
Pr   18:12  Before a **d** the heart is haughty,
Hos  14: 1  Your sins have been your **d**!

## DRAGON

Rev  12: 3  an enormous red **d** with seven heads
     13: 2  The **d** gave the beast his power
     16:13  they came out of the mouth of the **d**,
     20: 2  He seized the **d**, that ancient

## DRANK [DRINK]

Ge    9:21  When he **d** some of its wine,
Ex   24:11  they saw God, and they ate and **d**.
Dt    9: 9  I ate no bread and **d** no water.
Jer  51: 7  The nations **d** her wine;
Da    5: 4  As they **d** the wine, they praised
Ob    1:16  Just as you **d** on my holy hill, so all
Mk   14:23  it to them, and they all **d** from it.
1Co  10: 4  and **d** the same spiritual drink;
     10: 4  for they **d** from the spiritual rock

## DRAW [DRAWING, DRAWS]

Ge   24:11  time the women go out to **d** water.

Ex    2:16  and they came to **d** water and fill
1Sa  31: 4  "**D** your sword and run me through,
Isa  12: 3  joy you will **d** water from the wells
Zep   3: 2  she does not **d** near to her God.
Mt   26:52  "for all who **d** the sword will die
Jn    2: 8  "Now **d** some out and take it
      4: 7  Samaritan woman came to **d** water,
     12:32  earth, will **d** all people to myself."
Heb   7:19  by which we **d** near to God.
     10:22  let us **d** near to God with a sincere

## DRAWING [DRAW]

Lk   21:28  because your redemption is **d** near."

## DRAWS [DRAW]

Isa  51: 5  My righteousness **d** near speedily,
Jn    6:44  the Father who sent me **d** them,

## DREAD [DREADED, DREADFUL]

Ex    1:12  Egyptians came to **d** the Israelites
Nu   22: 3  Moab was filled with **d** because
Ps   53: 5  **d**, where there was nothing to **d**.
Isa   8:13  to fear, he is the one you are to **d**.

## DREADED [DREAD]

Dt   28:60  all the diseases of Egypt that you **d**,
Job   3:25  what I **d** has happened to me.

## DREADFUL [DREAD]

Joel  2:11  day of the LORD is great; it is **d**.
Mal   4: 5  and **d** day of the LORD comes.
Mt   24:19  How **d** it will be in those days
Heb  10:31  It is a **d** thing to fall into the hands

## DREAM [DREAMED, DREAMER, DREAMS]

Ge   20: 3  came to Abimelek in a **d** one night
     28:12  He had a **d** in which he saw
     31:11  angel of God said to me in the **d**,
     37: 5  Joseph had a **d**, and when he told it
     40: 5  had a **d** the same night, and each **d**
     41: 1  years had passed, Pharaoh had a **d**:
Jdg   7:13  his **d**. "I had a **d**," he was saying.
1Ki   3: 5  to Solomon during the night in a **d**,
Ecc   5: 3  A **d** comes when there are many
Da    2: 3  "I have had a **d** that troubles me
      4: 5  I had a **d** that made me afraid.
      7: 1  Daniel had a **d**, and visions passed
Joel  2:28  your old men will **d** dreams,
Mt    1:20  of the Lord appeared to him in a **d**
      2:12  having been warned in a **d** not to go
      2:13  the Lord appeared to Joseph in a **d**.
      2:19  the Lord appeared in a **d** to Joseph
      2:22  Having been warned in a **d**,
     27:19  a great deal today in a **d** because
Ac    2:17  visions, your old men will **d** dreams.

## DREAMED* [DREAM]

Ps  126: 1  of Zion, we were like those who **d**.
Da    2: 2  to tell him what he had **d**.

## DREAMER [DREAM]

Ge   37:19  "Here comes that **d**!" they said
Dt   13: 5  **d** tried to turn you from the way

## DREAMS [DREAM]
Nu   12: 6  in visions, I speak to them in **d**.
Dt   13: 1  or one who foretells by **d**,
1Sa  28: 6  LORD did not answer him by **d**
Jer  23:28  the prophets who have **d** tell their **d**,

## DREGS*
Ps   75: 8  the earth drink it down to its very **d**.
Isa  51:17  who have drained to its **d** the goblet
Jer  48:11  like wine left on its **d**, not poured
Zep   1:12  who are like wine left on its **d**,

## DRESS [DRESSED]
Ex   40:13  **d** Aaron in the sacred garments,
1Ti   2: 9  also want the women to **d** modestly,

## DRESSED [DRESS]
Ex   20:25  do not build it with **d** stones, for you
1Sa  17:38  Then Saul **d** David in his own tunic.
Zec   3: 3  Now Joshua was **d** in filthy clothes
Lk    7:25  out to see? A man **d** in fine clothes?
      8:35  Jesus' feet, **d** and in his right mind;
     12:27  in all his splendor was **d** like one
Rev   3: 4  They will walk with me, **d** in white,
      4: 4  They were **d** in white and had
     15: 6  They were **d** in clean, shining linen
     17: 4  The woman was **d** in purple
     19:13  He is **d** in a robe dipped in blood,
     21: 2  prepared as a bride beautifully **d**

## DRIED [DRY]
Ge    8:13  the water had **d** up from the earth.
Jos   5: 1  coast heard how the LORD had **d**
Ps   22:15  My mouth is **d** up like a potsherd,
     106: 9  rebuked the Red Sea, and it **d** up;
Isa  51:10  Was it not you who **d** up the sea,
Rev  16:12  its water was **d** up to prepare

## DRIFT*
Ac   27:32  the lifeboat and let it **d** away.
Heb   2: 1  heard, so that we do not **d** away.

## DRINK [DRANK, DRINKING, DRINKS, DRUNK, DRUNKARD, DRUNKARD'S, DRUNKARDS, DRUNKENNESS]
Ge   19:33  night they got their father to **d** wine,
Ex   15:23  they could not **d** its water because it
     17: 1  was no water for the people to **d**.
Lev  10: 9  are not to **d** wine or other fermented **d**
Nu    4: 7  bowls, and the jars for **d** offerings;
      6: 3  other fermented **d** and must not **d**
     20: 5  And there is no water to **d**!"
Jdg   7: 5  from those who kneel down to **d**."
     13: 4  Now see to it that you **d** no wine
2Sa  23:15  someone would get me a **d** of water
Ps   50:13  of bulls or **d** the blood of goats?
Pr    5:15  **D** water from your own cistern,
      7:18  let's **d** deep of love till morning;
     23:20  not join those who **d** too much wine
Ecc   2:24  do nothing better than to eat and **d**
      9: 7  and **d** your wine with a joyful heart,
Jer   8:14  and given us poisoned water to **d**,
     25:15  the nations to whom I send you **d** it.

Eze  23:32  "You will **d** your sister's cup, a cup
Da    1:12  but vegetables to eat and water to **d**.
Ob    1:16  they will **d** and **d** and be as if they
Mt   20:22  you **d** the cup I am going to **d**?"
     26:27  them, saying, "**D** from it, all of you.
     27:34  There they offered Jesus wine to **d**,
     27:34  but after tasting it, he refused to **d** it.
Lk   12:19  eat, **d** and be merry." '
Jn    7:37  who is thirsty come to me and **d**.
     18:11  Shall I not **d** the cup the Father has
1Co  10: 4  and drank the same spiritual **d**;
     10:21  You cannot **d** the cup of the Lord
     12:13  were all given the one Spirit to **d**.
Php   2:17  out like a **d** offering on the sacrifice
Col   2:16  judge you by what you eat or **d**,
2Ti   4: 6  being poured out like a **d** offering,
Heb   9:10  are only a matter of food and **d**
Rev  14: 8  all the nations **d** the maddening
     14:10  will **d** of the wine of God's fury,
     16: 6  them blood to **d** as they deserve."

## DRINK OFFERING  Ge 35:14; Ex 29:40, 41;
30:9; Lev 23:13; Nu 6:17; 15:5, 7, 10, 24; 28:7,
7, 8, 9, 10, 14, 15, 24; 29:16, 22, 25, 28, 31, 34,
38; 2Ki 16:13, 15; Php 2:17; 2Ti 4:6

## DRINK OFFERINGS  Ex 37:16; Lev 23:18,
37; Nu 4:7; 6:15; 28:31; 29:6, 11, 18, 19, 21, 24,
27, 30, 33, 37, 39; Dt 32:38; 1Ch 29:21; 2Ch
29:35; Ezr 7:17; Isa 57:6; Jer 7:18; 19:13; 32:29;
44:17, 18, 19, 19, 25; 52:19; Eze 20:28; 45:17;
Joel 1:9, 13; 2:14

## DRINKING [DRINK]
1Sa   1:15  I have not been **d** wine or beer;
Mt   11:19  The Son of Man came eating and **d**,
Lk   7:27  People were eating, **d**,
Ro   14:17  God is not a matter of eating and **d**,
1Ti   5:23  Stop **d** only water, and use a little

## DRINKS [DRINK]
Isa   5:22  wine and champions at mixing **d**,
Am    4: 1  your husbands, "Bring us some **d**!"
Jn    4:13  "Everyone who **d** this water will be
      6:54  and **d** my blood has eternal life,
1Co  11:27  bread or **d** the cup of the Lord

## DRIP* [DRIPPING]
Pr    5: 3  of the adulterous woman **d** honey,
Joel  3:18  day the mountains will **d** new wine,
Am    9:13  New wine will **d**

## DRIPPING [DRIP]
Pr   19:13  wife is like the constant **d** of a leaky
     27:15  A quarrelsome wife is like the **d**

## DRIVE [DRIVEN, DRIVER, DRIVES, DRIVING, DROVE]
Ex    6: 1  my mighty hand he will **d** them
     23:30  little I will **d** them out before you,
Nu   33:52  **d** out all the inhabitants of the land
Dt    7:17  How can we **d** them out?"
Jos  13:13  But the Israelites did not **d**
     23:13  LORD your God will no longer **d**
Jdg   1:19  but they were unable to **d** the people
Pr   22:10  **D** out the mocker, and out goes

Isa  22:23  I will **d** him like a peg into a firm
Jer  49: 2  Israel will **d** out those who drove
Mt  10: 1  gave them authority to **d** out evil
Lk  11:19  Now if I **d** out demons
      11:19  do your followers **d** them out?
      19:45  began to **d** out those who were selling.
Jn   6:37  comes to me I will never **d** away.

## DRIVEN [DRIVE]

Ex  12:39  yeast because they had been **d**
Dt  12:29  But when you have **d** them
Jn  12:31  prince of this world will be **d** out.

## DRIVER [DRIVE]

Ex  15: 1  and **d** he has hurled into the sea.

## DRIVES [DRIVE]

Mt  12:26  If Satan **d** out Satan, he is divided
1Jn  4:18  But perfect love **d** out fear,

## DRIVING [DRIVE]

Ex  14:25  so that they had difficulty **d**.
Ac  26:24  great learning is **d** you insane.”

## DROP [DROPS]

Pr  17:14  so **d** the matter before a dispute
Isa  40:15  Surely the nations are like a **d**
Zec  8:12  and the heavens will **d** their dew.

## DROPS [DROP]

Lk  22:44  his sweat was like **d** of blood falling

## DROSS

Ps 119:119  of the earth you discard like **d**;
Pr  25: 4  Remove the **d** from the silver,
Isa  1:22  Your silver has become **d**,
Eze  22:18  house of Israel has become **d** to me;

## DROUGHT

Dt  28:22  with scorching heat and **d**,
Jer  17: 8  It has no worries in a year of **d**
Hag  1:11  I called for a **d** on the fields

## DROVE [DRIVE]

Nu  11:31  LORD and **d** quail in from the sea.
Jos  24:18  the LORD **d** out before us all
Ps  44: 2  your hand you **d** out the nations
Jer  49: 2  will drive out those who **d** her out,”
Mt   8:16  and he **d** out the spirits with a word
      21:12  and **d** out all who were buying

## DROWN [DROWNED]

Mk   4:38  “Teacher, don’t you care if we **d**?”

## DROWNED [DROWN]

Ex  15: 4  Pharaoh’s officers are **d** in the Red
Mt  18: 6  they were **d** in the depths of the sea.
Lk   8:33  steep bank into the lake and was **d**.
Heb 11:29  tried to do so, they were **d**.

## DROWSINESS* [DROWSY]

Pr  23:21  poor, and **d** clothes them in rags.

## DROWSY* [DROWSINESS]

Mt  25: 5  they all became **d** and fell asleep.

## DRUNK [DRINK]

Ge   9:21  he became **d** and lay uncovered
Dt  32:42  I will make my arrows **d** with blood,
1Sa  1:13  Eli thought she was **d**
      25:36  He was in high spirits and very **d**.
2Sa  11:13  with him, and David made him **d**.
Isa  29: 9  be **d**, but not from wine, stagger,
Jer  51: 7  she made the whole earth **d**.
Na   3:11  You too will become **d**; you will go
Ac   2:15  These people are not **d**, as you
1Co 11:21  remains hungry and another gets **d**.
Eph  5:18  Do not get **d** on wine, which leads
Rev 17: 6  the woman was **d** with the blood
      18: 3  the nations have **d** the maddening

## DRUNKARD [DRINK]

Isa  24:20  The earth reels like a **d**, it sways
Mt  11:19  ‘Here is a glutton and a **d**, a friend

## DRUNKARD’S* [DRINK]

Pr  26: 9  a thornbush in a **d** hand is a proverb

## DRUNKARDS [DRINK]

Pr  23:21  for **d** and gluttons become poor,
Isa  19:14  as **d** stagger around in their vomit.
Isa  28: 1  the pride of Ephraim’s **d**,
1Co  5:11  or slanderers, **d** or swindlers.
      6:10  the greedy nor **d** nor slanderers nor

## DRUNKENNESS* [DRINK]

Ecc 10:17  for strength and not for **d**.
Jer  13:13  fill with **d** all who live in this land,
Eze  23:33  You will be filled with **d**
Lk  21:34  **d** and the anxieties of life,
Ro  13:13  not in carousing and **d**, not in sexual
Gal  5:21  and envy; **d**, orgies, and the like.
1Ti  3: 3  not given to **d**, not violent,
Tit  1: 7  not given to **d**, not violent,
1Pe  4: 3  living in debauchery, lust, **d**, orgies,

## DRY [DRIED]

Ge   1: 9  place, and let **d** ground appear.”
      7:22  Everything on **d** land that had
Ex  14:16  can go through the sea on **d** ground.
Jos  3:17  completed the crossing on **d** ground.
Jdg  6:37  on the fleece and all the ground is **d**,
2Ki  2: 8  of them crossed over on **d** ground.
Ps  66: 6  He turned the sea into **d** land,
      95: 5  it, and his hands formed the **d** land.
Isa  53: 2  and like a root out of **d** ground.
Eze  17:24  I **d** up the green tree and make the **d**
      37: 4  bones and say to them, ‘**D** bones,
Jnh  2:10  and it vomited Jonah onto **d** land.
Heb 11:29  through the Red Sea as on **d** land;

## DUE

Dt  32:35  In **d** time their foot will slip;
1Ch 16:29  to the LORD the glory **d** his name;
Ps  90:11  is as great as the fear that is your **d**.
Pr   3:27  good from those to whom it is **d**,
      11:31  If the righteous receive their **d**
Mal  1: 6  a father, where is the honor **d** me?

Mal  1: 6  master, where is the respect **d** me?"
Ro   1:27  in themselves the **d** penalty for their
1Pe  5: 6  that he may lift you up in **d** time.

## DUG [DIG]

Ps   57: 6  They **d** a pit in my path—
Isa   5: 2  He **d** it up and cleared it of stones
Jer  18:20  Yet they have **d** a pit for me.

## DULL

Isa   6:10  make their ears **d** and close their
     59: 1  to save, nor his ear too **d** to hear.
Mk   7:18  "Are you so **d**?" he asked.
2Co  3:14  But their minds were made **d**,

## DUNGEON

Ge   40:15  to deserve being put in a **d**."
Isa  42: 7  release from the **d** those who sit
Jer  37:16  was put into a vaulted cell in a **d**,

## DUST

Ge    2: 7  a man from the **d** of the ground
      3:14  you will eat **d** all the days of your
      3:19  for **d** you are and to **d** you will
     13:16  I will make your offspring like the **d**
     13:16  so that if anyone could count the **d**,
     28:14  Your descendants will be like the **d**
Nu   23:10  Who can count the **d** of Jacob
1Sa   2: 8  He raises the poor from the **d**
Job  42: 6  myself and repent in **d** and ashes."
Ps   22:15  you lay me in the **d** of death.
    103:14  he remembers that we are **d**.
Ecc   3:20  all come from **d**, and to **d** all return.
Isa  65:25  ox, but **d** will be the serpent's food.
Mt   10:14  shake the **d** off your feet when you
Ac   13:51  So they shook the **d** off their feet as
1Co  15:47  first man was of the **d** of the earth;
Rev  18:19  They will throw **d** on their heads,

## DUTIES [DUTY]

1Ki   3: 7  do not know how to carry out my **d**.
2Ti   4: 5  discharge all the **d** of your ministry.

## DUTY [DUTIES]

Ge   38: 8  wife and fulfill your **d** to her as
Ecc  12:13  this is the [**d**] of every human
Ac   23: 1  I have fulfilled my **d** to God in all
1Co   7: 3  husband should fulfill his marital **d**

## DWELL [DWELLING, DWELLINGS, DWELLS, DWELT]

Ex   25: 8  for me, and I will **d** among them.
2Sa   7: 5  the one to build me a house to **d** in?
1Ki   8:27  "But will God really **d** on earth?
Ezr   6:12  who has caused his Name to **d** there,
Ps   23: 6  I will **d** in the house of the LORD
     37: 3  **d** in the land and enjoy safe pasture.
     61: 4  I long to **d** in your tent forever
Pr    8:12  wisdom, **d** together with prudence;
Isa  26: 5  He humbles those who **d** on high,
     33:14  of us can **d** with the consuming fire?
     33:14  us can **d** with everlasting burning?"
     43:18  do not **d** on the past.
Jn    5:38  nor does his word **d** in you, for you
Ro    7:18  good itself does not **d** in me,

Eph   3:17  Christ may **d** in your hearts through
Col   1:19  to have all his fullness **d** in him,
      3:16  of Christ **d** among you richly as you
Rev  12:12  heavens and you who **d** in them!

## DWELLING [DWELL]

Lev  26:11  I will put my **d** place among you,
Dt   26:15  your holy **d** place, and bless your
1Ki   8:30  Hear from heaven, your **d** place,
Ps   90: 1  have been our **d** place throughout all
Isa  26:21  of his **d** to punish the people
La    2: 6  has laid waste his **d** like a garden;
Eze  37:27  My **d** place will be with them;
Mic   1: 3  LORD is coming from his **d** place;
Jn    1:14  flesh and made his **d** among us.
2Co   5: 2  to be clothed with our heavenly **d**,
Eph   2:22  built together to become a **d**
Rev  21: 3  God's **d** place is now among

## DWELLINGS [DWELL]

Lk   16: 9  will be welcomed into eternal **d**.

## DWELLS [DWELL]

Ps   46: 4  holy place where the Most High **d**.
     91: 1  Whoever **d** in the shelter
Isa   8:18  Almighty, who **d** on Mount Zion.
1Co   3:16  God's Spirit **d** in your midst?
Joel  3:21  I will not." The LORD **d** in Zion!

## DWELT [DWELL]

Dt   33:16  of him who **d** in the burning bush.
1Ch  17: 5  I have not **d** in a house from the day

## DYING [DIE]

Jn   11:37  man have kept this man from **d**?"
Ro    7: 6  now, by **d** to what once bound us,
2Co   6: 9  **d**, and yet we live on;

## DYNASTY

1Sa  25:28  God will certainly make a lasting **d**
1Ki   2:24  and has founded a **d** for me as he

---

# E

## EACH

Ge    1:24  animals, **e** according to its kind."
     49:28  giving **e** the blessing appropriate
Ex   12: 3  the tenth day of this month **e** man is
     12: 3  for his family, one for **e** household.
     25:20  The cherubim are to face **e** other,
Lev  25:14  do not take advantage of **e** other.
Nu   14:34  one year for **e** of the forty days your
1Sa  17:10  me a man and let us fight **e** other."
Eze  10:14  **E** of the cherubim had four faces:
Zec   7:10  Do not plot evil against **e** other.'
Mt    6:34  **E** day has enough trouble of its
Mk    9:50  and be at peace with **e** other."
Lk   11: 3  Give us **e** day our daily bread.
Jn   15:17  This is my command: Love **e** other.
Ac    2: 6  because **e** one heard their own
Ro   12: 5  **e** member belongs to all the others.

1Co 7: 7 But **e** of you has your own gift
 12: 7 Now to **e** one the manifestation
Gal 5:15 on biting and devouring **e** other,
 5:15 or you will be destroyed by **e** other.
 6: 2 Carry **e** other's burdens, and in this
Col 3: 9 Do not lie to **e** other, since you have
1Th 5:13 Live in peace with **e** other.
Jas 5:16 confess your sins to **e** other
 5:16 pray for **e** other so that you may be
1Pe 1:17 Father who judges **e** person's work
Rev 4: 8 **E** of the four living creatures had
 6:11 **e** of them was given a white robe,
 13: 1 and on **e** head a blasphemous name.

## EAGER [EAGERLY]

Pr 31:13 and flax and works with **e** hands.
Zep 3: 7 they were still **e** to act corruptly
Ro 8:19 The creation waits in **e** expectation
1Co 14:12 Since you are **e** for gifts
 14:39 and sisters, be **e** to prophesy, and do
1Ti 6:10 Some people, **e** for money,
Tit 2:14 his very own, **e** to do what is good.
1Pe 3:13 to harm you if you are **e** to do good?
 5: 2 dishonest gain, but **e** to serve;

## EAGERLY [EAGER]

Ro 8:23 groan inwardly as we wait **e** for our
1Co 12:31 Now **e** desire the greater gifts.
 14: 1 of love and **e** desire spiritual gifts,
Php 3:20 And we **e** await a Savior from there,

## EAGLE [EAGLE'S, EAGLES, EAGLES']

Dt 14:12 the **e**, the vulture, the black vulture,
 32:11 like an **e** that stirs up its nest
Pr 30:19 the way of an **e** in the sky, the way
Jer 48:40 An **e** is swooping down,
Eze 1:10 each also had the face of an **e**.
 17: 3 A great **e** with powerful wings,
Da 7: 4 a lion, and it had the wings of an **e**.
Hos 8: 1 An **e** is over the house
Ob 1: 4 Though you soar like the **e**
Rev 4: 7 man, the fourth was like a flying **e**.
 8:13 I heard an **e** that was flying
 12:14 given the two wings of a great **e**,

## EAGLE'S* [EAGLE]

Ps 103: 5 your youth is renewed like the **e**.
Jer 49:16 you build your nest as high as the **e**,

## EAGLES [EAGLE]

Isa 40:31 They will soar on wings like **e**;

## EAGLES'* [EAGLE]

Ex 19: 4 how I carried you on **e**' wings

## EAR [EARS]

Ex 21: 6 and pierce his **e** with an awl.
Lev 8:23 put it on the lobe of Aaron's right **e**,
2Ki 19:16 Give **e**, Lord, and hear;
Ne 1:11 let your **e** be attentive to the prayer
Job 12:11 Does not the **e** test words as
Ps 28: 1 Rock, do not turn a deaf **e** to me.
 116: 2 Because he turned his **e** to me, I will
Pr 2: 2 turning your **e** to wisdom
 25:12 of a wise judge to a listening **e**.

Pr 28: 9 If anyone turns a deaf **e** to my
Ecc 1: 8 seeing, nor the **e** its fill of hearing.
Isa 59: 1 to save, nor his **e** too dull to hear.
 64: 4 one has heard, no **e** has perceived,
Da 9:18 Give **e**, our God, and hear;
Mk 14:47 of the high priest, cutting off his **e**.
Lk 22:51 he touched the man's **e** and healed
1Co 2: 9 eye has seen, what no **e** has heard,
 12:17 If the whole body were an **e**,

## EARLIER [EARLY]

Zec 1: 4 to whom the **e** prophets proclaimed:
 7: 7 proclaimed through the **e** prophets
Heb 10:32 Remember those **e** days after you

## EARLY [EARLIER]

Ps 127: 2 In vain you rise **e** and stay up late,
Pr 27:14 anyone loudly blesses a neighbor **e**
Isa 5:11 to those who rise **e** in the morning
Hos 6: 4 mist, like the **e** dew that disappears.
 9:10 it was like seeing the **e** fruit
Mic 7: 1 eat, none of the **e** figs that I crave.
Mt 27: 1 **E** in the morning, all the chief
Lk 24:22 went to the tomb **e** this morning

## EARN [EARNINGS]

Pr 11:18 The wicked **e** deceptive wages,
Hag 1: 6 You **e** wages, only to put them
2Th 3:12 settle down and **e** the bread they eat.

## EARNEST* [EARNESTLY, EARNESTNESS]

Rev 3:19 So be **e**, and repent.

## EARNESTLY [EARNEST]

Ps 63: 1 God, are my God, **e** I seek you;
Hos 5:15 their misery they will **e** seek me."
Ro 11: 7 of Israel sought so **e** they did not
Heb 11: 6 he rewards those who **e** seek him.
Jas 5:17 He prayed **e** that it would not rain,

## EARNESTNESS [EARNEST]

2Co 7:11 what **e**, what eagerness to clear
 8: 7 in complete **e** and in the love we

## EARNINGS [EARN]

Pr 31:16 out of her **e** she plants a vineyard.

## EARRING [EARRINGS]

Pr 25:12 Like an **e** of gold or an ornament

## EARRINGS [EARRING]

Ex 32: 2 them, "Take off the gold **e** that your
SS 1:10 Your cheeks are beautiful with **e**,
Isa 3:19 the **e** and bracelets and veils,
Eze 16:12 **e** on your ears and a beautiful crown

## EARS [EAR]

Dt 29: 4 or eyes that see or **e** that hear.
Job 42: 5 My **e** had heard of you but now my
Ps 34:15 and his **e** are attentive to their cry.
 40: 6 but my **e** you have opened—
 115: 6 They have **e**, but cannot hear, noses,
Pr 20:12 **E** that hear and eyes that see—

Pr    21:13  Those who shut their **e** to the cry
      26:17  dog by the **e** is someone who rushes
Isa    6:10  make their **e** dull and close their
       6:10  hear with their **e**,
      35: 5  and the **e** of the deaf unstopped.
Jer    6:10  Their **e** are closed so they cannot
Mt    11:15  Whoever has **e**, let them hear.
Mk     8:18  but fail to see, and **e** but fail to hear?
Ac     7:51  hearts and **e** are still uncircumcised.
      28:27  they hardly hear with their **e**,
      28:27  hear with their **e**,
2Ti    4: 3  to say what their itching **e** want
1Pe    3:12  his **e** are attentive to their prayer,
Rev    2: 7  Whoever has **e**, let them hear what

## EARTH [EARTH'S, EARTHLY]

Ge     1: 1  God created the heavens and the **e**.
       1: 2  Now the **e** was formless and empty,
       4:12  be a restless wanderer on the **e**."
       6:11  Now the **e** was corrupt in God's
       6:17  on the **e** to destroy all life under
       6:17  Everything on **e** will perish.
       7:24  The waters flooded the **e**
       9:13  the covenant between me and the **e**.
      12: 3  on **e** will be blessed through you."
      14:19  Most High, Creator of heaven and **e**.
      24: 3  the God of heaven and the God of **e**,
      28:14  will be like the dust of the **e**,
      28:14  on **e** will be blessed through you
Ex    19: 5  Although the whole **e** is mine,
Nu    16:30  new, and the **e** opens its mouth
Jos    3:13  the Lord of all the **e**—set foot
1Ki    8:27  "But will God really dwell on **e**?
1Ch   16:23  Sing to the Lᴏʀᴅ, all the **e**;
      16:30  Tremble before him, all the **e**!
Job   26: 7  he suspends the **e** over nothing.
Ps     8: 1  majestic is your name in all the **e**!
      24: 1  The **e** is the Lᴏʀᴅ's,
      46: 6  he lifts his voice, the **e** melts.
      47: 2  the great King over all the **e**.
      73:25  **e** has nothing I desire besides you.
      97: 1  Lᴏʀᴅ reigns, let the **e** be glad;
     102:25  you laid the foundations of the **e**,
     108: 5  let your glory be over all the **e**.
Pr     8:26  its fields or any of the dust of the **e**.
Isa    6: 3  the whole **e** is full of his glory."
      24:20  The **e** reels like a drunkard, it sways
      37:16  the **e**. You have made heaven and **e**.
      40:22  enthroned above the circle of the **e**,
      51: 6  the heavens, look at the **e** beneath;
      51: 6  the **e** will wear out like a garment
      55: 9  the heavens are higher than the **e**,
      65:17  create new heavens and a new **e**.
      66: 1  throne, and the **e** is my footstool.
Jer   10:10  When he is angry, the **e** trembles;
      23:24  "Do not I fill heaven and **e**?"
      33:25  the laws of heaven and **e**,
Da     2:39  bronze, will rule over the whole **e**.
      12: 2  sleep in the dust of the **e** will awake:
Joel   2:30  in the heavens and on the **e**,
Am     9: 5  he touches the **e** and it melts, and all
Hab    2:20  let all the **e** be silent before him.
Zep    1:18  the whole **e** will be consumed,
Hag    2:21  to shake the heavens and the **e**.
Zec   14: 9  will be king over the whole **e**.
Mt     5: 5  the meek, for they will inherit the **e**.
       5:13  "You are the salt of the **e**.

Mt     5:18  until heaven and **e** disappear,
       5:35  or by the **e**, for it is his footstool;
       6:10  will be done, on **e** as it is in heaven.
      16:19  you bind on **e** will be bound
      16:19  you loose on **e** will be loosed
      24:35  Heaven and **e** will pass away,
      28:18  and on **e** has been given to me.
Mk     4:31  the smallest of all seeds on **e**.
Lk     2:14  on **e** peace to those on whom his
       5:24  of Man has authority on **e** to forgive
Jn    12:32  when I am lifted up from the **e**,
Ac     2:19  above and signs on the **e** below,
       4:24  the heaven and the **e** and the sea,
       7:49  throne, and the **e** is my footstool.
1Co   10:26  for, "The **e** is the Lord's,
      15:47  first man was of the dust of the **e**;
Eph    3:15  in heaven and on **e** derives its name.
Php    2:10  in heaven and on **e** and under the **e**,
Heb    1:10  you laid the foundations of the **e**,
2Pe    3:13  to a new heaven and a new **e**,
Rev    5: 3  on **e** or under the **e** could open
       8: 7  **e**. A third of the **e** was burned up,
      12:12  But woe to the **e** and the sea,
      20:11  The **e** and the heavens fled from his
      21: 1  I saw "a new heaven and a new **e**,"
      21: 1  and the first **e** had passed away,

## HEAVEN AND ... EARTH Ge 14:19, 22;
2Ki 19:15; 1Ch 21:16; 29:11; 2Ch 2:12; Ezr
5:11; Ps 69:34; 115:15; 121:2; 124:8; 134:3;
146:6; Isa 37:16; Jer 23:24; 33:25; 51:48; Zec
5:9; Mt 5:18; 11:25; 24:35; Mk 13:31; Lk 10:21;
16:17; 21:33; Ac 14:15; 17:24

## ENDS OF THE EARTH Dt 28:49; 33:17; 1Sa
2:10; Job 28:24; 37:3; Ps 2:8; 22:27; 46:9; 48:10;
59:13; 61:2; 65:5; 67:7; 72:8; 98:3; 135:7; Pr
17:24; 30:4; Isa 5:26; 24:16; 40:28; 41:5, 9;
42:10; 43:6; 45:22; 48:20; 49:6; 52:10; 62:11; Jer
6:22; 10:13; 16:19; 25:31, 32; 31:8; 50:41; 51:16;
Da 4:11; Mic 5:4; Zec 9:10; Mt 12:42; Mk 13:27;
Lk 11:31; Ac 1:8; 13:47

## EARTH'S [EARTH]

Job   38: 4  you when I laid the **e** foundation?
Pr     3:19  the Lᴏʀᴅ laid the **e** foundations,

## EARTHENWARE*

Pr    26:23  of silver dross on **e** are fervent lips

## EARTHLY [EARTH]

Jn     3:12  I have spoken to you of **e** things
Ro     1: 3  his **e** life was a descendant of David,
Eph    4: 9  descended to the lower, **e** regions?
Php    3:19  Their mind is set on **e** things.
Col    3: 2  on things above, not on **e** things.
       3: 5  whatever belongs to your **e** nature:
Jas    3:15  come down from heaven but is **e**,

## EARTHQUAKE [QUAKE]

1Ki   19:11  **e**, but the Lᴏʀᴅ was not in the **e**.
Isa   29: 6  will come with thunder and **e**
Eze   38:19  time there shall be a great **e**
Mt    28: 2  There was a violent **e**, for an angel
Ac    16:26  Suddenly there was such a violent **e**
Rev    6:12  There was a great **e**. The sun turned

Rev 11:13 that very hour there was a severe **e**
11:13 people were killed in the **e**,
16:18 peals of thunder and a severe **e**.
16:18 No **e** like it has ever occurred since

## EARTHQUAKES [QUAKE]
Mt 24: 7 be famines and **e** in various places.

## EASE [EASIER, EASILY, EASY]
Pr 1:33 to me will live in safety and be at **e**,

## EASIER [EASE]
Mt 9: 5 Which is **e**: to say, 'Your sins are
Lk 16:17 It is **e** for heaven and earth
18:25 it is **e** for a camel to go through

## EASILY [EASE]
Pr 22:24 with those who are **e** angered,
1Co 13: 5 it is not **e** angered, it keeps no
Heb 12: 1 and the sin that so **e** entangles.

## EAST
Ge 2: 8 God had planted a garden in the **e**,
Ex 14:21 the sea back with a strong **e** wind
Ps 103:12 as far as the **e** is from the west,
Eze 43: 2 the God of Israel coming from the **e**.
Hos 13:15 An **e** wind from the LORD will
Jnh 4: 8 God provided a scorching **e** wind,
Mt 2: 1 Magi from the **e** came to Jerusalem
8:11 you that many will come from the **e**
Rev 7: 2 another angel coming up from the **e**,

## EASY [EASE]
2Ki 3:18 This is an **e** thing in the eyes
Mt 11:30 For my yoke is **e** and my burden is
Lk 12:19 Take life **e**; eat, drink and be

## EAT [ATE, EATEN, EATER, EATING, EATS]
Ge 2:16 "You are free to **e** from any tree
2:17 you must not **e** from the tree
2:17 you **e** of it you will certainly die."
3:19 brow you will **e** your food until you
Ex 12:11 This is how you are to **e** it:
12:20 **E** nothing made with yeast.
16:12 'At twilight you will **e** meat,
16:32 can see the bread I gave you to **e**
32: 6 Afterward they sat down to **e**
Lev 11: 2 land, these are the ones you may **e**:
17:12 "None of you may **e** blood,
17:12 residing among you **e** blood."
Nu 11:13 wailing to me, 'Give us meat to **e**!'
Dt 8:16 He gave you manna to **e**
14: 4 These are the animals you may **e**:
Jdg 14:14 "Out of the eater, something to **e**;
2Sa 9: 7 and you will always **e** at my table."
Ps 22:26 The poor will **e** and be satisfied;
50:13 Do I **e** the flesh of bulls or drink
Pr 31:27 and does not **e** the bread of idleness.
Ecc 2:24 can do nothing better than to **e**
5:18 that it is appropriate for people to **e**,
Isa 11: 7 and the lion will **e** straw like the ox.
55: 1 have no money, come, buy and **e**!
65:25 and the lion will **e** straw like the ox,
Jer 19: 9 I will make them **e** the flesh of their

Jer 19: 9 and they will **e** one another's flesh
La 2:20 Should women **e** their offspring,
Eze 3: 1 **e** what is before you, **e** this scroll;
Da 1:12 vegetables to **e** and water to drink.
Hag 1: 6 You **e**, but never have enough.
Mt 14:16 You give them something to **e**."
15: 2 wash their hands before they **e**!"
25:35 and you gave me something to **e**,
26:26 his disciples, saying, "Take and **e**;
Mk 2:26 which is lawful only for priests to **e**
14:14 where I may **e** the Passover with my
Lk 10: 8 welcomed, **e** what is set before you.
12:19 **e**, drink and be merry." '
12:29 set your heart on what you will **e**
Jn 4:32 "I have food to **e** that you know
6:31 them bread from heaven to **e**.' "
6:53 unless you **e** the flesh of the Son
Ac 10:13 him, "Get up, Peter. Kill and **e**."
Ro 14: 2 faith allows them to **e** everything,
14: 6 who **e** meat do so to the Lord,
14:15 is distressed because of what you **e**,
14:20 a person to **e** anything that causes
14:23 have doubts are condemned if they **e**,
1Co 5:11 With such persons do not even **e**.
8:13 if what I **e** causes my brother
8:13 I will never **e** meat again, so that I
10:25 **E** anything sold in the meat market
10:31 So whether you **e** or drink
11:26 For whenever you **e** this bread
Col 2:16 let anyone judge you by what you **e**
2Th 3:10 is unwilling to work shall not **e**."
Rev 2: 7 I will give the right to **e**
3:20 I will come in and **e** with them,
10: 9 He said to me, "Take it and **e** it.

## EATEN [EAT]
Ge 3:11 Have you **e** from the tree that I
Jer 31:29 'The parents have **e** sour grapes,
Eze 4:14 I have never **e** anything found dead
Ac 10:14 "I have never **e** anything impure
12:23 and he was **e** by worms and died.
Rev 10:10 but when I had **e** it, my stomach

## EATER* [EAT]
Jdg 14:14 "Out of the **e**, something to eat;
Isa 55:10 for the sower and bread for the **e**,
Na 3:12 the figs fall into the mouth of the **e**.

## EATING [EAT]
Ex 34:28 and forty nights without **e** bread
Isa 7:15 He will be **e** curds and honey
Mt 15:20 but **e** with unwashed hands does not
Lk 7:34 The Son of Man came **e**
Ro 14:15 not by your **e** destroy your brother
14:17 kingdom of God is not a matter of **e**
14:23 eat, because their **e** is not from faith;
1Co 8: 4 about **e** food sacrificed to idols:
Heb 13: 9 not by the **e** of ceremonial foods,
Jude 1:12 **e** with you without the slightest

## EATS [EAT]
Lev 7:27 Anyone who **e** blood must be cut
1Sa 14:24 be anyone who **e** food before
Lk 15: 2 sinners and **e** with them."
Jn 6:51 Whoever **e** of this bread will live
6:54 Whoever **e** my flesh and drinks my

Ro   14: 2  faith is weak, **e** only vegetables.
1Co 11:27  whoever **e** the bread or drinks

## EBAL

Dt   11:29  and on Mount **E** the curses.
Jos   8:30  Joshua built on Mount **E** an altar

## EBED-MELEK*

A Cushite; saved Jeremiah from the cistern (Jer 38:1–13; 39:16).

## EBENEZER*

1Sa   4: 1  The Israelites camped at **E**,
        5: 1  God, they took it from **E** to Ashdod.
        7:12  He named it **E**, saying, "Thus far

## EBER

Ancestor of Abraham (Ge 11:14–17), of Jesus (Lk 3:35).

## EDEN

Ge   2: 8  planted a garden in the east, in **E**;
Eze 28:13  You were in **E**, the garden of God;

## EDGE  [DOUBLE-EDGED]

Jos   3:15  and their feet touched the water's **e**,
Jer 31:29  the children's teeth are set on **e**.'
Mt    9:20  him and touched the **e** of his cloak.
       14:36  to let the sick just touch the **e** of his

## EDICT

Est   4: 8  text of the **e** for their annihilation,
        8:11  The king's **e** granted the Jews
Da    6: 7  that the king should issue an **e**
Heb 11:23  they were not afraid of the king's **e**.

## EDIFICATION*  [EDIFIED, EDIFY]

Ro   14:19  what leads to peace and to mutual **e**.

## EDIFIED*  [EDIFICATION]

1Co 14: 5  so that the church may be **e**.
       14:17  enough, but the others are not **e**.

## EDIFY*  [EDIFICATION]

1Co 14: 4  speak in a tongue **e** themselves,
       14: 4  who prophesy **e** the church.

## EDOM  [EDOMITE, EDOMITES, ESAU]

Ge   25:30  (That is why he was also called **E**.)
       36: 1  the family line of Esau (that is, **E**).
Nu   20:18  But **E** answered: "You may not
1Ki 11:16  they had destroyed all the men in **E**.
Ps   60: 8  washbasin, on **E** I toss my sandal.
Isa   63: 1  Who is this coming from **E**,
Jer   49: 7  Concerning **E**: This is what
La     4:21  Daughter **E**, you who live
Eze 25:12  'Because **E** took revenge
Am    1:11  "For three sins of **E**, even for four,
Ob    1: 1  Sovereign LORD says about **E**—

## EDOMITE  [EDOM]

Dt   23: 7  Do not despise an **E**,

1Sa 22: 9  But Doeg the **E**, who was standing
Ps   52: T  *Doeg the E had gone to Saul*

## EDOMITES  [EDOM]

Ge   36:43  This was Esau the father of the **E**.
1Ch 18:13  the **E** became subject to David.
Ps   60: T  *and struck down twelve thousand E*
      137: 7  what the **E** did on the day Jerusalem

## EDUCATED*

Ac    7:22  Moses was **e** in all the wisdom

## EFFECT*  [EFFECTIVE]

Job 41:26  The sword that reaches it has no **e**,
Isa   32:17  its **e** will be quietness
Zep   2: 2  before the decree takes **e** and
1Co 15:10  his grace to me was not without **e**.
Eph   1:10  be put into **e** when the times reach
Heb   9:17  it never takes **e** while the one who
        9:18  was not put into **e** without blood.

## EFFECTIVE*  [EFFECT]

1Co 16: 9  a great door for **e** work has opened
Phm   : 6  partnership with us in the faith may be **e**
Jas   5:16  righteous person is powerful and **e**.

## EFFORT*  [EFFORTS]

Ecc   2:19  toil into which I have poured my **e**
Da    6:14  made every **e** until sundown to save
Lk   13:24  "Make every **e** to enter through
Ro    9:16  depend on human desire or **e**,
       14:19  Let us therefore make every **e** to do
Gal   3: 3  now trying to finish by human **e**?
        4:23  born as the result of human **e**,
        4:29  the son born by human **e** persecuted
Eph   4: 3  Make every **e** to keep the unity
1Th   2:16  in their **e** to keep us from speaking
        2:17  intense longing we made every **e**
Heb   4:11  make every **e** to enter that rest,
       12:14  Make every **e** to live in peace
2Pe   1: 5  make every **e** to add to your faith
        1:10  make every **e** to confirm your calling
        1:15  I will make every **e** to see
        3:14  make every **e** to be found spotless,

## EFFORTS  [EFFORT]

Gal   4:11  somehow I have wasted my **e**

## EGG*  [EGGS]

Lk   11:12  Or if he asks for an **e**, will give him

## EGGS  [EGG]

Dt   22: 6  is sitting on the young or on the **e**,
Isa   59: 5  They hatch the **e** of vipers and spin
        59: 5  Whoever eats their **e** will die,
Jer   17:11  that hatches **e** it did not lay are those

## EGLON

1. King of Moab killed by Ehud (Jdg 3:12–30).
2. City in Canaan (Jos 10).

## EGYPT  [EGYPTIAN, EGYPTIANS]

Ge   12:10  Abram went down to **E** to live there
       26: 2  and said, "Do not go down to **E**;

Ge 37:28 the Ishmaelites, who took him to E.
41:41 in charge of the whole land of E."
42: 3 went down to buy grain from E.
45: 9 God has made me lord of all E.
45:20 the best of all E will be yours.' "
46: 6 and all his offspring went to E,
47:27 Now the Israelites settled in E
Ex 1: 8 meant nothing, came to power in E.
3:11 and bring the Israelites out of E?"
7: 3 my signs and wonders in E,
11: 5 Every firstborn son in E will die,
12:12 same night I will pass through E
12:12 bring judgment on all the gods of E.
12:40 people lived in E was 430 years.
12:41 all the LORD's divisions left E.
32: 1 Moses who brought us up out of E,
Nu 11:18 We were better off in E!"
14: 4 choose a leader and go back to E."
24: 8 "God brought them out of E;
Dt 6:21 "We were slaves of Pharaoh in E,
6:21 us out of E with a mighty hand.
16:12 that you were slaves in E,
Jos 15:47 as far as the Wadi of E
1Ki 4:30 greater than all the wisdom of E.
10:28 horses were imported from E
11:40 but Jeroboam fled to E, to Shishak
14:25 king of E attacked Jerusalem.
2Ch 35:20 Necho king of E went up to fight
36: 3 The king of E dethroned him
Ne 9:18 who brought you up out of E,'
Ps 80: 8 You transplanted a vine from E;
Isa 19: 1 A prophecy concerning E:
19: 1 on a swift cloud and is coming to E.
19: 1 The idols of E tremble before him,
Jer 42:19 has told you, 'Do not go to E.'
44: 1 all the Jews living in Lower E—
46: 2 Concerning E: This is the message
46: 2 army of Pharaoh Necho king of E,
La 5: 6 We submitted to E and Assyria
Eze 29: 2 your face against Pharaoh king of E
30: 4 A sword will come against E,
Hos 11: 1 him, and out of E I called my son.
Mt 2:15 "Out of E I called my son."
Heb 11:22 the exodus of the Israelites from E
11:27 By faith he left E, not fearing
Rev 11: 8 is figuratively called Sodom and E,

**OUT OF EGYPT** Ge 45:25; 47:30; Ex 3:10,
11, 12; 6:13, 26, 27; 12:17, 39, 42, 51; 13:3, 8, 9,
14, 16, 18; 14:11; 16:1, 6, 32; 17:3; 18:1; 20:2;
23:15; 29:46; 32:1, 4, 7, 8, 11, 23; 33:1; 34:18;
Lev 11:45; 19:36; 22:33; 23:43; 25:38, 42, 55;
26:13, 45; Nu 1:1; 9:1; 15:41; 20:5, 16; 21:5;
22:5, 11; 23:22; 24:8; 26:4; 32:11; 33:1, 38; Dt
1:27; 4:20, 37, 45, 46; 5:6; 6:12, 21; 8:14; 9:12,
26; 13:5, 10; 16:1; 20:1; 23:4; 24:9; 25:17; 26:8;
29:25; Jos 2:10; 5:4; 24:6, 17; Jdg 2:1, 12; 6:8,
13; 11:13, 16; 19:30; 1Sa 8:8; 10:18; 12:6, 8;
15:6; 2Sa 7:6; 1Ki 6:1; 8:9, 16, 21, 51, 53; 9:9;
12:28; 2Ki 17:7, 36; 21:15; 1Ch 17:5; 2Ch 5:10;
6:5; 7:22; Ne 9:18; Ps 81:10; 114:1; Jer 2:6; 7:22;
11:4; 16:14; 23:7; 26:23; 31:32; 32:21; 34:13;
37:5; Eze 20:6, 9, 10; Da 9:15; Hos 2:15; 11:1;
12:9; 13:4; Am 2:10; 3:1; Mic 6:4; 7:15; Hag 2:5;
Mt 2:15; Ac 7:36, 40; Heb 3:16; 8:9; Jude 1:5

**KING OF EGYPT** See KING

## EGYPTIAN [EGYPT]

Ge 16: 1 she had an E servant named Hagar;
Ex 1:19 women are not like E women;
2:11 He saw an E beating a Hebrew,
Dt 11: 4 what he did to the E army, to its
23: 7 Do not despise an E, because you

## EGYPTIANS [EGYPT]

Ex 1:12 so the E came to dread the Israelites
3:22 And so you will plunder the E."
12:36 had made the E favorably disposed
12:36 so they plundered the E.
14: 4 and the E will know that I am
15:26 of the diseases I brought on the E,
Nu 14:13 "Then the E will hear about it!

## EHUD

Left-handed judge who delivered Israel from Moabite king, Eglon (Jdg 3:12–30).

## EIGHT [EIGHTH]

Ge 17:12 among you who is e days old must
21: 4 When his son Isaac was e days old,
2Ki 22: 1 Josiah was e years old when he
1Pe 3:20 In it only a few people, e in all,

## EIGHTEEN

Lk 13:11 been crippled by a spirit for e years.

## EIGHTH [EIGHT]

Lev 12: 3 On the e day the boy is to be
25:22 While you plant during the e year,
Lk 1:59 On the e day they came
2:21 On the e day, when it was time
Php 3: 5 circumcised on the e day,
Rev 17:11 was, and now is not, is an e king.

## EIGHTY

Ex 7: 7 Moses was e years old and Aaron
2Sa 19:35 I am now e years old. Can I tell
Ps 90:10 years, or e, if our strength endures;

## EIGHTY-FIVE

Jos 14:10 So here I am today, e years old!

## EITHER

Lk 16:13 E you will hate the one and love
Ro 11:21 branches, he will not spare you e.
Rev 3:15 I wish you were e one or the other!

## EKRON

Jos 13: 3 to the territory of E on the north,
1Sa 5:10 So they sent the ark of God to E.
5:10 E, the people of E cried out,
6:17 Gaza, Ashkelon, Gath and E.
2Ki 1: 2 the god of E, to see if I will recover

## EL BETHEL* [BETHEL]

Ge 35: 7 and he called the place E, because

## EL ELOHE ISRAEL* [ISRAEL]

Ge 33:20 he set up an altar and called it E.

## ELAH

1. Son of Baasha; king of Israel (1Ki 16:6–14).
2. Valley in which David fought Goliath (1Sa 17:2, 19; 21:9).

## ELAM

1Ch  1:17  **E**, Ashur, Arphaxad, Lud and Aram.
Jer  49:34  Jeremiah the prophet concerning **E**,

## ELATION*

Pr  28:12  righteous triumph, there is great **e**;

## ELDER  [ELDERLY, ELDERS]

Isa  3: 2  the prophet, the diviner and the **e**,
1Ti  5:19  accusation against an **e** unless it is
Tit  1: 6  An **e** must be blameless,
1Pe  5: 1  I appeal as a fellow **e** and a witness
2Jn  1: 1  The **e**, To the lady chosen by God
3Jn  1: 1  The **e**, To my dear friend Gaius,

## ELDERLY*  [ELDER]

Lev  19:32  show respect for the **e** and revere

## ELDERS  [ELDER]

Ex  3:16  assemble the **e** of Israel and say
     24: 1  and seventy of the **e** of Israel.
Dt  25: 7  she shall go to the **e** at the town gate
Jos  24: 1  He summoned the **e**, leaders,
Jdg  2: 7  of the **e** who outlived him and who
Ru  4: 2  Boaz took ten of the **e** of the town
2Ch 10:13  Rejecting the advice of the **e**,
Ps 105:22  he pleased and teach his **e** wisdom.
    119:100  have more understanding than the **e**,
Isa  3:14  enters into judgment against the **e**
La  5:14  The **e** are gone from the city gate;
Eze  8:11  them stood seventy **e** of the house
Mt  15: 2  break the tradition of the **e**?
Mk  7: 3  holding to the tradition of the **e**.
Lk  9:22  things and be rejected by the **e**,
Ac  4: 5  the **e** and the teachers of the law met
    11:30  their gift to the **e** by Barnabas
    14:23  Barnabas appointed **e** for them
    15: 2  apostles and **e** about this question.
    15: 6  and **e** met to consider this question.
    15:23  The apostles and **e**, your brothers,
    16: 4  and **e** in Jerusalem for the people
    20:17  to Ephesus for the **e** of the church.
    21:18  James, and all the **e** were present.
    23:14  the chief priests and the **e** and said,
    24: 1  to Caesarea with some of the **e**
    25:15  the **e** of the Jews brought charges
1Ti  4:14  the body of **e** laid their hands
     5:17  The **e** who direct the affairs
Tit  1: 5  and appoint **e** in every town, as I
Jas  5:14  Let them call the **e** of the church
1Pe  5: 1  To the **e** among you, I appeal as
     5: 5  submit yourselves to your **e**.
Rev  4: 4  seated on them were twenty-four **e**.
     4:10  the twenty-four **e** fall down before
     5: 6  the four living creatures and the **e**.
     7:11  and around the **e** and the four living
    11:16  And the twenty-four **e**, who were
    14: 3  the four living creatures and the **e**.
    19: 4  The twenty-four **e** and the four

## ELEAZAR

Third son of Aaron (Ex 6:23–25). Succeeded Aaron as high priest (Nu 20:26; Dt 10:6). Allotted land to tribes (Jos 14:1). Death (Jos 24:33).

## ELECT*  [ELECTION]

Mt  24:22  the **e** those days will be shortened.
    24:24  to deceive, if possible, even the **e**.
    24:31  they will gather his **e** from the four
Mk  13:20  But for the sake of the **e**, whom he
    13:22  to deceive, if possible, even the **e**.
    13:27  gather his **e** from the four winds,
Ro  11: 7  The **e** among them did,
1Ti  5:21  and Christ Jesus and the **e** angels,
2Ti  2:10  everything for the sake of the **e**,
Tit  1: 1  Christ to further the faith of God's **e**
1Pe  1: 1  Christ, To God's **e**, exiles scattered

## ELECTION*  [ELECT]

Ro  9:11  that God's purpose in **e** might stand:
    11:28  but as far as **e** is concerned, they are
2Pe  1:10  effort to confirm your calling and **e**.

## ELEMENTAL*  [ELEMENTS]

Gal  4: 3  the **e** spiritual forces of the world.
Col  2: 8  the **e** spiritual forces of this world
    2:20  you died with Christ to the **e** spiritual forces

## ELEMENTARY*  [ELEMENTS]

Heb  5:12  to teach you the **e** truths of God's
     6: 1  let us move beyond the **e** teachings

## ELEMENTS*  [ELEMENTAL, ELEMENTARY]

2Pe  3:10  the **e** will be destroyed by fire,
     3:12  fire, and the **e** will melt in the heat.

## ELEVATE*  [ELEVATED]

2Co  11: 7  in order to **e** you by preaching

## ELEVATED*  [ELEVATE]

Est  5:11  how he had **e** him above the other

## ELEVEN

Ge  32:22  two female servants and his **e** sons
    37: 9  **e** stars were bowing down to me."
Ex  26: 8  All **e** curtains are to be the same
Dt  1: 2  (It takes **e** days to go from Horeb
Mt  28:16  Then the **e** disciples went to Galilee,
Lk  24: 9  they told all these things to the **E**
    24:33  There they found the **E** and those
Ac  1:26  so he was added to the **e** apostles.
    2:14  Then Peter stood up with the **E**,

## ELI

1. High priest in youth of Samuel (1Sa 1–4). Blessed Hannah (1Sa 1:12–18); raised Samuel (1Sa 2:11–26). Prophesied against because of wicked sons (1Sa 2:27–36). Death of Eli and sons (1Sa 4:11–22).
2. Aramaic for "My God" in Jesus' last words on the cross.
Mt  27:46  loud voice, *"E, E, lema sabachthani?"*

## ELIAKIM [JEHOIAKIM]
1. Original name of king Jehoiakim (2Ki 23:34; 2Ch 36:4).
2. Hezekiah's palace administrator (2Ki 18:17–37; 19:2; Isa 36:1–22; 37:2).

## ELIASHIB
Ne    3: 1  E the high priest and his fellow

## ELIEZER
1. Servant of Abraham (Ge 15:2).
2. Son of Moses (Ex 18:4; 1Ch 23:15–17).

## ELIHU
A friend of Job (Job 32–37).

## ELIJAH
Prophet; predicted famine in Israel (1Ki 17:1; Jas 5:17). Fed by ravens (1Ki 17:2–6). Raised Sidonian widow's son (1Ki 17:7–24). Defeated prophets of Baal at Carmel (1Ki 18:16–46). Ran from Jezebel (1Ki 19:1–9). Prophesied death of Azariah (2Ki 1). Succeeded by Elishah (1Ki 19:19–21; 2Ki 2:1–18). Taken to heaven in whirlwind (2Ki 2:11–12).
Return prophesied (Mal 4:5–6); equated with John the Baptist (Mt 17:9–13; Mk 9:9–13; Lk 1:17). Appeared with Moses in transfiguration of Jesus (Mt 17:1–8; Mk 9:1–8).

## ELIM
Ex   15:27  Then they came to E, where there
Nu   33: 9  They left Marah and went to E,

## ELIMELEK
Ru    1: 3  Now E, Naomi's husband, died,
       4: 9  from Naomi all the property of E,

## ELIMINATE* [ELIMINATED]
Dt    7:22  will not be allowed to e them all

## ELIMINATED* [ELIMINATE]
Dt    2:15  them until he had completely e them

## ELIPHAZ
1. Firstborn of Esau (Ge 36).
2. A friend of Job (Job 4–5; 15; 22; 42:7, 9).

## ELISHA
Prophet; successor of Elijah (1Ki 19:16–21); inherited his cloak (2Ki 2:1–18). Purified bad water (2Ki 2:19–22). Cursed young men (2Ki 2:23–25). Aided Israel's defeat of Moab (2Ki 3). Provided widow with oil (2Ki 4:1–7). Raised Shunammite woman's son (2Ki 4:8–37). Purified food (2Ki 4:38–41). Fed 100 men (2Ki 4:42–44). Healed Naaman's leprosy (2Ki 5). Made axhead float (2Ki 6:1–7). Captured Arameans (2Ki 6:8–23). Political adviser to Israel (2Ki 6:24—8:6; 9:1–3; 13:14–19), Aram (2Ki 8:7–15). Death (2Ki 13:20).

## ELIZABETH*
Mother of John the Baptist (Lk 1:5–58).

## ELKANAH
Husband of Hannah, father of Samuel (1Sa 1–2).

## ELOI*
Mk   15:34  loud voice, "E, E, lema sabachthani?"

## ELON
Judge of Israel (Jdg 12:11–12).

## ELOQUENCE* [ELOQUENT]
1co   1:17  the gospel—not with wisdom and e,
       2: 1  I did not come with e or human

## ELOQUENT* [ELOQUENCE]
Ex    4:10  I have never been e,
Pr   17: 7  E lips are unsuited to a godless fool

## ELSE
Ex    4:13  Please send someone e."
Nu   12: 3  more humble than anyone e
Pr    4:23  Above all e, guard your heart,
      27: 2  Let someone e praise you, and not
Lk    7:19  or should we expect someone e?"
Jn    5:43  but if someone e comes in his own
Ac    4:12  Salvation is found in no one e,
Ro    8:39  depth, nor anything e in all creation,

## ELYMAS
Ac   13: 8  E the sorcerer (for that is what his

## EMASCULATE* [EMASCULATED]
Gal   5:12  go the whole way and e themselves!

## EMASCULATED* [EMASCULATE]
Dt   23: 1  No one who has been e by crushing

## EMBALMED*
Ge   50: 2  So the physicians e him,
      50:26  And after they e him, he was placed

## EMBEDDED*
Ecc  12:11  sayings like firmly e nails—

## EMBERS*
Ps  102: 3  my bones burn like glowing e.
Pr   26:21  As charcoal to e and as wood

## EMBITTER* [BITTER]
Col   3:21  Fathers, do not e your children,

## EMBLEM
Ex   39:30  They made the plate, the sacred e,

## EMBODIMENT* [BODY]
Ro    2:20  have in the law the e of knowledge

## EMBOLDENED* [BOLD]
Ps  138: 3  you greatly e me.
1Co   8:10  won't they be e to eat

## EMBRACE [EMBRACED, EMBRACES, EMBRACING]
Pr   5:20  Why **e** the bosom of a wayward
Ecc  3: 5  a time to **e** and a time to refrain,

## EMBRACED [EMBRACE]
Ge  48:10  his father kissed them and **e** them.
2Ch  7:22  and have **e** other gods,
Ac  20:37  They all wept as they **e** him

## EMBRACES* [EMBRACE]
SS   2: 6  my head, and his right arm **e** me.
     8: 3  my head and his right arm **e** me.

## EMBRACING* [EMBRACE]
Ecc  2: 3  myself with wine, and **e** folly—

## EMBROIDERED [EMBROIDERER]
Ps  45:14  In **e** garments she is led to the king;
Eze  16:10  I clothed you with an **e** dress

## EMBROIDERER [EMBROIDERED]
Ex  26:36  the work of an **e**.

## EMERALD
Ex  28:18  shall be turquoise, lapis lazuli and **e**;
Rev  4: 3  shone like an **e** encircled the throne.
     21:19  the third agate, the fourth **e**,

## EMMANUEL  See IMMANUEL

## EMMAUS*
Lk  24:13  were going to a village called **E**,

## EMPATHIZE*
Heb  4:15  unable to **e** with our weaknesses,

## EMPEROR*
Ac  25:25  made his appeal to the **E** I decided
1Pe  2:13  to the **e**, as the supreme authority,
     2:17  fear God, honor the **e**.

## EMPTIED [EMPTY]
Ne   5:13  such a person be shaken out and **e**!"
1Co  1:17  the cross of Christ be **e** of its power.

## EMPTY [EMPTIED, EMPTY-HANDED]
Ge   1: 2  Now the earth was formless and **e**,
Ru   1:21  the LORD has brought me back **e**.
2Ki  4: 3  and ask all your neighbors for **e** jars.
Job  26: 7  the northern [skies] over **e** space;
     35:16  So Job opens his mouth with **e** talk;
Isa  45:18  he did not create it to be **e**,
     55:11  It will not return to me **e**, but will
Jer  4:23  the earth, and it was formless and **e**;
Mt  12:36  for every **e** word they have spoken.
Lk   1:53  things but has sent the rich away **e**.
Eph  5: 6  no one deceive you with **e** words,
1Pe  1:18  you were redeemed from the **e** way
2Pe  2:18  For they mouth **e**, boastful words

## EMPTY-HANDED [EMPTY, HAND]
Ge  31:42  would surely have sent me away **e**.

Ex   3:21  when you leave you will not go **e**.
     23:15  "No one is to appear before me **e**.
Dt  15:13  them, do not send them away **e**.
Ru   3:17  back to your mother-in-law.' "
Mk  12: 3  him, beat him and sent him away **e**.

## EN GEDI
1Sa  24: 1  "David is in the Desert of **E**."

## ENABLE* [ABLE]
Lk   1:74  and to **e** us to serve him without fear
Ac   4:29  **e** your servants to speak your word

## ENABLED* [ABLE]
Ge  29:31  he **e** her to conceive,
     30:22  to her and **e** her to conceive.
Lev  26:13  **e** you to walk with heads held high.
Ru   4:13  her, the LORD **e** her to conceive,
1ch  28:19  **e** me to understand all the details
Jn   6:65  me unless the Father has **e** them."
Ac   2: 4  other tongues as the Spirit **e** them.
     7:10  and **e** him to gain the goodwill
Heb  11:11  was **e** to bear children because she

## ENABLES* [ABLE]
Hab  3:19  he **e** me to tread on the heights.
Php  3:21  by the power that **e** him to bring

## ENABLING* [ABLE]
Ac  14: 3  his grace by **e** them to perform signs

## ENCAMP [CAMP]
Ex  14: 2  to turn back and **e** near Pi Hahiroth,

## ENCAMPED [CAMP]
Nu   9:23  At the LORD's command they **e**,
     24: 2  out and saw Israel **e** tribe by tribe,

## ENCAMPS* [CAMP]
Ps  34: 7  the LORD **e** around those who fear

## ENCHANTER [ENCHANTERS]
Isa  3: 3  skilled worker and clever **e**.
Da   2:27  "No wise man, **e**,

## ENCHANTERS [ENCHANTER]
Da   1:20  and **e** in his whole kingdom.
     5: 7  The king summoned the **e**,

## ENCIRCLE [CIRCLE]
Ps  22:12  strong bulls of Bashan **e** me.

## ENCIRCLED [CIRCLE]
Rev  4: 3  shone like an emerald **e** the throne.
     5: 6  **e** by the four living creatures

## ENCLOSE* [CLOSE]
SS   8: 9  we will **e** her with panels of cedar.

## ENCLOSED [CLOSE]
SS   4:12  you are a spring **e**, a sealed

## ENCOURAGE* [ENCOURAGED, ENCOURAGEMENT, ENCOURAGES, ENCOURAGING]

| Dt | 1:38 | E him, because he will lead Israel |
| | 3:28 | Joshua, and e and strengthen him, |
| 2Sa | 11:25 | and destroy it.' Say this to e Joab." |
| | 19: 7 | Now go out and e your men. |
| Job | 16: 5 | But my mouth would e you; |
| Ps | 10:17 | you e them, and you listen to their |
| | 64: 5 | They e each other in evil plans, |
| Isa | 1:17 | Seek justice, e the oppressed. |
| Jer | 29: 8 | to the dreams you e them to have. |
| Ac | 15:32 | said much to e and strengthen |
| Ro | 12: 8 | if it is to e, then give |
| 2Co | 13:11 | e one another, be of one mind, |
| Eph | 6:22 | how we are, and that he may e you. |
| Col | 4: 8 | and that he may e your hearts. |
| 1Th | 3: 2 | strengthen and e you in your faith, |
| | 4:18 | Therefore e one another with these |
| | 5:11 | Therefore e one another and build |
| | 5:14 | and disruptive, e the disheartened, |
| 2Th | 2:17 | e your hearts and strengthen you |
| 2Ti | 4: 2 | correct, rebuke and e— |
| Tit | 1: 9 | he can e others by sound doctrine |
| | 2: 6 | Similarly, e the young men to be |
| | 2:15 | E and rebuke with all authority. |
| Heb | 3:13 | But e one another daily, as long as it |

## ENCOURAGED* [ENCOURAGE]

| Jdg | 7:11 | you will be e to attack the camp." |
| | 20:22 | But the Israelites e one another |
| 2Ch | 22: 3 | his mother e him to act wickedly. |
| | 32: 6 | gate and e them with these words: |
| | 35: 2 | and e them in the service |
| Eze | 13:22 | and because you e the wicked not |
| Ac | 9:31 | of the Lord and e by the Holy Spirit, |
| | 11:23 | e them all to remain true to the Lord |
| | 16:40 | met with the believers and e them. |
| | 18:27 | the believers e him and wrote |
| | 27:36 | They were all e and ate some food |
| | 28:15 | people Paul thanked God and was e. |
| Ro | 1:12 | I may be mutually e by each other's |
| 1Co | 14:31 | everyone may be instructed and e. |
| 2Co | 7: 4 | I am greatly e; in all our troubles |
| | 7:13 | By all this we are e. In addition |
| Col | 2: 2 | goal is that they may be e in heart |
| 1Th | 3: 7 | persecution we were e about you |
| Heb | 6:18 | hope set before us may be greatly e. |

## ENCOURAGEMENT*
[ENCOURAGE]

| Ac | 4:36 | (which means "son of e"), |
| | 20: 2 | speaking many words of e |
| Ro | 12: 8 | if it is to encourage, then give e; |
| | 15: 4 | the e they provide we might have |
| | 15: 5 | e give you the same attitude of mind |
| 1Co | 14: 3 | their strengthening, e and comfort. |
| 2Co | 7: 4 | In addition to our own e, we were |
| Php | 2: 1 | if you have any e from being united |
| 2Th | 2:16 | by his grace gave us eternal e |
| Phm | 1: 7 | love has given me great joy and e, |
| Heb | 12: 5 | completely forgotten this word of e |

## ENCOURAGES* [ENCOURAGE]

| Isa | 41: 7 | The metal worker e the goldsmith, |

## ENCOURAGING* [ENCOURAGE]

| Ac | 14:22 | e them to remain true to the faith. |
| | 15:31 | it and were glad for its e message. |
| | 20: 1 | after e them, said good-by and set |
| 1Th | 2:12 | e, comforting and urging you to live |
| Heb | 10:25 | but e one another—and all |
| 1Pe | 5:12 | e you and testifying that this is |

## ENCROACH

| Pr | 23:10 | or e on the fields of the fatherless, |

## END [ENDED, ENDLESS, ENDS, UNENDING]

| Ge | 6:13 | am going to put an e to all people, |
| Ex | 12:41 | At the e of the 430 years, to the very |
| Nu | 16:21 | this assembly so I can put an e |
| | 23:10 | and may my final e be like theirs!" |
| Dt | 8:16 | in the e it might go well with you. |
| | 31:24 | of this law from beginning to e, |
| Ne | 9:31 | great mercy you did not put an e |
| Job | 19:25 | in the e he will stand on the earth. |
| Ps | 48:14 | he will be our guide even to the e. |
| | 119:33 | that I may follow it to the e. |
| | 119:112 | keeping your decrees to the very e. |
| Pr | 5: 4 | but in the e she is bitter as gall, |
| | 5:11 | At the e of your life you will groan, |
| | 14:12 | right, but in the e it leads to death. |
| | 14:13 | ache, and rejoicing may e in grief. |
| | 16:25 | right, but in the e it leads to death. |
| | 19:20 | the e you will be counted among |
| | 20:21 | too soon will not be blessed at the e. |
| | 23:32 | In the e it bites like a snake |
| | 25: 8 | do in the e if your neighbor puts you |
| | 28:23 | the e gain favor rather than one who |
| Ecc | 3:11 | God has done from beginning to e. |
| | 7: 8 | The e of a matter is better than its |
| | 12:12 | making many books there is no e, |
| Isa | 9: 7 | and peace there will be no e. |
| Eze | 7: 2 | " 'The e! The e has come upon the four |
| Da | 4:34 | At the e of that time, I, |
| | 6:26 | his dominion will never e. |
| | 8:17 | vision concerns the time of the e." |
| | 9:26 | The e will come like a flood: |
| | 9:26 | War will continue until the e, |
| | 12:13 | "As for you, go your way till the e. |
| | 12:13 | at the e of the days you will rise |
| Mt | 10:22 | stand firm to the e will be saved. |
| | 24:13 | stands firm to the e will be saved. |
| | 24:14 | nations, and then the e will come. |
| Lk | 21: 9 | but the e will not come right away." |
| Jn | 13: 1 | he loved them to the e. |
| 1Co | 15:24 | Then the e will come, when he |
| 2Co | 3:13 | seeing the e of what was passing |
| Heb | 3:14 | we hold firmly till the e our original |
| | 6: 8 | In the e it will be burned. |
| 1Pe | 4: 7 | The e of all things is near. |
| 2Pe | 2:20 | are worse off at the e than they were |
| Rev | 2:26 | victorious and do my will to the e, |
| | 21: 6 | Omega, the Beginning and the E. |
| | 22:13 | the Last, the Beginning and the E. |

## ENDED [END]

| Pr | 10:19 | Sin is not e by multiplying words, |
| | 22:10 | quarrels and insults are e. |
| Rev | 20: 3 | until the thousand years were e. |

## ENDLESS [END]
Ps 106:31 as righteousness for e generations
Na   3:19 for who has not felt your e cruelty?

## ENDOR
1Sa 28: 7 "There is one in E," they said.

## ENDOW [ENDOWED]
Ps  72: 1 E the king with your justice, O God,

## ENDOWED [ENDOW]
Isa 55: 5 for he has e you with splendor."

## ENDS [END]
Ps   2: 8 the e of the earth your possession.
     19: 4 their words to the e of the world.
     67: 7 all the e of the earth will fear him.
Pr  20:17 but one e up with a mouth full
Isa 40:28 the Creator of the e of the earth.
     49: 6 may reach to the e of the earth."
     62:11 proclamation to the e of the earth:
Mic  5: 4 will reach to the e of the earth.
Lk  11:31 she came from the e of the earth
Ac  13:47 salvation to the e of the earth.' "
Ro  10:18 their words to the e of the world."

## ENDS OF THE EARTH See EARTH

## ENDURANCE⁺ [ENDURE]
Ro  15: 4 so that through the e taught
     15: 5 May the God who gives e
2Co  1: 6 you patient e of the same sufferings
     6: 4 in great e; in troubles,
Col  1:11 you may have great e and patience,
1Th  1: 3 your e inspired by hope in our Lord
1Ti  6:11 faith, love, e and gentleness.
2Ti  3:10 my purpose, faith, patience, love, e,
Tit  2: 2 and sound in faith, in love and in e.
Rev  1: 9 and patient e that are ours in Jesus,
     13:10 This calls for patient e
     14:12 This calls for patient e on the part

## ENDURE [ENDURANCE, ENDURED, ENDURES, ENDURING]
1Sa 13:14 But now your kingdom will not e;
2Sa  7:16 your kingdom will e forever before
Job 20:21 his prosperity will not e.
Ps  37:18 and their inheritance will e forever.
     49:12 despite their wealth, do not e;
     72:17 May his name e forever;
     89:29 his throne as long as the heavens e.
    104:31 the glory of the LORD e forever;
Pr  12:19 Truthful lips e forever, but a lying
     27:24 for riches do not e forever,
Ecc  3:14 everything God does will e forever;
Isa 55:13 an everlasting sign, that will e forever."
     66:22 earth that I make will e before me,"
     66:22 will your name and descendants e.
Jer 44:22 could no longer e your wicked
Da   2:44 to an end, but it will itself e forever.
Joel 2:11 it is dreadful. Who can e it?
Na   1: 6 Who can e his fierce anger?
Mal  3: 2 who can e the day of his coming?
1Co  4:12 when we are persecuted, we e it;
     10:13 provide a way out so that you can e it.

2Co  1: 8 far beyond our ability to e,
2Ti  2:10 Therefore I e everything
     2:12 if we e, we will also reign with him.
     4: 5 head in all situations, e hardship,
Heb 12: 7 E hardship as discipline;
1Pe  2:20 a beating for doing wrong and e it?
     2:20 suffer for doing good and you e it,
Rev  3:10 kept my command to e patiently,

## ENDURED* [ENDURE]
Ps 123: 3 for we have e no end of contempt.
    123: 4 We have e no end of ridicule
Ac  13:18 forty years he e their conduct
2Ti  3:11 and Lystra, the persecutions I e.
Heb 10:32 when you e in a great conflict
     12: 2 joy set before him he e the cross,
     12: 3 him who e such opposition
Rev  2: 3 and have e hardships for my name,

## ENDURES [ENDURE]
Ge   8:22 "As long as the earth e,
1Ch 16:41 LORD, "for his love e forever."
Ps 102:12 your renown e through all
    112: 9 poor, their righteousness e forever;
    136: 1 His love e forever.
    145:13 and your dominion e through all
Isa 40: 8 word of our God e forever."
Da   9:15 yourself a name that e to this day,
Jn   6:27 but for food that e to eternal life,
2Co  9: 9 their righteousness e forever."
1Pe  1:25 word of the Lord e forever."

## HIS LOVE ENDURES FOREVER See LOVE

## ENDURING [ENDURE]
Ps  19: 9 of the LORD is pure, e forever.
2Th  1: 4 the persecutions and trials you are e.
Heb 13:14 For here we do not have an e city,
1Pe  1:23 the living and e word of God.

## ENEMIES [ENEMY]
Ex   1:10 will join our e, fight against us
     23:22 I will be an enemy to your e
Lev 26:37 not be able to stand before your e.
Dt   6:19 thrusting out all your e before you,
     33:27 He will drive out your e before you,
Jos  5:13 "Are you for us or for our e?"
     21:44 Not one of their e withstood them;
     21:44 the LORD gave all their e
Jdg  2:14 into the hands of their e all around,
2Sa  7: 1 him rest from all his e around him,
Est  9: 5 The Jews struck down all their e
Job 19:11 he counts me among his e.
Ps   9: 6 Endless ruin has overtaken my e,
     23: 5 before me in the presence of my e.
     44: 7 but you give us victory over our e,
    110: 1 hand until I make your e a footstool
Pr  16: 7 he causes their e to make peace
     24:17 Do not gloat when your e fall;
     26:24 E disguise themselves with their lips,
     29:24 accomplices of thieves are their own e;
Isa 59:18 so will he repay wrath to his e
Jer 12: 7 one I love into the hands of her e.
Da   4:19 if only the dream applied to your e
Mic  7: 6 your e are the members of your own

Mt    5:44   love your **e** and pray for those who
     10:36   your **e** will be the members of your
Lk    6:35   But love your **e**, do good to them,
     20:43   until I make your **e** a footstool
Ro    5:10   if, while we were God's **e**, we were
1Co  15:25   he has put all his **e** under his feet.
Php   3:18   tears, many live as **e** of the cross
Col   1:21   were **e** in your minds because
Heb   1:13   hand until I make your **e** a footstool
     10:13   for his **e** to be made his footstool.
     10:27   fire that will consume the **e** of God.
Rev  11: 5   their mouths and devours their **e**.

## ENEMY [ENEMIES, ENMITY]

Ex   15: 9   The **e** boasted, 'I will pursue, I will
     23:22   I will be an **e** to your enemies
2Sa  22:18   He rescued me from my powerful **e**,
Est   3:10   the Agagite, the **e** of the Jews.
      9:24   the Agagite, the **e** of all the Jews,
Ps   74:10   How long will the **e** mock you,
Pr   25:21   If your **e** is hungry, give him food
     27: 6   trusted, but an **e** multiplies kisses.
Jer  30:14   I have struck you as an **e** would
La    2: 5   The Lord is like an **e**;
Mic   2: 8   my people have risen up like an **e**.
Mt   13:39   the **e** who sows them is the devil.
Lk   10:19   to overcome all the power of the **e**;
Ro   12:20   "If your **e** is hungry, feed him;
1Co  15:26   The last **e** to be destroyed is death.
1Ti   5:14   and to give the **e** no opportunity
1Pe   5: 8   Your **e** the devil prowls around like

## ENERGY*

Col   1:29   all the **e** Christ so powerfully works

## ENGRAVE [ENGRAVED, ENGRAVER]

Ex   28:11   **E** the names of the sons of Israel
Zec   3: 9   and I will **e** an inscription on it,'

## ENGRAVED [ENGRAVE]

Ex   32:16   the writing of God, **e** on the tablets.
Isa  49:16   I have **e** you on the palms of my
Jer  17: 1   "Judah's sin is **e** with an iron tool,
2Co   3: 7   which was **e** in letters on stone,

## ENGRAVER* [ENGRAVE]

Ex   38:23   an **e** and designer, and an embroiderer
Jer  10: 9   goldsmith and **e** have made is then
             dressed

## ENHANCES*

Ro    3: 7   my falsehood **e** God's truthfulness

## ENJOY [JOY]

Lev  26:34   the land will rest and **e** its sabbaths.
Nu   14:31   in to **e** the land you have rejected.
Dt    6: 2   you, and so that you may **e** long life.
Ps   37: 3   dwell in the land and **e** safe pasture.
Pr   28:16   ill-gotten gain will **e** a long reign.
Ecc   3:22   for people than to **e** their work,
      5:19   and the ability to **e** them, to accept
      6: 2   does not grant the ability to **e** them,
      9: 9   **E** life with your wife, whom you
Eph   6: 3   and that you may **e** long life
Heb  11:25   than to **e** the fleeting pleasures

3Jn   1: 2   I pray that you may **e** good health

## ENJOYED [JOY]

2Ch  36:21   The land **e** its sabbath rests;

## ENJOYMENT* [JOY]

Ecc   2:25   without him, who can eat or find **e**?
      4: 8   why am I depriving myself of **e**?"
      8:15   So I commend the **e** of life,
1Ti   6:17   us with everything for our **e**.

## ENLARGE* [LARGE]

Ex   34:24   before you and **e** your territory,
1Ch   4:10   would bless me and **e** my territory!
Isa  54: 2   "**E** the place of your tent,
2Co   9:10   seed and will **e** the harvest of your

## ENLARGED [LARGE]

Dt   12:20   your God has **e** your territory as he
Isa   9: 3   You have **e** the nation and increased
     26:15   You have **e** the nation, LORD;

## ENLARGES [LARGE]

Dt   19: 8   LORD your God **e** your territory,

## ENLIGHTEN* [LIGHT]

Isa  40:14   did the LORD consult to **e** him,

## ENLIGHTENED* [LIGHT]

Eph   1:18   eyes of your heart may be **e** in order
Heb   6: 4   for those who have once been **e**,

## ENMITY [ENEMY]

Ge    3:15   I will put **e** between you
Jas   4: 4   world means **e** against God?

## ENOCH

   1. Son of Cain (Ge 4:17–18).
   2. Descendant of Seth; walked with God and taken
by him (Ge 5:18–24; Heb 11:5). Prophet (Jude 14).

## ENOUGH

Dt    1: 6   "You have stayed long **e** at this
      9: 8   that he was angry **e** to destroy you.
2Sa   7:19   And as if this were not **e** in your sight,
Ezr   9:14   Would you not be angry **e** with us
Pr   30:15   satisfied, four that never say, '**E**!':
Ecc   1: 8   The eye never has **e** of seeing,
      5:10   who love money never have **e**;
Isa   7:13   Is it not **e** to try the patience
Joel  2:19   and olive oil, **e** to satisfy you fully;
Hag   1: 6   You eat, but never have **e**.

## ENRICH* [RICH]

Ps   65: 9   and water it; you **e** it abundantly.
Pr    5:10   and your toil **e** the house of another.

## ENRICHED [RICH]

1Co   1: 5   him you have been **e** in every way—

## ENSLAVE [SLAVE]

2Co  11:20   with any who **e** you or exploit you

## ENSLAVED [SLAVE]
Ge  15:13  that they will be **e** and mistreated
Gal  4: 9  wish to be **e** by them all over again?
Tit  3: 3  and **e** by all kinds of passions

## ENSLAVING* [SLAVE]
Ex   6: 5  whom the Egyptians are **e**, and I

## ENSNARE [SNARE]
Pr   5:22  evil deeds of the wicked **e** them;
Ecc  7:26  escape her, but the sinner she will **e**.

## ENSNARED* [SNARE]
Dt   7:25  or you will be **e** by it, for it is
     12:30  be careful not to be **e** by inquiring
Ps   9:16  the wicked are **e** by the work
Pr   6: 2  said, **e** by the words of your mouth.
     22:25  learn their ways and get yourself **e**.

## ENTANGLE* [ENTANGLED, ENTANGLES]
Ps  35: 8  may the net they hid **e** them,

## ENTANGLED [ENTANGLE]
Ps 116: 3  The cords of death **e** me,
2Pe  2:20  Jesus Christ and are again **e** in it

## ENTANGLES* [ENTANGLE]
Heb 12: 1  hinders and the sin that so easily **e**.

## ENTER [ENTERED, ENTERING, ENTERS, ENTRANCE]
Ge   6:18  with you, and you will **e** the ark—
Ex  40:35  Moses could not **e** the tent
Nu  20:24  He will not **e** the land I give
Dt   1:37  and said, "You shall not **e** it, either.
Ps  95:11  'They shall never **e** my rest.' "
    100: 4  **E** his gates with thanksgiving
    118:20  through which the righteous may **e**.
Pr   2:10  For wisdom will **e** your heart,
Isa 26: 2  that the righteous nation may **e**,
     35:10  They will **e** Zion with singing;
     51:11  They will **e** Zion with singing;
Eze 37: 5  I will make breath **e** you, and you
Joel  3: 2  There I will **e** into judgment against
Mt   5:20  you will certainly not **e** the kingdom
     7:13  "**E** through the narrow gate.
     7:21  will **e** the kingdom of heaven,
     18: 3  you will never **e** the kingdom
     18: 8  It is better for you to **e** life maimed
     19:17  If you want to **e** life,
Mk  10:15  like a little child will never **e** it."
     10:23  the rich to **e** the kingdom of God!"
Lk  13:24  effort to **e** through the narrow door,
     13:24  will try to **e** and will not be able to.
     24:26  these things and then **e** his glory?"
Jn   3: 5  no one can **e** the kingdom of God
Heb  3:11  'They shall never **e** my rest.' "
     4: 3  Now we who have believed **e**
     4:10  for those who **e** God's rest
     4:11  make every effort to **e** that rest,
     9:12  He did not **e** by means of the blood
     10:19  confidence to **e** the Most Holy Place
Rev 15: 8  no one could **e** the temple until

Rev 21:27  Nothing impure will ever **e** it,

## ENTERED [ENTER]
Ge   7: 9  came to Noah and **e** the ark, as God
Ex  24:18  Moses **e** the cloud as he went
Nu   7:89  When Moses **e** the tent of meeting
Dt  26: 1  you have **e** the land the LORD
2Ch 26:16  **e** the temple of the LORD to burn
Ps  73:17  till I **e** the sanctuary of God;
Isa 28:15  "We have **e** into a covenant
Eze  4:14  impure meat has ever **e** my mouth."
     37:10  commanded me, and breath **e** them;
     43: 4  of the LORD **e** the temple through
Lk   9:34  they were afraid as they **e** the cloud.
     22: 3  Then Satan **e** Judas, called Iscariot,
Jn  13:27  took the bread, Satan **e** into him.
Ac  11: 8  or unclean has ever **e** my mouth.'
Ro   5:12  just as sin **e** the world through one
Heb  6:20  Jesus, has **e** on our behalf.
     9:12  he **e** the Most Holy Place once
Rev 11:11  the breath of life from God **e** them,

## ENTERING [ENTER]
Nu  32: 9  **e** the land the LORD had given
Mt  21:31  the prostitutes are **e** the kingdom
Lk  11:52  have hindered those who were **e**."
Heb  4: 1  the promise of **e** his rest still stands,

## ENTERS [ENTER]
Mk   7:18  nothing that **e** you from the outside
Jn  10: 2  The one who **e** by the gate is

## ENTERTAIN* [ENTERTAINMENT]
Jdg 16:25  "Bring out Samson to **e** us."
Mt   9: 4  "Why do you **e** evil thoughts
1Ti  5:19  Do not **e** an accusation against

## ENTERTAINMENT* [ENTERTAIN]
Da   6:18  without any **e** being brought to him.

## ENTHRALLED*
Ps  45:11  Let the king be **e** by your beauty;

## ENTHRONED* [THRONE]
1Sa  4: 4  who is **e** between the cherubim.
2Sa  6: 2  who is **e** between the cherubim
2Ki 19:15  of Israel, **e** between the cherubim,
1Ch 13: 6  who is **e** between the cherubim—
Ps   2: 4  The One **e** in heaven laughs;
     7: 7  while you sit **e** over them
     9: 4  sitting **e** as the righteous judge.
     9:11  praises of the LORD, **e** in Zion;
     22: 3  Yet you are **e** as the Holy One;
     29:10  The LORD sits **e** over the flood;
     29:10  the LORD is **e** as King forever.
     55:19  God, who is **e** from of old,
     61: 7  May he be **e** in God's presence
     80: 1  You who sit **e** between
     99: 1  he sits **e** between the cherubim,
    102:12  But you, LORD, sit **e** forever;
    113: 5  God, the One who sits **e** on high,
    123: 1  to you who sit **e** in heaven.
    132:14  here I will sit **e**, for I have desired it.
Isa 14:13  I will sit **e** on the mount
     37:16  of Israel, **e** between the cherubim,

Isa  40:22  He sits **e** above the circle
      52: 2  rise up, sit **e**, Jerusalem.
Rev  18: 7  boasts, 'sit enthroned as **q**.

## ENTHRONES* [THRONE]
Job  36: 7  he **e** them with kings and exalts

## ENTHUSIASM*
2Co  8:17  but he is coming to you with much **e**
      9: 2  your **e** has stirred most of them

## ENTICE [ENTICED, ENTICES]
2Ch 18:19  'Who will **e** Ahab king of Israel
Pr    1:10  if sinful men **e** you, do not give
     16:29  The violent **e** their neighbors
2Pe  2:18  they **e** people who are just escaping
Rev  2:14  who taught Balak to **e** the Israelites

## ENTICED* [ENTICE]
Nu  31:16  **e** the Israelites to be unfaithful
Dt    4:19  do not be **e** into bowing down
     11:16  or you will be **e** to turn away
2Ki 17:21  Jeroboam **e** Israel away
Job  31: 9  my heart has been **e** by a woman,
     31:27  so that my heart was secretly **e**
Eze 14: 9  the prophet is **e** to utter a prophecy,
     14: 9  I the LORD have **e** that prophet,
Jas   1:14  away by your own evil desire and **e**.

## ENTICES* [ENTICE]
Dt   13: 6  or your closest friend secretly **e** you,
Job  36:18  careful that no one **e** you by riches;

## ENTIRE
Ex  14:28  the **e** army of Pharaoh that had
Dt    2:14  that **e** generation of fighting men
Jos  11:16  So Joshua took this **e** land:
Lk    2: 1  be taken of the **e** Roman world.
Ac   11:28  spread over the **e** Roman world.
     18: 8  and his **e** household believed
Gal   5:14  For the **e** law is fulfilled in keeping

## ENTRANCE [ENTER]
Ex  26:36  "For the **e** to the tent make a curtain
     27:16  "For the **e** to the courtyard,
Mt  27:60  stone in front of the **e** to the tomb
Mk  15:46  he rolled a stone against the **e**
     16: 3  away from the **e** of the tomb?"
Jn   11:38  a cave with a stone laid across the **e**.
     20: 1  stone had been removed from the **e**.
Ac   12: 6  and sentries stood guard at the **e**.

## ENTREAT [ENTREATY]
Zec  8:21  'Let us go at once to **e** the LORD

## ENTREATY [ENTREAT]
2Ch 33:19  and how God was moved by his **e**,

## ENTRUST [TRUST]
Jn    2:24  Jesus would not **e** himself to them,
2Ti   2: 2  many witnesses **e** to reliable people

## ENTRUSTED [TRUST]
Ge  39: 4  and he **e** to his care everything he

2Ki  22: 7  account for the money **e** to them,
Jer  13:20  is the flock that was **e** to you,
Lk   12:48  the one who has been **e** with much,
Jn    5:22  but has **e** all judgment to the Son,
Ro    3: 2  the Jews have been **e** with the very
1Co  4: 1  as those **e** with the mysteries God
Gal   2: 7  saw that I had been **e** with the task
1Th   2: 4  by God to be **e** with the gospel.
1Ti   1:11  the blessed God, which he **e** to me.
      6:20  guard what has been **e** to your care.
2Ti   1:12  to guard what I have **e** to him until
      1:14  the good deposit that was **e** to you—
Tit   1: 3  light through the preaching **e** to me
1Pe  2:23  he **e** himself to him who judges
      5: 3  not lording it over those **e** to you,
Jude  1: 3  the Lord has once for all **e** to us,

## ENVELOPED*
Isa  42:25  **e** them in flames, yet they did not
                understand;

## ENVIED [ENVY]
Ps   73: 3  For I **e** the arrogant when I saw

## ENVIOUS [ENVY]
Dt   32:21  I will make them **e** by those who are
Ps   37: 1  evil or be **e** of those who do wrong;
Pr   24:19  of evildoers or be **e** of the wicked,
Ro   10:19  "I will make you **e** by those who
     11:11  to the Gentiles to make Israel **e**.

## ENVOY
Pr   13:17  but a trustworthy **e** brings healing.

## ENVY [ENVIED, ENVIOUS, ENVYING]
Pr    3:31  Do not **e** the violent or choose any
     14:30  life to the body, but **e** rots the bones.
     23:17  Do not let your heart **e** sinners,
     24: 1  Do not **e** the wicked, do not desire
Ecc   4: 4  from one person's **e** of another.
Mt   27:18  of **e** that they had handed Jesus over
Mk    7:22  malice, deceit, lewdness, **e**, slander,
Ro    1:29  They are full of **e**, murder, strife,
     11:14  arouse my own people to **e** and save
1Co  13: 4  It does not **e**, it does not boast, it is
Gal   5:21  and **e**; drunkenness, orgies,
Php   1:15  true that some preach Christ out of **e**
1Ti   6: 4  quarrels about words that result in **e**,
Tit   3: 3  We lived in malice and **e**,
Jas   3:14  But if you harbor bitter **e** and selfish
      3:16  For where you have **e** and selfish
1Pe   2: 1  hypocrisy, **e**, and slander of every

## ENVYING* [ENVY]
Gal   5:26  provoking and **e** each other.

## EPAPHRAS*
Associate of Paul (Col 1:7; 4:12; Phm 23).

## EPAPHRODITUS*
Associate of Paul (Php 2:25; 4:18).

# EPHAH
Ex   16:36  (An omer is one-tenth of an **e**.)
Eze  45:10  an accurate **e** and an accurate bath.
Mic   6:10  and the short **e**, which is accursed?

# EPHESIANS  [EPHESUS]
Ac   19:28  "Great is Artemis of the **E**!"

# EPHESUS  [EPHESIANS]
Ac   18:19  They arrived at **E**, where Paul left
       19: 1  the interior and arrived at **E**.
       20:17  Paul sent to **E** for the elders
1Co 15:32  If I fought wild beasts in **E** with no
Eph   1: 1  God, To God's holy people in **E**,
Rev   2: 1  the angel of the church in **E** write:

# EPHOD
Ex   28: 6  "Make the **e** of gold, and of blue,
Jdg   8:27  Gideon made the gold into an **e**,
       17: 5  he made an **e** and some household
1Sa   2:18  a boy wearing a linen **e**.
1Ch 15:27  David also wore a linen **e**.
Hos   3: 4  stones, without **e** or household gods.

# EPHPHATHA*
Mk   7:34  a deep sigh said to him, *"E!"*

# EPHRAIM
    1. Second son of Joseph (Ge 41:52; 46:20).
Blessed as firstborn by Jacob (Ge 48). Tribe of numbered (Nu 1:33; 26:37), blessed (Dt 33:17), allotted
land (Jos 16:4–9; Eze 48:5), failed to fully possess
(Jos 16:10; Jdg 1:29).
    2. A term for the Northern Kingdom of Israel (Isa
7:17; Hos 5).

# EPHRATH  [BETHLEHEM,
    EPHRATHAH]
Ge   35:19  was buried on the way to **E** (that is,

# EPHRATHAH  [EPHRATH]
Ru   4:11  May you have standing in **E** and be
Mic   5: 2  Bethlehem **E**, though you are small

# EPHRON
    Hittite who sold Abraham a field (Ge 23).

# EPICUREAN*
Ac   17:18  A group of **E** and Stoic philosophers

# EPISTLE  See LETTER

# EQUAL  [EQUALED, EQUALITY,
    EQUITY]
Ge   44:18  though you are **e** to Pharaoh
Dt   33:25  and your strength will **e** your days.
1Ki   3:13  you will have no **e** among kings.
Isa   40:25  Or who is my **e**?" says the Holy
       46: 5  you compare me or count me **e**?
Da   1:19  and he found none **e** to Daniel,
Jn   5:18  Father, making himself **e** with God.
1Co 12:25  its parts should have **e** concern
2Co   2:16  And who is **e** to such a task?

# EQUALED  [EQUAL]
Mk   13:19  and never to be **e** again.

# EQUALITY*  [EQUAL]
2Co   8:13  pressed, but that there might be **e**.
       8:14  what you need. The goal is **e**,
Php   2: 6  God, did not consider **e** with God

# EQUIP*  [EQUIPMENT, EQUIPPED]
Eph   4:12  to **e** his people for works of service,
Heb 13:21  **e** you with everything good

# EQUIPMENT  [EQUIP]
Nu   3:36  all its **e**, and everything related
Zec 11:15  me, "Take again the **e** of a foolish

# EQUIPPED  [EQUIP]
2Ti   3:17  God's people may be thoroughly **e**

# EQUITY*  [EQUAL]
Ps   9: 8  and judges the peoples with **e**.
       58: 1  Do you judge people with **e**?
       67: 4  for you rule the peoples with **e**
       75: 2  it is I who judge with **e**.
       96:10  he will judge the peoples with **e**.
       98: 9  and the peoples with **e**.
       99: 4  you have established **e**; in Jacob you

# ER
Ge   38: 6  Judah got a wife for **E**, his firstborn,

# ERASTUS*
    Associate(s) of Paul (Ac 19:22; Ro 16:23; 2Ti
4:20).

# ERECT  [ERECTED]
Dt   16:22  and do not **e** a sacred stone,

# ERECTED  [ERECT]
1Ki   7:21  He **e** the pillars at the portico
2Ki 21: 3  he also **e** altars to Baal and made

# ERODES*
Job 14:18  "But as a mountain **e** and crumbles

# ERRED*  [ERROR]
Nu   15:28  for the one who **e** by sinning

# ERROR  [ERRED, ERRORS]
Job   4:18  if he charges his angels with **e**,
Isa   47:15  All of them go on in their **e**;
Mt   22:29  in **e** because you do not know
Ro   1:27  the due penalty for their **e**.
Jas   5:20  the way of **e** will save them
2Pe   2:18  escaping from those who live in **e**.
       3:17  carried away by the **e** of the lawless
Jude   1:11  rushed for profit into Balaam's **e**;

# ERRORS*  [ERROR]
Ps   19:12  But who can discern their own **e**?

# ESAU  [EDOM]
    Firstborn of Isaac, twin of Jacob (Ge 25:21–26).

Also called Edom (Ge 25:30). Sold Jacob his birthright (Ge 25:29–34); lost blessing (Gen 27). Married Hittites (Ge 26:34), Ishmaelites (Ge 28:6–9). Reconciled to Jacob (Gen 33). Genealogy (Ge 36). The LORD chose Jacob over Esau (Mal 1:2–3), but gave Esau land (Dt 2:2–12). Descendants eventually obliterated (Ob 1–21; Jer 49:7–22).

## ESCAPE [ESCAPED, ESCAPES, ESCAPING]

| | | |
|---|---|---|
| Ge | 7: 7 | wives entered the ark to e the waters |
| 1Sa | 19:10 | That night David made good his e. |
| 2Sa | 15:14 | or none of us will e from Absalom. |
| Job | 11:20 | will fail, and e will elude them; |
| Ps | 68:20 | the Sovereign LORD comes e |
| | 89:48 | who can e the power of the grave? |
| Pr | 11: 9 | through knowledge the righteous e. |
| | 12:13 | so the innocent e trouble. |
| Ecc | 7:26 | man who pleases God will e her, |
| Jer | 11:11 | on them a disaster they cannot e. |
| Eze | 6: 9 | those who e will remember me— |
| Mt | 23:33 | How will you e being condemned |
| Ro | 2: 3 | think you will e God's judgment? |
| 1Th | 5: 3 | woman, and they will not e. |
| 2Ti | 2:26 | and e from the trap of the devil, |
| Heb | 2: 3 | how shall we e if we ignore so great |
| | 12:25 | If they did not e when they refused |

## ESCAPED [ESCAPE]

| | | |
|---|---|---|
| 1Sa | 22: 1 | Gath and e to the cave of Adullam. |
| Ps | 124: 7 | We have e like a bird |
| | 124: 7 | has been broken, and we have e. |
| La | 2:22 | day of the LORD's anger no one e |
| Jn | 10:39 | to seize him, but he e their grasp. |
| Heb | 11:34 | flames, and the edge of the sword; |
| 2Pe | 1: 4 | having e the corruption in the world |
| | 2:20 | If they have e the corruption |

## ESCAPES* [ESCAPE]

| | | |
|---|---|---|
| Ps | 33:16 | no warrior e by his great strength. |
| Joel | 2: 3 | a desert waste—nothing e them. |

## ESCAPING [ESCAPE]

| | | |
|---|---|---|
| 1Co | 3:15 | only as one e through the flames. |
| 2Pe | 2:18 | they entice people who are just e |

## ESHKOL

| | | |
|---|---|---|
| Nu | 13:23 | they reached the Valley of E, |

## ESTABLISH [ESTABLISHED, ESTABLISHES]

| | | |
|---|---|---|
| Ge | 6:18 | But I will e my covenant with you, |
| | 9: 9 | "I now e my covenant with you |
| | 17:21 | But my covenant I will e with Isaac, |
| Ex | 23:31 | "I will e your borders from the Red |
| Dt | 28: 9 | The LORD will e you as his holy |
| 2Sa | 7:11 | the LORD himself will e a house |
| 1Ki | 9: 5 | I will e your royal throne over Israel |
| 1Ch | 28: 7 | I will e his kingdom forever if he is |
| Ps | 89: 4 | 'I will e your line forever and make |
| | 90:17 | e the work of our hands for us— |
| Pr | 16: 3 | and he will e your plans. |
| Isa | 26:12 | LORD, you e peace for us; |
| Eze | 16:60 | I will e an everlasting covenant |
| Ro | 10: 3 | of God and sought to e their own, |

| | | |
|---|---|---|
| Ro | 16:25 | Now to him who is able to e you |
| Heb | 10: 9 | sets aside the first to e the second. |

## ESTABLISHED [ESTABLISH]

| | | |
|---|---|---|
| Ge | 9:17 | the covenant I have e between me |
| Ex | 6: 4 | e my covenant with them to give |
| Dt | 19:15 | A matter must be e by the testimony |
| 2Sa | 7:16 | your throne will be e forever.' " |
| 1Ki | 2:46 | The kingdom was now e |
| Ps | 8: 2 | infants you have e a stronghold |
| | 78:69 | like the earth that he e forever. |
| | 93: 2 | Your throne was e long ago; |
| | 96:10 | The world is firmly e, it cannot be |
| | 103:19 | The LORD has e his throne |
| | 111: 8 | They are e for ever and ever, |
| Pr | 16:12 | a throne is e through righteousness. |
| | 20:18 | Plans are e by seeking advice; |
| Isa | 2: 2 | temple will be e as the highest |
| | 54:14 | In righteousness you will be e: |
| Jer | 33: 2 | the LORD who formed it and e it— |
| | 33:25 | and e the laws of heaven and earth, |
| Ro | 13: 1 | except that which God has e. |
| | 13: 1 | that exist have been e by God. |
| 2Co | 13: 1 | "Every matter must be e |
| Gal | 3:17 | set aside the covenant previously e |
| Eph | 3:17 | that you, being rooted and e in love, |
| Col | 1:23 | continue in your faith, e and firm, |
| Heb | 8: 6 | new covenant is e on better promises. |
| 2Pe | 1:12 | are firmly e in the truth you now |

## ESTABLISHES [ESTABLISH]

| | | |
|---|---|---|
| Job | 25: 2 | he e order in the heights of heaven. |
| Pr | 16: 9 | but the LORD e their steps. |
| Isa | 42: 4 | or be discouraged till he e justice |
| | 62: 7 | give him no rest till he e Jerusalem |

## ESTATE

| | | |
|---|---|---|
| Ge | 15: 2 | one who will inherit my e is Eliezer |
| Ru | 4: 6 | I might endanger my own e. |
| Est | 8: 7 | Jews, I have given his e to Esther, |
| Ps | 136:23 | He remembered us in our low e |
| Lk | 15:12 | 'Father, give me my share of the e.' |

## ESTEEM* [ESTEEMED]

| | | |
|---|---|---|
| Est | 10: 3 | in high e by his many fellow Jews, |
| Isa | 2:22 | Why hold them in e? |
| | 53: 3 | and we held him in low e. |
| Gal | 2: 6 | those who were held in high e— |

## ESTEEMED [ESTEEM]

| | | |
|---|---|---|
| Pr | 22: 1 | to be e is better than silver or gold. |
| Da | 10:11 | you who are highly e, |

## ESTHER [HADASSAH]

Jewess, originally named Hadassah, who lived in Persia; cousin of Mordecai (Est 2:7). Chosen queen of Xerxes (Est 2:8–18). Persuaded by Mordecai to foil Haman's plan to exterminate the Jews (Est 3–4). Revealed Haman's plans to Xerxes, resulting in Haman's death (Est 7), the Jews' preservation (Est 8–9), Mordecai's exaltation (Est 8:15; 9:4; 10). Decreed celebration of Purim (Est 9:18–32).

## ETERNAL* [ETERNITY]

| | | |
|---|---|---|
| Ge | 21:33 | the name of the LORD, the E God. |

Dt    33:27  The **e** God is your refuge,
1Ki   10: 9  of the LORD's **e** love for Israel,
Ps    16:11  with **e** pleasures at your right hand.
      111:10  To him belongs **e** praise.
      119:89  Your word, LORD, is **e**;
      119:160 all your righteous laws are **e**.
Ecc   12: 5  Then people go to their **e** home
Isa   26: 4  LORD, the LORD, is the Rock **e**.
      47: 7  said, 'I am forever—the **e** queen!'
Jer   10:10  he is the living God, the **e** King.
Da     4: 3  His kingdom is an **e** kingdom,
       4:34  His dominion is an **e** dominion;
Mt    18: 8  two feet and be thrown into **e** fire.
      19:16  good thing must I do to get **e** life?"
      19:29  times as much and will inherit **e** life.
      25:41  into the **e** fire prepared for the devil
      25:46  they will go away to **e** punishment,
      25:46  but the righteous to **e** life."
Mk     3:29  forgiven, but is guilty of an **e** sin."
      10:17  "what must I do to inherit **e** life?"
      10:30  and in the age to come **e** life.
Lk    10:25  "what must I do to inherit **e** life?"
      16: 9  will be welcomed into **e** dwellings.
      18:18  what must I do to inherit **e** life?"
      18:30  age, and in the age to come **e** life."
Jn     3:15  who believes may have **e** life
       3:16  him shall not perish but have **e** life.
       3:36  believes in the Son has **e** life,
       4.14  of water welling up to **e** life."
       4:36  now they harvest the crop for **e** life,
       5:24  believes him who sent me has **e** life
       5:39  think that in them you possess **e** life
       6:27  but for food that endures to **e** life,
       6:40  and believes in him shall have **e** life,
       6:47  whoever believes has **e** life.
       6:54  flesh and drinks my blood has **e** life,
       6:68  You have the words of **e** life.
      10:28  I give them **e** life, and they shall
      12:25  in this world will keep it for **e** life.
      12:50  that his command leads to **e** life.
      17: 2  he might give **e** life to all those you
      17: 3  Now this is **e** life: that they know
Ac    13:46  consider yourselves worthy of **e** life,
      13:48  were appointed for **e** life believed.
Ro     1:20  his **e** power and divine nature—
       2: 7  and immortality, he will give **e** life.
       5:21  bring **e** life through Jesus Christ our
       6:22  to holiness, and the result is **e** life.
       6:23  of God is **e** life in Christ Jesus our
      16:26  by the command of the **e** God,
2Co    4:17  for us an **e** glory that far outweighs
       4:18  temporary, but what is unseen is **e**.
       5: 1  from God, an **e** house in heaven,
Gal    6: 8  from the Spirit will reap **e** life.
Eph    3:11  according to his **e** purpose that he
2Th    2:16  his grace gave us **e** encouragement
1Ti    1:16  believe in him and receive **e** life.
       1:17  Now to the King **e**, immortal,
       6:12  Take hold of the **e** life to which you
2Ti    2:10  that is in Christ Jesus, with **e** glory.
Tit    1: 2  in the hope of **e** life, which God,
       3: 7  heirs having the hope of **e** life.
Heb    5: 9  he became the source of **e** salvation
       6: 2  of the dead, and **e** judgment.
       9:12  blood, thus obtaining **e** redemption.
       9:14  who through the **e** Spirit offered
       9:15  receive the promised **e** inheritance—

Heb   13:20  of the **e** covenant brought back
1Pe    5:10  who called you to his **e** glory
2Pe    1:11  a rich welcome into the **e** kingdom
1Jn    1: 2  it, and we proclaim to you the **e** life,
       2:25  this is what he promised us—**e** life.
       3:15  no murderers have **e** life in them.
       5:11  God has given us **e** life, and this life
       5:13  you may know that you have **e** life.
       5:20  He is the true God and **e** life.
Jude   1: 7  who suffer the punishment of **e** fire.
       1:21  Jesus Christ to bring you to **e** life.
Rev   14: 6  he had the **e** gospel to proclaim

## ETERNAL LIFE  Mt 19:16, 29; 25:46; Mk 10:17,
30; Lk 10:25; 18:18, 30; Jn 3:15, 16, 36; 4:14,
36; 5:24, 39; 6:27, 40, 47, 54, 68; 10:28; 12:25,
50; 17:2, 3; Ac 13:46, 48; Ro 2:7; 5:21; 6:22, 23;
Gal 6:8; 1Ti 1:16; 6:12; Tit 1:2; 3:7; 1Jn 1:2;
2:25; 3:15; 5:11, 13, 20; Jude 1:21

## ETERNITY* [ETERNAL]
Ps    93: 2  you are from all **e**.
Ecc    3:11  has also set **e** in the human heart;

## ETHAN
1Ki    4:31  else, including **E** the Ezrahite—
1Ch   15:19  and **E** were to sound the bronze
Ps    89: T  *A maskil of **E** the Ezrahite.*

## ETHIOPIAN*
Jer   13:23  Can an **E** change his skin
Ac     8:27  and on his way he met an **E** eunuch,

## EUNICE*
2Ti    1: 5  Lois and in your mother **E** and, I am

## EUNUCH [EUNUCHS]
Est    2:14  the king's **e** who was in charge
Isa   56: 3  And let no **e** complain, "I am only
Ac     8:27  on his way he met an Ethiopian **e**,

## EUNUCHS [EUNUCH]
2Ki   20:18  they will become **e** in the palace
Isa   56: 4  "To the **e** who keep my Sabbaths,
Mt    19:12  some are **e** because they were born
      19:12  others have been made **e**;

## EUODIA*
Php    4: 2  I plead with **E** and I plead

## EUPHRATES
Ge     2:14  And the fourth river is the **E**.
      15:18  of Egypt to the great river, the **E**—
Dt    11:24  and from the **E** River
2Ki   24: 7  the Wadi of Egypt to the **E** River.
Rev    9:14  who are bound at the great river **E**."
      16:12  out his bowl on the great river **E**,

## EUTYCHUS*
Ac    20: 9  window was a young man named **E**,

## EVANGELIST* [EVANGELISTS]
Ac    21: 8  stayed at the house of Philip the **e**,
2Ti    4: 5  do the work of an **e**, discharge all

## EVANGELISTS* [EVANGELIST]
Eph 4:11 the e, the pastors and teachers,

## EVE*
Ge 3:20 Adam named his wife **E**,
4: 1 Adam made love to his wife **E**,
2Co 11: 3 afraid that just as **E** was deceived
1Ti 2:13 For Adam was formed first, then **E**.

## EVEN
Ru 1:17 if e death separates you and me."

## EVEN-TEMPERED* [TEMPER]
Pr 17:27 those who have understanding are e.

## EVENING [EVENINGS]
Ge 1: 5 And there was e, and there was
8:11 the dove returned to him in the e,
24:11 it was toward e, the time the women
Ps 102:11 My days are like the e shadow;
Ecc 11: 6 and at e let your hands not be idle,
Zec 14: 7 When e comes, there will be light.

## EVENINGS* [EVENING]
Da 8:14 "It will take 2,300 e and mornings;
8:26 "The vision of the e and mornings

## EVENTS
2Ch 10:15 for this turn of e was from God,
Est 9:20 Mordecai recorded these e, and he
Lk 21:11 and fearful e and great signs
Ac 5:11 and all who heard about these e.

## EVER [EVERLASTING, FOREVER, FOREVERMORE]
Ex 9:18 the worst hailstorm that has e fallen
11: 6 worse than there has e been or e will
15:18 "The LORD reigns for e and e."
Dt 4:32 as this e happened, or has anything like
it e
8:19 you e forget the LORD your God
1Ki 3:12 anyone like you, nor will there e be.
2Ch 32:13 those nations e able to deliver their
Job 4: 7 being innocent, has e perished?
4: 7 were the upright e destroyed?
Ps 5:11 you be glad; let them e sing for joy.
10:16 The LORD is King for e and e;
25: 3 one who hopes in you will e be put
25:15 My eyes are e on the LORD,
38:17 to fall, and my pain is e with me.
45: 6 throne, O God, will last for e and e;
45:17 nations will praise you for e and e.
48:14 For this God is our God for e and e;
49: 8 is costly, no payment is e enough—
52: 8 in God's unfailing love for e and e.
61: 8 I will e sing in praise of your name
71: 6 I will e praise you.
83:17 May they e be ashamed
84: 4 they are e praising you.
89:33 nor will I e betray my faithfulness.
111: 8 They are established for e and e,
132:12 will sit on your throne for e and e."
145: 1 I will praise your name for e and e.
145: 2 and extol your name for e and e.

Ps 145:21 praise his holy name for e and e.
148: 6 he established them for e and e—
Pr 4:18 shining e brighter till the full light
5:19 may you e be intoxicated with her
Ecc 1: 6 it goes, e returning on its course.
Isa 6: 9 " 'Be e hearing, but never
6: 9 be e seeing, but never perceiving.'
66: 8 Who has e heard of such things?
66: 8 Who has e seen things like this?
Jer 2:11 Has a nation e changed its gods?
7: 7 I gave your ancestors for e and e.
25: 5 you and your ancestors for e and e.
31:36 the descendants of Israel e cease
Da 2:20 be to the name of God for e and e;
7:18 possess it forever—yes, for e and e.'
12: 3 like the stars for e and e.
Joel 2: 2 as never was of old nor e will be
Mic 4: 5 of the LORD our God for e and e.
Mt 9:33 "Nothing like this has e been seen
13:14 you will be e seeing but never
Mk 11: 2 there, which no one has e ridden.
Jn 1:18 No one has e seen God, but the one
3:13 No one has e gone into heaven
7:46 "No one e spoke the way this man
Ac 28:26 "You will be e hearing but never
28:26 you will be e seeing but never
Gal 1: 5 to whom be glory for e and e.
Eph 3:21 all generations, for e and e! Amen.
Php 4:20 God and Father be glory for e and e.
1Ti 1:17 God, be honor and glory for e and e.
2Ti 4:18 To him be glory for e and e. Amen.
Heb 1: 8 throne, O God, will last for e and e;
13:21 to whom be glory for e and e.
1Pe 4:11 the glory and the power for e and e.
5:11 To him be the power for e and e.
1Jn 4:12 No one has e seen God; but if we
Rev 1: 6 him be glory and power for e and e!
1:18 now look, I am alive for e and e!
4: 9 the throne and who lives for e and e,
7:12 strength be to our God for e and e.
10: 6 swore by him who lives for e and e,
11:15 and he will reign for e and e."
14:11 of their torment will rise for e and e.
20:10 tormented day and night for e and e.
21:27 Nothing impure will e enter it,
22: 5 And they will reign for e and e.

## FOR EVER AND EVER
Ex 15:18; Ps 9:5;
10:16; 21:4; 45:6, 17; 48:14; 52:8; 111:8; 119:44;
132:12, 14; 145:1, 2, 21; 148:6; Jer 7:7; 25:5; Da
2:20; 7:18; 12:3; Mic 4:5; Gal 1:5; Eph 3:21; Php
4:20; 1Ti 1:17; 2Ti 4:18; Heb 1:8; 13:21; 1Pe
4:11; 5:11; Rev 1:6, 18; 4:9, 10; 5:13; 7:12; 10:6;
11:15; 14:11; 15:7; 19:3; 20:10; 22:5

## EVER-INCREASING* [INCREASE]
Ro 6:19 to impurity and to e wickedness,
2Co 3:18 into his image with e glory,

## EVER-PRESENT* [PRESENT]
Ps 46: 1 and strength, an e help in trouble.

## EVERLASTING* [EVER]
Ge 9:16 remember the e covenant between
17: 7 covenant as an e covenant between
17: 8 I will give as an e possession to you

| Ge | 17:13 | in your flesh is to be an e covenant. |
| | 17:19 | with him as an e covenant for his |
| | 48: 4 | give this land as an e possession |
| Nu | 18:19 | It is an e covenant of salt before |
| Dt | 33:15 | and the fruitfulness of the e hills; |
| | 33:27 | and underneath are the e arms. |
| 2Sa | 23: 5 | have made with me an e covenant, |
| 1Ch | 16:17 | a decree, to Israel as an e covenant: |
| | 16:36 | the God of Israel, from e to e. |
| | 29:10 | God of our father Israel, from e to e. |
| Ezr | 9:12 | your children as an e inheritance.' |
| Ne | 9: 5 | your God, who is from e to e." |
| Ps | 41:13 | the God of Israel, from e to e. |
| | 52: 5 | God will bring you down to e ruin: |
| | 74: 3 | your steps toward these e ruins, |
| | 78:66 | he put them to e shame. |
| | 90: 2 | world, from e to e you are God. |
| | 103:17 | But from e to e the LORD's love is |
| | 105:10 | a decree, to Israel as an e covenant: |
| | 106:48 | the God of Israel, from e to e. |
| | 119:142 | Your righteousness is e and your |
| | 139:24 | in me, and lead me in the way e. |
| | 145:13 | Your kingdom is an e kingdom, |
| Isa | 9: 6 | Mighty God, E Father, |
| | 24: 5 | statutes and broken the e covenant. |
| | 30: 8 | to come it may be an e witness. |
| | 33:14 | of us can dwell with e burning?" |
| | 35:10 | e joy will crown their heads. |
| | 40:28 | The LORD is the e God, |
| | 45:17 | by the LORD with an e salvation; |
| | 45:17 | put to shame or disgraced, to ages e. |
| | 51:11 | e joy will crown their heads. |
| | 54: 8 | e kindness I will have compassion |
| | 55: 3 | I will make an e covenant with you, |
| | 55:13 | for an e sign, that will endure |
| | 56: 5 | I will give them an e name that will |
| | 60:15 | I will make you the e pride |
| | 60:19 | for the LORD will be your e light, |
| | 60:20 | the LORD will be your e light, |
| | 61: 7 | your land, and e joy will be yours. |
| | 61: 8 | and make an e covenant with them. |
| | 63:12 | them, to gain for himself e renown, |
| Jer | 5:22 | the sea, an e barrier it cannot cross. |
| | 23:40 | I will bring on you e disgrace—e shame |
| | 25: 9 | of horror and scorn, and an e ruin. |
| | 31: 3 | "I have loved you with an e love; |
| | 32:40 | I will make an e covenant |
| | 50: 5 | to the LORD in an e covenant |
| Eze | 16:60 | I will establish an e covenant |
| | 37:26 | it will be an e covenant. |
| Da | 7:14 | His dominion is an e dominion |
| | 7:27 | His kingdom will be an e kingdom, |
| | 9:24 | to bring in e righteousness, to seal |
| | 12: 2 | some to e life, others to shame and e |
| Mic | 6: 2 | you e foundations of the earth. |
| Hab | 1:12 | LORD, are you not from e? |
| 2Th | 1: 9 | will be punished with e destruction |
| Jude | 1: 6 | bound with e chains for judgment |

## EVERLASTING COVENANT Ge 9:16;
17:7, 13, 19; Nu 18:19; 2Sa 23:5; 1Ch 16:17; Ps
105:10; Isa 24:5; 55:3; 61:8; Jer 32:40; 50:5; Eze
16:60; 37:26

## EVERY [EVERYONE, EVERYONE'S, EVERYTHING, EVERYWHERE]
| Ge | 1:29 | "I give you e seed-bearing plant |

| Ge | 1:29 | e tree that has fruit with seed in it. |
| | 6: 5 | that e inclination of the thoughts |
| | 7: 4 | of the earth e living creature I have |
| | 7:23 | E living thing on the face |
| | 24: 1 | LORD had blessed him in e way. |
| Ex | 11: 5 | E firstborn son in Egypt will die, |
| | 13: 2 | "Consecrate to me e firstborn male. |
| | 13: 2 | of e womb among the Israelites |
| Lev | 17:14 | the life of e creature is its blood. |
| Dt | 7:15 | will keep you free from e disease. |
| | 8: 1 | follow e command I am giving you |
| | 8: 3 | but on e word that comes |
| Jos | 21:45 | of Israel failed; e one was fulfilled. |
| | 23:14 | E promise has been fulfilled; |
| 1Ch | 28: 9 | e heart and understands e desire and e thought. |
| Ps | 7:11 | a God who displays his wrath e day. |
| | 50:10 | for e animal of the forest is mine, |
| | 136:25 | He gives food to e creature. |
| | 145: 2 | E day I will praise you and extol |
| | 145:21 | Let e creature praise his holy name |
| Pr | 16:33 | its e decision is from the LORD. |
| | 30: 5 | "E word of God is flawless; he is |
| Ecc | 3: 1 | for e activity under the heavens: |
| | 12:14 | For God will bring e deed |
| | 12:14 | judgment, including e hidden thing, |
| Isa | 40: 4 | E valley shall be raised up, |
| | 45:23 | Before me e knee will bow; by me e |
| Jer | 2:20 | on e high hill and under e spreading |
| La | 3:23 | They are new e morning; |
| Eze | 21: 7 | E heart will melt and e hand go |
| | 21: 7 | e spirit will become faint and e knee |
| Mt | 4: 4 | but on e word that comes |
| | 7:17 | e good tree bears good fruit, |
| | 12:25 | "E kingdom divided against itself |
| | 12:25 | and e city or household divided |
| Jn | 13:11 | why he said not e one was clean. |
| | 15: 2 | He cuts off e branch in me |
| | 15: 2 | while e branch that does bear fruit |
| Ro | 14:11 | Lord, 'e knee will bow before me; |
| Php | 2:10 | name of Jesus e knee should bow, |
| 1Jn | 4: 1 | do not believe e spirit, but test |
| Rev | 1: 7 | and "e eye will see him, even those |
| | 7:17 | God will wipe away e tear |
| | 21: 4 | 'He will wipe e tear from their eyes, |
| | 22: 2 | of fruit, yielding its fruit e month. |

## EVERYONE [EVERY, ONE]
| Dt | 12: 8 | here today, e doing as they see fit, |
| Jdg | 17: 6 | had no king; e did as they saw fit. |
| | 21:25 | had no king; e did as they saw fit. |
| 1Ki | 8:39 | deal with e according to all they do, |
| Ps | 11: 4 | He observes e on earth; |
| | 39: 5 | E is but a breath, |
| | 53: 3 | E has turned away, all have become |
| | 62:12 | "You reward e according to |
| Pr | 24:12 | Will he not repay e according |
| Ecc | 7: 2 | death is the destiny of e; |
| Jer | 31:30 | Instead, e will die for their own sin; |
| Joel | 2:32 | And e who calls on the name |
| Jnh | 3: 8 | Let e call urgently on God. |
| Mt | 16:27 | reward e according to what they have |
| Lk | 11: 4 | also forgive e who sins against us. |
| | 11:10 | For e who asks receives; |
| Jn | 3:15 | e who believes may have eternal life |
| | 13:35 | e will know that you are my disciples, |
| Ac | 2:21 | e who calls on the name of the Lord |

Ro    2: 6  God "will repay e according to
     10:13  "E who calls on the name
1Co  10:33  even as I try to please e in every way.
Heb  12:14  live in peace with e and to be holy;
1Pe   2:17  Show proper respect to e, love your
2Pe   3: 9  perish, but e to come to repentance.
1Jn   3: 4  E who sins breaks the law;
      4: 7  E who loves has been born of God
      5: 4  for e born of God overcomes
Rev  20:13  e was judged according to what
     22:12  I will give to e according to what

## EVERYONE'S  [EVERY, ONE]
Ac    1:24  prayed, "Lord, you know e heart.
Ro    2:16  God judges e secrets through Jesus

## EVERYTHING  [EVERY, THING]
Ge    6:17  of life in it. E on earth will perish.
     39: 6  So Potiphar left e he had in Joseph's
Ex    7: 2  You are to say e I command you,
     19: 8  "We will do e the LORD has
     23:13  "Be careful to do e I have said
     24: 3  "E the LORD has said we will
Dt   15:18  your God will bless you in e you do.
     18:18  He will tell them e I command him.
     28:29  will be unsuccessful in e you do;
     29: 9  so that you may prosper in e you do.
1Ch  29:14  E comes from you, and we have
Ne    9: 6  You give life to e,
Job   1:11  out your hand and strike e he has,
Ps   24: 1  the LORD's, and e in it, the world,
    150: 6  Let e that has breath praise
Ecc   1: 2  E is meaningless."
      3: 1  There is a time for e, and a season
      3:11  He has made e beautiful in its time.
      3:14  that e God does will endure forever;
     10:19  and money is the answer for e.
Da    4:37  because e he does is right and all his
Mt    5:18  the Law until e is accomplished.
     28:20  to obey e I have commanded you.
Mk    9:23  "E is possible for one who
Lk   18:22  Sell e you have and give
Jn   14:26  will remind you of e I have said
Ac    2:44  were together and had e in common.
      3:22  you must listen to e he tells you.
      4:32  own, but they shared e they had.
Ro   14: 2  person's faith allows them to eat e,
1Co   6:12  but not e is beneficial.
     10:23  but not e is beneficial.
     10:23  but not e is constructive.
     15:27  For he "has put e under his feet."
     15:27  that "e" has been put under him,
     15:27  himself, who put e under Christ.
     16:14  Do e in love.
Gal   3:22  locked up e under the control of sin,
1Ti   4: 4  For e God created is good,
2Pe   1: 3  power has given us e we need
Rev  21: 5  throne said, "I am making e new!"

## EVERYWHERE  [EVERY, WHERE]
Pr   15: 3  The eyes of the LORD are e,

## EVIDENCE  [EVIDENT]
Mk   14:55  were looking for e against Jesus so
Jn   14:11  on the e of the works themselves.
2Th   1: 5  All this is e that God's judgment is

Jas   2:20  do you want e that faith without

## EVIDENT  [EVIDENCE]
Php   4: 5  Let your gentleness be e to all.

## EVIL  [EVILDOER, EVILDOERS, EVILS]
Ge    2: 9  of the knowledge of good and e.
      3: 5  be like God, knowing good and e."
      6: 5  human heart was only e all the time.
     44: 4  'Why have you repaid good with e?
Ex   32:22  how prone these people are to e.
Nu   32:13  of those who had done e in his sight
Dt    1:35  this e generation shall see the good
     13: 5  You must purge the e from among
     28:20  ruin because of the e you have done
Jos  23:15  bring on you all the e things he has
Jdg   2:11  the Israelites did e in the eyes
      3: 7  The Israelites did e in the eyes
      3:12  Again the Israelites did e in the eyes
      3:12  they did this e the LORD gave
      4: 1  Again the Israelites did e in the eyes
      6: 1  The Israelites did e in the eyes
     10: 6  Again the Israelites did e in the eyes
     13: 1  Again the Israelites did e in the eyes
1Sa  12:20  "You have done all this e;
     16:14  and an e spirit from the LORD
     18:10  The next day an e spirit from God
     19: 9  an e spirit from the LORD came
1Ki  11: 6  So Solomon did e in the eyes
     16:25  But Omri did e in the eyes
2Ki  15:24  Pekahiah did e in the eyes
Job   1: 1  he feared God and shunned e.
      1: 8  a man who fears God and shuns e."
      2: 3  a man who fears God and shuns e.
     15:35  conceive trouble and give birth to e;
     28:28  and to shun e is understanding."
     34:10  Far be it from God to do e,
     36:21  Beware of turning to e, which you
Ps    5: 4  with you, e people are not welcome.
     23: 4  I will fear no e, for you are with me;
     28: 4  for their deeds and for their e work;
     34:13  keep your tongue from e and your
     34:14  Turn from e and do good;
     34:16  LORD is against those who do e,
     37: 1  not fret because of those who are e
     37: 8  do not fret—it leads only to e.
     37:27  Turn from e and do good;
     49: 5  should I fear when e days come,
     51: 4  and done what is e in your sight;
     97:10  those who love the LORD hate e,
    101: 4  have nothing to do with what is e.
    141: 4  drawn to what is e so that I take part
Pr    3: 7  fear the LORD and shun e.
      4:27  or the left; keep your foot from e.
      8:13  To fear the LORD is to hate e;
      8:13  e behavior and perverse speech.
     11:19  but those who pursue e go to their
     11:27  e comes to those who search for it.
     14:16  wise fear the LORD and shun e,
     14:22  Do not those who plot e go astray?
     16: 6  the fear of the LORD e is avoided.
     17:13  of one who pays back e for good.
     20:30  Blows and wounds cleanse away e,
     26:23  are fervent lips with an e heart.
Ecc   4: 3  who has not seen the e that is done
     12:14  thing, whether it is good or e.

Isa    5:20  those who call **e** good and good **e**,
      13:11  I will punish the world for its **e**,
Jer    4:14  wash the **e** from your heart and be
      18: 8  that nation I warned repents of its **e**,
      18:10  if it does **e** in my sight and does not
Eze    3:18  dissuade them from their **e** ways
      33:11  Turn from your **e** ways!
      33:13  trust in their righteousness and do **e**,
      33:13  will die for the **e** they have done.
      33:15  and do no **e**, they will surely live;
Hos   10.13  you have reaped **e**, you have eaten
Am     5:13  in such times, for the times are **e**.
       5:14  Seek good, not **e**, that you may live.
Jnh    3: 8  Let them give up their **e** ways
Mic    3: 2  you who hate good and love **e**;
Hab    1:13  Your eyes are too pure to look on **e**;
Zec    8:17  do not plot **e** against each other,
Mal    2:17  "All who do **e** are good in the eyes
Mt     5:45  He causes his sun to rise on the **e**
       6:13  but deliver us from the **e** one.'
       7:11  though you are **e**, know how to give
      12:35  **e** people bring **e** things out of the **e**
      12:43  "When an **e** spirit comes
      13:38  weeds are the people of the **e** one,
      15:19  out of the heart come **e** thoughts,
Mk     7:21  out of your hearts, come **e** thoughts,
Lk     6: 9  to do good or to do **e**, to save life
      11:13  though you are **e**, know how to give
Jn     3:19  of light because their deeds were **e**.
       3:20  All those who do **e** hate the light,
      17:15  you protect them from the **e** one.
Ro     1:30  they invent ways of doing **e**;
       2: 8  who reject the truth and follow **e**,
       2: 9  for every human being who does **e**:
       3: 8  "Let us do **e** that good may
       6:12  body so that you obey its **e** desires.
       7:19  to do, but the **e** I do not want to do—
       7:21  to do good, **e** is right there with me.
      12: 9  Hate what is **e**; cling to what is
      12:17  Do not repay anyone **e** for **e**.
      12:21  by **e**, but overcome **e** with good.
      14:16  you know is good be spoken of as **e**.
      16:19  good, and innocent about what is **e**.
1Co   10: 6  our hearts on **e** things as they did.
      13: 6  Love does not delight in **e**
      14:20  In regard to **e** be infants, but in your
Gal    1: 4  to rescue us from the present **e** age,
Eph    5:16  opportunity, because the days are **e**.
       6:12  against the spiritual forces of **e**
       6:16  all the flaming arrows of the **e** one.
Col    1:21  minds because of your **e** behavior.
       3: 5  lust, **e** desires and greed, which is
2Th    3: 3  you and protect you from the **e** one.
1Ti    6:10  of money is a root of all kinds of **e**.
2Ti    2:22  Flee the **e** desires of youth
       3: 6  are swayed by all kinds of **e** desires,
Heb    5:14  to distinguish good from **e**.
Jas    1:13  For God cannot be tempted by **e**,
       1:21  filth and the **e** that is so prevalent
       2: 4  and become judges with **e** thoughts?
       3: 6  a world of **e** among the parts
       3: 8  It is a restless **e**, full of deadly
       4:16  All such boasting is **e**.
1Pe    1:14  not conform to the **e** desires you had
       2:16  your freedom as a cover-up for **e**;
       3: 9  Do not repay **e** with **e** or insult
       3: 9  the contrary, repay **e** with blessing,

1Pe    3:10  days must keep your tongue from **e**
       3:12  the Lord is against those who do **e**."
       3:17  for doing good than for doing **e**.
2Pe    1: 4  in the world caused by **e** desires.
       3: 3  and following their own **e** desires.
1Jn    2:13  you have overcome the **e** one.
       2:14  and you have overcome the **e** one.
       3:12  Cain, who belonged to the **e** one
       3:12  Because his own actions were **e**
       5:18  and the **e** one cannot harm them.
       5:19  is under the control of the **e** one.
3Jn    1:11  do not imitate what is **e** but what is
       1:11  who does what is **e** has not seen
Jude   1:16  they follow their own **e** desires;
Rev   16:13  I saw three **e** spirits that looked like
      18: 2  and a haunt for every **e** spirit,

**EVIL SPIRIT** 1Sa 16:14, 15, 16, 23; 18:10; 19:9;
    Mt 12:43; Mk 1:23, 26; 3:30; 5:2, 8; 7:25; 9:25;
    Lk 4:33; 8:29; 9:42; 11:24; Ac 19:15, 16; Rev
    18:2

**EVIL SPIRITS** Mt 10:1; Mk 1:27; 3:11; 5:13;
    6:7; Lk 4:36; 6:18; 7:21; 8:2; Ac 5:16; 8:7;
    19:12, 13; Rev 16:13

**EVIL IN THE EYES OF THE †LORD** See
    EYES

**EVILDOER\*** [FVII]
2Sa    3:39  the Lord repay the **e** according
Ps   101: 8  I will cut off every **e** from the city
Pr    24:20  for the **e** has no future hope,
Mal    4: 1  arrogant and every **e** will be stubble,

**EVILDOERS** [EVIL]
1Sa   24:13  'From **e** come evil deeds,' so my
Job    8:20  or strengthen the hands of **e**.
      34: 8  He keeps company with **e**;
      34:22  no utter darkness, where **e** can hide.
Ps    14: 4  Do all these **e** know nothing?
      14: 6  You **e** frustrate the plans
      26: 5  I abhor the assembly of **e** and refuse
      36:12  See how the **e** lie fallen—
      53: 4  Do all these **e** know nothing?
      59: 2  Deliver me from **e** and save me
      64: 2  of the wicked, from the plots of **e**.
      92: 7  up like grass and all **e** flourish,
      92: 9  all **e** will be scattered.
      94: 4  all the **e** are full of boasting.
      94:16  will take a stand for me against **e**?
     119:115  from me, you **e**, that I may keep
     125: 5  the Lord will banish with the **e**.
     141: 4  deeds along with those who are **e**;
     141: 5  will still be against the deeds of **e**.
     141: 9  me safe from the traps set by **e**,
Pr    21:15  joy to the righteous but terror to **e**.
      24:19  Do not fret because of **e**
      28: 5  **E** do not understand what is right,
      29: 6  **E** are snared by their own sin,
Isa    1: 4  great, a brood of **e**, children given
      31: 2  wicked, against those who help **e**.
Jer   23:14  They strengthen the hands of **e**,
Hos   10: 9  Will not war again overtake the **e**
Mal    3:15  Certainly **e** prosper, and even
Mt     7:23  Away from me, you **e**!'
Lk    13:27  Away from me, all you **e**!'

Lk     18:11   robbers, e, adulterers—
2Ti     3:13   while e and impostors will go

## EVILS* [EVIL]
Mk     7:23   All these e come from inside

## EWE
2Sa   12: 3   except one little e lamb he had

## EXACT*
Ge    43:21   us found his silver—the e weight—
Est     4: 7   including the e amount of money
Pr    22:23   and will e life for life.
Mt     2: 7   from them the e time the star had
Jn     4:53   realized that this was the e time
Heb    1: 3   the e representation of his being,

## EXALT* [EXALTED, EXALTS]
Ex     15: 2   my father's God, and I will e him.
Jos     3: 7   "Today I will begin to e you
1Sa     2:10   and e the horn of his anointed."
1Ch   25: 5   the promises of God to e him.
       29:12   power to e and give strength to all.
Job    19: 5   If indeed you would e yourselves
Ps     30: 1   I will e you, LORD, for you lifted
       34: 3   let us e his name together.
       35:26   may all who e themselves over me
       37:34   He will e you to inherit the land;
       38:16   e themselves over me when my feet
       75: 6   or from the desert can e themselves.
       89:17   and by your favor you e our horn.
       99: 5   E the LORD our God and worship
       99: 9   E the LORD our God and worship
      107:32   Let them e him in the assembly
      118:28   you are my God, and I will e you.
      145: 1   I will e you, my God the King;
Pr      4: 8   Cherish her, and she will e you;
       25: 6   Do not e yourself in the king's
       30:32   "If you play the fool and e yourself,
Isa    24:15   e the name of the LORD, the God
       25: 1   I will e you and praise your name,
Eze   29:15   will never again e itself
Da     4:37   praise and e and glorify the King
       11:36   He will e and magnify himself
       11:37   but will e himself above them all.
Hos   11: 7   High, I will by no means e them.
Mt    23:12   who e themselves will be humbled,
Lk    14:11   who e themselves will be humbled,
       18:14   who e themselves will be humbled,
2Th    2: 4   will e himself over everything

## EXALTED* [EXALT]
Ex     15: 1   to the LORD, for he is highly e.
       15:21   to the LORD, for he is highly e.
Nu     24: 7   their kingdom will be e.
Jos     4:14   day the LORD e Joshua
2Sa     5:12   had e his kingdom for the sake
       22:47   E be my God, the Rock, my Savior!
       22:49   You e me above my foes;
       23: 1   of the man e by the Most High,
1Ch   14: 2   his kingdom had been highly e
       17:17   me as though I were the most e
       29:11   you are e as head over all.
       29:25   The LORD highly e Solomon
Ne     9: 5   and may it be e above all blessing
Job   24:24   For a little while they are e,

Job   36:22   "God is e in his power. Who is
       37:23   is beyond our reach and e in power;
Ps     18:46   to my Rock! E be God my Savior!
       18:48   You e me above my foes;
       21:13   Be e in your strength, LORD;
       27: 6   Then my head will be e
       35:27   "The LORD be e, who delights
       46:10   be e among the nations, I will be e in
               the earth."
       47: 9   earth belong to God; he is greatly e.
       57: 5   Be e, O God, above the heavens;
       57:11   Be e, O God, above the heavens;
       89:13   hand is strong, your right hand e.
       89:24   through my name his horn will be e.
       89:27   the most e of the kings of the earth.
       89:42   You have e the right hand of his
       92: 8   But you, LORD, are forever e.
       92:10   You have e my horn like
       97: 9   you are e far above all gods.
       99: 2   he is e over all the nations.
      108: 5   Be e, O God, above the heavens;
      113: 4   The LORD is e over all
      138: 2   you have so e your solemn decree
      138: 6   Though the LORD is e, he looks
      148:13   the LORD, for his name alone is e;
Pr     11:11   blessing of the upright a city is e,
Isa     2: 2   it will be e above the hills,
        2:11   the LORD alone will be e
        2:12   for all that is e (and they will be
        2:17   the LORD alone will be e
        5:16   the LORD Almighty will be e
        6: 1   high and e, and the train of his robe
       12: 4   and proclaim that his name is e.
       33: 5   The LORD is e, for he dwells
       33:10   "Now will I be e; now will I be
       52:13   be raised and lifted up and highly e.
       57:15   the high and e One says—
Jer    17:12   throne, e from the beginning,
La      2:17   you, he has e the horn of your foes;
Eze    21:26   The lowly will be e and the e will
Hos   13: 1   he was e in Israel.
Mic     6: 6   and bow down before the e God?
Mt    23:12   who humble themselves will be e.
Lk    14:11   who humble themselves will be e."
       18:14   who humble themselves will be e."
Ac     2:33   E to the right hand of God, he has
        5:31   God e him to his own right hand as
Php    1:20   now as always Christ will be e
        2: 9   Therefore God e him to the highest
Heb    7:26   from sinners, e above the heavens.

## EXALTS* [EXALT]
1Sa     2: 7   he humbles and he e.
Job    36: 7   them with kings and e them forever.
Ps     75: 7   He brings one down, he e another.
Pr     14:34   Righteousness e a nation, but sin

## EXAMINE [EXAMINED, EXAMINES]
Job   34:23   God has no need to e people further,
Ps     11: 4   everyone on earth; his eyes e them.
       17: 3   though you e me at night and test
       26: 2   try me, e my heart and my mind;
Jer    17:10   search the heart and e the mind,
       20:12   you who e the righteous and probe
La      3:40   Let us e our ways and test them,
1Co   11:28   to e themselves before they eat

2Co 13: 5 **E** yourselves to see whether you are

## EXAMINED* [EXAMINE]
Job  5:27 "We have **e** this, and it is true.
     13: 9 Would it turn out well if he **e** you?
Lk  23:14 I have **e** him in your presence
Ac  17:11 **e** the Scriptures every day to see
    28:18 They **e** me and wanted to release

## EXAMINES [EXAMINE]
Lev 13: 3 When the priest **e** them, he shall
Ps  11: 5 The LORD **e** the righteous,
Pr   5:21 the LORD, and he **e** all your paths.

## EXAMPLE* [EXAMPLES]
2Ki 14: 3 everything he followed the **e** of his
Ecc  9:13 saw under the sun this **e** of wisdom
Eze 14: 8 and make them an **e** and a byword.
Jn  13:15 I have set you an **e** that you should
Ro  6:19 I am using an **e** from everyday life
   7: 2 For **e**, by law a married woman is
1Co 11: 1 Follow my **e**, as I follow the **e** of Christ.
Gal  3:15 let me take an **e** from everyday life.
Eph  5: 1 Follow God's **e**, therefore,
Php  3:17 Join together in following my **e**,
2Th  3: 7 how you ought to follow our **e**.
1Ti  1:16 his immense patience as an **e**
   4:12 set an **e** for the believers in speech,
Tit   2: 7 everything set them an **e** by doing
Heb  4:11 following their **e** of disobedience.
Jas   3: 4 Or take ships as an **e**.
   5:10 as an **e** of patience in the face
1Pe  2:21 leaving you an **e**, that you should
2Pe  2: 6 made them an **e** of what is going
Jude 1: 7 They serve as an **e** of those who

## EXAMPLES* [EXAMPLE]
1Co 10: 6 Now these things occurred as **e**
   10:11 These things happened to them as **e**
1Pe  5: 3 to you, but being **e** to the flock.

## EXASPERATE*
Eph  6: 4 Fathers, do not **e** your children;

## EXCEEDED
1Ki 10: 7 wealth you have far **e** the report I

## EXCEL* [EXCELLENT]
Ge  49: 4 you will no longer **e**, for you went
1Co 14:12 try to **e** in those that build
2Co  8: 7 But since you **e** in everything—
   8: 7 you also **e** in this grace of giving.

## EXCELLENT [EXCEL]
Ps  45: 2 You are the most **e** of men and your
1Co 12:31 yet I will show you the most **e** way.
Php  4: 8 if anything is **e** or praiseworthy—
1Ti  3:13 have served well gain an **e** standing
Tit   3: 8 These things are **e** and profitable

## EXCEPT
Nu  14:30 **e** Caleb son of Jephunneh
Dt  16: 6 **e** in the place he will choose as
2Sa 22:32 And who is the Rock **e** our God?
1Ki 15: 5 **e** in the case of Uriah the Hittite.

Hos 13: 4 no God but me, no Savior **e** me.
Mt   5:32 his wife, **e** for sexual immorality,
   11:27 No one knows the Son **e** the Father,
   11:27 no one knows the Father **e** the Son
   19: 9 his wife, **e** for sexual immorality,
Mk  10:18 "No one is good—**e** God alone.
Lk  11:29 none will be given it **e** the sign
Jn   3:13 into heaven **e** the one who came
   6:46 has seen the Father **e** the one who is
  14: 6 comes to the Father **e** through me.
  17:12 has been lost **e** the one doomed
1Co 10:13 has overtaken you **e** what is

## EXCESSIVE
2Co  2: 7 not be overwhelmed by **e** sorrow.

## EXCHANGE [EXCHANGED, EXCHANGING]
Mt  16:26 Or what can you give in **e** for your
Mk  8:37 Or what can you give in **e** for your
2Co  6:13 As a fair **e**—I speak as to my

## EXCHANGED [EXCHANGE]
Ps  106:20 They **e** their glorious God
Jer  2:11 my people have **e** their glorious God
Hos  4: 7 they **e** their glorious God
Ro  1:23 **e** the glory of the immortal God
   1:25 They **e** the truth about God for a lie,
   1:26 Even their women **e** natural sexual

## EXCHANGING* [EXCHANGE]
Jn   2:14 and others sitting at tables **e** money.

## EXCLAIM
Ps  35:10 My whole being will **e**, "Who is

## EXCLUDE* [EXCLUDED]
Isa 56: 3 "The LORD will surely **e** me
   66: 5 you, and **e** you because of my name,
Lk   6:22 when they **e** you and insult you
Rev 11: 2 But **e** the outer court;

## EXCLUDED [EXCLUDE]
Eph  2:12 **e** from citizenship in Israel

## EXCREMENT
2Ki 18:27 their own **e** and drink their own urine?"

## EXCUSE* [EXCUSES]
Lk  14:18 I must go and see it. Please **e** me.'
   14:19 way to try them out. Please **e** me.'
Jn  15:22 but now they have no **e** for their sin.
Ro  1:20 made, so that people are without **e**.
   2: 1 have no **e**, you who pass judgment

## EXCUSES* [EXCUSE]
Lk  14:18 "But they all alike began to make **e**.

## EXECUTE [EXECUTED]
Isa 66:16 sword the LORD will **e** judgment
Eze 20:35 to face, I will **e** judgment upon you.
Da   2:24 had appointed to **e** the wise men
   2:24 "Do not **e** the wise men of Babylon.
Jn  18:31 we have no right to **e** anyone,"

## EXECUTED [EXECUTE]
Mt 27:20 for Barabbas and to have Jesus e.

## EXERTED*
Eph 1:20 he e when he raised Christ

## EXHAUST* [EXHAUSTED, EXHAUSTION]
Jer 51:58 the peoples e themselves
Hab 2:13 that the nations e themselves

## EXHAUSTED [EXHAUST]
Da 8:27 I lay e for several days.
Lk 22:45 found them asleep, e from sorrow.

## EXHAUSTION* [EXHAUST]
Pr 6: 3 Go—to the point of e

## EXHORT* [EXHORTATION]
1Ti 5: 1 but e him as if he were your father.

## EXHORTATION* [EXHORT]
Ac 13:15 you have a word of e for the people,
Heb 13:22 urge you to bear with my word of e,

## EXILE [EXILED, EXILES]
2Ki 17:23 their homeland into e in Assyria,
    25:11 into e the people who remained
Ezr 6:21 who had returned from the e ate it,
Ne 1: 2 remnant that had survived the e,
Est 2: 6 who had been carried into e
Isa 5:13 Therefore my people will go into e
Jer 13:19 All Judah will be carried into e,
    48: 7 and Chemosh will go into e,
    49: 3 for Molek will go into e,
La 1: 3 harsh labor, Judah has gone into e.
Am 9:14 bring my people Israel back from e.

## EXILED [EXILE]
Ne 1: 9 then even if your e people are

## EXILES [EXILE]
Ezr 6:19 the e celebrated the Passover.
Ps 147: 2 he gathers the e of Israel.
Isa 56: 8 he who gathers the e of Israel:
Jer 24: 5 I regard as good the e from Judah,
Eze 11:25 I told the e everything the LORD
Zep 3:19 rescue the lame; I will gather the e.
1Pe 2:11 as foreigners and e,

## EXISTS
Ecc 6:10 Whatever e has already been
Heb 2:10 and through whom everything e,
    11: 6 comes to him must believe that he e

## EXODUS*
Heb 11:22 spoke about the e of the Israelites

## EXPANSES*
Job 38:18 Have you comprehended the vast e

## EXPECT [EXPECTANTLY, EXPECTATION, EXPECTED, EXPECTING]
Isa 64: 3 awesome things that we did not e,
Mt 11: 3 or should we e someone else?"
    24:44 at an hour when you do not e him.
Lk 12:40 at an hour when you do not e him."
Php 1:20 I eagerly e and hope that I will in no

## EXPECTANTLY [EXPECT]
Ps 5: 3 requests before you and wait e.

## EXPECTATION* [EXPECT]
Eze 19: 5 her hope unfulfilled, her e gone,
Ro 8:19 waits in eager e for the children
Heb 10:27 but only a fearful e of judgment

## EXPECTED [EXPECT]
Ge 48:11 "I never e to see your face again,
Hag 1: 9 "You e much, but see, it turned

## EXPECTING [EXPECT]
Lk 6:35 to them without e to get anything

## EXPEL* [EXPELLED]
1Co 5:13 "E the wicked person from among

## EXPELLED* [EXPEL]
1Sa 28: 3 Saul had e the mediums
1Ki 15:12 He e the male shrine prostitutes
Ezr 10: 8 and would himself be e
Eze 28:16 God, and I e you, guardian cherub,
Ac 13:50 and e them from their region.

## EXPENSE* [EXPENSIVE]
Lk 10:35 you for any extra e you may have.'
1Co 9: 7 serves as a soldier at his own e?

## EXPENSIVE* [EXPENSE]
Mt 26: 7 an alabaster jar of very e perfume,
Mk 14: 3 an alabaster jar of very e perfume,
Lk 7:25 No, those who wear e clothes
Jn 12: 3 a pint of pure nard, an e perfume;
1Ti 2: 9 or gold or pearls or e clothes,

## EXPERIENCE [EXPERIENCED]
Heb 11: 5 this life, so that he did not e death:

## EXPERIENCED [EXPERIENCE]
Dt 11: 2 e the discipline of the LORD your
Jos 24:31 who had e everything the LORD
Gal 3: 4 Have you e so much in vain

## EXPERT [EXPERTS]
Mt 22:35 One of them, an e in the law,
Lk 10:25 one occasion an e in the law stood
    10:37 The e in the law replied, "The one

## EXPERTS [EXPERT]
Lk 11:52 "Woe to you e in the law,

## EXPLAIN [EXPLAINED, EXPLAINING, EXPLAINS, EXPLANATION]

Ge   41:24  but none of them could e it to me."
2Ch   9: 2  was too hard for him to e to her.
Job  15:17  "Listen to me and I will e to you;
Da    2: 6  if you tell me the dream and e it,
Mt   13:36  "E to us the parable of the weeds
     15:15  Peter said, "E the parable to us."
Jn    4:25  comes, he will e everything to us."
Rev  17· 7  I will e to you the mystery

## EXPLAINED [EXPLAIN]

Jdg  14:17  She in turn e the riddle to her
1Sa  10:25  Samuel e to the people the rights
Mk    4:34  his own disciples, he e everything.
Lk   24:27  he e to them what was said in all
Ac   18:26  and e to him the way of God more

## EXPLAINING* [EXPLAIN]

Jdg  14:15  your husband into e the riddle
Isa  28: 9  To whom is he e his message?
Ac   17: 3  e and proving that the Messiah had
     28:23  e about the kingdom of God,
1Co   2:13  e spiritual realities with Spirit-taught

## EXPLAINS* [EXPLAIN]

Ac    8:31  said, "unless someone e it to me?"

## EXPLANATION* [EXPLAIN]

Ecc   8: 1  Who knows the e of things?
Da    7:23  "He gave me this e:

## EXPLOIT* [EXPLOITED, EXPLOITING, EXPLOITS]

Pr   22:22  Do not e the poor because they are
Isa  58: 3  you please and e all your workers.
2Co  11:20  or e you or take advantage of you
     12:17  Did I e you through any of the men
     12:18  Titus did not e you, did he?
2Pe   2: 3  their greed these teachers will e you

## EXPLOITED* [EXPLOIT]

2Co   7: 2  corrupted no one, we have e no one.

## EXPLOITING* [EXPLOIT]

Jas   2: 6  Is it not the rich who are e you?

## EXPLOITS [EXPLOIT]

1Ch  11:19  Such were the e of the three mighty

## EXPLORE [EXPLORED]

Nu   13: 2  "Send some men to e the land
Jos  14: 7  from Kadesh Barnea to e the land.
Ecc   1:13  and to e by wisdom all that is done

## EXPLORED [EXPLORE]

Nu   13:21  e the land from the Desert of Zin as

## EXPOSE [EXPOSED]

Job  20:27  The heavens will e his guilt;
Pr   13:16  but fools e their folly.
Mt    1:19  and did not want to e her to public
1Co   4: 5  and will e the motives of people's

Eph   5:11  of darkness, but rather e them.

## EXPOSED [EXPOSE]

Ex   20:26  lest your nakedness be e on it.'
Pr   26:26  but their wickedness will be e
Eze  23:29  shame of your prostitution will be e.
Hab   2:16  Drink and let your nakedness be e!
Jn    3:20  for fear that their deeds will be e.
2Co  11:23  and been e to death again and again.
Eph   5:13  everything e by the light becomes
Heb  10:33  Sometimes you were publicly e
Rev  16:15  not go naked and be shamefully e."

## EXPOUND*

Dt    1: 5  Moses began to e this law, saying:
Ps   49: 4  with the harp I will e my riddle:

## EXPRESS [EXPRESSING]

2Sa  10: 2  sent a delegation to e his sympathy

## EXPRESSING* [EXPRESS]

Gal   5: 6  counts is faith e itself through love.

## EXTEND [EXTENDED, EXTENDS, EXTENT]

Ex   25:32  Six branches are to e from the sides
Dt   11:24  Your territory will e from the desert
Jos   1. 4  Your territory will e from the desert
Ps  110: 2  The LORD will e your mighty
Isa  66:12  "I will e peace to her like a river,
Zec   9:10  His rule will e from sea to sea

## EXTENDED [EXTEND]

Ezr   7:28  and who has e his good favor to me
Est   8: 4  the king e the gold scepter to Esther

## EXTENDS [EXTEND]

Pr   31:20  poor and e her hands to the needy.
Lk    1:50  His mercy e to those who fear him,

## EXTENT* [EXTEND]

1Co  11:18  and to some extent I believe it.
2Co   2: 5  grieved all of you to some extent

## EXTERMINATE* [EXTERMINATING]

1Ki   9:21  whom the Israelites could not e—
Eze  25: 7  and e you from the countries.

## EXTERMINATING* [EXTERMINATE]

Jos  11:20  them totally, e them without mercy,

## EXTERNAL*

Heb   9:10  e regulations applying until the time

## EXTINGUISH* [EXTINGUISHED]

Eph   6:16  you can e all the flaming arrows

## EXTINGUISHED* [EXTINGUISH]

2Sa  21:17  the lamp of Israel will not be e."
Isa  43:17  never to rise again, e,

## EXTOL*

1Ch  16: 4  to e, thank, and praise the LORD,

Job 36:24 Remember to **e** his work,
Ps 34: 1 I will **e** the LORD at all times;
68: 4 **e** him who rides on the clouds;
95: 2 thanksgiving and **e** him with music
109:30 mouth I will greatly **e** the LORD;
111: 1 I will **e** the LORD with all my
115:18 it is we who **e** the LORD,
117: 1 **e** him, all you peoples.
145: 2 praise you and **e** your name for ever
145:10 your faithful people **e** you.
147:12 **E** the LORD, Jerusalem;
Ro 15:11 let all the peoples **e** him.'"

## EXTORT* [EXTORTION]

Eze 22:12 **e** unjust gain from your neighbors.
Lk 3:14 "Don't **e** money and don't accuse

## EXTORTION [EXTORT]

Lev 6: 4 what they have stolen or taken by **e**,
Ps 62:10 Do not trust in **e** or put vain hope
Pr 28:16 A tyrannical ruler practices **e**,
Ecc 7: 7 **E** turns the wise into fools,
Isa 33:15 who reject gain from **e** and keep
Eze 22:29 The people of the land practice **e**
Hab 2: 6 and makes himself wealthy by **e**!

## EXTRAORDINARY*

Ac 19:11 God did **e** miracles through Paul,

## EXTREME

2Co 8: 2 and their **e** poverty welled up in rich

## EXULT*

Ps 89:16 they **e** in your righteousness.
Isa 14: 8 the cedars of Lebanon **e** over you

## EYE [EYES]

Ge 2: 9 trees that were pleasing to the **e**
3: 6 good for food and pleasing to the **e**,
Ex 21:24 **e** for **e**, tooth for tooth,
Lev 24:20 fracture for fracture, **e** for **e**,
Dt 19:21 life for life, **e** for **e**, tooth for tooth,
Ezr 5: 5 But the **e** of their God was watching
Ps 17: 8 Keep me as the apple of your **e**;
94: 9 Does he who formed the **e** not see?
Pr 7: 2 my teachings as the apple of your **e**.
30:17 "The **e** that mocks a father,
Ecc 1: 8 The **e** never has enough of seeing,
Isa 64: 4 no **e** has seen any God besides you,
Zec 2: 8 you touches the apple of his **e**—
12: 4 keep a watchful **e** over the house
Mt 5:29 If your right **e** causes you
5:38 have heard that it was said, '**E** for **e**,
6:22 "The **e** is the lamp of the body.
7: 3 of sawdust in someone else's **e**
7: 3 to the plank in your own **e**?
18: 9 if your **e** causes you to stumble,
Mk 10:25 to go through the **e** of a needle than
1Co 2: 9 "What no **e** has seen, what no ear
12:16 "Because I am not an **e**, I do not
15:52 in the twinkling of an **e**, at the last
Eph 6: 6 to win their favor when their **e** is
Col 3:22 not only when their **e** is on you
Rev 1: 7 and "every **e** will see him,

## EYES [EYE]

Ge 3: 7 the **e** of both of them were opened,
6: 8 found favor in the **e** of the LORD.
18: 3 "If I have found favor in your **e**,
Ex 15:26 God and do what is right in his **e**,
34: 9 "if I have found favor in your **e**,
Nu 11:15 if I have found favor in your **e**—
15:39 the lusts of your own hearts and **e**.
22:31 the LORD opened Balaam's **e**,
33:55 remain will become barbs in your **e**
Dt 11:12 the **e** of the LORD your God are
12:25 what is right in the **e** of the LORD.
16:19 for a bribe blinds the **e** of the wise
34: 4 I have let you see it with your **e**,
Jos 23:13 on your backs and thorns in your **e**,
Jdg 16:28 on the Philistines for my two **e**."
1Sa 15:17 you were once small in your own **e**,
1Ki 10: 7 I came and saw with my own **e**.
2Ki 6:17 prayed, "Open his **e**, LORD,
6:17 the LORD opened the servant's **e**,
9:30 she painted her **e**, arranged her hair
2Ch 16: 9 For the **e** of the LORD range
Job 31: 1 "I made a covenant with my **e** not
36: 7 does not take his **e** off the righteous;
42: 5 of you but now my **e** have seen you.
Ps 13: 3 Give light to my **e**, or I will sleep
19: 8 are radiant, giving light to the **e**.
25:15 My **e** are ever on the LORD,
36: 1 is no fear of God before their **e**.
36: 2 their own **e** they flatter themselves
66: 7 his power, his **e** watch the nations—
101: 6 My **e** will be on the faithful
115: 5 but cannot speak, **e**, but cannot see.
118:23 this, and it is marvelous in our **e**.
119:18 Open my **e** that I may see wonderful
119:37 Turn my **e** away from worthless
121: 1 I lift up my **e** to the mountains—
123: 1 I lift up my **e** to you, to you who sit
123: 2 As the **e** of slaves look to the hand
123: 2 so our **e** look to the LORD our
139:16 your **e** saw my unformed body.
141: 8 But my **e** are fixed on you,
Pr 3: 7 Do not be wise in your own **e**;
4:25 Let your **e** look straight ahead;
6:17 haughty **e**, a lying tongue,
15: 3 The **e** of the LORD are
15:30 Light in a messenger's **e** brings joy to
17:24 a fool's **e** wander to the ends
20: 8 he winnows out all evil with his **e**.
22:12 The **e** of the LORD keep watch
23:29 Who has bloodshot **e**?
26: 5 or they will be wise in their own **e**.
26:16 their own **e** than seven people who
28:11 The rich are wise in their own **e**;
Ecc 2:10 denied myself nothing my **e** desired;
SS 4: 1 Your **e** behind your veil are doves.
Isa 1:15 prayer, I will hide my **e** from you;
6: 5 and my **e** have seen the King,
6:10 their ears dull and close their **e**.
11: 3 judge by what he sees with his **e**,
33:17 Your **e** will see the king in his
42: 7 to open **e** that are blind, to free
Jer 9: 1 water and my **e** a fountain of tears!
24: 6 My **e** will watch over them for their
La 3:48 from my **e** because my people are
Eze 1:18 four rims were full of **e** all around.
24:16 from you the delight of your **e**.

Da    7: 8   This horn had **e** like the **e**
     10: 6   lightning, his **e** like flaming torches,
Am    9: 4   "I will fix my **e** on them for evil
Hab   1:13   Your **e** are too pure to look on evil;
Zec   3: 9   There are seven **e** on that one stone,
      4:10   since the seven **e** of the LORD
Mt    6:22   If your **e** are healthy, your whole
     13:15   ears, and they have closed their **e**.
     13:15   they might see with their **e**,
     21:42   this, and it is marvelous in our **e**'?
Mk    8:25   the man's **e**. Then his **e** were opened,
Lk   10:23   "Blessed are the **e** that see what
     16:15   justify yourselves in the **e** of others,
     24:31   Then their **e** were opened and they
Jn    4:35   open your **e** and look at the fields!
      9:10   "How then were your **e** opened?"
     12:40   "He has blinded their **e**
     12:40   so they can neither see with their **e**,
Ac    1: 9   he was taken up before their very **e**,
      4:19   "Which is right in God's **e**: to listen
      9: 8   when he opened his **e** he could see
     28:27   ears, and they have closed their **e**.
     28:27   they might see with their **e**,
Ro   11:10   May their **e** be darkened so they
2Co   4:18   So we fix our **e** not on what is seen,
      8:21   not only in the **e** of the Lord
      8:21   the Lord but also in the **e** of others.
Gal   4:15   you would have torn out your **e**
Eph   1:18   pray that the **e** of your heart may be
Php   3:17   your **e** on those who live as we do.
Heb   4:13   and laid bare before the **e** of him
     12: 2   fixing our **e** on Jesus, the pioneer
Jas   2: 5   who are poor in the **e** of the world
1Pe   3:12   For the **e** of the Lord are
1Jn   1: 1   which we have seen with our **e**,
      2:16   the lust of their **e** and their boasting
Rev   1:14   and his **e** were like blazing fire.
      2:18   whose **e** are like blazing fire
      4: 6   and they were covered with **e**,
      5: 6   Lamb had seven horns and seven **e**,
      7:17   away every tear from their **e**.' "
     19:12   His **e** are like blazing fire,
     21: 4   will wipe every tear from their **e**.

### EVIL IN THE EYES OF THE †LORD Dt
4:25; 17:2; Jdg 2:11; 3:7, 12; 4:1; 6:1; 10:6; 13:1;
1Sa 15:19; 1Ki 11:6; 14:22; 15:26, 34; 16:19, 25,
30; 21:20, 25; 22:52; 2Ki 3:2; 8:18, 27; 13:2, 11;
14:24; 15:9, 18, 24, 28; 17:2, 17; 21:2, 6, 16, 20;
23:32, 37; 24:9, 19; 2Ch 21:6; 22:4; 29:6; 33:2,
6, 22; 36:5, 9, 12; Jer 52:2

### RIGHT IN THE EYES OF THE †LORD
Dt 12:25, 28; 21:9; 1Ki 15:5, 11; 22:43; 2Ki
12:2; 14:3; 15:3, 34; 16:2; 18:3; 22:2; 2Ch 14:2;
20:32; 24:2; 25:2; 26:4; 27:2; 28:1; 29:2; 34:2

### FAVOR IN ... EYES Ge 6:8; 18:3; 19:19;
30:27; 32:5; 33:8, 10, 15; 34:11; 39:4, 21; 47:25,
29; 50:4; Ex 34:9; Nu 11:15; 32:5; Jdg 6:17; Ru
2:10, 13; 1Sa 1:18; 20:3, 29; 27:5; 2Sa 14:22;
15:25; 16:4

### EYEWITNESSES* [WITNESS]
Lk    1: 2   by those who from the first were **e**
2Pe   1:16   but we were **e** of his majesty.

## EZEKIEL
Priest called to be prophet to the exiles (Eze 1–3).
Symbolically acted out destruction of Jerusalem (Eze
4–5; 12; 24).

## EZION GEBER
1Ki   9:26   Solomon also built ships at **E**,
     22:48   they were wrecked at **E**.

## EZRA
Priest and teacher of the Law who led a return of
exiles to Israel to reestablish temple and worship (Ezr
7–8). Corrected intermarriage of priests (Ezr 9–10).
Read Law at celebration of Feast of Tabernacles (Ne
8). Participated in dedication of Jerusalem's walls (Ne
12).

# F

## FACE   [FACED, FACEDOWN, FACES]
Ge    4: 6   Why is your **f** downcast?
      7: 4   from the **f** of the earth every living
     11: 9   LORD scattered them over the **f**
     32:30  "It is because I saw God **f** to **f**,
Ex    3: 6   Moses hid his **f**, because he was
     33:11   would speak to Moses **f** to **f**, as one
     33:20  "you cannot see my **f**, for no one
     34:29   that his **f** was radiant because he had
Nu    6:25   the LORD make his **f** shine on you
     12: 8   With him I speak **f** to **f**,
     14:14   LORD, have been seen **f** to **f**,
Dt    5: 4   The LORD spoke to you **f** to **f**
     31:17   I will hide my **f** from them, and they
     34:10   whom the LORD knew **f** to **f**,
Jdg   6:22   the angel of the LORD **f** to **f**!"
2Sa  14:24   he must not see my **f**."
     14:24   and did not see the **f** of the king.
2Ki  14: 8   "Come, meet me **f** to **f**."
1Ch  16:11   and his strength; seek his **f** always.
2Ch   7:14   and seek my **f** and turn from their
     25:17   "Come, meet me **f** to **f**."
     30: 9   He will not turn his **f** from you
Ezr   9: 6   to lift up my **f** to you, because our
Ne    2: 2   "Why does your **f** look so sad
Est   7: 8   mouth, they covered Haman's **f**.
Job   1:11   he will surely curse you to your **f**."
Ps    4: 6   Let the light of your **f** shine on us.
     10:11   he covers his **f** and never sees."
     13: 1   How long will you hide your **f**
     27: 8   his **f**!" Your **f**, LORD, I will seek.
     31:16   Let your **f** shine on your servant;
     44: 3   and the light of your **f**, for you loved
     44:22   your sake we **f** death all day long;
     51: 9   Hide your **f** from my sins and blot
     67: 1   bless us and make his **f** shine on us—
     80: 3   make your **f** shine on us, that we
    104:29   When you hide your **f**, they are
    105: 4   and his strength; seek his **f** always.
    119:135  Make your **f** shine on your servant
Pr   15:13   A happy heart makes the **f** cheerful,
Ecc   7: 3   because a sad **f** is good for the heart.
      8: 1   Wisdom brightens the **f** and changes

SS      2:14  show me your f, let me hear your
        2:14  voice is sweet, and your f is lovely.
Isa     8:17  who is hiding his f from the house
       50: 7  Therefore have I set my f like flint,
       50: 8  Let us f each other!
       54: 8  a surge of anger I hid my f from you
Jer    32: 4  will speak with him f to f and see
       34: 3  and he will speak with you f to f.
Eze     1:10  the four had the f of a human being,
        1:10  each also had the f of an eagle.
       10:14  One f was that of a cherub,
       10:14  the second the f of a human being,
       10:14  the third the f of a lion,
       10:14  and the fourth the f of an eagle.
       39:23  So I hid my f from them and handed
       39:29  I will no longer hide my f
Da     10: 6  was like topaz, his f like lightning,
Hos     5:15  borne their guilt and seek my f—
Mt     17: 2  His f shone like the sun, and his
       18:10  in heaven always see the f of my
       26:67  they spit in his f and struck him
Lk      9:29  the appearance of his f changed,
Jn     19: 3  And they slapped him in the f.
Ac      6:15  they saw that his f was like the f
Ro      8:36  your sake we f death all day long;
1Co    13:12  in a mirror; then we shall see f to f.
2Co     3: 7  steadily at the f of Moses because
        4: 6  glory displayed in the f of Christ.
       10: 1  who am "timid" when f to f
1Pe     3:12  but the f of the Lord is against those
2Jn     1:12  to visit you and talk with you f to f,
3Jn     1:14  see you soon, and we will talk f to f.
Rev     1:16  His f was like the sun shining in all
        4: 7  ox, the third had a f like a man,
       10: 1  his f was like the sun, and his legs
       22: 4  They will see his f, and his name

## FACED  [FACE]
Ex     37: 9  The cherubim f each other,
Eze     1:17  of the four directions the creatures f;

## FACEDOWN  [FACE]
Ge     17: 3  Abram fell f, and God said to him,
Lev     9:24  it, they shouted for joy and fell f.
Nu     16: 4  When Moses heard this, he fell f.
Jos     5:14  Then Joshua fell f to the ground
        7: 6  fell f to the ground before the ark
Mt     17: 6  heard this, they fell f to the ground,

## FACES  [FACE]
1Ch    12: 8  Their f were the f of lions, and they
Ps     34: 5  their f are never covered
       83:16  Cover their f with shame, LORD,
Isa     6: 2  two wings they covered their f,
Eze     1: 6  but each of them had four f and four
       10:14  Each of the cherubim had four f:
       41:18  Each cherub had two f:
Mt      6:16  they disfigure their f to show others
2Co     3:18  unveiled f contemplate the Lord's
Jas     1:23  who look at their f in a mirror
Rev     9: 7  gold, and their f resembled human f.
       11:16  fell on their f and worshiped God,

## FACT  [FACTS]
Jn      4: 2  in f it was not Jesus who baptized,

## FACTIONS*
1Ki    16:21  of Israel were split into two f;
2Co    12:20  outbursts of anger, f, slander,
Gal     5:20  rage, selfish ambition, dissensions,

## FACTS*  [FACT]
Ac     19:36  since these f are undeniable,

## FADE  [FADING]
Ps    109:23  I f away like an evening shadow;
Jas     1:11  the rich will f away even while they
1Pe     1: 4  that can never perish, spoil or f.
        5: 4  of glory that will never f away.

## FADING  [FADE]
Isa     1:30  will be like an oak with f leaves,

## FAIL  [FAILED, FAILING, FAILINGS, FAILS]
Lev    26:15  and f to carry out all my commands
Nu     15:22  as a community unintentionally f
1Ki     2: 4  you will never f to have a successor
1Ch    28:20  He will not f you or forsake you
2Ch    34:33  they did not f to follow the LORD,
Ps     69: 3  My eyes f, looking for my God.
       89:28  my covenant with him will never f.
Pr      8:36  those who f to find me harm
               themselves;
       15:22  Plans f for lack of counsel,
Isa    51: 6  my righteousness will never f.
       58:11  like a spring whose waters never f.
Jer    33:17  'David will never f to have a man
La      3:22  for his compassions never f.
Eze     2: 5  whether they listen or f to listen—
       47:12  will not wither, nor will their fruit f.
Zep     3: 5  and every new day he does not f,
Mk      8:18  but f to see, and ears but f to hear?
Lk      1:37  For no word from God will ever f."
       12:33  treasure in heaven that will never f,
       22:32  Simon, that your faith may not f.
Ac      5:38  activity is of human origin, it will f.
2Co    13: 5  unless, of course, you f the test?

## FAILED  [FAIL]
Jos    21:45  promises to the house of Israel f;
       23:14  LORD your God gave you has f.
       23:14  has been fulfilled; not one has f.
1Ki     8:56  Not one word has f of all the good
       15: 5  and had not f to keep any
Ne      9:17  and f to remember the miracles you
Ps     77: 8  Has his promise f for all time?
Ro      9: 6  is not as though God's word had f.
2Co    13: 6  discover that we have not f the test.

## FAILING*  [FAIL]
Ge     48:10  Now Israel's eyes were f because
Dt      8:11  God, f to observe his commands,
1Sa    12:23  I should sin against the LORD by f

## FAILINGS*  [FAIL]
Ro     15: 1  ought to bear with the f of the weak

## FAILS  [FAIL]
Ps    143: 7  me quickly, LORD; my spirit f.

Joel  1:10  new wine is dried up, the olive oil **f**
Hab  3:17  though the olive crop **f**
1Co 13: 8  Love never **f**. But where there are

## FAINT [FAINTHEARTED, FAINTS]

Job 26:14  how **f** the whisper we hear of him!
Ps 142: 3  When my spirit grows **f** within me,
SS    2: 5  me with apples, for I am **f** with love.
Isa 40:31  weary, they will walk and not be **f**.
Jer 31:25  refresh the weary and satisfy the **f**."
La    5:17  Because of this our hearts are **f**,

## FAINTHEARTED* [FAINT, HEART]

Dt  20: 3  Do not be **f** or afraid; do not be
      20: 8  shall add, "Is anyone afraid or **f**?

## FAINTS* [FAINT]

Ps  84: 2  even **f**, for the courts of the LORD;
    119:81  My soul **f** with longing for your

## FAIR [FAIRLY, FAIRNESS]

Job 26:13  By his breath the skies became **f**;
Pr    1: 3  doing what is right and just and **f**;
Hos 10:11  so I will put a yoke on her **f** neck.
Mt  16: 2  'It will be **f** weather, for the sky is
Col   4: 1  your slaves with what is right and **f**,

## FAIRLY [FAIR]

Lev 19:15  the great, but judge your neighbor **f**.
Pr  31: 9  Speak up and judge **f**;
Eze 18: 8  and judges **f** between two parties.

## FAIRNESS* [FAIR]

Pr  29:14  If a king judges the poor with **f**,

## FAITH* [FAITHFUL, FAITHFULLY, FAITHFULNESS, FAITHLESS]

Ex  21: 8  because he has broken **f** with her.
Dt  32:51  because both of you broke **f** with me
Jos 22:16  'How could you break **f**
Jdg  9:16  good **f** by making Abimelek king?
      9:19  in good **f** toward Jerub-Baal and his
1Sa 14:33  "You have broken **f**," he said.
2Ch 20:20  Have **f** in the LORD your God
      20:20  have **f** in his prophets anD
Isa   7: 9  If you do not stand firm in your **f**,
      26: 2  may enter, the nation that keeps **f**.
Mt   6:30  more clothe you—you of little **f**
      8:10  anyone in Israel with such great **f**
      8:26  "You of little **f**, why are you so
      9: 2  When Jesus saw their **f**, he said
      9:22  he said, "your **f** has healed you."
      9:29  "According to your **f** let it be done
     13:58  there because of their lack of **f**.
     14:31  "You of little **f**," he said, "why did
     15:28  to her, "Woman, you have great **f**!
     16: 8  "You of little **f**, why are you talking
     17:20  "Because you have so little **f**.
     17:20  if you have **f** as small as a mustard
     21:21  you, if you have **f** and do not doubt,
     24:10  time many will turn away from the **f**
Mk   2: 5  When Jesus saw their **f**, he said
      4:40  Do you still have no **f**?"
      5:34  "Daughter, your **f** has healed you.
      6: 6  He was amazed at their lack of **f**.

Mk 10:52  said Jesus, "your **f** has healed you."
     11:22  "Have **f** in God," Jesus answered.
     16:14  *he rebuked them for their lack of f*
Lk   5:20  When Jesus saw their **f**, he said,
      7: 9  I have not found such great **f** even
      7:50  the woman, "Your **f** has saved you;
      8:25  "Where is your **f**?" he asked his
      8:48  "Daughter, your **f** has healed you.
     12:28  will he clothe you—you of little **f**!
     17: 5  said to the Lord, "Increase our **f**!"
     17: 6  "If you have **f** as small as a mustard
     17:19  your **f** has made you well."
     18: 8  comes, will he find **f** on the earth?"
     18:42  your **f** has healed you."
     22:32  you, Simon, that your **f** may not fail.
Jn   2:11  and his disciples put their **f** in him.
      7:31  in the crowd put their **f** in him.
      8:30  as he spoke, many put their **f** in him.
     11:45  what Jesus did, put their **f** in him.
     12:11  to Jesus and putting their **f** in him.
     12:42  not openly acknowledge their **f**
     14:12  all who have **f** in me will do
Ac   3:16  By **f** in the name of Jesus, this man
      3:16  the **f** that comes through him
      6: 5  a man full of **f** and of the Holy
      6: 7  of priests became obedient to the **f**.
     11:24  full of the Holy Spirit and **f**,
     13: 8  to turn the proconsul from the **f**.
     14: 9  him, saw that he had **f** to be healed
     14:22  them to remain true to the **f**.
     14:27  how he had opened a door of **f**
     15: 9  for he purified their hearts by **f**.
     16: 5  churches were strengthened in the **f**
     20:21  and have **f** in our Lord Jesus.
     24:24  to him as he spoke about **f** in Christ
     26:18  among those who are sanctified by **f**
     27:25  men, for I have **f** in God that it will
Ro   1: 5  to call all the Gentiles to **f**
      1: 8  because your **f** is being reported all
      1:12  encouraged by each other's **f**.
      1:17  that is by **f** from first to last,
      1:17  "The righteous will live by **f**."
      3:22  righteousness is given through **f**
      3:25  of his blood—to be received by **f**.
      3:26  one who justifies those who have **f**
      3:27  of the "law" that requires **f**.
      3:28  a person is justified by **f** apart
      3:30  will justify the circumcised by **f**
      3:30  uncircumcised through that same **f**.
      3:31  we, then, nullify the law by this **f**?
      4: 5  their **f** is credited as righteousness.
      4: 9  that Abraham's **f** was credited
      4:11  **f** while he was still uncircumcised.
      4:12  of the **f** that our father Abraham had
      4:13  the righteousness that comes by **f**.
      4:14  **f** means nothing and the promise is
      4:16  the promise comes by **f**, so that it
      4:16  to those who have the **f** of Abraham.
      4:19  Without weakening in his **f**, he
      4:20  was strengthened in his **f** and gave
      5: 1  we have been justified through **f**,
      5: 2  whom we have gained access by **f**
      9:30  it, a righteousness that is by **f**;
      9:32  Because they pursued it not by **f**
     10: 6  the righteousness that is by **f** says:
     10: 8  the message concerning **f** that we
     10:10  you profess your **f** and are saved.

Ro  10:17  f comes from hearing the message,
    11:20  of unbelief, and you stand by f.
    12: 3  with the f God has distributed
    12: 6  prophesy in accordance with your f;
    14: 1  Accept those whose f is weak,
    14: 2  One person's f allows them to eat
    14: 2  but another person, whose f is weak,
    14:23  because their eating is not from f;
    14:23  that does not come from f is sin.
    16:26  all the Gentiles might come to f and
           obedience—
1Co  2: 5  so that your f might not rest
     7:22  when called to f in the Lord
    12: 9  to another f by the same Spirit,
    13: 2  I have a f that can move mountains,
    13:13  these three remain: f, hope and love.
    15:14  preaching is useless and so is your f.
    15:17  has not been raised, your f is futile;
    16:13  stand firm in the f; be courageous;
2Co  1:24  Not that we lord it over your f,
     1:24  because it is by f you stand firm.
     4:13  Since we have that same spirit of f,
     5: 7  We live by f, not by sight.
     8: 7  in f, in speech, in knowledge,
    10:15  is that, as your f continues to grow,
    13: 5  to see whether you are in the f;
Gal  1:23  is now preaching the f he once tried
     2:16  the law, but by f in Jesus Christ.
     2:16  have put our f in Christ Jesus
     2:16  we may be justified by f in Christ
     2:20  body, I live by f in the Son of God,
     3: 7  who have f are children of Abraham.
     3: 8  God would justify the Gentiles by f,
     3: 9  who rely on f are blessed along with
           Abraham, the man of f.
     3:11  "the righteous will live by f."
     3:12  The law is not based on f;
     3:14  by f we might receive the promise
     3:22  being given through f in Jesus
     3:23  Before the coming of this f, we were
     3:23  law, locked up until the f that was
     3:24  came that we might be justified by f.
     3:25  Now that this f has come, we are no
     3:26  are all children of God through f,
     5: 5  f we eagerly await through the Spirit
     5: 6  counts is f expressing itself through
Eph  1:15  heard about your f in the Lord Jesus
     2: 8  you have been saved, through f—
     3:12  through f in him we may approach
     3:17  may dwell in your hearts through f.
     4: 5  one Lord, one f, one baptism;
     4:13  until we all reach unity in the f
     6:16  take up the shield of f,
     6:23  and love with f from God the Father
Php  1:25  for your progress and joy in the f,
     1:27  one accord for the f of the gospel
     2:17  and service coming from your f,
     3: 9  that which is through f in Christ—
     3: 9  comes from God on the basis of f.
Col  1: 4  have heard of your f in Christ Jesus
     1: 5  the f and love that spring
     1:23  if you continue in your f,
     2: 5  are and how firm your f in Christ is.
     2: 7  in the f as you were taught,
     2:12  him through your f in the working
1Th  1: 3  Father your work produced by f,
     1: 8  your f in God has become known

1Th  3: 2  and encourage you in your f,
     3: 5  I sent to find out about your f.
     3: 6  has brought good news about your f
     3: 7  about you because of your f.
     3:10  and supply what is lacking in your f.
     5: 8  be sober, putting on f and love as
2Th  1: 3  because your f is growing more
     1: 4  and f in all the persecutions
     1:11  and your every deed prompted by f.
     3: 2  evil people, for not everyone has f.
1Ti  1: 2  To Timothy my true son in the f:
     1: 4  which is by f.
     1: 5  a good conscience and a sincere f.
     1:14  along with the f and love that are
     1:19  holding on to f and a good
     1:19  shipwreck with regard to the f.
     2:15  if they continue in f,
     3: 9  of the f with a clear conscience.
     3:13  assurance in their f in Christ Jesus.
     4: 1  later times some will abandon the f
     4: 6  nourished on the truths of the f
     4:12  conduct, in love, in f and in purity.
     5: 8  has denied the f and is worse than
     6:10  have wandered from the f
     6:11  righteousness, godliness, f, love,
     6:12  Fight the good fight of the f.
     6:21  so doing have departed from the f.
2Ti  1: 5  I am reminded of your sincere f,
     1:13  with f and love in Christ Jesus.
     2:18  and they destroy the f of some.
     2:22  youth and pursue righteousness, f,
     3: 8  who, as far as the f is concerned,
     3:10  way of life, my purpose, f, patience,
     3:15  salvation through f in Christ Jesus.
     4: 7  finished the race, I have kept the f.
Tit  1: 1  Christ to further the f of God's elect
     1: 4  Titus, my true son in our common f:
     1:13  so that they will be sound in the f
     2: 2  and sound in f, in love
     3:15  Greet those who love us in the f.
Phm  1: 5  people and your f in the Lord Jesus.
     1: 6  with us in the f may be effective
Heb  4: 2  because they did not share the f
     4:14  us hold firmly to the f we profess.
     6: 1  that lead to death, and of f in God,
     6:12  to imitate those who through f
    10:22  a sincere heart in full assurance of f,
    10:38  my righteous one will live by f.
    11: 1  Now f is being sure of what we
    11: 3  By f we understand that the universe
    11: 4  f Abel brought God a better offering
    11: 4  f he was commended as righteous,
    11: 4  And by f Abel still speaks,
    11: 5  By f Enoch was taken from this life,
    11: 6  without f it is impossible to please
    11: 7  By f Noah, when warned
    11: 7  By his f he condemned the world
    11: 7  that is in keeping with f.
    11: 8  By f Abraham, when called to go
    11: 9  By f he made his home
    11:11  And by f even Sarah, who was past
    11:13  these people were still living by f
    11:17  By f Abraham, when God tested
    11:20  By f Isaac blessed Jacob and Esau
    11:21  By f Jacob, when he was dying,
    11:22  By f Joseph, when his end was near,
    11:23  By f Moses' parents hid him

Heb 11:24 By f Moses, when he had grown up,
    11:27 By f he left Egypt, not fearing
    11:28 By f he kept the Passover
    11:29 f the people passed through the Red
    11:30 By f the walls of Jericho fell,
    11:31 By f the prostitute Rahab,
    11:33 who through f conquered kingdoms,
    11:39 were all commended for their f,
    12: 2 Jesus, the pioneer and perfecter of f.
    13: 7 their way of life and imitate their f.
Jas  1: 3 of your f produces perseverance.
    2: 5 the eyes of the world to be rich in f
    2:14 if people claim to have f but have no
    2:14 Can such f save them?
    2:17 In the same way, f by itself, if it is
    2:18 But someone will say, "You have f;
    2:18 Show me your f without deeds,
    2:18 I will show you my f by what I do.
    2:20 that f without deeds is useless?
    2:22 You see that his f and his actions
    2:22 his f was made complete by what he
    2:24 by what they do and not by f alone.
    2:26 is dead, so f without deeds is dead.
    5:15 offered in f will make them well;
1Pe  1: 5 who through f are shielded by God's
    1: 7 These have come so that your f—
    1: 9 receiving the end result of your f,
    1:21 and so your f and hope are in God.
    5: 9 standing firm in the f, because you
2Pe  1: 1 have received a f as precious as
    1: 5 effort to add to your f goodness;
1Jn  5: 4 has overcome the world, even our f.
Jude  1: 3 for the f that the Lord has once
    1:20 yourselves up in your most holy f
Rev  2:13 You did not renounce your f in me,
    2:19 your love and f, your service

# FAITHFUL* [FAITH]

Nu  12: 7 he is f in all my house.
Dt   7: 9 he is the f God, keeping his
    32: 4 A f God who does no wrong,
    33: 8 he is f in all my house.
1Sa  2: 9 guard the feet of his f servants,
    2:35 I will raise up for myself a f priest,
2Sa 20:19 We are the peaceful and f in Israel.
    22:26 "To the f you show yourself f,
1Ki  3: 6 David, because he was f to you
2Ch  6:41 may your f people rejoice in
    31:18 For they were f in consecrating
    31:20 and f before the LORD his God.
Ne   9: 8 You found his heart f to you,
Ps   4: 3 has set apart his f servant for himself;
    12: 1 LORD, for no one is f anymore;
    16:10 let your f one see decay.
    18:25 To the f you show yourself f,
    25:10 and f toward those who keep
    30: 4 you his f people; praise
    31: 5 LORD, my f God.
    31:23 Love the LORD, all his f people!
    32: 6 Therefore let all the f pray to you
    33: 4 right and true; he is f in all he does.
    37:28 just and will not forsake his f ones.
    43: 3 Send me your light and your f care,
    52: 9 in the presence of your f people.
    78: 8 whose spirits were not f to him.
    78:37 him, they were not f to his covenant.
    85: 8 promises peace to his people, his f

Ps  86: 2 Guard my life, for I am f to you;
    89:19 a vision, to your f people you said:
    89:24 My f love will be with him,
    89:37 the moon, the f witness in the sky."
    97:10 for he guards the lives of his f ones
   101: 6 My eyes will be on the f in the land,
   111: 7 The works of his hands are f
   116:15 is the death of those f to him.
   132: 9 may your f people sing for joy.' "
   132:16 her f people will ever sing
   145:10 LORD; your f people extol you
   145:13 all he promises and f in all he does.
   145:17 his ways and f in all he does.
   146: 6 he remains f forever.
   148:14 praise of all his f servants,
   149: 5 his f people rejoice in this
   149: 9 the glory of all his f people.
Pr   2: 8 and protects the way of his f ones.
    20: 6 love, but a f person who can find?
    28:20 A f person will be richly blessed,
    31:26 and f instruction is on her tongue.
Isa  1:21 See how the f city has become
    1:26 City of Righteousness, the F City."
    49: 7 who is f, the Holy One of Israel,
    55: 3 you, my f love promised to David.
Jer  3:12 for I am f,' declares the LORD,
    42: 5 f witness against us if we do not act
Eze 43:11 so that they may be f to its design
    48:11 who were f in serving me and did
Hos 11:12 God, even against the f Holy One.
Mic  7: 2 The f have been swept from the land;
    7:20 You will be f to Jacob,
Zec  8: 8 I will be f and righteous to them as
Mt  24:45 then is the f and wise servant,
    25:21 'Well done, good and f servant!
    25:21 You have been f with a few things;
    25:23 'Well done, good and f servant!
    25:23 You have been f with a few things;
Lk  12:42 then is the f and wise manager,
Ro  12:12 patient in affliction, f in prayer.
1Co  1: 9 God is f, who has called you
    4: 2 been given a trust must prove f.
    4:17 whom I love, who is f in the Lord.
    10:13 And God is f; he will not let you be
2Co  1:18 But as surely as God is f,
Eph  1: 1 in Ephesus, the f in Christ Jesus:
    6:21 brother and f servant in the Lord,
Col  1: 2 the f brothers and sisters in Christ:
    1: 7 who is a f minister of Christ on our
    4: 7 a f minister and fellow servant
    4: 9 Onesimus, our f and dear brother,
1Th  5:24 The one who calls you is f, and he
2Th  3: 3 But the Lord is f, and he will
1Ti  2: 7 true and f teacher of the Gentiles.
    3: 2 above reproach, f to his wife,
    3:12 A deacon must be f to his wife
    5: 9 sixty, has been f to her husband,
2Ti  2:13 he remains f, for he cannot disown
Tit  1: 6 elder must be blameless, f to his wife,
Heb  2:17 and f high priest in service to God,
    3: 2 He was f to the one who appointed
    3: 2 just as Moses was f in all God's
    3: 5 "Moses was f as a servant in all
    3: 6 Christ is f as the Son over God's
    8: 9 because they did not remain f to my
    10:23 profess, for he who promised is f.
    11:11 she considered him f who had made

1Pe 4:10 as f stewards of God's grace
      4:19 themselves to their f Creator
      5:12 whom I regard as a f brother, I have
1Jn  1: 9 he is f and just and will forgive us
3Jn  1: 5 you are f in what you are doing
Rev  1: 5 who is the f witness, the firstborn
      2:10 Be f, even to the point of death,
      2:13 in the days of Antipas, my f witness,
      3:14 of the Amen, the f and true witness,
     14:12 commands and remain f to Jesus.
     17:14 his called, chosen and f followers."
     19:11 whose rider is called F and True.

## FAITHFULLY [FAITH]

Dt   11:13 So if you f obey the commands I am
Jos   2:14 and f when the LORD gives us
1Sa  12:24 and serve him f with all your heart;
1Ki   2: 4 and if they walk f before me with all
2Ki  20: 3 how I have walked before you f
2Ch  19: 9 "You must serve f
     31:12 they f brought in the contributions,
     31:15 and Shekaniah assisted him f
     32: 1 all that Hezekiah had so f done,
     34:12 The workers did their work f.
Ne    9:33 you have acted f, while we acted
     13:14 what I have so f done for the house
Isa  38: 3 how I have walked before you f
Jer  23:28 the one who has my word speak it f.
Eze  18: 9 my decrees and f keeps my laws.

## FAITHFULNESS* [FAITH]

Ge   24:27 his kindness and f to my master.
     24:49 show kindness and f to my master,
     32:10 and f you have shown your servant.
     47:29 you will show me kindness and f.
Ex   34: 6 to anger, abounding in love and f,
Jos  24:14 the LORD and serve him with all f.
1Sa  26:23 man for his righteousness and f.
2Sa   2: 6 now show you kindness and f, and I
     15:20 LORD show you kindness and f."
Ps   26: 3 lived in reliance on your f.
     30: 9 Will it proclaim your f?
     36: 5 to the heavens, your f to the skies.
     40:10 I speak of your f and your saving
     40:10 and your f from the great assembly.
     40:11 love and f always protect me.
     51: 6 you desired f even in the womb;
     54: 5 in your f destroy them.
     57: 3 God sends forth his love and his f.
     57:10 your f reaches to the skies.
     61: 7 your love and f to protect him.
     71:22 praise you with the harp for your f,
     85:10 Love and f meet together;
     85:11 F springs forth from the earth,
     86:11 that I may rely on your f;
     86:15 to anger, abounding in love and f.
     88:11 in the grave, your f in Destruction?
     89: 1 will make your f known through all
     89: 2 that you have established your f
     89: 5 LORD, your f too, in the assembly
     89: 8 mighty, and your f surrounds you.
     89:14 love and f go before you.
     89:33 him, nor will I ever betray my f.
     89:49 in your f you swore to David?
     91: 4 his f will be your shield
     92: 2 in the morning and your f at night,

Ps   96:13 and the peoples in his f.
     98: 3 love and his f to the house of Israel;
    100: 5 his f continues through all
    108: 4 your f reaches to the skies.
    111: 8 ever, enacted in f and uprightness.
    115: 1 glory, because of your love and f.
    117: 2 the f of the LORD endures forever.
    119:30 I have chosen the way of f;
    119:75 and that in f you have afflicted me.
    119:90 Your f continues through all
    138: 2 for your unfailing love and your f,
    143: 1 in your f and righteousness come
Pr    3: 3 Let love and f never leave you;
     14:22 plan what is good find love and f.
     16: 6 Through love and f sin is atoned for;
     20:28 Love and f keep a king safe;
Isa  11: 5 belt and f the sash around his waist.
     16: 5 in f a man will sit on it—
     25: 1 perfect f you have done wonderful
     38:18 to the pit cannot hope for your f.
     38:19 tell their children about your f.
     40: 6 human f is like the flowers of the field.
     42: 3 In f he will bring forth justice;
     61: 8 In my f I will reward my people
La    3:23 new every morning; great is your f.
Hos   2:20 I will betroth you in f, and you will
      4: 1 "There is no f, no love,
Hab   2: 4 the righteous will live by their f—
Mt   23:23 of the law—justice, mercy and f.
Ro    3: 3 their unfaithfulness nullify God's f?
Gal   5:22 patience, kindness, goodness, f,
3Jn   1: 3 and testify to your f to the truth,
Rev  13:10 and f on the part of God's people.

## FAITHLESS* [FAITH]

Ps   78:57 ancestors they were disloyal and f,
    101: 3 I hate what f people do; I will have
    119:158 I look on the f with loathing,
Pr   14:14 The f will be fully repaid for their
Jer   3: 6 you seen what f Israel has done?
      3: 8 I gave f Israel her certificate
      3:11 "F Israel is more righteous than
      3:12 " 'Return, f Israel,'
      3:14 "Return, f people,"
      3:22 "Return, f people; I will cure you
     12: 1 Why do all the f live at ease?
2Ti   2:13 if we are f, he remains faithful,

## FALL [DOWNFALL, FALLEN, FALLING, FALLS, FELL]

Ge    2:21 LORD God caused the man to f
     27:13 him, "My son, let the curse f on me.
Lev  26: 7 they will f by the sword before you.
Nu   14:29 this wilderness your bodies will f—
Dt   32: 2 Let my teaching f like rain and my
1Sa   3:19 of Samuel's words f to the ground.
1Ch  21:13 Let me f into the hands
     21:13 do not let me f into human hands."
Ps   13: 4 and my foes will rejoice when I f.
     37:24 they will not f, for the LORD
     46: 5 God is within her, she will not f;
     69: 9 of those who insult you f on me.
     91: 7 A thousand may f at your side,
    145:14 The LORD upholds all who f
Pr   11:28 who trust in their riches will f,
     16:18 a haughty spirit before a f.

Pr   24:16  though the righteous **f** seven times,
     24:17  Do not gloat when your enemies **f**;
     28:14  harden their hearts **f** into trouble.
Ecc   4:10  they **f** down, they can help each other
Ecc  10: 8  Whoever digs a pit may **f** into it;
Isa   8:14  and a rock that makes them **f**.
     40: 7  The grass withers and the flowers **f**,
     40:30  and young men stumble and **f**;
     65:12  and all of you will **f** in the slaughter;
Jer   6:15  So they will **f** among the fallen;
     34:17  'freedom' to **f** by the sword,
La    1: 9  Her **f** was astounding;
Hos  10: 8  and to the hills, "**F** on us!"
Mt    7:25  yet it did not **f**, because it had its
     13:21  they quickly **f** away.
Mk    4:17  of the word, they quickly **f** away.
     13:25  the stars will **f** from the sky,
     14:27  "You will all **f** away," Jesus told
Lk   10:18  "I saw Satan **f** like lightning
     11:17  a house divided against itself will **f**.
     23:30  say to the mountains, "**F** on us!"
Jn   16: 1  that you will not **f** away.
Ro    3:23  and **f** short of the glory of God,
      9:33  and a rock that makes them **f**,
     11:11  stumble so as to **f** beyond recovery?
     14: 4  To their own master they stand or **f**.
     14:21  will cause your brother or sister to **f**.
1Co   8:13  my brother or sister to **f** into sin,
      8:13  so that I will not cause them to **f**.
     10:12  firm, be careful that you don't **f**!
Heb  10:31  It is a dreadful thing to **f**
1Pe   2: 8  and a rock that makes them **f**."
Rev   6:16  "**F** on us and hide us from the face

## FALLEN  [FALL]

1Sa   5: 3  **f** on his face on the ground before
2Sa   1:19  How the mighty have **f**!
Ps   36:12  See how the evildoers lie **f**—
Isa  14:12  How you have **f** from heaven,
     21: 9  'Babylon has **f**, has **f**!
Am    9:11  day I will restore David's **f** shelter—
Jn   11:11  "Our friend Lazarus has **f** asleep;
Ac   15:16  return and rebuild David's **f** tent.
1Co  11:30  and a number of you have **f** asleep.
     15: 6  living, though some have **f** asleep.
     15:18  who have **f** asleep in Christ are lost.
     15:20  of those who have **f** asleep.
Gal   5: 4  you have **f** away from grace.
1Th   4:15  precede those who have **f** asleep.
Heb   4: 1  of you be found to have **f** short of it.
      6: 6  and who have **f** away,
Rev   9: 1  I saw a star that had **f** from the sky
     14: 8  angel followed and said, " '**F**!
     17:10  Five have **f**, one is, the other has not
     18: 2  " '**F**! **F** is Babylon the Great!'

## FALLING  [FALL]

Lk   22:44  like drops of blood **f** to the ground.

## FALLS  [FALL]

Pr   11:14  For lack of guidance a nation **f**,
Lk   20:18  Everyone who **f** on that stone will
     20:18  on whom it **f** will be crushed."
Jn   12:24  a kernel of wheat **f** to the ground
Heb  12:15  that no one **f** short of the grace of God

## FALSE  [FALSEHOOD, FALSELY]

Ex   20:16  shall not give **f** testimony against
     23: 1  "Do not spread **f** reports.
     23: 7  Have nothing to do with a **f** charge
Dt    5:20  shall not give **f** testimony against
Job  36: 4  Be assured that my words are not **f**;
Ps    4: 2  you love delusions and seek **f** gods?
Pr   12:17  the truth, but a **f** witness tells lies.
     13: 5  The righteous hate what is **f**,
     14: 5  but a **f** witness pours out lies.
     14:25  lives, but a **f** witness is deceitful.
     19: 5  A **f** witness will not go unpunished,
     21:28  Those who give **f** witness will
     25:18  one who gives **f** testimony against
Isa  44:25  who foils the signs of **f** prophets
Jer  14:14  are prophesying to you **f** visions,
     23:16  they fill you with **f** hopes.
     50:36  A sword against her **f** prophets!
Eze  13: 6  Their visions are **f** and their
Am    2: 4  they have been led astray by **f** gods,
Mt    7:15  "Watch out for **f** prophets.
     15:19  theft, **f** testimony, slander.
     24:11  and many **f** prophets will appear
     24:24  For **f** messiahs and **f** prophets will
Mk   10:19  you shall not give **f** testimony,
     13:22  For **f** messiahs and **f** prophets will
     14:57  gave this **f** testimony against him:
Lk    6:26  ancestors treated the **f** prophets.
     18:20  steal, you shall not give **f** testimony,
Ac    6:13  They produced **f** witnesses,
     13: 6  and **f** prophet named Bar-Jesus,
1Co  15:15  found to be **f** witnesses about God,
2Co  11:13  For such persons are **f** apostles,
     11:26  and in danger from **f** believers.
Gal   2: 4  arose because some **f** believers had
Php   1:18  whether from **f** motives or true,
Col   2:18  anyone who delights in **f** humility
      2:23  their **f** humility and their harsh
1Ti   1: 3  not to teach **f** doctrines any longer
2Pe   2: 1  also **f** prophets among the people,
      2: 1  there will be **f** teachers among you.
1Jn   4: 1  because many **f** prophets have gone
Rev  16:13  out of the mouth of the **f** prophet.
     19:20  and with him the **f** prophet who had
     20:10  and the **f** prophet had been thrown.

## FALSE PROPHET  Ac 13:6; Rev 16:13; 19:20; 20:10

## FALSE PROPHETS  Isa 44:25; Jer 50:36; Mt 7:15; 24:11, 24; Mk 13:22; Lk 6:26; 2Pe 2:1; 1Jn 4:1

## FALSEHOOD*  [FALSE]

Job  21:34  is left of your answers but **f**!"
     31: 5  "If I have walked with **f** or my foot
Ps   52: 3  **f** rather than speaking the truth.
    119:163  hate and detest **f** but I love your law.
Pr   30: 8  Keep **f** and lies far from me;
Isa  28:15  our refuge and **f** our hiding place."
Ro    3: 7  my **f** enhances God's truthfulness
Eph   4:25  Therefore each of you must put off **f**
1Jn   4: 6  the Spirit of truth and the spirit of **f**.
Rev  22:15  everyone who loves and practices **f**.

## FALSELY  [FALSE]

Lev  19:12  " 'Do not swear **f** by my name

Isa   59:  3  Your lips have spoken f,
Da     6:24  men who had f accused Daniel were
Zec    5:  3  everyone who swears f will be
Mt     5:11  f say all kinds of evil against you
Mk   14:56  Many testified f against him,
Lk     3:14  money and don't accuse people f—
1Ti    6:20  ideas of what is f called knowledge,

## FALTER* [FALTERED, FALTERING]

Pr    24:10  If you f in a time of trouble,
Isa   42:  4  he will not f or be discouraged till

## FALTERED* [FALTER]

Ps    26:  1  in the LORD and have not f.
       105:37  from among their tribes no one f.

## FALTERING* [FALTER]

Ex     6:12  to me, since I speak with f lips?"
       6:30  "Since I speak with f lips,
Job    4:  4  you have strengthened f knees.

## FAME [FAMOUS]

Dt    26:19  f and honor high above all
Jos    9:  9  of the f of the LORD your God.
1Ch  14:17  So David's f spread throughout
2Ch    9:  1  of Sheba heard of Solomon's f,
Isa   66:19  islands that have not heard of my f
Hab    3:  2  LORD, I have heard of your f;

## FAMILIAR

Isa   53:  3  a man of suffering, and f with pain.

## FAMILIES [FAMILY]

Ex     1:21  God, he gave them f of their own.
Nu     1:  2  community by their clans and f,
       26:  2  whole Israelite community by f—
Ps    68:  6  God sets the lonely in f, he leads
       107:41  and increased their f like flocks.
Jer   31:  1  be the God of all the f of Israel,
Am     3:  2  I chosen of all the f of the earth;

## FAMILY [FAMILIES]

Ge     7:  1  ark, you and your whole f, because I
       24:38  go to my father's f and to my own
Dt    25:  9  not build up his brother's f line."
Jos    6:23  They brought out her entire f
Ru     3:  9  since you are a f guardian."
       4:10  will not disappear from among his f
       4:14  not left you without a f guardian.
1Sa   18:18  what is my f or my clan in Israel,
2Ch  22:10  to destroy the whole royal f
Ezr    2:62  These searched for their f records,
Est    2:20  had kept secret her f background
Pr    31:15  she provides food for her f
Zec  11:14  breaking the f bond between Judah and
Lk     9:61  go back and say good-by to my f."
       12:52  in one f divided against each other,
Ac    10:  2  He and all his f were devout
Gal    6:10  who belong to the f of believers.
Eph    3:15  from whom every f in heaven
1Ti    3:  4  He must manage his own f well
       5:  4  practice by caring for their own f
Heb   11:  7  holy fear built an ark to save his f.

## FAMINE [FAMINES]

Ge    12:10  Now there was a f in the land,
       12:10  for a while because the f was severe.
       26:  1  Now there was a f in the land—
       26:  1  besides the previous f in Abraham's
       41:27  They are seven years of f.
       42:  5  for the f was in the land of Canaan
       43:  1  Now the f was still severe
Dt    32:24  I will send wasting f against them,
Ru     1:  1  ruled, there was a f in the land.
1Ki   18:  2  Now the f was severe in Samaria,
2Ki    4:38  and there was a f in that region.
       6:25  There was a great f in the city;
Ps    37:19  in days of f they will enjoy plenty.
Jer   14:15  'No sword or f will touch this land.'
       14:15  prophets will perish by sword and f.
Eze    5:16  deadly and destructive arrows of f,
       5:16  bring more and more f upon you
Am     8:11  I will send a f through the land—
       8:11  not a f of food or a thirst for water,
       8:11  but a f of hearing the words
Lk     4:25  was a severe f throughout the land.
Ac    11:28  a severe f would spread over
Ro     8:35  or persecution or f or nakedness
Rev   18:  8  death, mourning and f.

## FAMINES [FAMINE]

Lk    21:11  f and pestilences in various places,

## FAMOUS [FAME]

Ru     4:11  in Ephrathah and be f in Bethlehem.
2Sa    8:13  David became f after he returned
1Ki    1:47  Solomon's name more f than yours

## FAN*

2Ti    1:  6  this reason I remind you to f

## FANTASIES*

Ps    73:20  Lord, you will despise them as f.
Pr    12:11  those who chase f have no sense.
       28:19  those who chase f will have their fill

## FAR

Ge    18:25  F be it from you to do such a thing—
       18:25  the wicked alike. F be it from you!
Nu    16:  3  said to them, "You have gone too f!
Jos   24:16  "F be it from us to forsake
1Sa    7:12  "Thus f the LORD has helped
       12:23  me, f be it from me that I should sin
Ps    22:  1  Why are you so f from saving me,
       22:  1  me, so f from the words of my
       103:12  as f as the east is from the west, so f
       119:155  Salvation is f from the wicked,
Pr    31:10  She is worth f more than rubies.
Isa   29:13  lips, but their hearts are f from me.
       57:19  peace, to those f and near,"
Jer   23:23  LORD, "and not a God f away?
Mk     7:  6  lips, but their hearts are f from me.
Rev    2:  5  Consider how f you have fallen!

## FARMER

Mk     4:  3  A f went out to sow his seed.
2Ti    2:  6  The hardworking f should be
Jas    5:  7  See how the f waits for the land

## FASHIONED [FASHIONING]

Ex  39: 8  They **f** the breastpiece—the work
Ps  94: 9  he who **f** the ear not hear?
Isa 37:19  wood and stone, **f** by human hands.
    45:18  he who **f** and made the earth,

## FASHIONING* [FASHIONED, FASHIONS]

Ex  32: 4  the shape of a calf, **f** it with a tool.

## FASHIONS [FASHIONING]

Isa 44:15  But he also **f** a god and worships it;

## FAST [FASTED, FASTING]

Dt  10:20  Hold **f** to him and take your oaths
    11:22  to him and to hold **f** to him—
    13: 4  serve him and hold **f** to him.
    30:20  listen to his voice, and hold **f** to him.
Jos 22: 5  to hold **f** to him and to serve him
    23: 8  to hold **f** to the LORD your God,
1Ki 11: 2  Solomon held **f** to them in love.
2Ki 18: 6  He held **f** to the LORD and did not
2Ch 20: 3  and he proclaimed a **f** for all Judah.
Ezr  8:21  I proclaimed a **f**, so that we might
Est  4:16  Jews who are in Susa, and **f** for me.
    4:16  I and my attendants will **f** as you do.
Ps  119:31  I hold **f** to your statutes, LORD;
   139:10  me, your right hand will hold me **f**.
Isa 56: 4  me and hold **f** to my covenant—
    58: 5  Is this the kind of **f** I have chosen,
    58: 5  Is that what you call a **f**, a day
Joel 1:14  Declare a holy **f**; call a sacred
Jnh  3: 5  They declared a **f**, and all of them,
Mt   6:16  "When you **f**, do not look somber
    9:14  **f** often, but your disciples do not **f**?"
1Pe  5:12  the true grace of God. Stand **f** in it.

## FASTED [FAST]

Isa 58: 3  'Why have we **f**,' they say, 'and you
Zec  7: 5  'When you **f** and mourned
    7: 5  was it really for me that you **f**?
Ac  13: 3  So after they had **f** and prayed,

## FASTING [FAST]

Ps  35:13  and humbled myself with **f**.
Isa 58: 6  not this the kind of **f** I have chosen:
Da   9: 3  in **f**, and in sackcloth and ashes.
Mt   4: 2  After **f** forty days and forty nights,
    6:16  their faces to show others they are **f**.
Ac  13: 2  were worshiping the Lord and **f**,
    14:23  with prayer and **f**, committed them

## FAT [FATTENED]

Ge   4: 4  **f** portions from some of the firstborn
Lev  3:16  All the **f** is the LORD's.
Jdg  3:17  of Moab, who was a very **f** man.
Ps  66:15  I will sacrifice **f** animals to you
Eze 34:20  will judge between the **f** sheep

## FATAL

Ex  21:12  someone a **f** blow is to be put to death.
Na   3:19  can heal you; your wound is **f**.
Rev 13: 3  but the **f** wound had been healed.

## FATE

Job 20:29  Such is the **f** God allots the wicked,
Ps  49:13  This is the **f** of those who trust
Ecc  2:14  that the same **f** overtakes them both.

## FATHER [ANCESTOR, FATHER'S, FATHER-IN-LAW, FATHERLESS, FATHERS, FOREFATHER, FOREFATHERS, PARENT]

Ge   2:24  this reason a man will leave his **f**'
    17: 4  You will be the **f** of many nations.
    19:32  Let's get our **f** to drink wine
    26:24  "I am the God of your **f** Abraham.
    27:38  you have only one blessing, my **f**?
    27:38  Bless me too, my **f**!"
    31: 5  the God of my **f** has been with me.
    46: 3  God, the God of your **f**," he said.
Ex  20:12  "Honor your **f** and your mother,
    21:15  "Anyone who attacks their **f**
    21:17  "Anyone who curses their **f**
    22:17  If her **f** absolutely refuses to give
Lev 18: 7  " 'Do not dishonor your **f**
    19: 3  you must respect your mother and **f**,
    20: 9  " 'Anyone who curses their **f**
Dt   1:31  carried you, as a **f** carries his son,
    5:16  "Honor your **f** and your mother,
    21:18  son who does not obey his **f**
    32: 6  Is he not your **F**, your Creator,
Jdg 17:10  with me and be my **f** and priest,
    18:19  with us, and be our **f** and priest.
Ru   4:17  Obed the **f** of Jesse, and Jesse the **f**
2Sa  7:14  I will be his **f**, and he will be my
1Ki  2:12  sat on the throne of his **f** David,
1Ch 17:13  I will be his **f**, and he will be my
    22:10  will be my son, and I will be his **f**.
    28: 6  to be my son, and I will be his **f**.
    29:10  the God of our **f** Israel,
Job 38:28  Does the rain have a **f**?
Ps   2: 7  today I have become your **f**.
    27:10  Though my **f** and mother forsake
    68: 5  A **f** to the fatherless, a defender
    89:26  out to me, 'You are my **F**, my God,
   103:13  As a **f** has compassion on his
Pr   3:12  loves, as a **f** the son he delights in.
    10: 1  Wise children bring joy to their **f**,
    15:20  Wise children bring joy to their **f**,
    17:25  children bring grief to their **f**
    19:26  Whoever robs their **f** and drives
    20:20  If you curse your **f** or mother,
    23:22  Listen to your **f**, who gave you life,
    23:24  The **f** of a righteous child has great
    28:24  Whoever robs their **f** or mother
    29: 3  loves wisdom brings joy to his **f**,
Isa  8: 4  the boy knows how to say 'My **f**'
    9: 6  God, Everlasting **F**, Prince of Peace.
    43:27  Your first **f** sinned; those I sent
    45:10  Woe to those who say to their **f**,
    63:16  But you are our **F**, though Abraham
    63:16  are our **F**, our Redeemer from of old
Jer  2:27  wood, 'You are my **f**,' and to stone,
    3:19  I thought you would call me '**F**'
    31: 9  because I am Israel's **f**, and Ephraim
Eze 18:19  the son not share the guilt of his **f**?'
Mic  7: 6  For a son dishonors his **f**, a daughter
Mal  1: 6  "A son honors his **f**, and slaves
    2:10  Do we not all have one **F**?

| | | |
|---|---|---|
| Mt | 3: 9 | 'We have Abraham as our **f**.' |
| | 5:16 | deeds and glorify your **F** in heaven. |
| | 6: 9 | " 'Our **F** in heaven, hallowed be |
| | 6:14 | your heavenly **F** will also forgive |
| | 6:15 | your **F** will not forgive your sins. |
| | 6:26 | and yet your heavenly **F** feeds them. |
| | 10:37 | "Anyone who loves their **f** |
| | 11:27 | No one knows the Son except the **F**, |
| | 11:27 | no one knows the **F** except the Son |
| | 15: 4 | said, 'Honor your **f** and mother' |
| | 18:10 | see the face of my **F** in heaven. |
| | 19: 5 | this reason a man will leave his **f** |
| | 19:19 | honor your **f** and mother,' and 'love |
| | 19:29 | brothers or sisters or **f** or mother |
| | 23: 9 | And do not call anyone on earth '**f**,' |
| | 23: 9 | for you have one **F**, and he is |
| | 28:19 | baptizing them in the name of the **F** |
| Mk | 14:36 | "*Abba*, **F**," he said, |
| Lk | 1:32 | give him the throne of his **f** David, |
| | 6:36 | merciful, just as your **F** is merciful. |
| | 9:59 | first let me go and bury my **f**." |
| | 11: 2 | " 'F, hallowed be your name, |
| | 12:30 | your **F** knows that you need them. |
| | 12:53 | **f** against son and son against **f**, |
| | 14:26 | me and does not hate **f** and mother, |
| | 15:12 | The younger one said to his **f**, 'F, |
| | 16:24 | So he called to him, 'F Abraham, |
| | 18:20 | honor your **f** and mother.' " |
| | 23:34 | Jesus said, "F, forgive them, |
| Jn | 1:14 | who came from the **F**, full of grace |
| | 1:18 | closest relationship with the **F**, |
| | 3:35 | The **F** loves the Son and has placed |
| | 4:23 | true worshipers will worship the **F** |
| | 5:17 | "My **F** is always at his work to this |
| | 5:18 | he was even calling God his own **F**, |
| | 5:20 | For the **F** loves the Son and shows |
| | 6:44 | me unless the **F** who sent me draws |
| | 6:46 | one has seen the **F** except the one |
| | 6:46 | is from God; only he has seen the **F**. |
| | 8:19 | "You do not know me or my **F**," |
| | 8:28 | speak just what the **F** has taught me. |
| | 8:41 | are doing the works of your own **f**." |
| | 8:41 | "The only **F** we have is God |
| | 8:44 | You belong to your **f**, the devil, |
| | 8:44 | for he is a liar and the **f** of lies. |
| | 10:17 | The reason my **F** loves me is that I |
| | 10:30 | I and the **F** are one." |
| | 10:38 | that the **F** is in me, and I in the **F**." |
| | 12:27 | 'F, save me from this hour'? |
| | 14: 6 | comes to the **F** except through me. |
| | 14: 9 | who has seen me has seen the **F**. |
| | 14: 9 | How can you say, 'Show us the **F**'? |
| | 14:11 | I am in the **F** and the **F** is in me; |
| | 14:21 | loves me will be loved by my **F**, |
| | 14:28 | to the **F**, for the **F** is greater than I. |
| | 15: 9 | "As the **F** has loved me, so have I |
| | 15:23 | who hate me hate my **F** as well. |
| | 20:17 | for I have not yet ascended to the **F**. |
| | 20:17 | am ascending to my **F** and your **F**, |
| | 20:21 | As the **F** has sent me, I am sending |
| Ac | 1: 4 | but wait for the gift my **F** promised, |
| | 13:33 | today I have become your **f**.' |
| Ro | 4:11 | he is the **f** of all who believe |
| | 4:16 | He is the **f** of us all. |
| | 8:15 | And by him we cry, "*Abba*, **F**." |
| 1Co | 4:15 | I became your **f** through the gospel. |
| 2Co | 1: 3 | God and **F** of our Lord Jesus Christ, |

| | | |
|---|---|---|
| 2Co | 1: 3 | the **F** of compassion and the God |
| | 6:18 | And, "I will be a **F** to you, and you |
| Gal | 4: 6 | Spirit who calls out, "*Abba*, **F**." |
| Eph | 5:31 | this reason a man will leave his **f** |
| | 6: 2 | "Honor your **f** and mother"— |
| Php | 2:11 | is Lord, to the glory of God the **F**. |
| 1Th | 2:11 | of you as a **f** deals with his own |
| Heb | 1: 5 | today I have become your **F**"? |
| | 1: 5 | "I will be his **F**, and he will be my |
| | 12: 7 | are not disciplined by their **f**? |
| | 12: 9 | should we submit to the **F** of spirits |
| Jas | 1:17 | from the **F** of the heavenly lights, |
| 1Jn | 1: 3 | our fellowship is with the **F** |
| | 2:15 | world, love for the **F** is not in you. |
| | 2:22 | denying the **F** and the Son. |
| | 3: 1 | what great love the **F** has lavished |
| 2Jn | 1: 9 | in the teaching has both the **F** |
| Rev | 2:27 | have received authority from my **F**. |
| | 3: 5 | their names before my **F** and his |
| | 3:21 | sat down with my **F** on his throne. |

**FATHER ABRAHAM** Ge 22:7; 26:3, 15, 18, 24; 28:13; 32:9; Jos 24:3; Lk 1:73; 16:24, 30; Jn 8:53, 56; Ac 7:2; Ro 4:12; Jas 2:21

**FATHER IN HEAVEN** Mt 5:16, 45; 6:1, 9; 7:11; 10:32, 33; 12:50; 16:17; 18:10, 14, 19; Mk 11:25; Lk 11:13

**HEAVENLY FATHER** Mt 5:48; 6:14, 26, 32; 15:13; 18:35

**GOD AND FATHER**  See GOD

**GOD OF ... FATHER**  See GOD

**GOD THE FATHER**  See GOD

**FATHER'S**  [FATHER]

| | | |
|---|---|---|
| Ge | 12: 1 | your **f** household to the land I will |
| | 27:34 | When Esau heard his **f** words, |
| | 31:19 | Rachel stole her **f** household gods. |
| | 49: 4 | for you went up onto your **f** bed, |
| Ex | 15: 2 | and I will praise him, my **f** God, |
| | 18: 4 | he said, "My **f** God was my helper; |
| 2Sa | 16:21 | your **f** concubines whom he left |
| Est | 4:14 | you and your **f** family will perish. |
| Pr | 4: 1 | Listen, my sons, to a **f** instruction; |
| | 19:13 | A foolish child is a **f** ruin, |
| Eze | 18:17 | He will not die for his **f** sin; |
| Mt | 16:27 | come in his **F** glory with his angels, |
| Lk | 2:49 | know I had to be in my **F** house?" |
| Jn | 2:16 | Stop turning my **F** house |
| | 5:43 | I have come in my **F** name, and you |
| | 10:29 | can snatch them out of my **F** hand. |
| | 14: 2 | My **F** house has plenty of room; |
| | 15: 8 | This is to my **F** glory, that you bear |
| Rev | 14: 1 | and his **F** name written on their |

**FATHER'S HOUSE**  See HOUSE

**FATHER-IN-LAW**  [FATHER]

| | | |
|---|---|---|
| Ex | 18: 8 | Moses told his **f** about everything |
| Jn | 18:13 | Annas, who was the **f** of Caiaphas, |

**FATHERLESS**  [FATHER]

| | | |
|---|---|---|
| Dt | 10:18 | He defends the cause of the **f** |
| | 14:29 | the **f** and the widows who live |

Dt   24:17  the foreigner or the **f** of justice,
     24:19  the foreigner, the **f** and the widow,
     26:12  the foreigner, the **f** and the widow,
Ps   10:14  you are the helper of the **f**.
     68: 5  A father to the **f**, a defender
     82: 3  Defend the weak and the **f**;
Pr   23:10  or encroach on the fields of the **f**,
Isa   1:17  Defend the cause of the **f**,
Jer   5:28  do not promote the case of the **f**;
Hos  14: 3  for in you the **f** find compassion."
Mal   3: 5  who oppress the widows and the **f**,

## FATHERS  [FATHER]

Ex    3:15  'The LORD, the God of your **f**—
Isa  49:23  Kings will be your foster **f**, and their
Lk   11:11  "Which of you **f**, if your son asks
1Co   4:15  you do not have many **f**,
Eph   6: 4  **F**, do not exasperate your children;
Col   3:21  **F**, do not embitter your children,
1Ti   1: 9  for those who kill their **f** or mothers,
1Jn   2:13  I am writing to you, **f**, because you

## GOD OF ... FATHERS  See GOD

## FATHOM*  [FATHOMED]

Job  11: 7  "Can you **f** the mysteries of God?
Ps  145: 3  his greatness no one can **f**
Ecc   3:11  yet no one can **f** what God has done
Isa  40:13  Who can **f** the Spirit of the LORD,
     40:28  and his understanding no one can **f**.
1Co  13: 2  of prophecy and can **f** all mysteries

## FATHOMED*  [FATHOM]

Job   5: 9  performs wonders that cannot be **f**,
      9:10  performs wonders that cannot be **f**,

## FATTENED  [FAT]

2Sa   6:13  he sacrificed a bull and a **f** calf.
Pr   15:17  with love than a **f** calf with hatred.
Isa   1:11  of rams and the fat of **f** animals;
Lk   15:23  Bring the **f** calf and kill it.
Jas   5: 5  You have **f** yourselves in the day

## FAULT  [FAULTFINDERS, FAULTLESS, FAULTS, FAULTY]

1Sa  29: 3  now, I have found no **f** in him."
Job  33:10  Yet God has found **f** with me;
Jer   2: 5  "What **f** did your ancestors find
Jnh   1:12  it is my **f** that this great storm has
Mt   18:15  go and point out the **f**, just between
Php   2:15  of God without **f** in a warped
Jas   1: 5  generously to all without finding **f**,
      3: 2  Those who are never at **f** in what
Jude  1:24  his glorious presence without **f**

## FAULTFINDERS*  [FAULT, FIND]

Jude  1:16  These people are grumblers and **f**;

## FAULTLESS*  [FAULT]

Php   3: 6  righteousness based on the law, **f**.
Jas   1:27  Father accepts as pure and **f** is this:

## FAULTS*  [FAULT]

Job  10: 6  that you must search out my **f**
Ps   19:12  Forgive my hidden **f**.

## FAULTY*  [FAULT]

Ps   78:57  faithless, as unreliable as a **f** bow.
Hos   7:16  they are like a **f** bow.

## FAVOR  [FAVORABLE, FAVORABLY, FAVORED, FAVORITISM, FAVORS]

Ge    4: 4  The LORD looked with **f** on Abel
      6: 8  But Noah found **f** in the eyes
Ex   33:12  and you have found **f** with me.'
     34: 9  "if I have found **f** in your eyes,
Lev  26: 9  " 'I will look on you with **f**
Nu   11:15  if I have found **f** in your eyes—
Jdg   2:26  "If now I have found **f** in your eyes,
1Sa   2:26  in stature and in **f** with the LORD
2Sa   2: 6  you the same **f** because you have
2Ki  13: 4  Jehoahaz sought the LORD's **f**,
2Ch  33:12  In his distress he sought the **f**
Ezr   7:28  who has extended his good **f** to me
Ne    5:19  Remember me with **f**, my God,
     13:31  Remember me with **f**, my God.
Est   2:15  Esther won the **f** of everyone who
      7: 3  "If I have found **f** with you,
Ps   30: 5  a moment, but his **f** lasts a lifetime;
     77: 7  Will he never show his **f** again?
     90:17  May the **f** of the Lord our God rest
Pr    3:34  but shows **f** to the humble and oppressed.
      8:35  life and receive **f** from the LORD.
     10:32  lips of the righteous know what finds **f**,
     11: 1  accurate weights find **f** with him.
     13:15  Good judgment wins **f**, but the way
     18:22  and receives **f** from the LORD.
     19: 6  Many curry **f** with a ruler,
Isa  49: 8  the time of my **f** I will answer you,
     61: 2  proclaim the year of the LORD's **f**
     66: 2  the ones I look on with **f**:
Eze  36: 9  for you and will look on you with **f**;
Zec  11: 7  called one **F** and the other Union,
Lk    1:30  you have found **f** with God.
      2:14  peace to those on whom his **f** rests."
      2:52  in wisdom and in **f** with God
      4:19  proclaim the year of the Lord's **f**."
Jn    5:32  is another who testifies in my **f**,
Ac    2:47  and enjoying the **f** of all the people.
2Co   6: 2  "In the time of my **f** I heard you,
      6: 2  now is the time of God's **f**, now is
1Pe   5: 5  but shows **f** to the humble and oppressed."

## FAVOR IN ... EYES  See EYES

## FAVORABLE  [FAVOR]

Jer  42: 6  Whether it is **f** or unfavorable,

## FAVORABLY  [FAVOR]

Ex    3:21  the Egyptians **f** disposed toward this
     11: 3  the Egyptians **f** disposed toward

## FAVORED  [FAVOR]

Ps   30: 7  when you **f** me, you made my royal
Lk    1:28  "Greetings, you who are highly **f**!
      1:43  But why am I so **f**, that the mother

## FAVORITISM*  [FAVOR]

Ex   23: 3  and do not show **f** to the poor

Lev 19:15 to the poor or **f** to the great,
Ac 10:34 true it is that God does not show **f**
Ro 2:11 For God does not show **f**.
Gal 2: 6 God does not show **f**—
Eph 6: 9 heaven, and there is no **f** with him.
Col 3:25 for their wrongs, and there is no **f**.
1Ti 5:21 partiality, and to do nothing out of **f**.
Jas 2: 1 Lord Jesus Christ must not show **f**.
2: 9 But if you show **f**, you sin and are

## FAVORS [FAVOR]

Eze 16:15 You lavished your **f** on anyone

## FAWNS

Ge 49:21 a doe set free that bears beautiful **f**.
SS 4: 5 **f**, like twin **f** of a gazelle that browse

## FEAR [AFRAID, FEARED, FEARFUL, FEARFULLY, FEARLESSLY, FEARS, FRIGHTEN, FRIGHTENED, GOD-FEARING]

Ge 9: 2 The **f** and dread of you will fall
22:12 Now I know that you **f** God,
31:42 God of Abraham and the **F** of Isaac,
Ex 9:30 still do not **f** the LORD God."
20:20 so that the **f** of God will be with you
Dt 2:25 and **f** of you on all the nations under
6:13 **F** the LORD your God, serve him
10:12 you but to **f** the LORD your God,
31:12 learn to **f** the LORD your God
Jos 2:24 the people are melting in **f** because
4:24 that you might always **f** the LORD
24:14 "Now **f** the LORD and serve him
1Sa 12:14 If you **f** the LORD and serve
12:24 be sure to **f** the LORD and serve
2Sa 23: 3 when he rules in the **f** of God,
1Ki 8:43 may know your name and **f** you,
2Ch 19: 7 Now let the **f** of the LORD be
26: 5 who instructed him in the **f** of God.
Ezr 3: 3 Despite their **f** of the peoples around
Est 8:17 nationalities became Jews because **f**
Job 1: 9 "Does Job **f** God for nothing?"
6:14 from a friend forsakes the **f**
Ps 2:11 Serve the LORD with **f**
3: 6 I will not **f** though tens of thousands
19: 9 The **f** of the LORD is pure,
23: 4 the darkest valley, I will **f** no evil,
27: 1 and my salvation—whom shall I **f**?
33: 8 Let all the earth **f** the LORD;
34: 7 encamps around those who **f** him,
34: 9 **F** the LORD, you his holy people,
34: 9 for those who **f** him lack nothing.
34:11 I will teach you the **f** of the LORD.
46: 2 Therefore we will not **f**,
55:19 because they have no **f** of God.
67: 7 all the ends of the earth will **f** him.
86:11 heart, that I may **f** your name.
90:11 Your wrath is as great as the **f** that is
91: 5 You will not **f** the terror of night,
111:10 The **f** of the LORD is
112: 1 Blessed are those who **f** the LORD,
118: 4 Let those who **f** the LORD say:
119:63 I am a friend to all who **f** you, to all
128: 1 Blessed are all who **f** the LORD,
145:19 the desires of those who **f** him;

Ps 147:11 LORD delights in those who **f** him,
Pr 1: 7 The **f** of the LORD is
1:29 and did not choose to **f** the LORD.
1:33 and be at ease, without **f** of harm."
3: 7 **f** the LORD and shun evil.
8:13 To **f** the LORD is to hate evil;
9:10 The **f** of the LORD is
10:27 The **f** of the LORD adds length
14:16 The wise **f** the LORD and shun evil,
14:26 who **f** the LORD have a secure fortress,
14:27 The **f** of the LORD is a fountain
15:33 instruction is to **f** the LORD,
16: 6 through the **f** of the LORD evil is
19:23 The **f** of the LORD leads to life;
22: 4 Humility is the **f** of the LORD;
29:25 To **f** anyone will prove to be
31:21 she has no **f** for her household;
Ecc 3:14 does it so that people will **f** him.
5: 7 Therefore **f** God.
8:12 those who **f** God, who are reverent
8:13 because the wicked do not **f** God,
12:13 of the matter: **F** God and keep his
Isa 8:12 do not **f** what they **f**, and do not
11: 3 will delight in the **f** of the LORD.
33: 6 the **f** of the LORD is the key to this
35: 4 fearful hearts, "Be strong, do not **f**;
41:10 So do not **f**, for I am with you;
41:13 right hand and says to you, Do not **f**;
43: 1 "Do not **f**, for I have redeemed you;
51: 7 Do not **f** the reproach of mere
54:14 you will have nothing to **f**.
Jer 5:22 Should you not **f** me?"
10: 7 Who should not **f** you, King of
17: 8 It does not **f** when heat comes;
Mic 6: 9 and to **f** your name is wisdom—
Zep 3:15 never again will you **f** any harm.
Lk 12: 5 you should **f**: **F** him who,
18: 4 'Even though I don't **f** God or care
Jn 12:42 their faith for **f** they would be put
20:19 the doors locked for **f** of the Jewish
Ac 5:11 Great **f** seized the whole church
Ro 8:15 slaves, so that you live in **f** again;
13: 3 want to be free from **f** of the one
2Co 5:11 we know what it is to **f** the Lord,
Gal 4:11 I **f** for you, that somehow I have
Php 1:14 to proclaim the gospel without **f**.
2:12 to work out your salvation with **f**
Heb 2:15 held in slavery by their **f** of death.
1Pe 1:17 time as foreigners here in reverent **f**.
3:14 "Do not **f** their threats; do not be
1Jn 4:18 There is no **f** in love.
4:18 But perfect love drives out **f**,
Jude 1:23 others show mercy, mixed with **f**—
Rev 14: 7 voice, "**F** God and give him glory,
15: 4 Who will not **f** you, Lord, and bring

## DO NOT FEAR Ex 9:30; Ecc 8:13; Isa 8:12;
35:4; 41:10, 13, 14; 51:7; 54:4; 57:11; Jer 10:5;
La 3:57; Zep 3:16; Hag 2:5; Mal 3:5; 1Pe 3:14

## FEAR GOD Ge 22:12; 42:18; Ex 18:21; Job 1:9;
Ps 66:16; Ecc 5:7; 8:12, 13; 12:13; Lk 18:4;
23:40; 1Pe 2:17; Rev 14:7

## FEAR OF GOD Ge 20:11; Ex 20:20; Dt 25:18;
2Sa 23:3; 2Ch 20:29; 26:5; Ps 36:1; 55:19; Ro
3:18; 1Pe 2:18

## FEAR OF THE †LORD 2Ch 17:10; 19:7, 9;
Ps 19:9; 34:11; 111:10; Pr 1:7; 2:5; 9:10; 10:27;
14:27; 15:16, 33; 16:6; 19:23; 22:4; 23:17; Isa
11:2, 3; 33:6

## FEAR THE †LORD Ex 9:30; Dt 6:2, 13, 24;
10:12, 20; 31:12, 13; Jos 4:24; 24:14; 1Sa 12:14,
24; Ps 22:23; 25:12; 33:8; 34:9; 40:3; 112:1;
115:13; 118:4; 128:1; Pr 1:29; 3:7; 8:13; 14:16,
26; 15:33; 24:21; Jer 5:24; 26:19

## FEARED [FEAR]
Ex     1:21  And because the midwives **f** God,
      14:31  the people **f** the LORD and put
Job    1: 1  he **f** God and shunned evil.
Ps    76: 7  It is you alone who are to be **f**.
      89: 7  of the holy ones God is greatly **f**;
Jnh    1:16  this the men greatly **f** the LORD,
Hag    1:12  And the people **f** the LORD.
Mal    1:14  name is to be **f** among the nations.
       3:16  those who **f** the LORD talked
       3:16  concerning those who **f** the LORD
Mk     6:20  because Herod **f** John and protected
Jn    19:38  but secretly because he **f** the Jewish

## FEARFUL [FEAR]
Heb 10:27  but only a **f** expectation of judgment

## FEARFULLY* [FEAR]
Ps 139:14  I praise you because I am **f**

## FEARLESSLY* [FEAR]
Ac     9:27  Damascus he had preached **f**
Eph    6:19  I will **f** make known the mystery
       6:20  Pray that I may declare it **f**, as I

## FEARS [FEAR]
Job    1: 8  a man who **f** God and shuns evil."
       2: 3  a man who **f** God and shuns evil.
Ps    15: 4  but honor whoever **f** the LORD;
      34: 4  he delivered me from all my **f**.
Pr    31:30  a woman who **f** the LORD is to be
Ecc    7:18  Whoever **f** God will avoid all
2Co    7: 5  conflicts on the outside, **f** within.
1Jn    4:18  The one who **f** is not made perfect

## FEAST [FEASTING, FEASTS; see also FESTIVAL]
Pr    15:15  the cheerful heart has a continual **f**.
Ecc   10:19  A **f** is made for laughter,
Isa   25: 6  LORD Almighty will prepare a **f**
Mt     8:11  their places at the **f** with Abraham,
Lk    14: 8  someone invites you to a wedding **f**,
2Pe    2:13  in their pleasures while they **f**

## FEASTING [FEAST]
Est    9:17  and made it a day of **f** and joy.
Job    1:13  daughters were **f** and drinking wine
Pr    17: 1  and quiet than a house full of **f**,
Zec    7: 6  were you not just **f** for yourselves?

## FEASTS [FEAST; see also FESTIVALS]
Nu    10:10  festivals and New Moon **f**—
Job    1: 4  sons used to hold **f** in their homes

Jude   1:12  people are blemishes at your love **f**,

## FEATHERS
Ps    91: 4  He will cover you with his **f**,
Eze   17: 3  long **f** and full plumage of varied
Da     4:33  heaven until his hair grew like the **f**

## FEATURES
1Sa   16:12  a fine appearance and handsome **f**.

## FED [FEED, WELL-FED]
Hos   13: 6  When I **f** them, they were satisfied;
Lk     6:25  Woe to you who are well **f** now,
Php    4:12  situation, whether well **f** or hungry,
Jas    2:16  keep warm and well **f**," but does

## FEEBLE
Job    4: 3  how you have strengthened **f** hands.
Ps    38: 8  I am **f** and utterly crushed;
Isa   35: 3  Strengthen the **f** hands,
Heb   12:12  strengthen your **f** arms and weak

## FEED [FED, FEEDS]
Isa    9:20  They will all **f** on the flesh of their
      11: 7  The cow will **f** with the bear,
      44:20  Such people **f** on ashes,
      65:25  wolf and the lamb will **f** together,
Eze   34:14  there they will **f** in a rich pasture
Hos   11: 4  cheek, and I bent down to **f** them.
Mic    3: 5  if you **f** them, they proclaim 'peace';
Mt    25:37  did we see you hungry and **f** you,
Mk     8: 4  get enough bread to **f** them?"
Jn    21:15  Jesus said, "**F** my lambs."
      21:17  Jesus said, "**F** my sheep.
Ro    12:20  "If your enemy is hungry, **f** him;
Jude   1:12  shepherds who **f** only themselves.

## FEEDS [FEED]
Pr    15:14  but the mouth of a fool **f** on folly.
Hos   12: 1  Ephraim **f** on the wind;
Mt     6:26  yet your heavenly Father **f** them.
Jn     6:57  so the one who **f** on me will live

## FEEL [FELT]
Jdg   16:26  "Put me where I can **f** the pillars
Ps   115: 7  They have hands, but cannot **f**, feet,
2Co   11:29  Who is weak, and I do not **f** weak?

## FEET [FOOT]
Ex    12:11  your sandals on your **f** and your
      24:10  Under his **f** was something like
      30:21  hands and **f** so that they will not die.
Dt     1:36  descendants the land he set his **f** on,
       8: 4  your **f** did not swell during these
Jos    3:15  and their **f** touched the water's edge,
Ru     3: 8  there was a woman lying at his **f**!
1Sa    2: 9  He will guard the **f** of his faithful
2Sa   22:34  He makes my **f** like the **f** of a deer
Ps     8: 6  you put everything under their **f**:
      22:16  they pierce my hands and my **f**
      40: 2  he set my **f** on a rock and gave me
      56:13  death and my **f** from stumbling,
      66: 9  lives and kept our **f** from slipping.
      73: 2  as for me, my **f** had almost slipped;
     110: 1  enemies a footstool for your **f**."

Ps 115: 7 but cannot feel, **f**, but cannot walk,
119:105 Your word is a lamp to my **f**
Pr 4:26 thought to the paths for your **f**
5: 5 Her **f** go down to death;
6:18 **f** that are quick to rush into evil,
Isa 6: 2 with two they covered their **f**,
52: 7 the mountains are the **f** of those who
Eze 34:18 the rest of your pasture with your **f**?
34:18 also muddy the rest with your **f**?
Da 2:33 iron, its **f** partly of iron and partly
Na 1: 3 and clouds are the dust of his **f**.
1:15 the **f** of one who brings good news,
Hab 3:19 he makes my **f** like the **f** of a deer,
Zec 14: 4 On that day his **f** will stand
Mt 7: 6 may trample them under their **f**,
10:14 shake the dust off your **f** when you
22:44 put your enemies under your **f**." '
Lk 1:79 death, to guide our **f** into the path
7:38 stood behind him at his **f** weeping,
7:38 she began to wet his **f** with her tears.
8:35 sitting at Jesus' **f**, dressed and in his
24:39 Look at my hands and my **f**. It is I
Jn 13: 5 and began to wash his disciples' **f**,
Ac 2:35 enemies a footstool for your **f**." '
4:35 and put it at the apostles' **f**, and it
Ro 3:15 "Their **f** are swift to shed blood;
10:15 "How beautiful are the **f** of those
16:20 will soon crush Satan under your **f**.
1Co 12:21 And the head cannot say to the **f**,
15:25 has put all his enemies under his **f**.
Eph 1:22 God placed all things under his **f**
6:15 with your **f** fitted with the readiness
1Ti 5:10 washing the **f** of the Lord's people,
Heb 1:13 enemies a footstool for your **f**"?
2: 8 and put everything under their **f**."
12:13 "Make level paths for your **f**,"
Rev 1:15 His **f** were like bronze glowing

# FELIX

Governor before whom Paul was tried (Ac 23:23—24:27).

# FELL [FALL]

Ge 7:12 And rain **f** on the earth forty days
15:12 setting, Abram **f** into a deep sleep,
1Sa 4:18 Eli **f** backward off his chair
31: 4 Saul took his own sword and **f** on it.
1Ki 18:38 the fire of the LORD **f** and burned
2Ki 1:10 Then fire **f** from heaven
Job 1:16 "The fire of God **f** from the sky
Mt 25: 5 all became drowsy and **f** asleep.
Mk 4: 8 Still other seed **f** on good soil.
Jn 18: 6 they drew back and **f** to the ground.
Ac 5: 5 heard this, he **f** down and died.
Heb 11:30 By faith the walls of Jericho **f**,
Rev 1:17 him, I **f** at his feet as though dead.
5:14 the elders **f** down and worshiped.
6:13 and the stars in the sky **f** to earth,

# FELLOW [FELLOWSHIP]

Lev 19:17 " 'Do not hate a **f** Israelite
Dt 10: 9 inheritance among their **f** Israelites;
Eph 2:19 but **f** citizens with God's people
1Co 5:11 claim to be **f** believers but are
2Th 3:15 but warn them as **f** believers.
1Pe 2:17 love your fellow **b**, fear God,

1Pe 5: 1 I appeal as a **f** elder and a witness
1Jn 2:10 Those who love their **f** believers
2:11 But those who hate a **f** believer
3:15 Anyone who hates a **f** believer
Rev 22: 9 I am a **f** servant with you
22: 9 with your **f** prophets and with all

# FELLOWSHIP [FELLOW]

Ex 20:24 your burnt offerings and **f** offerings,
Lev 3: 1 " 'If your offering is a **f** offering,
Ac 2:42 to the apostles' teaching and to **f**,
1Co 1: 9 who has called you into **f** with his
5: 2 your **f** the man who has been doing
2Co 6:14 what **f** can light have with darkness?
13:14 the **f** of the Holy Spirit be with you
Gal 2: 9 Barnabas the right hand of **f**
1Jn 1: 3 so that you also may have **f** with us.
1: 3 And our **f** is with the Father
1: 6 If we claim to have **f** with him
1: 7 light, we have **f** with one another,

# FELLOWSHIP OFFERING Lev 3:1, 3, 6, 9;
4:10, 26, 31, 35; 7:11, 13, 14, 15, 18, 20, 21, 29, 33, 37; 9:4, 18, 22; 19:5; 22:21; 23:19; Nu 6:14, 17, 18; 7:17, 23, 29, 35, 41, 47, 53, 59, 65, 71, 77, 83, 88; 15:8; Pr 7:14

# FELLOWSHIP OFFERINGS Ex 20:24;
24:5; 29:28; 32:6; Lev 6:12; 7:32, 34; 10:14; 17:5; Nu 10:10; 29:39; Dt 27:7; Jos 8:31; 22:23, 27; Jdg 20:26; 21:4; 1Sa 10:8; 11:15; 13:9; 2Sa 6:17, 18; 24:25; 1Ki 3:15; 8:63, 64, 64; 9:25; 2Ki 16:13; 1Ch 16:1, 2; 21:26; 2Ch 7:7; 29:35; 30:22; 31:2; 33:16; Eze 43:27; 45:15, 17; 46:2, 12, 12; Am 5:22

# FELT [FEEL]

Ex 10:21 darkness that can be **f**."
2Co 1: 9 we **f** we had received the sentence

# FEMALE

Ge 1:27 male and **f** he created them.
5: 2 He created them male and **f**
6:19 male and **f**, to keep them alive
Mt 19: 4 the Creator 'made them male and **f**,'
Mk 10: 6 God 'made them male and **f**.'
Ac 16:16 met by a **f** slave who had a spirit
Gal 3:28 neither male nor **f**, for you are all

# FERMENTED

Lev 10: 9 other **f** drink whenever you go
Nu 6: 3 abstain from wine and other **f** drink
Dt 14:26 wine or other **f** drink, or anything
Lk 1:15 never to take wine or other **f** drink,

# FEROCIOUS

Ge 37:33 Some **f** animal has devoured him.
Mt 7:15 but inwardly they are **f** wolves.

# FERTILE [FERTILIZE]

Isa 5: 1 one had a vineyard on a **f** hillside.
32:15 and the desert becomes a **f** field,
Jer 2: 7 I brought you into a **f** land to eat its

## FERTILIZE* [FERTILE]
Lk  13: 8  year, and I'll dig around it and **f** it.

## FERVENT* [FERVOR]
Pr  26:23  earthenware are **f** lips with an evil
Heb  5: 7  petitions with **f** cries and tears

## FERVOR* [FERVENT]
Ac  18:25  and he spoke with great **f** and taught
Ro  12:11  but keep your spiritual **f**,

## FESTIVAL [FESTIVALS]
Ex   5: 1  so that they may hold a **f** to me
     12:17  "Celebrate the **F** of Unleavened Bread,
     23:14  a year you are to celebrate a **f** to me.
     23:16  "Celebrate the **F** of Harvest with the
     34:18  "Celebrate the **F** of Unleavened Bread.
     34:22  "Celebrate the **F** of Weeks with the
Lev 23:34  the LORD's **F** of Tabernacles begins,
Dt  16:14  Be joyful at your **f**—you,
Ezr  3: 4  they celebrated the **F** of Tabernacles
Ne   8:18  celebrated the **f** for seven days,
Zec 14:16  and to celebrate the **F** of Tabernacles.
Mk  14: 2  "But not during the **f**," they said,
     15: 6  it was the custom at the **f** to release
Lk   2:41  Jerusalem for the **F** of the Passover.
Jn   2:23  he was in Jerusalem at the Passover **F**,
     7: 2  the Jewish **F** of Tabernacles was near,
     7:37  last and greatest day of the **f**,
     10:22  came the **F** of Dedication at Jerusalem.
     13: 1  It was just before the Passover **F**.
1Co  5: 8  Therefore let us keep the **F**,
Col  2:16  or with regard to a religious **f**,

### FESTIVAL OF TABERNACLES Lev 23:34;
Dt 16:13, 16; 31:10; 2Ch 8:13; Ezr 3:4; Zec
14:16, 18, 19; Jn 7:2

### FESTIVAL OF UNLEAVENED BREAD
Ex 12:17; 23:15; 34:18; Lev 23:6; Dt 16:16; 2Ch
8:13; 30:13, 21; 35:17; Ezr 6:22; Mt 26:17; Mk
14:1, 12; Lk 22:1; Ac 12:3; 20:6

## FESTIVALS [FESTIVAL]
Lev 23: 2  my appointed **f**, the appointed **f** of the
            LORD,
2Ch  8:13  and the three annual **f**—
La   1: 4  no one comes to her appointed **f**.
Hos  2:11  her yearly **f**, her New Moons,
Am   5:21  I despise your religious **f**;
Na   1:15  Celebrate your **f**, Judah, and fulfill
Zep  3:18  the loss of your appointed **f**,

### APPOINTED FESTIVALS See APPOINTED

## FESTUS [PORCIUS]
Governor who sent Paul to Caesar (Ac 25–26).

## FETTERS
Ps 149: 8  to bind their kings with **f**,

## FEVER
Lev 26:16  and **f** that will destroy your sight
Job 30:30  my body burns with **f**.
Mk   1:30  mother-in-law was in bed with a **f**,

Lk   4:39  he bent over her and rebuked the **f**,
Jn   4:52  one in the afternoon, the **f** left him."
Ac  28: 8  bed, suffering from **f** and dysentery.

## FEW [FEWEST]
Ge  47: 9  My years have been **f** and difficult,
Dt  26: 5  down into Egypt with a **f** people
1Ch 16:19  When they were but **f** in number,
Job 14: 1  are of **f** days and full of trouble.
Ecc  5: 2  are on earth, so let your words be **f**.
Mt   7:14  that leads to life, and only a **f** find it.
     22:14  many are invited, but **f** are chosen."
     25:21  have been faithful with a **f** things;
Lk  10: 2  is plentiful, but the workers are **f**.

## FEWEST* [FEW]
Dt   7: 7  for you were the **f** of all peoples.

## FIDELITY*
Ro   1:31  no **f**, no love, no mercy.
     16:10  whose **f** to Christ has stood the test.

## FIELD [AKELDAMA, FIELDS, GRAINFIELDS]
Ge   4: 8  Abel, "Let's go out to the **f**."
     4: 8  While they were in the **f**,
     23:17  So Ephron's **f** in Machpelah near
Lev 19: 9  not reap to the very edges of your **f**
     19:19  " 'Do not plant your **f** with two
Ru   2: 3  entered a **f** and began to glean
Ps  50:11  and the creatures of the **f** are mine.
     103:15  they flourish like a flower of the **f**;
Pr  24:30  I went past the **f** of a sluggard,
     31:16  She considers a **f** and buys it;
Isa  1: 8  like a hut in a **f** of melons,
     5: 8  and join **f** to **f** till no space is left
     40: 6  is like the flowers of the **f**.
Jer 32: 7  you and say, 'Buy my **f** at Anathoth,
Mt   6:28  See how the flowers of the **f** grow.
     6:30  how God clothes the grass of the **f**,
     13:38  The **f** is the world, and the good
     13:44  heaven is like treasure hidden in a **f**.
     24:40  Two men will be in the **f**;
     27: 8  is why it has been called the **F**
Lk  14:18  'I have just bought a **f**, and I must
Ac   1:18  his wickedness, Judas bought a **f**;
1Co  3: 9  you are God's **f**, God's building.
1Pe  1:24  glory is like the flowers of the **f**;

## FIELDS [FIELD]
Ex  23:10  "For six years you are to sow your **f**
Ru   2: 2  "Let me go to the **f** and pick
Ne   5: 3  "We are mortgaging our **f**,
Ps  96:12  Let the **f** be jubilant, and everything
     144:13  by tens of thousands in our **f**,
Isa 32:12  Beat your breasts for the pleasant **f**,
Mic  2: 2  They covet **f** and seize them,
Lk   2: 8  shepherds living out in the **f** nearby,
Jn   4:35  open your eyes and look at the **f**!

## FIERCE
Ge  49: 7  be their anger, so **f**, and their fury,
Ex  32:12  Turn from your **f** anger;
Nu  25: 4  the LORD's **f** anger may turn away
Jos  7:26  the LORD turned from his **f** anger.

Ps   85: 3  wrath and turned from your **f** anger.
Jer  30:24  The **f** anger of the LORD will not
Hos  11: 9  I will not carry out my **f** anger,
Jnh   3: 9  compassion turn from his **f** anger so
Na    1: 6  Who can endure his **f** anger?

## FIERY [FIRE]

Ps   11: 6  On the wicked he will rain **f** coals
Eze  21:31  breathe out my **f** anger against you;
1Pe   4:12  not be surprised at the **f** ordeal
Rev  10: 1  sun, and his legs were like **f** pillars.
     19:20  were thrown alive into the **f** lake
     21: 8  they will be consigned to the **f** lake

## FIFTIETH [FIFTY]

Lev  25:11  The **f** year shall be a jubilee for you;

## FIFTY [FIFTIETH]

Ge   18:24  What if there are **f** righteous people
Lev  23:16  Count off **f** days up to the day
Jn    8:57  "You are not yet **f** years old,"

## FIG [FIGS, SYCAMORE-FIG]

Ge    3: 7  so they sewed **f** leaves together
Jdg   9:10  the trees said to the **f** tree,
1Ki   4:25  under their own vine and **f** tree.
Pr   27:18  Those who guard a **f** tree will eat its
Hos   9:10  seeing the early fruit on the **f** tree.
Mic   4: 4  own vine and under their own **f** tree,
Na    3:12  All your fortresses are like **f** trees
Hab   3:17  Though the **f** tree does not bud
Zec   3:10  to sit under your vine and **f** tree,'
Mt   21:19  Seeing a **f** tree by the road, he went
     24:32  learn this lesson from the **f** tree:
Lk   13: 6  "A man had a **f** tree growing in his
Jn    1:48  still under the **f** tree before Philip
Jas   3:12  and sisters, can a **f** tree bear olives,
Rev   6:13  as figs drop from a **f** tree

## FIGHT [FIGHTING, FIGHTS, FOUGHT]

Ex   14:14  The LORD will **f** for you;
     17: 9  men and go out to **f** the Amalekites.
Dt    1:30  is going before you, will **f** for you,
      3:22  the LORD your God himself will **f**
Jdg   1: 1  first to **f** against the Canaanites?"
1Sa  17: 9  If he is able to **f** and kill me, we will
     25:28  because you **f** the LORD's battles,
Ne    4:20  Our God will **f** for us!"
Ps   35: 1  **f** against those who **f** against me.
Jer  21: 5  I myself will **f** against you
Zec  14: 3  go out and **f** against those nations,
Jn   18:36  my servants would **f** to prevent my
1Co   9:26  I do not **f** like a boxer beating
2Co  10: 4  The weapons we **f** with are not
1Ti   1:18  them you may **f** the battle well,
      6:12  **F** the good **f** of the faith.
2Ti   4: 7  I have fought the good **f**, I have
Rev   2:16  will **f** against them with the sword

## FIGHTING [FIGHT]

Ex    2:13  he went out and saw two Hebrews **f**.
     14:25  The LORD is **f** for them against
Jos  10:14  Surely the LORD was **f** for Israel!
Ac    5:39  find yourselves **f** against God."

## FIGHTS [FIGHT]

Jos  23:10  because the LORD your God **f**
Jas   4: 1  What causes **f** and quarrels among

## FIGS [FIG]

2Ki  20: 7  said, "Prepare a poultice of **f**."
Jer  24: 1  showed me two baskets of **f** placed
Mic   7: 1  eat, none of the early **f** that I crave.
Na    3:12  the **f** fall into the mouth of the eater.
Mk   11:13  because it was not the season for **f**.
Lk    6:44  People do not pick **f**
Jas   3:12  bear olives, or a grapevine bear **f**?
Rev   6:13  earth, as **f** drop from a fig tree

## FIGURATIVELY* [FIGURE]

Jn   16:25  "Though I have been speaking **f**,
Gal   4:24  I am taking these things **f**,
Rev  11: 8  which is **f** called Sodom and Egypt,

## FIGURE* [FIGURATIVELY, FIGURES]

Ge   29:17  but Rachel had a lovely **f**
1Sa  28:13  "I see a ghostly **f** coming up
Est   2: 7  Esther, had a lovely **f** and was
Eze   1:26  on the throne was a **f** like
      8: 2  and I saw a **f** like that of a man.
Jn    7: 4  to become a public **f** acts in secret.
     10: 6  Jesus used this **f** of speech,

## FIGURES* [FIGURE]

2Ch   4: 3  the rim, **f** of bulls encircled it—
Eze  23:14  **f** of Chaldeans portrayed in red,
Jn   16:29  clearly and without **f** of speech.

## FILL [FILLED, FILLING, FILLS, FULL, FULLNESS, FULLY]

Ge    1:28  **f** the earth and subdue it.
Lev  25:19  you will eat your **f** and live there
Dt   31:20  and when they eat their **f** and thrive,
Ps   16:11  you will **f** me with joy in your
     81:10  wide your mouth and I will **f** it.
Pr   12:21  the wicked have their **f** of trouble.
     28:19  who chase fantasies will have their **f**
Ecc   1: 8  seeing, nor the ear its **f** of hearing.
Isa  27: 6  and **f** all the world with fruit.
     33: 5  he will **f** Zion with his justice
Jer  23:24  "Do not I **f** heaven and earth?"
Eze  10: 2  **F** your hands with burning coals
Hag   1: 6  You drink, but never have your **f**.
      2: 7  and I will **f** this house with glory,'
Jn    2: 7  servants, "**F** the jars with water";
      6:26  you ate the loaves and had your **f**.
Ac    2:28  you will **f** me with joy in your
Ro   15:13  May the God of hope **f** you with all
Eph   4:10  in order to **f** the whole universe.)
Col   1: 9  We continually ask God to **f** you
      1:24  and I **f** up in my flesh what is still

## FILLED [FILL]

Ge    6:13  the earth is **f** with violence because
Ex    1: 7  that the land was **f** with them.
     31: 3  I have **f** him with the Spirit of God,
     35:31  he has **f** him with the Spirit of God,
     40:34  of the LORD **f** the tabernacle.
Lev  19:29  and be **f** with wickedness.
Dt    6:11  houses **f** with all kinds of good

| | | |
|---|---|---|
| Dt | 34: 9 | son of Nun was **f** with the spirit |
| 1Ki | 8:11 | glory of the LORD **f** his temple. |
| 2Ki | 3:17 | yet this valley will be **f** with water, |
| 2Ch | 5:14 | the glory of the LORD **f** the temple |
| | 7: 1 | glory of the LORD **f** the temple. |
| Ps | 71: 8 | My mouth is **f** with your praise, |
| | 72:19 | may the whole earth be **f** with his |
| | 119:64 | The earth is **f** with your love, |
| Pr | 8:30 | I was **f** with delight day after day, |
| Isa | 6: 4 | and the temple was **f** with smoke. |
| | 11: 9 | earth will be **f** with the knowledge |
| Jer | 25:15 | my hand this cup **f** with the wine |
| Eze | 10: 4 | The cloud **f** the temple, |
| | 43: 5 | glory of the LORD **f** the temple. |
| Da | 2:35 | mountain and **f** the whole earth. |
| Hab | 2:14 | For the earth will be **f** |
| | 3: 3 | heavens and his praise **f** the earth. |
| Mt | 5: 6 | for righteousness, for they will be **f**. |
| Lk | 1:15 | and he will be **f** with the Holy Spirit |
| | 1:41 | Elizabeth was **f** with the Holy Spirit. |
| | 1:67 | His father Zechariah was **f** |
| | 2:40 | he was **f** with wisdom, and the grace |
| Jn | 12: 3 | the house was **f** with the fragrance |
| Ac | 2: 4 | of them were **f** with the Holy Spirit |
| | 4: 8 | Then Peter, **f** with the Holy Spirit, |
| | 4:31 | they were all **f** with the Holy Spirit |
| | 5: 3 | Satan has so **f** your heart that you |
| | 9:17 | and be **f** with the Holy Spirit." |
| | 13: 9 | called Paul, **f** with the Holy Spirit, |
| | 13:52 | And the disciples were **f** with joy |
| Ro | 15:14 | **f** with knowledge and competent to |
| Eph | 5:18 | Instead, be **f** with the Spirit, |
| Php | 1:11 | **f** with the fruit of righteousness |
| Rev | 8: 5 | censer, **f** it with fire from the altar, |
| | 12:12 | He is **f** with fury, because he knows |
| | 15: 8 | the temple was **f** with smoke |
| | 16:19 | gave her the cup **f** with the wine |

## FILLING [FILL]
Eze 44: 4   the glory of the LORD **f** the temple

## FILLS [FILL]
Nu  14:21   of the LORD **f** the whole earth,
Ps 107: 9   and **f** the hungry with good things.
Eph  1:23   him who **f** everything in every way.

## FILTH [FILTHINESS, FILTHY]
Isa  4: 4   The Lord will wash away the **f**
Jas  1:21   get rid of all moral **f** and the evil
Rev 17: 4   things and the **f** of her adulteries.

## FILTHINESS* [FILTH]
La  1: 9   Her **f** clung to her skirts; she did not

## FILTHY* [FILTH]
Isa 64: 6   all our righteous acts are like **f** rags;
Zec  3: 3   in **f** clothes as he stood before
    3: 4   him, "Take off his **f** clothes."
Col  3: 8   and **f** language from your lips.
Jas  2: 2   a poor person in **f** old clothes

## FINAL [FINALITY]
Ps  73:17   then I understood their **f** destiny.
Isa 41:22   them and know their **f** outcome.
Lk  11:26   And the **f** condition of that person is

## FINALITY* [FINAL]
Ro  9:28   on earth with speed and **f**."

## FINANCIAL*
1Ti  6: 5   that godliness is a means to **f** gain.

## FIND [FAULTFINDERS, FINDING, FINDS, FOUND]

| | | |
|---|---|---|
| Ge | 18:26 | "If I **f** fifty righteous people |
| Ex | 33:13 | and continue to **f** favor with you. |
| Nu | 32:23 | be sure that your sin will **f** you out. |
| Dt | 4:29 | you will **f** him if you seek him |
| | 13: 3 | LORD your God is testing you to **f** |
| 1Sa | 23:16 | and helped him **f** strength in God. |
| | 28: 7 | "**F** me a woman who is a medium, |
| Job | 23: 3 | If only I knew where to **f** him; |
| Ps | 62: 5 | Yes, my soul, **f** rest in God; |
| | 91: 4 | under his wings you will **f** refuge; |
| | 112: 1 | who **f** great delight in his commands. |
| | 119:35 | commands, for there I **f** delight. |
| | 119:52 | laws, and I **f** comfort in them. |
| | 132: 5 | till I **f** a place for the LORD, |
| Pr | 2: 5 | and **f** the knowledge of God. |
| | 3:13 | Blessed are those who **f** wisdom, |
| | 4:22 | for they are life to those who **f** them |
| | 8:17 | me, and those who seek me **f** me. |
| | 8:35 | For those who **f** me **f** life |
| | 8:36 | who fail to **f** me harm themselves; |
| | 10:23 | Fools **f** pleasure in wicked schemes, |
| | 14:22 | those who plan what is good **f** love |
| | 20: 6 | but a faithful person who can **f**? |
| | 24:14 | If you **f** it, there is a future hope |
| | 31:10 | wife of noble character who can **f**? |
| Ecc | 2:24 | drink and **f** satisfaction in their toil. |
| | 12:10 | searched to **f** just the right words, |
| SS | 3: 2 | I looked for him but did not **f** him. |
| Isa | 58:14 | you will **f** your joy in the LORD, |
| Jer | 6:16 | it, and you will **f** rest for your souls. |
| | 29:13 | and **f** me when you seek me with all |
| Da | 6: 4 | and the satraps tried to **f** grounds |
| | 6: 4 | They could **f** no corruption in him, |
| Hos | 14: 3 | in you the fatherless **f** compassion." |
| Mt | 7: 7 | seek and you will **f**; |
| | 7: 8 | who seek **f**; and to those who knock, |
| | 11:29 | and you will **f** rest for your souls. |
| | 16:25 | loses their life for me will **f** it. |
| | 22: 9 | invite to the banquet anyone you **f**.' |
| Lk | 11: 9 | seek and you will **f**; |
| | 11:10 | who seek **f**; and to those who knock, |
| | 18: 8 | comes, will he **f** faith on the earth?" |
| | 23: 4 | "I **f** no basis for a charge against |
| | 24: 3 | they did not **f** the body of the Lord |
| Jn | 10: 9 | come in and go out, and **f** pasture. |
| Ac | 23: 9 | "We **f** nothing wrong with this |
| Eph | 5:10 | and **f** out what pleases the Lord. |

## FINDING [FIND]
Ex  15:22   in the desert without **f** water.
Hos  9:10   it was like **f** grapes in the desert;

## FINDS [FIND]
Ps  62: 1   Truly my soul **f** rest in God;
Ps 119:162  promise like one who **f** great spoil.
Pr  11:27   Whoever seeks good **f** favor,
    14: 6   mocker seeks wisdom and **f** none,

Pr    18:22  He who **f** a wife **f** what is good
Ecc    9:10  Whatever your hand **f** to do, do it
Mt    10:39  Whoever **f** their life will lose it,
Lk    12:37  whose master **f** them watching
      15: 4  go after the lost sheep until he **f** it?
      15: 8  and search carefully until she **f** it?

## FINE  [FINE-SOUNDING, FINEST]

Ex     2: 2  When she saw that he was a **f** child,
Pr     8:19  My fruit is better than **f** gold;
Ecc    7: 1  good name is better than **f** perfume,
Da    10: 5  belt of **f** gold from Uphaz around his
             waist.
Zec    3: 4  I will put **f** garments on you."
Lk     7:25  A man dressed in **f** clothes?

## FINE-SOUNDING*  [FINE, SOUND]

Col    2: 4  may deceive you by **f** arguments.

## FINEST  [FINE]

Job   28:15  It cannot be bought with the **f** gold,
Ps   147:14  satisfies you with the **f** of wheat.
Isa   25: 6  the best of meats and the **f** of wines.

## FINGER  [FINGERS]

Ex     8:19  to Pharaoh, "This is the **f** of God."
      31:18  of stone inscribed by the **f** of God.
Lev    4: 6  He is to dip his **f** into the blood
Dt     9:10  tablets inscribed by the **f** of God.
2Ch   10:10  them, 'My little **f** is thicker than my
Mt    23: 4  not willing to lift a **f** to move them.
Lk    11:20  I drive out demons by the **f** of God,
      16:24  to dip the tip of his **f** in water
Jn     8: 6  *to write on the ground with his f.*
      20:25  and put my **f** where the nails were,

## FINGERS  [FINGER]

Ps     8: 3  the work of your **f**, the moon
Pr     7: 3  Bind them on your **f**; write them
Da     5: 5  Suddenly the **f** of a human hand
Mk     7:33  Jesus put his **f** into the man's ears.

## FINISH  [FINISHED, UNFINISHED]

Ps    90: 9  we **f** our years with a moan.
Mt    10:23  you will not **f** going through
Jn     4:34  him who sent me and to **f** his work.
       5:36  that the Father has given me to **f**—
Ac    20:24  my only aim is to **f** the race
2Co    8:11  Now **f** the work, so that your eager
Gal    3: 3  now trying to **f** by human effort?
Jas    1: 4  Let perseverance **f** its work so

## FINISHED  [FINISH]

Ge     2: 2  seventh day God had **f** the work he
      24:15  Before he had **f** praying,
Ex    40:33  And so Moses **f** the work.
Dt    32:45  Moses **f** reciting all these words
Jos   19:51  And so they **f** dividing the land.
1Ki    8:54  Solomon had **f** all these prayers
Ezr    6:14  They **f** building the temple
Jn    19:28  everything had now been **f**,
      19:30  the drink, Jesus said, "It is **f**."
2Ti    4: 7  the good fight, I have **f** the race,
Heb    4: 3  work has been **f** since the creation
Rev   11: 7  when they have **f** their testimony,

## FINS

Lev   11: 9  streams you may eat any that have **f**

## FIRE  [FIERY, FIREPOT]

Ex     3: 2  in flames of **f** from within a bush.
       3: 2  the bush was on **f** it did not burn up.
      13:21  in a pillar of **f** to give them light,
      19:18  the LORD descended on it in **f**.
      40:38  and **f** was in the cloud by night,
Lev    6:12  The **f** on the altar must be kept
       6:12  arrange the burnt offering on the **f**
       9:24  **F** came out from the presence
      10: 1  put **f** in them and added incense;
      10: 1  offered unauthorized **f** before
Nu    11: 1  **f** from the LORD burned among
      16:35  And **f** came out from the LORD
Dt     4:12  LORD spoke to you out of the **f**.
Jdg    6:21  **F** flared from the rock,
1Ki   18:38  Then the **f** of the LORD fell
      19:12  After the earthquake came a **f**,
      19:12  but the LORD was not in the **f**.
2Ki    1:10  may **f** come down from heaven
       2:11  a chariot of **f** and horses of **f** appeared
       6:17  and chariots of **f** all around Elisha.
      16: 3  and even sacrificed his son in the **f**,
      25: 9  He set **f** to the temple
Ne     1: 3  its gates have been burned with **f**."
Ps    50: 3  a **f** devours before him, and around
      89:46  long will your wrath burn like **f**?
Pr     6:27  Can a man scoop **f** into his lap
Isa    5:24  as tongues of **f** lick up straw and as
      10:17  The Light of Israel will become a **f**,
      30:27  and his tongue is a consuming **f**.
      66:24  nor will their **f** be quenched,
Jer   23:29  "Is not my word like **f**,"
      36:23  the entire scroll was burned in the **f**.
Eze    1:13  creatures was like burning coals of **f**
       1:13  **F** moved back and forth among
Da     3:25  four men walking around in the **f**,
       7: 9  His throne was flaming with **f**,
Am     4:11  a burning stick snatched from the **f**,
Zec    2: 5  myself will be a wall of **f** around it,'
       3: 2  burning stick snatched from the **f**?"
Mal    3: 2  For he will be like a refiner's **f**.
Mt     3:11  you with the Holy Spirit and **f**.
       5:22  will be in danger of the **f** of hell.
      18: 8  feet and be thrown into eternal **f**.
      25:41  the eternal **f** prepared for the devil
Mk     9:43  into hell, where the **f** never goes out.
       9:48  not die, and the **f** is not quenched.'
       9:49  Everyone will be salted with **f**.
Lk     3:16  you with the Holy Spirit and **f**.
      12:49  have come to bring **f** on the earth,
Jn    15: 6  up, thrown into the **f** and burned.
Ac     2: 3  to be tongues of **f** that separated
1Co    3:13  It will be revealed with **f**, and the **f**
1Th    5:19  Do not put out the Spirit's **f**.
2Th    1: 7  blazing **f** with his powerful angels.
Heb   10:27  of raging **f** that will consume
      12:29  for our "God is a consuming **f**."
Jas    3: 6  The tongue also is a **f**, a world
       3: 6  life on **f**, and is itself set on **f** by hell.
1Pe    1: 7  perishes even though refined by **f**—
2Pe    3:10  the elements will be destroyed by **f**,
Jude   1: 7  suffer the punishment of eternal **f**.
       1:23  others by snatching them from the **f**;

Rev  1:14  and his eyes were like blazing **f**.
     8: 7  came hail and **f** mixed with blood,
     9:17  and out of their mouths came **f**,
    11: 5  **f** comes from their mouths
    15: 2  a sea of glass glowing with **f** and,
    20:14  were thrown into the lake of **f**.
    20:14  The lake of **f** is the second death.

## FIREPOT  [FIRE]

Ge  15:17  a smoking **f** with a blazing torch

## FIRM*  [FIRMLY]

Ex   14:13  Stand **f** and you will see
2Ch  20:17  stand **f** and see the deliverance
Ezr   9: 8  giving us a **f** place in his sanctuary,
Job  11:15  you will stand **f** and without fear.
     36: 5  he is mighty, and **f** in his purpose.
     41:23  they are **f** and immovable.
Ps   20: 8  and fall, but we rise up and stand **f**.
     30: 7  made my royal mountain stand **f**;
     33: 9  he commanded, and it stood **f**.
     33:11  plans of the Lord stand **f** forever,
     37:23  The Lord makes **f** the steps
     40: 2  rock and gave me a **f** place to stand.
     75: 3  quake, it is I who hold its pillars **f**.
     89: 2  that your love stands **f** forever,
     89: 4  and make your throne **f** through all
     93: 1  world is established, **f** and secure.
     93: 5  Your statutes, Lord, stand **f**;
    119:89  it stands **f** in the heavens.
Pr   10:25  but the righteous stand **f** forever.
     12: 7  the house of the righteous stands **f**.
Isa   7: 9  If you do not stand **f** in your faith,
     22:17  is about to take **f** hold of you
     22:23  drive him like a peg into a **f** place;
     22:25  into the **f** place will give way;
Eze  13: 5  so that it will stand **f** in the battle
Zec   8:23  nations will take **f** hold of one Jew
Mt   10:22  those who stand **f** to the end will be
     24:13  whoever stands **f** to the end will be
Mk   13:13  those who stand **f** to the end will be
Lk   21:19  Stand **f**, and you will win life.
1Co   1: 8  He will also keep you **f** to the end,
     10:12  if you think you are standing **f**,
     15:58  my dear brothers and sisters, stand **f**.
     16:13  on your guard; stand **f** in the faith;
2Co   1: 7  And our hope for you is **f**,
     1:21  both us and you stand **f** in Christ.
     1:24  because it is by faith you stand **f**.
Gal   5: 1  Stand **f**, then, and do not let
Eph   6:14  Stand **f** then, with the belt of truth
Php   1:27  that you stand **f** in the one Spirit,
     4: 1  stand **f** in the Lord in this way,
Col   1:23  established and **f**, and do not move
     2: 5  are and how **f** your faith in Christ is.
     4:12  that you may stand **f** in all the will
1Th   3: 8  since you are standing **f** in the Lord.
2Th   2:15  stand **f** and hold fast to the teachings
1Ti   6:19  themselves as a **f** foundation
2Ti   2:19  God's solid foundation stands **f**,
Heb   6:19  an anchor for the soul, **f** and secure.
Jas   5: 8  be patient and stand **f**,
1Pe   5: 9  Resist him, standing **f** in the faith,
     5:10  make you strong, **f** and steadfast.

## FIRMLY  [FIRM]

1Ch  16:30  The world is **f** established;
Ecc  12:11  sayings like **f** embedded nails—
1Co  15: 2  if you hold **f** to the word I preached
Heb   4:14  let us hold **f** to the faith we profess.

## FIRST  [FIRSTBORN, FIRSTFRUITS]

Ge    1: 5  and there was morning—the **f** day.
     13: 4  and where he had **f** built an altar.
Ex   12: 2  **f** month, the **f** month of your year.
     34: 1  out two stone tablets like the **f** ones,
     34: 1  the words that were on the **f** tablets,
     34:19  "The **f** offspring of every womb
     40:17  set up on the **f** day of the **f** month
Nu   18:15  The **f** offspring of every womb,
     28:11  " 'On the **f** of every month,
1Ki  22: 5  of Israel, "**F** seek the counsel
Pr    8:22  Lord brought me forth as the **f**
     18:17  a lawsuit the **f** to speak seems right,
Isa  44: 6  I am the **f** and I am the last;
     48:12  I am he; I am the **f** and I am the last.
Da    7: 4  "The **f** was like a lion, and it had
Mt    5:24  **F** go and be reconciled
     6:33  But seek **f** his kingdom and his
     7: 5  **f** take the plank out of your own
     8:21  **f** let me go and bury my father."
     19:30  But many who are **f** will be last,
     19:30  and many who are last will be **f**.
     22:38  This is the **f** and greatest
Mk    9:11  law say that Elijah must come **f**?"
     9:35  wants to be **f** must be the very last,
     10:31  are **f** will be last, and the last **f**."
     10:44  whoever wants to be **f** must be slave
     13:10  the gospel must **f** be preached to all
     16: 2  Very early on the **f** day of the week,
Lk   11:26  of that person is worse than the **f**."
Jn    8: 7  *who is without sin be the f to throw*
Ac   11:26  disciples were called Christians **f**
Ro    1:16  **f** to the Jew, then to the Gentile.
     1:17  that is by faith from **f** to last, just as
1Co  12:28  in the church **f** of all apostles,
     15:45  "The **f** Adam became a living
2Co   8: 5  having given themselves **f** of all
Eph   1:12  who were the **f** to put our hope
     6: 2  which is the **f** commandment
1Th   4:16  and the dead in Christ will rise **f**.
1Ti   2:13  For Adam was formed **f**, then Eve.
Heb   8:13  he has made the **f** one obsolete;
     10: 9  He sets aside the **f** to establish
Jas   3:17  comes from heaven is **f** of all pure;
1Jn   4:19  We love because he **f** loved us.
3Jn   1: 9  who loves to be **f**, will have nothing
Rev   1:17  I am the **F** and the Last.
     2: 4  have forsaken the love you had at **f**.
     4: 7  The **f** living creature was like a lion,
     6: 1  I watched as the Lamb opened the **f**
     8: 7  The **f** angel sounded his trumpet,
     9:12  The **f** woe is past; two other woes
     13:12  its inhabitants worship the **f** beast,
     20: 5  This is the **f** resurrection.
     21: 1  for the **f** heaven and the **f** earth had
     22:13  and the Omega, the **F** and the Last,

## FIRSTBORN  [FIRST, BEAR]

Ge   27:19  to his father, "I am Esau your **f**.
     48:18  "No, my father, this one is the **f**;

Ex   4:22  the LORD says: Israel is my **f** son,
      11: 5  Every **f** son in Egypt will die,
      11: 5  from the **f** son of Pharaoh,
      11: 5  to the **f** son of the female slave,
      11: 5  and all the **f** of the cattle as well.
      12:29  the LORD struck down all the **f**
      13: 2  "Consecrate to me every **f** male.
      34:20  Redeem the **f** donkey with a lamb,
      34:20  Redeem all your **f** sons. "No one is
Nu    3:41  in place of all the **f** of the Israelites,
Jos   6:26  his **f** son he will lay its foundations;
1Ki 16:34  at the cost of his **f** son Abiram,
Ps  89:27  And I will appoint him to be my **f**,
Mic   6: 7  Shall I offer my **f** for my
Zec 12:10  for him as one grieves for a **f** son.
Lk    2: 7  and she gave birth to her **f**, a son.
Ro    8:29  might be the **f** among many brothers
Col   1:15  God, the **f** over all creation.
      1:18  and the **f** from among the dead,
Heb   1: 6  God brings his **f** into the world,
      12:23  to the church of the **f**, whose names
Rev   1: 5  faithful witness, the **f** from the dead,

## FIRSTFRUITS  [FIRST, FRUIT]
Ex  23:16  with the **f** of the crops you sow
      34:22  with the **f** of the wheat harvest,
Pr    3: 9  wealth, with the **f** of all your crops;
Ro    8:23  who have the **f** of the Spirit,
1Co 15:23  Christ, the **f**; then, when he comes,
Jas   1:18  that we might be a kind of **f** of all he
Rev 14: 4  human race and offered as **f** to God

## FISH  [FISHERMEN, FISHHOOK]
Ge    1:26  they may rule over the **f** in the sea
Ex    7:18  The **f** in the Nile will die,
Nu  11: 5  We remember the **f** we ate in Egypt
Eze 47: 9  There will be large numbers of **f**,
Jnh   1:17  Now the LORD provided a huge **f**
      1:17  was in the belly of the **f** three days
      2: 1  From inside the **f** Jonah prayed
Mt    4:19  I will send you out to **f** for people."
      7:10  Or if he asks for a **f**, will give him
      12:40  three nights in the belly of a huge **f**,
      13:48  and collected the good **f** in baskets,
      14:17  five loaves of bread and two **f**,"
Mk    1:17  I will send you out to **f** for people."
      8: 7  They had a few small **f** as well;
Lk    5: 6  they caught such a large number of **f**
      5:10  from now on you will **f** for people."
Jn    6: 9  small barley loaves and two small **f**,
      21: 5  "Friends, haven't you any **f**?"
      21:11  It was full of large **f**, 153, but even

## FISHERMEN  [FISH]
Mk    1:16  a net into the lake, for they were **f**.

## FISHHOOK*  [FISH, HOOK]
Job 41: 1  you pull in the leviathan with a **f**

## FISTS
Isa  58: 4  in striking each other with wicked **f**.
Mt  26:67  his face and struck him with their **f**.

## FIT  [FITTING]
Dt   12: 8  today, everyone doing as they see **f**,

Jdg 17: 6  everyone did as they saw **f**.
      21:25  everyone did as they saw **f**.
Lk    9:62  and looks back is **f** for service

## FITTING*  [FIT]
Ps  33: 1  it is **f** for the upright to praise him.
      147: 1  how pleasant and **f** to praise him!
Pr   19:10  It is not **f** for a fool to live
      26: 1  in harvest, honor is not **f** for a fool.
1Co 14:40  everything should be done in a **f**
Col   3:18  to your husbands, as is **f** in the Lord.
Heb   2:10  to glory, it was **f** that God,

## FIVE
Lev 26: 8  **F** of you will chase a hundred,
1Sa   6: 4  "**F** gold tumors and **f** gold rats,
      6:16  The **f** rulers of the Philistines saw
      17:40  chose **f** smooth stones
Isa  30:17  the threat of **f** you will all flee away,
Mt  14:19  Taking the **f** loaves and the two fish
      16: 9  the **f** loaves for the **f** thousand,
      25: 2  **F** of them were foolish and **f** were
      25:15  To one he gave **f** bags of gold,
Jn    4:18  is, you have had **f** husbands,
1Co 14:19  rather speak **f** intelligible words
Rev   9: 5  only to torture them for **f** months.
      17:10  **F** have fallen, one is, the other has

## FIX*  [FIXED, FIXING]
Dt   11:18  **F** these words of mine in your
Job 14: 3  Do you **f** your eye on such as these?
Pr    4:25  **f** your gaze directly before you.
Am    9: 4  "I will **f** my eyes on them for evil
2Co   4:18  So we **f** our eyes not on what is
Heb   3: 1  calling, **f** your thoughts on Jesus,

## FIXED*  [FIX]
2Ki   8:11  him with a **f** gaze until Hazael was
Job 38:10  when I **f** limits for it and set its
Ps  141: 8  But my eyes are **f** on you,
Pr    8:28  **f** securely the fountains of the deep,

## FIXING*  [FIX]
Heb 12: 2  **f** our eyes on Jesus, the pioneer

## FLAME  [FLAMES, FLAMING]
Jdg 13:20  As the **f** blazed up from the altar
      13:20  of the LORD ascended in the **f**.
Isa  10:17  become a fire, their Holy One a **f**;
2Ti   1: 6  you to fan into **f** the gift of God,

## FLAMES  [FLAME]
Ex    3: 2  LORD appeared to him in **f** of fire
Da    3:22  the **f** of the fire killed the soldiers
1Co   3:15  only as one escaping through the **f**.
Heb 11:34  quenched the fury of the **f**,

## FLAMING  [FLAME]
Ge    3:24  and a **f** sword flashing back
Da    7: 9  His throne was **f** with fire, and its
      10: 6  his eyes like **f** torches, his arms
Eph   6:16  you can extinguish all the **f** arrows

## FLANK
Eze 34:21  Because you shove with **f**

## FLASH [FLASHED, FLASHES, FLASHING]
Eze 21:10  polished to f like lightning!
Lk    9:29  his clothes became as bright as a f
1Co 15:52  in a f, in the twinkling of an eye,

## FLASHED [FLASH]
Eze  1:13  was bright, and lightning f out of it.
Ac    9: 3  a light from heaven f around him.

## FLASHES [FLASH]
Eze  1:14  back and forth like f of lightning.
Lk  17:24  which f and lights up the sky
Rev  4: 5  From the throne came f of lightning,
       8: 5  f of lightning and an earthquake.
      11:19  And there came f of lightning,
      16:18  Then there came f of lightning,

## FLASHING [FLASH]
Ge    3:24  a flaming sword f back and forth
Dt  32:41  when I sharpen my f sword and my

## FLASK*
2Ki  9: 1  take this f of oil with you and go
       9: 3  take the f and pour the oil on his

## FLATTER* [FLATTERING, FLATTERY]
Job 32:21  no partiality, nor will I f anyone;
Ps  12: 2  f with their lips but harbor deception
      36: 2  In their own eyes they f themselves
      78:36  they would f him with their mouths,
Pr  29: 5  Those who f their neighbors
Jude 1:16  f others for their own advantage.

## FLATTERING* [FLATTER]
Ps  12: 3  May the LORD silence all f lips
Pr  26:28  it hurts, and a f mouth works ruin.
      28:23  rather than one who has a f tongue.
Eze 12:24  or f divinations among the people

## FLATTERY* [FLATTER]
Job 32:22  for if I were skilled in f, my Maker
Da  11:32  f he will corrupt those who have
Ro  16:18  f they deceive the minds of naive
1Th  2: 5  You know we never used f, nor did

## FLAW* [FLAWLESS]
Dt  15:21  or has any serious f, you must not
      17: 1  a sheep that has any defect or f in it,
SS    4: 7  are, my darling; there is no f in you.

## FLAWLESS* [FLAW]
2Sa 22:31  the LORD's word is f.
Job 11: 4  'My beliefs are f and I am pure
Ps  12: 6  And the words of the LORD are f,
      18:30  The LORD's word is f;
Pr  30: 5  "Every word of God is f; he is
SS    5: 2  my darling, my dove, my f one.

## FLAX
Jos   2: 6  under the stalks of f she had laid

## FLED [FLEE]
Ex    2:15  but Moses f from Pharaoh and went
1Sa 19:18  When David had f and made his
2Sa  4: 4  His nurse picked him up and f,
      19: 9  now he has f the country to escape
Ps    3: T  *When he f from his son Absalom.*
      57: T  *When he had f from Saul into the cave.*
     114: 3  The sea looked and f, the Jordan
Mk  14:50  Then everyone deserted him and f.
Rev 20:11  and the heavens f from his presence,

## FLEE [FLED, FLEES]
Ge  19:17  one of them said, "F for your lives!
Nu  35:11  killed someone accidentally may f.
Ps  68: 1  may his foes f before him.
     139: 7  Where can I f from your presence?
Pr  28: 1  The wicked f though no one pursues,
Isa 30:17  A thousand will f at the threat
      30:17  the threat of five you will all f away,
Jer 46: 6  "The swift cannot f nor the strong
      51: 6  "F from Babylon! Run for your
Jnh  1: 3  for Tarshish to f from the LORD.
Zec  2: 6  F from the land of the north,"
Lk    3: 7  Who warned you to f
1Co  6:18  F from sexual immorality.
      10:14  my dear friends, f from idolatry.
1Ti  6:11  man of God, f from all this,
2Ti  2:22  F the evil desires of youth
Jas  4: 7  the devil, and he will f from you.

## FLEECE
Jdg  6:37  look, I will place a wool f

## FLEES [FLEE]
Dt  19: 4  kills a person and f there for safety—

## FLEETING*
Job 14: 2  like f shadows, they do not endure.
Ps  39: 4  let me know how f my life is.
      89:47  Remember how f is my life.
     144: 4  their days are like a f shadow.
Pr  21: 6  made by a lying tongue is a f vapor
      31:30  Charm is deceptive, and beauty is f;
Heb 11:25  to enjoy the f pleasures of sin.

## FLESH  See also BODY, CREATURES, EARTHLY, HUMAN, HUMAN [NATURE], HUMAN [STANDARDS], MAN, MEAT, MORTAL, NATURAL, OUTWARDLY, PEOPLE, PHYSICAL, SENSUAL, SINFUL NATURE, WORLD, WORLDLY
Ge    2:23  bone of my bones and f of my f;
       2:24  wife, and they will become one f.
      17:13  My covenant in your f is to be
Lev 26:29  eat the f of your sons and the f of your daughters.
1Sa 17:44  "and I'll give your f to the birds
2Ch 32: 8  With him is only the arm of f,
Job 19:26  yet in my f I will see God;
Ps  50:13  Do I eat the f of bulls or drink
Jer  9:25  who are circumcised only in the f—
Eze 11:19  of stone and give them a heart of f.
      36:26  of stone and give you a heart of f.

Eze 37: 6 to you and make **f** come upon you
Mt 19: 5 and the two will become one **f**'?
26:41 but the **f** is weak."
Lk 24:39 a ghost does not have **f** and bones,
Jn 1:14 The Word became **f** and made his
3: 6 **F** gives birth to **f**, but the Spirit
6:51 This bread is my **f**, which I will give
1Co 6:16 said, "The two will become one **f**."
15:39 All **f** is not the same:
15:39 Human beings have one kind of **f**,
2Co 12: 7 I was given a thorn in my **f**,
Eph 2:15 setting aside in his **f** the law with its
5:31 and the two will become one **f**."
6:12 For our struggle is not against **f**
Php 3: 2 evildoers, those mutilators of the **f**.
Col 1:24 fill up in my **f** what is still lacking
1Jn 4: 2 that Jesus Christ has come in the **f** is
2Jn 1: 7 Jesus Christ as coming in the **f**,
Jude 1:23 the clothing stained by corrupted **f**.
Rev 19:18 so that you may eat the **f** of kings,
19:18 and the **f** of all people,

**FLESH AND BLOOD** Ge 29:14; 37:27; Jdg
9:2; 2Sa 5:1; 19:12, 13; 1Ki 8:19; 2Ki 20:18;
1Ch 11:1; 2Ch 6:9; Ne 5:5; Isa 39:7; 58:7; Mt
16:17; 1Co 15:50; Eph 6:12; Heb 2:14

**FLEW** [FLY]
Ps 18:10 He mounted the cherubim and **f**;
Isa 6: 6 one of the seraphs **f** to me

**FLIES** [FLY]
Ex 8:21 I will send swarms of **f** on you
8:21 of the Egyptians will be full of **f**;
Ps 91: 5 of night, nor the arrow that **f** by day,
Isa 7:18 day the LORD will whistle for **f**

**FLIGHT** [FLY]
Dt 32:30 or two put ten thousand to **f**,
Mt 24:20 Pray that your **f** will not take place

**FLINT**
Ex 4:25 But Zipporah took a **f** knife, cut off
Jos 5: 2 "Make **f** knives and circumcise
Isa 50: 7 Therefore have I set my face like **f**,
Zec 7:12 They made their hearts as hard as **f**

**FLIRTING**\*
Isa 3:16 outstretched necks, **f** with their eyes,

**FLOAT**\* [FLOATED]
1Ki 5: 9 I will **f** them as rafts by sea
2Ki 6: 6 threw it there, and made the iron **f**.
2Ch 2:16 will **f** them as rafts by sea down

**FLOATED**\* [FLOAT]
Ge 7:18 the ark **f** on the surface of the water.

**FLOCK** [FLOCKS]
Ex 2:17 to their rescue and watered their **f**.
3: 1 Now Moses was tending the **f**
3: 1 and he led the **f** to the far side
2Sa 7: 8 from tending the **f**, and appointed
Ps 77:20 You led your people like a **f**
78:52 he brought his people out like a **f**;

Ps 95: 7 of his pasture, the **f** under his care.
Isa 40:11 He tends his **f** like a shepherd:
Jer 10:21 prosper and all their **f** is scattered.
23: 2 "Because you have scattered my **f**
31:10 watch over his **f** like a shepherd.'
Eze 34: 2 not shepherds take care of the **f**?
Am 7:15 LORD took me from tending the **f**
Zec 11: 7 So I shepherded the **f** marked
11: 7 particularly the oppressed of the **f**.
Mt 26:31 the sheep of the **f** will be scattered.'
Lk 12:32 little **f**, for your Father has been
Jn 10:16 and there shall be one **f** and one
Ac 20:28 all the **f** of which the Holy Spirit has
1Co 9: 7 Who tends a **f** and does not drink
1Pe 5: 2 of God's **f** that is under your care,
5: 3 to you, but being examples to the **f**.

**FLOCKS** [FLOCK]
Ge 4: 2 Now Abel kept **f**, and Cain worked
Nu 32: 1 who had very large herds and **f**,
Lk 2: 8 keeping watch over their **f** at night.

**FLOG** [FLOGGED, FLOGGING]
Pr 19:25 **F** a mocker, and the simple will
Ac 22:25 As they stretched him out to **f** him,
22:25 **f** a Roman citizen who hasn't even

**FLOGGED** [FLOG]
Dt 25: 3 the guilty party is **f** more than that,
Mt 10:17 and be **f** in the synagogues.
Jn 19: 1 Pilate took Jesus and had him **f**.
Ac 5:40 the apostles in and had them **f**.
16:23 After they had been severely **f**,
22:24 He directed that he be **f**
2Co 11:23 frequently, been **f** more severely,

**FLOGGING**\* [FLOG]
Ps 89:32 with the rod, their iniquity with **f**;
Heb 11:36 Some faced jeers and **f**, and even

**FLOOD** [FLOODGATES,
FLOODWATERS]
Ge 7: 7 the ark to escape the waters of the **f**.
9:15 again will the waters become a **f**
Ps 29:10 LORD sits enthroned over the **f**;
Da 9:26 The end will come like a **f**:
Mal 2:13 You **f** the LORD's altar with tears.
Mt 24:38 For in the days before the **f**,
Lk 6:48 When a **f** came, the torrent struck
2Pe 2: 5 he brought the **f** on its ungodly

**FLOODGATES** [FLOOD]
Ge 7:11 the **f** of the heavens were opened.
Isa 24:18 The **f** of the heavens are opened,
Mal 3:10 I will not throw open the **f** of heaven

**FLOODWATERS** [FLOOD]
Ge 6:17 I am going to bring **f** on the earth
Isa 8: 7 bring against them the mighty **f**

**FLOOR**
Jdg 6:37 a wool fleece on the threshing **f**.
Ru 3: 3 Then go down to the threshing **f**,
1Ch 21:15 at the threshing **f** of Araunah
2Ch 3: 1 on the threshing **f** of Araunah

Hos  9: 1  of a prostitute at every threshing **f**.
Mt   3:12  and he will clear his threshing **f**,
Jas  2: 3  there" or "Sit on the **f** by my feet,"

# FLOUR
Lev  2: 1  your offering is to be of the finest **f**.
Nu   7:13  the finest **f** mixed with olive oil as
1Ki 17:12  only a handful of **f** in a jar
2Ki  4:41  Elisha said, "Get some **f**." He put it
Lk  13:21  of **f** until it worked all through

# FLOURISH [FLOURISHES, FLOURISHING]
Ps  72: 7  In his days may the righteous **f**
    92: 7  up like grass and all evildoers **f**,
    92:12  The righteous will **f** like a palm tree,
   103:15  they **f** like a flower of the field;
Pr  14:11  but the tent of the upright will **f**.
Isa 45: 8  let righteousness **f** with it;
    55:10  the earth and making it bud and **f**,
Eze 17:24  green tree and make the dry tree **f**.

# FLOURISHES* [FLOURISH]
Pr  12:12  but the root of the righteous **f**.

# FLOURISHING [FLOURISH]
Ps  37:35  and ruthless **f** like a luxuriant native
    52: 8  I am like an olive tree **f** in the house
Hos 14: 8  I am like a **f** juniper;

# FLOW [FLOWED, FLOWING, FLOWS]
Ex  14:26  that the waters may **f** back over
Nu  13:27  and it does **f** with milk and honey!
Ps  78:16  and made water **f** down like rivers.
   119:136  Streams of tears **f** from my eyes,
Ecc  1: 7  All streams **f** into the sea,
Joel 3:18  wine, and the hills will **f** with milk;
     3:18  A fountain will **f** out of the LORD's
Am   9:13  mountains and **f** from all the hills,
Zec 14: 8  that day living water will **f**
Jn   7:38  of living water will **f** from within
    19:34  bringing a sudden **f** of blood

# FLOWED [FLOW]
Ge   2:10  A river watering the garden **f**
Rev 14:20  and blood **f** out of the press,

# FLOWER [FLOWERS]
Ps  103:15  they flourish like a **f** of the field;
Jas  1:10  they will pass away like a wild **f**.

# FLOWERS [FLOWER]
Ex  25:33  Three cups shaped like almond **f**
1Ki  6:18  carved with gourds and open **f**.
Job 14: 2  They spring up like **f** and wither
Ps  37:20  enemies are like the **f** of the field,
Isa 40: 6  all human faithfulness is like the **f**
    40: 7  The grass withers and the **f** fall,
Lk  12:27  "Consider how the wild **f** grow.
1Pe  1:24  and all their glory is like the **f**
     1:24  the grass withers and the **f** fall,

# FLOWING [FLOW]
Ex   3: 8  land, a land **f** with milk and honey—
    33: 3  Go up to the land **f** with milk
Nu  16:14  brought us into a land **f** with milk
Jos  5: 6  us, a land **f** with milk and honey.
2Ki  4: 6  a jar left." Then the oil stopped **f**.
Ps 107:33  desert, **f** springs into thirsty ground,
Jer 32:22  a land **f** with milk and honey.
Eze 20: 6  them, a land **f** with milk and honey,
    32: 6  land with your **f** blood all the way
Da   7:10  A river of fire was **f**,
Rev 22: 1  **f** from the throne of God

# LAND FLOWING WITH MILK AND HONEY Ex 3:8, 17; 13:5; 33:3; Lev 20:24; Nu 14:8; 16:13, 14; Dt 6:3; 11:9; 26:9, 15; 27:3; 31:20; Jos 5:6; Jer 11:5; 32:22; Eze 20:6, 15

# FLOWS [FLOW]
Pr   4:23  everything you do **f** from it.
Eze 47: 9  will live wherever the river **f**.
    47: 9  because this water **f** there and makes

# FLUTE
Da   3: 5  as you hear the sound of the horn, **f**,

# FLY [FLEW, FLIES, FLIGHT, FLYING]
Ge   1:20  let birds **f** above the earth across
Pr  23: 5  and **f** off to the sky like an eagle.

# FLYING [FLY]
Ge   8: 7  and it kept **f** back and forth until
Dt  14:19  All **f** insects that swarm are unclean
Isa  6: 2  their feet, and with two they were **f**.
Zec  5: 1  and there before me was a **f** scroll.
Rev  4: 7  a man, the fourth was like a **f** eagle.
     8:13  an eagle that was **f** in midair call
    14: 6  I saw another angel **f** in midair,

# FOAL*
Zec  9: 9  donkey, on a colt, the **f** of a donkey.
Mt  21: 5  and on a colt, the **f** of a donkey.' "

# FOAM* [FOAMING]
Job 24:18  "Yet they are **f** on the surface
Ps  46: 3  though its waters roar and **f**

# FOAMING* [FOAM]
Dt  32:14  You drank the **f** blood of the grape.
Ps  75: 8  is a cup full of **f** wine mixed
Mk   9:20  and rolled around, **f** at the mouth.
Jude 1:13  waves of the sea, **f** up their shame;

# FOE [FOES]
Ps   8: 2  to silence the **f** and the avenger.
    61: 3  refuge, a strong tower against the **f**.

# FOES [FOE]
2Sa 22:49  You exalted me above my **f**;
Ps  44: 5  your name we trample our **f**.
    97: 3  and consumes his **f** on every side.
   106:41  nations, and their **f** ruled over them.
Na   1: 2  LORD takes vengeance on his **f**

## FOILS*

Ps   33:10  The LORD f the plans
Isa  44:25  who f the signs of false prophets

## FOLD [FOLDED, FOLDING, FOLDS]

Ecc   4: 5  Fools f their hands and ruin themselves.

## FOLDED [FOLD]

Ex   39: 9  a span wide — and f double.

## FOLDING* [FOLD]

Pr    6:10  a little f of the hands to rest—
     24:33  a little f of the hands to rest—

## FOLDS [FOLD]

Ne    5:13  I also shook out the f of my robe

## FOLLOW [FOLLOWED, FOLLOWERS, FOLLOWING, FOLLOWS]

Ex   16: 4  whether they will f my instructions.
     23: 2  "Do not f the crowd in doing
Lev  18: 4  laws and be careful to f my decrees.
Dt    4: 1  F them so that you may live
      5: 1  Learn them and be sure to f them.
      6:14  Do not f other gods, the gods
     17:19  f carefully all the words of this law
1Ki  11:10  forbidden Solomon to f other gods,
     18:21  f him; but if Baal is God, f him."
2Ch  34:33  they did not fail to f the LORD,
Ps   23: 6  love will f me all the days of my
    119:166  LORD, and I f your commands.
Jer  25: 6  Do not f other gods to serve
Eze  13: 3  the foolish prophets who f their own
Hos  11:10  They will f the LORD; he will roar
Mt    4:19  "Come, f me," Jesus said, "and I
      8:19  I will f you wherever you go."
      8:22  But Jesus told him, "F me, and let
     16:24  and take up their cross and f me.
     19:27  "We have left everything to f you!
Lk    9:23  take up their cross daily and f me.
      9:61  another said, "I will f you, Lord;
Jn   10: 4  his sheep f him because they know
     10: 5  But they will never f a stranger;
     10:27  I know them, and they f me.
     12:26  Whoever serves me must f me;
     13:36  you cannot f now, but you will f
     21:19  Then he said to him, "F me!"
1Co   1:12  One of you says, "I f Paul";
      1:12  another, "I f Apollos";
      1:12  still another, "I f Christ."
     11: 1  F my example, as I f the example
     14: 1  F the way of love and eagerly desire
Gal   2:14  force Gentiles to f Jewish customs?
Eph   5: 1  F God's example, therefore,
1Ti   5:15  fact already turned away to f Satan.
1Pe   2:21  that you should f in his steps.
2Pe   1:16  we did not f cleverly devised stories
      2:15  and wandered off to f the way
Jude  1:18  will be scoffers who will f their own
Rev  14: 4  They f the Lamb wherever he goes.

## FOLLOWED [FOLLOW]

Ex   14:23  and horsemen f them into the sea.

Nu   31:16  the ones who f Balaam's advice
     32:11  they have not f me wholeheartedly,
Dt    1:36  his feet on, because he f the LORD,
Jos  14:14  ever since, because he f the LORD,
Jdg   2:12  They f and worshiped various gods
2Ki  17: 8  and f the practices of the nations
2Ch  10:14  he f the advice of the young men
Pr    7:22  All at once he f her like an ox going
Jer   9:14  they have f the stubbornness of their
      9:14  they have f the Baals, as their
Eze  16:47  You not only f their ways
Mt    9: 9  him, and Matthew got up and f him.
     26:58  But Peter f him at a distance,
Mk    1:18  once they left their nets and f him.
Lk   18:43  he received his sight and f Jesus,
Jn    6:66  turned back and no longer f him.
Eph   2: 2  to live when you f the ways of this
Rev  13: 3  filled with wonder and f the beast.

## FOLLOWERS [FOLLOW]

Nu   16: 5  Then he said to Korah and all his f:
Ps  106:18  Fire blazed among their f;
Ac   17:34  of the people became f of Paul
Rev  17:14  be his called, chosen and faithful f."

## FOLLOWING [FOLLOW]

Nu   32:15  If you turn away from f him, he will
2Sa  15:12  and Absalom's f kept on increasing.
Ps  119:14  in f your statutes as one rejoices
Php   3:17  Join together in f my example,
Heb   4:11  one will perish by f their example

## FOLLOWS [FOLLOW]

Nu   14:24  spirit and f me wholeheartedly,
Jer   4:20  Disaster f disaster; the whole land
Eze  18: 9  He f my decrees and faithfully
Jn    8:12  Whoever f me will never walk

## FOLLY [FOOL]

1Sa  25:25  means Fool, and f goes with him.
Pr    9:13  F is an unruly woman; she is simple
     13:16  knowledge, but fools expose their f.
     14:18  The simple inherit f, but the prudent
     14:24  crown, but the f of fools yields f.
     14:29  but the quick-tempered display f.
     16:22  but f brings punishment to fools.
     19: 3  One's own f leads to ruin,
     22:15  F is bound up in the heart of a child,
     26: 4  answer fools according to their f,
     26: 5  Answer fools according to their f,
Ecc   2:13  I saw that wisdom is better than f,
     10: 1  so a little f outweighs wisdom
Mk    7:22  envy, slander, arrogance and f.
2Ti   3: 9  their f will be clear to everyone.

## FOOD [FOODS]

Ge    1:30  I give every green plant for f."
      3: 6  the fruit of the tree was good for f
      3:19  you will eat your f until you return
      9: 3  lives and moves will be f for you.
Lev   3:11  the altar as a f offering presented
     21: 8  they offer up the f of your God.
Nu   21: 5  And we detest this miserable f!"
Jos   5:12  after they ate this f from the land;
1Ki  17: 4  the ravens to supply you with f there."
Ps   42: 3  My tears have been my f day

Ps    78:18   test by demanding the **f** they craved.
  104:27   give them their **f** at the proper time.
Pr    12: 9   to be somebody and have no **f**.
  12:11   their land will have abundant **f**,
  20:13   awake and you will have **f** to spare.
  20:17   **F** gained by fraud tastes sweet,
  21:20   The wise store up choice **f** and olive
  22: 9   for they share their **f** with the poor.
  23: 3   his delicacies, for that **f** is deceptive.
  23: 6   Do not eat the **f** of a begrudging
  25:21   enemy is hungry, give him **f** to eat;
  31:14   ships, bringing her **f** from afar.
  31:15   she provides **f** for her family
Isa   58: 7   not to share your **f** with the hungry
  65:25   ox, but dust will be the serpent's **f**.
Eze   18: 7   robbery but gives his **f** to the hungry
Da     1: 8   not to defile himself with the royal **f**
Mt     3: 4   His **f** was locusts and wild honey.
  6:25   Is not life more important than **f**,
Jn     4:32   them, "I have **f** to eat that you know
  4:34   "My **f**," said Jesus, "is to do
  6:27   Do not work for **f** that spoils,
  6:27   but for **f** that endures to eternal life,
  6:55   For my flesh is real **f** and my blood
Ac    15:20   to abstain from **f** polluted by idols,
1Co    3: 2   not solid **f**, for you were not yet
  6:13   "**F** for the stomach and the stomach
  8: 1   Now about **f** sacrificed to idols:
  8: 8   But **f** does not bring us near to God;
2Co   11:27   thirst and have often gone without **f**;
1Ti    6: 8   But if we have **f** and clothing,
Heb    5:14   But solid **f** is for the mature,
Jas    2:15   sister is without clothes and daily **f**.

## FOODS [FOOD]

Mk     7:19   this, Jesus declared all **f** clean.)
1Ti    4: 3   order them to abstain from certain **f**,

## FOOL [FOLLY, FOOL'S, FOOLISH, FOOLISHNESS, FOOLS]

1Sa   25:25   his name means **F**, and folly goes
Pr    10:10   and a chattering **f** comes to ruin.
  10:18   lying lips and spreads slander is a **f**.
  14:16   but a **f** is hotheaded and yet feels
  15: 5   A **f** spurns a parent's discipline,
  17:12   of her cubs than a **f** bent on folly.
  17:21   To have a **f** for a child brings grief;
  17:21   no joy for the parent of a godless **f**.
  19:10   It is not fitting for a **f** to live
  20: 3   strife, but every **f** is quick to quarrel.
  26: 7   is a proverb in the mouth of a **f**.
  29:20   There is more hope for a **f** than
Ecc    2:16   the wise, like the **f**, will not be long
  2:16   Like the **f**, the wise too must die!
Hos    9: 7   great, the prophet is considered a **f**,
Mt     5:22   And anyone who says, 'You **f**!'
Lk    12:20   "But God said to him, 'You **f**!
2Co   11:21   I am speaking as a **f**—I also dare

## FOOL'S [FOOL]

Pr    12:23   but a **f** heart blurts out folly.
  14: 3   A **f** mouth lashes out with pride,

## FOOLISH [FOOL]

Pr     8: 5   you who are **f**, set your hearts on it.
  10: 1   but **f** children bring grief to their

Pr    14: 1   her own hands the **f** one tears hers
  14: 7   Stay away from the **f**,
  15:20   but **f** children despise their mother.
  17:25   **F** children bring grief to their father
  19:13   A **f** child is a father's ruin.
Jer    5:21   this, you **f** and senseless people,
Eze   13: 3   the **f** prophets who follow their own
Mt     7:26   practice is like a **f** man who built his
  25: 2   Five of them were **f** and five were
Lk    11:40   You **f** people! Did not the one who
  24:25   He said to them, "How **f** you are,
1Co    1:20   Has not God made **f** the wisdom
  1:27   God chose the **f** things of the world
Gal    3: 1   You **f** Galatians!
Eph    5: 4   be obscenity, **f** talk or coarse joking,
  5:17   Therefore do not be **f**,
2Ti    2:23   Don't have anything to do with **f**
Tit    3: 3   At one time we too were **f**,
  3: 9   But avoid **f** controversies

## FOOLISHNESS* [FOOL]

2Sa   15:31   turn Ahithophel's counsel into **f**."
1Co    1:18   of the cross is **f** to those who are
  1:21   God was pleased through the **f**
  1:23   block to Jews and **f** to Gentiles,
  1:25   the **f** of God is wiser than human
  2:14   Spirit of God but considers them **f**,
  3:19   of this world is **f** in God's sight.
2Co   11: 1   you will put up with me in a little **f**.

## FOOLS [FOOL]

Ps    14: 1   **F** say in their hearts, "There is no
Pr     1: 7   but **f** despise wisdom
  1:32   complacency of **f** will destroy them;
  3:35   inherit honor, but **f** get only shame.
  10:21   many, but **f** die for lack of sense.
  12:15   The way of **f** seems right to them,
  12:16   **F** show their annoyance at once,
  13:19   soul, but **f** detest turning from evil.
  13:20   for a companion of **f** suffers harm.
  14: 9   **F** mock at making amends for sin,
  14:24   crown, but the folly of **f** yields folly.
  16:22   but folly brings punishment to **f**.
  17:16   Why should **f** have money in hand
  17:28   Even **f** are thought wise if they keep
  18: 2   **F** find no pleasure in understanding
  18: 7   The mouths of **f** are their undoing,
  21:20   but **f** gulp theirs down.
  23: 9   Do not speak to **f**, for they will
  24: 7   Wisdom is too high for **f**;
  26: 4   Do not answer **f** according to their
  26: 5   Answer **f** according to their folly,
  26:11   to its vomit, so **f** repeat their folly.
  26:12   There is more hope for **f** than
  27:22   Though you grind **f** in a mortar,
  28:26   Those who trust in themselves are **f**,
  29:11   **F** give full vent to their rage,
Ecc    4: 5   **F** fold their hands and ruin
  5: 4   He has no pleasure in **f**;
  7: 4   but the heart of **f** is in the house
  7: 5   person than to listen to the song of **f**.
  7: 6   under the pot, so is the laughter of **f**.
  7: 7   Extortion turns the wise into **f**,
  10: 6   **F** are put in many high positions,
Mt    23:17   You blind **f**! Which is greater:
Ro     1:22   claimed to be wise, they became **f**

1Co  3:18  you should become "f" so that you
     4:10  We are f for Christ, but you are so
2Co 11:19  put up with f since you are so wise!

## FOOT  [BAREFOOT, FEET, FOOTHOLD, UNDERFOOT]

Ex  21:24  for tooth, hand for hand, f for f,
    32:19  to pieces at the f of the mountain.
Dt  11:24  where you set your f will be yours:
Jos   1: 3  every place where you set your f,
Ps  91:12  will not strike your f against a stone.
    121: 3  He will not let your f slip—
Pr   1:15  them, do not set f on their paths;
     3:23  safety, and your f will not stumble.
     4:27  or the left; keep your f from evil.
    25:17  Seldom set f in your neighbor's
Isa   1: 6  the sole of your f to the top of your
Mt    4: 6  you will not strike your f against
     18: 8  or your f causes you to stumble,
Lk    4:11  you will not strike your f against
1Co 12:15  Now if the f should say, "Because I
Rev 10: 2  He planted his right f on the sea
     10: 2  on the sea and his left f on the land,

## FOOTHOLD*  [FOOT]

Ps  69: 2  the miry depths, where there is no f.
    73: 2  I had nearly lost my f.
Eph  4:27  and do not give the devil a f.

## FOOTSTEPS  [STEP]

Ps 119:133  Direct my f according to your word;
Ro   4:12  follow in the f of the faith that our

## FOOTSTOOL

1Ch 28: 2  for the f of our God, and I made
Ps  99: 5  our God and worship at his f;
    110: 1  hand until I make your enemies a f
Isa  66: 1  is my throne, and the earth is my f.
La    2: 1  he has not remembered his f
Mt    5:35  or by the earth, for it is his f;
Ac    7:49  is my throne, and the earth is my f.
Heb   1:13  hand until I make your enemies a f
     10:13  for his enemies to be made his f.

## FORBEARANCE*

Ro   2: 4  riches of his kindness, f and patience,
     3:25  his f he had left the sins committed

## FORBID  [FORBIDDEN, FORBIDS]

1Co 14:39  and do not f speaking in tongues.
1Ti  4: 3  They f people to marry and order

## FORBIDDEN  [FORBID]

1Ki 11:10  Although he had f Solomon

## FORBIDS*  [FORBID]

Nu  30: 5  But if her father f her when he hears
    30: 8  if her husband f her when he hears
Jn   5:10  the law f you to carry your mat."

## FORCE  [FORCED, FORCEFUL, FORCEFULLY, FORCES, FORCING]

Ex  19:24  people must not f their way through
Jn   6:15  to come and make him king by f,

Ac  26:11  and I tried to f them to blaspheme.
Gal  2:14  that you f Gentiles to follow Jewish

## FORCED  [FORCE]

Ex   1:11  them to oppress them with f labor,
Jdg  1:28  pressed the Canaanites into f labor
1Ki  9:15  account of the f labor King Solomon
Mt  27:32  and they f him to carry the cross.
Phm  1:14  any favor you do would not seem f
Rev 13:16  It also f all people, great and small,

## FORCEFUL*  [FORCE]

2Co 10:10  "His letters are weighty and f,

## FORCEFULLY*  [FORCE]

1Sa 18:10  evil spirit from God came f on Saul.
Isa  28: 2  he will throw it f to the ground.

## FORCES  [FORCE]

Mt   5:41  If anyone f you to go one mile,
Gal  4: 3  elemental spiritual f of the world.
     4: 9  to those weak and miserable f?
Eph  6:12  against the spiritual f of evil
Col  2: 8  and the elemental spiritual f
     2:20  elemental spiritual f of this world,

## FORCING*  [FORCE]

Lk  16:16  and people are f their way into it.
Ac   7:19  oppressed our ancestors by f them

## FORDED*  [FORDS]

Jos  2:23  f the river and came to Joshua son

## FORDS  [FORDED]

Jos  2: 7  road that leads to the f of the Jordan,

## FOREFATHER  [FATHER]

1Ki 15: 3  as the heart of David his f had been.
Ro   4: 1  say that Abraham, the f of us Jews,

## FOREFATHERS*  [FATHER]

Da  11:24  neither his fathers nor his f did.

## FOREHEAD  [FOREHEADS]

Ex  13: 9  a reminder on your f that this law
    28:38  It will be on Aaron's f, and he will
    28:38  will be on Aaron's f continually so
1Sa 17:49  it and struck the Philistine on the f.
    17:49  The stone sank into his f, and he fell
Rev 14: 9  receives its mark on their f
     17: 5  This title was written on her f:

## FOREHEADS  [FOREHEAD]

Dt   6: 8  your hands and bind them on your f.
Rev  7: 3  we put a seal on the f of the servants
     9: 4  not have the seal of God on their f.
    13:16  on their right hands or on their f,
    14: 1  his Father's name written on their f.
    20: 4  had not received his mark on their f
    22: 4  face, and his name will be on their f.

## FOREIGN [FOREIGNER, FOREIGNERS]

Ge  35: 2  "Get rid of the **f** gods you have
Dt  32:12  no **f** god was with him.
Jos 24:23  "throw away the **f** gods that are
1Ki 11: 1  loved many **f** women besides
2Ch 14: 3  He removed the **f** altars and the high
     33:15  He got rid of the **f** gods
Ps  81: 9  You shall have no **f** god among you;
Isa 28:11  with **f** lips and strange tongues God
Jer  2:25  I love **f** gods, and I must go
Ac  17:18  seems to be advocating **f** gods."

## FOREIGNER [FOREIGN]

Ex  22:21  "Do not mistreat or oppress a **f**,
Lev 19:10  for the poor and the **f**.
     24:22  same law for the **f** and the native-born.
Dt  23:20  You may charge a **f** interest, but not
Ps 146: 9  The LORD watches over the **f**
Lk  17:18  give praise to God except this **f**?"
1Co 14:11  is saying, I am a **f** to the speaker,

## FOREIGNERS [FOREIGN]

Ge  31:15  Does he not regard us as **f**?
Ex  21: 8  He has no right to sell her to **f**,
     23: 9  feels to be **f**, because you were **f**
1Ki  8:41  "As for the **f** who do not belong
Jer  5:19  so now you will serve **f** in a land not
1Co 14:21  through the lips of **f** I will speak
Eph  2:12  **f** to the covenants of the promise,
     2:19  you are no longer **f** and strangers,
Heb 11:13  admitting that they were **f** and strangers
1Pe  2:11  I urge you, as **f** and exiles,

## FOREKNEW* [KNOW]

Ro   8:29  For those God **f** he also predestined
     11: 2  did not reject his people, whom he **f**.

## FOREKNOWLEDGE* [KNOW]

Ac   2:23  you by God's deliberate plan and **f**;
1Pe  1: 2  according to the **f** of God the Father,

## FORESAW* [FORESEE]

Gal  3: 8  Scripture **f** that God would justify

## FORESEE* [FORESAW]

Isa 47:11  you cannot **f** will suddenly come

## FORESKIN* [FORESKINS]

Ex   4:25  cut off her son's **f** and touched

## FORESKINS [FORESKIN]

1Sa 18:25  the bride than a hundred Philistine **f**,

## FOREST

2Sa 18: 8  the **f** swallowed up more men
1Ki  7: 2  the **F** of Lebanon a hundred cubits
1Ch 16:33  Let the trees of the **f** sing, let them
Ps  50:10  for every animal of the **f** is mine,
Jas  3: 5  Consider what a great **f** is set on fire

## FORETELL* [FORETELLS, FORETOLD]

Isa 44: 7  yes, let them **f** what will come.
     44: 8  I not proclaim this and **f** it long ago?

## FORETELLS* [FORETELL]

Dt  13: 1  or one who **f** by dreams,

## FORETOLD [FORETELL]

Ps 105:19  till what he **f** came to pass,
Isa 48: 3  I **f** the former things long ago,
Jude 1:17  apostles of our Lord Jesus Christ **f**.

## FOREVER [EVER]

Ge   3:22  the tree of life and eat, and live **f**."
      6: 3  not contend with human beings **f**,
Ex   3:15  "This is my name **f**, the name you
     31:17  sign between me and the Israelites **f**,
Dt  29:29  belong to us and to our children **f**,
2Sa  7:13  the throne of his kingdom **f**.
      7:26  so that your name will be great **f**.
1Ki  2:33  head of Joab and his descendants **f**.
      2:33  there be the LORD's peace **f**."
      9: 3  built, by putting my Name there **f**.
1Ch 16:15  He remembers his covenant **f**,
     16:41  LORD, "for his love endures **f**."
     17:24  and that your name will be great **f**.
2Ch  5:13  "He is good; his love endures **f**."
     33: 7  of Israel, I will put my Name **f**.
Ezr  3:11  his love toward Israel endures **f**."
Ps   9: 7  The LORD reigns **f**;
     19: 9  of the LORD is pure, enduring **f**.
     23: 6  dwell in the house of the LORD **f**.
     28: 9  be their shepherd and carry them **f**.
     29:10  the LORD is enthroned as King **f**.
     33:11  plans of the LORD stand firm **f**,
     44: 8  and we will praise your name **f**.
     44:23  Rouse yourself! Do not reject us **f**.
     61: 4  I long to dwell in your tent **f**
     72:19  Praise be to his glorious name **f**;
     73:26  of my heart and my portion **f**.
     74:10  Will the foe revile your name **f**?
     77: 8  Has his unfailing love vanished **f**?
     79:13  of your pasture, will praise you **f**;
     81:15  and their punishment would last **f**.
     86:12  I will glorify your name **f**.
     89: 1  sing of the LORD's great love **f**;
     92: 8  But you, LORD, are **f** exalted.
    100: 5  is good and his love endures **f**;
    102:12  But you, LORD, sit enthroned **f**;
    104:31  the glory of the LORD endure **f**;
    107: 1  for he is good; his love endures **f**.
    110: 4  "You are a priest **f**, in the order
    111: 3  and his righteousness endures **f**.
    112: 3  they will be remembered **f**.
    117: 2  of the LORD endures **f**.
    118: 1  for he is good; his love endures **f**.
    119:111  Your statutes are my heritage **f**;
    119:152  that you established them to last **f**.
    136: 1  *His love endures f.*
    146: 6  he remains faithful **f**.
Pr  10:25  gone, but the righteous stand firm **f**.
     27:24  for riches do not endure **f**,
Ecc  3:14  everything God does will endure **f**;
Isa 25: 8  he will swallow up death **f**.

Isa   26: 4  Trust in the LORD **f**,
      32:17  will be quietness and confidence **f**.
      40: 8  but the word of our God endures **f**."
      51: 6  But my salvation will last **f**,
      51: 8  But my righteousness will last **f**,
      57:15  he who lives **f**, whose name is holy:
      59:21  from this time on and **f**,"
Jer    3:12  the LORD, 'I will not be angry **f**.
      33:11  his love endures **f**."
La     5:19  You, LORD, reign **f**;
Eze   37:26  put my sanctuary among them **f**.
Da     2:44  to an end, but it will itself endure **f**.
       6:26  is the living God and he endures **f**;
Hos    2:19  I will betroth you to me **f**;
Jn     6:51  eats of this bread will live **f**.
      14:16  to help you and be with you **f**—
Ro     9: 5  who is God over all, **f** praised!
      16:27  God be glory **f** through Jesus Christ!
1Co    9:25  do it to get a crown that will last **f**.
1Th    4:17  And so we will be with the Lord **f**.
Heb    5: 6  "You are a priest **f**, in the order
       7:17  "You are a priest **f**, in the order
       7:24  but because Jesus lives **f**, he has
      13: 8  the same yesterday and today and **f**.
1Pe    1:25  but the word of the Lord endures **f**."
1Jn    2:17  does the will of God lives **f**.
2Jn    1: 2  lives in us and will be with us **f**:

## HIS LOVE ENDURES FOREVER See
   LOVE

## FOREVERMORE [EVER]

Ps   125: 2  his people both now and **f**.
     131: 3  hope in the LORD both now and **f**.

## FORFEIT

Mk     8:36  the whole world, yet **f** your soul?
Lk     9:25  and yet lose or **f** your very self?

## FORGAVE* [FORGIVE]

Ps    32: 5  And you **f** the guilt of my sin.
      65: 3  by sins, you **f** our transgressions.
      78:38  he **f** their iniquities and did not
      85: 2  You **f** the iniquity of your people
Lk     7:42  so he **f** the debts of both.
Eph    4:32  other, just as in Christ God **f** you.
Col    2:13  He **f** us all our sins,
       3:13  Forgive as the Lord **f** you.

## FORGET [FORGETS, FORGETTING, FORGOT, FORGOTTEN]

Dt     4:23  Be careful not to **f** the covenant
       6:12  that you do not **f** the LORD,
2Ki   17:38  Do not **f** the covenant I have made
Job    8:13  Such is the destiny of all who **f** God;
Ps     9:17  the dead, all the nations that **f** God.
      10:12  hand, O God. Do not **f** the helpless.
      50:22  you who **f** God, or I will tear you
      78: 7  in God and would not **f** his deeds
     103: 2  my soul, and **f** not all his benefits—
     119:93  I will never **f** your precepts,
     137: 5  If I **f** you, Jerusalem, may my right
             hand **f** its skill.
Pr     3: 1  My son, do not **f** my teaching,
       4: 5  do not **f** my words or turn away
      31: 5  drink and **f** what has been decreed,

Isa   49:15  Though she may **f**, I will not **f** you!
      51:13  that you **f** the LORD your Maker,
Jer    2:32  Does a young woman **f** her jewelry,
      23:39  I will surely **f** you and cast you
Heb    6:10  he will not **f** your work and the love
      13: 2  Do not **f** to show hospitality
      13:16  And do not **f** to do good
Jas    1:24  immediately **f** what they look like.
2Pe    3: 8  But do not **f** this one thing,

## FORGETS [FORGET]
Jn    16:21  is born she **f** the anguish because

## FORGETTING* [FORGET]
Php    3:13  **F** what is behind and straining
Jas    1:25  not **f** what they have heard,

## FORGIVE* [FORGAVE, FORGIVEN, FORGIVENESS, FORGIVES, FORGIVING]

Ge    50:17  I ask you to **f** your brothers the sins
      50:17  Now please **f** the sins of the servants
Ex    10:17  Now **f** my sin once more and pray
      23:21  he will not **f** your rebellion,
      32:32  But now, please **f** their sin—
      34: 9  **f** our wickedness and our sin,
Nu    14:19  great love, **f** the sin of these people,
Dt    29:20  will never be willing to **f** them;
Jos   24:19  He will not **f** your rebellion
1Sa   15:25  **f** my sin and come back with me,
      25:28  "Please **f** your servant's
1Ki    8:30  place, and when you hear, **f**.
       8:34  and **f** the sin of your people Israel
       8:36  and **f** the sin of your servants,
       8:39  **F** and act; deal with everyone
       8:50  And **f** your people, who have sinned
       8:50  **f** all the offenses they have
2Ki    5:18  may the LORD **f** your servant
       5:18  may the LORD **f** your servant
      24: 4  and the LORD was not willing to **f**.
2Ch    6:21  and when you hear, **f**.
       6:25  and **f** the sin of your people Israel
       6:27  and **f** the sin of your servants,
       6:30  **F**, and deal with everyone according
       6:39  And **f** your people, who have sinned
       7:14  and I will **f** their sin and will heal
Job    7:21  pardon my offenses and **f** my sins?
Ps    19:12  **F** my hidden faults.
      25:11  LORD, **f** my iniquity, though it is
      79: 9  and **f** our sins for your name's sake.
Isa    2: 9  do not **f** them.
Jer    5: 1  and seeks the truth, I will **f** this city.
       5: 7  "Why should I **f** you?
      18:23  Do not **f** their crimes or blot
      31:34  "For I will **f** their wickedness
      33: 8  and will **f** all their sins of rebellion
      36: 3  then I will **f** their wickedness
      50:20  for I will **f** the remnant I spare.
Da     9:19  Lord, **f**! Lord, hear and act!
Hos    1: 6  of Israel, that I should at all **f** them.
      14: 2  "**F** all our sins and receive us
Am     7: 2  I cried out, "Sovereign LORD, **f**!
Mt     6:12  And **f** us our debts, as we also have
       6:14  if you **f** others when they sin against
       6:14  heavenly Father will also **f** you.
       6:15  But if you do not **f** others their sins,

| | | |
|---|---|---|
| Mt | 6:15 | your Father will not f your sins. |
| | 9: 6 | has authority on earth to f sins." |
| | 18:21 | times shall I f someone who sins |
| | 18:35 | each of you unless you f a brother |
| Mk | 2: 7 | Who can f sins but God alone?" |
| | 2:10 | has authority on earth to f sins." |
| | 11:25 | anything against anyone, f them, |
| | 11:25 | in heaven may f you your sins." |
| Lk | 5:21 | Who can f sins but God alone?" |
| | 5:24 | has authority on earth to f sins." |
| | 6:37 | F, and you will be forgiven. |
| | 11: 4 | F us our sins, for we also f everyone |
| | 17: 3 | and if they repent, f them. |
| | 17: 4 | saying 'I repent,' you must f them." |
| | 23:34 | "Father, f them, for they do not |
| Jn | 20:23 | If you f the sins of anyone, |
| | 20:23 | if you do not f them, they are |
| Ac | 5:31 | repentance and f their sins. |
| | 8:22 | that he may f you for having such |
| 2Co | 2: 7 | you ought to f and comfort him, |
| | 2:10 | Anyone you f, I also f. |
| | 2:10 | if there was anything to f— |
| | 12:13 | a burden to you? F me this wrong! |
| Col | 3:13 | and f one another if any of you has |
| | 3:13 | F as the Lord forgave you. |
| Heb | 8:12 | For I will f their wickedness |
| 1Jn | 1: 9 | just and will f us our sins and purify |

## FORGIVEN [FORGIVE]

| | | |
|---|---|---|
| Lev | 4:20 | for them, and they will be f. |
| Nu | 14:20 | "I have f them, as you asked. |
| Ps | 32: 1 | are those whose transgressions are f, |
| Mk | 2: 9 | man, 'Your sins are f,' or to say, |
| | 3:29 | the Holy Spirit will never be f, |
| Lk | 7:47 | tell you, her many sins have been f— |
| | 7:47 | But whoever has been f little loves |
| Ro | 4: 7 | are those whose transgressions are f, |
| Jas | 5:15 | If they have sinned, they will be f. |

## FORGIVENESS [FORGIVE]

| | | |
|---|---|---|
| Ps | 130: 4 | But with you there is f, so that we |
| Mt | 26:28 | out for many for the f of sins. |
| Mk | 1: 4 | of repentance for the f of sins. |
| Lk | 1:77 | salvation through the f of their sins, |
| | 3: 3 | of repentance for the f of sins. |
| | 24:47 | for the f of sins will be preached |
| Ac | 10:43 | in him receives f of sins through his |
| | 13:38 | that through Jesus the f of sins is |
| | 26:18 | so that they may receive f of sins |
| Eph | 1: 7 | through his blood, the f of sins, |
| Col | 1:14 | we have redemption, the f of sins. |
| Heb | 9:22 | the shedding of blood there is no f. |

## FORGIVES* [FORGIVE]

| | | |
|---|---|---|
| Ps | 103: 3 | who f all your sins and heals all |
| Mic | 7:18 | f the transgression of the remnant |
| Lk | 7:49 | "Who is this who even f sins?" |

## FORGIVING* [FORGIVE]

| | | |
|---|---|---|
| Ex | 34: 7 | and f wickedness, rebellion and sin. |
| Nu | 14:18 | abounding in love and f sin |
| Ne | 9:17 | But you are a f God, |
| Ps | 86: 5 | Lord, are f and good, |
| | 99: 8 | you were to Israel a f God, |
| Da | 9: 9 | The Lord our God is merciful and f, |
| Eph | 4:32 | to one another, f each other, just as |

## FORGOT [FORGET]

| | | |
|---|---|---|
| Dt | 32:18 | you f the God who gave you birth. |
| 1Sa | 12: 9 | "But they f the LORD their God; |
| Ps | 78:11 | They f what he had done, |
| | 106:21 | They f the God who saved them, |
| Jer | 23:27 | just as their ancestors f my name |

## FORGOTTEN [FORGET]

| | | |
|---|---|---|
| Job | 11: 6 | God has even f some of your sin. |
| Ps | 44:20 | If we had f the name of our God |
| | 77: 9 | Has God f to be merciful? Has he |
| Isa | 17:10 | You have f God your Savior; |
| | 49:14 | forsaken me, the Lord has f me." |
| Jer | 2:32 | Yet my people have f me, |
| Hos | 8:14 | Israel has f their Maker and built |
| Lk | 12: 6 | Yet not one of them is f by God. |
| Heb | 12: 5 | have you completely f this word |
| 2Pe | 1: 9 | and you have f that you have been |

## FORM [FORMED, FORMLESS, FORMS]

| | | |
|---|---|---|
| Ex | 20: 4 | an image in the f of anything |
| Dt | 4:15 | You saw no f of any kind the day |
| Isa | 52:14 | and his f marred beyond human |
| Col | 2: 9 | of the Deity lives in bodily f, |
| 2Ti | 3: 5 | having a f of godliness but denying |

## FORMED [FORM]

| | | |
|---|---|---|
| Ge | 2: 7 | the LORD God f a man |
| Dt | 32: 6 | Creator, who made you and f you? |
| Ps | 94: 9 | Does he who f the eye not see? |
| | 103:14 | for he knows how we are f, |
| Pr | 8:23 | I was f long ages ago, |
| Ecc | 11: 5 | or how the body is f in a mother's |
| Isa | 29:16 | Shall what is f say to the one who f |
| | 43:10 | Before me no god was f, nor will |
| | 45:18 | be empty, but f it to be inhabited— |
| | 49: 5 | he who f me in the womb to be his |
| Jer | 1: 5 | "Before I f you in the womb I knew |
| | 18: 4 | so the potter f it into another pot, |
| Ro | 9:20 | what is f say to the one who f it, |
| Gal | 4:19 | of childbirth until Christ is f in you, |
| 1Ti | 2:13 | For Adam was f first, then Eve. |
| Heb | 11: 3 | that the universe was f at God's |
| 2Pe | 3: 5 | and the earth was f out of water |

## FORMER

| | | |
|---|---|---|
| Dt | 4:32 | Ask now about the f days, |
| Ezr | 3:12 | who had seen the f temple, |
| Ps | 77: 5 | I thought about the f days, the years |
| Isa | 46: 9 | Remember the f things, |
| Lk | 11:42 | latter without leaving the f undone. |

## FORMLESS* [FORM]

| | | |
|---|---|---|
| Ge | 1: 2 | Now the earth was f and empty, |
| Jer | 4:23 | at the earth, and it was f and empty; |

## FORMS [FORM]

| | | |
|---|---|---|
| Ps | 33:15 | he who f the hearts of all, |
| Am | 4:13 | He who f the mountains, |
| Zec | 12: 1 | who f the spirit in human beings, |

## FORSAKE [FORSAKEN, FORSAKING]

| | | |
|---|---|---|
| Dt | 31: 6 | he will never leave you nor f you." |

Jos  1: 5  I will never leave you nor **f** you.
    24:16  us to **f** the LORD to serve other
2Ch 15: 2  you, but if you **f** him, he will **f** you.
Ps  27:10  Though my father and mother **f** me,
    37:28  and will not **f** his faithful ones.
    94:14  he will never **f** his inheritance.
Pr   4: 6  Do not **f** wisdom, and she will
    27:10  Do not **f** your friend or a friend
Isa  1:28  those who **f** the LORD will perish.
    55: 7  Let the wicked **f** their ways
Jer 17:13  all who **f** you will be put to shame.
Heb 13: 5  will I leave you; never will I **f** you."

## FORSAKEN [FORSAKE]

Ezr  9: 9  our God has not **f** us in our bondage.
     9:10  For we have **f** the commands
Ps   9:10  have never **f** those who seek you.
    22: 1  God, my God, why have you **f** me?
    37:25  yet I have never seen the righteous **f**
Isa 49:14  "The LORD has **f** me, the Lord
Mt  27:46  my God, why have you **f** me?").
Rev  2: 4  You have **f** the love you had at first.

## FORSAKING [FORSAKE]

1Sa  8: 8  day, **f** me and serving other gods,

## FORTH

Ge   3:24  **f** to guard the way to the tree of life.
Ps  19: 2  Day after day they pour **f** speech;
    50: 2  perfect in beauty, God shines **f**.
Eph  4:14  tossed back and **f** by the waves,

## FORTIFIED [FORTRESS]

Nu  13:28  and the cities are **f** and very large.
Ne   9:25  They captured **f** cities and fertile
Pr  18:10  name of the LORD is a **f** tower;

## FORTRESS [FORTIFIED]

2Sa  5: 7  David captured the **f** of Zion—
    22: 2  is my rock, my **f** and my deliverer;
Ps  28: 8  a **f** of salvation for his anointed one.
    31: 2  of refuge, a strong **f** to save me.
    46: 7  is with us; the God of Jacob is our **f**.
    59:17  are my **f**, my God on whom I can
    71: 3  me, for you are my rock and my **f**.
Pr  14:26  fear the LORD have a secure **f**,
Isa 17:10  not remembered the Rock, your **f**.
Jer 16:19  my strength and my **f**, my refuge

## FORTUNE* [FORTUNE-TELLING, FORTUNES]

Ge  30:11  Then Leah said, "What good **f**!"
Job 31:25  wealth, the **f** my hands had gained,
Pr  21: 6  A **f** made by a lying tongue is
Isa 65:11  who spread a table for **F** and fill

## FORTUNE-TELLING* [FORTUNE]

Ac  16:16  deal of money for her owners by **f**.

## FORTUNES [FORTUNE]

Dt  30: 3  your God will restore your **f**
Ps 126: 1  When the LORD **r** the fortunes of Zion,
Jer 32:44  Negev, because I will restore their **f**,
Hos  6:11  "Whenever I would restore the **f**
Mic  3:11  and her prophets tell **f** for money.

## FORTY [40]

Ge   7: 4  on the earth for **f** days and **f** nights,
    18:29  "What if only **f** are found there?"
    18:29  "For the sake of **f**, I will not do it."
Ex  16:35  The Israelites ate manna **f** years,
    24:18  on the mountain **f** days and **f** nights.
Nu  14:34  For **f** years—one year for each
    14:34  of the **f** days you explored the land—
Dt  25: 3  must not impose more than **f** lashes.
Jos 14: 7  I was **f** years old when Moses
1Sa  4:18  He had led Israel **f** years.
2Sa  5: 4  became king, and he reigned **f** years.
1Ki 19: 8  he traveled **f** days and **f** nights until
2Ch  9:30  in Jerusalem over all Israel **f** years.
Ne   9:21  For **f** years you sustained them
Eze 29:12  cities will lie desolate **f** years among
Am   2:10  led you **f** years in the wilderness
Jnh  3: 4  "**F** more days and Nineveh will be
Mt   4: 2  After fasting **f** days and **f** nights,
Lk   4: 2  where for **f** days he was tempted
2Co 11:24  the Jews the **f** lashes minus one.
Heb  3:17  whom was he angry for **f** years?

## FORTY DAYS Ge 7:4, 12, 17; 8:6; 50:3; Ex
    24:18; 34:28; Nu 13:25; 14:34; Dt 9:9, 11, 18,
    25; 10:10; 1Sa 17:16; 1Ki 19:8; Mt 4:2; Mk 1:13;
    Lk 4:2; Ac 1:3

## FORTY YEARS Ge 25:20; 26:34; Ex 16:35; Nu
    14:33, 34; 32:13; Dt 2:7; 8:2, 4; 29:5; Jos 5:6;
    14:7; Jdg 3:11; 5:31; 8:28; 13:1; 1Sa 4:18; 2Sa
    2:10; 5:4; 1Ki 2:11; 11:42; 2Ki 12:1; 1Ch 29:27;
    2Ch 9:30; 24:1; Ne 9:21; Job 42:16; Ps 95:10;
    Eze 29:11, 12, 13; Am 2:10; 5:25; Ac 4:22; 7:23,
    30, 36, 42; 13:18, 21; Heb 3:9, 17

## FOSTER*

Pr  17: 9  would **f** love covers over an offense,
    17:11  Evildoers **f** rebellion against God;
Isa 49:23  Kings will be your **f** fathers,

## FOUGHT [FIGHT]

Jos 10:42  the God of Israel, **f** for Israel.
1Co 15:32  If I **f** wild beasts in Ephesus with no
2Ti  4: 7  I have **f** the good fight, I have
Rev 12: 7  and his angels **f** against the dragon,
    12: 7  the dragon and his angels **f** back.

## FOUND [FIND]

Ge   6: 8  But Noah **f** favor in the eyes
Ex  12:19  no yeast is to be **f** in your houses.
    33:12  and you have **f** favor with me.'
1Sa  9: 2  young man as could be **f** anywhere
2Ki 22: 8  "I have **f** the Book of the Law
1Ch 28: 9  If you seek him, he will be **f** by you;
2Ch 15:15  God eagerly, and he was **f** by them.
Ps  37:10  look for them, they will not be **f**.
Pr  10:13  Wisdom is **f** on the lips
    14: 9  but goodwill is **f** among the upright.
Isa 55: 6  Seek the LORD while he may be **f**;
    65: 1  I was **f** by those who did not seek
Jer 29:14  I will be **f** by you,"
Da   1:19  them, and he **f** none equal to Daniel,
     5:27  on the scales and **f** wanting.
    12: 1  everyone whose name is **f** written
Mt   1:18  she was **f** to be pregnant through

Lk    1:30  you have **f** favor with God.
      7: 9  I have not **f** such great faith even
     15: 6  I have **f** my lost sheep.'
     15: 9  I have **f** my lost coin.'
     15:24  is alive again; he was lost and is **f.**'
Ac    4:12  Salvation is **f** in no one else,
Ro   10:20  "I was **f** by those who did not seek
Php   2: 8  being **f** in appearance as a human
Col   2:17  the reality, however, is **f** in Christ.
Heb   3: 3  Jesus has been **f** worthy of greater
Jas   2: 8  If you really keep the royal law **f**
Rev   5: 4  no one was **f** who was worthy
     20:15  All whose names were not **f** written

## FOUNDATION [FOUNDATIONS, FOUNDED]

1Ki   6:37  The **f** of the temple of the LORD
Ezr   3: 6  though the **f** of the LORD's temple
Job  38: 4  were you when I laid the earth's **f?**
Ps   97: 2  and justice are the **f** of his throne.
Isa  28:16  a precious cornerstone for a sure **f;**
Mt    7:25  fall, because it had its **f** on the rock.
Lk   14:29  For if you lay the **f** and are not able
Ro   15:20  not be building on someone else's **f.**
1Co   3:10  me, I laid a **f** as a wise builder,
      3:11  one can lay any **f** other than the one
Eph   2:20  built on the **f** of the apostles
1Ti   3:15  God, the pillar and **f** of the truth.
2Ti   2:19  God's solid **f** stands firm,
Heb   6: 1  not laying again the **f** of repentance
Rev  21:19  The first **f** was jasper, the second

## FOUNDATIONS [FOUNDATION]

1Sa   2: 8  the **f** of the earth are the LORD's;
Ps  102:25  In the beginning you laid the **f**
    137: 7  they cried, "tear it down to its **f!**"
Pr    3:19  the LORD laid the earth's **f,**
Isa  48:13  My own hand laid the **f** of the earth,
Heb   1:10  Lord, you laid the **f** of the earth,
Rev  21:14  The wall of the city had twelve **f,**

## FOUNDED [FOUNDATION]

Jer  10:12  he **f** the world by his wisdom

## FOUNTAIN

Ps   36: 9  For with you is the **f** of life;
Pr    5:18  May your **f** be blessed, and may you
     14:27  The fear of the LORD is a **f** of life,
     18: 4  the **f** of wisdom is a rushing stream.
SS    4:12  are a spring enclosed, a sealed **f.**
Jer   9: 1  of water and my eyes a **f** of tears!
Joel  3:18  A **f** will flow out of the LORD's
Zec  13: 1  that day a **f** will be opened

## FOUR [FOURTH]

Ge    2:10  it was separated into **f** headwaters.
1Ki  18:19  And bring the **f** hundred and fifty
     18:19  the **f** hundred prophets of Asherah,
Isa  11:12  of Judah from the **f** quarters
Eze   1: 5  what looked like **f** living creatures,
     10: 9  I saw beside the cherubim **f** wheels,
     10:14  Each of the cherubim had **f** faces:
Da    1:17  To these **f** young men God gave
      7: 3  **F** great beasts, each different
      8: 8  in its place **f** prominent horns grew

Da    8: 8  up toward the **f** winds of heaven.
Zec   1:20  the LORD showed me **f** craftsmen.
      6: 5  "These are the **f** spirits of heaven,
Mt   15:38  those who ate was **f** thousand men,
Mk    8:20  the seven loaves for the **f** thousand,
Rev   4: 6  the throne, were **f** living creatures,
      9:14  "Release the **f** angels who are

## FOURTEEN

Mt    1:17  Thus there were **f** generations in all
2Co  12: 2  Christ who **f** years ago was caught
Gal   2: 1  Then after **f** years, I went up again

## FOURTH [FOUR]

Ge   15:16  In the **f** generation your descendants
Ex   20: 5  **f** generation of those who hate me,

## FOWLER* [FOWLER'S]

Pr    6: 5  like a bird from the snare of the **f.**

## FOWLER'S* [FOWLER]

Ps   91: 3  he will save you from the **f** snare
    124: 7  escaped like a bird from the **f** snare;

## FOX* [FOXES]

Ne    4: 3  even a **f** climbing up on it would
Lk   13:32  "Go tell that **f,** 'I will keep

## FOXES [FOX]

Jdg  15: 4  and caught three hundred **f** and tied
SS    2:15  Catch for us the **f,** the little **f**
Lk    9:58  "**F** have holes and birds have nests,

## FRACTURE*

Lev  24:20  **f** for **f,** eye for eye, tooth for tooth.

## FRAGRANCE [FRAGRANT]

Ex   30:38  like it to enjoy its **f** must be cut off
SS    4:10  the **f** of your perfume more than any
Jn   12: 3  was filled with the **f** of the perfume.

## FRAGRANT [FRAGRANCE]

Ex   25: 6  anointing oil and for the **f** incense;
     30: 7  "Aaron must burn **f** incense
Eph   5: 2  himself up for us as a **f** offering
Php   4:18  They are a **f** offering, an acceptable

## FRAME [DOORFRAME, DOORFRAMES, FRAMES]

Ps  139:15  My **f** was not hidden from you

## FRAMES [FRAME]

Ex   26:15  "Make upright **f** of acacia wood
Nu    3:36  take care of the **f** of the tabernacle,

## FRANKINCENSE

Mt    2:11  gifts of gold, **f** and myrrh.

## FRAUD* [DEFRAUD]

Pr   20:17  Food gained by **f** tastes sweet,
Jer  10:14  Their images are a **f;** they have no
     51:17  Their images are a **f;** they have no

## FREE [FREED, FREEDMEN, FREEDOM, FREELY]

| | | |
|---|---|---|
| Ge | 2:16 | "You are f to eat from any tree |
| | 49:21 | "Naphtali is a doe set f that bears |
| Ex | 21: 2 | year, he shall go f, without paying |
| Ps | 73:12 | always f of care, |
| | 119:32 | for you have set my heart f. |
| | 146: 7 | The LORD sets prisoners f, |
| Pr | 6: 3 | to f yourself, since you have fallen |
| Isa | 42: 7 | to f captives from prison |
| Lk | 13:12 | you are set f from your infirmity." |
| Jn | 8:32 | truth, and the truth will set you f." |
| | 8:36 | Son sets you f, you will be f indeed. |
| | 19:12 | on, Pilate tried to set Jesus f, |
| Ac | 13:39 | who believes is set f from every sin, |
| Ro | 6: 7 | who has died has been set f from sin. |
| | 6:18 | You have been set f from sin |
| | 8: 2 | Spirit who gives life has set you f |
| 1Co | 9:21 | having the law (though I am not f |
| | 12:13 | Jews or Gentiles, slave or f— |
| Gal | 3:28 | neither slave nor f, neither male nor |
| | 5: 1 | for freedom that Christ has set us f. |
| 1Pe | 2:16 | Live as f people, but do not use your |
| Rev | 20: 3 | he must be set f for a short time. |
| | 22:17 | let all who wish take the f gift |

## FREED [FREE]

| | | |
|---|---|---|
| Mk | 5:34 | and be f from your suffering." |
| 1Co | 7:22 | are the Lord's f people; |
| Rev | 1: 5 | has f us from our sins by his blood, |

## FREEDMEN* [FREE]

| | | |
|---|---|---|
| Ac | 6: 9 | members of the Synagogue of the F |

## FREEDOM [FREE]

| | | |
|---|---|---|
| Ps | 119:45 | I will walk about in f, for I have |
| Isa | 61: 1 | to proclaim f for the captives |
| Lk | 4:18 | me to proclaim f for the prisoners |
| Ro | 8:21 | brought into the f and glory |
| 1Co | 7:21 | although if you can gain your f, |
| | 10:29 | For why is my f being judged |
| 2Co | 3:17 | the Spirit of the Lord is, there is f. |
| Gal | 2: 4 | spy on the f we have in Christ Jesus |
| | 5: 1 | It is for f that Christ has set us free. |
| | 5:13 | But do not use your f to indulge |
| Jas | 1:25 | into the perfect law that gives f, |
| 1Pe | 2:16 | do not use your f as |

## FREELY [FREE]

| | | |
|---|---|---|
| Isa | 55: 7 | and to our God, for he will f pardon. |
| Mt | 10: 8 | F you have received, f give. |
| Ro | 3:24 | and all are justified f by his grace |
| Eph | 1: 6 | which he has f given us in the One |

## FREEWILL [WILL]

| | | |
|---|---|---|
| Ex | 35:29 | to the LORD f offerings for all |
| Ezr | 1: 4 | with f offerings for the temple |
| Ps | 54: 6 | I will sacrifice a f offering to you; |

## FRESH

| | | |
|---|---|---|
| Eze | 47: 8 | sea, the salty water there becomes f. |
| Jas | 3:11 | Can both f water and salt water flow |

## FRET*

| | | |
|---|---|---|
| Ps | 37: 1 | Do not f because of those who are |
| | 37: 7 | do not f when people succeed |
| | 37: 8 | do not f—it leads only to evil. |
| Pr | 24:19 | Do not f because of evildoers or be |

## FRICTION*

| | | |
|---|---|---|
| 1Ti | 6: 5 | constant f between people of corrupt |

## FRIEND [FRIENDS, FRIENDSHIP]

| | | |
|---|---|---|
| Ex | 33:11 | face to face, as one speaks to a f. |
| Dt | 13: 6 | your closest f secretly entices you, |
| 2Sa | 16:17 | f? If he's your f, why didn't you go |
| 2Ch | 20: 7 | the descendants of Abraham your f? |
| Ps | 41: 9 | Even my close f, someone I trusted, |
| | 88:18 | taken from me f and neighbor— |
| Pr | 17:17 | A f loves at all times, and a brother |
| | 18:24 | there is a f who sticks closer than |
| | 27: 6 | Wounds from a f can be trusted, |
| | 27:10 | Do not forsake your f or a f of your |
| SS | 5:16 | this is my f, daughters of Jerusalem. |
| Isa | 41: 8 | you descendants of Abraham my f, |
| Jer | 9: 5 | F deceives f, and no one speaks |
| Mt | 11:19 | a f of tax collectors and sinners.' |
| Jn | 19:12 | this man go, you are no f of Caesar. |
| Jas | 2:23 | and he was called God's f. |
| | 4: 4 | to be a f of the world becomes |

## FRIENDS [FRIEND]

| | | |
|---|---|---|
| Job | 2:11 | When Job's three f, |
| | 42:10 | After Job had prayed for his f, |
| Pr | 16:28 | and gossips separate close f. |
| | 17: 9 | repeats the matter separates close f. |
| | 18:24 | has unreliable f soon comes to ruin, |
| La | 1: 2 | All her f have betrayed her; |
| Zec | 13: 6 | I was given at the house of my f.' |
| Jn | 15:13 | to lay down one's life for one's f. |
| | 15:14 | You are my f if you do what I |

## FRIENDSHIP [FRIEND]

| | | |
|---|---|---|
| Dt | 23: 6 | Do not seek a treaty of f with them |
| Ezr | 9:12 | Do not seek a treaty of f with them |
| Lk | 11: 8 | give you the bread because of f, |
| Jas | 4: 4 | don't you know that f |

## FRIGHTEN [FEAR]

| | | |
|---|---|---|
| Dt | 28:26 | there will be no one to f them away. |
| Ne | 6: 9 | They were all trying to f us, |

## FRIGHTENED [FEAR]

| | | |
|---|---|---|
| Php | 1:28 | without being f in any way by those |
| 1Pe | 3:14 | not fear their threats; do not be f." |

## FROGS

| | | |
|---|---|---|
| Ex | 8: 2 | go, I will send a plague of f on your |
| Rev | 16:13 | three evil spirits that looked like f; |

## FROLIC

| | | |
|---|---|---|
| Mal | 4: 2 | and f like well-fed calves. |

## FRONT

| | | |
|---|---|---|
| Ex | 14:19 | God, who had been traveling in f |
| | 14:19 | moved from in f and stood behind |
| | 32:15 | inscribed on both sides, f and back. |

Lev 19:14 or put a stumbling block in **f**
Mt   5:24 leave your gift there in **f** of the altar.

## FROST [FROSTY]
Ex 16:14 thin flakes like **f** on the ground

## FROSTY* [FROST]
Zec 14: 6 no sunlight, no cold, **f** darkness.

## FRUIT [FIRSTFRUITS, FRUITFUL, FRUITION, FRUITLESS]
Ge   1:11 the land that bear **f** with seed in it,
     3: 3 'You must not eat **f** from the tree
Lev 19:23 of **f** tree, regard its **f** as forbidden.
Dt  28: 4 The **f** of your womb will be blessed,
    28:53 you will eat the **f** of the womb,
Jdg  9:11 'Should I give up my **f**, so good
Ps   1: 3 which yields its **f** in season
Pr   8:19 My **f** is better than fine gold;
    11:30 The **f** of the righteous is a tree
    12:14 the **f** of their lips people are filled
    27:18 who guard a fig tree will eat its **f**,
Isa 11: 1 from his roots a Branch will bear **f**.
    27: 6 blossom and fill all the world with **f**.
    32:17 The **f** of that righteousness will be
Jer 17: 8 drought and never fails to bear **f**."
Eze 47:12 **F** trees of all kinds will grow
    47:12 **f** fail. Every month they will bear **f**,
Hos  9:10 it was like seeing the early **f**
    10:12 reap the **f** of unfailing love,
    14: 2 that we may offer the **f** of our lips.
Am   8: 1 a basket of ripe **f**.
Mt   3: 8 Produce **f** in keeping
     3:10 does not produce good **f** will be cut
     7:16 By their **f** you will recognize them.
     7:17 good **f**, but a bad tree bears bad **f**.
Lk   6:44 Each tree is recognized by its own **f**.
    13: 6 he went to look for **f** on it but did
Jn  15: 2 every branch in me that bears no **f**,
    15: 2 branch that does bear **f** he prunes so
    15:16 so that you might go and bear **f**—
Ro   7: 4 order that we might bear **f** for God.
Gal  5:22 But the **f** of the Spirit is love, joy,
Eph  5: 9 (for the **f** of the light consists in all
Php  1:11 filled with the **f** of righteousness
Col  1:10 bearing **f** in every good work,
Heb 13:15 the **f** of lips that openly profess his
Jas  3:17 full of mercy and good **f**,
Jude 1:12 trees, without **f** and uprooted—
Rev 22: 2 of **f**, yielding its **f** every month.

## FRUITFUL [FRUIT]
Ge   1:22 "Be **f** and increase in number
     9: 1 "Be **f** and increase in number
    17: 6 I will make you very **f**; I will make
    35:11 be **f** and increase in number.
Ex   1: 7 the Israelites were exceedingly **f**;
Ps 105:24 The LORD made his people very **f**;
   128: 3 wife will be like a **f** vine within your
Isa 27: 2 "Sing about a **f** vineyard:
Jn  15: 2 prunes so that it will be even more **f**.
Php  1:22 body, this will mean **f** labor for me.

## FRUITION [FRUIT]
2Th  1:11 he may bring to **f** your every desire

## FRUITLESS* [FRUIT]
Eph  5:11 to do with the **f** deeds of darkness,

## FRUSTRATE* [FRUSTRATES, FRUSTRATION]
2Sa 17:14 had determined to **f** the good advice
Ezr  4: 5 **f** their plans during the entire reign
Ps  14: 6 You evildoers **f** the plans
Ecc  7: 3 **F** is better than laughter,
1Co  1:19 of the intelligent I will **f**."

## FRUSTRATES* [FRUSTRATE]
Ps 146: 9 but he **f** the ways of the wicked.
Pr  22:12 but he **f** the words of the unfaithful.

## FRUSTRATION* [FRUSTRATE]
Ecc  5:17 with great **f**, affliction and anger.
Ro   8:20 For the creation was subjected to **f**,

## FUEL
Isa 44:19 to say, "Half of it I used for **f**;
Eze 21:32 You will be **f** for the fire,

## FULFILL [FULFILLED, FULFILLMENT, FULFILLS]
Ge  38: 8 wife and **f** your duty to her as
Nu  23:19 Does he promise and not **f**?
Dt  25: 7 He will not **f** the duty
2Ch 10:15 **f** the word the LORD had spoken
    36:22 in order to **f** the word of the LORD
Ps  61: 8 name and **f** my vows day after day.
   116:14 I will **f** my vows to the LORD
Ecc  5: 5 a vow than to make one and not **f** it.
Isa 46:11 far-off land, a man to **f** my purpose.
Jer 11: 5 I will **f** the oath I swore to your
    33:14 I will **f** the good promise I made
Mt   1:22 **f** what the Lord had said through
     3:15 us to do this to **f** all righteousness."
     4:14 **f** what was said through the prophet
     5:17 come to abolish them but to **f** them.
     8:17 to **f** what was spoken through
    12:17 to **f** what was spoken through
    21: 4 to **f** what was spoken through
Jn  12:38 This was to **f** the word of Isaiah
    13:18 this is to **f** this passage of Scripture:
    15:25 this is to **f** what is written in their
1Co  7: 3 The husband should **f** his marital
Gal  6: 2 and in this way you will **f** the law

## FULFILLED [FULFILL]
Jos 21:45 of Israel failed; every one was **f**.
    23:14 Every promise has been **f**;
2Ch  6:15 and with your hand you have **f** it—
Pr  13:12 sick, but a longing **f** is a tree of life.
    13:19 A longing **f** is sweet to the soul,
Jer 25:12 "But when the seventy years are **f**,
Da  12: 6 these astonishing things are **f**?"
Mt   2:15 And so was **f** what the Lord had said
     2:17 through the prophet Jeremiah was **f**:
     2:23 So was **f** what was said through
    13:14 In them is **f** the prophecy of Isaiah:
    13:35 So was **f** what was spoken through
    26:54 would the Scriptures be **f** that say it
    26:56 of the prophets might be **f**."

Mt 27: 9 by Jeremiah the prophet was **f**:
Mk 13: 4 sign that they are all about to be **f**?"
 14:49 But the Scriptures must be **f**."
Lk 1: 1 things that have been **f** among us,
 4:21 "Today this scripture is **f** in your
 18:31 about the Son of Man will be **f**.
 24:44 Everything must be **f** that is written
Jn 17:12 so that Scripture would be **f**.
 18: 9 words he had spoken would be **f**:
 19:24 the scripture might be **f** that said,
 19:28 and so that Scripture would be **f**,
 19:36 so that the scripture would be **f**:
Ac 1:16 the Scripture had to be **f**
 3:18 But this is how God **f** what he had
Ro 13: 8 whoever loves others has **f** the law.
Gal 5:14 entire law is **f** in keeping this one
 command:
Jas 2:23 And the scripture was **f** that says,
Rev 17:17 to rule, until God's words are **f**.

## FULFILLMENT [FULFILL]
2Ch 36:21 seventy years were completed in **f**
Lk 22:16 I will not eat it again until it finds **f**
Ro 13:10 Therefore love is the **f** of the law.
Eph 1:10 effect when the times reach their **f**—

## FULFILLS* [FULFILL]
Ps 145:19 He **f** the desires of those who fear
Isa 44:26 **f** the predictions of his messengers,

## FULL [FILL]
Ge 6:11 God's sight and was **f** of violence.
 15:16 has not yet reached its **f** measure."
2Ki 4: 6 When all the jars were **f**, she said
2Ch 24:10 them into the chest until it was **f**.
Job 14: 1 are of few days and **f** of trouble.
Ps 31:23 him, but the proud he pays back in **f**.
 116: 5 our God is **f** of compassion.
 127: 5 Blessed is the man whose quiver is **f**
Pr 27: 7 One who is **f** loathes honey
 31:11 Her husband has **f** confidence in her
Isa 1:15 Your hands are **f** of blood;
 6: 3 the whole earth is **f** of his glory."
Jer 51:56 he will repay in **f**.
La 1: 1 lies the city, once so **f** of people!
Eze 10:12 wings, were completely **f** of eyes,
Lk 4: 1 Jesus, **f** of the Holy Spirit,
 11:34 your whole body also is **f** of light.
 11:34 your body also is **f** of darkness.
Jn 10:10 may have life, and have it to the **f**.
Ac 6: 3 who are known to be **f** of the Spirit
 6: 5 a man **f** of faith and of the Holy
 7:55 But Stephen, **f** of the Holy Spirit,
 11:24 man, **f** of the Holy Spirit and faith,
Eph 4:19 and they are **f** of greed.
 6:11 Put on the **f** armor of God,
1Ti 3: 4 in a manner worthy of **f** respect.

## FULL-GROWN* [GROW]
Jas 1:15 sin, when it is **f**, gives birth to death.

## FULLNESS* [FILL]
Dt 33:16 its **f** and the favor of him who dwelt
Jn 1:16 of his **f** we have all received grace
Ro 11:12 greater riches will their **f** bring!
Eph 1:23 the **f** of him who fills everything

Eph 3:19 to the measure of all the **f** of God.
 4:13 the whole measure of the **f** of Christ.
Col 1:19 to have all his **f** dwell in him,
 1:25 to you the word of God in its **f**—
 2: 9 in Christ all the **f** of the Deity lives
 2:10 Christ you have been brought to **f**.

## FULLY [FILL]
Ex 19: 5 Now if you obey me **f** and keep my
Dt 28: 1 If you **f** obey the LORD your God
1Ki 8:61 may your hearts be **f** committed
2Ch 16: 9 those whose hearts are **f** committed
Ps 119: 4 precepts that are to be **f** obeyed.
 119:138 they are **f** trustworthy.
Pr 13: 4 desires of the diligent are **f** satisfied.
Lk 6:40 but all who are **f** trained will be like
Ro 4:21 being **f** persuaded that God had
 8: 4 of the law might be **f** met in us,
 14: 5 Everyone should be **f** convinced
1Co 13:12 then I shall know **f**, even as I am **f**
 15:58 Always give yourselves **f**
Gal 4: 4 But when the set time had **f** come,
2Ti 4:17 the message might be **f** proclaimed
2Jn 1: 8 for, but that you may be rewarded **f**.

## FURIOUS [FURY]
Dt 29:28 In **f** anger and in great wrath
Jer 21: 5 in **f** anger and in great wrath.
 32:37 where I banish them in my **f** anger

## FURNACE
Dt 4:20 you out of the iron-smelting **f**,
1Ki 8:51 of Egypt, out of that iron-smelting **f**.
Isa 48:10 have tested you in the **f** of affliction.
Jer 11: 4 of Egypt, out of that iron-smelting **f**.'
Da 3: 6 be thrown into a blazing **f**."
Mal 4: 1 day is coming; it will burn like a **f**.
Mt 13:42 will throw them into the blazing **f**,
Rev 1:15 feet were like bronze glowing in a **f**,

## FURNISHED [FURNISHINGS]
Mk 14:15 a large room upstairs, **f** and ready.

## FURNISHINGS [FURNISHED]
Ex 25: 9 all its **f** exactly like the pattern I will
1Ki 7:48 also made all the **f** that were

## FURTHER
Job 34:23 has no need to examine people **f**,

## FURY [FURIOUS]
Isa 14: 6 in **f** subdued nations with relentless
Rev 12:12 He is filled with **f**, because he
 14:10 will drink of the wine of God's **f**,
 16:19 with the wine of the **f** of his wrath.
 19:15 the winepress of the **f** of the wrath

## FUTILE [FUTILITY]
Mal 3:14 have said, 'It is **f** to serve God.
Ro 1:21 but their thinking became **f** and their
1Co 3:20 that the thoughts of the wise are **f**."

## FUTILITY [FUTILE]
Ps 78:33 So he ended their days in **f** and their
Eph 4:17 do, in the **f** of their thinking.

## FUTURE

| | | |
|---|---|---|
| Dt | 6:20 | In the **f**, when your children ask |
| 1Ch | 17:17 | have spoken about the **f** of the house |
| Ps | 37:37 | a **f** awaits those who seek peace. |
| Pr | 23:18 | There is surely a **f** hope for you, |
| | 24:20 | for the evildoer has no **f** hope, |
| Ecc | 7:14 | discover anything about your **f**. |
| | 8: 7 | Since no one knows the **f**, who can |
| Jer | 29:11 | you, plans to give you hope and a **f**. |
| Da | 8:26 | vision, for it concerns the distant **f**." |
| Ro | 8:38 | neither the present nor the **f**, nor any |
| 1Co | 3:22 | life or death or the present or the **f**— |

---

# G

---

## GABBATHA*

Jn   19:13   Pavement (which in Aramaic is **G**).

## GABRIEL*

Angel who interpreted Daniel's visions (Da 8:16–26; 9:20–27); announced births of John (Lk 1:11–20), Jesus (Lk 1:26–38).

## GAD

1. Son of Jacob by Zilpah (Ge 30:9–11; 35:26; 1Ch 2:2). Tribe of blessed (Ge 49:19; Dt 33:20–21), numbered (Nu 1:25; 26:18), allotted land east of the Jordan (Nu 32; 34:14; Jos 18:7; 22), west (Eze 48:27–28), 12,000 from (Rev 7:5).

2. Prophet; seer of David (1Sa 22:5; 2Sa 24:11–19; 1Ch 29:29).

## GADARENES*

Mt   8:28   the other side in the region of the **G**,

## GAIN   [GAINED, GAINING, GAINS]

| | | |
|---|---|---|
| Ge | 15: 8 | that I will **g** possession of it?" |
| Ex | 14:17 | And I will **g** glory through Pharaoh |
| 1Sa | 3: 3 | They turned aside after dishonest **g** |
| Ps | 60:12 | With God we will **g** the victory, |
| | 90:12 | that we may **g** a heart of wisdom. |
| Pr | 1:19 | of all who go after ill-gotten **g**; |
| | 3:13 | those who **g** understanding, |
| | 4: 1 | pay attention and **g** understanding. |
| | 8: 5 | You who are simple, **g** prudence; |
| | 15:32 | who heed correction **g** understanding. |
| | 16: 8 | righteousness than much **g** |
| | 28:16 | who hates ill-gotten **g** will enjoy |
| | 28:23 | the end **g** favor rather than one who |
| | 29:23 | but the lowly in spirit **g** honor. |
| Ecc | 1: 3 | What does anyone **g** from all their |
| Isa | 63:12 | to **g** for himself everlasting renown, |
| Jer | 17:11 | are those who **g** riches by unjust means. |
| Da | 2: 8 | certain that you are trying to **g** time, |
| Mt | 16:26 | will it be for you to **g** the whole world, |
| Mk | 8:36 | is it for you to **g** the whole world, |
| Lk | 9:25 | is it for you to **g** the whole world, |
| 1Co | 13: 3 | but do not have love, I **g** nothing. |
| Php | 1:21 | me, to live is Christ and to die is **g**. |
| | 3: 8 | them garbage, that I may **g** Christ |
| 1Ti | 3: 8 | wine, and not pursuing dishonest **g**. |

| | | |
|---|---|---|
| 1Ti | 3:13 | who have served well **g** an excellent |
| | 6: 5 | godliness is a means to financial **g**. |
| | 6: 6 | with contentment is great **g**. |
| 2Ti | 3: 6 | and **g** control over gullible women, |
| Tit | 1: 7 | violent, not pursuing dishonest **g**. |
| 1Pe | 5: 2 | not pursuing dishonest **g**, but eager to |

## GAINED   [GAIN]

| | | |
|---|---|---|
| Ps | 30: 9 | "What is **g** if I am silenced, if I go |
| Ecc | 2:11 | nothing was **g** under the sun. |
| Jer | 32:20 | have **g** the renown that is still yours. |
| Ro | 5: 2 | through whom we have **g** access |
| Gal | 2:21 | could be **g** through the law, |
| Heb | 11:33 | justice, and **g** what was promised; |

## GAINING   [GAIN]

| | | |
|---|---|---|
| Ge | 3: 6 | and also desirable for **g** wisdom, |
| Pr | 1: 2 | for **g** wisdom and instruction; |
| Jn | 4: 1 | Pharisees had heard that he was **g** |

## GAINS*   [GAIN]

| | | |
|---|---|---|
| Pr | 11:16 | A kindhearted woman **g** honor, |
| | 11:24 | gives freely, yet **g** even more; |
| Mic | 4:13 | You will devote their ill-gotten **g** |
| Php | 3: 7 | were **g** to me I now consider loss |

## GAIUS

| | | |
|---|---|---|
| Ro | 16:23 | **G**, whose hospitality I |
| 3Jn | 1: 1 | To my dear friend **G**, whom I love |

## GALATIA   [GALATIANS]

| | | |
|---|---|---|
| Ac | 16: 6 | the region of Phrygia and **G**, |
| Gal | 1: 2 | with me, To the churches in **G**: |

## GALATIANS*   [GALATIA]

Gal   3: 1   You foolish **G**! Who has bewitched

## GALILEAN*   [GALILEE]

| | | |
|---|---|---|
| Mk | 14:70 | are one of them, for you are a **G**." |
| Lk | 22:59 | fellow was with him, for he is a **G**." |
| | 23: 6 | Pilate asked if the man was a **G**. |
| Ac | 5:37 | Judas the **G** appeared in the days |

## GALILEANS   [GALILEE]

| | | |
|---|---|---|
| Lk | 13: 1 | the **G** whose blood Pilate had mixed |
| Jn | 4:45 | in Galilee, the **G** welcomed him. |
| Ac | 2: 7 | all these who are speaking **G**? |

## GALILEE   [GALILEAN, GALILEANS, TIBERIAS]

| | | |
|---|---|---|
| Isa | 9: 1 | in the future he will honor **G** |
| Mt | 3:13 | Jesus came from **G** to the Jordan |
| | 4:15 | the Jordan, **G** of the Gentiles— |
| | 21:11 | the prophet from Nazareth in **G**." |
| | 26:32 | I will go ahead of you into **G**." |
| | 28:10 | Go and tell my brothers to go to **G**; |
| Lk | 23:49 | who had followed him from **G**, |
| Jn | 2: 1 | a wedding took place at Cana in **G**. |
| | 7:41 | can the Messiah come from **G**? |

## GALL

| | | |
|---|---|---|
| Ps | 69:21 | They put **g** in my food and gave me |
| Mt | 27:34 | Jesus wine to drink, mixed with **g**; |

## GALLIO*

Proconsul of Achaia, who refused to hear complaints against Paul (Ac 18:12–17).

## GAMALIEL

Ac　5:34　But a Pharisee named **G**, a teacher
　　22: 3　I studied under **G** and was

## GAME [GAMES]

Ge　25:28　who had a taste for wild **g**,
　　27: 3　country to hunt some wild **g** for me.

## GAMES* [GAME]

1Co　9:25　who competes in the **g** goes

## GANGRENE*

2Ti　2:17　Their teaching will spread like **g**.

## GAP [GAPS]

Ne　6: 1　the wall and not a **g** was left in it—
Eze 22:30　stand before me in the **g** on behalf

## GAPS* [GAP]

Ne　4: 7　and that the **g** were being closed,

## GARBAGE*

1Co　4:13　the **g** of the world—right up
Php　3: 8　consider them **g**, that I may gain Christ

## GARDEN [GARDENER, GARDENS]

Ge　2: 8　the LORD God had planted a **g**
　　2:15　put him in the **G** of Eden to work it
　　3:23　banished him from the **G** of Eden
　　13:10　watered, like the **g** of the LORD,
SS　4:12　You are a **g** locked up, my sister,
Isa 58:11　You will be like a well-watered **g**,
Jer 31:12　They will be like a well-watered **g**,
Eze 28:13　You were in Eden, the **g** of God;
　　31: 9　all the trees of Eden in the **g** of God.
Mk　4:32　becomes the largest of all **g** plants,
Jn　18: 3　So Judas came to the **g**,
　　19:41　there was a **g**, and in the **g** a new

## GARDENER* [GARDEN]

Jn　15: 1　true vine, and my Father is the **g**.
　　20:15　Thinking he was the **g**, she said,

## GARDENS [GARDEN]

Am　4: 9　"Many times I struck your **g**

## GARLAND*

Pr　1: 9　They are a **g** to grace your head
　　4: 9　She will give you a **g** to grace your

## GARMENT [GARMENTS]

Ge　9:23　Japheth took a **g** and laid it across
　　25:25　his whole body was like a hairy **g**;
Ru　3: 9　the corner of your **g** over me,
2Ki　1: 8　"He had a **g** of hair and had
Ps 102:26　they will all wear out like a **g**.
Pr　25:20　Like one who takes away a **g**
Isa 50: 9　They will all wear out like a **g**;
　　51: 6　the earth will wear out like a **g**

Isa 61: 3　a **g** of praise instead of a spirit
Mt　9:16　patch of unshrunk cloth on an old **g**,
Mk 14:52　he fled naked, leaving his **g** behind.
Jn　19:23　This **g** was seamless, woven in one
　　19:24　and cast lots for my **g**."
Heb　1:11　they will all wear out like a **g**.

## GARMENTS [GARMENT]

Ge　3:21　The LORD God made **g** of skin
Ex　28: 2　Make sacred **g** for your brother
Lev　8: 2　his sons, their **g**, the anointing oil, ·
　　16: 4　These are sacred **g**; so he must
Job 31:19　of clothing, or the needy without **g**,
Pr　31:24　She makes linen **g** and sells them,
Isa 52: 1　Put on your **g** of splendor,
　　61:10　For he has clothed me with **g**
　　63: 1　Bozrah, with his **g** stained crimson?
Eze 16:10　linen and covered you with costly **g**.
Joel　2:13　Rend your heart and not your **g**.
Zec　3: 4　sin, and I will put fine **g** on you."

## GATE [GATES, GATEWAY]

Dt　21:19　to the elders at the **g** of his town.
Jos　2: 5　when it was time to close the city **g**,
Ru　4:11　and all the people at the **g** said,
Est　2:19　Mordecai was sitting at the king's **g**.
Job 29: 7　"When I went to the **g** of the city
Ps　69:12　Those who sit at the **g** mock me,
　 118:20　This is the **g** of the LORD through
Pr　31:23　husband is respected at the city **g**,
　　31:31　works bring her praise at the city **g**.
Mt　7:13　"Enter through the narrow **g**. For wide
　　　　　is the **g**
Jn　10: 2　who enters by the **g** is the shepherd
　　10: 7　I tell you, I am the **g** for the sheep.
　　10: 9　I am the **g**; whoever enters through
Ac　3: 2　to the temple **g** called Beautiful,
Heb 13:12　suffered outside the city **g** to make
Rev 21:21　each **g** made of a single pearl.

## GATES [GATE]

Dt　6: 9　of your houses and on your **g**.
Ne　1: 3　its **g** have been burned with fire."
Ps　24: 7　Lift up your heads, you **g**;
　　87: 2　The LORD loves the **g** of Zion
　 100: 4　Enter his **g** with thanksgiving
　 118:19　Open for me the **g** of the righteous;
Isa 60:11　Your **g** will always stand open,
　　60:18　walls Salvation and your **g** Praise.
　　62:10　Pass through, pass through the **g**!
La　4:12　foes could enter the **g** of Jerusalem.
Eze 48:31　the **g** of the city will be named
Mt　16:18　the **g** of death will not overcome it.
Rev 21:12　**g**, and with twelve angels at the **g**.
　　21:12　On the **g** were written the names
　　21:21　The twelve **g** were twelve pearls,
　　21:25　On no day will its **g** ever be shut,
　　22:14　may go through the **g** into the city.

## GATEWAY [GATE, WAY]

Ge　19: 1　Lot was sitting in the **g** of the city.
1Sa　9:18　Saul approached Samuel in the **g**
2Sa 19: 8　got up and took his seat in the **g**.
　　19: 8　"The king is sitting in the **g**,"

# GATH

| | | |
|---|---|---|
| 1Sa | 5: 8 | of the god of Israel moved to **G**." |
| | 17: 4 | Goliath, who was from **G**, |
| | 21:10 | Saul and went to Achish king of **G**. |
| 2Sa | 1:20 | "Tell it not in **G**, proclaim it not |
| Mic | 1:10 | Tell it not in **G**; weep not at all. |

# GATHER [GATHERED, GATHERS, INGATHERING]

| | | |
|---|---|---|
| Ex | 16: 4 | each day and **g** enough for that day. |
| Lev | 19: 9 | or **g** the gleanings of your harvest. |
| Dt | 30: 4 | the LORD your God will **g** you |
| Ru | 2: 7 | and **g** among the sheaves behind |
| Ne | 1: 9 | I will **g** them from there and bring |
| Ps | 106:47 | and **g** us from the nations, that we |
| Isa | 11:12 | nations and **g** the exiles of Israel; |
| | 34:16 | and his Spirit will **g** them together. |
| Jer | 3:17 | all nations will **g** in Jerusalem |
| | 23: 3 | "I myself will **g** the remnant of my |
| | 31:10 | 'He who scattered Israel will **g** them |
| Eze | 39:28 | I will **g** them to their own land, |
| Zep | 2: 1 | **G** together, **g** yourselves together, |
| | 3:20 | At that time I will **g** you; |
| Zec | 14: 2 | I will **g** all the nations to Jerusalem |
| Mt | 12:30 | and whoever does not **g** with me |
| | 13:30 | then **g** the wheat and bring it |
| | 23:37 | longed to **g** your children together, |
| | 25:26 | **g** where I have not scattered seed? |
| Mk | 13:27 | and **g** his elect from the four winds, |
| Lk | 3:17 | and to **g** the wheat into his barn, |
| | 11:23 | and whoever does not **g** with me |
| | 13:34 | longed to **g** your children together, |
| | 17:37 | body, there the vultures will **g**." |
| Rev | 14:18 | and **g** the clusters of grapes |
| | 19:17 | **g** together for the great supper |
| | 20: 8 | and to **g** them for battle. |

# GATHERED [GATHER]

| | | |
|---|---|---|
| Ge | 1: 9 | "Let the water under the sky be **g** |
| Ex | 16:18 | the one who **g** much did not have |
| | 16:18 | the one who **g** little did not have too |
| | 16:18 | Each one had **g** just as much as they |
| Nu | 11:32 | day the people went out and **g** quail. |
| | 16:19 | When Korah had **g** all his followers |
| Ru | 2:18 | saw how much she had **g**. |
| Pr | 30: 4 | Whose hands have **g** up the wind? |
| Mt | 16: 9 | and how many basketfuls you **g**? |
| | 25:32 | All the nations will be **g** before him, |
| 2Co | 8:15 | "The one who **g** much did not have |
| 2Th | 2: 1 | Jesus Christ and our being **g** to him, |
| Rev | 14:19 | **g** its grapes and threw them |
| | 16:16 | they **g** the kings together |
| | 19:19 | their armies **g** together to make war |

# GATHERS [GATHER]

| | | |
|---|---|---|
| Ps | 147: 2 | he **g** the exiles of Israel. |
| Pr | 10: 5 | He who **g** crops in summer is |
| | 13:11 | but whoever **g** money little by little |
| Isa | 40:11 | He **g** the lambs in his arms |
| | 56: 8 | he who **g** the exiles of Israel: |
| Mt | 23:37 | as a hen **g** her chicks under her |

# GAUNT

| | | |
|---|---|---|
| Ge | 41: 3 | ugly and **g**, came up out of the Nile |

# GAVE [GIVE]

| | | |
|---|---|---|
| Ge | 2:20 | So the man **g** names to all |
| | 3: 6 | She also **g** some to her husband, |
| | 14:20 | Abram **g** him a tenth of everything. |
| | 16:13 | She **g** this name to the LORD who |
| | 28: 4 | the land God **g** to Abraham." |
| | 35:12 | The land I **g** to Abraham and Isaac I |
| | 39:23 | **g** him success in whatever he did. |
| | 47:11 | **g** them property in the best part |
| Ex | 4:11 | to him, "Who **g** human beings their |
| | 31:18 | he **g** him the two tablets |
| | 34:32 | and he **g** them all the commands |
| Nu | 22:18 | "Even if Balak **g** me all the silver |
| Dt | 2:12 | the land the LORD **g** them as their |
| | 2:36 | The LORD our God **g** us all |
| | 3:12 | I **g** the Reubenites and the Gadites |
| | 8:16 | He **g** you manna to eat |
| | 9:10 | The LORD **g** me two stone tablets |
| | 26: 9 | us to this place and **g** us this land, |
| | 31: 9 | down this law and **g** it to the priests, |
| | 32: 8 | the Most High **g** the nations their |
| Jos | 11:23 | he **g** it as an inheritance to Israel |
| | 13:14 | the tribe of Levi he **g** no inheritance, |
| | 15:13 | Joshua **g** to Caleb son of Jephunneh |
| | 19:49 | the Israelites **g** Joshua son of Nun |
| | 21:44 | the LORD **g** them rest on every side |
| | 24:13 | So I **g** you a land on which you did |
| Jdg | 2:14 | LORD **g** them into the hands of raiders |
| | 3: 6 | **g** their own daughters to their sons, |
| 1Sa | 1: 5 | But to Hannah he **g** a double portion |
| | 27: 6 | So on that day Achish **g** him Ziklag, |
| 2Sa | 8: 6 | The LORD **g** David victory |
| | 12: 8 | I **g** your master's house to you, |
| | 12: 8 | I **g** you the house of Israel |
| 1Ki | 4:29 | God **g** Solomon wisdom and very |
| | 5:12 | The LORD **g** Solomon wisdom, |
| 2Ch | 36:17 | God **g** them all into the hands of |
| Ezr | 2:69 | to their ability they **g** to the treasury |
| Ne | 9:15 | their hunger you **g** them bread |
| | 9:20 | You **g** your good Spirit to instruct |
| | 9:22 | "You **g** them kingdoms |
| | 9:27 | compassion you **g** them deliverers, |
| Job | 1:21 | The LORD **g** and the LORD has |
| | 42:10 | and **g** him twice as much as he had |
| Ps | 69:21 | food and **g** me vinegar for my thirst. |
| | 106:41 | He **g** them into the hands of the nations, |
| | 135:12 | he **g** their land as an inheritance, |
| Pr | 8:29 | he **g** the sea its boundary so |
| Ecc | 12: 7 | the spirit returns to God who **g** it. |
| Jer | 3: 8 | I **g** faithless Israel her certificate |
| Eze | 3: 2 | mouth, and he **g** me the scroll to eat. |
| Da | 1: 7 | The chief official **g** them new |
| | 1:17 | four young men God **g** knowledge |
| Mt | 1:25 | with her until she **g** birth to a son. |
| | 1:25 | And he **g** him the name Jesus. |
| | 2:16 | he **g** orders to kill all the boys |
| | 25:35 | and you **g** me something to eat, |
| | 25:35 | and you **g** me something to drink, |
| | 25:42 | hungry and you **g** me nothing to eat, |
| | 25:42 | and you **g** me nothing to drink, |
| | 26:26 | he broke it and **g** it to his disciples, |
| | 27:50 | in a loud voice, he **g** up his spirit. |
| Mk | 6: 7 | **g** them authority over evil spirits. |
| | 11:28 | who **g** you authority to do this?" |
| Jn | 1:12 | he **g** the right to become children |
| | 3:16 | so loved the world that he **g** his one |
| | 17: 4 | finishing the work you **g** me to do. |

Jn   17: 6   you to those whom you **g** me
    19:30   bowed his head and **g** up his spirit.
Ac   1: 3   **g** many convincing proofs that he
    11:17   if God **g** them the same gift he **g** us
Ro   1:24   Therefore God **g** them over
    1:26   God **g** them over to shameful lusts.
    1:28   so God **g** them over to a depraved
    8:32   own Son, but **g** him up for us all—
1Co   3: 2   I **g** you milk, not solid food, for you
2Co   5:18   **g** us the ministry of reconciliation:
    8: 3   they **g** as much as they were able,
    8: 5   they **g** themselves by the will
Gal   1: 4   who **g** himself for our sins to rescue
    2:20   who loved me and **g** himself for me.
Eph   4: 8   captives and **g** gifts to his people."
    4:11   So Christ himself **g** the apostles,
    5: 2   and **g** himself up for us as a fragrant
    5:25   the church and **g** himself up for her
Php   2: 9   **g** him the name that is above every
2Th   2:16   us and by his grace **g** us eternal
1Ti   2: 6   who **g** himself as a ransom for all
Tit   2:14   who **g** himself for us to redeem us
Heb   7: 2   and Abraham **g** him a tenth
1Jn   3:24   We know it by the Spirit he **g** us.
Rev   11:13   and **g** glory to the God of heaven.
    13: 2   The dragon **g** the beast his power
    16:19   **g** her the cup filled with the wine
    20:13   The sea **g** up the dead that were
    20:13   Hades **g** up the dead that were

## GAVE THANKS See THANKS

## GAZA

Jdg   16: 1   One day Samson went to **G**,
1Sa   6:17   one each for Ashdod, **G**, Ashkelon,
Am   1: 6   "For three sins of **G**, even for four,

## GAZE [GAZING]

Ps   27: 4   to **g** on the beauty of the LORD
Pr   4:25   fix your **g** directly before you.
    23:31   Do not **g** at wine when it is red,
Rev   11: 9   and nation will **g** on their bodies

## GAZELLE

2Sa   1:19   "A **g** lies slain on your heights,
    2:18   was as fleet-footed as a wild **g**.
SS   2: 9   My beloved is like a **g** or a young
    7: 3   two fawns, like twin fawns of a **g**.

## GAZING* [GAZE]

SS   2: 9   **g** through the windows, peering through
Da   10: 8   So I was left alone, **g** at this great
        vision;

## GEDALIAH

Governor of Judah appointed by Nebuchadnezzar
(2Ki 25:22–26; Jer 39–41).

## GEHAZI*

Servant of Elisha (2Ki 4:12—5:27; 8:4–5).

## GEMS

Ex   25: 7   other **g** to be mounted on the ephod

## GENEALOGIES [GENEALOGY]

1Ch   9: 1   Israel was listed in the **g** recorded
1Ti   1: 4   themselves to myths and endless **g**.
Tit   3: 9   avoid foolish controversies and **g**

## GENEALOGY [GENEALOGIES]

Mt   1: 1   This is the **g** of Jesus the Messiah
Heb   7: 3   without **g**, without beginning

## GENERATION [GENERATIONS]

Ge   7: 1   I have found you righteous in this **g**.
    15:16   the fourth **g** your descendants will
Ex   1: 6   all his brothers and all that **g** died,
    3:15   name you shall call me from **g** to **g**.
    20: 5   and fourth **g** of those who hate me,
    34: 7   parents to the third and fourth **g**."
Nu   32:13   until the whole **g** of those who had
Dt   1:35   this evil **g** shall see the good land I
Jdg   2:10   that whole **g** had been gathered
Job   8: 8   "Ask the former **g** and find out
Ps   24: 6   Such is the **g** of those who seek
    48:13   you may tell of them to the next **g**.
    71:18   I declare your power to the next **g**,
    78: 4   will tell the next **g** the praiseworthy
    102:18   Let this be written for a future **g**,
    112: 2   the **g** of the upright will be blessed.
    145: 4   One **g** commends your works
Isa   34:17   forever and dwell there from **g** to **g**.
    53: 8   Yet who of his **g** protested?
La   5:19   your throne endures from **g** to **g**.
Da   4: 3   his dominion endures from **g** to **g**.
    4:34   his kingdom endures from **g** to **g**.
Joel   1: 3   and their children to the next **g**.
Mt   12:39   and adulterous **g** asks for a sign!
    17:17   "You unbelieving and perverse **g**,"
    23:36   tell you, all this will come on this **g**.
    24:34   this **g** will certainly not pass away
Mk   9:19   "You unbelieving **g**,"
    13:30   this **g** will certainly not pass away
Lk   1:50   to those who fear him, from **g** to **g**.
    7:31   can I compare the people of this **g**?
    11:29   Jesus said, "This is a wicked **g**.
    11:50   Therefore this **g** will be held
    21:32   this **g** will certainly not pass away
Ac   2:40   yourselves from this corrupt **g**."
Php   2:15   fault in a warped and crooked **g**."
Heb   3:10   That is why I was angry with that **g**;

## GENERATIONS [GENERATION]

Ge   9:12   you, a covenant for all **g** to come:
    17: 7   after you for the **g** to come, to be
Ex   12:17   lasting ordinance for the **g** to come.
    30:21   his descendants for the **g** to come."
    31:13   me and you for the **g** to come,
    40:15   will continue throughout their **g**."
Dt   7: 9   a thousand **g** of those who love him
    32: 7   consider the **g** long past.
1Ch   16:15   promise he made, for a thousand **g**,
Ps   22:30   future **g** will be told about the Lord.
    33:11   purposes of his heart through all **g**.
    45:17   your memory through all **g**;
    89: 1   faithfulness known through all **g**.
    90: 1   our dwelling place throughout all **g**.
    100: 5   faithfulness continues through all **g**.
    102:12   your renown endures through all **g**.
    105: 8   promise he made, for a thousand **g**,

Ps 119:90 faithfulness continues through all **g**;
   135:13 renown, LORD, through all **g**.
   145:13 dominion endures through all **g**.
   146:10 forever, your God, O Zion, for all **g**.
Pr 27:24 and a crown is not secure for all **g**.
Ecc 1: 4 **G** come and **g** go, but the earth
Isa 41: 4 through, calling forth the **g**
   51: 8 my salvation through all **g**."
Mt 1:17 Thus there were fourteen **g** in all
Lk 1:48 now on all **g** will call me blessed,
Eph 3: 5 other **g** as it has now been revealed
   3:21 and in Christ Jesus throughout all **g**,
Col 1:26 has been kept hidden for ages and **g**,

## GENEROSITY* [GENEROUS]

2Co 8: 2 extreme poverty welled up in rich **g**.
   9:11 and through us your **g** will result
   9:13 and for your **g** in sharing with them

## GENEROUS* [GENEROSITY, GENEROUSLY]

Ps 37:26 They are always **g** and lend freely;
   112: 5 Good will come to those who are **g**
Pr 11:25 A **g** person will prosper;
   22: 9 The **g** will themselves be blessed,
Mt 20:15 are you envious because I am **g**?'
Lk 11:41 be **g** to the poor,
Ac 28: 7 showed us **g** hospitality for three days.
2Co 9: 5 for the **g** gift you had promised.
   9: 5 Then it will be ready as a **g** gift,
   9:11 that you can be **g** on every occasion,
1Ti 6:18 and to be **g** and willing to share.

## GENEROUSLY [GENEROUS]

Dt 15:10 Give **g** to them and do so without
1Ch 29:14 should be able to give as **g** as this?
Ps 37:21 not repay, but the righteous give **g**;
2Co 9: 6 whoever sows **g** will also reap **g**.
Jas 1: 5 who gives **g** to all without finding

## GENITALS

Eze 16:26 Egyptians, your neighbors with large **g**,

## GENTILE [GENTILES]

Ezr 6:21 practices of their **G** neighbors
Ne 5: 9 the reproach of our **G** enemies?
Ac 21:25 As for the **G** believers, we have
Ro 1:16 first to the Jew, then to the **G**.
   2: 9 first for the Jew, then for the **G**;
   2:10 first for the Jew, then for the **G**.
   10:12 no difference between Jew and **G**—
Gal 3:28 There is neither Jew nor **G**,
Col 3:11 Here there is no **G** or Jew,

## GENTILES [GENTILE]

Isa 42: 6 for the people and a light for the **G**,
   49: 6 will also make you a light for the **G**,
Mt 4:15 the Jordan, Galilee of the **G**—
Lk 2:32 a light for revelation to the **G**,
   21:24 by the **G** until the times of the **G** are
   22:25 kings of the **G** lord it over them;
Ac 9:15 to proclaim my name to the **G**
   10:45 had been poured out even on **G**.
   11: 1 throughout Judea heard that the **G**
   11:18 to **G** God has granted repentance

Ac 13:16 Israel and you **G** who worship God,
   13:46 of eternal life, we now turn to the **G**.
   13:47 have made you a light for the **G**,
   14:27 had opened a door of faith to the **G**.
   15: 5 "The **G** must be circumcised
   15:19 it difficult for the **G** who are turning
   18: 6 From now on I will go to the **G**."
   22:21 send you far away to the **G**.' "
   26:20 and then to the **G**, I preached
   28:28 salvation has been sent to the **G**,
Ro 2:14 when **G**, who do not have the law,
   3: 9 **G** alike are all under the power
   3:29 the God of **G** too? Yes, of **G** too,
   9:24 from the Jews but also from the **G**?
   11:11 to the **G** to make Israel envious.
   11:12 their loss means riches for the **G**,
   11:13 I am talking to you **G**.
   11:13 as I am the apostle to the **G**, I make
   15: 9 that the **G** might glorify God for his
   15: 9 I will praise you among the **G**;
   15:27 For if the **G** have shared in the Jews'
1Co 1:23 block to Jews and foolishness to **G**,
   12:13 whether Jews or **G**, slave or free
2Co 11:26 my own people, in danger from **G**;
Gal 1:16 I might preach him among the **G**,
   2: 2 gospel that I preach among the **G**.
   2: 8 at work in me as an apostle to the **G**.
   2:14 that you force **G** to follow Jewish
   3: 8 God would justify the **G** by faith,
   3:14 come to the **G** through Christ Jesus,
Eph 3: 6 the gospel the **G** are heirs together
   3: 8 preach to the **G** the boundless riches
   4:17 you must no longer live as the **G** do,
Col 1:27 known among the **G** the glorious
1Ti 2: 7 a true and faithful teacher of the **G**.
2Ti 4:17 and all the **G** might hear it.
Rev 11: 2 because it has been given to the **G**.

## GENTLE* [GENTLENESS, GENTLY]

Dt 28:54 Even the most **g** and sensitive man
   28:56 The most **g** and sensitive woman among
           you—so sensitive and **g**
2Sa 18: 5 "Be **g** with the young man Absalom
1Ki 19:12 And after the fire came a **g** whisper.
Job 41: 3 Will it speak to you with **g** words?
Pr 15: 1 A **g** answer turns away wrath,
   25:15 and a **g** tongue can break a bone.
Jer 11:19 I had been like a **g** lamb led
Mt 11:29 me, for I am **g** and humble in heart,
   21: 5 to you, **g** and riding on a donkey,
Ac 27:13 When a **g** south wind began
1Co 4:21 I come in love and with a **g** spirit?
Eph 4: 2 Be completely humble and **g**,
1Ti 3: 3 not violent but **g**, not quarrelsome,
Tit 3: 2 always to be **g** toward everyone.
1Pe 3: 4 the unfading beauty of a **g** and quiet

## GENTLENESS* [GENTLE]

2Co 10: 1 By the meekness and **g** of Christ,
Gal 5:23 **g** and self-control.
Php 4: 5 Let your **g** be evident to all.
Col 3:12 kindness, humility, **g** and patience.
1Ti 6:11 faith, love, endurance and **g**.
1Pe 3:15 But do this with **g** and respect,

## GENTLY [GENTLE]
Isa 40:11 he **g** leads those that have young.
Gal  6: 1 Spirit should restore that person **g**.
2Ti  2:25 Opponents must be **g** instructed,
Heb  5: 2 deal **g** with those who are ignorant

## GENUINE*
2Co  6: 8 **g**, yet regarded as impostors;
Php  2:20 who will show **g** concern for your
1Pe  1: 7 may be proved **g** and may result

## GERAHS
Eze 45:12 The shekel is to consist of twenty **g**.

## GERAR
Ge  20: 2 Abimelek king of **G** sent for Sarah
    26: 6 So Isaac stayed in **G**.

## GERASENES
Lk   8:26 They sailed to the region of the **G**,

## GERIZIM
Dt  27:12 on Mount **G** to bless the people:
Jos  8:33 people stood in front of Mount **G**

## GERSHOM
Ex   2:22 and Moses named him **G**, saying,
1Ch 23:15 The sons of Moses: **G** and Eliezer.

## GERSHON [GERSHONITE, GERSHONITES]
Ge  46:11 sons of Levi: **G**, Kohath and Merari.

## GERSHONITE [GERSHON]
Nu   4:24 "This is the service of the **G** clans

## GERSHONITES [GERSHON]
Nu   3:25 of meeting the **G** were responsible
1Ch  6:71 The **G** received the following:

## GESHEM
Ne   6: 1 **G** the Arab and the rest of our

## GESHUR
2Sa 13:38 After Absalom fled and went to **G**,

## GET [GETS, GOT, ILL-GOTTEN]
Ge  24: 4 and **g** a wife for my son Isaac."
    29:20 served seven years to **g** Rachel,
Nu  16:10 are trying to **g** the priesthood too.
Dt  30:12 will ascend into heaven to **g** it
Jdg 16:28 me with one blow **g** revenge
Pr   1: 5 and let the discerning **g** guidance—
     3:35 but fools **g** only shame.
     4: 5 **G** wisdom, **g** understanding;
    16:16 better to **g** wisdom than gold, to
          **g** insight
    19: 8 Those who **g** wisdom love their own
          lives;
    23: 4 Do not wear yourself out to **g** rich;
Eze 18:31 and **g** a new heart and a new spirit.
Mt  16:23 and said to Peter, "**G** behind me,
Mk   6: 2 did this man **g** these things?"

Mk  13:16 in the field go back to **g** their cloak.
Jn  19:24 "Let's decide by lot who will **g** it."
1Co  9:24 Run in such a way as to **g** the prize.

## GETHSEMANE*
Mt  26:36 his disciples to a place called **G**,
Mk  14:32 They went to a place called **G**,

## GETS [GET]
Ac  23:15 ready to kill him before he **g** here."

## GEZER
Jos 16:10 dislodge the Canaanites living in **G**;
1Ch 14:16 army, all the way from Gibeon to **G**.

## GHOST
Mt  14:26 "It's a **g**," they said, and cried
Lk  24:39 a **g** does not have flesh and bones,

## [GIVE UP THE] GHOST (KJV) See BREATHED [HIS LAST], DIE, DIED, DYING, GAVE [UP HIS SPIRIT], PERISHED

## [HOLY] GHOST (KJV) See [HOLY] SPIRIT

## GIBEAH
Jdg 19:12 We will go on to **G**."
1Sa 10:26 Saul also went to his home in **G**,
2Sa 21: 6 exposed before the LORD at **G**
Hos 10: 9 "Since the days of **G**, you have

## GIBEON [GIBEONITES]
Jos 10:12 "Sun, stand still over **G**, and you,
2Sa  2:13 out and met them at the pool of **G**.
1Ki  3: 5 At **G** the LORD appeared

## GIBEONITES [GIBEON]
Jos  9:16 they made the treaty with the **G**,
2Sa 21: 1 it is because he put the **G** to death."

## GIDEON [JERUB-BAAL]
Judge, also called Jerub-Baal; freed Israel from Midianites (Jdg 6–8; Heb 11:32). Given sign of fleece (Jdg 8:36–40).

## GIFT [GIFTED, GIFTS]
Ge  30:20 has presented me with a precious **g**.
Nu  18: 7 the service of the priesthood as a **g**.
Dt  16:17 of you must bring a **g** in proportion
2Ch  9:24 everyone who came brought a **g**—
Pr  18:16 A **g** opens the way and ushers
    21:14 A **g** given in secret soothes anger,
Ecc  3:13 in all their toil—this is the **g** of God.
     5:19 in their toil—this is a **g** of God.
Mt   5:23 if you are offering your **g** at the altar
     8: 4 and offer the **g** Moses commanded,
Jn   4:10 "If you knew the **g** of God and who
Ac   1: 4 wait for the **g** my Father promised,
     2:38 you will receive the **g** of the Holy
     8:20 you thought you could buy the **g**
    11:17 gave them the same **g** he gave us

Ro   1:11   to you some spiritual **g** to make you
     5:15   But the **g** is not like the trespass.
     6:23   the **g** of God is eternal life in Christ
    12: 6   If your **g** is prophesying,
1Co  7: 7   of you has your own **g** from God;
    14: 1   gifts, especially the **g** of prophecy.
2Co  8:12   the **g** is acceptable according
     9:15   be to God for his indescribable **g**!
Eph  2: 8   from yourselves, it is the **g** of God—
1Ti  4:14   Do not neglect your **g**, which was
2Ti  1: 6   you to fan into flame the **g** of God,
Heb  6: 4   who have tasted the heavenly **g**,
Jas  1:17   good and perfect **g** is from above,
1Pe  3: 7   with you of the gracious **g** of life,
    4:10   you should use whatever **g** you have
Rev 22:17   let all who wish take the free **g**

## GIFTED* [GIFT]
1Co 14:37   or otherwise **g** by the Spirit,

## GIFTS [GIFT]
Nu   8:19   I have given the Levites as **g**
Dt  12: 6   your tithes and special **g**, what you
Ezr  1: 6   and with valuable **g**, in addition
Ps  68:18   you received **g** from people,
   76:11   let all the neighboring lands bring **g**
  112: 9   They have scattered abroad their **g**
Pr  25:14   is one who boasts of **g** never given.
Mt   2:11   and presented him with **g** of gold,
    7:11   how to give good **g** to your children,
    7:11   in heaven give good **g** to those who
Lk  11:13   how to give good **g** to your children,
   21: 1   he saw the rich putting their **g**
Ac  10: 4   and to the poor have come up as
Ro  11:29   for God's **g** and his call are
   12: 6   We have different **g**,
1Co 12: 1   Now about the **g** of the Spirit,
   12: 4   There are different kinds of **g**,
  12:28   then **g** of healing, of helping,
  12:30   Do all have **g** of healing?
  12:31   Now eagerly desire the greater **g**.
  14: 1   love and eagerly desire spiritual **g**,
  14:12   Since you are eager for **g**
2Co  9: 9   "They have scattered abroad their **g**
Eph  4: 8   captives and gave **g** to his people."
Php  4:17   Not that I desire your **g**;
Heb  2: 4   by **g** of the Holy Spirit distributed
    9: 9   indicating that the **g** and sacrifices

## GIHON
Ge   2:13   name of the second river is the **G**;
2Ch 32:30   the upper outlet of the **G** spring

## GILBOA
1Ch 10: 8   and his sons fallen on Mount **G**.

## GILEAD [GILEADITE, JABESH
    GILEAD, RAMOTH GILEAD]
Nu  32:29   the land of **G** as their possession.
Dt  34: 1   the whole land—from **G** to Dan,
Jdg  11: 1   His father was **G**; his mother was
2Sa  2: 9   He made him king over **G**,
1Ch 27:21   the half-tribe of Manasseh in **G**:
Jer  8:22   Is there no balm in **G**? Is there no
  46:11   "Go up to **G** and get balm,

Hos  6: 8   **G** is a city of wicked people,
Mic  7:14   Bashan and **G** as in days long ago.

## GILEADITE [GILEAD]
Jdg  11: 1   Jephthah the **G** was a mighty
2Sa 19:31   Barzillai the **G** also came down

## GILGAL
Jos  4:20   **G** the twelve stones they had taken
    5: 9   So the place has been called **G**
Jdg  2: 1   LORD went up from **G** to Bokim
1Sa  7:16   circuit from Bethel to **G** to Mizpah,

## GIRD*
Ps  45: 3   **G** your sword on your side,

## GIRGASHITES
Dt  7: 1   the Hittites, **G**, Amorites,

## GIRL [GIRLS]
Ge  24:16   The **g** was very beautiful, a virgin;
Ex  1:16   but if it is a **g**, let her live."
2Ki  5: 2   had taken captive a young **g**
Mk  5:41   (which means "Little **g**, I say
    6:22   The king said to the **g**, "Ask me

## GIRLS [GIRL]
Joel  3: 3   they sold **g** for wine that they might
Zec  8: 5   with boys and **g** playing there."

## GIVE [GAVE, GIVEN, GIVER, GIVES,
    GIVING, LIFE-GIVING]
Ge   1:29   "I **g** you every seed-bearing plant
    9: 3   plants, I now **g** you everything.
   12: 7   your offspring I will **g** this land."
   27: 4   I may **g** you my blessing before I
   28: 4   May he **g** you and your descendants
  28:22   that you **g** me I will **g** you a tenth."
Ex  13: 5   he swore to your ancestors to **g** you,
   17: 2   and said, "**G** us water to drink."
  20:16   "You shall not **g** false testimony
  30:15   are not to **g** more than a half shekel
Lev 18:21   " 'Do not **g** any of your children
Nu  6:26   toward you and **g** you peace." '
  11:13   wailing to me, '**G** us meat to eat!'
Dt   5:20   "You shall not **g** false testimony
  15:10   **G** generously to them and do so
  28: 1   all his commands I **g** you today,
Jos  1: 6   I swore to their ancestors to **g** them.
Jdg  6:17   eyes, **g** me a sign that it is really you
1Sa  1:11   forget your servant but **g** her a son,
    1:11   I will **g** him to the LORD for all
    1:28   So now I **g** him to the LORD.
    8: 6   they said, "**G** us a king to lead us,"
1Ki  3: 5   whatever you want me to **g** you."
  11:13   will **g** him one tribe for the sake
2Ch  1:10   **G** me wisdom and knowledge, that I
  15: 7   be strong and do not **g** up, for your
Ne  9: 6   You **g** life to everything,
Job  2: 4   "A man will **g** all he has for his
Ps  13: 3   **G** light to my eyes, or I will sleep
Pr  4:26   **G** careful thought to the paths
  21:26   but the righteous **g** without sparing.
  23:26   **g** me your heart and let your eyes
  25:21   enemy is hungry, **g** him food to eat;

Pr 25:26 the righteous who **g** way to the wicked.
28:27 who **g** to the poor will lack nothing,
30: 8 **g** me neither poverty nor riches,
30: 8 but **g** me only my daily bread.
30:15 has two daughters. '**G! G!**' they cry.
Ecc 3: 6 a time to search and a time to **g** up,
SS 8: 7 one were to **g** all the wealth of one's
Isa 7:14 the Lord himself will **g** you a sign:
7:14 will conceive and **g** birth to a son,
Eze 36:26 I will **g** you a new heart and put
36:26 of stone and **g** you a heart of flesh.
Mt 6:11 **G** us today our daily bread.
7: 6 "Do not **g** dogs what is sacred;
7:11 know how to **g** good gifts to your
7:11 your Father in heaven **g** good gifts
10: 8 Freely you have received, freely **g**.
16:19 I will **g** you the keys of the kingdom
22:21 "**G** back to Caesar what is Caesar's,
Mk 6:23 "Whatever you ask I will **g** you,
8:37 Or what can you **g** in exchange
10:19 you shall not **g** false testimony,
10:45 to **g** his life as a ransom for many."
Lk 6:38 **G**, and it will be given to you.
11: 3 **G** us each day our daily bread.
11:13 Father in heaven **g** the Holy Spirit
14:33 you who do not **g** up everything you
Jn 4:14 drink the water I **g** them will never
6:52 "How can this man **g** us his flesh
10:28 I **g** them eternal life, and they shall
13:34 "A new command I **g** you:
14:16 he will **g** you another advocate
14:27 I leave with you; my peace I **g** you.
14:27 I do not **g** to you as the world gives.
17: 2 people that he might **g** eternal life
Ac 2:45 to **g** to anyone who had need.
3: 6 have, but what I do have I **g** you.
20:35 'It is more blessed to **g** than
Ro 2: 7 immortality, he will **g** eternal life.
8:32 with him, graciously **g** us all things?
12: 8 encourage, then **g** encouragement;
12: 8 if it is giving, then **g** generously;
13: 7 **G** to everyone what you owe:
14:12 So then, we will all **g** an account
1Co 13: 3 If I **g** all I possess to the poor and **g**
2Co 9: 7 you should **g** what you have decided in
your heart to **g**,
Gal 2: 5 We did not **g** in to them
6: 9 reap a harvest if we do not **g** up.
Eph 4:27 and do not **g** the devil a foothold.
Heb 13:17 as those who must **g** an account.
1Pe 3:15 Always be prepared to **g** an answer
Rev 2: 7 I will **g** the right to eat from the tree
2:10 and I will **g** you life as your victor's
2:17 I will **g** some of the hidden manna.
2:26 I will **g** authority over the nations—
2:28 I will also **g** them the morning star.
3:21 I will **g** the right to sit with me
14: 7 voice, "Fear God and **g** him glory,
18: 6 **G** back to her as she has given;
22:12 I will **g** to everyone according

## GIVE ... THANKS See THANKS

## GIVEN [GIVE]

Ex 4:21 the wonders I have **g** you the power
16:15 is the bread the LORD has **g** you
Nu 8:16 the Israelites who are to be **g** wholly

Dt 1:21 your God has **g** you the land.
26:11 things the LORD your God has **g**
Job 3:23 Why is life **g** to a man whose way is
Ps 31: 8 not **g** me into the hands of the enemy
105:42 he remembered his holy promise **g**
115:16 but the earth he has **g** to humankind.
118:18 but he has not **g** me over to death.
Pr 25:11 settings of silver is a ruling rightly **g**.
Isa 9: 6 to us a son is **g**, and the government
La 2: 7 He has **g** the walls of her palaces into
Am 9:15 from the land I have **g** them,"
Mt 6:33 all these things will be **g** to you as
7: 7 "Ask and it will be **g** to you;
22:30 people will neither marry nor be **g**
25:29 For those who have will be **g** more,
Mk 4:25 Those who have will be **g** more;
8:12 I tell you, no sign will be **g** to it."
Lk 6:38 Give, and it will be **g** to you.
8:10 kingdom of God has been **g** to you,
11: 9 Ask and it will be **g** to you;
22:19 saying, "This is my body **g** for you;
Jn 1:16 grace in place of grace already **g**.
1:17 For the law was **g** through Moses;
3:27 person can receive only what is **g**
6:39 lose none of all those he has **g** me,
17:24 I want those you have **g** me to be
17:24 glory you have **g** me because you
18:11 drink the cup the Father has **g** me?"
Ac 5:32 whom God has **g** to those who obey
7:53 law that was **g** through angels
20:24 the task the Lord Jesus has **g** me—
Ro 5: 5 Holy Spirit, who has been **g** to us.
11:35 "Who has ever **g** to God, that God
1Co 4: 2 those who have been **g** a trust must
11:24 and when he had **g** thanks, he broke
12:13 and we were all **g** the one Spirit
2Co 5: 5 who has **g** us the Spirit as a deposit,
12: 7 I was **g** a thorn in my flesh,
Gal 3:19 law was **g** through angels
3:22 being **g** through faith in Jesus
3:22 might be **g** to those who believe.
Eph 1: 6 he has freely **g** us in the One he
4: 7 one of us grace has been **g** as Christ
1Ti 4:14 which was **g** you through prophecy
1Pe 1: 3 great mercy he has **g** us new birth
2Pe 1: 3 divine power has **g** us everything
1Jn 4:13 he in us: He has **g** us of his Spirit.
5:20 come and has **g** us understanding,
Rev 6: 2 and he was **g** a crown, and he rode
15: 2 They held harps **g** them by God
20: 4 those who had been **g** authority

## GIVER* [GIVE]

Pr 18:16 ushers the **g** into the presence
2Co 9: 7 for God loves a cheerful **g**.

## GIVES [GIVE]

Ex 4:11 Who **g** them sight or makes them
Job 33: 4 breath of the Almighty **g** me life.
35:10 Maker, who **g** songs in the night,
Ps 29:11 The LORD **g** strength to his
119:130 unfolding of your words **g** light; it **g**
136:25 He **g** food to every creature.
Pr 2: 6 For the LORD **g** wisdom;
11:24 One person **g** freely, yet gains even
14:30 A heart at peace **g** life to the body,

| | | |
|---|---|---|
| Pr | 15:30 | good news **g** health to the bones. |
| | 19: 6 | is the friend of one who **g** gifts. |
| | 29: 4 | justice a king **g** a country stability, |
| Ecc | 2:26 | who pleases him, God **g** wisdom, |
| | 2:26 | the sinner he **g** the task of gathering |
| Isa | 40:29 | He **g** strength to the weary |
| Hab | 2:15 | to him who **g** drink to his neighbors, |
| Mt | 10:42 | if anyone **g** even a cup of cold water |
| Jn | 3:34 | for God **g** the Spirit without limit. |
| | 5:21 | raises the dead and **g** them life, |
| | 5:21 | even so the Son **g** life to whom he is |
| | 6:37 | whom the Father **g** me will come |
| | 6:63 | The Spirit **g** life; the flesh counts |
| | 14:27 | I do not give to you as the world **g**. |
| 1Co | 15:57 | He **g** us the victory through our |
| 2Co | 3: 6 | the letter kills, but the Spirit **g** life. |
| 1Th | 4: 8 | the very God who **g** you his Holy |
| Jas | 1:25 | into the perfect law that **g** freedom, |
| | 4: 6 | But he **g** us more grace. That is why |
| Rev | 21:23 | for the glory of God **g** it light, |

## GIVING [GIVE]

| | | |
|---|---|---|
| Ge | 13:17 | of the land, for I am **g** it to you." |
| Dt | 11: 8 | all the commands I am **g** you today, |
| Jos | 1:13 | give you rest by **g** you this land.' |
| Ne | 8: 8 | **g** the meaning so that the people |
| Est | 9:19 | a day for **g** presents to each other. |
| Ps | 19: 8 | LORD are right, **g** joy to the heart. |
| | 19: 8 | are radiant, **g** light to the eyes. |
| Pr | 1: 4 | for **g** prudence to those who are |
| | 15:23 | person finds joy in **g** an apt reply— |
| Mt | 6: 4 | so that your **g** may be in secret. |
| | 24:38 | marrying and **g** in marriage, |
| Ac | 15: 8 | accepted them by **g** the Holy Spirit |
| Ro | 12: 8 | if it is **g**, then give generously; |
| 2Co | 8: 7 | you also excel in this grace of **g**. |
| Php | 4:15 | shared with me in the matter of **g** |
| Heb | 10:25 | not **g** up meeting together, |

## GLAD* [GLADDENS, GLADNESS]

| | | |
|---|---|---|
| Ex | 4:14 | and his heart will be **g** when he sees |
| Jos | 22:33 | They were **g** to hear the report |
| Jdg | 8:25 | "We'll be **g** to give them." |
| 1Sa | 19: 5 | Israel, and you saw it and were **g**. |
| 2Sa | 1:20 | the daughters of the Philistines be **g**, |
| 1Ki | 8:66 | **g** in heart for all the good things |
| 1Ch | 16:31 | heavens rejoice, let the earth be **g**; |
| 2Ch | 7:10 | **g** in heart for the good things |
| Ps | 5:11 | let all who take refuge in you be **g**; |
| | 9: 2 | I will be **g** and rejoice in you; |
| | 14: 7 | let Jacob rejoice and Israel be **g**! |
| | 16: 9 | Therefore my heart is **g** and my |
| | 21: 6 | and made him **g** with the joy of your |
| | 31: 7 | I will be **g** and rejoice in your love, |
| | 32:11 | Rejoice in the LORD and be **g**, |
| | 40:16 | seek you rejoice and be **g** in you; |
| | 45: 8 | music of the strings makes you **g**. |
| | 46: 4 | river whose streams make **g** the city |
| | 48:11 | of Judah are **g** because of your |
| | 53: 6 | let Jacob rejoice and Israel be **g**! |
| | 58:10 | The righteous will be **g** when they |
| | 67: 4 | May the nations be **g** and sing |
| | 68: 3 | may the righteous be **g** and rejoice |
| | 69:32 | The poor will see and be **g**— |
| | 70: 4 | seek you rejoice and be **g** in you; |
| | 90:14 | sing for joy and be **g** all our days. |

| | | |
|---|---|---|
| Ps | 90:15 | Make us **g** for as many days as you |
| | 92: 4 | For you make me **g** by your deeds, |
| | 96:11 | heavens rejoice, let the earth be **g**; |
| | 97: 1 | LORD reigns, let the earth be **g**; |
| | 97: 8 | of Judah are **g** because of your |
| | 105:38 | Egypt was **g** when they left, |
| | 107:30 | They were **g** when it grew calm, |
| | 118:24 | let us rejoice today and be **g**. |
| | 149: 2 | people of Zion be **g** in their King. |
| Pr | 23:15 | then my heart will be **g** indeed; |
| | 29: 6 | righteous shout for joy and are **g**. |
| Ecc | 8:15 | sun than to eat and drink and be **g**. |
| Isa | 25: 9 | rejoice and be **g** in his salvation." |
| | 35: 1 | and the parched land will be **g**; |
| | 65:18 | be **g** and rejoice forever in what I |
| | 66:10 | with Jerusalem and be **g** for her, |
| Jer | 20:15 | who made him very **g**, saying, |
| | 31:13 | young women will dance and be **g**, |
| | 41:13 | who were with him, they were **g**. |
| | 50:11 | "Because you rejoice and are **g**, |
| La | 4:21 | Rejoice and be **g**, Daughter Edom, |
| Joel | 2:21 | land of Judah; be **g** and rejoice. |
| | 2:23 | Be **g**, people of Zion, |
| Hab | 1:15 | and so he rejoices and is **g**. |
| Zep | 3:14 | Be **g** and rejoice with all your heart, |
| Zec | 2:10 | "Shout and be **g**, Daughter Zion. |
| | 8:19 | will become joyful and **g** occasions |
| | 10: 7 | their hearts will be **g** as with wine. |
| Mt | 5:12 | Rejoice and be **g**, because great is |
| Lk | 15:32 | But we had to celebrate and be **g**, |
| Jn | 4:36 | and the reaper may be **g** together. |
| | 8:56 | he saw it and was **g**." |
| | 11:15 | for your sake I am **g** I was not there, |
| | 14:28 | you would be **g** that I am going |
| Ac | 2:26 | Therefore my heart is **g** and my |
| | 2:46 | and ate together with **g** and sincere |
| | 11:23 | he was **g** and encouraged them all |
| | 13:48 | they were **g** and honored the word |
| | 15: 3 | news made all the believers very **g**. |
| | 15:31 | were **g** for its encouraging message. |
| 1Co | 16:17 | I was **g** when Stephanas, |
| 2Co | 2: 2 | who is left to make me **g** but you |
| | 7:16 | I am **g** I can have complete |
| | 13: 9 | We are **g** whenever we are weak |
| Gal | 4:27 | "Be **g**, barren woman, you who |
| Php | 2:17 | I am **g** and rejoice with all of you. |
| | 2:18 | So you too should be **g** and rejoice |
| | 2:28 | you see him again you may be **g** |
| Rev | 19: 7 | rejoice and be **g** and give him glory! |

## GLADDENS* [GLAD]

| | | |
|---|---|---|
| Ps | 104:15 | wine that **g** human hearts, |

## GLADNESS* [GLAD]

| | | |
|---|---|---|
| 2Ch | 29:30 | So they sang praises with **g** |
| Est | 8:16 | of happiness and joy, **g** and honor. |
| | 8:17 | was joy and **g** among the Jews, |
| Job | 3:22 | who are filled with **g** and rejoice |
| Ps | 35:27 | my vindication shout for joy and **g**; |
| | 45:15 | Led in with joy and **g**, they enter |
| | 51: 8 | Let me hear joy and **g**; let the bones |
| | 65:12 | the hills are clothed with **g**. |
| | 100: 2 | Worship the LORD with **g**; |
| Ecc | 5:20 | God keeps them occupied with **g** |
| | 9: 7 | eat your food with **g**, and drink your |
| Isa | 16:10 | **g** are taken away from the orchards; |

Isa 35:10 **G** and joy will overtake them,
51: 3 Joy and **g** will be found in her,
51:11 **G** and joy will overtake them,
Jer 7:34 an end to the sounds of joy and **g**
16: 9 an end to the sounds of joy and **g**
25:10 from them the sounds of joy and **g**,
31:13 I will turn their mourning into **g**;
33:11 the sounds of joy and **g**, the voices
48:33 and **g** are gone from the orchards
Joel 1:16 and **g** from the house of our God?

## GLASS*

Rev 4: 6 was what looked like a sea of **g**,
15: 2 what looked like a sea of **g** glowing
21:18 the city of pure gold, as pure as **g**.
21:21 of gold, as pure as transparent **g**.

## GLEAM* [GLEAMED]

Da 10: 6 legs like the **g** of burnished bronze,

## GLEAMED* [GLEAM]

Eze 1: 7 a calf and **g** like burnished bronze.
Lk 24: 4 **g** like lightning stood beside them.

## GLEAN [GLEANED, GLEANINGS]

Ru 2: 3 began to **g** behind the harvesters.

## GLEANED* [GLEAN]

Ru 2:17 So Ruth **g** in the field until evening.

## GLEANINGS [GLEAN]

Lev 19: 9 field or gather the **g** of your harvest.

## GLIDE* [GLIDED, GLIDING]

Dt 32:24 venom of vipers that **g** in the dust.

## GLIDED* [GLIDE]

Job 4:15 A spirit **g** past my face, and the hair

## GLIDING* [GLIDE]

Job 26:13 his hand pierced the **g** serpent.
Isa 27: 1 Leviathan the **g** serpent,

## GLOAT [GLOATS]

Ps 22:17 people stare and **g** over me.
30: 1 did not let my enemies **g** over me.
Pr 24:17 Do not **g** when your enemies fall;
La 2:17 he has let the enemy **g** over you,
Rev 11:10 of the earth will **g** over them

## GLOATS* [GLOAT]

Pr 17: 5 whoever **g** over disaster will not go

## GLOOM

Isa 9: 1 there will be no more **g** for those
Joel 2: 2 a day of darkness and **g**, a day
Zep 1:15 a day of darkness and **g**, a day
Heb 12:18 to darkness, **g** and storm;

## GLORIES* [GLORY]

1Pe 1:11 Christ and the **g** that would follow.

## GLORIFIED* [GLORY]

Isa 66: 5 'Let the LORD be **g**, that we may
Da 4:34 and **g** him who lives forever.
Jn 7:39 since Jesus had not yet been **g**.
11: 4 God's Son may be **g** through it."
12:16 after Jesus was **g** did they realize
12:23 come for the Son of Man to be **g**.
12:28 "I have **g** it, and will glorify it
13:31 Son of Man **g** and God is **g** in him.
13:32 If God is **g** in him, God will glorify
14:13 so that the Father may be **g** in the Son.
Ac 3:13 our fathers, has **g** his servant Jesus.
Ro 1:21 they neither **g** him as God nor gave
8:30 those he justified, he also **g**.
2Th 1:10 he comes to be **g** in his holy people
1:12 of our Lord Jesus may be **g** in you,
1Pe 1:21 raised him from the dead and **g** him,

## GLORIFIES* [GLORY]

Lk 1:46 "My soul **g** the Lord
Jn 8:54 as your God, is the one who **g** me.

## GLORIFY* [GLORY]

Ps 34: 3 **G** the LORD with me; let us exalt
63: 3 better than life, my lips will **g** you.
69:30 song and **g** him with thanksgiving.
86:12 I will **g** your name forever.
Isa 60:13 and I will **g** the place for my feet.
Da 4:37 and exalt and **g** the King of heaven,
Mt 5:16 and **g** your Father in heaven.
Jn 8:54 "If I **g** myself, my glory means
12:28 Father, **g** your name!" Then a voice
12:28 glorified it, and will **g** it again."
13:32 God will **g** the Son in himself, and will
**g** him at once.
16:14 He will **g** me because it is from me
17: 1 **G** your Son, that your Son may **g**
17: 5 **g** me in your presence
21:19 death by which Peter would **g** God.
Ro 15: 6 one voice you may **g** the God
15: 9 the Gentiles might **g** God for his
1Pe 2:12 and **g** God on the day he visits us.
Rev 16: 9 they refused to repent and **g** him.

## GLORIFYING* [GLORY]

Lk 2:20 **g** and praising God for all the things

## GLORIOUS* [GLORY]

Dt 28:58 do not revere this **g** and awesome
33:29 shield and helper and your **g** sword.
1Ch 29:13 you thanks, and praise your **g** name.
Ne 9: 5 "Blessed be your **g** name, and may
Ps 45:13 All **g** is the princess within her
66: 2 of his name; make his praise **g**.
72:19 Praise be to his **g** name forever;
87: 3 **G** things are said of you,
106:20 exchanged their **g** God for an image
111: 3 **G** and majestic are his deeds,
145: 5 They speak of the **g** splendor
145:12 and the **g** splendor of your kingdom.
Pr 4: 9 present you with a **g** crown."
Isa 3: 8 the LORD, defying his **g** presence.
4: 2 the LORD will be beautiful and **g**,
11:10 him, and his resting place will be **g**.
12: 5 LORD, for he has done **g** things;

| | | |
|---|---|---|
| Isa | 28: 1 | to the fading flower, his **g** beauty, |
| | 28: 4 | That fading flower, his **g** beauty, |
| | 28: 5 | Almighty will be a **g** crown, |
| | 42:21 | to make his law great and **g**. |
| | 60: 7 | altar, and I will adorn my **g** temple. |
| | 63:12 | who sent his **g** arm of power to be |
| | 63:14 | to make for yourself a **g** name. |
| | 63:15 | from your lofty throne, holy and **g**. |
| | 64:11 | Our holy and **g** temple, where our |
| Jer | 2:11 | their **g** God for worthless idols. |
| | 13:18 | for your **g** crowns will fall |
| | 14:21 | do not dishonor your **g** throne. |
| | 17:12 | A **g** throne, |
| | 48:17 | scepter, how broken the **g** staff!' |
| Hos | 4: 7 | their **g** God for something disgraceful. |
| Zec | 2: 8 | "After the **G** One has sent me against |
| Mt | 19:28 | the Son of Man sits on his **g** throne, |
| | 25:31 | he will sit on his **g** throne. |
| Lk | 9:31 | appeared in **g** splendor, |
| Ac | 2:20 | of the great and **g** day of the Lord. |
| 2Co | 3: 8 | of the Spirit be even more **g**? |
| | 3: 9 | brought condemnation was **g**, how |
| | | much more **g** is the ministry |
| | 3:10 | For what was **g** has no glory now |
| Eph | 1: 6 | to the praise of his **g** grace, |
| | 1:17 | our Lord Jesus Christ, the **g** Father, |
| | 1:18 | the riches of his **g** inheritance in his |
| | 3:16 | his **g** riches he may strengthen you |
| Php | 3:21 | so that they will be like his **g** body. |
| Col | 1:11 | power according to his **g** might so |
| | 1:27 | among the Gentiles the **g** riches |
| Jas | 2: 1 | in our **g** Lord Jesus Christ must not |
| 1Pe | 1: 8 | with an inexpressible and **g** joy, |
| Jude | 1:24 | you before his **g** presence without |

## GLORY [GLORIES, GLORIFIED, GLORIFIES, GLORIFY, GLORIFYING, GLORIOUS]

| | | |
|---|---|---|
| Ex | 14: 4 | But I will gain **g** for myself through |
| | 14:17 | I will gain **g** through Pharaoh |
| | 14:18 | when I gain **g** through Pharaoh, |
| | 15:11 | awesome in **g**, working wonders? |
| | 16: 7 | in the morning you will see the **g** |
| | 16:10 | and there was the **g** of the Lord |
| | 24:16 | and the **g** of the Lord settled |
| | 24:17 | the Israelites the **g** of the Lord |
| | 29:43 | place will be consecrated by my **g**. |
| | 33:18 | said, "Now show me your **g**." |
| | 33:22 | When my **g** passes by, I will put |
| | 40:34 | and the **g** of the Lord filled |
| | 40:35 | it, and the **g** of the Lord filled |
| Lev | 9: 6 | the **g** of the Lord may appear |
| | 9:23 | the **g** of the Lord appeared to all |
| Nu | 14:10 | the **g** of the Lord appeared |
| | 14:21 | and as surely as the **g** of the Lord |
| | 14:22 | not one of those who saw my **g** |
| | 16:19 | the **g** of the Lord appeared |
| | 16:42 | it and the **g** of the Lord appeared. |
| | 20: 6 | and the **g** of the Lord appeared |
| Dt | 5:24 | Lord our God has shown us his **g** |
| Jos | 7:19 | "My son, give **g** to the Lord, |
| 1Sa | 4:21 | "The **G** has departed from Israel"— |
| | 6: 5 | and give **g** to Israel's god. |
| | 15:29 | He who is the **G** of Israel does not |
| 1Ki | 8:11 | for the **g** of the Lord filled his |
| 1Ch | 16:10 | **G** in his holy name; let the hearts |

| | | |
|---|---|---|
| 1Ch | 16:24 | Declare his **g** among the nations, |
| | 16:28 | ascribe to the Lord **g** |
| | 29:11 | the power and the **g** and the majesty |
| 2Ch | 5:14 | for the **g** of the Lord filled |
| | 7: 1 | and the **g** of the Lord filled |
| Ps | 3: 3 | my **g**, the one who lifts my head high. |
| | 4: 2 | How long will you men turn my **g** |
| | 8: 1 | You have set your **g** |
| | 8: 5 | crowned them with **g** and honor. |
| | 19: 1 | The heavens declare the **g** of God; |
| | 24: 7 | that the King of **g** may come in. |
| | 26: 8 | live, the place where your **g** dwells. |
| | 29: 1 | beings, ascribe to the Lord **g** |
| | 29: 3 | the God of **g** thunders, the Lord |
| | 29: 9 | And in his temple all cry, "**G**!" |
| | 34: 2 | I will **g** in the Lord; |
| | 57: 5 | let your **g** be over all the earth. |
| | 63: 2 | and behold your power and your **g**. |
| | 66: 2 | Sing the **g** of his name; |
| | 72:19 | the whole earth be filled with his **g**. |
| | 73:24 | afterward you will take me into **g**. |
| | 85: 9 | that his **g** may dwell in our land. |
| | 89:17 | For you are their **g** and strength, |
| | 96: 3 | Declare his **g** among the nations, |
| | 96: 6 | strength and **g** are in his sanctuary. |
| | 96: 8 | to the Lord the **g** due his name; |
| | 97: 6 | and all peoples see his **g**. |
| | 102:15 | kings of the earth will revere your **g**. |
| | 104:31 | May the **g** of the Lord endure |
| | 108: 5 | let your **g** be over all the earth. |
| | 138: 5 | for the **g** of the Lord is great. |
| | 149: 9 | this is the **g** of all his faithful |
| Pr | 19:11 | is to one's **g** to overlook an offense. |
| | 20:29 | The **g** of young men is their |
| | 25: 2 | It is the **g** of God to conceal |
| | 25: 2 | search out a matter is the **g** of kings. |
| Isa | 4: 5 | over everything the **g** will be |
| | 6: 3 | the whole earth is full of his **g**." |
| | 24:16 | "**G** to the Righteous One." |
| | 24:23 | before its elders—with great **g**. |
| | 26:15 | You have gained **g** for yourself; |
| | 35: 2 | The **g** of Lebanon will be given |
| | 35: 2 | they will see the **g** of the Lord, |
| | 40: 5 | And the **g** of the Lord will be |
| | 42: 8 | I will not yield my **g** to another |
| | 42:12 | Let them give **g** to the Lord |
| | 43: 7 | whom I created for my **g**, whom I |
| | 44:23 | Jacob, he displays his **g** in Israel. |
| | 48:11 | I will not yield my **g** to another. |
| | 60:19 | light, and your God will be your **g**. |
| | 66:18 | and they will come and see my **g**. |
| | 66:19 | not heard of my fame or seen my **g**. |
| | 66:19 | They will proclaim my **g** among |
| Eze | 1:28 | the likeness of the **g** of the Lord. |
| | 3:23 | the **g** of the Lord was standing |
| | 3:23 | like the **g** I had seen by the Kebar |
| | 8: 4 | there before me was the **g** |
| | 9: 3 | Now the **g** of the God of Israel went |
| | 10: 4 | Then the **g** of the Lord rose |
| | 10: 4 | the radiance of the **g** of the Lord. |
| | 10:18 | the **g** of the Lord departed |
| | 11:23 | The **g** of the Lord went |
| | 39:13 | I display my **g** will be a memorable day |
| | 43: 2 | and I saw the **g** of the God of Israel |
| | 43: 2 | and the land was radiant with his **g**. |
| | 43: 5 | and the **g** of the Lord filled |
| | 44: 4 | saw the **g** of the Lord filling |

| | | |
|---|---|---|
| Hab | 2:14 | of the **g** of the LORD as the waters |
| | 3: 3 | His **g** covered the heavens and his |
| Hag | 2: 7 | and I will fill this house with **g**,' |
| Zec | 2: 5 | LORD, 'and I will be its **g** within.' |
| Mt | 16:27 | in his Father's **g** with his angels, |
| | 24:30 | of heaven, with power and great **g**. |
| | 25:31 | the Son of Man comes in his **g**, |
| Mk | 8:38 | in his Father's **g** with the holy |
| | 10:37 | the other at your left in your **g**." |
| | 13:26 | in clouds with great power and **g**. |
| Lk | 2: 9 | and the **g** of the Lord shone around |
| | 2:14 | "**G** to God in the highest heaven, |
| | 2:32 | and the **g** of your people Israel." |
| | 9:26 | of you when he comes in his **g** |
| | 9:26 | and in the **g** of the Father |
| | 9:32 | they saw his **g** and the two men |
| | 19:38 | in heaven and **g** in the highest!" |
| | 21:27 | in a cloud with power and great **g**. |
| | 24:26 | these things and then enter his **g**?" |
| Jn | 1:14 | We have seen his **g**, the **g** of the one |
| | 2:11 | through which he revealed his **g**; |
| | 5:41 | "I do not accept **g** from human |
| | 5:44 | since you accept **g** from one another |
| | 7:18 | seeks the **g** of the one who sent him |
| | 8:50 | I am not seeking **g** for myself; |
| | 8:54 | glorify myself, my **g** means nothing. |
| | 11: 4 | it is for God's **g** so that God's Son |
| | 11:40 | believe, you will see the **g** of God?" |
| | 12:41 | said this because he saw Jesus' **g** |
| | 12:43 | loved human **g** more than the **g** of God. |
| | 15: 8 | This is to my Father's **g**, that you |
| | 17: 4 | I have brought you **g** on earth |
| | 17: 5 | your presence with the **g** I had |
| | 17:10 | **g** has come to me through them. |
| | 17:22 | I have given them the **g** that you |
| | 17:24 | am, and to see my **g**, the **g** you have |
| Ac | 7: 2 | The God of **g** appeared to our father |
| | 7:55 | up to heaven and saw the **g** of God, |
| Ro | 1:23 | exchanged the **g** of the immortal |
| | 2: 7 | by persistence in doing good seek **g**, |
| | 2:10 | but **g**, honor and peace for everyone |
| | 3: 7 | truthfulness and so increases his **g**, |
| | 3:23 | and fall short of the **g** of God, |
| | 4:20 | in his faith and gave **g** to God, |
| | 5: 2 | boast in the hope of the **g** of God. |
| | 8:17 | that we may also share in his **g**. |
| | 8:18 | with the **g** that will be revealed |
| | 8:21 | and **g** of the children of God. |
| | 9: 4 | theirs the divine **g**, the covenants, |
| | 9:23 | to make the riches of his **g** known |
| | 9:23 | he prepared in advance for **g**— |
| | 11:36 | To him be the **g** forever! Amen. |
| | 15:17 | Therefore I **g** in Christ Jesus in my |
| | 16:27 | wise God be **g** forever through Jesus |
| 1Co | 2: 7 | for our **g** before time began. |
| | 2: 8 | not have crucified the Lord of **g**. |
| | 10:31 | you do, do it all for the **g** of God. |
| | 11: 7 | since he is the image and **g** of God; |
| | 11: 7 | but woman is the **g** of man. |
| | 11:15 | if a woman has long hair, it is her **g**? |
| | 15:43 | is sown in dishonor, it is raised in **g**; |
| 2Co | 1:20 | is spoken by us to the **g** of God. |
| | 3: 7 | came with **g**, so that the Israelites |
| | 3: 7 | the face of Moses because of its **g**, |
| | 3:10 | what was glorious has no **g** now |
| | 3:10 | comparison with the surpassing **g**. |
| | 3:11 | **g**, how much greater is the **g** |

| | | |
|---|---|---|
| 2Co | 3:18 | faces contemplate the Lord's **g**, |
| | 3:18 | his image with ever-increasing **g**, |
| | 4: 4 | gospel that displays the **g** of Christ, |
| | 4: 6 | the knowledge of God's **g** displayed |
| | 4:15 | to overflow to the **g** of God. |
| | 4:17 | us an eternal **g** that far outweighs |
| Gal | 1: 5 | to whom be **g** for ever and ever. |
| Eph | 1:12 | might be for the praise of his **g**. |
| | 1:14 | to the praise of his **g**. |
| | 3:13 | for you, which are your **g**. |
| | 3:21 | to him be **g** in the church |
| Php | 1:11 | to the **g** and praise of God. |
| | 2:11 | is Lord, to the **g** of God the Father. |
| | 3:19 | and their **g** is in their shame. |
| | 4:19 | the riches of his **g** in Christ Jesus. |
| | 4:20 | To our God and Father be **g** for ever |
| Col | 1:27 | is Christ in you, the hope of **g**. |
| | 3: 4 | you also will appear with him in **g**. |
| 1Th | 2:12 | calls you into his kingdom and **g**. |
| | 2:19 | which we will **g** in the presence |
| | 2:20 | Indeed, you are our **g** and joy. |
| 2Th | 1: 9 | and from the **g** of his might |
| | 2:14 | in the **g** of our Lord Jesus Christ. |
| 1Ti | 1:11 | concerning the **g** of the blessed God, |
| | 1:17 | be honor and **g** for ever and ever. |
| | 3:16 | on in the world, was taken up in **g**. |
| 2Ti | 2:10 | is in Christ Jesus, with eternal **g**. |
| | 4:18 | To him be **g** for ever and ever. |
| Tit | 2:13 | the appearing of the **g** of our great God |
| Heb | 1: 3 | The Son is the radiance of God's **g** |
| | 2: 7 | you crowned them with **g** and honor |
| | 2: 9 | now crowned with **g** and honor |
| | 2:10 | many sons and daughters to **g**, |
| | 3: 6 | and the hope in which we **g**. |
| | 5: 5 | on himself the **g** of becoming a high |
| | 9: 5 | the ark were the cherubim of the **G**, |
| | 13:21 | to whom be **g** for ever and ever. |
| 1Pe | 1: 7 | **g** and honor when Jesus Christ is |
| | 1:24 | all their **g** is like the flowers |
| | 4:11 | To him be the **g** and the power |
| | 4:13 | be overjoyed when his **g** is revealed. |
| | 4:14 | for the Spirit of **g** and of God rests |
| | 5: 1 | will share in the **g** to be revealed: |
| | 5: 4 | you will receive the crown of **g** |
| | 5:10 | called you to his eternal **g** in Christ, |
| 2Pe | 1: 3 | of him who called us by his own **g** |
| | 1:17 | and **g** from God the Father |
| | 1:17 | came to him from the Majestic **G**, |
| | 3:18 | To him be **g** both now and forever! |
| Jude | 1:25 | to the only God our Savior be **g**, |
| Rev | 1: 6 | to him be **g** and power for ever |
| | 4: 9 | the living creatures give **g**, |
| | 4:11 | to receive **g** and honor and power, |
| | 5:12 | and honor and **g** and praise!" |
| | 5:13 | praise and honor and **g** and power, |
| | 7:12 | Praise and **g** and wisdom and thanks |
| | 11:13 | and gave **g** to the God of heaven. |
| | 14: 7 | "Fear God and give him **g**, |
| | 15: 4 | Lord, and bring **g** to your name? |
| | 15: 8 | filled with smoke from the **g** of God |
| | 18: 7 | grief as the **g** and luxury she gave |
| | 19: 1 | Salvation and **g** and power belong |
| | 19: 7 | rejoice and be glad and give him **g**! |
| | 21:11 | It shone with the **g** of God, and its |
| | 21:23 | for the **g** of God gives it light, |
| | 21:26 | The **g** and honor of the nations will |

**GLORY OF ... GOD** Ps 19:1; Pr 25:2; Eze
8:4; 9:3; 10:19; 11:22; 43:2; Jn 11:40; 12:43; Ac
7:55; Ro 3:23; 5:2; 1Co 10:31; 11:7; 2Co 1:20;
4:15; Php 2:11; Rev 15:8; 21:11, 23

**GLORY OF THE †LORD** Ex 16:7, 10;
24:16, 17; 40:34, 35; Lev 9:6, 23; Nu 14:10, 21;
16:19, 42; 20:6; 1Ki 8:11; 2Ch 5:14; 7:1, 2, 3; Ps
104:31; 138:5; Isa 35:2; 40:5; 58:8; 60:1; Eze
1:28; 3:12, 23; 10:4, 4, 18; 11:23; 43:4, 5; 44:4;
Hab 2:14

## GLOWING

| | | |
|---|---|---|
| 1Sa | 16:12 | He was **g** with health |
| Eze | 1:27 | his waist up he looked like **g** metal, |
| | 8: 2 | appearance was as bright as **g** metal. |
| Rev | 1:15 | His feet were like bronze **g** |
| | 15: 2 | looked like a sea of glass **g** with fire |

## GLUTTON* [GLUTTONS, GLUTTONY]

| | | |
|---|---|---|
| Mt | 11:19 | say, 'Here is a **g** and a drunkard, |
| Lk | 7:34 | say, 'Here is a **g** and a drunkard, |

## GLUTTONS* [GLUTTON]

| | | |
|---|---|---|
| Pr | 23:21 | for drunkards and **g** become poor, |
| | 28: 7 | of **g** disgrace their parents. |
| Tit | 1:12 | always liars, evil brutes, lazy **g**." |

## GLUTTONY* [GLUTTON]

| | | |
|---|---|---|
| Pr | 23: 2 | to your throat if you are given to **g**. |

## GNASH* [GNASHED, GNASHING]

| | | |
|---|---|---|
| Ps | 37:12 | righteous and **g** their teeth at them; |
| | 112:10 | they will **g** their teeth and waste |
| La | 2:16 | they scoff and **g** their teeth and say, |

## GNASHED* [GNASH]

| | | |
|---|---|---|
| Ps | 35:16 | they **g** their teeth at me. |
| Ac | 7:54 | furious and **g** their teeth at him. |

## GNASHING* [GNASH]

| | | |
|---|---|---|
| Mt | 8:12 | will be weeping and **g** of teeth." |
| | 13:42 | there will be weeping and **g** of teeth. |
| | 13:50 | there will be weeping and **g** of teeth. |
| | 22:13 | will be weeping and **g** of teeth.' |
| | 24:51 | there will be weeping and **g** of teeth. |
| | 25:30 | will be weeping and **g** of teeth.' |
| Lk | 13:28 | there, and **g** of teeth, when you see |

## GNAT* [GNATS]

| | | |
|---|---|---|
| Mt | 23:24 | You strain out a **g** but swallow |

## GNATS [GNAT]

| | | |
|---|---|---|
| Ex | 8:16 | of Egypt the dust will become **g**." |
| Ps | 105:31 | and **g** throughout their country. |

## GO [GOES, GOING, GONE]

| | | |
|---|---|---|
| Ge | 4: 8 | Abel, "Let's **g** out to the field." |
| | 7: 1 | then said to Noah, "**G** into the ark, |
| | 11: 7 | let us **g** down and confuse their |
| | 12: 1 | "**G** from your country, your people |
| | 13:17 | **G**, walk through the length |
| | 18:21 | that I will **g** down and see if what |

| | | |
|---|---|---|
| Ge | 46: 4 | I will **g** down to Egypt with you, |
| Ex | 3:10 | So now, **g**. I am sending you |
| | 3:19 | will not let you **g** unless a mighty |
| | 5: 1 | 'Let my people **g**, so that they may |
| | 12:31 | **G**, worship the LORD as you have |
| | 13:15 | stubbornly refused to let us **g**, |
| | 32: 1 | make us gods who will **g** before us. |
| | 33: 3 | **G** up to the land flowing with milk |
| | 33: 3 | But I will not **g** with you, |
| | 34: 9 | eyes, then let the Lord **g** with us. |
| Nu | 13:30 | and said, "We should **g** up and take |
| | 14: 3 | better for us to **g** back to Egypt?" |
| Dt | 1:26 | But you were unwilling to **g** up; |
| | 4:40 | so that it may **g** well with you |
| Jos | 1: 9 | will be with you wherever you **g**." |
| Ru | 1:16 | Where you **g** I will **g**, and where |
| Ps | 30: 1 | if I am silenced, if I **g** down to the pit? |
| | 42: 4 | I used to **g** to the house of God |
| | 122: 1 | to me, "Let us **g** to the house |
| | 139: 7 | Where can I **g** from your Spirit? |
| Pr | 6: 6 | **G** to the ant, you sluggard; |
| | 11:19 | those who pursue evil **g** to their death. |
| | 22: 6 | off on the way they should **g**, |
| | 31:18 | her lamp does not **g** out at night. |
| Ecc | 12: 5 | Then people **g** to their eternal home |
| Isa | 2: 3 | let us **g** up to the mountain |
| | 2: 3 | The law will **g** out from Zion, |
| | 55:12 | You will **g** out in joy and be led |
| Jer | 7:23 | you, that it may **g** well with you. |
| Eze | 1:12 | the spirit would **g**, they would **g**, |
| Mic | 4: 2 | let us **g** up to the mountain |
| | 4: 2 | The law will **g** out from Zion, |
| Zec | 14: 3 | Then the LORD will **g** |
| Mal | 4: 2 | And you will **g** out and frolic like |
| Mt | 5:41 | **g** one mile, **g** with them two miles. |
| | 6: 6 | when you pray, **g** into your room, |
| | 28:19 | Therefore **g** and make disciples |
| Mk | 10:25 | for a camel to **g** through the eye |
| Lk | 9:57 | will follow you wherever you **g**." |
| Jn | 6:68 | him, "Lord, to whom shall we **g**? |
| | 8:21 | Where I **g**, you cannot come." |
| | 14: 3 | if I **g** and prepare a place for you, |
| Rev | 22:14 | and may **g** through the gates |

## GOADS

| | | |
|---|---|---|
| Ecc | 12:11 | The words of the wise are like **g**, |
| Ac | 26:14 | hard for you to kick against the **g**.' |

## GOAL

| | | |
|---|---|---|
| Lk | 13:32 | on the third day I will reach my **g**.' |
| 2Co | 5: 9 | So we make it our **g** to please him, |
| Php | 3:14 | on toward the **g** to win the prize |
| 1Ti | 1: 5 | The **g** of this command is love, |

## GOAT [GOATS, SCAPEGOAT]

| | | |
|---|---|---|
| Ge | 15: 9 | "Bring me a heifer, a **g** and a ram, |
| | 30:32 | and every spotted or speckled **g**. |
| | 37:31 | slaughtered a **g** and dipped the robe |
| Ex | 26: 7 | "Make curtains of **g** hair |
| Lev | 16: 9 | shall bring the **g** whose lot falls |
| | 16:22 | The **g** will carry on itself all their |
| | 17: 7 | any of their sacrifices to the **g** idols |
| Nu | 7:16 | one male **g** for a sin offering; |
| Isa | 11: 6 | the leopard will lie down with the **g**, |
| Da | 8: 5 | suddenly a **g** with a prominent horn |
| | 8:21 | The shaggy **g** is the king of Greece, |

## GOATS [GOAT]
Lev 16: 5 to take two male **g** for a sin offering
Nu  7:17 five male **g** and five male lambs
Ps  50:13 of bulls or drink the blood of **g**?
Eze 34:17 another, and between rams and **g**.
Mt  25:32 separates the sheep from the **g**.
Heb  9:12 not enter by means of the blood of **g**
   10: 4 of bulls and **g** to take away sins.

## GOBLET [GOBLETS]
Isa  51:22 from that cup, the **g** of my wrath,

## GOBLETS [GOBLET]
1Ki 10:21 All King Solomon's **g** were gold,
Da   5: 2 silver **g** that Nebuchadnezzar his

## GOD [GOD'S, GOD-BREATHED, GOD-FEARING, GOD-HATERS, GODDESS, GODLESS, GODLESSNESS, GODLINESS, GODLY, GODS]
Ge   1: 1 the beginning **G** created the heavens
    1: 2 of **G** was hovering over the waters.
    1: 3 And **G** said, "Let there be light,"
    1: 7 So **G** made the vault and separated
    1: 9 And **G** said, "Let the water under
   1:11 Then **G** said, "Let the land produce
   1:21 So **G** created the great creatures
   1:21 And **G** saw that it was good.
   1:22 **G** blessed them and said,
   1:25 **G** made the wild animals according
   1:25 And **G** saw that it was good.
   1:26 Then **G** said, "Let us make human
   1:27 So **G** created human beings in his
   1:27 in the image of **G** he created them;
   1:28 **G** blessed them and said to them,
   1:31 **G** saw all that he had made, and it
    2: 3 Then **G** blessed the seventh day
    2: 4 when the LORD **G** made the earth
    2: 7 the LORD **G** formed a man
    2: 8 Now the LORD **G** had planted
   2:16 the LORD **G** commanded the man,
   2:22 the LORD **G** made a woman
    3: 1 to the woman, "Did **G** really say,
    3: 5 "For **G** knows that when you eat
    3: 5 and you will be like **G**,
    3: 8 of the LORD **G** as he was walking
    3: 8 from the LORD **G** among the trees
    3: 9 the LORD **G** called to the man,
   3:13 the LORD **G** said to the woman,
   3:14 So the LORD **G** said
   3:21 The LORD **G** made garments
   3:23 So the LORD **G** banished him
    5: 1 When **G** created human beings,
    5: 1 he made them in the likeness of **G**.
   5:24 Enoch walked faithfully with **G**;
   5:24 no more, because **G** took him away.
    6: 2 the sons of **G** saw that these
    6: 9 and he walked faithfully with **G**.
   6:12 **G** saw how corrupt the earth had
    8: 1 But **G** remembered Noah and all
    9: 1 Then **G** blessed Noah and his sons,
    9: 6 image of **G** has **G** made humankind.
   9:16 the everlasting covenant between **G**
  14:18 He was priest of **G** Most High,

Ge  14:19 be Abram by **G** Most High,
  16:13 "You are the **G** who sees me,"
  17: 1 to him and said, "I am **G** Almighty;
  17: 7 to be your **G** and the **G** of your
  19:29 So when **G** destroyed the cities
  21: 2 the very time **G** had promised him.
  21: 6 said, "**G** has brought me laughter,
  21:17 **G** heard the boy crying,
  21:17 the angel of **G** called to Hagar
  21:20 **G** was with the boy as he grew up.
  21:22 "**G** is with you in everything you
  21:33 name of the LORD, the Eternal **G**.
  22: 1 Some time later **G** tested Abraham.
  22: 8 "**G** himself will provide the lamb
  22:12 Now I know that you fear **G**,
  25:11 death, **G** blessed his son Isaac,
  26:24 and said, "I am the **G** of your father
  28:12 the angels of **G** were ascending
  28:17 is none other than the house of **G**;
  30: 2 "Am I in the place of **G**, who has
  31:13 I am the **G** of Bethel, where you
  31:42 If the **G** of my father, the **G**
  31:42 But **G** has seen my hardship
  31:50 that **G** is a witness between you
  32: 1 way, and the angels of **G** met him.
  32:28 because you have struggled with **G**
  32:30 "It is because I saw **G** face to face,
  33:11 for **G** has been gracious to me and I
  35: 1 Then **G** said to Jacob,
  35: 1 and build an altar there to **G**,
  35: 5 the terror of **G** fell on the towns all
  35:10 **G** said to him, "Your name is
  35:11 And **G** said to him, "I am **G**
  41:38 one in whom is the spirit of **G**?"
  41:51 said, "It is because **G** has made me
  41:52 said, "It is because **G** has made me
  46: 2 **G** spoke to Israel in a vision at night
  48:15 the **G** who has been my shepherd all
  50:19 Am I in the place of **G**?
  50:20 me, but **G** intended it for good
  50:24 But **G** will surely come to your aid
Ex   1:17 feared **G** and did not do what
   2:24 **G** heard their groaning and he
   3: 4 **G** called to him from within
   3: 5 "Do not come any closer," **G** said.
   3: 6 **G** of your father, the **G** of Abraham,
   3: 6 the **G** of Isaac and the **G** of Jacob."
   3: 6 because he was afraid to look at **G**.
   3:12 And **G** said, "I will be with you.
   3:14 **G** said to Moses, "I AM WHO I AM.
   3:18 LORD, the **G** of the Hebrews,
   4:27 he met Moses at the mountain of **G**
   6: 7 own people, and I will be your **G**.
   6: 7 know that I am the LORD your **G**,
   7: 1 I have made you like **G** to Pharaoh,
   8:10 is no one like the LORD our **G**.
   8:19 Pharaoh, "This is the finger of **G**."
  10:16 sinned against the LORD your **G**
  13:19 "**G** will surely come to your aid,
  14:19 Then the angel of **G**, who had been
  15: 2 He is my **G**, and I will praise him,
  15: 2 my father's **G**, and I will exalt him.
  16:12 that I am the LORD your **G**.' "
  17: 9 with the staff of **G** in my hands."
  18: 4 "My father's **G** was my helper;
  18: 5 camped near the mountain of **G**.
  19: 3 Then Moses went up to **G**,

Ex  20: 1  And **G** spoke all these words:
    20: 2  "I am the LORD your **G**,
    20: 5  the LORD your **G**, am a jealous **G**,
    20: 7  the name of the LORD your **G**,
    20:10  is a sabbath to the LORD your **G**.
    20:12  the LORD your **G** is giving you.
    20:19  But do not have **G** speak to us or we
    20:20  **G** has come to test you,
    20:20  that the fear of **G** will be with you
    22:20  any **g** other than the LORD must
    22:28  "Do not blaspheme **G** or curse
    23:19  to the house of the LORD your **G**.
    24:10  and saw the **G** of Israel.
    31:18  stone inscribed by the finger of **G**.
    34: 6  the compassionate and gracious **G**,
    34:14  Do not worship any other **g**,
    34:14  name is Jealous, is a jealous **G**.
Lev  2:13  the covenant of your **G** out of your
    11:44  I am the LORD your **G**;
    18:21  not profane the name of your **G**.
    19: 2  I, the LORD your **G**, am holy.
    20: 7  because I am the LORD your **G**.
    21: 6  They must be holy to their **G**
    21: 6  not profane the name of their **G**.
    22:33  you out of Egypt to be your **G**.
    26:12  walk among you and be your **G**,
Nu  15:40  and will be consecrated to your **G**.
    16:22  out, "O **G**, **G** of every human spirit,
    22: 9  **G** came to Balaam and asked,
    22:18  the command of the LORD my **G**.
    22:38  I must speak only what **G** puts
    23:19  **G** is not a human, that he should lie,
    25:13  was zealous for the honor of his **G**
    27:16  the **G** of every human spirit,
Dt   1:17  anyone, for judgment belongs to **G**.
    1:21  the LORD your **G** has given you
    1:32  did not trust in the LORD your **G**,
    3:22  the LORD your **G** himself will
    3:24  For what **g** is there in heaven
    4: 7  way the LORD our **G** is near us
    4:24  **G** is a consuming fire, a jealous **G**.
    4:29  there you seek the LORD your **G**,
    4:31  the LORD your **G** is a merciful **G**;
    4:39  day that the LORD is **G** in heaven
    5: 9  the LORD your **G**, am a jealous **G**,
    5:11  the name of the LORD your **G**,
    5:12  the LORD your **G** has commanded
    5:14  is a sabbath to the LORD your **G**.
    5:15  the LORD your **G** brought you
    5:15  the LORD your **G** has commanded
    5:16  the LORD your **G** is giving you.
    5:24  "The LORD our **G** has shown us
    5:26  voice of the living **G** speaking
    6: 2  fear the LORD your **G** as long as
    6: 4  The LORD our **G**, the LORD is
    6: 5  Love the LORD your **G** with all
    6:13  Fear the LORD your **G**, serve him
    6:16  Do not put the LORD your **G**
    7: 6  people holy to the LORD your **G**.
    7: 6  The LORD your **G** has chosen you
    7: 9  LORD your **G** is **G**; he is the faithful **G**,
    7:12  the LORD your **G** will keep his
    7:19  the LORD your **G** brought you
    7:21  you, is a great and awesome **G**.
    8: 5  the LORD your **G** disciplines you.
    8:11  do not forget the LORD your **G**,
    8:18  But remember the LORD your **G**,

Dt   9:10  tablets inscribed by the finger of **G**.
    10:12  what does the LORD your **G** ask
    10:12  you but to fear the LORD your **G**,
    10:12  to serve the LORD your **G** with all
    10:14  To the LORD your **G** belong
    10:17  For the LORD your **G** is **G** of gods
    10:17  the great **G**, mighty and awesome,
    10:21  he is your **G**, who performed
    11: 1  Love the LORD your **G** and keep
    11:13  to love the LORD your **G**
    12:12  rejoice before the LORD your **G**—
    12:28  in the eyes of the LORD your **G**.
    13: 3  The LORD your **G** is testing you
    13: 4  It is the LORD your **G** you must
    14: 1  the children of the LORD your **G**.
    14: 2  people holy to the LORD your **G**.
    15: 6  the LORD your **G** will bless you
    15:19  the LORD your **G** every firstborn
    16:11  rejoice before the LORD your **G**
    16:17  the LORD your **G** has blessed you.
    16:22  for these the LORD your **G** hates.
    18:13  before the LORD your **G**.
    18:15  The LORD your **G** will raise
    19: 9  to love the LORD your **G**
    22: 5  the LORD your **G** detests anyone
    23: 5  the LORD your **G** would not listen
    23: 5  the LORD your **G** loves you.
    23:14  the LORD your **G** moves
    23:21  make a vow to the LORD your **G**,
    25:16  the LORD your **G** detests anyone
    26: 5  declare before the LORD your **G**:
    27: 5  there an altar to the LORD your **G**,
    28: 1  you fully obey the LORD your **G**
    28:15  you do not obey the LORD your **G**
    29:13  he may be your **G** as he promised
    29:29  things belong to the LORD our **G**,
    30: 2  return to the LORD your **G**
    30: 4  the LORD your **G** will gather you
    30: 6  The LORD your **G** will circumcise
    30:16  today to love the LORD your **G**,
    30:16  the LORD your **G** will bless you
    30:20  you may love the LORD your **G**,
    31: 6  the LORD your **G** goes with you;
    32: 3  Oh, praise the greatness of our **G**!
    32: 4  A faithful **G** who does no wrong,
    32:18  you forgot the **G** who gave you
    32:39  There is no **g** besides me. I put
    33:27  The eternal **G** is your refuge,
Jos  1: 9  the LORD your **G** will be with you
    1:13  'The LORD your **G** will give you
    14: 8  the LORD my **G** wholeheartedly.
    14:14  the LORD, the **G** of Israel,
    22: 5  to love the LORD your **G**, to walk
    22:22  "The Mighty One, **G**, the LORD!
    22:34  that the LORD is **G**.
    23: 3  the LORD your **G** has done to all
    23: 3  was the LORD your **G** who fought
    23: 8  to hold fast to the LORD your **G**,
    23:11  careful to love the LORD your **G**.
    23:14  the LORD your **G** gave you has
    23:15  the LORD your **G** has promised
    23:15  the LORD your **G** has destroyed
    24:19  He is a holy **G**; he is a jealous **G**.
Jdg  1: 7  Now **G** has paid me back for what I
    5: 5  before the LORD, the **G** of Israel.
    6:20  The angel of **G** said to him,
    6:31  If Baal really is a **g**, he can defend

| | | | | |
|---|---|---|---|---|

Jdg 8:33 They set up Baal-Berith as their **g**
13: 6 told him, "A man of **G** came to me.
13: 6 He looked like an angel of **G**,
16:23 a great sacrifice to Dagon their **g**
16:23 "Our **g** has delivered Samson,
16:28 Please, **G**, strengthen me just once
20:27 ark of the covenant of **G** was there,
Ru 1:16 be my people and your **G** my **G**.
1Sa 2: 2 there is no Rock like our **G**.
2: 3 for the LORD is a **G** who knows,
2:25 **G** may mediate for the offender;
3: 3 The lamp of **G** had not yet gone out,
4:11 The ark of **G** was captured,
5:11 the ark of the **g** of Israel away;
10: 9 Samuel, **G** changed Saul's heart,
10:26 men whose hearts **G** had touched.
11: 6 the Spirit of **G** came on him
12:12 the LORD your **G** was your king.
14:15 It was a panic sent by **G**.
16:15 evil spirit from **G** is tormenting you.
17:36 defied the armies of the living **G**.
17:45 the **G** of the armies of Israel,
17:46 will know that there is a **G** in Israel.
19:23 the Spirit of **G** came even on him,
23:16 and helped him find strength in **G**.
28:15 me, and **G** has departed from me.
30: 6 found strength in the LORD his **G**.
2Sa 6: 7 therefore **G** struck him down,
6: 7 he died there beside the ark of **G**.
7:22 and there is no **G** but you, as we
7:23 one nation on earth that **G** went
7:27 "LORD Almighty, **G** of Israel,
14:14 But that is not what **G** desires;
14:17 lord the king is like an angel of **G**
21:14 **G** answered prayer in behalf
22: 3 my **G** is my rock, in whom I take
22:31 "As for **G**, his way is perfect;
22:32 For who is **G** besides the LORD?
22:32 And who is the Rock except our **G**?
22:33 It is **G** who arms me with strength
22:47 Exalted be my **G**, the Rock,
1Ki 2: 3 what the LORD your **G** requires:
4:29 **G** gave Solomon wisdom and very
5: 5 for the Name of the LORD my **G**,
8:23 **G** of Israel, there is no **G** like you in heaven
8:27 "But will **G** really dwell on earth?
8:60 may know that the LORD is **G**
8:61 committed to the LORD our **G**,
10:24 to hear the wisdom **G** had put in his
11: 4 fully devoted to the LORD his **G**,
11:33 Chemosh the **g** of the Moabites,
15:30 of the LORD, the **G** of Israel.
18:21 If the LORD is **G**, follow him;
18:21 but if Baal is **G**, follow him."
18:24 you call on the name of your **g**,
18:24 The **g** who answers by fire—
18:36 today that you are **G** in Israel
18:39 he is **G**! The LORD—he is **G**!"
20:28 The man of **G** came up and told
2Ki 1: 2 consult Baal-Zebub, the **g** of Ekron,
5:15 there is no **G** in all the world except
17: 7 sinned against the LORD their **G**,
19: 4 the LORD your **G** will hear all
19: 4 has sent to ridicule the living **G**,
19:15 you alone are **G** over all
19:19 that you alone, LORD, are **G**."

1Ch 12:18 you, for your **G** will help you."
13: 2 if it is the will of the LORD our **G**,
16:35 Cry out, "Save us, **G** our Savior;
17:20 and there is no **G** but you, as we
17:24 the **G** over Israel, is Israel's **G**!'
21: 8 Then David said to **G**, "I have
21:15 And **G** sent an angel to destroy
22: 1 of the LORD **G** is to be here,
22:19 soul to seeking the LORD your **G**.
28: 2 for the footstool of our **G**, and I
28: 9 acknowledge the **G** of your father,
28:20 for the LORD **G**, my **G**,
29: 1 the one whom **G** has chosen,
29: 2 provided for the temple of my **G**—
29:10 LORD, the **G** of our father Israel,
29:13 Now, our **G**, we give you thanks,
29:18 the **G** of our fathers Abraham,
2Ch 1: 7 That night **G** appeared to Solomon
2: 4 for the Name of the LORD my **G**
2: 5 because our **G** is greater than all
5:14 the LORD filled the temple of **G**.
6:14 the **G** of Israel, there is no **G** like you in heaven
6:18 will **G** really dwell on earth
10:15 for this turn of events was from **G**,
13:12 **G** is with us; he is our leader.
15: 3 time Israel was without the true **G**,
15:12 LORD, the **G** of their ancestors,
15:15 They sought **G** eagerly, and he was
18:13 can tell him only what my **G** says."
19: 3 have set your heart on seeking **G**."
19: 7 with the LORD our **G** there is no
20: 6 are you not the **G** who is in heaven?
20:20 Have faith in the LORD your **G**
25: 8 **G** will overthrow you before
25: 8 for **G** has the power to help
26: 5 who instructed him in the fear of **G**.
30: 9 for the LORD your **G** is gracious
30:19 who sets their heart on seeking **G**—
31:21 he sought his **G** and worked
32:15 much less will your **g** deliver you
32:17 so the **g** of Hezekiah will not rescue
32:31 **G** left him to test him and to know
33:12 the favor of the LORD his **G**
33:19 how **G** was moved by his entreaty,
34:33 in Israel serve the LORD their **G**.
Ezr 1: 3 may their **G** be with them, and let
2:68 of the house of **G** on its site.
6:16 of the house of **G** with joy.
7: 9 the gracious hand of his **G** was
7:18 accordance with the will of your **G**.
7:23 for the temple of the **G** of heaven.
8:22 "The gracious hand of our **G** is
8:31 The hand of our **G** was on us,
9: 6 my **G**, to lift up my face to you,
9: 9 our **G** has not forsaken us in our
9: 9 life to rebuild the house of our **G**
10: 3 let us make a covenant before our **G**
10: 3 who fear the commands of our **G**.
Ne 1: 5 the great and awesome **G**,
4:20 Our **G** will fight for us!"
5:15 for **G** I did not act like that.
7: 2 feared **G** more than most people do.
8: 8 from the Book of the Law of **G**,
8:18 from the Book of the Law of **G**.
9: 5 up and praise the LORD your **G**,
9:17 But you are a forgiving **G**,

Ne    9:31  you are a gracious and merciful **G**.
      9:32  "Now therefore, our **G**, the great **G**,
     10:29  through Moses the servant of **G**
     10:39  not neglect the house of our **G**."
     12:43  rejoicing because **G** had given them
     13: 2  (Our **G**, however, turned the curse
     13:11  is the house of **G** neglected?"
     13:26  He was loved by his **G**, and **G** made
     13:31  Remember me with favor, my **G**.
Job   1: 1  he feared **G** and shunned evil.
      1: 9  "Does Job fear **G** for nothing?"
      1:22  sin by charging **G** with wrongdoing.
      2:10  Shall we accept good from **G**,
      4:17  a mortal be more righteous than **G**?
      5:17  are those whom **G** corrects;
      8: 3  Does **G** pervert justice?
      8:20  "Surely **G** does not reject
      9: 2  prove their innocence before **G**?
     11: 7  you fathom the mysteries of **G**?
     12:13  "To **G** belong wisdom and power;
     16: 7  Surely, **G**, you have worn me out;
     19:26  yet in my flesh I will see **G**;
     20:29  Such is the fate **G** allots the wicked,
     21:19  '**G** stores up the punishment
     21:22  anyone teach knowledge to **G**,
     22:12  "Is not **G** in the heights of heaven?
     22:13  Yet you say, 'What does **G** know?'
     22:21  "Submit to **G** and be at peace
     25: 2  "Dominion and awe belong to **G**;
     25: 4  can a mortal be righteous before **G**?
     26: 6  Death is naked before **G**;
     30:20  "I cry out to you, **G**, but you do not
     31: 6  let **G** weigh me in honest scales
     31:14  will I do when **G** confronts me?
     32:13  let **G** refute him, not a mere mortal.'
     33:14  For **G** does speak—now one way,
     33:26  they can pray to **G** and find favor
     34:10  Far be it from **G** to do evil,
     34:23  **G** has no need to examine people
     34:33  Should **G** then reward you on your
     36: 5  "**G** is mighty, but despises no one;
     36:26  How great is **G**—
     40: 2  him who accuses **G** answer him!"
Ps    5: 2  my King and my **G**, for to you I
      5: 4  you are not a **G** who is pleased
      7:10  My shield is **G** Most High,
      7:11  **G** is a righteous judge, a **G** who
     10:14  But you, **G**, see the trouble
     14: 5  for **G** is present in the company
     18: 2  my **G** is my rock, in whom I take
     18:21  am not guilty of turning from my **G**.
     18:28  my **G** turns my darkness into light.
     18:30  As for **G**, his way is perfect:
     18:31  For who is **G** besides the Lord?
     18:31  And who is the Rock except our **G**?
     18:32  It is **G** who arms me with strength
     18:46  Exalted be **G** my Savior!
     19: 1  The heavens declare the glory of **G**;
     22: 1  My **G**, my **G**, why have you
     22:10  womb you have been my **G**.
     27: 9  me or forsake me, **G** my Savior.
     29: 3  the **G** of glory thunders, the Lord
     31: 5  redeem me, Lord, my faithful **G**.
     31:14  I say, "You are my **G**."
     33:12  the nation whose **G** is the Lord,
     35:23  Contend for me, my **G** and Lord.
     37:31  The law of their **G** is in their hearts;

Ps   40: 3  mouth, a hymn of praise to our **G**.
     40: 8  I desire to do your will, my **G**;
     42: 1  so my soul pants for you, my **G**.
     42: 2  soul thirsts for **G**, for the living **G**.
     42: 5  Put your hope in **G**, for I will yet
     42: 8  a prayer to the **G** of my life.
     42:11  Put your hope in **G**, for I will yet
     43: 4  I will go to the altar of **G**, to **G**, my joy
     44: 8  **G** we make our boast all day long,
     45: 6  O **G**, will last for ever and ever;
     45: 7  therefore **G**, your **G**, has set you
     46: 1  **G** is our refuge and strength,
     46: 5  **G** is within her, she will not fall;
     46:10  "Be still, and know that I am **G**;
     47: 1  shout to **G** with cries of joy.
     47: 6  Sing praises to **G**, sing praises;
     47: 7  For **G** is the King of all the earth;
     48: 9  O **G**, we meditate on your unfailing
     48:14  For this **G** is our **G** for ever
     49: 7  or give to **G** a sufficient ransom—
     50: 2  perfect in beauty, **G** shines forth.
     50: 3  Our **G** comes and will not be silent;
     51: 1  O **G**, according to your unfailing
     51:10  O **G**, and renew a steadfast spirit
     51:17  sacrifice, O **G**, is a broken spirit;
     53: 2  **G** looks down from heaven
     53: 2  who understand, any who seek **G**.
     54: 4  Surely **G** is my help; the Lord is
     55:19  because they have no fear of **G**.
     56: 4  In **G**, whose word I praise—in **G** I
     56:11  in **G** I trust and am not afraid.
     56:13  that I may walk before **G** in the light
     57: 3  **G** sends forth his love and his
     57: 7  My heart, O **G**, is steadfast,
     59:17  you, **G**, are my fortress, my **G**
     62: 1  Truly my soul finds rest in **G**;
     62: 7  and my honor depend on **G**;
     62: 8  hearts to him, for **G** is our refuge.
     62:11  "Power belongs to you, **G**,
     63: 1  You, **G**, are my **G**, earnestly I seek
     65: 5  and righteous deeds, **G** our Savior,
     66: 1  Shout for joy to **G**, all the earth!
     66: 3  Say to **G**, "How awesome are your
     66: 5  Come and see what **G** has done,
     66:16  Come and hear, all you who fear **G**;
     66:20  Praise be to **G**, who has not rejected
     68: 4  Sing to **G**, sing in praise of his
     68: 6  **G** sets the lonely in families,
     68:20  Our **G** is a **G** who saves;
     68:26  Praise **G** in the great congregation;
     68:35  You, **G**, are awesome in your
     69: 5  You, **G**, know my folly; my guilt is
     70: 1  Hasten, O **G**, to save me;
     70: 5  come quickly to me, O **G**.
     71:17  Since my youth, **G**, you have taught
     71:18  my **G**, till I declare your power
     71:19  Who is like you, **G**?
     71:22  harp for your faithfulness, my **G**;
     73:17  till I entered the sanctuary of **G**;
     73:26  but **G** is the strength of my heart
     76:11  Make vows to the Lord your **G**
     77:13  Your ways, **G**, are holy.
     77:13  What **g** is as great as our **G**?
     77:14  You are the **G** who performs
     78:19  They spoke against **G**;
     78:59  When **G** heard them, he was
     79: 9  Help us, **G** our Savior, for the glory

Ps 81: 1 Sing for joy to **G** our strength;
82: 1 **G** presides in the great assembly;
84: 2 my flesh cry out for the living **G**.
84:10 the house of my **G** than dwell
84:11 For the LORD **G** is a sun
86:12 you, Lord my **G**, with all my heart;
86:15 are a compassionate and gracious **G**,
87: 3 things are said of you, city of **G**:
89: 7 of the holy ones **G** is greatly feared;
90: 2 everlasting to everlasting you are **G**.
91: 2 fortress, my **G**, in whom I trust."
94: 1 The LORD is a **G** who avenges.
94:22 and my **G** the rock in whom I take
95: 3 For the LORD is the great **G**,
95: 7 for he is our **G** and we are
99: 8 LORD our **G**, you answered them;
99: 8 you were to Israel a forgiving **G**,
99: 9 Exalt the LORD our **G**
99: 9 for the LORD our **G** is holy.
100: 3 Know that the LORD is **G**. It is he
106:21 They forgot the **G** who saved them,
106:33 they rebelled against the Spirit of **G**,
108: 1 My heart, O **G**, is steadfast;
108: 5 Be exalted, O **G**, above the heavens;
113: 5 Who is like the LORD our **G**,
115: 3 Our **G** is in heaven;
116: 5 our **G** is full of compassion.
123: 2 our eyes look to the LORD our **G**,
136: 2 Give thanks to the **G** of gods.
136:26 Give thanks to the **G** of heaven.
139:17 to me are your thoughts, **G**!
139:23 Search me, **G**, and know my heart;
143:10 to do your will, for you are my **G**;
144: 2 He is my loving **G** and my fortress,
145: 1 I will exalt you, my **G** the King;
147: 1 good it is to sing praises to our **G**,
150: 1 Praise **G** in his sanctuary;
Pr 2: 5 and find the knowledge of **G**.
3: 4 a good name in the sight of **G**
14:31 is kind to the needy honors **G**.
25: 2 It is the glory of **G** to conceal
28:14 who always tremble before **G**,
30: 5 "Every word of **G** is flawless;
Ecc 1:13 What a heavy burden **G** has laid
2:26 who pleases him, **G** gives wisdom,
3:11 no one can fathom what **G** has done
3:13 in all their toil—this is the gift of **G**.
3:14 that everything **G** does will endure
3:14 **G** does it so that people will fear
5: 2 heart to utter anything before **G**.
5: 4 When you make a vow to **G**, do not
5:19 when **G** gives people wealth
5:19 in their toil—this is a gift of **G**.
7:18 Whoever fears **G** will avoid all
8:12 go better with those who fear **G**,
11: 5 cannot understand the work of **G**,
12: 7 the spirit returns to **G** who gave it.
12:13 of the matter: Fear **G** and keep his
Isa 5:16 the holy **G** will be proved holy
7:11 "Ask the LORD your **G** for a sign,
9: 6 Mighty **G**, Everlasting Father,
12: 2 Surely **G** is my salvation; I will trust
17:10 You have forgotten **G** your Savior;
25: 9 they will say, "Surely this is our **G**;
28:11 strange tongues **G** will speak to this
29:23 will stand in awe of the **G** of Israel.
30:18 For the LORD is a **G** of justice.

Isa 35: 4 your **G** will come, he will come
37:16 "LORD Almighty, the **G** of Israel,
37:16 you alone are **G** over all
40: 1 comfort my people, says your **G**.
40: 3 in the desert a highway for our **G**.
40: 8 the word of our **G** endures forever."
40:18 whom, then, will you compare **G**?
40:28 The LORD is the everlasting **G**,
41:10 not be dismayed, for I am your **G**.
41:13 the LORD your **G** who takes hold
43:10 Before me no **g** was formed,
44: 6 apart from me there is no **G**.
44:15 he also fashions a **g** and worships it;
45:18 he who created the heavens, he is **G**;
48:17 "I am the LORD your **G**,
49: 4 and my reward is with my **G**."
52: 7 who say to Zion, "Your **G** reigns!"
52:12 the **G** of Israel will be your rear
53: 4 we considered him punished by **G**,
55: 7 and to our **G**, for he will freely
57:21 says my **G**, "for the wicked."
59: 2 have separated you from your **G**;
60:19 light, and your **G** will be your glory.
61: 2 and the day of vengeance of our **G**,
61:10 my soul rejoices in my **G**.
62: 5 so will your **G** rejoice over you.
Jer 3:23 in the LORD our **G** is the salvation
7:23 I will be your **G** and you will be my
10:10 But the LORD is the true **G**;
10:10 he is the living **G**, the eternal King.
10:12 But **G** made the earth by his power;
23:23 "Am I only a **G** nearby,"
23:23 LORD, "and not a **G** far away?
23:36 word becomes a message from **G**.
23:36 distort the words of the living **G**,
31:33 I will be their **G**, and they will be
32:27 the **G** of the whole human race.
42: 6 we will obey the LORD our **G**,
42:13 and so disobey the LORD your **G**,
51:10 what the LORD our **G** has done.'
51:56 the LORD is a **G** of retribution;
Eze 1: 1 were opened and I saw visions of **G**.
11:20 be my people, and I will be their **G**.
28: 2 of your heart you say, "I am a **g**;
28: 2 But you are a mortal and not a **g**,
28:13 You were in Eden, the garden of **G**;
34:31 and I am your **G**,
43: 2 the glory of the **G** of Israel coming
Da 2:19 Daniel praised the **G** of heaven
2:28 there is a **G** in heaven who reveals
3:17 If the **G** we serve is able to deliver
3:29 who say anything against the **G**
6:12 days anyone who prays to any **g**
6:16 "May your **G**, whom you serve
9: 4 I prayed to the LORD my **G**
10:12 to humble yourself before your **G**,
11:32 who know their **G** will firmly resist
11:36 magnify himself above every **g**
Hos 1: 9 not my people, and I am not your **G**.
1:10 be called 'children of the living **G**.'
4: 6 you have ignored the law of your **G**,
6: 6 of **G** rather than burnt offerings.
9: 8 and hostility in the house of his **G**.
12: 6 But you must return to your **G**;
13: 4 You shall acknowledge no **G**
Joel 2:13 Return to the LORD your **G**, for he
2:23 rejoice in the LORD your **G**, for he

| | | |
|---|---|---|
| Am | 4:12 | Israel, prepare to meet your **G**.” |
| | 4:13 | the Lord **G** Almighty is his |
| | 5:26 | of your idols, the star of your **g**— |
| Jnh | 1: 6 | Get up and call on your **g**! |
| | 3: 5 | The Ninevites believed **G**. |
| | 4: 2 | are a gracious and compassionate **G**, |
| Mic | 6: 8 | and to walk humbly with your **G**. |
| | 7: 7 | **G** my Savior; my **G** will hear me. |
| | 7:18 | Who is a **G** like you, who pardons |
| Na | 1: 2 | is a jealous and avenging **G**; |
| Hab | 1:11 | whose own strength is their **g**.” |
| | 3:18 | I will be joyful in **G** my Savior. |
| Zep | 3:17 | The Lord your **G** is with you, |
| Hag | 1:14 | of the Lord Almighty, their **G**, |
| Zec | 4: 7 | shouts of ‘**G** bless it! **G** bless it!’ ” |
| | 12: 8 | the house of David will be like **G**, |
| | 14: 5 | Then the Lord my **G** will come, |
| Mal | 2:10 | Did not one **G** create us? |
| | 2:11 | women who worship a foreign **g**. |
| | 3: 8 | “Will a mere mortal rob **G**? |
| Mt | 1:23 | (which means “**G** with us”). |
| | 4: 4 | comes from the mouth of **G**.’ ” |
| | 4: 7 | ‘Do not put the Lord your **G** |
| | 4:10 | ‘Worship the Lord your **G**, |
| | 5: 8 | pure in heart, for they will see **G**. |
| | 5: 9 | for they will be called children of **G**. |
| | 6:24 | You cannot serve both **G** |
| | 12:28 | the kingdom of **G** has come |
| | 16:16 | Messiah, the Son of the living **G**.” |
| | 19: 6 | Therefore what **G** has joined |
| | 19:26 | but with **G** all things are possible.” |
| | 22:21 | Caesar’s, and to **G** what is God’s.” |
| | 22:32 | the **G** of Isaac, and the **G** of Jacob’? |
| | 22:32 | He is not the **G** of the dead |
| | 22:37 | “ ‘Love the Lord your **G** with all |
| | 27:40 | the cross, if you are the Son of **G**!” |
| | 27:46 | (which means “My **G**, my **G**, |
| | 27:54 | “Surely he was the Son of **G**!” |
| Mk | 1:24 | who you are—the Holy One of **G**!” |
| | 2: 7 | Who can forgive sins but **G** alone?” |
| | 7:13 | Thus you nullify the word of **G** |
| | 10: 6 | of creation **G** ‘made them male |
| | 10: 9 | Therefore what **G** has joined |
| | 10:18 | “No one is good—except **G** alone. |
| | 10:24 | hard it is to enter the kingdom of **G**! |
| | 10:27 | this is impossible, but not with **G**; |
| | 10:27 | all things are possible with **G**.” |
| | 11:22 | “Have faith in **G**,” Jesus answered. |
| | 12:17 | Caesar’s and to **G** what is God’s.” |
| | 12:29 | The Lord our **G**, the Lord is one. |
| | 12:30 | Love the Lord your **G** with all your |
| | 15:34 | (which means “My **G**, my **G**, |
| | 15:39 | this man was the Son of **G**!” |
| Lk | 1:19 | I stand in the presence of **G**, and I |
| | 1:30 | you have found favor with **G**. |
| | 1:35 | be born will be called the Son of **G**. |
| | 1:37 | For no word from **G** will ever fail.” |
| | 1:47 | my spirit rejoices in **G** my Savior, |
| | 2:14 | “Glory to **G** in the highest heaven, |
| | 2:40 | and the grace of **G** was on him. |
| | 2:52 | and in favor with **G** and people. |
| | 3:38 | Seth, the son of Adam, the son of **G**. |
| | 4: 3 | “If you are the Son of **G**, tell this |
| | 4: 8 | ‘Worship the Lord your **G** and serve |
| | 4:41 | shouting, “You are the Son of **G**!” |
| | 5:21 | Who can forgive sins but **G** alone?” |
| | 8:39 | tell how much **G** has done for you.” |

| | | |
|---|---|---|
| Lk | 10: 9 | ‘The kingdom of **G** has come near |
| | 10:27 | “ ‘Love the Lord your **G** with all |
| | 11:42 | because you give **G** a tenth of your |
| | 13:18 | “What is the kingdom of **G** like? |
| | 18:13 | but beat his breast and said, ‘**G**, |
| | 18:19 | “No one is good—except **G** alone. |
| | 18:27 | human beings is possible with **G**.” |
| | 20:25 | Caesar’s, and to **G** what is God’s.” |
| | 20:37 | and the **G** of Isaac, and the **G** |
| | 22:69 | at the right hand of the mighty **G**.” |
| | 22:70 | “Are you then the Son of **G**?” |
| Jn | 1: 1 | was with **G**, and the Word was **G**. |
| | 1:12 | the right to become children of **G**— |
| | 1:18 | No one has ever seen **G**, but the one |
| | 1:29 | the Lamb of **G**, who takes away |
| | 1:49 | “Rabbi, you are the Son of **G**; |
| | 3: 2 | are a teacher who has come from **G**. |
| | 3:16 | For **G** so loved the world that he |
| | 3:34 | **G** has sent speaks the words of **G**, |
| | 4:24 | **G** is spirit, and his worshipers must |
| | 5:18 | was even calling **G** his own Father, |
| | 5:18 | making himself equal with **G**. |
| | 5:44 | glory that comes from the only **G**? |
| | 6:29 | answered, “The work of **G** is this: |
| | 6:33 | For the bread of **G** is the bread |
| | 6:69 | that you are the Holy One of **G**.” |
| | 7:17 | to do the will of **G** will find |
| | 7:17 | whether my teaching comes from **G** |
| | 8:42 | “If **G** were your Father, you would |
| | 8:42 | for I came from **G** and now am |
| | 8:47 | belongs to **G** hears what **G** says. |
| | 11:40 | you will see the glory of **G**?” |
| | 13: 3 | from **G** and was returning to **G**; |
| | 13:31 | glorified and **G** is glorified in him. |
| | 14: 1 | Trust in **G**; trust also in me. |
| | 17: 3 | the only true **G**, and Jesus Christ, |
| | 20:17 | Father, to my **G** and your **G**.’ ” |
| | 20:28 | said to him, “My Lord and my **G**!” |
| | 20:31 | the Son of **G**, and that by believing |
| Ac | 1: 3 | and spoke about the kingdom of **G**. |
| | 2:11 | them declaring the wonders of **G**. |
| | 2:22 | was a man accredited by **G** to you |
| | 2:24 | But **G** raised him from the dead, |
| | 2:33 | Exalted to the right hand of **G**, |
| | 2:36 | **G** has made this Jesus, whom you |
| | 3:15 | life, but **G** raised him from the dead. |
| | 3:19 | and turn to **G**, so that your sins may |
| | 4:31 | and spoke the word of **G** boldly. |
| | 5: 4 | lied just to human beings but to **G**.” |
| | 5:29 | “We must obey **G** rather than |
| | 5:31 | **G** exalted him to his own right hand |
| | 5:32 | whom **G** has given to those who |
| | 5:39 | find yourselves fighting against **G**.” |
| | 6: 7 | So the word of **G** spread. |
| | 7:55 | to heaven and saw the glory of **G**, |
| | 7:55 | standing at the right hand of **G**. |
| | 8:21 | your heart is not right before **G**. |
| | 10:46 | speaking in tongues and praising **G**. |
| | 11: 9 | impure that **G** has made clean.” |
| | 12:24 | the word of **G** continued to increase |
| | 13:32 | What **G** promised our ancestors |
| | 14:22 | to enter the kingdom of **G**,” |
| | 15:10 | why do you try to test **G** by putting |
| | 17:23 | this inscription: TO AN UNKNOWN **G**. |
| | 17:30 | In the past **G** overlooked such |
| | 20:27 | proclaim to you the whole will of **G**. |
| | 20:32 | “Now I commit you to **G** |

Ac 24:16 keep my conscience clear before **G**
28: 6 their minds and said he was a **g**.
Ro 1: 4 holiness was appointed the Son of **G**
1:16 because it is the power of **G**
1:17 the righteousness of **G** is revealed—
1:18 The wrath of **G** is being revealed
1:24 Therefore **G** gave them over
1:26 **G** gave them over to shameful lusts.
2:11 For **G** does not show favoritism.
2:16 **G** judges everyone's secrets through
3: 4 Let **G** be true, and every human
3:19 whole world held accountable to **G**.
3:23 and fall short of the glory of **G**,
3:29 Is **G** the **G** of Jews only? Is he not
4: 3 "Abraham believed **G**, and it was
4: 6 whom **G** credits righteousness apart
4:17 He is our father in the sight of **G**,
4:17 the **G** who gives life to the dead
4:24 whom **G** will credit righteousness—
5: 1 **G** through our Lord Jesus Christ,
5: 8 **G** demonstrates his own love for us
6:22 sin and have become slaves of **G**,
6:23 the gift of **G** is eternal life in Christ
7: 4 order that we might bear fruit for **G**.
8: 7 The sinful mind is hostile to **G**;
8: 8 the sinful nature cannot please **G**.
8:17 heirs of **G** and co-heirs with Christ,
8:28 in all things **G** works for the good
8:31 If **G** is for us, who can be against
9:14 then shall we say? Is **G** unjust?
9:18 Therefore **G** has mercy on whom he
10: 9 in your heart that **G** raised him
11: 2 **G** did not reject his people,
11: 2 how he appealed to **G** against Israel:
11:22 the kindness and sternness of **G**:
11:32 For **G** has bound everyone over
13: 1 except that which **G** has established.
14:12 give an account of ourselves to **G**.
16:20 The **G** of peace will soon crush
1Co 1:18 are being saved it is the power of **G**.
1:20 Has not **G** made foolish the wisdom
1:24 but to those whom **G** has called,
1:24 power of **G** and the wisdom of **G**.
1:25 of **G** is wiser than human wisdom,
1:25 **G** is stronger than human strength.
1:27 **G** chose the foolish things
1:27 **G** chose the weak things
2: 9 these things **G** has prepared
2:11 thoughts of **G** except the Spirit of **G**.
3: 6 it, but **G** has been making it grow.
3:17 temple, **G** will destroy that person;
6:20 Therefore honor **G** with your
7: 7 of you has your own gift from **G**;
7:15 **G** has called us to live in peace.
7:20 you were in when **G** called you.
7:24 as responsible to **G**, should remain
7:24 the situation in which **G** called you.
8: 3 whoever loves **G** is known by **G**.
8: 8 food does not bring us near to **G**;
10:13 And **G** is faithful; he will not let you
10:31 you do, do it all for the glory of **G**.
12:24 But **G** has put the body together,
14:25 they will fall down and worship **G**,
14:25 "**G** is really among you!"
14:33 For **G** is not a **G** of disorder
15:24 over the kingdom to **G** the Father
15:28 him, so that **G** may be all in all.

1Co 15:34 are some who are ignorant of **G**—
15:57 But thanks be to **G**! He gives us
2Co 1: 9 not rely on ourselves but on **G**,
2:14 But thanks be to **G**, who always
2:15 we are to **G** the pleasing aroma
2:17 we do not peddle the word of **G**
2:17 in Christ we speak before **G**
2:17 with sincerity, as those sent from **G**.
3: 5 but our competence comes from **G**.
4: 2 nor do we distort the word of **G**.
4: 4 The **g** of this age has blinded
4: 4 of Christ, who is the image of **G**.
4: 7 this all-surpassing power is from **G**
5: 5 us for this very purpose is **G**,
5:19 that **G** was reconciling the world
5:20 as though **G** were making his appeal
5:20 Be reconciled to **G**.
5:21 **G** made him who had no sin to be
5:21 become the righteousness of **G**.
6:16 we are the temple of the living **G**.
6:16 and I will be their **G**, and they will
9: 7 for **G** loves a cheerful giver.
9: 8 **G** is able to bless you abundantly,
10:13 of service **G** himself has assigned
Gal 2: 6 **G** does not show favoritism—
3: 5 Does **G** give you his Spirit
3: 6 So also Abraham "believed **G**,
3:11 Clearly no one is justified before **G**
3:26 are all children of **G** through faith,
4: 4 time had fully come, **G** sent his Son,
6: 7 **G** cannot be mocked.
6:16 follow this rule—to the Israel of **G**.
Eph 1:22 **G** placed all things under his feet
2: 8 from yourselves, it is the gift of **G**—
2:10 which **G** prepared in advance for us
2:22 in which **G** lives by his Spirit.
4: 6 one **G** and Father of all, who is over
4:24 to be like **G** in true righteousness
6: 6 doing the will of **G** from your heart.
Php 2: 6 being in very nature **G**, did not
2: 6 consider equality with **G** something
2: 9 Therefore **G** exalted him
2:13 for it is **G** who works in you to will
3:14 which **G** has called me heavenward
3:19 destruction, their **g** is their stomach,
4: 7 And the peace of **G**,
4:19 And my **G** will meet all your needs
Col 1:19 For **G** was pleased to have all his
2:13 **G** made you alive with Christ.
3: 1 is seated at the right hand of **G**.
1Th 2: 4 we speak as those approved by **G**
2: 4 not trying to please people but **G**,
2:13 when you received the word of **G**,
3: 9 How can we thank **G** enough
4: 1 how to live in order to please **G**,
4: 7 For **G** did not call us to be impure,
4: 9 yourselves have been taught by **G**
5: 9 For **G** did not appoint us to suffer
2Th 1: 8 punish those who do not know **G**
1Ti 1:17 the only **G**, be honor and glory
2: 5 is one **G** and one mediator between
**G** and human
4: 4 For everything **G** created is good,
5: 4 for this is pleasing to **G**.
2Ti 1: 6 you to fan into flame the gift of **G**,
Tit 1: 2 life, which **G**, who does not lie,
2:13 of the glory of our great **G**

| | | |
|---|---|---|
| Heb | 1: 1 | In the past **G** spoke to our ancestors |
| | 3: 4 | but **G** is the builder of everything. |
| | 4: 4 | the seventh day **G** rested from all |
| | 4:12 | For the word of **G** is alive |
| | 5: 5 | But **G** said to him, "You are my |
| | 6:10 | **G** is not unjust; he will not forget |
| | 6:18 | **G** did this so that, by two |
| | 6:18 | which it is impossible for **G** to lie, |
| | 7:19 | by which we draw near to **G**. |
| | 7:25 | those who come to **G** through him, |
| | 10: 7 | come to do your will, my **G**.' " |
| | 10:22 | let us draw near to **G** with a sincere |
| | 10:31 | to fall into the hands of the living **G**. |
| | 11: 5 | because **G** had taken him away." |
| | 11: 5 | commended as one who pleased **G**. |
| | 11: 6 | faith it is impossible to please **G**, |
| | 11:16 | **G** is not ashamed to be called their **G**, |
| | 12: 7 | **G** is treating you as his children. |
| | 12:10 | but **G** disciplines us for our good, |
| | 12:29 | for our "**G** is a consuming fire." |
| | 13:15 | us continually offer to **G** a sacrifice |
| Jas | 1:12 | of life that **G** has promised to those |
| | 1:13 | should say, "**G** is tempting me." |
| | 1:13 | For **G** cannot be tempted by evil, |
| | 1:27 | that **G** our Father accepts as pure |
| | 2:19 | You believe that there is one **G**. |
| | 2:23 | "Abraham believed **G**, and it was |
| | 4: 4 | the world becomes an enemy of **G**. |
| | 4: 6 | "**G** opposes the proud but shows |
| | 4: 8 | Come near to **G** and he will come |
| 1Pe | 1:21 | Through him you believe in **G**, |
| | 1:21 | and so your faith and hope are in **G**. |
| | 1:23 | the living and enduring word of **G**. |
| | 2: 4 | chosen by **G** and precious to him— |
| | 2:10 | but now you are the people of **G**; |
| | 2:20 | it, this is commendable before **G**. |
| | 3:18 | the unrighteous, to bring you to **G**. |
| | 4: 2 | desires, but rather for the will of **G**. |
| | 4:11 | who speaks the very words of **G**. |
| | 4:11 | do so with the strength **G** provides, |
| | 4:11 | all things **G** may be praised through |
| | 4:17 | who do not obey the gospel of **G**? |
| | 5: 5 | "**G** opposes the proud but shows |
| 2Pe | 1:21 | from **G** as they were carried along |
| | 2: 4 | if **G** did not spare angels when they |
| 1Jn | 1: 5 | him and declare to you: **G** is light; |
| | 2: 5 | love for **G** is truly made complete in |
| | 2:14 | and the word of **G** lives in you, |
| | 2:17 | does the will of **G** lives forever. |
| | 3: 1 | we should be called children of **G**! |
| | 3: 9 | who are born of **G** will not continue |
| | 3: 9 | because they have been born of **G**. |
| | 3:10 | we know who the children of **G** are |
| | 3:17 | how can the love of **G** be in you? |
| | 3:20 | that **G** is greater than our hearts, |
| | 4: 2 | you can recognize the Spirit of **G**: |
| | 4: 2 | has come in the flesh is from **G**, |
| | 4: 7 | one another, for love comes from **G**. |
| | 4: 7 | has been born of **G** and knows **G**. |
| | 4: 8 | does not know **G**, because **G** is love. |
| | 4: 9 | This is how **G** showed his love |
| | 4:11 | Dear friends, since **G** so loved us, |
| | 4:12 | No one has ever seen **G**; but if we |
| | 4:12 | **G** lives in us and his love is made |
| | 4:15 | of **G**, **G** lives in them and they in **G**. |
| | 4:16 | and rely on the love **G** has for us. |
| | 4:16 | in love lives in **G**, and **G** in them. |

| | | |
|---|---|---|
| 1Jn | 4:20 | we say we love **G** yet hate a brother |
| | 4:20 | we cannot love **G**, whom we have |
| | 5: 2 | **G**: by loving **G** and carrying out his |
| | 5: 3 | In fact, this is love for **G**: |
| | 5: 4 | born of **G** overcomes the world. |
| | 5:10 | the Son of **G** accepts this testimony. |
| | 5:10 | does not believe **G** has made him |
| | 5:10 | believed the testimony **G** has given |
| | 5:11 | **G** has given us eternal life, and this |
| | 5:14 | we have in approaching **G**: |
| | 5:18 | who was born of **G** keeps them safe, |
| 2Jn | 1: 9 | teaching of Christ does not have **G**; |
| 3Jn | 1:11 | who does what is good is from **G**. |
| | 1:11 | does what is evil has not seen **G**. |
| Jude | 1: 4 | the grace of our **G** into a license |
| Rev | 2:18 | are the words of the Son of **G**, |
| | 3: 1 | who holds the seven spirits of **G** |
| | 4: 5 | These are the seven spirits of **G**. |
| | 4: 8 | holy is the Lord **G** Almighty,' |
| | 6: 9 | been slain because of the word of **G** |
| | 7: 2 | east, having the seal of the living **G**. |
| | 7:10 | "Salvation belongs to our **G**, |
| | 7:12 | strength be to our **G** for ever |
| | 7:17 | **G** will wipe away every tear |
| | 11:16 | seated on their thrones before **G**, |
| | 11:16 | fell on their faces and worshiped **G**, |
| | 12: 5 | her child was snatched up to **G** |
| | 13: 6 | It opened its mouth to blaspheme **G**, |
| | 14: 7 | voice, "Fear **G** and give him glory, |
| | 15: 3 | are your deeds, Lord **G** Almighty. |
| | 15: 7 | bowls filled with the wrath of **G**, |
| | 16:14 | on the great day of **G** Almighty. |
| | 17:17 | For **G** has put it into their hearts |
| | 18:20 | Rejoice, you people of **G**! |
| | 18:20 | For **G** has judged her |
| | 19: 1 | glory and power belong to our **G**, |
| | 19: 6 | For our Lord **G** Almighty reigns. |
| | 19: 9 | "These are the true words of **G**." |
| | 19:13 | and his name is the Word of **G**. |
| | 21: 3 | and **G** himself will be with them and be their **G**. |
| | 21:11 | It shone with the glory of **G**, and its |
| | 21:23 | for the glory of **G** gives it light, |
| | 22: 5 | for the Lord **G** will give them light. |

**ANGEL OF GOD** See ANGEL

**ARK OF GOD** See ARK

**FEAR GOD** See FEAR

**FEAR OF GOD** See FEAR

**GLORY OF ... GOD** See GLORY

**GOD AND FATHER** Ro 15:6; 2Co 1:3; 11:31; Gal 1:4; Eph 1:3; 4:6; Php 4:20; 1Th 1:3; 3:11, 13; 1Pe 1:3; Rev 1:6

**GOD OF ABRAHAM** Ge 31:42, 53; Ex 3:6, 15, 16; 4:5; 1Ki 18:36; 2Ch 30:6; Ps 47:9; Mt 22:32; Mk 12:26; Lk 20:37; Ac 3:13; 7:32

**GOD OF ... ANCESTORS** Dt 1:11, 21; 4:1; 6:3; 12:1; 26:7; 27:3; 29:25; Jos 18:3; Jdg 2:12; 2Ki 21:22; 1Ch 5:25; 12:17; 2Ch 7:22; 11:16; 13:12, 18; 14:4; 15:12; 19:4; 20:6, 33; 21:10; 24:18, 24; 28:6, 9, 25; 29:5; 30:7, 19, 22; 33:12;

34:32, 33; 36:15; Ezr 7:27; 8:28; 10:11; Da 2:23; Ac 5:30; 22:14; 24:14

**GOD OF HEAVEN** Ge 24:3, 7; 2Ch 36:23; Ezr 1:2; 5:11, 12; 6:9, 10; 7:12, 21, 23, 23; Ne 1:4, 5; 2:4, 20; Ps 136:26; Da 2:18, 19, 37, 44; Jnh 1:9; Rev 11:13; 16:11

**GOD OF ISRAEL** Ex 5:1; 24:10; 32:27; 34:23; Nu 16:9; Jos 7:13, 19, 20; 8:30; 9:18, 19; 10:40, 42; 13:14, 33; 14:14; 22:16, 24; 24:2, 23; Jdg 4:6; 5:3, 5; 6:8; 11:21, 23; 21:3; Ru 2:12; 1Sa 1:17; 2:30; 5:7, 8, 8, 8, 10, 11; 6:3; 10:18; 14:41; 20:12; 23:10, 11; 25:32, 34; 2Sa 7:27; 12:7; 23:3; 1Ki 1:30, 48; 8:15, 17, 20, 23, 25, 26; 11:9, 31; 14:7, 13; 15:30; 16:13, 26, 33; 17:1, 14; 22:53; 2Ki 9:6; 10:31; 14:25; 18:5; 19:15, 20; 21:12; 22:15, 18; 1Ch 4:10; 5:26; 15:12, 14; 16:4, 36; 22:6; 23:25; 24:19; 28:4; 2Ch 2:12; 6:4, 7, 10, 14, 16, 17; 11:16; 13:5; 15:4, 13; 20:19; 29:7, 10; 30:1, 5; 32:17; 33:16, 18; 34:23, 26; 36:13; Ezr 1:3; 3:2; 4:1, 3; 5:1; 6:14, 21, 22; 7:6, 15; 8:35; 9:4, 15; Ps 41:13; 59:5; 68:8, 35; 69:6; 72:18; 106:48; Isa 17:6; 21:10, 17; 24:15; 29:23; 37:16, 21; 41:17; 45:3; 48:1, 2; 52:12; Jer 7:3, 21; 9:15; 11:3; 13:12; 16:9; 19:3, 15; 21:4; 23:2; 24:5; 25:15, 27; 27:4, 21; 28:2, 14; 29:4, 8, 21, 25; 30:2; 31:23; 32:14, 15, 36; 33:4; 34:2, 13; 35:13, 17, 18, 19; 37:7; 38:17; 39:16; 42:9, 15, 18; 43:10; 44:2, 7, 11, 25; 45:2; 46:25; 48:1; 50:18; 51:33; Eze 8:4; 9:3; 10:19, 20; 11:22; 43:2; 44:2; Zep 2:9; Mal 2:16; Mt 15:31; Lk 1:68

**GOD OF JACOB** Ex 3:6, 15; 4:5; 2Sa 23:1; Ps 20:1; 24:6; 46:7, 11; 75:9; 76:6; 81:1, 4; 84:8; 94:7; 114:7; 146:5; Isa 2:3; Mic 4:2; Mt 22:32; Mk 12:26; Lk 20:37; Ac 7:46

**GOD OF ... FATHER** Ge 26:24; 28:13; 31:5, 29, 42, 53; 32:9, 9; 43:23; 46:1, 3; 50:17; Ex 3:6; 2Ki 20:5; 1Ch 28:9; 29:10; 2Ch 17:4; 21:12; 34:3; Isa 38:5

**GOD OF ... FATHERS** Ex 3:13, 15, 16; 4:5; 1Ch 29:18, 20; Ac 3:13; 7:32

**GOD THE FATHER** Jn 6:27; 1Co 8:6; 15:24; Gal 1:1; Eph 5:20; 6:23; Php 2:11; Col 3:17; 1Th 1:1; 2Th 1:2; 1Ti 1:2; 2Ti 1:2; Tit 1:4; 1Pe 1:2; 2Pe 1:17; 2Jn 1:3; Jude 1:1

**GRACE OF ... GOD** See GRACE

**HAND OF GOD** See HAND

**HOUSE OF ... GOD** See HOUSE

**KINGDOM OF GOD** See KINGDOM

**LIVING GOD** Dt 5:26; Jos 3:10; 1Sa 17:26, 36; 2Ki 19:4, 16; Ps 42:2; 84:2; Isa 37:4, 17; Jer 10:10; 23:36; Da 6:20, 26; Hos 1:10; Mt 16:16; 26:63; Ac 14:15; Ro 9:26; 2Co 3:3; 6:16; 1Ti 3:15; 4:10; Heb 3:12; 9:14; 10:31; 12:22; Rev 7:2

**†LORD GOD** Ge 2:4, 5, 7, 8, 9, 15, 16, 18, 19, 21, 22; 3:1, 8, 8, 9, 13, 14, 21, 22, 23; Ex 9:30; 2Sa 5:10; 7:25; 1Ki 19:10, 14; 1Ch 17:16, 17; 22:1, 19; 28:20; 29:1; 2Ch 1:9; 6:41, 41, 42;

26:18; 32:16; Ne 9:7; Ps 59:5; 68:18; 72:18; 80:4, 19; 84:8, 11; 89:8; Jer 5:14; 15:16; 35:17; 38:17; 44:7; Hos 12:5; Am 3:13; 4:13; 5:14, 15, 16; 6:8, 14; Jnh 4:6; Mal 2:16

**LORD GOD** Da 9:3; Lk 1:32; Rev 1:8; 4:8; 11:17; 15:3; 16:7; 18:8; 19:6; 21:22; 22:5

**†LORD GOD ALMIGHTY** 2Sa 5:10; 1Ki 19:10, 14; Ps 59:5; 80:4, 19; 84:8; 89:8; Jer 5:14; 15:16; 35:17; 38:17; 44:7; Hos 12:5; Am 3:13; 4:13; 5:14, 15, 16; 6:8, 14

**†LORD HIS/MY/OUR/THEIR/YOUR GOD** See †LORD

**MAN OF GOD** See MAN

**SON OF GOD** See SON

**SPIRIT OF GOD** See SPIRIT

**TEMPLE OF ... GOD** See TEMPLE

**WORD OF GOD** See WORD

## GOD'S [GOD]

| | | |
|---|---|---|
| Ge | 6:11 | the earth was corrupt in **G** sight. |
| Dt | 21:23 | is hung on a pole is under **G** curse. |
| 2Ch | 20:15 | For the battle is not yours, but **G**. |
| | 36:19 | They set fire to **G** temple and broke |
| Job | 15: 8 | Do you listen in on **G** council? |
| | 33: 6 | I am the same as you in **G** sight; |
| | 37:14 | stop and consider **G** wonders. |
| Ps | 52: 8 | I trust in **G** unfailing love for ever |
| | 69:30 | I will praise **G** name in song |
| Ecc | 9: 1 | and what they do are in **G** hands, |
| Mk | 3:35 | Whoever does **G** will is my brother |
| Lk | 3: 6 | all people will see **G** salvation.' " |
| | 9:20 | Peter answered, "**G** Messiah." |
| | 20:25 | is Caesar's, and to God what is **G**." |
| Jn | 10:36 | because I said, 'I am **G** Son'? |
| Ro | 2: 3 | think you will escape **G** judgment? |
| | 2: 4 | realizing that **G** kindness is intended |
| | 3: 3 | nullify **G** faithfulness? |
| | 5: 5 | because **G** love has been poured out |
| | 7:22 | my inner being I delight in **G** law; |
| | 8:16 | our spirit that we are **G** children. |
| | 9: 6 | is not as though **G** word had failed. |
| | 9:16 | desire or effort, but on **G** mercy. |
| | 11:29 | for **G** gifts and his call are |
| | 12: 2 | to test and approve what **G** will is— |
| | 13: 6 | for the authorities are **G** servants, |
| 1Co | 2: 7 | we declare **G** wisdom, a mystery |
| | 3: 9 | For we are **G** co-workers; you are **G** |
| | 3:16 | that you yourselves are **G** temple |
| | 3:16 | that **G** Spirit dwells in your midst? |
| | 7:19 | Keeping **G** commands is what |
| | 9:21 | (though I am not free from **G** law |
| 2Co | 6: 2 | now is the time of **G** favor, now is |
| Eph | 1: 7 | with the riches of **G** grace |
| | 2:10 | For we are **G** handiwork, |
| | 5: 1 | Follow **G** example, therefore, |
| 1Th | 4: 3 | It is **G** will that you should be |
| | 5:18 | for this is **G** will for you in Christ |
| 1Ti | 6: 1 | so that **G** name and our teaching |
| 2Ti | 2: 9 | But **G** word is not chained. |
| | 2:19 | **G** solid foundation stands firm, |
| Tit | 1: 7 | an overseer manages **G** household, |

Heb  1: 3   The Son is the radiance of **G** glory
     3: 6   is faithful as the Son over **G** house.
    9:24   now to appear for us in **G** presence.
   11: 3   was formed at **G** command,
Jas   2:23   and he was called **G** friend.
1Pe  2:15   For it is **G** will that by doing good
    3: 4   which is of great worth in **G** sight.
2Pe  3: 5   ago by **G** word the heavens came
1Jn  5: 9   **G** testimony is greater because it is
Rev  3:14   true witness, the ruler of **G** creation.
  11:19   **G** temple in heaven was opened,
  14:10   will drink of the wine of **G** fury,
  14:19   into the great winepress of **G** wrath.
  16: 1   the seven bowls of **G** wrath
  22:21   of the Lord Jesus be with **G** people.

## GOD-BREATHED* [BREATH, GOD]
2Ti  3:16   All Scripture is **G** and is useful

## GOD-FEARING* [FEAR, GOD]
Ac   2: 5   were staying in Jerusalem **G** Jews
  10: 2   all his family were devout and **G**;
  10:22   He is a righteous and **G** man, who is
  13:26   of Abraham and you **G** Gentiles,
  13:50   Jewish leaders incited the **G** women
  17: 4   as did a large number of **G** Greeks
  17:17   with both Jews and **G** Greeks,

## GOD-HATERS* [GOD, HATE]
Ro   1:30   slanderers, **G**, insolent,

## GODDESS [GOD]
1Ki  11: 5   He followed Ashtoreth the **g**
Ac  19:27   of the great **g** Artemis will be
  19:27   and the **g** herself, who is worshiped

## GODHEAD (KJV) See DEITY, DIVINE

## GODLESS [GOD]
Job  20: 5   the joy of the **g** lasts but a moment.
Pr   11: 9   their mouths the **g** destroy their
Jer  23:11   "Both prophet and priest are **g**;
1Ti  4: 7   Have nothing to do with **g** myths
  6:20   Turn away from **g** chatter
2Ti  2:16   Avoid **g** chatter, because those who
Heb 12:16   or is **g** like Esau, who for a single

## GODLESSNESS* [GOD]
Ro   1:18   from heaven against all the **g**
  11:26   he will turn **g** away from Jacob.

## GODLINESS* [GOD]
Ac   3:12   or **g** we had made this man walk?
1Ti  2: 2   and quiet lives in all **g** and holiness.
  3:16   from which true **g** springs is great:
  4: 8   value, but **g** has value for all things,
  6: 5   and who think that **g** is a means
  6: 6   **g** with contentment is great gain.
  6:11   and pursue righteousness, **g**, faith,
2Ti  3: 5   having a form of **g** but denying its
Tit   1: 1   of the truth that leads to **g**—
2Pe  1: 6   and to perseverance, **g**;
  1: 7   and to **g**, mutual affection;

## GODLY* [GOD]
Ps   16: 3   the **g** who are in the land,
Mal  2:15   Because he was seeking **g** offspring.
Jn   9:31   to the **g** person who does his will.
Ac   8: 2   **G** men buried Stephen and mourned
2Co  1:12   with integrity and **g** sincerity.
  7:10   **G** sorrow brings repentance
  7:11   See what this **g** sorrow has
  11: 2   jealous for you with a **g** jealousy.
1Ti  4: 7   rather, train yourself to be **g**.
  6: 3   Lord Jesus Christ and to **g** teaching,
2Ti  3:12   live a **g** life in Christ Jesus will be
Tit   2:12   and **g** lives in this present age,
2Pe  1: 3   need for a **g** life through our knowledge
2Pe  2: 9   how to rescue the **g** from trials
  3:11   You ought to live holy and **g** lives

## GODS [GOD]
Ge  31:19   stole her father's household **g**.
  35: 4   Jacob all the foreign **g** they had
Ex  12:12   judgment on all the **g** of Egypt.
  15:11   Who among the **g** is like you,
  20: 3   shall have no other **g** before me.
  23:13   Do not invoke the names of other **g**;
  32: 4   they said, "These are your **g**, Israel,
Dt   5: 7   shall have no other **g** before me.
  7:25   The images of their **g** you are
  13: 2   us follow other **g**" (**g** you have not
Jos  24:14   Throw away the **g** your ancestors
Jdg  2:17   but prostituted themselves to other **g**
1Sa  17:43   the Philistine cursed David by his **g**.
1Ki  20:23   him, "Their **g** are **g** of the hills.
1Ch  16:26   For all the **g** of the nations are idols,
2Ch  2: 5   our God is greater than all other **g**.
Ps   82: 6   "I said, 'You are "**g**"; you are all
  135: 5   that our Lord is greater than all **g**.
Isa  45:20   who pray to **g** that cannot save.
Jer   2:11   ever changed its **g**? (Yet they are not
            **g** at all.)
  10:11   'These **g**, who did not make
  16:20   people make their own **g**? Yes, but they
            are not **g**!"
Da   5: 4   they praised the **g** of gold and silver,
Hos  14: 3   We will never again say 'Our **g**'
Jn  10:34   Law, 'I have said you are "**g**" '?
Ac  19:26   **g** made by human hands are no **g** at all.
1Co  8: 5   For even if there are so-called **g**,

## GOES [GO]
Ex  12:23   the Lᴏʀᴅ **g** through the land
Nu   5:12   'If a man's wife **g** astray and is
Dt  31: 6   the Lᴏʀᴅ your God **g** with you;
2Ch 23: 7   close to the king wherever he **g**."
Pr   16:18   Pride **g** before destruction,
Da   9:25   the word **g** out to restore and rebuild
Rev  14: 4   follow the Lamb wherever he **g**.

## GOG
Eze  38: 2   set your face against **G**, of the land
  38:18   When **G** attacks the land of Israel,
Rev  20: 8   of the earth—**G** and Magog—

## GOING [GO]
Ge   6:17   I am **g** to bring floodwaters
Ps  144:14   of walls, no **g** into captivity, no cry

Pr   7:22  once he followed her like an ox g
Jn  13:21  you, one of you is g to betray me."
    13:36  him, "Lord, where are you g?"
    13:36  "Where I am g, you cannot follow
    14: 2  that I am g there to prepare a place
    16:10  because I am g to the Father,
1Pe  2:25  For "you were like sheep g astray,"

## GOLD [GOLD-COVERED, GOLDEN, GOLDSMITH, GOLDSMITHS]

Ex   3:22  her house for articles of silver and g
    12:35  Egyptians for articles of silver and g
    20:23  gods of silver or gods of g.
    25:17  an atonement cover of pure g—
    25:31  "Make a lampstand of pure g.
    28: 6  "Make the ephod of g, and of blue,
    32:31  have made themselves gods of g.
Dt  17:17  large amounts of silver and g.
Jos  7:21  a bar of g weighing fifty shekels,
Jdg  8:27  Gideon made the g into an ephod,
1Sa  6: 4  "Five g tumors and five g rats,
1Ki  6:21  the inside of the temple with pure g,
    20: 3  'Your silver and g are mine,
2Ch  9:13  the g that Solomon received yearly
Ezr  1: 6  them with articles of silver and g,
Job 22:25  then the Almighty will be your g,
    23:10  tested me, I will come forth as g.
    28:15  cannot be bought with the finest g,
    31:24  put my trust in g or said to pure g,
Ps  19:10  precious than g, than much pure g;
   115: 4  But their idols are silver and g,
  119:127  more than g, more than pure g,
Pr   3:14  and yields better returns than g.
     8:19  My fruit is better than fine g;
    22: 1  esteemed is better than silver or g.
    25:11  Like apples of g in settings of silver
Isa 60:17  Instead of bronze I will bring you g,
Da   2:32  of the statue was made of pure g,
     3: 1  made an image of g, sixty cubits
Hag  2: 8  silver is mine and the g is mine,'
Zec  4: 2  "I see a solid g lampstand
     6:11  Take the silver and g and make
Mt   2:11  and presented him with gifts of g,
Ac   3: 6  "Silver or g I do not have, but what
1Pe  1: 7  of greater worth than g,
Rev  3:18  to buy from me g refined in the fire,
     4: 4  and had crowns of g on their heads.
    14:14  man with a crown of g on his head
    21:18  and the city of pure g, as pure as
    21:21  The great street of the city was of g,

## GOLD-COVERED* [GOLD, COVER]
Heb  9: 4  and the g ark of the covenant.

## GOLDEN [GOLD]
1Ki 12:28  advice, the king made two g calves.
Rev  1:12  I turned I saw seven g lampstands,
     1:13  and with a g sash around his chest.
     5: 8  they were holding g bowls full
    15: 7  seven angels seven g bowls filled

## GOLDSMITH [GOLD]
Isa 46: 6  they hire a g to make it into a god,

## GOLDSMITHS [GOLD]
Jer 10:14  all g are shamed by their idols.

## GOLGOTHA*
Mt  27:33  a place called G (which means
Mk  15:22  to the place called G (which means
Jn  19:17  (which in Aramaic is called G).

## GOLIATH
Philistine giant killed by David (1Sa 17; 21:9).

## GOMER
Hos  1: 3  So he married G daughter

## GOMORRAH
Ge  13:10  LORD destroyed Sodom and G.)
    18:20  against Sodom and G is so great
    19:24  burning sulfur on Sodom and G—
Dt  29:23  the destruction of Sodom and G,
Isa  1: 9  Sodom, we would have been like G.
Jer 23:14  the people of Jerusalem are like G."
Mt  10:15  G on the day of judgment than
Ro   9:29  we would have been like G."
2Pe  2: 6  and G by burning them to ashes,
Jude 1: 7  Sodom and G and the surrounding

## GONE [GO]
Dt  34: 7  were not weak nor his strength g.
Jdg  4:14  Has not the LORD g ahead
Job 19: 4  If it is true that I have g astray,
Ps  90: 4  are like a day that has just g by,
Pr  30: 4  Who has g up to heaven and come
Isa 53: 6  like sheep, have g astray, each of us
La   1: 3  harsh labor, Judah has g into exile.
Mk   5:30  Jesus realized that power had g
Jn   2: 3  When the wine was g, Jesus' mother
2Co  5:17  The old has g, the new is here!
1Pe  3:22  who has g into heaven and is
1Jn  4: 1  because many false prophets have g
2Jn  1: 7  the flesh, have g out into the world.
Rev 12:12  sea, because the devil has g down

## GONG*
1Co 13: 1  love, I am only a resounding g

## GOOD [BEST, BETTER, GOODNESS]
Ge   1: 4  God saw that the light was g, and he
     1:10  And God saw that it was g.
     1:12  And God saw that it was g.
     1:18  And God saw that it was g.
     1:21  And God saw that it was g.
     1:25  And God saw that it was g.
     1:31  that he had made, and it was very g.
     2: 9  pleasing to the eye and g for food.
     2: 9  the tree of the knowledge of g
     2:17  from the tree of the knowledge of g
     2:18  "It is not g for the man to be alone.
     3: 6  the fruit of the tree was g for food
     3:22  like one of us, knowing g and evil.
    41:26  The seven g cows are seven years,
    50:20  God intended it for g to accomplish
Ex   3: 8  them up out of that land into a g
    18: 9  all the g things the LORD had
Nu  10:29  the LORD has promised g things
Dt   6:18  is right and g in the LORD's sight,

| | | |
|---|---|---|
| Dt | 6:18 | and take over the **g** land the LORD |
| | 10:13 | giving you today for your own **g**? |
| Jos | 21:45 | all the LORD's **g** promises |
| | 23:15 | just as all the **g** things the LORD |
| | 23:15 | from this **g** land he has given you. |
| 1Sa | 25:21 | He has paid me back evil for **g**. |
| 2Sa | 14:17 | like an angel of God in discerning **g** |
| 1Ki | 8:56 | all the **g** promises he gave through |
| 2Ch | 7: 3 | to the LORD, saying, "He is **g**; |
| | 31:20 | doing what was **g** and right |
| Ne | 2:18 | So they began this **g** work. |
| | 9:20 | You gave your **g** Spirit to instruct |
| Job | 2:10 | Shall we accept **g** from God, |
| Ps | 14: 1 | there is no one who does **g**. |
| | 25: 7 | me, for you, LORD, are **g**. |
| | 34: 8 | Taste and see that the LORD is **g**; |
| | 34:14 | Turn from evil and do **g**; |
| | 37: 3 | Trust in the LORD and do **g**; |
| | 37:27 | Turn from evil and do **g**; |
| | 52: 9 | in your name, for your name is **g**. |
| | 73: 1 | Surely God is **g** to Israel, to those |
| | 84:11 | no **g** thing does he withhold |
| | 86: 5 | are forgiving and **g**, |
| | 100: 5 | For the LORD is **g** and his love |
| | 103: 5 | your desires with **g** things so |
| | 109: 5 | They repay me evil for **g**, and hatred |
| | 112: 5 | **G** will come to those who are |
| | 119:68 | You are **g**, and what you do is **g**; |
| | 133: 1 | How **g** and pleasant it is |
| | 145: 9 | The LORD is **g** to all; |
| | 147: 1 | How **g** it is to sing praises to our |
| Pr | 3: 4 | and a **g** name in the sight of God |
| | 3:27 | Do not withhold **g** from those |
| | 11:27 | Whoever seeks **g** finds favor, |
| | 13:21 | righteous are rewarded with **g** things. |
| | 13:22 | **G** people leave an inheritance |
| | 14:22 | those who plan what is **g** find love |
| | 15: 3 | watch on the wicked and the **g**. |
| | 15:23 | and how **g** is a timely word! |
| | 15:30 | **g** news gives health to the bones. |
| | 17:22 | A cheerful heart is **g** medicine, |
| | 18:22 | He who finds a wife finds what is **g** |
| | 19: 2 | Desire without knowledge is not **g**— |
| | 22: 1 | A **g** name is more desirable than |
| | 31:12 | She brings him **g**, not harm, |
| Ecc | 3:12 | happy and to do **g** while they live. |
| | 12:14 | hidden thing, whether it is **g** or evil. |
| Isa | 5: 4 | When I looked for **g** grapes, |
| | 5:20 | Woe to those who call evil **g** and **g** |
| | 40: 9 | You who bring **g** news to Zion, |
| | 52: 7 | the feet of those who bring **g** news, |
| | 61: 1 | has anointed me to proclaim **g** news |
| Jer | 6:16 | ask where the **g** way is, and walk |
| | 13:23 | can you do **g** who are accustomed |
| | 16:19 | worthless idols that did them no **g**. |
| | 24: 2 | One basket had very **g** figs, |
| | 33:14 | 'when I will fulfill the **g** promise I made |
| La | 3:26 | it is **g** to wait quietly |
| Eze | 34:14 | I will tend them in a **g** pasture, |
| | 34:14 | they will lie down in **g** grazing land, |
| Hos | 8: 3 | But Israel has rejected what is **g**; |
| Am | 5:14 | Seek **g**, not evil, that you may live. |
| Mic | 6: 8 | has shown all you people what is **g**. |
| Na | 1:15 | the feet of one who brings **g** news, |
| Zec | 8:15 | I have determined to do **g** again |
| Mt | 5:13 | It is no longer **g** for anything, |
| | 5:45 | his sun to rise on the evil and the **g**, |

| | | |
|---|---|---|
| Mt | 7:11 | heaven give **g** gifts to those who ask |
| | 7:17 | Likewise, every **g** tree bears **g** fruit, |
| | 12:35 | **G** people bring **g** things out of the **g** |
| | 13: 8 | Still other seed fell on **g** soil, |
| | 13:24 | is like a man who sowed **g** seed |
| | 13:48 | and collected the **g** fish in baskets, |
| | 25:21 | 'Well done, **g** and faithful servant! |
| Mk | 1:15 | Repent and believe the **g** news!" |
| | 3: 4 | to do **g** or to do evil, to save life |
| | 4: 8 | Still other seed fell on **g** soil. |
| | 8:36 | What **g** is it for you to gain |
| | 10:18 | "Why do you call me **g**?" |
| | 10:18 | "No one is **g**—except God alone. |
| Lk | 2:10 | I bring you **g** news of great joy |
| | 3: 9 | does not produce **g** fruit will be cut |
| | 6:27 | do **g** to those who hate you, |
| | 6:35 | love your enemies, do **g** to them, |
| | 6:43 | "No **g** tree bears bad fruit, nor does a |
| | | bad tree bear **g** fruit. |
| | 7:22 | and the **g** news is proclaimed |
| | 8: 8 | Still other seed fell on **g** soil. |
| | 9:25 | What **g** is it for you to gain |
| | 14:34 | "Salt is **g**, but if it loses its |
| | 18:19 | "Why do you call me **g**?" |
| | 19:17 | " 'Well done, my **g** servant!' |
| Jn | 1:46 | Can anything **g** come from there?" |
| | 10:11 | "I am the **g** shepherd. The **g** |
| | 10:14 | "I am the **g** shepherd; I know my |
| Ac | 11:20 | telling them the **g** news |
| Ro | 3:12 | there is no one who does **g**, not even |
| | 7:12 | is holy, righteous and **g**. |
| | 7:16 | want to do, I agree that the law is **g**. |
| | 7:18 | I know that **g** itself does not dwell |
| | 7:18 | For I have the desire to do what is **g**, |
| | 8:28 | for the **g** of those who love him, |
| | 10:15 | feet of those who bring **g** news!" |
| | 12: 2 | his **g**, pleasing and perfect will. |
| | 12: 9 | Hate what is evil; cling to what is **g**. |
| | 12:21 | by evil, but overcome evil with **g**. |
| | 13: 4 | is God's servant for your **g**. |
| | 16:19 | want you to be wise about what is **g**, |
| 1Co | 7: 1 | "It is **g** for a man not to have sexual |
| | 10:24 | seek their own **g**, but the **g** of others. |
| | 10:33 | my own **g** but the **g** of many, |
| | 15:33 | company corrupts **g** character." |
| 2Co | 9: 8 | you will abound in every **g** work. |
| Gal | 4:18 | provided the purpose is **g**, and to be |
| | 5: 7 | You were running a **g** race. |
| | 6: 9 | Let us not become weary in doing **g**, |
| | 6:10 | let us do **g** to all people, |
| Eph | 2:10 | in Christ Jesus to do **g** works, |
| | 6: 8 | one of you for whatever **g** you do, |
| Php | 1: 6 | he who began a **g** work in you will |
| | 2:13 | act in order to fulfill his **g** purpose. |
| Col | 1:10 | bearing fruit in every **g** work, |
| 1Th | 5:15 | strive to do what is **g** for each other |
| | 5:21 | test them all; hold on to what is **g**, |
| 2Th | 2:17 | strengthen you in every **g** deed |
| | 3:13 | never tire of doing what is **g**. |
| 1Ti | 1: 5 | a pure heart and a **g** conscience |
| | 1: 8 | the law is **g** if one uses it properly. |
| | 3: 7 | have a **g** reputation with outsiders, |
| | 4: 4 | For everything God created is **g**, |
| | 6:12 | Fight the **g** fight of the faith. |
| | 6:12 | you made your **g** confession |
| | 6:18 | do **g**, to be rich in **g** deeds, to be |
| 2Ti | 2: 3 | like a **g** soldier of Christ Jesus. |

2Ti  3:17  equipped for every **g** work.
     4: 7  I have fought the **g** fight, I have
Tit   1: 8  one who loves what is **g**, who is
     2: 3  much wine, but to teach what is **g**.
     2: 7  an example by doing what is **g**.
    2:14  his very own, eager to do what is **g**.
Heb  5:14  to distinguish **g** from evil.
    10: 1  law is only a shadow of the **g** things
    10:24  another on toward love and **g** deeds,
    12:10  but God disciplines us for our **g**,
    13:16  do not forget to do **g** and to share
Jas   1:17  Every **g** and perfect gift is
    4:17  if you know the **g** you ought to do
1Pe  2: 3  you have tasted that the Lord is **g**.
    2:12  Live such **g** lives among the pagans
    2:12  they may see your **g** deeds
    2:18  not only to those who are **g**
    3:17  to suffer for doing **g** than for doing
3Jn  1: 2  I pray that you may enjoy **g** health
    1:11  imitate what is evil but what is **g**.

## GOOD NEWS
2Sa 4:10; 18:25, 26, 27, 31;
1Ki 1:42; 2Ki 7:9; Pr 15:30; 25:25; Isa 40:9, 9;
41:27; 52:7; 61:1; Na 1:15; Mt 4:23; 9:35; 11:5;
Mk 1:1, 14, 15; Lk 1:19; 2:10; 3:18; 4:18, 43;
7:22; 8:1; 9:6; 16:16; 20:1; Ac 5:42; 8:12, 35;
10:36; 11:20; 13:32; 14:15; 17:18; 20:24; Ro
10:15, 16; 1Th 3:6; Heb 4:2, 6

## GOODNESS [GOOD]
Ex  33:19  "I will cause all my **g** to pass
2Ch  6:41  faithful people rejoice in your **g**.
Ps   23: 6  Surely your **g** and love will follow
  116:12  to the Lord for all his **g** to me?
Eph  5: 9  the fruit of the light consists in all **g**,
Heb  6: 5  who have tasted the **g** of the word
2Pe  1: 5  to your faith **g**; and to **g**, knowledge;

## GOODS
Ps  62:10  or put vain hope in stolen **g**;
Ecc  5:11  As **g** increase, so do those who
Hab  2: 6  to him who piles up stolen **g**

## GOODWILL*
Est   9:30  words of **g** and assurance—
Pr   14: 9  but **g** is found among the upright.
Ac   7:10  him to gain the **g** of Pharaoh king
Php  1:15  and rivalry, but others out of **g**.

## GOPHER [WOOD] (KJV) See
CYPRESS

## GORGE [GORGED]
Pr   23:20  wine or **g** themselves on meat,
Eze  32: 4  of the wild **g** themselves on you.

## GORGED [GORGE]
Rev  19:21  all the birds **g** themselves on their

## GOSHEN
Ge  45:10  You shall live in the region of **G**
Ex   8:22  deal differently with the land of **G**,

## GOSPEL
Mt  24:14  And this **g** of the kingdom will be

Mk  13:10  the **g** must first be preached to all
Ac   14: 7  they continued to preach the **g**.
    14:21  They preached the **g** in that city
Ro   1:16  I am not ashamed of the **g**,
    15:16  duty of proclaiming the **g** of God,
    15:20  preach the **g** where Christ was not
1Co  1:17  me to baptize, but to preach the **g**—
    9:12  anything rather than hinder the **g**
    9:14  who preach the **g** should receive
    9:14  receive their living from the **g**.
    9:16  Woe to me if I do not preach the **g**!
    15: 1  to remind you of the **g** I preached
    15: 2  By this **g** you are saved, if you hold
2Co  4: 3  And even if our **g** is veiled, it is
    4: 4  light of the **g** that displays the glory
    9:13  your confession of the **g** of Christ,
    11: 4  or a different **g** from the one you
Gal   1: 6  and are turning to a different **g**—
    1: 7  which is really no **g** at all.
    1: 7  are trying to pervert the **g** of Christ.
    3: 8  and announced the **g** in advance
Eph  3: 6  through the **g** the Gentiles are heirs
    6:15  that comes from the **g** of peace.
Php  1: 7  or defending and confirming the **g**,
    1:27  a manner worthy of the **g** of Christ.
    1:27  one accord for the faith of the **g**
Col   1: 6  the **g** is bearing fruit and growing
    1:23  from the hope held out in the **g**.
    1:23  This is the **g** that you heard
1Th  2: 4  by God to be entrusted with the **g**.
2Th  1: 8  do not obey the **g** of our Lord Jesus.
2Ti   1: 8  join with me in suffering for the **g**,
Phm  1:13  me while I am in chains for the **g**.
Rev  14: 6  he had the eternal **g** to proclaim

## GOSSIP* [GOSSIPS]
Pr   18: 8  of a **g** are like choice morsels;
    20:19  A **g** betrays a confidence;
    26:20  without a **g** a quarrel dies down.
    26:22  of a **g** are like choice morsels;
2Co  12:20  slander, **g**, arrogance and disorder.

## GOSSIPS* [GOSSIP]
Pr   11:13  **G** betray a confidence,
    16:28  and **g** separate close friends.
Ro   1:29  strife, deceit and malice. They are **g**,

## GOT [GET]
Ex  32: 6  drink and **g** up to indulge in revelry.
1Co  10: 7  and **g** up to indulge in revelry."

## GOUGE
Mt   5:29  stumble, **g** it out and throw it away.

## GOURD [GOURDS]
Jnh  4: 6  God provided a **g** and made it grow

## GOURDS [GOURD]
1Ki  6:18  carved with **g** and open flowers.
2Ki  4:39  He gathered some of its **g** and filled

## GOVERN [GOVERNING,
GOVERNMENT, GOVERNOR,
GOVERNORS]
Ge   1:16  the greater light to **g** the day

| | | |
|---|---|---|
| Ge | 1:16 | and the lesser light to **g** the night. |
| 1Sa | 9:17 | to you about; he will **g** my people." |
| 1Ki | 3: 9 | a discerning heart to **g** your people |
| 2Ch | 1:11 | to **g** my people over whom I have |
| Job | 34:17 | Can one who hates justice **g**? |
| Ps | 136: 8 | the sun to **g** the day, *His love endures* |

## GOVERNING [GOVERN]
Ro 13: 1 be subject to the **g** authorities,

## GOVERNMENT [GOVERN]
Isa 9: 6 and the **g** will be on his shoulders.

## GOVERNOR [GOVERN]

| | | |
|---|---|---|
| Ge | 42: 6 | Now Joseph was the **g** of the land, |
| Ne | 5:14 | appointed to be their **g** in the land |
| | 12:26 | in the days of Nehemiah the **g** |
| Isa | 60:17 | I will make peace your **g** |
| Hag | 2:21 | "Tell Zerubbabel **g** of Judah that I |
| Mal | 1: 8 | Try offering them to your **g**! |
| Lk | 3: 1 | when Pontius Pilate was **g** of Judea, |

## GOVERNORS [GOVERN]
Mk 13: 9 of me you will stand before **g**

## GRACE* [GRACIOUS, GRACIOUSLY]

| | | |
|---|---|---|
| Ps | 45: 2 | your lips have been anointed with **g**, |
| Pr | 1: 9 | They are a garland to **g** your head |
| | 3:22 | you, an ornament to **g** your neck. |
| | 4: 9 | give you a garland to **g** your head |
| | 22:11 | who speaks with **g** will have the king |
| Isa | 26:10 | But when **g** is shown to the wicked, |
| Zec | 12:10 | inhabitants of Jerusalem a spirit of **g** |
| Lk | 2:40 | and the **g** of God was on him. |
| Jn | 1:14 | from the Father, full of **g** and truth. |
| | 1:16 | **g** in place of **g** already given. |
| | 1:17 | **g** and truth came through Jesus |
| Ac | 4:33 | God's **g** was so powerfully at work |
| | 6: 8 | a man full of God's **g** and power, |
| | 11:23 | saw what the **g** of God had done, |
| | 13:43 | them to continue in the **g** of God |
| | 14: 3 | message of his **g** by enabling them |
| | 14:26 | had been committed to the **g** of God |
| | 15:11 | We believe it is through the **g** of our |
| | 15:40 | by the believers to the **g** of the Lord. |
| | 18:27 | to those who by **g** had believed. |
| | 20:24 | to the good news of God's **g**. |
| | 20:32 | you to God and to the word of his **g**, |
| Ro | 1: 5 | Through him we received **g** |
| | 1: 7 | **G** and peace to you from God our |
| | 3:24 | by his **g** through the redemption |
| | 4:16 | so that it may be by **g** and may be |
| | 5: 2 | by faith into this **g** in which we now |
| | 5:15 | how much more did God's **g** |
| | 5:15 | that came by the **g** of the one man, |
| | 5:17 | God's abundant provision of **g** |
| | 5:20 | increased, **g** increased all the more, |
| | 5:21 | **g** might reign through righteousness |
| | 6: 1 | on sinning so that **g** may increase? |
| | 6:14 | are not under the law, but under **g**. |
| | 6:15 | are not under the law but under **g**? |
| | 11: 5 | time there is a remnant chosen by **g**. |
| | 11: 6 | And if by **g**, then it cannot be |
| | 11: 6 | if it were, **g** would no longer be **g**. |
| | 12: 3 | by the **g** given me I say to every one |
| | 12: 6 | according to the **g** given to each |

| | | |
|---|---|---|
| Ro | 15:15 | because of the **g** God gave me |
| | 16:20 | The **g** of our Lord Jesus be |
| 1Co | 1: 3 | **G** and peace to you from God our |
| | 1: 4 | you because of his **g** given you |
| | 3:10 | By the **g** God has given me, I laid |
| | 15:10 | But by the **g** of God I am what I am, |
| | 15:10 | his **g** to me was not without effect. |
| | 15:10 | but the **g** of God that was with me. |
| | 16:23 | The **g** of the Lord Jesus be |
| 2Co | 1: 2 | **G** and peace to you from God our |
| | 1:12 | on worldly wisdom but on God's **g**. |
| | 4:15 | so that the **g** that is reaching more |
| | 6: 1 | you not to receive God's **g** in vain. |
| | 8: 1 | about the **g** that God has given |
| | 8: 6 | to completion this act of **g** on your |
| | 8: 7 | you also excel in this **g** of giving. |
| | 8: 9 | you know the **g** of our Lord Jesus |
| | 9:14 | the surpassing **g** God has given you. |
| | 12: 9 | to me, "My **g** is sufficient for you, |
| | 13:14 | May the **g** of the Lord Jesus Christ, |
| Gal | 1: 3 | **G** and peace to you from God our |
| | 1: 6 | who called you by the **g** of Christ |
| | 1:15 | from birth and called me by his **g**, |
| | 2: 9 | they recognized the **g** given to me. |
| | 2:21 | I do not set aside the **g** of God, |
| | 3:18 | but God in his **g** gave it to Abraham |
| | 5: 4 | you have fallen away from **g**. |
| | 6:18 | The **g** of our Lord Jesus Christ be |
| Eph | 1: 2 | **G** and peace to you from God our |
| | 1: 6 | to the praise of his glorious **g**, |
| | 1: 7 | with the riches of God's **g** |
| | 2: 5 | it is by **g** you have been saved. |
| | 2: 7 | the incomparable riches of his **g**, |
| | 2: 8 | For it is by **g** you have been saved, |
| | 3: 2 | of God's **g** that was given to me |
| | 3: 7 | of God's **g** given me through |
| | 3: 8 | Lord's people, this **g** was given me: |
| | 4: 7 | one of us **g** has been given as Christ |
| | 6:24 | **G** to all who love our Lord Jesus |
| Php | 1: 2 | **G** and peace to you from God our |
| | 1: 7 | all of you share in God's **g** with me. |
| | 4:23 | The **g** of the Lord Jesus Christ be |
| Col | 1: 2 | **G** and peace to you from God our |
| | 1: 6 | it and truly understood God's **g**. |
| | 4: 6 | conversation be always full of **g**, |
| | 4:18 | **G** be with you. |
| 1Th | 1: 1 | **G** and peace to you. |
| | 5:28 | The **g** of our Lord Jesus Christ be |
| 2Th | 1: 2 | **G** and peace to you from God our |
| | 1:12 | according to the **g** of our God |
| | 2:16 | his **g** gave us eternal encouragement |
| | 3:18 | The **g** of our Lord Jesus Christ be |
| 1Ti | 1: 2 | **G**, mercy and peace from God |
| | 1:14 | The **g** of our Lord was poured |
| | 6:21 | from the faith. **G** be with you all. |
| 2Ti | 1: 2 | **G**, mercy and peace from God |
| | 1: 9 | because of his own purpose and **g**. |
| | 1: 9 | This **g** was given us in Christ Jesus |
| | 2: 1 | be strong in the **g** that is in Christ |
| | 4:22 | with your spirit. **G** be with you all. |
| Tit | 1: 4 | **G** and peace from God the Father |
| | 2:11 | For the **g** of God has appeared |
| | 3: 7 | having been justified by his **g**, |
| | 3:15 | us in the faith. **G** be with you all. |
| Phm | 1: 3 | **G** and peace to you from God our |
| | 1:25 | The **g** of the Lord Jesus Christ be |
| Heb | 2: 9 | by the **g** of God he might taste death |

Heb 4:16 approach God's throne of **g**
 4:16 find **g** to help us in our time of need.
 10:29 who have insulted the Spirit of **g**?
 12:15 no one falls short of the **g** of God
 13: 9 our hearts to be strengthened by **g**,
 13:25 **G** be with you all.
Jas 4: 6 But he gives us more **g**. That is why
1Pe 1: 2 **G** and peace be yours in abundance.
 1:10 who spoke of the **g** that was to come
 1:13 set your hope on the **g** to be brought
 4:10 of God's **g** in its various forms.
 5:10 And the God of all **g**, who called
 5:12 that this is the true **g** of God.
2Pe 1: 2 **G** and peace be yours in abundance
 3:18 grow in the **g** and knowledge of our
2Jn 1: 3 **G**, mercy and peace from God
Jude 1: 4 who pervert the **g** of our God
Rev 1: 4 **G** and peace to you from him who
 22:21 The **g** of the Lord Jesus be

## GRACE AND PEACE Ro 1:7; 1Co 1:3; 2Co
1:2; Gal 1:3; Eph 1:2; Php 1:2; Col 1:2; 1Th 1:1;
2Th 1:2; Tit 1:4; Phm 3; 1Pe 1:2; 2Pe 1:2; Rev
1:4

## GRACE OF ... GOD Lk 2:40; Ac 11:23;
13:43; 14:26; 1Co 15:10, 10; Gal 2:21; 2Th 1:12;
Tit 2:11; Heb 2:9; 12:15; 1Pe 5:12; Jude 1:4

## GRACIOUS [GRACE]
Ge 21: 1 Now the LORD was **g** to Sarah as
Ex 34: 6 the compassionate and **g** God,
Nu 6:25 face shine on you and be **g** to you;
1Sa 2:21 And the LORD was **g** to Hannah;
2Ki 13:23 But the LORD was **g** to them
2Ch 30: 9 for the LORD your God is **g**
Ezr 7: 9 for the **g** hand of his God was
 8:22 king, "The **g** hand of our God is
Ne 2: 8 because the **g** hand of my God was
 9:17 God, **g** and compassionate,
 9:31 for you are a **g** and merciful God.
Ps 67: 1 May God be **g** to us and bless us
 86:15 are a compassionate and **g** God,
 103: 8 LORD is compassionate and **g**,
 145: 8 The LORD is **g**
Pr 16:21 and **g** words promote instruction.
 16:24 **G** words are a honeycomb,
Isa 30:18 the LORD longs to be **g** to you;
Joel 2:13 God, for he is **g** and compassionate,
Jnh 4: 2 I knew that you are a **g**
1Pe 3: 7 heirs with you of the **g** gift of life,

## GRACIOUSLY [GRACE]
Hos 14: 2 all our sins and receive us **g**, that we

## GRAFT* [GRAFTED]
Ro 11:23 for God is able to **g** them in again.

## GRAFTED [GRAFT]
Ro 11:17 have been **g** in among the others

## GRAIN [GRAINS]
Ge 41: 5 Seven heads of **g**, healthy and good,
Lev 2: 1 anyone brings a **g** offering
 2:13 Season all your **g** offerings
Dt 25: 4 an ox while it is treading out the **g**.

Ru 2: 2 up the leftover **g** behind anyone
Ps 78:24 eat, he gave them the **g** of heaven.
Ecc 11: 1 Ship your **g** across the sea;
Hos 14: 7 they will flourish like the **g**,
Joel 2:19 "I am sending you **g**, new wine
Mk 2:23 they began to pick some heads of **g**.
Lk 17:35 women will be grinding **g** together;
1Co 9: 9 an ox while it is treading out the **g**."
1Ti 5:18 an ox while it is treading out the **g**,"

## GRAIN OFFERING Ex 29:41; 30:9; Lev 2:1,
3, 4, 5, 6, 7, 8, 9, 10, 11, 14, 15; 5:13; 6:14, 15,
20, 21, 23; 7:9, 10, 37; 9:4, 17; 10:12; 14:10, 20,
21, 31; 23:13; Nu 4:16; 5:15, 18, 25, 26; 6:17;
7:13, 19, 25, 31, 37, 43, 49, 55, 61, 67, 73, 79,
87; 8:8; 15:4, 6, 9, 24; 28:5, 8, 9, 12, 12, 13, 20,
28, 31; 29:3, 9, 11, 14, 16, 19, 22, 25, 28, 31, 34,
38; Jdg 13:19, 23; 2Ki 16:13, 15, 15, 15; 1Ch
21:23; Isa 66:3; Eze 45:24; 46:5, 5, 7, 11, 14, 14,
15, 20

## GRAIN OFFERINGS Ex 40:29; Lev 2:13, 13;
23:18, 37; Nu 6:15; 29:6, 18, 21, 24, 27, 30, 33,
37, 39; Jos 22:23, 29; 1Ki 8:64, 64; 1Ch 23:29;
2Ch 7:7; Ezr 7:17; Ne 10:33; 13:5, 9; Isa 19:21;
43:23; 57:6; 66:20; Jer 14:12; 17:26; 33:18; 41:5;
Eze 42:13; 44:29; 45:15, 17, 17, 25; Joel 1:9, 13;
2:14; Am 5:22

## GRAINFIELDS [FIELD]
Lk 6: 1 Jesus was going through the **g**,

## GRAINS* [GRAIN]
Job 29:18 my days as numerous as the **g**
Ps 139:18 they would outnumber the **g**
Isa 48:19 your children like its numberless **g**;

## GRANDCHILDREN [CHILD]
Ex 10: 2 and **g** how I dealt harshly
1Ti 5: 4 But if a widow has children or **g**,

## GRANDMOTHER [MOTHER]
2Ti 1: 5 which first lived in your **g** Lois

## GRANT [GRANTED, GRANTS]
Lev 26: 6 " 'I will **g** peace in the land,
Dt 28:11 The LORD will **g** you abundant
Est 7: 3 and if it pleases you, **g** me my life—
Ps 20: 5 May the LORD **g** all your
 51:12 salvation and **g** me a willing spirit,
 85: 7 LORD, and **g** us your salvation.
 140: 8 Do not **g** the wicked their desires,
Ecc 6: 2 God does not **g** the ability to enjoy
Isa 46:13 I will **g** salvation to Zion,
Hag 2: 9 'And in this place I will **g** peace,'
Mk 10:40 at my right or left is not for me to **g**.

## GRANTED [GRANT]
1Sa 1:27 the LORD has **g** me what I asked
Est 7: 2 to half the kingdom, it will be **g**."
Ps 21: 6 Surely you have **g** him unending
Pr 10:24 what the righteous desire will be **g**.
Mt 15:28 Your request is **g**."
Ac 11:18 Gentiles God has **g** repentance
Php 1:29 For it has been **g** to you on behalf

## GRANTS* [GRANT]
Ps 127: 2  for he **g** sleep to those he loves.
147:14  He **g** peace to your borders

## GRAPE [GRAPES]
Nu   6: 3  They must not drink **g** juice or eat
Ob   1: 5  If **g** pickers came to you,

## GRAPES [GRAPE]
Lev 19:10  or pick up the **g** that have fallen.
Nu 13:23  branch bearing a single cluster of **g**.
Dt 32:32  Their **g** are filled with poison,
Isa   5: 2  he looked for a crop of good **g**,
Jer 31:29  'The parents have eaten sour **g**,
Eze 18: 2  " 'The parents eat sour **g**,
Mic   6:15  you will crush **g** but not drink
Hab   3:17  bud and there are no **g** on the vines,
Mt   7:16  Do people pick **g** from thornbushes,
Rev 14:18  earth's vine, because its **g** are ripe."

## GRASP [GRASPED, GRASPING]
Ecc   7:18  It is good to **g** the one and not let go
Jn 10:39  to seize him, but he escaped their **g**.

## GRASPED [GRASP]
Hos 12: 3  In the womb he **g** his brother's heel;

## GRASPING [GRASP]
Ge 25:26  out, with his hand **g** Esau's heel;

## GRASS
Ps 37: 2  for like the **g** they will soon wither,
103:15  their days are like **g**, they flourish
104:14  He makes **g** grow for the cattle,
Pr 19:12  but his favor is like dew on the **g**.
Isa 40: 6  "All people are like **g**, and all
Mt   6:30  that is how God clothes the **g**
1Pe   1:24  "All people are like **g**, and all their
1:24  the **g** withers and the flowers fall,
Rev   8: 7  and all the green **g** was burned up.

## GRASSHOPPERS
Nu 13:33  We seemed like **g** in our own eyes,
Isa 40:22  the earth, and its people are like **g**.

## GRATIFY* [GRATIFYING]
Ro 13:14  how to **g** the desires of the sinful
Gal   5:16  and you will not **g** the desires

## GRATIFYING* [GRATIFY]
Eph   2: 3  **g** the cravings of our sinful nature

## GRATITUDE
Col   3:16  to God with **g** in your hearts.

## GRAVE [GRAVES]
Nu 19:16  who touches a human bone or a **g**,
Dt 34: 6  day no one knows where his **g** is.
Ps   5: 9  Their throat is an open **g**;
6: 5  Who praises you from the **g**?
Pr   7:27  Her house is a highway to the **g**,
SS   8: 6  its jealousy unyielding as the **g**.
Hos 13:14  them from the power of the **g**;
13:14  Where, O **g**, is your destruction?

Jn 11:44  "Take off the **g** clothes and let him

## GRAVES [GRAVE]
Ex 14:11  "Was it because there were no **g**
Eze 37:12  I am going to open your **g** and bring
Mt 23:29  and decorate the **g** of the righteous.
Lk 11:44  because you are like unmarked **g**,
Jn   5:28  are in their **g** will hear his voice
Ro   3:13  "Their throats are open **g**;

## GRAY
Ps 71:18  Even when I am old and **g**, do not
Pr 16:31  **G** hair is a crown of splendor;
20:29  **g** hair the splendor of the old.

## GREAT [GREATER, GREATEST, GREATLY, GREATNESS]
Ge   1:16  God made two **g** lights—
6: 5  LORD saw how **g** the wickedness
12: 2  "I will make you into a **g** nation,
12: 2  I will make your name **g**, and you
15: 1  your shield, your very **g** reward."
15:18  the Wadi of Egypt to the **g** river,
46: 3  will make you into a **g** nation there.
Ex 32:10  I will make you into a **g** nation."
32:11  brought out of Egypt with **g** power
Nu 14:19  In accordance with your **g** love,
Dt   4:32  Has anything so **g** as this ever
7:21  you, is a **g** and awesome God.
10:17  gods and Lord of lords, the **g** God,
29:28  **g** wrath the LORD uprooted them
Jos   7: 9  will you do for your own **g** name?"
Jdg 16: 5  you the secret of his **g** strength
1Sa 18:14  everything he did he had **g** success,
2Sa   7: 9  Now I will make your name **g**,
7:22  "How **g** you are,
22:36  your help has made me **g**.
24:14  of the LORD, for his mercy is **g**;
1Ch 16:25  For **g** is the LORD and most
17:19  will, you have done this **g** thing
17:19  made known all these **g** promises.
Ne   1: 5  of heaven, the **g** and awesome God,
8: 6  praised the LORD, the **g** God;
Ps 18:35  your help has made me **g**.
19:11  in keeping them there is **g** reward.
25:11  forgive my iniquity, though it is **g**.
36: 6  your justice like the **g** deep.
40:16  always say, "The LORD is **g**!"
47: 2  the **g** King over all the earth.
48: 2  Mount Zion, the city of the **G** King.
57:10  For **g** is your love,
68:11  **g** was the company of those who
70: 4  always say, "The LORD is **g**!"
89: 1  sing of the LORD's **g** love forever;
95: 3  For the LORD is the **g** God, the **g**
103:11  so **g** is his love for those who fear
108: 4  For **g** is your love, higher than
117: 2  For **g** is his love toward us,
119:165  **G** peace have those who love your
145: 3  **G** is the LORD and most worthy
Pr 22: 1  is more desirable than **g** riches;
23:24  father of a righteous child has **g** joy;
Isa   1: 4  a people whose guilt is **g**,
42:21  his righteousness to make his law **g**
Jer 10: 6  you are **g**, and your name is mighty
27: 5  With my **g** power and outstretched

Jer 32:19 **g** are your purposes and mighty are
La 3:23 **g** is your faithfulness.
Eze 17: 3 A **g** eagle with powerful wings,
Da 2:45 "The **g** God has shown the king
7: 3 Four **g** beasts, each different
9: 4 "Lord, the **g** and awesome God,
Joel 2:11 The day of the LORD is **g**;
2:20 Surely he has done **g** things!
Na 1: 3 is slow to anger but **g** in power;
Zep 1:14 The **g** day of the LORD is near—
Mal 1:11 name will be **g** among the nations,
4: 5 prophet Elijah to you before that **g**
Mt 4:16 in darkness have seen a **g** light;
13:46 When he found one of **g** value,
20:26 become **g** among you must be your
Mk 13:26 Man coming in clouds with **g** power
Lk 2:10 I bring you good news of **g** joy
6:23 because **g** is your reward in heaven.
6:35 Then your reward will be **g**, and you
21:23 There will be **g** distress in the land
21:27 in a cloud with power and **g** glory.
Ac 8:10 is rightly called the **G** Power of God."
Eph 1:19 his incomparable **g** power for us
2: 4 But because of his **g** love for us,
1Ti 3:16 which true godliness springs is **g**:
6: 6 with contentment is **g** gain.
Tit 2:13 appearing of the glory of our **g** God
Heb 2: 3 if we ignore so **g** a salvation?
10:21 since we have a **g** priest over
12: 1 by such a **g** cloud of witnesses,
13:20 Jesus, that **g** Shepherd of the sheep,
1Pe 1: 3 In his **g** mercy he has given us new
1Jn 3: 1 See what **g** love the Father has
Jude 1: 6 chains for judgment on the **g** Day.
Rev 6:17 For the **g** day of their wrath has
7:14 have come out of the **g** tribulation;
12: 9 The **g** dragon was hurled down—
14: 8 Fallen is Babylon the **G**,'
16:14 for the battle on the **g** day of God
17: 1 the punishment of the **g** prostitute,
18:10 Woe to you, **g** city, you mighty city
20:11 I saw a **g** white throne and him who
21:21 The **g** street of the city was of gold,

**GREAT KING** 2Ki 18:19, 28; Ezr 5:11; Ps 47:2; 48:2; 95:3; Isa 36:4, 13; Hos 5:13; 10:6; Mal 1:14; Mt 5:35

## GREATER [GREAT]

Ge 1:16 the **g** light to govern the day
Ex 18:11 the LORD is **g** than all other gods,
2Ch 2: 5 because our God is **g** than all other
Mt 11:11 has not risen anyone **g** than John
11:11 the kingdom of heaven is **g** than he.
12: 6 that one **g** than the temple is here.
Mk 12:31 is no commandment **g** than these."
Lk 11:31 now one **g** than Solomon is here.
11:32 and now one **g** than Jonah is here.
Jn 1:50 You will see **g** things than that."
3:30 He must become **g**; I must become
14:12 will do even **g** things than these,
15:13 **G** love has no one than this:
1Co 12:31 Now eagerly desire the **g** gifts.
2Co 3:11 how much **g** is the glory
Heb 3: 3 worthy of **g** honor than Moses,
7: 7 doubt the lesser is blessed by the **g**.
11:26 as of **g** value than the treasures

1Pe 1: 7 of **g** worth than gold,
1Jn 3:20 know that God is **g** than our hearts,
4: 4 is in you is **g** than the one who is

## GREATEST [GREAT]

2Sa 7: 9 like the names of the **g** men
Mt 18: 4 is the **g** in the kingdom of heaven.
22:38 is the first and **g** commandment.
23:11 The **g** among you will be your
Lk 9:48 is least among you all is the **g**."
22:24 of them was considered to be **g**.
Jn 7:37 On the last and **g** day of the festival,
1Co 13:13 But the **g** of these is love.

## GREATLY [GREAT]

2Ch 33:12 humbled himself **g** before the God
Ezr 10:13 because we have sinned **g** in this
Ps 47: 9 earth belong to God; he is **g** exalted.
Isa 61:10 I delight **g** in the LORD;
Jnh 1:16 this the men **g** feared the LORD,

## GREATNESS* [GREAT]

Ex 15: 7 "In the **g** of your majesty you threw
Dt 3:24 to show to your servant your **g**
32: 3 Oh, praise the **g** of our God!
1Ch 29:11 is the **g** and the power and the glory
2Ch 9: 6 not even half the **g** of your wisdom
Est 10: 2 a full account of the **g** of Mordecai
Ps 145: 3 his **g** no one can fathom.
150: 2 praise him for his surpassing **g**.
Isa 63: 1 forward in the **g** of his strength?
Eze 38:23 And so I will show my **g** and my
Da 4:22 your **g** has grown until it reaches
5:18 Nebuchadnezzar sovereignty and **g**
7:27 **g** of all the kingdoms under heaven
Mic 5: 4 his **g** will reach to the ends
Lk 9:43 were all amazed at the **g** of God.

## GREECE [GREEK, GREEKS]

Da 8:21 The shaggy goat is the king of **G**,
10:20 I go, the prince of **G** will come;

## GREED [GREEDY]

Mk 7:22 adultery, **g**, malice, deceit,
Lk 12:15 on your guard against all kinds of **g**;
Ro 1:29 wickedness, evil, **g** and depravity.
Eph 4:19 and they are full of **g**.
5: 3 or of **g**, because these are improper
Col 3: 5 evil desires and **g**, which is idolatry.
2Pe 2: 3 In their **g** these teachers will exploit
2:14 they are experts in **g**—

## GREEDY [GREED]

Pr 15:27 The **g** bring ruin to their
28:25 The **g** stir up dissension, but those
Eze 33:31 but their hearts are **g** for unjust gain.
1Co 5:11 but are sexually immoral or **g**,
6:10 thieves nor the **g** nor drunkards nor
Eph 5: 5 No immoral, impure or **g** person—

## GREEK [GREECE]

Jn 19:20 written in Aramaic, Latin and **G**.
Ac 16: 1 a believer but whose father was a **G**.
17:12 **G** women and many **G** men.
21:37 "Do you speak **G**?" he replied.

## GREEKS [GREECE]
Jn 12:20 there were some **G** among those
Ac 14: 1 great number of Jews and **G** believed.
     18: 4 trying to persuade Jews and **G**.
     20:21 and **G** that they must turn to God
1Co 1:22 signs and **G** look for wisdom,

## GREEN
Ge 1:30 I give every **g** plant for food."
     9: 3 Just as I gave you the **g** plants,
Ps 23: 2 makes me lie down in **g** pastures,
Jer 17: 8 its leaves are always **g**.
Mk 6:39 sit down in groups on the **g** grass.

## GREET [GREETED, GREETING, GREETINGS]
Mt 5:47 And if you **g** only your own people,
1Co 16:20 **G** one another with a holy kiss.

## GREETED [GREET]
Mt 23: 7 they love to be **g** with respect

## GREETING [GREET]
Lk 1:29 what kind of **g** this might be.
1Co 16:21 I, Paul, write this **g** in my own hand.
Col 4:18 I, Paul, write this **g** in my own hand.
2Th 3:17 I, Paul, write this **g** in my own hand,

## GREETINGS [GREET]
Mt 26:49 to Jesus, Judas said, "**G**, Rabbi!"
Lk 1:28 The angel went to her and said, "**G**,

## GREW [GROW]
Ge 21:20 God was with the boy as he **g** up.
Jdg 13:24 He **g** and the LORD blessed him,
1Sa 2:21 the boy Samuel **g** up in the presence
     3:19 was with Samuel as he **g** up, and he
2Sa 3: 1 David **g** stronger and stronger,
     3: 1 while the house of Saul **g** weaker
Isa 53: 2 He **g** up before him like a tender
Lk 1:80 the child **g** and became strong
     2:40 And the child **g** and became strong;
     2:52 And as Jesus **g** up, he increased
     13:19 It **g** and became a tree, and the birds
Ac 16: 5 in the faith and **g** daily in numbers.

## GRIEF [GRIEFS, GRIEVANCE, GRIEVE, GRIEVED, GRIEVES, GRIEVOUS]
Ps 10:14 you consider their **g** and take it
Pr 10: 1 but foolish children bring **g** to their
     14:13 ache, and rejoicing may end in **g**.
     17:21 To have a fool for a child brings **g**;
Ecc 1:18 the more knowledge, the more **g**.
La 3:32 Though he brings **g**, he will show
Jn 16:20 grieve, but your **g** will turn to joy.
1Pe 1: 6 may have had to suffer **g** in all kinds

## GRIEFS* [GRIEF]
1Ti 6:10 pierced themselves with many **g**.

## GRIEVANCE* [GRIEF]
Job 31:13 they had a **g** against me,

Ac 19:38 Demetrius and his associates have a **g**
Col 3:13 of you has a **g** against someone.

## GRIEVE [GRIEF]
2Sa 1:26 I **g** for you, Jonathan my brother;
Eph 4:30 do not **g** the Holy Spirit of God,
1Th 4:13 so that you do not **g** like the rest,

## GRIEVED [GRIEF]
Isa 63:10 they rebelled and **g** his Holy Spirit.

## GRIEVES* [GRIEF]
Zec 12:10 for him as one **g** for a firstborn son.

## GRIEVOUS [GRIEF]
Ge 18:20 is so great and their sin so **g**
Ecc 5:13 I have seen a **g** evil under the sun:
Jer 15:18 and my wound **g** and incurable?

## GRIND [GRINDING]
Job 31:10 may my wife **g** another man's grain,

## GRINDING [GRIND]
Jdg 16:21 they set him to **g** grain in the prison.
Lk 17:35 women will be **g** grain together;

## GROAN [GROANED, GROANING, GROANS]
Pr 29: 2 when the wicked rule, the people **g**.
Ro 8:23 **g** inwardly as we wait eagerly
2Co 5: 2 Meanwhile we **g**, longing to be
     5: 4 in this tent, we **g** and are burdened,

## GROANED* [GROAN]
Ex 2:23 The Israelites **g** in their slavery
Ps 77: 3 I remembered you, God, and I **g**;

## GROANING [GROAN]
Ex 2:24 God heard their **g** and he
     6: 5 I have heard the **g** of the Israelites,
Jdg 2:18 LORD relented because of their **g**
Ps 22: 1 me, so far from the words of my **g**?
Eze 21: 7 they ask you, 'Why are you **g**?'
Ro 8:22 the whole creation has been **g** as

## GROANS [GROAN]
Ro 8:26 for us through wordless **g**.

## GROPE
Dt 28:29 midday you will **g** about like a blind
La 4:14 Now they **g** through the streets as

## GROUND [GROUNDS]
Ge 1:10 God called the dry **g** "land,"
     2: 7 formed a man from the dust of the **g**
     3:17 it,' "Cursed is the **g** because of you;
     4:10 blood cries out to me from the **g**.
Ex 3: 5 where you are standing is holy **g**."
     15:19 walked through the sea on dry **g**.
Jos 3:17 of the Jordan and stood on dry **g**,
     3:17 completed the crossing on dry **g**.
Jdg 6:37 on the fleece and all the **g** is dry,
1Sa 5: 3 his face on the **g** before the ark

2Ki   2: 8  two of them crossed over on dry **g**.
Job   3:16  away in the **g** like a stillborn child,
Ps   26:12  My feet stand on level **g**;
     73:18  you place them on slippery **g**;
    143:10  your good Spirit lead me on level **g**.
    147: 6  but casts the wicked to the **g**.
Ecc  12: 7  dust returns to the **g** it came from,
Isa  53: 2  shoot, and like a root out of dry **g**.
Ob   1: 3  'Who can bring me down to the **g**?'
Mt   10:29  to the **g** outside your Father's care.
     25:25  went out and hid your gold in the **g**.
Lk   22:44  like drops of blood falling to the **g**.
Jn    8: 6  *to write on the **g** with his finger.*
     12:24  a kernel of wheat falls to the **g**
Eph   6:13  you may be able to stand your **g**,

## GROUNDS [GROUND]
Da    6: 4  to find **g** for charges against Daniel
Lk   23:22  in him no **g** for the death penalty.

## GROUP [GROUPS]
Nu   16: 3  They came as a **g** to oppose Moses

## GROUPS [GROUP]
Mk    6:39  have all the people sit down in **g**

## GROVE* [GROVES]
Ex   23:11  with your vineyard and your olive **g**.
SS    6:11  I went down to the **g** of nut trees to look

## GROVES [GROVE]
Dt    6:11  and olive **g** you did not plant—

## GROW [FULL-GROWN, GREW, GROWING, GROWN, GROWS]
Ge    2: 9  God made all kinds of trees **g**
Nu    6: 5  they must let their hair **g** long.
Jdg  16:22  on his head began to **g** again after it
1Sa   2:26  the boy Samuel continued to **g**
Ps   92:12  they will **g** like a cedar of Lebanon;
Pr   13:11  money little by little makes it **g**.
     20:13  not love sleep or you will **g** poor;
Isa  40:31  they will run and not **g** weary,
Eze  47:12  of all kinds will **g** on both banks
Jnh   4:10  you did not tend it or make it **g**.
Mt    6:28  See how the flowers of the field **g**.
1Co   3: 6  it, but God has been making it **g**.
2Co  10:15  as your faith continues to **g**,
1Pe   2: 2  so that by it you may **g** up in your
2Pe   3:18  But **g** in the grace and knowledge

## GROWING [GROW]
Lk   13: 6  fig tree **g** in his vineyard,
Col   1: 6  and **g** throughout the whole world—
      1:10  work, **g** in the knowledge of God,
2Th   1: 3  so, because your faith is **g** more

## GROWN [GROW]
Ex    2:11  after Moses had **g** up, he went
2Ch  10:10  The young men who had **g**
Heb  11:24  when he had **g** up, refused to be

## GROWS [GROW]
Ps  142: 3  When my spirit **g** faint within me,

Mk    4:32  it **g** and becomes the largest of all
Eph   4:16  **g** and builds itself up in love,
Col   2:19  sinews, **g** as God causes it to grow.
Heb  12:15  and that no bitter root **g** up to cause

## GRUDGE* [GRUDGING, GRUDGINGLY]
Ge   27:41  Esau held a **g** against Jacob because
     50:15  if Joseph holds a **g** against us
Lev  19:18  bear a **g** against anyone among your
Mk    6:19  So Herodias nursed a **g** against John

## GRUDGING* [GRUDGE]
Dt   15:10  to them and do so without a **g** heart;

## GRUDGINGLY* [GRUDGE]
2Co   9: 5  a generous gift, not as one **g** given.

## GRUMBLE [GRUMBLED, GRUMBLERS, GRUMBLING]
Ex   16: 7  we, that you should **g** against us?"
Nu   14:27  wicked community **g** against me?
     16:11  that you should **g** against him?"
1Co  10:10  And do not **g**, as some of them did—
Jas   5: 9  Don't **g** against one another,

## GRUMBLED [GRUMBLE]
Ex   15:24  So the people **g** against Moses,
     16: 2  whole community **g** against Moses
     17: 3  there, and they **g** against Moses.
Nu   14: 2  All the Israelites **g** against Moses
     16:41  whole Israelite community **g** against
Ps  106:25  They **g** in their tents and did not

## GRUMBLERS* [GRUMBLE]
Jude  1:16  These people are **g** and faultfinders;

## GRUMBLING [GRUMBLE]
Ex   16: 7  he has heard your **g** against him.
Nu   14:27  the complaints of these **g** Israelites.
     17: 5  of this constant **g** against you
Jn    6:43  "Stop **g** among yourselves,"
Php   2:14  Do everything without **g** or arguing,
1Pe   4: 9  hospitality to one another without **g**.

## GUARANTEE* [GUARANTEED, GUARANTEEING, GUARANTOR]
Ge   43: 9  I myself will **g** his safety;

## GUARANTEED* [GUARANTEE]
Ge   44:32  Your servant **g** the boy's safety
Ro    4:16  and may be **g** to all Abraham's

## GUARANTEEING* [GUARANTEE]
2Co   1:22  as a deposit, **g** what is to come.
      5: 5  as a deposit, **g** what is to come.
Eph   1:14  is a deposit **g** our inheritance until

## GUARANTOR* [GUARANTEE]
Heb   7:22  Jesus has become the **g** of a better
            covenant.

## GUARD [GUARDED, GUARDIAN, GUARDIANS, GUARDING, GUARDS, SAFEGUARD]

Ge  3:24  forth to **g** the way to the tree of life.
1Sa  2: 9  He will **g** the feet of his faithful
     26:15  Why didn't you **g** your lord
Ne  4: 9  posted a **g** day and night to meet
Ps  25:20  **G** my life and rescue me; do not let
     91:11  his angels concerning you to **g** you
    141: 3  Set a **g** over my mouth, Lᴏʀᴅ,
Pr  2:11  you, and understanding will **g** you.
     4:13  let it go; **g** it well, for it is your life.
     4:23  Above all else, **g** your heart,
     7: 2  **g** my teachings as the apple of your
    13: 3  who **g** their lips preserve their lives,
    21:23  Those who **g** their mouths
Isa 52:12  God of Israel will be your rear **g**.
Mal 2:15  So be on your **g**, and do not be
Mt  27:66  seal on the stone and posting the **g**.
Mk  13:33  Be on **g**! Be alert! You do not know
Lk  4:10  concerning you to **g** you carefully;
     12: 1  "Be on your **g** against the yeast
    12:15  Be on your **g** against all kinds
Ac  20:31  So be on your **g**!
1Co 16:13  Be on your **g**; stand firm
Php  4: 7  will **g** your hearts and your minds
1Ti  6:20  **g** what has been entrusted to your
2Ti  1:12  he is able to **g** what I have entrusted
     1:14  **g** it with the help of the Holy Spirit
2Pe  3:17  be on your **g** so that you may not be

## GUARDED [GUARD]

Dt  32:10  he **g** him as the apple of his eye,
    33: 9  your word and **g** your covenant.
Eze 44:15  who **g** my sanctuary when the Israelites

## GUARDIAN [GUARD]

Eze 28:14  You were anointed as a **g** cherub,

## GUARDIANS [GUARD]

1Co  4:15  if you had ten thousand **g** in Christ,
Gal  4: 2  They are subject to **g** and trustees

## GUARDING [GUARD]

Lk  22:63  The men who were **g** Jesus began

## GUARDS [GUARD]

Ne  4:22  so they can serve us as **g** by night
Ps  97:10  for he **g** the lives of his faithful ones
Mt  28: 4  The **g** were so afraid of him

## GUEST [GUESTS]

Mk  14:14  Where is my **g** room, where I may
Lk  19: 7  has gone to be the **g** of a sinner."

## GUESTS [GUEST]

Pr  9:18  that her **g** are deep in the realm
Mt  9:15  "How can the **g** of the bridegroom
Lk  14: 7  noticed how the **g** picked the places

## GUIDANCE [GUIDE]

1Ch 10:13  and even consulted a medium for **g**,
Pr  1: 5  and let the discerning get **g**—
    11:14  For lack of **g** a nation falls,

---

Hab  2:19  Can it give **g**? It is covered

## GUIDE [GUIDANCE, GUIDED, GUIDES]

Ex  13:21  of cloud to **g** them on their way
    15:13  In your strength you will **g** them
Ne  9:19  of cloud did not cease to **g** them
Ps  25: 5  **G** me in your truth and teach me,
    48:14  he will be our **g** even to the end.
    67· 4  equity and **g** the nations of the earth.
    73:24  You **g** me with your counsel,
   139:10  even there your hand will **g** me,
Pr  6:22  When you walk, they will **g** you;
Isa  9:16  Those who **g** this people mislead
    58:11  The Lᴏʀᴅ will **g** you always;
Lk  1:79  death, to **g** our feet into the path
Jn  16:13  he will **g** you into all the truth.

## GUIDED [GUIDE]

Job 31:18  and from my birth I **g** the widow—
Ps 107:30  he **g** them to their desired haven.

## GUIDES* [GUIDE]

Ps  23: 3  He **g** me along the right paths
    25: 9  He **g** the humble in what is right
Pr  11: 3  The integrity of the upright **g** them,
Isa  3:12  My people, your **g** lead you astray;
Mt  15:14  Leave them; they are blind **g**.
    23:16  "Woe to you, blind **g**! You say,
    23:24  You blind **g**! You strain out a gnat

## GUILT [BLOODGUILT, GUILTLESS, GUILTY]

Ge  44:16  God has uncovered your servants' **g**.
Lev  5:15  It is a **g** offering.
1Sa  6: 4  "What **g** offering should we send
Ezr  9: 6  our **g** has reached to the heavens.
Ps  32: 5  And you forgave the **g** of my sin.
    38: 4  My **g** has overwhelmed me like
Isa  1: 4  a people whose **g** is great, a brood
    6: 7  your **g** is taken away and your sin
Jer  2:22  stain of your **g** is still before me,"
Eze 18:19  'Why does the son not share the **g**
Hos  5:15  my lair until they have borne their **g**
Jn  9:41  claim you can see, your **g** remains.

## GUILT OFFERING
Lev 5:15, 16, 18, 19; 6:5, 6, 17; 7:1, 2, 5, 7, 37; 14:12, 13, 14, 17, 21, 24, 25, 28; 19:21, 22; Nu 6:12; 1Sa 6:3, 4, 8, 17; Ezr 10:19; Eze 46:20

## GUILT OFFERINGS
Nu 18:9; 2Ki 12:16; Eze 40:39; 42:13; 44:29

## GUILTLESS [GUILT]

Ex  20: 7  not hold anyone **g** who misuses his

## GUILTY [GUILT]

Ex  23: 1  Do not help a **g** person
    23: 7  to death, for I will not acquit the **g**.
    34· 7  he does not leave the **g** unpunished;
Nu  14:18  he does not leave the **g** unpunished;
Job 10: 2  Do not declare me **g**,
Pr  21: 8  The way of the **g** is devious,
Isa  5:23  who acquit the **g** for a bribe,

Na    1: 3   will not leave the **g** unpunished.
Mk    3:29   forgiven, but is **g** of an eternal sin."
Jn    8:46   Can any of you prove me **g** of sin?
      19:11   over to you is **g** of a greater sin."
1Co  11:27   in an unworthy manner will be **g**
Heb  10: 2   would no longer have felt **g** for their
      10:22   to cleanse us from a **g** conscience
Jas   2:10   at just one point is **g** of breaking all

## GULLIBLE*

2Ti   3: 6   gain control over **g** women,

## GULP*

Pr   21:20   but fools **g** theirs down.

## GUSH* [GUSHED, GUSHES]

Isa   35: 6   Water will **g** forth in the wilderness

## GUSHED* [GUSH]

Nu   20:11   Water **g** out, and the community
Ps   78:20   and water **g** out, streams flowed
     105:41   opened the rock, and water **g** out;
Isa   48:21   he split the rock and water **g** out.

## GUSHES* [GUSH]

Pr   15: 2   but the mouth of the fool **g** folly.
      15:28   but the mouth of the wicked **g** evil.

---

# H

---

## HABAKKUK*

Prophet to Judah (Hab 1:1; 3:1).

## HABIT

Nu   22:30   Have I been in the **h** of doing this
1Ti    5:13   they get into the **h** of being idle
Heb  10:25   as some are in the **h** of doing,

## HAD [HAVE]

Ge   11: 1   the whole world **h** one language
Ex   36: 7   what they already **h** was more than
Nu   11: 4   and said, "If only we **h** meat to eat!
Jdg   1:19   because they **h** chariots fitted
1Sa   2:12   they **h** no regard for the LORD.
2Sa  12: 3   the poor man **h** nothing except one
2Ch  26:21   King Uzziah **h** leprosy until the day
Job  28:17   it, nor can it be **h** for jewels of gold.
      42:10   After Job **h** prayed for his friends,
Ps   55: 6   "Oh, that I **h** the wings of a dove!
Isa    5: 1   My loved one **h** a vineyard
      53: 2   He **h** no beauty or majesty to attract
Eze    1: 6   each of them **h** four faces and four
      10:14   Each of the cherubim **h** four faces:
      41:18   Each cherub **h** two faces:
Mt    7:29   he taught as one who **h** authority,
      13:44   sold all he **h** and bought that field.
      13:46   sold everything he **h** and bought it.
Mk    4: 6   withered because they **h** no root.
      10:22   sad, because he **h** great wealth.
Jn   20: 9   Scripture that Jesus **h** to rise
Ac    1:16   the Scripture **h** to be fulfilled

Ac    2:13   "They have **h** too much wine."
      2:45   to give to anyone who **h** need.
      13:46   "We **h** to speak the word of God
      14: 9   him, saw that he **h** faith to be healed
      17: 3   proving that the Messiah **h** to suffer
Ro    4:21   **h** power to do what he **h** promised.
2Co   5:21   God made him who **h** no sin to be
Rev   4: 8   the four living creatures **h** six wings
      5: 6   a Lamb, looking as if it **h** been slain,
      13: 1   It **h** ten horns and seven heads,
      13: 3   seemed to have **h** a fatal wound,
      13: 3   but the fatal wound **h** been healed.
      14: 1   with him 144,000 who **h** his name

## HADAD [BEN-HADAD]

Edomite adversary of Solomon (1Ki 11:14–25).

## HADADEZER

2Sa   8: 3   David defeated **H** son of Rehob,

## HADASSAH* [ESTHER]

Est    2: 7   Mordecai had a cousin named **H**,

## HADES*

Lk   16:23   In **H**, where he was in torment,
Rev   1:18   And I hold the keys of death and **H**.
      6: 8   **H** was following close behind him.
      20:13   and **H** gave up the dead that were
      20:14   **H** were thrown into the lake of fire.

## HAGAR*

Servant of Sarah, wife of Abraham, mother of Ishmael (Ge 16:1–6; 25:12). Driven away by Sarah
while pregnant (Ge 16:5–16); after birth of Isaac (Ge
21:9–21; Gal 4:21–31).

## HAGGAI*

Post-exilic prophet who encouraged rebuilding of
the temple (Ezr 5:1; 6:14; Hag 1–2).

## HAGGITH

1Ki   1: 5   whose mother was **H**, put himself

## HAIL [HAILSTONES]

Ex    9:19   because the **h** will fall on every
      9:26   only place it did not **h** was the land
Ps   78:47   He destroyed their vines with **h**
     147:17   He hurls down his **h** like pebbles.
Jn   19: 3   saying, "**H**, king of the Jews!"
Rev   8: 7   there came **h** and fire mixed
      16:21   God on account of the plague of **h**,

## HAILSTONES [HAIL]

Jos   10:11   the LORD hurled large **h** down
Eze  13:11   and I will send **h** hurtling down,
Rev  16:21   From the sky huge **h**, each weighing

## HAIR [HAIRS, HAIRSTYLES, HAIRY]

Ex   26: 7   of goat **h** for the tent over
Lev  19:27   " 'Do not cut the **h** at the sides
Nu    6: 5   they must let their **h** grow long.
Jdg  16:19   shave off the seven braids of his **h**,
      16:22   But the **h** on his head began to grow
      20:16   of whom could sling a stone at a **h**

2Sa 14:26 Whenever he cut the **h** of his head—
    18: 9 Absalom's **h** got caught in the tree.
2Ki  1: 8 "He had a garment of **h** and had
Pr  16:31 Gray **h** is a crown of splendor;
    20:29 gray **h** the splendor of the old.
SS   7: 5 Your **h** is like royal tapestry;
Isa  3:24 instead of well-dressed **h**, baldness;
Eze  8: 3 and took me by the **h** of my head.
Da   4:33 of heaven until his **h** grew like
     7: 9 the **h** of his head was white like
Mt   3: 4 clothes were made of camel's **h**,
Lk   7:44 her tears and wiped them with her **h**.
    21:18 But not a **h** of your head will perish.
Jn  11: 2 Lord and wiped his feet with her **h**.)
    12: 3 feet and wiped his feet with her **h**.
1Co 11: 6 she might as well have her **h** cut off;
    11:14 teach you that if a man has long **h**,
    11:15 but that if a woman has long **h**, it is
Rev  1:14 The **h** on his head was white like

## HAIRS [HAIR]
Ps  40:12 They are more than the **h** of my
Mt  10:30 even the very **h** of your head are all
Lk  12: 7 the very **h** of your head are all

## HAIRSTYLES* [HAIR]
1Ti  2: 9 not with elaborate **h**
1Pe  3: 3 such as elaborate **h**

## HAIRY [HAIR]
Ge  27:11 brother Esau is a **h** man while I have

## HALAH
2Ki 18:11 to Assyria and settled them in **H**,

## HALF [HALF-TRIBE, HALVES]
Ge  15:10 birds, however, he did not cut in **h**.
Ex  24: 6 Moses took **h** of the blood and put it
    30:13 This **h** shekel is an offering
Nu  34:13 it be given to the nine and a **h** tribes,
Jos  8:33 **H** of the people stood in front
2Sa 10: 4 shaved off **h** of each man's beard,
1Ki  3:25 give **h** to one and **h** to the other."
    10: 7 Indeed, not even **h** was told me;
Ne   4:16 day on, **h** of my men did the work,
    13:24 **H** of their children spoke
Est  5: 3 Even up to **h** the kingdom, it will be
Isa 44:19 to say, "**H** of it I used for fuel;
Eze 16:51 did not commit **h** the sins you did.
Da   7:25 hands for a time, times and **h** a time.
    12: 7 be for a time, times and **h** a time.
Mk   6:23 give you, up to **h** my kingdom."
Lk  19: 8 now I give **h** of my possessions
Rev  8: 1 in heaven for about **h** an hour.
    11:11 a **h** days the breath of life from God
    12:14 time, times and **h** a time,

## HALF-TRIBE [HALF, TRIBE]
Nu  32:33 the **h** of Manasseh son of Joseph
Jos  4:12 and the **h** of Manasseh crossed over,

## HALL
1Ki  7: 7 He built the throne **h**, the **H**
SS   2: 4 Let him lead me to the banquet **h**,
Eze 41: 1 brought me to the main **h**

Da   5:10 his nobles, came into the banquet **h**.
Mt  22:10 and the wedding **h** was filled
Ac  19: 9 daily in the lecture **h** of Tyrannus.

## HALLELUJAH* [See also PRAISE THE †LORD]
Rev 19: 1 multitude in heaven shouting: "**H**!
    19: 3 And again they shouted: "**H**!
    19: 4 And they cried: "Amen, **H**!"
    19: 6 peals of thunder, shouting: "**H**!

## HALLOW, HALLOWED (KJV) See CONSECRATE, CONSECRATED, HOLY, SACRED, SET [APART]

## HALLOWED* [HOLY]
Mt   6: 9 Father in heaven, **h** be your name,
Lk  11: 2 " 'Father, **h** be your name,

## HALT
Job 38:11 here is where your proud waves **h**'?

## HALVES [HALF]
Ge  15:10 arranged the **h** opposite each other;

## HAM
Son of Noah (Ge 5:32; 1Ch 1:4), father of Canaan (Ge 9:18; 10:6–20; 1Ch 1:8–16). Saw Noah's nakedness (Ge 9:20–27).

## HAMAN
Agagite nobleman honored by Xerxes (Est 3:1–2). Plotted to exterminate the Jews because of Mordecai (Est 3:3–15). Forced to honor Mordecai (Est 5–6). Plot exposed by Esther (Est 5:1–8; 7:1–8). Hanged (Est 7:9–10).

## HAMATH [LEBO HAMATH]
2Sa  8: 9 Tou king of **H** heard that David had
2Ki 14:28 for Israel both Damascus and **H**,
    18:34 Where are the gods of **H**

## HAMMER [HAMMERED]
Ex  25:31 **H** out its base and shaft, and make
Nu  16:38 **H** the censers into sheets to overlay
Jdg  4:21 a **h** and went quietly to him while he
Jer 10: 4 they fasten it with **h** and nails so it

## HAMMERED [HAMMER]
Ex  25:18 cherubim out of **h** gold at the ends
2Ch  9:15 two hundred large shields of **h** gold;
     9:16 hundred small shields of **h** gold,

## HAMOR
Ge  34: 2 When Shechem son of **H** the Hivite,

## HAMPERED*
Pr   4:12 you walk, your steps will not be **h**;

## HAMSTRING* [HAMSTRUNG]
Jos 11: 6 You are to **h** their horses and burn

## HAMSTRUNG [HAMSTRING]

Jos  11: 9  He **h** their horses and burned their
1Ch 18: 4  He **h** all but a hundred of the chariot

## HANAMEL

Jer  32: 7  **H** son of Shallum your uncle is

## HANANEL

Ne   3: 1  and as far as the Tower of **H**.
Jer  31:38  the Tower of **H** to the Corner Gate.

## HANANI

Ne   7: 2  charge of Jerusalem my brother **H**,

## HANANIAH [SHADRACH]

1. False prophet; adversary of Jeremiah (Jer 28).
2. Original name of Shadrach (Da 1:6–19; 2:17).

## HAND [EMPTY-HANDED, HANDED, HANDFUL, HANDIWORK, HANDS, LEFT-HANDED, OPENHANDED, RIGHT-HANDED]

Ge   3:22  not be allowed to reach out his **h**
      4:11  your brother's blood from your **h**.
     14:12  raised **h** I have sworn an oath
     16:12  his **h** will be against everyone
     22:12  "Do not lay a **h** on the boy,"
     24: 2  he had, "Put your **h** under my thigh.
     25:26  out, with his **h** grasping Esau's heel;
     37:22  but don't lay a **h** on him."
     47:29  eyes, put your **h** under my thigh
     48:14  Israel reached out his right **h**
Ex   3:19  go unless a mighty **h** compels him.
      4: 6  "Put your **h** inside your cloak."
      6: 1  of my mighty **h** he will let them go;
     13: 3  you out of it with a mighty **h**.
     15: 6  Your right **h**, LORD, was majestic
     21:24  tooth for tooth, **h** for **h**, foot for foot,
     33:22  with my **h** until I have passed by.
Lev   1: 4  You are to lay your **h** on the head
      3: 2  You are to lay your **h** on the head
      4: 4  He is to lay his **h** on its head
Nu   14:30  with uplifted **h** to make your home,
Dt    3:24  your greatness and your strong **h**.
      4:34  by a mighty **h** and an outstretched
     12: 7  everything you have put your **h** to,
     19:21  tooth for tooth, **h** for **h**, foot for foot.
     32:39  and no one can deliver out of my **h**.
Jos   8: 7  your God will give it into your **h**.
Jdg   2:15  the **h** of the LORD was against
1Sa  17:50  his **h** he struck down the Philistine
     24:10  'I will not lay my **h** on my lord,
     26: 9  Who can lay a **h** on the LORD's
2Sa   1:14  lift your **h** to destroy the LORD's
     18:12  I would not lay a **h** on the king's
1Ki   8:24  with your **h** you have fulfilled it—
      8:42  your mighty **h** and your outstretched
     13: 4  the **h** he stretched out toward
     18:44  cloud as small as a man's **h** is rising
1Ch  21:17  let your **h** fall on me and my family,
     29:14  you only what comes from your **h**.
     29:16  Holy Name comes from your **h**,
2Ch   6:15  with your **h** you have fulfilled it—
     32:15  your god deliver you from my **h**!"

2Ch  32:22  from the **h** of Sennacherib king
Ezr   7: 9  for the gracious **h** of his God was
Ne    2: 8  because the gracious **h** of my God
      4:17  materials did their work with one **h**
Job  40: 4  I put my **h** over my mouth.
Ps   10:12  Lift up your **h**, O God.
     16: 8  With him at my right **h**, I will not be
     32: 4  and night your **h** was heavy on me;
     37:24  LORD upholds them with his **h**.
     44: 3  it was your right **h**, your arm,
     45: 9  at your right **h** is the royal bride
     63: 8  your right **h** upholds me.
     74:11  you hold back your **h**, your right **h**?
     75: 8  In the **h** of the LORD is a cup full
Ps   80:17  your **h** rest on the man at your right **h**,
     91: 7  ten thousand at your right **h**, but it
     95: 4  In his **h** are the depths of the earth,
     98: 1  his right **h** and his holy arm have
    109:31  he stands at the right **h** of the needy,
    110: 1  "Sit at my right **h** until I make your
    137: 5  may my right **h** forget its skill.
    139:10  even there your **h** will guide me,
    145:16  You open your **h** and satisfy
Pr    3:16  Long life is in her right **h**; in her left
             **h** are riches and honor.
     21: 1  the LORD's **h** the king's heart is
     27:16  the wind or grasping oil with the **h**.
Ecc   2:24  This too, I see, is from the **h** of God,
      9:10  Whatever your **h** finds to do, do it
Isa   1:25  I will turn my **h** against you;
      5:25  his **h** is still upraised.
     40:12  the waters in the hollow of his **h**,
     41:13  God who takes hold of your right **h**
     44: 5  still others will write on their **h**,
     48:13  My own **h** laid the foundations
     53:10  of the LORD will prosper in his **h**.
     64: 8  we are all the work of your **h**.
Jer  22:24  were a signet ring on my right **h**,
     31:32  I took them by the **h** to lead them
     51: 7  was a gold cup in the LORD's **h**;
La    3: 3  he has turned his **h** against me again
Eze   1: 3  There the **h** of the LORD was
      2: 9  and I saw a **h** stretched out to me.
     20: 5  With uplifted **h** I said to them,
Da    3:17  furnace and from Your Majesty's **h**.
      5: 5  the fingers of a human **h** appeared
     10:10  A **h** touched me and set me
Am    7: 7  to plumb, with a plumb line in his **h**.
Jnh   4:11  people who cannot tell their right **h**
Hab   2:16  the LORD's right **h** is coming
      3: 4  rays flashed from his **h**, where his
Mt    3:12  His winnowing fork is in his **h**,
      5:30  And if your right **h** causes you
      6: 3  not let your left **h** know what your right
             **h** is doing,
     12:10  a man with a shriveled **h** was there.
     18: 8  If your **h** or your foot causes you
     22:44  my right **h** until I put your enemies
     26:64  at the right **h** of the Mighty One
Mk    1:31  to her, took her **h** and helped her up.
      3: 1  a man with a shriveled **h** was there.
      5:41  He took her by the **h** and said to her,
      9:43  If your **h** causes you to stumble,
     12:36  my right **h** until I put your enemies
     14:62  at the right **h** of the Mighty One
Lk    5:13  Jesus reached out his **h** and touched
      9:62  "No one who puts a **h** to the plow

Lk 20:42 said to my Lord: "Sit at my right **h**
22:69 at the right **h** of the mighty God."
Jn 7:30 but no one laid a **h** on him,
10:28 one will snatch them out of my **h**.
20:27 Reach out your **h** and put it into my
Ac 2:34 said to my Lord: "Sit at my right **h**
7:55 Jesus standing at the right **h** of God.
Ro 8:34 is at the right **h** of God and is
1Co 12:15 say, "Because I am not a **h**, I do not
Eph 1:20 at his right **h** in the heavenly realms,
Col 3: 1 is seated at the right **h** of God.
Heb 1:13 "Sit at my right **h** until I make your
8: 1 sat down at the right **h** of the throne
10:12 he sat down at the right **h** of God,
1Pe 3:22 into heaven and is at God's right **h**—
Rev 1:16 In his right **h** he held seven stars,
5: 1 I saw in the right **h** of him who sat

**HAND OF GOD** 2Ch 30:12; Job 19:21; Ecc
2:24; Mk 16:19; Ac 2:33; 7:55, 56; Ro 8:34; Col
3:1; Heb 10:12

**HAND OF THE †LORD** Ex 9:3; Jos 4:24;
Jdg 2:15; 1Sa 7:13; 2Ki 3:15; Ezr 7:6, 28; Job
12:9; Ps 75:8; Isa 25:10; 41:20; 51:17; 66:14;
Eze 1:3; 3:14, 22; 33:22; 37:1; 40:1

**MIGHTY HAND** Ex 3:19; 6:1, 1; 13:3, 9, 14,
16; 32:11; Dt 4:34; 5:15; 6:21; 7:8, 19; 9:26;
11:2; 26:8; 1Ki 8:42; 2Ch 6:32; Ne 1:10; Ps
136:12; Jer 32:21; Eze 20:33, 34; Da 9:15; 1Pe
5:6

**RIGHT HAND** Ge 48:13, 14, 17, 18; Ex 15:6,
6, 12; Lev 8:23; 14:14, 17, 25, 28; Jdg 5:26;
16:29; 2Sa 20:9; 1Ki 2:19; 1Ch 6:39; Job 40:14;
Ps 16:8, 11; 17:7; 18:35; 20:6; 21:8; 44:3; 45:4,
9; 48:10; 60:5; 63:8; 73:23; 74:11; 77:10; 78:54;
80:15, 17; 89:13, 25, 42; 91:7; 98:1; 108:6;
109:6, 31; 110:1, 5; 118:15, 16, 16; 121:5; 137:5;
138:7; 139:10; 142:4; Pr 3:16; Isa 41:10, 13;
44:20; 45:1; 48:13; 62:8; 63:12; Jer 22:24; La
2:3, 4; Eze 21:22; 39:3; Da 12:7; Jnh 4:11; Hab
2:16; Mt 5:30; 6:3; 22:44; 26:64; 27:29; Mk
12:36; 14:62; 16:19; Lk 6:6; 20:42; 22:69; Ac
2:25, 33, 34; 3:7; 5:31; 7:55, 56; 25:11; Ro 8:34;
2Co 6:7; Gal 2:9; Eph 1:20; Col 3:1; Heb 1:3,
13; 8:1; 10:12; 12:2; 1Pe 3:22; Rev 1:16, 17, 20;
2:1; 5:1, 7; 10:5

# HANDED [HAND]
Mt 26: 2 Man will be **h** over to be crucified."
Mk 15:15 and **h** him over to be crucified.
Ac 3:13 You **h** him over to be killed,
1Ti 1:20 whom I have **h** over to Satan to be

# HANDFUL [HAND]
Ecc 4: 6 Better one **h** with tranquillity than

# HANDIWORK* [HAND, WORK]
Isa 19:25 Assyria my **h**, and Israel my inheritance
Eph 2:10 For we are God's **h**,

# HANDKERCHIEFS*
Ac 19:12 so that even **h** and aprons that had

# HANDLE [HANDLES]
Ex 18:18 you cannot **h** it alone.
Col 2:21 "Do not **h**! Do not taste!

# HANDLES [HANDLE]
2Ti 2:15 who correctly **h** the word of truth.

# HANDS [HAND]
Ge 5:29 painful toil of our **h** caused
27:22 Jacob, but the **h** are the **h** of Esau."
Ex 17:11 As long as Moses held up his **h**,
29:10 his sons shall lay their **h** on its head.
32:15 tablets of the covenant in his **h**.
34: 4 the two stone tablets in his **h**.
Dt 6: 8 Tie them as symbols on your **h**
11:18 tie them as symbols on your **h**
23:25 you may pick kernels with your **h**,
Jos 24:11 but I gave them into your **h**.
Jdg 2:16 them out of the **h** of these raiders.
7: 6 lapped with their **h** to their mouths.
14: 6 his bare **h** as he might have torn
1Sa 5: 4 His head and **h** had been broken off
2Sa 24:14 Let us fall into the **h** of the LORD,
2Ki 11:12 and the people clapped their **h**
22:17 by all the idols their **h** have made,
2Ch 6: 4 his **h** has fulfilled what he promised
Job 2: 6 "Very well, then, he is in your **h**;
Ps 22:16 they pierce my **h** and my feet.
24: 4 Those who have clean **h** and a pure
31: 5 Into your **h** I commit my spirit;
31:15 My times are in your **h**;
47: 1 Clap your **h**, all you nations;
63: 4 and in your name I will lift up my **h**.
90:17 establish the work of our **h** for us—
115: 7 They have **h**, but cannot feel, feet,
138: 8 do not abandon the works of your **h**.
Pr 10: 4 Lazy **h** make for poverty, but diligent
**h** bring wealth.
12:24 Diligent **h** will rule, but laziness
19:24 Sluggards bury their **h** in the dish
21:25 because their **h** refuse to work.
24:33 a little folding of the **h** to rest—
31:13 and flax and works with eager **h**.
31:20 poor and extends her **h** to the needy.
Ecc 4: 5 Fools fold their **h** and ruin
5:15 toil that they can carry in their **h**.
10:18 because of idle **h**, the house leaks.
11: 6 at evening let your **h** not be idle,
Isa 5:12 no respect for the work of his **h**.
11: 8 young children will put their **h**
35: 3 Strengthen the feeble **h**,
37:19 and stone, fashioned by human **h**.
45:12 My own **h** stretched
49:16 engraved you on the palms of my **h**;
55:12 trees of the field will clap their **h**.
65: 2 out my **h** to an obstinate people,
Jer 1:16 worshiping what their **h** have made.
20:13 the needy from the **h** of the wicked.
26:14 As for me, I am in your **h**;
La 3:41 hearts and our **h** to God in heaven,
Eze 8: 1 their four sides they had human **h**.
10: 8 be seen what looked like human **h**.)
Da 2:45 of a mountain, but not by human **h**—
Hos 14: 3 gods' to what our own **h** have made,
Mic 7: 3 Both **h** are skilled in doing evil;
Zec 8:13 be afraid, but let your **h** be strong."

Mal  1:10  will accept no offering from your **h**.
Mk   7: 5  of eating their food with defiled **h**?"
     10:16  placed his **h** on them and blessed
     14:41  is delivered into the **h** of sinners.
Lk   23:46  into your **h** I commit my spirit."
     24:40  this, he showed them his **h** and feet.
Jn   20:27  "Put your finger here; see my **h**.
Ac    6: 6  prayed and laid their **h** on them.
      8:18  at the laying on of the apostles' **h**,
     13: 3  they placed their **h** on them and sent
     19: 6  When Paul placed his **h** on them,
     28: 8  placed his **h** on him and healed him.
Ro   10:21  have held out my **h** to a disobedient
1Co  15:24  when he **h** over the kingdom to God
1Th   4:11  own business and work with your **h**,
1Ti   2: 8  lifting up holy **h** without anger
      4:14  body of elders laid their **h** on you.
      5:22  not be hasty in the laying on of **h**,
2Ti   1: 6  you through the laying on of my **h**.
Heb   6: 2  the laying on of **h**, the resurrection
     10:31  to fall into the **h** of the living God.
1Jn   1: 1  looked at and our **h** have touched—
Rev  13:16  to receive a mark on their right **h**
     20: 4  mark on their foreheads or their **h**.

## HANDSOME*

Ge   39: 6  Now Joseph was well-built and **h**,
1Sa   9: 2  Saul, as **h** a young man as could
     16:12  a fine appearance and **h** features.
     17:42  glowing with health and **h**, and he
2Sa  14:25  for his **h** appearance as Absalom.
1Ki   1: 6  also very **h** and was born next
SS    1:16  How **h** you are, my beloved!
Eze  23: 6  all of them **h** young men,
     23:12  horsemen, all **h** young men.
     23:23  Assyrians with them, **h** young men,
Da    1: 4  men without any physical defect, **h**,
Zec  11:13  the **h** price at which they valued me!

## HANG [HANGED, HANGING, HUNG]

Mt   22:40  and the Prophets **h** on these two

## HANGED* [HANG]

2Sa  17:23  house in order and then **h** himself.
Mt   27: 5  Then he went away and **h** himself.

## HANGING [HANG]

Jos  10:26  left **h** on the poles until evening.
2Sa  18: 9  He was left **h** in midair,
Ac   10:39  They killed him by **h** him

## HANNAH

Wife of Elkanah, mother of Samuel (1Sa 1). Prayer at dedication of Samuel (1Sa 2:1–10). Blessed (1Sa 2:18–21).

## HANUN

1Ch  19: 2  "I will show kindness to **H** son

## HAPPEN [HAPPENED, HAPPENING, HAPPENS]

Ge   49: 1  around so I can tell you what will **h**
Ecc   6:12  tell them what will **h** under the sun
Da    8:19  tell you what will **h** later in the time

Da   10:14  to you what will **h** to your people
Jnh   4: 5  to see what would **h** to the city.
Mk   10:32  told them what was going to **h**
Jn   13:19  when it does **h** you will believe
     14:29  that when it does **h** you will believe.
     18: 4  all that was going to **h** to him,
Ac    4:28  had decided beforehand should **h**.

## HAPPENED [HAPPEN]

Dt    4:32  Has anything so great as this ever **h**,
1Sa   4: 7  Nothing like this has **h** before.
2Ki  24:20  anger that all this **h** to Jerusalem
Ezr   9:13  "What has **h** to us is a result of our
Ne    9:33  In all that has **h** to us, you have
Jer  40: 3  All this **h** because you people

## HAPPENING [HAPPEN]

Lk   21:31  so, when you see these things **h**,
1Pe   4:12  as though something strange were **h**

## HAPPENS [HAPPEN]

Jn   13:19  "I am telling you now before it **h**,
     14:29  I have told you now before it **h**,

## HAPPIER* [HAPPY]

Ecc   4: 2  already died, are **h** than the living,
Mt   18:13  he is **h** about that one sheep than
1Co   7:40  she is **h** if she stays as she is—

## HAPPINESS* [HAPPY]

Dt   24: 5  bring **h** to the wife he has married.
Est   8:16  For the Jews it was a time of **h**
Job   7: 7  my eyes will never see **h** again.
Ecc   2:26  knowledge and **h**, but to the sinner
Mt   25:21  Come and share your master's **h**!'
     25:23  Come and share your master's **h**!'

## HAPPY* [HAPPIER, HAPPINESS]

Ge   30:13  Then Leah said, "How **h** I am! The women will call me **h**."
1Ki   4:20  ate, they drank and they were **h**.
     10: 8  How **h** your people must be! How **h** your officials,
2Ch   9: 7  How **h** your people must be! How **h** your officials,
Est   5: 9  Haman went out that day **h**
Ps   68: 3  may they be **h** and joyful.
     113: 9  her home as a **h** mother of children.
     137: 8  **h** are those who repay you
     137: 9  **H** are those who seize your infants
Pr   15:13  A **h** heart makes the face cheerful,
Ecc   3:12  better for people than to be **h**
      5:19  their lot and be **h** in their toil—
      7:14  When times are good, be **h**;
     11: 9  young, be **h** while you are young,
Jnh   4: 6  Jonah was very **h** about the gourd.
Zec   8:19  occasions and **h** festivals for Judah.
1Co   7:30  those who are **h**, as if they were not;
2Co   7: 9  yet now I am **h**, not because you
      7:13  delighted to see how **h** Titus was,
Jas   5:13  Is anyone **h**? Let them sing songs

## HARAN

Ge   11:26  the father of Abram, Nahor and **H**.
     11:27  And **H** became the father of Lot.

## HARASS* [HARASSED]
Dt   2: 9  "Do not **h** the Moabites or provoke
     2:19  do not **h** them or provoke them

## HARASSED* [HARASS]
Mt   9:36  because they were **h** and helpless,
2Co  7: 5  rest, but we were **h** at every turn—

## HARBOR
Dt  15: 9  careful not to **h** this wicked thought:
Job  36:13  "The godless in heart **h** resentment;
Ps  103: 9  nor will he **h** his anger forever;
Pr  26:24  but in their hearts they **h** deceit.
Jas   3:14  But if you **h** bitter envy and selfish

## HARD [HARDEN, HARDENED, HARDENING, HARDENS, HARDER, HARDSHIP, HARDSHIPS]
Ge  18:14  Is anything too **h** for the LORD?
Ex   7:13  Yet Pharaoh's heart became **h**
1Ki  10: 1  to test Solomon with **h** questions.
Pr  14:23  All **h** work brings a profit, but mere
Isa  40: 2  her **h** service has been completed,
Jer  32:17  Nothing is too **h** for you.
Zec   7:12  They made their hearts as **h** as flint
Mt  19:23  you, it is **h** for the rich to enter
Mk  10: 5  "It was because your hearts were **h**
Jn   6:60  disciples said, "This is a **h** teaching.
Ac  20:35  of **h** work we must help the weak,
     26:14  It is **h** for you to kick against
Ro  16:12  those women who work **h**
     16:12  woman who has worked very **h**
1Co  4:12  We work **h** with our own hands.
2Co  4: 8  We are **h** pressed on every side,
     6: 5  in **h** work, sleepless nights
1Th  5:12  those who work **h** among you,
1Pe  4:18  "If it is **h** for the righteous to be
2Pe  3:16  things that are **h** to understand,
Rev  2: 2  your **h** work and your perseverance.

## HARDEN [HARD]
Ex   4:21  I will **h** his heart so that he will not
     14:17  I will **h** the hearts of the Egyptians
1Sa  6: 6  Why do you **h** your hearts as
Ps  95: 8  "Do not **h** your hearts as you did
Pr  28:14  who **h** their hearts fall into trouble.
Ro   9:18  and he hardens whom he wants to **h**.
Heb  3: 8  do not **h** your hearts as you did
     4: 7  his voice, do not **h** your hearts."

## HARDENED [HARD]
Ex   8:32  this time also Pharaoh **h** his heart
     10:20  But the LORD **h** Pharaoh's heart,
Jos  11:20  LORD himself who **h** their hearts
Mk  8:17  Are your hearts **h**?
Jn  12:40  "He has blinded their eyes and **h** their hearts,
Ro  11: 7  them did, but the others were **h**,
Heb  3:13  you may be **h** by sin's deceitfulness.

## HARDENING* [HARD]
Ro  11:25  Israel has experienced a **h** in part
Eph  4:18  in them due to the **h** of their hearts.

## HARDENS* [HARD]
Ro  9:18  and he **h** whom he wants to harden.

## HARDER [HARD]
Jer  5: 3  They made their faces **h** than stone
1Co 15:10  No, I worked **h** than all of them—
2Co 11:23  I have worked much **h**,

## HARDHEARTED* [HEART]
Dt  15: 7  do not be **h** or tightfisted toward

## HARDSHIP [HARD]
Dt  15:18  Do not consider it a **h** to set your
Ne   9:32  do not let all this **h** seem trifling
Ro   8:35  Shall trouble or **h** or persecution
1Co 13: 3  my body [to **h**] that I may boast,
2Ti  4: 5  endure **h**, do the work
Heb 12: 7  Endure **h** as discipline;

## HARDSHIPS [HARD]
Nu  11: 1  about their **h** in the hearing
Ac  14:22  "We must go through many **h**
2Co  6: 4  in troubles, **h** and distresses;
     12:10  in insults, in **h**, in persecutions,
Rev  2: 3  and have endured **h** for my name,

## HARDWORKING* [WORK]
2Ti  2: 6  The **h** farmer should be the first

## HAREM
Est  2: 9  into the best place in the **h**.

## HARLOT (KJV) See PROSTITUTE

## HARLOTS*
Hos  4:14  the men themselves consort with **h**

## HARM [HARMED, HARMFUL, HARMING, HARMS]
Ge  31: 7  God has not allowed him to **h** me.
     31:52  past this heap to your side to **h** you
     48:16  who has delivered me from all **h**—
     50:20  You intended to **h** me, but God
1Sa 26:21  today, I will not try to **h** you again.
1Ch 16:22  do my prophets no **h**."
Ne   6: 2  But they were scheming to **h** me;
Ps  71:13  those who want to **h** me be covered
   121: 6  the sun will not **h** you by day,
Pr   3:29  Do not plot **h** against your neighbor,
     8:36  those who fail to find me **h** themselves;
     12:21  No **h** overtakes the righteous,
     13:20  for a companion of fools suffers **h**.
     31:12  good, not **h**, all the days of her life.
Isa  11: 9  They will neither **h** nor destroy
Jer  7: 6  follow other gods to your own **h**,
     10: 5  they can do no **h** nor can they do
     29:11  to prosper you and not to **h** you,
Zep  3:15  never again will you fear any **h**.
Ac       all the **h** he has done to your people
Ro  13:10  Love does no **h** to its neighbor.
1Co 11:17  your meetings do more **h** than good.
1Pe  3:13  Who is going to **h** you if you are
2Pe  2:13  paid back with **h** for the **h** they have done.

1Jn   5:18  and the evil one cannot **h** them.
Rev  11: 5  If anyone tries to **h** them,

## HARMED [HARM]
Da    3:27  that the fire had not **h** their bodies,

## HARMFUL [HARM]
1Th   5:22  reject whatever is **h**.

## HARMING [HARM]
1Sa  25:34  who has kept me from **h** you, if you

## HARMONY*
Zec   6:13  there will be **h** between the two.'
Ro   12:16  Live in **h** with one another.
2Co   6:15  What **h** is there between Christ

## HARMS* [HARM]
Ge   26:11  "Anyone who **h** this man or

## HARP [HARPIST, HARPISTS, HARPS]
1Ch  25: 3  using the **h** in thanking and praising
Ps   33: 2  Praise the LORD with the **h**;
     98: 5  music to the LORD with the **h**,
    108: 2  Awake, **h** and lyre! I will awaken
    150: 3  praise him with the **h** and lyre,
Da    3: 5  lyre, **h**, pipe and all kinds of music,
Rev   5: 8  Each one had a **h** and they were

## HARPIST [HARP]
2Ki   3:15  But now bring me a **h**." While the **h**

## HARPISTS* [HARP]
Rev  14: 2  like that of **h** playing their harps.
     18:22  The music of **h** and musicians,

## HARPS [HARP]
1Sa  10: 5  and **h** being played before them,
1Ch  15:16  lyres, **h** and cymbals.
     25: 1  accompanied by **h**,
Ps  137: 2  There on the poplars we hung our **h**,
Rev  15: 2  They held **h** given them by God

## HARSH [HARSHLY]
Ex    1:14  with **h** labor in brick and mortar
      6: 9  their discouragement and **h** labor.
2Ch  10: 4  but now lighten the **h** labor
Pr   15: 1  wrath, but a **h** word stirs up anger.
2Co  13:10  I may not have to be **h** in my use
Col   2:23  and their **h** treatment of the body,
      3:19  wives and do not be **h** with them.
1Pe   2:18  but also to those who are **h**.

## HARSHLY [HARSH]
Ge   42: 7  be a stranger and spoke **h** to them.
2Ch  10:13  The king answered them **h**.
1Ti   5: 1  Do not rebuke an older man **h**,

## HARVEST [HARVESTED,
   HARVESTERS, HARVESTS]
Ge    8:22  seedtime and **h**, cold and heat,
Ex   23:16  "Celebrate the Festival of **H**
Lev  19: 9  you reap the **h** of your land,

Dt   16:15  God will bless you in all your **h**
Pr   10: 5  who sleeps during **h** is a disgraceful
     20: 4  so at **h** time they look but find
Jer   8:20  "The **h** is past, the summer has
Joel  3:13  Swing the sickle, for the **h** is ripe.
Mic   6:15  You will plant but not **h**;
Mt    9:37  "The **h** is plentiful but the workers
     13:39  The **h** is the end of the age,
Lk   10: 2  Ask the Lord of the **h**, therefore,
Jn    4:35  They are ripe for **h**.
      4:36  now they **h** the crop for eternal life,
1Co   9:11  if we reap a material **h** from you?
2Co   9:10  seed and will enlarge the **h** of your
Gal   6: 9  at the proper time we will reap a **h**
Heb  12:11  it produces a **h** of righteousness
Jas   3:18  in peace reap a **h** of righteousness.
Rev  14:15  come, for the **h** of the earth is ripe."

## HARVESTED [HARVEST]
Hag   1: 6  have planted much, but have **h** little.
Rev  14:16  over the earth, and the earth was **h**.

## HARVESTERS [HARVEST]
Ru    2: 3  and began to glean behind the **h**.
Mt   13:39  end of the age, and the **h** are angels.

## HARVESTS [HARVEST]
Jer   5:17  devour your **h** and food, devour your
   sons

## HAS [HAVE]
Ge   31:32  if you find anyone who **h** your gods,
Nu   14:24  my servant Caleb **h** a different spirit
Dt   21:15  If someone **h** two wives, and he
2Ch  25: 8  for God **h** the power to help
Job   1:12  everything he **h** is in your power,
      2: 4  "A man will give all he **h** for his
     11: 6  for true wisdom **h** two sides.
     42: 8  what is right, as my servant Job **h**."
Ps   73:25  earth **h** nothing I desire besides you.
Pr   18:21  The tongue **h** the power of life
     23:29  Who **h** needless bruises?
Isa  34: 8  For the LORD **h** a day
Jer  23:28  let the one who **h** my word speak it
Eze   9: 6  not touch anyone who **h** the mark.
Mk    2:10  the Son of Man **h** authority on earth
      4: 9  said, "Whoever **h** ears to hear,
Lk    9:58  the Son of Man **h** no place to lay his
     12: 5  after your body **h** been killed,
Jn    3:36  believes in the Son **h** eternal life,
     15:13  Greater love **h** no one than this:
Ro    6: 9  death no longer **h** mastery over him.
1Co   7: 7  each of you **h** your own gift
      7:13  a woman **h** a husband who is not
     11:14  teach you that if a man **h** long hair,
1Ti   4: 8  but godliness **h** value for all things,
1Jn   2:23  acknowledges the Son **h** the Father
      5:12  Whoever **h** the Son **h** life;
Rev  20: 6  The second death **h** no power over

## HASTE [HASTEN, HASTILY, HASTY]
Ex   12:11  Eat it in **h**; it is the LORD's
Dt   16: 3  because you left Egypt in **h**—
Pr   21: 5  lead to profit as surely as **h** leads
     29:20  you see someone who speaks in **h**?

## HASTEN [HASTE]

| | | |
|---|---|---|
| Ps | 70: 1 | **H**, O God, to save me; |
| | 119:60 | I will **h** and not delay to obey your |
| Isa | 49:17 | Your children **h** back, and those |

## HASTILY* [HASTE]

Pr   25: 8   do not bring **h** to court, for what

## HASTY* [HASTE]

| | | |
|---|---|---|
| Pr | 19: 2 | how much more will **h** feet miss |
| Ecc | 5: 2 | do not be **h** in your heart to utter |
| 1Ti | 5:22 | Do not be **h** in the laying |

## HATE [GOD-HATERS, HATED, HATES, HATING, HATRED]

| | | |
|---|---|---|
| Ex | 18:21 | men who **h** dishonest gain— |
| | 20: 5 | generation of those who **h** me, |
| Lev | 19:17 | " 'Do not **h** a fellow Israelite |
| Dt | 7:10 | those who **h** him he will repay |
| 2Ch | 18: 7 | I **h** him because he never prophesies |
| Ps | 5: 5 | You **h** all who do wrong; |
| | 36: 2 | too much to detect or **h** their sin. |
| | 45: 7 | righteousness and **h** wickedness; |
| | 97:10 | those who love the LORD **h** evil, |
| | 119:104 | therefore I **h** every wrong path. |
| | 119:163 | I **h** and detest falsehood but I love |
| | 129: 5 | May all who **h** Zion be turned back |
| | 139:21 | Do I not **h** those who **h** you, |
| Pr | 1:22 | in mockery and fools **h** knowledge? |
| | 8:13 | To fear the LORD is to **h** evil; I **h** |
| | 9: 8 | rebuke mockers or they will **h** you; |
| | 13: 5 | The righteous **h** what is false, |
| | 13:24 | who spare the rod **h** their children, |
| | 15:27 | those who **h** bribes will live. |
| | 29:10 | The bloodthirsty **h** people |
| Ecc | 3: 8 | a time to love and a time to **h**, |
| Isa | 61: 8 | I **h** robbery and wrongdoing. |
| Jer | 44: 4 | not do this detestable thing that I **h**!' |
| Eze | 35: 6 | Since you did not **h** bloodshed, |
| Am | 5:15 | **H** evil, love good; |
| Mal | 2:16 | "I **h** divorce," says the LORD |
| Mt | 5:43 | your neighbor and **h** your enemy.' |
| | 10:22 | Everyone will **h** you because of me, |
| Lk | 6:22 | Blessed are you when people **h** you, |
| | 6:27 | do good to those who **h** you, |
| | 14:26 | and does not **h** father and mother, |
| | 16:13 | Either you will **h** the one and love |
| Jn | 3:20 | those who do evil **h** the light, |
| | 7: 7 | The world cannot **h** you, but it hates |
| | 12:25 | those who **h** their life in this world |
| Ro | 7:15 | to do I do not do, but what I **h** I do. |
| | 12: 9 | **H** what is evil; cling to what is |
| 1Jn | 2: 9 | in the light but **h** a fellow believer |
| | 4:20 | love God yet **h** a brother or sister, |

## HATED [HATE]

| | | |
|---|---|---|
| Ge | 37: 4 | they **h** him and could not speak |
| Est | 9: 1 | upper hand over those who **h** them. |
| Pr | 25:17 | and you will be **h**. |
| Ecc | 2:17 | So I **h** life, because the work that is |
| Mal | 1: 3 | but Esau I have **h**, and I have turned |
| Jn | 15:18 | you, keep in mind that it **h** me first. |
| Ro | 9:13 | "Jacob I loved, but Esau I **h**." |
| Eph | 5:29 | all, people have never **h** their own |
| Heb | 1: 9 | righteousness and **h** wickedness; |

## HATES [HATE]

| | | |
|---|---|---|
| Pr | 6:16 | There are six things the LORD **h**, |
| | 12: 1 | but whoever **h** correction is stupid. |
| | 26:28 | A lying tongue **h** those it hurts, |
| Jn | 15:19 | That is why the world **h** you. |

## HATING* [HATE]

| | | |
|---|---|---|
| Tit | 3: 3 | being hated and **h** one another. |
| Jude | 1:23 | **h** even the clothing stained |

## HATRED [HATE]

| | | |
|---|---|---|
| Pr | 10:12 | **H** stirs up dissension, but love |
| | 15:17 | love than a fattened calf with **h**. |
| Gal | 5:20 | **h**, discord, jealousy, fits of rage, |

## HAUGHTY

| | | |
|---|---|---|
| Job | 41:34 | It looks down on all that are **h**; |
| Ps | 18:27 | bring low those whose eyes are **h**. |
| | 131: 1 | proud, LORD, my eyes are not **h**; |
| Pr | 6:17 | **h** eyes, a lying tongue, |
| | 16:18 | destruction, a **h** spirit before a fall. |
| | 18:12 | downfall the heart is **h**, |
| Isa | 13:11 | put an end to the arrogance of the **h** |
| Zep | 3:11 | Never again will you be **h** on my |

## HAUNT

| | | |
|---|---|---|
| Jer | 10:22 | of Judah desolate, a **h** of jackals. |
| | 51:37 | be a heap of ruins, a **h** of jackals, |
| Rev | 18: 2 | demons and a **h** for every evil spirit, |

## HAVE [HAD, HAS, HAVING]

| | | |
|---|---|---|
| Ge | 18:10 | and Sarah your wife will **h** a son." |
| | 27:38 | "Do you **h** only one blessing, |
| Ex | 16:18 | gathered much did not **h** too much, |
| | 20: 3 | "You shall **h** no other gods before |
| | 33:19 | I will **h** mercy on whom I will **h** |
| Dt | 5: 7 | "You shall **h** no other gods before |
| Jos | 22:25 | You **h** no share in the LORD." |
| Ezr | 4: 3 | "You **h** no part with us in building |
| Job | 40: 9 | Do you **h** an arm like God's, |
| Ps | 73:25 | Whom **h** I in heaven but you? |
| | 115: 5 | They **h** mouths, but cannot speak, |
| | 119:99 | I **h** more insight than all my |
| Pr | 4: 7 | Though it cost all you **h**, |
| Ecc | 5:10 | who love money never **h** enough; |
| | 6: 8 | What advantage **h** the wise over fools? |
| Jer | 2:28 | **h** as many gods as you **h** towns. |
| | 5:21 | who **h** eyes but do not see, |
| Mal | 2:10 | Do we not all **h** one Father? |
| Mt | 3: 9 | 'We **h** Abraham as our father.' |
| | 21:21 | you, if you **h** faith and do not doubt, |
| Mk | 4:25 | Those who **h** will be given more; |
| | 10:21 | and you will **h** treasure in heaven. |
| | 14: 7 | But you will not always **h** me. |
| Lk | 14:33 | not give up everything you **h** |
| | 17: 6 | you **h** faith as small as a mustard |
| Jn | 3:16 | shall not perish but **h** eternal life. |
| | 4:32 | "I **h** food to eat that you know |
| | 4:44 | prophets **h** no honor in their own country.) |
| | 8:12 | but will **h** the light of life." |
| | 16:12 | "I **h** much more to say to you, |
| | 16:33 | In this world you will **h** trouble. |
| Ac | 3: 6 | "Silver or gold I do not **h**, but what |
| Ro | 2:14 | even though they do not **h** the law. |

Ro 5: 1 we **h** peace with God through
8: 9 if anyone does not **h** the Spirit
12: 6 We **h** different gifts,
1Co 2:16 But we **h** the mind of Christ.
13: 2 but do not **h** love, I am nothing.
2Co 4: 7 we **h** this treasure in jars of clay
8:15 gathered much did not **h** too much,
Eph 1: 7 In him we **h** redemption through his
2:18 through him we both **h** access
Heb 4:14 since we **h** a great high priest who
6:19 We **h** this hope as an anchor
Jas 2:14 claim to **h** faith but have no deeds?
1Jn 2:20 you **h** an anointing from the Holy
3: 3 All who **h** this hope in him
5:12 not **h** the Son of God does not **h** life.
Jude 1:19 instincts and do not **h** the Spirit.
Rev 20: 6 holy are those who **h** part in the first
22:14 that they may **h** the right to the tree

## HAVEN
Ps 107:30 he guided them to their desired **h**.

## HAVING [HAVE]
1Co 9:21 so as to win those not **h** the law.
2Co 6:10 **h** nothing, and yet possessing
2Ti 3: 5 **h** a form of godliness but denying

## HAVOC
Ac 9:21 "Isn't he the man who raised **h**

## HAY
1Co 3:12 costly stones, wood, **h** or straw,

## HAZAEL
1Ki 19:15 get there, anoint **H** king over Aram.
2Ki 8: 9 **H** went to meet Elisha,

## HAZOR
Jos 11:11 breathed, and he burned **H** itself.
Jer 49:33 "**H** will become a haunt of jackals,

## HEAD [AHEAD, HEADS, HOTHEADED]
Ge 3:15 he will crush your **h**, and you will
28:18 the stone he had placed under his **h**
48:18 put your right hand on his **h**."
Lev 1: 4 hand on the **h** of the burnt offering,
19:27 cut the hair at the sides of your **h**
Nu 6: 5 no razor may be used on their **h**.
Dt 28:13 The LORD will make you the **h**,
Jdg 16:17 If my **h** were shaved, my strength
1Sa 1:11 razor will ever be used on his **h**."
9: 2 he was a **h** taller than anyone else.
17:51 him, he cut off his **h** with the sword.
Ps 23: 5 You anoint my **h** with oil;
133: 2 is like precious oil poured on the **h**,
Pr 1: 9 They are a garland to grace your **h**
10: 6 Blessings crown the **h**
25:22 will heap burning coals on his **h**,
Isa 59:17 and the helmet of salvation on his **h**;
Jer 9: 1 that my **h** were a spring of water
Eze 8: 3 and took me by the hair of my **h**.
33: 4 their blood will be on their own **h**.
Da 2:32 The **h** of the statue was made
7: 9 hair of his **h** was white like wool.

Mt 8:20 of Man has no place to lay his **h**."
Mk 6:28 and brought back his **h** on a platter.
Jn 19: 2 crown of thorns and put it on his **h**.
Ro 12:20 will heap burning coals on his **h**."
1Co 11: 3 that the **h** of every man is Christ, and the **h** of the woman is man, and the **h** of Christ is God.
11: 4 with his **h** covered dishonors his **h**.
11: 5 her **h** uncovered dishonors her **h**—
12:21 And the **h** cannot say to the feet,
Eph 1:22 him to be **h** over everything
5:23 the husband is the **h** of the wife as Christ is the **h**
Col 1:18 And he is the **h** of the body,
2Ti 4: 5 you, keep your **h** in all situations,
Rev 1:14 hair on his **h** was white like wool,
10: 1 a cloud, with a rainbow above his **h**;
12: 1 a crown of twelve stars on her **h**.
13: 1 and on each **h** a blasphemous name.
14:14 man with a crown of gold on his **h**
19:12 fire, and on his **h** are many crowns.

## HEADLONG
Ac 1:18 there he fell **h**, his body burst open

## HEADS [HEAD]
Ge 41: 5 Seven **h** of grain, healthy and good,
Lev 26:13 you to walk with **h** held high.
Ne 4: 4 their insults back on their own **h**.
Ps 7:16 comes down on their own **h**.
22: 7 they hurl insults, shaking their **h**.
24: 7 Lift up your **h**, you gates;
Isa 35:10 everlasting joy will crown their **h**.
51:11 everlasting joy will crown their **h**.
Eze 11:21 on their own **h** what they have done,
Da 7: 6 This beast had four **h**, and it was
Mt 27:39 insults at him, shaking their **h**
Mk 2:23 they began to pick some **h** of grain.
Lk 21:28 stand up and lift up your **h**,
Ac 18: 6 "Your blood be on your own **h**!
Rev 4: 4 and had crowns of gold on their **h**.
12: 3 enormous red dragon with seven **h**
17: 9 The seven **h** are seven hills

## HEAL* [HEALED, HEALING, HEALS]
Nu 12:13 the LORD, "Please, God, **h** her!"
Dt 32:39 I have wounded and I will **h**, and no
2Ki 20: 5 and seen your tears; I will **h** you.
20: 8 the sign that the LORD will **h** me
2Ch 7:14 their sin and will **h** their land.
Job 5:18 he injures, but his hands also **h**.
Ps 6: 2 **h** me, LORD, for my bones are
41: 4 **h** me, for I have sinned against
Ecc 3: 3 a time to kill and a time to **h**, a time
Isa 19:22 he will strike them and **h**
19:22 respond to their pleas and **h** them.
57:18 seen their ways, but I will **h** them;
57:19 "And I will **h** them."
Jer 17:14 **H** me, LORD, and I will be healed;
30:17 you to health and **h** your wounds,'
33: 6 I will **h** my people and will let them
La 2:13 as deep as the sea. Who can **h** you?
Hos 5:13 to cure you, not able to **h** your sores.
6: 1 torn us to pieces but he will **h** us;
7: 1 whenever I would **h** Israel, the sins
14: 4 "I will **h** their waywardness

| | | |
|---|---|---|
| Na | 3:19 | Nothing can **h** you; your wound is |
| Zec | 11:16 | or **h** the injured, or feed the healthy, |
| Mt | 8: 7 | to him, "Shall I come and **h** him?" |
| | 10: 1 | and to **h** every disease and sickness. |
| | 10: 8 | **H** the sick, raise the dead, |
| | 12:10 | "Is it lawful to **h** on the Sabbath?" |
| | 13:15 | and turn, and I would **h** them.' |
| | 17:16 | but they could not **h** him." |
| Mk | 3: 2 | if he would **h** him on the Sabbath. |
| | 6: 5 | on a few sick people and **h** them. |
| Lk | 4:23 | 'Physician, **h** yourself!' |
| | 5:17 | Lord was with Jesus to **h** the sick. |
| | 6: 7 | to see if he would **h** on the Sabbath. |
| | 7: 3 | him to come and **h** his servant. |
| | 8:43 | years, but no one could **h** her. |
| | 9: 2 | kingdom of God and to **h** the sick. |
| | 10: 9 | **H** the sick who are there and tell |
| | 14: 3 | "Is it lawful to **h** on the Sabbath |
| Jn | 4:47 | begged him to come and **h** his son, |
| | 12:40 | and I would **h** them." |
| Ac | 4:30 | Stretch out your hand to **h** |
| | 28:27 | and turn, and I would **h** them.' |

## HEALED* [HEAL]

| | | |
|---|---|---|
| Ge | 20:17 | and God **h** Abimelek, his wife |
| Ex | 21:19 | see that the victim is completely **h**. |
| Lev | 13:37 | grown in it, the affected person is **h**. |
| | 14: 3 | If they have been **h** of their defiling |
| Jos | 5: 8 | they were in camp until they were **h**. |
| 1Sa | 6: 3 | Then you will be **h**, and you will |
| 2Ki | 2:21 | 'I have **h** this water. |
| 2Ch | 30:20 | heard Hezekiah and **h** the people. |
| Ps | 30: 2 | to you for help, and you **h** me. |
| | 107:20 | He sent out his word and **h** them; |
| Isa | 6:10 | their hearts, and be **h**.' |
| | 53: 5 | him, and by his wounds we are **h**. |
| Jer | 14:19 | afflicted us so that we cannot be **h**? |
| | 17:14 | Heal me, LORD, and I will be **h**; |
| | 51: 8 | for her pain; perhaps she can be **h**. |
| | 51: 9 | " 'We would have **h** Babylon, |
| | 51: 9 | but she cannot be **h**; |
| Eze | 30:21 | It has not been bound up to be **h** |
| | 34: 4 | strengthened the weak or **h** the sick |
| Hos | 11: 3 | did not realize it was I who **h** them. |
| Mt | 4:24 | and the paralyzed; and he **h** them. |
| | 8: 8 | the word, and my servant will be **h**. |
| | 8:13 | his servant was **h** at that very hour. |
| | 8:16 | with a word and **h** all the sick. |
| | 9:21 | I only touch his cloak, I will be **h**." |
| | 9:22 | he said, "your faith has **h** you." |
| | 9:22 | And the woman was **h** |
| | 12:15 | him, and he **h** all who were ill. |
| | 12:22 | and Jesus **h** him, so that he could |
| | 14:14 | on them and **h** their sick. |
| | 14:36 | and all who touched him were **h**. |
| | 15:28 | her daughter was **h** from that very |
| | 15:30 | laid them at his feet; and he **h** them. |
| | 17:18 | and he was **h** from that moment. |
| | 19: 2 | followed him, and he **h** them there. |
| | 21:14 | to him at the temple, and he **h** them. |
| Mk | 1:34 | and Jesus **h** many who had various |
| | 3:10 | For he had **h** many, so that those |
| | 5:23 | hands on her so that she will be **h** |
| | 5:28 | I just touch his clothes, I will be **h**." |
| | 5:34 | "Daughter, your faith has **h** you. |
| | 6:13 | sick people with oil and **h** them. |
| | 6:56 | and all who touched him were **h**. |

| | | |
|---|---|---|
| Mk | 10:52 | said Jesus, "your faith has **h** you." |
| Lk | 4:40 | his hands on each one, he **h** them. |
| | 5:15 | him and to be **h** of their sicknesses. |
| | 6:18 | him and to be **h** of their diseases. |
| | 7: 7 | the word, and my servant will be **h**. |
| | 8:47 | and how she had been instantly **h**. |
| | 8:48 | "Daughter, your faith has **h** you. |
| | 8:50 | just believe, and she will be **h**." |
| | 9:11 | and **h** those who needed healing. |
| | 9:42 | **h** the boy and gave him back to his |
| | 13:14 | Indignant because Jesus had **h** |
| | 13:14 | So come and be **h** on those days, |
| | 14: 4 | he **h** him and sent him on his way. |
| | 17:15 | when he saw he was **h**, came back, |
| | 18:42 | your faith has **h** you." |
| | 22:51 | he touched the man's ear and **h** him. |
| Jn | 5:10 | said to the man who had been **h**, |
| | 5:13 | The man who was **h** had no idea |
| Ac | 3:16 | him that has completely **h** him, |
| | 4: 9 | and are being asked how he was **h**, |
| | 4:10 | that this man stands before you **h**. |
| | 4:14 | man who had been **h** standing there |
| | 4:22 | who was miraculously **h** was over |
| | 5:16 | evil spirits, and all of them were **h**. |
| | 8: 7 | who were paralyzed or lame were **h**. |
| | 14: 9 | at him, saw that he had faith to be **h** |
| | 28: 8 | placed his hands on him and **h** him. |
| Heb | 12:13 | may not be disabled, but rather **h**. |
| Jas | 5:16 | for each other so that you may be **h**. |
| 1Pe | 2:24 | "by his wounds you have been **h**." |
| Rev | 13: 3 | but the fatal wound had been **h**. |
| | 13:12 | whose fatal wound had been **h**. |

## HEALING* [HEAL]

| | | |
|---|---|---|
| 2Ch | 28:15 | sandals, food and drink, and **h** balm. |
| Pr | 12:18 | but the tongue of the wise brings **h**. |
| | 13:17 | but a trustworthy envoy brings **h**. |
| | 16:24 | sweet to the soul and **h** to the bones. |
| Isa | 58: 8 | and your **h** will quickly appear; |
| Jer | 8:15 | for a time of **h** but there is only |
| | 8:22 | is there no **h** for the wound of my |
| | 14:19 | for a time of **h** but there is only |
| | 30:12 | is incurable, your injury beyond **h**. |
| | 30:13 | remedy for your sore, no **h** for you. |
| | 33: 6 | I will bring health and **h** to it; |
| | 46:11 | there is no **h** for you. |
| Eze | 47:12 | for food and their leaves for **h**." |
| Mal | 4: 2 | righteousness will rise with **h** in its |
| Mt | 4:23 | and **h** every disease and sickness |
| | 9:35 | of the kingdom and **h** every disease |
| Lk | 6:19 | coming from him and **h** them all. |
| | 9: 6 | news and **h** people everywhere. |
| | 9:11 | and healed those who needed **h**. |
| | 13:32 | out demons and **h** people today |
| Jn | 6: 2 | he had performed by **h** the sick. |
| | 7:23 | me for **h** a man's whole body |
| Ac | 10:38 | **h** all who were under the power |
| 1Co | 12: 9 | to another gifts of **h** by that one |
| | 12:28 | miracles, then gifts of **h**, of helping, |
| | 12:30 | Do all have gifts of **h**? Do all speak |
| Rev | 22: 2 | the tree are for the **h** of the nations. |

## HEALS* [HEAL]

| | | |
|---|---|---|
| Ex | 15:26 | for I am the LORD, who **h** you." |
| Lev | 13:18 | has a boil on their skin and it **h**, |
| Ps | 103: 3 | all your sins and **h** all your diseases, |

Ps 147: 3 He **h** the brokenhearted and binds
Isa 30:26 and **h** the wounds he inflicted.
Ac 9:34 said to him, "Jesus Christ **h** you.

## HEALTH* [HEALTHIER, HEALTHY]

1Sa 16:12 He was glowing with **h** and had
17:42 glowing with **h** and handsome,
25: 6 Good **h** to you and your household!
25: 6 And good **h** to all that is yours!
Ps 38: 3 your wrath there is no **h** in my body;
38: 7 there is no **h** in my body.
Pr 3: 8 This will bring **h** to your body
4:22 them and **h** to one's whole body.
15:30 and good news gives **h** to the bones.
Isa 38:16 You restored me to **h** and let me
Jer 30:17 I will restore you to **h** and heal your
33: 6 I will bring **h** and healing to it;
3Jn 1: 2 I pray that you may enjoy good **h**

## HEALTHIER* [HEALTH]

Da 1:15 end of the ten days they looked **h**

## HEALTHY* [HEALTH]

Ge 41: 5 Seven heads of grain, **h** and good,
41: 7 of grain swallowed up the seven **h**,
Ps 73: 4 their bodies are **h** and strong.
Zec 11:16 or feed the **h**, but will eat the meat
Mt 6:22 If your eyes are **h**, your whole
9:12 "It is not the **h** who need a doctor,
Mk 2:17 "It is not the **h** who need a doctor,
Lk 5:31 "It is not the **h** who need a doctor,
11:34 When your eyes are **h**, your whole

## HEAP [HEAPED, HEAPING]

Ge 31:48 "This **h** is a witness between you
Dt 32:23 "I will **h** calamities on them
Jos 3:13 will be cut off and stand up in a **h**."
1Sa 2: 8 and lifts the needy from the ash **h**;
Pr 25:22 this, you will **h** burning coals on his
Ro 12:20 this, you will **h** burning coals on his
1Th 2:16 this way they always **h** up their sins
1Pe 4: 4 living, and they **h** abuse on you.

## HEAPED [HEAP]

Mt 27:44 with him also **h** insults on him.

## HEAPING* [HEAP]

Ps 39: 6 **h** up wealth without knowing
110: 6 **h** up the dead and crushing
Isa 30: 1 but not by my Spirit, **h** sin upon sin;

## HEAR [HEARD, HEARERS, HEARING, HEARS]

Ex 15:14 The nations will **h** and tremble;
18: 9 Jethro was delighted to **h** about all
22:27 I will **h**, for I am compassionate.
Nu 14:13 "Then the Egyptians will **h** about it!
Dt 1:17 **h** both small and great alike.
4:36 heaven he made you **h** his voice
5: 1 **H**, Israel, the decrees and laws I
6: 3 **H**, Israel, and be careful to obey so
6: 4 **H**, O Israel: The LORD our God,
9: 1 **H**, Israel: You are now
13:11 Then all Israel will **h** and be afraid,
19:20 The rest of the people will **h** of this

Dt 20: 3 He shall say: "**H**, Israel:
31:13 law, must **h** it and learn to fear
Jos 7: 9 of the country will **h** about this
1Ki 8:30 **H** from heaven, your dwelling place,
10: 8 before you and **h** your wisdom!
2Ki 19:16 Give ear, LORD, and **h**;
2Ch 7:14 then I will **h** from heaven, and I will
Job 5:27 So **h** it and apply it to yourself."
20: 3 I **h** a rebuke that dishonors me,
26:14 how faint the whisper we **h** of him!
31:35 ("Oh, that I had someone to **h** me!
Ps 5: 2 **H** my cry for help, my King and my
30:10 **H**, LORD, and be merciful to me;
51: 8 Let me **h** joy and gladness;
80: 1 **H** us, Shepherd of Israel, you who
94: 9 he who fashioned the ear not **h**?
95: 7 if only you would **h** his voice,
135:17 but cannot **h**, nor is there breath
Ecc 7:21 or you may **h** your servant cursing
Isa 1:10 **H** the word of the LORD,
21: 3 I am staggered by what I **h**, I am
29:18 day the deaf will **h** the words
30:21 your ears will **h** a voice behind you,
51: 7 "**H** me, you who know what is
59: 1 to save, nor his ear too dull to **h**.
65:24 while they are still speaking I will **h**.
Jer 5:21 **H** this, you foolish and senseless
5:21 who have ears but do not **h**:
Eze 33: 7 so **h** the word I speak and give them
37: 4 bones, **h** the word of the LORD!
Da 3: 5 As soon as you **h** the sound
Mic 6: 2 "**H**, you mountains, the LORD's
Mt 11: 5 the deaf **h**, the dead are raised,
11:15 Whoever has ears, let them **h**.
13:17 and to **h** what you **h** but did not **h** it.
Mk 12:29 Jesus, "is this: '**H**, O Israel:
Lk 6:47 **h** my words and put them into practice,
7:22 the deaf **h**, the dead are raised,
Jn 5:25 the dead will **h** the voice of the Son
8:47 The reason you do not **h** is that you
Ac 13: 7 because he wanted to **h** the word
13:44 whole city gathered to **h** the word
17:32 "We want to **h** you again on this
Ro 2:13 is not those who **h** the law who are
10:14 how can they **h** without someone
2Ti 4: 3 what their itching ears want to **h**.
Heb 3: 7 "Today, if you **h** his voice,
Rev 1: 3 blessed are those who **h** it and take

## HEARD [HEAR]

Ge 3: 8 his wife **h** the sound of the LORD
21:17 God **h** the boy crying, and the angel
Ex 2:24 God **h** their groaning and he
6: 5 I have **h** the groaning
16: 7 because he has **h** your grumbling
Nu 12: 2 And the LORD **h** this.
14:27 I have **h** the complaints of these
Dt 4:32 has anything like it ever been **h** of?
Jos 24:27 It has **h** all the words the LORD
2Sa 7:22 as we have **h** with our own ears.
1Ki 4:34 world, who had **h** of his wisdom.
10: 1 the queen of Sheba **h** about the fame
Ne 9:27 From heaven you **h** them,
Job 42: 5 My ears had **h** of you but now my
Ps 18: 6 From his temple he **h** my voice;
62:11 has spoken, two things I have **h**:
66:19 listened and has **h** my prayer.

Ps   78:59  When God **h** them, he was furious;
    116:  1  love the LORD, for he **h** my voice;
Isa  40:21  Have you not **h**? Has it not been
     40:28  Have you not **h**? The LORD is
     66:  8  Who has ever **h** of such things?
Jer  18:13  Who has ever **h** anything like this?
La    3:56  You **h** my plea: "Do not close your
Eze  10:  5  the cherubim could be **h** as far away
Da   10:12  your words were **h**, and I have come
     12:  8  I **h**, but I did not understand.
Hab   3:16  I **h** and my heart pounded, my lips
Mt    2:  3  King Herod **h** this he was disturbed,
      5:21  "You have **h** that it was said
      5:27  "You have **h** that it was said,
      5:33  you have **h** that it was said
      5:38  "You have **h** that it was said,
      5:43  "You have **h** that it was said,
Mk    6:  2  and many who **h** him were amazed.
     14:64  "You have **h** the blasphemy.
Lk   12:  3  in the dark will be **h** in the daylight,
Jn    6:45  Everyone who has **h** the Father
      8:26  what I have **h** from him I tell
Ac    2:  6  because each one **h** their own
     10:44  came on all who **h** the message.
Ro   10:14  in the one of whom they have not **h**?
1Co   2:  9  what no ear has **h**, and what no
2Co  12:  4  paradise and **h** inexpressible things,
Gal   3:  2  the law, or by believing what you **h**?
1Th   2:13  which you **h** from us, you accepted
2Ti   1:13  What you **h** from me, keep as
Heb   4:  2  the message they **h** was of no value
Jas   1:25  not forgetting what they have **h**,
2Pe   1:18  We ourselves **h** this voice that came
1Jn   1:  3  to you what we have seen and **h**,
      3:11  this is the message you **h**
2Jn   1:  6  As you have **h** from the beginning,
Rev   1:10  I **h** behind me a loud voice like
     22:  8  am the one who **h** and saw these

## HEARERS* [HEAR]

1Ti   4:16  will save both yourself and your **h**.

## HEARING [HEAR]

Nu   11:  1  hardships in the **h** of the LORD,
Dt   31:11  read this law before them in their **h**.
2Ch  34:30  He read in their **h** all the words
Isa   6:  9  " 'Be ever **h**, but never
Am    8:11  but a famine of **h** the words
Mt   13:14  " 'You will be ever **h** but never
Mk    4:12  and ever **h** but never understanding;
Lk    4:21  this scripture is fulfilled in your **h**."
Jn    7:51  condemn a man without first **h** him
Ac   28:26  say, "You will be ever **h** but never
Ro   10:17  faith comes from **h** the message,
1Co  12:17  eye, where would the sense of **h** be?

## HEARS [HEAR]

Ps   69:33  The LORD **h** the needy and does
Pr   15:29  but he **h** the prayer of the righteous.
Isa  30:19  As soon as he **h**, he will answer you.
Mt    7:24  everyone who **h** these words
Jn    5:24  whoever **h** my word and believes
1Jn   5:14  according to his will, he **h** us.
Rev   3:20  If anyone **h** my voice and opens
     22:18  I warn everyone who **h** the words

## HEART [BROKENHEARTED, DISHEARTENED, FAINTHEARTED, HARDHEARTED, HEART'S, HEARTACHE, HEARTFELT, HEARTLESS, HEARTS, HEARTS', KINDHEARTED, WHOLEHEARTED, WHOLEHEARTEDLY]

Ge    6:  5  of the human **h** was only evil all
      6:  6  and his **h** was deeply troubled.
     24:45  "Before I finished praying in my **h**,
Ex    4:21  I will harden his **h** so that he will
      7:13  Yet Pharaoh's **h** became hard
      7:22  arts, and Pharaoh's **h** became hard;
      8:15  he hardened his **h** and would not
      8:19  But Pharaoh's **h** was hard and he
      8:32  Pharaoh hardened his **h** and would
      9:  7  Yet his **h** was unyielding and he
      9:12  the LORD hardened Pharaoh's **h**
      9:35  So Pharaoh's **h** was hard and he
     10:20  the LORD hardened Pharaoh's **h**,
     10:27  the LORD hardened Pharaoh's **h**,
     11:10  the LORD hardened Pharaoh's **h**,
     14:  4  And I will harden Pharaoh's **h**,
     25:  2  everyone whose **h** prompts them
     28:30  may be over Aaron's **h** whenever he
     35:21  and whose **h** moved them came
Lev  19:17  not hate a fellow Israelite in your **h**.
Dt    4:  9  slip from your **h** as long as you live.
      4:29  him if you seek him with all your **h**
      6:  5  LORD your God with all your **h**
      8:14  then your **h** will become proud
     10:12  LORD your God with all your **h**
     11:13  and to serve him with all your **h**
     13:  3  you love him with all your **h**
     15:10  and do so without a grudging **h**;
     26:16  observe them with all your **h**
     29:18  you today whose **h** turns away
     30:  2  obey him with all your **h**
     30:  6  you may love him with all your **h**
     30:10  LORD your God with all your **h**
     30:14  and in your **h** so you may obey it.
Jos  22:  5  and to serve him with all your **h**
     23:14  You know with all your **h** and soul
1Sa  10:  9  God changed Saul's **h**, and all these
     12:20  serve the LORD with all your **h**.
     12:24  serve him faithfully with all your **h**;
     13:14  sought out a man after his own **h**
     14:  7  I am with you **h** and soul."
     16:  7  but the LORD looks at the **h**."
     17:32  "Let no one lose **h** on account
2Sa   6:16  LORD, she despised him in her **h**.
1Ki   2:  4  faithfully before me with all their **h**
      3:  9  So give your servant a discerning **h**
      8:17  had it in his **h** to build a temple
      8:48  they turn back to you with all their **h**
      9:  3  eyes and my **h** will always be there.
      9:  4  me faithfully with integrity of **h**
     10:24  the wisdom God had put in his **h**.
     11:  4  his wives turned his **h** after other
     14:  8  and followed me with all his **h**,
     15:14  Asa's **h** was fully committed
2Ki  22:19  Because your **h** was responsive
     23:  3  and decrees with all his **h** and all his
1Ch  28:  9  for the LORD searches every **h**
2Ch   6:38  they turn back to you with all their **h**

| | | |
|---|---|---|
| 2Ch | 7:16 | eyes and my **h** will always be there. |
| | 15:12 | ancestors, with all their **h** and soul. |
| | 15:17 | Asa's **h** was fully committed |
| | 17: 6 | His **h** was devoted to the ways |
| | 22: 9 | sought the Lord with all his **h**." |
| | 32:25 | But Hezekiah's **h** was proud and he |
| | 34:31 | and decrees with all his **h** and all his |
| | 36:13 | hardened his **h** and would not turn |
| Ezr | 1: 1 | the Lord moved the **h** of Cyrus |
| | 1: 5 | everyone whose **h** God had moved— |
| Ne | 4: 6 | the people worked with all their **h**. |
| Job | 19:27 | How my **h** yearns within me! |
| | 22:22 | and lay up his words in your **h**. |
| | 31: 7 | if my **h** has been led by my eyes, |
| | 37: 1 | "At this my **h** pounds and leaps |
| Ps | 7:10 | High, who saves the upright in **h**. |
| | 9: 1 | praise you, Lord, with all my **h**; |
| | 16: 9 | Therefore my **h** is glad and my |
| | 19:14 | this meditation of my **h** be pleasing |
| | 20: 4 | he give you the desire of your **h** |
| | 24: 4 | who have clean hands and a pure **h**, |
| | 26: 2 | try me, examine my **h** and my mind; |
| | 28: 7 | My **h** leaps for joy, and with my |
| | 37: 4 | will give you the desires of your **h**. |
| | 44:21 | since he knows the secrets of the **h**? |
| | 45: 1 | My **h** is stirred by a noble theme as |
| | 51:10 | Create in me a pure **h**, O God, |
| | 51:17 | a broken and contrite **h** you, God, |
| | 66:18 | If I had cherished sin in my **h**, |
| | 73: 1 | to Israel, to those who are pure in **h**. |
| | 73:26 | My flesh and my **h** may fail, |
| | 73:26 | God is the strength of my **h** and my |
| | 86:11 | give me an undivided **h**, that I may |
| | 90:12 | that we may gain a **h** of wisdom. |
| | 97:11 | and joy on the upright in **h**. |
| | 108: 1 | My **h**, O God, is steadfast; |
| | 109:22 | and my **h** is wounded within me. |
| | 111: 1 | Lord with all my **h** in the council |
| | 119: 2 | and seek him with all their **h**— |
| | 119:10 | I seek you with all my **h**; do not let |
| | 119:11 | in my **h** that I might not sin against |
| | 119:30 | I have set my **h** on your laws. |
| | 119:32 | for you have set my **h** free. |
| | 119:34 | your law and obey it with all my **h**. |
| | 119:36 | Turn my **h** toward your statutes |
| | 119:58 | sought your face with all my **h**; |
| | 119:69 | I keep your precepts with all my **h**. |
| | 119:111 | they are the joy of my **h**. |
| | 119:112 | My **h** is set on keeping your decrees |
| | 119:145 | I call with all my **h**; |
| | 119:161 | but my **h** trembles at your word. |
| | 125: 4 | good, to those who are upright in **h**. |
| | 138: 1 | I praise you, Lord, with all my **h**; |
| | 139:23 | Search me, God, and know my **h**; |
| | 141: 4 | Do not let my **h** be drawn to what is |
| | 148:14 | of Israel, the people close to his **h**. |
| Pr | 2: 2 | applying your **h** to understanding— |
| | 3: 1 | but keep my commands in your **h**, |
| | 3: 3 | write them on the tablet of your **h**. |
| | 3: 5 | Trust in the Lord with all your **h** |
| | 4: 4 | hold of my words with all your **h**; |
| | 4:21 | your sight, keep them within your **h**; |
| | 4:23 | guard your **h**, for everything you do |
| | 6:21 | Bind them always on your **h**; |
| | 6:25 | not lust in your **h** after her beauty |
| | 7: 3 | write them on the tablet of your **h**. |
| | 10: 8 | The wise in **h** accept commands, |

| | | |
|---|---|---|
| Pr | 12:23 | but a fool's **h** blurts out folly. |
| | 12:25 | Anxiety weighs down the **h**, |
| | 13:12 | Hope deferred makes the **h** sick, |
| | 14:13 | Even in laughter the **h** may ache, |
| | 14:30 | A **h** at peace gives life to the body, |
| | 15:13 | A happy **h** makes the face cheerful, |
| | 15:15 | the cheerful **h** has a continual feast. |
| | 15:28 | The **h** of the righteous weighs its |
| | 15:30 | eyes brings joy to the **h**, and good |
| | 16: 5 | Lord detests all the proud of **h**. |
| | 17: 3 | for gold, but the Lord tests the **h**. |
| | 17:20 | One whose **h** is corrupt does not |
| | 17:22 | A cheerful **h** is good medicine, |
| | 19:21 | Many are the plans in a human **h**, |
| | 20: 9 | can say, "I have kept my **h** pure; |
| | 21: 1 | hand the king's **h** is a stream |
| | 21: 2 | right, but the Lord weighs the **h**. |
| | 22:11 | One who loves a pure **h** and who |
| | 22:15 | Folly is bound up in the **h** of a child, |
| | 22:17 | apply your **h** to what I teach, |
| | 22:18 | when you keep them in your **h** |
| | 23:15 | if your **h** is wise, then my **h** will be |
| | 23:17 | Do not let your **h** envy sinners, |
| | 23:19 | and set your **h** on the right path: |
| | 23:26 | give me your **h** and let your eyes |
| | 24:17 | stumble, do not let your **h** rejoice, |
| | 27:19 | the face, so one's life reflects the **h**. |
| Ecc | 2:10 | My **h** took delight in all my labor, |
| | 3:11 | set eternity in the human **h**; |
| | 5: 2 | your **h** to utter anything before God. |
| | 7: 7 | fools, and a bribe corrupts the **h**. |
| | 8: 5 | and the wise **h** will know the proper |
| | 9: 7 | and drink your wine with a joyful **h**, |
| | 11:10 | banish anxiety from your **h** and cast |
| SS | 3: 1 | bed I looked for the one my **h** loves; |
| | 4: 9 | You have stolen my **h**, my sister, |
| | 5: 2 | I slept but my **h** was awake. Listen! |
| | 8: 6 | Place me like a seal over your **h**, |
| Isa | 6:10 | Make the **h** of this people calloused; |
| | 40:11 | arms and carries them close to his **h**, |
| | 51: 7 | who have taken my instruction to **h**: |
| | 57:15 | and to revive the **h** of the contrite. |
| | 66:14 | this, your **h** will rejoice and you will |
| Jer | 3:10 | did not return to me with all her **h**, |
| | 3:15 | give you shepherds after my own **h**, |
| | 4:14 | wash the evil from your **h** and be |
| | 9:26 | of Israel is uncircumcised in **h**." |
| | 17: 9 | The **h** is deceitful above all things |
| | 17:10 | "I the Lord search the **h** |
| | 20: 9 | his word is in my **h** like a fire, a fire |
| | 24: 7 | I will give them a **h** to know me, |
| | 29:13 | when you seek me with all your **h**. |
| | 32:39 | I will give them singleness of **h**; |
| | 32:41 | plant them in this land with all my **h** |
| | 51:46 | Do not lose **h** or be afraid |
| Eze | 11:19 | remove from them their **h** of stone and give them a **h** of flesh. |
| | 18:31 | and get a new **h** and a new spirit. |
| | 28: 2 | " 'In the pride of your **h** you say, |
| | 36:26 | I will give you a new **h** and put |
| | 44: 7 | foreigners uncircumcised in **h** |
| Hos | 11: 8 | My **h** is changed within me; |
| Joel | 2:12 | "return to me with all your **h**, |
| | 2:13 | Rend your **h** and not your garments. |
| Ob | 1: 3 | pride of your **h** has deceived you, |
| Zep | 3:14 | Be glad and rejoice with all your **h**, |
| Mt | 5: 8 | Blessed are the pure in **h**, for they |

| Mt | 5:28 | adultery with her in his **h**. |
| | 6:21 | treasure is, there your **h** will be also. |
| | 11:29 | for I am gentle and humble in **h**, |
| | 12:34 | overflow of the **h** the mouth speaks. |
| | 13:15 | For this people's **h** has become |
| | 15:18 | out of the mouth come from the **h**, |
| | 15:19 | For out of the **h** come evil thoughts, |
| | 18:35 | a brother or sister from your **h**." |
| | 22:37 | the Lord your God with all your **h** |
| Mk | 11:23 | do not doubt in your **h** but believe |
| | 12:30 | the Lord your God with all your **h** |
| | 12:33 | To love him with all your **h**, with all |
| Lk | 2:19 | things and pondered them in her **h**. |
| | 2:51 | treasured all these things in her **h**. |
| | 6:45 | overflow of the **h** the mouth speaks. |
| | 8:15 | for those with a noble and good **h**, |
| | 10:27 | the Lord your God with all your **h** |
| | 12:34 | treasure is, there your **h** will be also. |
| Ac | 1:24 | "Lord, you know everyone's **h**. |
| | 2:37 | they were cut to the **h** and said |
| | 4:32 | All the believers were one in **h** |
| | 5: 3 | Satan has so filled your **h** that you |
| | 8:21 | because your **h** is not right before |
| | 15: 8 | who knows the **h**, showed that he |
| | 16:14 | The Lord opened her **h** to respond |
| | 28:27 | For this people's **h** has become |
| Ro | 2:29 | is circumcision of the **h**, |
| | 6:17 | come to obey from your **h** the pattern |
| | 10: 8 | it is in your mouth and in your **h**," |
| | 10: 9 | in your **h** that God raised him |
| 2Co | 2: 4 | anguish of **h** and with many tears, |
| | 4: 1 | have this ministry, we do not lose **h**. |
| | 4:16 | Therefore we do not lose **h**. |
| | 9: 7 | you have decided in your **h** to give, |
| Eph | 1:18 | eyes of your **h** may be enlightened |
| | 5:19 | music from your **h** to the Lord, |
| | 6: 5 | and with sincerity of **h**, just as you |
| | 6: 6 | doing the will of God from your **h**. |
| Php | 1: 7 | you, since I have you in my **h** and, |
| Col | 2: 2 | is that they may be encouraged in **h** |
| | 3:22 | with sincerity of **h** and reverence |
| | 3:23 | you do, work at it with all your **h**, |
| 1Ti | 1: 5 | which comes from a pure **h** |
| 2Ti | 2:22 | call on the Lord out of a pure **h**. |
| Phm | 1:12 | who is my very **h**—back to you. |
| | 1:20 | in the Lord; refresh my **h** in Christ. |
| Heb | 3:12 | unbelieving **h** that turns away |
| | 4:12 | the thoughts and attitudes of the **h**. |
| | 10:22 | with a sincere **h** in full assurance |
| | 12: 5 | do not lose **h** when he rebukes you, |
| 1Pe | 1:22 | love one another deeply, from the **h**. |
| Rev | 18: 7 | In her **h** she boasts, 'I sit enthroned |

**ALL ... HEART** Dt 4:29; 6:5; 10:12; 11:13;
13:3; 26:16; 30:2, 6, 10; Jos 22:5; 23:14; 1Sa
12:20, 24; 2Sa 3:21; 22:46; 1Ki 2:4; 8:48; 11:37;
14:8; 2Ki 10:31; 23:3, 25; 2Ch 6:38; 15:12; 22:9;
34:31; Ne 4:6; Ps 9:1; 18:45; 86:12; 111:1; 119:2,
10, 34, 58, 69, 145; 138:1; Pr 3:5; 4:4; Jer 3:10;
24:7; 29:13; 32:41; Joel 2:12; Zep 3:14; Mt
22:37; Mk 12:30, 33; Lk 10:27; Col 3:23

## HEART'S* [HEART]

| 2Ch | 1:11 | "Since this is your **h** desire and you |
| Ps | 21: 2 | granted him his **h** desire |
| Jer | 15:16 | they were my joy and my **h** delight, |
| Eze | 24:25 | delight of their eyes, their **h** desire, |

| Ro | 10: 1 | my **h** desire and prayer to God |

## HEARTACHE* [HEART]

| Pr | 15:13 | cheerful, but **h** crushes the spirit. |

## HEARTFELT* [HEART]

| Pr | 27: 9 | springs from their **h** advice. |

## HEARTLESS* [HEART]

| La | 4: 3 | people have become **h** like ostriches |

## HEARTS [HEART]

| Ex | 9:34 | and his officials hardened their **h**. |
| | 14:17 | I will harden the **h** of the Egyptians |
| Lev | 26:36 | I will make their **h** so fearful |
| | 26:41 | their uncircumcised **h** are humbled |
| Nu | 15:39 | chasing after the lusts of your own **h** |
| Dt | 1:28 | Our brothers have made our **h** melt |
| | 5:29 | that their **h** would be inclined to fear |
| | 6: 6 | I give you today are to be on your **h**. |
| | 10:16 | Circumcise your **h**, therefore, |
| | 11:18 | Fix these words of mine in your **h** |
| | 30: 6 | will circumcise your **h** and the **h** |
| Jos | 5: 1 | their **h** melted in fear and they no |
| | 7: 5 | At this the **h** of the people melted |
| | 11:20 | himself who hardened their **h** |
| | 14: 8 | me made the **h** of the people melt |
| | 24:23 | you and yield your **h** to the Lᴏʀᴅ, |
| 1Sa | 6: 6 | you harden your **h** as the Egyptians |
| | 7: 3 | to the Lᴏʀᴅ with all your **h**, |
| | 10:26 | by valiant men whose **h** God had |
| 2Sa | 15: 6 | so he stole the **h** of the people |
| 1Ki | 8:39 | do, since you know their **h** (for you |
| | 8:61 | may your **h** be fully committed |
| | 18:37 | you are turning their **h** back again." |
| 1Ch | 29:18 | in the **h** of your people forever, |
| | 29:18 | and keep their **h** loyal to you. |
| 2Ch | 6:30 | do, since you know their **h** (for you |
| | 11:16 | Israel who set their **h** on seeking |
| | 29:31 | all whose **h** were willing brought |
| Job | 1: 5 | sinned and cursed God in their **h**." |
| Ps | 4: 4 | beds, search your **h** and be silent. |
| | 7: 9 | God who probes minds and **h**. |
| | 14: 1 | Fools say in their **h**, "There is no |
| | 33:15 | he who forms the **h** of all, |
| | 33:21 | In him our **h** rejoice, for we trust |
| | 37:31 | The law of their God is in their **h**; |
| | 53: 1 | Fools say in their **h**, "There is no |
| | 62: 8 | pour out your **h** to him, for God is |
| | 78: 8 | whose **h** were not loyal to God, |
| | 81:12 | their stubborn **h** to follow their own |
| | 95: 8 | "Do not harden your **h** as you did |
| | 104:15 | wine that gladdens human **h**, |
| | 112: 7 | their **h** are steadfast, |
| | 112: 8 | Their **h** are secure, they will have no |
| Pr | 6:14 | who plot evil with deceit in their **h**— |
| | 16:23 | The **h** of the wise make their |
| Ecc | 9: 3 | madness in their **h** while they live, |
| Isa | 26: 8 | and renown are the desire of our **h**. |
| | 29:13 | lips, but their **h** are far from me. |
| | 35: 4 | say to those with fearful **h**, |
| | 59:13 | uttering lies our **h** have conceived. |
| | 63:17 | harden our **h** so we do not revere |
| | 65:14 | will sing out of the joy of their **h**, |
| Jer | 4: 4 | circumcise your **h**, you people |
| | 12: 2 | on their lips but far from their **h**. |

Jer  17: 1  on the tablets of their **h**
     31:33  their minds and write it on their **h**.
La    5:15  Joy is gone from our **h**;
Eze  14: 3  men have set up idols in their **h**
     20:16  For their **h** were devoted to their
Mal   4: 6  the **h** of the children to their parents;
Mt   15: 8  lips, but their **h** are far from me.
     19: 8  wives because your **h** were hard.
Mk    6:52  their **h** were hardened.
      7: 6  lips, but their **h** are far from me.
      7:21  out of your **h**, come evil thoughts,
Lk    1:17  to turn the **h** of the parents to their
     16:15  of others, but God knows your **h**.
     24:32  "Were not our **h** burning within us
Jn    5:42  not have the love of God in your **h**.
     12:40  their eyes and hardened their **h**,
     14: 1  "Do not let your **h** be troubled.
     14:27  Do not let your **h** be troubled and do
Ac    2:46  ate together with glad and sincere **h**,
      7:51  Your **h** and ears are still
     11:23  true to the Lord with all their **h**.
     15: 9  for he purified their **h** by faith.
     28:27  understand with their **h** and turn,
Ro    1:21  and their foolish **h** were darkened.
      2:15  of the law are written on their **h**,
      5: 5  into our **h** through the Holy Spirit,
      8:27  who searches our **h** knows the mind
1Co   4: 5  expose the motives of people's **h**.
     14:25  the secrets of their **h** are laid bare.
2Co   1:22  put his Spirit in our **h** as a deposit,
      3: 2  written on our **h**, known and read
      3: 3  of stone but on tablets of human **h**.
      3:15  Moses is read, a veil covers their **h**.
      4: 6  shine in our **h** to give us the light
      6:11  and opened wide our **h** to you.
      6:13  open wide your **h** also.
      7: 2  Make room for us in your **h**.
Gal   4: 6  sent the Spirit of his Son into our **h**,
Eph   3:17  may dwell in your **h** through faith.
Php   4: 7  will guard your **h** and your minds
Col   3: 1  Christ, set your **h** on things above,
      3:15  the peace of Christ rule in your **h**,
      3:16  to God with gratitude in your **h**.
1Th   2: 4  people but God, who tests our **h**.
      3:13  May he strengthen your **h** so
2Th   2:17  encourage your **h** and strengthen
Phm   1: 7  have refreshed the **h** of the Lord's
Heb   3: 8  do not harden your **h** as you did
      8:10  minds and write them on their **h**.
     10:16  I will put my laws in their **h**, and I
     10:22  having our **h** sprinkled to cleanse us
     13: 9  is good for our **h** to be strengthened
Jas   4: 8  you sinners, and purify your **h**,
1Pe   3:15  But in your **h** revere Christ as Lord.
2Pe   1:19  and the morning star rises in your **h**.
1Jn   3:20  If our **h** condemn us,
      3:20  know that God is greater than our **h**,
Rev   2:23  know that I am he who searches **h**
     17:17  their **h** to accomplish his purpose

# HEARTS'* [HEART]
Pr   13:25  The righteous eat to their **h**' content,

# HEAT
Ge    8:22  cold and **h**, summer and winter,
2Pe   3:12  and the elements will melt in the **h**.

Rev  16: 9  They were seared by the intense **h**

## HEAVE [OFFERING] (KJV) See WAVE [OFFERING]

## HEAVEN [HEAVENLY, HEAVENS, HEAVENWARD]
Ge   14:19  Most High, Creator of **h** and earth.
     21:17  angel of God called to Hagar from **h**
     22:11  LORD called out to him from **h**,
     24: 3  the God of **h** and the God of earth,
     28:12  with its top reaching to **h**,
Ex   16: 4  "I will rain down bread from **h**
     20:22  that I have spoken to you from **h**:
Dt    3:24  For what god is there in **h**
     26:15  Look down from **h**, your holy
     30:12  It is not up in **h**,
Jos   2:11  the LORD your God is God in **h**
1Ki   8:23  there is no God like you in **h**
      8:27  even the highest **h**, cannot contain
      8:30  Hear from **h**, your dwelling place,
     22:19  the host of **h** standing around him
2Ki   1:10  fire fell from **h** and consumed
      2: 1  take Elijah up to **h** in a whirlwind,
     19:15  You have made **h** and earth.
1Ch  29:11  for everything in **h** and earth is
2Ch   6:14  there is no God like you in **h**
      7:14  then I will hear from **h**, and I will
Ezr   7:12  teacher of the Law of the God of **h**:
Job  16:19  Even now my witness is in **h**;
     41:11  Everything under **h** belongs to me.
Ps    2: 4  The One enthroned in **h** laughs;
     73:25  Whom have I in **h** but you?
     75: 5  Do not lift your horns against **h**;
    115: 3  Our God is in **h**; he does whatever
    121: 2  LORD, the Maker of **h** and earth.
Pr   30: 4  Who has gone up to **h** and come
Isa  14:12  How you have fallen from **h**,
     66: 1  "**H** is my throne, and the earth is
Jer  23:24  "Do not I fill **h** and earth?"
Da    2:19  Then Daniel praised the God of **h**
      7:13  man, coming with the clouds of **h**.
Mt    3: 2  the kingdom of **h** has come near."
      3:16  At that moment **h** was opened,
      4:17  the kingdom of **h** has come near."
      5:12  because great is your reward in **h**,
      5:19  be called least in the kingdom of **h**,
      6: 9  " 'Our Father in **h**, hallowed be
      6:10  will be done, on earth as it is in **h**.
      6:20  up for yourselves treasures in **h**,
      7:21  will enter the kingdom of **h**,
      7:21  do the will of my Father who is in **h**.
     16:19  you the keys of the kingdom of **h**;
     18: 3  will never enter the kingdom of **h**.
     18:18  bind on earth will be bound in **h**,
     19:14  the kingdom of **h** belongs to such as
     19:21  and you will have treasure in **h**.
     19:23  the rich to enter the kingdom of **h**.
     23:13  the kingdom of **h** in people's faces.
     24:35  **H** and earth will pass away, but my
     26:64  and coming on the clouds of **h**."
     28:18  "All authority in **h** and on earth has
Mk    1:10  he saw **h** being torn open
      8:11  they asked him for a sign from **h**.
     10:21  and you will have treasure in **h**.
     11:30  was it from **h**, or of human origin?

| | | |
|---|---|---|
| Mk | 13:31 | **H** and earth will pass away, but my |
| | 14:62 | and coming on the clouds of **h**." |
| Lk | 3:21 | as he was praying, **h** was opened |
| | 9:54 | to call fire down from **h** to destroy |
| | 10:18 | saw Satan fall like lightning from **h**. |
| | 10:20 | that your names are written in **h**." |
| | 12:33 | a treasure in **h** that will never fail, |
| | 15: 7 | **h** over one sinner who repents than |
| | 18:22 | and you will have treasure in **h**. |
| | 19:38 | "Peace in **h** and glory |
| | 21:33 | **H** and earth will pass away, but my |
| | 24:51 | left them and was taken up into **h**. |
| Jn | 3:13 | into **h** except the one who came from **h** |
| | 6:31 | 'He gave them bread from **h** |
| | 6:38 | I have come down from **h** not to do |
| | 12:28 | Then a voice came from **h**, "I have |
| Ac | 1:11 | who has been taken from you into **h**, |
| | 7:49 | " 'H is my throne, and the earth is |
| | 7:55 | looked up to **h** and saw the glory |
| | 9: 3 | a light from **h** flashed around him. |
| | 11: 5 | a large sheet being let down from **h** |
| | 26:19 | not disobedient to the vision from **h**. |
| Ro | 10: 6 | heart, 'Who will ascend into **h**?' " |
| 1Co | 15:47 | of the earth; the second man is of **h**. |
| 2Co | 5: 1 | an eternal house in **h**, not built |
| | 12: 2 | ago was caught up to the third **h**. |
| Gal | 1: 8 | **h** should preach a gospel other than |
| Eph | 1:10 | to bring unity to all things in **h** |
| Php | 2:10 | in **h** and on earth and under |
| | 3:20 | But our citizenship is in **h**. |
| Col | 1: 5 | from the hope stored up for you in **h** |
| | 1:16 | things in **h** and on earth, |
| | 4: 1 | that you also have a Master in **h**. |
| 1Th | 1:10 | and to wait for his Son from **h**, |
| | 4:16 | himself will come down from **h**, |
| Heb | 1: 3 | at the right hand of the Majesty in **h**. |
| | 4:14 | who has ascended into **h**, |
| | 8: 5 | a copy and shadow of what is in **h**. |
| | 9:24 | he entered it itself, now to appear |
| | 12:23 | whose names are written in **h**. |
| Jas | 3:17 | comes from **h** is first of all pure; |
| 1Pe | 1: 4 | This inheritance is kept in **h** for you, |
| | 3:22 | who has gone into **h** and is at God's |
| 2Pe | 1:18 | that came from **h** when we were |
| | 3:13 | we are looking forward to a new **h** |
| Rev | 4: 1 | me was a door standing open in **h**. |
| | 5:13 | I heard every creature in **h** |
| | 11:19 | God's temple in **h** was opened, |
| | 12: 1 | and wondrous sign appeared in **h**: |
| | 12: 7 | And there was war in **h**. |
| | 15: 5 | I looked, and I saw in **h** the temple— |
| | 19: 1 | of a great multitude in **h** shouting: |
| | 19:11 | I saw **h** standing open and there |
| | 19:14 | armies of **h** were following him, |
| | 21: 1 | I saw "a new **h** and a new earth," |
| | 21: 2 | coming down out of **h** from God, |
| | 21:10 | coming down out of **h** from God. |

## GOD OF HEAVEN See GOD

## HEAVEN AND ... EARTH See EARTH

## KINGDOM OF HEAVEN See KINGDOM

## HEAVENLY [HEAVEN]

| | | |
|---|---|---|
| Ps | 8: 5 | them a little lower than the **h** beings |
| | 11: 4 | the LORD is on his **h** throne. |
| | 29: 1 | Ascribe to the LORD, you **h** beings, |

| | | |
|---|---|---|
| Ps | 89: 6 | the LORD among the **h** beings? |
| | 103:21 | all his **h** hosts, you his servants who |
| Mt | 5:48 | as your **h** Father is perfect. |
| Mk | 13:25 | and the **h** bodies will be shaken.' |
| Lk | 2:13 | company of the **h** host appeared |
| 2Co | 5: 2 | to be clothed with our **h** dwelling, |
| Eph | 1: 3 | who has blessed us in the **h** realms |
| | 1:20 | at his right hand in the **h** realms, |
| | 6:12 | forces of evil in the **h** realms. |
| 2Ti | 4:18 | bring me safely to his **h** kingdom. |
| Heb | 3: 1 | who share in the **h** calling, fix your |
| | 6. 4 | who have tasted the **h** gift, |
| | 9:23 | for the copies of the **h** things to be |
| | 12:22 | of the living God, the **h** Jerusalem. |

## HEAVENS [HEAVEN]

| | | |
|---|---|---|
| Ge | 1: 1 | In the beginning God created the **h** |
| | 2: 1 | Thus the **h** and the earth were |
| | 6:17 | earth to destroy all life under the **h**, |
| | 7:11 | the floodgates of the **h** were opened. |
| | 11: 4 | with a tower that reaches to the **h**, |
| Ex | 20:11 | in six days the LORD made the **h** |
| Dt | 4:26 | I call the **h** and the earth as |
| | 10:14 | the LORD your God belong the **h**, |
| | 28:12 | The LORD will open the **h**, |
| | 31:28 | and call the **h** and the earth to testify |
| | 33:26 | who rides on the **h** to help you |
| 2Sa | 22:10 | He parted the **h** and came down; |
| 1Ki | 8:27 | The **h**, even the highest heaven, |
| 2Ch | 2: 6 | him, since the **h**, even the highest **h**, |
| Ezr | 9: 6 | and our guilt has reached to the **h**. |
| Ne | 9: 6 | You made the **h**, even the highest **h**, |
| Job | 11: 8 | They are higher than the **h** above— |
| | 38:33 | Do you know the laws of the **h**? |
| Ps | 8: 3 | When I consider your **h**, the work |
| | 19: 1 | The **h** declare the glory of God; |
| | 33: 6 | of the LORD the **h** were made, |
| | 57: 5 | Be exalted, O God, above the **h**; |
| | 102:25 | the **h** are the work of your hands. |
| | 103:11 | as high as the **h** are above the earth, |
| | 108: 4 | great is your love, higher than the **h**; |
| | 115:16 | The highest **h** belong |
| | 119:89 | it stands firm in the **h**. |
| | 135: 6 | him, in the **h** and on the earth, |
| | 136: 5 | by his understanding made the **h**, |
| | 139: 8 | If I go up to the **h**, you are there; |
| | 148: 1 | Praise the LORD from the **h**; |
| Pr | 3:19 | understanding he set the **h** in place; |
| Ecc | 3: 1 | for every activity under the **h**: |
| Isa | 1: 2 | Hear me, you **h**! Listen, earth! |
| | 24: 4 | the **h** languish with the earth. |
| | 24:18 | The floodgates of the **h** are opened, |
| | 40:26 | Lift up your eyes and look to the **h**: |
| | 45: 8 | "You **h** above, rain down my |
| | 51: 6 | the **h** will vanish like smoke, |
| | 55: 9 | "As the **h** are higher than the earth, |
| | 65:17 | I will create new **h** and a new earth. |
| Jer | 10:11 | who did not make the **h** |
| | 31:37 | if the **h** above can be measured |
| | 32:17 | you have made the **h** and the earth |
| Eze | 1: 1 | the **h** were opened and I saw visions |
| Da | 12: 3 | shine like the brightness of the **h**, |
| Joel | 2:30 | I will show wonders in the **h** |
| Hab | 3:11 | moon stood still in the **h** at the glint |
| Mt | 24:31 | from one end of the **h** to the other. |
| Mk | 13:27 | of the earth to the ends of the **h**. |
| Eph | 4:10 | who ascended higher than all the **h**, |

Heb 7:26 from sinners, exalted above the **h**.
Jas 5:18 and the **h** gave rain, and the earth
2Pe 3: 5 God's word the **h** came into being
3:10 The **h** will disappear with a roar;
Rev 14: 7 Worship him who made the **h**,
20:11 and the **h** fled from his presence,

## HEAVENWARD* [HEAVEN]
Php 3:14 God has called me **h** in Christ Jesus.

## HEAVIER [HEAVY]
2Ch 10:14 I will make it even **h**.
Pr 27: 3 a fool's provocation is **h** than both.

## HEAVY [HEAVIER]
Ex 18:18 The work is too **h** for you;
Dt 25:13 in your bag—one **h**, one light.
1Ki 12: 4 "Your father put a **h** yoke on us,
Ecc 1:13 What a **h** burden God has laid
Isa 47: 6 on the aged you laid a very **h** yoke.
Mt 23: 4 They tie up **h**, cumbersome loads

## HEBREW [HEBREWS]
Ge 14:13 and reported this to Abram the **H**.
41:12 Now a young **H** was there with us,
Ex 1:19 "**H** women are not like Egyptian
2: 6 "This is one of the **H** babies,"
2:11 He saw an Egyptian beating a **H**,
21: 2 "If you buy a **H** servant, he is
2Ki 18:26 speak to us in **H** in the hearing
Jer 34: 9 Everyone was to free their **H** slaves,
Jnh 1: 9 "I am a **H** and I worship
Php 3: 5 tribe of Benjamin, a **H** of Hebrews;

## HEBREWS [HEBREW]
Ex 3:18 the God of the **H**, has met with us.
9: 1 the LORD, the God of the **H**, says:
2Co 11:22 Are they **H**? So am I.
Php 3: 5 tribe of Benjamin, a Hebrew of **H**;

## HEBRON [KIRIATH ARBA]
Ge 13:18 near the great trees of Mamre at **H**,
23: 2 (that is, **H**) in the land of Canaan,
Jos 14:13 and gave him **H** as his inheritance.
20: 7 is, **H**) in the hill country of Judah.
21:13 Aaron the priest they gave **H** (a city
Jdg 16: 3 to the top of the hill that faces **H**.
2Sa 2:11 David was king in **H** over the house
3: 2 Sons were born to David in **H**:
1Ch 2:43 The sons of **H**:
11: 1 Israel came together to David at **H**

## HEDGE* [HEDGED]
Job 1:10 "Have you not put a **h** around him
Isa 5: 5 I will take away its **h**, and it will be
Mic 7: 4 most upright worse than a thorn **h**.

## HEDGED* [HEDGE]
Job 3:23 way is hidden, whom God has **h** in?

## HEED [HEEDS]
1Sa 15:22 to **h** is better than the fat of rams.
Pr 15:32 who **h** correction gain understanding.
16:20 Those who give **h** to instruction
28: 7 who **h** instruction are discerning

Pr 29:18 blessed are those who **h** wisdom's
Ecc 7: 5 It is better to **h** the rebuke of a wise

## HEEDS* [HEED]
Pr 10:17 Whoever **h** discipline shows
13: 1 A wise child **h** a parent's
13:18 whoever **h** correction is honored.
15: 5 but whoever **h** correction shows
15:31 Whoever **h** life-giving correction

## HEEL
Ge 3:15 head, and you will strike his **h**."
25:26 with his hand grasping Esau's **h**;
Ps 41: 9 has lifted up his **h** against me.
Jn 13:18 has lifted up his **h** against me.'

## HEGAI
Est 2: 3 them be placed under the care of **H**,

## HEIFER
Ge 15: 9 "Bring me a **h**, a goat and a ram,
Nu 19: 2 to bring you a red **h** without defect
Jdg 14:18 "If you had not plowed with my **h**,
Heb 9:13 the ashes of a **h** sprinkled on those

## HEIGHT [HEIGHTS]
Nu 23: 3 Then he went off to a barren **h**.
1Sa 16: 7 not consider his appearance or his **h**,
17: 4 His **h** was six cubits and a span.
Ro 8:39 neither **h** nor depth, nor anything

## HEIGHTS [HEIGHT]
Dt 33:29 you will tread on their **h**."
2Sa 1:19 "A gazelle lies slain on your **h**,
Job 22:12 "Is not God in the **h** of heaven?
Ps 18:33 he causes me to stand on the **h**.
148: 1 praise him in the **h** above.
Ob 1: 3 rocks and make your home on the **h**,
Mic 1: 3 treads on the **h** of the earth.
Hab 3:19 he enables me to tread on the **h**.

## HEIR [INHERIT]
Ge 15: 4 your own body will be your **h**."
Lk 20:14 'This is the **h**,' they said.
Ro 4:13 that he would be **h** of the world,
Heb 1: 2 whom he appointed **h** of all things,
1: 7 became **h** of the righteousness

## HEIRS [INHERIT]
Ro 4:14 those who depend on the law are **h**,
8:17 if we are children, then we are **h**—
8:17 **h** of God and co-heirs with Christ,
Gal 3:29 and **h** according to the promise.
4: 1 saying is that as long as **h** are underage
4: 7 children, he has made you also **h**.
Eph 3: 6 gospel the Gentiles are **h** together
Tit 3: 7 we might become **h** having the hope
Heb 11: 9 who were **h** with him of the same
1Pe 3: 7 as **h** with you of the gracious gift

## HELD [HOLD]
Ex 17:11 As long as Moses **h** up his hands,
Dt 4: 4 you who **h** fast to the LORD your
1Sa 7:17 there he also **h** court for Israel.
1Ki 11: 2 Solomon **h** fast to them in love.

2Ki 18: 6 He **h** fast to the LORD and did not
Ps 17: 5 My steps have **h** to your paths;
SS 3: 4 I **h** him and would not let him go till
Isa 40:12 Who has **h** the dust of the earth
65: 2 All day long I have **h** out my hands
Ro 10:21 says, "All day long I have **h** out my
Gal 3:23 we were **h** in custody under the law,
Col 2:19 and **h** together by its ligaments
Rev 1:16 In his right hand he **h** seven stars,
6· 2 Its rider **h** a bow, and he was given
15: 2 They **h** harps given them by God
17: 4 She **h** a golden cup in her hand,

## HELDAI

Zec 6:14 The crown will be given to **H**,

## HELL*

Mt 5:22 will be in danger of the fire of **h**.
5:29 whole body to be thrown into **h**.
5:30 for your whole body to go into **h**.
10:28 can destroy both soul and body in **h**.
18: 9 and be thrown into the fire of **h**.
23:15 as much a child of **h** as you are.
23:33 you escape being condemned to **h**?
Mk 9:43 than with two hands to go into **h**,
9:45 have two feet and be thrown into **h**.
9:47 have two eyes and be thrown into **h**,
Lk 12: 5 has authority to throw you into **h**.
Jas 3: 6 on fire, and is itself set on fire by **h**.
2Pe 2: 4 but sent them to **h**, putting them

## HELLENISTIC*

Ac 6: 1 the **H** Jews among them complained
9:29 He talked and debated with the **H** Jews,

## HELMET

Ps 108: 8 Ephraim is my **h**, Judah is my
Isa 59:17 and the **h** of salvation on his head;
Eph 6:17 Take the **h** of salvation
1Th 5: 8 and the hope of salvation as a **h**.

## HELP [HELPED, HELPER, HELPFUL, HELPING, HELPLESS, HELPS]

Ge 4: 1 the **h** of the LORD I have brought
Ex 2:23 and their cry for **h** because of their
4:12 I will **h** you speak and will teach
23: 5 be sure you **h** your enemy with it.
Lev 25:35 **h** them as you would a foreigner
Dt 33:26 who rides on the heavens to **h** you
Jos 24: 7 But they cried to the LORD for **h**,
2Sa 22:36 your **h** has made me great.
1Ch 12:22 Day after day men came to **h** David,
2Ch 16:12 in his illness he did not seek **h**
28:16 sent to the kings of Assyria for **h**.
Ezr 4: 2 said, "Let us **h** you build because,
Ne 6:16 been done with the **h** of our God.
Job 29:12 I rescued the poor who cried for **h**,
Ps 18: 6 I cried to my God for **h**.
22:24 him but has listened to his cry for **h**.
30: 2 I called to you for **h**, and you healed
33:20 he is our **h** and our shield.
40:17 You are my **h** and my deliverer;
46: 1 an ever-present **h** in trouble.
72:12 the afflicted who have no one to **h**.
79: 9 **H** us, God our Savior, for the glory

Ps 108:12 enemy, for human **h** is worthless.
109:21 **h** me for your name's sake;
115: 9 he is their **h** and shield.
121: 1 where does my **h** come from?
146: 5 are those whose **h** is the God
Ecc 4:10 fall down, they can **h** each other up.
Isa 41:10 I will strengthen you and **h** you;
49: 8 in the day of salvation I will **h** you;
La 1: 7 hands, there was no one to **h** her.
Jnh 2: 2 the realm of the dead I called for **h**,
Mk 7:11 have been used to **h** their father
9:24 **h** me overcome my unbelief!"
Lk 11:46 will not lift one finger to **h** them.
Ac 16: 9 over to Macedonia and **h** us."
18:27 he was a great **h** to those who
20:35 of hard work we must **h** the weak,
2Co 9: 2 For I know your eagerness to **h**,
1Th 5:14 the disheartened, **h** the weak,
1Ti 5:16 the church can **h** those widows who
Heb 2:18 to **h** those who are being tempted.
4:16 and find grace to **h** us in our time

## HELPED [HELP]

1Sa 7:12 "Thus far the LORD has **h** us."
Ps 118:13 about to fall, but the LORD **h** me.
Mk 1:31 to her, took her hand and **h** her up.
Lk 1:54 He has **h** his servant Israel,
Ac 26:22 But God has **h** me to this very day;
2Co 6: 2 and in the day of salvation I **h** you."

## HELPER [HELP]

Ge 2:18 I will make a **h** suitable for him."
Ex 18: 4 said, "My father's God was my **h**;
Dt 33:29 He is your shield and **h** and your
Ps 10:14 you are the **h** of the fatherless.
118: 7 The LORD is with me; he is my **h**.
Heb 13: 6 confidence, "The Lord is my **h**;

## HELPFUL [HELP]

Eph 4:29 only what is **h** for building others

## HELPING [HELP]

Lk 8: 3 These women were **h** to support
Ac 9:36 always doing good and **h** the poor.
1Co 12:28 gifts of healing, of **h**, of guidance,
1Ti 5:10 **h** those in trouble and devoting

## HELPLESS [HELP]

Ps 10:12 hand, O God. Do not forget the **h**.
Pr 28:15 is a wicked ruler over a **h** people.
Mt 9:36 because they were harassed and **h**,

## HELPS [HELP]

Ps 37:40 The LORD **h** them and delivers
Isa 50: 7 the Sovereign LORD **h** me, I will
Ro 8:26 the Spirit **h** us in our weakness.
Heb 2:16 For surely it is not angels he **h**,

## HEM

1Sa 15:27 caught hold of the **h** of his robe,
Ps 139: 5 You **h** me in behind and before,
Hab 1: 4 The wicked **h** in the righteous,

## HEMAN

1Ki 4:31 wiser than **H**, Kalkol and Darda,

1Ch 15:19 The musicians **H**, Asaph and Ethan
Ps   88: T  *A maskil of **H** the Ezrahite.*

## HEN
Mt  23:37 as a **h** gathers her chicks under her
Lk  13:34 as a **h** gathers her chicks under her

## HEPHZIBAH
Isa  62: 4 But you will be called **H**, and your

## HERALD
Hab  2: 2 tablets so that a **h** may run with it.
1Ti   2: 7 for this purpose I was appointed a **h**
2Ti   1:11 of this gospel I was appointed a **h**

## HERBS
Ex  12: 8 along with bitter **h**, and bread made
Nu   9:11 with unleavened bread and bitter **h**.
La    3:15 He has filled me with bitter **h**

## HERD [HERDERS, HERDS]
Lev 27:32 Every tithe of the **h** and flock—
Mt   8:31 us out, send us into the **h** of pigs."

## HERDERS [HERD]
Ge  13: 7 quarreling arose between Abram's **h**
    26:20 the **h** of Gerar quarreled with those

## HERDS [HERD]
Nu  32: 1 who had very large **h** and flocks,
Dt    8:13 when your **h** and flocks grow large
    12: 6 the firstborn of your **h** and flocks.

## HERE
Ge   3:12 "The woman you put **h** with me—
    22: 1 "**H** I am," he replied.
Ex   3: 4 And Moses said, "**H** I am."
1Sa  3: 4 Samuel answered, "**H** I am."
Ps  40: 7 Then I said, "**H** I am, I have come—
Isa   6: 8 And I said, "**H** am I. Send me!"
    40: 9 towns of Judah, "**H** is your God!"
Mt  12:42 now one greater than Solomon is **h**.
    24:23 to you, 'Look, **h** is the Messiah!'
Mk  14:42 Let us go! **H** comes my betrayer!"
    16: 6 He is not **h**. See the place where
Lk  24: 6 He is not **h**; he has risen!
Heb 10: 7 Then I said, '**H** I am—it is written
Rev  3:20 **H** I am! I stand at the door
    4: 1 "Come up **h**, and I will show you
    11:12 saying to them, "Come up **h**."

## HERESIES*
2Pe  2: 1 will secretly introduce destructive **h**,

## HERITAGE [INHERIT]
Ps  61: 5 you have given me the **h** of those
    119:111 Your statutes are my **h** forever;
    127: 3 Children are a **h** from the LORD,
Isa  54:17 This is the **h** of the servants

## HERMON
Dt   3: 8 the Arnon Gorge as far as Mount **H**.
Ps 133: 3 the dew of **H** were falling on Mount

## HERO* [HEROES]
1Sa 17:51 saw that their **h** was dead,
2Sa 23: 1 the **h** of Israel's songs:
Ps  52: 1 boast of evil, you mighty **h**?
Isa   3: 2 the **h** and the warrior, the judge

## HEROD [ANTIPAS, HERODIANS]
1. King of Judea who tried to kill Jesus (Mt 2; Lk 1:5).
2. Son of 1. Tetrarch of Galilee who arrested and beheaded John the Baptist (Mt 14:1–12; Mk 6:14–29; Lk 3:1, 19–20; 9:7–9); tried Jesus (Lk 23:6–15).
3. Grandson of 1. King of Judea who killed James (Ac 12:2); arrested Peter (Ac 12:3–19). Death (Ac 12:19–23).

## HERODIANS* [HEROD]
Mt  22:16 disciples to him along with the **H**.
Mk   3: 6 the **H** how they might kill Jesus.
    12:13 and **H** to Jesus to catch him in his

## HERODIAS
Wife of Herod the Tetrarch who persuaded her daughter to ask for John the Baptist's head (Mt 14:1–12; Mk 6:14–29).

## HEROES [HERO]
Isa   5:22 to those who are **h** at drinking wine

## HESHBON
Nu  21:26 **H** was the city of Sihon king
Dt    3: 6 we had done with Sihon king of **H**,

## HESITATED
Ge  19:16 When he **h**, the men grasped his
Ac  20:27 For I have not **h** to proclaim to you

## HEWN*
Isa  51: 1 the quarry from which you were **h**;

## HEZEKIAH
King of Judah. Restored the temple and worship (2Ch 29–31). Sought the LORD for help against Assyria (2Ki 18–19; 2Ch 32:1–23; Isa 36–37). Illness healed (2Ki 20:1–11; 2Ch 32:24–26; Isa 38). Judged for showing Babylonians his treasures (2Ki 20:12–21; 2Ch 32:31; Isa 39).

## HEZRON
Ru   4:18 Perez was the father of **H**,
Mt   1: 3 Perez the father of **H**, **H** the father

## HID [HIDE]
Ge   3: 8 they **h** from the LORD God among
Ex   2: 2 child, she **h** him for three months.
    3: 6 At this, Moses **h** his face,
Jos  6:17 because she **h** the spies we sent.
1Ki 18:13 I **h** a hundred of the LORD's
2Ch 22:11 she **h** the child from Athaliah so she
Isa  49: 2 in the shadow of his hand he **h** me;
    54: 8 In a surge of anger I **h** my face
Eze 39:23 So I **h** my face from them
Mt  13:44 When a man found it, he **h** it again,
    25:25 out and **h** your gold in the ground.

Heb 11:23  faith Moses' parents **h** him for three

## HIDDEN [HIDE]

Ge   4:14  and I will be **h** from your presence;
Jos   2: 6  **h** them under the stalks of flax she
       7:22  and there it was, **h** in his tent,
1Sa 10:22  "Yes, he has **h** himself among
2Ki  11: 3  He remained **h** with his nurse
Job 28:11  the rivers and bring **h** things to light.
Ps  19:12  Forgive my **h** faults.
      69: 5  my guilt is not **h** from you.
    119:11  I have **h** your word in my heart
    142: 3  where I walk people have **h** a snare
Pr   2: 4  and search for it as for **h** treasure,
      27: 5  Better is open rebuke than **h** love.
Ecc 12:14  including every **h** thing, whether it
Isa 40:27  "My way is **h** from the LORD;
      59: 2  your sins have **h** his face from you,
Da   2:22  He reveals deep and **h** things;
Mt   5:14  A city on a hill cannot be **h**.
     10:26  or **h** that will not be made known.
     13:35  will utter things **h** since the creation
     13:44  heaven is like treasure **h** in a field.
Mk   4:22  For whatever is **h** is meant to be
Lk  10:21  because you have **h** these things
     18:34  Its meaning was **h** from them,
Ro  16:25  of the mystery **h** for long ages past,
1Co  2: 7  a mystery that has been **h**
       4: 5  bring to light what is **h** in darkness
Eph   3: 9  for ages past was kept **h** in God,
Col   1:26  that has been kept **h** for ages
       2: 3  in whom are **h** all the treasures
       3: 3  and your life is now **h** with Christ
Heb   4:13  in all creation is **h** from God's sight.
Rev   2:17  I will give some of the **h** manna.

## HIDE [HID, HIDDEN, HIDES, HIDING]

Ge  18:17  "Shall I **h** from Abraham what I am
Ex   2: 3  when she could **h** him no longer,
Lev  4:11  But the **h** of the bull and all its flesh,
Nu  19: 5  its **h**, flesh, blood and intestines.
Dt  31:17  I will **h** my face from them,
Ps  13: 1  How long will you **h** your face
      17: 8  **h** me in the shadow of your wings
      27: 5  he will **h** me in the shelter of his
      51: 9  **H** your face from my sins and blot
    143: 9  LORD, for I **h** myself in you.
Isa  53: 3  whom people **h** their faces he was
Eze 39:29  I will no longer **h** my face
Rev  6:16  **h** us from the face of him who sits

## HIDES [HIDE]

Lk   8:16  lights a lamp and **h** it in a clay jar

## HIDING [HIDE]

Ps  32: 7  You are my **h** place;
Pr  28:12  rise to power, people go into **h**.
Isa 45:15  God who has been **h** himself,

## HIGH [HIGHER, HIGHEST, HIGHLY]

Ge  14:18  He was priest of God Most **H**,
     14:22  God Most **H**, Creator of heaven
Lev 16:32  to succeed his father as **h** priest is
     26:30  I will destroy your **h** places,

1Sa   2: 1  in the LORD my horn is lifted **h**.
1Ki   3: 2  were still sacrificing at the **h** places,
      11: 7  Solomon built a **h** place
     12:31  Jeroboam built shrines on **h** places
Ps   7: 7  you sit enthroned over them on **h**.
      7:10  My shield is God Most **H**,
      21: 7  of the Most **H** he will not be shaken.
     46: 4  place where the Most **H** dwells.
     82: 6  you are all sons of the Most **H**.'
    103:11  For as **h** as the heavens are
    113: 5  the One who sits enthroned on **h**,
Pr  24: 7  Wisdom is too **h** for fools;
Isa 14:14  will make myself like the Most **H**."
Jer   2:20  on every **h** hill and under every
Eze  1:26  **h** above on the throne was a figure
Da   4:17  the Most **H** is sovereign over
Mt   4: 8  devil took him to a very **h** mountain
     17: 1  and led them up a **h** mountain
Mk   5: 7  me, Jesus, Son of the Most **H** God?
     14:53  They took Jesus to the **h** priest,
Jn  18:22  the way you answer the **h** priest?"
Ac  23: 4  dare you insult God's **h** priest!"
Eph   3:18  long and **h** and deep is the love
       4: 8  "When he ascended on **h**, he took
Heb   2:17  faithful **h** priest in service to God,
       7: 1  of Salem and priest of God Most **H**,
       7:26  Such a **h** priest truly meets our

**HIGH PLACE** 1Sa 9:12, 13, 14, 19, 25; 10:5, 13; 1Ki 3:4; 11:7; 2Ki 17:11; 23:15, 15, 15; 1Ch 16:39; 21:29; 2Ch 1:3, 13; Isa 16:12; Eze 20:29; Mic 1:5; Lk 4:5

**HIGH PLACES** Lev 26:30; Nu 33:52; 1Ki 3:2, 3; 12:31, 32; 13:2, 32, 33, 33; 14:23; 15:14; 22:43; 2Ki 12:3; 14:4; 15:4, 35; 16:4; 17:9, 29, 32; 18:4, 22; 21:3; 23:5, 8, 9, 13, 19, 20; 2Ch 11:15; 14:3, 5; 15:17; 17:6; 20:33; 21:11; 28:4, 25; 31:1; 32:12; 33:3, 17, 19; 34:3; Ps 78:58; Isa 15:2; 36:7; Jer 7:31; 17:3; 19:5; 32:35; 48:35; Eze 6:3, 6; 16:16; Hos 10:8; Am 7:9

**HIGH PRIEST** Lev 16:32; 21:10; Nu 35:25, 28, 28, 32; Jos 20:6; 2Ki 12:10; 22:4, 8; 23:4; 2Ch 34:9; Ne 3:1, 20; 13:28; Hag 1:1, 12, 14; 2:2, 4; Zec 3:1, 8; 6:11; Mt 26:3, 51, 57, 58, 62, 63, 65; Mk 2:26; 14:47, 53, 54, 60, 61, 63, 66; Lk 22:50, 54; Jn 11:49, 51; 18:13, 15, 16, 19, 22, 24; Ac 4:6; 5:17, 21, 27; 7:1; 9:1; 22:5; 23:2, 4, 5; 24:1; Heb 2:17; 3:1; 4:14, 15; 5:1, 5, 10; 6:20; 7:26; 8:1, 3; 9:7, 11, 25; 13:11

**MOST HIGH** Ge 14:18, 19, 20, 22; Nu 24:16; Dt 32:8; 1Sa 2:10; 2Sa 22:14; 23:1; Ps 7:8, 10, 17; 9:2; 18:13; 21:7; 46:4; 47:2; 50:14; 57:2; 73:11; 77:10; 78:17, 35, 56; 82:6; 83:18; 87:5; 91:1, 9; 92:1; 97:9; 107:11; Isa 14:14; La 3:35, 38; Da 3:26; 4:2, 17, 24, 25, 32, 34; 5:18, 21; 7:18, 22, 25, 27; Hos 7:16; 11:7; Mk 5:7; Lk 1:32, 35, 76; 6:35; 8:28; Ac 7:48; 16:17; Heb 7:1

## HIGHER [HIGH]

Dt  28:43  you will rise above you **h** and **h**,
Ps  61: 2  lead me to the rock that is **h** than I.
    108: 4  is your love, **h** than the heavens;
Isa 55: 9  the heavens are **h** than the earth,

## HIGHEST [HIGH]

1Ki   8:27  even the **h** heaven, cannot contain
Ps  115:16  The **h** heavens belong
Pr    9: 3  and she calls from the **h** point
Isa   2: 2  established as the **h** of the mountains;
Mt    4: 5  had him stand on the **h** point
     21: 9  "Hosanna in the **h** heaven!"
Lk    2:14  "Glory to God in the **h** heaven,
     19:38  in heaven and glory in the **h**!"
Php   2: 9  God exalted him to the **h** place

## HIGHLY [HIGH]

Ex   15: 1  to the LORD, for he is **h** exalted.
1Ch 29:25  The LORD **h** exalted Solomon
Da   10:11  you who are **h** esteemed,
Lk    1:28  "Greetings, you who are **h** favored!
Ro   12: 3  of yourself more **h** than you ought,

## HIGHWAY

Pr    7:27  Her house is a **h** to the grave,
     16:17  The **h** of the upright avoids evil;
Isa  40: 3  in the desert a **h** for our God.

## HILKIAH

2Ki  22:10  king, "**H** the priest has given me
2Ch 34:14  **H** the priest found the Book

## HILL [HILLS]

Ex   17: 9  on top of the **h** with the staff of God
1Sa  17: 3  The Philistines occupied one **h**
1Ki  16:24  He bought the **h** of Samaria
Isa  40: 4  every mountain and **h** made low;
Jer  26:18  the temple **h** a mound overgrown
Da    9:16  Jerusalem, your city, your holy **h**.
Mic   3:12  the temple **h** a mound overgrown
Mt    5:14  A city on a **h** cannot be hidden.
Lk    3: 5  in, every mountain and **h** made low.

## HILL COUNTRY  Ge 10:30; 14:6; 31:21, 23,
25, 54; 36:8, 9; Nu 13:17, 29; 14:40, 44, 45; Dt
1:7, 19, 20, 24, 41, 43; 2:1, 3, 5; 3:12, 25; Jos
9:1; 10:6, 40; 11:3, 16, 21, 21, 21; 12:8; 14:12;
15:48; 16:1; 17:15, 16, 18; 18:12; 19:50; 20:7, 7,
7; 21:11, 21; 24:4, 30, 33; Jdg 1:9, 19, 34; 2:9;
3:27; 4:5; 7:24; 10:1; 12:15; 17:1, 8; 18:2, 13;
19:1, 16, 18; 1Sa 1:1; 9:4; 13:2; 14:22; 2Sa
20:21; 1Ki 4:8; 12:25; 2Ki 5:22; 1Ch 4:42; 6:67;
2Ch 13:4; 19:4; 27:4; Ne 8:15; Ps 78:54; Jer
17:26; 32:44; 33:13; Mal 1:3; Lk 1:39, 65

## HOLY HILL  See HOLY

## HILLS [HILL]

1Ki  20:23  him, "Their gods are gods of the **h**.
2Ch  18:16  the **h** like sheep without a shepherd,
Ps   50:10  and the cattle on a thousand **h**.
    114: 6  leap like rams, you **h**, like lambs?
Pr    8:25  before the **h**, I was given birth,
Isa   2: 2  it will be exalted above the **h**,
Hos  10: 8  and to the **h**, "Fall on us!"
Joel  3:18  wine, and the **h** will flow with milk;
Am    9:13  mountains and flow from all the **h**,
Lk   23:30  and to the **h**, "Cover us!" '
Rev  17: 9  The seven heads are seven **h**

## HINDER [HINDERED, HINDERS, HINDRANCE]

1Sa  14: 6  Nothing can **h** the LORD
Mt   19:14  and do not **h** them, for the kingdom
1Co   9:12  anything rather than **h** the gospel
1Pe   3: 7  so that nothing will **h** your prayers.

## HINDERED* [HINDER]

Lk   11:52  and you have **h** those who were
Ro   15:22  This is why I have often been **h**

## HINDERS* [HINDER]

Heb  12: 1  let us throw off everything that **h**

## HINDRANCE* [HINDER]

Ac   28:31  with all boldness and without **h**!

## HINGES*

Pr   26:14  As a door turns on its **h**,

## HINT*

Eph   5: 3  you there must not be even a **h**

## HIP

Ge   32:25  touched the socket of Jacob's **h** so
     32:25  his **h** was wrenched as he wrestled

## HIRAM

King of Tyre; helped David build his palace (2Sa
5:11–12; 1Ch 14:1); helped Solomon build the temple
(1Ki 5; 2Ch 2) and his navy (1Ki 9:10–27; 2Ch 8).

## HIRE [HIRED, HIRES]

1Sa   2: 5  Those who were full **h** themselves
Mt   20: 1  in the morning to **h** workers for his

## HIRED [HIRE]

Lev  19:13  the wages of a **h** worker overnight.
Dt   23: 4  and they **h** Balaam son of Beor
     24:14  of a **h** worker who is poor
Ne    6:13  He had been **h** to intimidate me so
Lk   15:15  and **h** himself out to a citizen
Jn   10:12  The **h** hand is not the shepherd

## HIRES* [HIRE]

Pr   26:10  at random is one who **h** a fool

## HISTORY

Ezr   4:19  that this city has a long **h** of revolt

## HIT [HITS]

Ex   21:22  a pregnant woman is **h** and gives
Dt   19: 5  head may fly off and **h** his neighbor
Pr   23:35  "They **h** me," you will say,
Lk   22:64  Who **h** you?"

## HITS [HIT]

Ex   21:26  "An owner who **h** a male or female

## HITTITE [HITTITES]

Ge   23:10  Ephron the **H** was sitting among his
     27:46  living because of these **H** women.

Jos  1: 4  all the **H** country—
2Sa 11: 3  Eliam and the wife of Uriah the **H**."
    11:17  moreover, Uriah the **H** died.

## HITTITES [HITTITE]
Ge  25:10  Abraham had bought from the **H**.
Dt  20:17  the **H**, Amorites, Canaanites,
Ezr  9: 1  like those of the Canaanites, **H**,

## HIVITES
Ex  23:28  hornet ahead of you to drive the **H**,
Jos  9: 7  The Israelites said to the **H**,

## HOARD* [HOARDED]
Pr  11:26  People curse those who **h** grain,

## HOARDED* [HOARD]
Ecc  5:13  wealth **h** to the harm of its owners,
Isa 23:18  not be stored up or **h**.
Jas  5: 3  You have **h** wealth in the last days.

## HOBAB
Nu 10:29  Now Moses said to **H** son of Reuel

## HOLD [HELD, HOLDING, HOLDS]
Ex  4: 4  reached out and took **h** of the snake
    9: 2  go and continue to **h** them back,
    20: 7  LORD will not **h** anyone guiltless
Lev 19:13  " 'Do not **h** back the wages
Dt  5:11  LORD will not **h** anyone guiltless
    11:22  to him and to **h** fast to him—
    13: 4  serve him and **h** fast to him.
    30:20  listen to his voice, and **h** fast to him.
Jos 22: 5  to **h** fast to him and serve him
2Sa  6: 6  out and took **h** of the ark of God,
2Ki  4:16  "you will **h** a son in your arms."
Ps  18:16  from on high and took **h** of me;
    73:23  you **h** me by my right hand.
   119:31  I **h** fast to your statutes, LORD;
Pr  3:18  those who **h** her fast will be blessed.
    4: 4  "Take **h** of my words with all your
    5:22  the cords of their sins **h** them fast.
    10:19  but the prudent **h** their tongues.
    17:28  discerning if they **h** their tongues.
Isa 22:17  is about to take firm **h** of you
    41:13  the LORD your God who takes **h**
    54: 2  tent curtains wide, do not **h** back;
Jer  6:11  of the LORD, and I cannot **h** it in.
Eze  3:18  I will **h** you accountable for their
    3:20  I will **h** you accountable for their
    33: 6  I will **h** the watchman accountable
Zec  8:23  nations will take firm **h** of one Jew
Mk 11:25  if you **h** anything against anyone,
Jn  8:31  "If you **h** to my teaching, you are
    20:17  Jesus said, "Do not **h** on to me,
Ac  2:24  for death to keep its **h** on him.
    7:60  do not **h** this sin against them."
1Co 15: 2  saved, if you **h** firmly to the word I
Php 2:16  as you **h** firmly to the word of life.
    3:12  I press on to take **h**
    3:12  for which Christ Jesus took **h** of me.
Col  1:17  and in him all things **h** together.
1Th  5:21  test them all; **h** on to what is good,
2Th  2:15  **h** fast to the teachings we passed
1Ti  3: 9  They must keep **h** of the deep truths

1Ti  6:12  Take **h** of the eternal life
    6:19  so that they may take **h** of the life
Tit  1: 9  He must **h** firmly to the trustworthy
Heb  3:14  if indeed we **h** firmly till the end our
    4:14  God, let us **h** firmly to the faith we
    6:18  take **h** of the hope set before us may
    10:23  Let us **h** unswervingly to the hope
Rev  1:18  And I **h** the keys of death
    12:17  **h** fast their testimony about Jesus.
    19:10  sisters who **h** to Jesus' testimony.

## HOLDING [HOLD]
Ne  4:21  the work with half the men **h** spears,
Jer 15: 6  destroy you; I am tired of **h** back.
Mk  7: 3  **h** to the tradition of the elders.
1Co 11: 2  and for **h** to the traditions just as I

## HOLDS [HOLD]
2Th  2: 7  but the one who now **h** it back will
Heb  2:14  the power of him who **h** the power
Rev  2: 1  words of him who **h** the seven stars
    3: 1  of him who **h** the seven spirits
    3: 7  and true, who **h** the key of David.

## HOLE [HOLES]
Isa 11: 8  Infants will play near the **h**

## HOLES [HOLE]
Hag  1: 6  to put them in a purse with **h** in it."
Mt  8:20  "Foxes have **h** and birds have nests,

## HOLIEST* [HOLY]
Nu 18:29  **h** part of everything given to you.'

## HOLINESS* [HOLY]
Ex  15:11  majestic in **h**, awesome in glory,
Dt  32:51  you did not uphold my **h** among
1Ch 16:29  the LORD in the splendor of his **h**.
2Ch 20:21  the splendor of his **h** as they went
Ps  29: 2  the LORD in the splendor of his **h**.
    89:35  for all, I have sworn by my **h**—
    93: 5  **h** adorns your house for endless
    96: 9  the LORD in the splendor of his **h**;
Isa 29:23  they will acknowledge the **h**
    35: 8  it will be called the Way of **H**;
Eze 36:23  I will show the **h** of my great name,
    38:23  I will show my greatness and my **h**,
Am  4: 2  LORD has sworn by his **h**:
Lk  1:75  in **h** and righteousness before him
Ro  1: 4  Spirit of **h** was appointed the Son
    6:19  slaves to righteousness leading to **h**.
    6:22  the benefit you reap leads to **h**,
1Co  1:30  righteousness, **h** and redemption.
2Co  7: 1  perfecting **h** out of reverence
Eph  4:24  God in true righteousness and **h**.
1Ti  2: 2  quiet lives in all godliness and **h**.
    2:15  in faith, love and **h** with propriety.
Heb 12:10  good, that we may share in his **h**.
    12:14  without **h** no one will see the Lord.

## HOLLOW
Ex  27: 8  Make the altar **h**, out of boards.
Isa 40:12  the waters in the **h** of his hand,
Col  2: 8  no one takes you captive through **h**

## HOLY [HALLOWED, HOLIEST, HOLINESS]

| | | |
|---|---|---|
| Ge | 2: 3 | the seventh day and made it **h**, |
| Ex | 3: 5 | you are standing is **h** ground." |
| | 16:23 | rest, a **h** sabbath to the LORD. |
| | 19: 6 | kingdom of priests and a **h** nation.' |
| | 20: 8 | the Sabbath day by keeping it **h**. |
| | 26:33 | curtain will separate the **H** Place from the Most **H** Place. |
| | 28:36 | on it as on a seal: H TO THE LORD. |
| | 29:37 | Then the altar will be most **h**, and whatever touches it will be **h**. |
| | 30:10 | It is most **h** to the LORD." |
| | 30:29 | them so they will be most **h**, |
| | 31:13 | I am the LORD, who makes you **h**. |
| | 40: 9 | all its furnishings, and it will be **h**. |
| Lev | 10: 3 | approach me I will be proved **h**; |
| | 10:10 | you can distinguish between the **h** |
| | 11:44 | and be **h**, because I am **h**. |
| | 11:45 | therefore be **h**, because I am **h**. |
| | 19: 2 | 'Be **h** because I, the LORD your God, am **h**. |
| | 19: 8 | they have desecrated what is **h** |
| | 19:24 | the fourth year all its fruit will be **h**, |
| | 20: 3 | sanctuary and profaned my **h** name. |
| | 20: 7 | yourselves and be **h**, because I am |
| | 20: 8 | I am the LORD, who makes you **h** |
| | 20:26 | You are to be **h** to me because I, |
| | 20:26 | am **h**, and I have set you apart |
| | 21: 6 | They must be **h** to their God |
| | 21: 8 | Consider them **h**, because the LORD am **h**—I who make you **h**. |
| | 22: 9 | am the LORD, who makes them **h**. |
| | 22:32 | Do not profane my **h** name, for I |
| | 22:32 | I must be acknowledged as **h** |
| | 25:12 | it is a jubilee and is to be **h** for you; |
| | 27: 9 | given to the LORD becomes **h**. |
| Nu | 4:15 | they must not touch the **h** things |
| | 6: 5 | They must be **h** until the period |
| | 16: 7 | chooses will be the one who is **h**. |
| | 20:12 | enough to honor me as **h** in the sight |
| | 20:13 | he was proved **h** among them. |
| Dt | 5:12 | the Sabbath day by keeping it **h**, |
| | 23:14 | Your camp must be **h**, so that he |
| | 26:15 | from heaven, your **h** dwelling place. |
| | 33: 2 | myriads of **h** ones from the south, |
| Jos | 5:15 | place where you are standing is **h**." |
| | 24:19 | He is a **h** God; he is a jealous God. |
| 1Sa | 2: 2 | "There is no one **h** like the LORD; |
| | 6:20 | of the LORD, this **h** God? |
| | 21: 5 | men's bodies are **h** even on missions that are not **h**. |
| 2Ki | 4: 9 | often comes our way is a **h** man |
| 1Ch | 16:10 | Glory in his **h** name; let the hearts |
| | 16:35 | we may give thanks to your **h** name, |
| | 29: 3 | I have provided for this **h** temple: |
| 2Ch | 3: 1 | He built the Most **H** Place, its length |
| | 30:27 | heaven, his **h** dwelling place. |
| Ezr | 9: 2 | have mingled the **h** race |
| Ne | 8:10 | This day is **h** to our Lord. |
| | 11: 1 | them to live in Jerusalem, the **h** city, |
| Job | 6:10 | not denied the words of the **H** One. |
| Ps | 2: 6 | my king on Zion, my **h** mountain." |
| | 5: 7 | I bow down toward your **h** temple. |
| | 11: 4 | The LORD is in his **h** temple; |
| | 22: 3 | you are enthroned as the **H** One; |

| | | |
|---|---|---|
| Ps | 24: 3 | Who may stand in his **h** place? |
| | 30: 4 | praise his **h** name. |
| | 33:21 | rejoice, for we trust in his **h** name. |
| | 47: 8 | God is seated on his **h** throne. |
| | 77:13 | Your ways, God, are **h**. What god is |
| | 78:54 | them to the border of his **h** land, |
| | 89: 5 | too, in the assembly of the **h** ones. |
| | 89:18 | our king to the **H** One of Israel. |
| | 99: 3 | great and awesome name—he is **h**. |
| | 99: 9 | God and worship at his **h** mountain, |
| | 105: 3 | Glory in his **h** name; let the hearts |
| | 111: 9 | **h** and awesome is his name. |
| Pr | 9:10 | of the **H** One is understanding. |
| Isa | 1: 4 | they have spurned the **H** One |
| | 5:16 | the **h** God will be proved **h** by his |
| | 6: 3 | "**H**, **h**, **h** is the LORD Almighty; |
| | 6:13 | so the **h** seed will be the stump |
| | 8:13 | is the one you are to regard as **h**, |
| | 29:23 | the holiness of the **H** One of Jacob, |
| | 40:25 | who is my equal?" says the **H** One. |
| | 43: 3 | your God, the **H** One of Israel, |
| | 52:10 | The LORD will lay bare his **h** arm |
| | 54: 5 | the **H** One of Israel is your |
| | 57:15 | who lives forever, whose name is **h**: |
| | 58:13 | doing as you please on my **h** day, |
| Jer | 2: 3 | Israel was **h** to the LORD, |
| | 17:22 | but keep the Sabbath day **h**, as I |
| Eze | 20:41 | I will be proved **h** through you |
| | 22:26 | do not distinguish between the **h** |
| | 28:22 | and within you am proved to be **h**. |
| | 28:25 | I will be proved **h** through them |
| | 36:20 | nations they profaned my **h** name, |
| | 38:16 | I am proved **h** through you before |
| | 44:23 | people the difference between the **h** |
| Da | 4:13 | and there before me was a **h** one, |
| | 8:13 | Then I heard a **h** one speaking, |
| | 9:24 | and to anoint the Most **H** Place. |
| | 11:28 | will be set against the **h** covenant. |
| Jnh | 2: 4 | look again toward your **h** temple.' |
| Hab | 2:20 | The LORD is in his **h** temple; |
| Zec | 8: 3 | will be called the **H** Mountain." |
| | 14: 5 | come, and all the **h** ones with him. |
| | 14:20 | On that day H TO THE LORD will be |
| Mt | 1:18 | to be pregnant through the **H** Spirit. |
| | 3:11 | will baptize you with the **H** Spirit |
| | 4: 5 | the devil took him to the **h** city |
| | 24:15 | in the **h** place 'the abomination |
| | 27:52 | many **h** people who had died were |
| | 28:19 | and of the Son and of the **H** Spirit, |
| Mk | 1:24 | who you are—the **H** One of God!" |
| | 3:29 | blasphemes against the **H** Spirit will |
| Lk | 1:15 | the **H** Spirit even before he is born. |
| | 1:35 | "The **H** Spirit will come on you, |
| | 1:35 | So the **h** one to be born will be |
| | 1:49 | great things for me—**h** is his name. |
| | 3:22 | the **H** Spirit descended on him |
| | 4: 1 | full of the **H** Spirit, left the Jordan |
| | 10:21 | full of joy through the **H** Spirit, |
| | 11:13 | in heaven give the **H** Spirit to those |
| Jn | 6:69 | that you are the **H** One of God." |
| | 14:26 | But the Advocate, the **H** Spirit, |
| | 20:22 | and said, "Receive the **H** Spirit. |
| Ac | 1: 5 | will be baptized with the **H** Spirit." |
| | 2: 4 | of them were filled with the **H** Spirit |
| | 2:27 | will not let your **h** one see decay. |
| | 2:38 | will receive the gift of the **H** Spirit. |
| | 4:27 | against your **h** servant Jesus, |

| | | |
|---|---|---|
| Ac | 5: 3 | that you have lied to the **H** Spirit |
| | 8:15 | that they might receive the **H** Spirit, |
| | 10:44 | the **H** Spirit came on all who heard |
| | 13:35 | will not let your **h** one see decay.' |
| | 15: 8 | them by giving the **H** Spirit to them, |
| | 19: 2 | even heard that there is a **H** Spirit." |
| Ro | 1: 2 | his prophets in the **H** Scriptures |
| | 7:12 | the law is **h**, |
| | 11:16 | then the whole batch is **h**; |
| | 12: 1 | sacrifice, **h** and pleasing to God— |
| | 15:16 | to God, sanctified by the **H** Spirit. |
| | 16:16 | Greet one another with a **h** kiss. |
| 1Co | 1: 2 | Jesus and called to be his **h** people, |
| | 7:14 | be unclean, but as it is, they are **h**. |
| Eph | 1: 4 | the creation of the world to be **h** |
| | 2:21 | to become a **h** temple in the Lord. |
| | 3: 5 | by the Spirit to God's **h** apostles |
| | 4:30 | do not grieve the **H** Spirit of God, |
| | 5:26 | to make her **h**, cleansing her |
| Col | 1:22 | death to present you **h** in his sight, |
| 1Th | 2:10 | of how **h**, righteous and blameless |
| | 3:13 | Jesus comes with all his **h** ones. |
| | 4: 7 | us to be impure, but to live a **h** life. |
| 2Th | 1:10 | comes to be glorified in his **h** people |
| 1Ti | 2: 8 | lifting up **h** hands without anger |
| 2Ti | 1: 9 | saved us and called us to a **h** life— |
| | 2:21 | made **h**, useful to the Master |
| | 3:15 | you have known the **H** Scriptures, |
| Tit | 1: 8 | upright, **h** and disciplined. |
| | 3: 5 | rebirth and renewal by the **H** Spirit, |
| Heb | 2: 4 | of the **H** Spirit distributed according |
| | 2:11 | Both the one who makes people **h** |
| | 6: 4 | who have shared in the **H** Spirit, |
| | 7:26 | one who is **h**, blameless, pure, |
| | 9:12 | he entered the Most **H** Place once |
| | 10:10 | we have been made **h** through |
| | 10:14 | forever those who are being made **h**. |
| | 10:19 | enter the Most **H** Place by the blood |
| | 12:14 | in peace with everyone and to be **h**; |
| | 13:12 | make the people **h** through his own |
| 1Pe | 1:15 | But just as he who called you is **h**, so be |
| | | **h** in all you do; |
| | 1:16 | "Be **h**, because I am **h**." |
| | 2: 5 | spiritual house to be a **h** priesthood, |
| | 2: 9 | a royal priesthood, a **h** nation, |
| | 3: 5 | this is the way the **h** women |
| 2Pe | 1:21 | were carried along by the **H** Spirit. |
| | 3:11 | You ought to live **h** and godly lives |
| 1Jn | 2:20 | have an anointing from the **H** One, |
| Jude | 1:14 | upon thousands of his **h** ones |
| | 1:20 | yourselves up in your most **h** faith and |
| | | praying in the **H** Spirit, |
| Rev | 3: 7 | These are the words of him who is **h** |
| | 4: 8 | " '**H, h, h** is the Lord God |
| | 11: 2 | They will trample on the **h** city |
| | 15: 4 | For you alone are **h**. All nations will |
| | 20: 6 | **h** are those who have part in the first |
| | 21: 2 | I saw the **H** City, the new |
| | 21:10 | high, and showed me the **H** City, |
| | 22:11 | those who are **h** continue to be **h**." |
| | 22:19 | in the tree of life and in the **H** City, |

**HOLY CITY** Ne 11:1, 18; Isa 48:2; 52:1; Da
9:24; Mt 4:5; 27:53; Rev 11:2; 21:2, 10; 22:19

**HOLY HILL** Da 9:16, 20; Joel 2:1; 3:17; Ob
1:16; Zep 3:11

**HOLY MOUNTAIN** Ps 2:6; 3:4; 15:1; 43:3;
48:1; 87:1; 99:9; Isa 11:9; 27:13; 56:7; 57:13;
65:11, 25; 66:20; Eze 20:40; Da 11:45; Zec 8:3

**HOLY NAME** Lev 20:3; 22:2, 32; 1Ch 16:10,
35; 29:16; Ps 30:4; 33:21; 97:12; 103:1; 105:3;
106:47; 145:21; Eze 20:39; 36:20, 21, 22; 39:7,
7, 25; 43:7, 8; Am 2:7

**HOLY ONE** 2Ki 19:22; Job 6:10; Ps 22:3;
71:22; 78:41; 89:18; Pr 9:10; 30:3; Isa 1:4; 5:19,
24; 10:17, 20; 12:6; 17:7; 29:19, 23; 30:11, 12,
15; 31:1; 37:23; 40:25; 41:14, 16, 20; 43:3, 14,
15; 45:11; 47:4; 48:17; 49:7, 7; 54:5; 55:5; 60:9,
14; Jer 50:29; 51:5; Eze 39:7; Da 4:13, 23; 8:13,
13; Hos 11:9, 12; Hab 1:12; 3:3; Mk 1:24; Lk
1:35; 4:34; Jn 6:69; Ac 2:27; 13:35; 1Jn 2:20;
Rev 16:5

**HOLY ONES** Dt 33:2, 3; Job 5:1; 15:15; Ps
89:5, 7; Isa 13:3; Da 4:17; Zec 14:5; 1Th 3:13;
Jude 1:14

**HOLY PLACE** Ex 26:33, 33, 34; 28:29, 35, 43;
29:30; 31:11; Lev 6:30; 10:18; 16:2, 3, 16, 17,
20, 23, 27, 33; Jos 24:26; 1Ki 6:16; 7:50; 8:6, 8,
8, 10; 1Ch 6:49; 23:32; 2Ch 3:8, 10; 4:22; 5:7, 9,
11; 35:5; Ps 24:3; 28:2; 46:4; Ecc 8:10; Isa 8:14;
57:15; 63:18; Eze 41:4, 21, 23; 45:3, 4; Da 9:24;
Mt 24:15; Ac 6:13, 21:28; Heb 9:2, 3, 8, 12, 25;
10:19; 13:11

**HOLY SPIRIT** Ps 51:11; Isa 63:10, 11; Mt 1:18,
20; 3:11; 12:32; 28:19; Mk 1:8; 3:29; 12:36;
13:11; Lk 1:15, 35, 41, 67; 2:25, 26; 3:16, 22;
4:1; 10:21; 11:13; 12:10, 12; Jn 1:33; 14:26;
20:22; Ac 1:2, 5, 8, 16; 2:4, 33, 38; 4:8, 25, 31;
5:3, 32; 6:5; 7:51, 55; 8:15, 16, 17, 19; 9:17, 31;
10:38, 44, 45, 47; 11:15, 16, 24; 13:2, 4, 9, 52;
15:8, 28; 16:6; 19:2, 2, 6; 20:23, 28; 21:11;
28:25; Ro 5:5; 9:1; 14:17; 15:13, 16; 1Co 6:19;
12:3; 2Co 6:6; 13:14; Eph 1:13; 4:30; 1Th 1:5, 6;
4:8; 2Ti 1:14; Tit 3:5; Heb 2:4; 3:7; 6:4; 9:8;
10:15; 1Pe 1:12; 2Pe 1:21; Jude 1:20

**HOLY TO THE †LORD** Ex 28:36; 30:10, 37;
31:15; 39:30; Lev 19:8; 27:14, 23, 28, 30, 32; Dt
7:6; 14:2, 21; 26:19; Ne 8:9; Jer 2:3; 31:40; Eze
48:14; Zec 14:20, 21

**MOST HOLY** Ex 26:33, 34; 29:37; 30:10, 29,
36; 40:10; Lev 2:3, 10; 6:17, 25, 29; 7:1, 6;
10:12, 17; 14:13; 16:2, 3, 16, 17, 20, 23, 27, 33;
21:22; 24:9; 27:28; Nu 4:4, 19; 18:9, 9, 10; 1Ki
6:16; 7:50; 8:6; 1Ch 6:49; 23:13; 2Ch 3:8, 10;
4:22; 5:7; Ps 28:2; Eze 41:4, 21, 23; 42:13, 13;
43:12; 44:13; 45:3; 48:12; Da 9:24; Heb 9:3, 8,
12, 25; 10:19; 13:11; Jude 1:20

# HOME [HOMELAND, HOMELESS, HOMES]

| | | |
|---|---|---|
| Nu | 14:30 | with uplifted hand to make your **h**, |
| Dt | 6: 7 | Talk about them when you sit at **h** |
| | 11:19 | talking about them when you sit at **h** |
| | 20: 5 | Let him go **h**, or he may die in battle |
| | 24: 5 | one year he is to be free to stay at **h** |
| Jos | 22: 7 | When Joshua sent them **h**, |

| | | |
|---|---|---|
| Ru | 1:11 | said, "Return **h**, my daughters. |
| 2Sa | 7:10 | that they can have a **h** of their own |
| 1Ch | 16:43 | David returned **h** to bless his family. |
| 2Ch | 10:16 | So all the Israelites went **h**. |
| Ps | 84: 3 | Even the sparrow has found a **h**, |
| | 113: 9 | woman in her **h** as a happy mother |
| Pr | 3:33 | but he blesses the **h** of the righteous. |
| | 7:11 | and defiant, her feet never stay at **h**; |
| | 27: 8 | its nest is anyone who flees from **h**. |
| Ecc | 12: 5 | people go to their eternal **h** |
| Eze | 36: 8 | Israel, for they will soon come **h**. |
| Hag | 1: 9 | What you brought **h**, I blew away. |
| Mt | 1:20 | afraid to take Mary **h** as your wife, |
| Mk | 2:11 | get up, take your mat and go **h**." |
| | 5:19 | "Go **h** to your own people and tell |
| | 10:29 | "no one who has left **h** or brothers |
| Lk | 10:38 | woman named Martha opened her **h** |
| Jn | 9: 7 | and washed, and came **h** seeing. |
| | 14:23 | to them and make our **h** with them. |
| | 19:27 | on, this disciple took her into his **h**. |
| Ac | 10:32 | a guest in the **h** of Simon the tanner, |
| | 16:15 | baptized, she invited us to her **h**. |
| 1Co | 11:34 | hungry should eat something at **h**, |
| 2Co | 5: 8 | the body and at **h** with the Lord. |
| Tit | 2: 5 | and pure, to be busy at **h**, to be kind, |

## HOMELAND [HOME]

| | | |
|---|---|---|
| Ge | 30:25 | way so I can go back to my own **h**. |
| Ru | 2:11 | and your **h** and came to live |
| 2Ki | 17:23 | were taken from their **h** into exile |
| Ps | 79: 7 | Jacob and devastated his **h**. |

## HOMELESS* [HOME]

| | | |
|---|---|---|
| 1Co | 4:11 | we are brutally treated, we are **h**. |

## HOMES [HOME]

| | | |
|---|---|---|
| Nu | 32:18 | to our **h** until all the Israelites have |
| Jos | 22: 6 | them away, and they went to their **h**. |
| Ne | 4:14 | daughters, your wives and your **h**." |
| Isa | 32:18 | in secure **h**, in undisturbed places |
| Hos | 11:11 | I will settle them in their **h**," |
| Mic | 2: 2 | They defraud people of their **h**, |
| Mt | 13:57 | own **h** are prophets without honor." |
| Mk | 10:30 | **h**, brothers, sisters, mothers, |
| 1Ti | 5:14 | to manage their **h** and to give |
| 2Ti | 3: 6 | the kind who worm their way into **h** |

## HOMETOWN [TOWN]

| | | |
|---|---|---|
| Mt | 13:54 | Coming to his **h**, he began teaching the |

## HOMETOWNS* [TOWN]

| | | |
|---|---|---|
| Lk | 4:24 | are not accepted in their **h**. |

## HOMOSEXUALITY*
### [HOMOSEXUALS}

| | | |
|---|---|---|
| 1Ti | 1:10 | practicing **h**, for slave traders |

## HOMOSEXUALS*
### [HOMOSEXUALITY]

| | | |
|---|---|---|
| 1Co | 6: 9 | nor male prostitutes nor practicing **h** |

## HONEST [HONESTLY, HONESTY]

| | | |
|---|---|---|
| Ex | 23: 7 | put an innocent or **h** person to death, |

| | | |
|---|---|---|
| Lev | 19:36 | Use **h** scales and **h** weights, an **h** ephah |
| | | and an **h** hin. |
| Dt | 25:15 | must have accurate and **h** weights |
| 2Ki | 22: 7 | because they are **h** in their dealings." |
| Job | 31: 6 | let God weigh me in **h** scales and he |
| Pr | 12:17 | An **h** witness tells the truth, |
| | 14: 5 | An **h** witness does not deceive, |
| | 16:11 | **H** scales and balances belong |
| | 17:26 | to flog **h** officials is not right. |

## HONESTLY* [HONEST]

| | | |
|---|---|---|
| Jer | 5: 1 | one person who deals **h** and seeks |

## HONESTY* [HONEST]

| | | |
|---|---|---|
| Ge | 30:33 | And my **h** will testify for me |
| 2Ki | 12:15 | because they acted with complete **h**. |
| Isa | 59:14 | in the streets, **h** cannot enter. |

## HONEY [HONEYCOMB]

| | | |
|---|---|---|
| Ex | 3: 8 | a land flowing with milk and **h**— |
| | 16:31 | and tasted like wafers made with **h**. |
| Lev | 2:11 | **h** in a food offering presented |
| Jdg | 14: 8 | he saw a swarm of bees and some **h**. |
| 1Sa | 14:26 | woods, they saw the **h** oozing out; |
| Ps | 19:10 | they are sweeter than **h**, than **h** |
| | 119:103 | taste, sweeter than **h** to my mouth! |
| Pr | 5: 3 | lips of the adulterous woman drip **h**, |
| | 24:14 | Know also that wisdom is like **h** for you |
| | 25:16 | If you find **h**, eat just enough— |
| SS | 4:11 | milk and **h** are under your tongue. |
| Isa | 7:15 | **h** when he knows enough to reject |
| Eze | 3: 3 | it tasted as sweet as **h** in my mouth. |
| Mt | 3: 4 | His food was locusts and wild **h**. |
| Rev | 10: 9 | mouth it will be as sweet as **h**.' " |

## HONEYCOMB* [HONEY]

| | | |
|---|---|---|
| 1Sa | 14:27 | in his hand and dipped it into the **h**. |
| Ps | 19:10 | than honey from the **h**. |
| Pr | 16:24 | Gracious words are a **h**, |
| SS | 4:11 | Your lips drop sweetness as the **h**, |
| | 5: 1 | I have eaten my **h** and my honey; |

## HONOR [HONORABLE, HONORABLY, HONORED, HONORS]

| | | |
|---|---|---|
| Ex | 12:42 | to keep vigil to **h** the LORD |
| | 20:12 | "**H** your father and your mother, |
| Nu | 20:12 | in me enough to **h** me as holy |
| | 25:13 | he was zealous for the **h** of his God |
| Dt | 5:16 | "**H** your father and your mother, |
| Jdg | 4: 9 | are taking, the **h** will not be yours, |
| 1Sa | 2: 8 | and has them inherit a throne of **h**. |
| | 2:30 | Those who **h** me I will **h**, but those |
| 2Ki | 10:20 | "Call an assembly in **h** of Baal." |
| 1Ch | 29:12 | Wealth and **h** come from you; |
| 2Ch | 1:11 | possessions or **h**, nor for the death |
| | 18: 1 | Jehoshaphat had great wealth and **h**, |
| Ezr | 10:11 | **h** the LORD, the God of your ancestors, |
| Est | 6: 6 | for the man the king delights to **h**?" |
| Ps | 8: 5 | and crowned them with glory and **h**. |
| | 15: 4 | but **h** whoever fears the LORD; |
| | 45:11 | **h** him, for he is your lord. |
| | 50:23 | sacrifice thank offerings **h** me, |
| | 84:11 | the LORD bestows favor and **h**; |
| | 112: 9 | their horn will be lifted high in **h**. |

Pr     3: 9  **H** the LORD with your wealth,
       3:35  The wise inherit **h**, but fools get
      11:16  A kindhearted woman gains **h**,
      15:33  and humility comes before **h**.
      18:12  but humility comes before **h**.
      20: 3  It is to one's **h** to avoid strife,
      22: 4  its wages are riches and life.
      29:23  low, but the lowly in spirit gain **h**.
      31:31  **H** her for all that her hands
Ecc   10: 1  little folly outweighs wisdom and **h**.
Isa    9: 1  in the future he will **h** Galilee
      29:13  their mouth and **h** me with their lips,
Jer   33: 9  **h** before all nations on earth
Da     2:46  and paid him **h** and ordered
       5:23  you did not **h** the God who holds
Mal    1: 6  am a father, where is the **h** due me?
Mt    13:57  homes are prophets without **h**."
      15: 4  '**H** your father and mother'
      15: 8  " 'These people **h** me with their
      19:19  **h** your father and mother,' and 'love
      23: 6  they love the place of **h** at banquets
Mk     6: 4  homes are prophets without **h**."
Lk    14: 8  do not take the place of **h**,
Jn     4:44  that prophets have no **h** in their own
       5:23  all may **h** the Son just as they **h**
       8:49  Jesus, "but I **h** my Father and you
      12:26  My Father will **h** the one who
Ro    12:10  **H** one another above yourselves.
      13: 7  if respect, then respect; if **h**, then **h**.
1Co    6:20  Therefore **h** God with your bodies.
      12:23  honorable we treat with special **h**.
Eph    6: 2  "**H** your father and mother"—
1Ti    5:17  church well are worthy of double **h**,
Heb    2: 7  you crowned them with glory and **h**
       3: 3  worthy of greater **h** than Moses,
1Pe    1: 7  and **h** when Jesus Christ is revealed.
2Pe    1:17  He received **h** and glory from God
Rev    4: 9  **h** and thanks to him who sits
       4:11  to receive glory and **h** and power,
       5:12  and strength and **h** and glory
       7:12  wisdom and thanks and **h** and power
      13:14  an image in **h** of the beast who was
      21:26  **h** of the nations will be brought

## HONORABLE [HONOR]

Pr    25:27  nor is it **h** to search out matters
1Th    4: 4  body in a way that is holy and **h**,

## HONORABLY [HONOR]

Heb  13:18  and desire to live **h** in every way.

## HONORED [HONOR]

Ex    20:24  Wherever I cause my name to be **h**,
Ps    12: 8  while depravity is **h** by the human
Pr    13:18  but whoever heeds correction is **h**.
      27:18  who protect their masters will be **h**.
Da     4:34  I **h** and glorified him who lives
Hag    1: 8  I may take pleasure in it and be **h**,"
Lk    14:10  you will be **h** in the presence of all
1Co   12:26  if one part is **h**, every part rejoices
Heb   13: 4  Marriage should be **h** by all,

## HONORS* [HONOR]

Pr    14:31  whoever is kind to the needy **h** God.
Mal    1: 6  "A son **h** his father, and slaves

## HOOF

Ex    10:26  not a **h** is to be left behind.
Lev   11: 3  eat any animal that has a divided **h**

## HOOK [FISHHOOK, HOOKS]

2Ch   33:11  prisoner, put a **h** in his nose,
Isa   37:29  I will put my **h** in your nose and my

## HOOKS [HOOK]

Ex    26:37  Make gold **h** for this curtain
Isa    2: 4  and their spears into pruning **h**.
Joel   3:10  and your pruning **h** into spears.
Am     4: 2  you will be taken away with **h**,
Mic    4: 3  and their spears into pruning **h**.

## HOPE [HOPED, HOPELESS, HOPES]

Ru     1:12  if I thought there was still **h** for me—
Ezr   10: 2  of this, there is still **h** for Israel.
Job    6: 8  that God would grant what I **h** for,
      13:15  he slay me, yet will I **h** in him;
      17:15  is my **h**—who can see any **h** for me?
Ps     9:18  the **h** of the afflicted will never
      31:24  heart, all you who **h** in the LORD.
      33:17  A horse is a vain **h** for deliverance;
      33:18  on those whose **h** is in his unfailing
      33:22  even as we put our **h** in you.
      37:34  **H** in the LORD and keep
      39: 7  what do I look for? My **h** is in you
      42: 5  Put your **h** in God, for I will yet
      52: 9  And I will **h** in your name, for your
      62: 5  rest in God; my **h** comes from him.
      65: 5  the **h** of all the ends of the earth
      71:14  As for me, I will always have **h**;
     119:43  for I have put my **h** in your laws.
     119:74  for I have put my **h** in your word.
     130: 5  waits, and in his word I put my **h**.
     130: 7  Israel, put your **h** in the LORD,
     146: 5  whose **h** is in the LORD their God.
     147:11  who put their **h** in his unfailing love.
Pr    13:12  **H** deferred makes the heart sick,
      23:18  There is surely a future for you,
      24:14  you, and your **h** will not be cut off.
      26:12  There is more **h** for fools than
Ecc    9: 4  who is among the living has **h**—
Isa   40:31  but those who **h** in the LORD will
      49:23  those who **h** in me will not be
Jer   14: 8  You who are the **h** of Israel,
      29:11  plans to give you **h** and a future.
La     3:21  call to mind and therefore I have **h**:
Eze   37:11  are dried up and our **h** is gone;
Mic    7: 7  for me, I watch in **h** for the LORD,
Zec    9:12  to your fortress, you prisoners of **h**;
Mt    12:21  name the nations will put their **h**."
Ac     2:26  my body also will rest in **h**,
      23: 6  because of the **h** of the resurrection
Ro     4:18  Against all **h**, Abraham in **h**
       5: 4  and character, **h**.
       5: 5  And **h** does not put us to shame,
       8:20  of the one who subjected it, in **h**
       8:24  But **h** that is seen is no **h** at all.
       8:25  if we **h** for what we do not yet have,
      12:12  Be joyful in **h**, patient in affliction,
      15: 4  they provide we might have **h**.
      15:12  in him the Gentiles will **h**."
      15:13  May the God of **h** fill you with all
1Co   13:13  these three remain: faith, **h** and love.

1Co 15:19 for this life we have **h** in Christ,
2Co  1:10 him we have set our **h** that he will
Gal  5: 5 the righteousness for which we **h**.
Eph  1:12 were the first to put our **h** in Christ,
     2:12 without **h** and without God
     4: 4 to one **h** when you were called;
Col  1: 5 love that spring from the **h** stored
     1:23 do not move from the **h** held
     1:27 is Christ in you, the **h** of glory.
1Th  1: 3 your endurance inspired by **h** in our
     4:13 grieve like the rest, who have no **h**.
     5: 8 and the **h** of salvation as a helmet.
1Ti  1: 1 our Savior and of Christ Jesus our **h**,
     4:10 because we have put our **h**
     6:17 arrogant nor to put their **h** in wealth,
Tit  1: 2 in the **h** of eternal life, which God,
     2:13 while we wait for the blessed **h**—
Heb  3: 6 and the **h** in which we glory.
     6:11 end, in order to make your **h** sure.
     6:19 We have this **h** as an anchor
     7:19 and a better **h** is introduced,
    10:23 unswervingly to the **h** we profess,
    11: 1 faith is being sure of what we **h**
1Pe  1: 3 a living **h** through the resurrection
     1:21 and so your faith and **h** are in God.
     3: 5 the past who put their **h** in God used
     3:15 the reason for the **h** that you have.
1Jn  3: 3 All who have this **h** in him purify

## HOPED [HOPE]

Job 30:26 Yet when I **h** for good, evil came;
Jer  8:15 We **h** for peace but no good has
Lk  20:20 They **h** to catch Jesus in something

## HOPELESS* [HOPE]

Isa 57:10 but you would not say, 'It is **h**.'

## HOPES [HOPE]

2Ki  4:28 I tell you, 'Don't raise my **h**'?"
Ps  25: 3 No one who **h** in you will ever be
   119:116 do not let my **h** be dashed.
Pr  10:28 joy, but the **h** of the wicked come
    11: 7 **H** placed in mortals die with them;
Jer 23:16 they fill you with false **h**.
Jn   5:45 is Moses, on whom your **h** are set.
Ro   8:24 Who **h** for what they already have?
1Co 13: 7 trusts, always **h**, always perseveres.

## HOPHNI*

A wicked priest (1Sa 1:3; 2:34; 4:4–17).

## HOR

Nu 33:38 Aaron the priest went up Mount **H**,
Dt  32:50 brother Aaron died on Mount **H**

## HOREB

Ex   3: 1 of the wilderness and came to **H**,
    17: 6 there before you by the rock at **H**.
Dt   5: 2 God made a covenant with us at **H**.
1Ki 19: 8 and forty nights until he reached **H**,
Ps 106:19 At **H** they made a calf

## HORIZON*

Ne   1: 9 exiled people are at the farthest **h**,
Job 26:10 He marks out the **h** on the face

Pr   8:27 he marked out the **h** on the face

## HORMAH

Nu 14:45 beat them down all the way to **H**.
    21: 3 so the place was named **H**.

## HORN [HORNS]

Ex  19:13 the ram's **h** sounds a long blast may
    27: 2 Make a **h** at each of the four
1Sa  2: 1 in the LORD my **h** is lifted high.
    16: 1 Fill your **h** with oil and be on your
Ps  18: 2 my shield and the **h** of my salvation,
    92:10 You have exalted my **h** like
   148:14 he has raised up for his people a **h**,
La   2: 3 fierce anger he has cut off every **h**
Da   3: 5 soon as you hear the sound of the **h**,
     7: 8 This **h** had eyes like the eyes
     8: 5 with a prominent **h** between its eyes
Lk   1:69 He has raised up a **h** of salvation

## HORNET*

Ex  23:28 I will send the **h** ahead of you
Dt   7:20 will send the **h** among them until
Jos 24:12 I sent the **h** ahead of you,

## HORNS [HORN]

Ge  22:13 thicket he saw a ram caught by its **h**.
Ex  27: 2 so that the **h** and the altar are of one
Lev  4: 7 of the blood on the **h** of the altar
Jos  6: 4 carry trumpets of rams' **h** in front
Ps  75: 5 Do not lift your **h** against heaven;
Da   7: 7 the former beasts, and it had ten **h**.
     7:24 The ten **h** are ten kings who will
     8: 3 before me was a ram with two **h**,
Rev  5: 6 The Lamb had seven **h** and seven
     9:13 from the four **h** of the golden altar
    12: 3 ten **h** and seven crowns on its heads.
    13: 1 It had ten **h** and seven heads, with ten
         crowns on its **h**,
    13:11 It had two **h** like a lamb, but it
    17: 3 and had seven heads and ten **h**.

## HORRIBLE [HORROR]

Dt   7:15 on you the **h** diseases you knew
Jer  5:30 "A **h** and shocking thing has
Hos  6:10 I have seen a **h** thing in the house

## HORRIFIED*

Pr  25:23 sly tongue—which provokes a **h** look.
Jer  4: 9 the priests will be **h**,

## HORROR [HORRIBLE]

Dt  28:25 you will become a thing of **h** to all
2Ch 29: 8 made them an object of dread and **h**
Ps  55: 5 **h** has overwhelmed me.
Jer  2:12 and shudder with great **h**,"
    25:18 a ruin and an object of **h** and scorn,
Eze 20:26 fill them with **h** so they would know

## HORSE [HORSEMAN, HORSEMEN, HORSES, HORSES']

Ex  15: 1 Both **h** and driver he has hurled
Est  6: 8 worn and a **h** the king has ridden,
Ps  32: 9 Do not be like the **h** or the mule,
    33:17 A **h** is a vain hope for deliverance;

Ps 147:10 is not in the strength of the **h**,
Pr   26: 3 A whip for the **h**, a bridle
Jer 51:21 with you I shatter **h** and rider,
Zec   1: 8 me was a man mounted on a red **h**.
Rev   6: 2 and there before me was a white **h**!
        6: 4 Then another **h** came out, a fiery red
        6: 5 and there before me was a black **h**!
        6: 8 and there before me was a pale **h**!
      19:11 and there before me was a white **h**,

## HORSEMAN [HORSE, MAN]
Am   2:15 and the **h** will not save his life.

## HORSEMEN [HORSE, MAN]
Ex 14:28 and covered the chariots and **h**—
      15:19 chariots and **h** went into the sea,
2Ki   2:12 The chariots and **h** of Israel!"
      18:24 on Egypt for chariots and **h**?
Isa 31: 1 and in the great strength of their **h**,

## HORSES [HORSE]
Ge 47:17 them food in exchange for their **h**,
Ex 14:23 and all Pharaoh's **h** and chariots
Dt 17:16 must not acquire great numbers of **h**
Jos 11: 6 You are to hamstring their **h**
1Ki 4:26 four thousand stalls for chariot **h**,
      10:26 accumulated chariots and **h**;
2Ki 2:11 chariot of fire and **h** of fire appeared
      6:17 saw the hills full of **h** and chariots
Ps 20: 7 trust in chariots and some in **h**,
Isa 31: 3 their **h** are flesh and not spirit.
Jer 12: 5 out, how can you compete with **h**?
Joel 2: 4 They have the appearance of **h**;
Zec 6: 2 The first chariot had red **h**,
Rev 9: 7 The locusts looked like **h** prepared
      19:14 riding on white **h** and dressed

## HORSES' [HORSE]
Rev 14:20 rising as high as the **h'** bridles

## HOSANNA*
Mt 21: 9 shouted, "**H** to the Son of David!"
      21: 9 "**H** in the highest heaven!"
      21:15 courts, "**H** to the Son of David,"
Mk 11: 9 those who followed shouted, "**H!**"
      11:10 "**H** in the highest heaven!"
Jn 12:13 out to meet him, shouting, "**H!**"

## HOSEA
Prophet whose wife and family pictured the unfaithfulness of Israel (Hos 1–3).

## HOSHEA [JOSHUA]
  1. Original name of Joshua (Nu 13:8, 16).
  2. Last king of Israel (2Ki 15:30; 17:1–6).

## HOSPITABLE* [HOSPITALITY]
1Ti 3: 2 respectable, **h**, able to teach,
Tit 1: 8 he must be **h**, one who loves what is

## HOSPITALITY* [HOSPITABLE]
Ac 28: 7 showed us generous **h** for three days.
Ro 12:13 people who are in need. Practice **h**.
      16:23 whose **h** I and the whole church
1Ti 5:10 showing **h**, washing the feet

Heb 13: 2 Do not forget to show **h** to strangers,
      13: 2 shown **h** to angels without knowing it.
1Pe 4: 9 Offer **h** to one another without
3Jn 1: 8 to show **h** to such people so that we

## HOST [HOSTS]
1Ki 22:19 all the **h** of heaven standing around
Ne 9: 6 and all their starry **h**, the earth
Isa 34: 4 all the starry **h** will fall like
      40:26 brings out the starry **h** one by one,
Da 8:10 of the starry **h** down to the earth
Lk 2:13 of the heavenly **h** appeared

## HOSTILE [HOSTILITY]
Lev 26:21 " 'If you remain **h** toward me
Ro 8: 7 The sinful mind is **h** to God;
1Th 2:15 displease God and are **h** to everyone

## HOSTILITY [HOSTILE]
Ge 16:12 live in **h** toward all his brothers."
      25:18 in **h** toward all the tribes related
Hos 9: 8 paths, and **h** in the house of his God.
Eph 2:14 the barrier, the dividing wall of **h**,
      2:16 by which he put to death their **h**.

## HOSTS [HOST]
2Ki 17:16 bowed down to all the starry **h**,
2Ch 33: 5 he built altars to all the starry **h**.
Ps 103:21 all his heavenly **h**, you his servants
      148: 2 praise him, all his heavenly **h**.
Isa 45:12 I marshaled their starry **h**.

## HOT [HOT-TEMPERED, HOTHEADED, HOTTER]
Ex 11: 8 Then Moses, **h** with anger,
Ps 39: 3 my heart grew **h** within me.
Pr 6:28 on **h** coals without his feet being
Eze 38:18 Israel, my **h** anger will be aroused,
Da 3:22 the furnace so **h** that the flames
1Ti 4: 2 have been seared as with a **h** iron.
Rev 3:15 that you are neither cold nor **h**.

## HOT-TEMPERED* [HOT, TEMPER]
Pr 15:18 The **h** stir up dissension, but those
      19:19 The **h** must pay the penalty;
      22:24 Do not make friends with the **h**,
      29:22 and a **h** person commits many sins.

## HOTHEADED* [HOT, HEAD]
Pr 14:16 but a fool is **h** and yet feels secure.

## HOTTER* [HOT]
Da 3:19 heated seven times **h** than usual

## HOUNDED*
Ps 109:16 but **h** to death the poor

## HOUR
Ecc 9:12 one knows when their **h** will come:
Mt 6:27 worrying add a single **h** to your life?
      8:13 servant was healed at that very **h**.
      24:36 about that day or **h** no one knows,
Mk 14:35 if possible the **h** might pass
      14:37 you not keep watch for one **h**?

| | | |
|---|---|---|
| Lk | 12:40 | an **h** when you do not expect him." |
| Jn | 2: 4 | Jesus replied. "My **h** has not yet come." |
| | 12:23 | "The **h** has come for the Son |
| | 12:27 | for this very reason I came to this **h**. |
| | 17: 1 | and prayed: "Father, the **h** has come. |
| 1Jn | 2:18 | Dear children, this is the last **h**; |
| Rev | 3:10 | keep you from the **h** of trial that is |
| | 8: 1 | in heaven for about half an **h**. |
| | 14: 7 | because the **h** of his judgment has |
| | 17:12 | one **h** will receive authority as kings |
| | 18:10 | In one **h** your doom has come!' |

## HOUSE [HOUSEHOLD, HOUSEHOLDS, HOUSES, STOREHOUSE, STOREHOUSES]

| | | |
|---|---|---|
| Ge | 19: 2 | turn aside to your servant's **h**. |
| | 24:23 | there room in your father's **h** for us |
| | 28:17 | This is none other than the **h** |
| Ex | 12:22 | of the door of your **h** until morning. |
| | 20:17 | shall not covet your neighbor's **h**. |
| Lev | 27:14 | dedicates their **h** as something holy |
| Nu | 12: 7 | he is faithful in all my **h**. |
| Dt | 5:21 | set your desire on your neighbor's **h** |
| Jos | 2: 1 | entered the **h** of a prostitute named |
| | 6:22 | land, "Go into the prostitute's **h** |
| 1Sa | 1: 7 | went up to the **h** of the LORD, |
| | 3: 3 | Samuel was lying down in the **h** |
| 2Sa | 2:10 | The **h** of Judah, however, |
| | 3: 1 | while the **h** of Saul grew weaker |
| | 7: 2 | living in a **h** of cedar, |
| | 7: 5 | the one to build me a **h** to dwell in? |
| | 7:11 | LORD himself will establish a **h** |
| | 23: 5 | "If my **h** were not right with God, |
| 1Ki | 8:43 | this **h** I have built bears your Name. |
| 2Ki | 15: 5 | he died, and he lived in a separate **h**. |
| 1Ch | 9:23 | the **h** called the tent of meeting. |
| | 17:12 | He is the one who will build a **h** |
| | 22: 1 | "The **h** of the LORD God is to be |
| Ezr | 1: 5 | up and build the **h** of the LORD |
| | 3:11 | of the **h** of the LORD was laid. |
| Ne | 10:39 | "We will not neglect the **h** of our |
| Ps | 23: 6 | in the **h** of the LORD forever. |
| | 27: 4 | in the **h** of the LORD all the days |
| | 52: 8 | tree flourishing in the **h** of God; |
| | 69: 9 | for zeal for your **h** consumes me, |
| | 84:10 | in the **h** of my God than dwell |
| | 122: 1 | "Let us go to the **h** of the LORD." |
| | 127: 1 | Unless the LORD builds the **h**, |
| Pr | 7:27 | Her **h** is a highway to the grave, |
| | 9: 1 | Wisdom has built her **h**; she has set |
| | 9: 4 | all who are simple come to my **h**!" |
| | 14: 1 | The wise woman builds her **h**, |
| | 14:11 | The **h** of the wicked will be |
| | 21: 9 | of the roof than share a **h** |
| Ecc | 10:18 | because of idle hands, the **h** leaks. |
| Isa | 5: 8 | Woe to you who add **h** to **h** and join |
| | 7:13 | said, "Hear now, you **h** of David! |
| | 56: 7 | for my **h** will be called a **h** of prayer |
| Jer | 3:18 | those days the **h** of Judah will join the **h** of Israel, |
| | 7:11 | Has this **h**, which bears my Name, |
| | 18: 2 | "Go down to the potter's **h**, |
| | 31:31 | a new covenant with the **h** of Israel |
| | 32:34 | images in the **h** that bears my Name |
| Eze | 2: 8 | Do not rebel like that rebellious **h**; |
| | 33: 7 | you a watchman for the **h** of Israel; |

| | | |
|---|---|---|
| Eze | 39:29 | out my Spirit on the **h** of Israel, |
| Joel | 3:18 | will flow out of the LORD's **h** |
| Hab | 2: 9 | "Woe to him who builds his **h** by unjust |
| Hag | 1: 4 | while this **h** remains a ruin?" |
| | 2: 7 | and I will fill this **h** with glory,' |
| Zec | 8: 9 | for the **h** of the LORD Almighty. |
| | 13: 6 | I was given at the **h** of my friends.' |
| Mt | 7:24 | is like a wise man who built his **h** |
| | 10:11 | at that person's **h** until you leave. |
| | 12:29 | can anyone enter a strong man's **h** |
| | 21:13 | " 'My **h** will be called a **h** |
| Mk | 3:25 | If a **h** is divided against itself, that **h** |
| | 11:17 | 'My **h** will be called a **h** of prayer |
| Lk | 6:48 | They are like a man building a **h**, |
| | 10: 7 | Do not move around from **h** to **h**. |
| | 11:17 | a **h** divided against itself will fall. |
| | 11:24 | it says, 'I will return to the **h** I left.' |
| | 15: 8 | sweep the **h** and search carefully |
| | 19: 9 | salvation has come to this **h**, |
| Jn | 2:16 | Stop turning my Father's **h** |
| | 2:17 | for your **h** will consume me." |
| | 12: 3 | the **h** was filled with the fragrance |
| | 14: 2 | My Father's **h** has plenty of room; |
| Ac | 5:42 | in the temple courts and from **h** to **h**, |
| | 16:15 | she said, "come and stay at my **h**." |
| | 20:20 | taught you publicly and from **h** to **h**. |
| | 28:30 | stayed there in his own rented **h** |
| Ro | 16: 5 | also the church that meets at their **h**. |
| 2Co | 5: 1 | from God, an eternal **h** in heaven, |
| Heb | 3: 2 | Moses was faithful in all God's **h**. |
| | 8: 8 | a new covenant with the **h** of Israel |
| | 10:21 | we have a great priest over the **h** |
| 1Pe | 2: 5 | a spiritual **h** to be a holy priesthood, |
| 2Jn | 1:10 | do not take them into your **h** |

**FATHER'S HOUSE** Ge 24:23; Dt 22:21, 21; Jdg 11:7; Ps 45:10; Isa 3:6; Lk 2:49; Jn 2:16; 14:2

**HOUSE OF DAVID** 1Sa 20:16; 2Sa 3:1, 6; 1Ki 12:19, 20, 26; 13:2; 14:8; 2Ki 17:21; 2Ch 10:19; 21:7; Ps 122:5; Isa 7:2, 13; 16:5; 22:22; Jer 21:12; Zec 12:7, 8, 10, 12; 13:1

**HOUSE OF ... GOD** Ge 28:17; Jos 9:23; Jdg 18:31; 1Ch 6:48; 9:11, 13, 26, 27; 22:1, 2; 23:28; 25:6; 26:20; Ezr 2:68; 3:8, 9; 4:24; 5:2, 13, 14, 15, 16, 17; 6:5, 5, 7, 8, 16, 17, 22; 7:24; 8:17, 25, 30, 33, 36; 9:9; 10:1, 6, 9; Ne 6:10; 8:16; 10:32, 33, 34, 36, 37, 38, 39; 11:11, 16, 22; 12:40; 13:4, 7, 9, 11, 14; Ps 42:4; 52:8; 55:14; 84:10; 135:2; Ecc 5:1; Isa 2:3; Da 1:2; Hos 9:8; Joel 1:13, 16; Am 2:8; Mic 4:2; Mt 12:4; Mk 2:26; Lk 6:4; Heb 10:21

**HOUSE OF ISRAEL** Ex 40:38; Lev 10:6; Nu 20:29; Jos 21:45; Ru 4:11; 1Sa 7:3; 2Sa 1:12; 6:5, 15; 12:8; 16:3; 1Ki 12:21; 20:31; Ps 98:3; 115:9, 12; 135:19; Isa 5:7; 14:2; 46:3; 63:7; Jer 2:4, 26; 3:18, 20; 5:11, 15; 9:26; 10:1; 11:10, 17; 13:11; 18:6, 6; 31:27, 31, 33; 33:14, 17; 48:13; Eze 3:1, 4, 5, 7, 7, 17; 4:3, 4, 5; 5:4; 6:11; 8:6, 10, 11, 12; 9:9; 11:5, 15; 12:6, 9, 10, 27; 13:5, 9; 14:6; 17:2; 18:6, 15, 25, 29, 29, 30, 31; 20:30, 31, 39, 40, 44; 22:18; 24:21; 29:6, 21; 33:7, 10, 11, 20; 34:30; 35:15; 36:10, 21, 22, 22, 32, 37; 37:11, 16; 39:12, 22, 29; 40:4; 43:7; 44:6, 6, 12;

45:6, 8, 17, 17; Hos 1:6; 6:10; 11:12; Am 5:1, 3, 4, 25; 6:14; 9:9; Mic 1:5; 3:1, 9; Ac 7:42; Heb 8:8, 10

## HOUSE OF JACOB Ex 19:3; Ps 114:1; Isa 2:5, 6; 8:17; 10:20; 14:1; 29:22; 46:3; 48:1; 58:1; Jer 2:4; 5:20; Eze 20:5; Am 3:13; 9:8; Ob 1:17, 18; Mic 2:7; 3:9; Lk 1:33

## HOUSE OF JUDAH 2Sa 2:4, 7, 10, 11; 1Ki 12:21, 23; 2Ki 19:30; 1Ch 28:4; 2Ch 11:1; 22:10; Isa 22:21; 37:31; Jer 3:18; 5:11; 11:10, 17; 12:14; 13:11; 21:11; 31:27, 31; 33:14; Eze 4:6; 8:17; 25:8, 12; Hos 1:7; Zep 2:7; Zec 10:3, 6; 12:4; Heb 8:8

## HOUSE OF THE †LORD Ex 23:19; 34:26; Dt 23:18; Jdg 19:18; 1Sa 1:7, 24; 3:3, 15; 2Sa 12:20; 1Ch 6:31; 9:23; 22:1, 11; Ezr 1:5; 2:68; 3:8, 11; 7:27; 8:29; Ne 10:35; Ps 23:6; 27:4; 92:13; 116:19; 118:26; 122:1, 9; 134:1; 135:2; Jer 17:26; 26:2, 7, 9, 10; 27:18, 21; 28:1, 5; 29:26; 33:11; 35:2, 4; 36:6; 41:5; La 2:7; Eze 8:14, 16; 11:1; Hos 8:1; Joel 1:9, 14; Hag 1:14; Zec 7:3; 8:9; 11:13; 14:21

## HOUSEHOLD [HOUSE]
| | | |
|---|---|---|
| Ge | 12: 1 | and your father's **h** to the land I will |
| | 15: 3 | a servant in my **h** will be my heir." |
| | 17:12 | including those born in your **h** |
| | 31:19 | Rachel stole her father's **h** gods. |
| | 39: 4 | Potiphar put him in charge of his **h**, |
| Ex | 12: 3 | lamb for his family, one for each **h**. |
| Lev | 16: 6 | atonement for himself and his **h**. |
| Jos | 24:15 | But as for me and my **h**, we will |
| Jdg | 18:14 | some **h** gods and an image overlaid with |
| Pr | 31:21 | it snows, she has no fear for her **h**; |
| | 31:27 | watches over the affairs of her **h** |
| Mic | 7: 6 | are the members of your own **h**. |
| Mt | 10:36 | will be the members of your own **h**.' |
| | 12:25 | or **h** divided against itself will not |
| Jn | 4:53 | So he and his whole **h** believed. |
| Ac | 16:31 | will be saved—you and your **h**." |
| | 16:33 | he and all his **h** were baptized. |
| Eph | 2:19 | people and also members of his **h**, |
| 1Ti | 3:12 | manage his children and his **h** well. |
| | 3:15 | to conduct themselves in God's **h**, |
| | 5: 8 | especially for their own **h**, |
| 1Pe | 4:17 | judgment to begin with God's **h**; |

## HOUSEHOLDS [HOUSE]
| | | |
|---|---|---|
| Nu | 16:32 | and swallowed them and their **h**, |
| Dt | 11: 6 | and swallowed them up with their **h**, |
| Pr | 15:27 | greedy bring ruin to their **h**, |
| Tit | 1:11 | because they are disrupting whole **h** |

## HOUSES [HOUSE]
| | | |
|---|---|---|
| Ex | 12: 7 | of the **h** where they eat the lambs. |
| | 12:27 | who passed over the **h** |
| Dt | 6: 9 | them on the doorframes of your **h** |
| | 11:20 | them on the doorframes of your **h** |
| Ps | 112: 3 | Wealth and riches are in their **h**, |
| Isa | 65:21 | They will build **h** and dwell |
| Jer | 29:28 | Therefore build **h** and settle down; |
| Eze | 11: 3 | say, 'Haven't our **h** been recently |
| Mt | 19:29 | everyone who has left **h** or brothers |

| | | |
|---|---|---|
| Mk | 12:40 | They devour widows' **h** |
| Ac | 4:34 | who owned land or **h** sold them, |

## HOVERING* [HOVERS]
| | | |
|---|---|---|
| Ge | 1: 2 | Spirit of God was **h** over the waters. |
| Isa | 31: 5 | Like birds **h** overhead, the LORD |

## HOVERS* [HOVERING]
| | | |
|---|---|---|
| Dt | 32:11 | up its nest and **h** over its young, |

## HOW [HOWEVER, SOMEHOW]
| | | |
|---|---|---|
| Ge | 6:12 | God saw **h** corrupt the earth had |
| | 6:15 | This is **h** you are to build it: |
| | 28:17 | and said, "**H** awesome is this place! |
| | 39: 9 | **H** then could I do such a wicked |
| Ex | 12:11 | This is **h** you are to eat it: |
| Nu | 6:23 | sons, 'This is **h** you are to bless |
| | 23: 8 | **H** can I curse those whom God has |
| Dt | 31:27 | For I know **h** rebellious |
| 2Sa | 1:19 | **H** the mighty have fallen! |
| | 7:22 | "**H** great you are, |
| 1Ki | 3: 7 | and do not know **h** to carry out my |
| 2Ch | 6:18 | **H** much less this temple I have |
| | 32:14 | **H** then can your god deliver you |
| Job | 2:13 | to him, because they saw **h** great his |
| | 25: 4 | **H** can one born of woman be pure? |
| | 40: 4 | **h** can I reply to you? |
| Ps | 6: 3 | **H** long, LORD, **h** long? |
| | 8: 1 | **h** majestic is your name in all |
| | 31:19 | **H** great is your goodness, |
| | 36: 7 | **H** priceless is your unfailing love, |
| | 92: 5 | **H** great are your works, LORD, |
| | 119: 9 | **H** can those who are young keep |
| | 147: 1 | **h** pleasant and fitting to praise him! |
| Pr | 15:23 | and **h** good is a timely word! |
| SS | 1:15 | **H** beautiful you are, my darling! |
| | 1:16 | **H** handsome you are, my beloved! |
| Isa | 1:21 | See **h** the faithful city has become |
| | 14:12 | **H** you have fallen from heaven, |
| Jer | 1: 6 | I said, "I do not know **h** to speak; |
| | 38:28 | This is **h** Jerusalem was taken: |
| La | 1: 1 | **H** deserted lies the city, once so full |
| Eze | 33:10 | **H** then can we live?" ' |
| Hos | 11: 8 | "**H** can I give you up, Ephraim? |
| Mal | 1: 2 | you ask, '**H** have you loved us?' |
| Mk | 9:50 | **h** can you make it salty again? |
| | 10:23 | "**H** hard it is for the rich to enter |
| Lk | 12:27 | "Consider **h** the wild flowers grow. |
| | 20:44 | **H** then can he be his son?" |
| Jn | 3: 4 | "**H** can anyone be born when they |
| | 7:15 | "**H** did this man get such learning |
| Eph | 5:15 | Be very careful, then, **h** you live— |
| 1Ti | 3: 5 | **h** can he take care of God's |
| Heb | 2: 3 | **h** shall we escape if we ignore so |
| 2Pe | 2: 9 | then the Lord knows **h** to rescue |

## HOW LONG Ex 10:3, 7; 16:28; Nu 14:11, 11, 27; Jos 18:3; 1Sa 1:14; 16:1; 2Sa 2:26; 1Ki 18:21; Ne 2:6; Job 7:4; 8:2; 19:2; Ps 4:2, 2; 6:3, 3; 13:1, 1, 2, 2; 35:17; 62:3; 74:9, 10; 79:5, 5; 80:4; 82:2; 89:46, 46; 90:13; 94:3, 3; 119:84; Pr 1:22, 22; 6:9; Ecc 6:3; Isa 6:11; Jer 4:14, 21; 12:4; 13:27; 23:26; 31:22; 47:5, 6; Da 8:13; 12:6; Hos 8:5; Hab 1:2; 2:6; Zec 1:12; 2:2; Mt 17:17, 17; Mk 9:19, 19, 21; Lk 9:41; Jn 10:24; Rev 6:10

### HOW MUCH MORE
Dt 31:27; 1Sa 21:5; 23:3; 2Sa 4:11; 16:11; 2Ki 5:13; Job 4:19; Pr 11:31; 15:11; 19:2, 7; 21:27; SS 4:10; Mt 7:11; 10:25; 12:12; Lk 11:13; 12:24, 28; Ro 5:9, 10, 15, 17; 11:24; 1Co 6:3; 2Co 3:9; Heb 9:14; 10:29; 12:9

### HOWEVER [HOW]
| | | |
|---|---|---|
| Ex | 16:20 | **H**, some of them paid no attention |
| Dt | 15: 4 | **H**, there need be no poor people |
| | 28:15 | **H**, if you do not obey the LORD |
| Jos | 14: 8 | I, **h**, followed the LORD my God |
| Jer | 34:14 | Your ancestors, **h**, did not listen |
| Lk | 18: 8 | **H**, when the Son of Man comes, |
| Ro | 8: 9 | You, **h**, are not controlled |
| 1Pe | 4:16 | **H**, if you suffer as a Christian, |

### HUGE
| | | |
|---|---|---|
| 2Sa | 21:20 | there was a **h** man with six fingers |
| | 23:21 | And he struck down a **h** Egyptian. |
| Da | 2:35 | the statue became a **h** mountain |
| Jnh | 1:17 | provided a **h** fish to swallow Jonah, |
| Rev | 8: 8 | and something like a **h** mountain, |
| | 16:21 | From the sky **h** hailstones, |

### HULDAH
Female prophet consulted by Hilkiah the priest for King Josiah (2Ki 22; 2Ch 34:14–28).

### HUMAN [HUMANITY]
| | | |
|---|---|---|
| Ge | 1:26 | "Let us make **h** beings in our image, |
| | 6: 3 | Spirit will not contend with **h** beings |
| | 6: 6 | regretted that he had made **h** beings |
| | 6: 7 | of the earth the **h** race I have created— |
| | 9: 6 | "Whoever sheds **h** blood, by **h** beings shall their blood be shed; |
| Ex | 4:11 | "Who gave **h** beings their mouths? |
| Lev | 24:17 | who takes the life of a **h** being is |
| | 24:21 | kills a **h** being is to be put to death. |
| Nu | 16:22 | God of every **h** spirit, |
| | 19:16 | anyone who touches a **h** bone |
| | 23:19 | God is not a **h**, that he should lie, |
| | 27:16 | the LORD, the God of every **h** spirit, |
| Dt | 4:28 | and stone made by **h** hands, |
| | 32: 8 | when he divided all the **h** race, |
| Jos | 10:14 | the LORD listened to a **h** being. |
| 1Sa | 2:25 | anyone sins against another **h** being, |
| | 15:29 | for he is not a **h** being, |
| | 16: 7 | does not look at the things **h** beings |
| 2Sa | 7:19 | Sovereign LORD, is for a **h** being! |
| 1Ki | 8:39 | (for you alone know every **h** heart), |
| | 13: 2 | **h** bones will be burned on you.' " |
| 2Ki | 19:18 | fashioned by **h** hands. |
| | 23:14 | and covered the sites with **h** bones. |
| 1Ch | 21:13 | do not let me fall into **h** hands." |
| | 29: 1 | not for **h** beings but for the LORD |
| 2Ch | 32:19 | the work of **h** hands. |
| Job | 4:17 | **h** beings be more pure than their Maker |
| | 5: 7 | Yet **h** beings are born to trouble |
| Ps | 94:11 | The LORD knows all **h** plans; |
| Ecc | 1:13 | God has laid on the **h** race! |
| | 3:11 | He has also set eternity in the **h** heart; |
| | 3:19 | **h** beings is like that of the animals; |
| | 12:13 | this is the [duty] of every **h** being. |
| Isa | 2:22 | Stop trusting in **h** beings, |
| | 29:13 | based on merely **h** rules |
| | 37:19 | and stone, fashioned by **h** hands. |
| | 45:12 | made the earth and created **h** beings |
| | 52:14 | his form marred beyond **h** likeness— |
| Jer | 32:27 | the God of the whole **h** race. |
| Da | 2:34 | was cut out, but not by **h** hands. |
| | 5: 5 | the fingers of a **h** hand appeared |
| | 7: 4 | human being, and a **h** mind was given |
| | 8:25 | be destroyed, but not by **h** power. |
| Hos | 11: 4 | I led them with cords of **h** kindness, |
| | 11: 9 | For I am God, and not a **h** being— |
| Hab | 2: 8 | you have shed **h** blood; |
| | 2:17 | you have shed **h** blood; |
| Mt | 12:12 | more valuable is a **h** being than a sheep! |
| | 15: 9 | teachings are merely **h** rules.' " |
| | 19:26 | "With **h** beings this is impossible, |
| Mk | 7: 7 | their teachings are merely **h** rules.' |
| | 11:30 | was it from heaven, or of **h** origin? |
| | 14:58 | destroy this temple made with **h** hands |
| Jn | 1:13 | nor of **h** decision or a husband's |
| | 2:25 | did not need **h** testimony about them, |
| | 5:34 | Not that I accept **h** testimony; |
| | 8:15 | You judge by **h** standards; |
| Ac | 5:38 | purpose or activity is of **h** origin, |
| | 10:26 | he said, "I am only **h** myself." |
| | 19:26 | gods made by **h** hands are no gods |
| Ro | 3: 4 | and every **h** being a liar. |
| | 6:19 | life because of your **h** limitations. |
| | 9: 5 | them is traced the **h** ancestry |
| | 9:20 | who are you, a mere **h** being, |
| 1Co | 1:25 | of God is wiser than **h** wisdom, |
| | 1:26 | of you were wise by **h** standards; |
| | 2: 5 | faith might not rest on **h** wisdom, |
| | 2:13 | not in words taught us by **h** wisdom |
| | 13: 1 | speak in **h** or angelic tongues, |
| | 15:21 | since death came through a **h** being, |
| 2Co | 3: 3 | of stone but on tablets of **h** hearts. |
| | 5: 1 | in heaven, not built by **h** hands. |
| Gal | 1: 1 | Paul, an apostle—sent not with a **h** |
| | 1:10 | now trying to win **h** approval, |
| | 3: 3 | you now trying to finish by **h** effort? |
| Php | 2: 7 | a servant, being made in **h** likeness. |
| | 2: 8 | found in appearance as a **h** being, |
| Col | 2: 8 | which depends on **h** tradition |
| | 2:22 | are based on merely **h** commands |
| 1Th | 2:13 | you accepted it not as a **h** word, |
| 1Ti | 2: 5 | Christ Jesus, himself **h**, |
| Heb | 9:11 | that is not made with **h** hands, |
| | 9:24 | not enter a sanctuary made with **h** hands |
| | 13: 6 | What can **h** beings do to me?" |
| Jas | 5:17 | Elijah was a **h** being, even as we are. |
| 2Pe | 1:21 | never had its origin in the **h** will, |
| | 1:21 | though **h**, spoke from God |
| 2Pe | 2:18 | the lustful desires of sinful **h** nature, |
| Rev | 9: 7 | and their faces resembled **h** faces. |
| | 18:13 | and **h** beings sold as slaves. |

### HUMANITY [HUMAN, HUMANKIND, MAN]
| | | |
|---|---|---|
| Eph | 2:15 | create in himself one new **h** |
| Heb | 2:14 | he too shared in their **h** so |

### HUMANKIND [HUMAN]
| | | |
|---|---|---|
| Ps | 33:13 | LORD looks down and sees all **h**; |
| | 66: 5 | his awesome deeds for **h**! |
| | 107: 8 | his wonderful deeds for **h**, |

Pr    8:31  whole world and delighting in **h**.
Ecc   7:29  God created **h** upright,

## HUMBLE* [HUMBLED, HUMBLES, HUMBLY, HUMILIATE, HUMILIATED, HUMILIATING, HUMILIATION, HUMILITY]

Ex   10: 3  you refuse to **h** yourself before me?
Nu   12: 3  (Now Moses was a very **h** man, more **h**
Dt    8: 2  to **h** and test you in order to know
      8:16  to **h** and test you so that in the end it
2Sa  22:28  You save the **h**, but your eyes are
1Ki  11:39  I will **h** David's descendants
2Ch   7:14  will **h** themselves and pray and seek
     33:23  he did not **h** himself before
     36:12  did not **h** himself before Jeremiah
Ezr   8:21  we might **h** ourselves before our
Job   8: 7  Your beginnings will seem **h**,
     40:12  at all who are proud and **h** them,
Ps   18:27  You save the **h** but bring low those
     25: 9  He guides the **h** in what is right
     55:19  he will hear them and **h** them,
    147: 6  The LORD sustains the **h** but casts
    149: 4  he crowns the **h** will victory.
Pr    3:34  shows favor to the **h** and oppressed.
Isa  13:11  and will **h** the pride of the ruthless.
     23: 9  to **h** all who are renowned
     29.19  Once more the **h** will rejoice
     58: 5  a day for people to **h** themselves?
     66: 2  those who are **h** and contrite
Da    4:37  who walk in pride he is able to **h**.
      5:19  and those he wanted to **h**,
     10:12  and to **h** yourself before your God,
Zep   2: 3  the LORD, all you **h** of the land,
      3:12  leave within you the meek and **h**.
Mt   11:29  for I am gentle and **h** in heart,
     18: 4  Therefore, whoever takes a **h** place
     23:12  who **h** themselves will be exalted.
Lk    1:48  he has been mindful of the **h** state
      1:52  their thrones but has lifted up the **h**.
     14:11  who **h** themselves will be exalted."
     18:14  who **h** themselves will be exalted."
2Co  12:21  again my God will **h** me before you,
Eph   4: 2  Be completely **h** and gentle;
Jas   1: 9  Believers in **h** circumstances ought
      4: 6  proud but shows favor to the **h**
      4:10  **H** yourselves before the Lord,
1Pe   3: 8  another, be compassionate and **h**.
      5: 5  proud but shows favor to the **h**
      5: 6  **H** yourselves, therefore,

## HUMBLED [HUMBLE]

Lev  26:41  their uncircumcised hearts are **h**
Dt    8: 3  He **h** you, causing you to hunger
1Ki  21:29  Because he has **h** himself, I will not
2Ch  12: 7  "Since they have **h** themselves,
     33:12  **h** himself greatly before the God
     34:27  you **h** yourself before God
Ps   35:13  sackcloth and **h** myself with fasting.
     44: 9  But now you have rejected and **h** us;
    107:39  and they were **h** by oppression,
Isa   2: 9  be brought low and everyone **h**—
Jer  44:10  this day they have not **h** themselves
Da    5:22  son, have not **h** yourself, though you
Mt   23:12  who exalt themselves will be **h**,
Lk   14:11  who exalt themselves will be **h**,

Php   2: 8  he **h** himself by becoming obedient

## HUMBLES* [HUMBLE]

1Sa   2: 7  he **h** and he exalts.
Isa  26: 5  He **h** those who dwell on high,

## HUMBLY [HUMBLE]

Mic   6: 8  mercy and to walk **h** with your God.
Jas   1:21  **h** accept the word planted in you,

## HUMILIATE* [HUMBLE]

Pr   25: 7  for him to **h** you before his nobles.

## HUMILIATED [HUMBLE]

Isa  54: 4  not fear disgrace; you will not be **h**.
Jer  31:19  **h** because I bore the disgrace of my
Lk   13:17  all his opponents were **h**,
     14: 9  Then, **h**, you will have to take

## HUMILIATING* [HUMBLE]

1Co  11:22  despise the church of God by **h** those

## HUMILIATION [HUMBLE]

Jas   1:10  should take pride in their **h**—

## HUMILITY* [HUMBLE]

Ps   45: 4  in the cause of truth, **h** and justice;
Pr   11: 2  disgrace, but with **h** comes wisdom.
     15:33  LORD, and **h** comes before honor.
     18:12  haughty, but **h** comes before honor.
     22: 4  **H** is the fear of the LORD;
Zep   2: 3  Seek righteousness, seek **h**;
Ac   20:19  I served the Lord with great **h**
Php   2: 3  in **h** value others above yourselves,
Col   2:18  let anyone who delights in false **h**
      2:23  their false **h** and their harsh
      3:12  kindness, **h**,
Jas   3:13  deeds done in the **h** that comes
1Pe   5: 5  with **h** toward one another, because,

## HUNDRED [HUNDREDFOLD]

Ge    6: 3  their days will be a **h** and twenty
     15:13  four **h** years your descendants will
     17:17  son be born to a man a **h** years old?
Lev  26: 8  Five of you will chase a **h**, and a **h**
1Ki  18:13  I hid a **h** of the LORD's prophets
Isa  65:20  at a **h** will be thought mere youths;
Mt   13:23  yielding a **h**, sixty or thirty times
     18:12  If a man owns a **h** sheep, and one
Lk    7:41  One owed him five **h** denarii,
Ac    1:15  (a group numbering about a **h**

## HUNDREDFOLD* [HUNDRED]

Ge   26:12  land and the same year reaped a **h**,

## HUNG [HANG]

Dt   21:23  because anyone who is **h** on a pole
Ps  137: 2  on the poplars we **h** our harps,
Mt   18: 6  large millstone were **h** around their
Mk    9:42  large millstone were **h** around
Lk   19:48  do it, because all the people **h** on his
     23:39  of the criminals who **h** there hurled
Gal   3:13  "Cursed is everyone who is **h**

# HUNGER [HUNGRY]

| | | |
|---|---|---|
| Dt | 8: 3 | causing you to **h** and then feeding |
| Ne | 9:15 | In their **h** you gave them bread |
| Pr | 6:30 | to satisfy his **h** when he is starving. |
| Isa | 49:10 | They will neither **h** nor thirst, |
| Mt | 5: 6 | Blessed are those who **h** and thirst |
| Lk | 6:21 | Blessed are you who **h** now, for you |
| 2Co | 6: 5 | in hard work, sleepless nights and **h**; |
| | 11:27 | I have known **h** and thirst and have |
| Rev | 7:16 | 'Never again will they **h**; |

# HUNGRY [HUNGER]

| | | |
|---|---|---|
| 1Sa | 2: 5 | who were **h** are **h** no more. |
| Job | 24:10 | carry the sheaves, but still go **h**. |
| Ps | 50:12 | If I were **h** I would not tell you, |
| | 107: 9 | and fills the **h** with good things. |
| | 146: 7 | oppressed and gives food to the **h**. |
| Pr | 10: 3 | does not let the righteous go **h**, |
| | 19:15 | deep sleep, and the shiftless go **h**. |
| | 25:21 | If your enemy is **h**, give him food |
| | 27: 7 | but to the **h** even what is bitter tastes |
| Isa | 29: 8 | **h** people dream they are eating, |
| | 58: 7 | it not to share your food with the **h** |
| Eze | 18: 7 | gives his food to the **h** and provides |
| Mt | 4: 2 | days and forty nights, he was **h**. |
| | 12: 1 | His disciples were **h** and began |
| | 15:32 | I do not want to send them away **h**, |
| | 25:35 | For I was **h** and you gave me |
| | 25:42 | For I was **h** and you gave me |
| Mk | 11:12 | were leaving Bethany, Jesus was **h**. |
| Lk | 1:53 | He has filled the **h** with good things |
| Jn | 6:35 | comes to me will never go **h**, |
| Ro | 12:20 | "If your enemy is **h**, feed him; |
| 1Co | 4:11 | To this very hour we go **h** |
| | 11:34 | Those who are **h** should eat |
| Php | 4:12 | whether well fed or **h**, |

# HUNT [HUNTED, HUNTER, HUNTS]

| | | |
|---|---|---|
| Ge | 27: 3 | open country to **h** some wild game |
| Ps | 10: 2 | the wicked **h** down the weak, |
| Am | 9: 3 | there I will **h** them down and seize |
| Mic | 7: 2 | they **h** each other with nets. |

# HUNTED [HUNT]

| | | |
|---|---|---|
| La | 3:52 | enemies without cause **h** me like |

# HUNTER [HUNT]

| | | |
|---|---|---|
| Ge | 10: 9 | was a mighty **h** before the LORD; |
| | 25:27 | and Esau became a skillful **h**, a man |

# HUNTS [HUNT]

| | | |
|---|---|---|
| Lev | 17:13 | foreigner residing among you who **h** |

# HUR

| | | |
|---|---|---|
| Ex | 17:12 | Aaron and **H** held his hands up— |

# HURAM [HURAM-ABI]

| | | |
|---|---|---|
| 1Ki | 7:14 | **H** was filled with wisdom, |
| 2Ch | 4:11 | So **H** finished the work he had |

# HURAM-ABI [HURAM]

| | | |
|---|---|---|
| 2Ch | 2:13 | "I am sending you **H**, a man |

# HURL [HURLED]

| | | |
|---|---|---|
| 1Sa | 25:29 | of your enemies he will **h** away as |
| 2Ch | 26:15 | and **h** large stones from the walls. |
| Ps | 22: 7 | they **h** insults, shaking their heads. |
| Mic | 7:19 | **h** all our iniquities into the depths |

# HURLED [HURL]

| | | |
|---|---|---|
| Ex | 15: 1 | and driver he has **h** into the sea. |
| Jos | 10:11 | the LORD **h** large hailstones down |
| 1Sa | 20:33 | Saul **h** his spear at him to kill him. |
| La | 2: 1 | He has **h** down the splendor |
| Jnh | 2: 3 | You **h** me into the deep, |
| Mk | 15:29 | Those who passed by **h** insults |
| 1Pe | 2:23 | When they **h** their insults at him, |
| Rev | 8: 5 | from the altar, and **h** it on the earth; |
| | 12: 9 | The great dragon was **h** down— |

# HURRIED [HURRY]

| | | |
|---|---|---|
| Ge | 18: 6 | So Abraham **h** into the tent to Sarah. |
| | 24:17 | The servant **h** to meet her and said, |
| 2Ki | 5:21 | So Gehazi **h** after Naaman. |
| Da | 6:19 | king got up and **h** to the lions' den. |
| Mt | 28: 8 | So the women **h** away |
| Lk | 2:16 | So they **h** off and found Mary |

# HURRIES* [HURRY]

| | | |
|---|---|---|
| Ecc | 1: 5 | sets, and **h** back to where it rises. |

# HURRY [HURRIED, HURRIES]

| | | |
|---|---|---|
| Ge | 19:15 | the angels urged Lot, saying, "**H**! |
| Ex | 12:33 | The Egyptians urged the people to **h** |

# HURT [HURTS]

| | | |
|---|---|---|
| Ecc | 8: 9 | lords it over others to his own **h**. |
| Da | 6:22 | They have not **h** me, because I was |
| Mk | 16:18 | it will not **h** them at all; |
| Jn | 21:17 | Peter was **h** because Jesus asked |
| 2Co | 7: 8 | I see that my letter **h** you, but only |
| Rev | 2:11 | who are victorious will not be **h** |

# HURTS* [HURT]

| | | |
|---|---|---|
| Ps | 15: 4 | keep their oaths even when it **h**; |
| Pr | 26:28 | A lying tongue hates those it **h**, |

# HUSBAND [HUSBAND'S, HUSBANDS]

| | | |
|---|---|---|
| Ge | 3: 6 | She also gave some to her **h**, |
| | 3:16 | Your desire will be for your **h**, |
| | 16: 3 | and gave her to her **h** to be his wife. |
| Nu | 30: 8 | if her **h** forbids her when he hears |
| Dt | 24: 4 | then her first **h**, who divorced her, |
| Pr | 7:19 | My **h** is not at home; he has gone |
| | 31:11 | Her **h** has full confidence in her |
| | 31:23 | Her **h** is respected at the city gate, |
| | 31:28 | her **h** also, and he praises her: |
| Isa | 54: 1 | woman than of her who has a **h**," |
| | 54: 5 | For your Maker is your **h**— |
| Jer | 3:14 | the LORD, "for I am your **h**. |
| | 3:20 | like a woman unfaithful to her **h**, |
| | 31:32 | though I was a **h** to them," |
| Hos | 2:16 | LORD, "you will call me 'my **h**'; |
| Mt | 1:19 | Because Joseph her **h** was |
| | 19:10 | "If this is the situation between a **h** |
| Mk | 10:12 | if she divorces her **h** and marries |

Jn     4:17  "I have no **h**," she replied.
Ro     7: 2  bound to her **h** as long as he is alive,
1Co    7: 2  and each woman with her own **h**.
       7: 3  The **h** should fulfill his marital duty
       7: 4  **h** does not have authority over his own body
       7:10  wife must not separate from her **h**.
       7:11  And a **h** must not divorce his wife.
       7:14  sanctified through her believing **h**.
       7:39  is bound to her **h** as long as he lives.
2Co   11: 2  I promised you to one **h**, to Christ,
Gal    4:27  woman than of her who has a **h**."
Eph    5:23  For the **h** is the head of the wife as
       5:33  and the wife must respect her **h**.
1Ti    5: 9  sixty, has been faithful to her **h**,
Rev   21: 2  a bride beautifully dressed for her **h**.

## HUSBAND'S  [HUSBAND]

Dt    25: 5  Her **h** brother shall take her
Ru     2: 1  Naomi had a relative on her **h** side,
Pr    12: 4  of noble character is her **h** crown,
Jn     1:13  nor of human decision or a **h** will,

## HUSBANDMAN  (KJV) See FARMER, GARDENER

## HUSBANDS  [HUSBAND]

Jn     4:18  is, you have had five **h**, and the man
1Co   14:35  they should ask their own **h**
Eph    5:22  yourselves to your own **h** as you do
       5:25  **H**, love your wives, just as Christ
       5:28  **h** ought to love their wives as their
Col    3:18  submit yourselves to your **h**, as is
       3:19  **H**, love your wives and do not be
Tit    2: 4  the younger women to love their **h**
       2: 5  and to be subject to their **h**,
1Pe    3: 1  yourselves to your own **h** so that,
       3: 7  **H**, in the same way be considerate

## HUSHAI

Wise man of David who frustrated Ahithophel's advice and foiled Absalom's revolt (2Sa 15:32–37; 16:15—17:16; 1Ch 27:33).

## HUT*

Job   27:18  like a **h** made by a watchman.
Isa    1: 8  like a **h** in a field of melons,
      24:20  it sways like a **h** in the wind;

## HYMENAEUS*

A false teacher (1Ti 1:20; 2Ti 2:17).

## HYMN*  [HYMNS]

Ps    40: 3  my mouth, a **h** of praise to our God.
Mt    26:30  When they had sung a **h**, they went
Mk    14:26  When they had sung a **h**, they went
1Co   14:26  each of you has a **h**, or a word

## HYMNS*  [HYMN]

Ac    16:25  were praying and singing **h** to God,
Eph    5:19  psalms, **h** and songs from the Spirit,
Col    3:16  psalms, **h** and songs from the Spirit,

## HYPOCRISY*  [HYPOCRITE, HYPOCRITES, HYPOCRITICAL]

Mt    23:28  on the inside you are full of **h**
Mk    12:15  But Jesus knew their **h**.
Lk    12: 1  yeast of the Pharisees, which is **h**.
Gal    2:13  The other Jews joined him in his **h**, so that by their **h**
1Pe    2: 1  of all malice and all deceit, **h**, envy,

## HYPOCRITE*  [HYPOCRISY]

Mt     7: 5  You **h**, first take the plank
Lk     6:42  You **h**, first take the plank

## HYPOCRITES*  [HYPOCRISY]

Ps    26: 4  deceitful, nor do I associate with **h**.
Mt     6: 2  as the **h** do in the synagogues
       6: 5  do not be like the **h**, for they love
       6:16  do not look somber as the **h** do,
      15: 7  You **h**! Isaiah was right when he
      22:18  "You **h**, why are you trying to trap
      23:13  of the law and Pharisees, you **h**!
      23:15  of the law and Pharisees, you **h**!
      23:23  of the law and Pharisees, you **h**!
      23:25  of the law and Pharisees, you **h**!
      23:27  of the law and Pharisees, you **h**!
      23:29  of the law and Pharisees, you **h**!
      24:51  and assign him a place with the **h**,
Mk     7: 6  when he prophesied about you **h**;
Lk    12:56  **H**! You know how to interpret
      13:15  The Lord answered him, "You **h**!

## HYPOCRITICAL*  [HYPOCRISY]

1Ti    4: 2  teachings come through **h** liars,

## HYSSOP

Ex    12:22  Take a bunch of **h**, dip it
Lev   14: 4  **h** be brought for the person to be
Nu    19: 6  **h** and scarlet wool and throw them
Ps    51: 7  Cleanse me with **h**, and I will be
Jn    19:29  the sponge on a stalk of the **h** plant,
Heb    9:19  scarlet wool and branches of **h**,

---

# I

## I AM

Ge    15: 1  **I am** your shield,
      17: 1  "**I am** God Almighty; walk before me
Ex     3:14  God said to Moses, "**I AM WHO I AM**.
       3:14  '**I AM** has sent me to you.' "
Ps    35: 3  "**I am** your salvation."
      46:10  "Be still, and know that **I am** God;
Isa   41:10  do not fear, for **I am** with you;
      41:10  do not be dismayed, for **I am** your God.
      43: 3  For **I am** the LORD your God,
      43:15  **I am** the LORD, your Holy One,
      44: 6  **I am** the first and **I am** the last;
      48:12  **I am** the first and **I am** the last.
Jer    3:14  the LORD, "for **I am** your husband.
      32:27  "**I am** the LORD, the God of the whole
Mt    16:15  he asked. "Who do you say **I am**?"
      28:20  And surely **I am** with you always,

Mk    8:29  he asked. "Who do you say **I am**?"
     14:62  "**I am**," said Jesus. "And you will see
Jn    6:35  Jesus declared, "**I am** the bread of life.
      6:41  "**I am** the bread that came down from
            heaven.
      6:48  **I am** the bread of life.
      6:51  **I am** the living bread that came down
            from heaven.
      8:12  he said, "**I am** the light of the world.
      8:24  if you do not believe that **I am** he,
      8:28  then you will know that **I am** he
      8:58  "before Abraham was born, **I am**!"
      9: 5  **I am** the light of the world."
     10: 7  **I am** the gate for the sheep.
     10: 9  **I am** the gate; whoever enters through
     10:11  "**I am** the good shepherd.
     10:14  "**I am** the good shepherd;
     10:36  because I said, '**I am** God's Son'?
     11:25  "**I am** the resurrection and the life.
     13:19  you will believe that **I am** who **I am**.
     14: 6  "**I am** the way and the truth and the life.
     14:10  believe that **I am** in the Father,
     14:11  when I say that **I am** in the Father
     14:20  that **I am** in my Father, and you are in
            me, and **I am** in you.
     15: 1  "**I am** the true vine, and my Father
     15: 5  "**I am** the vine; you are the branches.
     18: 5  "**I am** he," Jesus said.
     18: 6  When Jesus said, "**I am** he,"
     18: 8  answered, "I told you that **I am** he.
Ac    9: 5  "**I am** Jesus, whom you are persecuting
     18:10  For **I am** with you, and no one
     22: 8  " '**I am** Jesus of Nazareth, whom you
     26:15  '**I am** Jesus, whom you are persecuting,
Rev   1: 8  "**I am** the Alpha and the Omega,"
      1:17  **I am** the First and the Last.
      1:18  **I am** the Living One;
      3:11  **I am** coming soon.
     21: 6  **I am** the Alpha and the Omega,
     22: 7  "Look, **I am** coming soon!
     22:12  "Look, **I am** coming soon!
     22:13  **I am** the Alpha and the Omega,
     22:16  **I am** the Root and the Offspring of
            David,
     22:20  "Yes, **I am** coming soon." Amen.

**I AM THE †LORD**  Ge 15:7; 28:13; Ex 6:2, 6,
     7, 8, 29; 7:5, 17; 10:2; 12:12; 14:4, 18; 15:26;
     16:12; 20:2; 29:46, 46; 31:13; Lev 11:44, 45;
     18:2, 4, 5, 6, 21, 30; 19:3, 4, 10, 12, 14, 16, 18,
     25, 28, 30, 31, 32, 34, 36, 37; 20:7, 8, 24; 21:12,
     15, 23; 22:2, 3, 8, 9, 16, 30, 31, 32, 33; 23:22,
     43; 24:22; 25:17, 38, 55; 26:1, 2, 13, 44, 45; Nu
     3:13, 41, 45; 10:10; 15:41, 41; Dt 5:6; 29:6; Jdg
     6:10; 1Ki 20:13, 28; Ps 81:10; Isa 41:13; 42:8;
     43:3, 11, 15; 44:24; 45:3, 5, 6, 18; 48:17; 49:23;
     51:15; 60:22; Jer 9:24; 24:7; 32:27; Eze 6:7, 10,
     13, 14; 7:4, 27; 11:10, 12; 12:15, 16, 20; 13:14,
     21, 23; 14:8; 15:7; 16:62; 20:5, 7, 19, 20, 26, 38,
     42, 44; 22:16; 24:27; 25:5, 7, 11, 17; 26:6; 28:22,
     23, 26; 29:6, 9, 21; 30:8, 19, 25, 26; 32:15;
     33:29; 34:27; 35:4, 9, 15; 36:11, 23, 38; 37:6, 13;
     38:23; 39:6, 22, 28; Joel 2:27; Zec 10:6

**I AM WITH YOU**  See WITH

## IBZAN*
Judge of Israel (Jdg 12:8–10).

## ICE  [ICY]
Job  37:10  The breath of God produces **i**,

## ICHABOD*
1Sa  4:21  She named the boy **I**, saying,

## ICONIUM
Ac   14: 1  At **I** Paul and Barnabas went as
2Ti   3:11  to me in Antioch, **I** and Lystra,

## ICY*  [ICE]
Ps  147:17  Who can withstand his **i** blast?

## IDDO
2Ch  9:29  **I** the seer concerning Jeroboam son
     12:15  and of **I** the seer that deal
     13:22  in the annotations of the prophet **I**.

## IDEA  [IDEAS]
Jn   18:34  "Is that your own **i**," Jesus asked,
2Pe   2:13  Their **i** of pleasure is to carouse

## IDEAS  [IDEA]
Ac   17:21  about and listening to the latest **i**.)

## IDLE*  [IDLENESS, IDLERS]
Dt   32:47  They are not just **i** words for you—
Job  11: 3  Will your **i** talk reduce others
Ecc  10:18  because of **i** hands, the house leaks.
     11: 6  at evening let your hands not be **i**,
Isa  58:13  as you please or speaking **i** words,
Col   2:18  minds puff them up with **i** notions.
1Th   5:14  warn those who are **i** and disruptive,
2Th   3: 6  away from every believer who is **i**
      3: 7  We were not **i** when we were
      3:11  We hear that some among you are **i**
1Ti   5:13  they get into the habit of being **i**

## IDLENESS*  [IDLE]
Pr   31:27  and does not eat the bread of **i**.

## IDLERS*  [IDLE]
1Ti   5:13  And not only do they become **i**,

## IDOL  [CALF-IDOL, IDOL'S,
     IDOLATER, IDOLATERS,
     IDOLATRIES, IDOLATROUS,
     IDOLATRY, IDOLS]
Ex   32: 4  made it into an **i** cast in the shape
Dt   27:15  is anyone who makes an **i**—
Ps  106:19  and worshiped an **i** cast from metal.
Isa  40:19  As for an **i**, a metal worker casts it,
     41: 7  other nails down the **i** so it will not
     44:15  he makes an **i** and bows down to it.
     44:17  From the rest he makes a god, his **i**;
Eze   8: 3  court, where the **i** that provokes
Hos   4:12  My people consult a wooden **i**
Hab   2:18  what value is an **i** that someone has
1Co   8: 4  We know that "An **i** is nothing
1Co  10:19  food sacrificed to an **i** is anything,

## IDOL'S* [IDOL]

1Co  8:10  eating in an **i** temple, won't they be

## IDOLATER* [IDOL]

Eph  5: 5  such a person is an **i**—

## IDOLATERS* [IDOL]

1Co  5:10  or the greedy and swindlers, or **i**.
     5:11  immoral or greedy, **i** or slanderers,
     6: 9  immoral nor **i** nor adulterers nor
     10: 7  Do not be **i**, as some of them were;
Rev 21: 8  magic arts, the **i** and all liars—
    22:15  the **i** and everyone who loves

## IDOLATRIES* [IDOL]

Jer 14:14  **i** and the delusions of their own

## IDOLATROUS [IDOL]

2Ki 23: 5  the **i** priests appointed by the kings

## IDOLATRY [IDOL]

1Sa 15:23  and arrogance like the evil of **i**.
Eze 23:49  the consequences of your sins of **i**.
1Co 10:14  my dear friends, flee from **i**.
Gal  5:20  **i** and witchcraft;
Col  3: 5  evil desires and greed, which is **i**.
1Pe  4: 3  orgies, carousing and detestable **i**.

## IDOLS [IDOL]

Ex  34:17  "Do not make any **i**.
Lev 26:30  on the lifeless forms of your **i**, and I
Dt   7: 5  poles and burn their **i** in the fire.
    32:16  angered him with their detestable **i**.
1Ki 15:12  of all the **i** his ancestors had made.
2Ki 17:15  They followed worthless **i**
1Ch 16:26  For all the gods of the nations are **i**,
Ps  31: 6  hate those who cling to worthless **i**;
    78:58  aroused his jealousy with their **i**.
   115: 4  But their **i** are silver and gold,
Isa 42: 8  glory to another or my praise to **i**.
    44: 9  All who make **i** are nothing,
Jer 10: 5  a melon patch, their **i** cannot speak;
    16:19  worthless **i** that did them no good.
Eze 14: 3  these men have set up **i** in their
    23:37  committed adultery with their **i**;
    23:39  sacrificed their children to their **i**,
Mic  5:13  destroy your **i** and your sacred stones
Hab  2:18  they make **i** that cannot speak.
Zec 10: 2  The **i** speak deceitfully, diviners see
Ac  15:20  to abstain from food polluted by **i**,
    21:25  abstain from food sacrificed to **i**,
1Co  8: 1  Now about food sacrificed to **i**:
2Co  6:16  between the temple of God and **i**?
1Jn  5:21  children, keep yourselves from **i**.
Rev  2:14  so that they ate food sacrificed to **i**

## IF

Ge   4: 7  **I** you do what is right, will you not
Ex  19: 5  Now **i** you obey me fully and keep
    33:15  "**I** your Presence does not go
Dt  11:27  the blessing **i** you obey
    11:28  the curse **i** you disobey
1Ki 18:21  **I** the LORD is God, follow him;
1Ch 28: 9  **I** you seek him, he will be found
Ps  95: 7  **i** only you would hear his voice,

Pr  17:28  are thought wise **i** they keep silent,
Jer 18: 8  **i** that nation I warned repents of its
Eze 18:21  **i** the wicked turn away from all
Mt   4: 3  and said, "**I** you are the Son of God,
    27:40  cross, **i** you are the Son of God!"
Mk   3:24  **I** a kingdom is divided against itself,
     5:28  thought, "**I** I just touch his clothes,
     8:38  **I** any of you are ashamed of me
Lk   6:32  "**I** you love those who love you,
Jn  13:17  you will be blessed **i** you do them.
    14:15  "**I** you love me, keep my
    15: 5  **I** you remain in me and I in you,
    15:10  **I** you keep my commands, you will
Ro   6: 8  Now **i** we died with Christ,
     8:31  **I** God is for us, who can be against
Heb  3: 7  "Today, **i** you hear his voice,
Jas  1: 5  **I** any of you lacks wisdom,
1Pe  4:16  **i** you suffer as a Christian, do not be
1Jn  1: 9  **I** we confess our sins, he is faithful
     3:20  **I** our hearts condemn us,
Rev  3:20  **I** anyone hears my voice and opens

## IGNORANCE [IGNORE]

Ac   3:17  I know that you acted in **i**, as did
    17:30  In the past God overlooked such **i**,
1Ti  1:13  shown mercy because I acted in **i**
Heb  9: 7  sins the people had committed in **i**.

## IGNORANT [IGNORE]

Isa 45:20  **I** are those who carry about idols
1Co 15:34  there are some who are **i** of God—
Heb  5: 2  to deal gently with those who are **i**
1Pe  2:15  good you should silence the **i** talk
2Pe  3:16  which **i** and unstable people distort,

## IGNORE [IGNORANCE, IGNORANT, IGNORED, IGNORES]

Dt  22: 1  do not **i** it but be sure to take it back
Ps   9:12  he does not **i** the cries
1Co 14:38  who **i** this will themselves be ignored.
Heb  2: 3  escape if we **i** so great a salvation?

## IGNORED [IGNORE]

Hos  4: 6  because you have **i** the law of your
1Co 14:38  ignore this will themselves be **i**.

## IGNORES* [IGNORE]

Pr  10:17  whoever **i** correction leads others

## ILL [ILLNESS, ILLNESSES]

2Ch 32:24  In those days Hezekiah became **i**
Mt   4:24  to him all who were **i** with various

## ILL-GOTTEN [GET]

Pr   1:19  the paths of all who go after **i** gain;
    10: 2  **I** treasures have no lasting value,
Mic  4:13  You will devote their **i** gains

## ILLEGITIMATE*

Hos  5: 7  they give birth to **i** children.
Jn   8:41  "We are not **i** children,"

## ILLNESS [ILL]

2Ki  8: 9  ask, 'Will I recover from this **i**?' "

2Ch 16:12 even in his i he did not seek help
Ps 41: 3 restores them from their bed of i.
Isa 38: 9 of Hezekiah king of Judah after his i
Gal 4:13 an i that I first preached the gospel

## ILLNESSES* [ILL]

Dt 28:59 disasters, and severe and lingering i.
Ac 19:12 and their i were cured and the evil
1Ti 5:23 your stomach and your frequent i.

## ILLUMINATED*

Eph 5:13 that is i becomes a light.
Rev 18: 1 and the earth was i by his splendor.

## ILLUSIONS*

Isa 30:10 Tell us pleasant things, prophesy i.

## ILLUSTRATION*

Heb 9: 9 This is an i for the present time,

## IMAGE [IMAGES]

Ge 1:26 us make human beings in our i,
1:27 created human beings in his own i,
9: 6 for in the i of God has God made
Ex 20: 4 not make for yourself an i
Lev 26: 1 or set up an i or a sacred stone
Ps 106:20 their glorious God for an i of a bull,
Isa 40:18 To what i will you liken him?
Da 3: 1 King Nebuchadnezzar made an i
Lk 20:24 Whose i and inscription are on it?"
Ro 8:29 to be conformed to the i of his Son,
1Co 11: 7 since he is the i and glory of God;
15:49 we have borne the i of the earthly man,
2Co 3:18 being transformed into his i
4: 4 glory of Christ, who is the i of God.
Col 1:15 The Son is the i of the invisible
3:10 in knowledge in the i of its Creator.
Rev 13:14 set up an i in honor of the beast who
14:11 who worship the beast and its i,
20: 4 his i and had not received his mark

## IMAGES [IMAGE]

Nu 33:52 Destroy all their carved i and their
Ps 97: 7 All who worship i are put to shame,
Isa 42:17 who say to i, 'You are our gods,'
Jer 10:14 Their i are a fraud; they have no
Eze 5:11 my sanctuary with all your vile i
Ro 1:23 the immortal God for i made to look

## IMAGINATION* [IMAGINE]

Eze 13: 2 who prophesy out of their own i:
13:17 who prophesy out of their own i.

## IMAGINE [IMAGINATION]

Eph 3:20 more than all we ask or i,

## IMITATE* [IMITATED, IMITATORS]

Dt 18: 9 do not learn to i the detestable ways
Eze 23:48 may take warning and not i you.
1Co 4:16 Therefore I urge you to i me.
2Th 3: 9 as a model for you to i.
Heb 6:12 but to i those who through faith
13: 7 of their way of life and i their faith.
3Jn 1:11 do not i what is evil but what is

## IMITATED* [IMITATE]

2Ki 17:15 They i the nations around them

## IMITATORS* [IMITATE]

1Th 1: 6 You became i of us and of the Lord,
2:14 became i of God's churches

## IMMANUEL*

Isa 7:14 birth to a son, and will call him I.
8: 8 cover the breadth of your land, I!"
Mt 1:23 they will call him I" (which means

## IMMEASURABLY* [MEASURE]

Eph 3:20 is able to do i more than all we ask

## IMMENSE

1Ti 1:16 Jesus might display his i patience

## IMMORAL* [IMMORALITY]

1Co 5: 9 to associate with sexually i people—
5:10 the people of this world who are i,
5:11 but are sexually i or greedy,
6: 9 Neither the sexually i nor idolaters
Eph 5: 5 No i, impure or greedy person—
1Ti 1:10 for the sexually i,
Heb 12:16 See that no one is sexually i, or is
13: 4 the adulterer and all the sexually i.
Rev 21: 8 the sexually i, those who practice
22:15 arts, the sexually i, the murderers,

## IMMORALITY* [IMMORAL]

Nu 25: 1 in sexual i with Moabite women,
Jer 3: 9 Because Israel's i mattered so little
Mt 5:32 except for sexual i,
15:19 adultery, sexual i, theft,
19: 9 except for sexual i,
Mk 7:21 come evil thoughts, sexual i, theft,
Ac 15:20 from sexual i, from the meat
15:29 strangled animals and from sexual i.
21:25 animals and from sexual i."
Ro 13:13 not in sexual i and debauchery,
1Co 5: 1 that there is sexual i among you,
6:13 is not meant for sexual i
6:18 Flee from sexual i. All other sins
7: 2 But since sexual i is occurring,
10: 8 We should not commit sexual i,
Gal 5:19 sexual i, impurity and debauchery;
Eph 5: 3 must not be even a hint of sexual i,
Col 3: 5 sexual i, impurity, lust, evil desires
1Th 4: 3 that you should avoid sexual i;
Jude 1: 4 grace of our God into a license for i
1: 7 gave themselves up to sexual i
Rev 2:14 to idols and committed sexual i.
2:20 misleads my servants into sexual i
2:21 given her time to repent of her i,
9:21 arts, their sexual i or their thefts.

## IMMORTAL* [IMMORTALITY]

Ro 1:23 exchanged the glory of the i God
1Ti 1:17 Now to the King eternal, i,
6:16 who alone is i and who lives

## IMMORTALITY* [IMMORTAL]

Pr 12:28 there is life; along that path is i.

Ro    2: 7  honor and i, he will give eternal life.
1Co 15:53  imperishable, and the mortal with i.
       15:54  and the mortal with i,
2Ti    1:10  life and i to light through the gospel.

## IMMOVABLE
Zec 12: 3  I will make Jerusalem an i rock

## IMPALE* [IMPALED]
Ge   40:19  and i your body on a pole.
Est    7: 9  The king said, "I him on it!"

## IMPALED [IMPALE]
Ge   40:22  but he i the chief baker,
Jos    8:29  He i the body of the king of Ai
Est    2:23  the two officials were i on poles.
       7:10  So they i Haman on the pole

## IMPART*
Pr   29:15  rod and a reprimand i wisdom,
Ro    1:11  I may i to you some spiritual gift
Gal    3:21  law had been given that could i life,

## IMPARTIAL* [IMPARTIALLY]
Jas    3:17  mercy and good fruit, i and sincere.

## IMPARTIALLY [IMPARTIAL]
1Pe    1:17  who judges each person's work i,

## IMPATIENT
Nu   21: 4  But the people grew i on the way;

## IMPERISHABLE
1Co 15:42  is sown is perishable, it is raised i;
       15:50  nor does the perishable inherit the i.
1Pe    1:23  seed, but of i, through the living

## IMPLORE*
Mal    1: 9  "Now i God to be gracious to us.
2Co    5:20  We i you on Christ's behalf:

## IMPORTANCE* [IMPORTANT]
1Co 15: 3  I passed on to you as of first i:

## IMPORTANT [IMPORTANCE]
1Ki    3: 4  for that was the most i high place,
Jer   52:13  Every i building he burned down.
Mt     6:25  Is not life more i than food,
       23:23  have neglected the more i matters
Mk   12:29  "The most i one," answered Jesus,
       12:33  as yourself is more i than all burnt
Lk   11:43  because you love the most i seats
Php    1:18  The i thing is that in every way,

## IMPOSED
Rev  18:20  with the judgment she i on you."

## IMPOSING
Jos   22:10  of Manasseh built an i altar there
Pr   17:26  i a fine on the innocent is not good,

## IMPOSSIBLE
Ge   11: 6  they plan to do will be i for them.

Mt   17:20  Nothing will be i for you."
       19:26  "With human beings this is i,
Mk   10:27  "With human beings this is i,
Lk   18:27  "What is i with human beings is
Ac     2:24  because it was i for death to keep its
Heb   6: 4  It is i for those who have once been
       6:18  things in which it is i for God to lie,
       10: 4  It is i for the blood of bulls
       11: 6  without faith it is i to please God,

## IMPOSTORS*
2Co    6: 8  genuine, yet regarded as i;
2Ti    3:13  and i will go from bad to worse,

## IMPRESS* [IMPRESSED, IMPRESSES]
Dt     6: 7  I them on your children.
Gal    6:12  who want to i others by means

## IMPRESSED [IMPRESS]
Ecc    9:13  of wisdom that greatly i me:

## IMPRESSES* [IMPRESS]
Pr   17:10  A rebuke i a discerning person more

## IMPRISON* [PRISON]
Ac   22:19  from one synagogue to another to i

## IMPRISONED [PRISON]
Jer   37:15  and i in the house of Jonathan
1Pe    3:19  made proclamation to the i spirits—

## IMPRISONMENT [PRISON]
Ac   23:29  against him that deserved death or i.
       26:31  anything that deserves death or i."
Heb 11:36  and even chains and i.

## IMPRISONMENTS* [PRISON]
2Co    6: 5  in beatings, i and riots;

## IMPROPER*
Eph    5: 3  because these are i for the Lord's

## IMPURE [IMPURITIES, IMPURITY]
Nu     5:14  he suspects his wife and she is i—
Ac   10:15  "Do not call anything i that God
       11: 9  'Do not call anything i that God has
Eph    5: 5  No immoral, i or greedy person—
1Th    2: 3  not spring from error or i motives,
       4: 7  For God did not call us to be i,
Rev  21:27  Nothing i will ever enter it, nor will

## IMPURITIES [IMPURE]
Isa    1:25  your dross and remove all your i.
Eze   36:25  I will cleanse you from all your i

## IMPURITY [IMPURE]
Zec  13: 1  to cleanse them from sin and i.
Ro    1:24  hearts to sexual i for the degrading
       6:19  to offer yourselves as slaves to i
Gal    5:19  immorality, i and debauchery;
Eph    4:19  so as to indulge in every kind of i,
       5: 3  or of any kind of i, or of greed,
Col    3: 5  sexual immorality, i, lust,

## INCENSE

Ex 30: 1 altar of acacia wood for burning i.
40: 5 Place the gold altar of i in front
Lev 10: 1 put fire in them and added i;
Nu 16:17 is to take his censer and put i in it—
2Ch 26:16 to burn i on the altar of i.
Ps 141: 2 my prayer be set before you like i;
Isa 1:13 Your i is detestable to me.
Jer 1:16 me, in burning i to other gods
Hos 2:13 the days she burned i to the Baals;
Lk 1:10 the time for the burning of i came,
Heb 9: 4 which had the golden altar of i
Rev 5: 8 were holding golden bowls full of i,
8: 4 The smoke of the i,

## INCITED [INCITING]

1Sa 26:19 If the LORD has i you against me,
1Ch 21: 1 i David to take a census of Israel.

## INCITING [INCITED]

Dt 13: 5 for i rebellion against the LORD

## INCLINATION* [INCLINATIONS, INCLINED, INCLINES]

Ge 6: 5 that every i of the thoughts
8:21 even though every i of the human

## INCLINATIONS* [INCLINATION]

Jer 7:24 they followed the stubborn i of their

## INCLINED [INCLINATION]

Dt 5:29 their hearts would be i to fear me

## INCLINES* [INCLINATION]

Ecc 10: 2 The heart of the wise i to the right,

## INCOME

Ecc 5:10 are never satisfied with their i.
1Co 16: 2 of money in keeping with your i,

## INCOMPARABLE*
[INCOMPARABLY]

Eph 2: 7 ages he might show the i riches

## INCOMPARABLY*
[INCOMPARABLE]

Eph 1:19 his i great power for us who believe.

## INCREASE [EVER-INCREASING, INCREASED, INCREASES, INCREASING]

Ge 1:22 "Be fruitful and i in number and fill
1:28 them, "Be fruitful and i in number;
8:17 be fruitful and i in number on it."
16:10 "I will i your descendants so much
Dt 1:11 i you a thousand times and bless
Ps 62:10 though your riches i, do not set your
Pr 22:16 oppress the poor to i their wealth
Isa 9: 7 Of the i of his government
Jer 23: 3 they will be fruitful and i in number.
Mt 24:12 Because of the i of wickedness,
Lk 17: 5 said to the Lord, "I our faith!"
Ac 12:24 the word of God continued to i

Ro 5:20 in so that the trespass might i.
6: 1 go on sinning so that grace may i?
1Th 3:12 May the Lord make your love i

## INCREASED [INCREASE]

Ge 7:17 as the waters i they lifted the ark
Ex 1:20 the people i and became even more
Dt 1:10 your God has i your numbers so
Ac 6: 7 of disciples in Jerusalem i rapidly,
9:31 by the Holy Spirit, it i in numbers.
Ro 5:20 But where sin i, grace i all the more,

## INCREASES [INCREASE]

Isa 40:29 weary and i the power of the weak.

## INCREASING [INCREASE]

Ac 6: 1 when the number of disciples was i,
2Th 1: 3 all of you have for one another is i.
2Pe 1: 8 possess these qualities in i measure,

## INCREDIBLE*

Ac 26: 8 you consider it i that God raises

## INCURABLE

2Ch 21:18 afflicted Jehoram with an i disease
Jer 10:19 My wound is i! Yet I said to myself,
Mic 1: 9 For Samaria's wound is i;

## INDECENT

Dt 24: 1 to him because he finds something i

## INDEPENDENT*

1Co 11:11 woman is not i of man, nor is man i of woman.

## INDESCRIBABLE*

2Co 9:15 Thanks be to God for his i gift!

## INDESTRUCTIBLE*

Heb 7:16 the basis of the power of an i life.

## INDIGNANT [INDIGNATION]

Mt 20:24 they were i with the two brothers.
Mk 1:41 Jesus was i. He reached out his hand
10:14 When Jesus saw this, he was i.
Lk 13:14 I because Jesus had healed

## INDIGNATION [INDIGNANT]

Ps 90: 7 your anger and terrified by your i.
Na 1: 6 Who can withstand his i?

## INDISPENSABLE*

1Co 12:22 body that seem to be weaker are i,

## INDULGE [INDULGED, INDULGENCE, INDULGING, SELF-INDULGENCE]

Ex 32: 6 and drink and got up to i in revelry.
Nu 25: 1 the men began to i in sexual
1Co 10: 7 drink and got up to i in revelry."
Gal 5:13 your freedom to i the sinful nature;

## INDULGED* [INDULGE]
2Co 12:21 debauchery in which they have **i**.

## INDULGENCE* [INDULGE]
Col 2:23 any value in restraining sensual **i**.

## INDULGING* [INDULGE]
1Ti 3: 8 sincere, not **i** in much wine, and not

## INEFFECTIVE*
2Pe 1: 8 they will keep you from being **i**

## INEXPRESSIBLE*
2Co 12: 4 up to paradise and heard **i** things,
1Pe 1: 8 are filled with an **i** and glorious joy,

## INFANCY* [INFANT]
2Ti 3:15 from **i** you have known the Holy

## INFANT [INFANCY, INFANTS]
Nu 11:12 as a nurse carries an **i**, to the land

## INFANTS [INFANT]
Ps 8: 2 **i** you have established a stronghold
Isa 11: 8 **i** will play near the hole
65:20 again will there be in it **i** who live
Mt 21:16 and **i** you have ordained praise'?"
1Co 3: 1 but as worldly—mere **i** in Christ.
14:20 In regard to evil be **i**, but in your
Eph 4:14 Then we will no longer be **i**,

## INFILTRATED*
Gal 2: 4 some false believers had **i** our ranks

## INFIRMITIES* [INFIRMITY]
Mt 8:17 "He took up our **i** and bore our

## INFIRMITY* [INFIRMITIES]
Lk 13:12 you are set free from your **i**."

## INFLAMED
Ro 1:27 and were **i** with lust for one another.

## INFLICT [INFLICTED]
Dt 7:15 He will not **i** on you the horrible
Ps 149: 7 to **i** vengeance on the nations
Jer 18: 8 not **i** on it the disaster I had planned.
26: 3 I will relent and not **i** on them

## INFLICTED [INFLICT]
Ge 12:17 the LORD **i** serious diseases
Isa 30:26 people and heals the wounds he **i**.

## INFLUENCED* [INFLUENTIAL]
1Co 12: 2 or other you were **i** and led astray

## INFLUENTIAL* [INFLUENCED]
1Co 1:26 not many were **i**; not many were

## INGATHERING* [GATHER]
Ex 23:16 "Celebrate the Festival of **I**
34:22 the Festival of **I** at the turn

## INHABITANT [INHABITANTS, INHABITED]
Isa 6:11 the cities lie ruined and without **i**,
Jer 4: 7 towns will lie in ruins without **i**.

## INHABITANTS [INHABITANT]
Lev 18:25 sin, and the land vomited out its **i**.
Nu 33:55 do not drive out the **i** of the land,
Jos 9:24 to wipe out all its **i** from before you.
Rev 6:10 until you judge the **i** of the earth
8:13 Woe to the **I** of the earth,
13: 8 All **i** of the earth will worship

## INHABITED [INHABITANT]
Isa 45:18 to be empty, but formed it to be **i**—
Joel 3:20 Judah will be **i** forever
Zec 14:11 It will be **i**; never again will it be

## INHERIT [CO-HEIRS, HEIR, HEIRS, HERITAGE, INHERITANCE, INHERITED]
Ge 15: 2 and the one who will **i** my estate is
Dt 1:38 because he will lead Israel to **i** it.
Jos 1: 6 these people to **i** the land I swore
2Ki 2: 9 "Let me **i** a double portion of your
Ps 37:11 the meek will **i** the land and enjoy
37:29 The righteous will **i** the land
Pr 3:35 The wise **i** honor, but fools get only
11:29 on their families will **i** only wind,
14:18 The simple **i** folly, but the prudent
Isa 61: 7 so you will **i** a double portion
Zec 2:12 The LORD will **i** Judah as his
Mt 5: 5 the meek, for they will **i** the earth.
19:29 times as much and will **i** eternal life.
Mk 10:17 "what must I do to **i** eternal life?"
Lk 10:25 "what must I do to **i** eternal life?"
18:18 what must I do to **i** eternal life?"
1Co 6: 9 wrongdoers will not **i** the kingdom
15:50 blood cannot **i** the kingdom of God,
Gal 5:21 live like this will not **i** the kingdom
Heb 1:14 to serve those who will **i** salvation?
Rev 21: 7 who are victorious will **i** all this,

## INHERITANCE [INHERIT]
Ge 21:10 share in the **i** with my son Isaac."
Ex 34: 9 and our sin, and take us as your **i**."
Lev 20:24 I will give it to you as an **i**, a land
Nu 18:20 "You will have no **i** in their land,
Dt 4:20 to be the people of his **i**, as you now
10: 9 the LORD is their **i**,
Jos 14: 1 areas the Israelites received as an **i**
14: 3 the two-and-a-half tribes their **i** east
Ps 2: 8 and I will make the nations your **i**,
16: 6 surely I have a delightful **i**.
33:12 the people he chose for his **i**.
136:21 and gave their land as an **i**,
Pr 13:22 Good people leave an **i** for their
Jer 3:19 the most beautiful **i** of any nation.'
Da 12:13 will rise to receive your allotted **i**."
Joel 2:17 Do not make your **i** an object
Mt 25:34 take your **i**, the kingdom prepared
Lk 12:13 my brother to divide the **i** with me."
Gal 3:18 For if the **i** depends on the law,
4:30 in the **i** with the free woman's son."
Eph 1:14 deposit guaranteeing our **i** until

Eph 5: 5 has any **i** in the kingdom of Christ
Col 1:12 to share in the **i** of his people
     3:24 you will receive an **i** from the Lord
Heb 9:15 may receive the promised eternal **i**—
1Pe 1: 4 and into an **i** that can never perish,

## INHERITED [INHERIT]
Heb 1: 4 as the name he has **i** is superior

## INIQUITIES [INIQUITY]
Ps 78:38 he forgave their **i** and did not
     90: 8 You have set our **i** before you,
  103:10 or repay us according to our **i**.
Isa 53: 5 he was crushed for our **i**;
   53:11 many, and he will bear their **i**.
   59: 2 your **i** have separated you from your
Mic 7:19 hurl all our **i** into the depths

## INIQUITY [INIQUITIES]
Ps 25:11 forgive my **i**, though it is great.
   32: 5 to you and did not cover up my **i**.
   38:18 I confess my **i**; I am troubled by my
   51: 2 Wash away all my **i** and cleanse me
   51: 9 from my sins and blot out all my **i**.
Isa 53: 6 has laid on him the **i** of us all.
Mic 2: 1 Woe to those who plan **i**, to those

## INJURED [INJURY]
Isa 1: 5 Your whole head is **i**, your whole
Eze 34:16 I will bind up the **i** and strengthen
Zec 11:16 or heal the **i**, or feed the healthy,
Mal 1:13 "When you bring **i**,

## INJURES [INJURY]
Lev 24:19 Anyone who **i** a neighbor is to be
Job 5:18 he **i**, but his hands also heal.

## INJURY [INJURED, INJURES]
Ex 21:23 But if there is serious **i**, you are
Jer 30:12 is incurable, your **i** beyond healing.
Rev 9:19 heads with which they inflict **i**.

## INJUSTICE
2Ch 19: 7 the LORD our God there is no **i**
Pr 13:23 for the poor, but **i** sweeps it away.
  16: 8 than much gain with **i**.
Hab 2:12 establishes a town by **i**!
Mal 2:16 people clothe themselves with **i**,"

## INK*
Jer 36:18 and I wrote them in **i** on the scroll."
2Co 3: 3 written not with **i** but with the Spirit
2Jn 1:12 but I do not want to use paper and **i**.
3Jn 1:13 do not want to do so with pen and **i**.

## INMOST [INNER]
Ps 139:13 For you created my **i** being;

## INN*
Lk 10:34 brought him to an **i** and took care

## INNER [INMOST]
2Sa 18:24 David was sitting between the **i**
1Ki 6:16 within the temple an **i** sanctuary,

Ro 7:22 in my **i** being I delight in God's law;

## INNOCENCE [INNOCENT]
Job 27: 6 maintain my **i** and never let go
Ps 26: 6 I wash my hands in **i**, and go

## INNOCENT [INNOCENCE]
Ex 23: 7 do not put an **i** or honest person
Dt 19:10 this so that **i** blood will not be shed
  25: 1 acquitting the **i** and condemning
Job 34: 5 'I am **i**, but God denies me justice.
Ps 19:13 blameless, **i** of great transgression.
Pr 6:17 tongue, hands that shed **i** blood,
  17:26 imposing a fine on the **i** is not good,
Isa 59: 7 they are swift to shed **i** blood.
Mt 10:16 shrewd as snakes and as **i** as doves.
  12: 7 would not have condemned the **i**.
  27: 4 said, "for I have betrayed **i** blood."
  27:24 "I am **i** of this man's blood,"
Ac 18: 6 on your own heads! I am **i** of it.
  20:26 you today that I am **i** of the blood
Ro 16:19 is good, and **i** about what is evil.
1Co 4: 4 clear, but that does not make me **i**.

## INQUIRE [INQUIRED, INQUIRING]
Jos 9:14 but did not **i** of the LORD.
1Sa 28: 7 medium, so I may go and **i** of her."
1Ch 10:14 and did not **i** of the LORD.
2Ch 20: 3 Jehoshaphat resolved to **i**
Isa 8:19 should not a people **i** of their God?
Eze 14: 3 Should I let them **i** of me at all?

## INQUIRED [INQUIRE]
1Sa 22:10 Ahimelek **i** of the LORD for him;
  28: 6 He **i** of the LORD, but the LORD

## INQUIRING [INQUIRE]
Nu 27:21 for him by **i** of the Urim before
Dt 12:30 to be ensnared by **i** about their gods,

## INSANE
1Sa 21:13 pretended to be **i** in their presence;
Ps 34: T *Of David. When he pretended to be i*
Ac 26:24 great learning is driving you **i**."

## INSCRIBE* [INSCRIBED, INSCRIPTION]
Isa 30: 8 on a tablet for them, **i** it on a scroll,

## INSCRIBED [INSCRIBE]
Ex 31:18 the tablets of stone **i** by the finger
Dt 9:10 LORD gave me two stone tablets **i**
Zec 14:20 LORD will be **i** on the bells

## INSCRIPTION [INSCRIBE]
Da 5:24 he sent the hand that wrote the **i**.
Mt 22:20 image is this? And whose **i**?"
2Ti 2:19 stands firm, sealed with this **i**:

## INSECTS
Lev 11:20 " 'All flying **i** that walk on all
Dt 14:19 All flying **i** that swarm are unclean

## INSIDE

Ge   6:14  in it and coat it with pitch **i** and out.
Ex    4: 6  said, "Put your hand **i** your cloak."
      12:46  "It must be eaten **i** one house;
1Ki  6:20  He overlaid the **i** with pure gold,
Mt  23:26  First clean the **i** of the cup and dish,
      23:27  on the **i** are full of the bones
Mk   7:23  All these evils come from **i**
1Co  5:12  Are you not to judge those **i**?
Rev   5: 4  worthy to open the scroll or look **i.**

## INSIGHT [INSIGHTS]

1Ki  4:29  Solomon wisdom and very great **i,**
Ps 119:99  I have more **i** than all my teachers,
Pr    5: 1  turn your ear to my words of **i,**
       7: 4  and to **i,** "You are my relative."
     16:16  to get **i** rather than silver!
     20: 5  those who have **i** draw them out.
     21:30  no **i,** no plan that can succeed
     23:23  wisdom, instruction and **i** as well.
Da   5:11  your father he was found to have **i**
     9:22  I have now come to give you **i**
Eph  3: 4  to understand my **i** into the mystery
Php  1: 9  more in knowledge and depth of **i,**
2Ti   2: 7  the Lord will give you **i** into all this.
Rev 13:18  Let those who have **i** calculate

## INSIGHTS* [INSIGHT]

Job 15: 9  What **i** do you have that we do not

## INSOLENT

Pr  29:21  youth will turn out to be **i.**
Ro   1:30  God-haters, **i,** arrogant and boastful;

## INSPIRE [INSPIRED, INSPIRES]

Jer  32:40  and I will **i** them to fear me,

## INSPIRED* [INSPIRE]

2Sa 23: 1  "The **i** utterance of David
Pr  30: 1  Agur son of Jakeh—an **i** utterance.
     31: 1  an **i** utterance his mother taught him.
Hos  9: 7  a fool, anyone who is **i** a maniac.
1Th  1: 3  and your endurance **i** by hope in our

## INSPIRES [INSPIRE]

Rev 22: 6  the God who **i** the prophets,

## INSTALLED

Ps   2: 6  "I have **i** my king on Zion, my holy

## INSTANT [INSTANTLY]

Pr   6:15  disaster will overtake them in an **i;**
Lk   4: 5  showed him in an **i** all the kingdoms

## INSTANTLY* [INSTANT]

Lk   8:47  him and how she had been **i** healed.
Ac   3: 7  up, and **i** the man's feet and ankles

## INSTEAD

Ge  22:13  sacrificed it as a burnt offering **i**
2Ch 28:20  but he gave him trouble **i** of help.
Pr   8:10  Choose my instruction **i** of silver,
Isa 60:17  **I** of bronze I will bring you gold,
     61: 7  **i** of disgrace you will rejoice in your

Jer   7:24  **i,** they followed the stubborn
Jn   3:19  but people loved darkness **i** of light
    15:15  **I,** I have called you friends,

## INSTINCT* [INSTINCTS]

2Pe  2:12  creatures of **i,** born only to be
Jude 1:10  what things they do understand by **i,**

## INSTINCTS* [INSTINCT]

Jude 1:19  who follow mere natural **i** and do

## INSTITUTED

Ro  13: 2  is rebelling against what God has **i,**

## INSTRUCT [INSTRUCTED, INSTRUCTION, INSTRUCTIONS, INSTRUCTOR, INSTRUCTS]

Dt  17:10  do everything they **i** you to do.
Ne   9:20  gave your good Spirit to **i** them.
Ps  32: 8  I will **i** you and teach you
   105:22  to **i** his princes as he pleased
Pr   9: 9  **I** the wise and they will be wiser
Isa 40:13  or **i** the Lᴏʀᴅ as his counselor?
Da  11:33  "Those who are wise will **i** many,
Ro  15:14  and competent to **i** one another.
1Co  2:16  mind of the Lord so as to **i** him?"
    14:19  to **i** others than ten thousand words

## INSTRUCTED [INSTRUCT]

2Ch 26: 5  who **i** him in the fear of God.
Isa 50: 4  Lᴏʀᴅ has given me an **i** tongue,
Mt  13:52  of the law who has been **i**
    21: 6  went and did as Jesus had **i** them.
Ac  18:25  He had been **i** in the way
1Co 14:31  in turn so that everyone may be **i**
2Ti   2:25  Opponents must be gently **i,**

## INSTRUCTION [INSTRUCT]

Ex 15:25  Lᴏʀᴅ issued a ruling and **i** for them
    24:12  I have written for their **i."**
Pr   1: 2  for gaining wisdom and **i;**
    1: 3  for receiving **i** in prudent behavior,
    1: 7  but fools despise wisdom and **i**
    1: 8  to your father's **i** and do not forsake
    4: 1  Listen, my sons, to a father's **i;**
    4:13  Hold on to **i,** do not let it go;
    6:23  correction and **i** are the way to life,
    8:10  Choose my **i** instead of silver,
    8:33  Listen to my **i** and be wise;
   13: 1  A wise child heeds a parent's **i,**
   13:13  Whoever scorns **i** will pay for it,
   15:33  Wisdom's **i** is to fear the Lᴏʀᴅ,
   16:20  Those who give heed to **i** prosper,
   16:21  and gracious words promote **i.**
   23:12  Apply your heart to **i** and your ears
   23:23  wisdom, **i** and insight as well.
   28: 9  If anyone turns a deaf ear to my **i,**
   29:18  blessed are those who heed wisdom's **i.**
   31:26  and faithful **i** is on her tongue.
Isa  8:20  Consult God's **i** and the testimony of
   29:24  those who complain will accept **i."**
1Co 14: 6  or prophecy or word of **i?**
    14:26  a hymn, or a word of **i,** a revelation,
Gal  6: 6  those who receive **i** in the word
Eph  6: 4  up in the training and **i** of the Lord.

1Th  4: 8  who rejects this i does not reject
2Th  3:14  those who do not obey our i in this
1Ti  6: 3  the sound i of our Lord Jesus Christ
2Ti  4: 2  with great patience and careful i.

## INSTRUCTIONS [INSTRUCT]
Ge  26: 5  my decrees and my i."
Ex  12:24  "Obey these i as a lasting ordinance
Jos  8:33  when he gave i to bless the people
1Ki  3: 3  walking according to the i
Ac  1: 2  giving i through the Holy Spirit
1Ti  3:14  I am writing you these i so that,

## INSTRUCTOR* [INSTRUCT]
Ro  2:20  an i of the foolish, a teacher
Gal  6: 6  share all good things with their i.

## INSTRUCTS* [INSTRUCT]
Ps  16: 7  even at night my heart i me.
    25: 8  therefore he i sinners in his ways.
Isa  28:26  Their God i them and teaches them

## INSTRUMENT* [INSTRUMENTS]
Eze  33:32  beautiful voice and plays an i well,
Ac  9:15  This man is my chosen i to proclaim
Ro  6:13  to sin as an i of wickedness,
    6:13  to him as an i of righteousness.

## INSTRUMENTS [INSTRUMENT]
1Ch  15:16  make a joyful sound with musical i:
     23: 5  with the musical i I have provided
2Ch  23:13  musicians with their i were leading
2Ti  2:21  from the latter will be i for noble

## INSULT [INSULTED, INSULTS]
Ps  69: 9  the insults of those who i you fall
Pr  12:16  once, but the prudent overlook an i.
Jer  20: 8  of the LORD has brought me i
Mt  5:11  are you when people i you,
Lk  6:22  when they exclude you and i you
    18:32  mock him, i him and spit on him;
Heb  10:33  you were publicly exposed to i
1Pe  3: 9  not repay evil with evil or i with i.

## INSULTED [INSULT]
Heb  10:29  and who have i the Spirit of grace?
1Pe  4:14  If you are i because of the name

## INSULTS [INSULT]
Ne  4: 4  Turn their i back on their own
Ps  22: 7  they hurl i, shaking their heads.
    69: 9  the i of those who insult you fall
Pr  9: 7  corrects a mocker invites i;
    22:10  quarrels and i are ended.
La  3:61  you have heard their i, all their plots
Mk  15:29  who passed by hurled i at him,
Jn  9:28  Then they hurled i at him and said,
Ro  15: 3  "The i of those who insult you have
2Co  12:10  in weaknesses, in i, in hardships,
1Pe  2:23  When they hurled their i at him,

## INTEGRITY*
Dt  9: 5  your i that you are going in to take
1Ki  9: 4  you walk before me faithfully with i
1Ch  29:17  test the heart and are pleased with i.

Job  2: 3  And he still maintains his i,
    2: 9  "Are you still maintaining your i?
    6:29  reconsider, for my i is at stake.
    27: 5  till I die, I will not deny my i.
Ps  7: 8  according to my i, O Most High.
    25:21  May i and uprightness protect me,
    41:12  In my i you uphold me and set me
    78:72  David shepherded them with i
Pr  10: 9  Whoever walks in i walks securely,
    11: 3  The i of the upright guides them,
    13: 6  guards the person of i,
    29:10  The bloodthirsty hate people of i
Isa  45:23  my mouth has uttered in all i a word
    59: 4  no one pleads their case with i.
Mt  22:16  "we know that you are a man of i
Mk  12:14  we know that you are a man of i.
2Co  1:12  with i and godly sincerity.
Tit  2: 7  In your teaching show i,

## INTELLIGENCE [INTELLIGENT]
Isa  29:14  the i of the intelligent will vanish."
Da  5:11  he was found to have insight and i
1Co  1:19  the i of the intelligent I will

## INTELLIGENT [INTELLIGENCE]
1Sa  25: 3  She was an i and beautiful woman,

## INTELLIGIBLE*
1Co  14: 9  Unless you speak i words with your
    14:19  I would rather speak five i words

## INTEND [INTENDED, INTENT,
INTENTIONAL, INTENTIONALLY,
INTENTLY]
1Ki  5: 5  I i, therefore, to build a temple
2Ch  29:10  Now I i to make a covenant

## INTENDED [INTEND]
Ge  50:20  You i to harm me, but God i it
Jer  18:10  I will reconsider the good I had i
Ro  7:10  was i to bring life actually brought

## INTENSE [INTENSELY]
1Th  2:17  our i longing we made every effort
Rev  16: 9  They were seared by the i heat

## INTENSELY [INTENSE]
Gal  1:13  how i I persecuted the church

## INTENT [INTEND]
Ex  32:12  with evil i that he brought them out,
Pr  7:10  like a prostitute and with crafty i.
Mt  22:18  But Jesus, knowing their evil i, said,

## INTENTIONAL* [INTEND]
Nu  15:25  for it was not i and they have

## INTENTIONALLY* [INTEND]
Ex  21:13  if it is not done i, but God lets it
Nu  35:20  throws something at them i so

## INTENTLY* [INTEND]
Ac  1:10  They were looking i up into the sky

Ac    6:15   the Sanhedrin looked **i** at Stephen,
Jas   1:25   those who look **i** into the perfect
1Pe   1:10   you, searched **i** and with the greatest

## INTERCEDE [INTERCEDES, INTERCEDING, INTERCESSION, INTERCESSOR]
1Sa   2:25   the LORD, who will **i** for them?"
Heb   7:25   him, because he always lives to **i**

## INTERCEDES* [INTERCEDE]
Ro    8:26   the Spirit himself **i** for us through
      8:27   Spirit, because the Spirit **i** for God's

## INTERCEDING* [INTERCEDE]
Ro    8:34   hand of God and is also **i** for us.

## INTERCESSION* [INTERCEDE]
Isa  53:12   and made **i** for the transgressors.
1Ti   2: 1   **i** and thanksgiving be made

## INTERCESSOR* [INTERCEDE]
Job  16:20   My **i** is my friend as my eyes pour

## INTEREST [INTERESTS]
Lev  25:36   Do not take **i** or any profit
Dt   23:19   Do not charge an Israelite **i**,
     23:20   You may charge a foreigner **i**,
Ne    5:10   let us stop charging **i**!
Ps   15: 5   lend money to the poor without **i**
Eze  18: 8   He does not lend to them at **i**
Lk   19:23   I could have collected it with **i**?'
1Ti   6: 4   They have an unhealthy **i**

## INTERESTS [INTEREST]
1Co   7:34   and his **i** are divided.
Php   2: 4   your own **i** but each of you to the **i** of
              the others.
      2:21   everyone looks out for their own **i**,

## INTERFERE
Ezr   6: 7   Do not **i** with the work on this

## INTERMARRY* [MARRY]
Ge   34: 9   **I** with us; give us your daughters
Dt    7: 3   Do not **i** with them. Do not give
Jos  23:12   and if you **i** with them and associate
1Ki  11: 2   "You must not **i** with them,
Ezr   9:14   **i** with the peoples who commit such

## INTERPRET [INTERPRETATION, INTERPRETATIONS, INTERPRETER, INTERPRETS]
Ge   41:15   "I had a dream, and no one can **i** it.
Da    2: 6   tell me the dream and **i** it for me."
      4: 9   Here is my dream; **i** it for me.
Mt   16: 3   you cannot **i** the signs of the times.
1Co  12:30   Do all speak in tongues? Do all **i**?
     14: 5   speak in tongues, unless they **i**,
     14:13   pray that they may **i** what they say.
     14:27   one at a time, and someone must **i**.

## INTERPRETATION [INTERPRET]
Ge   40:16   that Joseph had given a favorable **i**,
Jdg   7:15   Gideon heard the dream and its **i**,
1Co  12:10   and to still another the **i** of tongues.
     14:26   a revelation, a tongue or an **i**.
2Pe   1:20   by the prophet's own **i** of things.

## INTERPRETATIONS* [INTERPRET]
Ge   40: 8   to them, "Do not **i** belong to God?
Da    5:16   heard that you are able to give **i**

## INTERPRETER [INTERPRET]
1Co  14:28   If there is no **i**, the speaker should

## INTERPRETS* [INTERPRET]
Dt   18:10   divination or sorcery, **i** omens,

## INTERVENED
Ac   15:14   how God first **i** to choose a people

## INTOXICATED*
Pr    5:19   may you ever be **i** with her love.
      5:20   be **i** with another man's wife?
Rev  17: 2   of the earth were **i** with the wine

## INVADE [INVADED, INVADING]
Dt   12:29   you the nations you are about to **i**
Da   11:41   He will also **i** the Beautiful Land.
Na    1:15   No more will the wicked **i** you;

## INVADED [INVADE]
2Ki  17: 5   king of Assyria **i** the entire land,
     24: 1   king of Babylon **i** the land,

## INVADING [INVADE]
Hab   3:16   calamity to come on the nation **i** us.

## INVENT*
Ro    1:30   they **i** ways of doing evil;

## INVESTIGATED
Lk    1: 3   I myself have carefully **i** everything

## INVISIBLE*
Ro    1:20   of the world God's **i** qualities—
Col   1:15   The Son is the image of the **i** God,
      1:16   visible and **i**, whether thrones
1Ti   1:17   eternal, immortal, **i**, the only God,
Heb  11:27   because he saw him who is **i**.

## INVITE [INVITED, INVITES]
Pr   18: 6   and their mouths **i** a beating.
Mt   22: 9   **i** to the banquet anyone you find.'
     25:38   we see you a stranger and **i** you in,
Lk   14:12   do not **i** your friends,
     14:13   when you give a banquet, **i** the poor,

## INVITED [INVITE]
Zep   1: 7   he has consecrated those he has **i**.
Mt   22:14   "For many are **i**, but few are
     25:35   I was a stranger and you **i** me in,
Lk    7:36   the Pharisees **i** Jesus to have dinner
     11:37   a Pharisee **i** him to eat with him;

Lk  14:10  But when you are i, take the lowest
Rev 19: 9  'Blessed are those who are i

## INVITES [INVITE]
Pr   9: 7  corrects a mocker i insults;
    10:14  but the mouth of a fool i ruin.
1Co 10:27  If an unbeliever i you to a meal

## INVOKE [INVOKED]
Ex  23:13  Do not i the names of other gods;
Ac  19:13  evil spirits tried to i the name

## INVOKED* [INVOKE]
Hos  2:17  no longer will their names be i.
Eph  1:21  every name that can be i,

## INVOLVED
2Ti  2: 4  No one serving as a soldier gets i

## INWARDLY
Mt   7:15  but i they are ferocious wolves.
Ro   2:29  No, a person is a Jew who is one i;
     8:23  groan i as we wait eagerly for our
2Co  4:16  yet i we are being renewed day

## IRON [IRON-SMELTING]
Ge   4:22  kinds of tools out of bronze and i.
Lev 26:19  make the sky above you like i
2Ki  6: 6  threw it there, and made the i float.
Ps   2: 9  You will break them with a rod of i;
Pr  27:17  As i sharpens i, so one person
Isa 60:17  and silver in place of i.
Da   2:33  its legs of iron, its feet partly of i
     7: 7  It had large i teeth; it crushed
1Ti  4: 2  have been seared as with a hot i.
Rev  2:27  'will rule them with an i scepter
    12: 5  all the nations with an i scepter."
    19:15  will rule them with an i scepter."

## IRON-SMELTING [IRON]
Dt   4:20  brought you out of the i furnace,

## IRRELIGIOUS*
1Ti  1: 9  the unholy and i, for those who kill

## IRREVOCABLE*
Ro  11:29  for God's gifts and his call are i.

## ISAAC
Son of Abraham by Sarah (Ge 17:19; 21:1–7; 1Ch 1:28). Abrahamic covenant perpetuated through (Ge 17:21; 26:2–5). Offered up by Abraham (Ge 22; Heb 11:17–19). Rebekah taken as wife (Ge 24). Inherited Abraham's estate (Ge 25:5). Fathered Esau and Jacob (Ge 25:19–26; 1Ch 1:34). Nearly lost Rebekah to Abimelech (Ge 26:1–11). Covenant with Abimelech (Ge 26:12–31). Tricked into blessing Jacob (Ge 27). Death (Ge 35:27–29). Father of Israel (Ex 3:6; Dt 29:13; Ro 9:10).

## ISAIAH
Prophet to Judah (Isa 1:1). Called by the LORD (Isa 6). Announced judgment to Ahaz (Isa 7), deliverance from Assyria to Hezekiah (2Ki 19; Isa 36–37), deliv-

erance from death to Hezekiah (2Ki 20:1–11; Isa 38). Chronicler of Judah's history (2Ch 26:22; 32:32).

## ISCARIOT [JUDAS]
Mt  10: 4  Simon the Zealot and Judas I,
Lk  22: 3  Judas, called I, one of the Twelve.

## ISH-BOSHETH
Son of Saul who attempted to succeed him as king (2Sa 2:8—4:12; 1Ch 8:33).

## ISHMAEL [ISHMAELITES]
Son of Abraham by Hagar (Ge 16; 1Ch 1:28). Blessed, but not son of covenant (Ge 17:18–21; Gal 4:21–31). Sent away by Sarah (Ge 21:8–21). Children (Ge 25:12–18; 1Ch 1:29–31). Death (Ge 25:17).

## ISHMAELITES [ISHMAEL]
Ge  37:27  let's sell him to the I and not lay our

## ISLAND [ISLANDS]
Rev  1: 9  was on the i of Patmos because
    16:20  Every i fled away

## ISLANDS [ISLAND]
Isa 42: 4  In his teaching the i will put their
    66:19  to the distant i that have not heard

## ISRAEL [EL ELOHE ISRAEL, ISRAEL'S, ISRAELITE, ISRAELITES, JACOB]
1. Name given to Jacob (Ge 32:28; 35:10; see JACOB).
2. Corporate name of Jacob's descendants; often specifically Northern Kingdom.
Ge  49:24  of the Shepherd, the Rock of I,
    49:28  All these are the twelve tribes of I,
Ex  28:11  the sons of I on the two stones
    28:29  of the sons of I over his heart
Nu  19:13  They must be cut off from I.
    24:17  a scepter will rise out of I.
Dt   6: 4  Hear, O I: The LORD our God,
    10:12  And now, I, what does the LORD
    18: 1  no allotment or inheritance with I.
Jos  4:22  them, 'I crossed the Jordan on dry
    24:31  I served the LORD throughout
Jdg 17: 6  In those days I had no king;
    21: 3  cried, "why has this happened to I?
Ru   4:14  he become famous throughout I!
1Sa  3:20  And all I from Dan to Beersheba
     4:21  "The Glory has departed from I"—
    14:23  So on that day the LORD saved I,
    15:26  has rejected you as king over I!"
    17:46  will know that there is a God in I.
    18:16  But all I and Judah loved David,
2Sa  5: 2  'You will shepherd my people I,
     5: 3  they anointed David king over I.
     7:26  LORD Almighty is God over I!'
    14:25  all I there was not a man so highly
1Ki  1:35  I have appointed him ruler over I
     8:25  to sit before me on the throne of I,
    10: 9  of the LORD's eternal love for I,
    12: 1  all I had gone there to make him king.
    12:19  So I has been in rebellion against
    18:17  "Is that you, you troubler of I?"
    19:18  Yet I reserve seven thousand in I—

2Ki  5: 8  know that there is a prophet in **I**."
     17:20  LORD rejected all the people of **I**;
1Ch 17:22  made your people **I** your very own
     21: 1  Satan rose up against **I** and incited
     29:25  as no king over **I** ever had before.
2Ch  9: 8  of the love of your God for **I** and his
Ps   22: 3  you are the praise of **I**.
     73: 1  Surely God is good to **I**, to those
     78:21  Jacob, and his wrath rose against **I**,
     81: 8  if you would only listen to me, **I**!
     98: 3  his faithfulness to the house of **I**;
     99: 8  you were to **I** a forgiving God,
    125: 5  with the evildoers. Peace be on **I**.
Isa   1: 3  but **I** does not know, my people do
     11:12  nations and gather the exiles of **I**;
     27: 6  **I** will bud and blossom and fill all
     44:21  for you, **I**, are my servant.
     46:13  salvation to Zion, my splendor to **I**.
Jer   2: 3  **I** was holy to the LORD,
     23: 6  be saved and **I** will live in safety.
     31: 2  **I** will come to give rest to **I**."
     31:10  'He who scattered **I** will gather
     31:31  a new covenant with the house of **I**
     33:17  to sit on the throne of the house of **I**,
La    2: 5  he has swallowed up **I**.
Eze   3:17  you a watchman for the house of **I**;
     33: 7  you a watchman for the house of **I**;
     34: 2  prophesy against the shepherds of **I**;
     36: 1  'Mountains of **I**, hear the word
     37:28  that I the LORD make **I** holy,
     39:23  that the people of **I** went into exile
Da    9:20  the sin of my people **I** and making
Hos   7: 1  whenever I would heal **I**, the sins
     11: 1  "When **I** was a child, I loved him,
Am    4:12  this is what I will do to you, **I**,
      7:11  and **I** will surely go into exile,
      8: 2  "The time is ripe for my people **I**;
      9:14  I will bring my people **I** back
Mic   5: 2  for me one who will be ruler over **I**,
Zec  11:14  family bond between Judah and **I**.
Mal   1: 5  even beyond the borders of **I**!'
Mt    2: 6  who will shepherd my people **I**.' "
     10: 6  Go rather to the lost sheep of **I**.
     15:24  sent only to the lost sheep of **I**."
Mk   12:29  'Hear, O **I**: The Lord our God,
     15:32  this king of **I**, come down now
Lk    1:54  He has helped his servant **I**,
      2:34  the falling and rising of many in **I**,
     22:30  judging the twelve tribes of **I**.
Jn   12:13  "Blessed is the king of **I**!"
Ac    1: 6  going to restore the kingdom to **I**?"
      9:15  their kings and to the people of **I**.
Ro    9: 6  all who are descended from **I** are **I**.
      9:31  but the people of **I**, who pursued
     11: 7  of **I** sought so earnestly they did not
     11:26  and in this way all **I** will be saved.
Gal   6:16  follow this rule—to the **I** of God.
Eph   2:12  excluded from citizenship in **I**
      3: 6  Gentiles are heirs together with **I**,
Heb   8: 8  a new covenant with the house of **I**
Rev   7: 4  144,000 from all the tribes of **I**.
     21:12  the names of the twelve tribes of **I**.

**ALL ISRAEL** Ex 18:25; Dt 1:1; 5:1; 11:6; 13:11;
     21:21; 27:9; 31:1, 7, 11; 32:45; 34:12; Jos 3:7,
     17; 4:14; 7:24, 25; 8:15, 21; 10:15, 29, 31, 34,
     36, 38, 43; 23:2; Jdg 8:27; 1Sa 2:22; 3:20; 4:1, 5;

7:5; 10:20; 11:2; 12:1; 13:4, 20; 18:16; 19:5;
24:2; 25:1; 28:3, 4; 2Sa 2:9; 3:12, 21, 37; 4:1;
5:5; 8:15; 10:17; 12:12; 14:25; 16:21, 22; 17:10,
11, 13; 1Ki 1:20; 2:15; 3:28; 4:1, 7; 5:13; 8:62,
65; 11:42; 12:1, 16, 18, 20; 14:13, 18; 15:27, 33;
18:20; 22:17; 2Ki 3:6; 9:14; 1Ch 9:1; 11:1, 10;
12:38; 13:5, 6; 14:8; 15:3, 28; 18:14; 19:17; 21:5;
28:4, 8; 29:21, 23, 25, 26; 2Ch 1:2; 7:8; 9:30;
10:1, 3, 16; 11:3; 12:1; 13:4, 15; 18:16; 24:5;
28:23; 29:24, 24; 30:1; 35:3; Ezr 6:17; 8:25, 35;
10:5; Ne 12:47; 13:26; Da 9:7, 11; Mal 4:4; Ac
2:36; Ro 11:26

**CHILDREN OF ISRAEL** (KJV) See
ISRAELITES

**GOD OF ISRAEL** See GOD

**HOLY ONE OF ISRAEL** 2Ki 19:22; Ps
71:22; 78:41; 89:18; Isa 1:4; 5:19, 24; 10:20;
12:6; 17:7; 29:19; 30:11, 12, 15; 31:1; 37:23;
41:14, 16, 20; 43:3, 14; 45:11; 47:4; 48:17; 49:7,
7; 54:5; 55:5; 60:9, 14; Jer 50:29; 51:5

**HOUSE OF ISRAEL** See HOUSE

**ISRAEL AND JUDAH** 1Sa 17:52; 18:16; 2Sa
3:10; 5:5; 11:11; 12:8; 21:2; 24:1; 1Ki 1:35; 2Ki
17:13; 1Ch 9:1; 2Ch 27:7; 30:1, 6; 31:6; 34:21;
35:27; 36:8; Jer 30:3, 4; 32:30, 32; 51:5; Eze 9:9

**KING OF ISRAEL** See KING

**KINGS OF ISRAEL** See KINGS

**MEN OF ISRAEL** Nu 26:51; Dt 29:10; Jos
10:24; Jdg 20:33, 36, 48; 21:1; 1Sa 7:11; 11:8;
14:41; 17:19, 52; 2Sa 6:1; 16:15, 18; 17:14, 24;
19:41, 42, 43, 43; 20:2; 24:4; 1Ch 21:14; 2Ch
28:8; Ne 7:7; Ps 78:31; Ac 5:35

**PEOPLE OF ISRAEL** Ex 16:31; 19:3; Nu 32:4;
Dt 27:14; 32:52; Jos 4:7; 8:33; 1Sa 7:2; 10:17;
2Sa 15:6, 13; 1Ki 16:21; 2Ki 17:20, 23; 2Ch
6:11; 13:12; 30:6; 31:6; Ezr 2:2; 6:16; 9:1; Ne
1:6; 10:39; Ps 103:7; Jer 3:21; 32:30, 30, 32;
50:4, 33; Eze 4:13; 12:24; 14:5, 11; 20:13, 27;
28:24, 25; 29:16; 36:17; 39:23, 25; 43:10; Hos
1:11; Joel 3:16; Am 2:11; 3:1; 6:1; Mt 27:9; Lk
1:16; Ac 2:22; 3:12; 4:10, 27; 9:15; 10:36; 13:16,
17, 24; 21:28; Ro 9:4, 31; 11:7; 1Co 10:18; Php
3:5

**TRIBES OF ISRAEL** Ge 49:16, 28; Ex 24:4;
Nu 30:1; 31:4; Dt 29:21; 33:5; Jos 3:12; 12:7;
22:14; 24:1; Jdg 18:1; 20:2, 10, 12; 21:5, 8, 15;
1Sa 2:28; 15:17; 2Sa 5:1; 15:2, 10; 19:9; 20:14;
24:2; 1Ki 11:32; 14:21; 2Ki 21:7; 1Ch 27:16, 22;
29:6; 2Ch 12:13; 33:7; Ezr 6:17; Ps 78:55; Eze
47:13, 21, 22; 48:19, 29, 31; Hos 5:9; Zec 9:1;
Mt 19:28; Lk 22:30; Rev 7:4; 21:12

## ISRAEL'S [ISRAEL]
Jdg  10:16  he could bear **I** misery no longer.
2Sa  23: 1  God of Jacob, the hero of **I** songs:
Isa  44: 6  **I** King and Redeemer, the LORD
Jer   3: 9  Because **I** immorality mattered so
     31: 9  because I am **I** father, and Ephraim

Hos  5: 5  I arrogance testifies against them;
Jn   3:10  "You are I teacher," said Jesus,

## ISRAELITE [ISRAEL]

Ex   16: 1  The whole I community set
     35:29  All the I men and women who were
Nu    8:16  male offspring from every I woman.
     20: 1  the whole I community arrived
     20:22  The whole I community set
Dt   23:19  Do not charge an I interest,
Ne    9: 2  I descent had separated themselves
Jn    1:47  "Here truly is an I in whom there is
Ro   11: 1  I am an I myself, a descendant

## ISRAELITES [ISRAEL]

Ex    1: 7  but the I were exceedingly fruitful;
      2:23  The I groaned in their slavery
      3: 9  now the cry of the I has reached me,
     12:35  The I did as Moses instructed
     12:37  The I journeyed from Rameses
     14:22  the I went through the sea on dry
     16:12  have heard the grumbling of the I.
     16:35  The I ate manna forty years,
     24:17  To the I the glory of the LORD
     28:30  for the I over his heart before
     29:45  I will dwell among the I and be their
     31:16  The I are to observe the Sabbath,
     33: 5  "Tell the I, 'You are a stiff-necked
     39:42  The I had done all the work just as
Lev  22:32  be acknowledged as holy by the I.
     25:46  rule over your fellow I ruthlessly.
     25:55  for the I belong to me as servants.
Nu    2:32  These are the I, counted according
      6:23  'This is how you are to bless the I.
      9: 2  "Have the I celebrate the Passover
      9:17  the cloud settled, the I encamped.
     10:12  the I set out from the Desert of Sinai
     14: 2  All the I grumbled against Moses
     20:12  me as holy in the sight of the I,
     21: 6  they bit the people and many I died.
     26:65  had told those I they would surely
     27:12  and see the land I have given the I.
     33: 3  The I set out from Rameses
     35:10  "Speak to the I and say to them:
Dt    4:44  is the law Moses set before the I.
     33: 1  on the I before his death.
Jos   1: 2  I am about to give to them—to the I.
      1:14  must cross over ahead of the other I.
      5: 6  The I had moved
      7: 1  the I were unfaithful in regard
      8:32  in the presence of the I,
     18: 1  whole assembly of the I gathered
     21: 3  the I gave the Levites the following
     22: 9  of Manasseh left the I at Shiloh
Jdg   2:11  Then the I did evil in the eyes
      3:12  Again the I did evil in the eyes
      4: 1  Again the I did evil in the eyes
      6: 1  The I did evil in the eyes
     10: 6  Again the I did evil in the eyes
     13: 1  Again the I did evil in the eyes
1Sa   7: 4  So the I put away their Baals
     17: 2  Saul and the I assembled
1Ki   8:63  all the I dedicated the temple
      9:22  did not make slaves of any of the I;
     12:17  as for the I who were living
2Ki  17: 7  took place because the I had sinned

1Ch   9: 2  in their own towns were some I,
     10: 1  the I fled before them, and many
     11: 4  all the I marched to Jerusalem
     21: 2  count the I from Beersheba to Dan.
2Ch   7: 6  and all the I were standing.
Ezr   2:70  and the rest of the I settled in their
Ne    1: 6  I confess the sins we I,
      8:17  the I had not celebrated it like this.
Jer  16:14  who brought the I up out of Egypt,'
Hos   1:10  "Yet the I will be like the sand
      3: 1  Love her as the LORD loves the I,
Am    4: 5  you I, for this is what you love
Mic   5: 3  of his brothers return to join the I.
Ro    9:27  the number of the I be like the sand
     10: 1  to God for the I is that they may be
     10:16  not all the I accepted the good news.
2Co  11:22  So am I. Are they I? So am I.

## ISSACHAR

Son of Jacob by Leah (Ge 30:18; 35:23; 1Ch 2:1).
Tribe of blessed (Ge 49:14–15; Dt 33:18–19), num-
bered (Nu 1:29; 26:25), allotted land (Jos 19:17–23;
Eze 48:25), assisted Deborah (Jdg 5:15), 12,000 from
(Rev 7:7).

## ISSUED [ISSUES]

Ex   15:25  There the LORD i a ruling
Lk    2: 1  days Caesar Augustus i a decree

## ISSUES* [ISSUED]

Da    6:15  that the king i can be changed."

## ITALIAN* [ITALY]

Ac   10: 1  what was known as the I Regiment.

## ITALY [ITALIAN]

Ac   27: 1  decided that we would sail for I,
Heb  13:24  from I send you their greetings.

## ITCHING*

2Ti   4: 3  to say what their i ears want to hear.

## ITHAMAR

Son of Aaron (Ex 6:23; 1Ch 6:3). Duties at tabernacle (Ex 38:21; Nu 4:21–33; 7:8).

## ITTAI

2Sa  15:19  The king said to I the Gittite,

## IVORY

1Ki  10:22  silver and i, and apes and baboons.
     22:39  the palace he built and inlaid with i,
Am    3:15  adorned with i will be destroyed
Rev  18:12  and articles of every kind made of i,

# J

## JABBOK

Ge   32:22  sons and crossed the ford of the J.
Dt    3:16  the border) and out to the J River,

## JABESH [JABESH GILEAD]
1Sa 11: 1 And all the men of **J** said to him,
    31:12 the wall of Beth Shan and went to **J**,
1Ch 10:12 their bones under the great tree in **J**,

## JABESH GILEAD [GILEAD, JABESH]
2Sa 2: 4 men from **J** who had buried Saul,

## JABIN
Jos 11: 1 When **J** king of Hazor heard of this,
Jdg 4:23 day God subdued **J** king of Canaan

## JACKALS
Ps 63:10 to the sword and become food for **j**.
Isa 13:21 will lie there, **j** will fill her houses;
    35: 7 In the haunts where **j** once lay,
Mal 1: 3 left his inheritance to the desert **j**."

## JACOB [ISRAEL]
1. Second son of Isaac, twin of Esau (Ge 26:21–26; 1Ch 1:34). Bought Esau's birthright (Ge 26:29–34); tricked Isaac into blessing him (Ge 27:1–37). Fled to Haran (Ge 28:1–5). Abrahamic covenant perpetuated through (Ge 28:13–15; Mal 1:2). Vision at Bethel (Ge 28:10–22). Served Laban for Rachel and Leah (Ge 29:1–30). Children (Ge 29:31—30:24; 35:16–26; 1Ch 2–9). Flocks increased (Ge 30:25–43). Returned to Canaan (Ge 31). Wrestled with God; name changed to Israel (Ge 32:22–32). Reconciled to Esau (Ge 33). Returned to Bethel (Ge 35:1–15). Favored Joseph (Ge 37:3). Sent sons to Egypt during famine (Ge 42–43). Settled in Egypt (Ge 46). Blessed Ephraim and Manasseh (Ge 48). Blessed sons (Ge 49:1–28; Heb 11:21). Death (Ge 49:29–33). Burial (Ge 50:1–14).
2. Corporate name of Jacob's descendants; often specifically Northern Kingdom.
Ps 53: 6 let **J** rejoice and Israel be glad!
    59:13 of the earth that God rules over **J**.
   135: 4 the LORD has chosen **J** to be his
Isa 44: 1 "But now listen, **J**, my servant,
Jer 30:10 do not be afraid, **J** my servant;
Eze 39:25 I will now restore the fortunes of **J**
Mic 7:20 You will be faithful to **J**, and show
Mal 1: 2 "Yet I have loved **J**,
Ro 9:13 "**J** I loved, but Esau I hated."

### GOD OF JACOB See GOD

### HOUSE OF JACOB See HOUSE

## JAEL*
Woman who killed Canaanite general, Sisera (Jdg 4:17–22; 5:6, 24–27).

## JAH (KJV) See †LORD

## JAIL [JAILER]
Ac 4: 3 they put them in **j** until the next day.
    5:18 and put them in the public **j**.

## JAILER [JAIL]
Ac 16:34 The **j** brought them into his house

## JAIR
Judge from Gilead (Jdg 10:3–5).

## JAIRUS*
Synagogue ruler whose daughter Jesus raised (Mk 5:22–43; Lk 8:41–56).

## JAKIN
1Ki 7:21 The pillar to the south he named **J**

## JAMBRES*
2Ti 3: 8 as Jannes and **J** opposed Moses,

## JAMES
1. Apostle; brother of John (Mt 4:21–22; 10:2; Mk 3:17; Lk 5:1–10). At transfiguration (Mt 17:1–13; Mk 9:1–13; Lk 9:28–36). Killed by Herod (Ac 12:2).
2. Apostle; son of Alphaeus (Mt 10:3; Mk 3:18; Lk 6:15).
3. Brother of Jesus (Mt 13:55; Mk 6:3; Lk 24:10; Gal 1:19) and Judas (Jude 1). With believers before Pentecost (Ac 1:13). Leader of church at Jerusalem (Ac 12:17; 15; 21:18; Gal 2:9, 12). Author of epistle (Jas 1:1).

## JANNES*
2Ti 3: 8 Just as **J** and Jambres opposed

## JAPHETH
Son of Noah (Ge 5:32; 1Ch 1:4–5). Blessed (Ge 9:18–28). Sons of (Ge 10:2–5).

## JAR [JARS]
Ge 24:14 'Please let down your **j** that I may
Ex 16:33 "Take a **j** and put an omer of manna
1Ki 17:14 'The **j** of flour will not be used
Jer 19: 1 "Go and buy a clay **j** from a potter.
Mk 14: 3 an alabaster **j** of very expensive
Lk 8:16 hides it in a clay **j** or puts it under
    22:10 city, a man carrying a **j** of water will
Heb 9: 4 This ark contained the gold **j**

## JARS [JAR]
Jdg 7:19 broke the **j** that were in their hands.
Jn 2: 6 Nearby stood six stone water **j**,
2Co 4: 7 we have this treasure in **j** of clay

## JASHAR*
Jos 10:13 as it is written in the Book of **J**.
2Sa 1:18 bow (it is written in the Book of **J**):

## JASON
Ac 17: 7 and **J** has welcomed them into his

## JASPER
Ex 28:20 row shall be topaz, onyx and **j**.
Eze 28:13 topaz, onyx and **j**, lapis lazuli,
Rev 4: 3 sat there had the appearance of **j**
    21:19 The first foundation was **j**,

## JAVELIN
Jos 8:18 "Hold out toward Ai the **j** that is
1Sa 17:45 me with sword and spear and **j**, but I

## JAWBONE
Jdg 15:15 Finding a fresh **j** of a donkey,

## JAZER

Nu 21:32 After Moses had sent spies to **J**,
32: 1 saw that the lands of **J** and Gilead

## JEALOUS* [JEALOUSLY, JEALOUSY]

Ge 30: 1 children, she became **j** of her sister.
37:11 His brothers were **j** of him, but his
Ex 20: 5 am a **j** God, punishing the children
34:14 whose name is **J**, is a **j** God.
Nu 5:14 or if he is **j** and suspects her even
11:29 replied, "Are you **j** for my sake?
Dt 4:24 God is a consuming fire, a **j** God.
5: 9 am a **j** God, punishing the children
6:15 is a **j** God and his anger will burn
32:16 They made him **j** with their foreign
32:21 They made me **j** by what is no god
Jos 24:19 He is a holy God; he is a **j** God.
1Ki 14:22 up his **j** anger more than those who
Isa 11:13 Ephraim will not be **j** of Judah,
Eze 16:38 vengeance of my wrath and **j** anger.
16:42 my **j** anger will turn away from you;
23:25 I will direct my **j** anger against you,
36: 6 in my **j** wrath because you have
Joel 2:18 Then the LORD was **j** for his land
Na 1: 2 The LORD is a **j** and avenging
Zep 3: 8 consumed by the fire of my **j** anger.
Zec 1:14 'I am very **j** for Jerusalem and Zion,
8: 2 "I am very **j** for Zion;
Ac 7: 9 "Because the patriarchs were **j**
17: 5 But other Jews were **j**;
2Co 11: 2 I am **j** for you with a godly jealousy.

## JEALOUSLY* [JEALOUS]

Jas 4: 5 he **j** longs for the spirit

## JEALOUSY [JEALOUS]

Nu 5:14 feelings of **j** come over her husband
Ps 79: 5 How long will your **j** burn like fire?
Pr 6:34 For **j** arouses a husband's fury,
27: 4 but who can stand before **j**?
SS 8: 6 death, its **j** unyielding as the grave.
Eze 8: 3 the idol that provokes to **j** stood.
35:11 **j** you showed in your hatred of them
Zep 1:18 fire of his **j** the whole earth will be
Zec 8: 2 I am burning with **j** for her."
Ac 5:17 of the Sadducees, were filled with **j**.
13:45 the crowds, they were filled with **j**.
Ro 13:13 debauchery, not in dissension and **j**.
1Co 3: 3 For since there is **j** and quarreling
10:22 we trying to arouse the Lord's **j**?
2Co 11: 2 I am jealous for you with a godly **j**.
12:20 fear that there may be quarreling, **j**,
Gal 5:20 hatred, discord, **j**, fits of rage,

## JEBUS [JEBUSITE, JEBUSITES, JERUSALEM]

1Ch 11: 4 marched to Jerusalem (that is, **J**).

## JEBUSITE [JEBUS]

Jos 18:28 Zelah, Haeleph, the **J** city (that is,
2Sa 24:18 threshing floor of Araunah the **J**."
2Ch 3: 1 the threshing floor of Araunah the **J**,

## JEBUSITES [JEBUS]

Ge 15:21 Canaanites, Girgashites and **J**."

Ex 3: 8 Amorites, Perizzites, Hivites and **J**.
Jos 15:63 Judah could not dislodge the **J**,
2Sa 5: 6 to Jerusalem to attack the **J**,

## JECONIAH* [JEHOIACHIN]

A form of Jehoiachin (Mt 1:11–12).

## JEDIDIAH* [SOLOMON]

2Sa 12:25 Nathan the prophet to name him **J**.

## JEDUTHUN

1Ch 16:41 With them were Heman and **J**
2Ch 35:15 Heman and **J** the king's seer.
Ps 39: T *For the director of music. For J.*
62: T *For J. A psalm of David.*

## JEER* [JEERED, JEERS]

Job 16:10 People open their mouths to **j** at me;

## JEERED* [JEER]

2Ki 2:23 came out of the town and **j** at him.

## JEERS* [JEER]

Heb 11:36 Some faced **j** and flogging,

## JEHOAHAZ

1. Son of Jehu; king of Israel (2Ki 13:1–9).
2. Son of Josiah; king of Judah (2Ki 23:31–34; 2Ch 36:1–4).

## JEHOASH [JOASH]

1. See JOASH.
2. Son of Jehoahaz; king of Israel. Defeat of Aram prophesied by Elisha (2Ki 13:10–25). Defeated Amaziah in Jerusalem (2Ki 14:1–16; 2Ch 25:17–24).

## JEHOIACHIN [JECONIAH]

Son of Jehoiakim; king of Judah exiled by Nebuchadnezzar (2Ki 24:8–17; 2Ch 36:8–10; Jer 22:24–30; 24:1). Raised from prisoner status (2Ki 25:27–30; Jer 52:31–34).

## JEHOIADA

Priest who sheltered Joash from Athaliah (2Ki 11–12; 2Ch 22:11—24:16).

## JEHOIAKIM [ELIAKIM]

Son of Josiah; made king of Judah by Nebu-chadnezzar (2Ki 23:34—24:6; 2Ch 36:4–8; Jer 22:18–23). Burned scroll of Jeremiah's prophecies (Jer 36).

## JEHONADAB

Jer 35: 8 our ancestor **J** son of Rekab commanded

## JEHORAM [JORAM]

1. Son of Jehoshaphat; king of Judah (2Ki 8:16–24). Prophesied against by Elijah; killed by the LORD (2Ch 21).
2. See JORAM.

## JEHOSHAPHAT

1. Son of Asa; king of Judah. Strengthened his

kingdom (2Ch 17). Joined with Ahab against Aram (2Ki 22; 2Ch 18). Established judges (2Ch 19). Joined with Joram against Moab (2Ki 3; 2Ch 20).
2. Valley of judgment (Joel 3:2, 12).

## JEHOVAH (KJV) See †LORD

## JEHU
1. Prophet against Baasha (2Ki 16:1–7).
2. King of Israel. Anointed by Elijah to obliterate house of Ahab (1Ki 19:16–17); anointed by servant of Elisha (2Ki 9:1–13). Killed Joram and Ahaziah (2Ki 9:14–29; 2Ch 22:7–9), Jezebel (2Ki 9:30–37), relatives of Ahab (2Ki 10:1–17; Hos 1:4), ministers of Baal (2Ki 10:18–29). Death (2Ki 10:30–36).

## JEPHTHAH
Judge from Gilead who delivered Israel from Ammon (Jdg 10:6—12:7). Made rash vow concerning his daughter (Jdg 11:30–40).

## JEREMIAH
Prophet to Judah (Jer 1:1–3). Called by the LORD (Jer 1). Put in stocks (Jer 20:1–3). Threatened for prophesying (Jer 11:18–23; 26). Opposed by Hananiah (Jer 28). Scroll burned (Jer 36). Imprisoned (Jer 37). Thrown into cistern (Jer 38). Forced to Egypt with those fleeing Babylonians (Jer 43).

## JERICHO
Nu   22: 1   along the Jordan across from J.
Dt   34: 3   whole region from the Valley of J,
Jos   3:16   the people crossed over opposite J.
        5:10   camped at Gilgal on the plains of J,
        6: 2   I have delivered J into your hands,
        6:26   undertakes to rebuild this city, J:
1Ki 16:34   time, Hiel of Bethel rebuilt J.
2Ki 25: 5   and overtook him in the plains of J.
Lk  10:30   going down from Jerusalem to J,
      18:35   As Jesus approached J, a blind man
      19: 1   Jesus entered J and was passing
Heb 11:30   By faith the walls of J fell,

## JEROBOAM
1. Official of Solomon; rebelled to become first king of Israel (1Ki 11:26–40; 12:1–20; 2Ch 10). Idolatry (1Ki 12:25–33); judgment for (1Ki 13–14; 2Ch 13).
2. Son of Jehoash; king of Israel (1Ki 14:23–29).

## JERUB-BAAL [GIDEON]
Jdg   6:32   day they gave Gideon the name J,
1Sa 12:11   Then the LORD sent J, Barak,

## JERUSALEM [JEBUS]
Jos  10: 1   Now Adoni-Zedek king of J heard
      15: 8   slope of the Jebusite city (that is, J).
Jdg   1: 8   The men of Judah attacked J
1Sa 17:54   Philistine's head and brought it to J;
2Sa   5: 5   in J he reigned over all Israel
        9:13   And Mephibosheth lived in J,
      11: 1   But David remained in J.
      15:29   took the ark of God back to J
      24:16   stretched out his hand to destroy J,
1Ki   3: 1   the LORD, and the wall around J.

1Ki   9:15   terraces, the wall of J, and Hazor,
        9:19   whatever he desired to build in J,
      10:26   chariot cities and also with him in J.
      10:27   silver as common in J as stones,
      11: 7   On a hill east of J, Solomon built
      11:13   my servant and for the sake of J,
      11:36   always have a lamp before me in J,
      11:42   in J over all Israel forty years.
      12:27   at the temple of the LORD in J,
      14:21   and he reigned seventeen years in J,
      14:25   Shishak king of Egypt attacked J.
      15: 2   and he reigned in J three years.
      15:10   and he reigned in J forty-one years.
      22:42   he reigned in J twenty-five years.
2Ki   8:17   and he reigned in J eight years.
        8:26   king, and he reigned in J one year.
      12: 1   and he reigned in J forty years.
      12:17   Then he turned to attack J.
      14: 2   he reigned in J twenty-nine years.
      14: 2   she was from J.
      14:13   Jehoash went to J and broke down the wall of J
      15: 2   and he reigned in J fifty-two years.
      15: 2   name was Jekoliah; she was from J.
      15:33   and he reigned in J sixteen years.
      16: 2   and he reigned in J sixteen years.
      16: 5   Israel marched up to fight against J
      18: 2   he reigned in J twenty-nine years.
      18:17   from Lachish to King Hezekiah at J.
      18:35   can the LORD deliver J from my
      19:31   For out of J will come a remnant,
      21: 1   and he reigned in J fifty-five years.
      21: 4   said, "In J I will put my Name."
      21:12   am going to bring such disaster on J
      21:19   king, and he reigned in J two years.
      22: 1   and he reigned in J thirty-one years.
      23:27   and I will reject J, the city I chose,
      23:31   and he reigned in J three months.
      23:36   and he reigned in J eleven years.
      24: 8   and he reigned in J three months.
      24: 8   she was from J.
      24:10   king of Babylon advanced on J
      24:14   He carried all J into exile:
      24:18   and he reigned in J eleven years.
      24:20   anger that all this happened to J
      25: 1   Babylon marched against J with his
      25:10   broke down the walls around J.
1Ch 11: 4   all the Israelites marched to J
      21:16   sword in his hand extended over J.
2Ch   1: 4   he had pitched a tent for it in J.
        3: 1   the LORD in J on Mount Moriah,
        6: 6   now I have chosen J for my Name
        9: 1   she came to J to test him with hard
      20:15   and all who live in Judah and J!
      20:27   Judah and J returned joyfully to J,
      29: 8   LORD has fallen on Judah and J;
      36:19   and broke down the wall of J;
Ezr   1: 2   build a temple for him at J in Judah.
        2: 1   to Babylon (they returned to J
        3: 1   assembled with one accord in J.
        4:12   up to us from you have gone to J
        4:24   of God in J came to a standstill until
        6:12   decree or to destroy this temple in J.
        7: 8   Ezra arrived in J in the fifth month
        9: 9   a wall of protection in Judah and J.
      10: 7   J for all the exiles to assemble in J.
Ne    1: 2   survived the exile, and also about J.

Ne  1: 3  The wall of J is broken down,
2:11  I went to J, and after staying there
2:17  let us rebuild the wall of J,
2:20  you have no share in J or any claim
3: 8  They restored J as far as the Broad
4: 8  fight against J and stir up trouble
11: 1  the leaders of the people settled in J.
12:27  At the dedication of the wall of J,
12:43  in J could be heard far away.
Ps  51:18  Zion, to build up the walls of J.
79: 1  they have reduced J to rubble.
122: 2  feet are standing in your gates, J.
122: 3  J is built like a city that is closely
122: 6  Pray for the peace of J:
125: 2  As the mountains surround J,
128: 5  see the prosperity of J all the days
137: 5  If I forget you, J, may my right
147: 2  The LORD builds up J;
147:12  Extol the LORD, J;
Ecc  1:12  Teacher, was king over Israel in J.
SS  6: 4  as lovely as J, as majestic as troops
Isa  1: 1  and J that Isaiah son of Amoz saw
2: 1  Amoz saw concerning Judah and J:
3: 1  is about to take from J and Judah
3: 8  J staggers, Judah is falling;
4: 3  who remain in J, will be called
8:14  for the people of J he will be a trap
27:13  LORD on the holy mountain in J.
31: 5  the LORD Almighty will shield J;
33:20  your eyes will see J, a peaceful
40: 2  Speak tenderly to J, and proclaim
40: 9  You who bring good news to J,
52: 1  Put on your garments of splendor, J,
52: 2  rise up, sit enthroned, J.
62: 6  posted watchmen on your walls, J;
62: 7  give him no rest till he establishes J
65:18  for I will create J to be a delight
66:13  and you will be comforted over J."
Jer  2: 2  and proclaim in the hearing of J:
3:17  time they will call J The Throne
4: 5  in Judah and proclaim in J and say:
4:14  J, wash the evil from your heart
5: 1  "Go up and down the streets of J,
6: 6  and build siege ramps against J.
8: 5  Why does J always turn away?
9:11  "I will make J a heap of ruins,
13:27  Woe to you, J! How long will you
23:14  the people of J are like Gomorrah."
24: 1  carried into exile from J to Babylon
26:18  J will become a heap of rubble,
32: 2  of Babylon was then besieging J,
33:10  and the streets of J that are deserted,
39: 1  Babylon marched against J with his
51:50  a distant land, and call to mind J."
52:14  broke down all the walls around J.
La  1: 8  J has sinned greatly and so has
Eze  8: 3  in visions of God he took me to J,
14:21  I send against J my four dreadful
16: 2  man, confront J with her detestable
21: 2  set your face against J and preach
23: 4  is Samaria, and Oholibah is J.
Da  5: 3  taken from the temple of God in J,
6:10  the windows opened toward J.
9: 2  of J would last seventy years.
9:12  done like what has been done to J.
9:25  rebuild J until the Anointed One,
Joel  3: 1  I restore the fortunes of Judah and J,

Joel  3:16  roar from Zion and thunder from J;
3:17  J will be holy; never again will
Am  2: 5  will consume the fortresses of J."
Ob  1:11  entered his gates and cast lots for J,
Mic  1: 5  is Judah's high place? Is it not J?
4: 2  the word of the LORD from J.
Zep  3:16  On that day they will say to J,
Zec  1:14  'I am very jealous for J and Zion,
1:17  comfort Zion and choose J.' "
2: 2  me, "To measure J, to find out how
2: 4  man, 'J will be a city without walls
8: 3  J will be called the City of Truth,
8: 8  I will bring them back to live in J;
8:15  determined to do good again to J
8:22  powerful nations will come to J
9: 9  Shout, Daughter J! See, your king
9:10  Ephraim and the warhorses from J,
12: 3  I will make J an immovable rock
12:10  the inhabitants of J a spirit of grace
14: 2  I will gather all the nations to J
14: 8  living water will flow out from J,
14:16  nations that have attacked J will go
Mt  2: 1  Magi from the east came to J
16:21  to his disciples that he must go to J
20:18  "We are going up to J, and the Son
21:10  When Jesus entered, the whole
23:37  "J, J, you who kill the prophets
Mk  10:33  "We are going up to J," he said,
15:41  had come up with him to J were
Lk  2:22  Mary took him to J to present him
2:41  Every year Jesus' parents went to J
2:43  the boy Jesus stayed behind in J,
4: 9  The devil led him to J and had him
9:31  about to bring to fulfillment at J.
9:51  Jesus resolutely set out for J.
13:34  "J, J, you who kill the prophets
18:31  them, "We are going up to J,
19:41  As he approached J and saw
21:20  "When you see J being surrounded
21:24  J will be trampled
23:28  "Daughters of J, do not weep
24:47  name to all nations, beginning at J.
Jn  1:19  the Jewish leaders in J sent priests
4:20  where we must worship is in J."
5: 1  Jesus went up to J for one
10:22  the Festival of Dedication at J.
Ac  1: 4  "Do not leave J, but wait
1: 8  and you will be my witnesses in J,
6: 7  of disciples in J increased rapidly,
9:13  he has done to your people in J,
9:28  them and moved about freely in J,
11:27  some prophets came down from J
15: 2  to go up to J to see the apostles
20:22  I am going to J, not knowing what
21: 4  they urged Paul not to go on to J.
23:11  As you have testified about me in J,
Ro  15:19  So from J all the way around
Gal  1:17  to J to see those who were apostles
2: 1  I went up again to J, this time
4:25  corresponds to the present city of J,
4:26  But the J that is above is free,
Heb  12:22  of the living God, the heavenly J.
Rev  3:12  the new J, which is coming down
21: 2  the new J, coming down
21:10  and showed me the Holy City, J,

## DAUGHTER JERUSALEM See
DAUGHTER

## DAUGHTERS OF JERUSALEM See
DAUGHTERS

## PEOPLE OF JERUSALEM 2Ch 20:20; 21:11,
13; 22:1; 32:18, 22, 26, 33; 33:9; 34:32; 35:18;
Isa 8:14; Jer 1:3; 8:1; 11:12; 19:3; 23:14; Eze
11:15; Zec 12:5; Mk 1:5; Jn 7:25; Ac 13:27

## JESHUA
Ezr    2:36  of Jedaiah (through the family of J)

## JESSE
Father of David (Ru 4:17–22; 1Sa 16; 1Ch
2:12–17).

## SON OF JESSE See SON

## JESUS [JESUS'; see also JUSTUS]
**LIFE:** Genealogy (Mt 1:1–17; Lk 3:21–37). Birth
announced (Mt 1:18–25; Lk 1:26–45). Birth (Mt
2:1–12; Lk 2:1–40). Escape to Egypt (Mt 2:13–23).
As a boy in the temple (Lk 2:41–52). Baptism (Mt
3:13–17; Mk 1:9–11; Lk 3:21–22; Jn 1:32–34).
Temptation (Mt 4:1–11; Mk 1:12–13; Lk 4:1–13).
Ministry in Galilee (Mt 4:12—18:35; Mk 1:14—
9:50; Lk 4:14—13:9; Jn 1:35—2:11; 4; 6), Transfiguration (Mt 17:1–8; Mk 9:2–8; Lk 9:28–36), on the
way to Jerusalem (Mt 19–20; Mk 10; Lk 13:10—
19:27), in Jerusalem (Mt 21–25; Mk 11–13; Lk
19:28—21:38; Jn 2:12—3:36; 5; 7–12). Last supper
(Mt 26:17–35; Mk 14:12–31; Lk 22:1–38; Jn 13–17).
Arrest and trial (Mt 26:36—27:31; Mk 14:43—15:20;
Lk 22:39—23:25; Jn 18:1—19:16). Crucifixion (Mt
27:32–66; Mk 15:21–47; Lk 23:26–55; Jn 19:28–42).
Resurrection and appearances (Mt 28; Mk 16; Lk 24;
Jn 20–21; Ac 1:1–11; 7:56; 9:3–6; 1Co 15:1–8; Rev
1:1–20).
**MIRACLES.** *Healings:* official's son (Jn
4:43–54), demoniac in Capernaum (Mk 1:23–26; Lk
4:33–35), Peter's mother-in-law (Mt 8:14–17; Mk
1:29–31; Lk 4:38–39), leper (Mt 8:2–4; Mk 1:40–45;
Lk 5:12–16), paralytic (Mt 9:1–8; Mk 2:1–12; Lk
5:17–26), cripple (Jn 5:1–9), shriveled hand (Mt
12:10–13; Mk 3:1–5; Lk 6:6–11), centurion's servant
(Mt 8:5–13; Lk 7:1–10), widow's son raised (Lk
7:11–17), demoniac (Mt 12:22–23; Lk 11:14),
Gadarene demoniacs (Mt 8:28–34; Mk 5:1–20; Lk
8:26–39), woman's bleeding and Jairus' daughter (Mt
9:18–26; Mk 5:21–43; Lk 8:40–56), blind man (Mt
9:27–31), mute man (Mt 9:32–33), Canaanite
woman's daughter (Mt 15:21–28; Mk 7:24–30), deaf
man (Mk 7:31–37), blind man (Mk 8:22–26), demoniac boy (Mt 17:14–18; Mk 9:14–29; Lk 9:37–43),
ten lepers (Lk 17:11–19), man born blind (Jn 9:1–7),
Lazarus raised (Jn 11), crippled woman (Lk
13:11–17), man with dropsy (Lk 14:1–6), two blind
men (Mt 20:29–34; Mk 10:46–52; Lk 18:35–43),
Malchus' ear (Lk 22:50–51). *Other Miracles:* water to
wine (Jn 2:1–11), catch of fish (Lk 5:1–11), storm
stilled (Mt 8:23–27; Mk 4:37–41; Lk 8:22–25), 5,000
fed (Mt 14:15–21; Mk 6:35–44; Lk 9:10–17; Jn
6:1–14), walking on water (Mt 14:25–33; Mk
6:48–52; Jn 6:15–21), 4,000 fed (Mt 15:32–39; Mk
8:1–9), money from fish (Mt 17:24–27), fig tree

cursed (Mt 21:18–22; Mk 11:12–14), catch of fish (Jn
21:1–14).
**MAJOR TEACHING:** Sermon on the Mount (Mt
5–7; Lk 6:17–49), to Nicodemus (Jn 3), to Samaritan
woman (Jn 4), Bread of Life (Jn 6:22–59), at Feast of
Tabernacles (Jn 7–8), woes to Pharisees (Mt 23; Lk
11:37–54), Good Shepherd (Jn 10:1–18), Olivet Discourse (Mt 24–25; Mk 13; Lk 21:5–36), Upper Room
Discourse (Jn 13–16).
**PARABLES:** Sower (Mt 13:3–23; Mk 4:3–25; Lk
8:5–18), seed's growth (Mk 4:26–29), wheat and
weeds (Mt 13:24–30, 36–43), mustard seed (Mt
13:31–32; Mk 4:30–32), yeast (Mt 13:33; Lk
13:20–21), hidden treasure (Mt 13:44), valuable pearl
(Mt 13:45–46), net (Mt 13:47–51), house owner (Mt
13:52), good Samaritan (Lk 10:25–37), unmerciful
servant (Mt 18:15–35), lost sheep (Mt 18:10–14; Lk
15:4–7), lost coin (Lk 15:8–10), prodigal son (Lk
15:11–32), dishonest manager (Lk 16:1–13), rich man
and Lazarus (Lk 16:19–31), persistent widow (Lk
18:1–8), Pharisee and tax collector (Lk 18:9–14),
payment of workers (Mt 20:1–16), tenants and the
vineyard (Mt 21:28–46; Mt 12:1–12; Lk 20:9–19),
wedding banquet (Mt 22:1–14), faithful servant (Mt
24:45–51), ten virgins (Mt 25:1–13), talents (Mt
25:1–30; Lk 19:12–27).
**DISCIPLES:** Call (Jn 1:35–51; Mt 4:18–22; 9:9;
Mk 1:16–20; 2:13–14; Lk 5:1–11, 27–28). Named
Apostles (Mk 3:13–19; Lk 6:12–16). Twelve sent out
(Mt 10; Mk 6:7–11; Lk 9:1–5). Seventy sent out (Lk
10:1–24). Defection of (Jn 6:60–71; Mt 26:56; Mk
14:50–52). Final commission (Mt 28:16–20; Jn
21:15–23; Ac 1:3–8).See also APOSTLES.

| | | |
|---|---|---|
| Ac | 2:32 | God has raised this **J** to life, and we |
| | 9: 5 | Saul asked. "I am **J**, whom you are |
| | 9:34 | said to him, "**J** Christ heals you. |
| | 15:11 | of our Lord **J** that we are saved, |
| | 16:31 | "Believe in the Lord **J**, and you will |
| | 20:24 | the task the Lord **J** has given me— |
| Ro | 3:24 | redemption that came by Christ **J**. |
| | 5:17 | life through the one man, **J** Christ! |
| | 8: 1 | for those who are in Christ **J**, |
| 1Co | 1: 7 | for our Lord **J** Christ to be revealed. |
| | 2: 2 | I was with you except **J** Christ |
| | 6:11 | in the name of the Lord **J** Christ |
| | 8: 6 | and there is but one Lord, **J** Christ, |
| | 12: 3 | Spirit of God says, "**J** be cursed," |
| | 12: 3 | and no one can say, "**J** is Lord," |
| 2Co | 4: 5 | but **J** Christ as Lord, and ourselves |
| | 13: 5 | Do you not realize that Christ **J** is |
| Gal | 2:16 | but by faith in **J** Christ. |
| | 2:16 | in Christ **J** that we may be justified |
| | 3:28 | for you are all one in Christ **J**. |
| | 5: 6 | in Christ **J** neither circumcision nor |
| | 6:17 | I bear on my body the marks of **J**. |
| Eph | 1: 5 | to sonship through **J** Christ, |
| | 2:10 | in Christ **J** to do good works, |
| | 2:20 | with Christ **J** himself as the chief |
| Php | 1: 6 | completion until the day of Christ **J**. |
| | 2: 5 | same attitude of mind Christ **J** had: |
| | 2:10 | name of **J** every knee should bow, |
| Col | 3:17 | do it all in the name of the Lord **J**, |
| 1Th | 1:10 | **J**, who rescues us from the coming |
| | 4:14 | with **J** those who have fallen asleep |
| | 5:23 | at the coming of our Lord **J** Christ. |
| 2Th | 1: 7 | happen when the Lord **J** is revealed |
| | 2: 1 | the coming of our Lord **J** Christ |

1Ti 1:15 Christ **J** came into the world to save
2Ti 1:10 Christ **J**, who has destroyed death
2: 3 like a good soldier of Christ **J**.
3:12 life in Christ **J** will be persecuted,
Tit 2:13 our great God and Savior, **J** Christ,
Heb 2: 9 But we do see **J**, who was made
2:11 So **J** is not ashamed to call them
3: 1 fix your thoughts on **J**, whom we
3: 3 **J** has been found worthy of greater
4:14 into heaven, **J** the Son of God, let us
6:20 where our forerunner, **J**, has entered
7:22 **J** has become the guarantor
7:24 but because **J** lives forever, he has
8: 6 fact the ministry **J** has received is as
12: 2 fixing our eyes on **J**, the pioneer
12:24 to **J** the mediator of a new covenant,
13: 8 **J** Christ is the same yesterday
1Pe 1: 3 through the resurrection of **J** Christ
2Pe 1:16 of our Lord **J** Christ in power,
1Jn 1: 7 another, and the blood of **J**, his Son,
2: 1 **J** Christ, the Righteous One.
2: 6 to live in him must live as **J** did.
4:15 acknowledges that **J** is the Son
Rev 1: 1 The revelation from **J** Christ,
12:17 hold fast their testimony about **J**.
17: 6 of those who bore testimony to **J**.
22:16 "I, **J**, have sent my angel to give
22:20 Amen. Come, Lord **J**.

**CHRIST JESUS** Ac 24:24; Ro 1:1; 3:24; 6:3, 11, 23; 8:1, 2, 34, 39; 15:5, 16, 17; 16:3; 1Co 1:1, 2, 4, 30; 4:15, 17; 15:31; 16:24; 2Co 1:1; 13:5; Gal 2:4, 16; 3:14, 26, 28; 4:14; 5:6, 24; Eph 1:1, 1; 2:6, 7, 10, 13, 20; 3:1, 6, 11, 21; Php 1:1, 1, 6, 8, 26; 2:5; 3:3, 8, 12, 14; 4:7, 19, 21; Col 1:1, 4; 2:6; 4:12; 1Th 2:14; 5:18; 1Ti 1:1, 1, 2, 12, 14, 15, 16; 2:5; 3:13; 4:6; 5:21; 6:13; 2Ti 1:1, 1, 2, 9, 10, 13; 2:1, 3, 10; 3:12, 15; 4:1; Tit 1:4; Phm 1:1, 9, 23

**JESUS CHRIST** Jn 1:17; 17:3; Ac 2:38; 3:6; 4:10; 8:12; 9:34; 10:36, 48; 11:17; 15:26; 16:18; 28:31; Ro 1:4, 6, 7, 8; 2:16; 3:22; 5:1, 11, 15, 17, 21; 7:25; 13:14; 15:6, 30; 16:25, 27; 1Co 1:2, 3, 7, 8, 9, 10; 2:2; 3:11; 6:11; 8:6; 15:57; 2Co 1:2, 3, 19; 4:5; 8:9; 13:14; Gal 1:1, 3, 12; 2:16; 3:1, 22; 6:14, 18; Eph 1:2, 3, 5, 17; 5:20; 6:23, 24; Php 1:2, 11, 19; 2:11, 21; 3:20; 4:23; Col 1:3; 1Th 1:1, 3; 5:9, 23, 28; 2Th 1:1, 2, 12; 2:1, 14, 16; 3:6, 12, 18; 1Ti 6:3, 14; 2Ti 2:8; Tit 1:1; 2:13; 3:6; Phm 1:3, 25; Heb 10:10; 13:8, 21; Jas 1:1; 2:1; 1Pe 1:1, 2, 3, 3, 7, 13; 2:5; 3:21; 4:11; 2Pe 1:1, 1, 8, 11, 14, 16; 2:20; 3:18; 1Jn 1:3; 2:1; 3:16, 23; 4:2; 5:6, 20; 2Jn 1:3, 7; Jude 1:1, 1, 4, 17, 21, 25; Rev 1:1, 2, 5

**JESUS ... MESSIAH** Mt 1:1, 16, 18; 27:17, 22; Mk 1:1; Jn 9:22; 20:31; Ac 5:42; 9:22; 18:5, 28; 1Jn 2:22; 5:1

**JESUS OF NAZARETH** Mt 26:71; Mk 1:24; 10:47; Lk 4:34; 18:37; 24:19; Jn 1:45; 18:5, 7; 19:19; Ac 2:22; 6:14; 10:38; 22:8; 26:9

**LORD JESUS** Mk 16:19; Lk 24:3; Ac 1:21; 4:33; 7:59; 8:16; 9:17; 11:17, 20; 15:11, 26; 16:31; 19:5, 13, 17; 20:21, 24, 35; 21:13; 28:31;

Ro 1:7; 5:1, 11; 13:14; 14:14; 15:6, 30; 16:20; 1Co 1:2, 3, 7, 8, 10; 5:4, 4; 6:11; 8:6; 11:23; 15:57; 16:23; 2Co 1:2, 3, 14; 4:14; 8:9; 11:31; 13:14; Gal 1:3; 6:14, 18; Eph 1:2, 3, 15, 17; 5:20; 6:23, 24; Php 1:2; 2:19; 3:20; 4:23; Col 1:3; 3:17; 1Th 1:1, 3; 2:15, 19; 3:11, 13; 4:1, 2; 5:9, 23, 28; 2Th 1:1, 2, 7, 8, 12, 12; 2:1, 8, 14, 16; 3:6, 12, 18; 1Ti 6:3, 14; Phm 1:3, 5, 25; Heb 13:20; Jas 1:1; 2:1; 1Pe 1:3; 2Pe 1:8, 14, 16; Jude 1:17, 21; Rev 22:20, 21

**LORD JESUS CHRIST** Ac 11:17; 15:26; 28:31; Ro 1:7; 5:1, 11; 13:14; 15:6, 30; 1Co 1:2, 3, 7, 8, 10; 6:11; 8:6; 15:57; 2Co 1:2, 3; 8:9; 13:14; Gal 1:3; 6:14, 18; Eph 1:2, 3, 17; 5:20; 6:23, 24; Php 1:2; 3:20; 4:23; Col 1:3; 1Th 1:1, 3; 5:9, 23, 28; 2Th 1:1, 2, 12; 2:1, 14, 16; 3:6, 12, 18; 1Ti 6:3, 14; Phm 1:3, 25; Jas 1:1; 2:1; 1Pe 1:3; 2Pe 1:8, 14, 16; Jude 1:17, 21

**NAME OF JESUS** See NAME

**JESUS'** [JESUS]
Mt 27:58 he asked for **J'** body, and Pilate
Lk 8:35 sitting at **J'** feet, dressed and in his
Jn 12:41 said this because he saw **J'** glory
19:34 of the soldiers pierced **J'** side
Ac 3:16 It is **J'** name and the faith

**JETHRO**\*
Father-in-law and adviser of Moses (Ex 3:1; 4:18; 18). Also known as Reuel (Ex 2:18).

**JEW** [JEWISH, JEWS, JEWS', JUDAISM]
Est 2: 5 the citadel of Susa a **J** of the tribe
10: 3 Mordecai the **J** was second in rank
Zec 8:23 take firm hold of one **J** by the hem
Jn 4: 9 "You are a **J** and I am a Samaritan
18:35 "Am I a **J**?" Pilate replied.
Ac 21:39 "I am a **J**, from Tarsus in Cilicia,
Ro 1:16 first to the **J**, then to the Gentile.
2: 9 first for the **J**, then for the Gentile;
2:29 a person is a **J** who is one inwardly;
10:12 For there is no difference between **J**
1Co 9:20 To the Jews I became like a **J**,
Gal 2:14 "You are a **J**, yet you live like a Gentile and not like a **J**.
3:28 There is neither **J** nor Gentile,
Col 3:11 Here there is no Gentile or **J**,

**JEWEL**\* [JEWELRY, JEWELS]
Pr 20:15 that speak knowledge are a rare **j**.
SS 4: 9 eyes, with one **j** of your necklace.
Isa 13:19 Babylon, the **j** of kingdoms,
Rev 21:11 was like that of a very precious **j**,

**JEWELRY** [JEWEL]
Ex 35:22 and brought gold **j** of all kinds:
Jer 2:32 Does a young woman forget her **j**,
Eze 16:11 I adorned you with **j**: I put bracelets
1Pe 3: 3 and the wearing of gold **j** and fine

**JEWELS** [JEWEL]
Job 28:17 it, nor can it be had for **j** of gold.

Isa 54:12 your gates of sparkling **j**, and all
    61:10 as a bride adorns herself with her **j**.
Zec  9:16 sparkle in his land like **j** in a crown.

## JEWISH [JEW]

Ezr  6: 7 the **J** elders rebuild this house
Ne  1: 2 them about the **J** remnant that had
Jn   3: 1 a member of the **J** ruling council.
  11:51 Jesus would die for the **J** nation,
Ac  3: 6 There they met a **J** sorcerer
  16: 1 mother was **J** and a believer
  24:24 his wife Drusilla, who was **J**.
Gal  2:14 force Gentiles to follow **J** customs?

## JEWS [JEW]

Ezr  5: 5 watching over the elders of the **J**,
Ne  4: 1 He ridiculed the **J**,
Est  3:13 kill and annihilate all the **J**—
  4:14 deliverance for the **J** will arise
  10: 3 spoke up for the welfare of all the **J**.
Da   3: 8 came forward and denounced the **J**.
Mt   2: 2 who has been born king of the **J**?
  27:11 him, "Are you the king of the **J**?"
  27:37 THIS IS JESUS, THE KING OF THE **J**.
Jn   4: 9 (For **J** do not associate
  4:22 do know, for salvation is from the **J**.
  19: 3 saying, "Hail, king of the **J**!"
  19:21 "Do not write 'The King of the **J**,'
Ac  17· 4 Some of the **J** were persuaded
  20:21 I have declared to both **J**
  21:20 many thousands of **J** have believed,
Ro   3:29 Is God the God of **J** only? Is he not
  9:24 not only from the **J**
  15:27 they owe it to the **J** to share
1Co  1:22 **J** demand signs and Greeks look
  9:20 To the **J** I became like a Jew, to win the **J**.
  12:13 whether **J** or Gentiles,
Gal  2: 8 work in Peter as an apostle to the **J**,
1Th  2:14 those churches suffered from the **J**,
Rev  2: 9 slander of those who say they are **J**
  3: 9 claim to be **J** though they are not,

### KING OF THE JEWS See KING

## JEWS'* [JEW]

Ro  15:27 shared in the **J'** spiritual blessings,

## JEZEBEL*

Sidonian wife of Ahab (1Ki 16:31). Promoted Baal worship (1Ki 16:32–33). Killed prophets of the LORD (1Ki 18:4, 13). Opposed Elijah (1Ki 19:1–2). Had Naboth killed (1Ki 21). Death prophesied (1Ki 21:17–24). Killed by Jehu (2Ki 9:30–37). Metaphor of immorality (Rev 2:20).

## JEZREEL [JEZREELITE]

1Ki 21:23 devour Jezebel by the wall of **J**.'
2Ki  9:36 **J** dogs will devour Jezebel's flesh.
  10: 7 baskets and sent them to Jehu in **J**.
Hos  1: 4 "Call him **J**, because I will soon
  1:11 land, for great will be the day of **J**.
  2:22 olive oil, and they will respond to **J**.

## JEZREELITE [JEZREEL]

1Ki 21: 1 vineyard belonging to Naboth the **J**.

2Ki  9:25 field that belonged to Naboth the **J**.

## JOAB

Nephew of David (1Ch 2:16). Commander of his army (2Sa 8:16). Victorious over Ammon (2Sa 10; 1Ch 19), Rabbah (2Sa 11; 1Ch 20), Jerusalem (1Ch 11:6), Absalom (2Sa 18), Sheba (2Sa 20). Killed Abner (2Sa 3:22–39), Amasa (2Sa 20:1–13). Numbered David's army (2Sa 24; 1Ch 21). Sided with Adonijah (1Ki 1:17, 19). Killed by Benaiah (1Ki 2:5–6, 28–35).

## JOANNA*

Lk   8: 3 **J** the wife of Chuza, the manager
  24:10 It was Mary Magdalene, **J**,

## JOASH [JEHOASH]

1. Son of Ahaziah; king of Judah. Sheltered from Athaliah by Jehoiada (2Ki 11; 2Ch 22:10—23:21). Repaired temple (2Ki 12; 2Ch 24).
2. See JEHOASH.

## JOB

Wealthy man from Uz; feared God (Job 1:1–5). Integrity tested by disaster (Job 1:6–22), personal affliction (Job 2). Maintained innocence in debate with three friends (Job 3–31), Elihu (Job 32–37). Rebuked by the LORD (Job 38–41). Vindicated and restored to greater stature by the LORD (Job 42). Example of righteousness (Eze 14:14, 20).

## JOCHEBED*

Mother of Moses and Aaron (Ex 6:20; Nu 26:59).

## JOEL

1. Son of Samuel (1Sa 8:2; 1Ch 6:28).
2. Prophet (Joel 1:1; Ac 2:16).

## JOHANAN

1. First high priest in Solomon's temple (1Ch 6:9–10).
2. Jewish leader who tried to save Gedaliah from assassination (Jer 40:13–14); took Jews, including Jeremiah, to Egypt (Jer 40–43).

## JOHN

1. Son of Zechariah and Elizabeth (Lk 1). Called the Baptist (Mt 3:1–12; Mk 1:2–8). Witness to Jesus (Mt 3:11–12; Mk 1:7–8; Lk 3:15–18; Jn 1:6–35; 3:27–30; 5:33–36). Doubts about Jesus (Mt 11:2–6; Lk 7:18–23). Arrest (Mt 4:12; Mk 1:14). Execution (Mt 14:1–12; Mk 6:14–29; Lk 9:7–9). Ministry compared to Elijah (Mt 11:7–19; Mk 9:11–13; Lk 7:24–35).
2. Apostle; brother of James (Mt 4:21–22; 10:2; Mk 3:17; Lk 5:1–10). At transfiguration (Mt 17:1–13; Mk 9:1–13; Lk 9:28–36). Desire to be greatest (Mk 10:35–45). Leader of church at Jerusalem (Ac 4:1–3; Gal 2:9). Elder who wrote epistles (2Jn 1; 3Jn 1). Prophet who wrote Revelation (Rev 1:1; 22:8).
3. Cousin of Barnabas, co-worker with Paul, (Ac 12:12—13:13; 15:37; see MARK).

## JOIN [JOINED, JOINS]

Ex   1:10 war breaks out, will **j** our enemies,

Ne  10:29  all these now **j** their fellow Israelites
Pr  23:20  Do not **j** those who drink too much
    24:21  do not **j** with rebellious officials,
Jer  3:18  the house of Judah will **j** the house
Eze 37:17  **J** them together into one stick so
Da  11:34  who are not sincere will **j** them.
Ac   5:13  No one else dared **j** them,
     9:26  he tried to **j** the disciples, but they
Ro  15:30  to **j** me in my struggle by praying
2Ti  1: 8  But **j** with me in suffering
     2: 3  **J** with me in suffering,
1Pe  4: 4  not **j** them in their reckless,

## JOINED [JOIN]

1Sa 10:10  and he **j** in their prophesying.
Hos  4:17  Ephraim is **j** to idols;
Zec  2:11  "Many nations will be **j**
Mt  19: 6  Therefore what God has **j** together,
Mk  10: 9  Therefore what God has **j** together,
Ac   1:14  They all **j** together constantly
Eph  2:21  him the whole building is **j** together
     4:16  body, **j** and held together by every

## JOINS* [JOIN]

Hos  7: 5  and he **j** hands with the mockers.
1Co 16:16  to everyone who **j** in the work

## JOINT* [JOINTS]

Job 31:22  shoulder, let it be broken off at the **j**.
Ps  22:14  water, and all my bones are out of **j**.

## JOINTS* [JOINT]

Heb  4:12  soul and spirit, **j** and marrow;

## JOKING*

Ge  19:14  his sons-in-law thought he was **j**.
Pr  26:19  neighbor and says, "I was only **j**!"
Eph  5: 4  foolish talk or coarse **j**, which are

## JONADAB  See also JEHONADAB

2Sa 13: 3  Amnon had an adviser named **J** son

## JONAH

Prophet in days of Jeroboam II (2Ki 14:25). Called to Nineveh; fled to Tarshish (Jnh 1:1–3). Cause of storm; thrown into sea (Jnh 1:4–16). Swallowed by fish (Jnh 1:17). Prayer (Jnh 2). Preached to Nineveh (Jnh 3). Attitude reproved by the LORD (Jnh 4). Sign of (Mt 12:39–41; Lk 11:29–32).

## JONATHAN

Son of Saul (1Sa 13:16; 1Ch 8:33). Valiant warrior (1Sa 13–14). Relation to David (1Sa 18:1–4; 19–20; 23:16–18). Killed at Gilboa (1Sa 31). Mourned by David (2Sa 1).

## JOPPA

2Ch  2:16  float them as rafts by sea down to **J**.
Ezr  3: 7  logs by sea from Lebanon to **J**,
Jnh  1: 3  He went down to **J**, where he found
Ac   9:43  Peter stayed in **J** for some time

## JORAM

1. Son of Ahab; king of Israel. With Jehoshaphat fought against Moab (2Ki 3). Killed with Ahaziah by Jehu (2Ki 8:25–29; 9:14–26; 2Ch 22:5–9).
2. See JEHORAM.

## JORDAN

Ge  13:10  plain of the **J** was well watered,
Nu  22: 1  and camped along the **J** across
    34:12  boundary will go down along the **J**
Dt   1: 1  in the wilderness east of the **J**—
     3:27  you are not going to cross this **J**.
Jos  1: 2  cross the **J** River into the land I am
     3:11  all the earth will go into the **J** ahead
     3:17  stopped in the middle of the **J**
     4: 8  stones from the middle of the **J**,
     4:22  'Israel crossed the **J** on dry ground.'
    23: 4  between the **J**
2Ki  2: 7  and Elisha had stopped at the **J**.
     2:13  back and stood on the bank of the **J**.
     5:10  wash yourself seven times in the **J**
     6: 4  They went to the **J** and began to cut
Ps  114: 3  looked and fled, the **J** turned back;
Isa  9: 1  the Way of the Sea, beyond the **J**—
Jer  12: 5  you manage in the thickets by the **J**?
Mt   3: 6  were baptized by him in the **J** River.
     4:15  the Sea, beyond the **J**,
Mk   1: 9  and was baptized by John in the **J**.
Jn   1:28  Bethany on the other side of the **J**,

## JOSEPH [BARNABAS, JUSTUS]

1. Son of Jacob by Rachel (Ge 30:24; 1Ch 2:2). Favored by Jacob, hated by brothers (Ge 37:3–4). Dreams (Ge 37:5–11). Sold by brothers (Ge 37:12–36). Served Potiphar; imprisoned by false accusation (Ge 39). Interpreted dreams of Pharaoh's servants (Ge 40), of Pharaoh (Ge 41:4–40). Made greatest in Egypt (Ge 41:41–57). Sold grain to brothers (Ge 42–45). Brought Jacob and sons to Egypt (Ge 46–47). Sons Ephraim and Manasseh blessed (Ge 48). Blessed (Ge 49:22–26; Dt 33:13–17). Death (Ge 50:22–26; Ex 13:19; Heb 11:22). 12,000 from (Rev 7:8).
2. Husband of Mary mother of Jesus (Mt 1:16–24; 2:13–19; Lk 1:27; 2; Jn 1:45).
3. Disciple from Arimathea, who gave his tomb for Jesus' burial (Mt 27:57–61; Mk 15:43–47; Lk 23:50–52).
4. Disciple, also known as Barsabbas and Justus, proposed as a replacement for Judas (Ac 1:23).
5. Original name of Barnabas (Ac 4:36).

## JOSHUA [HOSHEA]

1. Son of Nun; name changed from Hoshea (Nu 13:8, 16; 1Ch 7:27). Fought Amalekites under Moses (Ex 17:9–14). Servant of Moses on Sinai (Ex 24:13; 32:17). Spied Canaan (Nu 13). With Caleb, allowed to enter land (Nu 14:6, 30). Succeeded Moses (Dt 1:38; 31:1–8; 34:9).

Charged Israel to conquer Canaan (Jos 1). Crossed Jordan (Jos 3–4). Circumcised sons of wilderness wanderings (Jos 5). Conquered Jericho (Jos 6), Ai (Jos 7–8), five kings at Gibeon (Jos 10:1–28), southern Canaan (Jos 10:29–43), northern Canaan (Jos 11–12). Defeated at Ai (Jos 7). Deceived by Gibeonites (Jos 9). Renewed covenant (Jos 8:30–35; 24:1–27). Divided land among tribes (Jos 13–22). Last words (Jos 23). Death (Jos 24:28–31).

2. High priest during rebuilding of temple (Hag 1–2; Zec 3:1–9; 6:11).

Ezr   4: 3   **J** and the rest of the heads of the
       10:18   the descendants of **J** son of Jozadak,
Ne   12: 1   and with **J**: Seraiah, Jeremiah, Ezra,

## JOSIAH

Son of Amon; king of Judah (2Ki 21:26; 1Ch 3:14). Prophesied (1Ki 13:2). Book of the Law discovered during his reign (2Ki 22; 2Ch 34:14–31). Reforms (2Ki 23:1–25; 2Ch 34:1–13; 35:1–19). Killed by Pharaoh Neco (2Ki 23:29–30; 2Ch 35:20–27).

## JOTHAM

1. Son of Gideon (Jdg 9).
2. Son of Azariah (Uzziah); king of Judah (2Ki 15:32–38; 2Ch 26:21—27:9).

## JOURNEY

Ge   24:21   LORD had made his **j** successful.
Ex    3:18   Let us take a three-day **j**
Nu   33: 1   the stages in the **j** of the Israelites
Dt    1:33   who went ahead of you on your **j**,
       2: 7   has watched over your **j** through this
Jdg  18: 6   Your **j** has the LORD's approval."
Ezr   8:21   ask him for a safe **j** for us and our
Isa  35: 8   The unclean will not **j** on it;
Mt   25:14   it will be like a man going on a **j**,
Lk    9. 3   "Take nothing for the **j**
Ac    9:27   how Saul on his **j** had seen the Lord
Ro   15:24   to have you assist me on my **j** there,

## JOY* [ENJOY, ENJOYED, ENJOYMENT, JOYFUL, JOYFULLY, JOYOUS, OVERJOYED, REJOICE, REJOICED, REJOICES, REJOICING]

Ge   31:27   so I could send you away with **j**
Lev   9:24   saw it, they shouted for **j** and fell
Dt   16:15   hands, and your **j** will be complete.
Jdg   9:19   may Abimelek be your **j**, and may
1Ch  12:40   and sheep, for there was **j** in Israel.
      16:27   and **j** are in his dwelling place.
      16:33   them sing for **j** before the LORD,
      29:17   **j** how willingly your people who are
      29:22   drank with great **j** in the presence
2Ch  30:26   There was great **j** in Jerusalem.
Ezr   3:12   while many others shouted for **j**.
       3:13   of the shouts of **j** from the sound
       6:16   of the house of God with **j**.
       6:22   they celebrated with **j** the Festival
       6:22   the LORD had filled them with **j**
Ne    8:10   for the **j** of the LORD is your
       8:12   of food and to celebrate with great **j**,
       8:17   And their **j** was very great.
      12:43   because God had given them great **j**.
Est   8:16   it was a time of happiness and **j**,
       8:17   there was **j** and gladness among
       9:17   and made it a day of feasting and **j**.
       9:18   and made it a day of feasting and **j**
       9:19   of the month of Adar as a day of **j**
       9:22   when their sorrow was turned into **j**
       9:22   the days as days of feasting and **j**
Job   3: 7   may no shout of **j** be heard in it.
       6:10   my **j** in unrelenting pain—that I had
       8:21   and your lips with shouts of **j**.

Job   9:25   fly away without a glimpse of **j**.
      10:20   from me so I can have a moment's **j**
      20: 5   brief, the **j** of the godless lasts
      33:26   will see God's face and shout for **j**;
      38: 7   and all the angels shouted for **j**?
Ps    4: 7   Fill my heart with **j** when their grain
       5:11   you be glad; let them ever sing for **j**.
      16:11   you will fill me with **j** in your
      19: 8   are right, giving **j** to the heart.
      20: 5   we shout for **j** over your victory
      21: 1   How great is his **j** in the victories
      21. 6   glad with the **j** of your presence.
      27: 6   I will sacrifice with shouts of **j**;
      28: 7   My heart leaps for **j**, and with my
      30:11   my sackcloth and clothed me with **j**,
      33: 3   play skillfully, and shout for **j**.
      35:27   delight in my vindication shout for **j**
      42: 4   of the Mighty One with shouts of **j**.
      43: 4   God, to God, my **j** and my delight.
      45: 7   by anointing you with the oil of **j**.
      45:15   Led in with **j** and gladness,
      47: 1   shout to God with cries of **j**.
      47: 5   God has ascended amid shouts of **j**,
      48: 2   its loftiness, the **j** of the whole earth,
      51: 8   Let me hear **j** and gladness;
      51:12   Restore to me the **j** of your salvation
      65: 8   fades, you call forth songs of **j**.
      65:13   they shout for **j** and sing.
      66: 1   Shout for **j** to God, all the earth!
      67: 4   the nations be glad and sing for **j**,
      71:23   My lips will shout for **j** when I sing
      81: 1   Sing for **j** to God our strength;
      86: 4   Bring **j** to your servant, Lord, for I
      89:12   and Hermon sing for **j** at your name.
      90:14   that we may sing for **j** and be glad
      92: 4   I sing for **j** at what your hands have
      94:19   me, your consolation brought me **j**.
      95: 1   let us sing for **j** to the LORD;
      96:12   all the trees of the forest sing for **j**.
      97:11   and **j** on the upright in heart.
      98: 4   Shout for **j** to the LORD,
      98: 6   shout for **j** before the LORD,
      98: 8   let the mountains sing together for **j**;
     100: 1   Shout for **j** to the LORD,
     105:43   his chosen ones with shouts of **j**;
     106: 5   I may share in the **j** of your nation
     107:22   and tell of his works with songs of **j**.
     118:15   Shouts of **j** and victory resound
     119:111   they are the **j** of my heart.
     126: 2   our tongues with songs of **j**.
     126: 3   for us, and we are filled with **j**.
     126: 5   with tears will reap with songs of **j**.
     126: 6   will return with songs of **j**,
     132: 9   your faithful people sing for **j**.' "
     132:16   faithful people will ever sing for **j**.
     137: 3   tormentors demanded songs of **j**;
     137: 6   not consider Jerusalem my highest **j**.
     149: 5   honor and sing for **j** on their beds.
Pr   10: 1   Wise children bring **j** to their father,
      10:28   The prospect of the righteous is **j**.
      11:10   wicked perish, there are shouts of **j**.
      12:20   those who promote peace have **j**.
      14:10   and no one else can share its **j**.
      15:20   Wise children bring **j** to their father,
      15:21   Folly brings **j** to those who have no
      15:23   A person finds **j** in giving an apt
      15:30   in a messenger's eyes brings **j**

| | | |
|---|---|---|
| Pr | 17:21 | there is no **j** for the parent |
| | 21:15 | it brings **j** to the righteous but terror |
| | 23:24 | of a righteous child has great **j**; |
| | 27: 9 | and incense bring **j** to the heart, |
| | 27:11 | my child, and bring **j** to my heart; |
| | 29: 3 | A man who loves wisdom brings **j** |
| | 29: 6 | righteous shout for **j** and are glad. |
| Ecc | 8:15 | **j** will accompany them in their toil |
| | 11: 9 | let your hearts give you **j** in the days |
| Isa | 9: 3 | the nation and increased their **j**; |
| | 12: 3 | With **j** you will draw water |
| | 12: 6 | Shout aloud and sing for **j**, |
| | 16: 9 | shouts of **j** over your ripened fruit |
| | 16:10 | **J** and gladness are taken away |
| | 22:13 | But see, there is **j** and revelry, |
| | 24:11 | all **j** turns to gloom, all gaiety is |
| | 24:14 | raise their voices, they shout for **j**; |
| | 26:19 | in the dust wake up and shout for **j**— |
| | 35: 2 | will rejoice greatly and shout for **j**. |
| | 35: 6 | and the mute tongue shout for **j**. |
| | 35:10 | everlasting **j** will crown their heads. |
| | 35:10 | Gladness and **j** will overtake them, |
| | 42:11 | Let the people of Sela sing for **j**; |
| | 44:23 | Sing for **j**, you heavens, |
| | 48:20 | Announce this with shouts of **j** |
| | 49:13 | Shout for **j**, you heavens; |
| | 51: 3 | **J** and gladness will be found in her, |
| | 51:11 | everlasting **j** will crown their heads. |
| | 51:11 | Gladness and **j** will overtake them, |
| | 52: 8 | together they shout for **j**. |
| | 52: 9 | Burst into songs of **j** together, |
| | 54: 1 | shout for **j**, you who were never |
| | 55:12 | You will go out in **j** and be led forth |
| | 56: 7 | give them **j** in my house of prayer. |
| | 58:14 | you will find your **j** in the LORD, |
| | 60: 5 | heart will throb and swell with **j**; |
| | 60:15 | pride and the **j** of all generations. |
| | 61: 3 | the oil of **j** instead of mourning, |
| | 61: 7 | land, and everlasting **j** will be yours. |
| | 65:14 | will sing out of the **j** of their hearts, |
| | 65:18 | to be a delight and its people a **j**. |
| | 66: 5 | glorified, that we may see your **j**!' |
| Jer | 7:34 | I will bring an end to the sounds of **j** |
| | 15:16 | they were my **j** and my heart's |
| | 16: 9 | I will bring an end to the sounds of **j** |
| | 25:10 | banish from them the sounds of **j** |
| | 31: 7 | "Sing with **j** for Jacob; |
| | 31:12 | shout for **j** on the heights of Zion; |
| | 31:13 | comfort and **j** instead of sorrow. |
| | 33: 9 | this city will bring me renown, **j**, |
| | 33:11 | the sounds of **j** and gladness, |
| | 48:33 | **J** and gladness are gone |
| | 48:33 | no one treads them with shouts of **j**. |
| | 48:33 | they are not shouts of **j**. |
| | 51:48 | them will shout for **j** over Babylon, |
| La | 2:15 | of beauty, the **j** of the whole earth?" |
| | 5:15 | **J** is gone from our hearts; |
| Eze | 7: 7 | is panic, not **j**, on the mountains. |
| | 24:25 | their stronghold, their **j** and glory, |
| Joel | 1:12 | Surely the people's **j** is withered |
| | 1:16 | **j** and gladness from the house of our |
| Mt | 13:20 | word and at once receive it with **j**. |
| | 13:44 | in his **j** went and sold all he had |
| | 28: 8 | afraid yet filled with **j**, and ran |
| Mk | 4:16 | word and at once receive it with **j**. |
| Lk | 1:14 | He will be a **j** and delight to you, |
| | 1:44 | the baby in my womb leaped for **j**. |

| | | |
|---|---|---|
| Lk | 1:58 | great mercy, and they shared her **j**. |
| | 2:10 | good news of great **j** that will be |
| | 6:23 | "Rejoice in that day and leap for **j**, |
| | 8:13 | ones who receive the word with **j** |
| | 10:17 | The seventy-two returned with **j** |
| | 10:21 | full of **j** through the Holy Spirit, |
| | 24:41 | still did not believe it because of **j** |
| | 24:52 | returned to Jerusalem with great **j**. |
| Jn | 3:29 | and is full of **j** when he hears |
| | 3:29 | That **j** is mine, and it is now |
| | 15:11 | told you this so that my **j** may be |
| | 15:11 | and that your **j** may be complete. |
| | 16:20 | grieve, but your grief will turn to **j**. |
| | 16:21 | because of her **j** that a child is born |
| | 16:22 | and no one will take away your **j**. |
| | 16:24 | receive, and your **j** will be complete. |
| | 17:13 | full measure of my **j** within them. |
| Ac | 2:28 | you will fill me with **j** in your |
| | 8: 8 | So there was great **j** in that city. |
| | 13:52 | the disciples were filled with **j** |
| | 14:17 | of food and fills your hearts with **j**." |
| | 16:34 | filled with **j** because he had come |
| Ro | 14:17 | peace and **j** in the Holy Spirit, |
| | 15:13 | the God of hope fill you with all **j** |
| | 15:32 | God's will I may come to you with **j** |
| 2Co | 1:24 | but we work with you for your **j**, |
| | 2: 3 | you, that you would all share my **j**. |
| | 7: 4 | our troubles my **j** knows no bounds. |
| | 7: 7 | so that my **j** was greater than ever. |
| | 8: 2 | trial, their overflowing **j** and their |
| Gal | 4:15 | What has happened to all your **j**? |
| | 4:27 | shout for **j** and cry aloud, |
| | 5:22 | But the fruit of the Spirit is love, **j**, |
| Php | 1: 4 | for all of you, I always pray with **j** |
| | 1:25 | for your progress and **j** in the faith, |
| | 2: 2 | then make my **j** complete by being |
| | 2:29 | him in the Lord with great **j**, |
| | 4: 1 | I love and long for, my **j** and crown, |
| 1Th | 1: 6 | severe suffering with the **j** given |
| | 2:19 | our **j**, or the crown in which we will |
| | 2:20 | Indeed, you are our glory and **j**. |
| | 3: 9 | in return for all the **j** we have |
| 2Ti | 1: 4 | you, so that I may be filled with **j**. |
| Phm | 1: 7 | Your love has given me great **j** |
| Heb | 1: 9 | by anointing you with the oil of **j**." |
| | 12: 2 | the **j** set before him he endured |
| | 13:17 | this so that their work will be a **j**, |
| Jas | 1: 2 | Consider it pure **j**, my brothers |
| | 4: 9 | to mourning and your **j** to gloom. |
| 1Pe | 1: 8 | with an inexpressible and glorious **j**, |
| 1Jn | 1: 4 | write this to make our **j** complete. |
| 2Jn | 1: 4 | It has given me great **j** to find some |
| | 1:12 | face, so that our **j** may be complete. |
| 3Jn | 1: 3 | It gave me great **j** to have some |
| | 1: 4 | I have no greater **j** than to hear |
| Jude | 1:24 | without fault and with great **j**— |

## JOYFUL* [JOY]

| | | |
|---|---|---|
| Dt | 16:14 | Be **j** at your festival— |
| 1Sa | 18: 6 | with **j** songs and with timbrels |
| 1Ki | 8:66 | **j** and glad in heart for all the good |
| 1Ch | 15:16 | to make a **j** sound with musical |
| 2Ch | 7:10 | **j** and glad in heart for the good |
| Ps | 68: 3 | may they be happy and **j**. |
| | 100: 2 | come before him with **j** songs. |
| Pr | 23:25 | may she who gave you birth be **j**! |
| Ecc | 9: 7 | and drink your wine with a **j** heart, |

Isa 24: 8 has stopped, the **j** harp is silent.
Jer 31: 4 and go out to dance with the **j**.
Hab 3:18 I will be **j** in God my Savior.
Zec 8:19 tenth months will become **j** and glad
    10: 7 Their children will see it and be **j**;
Ro 12:12 Be **j** in hope, patient in affliction,
Col 1:12 and giving **j** thanks to the Father,
Heb 12:22 thousands of angels in **j** assembly,

## JOYFULLY* [JOY]

Dt 28:47 not serve the LORD your God **j**
2Ch 20:27 Jerusalem returned **j** to Jerusalem,
    30:23 seven days they celebrated **j**.
Ne 12:27 to celebrate **j** the dedication
Job 39:13 "The wings of the ostrich flap **j**,
Ps 33: 1 Sing **j** to the LORD, you righteous;
    145: 7 and **j** sing of your righteousness.
Lk 15: 5 finds it, he **j** puts it on his shoulders
    19:37 of disciples began **j** to praise God
Heb 10:34 **j** accepted the confiscation of your

## JOYOUS* [JOY]

Est 8:15 the city of Susa held a **j** celebration.

## JOZABAD

2Ki 12:21 who murdered him were **J** son
Ezr 8:33 so were the Levites **J** son of Jeshua

## JOZADAK

1Ch 6:15 **J** was deported when the LORD
Hag 1:12 Joshua son of **J**, the high priest,

## JUBILANT*

1Ch 16:32 let the fields be **j**, and everything
Ps 94: 3 how long will the wicked be **j**?
    96:12 Let the fields be **j**, and everything
    98: 4 earth, burst into **j** song with music;
Hos 9: 1 do not be **j** like the other nations.

## JUBILEE

Lev 25:11 The fiftieth year shall be a **j** for you;
    27:17 a field during the Year of **J**,
Nu 36: 4 When the Year of **J** for the Israelites

## JUDAH [JUDEA, JUDEAN]

1. Son of Jacob by Leah (Ge 29:35; 35:23; 1Ch 2:1). Did not want to kill Joseph (Ge 37:26–27). Among Canaanites, fathered Perez by Tamar (Ge 38). Tribe of blessed as ruling tribe (Ge 49:8–12; Dt 33:7), numbered (Nu 1:27; 26:22), allotted land (Jos 15; Eze 48:7), failed to fully possess (Jos 15:63; Jdg 1:1–20).
2. Name used for people and land of Southern Kingdom.
Ru 1: 7 take them back to the land of **J**.
2Sa 2: 4 David king over the house of **J**.
    5: 5 he reigned over **J** seven years
    24: 1 and take a census of Israel and **J**."
1Ch 28: 4 He chose **J** as leader,
    28: 4 the house of **J** he chose my family,
Ne 6: 7 'There is a king in **J**!'
Isa 1: 1 The vision concerning **J**
    3: 8 Jerusalem staggers, **J** is falling;
Jer 2:28 For you, **J**, have as many gods as
    13:19 All **J** will be carried into exile,
    30: 3 Israel and **J** back from captivity

Jer 31:31 of Israel and with the house of **J**.
La 1: 3 harsh labor, **J** has gone into exile.
Hos 1: 7 I will show love to the house of **J**;
Joel 3: 1 when I restore the fortunes of **J**
Mic 5: 2 you are small among the clans of **J**,
Zec 1:19 are the horns that scattered **J**,
    8:15 to do good again to Jerusalem and **J**.
    10: 4 From **J** will come the cornerstone,
    11:14 breaking the family bond between **J**
Mal 2:11 **J** has been unfaithful.
Mt 2: 6 in the land of **J**, are by no means
Heb 7:14 that our Lord descended from **J**,
    8: 8 of Israel and with the house of **J**.
Rev 5: 5 the Lion of the tribe of **J**, the Root

## HOUSE OF JUDAH See HOUSE

## ISRAEL AND JUDAH See ISRAEL

## KING OF JUDAH See KING

## KINGS OF JUDAH See KINGS

## MEN OF JUDAH Jdg 1:3, 8, 17, 19; 2Sa 2:4;
    19:14, 15, 16, 41, 42, 43, 43; 20:2, 4; 2Ki 25:25;
    2Ch 13:15, 18; 14:13; 16:6; 20:13, 24, 27; 23:8;
    Ezr 10:9; Ne 13:23; Jer 17:25; 41:3

## PEOPLE OF JUDAH Nu 2:3; Jos 14:6; 15:12,
    63; 18:14; Jdg 1:16; 15:10; 2Sa 1:18; 1Ki 4:20;
    2Ki 14:21; 16:6; 23:2; 1Ch 2:10; 4:27; 2Ch 20:4,
    18; 25:5; 26:1; 32:9; 34:9, 30; Ezr 4:4, 6; Ne
    4:16; 11:25; 13:16; Isa 5:3, 7; 11:12; Jer 4:3, 4;
    7:2, 30; 11:2, 9; 17:20; 18:11; 25:1, 2; 26:18;
    32:32; 35:13; 36:3, 6, 31; 44:24; 50:4, 33; Eze
    25:3; Da 9:7; Hos 1:11; 5:12; Joel 3:6, 8, 19; Ob
    1:12

## TRIBE OF JUDAH Ex 31:2; 35:30; 38:22; Nu
    1:27; 7:12; 13:6; 34:19; Jos 7:1, 18; 15:1, 20, 21;
    1Ki 12:20; 2Ki 17:18; 1Ch 4:18; 2Ch 19:11; Ps
    78:68; Rev 5:5; 7:5

## JUDAISM* [JEW]

Ac 2:11 (both Jews and converts to **J**);
    6: 5 from Antioch, a convert to **J**.
    13:43 devout converts to **J** followed Paul
Gal 1:13 of my previous way of life in **J**,
    1:14 I was advancing in **J** beyond many

## JUDAS [ISCARIOT]

1. Apostle; son of James (Lk 6:16; Jn 14:22; Ac 1:13). Probably also called Thaddaeus (Mt 10:3; Mk 3:18).
2. Brother of James and Jesus (Mt 13:55; Mk 6:3), also called Jude (Jude 1).
3. Christian prophet (Ac 15:22–32).
4. Apostle, also called Iscariot, who betrayed Jesus (Mt 10:4; 26:14–56; Mk 3:19; 14:10–50; Lk 6:16; 22:3–53; Jn 6:71; 12:4; 13:2–30; 18:2–11). Suicide of (Mt 27:3–5; Ac 1:16–25).

## JUDE*

Jude 1: 1 **J**, a servant of Jesus Christ

## JUDEA [JUDAH]

Mt 2: 1 Jesus was born in Bethlehem in **J**,
    3: 1 preaching in the wilderness of **J**

| | | |
|---|---|---|
| Mt | 24:16 | let those who are in **J** flee |
| Mk | 3: 8 | many people came to him from **J**, |
| Lk | 1: 5 | king of **J** there was a priest named |
| | 3: 1 | Pontius Pilate was governor of **J**, |
| | 7:17 | about Jesus spread throughout **J** |
| Ac | 1: 8 | and in all **J** and Samaria, |
| | 8: 1 | apostles were scattered throughout **J** |
| | 9:31 | Then the church throughout **J**, |
| 1Th | 2:14 | imitators of God's churches in **J**, |

## JUDEAN [JUDAH]

| | | |
|---|---|---|
| Mk | 1: 5 | The whole **J** countryside and all |

## JUDGE [JUDGE'S, JUDGED, JUDGES, JUDGING, JUDGMENT, JUDGMENTS]

| | | |
|---|---|---|
| Ge | 16: 5 | May the LORD **j** between you |
| | 18:25 | Will not the **J** of all the earth do |
| | 19: 9 | and now he wants to play the **j**! |
| | 31:53 | God of their father, **j** between us." |
| Ex | 2:14 | made you ruler and **j** over us? |
| | 18:14 | Why do you alone sit as **j**, while all |
| Lev | 19:15 | the great, but **j** your neighbor fairly. |
| Dt | 1:16 | between your people and **j** fairly, |
| | 17: 9 | to the **j** who is in office at that time. |
| Jdg | 2:18 | the LORD raised up a **j** for them, |
| | 11:27 | the **J**, decide the dispute this day |
| 1Sa | 2:10 | the LORD will **j** the ends |
| | 3:13 | I would **j** his family forever because |
| | 24:12 | May the LORD **j** between you |
| 1Ki | 8:32 | **J** between your servants, |
| 1Ch | 16:33 | LORD, for he comes to **j** the earth. |
| 2Ch | 6:23 | **J** between your servants, |
| | 19: 7 | **J** carefully, for with the LORD our |
| Job | 9:15 | only plead with my **J** for mercy. |
| Ps | 7: 8 | Let the LORD **j** the peoples. |
| | 7:11 | God is a righteous **j**, a God who |
| | 9: 4 | sitting enthroned as the righteous **j**. |
| | 51: 4 | verdict and justified when you **j**. |
| | 75: 2 | it is I who **j** with equity. |
| | 76: 9 | rose up to **j**, to save all the afflicted |
| | 82: 8 | up, O God, **j** the earth, for all |
| | 94: 2 | Rise up, **J** of the earth; pay back |
| | 96:10 | he will **j** the peoples with equity. |
| | 96:13 | he comes, he comes to **j** the earth. |
| | 96:13 | He will **j** the world in righteousness |
| | 98: 9 | for he comes to **j** the earth. |
| | 98: 9 | He will **j** the world in righteousness |
| | 110: 6 | He will **j** the nations, |
| Pr | 31: 9 | Speak up and **j** fairly; |
| Isa | 2: 4 | He will **j** between the nations |
| | 3:13 | he rises to **j** the people. |
| | 11: 3 | He will not **j** by what he sees |
| | 33:22 | For the LORD is our **j**, the LORD |
| Jer | 11:20 | who **j** righteously and test the heart |
| Eze | 7: 3 | I will **j** you according to your |
| | 7:27 | by their own standards I will **j** them. |
| | 18:30 | I will **j** each of you according |
| | 20:36 | Egypt, so I will **j** you, |
| | 22: 2 | Will you **j** this city of bloodshed? |
| | 33:20 | But I will **j** each of you according |
| | 34:17 | I will **j** between one sheep |
| Joel | 3:12 | there I will sit to **j** all the nations |
| Mic | 3:11 | Her leaders **j** for a bribe, her priests |
| | 4: 3 | He will **j** between many peoples |
| Mt | 7: 1 | "Do not **j**, or you too will be |

| | | |
|---|---|---|
| Lk | 6:37 | "Do not **j**, and you will not be |
| | 12:14 | who appointed me a **j** or an arbiter |
| | 18: 2 | there was a **j** who neither feared |
| | 19:22 | 'I will **j** you by your own words, |
| Jn | 5:27 | authority to **j** because he is the Son |
| | 5:30 | I **j** only as I hear, and my judgment |
| | 7:24 | but instead **j** correctly." |
| | 8:16 | But if I do **j**, my decisions are true, |
| | 12:47 | For I did not come to **j** the world, |
| | 12:48 | There is a **j** for those who reject me |
| | 18:31 | and **j** him by your own law." |
| Ac | 7:27 | 'Who made you ruler and **j** over us? |
| | 10:42 | is the one whom God appointed as **j** |
| | 17:31 | set a day when he will **j** the world |
| Ro | 2: 1 | for at whatever point you **j** another, |
| | 3: 4 | you speak and prevail when you **j**." |
| | 3: 6 | so, how could God **j** the world? |
| | 14:10 | why do you **j** your brother or sister? |
| 1Co | 4: 3 | indeed, I do not even **j** myself. |
| | 4: 5 | Therefore **j** nothing before |
| | 5:12 | Are you not to **j** those inside? |
| | 6: 2 | the Lord's people will **j** the world? |
| | 6: 3 | you not know that we will **j** angels? |
| Col | 2:16 | Therefore do not let anyone **j** you |
| 2Ti | 4: 1 | who will **j** the living and the dead, |
| | 4: 8 | the righteous **J**, will award to me |
| Heb | 10:30 | "The Lord will **j** his people." |
| | 12:23 | You have come to God, the **J** of all, |
| | 13: 4 | for God will **j** the adulterer and all |
| Jas | 4:12 | There is only one Lawgiver and **J**, |
| | 4:12 | who are you to **j** your neighbor? |
| | 5: 9 | The **J** is standing at the door! |
| 1Pe | 4: 5 | to him who is ready to **j** the living |
| Jude | 1:15 | to **j** everyone, and to convict all |
| Rev | 6:10 | until you **j** the inhabitants |
| | 20: 4 | who had been given authority to **j**. |

## JUDGE'S* [JUDGE]

| | | |
|---|---|---|
| Mt | 27:19 | Pilate was sitting on the **j** seat, |
| Jn | 19:13 | and sat down on the **j** seat at a place |

## JUDGED [JUDGE]

| | | |
|---|---|---|
| Ps | 9:19 | let the nations be **j** in your presence. |
| Eze | 20:36 | As I **j** your ancestors |
| | 24:14 | You will be **j** according to your |
| Mt | 7: 1 | "Do not judge, or you too will be **j**. |
| Jn | 5:24 | will not be **j** but has crossed over |
| Ro | 2:12 | all who sin under the law will be **j** |
| 1Co | 4: 3 | I care very little if I am **j** by you |
| | 10:29 | For why is my freedom being **j** |
| Jas | 2:12 | who are going to be **j** by the law |
| | 3: 1 | we who teach will be **j** more strictly. |
| | 5: 9 | brothers and sisters, or you will be **j**. |
| Rev | 16: 5 | Holy One, because you have so **j**; |
| | 18:20 | God has **j** her with the judgment she |
| | 20:12 | The dead were **j** according to what |

## JUDGES [JUDGE]

### The Judges of Israel

| Judge | Oppressor | Peace | Text |
|---|---|---|---|
| Othniel | Aram | 40 years | Jdg 3:7–11 |
| Ehud | Moab | 80 years | Jdg 3:12–30 |
| Shamgar | Philistia | | Jdg 3:31 |
| Deborah | Canaan | 40 years | Jdg 4–5 |

| | | | |
|---|---|---|---|
| Gideon | Midian | 40 years | Jdg 6–8 |
| Tola | | 23 years | Jdg 10:1–2 |
| Jair | | 22 years | Jdg 10:3–5 |
| Jephthah | Ammon | 6 years | Jdg 10:6—12:7 |
| Ibzan | | 7 years | Jdg 12:8–10 |
| Elon | | 10 years | Jdg 12:11–12 |
| Abdon | | 8 years | Jdg 12:13–15 |
| Samson | Philistia | 20 years | Jdg 13–16 |

See also each judge by name

| | | |
|---|---|---|
| Ex | 18.22 | Have them serve as **j** for the people |
| Jdg | 2:16 | Then the LORD raised up **j**, |
| Ru | 1: 1 | In the days when the **j** ruled, |
| Job | 9:24 | of the wicked, he blindfolds its **j**. |
| Ps | 9: 8 | and **j** the peoples with equity. |
| | 58:11 | there is a God who **j** the earth." |
| | 75: 7 | It is God who **j**: He brings one |
| Pr | 29:14 | If a king **j** the poor with fairness, |
| Lk | 11:19 | So then, they will be your **j**. |
| Jn | 5:22 | Moreover, the Father **j** no one, |
| Ac | 4:19 | to you, or to him? You be the **j**! |
| Ro | 2:16 | God **j** everyone's secrets through |
| 1Co | 4: 4 | It is the Lord who **j** me. |
| Heb | 4:12 | it **j** the thoughts and attitudes |
| Jas | 4:11 | **j** them speaks against the law and **j** it. |
| 1Pe | 1:17 | a Father who **j** each person's work |
| | 2:23 | himself to him who **j** justly. |
| Rev | 18: 8 | mighty is the Lord God who **j** her. |
| | 19:11 | With justice he **j** and makes war. |

## JUDGING [JUDGE]

| | | |
|---|---|---|
| Dt | 1:17 | Do not show partiality in **j**; |
| Pr | 24:23 | To show partiality in **j** is not good: |
| Isa | 16: 5 | one who in **j** seeks justice |
| Mt | 19:28 | thrones, **j** the twelve tribes of Israel. |
| Jn | 7:24 | Stop **j** by mere appearances, |
| 2Co | 10: 7 | You are **j** by appearances. |
| Rev | 11:18 | The time has come for **j** the dead, |

## JUDGMENT [JUDGE]

| | | |
|---|---|---|
| Ex | 6: 6 | arm and with mighty acts of **j**. |
| | 12:12 | and I will bring **j** on all the gods |
| Nu | 33: 4 | the LORD had brought **j** on their |
| Dt | 1:17 | of anyone, for **j** belongs to God. |
| | 32:41 | sword and my hand grasps it in **j**, |
| 1Sa | 25:33 | May you be blessed for your good **j** |
| Job | 24: 1 | the Almighty not set times for **j**? |
| Ps | 1: 5 | the wicked will not stand in the **j**, |
| | 9: 7 | he has established his throne for **j**. |
| | 76: 8 | From heaven you pronounced **j**, |
| | 82: 1 | he gives **j** among the "gods": |
| | 119:66 | Teach me knowledge and good **j**, |
| | 122: 5 | There stand the thrones for **j**, |
| | 143: 2 | Do not bring your servant into **j**, |
| Pr | 3:21 | preserve sound **j** and discretion; |
| | 8:14 | Counsel and sound **J** are mine; |
| | 18: 1 | against all sound **j** starts quarrels. |
| Ecc | 3:17 | will bring into **j** both the righteous |
| | 11: 9 | things God will bring you into **j**. |
| | 12:14 | God will bring every deed into **j**, |
| Isa | 3:14 | enters into **j** against the elders |
| | 28: 6 | spirit of justice to those who sit in **j**, |
| | 53: 8 | oppression and **j** he was taken away. |
| | 66:16 | his sword the LORD will execute **j** |
| Jer | 2:35 | But I will pass **j** on you because you |
| | 25:31 | he will bring **j** on all humankind |

| | | |
|---|---|---|
| Jer | 51:18 | when their **j** comes, they will perish. |
| Eze | 11:10 | and I will execute **j** on you |
| Da | 7:22 | pronounced **j** in favor of the holy |
| Joel | 3: 2 | into **j** against them concerning my |
| Am | 7: 4 | Sovereign LORD was calling for **j** |
| Hab | 1:12 | have appointed them to execute **j**; |
| Zec | 8:16 | true and sound **j** in your courts; |
| Mt | 5:21 | who murders will be subject to **j**.' |
| | 5:22 | brother or sister will be subject to **j**. |
| | 10:15 | Gomorrah on the day of **j** than |
| | 11:24 | on the day of **j** than for you." |
| | 12:36 | the day of **j** for every empty word |
| | 12:41 | stand up at the **j** with this generation |
| Jn | 5:22 | but has entrusted all **j** to the Son, |
| | 5:30 | and my **j** is just, for I seek not |
| | 8:26 | "I have much to say in **j** of you. |
| | 9:39 | "For **j** I have come into this world, |
| | 12:31 | Now is the time for **j** on this world; |
| | 16: 8 | about sin and righteousness and **j**: |
| | 16:11 | and about **j**, because the prince |
| Ac | 24:25 | self-control and the **j** to come, |
| Ro | 2: 1 | because you who pass **j** do the same |
| | 2: 2 | God's **j** against those who do such |
| | 5:16 | The **j** followed one sin and brought |
| | 12: 3 | rather think of yourself with sober **j**, |
| | 14:10 | will all stand before God's **j** seat. |
| | 14:13 | Therefore let us stop passing **j** |
| 1Co | 7:40 | In my **j**, she is happier if she stays |
| | 11:29 | eat and drink **j** on themselves. |
| | 14:24 | are brought under **j** by all, |
| 2Co | 5:10 | we must all appear before the **j** seat |
| 2Th | 1: 5 | this is evidence that God's **j** is right, |
| 1Ti | 3: 6 | fall under the same **j** as the devil. |
| | 5:12 | Thus they bring **j** on themselves, |
| Heb | 6: 2 | of the dead, and eternal **j**. |
| | 9:27 | to die once, and after that to face **j**, |
| | 10:27 | only a fearful expectation of **j** |
| Jas | 2:13 | Mercy triumphs over **j**. |
| | 4:11 | not keeping it, but sitting in **j** on it. |
| 1Pe | 4:17 | For it is time for **j** to begin |
| 2Pe | 2: 4 | chains of darkness to be held for **j**; |
| | 2: 9 | for punishment on the day of **j**. |
| | 3: 7 | fire, being kept for the day of **j** |
| 1Jn | 4:17 | have confidence on the day of **j**: |
| Jude | 1: 6 | everlasting chains for **j** on the great |
| Rev | 14: 7 | because the hour of his **j** has come. |

## JUDGMENTS [JUDGE]

| | | |
|---|---|---|
| 1Ch | 16:14 | his **j** are in all the earth. |
| Jer | 1:16 | I will pronounce my **j** on my people |
| Eze | 14:21 | Jerusalem my four dreadful **j**— |
| Da | 9:11 | and sworn **j** written in the Law |
| Hos | 6: 5 | then my **j** go forth like the sun. |
| Ro | 11:33 | How unsearchable his **j**, and his |
| 1Co | 2:15 | the Spirit makes **j** about all things, |
| Rev | 16: 5 | "You are just in these **j**, you who |
| | 16: 7 | Almighty, true and just are your **j**." |
| | 19: 2 | for true and just are his **j**. |

## JUG

| | | |
|---|---|---|
| 1Sa | 26:12 | spear and water **j** near Saul's head, |
| 1Ki | 17:12 | in a jar and a little olive oil in a **j**. |

## JUICE

| | | |
|---|---|---|
| Nu | 6: 3 | They must not drink grape **j** or eat |

## JUMPED* [JUMPING]

| | | |
|---|---|---|
| Mk | 10:50 | he **j** to his feet and came to Jesus. |
| Jn | 21: 7 | taken it off) and **j** into the water. |
| Ac | 3: 8 | He **j** to his feet and began to walk. |
| | 14:10 | the man **j** up and began to walk. |
| | 19:16 | the man who had the evil spirit **j** |

## JUMPING* [JUMPED]

| | | |
|---|---|---|
| Ac | 3: 8 | walking and **j**, and praising God. |

## JUNIPER

| | | |
|---|---|---|
| 1Ki | 5: 8 | providing the cedar and **j** logs. |
| Isa | 60:13 | **j**, the fir and the cypress together, |
| Hos | 14: 8 | I am like a flourishing **j**; |

## JUPITER (KJV) See ZEUS

## JUST [JUSTICE, JUSTIFICATION, JUSTIFIED, JUSTIFIES, JUSTIFY, JUSTIFYING, JUSTLY]

| | | |
|---|---|---|
| Ge | 18:19 | by doing what is right and **j**, |
| Dt | 32: 4 | and all his ways are **j**. |
| | 32: 4 | upright and **j** is he. |
| | 32:47 | They are not **j** idle words for you— |
| 2Sa | 8:15 | doing what was **j** and right for all |
| 1Ch | 18:14 | doing what was **j** and right for all |
| 2Ch | 12: 6 | and said, "The Lord is **j**." |
| Ne | 9:13 | and laws that are **j** and right, |
| Job | 34:17 | Will you condemn the **j** and mighty |
| | 35: 2 | "Do you think this is **j**? You say, |
| Ps | 37:28 | For the Lord loves the **j** and will |
| | 37:30 | and their tongues speak what is **j**. |
| | 99: 4 | in Jacob you have done what is **j** |
| | 111: 7 | of his hands are faithful and **j**; |
| | 119:121 | I have done what is righteous and **j**; |
| Pr | 1: 3 | doing what is right and **j** and fair; |
| | 2: 8 | for he guards the course of the **j** |
| | 2: 9 | will understand what is right and **j** |
| | 8: 8 | All the words of my mouth are **j**; |
| | 8:15 | and rulers issue decrees that are **j**; |
| | 12: 5 | The plans of the righteous are **j**, |
| | 21: 3 | **j** is more acceptable to the Lord |
| Isa | 32: 7 | even when the plea of the needy is **j**. |
| | 58: 2 | They ask me for **j** decisions |
| Jer | 4: 2 | **j** and righteous way you swear, |
| | 22: 3 | Do what is **j** and right. |
| | 22:15 | He did what was right and **j**, so all |
| | 23: 5 | do what is **j** and right in the land. |
| | 33:15 | he will do what is **j** and right |
| Eze | 18: 5 | a righteous man who does what is **j** |
| | 18:19 | Since the son has done what is **j** |
| | 18:21 | decrees and do what is **j** and right, |
| | 18:25 | say, 'The way of the Lord is not **j**.' |
| | 18:27 | and do what is **j** and right, they will |
| | 18:29 | says, 'The way of the Lord is not **j**.' |
| | 33:14 | sins and do what is **j** and right— |
| | 33:16 | They have done what is **j** and right; |
| | 33:17 | say, 'The way of the Lord is not **j**.' |
| | 33:17 | But it is their way that is not **j**. |
| | 33:19 | and do what is **j** and right, they will |
| | 33:20 | 'The way of the Lord is not **j**.' |
| | 45: 9 | and do what is **j** and right. |
| Da | 4:37 | does right and all his ways are **j**. |
| Lk | 8:50 | **j** believe, and she will be healed." |
| Jn | 5:30 | and my judgment is **j**, for I seek not |

| | | |
|---|---|---|
| Ro | 3: 8 | Their condemnation is **j**! |
| | 3:26 | time, so as to be **j** and the one who |
| 2Th | 1: 6 | God is **j**: He will pay back trouble |
| Heb | 2: 2 | received its **j** punishment, |
| 1Jn | 1: 9 | he is faithful and **j** and will forgive |
| Rev | 15: 3 | **J** and true are your ways, |
| | 16: 5 | "You are **j** in these judgments, |
| | 16: 7 | true and **j** are your judgments." |
| | 19: 2 | for true and **j** are his judgments. |

## JUSTICE* [JUST]

| | | |
|---|---|---|
| Ge | 49:16 | "Dan will provide **j** for his people |
| Ex | 23: 2 | do not pervert **j** by siding |
| | 23: 6 | "Do not deny **j** to your poor people |
| Lev | 19:15 | " 'Do not pervert **j**; do not show |
| Dt | 16:19 | Do not pervert **j** or show partiality. |
| | 16:20 | Follow **j** and **j** alone, so that you |
| | 24:17 | the foreigner or the fatherless of **j**, |
| | 27:19 | "Cursed is anyone who withholds **j** |
| 1Sa | 8: 3 | and accepted bribes and perverted **j**. |
| 2Sa | 15: 4 | and I would see that they receive **j**." |
| | 15: 6 | who came to the king asking for **j**, |
| 1Ki | 3:11 | for discernment in administering **j**, |
| | 3:28 | wisdom from God to administer **j**. |
| | 7: 7 | hall, the Hall of **J**, where he was |
| | 10: 9 | he has made you king to maintain **j** |
| 2Ch | 9: 8 | to maintain **j** and righteousness." |
| Ezr | 7:25 | to administer **j** to all the people |
| Est | 1:13 | experts in matters of law and **j**, |
| Job | 8: 3 | Does God pervert **j**? |
| | 9:19 | And if it is a matter of **j**, who can |
| | 19: 7 | though I call for help, there is no **j**. |
| | 27: 2 | who has denied me **j**, the Almighty, |
| | 29:14 | **j** was my robe and my turban. |
| | 31:13 | "If I have denied **j** to any of my |
| | 34: 5 | am innocent, but God denies me **j**. |
| | 34:12 | that the Almighty would pervert **j**. |
| | 34:17 | Can one who hates **j** govern? |
| | 36: 3 | I will ascribe **j** to my Maker. |
| | 36:17 | and **j** have taken hold of you. |
| | 37:23 | in his **j** and great righteousness, |
| | 40: 8 | "Would you discredit my **j**? |
| Ps | 7: 6 | Awake, my God; decree **j**. |
| | 9:16 | Lord is known by his acts of **j**; |
| | 11: 7 | the Lord is righteous, he loves **j**; |
| | 33: 5 | Lord loves righteousness and **j**; |
| | 36: 6 | your **j** like the great deep. |
| | 45: 4 | the cause of truth, humility and **j**; |
| | 45: 6 | a scepter of **j** will be the scepter |
| | 50: 6 | for he is a God of **j**. |
| | 72: 1 | Endow the king with your **j**, O God, |
| | 72: 2 | your afflicted ones with **j**. |
| | 89:14 | **j** are the foundation of your throne; |
| | 97: 2 | **j** are the foundation of his throne. |
| | 99: 4 | The King is mighty, he loves **j**— |
| | 101: 1 | I will sing of your love and **j**; |
| | 103: 6 | and **j** for all the oppressed. |
| | 112: 5 | who conduct their affairs with **j**. |
| | 140:12 | the Lord secures **j** for the poor |
| Pr | 8:20 | righteousness, along the paths of **j**, |
| | 16:10 | and his mouth does not betray **j**. |
| | 17:23 | in secret to pervert the course of **j**. |
| | 18: 5 | and so deprive the innocent of **j**. |
| | 19:28 | A corrupt witness mocks at **j**, |
| | 21:15 | When **j** is done, it brings joy |
| | 29: 4 | By **j** a king gives a country stability, |
| | 29: 7 | The righteous care about **j** |

Pr   29:26  is from the LORD that one gets **j**.
Ecc   3:16  was there, in the place of **j**—
      5: 8  in a district, and **j** and rights denied,
Isa   1:17  Seek **j**, encourage the oppressed.
      1:21  She once was full of **j**;
      1:27  Zion will be delivered with **j**,
      5: 7  And he looked for **j**, but saw
      5:16  Almighty will be exalted by his **j**,
      5:23  a bribe, but deny **j** to the innocent.
      9: 7  and upholding it with **j**
     10: 2  withhold **j** from the oppressed of my
     11: 4  with **j** he will give decisions
     16: 5  one who in judging seeks **j**
     28: 6  He will be a spirit of **j** to those who
     28:17  I will make **j** the measuring line
     29:21  testimony deprive the innocent of **j**.
     30:18  For the LORD is a God of **j**.
     32: 1  and rulers will rule with **j**.
     32:16  The LORD's **j** will dwell
     33: 5  he will fill Zion with his **j**
     42: 1  and he will bring **j** to the nations.
     42: 3  In faithfulness he will bring forth **j**;
     42: 4  be discouraged till he establishes **j**
     51: 4  my **j** will become a light
     51: 5  my arm will bring **j** to the nations.
     56: 1  "Maintain **j** and do what is right,
     59: 4  No one calls for **j**; no one pleads
     59: 8  there is no **j** in their paths.
     59: 9  So **j** is far from us,
     59:11  We look for **j**, but find none;
     59:14  So **j** is driven back,
     59:15  was displeased that there was no **j**.
     61: 8  "For I, the LORD, love **j**;
Jer   5:28  no limit; they do not seek **j**.
      9:24  **j** and righteousness on earth,
     12: 1  would speak with you about your **j**:
     21:12  " 'Administer **j** every morning;
La    3:36  to deprive them of **j**—would not
Eze  22:29  the foreigner, denying them **j**.
     34:16  I will shepherd the flock with **j**.
Hos   2:19  betroth you in righteousness and **j**,
     12: 6  maintain love and **j**, and wait
Am    2: 7  ground and deny **j** to the oppressed.
      5: 7  There are those who turn **j**
      5:12  deprive the poor of **j** in the courts.
      5:15  maintain **j** in the courts.
      5:24  But let **j** roll on like a river,
      6:12  But you have turned **j** into poison
Mic   3: 1  Should you not know **j**,
      3: 8  and with **j** and might, to declare
      3: 9  who despise **j** and distort all that is
Hab   1: 4  and **j** never prevails.
      1: 4  so that **j** is perverted.
Zep   3: 5  by morning dispenses his **j**,
Zec   7: 9  'Administer true **j**; show mercy
Mal   2:17  them" or "Where is the God of **j**?"
      3: 5  the foreigners among you of **j**,
Mt   12:18  he will proclaim **j** to the nations.
     12:20  snuff out, till he leads **j** to victory.
     23:23  **j**, mercy and faithfulness.
Lk   11:42  you neglect **j** and the love of God.
     18: 3  'Grant me **j** against my adversary.'
     18: 5  I will see that she gets **j**, so that she
     18: 7  will not God bring about **j** for his
     18: 8  you, he will see that they get **j**,
Ac    8:33  humiliation he was deprived of **j**.
     17:31  he will judge the world with **j**

Ac   28: 4  the goddess **J** has not allowed him
Ro    3:25  He did this to demonstrate his **j**,
      3:26  it to demonstrate his **j** at the present
2Co   7:11  what readiness to see **j** done.
Heb   1: 8  scepter of **j** will be the scepter
     11:33  administered **j**, and gained what was
Rev  19:11  With **j** he judges and makes war.

## JUSTIFICATION* [JUST]

Eze  16:52  you have furnished some **j** for your
Ac   13:39  a **j** you were not able to obtain under
                 the law
Ro    4:25  sins and was raised to life for our **j**.
      5:16  many trespasses and brought **j**.
      5:18  one righteous act resulted in **j**

## JUSTIFIED* [JUST]

Ps   51: 4  your verdict and **j** when you judge.
Lk   18:14  the other, went home **j** before God.
Ro    3:24  all are **j** freely by his grace through
      3:28  that a person is **j** by faith apart
      4: 2  in fact, Abraham was **j** by works,
      5: 1  since we have been **j** through faith,
      5: 9  Since we have now been **j** by his
      8:30  those he called, he also **j**; those he **j**, he
                 also glorified.
     10:10  heart that you believe and are **j**,
1Co   6:11  you were **j** in the name of the Lord
Gal   2:16  a person is not **j** by observing
      2:16  Jesus that we may be **j** by faith
      2:16  observing the law no one will be **j**.
      2:17  in seeking to be **j** in Christ, we Jews
      3:11  Clearly no one is **j** before God
      3:24  came that we might be **j** by faith.
      5: 4  be **j** by the law have been alienated
Tit   3: 7  so that, having been **j** by his grace,
Jas   2:24  see that people are **j** by what they do

## JUSTIFIES* [JUST]

Ro    3:26  the one who **j** those who have faith
      4: 5  but trusts God who **j** the ungodly,
      8:33  God has chosen? It is God who **j**.

## JUSTIFY* [JUST]

Est   7: 4  such distress would **j** disturbing
Job  40: 8  you condemn me to **j** yourself?
Isa  53:11  my righteous servant will **j** many,
Lk   10:29  But he wanted to **j** himself, so he
     16:15  "You are the ones who **j** yourselves
Ro    3:30  who will **j** the circumcised by faith
Gal   3: 8  that God would **j** the Gentiles

## JUSTIFYING* [JUST]

Job  32: 2  Job for **j** himself rather than God.

## JUSTLY* [JUST]

Ps   58: 1  Do you rulers indeed speak **j**?
    106: 3  Blessed are those who act **j**,
Jer   7: 5  actions and deal with each other **j**,
Mic   6: 8  To act **j** and to love mercy
Lk   23:41  We are punished **j**, for we are
1Pe   2:23  himself to him who judges **j**.

## JUSTUS* [JOSEPH]

Ac    1:23  Joseph called Barsabbas (also known as **J**)

Ac 18: 7 next door to the house of Titius **J**,
Col 4:11 Jesus, who is called **J**, also sends

# K

## KADESH [KADESH BARNEA, MERIBAH KADESH]
Nu 20: 1 Desert of Zin, and they stayed at **K**.
Dt 1:46 And so you stayed in **K** many days—

## KADESH BARNEA [KADESH]
Nu 32: 8 from **K** to look over the land.

## KEBAR
Eze 1: 1 among the exiles by the **K** River,
3:23 the glory I had seen by the **K** River,
43: 3 visions I had seen by the **K** River,

## KEDESH
Jos 12:22 the king of **K** one the king
Jdg 4: 6 son of Abinoam from **K** in Naphtali

## KEDORLAOMER
Ge 14:17 Abram returned from defeating **K**

## KEEP [DOORKEEPER, KEEPER, KEEPING, KEEPS, KEPT]
Ge 6:19 female, to **k** them alive with you.
17: 9 for you, you must **k** my covenant,
31:49 "May the LORD **k** watch between
Ex 15:26 his commands and **k** all his decrees,
19: 5 obey me fully and **k** my covenant,
20: 6 love me and **k** my commandments.
Lev 15:31 " 'You must **k** the Israelites
Nu 6:24 LORD bless you and **k** you;
Dt 4: 2 **k** the commands of the LORD your
5:10 love me and **k** my commandments.
6:17 Be sure to **k** the commands
7: 9 love him and **k** his commandments.
7:12 your God will **k** his covenant
11: 1 your God and **k** his requirements,
13: 4 **K** his commands and obey him;
30:10 your God and **k** his commands
30:16 and to **k** his commands,
Jos 1: 8 **K** this Book of the Law always on your lips;
22: 5 very careful to **k** the commandment
2Sa 7:25 **k** forever the promise you have
1Ki 8:25 **k** for your servant David my father
8:58 to him and **k** the commands,
2Ki 17:19 even Judah did not **k** the commands
23: 3 the LORD and **k** his commands,
1Ch 29:18 and **k** their hearts loyal to you.
2Ch 6:14 you who **k** your covenant of love
34:31 the LORD and **k** his commands,
Ne 1: 5 love him and **k** his commandments,
Job 14:16 my steps but not **k** track of my sin.
Ps 15: 4 who **k** their oaths even when it hurts;
18:28 You, LORD, **k** my lamp burning;
19:13 **K** your servant also from willful
37:34 Hope in the LORD and **k** his way.

Ps 78:10 they did not **k** God's covenant
119: 2 Blessed are those who **k** his statutes
119: 9 who are young **k** their way pure?
121: 7 The LORD will **k** you from all
141: 3 **k** watch over the door of my lips.
Pr 4:21 sight, **k** them within your heart;
4:24 **K** your mouth free of perversity;
7: 2 **K** my commands and you will live;
7: 5 They will **k** you from the adulterous
11:13 but the trustworthy **k** a secret.
12:23 prudent **k** their knowledge to themselves,
15:21 have understanding **k** a straight course.
17:28 fools are thought wise if they **k** silent,
30: 8 **K** falsehood and lies far from me;
Ecc 3: 6 up, a time to **k** and a time to throw
12:13 Fear God and **k** his commandments,
Isa 26: 3 You will **k** in perfect peace those
33:15 and **k** their hands from accepting bribes,
42: 6 I will **k** you and will make you to be
46: 8 "Remember this, **k** it in mind,
56: 2 who **k** the Sabbath without desecrating it,
58:13 "If you **k** your feet from breaking
Jer 16:11 forsook me and did not **k** my law.
Eze 20:19 decrees and be careful to **k** my laws.
Da 9: 4 love him and **k** his commandments,
Am 5:13 the prudent **k** quiet in such times,
Mt 10:10 staff, for workers are worth their **k**.
19:17 want to enter life, **k** the commandments."
Lk 12:35 service and **k** your lamps burning,
17:33 tries to **k** their life will lose it,
Jn 9:16 for he does not **k** the Sabbath."
10:24 saying, "How long will you **k** us
12:25 in this world will **k** it for eternal life.
14:15 "If you love me, **k** my commands.
15:10 If you **k** my commands,
Ac 2:24 for death to **k** its hold on him.
15: 5 and required to **k** the law of Moses."
18: 9 **k** on speaking, do not be silent.
Ro 7:19 not want to do—this I **k** on doing.
12:11 but **k** your spiritual fervor,
14:22 these things **k** between yourself
16:17 **K** away from them.
1Co 1: 8 He will also **k** you firm to the end,
2Co 12: 7 in order to **k** me from becoming
Gal 5:25 let us **k** in step with the Spirit.
Eph 4: 3 Make every effort to **k** the unity
2Th 3: 6 to **k** away from every believer who
1Ti 5:22 the sins of others. **K** yourself pure.
2Ti 1:13 **k** as the pattern of sound teaching,
4: 5 you, **k** your head in all situations,
Heb 9:20 God has commanded you to **k**."
10:26 If we deliberately **k** on sinning
13: 1 **K** on loving one another as brothers
13: 5 **K** your lives free from the love
Jas 1:26 and yet do not **k** a tight rein on their
2: 8 If you really **k** the royal law found
3: 2 able to **k** their whole body in check.
1Pe 3:10 see good days must **k** your tongue
2Pe 1: 8 measure, they will **k** you from being
1Jn 3:24 who **k** his commands live in him,
5: 3 love for God: to **k** his commands.
5:21 children, **k** yourselves from idols.
Jude 1: 6 angels who did not **k** their positions
1:21 **k** yourselves in God's love as you

Jude  1:24  To him who is able to **k** you
Rev   3:10  **k** you from the hour of trial that is
     12:17  those who **k** God's commands
     14:12  people of God who **k** his commands
     22: 7  Blessed are those who **k** the words
     22: 9  and with all who **k** the words of this

## KEEPER [KEEP]

Ge    4: 9  "Am I my brother's **k**?"
Jn   12: 6  as **k** of the money bag, he used

## KEEPING [KEEP]

Ex   20: 8  the Sabbath day by **k** it holy.
Dt    5:12  the Sabbath day by **k** it holy,
      6: 2  long as you live by **k** all his decrees
     13:18  **k** all his commands that I am giving
Ps   19:11  in **k** them there is great reward.
    119:112  My heart is set on **k** your decrees
Pr    6:24  **k** you from your neighbor's wife,
     15: 3  **k** watch on the wicked and the good.
Mt    3: 8  Produce fruit in **k** with repentance.
Lk    2: 8  **k** watch over their flocks at night.
      3: 8  Produce fruit in **k** with repentance.
1Co   7:19  **K** God's commands is what counts.
     16: 2  of money in **k** with your income,
Jas   4:11  law, you are not **k** it, but sitting
1Pe   3:16  **k** a clear conscience, so that those
2Pe   3: 9  Lord is not slow in **k** his promise,
      3:13  in **k** with his promise we are looking

## KEEPS [KEEP]

Ne    1: 5  who **k** his covenant of love
      9:32  who **k** his covenant of love, do not
Pr   17:24  A discerning person **k** wisdom
Da    9: 4  who **k** his covenant of love
Jn    7:19  Yet not one of you **k** the law.
     14:21  and **k** them is the one who loves me.
1Co  13: 5  angered, it **k** no record of wrongs.
Jas   2:10  For whoever **k** the whole law
1Jn   3: 6  one who lives in him **k** on sinning.

## KEILAH

1Sa  23: 5  So David and his men went to **K**,

## KENITE

Jdg   1:16  the **K**, went up from the City
      4:17  the wife of Heber the **K**,

## KEPT [KEEP]

Ge    4: 2  Now Abel **k** flocks, and Cain
      7:17  forty days the flood **k** coming
     20:18  LORD had **k** all the women in
     37:11  but his father **k** the matter in mind.
Ex   12:42  Because the LORD **k** vigil
     16:33  LORD to be **k** for the generations
Lev   6: 9  the fire must be **k** burning
Nu   17:10  to be **k** as a sign to the rebellious.
Dt    7: 8  you and **k** the oath he swore to your
2Sa  22:22  For I have **k** the ways
2Ki   9: 8  he **k** the commands the LORD had
Ne    9: 8  You have **k** your promise because
Ps  130: 3  LORD, **k** a record of sins, Lord,
Pr   28:18  whose walk is blameless are **k** safe,
     28:26  who walk in wisdom are **k** safe.
     29:25  trusts in the LORD is **k** safe.

Isa  38:17  In your love you **k** me from the pit
Mt   19:20  "All these I have **k**," the young
2Co  11: 9  I have **k** myself from being a burden
2Ti   4: 7  finished the race, I have **k** the faith.
Heb  13: 4  all, and the marriage bed **k** pure,
1Pe   1: 4  This inheritance is **k** in heaven
2Pe   3: 7  being **k** for the day of judgment
Rev   3: 8  yet you have **k** my word and have
      3:10  Since you have **k** my command
      9:15  four angels who had been **k** ready

## KERNEL* [KERNELS]

Mk    4:28  the head, then the full **k** in the head.
Jn   12:24  you, unless a **k** of wheat falls

## KERNELS [KERNEL]

Dt   23:25  you may pick **k** with your hands,
Lk    6: 1  them in their hands and eat the **k**.

## KETTLES*

Mk    7: 4  the washing of cups, pitchers and **k**.)

## KETURAH*

Wife of Abraham (Ge 25:1-4; 1Ch 1:32-33).

## KEY [KEYS]

Isa  22:22  on his shoulder the **k** to the house
     33: 6  the LORD is the **k** to this treasure.
Lk   11:52  because you have taken away the **k**
Rev   3: 7  and true, who holds the **k** of David.
      9: 1  The star was given the **k** to the shaft
     20: 1  having the **k** to the Abyss

## KEYS* [KEY]

Mt   16:19  I will give you the **k** of the kingdom
Rev   1:18  And I hold the **k** of death

## KICK*

Ac   26:14  hard for you to **k** against the goads.'

## KIDNAPPER* [KIDNAPS]

Dt   24: 7  Israelite as a slave, the **k** must die.

## KIDNAPS* [KIDNAPPER]

Ex   21:16  "Anyone who **k** someone is to be

## KIDRON

2Sa  15:23  The king also crossed the **K** Valley,
Jn   18: 1  disciples and crossed the **K** Valley.

## KILION

Ru    1: 5  both Mahlon and **K** also died,

## KILL [KILLED, KILLING, KILLS]

Ge    4:14  and whoever finds me will **k** me."
     12:12  they will **k** me but will let you live.
     20:11  they will **k** me because of my wife.'
     26: 7  of this place might **k** me on account
     37:18  reached them, they plotted to **k** him.
Ex    2:15  he tried to **k** Moses, but Moses fled
      4:19  who wanted to **k** you are dead."
      4:23  so I will **k** your firstborn son.' "
1Sa  19: 1  and all the attendants to **k** David.
     20:33  that his father intended to **k** David.

1Ki 11:40 Solomon tried to **k** Jeroboam,
Pr 1:32 of the simple will **k** them,
Ecc 3: 3 a time to **k** and a time to heal, a time
Mt 2:13 to search for the child to **k** him."
10:28 be afraid of those who **k** the body but cannot **k** the soul.
14: 5 Herod wanted to **k** John, but he was
Mk 14: 1 sly way to arrest Jesus and **k** him.
Jn 10:10 The thief comes only to steal and **k**

## KILLED [KILL]
Ge 4: 8 attacked his brother Abel and **k** him.
Ex 2:12 he **k** the Egyptian and hid him
13:15 the LORD **k** the firstborn of both
Nu 35:11 who has **k** someone accidentally
1Sa 17:50 down the Philistine and **k** him.
Ne 9:26 They **k** your prophets, who had
Hos 6: 5 I **k** you with the words of my
Mt 17:23 He will be **k**, and on the third day he
Mk 8:31 and that he must be **k** and after three
9:31 He will be **k**, and after three days he
Lk 11:48 they **k** the prophets, and you build
Ac 3:15 You **k** the author of life, but God
23:12 to eat or drink until they had **k** Paul.
2Co 6: 9 we live on; beaten, and yet not **k**;
Rev 9:18 of the people were **k** by the three
19:21 The rest were **k** with the sword

## KILLING [KILL]
1Ki 18: 4 While Jezebel was **k** off
Est 3: 6 the idea of **k** only Mordecai.
Ac 8: 1 And Saul approved of their **k** him.

## KILLS [KILL]
Ge 4:15 anyone who **k** Cain will suffer
Lev 24:21 Whoever **k** an animal must make
24:21 whoever **k** a human being is to be
2Co 3: 6 for the letter **k**, but the Spirit gives

## KIND [KINDEST, KINDHEARTED, KINDNESS, KINDNESSES, KINDS]
Ge 1:24 animals, each according to its **k**."
6:20 Two of every **k** of bird,
7: 2 pairs of every **k** of clean animal,
Ex 1:20 So God was **k** to the midwives
2Ch 10: 7 "If you will be **k** to these people
Pr 11:17 Those who are **k** benefit themselves,
12:25 the heart, but a **k** word cheers it up.
14:21 blessed are those who are **k**
14:31 whoever is **k** to the needy honors
19:17 Those who are **k** to the poor lend
Isa 58: 5 Is this the **k** of fast I have chosen,
Da 4:27 by being **k** to the oppressed.
Zec 1:13 So the LORD spoke **k**
Mt 8:27 and asked, "What **k** of man is this?
Lk 6:35 because he is **k** to the ungrateful
Jn 4:23 for they are the **k** of worshipers
1Co 13: 4 Love is patient, love is **k**. It does not
15:35 what **k** of body will they come?"
Eph 4:32 Be **k** and compassionate to one
2Ti 2:24 but must be **k** to everyone,
Tit 2: 5 to be **k**, and to be subject to their
2Pe 3:11 what **k** of people ought you to be?

## KINDEST* [KIND]
Pr 12:10 the **k** acts of the wicked are cruel.

## KINDHEARTED* [KIND, HEART]
Pr 11:16 A **k** woman gains honor,

## KINDLE [KINDLED]
Jer 15:14 my anger will **k** a fire that will burn

## KINDLED [KINDLE]
Dt 32:22 For a fire will be **k** by my wrath,
Lk 12:49 and how I wish it were already **k**!

## KINDNESS [KIND]
Ge 19:19 shown great **k** to me in sparing my life.
21:23 the same **k** I have shown to you."
24:12 and show **k** to my master Abraham.
24:27 not abandoned his **k** and faithfulness
32:10 I am unworthy of all the **k**
39:21 he showed him **k** and granted him
40:14 remember me and show me **k**;
47:29 you will show me **k** and faithfulness.
Jos 2:12 because I have shown **k** to you.
Ru 1: 8 May the LORD show you **k**,
2:20 "He has not stopped showing his **k**
1Sa 15: 6 for you showed **k** to all the Israelites
20: 8 As for you, show **k** to your servant,
20:14 But show me unfailing **k** like the LORD's **k** as long as I live,
2Sa 2: 6 May the LORD now show you **k**
9: 3 to whom I can show God's **k**?"
22:51 he shows unfailing **k** to his
Job 6:14 "Anyone who withholds **k** from a friend
Ps 141: 5 that is a **k**; let him rebuke me—
Isa 54: 8 everlasting **k** I will have compassion
Jer 9:24 who exercises **k**,
31: 3 drawn you with unfailing **k**.
Hos 11: 4 I led them with cords of human **k**,
Ac 14:17 He has shown **k** by giving you rain
Ro 2: 4 realizing that God's **k** is intended
11:22 Consider therefore the **k**
2Co 6: 6 understanding, patience and **k**;
Gal 5:22 joy, peace, patience, **k**, goodness,
Eph 2: 7 expressed in his **k** to us in Christ
Col 3:12 yourselves with compassion, **k**,
Tit 3: 4 But when the **k** and love of God our

## KINDNESSES* [KIND]
Ps 106: 7 they did not remember your many **k**,
Isa 63: 7 I will tell of the **k** of the LORD,
63: 7 to his compassion and many **k**.

## KINDS [KIND]
Ge 1:11 in it, according to their various **k**."
1:21 according to their **k**, and every
1:24 living creatures according to their **k**:
Lev 19:19 " 'Do not mate different **k**
Dt 12:31 they do all **k** of detestable things
Jer 15: 3 "I will send four **k** of destroyers
Da 3: 5 pipe and all **k** of music, you must
Mt 5:11 falsely say all **k** of evil against you
1Co 12: 4 There are different **k** of gifts,
1Ti 6:10 of money is a root of all **k** of evil.
Jas 1: 2 whenever you face trials of many **k**,
1Pe 1: 6 had to suffer grief in all **k** of trials.

## KING [KING'S, KINGDOM, KINGDOMS, KINGS, KINGSHIP]

### The Kings of the United Kingdom

| Name | Ruled | Dates B.C. |
|------|-------|-----------|
| 1. Saul | 40 years | 1050-1010 |
| 2. David | 40 years | 1010-970 |
| 3. Solomon | 40 years | 970-930 |

### The Kings of Israel

| Name | Ruled | Dates B.C. |
|------|-------|-----------|
| 1. Jeroboam I | 22 years | 930-909 |
| 2. Nadab | 2 years | 909-908 |
| 3. Baasha | 24 years | 908-886 |
| 4. Elah | 2 years | 886-885 |
| 5. Zimri | 7 days | 885 |
| 6. Omri | 12 years | 885-874 |
| 7. Ahab | 22 years | 874-853 |
| 8. Ahaziah | 2 years | 853-852 |
| 9. Joram | 12 years | 852-841 |
| 10. Jehu | 28 years | 841-814 |
| 11. Jehoahaz | 17 years | 814-798 |
| 12. Jehoash | 16 years | 798-782 |
| 13. Jeroboam II | 41 years | 793-753 |
| 14. Zechariah | 6 months | 753 |
| 15. Shallum | 1 month | 752 |
| 16. Menahem | 10 years | 752-742 |
| 17. Pekahiah | 2 years | 742-740 |
| 18. Pekah | 20 years | 752-732 |
| 19. Hoshea | 9 years | 732-722 |

### The Kings (and Queen) of Judah

| Name | Ruled | Dates B.C. |
|------|-------|-----------|
| 1. Rehoboam | 17 years | 930-913 |
| 2. Abijah | 3 years | 913-910 |
| 3. Asa | 41 years | 910-869 |
| 4. Jehoshaphat | 25 years | 872-848 |
| 5. Jehoram | 8 years | 848-841 |
| 6. Ahaziah | 1 year | 841 |
| 7. Queen Athaliah | 6 years | 841-835 |
| 8. Joash | 40 years | 835-796 |
| 9. Amaziah | 29 years | 796-767 |
| 10. Uzziah / Azariah | 52 years | 792-740 |
| 11. Jotham | 16 years | 750-735 |
| 12. Ahaz | 16 years | 732-715 |
| 13. Hezekiah | 29 years | 715-686 |
| 14. Manasseh | 55 years | 697-642 |
| 15. Amon | 2 years | 642-640 |
| 16. Josiah | 31 years | 640-609 |
| 17. Jehoahaz | 3 months | 609 |
| 18. Jehoiakim | 11 years | 609-598 |
| 19. Jehoiachin | 3 months | 598-597 |
| 20. Zedekiah / Mattaniah | 11 years | 597-586 |

See also each king by name.

Ge 14:18 Melchizedek **k** of Salem brought
20: 2 Abimelek **k** of Gerar sent for Sarah
26: 8 Abimelek **k** of the Philistines looked
Ex 1: 8 Then a new **k**, to whom Joseph
Nu 21:26 the city of Sihon **k** of the Amorites,
21:33 and Og **k** of Bashan and his whole
22:10 "Balak son of Zippor, **k** of Moab,
23:21 the shout of the **K** is among them.

Dt 17:14 "Let us set a **k** over us like all
Jdg 9: 8 out to anoint a **k** for themselves.
17: 6 In those days Israel had no **k**;
18: 1 In those days Israel had no **k**;
19: 1 In those days Israel had no **k**.
21:25 In those days Israel had no **k**;
1Sa 8: 5 now appoint a **k** to lead us, such as
11:15 made Saul **k** in the presence
12:12 the LORD your God was your **k**.
15:11 "I regret that I have made Saul **k**,
16: 1 chosen one of his sons to be **k**."
2Sa 2: 4 there they anointed David **k** over
1Ki 1:30 Solomon your son shall be **k**
Ps 2: 6 "I have installed my **k** on Zion,
10:16 The LORD is **K** for ever and ever;
24: 7 that the **K** of glory may come in.
33:16 No **k** is saved by the size of his
44: 4 You are my **K** and my God,
47: 7 For God is the **K** of all the earth;
48: 2 Mount Zion, the city of the Great **K**.
Isa 6: 5 and my eyes have seen the **K**,
32: 1 a **k** will reign in righteousness
43:15 One, Israel's Creator, your **K**."
Jer 10:10 he is the living God, the eternal **K**.
30: 9 their God and David their **k**, whom I
Eze 37:24 servant David will be **k** over them,
Da 2: 4 Then the astrologers answered the **k**,
Hos 3: 5 their God and David their **k**.
Mic 2:13 Their **K** will pass through before
Zep 3:15 The LORD, the **K** of Israel,
Zec 9: 9 See, your **k** comes to you,
14: 9 LORD will be **k** over the whole
Mal 1:14 For I am a great **k**,"
Mt 2: 2 is the one who has been born **k**
21: 5 'See, your **k** comes to you,
27:11 him, "Are you the **k** of the Jews?"
27:37 THIS IS JESUS, THE **K** OF THE JEWS.
Mk 15:32 Let this Messiah, this **k** of Israel,
Lk 19:38 "Blessed is the **k** who comes
23: 3 Jesus, "Are you the **k** of the Jews?"
Jn 1:49 you are the **k** of Israel."
12:13 "Blessed is the **k** of Israel!"
18:37 answered, "You say that I am a **k**.
19:15 "We have no **k** but Caesar,"
19:21 "Do not write 'The **K** of the Jews,'
Ac 17: 7 saying that there is another **k**,
1Ti 1:17 Now to the **K** eternal, immortal,
6:15 the **K** of kings and Lord of lords,
Heb 7: 1 This Melchizedek was **k** of Salem
Rev 15: 3 true are your ways, **K** of the nations.
17:14 he is Lord of lords and **K** of kings—
19:16 **K** OF KINGS AND LORD OF LORDS.

**GREAT KING** See GREAT

**KING OF ASSYRIA** 2Ki 15:19, 20, 20, 29;
16:7, 8, 9, 10, 18; 17:3, 4, 4, 5, 6, 24, 26, 27;
18:7, 9, 11, 13, 14, 16, 17, 19, 23, 28, 30, 31,
33; 19:4, 6, 8, 10, 20, 32, 36; 20:6; 23:29; 1Ch
5:6, 26, 26; 2Ch 28:20, 21; 32:1, 7, 9, 10, 11, 22;
33:11; Ezr 4:2; 6:22; Isa 7:17, 20; 8:4, 7; 10:12;
20:1, 4, 6; 36:1, 2, 4, 8, 13, 15, 16, 18; 37:4, 6, 8,
10, 21, 33, 37; 38:6; Jer 50:17, 18; Na 3:18

**KING OF BABYLON** 2Ki 20:12, 18; 24:1, 7,
10, 12, 16, 20; 25:1, 6, 8, 8, 11, 20, 22, 23, 24,
27; 2Ch 36:6; Ezr 2:1; 5:12, 13; Ne 7:6; 13:6; Est
2:6; Isa 14:4; 39:1, 7; Jer 20:4; 21:2, 4, 7, 10;

22:25; 24:1; 25:1, 9, 11, 12; 27:6, 8, 9, 11, 12, 13, 14, 17, 20; 28:2, 3, 4, 11, 14; 29:21, 22; 32:2, 3, 4, 28, 36; 34:1, 2, 3, 7, 21; 35:11; 36:29; 37:1, 17, 19; 38:3, 17, 18, 22, 23; 39:1, 3, 3, 5, 6, 11, 13; 40:5, 7, 9, 11; 41:2, 18; 42:11; 43:10; 44:30; 46:2, 13, 26; 49:28, 30; 50:17, 18, 43; 51:31, 34; 52:3, 4, 9, 10, 12, 12, 15, 26, 31, 34; Eze 17:12; 19:9; 21:19, 21; 24:2; 26:7; 29:18, 19; 30:10, 24, 25, 25; 32:11; Da 1:1; 7:1

## KING OF EGYPT Ge 40:1, 1, 5; 41:46; Ex

1:15, 17, 18; 2:23; 3:18, 19; 5:4; 6:11, 13, 27, 29; 14:5, 8; Dt 7:8; 11:3; 1Ki 3:1; 9:16; 11:18; 14:25; 2Ki 17:4, 7; 18:21; 23:29; 24:7; 2Ch 12:2, 9; 35:20; 36:3, 4; Isa 36:6; Jer 25:19; 44:30; 46:2, 17; Eze 29:2, 3; 30:21, 22; 31:2; 32:2; Ac 7:10

## KING OF ISRAEL 1Sa 24:14; 26:20; 29:3; 2Sa

6:20; 1Ki 15:9, 16, 17, 19, 25, 32; 16:8, 23, 29; 20:2, 4, 7, 11, 13, 21, 22, 28, 31, 32, 40, 41, 43; 21:18; 22:2, 3, 4, 5, 6, 8, 9, 10, 18, 26, 29, 30, 30, 31, 32, 33, 34, 41, 44, 51; 2Ki 3:1, 4, 5, 9, 10, 11, 12, 13, 13; 5:5, 6, 7, 8; 6:9, 10, 11, 12, 21, 26; 7:6; 8:16, 25, 26; 9:21; 13:1, 10, 14, 16; 14:1, 8, 9, 11, 13, 17, 23; 15:1, 8, 17, 23, 27, 29, 32; 16:5, 7; 17:1; 18:1, 9, 10; 21:3; 23:13; 24:13; 1Ch 5:17; 2Ch 8:11; 16:1, 3; 18:3, 4, 5, 7, 8, 9, 17, 19, 25, 28, 29, 29, 30, 31, 32, 33, 34; 20:35; 21:2; 22:5; 25:17, 18, 21, 23, 25; 28:5, 19; 29:27; 30:26; 35:3, 4; Ezr 3:10; 5:11; Ne 13:26; Pr 1:1; Isa 7:1; Jer 41:9; Hos 1:1; 10:15; Am 1:1; 7:10; Zep 3:15; Mt 27:42; Mk 15:32; Jn 1:49; 12:13

## KING OF JUDAH 1Ki 12:23, 27; 15:1, 9, 17,

25, 28, 33; 16:8, 10, 15, 23, 29; 22:2, 10, 29, 41, 51; 2Ki 1:17; 3:1, 7, 9, 14; 8:16, 16, 25, 29; 9:16, 21, 27, 29; 10:13; 12:18; 13:1, 10, 12; 14:1, 9, 11, 13, 15, 17, 23; 15:1, 8, 13, 17, 23, 27, 32; 16:1; 17:1; 18:1, 14, 14, 16; 19:10; 21:11; 22:16, 18; 24:12; 25:27, 27; 1Ch 4:41; 5:17; 2Ch 11:3; 13:1; 16:1, 7; 18:3, 9, 28; 19:1; 20:31, 35; 21:12; 22:1, 6; 25:17, 18, 21, 23, 25; 30:24; 32:8, 9, 23; 34:24, 26; 35:21; Est 2:6; Pr 25:1; Isa 7:1; 37:10; 38:9; Jer 1:2, 3, 3; 15:4; 21:7; 22:1, 2, 6, 11, 18, 24; 24:1, 8; 25:1, 3; 26:1, 18, 19; 27:1, 3, 12, 18, 20, 21; 28:1, 4; 29:3; 32:1, 3, 4; 34:2, 4, 6, 21; 35:1; 36:1, 9, 28, 29, 30, 32; 37:1, 7; 38:22; 39:1, 4; 44:30; 45:1; 46:2; 49:34; 51:59; 52:31, 31; Da 1:1, 2; Am 1:1; Zep 1:1; Zec 14:5

## KING OF KINGS Ezr 7:12; Eze 26:7; Da

2:37; 1Ti 6:15; Rev 17:14; 19:16

## KING OF THE JEWS Mt 2:2; 27:11, 29, 37;

Mk 15:2, 9, 12, 18, 26; Lk 23:3, 37, 38; Jn 18:33, 39; 19:3, 19, 21, 21

## KING'S [KING]

| | | |
|---|---|---|
| Nu | 20:17 | We will travel along the **K** Highway |
| 1Sa | 18:18 | I should become the **k** son-in-law?" |
| 2Sa | 9:13 | because he always ate at the **k** table; |
| Pr | 21: 1 | the LORD's hand the **k** heart is |
| Ecc | 8: 2 | Obey the **k** command, I say, |
| Jer | 52:33 | his life ate regularly at the **k** table. |
| Heb | 11:23 | they were not afraid of the **k** edict. |

## KINGDOM [KING]

| | | |
|---|---|---|
| Ex | 19: 6 | you will be for me a **k** of priests |
| Dt | 17:18 | When he takes the throne of his **k**, |
| 1Sa | 13:14 | But now your **k** will not endure; |
| | 28:17 | The LORD has torn the **k** |
| 2Sa | 7:12 | own body, and I will establish his **k**. |
| 1Ki | 11:31 | 'See, I am going to tear the **k** |
| 1Ch | 17:11 | own sons, and I will establish his **k**. |
| | 29:11 | Yours, LORD, is the **k**; |
| Ps | 45: 6 | justice will be the scepter of your **k**. |
| | 103:19 | in heaven, and his **k** rules over all. |
| | 145:13 | Your **k** is an everlasting **k**, and your |
| Isa | 9: 7 | on David's throne and over his **k**, |
| Jer | 18: 7 | that a nation or **k** is to be uprooted, |
| Eze | 29:14 | There they will be a lowly **k**. |
| Da | 2:39 | "After you, another **k** will arise, |
| | 2:44 | up a **k** that will never be destroyed, |
| | 4: 3 | His **k** is an eternal **k**; |
| | 5:28 | Your **k** is divided and given |
| | 7:18 | of the Most High will receive the **k** |
| | 7:27 | His **k** will be an everlasting **k**, |
| Ob | 1:21 | And the **k** will be the LORD's. |
| Mt | 3: 2 | for the **k** of heaven has come near." |
| | 4:17 | for the **k** of heaven has come near." |
| | 4:23 | proclaiming the good news of the **k**, |
| | 5: 3 | spirit, for theirs is the **k** of heaven. |
| | 5:10 | for theirs is the **k** of heaven. |
| | 5:19 | be called least in the **k** of heaven, |
| | 5:20 | you will certainly not enter the **k** |
| | 6:10 | your **k** come, your will be done, |
| | 6:33 | But seek first his **k** and his |
| | 7:21 | Lord,' will enter the **k** of heaven, |
| | 8:12 | of the **k** will be thrown outside, |
| | 9:35 | proclaiming the good news of the **k** |
| | 10: 7 | 'The **k** of heaven has come near.' |
| | 11:11 | in the **k** of heaven is greater than he. |
| | 11:12 | the **k** of heaven has been subjected |
| | 12:25 | "Every **k** divided against itself will |
| | 12:28 | the **k** of God has come upon you. |
| | 13:11 | of the **k** of heaven has been given |
| | 13:19 | people hear the message about the **k** |
| | 13:24 | "The **k** of heaven is like a man who |
| | 13:31 | "The **k** of heaven is like a mustard |
| | 13:33 | "The **k** of heaven is like yeast |
| | 13:38 | seed stands for the people of the **k**. |
| | 13:44 | "The **k** of heaven is like treasure |
| | 13:45 | the **k** of heaven is like a merchant |
| | 13:47 | the **k** of heaven is like a net that was |
| | 13:52 | the **k** of heaven is like the owner |
| | 16:19 | you the keys of the **k** of heaven; |
| | 16:28 | the Son of Man coming in his **k**." |
| | 18: 1 | is the greatest in the **k** of heaven?" |
| | 18: 3 | you will never enter the **k** of heaven. |
| | 18: 4 | is the greatest in the **k** of heaven. |
| | 18:23 | the **k** of heaven is like a king who |
| | 19:12 | because of the **k** of heaven. |
| | 19:14 | for the **k** of heaven belongs to such |
| | 19:23 | for the rich to enter the **k** of heaven. |
| | 20: 1 | the **k** of heaven is like a landowner |
| | 20:21 | and the other at your left in your **k**." |
| | 21:31 | the prostitutes are entering the **k** |
| | 21:43 | that the **k** of God will be taken away |
| | 22: 2 | "The **k** of heaven is like a king who |
| | 23:13 | You shut the door of the **k** of heaven |
| | 24:14 | this gospel of the **k** will be preached |
| | 25: 1 | time the **k** of heaven will be like ten |
| | 25:34 | the **k** prepared for you since |

Mt   26:29   it new with you in my Father's **k**."
Mk   1:15   "The **k** of God has come near.
      3:24   If a **k** is divided against itself, that **k**
      4:11   of the **k** of God has been given
      4:26   "This is what the **k** of God is like.
      6:23   I will give you, up to half my **k**."
      9: 1   they see that the **k** of God has come
      9:47   you to enter the **k** of God with one
    10:14   for the **k** of God belongs to such as
    10:15   anyone who will not receive the **k**
    10:23   for the rich to enter the **k** of God!"
    10:24   how hard it is to enter the **k** of God!
    11:10   "Blessed is the coming **k** of our
    12:34   are not far from the **k** of God."
    13: 8   rise against nation, and **k** against **k**.
    14:25   I drink it new in the **k** of God."
    15:43   himself waiting for the **k** of God,
Lk   1:33   his **k** will never end."
    4:43   the good news of the **k** of God
    6:20   are poor, for yours is the **k** of God.
    7:28   in the **k** of God is greater than he."
    8: 1   the good news of the **k** of God.
    8:10   of the **k** of God has been given
    9: 2   them out to proclaim the **k** of God
    9:11   spoke to them about the **k** of God,
    9:27   not taste death before they see the **k**
    9:60   you go and proclaim the **k** of God."
    9:62   is fit for service in the **k** of God."
   10: 9   'The **k** of God has come near
   10:11   The **k** of God has come near.'
   11: 2   be your name, your **k** come.
   11:18   himself, how can his **k** stand?
   11:20   the **k** of God has come upon you.
   12:31   But seek his **k**, and these things will
   12:32   has been pleased to give you the **k**.
   13:18   asked, "What is the **k** of God like?
   13:29   places at the feast in the **k** of God.
   14:15   eat at the feast in the **k** of God."
   16:16   of the **k** of God is being preached,
   17:20   when the **k** of God would come,
   17:21   is,' because the **k** of God is in your
   18:16   for the **k** of God belongs to such as
   18:24   is for the rich to enter the **k** of God!
   18:29   children for the sake of the **k** of God
   19:11   thought that the **k** of God was going
   21:31   you know that the **k** of God is near.
   22:16   it finds fulfillment in the **k** of God."
   22:18   the vine until the **k** of God comes."
   22:29   And I confer on you a **k**, just as my
   22:30   drink at my table in my **k** and sit
   23:42   me when you come into your **k**."
   23:51   was waiting for the **k** of God.
Jn   3: 3   no one can see the **k** of God without
   3: 5   you, no one can enter the **k** of God
   18:36   said, "My **k** is not of this world.
Ac   1: 3   days and spoke about the **k** of God.
   1: 6   going to restore the **k** to Israel?"
   8:12   the good news of the **k** of God
   14:22   hardships to enter the **k** of God,"
   19: 8   persuasively about the **k** of God.
   20:25   preaching the **k** will ever see me
   28:23   explaining about the **k** of God,
   28:31   He proclaimed the **k** of God
Ro   14:17   For the **k** of God is not a matter
1Co   4:20   For the **k** of God is not a matter
   6: 9   wrongdoers will not inherit the **k**
   15:24   when he hands over the **k** to God

1Co   15:50   blood cannot inherit the **k** of God,
Gal   5:21   live like this will not inherit the **k**
Eph   2: 2   and of the ruler of the **k** of the air,
   5: 5   any inheritance in the **k** of Christ
Col   1:12   of his people in the **k** of light.
   1:13   us into the **k** of the Son he loves,
   4:11   my co-workers for the **k** of God,
1Th   2:12   who calls you into his **k** and glory.
2Th   1: 5   be counted worthy of the **k** of God,
2Ti   4: 1   in view of his appearing and his **k**,
   4:18   bring me safely to his heavenly **k**.
Heb   1: 8   justice will be the scepter of your **k**.
   12:28   since we are receiving a **k**
Jas   2: 5   inherit the **k** he promised those who
2Pe   1:11   into the eternal **k** of our Lord
Rev   1: 6   has made us to be a **k** and priests
   1: 9   companion in the suffering and **k**
   5:10   You have made them to be a **k**
   11:15   "The **k** of the world has become the
           **k** of our
   12:10   and the power and the **k** of our God,
   16:10   and its **k** was plunged into darkness.
   17:12   kings who have not yet received a **k**,

## KINGDOM OF HEAVEN Mt 3:2; 4:17; 5:3,
10, 19, 19, 20; 7:21; 8:11; 10:7; 11:11, 12; 13:11,
24, 31, 33, 44, 45, 47, 52; 16:19; 18:1, 3, 4, 23;
19:12, 14, 23; 20:1; 22:2; 23:13; 25:1

## KINGDOM OF GOD Mt 12:28; 19:24;
21:31, 43; Mk 1:15; 4:11, 26, 30; 9:1, 47; 10:14,
15, 23, 24, 25; 12:34; 14:25; 15:43; Lk 4:43;
6:20; 7:28; 8:1, 10; 9:2, 11, 27, 60, 62; 10:9, 11;
11:20; 13:18, 20, 28, 29; 14:15; 16:16; 17:20, 20,
21; 18:16, 17, 24, 25, 29; 19:11; 21:31; 22:16,
18; 23:51; Jn 3:3, 5; Ac 1:3; 8:12; 14:22; 19:8;
28:23, 31; Ro 14:17; 1Co 4:20; 6:9, 10; 15:50;
Gal 5:21; Col 4:11; 2Th 1:5

## KINGDOMS [KING]
Dt   3:21   to all the **k** over there where you are
1Ki   4:21   Solomon ruled over all the **k**
2Ki   19:15   you alone are God over all the **k**
   19:19   that all the **k** of the earth may know
2Ch   20: 6   You rule over all the **k**
Ps   68:32   Sing to God, you **k** of the earth,
Isa   37:16   you alone are God over all the **k**
   37:20   that all the **k** of the earth may know
Jer   33:24   has rejected the two **k** he chose'?
Eze   37:22   nations or be divided into two **k**.
Da   2:44   It will crush all those **k** and bring
   4:17   Most High is sovereign over the **k**
Zep   3: 8   to gather the **k** and to pour out my
Lk   4: 5   in an instant all the **k** of the world.
Heb   11:33   who through faith conquered **k**,

## KINGS [KING]
Ge   14: 9   king of Ellasar—four **k** against five.
   17: 6   of you, and **k** will come from you.
Jos   12: 1   These are the **k** of the land whom
2Sa   11: 1   at the time when **k** go off to war,
1Ki   10:23   wisdom than all the other **k**
Ps   2: 2   The **k** of the earth rise
   47: 9   for the **k** of the earth belong to God;
   68:29   at Jerusalem **k** will bring you gifts.
   72:11   May all **k** bow down to him and all
   89:27   most exalted of the **k** of the earth.

Ps 110: 5 he will crush **k** on the day of his
138: 4 May all the **k** of the earth praise
149: 8 to bind their **k** with fetters,
Pr 8:15 By me **k** reign and rulers issue
16:12 **K** detest wrongdoing, for a throne is
31: 4 it is not for **k** to drink wine,
Isa 24:21 above and the **k** on the earth below.
52:15 **k** will shut their mouths because
60:11 their **k** led in triumphal procession.
Da 2:21 he deposes **k** and raises up others.
2:47 and the Lord of **k** and a revealer
7:17 four **k** that will rise from the earth.
7:24 ten horns are ten **k** who will come
Lk 10:24 and **k** wanted to see what you see
21:12 you will be brought before **k**
Ac 4:26 The **k** of the earth rise
1Ti 2: 2 for **k** and all those in authority,
6:15 the King of **k** and Lord of lords,
Rev 1: 5 and the ruler of the **k** of the earth.
16:16 they gathered the **k** together
17: 2 her the **k** of the earth committed
17:12 you saw are ten **k** who have not yet
17:14 he is Lord of lords and King of **k**—
19:16 KING OF **K** AND LORD OF LORDS.
19:19 I saw the beast and the **k** of the earth
21:24 the **k** of the earth will bring their

**KING OF KINGS** See KING

**KINGS OF ISRAEL** 1Ki 14:19; 15:31; 16:5,
14, 20, 27, 33; 22:39; 2Ki 1:18; 8:18; 10:34;
13:8, 12, 13; 14:15, 16, 28, 29; 15:11, 15, 21, 26,
31; 16:3; 17:2, 8; 23:19, 22; 1Ch 9:1; 2Ch 20:34;
21:6, 13; 27:7; 28:2, 27; 33:18; 35:18, 27; 36:8;
Mic 1:14

**KINGS OF JUDAH** 1Sa 27:6; 1Ki 14:29;
15:7, 23; 22:45; 2Ki 8:23; 12:18, 19; 14:18; 15:6,
36; 16:19; 18:5; 20:20; 21:17, 25; 23:5, 11, 12,
22, 28; 24:5; 2Ch 16:11; 25:26; 28:26; 32:32;
34:11; Isa 1:1; Jer 1:18; 17:19, 20; 19:3, 4, 13;
20:5; Hos 1:1; Mic 1:1

**KINGS OF THE EARTH** 1Ki 10:23; 2Ch
9:22, 23; Ps 2:2; 47:9; 76:12; 89:27; 102:15;
138:4; 148:11; La 4:12; Eze 27:33; Mt 17:25; Ac
4:26; Rev 1:5; 6:15; 17:2, 18; 18:3, 9; 19:19;
21:24

**KINGSHIP** [KING]
1Sa 10:25 the people the rights and duties of **k**.
1Ch 11:10 gave his **k** strong support to extend
Mic 4: 8 **k** will come to Daughter

**KIRIATH ARBA** [HEBRON]
Ge 23: 2 She died at **K** (that is, Hebron)
35:27 to his father Isaac in Mamre, near **K**
Jos 21:11 They gave them **K** (that is, Hebron),

**KIRIATH JEARIM**
1Sa 7: 1 So the men of **K** came and took up
1Ch 13: 5 to bring the ark of God from **K**.

**KISH**
1Sa 10:21 Finally Saul son of **K** was taken.

**KISHON**
Jdg 5:21 The river **K** swept them away,
Ps 83: 9 to Sisera and Jabin at the river **K**,

**KISS** [KISSED, KISSES, KISSING]
Ge 27:26 "Come here, my son, and **k** me."
31:28 even let me **k** my grandchildren
1Ki 19:20 "Let me **k** my father and mother
Ps 2:12 **K** his son, or he will be angry
85:10 and peace **k** each other.
Pr 24:26 An honest answer is like a **k**
SS 1: 2 Let him **k** me with the kisses of his
8: 1 I would **k** you, and no one would
Hos 13: 2 They **k** calf-idols!"
Mt 26:48 "The one I **k** is the man;
Lk 7:45 You did not give me a **k**, but this
22:48 the Son of Man with a **k**?"
Ro 16:16 Greet one another with a holy **k**.
1Co 16:20 Greet one another with a holy **k**.
2Co 13:12 Greet one another with a holy **k**.
1Th 5:26 all God's people with a holy **k**.
1Pe 5:14 Greet one another with a **k** of love.

**KISSED** [KISS]
Ge 29:11 Then Jacob **k** Rachel and began
33: 4 his arms around his neck and **k** him.
45:15 And he **k** all his brothers and wept
50: 1 father and wept over him and **k** him.
Ex 4:27 at the mountain of God and **k** him.
Ru 1: 9 Then she **k** them good-by and they
1Sa 10: 1 poured it on Saul's head and **k** him,
20:41 Then they **k** each other and wept
1Ki 19:18 and whose mouths have not **k** him."
Pr 7:13 She took hold of him and **k** him
Mk 14:45 Judas said, "Rabbi!" and **k** him.
Lk 7:38 hair, **k** them and poured perfume

**KISSES**\* [KISS]
Pr 27: 6 trusted, but an enemy multiplies **k**.
SS 1: 2 kiss me with the **k** of his mouth—

**KISSING**\* [KISS]
Lk 7:45 I entered, has not stopped **k** my feet.

**KNEADING**
Dt 28: 5 and your **k** trough will be blessed.
28:17 and your **k** trough will be cursed.

**KNEE** [KNEES]
Isa 45:23 Before me every **k** will bow;
Ro 11: 4 thousand who have not bowed the **k**
14:11 Lord, 'every **k** will bow before me;
Php 2:10 name of Jesus every **k** should bow,

**KNEEL** [KNELT]
Est 3: 2 Mordecai would not **k** down or pay
Ps 95: 6 let us **k** before the LORD our
Eph 3:14 For this reason I **k** before the Father,

**KNEES** [KNEE]
Jdg 7: 6 the rest got down on their **k** to drink.
1Ki 19:18 all whose **k** have not bowed down
Isa 35: 3 hands, steady the **k** that give way;
Da 6:10 times a day he got down on his **k**

Lk　5: 8　saw this, he fell at Jesus' **k** and said,
Heb 12:12　your feeble arms and weak **k**.

## KNELT* [KNEEL]

2Ch　6:13　**k** down before the whole assembly
　　　7: 3　they **k** on the pavement with their
　　29:29　everyone present with him **k** down
Est　3: 2　officials at the king's gate **k** down
Mt　8: 2　with leprosy came and **k** before him
　　9:18　leader came and **k** before him
　　15:25　The woman came and **k** before him.
　　17:14　approached Jesus and **k** before him
　　27:29　Then they **k** in front of him
Lk　22:41　beyond them, **k** down and prayed,
Ac　20:36　he **k** down with all of them
　　21: 5　and there on the beach we **k** to pray.

## KNEW [KNOW]

Dt　34:10　whom the Lord **k** face to face,
Jdg　2:10　who **k** neither the Lord nor what
2Ch 33:13　Manasseh **k** that the Lord is God.
Job　23: 3　If only I **k** where to find him;
Pr　24:12　say, "But we **k** nothing about this,"
Jer　1: 5　I formed you in the womb I **k** you,
　　19: 4　nor the kings of Judah ever **k**,
Jnh　4: 2　I **k** that you are a gracious
Mt　7:23　tell them plainly, 'I never **k** you.
　　12:25　Jesus **k** their thoughts and said
Lk　4:41　because they **k** he was the Messiah.
Jn　2:24　himself to them, for he **k** all people.
　　4:10　"If you **k** the gift of God and who it
　　8:19　"If you **k** me, you would know my
　　13: 1　Jesus **k** that the hour had come
　　13:11　For he **k** who was going to betray
Ro　1:21　For although they **k** God,

## KNIFE [KNIVES]

Ge　22:10　hand and took the **k** to slay his son.
Ex　4:25　But Zipporah took a flint **k**, cut off
Pr　23: 2　and put a **k** to your throat if you are

## KNIT*

Job　10:11　flesh and **k** me together with bones
Ps 139:13　you **k** me together in my mother's

## KNIVES [KNIFE]

Jos　5: 2　"Make flint **k** and circumcise

## KNOCK* [KNOCKING, KNOCKS]

Mt　7: 7　**k** and the door will be opened
　　7: 8　those who **k**, the door will be opened.
Lk　11: 9　**k** and the door will be opened
Lk　11:10　to those who **k**, the door will
Rev　3:20　I stand at the door and **k**.

## KNOCKING* [KNOCK]

SS　5: 2　My beloved is **k**: "Open to me,
Da　5: 6　became weak and his knees were **k**.
Lk　13:25　door, you will stand outside **k**
Ac　12:16　But Peter kept on **k**, and when they

## KNOCKS [KNOCK]

Lk　12:36　**k** they can immediately open

## KNOW [FOREKNEW, FOREKNOWLEDGE, KNEW, KNOWING, KNOWLEDGE, KNOWN, KNOWS, WELL-KNOWN]

Ge　15: 8　Lord, how can I **k** that I will gain
　　22:12　Now I **k** that you fear God,
Ex　3:19　I **k** that the king of Egypt will not let
　　6: 7　you will **k** that I am the Lord
　　7: 5　the Egyptians will **k** that I am
　　14: 4　the Egyptians will **k** that I am
　　18:11　Now I **k** that the Lord is greater
　　33:12　'I **k** you by name and you have
　　33:13　teach me your ways so I may **k** you
Nu　16:28　"This is how you will **k**
Dt　7: 9　**K** therefore that the Lord your
　　8: 2　in order to **k** what was in your heart,
　　18:21　"How can we **k** when a message
Jos　3: 7　so they may **k** that I am with you as
　　4:24　of the earth might **k** that the hand
　　23:14　You **k** with all your heart and soul
1Sa 17:46　the whole world will **k** that there is
1Ki　8:39　you alone **k** every human heart),
Job　11: 6　**K** this: God has even forgotten some
　　19:25　I **k** that my redeemer lives,
　　42: 2　"I **k** that you can do all things;
　　42: 3　things too wonderful for me to **k**.
Ps　9:10　Those who **k** your name trust
　　14: 4　Do all these evildoers **k** nothing?
　　36:10　your love to those who **k** you,
　　46:10　"Be still, and **k** that I am God;
　　73:11　God **k**? Does the Most High **k**
　　100: 3　**K** that the Lord is God. It is he
　　139: 1　me, Lord, and you **k** me.
　　139:23　Search me, God, and **k** my heart;
　　145:12　that all people may **k** of your mighty
Pr　27: 1　you do not **k** what a day may bring.
　　30: 4　the name of his son? Surely you **k**!
Ecc　8: 5　the wise heart will **k** the proper time
　　8:16　I applied my mind to **k** wisdom
　　8:17　Even if the wise claim they **k**,
Isa　1: 3　but Israel does not **k**, my people do
　　29:15　think, "Who sees us? Who will **k**?"
　　29:16　pot say to the potter, "You **k** nothing"?
　　40:21　Do you not **k**? Have you not heard?
　　44: 8　there is no other Rock; I **k** not one."
Jer　4:22　they **k** not how to do good.
　　6:15　they do not even **k** how to blush.
　　9:24　that they understand and **k** me,
　　22:16　Is that not what it means to **k** me?"
　　24: 7　I will give them a heart to **k** me,
　　31:34　because they will all **k** me,
　　33: 3　unsearchable things you do not **k**.'
Eze　2: 5　they will **k** that a prophet has been
　　6:10　they will **k** that I am the Lord;
Da　11:32　but the people who **k** their God will
Mt　6: 3　let your left hand **k** what your right
　　7:11　**k** how to give good gifts to your
　　9: 6　I want you to **k** that the Son of Man
　　22:29　because you do not **k** the Scriptures
　　24:42　because you do not **k** on what day
　　26:74　to them, "I don't **k** the man!"
Mk　12:24　because you do not **k** the Scriptures
Lk　1: 4　so that you may **k** the certainty
　　11:13　**k** how to give good gifts to your
　　12:48　the one who does not **k** and does
　　13:25　'I don't **k** you or where you come

| | | |
|---|---|---|
| Lk | 18:20 | You **k** the commandments: |
| | 21:31 | you **k** that the kingdom of God is |
| | 22:34 | deny three times that you **k** me." |
| | 23:34 | they do not **k** what they are doing." |
| Jn | 1:26 | among you stands one you do not **k**. |
| | 3:11 | you, we speak of what we **k**, and we |
| | 4:22 | worship what you do not **k**; |
| | 4:42 | and we **k** that this man really is |
| | 6:69 | to **k** that you are the Holy One |
| | 7:28 | "Yes, you **k** me, and you **k** where I |
| | 8:14 | valid, for I **k** where I came |
| | 8:19 | "You do not **k** me or my Father," |
| | 8:32 | Then you will **k** the truth, |
| | 8:55 | Though you do not **k** him, I **k** him. |
| | 9:25 | One thing I do **k**. I was blind |
| | 10: 4 | follow him because they **k** his voice. |
| | 10:14 | I **k** my sheep and my sheep **k** me— |
| | 10:27 | I **k** them, and they follow me. |
| | 12:35 | in the dark do not **k** where they are |
| | 13:17 | Now that you **k** these things, |
| | 13:35 | this everyone will **k** that you are my |
| | 14: 7 | really **k** me, you will **k** my Father |
| | 14:17 | But you **k** him, for he lives with you |
| | 15:21 | they do not **k** the one who sent me. |
| | 16:30 | we can see that you **k** all things |
| | 17: 3 | that they **k** you, the only true God, |
| | 17:23 | the world will **k** that you sent me |
| | 21:15 | he said, "you **k** that I love you." |
| | 21:24 | We **k** that his testimony is true. |
| Ac | 1: 7 | "It is not for you to **k** the times |
| | 1:24 | "Lord, you **k** everyone's heart. |
| Ro | 3:17 | the way of peace they do not **k**." |
| | 6: 3 | don't you **k** that all of us who were |
| | 6: 6 | we **k** that our old self was crucified |
| | 6:16 | Don't you **k** that when you offer |
| | 7: 1 | Do you not **k**, brothers and sisters— |
| | 7:14 | We **k** that the law is spiritual; |
| | 7:18 | I **k** that good itself does not dwell |
| | 8:22 | We **k** that the whole creation has |
| | 8:26 | We do not **k** what we ought to pray |
| | 8:28 | we **k** that in all things God works |
| | 11: 2 | Don't you **k** what Scripture says |
| 1Co | 1:21 | through its wisdom did not **k** him, |
| | 2: 2 | I resolved to **k** nothing while I was |
| | 3:16 | Don't you **k** that you yourselves are |
| | 5: 6 | Don't you **k** that a little yeast |
| | 6: 2 | do you not **k** that the Lord's people |
| | 6:15 | Do you not **k** that your bodies are |
| | 6:16 | Do you not **k** that he who unites |
| | 6:19 | Do you not **k** that your bodies are |
| | 7:16 | How do you **k**, wife, whether you |
| | 8: 2 | do not yet **k** as they ought to **k**. |
| | 8: 4 | We **k** that "An idol is nothing at all |
| | 9:13 | Don't you **k** that those who serve |
| | 9:24 | Do you not **k** that in a race all |
| | 12: 2 | You **k** that when you were pagans, |
| | 13: 9 | For we **k** in part and we prophesy |
| | 13:12 | Now I **k** in part; then I shall **k** fully, |
| | 14: 9 | how will anyone **k** what you are |
| | 14:16 | they do not **k** what you are saying? |
| | 15:58 | because you **k** that your labor |
| 2Co | 4:14 | because we **k** that the one who |
| | 5: 1 | For we **k** that if the earthly tent we |
| | 5: 6 | **k** that as long as we are at home |
| | 5:11 | we **k** what it is to fear the Lord, |
| | 8: 9 | For you **k** the grace of our Lord |
| | 12: 2 | I **k** a man in Christ who fourteen |

| | | |
|---|---|---|
| Gal | 1:11 | I want you to **k**, brothers and sisters, |
| | 2:16 | **k** that a person is not justified |
| | 4: 9 | But now that you **k** God— |
| Eph | 1:17 | so that you may **k** him better. |
| | 1:18 | in order that you may **k** the hope |
| | 3:19 | and to **k** this love that surpasses |
| | 6: 8 | because you **k** that the Lord will |
| Php | 3:10 | I want to **k** Christ—yes, to **k** |
| | 4:12 | I **k** what it is to be in need, and I **k** |
| Col | 2: 2 | order that they may **k** the mystery |
| | 4: 1 | because you **k** that you also have |
| | 4: 6 | you may **k** how to answer everyone. |
| 1Th | 3: 3 | You **k** quite well that we are |
| | 5: 2 | for you **k** very well that the day |
| 2Th | 1: 8 | will punish those who do not **k** God |
| | 2: 6 | And now you **k** what is holding him |
| 1Ti | 1: 7 | they do not **k** what they are talking |
| | 3: 5 | anyone does not **k** how to manage |
| | 3:15 | you will **k** how people ought |
| 2Ti | 1:12 | because I **k** whom I have believed, |
| | 2:23 | because you **k** they produce |
| | 3:14 | of, because you **k** those from whom |
| Tit | 1:16 | They claim to **k** God, but by their |
| Heb | 8:11 | because they will all **k** me, |
| | 11: 8 | though he did not **k** where he was |
| Jas | 1: 3 | because you **k** that the testing |
| | 3: 1 | because you **k** that we who teach |
| | 4: 4 | don't you **k** that friendship |
| | 4:14 | you do not even **k** what will happen |
| | 4:17 | if you **k** the good you ought to do |
| 1Pe | 1:18 | For you **k** that it was not |
| 2Pe | 1:12 | even though you **k** them and are |
| 1Jn | 2: 3 | We **k** that we have come to **k** him |
| | 2: 4 | Those who say, "I **k** him," but do |
| | 2: 5 | This is how we **k** we are in him: |
| | 2:11 | they do not **k** where they are going, |
| | 2:18 | This is how we **k** it is the last hour. |
| | 2:20 | Holy One, and all of you **k** the truth. |
| | 2:29 | If you **k** that he is righteous, you **k** |
| | 3: 1 | does not **k** us is that it did not **k** him. |
| | 3: 2 | But we **k** that when Christ appears, |
| | 3:10 | This is how we **k** who the children |
| | 3:14 | We **k** that we have passed |
| | 3:16 | This is how we **k** what love is: |
| | 3:19 | This is how we **k** that we belong |
| | 3:24 | this is how we **k** that he lives in us: |
| | 4: 8 | does not love does not **k** God, |
| | 4:13 | This is how we **k** that we live in him |
| | 4:16 | so we **k** and rely on the love God |
| | 5: 2 | This is how we **k** that we love |
| | 5:13 | you may **k** that you have eternal life. |
| | 5:15 | And if we **k** that he hears us— |
| | 5:18 | We **k** that anyone born of God does |
| | 5:20 | We **k** also that the Son of God has |
| | 5:20 | so that we may **k** him who is true. |
| 2Jn | 1: 1 | I only, but also all who **k** the truth— |
| 3Jn | 1:12 | and you **k** that our testimony is true. |
| Jude | 1: 5 | Though you already **k** all this, |
| Rev | 2: 2 | I **k** your deeds, your hard work |
| | 2: 9 | I **k** your afflictions and your |
| | 2:13 | I **k** where you live— |
| | 2:19 | I **k** your deeds, your love and faith, |
| | 3: 3 | you will not **k** at what time I will |
| | 3: 8 | I **k** that you have little strength, |
| | 3:15 | I **k** your deeds, that you are neither |

## KNOW THAT I AM THE †LORD Ex 6:7;
7:5, 17; 10:2; 14:4, 18; 16:12; 29:46; 31:13; Dt
29:6; 1Ki 20:13, 28; Isa 45:3; 49:23; Eze 6:7, 10,
13, 14; 7:4, 27; 11:10, 12; 12:15, 16, 20; 13:9,
14, 21, 23; 14:8; 15:7; 16:62; 20:20, 26, 38, 42,
44; 22:16; 23:49; 24:24, 27; 25:5, 7, 11, 17; 26:6;
28:22, 23, 24, 26; 29:6, 9, 16, 21; 30:8, 19, 25,
26; 32:15; 33:29; 34:27; 35:4, 9, 15; 36:11, 23,
38; 37:6, 13; 38:23; 39:6, 22, 28

## KNOW THAT I THE †LORD Ex 8:22; Isa
49:26; 60:16; Eze 5:13; 17:21, 24; 20:12; 21:5;
22:22; 34:30; 35:12; 36:36; 37:14, 28; 39:7; Joel
3:17

## KNOW THAT THE †LORD Ex 11:7; 18:11;
Nu 16:28; Dt 4:35; Jos 2:9; 22:31; Jdg 16:20;
17:13; 1Ki 8:60; 2Ki 2:3, 5; 2Ch 13:5; Ps 4:3;
100:3; 135:5; 140:12; Zec 2:9, 11; 4:9; 6:15

# KNOWING [KNOW]
| | | |
|---|---|---|
| Ge | 3: 5 | will be like God, **k** good and evil." |
| | 3:22 | like one of us, **k** good and evil. |
| Pr | 7:23 | little **k** it will cost him his life. |
| Mt | 22:18 | But Jesus, **k** their evil intent, said, |
| Lk | 9:47 | Jesus, **k** their thoughts, took a little |
| Jn | 18: 4 | **k** all that was going to happen |
| | 19:28 | **k** that everything had now been |
| Php | 3: 8 | worth of **k** Christ Jesus my Lord, |
| Phm | 1:21 | **k** that you will do even more than I |
| Heb | 13: 2 | hospitality to angels without **k** it. |

# KNOWLEDGE [KNOW]
| | | |
|---|---|---|
| Ge | 2: 9 | the tree of the **k** of good and evil. |
| | 2:17 | eat from the tree of the **k** of good |
| Nu | 24:16 | who has **k** from the Most High, |
| 2Ch | 1:10 | Give me wisdom and **k**, that I may |
| Job | 21:22 | "Can anyone teach **k** to God, |
| | 38: 2 | my plans with words without **k**? |
| | 42: 3 | that obscures my plans without **k**?' |
| Ps | 19: 2 | night after night they display **k**. |
| | 94:10 | who teaches human beings lack **k**? |
| | 119:66 | Teach me **k** and good judgment, |
| | 139: 6 | Such **k** is too wonderful for me, |
| Pr | 1: 4 | **k** and discretion to the young— |
| | 1: 7 | of the LORD is the beginning of **k**, |
| | 1:29 | since they hated **k** and did not |
| | 2: 5 | the LORD and find the **k** of God. |
| | 2: 6 | from his mouth come **k** |
| | 2:10 | and **k** will be pleasant to your soul. |
| | 3:20 | by his **k** the deeps were divided, |
| | 8:10 | of silver, **k** rather than choice gold, |
| | 8:12 | I possess **k** and discretion. |
| | 9:10 | **k** of the Holy One is understanding. |
| | 10:14 | The wise store up **k**, but the mouth |
| | 11: 9 | but through **k** the righteous escape. |
| | 12: 1 | Whoever loves discipline loves **k**, |
| | 12:23 | The prudent keep their **k** |
| | 13:16 | All who are prudent act with **k**, |
| | 14: 6 | but **k** comes easily to the discerning. |
| | 15: 7 | The lips of the wise spread **k**, |
| | 15:14 | The discerning heart seeks **k**, |
| | 17:27 | Those who have **k** use words |
| | 18:15 | heart of the discerning acquires **k**, |
| | 19: 2 | Desire without **k** is not good— |
| | 19:25 | the discerning, and they will gain **k**. |

| | | |
|---|---|---|
| Pr | 20:15 | but lips that speak **k** are a rare jewel. |
| | 21:11 | the wise they get **k**. |
| | 23:12 | and your ears to words of **k**. |
| | 24: 4 | through **k** its rooms are filled |
| | 24: 5 | and those who have **k** muster their |
| Ecc | 1:18 | the more **k**, the more grief. |
| | 2:26 | God gives wisdom, **k** and happiness, |
| | 7:12 | but the advantage of **k** is this: |
| Isa | 11: 2 | the Spirit of the **k** and fear |
| | 11: 9 | the **k** of the LORD as the waters |
| | 40:14 | Who was it that taught him **k**, |
| | 53:11 | by his **k** my righteous servant will |
| Jer | 3:15 | heart, who will lead you with **k** |
| | 10:14 | is senseless and without **k**; |
| Da | 1:17 | these four young men God gave **k** |
| Hos | 4: 6 | "Because you have rejected **k**, |
| Hab | 2:14 | will be filled with the **k** of the glory |
| Mal | 2: 7 | lips of a priest ought to preserve **k**, |
| Mt | 13:11 | replied, "The **k** of the secrets |
| Lk | 1:77 | to give his people the **k** of salvation |
| | 8:10 | He said, "The **k** of the secrets |
| | 11:52 | you have taken away the key to **k**. |
| Ac | 18:24 | with a thorough **k** of the Scriptures. |
| Ro | 1:28 | it worthwhile to retain the **k** of God, |
| | 2:20 | have in the law the embodiment of **k** |
| | 10: 2 | God, but their zeal is not based on **k**. |
| | 11:33 | riches of the wisdom and **k** of God! |
| | 15:14 | filled with **k** and competent |
| 1Co | 8: 1 | But **k** puffs up while love builds up. |
| | 8:10 | with all your **k**, eating in an idol's |
| | 8:11 | Christ died, is destroyed by your **k**. |
| | 12: 8 | to another a message of **k** by means |
| | 13: 2 | can fathom all mysteries and all **k**, |
| | 13: 8 | where there is **k**, it will pass away. |
| 2Co | 2:14 | aroma of the **k** of him everywhere. |
| | 4: 6 | of the **k** of God's glory displayed |
| | 8: 7 | in **k**, in complete earnestness |
| | 10: 5 | sets itself up against the **k** of God, |
| | 11: 6 | as a speaker, but I do have **k**. |
| Eph | 3:19 | to know this love that surpasses **k**— |
| | 4:13 | faith and in the **k** of the Son of God |
| Php | 1: 9 | and more in **k** and depth of insight, |
| Col | 1:10 | work, growing in the **k** of God, |
| | 2: 3 | all the treasures of wisdom and **k**. |
| | 3:10 | is being renewed in **k** in the image |
| 1Ti | 2: 4 | and to come to a **k** of the truth. |
| | 6:20 | ideas of what is falsely called **k**, |
| 2Ti | 2:25 | leading them to a **k** of the truth, |
| | 3: 7 | never able to come to a **k** of the truth. |
| Heb | 10:26 | we have received the **k** of the truth, |
| 2Pe | 1: 3 | for a godly life through our **k** of him |
| | 1: 5 | and to goodness, **k**; |
| | 3:18 | grow in the grace and **k** of our Lord |

# KNOWN [KNOW]
| | | |
|---|---|---|
| Ex | 6: 3 | the LORD I did not make myself **k** |
| Dt | 13: 2 | other gods" (gods you have not **k**) |
| Ps | 9:16 | The LORD is **k** by his acts |
| | 16:11 | You make **k** to me the path of life; |
| | 67: 2 | that your ways may be **k** on earth, |
| | 89: 1 | make your faithfulness **k** through all |
| | 98: 2 | LORD has made his salvation **k** |
| | 105: 1 | make **k** among the nations what he |
| | 119:168 | for all my ways are **k** to you. |
| Pr | 20:11 | Even small children are **k** by their |
| Isa | 12: 4 | make **k** among the nations what he |
| | 46:10 | I make **k** the end |

Isa   61: 9  descendants will be **k** among
Jer    7: 9  follow other gods you have not **k**,
Eze  38:23  I will make myself **k** in the sight
      39: 7  " 'I will make **k** my holy name
Zec  14: 7  a day **k** only to the LORD—
Mt   10:26  or hidden that will not be made **k**.
     24:43  of the house had **k** at what time
Mk    6:14  for Jesus' name had become well **k**.
Lk   19:42  had only **k** on this day what would
Jn     1:18  with the Father, has made him **k**.
     15:15  my Father I have made **k** to you.
     16:14  he will receive what he will make **k**
     17:26  I have made you **k** to them,
Ac     2:28  You have made **k** to me the paths
Ro     1:19  since what may be **k** about God is
       3:21  of God has been made **k**,
       7: 7  I would not have **k** what sin was had
       9:22  his wrath and make his power **k**,
     11:34  "Who has **k** the mind of the Lord?
     15:20  the gospel where Christ was not **k**,
     16:26  and made **k** through the prophetic
1Co   2:16  "Who has **k** the mind of the Lord so
       8: 3  But whoever loves God is **k** by God.
     13:12  know fully, even as I am fully **k**.
2Co   3: 2  our hearts, **k** and read by everyone.
       6: 9  **k**, yet regarded as unknown;
Gal    4: 9  or rather are **k** by God—how is it
Eph    1: 9  he made **k** to us the mystery of his
       3: 3  that is, the mystery made **k** to me
       6:19  I will fearlessly make **k** the mystery
2Ti    3:15  from infancy you have **k** the Holy
Heb   3:10  and they have not **k** my ways.'
2Pe    2:21  for them not to have **k** the way
1Jn    3: 2  we will be has not yet been made **k**.
Rev    1: 1  He made it **k** by sending his angel

# KNOWS [KNOW]

Ge     3: 5  "For God **k** that when you eat of it
1Sa    2: 3  for the LORD is a God who **k**,
Est    4:14  who **k** but that you have come
Job  23:10  But he **k** the way that I take;
Ps   44:21  since he **k** the secrets of the heart?
     94:11  The LORD **k** all human plans; he **k**
    103:14  for he **k** how we are formed,
Pr     9:13  she is simple and **k** nothing.
     14:10  Each heart **k** its own bitterness,
Ecc    2:19  who **k** whether that person will be
       8: 7  Since no one **k** the future, who can
       9:12  no one **k** when their hour will come:
Mt     6: 8  your Father **k** what you need before
       6:32  and your heavenly Father **k** that you
     11:27  No one **k** the Son except the Father,
     24:36  about that day or hour no one **k**,
Lk   12:47  "The servant who **k** the master's
     16:15  of others, but God **k** your hearts.
Ac   15: 8  God, who **k** the heart,
Ro     8:27  who searches our hearts **k** the mind
1Co   2:11  who **k** a person's thoughts except
       3:20  "The Lord **k** that the thoughts
2Ti    2:19  "The Lord **k** those who are his,"
2Pe    2: 9  the Lord **k** how to rescue the godly
1Jn    4: 6  and whoever **k** God listens to us;
       4: 7  has been born of God and **k** God.
Rev  19:12  a name written on him that no one **k**

## KOHATH [KOHATHITE, KOHATHITES]

Ge   46:11  Gershon, **K** and Merari.
Nu   26:58  (**K** was the forefather of Amram;
1Ch  23: 6  Gershon, **K** and Merari.

## KOHATHITE [KOHATH]

Nu     3:29  The **K** clans were to camp

## KOHATHITES [KOHATH]

Nu     3:28  The **K** were responsible for the care
       4:15  The **K** are to carry those things
1Ch   9:32  Some of the **K**, their fellow Levites,

## KORAH

  1. Levite who led rebellion against Moses and Aaron (Nu 16; Jude 11).
  2. Psalms of the sons of Korah: Pss 42; 44-49; 84; 85; 87; 88

## SONS OF KORAH  See SONS

## KORAZIN  (NIV) See CHORAZIN

## KOUM*

Mk     5:41  and said to her, *"Talitha k!"*

---

# L

## LABAN

  Brother of Rebekah (Ge 24:29), father of Rachel and Leah (Ge 29:16). Received Abraham's servant (Ge 24:29–51). Provided daughters as wives for Jacob in exchange for Jacob's service (Ge 29:1–30). Provided flocks for Jacob's service (Ge 30:25–43). After Jacob's departure, pursued and covenanted with him (Ge 31).

## LABOR [LABORER, LABORER'S, LABORERS, LABORING, LABORS]

Ex     1:11  them to oppress them with forced **l**,
       6: 9  their discouragement and harsh **l**.
     20: 9  Six days you shall **l** and do all your
Dt     5:13  Six days you shall **l** and do all your
Jdg    1:30  did subject them to forced **l**.
       1:35  they too were pressed into forced **l**.
1Ki  12: 4  but now lighten the harsh **l**
Ps   48: 6  there, pain like that of a woman in **l**.
    107:12  So he subjected them to bitter **l**;
    127: 1  the house, the builders **l** in vain.
    128: 2  You will eat the fruit of your **l**;
Pr   12:24  rule, but laziness ends in forced **l**.
Ecc    2:10  heart took delight in all my **l**,
       5:18  their toilsome **l** under the sun during
Isa  54: 1  for joy, you who were never in **l**;
     55: 2  and your **l** on what does not satisfy?
Jer  51:58  the nations' **l** is only fuel
Hab   2:13  the people's **l** is only fuel
Mt     6:28  They do not **l** or spin.
Jn     4:38  have reaped the benefits of their **l**."
1Co   3: 8  rewarded according to their own **l**.
     15:58  know that your **l** in the Lord is not

Gal   4:27   cry aloud, you who were never in l;
Php   2:16   Christ that I did not run or l in vain.
Rev 14:13   "they will rest from their l, for their

## LABORER* [LABOR]
Job   7: 2   evening shadows, or a hired l waiting

## LABORER'S* [LABOR]
Jdg   5:26   tent peg, her right hand for the l

## LABORERS [LABOR]
Ne    4:10   "The strength of the l is giving out,
Pr   16:26   The appetite of l works for them;
Ecc   5:12   The sleep of l is sweet, whether they
Mal   3: 5   against those who defraud l of their

## LABORING* [LABOR]
2Th   3: 8   l and toiling so that we would not be

## LABORS* [LABOR]
Ecc   1: 3   does anyone gain from all their l
1Co 16:16   joins in the work and l at it.
1Th   3: 5   our l might have been in vain.

## LACHISH
Jos 10:32   The LORD gave L into Israel's
2Ch 25:27   but they sent men after him to L

## LACK [LACKED, LACKING, LACKS]
Dt    8: 9   not be scarce and you will l nothing;
Ps   23: 1   LORD is my shepherd, I l nothing.
     34: 9   for those who fear him l nothing.
     94:10   teaches human beings l knowledge?
Pr    5:23   For l of discipline they will die,
     10:21   many, but fools die for l of sense.
     11:14   For l of guidance a nation falls,
     15:22   Plans fail for l of counsel,
     28:27   who give to the poor will l nothing,
Ecc  10: 3   they l sense and show everyone
Isa   5:13   go into exile for l of understanding;
Hos   4: 6   my people are destroyed from l
Zec  10: 2   wander like sheep oppressed for l
Mt   13:58   there because of their l of faith.
Mk    6: 6   He was amazed at their l of faith.
     16:14   he rebuked them for their l of faith
Lk   18:22   said to him, "You still l one thing.
1Co   1: 7   you do not l any spiritual gift as you
      7: 5   because of your l of self-control.
Col   2:23   but they l any value in restraining

## LACKED [LACK]
Dt    2: 7   you, and you have not l anything.
Ne    9:21   they l nothing, their clothes did not
1Co 12:24   greater honor to the parts that l it,

## LACKING [LACK]
Ecc   1:15   what is l cannot be counted.
Ro   12:11   Never be l in zeal, but keep your
Col   1:24   in my flesh what is still l in regard
Jas   1: 4   and complete, not l anything.

## LACKS [LACK]
Pr   25:28   is a person who l self-control.
     31:11   in her and l nothing of value.

Eze 34: 8   because my flock l a shepherd
Jas   1: 5   If any of you l wisdom, you should

## LADY*
2Jn   1: 1   To the l chosen by God and to her
      1: 5   dear l, I am not writing you a new

## LAID [LAY]
Ge   22: 9   his son Isaac and l him on the altar,
Nu   27:23   Then he l his hands on him
Dt   34: 9   because Moses had l his hands
1Ki   6:37   the LORD was l in the fourth year,
Ezr   3:11   of the house of the LORD was l.
Job  38: 4   you when I l the earth's foundation?
Ps   18:15   of the earth l bare at your rebuke,
    102:25   the beginning you l the foundations
Pr    3:19   By wisdom the LORD l the earth's
Ecc   1:13   What a heavy burden God has l
Isa  14: 8   "Now that you have been l low,
     44:28   "Let its foundations be l." '
     53: 6   and the LORD has l on him
Eze  24: 2   of Babylon has l siege to Jerusalem
Zec   4: 9   of Zerubbabel have l the foundation
Mk    6:29   and took his body and l it in a tomb.
     16: 6   See the place where they l him.
Lk    6:48   deep and l the foundation on rock.
Jn   11:38   with a stone l across the entrance.
     19:42   tomb was nearby, they l Jesus there.
Ac    6: 6   prayed and l their hands on them.
      7:58   the witnesses l their coats at the feet
1Co   3:11   other than the one already l,
     14:25   the secrets of their hearts are l bare.
1Ti   4:14   the body of elders l their hands
Heb   1:10   you l the foundations of the earth,
      4:13   and l bare before the eyes of him
2Pe   3:10   everything done in it will be l bare.
1Jn   3:16   Jesus Christ l down his life for us.

## LAKE
Mt    4:18   They were casting a net into the l,
      8:24   a furious storm came up on the l,
     14:25   went out to them, walking on the l.
Mk    4: 1   Again Jesus began to teach by the l.
Lk    8:33   down the steep bank into the l
Jn    6:25   found him on the other side of the l,
Rev  19:20   into the fiery l of burning sulfur.
     20:10   thrown into the l of burning sulfur,
     20:14   Hades were thrown into the l of fire.
     20:14   The l of fire is the second death.

## LAMB [LAMB'S, LAMBS]
Ge   22: 8   "God himself will provide the l
     30:32   every dark-colored l and every
Ex   12:21   and slaughter the Passover l.
Lev   3: 7   If you offer a l, you are to present it
      4:32   they bring a l as their sin offering
      5: 7   who cannot afford a l is to bring two
Nu    9:11   They are to eat the l,
2Sa  12: 6   must pay for that l four times over,
Isa  11: 6   The wolf will live with the l,
     53: 7   he was led like a l to the slaughter,
     65:25   wolf and the l will feed together,
Jer  11:19   I had been like a gentle l led
Mk   14:12   to sacrifice the Passover l.
Jn    1:29   "Look, the L of God, who takes
Ac    8:32   and as a l before its shearer is silent,

1Co 5: 7 our Passover l, has been sacrificed.
1Pe 1:19 a l without blemish or defect.
Rev 5: 6 Then I saw a L, looking as if it had
    5:12 "Worthy is the L, who was slain,
    6: 1 I watched as the L opened the first
    7:14 them white in the blood of the L.
    12:11 over him by the blood of the L
    13: 8 of life, the L who was slain
    14: 1 and there before me was the L,
    15: 3 God's servant Moses and of the L:
    17:14 They will make war against the L,
    19: 7 For the wedding of the L has come,
    21: 9 you the bride, the wife of the L."
    21:14 of the twelve apostles of the L.
    21:23 gives it light, and the L is its lamp.
    22: 1 from the throne of God and of the L

## LAMB'S* [LAMB]
Rev 13: 8 written in the L's book of life,
    21:27 names are written in the L book

## LAMBS [LAMB]
Ex 29:38 regularly each day: two l a year old.
Ps 114: 4 leaped like rams, the hills like l.
Isa 40:11 He gathers the l in his arms
Lk 10: 3 you out like l among wolves.
Jn 21:15 Jesus said, "Feed my l."

## LAME
2Sa 4: 4 of Saul had a son who was l in both
    5: 6 blind and the l can ward you off."
    9: 3 a son of Jonathan; he is l in both feet."
Isa 33:23 even the l will carry off plunder.
    35: 6 Then will the l leap like a deer,
Mic 4: 6 the LORD, "I will gather the l;
Zep 3:19 I will rescue the l; I will gather
Mal 1: 8 you sacrifice l or diseased animals,
Mt 11: 5 The blind receive sight, the l walk,
    15:31 the l walking and the blind seeing.
Lk 14:13 poor, the crippled, the l, the blind,
Ac 3: 2 Now a man who was l from birth
    4: 9 a man who was l and are being asked
    14: 8 In Lystra there sat a man who was l.

## LAMECH
Ge 4:19 L married two women, one named

## LAMENT [LAMENTATION, LAMENTS]
2Sa 1:17 took up this l concerning Saul
    3:33 The king sang this l for Abner:
Ps 5: 1 LORD, consider my l.
Eze 19: 1 "Take up a l concerning the princes

## LAMENTATION [LAMENT]
La 2: 5 mourning and l for Daughter Judah.

## LAMENTS [LAMENT]
2Ch 35:25 Jeremiah composed l for Josiah,

## LAMP [LAMPS, LAMPSTAND, LAMPSTANDS]
1Sa 3: 3 The l of God had not yet gone out,
2Sa 22:29 You, LORD, are my l;

1Ki 11:36 may always have a l before me
    15: 4 the LORD his God gave him a l
2Ki 8:19 promised to maintain a l for David
Job 18: 5 "The l of a wicked man is snuffed
Ps 18:28 You, LORD, keep my l burning;
    119:105 Your word is a l to my feet
    132:17 and set up a l for my anointed one.
Pr 6:23 For this command is a l,
    20:27 The human spirit is the l
    31:18 and her l does not go out at night.
Mt 5:15 Neither do people light a l and put it
    6:22 "The eye is the l of the body.
Lk 8:16 "No one lights a l and hides it
Jn 5:35 John was a l that burned and gave
Rev 21:23 gives it light, and the Lamb is its l.
    22: 5 They will not need the light of a l

## LAMPS [LAMP]
Ex 27:21 are to keep the l burning before
Mt 25: 1 be like ten virgins who took their l
Lk 12:35 for service and keep your l burning,
Rev 4: 5 the throne, seven l were blazing.

## LAMPSTAND [LAMP]
Ex 25:31 "Make a l of pure gold.
Nu 3:31 ark, the table, the l, the altars,
Zec 4: 2 "I see a solid gold l with a bowl
    4:11 on the right and the left of the l?"
Heb 9: 2 In its first room were the l
Rev 2: 5 and remove your l from its place.

## LAMPSTANDS [LAMP]
2Ch 4: 7 He made ten gold l according
Rev 1:12 when I turned I saw seven golden l,
    1:20 the seven l are the seven churches.
    11: 4 "the two olive trees" and the two l,

## LAND [LANDOWNER, LANDS, WASTELAND, WASTELANDS]
Ge 1:10 God called the dry ground "l,"
    1:11 said, "Let the l produce vegetation:
    1:24 "Let the l produce living creatures
    7:22 on dry l that had the breath of life
    12: 1 household to the l I will show you.
    12: 7 your offspring I will give this l."
    12:10 Now there was a famine in the l,
    13:15 All the l that you see I will give
    15:18 "To your descendants I give this l,
    17: 8 The whole l of Canaan, where you
    24: 7 your offspring I will give this l'—
    26: 1 Now there was a famine in the l—
    28:15 and I will bring you back to this l.
    31:13 and go back to your native l.' "
    40:15 off from the l of the Hebrews,
    41:30 and the famine will ravage the l.
    42: 6 Joseph was the governor of the l,
    50:24 of this l to the l he promised on oath
Ex 1: 7 so numerous that the l was filled
    3: 8 a l flowing with milk and honey—
    6: 8 I will bring you to the l I swore
    8:22 that I, the LORD, am in this l.
    20: 2 out of Egypt, out of the l of slavery.
    20:12 the l the LORD your God is giving
    34:12 live in the l where you are going,
Lev 18:25 and the l vomited out its inhabitants.
    25: 5 The l is to have a year of rest.

Lev 25:23 the l is mine and you reside in my l as foreigners
26:34 the l will enjoy its sabbath years all
Nu 13: 2 men to explore the l of Canaan,
13:30 go up and take possession of the l,
14: 9 not be afraid of the people of the l,
14:23 them will ever see the l l promised
26:55 Be sure that the l is distributed
35:33 Bloodshed pollutes the l,
Dt 1: 8 See, I have given you this l.
8: 7 God is bringing you into a good l—
11:10 The l you are entering to take over is not like the l of Egypt,
28:21 you from the l you are entering
29:24 has the LORD done this to this l?
34: 1 LORD showed him the whole l—
Jos 1: 6 these people to inherit the l l swore
2: 1 "Go, look over the l," he said,
5:12 after they ate this food from the l;
11:23 So Joshua took the entire l,
13: 2 "This is the l that remains:
14: 4 Levites received no share of the l
14: 9 me, 'The l on which your feet have
Jdg 1:27 were determined to live in that l.
Ru 1: 1 ruled, there was a famine in the l.
2Sa 21:14 answered prayer in behalf of the l.
24:25 his prayer in behalf of the l,
1Ki 8:34 bring them back to the l you gave
17: 7 there had been no rain in the l.
2Ki 17: 5 king of Assyria invaded the entire l,
24: 1 king of Babylon invaded the l,
25:21 went into captivity, away from her l.
1Ch 14:17 fame spread throughout every l,
2Ch 7:14 their sin and will heal their l.
7:20 then I will uproot Israel from my l,
32:21 withdrew to his own l in disgrace.
36:21 The l enjoyed its sabbath rests;
Ezr 9:11 'The l you are entering to possess is
Ne 9:36 the l you gave our ancestors so they
Ps 25:13 their descendants will inherit the l.
37:11 the meek will inherit the l and enjoy
37:29 The righteous will inherit the l
44: 3 by their sword that they won the l,
65: 9 You care for the l and water it;
136:21 and gave their l as an inheritance
142: 5 my portion in the l of the living."
Pr 2:21 For the upright will live in the l,
12:11 who work their l will have abundant
Isa 2: 8 Their l is full of idols;
6:13 seed will be the stump in the l."
9: 2 in the l of deep darkness a light has
53: 8 was cut off from the l of the living;
Jer 2: 7 you into a fertile l to eat its fruit
2: 7 came and defiled my l
22:29 O l, l, l, hear the word
31:17 children will return to their own l.
Eze 7:23 For the l is full of bloodshed,
36:24 and bring you back into your own l.
39:28 I will gather them to their own l,
43: 2 and the l was radiant with his glory.
Da 11:41 He will also invade the Beautiful L.
Hos 2:23 I will plant her for myself in the l;
Zec 3: 9 the sin of this l in a single day.
Mal 4: 6 strike the l with total destruction."
Mt 4:16 those living in the l of the shadow
Mk 15:33 came over the whole l until three
Lk 21:23 There will be great distress in the l

Jas 5:17 it did not rain on the l for three
Rev 7: 3 "Do not harm the l or the sea
16: 2 and poured out his bowl on the l,

## LAND FLOWING WITH MILK AND HONEY See FLOWING

## LANDOWNER* [LAND]

Mt 20: 1 of heaven is like a l who went
20:11 they began to grumble against the l.
21:33 There was a l who planted

## LANDS [LAND]

Ge 26: 3 descendants I will give all these l
Ps 106:27 and scatter them throughout the l.
107: 3 those he gathered from the l,
111: 6 giving them the l of other nations.
Isa 36:18 of any nations ever delivered their l
Eze 20: 6 honey, the most beautiful of all l.
Hab 2: 8 you have destroyed l and cities
2:17 you have destroyed l and cities
Zec 10: 9 in distant l they will remember me.

## LANGUAGE [LANGUAGES]

Ge 11: 1 Now the whole world had one l
11: 9 there the LORD confused the l
Dt 28:49 down, a nation whose l you will not
Ne 13:24 know how to speak the l of Judah.
Jer 5:15 a people whose l you do not know,
Jn 8:44 he speaks his native l, for he is a liar
Ac 2: 6 one heard their own l being spoken.
Col 3: 8 slander, and filthy l from your lips.
Rev 5: 9 God members of every tribe and l
7: 9 people and l, standing before
13: 7 every tribe, people, l and nation.
14: 6 to every nation, tribe, l and people.

## LANGUAGES [LANGUAGE]

Isa 66:18 people of all nations and l,
Zec 8:23 "In those days ten people from all l

## LANTERNS*

Jn 18: 3 carrying torches, l and weapons.

## LAODICEA

Col 4:16 you in turn read the letter from L.
Rev 3:14 the angel of the church in L write:

## LAP

Jdg 7: 5 "Separate those who l the water
Pr 6:27 into his l without his clothes being
16:33 The lot is cast into the l, but its
Lk 6:38 over, will be poured into your l.

## LAPIS [LAZULI]

Ex 24:10 pavement made of l lazuli, as bright
28:18 shall be turquoise, l lazuli and emerald;
Eze 1:26 what looked like a throne of l lazuli,
10: 1 the likeness of a throne of l lazuli above

## LARGE [ENLARGE, ENLARGED, ENLARGES, LARGER, LARGEST]

Nu 13:28 the cities are fortified and very l.
Dt 6:10 a land with l, flourishing cities you
17:17 He must not accumulate l amounts

Jos 10:11 LORD hurled l hailstones down
Eze 23:32 your sister's cup, a cup l and deep;
Da 2:31 there before you stood a l statue—
4:11 The tree grew l and strong and its
7: 7 It had l iron teeth; it crushed
8:21 the l horn between its eyes is
Mk 14:15 He will show you a l room upstairs,
Gal 6:11 See what l letters I use as I write
Rev 6: 4 To him was given a l sword.
18:21 up a boulder the size of a l millstone

## LARGER [LARGE]

Nu 33:54 To a l group give a l inheritance,
Dt 11:23 you will dispossess nations l

## LARGEST* [LARGE]

Mt 13:32 it is the l of garden plants
Mk 4:32 becomes the l of all garden plants,

## LASHES

Dt 25: 3 must not impose more than forty l.
Pr 17:10 person more than a hundred l a fool.
2Co 11:24 from the Jews the forty l minus one.

## LAST [LASTING, LASTS, LATTER]

Ex 14:24 During the l watch of the night
2Sa 23: 1 These are the l words of David:
1Ch 23:27 According to the l instructions
Ps 45: 6 O God, will l for ever and ever;
119:152 you established them to l forever.
Isa 2: 2 In the l days the mountain
41: 4 the first of them and with the l—
44: 6 I am the first and I am the l;
48:12 I am the first and I am the l.
51: 6 But my salvation will l forever,
Da 9: 2 of Jerusalem would l seventy years.
Hos 3: 5 and to his blessings in the l days.
Mic 4: 1 In the l days the mountain
Mt 19:30 who are first will be l, and many who
are l will be first.
20: 8 beginning with the l ones hired
21:37 L of all, he sent his son to them.
27:64 This l deception will be worse than
Mk 9:35 wants to be first must be the very l,
10:31 who are first will be l, and the l first."
15:37 a loud cry, Jesus breathed his l.
Jn 6:40 I will raise them up at the l day."
7:37 On the l and greatest day
11:24 in the resurrection at the l day."
15:16 fruit that will l—and so
Ac 2:17 " 'In the l days, God says, I will
Ro 1:17 that is by faith from first to l, just as
1Co 9:25 it to get a crown that will l forever.
15: 8 and l of all he appeared to me also,
15:26 The l enemy to be destroyed is
15:52 twinkling of an eye, at the l trumpet.
2Ti 3: 1 will be terrible times in the l days.
Heb 1: 2 in these l days he has spoken to us
1: 8 O God, will l for ever and ever;
1Pe 1: 5 is ready to be revealed in the l time.
2Pe 3: 3 that in the l days scoffers will come,
1Jn 2:18 Dear children, this is the l hour;
Jude 1:18 "In the l times there will be scoffers
Rev 1:17 I am the First and the L.
2: 8 of him who is the First and the L,
15: 1 angels with the seven l plagues—l,

Rev 21: 9 full of the seven l plagues came
22:13 the First and the L, the Beginning

## LASTING [LAST]

Ex 12:14 to the LORD—a l ordinance.
28:43 is to be a l ordinance for Aaron
Lev 24: 8 of the Israelites, as a l covenant.
Nu 25:13 have a covenant of a l priesthood,
Heb 10:34 had better and l possessions.

## A LASTING ORDINANCE Ex 12:14, 17,
24; 27:21; 28:43; 29:9; 30:21; Lev 3:17; 10:9;
16:29, 31, 34; 17:7; 23:14, 21, 31, 41; 24:3; Nu
10:8; 15:15; 18:23; 19:10, 21; 2Ch 2:4; Eze
46:14

## LASTS [LAST]

Job 20: 5 is brief, the joy of the godless l
Ps 30: 5 For his anger l only a moment, but his
favor l a lifetime;
Pr 12:19 but a lying tongue l only a moment.
2Co 3:11 greater is the glory of that which l!

## LATE [LATER]

Ps 127: 2 In vain you rise early and stay up l,

## LATER [LATE]

Mk 10:34 Three days l he will rise."
Jn 13: 7 doing, but l you will understand."
Gal 3:17 introduced 430 years l, does not set
1Ti 4: 1 l times some will abandon the faith
Rev 1:19 is now and what will take place l.

## LATIN*

Jn 19:20 written in Aramaic, L and Greek.

## LATTER [LAST]

Job 42:12 The LORD blessed the l part
Mt 23:23 You should have practiced the l,
Php 1:16 The l do so out of love,

## LAUD (KJV) See SING ... PRAISE,
SING ... PRAISES

## LAUGH [LAUGHED,
LAUGHINGSTOCK, LAUGHS,
LAUGHTER]

Ge 18:13 "Why did Sarah l and say, 'Will I
21: 6 hears about this will l with me."
Ps 59: 8 But you l at them, LORD;
Pr 31:25 she can l at the days to come.
Ecc 3: 4 a time to weep and a time to l,
Lk 6:21 you who weep now, for you will l.
6:25 Woe to you who l now, for you will

## LAUGHED [LAUGH]

Ge 17:17 he l and said to himself, "Will a son
18:12 So Sarah l to herself as she thought,
La 1: 7 at her and l at her destruction.
Lk 8:53 They l at him, knowing that she was

## LAUGHINGSTOCK [LAUGH]

La 3:14 I became the l of all my people;

## LAUGHS [LAUGH]

Ps   2: 4   The One enthroned in heaven l;
     37:13   but the Lord l at the wicked, for he

## LAUGHTER [LAUGH]

Ge  21: 6   said, "God has brought me l,
Ps  126: 2   Our mouths were filled with l,
Pr   14:13   Even in l the heart may ache,
Ecc   7: 3   Frustration is better than l,
     10:19   A feast is made for l, wine makes
Jas   4: 9   Change your l to mourning and your

## LAUNDERER'S

Mal  3: 2   be like a refiner's fire or a l soap.

## LAVER (KJV) See BASIN

## LAVISHED

Eph  1: 8   that he l on us. With all wisdom
1Jn  3: 1   See what great love the Father has l

## LAW [LAW'S, LAWFUL, LAWGIVER, LAWS, LAWSUITS]

Ex  16:34   with the tablets of the covenant l,
    25:16   ark the tablets of the covenant l,
    31:18   the two tablets of the covenant l,
Lev  24:22   to have the same l for the foreigner
Nu   5.29   is the l of jealousy when a woman
    6:13   " 'Now this is the l
Dt   1: 5   Moses began to expound this l,
    6:25   to obey all this l before the LORD
    17:18   himself on a scroll a copy of this l,
    27:26   of this l by carrying them out."
    31: 9   So Moses wrote down this l
    31:11   you shall read this l before them
    31:26   "Take this Book of the L and place
Jos   1: 7   to obey all the l my servant Moses
    1: 8   Keep this Book of the L always
    8:32   copied on stones the l of Moses,
    22: 5   the l that Moses the servant
2Ki  22: 8   the Book of the L in the temple
2Ch  6:16   walk before me according to my l,
    17: 9   the Book of the L of the LORD;
    34:14   the Book of the L of the LORD
Ezr   7: 6   well versed in the L of Moses,
Ne   8: 2   the priest brought the L before
    8: 8   read from the Book of the L of God,
Ps   1: 2   who delight in the l of the LORD
    1: 2   and meditate on his l day and night.
    19: 7   The l of the LORD is perfect,
    37:31   The l of their God is in their hearts;
    40: 8   your l is within my heart."
    89:30   "If his sons forsake my l and do not
    119:18   may see wonderful things in your l.
    119:70   unfeeling, but I delight in your l.
    119:72   The l from your mouth is more
    119:77   I may live, for your l is my delight.
    119:97   Oh, how I love your l! I meditate
    119:142   is everlasting and your l is true.
    119:163   detest falsehood but I love your l.
    119:165   peace have those who love your l,
Isa   2: 3   The l will go out from Zion,
    42:21   his righteousness to make his l great
Jer   2: 8   deal with the l did not know me;
    8: 8   for we have the l of the LORD,"

Jer  31:33   "I will put my l in their minds
La   2: 9   among the nations, the l is no more,
Da   9:11   All Israel has transgressed your l
Hos   4: 6   because you have ignored the l
Mic   4: 2   The l will go out from Zion,
Hab   1: 4   Therefore the l is paralyzed,
    1: 7   they are a l to themselves
Zec   7:12   would not listen to the l
Mal   2: 9   partiality in matters of the l."
Mt   5:17   that I have come to abolish the L
    7:12   you, for this sums up the L
    22:36   greatest commandment in the L?"
    22:40   All the L and the Prophets hang
    23:23   the more important matters of the l—
Lk   2:23   (as it is written in the L of the Lord,
    2:39   required by the L of the Lord,
    10:26   "What is written in the L?"
    11:52   "Woe to you experts in the l,
    16:17   stroke of a pen to drop out of the L.
    24:44   written about me in the L of Moses,
Jn   1:17   For the l was given through Moses;
    7:19   Yet not one of you keeps the l.
    18:31   and judge him by your own l."
Ac   6:13   this holy place and against the l.
    13:39   able to obtain under the l of Moses.
    15: 5   required to keep the l of Moses."
    28:23   from the L of Moses
Ro   2:12   All who sin apart from the l
    2:12   under the l will be judged by the l.
    2:15   the requirements of the l are written
    2:20   you have in the l the embodiment
    2:25   has value if you observe the l,
    3:19   we know that whatever the l says,
    3:20   through the l we become conscious
    3:21   apart from the l the righteousness
    3:28   by faith apart from observing the l.
    3:31   nullify the l by this faith?
    4:13   It was not through the l
    4:15   because the l brings wrath.
    4:15   And where there is no l there is no
    5:13   account where there is no l.
    5:20   The l was brought in so
    6:14   because you are not under the l,
    6:15   sin because we are not under the l
    7: 1   the l has authority over someone
    7: 4   died to the l through the body
    7: 5   passions aroused by the l were
    7: 6   we have been released from the l so
    7: 7   Is the l sinful?
    7: 8   For apart from the l, sin was dead.
    7: 9   Once I was alive apart from the l;
    7:12   So then, the l is holy,
    7:14   We know that the l is spiritual;
    7:22   my inner being I delight in God's l;
    7:25   in my mind am a slave to God's l,
    8: 2   life has set you free from the l of sin
    8: 3   For what the l was powerless to do
    8: 4   of the l might be fully met in us,
    8: 7   it does not submit to God's l,
    9: 4   the receiving of the l, the temple
    9:31   who pursued the l as the way
    10: 4   Christ is the culmination of the l so
    13: 8   loves others has fulfilled the l.
    13:10   love is the fulfillment of the l.
1Co   6: 6   brother goes to l against another—
    9: 9   For it is written in the L of Moses:

1Co  9:20  those under the l I became like one
           under the l
     9:21  so as to win those not having the l.
    15:56  is sin, and the power of sin is the l.
Gal  2:16  is not justified by observing the l,
     2:16  by observing the l no one will be
     2:19  "For through the l I died to the l so
     3: 2  receive the Spirit by observing the l,
     3: 5  among you by your observing the l,
     3:10  on observing the l are under a curse,
     3:11  one is justified before God by the l,
     3:13  curse of the l by becoming a curse
     3:19  then, was the purpose of the l?
     3:21  Is the l, therefore,
     3:23  we were held in custody under the l,
     3:24  So the l was put in charge of us
     4: 4  born of a woman, born under the l,
     4:21  you who want to be under the l,
     5: 3  he is obligated to obey the whole l.
     5: 4  by the l have been alienated
     5:14  For the entire l is fulfilled
     5:18  the Spirit, you are not under the l.
     6: 2  in this way you will fulfill the l
Eph  2:15  in his flesh the l with its commands
Php  3: 5  in regard to the l, a Pharisee;
     3: 6  righteousness based on the l, faultless.
     3: 9  of my own that comes from the l,
1Ti  1: 8  We know that the l is good if one
Tit  3: 9  arguments and quarrels about the l,
Heb  7:12  the l must be changed also.
     7:19  (for the l made nothing perfect),
    10: 1  The l is only a shadow of the good
Jas  1:25  into the perfect l that gives freedom,
     2: 8  you really keep the royal l found
     2:10  For whoever keeps the whole l
     4:11  judges them speaks against the l
1Jn  3: 4  Everyone who sins breaks the l;
Rev 15: 5  the tabernacle of the covenant l—

**BOOK OF THE LAW** Dt 28:61; 29:21; 30:10;
    31:26; Jos 1:8; 8:31, 34; 23:6; 24:26; 2Ki 14:6;
    22:8, 11; 2Ch 17:9; 34:14, 15; Ne 8:1, 3, 8, 18;
    9:3; Gal 3:10

**LAW OF MOSES** Jos 8:31, 32; 23:6; 1Ki 2:3;
    2Ki 14:6; 23:25; 2Ch 23:18; 30:16; Ezr 3:2; 7:6;
    Ne 8:1; Da 9:11, 13; Lk 2:22; 24:44; Jn 7:23; Ac
    13:39; 15:5, 21; 28:23; 1Co 9:9; Heb 10:28

**LAW OF THE †LORD** Ex 13:9; 2Ki 10:31;
    1Ch 16:40; 22:12; 2Ch 12:1; 17:9; 19:8; 31:3, 4;
    34:14; 35:26; Ezr 7:10; Ne 9:3; Ps 1:2; 19:7;
    119:1; Isa 5:24; Jer 8:8; Am 2:4

**TEACHER OF THE LAW** Ezr 7:11, 12, 21;
    Ne 8:1, 4, 9; 12:26, 36; Mt 8:19; 13:52; Ac 5:34;
    1Co 1:20

**TEACHERS OF THE LAW** Mt 2:4; 5:20;
    7:29; 9:3; 12:38; 15:1; 16:21; 17:10; 20:18;
    21:15; 23:2, 13, 15, 23, 25, 27, 29; 26:57; 27:41;
    Mk 1:22; 2:6, 16; 3:22; 7:1, 5; 8:31; 9:11, 14;
    10:33; 11:18, 27; 12:12, 28, 35, 38; 14:1, 43, 53;
    15:1, 31; Lk 5:17, 21, 30; 6:7, 11; 9:22; 11:53;
    15:2; 19:47; 20:1, 19, 39, 46; 22:2, 66; 23:10; Jn
    8:3; Ac 4:5; 6:12; 23:9; 1Ti 1:7

**LAW'S**\* [LAW]
Ro   2:26  keep the l requirements, will they

**LAWBREAKER**\* [BREAK]
Ro   2:27  code and circumcision, are a l.
Gal  2:18  then I really would be a l.
Jas  2:11  murder, you have become a l.

**LAWBREAKERS**\* [BREAK]
1Ti  1: 9  the righteous but for l and rebels,
Jas  2: 9  and are convicted by the law as l.

**LAWFUL** [LAW]
Mt  12:12  Therefore it is l to do good
    19: 3  "Is it l for a man to divorce his wife
Mk   2:26  which is l only for priests to eat.
Lk  14: 3  "Is it l to heal on the Sabbath

**LAWGIVER**\* [LAW]
Isa 33:22  the LORD is our l, the LORD is
Jas  4:12  There is only one L and Judge,

**LAWLESS** [LAWLESSNESS]
2Th  2: 8  And then the l one will be revealed,
Heb 10:17  l acts I will remember no more."
2Pe  3:17  be carried away by the error of the l

**LAWLESSNESS**\* [LAWLESS]
2Th  2: 3  occurs and the man of l is revealed,
     2: 7  the secret power of l is already
1Jn  3: 4  sins breaks the law; in fact, sin is l.

**LAWS** [LAW]
Ex  21: 1  "These are the l you are to set
Lev 25:18  decrees and be careful to obey my l,
    26:43  their sins because they rejected my l
Dt   4: 1  and l I am about to teach you.
    30:16  keep his commands, decrees and l;
Jos 24:25  reaffirmed for them decrees and l
1Ki 11:33  nor kept my decrees and l as David,
Ezr  7:10  teaching its decrees and l in Israel.
Job 38:33  Do you know the l of the heavens?
Ps  18:22  All his l are before me; I have not
   119:30  I have set my heart on your l.
   119:43  for I have put my hope in your l.
   119:120 fear of you; I stand in awe of your l.
   119:164 I praise you for your righteous l.
   119:175 you, and may your l sustain me.
   147:20  they do not know his l.
Isa 10: 1  Woe to those who make unjust l,
Eze  5: 6  She has rejected my l and has not
    36:27  decrees and be careful to keep my l.
Heb  8:10  I will put my l in their minds
    10:16  I will put my l in their hearts, and I

**LAWSUITS** [LAW]
Hos 10: 4  therefore l spring up like poisonous
1Co  6: 7  you have l among you means you

**LAY** [LAID, LAYING, LAYS]
Ge  22:12  "Do not l a hand on the boy,"
Ex   7: 4  Then I will l my hand on Egypt
    29:10  his sons shall l their hands on its
Lev  1: 4  You are to l your hand on the head

| Lev | 4:15 | the community are to l their hands |
|---|---|---|
| Nu | 8:10 | the Israelites are to l their hands |
| | 27:18 | leadership, and l your hand on him. |
| Dt | 9:25 | I l prostrate before the LORD |
| 1Sa | 26: 9 | Who can l a hand on the LORD's |
| Job | 1:12 | the man himself do not l a finger." |
| | 22:22 | and l up his words in your heart. |
| Ecc | 10: 4 | calmness can l great offenses |
| Isa | 28:16 | "See, I l a stone in Zion, a tested |
| Mt | 8:20 | of Man has no place to l his head." |
| | 28. 6 | Come and see the place where he l. |
| Mk | 6: 5 | except l his hands on a few sick |
| Lk | 9:58 | of Man has no place to l his head." |
| Jn | 10:15 | and I l down my life for the sheep. |
| | 10:18 | but I l it down of my own accord. |
| | 13:37 | I will l down my life for you." |
| | 15:13 | to l down one's life for one's |
| Ac | 8:19 | whom I l my hands may receive |
| Ro | 9:33 | I l in Zion a stone that causes people |
| 1Co | 3:11 | no one can l any foundation other |
| | 7:17 | This is the rule I l down in all |
| 1Ti | 6:19 | In this way they will l up treasure |
| 1Pe | 2: 6 | "See, I l a stone in Zion, a chosen |
| 1Jn | 3:16 | we ought to l down our lives for one |
| Rev | 4:10 | They l their crowns before |

## LAYING [LAY]

| Lk | 4:40 | and l his hands on each one, |
|---|---|---|
| Ac | 8:18 | the Spirit was given at the l |
| 1Ti | 5:22 | Do not be hasty in the l on of hands, |
| 2Ti | 1: 6 | is in you through the l on of my |
| Heb | 6: 1 | not l again the foundation |
| | 6: 2 | cleansing rites, the l on of hands, |

## LAYS [LAY]

| Jn | 10:11 | The good shepherd l down his life |
|---|---|---|

## LAZARUS*

1. Poor man in Jesus' parable (Lk 16:19–31).
2. Brother of Mary and Martha whom Jesus raised
from the dead (Jn 11:1—12:19).

## LAZINESS* [LAZY]

| Pr | 12:24 | will rule, but l ends in forced labor. |
|---|---|---|
| | 19:15 | L brings on deep sleep, |
| Ecc | 10:18 | Through l, the rafters sag; |

## LAZULI [LAPIS]

| Job | 28: 6 | lapis l comes from its rocks, |
|---|---|---|
| SS | 5:14 | decorated with lapis l. |
| Isa | 54:11 | turquoise, your foundations with lapis l. |
| La | 4: 7 | rubies, their appearance like lapis l. |

## LAZY* [LAZINESS]

| Ex | 5: 8 | They are l; that is why they are |
|---|---|---|
| | 5:17 | Pharaoh said, "L, that's what you |
| | | are—l!" |
| Pr | 10: 4 | L hands make for poverty, |
| | 12:27 | The l do not roast any game, |
| | 26:15 | are too l to bring them back to their |
| Mt | 25:26 | replied, 'You wicked, l servant! |
| Tit | 1:12 | always liars, evil brutes, l gluttons." |
| Heb | 6:12 | We do not want you to become l, |

## LEAD [LEADER, LEADERS, LEADERSHIP, LEADING, LEADS, LED]

| Ex | 15:13 | love you will l the people you have |
|---|---|---|
| | 32:34 | l the people to the place I spoke of, |
| Nu | 14: 8 | with us, he will l us into that land, |
| Dt | 31: 2 | old and I am no longer able to l you. |
| Jos | 1: 6 | because you will l these people |
| 1Sa | 8: 5 | now appoint a king to l us, such as |
| 2Ch | 1:10 | that I may l this people, for who is |
| | 8:14 | and the Levites to l the praise |
| Ps | 27:11 | l me in a straight path because |
| | 43: 3 | let them l me; let them bring me |
| | 61: 2 | l me to the rock that is higher than I. |
| | 139:24 | me, and l me in the way everlasting. |
| | 143:10 | may your good Spirit l me on level |
| Pr | 4:11 | and l you along straight paths. |
| | 5: 5 | her steps l straight to the grave. |
| | 20: 7 | The righteous l blameless lives; |
| | 21: 5 | of the diligent l to profit as surely as |
| Ecc | 5: 6 | Do not let your mouth l you |
| Isa | 3:12 | people, your guides l you astray; |
| | 11: 6 | and a little child will l them. |
| | 49:10 | and l them beside springs of water. |
| Jer | 31: 9 | I will l them beside streams of water |
| Da | 12: 3 | those who l many to righteousness, |
| Mt | 6:13 | And l us not into temptation, |
| | 15:14 | blind l the blind, both will fall into a pit. |
| Lk | 6:39 | "Can the blind l the blind? |
| | 11: 4 | And l us not into temptation.' " |
| Ro | 2: 4 | is intended to l you to repentance? |
| | 12: 8 | if it is to l, do it diligently; |
| 1Th | 4:11 | it your ambition to l a quiet life: |
| 1Jn | 2:26 | those who are trying to l you astray. |
| | 3: 7 | do not let anyone l you astray. |
| | 5:16 | a sin that does not l to death, |
| Rev | 7:17 | 'he will l them to springs of living |

## LEADER [LEAD]

| Lev | 4:22 | " 'When a l sins unintentionally |
|---|---|---|
| 1Sa | 7: 6 | Now Samuel was serving as l |
| | 7:15 | Samuel continued as Israel's l |
| | 12: 2 | Now you have a king as your l. |
| 1Ch | 28: 4 | He chose Judah as l, |
| Lk | 8:41 | man named Jairus, a synagogue l, |

## LEADERS [LEAD]

| Nu | 1:16 | the l of their ancestral tribes. |
|---|---|---|
| | 7:10 | the l brought their offerings for its |
| 1Sa | 8: 1 | he appointed his sons as Israel's l. |
| 1Ch | 29: 9 | at the willing response of their l, |
| Isa | 3:14 | the elders and l of his people: |
| Jer | 25:34 | roll in the dust, you l of the flock. |
| Mic | 3: 1 | "Listen, you l of Jacob, you rulers |
| Jn | 7:13 | about him for fear of the l. |
| | 9:22 | they were afraid of the Jewish l, |
| 1Co | 3:21 | no more boasting about human l! |
| Heb | 13: 7 | Remember your l, who spoke |
| | 13:17 | Have confidence in your l |

## LEADERSHIP* [LEAD]

| Nu | 33: 1 | by divisions under the l of Moses |
|---|---|---|
| | 27:18 | in whom is the spirit of l, |
| Ps | 109: 8 | may another take his place of l. |
| Ac | 1:20 | another take his place of l.' |

## LEADING [LEAD]

| | | |
|---|---|---|
| Dt | 1:15 | So I took the l men of your tribes, |
| Mk | 14:48 | "Am I l a rebellion," said Jesus, |
| Ro | 6:19 | slaves to righteousness l to holiness. |
| 2Ti | 2:25 | will grant them repentance l them |

## LEADS [LEAD]

| | | |
|---|---|---|
| Dt | 27:18 | is anyone who l the blind astray |
| Ps | 23: 2 | he l me beside quiet waters, |
| | 37: 8 | do not fret—it l only to evil. |
| | 68: 6 | he l out the prisoners with singing; |
| Pr | 2:18 | Surely her house l down to death |
| | 10:17 | ignores correction l others astray. |
| | 12:26 | the way of the wicked l them astray. |
| | 14:12 | be right, but in the end it l to death. |
| | 14:23 | but mere talk l only to poverty. |
| | 16:25 | be right, but in the end it l to death. |
| | 19:23 | The fear of the LORD l to life; |
| | 21: 5 | profit as surely as haste l to poverty. |
| Isa | 40:11 | he gently l those that have young. |
| Mt | 7:13 | gate and broad is the road that l |
| | 7:14 | and narrow the road that l to life, |
| | 12:20 | snuff out, till he l justice to victory. |
| Jn | 10: 3 | own sheep by name and l them out. |
| Ro | 6:16 | which l to righteousness? |
| | 6:22 | the benefit you reap l to holiness, |
| | 14:19 | every effort to do what l to peace |
| 2Co | 2:14 | God, who always l us as captives |
| | 7:10 | sorrow brings repentance that l |
| Tit | 1: 1 | of the truth that l to godliness— |
| 1Jn | 5:16 | There is a sin that l to death. |
| Rev | 12: 9 | Satan, who l the whole world astray. |

## LEAF [LEAVES]

| | | |
|---|---|---|
| Ge | 8:11 | beak was a freshly plucked olive l! |
| Ps | 1: 3 | and whose l does not wither— |
| Pr | 11:28 | righteous will thrive like a green l. |

## LEAH

Wife of Jacob (Ge 29:16–30); bore six sons and one daughter (Ge 29:31—30:21; 34:1; 35:23).

## LEAN [LEANED, LEANING]

| | | |
|---|---|---|
| Ge | 41:20 | The l, ugly cows ate up the seven |
| Pr | 3: 5 | l not on your own understanding; |

## LEANED [LEAN]

| | | |
|---|---|---|
| Ge | 47:31 | Israel worshiped as he l on the top |
| Jn | 21:20 | one who had l back against Jesus |
| Heb | 11:21 | worshiped as he l on the top of his |

## LEANING [LEAN]

| | | |
|---|---|---|
| Jn | 13:25 | L back against Jesus, he asked him, |

## LEAP [LEAPED, LEAPS]

| | | |
|---|---|---|
| Ps | 29: 6 | He makes Lebanon l like a calf, |
| Isa | 35: 6 | Then will the lame l like a deer, |
| Lk | 6:23 | "Rejoice in that day and l for joy, |

## LEAPED [LEAP]

| | | |
|---|---|---|
| Ps | 114: 4 | the mountains l like rams, |
| Lk | 1:41 | greeting, the baby l in her womb, |

## LEAPS* [LEAP]

| | | |
|---|---|---|
| Job | 37: 1 | heart pounds and l from its place. |
| Ps | 28: 7 | My heart l for joy, and with my |

## LEARN [LEARNED, LEARNING]

| | | |
|---|---|---|
| Dt | 4:10 | they may l to revere me as long as |
| | 5: 1 | L them and be sure to follow them. |
| | 18: 9 | do not l to imitate the detestable |
| | 31:12 | and l to fear the LORD your God |
| Ps | 119: 7 | heart as I l your righteous laws. |
| Pr | 19:25 | and the simple will l prudence; |
| Isa | 1:17 | l to do right! |
| | 26: 9 | people of the world l righteousness. |
| Jer | 35:13 | 'Will you not l a lesson and obey |
| Mt | 11:29 | my yoke upon you and l from me, |
| Mk | 13:28 | "Now l this lesson from the fig |
| Jn | 14:31 | that the world may l that I love |
| 1Th | 4: 4 | of you should l to control your own |
| 1Ti | 2:11 | A woman should l in quietness |
| | 5: 4 | these should l first of all to put their |
| Tit | 3:14 | Our people must l to devote |
| Rev | 14: 3 | No one could l the song except |

## LEARNED [LEARN]

| | | |
|---|---|---|
| Ps | 119:152 | Long ago I l from your statutes |
| Pr | 24:32 | and l a lesson from what I saw: |
| Ecc | 1:17 | and folly, but I l that this, too, |
| | 9:11 | to the brilliant or favor to the l; |
| Mt | 11:25 | these things from the wise and l, |
| Jn | 6:45 | and l from him comes to me. |
| | 15:15 | that I l from my Father I have made |
| Eph | 4:20 | not the way of life you l |
| Php | 4: 9 | Whatever you have l or received |
| | 4:11 | I have l to be content whatever |
| 2Ti | 3:14 | continue in what you have l |
| Heb | 5: 8 | he was, he l obedience from what he |
| Rev | 2:24 | have not l Satan's so-called deep |

## LEARNING [LEARN]

| | | |
|---|---|---|
| Pr | 1: 5 | let the wise listen and add to their l, |
| | 4: 2 | I give you sound l, so do not forsake |
| | 9: 9 | and they will add to their l. |
| Isa | 44:25 | who overthrows the l of the wise |
| Jn | 7:15 | man get such l without having been |
| Ac | 26:24 | "Your great l is driving you |
| 2Ti | 3: 7 | always l but never able to come |

## LEAST [LESS]

| | | |
|---|---|---|
| 1Sa | 9:21 | is not my clan the l of all the clans |
| Isa | 60:22 | The l of you will become |
| Mt | 5:18 | letter, not the l stroke of a pen, |
| | 5:19 | others accordingly will be called l |
| | 25:40 | did for one of the l of these brothers |
| Lk | 7:28 | yet the one who is l in the kingdom |
| | 9:48 | whoever is l among you all is |
| 1Co | 15: 9 | For I am the l of the apostles and do |
| 2Co | 11: 5 | I do not think I am in the l inferior |
| Eph | 3: 8 | Although I am less than the l of all |

## LEATHER

| | | |
|---|---|---|
| Ex | 25: 5 | skins dyed red and another durable l; |
| Lev | 13:48 | wool, any l or anything made of l— |
| Nu | 4: 6 | cover the curtain with a durable l, |
| 2Ki | 1: 8 | and had a l belt around his waist." |
| Mt | 3: 4 | and he had a l belt around his waist. |

## LEAVE [LEAVES]

| | | |
|---|---|---|
| Ge | 2:24 | this reason a man will l his father |
| Ex | 12:10 | Do not l any of it till morning; |
| | 12:33 | people to hurry and l the country. |
| | 34: 7 | he does not l the guilty unpunished; |
| Lev | 19:10 | L them for the poor |
| Nu | 11:20 | did we ever l Egypt?" ' " |
| Dt | 31: 6 | he will never l nor forsake |
| Jos | 1: 5 | I will never l you nor forsake you. |
| Ru | 1:16 | "Don't urge me to l you or to turn |
| Pr | 13:22 | Good people l an inheritance |
| | 15:10 | discipline awaits those who l the path; |
| Mk | 10: 7 | this reason a man will l his father |
| Jn | 8:11 | *"Go now and l your life of sin."* |
| | 14:18 | I will not l you as orphans; |
| | 14:27 | Peace I l with you; my peace I give |
| Eph | 5:31 | this reason a man will l his father |
| Heb | 13: 5 | God has said, "Never will I l you; |

## LEAVEN (KJV) See YEAST

## LEAVENS*

| | | |
|---|---|---|
| 1Co | 5: 6 | a little yeast l the whole batch |

## LEAVES [LEAF, LEAVE]

| | | |
|---|---|---|
| Ge | 3: 7 | so they sewed fig l together |
| Jer | 17: 8 | its l are always green. |
| Eze | 47:12 | for food and their l for healing." |
| Mk | 11:13 | it, he found nothing but l, because it |
| 1Co | 7:15 | But if the unbeliever l, let it be so. |
| Rev | 22: 2 | the l of the tree are for the healing |

## LEBANON

| | | |
|---|---|---|
| Dt | 11:24 | will extend from the desert to L, |
| 1Ki | 4:33 | from the cedar of L to the hyssop |
| | 5: 6 | that cedars of L be cut for me. |
| 2Ki | 14: 9 | "A thistle in L sent a message |
| Ps | 29: 6 | He makes L leap like a calf, |
| | 92:12 | they will grow like a cedar of L; |
| Isa | 40:16 | L is not sufficient for altar fires, |
| Hab | 2:17 | have done to L will overwhelm you, |

## LEBBAEUS (KJV) See THADDAEUS

## LEBO HAMATH [HAMATH]

| | | |
|---|---|---|
| Nu | 34: 8 | and from Mount Hor to L. |
| 2Ki | 14:25 | the boundaries of Israel from L |

## LECTURE*

| | | |
|---|---|---|
| Jn | 9:34 | in sin at birth; how dare you l us!" |
| Ac | 19: 9 | had discussions daily in the l hall |

## LED [LEAD]

| | | |
|---|---|---|
| Ex | 3: 1 | he l the flock to the far side |
| | 32:21 | you, that you l them into such great |
| Dt | 8: 2 | the LORD your God l you all |
| | 17:17 | wives, or his heart will be l astray. |
| 1Ki | 11: 3 | and his wives l him astray. |
| 2Ki | 21: 9 | Manasseh l them astray, so that they |
| 2Ch | 26:16 | powerful, his pride l to his downfall. |
| Ne | 13:26 | but even he was l into sin by foreign |
| Job | 31: 7 | if my heart has been l by my eyes, |
| Ps | 77:19 | Your path l through the sea, |
| | 78:52 | he l them like sheep through |

| | | |
|---|---|---|
| Pr | 7:21 | persuasive words she l him astray; |
| | 20: 1 | whoever is l astray by them is not |
| Isa | 53: 7 | he was l like a lamb |
| | 55:12 | go out in joy and be l forth in peace; |
| Jer | 11:19 | I had been like a gentle lamb l |
| | 50: 6 | their shepherds have l them astray |
| Hos | 11: 4 | I l them with cords of human |
| Am | 2:10 | I you forty years in the wilderness |
| Mt | 4: 1 | Jesus was l by the Spirit |
| | 27:31 | they l him away to crucify him. |
| Lk | 4: 1 | and was l by the Spirit |
| | 4: 5 | The devil l him up to a high place |
| | 4: 9 | The devil l him to Jerusalem |
| Ac | 8:32 | "He was l like a sheep |
| Ro | 8:14 | For those who are l by the Spirit |
| 2Co | 7: 9 | but because your sorrow l you |
| Gal | 5:18 | But if you are l by the Spirit, |

## LEECH*

| | | |
|---|---|---|
| Pr | 30:15 | "The l has two daughters. 'Give! |

## LEEKS*

| | | |
|---|---|---|
| Nu | 11: 5 | melons, l, onions and garlic. |

## LEFT [LEFT-HANDED, LEFTOVER]

| | | |
|---|---|---|
| Ge | 7:23 | Only Noah was l, and those |
| | 13: 9 | If you go to the l, I'll go to the right; |
| Ex | 12:41 | all the LORD's divisions l Egypt. |
| Nu | 26:65 | one of them was l except Caleb son |
| Dt | 28:14 | to the right or to the l, |
| Jos | 1: 7 | turn from it to the right or to the l, |
| | 23: 6 | turning aside to the right or to the l. |
| Jdg | 3: 4 | They were l to test the Israelites |
| 2Ki | 22: 2 | turning aside to the right or to the l. |
| Pr | 4:27 | Do not turn to the right or the l; |
| Isa | 30:21 | you turn to the right or to the l, |
| Mt | 6: 3 | do not let your l hand know what |
| | 25:33 | on his right and the goats on his l. |
| Mk | 8: 8 | of broken pieces that were l over. |
| | 10:28 | "We have l everything to follow |
| | 10:40 | my right or l is not for me to grant. |
| Lk | 17:34 | one will be taken and the other l. |
| 1Th | 4:15 | who are l till the coming |
| Heb | 10:26 | of the truth, no sacrifice for sins is l, |
| 2Pe | 2:15 | They have l the straight way |

## LEFT-HANDED* [HAND, LEFT]

| | | |
|---|---|---|
| Jdg | 3:15 | Ehud, a l man, the son of Gera |
| | 20:16 | were seven hundred who were l; |
| 1Ch | 12: 2 | or to sling stones right-handed or l; |

## LEFTOVER* [LEFT]

| | | |
|---|---|---|
| Ru | 2: 2 | pick up the l grain behind anyone |

## LEGAL

| | | |
|---|---|---|
| Col | 2:14 | the charge of our l indebtedness, |

## LEGION [LEGIONS]

| | | |
|---|---|---|
| Mk | 5: 9 | "My name is L," he replied, |

## LEGIONS* [LEGION]

| | | |
|---|---|---|
| Mt | 26:53 | at my disposal more than twelve l |

## LEGITIMATE*

| | | |
|---|---|---|
| Heb | 12: 8 | you are not l children at all. |

## LEGS

Ps 147:10 his delight in the power of human l;
Da  2:33 its l of iron, its feet partly of iron
    10: 6 and l like the gleam of burnished
Jn  19:33 dead, they did not break his l.
Rev 10: 1 sun, and his l were like fiery pillars.

## LEMA*

Mt 27:46 *"Eli, Eli, l sabachthani?"*
Mk 15:34 *"Eloi, Eloi, l sabachthani?"*

## LEMUEL*

Pr 31: 1 The sayings of King L—
   31: 4 It is not for kings, L—it is not

## LEND [LENDER, LENDS, MONEYLENDER]

Ex  22:25 "If you l money to one of my people
Lev 25:37 You must not l them money
Dt  15: 8 freely l them whatever they need.
    28:12 You will l to many nations but will
    28:44 They will l to you, but you will not l
Ps  15: 5 l money to the poor without interest
    37:26 are always generous and l freely;
    112: 5 those who are generous and l freely,
Pr  19:17 kind to the poor l to the LORD,
Eze 18: 8 He does not l to them at interest
Lk   6:34 Even sinners l to sinners,

## LENDER* [LEND]

Pr  22: 7 and the borrower is slave to the l.
Isa 24: 2 for borrower as for l, for debtor as

## LENDS* [LEND]

Eze 18:13 He l at interest and takes a profit.

## LENGTH [LONG]

Ge 13:17 walk through the l and breadth
Pr 10:27 fear of the LORD adds l to life,

## LENGTHY* [LONG]

Mk 12:40 and for a show make l prayers.
Lk 20:47 and for a show make l prayers.

## LEOPARD

Isa 11: 6 the l will lie down with the goat,
Jer 13:23 change his skin or a l its spots?
Da   7: 6 beast, one that looked like a l.
Rev 13: 2 The beast I saw resembled a l,

## LEPROSY [LEPROUS]

2Ki  5: 1 was a valiant soldier, but he had l.
     7: 3 Now there were four men with l
2Ch 26:21 King Uzziah had l until the day he
Mt   8: 3 he was cleansed of his l.
    11: 5 those who have l are cleansed,
Lk   4:27 many in Israel with l in the time
    17:12 village, ten men who had l met him.

## LEPROUS [LEPROSY]

Ex  4: 6 when he took it out, the skin was l—
Nu 12:10 Miriam's skin was l—

## LESS [LEAST]

Ex  30:15 give l when you make the offering
2Ch  6:18 How much l this temple I have
    32:15 How much l will your god deliver
Ezr  9:13 you have punished us l than our sins
Jn   3:30 I must become l."

## LESSON

Mk 13:28 "Now learn this l from the fig tree:

## LEST

Pr   31: 5 l they drink and forget what has
1Co  1:17 l the cross of Christ be emptied

## LET

Ge   1: 3 And God said, "L there be light,"
     1: 6 "L there be a vault between
     1: 9 and l dry ground appear."
    1:11 "L the land produce vegetation:
    1:14 "L there be lights in the vault
    1:20 said, "L the water teem with living
    1:24 "L the land produce living creatures
    1:26 "L us make human beings in our
    11: 7 l us go down and confuse their
Ex   1:16 but if it is a girl, l her live."
     5: 1 'L my people go, so that they may
     5: 2 LORD and I will not l Israel go."
    13:17 When Pharaoh l the people go,
Ps  22: 8 they say, "l the LORD rescue him.
    25: 2 do not l me be put to shame, nor l
    33: 8 L all the earth fear the LORD; l all
    95: 1 l us sing for joy to the LORD; l us
   118:24 l us rejoice today and be glad.
Jer  9:24 l those who boast boast about this:
La   3:40 and l us return to the LORD.
Joel 3:10 L the weakling say, "I am strong!"
Mt  27:43 L God rescue him now if he wants
Mk   4: 9 has ears to hear, l them hear."
    10: 9 joined together, l no one separate."
Jn   7:37 "L anyone who is thirsty come
    14: 1 "Do not l your hearts be troubled.
Ro   3: 4 L God be true, and every human
2Co 10:17 "L those who boast boast
Eph  4:26 Do not l the sun go down while you
Col  3:15 L the peace of Christ rule in your
     3:16 L the message of Christ dwell
Heb 10:22 l us draw near to God with a sincere
1Jn  4: 7 Dear friends, l us love one another,
Rev 22:17 L those who are thirsty come;

## LETTER [LETTERS]

Mt   5:18 not the smallest l, not the least
2Co  3: 2 You yourselves are our l,
     3: 6 not of the l but of the Spirit; for the l
2Th  3:14 do not obey our instruction in this l.

## LETTERS [LETTER]

2Ch 32:17 also wrote l ridiculing the LORD,
2Co  3: 7 which was engraved in l on stone,
    10:10 "His l are weighty and forceful,
Gal  6:11 See what large l I use as I write
2Th  3:17 the distinguishing mark in all my l.
2Pe  3:16 His l contain some things that are

## LEVEL

Ps 143:10  good Spirit lead me on l ground.
Isa 26: 7  The path of the righteous is l;
     40: 4  the rough ground shall become l,
     45: 2  before you and will l the mountains;
Jer 31: 9  a l path where they will not stumble,
Lk  6:17  with them and stood on a l place.
Heb 12:13  "Make l paths for your feet,"

## LEVI  [l FVITE, LEVITES, LEVITICAL]

1. Son of Jacob by Leah (Ge 29:34; 46:11; 1Ch
2:1). With Simeon avenged rape of Dinah (Ge 34).
Tribe of blessed (Ge 49:5–7; Dt 33:8–11), chosen as
priests (Nu 3–4), numbered (Nu 3:39; 26:62), given
cities, but not land (Nu 18; 35; Dt 10:9; Jos 13:14;
21), land (Eze 48:8–22), 12,000 from (Rev 7:7).
2. See MATTHEW.

## LEVIATHAN*

Job  3: 8  day, those who are ready to rouse L.
     41: 1  you pull in the l with a fishhook
Ps  74:14  was you who crushed the heads of L
    104:26  fro, and the l, which you formed
Isa 27: 1  L the gliding serpent, L the coiling
             serpent;

## LEVITE  [LEVI]

Nu  3:20  These were the L clans,
Dt  26:12  tithe, you shall give it to the L,
Jdg 19: 1  Now a L who lived in a remote area
Ac  4:36  Joseph, a L from Cyprus,

## LEVITES  [LEVI]

Ex  32:26  And all the L rallied to him.
Nu  1:53  The L, however, are to set up their
     1:53  The L are to be responsible
     3:12  The L are mine,
     8: 6  "Take the L from among all
    16: 7  You L have gone too far!"
    18:21  "I give to the L all the tithes
    35: 7  must give the L forty-eight towns,
Jos 14: 4  The L received no share of the land
1Ch 15: 2  but the L may carry the ark of God,
     23: 6  David separated the L into divisions
2Ch 31: 2  to their duties as priests or L—
Ezr  6:18  the L in their groups for the service
Ne  8: 9  and the L who were instructing
Mal  3: 3  he will purify the L and refine them

## PRIESTS AND LEVITES  See PRIESTS

## LEVITICAL  [LEVI]

Heb  7:11  attained through the L priesthood—

## LEVY

Am  5:11  You l a straw tax on the poor

## LEWD  [LEWDNESS]

Jdg 20: 6  because they committed this l

## LEWDNESS  [LEWD]

Eze 16:58  will bear the consequences of your l
     23:48  "So I will put an end to l
Mk  7:22  malice, deceit, l, envy, slander,

## LIAR*  [LIE]

Dt  19:18  and if the witness proves to be a l,
Job 34: 6  I am right, I am considered a l;
Ps 116:11  I said, "Everyone is a l."
Pr  17: 4  a l pays attention to a destructive
     19:22  better to be poor than a l.
     30: 6  will rebuke you and prove you a l.
Jn   8:44  for he is a l and the father of lies.
     8:55  not, I would be a l like you, but I do
Ro   3: 4  be true, and every human being a l.
1Jn  1:10  we make him out to be a l and his
     2:22  Who is the l? It is whoever denies
     5:10  God has made him out to be a l,

## LIARS*  [LIE]

Ps  63:11  the mouths of l will be silenced.
Isa 57: 4  a brood of rebels, the offspring of l?
Mic  2:11  If l and deceivers come and say,
     6:12  her inhabitants are l and their
1Ti  1:10  for slave traders and l and perjurers.
     4: 2  come through hypocritical l,
Tit  1:12  "Cretans are always l, evil brutes,
1Jn  2: 4  do not do what he commands are l,
     4:20  yet hate a brother or sister, we are l.
Rev  3: 9  Jews though they are not, but are l—
     21: 8  magic arts, the idolaters and all l—

## LIBATIONS*

Ps  16: 4  I will not pour out their l of blood

## LIBERAL*  [LIBERALLY]

2Co  8:20  of the way we administer this l gift.

## LIBERALLY*  [LIBERAL]

Dt  15:14  Supply them l from your flock,

## LIBERATED*  [LIBERTY]

Ro   8:21  the creation itself will be l from its

## LIBERTY*  [LIBERATED]

Lev 25:10  proclaim l throughout the land to all

## LICE  (KJV) See GNATS

## LICENSE*

Jude 1: 4  of our God into a l for immorality

## LICK

Ps  72: 9  him and his enemies l the dust.
Isa 49:23  they will l the dust at your feet.
Mic  7:17  They will l dust like a snake,

## LIE  [LIAR, LIARS, LIED, LIES, LYING]

Lev  6: 3  if they find lost property and l about it,
     19:11  " 'Do not l. " 'Do not deceive
Nu  23:19  that he should l, not a human being,
Dt   6: 7  when you l down and when you get
     11:19  when you l down and when you get
Ru   3: 4  go and uncover his feet and l down.
1Sa 15:29  who is the Glory of Israel does not l
Ps   4: 8  In peace I will l down and sleep,
     23: 2  He makes me l down in green
     38:12  all day long they scheme and l.
     89:35  and I will not l to David—

Pr    3:24   When you l down, you will not be
Isa   11: 6   the leopard will l down
      28:15   for we have made a l our refuge
Jer    9: 5   They have taught their tongues to l;
      23:14   They commit adultery and live a l.
Eze   13: 6   are false and their divinations a l.
      34:14   There they will l down in good
Zep    3:13   They will eat and l down and no one
Ro     1:25   the truth about God for a l,
Col    3: 9   Do not l to each other, since you
2Th    2: 9   signs and wonders that serve the l,
       2:11   so that they will believe the l
Tit    1: 2   who does not l, promised before
Heb    6:18   which it is impossible for God to l,
1Jn    1: 6   we l and do not live out the truth.
       2:21   because no l comes from the truth.
Rev   14: 5   No l was found in their mouths;

## LIED [LIE]

Ge    18:15   Sarah was afraid, so she l and said,
Jer    5:12   They have l about the LORD;
Ac     5: 4   You have not l just to human beings

## LIES [LIE]

Job   27: 4   and my tongue will not utter l.
Ps     5: 6   you destroy those who tell l.
       5: 9   with their tongues they tell l.
      10: 7   Their mouths are full of l
      12: 2   Everyone l to their neighbor;
      34:13   evil and your lips from telling l.
      58: 3   they are wayward, spreading l.
     144: 8   whose mouths are full of l,
Pr     6:19   a false witness who pours out l
      12:17   the truth, but a false witness tells l.
      19: 5   whoever pours out l will not go free.
      19: 9   and whoever pours out l will perish.
      29:12   If a ruler listens to l, all his officials
      30: 8   Keep falsehood and l far from me;
Jer    5:31   The prophets prophesy l, the priests
       9: 3   their tongue like a bow, to shoot l;
      14:14   "The prophets are prophesying l
La     1: 1   How deserted l the city, once so full
Eze   13:22   the righteous with your l, when l
Hos   11:12   Ephraim has surrounded me with l,
Na     3: 1   of blood, full of l, full of plunder,
Hab    2:18   Or an image that teaches l?
Zep    3:13   do no wrong; they will tell no l.
Jn     8:44   for he is a liar and the father of l.

## LIFE [LIVE]

Ge    1:30   that has the breath of l in it—
      2: 7   into his nostrils the breath of l,
      2: 9   of the garden were the tree of l
      6:17   to destroy all l under the heavens,
      9: 5   for the l of another human being.
      9:11   Never again will all l be destroyed
Ex    21: 6   Then he will be his servant for l.
      21:23   serious injury, you are to take l for l,
      23:26   I will give you a full l span.
Lev   17:14   because the l of every creature is its
      24:17   " 'Anyone who takes the l
      24:18   Anyone who takes the l
Nu    35:31   a ransom for the l of a murderer,
Dt     4:42   one of these cities and save their l.
      12:23   because the blood is the l,
      19:21   l for l, eye for eye, tooth for tooth,

Dt    30:15   See, I set before you today l
      30:19   Now choose l, so that you and your
      30:20   For the LORD is your l, and he
      32:39   I put to death and I bring to l, I have
      32:47   idle words for you—they are your l.
1Sa   19: 5   He took his l in his hands when he
Ne     9: 6   You give l to everything,
Job    2: 4   will give all he has for his own l.
       2: 6   but you must spare his l."
      10: 1   "I loathe my very l; therefore I will
      33: 4   breath of the Almighty gives me l.
      33:30   the light of l may shine on them.
      42:12   of Job's l more than the former part.
Ps    16:11   make known to me the path of l;
      17:14   this world whose reward is in this l.
      23: 6   will follow me all the days of my l,
      27: 1   LORD is the stronghold of my l—
      34:12   Whoever of you loves l and desires
      36: 9   For with you is the fountain of l;
      49: 7   No one can redeem the l of another
      49: 8   the ransom for a l is costly,
      63: 3   Because your love is better than l,
      69:28   they be blotted out of the book of l
      91:16   With long l I will satisfy them
     104:33   I will sing to the LORD all my l;
     119:25   preserve my l according to your
Pr     1:19   it takes away the l of those who get it.
       3: 2   they will prolong your l many years
       3:16   Long l is in her right hand;
       3:18   She is a tree of l to those who take
       6:23   and instruction are the way to l,
       6:26   man's wife preys on your very l.
       7:23   little knowing it will cost him his l.
       8:35   For those who find me find l
      10:11   of the righteous is a fountain of l,
      10:27   fear of the LORD adds length to l,
      11:30   fruit of the righteous is a tree of l,
      13:12   but a longing fulfilled is a tree of l.
      13:14   of the wise is a fountain of l,
      14:27   of the LORD is a fountain of l,
      15: 4   The soothing tongue is a tree of l,
      16:22   Prudence is a fountain of l
      18:21   The tongue has the power of l
      19:23   The fear of the LORD leads to l;
      21:21   righteousness and love finds l,
      22: 5   preserve their l stay far from them.
Ecc    2:17   So I hated l, because the work
       7:12   Wisdom preserves the l of its
       9: 9   Enjoy l with your wife,
       9: 9   wine makes l merry, and money is
Isa   53:10   the LORD makes his l an offering
      53:11   he will see the light of l and be
      53:12   he poured out his l unto death,
La     3:58   up my case; you redeemed my l.
Eze   37: 5   enter you, and you will come to l.
Da    12: 2   some to everlasting l,
Jnh    2: 6   God, brought my l up from the pit.
Mal    2: 5   with him, a covenant of l and peace,
Mt     6:25   do not worry about your l,
       7:14   and narrow the road that leads to l,
      10:39   Whoever finds their l will lose it,
      16:21   and on the third day be raised to l.
      16:25   but whoever loses their l for me will
      18: 8   It is better for you to enter l maimed
      19:16   thing must I do to get eternal l?"
      19:29   as much and will inherit eternal l.
      20:28   to give his l as a ransom for many."

Mt 25:46 but the righteous to eternal l."
Mk  3: 4 or to do evil, to save l or to kill?"
     8:35 wants to save their l will lose it,
     9:43 you to enter l maimed than with two
    10:17 must I do to inherit eternal l?"
    10:30 and in the age to come eternal l.
    10:45 to give his l as a ransom for many."
Lk  6: 9 do evil, to save l or to destroy it?"
     9:22 and on the third day be raised to l."
     9:24 but whoever loses their l for me will
    12:15 l does not consist in an abundance
    12:22 do not worry about your l, what you
    12:25 can add a single hour to your l?
    14:26 yes, even l itself—such a person
    17:33 whoever loses their l will preserve
    21:19 Stand firm, and you will win l.
Jn   1: 4 In him was l, and that l was the light
     3:15 who believes may have eternal l
     3:36 believes in the Son has eternal l,
     3:36 rejects the Son will not see l,
     4:14 of water welling up to eternal l."
     5:21 raises the dead and gives them l,
     5:24 but has crossed over from death to l.
     5:26 For as the Father has l in himself,
     5:39 that in them you possess eternal l.
     5:40 you refuse to come to me to have l.
     6:27 for food that endures to eternal l,
     6:33 heaven and gives l to the world."
     6:35 Jesus declared, "I am the bread of l.
     6:40 believes in him shall have eternal l,
     6:47 you, whoever believes has eternal l.
     6:48 I am the bread of l.
     6:51 I will give for the l of the world."
     6:53 his blood, you have no l in you.
     6:63 The Spirit gives l;
     6:68 You have the words of eternal l.
     8:12 but will have the light of l."
    10:10 I have come that they may have l,
    10:11 The good shepherd lays down his l
    10:15 and I lay down my l for the sheep.
    10:28 I give them eternal l, and they shall
    11:25 "I am the resurrection and the l.
    12:25 Those who love their l will lose it,
    12:50 that his command leads to eternal l.
    13:37 I will lay down my l for you."
    14: 6 am the way and the truth and the l.
    15:13 lay down one's l for one's friends.
    17: 2 he might give eternal l to all those
    17: 3 Now this is eternal l: that they know
    20:31 by believing you may have l in his
Ac   2:28 made known to me the paths of l;
     2:32 God has raised this Jesus to l,
     3:15 You killed the author of l, but God
    11:18 granted repentance that leads to l."
    13:48 appointed for eternal l believed.
Ro   2: 7 immortality, he will give eternal l.
     4:25 was raised to l for our justification.
     5:10 shall we be saved through his l!
     5:18 resulted in justification and l for all.
     5:21 bring eternal l through Jesus Christ
     6: 4 the Father, we too may live a new l.
     6:13 have been brought from death to l,
     6:22 holiness, and the result is eternal l.
     6:23 God is eternal l in Christ Jesus our
     7:10 to bring l actually brought death.
     8: 2 of the Spirit who gives l has set you
     8: 6 the mind controlled by the Spirit is l

Ro   8:11 give l to your mortal bodies because
     8:38 convinced that neither death nor l,
1Co 15:19 If only for this l we have hope
    15:36 does not come to l unless it dies.
2Co  2:16 to the other, an aroma that brings l.
     3: 6 the letter kills, but the Spirit gives l.
     4:10 so that the l of Jesus may also be
     5: 4 is mortal may be swallowed up by l.
Gal  2:20 The l I now live in the body, I live
     3:21 had been given that could impart l,
     6: 8 from the Spirit will reap eternal l.
Eph  4: 1 to live a l worthy of the calling you
     6: 3 you may enjoy long l on the earth."
Php  2:16 as you hold firmly to the word of l.
     4: 3 whose names are in the book of l.
Col  1:10 you may live a l worthy of the Lord
     3: 3 your l is now hidden with Christ
1Th  4:12 your daily l may win the respect
1Ti  1:16 believe in him and receive eternal l.
     4: 8 promise for both the present l and the
          l to come.
     4:16 Watch your l and doctrine closely.
     6:12 Take hold of the eternal l
     6:19 may take hold of the l that is truly l.
2Ti  1: 9 saved us and called us to a holy l—
     1:10 and has brought l and immortality
     3:12 live a godly l in Christ Jesus will be
Tit  1: 2 in the hope of eternal l, which God,
     3: 7 heirs having the hope of eternal l.
Heb  7:16 of the power of an indestructible l.
Jas  1:12 they will receive the crown of l
     3:13 Let them show it by their good l,
1Pe  3: 7 with you of the gracious gift of l,
     3:10 "Whoever among you would love l
2Pe  1: 3 for a godly l through our knowledge
1Jn  1: 1 proclaim concerning the Word of l.
     2:25 is what he promised us—eternal l.
     3:14 that we have passed from death to l,
     3:16 Jesus Christ laid down his l for us.
     5:11 God has given us eternal l, and this l
     5:20 He is the true God and eternal l.
Jude 1:21 Christ to bring you to eternal l.
Rev  2: 7 the right to eat from the tree of l,
     2: 8 Last, who died and came to l again.
     2:10 and I will give you l as your victor's
     3: 5 out their names from the book of l,
    11:11 a half days the breath of l from God
    13: 8 written in the Lamb's book of l,
    17: 8 in the book of l from the creation
    20: 4 They came to l and reigned
    20:12 was opened, which is the book of l.
    20:15 the book of l were thrown
    21: 6 from the spring of the water of l.
    21:27 are written in the Lamb's book of l.
    22: 1 me the river of the water of l,
    22: 2 side of the river stood the tree of l,
    22:14 may have the right to the tree of l
    22:17 take the free gift of the water of l.
    22:19 from you your share in the tree of l

**ETERNAL LIFE** Mt 19:16, 29; 25:46; Mk 10:17,
  30; Lk 10:25; 18:18, 30; Jn 3:15, 16, 36; 4:14,
  36; 5:24, 39; 6:27, 40, 47, 54, 68; 10:28; 12:25,
  50; 17:2, 3; Ac 13:46, 48; Ro 2:7; 5:21; 6:22, 23;
  Gal 6:8; 1Ti 1:16; 6:12; Tit 1:2; 3:7; 1Jn 1:2;
  2:25; 3:15; 5:11, 13, 20; Jude 1:21

## LIFE'S* [LIVE]
Ps 39: 4 my l end and the number of my
Lk 8:14 way they are choked by l worries,

## LIFE-GIVING* [GIVE]
Pr 15:31 Whoever heeds l correction will be
1Co 15:45 the last Adam, a l spirit.

## LIFEBLOOD [BLOOD]
Ge 9: 4 not eat meat that has its l still in it.

## LIFELESS [LIVE]
Ps 106:28 and ate sacrifices offered to l gods;
Jer 16:18 defiled my land with the l forms
Hab 2:19 Or to l stone, 'Wake up!'

## LIFETIME [LIVE]
1Ki 3:13 that in your l you will have no equal
Ps 30: 5 a moment, but his favor lasts a l;
Lk 16:25 in your l you received your good

## LIFT [LIFTED, LIFTING, LIFTS, UPLIFTED]
Dt 32:40 I l my hand to heaven and declare:
Ps 24: 7 L up your heads, you gates;
28: 2 as I l up my hands toward your
63: 4 in your name I will l up my hands.
91:12 they will l you up in their hands,
121: 1 I l up my eyes to the mountains—
123: 1 I l up my eyes to you, to you who
134: 2 L up your hands in the sanctuary
Isa 40: 9 l up your voice with a shout, l it up,
La 2:19 l up your hands to him for the lives
3:41 Let us l up our hearts and our hands
Mt 4: 6 they will l you up in their hands,
Lk 11:46 you yourselves will not l one finger
21:28 place, stand up and l up your heads,
Jas 4:10 the Lord, and he will l you up.
1Pe 5: 6 that he may l you up in due time.

## LIFTED [LIFT]
Ex 17:16 "Because hands were l up against
Nu 9:21 whenever the cloud l, they set out.
1Sa 2: 1 in the LORD my horn is l high.
Ne 8: 6 and all the people l their hands
Ps 30: 1 for you l me out of the depths
40: 2 He l me out of the slimy pit,
41: 9 bread, has l up his heel against me.
93: 3 The seas have l up, LORD,
112: 9 their horn will be l high in honor.
118:16 The LORD's right hand is l high;
Isa 52:13 he will be raised and l up and highly
63: 9 he l them up and carried them all
Eze 3:12 Then the Spirit l me up, and I heard
8: 3 The Spirit l me up between earth
11: 1 Then the Spirit l me up and brought
Mt 11:23 will you be l up to the skies?
Lk 24:50 he l up his hands and blessed them.
Jn 3:14 so the Son of Man must be l up,
8:28 "When you have l up the Son
12:32 I, when I am l up from the earth,
12:34 'The Son of Man must be l up'?
13:18 'He who shared my bread has l

## LIFTING [LIFT]
Ps 141: 2 may the l up of my hands be like
1Ti 2: 8 l up holy hands without anger

## LIFTS [LIFT]
1Sa 2: 8 and l the needy from the ash heap;
Ps 3: 3 glory, the one who l my head high.
113: 7 and l the needy from the ash heap;
145:14 and l up all who are bowed down.

## LIGAMENT* [LIGAMENTS]
Eph 4:16 held together by every supporting l,

## LIGAMENTS* [LIGAMENT]
Col 2:19 held together by its l and sinews,

## LIGHT [DAYLIGHT, ENLIGHTEN, ENLIGHTENED, LIGHTEN, LIGHTENED, LIGHTS, TWILIGHT]
Ge 1: 3 "Let there be l," and there was l.
1: 5 God called the l "day,"
1:16 the greater l to govern the day
Ex 13:21 in a pillar of fire to give them l,
25:37 on it so that they l the space in front
Dt 25:13 in your bag—one heavy, one l.
2Sa 22:29 LORD turns my darkness into l.
Ezr 9: 8 and so our God gives l to our eyes
Job 3:20 "Why is l given to those in misery,
38:19 "What is the way to the abode of l?
Ps 4: 6 Let the l of your face shine on us.
18:28 my God turns my darkness into l.
19: 8 are radiant, giving l to the eyes.
27: 1 The LORD is my l and my
36: 9 fountain of life; in your l we see l.
56:13 walk before God in the l of life.
76: 4 You are resplendent with l,
89:15 who walk in the l of your presence,
104: 2 The LORD wraps himself in l as
119:105 lamp to my feet and a l for my path.
119:130 unfolding of your words gives l;
139:12 the day, for darkness is as l to you.
Pr 4:18 shining ever brighter till the full l
13: 9 The l of the righteous shines
15:30 L in a messenger's eyes brings joy
Ecc 2:13 just as l is better than darkness.
Isa 2: 5 let us walk in the l of the LORD.
9: 2 in darkness have seen a great l;
42: 6 the people and a l for the Gentiles,
45: 7 I form the l and create darkness,
49: 6 also make you a l for the Gentiles,
53:11 he will see the l of life and be
58:10 then your l will rise in the darkness,
60: 1 for your l has come, and the glory
60:19 LORD will be your everlasting l,
Eze 1:27 and brilliant l surrounded him.
Am 5:18 That day will be darkness, not l.
Mic 7: 8 darkness, the LORD will be my l.
Mt 4:16 in darkness have seen a great l;
5:14 "You are the l of the world.
5:16 way, let your l shine before others,
6:22 your whole body will be full of l.
11:30 yoke is easy and my burden is l."
17: 2 his clothes became as white as the l.
24:29 and the moon will not give its l;
Mk 13:24 and the moon will not give its l;

| | | |
|---|---|---|
| Lk | 2:32 | a l for revelation to the Gentiles, |
| | 8:16 | those who come in can see the l. |
| | 11:33 | those who come in may see the l. |
| Jn | 1: 4 | and that life was the l of all people. |
| | 1: 5 | The l shines in the darkness, |
| | 1: 7 | witness to testify concerning that l, |
| | 1: 9 | The true l that gives l to everyone |
| | 3:19 | of l because their deeds were evil. |
| | 3:20 | All those who do evil hate the l, |
| | 5:35 | you chose for a time to enjoy his l. |
| | 8:12 | he said, "I am the l of the world. |
| | 8:12 | but will have the l of life." |
| | 9: 5 | the world, I am the l of the world." |
| | 12:35 | Walk while you have the l, |
| | 12:46 | I have come into the world as a l, |
| Ac | 9: 3 | suddenly a l from heaven flashed |
| | 13:47 | " 'I have made you a l |
| Ro | 13:12 | darkness and put on the armor of l. |
| 1Co | 3:13 | is, because the Day will bring it to l. |
| 2Co | 4: 6 | said, "Let l shine out of darkness," |
| | 4:17 | For our l and momentary troubles |
| | 6:14 | Or what fellowship can l have |
| | 11:14 | masquerades as an angel of l. |
| Eph | 5: 8 | but now you are l in the Lord. |
| | 5: 9 | (for the fruit of the l consists in all |
| Col | 1:12 | of his people in the kingdom of l. |
| 1Th | 5: 5 | You are all children of the l |
| 1Ti | 6:16 | and who lives in unapproachable l, |
| Heb | 12: 5 | son, do not make l of the Lord's |
| 1Pe | 2: 9 | out of darkness into his wonderful l. |
| 2Pe | 1:19 | it, as to a l shining in a dark place, |
| 1Jn | 1: 5 | God is l; in him there is no darkness |
| | 1: 7 | But if we walk in the l, as he is in the l, |
| | 2: 8 | and the true l is already shining. |
| | 2: 9 | Those who claim to be in the l |
| Rev | 8:12 | A third of the day was without l, |
| | 21:23 | for the glory of God gives it l, |
| | 22: 5 | They will not need the l of a lamp or the l of the sun, |

# LIGHTEN [LIGHT]

| | | |
|---|---|---|
| 2Ch | 10: 9 | 'L the yoke your father put on us'?" |
| Jnh | 1: 5 | the cargo into the sea to l the ship. |

# LIGHTENED* [LIGHT]

| | | |
|---|---|---|
| Ac | 27:38 | they l the ship by throwing the grain |

# LIGHTNING

| | | |
|---|---|---|
| Ex | 9:23 | and l flashed down to the ground. |
| | 19:16 | third day there was thunder and l, |
| | 20:18 | the people saw the thunder and l |
| 2Sa | 22:15 | with great bolts of l he routed them. |
| Job | 37:15 | the clouds and makes his l flash? |
| Ps | 18:12 | with hailstones and bolts of l. |
| | 97: 4 | His l lights up the world; |
| Jer | 10:13 | He sends l with the rain and brings |
| Eze | 1:13 | it was bright, and l flashed out of it. |
| Da | 10: 6 | his face like l, his eyes like flaming |
| Mt | 24:27 | For as l that comes from the east is |
| | 28: 3 | His appearance was like l, and his |
| Lk | 9:29 | became as bright as a flash of l. |
| | 10:18 | replied, "I saw Satan fall like l |
| Rev | 4: 5 | From the throne came flashes of l, |
| | 8: 5 | flashes of l and an earthquake. |
| | 11:19 | And there came flashes of l, |
| | 16:18 | Then there came flashes of l, |

# LIGHTS [LIGHT]

| | | |
|---|---|---|
| Ge | 1:14 | "Let there be l in the vault |
| | 1:16 | God made two great l— |
| Ps | 136: 7 | who made the great l— |
| Lk | 8:16 | "No one l a lamp and hides it |
| Jas | 1:17 | from the Father of the heavenly l, |

# LIKE [LIKE-MINDED, LIKENESS]

| | | |
|---|---|---|
| Ge | 3: 5 | and you will be l God, |
| | 3:22 | "The man has now become l one |
| | 13.16 | I will make your offspring l the dust |
| | 28:14 | Your descendants will be l the dust |
| Ex | 7: 1 | I have made you l God to Pharaoh, |
| | 8:10 | there is no one l the LORD our |
| | 15:11 | Who among the gods is l you, |
| | 24:17 | of the LORD looked l a consuming |
| | 34: 1 | out two stone tablets l the first ones, |
| Nu | 11: 7 | The manna was l coriander seed and looked l resin. |
| | 13:33 | We seemed l grasshoppers in our |
| Dt | 8:20 | L the nations the LORD destroyed |
| | 18:15 | for you a prophet l me from among |
| | 32:31 | For their rock is not l our Rock, |
| | 33:29 | Who is l you, a people saved |
| 1Sa | 2: 2 | is no one holy l the LORD; |
| | 25:25 | He is just l his name— |
| 2Sa | 7:22 | There is no one l you, and there is |
| 1Ki | 8:23 | there is no God l you in heaven |
| | 14. 8 | have not been l my servant David, |
| | 21:25 | (There was never anyone l Ahab, |
| 1Ch | 17:21 | And who is l your people Israel— |
| Job | 1: 8 | There is no one on earth l him; |
| | 9:32 | "He is not a mere mortal l me that I |
| | 40: 9 | Do you have an arm l God's, |
| Ps | 1: 3 | They are l a tree planted by streams |
| | 1: 4 | They are l chaff that the wind blows |
| | 18:33 | He makes my feet l the feet |
| | 22:14 | I am poured out l water, and all my |
| | 35:10 | exclaim, "Who is l you, LORD? |
| | 48:10 | L your name, O God, your praise |
| | 86: 8 | Among the gods there is none l you, |
| | 103:15 | their days are l grass, they flourish l |
| | 113: 5 | Who is l the LORD our God, |
| | 114: 4 | the mountains leaped l rams, |
| | 114: 4 | They are l a breath; their days are l |
| Pr | 7:22 | l a deer stepping into a noose |
| | 11:22 | L a gold ring in a pig's snout is |
| | 25:11 | L apples of gold in settings of silver |
| Ecc | 2:16 | For the wise, l the fool, |
| | 12:11 | The words of the wise are l goads, |
| SS | 2: 2 | L a lily among thorns is my darling |
| | 8: 6 | Place me l a seal over your heart, |
| Isa | 1: 9 | we would have become l Sodom, |
| | 1:18 | "Though your sins are l scarlet, |
| | 11: 7 | and the lion will eat straw l the ox. |
| | 40: 6 | "All people are l grass, |
| | 46: 9 | I am God, and there is none l me. |
| | 53: 2 | and l a root out of dry ground. |
| | 53: 6 | We all, l sheep, have gone astray, |
| | 64: 6 | our righteous acts are l filthy rags; |
| Jer | 10: 6 | No one is l you, LORD, |
| | 23:29 | "Is not my word l fire," |
| La | 1:12 | Is any suffering l my suffering |
| | 2: 5 | The Lord is l an enemy; |
| Eze | 1: 4 | of the fire looked l glowing metal, |
| | 1:10 | Their faces looked l this: |

Eze   1:26   on the throne was a figure l
      8: 2   and I saw a figure l that of a man.
Da    3:25   and the fourth looks l a son
      7: 4   "The first was l a lion,
      7:13   there before me was one l a son
     10: 6   His body was l topaz, his face l
Hos   1:10   "Yet the Israelites will be l the sand
      6: 4   Your love is l the morning mist,
     14: 5   I will be l the dew to Israel;
Mic   7:18   Who is a God l you, who pardons
Na    1: 6   His wrath is poured out l fire;
Zec   1: 4   Do not be l your ancestors, to whom
     13: 9   refine them l silver and test them l gold.
Mt    9:36   l sheep without a shepherd.
     10:16   you out l sheep among wolves.
Lk    6:48   They are l a man building a house,
     13:18   "What is the kingdom of God l?
     22:26   and the one who rules l the one who
Ac    3:22   for you a prophet l me from among
Ro    5:15   But the gift is not l the trespass.
      9:29   we would have become l Sodom,
1Co   9:20   To the Jews I became l a Jew,
     13:11   I was a child, I talked l a child,
1Pe   1:24   "All people are l grass, and all their
2Pe   3: 8   and a thousand years are l a day.
      3:10   day of the Lord will come l a thief.
Rev   1:13   the lampstands was someone l a son
      2:18   whose eyes are l blazing fire
      3: 3   I will come l a thief, and you will
      4: 7   The first living creature was l a lion,
     10: 1   his face was l the sun,
     13: 4   and asked, "Who is l the beast?
     16:15   "Look, I come l a thief!
     19:12   His eyes are l blazing fire,

## LIKE-MINDED* [LIKE, MIND]
Php   2: 2   make my joy complete by being l,
1Pe   3: 8   all of you, be l, be sympathetic,

## LIKENESS [LIKE]
Ge    1:26   in our l, so that they may rule over
      5: 1   he made them in the l of God.
Ps   17:15   I will be satisfied with seeing your l.
Isa  52:14   his form marred beyond human l—
Ro    8: 3   own Son in the l of sinful humanity
Php   2: 7   of a servant, being made in human l.
Jas   3: 9   who have been made in God's l.

## LILIES [LILY]
1Ki   7:22   on top were in the shape of l.
SS    2:16   I am his; he browses among the l.

## LILY [LILIES]
2Ch   4: 5   the rim of a cup, like a l blossom.
SS    2: 1   a rose of Sharon, a l of the valleys.
      2: 2   Like a l among thorns is my darling
Hos  14: 5   he will blossom like a l.

## LIMIT [LIMITS]
Ps  147: 5   his understanding has no l.
Jer   5:28   Their evil deeds have no l;
Jn    3:34   for God gives the Spirit without l.

## LIMITS [LIMIT]
Ex   19:23   'Put l around the mountain and set it

Job  11: 7   Can you probe the l
2Co  10:13   will not boast beyond proper l,

## LIMP
Isa  13: 7   this, all hands will go l, every man's
Zep   3:16   do not let your hands hang l.

## LINE
Ge   19:32   preserve our family l through our
Dt   25: 9   not build up his brother's family l."
Ru    4: 4   it except you, and I am next in l."
Ps   89:29   I will establish his l forever,
Isa  28:17   I will make justice the measuring l
Jer  33:15   Branch sprout from David's l;
Mt   17:27   go to the lake and throw out your l.
Lk    2: 4   to the house and l of David.

## LINEN
Ex   26: 1   with ten curtains of finely twisted l
     28:39   "Weave the tunic of fine l
Lev  16: 4   He is to put on the sacred l tunic,
Pr   31:22   she is clothed in fine l and purple.
     31:24   She makes l garments and sells
Jer  13: 1   buy a l belt and put it around your
Eze   9: 2   clothed in l who had a writing kit
Da   10: 5   before me was a man dressed in l,
Mk   15:46   wrapped it in the l, and placed it
Jn   20: 6   He saw the strips of l lying there,
Rev  15: 6   shining l and wore golden sashes
     19: 8   (Fine l stands for the righteous acts

## LINGER
Pr   23:30   Those who l over wine, who go
Hab   2: 3   Though it l, wait for it;

## LION [LION'S, LIONS, LIONS']
Ge   49: 9   Like a l he crouches and lies down,
Jdg  14: 6   that he tore the l apart with his bare
1Sa  17:34   When a l or a bear came and carried
Ps   91:13   You will tread on the l
Ecc   9: 4   a live dog is better off than a dead l!
Isa  11: 7   and the l will eat straw like the ox.
     65:25   and the l will eat straw like the ox,
Jer   4: 7   A l has come out of his lair;
     25:38   Like a l he will leave his lair,
Eze   1:10   right side each had the face of a l,
     10:14   the third the face of a l,
Da    7: 4   "The first was like a l, and it had
Hos  13: 7   So I will come upon them like a l,
1Pe   5: 8   around like a roaring l looking
Rev   4: 7   The first living creature was like a l,
      5: 5   See, the L of the tribe of Judah,
     13: 2   a bear and a mouth like that of a l.

## LION'S [LION]
Ge   49: 9   You are a l cub, Judah;
2Ti   4:17   I was delivered from the l mouth.

## LIONS [LION]
Ps   22:21   Rescue me from the mouth of the l;
Da    6:20   able to rescue you from the l?"

## LIONS' [LION]
Da    6: 7   shall be thrown into the l' den.
Na    2:11   Where now is the l' den, the place

## LIPS

| | | |
|---|---|---|
| Ex | 6:12 | me, since I speak with faltering l?" |
| Dt | 23:23 | Whatever your l utter you must be |
| Ps | 34: 1 | his praise will always be on my l. |
| | 40: 9 | I do not seal my l, LORD, as you |
| | 63: 3 | than life, my l will glorify you. |
| | 119:171 | May my l overflow with praise, |
| | 140: 3 | the poison of vipers is on their l. |
| | 141: 3 | keep watch over the door of my l. |
| Pr | 5: 3 | the l of the adulterous woman drip |
| | 10:13 | is found on the l of the discerning, |
| | 10:18 | conceals hatred with lying l |
| | 10:21 | The l of the righteous nourish many, |
| | 10:32 | The l of the righteous know what |
| | 12:22 | The LORD detests lying l, but he |
| | 13: 3 | who guard their l preserve their |
| | 14: 7 | will not find knowledge on their l. |
| | 15: 7 | The l of the wise spread knowledge, |
| | 24:26 | honest answer is like a kiss on the l. |
| | 26:23 | on earthenware are fervent l |
| | 27: 2 | an outsider, and not your own l. |
| Ecc | 10:12 | fools are consumed by their own l. |
| SS | 4:11 | Your l drop sweetness as |
| Isa | 6: 5 | For I am a man of unclean l, |
| | 28:11 | with foreign l and strange tongues |
| | 29:13 | mouth and honor me with their l, |
| Jer | 12: 2 | You are always on their l but far |
| Hos | 14: 2 | that we may offer the fruit of our l. |
| Mal | 2: 7 | "For the l of a priest ought |
| Mt | 15: 8 | people honor me with their l, |
| | 21:16 | read, " 'From the l of children |
| Lk | 4:22 | gracious words that came from his l. |
| Ro | 3:13 | "The poison of vipers is on their l." |
| 1Co | 14:21 | and through the l of foreigners I will |
| Col | 3: 8 | and filthy language from your l. |
| Heb | 13:15 | the fruit of l that openly profess his |
| 1Pe | 3:10 | and your l from deceitful speech. |

## LIPS

| | | |
|---|---|---|
| Jos | 1: 8 | Keep this Book of the Law always on your l; |

## LIQUOR (KJV) See JUICE, WINE

## LIST [LISTED]

| | | |
|---|---|---|
| 1Ch | 11:11 | this is the l of David's mighty |
| | 27: 1 | This is the l of the Israelites— |
| Ezr | 2: 2 | The l of the men of the people |
| Ne | 7: 7 | The l of the men of Israel: |
| Ps | 56: 8 | l my tears on your scroll— |
| 1Ti | 5: 9 | the l of widows unless she is over |

## LISTED [LIST]

| | | |
|---|---|---|
| Nu | 1:18 | years old or more were l by name, |

## LISTEN [LISTENED, LISTENING, LISTENS]

| | | |
|---|---|---|
| Ex | 4: 1 | if they do not believe me or l to me |
| | 6:30 | lips, why would Pharaoh l to me?" |
| | 7:13 | hard and he would not l to them, |
| | 15:26 | "If you l carefully to the LORD |
| | 23:22 | If you l carefully to what he says |
| Lev | 26:14 | if you will not l to me and carry |
| Dt | 18:15 | You must l to him. |
| | 30:20 | LORD your God, l to his voice, |

| | | |
|---|---|---|
| 1Ki | 4:34 | From all nations people came to l |
| 2Ki | 17:40 | They would not l, however, |
| | 21: 9 | But the people did not l. |
| Ps | 5: 1 | L to my words, LORD, |
| | 34:11 | Come, my children, l to me; |
| | 55: 1 | L to my prayer, O God, do not |
| | 143: 1 | my prayer, l to my cry for mercy; |
| Pr | 1: 5 | let the wise l and add to their |
| | 4: 1 | L, my sons, to a father's instruction; |
| | 8:33 | L to my instruction and be wise; |
| | 8:34 | Blessed are those who l to me, |
| | 12:15 | but the wise l to advice. |
| Ecc | 5: 1 | Go near to l rather than to offer |
| Isa | 44: 1 | "But now l, Jacob, my servant, |
| Jer | 7:24 | But they did not l or pay attention; |
| Eze | 2: 5 | And whether they l or fail to l— |
| | 40: 4 | look carefully and l closely and pay |
| Zec | 7:13 | " 'When I called, they did not l; |
| Mt | 12:42 | the earth to l to Solomon's wisdom, |
| Mk | 9: 7 | is my Son, whom I love. L to him!" |
| Jn | 10:27 | My sheep l to my voice; |
| Ac | 3:22 | you must l to everything he tells |
| Jas | 1:19 | Everyone should be quick to l, |
| | 1:22 | Do not merely l to the word, and so |
| 1Jn | 4: 6 | is not from God does not l to us. |

## LISTENED [LISTEN]

| | | |
|---|---|---|
| Ge | 3:17 | "Because you l to your wife and ate |
| | 30:17 | God l to Leah, and she became |
| | 30:22 | he l to her and enabled her |
| Nu | 21: 3 | The LORD l to Israel's plea |
| Dt | 9:19 | But again the LORD l to me. |
| | 10:10 | the LORD l to me at this time also. |
| | 34: 9 | So the Israelites l to him and did |
| Ne | 8: 3 | all the people l attentively |
| Isa | 66: 4 | answered, when I spoke, no one l. |
| Da | 9: 6 | We have not l to your servants |

## LISTENING [LISTEN]

| | | |
|---|---|---|
| 1Sa | 3:10 | said, "Speak, for your servant is l." |
| Pr | 18:13 | To answer before l—that is folly |
| Lk | 10:39 | at the Lord's feet l to what he said. |

## LISTENS [LISTEN]

| | | |
|---|---|---|
| Pr | 1:33 | whoever l to me will live in safety |
| | 17: 4 | A wicked person l to deceitful lips; |
| Lk | 10:16 | "Whoever l to you l to me; |
| Jn | 18:37 | on the side of truth l to me." |
| 1Jn | 4: 6 | and whoever knows God l to us; |

## LITTLE

| | | |
|---|---|---|
| Ex | 16:18 | who gathered l did not have too l. |
| | 23:30 | L by l I will drive them out before |
| 1Ki | 17:12 | in a jar and a l olive oil in a jug. |
| 2Ki | 4: 2 | she said, "except a l olive oil." |
| Ps | 8: 5 | have made them a l lower than |
| Pr | 6:10 | A l sleep, a l slumber, a l folding |
| | 13:11 | but whoever gathers money l by l |
| | 15:16 | Better a l with the fear |
| | 16: 8 | Better a l with righteousness than |
| Ecc | 10: 1 | so a l folly outweighs wisdom |
| Isa | 11: 6 | and a l child will lead them. |
| Mt | 6:30 | more clothe you—you of l faith? |
| | 8:26 | "You of l faith, why are you so |
| | 14:31 | "You of l faith," he said, "why did |
| | 16: 8 | "You of l faith, why are you talking |

| | | |
|---|---|---|
| Mt | 17:20 | "Because you have so l faith. |
| | 19:14 | "Let the l children come to me, |
| Mk | 9:37 | welcomes one of these l children |
| Lk | 7:47 | has been forgiven l loves l." |
| | 18:17 | of God like a l child will never enter |
| 1Co | 5: 6 | a l yeast leavens the whole batch |
| 2Co | 8:15 | who gathered l did not have too l." |
| Gal | 5: 9 | "A l yeast works through the whole |
| 1Ti | 5:23 | and use a l wine because of your |
| Heb | 2: 7 | You made them a l lower than |
| Rev | 3: 8 | I know that you have l strength, |
| | 10: 2 | He was holding a l scroll, which lay |

## LIVE [ALIVE, LIFE, LIFE'S, LIFELESS, LIFETIME, LIVED, LIVES, LIVING]

| | | |
|---|---|---|
| Ge | 3:22 | tree of life and eat, and l forever." |
| | 12:12 | they will kill me but will let you l. |
| Ex | 1:16 | but if it is a girl, let her l." |
| | 20:12 | that you may l long in the land |
| | 33:20 | face, for no one may see me and l." |
| Lev | 23:42 | L in temporary shelters for seven |
| Nu | 21: 8 | who is bitten can look at it and l." |
| Dt | 4: 1 | Follow them so that you may l |
| | 5:24 | that people can l even if God speaks |
| | 6: 2 | LORD your God as long as you l |
| | 8: 3 | that people do not l on bread alone |
| | 30: 6 | heart and with all your soul, and l. |
| Jdg | 1:27 | the Canaanites were determined to l |
| Job | 14:14 | If someone dies, will they l again? |
| Ps | 15: 1 | Who may l on your holy mountain? |
| | 24: 1 | in it, the world, and all who l in it; |
| | 26: 8 | I love the house where you l, |
| | 63: 4 | I will praise you as long as I l, |
| | 119:175 | Let me l that I may praise you, |
| Pr | 2:21 | For the upright will l in the land, |
| | 4: 4 | keep my commands, and you will l. |
| | 15:27 | but those who hate bribes will l. |
| | 21: 9 | Better to l on a corner of the roof |
| | 21:19 | Better to l in a desert than |
| Ecc | 3:12 | happy and to do good while they l. |
| | 9: 4 | even a l dog is better off than a dead |
| Isa | 6: 5 | I l among a people of unclean lips, |
| | 11: 6 | The wolf will l with the lamb, |
| | 26:19 | But your dead will l, LORD; |
| | 55: 3 | come to me; listen, that you may l. |
| | 65:20 | infants who l but a few days, |
| Eze | 18: 9 | he will surely l, |
| | 18:32 | Repent and l! |
| | 20:11 | people will l if they obey them. |
| | 37: 3 | "Son of man, can these bones l?" |
| Am | 5: 6 | Seek the LORD and l, or he will |
| Jnh | 4: 3 | it is better for me to die than to l." |
| | 4: 8 | be better for me to die than to l." |
| Hab | 2: 4 | but the righteous will l by their |
| Zec | 2:11 | I will l among you and you will |
| | 10:12 | in his name they will l securely," |
| Mt | 4: 4 | 'People do not l on bread alone, |
| Lk | 10:28 | "Do this and you will l." |
| Jn | 6:51 | eats of this bread will l forever. |
| | 6:58 | feeds on this bread will l forever." |
| | 11:25 | Anyone who believes in me will l, |
| | 14:19 | Because I l, you also will l. |
| Ac | 17:24 | does not l in temples built by hands. |
| | 17:28 | 'For in him we l and move and have |
| Ro | 1:17 | "The righteous will l by faith." |
| | 6: 8 | believe that we will also l with him. |

| | | |
|---|---|---|
| Ro | 8: 4 | who do not l according to the sinful |
| | 14: 7 | For we do not l to ourselves alone |
| | 14: 8 | If we l, we l to the Lord; |
| 1Co | 7:17 | each of you should l as a believer |
| | 8: 6 | came and through whom we l. |
| 2Co | 5: 7 | We l by faith, not by sight. |
| | 5:15 | that those who l should no longer l |
| | 6:16 | "I will l with them and walk among |
| Gal | 2:20 | The life I now l in the body, I l |
| | 3:11 | because "the righteous will l |
| | 3:12 | "Whoever does these things will l |
| | 5:25 | Since we l by the Spirit, let us keep |
| Eph | 4: 1 | I urge you to l a life worthy |
| | 4:17 | you must no longer l as the Gentiles |
| | 5: 8 | in the Lord. L as children of light |
| Php | 1:21 | me, to l is Christ and to die is gain. |
| | 1:27 | l in a manner worthy of the gospel |
| | 3:17 | eyes on those who l as we do. |
| Col | 1:10 | so that you may l a life worthy |
| 1Th | 4: 1 | we instructed you how to l in order |
| | 5:13 | L in peace with each other. |
| 1Ti | 2: 2 | that we may l peaceful and quiet |
| 2Ti | 3:12 | everyone who wants to l a godly life |
| Tit | 2:12 | and to l self-controlled, |
| Heb | 10:38 | my righteous one will l by faith. |
| | 12:14 | Make every effort to l in peace |
| 1Pe | 1:17 | l out your time as foreigners here |
| | 2:12 | L such good lives among the pagans |
| 2Pe | 3:11 | You ought to l holy and godly lives |
| 1Jn | 2:10 | their fellow believers l in the light, |
| | 3:24 | Those who keep his commands l |

**AS I LIVE** Nu 14:21, 28; Dt 32:40; 1Sa 20:14; Job 27:6; Ps 63:4; 104:33; 116:2; 146:2; Isa 49:18; Jer 22:24; 46:18; Eze 5:11; 14:16, 18, 20; 16:48; 17:16, 19; 18:3; 20:3, 31, 33; 33:11, 27; 34:8; 35:6, 11; Zep 2:9; Ro 14:11; 2Pe 1:13

## LIVED [LIVE]

| | | |
|---|---|---|
| Ex | 12:40 | time the Israelite people l in Egypt |
| Dt | 26: 5 | Egypt with a few people and l there |
| Jos | 24: 2 | l beyond the Euphrates River |
| | 24: 7 | you l in the wilderness for a long |
| Jdg | 1:30 | these Canaanites l among them, |
| | 3: 5 | The Israelites l among |
| Lk | 1:80 | and he l in the wilderness until he |
| Col | 3: 7 | in these ways, in the life you once l. |
| Tit | 3: 3 | We l in malice and envy, |

## LIVES [LIVE]

| | | |
|---|---|---|
| Ge | 9: 3 | Everything that l and moves will be |
| | 45: 7 | save your l by a great deliverance. |
| | 50:20 | being done, the saving of many l. |
| Ex | 1:14 | They made their l bitter with harsh |
| | 30:16 | making atonement for your l." |
| Job | 19:25 | I know that my redeemer l, |
| Ps | 18:46 | The LORD l! Praise be to my |
| Pr | 13: 3 | who guard their lips preserve their l, |
| | 14:25 | A truthful witness saves l, |
| | 19: 8 | get wisdom love their own l; |
| Isa | 57:15 | he who l forever, whose name is |
| Jer | 10:23 | I know that people's l are not their own; |
| Eze | 18:27 | they will save their l. |
| Da | 3:28 | to give up their l rather than serve |
| | 4:34 | and glorified him who l forever. |
| | 12: 7 | him swear by him who l forever, |
| Jn | 11:26 | whoever l by believing in me will |

Jn   14:17  for he I with you and will be in you.
Ro    6:10  but the life he I, he I to God.
      8: 9  if indeed the Spirit of God I in you.
Gal   2:20  I no longer live, but Christ I in me.
Eph   2:22  in which God I by his Spirit.
Col   2: 9  of the Deity I in bodily form,
1Th   2: 8  the gospel of God but our I as well.
      2:12  urging you to live I worthy of God,
1Ti   2: 2  peaceful and quiet I in all godliness
      6:16  and who I in unapproachable light,
2Ti   1:14  help of the Holy Spirit who I in us.
Tit   2:12  and godly I in this present age,
Heb   7:24  but because Jesus I forever, he has
      7:25  because he always I to intercede
     13: 5  Keep your I free from the love
1Pe   3: 2  the purity and reverence of your I.
      4: 2  not live the rest of their earthly I
2Pe   3:11  You ought to live holy and godly I
1Jn   2:14  and the word of God I in you,
      2:17  does the will of God I forever.
      3:16  to lay down our I for one another.
      4:16  Whoever I in love I in God,
Rev   4: 9  sits on the throne and who I for ever
      4:10  and worship him who I for ever
     10: 6  he swore by him who I for ever
     15: 7  of God, who I for ever and ever.

## AS SURELY AS THE †LORD ... LIVES
See †LORD

## LIVESTOCK
Ge    1:25  kinds, the I according to their kinds,
      2:20  So the man gave names to all the I,
      3:14  "Cursed are you above all I and all
Ex   34:19  all the firstborn males of your I,

## LIVING [LIVE]
Ge    2: 7  life, and the man became a I being.
      3:20  become the mother of all the I.
      6:19  into the ark two of all I creatures,
      8:21  again will I destroy all I creatures,
Dt    5:26  the voice of the I God speaking
Jos   3:10  know that the I God is among you
1Sa  17:26  defy the armies of the I God?"
2Ki  19: 4  has sent to ridicule the I God,
Ps   84: 2  and my flesh cry out for the I God.
     119: 9  By I according to your word.
     142: 5  my portion in the land of the I."
Ecc   9: 4  who is among the I has hope—
Isa  53: 8  was cut off from the land of the I;
Jer   2:13  the spring of I water, and have dug
     10:10  he is the I God, the eternal King.
     17:13  the LORD, the spring of I water.
Eze   1: 5  what looked like four I creatures.
     10:17  the spirit of the I creatures was
Da    6:26  "For he is the I God and he endures
Hos   1:10  be called 'children of the I God.'
Zec  14: 8  On that day I water will flow
Mt    4:16  the people I in darkness have seen
     16:16  the Messiah, the Son of the I God."
     22:32  the God of the dead but of the I."
Jn    4:10  he would have given you I water."
      6:51  I am the I bread that came down
      7:38  said, rivers of I water will flow
Ro    8:11  Jesus from the dead is I in you,
      9:26  called 'children of the I God.' "
     12: 1  to offer your bodies as a I sacrifice,

Ro   14: 9  the Lord of both the dead and the I.
1Co   9:14  the gospel should receive their I
2Co   6:16  For we are the temple of the I God.
1Ti   4:10  we have put our hope in the I God,
2Ti   4: 1  who will judge the I and the dead,
Heb  10:20  and I way opened for us through
     10:31  to fall into the hands of the I God.
     11:13  All these people were still I by faith
1Pe   1:23  through the I and enduring word
      2: 4  As you come to him, the I Stone—
Rev   1·18  I am the L One; I was dead,
      4: 6  were four I creatures, and they were
      7:17  will lead them to springs of I water.'

## LIVING GOD See GOD

## LIVING WATER Jer 2:13; 17:13; Zec 14:8; Jn
4:10, 11; 7:38; Rev 7:17

## LOAD [LOADED, LOADS]
Ne   13:19  gates so that no I could be brought
Jer  17:24  bring no I through the gates of this
Lk   11:46  because you I people down
Gal   6: 5  of you should carry your own I.

## LOADED [LOAD]
2Ti   3: 6  who are I down with sins and are

## LOADS [LOAD]
Mt   23: 4  cumbersome I and put them

## LOAF [LOAVES]
Jdg   7:13  "A round I of barley bread came
1Ki  17:13  But first make a small I of bread
Pr    6:26  can be had for a I of bread,
Hos   7: 8  Ephraim is a flat I not turned over.
1Co  10:17  for we all partake of the one I.

## LOAN
Dt   15: 2  shall cancel any I they have made
     24:10  When you make a I of any kind

## LOAVES [LOAF]
Ex   12:39  they baked I of unleavened bread.
Nu   11: 8  in a pot or made it into I.
Mk    6:41  Taking the five I and the two fish
      8: 6  When he had taken the seven I
      8:19  When I broke the five I for the five
      8:20  when I broke the seven I for the four
Lk   11: 5  'Friend, lend me three I of bread;

## LOBE
Dt   15:17  and push it through his ear I

## LOCKED
SS    4:12  You are a garden I up, my sister,
Lk    3:20  to them all: He I John up in prison.
Jn   20:19  with the doors I for fear
     20:26  Though the doors were I,
Ac    5:23  "We found the jail securely I,
Gal   3:22  I up everything under the control of sin,
      3:23  I up until the faith that was to come
Rev  20: 3  Abyss, and I and sealed it over him,

## LOCUSTS
Ex   10: 4  go, I will bring l into your country
2Ch  7:13  or command l to devour the land
Joel  2:25  you for the years the l have eaten—
Mt    3: 4  His food was l and wild honey.
Rev   9: 3  of the smoke l came down

## LOFTY
Ps  139: 6  for me, too l for me to attain.
Isa  26: 5  dwell on high, he lays the l city low;
Eze 16:24  and made a l shrine in every public

## LOGS
2Ch  2: 3  "Send me cedar l as you did for my
Ezr   3: 7  that they would bring cedar l by sea

## LOIS*
2Ti   1: 5  first lived in your grandmother L

## LONELY* [ALONE]
Ps   25:16  to me, for I am l and afflicted.
     68: 6  God sets the l in families, he leads
Mk    1:45  but stayed outside in l places.
Lk    5:16  Jesus often withdrew to l places

## LONG [LENGTH, LENGTHY, LONGED, LONGER, LONGING, LONGINGS, LONGS]
Ex   17:11  As l as Moses held up his hands,
     20:12  so that you may live l in the land
Nu    6: 5  they must let their hair grow l.
     14:11  How l will they refuse to believe
Dt    6: 2  and so that you may enjoy l life.
1Ki  18:21  "How l will you waver between
2Ch   1:11  since you have not asked for a l life
Ps   40:16  who l for your saving help always say,
     70: 4  those who l for your saving help
     93: 2  Your throne was established l ago;
    116: 2  me, I will call on him as l as I live.
    119:97  I meditate on it all day l.
   119:174  I l for your salvation, LORD,
Pr    3:16  L life is in her right hand; in her left
Isa  48: 3  I foretold the former things l ago,
Jer  44:14  to which they l to return and live;
La    5:20  Why do you forsake us so l?
Hos   7:13  I l to redeem them but they speak
Am    5:18  Woe to you who l for the day
Mt   25: 5  The bridegroom was a l time
Lk   10:13  they would have repented l ago,
Jn    9: 4  As l as it is day, we must do
1Co  11:14  teach you that if a man has l hair,
     11:15  but that if a woman has l hair,
Eph   3:18  to grasp how wide and l and high
Php   1: 8  God can testify how I l for all
1Pe   1:12  Even angels l to look into these
Rev   6:10  voice, "How l, Sovereign Lord,

**HOW LONG** See HOW

## LONG-SUFFERING* [SUFFER]
Jer  15:15  You are l—do not take me away;

## LONGED [LONG]
Mt   13:17  righteous people l to see what you

Mt   23:37  how often I have l to gather your
Lk   13:34  how often I have l to gather your
2Ti   4: 8  to all who have l for his appearing.

## LONGER [LONG]
Ge   17: 5  No l will you be called Abram;
     17:15  wife, you are no l to call her Sarai;
     32:28  "Your name will no l be Jacob,
Lev  26:13  that you would no l be slaves
Isa  29:22  "No l will Jacob be ashamed; no l
     62:12  After, the City No L Deserted.
Eze  14:11  of Israel will no l stray from me,
     39:29  I will no l hide my face from them,
Mt    5:13  It is no l good for anything,
Mk   10: 8  So they are no l two, but one.
Jn   13:33  I will be with you only a little l.
Ro    6: 6  that we should no l be slaves to sin—
Gal   2:20  crucified with Christ and I no l live,
      4: 7  So you are no l slaves, but God's
Eph   2:19  you are no l foreigners
      4:14  Then we will no l be infants,
Heb   8:11  No l will they teach their neighbors,
Rev  21: 1  away, and there was no l any sea.
     22: 3  No l will there be any curse.

## LONGING* [LONG]
Dt   28:65  eyes weary with l, and a despairing
Job   7: 2  Like a slave l for the evening
Ps  119:20  My soul is consumed with l for your
    119:81  My soul faints with l for your
   119:131  and pant, l for your commands.
Pr   13:12  sick, but a l fulfilled is a tree of life.
     13:19  A l fulfilled is sweet to the soul,
Eze  23:27  will not look on these things with l
Lk   16:21  and l to eat what fell from the rich
Ro   15:23  since I have been l for many years
2Co   5: 2  l to be clothed with our heavenly
      7: 7  He told us about your l for me,
      7:11  what alarm, what l, what concern,
1Th   2:17  our intense l we made every effort
Heb  11:16  they were l for a better country—

## LONGINGS* [LONG]
Ps   38: 9  All my l lie open before you, Lord;
    112:10  the l of the wicked will come

## LONGS* [LONG]
Ps   63: 1  for you, my whole being l for you,
Isa  26: 9  in the morning my spirit l for you.
     30:18  Yet the LORD l to be gracious
Php   2:26  For he l for all of you and is
Jas   4: 5  he jealously l for the spirit

## LONGSUFFERING (KJV) See PATIENCE

## LOOK [LOOKED, LOOKING, LOOKS]
Ge   13:14  "L around from where you are,
     15: 5  "L up at the heavens and count
     19:17  Don't l back, and don't stop
Ex    3: 6  because he was afraid to l at God.
Nu   21: 8  anyone who is bitten can l at it
     32: 8  Kadesh Barnea to l over the land.
Dt    3:27  L at the land with your own eyes,

| | | |
|---|---|---|
| Dt | 26:15 | **L** down from heaven, your holy |
| Jos | 2: 1 | "Go, **l** over the land," he said, |
| 1Sa | 16: 7 | not **l** at the things human beings **l** at. |
| 1Ch | 16:11 | **L** to the LORD and his strength; |
| Job | 31: 1 | my eyes not to **l** lustfully at a virgin. |
| Ps | 34: 5 | Those who **l** to him are radiant; |
| | 80:14 | **L** down from heaven and see! |
| | 105: 4 | **L** to the LORD and his strength; |
| | 113: 6 | who stoops down to **l** |
| | 123: 2 | so our eyes **l** to the LORD our |
| Pr | 1:28 | they will **l** for me but will not find |
| | 4:25 | Let your eyes **l** straight ahead; |
| Isa | 3: 9 | The **l** on their faces testifies against |
| | 17: 7 | that day people will **l** to their Maker |
| | 31: 1 | do not **l** to the Holy One of Israel, |
| | 40:26 | up your eyes and **l** to the heavens: |
| | 42:18 | **l**, you blind, and see! |
| | 60: 5 | Then you will **l** and be radiant, |
| Jer | 3: 3 | Yet you have the brazen **l** |
| | 6:16 | "Stand at the crossroads and **l**; |
| Eze | 5:11 | I will not **l** on you with pity or spare |
| | 34:11 | for my sheep and **l** after them. |
| | 34:12 | shepherds **l** after their scattered flocks |
| Da | 9:17 | Lord, **l** with favor on your desolate |
| Hab | 1:13 | Your eyes are too pure to **l** on evil; |
| Zec | 12:10 | They will **l** on me, the one they |
| Mt | 6:26 | **L** at the birds of the air; they do not |
| | 18:12 | go to **l** for the one that wandered |
| | 23:27 | which **l** beautiful on the outside |
| Mk | 8:24 | they **l** like trees walking around." |
| | 13:21 | is the Messiah!' or, '**L**, there he is!' |
| Lk | 6:41 | "Why do you **l** at the speck |
| | 24:39 | **L** at my hands and my feet. It is I |
| Jn | 1:36 | by, he said, "**L**, the Lamb of God!" |
| | 4:35 | open your eyes and **l** at the fields! |
| | 7:34 | You will **l** for me, but you will not |
| | 12:45 | When they **l** at me, |
| | 13:33 | You will **l** for me, and just as I told |
| | 19:37 | "They will **l** on the one they have |
| 1Ti | 4:12 | Don't let anyone **l** down on you |
| Jas | 1:25 | who **l** intently into the perfect law |
| | 1:27 | to **l** after orphans and widows |
| 1Pe | 1:12 | Even angels long to **l** into these |
| 2Pe | 3:12 | as you **l** forward to the day of God |
| Rev | 1:18 | and now **l**, I am alive for ever |
| | 16:15 | "Look, I come like a thief! |
| | 22: 7 | "**L**, I am coming soon! |
| | 22:12 | "**L**, I am coming soon! |

## LOOKED [LOOK]

| | | |
|---|---|---|
| Ge | 4: 4 | The LORD **l** with favor on Abel |
| | 19:26 | But Lot's wife **l** back, and she |
| Ex | 2:25 | So God **l** on the Israelites and was |
| | 24:17 | the LORD **l** like a consuming fire |
| 1Sa | 6:19 | to death because they **l** into the ark |
| Ps | 102:19 | "The LORD **l** down from his |
| SS | 3: 1 | on my bed I **l** for the one my heart |
| Eze | 1: 5 | the fire was what **l** like four living |
| | 1:26 | their heads was what **l** like a throne |
| | 10: 1 | I **l**, and I saw the likeness |
| | 22:30 | "I **l** for someone among them who |
| | 34: 6 | and no one searched or **l** for them. |
| | 37: 8 | I **l**, and tendons and flesh appeared |
| | 44: 4 | I **l** and saw the glory of the LORD |
| Da | 7: 2 | "In my vision at night I **l**, and there |
| | 7: 9 | "As I **l**, "thrones were set in place, |
| | 8: 3 | I **l** up, and there before me was |

| | | |
|---|---|---|
| Da | 10: 5 | I **l** up and there before me was |
| Hab | 3: 6 | he **l**, and made the nations tremble. |
| Zec | 1:18 | Then I **l** up, and there before me |
| | 2: 1 | Then I **l** up, and there before me |
| | 5: 1 | I **l** again, and there before me was |
| | 5: 9 | Then I **l** up—and there before me |
| | 6: 1 | I **l** up again, and there before me |
| Mt | 25:36 | I was sick and you **l** after me, I was |
| Mk | 10:21 | Jesus **l** at him and loved him. |
| Lk | 18: 9 | and **l** down on everyone else, |
| | 22:61 | Lord turned and **l** straight at Peter. |
| Ac | 7:55 | **l** up to heaven and saw the glory |
| 1Jn | 1: 1 | which we have **l** at and our hands |
| Rev | 4: 1 | After this I **l**, and there before me |
| | 5:11 | I **l** and heard the voice of many |
| | 6: 2 | I **l**, and there before me was a white |
| | 7: 9 | After this I **l**, and there before me |
| | 14: 1 | Then I **l**, and there before me was |
| | 15: 2 | And I saw what **l** like a sea of glass |

## LOOKING [LOOK]

| | | |
|---|---|---|
| Ps | 69: 3 | My eyes fail, **l** for my God. |
| | 119:82 | My eyes fail, **l** for your promise; |
| | 119:123 | My eyes fail, **l** for your salvation, |
| Mk | 3: 2 | Some of them were **l** for a reason |
| | 16: 6 | "You are **l** for Jesus the Nazarene, |
| Ac | 1:10 | They were **l** intently up into the sky |
| Php | 2: 4 | not **l** to your own interests but each |
| 1Th | 2: 6 | We were not **l** for praise from any |
| Heb | 11:26 | Egypt, because he was **l** ahead to his |
| | 13:14 | we are **l** for the city that is to come. |
| 1Pe | 5: 8 | prowls around like a roaring lion **l** |
| 2Pe | 3:13 | his promise we are **l** forward |
| Rev | 5: 6 | saw a Lamb, **l** as if it had been slain, |

## LOOKINGGLASSES (KJV) See
MIRROR

## LOOKS [LOOK]

| | | |
|---|---|---|
| 1Sa | 16: 7 | but the LORD **l** at the heart." |
| Ezr | 8:22 | God is on everyone who **l** to him, |
| Ps | 14: 2 | The LORD **l** down from heaven |
| | 33:13 | From heaven the LORD **l** down |
| | 85:11 | righteousness **l** down from heaven. |
| | 104:32 | he who **l** at the earth, and it |
| | 138: 6 | is exalted, he **l** kindly on the lowly, |
| Mt | 5:28 | anyone who **l** at a woman lustfully |
| | 16: 4 | adulterous generation **l** for a sign, |
| Lk | 9:62 | and **l** back is fit for service |
| Jn | 6:40 | is that everyone who **l** to the Son |
| Php | 2:21 | For everyone **l** out for their own |

## LOOSE [LOOSED]

| | | |
|---|---|---|
| Jdg | 16: 3 | posts, and tore them **l**, bar and all. |
| Isa | 33:23 | Your rigging hangs **l**: The mast is |
| Mt | 16:19 | and whatever you **l** on earth will be |
| | 18:18 | and whatever you **l** on earth will be |
| Ac | 16:26 | open, and everyone's chains came **l**. |

## LOOSED [LOOSE]

| | | |
|---|---|---|
| Ps | 116:16 | you have **l** my bonds of affliction. |

## LOOT

| | | |
|---|---|---|
| Isa | 42:24 | handed Jacob over to become **l**, |
| Eze | 39:10 | them and **l** those who looted them, |

## LORD [LORD'S, LORDED, LORDING, LORDS; see also †LORD (Yahweh)]

| | | |
|---|---|---|
| Ge | 18:27 | so bold as to speak to the L, |
| | 45: 8 | l of his entire household and ruler |
| Ex | 4:10 | the LORD, "Pardon your servant, L. |
| | 15:17 | sanctuary, L, your hands established. |
| | 34: 9 | "L," he said, "if I have found favor |
| Nu | 12:11 | my l, I ask you not to hold against us |
| | 16:13 | now you also want to l it over us! |
| Dt | 10:17 | God of gods and L of lords, |
| Jos | 3:11 | the ark of the covenant of the L |
| 1Sa | 24:10 | 'I will not lay my hand on my l, |
| 1Ki | 3:10 | L was pleased that Solomon had asked |
| Ne | 1:11 | L, let your ear be attentive to the prayer |
| | 4:14 | Remember the L, who is great and |
| | 10:29 | decrees of the LORD our L. |
| Job | 28:28 | "The fear of the L—that is wisdom, |
| Ps | 2: 4 | heaven laughs; the L scoffs at them. |
| | 8: 1 | LORD, our L, how majestic is your name |
| | 12: 4 | lips will defend us—who is l over us?" |
| | 16: 2 | my L; apart from you I have no good |
| | 30: 8 | to the L I cried for mercy: |
| | 35:23 | Contend for me, my God and L. |
| | 37:13 | but the L laughs at the wicked, |
| | 38:22 | help me, my L and my Savior. |
| | 40:17 | may the L think of me. You are my help |
| | 54: 4 | the L is the one who sustains me. |
| | 57: 9 | I will praise you, L, among the nations; |
| | 62:12 | and with you, L, is unfailing love"; |
| | 69: 6 | L, the LORD Almighty, |
| | 86: 5 | You, L, are forgiving and good, |
| | 86: 8 | L; no deeds can compare with yours. |
| | 97: 5 | before the L of all the earth. |
| | 110: 1 | The LORD says to my l: |
| | 135: 5 | that our L is greater than all gods. |
| | 136: 3 | Give thanks to the L of lords: |
| | 147: 5 | Great is our L and mighty in power; |
| Isa | 6: 1 | I saw the L seated on a throne, |
| | 7:14 | the L himself will give you a sign: |
| | 49:14 | the L has forgotten me." |
| Jer | 46:10 | belongs to the L, the LORD Almighty |
| La | 3:31 | people are not cast off by the L forever. |
| Eze | 18:25 | 'The way of the L is not just.' |
| Da | 2:47 | God of gods and the L of kings |
| | 5:23 | set yourself up against the L of heaven. |
| | 9: 3 | I turned to the L God and pleaded |
| | 9: 7 | "L, you are righteous, |
| | 9: 9 | The L our God is merciful and |
| | 9:19 | L, forgive! L, hear and act! |
| Am | 9: 1 | I saw the L standing by the altar, |
| Mic | 1: 2 | the L from his holy temple. |
| Mal | 3: 1 | L you are seeking will come to his |
| Mt | 1:20 | an angel of the L appeared to him |
| | 3: 3 | 'Prepare the way for the L, |
| | 4: 7 | 'Do not put the L your God to the test.' |
| | 4:10 | 'Worship the L your God, |
| | 7:21 | everyone who says to me, 'L, L,' |
| | 9:38 | Ask the L of the harvest, |
| | 12: 8 | Son of Man is L of the Sabbath." |
| | 20:25 | the rulers of the Gentiles l it over them, |
| | 21: 9 | he who comes in the name of the L!" |
| | 21:42 | the L has done this, |
| | 22:37 | " 'Love the L your God with all your |
| | 22:44 | " 'The L said to my L: |
| | 23:39 | who comes in the name of the L' " |
| Mk | 1: 3 | 'Prepare the way for the L, |
| | 5:19 | tell them how much the L has done |
| | 12:11 | the L has done this, |
| | 12:29 | The L our God, the L is one. |
| | 12:30 | Love the L your God with all your heart |
| | 12:37 | David himself calls him 'L.' |
| Lk | 1:11 | an angel of the L appeared to him, |
| | 1:32 | The L God will give him the throne |
| | 1:46 | Mary said: "My soul glorifies the L |
| | 2: 9 | the glory of the L shone around them, |
| | 2:11 | born to you; he is the Messiah, the L. |
| | 4:18 | "The Spirit of the L is on me, |
| | 5:12 | "L, if you are willing, |
| | 5:17 | power of the L was with Jesus to heal |
| | 6: 5 | "The Son of Man is L of the Sabbath." |
| | 6:46 | "Why do you call me, 'L, L,' |
| | 10:21 | Father, L of heaven and earth, |
| | 10:27 | " 'Love the L your God with all your |
| | 19:31 | say, 'The L needs it.' " |
| | 19:38 | king who comes in the name of the L!" |
| | 24:34 | L has risen and has appeared to Simon." |
| Jn | 1:23 | 'Make straight the way for the L' " |
| | 9:38 | Then the man said, "L, I believe," |
| | 13:13 | "You call me 'Teacher' and 'L,' |
| | 20:18 | "I have seen the L!" |
| | 20:28 | "My L and my God!" |
| | 21:17 | "L, you know all things; |
| Ac | 2:21 | on the name of the L will be saved.' |
| | 2:34 | " 'The L said to my L: |
| | 2:36 | you crucified, both L and Messiah." |
| | 4:26 | rulers band together against the L |
| | 5:19 | an angel of the L opened the doors of |
| | 7:59 | "L Jesus, receive my spirit." |
| | 8:16 | baptized into the name of the L Jesus. |
| | 9: 5 | "Who are you, L?" Saul asked. |
| | 9:31 | Living in the fear of the L |
| | 10:36 | Jesus Christ, who is L of all. |
| | 11:23 | true to the L with all their hearts. |
| | 16:31 | "Believe in the L Jesus, and you will be |
| | 22:10 | " 'What shall I do, L?' I asked. |
| Ro | 4:24 | raised Jesus our L from the dead. |
| | 5: 1 | peace with God through our L Jesus |
| | 6:23 | eternal life in Christ Jesus our L. |
| | 8:39 | love of God that is in Christ Jesus our L |
| | 10: 9 | declare with your mouth, "Jesus is L," |
| | 10:12 | the same L is L of all |
| | 10:13 | calls on the name of the L will be saved |
| | 12:11 | your spiritual fervor, serving the L. |
| | 13:14 | yourselves with the L Jesus Christ, |
| | 14: 4 | the L is able to make them stand. |
| | 14: 8 | If we live, we live to the L; |
| | 14: 9 | the L of both the dead and the living. |
| 1Co | 1:31 | those who boast boast in the L." |
| | 2: 8 | would not have crucified the L of glory. |
| | 2:16 | "Who has known the mind of the L |
| | 3: 5 | as the L has assigned to each his task. |
| | 4: 4 | It is the L who judges me. |
| | 6:13 | but for the L, and the L for the body. |
| | 6:14 | God raised the L from the dead, |
| | 7:10 | this command (not I, but the L): |
| | 7:12 | To the rest I say this (I, not the L): |
| | 7:25 | I have no command from the L, |
| | 7:32 | how he can please the L. |
| | 7:34 | devoted to the L in both body and spirit. |
| | 7:39 | but he must belong to the L. |
| | 8: 6 | but one L, Jesus Christ, |
| | 10:21 | cup of the L and the cup of demons too; |

1Co 11:23 For I received from the **L** what I also
    11:27 cup of the **L** in an unworthy manner
    12: 3 no one can say, "Jesus is **L**,"
    15:57 victory through our **L** Jesus Christ.
    15:58 yourselves fully to the work of the **L**,
    16:22 If anyone does not love the **L**, let that
         person be cursed! Come, **L**!
2Co 1:24 Not that we **l** it over your faith,
    2:12 found that the **L** had opened a door
    3:17 Now the **L** is the Spirit,
    4: 5 but Jesus Christ as **L**,
    5: 8 from the body and at home with the **L**.
    8: 5 given themselves first of all to the **L**,
    10:17 "Let those who boast boast in the **L**."
    10:18 but those whom the **L** commends.
    13:10 the authority the **L** gave me
Gal 6:14 in the cross of our **L** Jesus Christ,
Eph 2:21 rises to become a holy temple in the **L**.
    4: 5 one **L**, one faith, one baptism;
    5: 8 but now you are light in the **L**.
    5:10 and find out what pleases the **L**.
    5:19 music from your heart to the **L**,
    5:22 own husbands as you do to the **L**.
    6: 1 Children, obey your parents in the **L**,
    6: 8 the **L** will reward each one of you
    6:10 Finally, be strong in the **L**
Php 2:11 acknowledge that Jesus Christ is **L**,
    3: 1 rejoice in the **L**!
    3: 8 worth of knowing Christ Jesus my **L**,
    4: 1 stand firm in the **L** in this way,
    4: 4 Rejoice in the **L** always.
    4: 5 evident to all. The **L** is near.
Col 1:10 live a life worthy of the **L**
    2: 6 just as you received Christ Jesus as **L**,
    3:13 Forgive as the **L** forgave you.
    3:17 do it all in the name of the **L** Jesus,
    3:18 as is fitting in the **L**.
    3:20 for this pleases the **L**.
    3:23 working for the **L**, not for human
    3:24 inheritance from the **L** as a reward.
    4:17 the work you have received in the **L**."
1Th 1: 6 became imitators of us and of the **L**,
    3: 8 since you are standing firm in the **L**.
    3:12 May the **L** make your love increase
    4: 1 we ask you and urge you in the **L** Jesus
    4: 6 **L** will punish all those who commit
    4:15 who are left till the coming of the **L**,
    4:17 so we will be with the **L** forever.
    5: 2 day of the **L** will come like a thief
    5:23 blameless at the coming of our **L**
2Th 1: 7 **L** Jesus is revealed from heaven
    1:12 name of our **L** Jesus may be glorified
    2: 1 the coming of our **L** Jesus Christ
    2: 8 the **L** Jesus will overthrow
    3: 3 But the **L** is faithful,
    3: 5 May the **L** direct your hearts
1Ti 1:14 grace of our **L** was poured out on me
    6:14 the appearing of our **L** Jesus Christ,
    6:15 the King of kings and **L** of lords,
2Ti 1: 8 testimony about our **L** or of me
    2:19 "The **L** knows those who are his,"
    4: 8 which the **L**, the righteous Judge,
    4:17 But the **L** stood at my side
Phm 1:25 grace of the **L** Jesus Christ be with your
Heb 1:10 **L**, you laid the foundations of the earth,
    8: 2 true tabernacle set up by the **L**,
    8:11 say to one another, 'Know the **L**,'

Heb 10:30 "The **L** will judge his people."
    12: 6 the **L** disciplines those he loves,
    12:14 without holiness no one will see the **L**.
    13: 6 The **L** is my helper; I will not be afraid.
Jas 1: 7 will receive anything from the **L**;
    3: 9 the tongue we praise our **L** and Father,
    4:10 Humble yourselves before the **L**,
    5:11 The **L** is full of compassion and mercy.
    5:15 the **L** will raise them up.
1Pe 1:25 but the word of the **L** endures forever."
    2: 3 you have tasted that the **L** is good.
    3:12 the **L** is against those who do evil."
    3:15 But in your hearts revere Christ as **L**.
2Pe 1:11 eternal kingdom of our **L** and Savior
    1:16 coming of our **L** Jesus Christ in power,
    2: 1 denying the sovereign **L** who bought
    2: 9 the **L** knows how to rescue the godly
    3: 9 **L** is not slow in keeping his promise.
    3:10 day of the **L** will come like a thief.
    3:18 of our **L** and Savior Jesus Christ.
Jude 1: 4 Jesus Christ our only Sovereign and **L**.
    1:14 "See, the **L** is coming with thousands
Rev 4: 8 Holy, holy, holy is the **L** God Almighty,
    6:10 "How long, Sovereign **L**, holy and true,
    11: 8 where also their **L** was crucified.
    11:15 kingdom of our **L** and of his Messiah,
    11:17 give thanks to you, **L** God Almighty,
    14:13 dead who die in the **L** from now on."
    15: 4 Who will not fear you, **L**,
    17:14 will triumph over them because he is **L**
    19: 6 For our **L** God Almighty reigns.
    19:16 KING OF KINGS AND **L** OF LORDS.
    21:22 because the **L** God Almighty
    22: 5 the **L** God will give them light.
    22:20 Amen. Come, **L** Jesus.

## ANGEL OF THE LORD See ANGEL

## LORD GOD Da 9:3; Lk 1:32; Rev 1:8; 4:8;
11:17; 15:3; 16:7; 18:8; 19:6; 21:22; 22:5

## LORD JESUS See JESUS

## LORD JESUS CHRIST See JESUS

## THE LORD THE †LORD ALMIGHTY
Ps 69:6; Isa 1:24; 3:1, 15; 10:16, 23, 24, 33;
19:4; 22:5, 12, 14, 15; 28:22; Jer 2:19; 46:10, 10;
49:5; 50:31; Am 9:5

## MY/OUR LORD THE KING 1Sa 24:8;
26:15, 15, 17, 19; 29:8; 2Sa 3:21; 4:8; 9:11;
13:33; 14:9, 12, 15, 17, 17, 18, 19, 19, 22; 15:15,
21, 21; 16:4, 9; 18:28, 31, 32; 19:19, 20, 26, 27,
27, 28, 30, 35, 37; 24:3, 3, 21, 22; 1Ki 1:2, 13,
18, 20, 20, 21, 24, 27, 27, 36, 37; 2:38; 20:4, 9;
2Ki 6:12, 26; 8:5; 1Ch 21:3, 23; Jer 37:20; 38:9;
Da 1:10; 4:24

## NAME OF THE LORD See NAME

## LORD'S [LORD; see also †LORD'S (Yahweh's)]
Nu 14:17 may the **L** strength be displayed,
Mal 1:12 'The **L** table is defiled,'
Lk 1:38 "I am the **L** servant,"
    1:66 the **L** hand was with him.
    4:19 proclaim the year of the **L** favor."

Lk    10:39  sat at the **L** feet listening
Ac    11:21  **L** hand was with them,
      21:14  "The **L** will be done."
Ro    12:13  Share with the **L** people who are in
1Co    7:32  concerned about the **L** affairs
      10:21  part in both the **L** table
      10:22  trying to arouse the **L** jealousy?
      10:26  "The earth is the **L**, and everything
      11:20  it is not the **L** Supper you eat,
      11:26  the **L** death until he comes.
2Co    3:18  faces contemplate the **L** glory,
Gal    1:19  only James, the **L** brother.
Eph    5:17  understand what the **L** will is.
2Ti    2:24  the **L** servant must not be quarrelsome
Heb   12: 5  make light of the **L** discipline,
Jas    4:15  "If it is the **L** will,
       5: 8  because the **L** coming is near.
1Pe    2:13  Submit yourselves for the **L** sake
2Pe    3:15  our **L** patience means salvation,
Rev    1:10  On the **L** Day I was in the Spirit,

## ✝LORD (Yahweh) [✝LORD'S (Yahweh's); see also LORD]

Ge     2: 4  **L** God made the earth and the heavens.
       2: 7  **L** God formed a man from the dust
       2:16  the **L** God commanded the man,
       2:22  the **L** God made a woman from the rib
       3: 9  the **L** God called to the man,
       3:13  Then the **L** God said to the woman,
       3:14  the **L** God said to the serpent,
       3:23  So the **L** God banished him
       4: 4  **L** looked with favor on Abel
       4:15  the **L** put a mark on Cain
       4:26  began to call on the name of the **L**.
       6: 6  **L** regretted that he had made human
       6: 8  found favor in the eyes of the **L**.
       7:16  the **L** shut him in.
       8:20  Noah built an altar to the **L** and,
       9:26  "Praise be to the **L**, the God of Shem!
      10: 9  mighty hunter before the **L**;
      11: 9  the **L** confused the language
      12: 1  The **L** had said to Abram,
      12: 7  built an altar there to the **L**,
      13: 4  Abram called on the name of the **L**.
      15: 6  Abram believed the **L**,
      15:18  On that day the **L** made a covenant
      17: 1  the **L** appeared to him and said,
      18: 1  **L** appeared to Abraham near the great
      18:14  anything too hard for the **L**?
      18:19  keep the way of the **L** by doing
      19:14  the **L** is about to destroy the city!"
      21: 1  the **L** was gracious to Sarah
      22:14  called that place The **L** Will Provide.
      24: 1  the **L** had blessed him in every way.
      25:21  Isaac prayed to the **L** on behalf of his
      26: 2  **L** appeared to Isaac and said,
      26:25  called on the name of the **L**.
      28:16  "Surely the **L** is in this place,
      31:49  the **L** keep watch between you and me
      39: 2  The **L** was with Joseph so that he
      39:23  because the **L** was with Joseph
Ex     3: 2  angel of the **L** appeared to him in
       3:15  'The **L**, the God of your fathers
       4:11  Is it not I, the **L**?
       4:31  heard that the **L** was concerned
       5: 2  Pharaoh said, "Who is the **L**,

Ex     6: 2  said to Moses, "I am the **L**.
       6: 7  know that I am the **L** your God,
       8:10  no one like the **L** our God.
       9:12  But the **L** hardened Pharaoh's heart
       9:30  still do not fear the **L** God."
      10:16  "I have sinned against the **L** your God
      10:20  But the **L** hardened Pharaoh's heart,
      10:27  But the **L** hardened Pharaoh's heart,
      11:10  but the **L** hardened Pharaoh's heart,
      12:27  the Passover sacrifice to the **L**,
      12:29  **L** struck down all the firstborn in Egypt,
      13: 9  **L** brought you out of Egypt
      13:12  give over to the **L** the first offspring
      13:21  **L** went ahead of them in a pillar of
      14: 8  **L** hardened the heart of Pharaoh
      14:13  deliverance the **L** will bring you today.
      14:18  Egyptians will know that I am the **L**
      14:30  **L** saved Israel from the hands of the
      15: 3  **L** is a warrior; the **L** is his name.
      15:11  Who among the gods is like you, **L**?
      15:26  If you listen carefully to the **L** your God
      16:12  know that I am the **L** your God.' "
      16:29  the **L** has given you the Sabbath;
      17: 7  tested the **L** saying, "Is the **L** among
      17:15  called it The **L** is my Banner.
      18:10  He said, "Praise be to the **L**,
      19: 8  "We will do everything the **L** has said."
      19: 8  brought their answer back to the **L**.
      19:20  **L** descended to the top of Mount Sinai
      20: 2  "I am the **L** your God,
      20: 5  the **L** your God, am a jealous God,
      20: 7  not misuse the name of the **L** your God,
      20: 7  for the **L** will not hold anyone guiltless
      20:10  seventh day is a sabbath to the **L**
      20:11  For in six days the **L** made the heavens
      20:11  **L** blessed the Sabbath day and made it
      20:12  land the **L** your God is giving you.
      23:25  Worship the **L** your God,
      24: 3  "Everything the **L** has said we will do."
      24:12  The **L** said to Moses, "Come up
      24:16  glory of the **L** settled on Mount Sinai.
      24:16  the **L** called to Moses from within the
      25: 1  The **L** said to Moses,
      28:36  on a seal: HOLY TO THE **L**.
      30:11  Then the **L** said to Moses,
      31:13  I am the **L**, who makes you holy.
      31:18  When the **L** finished speaking to Moses
      32:11  favor of the **L** his God. "**L**," he said,
      33: 9  while the **L** spoke with Moses.
      34: 5  Then the **L** came down in the cloud
      34: 5  proclaimed his name, the **L**.
      34: 6  "The **L**, the **L**, the compassionate
      34:10  the **L** said: "I am making a covenant
      34:10  the **L**, will do for you.
      34:14  any other god, for the **L**,
      34:29  because he had spoken with the **L**.
      40:34  glory of the **L** filled the tabernacle.
      40:38  cloud of the **L** was over the tabernacle
Lev    1: 2  bring an offering to the **L**,
       1: 9  an aroma pleasing to the **L**.
       8:36  everything the **L** commanded
       9:23  glory of the **L** appeared to all the people
      10: 2  fire came out from the presence of the **L**
      10: 2  and they died before the **L**.
      19: 2  holy because I, the **L** your God,
      20: 8  I am the **L**, who makes you holy.
      20:26  holy to me because I, the **L**,

| | | |
|---|---|---|
| Lev | 23:40 | and rejoice before the **L** your God |
| | 24:16 | who blasphemes the name of the **L** |
| Nu | 6:24 | **L** bless you and keep you; |
| | 8: 5 | The **L** said to Moses: |
| | 10:29 | place about which the **L** said, |
| | 10:29 | **L** has promised good things to Israel." |
| | 11: 1 | hardships in the hearing of the **L**, |
| | 11: 1 | fire from the **L** burned among them |
| | 14:14 | have already heard that you, **L**, |
| | 14:14 | **L**, have been seen face to face, |
| | 14:18 | 'The **L** is slow to anger, |
| | 14:21 | glory of the **L** fills the whole earth, |
| | 16: 7 | incense in them before the **L**. |
| | 16: 7 | man the **L** chooses will be the one |
| | 20:13 | Israelites quarreled with the **L** |
| | 21: 6 | the **L** sent venomous snakes among |
| | 21:14 | why the Book of the Wars of the **L** says: |
| | 22:31 | Then the **L** opened Balaam's eyes, |
| | 22:31 | he saw the angel of the **L** standing |
| | 23:12 | not speak what the **L** puts in my mouth? |
| | 30: 2 | When a man makes a vow to the **L** |
| | 32:12 | followed the **L** wholeheartedly.' |
| Dt | 1:21 | the **L** your God has given you the land. |
| | 1:21 | and take possession of it as the **L**, |
| | 2: 7 | **L** your God has blessed you in all the |
| | 2: 7 | the **L** your God has been with you, |
| | 4:29 | if from there you seek the **L** your God, |
| | 4:39 | **L** is God in heaven above |
| | 5: 6 | "I am the **L** your God, who brought |
| | 5: 9 | the **L** your God, am a jealous God, |
| | 5:11 | name of the **L** your God, for the **L** |
| | 5:14 | seventh day is a sabbath to the **L** |
| | 6: 4 | The **L** our God, the **L** is one. |
| | 6: 5 | Love the **L** your God with all your heart |
| | 6:16 | Do not put the **L** your God to the test |
| | 6:25 | obey all this law before the **L** our God, |
| | 7: 1 | the **L** your God brings you into the land |
| | 7: 6 | holy to the **L** your God. The **L** your |
| | 7: 8 | because the **L** loved you |
| | 7: 9 | the **L** your God is God; |
| | 7:12 | the **L** your God will keep his covenant |
| | 7:22 | **L** your God will drive out those nations |
| | 8: 5 | so the **L** your God disciplines you. |
| | 9:10 | The **L** gave me two stone tablet |
| | 9:10 | commandments the **L** proclaimed to you |
| | 10:12 | what does the **L** your God ask of you |
| | 10:12 | but to fear the **L** your God, |
| | 10:12 | serve the **L** your God with all your heart |
| | 10:14 | **L** your God belong the heavens, |
| | 10:17 | For the **L** your God is God of gods |
| | 10:20 | Fear the **L** your God and serve him. |
| | 10:22 | **L** your God has made you as numerous |
| | 11: 1 | Love the **L** your God |
| | 11:13 | love the **L** your God and to serve |
| | 13: 3 | The **L** your God is testing you |
| | 14: 1 | the children of the **L** your God. |
| | 16: 1 | the Passover of the **L** your God, |
| | 17:15 | the king the **L** your God chooses. |
| | 18: 2 | the **L** is their inheritance. |
| | 18:15 | The **L** your God will raise up |
| | 28: 1 | If you fully obey the **L** your God |
| | 28: 1 | the **L** your God will set you high |
| | 28:15 | if you do not obey the **L** your God |
| | 29: 1 | covenant the **L** commanded Moses |
| | 29:29 | secret things belong to the **L** |
| | 30: 4 | **L** your God will gather you |
| | 30: 6 | **L** your God will circumcise your hearts |

| | | |
|---|---|---|
| Dt | 30:10 | if you obey the **L** your God |
| | 30:10 | turn to the **L** your God |
| | 30:16 | to love the **L** your God, |
| | 30:16 | the **L** your God will bless you |
| | 30:20 | that you may love the **L** your God, |
| | 30:20 | For the **L** is your life, |
| | 31: 6 | for the **L** your God goes with you; |
| | 34: 5 | servant of the **L** died there |
| | 34: 5 | as the **L** had said. |
| Jos | 1:13 | Moses the servant of the **L** gave |
| | 1:13 | **L** your God will give you rest |
| | 2:11 | the **L** your God is God in heaven |
| | 7:20 | I have sinned against the **L**, the God |
| | 10:14 | when the **L** listened to a human being. |
| | 10:14 | Surely the **L** was fighting for Israel! |
| | 21:44 | The **L** gave them rest on every side, |
| | 21:44 | **L** gave all their enemies into their hands |
| | 22: 5 | of the **L** gave you: to love the **L** |
| | 22:22 | **L**! The Mighty One, God, the **L**! |
| | 22:22 | disobedience to the **L**, do not spare us |
| | 22:34 | Between Us—that the **L** is God. |
| | 23:11 | careful to love the **L** your God. |
| | 24:15 | serving the **L** seems undesirable |
| | 24:15 | my household, we will serve the **L**." |
| | 24:18 | And the **L** drove out before us |
| | 24:18 | We too will serve the **L**, |
| Jdg | 2:12 | They forsook the **L**, |
| | 3: 9 | when they cried out to the **L**, |
| Ru | 1: 8 | May the **L** show you kindness, |
| | 4:13 | the **L** enabled her to conceive, |
| 1Sa | 1:11 | "**L** Almighty, if you will only look |
| | 1:11 | the **L** for all the days of his life, |
| | 1:19 | worshiped before the **L** |
| | 1:19 | and the **L** remembered her. |
| | 1:28 | now I give him to the **L**. |
| | 1:28 | the **L**." And he worshiped the **L** |
| | 2: 2 | no one holy like the **L**; |
| | 2:25 | if anyone sins against the **L**, |
| | 2:26 | favor with the **L** and with people. |
| | 3: 1 | ministered before the **L** under Eli. |
| | 3: 1 | the word of the **L** was rare; |
| | 3: 8 | time the **L** called, "Samuel!" |
| | 3: 8 | that the **L** was calling the boy. |
| | 3:19 | The **L** was with Samuel as he grew |
| | 4: 3 | "Why did the **L** bring defeat on us |
| | 5: 3 | before the ark of the **L**! |
| | 7:12 | "Thus far the **L** has helped us." |
| | 10: 1 | "Has not the **L** anointed you ruler |
| | 11:15 | Saul king in the presence of the **L**. |
| | 11:15 | fellowship offerings before the **L**, |
| | 12: 5 | "The **L** is witness against you, |
| | 12:18 | Then Samuel called on the **L**, |
| | 12:18 | same day the **L** sent thunder and rain. |
| | 12:18 | stood in awe of the **L** and of Samuel. |
| | 12:22 | sake of his great name the **L** |
| | 12:22 | the **L** was pleased to make you his own. |
| | 12:24 | be sure to fear the **L** and serve him |
| | 13:14 | the **L** has sought out a man |
| | 14: 6 | Perhaps the **L** will act in our behalf. |
| | 14: 6 | Nothing can hinder the **L** from |
| | 15:22 | "Does the **L** delight in burnt offerings |
| | 15:22 | as much as in obeying the **L**? |
| | 15:28 | "The **L** has torn from the kingdom |
| | 16:13 | Spirit of the **L** came on David |
| | 17:45 | in the name of the **L** Almighty, |
| 2Sa | 5:10 | the **L** God Almighty was with him. |
| | 6:14 | dancing before the **L** with all his |

| | | |
|---|---|---|
| 2Sa | 7:22 | "How great you are, Sovereign L! |
| | 8: 6 | The L gave David victory wherever |
| | 12:13 | "I have sinned against the L." |
| | 12:13 | "The L has taken away your sin. |
| | 22: 2 | "The L is my rock, my fortress |
| | 22:29 | L, are my lamp; the L turns |
| | 24:14 | fall into the hands of the L, |
| 1Ki | 1:30 | I swore to you by the L, |
| | 2: 3 | observe what the L your God requires: |
| | 3: 3 | Solomon showed his love for the L |
| | 5: 5 | Name of the L my God, as the L |
| | 5:12 | The L gave Solomon wisdom, |
| | 8:11 | glory of the L filled his temple. |
| | 8:23 | "L, the God of Israel, |
| | 8:61 | fully committed to the L our God, |
| | 9: 3 | The L said to him: "I have heard |
| | 10: 9 | Praise be to the L your God, |
| | 11: 4 | not fully devoted to the L his God, |
| | 15:14 | fully committed to the L all his life. |
| | 18:21 | If the L is God, follow him; |
| | 18:36 | "L, the God of Abraham, |
| | 18:39 | "The L—he is God! The L |
| | 19:11 | The L said, "Go out and stand |
| | 19:11 | presence of the L, for the L |
| | 19:11 | before the L, but the L was not |
| | 19:11 | the L was not in the earthquake. |
| | 21:23 | L says: 'Dogs will devour Jezebel |
| | 22: 5 | "First seek the counsel of the L." |
| 2Ki | 3:18 | easy thing in the eyes of the L; |
| | 13:23 | But the L was gracious to them |
| | 17:20 | the L rejected all the people |
| | 18: 5 | Hezekiah trusted in the L, |
| | 19: 1 | went into the temple of the L. |
| | 19:31 | zeal of the L Almighty will accomplish |
| | 20:11 | called on the L, and the L made |
| | 21:12 | this is what the L, the God of Israel, |
| | 22: 2 | right in the eyes of the L |
| | 22: 8 | Book of the Law in the temple of the L. |
| | 23: 3 | presence of the L—to follow the L |
| | 23:21 | "Celebrate the Passover to the L |
| | 23:25 | who turned to the L as he did— |
| | 24: 2 | The L sent Babylonian, Aramean, |
| | 24: 2 | the word of the L proclaimed |
| | 24: 4 | L was not willing to forgive. |
| | 25: 9 | He set fire to the temple of the L, |
| 1Ch | 10:13 | he was unfaithful to the L; |
| | 10:13 | did not keep the word of the L |
| | 11: 3 | Hebron before the L, |
| | 11: 3 | the L had promised through Samuel. |
| | 11: 9 | because the L Almighty was with him. |
| | 13: 6 | ark of God the L, who is enthroned |
| | 16: 8 | Give praise to the L, |
| | 16:11 | Look to the L and his strength; |
| | 16:23 | Sing to the L, all the earth; |
| | 17: 1 | ark of the covenant of the L is under |
| | 17:20 | "There is no one like you, L, |
| | 21:24 | not take for the L what is yours, |
| | 22: 1 | house of the L God is to be here, |
| | 22:11 | my son, the L be with you, |
| | 22:11 | build the house of the L your God, |
| | 22:13 | and laws that the L gave Moses |
| | 22:16 | the L be with you." |
| | 22:19 | heart and soul to seeking the L |
| | 22:19 | build the sanctuary of the L God, |
| | 22:19 | bring the ark of the covenant of the L |
| | 22:19 | built for the Name of the L." |
| | 25: 7 | trained and skilled in music for the L— |

| | | |
|---|---|---|
| 1Ch | 28: 9 | L searches every heart and understands |
| | 28:20 | the L God, my God, is with you. |
| | 28:20 | temple of the L is finished. |
| | 29: 1 | human beings but for the L God. |
| | 29:11 | Yours, L, is the greatness and the power |
| | 29:11 | L, is the kingdom; you are exalted |
| | 29:25 | The L highly exalted Solomon |
| 2Ch | 1: 1 | the L his God was with him |
| | 2:11 | "Because the L loves his people, |
| | 5:14 | glory of the L filled the temple of God. |
| | 6:17 | And now, L, the God of Israel, |
| | 7: 1 | the glory of the L filled the temple. |
| | 7:12 | the L appeared to him at night |
| | 7:21 | 'Why has the L done such a thing |
| | 9: 8 | Praise be to the L your God, |
| | 9: 8 | as king to rule for the L your God. |
| | 13:12 | do not fight against the L, |
| | 14: 6 | for the L gave him rest. |
| | 15:15 | the L gave them rest on every side. |
| | 16: 9 | For the eyes of the L range throughout |
| | 17: 9 | Book of the Law of the L; |
| | 18:15 | truth in the name of the L?" |
| | 19: 6 | judging for mere mortals but for the L, |
| | 19: 9 | wholeheartedly in the fear of the L. |
| | 20:15 | what the L says to you: |
| | 20:20 | Have faith in the L your God |
| | 21: 7 | L had made with David, the L |
| | 26: 5 | As long as he sought the L, |
| | 26:16 | He was unfaithful to the L his God, |
| | 26:16 | and entered the temple of the L |
| | 29:31 | dedicated yourselves to the L. |
| | 29:31 | thank offerings to the temple of the L." |
| | 30: 9 | If you return to the L, |
| | 30: 9 | the L your God is gracious |
| | 31:20 | faithful before the L his God. |
| | 32: 8 | but with us is the L our God |
| | 33:13 | the L was moved by his entreaty |
| | 33:13 | Manasseh knew that the L is God. |
| | 34:14 | taken into the temple of the L, |
| | 34:14 | Book of the Law of the L |
| | 34:31 | presence of the L—to follow the L |
| | 36:22 | of the L spoken by Jeremiah, the L |
| Ezr | 3:10 | foundation of the temple of the L, |
| | 3:10 | took their places to praise the L, |
| | 7: 6 | which the L, the God of Israel, |
| | 7: 6 | the L his God was on him. |
| | 7:10 | observance of the Law of the L, |
| | 9: 5 | hands spread out to the L my God |
| | 9: 8 | the L our God has been gracious |
| Ne | 1: 5 | "L, the God of heaven, |
| | 8: 1 | the L had commanded for Israel. |
| | 8:10 | joy of the L is your strength." |
| | 9: 6 | You alone are the L. |
| Job | 1: 6 | present themselves before the L, |
| | 1:21 | L gave and the L has taken away; |
| | 1:21 | may the name of the L be praised." |
| | 38: 1 | L spoke to Job out of the storm. |
| | 42:12 | L blessed the latter part of Job's life |
| Ps | 1: 2 | who delight in the law of the L |
| | 1: 6 | L watches over the way of the righteous |
| | 2: 2 | rulers band together against the L |
| | 3: 8 | From the L comes deliverance. |
| | 4: 6 | Many, L, are asking, |
| | 5: 3 | In the morning, L, you hear my voice; |
| | 6: 1 | L, do not rebuke me in your anger |
| | 7: 1 | L my God, I take refuge in you; |
| | 8: 1 | L, our Lord, how majestic is your name |

| | | |
|---|---|---|
| Ps | 9: 9 | The **L** is a refuge for the oppressed, |
| | 9:19 | **L**, do not let mortals triumph; |
| | 10:16 | The **L** is King for ever and ever; |
| | 11: 5 | The **L** examines the righteous, |
| | 12: 6 | And the words of the **L** are flawless, |
| | 13: 1 | How long, **L**? Will you forget me |
| | 14: 6 | but the **L** is their refuge. |
| | 15: 4 | but honor whoever fears the **L**; |
| | 16: 2 | I say to the **L**, "You are my Lord; |
| | 16: 8 | my eyes always on the **L**. |
| | 17: 1 | Hear me, **L**, my plea is just; |
| | 18: 1 | I love you, **L**, my strength. |
| | 18: 6 | In my distress I called to the **L**; |
| | 18:31 | who is God besides the **L**? |
| | 19: 7 | The law of the **L** is perfect, |
| | 19: 7 | statutes of the **L** are trustworthy, |
| | 19:14 | heart be pleasing in your sight, **L**, |
| | 20: 5 | May the **L** grant all your requests. |
| | 20: 7 | trust in the name of the **L** our God. |
| | 21:13 | Be exalted in your strength, **L**; |
| | 22: 8 | in the **L**," they say, "let the **L** |
| | 23: 1 | The **L** is my shepherd, |
| | 23: 6 | dwell in the house of the **L** forever. |
| | 24: 3 | ascend the mountain of the **L**? |
| | 24: 8 | **L** strong and mighty, the **L** |
| | 25:10 | the ways of the **L** are loving |
| | 26: 2 | Test me, **L**, and try me, |
| | 27: 1 | The **L** is my light and my salvation |
| | 27: 1 | **L** is the stronghold of my life— |
| | 27: 4 | One thing I ask from the **L**, |
| | 27: 4 | dwell in the house of the **L** |
| | 27: 4 | gaze on the beauty of the **L** |
| | 27: 6 | I will sing and make music to the **L**. |
| | 28: 7 | The **L** is my strength and my shield; |
| | 29: 1 | Ascribe to the **L**, |
| | 29: 1 | ascribe to the **L** glory and strength. |
| | 29: 4 | **L** is powerful; the voice of the **L** |
| | 30: 4 | Sing the praises of the **L**, |
| | 31: 5 | redeem me, **L**, my faithful God. |
| | 32: 2 | Blessed are those whose sin the **L** |
| | 33: 1 | Sing joyfully to the **L**, |
| | 33: 6 | By the word of the **L** the heavens |
| | 33:12 | nation whose God is the **L**, |
| | 33:20 | We wait in hope for the **L**; |
| | 34: 1 | I will extol the **L** at all times; |
| | 34: 4 | I sought the **L**, |
| | 34: 7 | The angel of the **L** encamps |
| | 34: 8 | Taste and see that the **L** is good; |
| | 34: 9 | Fear the **L**, you his holy people, |
| | 34:15 | The eyes of the **L** are on the righteous |
| | 34:18 | The **L** is close to the brokenhearted |
| | 35:10 | "Who is like you, **L**? You rescue |
| | 36: 6 | **L**, preserve both people and animals. |
| | 37: 4 | Take delight in the **L** |
| | 37: 5 | Commit your way to the **L**; |
| | 38:21 | **L**, do not forsake me; |
| | 40: 1 | I waited patiently for the **L**; |
| | 40:13 | **L**; come quickly, **L**, |
| | 41:10 | may you have mercy on me, **L**; |
| | 46: 7 | The **L** Almighty is with us; |
| | 47: 2 | For the **L** Most High is awesome, |
| | 48: 1 | Great is the **L**, and most worthy |
| | 50: 1 | **L**, speaks and summons the earth |
| | 55:22 | Cast your cares on the **L** |
| | 59: 8 | But you laugh at them, **L**; |
| | 68: 4 | his name is the **L**. |
| | 68:20 | **L** comes escape from death. |

| | | |
|---|---|---|
| Ps | 69:31 | This will please the **L** more |
| | 70: 5 | my help and my deliverer; **L**, |
| | 71: 1 | In you, **L**, I have taken refuge; |
| | 73:28 | I have made the Sovereign **L** my refuge; |
| | 75: 8 | In the hand of the **L** is a cup |
| | 78: 4 | praiseworthy deeds of the **L**, |
| | 81:10 | I am the **L** your God, |
| | 83:18 | whose name is the **L**— |
| | 84:11 | **L** God is a sun and shield; the **L** |
| | 85: 7 | Show us your unfailing love, **L**, |
| | 86:11 | Teach me your way, **L**, |
| | 87: 2 | The **L** loves the gates of Zion |
| | 88: 1 | **L**, you are the God who saves me; |
| | 89: 6 | the **L**? Who is like the **L** |
| | 91: 2 | They say of the **L**, |
| | 92: 1 | It is good to praise the **L** |
| | 92: 4 | you make me glad by your deeds, **L**; |
| | 93: 1 | **L** reigns, he is robed in majesty; the **L** |
| | 93: 5 | Your statutes, **L**, stand firm; |
| | 94: 1 | The **L** is a God who avenges; |
| | 94:12 | Blessed are those you discipline, **L**, |
| | 94:18 | your unfailing love, **L**, supported me. |
| | 95: 1 | Come, let us sing for joy to the **L**; |
| | 95: 3 | For the **L** is the great God, |
| | 96: 1 | **L** a new song; sing to the **L**, |
| | 96: 5 | but the **L** made the heavens. |
| | 96: 9 | Worship the **L** in the splendor |
| | 97: 1 | The **L** reigns, let the earth be glad; |
| | 97:10 | Let those who love the **L** hate evil, |
| | 98: 2 | The **L** has made his salvation known |
| | 99: 1 | The **L** reigns, let the nations tremble; |
| | 99: 5 | Exalt the **L** our God and worship |
| | 100: 2 | Worship the **L** with gladness; |
| | 101: 1 | to you, **L**, I will sing praise. |
| | 102:12 | But you, **L**, sit enthroned forever; |
| | 103: 1 | Praise the **L**, my soul; |
| | 103: 8 | The **L** is compassionate and gracious, |
| | 103:19 | The **L** has established his throne |
| | 104: 1 | Praise the **L**, my soul. **L** my God, |
| | 104:24 | How many are your works, **L**! |
| | 104:33 | I will sing to the **L** all my life; |
| | 105: 4 | Look to the **L** and his strength; |
| | 105:24 | The **L** made his people very fruitful; |
| | 106:47 | Save us, **L** our God, |
| | 107: 1 | Give thanks to the **L**, |
| | 107: 8 | thanks to the **L** for his unfailing love |
| | 107:43 | ponder the loving deeds of the **L**. |
| | 108: 3 | I will praise you, **L**, among the nations; |
| | 109:26 | Help me, **L** my God; |
| | 110: 1 | The **L** says to my lord: |
| | 110: 4 | The **L** has sworn and will not change |
| | 111: 2 | Great are the works of the **L**; |
| | 111: 4 | the **L** is gracious and compassionate. |
| | 111:10 | fear of the **L** is the beginning of wisdom |
| | 112: 1 | Praise the **L**. Blessed are those |
| | 113: 1 | Praise the **L**. Praise the **L**, |
| | 113: 1 | praise the name of the **L**. |
| | 113: 5 | Who is like the **L** our God, |
| | 115: 1 | Not to us, **L**, not to us but to your name |
| | 115:18 | it is we who extol the **L**, |
| | 115:18 | both now and forevermore. Praise the **L**. |
| | 116: 5 | The **L** is gracious and righteous; |
| | 116:12 | What shall I return to the **L** |
| | 116:15 | Precious in the sight of the **L** |
| | 117: 1 | Praise the **L**, all you nations; |
| | 118: 7 | The **L** is with me; he is my helper. |
| | 118: 8 | better to take refuge in the **L** |

Ps 118:18 The L has chastened me severely,
118:24 The L has done it this very day;
118:26 L. From the house of the L
119: 1 walk according to the law of the L.
119:64 L; teach me your decrees.
119:89 Your word, L, is eternal;
119:126 It is time for you to act, L;
119:159 preserve my life, L,
120: 1 I call on the L in my distress,
121: 2 My help comes from the L,
121: 5 L watches over you—the L
122: 1 go to the house of the L."
123: 2 eyes look to the L our God,
124: 1 If the L had not been on our side—
124: 8 Our help is in the name of the L,
125: 2 so the L surrounds his people
126: 3 L has done great things for us,
127: 1 Unless the L builds the house,
127: 1 Unless the L watches over the city,
127: 3 Children are a heritage from the L,
128: 1 Blessed are all who fear the L,
129: 4 But the L is righteous;
130: 3 If you, L, kept a record of sins,
130: 5 I wait for the L, my whole being
131: 3 put your hope in the L both now
132: 1 L, remember David
132:13 For the L has chosen Zion,
133: 3 the L bestows his blessing,
134: 3 May the L bless you from Zion,
135: 3 Praise the L, for the L is good;
135: 6 The L does whatever pleases him,
136: 1 Give thanks to the L, for he is good.
137: 4 How can we sing the songs of the L
138: 1 I will praise you, L, with all my heart;
138: 8 L will vindicate me; your love, L,
139: 1 You have searched me, L,
140: 1 Rescue me, L, from evildoers;
141: 1 I call to you, L, come quickly to me;
141: 3 Set a guard over my mouth, L;
142: 5 I cry to you, L; I say,
143: 9 Rescue me from my enemies, L,
144: 3 L, what are human beings that you care
145: 3 Great is the L and most worthy of
145: 8 The L is gracious and compassionate,
145: 9 The L is good to all;
145:17 The L is righteous in all his ways
145:18 The L is near to all who call on him,
146: 5 hope is in the L their God.
146: 7 The L sets prisoners free,
147: 2 The L builds up Jerusalem;
147: 7 Sing to the L with grateful praise;
148: 1 Praise the L. Praise the L
148: 7 Praise the L from the earth,
149: 4 For the L takes delight in his people;
150: 1 Praise the L. Praise God in his
150: 6 praise the L. Praise the L.
Pr 1: 7 fear of the L is the beginning
1:29 did not choose to fear the L.
2: 5 fear of the L and find the knowledge
2: 6 For the L gives wisdom;
3: 5 Trust in the L with all your heart
3: 7 fear the L and shun evil.
3: 9 Honor the L with your wealth,
3:12 the L disciplines those he loves,
3:19 the L laid the earth's foundations,
5:21 ways are in full view of the L,
6:16 six things the L hates,

Pr 8:13 To fear the L is to hate evil;
8:35 receive favor from the L.
9:10 The fear of the L is the beginning
10:22 blessing of the L brings wealth,
10:27 The fear of the L adds length to life,
10:29 of the L is a refuge for the blameless,
11: 1 The L detests dishonest scales,
12: 2 obtain favor from the L,
12:22 The L detests lying lips,
14: 2 Whoever fears the L walks uprightly,
14:16 wise fear the L and shun evil,
14:26 who fear the L have a secure fortress,
14:27 fear of the L is a fountain of life,
15: 3 eyes of the L are everywhere,
15:16 Better a little with the fear of the L
15:29 The L is far from the wicked,
15:33 Wisdom's instruction is to fear the L,
16: 1 from the L comes the proper answer
16: 2 motives are weighed by the L.
16: 3 Commit to the L whatever you do,
16: 4 The L works out everything
16: 5 The L detests all the proud of heart.
16: 6 fear of the L evil is avoided.
16: 9 but the L establishes their steps.
16:20 blessed are those who trust in the L.
16:33 every decision is from the L.
17: 3 the L tests the heart.
18:10 name of the L is a fortified tower;
18:22 receives favor from the L.
19:14 but a prudent wife is from the L.
19:17 who are kind to the poor lend to the L,
19:23 The fear of the L leads to life;
20:10 the L detests them both.
20:12 the L has made them both.
20:22 Wait for the L, and he will avenge you.
20:23 L detests differing weights,
20:24 person's steps are directed by the L.
20:27 human spirit is the lamp of the L
21: 2 but the L weighs the heart.
21: 3 acceptable to the L than sacrifice.
21:30 no plan that can succeed against the L.
21:31 but victory rests with the L.
22: 2 The L is the Maker of them all.
22: 4 Humility is the fear of the L;
22:12 of the L keep watch over knowledge,
22:19 your trust may be in the L,
22:23 for the L will take up their case
23:17 always be zealous for the fear of the L.
24:21 Fear the L and the king,
25:22 and the L will reward you.
28: 5 who seek the L understand it fully.
28:25 who trust in the L will prosper.
29:25 whoever trusts in the L is kept safe.
29:26 from the L that one gets justice.
31:30 who fears the L is to be praised.
Isa 1: 4 They have forsaken the L;
1:18 let us reason together," says the L.
2: 3 let us go up to the mountain of the L,
2: 3 the word of the L from Jerusalem.
2:11 the L alone will be exalted in that day.
3:13 The L takes his place in court;
4: 2 the L will be beautiful and glorious,
5: 7 vineyard of the L Almighty is the house
5:16 L Almighty will be exalted by his
6: 3 "Holy, holy, holy is the L Almighty;
7:11 "Ask the L your God for a sign,
9: 7 zeal of the L Almighty will accomplish

Isa 11: 2 Spirit of the **L** will rest on him—
11: 2 the knowledge and fear of the **L**—
11: 9 the knowledge of the **L** as the waters
12: 2 The **L**, the **L**, is my strength
13: 9 See, the day of the **L** is coming—
18: 7 gifts will be brought to the **L** Almighty
18: 7 place of the Name of the **L** Almighty.
24: 1 See, the **L** is going to lay waste
25: 1 **L**, you are my God; I will exalt you
25: 6 On this mountain the **L** Almighty
25: 8 Sovereign **L** will wipe away the tears
25: 8 The **L** has spoken.
26: 4 Trust in the **L** forever, for the **L**, the **L**,
26: 8 **L**, walking in the way of your laws,
26:13 **L** our God, other lords besides you
26:21 See, the **L** is coming out of his dwelling
27: 1 the **L** will punish with his sword—
27:12 the **L** will thresh from the flowing
28: 5 **L** Almighty will be a glorious crown,
29: 6 the **L** Almighty will come with thunder
29:15 hide their plans from the **L**,
29:19 the humble will rejoice in the **L**;
30:18 Yet the **L** longs to be gracious to you;
30:18 For the **L** is a God of justice.
30:26 when the **L** binds up the bruises
30:30 The **L** will cause people to hear
33: 2 **L**, be gracious to us; we long for you.
33: 6 fear of the **L** is the key to this treasure.
33:22 For the **L** is our judge, the **L**
33:22 the **L** is our king;
34: 2 The **L** is angry with all nations;
35: 2 they will see the glory of the **L**,
35:10 and those the **L** has rescued will return.
37:15 And Hezekiah prayed to the **L**:
40: 3 wilderness prepare the way for the **L**;
40: 5 And the glory of the **L** will be revealed,
40: 5 For the mouth of the **L** has spoken."
40: 7 the breath of the **L** blows on them.
40:10 See, the Sovereign **L** comes with power,
40:14 did the **L** consult to enlighten him,
40:27 "My way is hidden from the **L**;
40:28 The **L** is the everlasting God,
40:31 hope in the **L** will renew their strength.
41:14 declares the **L**, your Redeemer, the Holy
41:20 the hand of the **L** has done this,
42: 8 "I am the **L**; that is my name!
42:10 Sing to the **L** a new song, his praise
42:13 The **L** will march out like a champion,
42:21 It pleased the **L** for the sake of his
43: 3 For I am the **L** your God, the Holy One
43:11 **L**, and apart from me there is no savior.
44: 6 **L** says—Israel's King and Redeemer,
       the **L**
44:23 for the **L** has done this; shout aloud,
44:23 for the **L** has redeemed Jacob,
45: 5 I am the **L**, and there is no other;
45: 7 I, the **L**, do all these things.
45:17 But Israel will be saved by the **L**
45:21 Was it not I, the **L**? And there is no God
48:17 what the **L** says—your Redeemer,
48:17 "I am the **L** your God, who teaches you
49: 7 This is what the **L** says—
49: 7 the **L**, who is faithful, the Holy One
49:14 "The **L** has forsaken me, the Lord has
50: 5 The Sovereign **L** has opened my ears;
50:10 Who among you fears the **L** and obeys
50:10 trust in the name of the **L** and rely on

Isa 51: 1 righteousness and who seek the **L**:
51:11 Those the **L** has rescued will return.
51:15 For I am the **L** your God, who stirs up
51:15 the **L** Almighty is his name.
52:10 The **L** will lay bare his holy arm
53: 1 the arm of the **L** been revealed?
53: 6 the **L** has laid on him the iniquity
53:10 though the **L** makes his life an offering
53:10 will of the **L** will prosper in his hand.
54: 5 is your husband—the **L** Almighty
55: 6 Seek the **L** while he may be found;
55: 7 turn to the **L**, and he will have mercy
56: 6 bind themselves to the **L** to minister
56: 6 to love the name of the **L**,
58: 5 a day acceptable to the **L**?
58:11 The **L** will guide you always;
59: 1 arm of the **L** is not too short to save,
59:19 people will fear the name of the **L**,
59:19 that the breath of the **L** drives along.
60: 1 the glory of the **L** rises upon you.
60:19 for the **L** will be your everlasting light,
61: 1 **L** is on me, because the **L** has anointed
61: 3 the **L** for the display of his splendor.
61: 8 "For I, the **L**, love justice;
61:10 I delight greatly in the **L**;
62: 4 for the **L** will take delight in you,
63: 7 kindnesses of the **L**,
63: 7 according to all the **L** has done for us—
64: 8 Yet you, **L**, are our Father.
65:23 people blessed by the **L**,
66:15 See, the **L** is coming with fire,
Jer 1: 9 the **L** reached out his hand
2:19 when you forsake the **L** your God
2:19 declares the Lord, the **L** Almighty
3:12 'Return, faithless Israel,' declares the **L**,
3:12 for I am faithful,' declares the **L**,
3:25 We have sinned against the **L**,
3:25 not obeyed the **L** our God."
4: 4 Circumcise yourselves to the **L**,
6:10 The word of the **L** is offensive to them;
8: 7 do not know the requirements of the **L**.
9:24 that I am the **L**,
9:24 these I delight," declares the **L**.
10: 6 No one is like you, **L**;
10:10 But the **L** is the true God;
10:21 do not inquire of the **L**;
12: 1 You are always righteous, **L**,
14: 7 **L**, for the sake of your name.
14:20 We acknowledge our wickedness, **L**,
16:19 **L**, my strength and my fortress,
17: 7 blessed are those who trust in the **L**,
17:10 "I the **L** search the heart
17:13 **L**, you are the hope of Israel;
17:13 forsaken the **L**, the spring of living
20:11 the **L** is with me like a mighty warrior;
23: 6 called: The **L** Our Righteous Savior.
24: 7 know me, that I am the **L**.
28: 9 one truly sent by the **L** only if
31:11 For the **L** will deliver Jacob
31:22 The **L** will create a new thing on earth
31:34 to one another, 'Know the **L**,'
31:34 of them to the greatest," declares the **L**.
32:27 the **L**, the God of the whole human race
33:16 The **L** Our Righteous Savior.'
36: 6 go to the house of the **L**
36: 6 scroll the words of the **L** that you wrote
40: 3 now the **L** has brought it about;

| | | |
|---|---|---|
| Jer | 40: 3 | people sinned against the **L** |
| | 42: 3 | Pray that the **L** your God |
| | 42: 4 | "I will certainly pray to the **L** your God |
| | 42: 4 | tell you everything the **L** says |
| | 42: 6 | we will obey the **L** our God, |
| | 42: 6 | will obey the **L** our God." |
| | 50: 4 | those days, at that time," declares the **L**, |
| | 50: 4 | go in tears to seek the **L** their God. |
| | 51:10 | " 'The **L** has vindicated us; |
| | 51:10 | in Zion what the **L** our God has done.' |
| | 51:56 | the **L** is a God of retribution; |
| La | 1: 5 | The **L** has brought her grief |
| | 3:24 | "The **L** is my portion; |
| | 3:25 | The **L** is good to those whose hope |
| | 3:26 | quietly for the salvation of the **L**. |
| | 3:40 | and let us return to the **L**. |
| Eze | 1: 3 | the word of the **L** came to Ezekiel |
| | 1: 3 | the hand of the **L** was on him. |
| | 1:28 | the likeness of the glory of the **L**. |
| | 3:23 | glory of the **L** was standing there, |
| | 4:14 | "Not so, Sovereign **L**! |
| | 10: 4 | glory of the **L** rose from above |
| | 10: 4 | radiance of the glory of the **L**. |
| | 10:18 | the glory of the **L** departed |
| | 15: 7 | you will know that I am the **L**. |
| | 30: 3 | the day of the **L** is near— |
| | 34:24 | I the **L** will be their God, |
| | 34:24 | I the **L** have spoken. |
| | 36:23 | I am the **L**, declares the Sovereign **L**, |
| | 37: 4 | 'Dry bones, hear the word of the **L**! |
| | 43: 4 | The glory of the **L** entered the temple |
| | 44: 4 | **L** filling the temple of the **L**, |
| | 48:35 | on will be: THE **L** IS THERE." |
| Da | 9: 2 | word of the **L** given to Jeremiah |
| | 9:14 | The **L** did not hesitate to bring |
| | 9:14 | disaster on us, for the **L** our God |
| Hos | 1: 7 | but by the **L** their God." |
| | 2:13 | but me she forgot," declares the **L**. |
| | 2:20 | and you will acknowledge the **L**. |
| | 3: 1 | The **L** said to me, "Go, show |
| | 3: 1 | Love her as the **L** loves the Israelites, |
| | 3: 5 | Israelites will return and seek the **L** |
| | 3: 5 | They will come trembling to the **L** |
| | 4: 1 | Hear the word of the **L**, you Israelites, |
| | 4: 1 | because the **L** has a charge to bring |
| | 6: 1 | "Come, let us return to the **L**. |
| | 6: 3 | Let us acknowledge the **L**; |
| | 10:12 | it is time to seek the **L**, |
| | 12: 5 | **L** God Almighty, the **L** is his name! |
| | 14: 1 | Return, Israel, to the **L** your God. |
| Joel | 1:15 | For the day of the **L** is near; |
| | 2:11 | The **L** thunders at the head of his army; |
| | 2:11 | day of the **L** is great; it is dreadful. |
| | 2:13 | Return to the **L** your God, |
| | 2:21 | Surely the **L** has done great things! |
| | 2:23 | rejoice in the **L** your God, |
| | 2:31 | great and dreadful day of the **L**. |
| | 2:32 | name of the **L** will be saved; |
| | 2:32 | as the **L** has said, |
| | 2:32 | among the survivors whom the **L** calls. |
| | 3:14 | day of the **L** is near in the valley of |
| | 3:16 | The **L** will roar from Zion |
| | 3:16 | the **L** will be a refuge for his people, |
| Am | 1: 2 | "The **L** roars from Zion |
| | 4:13 | the **L** God Almighty is his name. |
| | 5: 6 | Seek the **L** and live, or he will sweep |
| | 5:15 | the **L** God Almighty will have mercy |

| | | |
|---|---|---|
| Am | 5:18 | who long for the day of the **L**! |
| | 5:18 | Why do you long for the day of the **L**? |
| | 7:15 | the **L** took me from tending the flock |
| | 8:11 | are coming," declares the Sovereign **L**, |
| | 8:11 | a famine of hearing the words of the **L**. |
| | 9: 5 | The Lord, the **L** Almighty— |
| Ob | 1:15 | "The day of the **L** is near for all nations. |
| Jnh | 1: 3 | But Jonah ran away from the **L** |
| | 1: 3 | sailed for Tarshish to flee from the **L**. |
| | 1: 4 | Then the **L** sent a great wind on the sea, |
| | 1:17 | **L** provided a huge fish to swallow |
| | 2: 9 | 'Salvation comes from the **L**.' " |
| | 4: 2 | the **L**, "Isn't this what I said, **L**, |
| | 4: 6 | Then the **L** God provided a gourd |
| Mic | 1:12 | disaster has come from the **L**, |
| | 4: 2 | go up to the mountain of the **L**, |
| | 4: 2 | the word of the **L** from Jerusalem. |
| | 5: 4 | in the strength of the **L**, |
| | 5: 4 | majesty of the name of the **L** his God. |
| | 6: 2 | **L** has a case against his people; |
| | 6: 8 | what does the **L** require of you? |
| | 7: 7 | I watch in hope for the **L**, |
| Na | 1: 2 | **L** is a jealous and avenging God; |
| | 1: 2 | **L** takes vengeance and is filled with |
| | 1: 2 | **L** takes vengeance on his foes |
| | 1: 3 | **L** is slow to anger but great in power; |
| | 1: 3 | the **L** will not leave the guilty |
| Hab | 1:12 | **L**, are you not from everlasting? |
| | 1:12 | You, **L**, have appointed them |
| | 2:14 | knowledge of the glory of the **L** |
| | 2:20 | The **L** is in his holy temple; |
| | 3: 2 | **L**, I have heard of your fame; |
| | 3: 2 | I stand in awe of your deeds, **L**. |
| Zep | 1: 7 | Sovereign **L**, for the day of the **L** is near. |
| | 1: 7 | The **L** has prepared a sacrifice; |
| | 1:14 | great day of the **L** is near— |
| | 1:14 | cry on the day of the **L** is bitter; |
| | 3:17 | The **L** your God is with you, |
| Hag | 1:12 | voice of the **L** their God |
| | 1:12 | because the **L** their God had sent him. |
| | 1:12 | And the people feared the **L**. |
| | 2:23 | 'On that day,' declares the **L** Almighty, |
| | 2:23 | son of Shealtiel,' declares the **L**, |
| | 2:23 | chosen you,' declares the **L** Almighty." |
| Zec | 1: 2 | "The **L** was very angry with your |
| | 1:17 | This is what the **L** Almighty says: |
| | 1:17 | the **L** will again comfort Zion |
| | 3: 1 | standing before the angel of the **L**, |
| | 3: 2 | The **L** said to Satan, "The **L** rebuke you, Satan! The **L**, who has chosen Jerusalem, |
| | 4: 6 | This is the word of the **L** to Zerubbabel: |
| | 4: 6 | but by my Spirit,' says the **L** Almighty. |
| | 6:12 | this is what the **L** Almighty says: |
| | 6:12 | build the temple of the **L**. |
| | 8:21 | entreat the **L** and seek the **L** |
| | 9:16 | The **L** their God will save his people |
| | 14: 5 | The **L** my God will come, |
| | 14: 7 | a day known only to the **L**— |
| | 14: 9 | **L** will be king over the whole earth. |
| | 14: 9 | On that day there will be one **L**, |
| | 14:20 | On that day HOLY TO THE **L** |
| Mal | 1: 2 | "I have loved you," says the **L**. |
| | 1: 2 | Esau Jacob's brother?" declares the **L**. |
| | 3: 6 | "I the **L** do not change. |
| | 4: 5 | great and dreadful day of the **L** comes. |

**ANGEL OF THE †LORD** See ANGEL

**ANGER OF THE †LORD** See ANGER

**ARK OF THE †LORD** See ARK

**AS SURELY AS THE †LORD ... LIVES**
Jdg 8:19; Ru 3:13; 1Sa 14:45; 19:6; 20:3, 21; 25:26; 26:10, 16; 28:10; 29:6; 2Sa 4:9; 12:5; 14:11; 15:21; 1Ki 1:29; 2:24; 17:12; 18:10; 22:14; 2Ki 2:2, 4, 6; 3:14; 4:30; 5:16, 20; 2Ch 18:13; Jer 4:2; 5:2; 12:16; 16:14, 15; 23:7, 8; 38:16; Hos 4:15

**AS THE †LORD ... COMMANDED** Ex
7:6, 10, 20; 16:34; 17:1; 34:4; 36:1; 39:1, 5, 7, 21, 26, 29, 31, 32, 42, 43; 40:16, 19, 21, 23, 25, 27, 29, 32; Lev 8:4, 9, 13, 17, 21, 29; 9:7, 10; 10:15; 16:34; 24:23; Nu 1:19, 54; 2:33; 3:42; 4:49; 8:3, 20, 22; 9:5; 15:36; 17:11; 20:27; 26:4; 27:11, 22; 31:7, 31, 41, 47; 36:10; Dt 10:5; Jos 11:15, 20; 14:2, 5; 19:50; 21:3, 8; 2Sa 5:25; 24:19; Ps 106:34

**COMMANDS OF THE †LORD** See COMMANDS

**COVENANT OF THE †LORD** See COVENANT

**DAY OF THE †LORD** See DAY

**DECLARES THE †LORD** Ge 22:16; Nu
14:28; 2Ki 9:26, 26; 19:33; 22:19; 2Ch 34:27; Isa 14:22, 22, 23; 17:3, 6; 22:25; 30:1; 31:9; 37:34; 41:14; 43:10, 12; 49:18; 52:5, 5; 54:17; 55:8; 59:20; 66:2, 17, 22; Jer 1:8, 15, 19; 2:3, 9, 12, 29; 3:1, 10, 12, 12, 13, 14, 16, 20; 4:1, 9, 17; 5:9, 11, 15, 18, 22, 29; 6:12; 7:11, 13, 19, 30, 32; 8:1, 3, 13, 17; 9:3, 6, 9, 24, 25; 12:17; 13:11, 14, 25; 15:3, 6, 9, 20; 16:5, 11, 14, 16; 17:24; 18:6; 19:6, 12; 21:7, 10, 13, 14; 22:5, 16, 24; 23:1, 2, 4, 5, 7, 11, 12, 23, 24, 24, 28, 29, 30, 31, 32, 32, 33; 25:7, 9, 12, 29, 31; 27:8, 11, 15, 22; 28:4; 29:9, 11, 14, 14, 19, 19, 23, 32; 30:3, 8, 10, 11, 17, 21; 31:1, 14, 16, 17, 20, 27, 28, 31, 32, 33, 34, 36, 37, 38; 32:5, 30, 44; 33:14; 34:5, 17, 22; 35:13; 39:17, 18; 42:11; 44:29; 45:5; 46:5, 23, 26, 28; 48:12, 25, 30, 35, 38, 43, 44, 47; 49:2, 6, 13, 16, 26, 30, 31, 32, 37, 38, 39; 50:4, 10, 20, 21, 30, 35, 40; 51:24, 25, 26, 39, 48, 52, 53; Eze 16:58; 37:14; Hos 2:13, 16, 21; 11:11; Joel 2:12; Am 2:11, 16; 3:10, 15; 4:3, 6, 8, 9, 10, 11; 9:7, 8, 12, 13; Ob 1:4, 8; Mic 4:6; 5:10; Na 2:13; 3:5; Zep 1:2, 3, 10; 2:9; 3:8; Hag 1:9, 13; 2:4, 4, 4, 8, 9, 14, 17, 23, 23, 23; Zec 1:3, 4, 16; 2:5, 6, 6, 10; 3:10; 8:6, 11, 17; 10:12; 11:6; 12:4; 13:2, 7, 8; Mal 1:2

**DECLARES THE SOVEREIGN †LORD**
Jer 2:22; Eze 5:11; 11:8, 21; 12:25, 28; 13:8, 16; 14:11, 14, 16, 18, 20, 23; 15:8; 16:8, 14, 19, 23, 30, 43, 48, 63; 17:16; 18:3, 9, 23, 30, 32; 20:3, 31, 33, 36, 40, 44; 21:7, 13; 22:12, 31; 23:34; 24:14; 25:14; 26:5, 14, 21; 28:10; 29:20; 30:6; 31:18; 32:8, 14, 16, 31, 32; 33:11; 34:8, 15, 30, 31; 35:6, 11; 36:14, 15, 23, 32; 38:18, 21; 39:5,

8, 10, 13, 20, 29; 43:19, 27; 44:12, 15, 27; 45:9, 15; 47:23; 48:29; Am 4:5; 8:3, 9, 11

**EVIL IN THE EYES OF THE †LORD** See EYES

**FEAR OF THE †LORD** See FEAR

**FEAR THE †LORD** See FEAR

**GIVE THANKS TO THE †LORD** 1Ch
16:34, 41; 2Ch 20:21; Ps 7:17; 106:1; 107:1, 8, 15, 21, 31; 118:1, 19, 29; 136:1; Jer 33:11

**GLORY OF THE †LORD** See GLORY

**HAND OF THE †LORD** See HAND

**HOLY TO THE †LORD** See HOLY

**HOUSE OF THE †LORD** See HOUSE

**I AM THE †LORD** See I AM

**KNOW THAT I AM THE †LORD** See KNOW

**KNOW THAT I THE †LORD** See KNOW

**KNOW THAT THE †LORD** See KNOW

**LAW OF THE †LORD** See LAW

**THE LORD THE †LORD ALMIGHTY**
See LORD

**†LORD ALMIGHTY** 1Sa 1:3, 11; 4:4; 15:2;
17:45; 2Sa 6:2, 18; 7:8, 26, 27; 1Ki 18:15; 2Ki 3:14; 19:31; 1Ch 11:9; 17:7, 24; Ps 24:10; 46:7, 11; 48:8; 69:6; 84:1, 3, 12; Isa 1:9, 24; 2:12; 3:1, 15; 5:7, 9, 16, 24; 6:3, 5; 8:13, 18; 9:7, 13, 19; 10:16, 23, 24, 26, 33; 13:4, 13; 14:22, 23, 24, 27; 17:3; 18:7, 7; 19:4, 12, 16, 17, 18, 20, 25; 21:10; 22:5, 12, 14, 14, 15, 25; 23:9; 24:23; 25:6; 28:5, 22, 29; 29:6; 31:4, 5; 37:16, 32; 39:5; 44:6; 45:13; 47:4; 48:2; 51:15; 54:5; Jer 2:19; 6:6, 9; 7:3, 21; 8:3; 9:7, 15, 17; 10:16; 11:17, 20, 22; 16:9; 19:3, 11, 15; 20:12; 23:15, 16, 36; 25:8, 27, 28, 29, 32; 26:18; 27:4, 18, 19, 21; 28:2, 14; 29:4, 8, 17, 21, 25; 30:8; 31:23, 35; 32:14, 15, 18; 33:11, 12; 35:13, 18, 19; 39:16; 42:15, 18; 43:10; 44:2, 11, 25; 46:10, 10, 18, 25; 48:1, 15; 49:5, 7, 26, 35; 50:18, 25, 31, 33, 34; 51:5, 14, 19, 33, 57, 58; Am 9:5; Mic 4:4; Na 2:13; 3:5; Hab 2:13; Zep 2:9, 10; Hag 1:2, 5, 7, 9, 14; 2:4, 6, 7, 8, 9, 9, 11, 23, 23; Zec 1:3, 3, 3, 4, 6, 12, 14, 16, 17; 2:8, 9, 11; 3:7, 9, 10; 4:6, 9; 5:4; 6:12, 15; 7:3, 4, 9, 12, 12, 13; 8:1, 2, 3, 4, 6, 6, 7, 9, 9, 11, 14, 14, 18, 19, 20, 21, 22, 23; 9:15; 10:3; 12:5; 13:2, 7; 14:16, 17, 21, 21; Mal 1:4, 6, 8, 9, 10, 11, 13, 14; 2:2, 4, 7, 8, 12, 16; 3:1, 5, 7, 10, 11, 12, 14, 17; 4:1, 3

**†LORD ALMIGHTY SAYS** 1Sa 15:2; 2Sa
7:8; 1Ch 17:7; Isa 10:24; 22:15; Jer 6:6, 9; 9:7, 17; 11:22; 19:11; 23:15, 16; 25:8, 28, 32; 26:18; 27:19; 29:17; 33:12; 49:7, 35; 50:33; 51:58; Hag 1:2, 5, 7; 2:6, 11; Zec 1:3, 4, 14, 17; 2:8; 3:7; 6:12; 8:2, 4, 6, 7, 9, 14, 19, 20, 23; Mal 1:4

**†LORD GOD** Ge 2:4, 5, 7, 8, 9, 15, 16, 18, 19, 21, 22; 3:1, 8, 8, 9, 13, 14, 21, 22, 23; 14:22; 24:12, 42; Ex 9:30; Jdg 21:3; 1Sa 23:10, 11; 2Sa 5:10; 7:25; 1Ki 19:10, 14; 1Ch 17:16, 17; 22:1, 19; 28:20; 29:1; 2Ch 1:9; 6:41, 41, 42; 26:5, 18; 32:16; Ne 9:7; Ps 59:5; 68:18; 72:18; 80:4, 19; 84:8, 11; 89:8; Jer 5:14; 15:16; 35:17; 38:17; 44:7; Hos 12:5; Am 3:13; 4:13; 5:14, 15, 16; 6:8, 14; Jnh 4:6; Mal 2:16

**†LORD GOD ALMIGHTY** 2Sa 5:10; 1Ki 19:10, 14; Ps 59:5; 80:4, 19; 84:8; 89:8; Jer 5:14; 15:16; 35:17; 38:17; 44:7; Hos 12:5; Am 3:13; 4:13; 5:14, 15, 16; 6:8, 14

**†LORD HIS GOD** Ex 32:11; Lev 4:22; Dt 17:19; 18:7; 1Sa 30:6; 2Sa 14:11; 1Ki 5:3; 11:4; 15:3, 4; 2Ki 5:11; 16:2; 2Ch 1:1; 14:2, 11; 15:9; 26:16; 27:6; 28:5; 31:20; 33:12; 34:8; 36:5, 12; Ezr 7:6; Hos 7:10; Jnh 2:1; Mic 5:4

**†LORD MY GOD** Nu 22:18; Dt 4:5; 26:14; Jos 14:8, 9; 2Sa 24:24; 1Ki 3:7; 5:4, 5; 8:28; 17:20, 21; 1Ch 21:17; 22:7; 2Ch 2:4; 6:19; Ezr 7:28; 9:5; Ps 7:1, 3; 13:3; 25:1; 30:2, 12; 35:24; 40:5; 104:1; 109:26; Jer 31:18; Da 9:4, 20; Jnh 2:6; Zec 11:4; 14:5

**†LORD OUR GOD** Ex 3:18; 5:3; 8:10, 26, 27; 10:25, 26; Dt 1:6, 19, 20, 25, 41; 2:29, 33, 36, 37; 3:3; 4:7; 5:2, 24, 25, 27, 27; 6:4, 20, 24, 25; 18:16; 29:15, 18, 29; Jos 18:6; 22:19, 29; 24:17, 24; Jdg 11:24; 1Sa 7:8; 1Ki 8:57, 59, 61, 65; 2Ki 18:22; 19:19; 1Ch 13:2; 15:13; 16:14; 29:16; 2Ch 2:4; 13:11; 14:7, 11; 19:7; 29:6; 32:8, 11; Ezr 9:8; Ne 10:34; Ps 20:7; 94:23; 99:5, 8, 9, 9; 105:7; 106:47; 113:5; 122:9; 123:2; Isa 26:13; 36:7; 37:20; Jer 3:22, 23, 25, 25; 5:19, 24; 8:14; 14:22; 16:10; 26:16; 31:6; 37:3; 42:6, 6, 20; 43:2; 50:28; 51:10; Da 9:10, 13, 14; Mic 4:5; 7:17

**†LORD THEIR GOD** Ex 10:7; 29:46, 46; Lev 26:44; Nu 23:21; Jdg 3:7; 8:34; 1Sa 12:9; 1Ki 9:9; 2Ki 17:7, 9, 14, 16, 19; 18:12; 2Ch 31:6; 33:17; 34:33; 36:23; Ne 9:3, 3, 4; Ps 146:5; Jer 3:21; 22:9; 30:9; 43:1; 50:4; Eze 28:26; 34:30; 39:22, 28; Hos 1:7; 3:5; Zep 2:7; Hag 1:12, 12; Zec 9:16; 10:6

**†LORD YOUR GOD** Ge 27:20; Ex 6:7; 8:28; 10:8, 16, 17; 15:26; 16:12; 20:2, 5, 7, 10, 12; 23:19, 25; 34:24, 26; Lev 11:44; 18:2, 4, 30; 19:2, 3, 4, 10, 25, 31, 34, 36; 20:7, 24; 23:22, 28, 40, 43; 24:22; 25:17, 38, 55; 26:1, 13; Nu 10:9, 10; 15:41, 41; Dt 1:10, 21, 26, 30, 31, 32; 2:7, 7, 30; 3:18, 20, 21, 22; 4:2, 3, 4, 10, 19, 21, 23, 23, 24, 25, 29, 30, 31, 34, 40; 5:6, 9, 11, 12, 14, 15, 15, 16, 16, 32, 33; 6:1, 2, 5, 10, 13, 15, 16, 17; 7:1, 2, 6, 6, 9, 12, 16, 18, 19, 19, 20, 21, 22, 23, 25; 8:2, 5, 6, 7, 10, 11, 14, 18, 19, 20; 9:3, 4, 5, 6, 7, 16, 23; 10:9, 12, 12, 12, 14, 17, 20, 22; 11:1, 2, 12, 12, 13, 22, 25, 27, 28, 29, 31; 12:4, 5, 7, 7, 9, 10, 11, 12, 15, 18, 18, 18, 20, 21, 27, 27, 28, 29, 31; 13:3, 4, 5, 5, 10, 12, 16, 18; 14:1, 2, 21, 23, 23, 24, 25, 26, 29; 15:4, 5, 6, 7, 10, 14, 15, 18, 19, 20, 21; 16:1, 2, 5, 7, 8, 10, 10, 11, 15,

15, 16, 17, 18, 20, 21, 22; 17:1, 2, 8, 12, 14, 15; 18:5, 9, 12, 13, 14, 15, 16; 19:1, 2, 3, 8, 9, 10, 14; 20:1, 4, 13, 14, 16, 17, 18; 21:1, 5, 10, 23; 22:5; 23:5, 5, 14, 18, 18, 20, 21, 21, 23; 24:4, 9, 13, 18, 19; 25:15, 16, 19; 26:1, 2, 2, 3, 4, 5, 10, 11, 13, 16, 19; 27:2, 3, 5, 6, 6, 7, 9, 10; 28:1, 1, 2, 8, 9, 13, 15, 45, 47, 52, 53, 58, 62; 29:6, 10, 12; 30:1, 2, 3, 4, 6, 7, 9, 10, 10, 16, 16, 20; 31:3, 6, 11, 12, 13, 26; Jos 1:9, 11, 13, 15, 17; 2:11; 3:3, 9; 4:5, 23, 23, 24; 8:7; 9:9, 24; 10:19; 22:3, 4, 5; 23:3, 3, 5, 5, 8, 10, 11, 13, 13, 14, 15, 15, 16; Jdg 6:10, 26; 1Sa 12:12, 14, 19; 13:13; 15:15, 21, 30; 25:26, 28, 29, 31; 2Sa 14:17; 18:28; 24:3, 23; 1Ki 1:17; 2:3; 10:9; 13:6, 21; 17:12; 18:10; 2Ki 17:39; 19:4, 4; 23:21; 1Ch 11:2; 22:11, 12, 18, 19; 28:8; 29:20; 2Ch 9:8, 8; 16:7; 20:20; 28:10; 30:8, 9; 35:3; Ne 8:9; 9:5; Ps 76:11; 81:10; Isa 7:11; 37:4, 4; 41:13; 43:3; 48:17; 51:15; 55:5; 60:9; Jer 2:17, 19; 3:13; 13:16; 26:13; 40:2; 42:2, 3, 4, 5, 13, 20, 21; Eze 20:5, 7, 19, 20; Hos 12:9; 13:4; 14:1; Joel 1:14; 2:13, 14, 23, 26, 27; 3:17; Am 9:15; Mic 7:10; Zep 3:17; Zec 6:15

**LOVE THE †LORD** See LOVE

**NAME OF THE †LORD** See NAME

**PRAISE BE TO THE †LORD** See PRAISE

**PRAISE THE †LORD** See PRAISE

**PRESENCE OF THE †LORD** See PRESENCE

**SAYS THE †LORD** 2Ki 20:17; Ps 12:5; 91:14; Isa 1:11, 18; 33:10; 39:6; 41:21; 45:13; 48:22; 54:1, 8, 10; 57:19; 59:21, 21; 65:7, 25; 66:9, 20, 21, 23; Jer 6:15; 8:12; 24:8; 30:3; 33:11, 13; 44:26; 49:2, 18; Am 1:5, 15; 2:3; 5:17, 27; 9:15; Zep 3:20; Hag 1:8; 2:7, 9; Zec 1:3; 3:9; 4:6; 7:13; 8:14; Mal 1:2, 6, 8, 9, 10, 11, 13, 13, 14; 2:2, 4, 8, 16, 16; 3:1, 5, 7, 10, 11, 12, 13, 17; 4:1, 3

**SERVANT OF THE †LORD** See SERVANT

**SOVEREIGN †LORD** Ge 15:2, 8; Ex 23:17; 34:23; Dt 3:24; 9:26; Jos 7:7; Jdg 6:22; 16:28; 2Sa 7:18, 19, 19, 20, 22, 28, 29; 1Ki 2:26; 8:53; Ps 68:20; 71:5, 16; 73:28; 109:21; 140:7; 141:8; Isa 7:7; 25:8; 28:16; 30:15; 40:10; 48:16; 49:22; 50:4, 5, 7, 9; 51:22; 52:4; 56:8; 61:1, 11; 65:13, 15; Jer 1:6; 2:22; 4:10; 7:20; 14:13; 32:17, 25; 44:26; 50:25; Eze 2:4; 3:11, 27; 4:14; 5:5, 7, 8, 11; 6:3, 3, 11; 7:2, 5; 8:1; 9:8; 11:7, 8, 13, 16, 17, 21; 12:10, 19, 23, 25, 28, 28; 13:3, 8, 8, 9, 13, 16, 18, 20; 14:4, 6, 11, 14, 16, 18, 20, 21, 23; 15:6, 8; 16:3, 8, 14, 19, 23, 30, 36, 43, 48, 59, 63; 17:3, 9, 16, 19, 22; 18:3, 9, 23, 30, 32; 20:3, 3, 5, 27, 30, 31, 33, 36, 39, 40, 44, 47, 49; 21:7, 13, 24, 26, 28; 22:3, 12, 19, 28, 31; 23:22, 28, 32, 34, 35, 46, 49; 24:3, 6, 9, 14, 21, 24; 25:3, 3, 6, 8, 12, 13, 14, 15, 16; 26:3, 5, 7, 14, 15, 19, 21; 27:3; 28:2, 6, 10, 12, 22, 24, 25; 29:3, 8, 13, 16, 19, 20; 30:2, 6, 10, 13, 22; 31:10, 15, 18; 32:3, 8, 11, 14, 16, 31, 32; 33:11, 25, 27; 34:2, 8, 10, 11,

15, 17, 20, 30, 31; 35:3, 6, 11, 14; 36:2, 3, 4, 4, 5, 6, 7, 13, 14, 15, 22, 23, 32, 33, 37; 37:3, 5, 9, 12, 19, 21; 38:3, 10, 14, 17, 18, 21; 39:1, 5, 8, 10, 13, 17, 20, 25, 29; 43:18, 19, 27; 44:6, 9, 12, 15, 27; 45:9, 9, 15, 18; 46:1, 16; 47:13, 23; 48:29; Am 1:8; 3:7, 8, 11; 4:2, 5; 5:3; 6:8; 7:1, 2, 4, 4, 5, 6; 8:1, 3, 9, 11; 9:8; Ob 1:1; Mic 1:2; Hab 3:19; Zep 1:7; Zec 9:14

## SPIRIT OF THE †LORD  See SPIRIT

## TEMPLE OF THE †LORD  See TEMPLE

## VOICE OF THE †LORD  See VOICE

## WHAT THE †LORD SAYS  Ex 4:22; 7:17;
8:1, 20; 11:4; Nu 24:13; 1Sa 2:27; 2Sa 7:5; 12:11; 24:12; 1Ki 12:24; 13:2, 21; 20:13, 14, 28, 42; 21:19, 19; 22:11; 2Ki 1:4, 6, 16; 2:21; 3:16, 17; 4:43; 7:1; 9:3, 12; 19:6, 32; 20:1; 22:16; 1Ch 17:4; 21:10, 11; 2Ch 11:4; 12:5; 18:10; 20:15; 34:24; Isa 8:11; 18:4; 31:4; 37:6, 33; 38:1; 43:1, 14, 16; 44:2, 6, 24; 45:1, 11, 14, 18; 48:17; 49:7, 8, 25; 50:1; 52:3; 56:1, 4; 65:8; 66:1, 12; Jer 2:2, 5; 4:3, 27; 6:16, 21, 22; 8:4; 9:23; 10:1, 2, 18; 11:11, 21; 12:14; 13:9, 13; 14:10, 15; 15:2, 19; 16:3, 5; 17:5, 21; 18:11, 13; 19:1; 20:4; 21:8, 12; 22:1, 3, 6, 11, 18, 30; 23:38; 26:2, 4; 27:16; 28:11, 13, 16; 29:10, 16, 31, 32; 30:5, 12, 18; 31:2, 7, 15, 16, 35, 37; 32:3, 28, 42; 33:2, 10, 17, 20, 25; 34:2, 4, 17; 36:29, 30; 37:9; 38:2, 3; 44:30; 45:4; 47:2; 48:40; 49:1, 12, 28; 51:1, 36; Eze 11:5; 21:3; 30:6; Am 1:3, 6, 9, 11, 13; 2:1, 4, 6; 3:12; 5:4; 7:17; Mic 3:5; 6:1; Na 1:12; Zec 1:16; 8:3

## WHAT THE SOVEREIGN †LORD SAYS
Isa 7:7; 28:16; 49.22; 52:4; 65:13; Jer 7:20; Eze 2:4; 3:11, 27; 5:5, 7, 8; 6:3, 11; 7:2, 5; 11:7, 16, 17; 12:10, 19, 23, 28; 13:3, 8, 13, 18, 20; 14:4, 6, 21; 15:6; 16:3, 36, 59; 17:3, 9, 19, 22; 20:3, 5, 27, 30, 39, 47; 21:24, 26, 28; 22:3, 19, 28; 23:22, 28, 32, 35, 46; 24:3, 6, 9, 21; 25:3, 6, 8, 12, 13, 15, 16; 26:3, 7, 15, 19; 27:3; 28:2, 6, 12, 22, 25; 29:3, 8, 13, 19; 30:2, 10, 13, 22; 31:10, 15; 32:3, 11; 33:25, 27; 34:2, 10, 11, 17, 20; 35:3, 14; 36:2, 3, 4, 5, 6, 7, 13, 22, 33, 37; 37:5, 9, 12, 19, 21; 38:3, 10, 14, 17; 39:1, 17, 25; 43:18; 44:6, 9; 45:9, 18; 46:1, 16; 47:13; Am 3:11; 5:3; Ob 1:1

## WORD OF THE †LORD  See WORD

## †LORD'S  (Yahweh's) [†LORD (Yahweh); see also LORD'S]
Ex    4:14  the L anger burned against Moses
        9:29  know that the earth is the L.
       12:11  Eat it in haste; it is the L Passover.
       24: 3  all the L words and laws,
       34:34  he entered the L presence
Lev 23: 4  " 'These are the L appointed festivals,
Nu    9:23  At the L command they encamped, and at the L command they set out. They obeyed the L order,
       11:23  "Is the L arm too short?
       14:41  are you disobeying the L command?
       31: 3  carry out the L vengeance on them.
       32:13  The L anger burned against Israel

Dt    6:18  right and good in the L sight,
       10:13  and to observe the L commands
       32: 9  For the L portion is his people,
       33:21  he carried out the L righteous will,
Jos 21:45  Not one of all the L good promises
Jdg   2:12  They aroused the L anger
        3: 4  they would obey the L commands,
1Sa   2:25  the L will to put them to death.
        4: 3  Let us bring the ark of the L covenant
       13:14  have not kept the L command."
       17:47  for the battle is the L,
       24:10  because he is the L anointed.'
2Sa 22:31  the L word is flawless,
1Ki 10: 9  the L eternal love for Israel,
Ps   24: 1  The earth is the L, and everything in it,
       32:10  but the L unfailing love surrounds those
       89: 1  I will sing of the L great love forever;
      103:17  the L love is with those who fear him,
      118:15  "The L right hand has done mighty
Pr     3:11  do not despise the L discipline,
        3:33  The L curse is on the house of the
       19:21  but it is the L purpose that prevails.
       21: 1  In the L hand the king's heart
Isa    2: 2  mountain of the L temple will be
       24:14  the west they acclaim the L majesty.
       30: 9  unwilling to listen to the L instruction.
       38: 7  L sign to you that the L will do what
       40: 2  from the L hand double for all her sins.
       49: 4  what is due me is in the L hand,
       53:10  Yet it was the L will to crush him
       55:13  the L renown, for an everlasting sign,
       61: 2  to proclaim the year of the L favor
       62: 3  crown of splendor in the L hand,
Jer  13:17  the L flock will be taken captive.
       25:17  I took the cup from the L hand
       48:10  those who are lax in doing the L work!
       51: 6  It is time for the L vengeance;
La     3:22  the L great love we are not consumed,
Eze   7:19  deliver them in the day of the L wrath.
Joel  3:18  fountain will flow out of the L house
Ob    1:21  And the kingdom will be the L.
Mic   4: 1  mountain of the L temple will be
        6: 2  the L accusation; listen,
Hab   2:16  cup from the L right hand is coming
Zep   2: 3  be sheltered on the day of the L anger.
Zec 14:20  cooking pots in the L house

## LORDED*  [LORD]
Ne    5:15  assistants also l it over the people.

## LORDING*  [LORD]
1Pe   5: 3  not l it over those entrusted to you,

## LORDS  [LORD]
Dt   10:17  God is God of gods and Lord of l,
Ps  136: 3  Give thanks to the Lord of l:
Isa  26:13  other l besides you have ruled over
1Co   8: 5  are many "gods" and many "l"),
Rev 17:14  over them because he is Lord of l
       19:16  KING OF KINGS AND LORD OF L.

## LOSE  [LOSES, LOSS, LOST]
Ge   26: 9  I thought I might l my life
1Sa 17:32  "Let no one l heart on account
Isa    7: 4  Do not l heart because of these two
Mt   10:39  Whoever finds their life will l it,

| | | |
|---|---|---|
| Mk | 8:35 | wants to save their life will l it, |
| Lk | 9:25 | and yet l or forfeit your very self? |
| Jn | 6:39 | that I shall l none of all those he has |
| | 12:25 | Those who love their life will l it, |
| 2Co | 4: 1 | this ministry, we do not l heart. |
| | 4:16 | Therefore we do not l heart. |
| Heb | 12: 3 | you will not grow weary and l heart. |
| | 12: 5 | do not l heart when he rebukes you, |
| 2Jn | 1: 8 | you do not l what we have worked |

## LOSES [LOSE]

| | | |
|---|---|---|
| Mt | 5:13 | But if the salt l its saltiness, |
| Mk | 8:35 | but whoever l their life for me |
| Lk | 15: 4 | a hundred sheep and l one of them. |
| | 15: 8 | has ten silver coins and l one. |

## LOSS [LOSE]

| | | |
|---|---|---|
| Ro | 11:12 | their l means riches for the Gentiles, |
| 1Co | 3:15 | the builder will suffer l but yet will |
| Php | 3: 8 | I consider everything a l because |
| Heb | 6: 6 | their l they are crucifying the Son |

## LOST [LOSE]

| | | |
|---|---|---|
| Nu | 17:12 | "We will die! We are l, we are all l! |
| Ps | 73: 2 | I had nearly l my foothold. |
| | 119:176 | I have strayed like a l sheep. |
| Jer | 50: 6 | "My people have been l sheep; |
| Eze | 34: 4 | back the strays or searched for the l. |
| | 34:16 | I will search for the l and bring back |
| Mt | 10: 6 | Go rather to the l sheep of Israel. |
| | 15:24 | "I was sent only to the l sheep |
| Lk | 15: 4 | go after the l sheep until he finds it? |
| | 15: 6 | I have found my l sheep.' |
| | 15: 9 | I have found my l coin.' |
| | 15:24 | he was l and is found.' |
| | 19:10 | to seek and to save what was l." |
| Jn | 17:12 | None has been l except the one |
| | 18: 9 | "I have not l one of those you gave |
| Php | 3: 8 | for whose sake I have l all things. |
| Col | 2:19 | They have l connection |

## LOT [LOT'S, LOTS, PUR]

Nephew of Abraham (Ge 11:27; 12:5). Chose to live in Sodom (Ge 13). Rescued from four kings (Ge 14). Rescued from Sodom (Ge 19:1–29; 2Pe 2:7). Fathered Moab and Ammon by his daughters (Ge 19:30–38).

| | | |
|---|---|---|
| Lev | 16: 9 | shall bring the goat whose l falls |
| Nu | 33:54 | Distribute the land by l, |
| 1Sa | 14:42 | said, "Cast the l between me |
| Est | 3: 7 | And the l fell on the twelfth month, |
| | 9:24 | the l) for their ruin and destruction. |
| Job | 31: 2 | For what is our l from God above, |
| Ps | 16: 5 | you have made my l secure. |
| Pr | 16:33 | The l is cast into the lap, but its |
| | 18:18 | Casting the l settles disputes |
| Ecc | 3:22 | their work, because that is their l. |
| | 5:19 | to accept their l and be happy |
| Jnh | 1: 7 | cast lots and the l fell on Jonah. |
| Ac | 1:26 | cast lots, and the l fell to Matthias; |

## LOT'S* [LOT]

| | | |
|---|---|---|
| Ge | 19:26 | But L wife looked back, and she |
| | 19:36 | of L daughters became pregnant |
| Ps | 83: 8 | joined them to reinforce L descendants. |
| Lk | 17:32 | Remember L wife! |

## LOTS [LOT]

| | | |
|---|---|---|
| Lev | 16: 8 | He is to cast l for the two goats— |
| Jos | 18:10 | then cast l for them in Shiloh |
| 1Ch | 25: 8 | as student, cast l for their duties. |
| Ps | 22:18 | them and cast l for my garment. |
| Joel | 3: 3 | They cast l for my people |
| Ob | 1:11 | his gates and cast l for Jerusalem, |
| Mt | 27:35 | divided up his clothes by casting l. |
| Ac | 1:26 | Then they cast l, and the lot fell |

## LOUD

| | | |
|---|---|---|
| Ex | 12:30 | and there was l wailing in Egypt, |
| | 19:16 | and a very l trumpet blast. |
| Jos | 6: 5 | have the whole army give a l shout; |
| Eze | 9: 1 | I heard him call out in a l voice, |
| Da | 4:14 | He called in a l voice: |
| Mk | 15:34 | Jesus cried out in a l voice, "Eloi, |
| Jn | 11:43 | Jesus called in a l voice, "Lazarus, |
| Rev | 1:10 | I heard behind me a l voice like |
| | 21: 3 | I heard a l voice from the throne |

## LOVE* [BELOVED, BELOVED'S, LOVED, LOVELY, LOVER, LOVERS, LOVES, LOVING]

| | | |
|---|---|---|
| Ge | 4: 1 | Adam made l to his wife Eve, |
| | 4:17 | Cain made l to his wife, and she |
| | 4:25 | Adam made l to his wife again, |
| | 20:13 | 'This is how you can show your l |
| | 22: 2 | son, your only son, whom you l— |
| | 29:18 | Jacob was in l with Rachel and said, |
| | 29:20 | days to him because of his l for her. |
| | 29:21 | and I want to make l to her." |
| | 29:23 | to Jacob, and Jacob made l to her. |
| | 29:30 | Jacob made l to Rachel also, and his l for Rachel was greater than his l for Leah. |
| | 29:32 | Surely my husband will l me now." |
| | 38: 2 | He married her and made l to her; |
| Ex | 15:13 | In your unfailing l you will lead |
| | 20: 6 | showing l to a thousand generations of those who l me |
| | 21: 5 | 'I l my master and my wife |
| | 34: 6 | abounding in l and faithfulness, |
| | 34: 7 | maintaining l to thousands, |
| Lev | 19:18 | but l your neighbor as yourself. |
| | 19:34 | L them as yourself, for you were |
| Nu | 14:18 | abounding in l and forgiving sin |
| | 14:19 | In accordance with your great l, |
| Dt | 5:10 | showing l to a thousand generations of those who l me |
| | 6: 5 | L the Lord your God with all |
| | 7: 9 | God, keeping his covenant of l |
| | 7: 9 | generations of those who l him |
| | 7:12 | God will keep his covenant of l |
| | 7:13 | He will l you and bless you |
| | 10:12 | to l him, to serve the Lord your |
| | 10:19 | are to l those who are foreigners, |
| | 11: 1 | L the Lord your God and keep |
| | 11:13 | to l the Lord your God, |
| | 11:22 | to l the Lord your God, to walk |
| | 13: 3 | out whether you l him with all your |
| | 13: 6 | or the wife you l, or your closest |
| | 19: 9 | to l the Lord your God |
| | 21:15 | is the son of the wife he does not l, |
| | 21:16 | the son of the wife he does not l. |

| | | | | | |
|---|---|---|---|---|---|
| Dt | 30: 6 | you may l him with all your heart | Ps | 31:16 | save me in your unfailing l. |
| | 30:16 | today to l the LORD your God, | | 31:21 | me the wonders of his l when I was |
| | 30:20 | you may l the LORD your God, | | 31:23 | L the LORD, all his faithful |
| | 33: 3 | Surely it is you who l the people; | | 32:10 | the LORD's unfailing l surrounds |
| Jos | 22: 5 | to l the LORD your God, to walk | | 33: 5 | the earth is full of his unfailing l. |
| | 23:11 | careful to l the LORD your God. | | 33:18 | whose hope is in his unfailing l, |
| Jdg | 5:31 | may all who l you be like the sun | | 33:22 | May your unfailing l be with us, |
| | 14:16 | You don't really l me. | | 36: 5 | Your l, LORD, |
| | 16: 4 | he fell in l with a woman | | 36: 7 | How priceless is your unfailing l, |
| | 16:15 | "How can you say, 'I l you,' | | 36:10 | Continue your l to those who know |
| Ru | 4:13 | When he made l to her, | | 40:10 | I do not conceal your l and your |
| 1Sa | 1:19 | Elkanah made l to his wife Hannah, | | 40:11 | may your l and faithfulness always |
| | 18:20 | Saul's daughter Michal was in l | | 42: 8 | By day the LORD directs his l, |
| | 18:22 | and his attendants all l you; | | 44:26 | us because of your unfailing l. |
| | 20:17 | reaffirm his oath out of l for him, | | 45: 7 | You l righteousness and hate |
| 2Sa | 1:26 | Your l for me was wonderful, | | 48: 9 | we meditate on your unfailing l. |
| | 7:15 | my l will never be taken away | | 51: 1 | God, according to your unfailing l; |
| | 11:11 | drink and make l to my wife? | | 52: 3 | You l evil rather than good, |
| 2Sa | 12:24 | went to her and made l to her. | | 52: 4 | You l every harmful word, |
| | 13: 1 | son of David fell in l with Tamar, | | 52: 8 | I trust in God's unfailing l for ever |
| | 13: 4 | said to him, "I'm in l with Tamar, | | 57: 3 | God sends forth his l and his |
| | 16:17 | "So this is the l you show your | | 57:10 | For great is your l, |
| | 19: 6 | You l those who hate you and hate those | | 59:16 | in the morning I will sing of your l; |
| | | who l you. | | 60: 5 | that those you l may be delivered. |
| 1Ki | 3: 3 | Solomon showed his l for the | | 61: 7 | appoint your l and faithfulness |
| | 3:26 | deeply moved out of l for her son | | 62:12 | with you, Lord, is unfailing l"; |
| | 8:23 | you who keep your covenant of l | | 63: 3 | Because your l is better than life, |
| | 10: 9 | of the LORD's eternal l for Israel, | | 66:20 | prayer or withheld his l from me! |
| | 11: 2 | Solomon held fast to them in l. | | 69:13 | in your great l, O God, answer me |
| 1Ch | 2:21 | He made l to her, and she bore | | 69:16 | out of the goodness of your l; |
| | 7:23 | Then he made l to his wife again, | | 69:36 | and those who l his name will dwell |
| | 16:34 | for he is good; his l endures forever. | | 77: 8 | his unfailing l vanished forever? |
| | 16:41 | "for his l endures forever." | | 85: 7 | Show us your unfailing l, LORD, |
| | 17:13 | I will never take my l away | | 85:10 | L and faithfulness meet together; |
| 2Ch | 5:13 | his l endures forever." | | 86: 5 | abounding in l to all who call |
| | 6:14 | you who keep your covenant of l | | 86:13 | For great is your l toward me; |
| | 6:42 | Remember the great l promised | | 86:15 | abounding in l and faithfulness. |
| | 7: 3 | his l endures forever." | | 88:11 | Is your l declared in the grave, |
| | 7: 6 | saying, "His l endures forever." | | 89: 1 | sing of the LORD's great l forever; |
| | 9: 8 | Because of the l of your God | | 89: 2 | that your l stands firm forever, |
| | 19: 2 | and l those who hate the LORD? | | 89:14 | l and faithfulness go before you. |
| | 20:21 | LORD, for his l endures forever." | | 89:24 | My faithful l will be with him, |
| Ezr | 3:11 | his l toward Israel endures forever." | | 89:28 | I will maintain my l to him forever, |
| Ne | 1: 5 | who keeps his covenant of l with those | | 89:33 | but I will not take my l from him, |
| | | who l him | | 89:49 | where is your former great l, |
| | 9:17 | slow to anger and abounding in l. | | 90:14 | the morning with your unfailing l, |
| | 9:32 | who keeps his covenant of l, do not | | 91:14 | "Because they l me," |
| | 13:22 | to me according to your great l. | | 92: 2 | proclaiming your l in the morning |
| Job | 15:34 | the tents of those who l bribes. | | 94:18 | slipping," your unfailing l, LORD, |
| | 19:19 | those I l have turned against me. | | 97:10 | Let those who l the LORD hate |
| | 37:13 | or to water his earth and show his l. | | 98: 3 | He has remembered his l and his |
| Ps | 4: 2 | How long will you l delusions | | 100: 5 | is good and his l endures forever; |
| | 5: 7 | But I, by your great l, | | 101: 1 | I will sing of your l and justice; |
| | 5:11 | those who l your name may rejoice | | 103: 4 | crowns you with l and compassion, |
| | 6: 4 | save me because of your unfailing l. | | 103: 8 | slow to anger, abounding in l. |
| | 11: 5 | those who l violence, he hates | | 103:11 | so great is his l for those who fear |
| | 13: 5 | But I trust in your unfailing l; | | 103:17 | to everlasting the LORD's l is |
| | 17: 7 | me the wonders of your great l, | | 106: 1 | for he is good; his l endures forever. |
| | 18: 1 | I l you, LORD, my strength. | | 106:45 | and out of his great l he relented. |
| | 18:50 | shows unfailing l to his anointed, | | 107: 1 | for he is good; his l endures forever. |
| | 21: 7 | through the unfailing l of the Most | | 107. 8 | to the LORD for his unfailing l |
| | 23: 6 | l will follow me all the days of my | | 107:15 | to the LORD for his unfailing l |
| | 25: 6 | your great mercy and l, for they are | | 107:21 | to the LORD for his unfailing l |
| | 25: 7 | according to your l remember me, | | 107:31 | to the LORD for his unfailing l |
| | 26: 3 | been mindful of your unfailing l | | 108: 4 | For great is your l, higher than |
| | 26: 8 | I l the house where you live, | | 108: 6 | that those you l may be delivered. |
| | 31: 7 | I will be glad and rejoice in your l, | | 109:21 | out of the goodness of your l, |

Ps 109:26 me according to your unfailing l.
115: 1 because of your l and faithfulness.
116: 1 I l the LORD, for he heard my
117: 2 For great is his l toward us,
118: 1 for he is good; his l endures forever.
118: 2 "His l endures forever."
118: 3 "His l endures forever."
118: 4 "His l endures forever."
118:29 for he is good; his l endures forever.
119:41 May your unfailing l come to me,
119:47 in your commands because I l them.
119:48 which I l, that I may meditate
119:64 The earth is filled with your l,
119:76 May your unfailing l be my
119:88 In your unfailing l preserve my life,
119:97 Oh, how I l your law! I meditate
119:113 people, but I l your law.
119:119 therefore I l your statutes.
119:124 your servant according to your l
119:127 Because I l your commands more
119:132 do to those who l your name.
119:149 my voice in accordance with your l;
119:159 See how I l your precepts;
119:159 LORD, in accordance with your l.
119:163 detest falsehood but I l your law.
119:165 peace have those who l your law,
119:167 your statutes, for I l them greatly.
122: 6 "May those who l you be secure.
130: 7 for with the LORD is unfailing l
136: 1 His l endures forever.
136: 2 His l endures forever.
136: 3 His l endures forever.
136: 4 His l endures forever.
136: 5 His l endures forever.
136: 6 His l endures forever.
136: 7 His l endures forever.
136: 8 His l endures forever.
136: 9 His l endures forever.
136:10 His l endures fovever.
136:11 His l endures forever.
136:12 His l endures forever.
136:13 His l endures fovever.
136:14 His l endures forever.
136:15 His l endures forever.
136:16 His l endures forever.
136:17 His l endures forever.
136:18 His l endures forever.
136:19 His l endures fovever.
136:20 His l endures forever.
136:21 His l endures forever.
136:22 His l endures forever.
136:23 His l endures fovever.
136:24 His l endures forever.
136:25 His l endures forever.
136:26 His l endures forever.
138: 2 your name for your unfailing l
138: 8 your l, LORD, endures forever—
143: 8 bring me word of your unfailing l,
143:12 In your unfailing l, silence my
145: 8 slow to anger and rich in l.
145:20 LORD watches over all who l him,
147:11 who put their hope in his unfailing l.
Pr 1:22 who are simple l your simple ways?
3: 3 Let l and faithfulness never leave
4: 6 l her, and she will watch over you.
5:19 you ever be intoxicated with her l.
7:18 let's drink deep of l till morning;

Pr 7:18 let's enjoy ourselves with l!
8:17 I l those who l me, and those
8:21 a rich inheritance on those who l me
8:36 all who hate me l death."
9: 8 rebuke the wise and they will l you.
10:12 but l covers over all wrongs.
13:24 who l them are careful to discipline
14:22 those who plan what is good find l
15:17 with l than a fattened calf
16: 6 Through l and faithfulness sin is
17: 9 Whoever would foster l covers over
18:21 and those who l it will eat its fruit.
19: 8 who get wisdom l their own lives;
19:22 What a person desires is unfailing l;
20: 6 Many claim to have unfailing l,
20:13 Do not l sleep or you will grow
20:28 L and faithfulness keep a king safe;
20:28 through l his throne is made secure.
21:21 righteousness and l finds life,
27: 5 Better is open rebuke than hidden l.
Ecc 3: 8 a time to l and a time to hate, a time
5:10 who l money never have enough; those
who l wealth
9: 1 but no one knows whether l or hate
9: 6 Their l, their hate and their jealousy
9: 9 whom you l, all the days of this
SS 1: 2 your l is more delightful than wine.
1: 3 No wonder the young women l you!
1: 4 will praise your l more than wine.
1: 7 you whom I l, where you graze your
2: 4 hall, and let his banner over me be l.
2: 5 with apples, for I am faint with l.
2: 7 or awaken l until it so desires.
3: 5 or awaken l until it so desires.
3:10 its interior inlaid with l.
4:10 How delightful is your l, my sister,
4:10 more pleasing is your l than wine,
5: 1 and drink; drink your fill of l.
5: 8 Tell him I am faint with l.
7: 6 pleasing, my l, with your delights!
7:12 there I will give you my l.
8: 4 or awaken l until it so desires.
8: 6 for l is as strong as death,
8: 7 Many waters cannot quench l;
8: 7 all the wealth of one's house for l,
Isa 1:23 they all l bribes and chase
5: 1 sing for the one I l a song about his
8: 3 Then I made l to the prophetess,
16: 5 In l a throne will be established;
38:17 In your l you kept me from the pit
43: 4 and because I l you, I will give
54:10 yet my unfailing l for you will not
55: 3 my faithful l promised to David.
56: 6 to him, to l the name of the LORD,
56:10 around and dream, they l to sleep.
57: 8 a pact with those whose beds you l,
61: 8 "For I, the LORD, l justice;
63: 9 In his l and mercy he redeemed
66:10 be glad for her, all you who l her;
Jer 2:25 I l foreign gods, and I must go
2:33 How skilled you are at pursuing l!
5:31 and my people l it this way.
12: 7 I will give the one I l into the hands
14:10 "They greatly l to wander;
16: 5 my l and my pity from this people,"
31: 3 loved you with an everlasting l;
32:18 You show l to thousands but bring

| | | |
|---|---|---|
| Jer | 33:11 | his l endures forever." |
| La | 3:22 | of the LORD's great l we are not |
| | 3:32 | so great is his unfailing l. |
| Eze | 16: 8 | saw that you were old enough for l, |
| | 23:17 | to the bed of l, and in their lust they |
| | 33:31 | Their mouths speak of l, |
| | 33:32 | more than one who sings l songs |
| Da | 9: 4 | keeps his covenant of l with those who l him |
| Hos | 1: 6 | I will no longer show l to the house |
| | 1: 7 | Yet I will show l to the house |
| | 2: 4 | I will not show my l to her children, |
| | 2:19 | and justice, in l and compassion. |
| | 2:23 | I will show my l to the one I called |
| | 3: 1 | show your l to your wife again, |
| | 3: 1 | L her as the LORD loves |
| | 3: 1 | gods and l the sacred raisin cakes." |
| | 4: 1 | no l, no acknowledgment of God |
| | 4:18 | their rulers dearly l shameful ways. |
| | 6: 4 | Your l is like the morning mist, |
| | 9: 1 | you l the wages of a prostitute |
| | 9:15 | I will no longer l them; |
| | 10:12 | reap the fruit of unfailing l, |
| | 11: 4 | of human kindness, with ties of l. |
| | 12: 6 | maintain l and justice, and wait |
| | 12: 7 | dishonest scales; they l to defraud. |
| | 14: 4 | waywardness and l them freely, |
| Joel | 2:13 | slow to anger and abounding in l, |
| Am | 4: 5 | for this is what you l to do," |
| | 5:15 | Hate evil, l good; maintain justice |
| Jnh | 2: 8 | worthless idols forfeit God's l for them. |
| | 4: 2 | slow to anger and abounding in l, |
| Mic | 3: 2 | you who hate good and l evil; |
| | 6: 8 | to l mercy and to walk humbly |
| | 7:20 | and show l to Abraham, |
| Zep | 3:17 | his l he will no longer rebuke you, |
| Zec | 8:17 | other, and do not l to swear falsely. |
| | 8:19 | Therefore l truth and peace." |
| Mt | 3:17 | said, "This is my Son, whom I l; |
| | 5:43 | said, 'L your neighbor and hate your |
| | 5:44 | l your enemies and pray for those |
| | 5:46 | If you l those who l you, |
| | 6: 5 | for they l to pray standing |
| | 6:24 | will hate the one and l the other, |
| | 12:18 | the one I l, in whom I delight; |
| | 17: 5 | said, "This is my Son, whom I l; |
| | 19:19 | 'l your neighbor as yourself.' " |
| | 22:37 | " 'L the Lord your God with all |
| | 22:39 | 'L your neighbor as yourself.' |
| | 23: 6 | they l the place of honor at banquets |
| | 23: 7 | they l to be greeted with respect |
| | 24:12 | the l of most will grow cold, |
| Mk | 1:11 | "You are my Son, whom I l; |
| | 9: 7 | "This is my Son, whom I l. |
| | 12:30 | L the Lord your God with all your |
| | 12:31 | 'L your neighbor as yourself.' |
| | 12:33 | To l him with all your heart, |
| | 12:33 | l your neighbor as yourself is more |
| Lk | 3:22 | "You are my Son, whom I l; |
| | 6:27 | L your enemies, do good to those |
| | 6:32 | "If you l those who l you, |
| | 6:32 | Even sinners l those who l them. |
| | 6:35 | But l your enemies, do good |
| | 7:42 | which of them will l him more?" |
| | 7:47 | as her great l has shown. |
| | 10:27 | " 'L the Lord your God with all |
| | 10:27 | 'L your neighbor as yourself.' " |

| | | |
|---|---|---|
| Lk | 11:42 | you neglect justice and the l of God. |
| | 11:43 | because you l the most important |
| | 16:13 | will hate the one and l the other, |
| | 20:13 | I will send my son, whom I l; |
| | 20:46 | l to be greeted with respect |
| Jn | 5:42 | that you do not have the l of God |
| | 8:42 | you would l me, for I came |
| | 11: 3 | Jesus, "Lord, the one you l is sick." |
| | 12:25 | Those who l their life will lose it, |
| | 13:34 | command I give you: L one another. |
| | 13:34 | so you must l one another. |
| | 13:35 | my disciples, if you l one another." |
| | 14:15 | "If you l me, keep my commands. |
| | 14:21 | I too will l them and show myself |
| | 14:23 | My Father will l them, and we will |
| | 14:24 | Anyone who does not l me will not |
| | 14:31 | world may learn that I l the Father |
| | 15: 9 | I loved you. Now remain in my l. |
| | 15:10 | you will remain in my l, just as I |
| | 15:10 | commands and remain in his l. |
| | 15:12 | L each other as I have loved you. |
| | 15:13 | Greater l has no one than this: |
| | 15:17 | This is my command: L each other. |
| | 15:19 | the world, it would l you as its own. |
| | 17:26 | order that the l you have for me may |
| | 21:15 | do you l me more than these?" |
| | 21:15 | he said, "you know that I l you." |
| | 21:16 | "Simon son of John, do you l me?" |
| | 21:16 | Lord, you know that I l you." |
| | 21:17 | "Simon son of John, do you l me?" |
| | 21:17 | him the third time, "Do you l me?" |
| | 21:17 | you know that I l you." |
| Ro | 1:31 | no fidelity, no l, no mercy. |
| | 5: 5 | because God's l has been poured |
| | 5: 8 | God demonstrates his own l for us |
| | 8:28 | for the good of those who l him, |
| | 8:35 | separate us from the l of Christ? |
| | 8:39 | separate us from the l of God that is |
| | 12: 9 | L must be sincere. Hate what is evil; |
| | 12:10 | Be devoted to one another in l. |
| | 13: 8 | the continuing debt to l one another, |
| | 13: 9 | "L your neighbor as yourself." |
| | 13:10 | L does no harm to its neighbor. |
| | 13:10 | Therefore l is the fulfillment |
| | 14:15 | eat, you are no longer acting in l. |
| | 15:30 | Christ and by the l of the Spirit, |
| 1Co | 2: 9 | has prepared for those who l him"— |
| | 4:17 | my son whom I l, who is faithful |
| | 4:21 | shall I come in l and with a gentle |
| | 8: 1 | puffs up while l builds up. |
| | 13: 1 | but do not have l, I am only |
| | 13: 2 | but do not have l, I am nothing. |
| | 13: 3 | but do not have l, I gain nothing. |
| | 13: 4 | L is patient, l is kind. |
| | 13: 6 | L does not delight in evil |
| | 13: 8 | L never fails. But where there are |
| | 13:13 | these three remain: faith, hope and l. |
| | 13:13 | But the greatest of these is l. |
| | 14: 1 | Follow the way of l and eagerly |
| | 16:14 | Do everything in l. |
| | 16:22 | If anyone does not l the Lord, |
| | 16:24 | My l to all of you in Christ Jesus. |
| 2Co | 2: 4 | you know the depth of my l for you. |
| | 2: 8 | therefore, to reaffirm your l for him. |
| | 5:14 | For Christ's l compels us, |
| | 6: 6 | in the Holy Spirit and in sincere l; |
| | 8: 7 | in the l we have kindled in you— |

| | | |
|---|---|---|
| 2Co | 8: 8 | sincerity of your l by comparing it |
| | 8:24 | show these men the proof of your l |
| | 11:11 | Because I do not l you? |
| | 12:15 | If I l you more, will you l me less? |
| | 13:11 | the God of l and peace will be |
| | 13:14 | and the l of God, and the fellowship |
| Gal | 5: 6 | is faith expressing itself through l. |
| | 5:13 | serve one another humbly in l. |
| | 5:14 | "L your neighbor as yourself." |
| | 5:22 | But the fruit of the Spirit is l, joy, |
| Eph | 1: 4 | holy and blameless in his sight. In l |
| | 1:15 | Jesus and your l for all his people, |
| | 2: 4 | But because of his great l for us, |
| | 3:17 | being rooted and established in l, |
| | 3:18 | and high and deep is the l of Christ, |
| | 3:19 | and to know this l that surpasses |
| | 4: 2 | bearing with one another in l. |
| | 4:15 | speaking the truth in l, we will in all |
| | 4:16 | grows and builds itself up in l, |
| | 5: 2 | and walk in the way of l, just as |
| | 5:25 | Husbands, l your wives, just as |
| | 5:28 | to l their wives as their own bodies. |
| | 5:33 | must l his wife as he loves himself, |
| | 6:23 | and l with faith from God the Father |
| | 6:24 | to all who l our Lord Jesus Christ |
| | 6:24 | Lord Jesus Christ with an undying l. |
| Php | 1: 9 | that your l may abound more |
| | 1:16 | The latter do so out of l, |
| | 2: 1 | if any comfort from his l, if any |
| | 2: 2 | having the same l, being one |
| | 4: 1 | sisters, you whom I l and long for, |
| Col | 1: 4 | of the l you have for all his people— |
| | 1: 5 | l that spring from the hope stored |
| | 1: 8 | also told us of your l in the Spirit. |
| | 2: 2 | encouraged in heart and united in l, |
| | 3:14 | And over all these virtues put on l, |
| | 3:19 | l your wives and do not be harsh |
| 1Th | 1: 3 | your labor prompted by l, and your |
| | 3: 6 | good news about your faith and l. |
| | 3:12 | May the Lord make your l increase |
| | 4: 9 | your l for one another we do not |
| | 4: 9 | been taught by God to l each other. |
| | 4:10 | you do l all the brothers and sisters |
| | 5: 8 | on faith and l as a breastplate, |
| | 5:13 | in the highest regard in l because |
| 2Th | 1: 3 | the l all of you have for one another |
| | 2:10 | because they refused to l the truth |
| | 3: 5 | Lord direct your hearts into God's l |
| 1Ti | 1: 5 | The goal of this command is l, |
| | 1:14 | faith and l that are in Christ Jesus. |
| | 2:15 | faith, l and holiness with propriety. |
| | 4:12 | conduct, in l, in faith and in purity. |
| | 6:10 | For the l of money is a root of all |
| | 6:11 | faith, l, endurance and gentleness. |
| 2Ti | 1: 7 | us power, l and self-discipline. |
| | 1:13 | with faith and l in Christ Jesus. |
| | 2:22 | faith, l and peace, along with those |
| | 3: 3 | without l, unforgiving, slanderous, |
| | 3:10 | faith, patience, l, endurance, |
| Tit | 2: 2 | in faith, in l and in endurance. |
| | 2: 4 | younger women to l their husbands |
| | 3: 4 | and l of God our Savior appeared, |
| | 3:15 | Greet those who l us in the faith. |
| Phm | 1: 5 | I hear about your l for all his people |
| | 1: 7 | Your l has given me great joy |
| | 1: 9 | to appeal to you on the basis of l. |
| Heb | 4:21 | who l God must also l one another. |

| | | |
|---|---|---|
| Heb | 6:10 | the l you have shown him as you |
| | 10:24 | may spur one another on toward l |
| | 13: 5 | your lives free from the l of money |
| Jas | 1:12 | has promised to those who l him. |
| | 2: 5 | he promised those who l him? |
| | 2: 8 | "L your neighbor as yourself," |
| 1Pe | 1: 8 | you have not seen him, you l him; |
| | 1:22 | have sincere l for each other, l one |
| | | another deeply, |
| | 2:17 | to everyone, l your fellow believers, |
| | 3: 8 | be sympathetic, l one another, |
| | 3:10 | "Whoever among you would l life |
| | 4: 8 | Above all, l each other deeply, |
| | 4: 8 | because l covers over a multitude |
| | 5:14 | Greet one another with a kiss of l. |
| 2Pe | 1: 7 | and to mutual affection, l. |
| | 1:17 | saying, "This is my Son, whom I l; |
| 1Jn | 2: 5 | l for God is truly made complete |
| | 2:10 | Those who l their fellow believers |
| | 2:15 | Do not l the world or anything |
| | 2:15 | If you l the world, l for the Father is |
| | 3: 1 | See what great l the Father has |
| | 3:10 | are those who do not l their brothers |
| | 3:11 | We should l one another. |
| | 3:14 | to life, because we l each other. |
| | 3:14 | Anyone who does not l remains |
| | 3:16 | This is how we know what l is: |
| | 3:17 | how can the l of God be in you? |
| | 3:18 | let us not l with words or tongue |
| | 3:23 | l one another as he commanded us. |
| | 4: 7 | Dear friends, let us l one another, |
| | 4: 7 | for l comes from God. |
| | 4: 8 | Whoever does not l does not know God, |
| | | because God is l. |
| | 4: 9 | is how God showed his l among us: |
| | 4:10 | This is l: not that we loved God, |
| | 4:11 | us, we also ought to l one another. |
| | 4:12 | but if we l one another, |
| | 4:12 | and his l is made complete in us. |
| | 4:16 | and rely on the l God has for us. |
| | 4:16 | God is l. Whoever lives in l lives in God |
| | 4:17 | This is how l is made complete |
| | 4:18 | There is no fear in l. But perfect l drives |
| | | out fear, |
| | 4:18 | who fears is not made perfect in l. |
| | 4:19 | We l because he first loved us. |
| | 4:20 | we say we l God yet hate a brother |
| | 4:20 | For if we do not l a fellow believer, |
| | 4:20 | we cannot l God, whom we have |
| | 4:21 | who l God must also l one another. |
| | 5: 2 | how we know that we l the children |
| | 5: 3 | In fact, this is l for God: to keep his |
| 2Jn | 1: 1 | her children, whom I l in the truth— |
| | 1: 3 | Son, will be with us in truth and l. |
| | 1: 5 | I ask that we l one another. |
| | 1: 6 | And this is l: that we walk |
| | 1: 6 | his command is that you walk in l. |
| 3Jn | 1: 1 | friend Gaius, whom I l in the truth. |
| | 1: 6 | have told the church about your l. |
| Jude | 1: 2 | peace and l be yours in abundance. |
| | 1:12 | are blemishes at your l feasts, |
| | 1:21 | yourselves in God's l as you wait |
| Rev | 2: 4 | You have forsaken the l you had |
| | 2:19 | I know your deeds, your l and faith, |
| | 3:19 | Those whom I l I rebuke |
| | 12:11 | they did not l their lives so much as |

## HIS LOVE ENDURES FOREVER 1Ch

16:34, 41; 2Ch 5:13; 7:3, 6; 20:21; Ezr 3:11; Ps
100:5; 106:1; 107:1; 118:1, 2, 3, 4, 29; 136:1, 2,
3, 4, 5, 6, 7, 8, 9, 10, 11, 12, 13, 14, 15, 16, 17,
18, 19, 20, 21, 22, 23, 24, 25, 26; Jer 33:11

## LOVE THE †LORD Dt 6:5; 11:1, 13, 22; 19:9;

30:16, 20; Jos 22:5; 23:11; Ps 31:23; 97:10;
116:1

## LOVE YOUR NEIGHBOR Lev 19:18; Mt

5.43; 19:19; 22:39; Mk 12:31, 33; Lk 10:27; Ro
13:9; Gal 5:14; Jas 2:8

## UNFAILING LOVE Ex 15:13; Ps 6:4; 13:5;

18:50; 21:7; 26:3; 31:16; 32:10; 33:5, 18, 22;
36:7; 44:26; 48:9; 51:1; 52:8; 62:12; 77:8; 85:7;
90:14; 94:18; 107:8, 15, 21, 31; 109:26; 119:41,
76, 88; 130:7; 138:2; 143:8, 12; 147:11; Pr
19:22; 20:6; Isa 54:10; La 3:32; Hos 10:12

## LOVED* [LOVE]

| | | |
|---|---|---|
| Ge | 24:67 | she became his wife, and he l her; |
| | 25:28 | l Esau, but Rebekah l Jacob. |
| | 29:31 | the LORD saw that Leah was not l, |
| | 29:33 | the LORD heard that I am not l, |
| | 34: 3 | he l the young woman and spoke |
| | 37: 3 | Now Israel l Joseph more than any |
| | 37: 4 | that their father l him more than any |
| Dt | 4:37 | Because he l your ancestors |
| | 7: 8 | it was because the LORD l you |
| | 10:15 | on your ancestors and l them, |
| 1Sa | 1: 5 | a double portion because he l her, |
| | 18: 1 | with David, and he l him as himself. |
| | 18: 3 | David because he l him as himself. |
| | 18:16 | But all Israel and Judah l David, |
| | 18:28 | that his daughter Michal l David, |
| | 20:17 | because he l him as he l himself. |
| 2Sa | 1:23 | in life they were l and admired, |
| | 12:24 | The LORD l him; |
| | 12:25 | and because the LORD l him, |
| | 13:15 | he hated her more than he had l her. |
| 1Ki | 11: 1 | l many foreign women besides |
| 2Ch | 11:21 | Rehoboam l Maakah daughter |
| | 26:10 | in the fertile lands, for he l the soil. |
| Ne | 13:26 | He was l by his God, and God made |
| Ps | 44: 3 | light of your face, for you l them. |
| | 47: 4 | us, the pride of Jacob, whom he l. |
| | 78:68 | of Judah, Mount Zion, which he l. |
| | 109:17 | He l to pronounce a curse— |
| Isa | 5: 1 | My l one had a vineyard on a fertile |
| Jer | 2: 2 | youth, how as a bride you l me |
| | 8: 2 | which they have l and served |
| | 31: 3 | "I have l you with an everlasting |
| Eze | 16:37 | those you l as well as those you |
| Hos | 1: 6 | Lo-Ruhamah (which means "not l"), |
| | 2: 1 | and of your sisters, 'My l one.' |
| | 2:23 | to the one I called 'Not my l one.' |
| | 3: 1 | though she is l by another and is |
| | 9:10 | became as vile as the thing they l. |
| | 11: 1 | "When Israel was a child, I l him, |
| Mal | 1: 2 | "I have l you," says the LORD. |
| | 1: 2 | "But you ask, 'How have you l us?' |
| | 1: 2 | "Yet I have l Jacob, |
| Mk | 10:21 | Jesus looked at him and l him. |
| | 12: 6 | one left to send, a son, whom he l. |
| Lk | 16:14 | The Pharisees, who l money, |

| | | |
|---|---|---|
| Jn | 3:16 | For God so l the world that he gave |
| | 3:19 | people l darkness instead of light |
| | 11: 5 | Now Jesus l Martha and her sister |
| | 11:36 | the Jews said, "See how he l him!" |
| | 12:43 | they l human glory more than |
| | 13: 1 | Having l his own who were |
| | 13: 1 | he l them to the end. |
| | 13:23 | the disciple whom Jesus l, |
| | 13:34 | As I have l you, so you must love |
| | 14:21 | Anyone who loves me will be l |
| | 14:28 | If you l me, you would be glad |
| | 15: 9 | "As the Father has l me, so have I l you. |
| | 15:12 | Love each other as I have l you. |
| | 16:27 | loves you because you have l me |
| | 17:23 | have l them even as you have l me. |
| | 17:24 | me because you l me before |
| | 19:26 | disciple whom he l standing nearby, |
| | 20: 2 | disciple, the one Jesus l, and said, |
| | 21: 7 | The disciple whom Jesus l said |
| | 21:20 | whom Jesus l was following them. |
| Ro | 1: 7 | To all in Rome who are l by God |
| | 8:37 | conquerors through him who l us. |
| | 9:13 | "Jacob I l, but Esau I hated." |
| | 9:25 | I will call her 'my l one' who is not my l one," |
| | 11:28 | they are l on account |
| Gal | 2:20 | who l me and gave himself for me. |
| Eph | 5: 1 | therefore, as dearly l children |
| | 5: 2 | just as Christ l us and gave himself |
| | 5:25 | just as Christ l the church and gave |
| Col | 3:12 | holy and dearly l, clothe yourselves |
| 1Th | 1: 4 | brothers and sisters l by God, |
| | 2: 8 | Because we l you so much, we were |
| 2Th | 2:13 | brothers and sisters l by the Lord, |
| | 2:16 | who l us and by his grace gave us |
| 2Ti | 4:10 | for Demas, because he l this world, |
| Heb | 1: 9 | You have l righteousness and hated |
| 2Pe | 2:15 | who l the wages of wickedness. |
| 1Jn | 4:10 | not that we l God, but that he l us |
| | 4:11 | since God so l us, we also ought |
| | 4:19 | We love because he first l us. |
| Jude | 1: 1 | who are l in God the Father |
| Rev | 3: 9 | and acknowledge that I have l you. |

## LOVELY* [LOVE]

| | | |
|---|---|---|
| Ge | 29:17 | but Rachel had a l figure and was |
| Est | 1:11 | and nobles, for she was l to look at. |
| | 2: 7 | had a l figure and was beautiful. |
| Ps | 84: 1 | How l is your dwelling place, |
| SS | 1: 5 | am I, yet l, daughters of Jerusalem, |
| | 2:14 | voice is sweet, and your face is l. |
| | 4: 3 | a scarlet ribbon; your mouth is l. |
| | 5:16 | is sweetness itself; he is altogether l. |
| | 6: 4 | my darling, as l as Jerusalem, |
| Am | 8:13 | "In that day "the l young women |
| Php | 4: 8 | is pure, whatever is l, whatever is |

## LOVER* [LOVE]

| | | |
|---|---|---|
| Isa | 47: 8 | listen, you l of pleasure, |
| 1Ti | 3: 3 | not quarrelsome, not a l of money. |

## LOVERS* [LOVE]

| | | |
|---|---|---|
| Jer | 3: 1 | lived as a prostitute with many l— |
| | 3: 2 | the roadside you sat waiting for l, |
| | 4:30 | Your l despise you; they seek your |
| La | 1: 2 | Among all her l there is none |

Eze 16:33 gifts, but you give gifts to all your l,
16:36 in your promiscuity with your l,
16:37 I am going to gather all your l,
16:39 deliver you into the hands of your l,
16:41 and you will no longer pay your l.
23: 5 and she lusted after her l,
23: 9 delivered her into the hands of her l,
23:20 There she lusted after her l,
23:22 I will stir up your l against you,
Hos 2: 5 'I will go after my l, who give me
2: 7 She will chase after her l but not
2:10 lewdness before the eyes of her l;
2:12 she said were her pay from her l;
2:13 and went after her l, but me she
8: 9 Ephraim has sold herself to l.
2Ti 3: 2 will be l of themselves, l of money,
3: 3 brutal, not l of the good,
3: 4 l of pleasure rather than l of God—

## LOVES* [LOVE]
Ge 44:20 sons left, and his father l him.'
Dt 10:18 l the foreigners residing among you,
15:16 because he l you and your family
21:15 and he l one but not the other,
21:16 son of the wife he l in preference
23: 5 the LORD your God l you.
28:54 or the wife he l or his surviving
28:56 will begrudge the husband she l
33:12 one the LORD l rests between his
Ru 4:15 who l you and who is better to you
2Ch 2:11 "Because the LORD l his people,
Ps 11: 7 LORD is righteous, he l justice;
33: 5 The LORD l righteousness
34:12 Whoever of you l life and desires
37:28 For the LORD l the just and will
87: 2 The LORD l the gates of Zion
99: 4 The King is mighty, he l justice—
119:140 tested, and your servant l them.
127: 2 for he grants sleep to those he l.
146: 8 down, the LORD l the righteous.
Pr 3:12 the LORD disciplines those he l,
12: 1 Whoever l discipline l knowledge,
15: 9 wicked, but he l those who pursue
17:17 A friend l at all times, and a brother
17:19 Whoever l a quarrel l sin;
21:17 Whoever l pleasure will become
21:17 whoever l wine and olive oil will
22:11 One who l a pure heart and who
29: 3 A man who l wisdom brings joy
SS 3: 1 bed I looked for the one my heart l;
3: 2 I will search for the one my heart l.
3: 3 you seen the one my heart l?"
3: 4 when I found the one my heart l.
Hos 3: 1 her as the LORD l the Israelites,
10:11 Ephraim is a trained heifer that l
Mal 2:11 the sanctuary the LORD l
Mt 10:37 "Anyone who l their father
10:37 anyone who l a son or daughter
Lk 7: 5 because he l our nation and has built
7:47 has been forgiven little l little."
10: 6 If the head of the house l peace,
Jn 3:35 The Father l the Son and has placed
5:20 For the Father l the Son and shows
10:17 The reason my Father l me is that I
14:21 and keeps them is the one who l me.
14:21 Anyone who l me will be loved
14:23 "Anyone who l me will obey my

Jn 16:27 the Father himself l you because
Ro 13: 8 for whoever l others has fulfilled
1Co 8: 3 whoever l God is known by God.
2Co 9: 7 for God l a cheerful giver.
Eph 1: 6 has freely given us in the One he l.
5:28 He who l his wife l himself.
5:33 must love his wife as he l himself,
Col 1:13 us into the kingdom of the Son he l,
Tit 1: 8 hospitable, one who l what is good,
Heb 12: 6 the Lord disciplines those he l,
1Jn 4: 7 who l has been born of God
5: 1 everyone who l the father l his child
3Jn 1: 9 but Diotrephes, who l to be first,
Rev 1: 5 To him who l us and has freed us
20: 9 camp of God's people, the city he l.
22:15 and everyone who l and practices

## LOVING* [LOVE]
Ps 25:10 All the ways of the LORD are l
32: 8 counsel you with my l eye on you.
107:43 ponder the l deeds of the LORD.
144: 2 He is my l God and my fortress,
Pr 5:19 A l doe, a graceful deer—
Heb 13: 1 Keep on l one another as brothers
1Jn 5: 2 by l God and carrying out his

## LOVINGKINDNESS (KJV) See [UNFAILING] LOVE

## LOW [BELOW, LOWER, LOWERED, LOWEST, LOWLY]
2Sa 22:28 are on the haughty to bring them l.
Job 40:11 all who are proud and bring them l,
Ps 116: 6 when I was brought l,
136:23 He remembered us in our l estate
Pr 29:23 Pride brings a person l,
Isa 2:11 and human pride brought l;
40: 4 up, every mountain and hill made l;
Lk 3: 5 in, every mountain and hill made l.
Ro 12:16 associate with people of l position.

## LOWER [LOW]
Dt 28:43 and higher, but you will sink l and l.
Ps 8: 5 them a little l than the heavenly
2Co 11: 7 it a sin for me to l myself in order
Eph 4: 9 that he also descended to the l,
Heb 2: 7 made them a little l than the angels;

## LOWERED [LOW]
Ex 17:11 but whenever he l his hands,
Jer 38: 6 They l Jeremiah by ropes
Mk 2: 4 then l the mat the man was lying on.
Ac 9:25 and l him in a basket through
2Co 11:33 I was l in a basket from a window

## LOWEST [LOW]
Ge 9:25 The l of slaves will he be to his
Ps 88: 6 You have put me in the l pit,
Lk 14:10 take the l place, so that when your

## LOWING
1Sa 15:14 What is this l of cattle that I hear?"

## LOWLY [LOW]

| | | |
|---|---|---|
| Job | 5:11 | The l he sets on high, and those who |
| Ps | 119:141 | Though I am l and despised, I do |
| | 138: 6 | he looks kindly on the l, but he |
| Pr | 16:19 | Better to be l in spirit along |
| | 29:23 | low, but the l in spirit gain honor. |
| Isa | 57:15 | who are contrite and l in spirit, |
| | 57:15 | to revive the spirit of the l |
| Eze | 21:26 | The l will be exalted and the exalted |
| Zec | 9: 9 | l and riding on a donkey, |
| 1Co | 1:28 | God chose the l things of this world |
| Php | 3:21 | will transform our l bodies so |

## LOYAL [LOYALTY]

| | | |
|---|---|---|
| 1Ki | 12:20 | of Judah remained l to the house |
| 1Ch | 29:18 | and keep their hearts l to you. |
| Ps | 78: 8 | whose hearts were not l to God, |

## LOYALTY* [LOYAL]

| | | |
|---|---|---|
| Jdg | 8:35 | show any l to the family of Jerub-Baal |
| 1Ch | 12:33 | to help David with undivided l— |

## LUCIFER (KJV) See MORNING STAR

## LUCRE (KJV) See DISHONEST GAIN, MONEY

## LUKE*

Associate of Paul (Col 4:14; 2Ti 4:11; Phm 24).

## LUKEWARM* [WARM]

| | | |
|---|---|---|
| Rev | 3:16 | So, because you are l— |

## LUMP*

| | | |
|---|---|---|
| Ro | 9:21 | of the same l of clay some pottery |

## LURK* [LURKED, LURKS]

| | | |
|---|---|---|
| Ps | 56: 6 | they l, they watch my steps, |
| Pr | 24:15 | Do not l like a thief near the house |
| Hos | 13: 7 | like a leopard I will l by the path. |

## LURKED* [LURK]

| | | |
|---|---|---|
| Job | 31: 9 | or if I have l at my neighbor's door, |

## LURKS* [LURK]

| | | |
|---|---|---|
| Pr | 7:12 | the squares, at every corner she l.) |

## LUST* [LUSTED, LUSTFUL, LUSTFULLY, LUSTS]

| | | |
|---|---|---|
| Pr | 6:25 | Do not l in your heart after her |
| Isa | 57: 5 | You burn with l among the oaks |
| Eze | 16:36 | Because you poured out your l |
| | 20:30 | did and l after their vile images? |
| | 23: 8 | bosom and poured out their l on her. |
| | 23:11 | yet in her l and prostitution she was |
| | 23:17 | love, and in their l they defiled her. |
| Na | 3: 4 | of the wanton l of a prostitute, |
| Ro | 1:27 | and were inflamed with l for one |
| Col | 3: 5 | impurity, l, evil desires and greed, |
| 1Th | 4: 5 | not in passionate l like the pagans, |
| 1Pe | 4: 3 | living in debauchery, l, |
| 1Jn | 2:16 | the l of their eyes and their boasting |

## LUSTED [LUST]

| | | |
|---|---|---|
| Eze | 6: 9 | eyes, which have l after their idols. |
| | 23: 5 | and she l after her lovers, |

## LUSTFUL* [LUST]

| | | |
|---|---|---|
| Jer | 13:27 | your adulteries and l neighings, |
| 2Pe | 2:18 | appealing to the l desires of sinful |

## LUSTFULLY* [LUST]

| | | |
|---|---|---|
| Job | 31: 1 | my eyes not to look l at a virgin. |
| Mt | 5:28 | at a woman l has already committed |

## LUSTS* [LUST]

| | | |
|---|---|---|
| Nu | 15:39 | after the l of your own hearts |
| Ro | 1:26 | God gave them over to shameful l. |

## LUXURY

| | | |
|---|---|---|
| Pr | 19:10 | is not fitting for a fool to live in l— |
| Lk | 16:19 | fine linen and lived in l every day. |
| Jas | 5: 5 | You have lived on earth in l |
| Rev | 18: 7 | as the glory and l she gave herself. |

## LUZ [BETHEL]

| | | |
|---|---|---|
| Ge | 28:19 | though the city used to be called L. |
| | 48: 3 | appeared to me at L in the land |

## LYDDA

| | | |
|---|---|---|
| Ac | 9:32 | the Lord's people who lived in L. |

## LYDIA [LYDIA'S]

| | | |
|---|---|---|
| Jer | 46: 9 | men of L who draw the bow. |
| Ac | 16:14 | from the city of Thyatira named L, |

## LYDIA'S* [LYDIA]

| | | |
|---|---|---|
| Ac | 16:40 | they went to L house, where they |

## LYING [LIE]

| | | |
|---|---|---|
| Ge | 28:13 | the land on which you are l. |
| Ex | 14:30 | Israel saw the Egyptians l dead |
| Jdg | 16:13 | making a fool of me and l to me. |
| Ru | 3: 8 | and there was a woman l at his feet! |
| 1Sa | 3: 3 | Samuel was l down in the house |
| | 5: 4 | off and were l on the threshold; |
| | 26: 5 | Saul was l inside the camp, |
| 1Ki | 22:23 | now the LORD has put a l spirit |
| Ps | 31:18 | Let their l lips be silenced, |
| | 120: 2 | from l lips and from deceitful |
| Pr | 6:17 | haughty eyes, a l tongue, |
| | 12:19 | but a l tongue lasts only a moment. |
| | 12:22 | The LORD detests l lips, but he |
| | 21: 6 | by a l tongue is a fleeting vapor |
| | 26:28 | A l tongue hates those it hurts, |
| Jer | 23:26 | in the hearts of these l prophets, |
| Eze | 13: 9 | false visions and utter l divinations. |
| Da | 4:10 | These are the visions I saw while l |
| Hos | 4: 2 | There is only cursing, l and murder, |
| Mt | 8:14 | he saw Peter's mother-in-law l |
| Mk | 2: 4 | lowered the mat the man was l on. |
| | 7:30 | and found her child l on the bed, |
| Lk | 2:12 | in cloths and l in a manger." |
| Jn | 5: 6 | When Jesus saw him l there |
| | 20: 6 | He saw the strips of linen l there, |
| Ro | 9: 1 | I am not l, my conscience confirms |

## LYRE [LYRES]

| | | |
|---|---|---|
| 1Sa | 16:23 | David would take up his **l** and play. |
| | 18:10 | while David was playing the **l**, |
| | 19: 9 | While David was playing the **l**, |
| Job | 30:31 | My **l** is tuned to mourning, |
| Ps | 33: 2 | music to him on the ten-stringed **l**. |
| | 57: 8 | Awake, harp and **l**! I will awaken |
| | 150: 3 | praise him with the harp and **l**, |
| Da | 3: 7 | flute, zither, **l**, harp and all kinds |

## LYRES [LYRE]

| | | |
|---|---|---|
| 1Sa | 10: 5 | down from the high place with **l**, |
| | 18: 6 | songs and with timbrels and **l**. |
| 1Ch | 15:16 | **l**, harps and cymbals. |
| 2Ch | 20:28 | with harps and **l** and trumpets. |

## LYSTRA

| | | |
|---|---|---|
| Ac | 14: 8 | In **L** there sat a man who was lame. |
| 2Ti | 3:11 | Iconium and **L**, the persecutions I |

---

# M

---

## MAAKAH

| | | |
|---|---|---|
| 2Sa | 3: 3 | Absalom the son of **M** daughter |
| 1Ki | 15: 2 | His mother's name was **M** |
| | 15:10 | His grandmother's name was **M** |

## MACEDONIA

| | | |
|---|---|---|
| Ac | 16: 9 | had a vision of a man of **M** standing |
| | 18: 5 | Silas and Timothy came from **M**, |
| | 20: 3 | he decided to go back through **M**. |

## MACHPELAH

| | | |
|---|---|---|
| Ge | 23: 9 | so he will sell me the cave of **M**, |
| | 49:30 | the cave in the field of **M**, |
| | 50:13 | him in the cave in the field of **M**, |

## MAD [MADDENING, MADMAN, MADMEN, MADNESS]

| | | |
|---|---|---|
| Dt | 28:34 | The sights you see will drive you **m**. |
| Jer | 51: 7 | therefore they have now gone **m**. |
| Jn | 10:20 | is demon-possessed and raving **m**. |

## MADDENING* [MAD]

| | | |
|---|---|---|
| Rev | 14: 8 | all the nations drink the **m** wine |
| | 18: 3 | the nations have drunk the **m** wine |

## MADE [MAKE]

| | | |
|---|---|---|
| Ge | 1: 7 | So God **m** the vault and separated |
| | 1:16 | God **m** two great lights— |
| | 1:16 | He also **m** the stars. |
| | 1:25 | God **m** the wild animals according |
| | 1:31 | God saw all that he had **m**, and it |
| | 2: 3 | the seventh day and **m** it holy, |
| | 2:22 | the LORD God **m** a woman |
| | 3:21 | The LORD God **m** garments |
| | 6: 6 | that he had **m** human beings |
| | 9: 6 | of God has God **m** humankind. |
| | 15:18 | day the LORD **m** a covenant |
| | 24:21 | not the LORD had **m** his journey |

| | | |
|---|---|---|
| Ge | 45: 9 | God has **m** me lord of all Egypt. |
| Ex | 1:14 | They **m** their lives bitter with harsh |
| | 2:14 | "Who **m** you ruler and judge over |
| | 7: 1 | I have **m** you like God to Pharaoh, |
| | 12: 8 | herbs, and bread **m** without yeast. |
| | 12:36 | The LORD had **m** the Egyptians |
| | 20:11 | the Sabbath day and **m** it holy. |
| | 24: 8 | that the LORD has **m** with you |
| | 32: 4 | **m** it into an idol cast in the shape |
| | 36: 8 | among the workers **m** the tabernacle |
| | 37: 1 | Bezalel **m** the ark of acacia wood— |
| | 37:10 | They **m** the table of acacia wood— |
| | 37:17 | They **m** the lampstand of pure gold. |
| | 37:25 | They **m** the altar of incense |
| | 37:29 | They also **m** the sacred anointing oil |
| | 38: 9 | Next they **m** the courtyard. |
| | 39: 1 | also **m** sacred garments for Aaron, |
| Lev | 16:34 | Atonement is to be **m** once a year |
| Nu | 14:36 | the whole community grumble |
| | 21: 2 | Israel **m** this vow to the LORD: |
| | 21: 9 | So Moses **m** a bronze snake and put |
| Dt | 1:28 | Our brothers have **m** our hearts melt |
| | 5: 2 | The LORD our God **m** a covenant |
| | 32: 6 | who **m** you and formed you? |
| | 32:21 | They **m** me jealous by what is no |
| Jos | 24:25 | that day Joshua **m** a covenant |
| Jdg | 11:30 | Jephthah **m** a vow to the LORD: |
| 1Sa | 1:11 | And she **m** a vow, saying, |
| | 15:11 | "I regret that I have **m** Saul king, |
| | 20:16 | So Jonathan **m** a covenant |
| 2Sa | 23: 5 | surely he would not have **m** with me |
| 1Ki | 12:28 | the king **m** two golden calves. |
| 2Ki | 17:38 | Do not forget the covenant I have **m** |
| | 18: 4 | the bronze snake Moses had **m**, |
| | 19:15 | You have **m** heaven and earth. |
| 1Ch | 22: 5 | So David **m** extensive preparations |
| 2Ch | 2:12 | of Israel, who **m** heaven and earth! |
| | 3:10 | the Most Holy Place he **m** a pair |
| | 4:19 | **m** all the furnishings that were |
| Ne | 9: 6 | You **m** the heavens, |
| | 9:10 | You **m** a name for yourself, |
| Job | 7:20 | Why have you **m** me your target? |
| | 31: 1 | "I **m** a covenant with my eyes not |
| | 33: 4 | The Spirit of God has **m** me; |
| Ps | 8: 5 | You have **m** them a little lower than |
| | 33: 6 | of the LORD the heavens were **m**, |
| | 73:28 | I have **m** the Sovereign LORD my |
| | 95: 5 | for he **m** it, and his hands formed |
| | 96: 5 | but the LORD **m** the heavens. |
| | 98: 2 | The LORD has **m** his salvation |
| | 100: 3 | It is he who **m** us, and we are his; |
| | 136: 7 | who **m** the great lights— |
| | 139:14 | I am fearfully and wonderfully **m**; |
| Pr | 8:26 | before he **m** the world or its fields |
| Ecc | 3:11 | He has **m** everything beautiful in its |
| | 7:13 | straighten what he has **m** crooked? |
| Isa | 22:11 | did not look to the One who **m** it, |
| | 43: 7 | my glory, whom I formed and **m**." |
| | 44:21 | I have **m** you, you are my servant; |
| | 45:12 | It is I who **m** the earth and created |
| | 53:12 | **m** intercession for the transgressors. |
| | 66: 2 | Has not my hand **m** all these things, |
| Jer | 10:12 | But God **m** the earth by his power; |
| | 25: 6 | anger with what your hands have **m**. |
| | 27: 5 | outstretched arm I **m** the earth |
| | 31:32 | It will not be like the covenant I **m** |
| | 33: 2 | LORD says, he who **m** the earth, |

Jer 51:15 "He **m** the earth by his power;
La    3:12 and **m** me the target for his arrows.
Eze   3:17 I have **m** you a watchman
     16:60 I will remember the covenant I **m**
     33: 7 I have **m** you a watchman
Da   2:38 he has **m** you ruler over them all.
     3: 1 King Nebuchadnezzar **m** an image
Hos 14: 3 to what our own hands have **m**,
Am   5: 8 He who **m** the Pleiades and Orion,
Jnh   1: 9 who **m** the sea and the dry land."
Mt   5:33 to the Lord the vows you have **m**.'
Mk   1: 6 John wore clothing **m** of camel's
     2:27 "The Sabbath was **m** for people,
     15: 5 But Jesus still **m** no reply, and Pilate
Lk   17:19 your faith has **m** you well."
     19:46 but you have **m** it 'a den
Jn   1: 3 Through him all things were **m**;
     1:18 with the Father, has **m** him known.
     9: 6 **m** some mud with the saliva,
Ac   2:36 God has **m** this Jesus, whom you
     10:15 impure that God has **m** clean."
     17:24 "The God who **m** the world
Ro   1:19 because God has **m** it plain to them.
1Co   1:20 Has not God **m** foolish the wisdom
     12:14 Even so the body is not **m** up of one
     15:22 die, so in Christ all will be **m** alive.
     15:28 the Son himself will be **m** subject
2Co   3: 6 He has **m** us competent as ministers
     5:21 God **m** him who had no sin to be sin
     12: 9 you, for my power is **m** perfect
Eph   2: 5 **m** us alive with Christ even
     2:14 who has **m** the two one and has
Php   2: 7 being **m** in human likeness.
Heb   1: 2 whom also he **m** the universe.
     2: 7 You **m** them a little lower than
     8: 9 It will not be like the covenant I **m**
Jas   2:22 his faith was **m** complete by what he
     3: 9 who have been **m** in God's likeness.
1Jn   2: 5 for God is truly **m** complete in them.
Rev   5:10 You have **m** them to be a kingdom
     14: 7 Worship him who **m** the heavens,
     19: 7 and his bride has **m** herself ready.

## MADMAN* [MAD]
1Sa 21:13 was in their hands he acted like a **m**,

## MADMEN [MAD]
1Sa 21:15 Am I so short of **m** that you have

## MADNESS [MAD]
Dt   28:28 The LORD will afflict you with **m**,
Ecc   7:25 of wickedness and the **m** of folly.
     9: 3 there is **m** in their hearts while they

## MAGDALENE
Mt   27:56 Among them were Mary **M**,
Mk   16: 1 Mary **M**, Mary the mother of James,
Lk   8: 2 Mary (called **M**) from whom seven
Jn   20: 1 Mary **M** went to the tomb and saw

## MAGI
Mt   2: 1 **M** from the east came to Jerusalem

## MAGIC* [MAGICIAN, MAGICIANS]
Isa   47:12 with your **m** spells and with your

Eze 13:18 to the women who sew **m** charms
     13:20 I am against your **m** charms
Rev   9:21 repent of their murders, their **m** arts,
     18:23 your **m** spell all the nations were led
     21: 8 those who practice **m** arts,
     22:15 dogs, those who practice **m** arts,

## MAGICIAN* [MAGIC]
Da   2:10 ever asked such a thing of any **m**
     2:27 **m** or diviner can explain to the king

## MAGICIANS [MAGIC]
Ge   41: 8 so he sent for all the **m** and wise
Ex   7:11 the Egyptian **m** also did the same
     7:22 the Egyptian **m** did the same things
     8: 7 the **m** did the same things by their
     8:18 when the **m** tried to produce gnats
     9:11 The **m** could not stand before Moses
Da   2: 2 So the king summoned the **m**,
     5:11 appointed him chief of the **m**,

## MAGNIFICENCE* [MAGNIFY]
1Ch 22: 5 for the LORD should be of great **m**

## MAGNIFICENT* [MAGNIFY]
1Ki   8:13 I have indeed built a **m** temple
2Ch   2: 9 temple I build must be large and **m**.
     6: 2 I have built a **m** temple for you,
Isa   28:29 is wonderful, whose wisdom is **m**.
Mk   13: 1 What **m** buildings!"

## MAGNIFY* [MAGNIFICENCE, MAGNIFICENT]
Da   11:36 and **m** himself above every god

## MAGOG
Eze 38: 2 of the land of **M**, the chief prince
     39: 6 I will send fire on **M** and on those
Rev 20: 8 Gog and **M**—and to gather them

## MAHANAIM
Ge   32: 2 So he named that place **M**.
2Sa 17:24 David went to **M**, and Absalom

## MAHER-SHALAL-HASH-BAZ
Isa   8: 3 LORD said to me, "Name him **M**.

## MAHLON [MAHLON'S]
Ru   1: 5 both **M** and Kilion also died,

## MAHLON'S* [MAHLON]
Ru   4:10 Ruth the Moabite, **M** widow, as my

## MAIMED
Mk   9:43 to enter life **m** than with two hands

## MAIN
1Ki   7:50 for the doors of the **m** hall

## MAINTAIN [MAINTAINED, MAINTAINING, MAINTAINS]
Ru   4: 5 in order to **m** the name of the dead
1Ki 10: 9 he has made you king to **m** justice

2Ki 8:19 He had promised to **m** a lamp
Isa 56: 1 "**M** justice and do what is right,
Hos 12: 6 **m** love and justice, and wait
Am 5:15 **m** justice in the courts.
Ro 3:28 For we **m** that a person is justified

## MAINTAINED* [MAINTAIN]
Rev 6: 9 God and the testimony they had **m**.

## MAINTAINING [MAINTAIN]
Ex 34: 7 **m** love to thousands, and forgiving

## MAINTAINS [MAINTAIN]
Job 2: 3 And he still **m** his integrity,

## MAJESTIC* [MAJESTY]
Ex 15: 6 hand, LORD, was **m** in power.
    15:11 **m** in holiness, awesome in glory,
Job 37: 4 he thunders with his **m** voice.
Ps 8: 1 how **m** is your name in all the earth!
    8: 9 how **m** is your name in all the earth!
    29: 4 the voice of the LORD is **m**.
    68:15 Mount Bashan, **m** mountain,
    76: 4 more **m** than mountains rich
    111: 3 Glorious and **m** are his deeds,
SS 6: 4 as **m** as troops with banners.
    6:10 sun, **m** as the stars in procession?
Isa 30:30 cause people to hear his **m** voice
Eze 31: 7 It was **m** in beauty, with its
2Pe 1:17 came to him from the **M** Glory,

## MAJESTY [MAJESTIC]
Ex 15: 7 your **m** you threw down those who
Dt 5:24 has shown us his glory and his **m**,
    11: 2 his **m**, his mighty hand,
    33:17 In **m** he is like a firstborn bull;
    33:26 help you and on the clouds in his **m**.
1Ch 16:27 Splendor and **m** are before him;
    29:11 glory and the **m** and the splendor,
Est 1: 4 and the splendor and glory of his **m**.
    7: 3 you, Your **M**, and if it pleases you,
Job 37:22 God comes in awesome **m**.
    40:10 and clothe yourself in honor and **m**.
Ps 21: 5 bestowed on him splendor and **m**.
    45: 3 clothe yourself with splendor and **m**.
    45: 4 In your **m** ride forth victoriously
    68:34 of God, whose **m** is over Israel,
    93: 1 LORD reigns, he is robed in **m**; the LORD
        is robed in **m**
    96: 6 Splendor and **m** are before him;
    104: 1 are clothed with splendor and **m**.
    145: 5 of the glorious splendor of your **m**—
Isa 2:10 LORD and the splendor of his **m**!
    2:19 LORD and the splendor of his **m**,
    2:21 LORD and the splendor of his **m**,
    24:14 west they acclaim the LORD's **m**.
    26:10 do not regard the **m** of the LORD.
    53: 2 no beauty or **m** to attract us to him,
Eze 31: 2 can be compared with you in **m**?
    31:18 with you in splendor and **m**?
Da 4:30 power and for the glory of my **m**?"
Mic 5: 4 in the **m** of the name of the LORD
Zec 6:13 he will be clothed with **m** and will
Ac 19:27 will be robbed of her divine **m**."
    25:26 to write to His **M** about him.
Heb 1: 3 at the right hand of the **M** in heaven.

Heb 8: 1 of the throne of the **M** in heaven,
2Pe 1:16 but we were eyewitnesses of his **m**.
Jude 1:25 only God our Savior be glory, **m**,

## MAKE [MADE, MAKER, MAKERS, MAKES, MAKING]
Ge 1:26 "Let us **m** human beings in our
    2:18 I will **m** a helper suitable for him."
    3:16 "I will **m** your pains in childbearing
    6:14 So **m** yourself an ark of cypress
    11: 4 so that we may **m** a name
    12: 2 "I will **m** you into a great nation,
    12: 2 I will **m** your name great,
    13:16 I will **m** your offspring like the dust
    17: 2 Then I will **m** my covenant between me
    17: 6 I will **m** you very fruitful; I will **m**
    21:18 I will **m** him into a great nation.
    22:17 **m** your descendants as numerous as
    24:40 you and **m** your journey a success,
    26: 4 I will **m** your descendants as
    28: 3 bless you and **m** you fruitful
    32: 9 relatives, and I will **m** you prosper,'
    46: 3 for I will **m** you into a great nation
    48: 4 'I am going to **m** you fruitful
Ex 6: 3 LORD I did not **m** myself known
    9: 4 But the LORD will **m** a distinction
    20: 4 "You shall not **m** for yourself
    20:23 Do not **m** any gods to be alongside
    22: 3 steals must certainly **m** restitution,
    25: 9 **M** this tabernacle and all its
    25:10 "Have them **m** an ark of acacia
    25:23 "**M** a table of acacia wood—
    25:31 "**M** a lampstand of pure gold.
    25:40 See that you **m** them according
    28: 2 **M** sacred garments for your brother
    32: 1 **m** us gods who will go before us.
    32:10 I will **m** you into a great nation."
    34:17 "Do not **m** any idols.
Lev 1: 4 your behalf to **m** atonement for you.
    4:20 this way the priest will **m** atonement
    8:15 So he consecrated it to **m** atonement
    20:25 must therefore **m** a distinction
Nu 6:25 the LORD **m** his face shine on you
    21: 8 "**M** a snake and put it up on a pole;
Dt 7: 2 **M** no treaty with them, and show
    30: 9 LORD your God will **m** you most
Jos 9: 7 us, so how can we **m** a treaty
2Sa 7: 9 Now I will **m** your name great,
    22:36 You **m** your saving help my shield;
Ezr 10: 3 Now let us **m** a covenant before our
Job 7:17 human beings that you **m** so much
Ps 4: 8 LORD, **m** me dwell in safety.
    20: 4 heart and **m** all your plans succeed.
    27: 6 sing and **m** music to the LORD.
    40: 4 Blessed are those who **m** the LORD
    80: 7 **m** your face shine on us, that we
    108: 1 sing and **m** music with all my soul.
    110: 1 right hand until I **m** your enemies
    115: 8 Those who **m** them will be like
    119:165 and nothing can **m** them stumble.
Pr 3: 6 and he will **m** your paths straight.
    10: 4 Lazy hands **m** for poverty,
    13: 5 the wicked **m** themselves a stench
    16: 7 causes their enemies to **m** peace with
    16:23 of the wise **m** their mouths prudent,
Ecc 5: 4 When you **m** a vow to God, do not

| | | |
|---|---|---|
| Isa | 6:10 | **M** the heart of this people calloused; **m** their ears dull |
| | 14:14 | I will **m** myself like the Most |
| | 29:16 | formed it, "You did not **m** me"? |
| | 40: 3 | **m** straight in the desert a highway |
| | 44: 9 | All who **m** idols are nothing, |
| | 49: 6 | also **m** you a light for the Gentiles, |
| | 49: 8 | will **m** you to be a covenant |
| | 55: 3 | I will **m** an everlasting covenant |
| | 61: 8 | and **m** an everlasting covenant |
| | 66:22 | that I **m** will endure before me," |
| Jer | 10:11 | who did not **m** the heavens |
| | 16:20 | Do people **m** their own gods? |
| | 30:10 | and no one will **m** him afraid. |
| | 31:31 | "when I will **m** a new covenant |
| | 32:40 | I will **m** an everlasting covenant |
| | 33:15 | time I will **m** a righteous Branch |
| Eze | 34:25 | " 'I will **m** a covenant of peace |
| | 37: 5 | I will **m** breath enter you, and you |
| | 37:26 | I will **m** a covenant of peace |
| | 39: 7 | " 'I will **m** known my holy name |
| Hos | 2:18 | day I will **m** a covenant for them |
| Jnh | 2: 9 | What I have vowed I will **m** good. |
| Mt | 3: 3 | Lord, **m** straight paths for him.' " |
| | 27:65 | **m** the tomb as secure as you know |
| | 28:19 | go and **m** disciples of all nations, |
| Lk | 1:17 | to **m** ready a people prepared |
| | 13:24 | "**M** every effort to enter through |
| Jn | 1:23 | '**M** straight the way |
| Ac | 2:35 | until I **m** your enemies a footstool |
| Ro | 9:20 | 'Why did you **m** me like this?' " |
| | 14: 4 | for the Lord is able to **m** them stand. |
| | 14:19 | Let us therefore **m** every effort to do |
| 1Co | 9:27 | **m** it my slave so that after I have |
| 2Co | 5: 9 | So we **m** it our goal to please him, |
| Eph | 4: 3 | **M** every effort to keep the unity |
| | 5:19 | and **m** music from your heart |
| Col | 4: 5 | **m** the most of every opportunity. |
| 1Th | 4:11 | to **m** it your ambition to lead a quiet |
| 2Th | 1:11 | God may **m** you worthy of his calling, |
| 2Ti | 3:15 | are able to **m** you wise for salvation |
| Heb | 1:13 | right hand until I **m** your enemies |
| | 2:17 | he might **m** atonement for the sins |
| | 4:11 | **m** every effort to enter that rest, |
| | 8: 8 | when I will **m** a new covenant |
| | 12: 5 | son, do not **m** light of the Lord's |
| | 12:14 | **M** every effort to live in peace |
| 2Pe | 1: 5 | **m** every effort to add to your faith |
| | 1:10 | **m** every effort to confirm your |
| | 3:14 | **m** every effort to be found spotless, |
| 1Jn | 1:10 | we **m** him out to be a liar and his |
| Rev | 17:14 | They will **m** war against the Lamb, |
| | 19:19 | together to **m** war against the rider |

## MAKER* [MAKE]

| | | |
|---|---|---|
| Job | 4:17 | beings be more pure than their **M**? |
| | 9: 9 | He is the **M** of the Bear and Orion, |
| | 32:22 | my **M** would soon take me away. |
| | 35:10 | 'Where is God my **M**, who gives |
| | 36: 3 | I will ascribe justice to my **M**. |
| | 40:19 | yet its **M** can approach it with his |
| Ps | 95: 6 | us kneel before the Lord our **M**; |
| | 115:15 | Lord, the **M** of heaven and earth. |
| | 121: 2 | Lord, the **M** of heaven and earth. |
| | 124: 8 | Lord, the **M** of heaven and earth. |
| | 134: 3 | he who is the **M** of heaven |
| | 146: 6 | He is the **M** of heaven and earth, |

| | | |
|---|---|---|
| Ps | 149: 2 | Let Israel rejoice in their **M**; |
| Pr | 14:31 | poor shows contempt for their **M**, |
| | 17: 5 | poor shows contempt for their **M**; |
| | 22: 2 | The Lord is the **M** of them all. |
| Ecc | 11: 5 | work of God, the **M** of all things. |
| Isa | 17: 7 | that day people will look to their **M** |
| | 27:11 | so their **M** has no compassion |
| | 45: 9 | to those who quarrel with their **M**, |
| | 45:11 | the Holy One of Israel, and its **M**: |
| | 51:13 | that you forget the Lord your **M**, |
| | 54: 5 | For your **M** is your husband— |
| Jer | 10:16 | these, for he is the **M** of all things, |
| | 51:19 | these, for he is the **M** of all things, |
| Hos | 8:14 | Israel has forgotten their **M** |

## MAKERS* [MAKE]

| | | |
|---|---|---|
| Isa | 45:16 | All the **m** of idols will be put |

## MAKES [MAKE]

| | | |
|---|---|---|
| Ex | 4:11 | Who **m** them deaf or mute? |
| | 11: 7 | the Lord **m** a distinction between |
| Lev | 20: 8 | I am the Lord, who **m** you holy. |
| Dt | 27:15 | "Cursed is anyone who **m** an idol |
| 1Sa | 2: 6 | Lord brings death and **m** alive; |
| 2Sa | 22:34 | He **m** my feet like the feet of a deer |
| Ps | 18:33 | He **m** my feet like the feet of a deer; |
| | 23: 2 | He **m** me lie down in green pastures, |
| Pr | 13:12 | Hope deferred **m** the heart sick, |
| | 15:13 | A happy heart **m** the face cheerful, |
| Ecc | 10:19 | for laughter, wine **m** life merry, |
| Isa | 8:14 | stumble and a rock that **m** them fall. |
| | 53:10 | and though the Lord **m** his life |
| Mk | 7:37 | "He even **m** the deaf hear |
| Ro | 9:33 | stumble and a rock that **m** them fall, |
| 1Co | 3: 7 | but only God, who **m** things grow. |
| 1Pe | 2: 8 | and a rock that **m** them fall." |

## MAKING [MAKE]

| | | |
|---|---|---|
| Ne | 8: 8 | **m** it clear and giving the meaning so |
| Ps | 19: 7 | are trustworthy, **m** wise the simple. |
| Ecc | 12:12 | Of **m** many books there is no end, |
| Isa | 43:19 | I am **m** a way in the wilderness |
| Mt | 21:13 | you are **m** it 'a den of robbers.' " |
| Mk | 2:21 | from the old, **m** the tear worse. |
| Jn | 5:18 | Father, **m** himself equal with God. |
| 1Co | 3: 6 | but God has been **m** it grow. |
| Eph | 5:16 | **m** the most of every opportunity, |
| Col | 1:20 | by **m** peace through his blood, |
| Rev | 21: 5 | said, "I am **m** everything new!" |

## MALACHI*

| | | |
|---|---|---|
| Mal | 1: 1 | of the Lord to Israel through **M**. |

## MALE [MALES]

| | | |
|---|---|---|
| Ge | 1:27 | **m** and female he created them. |
| | 5: 2 | He created them **m** and female |
| | 6:19 | all living creatures, **m** and female, |
| | 17:10 | Every **m** among you shall be |
| Ex | 13: 2 | to me every firstborn **m**. |
| | 20:10 | nor your **m** or female servant, |
| Nu | 8:16 | the first **m** offspring from every |
| Dt | 5:14 | nor your **m** or female servant, |
| 2Ki | 23: 7 | quarters of the **m** shrine prostitutes |
| Mt | 19: 4 | the Creator 'made them **m** |
| Lk | 2:23 | Lord, "Every firstborn **m** is to be |
| 1Co | 6: 9 | nor adulterers nor **m** prostitutes nor |

Gal 3:28 slave nor free, neither **m** nor female,
Rev 12: 5 She gave birth to a son, a **m** child,

## MALES [MALE]

Ex 12:48 Passover must have all the **m** in his
34:19 including all the firstborn **m** of your

## MALICE [MALICIOUS]

Nu 35:20 with **m** aforethought shoves another
Dt 4:42 a neighbor without **m** aforethought.
Mk 7:22 adultery, greed, **m**, deceit, lewdness,
Ro 1:29 envy, murder, strife, deceit and **m**.
1Co 5: 8 with the old bread leavened with **m**
Eph 4:31 slander, along with every form of **m**.
Col 3: 8 anger, rage, **m**, slander, and filthy
Tit 3: 3 We lived in **m** and envy,
1Pe 2: 1 rid yourselves of all **m** and all

## MALICIOUS [MALICE]

Ex 23: 1 guilty person by being a **m** witness.
Dt 19:16 If a **m** witness takes the stand
1Ti 3:11 not **m** talkers but temperate
6: 4 envy, strife, **m** talk, evil suspicions

## MALIGN*

Ps 12: 5 them from those who **m** them."
Tit 2: 5 that no one will **m** the word of God.

## MAMMON (KJV) See MONEY, WEALTH

## MAMRE

Ge 13:18 to live near the great trees of **M**
25: 9 in the cave of Machpelah near **M**,

## MALLOW*

Job 6: 6 flavor in the sap of the **m**?

## MAN [HORSEMAN, HORSEMEN, HUMANITY, MAN'S, MEN, MEN'S, PEOPLE, PERSON]

Ge 2: 7 the Lord God formed a **m**
2: 7 and the **m** became a living being.
2:15 The Lord God took the **m**
2:18 is not good for the **m** to be alone.
2:20 So the **m** gave names to all
2:23 for she was taken out of **m**."
2:25 The **m** and his wife were both
3: 9 the Lord God called to the **m**,
3:22 "The **m** has now become like one
4: 1 Lord I have brought forth a **m**."
32:24 a **m** wrestled with him till daybreak.
Lev 20:10 " 'If a **m** commits adultery
20:13 " 'If a **m** has sexual relations with a **m**
Nu 1: 2 families, listing every **m** by name,
Dt 22: 5 nor a **m** wear women's clothing,
32:30 How could one **m** chase a thousand,
Jdg 8:21 'As is the **m**, so is his strength.' "
16: 7 become as weak as any other **m**."
1Sa 13:14 sought out a **m** after his own heart
Est 6: 7 "For the **m** the king delights
Job 2: 4 "A **m** will give all he has for his
Ps 127: 5 Blessed is the **m** whose quiver is
Pr 6:32 a **m** who commits adultery has no

Pr 30:19 way of a **m** with a young woman.
Isa 53: 3 rejected by others, a **m** of suffering,
Da 7:13 before me was one like a son of **m**,
Zec 6:12 'Here is the **m** whose name is
Mt 9: 6 the Son of **M** has authority on earth
19: 5 this reason a **m** will leave his father
Mk 9:12 that the Son of **M** must suffer much
Lk 6: 5 them, "The Son of **M** is Lord
Jn 9:35 "Do you believe in the Son of **M**?"
Ac 3:11 While the **m** held on to Peter and John,
7:56 the Son of **M** standing at the right
16: 9 vision of a **m** of Macedonia standing
Ro 5:12 entered the world through one **m**,
1Co 7: 1 "It is good for a **m** not to have
7: 2 each **m** should have sexual relations
11: 3 that the head of every **m** is Christ,
11: 7 A **m** ought not to cover his head,
11:14 teach you that if a **m** has long hair,
13:11 When I became a **m**, I put the ways
15:47 The first **m** was of the dust
15:49 bear the image of the heavenly **m**.
2Co 12: 2 I know a **m** in Christ who fourteen
Eph 5:31 this reason a **m** will leave his father
Rev 1:13 was someone like a son of **m**,
4: 7 ox, the third had a face like a **m**,
13:18 number of a **m**. That number is 666.
14:14 on the cloud was one like a son of **m**

## MAN OF GOD Dt 33:1; Jos 14:6; Jdg 13:6, 8;

1Sa 2:27; 9:6, 7, 8, 10; 1Ki 12:22; 13:1, 3, 4, 5, 6, 6, 7, 8, 11, 12, 14, 14, 16, 19, 21, 23, 26, 29, 31; 17:18, 24; 20:28; 2Ki 1:9, 10, 11, 12, 13; 4:7, 9, 16, 21, 22, 25, 25, 27, 27, 40, 42; 5:8, 14, 15, 20; 6:6, 9, 10, 15; 7:2, 17, 18, 19, 19; 8:2, 4, 7, 8, 11; 13:19; 23:16, 17; 1Ch 23:14; 2Ch 8:14; 11:2; 25:7, 9, 9; 30:16; Ezr 3:2; Ne 12:24, 36; Ps 90:Heading; Jer 35:4; 1Ti 6:11

## SON OF MAN See SON

## MAN'S [MAN]

Ge 2:21 he took one of the **m** ribs

## MANAGE* [MANAGER, MANAGES]

Jer 12: 5 how will you **m** in the thickets
1Ti 3: 4 He must **m** his own family well
3: 5 not know how to **m** his own family,
3:12 to his wife and must **m** his children
5:14 to **m** their homes and to give

## MANAGER [MANAGE]

Lk 12:42 then is the faithful and wise **m**,
16: 1 a rich man whose **m** was accused

## MANAGES* [MANAGE]

Tit 1: 7 Since an overseer **m** God's household,

## MANASSEH

1. Firstborn of Joseph (Ge 41:51; 46:20). Blessed by Jacob but not as firstborn (Ge 48). Tribe of blessed (Dt 33:17), numbered (Nu 1:35; 26:34), half allotted land east of Jordan (Nu 32; Jos 13:8–33), half west (Jos 16; Eze 48:4), failed to fully possess (Jos 17:12–13; Jdg 1:27), 12,000 from (Rev 7:6).
2. Son of Hezekiah; king of Judah (2Ki 21:1–18;

2Ch 33:1–20). Judah exiled for his detestable sins (2Ki 21:10–15). Repentance (2Ch 33:12–19).

## MANDRAKES
Ge  30:14  give me some of your son's **m**."
SS   7:13  The **m** send out their fragrance,

## MANGER
Isa   1: 3  the donkey its owner's **m**, but Israel
Lk   2:12  in cloths and lying in a **m**."

## MANIFESTATION*
1Co 12: 7  each one the **m** of the Spirit is given

## MANNA
Ex  16:31  people of Israel called the bread **m**.
Nu  11: 6  we never see anything but this **m**!"
Dt   8:16  He gave you **m** to eat
Jos   5:12  The **m** stopped the day after they ate
Ps  78:24  he rained down **m** for the people
Jn   6:49  Your ancestors ate the **m**
Heb  9: 4  This ark contained the gold jar of **m**,
Rev  2:17  I will give some of the hidden **m**.

## MANNER
1Co 11:27  in an unworthy **m** will be guilty
Php  1:27  of heaven live in a **m** worthy
Heb 11:19  in a **m** of speaking he did receive

## MANOAH*
Father of Samson (Jdg 13:2–21; 16:31).

## MANSIONS*
Ps  49:14  the grave, far from their princely **m**.
Isa   5: 9  the fine **m** left without occupants.
Am   3:15  and the **m** will be demolished,"
     5:11  though you have built stone **m**,

## MANY
Ge  17: 4  You will be the father of **m** nations.
    50:20  being done, the saving of **m** lives.
Dt   1:10  today you are as **m** as the stars
    15: 6  you will lend to **m** nations but will
    15: 6  You will rule over **m** nations
    17:17  He must not take **m** wives, or his
Jdg  16:30  Thus he killed **m** more when he died
1Ki   8: 5  sacrificing so **m** sheep and cattle
    11: 1  loved **m** foreign women besides
Ps  32:10  **M** are the woes of the wicked,
    34:12  life and desires to see **m** good days,
  104:24  How **m** are your works, Lord!
Pr   3: 2  they will prolong your life **m** years
    9:11  wisdom your days will be **m**,
    11:14  victory is won through **m** advisers.
    15:22  but with **m** advisers they succeed.
    31:29  "**M** women do noble things,
Ecc   5: 3  comes when there are **m** cares,
    12:12  Of making **m** books there is no end,
SS   8: 7  **M** waters cannot quench love;
Isa  52:14  as there were **m** who were appalled
    52:15  so he will sprinkle **m** nations,
    53:11  my righteous servant will justify **m**,
    53:12  For he bore the sin of **m**, and made
Jer  11:13  have as **m** gods as you have towns;
Da   9:27  He will confirm a covenant with **m**

Da  12: 3  those who lead **m** to righteousness,
Mt  10:31  are worth more than **m** sparrows.
    18:21  "Lord, how **m** times shall I forgive
    22:14  "For **m** are invited, but few are
    24: 5  For **m** will come in my name,
    26:28  poured out for **m** for the forgiveness
Mk  10:31  But **m** who are first will be last,
    10:45  to give his life as a ransom for **m**."
Lk   2:34  the falling and rising of **m** in Israel,
    10:41  worried and upset about **m** things,
Jn  20:30  Jesus performed **m** other signs
    21.25  Jesus did **m** other things as well.
Ac   1: 3  gave **m** convincing proofs that he
    5:12  The apostles performed **m** signs
    14:22  "We must go through **m** hardships
Ro   5:19  of the one man the **m** will be made
    12: 5  we, though **m**, form one body,
1Co  1:26  Not **m** of you were wise by human
    12:12  **m** parts, but all its **m** parts form one body,
Heb  2:10  In bringing **m** sons and daughters
    9:28  once to take away the sins of **m**;
Jas   1: 2  whenever you face trials of **m** kinds,
    3: 1  Not **m** of you should presume to be
1Jn  2:18  even now **m** antichrists have come.
2Jn  1: 7  **M** deceivers, who do not
Rev  5:11  and heard the voice of **m** angels,
    19:12  fire, and on his head are **m** crowns.

## MAON
1Sa 23:24  his men were in the Desert of **M**,

## MARA*
Ru  1:20  "Call me **M**, because the Almighty

## MARAH
Ex  15:23  When they came to **M**, they could

## MARANATHA (KJV) See COME, LORD (1Co 16:22)

## MARCH [MARCHED, MARCHING]
Jos   6: 4  day, **m** around the city seven times,
Isa  42:13  The Lord will **m** out like

## MARCHED [MARCH]
Nu  33: 3  They **m** out defiantly in full view

## MARCHING [MARCH]
Ex  14: 8  Israelites, who were **m** out boldly.
Jos   6:13  **m** before the ark of the Lord
2Sa  5:24  As soon as you hear the sound of **m**

## MARITAL* [MARRY]
Ex  21:10  of her food, clothing and **m** rights.
1Co  7: 3  husband should fulfill his **m** duty

## MARK [MARKED, MARKS]
Cousin of Barnabas (Ac 12:12; 15:37–39; Col 4:10; 2Ti 4:11; Phm 24; 1Pe 5:13), see JOHN.
Ge   1:14  let them serve as signs to **m** seasons
    4:15  the Lord put a **m** on Cain so
Eze   9: 6  do not touch anyone who has the **m**.
Rev  13:16  to receive a **m** on their right hands

Rev 14: 9  and receives its **m** on their forehead
16: 2  on the people who had the **m**
19:20  those who had received the **m**
20: 4  and had not received his **m** on their

## MARKED [MARK]

Job 38: 5  Who **m** off its dimensions?
Pr   8:27  when he **m** out the horizon
Ac  17:26  **m** out their appointed times in history
Eph  1:13  you were **m** in him with a seal,
Heb 12: 1  with perseverance the race **m**

## MARKET [MARKETPLACE, MARKETPLACES]

Jn   2:16  my Father's house into a **m**!"

## MARKETPLACE [MARKET]

Lk   7:32  are like children sitting in the **m**

## MARKETPLACES [MARKET]

Mt  23: 7  to be greeted with respect in the **m**

## MARKS [MARK]

Lev 19:28  dead or put tattoo **m** on yourselves.
Jn  20:25  "Unless I see the nail **m** in his
Gal  6:17  I bear on my body the **m** of Jesus.

## MARRED*

Isa 52:14  and his form **m** beyond human
Jer 18: 4  from the clay was **m** in his hands;

## MARRIAGE [MARRY]

Ge  29:26  daughter in **m** before the older one.
Dt  23: 2  of a forbidden **m** nor any offspring
Jdg  3: 6  They took their daughters in **m**
Ezr  9:12  do not give your daughters in **m**
Ne  13:25  to give your daughters in **m** to their
Mt  22:30  neither marry nor be given in **m**;
24:38  marrying and giving in **m**,
Heb 13: 4  **M** should be honored by all, and the
**m** bed kept pure,

## MARRIAGES* [MARRY]

Ne  13:26  Was it not because of **m** like these

## MARRIED [MARRY]

Ge   4:19  Lamech **m** two women, one named
Dt  24: 5  If a man has recently **m**, he must not
Ezr 10:10  you have **m** foreign women,
Pr  30:23  a contemptible woman who gets **m**,
Isa 62: 4  in you, and your land will be **m**.
Mt   1:18  was pledged to be **m** to Joseph,
Mk  12:23  be, since the seven were **m** to her?"
Lk   1:27  to be **m** to a man named Joseph,
Ro   7: 2  by law a woman is bound to her
1Co  7:10  the **m** I give this command (not I,
7:33  But a **m** man is concerned
7:36  is not sinning. They should get **m**.

## MARRIES [MARRY]

Dt  24: 1  If a man **m** a woman who becomes
Jer  3: 1  she leaves him and **m** another man,
Mt   5:32  anyone who **m** the divorced woman
19: 9  and **m** another woman commits

Mk  10:11  **m** another woman commits adultery
Lk  16:18  wife and **m** another woman commits
Ro   7: 3  then, if she **m** another man while her
1Co  7:28  and if a virgin **m**, she has not

## MARROW

Heb  4:12  soul and spirit, joints and **m**;

## MARRY [INTERMARRY, MARITAL, MARRIAGE, MARRIAGES, MARRIED, MARRIES, MARRYING]

Dt  25: 5  his widow must not **m** outside
Jdg 11:37  friends, because I will never **m**."
Hos  1: 2  "Go, **m** a promiscuous woman
Mt  19:10  and wife, it is better not to **m**."
22:30  people will neither **m** nor be given
Mk  12:19  the man must **m** the widow
1Co  7: 9  they should **m**, for it is better to **m**
7:28  But if you do **m**, you have not
1Ti  4: 3  They forbid people to **m** and order
5:14  So I counsel younger widows to **m**,

## MARRYING* [MARRY]

Ezr 10: 2  our God by **m** foreign women
Ne  13:27  to our God by **m** foreign women?"
Mal  2:11  by **m** women who worship a foreign
Mt  24:38  drinking, **m** and giving in marriage,
Lk  17:27  **m** and being given in marriage
1Co  7:36  getting beyond the usual age for **m**

## MARS' (KJV) See AREOPAGUS

## MARTHA*

Sister of Mary and Lazarus (Lk 10:38–42; Jn 11; 12:2).

## MARTYR*

Ac  22:20  blood of your **m** Stephen was shed,

## MARVELED* [MARVELOUS]

Lk   2:33  mother **m** at what was said
2Th  1:10  to be **m** at among all those who have

## MARVELING* [MARVELOUS]

Lk   9:43  While everyone was **m** at all

## MARVELOUS* [MARVELED, MARVELING]

1Ch 16:24  his **m** deeds among all peoples.
Job 37: 5  God's voice thunders in **m** ways;
Ps  71:17  to this day I declare your **m** deeds.
72:18  of Israel, who alone does **m** deeds.
86:10  For you are great and do **m** deeds;
96: 3  his **m** deeds among all peoples.
98: 1  new song, for he has done **m** things;
118:23  done this, and it is **m** in our eyes.
Zec  8: 6  "It may seem **m** to the remnant
8: 6  but will it seem **m** to me?"
Mt  21:42  done this, and it is **m** in our eyes'?
Mk  12:11  done this, and it is **m** in our eyes'?"
Rev 15: 1  in heaven another great and **m** sign:
15: 3  "Great and **m** are your deeds,

## MARY

1. Mother of Jesus (Mt 1:16–25; Lk 1:27–56; 2:1–40). With Jesus at temple (Lk 2:41–52), at the wedding in Cana (Jn 2:1–5), questioning his sanity (Mk 3:21), at the cross (Jn 19:25–27). Among disciples after Ascension (Ac 1:14).

2. Magdalene; former demoniac (Lk 8:2). Helped support Jesus' ministry (Lk 8:1–3). At the cross (Mt 27:56; Mk 15:40; Jn 19:25), burial (Mt 27:61; Mk 15:47). Saw angel after resurrection (Mt 28:1–10; Mk 16:1–9; Lk 24:1–12); also Jesus (Jn 20:1–18).

3. Sister of Martha and Lazarus (Jn 11). Washed Jesus' feet (Jn 12:1–8).

4. Mother of James and Joses; witnessed crucifixion (Mt 27:56; Mk 15:40) and empty tomb (Mk 16:1; Lk 24:10).

## MASONS

| | | |
|---|---|---|
| 1Ch | 22:15 | stonecutters, **m** and carpenters, |
| 2Ch | 24:12 | They hired **m** and carpenters |
| Ezr | 3: 7 | Then they gave money to the **m** |

## MASQUERADE* [MASQUERADES, MASQUERADING]

2Co 11:15  also **m** as servants of righteousness.

## MASQUERADES* [MASQUERADE]

2Co 11:14  for Satan himself **m** as an angel

## MASQUERADING*

[MASQUERADE]

2Co 11:13  workers, **m** as apostles of Christ.

## MASSAH

| | | |
|---|---|---|
| Ex | 17: 7 | he called the place **M** and Meribah |
| Dt | 33: 8 | You tested him at **M**; |
| Ps | 95: 8 | did that day at **M** in the wilderness, |

## MASTER [MASTER'S, MASTERED, MASTERS, MASTERY]

| | | |
|---|---|---|
| Ge | 24:12 | God of my **m** Abraham, make me |
| Ex | 21: 5 | 'I love my **m** and my wife |
| Pr | 25:13 | the spirit of his **m**. |
| Isa | 1: 3 | The ox knows its **m**, the donkey its |
| Hos | 2:16 | you will no longer call me 'my **m**.' |
| Mal | 1: 6 | If I am a **m**, where is the respect due |
| Mt | 10:24 | teacher, nor servants above their **m**. |
| | 23: 8 | for you have only one **M** and you |
| | 24:46 | servant whose **m** finds him doing so |
| | 25:21 | "His **m** replied, 'Well done, |
| | 25:23 | "His **m** replied, 'Well done, |
| Jn | 13:16 | servants are not greater than their **m**, |
| | 15:20 | are not greater than their **m**.' |
| Ro | 6:14 | For sin shall no longer be your **m**, |
| | 14: 4 | To their own **m** they stand or fall. |
| Eph | 6: 9 | know that he who is both their **M** |
| Col | 4: 1 | that you also have a **M** in heaven. |
| 2Ti | 2:21 | useful to the **M** and prepared to do |

## MASTER'S [MASTER]

| | | |
|---|---|---|
| Mt | 25:21 | Come and share your **m** happiness!' |
| Lk | 12:47 | "The servant who knows the **m** will |

## MASTERED* [MASTER]

| | | |
|---|---|---|
| 1Co | 6:12 | but I will not be **m** by anything. |
| 2Pe | 2:19 | are slaves to whatever has **m** them." |

## MASTERS [MASTER]

| | | |
|---|---|---|
| Ex | 1:11 | So they put slave **m** over them |
| Mt | 6:24 | "No one can serve two **m**. |
| Lk | 16:13 | "No one can serve two **m**. |
| Eph | 6: 5 | obey your earthly **m** with respect |
| | 6: 9 | And **m**, treat your slaves in the same |
| Col | 3:22 | obey your earthly **m** in everything; |
| | 4: 1 | **M**, provide your slaves with what is |
| 1Ti | 6: 1 | should consider their **m** worthy |
| | 6: 2 | who have believing **m** should not |
| Tit | 2: 9 | be subject to their **m** in everything, |
| 1Pe | 2:18 | God submit yourselves to your **m**, |

## MASTERY* [MASTER]

Ro 6: 9  death no longer has **m** over him.

## MAT [MATS]

| | | |
|---|---|---|
| Mk | 2: 9 | 'Get up, take your **m** and walk'? |
| Jn | 5: 8 | Pick up your **m** and walk." |
| Ac | 9:34 | Get up and roll up your **m**." |

## MATCHED*

2Co 8:11  do it may be **m** by your completion

## MATERIAL

| | | |
|---|---|---|
| Ro | 15:27 | share with them their **m** blessings. |
| 1Co | 9:11 | if we reap a **m** harvest from you? |
| 1Jn | 3:17 | If any one of you has **m** possessions |

## MATS* [MAT]

| | | |
|---|---|---|
| Mk | 6:55 | carried the sick on **m** to wherever |
| Ac | 5:15 | **m** so that at least Peter's shadow |

## MATTANIAH [ZEDEKIAH]

Original name of King Zedekiah (2Ki 24:17).

## MATTER [MATTERS]

| | | |
|---|---|---|
| Dt | 19:15 | A **m** must be established |
| Ecc | 12:13 | here is the conclusion of the **m**: |
| Mt | 18:16 | so that 'every **m** may be established |
| 2Co | 13: 1 | "Every **m** must be established |

## MATTERS [MATTER]

Mt 23:23  neglected the more important **m**

## MATTHEW

Apostle; former tax collector (Mt 9:9–13; 10:3; Mk 3:18; Lk 6:15; Ac 1:13). Also called Levi (Mk 2:14–17; Lk 5:27–32).

## MATTHIAS*

Disciple chosen to replace Judas (Ac 1:23–26).

## MATURE* [MATURITY, PREMATURELY]

| | | |
|---|---|---|
| Lk | 8:14 | and pleasures, and they do not **m**. |
| 1Co | 2: 6 | a message of wisdom among the **m**, |
| Eph | 4:13 | of the Son of God and become **m**, |
| Php | 3:15 | who are **m** should take such a view |

Col   1:28   everyone fully **m** in Christ.
      4:12   will of God, **m** and fully assured.
Heb   5:14   But solid food is for the **m**,
Jas   1: 4   finish its work so that you may be **m**

## MATURITY* [MATURE]
Heb   6: 1   Christ and be taken forward to **m**,

## MEAL
Lk    11:38   did not first wash before the **m**.
1Co   10:27   If an unbeliever invites you to a **m**
Heb   12:16   a single **m** sold his inheritance rights

## MEAN [MEANING, MEANINGLESS, MEANS]
Ex    12:26   you, 'What does this ceremony **m**
Jos    4: 6   ask you, 'What do these stones **m**?'
Da     5:26   "This is what these words **m**:
Mt    12: 7   you had known what these words **m**,

## MEANING [MEAN]
Ne     8: 8   and giving the **m** so that the people
Ecc    6:11   the less the **m**, and how does

## MEANINGLESS [MEAN]
Ecc    1: 2   "**M**! **M**!" says the Teacher. "Utterly **m**!
             Everything is **m**."
       2:11   everything was **m**, a chasing
      12: 8   "**M**! **M**!" says the Teacher. "Everything
             is **m**!"
1Ti    1: 6   these and have turned to **m** talk.

## MEANS [MEAN]
Ge    40:12   "This is what it **m**," Joseph said
Da     2:25   tell the king what his dream **m**."
       4:18   tell me what it **m**, for none
       5:17   for the king and tell him what it **m**.
Mt    13:18   to what the parable of the sower **m**:
1Co    9:22   by all possible **m** I might save some.
Heb    9:12   He did not enter by **m** of the blood
2Pe    3:15   our Lord's patience **m** salvation,

## MEASURE [IMMEASURABLY, MEASURED, MEASURES]
Ge    15:16   has not yet reached its full **m**."
Jer   10:24   Discipline me, LORD, but only in due **m**
      30:11   I will discipline you but only in due **m**;
      46:28   I will discipline you but only in due **m**;
Eze   45: 3   m off a section 25,000 cubits long
Zec    2: 2   "To **m** Jerusalem, to find out how
Mk     4:24   "With the **m** you use, it will be
Lk     6:38   A good **m**, pressed down,
Eph    3:19   be filled to the **m** of all the fullness
       4:13   to the whole **m** of the fullness
2Pe    1: 8   these qualities in increasing **m**,
Rev   11: 1   "Go and **m** the temple of God

## MEASURED [MEASURE]
Isa   40:12   Who has **m** the waters in the hollow
Jer   31:37   if the heavens above can be **m**
Mk     4:24   you use, it will be **m** to you—

## MEASURES [MEASURE]
Dt    25:14   Do not have two differing **m** in your

Pr    20:10   Differing weights and differing **m**—

## MEAT
Ge     9: 4   "But you must not eat **m** that has its
Ex    16:12   'At twilight you will eat **m**,
Nu    11:13   wailing to me, 'Give us **m** to eat!'
Pr    23:20   wine or gorge themselves on **m**,
Ac    15:20   from the **m** of strangled animals
Ro    14: 6   Those who eat **m** do so to the Lord,
      14:21   It is better not to eat **m** or drink
1Co    8:13   I will never eat **m** again, so that I
      10:25   sold in the **m** market without raising

## MEDAD
Nu    11:27   **M** are prophesying in the camp."

## MEDDLER*
1Pe    4:15   kind of criminal, or even as a **m**.

## MEDE [MEDIA]
Da     5:31   and Darius the **M** took over

## MEDES [MEDIA]
Da     5:28   and given to the **M** and Persians."
       6: 8   in accordance with the law of the **M**
Ac     2: 9   Parthians, **M** and Elamites;

## MEDIA [MEDE, MEDES]
Ezr    6: 2   of Ecbatana in the province of **M**,
Da     8:20   you saw represents the kings of **M**

## MEDIATE* [MEDIATOR]
1Sa    2:25   being, God may **m** for the offender;

## MEDIATOR [MEDIATE]
Gal    3:19   through angels and entrusted to a **m**.
1Ti    2: 5   is one God and one **m** between God
Heb    8: 6   which he is **m** is superior to the old
       9:15   this reason Christ is the **m** of a new
      12:24   to Jesus the **m** of a new covenant,

## MEDICINE*
Pr    17:22   A cheerful heart is good **m**,

## MEDITATE* [MEDITATED, MEDITATION]
Ge    24:63   out to the field one evening to **m**,
Jos    1: 8   **m** on it day and night, so that you
Ps     1: 2   and **m** on his law day and night.
      48: 9   God, we **m** on your unfailing love.
      77:12   and **m** on all your mighty deeds."
     119:15   I **m** on your precepts and consider
     119:23   your servant will **m** on your decrees.
     119:27   I may **m** on your wonderful deeds.
     119:48   love, that I may **m** on your decrees.
     119:78   but I will **m** on your precepts.
     119:97   I **m** on it all day long.
     119:99   teachers, for I **m** on your statutes.
    119:148   that I may **m** on your promises.
     143: 5   I **m** on all your works and consider
     145: 5   I will **m** on your wonderful works.

## MEDITATED* [MEDITATE]
Ps    39: 3   While I **m**, the fire burned;

Ps   77: 3  I groaned; I **m**, and my spirit grew
      77: 6  My heart **m** and my spirit asked:

## MEDITATION* [MEDITATE]

Ps   19:14  this **m** of my heart be pleasing
      49: 3  the **m** of my heart will give
     104:34 May my **m** be pleasing to him, as I

## MEDITERRANEAN

Ex   23:31  the Red Sea to the **M** Sea,

## MEDIUM* [MEDIUMS]

Lev  20:27  or woman who is a **m** or spiritist
Dt   18:11  or who is a **m** or spiritist or who
1Sa  28: 7  "Find me a woman who is a **m**, so I
1Ch  10:13  even consulted a **m** for guidance,

## MEDIUMS [MEDIUM]

Lev  19:31  " 'Do not turn to **m** or seek
2Ki  21: 6  and consulted **m** and spiritists.
     23:24  Josiah got rid of the **m** and spiritists,
Isa   8:19  someone tells you to consult **m**

## MEEK* [MEEKNESS]

Ps   37:11  But the **m** will inherit the land
Zep   3:12  I will leave within you the **m**
Mt    5: 5  Blessed are the **m**, for they will

## MEEKNESS* [MEEK]

2Co  10: 1  By the **m** and gentleness of Christ,

## MEET [MEETING, MEETINGS, MEETS, MET]

Ex   19:17  out of the camp to **m** with God,
     30:36  meeting, where I will **m** with you.
Ps   42: 2  When can I go and **m** with God?
      79: 8  your mercy come quickly to **m** us,
      85:10 Love and faithfulness **m** together;
Pr    7:10  Then out came a woman to **m** him,
Am    4:12  Israel, prepare to **m** your God."
Ac    2:46  day they continued to **m** together
      5:12  all the believers used to **m** together
1Co  11:34  you **m** together it may not result
1Th   4:17  the clouds to **m** the Lord in the air.

## MEETING [MEET]

Ex   27:21  In the tent of **m**, outside the curtain
     29:44  "So I will consecrate the tent of **m**
     33: 7  away, calling it the "tent of **m**."
     40:34  the cloud covered the tent of **m**,
Jos  18: 1  and set up the tent of **m** there.
Heb  10:25  not giving up **m** together, as some

## TENT OF MEETING See TENT

## MEETINGS* [MEET]

1Co  11:17  for your **m** do more harm than good.

## MEETS [MEET]

Ro   16: 5  the church that **m** at their house.
1Co  16:19  so does the church that **m** at their
Phm   1: 2  to the church that **m** in your home:
Heb   7:26  a high priest truly **m** our need—

## MEGIDDO

Jos  12:21  of Taanach one the king of **M** one
Jdg   1:27  Ibleam or **M** and their surrounding

## MELCHIZEDEK

Ge   14:18  **M** king of Salem brought out bread
Ps   110: 4  a priest forever, in the order of **M**."
Heb   5:10  to be high priest in the order of **M**.
      6:20  priest forever, in the order of **M**.
      7: 1  This **M** was king of Salem
      7:11  one in the order of **M**,

## MELON* [MELONS]

Jer  10: 5  Like a scarecrow in a **m** patch,

## MELONS* [MELON]

Nu   11: 5  also the cucumbers, **m**, leeks,
Isa   1: 8  like a hut in a field of **m**, like a city

## MELT [MELTED, MELTS]

Ex   15:15  the people of Canaan will **m** away;
Dt    1:28  brothers have made our hearts **m** in fear.
Jos  14: 8  the hearts of the people **m** in fear.
Mic   1: 4  The mountains **m** beneath him
Na    1: 5  before him and the hills **m** away.
2Pe   3:12  and the elements will **m** in the heat.

## MELTED [MELT]

Jos   2:11  our hearts **m** in fear and everyone's

## MELTS [MELT]

Ps   147:18 He sends his word and **m** them;
Am    9: 5  he touches the earth and it **m**,

## MEMBER [MEMBERS]

Mk   15:43  a prominent **m** of the Council,
Jn    3: 1  named Nicodemus who was a **m**
Ac   17:34  Dionysius, a **m** of the Areopagus,
Ro   12: 5  and each **m** belongs to all the others.

## MEMBERS [MEMBER]

Mic   7: 6  your enemies are the **m** of your own
Mt   10:36  your enemies will be the **m** of your
Ro   12: 4  of us has one body with many **m**,
1Co   6:15  your bodies are **m** of Christ himself?
Eph   2:19  people and also **m** of his household,
      3: 6  with Israel, **m** together of one body,
      4:25  for we are all **m** of one body.
      5:30  for we are **m** of his body.
Col   3:15  since as **m** of one body you were
Rev   5: 9  your blood you purchased for God **m**

## MEMORABLE* [MEMORY]

Eze  39:13  I display my glory will be a **m** day

## MEMORIAL [MEMORY]

Ex   28:12  the ephod as **m** stones for the sons
Lev   2: 2  burn this as a **m** portion on the altar,
Jos   4: 7  stones are to be a **m** to the people

## MEMORIES* [MEMORY]

1Th   3: 6  you always have pleasant **m** of us

## MEMORY [MEMORABLE, MEMORIAL, MEMORIES]

Mt  26:13  done will also be told, in **m** of her."

## MEN [MAN]

Ge    6: 4  the heroes of old, **m** of renown.
     18: 2  up and saw three **m** standing nearby.
Nu    1:44  These were the **m** counted by Moses
     13: 2  "Send some **m** to explore the land
     16:29  If these **m** die a natural death
     26:51  of the **m** of Israel was 601,730.
Dt   16:16  year all your **m** must appear before
Jdg  15:15  it and struck down a thousand **m**.
2Sa  18: 8  forest swallowed up more **m** that day
     23: 8  his spear against eight hundred **m**,
     24: 2  Beersheba and enroll the fighting **m**,
1Ki  12:10  The young **m** who had grown
2Ki   4:43  can I set this before a hundred **m**?"
1Ch  17:17  I were the most exalted of **m**.
Pr   11:16  but ruthless **m** gain only wealth.
Da    1:17  To these four young **m** God gave
      3:25  I see four **m** walking around
Mk    6:44  of the **m** who had eaten was five
Lk    9:30  Two **m**, Moses and Elijah,
Ac    4: 4  the number of **m** who believed grew
      4:13  they took note that these **m** had been
Ro    1:27  **M** committed shameful acts with
            other **m**,
1Co  16:18  Such **m** deserve recognition.
1Ti   2: 8  Therefore I want the **m** everywhere
Tit   2: 2  Teach the older **m** to be temperate,
      2: 6  encourage the young **m** to be
Heb   7:28  the law appoints as high priests **m**

## MEN OF ISRAEL See ISRAEL

## MEN OF JUDAH See JUDAH

## MEN'S [MAN]

Dt   22: 5  A woman must not wear **m** clothing,

## MENAHEM*

King of Israel (2Ki 15:14–23).

## MEND*

Ps   60: 2  **m** its fractures, for it is quaking.
Ecc   3: 7  a time to tear and a time to **m**,

## MENE*

Da    5:25  inscription that was written: M, M,
      5:26  is what these words mean: *M*:

## MENTION

Eph   5:12  even to **m** what the disobedient do

## MEPHIBOSHETH

Son of Jonathan shown kindness by David (2Sa 4:4; 9; 21:7). Accused of siding with Absalom (2Sa 16:1–4; 19:24–30).

## MERAB*

Daughter of Saul (1Sa 14:49; 18:17–19; 2Sa 21:8).

## MERARI [MERARITE, MERARITES]

Ge   46:11  Gershon, Kohath and **M**.
Jos  21: 7  The descendants of **M**,
1Ch   6:19  The sons of **M**: Mahli and Mushi.
2Ch  34:12  Levites descended from **M**,

## MERARITE [MERARI]

Nu    3:20  The **M** clans: Mahli and Mushi.
      4:45  the total of those in the **M** clans.

## MERARITES [MERARI]

Nu    3:36  The **M** were appointed to take care

## MERCHANDISE

Ne   10:31  the neighboring peoples bring **m**
Mk   11:16  carry **m** through the temple courts.

## MERCHANT [MERCHANTS]

Pr   31:14  She is like the **m** ships, bringing her
Mt   13:45  heaven is like a **m** looking for fine

## MERCHANTS [MERCHANT]

Ge   37:28  So when the Midianite **m** came by,
Ps  107:23  they were **m** on the mighty waters.
Hos  12: 7  The **m** use dishonest scales;
Na    3:16  of your **m** till they are more than
Rev  18:11  "The **m** of the earth will weep

## MERCIFUL* [MERCY]

Ge   19:16  city, for the LORD was **m** to them.
Dt    4:31  the LORD your God is a **m** God;
1Ki  20:31  kings of the house of Israel are **m**.
Ne    9:31  for you are a gracious and **m** God.
Ps   26:11  redeem me and be **m** to me.
     27: 7  be **m** to me and answer me.
     30:10  Hear, LORD, and be **m** to me;
     31: 9  Be **m** to me, LORD, for I am
     56: 1  Be **m** to me, my God, for my
     77: 9  Has God forgotten to be **m**?
     78:38  Yet he was **m**; he forgave their
Da    9: 9  The Lord our God is **m**
Mt    5: 7  Blessed are the **m**, for they will be
Lk    1:54  servant Israel, remembering to be **m**
      6:36  Be **m**, just as your Father is **m**.
Heb   2:17  in order that he might become a **m**
Jas   2:13  to anyone who has not been **m**.
Jude  1:22  Be **m** to those who doubt;

## MERCY* [MERCIFUL]

Ge   43:14  Almighty grant you **m** before
Ex   33:19  will have **m** on whom I will have **m**,
Dt    7: 2  with them, and show them no **m**.
     13:17  he will show you **m**,
Jos  11:20  exterminating them without **m**,
2Sa  24:14  of the LORD, for his **m** is great;
1Ki   8:28  servant's prayer and his plea for **m**,
      8:50  cause their captors to show them **m**;
1Ch  21:13  the LORD, for his **m** is very great;
2Ch   6:19  servant's prayer and his plea for **m**.
Ne    9:31  your great **m** you did not put an end
     13:22  and show **m** to me according to your
Est   4: 8  the king's presence to beg for **m**
Job   9:15  only plead with my Judge for **m**.
     27:22  against him without **m** as he flees
     41: 3  Will it keep begging you for **m**?

| | | |
|---|---|---|
| Ps | 4: 1 | have **m** on me and hear my prayer. |
| | 6: 2 | Have **m** on me, LORD, |
| | 6: 9 | LORD has heard my cry for **m**; |
| | 9:13 | Have **m** and lift me |
| | 25: 6 | LORD, your great **m** and love, |
| | 28: 2 | Hear my cry for **m** as I call to you |
| | 28: 6 | for he has heard my cry for **m**. |
| | 30: 8 | to the Lord I cried for **m**: |
| | 31:22 | Yet you heard my cry for **m** when I |
| | 40:11 | Do not withhold your **m** from me, |
| | 41: 4 | I said, "Have **m** on me, LORD; |
| | 41:10 | But may you have **m** on me, |
| | 51: 1 | Have **m** on me, O God, |
| | 57: 1 | Have **m** on me, my God, have **m** |
| | 59: 5 | show no **m** to wicked traitors. |
| | 69:16 | in your great **m** turn to me. |
| | 79: 8 | may your **m** come quickly to meet |
| | 86: 3 | have **m** on me, Lord, for I call |
| | 86: 6 | listen to my cry for **m**. |
| | 86:16 | Turn to me and have **m** on me; |
| | 106:46 | them captive to show them **m**. |
| | 116: 1 | he heard my cry for **m**. |
| | 119:132 | Turn to me and have **m** on me, |
| | 123: 2 | our God, till he shows us his **m**. |
| | 123: 3 | Have **m** on us, LORD, have **m** |
| | 130: 2 | ears be attentive to my cry for **m**. |
| | 140: 6 | Hear, LORD, my cry for **m**. |
| | 142: 1 | up my voice to the LORD for **m**. |
| | 143: 1 | my prayer, listen to my cry for **m**; |
| Pr | 6:34 | he will show no **m** when he takes |
| | 18:23 | The poor plead for **m**, but the rich |
| | 21:10 | their neighbors get no **m** from them. |
| | 28:13 | confess and renounce them find **m**. |
| Isa | 13:18 | they will have no **m** on infants, |
| | 47: 6 | hand, and you showed them no **m**. |
| | 55: 7 | and he will have **m** on them, |
| | 63: 9 | his love and **m** he redeemed them; |
| Jer | 6:23 | they are cruel and show no **m**. |
| | 13:14 | I will allow no pity or **m** |
| | 21: 7 | he will show them no **m** or pity |
| | 50:42 | they are cruel and without **m**. |
| Da | 2:18 | them to plead for **m** from the God |
| | 9:18 | but because of your great **m**. |
| Hos | 6: 6 | For I desire **m**, not sacrifice, |
| Am | 5:15 | LORD God Almighty will have **m** |
| Mic | 6: 8 | to love **m** and to walk humbly |
| | 7:18 | angry forever but delight to show **m**. |
| Hab | 1:17 | net, destroying nations without **m**? |
| | 3: 2 | in wrath remember **m**. |
| Zec | 1:12 | how long will you withhold **m** |
| | 1:16 | 'I will return to Jerusalem with **m**, |
| | 7: 9 | show **m** and compassion to one |
| Mt | 5: 7 | merciful, for they will be shown **m**. |
| | 9:13 | 'I desire **m**, not sacrifice.' |
| | 9:27 | calling out, "Have **m** on us, |
| | 12: 7 | mean, 'I desire **m**, not sacrifice,' |
| | 15:22 | Son of David, have **m** on me! |
| | 17:15 | "Lord, have **m** on my son," he said. |
| | 18:33 | Shouldn't you have had **m** on your |
| | 20:30 | Son of David, have **m** on us!" |
| | 20:31 | Son of David, have **m** on us!" |
| | 23:23 | justice, **m** and faithfulness. |
| Mk | 5:19 | and how he has had **m** on you." |
| | 10:47 | Son of David, have **m** on me!" |
| | 10:48 | "Son of David, have **m** on me!" |
| Lk | 1:50 | His **m** extends to those who fear |
| | 1:58 | the Lord had shown her great **m**, |

| | | |
|---|---|---|
| Lk | 1:72 | to show **m** to our ancestors |
| | 1:78 | because of the tender **m** of our God, |
| | 10:37 | "The one who had **m** on him." |
| | 18:13 | said, 'God, have **m** on me, a sinner.' |
| | 18:38 | Son of David, have **m** on me!" |
| | 18:39 | "Son of David, have **m** on me!" |
| Ro | 1:31 | no fidelity, no love, no **m**. |
| | 9:15 | "I will have **m** on whom I have **m**, |
| | 9:16 | desire or effort, but on God's **m**. |
| | 9:18 | has **m** on whom he wants to have **m**, |
| | 9:23 | glory known to the objects of his **m**, |
| | 11:30 | have now received **m** as a result |
| | 11:31 | **m** as a result of God's **m** to you. |
| | 11:32 | so that he may have **m** on them all. |
| | 12: 1 | in view of God's **m**, to offer your |
| | 12: 8 | if it is to show **m**, do it cheerfully. |
| | 15: 9 | might glorify God for his **m**. As it is |
| 1Co | 7:25 | who by the Lord's **m** is trustworthy. |
| 2Co | 4: 1 | since through God's **m** we have this |
| Gal | 6:16 | and **m** to all who follow this rule— |
| Eph | 2: 4 | love for us, God, who is rich in **m**, |
| Php | 2:27 | But God had **m** on him, and not |
| 1Ti | 1: 2 | **m** and peace from God the Father |
| | 1:13 | I was shown **m** because I acted |
| | 1:16 | very reason I was shown **m** so |
| 2Ti | 1: 2 | **m** and peace from God the Father |
| | 1:16 | May the Lord show **m** |
| | 1:18 | that he will find **m** from the Lord |
| Tit | 3: 5 | we had done, but because of his **m**. |
| Heb | 4:16 | so that we may receive **m** and find |
| | 10:28 | law of Moses died without **m** |
| Jas | 2:13 | because judgment without **m** will be |
| | 2:13 | **M** triumphs over judgment. |
| | 3:17 | submissive, full of **m** and good fruit, |
| | 5:11 | Lord is full of compassion and **m**. |
| 1Pe | 1: 3 | In his great **m** he has given us new |
| | 2:10 | you had not received **m**, but now you |
| | | have received **m**. |
| 2Jn | 1: 3 | **m** and peace from God the Father |
| Jude | 1: 2 | **M**, peace and love be yours |
| | 1:21 | for the **m** of our Lord Jesus Christ |
| | 1:23 | to others show **m**, mixed with fear— |

## MERCY SEAT, MERCYSEAT (KJV)
See ATONEMENT [COVER]

## MERELY
| | | |
|---|---|---|
| Ro | 2:28 | nor is circumcision **m** outward |
| Jas | 1:22 | Do not **m** listen to the word, and so |

## MERIBAH [MERIBAH KADESH]
| | | |
|---|---|---|
| Ex | 17: 7 | **M** because the Israelites quarreled |
| Nu | 20:13 | These were the waters of **M**, |
| Dt | 33: 8 | with him at the waters of **M**. |
| Ps | 95: 8 | harden your hearts as you did at **M**, |
| | 106:32 | of **M** they angered the LORD, |

## MERIBAH KADESH [KADESH, MERIBAH]
| | | |
|---|---|---|
| Nu | 27:14 | (These were the waters of **M**, |

## MERRY
| | | |
|---|---|---|
| Ecc | 10:19 | wine makes life **m**, and money is |
| Lk | 12:19 | eat, drink and be **m**.' ' |

## MESHACH* [MISHAEL]

Hebrew exiled to Babylon; name changed from Mishael (Da 1:6–7). Refused defilement by food (Da 1:8–20). Refused to worship idol (Da 3:1–18); saved from furnace (Da 3:19–30).

## MESHEK

| | | |
|---|---|---|
| Ge | 10: 2 | Madai, Javan, Tubal, **M** and Tiras. |
| | 10:23 | sons of Aram: Uz, Hul, Gether and **M**. |
| Ps | 120: 5 | Woe to me that I dwell in **M**, |
| Eze | 38: 3 | Gog, chief prince of **M** and Tubal. |
| | 39: 1 | chief prince of **M** and Tubal. |

## MESOPOTAMIA*

| | | |
|---|---|---|
| Ac | 2: 9 | residents of **M**, |
| | 7: 2 | Abraham while he was still in **M**, |

## MESSAGE [MESSENGER, MESSENGERS]

| | | |
|---|---|---|
| Nu | 23: 7 | Then Balaam spoke his **m**: |
| Dt | 18:22 | is a **m** the LORD has not spoken. |
| 2Ch | 25:18 | in Lebanon sent a **m** to a cedar |
| Ps | 36: 1 | I have a **m** from God in my heart |
| Isa | 9: 8 | Lord has sent a **m** against Jacob; |
| | 28: 9 | To whom is he explaining his **m**? |
| | 53: 1 | Who has believed our **m** |
| Jer | 23:21 | yet they have run with their **m**; |
| | 23:33 | 'What is the **m** from the LORD?' |
| | 49:14 | I have heard a **m** from the LORD; |
| Da | 10: 1 | The understanding of the **m** came |
| Mt | 10: 7 | As you go, proclaim this **m**: |
| Jn | 12:38 | who has believed our **m** |
| | 17:20 | will believe in me through their **m**, |
| Ac | 2:41 | who accepted his **m** were baptized, |
| | 4: 4 | many who heard the **m** believed; |
| | 10:36 | You know the **m** God sent |
| | 15:31 | were glad for its encouraging **m**. |
| | 17:11 | for they received the **m** with great |
| Ro | 10:16 | "Lord, who has believed our **m**?" |
| | 10:17 | faith comes from hearing the **m**, |
| 1Co | 1:18 | For the **m** of the cross is foolishness |
| | 2: 4 | My **m** and my preaching were not |
| | 12: 8 | there is given through the Spirit a **m** |
| | 12: 8 | to another a **m** of knowledge |
| 2Co | 5:19 | to us the **m** of reconciliation. |
| Col | 3:16 | Let the **m** of Christ dwell |
| 2Th | 3: 1 | that the **m** of the Lord may spread |
| Tit | 1: 9 | to the trustworthy **m** as it has been |
| Heb | 4: 2 | the **m** they heard was of no value |
| 1Pe | 2: 8 | because they disobey the **m**— |
| 2Pe | 1:19 | have the prophetic **m** |
| 1Jn | 1: 5 | This is the **m** we have heard |
| | 3:11 | For this is the **m** you heard |

## MESSENGER [MESSAGE]

| | | |
|---|---|---|
| Isa | 41:27 | to Jerusalem a **m** of good news. |
| | 42:19 | servant, and deaf like the **m** I send? |
| Da | 4:13 | a **m**, coming down from heaven. |
| Hag | 1:13 | the LORD's **m**, gave this message |
| Mal | 2: 7 | because he is the **m** of the LORD |
| | 3: 1 | "I will send my **m**, who will |
| Mt | 11:10 | " 'I will send my **m** ahead of you, |
| 2Co | 12: 7 | a thorn in my flesh, a **m** of Satan, |

## MESSENGERS [MESSAGE]

| | | |
|---|---|---|
| 2Sa | 15:10 | sent secret **m** throughout the tribes |
| 2Ch | 36:15 | word to them through his **m** again |
| Ps | 104: 4 | He makes winds his **m**, |
| Isa | 44:26 | and fulfills the predictions of his **m**, |
| Jn | 13:16 | nor are **m** greater than the one who |

## MESSIAH [CHRIST, MESSIAHS]

| | | |
|---|---|---|
| Mt | 1: 1 | This is the genealogy of Jesus the **M** |
| | 1:16 | mother of Jesus who is called the **M**. |
| | 16:16 | the **M**, the Son of the living God." |
| | 22:42 | "What do you think about the **M**? |
| | 23:10 | you have one Teacher, the **M**. |
| | 24: 5 | 'I am the **M**,' and will deceive many. |
| Mk | 1: 1 | the good news about Jesus the **M**, |
| | 8:29 | Peter answered, "You are the **M**." |
| | 14:61 | "Are you the **M**, the Son of the Blessed |
| Lk | 2:11 | he is the **M**, the Lord. |
| | 9:20 | Peter answered, "God's **M**." |
| | 23:39 | "Aren't you the **M**? Save yourself and |
| Jn | 1:20 | confessed freely, "I am not the **M**." |
| | 1:41 | "We have found the **M**" (that is, |
| | 4:25 | that **M**" (called Christ) "is coming. |
| | 7:41 | Others said, "He is the **M**." |
| | 20:31 | that Jesus is the **M**, the Son of God, |
| Ac | 2:36 | whom you crucified, both Lord and **M**." |
| | 5:42 | the good news that Jesus is the **M**. |
| | 8: 5 | and proclaimed the **M** there. |
| | 9:22 | by proving that Jesus is the **M**. |
| | 17: 3 | to you is the **M**," he said. |
| | 18:28 | the Scriptures that Jesus was the **M**. |
| | 26:23 | that the **M** would suffer and, |
| Ro | 9: 5 | the human ancestry of the **M**, |
| 1Jn | 2:22 | It is whoever denies that Jesus is the **M**. |
| | 5: 1 | who believes that Jesus is the **M** is born |
| Rev | 11:15 | kingdom of our Lord and of his **M**, |

## MESSIAHS* [MESSIAH]

| | | |
|---|---|---|
| Mt | 24:24 | For false **m** and false prophets |
| Mk | 13:22 | For false **m** and false prophets will |

## MET [MEET]

| | | |
|---|---|---|
| Ge | 32: 1 | way, and the angels of God **m** him. |
| Ex | 3:18 | God of the Hebrews, has **m** with us. |
| | 5: 3 | God of the Hebrews has **m** with us. |
| Mt | 28: 9 | Suddenly Jesus **m** them. |
| Jn | 18: 2 | because Jesus had often **m** there |

## METAL [METALWORKER]

| | | |
|---|---|---|
| Lev | 19: 4 | or make **m** gods for yourselves. |
| 1Ki | 14: 9 | other gods, idols made of **m**; |
| 2Ch | 4: 2 | He made the Sea of cast **m**, |
| Ps | 106:19 | and worshiped an idol cast from **m**. |
| Isa | 48: 5 | image and **m** god ordained them.' |
| Eze | 1:27 | waist up he looked like glowing **m**, |
| | 8: 2 | was as bright as glowing **m**. |

## METALWORKER [METAL, WORK]

| | | |
|---|---|---|
| Hos | 8: 6 | a **m** has made it; it is not God. |
| 2Ti | 4:14 | Alexander the **m** did me a great deal of harm. |

## METHUSELAH

| | | |
|---|---|---|
| Ge | 5:27 | **M** lived a total of 969 years, |

## MICAH
1. Idolater from Ephraim (Jdg 17–18).
2. Prophet from Moresheth (Jer 26:18–19; Mic 1:1).

## MICAIAH
Prophet of the LORD who spoke against Ahab (1Ki 22:1–28; 2Ch 18:1–27).

## MICHAEL
Archangel (Jude 9); warrior in angelic realm, protector of Israel (Da 10:13, 21; 12:1; Rev 12:7).

## MICHAL*
Daughter of Saul, wife of David (1Sa 14:49; 18:20–28). Warned David of Saul's plot (1Sa 19). Saul gave her to Paltiel (1Sa 25:44); David retrieved her (2Sa 3:13–16). Criticized David for dancing before the ark (2Sa 6:16–23; 1Ch 15:29).

## MIDAIR* [AIR]
| | | |
|---|---|---|
| 2Sa | 18: 9 | He was left hanging in **m**, |
| Rev | 8:13 | eagle that was flying in **m** call |
| | 14: 6 | I saw another angel flying in **m**, |
| | 19:17 | voice to all the birds flying in **m**, |

## MIDDAY [DAY]
| | | |
|---|---|---|
| Dt | 28.29 | At **m** you will grope about like |
| Isa | 59:10 | At **m** we stumble as if it were |

## MIDDLE [MIDST]
| | | |
|---|---|---|
| Ge | 2: 9 | In the **m** of the garden were the tree |
| Jos | 3:17 | stopped in the **m** of the Jordan, |
| | 4: 3 | stones from the **m** of the Jordan, |
| | 10:13 | The sun stopped in the **m** of the sky |
| Jdg | 16: 3 | Samson lay there only until the **m** |
| Ru | 3: 8 | In the **m** of the night something |
| Da | 9:27 | the **m** of the 'seven' he will put |
| Jn | 19:18 | one on each side and Jesus in the **m**. |

## MIDIAN [MIDIANITE, MIDIANITES]
| | | |
|---|---|---|
| Ex | 2:15 | from Pharaoh and went to live in **M**, |
| | 18: 1 | the priest of **M** and father-in-law |
| Jdg | 7: 2 | I cannot deliver **M** into their hands, |
| Ps | 83: 9 | Do to them as you did to **M**, as you |

## MIDIANITE [MIDIAN]
| | | |
|---|---|---|
| Ge | 37:28 | So when the **M** merchants came by, |
| Nu | 25: 6 | the camp a **M** woman right before |

## MIDIANITES [MIDIAN]
| | | |
|---|---|---|
| Ge | 37:36 | the **M** sold Joseph in Egypt |
| Nu | 31: 2 | on the **M** for the Israelites. |
| Jdg | 6:16 | strike down all the **M** together." |

## MIDNIGHT [NIGHT]
| | | |
|---|---|---|
| Ex | 11: 4 | **m** I will go throughout Egypt. |
| | 12:29 | **m** the LORD struck down all |
| Ps | 119:62 | At **m** I rise to give you thanks |
| Ac | 16:25 | About **m** Paul and Silas were |

## MIDST [MIDDLE]
| | | |
|---|---|---|
| Ps | 135: 9 | his signs and wonders into your **m**, |
| | 136:14 | brought Israel through the **m** of it, |

## MIDWIVES
| | | |
|---|---|---|
| Ex | 1:17 | The **m**, however, feared God |

## MIGHT [ALMIGHTY, MIGHTIER, MIGHTY]
| | | |
|---|---|---|
| Ex | 9:16 | that my name **m** be proclaimed |
| | 33: 3 | and I **m** destroy you on the way." |
| Dt | 5:29 | so that it **m** go well with them |
| Jos | 4:24 | you **m** always fear the LORD your |
| Jdg | 16:30 | Then he pushed with all his **m**, |
| 2Sa | 6: 5 | with all their **m** before the LORD, |
| | 6:14 | before the LORD with all his **m**, |
| 2Ch | 6:41 | place, you and the ark of your **m**. |
| | 20: 6 | Power and **m** are in your hand, |
| Ps | 21:13 | we will sing and praise your **m**. |
| | 54: 1 | vindicate me by your **m**. |
| | 59:11 | In your **m** uproot them and bring |
| | 80: 2 | Awaken your **m**; come and save us. |
| | 119:101 | heart that I **m** not sin against you. |
| | 119:71 | so that I **m** learn your decrees. |
| | 119:101 | path so that I **m** obey your word. |
| Ecc | 9:10 | do, do it with all your **m**, |
| Isa | 11: 2 | Spirit of counsel and of **m**, |
| | 63:15 | Where are your zeal and your **m**? |
| Jer | 16:21 | I will teach them my power and **m**. |
| Mic | 3: 8 | and with justice and **m**, to declare |
| Zec | 4: 6 | 'Not by **m** nor by power, but by my |
| Mt | 13:15 | Otherwise they **m** see with their |
| Mk | 14:35 | possible the hour **m** pass from him. |
| Lk | 22: 4 | with them how he **m** betray Jesus. |
| Jn | 1: 7 | so that through him all **m** believe. |
| Ac | 28:27 | Otherwise they **m** see with their |
| 1Co | 9:22 | all possible means I **m** save some. |
| 2Co | 8: 9 | through his poverty **m** become rich. |
| Col | 1:11 | his glorious **m** so that you may have |
| 1Ti | 6:16 | To him be honor and **m** forever. |
| 2Th | 1: 9 | and from the glory of his **m** |
| 1Pe | 2:24 | so that we **m** die to sins and live |
| 1Jn | 3: 5 | so that he **m** take away our sins. |

## MIGHTIER* [MIGHT]
| | | |
|---|---|---|
| Ps | 93: 4 | **M** than the thunder of the great |
| | 93: 4 | **m** than the breakers of the sea— |

## MIGHTY [MIGHT]
| | | |
|---|---|---|
| Ge | 10: 9 | a **m** hunter before the LORD." |
| | 49:24 | of the hand of the **M** One of Jacob, |
| Ex | 6: 1 | of my **m** hand he will let them go; |
| | 7: 4 | with **m** acts of judgment I will bring |
| | 13: 3 | brought you out of it with a **m** hand. |
| Dt | 3:24 | do the deeds and **m** works you do? |
| | 5:15 | you out of there with a **m** hand |
| | 7: 8 | he brought you out with a **m** hand |
| | 10:17 | the great God, **m** and awesome, |
| | 34:12 | no one has ever shown the **m** power |
| Jos | 22:22 | "The **M** One, God, the LORD! The **M** One, God, the LORD! |
| 2Sa | 1:19 | How the **m** have fallen! |
| | 23: 8 | the names of David's **m** warriors: |
| 2Ch | 14:11 | to help the powerless against the **m**. |
| Ne | 9:32 | the great God, **m** and awesome, |
| Job | 36: 5 | "God is **m**, but despises no one; |
| Ps | 24: 8 | The LORD strong and **m**, |
| | 45: 3 | sword on your side, you **m** one; |
| | 50: 1 | The **M** One, God, the LORD, |

Ps 62: 7 he is my **m** rock, my refuge.
68:33 above, who thunders with **m** voice.
71:16 will come and proclaim your **m** acts,
77:12 and meditate on all your **m** deeds."
77:15 your **m** arm you redeemed your
89: 8 are **m**, and your faithfulness
93: 4 the LORD on high is **m**.
99: 4 The King is **m**, he loves justice—
106: 2 Who can proclaim the **m** acts
110: 2 LORD will extend your **m** scepter
118:15 right hand has done **m** things!
136:12 with a **m** hand and outstretched arm;
145: 4 they tell of your **m** acts.
145:12 all people may know of your **m** acts
147: 5 Great is our Lord and **m** in power;
150: 1 praise him in his **m** heavens.
SS 8: 6 like blazing fire, like a **m** flame.
Isa 9: 6 Wonderful Counselor, **M** God,
33:21 the LORD will be our **M** One.
49:26 Redeemer, the **M** One of Jacob."
60:16 Redeemer, the **M** One of Jacob.
63: 1 in righteousness, **m** to save."
Jer 10: 6 great, and your name is **m** in power.
20:11 LORD is with me like a **m** warrior;
32:18 Great and **m** God, whose name
32:19 purposes and **m** are your deeds.
Eze 20:33 I will reign over you with a **m** hand
Da 4: 3 are his signs, how **m** his wonders!
11: 3 Then a **m** king will arise, who will
Zep 3:17 with you, the **M** Warrior who saves.
Mk 14:62 at the right hand of the **M** One
Lk 1:49 for the **M** One has done great things
Eph 1:19 power is the same as the **m** strength
6:10 in the Lord and in his **m** power.
1Pe 5: 6 under God's **m** hand, that he may
Rev 18: 8 **m** is the Lord God who judges her.

## MIGHTY HAND See HAND

## MIGHTY ONE Ge 49:24; Jos 22:22, 22; Job
34:17; Ps 42:4; 45:3; 50:1; 132:2, 5; Isa 1:24;
10:13, 34; 33:21; 49:26; 60:16; Mt 26:64; Mk
14:62; Lk 1:49

# MILDEW
Dt 28:22 with blight and **m**, which will
2Ch 6:28 to the land, or blight or **m**,
Am 4: 9 destroying them with blight and **m**.

# MILE*
Mt 5:41 If anyone forces you to go one **m**,

# MILETUS
2Ti 4:20 and I left Trophimus sick in **M**.

# MILK
Ex 3: 8 a land flowing with **m** and honey—
23:19 cook a young goat in its mother's **m**.
SS 4:11 **m** and honey are under your tongue.
Isa 55: 1 buy wine and **m** without money
Joel 3:18 wine, and the hills will flow with **m**;
1Co 3: 2 I gave you **m**, not solid food,
Heb 5:12 You need **m**, not solid food!
1Pe 2: 2 crave pure spiritual **m**, so that by it

# MILKAH
Ge 11:29 the father of both **M** and Iskah.

## LAND FLOWING WITH MILK AND HONEY See FLOWING

# MILL
Mt 24:41 will be grinding with a hand **m**;

## MILLSTONE [STONE]
Jdg 9:53 a woman dropped an upper **m** on his
Lk 17: 2 with a **m** tied around your neck than

## MILLSTONES [STONE]
Dt 24: 6 Do not take a pair of **m**—

## MIND [DOUBLE-MINDED, LIKE-MINDED, MINDFUL, MINDS]
Ge 37:11 but his father kept the matter in **m**.
Nu 23:19 being, that he should change his **m**.
Dt 28:65 LORD will give you an anxious **m**,
29: 4 the LORD has not given you a **m**
1Sa 15:29 that he should change his **m**."
1Ch 28: 9 devotion and with a willing **m**,
2Ch 30:12 to give them unity of **m** to carry
Ps 26: 2 me, examine my heart and my **m**;
110: 4 sworn and will not change his **m**:
Ecc 2: 3 my **m** still guiding me with wisdom.
Jer 17:10 search the heart and examine the **m**,
La 3:21 Yet this I call to **m** and therefore I
Da 4:16 Let his **m** be changed
7: 4 and a human **m** was given to it.
Mt 1:19 he had in **m** to divorce her quietly.
22:37 all your soul and with all your **m**.'
Mk 3:21 for they said, "He is out of his **m**."
5:15 there, dressed and in his right **m**;
12:30 with all your **m** and with all your
Lk 10:27 your strength and with all your **m**';
Ac 4:32 believers were one in heart and **m**.
Ro 1:28 gave them over to a depraved **m**,
7:25 then, I myself in my **m** am a slave
8: 6 The **m** controlled by the sinful
8: 6 the **m** controlled by the Spirit is life
8: 7 The sinful **m** is hostile to God;
11:34 "Who has known the **m**
12: 2 by the renewing of your **m**.
14:13 make up your **m** not to put any
15: 6 with one **m** and one voice you may
1Co 1:10 but that you be perfectly united in **m**
2: 9 what no human **m** has conceived—
2:16 "Who has known the **m** of the Lord
14:14 spirit prays, but my **m** is unfruitful.
2Co 5:13 If we are "out of our **m**," as some
5:13 if we are in our right **m**, it is for you.
13:11 another, be of one **m**, live in peace.
Php 2: 2 being one in spirit and of one **m**.
3:19 Their **m** is set on earthly things.
1Th 4:11 You should **m** your own business
Heb 7:21 sworn and will not change his **m**:
1Pe 4: 7 be alert and of sober **m**
Rev 17: 9 "This calls for a **m** with wisdom.

## MINDFUL* [MIND]
Ps 8: 4 mortals that you are **m** of them,
Ps 26: 3 always been **m** of your unfailing love

Lk    1:48  he has been **m** of the humble state
Heb   2: 6  mortals that you are **m** of them,

## MINDS [MIND]
Dt   11:18  words of mine in your hearts and **m**;
Ps    7: 9  the righteous God who probes **m**
Isa  26: 3  peace those whose **m** are steadfast,
Jer  23:16  speak visions from their own **m**,
     31:33  "I will put my law in their **m**
Lk   24:38  and why do doubts rise in your **m**?
     24:45  he opened their **m** so they could
Ro    8: 5  the sinful nature have their **m** set
      8: 5  the Spirit have their **m** set on what
2Co   3:14  But their **m** were made dull,
      4: 4  god of this age has blinded the **m**
Eph   4:23  made new in the attitude of your **m**;
Php   4: 7  hearts and your **m** in Christ Jesus.
Col   2:18  and their unspiritual **m** puff them
      3: 2  Set your **m** on things above,
Heb   8:10  I will put my laws in their **m**
     10:16  and I will write them on their **m**."
1Pe   1:13  with **m** that are alert and fully sober,
Rev   2:23  I am he who searches hearts and **m**,

## MINE
Ex   19: 5  Although the whole earth is **m**,
Nu    3:12  The Levites are **m**,
      3:13  for all the firstborn are **m**.
Dt   32:35  It is **m** to avenge; I will repay.
Job  28: 1  There is a **m** for silver and a place
Ps   50:10  for every animal of the forest is **m**,
Pr    8:14  Counsel and sound judgment are **m**;
SS    2:16  My beloved is **m** and I am his;
Isa  30: 1  who carry out plans that are not **m**,
Hag   2: 8  'The silver is **m** and the gold is **m**,'
Mt    7:24  who hears these words of **m**
     25:40  of these brothers and sisters of **m**,
Jn   16:15  All that belongs to the Father is **m**.
Ro   12:19  for it is written: "It is **m** to avenge;
Heb  10:30  him who said, "It is **m** to avenge;

## MINGLED*
Ezr   9: 2  and have **m** the holy race
Ps  106:35  but they **m** with the nations

## MINISTER [MINISTERED, MINISTERING, MINISTERS, MINISTRY]
Nu   16: 9  the community and **m** to them?
Dt   10: 8  to stand before the LORD to **m**
1Ch  15: 2  and to **m** before him forever."
Ps  101: 6  whose walk is blameless will **m**
    135: 2  you who **m** in the house
Ro   15:16  to be a **m** of Christ Jesus
1Ti   4: 6  you will be a good **m** of Christ

## MINISTERED* [MINISTER]
1Sa   2:11  the boy **m** before the LORD under
      3: 1  The boy Samuel **m** before
1Ch   6:32  They **m** with music before

## MINISTERING [MINISTER]
1Ch  24: 3  for their appointed order of **m**.
Heb   1:14  Are not all angels **m** spirits sent

## MINISTERS [MINISTER]
2Co   3: 6  He has made us competent as **m**

## MINISTRY [MINISTER]
Lk    3:23  years old when he began his **m**.
Ac    1:17  our number and shared in our **m**."
      6: 4  to prayer and the **m** of the word."
Ro   11:13  the Gentiles, I make much of my **m**
2Co   3: 7  Now if the **m** that brought death,
      4: 1  God's mercy we have this **m**, we do
      5:18  and gave us the **m** of reconciliation:
      6: 3  so that our **m** will not be discredited.
2Ti   4: 5  discharge all the duties of your **m**.
Heb   8: 6  in fact the **m** Jesus has received is as

## MIRACLE* [MIRACLES, MIRACULOUS]
Ex    7: 9  'Perform a **m**,' then say to Aaron,
Mk    9:39  "No one who does a **m** in my name
Jn    7:21  them, "I did one **m**, and you are all

## MIRACLES* [MIRACLE]
1Ch  16:12  done, his **m**, and the judgments he
Ne    9:17  to remember the **m** you performed
Job   5: 9  fathomed, **m** that cannot be counted.
      9:10  fathomed, **m** that cannot be counted.
Ps   77:11  I will remember your **m** of long ago.
     77:14  You are the God who performs **m**;
     78:12  He did **m** in the sight of their
    105: 5  done, his **m**, and the judgments he
    106: 7  they gave no thought to your **m**;
    106:22  **m** in the land of Ham and awesome
Mt    7:22  in your name perform many **m**?'
     11:20  most of his **m** had been performed,
     11:21  If the **m** that were performed in you
     11:23  If the **m** that were performed in you
     13:58  he did not do many **m** there because
Mk    6: 2  What are these remarkable **m** he is
      6: 5  He could not do any **m** there,
Lk   10:13  if the **m** that were performed in you
     19:37  voices for all the **m** they had seen:
Ac    2:22  man accredited by God to you by **m**,
      8:13  by the great signs and **m** he saw.
     19:11  did extraordinary **m** through Paul,
1Co  12:28  then **m**, then gifts of healing,
     12:29  Are all teachers? Do all work **m**?
2Co  12:12  including signs, wonders and **m**.
Gal   3: 5  and work **m** among you by your
Heb   2: 4  wonders and various **m**, and by gifts

## MIRACULOUS [MIRACLE]
Mt   13:54  this wisdom and these **m** powers?"
1Co  12:10  to another **m** powers, to another

## MIRE
Ps   40: 2  the slimy pit, out of the mud and **m**;
Isa  57:20  whose waves cast up **m** and mud.

## MIRIAM
Sister of Moses and Aaron (Nu 26:59); with them a leader of Israel (Mic 6:4). Prophet who led singing and dancing at Red Sea (Ex 15:20–21). Struck with leprosy for criticizing Moses (Nu 12). Death (Nu 20:1).

## MIRROR*
Job 37:18 skies, hard as a **m** of cast bronze?
1Co 13:12 we see only a reflection as in a **m**;
Jas 1:23 who look at their faces in a **m**

## MISCARRY
Ex 23:26 and none will **m** or be barren in your

## MISDEEDS*
Ps 99: 8 God, though you punished their **m**.
Ro 8:13 you put to death the **m** of the body,

## MISERABLE [MISERY]
Gal 4: 9 back to those weak and **m** forces?

## MISERY [MISERABLE]
Ex 3: 7 "I have indeed seen the **m** of my
Nu 23:21 in Jacob, no **m** observed in Israel.
Jdg 10:16 he could bear Israel's **m** no longer.
Ps 44:24 and forget our **m** and oppression?
56: 8 Record my **m**; list my tears
Ecc 8: 6 person may be weighed down by **m**.
Hos 5:15 in their **m** they will earnestly seek
Ro 3:16 ruin and **m** mark their ways,
Jas 5: 1 wail because of the **m** that is coming

## MISFORTUNE
Nu 23:21 "No **m** is seen in Jacob, no misery
Ob 1:12 your brother in the day of his **m**,

## MISHAEL [MESHACH]
Original name of Meshach (Da 1:6–19; 2:17).

## MISLEAD [MISLEADS, MISLED]
Pr 24:28 would you use your lips to **m**?
Isa 9:16 who guide this people **m** them,
47:10 knowledge **m** you when you say

## MISLEADS* [MISLEAD]
Isa 44:20 on ashes, a deluded heart **m** them;
Rev 2:20 her teaching she **m** my servants

## MISLED [MISLEAD]
1Co 15:33 Do not be **m**:

## MISS* [MISSES, MISSING]
Jdg 20:16 sling a stone at a hair and not **m**.
Pr 19: 2 more will hasty feet **m** the way!

## MISSES* [MISS]
1Sa 20: 6 If your father **m** me at all,

## MISSING [MISS]
Jdg 21: 3 Why should one tribe be **m**
Isa 40:26 strength, not one of them is **m**.

## MISSION
Isa 48:15 him, and he will succeed in his **m**.
Ac 12:25 and Saul had finished their **m**,

## MIST* [MISTS]
Isa 44:22 cloud, your sins like the morning **m**.
Hos 6: 4 Your love is like the morning **m**,

Hos 13: 3 they will be like the morning **m**,
Ac 13:11 Immediately **m** and darkness came
Jas 4:14 You are a **m** that appears for a little

## MISTAKE
Ecc 5: 6 messenger, "My vow was a **m**."

## MISTREAT [MISTREATED]
Ex 22:21 "Do not **m** or oppress a foreigner,
Eze 22:29 poor and needy and **m** the foreigner,
Lk 6:28 you, pray for those who **m** you.

## MISTREATED [MISTREAT]
Ge 15:13 they will be enslaved and **m** there.
16: 6 Then Sarai **m** Hagar; so she fled
Nu 20:15 The Egyptians **m** us and our
Eze 22: 7 the foreigner and **m** the fatherless
Heb 11:25 He chose to be **m** along
11:37 destitute, persecuted and **m**—
13: 3 and those who are **m** as if you

## MISTRESS
Ge 16: 4 she began to despise her **m**.
Ps 123: 2 slave look to the hand of her **m**,

## MISTS* [MIST]
2Pe 2:17 water and **m** driven by a storm.

## MISUSE* [MISUSES]
Ex 20: 7 "You shall not **m** the name
Dt 5:11 "You shall not **m** the name
Ps 139:20 your adversaries **m** your name.
1Co 9:18 not **m** my rights as a preacher

## MISUSES* [MISUSE]
Ex 20: 7 anyone guiltless who **m** his name.
Dt 5:11 anyone guiltless who **m** his name.

## MITE(S) (KJV) See PENNY, [SMALL] COPPER [COINS]

## MIXED [MIXES, MIXING, MIXTURE, WELL-MIXED]
Ex 29: 2 yeast and with olive oil **m** in,
Lev 7:10 offering, whether **m** with oil or dry,
Ps 75: 8 full of foaming wine **m** with spices;
Pr 9: 5 food and drink the wine I have **m**.
Da 2:41 it, even as you saw iron **m** with clay.
Mk 15:23 Then they offered him wine **m**
Jude 1:23 to others show mercy, **m** with fear—
Rev 8: 7 came hail and fire **m** with blood,

## MIXES* [MIXED]
Da 2:43 any more than iron **m** with clay.
Hos 7: 8 "Ephraim **m** with the nations;

## MIXING [MIXED]
Isa 5:22 wine and champions at **m** drinks,

## MIXTURE [MIXED]
Jn 19:39 Nicodemus brought a **m** of myrrh and

## MIZPAH
Ge 31:49 It was also called **M**, because he
1Sa 7: 6 was serving as leader of Israel at **M**.
Jer 41: 1 to Gedaliah son of Ahikam at **M**.

## MOAB [MOABITE, MOABITES]
Ge 19:37 had a son, and she named him **M**;
Nu 22: 3 **M** was filled with dread because
Dt 34: 5 of the LORD died there in **M**,
Jdg 3:12 Eglon king of **M** power over Israel.
Ru 1: 1 live for a while in the country of **M**.
1Sa 22: 4 So he left them with the king of **M**,
2Ki 1: 1 death, **M** rebelled against Israel.
23:13 for Chemosh the vile god of **M**,
Isa 15: 1 A prophecy concerning **M**: Ar in **M**
Jer 48: 1 Concerning **M**: This is what
48:16 "The fall of **M** is at hand;
Eze 25: 8 'Because **M** and Seir said, "Look,
Am 2: 1 "For three sins of **M**, even for four,
Zep 2: 9 "surely **M** will become like Sodom,

## MOABITE [MOAB]
Nu 25: 1 sexual immorality with **M** women,
Dt 23: 3 No Ammonite or **M** or any of their
Ru 1:22 accompanied by Ruth the **M**,
Ne 13: 1 **M** should ever be admitted

## MOABITES [MOAB]
Ge 19:37 he is the father of the **M** of today.

## MOAN
Ps 90: 9 we finish our years with a **m**.
Isa 59:11 we **m** mournfully like doves.

## MOCK [MOCKED, MOCKER, MOCKERS, MOCKERY, MOCKING, MOCKS]
Ps 22: 7 All who see me **m** me;
74:22 remember how fools **m** you all day
119:51 The arrogant **m** me unmercifully,
Pr 1:26 I will **m** when calamity overtakes
14: 9 Fools **m** at making amends for sin,
La 3:63 standing, they **m** me in their songs.
Hab 1:10 They **m** kings and scoff at rulers.
Mk 10:34 who will **m** him and spit on him,

## MOCKED [MOCK]
2Ch 36:16 But they **m** God's messengers,
Ps 74:18 how the enemy has **m** you, LORD,
89:51 have **m**, with which they have **m**
Mt 27:29 knelt in front of him and **m** him,
27:41 of the law and the elders **m** him.
Lk 23:11 his soldiers ridiculed and **m** him.
Gal 6: 7 not be deceived: God cannot be **m**.

## MOCKER [MOCK]
Pr 9: 7 corrects a **m** invites insults;
9:12 if you are a **m**, you alone will suffer.
20: 1 Wine is a **m** and beer a brawler;
22:10 Drive out the **m**, and out goes strife;
24: 9 folly are sin, and people detest a **m**.

## MOCKERS [MOCK]
Ps 1: 1 take or sit in the company of **m**,

Pr 3:34 He mocks proud **m** but shows favor
29: 8 **M** stir up a city, but the wise turn

## MOCKERY* [MOCK]
Pr 1:22 How long will mockers delight in **m**
Jer 10:15 are worthless, the objects of **m**;
51:18 are worthless, the objects of **m**;

## MOCKING [MOCK]
Isa 50: 6 I did not hide my face from **m**
Lk 22:63 who were guarding Jesus began **m**

## MOCKS [MOCK]
Pr 17: 5 Whoever **m** the poor shows
19:28 A corrupt witness **m** at justice,
30:17 "The eye that **m** a father,

## MODEL*
Php 3:17 and just as you have us as a **m**,
1Th 1: 7 And so you became a **m** to all
2Th 3: 9 to offer ourselves as a **m** for you

## MODESTLY* [MODESTY]
1Ti 2: 9 I also want the women to dress **m**,

## MODESTY* [MODESTLY]
1Co 12:23 are treated with special **m**,

## MOLDED*
Job 10: 9 Remember that you **m** me like clay.

## MOLDY
Jos 9: 5 of their food supply was dry and **m**.

## MOLEK
Lev 20: 2 sacrifices any of his children to **M**
1Ki 11:33 and **M** the god of the Ammonites,
2Ki 23:10 their son or daughter in the fire to **M**.
Jer 32:35 sacrifice their sons and daughters to **M**,

## MOMENT [MOMENTARY]
Ex 33: 5 I were to go with you even for a **m**,
Nu 4:20 even for a **m**, or they will die."
Job 20: 5 the joy of the godless lasts but a **m**.
Ps 2:12 for his wrath can flare up in a **m**.
30: 5 For his anger lasts only a **m**, but his
Pr 12:19 but a lying tongue lasts only a **m**.
Isa 54: 7 "For a brief **m** I abandoned you,
66: 8 or a nation be brought forth in a **m**?
Mt 9:22 the woman was healed from that **m**.
Jn 18:27 at that **m** a rooster began to crow.
Ac 5:10 At that **m** she fell down at his feet
Gal 2: 5 We did not give in to them for a **m**,

## MOMENTARY* [MOMENT]
2Co 4:17 **m** troubles are achieving for us

## MONEY
Ex 22:25 "If you lend **m** to one of my people
30:16 Receive the atonement **m**
2Ki 12: 4 "Collect all the **m** that is brought as
Ps 15: 5 who lend **m** to the poor without
Pr 13:11 Dishonest **m** dwindles away,
13:11 but whoever gathers **m** little by little

| | | |
|---|---|---|
| Ecc | 5:10 | Those who love **m** never have |
| | 7:12 | is a shelter as **m** is a shelter, |
| | 10:19 | and **m** is the answer for everything. |
| Isa | 55: 1 | and you who have no **m**, come, |
| Mic | 3:11 | and her prophets tell fortunes for **m**. |
| Mt | 6:24 | You cannot serve both God and **m**. |
| | 27: 5 | So Judas threw the **m** |
| Lk | 3:14 | "Don't extort **m** and don't accuse |
| | 9: 3 | bag, no bread, no **m**, no extra shirt. |
| | 16:13 | You cannot serve both God and **m**." |
| Jn | 2:14 | sitting at tables exchanging **m**. |
| | 12: 6 | as keeper of the **m** bag, he used |
| Ac | 5: 2 | kept back part of the **m** for himself, |
| 1Co | 16: 2 | you should set aside a sum of **m** |
| 1Ti | 3: 3 | not quarrelsome, not a lover of **m**. |
| | 6:10 | the love of **m** is a root of all kinds |
| 2Ti | 3: 2 | of themselves, lovers of **m**, boastful, |
| Heb | 13: 5 | your lives free from the love of **m** |

## MONEYLENDER* [LEND]

| | | |
|---|---|---|
| Lk | 7:41 | people owed money to a certain **m**. |

## MONOPOLY*

| | | |
|---|---|---|
| Job | 15: 8 | Do you have a **m** on wisdom? |

## MONSTER*

| | | |
|---|---|---|
| Job | 7:12 | or the **m** of the deep, that you put |
| Ps | 74:13 | the heads of the **m** in the waters. |
| Isa | 27: 1 | he will slay the **m** of the sea. |
| | 51: 9 | pieces, who pierced that **m** through? |
| Eze | 29: 3 | you great **m** lying among your |
| | 32: 2 | you are like a **m** in the seas |

## MONTH [MONTHLY, MONTHS]

| | | |
|---|---|---|
| Ex | 12: 2 | "This **m** is to be for you the first **m**, |
| | 40: 2 | on the first day of the first **m**. |
| Lev | 23:24 | first day of the seventh **m** you are |
| | 23:27 | day of this seventh **m** is the Day |
| | 23:34 | the seventh **m** the LORD's Festival |
| | 25: 9 | on the tenth day of the seventh **m**; |
| Nu | 3:15 | Count every male a **m** old or more." |
| | 11:21 | them meat to eat for a whole **m**!' |
| Ezr | 6:19 | On the fourteenth day of the first **m**, |
| Ne | 8: 2 | day of the seventh **m** Ezra the priest |
| Est | 9:21 | and fifteenth days of the **m** of Adar |
| Eze | 47:12 | Every **m** they will bear fruit, |
| Rev | 9:15 | day and **m** and year were released |
| | 22: 2 | of fruit, yielding its fruit every **m**. |

## MONTHLY [MONTH]

| | | |
|---|---|---|
| Lev | 15:19 | of her **m** period will last seven days, |
| Nu | 28:14 | This is the **m** burnt offering to be |

## MONTHS [MONTH]

| | | |
|---|---|---|
| Ex | 2: 2 | a fine child, she hid him for three **m**. |
| Jdg | 11:37 | "Give me two **m** to roam the hills |
| 1Sa | 6: 1 | been in Philistine territory seven **m**, |
| 1Ch | 13:14 | in his house for three **m**, |
| Jn | 4:35 | 'It's still four **m** until harvest'? |
| Gal | 4:10 | are observing special days and **m** |
| Rev | 9: 5 | but only to torture them for five **m**. |
| | 11: 2 | trample on the holy city for 42 **m**. |
| | 13: 5 | its authority for forty-two **m**. |

## MOON [MOONS]

| | | |
|---|---|---|
| Ge | 37: 9 | this time the sun and **m** and eleven |
| Nu | 28:14 | at each new **m** during the year. |
| Dt | 17: 3 | sun or the **m** or the stars in the sky, |
| Jos | 10:13 | and the **m** stopped, till the nation |
| Ps | 8: 3 | of your fingers, the **m** and the stars, |
| | 72: 7 | abound till the **m** is no more. |
| | 74:16 | you established the sun and **m**. |
| | 89:37 | be established forever like the **m**, |
| | 104:19 | He made the **m** to mark the seasons, |
| | 121: 6 | you by day, nor the **m** by night. |
| | 136: 9 | the **m** and stars to govern the night; |
| | 148: 3 | Praise him, sun and **m**; |
| SS | 6:10 | fair as the **m**, bright as the sun, |
| Isa | 13:10 | and the **m** will not give its light. |
| Jer | 31:35 | who decrees the **m** and stars to shine |
| Eze | 32: 7 | and the **m** will not give its light. |
| Joel | 2:31 | the **m** to blood before the coming |
| Hab | 3:11 | **m** stood still in the heavens |
| Mt | 24:29 | and the **m** will not give its light; |
| Ac | 2:20 | the **m** to blood before the coming |
| 1Co | 15:41 | the **m** another and the stars another; |
| Col | 2:16 | a New **M** celebration or a Sabbath |
| Rev | 6:12 | hair, the whole **m** turned blood red, |
| | 8:12 | a third of the **m**, and a third |
| | 12: 1 | sun, with the **m** under her feet |
| | 21:23 | need the sun or the **m** to shine on it, |

## MOONS [MOON]

| | | |
|---|---|---|
| 2Ch | 8:13 | the New **M** and the three annual |
| | 31: 3 | at the New **M** and at the appointed |
| Isa | 1:13 | New **M**, Sabbaths and convocations— |

## MORAL*

| | | |
|---|---|---|
| Jas | 1:21 | get rid of all **m** filth and the evil |

## MORDECAI

Benjamite exile who raised Esther (Est 2:5–15). Exposed plot to kill Xerxes (Est 2:19–23). Refused to honor Haman (Est 3:1–6; 5:9–14). Charged Esther to foil Haman's plot against the Jews (Est 4). Xerxes forced Haman to honor Mordecai (Est 6). Mordecai exalted (Est 8–10). Established Purim (Est 9:18–32).

## MORE [MUCH]

| | | |
|---|---|---|
| Ge | 3: 1 | the serpent was **m** crafty than any |
| | 4:13 | "My punishment is **m** than I can |
| | 5:24 | then he was no **m**, because God took |
| | 37: 3 | Now Israel loved Joseph **m** than any |
| Ex | 1:12 | But the **m** they were oppressed, the |
| | | **m** they multiplied and spread; |
| Nu | 1:18 | years old or **m** were listed by name, |
| | 3:15 | every male a month old or **m**." |
| | 12: 3 | **m** humble than anyone else |
| Dt | 7:14 | will be blessed **m** than any other |
| Jos | 10:11 | **m** of them died from the hail than |
| Jdg | 16:30 | Thus he killed many **m** when he |
| 2Sa | 1:26 | **m** wonderful than that of women. |
| | 18: 8 | the forest swallowed up **m** men |
| 1Ki | 16:33 | and did **m** to arouse the anger |
| 2Ki | 2:12 | And Elisha saw him no **m**. |
| 1Ch | 11: 9 | David became **m** and **m** powerful, |
| Job | 4:17 | a mortal be **m** righteous than God? |
| | 42:12 | of Job's life **m** than the former part. |
| Ps | 19:10 | They are **m** precious than gold, |

Ps   37:10   while, and the wicked will be no **m**;
    69:31   please the LORD **m** than an ox,
    71:14   I will praise you **m** and **m**.
  119:127   I love your commands **m** than gold,
   130: 6   for the Lord **m** than watchmen wait
Pr    3:14   for she is **m** profitable than silver
    8:11   wisdom is **m** precious than rubies,
   21: 3   just is **m** acceptable to the LORD
   22: 1   good name is **m** desirable than great
  31:10   She is worth far **m** than rubies.
Ecc   1:18   the **m** knowledge, the **m** grief.
SS    1: 2   your love is **m** delightful than wine.
Isa   54: 1   because **m** are the children
  60:19   The sun will no **m** be your light
Jer   31:34   and will remember their sins no **m**."
La    5: 7   Our parents sinned and are no **m**,
Hos 13: 2   Now they sin **m** and **m**;
Jnh   3: 4   "Forty **m** days and Nineveh will be
Na    1:15   No **m** will the wicked invade you;
Mt   2:18   comforted, because they are no **m**."
Mk   4:25   Those who have will be given **m**;
  12:43   this poor widow has put **m**
Lk    3:16   one who is **m** powerful than I will
  12:23   Life is **m** than food, and the body **m**
Jn   16:12   "I have much **m** to say to you,
  16:16   a little while you will see me no **m**,
  21:15   do you love me **m** than these?"
Ac   17:11   of **m** noble character than those
Ro    5: 9   how much **m** shall we be saved
   8:37   things we are **m** than conquerors
  14: 5   consider one day **m** sacred than
2Co   3: 9   how much **m** glorious is
Heb   8:12   and will remember their sins no **m**."
  10:17   lawless acts I will remember no **m**."
Jas    4: 6   But he gives us **m** grace.
Rev 10: 6   said, "There will be no **m** delay!
  21: 4   There will be no **m** death'
  22: 5   There will be no **m** night.

## HOW MUCH MORE   See HOW

## MORIAH*

Ge   22: 2   Isaac—and go to the region of **M**.
2Ch   3: 1   LORD in Jerusalem on Mount **M**,

## MORNING   [MORNINGS]

Ge    1: 5   was evening, and there was **m**—
Ex   12:10   Do not leave any of it till **m**;
  16:12   and in the **m** you will be filled
  29:39   Offer one in the **m** and the other
Dt   28:67   In the **m** you will say, "If only it
2Sa 23: 4   he is like the light of **m** at sunrise on a
         cloudless **m**,
Ezr    3: 3   both the **m** and evening sacrifices.
Job 38: 7   while the **m** stars sang together
Ps    5: 3   In the **m**, LORD, you hear my
   5: 3   the **m** I lay my requests before you
  30: 5   night, but rejoicing comes in the **m**.
  130: 6   more than watchmen wait for the **m**,
Pr   27:14   blesses a neighbor early in the **m**,
Ecc 11: 6   Sow your seed in the **m**,
Isa   14:12   you have fallen from heaven, **m** star,
  50: 4   He wakens me **m** by **m**, wakens my
La    3:23   They are new every **m**; great is your
Hos   6: 4   Your love is like the **m** mist,
  13: 3   they will be like the **m** mist,
Zep   3: 5   **M** by **m** he dispenses his justice,

Lk   24: 1   very early in the **m**, the women took
  24:22   They went to the tomb early this **m**
Ac    2:15   It's only nine in the **m**!
2Pe   1:19   and the **m** star rises in your hearts.
Rev   2:28   I will also give them the **m** star.
  22:16   of David, and the bright **M** Star."

## MORNINGS*   [MORNING]

Da   8:14   "It will take 2,300 evenings and **m**;
   8:26   **m** that has been given you is true,

## MORTAL   [MORTALS]

Ge    6: 3   beings forever, for they are **m**;
Dt    5:26   For what **m** has ever heard the voice
Job   4:17   'Can a **m** be more righteous than
   9:32   "He is not a mere **m** like me
  10: 4   Do you see as a **m** sees?
Mal   3: 8   "Will a mere **m** rob God?
Ro    1:23   made to look like **m** human beings
   6:12   not let sin reign in your **m** body so
   8:11   give life to your **m** bodies because
1Co 15:53   and the **m** with immortality.
2Co   5: 4   so that what is **m** may be swallowed

## MORTALS   [MORTAL]

Job 13: 9   as you might deceive **m**?
  14: 1   "**M**, born of woman,
Ps    8: 4   are mere **m** that you are mindful
   9:20   the nations know they are only **m**.
  56: 4   What can mere **m** do to me?
  103:15   As for **m**, their days are like grass,
  144: 3   mere **m** that you think of them?
Isa   51:12   Who are you that you fear mere **m**,
Jer   17: 5   "Cursed are those who trust in **m**,
Heb   2: 6   are mere **m** that you are mindful

## MORTGAGING*

Ne    5: 3   were saying, "We are **m** our fields,

## MOSES

Levite; brother of Aaron (Ex 6:20; 1Ch 6:3). Put in basket into Nile; discovered and raised by Pharaoh's daughter (Ex 2:1–10). Fled to Midian after killing Egyptian (Ex 2:11–15). Married to Zipporah, fathered Gershom (Ex 2:16–22).

Called by the LORD to deliver Israel (Ex 3–4). Pharaoh's resistance (Ex 5). Ten plagues (Ex 7–11). Passover and Exodus (Ex 12–13). Led Israel through Red Sea (Ex 14). Song of deliverance (Ex 15:1–21). Brought water from rock (Ex 17:1–7). Raised hands to defeat Amalekites (Ex 17:8–16). Delegated judges (Ex 18; Dt 1:9–18).

Received Law at Sinai (Ex 19–23; 25–31; Jn 1:17). Announced Law to Israel (Ex 19:7–8; 24; 35). Broke tablets because of golden calf (Ex 32; Dt 9). Saw glory of the LORD (Ex 33–34). Supervised building of tabernacle (Ex 36–40). Set apart Aaron and priests (Lev 8–9). Numbered tribes (Nu 1–4; 26). Opposed by Aaron and Miriam (Nu 12). Sent spies into Canaan (Nu 13). Announced forty years of wandering for failure to enter land (Nu 14). Opposed by Korah (Nu 16). Forbidden to enter land for striking rock (Nu 20:1–13; Dt 1:37). Lifted bronze snake for healing (Nu 21:4–9; Jn 3:14). Final address to Israel (Dt 1–33). Succeeded by Joshua (Nu 27:12–23; Dt 34). Death and burial by God (Dt 34:5–12).

"Law of Moses" (1Ki 2:3; Ezr 3:2; Mk 12:26; Lk 24:44). "Book of Moses" (2Ch 25:12; Ne 13:1). "Song of Moses" (Ex 15:1–21; Rev 15:3). "Prayer of Moses" (Ps 90).

## LAW OF MOSES See LAW

## MOST [INMOST, MUCH]

Ge 14:18 He was priest of God **M** High,
Ex 26:33 Holy Place from the **M** Holy Place.
Nu 4: 4 the care of the **m** holy things.
24:16 has knowledge from the **M** High,
Jdg 5:24 "**M** blessed of women be Jael,
1Ki 3: 4 that was the **m** important high place,
1Ch 16:25 the LORD and **m** worthy of praise;
Ps 7:10 My shield is God **M** High,
46: 4 place where the **M** High dwells.
48: 1 and **m** worthy of praise, in the city
78:35 God **M** High was their Redeemer.
91: 1 the shelter of the **M** High will rest
SS 1: 8 do not know, **m** beautiful of women,
Isa 14:14 will make myself like the **M** High."
Jer 3:19 the **m** beautiful inheritance of any
Eze 20: 6 honey, the **m** beautiful of all lands.
Da 4:17 the **M** High is sovereign over
7:25 He will speak against the **M** High
Mk 5: 7 me, Jesus, Son of the **M** High God?
12:28 which is the **m** important?"
Lk 1:32 be called the Son of the **M** High.
1:76 be called a prophet of the **M** High;
20:47 men will be punished **m** severely."
Eph 5:16 making the **m** of every opportunity,
Col 4: 5 make the **m** of every opportunity.
Jude 1:20 yourselves up in your **m** holy faith

## MOST HIGH See HIGH

## MOST HOLY See HOLY

## MOTH

Ps 39:11 you consume their wealth like a **m**—
Isa 51: 8 For the **m** will eat them up like
Mt 6:19 on earth, where **m** and rust destroy,

## MOTHER [GRANDMOTHER, MOTHER'S, MOTHER-IN-LAW, MOTHERS]

Ge 2:24 a man will leave his father and **m**
3:20 because she would become the **m**
17:16 so that she will be the **m** of nations;
Ex 20:12 "Honor your father and your **m**,
21:15 father or **m** is to be put to death.
21:17 father or **m** is to be put to death.
Lev 18: 7 having sexual relations with your **m**.
19: 3 of you must respect your **m**
20: 9 father or **m** is to be put to death.
Dt 5:16 "Honor your father and your **m**,
21:18 who does not obey his father and **m**
22: 6 do not take the **m** with the young.
27:16 who dishonors their father or **m**."
Jdg 5: 7 arose, until I arose, a **m** in Israel.
1Sa 2:19 Each year his **m** made him a little
2Sa 20:19 to destroy a city that is a **m** in Israel.
1Ki 19:20 me kiss my father and **m** good-by,"
Ps 27:10 my father and **m** forsake me,
51: 5 from the time my **m** conceived me.
113: 9 her home as a happy **m** of children.

Pr 10: 1 children bring grief to their **m**.
15:20 but foolish children despise their **m**.
20:20 If you curse your father or **m**,
23:22 do not despise your **m** when she is
23:25 May your father and **m** rejoice;
29:15 left to themselves disgrace their **m**.
30:17 that scorns an aged **m**, will be
31: 1 inspired utterance his **m** taught him.
SS 6: 9 the only daughter of her **m**,
Isa 8: 4 how to say 'My father' or 'My **m**,'
49:15 "Can a **m** forget the baby at her
66:13 As a **m** comforts her child, so will I
Jer 20:17 with my **m** as my grave, her womb
Hos 2: 2 "Rebuke your **m**, rebuke her,
Mic 7: 6 a daughter rises up against her **m**,
Mt 1:16 and Mary was the **m** of Jesus
2:11 they saw the child with his **m** Mary,
10:35 father, a daughter against her **m**,
10:37 or **m** more than me is not worthy
12:48 "Who is my **m**, and who are my
19: 5 a man will leave his father and **m**
19:19 honor your father and **m**,' and 'love
Mk 7:10 'Honor your father and **m**,' and,
10:19 honor your father and **m**.' "
Lk 11:27 "Blessed is the **m** who gave you
12:53 **m** against daughter and daughter against **m**,
14:26 me and does not hate father and **m**,
18:20 honor your father and **m**.' "
Jn 19:27 to the disciple, "Here is your **m**."
Gal 4:26 is above is free, and she is our **m**.
Eph 5:31 a man will leave his father and **m**
6: 2 "Honor your father and **m**"—
1Th 2: 7 Just as a nursing **m** cares for her
2Ti 1: 5 Lois and in your **m** Eunice and, I am
Heb 7: 3 Without father or **m**,
Rev 17: 5 THE GREAT THE **M** OF PROSTITUTES

## MOTHER'S [MOTHER]

Ex 23:19 not cook a young goat in its **m** milk.
Job 1:21 "Naked I came from my **m** womb,
Ps 22:10 my **m** womb you have been my
Pr 1: 8 and do not forsake your **m** teaching.
6:20 and do not forsake your **m** teaching.
Ecc 5:15 comes naked from their **m** womb,
11: 5 the body is formed in a **m** womb,
Isa 50: 1 "Where is your **m** certificate
Jn 3: 4 a second time into their **m** womb

## MOTHER-IN-LAW [MOTHER]

Dt 27:23 is anyone who sleeps with his **m**."
Ru 2:11 done for your **m** since the death
Mic 7: 6 a daughter-in-law against her **m**—
Mt 10:35 a daughter-in-law against her **m**—
Mk 1:30 Simon's **m** was in bed with a fever,

## MOTHERS [MOTHER]

Pr 30:11 fathers and do not bless their **m**;
Hos 10:14 when **m** were dashed to the ground
Mk 13:17 for pregnant women and nursing **m**!
1Ti 1: 9 for those who kill their fathers or **m**,
5: 2 older women as **m**, and younger

## MOTIONED

Jn 13:24 Simon Peter **m** to this disciple
Ac 12:17 Peter **m** with his hand for them to be

Ac  13:16  up, Paul **m** with his hand and said:
    19:33  He **m** for silence in order to make
    26: 1  So Paul **m** with his hand and began

## MOTIVES*

Pr   16: 2  but **m** are weighed by the LORD.
1Co   4: 5  and will expose the **m** of people's
Php   1:18  way, whether from false **m** or true,
1Th   2: 3  not spring from error or impure **m**,
Jas   4: 3  because you ask with wrong **m**,

## MOUND

Jer  26:18  the temple hill a **m** overgrown
Mic   3:12  the temple hill a **m** overgrown

## MOUNT [MOUNTAIN, MOUNTAINS, MOUNTAINSIDE, MOUNTAINTOPS, MOUNTED]

Ex   19:20  descended to the top of **M** Sinai
    34:29  Moses came down from **M** Sinai
Nu   33:39  years old when he died on **M** Hor.
Dt   11:29  on **M** Gerizim the blessings, and on
            **M** Ebal the curses.
    34: 1  Moses climbed **M** Nebo
Jos   8:30  Joshua built on **M** Ebal an altar
1Ch  10: 8  and his sons fallen on **M** Gilboa.
2Ch   3: 1  LORD in Jerusalem on **M** Moriah,
Ps   78:68  he chose the tribe of Judah, **M** Zion,
    89: 9  when its waves **m** up, you still them.
Isa  14:13  sit enthroned on the **m** of assembly,
Eze  28:14  You were on the holy **m** of God;
Ob    1:17  But on **M** Zion will be deliverance;
Mic   4: 7  will rule over them in **M** Zion
Zec  14: 4  the **M** of Olives will be split in two
Mk   13: 3  the **M** of Olives opposite the temple,
Gal   4:24  One covenant is from **M** Sinai
Heb  12:22  But you have come to **M** Zion,
Rev  14: 1  standing on **M** Zion, and with him

## MOUNT OF OLIVES 2Sa 15:30; Zec 14:4, 4; Mt 21:1; 24:3; 26:30; Mk 11:1; 13:3; 14:26; Lk 19:29, 37; 21:37; 22:39; Jn 8:1; Ac 1:12

## MOUNT SINAI Ex 19:11, 18, 20, 23; 24:16; 31:18; 34:2, 4, 29, 32; Lev 7:38; 25:1; 26:46; 27:34; Nu 3:1; 28:6; Ne 9:13; Ac 7:30, 38; Gal 4:24, 25

## MOUNT ZION 2Ki 19:31; Ps 48:2, 11; 74:2; 78:68; 125:1; 133:3; Isa 4:5; 8:18; 10:12; 18:7; 24:23; 29:8; 31:4; 37:32; La 5:18; Joel 2:32; Ob 1:17, 21; Mic 4:7; Heb 12:22; Rev 14:1

## MOUNTAIN [MOUNT]

Ge   22:14  "On the **m** of the LORD it will be
Ex    3: 1  and came to Horeb, the **m** of God.
    19: 2  there in the desert in front of the **m**.
    19:20  called Moses to the top of the **m**.
    24:18  he stayed on the **m** forty days
    32:19  them to pieces at the foot of the **m**.
Dt    5: 4  face to face out of the fire on the **m**.
1Ki  19: 8  he reached Horeb, the **m** of God.
Job  14:18  "But as a **m** erodes and crumbles
Ps   15: 1  may live on your holy **m**?
    24: 3  may ascend the **m** of the LORD?
    48: 1  in the city of our God, his holy **m**.

Ps   68:16  you rugged **m**, at the **m** where God
Isa   2: 2  the last days the **m** of the LORD's
    11: 9  harm nor destroy on all my holy **m**,
    40: 4  up, every **m** and hill made low;
    65:25  nor destroy on all my holy **m**,"
Da    2:45  the vision of the rock cut out of a **m**,
Mic   4: 1  the last days the **m** of the LORD's
Zec  14: 4  with half of the **m** moving north
Mt    4: 8  the devil took him to a very high **m**
    17:20  you can say to this **m**,
Mk    9: 2  with him and led them up a high **m**,
Lk    3: 5  filled in, every **m** and hill made low.
Jn    4:21  the Father neither on this **m** nor
2Pe   1:18  we were with him on the sacred **m**.
Rev   6:14  every **m** and island was removed
     8: 8  and something like a huge **m**,
    21:10  me away in the Spirit to a **m** great

## HOLY MOUNTAIN See HOLY

## MOUNTAINS [MOUNT]

Ge    7:20  covered the **m** to a depth of more
     8: 4  ark came to rest on the **m** of Ararat.
Ps   36: 6  righteousness is like the highest **m**,
    46: 2  the **m** fall into the heart of the sea,
    90: 2  Before the **m** were born or you
    97: 5  The **m** melt like wax before
    98: 8  let the **m** sing together for joy;
    121: 1  I lift up my eyes to the **m**
    125: 2  As the **m** surround Jerusalem,
Isa   2: 2  established as the highest of the **m**,
    52: 7  How beautiful on the **m** are the feet
    54:10  Though the **m** be shaken
    55:12  the **m** and hills will burst into song
Eze  34: 6  My sheep wandered over all the **m**
    39: 4  On the **m** of Israel you will fall,
Hos  10: 8  Then they will say to the **m**,
Mic   4: 1  established as chief among the **m**;
Na    1:15  there on the **m**, the feet of one who
Mk   13:14  those who are in Judea flee to the **m**.
Lk   23:30  Then " 'they will say to the **m**,
1Co  13: 2  if I have a faith that can move **m**,
Rev   6:16  They called to the **m** and the rocks,
    16:20  away and the **m** could not be found.

## MOUNTAINSIDE [MOUNT]

Mt    5: 1  he went up on a **m** and sat down.
Mk    6:46  them, he went up on a **m** to pray.

## MOUNTAINTOPS [MOUNT]

Isa  42:11  let them shout from the **m**.
Eze   6:13  on every high hill and on all the **m**,

## MOUNTED [MOUNT]

Ex   25: 7  other gems to be **m** on the ephod
2Sa  22:11  He **m** the cherubim and flew;
SS    5:12  washed in milk, **m** like jewels.

## MOURN [MOURNED, MOURNING, MOURNS]

Ge   23: 2  and Abraham went to **m** for Sarah
Ezr  10: 6  to **m** over the unfaithfulness
Ne    8: 9  Do not **m** or weep."
Ecc   3: 4  a time to **m** and a time to dance,
Isa  61: 2  of our God, to comfort all who **m**,
Zec  12:10  they will **m** for him as one mourns

Mt    5: 4  Blessed are those who **m**, for they
      9:15  of the bridegroom **m** while he is
Lk    6:25  now, for you will **m** and weep.
Ro   12:15  **m** with those who **m**.
1Co   7:30  those who **m**, as if they did not;
Rev   1: 7  on earth "will **m** because of him."
     18: 7  I am not a widow; I will never **m**.'

## MOURNED [MOURN]

Nu   14:39  to all the Israelites, they **m** bitterly.
Ne    1: 4  For some days I **m** and fasted
Da   10: 2  time I, Daniel, **m** for three weeks.
Lk   23:27  including women who **m** and wailed
Ac    8: 2  Stephen and **m** deeply for him.

## MOURNING [MOURN]

Est   4: 3  there was great **m** among the Jews,
      9:22  their **m** into a day of celebration.
Ecc   7: 2  to go to a house of **m** than to go
Isa  61: 3  the oil of joy instead of **m**,
Jer  31:13  I will turn their **m** into gladness;
La    5:15  our dancing has turned to **m**.
Rev  21: 4  There will be no more death' or **m**

## MOURNS [MOURN]

Zec  12:10  for him as one **m** for an only child,

## MOUTH [MOUTHS]

Nu   16:30  the earth opens its **m** and swallows
     22:38  only what God puts in my **m**."
Dt    8: 3  comes from the **m** of the LORD.
     18:18  and I will put my words in his **m**.
     30:14  it is in your **m** and in your heart so
2Ki   4:34  the bed and lay on the boy, **m** to **m**,
Job  23:12  of his **m** more than my daily bread.
     40: 4  I put my hand over my **m**.
Ps   17: 3  my **m** has not transgressed.
     19:14  May these words of my **m** and this
     40: 3  He put a new song in my **m**, a hymn
     71: 8  My **m** is filled with your praise,
     78: 2  I will open my **m** with a parable;
    119:103 taste, sweeter than honey to my **m**!
     141: 3  Set a guard over my **m**, LORD;
Pr    2: 6  from his **m** come knowledge
      4:24  Keep your **m** free of perversity;
      8: 7  My **m** speaks what is true, for my
     10:11  The **m** of the righteous is a fountain
     10:31  the **m** of the righteous comes
     14: 3  A fool's **m** lashes out with pride,
     15: 2  but the **m** of the fool gushes folly.
     26:28  hurts, and a flattering **m** works ruin.
     27: 2  praise you, and not your own **m**;
Ecc   5: 2  Do not be quick with your **m**, do not
      6: 7  Everyone's toil is for the **m**,
SS    1: 2  kiss me with the kisses of his **m**—
      5:16  His **m** is sweetness itself;
Isa  29:13  come near to me with their **m**
     40: 5  the **m** of the LORD has spoken."
     45:23  my **m** has uttered in all integrity
     48: 3  my **m** announced them and I made
     49: 2  He made my **m** like a sharpened
     51:16  I have put my words in your **m**
     53: 7  afflicted, yet he did not open his **m**;
     55:11  my word that goes out from my **m**:
     59:21  I have put in your **m** will not depart
Jer   1: 9  "I have put my words in your **m**.

Eze   3: 2  So I opened my **m**, and he gave me
Da    7: 8  being and a **m** that spoke boastfully.
Hos   6: 5  killed you with the words of my **m**—
Mal   2: 7  people seek instruction from his **m**.
Mt    4: 4  that comes from the **m** of God.' "
     12:34  overflow of the heart the **m** speaks.
     15:11  but what comes out of your **m**,
Lk    6:45  overflow of the heart the **m** speaks.
Ac    8:32  is silent, so he did not open his **m**.
Ro   10: 8  it is in your **m** and in your heart,"
     10: 9  If you declare with your **m**,
2Th   2: 8  overthrow with the breath of his **m**
Jas   3:10  Out of the same **m** come praise
1Pe   2:22  and no deceit was found in his **m**."
Rev   1:16  coming out of his **m** was a sharp,
      2:16  them with the sword of my **m**.
      3:16  I am about to spit you out of my **m**.
     10:10  It tasted as sweet as honey in my **m**,
     13: 6  It opened its **m** to blaspheme God,
     19:15  out of his **m** is a sharp sword

## MOUTHS [MOUTH]

Ex    4:11  "Who gave human beings their **m**?
Ps   10: 7  Their **m** are full of lies and threats;
     37:30  The **m** of the righteous utter
     73: 9  Their **m** lay claim to heaven,
     78:36  they would flatter him with their **m**,
     115: 5  They have **m**, but cannot speak,
    135:17  hear, nor is there breath in their **m**.
Pr   16:23  of the wise make their **m** prudent,
     18: 7  The **m** of fools are their undoing,
Isa  52:15  kings will shut their **m** because
Eze  33:31  Their **m** speak of love, but their
Da    6:22  and he shut the **m** of the lions.
Ro    3:14  "Their **m** are full of cursing
Eph   4:29  talk come out of your **m**, but only
Jas   3: 3  we put bits into the **m** of horses
Rev   9:17  and out of their **m** came fire,
     11: 5  fire comes from their **m** and devours
     14: 5  No lie was found in their **m**;

## MOVE [MOVED, MOVES]

Ge    1:24  creatures that **m** along the ground,
Lev  11:29  " 'Of the animals that **m**
Nu    1:51  Whenever the tabernacle is to **m**,
Dt   19:14  Do not **m** your neighbor's boundary
Job  24: 2  are those who **m** boundary stones;
Pr   23:10  Do not **m** an ancient boundary stone
Isa  46: 7  From that spot it cannot **m**.
Mt   17:20  'M from here to there,' and it will **m**.
Ac   17:28  'For in him we live and **m** and have
1Co  13: 2  I have a faith that can **m** mountains,
     15:58  Let nothing **m** you.
Col   1:23  do not **m** from the hope held out

## MOVED [MOVE]

Ge    7:21  Every living thing that **m**
Ex   35:21  and whose heart **m** them came
1Ki   3:26  woman whose son was alive was deeply
            **m**
1Ch  16:30  is firmly established; it cannot be **m**.
2Ch  33:19  and how God was **m** by his entreaty,
     36:22  the LORD **m** the heart of Cyrus
Ezr   1: 5  everyone whose heart God had **m**—
Isa  33:20  abode, a tent that will not be **m**;
Eze   1:19  When the living creatures **m**,

Jn  11:33  he was deeply **m** in spirit

## MOVES  [MOVE]
Ge   9: 3  lives and **m** will be food for you.
Lev 11:41  " 'Every creature that **m**
Dt  23:14  For the LORD your God **m**
    27:17  is anyone who **m** their neighbor's

## MUCH  [MORE, MOST]
Ex  16:18  gathered just as **m** as they needed.
Dt  28:38  You will sow **m** seed in the field
1Ki  8:27  How **m** less this temple I have built!
Job  7:17  beings that you make so **m** of them,
    42:10  and gave him twice as **m** as he had
Ps  19:10  than gold, than **m** pure wisdom;
Pr  16:16  How **m** better to get wisdom than
    23:20  not join those who drink too **m** wine
Ecc  1:18  with **m** wisdom comes **m** sorrow;
     9:18  but one sinner destroys **m** good.
    12:12  end, and **m** study wearies the body.
Hag  1: 9  "You expected **m**, but see, it turned
Mt   6:26  Are you not **m** more valuable than
    23:15  convert twice as **m** a child of hell as
Mk   9:12  that the Son of Man must suffer **m**
Lk  12:48  one who has been entrusted with **m**,
           **m** more will be asked.
    16:10  little will also be dishonest with **m**.
Jn   8:26  "I have **m** to say in judgment
    15: 5  and I in you, you will bear **m** fruit;
    16:12  "I have **m** more to say to you,
Ac   2:13  said, "They have had too **m** wine."
2Co  3:11  how **m** greater is the glory
     8:15  who gathered **m** did not have too **m**,
1Ti  3: 8  not indulging in **m** wine, and not
Tit  2: 3  be slanderers or addicted to **m** wine,
Heb  1: 4  So he became as **m** superior
Rev 12:11  they did not love their lives so **m** as
    18: 7  Give her as **m** torment and grief as

## HOW MUCH MORE  See HOW

## MUD  [MUDDIED]
Ps  40: 2  the slimy pit, out of the **m** and mire;
Isa 57:20  whose waves cast up mire and **m**.
Jer 38: 6  and Jeremiah sank down into the **m**.
Jn   9: 6  made some **m** with the saliva,
2Pe  2:22  returns to her wallowing in the **m**."

## MUDDIED*  [MUD]
Pr  25:26  Like a **m** spring or a polluted well
Eze 32:13  feet or **m** by the hooves of cattle.
    34:19  drink what you have **m** with your

## MULBERRY*
Lk  17: 6  seed, you can say to this **m** tree,

## MULE
2Sa 18: 9  He was riding his **m**, and as the **m**
1Ki  1:38  Solomon mount King David's **m**,
Ps  32: 9  Do not be like the horse or the **m**,

## MULTIPLIED  [MULTIPLY]
Ex   1: 7  they **m** greatly,
    11: 9  my wonders may be **m** in Egypt."

## MULTIPLIES  [MULTIPLY]
Pr  27: 6  be trusted, but an enemy **m** kisses.

## MULTIPLY  [MULTIPLIED,
   MULTIPLIES, MULTIPLYING]
Ge   9: 7  **m** on the earth and increase
Ex   7: 3  heart, and though I **m** my signs
Lev 26:21  I will **m** your afflictions seven times
Ecc 10:14  and fools **m** words.

## MULTIPLYING*  [MULTIPLY]
Pr  10:19  Sin is not ended by **m** words,
Mk   4: 8  and produced a crop, some **m** thirty,

## MULTITUDE  [MULTITUDES]
Isa 31: 1  who trust in the **m** of their chariots
Da  10: 6  and his voice like the sound of a **m**.
Jas  5:20  death and cover over a **m** of sins.
1Pe  4: 8  because love covers over a **m**
Rev  7: 9  there before me was a great **m**
    19: 6  I heard what sounded like a great **m**,

## MULTITUDES  [MULTITUDE]
Ne   9: 6  and the **m** of heaven worship you.
Da  12: 2  **M** who sleep in the dust of the earth
Joel 3:14  **M**, **m** in the valley of decision!

## MURDER  [MURDERED, MURDERER,
   MURDERERS, MURDEROUS,
   MURDERS]
Ex  20:13  "You shall not **m**.
Nu  35:12  **m** may not die before standing trial
Dt   5:17  "You shall not **m**.
Hos  4: 2  lying and **m**, stealing and adultery;
Mt   5:21  'You shall not **m**, and anyone who
    15:19  of the heart come evil thoughts, **m**,
Mk  10:19  'You shall not **m**, you shall not
Ro   1:29  They are full of envy, **m**, strife,
    13: 9  "You shall not **m**," "You shall not
Jas  2:11  also said, "You shall not **m**."
1Jn  3:12  And why did he **m** him?

## MURDERED  [MURDER]
Jdg  9:18  You have **m** his seventy sons
Mt  23:31  of those who **m** the prophets.
Ac   7:52  now you have betrayed and **m** him—
1Jn  3:12  to the evil one and **m** his brother.

## MURDERER  [MURDER]
Nu  35:16  the **m** is to be put to death.
    35:31  accept a ransom for the life of a **m**,
Jn   8:44  He was a **m** from the beginning,
Ac   3:14  asked that a **m** be released to you.
1Jn  3:15  who hates a fellow believer is a **m**,

## MURDERERS  [MURDER]
1Ti  1: 9  kill their fathers or mothers, for **m**,
Rev 21: 8  vile, the **m**, the sexually immoral,
    22:15  the **m**, the idolaters and everyone

## MURDEROUS*  [MURDER]
Ac   9: 1  out **m** threats against the Lord's

## MURDERS [MURDER]

| Mt | 5:21 | anyone who **m** will be subject |
| Rev | 9:21 | Nor did they repent of their **m**, |

## MUSHI

| Nu | 3:20 | The Merarite clans: Mahli and **M**. |

## MUSIC [MUSICAL, MUSICIAN, MUSICIANS]

| Ge | 31:27 | and singing to the **m** of timbrels |
| 1Ch | 6:31 | charge of the **m** in the house |
| | 6:32 | with **m** before the tabernacle, |
| | 25: 6 | their father for the **m** of the temple |
| | 25: 7 | and skilled in **m** for the LORD— |
| Ne | 12:27 | and with the **m** of cymbals, |
| Job | 21:12 | They sing to the **m** of timbrel |
| Ps | 27: 6 | sing and make **m** to the LORD. |
| | 33: 2 | make **m** to him on the ten-stringed |
| | 45: 8 | ivory the **m** of the strings makes you |
| | 57: 7 | I will sing and make **m**. |
| | 81: 2 | Begin the **m**, strike the timbrel, |
| | 87: 7 | As they make **m** they will sing, |
| | 92: 1 | LORD and make **m** to your name, |
| | 92: 3 | to the **m** of the ten-stringed lyre |
| | 95: 2 | and extol him with **m** and song. |
| | 98: 4 | burst into jubilant song with **m**; |
| | 98: 5 | make **m** to the LORD |
| | 108: 1 | sing and make **m** with all my soul. |
| | 144: 9 | the ten-stringed lyre I will make **m** |
| | 147: 7 | make **m** to our God on the harp. |
| | 149: 3 | and make **m** to him with timbrel |
| Isa | 30:32 | club will be to the **m** of timbrels |
| La | 5:14 | young men have stopped their **m**. |
| Eze | 26:13 | the **m** of your harps will be heard no |
| Da | 3: 5 | pipe and all kinds of **m**, you must |
| | 3: 7 | lyre, harp and all kinds of **m**, |
| | 3:10 | all kinds of **m** must fall down |
| | 3:15 | pipe and all kinds of **m**, if you are |
| Am | 5:23 | not listen to the **m** of your harps. |
| Lk | 15:25 | the house, he heard **m** and dancing. |
| Eph | 5:19 | make **m** from your heart to the Lord, |
| Rev | 18:22 | The **m** of harpists and musicians, |

## FOR THE DIRECTOR OF MUSIC Ps 4:T;

5:T; 6:T; 8:T; 9:T; 11:T; 12:T; 13:T; 14:T; 18:T;
19:T; 20:T; 21:T; 22:T; 31:T; 36:T; 39:T; 40:T;
41:T; 42:T; 44:T; 45:T; 46:T; 47:T; 49:T; 51:T;
52:T; 53:T; 54:T; 55:T; 56:T; 57:T; 58:T; 59:T;
60:T; 61:T; 62:T; 64:T; 65:T; 66:T; 67:T; 68:T;
69:T; 70:T; 75:T; 76:T; 77:T; 80:T; 81:T; 84:T;
85:T; 88:T; 109:T; 139:T; 140:T; Hab 3:19

## MUSICAL* [MUSIC]

| 1Ch | 15:16 | a joyful sound with **m** instruments: |
| | 23: 5 | the **m** instruments I have provided |
| 2Ch | 7: 6 | with the LORD's **m** instruments, |
| | 34:12 | skilled in playing **m** instruments— |
| Ne | 12:36 | with **m** instruments [prescribed |
| Am | 6: 5 | and improvise on **m** instruments. |

## MUSICIAN* [MUSIC]

| 1Ch | 6:33 | Heman, the **m**, the son of Joel, |

## MUSICIANS [MUSIC]

| 1Ki | 10:12 | to make harps and lyres for the **m**. |

| 1Ch | 9:33 | Those who were **m**, heads of Levite |
| | 15:16 | as **m** to make a joyful sound |
| | 15:19 | The **m** Heman, Asaph and Ethan |
| 2Ch | 5:12 | All the Levites who were **m**— |
| | 9:11 | to make harps and lyres for the **m**. |
| | 35:15 | The **m**, the descendants of Asaph, |
| Ezr | 2:70 | the Levites, the **m**, the gatekeepers |
| Ps | 68:25 | are the singers, after them the **m**; |
| Rev | 18:22 | The music of harpists and **m**, |

## MUST

| Ge | 2:17 | you **m** not eat from the tree |
| | 3: 1 | 'You **m** not eat from any tree |
| | 4: 7 | have you, but you **m** rule over it." |
| | 9: 4 | "But you **m** not eat meat that has its |
| | 17:12 | is eight days old **m** be circumcised, |
| Ex | 22: 3 | who steals **m** certainly make |
| Dt | 7: 2 | then you **m** destroy them totally. |
| | 13: 4 | the LORD your God you **m** follow, |
| | 18:13 | You **m** be blameless before |
| 1Sa | 26:16 | you and your men **m** die, |
| 2Sa | 12: 5 | the man who did this **m** die! |
| Ps | 119:84 | How long **m** your servant wait? |
| Pr | 19:19 | The hot-tempered **m** pay |
| Hos | 12: 6 | But you **m** return to your God; |
| Mt | 16:21 | that he **m** be killed and on the third |
| Mk | 8:34 | be my disciple **m** deny themselves |
| | 10:17 | "what **m** I do to inherit eternal |
| | 13: 7 | Such things **m** happen, but the end |
| | 14:49 | But the Scriptures **m** be fulfilled." |
| Lk | 9:22 | Son of Man **m** suffer many things |
| Jn | 3: 7 | my saying, 'You **m** be born again.' |
| | 3:14 | so the Son of Man **m** be lifted up, |
| | 4:24 | and his worshipers **m** worship |
| | 13:34 | you, so you **m** love one another. |
| | 15: 4 | it **m** remain in the vine. |
| Ac | 20:21 | Greeks that they **m** turn to God |
| Ro | 12: 9 | Love **m** be sincere. Hate what is |
| 1Co | 7:10 | A wife **m** not separate from her |
| | 7:11 | a husband **m** not divorce his wife. |
| 2Co | 5:10 | we **m** all appear before the judgment |
| Eph | 5:33 | **m** love his wife as he loves himself, |
| | 5:33 | and the wife **m** respect her husband. |
| 1Ti | 3:12 | A deacon **m** be faithful to his wife |
| Tit | 1: 6 | An elder **m** be blameless, |
| Heb | 11: 6 | anyone who comes to him **m** believe |
| Rev | 4: 1 | I will show you what **m** take place |
| | 22: 6 | the things that **m** soon take place." |

## MUST BE CUT OFF Ex 12:15, 19; 30:33, 38;

31:14; Lev 7:20, 21, 25, 27; 17:4, 9, 14; 18:29;
19:8; 22:3; 23:29; Nu 9:13; 15:30; 19:13, 20

## MUST DIE Nu 15:35; Dt 22:22; 24:7; Jdg 6:30;

1Sa 14:39, 43; 20:31; 26:16; 2Sa 12:5; 14:14;
Ecc 2:16; Jer 26:8; Zec 13:3; Jn 19:7; Rev 11:5

## MUST NOT EAT Ge 2:17; 3:1, 3, 17; 9:4; Lev

3:17; 7:24, 26; 11:4, 8, 11; 17:14; 22:6, 8; 23:14;
Nu 6:4; Dt 12:16, 17, 23, 24; 15:23; Jdg 13:14;
1Ki 13:9, 17; Eze 44:31

## MUST PURGE Dt 13:5; 17:7, 12; 19:13, 19;

21:21; 22:21, 22, 24; 24:7

## MUST WASH Lev 6:27; 11:25, 28, 40, 40;

13:6, 34; 14:8, 9, 47; 15:5, 6, 7, 8, 10, 11, 13, 21,
22, 27; 16:26, 28; 17:15; Nu 19:7, 19

## MUSTARD*

| | | |
|---|---|---|
| Mt | 13:31 | kingdom of heaven is like a **m** seed, |
| | 17:20 | you have faith as small as a **m** seed, |
| Mk | 4:31 | It is like a **m** seed, which is |
| Lk | 13:19 | It is like a **m** seed, which a man took |
| | 17: 6 | you have faith as small as a **m** seed, |

## MUSTER

| | | |
|---|---|---|
| Pr | 24: 5 | have knowledge **m** their strength. |

## MUTE

| | | |
|---|---|---|
| Ex | 4:11 | Who makes them deaf or **m**? |
| Isa | 35: 6 | and the **m** tongue shout for joy. |
| Mt | 9:33 | out, the man who had been **m** spoke. |
| Mk | 7:37 | the deaf hear and the **m** speak." |
| 1Co | 12: 2 | influenced and led astray to **m** idols. |

## MUTILATORS*

| | | |
|---|---|---|
| Php | 3: 2 | those evildoers, those **m** of the flesh. |

## MUTTER

| | | |
|---|---|---|
| Isa | 8:19 | who whisper and **m**, should not |

## MUTUAL* [MUTUALLY]

| | | |
|---|---|---|
| Ro | 14:19 | leads to peace and to **m** edification. |
| 1Co | 7: 5 | other except perhaps by **m** consent |
| 2Pe | 1: 7 | and to godliness, **m** affection; and to **m** affection, love. |

## MUTUALLY* [MUTUAL]

| | | |
|---|---|---|
| Ro | 1:12 | and I may be **m** encouraged by each |

## MUZZLE*

| | | |
|---|---|---|
| Dt | 25: 4 | Do not **m** an ox while it is treading |
| Ps | 39: 1 | I will put a **m** on my mouth while |
| 1Co | 9: 9 | "Do not **m** an ox while it is treading |
| 1Ti | 5:18 | "Do not **m** an ox while it is treading |

## MYRRH

| | | |
|---|---|---|
| Ps | 45: 8 | All your robes are fragrant with **m** |
| SS | 1:13 | of **m** resting between my breasts. |
| Mt | 2:11 | gifts of gold, frankincense and **m**. |
| Mk | 15:23 | offered him wine mixed with **m**, |
| Jn | 19:39 | Nicodemus brought a mixture of **m** |
| Rev | 18:13 | of incense, **m** and frankincense, |

## MYRTLE

| | | |
|---|---|---|
| Isa | 55:13 | instead of briers the **m** will grow. |
| Zec | 1: 8 | He was standing among the **m** trees |

## MYSTERIES* [MYSTERY]

| | | |
|---|---|---|
| Job | 11: 7 | "Can you fathom the **m** of God? |
| Da | 2:28 | is a God in heaven who reveals **m**. |
| | 2:29 | of **m** showed you what is going |
| | 2:47 | Lord of kings and a revealer of **m**, |
| 1Co | 4: 1 | entrusted with the **m** God has revealed. |
| | 13: 2 | can fathom all **m** and all knowledge, |
| | 14: 2 | they utter **m** by the Spirit. |

## MYSTERY* [MYSTERIES]

| | | |
|---|---|---|
| Da | 2:18 | God of heaven concerning this **m**, |
| | 2:19 | During the night the **m** was revealed |
| | 2:27 | the king the **m** he has asked about, |
| | 2:30 | me, this **m** has been revealed to me, |
| | 2:47 | for you were able to reveal this **m**." |
| | 4: 9 | and no **m** is too difficult for you. |
| Ro | 11:25 | want you to be ignorant of this **m**, |
| | 16:25 | the revelation of the **m** hidden |
| 1Co | 2: 7 | a **m** that has been hidden |
| | 15:51 | Listen, I tell you a **m**: We will not |
| Eph | 1: 9 | to us the **m** of his will according |
| | 3: 3 | that is, the **m** made known to me |
| | 3: 4 | my insight into the **m** of Christ, |
| | 3: 6 | This **m** is that through the gospel |
| | 3: 9 | the administration of this **m**, |
| | 5:32 | This is a profound **m**—but I am |
| | 6:19 | I will fearlessly make known the **m** |
| Col | 1:26 | the **m** that has been kept hidden |
| | 1:27 | the glorious riches of this **m**, |
| | 2: 2 | that they may know the **m** of God, |
| | 4: 3 | we may proclaim the **m** of Christ, |
| 1Ti | 3:16 | the **m** from which true godliness |
| Rev | 1:20 | The **m** of the seven stars that you |
| | 10: 7 | the **m** of God will be accomplished, |
| | 17: 5 | title was written on her forehead: M |
| | 17: 7 | explain to you the **m** of the woman |

## MYTHS*

| | | |
|---|---|---|
| 1Ti | 1: 4 | or to devote themselves to **m** |
| | 4: 7 | Have nothing to do with godless **m** |
| 2Ti | 4: 4 | from the truth and turn aside to **m**. |
| Tit | 1:14 | will pay no attention to Jewish **m** |

# N

## NAAMAN

Aramean general whose leprosy was cleansed by Elisha (2Ki 5; Lk 4:27).

## NABAL

Wealthy Carmelite the LORD killed for refusing to help David (1Sa 25). David married Abigail, his widow (1Sa 25:39–42).

## NABOTH*

Jezreelite killed by Jezebel for his vineyard (1Ki 21). Ahab's family destroyed for this (1Ki 21:17–24; 2Ki 9:21–37).

## NADAB

1. Firstborn of Aaron (Ex 6:23); killed with Abihu for offering unauthorized fire (Lev 10; Nu 3:4).
2. Son of Jeroboam I; king of Israel (1Ki 15:25–32).

## NAGGING*

| | | |
|---|---|---|
| Jdg | 16:16 | such **n** she prodded him day after day |
| Pr | 21:19 | with a quarrelsome and **n** wife. |

## NAHASH

| | | |
|---|---|---|
| 1Sa | 11: 1 | **N** the Ammonite went |

## NAHOR

| | | |
|---|---|---|
| Ge | 11:26 | the father of Abram, **N** and Haran. |
| | 22:23 | eight sons to Abraham's brother **N**. |

Ge 24:15 the wife of Abraham's brother **N**.

## NAHUM

Prophet against Nineveh (Na 1:1).

## NAIL* [NAILING, NAILS]

Jn 20:25 "Unless I see the **n** marks in his

## NAILING* [NAIL]

Ac 2:23 him to death by **n** him to the cross.
Col 2:14 has taken it away, **n** it to the cross.

## NAILS [NAIL]

Ecc 12:11 sayings like firmly embedded **n**—
Isa 41: 7 The other **n** down the idol so it will
Jn 20:25 and put my finger where the **n** were,

## NAIOTH

1Sa 19:18 Samuel went to **N** and stayed there.

## NAIVE*

Ro 16:18 they deceive the minds of **n** people.

## NAKED [NAKEDNESS]

Ge 2:25 The man and his wife were both **n**,
Job 1:21 "**N** I came from my mother's womb,
          and **n** I will depart.
Ecc 5:15 Everyone comes **n** from their
Isa 58: 7 when you see the **n**, to clothe them,
Eze 16: 7 yet you were stark **n**.
    23:29 They will leave you stark **n**,
Mk 14:52 he fled **n**, leaving his garment
2Co 5: 3 are clothed, we will not be found **n**.
    11:27 I have been cold and **n**.
Rev 3:17 wretched, pitiful, poor, blind and **n**.

## NAKEDNESS [NAKED]

Ge 9:22 saw his father's **n** and told his two
Ex 20:26 steps, lest your **n** be exposed on it.'
Eze 16: 8 over you and covered your **n**.
Ro 8:35 persecution or famine or **n** or danger
Rev 3:18 so you can cover your shameful **n**;

## NAME [NAME'S, NAMED, NAMES]

Ge 2:19 man to see what he would **n** them;
    4:26 to call on the **n** of the LORD.
    11: 4 that we may make a **n** for ourselves
    12: 2 I will make your **n** great, and you
    12: 8 and called on the **n** of the LORD.
    13: 4 called on the **n** of the LORD.
    16:13 She gave this **n** to the LORD who
    17: 5 your **n** will be Abraham, for I have
    17:15 call her Sarai; her **n** will be Sarah.
    21:33 he called on the **n** of the LORD,
    26:25 and called on the **n** of the LORD.
    32:28 "Your **n** will no longer be Jacob,
    32:29 Jacob said, "Please tell me your **n**."
Ex 3:15 "This is my **n** forever, the **n** you
    6: 3 by my **n** the LORD I did not make
    17:14 completely blot out the **n** of Amalek
    20: 7 "You shall not misuse the **n**
    33:17 with you and I know you by **n**."
    33:19 you, and I will proclaim my **n**,
    34: 5 with him and proclaimed his **n**,
    34:14 for the LORD, whose **n** is Jealous,

Lev 19:12 " 'Do not swear falsely by my **n** and so
          profane the **n** of your God.
    24:11 Israelite woman blasphemed the **N**
Nu 1: 2 listing every man by **n**, one by one.
    17: 2 Write the **n** of each man on his staff.
Dt 5:11 "You shall not misuse the **n**
    10: 8 and to pronounce blessings in his **n**,
    12:11 will choose as a dwelling for his **N**—
    18: 5 minister in the LORD's **n** always.
    25: 6 so that his **n** will not be blotted
    28:58 this glorious and awesome **n**—
Jos 7: 9 will you do for your own great **n**?"
Jdg 13:17 "What is your **n**, so that we may
Ru 4: 5 order to maintain the **n** of the dead
1Sa 12:22 of his great **n** the LORD will not
    17:45 in the **n** of the LORD Almighty,
    25:25 He is just like his **n**—his **n** means
2Sa 6: 2 which is called by the **N**, the **n**
    7: 9 Now I will make your **n** great,
1Ki 5: 5 will build the temple for my **N**.'
    8:29 you said, 'My **N** shall be there,'
    18:24 I will call on the **n** of the LORD.
1Ch 17: 8 I will make your **n** like the names
2Ch 7:14 people, who are called by my **n**,
Ezr 6:12 who has caused his **N** to dwell there,
Ne 9:10 You made a **n** for yourself,
Ps 5:11 those who love your **n** may rejoice
    8: 1 how majestic is your **n** in all
    9: 5 you have blotted out their **n** for ever
    9:10 Those who know your **n** trust
    20: 7 in the **n** of the LORD our God.
    29: 2 to the LORD the glory due his **n**;
    34: 3 let us exalt his **n** together.
    44:20 If we had forgotten the **n** of our God
    54: 1 Save me, O God, by your **n**;
    66: 2 Sing the glory of his **n**;
    68: 4 his **n** is the LORD.
    74:10 Will the foe revile your **n** forever?
    74:21 the poor and needy praise your **n**.
    79: 9 our Savior, for the glory of your **n**;
    96: 8 to the LORD the glory due his **n**;
    103: 1 my inmost being, praise his holy **n**.
    113: 1 praise the **n** of the LORD.
    115: 1 not to us but to your **n** be the glory,
    124: 8 Our help is in the **n** of the LORD,
    138: 2 will praise your **n** for your unfailing
    145: 1 I will praise your **n** for ever
    147: 4 the stars and calls them each by **n**.
    149: 3 Let them praise his **n** with dancing
Pr 3: 4 and a good **n** in the sight of God
    10: 7 but the **n** of the wicked will rot.
    18:10 The **n** of the LORD is a fortified
    22: 1 A good **n** is more desirable than
    30: 4 What is his **n**, and what is the **n**
Ecc 7: 1 A good **n** is better than fine
SS 1: 3 your **n** is like perfume poured out.
Isa 12: 4 and proclaim that his **n** is exalted.
    26: 8 your **n** and renown are the desire
    40:26 by one, and calls them each by **n**.
    42: 8 "I am the LORD; that is my **n**!
    50:10 trust in the **n** of the LORD and rely
    56: 5 a memorial and a **n** better than sons
    57:15 who lives forever, whose **n** is holy:
    63:14 to make for yourself a glorious **n**.
Jer 7:11 which bears my **N**, become a den
    10: 6 and your **n** is mighty in power.
    14: 7 LORD, for the sake of your **n**.

| | | |
|---|---|---|
| Jer | 15:16 | for I bear your **n**, LORD God |
| | 27:15 | 'They are prophesying lies in my **n**. |
| Eze | 20: 9 | But for the sake of my **n**, I brought |
| | 20:14 | of my **n** I did what would keep it |
| | 20:22 | of my **n** I did what would keep it |
| | 36:22 | but for the sake of my holy **n**, |
| | 48:35 | the **n** of the city from that time |
| Da | 2:20 | "Praise be to the **n** of God for ever |
| | 12: 1 | everyone whose **n** is found written |
| Hos | 12: 5 | God Almighty, the LORD is his **n**! |
| Joel | 2:32 | the **n** of the LORD will be saved; |
| Am | 9:12 | and all the nations that bear my **n**," |
| Mic | 5: 4 | of the **n** of the LORD his God. |
| | 6: 9 | and to fear your **n** is wisdom— |
| Zep | 3: 9 | may call on the **n** of the LORD |
| Zec | 6:12 | is the man whose **n** is the Branch, |
| | 13: 9 | They will call on my **n** and I will |
| | 14: 9 | one LORD, and his **n** the only **n**. |
| Mal | 1: 6 | who show contempt for my **n**. |
| | 4: 2 | But for you who revere my **n**, |
| Mt | 1:21 | and you are to give him the **n** Jesus, |
| | 6: 9 | in heaven, hallowed be your **n**, |
| | 7:22 | did we not prophesy in your **n** |
| | 12:21 | In his **n** the nations will put their |
| | 18:20 | two or three come together in my **n**, |
| | 24: 5 | For many will come in my **n**, |
| | 28:19 | baptizing them in the **n** of the Father |
| Mk | 9:41 | water in my **n** because you belong |
| | 11: 9 | who comes in the **n** of the Lord!" |
| Lk | 11: 2 | hallowed be your **n**, your kingdom |
| | 19:38 | who comes in the **n** of the Lord!" |
| Jn | 1:12 | to those who believed in his **n**, |
| | 5:43 | I have come in my Father's **n**, |
| | 10: 3 | He calls his own sheep by **n** |
| | 12:28 | Father, glorify your **n**!" |
| | 14:13 | I will do whatever you ask in my **n**, |
| | 15:16 | in my **n** the Father will give you. |
| | 16:23 | give you whatever you ask in my **n**. |
| | 16:24 | not asked for anything in my **n**. |
| | 17:11 | them by the power of your **n**, the **n** |
| | 20:31 | believing you may have life in his **n**. |
| Ac | 2:21 | on the **n** of the Lord will be saved.' |
| | 3:16 | By faith in the **n** of Jesus, this man |
| | 4:12 | is no other **n** given under heaven |
| | 4:17 | no longer to anyone in this **n**." |
| | 5:40 | them not to speak in the **n** of Jesus, |
| | 15:17 | all the Gentiles who bear my **n**, |
| Ro | 10:13 | on the **n** of the Lord will be saved." |
| 1Co | 6:11 | in the **n** of the Lord Jesus Christ |
| Eph | 1:21 | every **n** that can be invoked, |
| | 3:15 | in heaven and on earth derives its **n**. |
| Php | 2: 9 | gave him the **n** that is above every **n**, |
| | 2:10 | at the **n** of Jesus every knee should |
| Col | 3:17 | do it all in the **n** of the Lord Jesus, |
| 2Ti | 2:19 | "Everyone who confesses the **n** |
| Heb | 1: 4 | the angels as the **n** he has inherited |
| | 13:15 | of lips that openly profess his **n**. |
| Jas | 5:14 | them with oil in the **n** of the Lord. |
| 1Pe | 4:16 | but praise God that you bear that **n**. |
| 1Jn | 2:12 | been forgiven on account of his **n**. |
| | 3:23 | to believe in the **n** of his Son, |
| | 5:13 | you who believe in the **n** of the Son |
| Rev | 2: 3 | have endured hardships for my **n**, |
| | 2:13 | Yet you remain true to my **n**. |
| | 2:17 | stone with a new **n** written on it, |
| | 3: 8 | my word and have not denied my **n**. |
| | 3:12 | will write on them the **n** of my God |

| | | |
|---|---|---|
| Rev | 11:18 | and your people who revere your **n**, |
| | 13: 1 | and on each head a blasphemous **n**. |
| | 13:17 | which is the **n** of the beast or the |
| | | number of its **n**. |
| | 14: 1 | **n** and his Father's **n** written on their |
| | 16: 9 | heat and they cursed the **n** of God, |
| | 19:12 | He has a **n** written on him that no |
| | 19:13 | blood, and his **n** is the Word of God. |
| | 19:16 | on his thigh he has this **n** written: |
| | 22: 4 | and his **n** will be on their foreheads. |

## HOLY NAME See HOLY

## NAME OF JESUS
Ac 2:38; 3:6, 16; 4:10, 18;
5:40; 8:12; 9:27; 10:48; 16:18; 19:13; 26:9; Php
2:10

## NAME OF THE LORD
Mt 21:9; 23:39; Mk
11:9; Lk 13:35; 19:38; Jn 12:13; Ac 2:21; 8:16;
9:28; 19:5, 13, 17; 21:13; Ro 10:13; 1Co 6:11;
Col 3:17; 2Th 3:6; 2Ti 2:19; Jas 5:10, 14

## NAME OF THE †LORD
Ge 4:26; 12:8; 13:4;
21:33; 26:25; Ex 20:7; Lev 24:16; Dt 5:11; 18:7,
22; 21:5; 28:10; 32:3; 1Sa 17:45; 20:42; 2Sa 6:2,
18; 1Ki 3:2; 5:3, 5; 8:17, 20; 18:24, 32; 22:16;
2Ki 2:24; 5:11; 1Ch 16:2; 21:19; 22:7, 19; 2Ch
2:1, 4; 6:7, 10; 18:15; 33:18; Job 1:21; Ps 7:17;
20:7; 102:15, 21; 113:1, 2, 3; 116:4, 13, 17;
118:10, 11, 12, 26; 122:4; 124:8; 129:8; 135:1;
148:5, 13; Pr 18:10; Isa 18:7; 24:15; 30:27; 48:1;
50:10; 56:6; 59:19; Jer 3:17; 11:21; 26:16, 20;
44:16; Joel 2:26, 32; Am 6:10; Mic 4:5; 5:4; Zep
3:9, 12

## NAME'S [NAME]
| | | |
|---|---|---|
| Ps | 23: 3 | along the right paths for his **n** sake. |
| | 79: 9 | and forgive our sins for your **n** sake. |
| | 106: 8 | Yet he saved them for his **n** sake, |
| Eze | 20:44 | when I deal with you for my **n** sake |

## NAMED [NAME]
| | | |
|---|---|---|
| Ge | 3:20 | Adam **n** his wife Eve, because she |
| | 5:29 | He **n** him Noah and said, "He will |
| | 27:36 | said, "Isn't he rightly **n** Jacob? |
| Ex | 2:10 | She **n** him Moses, saying, "I drew |
| 1Sa | 4:21 | She **n** the boy Ichabod, saying, |
| | 7:12 | He **n** it Ebenezer, saying, "Thus far |
| Lk | 2:21 | he was **n** Jesus, the name the angel |

## NAMES [NAME]
| | | |
|---|---|---|
| Ge | 2:20 | So the man gave **n** to all |
| Ex | 28: 9 | engrave on them the **n** of the sons |
| Dt | 7:24 | wipe out their **n** from under heaven. |
| 2Sa | 7: 9 | like the **n** of the greatest men |
| Hos | 2:17 | I will remove the **n** of the Baals |
| Mt | 10: 2 | These are the **n** of the twelve |
| Lk | 10:20 | but rejoice that your **n** are written |
| Php | 4: 3 | whose **n** are in the book of life. |
| Heb | 12:23 | whose **n** are written in heaven. |
| Rev | 3: 5 | never blot out their **n** from the book |
| | 3: 5 | will acknowledge their **n** before my |
| | 17: 3 | was covered with blasphemous **n** |
| | 17: 8 | of the earth whose **n** have not been |
| | 20:15 | All whose **n** were not found written |
| | 21:12 | the gates were written the **n** |
| | 21:14 | on them were the **n** of the twelve |

Rev 21:27 only those whose **n** are written

## NAOMI

Wife of Elimelech, mother-in-law of Ruth (Ru 1:2, 4). Left Bethlehem for Moab during famine (Ru 1:1). Returned a widow, with Ruth (Ru 1:6–22). Advised Ruth to seek marriage with Boaz (Ru 2:17—3:4). Cared for Ruth's son Obed (Ru 4:13–17).

## NAPHTALI [NAPHTALITES]

Son of Jacob by Bilhah (Ge 30:8; 35:25; 1Ch 2:2). Tribe of blessed (Ge 49:21; Dt 33:23), numbered (Nu 1:43; 26:50), allotted land (Jos 19:32–39; Eze 48:3), failed to fully possess (Jdg 1:33), supported Deborah (Jdg 4:10; 5:18), David (1Ch 12:34), 12,000 from (Rev 7:6).

## NAPHTALITES* [NAPHTALI]

Jdg 1:33 the **N** too lived among the Canaanite

## NARD

Jn 12: 3 Mary took about a pint of pure **n**,

## NARROW

Nu 22:24 in a **n** path through the vineyards,
Mt 7:13 "Enter through the **n** gate,
Lk 13:24 effort to enter through the **n** door,

## NATHAN

Prophet and chronicler of Israel's history (1Ch 29:29; 2Ch 9:29). Announced the Davidic covenant (2Sa 7; 1Ch 17). Denounced David's sin with Bathsheba (2Sa 12). Supported Solomon (1Ki 1).

## NATHANAEL*

Apostle (Jn 1:45–49; 21:2). Probably also called Bartholomew (Mt 10:3).

## NATION [NATIONAL, NATIONALITY, NATIONS]

Ge 12: 2 "I will make you into a great **n**,
    15:14 But I will punish the **n** they serve as
    35:11 A **n** and a community of nations
Ex 19: 6 a kingdom of priests and a holy **n**.'
    32:10 I will make you into a great **n**."
Nu 14:12 I will make you into a **n** greater
Dt 4: 7 What other **n** is so great as to have
Jos 4: 1 the whole **n** had finished crossing
    5: 8 the whole **n** had been circumcised,
2Sa 7:23 the one **n** on earth that God went
2Ki 18:33 god of any **n** ever delivered his land
1Ch 16:20 they wandered from **n** to **n**,
Ps 33:12 Blessed is the **n** whose God is
    147:20 He has done this for no other **n**;
Pr 11:14 For lack of guidance a **n** falls,
    14:34 Righteousness exalts a **n**, but sin
Isa 2: 4 **N** will not take up sword against **n**,
    9: 3 You have enlarged the **n**
    26: 2 gates that the righteous **n** may enter,
    60:12 For the **n** or kingdom that will not
    65: 1 To a **n** that did not call on my name,
    66: 8 a **n** be brought forth in a moment?
Jer 2:11 Has a **n** ever changed its gods?
    18: 8 if that **n** I warned repents of its evil,
Eze 37:22 I will make them one **n** in the land,

Mic 4: 3 **N** will not take up sword against **n**,
Mal 3: 9 your whole **n**—because you are
Mt 24: 7 **N** will rise against **n**, and kingdom
Jn 11:50 than that the whole **n** perish."
1Pe 2: 9 a holy **n**, God's special possession,
Rev 5: 9 and language and people and **n**.
    7: 9 could count, from every **n**, tribe,
    14: 6 to every **n**, tribe,

## NATIONAL* [NATION]

2Ki 17:29 each **n** group made its own gods

## NATIONALITY [NATION]

Est 2:10 Esther had not revealed her **n**

## NATIONS [NATION]

Ge 17: 4 You will be the father of many **n**.
    18:18 and all **n** on earth will be blessed
    22:18 through your offspring all **n** on earth
Ex 19: 5 out of all **n** you will be my treasured
    34:24 I will drive out **n** before you
Lev 18:28 out the **n** that were before you.
    20:26 you apart from the **n** to be my own.
Dt 7: 1 seven **n** larger and stronger than
    15: 6 You will rule over many **n** but none
    32:43 Rejoice, you **n**, with his people,
Jos 23: 7 with these **n** that remain among you;
Jdg 3: 1 These are the **n** the LORD left
1Sa 8:20 Then we will be like all the other **n**,
1Ki 4:34 From all **n** people came to listen
2Ki 17:15 They imitated the **n** around them
2Ch 20: 6 rule over all the kingdoms of the **n**.
Ne 1: 8 I will scatter you among the **n**,
Ps 2: 1 Why do the **n** conspire
    2: 8 I will make the **n** your inheritance,
    9: 5 You have rebuked the **n**
    22:28 the LORD and he rules over the **n**.
    33:10 The LORD foils the plans of the **n**;
    46:10 I will be exalted among the **n**, I will
    47: 8 God reigns over the **n**; God is seated
    66: 7 by his power, his eyes watch the **n**—
    67: 2 earth, your salvation among all **n**.
    68:30 Scatter the **n** who delight in war.
    72:17 all **n** will be blessed through him,
    96: 5 For all the gods of the **n** are idols,
    99: 2 he is exalted over all the **n**.
    106:35 they mingled with the **n** and adopted
    110: 6 He will judge the **n**,
    113: 4 LORD is exalted over all the **n**,
Isa 2: 2 the hills, and all **n** will stream to it.
    5:26 lifts up a banner for the distant **n**,
    11:10 the **n** will rally to him, and his
    12: 4 known among the **n** what he has
    40:15 Surely the **n** are like a drop
    42: 1 and he will bring justice to the **n**.
    49:22 I will beckon to the **n**,
    51: 4 justice will become a light to the **n**.
    52:15 so he will sprinkle many **n**,
    56: 7 called a house of prayer for all **n**."
    60: 3 **N** will come to your light, and kings
    66:18 and gather the people of all **n**
Jer 1: 5 you as a prophet to the **n**."
    3:17 and all **n** will gather in Jerusalem
    31:10 the word of the LORD, you **n**;
    33: 9 honor before all **n** on earth that hear
    46:28 completely destroy all the **n** among

La 1: 1 who once was great among the **n**!
Eze 22: 4 make you an object of scorn to the **n**
34:13 I will bring them out from the **n**
36:23 Then the **n** will know that I am
37:22 they will never again be two **n** or be
39:21 will display my glory among the **n**,
Hos 7: 8 "Ephraim mixes with the **n**;
Joel 2:17 of scorn, a byword among the **n**.
3: 2 I will gather all **n** and bring them
Am 9:12 and all the **n** that bear my name,"
Ob 1:15 day of the LORD is near for all **n**.
Zep 3· 8 I have decided to assemble the **n**,
Hag 2: 7 what is desired by all **n** will come,
Zec 8:13 have been a curse among the **n**, so I
8:23 **n** will take firm hold of one Jew
9:10 He will proclaim peace to the **n**.
14: 2 I will gather all the **n** to Jerusalem
Mal 1:11 My name will be great among the **n**,
3:12 all the **n** will call you blessed,
Mt 12:18 and he will proclaim justice to the **n**.
24: 9 you will be hated by all **n** because
24:14 whole world as a testimony to all **n**,
25:32 All the **n** will be gathered before
28:19 go and make disciples of all **n**,
Mk 11:17 called a house of prayer for all **n**'?
Ac 4:25 " 'Why do the **n** rage
17:26 From one man he made all the **n**,
Ro 4:18 and so became the father of many **n**,
15:12 who will arise to rule over the **n**;
Gal 3: 8 "All **n** will be blessed through
1Ti 3:16 was preached among the **n**,
Rev 2:26 I will give authority over the **n**—
12: 5 who "will rule all the **n** with an iron
15: 3 King of the **n**.
15: 4 All **n** will come and worship before
18:23 magic spell all the **n** were led astray.
19:15 with which to strike down the **n**.
20: 8 to deceive the **n** in the four corners
21:24 The **n** will walk by its light,
22: 2 the tree are for the healing of the **n**.

## NATIVE [NATIVE-BORN]
Jn 8:44 he speaks his **n** language, for he is
Ac 2: 8 of us hears them in our **n** language?

## NATIVE-BORN [BEAR, NATIVE]
Ex 12:49 The same law applies both to the **n**

## NATURAL [NATURE]
Nu 16:29 If these men die a **n** death and suffer
Jn 1:13 children born not of **n** descent,
Ro 1:26 their women exchanged **n** sexual
11:21 if God did not spare the **n** branches,
1Co 15:44 it is sown a **n** body, it is raised

## NATURE [NATURAL]
Ro 1:20 his eternal power and divine **n**—
7:18 dwell in me, that is, in my sinful **n**.
7:25 in my sinful **n** a slave to the law
8: 4 do not live according to the sinful **n**
8: 5 minds set on what that **n** desires;
8: 8 by the sinful **n** cannot please God.
13:14 to gratify the desires of the sinful **n**.
Gal 5:13 freedom to indulge the sinful **n**;
5:19 The acts of the sinful **n** are obvious:
5:24 Jesus have crucified the sinful **n**

Eph 2: 3 we were by **n** deserving of wrath.
Php 2: 6 Who, being in very **n** God, did not
Col 2:11 Your sinful **n** was put off when you
3: 5 whatever belongs to your earthly **n**:
2Pe 1: 4 you may participate in the divine **n**,

## SINFUL NATURE See SINFUL

## NAZARENE* [NAZARETH]
Mt 2:23 "He will be called a **N**."
Mk 14:67 "You also were with that **N**,
16: 6 "You are looking for Jesus the **N**,
Ac 24: 5 He is a ringleader of the **N** sect

## NAZARETH [NAZARENE]
Mt 2:23 went and lived in a town called **N**.
Mk 1:24 do you want with us, Jesus of **N**?
Lk 1:26 God sent the angel Gabriel to **N**,
4:16 He went to **N**, where he had been
Jn 1:46 "**N**! Can anything good come
19:19 It read: JESUS OF **N**, THE KING OF
Ac 2:22 Jesus of **N** was a man accredited
10:38 how God anointed Jesus of **N**

## JESUS OF NAZARETH See JESUS

## NAZIRITE [NAZIRITES]
Nu 6: 2 of dedication to the LORD as a **N**,
Jdg 13: 5 a razor because the boy is to be a **N**,

## NAZIRITES [NAZIRITE]
Am 2:12 you made the **N** drink wine

## NEAR [NEARBY, NEARER, NEARSIGHTED]
Dt 4: 7 have their gods **n** them the way
4: 7 our God is **n** us whenever we pray
30:14 No, the word is very **n** you; it is
Ps 69:18 Come **n** and rescue me;
73:28 as for me, it is good to be **n** God.
85: 9 his salvation is to those who fear
145:18 The LORD is **n** to all who call
Isa 11: 8 Infants will play **n** the hole
55: 6 call on him while he is **n**.
Eze 7: 7 The day is **n**! There is panic,
Joel 1:15 For the day of the LORD is **n**;
Zep 1: 7 for the day of the LORD is **n**.
Mk 1:15 "The kingdom of God has come **n**.
Lk 10: 9 of God has come **n** to you.'
21:28 your redemption is drawing **n**."
Ro 10: 8 "The word is **n** you; it is in your
1Co 8: 8 food does not bring us **n** to God;
Php 4: 5 be evident to all. The Lord is **n**.
Heb 10:22 let us draw **n** to God with a sincere
Jas 4: 8 Come **n** to God and he will come **n**
1Pe 4: 7 The end of all things is **n**.
Rev 1: 3 written in it, because the time is **n**.
22:10 of this scroll, because the time is **n**.

## NEARBY [NEAR]
Jer 23:23 "Am I only a God **n**,"

## NEARER* [NEAR]
Ro 13:11 because our salvation is **n** now than

## NEARSIGHTED* [NEAR, SEE]

2Pe  1: 9  not have them, you are **n** and blind,

## NEBO

Dt  34: 1  Moses climbed Mount **N**
Isa  46: 1  Bel bows down, **N** stoops low;

## NEBUCHADNEZZAR

Babylonian king. Subdued and exiled Judah (2Ki 24–25; 2Ch 36; Jer 39). Dreams interpreted by Daniel (Da 2; 4). Worshiped God (Da 3:28–29; 4:34–37).

## NEBUZARADAN

2Ki  25: 8  **N** commander of the imperial guard,
Jer  52:12  **N** commander of the imperial guard,

## NECESSARY*

Ac   1:21  Therefore it is **n** to choose one
Ro  13: 5  it is **n** to submit to the authorities,
2Co  9: 5  So I thought it **n** to urge the brothers
Php  1:24  it is more **n** for you that I remain
     2:25  I think it is **n** to send back to you
Heb  8: 3  and so it was **n** for this one
     9:16  it is **n** to prove the death of the one
     9:23  It was **n**, then, for the copies
    10:18  sacrifice for sin is no longer **n**.

## NECHO

Pharaoh who killed Josiah (2Ki 23:29–30; 2Ch 35:20–22), deposed Jehoahaz (2Ki 23:33–35; 2Ch 36:3–4).

## NECK [NECKS, STIFF-NECKED]

Ge  27:16  part of his **n** with the goatskins.
Ps  75: 5  not speak with outstretched **n**.' ”
Pr   1: 9  head and a chain to adorn your **n**.
     3:22  you, an ornament to grace your **n**.
     6:21  fasten them around your **n**.
SS   7: 4  Your **n** is like an ivory tower.
Jer  28:10  Hananiah took the yoke off the **n**
Hos 10:11  so I will put a yoke on her fair **n**.
Mt  18: 6  millstone were hung around their **n**

## NECKS [NECK]

Isa  3:16  walking along with outstretched **n**,

## NEED [NEEDED, NEEDS, NEEDY]

Ex  14:14  you **n** only to be still.”
    16:16  gather as much as they **n**.
Dt  15: 8  lend them whatever they **n**.
1Ki  8:59  Israel according to each day's **n**,
Job 34:23  God has no **n** to examine people
Ps  50: 9  I have no **n** of a bull from your stall
    79: 8  meet us, for we are in desperate **n**.
   142: 6  to my cry, for I am in desperate **n**;
Mt   3:14  saying, “I **n** to be baptized by you,
     6: 8  knows what you **n** before you ask
Mk   2:17  is not the healthy who **n** a doctor,
Lk  12:30  your Father knows that you **n** them.
    15:14  country, and he began to be in **n**.
Jn   2:25  He did not **n** human testimony
    13:10  had a bath **n** only to wash their feet;
Ac   2:45  to give to anyone who had **n**.
     4:35  distributed to anyone who had **n**.

Ro  12:13  with the Lord's people who are in **n**.
1Co 12:21  say to the hand, “I don't **n** you!”
2Co  8:14  their plenty will supply what you **n**.
Eph  4:28  something to share with those in **n**.
1Th  5: 1  dates we do not **n** to write to you,
1Ti  5: 3  to those widows who are really in **n**.
2Ti  2:15  a worker who does not **n** to be
Heb  4:16  grace to help us in our time of **n**.
     7:26  a high priest truly meets our **n**—
2Pe  1: 3  power has given us everything we **n**
1Jn  2:27  you do not **n** anyone to teach you.
     3:17  sister in **n** but has no pity on them,
Rev 21:23  The city does not **n** the sun
    22: 5  They will not **n** the light of a lamp

## NEEDED [NEED]

Ex  16:18  had gathered just as much as they **n**.
Mt  25:36  I **n** clothes and you clothed me,
Ac  17:25  human hands, as if he **n** anything.

## NEEDLE

Lk  18:25  to go through the eye of a **n** than

## NEEDS [NEED]

Pr  12:10  care for the **n** of their animals,
Isa 58:11  he will satisfy your **n**
Mk  15:41  followed him and cared for his **n**.
Eph  4:29  others up according to their **n**, that it
Php  2:25  whom you sent to take care of my **n**.
     4:19  God will meet all your **n** according
Tit  3:14  in order to provide for urgent **n**
Jas  2:16  does nothing about their physical **n**,

## NEEDY [NEED]

Ex  22:25  of my people among you who is **n**,
Dt  15:11  who are poor and **n** in your land.
1Sa  2: 8  and lifts the **n** from the ash heap;
Job 29:16  I was a father to the **n**; I took
Ps   9:18  But God will never forget the **n**;
    35:10  and **n** from those who rob them.”
    69:33  The LORD hears the **n** and does
    70: 5  But as for me, I am poor and **n**;
    72:12  he will deliver the **n** who cry out,
    74:21  the poor and **n** praise your name.
   113: 7  and lifts the **n** from the ash heap;
   140:12  poor and upholds the cause of the **n**.
Pr  14:21  are those who are kind to the **n**.
    14:31  is kind to the **n** honors God.
    22:22  poor and do not crush the **n** in court,
    31: 9  defend the rights of the poor and **n**.
    31:20  poor and extends her hands to the **n**.
Isa 11: 4  righteousness he will judge the **n**,
Am   8: 4  you who trample the **n** and do away
Mt   6: 2  “So when you give to the **n**, do not

## NEGEV

Ge  13: 1  went up from Egypt to the **N**,
    24:62  Roi, for he was living in the **N**.
Jos 11:16  all the **N**, the whole region
Ps 126: 4  LORD, like streams in the **N**.

## NEGLECT* [NEGLECTED]

Dt  12:19  to **n** the Levites as long as you live
    14:27  do not **n** the Levites living in your
Ezr  4:22  Be careful not to **n** this matter.

Ne  10:39  "We will not **n** the house of our
Est   6:10  Do not **n** anything you have
Ps 119:16  I will not **n** your word.
SS    1: 6  my own vineyard I had to **n**.
Lk  11:42  but you **n** justice and the love
Ac    6: 2  for us to **n** the ministry of the word
1Ti   4:14  Do not **n** your gift, which was given

## NEGLECTED* [NEGLECT]
Ne  13:11  "Why is the house of God **n**?"
Mt  23:23  But you have **n** the more important

## NEHEMIAH
Cupbearer of Artaxerxes (Ne 2:1); governor of Israel (Ne 8:9). Returned to Jerusalem to rebuild walls (Ne 2–6). With Ezra, reestablished worship (Ne 8). Prayer confessing nation's sin (Ne 9). Dedicated wall (Ne 12).

## NEHUSHTAN*
2Ki 18: 4  incense to it. (It was called **N**.)

## NEIGHBOR  [NEIGHBOR'S, NEIGHBORS]
Ex  20:16  give false testimony against your **n**.
      20:17  or anything that belongs to your **n**."
Lev 19:17  Rebuke your **n** frankly so you will
      19:18  people, but love your **n** as yourself
Dt    4:42  killed a **n** without malice
      5:20  give false testimony against your **n**.
      19:11  assaults and kills a **n**, and then flees
2Ch  6:22  "When anyone wrongs their **n**
Pr    3:29  Do not plot harm against your **n**,
      14:21  It is a sin to despise one's **n**,
      24:28  against your **n** without cause—
      25:18  gives false testimony against a **n**.
      27:10  better a **n** nearby than a relative far
      27:14  If anyone loudly blesses a **n** early
Isa  19: 2  fight against brother, **n** against **n**,
Mt    5:43  'Love your **n** and hate your enemy.'
      19:19  and 'love your **n** as yourself.' "
Mk  12:31  'Love your **n** as yourself.'
Lk  10:27  and, 'Love your **n** as yourself.' "
      10:29  asked Jesus, "And who is my **n**?"
Ro  13: 9  "Love your **n** as yourself."
      13:10  Love does no harm to its **n**.
Gal   5:14  "Love your **n** as yourself."
Eph   4:25  and speak truthfully to your **n**,
Jas   2: 8  "Love your **n** as yourself," you are

## LOVE YOUR NEIGHBOR  See LOVE

## NEIGHBOR'S [NEIGHBOR]
Ex  20:17  "You shall not covet your **n** house.
      20:17  You shall not covet your **n** wife,
      22:26  If you take your **n** cloak as a pledge,
Lev 19:16  anything that endangers your **n** life.
Dt    5:21  "You shall not covet your **n** wife.
      5:21  not set your desire on your **n** house
      19:14  not move your **n** boundary stone set
      27:17  moves their **n** boundary stone."
Pr  25:17  Seldom set foot in your **n** house—

## NEIGHBORS  [NEIGHBOR]
Ex  11: 2  alike are to ask their **n** for articles

Lev 19:13  " 'Do not defraud your **n** or rob
1Sa 15:28  and has given it to one of your **n**—
2Ki  4: 3  and ask all your **n** for empty jars.
Ezr   1: 6  All their **n** assisted them
      6:21  practices of their Gentile **n** in order
Ps  15: 3  who do their **n** no wrong, who cast
      79: 4  We are objects of contempt to our **n**,
      79:12  our **n** seven times the contempt they
Pr  11:12  who have no sense deride their **n**,
      16:29  The violent entice their **n** and lead
      29: 5  who flatter their **n** are spreading
Jer  31:34  No longer will they teach their **n**,
Ro  15: 2  We should all please our **n** for their
Heb  8:11  No longer will they teach their **n**,

## NEPHEW*
Ge  12: 5  He took his wife Sarai, his **n** Lot,
      14:12  carried off Abram's **n** Lot and his

## NEST  [NESTED, NESTING, NESTS]
Dt  22: 6  across a bird's **n** beside the road,
Isa  11: 8  put their hands into the viper's **n**.
Ob    1: 4  and make your **n** among the stars,
Hab   2: 9  setting his **n** on high to escape

## NESTED* [NEST]
Eze 31: 6  the birds of the sky **n** in its boughs,

## NESTING* [NEST]
Da    4:21  having **n** places in its branches

## NESTS  [NEST]
Mt    8:20  have holes and birds have **n**,

## NET  [NETS]
Ps  35: 8  may the **n** they hid entangle them,
Pr    1:17  spread a **n** where every bird can see
La    1:13  He spread a **n** for my feet
Hab   1:15  he catches them in his **n**, he gathers
Mt  13:47  heaven is like a **n** that was let down
Mk    1:16  his brother Andrew casting a **n**
Jn  21: 6  "Throw your **n** on the right side

## NETS  [NET]
Ps 141:10  Let the wicked fall into their own **n**,
Mt    4:20  At once they left their **n**
Lk    5: 4  and let down the **n** for a catch."

## NEVER
Ge    8:21  And **n** again will I destroy all living
Dt    9: 7  **n** forget how you aroused the anger
      31: 6  he will **n** leave you nor forsake
Jdg   1:28  but **n** drove them out completely.
2Sa   7:15  my love will **n** be taken away
1Ki   2: 4  you will **n** fail to have a successor
      8:25  'You shall **n** fail to have a successor
      9: 5  'You shall **n** fail to have a successor
2Ch 18: 7  because he **n** prophesies anything
Ps    9:18  hope of the afflicted will **n** perish.
      14: 4  they **n** call on the LORD.
      30: 6  secure, I said, "I will **n** be shaken."
      89:28  my covenant with him will **n** fail.
      95:11  'They shall **n** enter my rest.' "
Pr    3: 3  love and faithfulness **n** leave you;
      13: 4  A sluggard's appetite is **n** filled,

Pr 30:15 satisfied, four that **n** say, 'Enough!':
Ecc 1: 8 The eye **n** has enough of seeing,
 5:10 who love wealth are **n** satisfied
Isa 6: 9 ever hearing, but **n** understanding;
 28:16 who relies on it will **n** be stricken
 51: 6 my righteousness will **n** fail.
Jer 33:17 'David will **n** fail to have a man
La 3:22 for his compassions **n** fail.
Da 2:44 a kingdom that will **n** be destroyed,
 6:26 destroyed, his dominion will **n** end.
Hos 14: 3 We will **n** again say 'Our gods'
Mk 3:29 the Holy Spirit will **n** be forgiven,
 4:12 be ever seeing but **n** perceiving,
Lk 21:33 but my words will **n** pass away.
Jn 4:14 the water I give them will **n** thirst.
 6:35 comes to me will **n** go hungry,
 8:51 obeys my word will **n** see death."
 10:28 eternal life, and they shall **n** perish;
 11:26 lives by believing in me will **n** die.
Ro 9:33 who believes in him will **n** be put
1Co 13: 8 Love **n** fails. But where there are
Gal 6:14 May I **n** boast except in the cross
2Th 3:13 sisters, **n** tire of doing what is good.
Heb 3:11 'They shall **n** enter my rest.' "
 4: 3 'They shall **n** enter my rest.' "
 13: 5 God has said, "**N** will I leave you;
1Pe 1: 4 into an inheritance that can **n** perish,
 2: 6 one who trusts in him will **n** be put
 5: 4 of glory that will **n** fade away.
2Pe 1:10 do these things, you will **n** stumble,
Rev 7:16 '**N** again will they hunger; **n** again

## NEVER-FAILING*
Am 5:24 river, righteousness like a **n** stream!

## NEW
Ex 1: 8 Then a **n** king, to whom Joseph
Jdg 5: 8 God chose **n** leaders when war came
Ezr 9: 9 He has granted us **n** life to rebuild
Ne 13: 5 **n** wine and olive oil prescribed
Ps 33: 3 Sing to him a **n** song;
 40: 3 He put a **n** song in my mouth,
 98: 1 Sing to the LORD a **n** song, for he
Pr 3:10 vats will brim over with **n** wine.
Ecc 1: 9 there is nothing **n** under the sun.
Isa 42: 9 taken place, and **n** things I declare;
 42:10 Sing to the LORD a **n** song,
 43:19 See, I am doing a **n** thing!
 62: 2 you will be called by a **n** name
 65:17 I will create **n** heavens and a **n**
 66:22 "As the **n** heavens and the **n** earth
Jer 31:31 I will make a **n** covenant
La 3:23 They are **n** every morning;
Eze 11:19 heart and put a **n** spirit in them;
 18:31 and get a **n** heart and a **n** spirit.
 36:26 I will give you a **n** heart and put a **n**
Joel 3:18 day the mountains will drip **n** wine,
Am 9:13 **N** wine will drip from the mountains
Zep 3: 5 and every **n** day he does not fail,
Mt 9:17 they pour **n** wine into **n** wineskins,
 13:52 his storeroom **n** treasures as well as
Mk 1:27 A **n** teaching—and with authority!
Lk 5:39 old wine, wants the **n**, for you say,
 22:20 "This cup is the **n** covenant in my
Jn 13:34 "A **n** command I give you:
Ac 5:20 tell the people all about this **n** life."

Ac 17:19 we know what this **n** teaching is
Ro 6: 4 the Father, we too may live a **n** life.
1Co 5: 7 you may be a **n** unleavened batch—
 11:25 "This cup is the **n** covenant in my
2Co 3: 6 as ministers of a **n** covenant—
 5:17 is in Christ, the **n** creation has come:
Gal 6:15 what counts is the **n** creation.
Eph 2:15 in himself one **n** humanity
 4:23 to be made **n** in the attitude of your
 4:24 and to put on the **n** self,
Col 3:10 and have put on the **n** self, which is
Heb 8: 8 I will make a **n** covenant
 9:15 is the mediator of a **n** covenant,
 10:20 by a **n** and living way opened for us
 12:24 Jesus the mediator of a **n** covenant,
1Pe 1: 3 great mercy he has given us **n** birth
2Pe 3:13 forward to a **n** heaven and a **n** earth,
1Jn 2: 7 I am not writing you a **n** command
2Jn 1: 5 I am not writing you a **n** command
Rev 2:17 a white stone with a **n** name written
 3:12 the city of my God, the **n** Jerusalem.
 3:12 will also write on them my **n** name.
 5: 9 And they sang a **n** song, saying:
 14: 3 they sang a **n** song before the throne
 21: 1 I saw "a **n** heaven and a **n** earth,"
 21: 2 saw the Holy City, the **n** Jerusalem,
 21: 5 said, "I am making everything **n**!"

## NEW MOON
Nu 10:10; 28:14; 1Sa 20:5, 18, 24; 2Ki 4:23; 1Ch 23:31; Ezr 3:5; Ne 10:33; Ps 81:3; Isa 1:14; 66:23; Eze 46:1, 6; Hos 5:7; Am 8:5; Col 2:16

## NEW WINE
Ge 27:28, 37; Nu 18:12; Dt 7:13; 11:14; 12:17; 14:23; 18:4; 28:51; 33:28; 2Ki 18:32; 2Ch 31:5; 32:28; Ne 5:11; 10:37, 39; 13:5, 12; Ps 4:7; Pr 3:10; Isa 24:7; 36:17; 62:8; Jer 31:12; Hos 2:8, 9, 22; 4:11; 7:14; 9:2; Joel 1:5, 10; 2:19, 24; 3:18; Am 9:13; Hag 1:11; Zec 9:17; Mt 9:17, 17; Mk 2:22, 22; Lk 5:37, 37, 38

## NEWBORN [BEAR]
1Pe 2: 2 Like **n** babies, crave pure spiritual

## NEWS
2Ki 7: 9 This is a day of good **n** and we are
Ps 112: 7 They will have no fear of bad **n**;
Pr 15:30 good **n** gives health to the bones.
 25:25 to a weary soul is good **n**
Isa 40: 9 You who bring good **n** to Zion,
 52: 7 the feet of those who bring good **n**,
 61: 1 me to proclaim good **n** to the poor.
Na 1:15 the feet of one who brings good **n**,
Mt 4:23 proclaiming the good **n**
 9:35 proclaiming the good **n**
 11: 5 and the good **n** is proclaimed
Mk 1: 1 the good **n** about Jesus the Messiah,
 1:15 Repent and believe the good **n**!"
Lk 1:19 to you and to tell you this good **n**.
 2:10 I bring you good **n** of great joy
 3:18 and proclaimed the good **n** to them.
 4:43 "I must proclaim the good **n**
 8: 1 proclaiming the good **n**
 9: 6 proclaiming the good **n** and healing
 16:16 the good **n** of the kingdom of God is
Jn 20:18 went to the disciples with the **n**:
Ac 5:42 proclaiming the good **n** that Jesus is

Ac  10:36  announcing the good **n** of peace
    17:18  Paul was preaching the good **n**
Ro  10:15  feet of those who bring good **n**!"

## GOOD NEWS  See GOOD

## NEXT

Ge  18:10  return to you about this time **n** year,
Ps  78: 4  we will tell the **n** generation

## NICODEMUS*

Pharisee who visted Jesus at night (Jn 3). Argued for fair treatment of Jesus (Jn 7:50–52). With Joseph, prepared Jesus for burial (Jn 19:38–42).

## NICOLAITANS*

Rev  2: 6  You hate the practices of the **N**,
     2:15  who hold to the teaching of the **N**.

## NIGER*

Ac  13: 1  Simeon called **N**, Lucius of Cyrene,

## NIGHT  [MIDNIGHT, NIGHTS, OVERNIGHT]

Ge   1: 5  and the darkness he called "**n**."
     1:16  and the lesser light to govern the **n**.
     8:22  winter, day and **n** will never cease."
Ex  13:21  by **n** in a pillar of fire to give them
    40:38  and fire was in the cloud by **n**,
Dt  28:66  filled with dread both **n** and day,
Jos  1: 8  meditate on it day and **n**, so that you
Job 35:10  Maker, who gives songs in the **n**,
Ps   1: 2  and meditate on his law day and **n**.
    16: 7  even at **n** my heart instructs me.
    19: 2  **n** after **n** they display knowledge.
    42: 8  his love, at **n** his song is with me—
    63: 6  of you through the watches of the **n**.
    74:16  day is yours, and yours also the **n**;
    77: 6  I remembered my songs in the **n**.
    90: 4  gone by, or like a watch in the **n**.
    91: 5  You will not fear the terror of **n**,
   119:55  In the **n**, LORD, I remember your
   121: 6  you by day, nor the moon by **n**.
   136: 9  the moon and stars to govern the **n**;
Pr  31:15  She gets up while it is still **n**;
    31:18  and her lamp does not go out at **n**.
Ecc  2:23  even at **n** their minds do not rest.
Isa 21:11  "Watchman, what is left of the **n**?
    58:10  and your **n** will become like
Jer 33:20  **n** no longer come at their appointed
Zec 14: 7  no distinction between day and **n**.
Mt  24:43  time of **n** the thief was coming,
Lk   2: 8  keeping watch over their flocks at **n**.
     6:12  and spent the **n** praying to God.
Jn   3: 2  He came to Jesus at **n** and said,
     9: 4  **N** is coming, when no one can
    11:10  people walk at **n** that they stumble,
1Th  5: 2  Lord will come like a thief in the **n**.
     5: 5  We do not belong to the **n**
Rev  8:12  light, and also a third of the **n**.
    20:10  will be tormented day and **n** for ever
    21:25  be shut, for there will be no **n** there.
    22: 5  There will be no more **n**.

## NIGHTS  [NIGHT]

Ge   7:12  on the earth forty days and forty **n**.
Ex  24:18  the mountain forty days and forty **n**.
1Ki 19: 8  and forty **n** until he reached Horeb,
Jnh  1:17  of the fish three days and three **n**.
Mt   4: 2  After fasting forty days and forty **n**,
    12:40  three **n** in the belly of a huge fish,
2Co  6: 5  hard work, sleepless **n** and hunger;

## NILE

Ex   1.22  is born you must throw into the **N**,
     2: 5  went down to the **N** to bathe,
     7:17  hand I will strike the water of the **N**,

## NIMROD

Ge  10: 9  "Like **N**, a mighty hunter before

## NINE  [NINTH]

Nu  34:13  has ordered that it be given to the **n**
Jos 13: 7  as an inheritance among the **n** tribes
Ac   2:15  It's only **n** in the morning!

## NINETY

Ge  17:17  Sarah bear a child at the age of **n**?"

## NINETY-NINE

Ge  17: 1  When Abram was **n** years old,
Lk  15. 4  Doesn't he leave the **n** in the open

## NINEVEH  [NINEVITES]

Jnh  1: 2  "Go to the great city **N** and preach
Na   1: 1  A prophecy concerning **N**.
Mt  12:41  The people of **N** will stand

## NINEVITES*  [NINEVEH]

Jnh  3: 5  The **N** believed God.
Lk  11:30  For as Jonah was a sign to the **N**,

## NINTH  [NINE]

Jer 52: 6  **n** day of the fourth month the famine

## NO  [NONE, NOTHING]

Ex  20: 3  "You shall have **n** other gods
Dt   4:35  besides him there is **n** other.
     5: 7  "You shall have **n** other gods
    15: 4  there need be **n** poor people among
    32: 4  A faithful God who does **n** wrong,
1Ki  8:23  there is **n** God like you in heaven
Pr   6:32  who commits adultery has **n** sense;
     9: 4  those who have **n** sense she says,
    11:12  have **n** sense deride their neighbors,
    12:11  those who chase fantasies have **n** sense.
    15:21  brings joy to those who have **n** sense,
    17:18  One who has **n** sense shakes hands
    24:30  vineyard of someone who has **n** sense;
Ecc 12:12  making many books there is **n** end,
Isa 43:11  and apart from me there is **n** savior.
Jer 31:34  will remember their sins **n** more."
Eze 13:10  when there is **n** peace, and because,
Zec 14: 7  with a distinction between day
Mt   5:37  need to say is simply 'Yes' or '**N**';
    24:36  about that day or hour **n** one knows,
Mk   8:12  tell you, **n** sign will be given to it."
    10:18  "**N** one is good—except God alone.

Lk 1:37 For **n** word from God will ever fail."
16:13 "**N** one can serve two masters.
Jn 1:18 **N** one has ever seen God,
4:44 prophets have **n** honor in their own
Ro 8: 1 there is now **n** condemnation
Jas 5:12 to say is a simple "Yes" or "**N**."
Rev 21: 1 and there was **n** longer any sea.
21: 4 There will be **n** more death'
22: 3 **N** longer will there be any curse.
22: 5 There will be **n** more night.

## NOAH

Righteous man (Eze 14:14, 20) called to build ark (Ge 6–8; Heb 11:7; 1Pe 3:20; 2Pe 2:5). God's covenant with (Ge 9:1–17). Drunkenness of (Ge 9:18–23). Blessed sons, cursed Canaan (Ge 9:24–27).

## NOB

1Sa 21: 1 David went to **N**, to Ahimelek

## NOBLE

Ru 3:11 that you are a woman of **n** character.
Ps 16: 3 the **n** people in whom is all my delight."
45: 1 by a **n** theme as I recite my verses
Pr 12: 4 **n** character is her husband's crown,
31:10 A wife of **n** character who can find?
31:29 "Many women do **n** things, but you
Isa 32: 8 But the **n** make **n** plans, and by **n**
Lk 8:15 good soil stands for those with a **n**
Ac 17:11 were of more **n** character than those
Ro 9:21 of clay some pottery for **n** purposes
1Co 1:26 not many were of **n** birth.
Php 4: 8 whatever is **n**, whatever is right,
1Ti 3: 1 to be an overseer desires a **n** task.
2Ti 2:20 some are for **n** purposes and some
Jas 2: 7 who are blaspheming the **n** name

## NOBODY

Jn 9:32 **N** has ever heard of opening
1Th 5:15 Make sure that **n** pays back wrong

## NOISE

Ex 32:17 Joshua heard the **n** of the people
Isa 13: 4 Listen, a **n** on the mountains,
29: 6 thunder and earthquake and great **n**,

## NONE  [NO]

Dt 15: 6 nations but **n** will rule over you.
1Sa 3:19 he let **n** of Samuel's words fall
Ps 86: 8 Among the gods there is **n** like you,
Pr 2:19 **N** who go to her return or attain
Isa 46: 9 I am God, and there is **n** like me.
47: 8 'I am, and there is **n** besides me.
Mt 12:39 **n** will be given it except the sign
16: 4 **n** will be given it except the sign
Jn 6:39 that I shall lose **n** of all those he has
17:12 **N** has been lost except the one

## NONSENSE

3Jn 1:10 spreading malicious **n** about us.

## NOON

Mk 15:33 At **n**, darkness came over

## NORTH

Ge 13:14 where you are, to the **n** and south,
Nu 34: 9 This will be your boundary on the **n**.
Ps 89:12 You created the **n** and the south;
Isa 41:25 "I have stirred up one from the **n**,
Jer 4: 6 I am bringing disaster from the **n**,
Eze 1: 4 a windstorm coming out of the **n**—
Da 11: 6 king of the **N** to make an alliance,
Zec 2: 6 Come! Flee from the land of the **n**,"
14: 4 with half of the mountain moving **n**

## NOSE  [NOSES]

2Ki 19:28 I will put my hook in your **n** and my
2Ch 33:11 put a hook in his **n**, bound him

## NOSES*  [NOSE]

Ps 115: 6 but cannot hear, **n**, but cannot smell.
Eze 23:25 They will cut off your **n** and your

## NOSTRILS

Ge 2: 7 breathed into his **n** the breath of life,
7:22 had the breath of life in its **n** died.
Ex 15: 8 blast of your **n** the waters piled up.
Ps 18:15 at the blast of breath from your **n**.
Isa 2:22 who have but a breath in their **n**.

## NOTABLE*

Am 6: 1 you **n** men of the foremost nation,
Ac 4:16 they have performed a **n** sign,

## NOTE

Ac 4:13 they took **n** that these men had been

## NOTHING  [NO, THING]

Ge 14:23 I will accept **n** belonging to you,
Ex 1: 8 to whom Joseph meant **n**,
2Sa 24:24 burnt offerings that cost me **n**."
2Ch 9: 2 **n** was too hard for him to explain
Ne 9:21 they lacked **n**, their clothes did not
Job 1: 9 "Does Job fear God for **n**?"
Ps 34: 9 for those who fear him lack **n**.
73:25 earth has **n** I desire besides you.
82: 5 'gods' know **n**, they understand **n**.
Pr 8:11 **n** you desire can compare with her.
9:13 she is simple and knows **n**.
10:28 the hopes of the wicked come to **n**.
28:27 who give to the poor will lack **n**,
Ecc 1: 9 there is **n** new under the sun.
3:22 that there is **n** better for people than
8:15 because there is **n** better for people
Isa 44: 9 All who make idols are **n**,
53: 2 **n** in his appearance that we should
Jer 32:17 **N** is too hard for you.
Da 9:26 will be put to death and will have **n**.
Mt 17:20 **N** will be impossible for you."
Lk 23:15 see, he has done **n** to deserve death.
Jn 5:30 By myself I can do **n**; I judge only
15: 5 apart from me you can do **n**.
Ro 14:14 that **n** is unclean in itself.
1Co 8: 4 We know that "An idol is **n** at all
13: 2 but do not have love, I am **n**.
Gal 2:21 through the law, Christ died for **n**!"
Php 2: 7 he made himself **n** by taking
1Ti 6: 7 For we brought **n** into the world,
Heb 4:13 **N** in all creation is hidden

Heb  7:19  (for the law made **n** perfect),

## NOTICE
Ps  10:11  "God will never **n**; he covers his face

## NOURISH [NOURISHED,
   NOURISHING, NOURISHMENT]
Pr  10:21  The lips of the righteous **n** many,

## NOURISHED [NOURISH]
Dt  32:13  He **n** him with honey from the rock,
Da   1:15  better **n** than any of the young men

## NOURISHING* [NOURISH]
Ro  11:17  and now share in the **n** sap

## NOURISHMENT* [NOURISH]
Pr   3: 8  to your body and **n** to your bones.

## NOW
Ge  22:12  **N** I know that you fear God,
Ezr  9: 8  "But **n**, for a brief moment,
Ps  20: 6  **N** this I know: The LORD gives
    131: 3  put your hope in the LORD both **n**
Hab  2:16  instead of glory. **N** it is your turn!
Zec  1: 5  Where are your ancestors **n**?
Mt  12:42  **n** one greater than Solomon is here.
Lk   1:48  From **n** on all generations will call
Jn   2:10  but you have saved the best till **n**."
     5:25  has **n** come when the dead will hear
     9:25  I do know. I was blind but **n** I see!"
    13:19  am telling you **n** before it happens,
    13:36  you cannot follow **n**, but you will
    16:12  to you, more than you can **n** bear.
Ro   3:21  But **n** apart from the law
     5: 9  Since we have **n** been justified
     8: 1  there is **n** no condemnation for those
    13:11  our salvation is nearer **n** than
1Co 13:13  And **n** these three remain:
2Co  6: 2  you, **n** is the time of God's favor,
Gal  4: 9  But **n** that you know God—
Eph  2: 2  the spirit who is at work in those
     3: 5  generations as it has **n** been revealed
Col  1:26  is **n** disclosed to the Lord's people.
1Pe  1: 8  even though you do not see him **n**,
     2:10  but **n** you are the people of God;
1Jn  2:18  even **n** many antichrists have come.
Rev  1:19  both what is **n** and what will take
    21: 3  dwelling place is **n** among

## NULLIFY
Mt  15: 6  Thus you **n** the word of God
Ro   3: 3  Will their unfaithfulness **n** God's
     3:31  Do we, then, **n** the law by this faith?

## NUMBER [NUMBERED,
   NUMBERING, NUMBERLESS,
   NUMBERS, NUMEROUS,
   OUTNUMBER]
Ge   1:22  increase in **n** and fill the water
     1:28  "Be fruitful and increase in **n**;
     9: 1  and increase in **n** and fill the earth.
Nu  26:51  The total **n** of the men of Israel was
Dt  32: 8  according to the **n** of the sons

1Ki  3: 8  people, too numerous to count or **n**.
1Ch 21: 5  Joab reported the **n** of the fighting
Ps  90:12  Teach us to **n** our days, that we may
    105:12  When they were but few in **n**,
    147: 4  He determines the **n** of the stars
Jer  23: 3  will be fruitful and increase in **n**.
Mt  14:21  The **n** of those who ate was
    15:38  The **n** of those who ate was four
Jn  21: 6  net in because of the large **n** of fish.
Ac   2:47  their **n** daily those who were being
     5:14  the Lord and were added to their **n**.
     6: 1  the **n** of disciples was increasing,
    11:21  and a great **n** of people believed
Ro  11:25  part until the full **n** of the Gentiles
Rev  6:11  until the full **n** of their fellow
     7: 4  I heard the **n** of those who were
    13:18  **n** of a man. That **n** is 666.
    20: 8  In **n** they are like the sand

## NUMBERED [NUMBER]
Ex   1: 5  The descendants of Jacob **n** seventy
Nu  25: 9  those who died in the plague **n** 24,000.
Lk  12: 7  the very hairs of your head are all **n**.
    22:37  he was **n** with the transgressors';

## NUMBERING [NUMBER]
1Ch 27:24  came on Israel on account of this **n**,
Ac   1: 5  (a group **n** about a hundred and twenty)
Rev  5:11  angels, **n** thousands upon thousands,

## NUMBERLESS* [NUMBER]
Isa  48:19  sand, your children like its **n** grains;

## NUMBERS [NUMBER]
Ge  17: 2  and will greatly increase your **n**."
    28: 3  increase your **n** until you become
    48: 4  you fruitful and increase your **n**.
Lev 26: 9  you fruitful and increase your **n**,
Dt   1:10  your God has increased your **n** so

## NUMEROUS [NUMBER]
Ge  16:10  that they will be too **n** to count."
    22:17  your descendants as **n** as the stars
Ex   1: 9  Israelites have become far too **n**
    23:29  and the wild animals too **n** for you.
Ne   9:23  made their children as **n** as the stars
Zec 10: 8  they will be as **n** as before.
Heb 11:12  came descendants as **n** as the stars

## NURSE [NURSED, NURSING]
Ge  21: 7  that Sarah would **n** children?
Ex   2: 7  of the Hebrew women to **n** the baby
Nu  11:12  in my arms, as a **n** carries an infant,
2Sa  4: 4  His **n** picked him up and fled, but as
2Ki 11: 3  hidden with his **n** at the temple
Isa 66:11  For you will **n** and be satisfied

## NURSED [NURSE]
Ex   2: 9  the woman took the baby and **n** him.
Lk  11:27  who gave you birth and **n** you."

## NURSING [NURSE]
Isa 49:23  and their queens your **n** mothers.
Lk  21:23  for pregnant women and **n** mothers!
1Th  2: 7  as a **n** mother cares for her children,

# O

## OAK [OAKS]

| | | |
|---|---|---|
| Ge | 35: 4 | Jacob buried them under the **o** |
| 2Sa | 18:10 | saw Absalom hanging in an **o** tree." |
| Eze | 6:13 | spreading tree and every leafy **o**— |

## OAKS [OAK]

| | | |
|---|---|---|
| Ps | 29: 9 | voice of the LORD twists the **o** |
| Isa | 57: 5 | You burn with lust among the **o** |

## OATH [OATHS]

| | | |
|---|---|---|
| Ge | 21:31 | the two men swore an **o** there. |
| | 24: 7 | spoke to me and promised me on **o**, |
| | 26: 3 | will confirm the **o** I swore to your |
| Ex | 13:11 | as he promised on **o** to you and your |
| | 33: 1 | go up to the land I promised on **o** |
| Nu | 30: 2 | takes an **o** to obligate himself |
| Dt | 6:18 | land the LORD promised on **o** |
| | 7: 8 | you and kept the **o** he swore to your |
| | 29:12 | you this day and sealing with an **o**, |
| Jos | 2:17 | "This **o** you made us swear will not |
| | 6:22 | in accordance with your **o** to her." |
| 1Sa | 14:24 | had bound the people under an **o**, |
| | 24:22 | So David gave his **o** to Saul. |
| Ezr | 10: 5 | And they took the **o**. |
| Ne | 13:25 | I made them take an **o** in God's |
| Ps | 95:11 | So I declared on **o** in my anger, |
| | 119:106 | I have taken an **o** and confirmed it, |
| | 132:11 | The LORD swore an **o** to David, |
| Ecc | 8: 2 | because you took an **o** before God. |
| Mt | 5:33 | 'Do not break your **o**, but fulfill |
| Heb | 4: 3 | "So I declared on **o** in my anger, |
| | 7:20 | And it was not without an **o**! |

## OATHS [OATH]

| | | |
|---|---|---|
| Dt | 6:13 | only and take your **o** in his name. |
| Ps | 15: 4 | who keep their **o** even when it hurts; |

## OBADIAH

1. Believer who sheltered 100 prophets from Jezebel (1Ki 18:1-16).
2. Prophet against Edom (Ob 1).

## OBED

| | | |
|---|---|---|
| Ru | 4:22 | **O** the father of Jesse, and Jesse |
| Lk | 3:32 | Jesse, the son of **O**, the son of Boaz, |

## OBED-EDOM

| | | |
|---|---|---|
| 2Sa | 6:10 | took it to the house of **O** the Gittite. |
| 1Ch | 26: 5 | (For God had blessed **O**.) |

## OBEDIENCE [OBEY]

| | | |
|---|---|---|
| Ge | 49:10 | and the **o** of the nations be his. |
| Dt | 10:12 | to walk in **o** to him, to love him, |
| | 26:17 | that you will walk in **o** to him, |
| | 30:16 | to walk in **o** to him, |
| Jos | 22: 5 | to walk in **o** to him, |
| Jdg | 2:17 | the way of **o** to the LORD's |
| 1Ki | 8:58 | to walk in **o** to him and keep |
| 1Ch | 21:19 | So David went up in **o** to the word |

| | | |
|---|---|---|
| 2Ch | 31:21 | of God's temple and in **o** to the law |
| Lk | 23:56 | rested on the Sabbath in **o** |
| Ac | 21:24 | you yourself are living in **o** |
| Ro | 1: 5 | to faith and **o** for his name's sake. |
| | 5:19 | through the **o** of the one man |
| | 6:16 | to death, or to **o**, which leads |
| | 16:19 | Everyone has heard about your **o**, |
| | 16:26 | Gentiles might come to faith and **o**— |
| 2Co | 9:13 | God for the **o** that accompanies your |
| | 10: 6 | once your **o** is complete. |
| Phm | 1:21 | Confident of your **o**, I write to you, |
| Heb | 5: 8 | he learned **o** from what he suffered |
| 2Jn | 1: 6 | that we walk in **o** to his commands. |

## OBEDIENT* [OBEY]

| | | |
|---|---|---|
| Dt | 30:17 | heart turns away and you are not **o**, |
| Isa | 1:19 | If you are willing and **o**, you will |
| Lk | 2:51 | with them and was **o** to them. |
| Ac | 6: 7 | of priests became **o** to the faith. |
| Ro | 6:16 | offer yourselves to someone as **o** slaves, |
| 2Co | 2: 9 | the test and be **o** in everything. |
| | 7:15 | he remembers that you were all **o**, |
| | 10: 5 | every thought to make it **o** to Christ. |
| Php | 2: 8 | himself by becoming **o** to death— |
| Tit | 3: 1 | to be **o**, to be ready to do whatever |
| 1Pe | 1: 2 | to be **o** to Jesus Christ and sprinkled |
| | 1:14 | As **o** children, do not conform |

## OBEY [OBEDIENCE, OBEDIENT, OBEYED, OBEYING, OBEYS]

| | | |
|---|---|---|
| Ex | 12:24 | "**O** these instructions as a lasting |
| | 19: 5 | Now if you **o** me fully and keep my |
| | 24: 7 | the LORD has said; we will **o**." |
| Lev | 18: 4 | You must **o** my laws and be careful |
| | 25:18 | decrees and be careful to **o** my laws, |
| Nu | 15:40 | remember to **o** all my commands |
| Dt | 4:30 | to the LORD your God and **o** him. |
| | 5:27 | We will listen and **o**." |
| | 6: 3 | and be careful to **o** so that it may go |
| | 6:24 | commanded us to **o** all these decrees |
| | 11:13 | you faithfully **o** the commands I am |
| | 11:27 | the blessing if you **o** the commands |
| | 12:28 | **o** all these regulations I am giving |
| | 13: 4 | Keep his commands and **o** him; |
| | 21:18 | son who does not **o** his father |
| | 28: 1 | If you fully **o** the LORD your God |
| | 28:15 | you do not **o** the LORD your God |
| | 30: 2 | God and **o** him with all your heart |
| | 30:10 | if you **o** the LORD your God |
| | 30:14 | and in your heart so you may **o** it. |
| | 32:46 | children to **o** carefully all the words |
| Jos | 1: 7 | **o** all the law my servant Moses gave |
| | 24:24 | the LORD our God and **o** him." |
| Jdg | 3: 4 | whether they would **o** the LORD's |
| 1Sa | 12:14 | serve and **o** him and do not rebel |
| | 15:22 | To **o** is better than sacrifice, |
| 1Ki | 8:61 | by his decrees and **o** his commands, |
| 2Ki | 17:13 | I commanded your ancestors to **o** |
| 2Ch | 34:31 | and to **o** the words of the covenant |
| Ps | 103:18 | and remember to **o** his precepts. |
| | 103:20 | do his bidding, who **o** his word. |
| | 119:17 | while I live, that I may **o** your word. |
| | 119:34 | your law and **o** it with all my heart. |
| | 119:57 | I have promised to **o** your words. |
| | 119:67 | went astray, but now I **o** your word. |
| | 119:100 | the elders, for I **o** your precepts. |

Ps 119:129 therefore I **o** them.
    119:167 I **o** your statutes, for I love them
Pr   5:13 I would not **o** my teachers or turn
   19:16 who **o** instructions preserve their lives,
Jer   7:23 **O** me, and I will be your God
   11: 4 I said, '**O** me and do everything I
   11: 7 again and again, saying, "**O** me."
   18:10 evil in my sight and does not **o** me,
   42: 6 we will **o** the LORD our God,
Eze 20:11 people will live if they **o** them.
Mt   8:27 the winds and the waves **o** him!"
   28:20 to **o** everything I have commanded
Lk  11:28 hear the word of God and **o** it."
Jn  14:24 not love me will not **o** my teaching.
Ac   5:29 "We must **o** God rather than human
   5:32 God has given to those who **o** him."
Ro   2:13 it is those who **o** the law who will
   6:12 body so that you **o** its evil desires.
   6:16 you are slaves of the one you **o**—
   6:17 have come to **o** from your heart
  15:18 in leading the Gentiles to **o** God
Gal   5: 3 he is obligated to **o** the whole law.
Eph  6: 1 **o** your parents in the Lord, for this
   6: 5 just as you would **o** Christ.
Col  3:20 **o** your parents in everything,
   3:22 Slaves, **o** your earthly masters
2Th  3:14 those who do not **o** our instruction
1Ti   3: 4 well and see that his children **o** him,
Heb  5: 9 eternal salvation for all who **o** him
1Pe  4.17 for those who do not **o** the gospel

## OBEYED [OBEY]

Ge  22:18 blessed, because you have **o** me."
   26: 5 because Abraham **o** me and did
Jos   1:17 Just as we fully **o** Moses, so we will
2Ki 18:12 they had not **o** the LORD their
Ps  119: 4 down precepts that are to be fully **o**.
Jer   3:13 and have not **o** me,' "
Da   9:10 we have not **o** the LORD our God
Jnh   3: 3 Jonah **o** the word of the LORD
Mic  5:15 on the nations that have not **o** me."
Jn  15:20 If they **o** my teaching, they will
   15: 6 to me and they have **o** your word.
Ac   7:53 through angels but have not **o** it."
Php  2:12 dear friends, as you have always **o**—
Heb 11: 8 as his inheritance, **o** and went,
1Pe  3: 6 who **o** Abraham and called him her

## OBEYING* [OBEY]

Dt   8:20 for not **o** the LORD your God.
1Sa 15:22 as much as in **o** the LORD?
1Ki 11:38 by **o** my decrees and commands,
Ps  119: 5 were steadfast in **o** your decrees!
Jer  16:12 of your evil hearts instead of **o** me.
Gal   5: 7 you to keep you from **o** the truth?
1Pe  1:22 purified yourselves by **o** the truth so

## OBEYS [OBEY]

Lev 18: 5 for whoever **o** them will live
Ne   9:29 said, 'Whoever **o** them will live
Jn   8:51 **o** my word will never see death."
Ro   2:27 and yet **o** the law will condemn you
1Jn  2: 5 But if anyone **o** his word,

## OBJECT [OBJECTS]

Jer  18:16 land will be an **o** of horror

## OBJECTS [OBJECT]

Ro   9:23 glory known to the **o** of his mercy,

## OBLATION(S) (KJV) See GIFT(S), OFFERING(S), PORTION, SACRIFICE

## OBLIGATE* [OBLIGATED, OBLIGATION, OBLIGATIONS]

Nu  30: 2 or takes an oath to **o** himself

## OBLIGATED [OBLIGATE]

Ro   1:14 I am **o** both to Greeks
Gal   5: 3 that he is **o** to obey the whole law.

## OBLIGATION [OBLIGATE]

Ro   8:12 brothers and sisters, we have an **o**—

## OBLIGATIONS* [OBLIGATE]

Nu   3: 8 fulfilling the **o** of the Israelites
1Ki  9:25 them, and so fulfilled the temple **o**.

## OBSCENITY*

Eph  5: 4 Nor should there be **o**, foolish talk

## OBSCURES*

Job 38: 2 "Who is this that **o** my plans with words
   42: 3 **o** my plans without knowledge?'

## OBSERVANCE* [OBSERVE]

Ex  13: 9 This **o** will be for you like a sign
Ezr  7:10 and **o** of the Law of the LORD,

## OBSERVE [OBSERVANCE, OBSERVED, OBSERVER, OBSERVES, OBSERVING]

Ex  31:13 'You must **o** my Sabbaths.
Lev 25: 2 the land itself must **o** a sabbath
Dt   4: 6 **O** them carefully, for this will show
   5:12 "**O** the Sabbath day by keeping it
   8: 6 **O** the commands of the LORD
  11:22 you carefully **o** all these commands
  26:16 carefully **o** them with all your heart
Ps  37:37 the blameless, **o** the upright;
Mk  7: 9 in order to **o** your own traditions!
Ro   2:25 has value if you **o** the law,

## OBSERVED

Lk  17:20 is not something that can be **o**,

## OBSERVER* [OBSERVE]

Ac  22:12 He was a devout **o** of the law

## OBSERVES* [OBSERVE]

Ps  11: 4 He **o** everyone on earth;

## OBSERVING [OBSERVE]

Ro   3:20 in God's sight by **o** the law;
Gal   2:16 person is not justified by **o** the law,
   3: 2 you receive the Spirit by **o** the law,
   3: 5 miracles among you by your **o** the law,
   3:10 rely on **o** the law are under a curse,

## OBSOLETE*
Heb 8:13 "new," he has made the first one o;
8:13 what is o and outdated will soon

## OBSTACLE* [OBSTACLES]
Ro 14:13 block or o in the way of a brother

## OBSTACLES* [OBSTACLE]
Isa 57:14 Remove the o out of the way of my
Jer 6:21 "I will put o before this people.
Ro 16:17 put o in your way that are contrary

## OBSTINATE
Isa 65: 2 held out my hands to an o people,
Eze 3: 7 house of Israel is hardened and o.
Ro 10:21 to a disobedient and o people."

## OBTAIN [OBTAINED, OBTAINING]
Pr 12: 2 Good people o favor from the LORD,
Ro 11: 7 sought so earnestly they did not o.
2Ti 2:10 they too may o the salvation that is

## OBTAINED [OBTAIN]
Ro 9:30 not pursue righteousness, have o it,
Php 3:12 Not that I have already o all this,

## OBTAINING* [OBTAIN]
Heb 9:12 own blood, thus o eternal redemption.

## OBVIOUS*
Mt 6:18 so that it will not be o to others
Gal 5:19 The acts of the sinful nature are o:
1Ti 5:24 The sins of some are o,
5:25 good deeds are o, and even those that
are not o cannot

## OCCASIONS*
Zec 8:19 and glad o and happy festivals
Eph 6:18 the Spirit on all o with all kinds

## ODED
2Ch 28: 9 of the LORD named O was there,

## ODOR*
Jn 11:39 "by this time there is a bad o, for he

## OFFEND* [OFFENDED, OFFENDER,
OFFENSE, OFFENSES, OFFENSIVE]
Job 34:31 'I am guilty but will o no more.
Jn 6:61 said to them, "Does this o you?

## OFFENDED [OFFEND]
Mt 15:12 Pharisees were o when they heard

## OFFENDER [OFFEND]
Ex 21:22 serious injury, the o must be fined

## OFFENSE [OFFEND]
Dt 19:15 or o they may have committed.
21:22 anyone guilty of a capital o is put
Pr 17: 9 would foster love covers over an o,
19:11 it is to one's glory to overlook an o.

Mt 17:27 so that we may not cause o,
Mk 6: 3 And they took o at him.
Gal 5:11 that case the o of the cross has been

## OFFENSES [OFFEND]
Job 7:21 Why do you not pardon my o
Ecc 10: 4 calmness can lay great o to rest.
Isa 44:22 swept away your o like a cloud,
59:12 For our o are many in your sight,
Eze 18:30 Turn away from all your o;
33:10 "Our o and sins weigh us down,

## OFFENSIVE [OFFEND]
Ps 139:24 See if there is any o way in me,

## OFFER [OFFERED, OFFERING,
OFFERINGS, OFFERS]
Ex 29:38 "This is what you are to o
Dt 12:14 O them only at the place
Ps 4: 5 O the sacrifices of the righteous
Isa 1:15 even if you o many prayers, I will
Jer 7:16 pray for this people nor o any plea
Hos 14: 2 that we may o the fruit of our lips.
Mic 6: 7 Shall I o my firstborn for my
Mt 5:24 then come and o your gift.
Ro 6:13 Do not o any part of yourself to sin
12: 1 o your bodies as a living sacrifice,
Heb 9:25 he enter heaven to o himself again
13:15 let us continually o to God

## OFFERED [OFFER]
Lev 10: 1 they o unauthorized fire before
1Sa 13: 9 And Saul o up the burnt offering.
1Ki 3: 4 and Solomon o a thousand burnt
Ps 106:28 and ate sacrifices to lifeless gods;
Isa 50: 6 I o my back to those who beat me,
Mt 27:34 There they o Jesus wine to drink,
1Co 9:13 altar share in what is o on the altar?
10:20 of pagans are o to demons,
Heb 7:27 sins once for all when he o himself.
9:14 eternal Spirit o himself unblemished
11:17 tested him, o Isaac as a sacrifice.
Jas 5:15 the prayer o in faith will make them

## OFFERING [OFFER]
Ge 4: 4 with favor on Abel and his o,
22: 2 Sacrifice him there as a burnt o
22: 8 provide the lamb for the burnt o,
Ex 29:14 outside the camp. It is a sin o.
29:18 It is a burnt o to the LORD,
29:18 a food o presented to the LORD.
29:24 before the LORD as a wave o.
29:40 quarter of a hin of wine as a drink o.
Lev 1: 3 " 'If the o is a burnt o
2: 1 anyone brings a grain o
3: 1 " 'If your o is a fellowship o,
4: 3 young bull without defect as a sin o
5:15 the sanctuary shekel. It is a guilt o.
7:37 are the regulations for the burnt o, the
grain o, the sin o, the guilt o, the
ordination o and the fellowship o,
9:24 consumed the burnt o and the fat
1Sa 13: 9 And Saul offered up the burnt o.
1Ch 21:26 from heaven on the altar of burnt o.
2Ch 7: 1 and consumed the burnt o

Ezr 6:17 lambs and, as a sin **o** for all Israel,
Ps 40: 6 Sacrifice and **o** you did not desire—
116:17 I will sacrifice a thank **o** to you
Isa 53:10 the LORD makes his life an **o**
Mt 5:23 if you are **o** your gift at the altar
Ro 8: 3 of sinful humanity to be a sin **o**.
Eph 5: 2 himself up for us as a fragrant **o**
Php 2:17 out like a drink **o** on the sacrifice
4:18 They are a fragrant **o**, an acceptable
2Ti 4: 6 being poured out like a drink **o**,
Heb 10: 5 "Sacrifice and **o** you did not desire,
11: 4 Abel brought God a better **o** than Cain
1Pe 2: 5 **o** spiritual sacrifices acceptable

## BURNT OFFERING See BURNT

## DRINK OFFERING See DRINK

## FELLOWSHIP OFFERING See
FELLOWSHIP

## GRAIN OFFERING See GRAIN

## GUILT OFFERING See GUILT

## SIN OFFERING See SIN

## WAVE OFFERING See WAVE

## OFFERINGS [OFFER]
Ge 8:20 birds, he sacrificed burnt **o** on it.
Ex 40:29 offered on it burnt **o** and grain **o**,
1Sa 15:22 the LORD delight in burnt **o**
Ps 40: 6 burnt **o** and sin **o** you did not
50:14 "Sacrifice thank **o** to God,
Isa 1:13 Stop bringing meaningless **o**!
Jer 6:20 Your burnt **o** are not acceptable;
Hos 6: 6 of God rather than burnt **o**.
Mal 3: 8 we robbing you?' "In tithes and **o**.
Mk 12:33 is more important than all burnt **o**
Heb 10: 6 with burnt **o** and sin **o** you were not

## BURNT OFFERINGS See BURNT

## DRINK OFFERINGS See DRINK

## FELLOWSHIP OFFERINGS See
FELLOWSHIP

## GRAIN OFFERINGS See GRAIN

## GUILT OFFERINGS See GUILT

## SIN OFFERINGS See SIN

## OFFERS [OFFER]
Tit 2:11 that **o** salvation to all people.
Heb 10:11 and again he **o** the same sacrifices,

## OFFICER [OFFICERS, OFFICIALS]
2Ti 2: 4 try to please their commanding **o**.

## OFFICERS [OFFICER]
Ex 15: 4 best of Pharaoh's **o** are drowned

## OFFICIALS [OFFICER]
Ex 5:21 his **o** and have put a sword in their
9:20 Those **o** of Pharaoh who feared
Ezr 4: 5 They bribed **o** to work against them
Pr 17:26 surely to flog honest **o** is not right.

Pr 29:12 to lies, all his **o** become wicked.
Jer 52:10 he also killed all the **o** of Judah.
Mk 10:42 their high **o** exercise authority over

## OFFSPRING
Ge 3:15 and between your **o** and hers;
12: 7 "To your **o** I will give this land."
13:16 I will make your **o** like the dust
26: 4 through your **o** all nations on earth
28:14 be blessed through you and your **o**.
Ex 13:12 to the LORD the first **o** of every
Ru 4:12 Through the **o** the LORD gives
2Sa 7:12 will raise up your **o** to succeed you,
Isa 44: 3 I will pour out my Spirit on your **o**,
53:10 sin, he will see his **o** and prolong his
Mal 2:15 Because he was seeking godly **o**.
Ac 3:25 'Through your **o** all peoples
17:28 own poets have said, 'We are his **o**.'
17:29 "Therefore since we are God's **o**,
Ro 4:18 said to him, "So shall your **o** be."
9: 8 who are regarded as Abraham's **o**.
Rev 22:16 I am the Root and the **O** of David,

## OFTEN
Lk 13:34 how **o** I have longed to gather your
Jn 18: 2 because Jesus had **o** met there

## OG
Nu 21:33 and **O** king of Bashan and his whole
Dt 31: 4 to them what he did to Sihon and **O**,
Ps 136:20 and **O** king of Bashan—

## OHOLIAB*
Craftsman who worked on the tabernacle (Ex 31:6; 35:34; 36:1-2; 38:23).

## OIL
Ge 28:18 as a pillar and poured **o** on top of it.
35:14 he also poured **o** on it.
Ex 25: 6 olive **o** for the light; spices for the anointing **o**
29: 7 Take the anointing **o** and anoint him
30:25 It will be the sacred anointing **o**.
Dt 14:23 grain, new wine and olive **o**,
1Sa 10: 1 Samuel took a bottle of olive **o**
16:13 So Samuel took the horn of **o**,
1Ki 17:16 up and the jug of **o** did not run dry,
2Ki 4: 6 Then the **o** stopped flowing.
Ps 23: 5 You anoint my head with **o**;
45: 7 by anointing you with the **o** of joy.
104:15 hearts, **o** to make their faces shine,
133: 2 It is like precious **o** poured
Pr 5: 3 and her speech is smoother than **o**;
21:17 wine and olive **o** will never be rich.
Isa 1: 6 bandaged or soothed with olive **o**.
61: 3 the **o** of joy instead of mourning,
Joel 2:24 will overflow with new wine and **o**.
Mt 25: 3 but did not take any **o** with them.
Heb 1: 9 by anointing you with the **o** of joy."
Jas 5:14 anoint them with **o** in the name

## ANOINTING OIL Ex 25:6; 29:7, 21; 30:25, 25, 31; 31:11; 35:8, 15, 28; 37:29; 39:38; 40:9; Lev 8:2, 10, 12, 30; 10:7; 21:10, 12; Nu 4:16

**OLIVE OIL** Ex 25:6; 29:2, 2, 23; 30:24; 35:8,
28; Lev 2:1, 4, 4, 7; 6:15; 7:12, 12, 12; 8:26; 9:4;
14:10, 21; 23:13; Nu 4:9; 6:15, 15; 7:13, 19, 25,
31, 37, 43, 49, 55, 61, 67, 73, 79; 8:8; 11:8; 15:4,
6, 9; 18:12; 28:9; 29:3, 9, 14; Dt 7:13; 8:8; 11:14;
12:17; 14:23; 18:4; 28:51; 1Sa 10:1; 1Ki 5:11;
17:12; 2Ki 4:2; 20:13; 1Ch 27:28; 2Ch 2:10, 15;
11:11; 32:28; Ezr 3:7; 6:9; 7:22; Ne 5:11; 10:37,
39; 13:5, 12; Job 29:6; Pr 21:17, 20; Isa 1:6;
39:2; 57:9; Jer 31:12; 40:10; 41:8; Eze 16:13, 19;
23:41; 27:17; 45:14, 24; 46:5; Hos 2:5, 22; 12:1;
Joel 1:10; 2:19; Mic 6:7; Hag 1:11; 2:12; Lk
16:6; Rev 18:13

## OLD [AGE-OLD, OLDER]
Ge  17:12  is eight days o must be circumcised,
    17:17  be born to a man a hundred years o?
    21: 7  have borne him a son in his o age.”
Nu   1: 3  in Israel who are twenty years o
    14:29  every one of you twenty years o
Dt  32: 7  Remember the days of o;
Ps  71: 9  Do not cast me away when I am o;
Pr  20:29  gray hair the splendor of the o.
    22: 6  when they are o they will not turn
La   5:21  renew our days as of o
Joel 2:28  your o men will dream dreams,
Mic  5: 2  whose origins are from of o,
Mk   2:22  not pour new wine into o wineskins.
Jn   3: 4  anyone be born when they are o?”
Ac   2:17  your o men will dream dreams.
Ro   4:19  he was about a hundred years o—
1Co  5: 7  Get rid of the o yeast, so that you
2Co  5:17  The o has gone, the new is here!
Eph  4:22  to put off your o self, which is being
Heb  8: 6  is mediator is superior to the o one,
1Jn  2: 7  you a new command but an o one,
Rev 21: 4  for the o order of things has passed

## OLDER [OLD]
1Ti  5: 1  Do not rebuke an o man harshly,
     5: 2  o women as mothers, and younger
Tit  2: 2  Teach the o men to be temperate,
     2: 3  teach the o women to be reverent

## OLIVE [OLIVES]
Ge   8:11  beak was a freshly plucked o leaf!
Ex  25: 6  o oil for the light;
Jdg  9: 8  They said to the o tree, ‘Be our
Ps  52: 8  I am like an o tree flourishing
Jer 11:16  LORD called you a thriving o tree
Hab  3:17  though the o crop fails
Zec  4: 3  Also there are two o trees by it,
Ro  11:17  though a wild o shoot, have been
    11:24  were grafted into a cultivated o tree,
Rev 11: 4  They are “the two o trees”

## OLIVE OIL See OIL

## OLIVES [OLIVE]
Dt  24:20  you beat the o from your trees,
Zec 14: 4  the Mount of O will be split in two
Mt  24: 3  Jesus was sitting on the Mount of O,
Jas  3:12  can a fig tree bear o, or a grapevine

## MOUNT OF OLIVES See MOUNT

## OMEGA*
Rev  1: 8  “I am the Alpha and the O,”
    21: 6  I am the Alpha and the O,
    22:13  I am the Alpha and the O, the First

## OMENS
Dt  18:10  interprets o, engages in witchcraft,

## OMIT*
Jer 26: 2  I command you; do not o a word.

## OMNIPOTENT (KJV) See
ALMIGHTY

## OMRI
  King of Israel (1Ki 16:21-26).

## ONAN
Ge  38: 8  Then Judah said to O,
    46:12  Er, O, Shelah, Perez and Zerah

## ONCE [ONE]
Ge  18:32  angry, but let me speak just o more.
Ex  30:10  O a year Aaron shall make
Job 40: 5  I spoke o, but I have no answer—
La   1: 1  lies the city, o so full of people!
Ro   6:10  he died, he died to sin o for all;
     7: 9  O I was alive apart from the law;
Eph  5: 8  For you were o darkness, but now
Heb  7:27  He sacrificed for their sins o for all
     9:12  he entered the Most Holy Place o
     9:27  Just as people are destined to die o,
1Pe  2:10  O you were not a people,
     3:18  For Christ also suffered o for sins,

## ONE [EVERYONE, ONCE, ONES]
Ge   2:24  wife, and they will become o flesh.
Ex  12: 3  for his family, o for each household.
    33:11  face to face, as o speaks to a friend.
Nu   1: 2  listing every man by name, o by o.
Dt   6: 4  LORD our God, the LORD is o.
Jos 23:10  O of you routs a thousand,
Ps  14: 3  is no o who does good, not even o.
Ecc  4: 9  Two are better than o, because they
Isa 30:17  thousand will flee at the threat of o;
Eze 18: 4  The o who sins is the one
    34:23  I will place over them o shepherd,
    37:22  I will make them o nation
Zec 14: 9  On that day there will be o LORD,
Mal  2:10  Do we not all have o Father? Did not
           o God create us?
Mk  10: 8  and the two will become o flesh.’
    10: 9  joined together, let no o separate.”
    10:21  “O thing you lack,” he said.
    12:29  “The most important o,”
Lk  10:42  or indeed only o.
Jn   1:14  the glory of the o and only [Son],
     1:18  No o has ever seen God, but the o
     3:16  loved the world that he gave his o
    10:16  and there shall be o flock and o
    10:30  I and the Father are o.”
Ro   3:10  is no o righteous, not even o;
     5:15  that came by the grace of the o man,
    13: 9  are summed up in this o command:

1Co 6:16 "The two will become o flesh."
     8: 4 and that "There is no God but o."
    10:17 who are many, are o body, for we
    10:24 No o should seek their own good,
    12:12 Just as a body, though o,
    12:13 by o Spirit so as to form o body—
Gal  5:14 is fulfilled in keeping this o command:
Eph  4: 5 o Lord, o faith, o baptism;
1Ti  2: 5 For there is o God and o mediator
2Pe  3: 8 But do not forget this o thing,

## ANOINTED ONE See ANOINTED

## HOLY ONE See HOLY

## MIGHTY ONE See MIGHTY

## ONE ANOTHER Ge 42:21; Lev 19:11; 26:37;
Jdg 20:22; 2Ki 7:6; 2Ch 20:23; Est 9:22; Job
41:17; Isa 6:3; Jer 9:20; 22:8; 23:27, 30; 31:34;
Zec 7:9; 14:13; Mal 2:10; Mk 8:16; 12:7; 14:4;
Lk 2:15; 6:11; 8:25; 12:1; Jn 5:44; 7:35; 11:56;
12:19; 13:22, 34, 34, 35; 16:17, 19; 19:24; Ac
2:12; 26:31; Ro 1:24, 27; 12:10, 10, 16; 13:8;
14:13; 15:7, 14; 16:16; 1Co 1:10; 16:20; 2Co
13:11, 12; Gal 5:13; Eph 4:2, 32; 5:19, 21; Php
2:5; Col 3:13, 16; 1Th 4:9, 18; 5:11; 2Th 1:3; Tit
3:3; Heb 3:13; 8:11; 10:24, 25; 13:1; Jas 4:11;
5:9; 1Pe 1:22; 3:8; 4:9; 5:5, 14; 1Jn 1:7; 3:11, 16,
23; 4:7, 11, 12, 21; 2Jn 1:5

## ONES [ONE]
Dt   33: 3 all the holy o are in your hand.
1Ch 16:13 his chosen o, the children of Jacob.
Ps   17:14 there be leftovers for their little o.
     37:28 and will not forsake his faithful o.
    105:15 "Do not touch my anointed o;
Mt   18: 6 anyone causes one of these little o—
1Th   3:13 Jesus comes with all his holy o.
Jude  1:14 upon thousands of his holy o

## HOLY ONES See HOLY

## ONESIMUS*
Col  4: 9 He is coming with O, our faithful
Phm  1:10 that I appeal to you for my son O,

## ONESIPHORUS*
2Ti  1:16 show mercy to the household of O,
     4:19 and Aquila and the household of O.

## ONIONS*
Nu   11: 5 melons, leeks, o and garlic.

## ONLY
Ge    6: 5 of the human heart was o evil all
      7:23 O Noah was left, and those
     22: 2 "Take your son, your o son,
Nu   11: 4 and said, "If o we had meat to eat!
     14: 2 them, "If o we had died in Egypt!
     20: 3 said, "If o we had died when our
Dt   15: 5 if o you fully obey the LORD your
1Ki  18:22 "I am the o one of the LORD's
Job  23: 3 If o I knew where to find him; if o I
Ps   30: 5 For his anger lasts o a moment,
Pr   30: 8 but give me o my daily bread.
Jer  23:23 "Am I o a God nearby,"

Mt    4:10 your God, and serve him o.' "
      7:14 that leads to life, and o a few find it.
Mk   13:32 nor the Son, but o the Father.
Jn    1:14 the glory of the one and o [Son],
      1:18 but the one and o [Son], who is
      3:16 that he gave his one and o Son,
Ro    3:29 Is God the God of Jews o? Is he not
1Ti   1:17 invisible, the o God, be honor
1Jn   4: 9 o Son into the world that we might

## ONYX
Ex   28: 9 "Take two o stones and engrave
     28:20 row shall be topaz, o and jasper.

## OPEN [OPENED, OPENHANDED,
OPENING, OPENS]
Dt   28:12 The LORD will o the heavens,
Ps   78: 2 I will o my mouth with a parable;
    118:19 O for me the gates of the righteous;
    145:16 You o your hand and satisfy
Pr   15:11 and Destruction lie o before
     27: 5 Better is o rebuke than hidden love.
SS    5: 2 "O to me, my sister, my darling,
Isa  42: 7 to o eyes that are blind, to free
     53: 7 so he did not o his mouth.
Mal   3:10 I will not throw o the floodgates
Mt   13:35 "I will o my mouth in parables,
     17:27 o its mouth and you will find
Mk    1:10 he saw heaven being torn o
Ac    7:56 "I see heaven o and the Son of Man
Rev   3: 8 I have placed before you an o door
      4: 1 before me was a door standing o
      5: 2 to break the seals and o the scroll?"
     19:11 I saw heaven standing o and there

## OPENED [OPEN]
Ge    3: 7 the eyes of both of them were o,
Nu   16:32 and the earth o its mouth
Ne    8: 5 Ezra o the book.
Ps   40: 6 but my ears you have o—
    105:41 He o the rock, and water gushed
Isa  35: 5 will the eyes of the blind be o
     50: 5 Sovereign LORD has o my ears;
Da    7:10 was seated, and the books were o.
Zec  13: 1 day a fountain will be o to the house
Mt    3:16 At that moment heaven was o,
Lk   11: 9 knock and the door will be o to you.
     24:45 Then he o their minds so they could
Ac   10:11 He saw heaven o and something
Heb  10:20 and living way o for us through
Rev   6: 1 I watched as the Lamb o the first
     11:19 God's temple in heaven was o,
     20:12 before the throne, and books were o.

## OPENHANDED* [HAND, OPEN]
Dt   15: 8 be o and freely lend them whatever
     15:11 command you to be o toward those

## OPENING [OPEN]
Mk    2: 4 they made an o in the roof

## OPENS [OPEN]
Isa  22:22 what he o no one can shut, and what
Rev   3: 7 What he o no one can shut,
      3:20 hears my voice and o the door,

## OPHIR
1Ki 10:11  ships brought gold from O;
Isa 13:12  gold, more rare than the gold of O.

## OPINIONS*
1Ki 18:21  long will you waver between two o?
Pr 18: 2  but delight in airing their own o.

## OPPONENTS* [OPPOSE]
Ps 127: 5  they contend with their o in court.
Pr 18:18  disputes and keeps strong o apart.
Lk 13:17  said this, all his o were humiliated,
2Ti 2:25  O must be gently instructed,

## OPPORTUNE* [OPPORTUNITY]
Mk 6:21  Finally the o time came.
Lk 4:13  he left him until an o time.

## OPPORTUNITY [OPPORTUNE]
Mt 26:16  watched for an o to hand him over.
Ac 25:16  have had an o to defend themselves
Ro 7: 8  sin, seizing the o afforded
2Co 5:12  are giving you an o to take pride
11:12  under those who want an o to be
Gal 6:10  as we have o, let us do good to all
Eph 5:16  making the most of every o,
Php 4:10  but you had no o to show it.
Col 4: 5  make the most of every o.
1Ti 5:14  to give the enemy no o for slander.
Heb 11:15  they would have had o to return.

## OPPOSE [OPPONENTS, OPPOSED, OPPOSES, OPPOSING, OPPOSITION]
Ex 23:22  enemies and will o those who o you.
Nu 16: 3  They came as a group to o Moses
1Sa 2:10  those who o the LORD will be
Job 23:13  stands alone, and who can o him?
Ps 55:18  me, even though many o me.
2Ti 3: 8  so also these teachers o the truth.
Tit 1: 9  doctrine and refute those who o it.
2: 8  those who o you may be ashamed

## OPPOSED [OPPOSE]
Gal 2:11  came to Antioch, I o him to his face,
3:21  therefore, o to the promises of God?
2Ti 3: 8  as Jannes and Jambres o Moses,

## OPPOSES* [OPPOSE]
Mk 3:26  if Satan o himself and is divided,
Lk 23: 2  He o payment of taxes to Caesar
Jn 19:12  who claims to be a king o Caesar."
Jas 4: 6  "God o the proud but shows favor
1Pe 5: 5  "God o the proud but shows favor

## OPPOSING [OPPOSE]
1Ti 6:20  the o ideas of what is falsely called

## OPPOSITION [OPPOSE]
Nu 16:42  the assembly gathered in o to Moses
20: 2  the people gathered in o to Moses
Heb 12: 3  Consider him who endured such o

## OPPRESS [OPPRESSED, OPPRESSES, OPPRESSION, OPPRESSOR, OPPRESSORS]
Ex 1:11  slave masters over them to o them
22:21  "Do not mistreat or o a foreigner,
1Ch 17: 9  people will not o them anymore,
Ps 105:14  He allowed no one to o them;
Pr 22:16  o the poor to increase their wealth
Isa 3: 5  People will o each other—
Eze 22:29  they o the poor and needy
Da 7:25  the Most High and o his holy people
Am 5:12  There are those who o the innocent
Zec 7:10  Do not o the widow
Mal 3: 5  wages, who o the widows

## OPPRESSED [OPPRESS]
Ex 1:12  But the more they were o, the more
Jdg 2:18  of their groaning under those who o
Ne 9:27  when they were o they cried
Ps 9: 9  The LORD is a refuge for the o,
82: 3  the cause of the poor and the o.
103: 6  and justice for all the o.
146: 7  He upholds the cause of the o
Pr 16:19  spirit along with the o than to share
31: 5  and deprive all the o of their rights.
Isa 1:17  Seek justice, encourage the o.
53: 7  He was o and afflicted, yet he did
58:10  and satisfy the needs of the o,
Zep 3:19  time I will deal with all who o you.
Zec 10: 2  the people wander like sheep o
Lk 4:18  sight for the blind, to set the o free,

## OPPRESSES* [OPPRESS]
Pr 14:31  Whoever o the poor shows
28: 3  A ruler who o the poor is like
Eze 18:12  He o the poor and needy.

## OPPRESSION [OPPRESS]
Dt 26: 7  and saw our misery, toil and o.
Ps 72:14  He will rescue them from o
119:134  Redeem me from human o, that I
Isa 53: 8  By o and judgment he was taken
58: 9  "If you do away with the yoke of o,
Eze 45: 9  Give up your violence and o and do

## OPPRESSOR [OPPRESS]
Ps 72: 4  of the needy; may he crush the o.
Isa 51:13  For where is the wrath of the o?

## OPPRESSORS [OPPRESS]
Jdg 6: 9  you from the hand of all your o;
Jer 22: 3  their o those who have been robbed.
Zep 3: 1  Woe to the city of o,

## ORACLE*
Pr 16:10  The lips of a king speak as an o,

## ORDAIN [ORDAINED, ORDINATION]
Ex 29: 9  you shall o Aaron and his sons.

## ORDAINED [ORDAIN]
Ps 111: 9  he o his covenant forever—
139:16  All the days o for me were written

Isa  37:26  Long ago I **o** it. In days of old I
Eze  28:14  as a guardian cherub, for so I **o** you.
Hab   1:12  my Rock, have **o** them to punish.
Mt   21:16  and infants you have **o** praise'?"

## ORDEAL*
1Pe   4:12  do not be surprised at the fiery **o**

## ORDER [ORDERED, ORDERLY, ORDERS]
Nu    9:23  They obeyed the LORD's **o**,
Dt    8: 2  test you in **o** to know what was
2Ch  36:22  Persia, in **o** to fulfill the word
Ps  110: 4  forever, in the **o** of Melchizedek."
Mk    7: 9  of God in **o** to observe your own
Ro    7: 4  in **o** that we might bear fruit
1Co  15:23  But in this **o**: Christ, the firstfruits;
Heb   5:10  high priest in the **o** of Melchizedek.
      9:10  applying until the time of the new **o**.
Rev  21: 4  for the old **o** of things has passed

## ORDERED [ORDER]
2Ki  17:15  the LORD had **o** them,

## ORDERLY* [ORDER]
Lk    1: 3  to write an **o** account for you,
1Co  14:40  be done in a fitting and **o** way.

## ORDERS [ORDER]
Mk    1:27  He even gives **o** to evil spirits
      3:12  But he gave them strict **o** not to tell
      9: 9  Jesus gave them **o** not to tell anyone
Ac    5:28  "We gave you strict **o** not to teach

## ORDINANCE [ORDINANCES]
Ex   12:17  Celebrate this day as a lasting **o**
     29: 9  priesthood is theirs by a lasting **o**.

**A LASTING ORDINANCE** See LASTING

## ORDINANCES [ORDINANCE]
Ps   19: 9  The **o** of the LORD are sure,

## ORDINARY
Ac    4:13  that they were unschooled, **o** men,
Heb  11:23  because they saw he was no **o** child,

## ORDINATION [ORDAIN]
Ex   29:22  (This is the ram for the **o**.)

## OREB
Jdg   7:25  the Midianite leaders, **O** and Zeeb.
Ps   83:11  Make their nobles like **O** and Zeeb,

## ORGIES*
Gal   5:21  drunkenness, **o**, and the like.
1Pe   4: 3  lust, drunkenness, **o**,

## ORIGIN [ORIGINAL, ORIGINATE, ORIGINS]
Est   6:13  is of Jewish **o**, you cannot stand
Ac    5:38  purpose or activity is of human **o**,
2Pe   1:21  For prophecy never had its **o**

## ORIGINAL* [ORIGIN]
2Ch  24:13  of God according to its **o** design
Heb   3:14  hold firmly till the end our **o** conviction.

## ORIGINATE* [ORIGIN]
1Co  14:36  Or did the word of God **o** with you?

## ORIGINS* [ORIGIN]
Mic   5: 2  over Israel, whose **o** are from of old,

## ORION
Job   9: 9  He is the Maker of the Bear and **O**,

## ORNAMENT* [ORNAMENTED, ORNAMENTS]
Pr    3:22  life for you, an **o** to grace your neck.
     25:12  an **o** of fine gold is the rebuke

## ORNAMENTED [ORNAMENT]
Ge   37: 3  and he made a richly **o** robe for him.

## ORNAMENTS [ORNAMENT]
Ex   33: 6  So the Israelites stripped off their **o**

## ORPAH
Ru    1: 4  one named **O** and the other Ruth.

## ORPHAN* [ORPHANS]
Ex   22:22  take advantage of a widow or an **o**.

## ORPHANS* [ORPHAN]
Jn   14:18  I will not leave you as **o**;
Jas   1:27  to look after **o** and widows in their

## OTHER [OTHER'S, OTHERS, OTHERWISE]
Ge   28:17  This is none **o** than the house
Ex   20: 3  shall have no **o** gods before me.
     23:13  Do not invoke the names of **o** gods;
Dt    4:35  besides him there is no **o**.
Jdg   2:19  following **o** gods and serving
1Sa   8:20  we will be like all the **o** nations,
1Ki  11: 4  wives turned his heart after **o** gods,
2Ki  17: 7  They worshiped **o** gods
2Ch   2: 5  our God is greater than all **o** gods.
Ps  147:20  He has done this for no **o** nation;
Ecc   4:10  they can help each **o** up.
Isa  44: 8  No, there is no **o** Rock; I know not
     45: 5  I am the LORD, and there is no **o**;
Jer   7: 6  if you do not follow **o** gods to your
Da    3:29  for no **o** god can save in this way."
Zec   8:17  do not plot evil against each **o**,
Mt    6:24  you will hate the one and love the **o**,
Lk   17:34  one will be taken and the **o** left.
Jn   20:30  Jesus performed many **o** signs
     21:25  Jesus did many **o** things as well.
1Co  14:21  **o** tongues and through the lips of
1Pe   1:22  sincere love for each **o**,
      4: 8  all, love each **o** deeply, because love
2Pe   3:16  as they do the **o** Scriptures, to their
1Jn   3:14  because we love each **o**.
Rev   3:15  I wish you were either one or the **o**!

**NO OTHER** Ex 20:3; Nu 5:19; Dt 4:35, 39; 5:7; 1Sa 18:25; 1Ki 8:60; 1Ch 23:17; Ps 147:20; Isa 44:8; 45:5, 6, 14, 14, 18, 22; 46:9; Eze 31:14, 14; Da 3:29; Joel 2:27; Mk 12:32; Ac 4:12; 1Co 11:16; Gal 5:10

**OTHER GODS** Ex 18:11; 20:3; 23:13; Dt 5:7; 6:14; 7:4; 8:19; 11:16, 28; 13:2, 6, 13; 17:3; 18:20; 28:14, 36, 64; 29:26; 30:17; 31:18, 20; Jos 23:16; 24:2, 16; Jdg 2:17, 19; 10:13; 1Sa 8:8; 26:19; 1Ki 9:6, 9; 11:4, 10; 14:9; 2Ki 17:7, 35, 37, 38; 22:17; 2Ch 2:5; 7:19, 22; 28:25; 34:25; Ps 16:4; Jer 1:16; 7:6, 9, 18; 11:10; 13:10; 16:11, 13; 19:13; 22:9; 25:6; 32:29; 35:15; 44:3, 5, 8, 15; Hos 3:1

**OTHER'S\*** [OTHER]
Ro    1:12   encouraged by each **o** faith.
Gal   6: 2   Carry each **o** burdens, and in this

**OTHERS** [OTHER]
Ps    15: 3   who cast no slur on **o**;
Pr    10:17   ignores correction leads **o** astray.
SS    5: 9   How is your beloved better than **o**,
Da    12: 2   life, **o** to shame and everlasting
Mt    6:14   forgive **o** when they sin against you,
       7: 2   For in the same way you judge **o**,
       7:12   to **o** what you would have them do
Lk    6:31   Do to **o** as you would have them do
Ro    13: 8   whoever loves **o** has fulfilled the law.
2Co   8:21   but also in the eyes of **o**.
Php   2: 3   humility value **o** above yourselves,

**OTHERWISE** [OTHER]
Isa   6:10   **O** they might see with their eyes,
Mt    13:15   **O** they might see with their eyes,
Ac    28:27   **O** they might see with their eyes,
1Ti   6: 3   If anyone teaches **o** and does not

**OTHNIEL**
Nephew of Caleb (Jos 15:15-19; Jdg 1:12-15). Judge who freed Israel from Aram (Jdg 3:7-11).

**OUGHT**
Ro    1:28   that they do what **o** not to be done.
       12: 3   of yourself more highly than you **o**,
Jas   4:17   if you know the good you **o** to do
2Pe   3:11   what kind of people **o** you to be?
1Jn   3:16   we **o** to lay down our lives for one
3Jn   1: 8   We **o** therefore to show hospitality

**OUTBURSTS\***
2Co   12:20   jealousy, **o** of anger, factions,

**OUTCOME**
Isa   41:22   them and know their final **o**.
Da    12: 8   lord, what will the **o** of all this be?"
Heb   13: 7   Consider the **o** of their way of life
1Pe   4:17   what will the **o** be for those who do

**OUTNUMBER** [NUMBER]
Ps    139:18   they would **o** the grains of sand—

**OUTPOURED\*** [POUR]
Ps    79:10   that you avenge the **o** blood of your
Eze   20:33   outstretched arm and with **o** wrath.
       20:34   outstretched arm and with **o** wrath.

**OUTPOURING\*** [POUR]
Eze   9: 8   of Israel in this **o** of your wrath

**OUTRAGEOUS**
Jdg   19:23   don't do this **o** thing.

**OUTSIDE** [OUTSIDERS]
Pr    22:13   sluggard says, "There's a lion **o**!
Mt    22:13   and throw him **o**, into the darkness,
Lk    11:39   you Pharisees clean the **o** of the cup
       13:33   no prophet can die **o** Jerusalem!
1Co   5:13   God will judge those **o**.
Heb   13:12   suffered **o** the city gate to make
Rev   22:15   **O** are the dogs, those who practice

**OUTSIDE THE CAMP** See CAMP

**OUTSIDERS\*** [OUTSIDE]
Col   4: 5   wise in the way you act toward **o**;
1Th   4:12   daily life may win the respect of **o**
1Ti   3: 7   also have a good reputation with **o**,

**OUTSTANDING**
SS    5:10   and ruddy, **o** among ten thousand.
Ro    13: 8   Let no debt remain **o**,

**OUTSTRETCHED** [STRETCH]
Ex    6: 6   I will redeem you with an **o** arm
Dt    4:34   by a mighty hand and an **o** arm,
1Ki   8:42   your mighty hand and your **o** arm—
Ps    136:12   with a mighty hand and **o** arm;
Isa   3:16   walking along with **o** necks,
Jer   27: 5   power and **o** arm I made the earth
       32:17   by your great power and **o** arm.
Eze   20:33   with a mighty hand and an **o** arm

**OUTSTRETCHED ARM** Ex 6:6; Dt 4:34; 5:15; 7:19; 9:29; 11:2; 26:8; 1Ki 8:42; 2Ki 17:36; 2Ch 6:32; Ps 136:12; Jer 27:5; 32:17, 21; Eze 20:33, 34

**OUTWARD\*** [OUTWARDLY]
1Sa   16: 7   People look at the **o** appearance,
Ro    2:28   nor is circumcision merely **o**
1Pe   3: 3   should not come from **o** adornment,

**OUTWARDLY** [OUTWARD]
Ro    2:28   is not a Jew who is one only **o**,
2Co   4:16   Though **o** we are wasting away,

**OUTWEIGHS\*** [WEIGH]
Ecc   10: 1   so a little folly **o** wisdom and honor.
2Co   4:17   an eternal glory that far **o** them all.

**OUTWIT\*** [OUTWITTED]
2Co   2:11   in order that Satan might not **o** us.

**OUTWITTED\*** [OUTWIT]
Mt    2:16   that he had been **o** by the Magi,

# OVER

Ex  12:13  I see the blood, I will pass **o** you.
     12:23  and will pass **o** that doorway, and he
Ps   1: 6  the LORD watches **o** the way
     8: 6  You made them rulers **o** the works
   113: 4  LORD is exalted **o** all the nations,
   145:20  The LORD watches **o** all who love
Isa  31: 5  it, he will 'pass **o**' it and will rescue
Mk   15:15  and handed him **o** to be crucified.

# OVERAWED* [AWE]

Ps  49:16  Do not be **o** when others grow rich,

# OVERBEARING*

Tit   1: 7  not **o**, not quick-tempered, not given

# OVERCAME [OVERCOME]

Hos  12: 4  struggled with the angel and **o** him;

# OVERCOME [OVERCAME, OVERCOMES]

Ge  32:28  with human beings and have **o**."
Mt   16:18  and the gates of death will not **o** it.
Mk    9:24  help me **o** my unbelief!"
Lk   10:19  and to **o** all the power of the enemy;
Jn    1: 5  the darkness has not **o** it.
     16:33  But take heart! I have **o** the world."
Ro   12:21  Do not be **o** by evil, but **o** evil
1Ti   5:11  sensual desires **o** their dedication
2Pe   2:20  are again entangled in it and are **o**,
1Jn   2:13  because you have **o** the evil one.
      4: 4  are from God and have **o** them,
      5: 4  is the victory that has **o** the world,

# OVERCOMES* [OVERCOME]

1Jn   5: 4  everyone born of God **o** the world.
      5: 5  Who is it that **o** the world?

# OVERFLOW [OVERFLOWING, OVERFLOWS]

Ps  65:11  and your carts **o** with abundance.
   119:171  May my lips **o** with praise, for you
La    1:16  I weep and my eyes **o** with tears.
Mt   12:34  the **o** of the heart the mouth speaks.
Lk    6:45  the **o** of the heart the mouth speaks.
Ro    5:15  man, Jesus Christ, **o** to the many!
     15:13  so that you may **o** with hope
2Co   4:15  people may cause thanksgiving to **o**
1Th   3:12  love increase and **o** for each other

# OVERFLOWING [OVERFLOW]

Pr    3:10  then your barns will be filled to **o**,
2Co   8: 2  trial, their **o** joy and their extreme
      9:12  **o** in many expressions of thanks
Col   2: 7  taught, and **o** with thankfulness.

# OVERFLOWS* [OVERFLOW]

Ps  23: 5  anoint my head with oil; my cup **o**.

# OVERJOYED* [JOY]

Da    6:23  The king was **o** and gave orders
Mt   2:10  they saw the star, they were **o**.
Jn   20:20  The disciples were **o** when they saw
Ac   12:14  she was so **o** she ran back without

1Pe   4:13  that you may be **o** when his glory is

# OVERLOOK* [OVERLOOKED, OVERLOOKS]

Dt    9:27  **O** the stubbornness of this people,
     24:19  in your field and you **o** a sheaf,
Pr   12:16  but the prudent **o** an insult.
     19:11  it is to one's glory to **o** an offense.

# OVERLOOKED* [OVERLOOK]

Ac    6: 1  because their widows were being **o**
     17:30  In the past God **o** such ignorance,

# OVERLOOKS [OVERLOOK]

2Ch 20:24  me to the place that **o** the desert

# OVERNIGHT [NIGHT]

Lev  19:13  back the wages of a hired worker **o**.
Jnh   4:10  It sprang up **o** and died **o**.

# OVERPOWER [POWER]

Ge  32:25  man saw that he could not **o** him,
Rev  11: 7  attack them, and **o** and kill them.

# OVERRIGHTEOUS* [RIGHTEOUS]

Ecc   7:16  Do not be **o**, neither be overwise—

# OVERSEER [OVERSEERS]

Pr    6: 7  It has no commander, no **o** or ruler,
1Ti   3: 1  to be an **o** desires a noble task.
      3: 2  Now the **o** is to be above reproach,
Tit   1: 7  Since an **o** manages God's
1Pe   2:25  the Shepherd and **O** of your souls.

# OVERSEERS [OVERSEER]

Ac  20:28  the Holy Spirit has made you **o**.
Php   1: 1  together with the **o** and deacons:

# OVERSHADOW* [OVERSHADOWING]

1Ch 28:18  and **o** the ark of the covenant
Lk    1:35  power of the Most High will **o** you.

# OVERSHADOWING [OVERSHADOW]

Ex  25:20  upward, **o** the cover with them.
Heb   9: 5  of the Glory, **o** the atonement cover.

# OVERTAKE [OVERTAKES]

Ps  91:10  no harm will **o** you,

# OVERTAKES [OVERTAKE]

Pr   12:21  No harm **o** the righteous,

# OVERTHREW [OVERTHROW]

Ge  19:25  Thus he **o** those cities and the entire
Jer  50:40  As I **o** Sodom and Gomorrah along

# OVERTHROW [OVERTHREW, OVERTHROWN, OVERTHROWS]

2Th   2: 8  whom the Lord Jesus will **o**

## OVERTHROWN [OVERTHROW]
Isa 13:19 will be **o** by God like Sodom

## OVERTHROWS [OVERTHROW]
Pr 13: 6 but wickedness **o** the sinner.
Isa 44:25 who **o** the learning of the wise

## OVERTURNED
Mk 11:15 He **o** the tables of the money

## OVERWHELMED
[OVERWHELMING]
2Sa 22: 5 the torrents of destruction **o** me.
1Ki 10: 5 temple of the LORD, she was **o**.
Ps 38: 4 My guilt has **o** me like a burden too
65: 3 When we were **o** by sins,
Mt 26:38 "My soul is **o** with sorrow
Mk 7:37 People were **o** with amazement.
9:15 they were **o** with wonder and ran
2Co 2: 7 so that he will not be **o** by excessive

## OVERWHELMING
[OVERWHELMED]
Pr 27: 4 Anger is cruel and fury **o**, but who
Isa 10:22 has been decreed, **o** and righteous.
28:15 When an **o** scourge sweeps by,
Na 1: 8 with an **o** flood he will make an end

## OVERWICKED* [WICKED]
Ecc 7:17 Do not be **o**, and do not be a fool—

## OVERWISE* [WISE]
Ecc 7:16 not be overrighteous, neither be **o**—

## OWE [OWES]
Ro 13: 7 Give to everyone what you **o**:
Phm 1:19 that you **o** me your very self.

## OWES* [OWE]
Dt 15: 3 any debt one of your people **o** you.
Phm 1:18 you any wrong or **o** you anything,

## OWN [OWNER, OWNER'S, OWNERSHIP, OWNS]
Ge 1:27 human beings in his **o** image,
15: 4 your **o** body will be your heir."
Ex 6: 7 I will take you as my **o** people, and I
32:13 to whom you swore by your **o** self:
Dt 18:15 among you, from your **o** people.
24:16 each of you will die for your **o** sin.
1Sa 13:14 sought out a man after his **o** heart
Pr 3: 7 Do not be wise in your **o** eyes;
26:12 people who are wise in their **o** eyes?
Isa 48:11 For my **o** sake, for my **o** sake, I do
53: 6 each of us has turned to our **o** way;
Jer 10:23 that people's lives are not their **o**;
31:30 everyone will die for their **o** sin;
Eze 33: 4 their blood will be on their **o** head.
Jn 1:11 He came to that which was his **o**,
7:16 "My teaching is not my **o**.
10:12 and does not **o** the sheep.
10:18 but I lay it down of my **o** accord.
12:49 For I did not speak on my **o**,

Ro 8:32 He who did not spare his **o** Son,
1Co 6:19 You are not your **o**;
7: 7 of you has your **o** gift from God;
Gal 6: 5 of you should carry your **o** load.
Php 2: 4 not looking to your **o** interests

## OWNER [OWN]
Mt 21:40 when the **o** of the vineyard comes,
24:43 If the **o** of the house had known

## OWNER'S [OWN]
Isa 1: 3 the donkey its **o** manger, but Israel

## OWNERSHIP* [OWN]
2Co 1:22 set his seal of **o** on us, and put his

## OWNS [OWN]
Mt 18:12 If a man **o** a hundred sheep, and one

## OX [OXEN]
Ex 20:17 or female servant, his **o** or donkey,
Dt 22:10 Do not plow with an **o** and a donkey
25: 4 Do not muzzle an **o** while it is
Pr 7:22 he followed her like an **o** going
Isa 11: 7 and the lion will eat straw like the **o**.
65:25 and the lion will eat straw like the **o**,
Eze 1:10 lion, and on the left the face of an **o**;
Lk 13:15 of you on the Sabbath untie your **o**
1Co 9: 9 "Do not muzzle an **o** while it is
1Ti 5:18 "Do not muzzle an **o** while it is
Rev 4: 7 the second was like an **o**, the third

## OXEN [OX]
1Ki 19:20 then left his **o** and ran after Elijah.
Lk 14:19 'I have just bought five yoke of **o**,
1Co 9: 9 Is it about **o** that God is concerned?

---

# P

---

## PADDAN ARAM [ARAM]
Ge 28: 2 Go at once to **P**, to the house
35: 9 After Jacob returned from **P**,

## PAGAN [PAGANS]
Isa 57: 8 you have put your **p** symbols.
Mt 18:17 treat them as you would a **p** or a tax
Lk 12:30 For the **p** world runs after all such

## PAGANS* [PAGAN]
Isa 2: 6 Philistines and clasp hands with **p**.
Mt 5:47 Do not even **p** do that?
6: 7 do not keep on babbling like **p**,
6:32 For the **p** run after all these things,
1Co 5: 1 of a kind that even **p** do not tolerate:
10:20 but the sacrifices of **p** are offered
12: 2 You know that when you were **p**,
1Th 4: 5 not in passionate lust like the **p**,
1Pe 2:12 such good lives among the **p** that,
4: 3 the past doing what **p** choose to do—
3Jn 1: 7 out, receiving no help from the **p**.

## PAID [PAY]
Jdg 1: 7 Now God has **p** me back for what I
1Sa 25:21 He has **p** me back evil for good.
Ne 9:30 Yet they **p** no attention, so you gave
Isa 40: 2 that her sin has been **p** for, that she
Zec 11:12 So they **p** me thirty pieces of silver.
2Pe 2:13 They will be **p** back with harm

## PAIN [PAINFUL, PAINS]
Ge 3:16 with **p** you will give birth
Job 6:10 my joy in unrelenting **p**—that I had
33:19 on a bed of **p** with constant distress
Isa 26:18 we writhed in **p**, but we gave birth
53: 4 he took up our **p** and bore our suffering,
Jer 4:19 I writhe in **p**. Oh, the agony of my
15:18 Why is my **p** unending and my
Mt 4:24 those suffering severe **p**,
Jn 16:21 to a child has **p** because her time has
1Pe 2:19 up under the **p** of unjust suffering
Rev 21: 4 death' or mourning or crying or **p**,

## PAINFUL [PAIN]
Ge 3:17 through **p** toil you will eat of it all
5:29 **p** toil of our hands caused
Job 6:25 How **p** are honest words!
Eze 28:24 neighbors who are **p** briers
2Co 2: 1 I would not make another **p** visit
Heb 12:11 seems pleasant at the time, but **p**.

## PAINS [PAIN]
Ge 3:16 "I will make your **p** in childbearing
Mk 13: 8 These are the beginning of birth **p**.
Ro 8:22 as in the **p** of childbirth right
Gal 4:19 in the **p** of childbirth until Christ is
1Th 5: 3 as labor **p** on a pregnant woman,

## PAIRS
Ge 7: 8 **P** of clean and unclean animals,

## PALACE [PALACES]
2Sa 5:11 and they built a **p** for David.
1Ki 7: 2 He built the **P** of the Forest
9: 1 of the LORD and the royal **p**,
Est 9: 4 Mordecai was prominent in the **p**;
Jer 22:13 "Woe to him who builds his **p**
52:13 the royal **p** and all the houses
Jn 18:28 to the **p** of the Roman governor.
Ac 23:35 be kept under guard in Herod's **p**.

## PALACES [PALACE]
Hos 8:14 forgotten their Maker and built **p**;
Lk 7:25 and indulge in luxury are in **p**.

## PALE
Isa 29:22 no longer will their faces grow **p**.
Jer 30: 6 labor, every face turned deathly **p**?
Da 10: 8 my face turned deathly **p** and I was
Rev 6: 8 and there before me was a **p** horse!

## PALESTINE (KJV) See PHILISTIA, PHILISTINE

## PALM [PALMS]
Ex 15:27 twelve springs and seventy **p** trees,

Jdg 4: 5 She held court under the **P**
1Ki 6:29 cherubim, **p** trees and open flowers.
Ps 92:12 righteous will flourish like a **p** tree,
Jn 12:13 They took **p** branches and went
Rev 7: 9 and were holding **p** branches in their

## PALMS [PALM]
Lev 23:40 from **p**, willows and other leafy
Ne 8:15 and from myrtles, **p** and shade trees,
Isa 49:16 engraved you on the **p** of my hands;

## PAMPERED⁺
Pr 29:21 servant **p** from youth will turn

## PANELED [PANELING]
Hag 1: 4 to be living in your **p** houses,

## PANELING* [PANELED]
1Ki 6:15 **p** them from the floor of the temple
Ps 74: 6 They smashed all the carved **p**

## PANIC
Dt 20: 3 or give way to **p** before them.
1Sa 14:15 It was a **p** sent by God.
Isa 28:16 relies on it will never be stricken with **p**
Eze 7: 7 There is **p**, not joy,
Zec 14:13 by the LORD with great **p**.

## PANTS*
Ps 42: 1 As the deer **p** for streams of water, so my soul **p** for you,

## PAPER*
2Jn 1:12 but I do not want to use **p** and ink.

## PAPYRUS
Ex 2: 3 she got a **p** basket for him

## PARABLE [PARABLES]
Ps 78: 2 open my mouth with a **p**;
Eze 17: 2 tell it to the house of Israel as a **p**.
Mt 13:18 to what the **p** of the sower means:
15:15 Peter said, "Explain the **p** to us."
21:33 "Listen to another **p**: There was
Lk 20:19 he had spoken this **p** against them.

## PARABLES [PARABLE]
See also JESUS: PARABLES
Mt 13:35 "I will open my mouth in **p**, I will
Lk 8:10 but to others I speak in **p**, so that,

## PARADISE*
Lk 23:43 today you will be with me in **p**."
2Co 12: 4 was caught up to **p** and heard
Rev 2: 7 tree of life, which is in the **p** of God.

## PARALYZED
Hab 1: 4 Therefore the law is **p**, and justice
Mt 9: 2 men brought to him a **p** man,
Mk 2: 3 bringing to him a **p** man,
Jn 5: 3 the blind, the lame, the **p**.
Ac 9:33 was **p** and had been bedridden

## PARAN
Ge   21:21  he was living in the Desert of **P**,
Nu   10:12  came to rest in the Desert of **P**.
Hab   3: 3  the Holy One from Mount **P**.

## PARCHED
Ps  143: 6  I thirst for you like a **p** land.
Isa   41:18  and the **p** ground into springs.

## PARCHMENTS*
2Ti   4:13  and my scrolls, especially the **p**.

## PARDON  [PARDONED, PARDONS]
2Ch 30:18  LORD, who is good, **p** everyone
Job   7:21  Why do you not **p** my offenses
Isa   55: 7  and to our God, for he will freely **p**.

## PARDONED*  [PARDON]
Nu   14:19  just as you have **p** them

## PARDONS*  [PARDON]
Mic   7:18  like you, who **p** sin and forgives

## PARENT  [FATHER, PARENT'S,
    PARENTS]
Pr   17:21  no joy for the **p** of a godless fool.

## PARENT'S*  [PARENT]
Pr   13: 1  A wise child heeds a **p** instruction,
      15: 5  A fool spurns a **p** discipline,

## PARENTS  [PARENT]
Ex   20: 5  the children for the sin of the **p**
Dt   24:16  **P** are not to be put to death for their
      24:16  nor children put to death for their **p**;
Pr   17: 6  and **p** are the pride of their children.
      19:14  and wealth are inherited from **p**,
      28: 7  companions of gluttons disgrace their **p**.
Jer   31:29  'The **p** have eaten sour grapes,
La    5: 7  Our **p** sinned and are no more,
Eze   18: 2  " 'The **p** eat sour grapes,
Mal   4: 6  turn the hearts of the **p** to their children,
      4: 6  and the hearts of the children to their **p**;
Mk   13:12  Children will rebel against their **p**
Lk    1:17  turn the hearts of the **p** to their children
      2:27  When the **p** brought in the child
      18:29  sisters or **p** or children for the sake
      21:16  You will be betrayed even by **p**,
Jn    9: 3  this man nor his **p** sinned,"
Ro    1:30  of doing evil; they disobey their **p**;
2Co  12:14  not have to save up for their **p**, but **p**
Eph   6: 1  Children, obey your **p** in the Lord,
Col   3:20  Children, obey your **p** in everything,
1Ti   5: 4  family and so repaying their **p**
2Ti   3: 2  disobedient to their **p**, ungrateful,
Heb  12: 9  we have all had **p** who disciplined us

## PARSIN*  [PERES]
Da    5:25  MENE, MENE, TEKEL, **P**

## PART  [APART, PARTED, PARTLY,
    PARTS]
Nu   18:29  and holiest **p** of everything given

2Sa   20: 1  share in David, no **p** in Jesse's son!
1Ki   12:16  in David, what **p** in Jesse's son?
Job   42:12  LORD blessed the latter **p** of Job's life
Ps   144: 5  **P** your heavens, LORD, and come
Mt    5:29  you to lose one **p** of your body than
Jn    13: 8  wash you, you have no **p** with me."
1Co  12:14  so the body is not made up of one **p**
      13: 9  we know in **p** and we prophesy in **p**,
      13:10  what is in **p** disappears.
Rev   20: 6  holy are those who have **p**

## PARTAKE*
1Co  10:17  body, for we all **p** of the one loaf.

## PARTED  [PART]
Ge    13:11  The two men **p** company:
2Sa   22:10  He **p** the heavens and came down;
Ac    15:39  disagreement that they **p** company.

## PARTIAL*  [PARTIALITY]
Pr    18: 5  It is not good to be **p** to the wicked

## PARTIALITY*  [PARTIAL]
Lev   19:15  do not show **p** to the poor
Dt    1:17  Do not show **p** in judging;
      10:17  who shows no **p** and accepts no
      16:19  Do not pervert justice or show **p**.
2Ch  19: 7  our God there is no injustice or **p**
Job   13: 8  Will you show him **p**?
      13:10  to account if you secretly showed **p**.
      32:21  I will show no **p**, nor will I flatter
      34:19  who shows no **p** to princes and does
Ps    82: 2  unjust and show **p** to the wicked?
Pr    24:23  To show **p** in judging is not good:
      28:21  To show **p** is not good—
Mal   2: 9  but have shown **p** in matters
Lk    20:21  that you do not show **p** but teach
1Ti   5:21  to keep these instructions without **p**,

## PARTICIPANTS*  [PARTICIPATE]
1Co  10:20  not want you to be **p** with demons.

## PARTICIPATE*  [PARTICIPANTS,
    PARTICIPATION]
1Co  10:18  not those who eat the sacrifices **p**
1Pe   4:13  But rejoice inasmuch as you **p**
2Pe   1: 4  that through them you may **p**

## PARTICIPATION*  [PARTICIPATE]
1Co  10:16  we give thanks a **p** in the blood
      10:16  bread that we break a **p** in the body
Php   3:10  resurrection and **p** in his sufferings,

## PARTLY  [PART]
Da    2:33  its feet **p** of iron and **p** of baked

## PARTNER  [PARTNERS,
    PARTNERSHIP]
Pr    2:17  who has left the **p** of her youth
Mal   2:14  though she is your **p**, the wife
1Pe   3: 7  them with respect as the weaker **p**

## PARTNERS  [PARTNER]
Eph   5: 7  Therefore do not be **p** with them.

## PARTNERSHIP* [PARTNER]
Php 1: 5 because of your **p** in the gospel
Phm 1: 6 your **p** with us in the faith may be

## PARTS [PART]
Pr 18: 8 they go down to the inmost **p**.
1Co 12:20 is, there are many **p**, but one body.

## PASHHUR
Priest; opponent of Jeremiah (Jer 20:1–6).

## PASS [PASSED, PASSER-BY, PASSES, PASSING]
Ex 12:13 I see the blood, I will **p** over you.
12:23 and will **p** over that doorway,
33:19 "I will cause all my goodness to **p**
Nu 20:17 Please let us **p** through your
21:22 "Let us **p** through your country.
1Ki 9: 8 All who **p** by will be appalled
19:11 for the LORD is about to **p** by."
Ps 90:10 for they quickly **p**, and we fly away.
105:19 till what he foretold came to **p**,
Ecc 6:12 they **p** through like a shadow?
Isa 31: 5 it, he will '**p** over' it and will rescue
43: 2 When you **p** through the waters,
43: 2 and when you **p** through the rivers,
62:10 **P** through, **p** through the gates!
Jer 22: 8 many nations will **p** by this city
La 1:12 it nothing to you, all you who **p** by?
Da 7:14 dominion that will not **p** away,
Am 5:17 for I will **p** through your midst,"
Mt 24:35 Heaven and earth will **p** away, but my words will never **p** away.
Mk 14:35 possible the hour might **p** from him.
Ro 2: 1 because you who **p** judgment do
1Co 13: 8 there is knowledge, it will **p** away.
Jas 1:10 since they will **p** away like a wild
1Jn 2:17 The world and its desires **p** away,

## PASSED [PASS]
Ge 15:17 appeared and **p** between the pieces.
Ex 12:27 who **p** over the houses
33:22 you with my hand until I have **p** by.
34: 6 And he **p** in front of Moses,
Nu 33: 8 **p** through the sea into the desert,
Jos 3:17 while all Israel **p** by until the whole
2Ch 21:20 He **p** away, to no one's regret,
Ps 37:36 but they soon **p** away and were no
57: 1 your wings until the disaster has **p**.
Lk 10:32 and saw him, **p** by on the other side.
1Co 15: 3 For what I received I **p** on to you as
Heb 11:29 faith the people **p** through the Red
1Jn 3:14 We know that we have **p** from death
Rev 21: 1 and the first earth had **p** away,
21: 4 the old order of things has **p** away."

## PASSER-BY* [PASS]
Pr 26:10 is one who hires a fool or any **p**.

## PASSES [PASS]
Ex 33:22 When my glory **p** by, I will put you
Zep 2: 2 that day **p** like windblown chaff,

## PASSING [PASS]
Ro 14:13 Therefore let us stop **p** judgment
1Co 7:31 world in its present form is **p** away.
2Co 3:13 the end of what was **p** away.
1Jn 2: 8 because the darkness is **p**

## PASSION* [PASSIONATE, PASSIONS]
Ps 11: 5 who love violence, he hates with a **p**.
Hos 7: 6 Their **p** smolders all night;
1Co 7: 9 better to marry than to burn with **p**.

## PASSIONATE* [PASSION]
1Th 4: 5 not in **p** lust like the pagans, who do

## PASSIONS* [PASSION]
Ro 7: 5 the sinful **p** aroused by the law were
Gal 5:24 crucified the sinful nature with its **p**
Tit 2:12 to ungodliness and worldly **p**,
3: 3 and enslaved by all kinds of **p**

## PASSOVER
Ex 12:11 Eat it in haste; it is the LORD's **P**.
Lev 23: 5 The LORD's **P** begins at twilight
Nu 9: 2 "Have the Israelites celebrate the **P**
Dt 16: 1 celebrate the **P** of the LORD your
Jos 5:10 the Israelites celebrated the **P**.
2Ki 23:21 "Celebrate the **P** to the LORD
2Ch 30: 1 and celebrate the **P** to the LORD,
Ezr 6:19 month, the exiles celebrated the **P**.
Mk 14:12 customary to sacrifice the **P** lamb,
14:12 preparations for you to eat the **P**?"
Lk 22: 8 preparations for us to eat the **P**."
1Co 5: 7 For Christ, our **P** lamb, has been
Heb 11:28 By faith he kept the **P**

## PAST
Ge 18:11 Sarah was **p** the age of childbearing.
Ecc 3:15 and God will call the **p** to account.
Isa 43:18 do not dwell on the **p**.
65:16 For the **p** troubles will be forgotten
Ac 14:16 In the **p**, he let all nations go their
17:30 In the **p** God overlooked such
Ro 15: 4 was written in the **p** was written
16:25 the mystery hidden for long ages **p**,
Eph 3: 9 for ages **p** was kept hidden in God,
Heb 1: 1 In the **p** God spoke to our ancestors
11:11 Sarah, who was **p** childbearing age,
1Pe 3: 5 women of the **p** who put their hope
2Pe 1: 9 been cleansed from your **p** sins.

## PASTORS*
Eph 4:11 the evangelists, the **p** and teachers,

## PASTURE [PASTURELANDS, PASTURES]
Ps 37: 3 dwell in the land and enjoy safe **p**.
79:13 the sheep of your **p**, will praise you
95: 7 God and we are the people of his **p**,
100: 3 are his people, the sheep of his **p**.
Jer 23: 1 and scattering the sheep of my **p**!"
50: 7 their verdant **p**, the LORD,
Eze 34:13 I will **p** them on the mountains
Jn 10: 9 will come in and go out, and find **p**.

## PASTURELANDS [PASTURE]
Nu  35: 2  And give them **p** around the towns.

## PASTURES [PASTURE]
Ps  23: 2  He makes me lie down in green **p**,

## PATCH
Jer  10: 5  Like a scarecrow in a melon **p**,
Mk  2:21  "No one sews a **p** of unshrunk cloth

## PATH [PATHS]
Nu  22:24  in a narrow **p** through the vineyards,
2Sa  22:37  You provide a broad **p** for my feet,
Ne  9:19  not cease to guide them on their **p**,
Job  16:22  before I take the **p** of no return.
Ps  16:11  make known to me the **p** of life;
    27:11  me in a straight **p** because of my
    119:32  I run in the **p** of your commands,
    119:105  to my feet and a light for my **p**.
Pr  2: 9  and just and fair—every good **p**.
    5: 8  Keep to a **p** far from her, do not go
    12:28  along that **p** is immortality.
    15:10  awaits those who leave the **p**;
    15:19  the **p** of the upright is a highway.
    15:24  The **p** of life leads upward
    21:16  strays from the **p** of prudence comes
Isa  26: 7  The **p** of the righteous is level;
Jer  31: 9  on a level **p** where they will not
Mt  13: 4  some fell along the **p**, and the birds
Lk  1:79  guide our feet into the **p** of peace."
2Co  6: 3  no stumbling block in anyone's **p**,

## PATHS [PATH]
Ps  17: 5  My steps have held to your **p**;
    23: 3  He guides me along the right **p**
    25: 4  ways, LORD, teach me your **p**.
Pr  1:19  Such are the **p** of all who go after
    2:13  who have left the straight **p** to walk
    2:18  and her **p** to the spirits of the dead.
    3: 6  and he will make your **p** straight.
    4:11  and lead you along straight **p**.
    4:26  careful thought to the **p** for your feet
    5:21  and he examines all your **p**.
    8:20  righteousness, along the **p** of justice,
    22: 5  In the **p** of the wicked are snares
Isa  2: 3  so that we may walk in his **p**."
Jer  6:16  ask for the ancient **p**, ask where
Mic  4: 2  so that we may walk in his **p**."
Mt  3: 3  Lord, make straight **p** for him.' "
Ac  2:28  made known to me the **p** of life;
Ro  11:33  and his **p** beyond tracing out!
Heb  12:13  "Make level **p** for your feet,"

## PATIENCE* [PATIENT]
Pr  19:11  A person's wisdom yields **p**; it is
    25:15  Through **p** a ruler can be persuaded,
Ecc  7: 8  and **p** is better than pride.
Isa  7:13  to try the **p** of human beings?
    7:13  Will you try the **p** of my God also?
Ro  2: 4  forbearance and **p**, not realizing
    9:22  bore with great **p** the objects of his
2Co  6: 6  understanding, **p** and kindness;
Gal  5:22  joy, peace, **p**, kindness, goodness,
Col  1:11  may have great endurance and **p**,
    3:12  humility, gentleness and **p**.

1Ti  1:16  might display his immense **p** as
2Ti  3:10  of life, my purpose, faith, **p**, love,
    4: 2  with great **p** and careful instruction.
Heb  6:12  **p** inherit what has been promised.
Jas  5:10  as an example of **p** in the face
2Pe  3:15  that our Lord's **p** means salvation,

## PATIENT* [PATIENCE, PATIENTLY]
Ne  9:30  many years you were **p** with them.
Job  6:11  What prospects, that I should be **p**?
Pr  14:29  Those who are **p** have great
    15:18  but those who are **p** calm a quarrel.
    16:32  Better a **p** person than a warrior,
Mt  18:26  'Be **p** with me,' he begged, 'and I
    18:29  and begged him, 'Be **p** with me,
Ro  12:12  Be joyful in hope, **p** in affliction,
1Co  13: 4  Love is **p**, love is kind. It does not
2Co  1: 6  produces in you **p** endurance
Eph  4: 2  be **p**, bearing with one another
1Th  5:14  help the weak, be **p** with everyone.
Jas  5: 7  Be **p**, then, brothers and sisters,
    5: 8  You too, be **p** and stand firm,
2Pe  3: 9  Instead he is **p** with you,
Rev  1: 9  **p** endurance that are ours in Jesus,
    13:10  This calls for **p** endurance
    14:12  This calls for **p** endurance

## PATIENTLY* [PATIENT]
Ps  37: 7  the LORD and wait **p** for him;
    40: 1  I waited **p** for the LORD;
Isa  38:13  I waited **p** till dawn, but like a lion
Hab  3:16  Yet I will wait **p** for the day
Ac  26: 3  I beg you to listen to me **p**.
Ro  8:25  we do not yet have, we wait for it **p**.
Heb  6:15  And so after waiting **p**,
Jas  5: 7  **p** waiting for the autumn and spring
1Pe  3:20  ago when God waited **p** in the days
Rev  3:10  have kept my command to endure **p**,

## PATMOS*
Rev  1: 9  the island of **P** because of the word

## PATRIARCH* [PATRIARCHS]
Ac  2:29  we all know that the **p** David died
Heb  7: 4  Even the **p** Abraham gave him

## PATRIARCHS [PATRIARCH]
Jn  7:22  but from the **p**), you circumcise
Ro  9: 5  Theirs are the **p**, and from them is
    15: 8  made to the **p** might be confirmed

## PATTERN
Ex  25:40  them according to the **p** shown you
Nu  8: 4  exactly like the **p** the LORD had
Ro  5:14  who is a **p** of the one to come.
    12: 2  not conform to the **p** of this world,
2Ti  1:13  me, keep as the **p** of sound teaching,
Heb  8: 5  according to the **p** shown you

## PAUL [SAUL]
Also called Saul (Ac 13:9). Pharisee from Tarsus (Ac 9:11; Php 3:5). Apostle (Gal 1). At stoning of Stephen (Ac 8:1). Persecuted Church (Ac 9:1–2; Gal 1:13). Vision of Jesus on road to Damascus (Ac 9:4–9; 26:12–18). In Arabia (Gal 1:17). Preached in

Damascus; escaped death through the wall in a basket (Ac 9:19–25). In Jerusalem; sent back to Tarsus (Ac 9:26–30).

Brought to Antioch by Barnabas (Ac 11:22–26). First missionary journey to Cyprus and Galatia (Ac 13–14). Stoned at Lystra (Ac 14:19–20). At Jerusalem council (Ac 15). Split with Barnabas over Mark (Ac 15:36–41).

Second missionary journey with Silas (Ac 16–20). Called to Macedonia (Ac 16:6–10). Freed from prison in Philippi (Ac 16:16–40). In Thessalonica (Ac 17.1–9). Speech in Athens (Ac 17:16 33). In Corinth (Ac 18). In Ephesus (Ac 19). Return to Jerusalem (Ac 20). Farewell to Ephesian elders (Ac 20:13–38). Arrival in Jerusalem (Ac 21:1–26). Arrested (Ac 21:27–36). Addressed crowds (Ac 22), Sanhedrin (Ac 23:1–11). Sent to Caesarea (Ac 23:12–35). Trial before Felix (Ac 24), Festus (Ac 25:1–12). Before Agrippa (Ac 25:13—26:32). Voyage to Rome; shipwreck (Ac 27). Arrival in Rome (Ac 28).

Letters: Romans, 1 and 2 Corinthians, Galatians, Ephesians, Philippians, Colossians, 1 and 2 Thessalonians, 1 and 2 Timothy, Titus, Philemon.

## PAVEMENT

Ex 24:10 feet was something like a **p** made
Jn 19:13 seat at a place known as the Stone **P**

## PAW*

1Sa 17:37 the **p** of the lion and the **p** of the bear

## PAY [PAID, PAYING, PAYMENT, PAYS, REPAID, REPAY, REPAYING]

Ge 23:13 I will **p** the price of the field.
Ex 4: 8 you or **p** attention to the first sign,
 15:26 if you **p** attention to his commands
 22: 3 they must be sold to **p** for their
 22: 4 they must **p** back double.
 30:12 them, each one must **p** the LORD
Lev 26:43 They will **p** for their sins because
Dt 7:12 If you **p** attention to these laws
Ps 94: 2 **p** back to the proud what they
Pr 4: 1 **p** attention and gain understanding.
 4:20 My son, **p** attention to what I say;
 5: 1 My son, **p** attention to my wisdom,
 6:31 he must **p** sevenfold, though it costs
 19:19 hot-tempered must **p** the penalty;
 22:17 **P** attention and turn your ear
 24:29 I'll **p** them back for what they did."
Jer 7:24 they did not listen or **p** attention;
Eze 40: 4 **p** attention to everything I am going
Zec 11:12 "If you think it best, give me my **p**;
Mt 20: 4 and I will **p** you whatever is right.'
 22:16 because you **p** no attention to who
 22:17 Is it right to **p** the imperial tax
Lk 3:14 be content with your **p**."
 19: 8 I will **p** back four times
Ro 13: 6 This is also why you **p** taxes,
2Th 1: 6 He will **p** back trouble to those who
2Pe 1:19 you will do well to **p** attention to it,
Rev 18: 6 **p** her back double for what she has

## PAYING [PAY]

1Ch 21:24 "No, I insist on **p** the full price.
Mt 22:19 me the coin used for **p** the tax."

## PAYMENT [PAY]

Ps 49: 8 a life is costly, no **p** is ever enough—
Isa 65: 7 their laps the full **p** for their former
Php 4:18 I have received full **p** and have

## PAYS [PAY]

Ps 31:23 him, but the proud he **p** back in full.
Pr 17:13 the house of one who **p** back evil
1Th 5:15 sure that nobody **p** back wrong

## PEACE [PEACE-LOVING, PEACEABLE, PEACEFUL, PEACEMAKERS]

Lev 26: 6 " 'I will grant **p** in the land,
Nu 6:26 toward you and give you **p**." '
 25:12 him I am making my covenant of **p**.
Dt 20:10 a city, make its people an offer of **p**.
Jos 9:15 Joshua made a treaty of **p** with them
 11:19 not one city made a treaty of **p**
Jdg 3:11 So the land had **p** for forty years.
 3:30 and the land had **p** for eighty years.
 5:31 Then the land had **p** forty years.
 6:24 there and called it The LORD Is **P**.
 8:28 lifetime, the land had **p** forty years.
1Sa 1:17 "Go in **p**, and may the God of Israel
 7:14 And there was **p** between Israel
 20:42 David, "Go in **p**, for we have sworn
2Sa 10:19 they made **p** with the Israelites
1Ki 2:33 there be the LORD's **p** forever."
2Ki 9:17 and ask, 'Do you come in **p**?' "
1Ch 19:19 they made **p** with David and became
 22: 9 have a son who will be a man of **p**
2Ch 14: 1 his days the country was at **p** for ten
 20:30 kingdom of Jehoshaphat was at **p**,
Job 3:26 I have no **p**, no quietness; I have no
 22:21 to God and be at **p** with him;
Ps 29:11 LORD blesses his people with **p**.
 34:14 and do good; seek **p** and pursue it.
 37:11 the land and enjoy **p** and prosperity.
 37:37 a future awaits those who seek **p**.
 85: 8 he promises **p** to his people,
 85:10 righteousness and **p** kiss each other.
 119:165 Great **p** have those who love your
 120: 7 I am for **p**; but when I speak,
 122: 6 Pray for the **p** of Jerusalem:
 147:14 He grants **p** to your borders
Pr 3:17 ways, and all her paths are **p**.
 12:20 but those who promote **p** have joy.
 14:30 A heart at **p** gives life to the body,
 16: 7 their enemies to make **p** with them.
 17: 1 Better a dry crust with **p** and quiet
Ecc 3: 8 a time for war and a time for **p**.
Isa 9: 6 Everlasting Father, Prince of **P**.
 14: 7 All the lands are at rest and at **p**;
 26: 3 in perfect **p** those whose minds are
 32:17 fruit of that righteousness will be **p**;
 48:18 your **p** would have been like a river,
 48:22 "There is no **p**," says the LORD.
 52: 7 who proclaim **p**, who bring good
 53: 5 that brought us **p** was on him,
 54:10 nor my covenant of **p** be removed,"
 55:12 go out in joy and be led forth in **p**;
 57: 2 who walk uprightly enter into **p**;
 57:19 **P, p**, to those far and near,"
 57:21 "There is no **p**," says my God,
 59: 8 The way of **p** they do not know;
 59: 8 along them will know **p**.

Isa  66:12  "I will extend **p** to her like a river,
Jer   6:14  'P, p,' they say, when there is no **p**.
       8:11  "P, p," they say, when there is no **p**.
      30:10  Jacob will again have **p**
      33: 6  will let them enjoy abundant **p**
      46:27  Jacob will again have **p**
La    3:17  I have been deprived of **p**;
Eze  13:10  saying, "P," when there is no **p**,
      34:25  " 'I will make a covenant of **p**
      37:26  I will make a covenant of **p**
Mic   5: 5  he will be our **p** when the Assyrians
Na    1:15  brings good news, who proclaims **p**!
Hag   2: 9  'And in this place I will grant **p**,'
Zec   8:19  Therefore love truth and **p**."
       9:10  He will proclaim **p** to the nations.
Mal   2: 5  a covenant of life and **p**, and I gave
       2: 6  He walked with me in **p**
Mt   10:13  is deserving, let your **p** rest on it;
      10:34  I did not come to bring **p**,
Mk    9:50  and be at **p** with each other."
Lk    1:79  to guide our feet into the path of **p**."
       2:14  and on earth **p** to those on whom his
       7:50  faith has saved you; go in **p**."
      19:38  "P in heaven and glory
      19:42  this day what would bring you **p**—
Jn   14:27  P I leave with you; my **p** I give you.
      16:33  so that in me you may have **p**.
Ac   10:36  news of **p** through Jesus Christ,
Ro    2:10  and **p** for everyone who does good:
       3:17  the way of **p** they do not know."
       5: 1  we have **p** with God through our
       8: 6  controlled by the Spirit is life and **p**.
      12:18  on you, live at **p** with everyone.
      14:19  every effort to do what leads to **p**
      16:20  **p** will soon crush Satan under your
1Co   7:15  God has called us to live in **p**.
      14:33  is not a God of disorder but of **p**—
2Co  13:11  God of love and **p** will be with you.
Gal   5:22  of the Spirit is love, joy, **p**, patience,
       6:16  P and mercy to all who follow this
Eph   2:14  For he himself is our **p**, who has
       2:15  out of the two, thus making **p**,
       2:17  and preached **p** to you who were far
                away and **p** to those who were near.
       4: 3  of the Spirit through the bond of **p**.
       6:15  that comes from the gospel of **p**.
Php   4: 7  And the **p** of God, which transcends
Col   1:20  by making **p** through his blood,
       3:15  Let the **p** of Christ rule in your
       3:15  of one body you were called to **p**.
1Th   5: 3  people are saying, "P and safety,"
       5:13  Live in **p** with each other.
       5:23  the God of **p**, sanctify you through
2Th   3:16  the Lord of **p** himself give you **p**
2Ti   2:22  love and **p**, along with those who
Heb   7: 2  of Salem" means "king of **p**."
      12:11  **p** for those who have been trained
      12:14  effort to live in **p** with everyone
      13:20  Now may the God of **p**,
Jas   3:18  who sow in **p** reap a harvest
1Pe   3:11  and do good; seek **p** and pursue it.
2Pe   3:14  blameless and at **p** with him.
Rev   6: 4  given power to take **p** from the earth

**GRACE AND PEACE** See GRACE

## PEACE-LOVING* [PEACE, LOVE]
Jas   3:17  then **p**, considerate, submissive,

## PEACEABLE* [PEACE]
Tit   3: 2  no one, to be **p** and considerate,

## PEACEFUL [PEACE]
1Ti   2: 2  that we may live **p** and quiet lives

## PEACEMAKERS* [PEACE]
Mt    5: 9  Blessed are the **p**, for they will be
Jas   3:18  P who sow in peace reap a harvest

## PEARL* [PEARLS]
Rev  21:21  pearls, each gate made of a single **p**.

## PEARLS [PEARL]
Mt    7: 6  do not throw your **p** to pigs.
      13:45  is like a merchant looking for fine **p**.
1Ti   2: 9  or gold or **p** or expensive clothes,
Rev  21:21  The twelve gates were twelve **p**,

## PEBBLE*
2Sa  17:13  until not so much as a **p** is left."
Am    9: 9  and not a **p** will reach the ground.

## PEDDLE*
2Co   2:17  we do not **p** the word of God

## PEG
Jdg   4:21  She drove the **p** through his temple
Isa  22:23  I will drive him like a **p** into a firm
Zec  10: 4  from him the tent **p**, from him

## PEKAH
       King of Israel (2Ki 15:25–31; 2Ch 28:6; Isa 7:1).

## PEKAHIAH*
       Son of Menahem; king of Israel (2Ki 15:22–26).

## PELETHITES
2Sa  20: 7  and the Kerethites and **P** and all
1Ch  18:17  was over the Kerethites and **P**;

## PELTED*
2Sa  16: 6  He **p** David and all the king's officials
2Co  11:25  once I was **p** with stones,

## PEN [PENS]
Ps   45: 1  my tongue is the **p** of a skillful
Isa   8: 1  and write on it with an ordinary **p**:
Hab   3:17  though there are no sheep in the **p**
Mt    5:18  not the least stroke of a **p**,
Jn   10: 1  who does not enter the sheep **p**
3Jn   1:13  I do not want to do so with **p**

## PENALTIES* [PENALTY]
Pr   19:29  P are prepared for mockers,

## PENALTY [PENALTIES]
Lev   5: 6  and, as a **p** for the sin they have
Pr   19:19  The hot-tempered must pay the **p**;

Eze 23:49 You will suffer the **p** for your
Lk  23:22 in him no grounds for the death **p**.
Ro   1:27 themselves the due **p** for their error.

## PENETRATES*
Heb  4:12 it **p** even to dividing soul and spirit,

## PENIEL
Ge  32:30 So Jacob called the place **P**, saying,

## PENINNAH
1Sa  1: 2 was called Hannah and the other **P**.

## PENITENT* [REPENT]
Isa  1:27 her **p** ones with righteousness.

## PENNIES* [PENNY]
Lk  12: 6 not five sparrows sold for two **p**?

## PENNY* [PENNIES]
Mt   5:26 out until you have paid the last **p**.
    10:29 Are not two sparrows sold for a **p**?
Mk  12:42 coins, worth only a fraction of a **p**.
Lk  12:59 out until you have paid the last **p**."

## PENS [PEN]
Ps  50: 9 your stall or of goats from your **p**,
    78:70 and took him from the sheep **p**;

## PENTECOST*
Ac   2: 1 When the day of **P** came, they were
    20:16 if possible, by the day of **P**.
1Co 16: 8 I will stay on at Ephesus until **P**,

## PEOPLE [PEOPLE'S, PEOPLES]
Ge   4:26 **p** began to call on the name of the LORD
     6:13 "I am going to put an end to all **p**,
    11: 6 said, "If as one **p** speaking the same
    12: 1 your **p** and your father's household
    18:24 if there are fifty righteous **p**
Ex   3:10 Pharaoh to bring my **p** the Israelites
     5: 1 'Let my **p** go, so that they may hold
     6: 7 I will take you as my own **p**, and I
     8:23 distinction between my **p** and your **p**.
    13:17 When Pharaoh let the **p** go, God did
    15:13 will lead the **p** you have redeemed.
    15:24 So the **p** grumbled against Moses,
    19: 8 The **p** all responded together,
    24: 3 told the **p** all the LORD's words
    32: 1 When the **p** saw that Moses was so
    32: 9 "and they are a stiff-necked **p**.
    32:12 and do not bring disaster on your **p**.
    33:13 that this nation is your **p**."
Lev  9: 7 atonement for yourself and the **p**;
    16:24 and the burnt offering for the **p**,
    26:12 be your God, and you will be my **p**.
Nu  11:11 put the burden of all these **p** on me?
    14:11 "How long will these **p** treat me
    14:19 forgive the sin of these **p**, just as
    20: 2 and the **p** gathered in opposition
    21: 7 So Moses prayed for the **p**.
    22: 5 "A **p** has come out of Egypt;
Dt   4: 6 is a wise and understanding **p**."
     4:20 to be the **p** of his inheritance, as you
     5:28 "I have heard what this **p** said

Dt   7: 6 you are a **p** holy to the LORD your
     8: 3 that **p** do not live on bread alone
    18:18 prophet like you from among their **p**,
    26:18 declared this day that you are his **p**,
    31: 7 must go with this **p** into the land
    31:16 and these **p** will soon prostitute
    32: 9 For the LORD's portion is his **p**,
    32:43 with his **p**, for he will avenge
    32:43 make atonement for his land and **p**.
    33:29 like you, a **p** saved by the LORD?
Jos  1: 6 because you will lead these **p**
     3:16 So the **p** crossed over opposite
    24: 6 When I brought your **p** out of Egypt,
    24:25 Joshua made a covenant for the **p**,
Jdg  2: 7 The **p** served the LORD
     2:19 the **p** returned to ways even more
Ru   1:16 Your **p** will be my **p** and your God
1Sa  2:26 in favor with the LORD and with **p**.
     8: 7 to all that the **p** are saying to you;
    10:24 is no one like him among all the **p**."
    12:22 the LORD will not reject his **p**,
2Sa  5: 2 'You will shepherd my **p** Israel,
     7:10 will provide a place for my **p** Israel
     7:23 And who is like your **p** Israel—
    24:17 angel who was striking down the **p**,
1Ki  3: 8 here among the **p** you have chosen,
     4:34 **p** came to listen to Solomon's wisdom,
     8:30 and of your **p** Israel when they pray
     8:56 to his **p** Israel just as he promised.
    18:39 When all the **p** saw this, they fell
2Ki 17:23 So the **p** of Israel were taken
    23: 3 all the **p** pledged themselves
    25:11 into exile the **p** who remained
1Ch 17:21 went out to redeem a **p** for himself,
    29:11 how willingly your **p** who are here
2Ch  2:11 "Because the LORD loves his **p**,
     6:41 may your faithful **p** rejoice
     7: 5 and all the **p** dedicated the temple
     7:14 if my **p**, who are called by my
    30: 6 "**P** of Israel, return to the LORD,
    36:16 LORD was aroused against his **p**
Ezr  2: 1 Now these are the **p** of the province
     3: 1 the **p** assembled with one accord
Ne   1:10 "They are your servants and your **p**,
     4: 6 for the **p** worked with all their heart.
     4:14 and fight for your **p**,
     8: 1 all the **p** assembled with one accord
Est  3: 6 a way to destroy all Mordecai's **p**,
     7: 3 And spare my **p**—this is my request.
Job 12: 2 "Doubtless you are the **p**,
    34:23 God has no need to examine **p** further,
Ps   3: 8 May your blessing be on your **p**.
    22:22 I will declare your name to my **p**;
    29:11 the LORD blesses his **p**
    30: 4 you his faithful **p**; praise his
    31:23 Love the LORD, all his faithful **p**!
    33:12 the **p** he chose for his inheritance.
    34: 9 Fear the LORD, you his holy **p**,
    36: 7 **P** take refuge in the shadow
    50: 4 the earth, that he may judge his **p**:
    53: 6 When God restores his **p**, let Jacob
    81:13 "If my **p** would only listen to me,
    90: 3 You turn **p** back to dust, saying,
    94:14 For the LORD will not reject his **p**;
    95: 7 God and we are the **p** of his pasture,
    95:10 said, 'They are a **p** whose hearts go
   125: 2 LORD surrounds his **p** both now

| | | |
|---|---|---|
| Ps | 133: 1 | when God's **p** live together in unity! |
| | 135:14 | For the LORD will vindicate his **p** |
| | 144:15 | blessed is the **p** whose God is |
| | 149: 1 | in the assembly of his faithful **p**. |
| | 149: 4 | the LORD takes delight in his **p**; |
| | 149: 5 | Let his faithful **p** rejoice in this honor |
| | 149: 9 | the glory of all his faithful **p**. |
| Pr | 12: 8 | **P** are praised according to their prudence |
| | 12:22 | delights in **p** who are trustworthy. |
| | 14:34 | a nation, but sin condemns any **p**. |
| | 16: 2 | **P** may think all their ways are pure, |
| | 26:12 | see **p** who are wise in their own eyes? |
| | 29: 2 | the righteous thrive, the **p** rejoice; |
| | 29:18 | is no revelation, **p** cast off restraint; |
| Ecc | 3:12 | nothing better for **p** than to be happy |
| Isa | 1: 3 | not know, my **p** do not understand." |
| | 1: 4 | nation, a **p** whose guilt is great, |
| | 5:13 | Therefore my **p** will go into exile |
| | 6:10 | Make the heart of this **p** calloused; |
| | 9: 2 | The **p** walking in darkness have |
| | 19:25 | "Blessed be Egypt my **p**, |
| | 29:13 | "These **p** come near to me |
| | 40: 1 | comfort my **p**, says your God. |
| | 40: 5 | and all **p** will see it together. |
| | 40: 6 | "All **p** are like grass, |
| | 40: 7 | Surely the **p** are grass. |
| | 42: 6 | make you to be a covenant for the **p** |
| | 49: 8 | make you to be a covenant for the **p**, |
| | 49:13 | For the LORD comforts his **p** |
| | 51: 4 | "Listen to me, my **p**; hear me, |
| | 52: 6 | Therefore my **p** will know my |
| | 53: 3 | Like one from whom **p** hide their faces |
| | 53: 8 | of my **p** he was punished. |
| | 60:21 | will all your **p** be righteous and they |
| | 62:12 | They will be called the Holy P, |
| | 65: 2 | held out my hands to an obstinate **p**, |
| | 65:23 | for they will be a **p** blessed |
| Jer | 2:11 | my **p** have exchanged their glorious |
| | 2:13 | "My **p** have committed two sins: |
| | 2:32 | Yet my **p** have forgotten me, |
| | 4:22 | "My **p** are fools; they do not know |
| | 5:14 | and these **p** the wood it consumes. |
| | 5:31 | authority, and my **p** love it this way. |
| | 6:27 | a tester of metals and my **p** the ore, |
| | 7:16 | not pray for this **p** nor offer any plea |
| | 7:23 | be your God and you will be my **p**. |
| | 16:20 | Do **p** make their own gods? |
| | 18:15 | Yet my **p** have forgotten me; |
| | 23: 2 | to the shepherds who tend my **p**: |
| | 30: 3 | 'when I will bring my **p** Israel |
| | 31:33 | be their God, and they will be my **p**. |
| | 50: 6 | "My **p** have been lost sheep; |
| La | 1: 1 | lies the city, once so full of **p**! |
| | 3:31 | **p** are not cast off by the Lord forever. |
| Eze | 12: 2 | you are living among a rebellious **p**. |
| | 13:23 | I will save my **p** from your hands. |
| | 20:11 | which **p** will live if they obey them. |
| | 36: 8 | branches and fruit for my **p** Israel, |
| | 36:28 | you will be my **p**, and I will be your |
| | 36:38 | cities be filled with flocks of **p**. |
| | 37:13 | you, my **p**, will know that I am |
| | 38:14 | day, when my **p** Israel are living |
| | 39: 7 | my holy name among my **p** Israel. |
| Da | 7:18 | But the holy **p** of the Most High |
| | 7:21 | against the holy **p** and defeating them, |
| | 7:27 | over to the holy **p** of the Most High. |
| | 8:24 | the mighty warriors, the holy **p**. |

| | | |
|---|---|---|
| Da | 9:19 | city and your **p** bear your Name." |
| | 9:24 | 'sevens' are decreed for your **p** |
| | 9:26 | The **p** of the ruler who will come |
| | 10:14 | will happen to your **p** in the future, |
| | 11:32 | but the **p** who know their God will |
| | 12: 1 | great prince who protects your **p**, |
| Hos | 1:10 | 'You are not my **p**,' they will be |
| | 2:23 | will say to those called 'Not my **p**,' |
| | 4:14 | a **p** without understanding will |
| Joel | 2:18 | for his land and took pity on his **p**. |
| | 3:16 | a stronghold for the **p** of Israel. |
| Am | 9:14 | I will bring my **p** Israel back |
| Jnh | 4:11 | twenty thousand **p** who cannot tell |
| Mic | 3: 5 | the prophets who lead my **p** astray, |
| | 6: 2 | the LORD has a case against his **p**; |
| | 6: 8 | shown all you **p** what is good. |
| | 7:14 | Shepherd your **p** with your staff, |
| Zep | 2: 9 | remnant of my **p** will plunder them; |
| Hag | 1:12 | And the **p** feared the LORD. |
| Zec | 2:11 | in that day and will become my **p**. |
| | 2:13 | Be still before the LORD, all **p**, |
| | 8: 7 | "I will save my **p** |
| | 13: 9 | 'They are my **p**,' and they will say, |
| Mt | 1:21 | because he will save his **p** |
| | 2: 6 | who will shepherd my **p** Israel.' " |
| | 4: 4 | 'P do not live on bread alone, |
| | 4:16 | the **p** living in darkness have seen |
| | 4:19 | "and I will send you out to fish for **p**." |
| | 5:47 | if you greet only your own **p**, |
| | 12:31 | **p** will be forgiven every sin and blasphemy. |
| | 12:36 | tell you that **p** will have to give account |
| | 13:38 | seed stands for the **p** of the kingdom. |
| | 23: 5 | Everything they do is done for **p** to see: |
| Mk | 2:27 | Sabbath was made for **p**, not **p** for the Sabbath. |
| | 5:19 | "Go home to your own **p** and tell |
| | 7: 6 | " 'These **p** honor me with their |
| | 8:27 | asked them, "Who do **p** say I am?" |
| Lk | 1:17 | to make ready a **p** prepared |
| | 1:68 | because he has come to his **p** |
| | 2:10 | of great joy that will be for all the **p**. |
| Lk | 2:52 | in wisdom and in favor with God and **p**. |
| | 3: 6 | And all **p** will see God's salvation.' " |
| | 4: 4 | 'P do not live on bread alone.' " |
| | 6:22 | Blessed are you when **p** hate you, |
| | 13:23 | "Lord, are only a few **p** going to be |
| | 21:23 | in the land and wrath against this **p**. |
| Jn | 1: 4 | and that life was the light of all **p**. |
| | 2:24 | for he knew all **p**. |
| | 3:19 | but **p** loved darkness instead of light |
| | 7:43 | Thus the **p** were divided because |
| | 11:50 | one man die for the **p** than |
| | 12:32 | will draw all **p** to myself." |
| | 18:14 | be good if one man died for the **p**. |
| Ac | 2:17 | I will pour out my Spirit on all **p**. |
| | 2:47 | and enjoying the favor of all the **p**. |
| | 3:22 | like me from among your own **p**; |
| | 5:13 | they were highly regarded by the **p**. |
| | 9:13 | harm he has done to your **p** |
| | 15:14 | to choose a **p** for his name |
| | 18:10 | because I have many **p** in this city." |
| Ro | 5:12 | death came to all **p**, |
| | 5:18 | condemnation for all **p**, |
| | 8:27 | the Spirit intercedes for God's **p** |
| | 9: 3 | Christ for the sake of my **p**, |
| | 9: 4 | the **p** of Israel. Theirs is the adoption; |

| | | |
|---|---|---|
| Ro | 9:25 | call them 'my **p**' who are not my **p**; |
| | 11: 1 | I ask then: Did God reject his **p**? |
| | 15:10 | you Gentiles, with his **p**." |
| 1Co | 6: 2 | the Lord's **p** will judge the world? |
| | 9:22 | I have become all things to all **p** |
| 2Co | 5:11 | we try to persuade **p**. |
| | 6:16 | their God, and they will be my **p**." |
| | 11:26 | in danger from my own **p**, |
| Eph | 1:15 | and your love for all his **p**, |
| | 1:18 | his glorious inheritance in his **p**, |
| | 2:19 | but fellow citizens with God's **p** |
| | 4: 8 | and gave gifts to his **p**." |
| | 5: 3 | improper for the Lord's **p**. |
| | 6:18 | keep on praying for all the Lord's **p**. |
| Col | 1:12 | share in the inheritance of his **p** |
| | 1:26 | but is now disclosed to the Lord's **p**. |
| | 3:12 | as God's chosen **p**, holy and dearly |
| 1Th | 2: 4 | not trying to please **p** but God, |
| | 5:26 | Greet all God's **p** with a holy kiss. |
| 1Ti | 2: 4 | who wants all **p** to be saved |
| | 2: 6 | gave himself as a ransom for all **p**. |
| | 4:10 | who is the Savior of all **p**, |
| | 5:10 | washing the feet of the Lord's **p**, |
| | 6: 9 | desires that plunge **p** into ruin |
| 2Ti | 2: 2 | entrust to reliable **p** |
| | 3:17 | God's **p** may be thoroughly equipped |
| Tit | 1:10 | For there are many rebellious **p**, |
| | 2:11 | appeared that offers salvation to all **p**. |
| | 2:14 | himself a **p** that are his very own, |
| Phm | 1: 7 | refreshed the hearts of the Lord's **p**. |
| Heb | 2:17 | atonement for the sins of the **p**. |
| | 4: 9 | a Sabbath-rest for the **p** of God; |
| | 5: 1 | high priest is selected from among the **p** |
| | 5: 3 | sins, as well as for the sins of the **p**. |
| | 8:10 | be their God, and they will be my **p**. |
| | 9:27 | Just as **p** are destined to die once, |
| | 10:30 | again, "The Lord will judge his **p**." |
| | 11:13 | All these **p** were still living by faith |
| | 13:12 | to make the **p** holy through his own |
| 1Pe | 1:24 | "All **p** are like grass, |
| | 2: 8 | "A stone that causes **p** to stumble |
| | 2: 9 | But you are a chosen **p**, a royal |
| | 2:10 | Once you were not a **p**, but now you |
| 2Pe | 2: 1 | also false prophets among the **p**, |
| | 3:11 | what kind of **p** ought you to be? |
| Jude | 1: 3 | for all entrusted to us, his **p**. |
| Rev | 5: 8 | which are the prayers of God's **p**. |
| | 8: 3 | with the prayers of all God's **p**, |
| | 9:15 | released to kill a third of the world's **p**. |
| | 13: 4 | **P** worshiped the dragon |
| | 13: 7 | authority over every tribe, **p**, |
| | 14:12 | endurance on the part of the **p** |
| | 16: 6 | blood of your **p** and your prophets, |
| | 17: 6 | drunk with the blood of God's **p**, |
| | 18: 4 | my **p**,' so that you will not share |
| | 18:20 | Rejoice, you **p** of God! |
| | 19: 8 | the righteous acts of God's **p**.) |
| | 21: 3 | They will be his **p**, and God himself |
| | 22:21 | of the Lord Jesus be with God's **p**. |

**ALL PEOPLE** Ge 6:13; Job 34:15; Ps 64:9; 65:2; 145:12; Isa 2:17; 40:5, 6; 66:16, 23; Jer 17:20; 45:5; Eze 21:5; Da 2:38; Joel 2:28; Zep 1:3, 17; Zec 2:13; 9:1; 10:1; Lk 3:6; Jn 1:4; 2:24; 12:32; 17:2; Ac 2:17; 17:30; 22:15; 24:16; Ro 5:12, 18; 1Co 9:22; Gal 6:10; Eph 5:29; 1Ti 2:4, 6; 4:10; Tit 2:11; 1Pe 1:24; Rev 13:16; 19:18

**ALL THE PEOPLE** Ge 6:12; 26:11; 29:22; 35:6; Ex 11:8; 18:21; 19:11; 32:3; 33:8; Lev 9:23, 24; 10:3; Nu 13:32; 15:26; 24:17; Dt 13:9; 17:7, 13; 20:11; 27:14, 15, 16, 17, 18, 19, 20, 21, 22, 23, 24, 25, 26; Jos 2:24; 5:5, 5; 8:25; 11:14; 24:2, 27; Jdg 9:49, 51; 16:30; 20:2, 8; Ru 3:11; 4:9, 11; 1Sa 2:23; 7:2; 10:24, 24; 11:15; 12:18; 2Sa 6:19; 15:17, 23, 23, 24, 30; 16:14; 17:2, 3, 3, 16, 22; 19:9, 39; 20:22; 1Ki 1:39, 40; 4:30; 12:12; 18:24, 30, 39; 2Ki 10:9, 18; 11:14, 18, 19, 20; 14:21; 16:15; 17:20; 23:2, 3, 21; 25:26; 1Ch 13:4; 16:36, 43; 28:21, 2Ch 7:4, 5; 10:12; 20:18; 23:13, 17, 20, 21; 24:10; 26:1; 29:36; 32:9; 34:9, 30; 35:13; Ezr 3:11; 7:25; 10:9; Ne 4:16; 8:1, 3, 5, 6, 9, 11, 12; 9:10; Est 1:5; Job 1:3; Ps 33:8; 106:48; 122:8; Ecc 4:16; Isa 9:9; Jer 19:14; 25:1, 2; 26:2, 7, 8, 8, 9, 11, 12, 16, 18; 28:1, 5, 7, 11; 29:16, 25; 34:8, 19; 36:6, 9, 10; 38:1, 4; 41:13, 14, 16; 42:1, 8; 43:4; 44:15, 20, 24; Eze 38:20; 39:13, 25; 45:16, 22; Da 9:6; Am 9:1; Zec 7:5; Mal 2:9; Mt 12:23; 13:2; 22:10; 27:25; Mk 1:5; 4:1; 5:20; 6:39; 9:15; Lk 2:10; 3:21; 4:28, 36; 7:29; 8:37, 47, 52; 18:43; 19:7, 48; 20:6, 45; 21:38; 23:48; 24:19; Jn 8:2; Ac 2:47; 3:9, 11; 4:10, 21; 5:34; 8:9, 10; 10:41; 13:24; Heb 9:19, 19

**PEOPLE OF ISRAEL** See ISRAEL

**PEOPLE OF JERUSALEM** See JERUSALEM

**PEOPLE OF JUDAH** See JUDAH

**PEOPLE'S** [PEOPLE]

| | | |
|---|---|---|
| 2Ch | 25:15 | "Why do you consult this **p** gods, |
| Isa | 25: 8 | remove his **p** disgrace |
| Jer | 10:23 | I know that **p** lives are not their own; |
| Mt | 13:15 | this **p** heart has become calloused; |
| | 23: 4 | put them on other **p** shoulders, |
| Ac | 28:27 | this **p** heart has become calloused; |
| 2Co | 5:19 | not counting **p** sins against them. |

**PEOPLES** [PEOPLE]

| | | |
|---|---|---|
| Ge | 12: 3 | and all **p** on earth will be blessed |
| | 17:16 | kings of **p** will come from her." |
| | 25:23 | and two **p** from within you will be |
| | 27:29 | serve you and **p** bow down to you. |
| | 28: 3 | until you become a community of **p**. |
| | 48: 4 | I will make you a community of **p**, |
| Dt | 4:27 | will scatter you among the **p**, |
| | 7: 7 | for you were the fewest of all **p**. |
| | 14: 2 | of all the **p** on the face of the earth, |
| | 28:10 | all the **p** on earth will see that you |
| Jos | 4:24 | all the **p** of the earth might know |
| Jdg | 2:12 | various gods of the **p** around them. |
| 1Ki | 8:43 | all the **p** of the earth may know your |
| 2Ch | 7:20 | an object of ridicule among all **p**. |
| Ezr | 3: 3 | their fear of the **p** around them, |
| | 10: 2 | women from the **p** around us. |
| Ne | 10:30 | in marriage to the **p** around us |
| Ps | 2: 1 | conspire and the **p** plot in vain? |
| | 9: 8 | and judges the **p** with equity. |
| | 67: 3 | May the **p** praise you, God; |
| | 87: 6 | will write in the register of the **p**: |
| | 96:10 | he will judge the **p** with equity. |

Ps 117: 1 all you nations; extol him, all you **p**.
Isa 2: 4 and will settle disputes for many **p**.
11:10 will stand as a banner for the **p**;
17:12 Woe to the **p** who roar—
25: 6 prepare a feast of rich food for all **p**,
34: 1 pay attention, you **p**!
49:22 I will lift up my banner to the **p**;
55: 4 I have made him a witness to the **p**,
Jer 10: 3 the practices of the **p** are worthless;
Da 7:14 **p** of every language worshiped him.
Mic 4: 1 the hills, and **p** will stream to it.
5: 7 the midst of many **p** like dew
Zep 3: 9 "Then I will purify the lips of the **p**,
3:20 praise among all the **p** of the earth
Zec 8:20 "Many **p** and the inhabitants
12: 2 sends all the surrounding **p** reeling.
Ac 3:25 'Through your offspring all **p**
4:25 nations rage and the **p** plot in vain?
Rev 1: 7 all **p** on earth "will mourn because
10:11 must prophesy again about many **p**,

**ALL PEOPLES** Ge 12:3; 28:14; Dt 7:7; 1Ki 9:7;
1Ch 16:24; 2Ch 7:20; Ps 66:8; 96:3; 97:6; Isa
25:6, 7; Ac 3:25; Rev 1:7

**ALL THE PEOPLES** Dt 7:6, 16, 19; 14:2;
28:10, 37; Jos 4:24; 1Ki 8:43, 60; 2Ch 6:33;
32:13; Ps 67:3, 5; Jer 1:15; 25:9; Da 4:35; Hab
2:5; Zep 3:20; Mt 24:30; Ro 15:11

## PEOR
Nu 25: 3 yoked themselves to the Baal of **P**.
Dt 4: 3 who followed the Baal of **P**,
Jos 22:17 Was not the sin of **P** enough for us?

## PERCEIVE [PERCEIVED, PERCEIVING]
Ps 139: 2 you **p** my thoughts from afar.
Pr 24:12 not he who weighs the heart **p** it?

## PERCEIVED* [PERCEIVE]
Isa 64: 4 no ear has **p**, no eye has seen any

## PERCEIVING* [PERCEIVE]
Isa 6: 9 be ever seeing, but never **p**.'
Mt 13:14 you will be ever seeing but never **p**.
Mk 4:12 may be ever seeing but never **p**,
Ac 28:26 will be ever seeing but never **p**."

## PERCH
Ge 8: 9 the dove could find nowhere to **p**

## PERES* [PARSIN]
Da 5:28 **P**: Your kingdom is divided

## PEREZ
Ge 38:29 And he was named **P**.
Ru 4:12 may your family be like that of **P**,
Mt 1: 3 Judah the father of **P** and Zerah,

## PERFECT* [PERFECTER, PERFECTING, PERFECTION]
Dt 32: 4 his works are **p**, and all his ways are
2Sa 22:31 "As for God, his way is **p**;
Job 36: 4 one who has **p** knowledge is

Job 37:16 of him who has **p** knowledge?
Ps 18:30 As for God, his way is **p**:
19: 7 The law of the LORD is **p**,
50: 2 From Zion, **p** in beauty, God shines
64: 6 say, "We have devised a **p** plan!"
SS 6: 9 but my dove, my **p** one, is unique,
Isa 25: 1 for in **p** faithfulness you have done
26: 3 in **p** peace those whose minds are
Eze 16:14 had given you made your beauty **p**,
27: 3 say, Tyre, "I am **p** in beauty."
28:12 full of wisdom and **p** in beauty.
Mt 5:48 Be **p**, therefore, as your heavenly Father is **p**.
19:21 answered, "If you want to be **p**, go,
Ro 12: 2 his good, pleasing and **p** will.
2Co 12: 9 my power is made **p** in weakness."
Col 3:14 binds them all together in **p** unity.
Heb 2:10 of their salvation **p** through what he
5: 9 once made **p**, he became the source
7:19 (for the law made nothing **p**),
7:28 Son, who has been made **p** forever.
9:11 more **p** tabernacle that is not made
10: 1 make **p** those who draw near
10:14 he has made **p** forever those who
11:40 with us would they be made **p**.
12:23 the spirits of the righteous made **p**,
Jas 1:17 good and **p** gift is from above,
1:25 who look intently into the **p** law
3: 2 never at fault in what they say are **p**,
1Jn 4:18 But **p** love drives out fear,
4:18 The one who fears is not made **p**

## PERFECTER* [PERFECT]
Heb 12: 2 on Jesus, the pioneer and **p** of faith.

## PERFECTING* [PERFECT]
2Co 7: 1 **p** holiness out of reverence for God.

## PERFECTION* [PERFECT]
Ps 119:96 To all **p** I see a limit, but your
La 2:15 city that was called the **p** of beauty,
Eze 27: 4 builders brought your beauty to **p**.
27:11 they brought your beauty to **p**.
28:12 " 'You were the seal of **p**,
43:10 Let them consider its **p**,
Heb 7:11 **p** could have been attained through

## PERFORM [PERFORMED, PERFORMS]
Ex 3:20 wonders that I will **p** among them.
2Sa 7:23 to **p** great and awesome wonders
1Ki 8:11 the priests could not **p** their service
Jer 21: 2 Perhaps the LORD will **p** wonders
Mk 13:22 prophets will appear and **p** signs
Jn 3: 2 For no one could **p** the signs you are

## PERFORMED [PERFORM]
Ex 4:30 also **p** the signs before the people,
Nu 14:11 all the signs I have **p** among them?
Dt 11: 3 the signs he **p** and the things he did
Ne 9:17 the miracles you **p** among them.
Mt 11:21 that were **p** in you had been **p**
Jn 10:41 "Though John never **p** a sign,
Ac 5:12 The apostles **p** many signs
Rev 13:13 And it **p** great signs, even causing

Rev 19:20 false prophet who had **p** the signs

## PERFORMS [PERFORM]
Ps 77:14 You are the God who **p** miracles;

## PERFUME
Ex  30:33 Whoever makes **p** like it and puts it
Ecc  7: 1 A good name is better than fine **p**,
SS   1: 3 your name is like **p** poured out.
Mk  14: 3 an alabaster jar of very expensive **p**,
Jn  12: 7 she should save this **p** for the day

## PERGAMUM*
Rev  1:11 to Ephesus, Smyrna, **P**, Thyatira,
     2:12 the angel of the church in **P** write:

## PERIL
2Co  1:10 delivered us from such a deadly **p**,

## PERISH [PERISHABLE, PERISHED, PERISHES, PERISHING]
Ge   6:17 life in it. Everything on earth will **p**.
Lev 26:38 You will **p** among the nations;
Jos 23:13 until you **p** from this good land,
Est  4:16 is against the law. And if I **p**, I **p**."
Ps  37:20 But the wicked will **p**:
    73:27 Those who are far from you will **p**;
   102:26 They will **p**, but you remain;
Pr  11:10 when the wicked **p**, there are shouts
    19: 9 and whoever pours out lies will **p**.
    21:28 Those who give false witness will **p**,
    28:28 but when the wicked **p**,
Isa  1:28 who forsake the LORD will **p**.
    29:14 the wisdom of the wise will **p**,
    60:12 that will not serve you will **p**;
Jer 51:18 their judgment comes, they will **p**.
Jnh  1: 6 notice of us so that we will not **p**."
     3: 9 fierce anger so that we will not **p**."
Zec 11: 9 the dying die, and the perishing **p**.
Mt  18:14 any of these little ones should **p**.
Lk  13: 3 unless you repent, you too will all **p**.
    13: 5 you repent, you too will all **p**."
    21:18 But not a hair of your head will **p**.
Jn   3:16 whoever believes in him shall not **p**
    10:28 eternal life, and they shall never **p**;
    11:50 than that the whole nation **p**."
Ac   8:20 "May your money **p** with you,
Ro   2:12 law will also **p** apart from the law,
Col  2:22 that are all destined to **p** with use,
2Th  2:10 They **p** because they refused to love
Heb  1:11 They will **p**, but you remain;
1Pe  1: 4 into an inheritance that can never **p**,
2Pe  3: 9 you, not wanting anyone to **p**,

## PERISHABLE [PERISH]
1Co 15:42 The body that is sown is **p**, it is
1Pe  1:18 was not with **p** things such as silver
     1:23 not of **p** seed, but of imperishable,

## PERISHED [PERISH]
Ge   7:21 thing that moved on the earth **p**—
Dt   2:14 fighting men had **p** from the camp,
Job  4: 7 Who, being innocent, has ever **p**?
Ps 119:92 I would have **p** in my affliction.
Jer  7:28 Truth has **p**; it has vanished

## PERISHES [PERISH]
Job  8:13 so **p** the hope of the godless.
1Pe  1: 7 which **p** even though refined

## PERISHING [PERISH]
Ecc  7:15 the righteous **p** in their
1Co  1:18 is foolishness to those who are **p**,
2Co  2:15 being saved and those who are **p**.
     4: 3 it is veiled to those who are **p**.

## PERIZZITES
Ge  13: 7 The Canaanites and **P** were
Ex   3: 8 Amorites, **P**, Hivites and Jebusites.
Jos 24:11 you, as did also the Amorites, **P**,

## PERJURERS* [PERJURY]
Mal  3: 5 adulterers and **p**, against those who
1Ti  1:10 for slave traders and liars and **p**.

## PERJURY* [PERJURERS]
Jer  7: 9 commit adultery and **p**, burn incense

## PERMANENT* [PERMANENTLY]
Lev 25:34 not be sold; it is their **p** possession.
Jos  8:28 Ai and made it a **p** heap of ruins,
Jn   8:35 Now a slave has no **p** place
Heb  7:24 lives forever, he has a **p** priesthood.

## PERMANENTLY [PERMANENT]
Lev 25:23 " 'The land must not be sold **p**,

## PERMIT* [PERMITTED]
Ex  12:23 he will not **p** the destroyer to enter
Hos  5: 4 "Their deeds do not **p** them
Ac  24:23 and **p** his friends to take care of his
1Ti  2:12 I do not **p** a woman to teach

## PERMITTED [PERMIT]
Mt  19: 8 "Moses **p** you to divorce your
2Co 12: 4 things, things that no one is **p** to tell.

## PERPETUAL
Ex  29:28 This is always to be the **p** share

## PERPLEXED
2Co  4: 8 **p**, but not in despair;

## PERSECUTE [PERSECUTED, PERSECUTING, PERSECUTION, PERSECUTIONS, PERSECUTORS]
Dt  30: 7 your enemies who hate and **p** you.
Mt   5:11 **p** you and falsely say all kinds
     5:44 and pray for those who **p** you,
Lk  11:49 they will kill and others they will **p**.'
    21:12 will lay hands on you and **p** you.
Jn  15:20 persecuted me, they will **p** you also.
Ac   9: 4 "Saul, Saul, why do you **p** me?"
    22: 7 Saul! Why do you **p** me?'
Ro  12:14 Bless those who **p** you; bless and do

## PERSECUTED [PERSECUTE]
Ps 119:86 I am being **p** without cause.
Mt   5:10 Blessed are those who **p** because

Mt 5:12 same way they **p** the prophets who
Jn 15:20 If they **p** me, they will persecute
Ac 22: 4 I **p** the followers of this Way to their
1Co 4:12 when we are **p**, we endure it;
15: 9 because I **p** the church of God.
2Co 4: 9 **p**, but not abandoned;
Gal 1:13 how intensely I **p** the church of God
1Th 3: 4 kept telling you that we would be **p**.
2Ti 3:12 godly life in Christ Jesus will be **p**,
Heb 11:37 destitute, **p** and mistreated—

## PERSECUTING* [PERSECUTE]
Ac 9: 5 Jesus, whom you are **p**," he replied.
22: 8 whom you are **p**,' he replied.
26:11 so obsessed with **p** them
26:15 whom you are **p**,' the Lord replied.
Php 3: 6 as for zeal, **p** the church;

## PERSECUTION [PERSECUTE]
Mt 13:21 or **p** comes because of the word,
Ac 8: 1 day a great **p** broke out against
Ro 8:35 trouble or hardship or **p** or famine
Heb 10:33 publicly exposed to insult and **p**;

## PERSECUTIONS* [PERSECUTE]
Mk 10:30 along with **p**—and in the age
2Co 12:10 in hardships, in **p**, in difficulties.
2Th 1: 4 faith in all the **p** and trials you are
2Ti 3:11 **p**, sufferings—what kinds of things
3:11 Iconium and Lystra, the **p** I endured.

## PERSECUTORS [PERSECUTE]
Ps 119:84 When will you punish my **p**?
Jer 15:15 Avenge me on my **p**.

## PERSEVERANCE* [PERSEVERE]
Ro 5: 3 we know that suffering produces **p**;
5: 4 **p**, character; and character, hope.
2Th 1: 4 churches we boast about your **p**
3: 5 into God's love and Christ's **p**.
Heb 12: 1 let us run with **p** the race marked
Jas 1: 3 the testing of your faith produces **p**.
1: 4 Let **p** finish its work so that you
5:11 You have heard of Job's **p** and have
2Pe 1: 6 and to self-control, **p**; and to **p**,
Rev 2: 2 deeds, your hard work and your **p**.
2:19 your service and **p**, and that you are

## PERSEVERE* [PERSEVERANCE, PERSEVERED, PERSEVERES, PERSEVERING]
1Ti 4:16 **P** in them, because if you do,
Heb 10:36 You need to **p** so that when you
Jas 1:12 Blessed are those who **p** under trial,

## PERSEVERED* [PERSEVERE]
2Co 12:12 I **p** in demonstrating among you
Heb 11:27 he **p** because he saw him who is
Jas 5:11 count as blessed those who have **p**.
Rev 2: 3 You have **p** and have endured

## PERSEVERES* [PERSEVERE]
1Co 13: 7 trusts, always hopes, always **p**.

## PERSEVERING* [PERSEVERE]
Lk 8:15 retain it, and by **p** produce a crop.

## PERSIA [PERSIANS]
Ezr 1: 1 In the first year of Cyrus king of **P**,
Da 8:20 the kings of Media and **P**.
10:20 to fight against the prince of **P**,

## PERSIANS [PERSIA]
Da 6:15 law of the Medes and **P** no decree

## PERSIST [PERSISTENCE]
Isa 1: 5 Why do you **p** in rebellion?
Ro 11:23 And if they do not **p** in unbelief,

## PERSISTENCE* [PERSIST]
Ro 2: 7 those who by **p** in doing good seek

## PERSON [PERSON'S]
Ex 23: 7 put an innocent or honest **p** to death,
Pr 11:25 A generous **p** will prosper;
28:20 faithful **p** will be richly blessed,
Mt 5:24 be reconciled to that **p**;
1Co 2:15 **p** with the Spirit makes judgments

## PERSON'S [PERSON]
Pr 20:24 **p** steps are directed by the LORD.
Mt 7: 5 remove the speck from the other **p** eye.
1Co 3:13 fire will test the quality of each **p** work.
2:11 who knows a **p** thoughts except
1Pe 1:17 who judges each **p** work impartially,

## PERSUADE [PERSUADED, PERSUASIVE]
Ac 18: 4 trying to **p** Jews and Greeks.
26:28 in such a short time you can **p** me
28:23 he tried to **p** them about Jesus.
2Co 5:11 to fear the Lord, we try to **p** people.

## PERSUADED [PERSUADE]
Mt 27:20 and the elders **p** the crowd to ask
Ro 4:21 being fully **p** that God had power

## PERSUASIVE* [PERSUADE]
Pr 7:21 With **p** words she led him astray;
1Co 2: 4 were not with wise and **p** words,

## PERVERSE [PERVERT]
Dt 32:20 for they are a **p** generation,
Pr 3:32 For the LORD detests the **p**
15: 4 but a **p** tongue crushes the spirit.
17:20 one whose tongue is **p** falls
Lk 9:41 unbelieving and **p** generation,"

## PERVERSION* [PERVERT]
Lev 18:23 sexual relations with it; that is a **p**.
20:12 What they have done is a **p**;
Jude 1: 7 up to sexual immorality and **p**.

## PERVERT* [PERVERSE, PERVERSION, PERVERTED, PERVERTING]
Ex 23: 2 do not **p** justice by siding
Lev 19:15 " 'Do not **p** justice; do not show

Dt   16:19  Do not **p** justice or show partiality.
Job   8: 3  Does God **p** justice?
       8: 3  Does the Almighty **p** what is right?
      34:12  that the Almighty would **p** justice.
Pr   17:23  in secret to **p** the course of justice.
Gal   1: 7  are trying to **p** the gospel of Christ.
Jude  1: 4  who **p** the grace of our God

## PERVERTED [PERVERT]

1Sa   8: 3  and accepted bribes and **p** justice.
Jer   3:21  because they have **p** their ways

## PERVERTING* [PERVERT]

Ac   13:10  Will you never stop **p** the right ways

## PESTILENCE [PESTILENCES]

Dt   32:24  consuming **p** and deadly plague;
Ps   91: 6  nor the **p** that stalks in the darkness,

## PESTILENCES* [PESTILENCE]

Lk   21:11  famines and **p** in various places,

## PETER [CEPHAS, SIMON]

Apostle, brother of Andrew, also called Simon (Mt 10:2; Mk 3:16; Lk 6:14; Ac 1:13), and Cephas (Jn 1:42). Confession of Christ (Mt 16:13–20; Mk 8:27–30; Lk 9:18–27). At transfiguration (Mt 17:1–8; Mk 9:2–8; Lk 9:28–36; 2Pe 1:16–18). Caught fish with coin (Mt 17:24–27). Denial of Jesus predicted (Mt 26:31–35; Mk 14:27–31; Lk 22:31–34; Jn 13:31–38). Denied Jesus (Mt 26:69–75; Mk 14:66–72; Lk 22:54–62; Jn 18:15–27). Commissioned by Jesus to shepherd his flock (Jn 21:15–23). Speech at Pentecost (Ac 2). Healed beggar (Ac 3:1–10). Speech at temple (Ac 3:11–26), before Sanhedrin (Ac 4:1–22). In Samaria (Ac 8:14–25). Sent by vision to Cornelius (Ac 10). Announced salvation of Gentiles in Jerusalem (Ac 11; 15). Freed from prison (Ac 12). Inconsistency at Antioch (Gal 2:11–21). At Jerusalem Council (Ac 15).
Letters: 1–2 Peter.

## PETITION [PETITIONS]

Est   7: 3  you, grant me my life—this is my **p**.
Jer   7:16  nor offer any plea or **p** for them;
Da   9: 3  pleaded with him in prayer and **p**,
Php   4: 6  by prayer and **p**, with thanksgiving,

## PETITIONS* [PETITION]

Da   9:17  the prayers and **p** of your servant.
1Ti   2: 1  **p**, prayers, intercession and thanksgiving
Heb   5: 7  up prayers and **p** with fervent cries

## PHANTOM*

Ps   39: 6  everyone goes around like a mere **p**;

## PHARAOH [PHARAOH'S]

Ge   12:15  they praised her to **P**, and she was
      41:14  So **P** sent for Joseph,
      47:10  Jacob blessed **P** and went
Ex    1:22  **P** gave this order to all his people:
       2:15  When **P** heard of this,
       3:11  "Who am I that I should go to **P**
       5: 2  **P** said, "Who is the LORD, that I
      11: 1  "I will bring one more plague on **P**

Ex   14:17  I will gain glory through **P** and all
Dt    7: 8  from the power of **P** king of Egypt.
Isa  36: 6  Such is **P** king of Egypt to all who
Ro    9:17  For Scripture says to **P**:

## PHARAOH'S [PHARAOH]

Ex    2: 5  **P** daughter went down to the Nile
       7: 3  But I will harden **P** heart,
       7:13  Yet **P** heart became hard and he
       7:22  arts, and **P** heart became hard;
       8:19  But **P** heart was hard and he would
       9:12  the LORD hardened **P** heart and he
       9:35  So **P** heart was hard and he would
      10:20  But the LORD hardened **P** heart,
      10:27  But the LORD hardened **P** heart,
      11:10  but the LORD hardened **P** heart,
      14: 4  And I will harden **P** heart, and he
1Ki  11: 1  foreign women besides **P** daughter—
Heb  11:24  be known as the son of **P** daughter.

## PHARISEE [PHARISEES]

Lk   11:37  a **P** invited him to eat with him;
Jn    3: 1  Now there was a **P**, a man
Ac    5:34  But a **P** named Gamaliel, a teacher
      23: 6  I am a **P**, descended from Pharisees.
Php   3: 5  in regard to the law, a **P**;

## PHARISEES [PHARISEE]

Mt    5:20  surpasses that of the **P**
      16: 6  guard against the yeast of the **P**
      23:13  you, teachers of the law and **P**,
Mk    2:18  the disciples of the **P** are fasting,
Lk   11:42  "Woe to you **P**, because you give
Ac   23: 7  a dispute broke out between the **P**

## PHILADELPHIA*

Rev   1:11  Thyatira, Sardis, **P** and Laodicea."
       3: 7  the angel of the church in **P** write:

## PHILEMON*

Phm   1: 1  To **P** our dear friend and fellow

## PHILIP

1. Apostle (Mt 10:3; Mk 3:18; Lk 6:14; Jn 1:43–48; 14:8; Ac 1:13).
2. Deacon (Ac 6:1–7); evangelist in Samaria (Ac 8:4–25), to Ethiopian (Ac 8:26–40).
3. Herod Philip I (Mt 14:3; Mk 6:17).
4. Herod Philip II (Lk 3:1).

## PHILIPPI

Mt   16:13  came to the region of Caesarea **P**,
Ac   16:12  From there we traveled to **P**,
Php   1: 1  holy people in Christ Jesus at **P**,

## PHILISTIA [PHILISTINE]

Ex   15:14  anguish will grip the people of **P**.
Ps   60: 8  over **P** I shout in triumph."

## PHILISTINE [PHILISTIA, PHILISTINES]

Jos  13: 3  held by the five **P** rulers in Gaza,
1Sa   6: 1  been in **P** territory seven months,
      14: 1  let's go over to the **P** outpost

1Sa 17:23 Goliath, the **P** champion from Gath,
17:37 rescue me from the hand of this **P**."

## PHILISTINES [PHILISTINE]
Ge 21:34 in the land of the **P** for a long time.
26: 1 to Abimelek king of the **P** in Gerar.
Jdg 10: 7 He sold them into the hands of the **P**
13: 1 the hands of the **P** for forty years.
16: 5 The rulers of the **P** went to her
16:30 said, "Let me die with the **P**!"
1Sa 4: 1 went out to fight against the **P**.
5: 1 After the **P** had captured the ark
13:20 to the **P** to have their plowpoints,
17: 1 Now the **P** gathered their forces
17:51 When the **P** saw that their hero was
23: 1 the **P** are fighting against Keilah
27: 1 do is to escape to the land of the **P**.
31: 1 Now the **P** fought against Israel;
2Sa 5:17 When the **P** heard that David had
8: 1 David defeated the **P** and subdued
21:15 there was a battle between the **P**
2Ki 18: 8 he defeated the **P**, as far as Gaza
Isa 14:31 Melt away, all you **P**! A cloud
Jer 47: 4 LORD is about to destroy the **P**,
Eze 25:16 to stretch out my hand against the **P**,
Am 1: 8 till the last of the **P** are dead,"

## PHILOSOPHER* [PHILOSOPHY]
1Co 1:20 Where is the **p** of this age?

## PHILOSOPHERS* [PHILOSOPHY]
Ac 17:18 Stoic **p** began to debate with him.

## PHILOSOPHY* [PHILOSOPHER, PHILOSOPHERS]
Col 2: 8 through hollow and deceptive **p**,

## PHINEHAS
1. Grandson of Aaron (Ex 6:25; Jos 22:30–32). Zeal for the LORD stopped plague (Nu 25:7–13; Ps 106:30).
2. Son of Eli; a wicked priest (1Sa 1:3; 2:12–17; 4:1–19).

## PHOEBE*
Ro 16: 1 I commend to you our sister **P**,

## PHYLACTERIES*
Mt 23: 5 They make their **p** wide

## PHYSICAL*
Da 1: 4 young men without any **p** defect,
Ro 2:28 circumcision merely outward and **p**.
Col 1:22 by Christ's **p** body through death
1Ti 4: 8 For **p** training is of some value,
Jas 2:16 does nothing about their **p** needs,

## PHYSICIAN* [PHYSICIANS]
Jer 8:22 Is there no **p** there? Why then is
Lk 4:23 proverb to me: '**P**, heal yourself!'

## PHYSICIANS [PHYSICIAN]
Job 13: 4 you are worthless **p**, all of you!

## PICK [PICKED]
Lev 19:10 or **p** up the grapes that have fallen.
Dt 23:25 you may **p** kernels with your hands,
Ru 2:16 and leave them for her to **p** up,
Mk 2:23 they began to **p** some heads
Jn 5: 8 **P** up your mat and walk."

## PICKED [PICK]
Lk 14: 7 noticed how the guests **p** the places
Jn 5: 9 he **p** up his mat and walked.
8:59 this, they **p** up stones to stone him,

## PIECE [PIECES]
Ex 15:25 and the LORD showed him a **p**
1Sa 24:11 look at this **p** of your robe in my
1Ki 17:11 bring me, please, a **p** of bread."
Mk 2:21 the new **p** will pull away
Jn 13:26 to whom I will give this **p** of bread
19:23 woven in one **p** from top to bottom.

## PIECES [PIECE]
Ge 15:17 appeared and passed between the **p**.
Ex 32:19 breaking them to **p** at the foot
Jdg 20: 6 cut her into **p** and sent one piece
1Ki 11:30 wearing and tore it into twelve **p**.
2Ki 18: 4 into **p** the bronze snake Moses had
Ps 2: 9 will dash them to **p** like pottery."
Jer 34:18 two and then walked between its **p**.
Hos 6: 5 Therefore I cut you in **p** with my
Mic 1: 7 All her idols will be broken to **p**;
Zec 11:12 So they paid me thirty **p** of silver.
Mt 14:20 of broken **p** that were left over.
15:37 of broken **p** that were left over.
Lk 20:18 on that stone will be broken to **p**,
Rev 2:27 will dash them to **p** like pottery'—

## PIERCE [PIERCED]
Ex 21: 6 doorpost and **p** his ear with an awl.
Ps 22:16 they **p** my hands and my feet.
Pr 12:18 words of the reckless **p** like swords,
Lk 2:35 a sword will **p** your own soul too."

## PIERCED [PIERCE]
Isa 53: 5 But he was **p** for our transgressions,
Zec 12:10 the one they have **p**, and they will
Jn 19:37 will look on the one they have **p**."
Rev 1: 7 see him, even those who **p** him";

## PIG* [PIG'S, PIGS]
Lev 11: 7 And the **p**, though it has a divided
Dt 14: 8 The **p** is also unclean;

## PIG'S* [PIG]
Pr 11:22 a **p** snout is a beautiful woman who
Isa 66: 3 is like one who presents **p** blood,

## PIGEONS
Lev 5: 7 or two young **p** to the LORD as
12: 8 to bring two doves or two young **p**,
Lk 2:24 "a pair of doves or two young **p**."

## PIGS [PIG]
Isa 66:17 among those who eat the flesh of **p**,
Mt 7: 6 do not throw your pearls to **p**.

Mk   5:11  A large herd of **p** was feeding
Lk  15:16  with the pods that the **p** were eating,

## PILATE [PONTIUS]

Governor of Judea. Questioned Jesus (Mt 27:1–26; Mk 15:15; Lk 22:66—23:25; Jn 18:28—19:16); sent him to Herod (Lk 23:6–12); consented to his crucifixion when crowds chose Barabbas (Mt 27:15–26; Mk 15:6–15; Lk 23:13–25; Jn 19:1–10).

## PILGRIMS (KJV) See STRANGERS

## PILLAR [PILLARS]

Ge  19:26  back, and she became a **p** of salt.
    28:18  set it up as a **p** and poured oil on top
    31:52  and this **p** is a witness, that I will
Ex  13:21  them in a **p** of cloud to guide them
    13:21  by night in a **p** of fire to give them
Nu  14:14  you go before them in a **p** of cloud by day and a **p** of fire by night.
1Ti   3:15  the **p** and foundation of the truth.

## PILLARS [PILLAR]

Ex  24: 4  up twelve stone **p** representing
Jdg 16:29  reached toward the two central **p**
1Ki   7:15  He cast two bronze **p**, each eighteen
2Ki 25:13  Babylonians broke up the bronze **p**,
Ps  75: 3  quake, it is I who hold its **p** firm.
   144:12  our daughters will be like **p** carved
Pr   9: 1  she has set up its seven **p**.
SS   5:15  His legs are **p** of marble set on bases
Gal  2: 9  those esteemed as **p**, gave me
Rev  3:12  who are victorious I will make **p**
    10: 1  sun, and his legs were like fiery **p**.

## PINE*

Isa  19: 8  throw nets on the water will **p** away.
    44:14  planted a **p**, and the rain made it grow.

## PIONEER*

Heb  2:10  make the **p** of their salvation perfect
    12: 2  Jesus, the **p** and perfecter of faith.

## PIPE [PIPERS, PIPES]

Ps 150: 4  praise him with the strings and **p**,
Da   3: 5  harp, **p** and all kinds of music,
Mt  11:17  " 'We played the **p** for you,
1Co 14: 7  such as the **p** or harp,

## PIPERS* [PIPE]

Rev 18:22  harpists and musicians, **p** and trumpeters,

## PIPES [PIPE]

Ge   4:21  who play stringed instruments and **p**.

## PISGAH

Dt   3:27  Go up to the top of **P** and look west

## PIT

Ex  21:33  "If anyone uncovers a **p** or digs one
Ps   7:15  it out fall into the **p** they have made.
    35: 8  may they fall into the **p**, to their
    40: 2  He lifted me out of the slimy **p**,

Ps 103: 4  who redeems your life from the **p**
Pr  23:27  for an adulterous woman is a deep **p**
    26:27  If anyone digs a **p**, they themselves
Isa  24:17  Terror and **p** and snare await you,
    38:17  kept me from the **p** of destruction;
Eze 19: 4  him, and he was trapped in their **p**.
Jnh  2: 6  God, brought my life up from the **p**.
Mt  15:14  the blind, both will fall into a **p**."

## PITCH

Ge   6:14  it and coat it with **p** inside and out.
Ex   2: 3  for him and coated it with tar and **p**

## PITIED* [PITY]

1Co 15:19  we are to be **p** more than all others.

## PITIFUL* [PITY]

Rev  3:17  not realize that you are wretched, **p**,

## PITY [PITIED, PITIFUL]

Dt   7:16  Do not look on them with **p** and do
2Ch 36:15  because he had **p** on his people
Ps  72:13  He will take **p** on the weak
Ecc  4:10  But **p** those who fall and have no
Eze  7: 4  I will not look on you with **p**;
Lk  10:33  when he saw him, he took **p** on him.
1Jn  3:17  sister in need but has no **p** on them,

## PLACE [PLACED, PLACES]

Ge  22:14  that **p** The LORD Will Provide.
    28:16  "Surely the LORD is in this **p**,
    50:19  Am I in the **p** of God?
Ex   3: 5  the **p** where you are standing is holy
    26:33  The curtain will separate the Holy **P** from the Most Holy **P**.
    32:34  lead the people to the **p** I spoke of,
Lev 16: 3  Aaron is to enter the Most Holy **P**:
    26:11  will put my dwelling **p** among you,
Dt  12: 5  to seek the **p** the LORD your God
Jos  5:15  for the **p** where you are standing is
1Ki  8:13  you, a **p** for you to dwell forever."
2Ki 17:11  every high **p** they burned incense,
2Ch  6:21  Hear from heaven, your dwelling **p**;
Ezr  9: 8  giving us a firm **p** in his sanctuary,
Est  4:14  the Jews will arise from another **p**,
Ps  24: 3  Who may stand in his holy **p**?
    26: 8  live, the **p** where your glory dwells.
    32: 7  You are my hiding **p**;
    84: 1  How lovely is your dwelling **p**,
   118: 5  he brought me into a spacious **p**.
   132:14  "This is my resting **p** for ever
Pr   8:27  there when he set the heavens in **p**,
Ecc  6: 6  Do not all go to the same **p**?
SS   8: 6  **P** me like a seal over your heart,
Isa  8:14  He will be a holy **p**; for both houses
    42: 9  the former things have taken **p**,
Eze 37:27  My dwelling **p** will be with them;
Da   7: 9  "thrones were set in **p**,
Hag  2: 9  'And in this **p** I will grant peace,'
Mt   8:20  of Man has no **p** to lay his head."
    27:33  (which means "the **p** of the skull").
Lk  18:15  Jesus for him to **p** his hands on them.
Jn  14: 2  going there to prepare a **p** for you?
Ac  18:12  brought him to the **p** of judgment.
Php  2: 9  God exalted him to the highest **p**
2Pe  1:19  it, as to a light shining in a dark **p**,

Rev 1: 1 his servants what must soon take **p**.
20:11 and there was no **p** for them.
22: 6 the things that must soon take **p**."

## HIGH PLACE See HIGH

## HOLY PLACE See HOLY

## PLACED [PLACE]

Mk 15:46 and **p** it in a tomb cut out of rock.
Lk 2: 7 in cloths and **p** him in a manger,
Jn 6:27 him God the Father has **p** his seal
1Co 12:18 God has **p** the parts in the body,
12:28 And God has **p** in the church
Eph 1:22 And God **p** all things under his feet

## PLACES [PLACE]

1Ki 3: 2 were still sacrificing at the high **p**,
2Ki 18: 4 He removed the high **p**,
Ps 78:58 They angered him with their high **p**;
Jer 19: 5 They have built the high **p** of Baal
Mt 13: 5 Some fell on rocky **p**, where it did

## HIGH PLACES See HIGH

## PLAGUE [PLAGUED, PLAGUES]

Ex 11: 1 Moses, "I will bring one more **p**
32:35 struck the people with a **p** because
Nu 11:33 and he struck them with a severe **p**.
14:37 and died of a **p** before the LORD.
16:48 and the dead, and the **p** stopped.
25: 8 Then the **p** against the Israelites was
Dt 28:21 The LORD will **p** you
2Sa 24:13 Or three days of **p** in your land?
2Ch 6:28 famine or **p** comes to the land,
Ps 91: 6 nor the **p** that destroys at midday.
Jer 14:12 with the sword, famine and **p**."
Zec 14:12 This is the **p** with which the LORD
Rev 11: 6 kind of **p** as often as they want.
16:21 because the **p** was so terrible.

## PLAGUED* [PLAGUE]

Ps 73: 5 they are not **p** by human ills.

## PLAGUES [PLAGUE]

Hos 13:14 Where, O death, are your **p**?
Rev 9:18 were killed by the three **p** of fire,
15: 1 seven angels with the seven last **p**—
21: 9 bowls full of the seven last **p** came
22:18 to you the **p** described in this scroll.

## PLAIN [PLAINS]

Ge 13:12 Lot lived among the cities of the **p**
19:29 God destroyed the cities of the **p**,
Isa 40: 4 become level, the rugged places a **p**.
Ro 1:19 because God has made it **p** to them.

## PLAINS [PLAIN]

Dt 34: 8 Moses in the **p** of Moab thirty days,
1Ki 20:23 But if we fight them on the **p**,

## PLAN [PLANNED, PLANS]

Ge 11: 6 then nothing they **p** to do will be
Ex 26:30 according to the **p** shown you
Est 8: 3 to the evil **p** of Haman the Agagite,
Pr 14:22 those who **p** what is good find love

Pr 21:30 no **p** that can succeed against
Isa 8:10 propose your **p**, but it will not stand,
Isa 28:29 whose **p** is wonderful, whose wisdom
Am 3: 7 does nothing without revealing his **p**
Ac 2:23 God's deliberate **p** and foreknowledge;
Eph 1:11 to the **p** of him who works

## PLANK

Mt 7: 3 attention to the **p** in your own eye?
Lk 6:42 first take the **p** out of your eye,

## PLANNED [PLAN]

Ps 17: 3 I have **p** no evil; my mouth has not
40: 5 have done, the things you **p** for us.
Isa 14:24 "Surely, as I have **p**, so it will be,
23: 9 The LORD Almighty **p** it, to bring
46:11 what I have **p**, that I will do.
La 2:17 The LORD has done what he **p**;
Heb 11:40 God had **p** something better for us

## PLANS [PLAN]

Ps 20: 4 heart and make all your **p** succeed.
33:11 But the **p** of the LORD stand firm
94:11 The LORD knows all human **p**;
107:11 and despised the **p** of the Most High.
Pr 12: 5 The **p** of the righteous are just,
15:22 **P** fail for lack of counsel,
16: 3 you do, and he will establish your **p**.
19:21 Many are the **p** in a human heart,
20:18 **P** are established by seeking advice;
Isa 29:15 to hide their **p** from the LORD,
30: 1 those who carry out **p** that are not
32: 8 But the noble make noble **p**,
Jer 29:11 For I know the **p** I have for you,"
2Co 1:17 do I make my **p** in a worldly manner

## PLANT [PLANTED, PLANTING, PLANTS, REPLANTED]

Ge 1:29 "I give you every seed-bearing **p**
Ex 15:17 and **p** them on the mountain of your
Lev 19:19 " 'Do not **p** your field with two
Ecc 3: 2 die, a time to **p** and a time to uproot,
Eze 16: 7 I made you grow like a **p** of the field.
Hos 2:23 I will **p** her for myself in the land;
Am 9:15 I will **p** Israel in their own land,
Mt 15:13 "Every **p** that my heavenly Father
1Co 15:37 you do not **p** the body that will be,

## PLANTED [PLANT]

Ge 2: 8 the LORD God had **p** a garden
Ps 1: 3 They are like a tree **p** by streams
92:13 **p** in the house of the LORD,
Isa 60:21 They are the shoot I have **p**,
Jer 17: 8 They will be like a tree **p**
18: 9 or kingdom is to be built up and **p**,
Mt 15:13 Father has not **p** will be pulled
21:33 was a landowner who **p** a vineyard.
1Co 3: 6 I **p** the seed, Apollos watered it,
Jas 1:21 humbly accept the word **p** in you,

## PLANTING [PLANT]

Isa 61: 3 a **p** of the LORD for the display

## PLANTS [PLANT]

Ge 1:11 seed-bearing **p** and trees on the land

Ge    9: 3  Just as I gave you the green **p**, I now
Ps  144:12  youth will be like well-nurtured **p**,
Pr   31:16  out of her earnings she **p** a vineyard.
Mk    4:32  becomes the largest of all garden **p**,
1Co   3: 7  neither the one who **p** nor the one
      9: 7  Who **p** a vineyard and does not eat

## PLASTER

Dt   27: 2  large stones and coat them with **p**.
Da    5: 5  and wrote on the **p** of the wall,

## PLATE [PLATES, PLATTER]

Ex   28:36  "Make a **p** of pure gold

## PLATES [PLATE]

Ex   25:29  make its **p** and dishes of pure gold,

## PLATFORM

2Ch   6:13  Now he had made a bronze **p**,
Ne    8: 4  on a high wooden **p** built

## PLATTER [PLATE]

Mk    6:25  head of John the Baptist on a **p**."

## PLAY [PLAYED, PLAYING]

Ge   19: 9  and now he wants to **p** the judge!
1Sa  16:23  David would take up his lyre and **p**.
Ps   33: 3  **p** skillfully, and shout for joy.
Isa  11: 8  Infants will **p** near the hole

## PLAYED [PLAY]

Mt   11:17  " 'We **p** the pipe for you, and you
1Co  14: 7  what tune is being **p** unless there is

## PLAYING [PLAY]

1Sa  18:10  while David was **p** the lyre, as he
     19: 9  While David was **p** the lyre,
Zec   8: 5  filled with boys and girls **p** there."
Rev  14: 2  like that of harpists **p** their harps.

## PLEA [PLEAD, PLEADED, PLEADS, PLEAS]

1Ki   8:28  prayer and his **p** for mercy,
      9: 3  and **p** you have made before me;
Ps   17: 1  Hear me, LORD, my **p** is just;
    102:17  he will not despise their **p**.
Jer   7:16  pray for this people nor offer any **p**
La    3:56  You heard my **p**: "Do not close

## PLEAD [PLEA]

2Ch   6:37  and **p** with you in the land of their
Ps   43: 1  **p** my cause against an unfaithful
Isa   1:17  fatherless, **p** the case of the widow.
Jer  30:13  There is no one to **p** your cause,
Mic   6: 1  up, **p** my case before the mountains;

## PLEADED [PLEA]

Dt    3:23  At that time I **p** with the LORD:
Est   8: 3  Esther again **p** with the king,
Da    9: 3  Lord God and **p** with him in prayer
2Co  12: 8  Three times I **p** with the Lord

## PLEADS [PLEA]

Job  16:21  he **p** with God as one **p** for a friend.

## PLEAS* [PLEA]

2Ch   6:39  hear their prayer and their **p**,
Job  13: 6  listen to the **p** of my lips.
Isa  19:22  he will respond to their **p** and heal

## PLEASANT [PLEASE]

Ge   49:15  resting place and how **p** is his land,
Ps   16: 6  lines have fallen for me in **p** places;
    106:24  Then they despised the **p** land;
    133: 1  and **p** it is when God's people live
    135: 3  sing praise to his name, for that is **p**.
    147: 1  how **p** and fitting to praise him!
Pr    2:10  knowledge will be **p** to your soul.
      3:17  Her ways are **p** ways, and all her
Isa  30:10  Tell us **p** things, prophesy illusions.
Jer   3:19  and give you a **p** land,
Heb  12:11  No discipline seems **p** at the time,

## PLEASANTNESS* [PLEASE]

Pr   27: 9  the **p** of a friend springs from their

## PLEASE [PLEASANT, PLEASANTNESS, PLEASED, PLEASES, PLEASING, PLEASURE, PLEASURES]

Ex   21: 8  If she does not **p** the master who has
Dt   12:13  burnt offerings anywhere you **p**.
Job  10: 3  Does it **p** you to oppress me,
Ps   69:31  This will **p** the LORD more than
Pr   20:23  and dishonest scales do not **p** him.
Pr   21: 1  channels toward all who **p** him.
Isa  44:28  and will accomplish all that I **p**;
     46:10  will stand, and I will do all that I **p**.'
Jer   6:20  your sacrifices do not **p** me."
     27: 5  are on it, and I give it to anyone I **p**.
Hos  10:10  When I **p**, I will punish them;
Jn    5:30  for I seek not to **p** myself but him
Ro    8: 8  by the sinful nature cannot **p** God.
     15: 1  of the weak and not to **p** ourselves.
     15: 2  We should all **p** our neighbors
1Co   7:32  how he can **p** the Lord.
      7:33  how he can **p** his wife—
     10:33  even as I try to **p** everyone in every
2Co   5: 9  So we make it our goal to **p** him,
Gal   1:10  Or am I trying to **p** people?
      6: 8  those who sow to **p** the Spirit,
Col   1:10  of the Lord and **p** him in every way:
1Th   2: 4  We are not trying to **p** people
      4: 1  you how to live in order to **p** God,
2Ti   2: 4  try to **p** their commanding officer.
Tit   2: 9  to try to **p** them, not to talk back
Heb  11: 6  faith it is impossible to **p** God,

## PLEASED [PLEASE]

Ex   33:13  If you are **p** with me, teach me your
Nu   14: 8  If the LORD is **p** with us, he will
     24: 1  Balaam saw that it **p** the LORD
Dt   28:63  Just as it **p** the LORD to make you
Jdg  18:20  The priest was very **p**.
1Sa  12:22  because the LORD was **p** to make
1Ki   3:10  The Lord was **p** that Solomon had
1Ch  29:17  the heart and are **p** with integrity.
Ps    5: 4  not a God who is **p** with wickedness;

Ps 40:13 Be **p** to save me, LORD;
Isa 42:21 It **p** the LORD for the sake of his
Eze 18:23 am I not **p** when they turn from their
Da 8: 4 It did as it **p** and became great.
Mic 6: 7 Will the LORD be **p**
Mal 1:10 I am not **p** with you,"
Mt 3:17 with him I am well **p**."
17: 5 whom I love; with him I am well **p**.
Mk 1:11 with you I am well **p**."
Lk 3:22 with you I am well **p**."
Jn 5:21 gives life to whom he is **p** to give it.
1Co 1:21 God was **p** through the foolishness
10: 5 God was not **p** with most of them;
Col 1:19 God was **p** to have all his fullness
Heb 10: 6 and sin offerings you were not **p**.
10: 8 desire, nor were you **p** with them"—
11: 5 was commended as one who **p** God.
13:16 for with such sacrifices God is **p**.
2Pe 1:17 with him I am well **p**."

## PLEASES [PLEASE]
Job 23:13 He does whatever he **p**.
Ps 115: 3 he does whatever **p** him.
135: 6 The LORD does whatever **p** him,
Pr 15: 8 but the prayer of the upright **p** him.
Ecc 2:26 To the person who **p** him, God gives
2:26 hand it over to the one who **p** God.
7:26 The man who **p** God will escape
Isa 56: 4 who choose what **p** me and hold fast
Da 4:35 He does as he **p** with the powers
11: 3 with great power and do as he **p**.
11:36 "The king will do as he **p**.
Jn 3: 8 The wind blows wherever it **p**.
8:29 alone, for I always do what **p** him."
Eph 5:10 and find out what **p** the Lord.
Col 3:20 in everything, for this **p** the Lord.
1Ti 2: 3 This is good, and **p** God our Savior,
1Jn 3:22 his commands and do what **p** him.

## PLEASING [PLEASE]
Ge 2: 9 trees that were **p** to the eye
8:21 The LORD smelled the **p** aroma
Ex 29:18 offering to the LORD, a **p** aroma,
Lev 1: 9 offering, an aroma **p** to the LORD.
Ezr 6:10 they may offer sacrifices **p**
Ps 19:14 of my heart be **p** in your sight,
104:34 May my meditation be **p** to him, as I
SS 1: 3 **P** is the fragrance of your perfumes;
4:10 How much more **p** is your love than
7: 6 How beautiful you are and how **p**,
Ro 12: 1 living sacrifice, holy and **p** to God—
14:18 serves Christ in this way is **p** to God
Php 4:18 an acceptable sacrifice, **p** to God.
1Ti 5: 4 grandparents, for this is **p** to God.
Heb 13:21 may he work in us what is **p** to him,

## AROMA PLEASING Lev 1:9, 13, 17; 2:2, 9;
3:5; 4:31; 6:15, 21; 17:6; 23:18; Nu 15:3, 7, 10,
13, 14, 24; 18:17; 28:2, 8, 24, 27; 29:2, 8, 13, 36

## PLEASING AROMA Ge 8:21; Ex 29:18, 25,
41; Lev 2:12; 3:16; 8:21, 28; 23:13; 26:31; Nu
28:6, 13; 29:6; 2Co 2:15

## PLEASURE [PLEASE]
Ge 18:12 lord is old, will I now have this **p**?"
Ps 51:16 you do not take **p** in burnt offerings.

Ps 147:10 His **p** is not in the strength
Pr 10:23 Fools find **p** in wicked schemes,
16: 7 the LORD takes **p** in anyone's way,
18: 2 Fools find no **p** in understanding
21:17 Whoever loves **p** will become poor;
Ecc 2: 2 And what does **p** accomplish?"
7: 4 heart of fools is in the house of **p**.
Isa 1:11 I have no **p** in the blood of bulls
Jer 6:10 they find no **p** in it.
Eze 18:32 For I take no **p** in the death
33:11 I take no **p** in the death
Hag 1: 8 so that I may take **p** in it and be
Lk 10:21 Father, for this was your good **p**.
Eph 1: 5 in accordance with his **p** and will—
1: 9 of his will according to his good **p**,
1Ti 5: 6 for **p** is dead even while she lives.
2Ti 3: 4 lovers of **p** rather than lovers
Heb 10:38 take no **p** in the one who shrinks
2Pe 2:13 Their idea of **p** is to carouse

## PLEASURES* [PLEASE]
Ps 16:11 with eternal **p** at your right hand.
Lk 8:14 riches and **p**, and they do not
Tit 3: 3 by all kinds of passions and **p**.
Heb 11:25 than to enjoy the fleeting **p** of sin.
Jas 4: 3 may spend what you get on your **p**.
2Pe 2:13 reveling in their **p** while they feast

## PLEDGE [PLEDGED]
Ge 38:17 me something as a **p** until you send
Ex 22:26 take your neighbor's cloak as a **p**,
Nu 30: 2 an oath to obligate himself by a **p**,
Dt 24:17 take the cloak of the widow as a **p**.
Pr 6: 1 if you have shaken hands in a **p**
22:26 not be one who shakes hands in **p**
Eze 18: 7 returns what he took in **p** for a loan.
1Pe 3:21 the **p** of a clear conscience toward

## PLEDGED [PLEDGE]
Mt 1:18 His mother Mary was **p** to be
Lk 1:27 to a virgin **p** to be married to a man
1Co 7:27 Are you **p** to a woman?

## PLEIADES
Job 38:31 "Can you bind the chains of the **P**?
Am 5: 8 He who made the **P** and Orion,

## PLENTIFUL [PLENTY]
Mt 9:37 "The harvest is **p** but the workers
Lk 10: 2 "The harvest is **p**, but the workers

## PLENTY [PLENTIFUL]
Mic 2:11 will prophesy for you **p** of wine
2Co 8:14 in turn their **p** will supply what you
Php 4:12 whether living in **p** or in want.

## PLOT [PLOTS, PLOTTED]
Ne 4:15 heard that we were aware of their **p**
Est 2:22 Mordecai found out about the **p**
Ps 2: 1 conspire and the peoples **p** in vain?
64: 6 They **p** injustice and say, "We have
Pr 3:29 Do not **p** harm against your
6:14 who **p** evil with deceit
14:22 Do not those who **p** evil go astray?
Jer 11:18 the LORD revealed their **p** to me,

Na    1: 9  Whatever they **p** against
Zec   8:17  do not **p** evil against each other,
Mk    3: 6  began to **p** with the Herodians how
Ac    4:25  rage and the peoples **p** in vain?
      23:16  son of Paul's sister heard of this **p**,

## PLOTS [PLOT]
Na    1:11  come forth who **p** evil against

## PLOTTED [PLOT]
Est   9:24  had **p** against the Jews to destroy
Jn   11:53  that day on they **p** to take his life.

## PLOW [PLOWED, PLOWMEN, PLOWPOINTS, PLOWS, PLOWSHARES]
Dt   22:10  Do not **p** with an ox and a donkey
Pr   20: 4  Sluggards do not **p** in season;
Lk    9:62  "No one who puts a hand to the **p**
1Co   9:10  because when farmers **p** and thresh,

## PLOWED [PLOW]
Jdg  14:18  "If you had not **p** with my heifer,

## PLOWMEN* [PLOW]
Ps  129: 3  **P** have plowed my back and made

## PLOWPOINTS [PLOW]
1Sa  13:20  Philistines to have their **p**,

## PLOWS [PLOW]
Am    9:13  overtaken by the one who **p**

## PLOWSHARES* [PLOW]
Isa   2: 4  They will beat their swords into **p**
Joel  3:10  Beat your **p** into swords and your
Mic   4: 3  They will beat their swords into **p**

## PLUCK*
Ps   52: 5  and **p** you from your tent;
Mk    9:47  eye causes you to stumble, **p** it out.

## PLUMB
2Ki  21:13  the **p** line used against the house
Isa  28:17  line and righteousness the **p** line;
Am    7: 8  I am setting a **p** line among my

## PLUNDER [PLUNDERED]
Ex    3:22  And so you will **p** the Egyptians."
Nu   14:31  that you said would be taken as **p**,
Dt   20:14  you may take these as **p**
Jos   7:21  I saw in the **p** a beautiful robe
Est   3:13  month of Adar, and to **p** their goods.
      8:11  to **p** the property of their enemies.
      9:10  did not lay their hands on the **p**.
Pr   12:12  The wicked desire the **p**
Isa   3:14  the **p** from the poor is in your
Jer  30:16  Those who **p** you will be plundered;
Eze  39:10  they will **p** those who plundered
Mk    3:27  he can **p** the strong man's house.
Hab   2: 8  the peoples who are left will **p** you.
Zep   2: 9  remnant of my people will **p** them;

## PLUNDERED [PLUNDER]
Ex   12:36  so they **p** the Egyptians.
Jdg   2:14  the hands of raiders who **p** them.
Ps   12: 5  "Because the poor are **p**
Eze  34: 8  so has been **p** and has become food

## PLUNGE
1Ti   6: 9  harmful desires that **p** people

## POCKET*
1Sa  25:29  hurl away as from the **p** of a sling.

## PODS
Lk   15:16  with the **p** that the pigs were eating,

## POETS*
Nu   21:27  That is why the **p** say:
Ac   17:28  As some of your own **p** have said,

## POINT
Pr    9: 3  calls from the highest **p** of the city,
Mt    4: 5  stand on the highest **p** of the temple.
     26:38  with sorrow to the **p** of death.
Ro    2: 1  for at whatever **p** you judge another,
Heb  12: 4  to the **p** of shedding your blood.
Jas   2:10  yet stumbles at just one **p** is guilty
Rev   2:10  even to the **p** of death, and I will

## POISON
Dt   32:32  Their grapes are filled with **p**,
Ps  140: 3  the **p** of vipers is on their lips.
Am    6:12  you have turned justice into **p**
Mk   16:18  *and when they drink deadly p,*
Ro    3:13  "The **p** of vipers is on their lips."
Jas   3: 8  It is a restless evil, full of deadly **p**.

## POLE [POLES]
Nu   21: 8  "Make a snake and put it up on a **p**;
Dt   16:21  any wooden Asherah **p** beside
     21:23  not leave the body hanging on the **p**
Jdg   6:25  cut down the Asherah **p** beside it.
1Ki  16:33  made an Asherah **p** and did more
Est   7:10  impaled Haman on the **p** he had set up
Gal   3:13  everyone who is hung on a **p**."

## POLES [POLE]
Ex   25:13  Then make **p** of acacia wood
Dt   12: 3  and burn their Asherah **p** in the fire;
2Ki  17:10  and Asherah **p** on every high hill
Est   9:13  let Haman's ten sons be impaled on **p**."

## POLISHED
Isa  49: 2  he made me into a **p** arrow
Eze  21:11  " 'The sword is appointed to be **p**,

## POLLUTE* [POLLUTED, POLLUTES]
Nu   35:33  " 'Do not **p** the land where you
Jude  1: 8  these ungodly people **p** their own

## POLLUTED* [POLLUTE]
Ezr   9:11  possess is a land **p** by the corruption
Pr   25:26  a **p** well are the righteous who give
Ac   15:20  to abstain from food **p** by idols,
Jas   1:27  oneself from being **p** by the world.

## POLLUTES* [POLLUTE]
Nu 35:33 Bloodshed p the land,

## POMEGRANATES
Ex  28:33 Make p of blue, purple and scarlet
Dt   8: 8 vines and fig trees, p, olive oil
1Ki  7:18 He made p in two rows encircling
SS   8: 2 wine to drink, the nectar of my p.

## PONDER [PONDERED]
Ps  64: 9 of God and p what he has done.
107:43 and p the loving deeds of the LORD.
119:95 me, but I will p your statutes.

## PONDERED [PONDER]
Ps 111: 2 they are p by all who delight
Ecc 12: 9 He p and searched out and set
Lk   2:19 these things and p them in her heart.

## PONTIUS [PILATE]
Lk   3: 1 when P Pilate was governor

## POOL [POOLS]
2Sa  2:13 and met them at the p of Gibeon.
1Ki 22:38 chariot at a p in Samaria (where
Ps 114: 8 who turned the rock into a p,
Jn   5: 2 Jerusalem near the Sheep Gate a p,
     9: 7 the P of Siloam" (this word means

## POOLS [POOL]
Dt   8: 7 a land with streams and p of water,
Ps 107:35 He turned the desert into p of water

## POOR [POOREST, POVERTY]
Ex  23: 3 favoritism to the p in a lawsuit.
    23: 6 not deny justice to your p people
Lev 19:10 Leave them for the p
    23:22 Leave them for the p
    27: 8 anyone making the vow is too p
Dt  15: 4 need be no p people among you,
    15: 7 If anyone is p among your people
    15:11 There will always be p people
    24:12 If the neighbor is p, do not go
    24:14 of a hired worker who is p
1Sa  2: 8 He raises the p from the dust
2Sa 12: 1 town, one rich and the other p.
Job  5:16 So the p have hope, and injustice
    24: 4 and force all the p of the land
    30:25 Has not my soul grieved for the p?
Ps  14: 6 frustrate the plans of the p,
    34: 6 This p man called, and the LORD
    35:10 the p and needy from those who rob
    40:17 But as for me, I am p and needy;
    68:10 God, you provided for the p.
    69:32 The p will see and be glad—
    82: 3 uphold the cause of the p
   112: 9 scattered abroad their gifts to the p,
   113: 7 He raises the p from the dust
   140:12 the LORD secures justice for the p
Pr  13: 7 another pretends to be p, yet has
    14:20 The p are shunned even by their
    14:31 oppresses the p shows contempt
    17: 5 mocks the p shows contempt
    19: 1 Better the p whose walk is
    19:17 Those who are kind to the p lend

Pr  19:22 better to be p than a liar.
    20:13 not love sleep or you will grow p;
    21:13 their ears to the cry of the p will
    21:17 loves pleasure will become p;
    22: 2 Rich and p have this in common:
    22: 9 for they share their food with the p.
    22:22 not exploit the p because they are p
    28: 6 Better the p whose walk is
    28:27 who give to the p will lack nothing,
    29: 7 care about justice for the p,
    31: 9 defend the rights of the p and needy.
    31:20 She opens her arms to the p
Ecc  4:13 Better a p but wise youth than
Isa  3:14 the plunder from the p is in your
    10: 2 to deprive the p of their rights
    14:30 poorest of the p will find pasture,
    25: 4 You have been a refuge for the p,
    32: 7 schemes to destroy the p with lies,
    61: 1 me to proclaim good news to the p.
Jer 22:16 He defended the cause of the p
Eze 18:12 He oppresses the p and needy.
Am   2: 7 on the heads of the p as on the dust
     4: 1 you women who oppress the p
     5:11 You levy a straw tax on the p
Zec  7:10 the fatherless, the foreigner or the p.
Mt   5: 3 "Blessed are the p in spirit,
    11: 5 good news is proclaimed to the p.
Mk  10:21 you have and give to the p, and you
    12:42 But a p widow came and put in two
    14: 7 The p you will always have
Lk   4:18 me to proclaim good news to the p.
     6:20 "Blessed are you who are p,
    11:41 be generous to the p, and everything
    14:13 a banquet, invite the p, the crippled,
    19: 8 give half of my possessions to the p,
    21: 2 also saw a p widow put in two very
Jn  12: 8 will always have the p among you,
Ac   9:36 doing good and helping the p.
    10: 4 and gifts to the p have come up as
    24:17 to bring my people gifts for the p
Ro  15:26 for the p among the Lord's people
1Co 13: 3 If I give all I possess to the p
2Co  6:10 p, yet making many rich;
     8: 9 yet for your sake he became p,
     9: 9 scattered abroad their gifts to the p;
Gal  2:10 should continue to remember the p,
Jas  2: 2 and a p person in filthy old clothes
     2: 5 not God chosen those who are p
Rev  3:17 pitiful, p, blind and naked.

## POOREST [POOR]
2Ki 24:14 Only the p people of the land were
Jer 52:16 left behind the rest of the p people

## POPULATION*
Pr  14:28 A large p is a king's glory,

## PORCIUS* [FESTUS]
Ac  24:27 Felix was succeeded by P Festus,

## PORTENT*
Ps  71: 7 I have become like a p to many,
Isa 20: 3 as a sign and p against Egypt

## PORTICO
1Ki  6: 3 The p at the front of the main hall

1Ch 28:11 the plans for the **p** of the temple,

## PORTION [PORTIONS]

Lev  2: 2  and burn this as a memorial **p**
      5:12  take a handful of it as a memorial **p**
Nu 18:29  present as the LORD's **p** the best
Dt  32: 9  For the LORD's **p** is his people,
Jos 18: 7  do not get a **p** among you,
1Sa  1: 5  he gave a double **p** because he loved
2Ki  2: 9  "Let me inherit a double **p** of your
Ps  16: 5  you have assigned me my **p** and my
    73:26  of my heart and my **p** forever.
  119:57  You are my **p**, LORD;
  142: 5  my **p** in the land of the living."
Isa 53:12  I will give him a **p** among the great,
  61: 7  so you will inherit a double **p**
Jer 10:16  He who is the **P** of Jacob is not like
La   3:24  to myself, "The LORD is my **p**;
Zec  2:12  LORD will inherit Judah as his **p**
Rev 18: 6  Pour her a double **p** from her own

## PORTIONS [PORTION]

Ge   4: 4  fat **p** from some of the firstborn
Lev  9:24  offering and the fat **p** on the altar.
Jos 19:49  dividing the land into its allotted **p**,

## PORTRAYED

Gal   3: 1  Christ was clearly **p** as crucified.

## POSITION [POSITIONS]

Est  4:14  to royal **p** for such a time as this?"
Da   2:48  the king placed Daniel in a high **p**
Ro  12:16  to associate with people of low **p**.
2Pe  3:17  lawless and fall from your secure **p**.

## POSITIONS [POSITION]

2Ch 20:17  Take up your **p**; stand firm and see
Ecc 10: 6  Fools are put in many high **p**,
Jude  1: 6  the angels who did not keep their **p**

## POSSESS [DEMON-POSSESSED, POSSESSED, POSSESSING, POSSESSION, POSSESSIONS, POSSESSOR]

Lev 20:24  said to you, "You will **p** their land;
Nu 33:53  for I have given you the land to **p**.
Dt   4:14  you are crossing the Jordan to **p**.
  28:21  from the land you are entering to **p**.
Ezr  9:11  are entering to **p** is a land polluted
Pr   8:12  I **p** knowledge and discretion.
Isa 60:21  and they will **p** the land forever.
Da   7:18  the kingdom and will **p** it forever—
Jn   5:39  think that in them you **p** eternal life.
1Co 13: 3  If I give all I **p** to the poor and give
2Pe  1: 8  if you **p** these qualities in increasing

## POSSESSED [POSSESS]

Jer 16:19  "Our ancestors **p** nothing but false
Mk  3:22  said, "He is **p** by Beelzebul!
Lk  4:33  the synagogue there was a man **p**
Jn  8:49  "I am not **p** by a demon,"
  10:21  sayings of someone **p** by a demon.

## POSSESSING* [POSSESS]

2Co  6:10  nothing, and yet **p** everything.

## POSSESSION [POSSESS]

Ge  15: 7  give you this land to take **p** of it."
  17: 8  I will give as an everlasting **p** to you
Ex   6: 8  I will give it to you as a **p**. I am
  19: 5  nations you will be my treasured **p**.
Nu 13:30  should go up and take **p** of the land,
Dt   1: 8  take **p** of the land the LORD swore
  7: 6  to be his people, his treasured **p**.
Jos  1:11  take **p** of the land the LORD your
  21:43  and they took **p** of it and settled
Ps   2: 8  the ends of the earth your **p**.
  135: 4  his own, Israel to be his treasured **p**.
Isa 14: 2  Israel will take **p** of the nations
Eze 44:28  no **p** in Israel; I will be their **p**.
Mal  3:17  "they will be my treasured **p**.
Eph  1:14  of those who are God's **p**—
1Pe  2: 9  God's special **p**,

## POSSESSIONS [POSSESS]

Ge 15:14  they will come out with great **p**.
Ecc  5:19  God gives people wealth and **p**,
Mt 19:21  go, sell your **p** and give to the poor,
Lk 11:21  his own house, his **p** are safe.
  12:15  not consist in an abundance of **p**."
  19: 8  now I give half of my **p** to the poor,
Ac  4:32  that any of their **p** was their own,
2Co 12:14  because what I want is not your **p**
Heb 10:34  yourselves had better and lasting **p**.
1Jn  3:17  If any one of you has material **p**

## POSSESSOR* [POSSESS]

Ecc  7:12  Wisdom preserves the life of its **p**.

## POSSIBLE

Mt 19:26  but with God all things are **p**."
  26:39  if it is **p**, may this cup be taken
Mk  9:23  "Everything is **p** for one who
  10:27  all things are **p** with God."
  14:35  if **p** the hour might pass from him.
Lk 18:27  with human beings is **p** with God."
Ro 12:18  If it is **p**, as far as it depends on you,
1Co  9:19  to everyone, to win as many as **p**.
  9:22  by all **p** means I might save some.

## POSTS

Ex 27:17  All the **p** around the courtyard are
Jdg 16: 3  together with the two **p**, and tore

## POT [POTSHERD, POTSHERDS, POTTER, POTTER'S, POTTERY]

2Ki  4:40  of God, there is death in the **p**!"
Isa 29:16  Can the **p** say to the potter,
Jer  1:13  "I see a **p** that is boiling,"
  18: 4  the potter formed it into another **p**,
Eze 11: 3  This city is a **p**, and we are the meat

## POTIPHAR*

Egyptian who bought Joseph (Ge 37:36), set him over his house (Ge 39:1–6), sent him to prison (Ge 39:7–30).

## POTSHERD [POT]
Ps 22:15 My mouth is dried up like a **p**,

## POTSHERDS [POT]
Isa 45: 9 but **p** among the **p** on the ground.

## POTTER [POT]
Isa 29:16 Can the pot say to the **p**,
   45: 9 Does the clay say to the **p**,
   64: 8 We are the clay, you are the **p**;
Jer 18: 6 house of Israel, as this **p** does?"
Zec 11:13 said to me, "Throw it to the **p**"—
Ro 9:21 Does not the **p** have the right

## POTTER'S [POT]
Jer 18: 2 "Go down to the **p** house, and there
Mt 27: 7 to buy the **p** field as a burial place

## POTTERY [POT]
Ps 2: 9 will dash them to pieces like **p**."
Ro 9:21 of clay some **p** for noble purposes
Rev 2:27 will dash them to pieces like **p'**—

## POUR [OUTPOURED, OUTPOURING, POURED, POURING, POURS]
Lev 4: 7 of the bull's blood he shall **p**
Nu 20: 8 their eyes and it will **p** out its water.
Dt 12:16 **p** it out on the ground like water.
2Ki 4: 4 **P** oil into all the jars, and as each is
Ps 19: 2 Day after day they **p** forth speech;
  62: 8 **p** out your hearts to him, for God is
  79: 6 **P** out your wrath on the nations
Isa 44: 3 I will **p** out my Spirit on your
Eze 20: 8 So I said I would **p** out my wrath
  39:29 for I will **p** out my Spirit
Joel 2:28 I will **p** out my Spirit on all people.
Zec 12:10 I will **p** out on the house of David
Mal 3:10 **p** out so much blessing that there
Mt 9:17 No, they **p** new wine into new
Lk 5:37 people do not **p** new wine
Ac 2:17 I will **p** out my Spirit on all people.
Rev 16: 1 **p** out the seven bowls of God's
  18: 6 **P** her a double portion from her own cup

## POURED [POUR]
Ge 28:18 it up as a pillar and **p** oil on top of it.
  35:14 and he **p** out a drink offering on it;
Lev 8:12 He **p** some of the anointing oil
2Sa 23:16 he **p** it out before the LORD.
2Ch 34:25 my anger will be **p** out on this place
Ps 22:14 I am **p** out like water, and all my
  133: 2 It is like precious oil **p** on the head,
SS 1: 3 your name is like perfume **p** out.
Isa 19:14 The LORD has **p** into them a spirit
  32:15 till the Spirit is **p** on us
La 4:11 he has **p** out his fierce anger.
Mt 26:28 which is **p** out for many
Mk 14: 3 jar and **p** the perfume on his head.
Lk 6:38 over, will be **p** into your lap.
  22:20 in my blood, which is **p** out for you.
Ac 2:33 and has **p** out what you now see
  10:45 the Holy Spirit had been **p** out even
Ro 5: 5 because God's love has been **p**

Php 2:17 even if I am being **p** out like a drink
1Ti 1:14 The grace of our Lord was **p**
2Ti 4: 6 I am already being **p** out like a drink
Tit 3: 6 whom he **p** out on us generously
Rev 14:10 which has been **p** full strength
  16: 2 went and **p** out his bowl on the land,

## POURING [POUR]
1Sa 1:15 I was **p** out my soul to the LORD.
2Ki 4: 5 the jars to her and she kept **p**.
Lk 10:34 his wounds, **p** on oil and wine.

## POURS [POUR]
Pr 14: 5 but a false witness **p** out lies.

## POVERTY* [POOR]
Dt 28:48 in nakedness and dire **p**, you will
1Sa 2: 7 The LORD sends **p** and wealth;
Pr 6:11 and **p** will come on you like a thief
  10: 4 Lazy hands make for **p**,
  10:15 city, but **p** is the ruin of the poor.
  11:24 withholds unduly, but comes to **p**.
  13:18 disregards discipline comes to **p**
  14:23 profit, but mere talk leads only to **p**.
  21: 5 profit as surely as haste leads to **p**.
  22:16 gifts to the rich—both come to **p**.
  24:34 and **p** will come on you like a thief
  28:19 fantasies will have their fill of **p**.
  28:22 and are unaware that **p** awaits them.
  30: 8 give me neither **p** nor riches,
  31: 7 forget their **p** and remember their
Ecc 4:14 been born in **p** within his kingdom.
Mk 12:44 she, out of her **p**, put in everything—
Lk 21: 4 she out of her **p** put in all she had
2Co 8: 2 their extreme **p** welled up in rich
  8: 9 you through his **p** might become
Rev 2: 9 I know your afflictions and your **p**—

## POWDER
Ex 32:20 then he ground it to **p**, scattered it
2Ki 23:15 the high place and ground it to **p**,
Job 9:30 and my hands with cleansing **p**,

## POWER [OVERPOWER, POWERFUL, POWERLESS, POWERS]
Ex 9:16 that I might show you my **p**
  15: 6 hand, LORD, was majestic in **p**.
  32:11 brought out of Egypt with great **p**
Dt 8:17 "My **p** and the strength of my
  34:12 no one has ever shown the mighty **p**
Jdg 14:19 of the LORD came on him in **p**.
  15:14 of the LORD came on him in **p**.
1Sa 10:10 the Spirit of God came on him in **p**,
  11: 6 the Spirit of God came on him in **p**,
  16:13 of the LORD came on David in **p**.
1Ki 18:46 The **p** of the LORD came on Elijah
1Ch 29:11 greatness and the **p** and the glory
2Ch 20: 6 **P** and might are in your hand,
  32: 7 for there is a greater **p** with us
Job 1:12 everything he has is in your **p**,
  9: 4 wisdom is profound, his **p** is vast.
  12:13 "To God belong wisdom and **p**;
  36:22 "God is exalted in his **p**.
  37:23 beyond our reach and exalted in **p**;
Ps 20: 6 the victorious **p** of his right hand.

| | | |
|---|---|---|
| Ps | 37:17 | the **p** of the wicked will be broken, |
| | 62:11 | "**P** belongs to you, God, |
| | 63: 2 | and beheld your **p** and your glory. |
| | 66: 3 | So great is your **p** that your enemies |
| | 68:34 | Proclaim the **p** of God, |
| | 77:14 | you display your **p** among |
| | 89:13 | Your arm is endued with **p**; |
| | 145: 6 | of the **p** of your awesome works— |
| | 147: 5 | Great is our Lord and mighty in **p**; |
| | 150: 2 | Praise him for his acts of **p**; |
| Pr | 3:27 | it is due, when it is in your **p** to act. |
| | 8:14 | I have insight, I have **p**. |
| | 18:21 | The tongue has the **p** of life |
| | 24: 5 | The wise prevail through great **p**, |
| | 28:12 | but when the wicked rise to **p**, |
| Ecc | 8: 8 | As no one has **p** over the wind |
| Isa | 40:10 | Sovereign LORD comes with **p**, |
| | 40:26 | Because of his great **p** and mighty |
| | 40:29 | and increases the **p** of the weak. |
| | 63:12 | who sent his glorious arm of **p** to be |
| Jer | 10: 6 | great, and your name is mighty in **p**. |
| | 10:12 | But God made the earth by his **p**; |
| | 27: 5 | With my great **p** and outstretched |
| | 32:17 | and the earth by your great **p** |
| Da | 2:20 | wisdom and **p** are his. |
| | 6:27 | Daniel from the **p** of the lions." |
| | 11: 3 | who will rule with great **p** and do as |
| Hos | 13:14 | them from the **p** of the grave; |
| Mic | 3: 8 | I am filled with **p**, with the Spirit |
| Na | 1: 3 | is slow to anger but great in **p**; |
| Zec | 4: 6 | 'Not by might nor by **p**, but by my |
| Mt | 22:29 | know the Scriptures or the **p** of God. |
| | 24:30 | of heaven, with **p** and great glory. |
| Mk | 9: 1 | kingdom of God has come with **p**." |
| | 13:26 | Man coming in clouds with great **p** |
| Lk | 1:17 | in the spirit and **p** of Elijah, to turn |
| | 1:35 | you, and the **p** of the Most High will |
| | 4:14 | to Galilee in the **p** of the Spirit, |
| | 6:19 | because **p** was coming from him |
| | 8:46 | I know that **p** has gone |
| | 9: 1 | he gave them **p** and authority |
| | 10:19 | to overcome all the **p** of the enemy; |
| | 21:27 | of Man coming in a cloud with **p** |
| | 24:49 | until you have been clothed with **p** |
| Jn | 19:11 | "You would have no **p** over me if it |
| Ac | 1: 8 | you will receive **p** when the Holy |
| | 4:28 | They did what your **p** and will had |
| | 4:33 | With great **p** the apostles continued |
| | 8:10 | man is rightly called the Great **P** |
| | 10:38 | Nazareth with the Holy Spirit and **p**, |
| | 26:18 | and from the **p** of Satan to God, |
| Ro | 1:16 | because it is the **p** of God |
| | 1:20 | his eternal **p** and divine nature— |
| | 4:21 | that God had **p** to do what he had |
| | 9:17 | that I might display my **p** in you |
| | 15:13 | hope by the **p** of the Holy Spirit. |
| | 15:19 | by the **p** of signs and wonders, |
| | 15:19 | through the **p** of the Spirit of God. |
| 1Co | 1:17 | cross of Christ be emptied of its **p**. |
| | 1:18 | us who are being saved it is the **p** |
| | 1:24 | Christ the **p** of God and the wisdom |
| | 2: 4 | a demonstration of the Spirit's **p**, |
| | 6:14 | By his **p** God raised the Lord |
| | 15:24 | all dominion, authority and **p**. |
| | 15:56 | is sin, and the **p** of sin is the law. |
| 2Co | 4: 7 | this all-surpassing **p** is from God |
| | 6: 7 | truthful speech and in the **p** of God; |

| | | |
|---|---|---|
| 2Co | 10: 4 | they have divine **p** to demolish |
| | 12: 9 | so that Christ's **p** may rest on me. |
| | 13: 4 | weakness, yet he lives by God's **p**. |
| | 13: 4 | yet by God's **p** we will live |
| Eph | 1:19 | his incomparably great **p** for us who |
| | 1:19 | **p** is the same as the mighty strength |
| | 1:21 | rule and authority, **p** and dominion, |
| | 3:16 | you with **p** through his Spirit |
| | 3:20 | according to his **p** that is at work |
| | 6:10 | in the Lord and in his mighty **p**. |
| Php | 3:10 | to know the **p** of his resurrection |
| | 3:21 | by the **p** that enables him to bring |
| Col | 1:11 | strengthened with all **p** according |
| | 2:10 | He is the head over every **p** |
| 1Th | 1: 5 | simply with words but also with **p**, |
| 2Th | 2: 7 | For the secret **p** of lawlessness is |
| 2Ti | 1: 7 | us timid, but gives us **p**, |
| | 3: 5 | form of godliness but denying its **p**. |
| Heb | 2:14 | **p** of him who holds the **p** of death— |
| | 7:16 | of the **p** of an indestructible life. |
| 1Pe | 1: 5 | by God's **p** until the coming |
| 2Pe | 1: 3 | His divine **p** has given us everything |
| | 1:16 | of our Lord Jesus Christ in **p**, |
| Jude | 1:25 | majesty, **p** and authority, |
| Rev | 4:11 | to receive glory and honor and **p**, |
| | 5:12 | to receive **p** and wealth and wisdom |
| | 6: 4 | Its rider was given **p** to take peace |
| | 6: 8 | They were given **p** over a fourth |
| | 7: 2 | four angels who had been given **p** |
| | 11:17 | because you have taken your great **p** |
| | 12:10 | the **p** and the kingdom of our God, |
| | 13: 2 | The dragon gave the beast his **p** |
| | 17:17 | to give the beast their **p** to rule, |
| | 19: 1 | and glory and **p** belong to our God, |
| | 20: 6 | second death has no **p** over them, |

## POWERFUL [POWER]

| | | |
|---|---|---|
| Ge | 18:18 | surely become a great and **p** nation, |
| Nu | 13:28 | But the people who live there are **p**, |
| Jos | 4:24 | that the hand of the LORD is **p** |
| 1Ch | 11: 9 | David became more and more **p**, |
| 2Ch | 26:16 | But after Uzziah became **p**, |
| | 27: 6 | Jotham grew **p** because he walked |
| Est | 9: 4 | and he became more and more **p**. |
| Ps | 29: 4 | The voice of the LORD is **p**; |
| Ecc | 7:19 | wise person more **p** than ten rulers |
| Zec | 8:22 | **p** nations will come to Jerusalem |
| Mk | 1: 7 | me comes the one more **p** than I, |
| Lk | 24:19 | **p** in word and deed before God |
| Ac | 9:22 | more **p** and baffled the Jews living |
| 2Th | 1: 7 | in blazing fire with his **p** angels. |
| Heb | 1: 3 | sustaining all things by his **p** word. |
| Jas | 5:16 | prayer of a righteous person is **p** |

## POWERLESS [POWER]

| | | |
|---|---|---|
| 2Ch | 14:11 | you to help the **p** against the mighty. |
| Ro | 5: 6 | when we were still **p**, Christ died |
| | 8: 3 | what the law was **p** to do because it |

## POWERS [POWER]

| | | |
|---|---|---|
| Isa | 24:21 | day the LORD will punish the **p** |
| Da | 4:35 | as he pleases with the **p** of heaven |
| Mt | 13:54 | wisdom and these miraculous **p**?" |
| Ro | 8:38 | the present nor the future, nor any **p**, |
| 1Co | 12:10 | to another miraculous **p**, to another |
| Eph | 6:12 | against the **p** of this dark world |

Col  1:16  whether thrones or **p** or rulers
     2:15  And having disarmed the **p**
Heb  6: 5  of God and the **p** of the coming age
1Pe  3:22  and **p** in submission to him.

## PRACTICE [PRACTICED, PRACTICES]

Lev 19:26  " 'Do not **p** divination or seek
Ps 119:56  This has been my **p**: I obey your
Jer   6:13  and priests alike, all **p** deceit.
Eze 13:23  see false visions or **p** divination.
     33:31  but they do not put them into **p**.
Mt    7:24  **p** is like a wise man who built his
     23: 3  for they do not **p** what they preach.
Lk    8:21  hear God's word and put it into **p**."
Ro   12:13  who are in need. **P** hospitality.
Php   4: 9  me, or seen in me—put it into **p**.
1Ti   5: 4  to put their religion into **p** by caring
Rev  21: 8  immoral, those who **p** magic arts,
     22:15  the dogs, those who **p** magic arts,

## PRACTICED [PRACTICE]

Lev 18:30  that were **p** before you came and do
Mt   23:23  You should have **p** the latter,
Ac    8: 9  a man named Simon had **p** sorcery
     19:19  number who had **p** sorcery brought

## PRACTICES [PRACTICE]

Ex   23:24  or worship them or follow their **p**.
Lev  18: 3  Do not follow their **p**.
Jdg   2:19  They refused to give up their evil **p**
2Ki  17: 8  followed the **p** of the nations
Ps  101: 7  No one who **p** deceit will dwell
Pr   28:16  A tyrannical ruler **p** extortion,
Jer  10: 3  For the **p** of the peoples are worthless;
Eze   7: 3  repay you for all your detestable **p**.
Mt    5:19  but whoever **p** and teaches these
Col   3: 9  taken off your old self with its **p**
Rev  22:15  who loves and **p** falsehood.

## PRAETORIUM*

Mt   27:27  soldiers took Jesus into the **P**
Mk   15:16  the **P**) and called together the whole

## PRAISE [PRAISED, PRAISES, PRAISEWORTHY, PRAISING]

Ge    9:26  He also said, "**P** be to the LORD,
Ex   15: 2  and I will **p** him, my father's God,
Lev  19:24  an offering of **p** to the LORD.
Dt   10:21  He is the one you **p**; he is your God,
     26:19  declared that he will set you in **p**,
     32: 3  Oh, **p** the greatness of our God!
Ru    4:14  "**P** be to the LORD, who this day
2Sa  22: 4  who is worthy of **p**, and have been
     22:47  **P** be to my Rock!
1Ki   8:33  back to you and give **p** to your name,
      8:35  and give **p** to your name and turn
1Ch  16: 7  give **p** to the LORD in this manner:
     16: 8  Give **p** to the LORD,
     16:25  the LORD and most worthy of **p**;
     23: 5  four thousand are to **p** the LORD
     29:10  saying, "**P** be to you, LORD,
2Ch   5:13  the singers raised their voices in **p**
      6:24  turn back and give **p** to your name,
      6:26  this place and give **p** to your name
     20:21  and to **p** him for the splendor of his

2Ch  29:30  ordered the Levites to **p** the LORD
Ezr   3:10  took their places to **p** the LORD,
Ne    9: 5  be exalted above all blessing and **p**.
Ps    8: 2  Through the **p** of children
      9: 1  I will **p** you, LORD, with all my
     16: 7  I will **p** the LORD, who counsels
     22:23  You who fear the LORD, **p** him!
     26: 7  proclaiming aloud your **p**
     28: 7  with my song I **p** him.
     30: 4  his faithful people; **p** his holy name.
     30:12  my God, I will **p** you forever.
     33: 1  it is fitting for the upright to **p** him.
     34: 1  his **p** will always be on my lips.
     40: 3  my mouth, a hymn of **p** to our God.
     42: 5  for I will yet **p** him, my Savior
     43: 5  for I will yet **p** him, my Savior
     45:17  therefore the nations will **p** you
     47: 7  sing to him a psalm of **p**.
     48: 1  and most worthy of **p**, in the city
     51:15  and my mouth will declare your **p**.
     56: 4  In God, whose word I **p**—in God I
     57: 9  I will **p** you, Lord,
     63: 4  I will **p** you as long as I live,
     65: 1  **P** awaits you, our God, in Zion;
     66: 2  of his name; make his **p** glorious.
     66: 8  **P** our God, all peoples, let the sound
     68:19  **P** be to the Lord, to God our Savior,
     68:26  **P** God in the great congregation;
     69:30  I will **p** God's name in song
     69:34  Let heaven and earth **p** him, the seas
     71: 8  My mouth is filled with your **p**,
     71:14  I will **p** you more and more.
     71:22  I will **p** you with the harp for your
     74:21  the poor and needy **p** your name.
     75: 1  we **p** you, for your Name is near;
     86:12  I will **p** you, Lord my God, with all
     89: 5  The heavens **p** your wonders,
     92: 1  It is good to **p** the LORD and make
     96: 2  Sing to the LORD, **p** his name;
    100: 4  thanksgiving and his courts with **p**;
    100: 4  give thanks to him and **p** his name.
    101: 1  to you, LORD, I will sing **p**.
    102:18  not yet created may **p** the LORD:
    103: 1  my inmost being, **p** his holy name.
    103:20  **P** the LORD, you his angels,
    104: 1  **P** the LORD, my soul.
    106: 2  the LORD or fully declare his **p**?
    108: 3  I will **p** you, LORD,
    111:10  To him belongs eternal **p**.
    113: 1  **p** the name of the LORD.
    117: 1  **P** the LORD, all you nations;
    119:175  Let me live that I may **p** you,
    135: 1  **P** the LORD. **P** the name
    135:20  you who fear him, **p** the LORD.
    138: 1  the "gods" I will sing your **p**.
    139:14  I **p** you because I am fearfully
    144: 1  **P** be to the LORD my Rock,
    145: 3  the LORD and most worthy of **p**;
    145:10  All your works **p** you, LORD;
    145:21  Let every creature **p** his holy name
    146: 1  **P** the LORD. **P** the LORD,
    147: 1  **P** the LORD. How good it is
    147: 1  how pleasant and fitting to **p** him!
    148: 1  **P** the LORD. **P** the LORD
    148: 1  **p** him in the heights above.
    148:13  Let them **p** the name of the LORD,
    149: 1  his **p** in the assembly of his faithful

Ps 149: 6 May the **p** of God be in their mouths
   150: 2 **P** him for his acts of power; **p** him
   150: 6 that has breath **p** the LORD.
Pr  27: 2 Let someone else **p** you, and not
   27:21 but people are tested by their **p.**
   31:31 let her works bring her **p** at the city
SS   1: 4 we will **p** your love more than wine.
Isa 12: 1 "I will **p** you, LORD.
   38:18 For the grave cannot **p** you,
   42:10 his **p** from the ends of the earth,
   61: 3 a garment of **p** instead of a spirit
Jer 33: 9 **p** and honor before all nations
Da   2:20 "**P** be to the name of God for ever
   4:37 **p** and exalt and glorify the King
Jnh  2: 9 But I, with shouts of grateful **p,**
Hab  3: 3 heavens and his **p** filled the earth.
Mt  21:16 and infants you have ordained **p**'?"
Lk  19:37 disciples began joyfully to **p** God
Ac  12:23 because Herod did not give **p**
Ro   2:29 Such a person's **p** is not from other
   15: 7 you, in order to bring **p** to God.
   15:11 "**P** the Lord, all you Gentiles;
1Co  4: 5 time each will receive their **p**
2Co  1: 3 **P** be to the God and Father of our
Eph  1: 6 to the **p** of his glorious grace,
   1:12 might be for the **p** of his glory.
   1:14 to the **p** of his glory.
1Th  2: 6 We were not looking for **p** from any
Heb 13:15 offer to God a sacrifice of **p**—
Jas  3: 9 With the tongue we **p** our Lord
   5:13 Let them sing songs of **p.**
1Pe  4:16 but **p** God that you bear that name.
Rev  5:13 and to the Lamb be **p** and honor
   7:12 **P** and glory and wisdom and thanks
   19: 5 "**P** our God, all you his servants,

### PRAISE BE TO THE †LORD Ge 9:26;
   24:27; Ex 18:10; Ru 4:14; 1Sa 25:32, 39; 2Sa
   18:28; 1Ki 1:48; 5:7; 8:15, 56; 10:9; 1Ch 16:36;
   2Ch 2:12; 6:4; 9:8; Ezr 7:27; Ps 28:6; 31:21;
   41:13; 72:18; 89:52; 106:48; 124:6; 135:21;
   144:1

### PRAISE THE †LORD Ge 29:35; Dt 8:10; Jdg
   5:2, 3, 9; 1Ch 16:4, 36; 23:5, 30; 29:20; 2Ch
   29:30; Ezr 3:10; Ne 9:5; Ps 16:7; 26:12; 33:2;
   68:26; 92:1; 102:18; 103:1, 2, 20, 21, 22, 22;
   104:1, 35, 35; 105:45; 106:1, 48; 111:1; 112:1;
   113:1, 1, 9; 115:17, 18; 116:19; 117:1, 2; 134:1,
   2; 135:1, 3, 19, 19, 20, 20, 21; 146:1, 1, 2, 10;
   147:1, 20; 148:1, 1, 7, 14; 149:1, 9; 150:1, 6, 6;
   Isa 62:9; Zec 11:5

### SING ... PRAISE 1Ch 16:9; 2Ch 20:22; Ps
   21:13; 59:17; 61:8; 66:4; 68:4, 32; 71:22, 23;
   75:9; 101:1; 104:33; 135:3; 138:1; 146:2; Isa
   38:18

### PRAISED [PRAISE]
Ge  12:15 saw her, they **p** her to Pharaoh,
Jdg 16:24 people saw him, they **p** their god,
2Sa 14:25 there was not a man so highly **p**
1Ch 29:10 David **p** the LORD in the presence
Ne   8: 6 Ezra **p** the LORD, the great God;
Job  1:21 may the name of the LORD be **p.**"
Ps 113: 2 Let the name of the LORD be **p,**
Pr  12: 8 People are **p** according to their

Pr  31:30 who fears the LORD is to be **p.**
Isa 63: 7 the deeds for which he is to be **p,**
Da   2:19 Then Daniel **p** the God of heaven
   4:34 Then I **p** the Most High;
   5: 4 they **p** the gods of gold and silver,
Lk  18:43 the people saw it, they also **p** God.
   23:47 what had happened, **p** God and said,
Ro   1:25 than the Creator—who is forever **p.**
   9: 5 who is God over all, forever **p**!
Gal  1:24 And they **p** God because of me.
1Pe  4:11 God may be **p** through Jesus Christ.

### PRAISES [PRAISE]
2Sa 22:50 I will sing the **p** of your name.
2Ch 23:13 their instruments were leading the **p.**
   29:30 So they sang **p** with gladness
   31: 2 and to sing **p** at the gates
Ps   6: 5 Who **p** you from the grave?
   9:11 Sing the **p** of the LORD,
   9:14 I may declare your **p** in the gates
   18:49 I will sing the **p** of your name.
   35:28 righteousness, your **p** all day long.
   47: 6 Sing **p** to God, sing **p**; sing **p** to our
         King, sing **p.**
   147: 1 How good it is to sing **p** to our God,
   105: 2 Sing of him, sing his **p**; tell of all his
Pr  31:28 her husband also, and he **p** her:
Jer 31: 7 Make your **p** heard, and say,
Ro  15: 9 I will sing the **p** of your name."
Heb  2:12 in the assembly I will sing your **p.**"
1Pe  2: 9 you may declare the **p** of him who

### SING ... PRAISES 2Sa 22:50; 2Ch 31:2; Ps
   7:17; 9:2, 11; 18:49; 30:4, 12; 47:6, 6, 6; 66:4;
   105:2; 147:1; Ro 15:9; Heb 2:12

### PRAISEWORTHY* [PRAISE]
Ps  78: 4 tell the next generation the **p** deeds
Php  4: 8 if anything is excellent or **p**—

### PRAISING [PRAISE]
1Ch 25: 3 harp in thanking and **p** the LORD.
2Ch  7: 6 David had made for **p** the LORD
Lk   2:13 with the angel, **p** God and saying,
   2:20 **p** God for all the things they had
   24:53 continually at the temple, **p** God.
Ac   2:47 **p** God and enjoying the favor of all
   3: 8 walking and jumping, and **p** God.
   10:46 speaking in tongues and **p** God.
1Co 14:16 when you are **p** God in the Spirit,

### PRAY [PRAYED, PRAYER, PRAYERS, PRAYING, PRAYS]
Ex   8: 9 setting the time for me to **p** for you
Nu  21: 7 **P** that the LORD will take
Dt   4: 7 our God is near us whenever we **p**
1Sa 12:23 the LORD by failing to **p** for you.
1Ki  8:30 when they **p** toward this place.
2Ch  6:32 they come and **p** toward this temple,
   6:38 **p** toward the land you gave their
   7:14 will humble themselves and **p**
Ezr  6:10 and **p** for the well-being of the king
Job 42: 8 My servant Job will **p** for you, and I
Ps   5: 2 King and my God, for to you I **p.**
   32: 6 Therefore let all the faithful **p**
   122: 6 **P** for the peace of Jerusalem:

| | | |
|---|---|---|
| Isa | 37: 4 | Therefore **p** for the remnant that still |
| | 45:20 | who **p** to gods that cannot save. |
| Jer | 7:16 | "So do not **p** for this people nor |
| | 29: 7 | **P** to the LORD for it, because if it |
| | 29:12 | call on me and come and **p** to me, |
| | 42: 3 | **P** that the LORD your God will |
| Da | 9:23 | As soon as you began to **p**, a word |
| Mt | 5:44 | and **p** for those who persecute you, |
| | 6: 5 | "And when you **p**, do not be like |
| | 6: 9 | "This, then, is how you should **p**: |
| | 14:23 | on a mountainside by himself to **p**. |
| | 19:13 | his hands on them and **p** for them. |
| | 26:36 | here while I go over there and **p**." |
| Lk | 5:33 | "John's disciples often fast and **p**, |
| | 6:28 | you, **p** for those who mistreat you. |
| | 11: 1 | teach us to **p**, just as John taught his |
| | 18: 1 | them that they should always **p** |
| | 18:10 | men went up to the temple to **p**, |
| | 22:40 | them, "**P** that you will not fall |
| Jn | 17:20 | I **p** also for those who will believe |
| Ro | 8:26 | do not know what we ought to **p** for, |
| 1Co | 11:13 | Is it proper for a woman to **p** to God |
| | 14:13 | in a tongue should **p** that they may |
| | 14:15 | I will also **p** with my understanding; |
| Eph | 1:18 | I **p** that the eyes of your heart may |
| | 3:16 | I **p** that out of his glorious riches he |
| | 6:18 | **p** in the Spirit on all occasions |
| 1Th | 5:17 | **p** continually, |
| 2Th | 1:11 | in mind, we constantly **p** for you, |
| 1Ti | 2: 8 | want the men everywhere to **p**, |
| | 5: 5 | day to **p** and to ask God for help. |
| Jas | 5:13 | Let them **p**. Is anyone happy? |
| | 5:16 | **p** for each other so that you may be |
| 1Pe | 4: 7 | of sober mind so that you may **p**. |
| 1Jn | 5:16 | saying that you should **p** about that. |

## PRAYED [PRAY]

| | | |
|---|---|---|
| Ge | 20:17 | Then Abraham **p** to God, and God |
| | 24:12 | Then he **p**, "LORD, God of my |
| | 25:21 | Isaac **p** to the LORD on behalf |
| Nu | 11: 2 | he **p** to the LORD and the fire died |
| | 21: 7 | So Moses **p** for the people. |
| Jdg | 16:28 | Then Samson **p** to the LORD, |
| 1Sa | 1:27 | I **p** for this child, and the LORD |
| 1Ki | 18:36 | Elijah stepped forward and **p**: |
| | 19: 4 | under it and **p** that he might die. |
| 2Ki | 6:17 | And Elisha **p**, "Open his eyes, |
| 2Ch | 30:18 | But Hezekiah **p** for them, saying, |
| Ne | 1: 4 | and **p** before the God of heaven. |
| | 4: 9 | But we **p** to our God and posted |
| Job | 42:10 | After Job had **p** for his friends, |
| Da | 6:10 | day he got down on his knees and **p**, |
| | 9: 4 | I **p** to the LORD my God |
| Jnh | 2: 1 | From inside the fish Jonah **p** |
| Mt | 26:39 | with his face to the ground and **p**, |
| Mk | 1:35 | off to a solitary place, where he **p**. |
| | 14:35 | and **p** that if possible the hour might |
| Lk | 5:16 | withdrew to lonely places and **p**. |
| | 18:11 | Pharisee stood by himself and **p**: |
| | 22:41 | beyond them, knelt down and **p**, |
| Jn | 17: 1 | he looked toward heaven and **p**: |
| Ac | 1:24 | After they **p**, the place where they |
| | 6: 6 | who **p** and laid their hands on them. |
| | 8:15 | they **p** for the new believers there |
| | 13: 3 | So after they had fasted and **p**, |
| Jas | 5:17 | He **p** earnestly that it would not |

## PRAYER [PRAY]

| | | |
|---|---|---|
| Ge | 25:21 | The LORD answered his **p**, and his |
| 2Sa | 21:14 | God answered **p** in behalf |
| | 24:25 | Then the LORD answered his **p** |
| 1Ki | 8:49 | place, hear their **p** and their plea, |
| 2Ch | 7:12 | "I have heard your **p** and have |
| | 30:27 | for their **p** reached heaven, his holy |
| | 33:19 | His **p** and how God was moved |
| Ezr | 8:23 | about this, and he answered our **p**. |
| Job | 42: 8 | I will accept his **p** and not deal |
| Ps | 4: 1 | have mercy on me and hear my **p**. |
| | 6: 9 | the LORD accepts my **p**. |
| | 17: 1 | Hear my **p**—it does not rise |
| | 55: 1 | Listen to my **p**, O God, do not |
| | 65: 2 | You who answer **p**, to you all |
| | 66:20 | God, who has not rejected my **p** |
| | 86: T | *A p of David.* |
| Pr | 15: 8 | but the **p** of the upright pleases him. |
| | 15:29 | but he hears the **p** of the righteous. |
| Isa | 56: 7 | my house will be called a house of **p** |
| Hab | 3: 1 | A **p** of Habakkuk the prophet. |
| Mt | 21:13 | house will be called a house of **p**,' |
| | 21:22 | receive whatever you ask for in **p**." |
| Mk | 9:29 | kind can come out only by **p**." |
| | 11:24 | whatever you ask for in **p**, |
| Jn | 17:15 | My **p** is not that you take them |
| Ac | 1:14 | all joined together constantly in **p**, |
| | 2:42 | to the breaking of bread and to **p**. |
| | 6: 4 | will give our attention to **p** |
| | 10:31 | God has heard your **p** |
| | 16:13 | we expected to find a place of **p**. |
| Ro | 10: 1 | and **p** to God for the Israelites is |
| | 12:12 | patient in affliction, faithful in **p**. |
| 1Co | 7: 5 | you may devote yourselves to **p**. |
| 2Co | 13: 9 | and our **p** is that you may be fully |
| Php | 1: 9 | And this is my **p**: that your love |
| | 4: 6 | in every situation, by **p** and petition, |
| Col | 4: 2 | Devote yourselves to **p**, |
| 1Ti | 4: 5 | by the word of God and **p**. |
| Jas | 5:15 | And the **p** offered in faith will make |
| | 5:16 | The **p** of a righteous person is |
| 1Pe | 3:12 | and his ears are attentive to their **p**, |

## PRAYERS [PRAY]

| | | |
|---|---|---|
| 1Ch | 5:20 | He answered their **p**, because they |
| Ps | 35:13 | When my **p** returned to me |
| Isa | 1:15 | even if you offer many **p**, I will not |
| Mk | 12:40 | and for a show make lengthy **p**. |
| 2Co | 1:11 | as you help us by your **p**. |
| Eph | 6:18 | on all occasions with all kinds of **p** |
| 1Ti | 2: 1 | that petitions, **p**, |
| Heb | 5: 7 | he offered up **p** and petitions |
| 1Pe | 3: 7 | so that nothing will hinder your **p**. |
| Rev | 5: 8 | which are the **p** of God's people. |
| | 8: 3 | with the **p** of all God's people, |

## PRAYING [PRAY]

| | | |
|---|---|---|
| Ge | 24:45 | "Before I finished **p** in my heart, |
| 1Sa | 1:13 | Hannah was **p** in her heart, and her |
| 2Ch | 7: 1 | When Solomon finished **p**, |
| Da | 6:11 | found Daniel **p** and asking God |
| Mk | 11:25 | And when you stand **p**, if you hold |
| Lk | 3:21 | And as he was **p**, heaven was |
| | 6:12 | pray, and spent the night **p** to God. |
| | 9:29 | As he was **p**, the appearance of his |
| Jn | 17: 9 | I am not **p** for the world, |

Ac   9:11  from Tarsus named Saul, for he is **p**.
     16:25  Silas were **p** and singing hymns
Ro  15:30  join me in my struggle by **p** to God
Eph  6:18  always keep on **p** for all the Lord's
Jude  1:20  holy faith and **p** in the Holy Spirit,

## PRAYS [PRAY]

Da   6: 7  that anyone who **p** to any god
1Co 11: 4  Every man who **p** or prophesies
    14:14  tongue, my spirit **p**, but my mind is

## PREACH [PREACHED, PREACHER, PREACHING]

Mt   4:17  From that time on Jesus began to **p**,
    23: 3  for they do not practice what they **p**.
Ac   9:20  At once he began to **p**
   16:10  God had called us to **p** the gospel
Ro   1:15  is why I am so eager to **p** the gospel
   10:15  how can anyone unless they are
   15:20  to **p** the gospel where Christ was not
1Co  1:17  me to baptize, but to **p** the gospel—
    1:23  but we **p** Christ crucified:
    9:14  that those who **p** the gospel should
    9:16  Woe to me if I do not **p** the gospel!
2Co  4: 5  For what we **p** is not ourselves,
   10:16  so that we can **p** the gospel
Gal   1: 8  heaven should **p** a gospel other than
Php  1:15  It is true that some **p** Christ
2Ti   4: 2  **P** the word; be prepared in season

## PREACHED [PREACH]

Jer  28:16  you have **p** rebellion against
Mk   6:12  out and **p** that people should repent.
   13:10  And the gospel must first be **p** to all
   14: 9  the gospel is **p** throughout
Lk  24:47  of sins will be **p** in his name to all
Ac   8: 4  who had been scattered **p** the word
   15:21  of Moses has been **p** in every city
1Co  9:27  slave so that after I have **p** to others,
   15: 1  remind you of the gospel I **p** to you,
   15:12  if it is **p** that Christ has been raised
2Co 11: 4  a Jesus other than the Jesus we **p**,
Gal   1: 8  a gospel other than the one we **p**
Eph  2:17  **p** peace to you who were far away
Php  1:18  false motives or true, Christ is **p**.
1Ti   3:16  by angels, was **p** among the nations,
1Pe   1:25  this is the word that was **p** to you.

## PREACHER* [PREACH]

1Co  9:18  not misuse my rights as a **p** of the
          gospel.
2Pe   2: 5  Noah, a **p** of righteousness,

## PREACHING [PREACH]

Ezr   6:14  prosper under the **p** of Haggai
Am   7:16  stop **p** against the house of Isaac.'
Mt  12:41  for they repented at the **p** of Jonah,
Ac  18: 5  devoted himself exclusively to **p**,
Ro  10:14  can they hear without someone **p**
1Co  2: 4  and my **p** were not with wise
    9:18  in **p** the gospel I may offer it free
Gal   1: 9  anybody is **p** to you a gospel other
1Ti   4:13  of Scripture, to **p** and to teaching.
    5:17  especially those whose work is **p**

## PRECEDE*

1Th  4:15  will certainly not **p** those who have

## PRECEPTS*

Dt  33:10  He teaches your **p** to Jacob and your
Ps   19: 8  The **p** of the LORD are right,
  103:18  and remember to obey his **p**.
  105:45  that they might keep his **p**
  111: 7  all his **p** are trustworthy.
  111:10  all who follow his **p** have good
  119: 4  You have laid down **p** that are to be
  119:15  I meditate on your **p** and consider
  119:27  me to understand the way of your **p**,
  119:40  How I long for your **p**!
  119:45  for I have sought out your **p**.
  119:56  has been my practice: I obey your **p**.
  119:63  fear you, to all who follow your **p**.
  119:69  lies, I keep your **p** with all my heart.
  119:78  but I will meditate on your **p**.
  119:87  but I have not forsaken your **p**.
  119:93  I will never forget your **p**,
  119:94  I have sought out your **p**.
  119:100  than the elders, for I obey your **p**.
  119:104  I gain understanding from your **p**;
  119:110  but I have not strayed from your **p**.
  119:128  because I consider all your **p** right,
  119:134  oppression, that I may obey your **p**.
  119:141  and despised, I do not forget your **p**.
  119:159  See how I love your **p**;
  119:168  I obey your **p** and your statutes,
  119:173  help me, for I have chosen your **p**.

## PRECIOUS

Ex  28:17  mount four rows of **p** stones on it.
1Sa 26:21  you considered my life **p** today,
2Ch  3: 6  adorned the temple with **p** stones.
Ps  19:10  They are more **p** than gold,
    35:17  ravages, my **p** life from these lions.
    72:14  for **p** is their blood in his sight.
  116:15  **P** in the sight of the LORD is
  119:72  your mouth is more **p** to me than
  139:17  How **p** to me are your thoughts,
Pr   3:15  She is more **p** than rubies;
    8:11  for wisdom is more **p** than rubies,
Isa  28:16  stone, a **p** cornerstone for a sure
Eze 28:13  every **p** stone adorned you:
1Pe  1:19  but with the **p** blood of Christ,
    2: 4  but chosen by God and **p** to him—
    2: 6  a chosen and **p** cornerstone,
2Pe  1: 1  have received a faith as **p** as ours:
    1: 4  us his very great and **p** promises,
Rev 21:11  was like that of a very **p** jewel,
   21:19  with every kind of **p** stone.

## PREDESTINED* [DESTINE]

Ro  8:29  **p** to be conformed to the image
   8:30  And those he **p**, he also called;
Eph  1: 5  he **p** us for adoption to sonship
   1:11  having been **p** according to the plan

## PREDICTED* [PREDICTION]

1Sa 28:17  has done what he **p** through me.
Ac  7:52  even killed those who **p** the coming
  11:28  through the Spirit **p** that a severe
  16:16  a spirit by which she **p** the future.

1Pe  1:11  pointing when he **p** the sufferings

## PREDICTING* [PREDICTION]
1Ki  22:13  without exception are **p** success
2Ch  18:12  without exception are **p** success

## PREDICTION* [PREDICTED, PREDICTING, PREDICTIONS]
Jer  28: 9  LORD only if his **p** comes true."

## PREDICTIONS* [PREDICTION]
Isa  44:26  and fulfills the **p** of his messengers,
     47:13  those stargazers who make **p** month

## PREGNANT
Ge   19:36  Lot's daughters became **p** by their
     21: 2  Sarah became **p** and bore a son
     25:21  and his wife Rebekah became **p**.
Ex   21:22  are fighting and a **p** woman is hit
Ps    7:14  Those who are **p** with evil conceive
Mt   24:19  it will be in those days for **p** women
1Th   5: 3  as labor pains on a **p** woman,
Rev  12: 2  She was **p** and cried out in pain as

## PREMATURELY* [MATURE]
Ex   21:22  gives birth **p** but there is no serious

## PREPARATION [PREPARE]
Mt   27:62  the one after **P** Day, the chief priests
Jn   19:14  It was the day of **P** of the Passover;

## PREPARATIONS [PREPARE]
1Ch  22: 5  David made extensive **p** before his
Mk   14:12  to go and make **p** for you to eat

## PREPARE [PREPARATION, PREPARATIONS, PREPARED]
Job  38: 3  **P** to defend yourself;
     40: 7  "**P** to defend yourself;
Ps   23: 5  You **p** a table before me
Isa  25: 6  the LORD Almighty will **p** a feast
     40: 3  "In the wilderness **p** the way
Am    4:12  to you, Israel, **p** to meet your God."
Mal   3: 1  who will **p** the way before me.
Mt    3: 3  wilderness, '**P** the way for the Lord,
     11:10  who will **p** your way before you.'
     26:12  body, she did it to **p** me for burial.
Jn   14: 2  that I am going there to **p** a place

## PREPARED [PREPARE]
Ex   23:20  to bring you to the place I have **p**.
1Ch  15: 1  he **p** a place for the ark of God
2Ch   1: 4  Jearim to the place he had **p** for it,
Pr   19:29  Penalties are **p** for mockers,
Mt   20:23  for whom they have been **p** by my
     25:34  the kingdom **p** for you since
Lk    1:17  to make ready a people **p**
Ro    9:23  whom he **p** in advance for glory—
1Co   2: 9  these things God has **p** for those
Eph   2:10  which God **p** in advance for us
2Ti   2:21  Master and **p** to do any good work.
      4: 2  be **p** in season and out of season;
Heb  10: 5  not desire, but a body you **p** for me;
     11:16  God, for he has **p** a city for them.

1Pe   3:15  Always be **p** to give an answer
Rev  12: 6  the wilderness to a place **p** for her
     21: 2  **p** as a bride beautifully dressed

## PRESBYTERY (KJV) See ELDERS

## PRESCRIBED
1Ch  24:19  to the regulations **p** for them
2Ch  29:25  and lyres in the way **p** by David
Ezr   3: 4  of burnt offerings **p** for each day.
      3:10  as **p** by David king of Israel.
      7:23  Whatever the God of heaven has **p**,
Ne   12:24  as **p** by David the man of God.
Heb   8: 4  already priests who offer the gifts **p**

## PRESENCE [PRESENT]
Ex   18:12  father-in-law in the **p** of God.
     25:30  Put the bread of the **P** on this table
     33:14  replied, "My **P** will go with you,
     34:34  he entered the LORD's **p** to speak
Lev   9:24  came out from the **p** of the LORD
     10: 2  came out from the **p** of the LORD
Nu    4: 7  "Over the table of the **P** they are
Dt    4:37  brought you out of Egypt by his **P**
1Sa   2:21  grew up in the **p** of the LORD.
      6:20  can stand in the **p** of the LORD,
     21: 6  of the **P** that had been removed
2Sa  22:13  of the brightness of his **p** bolts
2Ki  17:23  LORD removed them from his **p**,
     23:27  also from my **p** as I removed Israel,
     24:20  in the end he thrust them from his **p**.
Ezr   9:15  not one of us can stand in your **p**."
Job   1:12  went out from the **p** of the LORD.
      2: 7  went out from the **p** of the LORD
Ps    5: 5  The arrogant cannot stand in your **p**.
     16:11  you will fill me with joy in your **p**,
     21: 6  him glad with the joy of your **p**.
     23: 5  before me in the **p** of my enemies.
     31:20  the shelter of your **p** you hide them
     41:12  me and set me in your **p** forever.
     51:11  Do not cast me from your **p** or take
     52: 9  you in the **p** of your faithful people.
     89:15  who walk in the light of your **p**,
     90: 8  our secret sins in the light of your **p**.
    114: 7  at the **p** of the Lord, at the **p**
    139: 7  Where can I flee from your **p**?
Isa  26:17  pain, so were we in your **p**, LORD.
     63: 9  and the angel of his **p** saved them.
Jer   5:22  "Should you not tremble in my **p**?
Eze  38:20  of the earth will tremble at my **p**.
Da    7:13  of Days and was led into his **p**.
Hos   6: 2  restore us, that we may live in his **p**.
Na    1: 5  The earth trembles at his **p**,
Mal   3:16  his **p** concerning those who feared
Jn    8:38  what I have seen in the Father's **p**,
     17: 5  me in your **p** with the glory I had
Ac    2:28  you will fill me with joy in your **p**.'
1Th   2:19  will glory in the **p** of our Lord Jesus
      3:13  holy in the **p** of our God and Father
2Th   1: 9  shut out from the **p** of the Lord
Heb   9:24  now to appear for us in God's **p**.
1Jn   3:19  we set our hearts at rest in his **p**:
Jude  1:24  before his glorious **p** without fault
Rev  14:10  sulfur in the **p** of the holy angels
     20:11  and the heavens fled from his **p**,

## PRESENCE OF THE †LORD Ge 27:7; Ex
28:30; Lev 9:24; 10:2; Dt 12:7, 18; 14:23, 26;
15:20; 18:7; 19:17; 27:7; 29:10, 15; Jos 18:6, 8,
10; 19:51; 1Sa 2:21; 6:20; 11:15; 12:3; 26:20;
1Ki 19:11; 2Ki 23:3; 1Ch 29:22; 2Ch 34:31; Job
1:12; 2:7; Isa 2:10, 19, 21; Eze 44:3; 46:3

## †LORD'S PRESENCE Ge 4:16; Ex 29:11;
34:34; Nu 17:9; 20:9

## PRESENT [EVER-PRESENT,
PRESENCE, PRESENTED]
Lev 18:23   A woman must not **p** herself
Nu  16:17   and **p** it before the LORD.
    18:29   You must **p** as the LORD's portion
Ezr  6: 3   be rebuilt as a place to **p** sacrifices,
Job  1: 6   to **p** themselves before the LORD,
     2: 1   to **p** themselves before the LORD,
     2: 1   with them to **p** himself before him.
Ps  14: 5   for God is **p** in the company
Isa 41:21   "**P** your case," says the LORD.
Mk 10:30   times as much in this **p** age:
Lk   2:22   to Jerusalem to **p** him to the Lord
Ro   8:18   that our **p** sufferings are not worth
     8:38   demons, neither the **p** nor the future,
1Co  3:22   life or death or the **p** or the future—
     7:26   Because of the **p** crisis, I think
     7:31   world in its **p** form is passing away.
2Co 11: 2   that I might **p** you as a pure virgin
Gal  1: 4   sins to rescue us from the **p** evil age,
Eph  1:21   not only in the **p** age
     5:27   and to **p** her to himself as a radiant
Col  1:22   body through death to **p** you holy
1Ti  4: 8   holding promise for both the **p** life
2Ti  2:15   Do your best to **p** yourself to God as
Tit  2:12   upright and godly lives in this **p** age,
2Pe  3: 7   By the same word the **p** heavens
Jude 1:24   **p** you before his glorious presence

## PRESENTED [PRESENT]
Mt   2:11   and **p** him with gifts of gold,
Ac   1: 3   After his suffering, he **p** himself
     9:41   the widows, and **p** her to them alive.
Ro   3:25   God **p** Christ as a sacrifice

## PRESERVE [PRESERVES]
Ge 19:32   and **p** our family line through our
Ps  36: 6   LORD, **p** both people and animals.
   119:25   **p** my life according to your word.
Pr   3:21   **p** sound judgment and discretion;
     5: 2   and your lips may **p** knowledge.
    19:16   who obey instructions **p** their lives,
    22: 5   would **p** their life stay far from them.
Eze  7:13   not one of them will **p** their life.
Lk  17:33   whoever loses their life will **p** it.

## PRESERVES* [PRESERVE]
Ps  31:23   The LORD **p** those who are true
    41: 2   The LORD protects and **p** them—
   119:50   Your promise **p** my life.
Ecc  7:12   Wisdom **p** the life of its possessor.

## PRESS [PRESSED, PRESSURE]
Php  3:12   I **p** on to take hold
     3:14   I **p** on toward the goal to win

## PRESSED [PRESS]
Ps 118: 5   When hard **p**, I cried to the LORD;
Lk   6:38   A good measure, **p** down,
2Co  4: 8   We are hard **p** on every side, but not

## PRESSURE [PRESS]
2Co  1: 8   We were under great **p**, far beyond
    11:28   I face daily the **p** of my concern

## PRESUME* [PRESUMES,
PRESUMPTION,
PRESUMPTUOUSLY]
Jas  3: 1   of you should **p** to be teachers,

## PRESUMES* [PRESUME]
Dt  18:20   But a prophet who **p** to speak in my

## PRESUMPTION* [PRESUME]
Nu  14:44   in their **p** they went up toward
1Sa 25:28   "Please forgive your servant's **p**.

## PRESUMPTUOUSLY* [PRESUME]
Dt  18:22   That prophet has spoken **p**.

## PRETENDED [PRETENSION]
Ge  42: 7   but he **p** to be a stranger and spoke
1Sa 21:13   So he **p** to be insane in their

## PRETENSION* [PRETENDED]
2Co 10: 5   every **p** that sets itself up against

## PREVAIL [PREVAILS]
2Ch 14:11   not let mere mortals **p** against you."
Isa 54:17   weapon forged against you will **p**,
Ro   3: 4   you speak and **p** when you judge."

## PREVAILS* [PREVAIL]
1Sa  2: 9   "It is not by strength that one **p**;
Pr  19:21   it is the LORD's purpose that **p**.
Hab  1: 4   is paralyzed, and justice never **p**.

## PREY [PREYS]
Ge  15:11   Then birds of **p** came down
Na   2:13   I will leave you no **p** on the earth.
Hab  2: 7   Then you will become their **p**.

## PREYS* [PREY]
Pr   6:26   another man's wife **p** on your very

## PRICE [PRICELESS]
Ge  23: 9   for the full **p** as a burial site among
Lev 25:50   The **p** for their release is to be based
1Ch 21:22   Sell it to me at the full **p**."
Job 28:18   the **p** of wisdom is beyond rubies.
Zec 11:13   the handsome **p** at which they
Mt  27: 9   the **p** set on him by the people
Ac   5: 8   is this the **p** you and Ananias got
1Co  6:20   you were bought at a **p**.
     7:23   You were bought at a **p**;

## PRICELESS* [PRICE]
Ps  36: 7   How **p** is your unfailing love,

## PRIDE [PROUD]

| | | |
|---|---|---|
| Lev | 26:19 | I will break down your stubborn **p** |
| 2Ch | 26:16 | powerful, his **p** led to his downfall. |
| | 32:26 | repented of the **p** of his heart, as did |
| Ps | 47: 4 | inheritance for us, the **p** of Jacob, |
| Pr | 8:13 | I hate **p** and arrogance, |
| | 11: 2 | When **p** comes, then comes |
| | 13:10 | there is **p**, but wisdom is found |
| | 14: 3 | fool's mouth lashes out with **p**, |
| | 16:18 | **P** goes before destruction, a haughty |
| | 17: 6 | parents are the **p** of their children. |
| | 29:23 | **P** brings a person low, but the lowly |
| Ecc | 7: 8 | and patience is better than **p**. |
| Isa | 2:11 | humbled and human **p** brought low; |
| | 25:11 | will bring down their **p** despite |
| | 60:15 | I will make you the everlasting **p** |
| Eze | 28: 2 | " 'In the **p** of your heart you say, |
| Da | 4:37 | those who walk in **p** he is able |
| Am | 8: 7 | sworn by himself, the **P** of Jacob: |
| 2Co | 5:12 | you can answer those who take **p** |
| | 7: 4 | I take great **p** in you. |
| Gal | 6: 4 | Then you can take **p** in yourself, |
| Jas | 1: 9 | to take **p** in their high position. |

## PRIEST [PRIEST'S, PRIESTHOOD, PRIESTLY, PRIESTS]

| | | |
|---|---|---|
| Ge | 14:18 | He was **p** of God Most High, |
| Ex | 2:16 | Now a **p** of Midian had seven |
| | 18: 1 | the **p** of Midian and father-in-law |
| | 28: 3 | so he may serve me as **p**. |
| Lev | 4: 3 | " 'If the anointed **p** sins, |
| | 4:20 | this way the **p** will make atonement |
| | 5: 6 | the **p** shall make atonement for them |
| | 5:13 | of the offering will belong to the **p**, |
| Nu | 5:10 | they give to the **p** will belong to the **p**.' |
| Jdg | 17:10 | with me and be my father and **p**, |
| 1Sa | 2:11 | before the Lord under Eli the **p**. |
| | 2:35 | will raise up for myself a faithful **p**, |
| | 21: 6 | So the **p** gave him the consecrated |
| 2Ch | 13: 9 | seven rams may become a **p** of what |
| Ne | 8: 9 | Ezra the **p** and teacher of the Law, |
| Ps | 110: 4 | "You are a **p** forever, in the order |
| Jer | 23:11 | "Both prophet and **p** are godless; |
| Eze | 1: 3 | the Lord came to Ezekiel the **p**, |
| Zec | 6:13 | And he will be a **p** on his throne. |
| Mk | 14:63 | The high **p** tore his clothes. |
| Heb | 2:17 | faithful high **p** in service to God, |
| | 3: 1 | as our apostle and high **p**. |
| | 4:14 | a great high **p** who has ascended |
| | 4:15 | do not have a high **p** who is unable |
| | 5: 6 | "You are a **p** forever, in the order |
| | 6:20 | He has become a high **p** forever, |
| | 7: 3 | Son of God, he remains a **p** forever. |
| | 7:15 | another **p** like Melchizedek appears, |
| | 7:26 | Such a high **p** truly meets our need— |
| | 8: 1 | We do have such a high **p**, who sat |
| | 9:11 | Christ came as high **p** of the good |
| | 10:21 | we have a great **p** over the house |
| | 13:11 | The high **p** carries the blood |

## HIGH PRIEST See HIGH

## PRIEST'S [PRIEST]

| | | |
|---|---|---|
| Lev | 6:29 | Any male in a **p** family may eat it; |
| | 21: 9 | " 'If a **p** daughter defiles herself |
| | 22:10 | one outside a **p** family may eat |

## PRIESTHOOD [PRIEST]

| | | |
|---|---|---|
| Ex | 29: 9 | The **p** is theirs by a lasting |
| Nu | 16:10 | now you are trying to get the **p** too. |
| | 25:13 | will have a covenant of a lasting **p**, |
| Ezr | 2:62 | excluded from the **p** as unclean. |
| Heb | 7:24 | lives forever, he has a permanent **p**. |
| 1Pe | 2: 5 | into a spiritual house to be a holy **p**, |
| | 2: 9 | people, a royal **p**, a holy nation, |

## PRIESTLY [PRIEST]

| | | |
|---|---|---|
| Jos | 18: 7 | because the **p** service of the Lord |
| Ro | 15:16 | He gave me the **p** duty |

## PRIESTS [PRIEST]

| | | |
|---|---|---|
| Ex | 19: 6 | you will be for me a kingdom of **p** |
| | 28: 1 | Ithamar, so they may serve me as **p**. |
| | 40:15 | father, so they may serve me as **p**. |
| Lev | 21: 7 | because **p** are holy to their God. |
| Dt | 31: 9 | down this law and gave it to the **p**, |
| Jos | 3:15 | as soon as the **p** who carried the ark |
| | 6: 4 | Have seven **p** carry trumpets |
| 1Sa | 22:17 | "Turn and kill the **p** of the Lord, |
| 2Ch | 5: 7 | The **p** then brought the ark |
| | 31: 2 | Hezekiah assigned the **p** and Levites |
| | 34: 5 | the bones of the **p** on their altars, |
| Ezr | 6:20 | The **p** and Levites had purified |
| | 10: 5 | up and put the leading **p** and Levites |
| Ne | 3:28 | the Horse Gate, the **p** made repairs, |
| | 13:30 | So I purified the **p** and the Levites |
| Ps | 99: 6 | and Aaron were among his **p**, |
| Isa | 28: 7 | **P** and prophets stagger from beer |
| Jer | 5:31 | the **p** rule by their own authority, |
| Eze | 22:26 | Her **p** do violence to my law |
| | 44:28 | be the only inheritance the **p** have. |
| Hos | 4: 6 | I also reject you as my **p**; |
| Mic | 3:11 | for a bribe, her **p** teach for a price, |
| Mal | 2: 1 | "It is you **p** who show contempt |
| Mt | 20:18 | will be delivered over to the chief **p** |
| | 27: 3 | thirty pieces of silver to the chief **p** |
| Mk | 2:26 | which is lawful only for **p** to eat. |
| | 15: 3 | The chief **p** accused him of many |
| Ac | 6: 7 | large number of **p** became obedient |
| Heb | 7:27 | Unlike the other high **p**, he does not |
| Rev | 1: 6 | a kingdom and **p** to serve his God |
| | 5:10 | a kingdom and **p** to serve our God, |
| | 20: 6 | but they will be **p** of God |

## CHIEF PRIESTS See CHIEF

## PRIESTS AND LEVITES 1Ki 8:4; 1Ch 13:2;
15:14; 23:2; 24:6, 31; 28:13, 21; 2Ch 11:13;
23:4, 6; 24:5; 29:4; 30:15, 25, 27; 31:2, 4, 9;
34:30; 35:8; Ezr 1:5; 3:8, 12; 6:20; 7:13; 8:29,
30; 9:1; 10:5; Ne 8:13; 11:20; 12:1, 30, 44, 44;
13:30; Isa 66:21; Jn 1:19

## PRINCE [PRINCES, PRINCESS]

| | | |
|---|---|---|
| Ge | 49:26 | brow of the **p** among his brothers. |
| Dt | 33:16 | brow of the **p** among his brothers. |
| Isa | 9: 6 | God, Everlasting Father, **P** of Peace. |
| Eze | 34:24 | David will be **p** among them. |
| | 37:25 | my servant will be their **p** forever. |
| | 45:17 | the **p** to provide the burnt offerings, |
| | 46: 8 | When the **p** enters, he is to go |
| Da | 8:25 | and take his stand against the **P** |
| | 10:20 | to fight against the **p** of Persia, |

Da 10:21 them except Michael, your **p**.
   11:22 it and a **p** of the covenant will be
   12: 1 the great **p** who protects your
Lk 11:15 "By Beelzebul, the **p** of demons,
Jn 12:31 now the **p** of this world will be
   14:30 for the **p** of this world is coming.
   16:11 because the **p** of this world now
Ac 5:31 him to his own right hand as **P**

## PRINCES [PRINCE]
Jdg 5: 9 My heart is with Israel's **p**,
1Sa 2: 8 he seats them with **p** and has them
Job 34:19 who shows no partiality to **p**
Ps 113: 8 he seats them with **p**, with the **p**
   118: 9 in the LORD than to trust in **p**.
   146: 3 Do not put your trust in **p**, in human
   148:11 you **p** and all rulers on earth,
Pr 8:16 by me **p** govern, and nobles—
Isa 40:23 He brings **p** to naught and reduces
Eze 19: 1 a lament concerning the **p** of Israel
Da 8:25 his stand against the Prince of **p**.
   10:13 one of the chief **p**, came to help me,
Rev 6:15 of the earth, the **p**, the generals,

## PRINCESS* [PRINCE]
Ps 45:13 All glorious is the **p** within her

## PRISCILLA
Wife of Aquila; co-worker with Paul (Ac 18; Ro 16:3; 1Co 16:19; 2Ti 4:19); instructor of Apollos (Ac 18:24–28).

## PRISON [IMPRISON, IMPRISONED, IMPRISONMENT, IMPRISONMENTS, PRISONER, PRISONERS]
Ge 39:20 But while Joseph was there in the **p**,
Jdg 16:25 So they called Samson out of the **p**,
2Ki 25:29 Jehoiachin put aside his **p** clothes
Ps 66:11 You brought us into **p** and laid
   142: 7 Set me free from my **p**, that I may
Isa 42: 7 blind, to free captives from **p**
Mt 4:12 heard that John had been put in **p**,
   14:10 and had John beheaded in the **p**.
   25:36 me, I was in **p** and you came to visit
Lk 22:33 I am ready to go with you to **p**
Ac 8: 3 men and women and put them in **p**.
   12: 5 So Peter was kept in **p**,
   16:26 At once all the **p** doors flew open,
2Co 11:23 been in **p** more frequently,
Heb 13: 3 remember those in **p** as if you were
Rev 2:10 put some of you in **p** to test you,
   20: 7 Satan will be released from his **p**

## PRISONER [PRISON]
Jdg 15:10 have come to take Samson **p**,"
2Ki 24:12 of Babylon, he took Jehoiachin **p**.
2Ch 33:11 who took Manasseh **p**, put a hook
Mk 15: 6 to release a **p** whom the people
Ro 7:23 making me a **p** of the law of sin
Eph 3: 1 the **p** of Christ Jesus for the sake

## PRISONERS [PRISON]
Ps 68: 6 he leads out the **p** with singing;
   79:11 groans of the **p** come before you;
   107:10 darkness, **p** suffering in iron chains,

Ps 146: 7 The LORD sets **p** free,
Isa 51:14 The cowering **p** will soon be set
   61: 1 and release from darkness for the **p**,
Zec 9:12 to your fortress, you **p** of hope;
Lk 4:18 me to proclaim freedom for the **p**
Ac 9: 2 women, he might take them as **p**

## PRIVATE
Mt 17:19 the disciples came to Jesus in **p**
Lk 9:18 Once when Jesus was praying in **p**

## PRIVILEGE*
2Co 8: 4 us for the **p** of sharing in this service

## PRIZE*
1Co 9:24 runners run, but only one gets the **p**?
   9:24 Run in such a way as to get the **p**.
   9:27 will not be disqualified for the **p**.
Php 3:14 on toward the goal to win the **p**

## PROBE [PROBES]
Job 11: 7 Can you **p** the limits
Ps 17: 3 Though you **p** my heart, though you
Jer 20:12 the righteous and **p** the heart

## PROBES* [PROBE]
Ps 7: 9 righteous God who **p** minds and hearts.

## PROBLEMS*
Dt 1:12 But how can I bear your **p** and your
Da 5:12 explain riddles and solve difficult **p**.
   5:16 and to solve difficult **p**. If you can

## PROCEDURE* [PROCESSION]
Ecc 8: 5 will know the proper time and **p**.
   8: 6 proper time and **p** for every matter,

## PROCESSION [PROCEDURE]
1Sa 10:10 at Gibeah, a **p** of prophets met him;
Ne 12:36 the teacher of the Law led the **p**.
Ps 68:24 Your **p**, God, has come into view,
   118:27 join in the festal **p** up to the horns
Isa 60:11 their kings led in triumphal **p**.
1Co 4: 9 on display at the end of the **p**,
2Co 2:14 as captives in Christ's triumphal **p**

## PROCLAIM [PROCLAIMED, PROCLAIMING, PROCLAIMS, PROCLAMATION]
Ex 33:19 and I will **p** my name, the LORD,
Lev 25:10 **p** liberty throughout the land to all
Dt 30:12 it and **p** it to us so we may obey it?"
   32: 3 I will **p** the name of the LORD.
2Sa 1:20 **p** it not in the streets of Ashkelon,
1Ch 16:23 **p** his salvation day after day.
Ne 8:15 and that they should **p** this word
Ps 2: 7 I will **p** the LORD's decree:
   9:11 **p** among the nations what he has
   19: 1 the skies **p** the work of his hands.
   22:31 They will **p** his righteousness,
   30: 9 Will it **p** your faithfulness?
   40: 9 I **p** your saving acts in the great
   50: 6 the heavens **p** his righteousness,
   64: 9 they will **p** the works of God

Ps  68:34  **P** the power of God, whose majesty
    71:16  I will come and **p** your mighty acts,
    79:13  to generation we will **p** your praise.
    96: 2  **p** his salvation day after day.
    97: 6  The heavens **p** his righteousness,
   106: 2  Who can **p** the mighty acts
   118:17  will **p** what the LORD has done.
   145: 6  and I will **p** your great deeds.
Isa 12: 4  done, and **p** that his name is exalted.
    40: 2  **p** to her that her hard service has
    42:12  and **p** his praise in the islands.
    43:21  myself that they may **p** my praise.
    44: 8  Did I not **p** this and foretell it long
    52: 7  who bring good news, who **p** peace,
    61: 1  to **p** good news to the poor.
    61: 1  to **p** freedom for the captives
    66:19  They will **p** my glory among
Jer  7: 2  house and there **p** this message:
    50: 2  and **p** among the nations,
Hos  5: 9  tribes of Israel I **p** what is certain.
Jnh  3: 2  and **p** to it the message I give you."
Mic  3: 5  if you feed them, they **p** 'peace';
Zec  9:10  He will **p** peace to the nations.
Mt  10: 7  As you go, **p** this message:
    10:27  in your ear, **p** from the roofs.
    12:18  and he will **p** justice to the nations.
Lk   4:18  anointed me to **p** good news
     4:19  to **p** the year of the Lord's favor."
     9:60  you go and **p** the kingdom of God."
Ac  17:23  this is what I am going to **p** to you.
    20:27  I have not hesitated to **p** to you
Ro  10: 8  message concerning faith that we **p**:
    16:25  message I **p** about Jesus Christ,
1Co 11:26  cup, you **p** the Lord's death until he
Php  1:14  dare all the more to **p** the gospel
Col  1:28  We **p** him, admonishing and teaching
     4: 4  Pray that I may **p** it clearly, as I
1Jn  1: 1  this we **p** concerning the Word
Rev 14: 6  and he had the eternal gospel to **p**

## PROCLAIMED [PROCLAIM]

Ex   9:16  my name might be **p** in all the earth.
    34: 5  there with him and **p** his name,
Dt  10: 4  the Ten Commandments he had **p**
Ps  68:11  was the company of those who **p** it:
Isa 43: 9  this and **p** to us the former things?
    43:12  I have revealed and saved and **p**—
Lk   7:22  good news is **p** to the poor.
    16:16  and the Prophets were **p** until John.
Ac  28:31  He **p** the kingdom of God and taught
Ro   9:17  that my name might be **p** in all
    15:19  I have fully **p** the gospel of Christ.
Col  1:23  has been **p** to every creature under
2Ti  4:17  me the message might be fully **p**

## PROCLAIMING [PROCLAIM]

Ex  34: 6  And he passed in front of Moses, **p**,
Ps  26: 7  **p** aloud your praise and telling of all
    92: 2  **p** your love in the morning and your
    92:15  **p**, "The LORD is upright;
Mk   1:14  Galilee, **p** the good news of God.
Lk   9: 6  **p** the good news and healing people
Ac   4: 2  **p** in Jesus the resurrection
     5:42  **p** the good news that Jesus is
    17: 3  "This Jesus I am **p** to you is
2Th  2: 4  God's temple, **p** himself to be God.

## PROCLAIMS* [PROCLAIM]

Dt  18:22  If what a prophet **p** in the name
Ps   6: 5  Among the dead no one **p** your name.
Na   1:15  brings good news, who **p** peace!

## PROCLAMATION [PROCLAIM]

Ezr  1: 1  to make a **p** throughout his realm
Isa 62:11  The LORD has made **p** to the ends
1Pe  3:19  made **p** to the imprisoned spirits—

## PROCONSUL

Ac  13:12  the **p** saw what had happened,

## PRODUCE [PRODUCED, PRODUCES]

Ge   1:11  said, "Let the land **p** vegetation:
     1:24  "Let the land **p** living creatures
     3:18  It will **p** thorns and thistles for you,
Dt  14:22  of all that your fields **p** each year.
Jos  5:11  they ate some of the **p** of the land:
Eze 36: 8  will **p** branches and fruit for my
Mt   3: 8  **P** fruit in keeping with repentance.
    13:23  They **p** a crop, yielding a hundred,
Lk   3: 9  that does not **p** good fruit will be cut
Jas  3:12  can a salt spring **p** fresh water.

## PRODUCED [PRODUCE]

Nu  17: 8  budded, blossomed and **p** almonds.
Mk   4: 8  It came up, grew and **p** a crop,

## PRODUCES [PRODUCE]

Pr  30:33  blood, so stirring up anger **p** strife."
Jn  12:24  But if it dies, it **p** many seeds.
Ro   5: 3  know that suffering **p** perseverance;
2Co  1: 6  which **p** in you patient endurance
Heb  6: 8  But land that **p** thorns and thistles is
    12:11  it **p** a harvest of righteousness

## PROFANE [PROFANED]

Lev 18:21  for you must not **p** the name of your
    19:12  and so **p** the name of your God.
    22:32  Do not **p** my holy name, for I must
Eze 20:39  and no longer **p** my holy name
Zep  3: 4  Her priests **p** the sanctuary and do
Mal  2:10  Why do we **p** the covenant of our

## PROFANED [PROFANE]

Jer 34:16  have turned around and **p** my name;
Eze 20: 9  my name from being **p** in the eyes
    36:20  the nations they **p** my holy name,
    39: 7  no longer let my holy name be **p**,

## PROFESS* [PROFESSED]

Ro  10:10  with your mouth that you **p** your faith
1Ti  2:10  for women who **p** to worship God.
Heb  4:14  let us hold firmly to the faith we **p**.
    10:23  hold unswervingly to the hope we **p**,
    13:15  lips that openly **p** his name.

## PROFESSED* [PROFESS]

1Ti  6:21  which some have **p** and in so doing

## PROFIT [PROFITABLE]

Lev 25:37  at interest or sell them food at a **p**.

| | | |
|---|---|---|
| Pr | 14:23 | All hard work brings a **p**, but mere |
| | 21: 5 | lead to **p** as surely as haste leads |
| Isa | 44:10 | casts an idol, which can **p** nothing? |
| Eze | 18: 8 | at interest or take a **p** from them. |
| 2Co | 2:17 | not peddle the word of God for **p**. |

## PROFITABLE* [PROFIT]

| | | |
|---|---|---|
| Pr | 3:14 | for she is more **p** than silver |
| | 31:18 | She sees that her trading is **p**, |
| Tit | 3: 8 | are excellent and **p** for everyone. |

## PROFOUND*

| | | |
|---|---|---|
| Job | 9: 4 | His wisdom is **p**, his power is vast. |
| Ps | 92: 5 | LORD, how **p** your thoughts! |
| Ecc | 7:24 | exists is far off and most **p**— |
| Ac | 24: 3 | acknowledge this with **p** gratitude. |
| Eph | 5:32 | This is a **p** mystery—but I am |

## PROGRESS*

| | | |
|---|---|---|
| Ezr | 5: 8 | and is making rapid **p** under their |
| Jn | 13: 2 | The evening meal was in **p**, |
| Php | 1:25 | continue with all of you for your **p** |
| 1Ti | 4:15 | so that everyone may see your **p**. |

## PROLONG*

| | | |
|---|---|---|
| Dt | 5:33 | **p** your days in the land that you will |
| Ps | 85: 5 | Will you **p** your anger through all |
| Pr | 3: 2 | for they will **p** your life many years |
| Isa | 53:10 | will see his offspring and **p** his days, |
| La | 4:22 | he will not **p** your exile. |

## PROMINENT

| | | |
|---|---|---|
| Est | 9: 4 | Mordecai was **p** in the palace; |
| Da | 8: 5 | with a **p** horn between its eyes came |
| Mk | 15:43 | a **p** member of the Council, |
| Lk | 14: 1 | to eat in the house of a **p** Pharisee, |
| Ac | 17: 4 | Greeks and not a few **p** women. |
| | 17:12 | a number of **p** Greek women |

## PROMISCUITY [PROMISCUOUS]

| | | |
|---|---|---|
| Eze | 16:25 | increasing **p** to anyone who passed |
| | 23:29 | Your lewdness and **p** |

## PROMISCUOUS* [PROMISCUITY]

| | | |
|---|---|---|
| Dt | 22:21 | in Israel by being **p** while still in her |
| Eze | 23:19 | more **p** as she recalled the days |
| Hos | 1: 2 | marry a **p** woman and have children |

## PROMISE [PROMISED, PROMISES]

| | | |
|---|---|---|
| Nu | 23:19 | Does he **p** and not fulfill? |
| | 30: 6 | after her lips utter a rash **p** |
| Jos | 9:21 | So the leaders' **p** to them was kept. |
| | 23:14 | Every **p** has been fulfilled; |
| 2Sa | 7:25 | keep forever the **p** you have made |
| 1Ki | 6:12 | will fulfill through you the **p** I gave |
| | 8:20 | LORD has kept the **p** he made: |
| | 8:24 | You have kept your **p** to your |
| Ne | 5:13 | anyone who does not keep this **p**. |
| | 9: 8 | have kept your **p** because you are |
| Ps | 77: 8 | Has his **p** failed for all time? |
| | 105:42 | he remembered his holy **p** given |
| | 106:24 | they did not believe his **p**. |
| | 119:41 | your salvation, according to your **p**; |
| | 119:50 | Your **p** preserves my life. |
| | 119:58 | gracious to me according to your **p**. |

| | | |
|---|---|---|
| Ps | 119:162 | in your **p** like one who finds great |
| Pr | 11: 7 | the **p** of their power comes to nothing. |
| Ac | 2:39 | The **p** is for you and your children |
| | 26: 7 | This is the **p** our twelve tribes are |
| Ro | 4:13 | his offspring received the **p** that he |
| | 4:20 | through unbelief regarding the **p** |
| | 9: 8 | of the **p** who are regarded as |
| Gal | 3:14 | faith we might receive the **p** |
| Eph | 2:12 | foreigners to the covenants of the **p**, |
| | 6: 2 | is the first commandment with a **p**— |
| 1Ti | 4: 8 | holding **p** for both the present life |
| 2Ti | 1: 1 | in keeping with the **p** of life that is |
| Heb | 4: 1 | since the **p** of entering his rest still |
| | 6:13 | When God made his **p** to Abraham, |
| | 11:11 | him faithful who had made the **p**. |
| 2Pe | 2:19 | They **p** them freedom, while they |
| | 3: 9 | Lord is not slow in keeping his **p**, |
| | 3:13 | with his **p** we are looking forward |

## PROMISED [PROMISE]

| | | |
|---|---|---|
| Ge | 18:19 | for Abraham what he has **p** him." |
| | 21: 1 | did for Sarah what he had **p**. |
| | 24: 7 | who spoke to me and **p** me on oath, |
| | 28:15 | I have done what I have **p** you." |
| Ex | 3:17 | I have **p** to bring you up out of your |
| | 32:13 | descendants all this land I **p** them, |
| Nu | 10:29 | for the LORD has **p** good things |
| | 14:23 | of them will ever see the land I **p** |
| Dt | 15: 6 | your God will bless you as he has **p**, |
| | 26:18 | his treasured possession as he **p**, |
| | 34: 4 | him, "This is the land I **p** on oath |
| Jos | 23: 5 | as the LORD your God **p** you. |
| 2Sa | 7:28 | and you have **p** these good things |
| 1Ki | 8:15 | his own hand has fulfilled what he **p** |
| | 9: 5 | as I **p** David your father when I |
| 2Ch | 6:15 | with your mouth you have **p** |
| Ps | 119:57 | I have **p** to obey your words. |
| Isa | 55: 3 | you, my faithful love **p** to David. |
| Mk | 6:23 | And he **p** her with an oath, |
| Lk | 24:49 | to send you what my Father has **p**; |
| Ac | 1: 4 | but wait for the gift my Father **p**, |
| | 2:33 | from the Father the **p** Holy Spirit |
| | 13:23 | to Israel the Savior Jesus, as he **p**. |
| | 13:32 | What God **p** our ancestors |
| Ro | 4:21 | God had power to do what he had **p**. |
| 2Co | 11: 2 | I **p** you to one husband, to Christ, |
| Eph | 1:13 | in him with a seal, the **p** Holy Spirit, |
| Tit | 1: 2 | lie, **p** before the beginning of time, |
| Heb | 6:15 | Abraham received what was **p**. |
| | 10:23 | we profess, for he who **p** is faithful. |
| | 10:36 | you will receive what he has **p**. |
| | 11:13 | They did not receive the things **p**; |
| Jas | 1:12 | God has **p** to those who love him. |
| | 2: 5 | the kingdom he **p** those who love |
| 2Pe | 3: 4 | say, "Where is this 'coming' he **p**? |
| 1Jn | 2:25 | And this is what he **p** us— |

## PROMISES [PROMISE]

| | | |
|---|---|---|
| Jos | 21:45 | of all the LORD's good **p** |
| | 23:14 | all the good **p** the LORD your God |
| 1Ki | 8:56 | all the good **p** he gave through his |
| 1Ch | 17:19 | and made known all these great **p**. |
| Ps | 85: 8 | he **p** peace to his people, his faithful |
| | 106:12 | they believed his **p** and sang his |
| | 119:140 | Your **p** have been thoroughly tested, |
| | 119:148 | that I may meditate on your **p**. |

Ps 145:13 LORD is trustworthy in all he **p**
Ro    9: 4 law, the temple worship and the **p**.
2Co 1:20 matter how many **p** God has made,
      7: 1 since we have these **p**, dear friends,
Gal  3:21 therefore, opposed to the **p** of God?
Heb  8: 6 covenant is established on better **p**.
2Pe  1: 4 us his very great and precious **p**,

## PROMOTE [PROMOTES]
Pr  12:20 but those who **p** peace have joy.
    16:21 and gracious words **p** instruction.
1Ti   1: 4 Such things **p** controversial

## PROMOTES* [PROMOTE]
Gal  2:17 doesn't that mean that Christ **p** sin?

## PROMPTED*
Mt   14: 8 **P** by her mother, she said,
Jn   13: 2 and the devil had already **p** Judas, .
1Th   1: 3 by faith, your labor **p** by love,
2Th   1:11 and your every deed **p** by faith.

## PRONE*
Ex  32:22 "You know how **p** these people are

## PRONOUNCE [PRONOUNCED]
Ge  48:20 name will Israel **p** this blessing:
Dt   10: 8 and to **p** blessings in his name,
Jdg  12: 6 he could not **p** the word correctly,
1Ch 23:13 to **p** blessings in his name forever.
Ps  109:17 He loved to **p** a curse—may it come
Jer    1:16 I will **p** my judgments on my people

## PRONOUNCED [PRONOUNCE]
1Ch 16:12 miracles, and the judgments he **p**,
Ps   76: 8 From heaven you **p** judgment,
Da    7:22 and **p** judgment in favor of the holy

## PROOF [PROVE]
Dt  22:14 I did not find **p** of her virginity,"
Ac  17:31 He has given **p** of this to everyone
2Co  8:24 Therefore show these men the **p**

## PROOFS* [PROVE]
Ac    1: 3 gave many convincing **p** that he was

## PROPER [PROPERLY]
Ps  104:27 give them their food at the **p** time.
    145:15 give them their food at the **p** time.
Ecc   8: 5 the wise heart will know the **p** time
Mt    3:15 it is **p** for us to do this to fulfill all
    24:45 give them their food at the **p** time?
1Co 11:13 Is it **p** for a woman to pray to God
2Co 10:13 will not boast beyond **p** limits,
Gal   6: 9 at the **p** time we will reap a harvest
2Th   2: 6 he may be revealed at the **p** time.
1Ti   2: 6 now been witnessed to at the **p** time.
      5: 3 Give **p** recognition to those widows
1Pe   2:17 Show **p** respect to everyone,

## PROPERLY* [PROPER]
1Ti   1: 8 that the law is good if one uses it **p**.

## PROPERTY
Ge  23: 4 Sell me some **p** for a burial site here
Lev 25:10 of you is to return to your family **p**
Ru    4: 5 the name of the dead with his **p**."
Lk  15:12 So he divided his **p** between them.
Ac    5: 1 Sapphira, also sold a piece of **p**.
Heb 10:34 accepted the confiscation of your **p**,

## PROPHECIES [PROPHESY]
La    2:14 **p** they gave you were false
1Co 13: 8 But where there are **p**, they will
1Th   5:20 Do not treat **p** with contempt

## PROPHECY [PROPHESY]
2Ki   9:25 LORD spoke this **p** against him:
Eze 14: 9 if the prophet is enticed to utter a **p**,
Da    9:24 to seal up vision and **p** and to anoint
1Co 12:10 powers, to another **p**, to another
    13: 2 If I have the gift of **p** and can
    14: 1 gifts, especially the gift of **p**.
    14: 6 or knowledge or **p** or word
    14:22 **p**, however, is not for unbelievers
2Th   2: 2 whether by a **p** or by word of mouth
2Pe   1:20 that no **p** of Scripture came
Rev   1: 3 who reads aloud the words of this **p**,
    19:10 of Jesus is the Spirit of **p**."
    22: 7 the words of the **p** in this scroll."
    22:18 the words of the **p** of this scroll:

## PROPHESIED [PROPHESY]
Nu  11:25 the Spirit rested on them, they **p**—
1Sa 19:24 and he too **p** in Samuel's presence.
Jer    2: 8 The prophets **p** by Baal,
    26:11 because he has **p** against this city.
Mt  11:13 Prophets and the Law **p** until John.
Mk    7: 6 when he **p** about you hypocrites;
Jn  11:51 that year he **p** that Jesus would die
Ac  19: 6 and they spoke in tongues and **p**.
    21: 9 four unmarried daughters who **p**.
Jude 1:14 seventh from Adam, **p** about them:

## PROPHESIES [PROPHESY]
2Ch 18: 7 because he never **p** anything good
Jer  28: 9 But the prophet who **p** peace will be
Eze 12:27 and he **p** about the distant future.'
1Co 11: 4 **p** with his head covered dishonors

## PROPHESY [PROPHECIES,
    PROPHECY, PROPHESIED,
    PROPHESIES, PROPHESYING,
    PROPHET, PROPHET'S,
    PROPHETESS, PROPHETIC,
    PROPHETS]
1Sa 10: 6 in power, and you will **p** with them;
Isa 30:10 Tell us pleasant things, **p** illusions.
Jer   5:31 The prophets **p** lies, the priests rule
Eze 13: 2 **p** against the prophets of Israel who
    13:17 **P** against them
    34: 2 **p** against the shepherds of Israel;
    37: 4 "**P** to these bones and say to them,
Joel  2:28 Your sons and daughters will **p**,
Am   2:12 commanded the prophets not to **p**.
      7:16 say, " 'Do not **p** against Israel,
Mic   2: 6 "Do not **p**," their prophets say.

Mt    7:22  did we not **p** in your name
Lk   22:64  blindfolded him and demanded, "**P**!
Ac    2:17  Your sons and daughters will **p**,
Ro   12: 6  **p** in accordance with your faith;
1Co  13: 9  we know in part and we **p** in part,
     14: 3  But those who **p** speak to people
     14: 5  but I would rather have you **p**.
     14:39  be eager to **p**, and do not forbid
Rev  11: 3  and they will **p** for 1,260 days,

## PROPHESYING [PROPHESY]

1Sa  10:13  After Saul stopped **p**, he went
     19:20  they saw a group of prophets **p**,
1Ki  18:29  continued their frantic **p** until
1Ch  25: 1  and Jeduthun for the ministry of **p**,
Jer  14:14  me, "The prophets are **p** lies in my
Ro   12: 6  If your gift is **p**, then prophesy
1Co  14:24  comes in while everyone is **p**,
Rev  11: 6  not rain during the time they are **p**;

## PROPHET [PROPHESY]

Ex    7: 1  your brother Aaron will be your **p**.
     15:20  Then Miriam the **p**, Aaron's sister,
Dt   13: 1  If a **p**, or one who foretells
     18:18  for them a **p** like you from among
     18:22  That **p** has spoken presumptuously.
     34:10  no **p** has risen in Israel like Moses,
Jdg   4: 4  Deborah, a **p**, the wife of Lappidoth,
1Sa   3:20  Samuel was attested as a **p**
      9: 9  because the **p** of today used to be
1Ki   1: 8  Nathan the **p**, Shimei and Rei
     18:36  the **p** Elijah stepped forward
     22: 7  asked, "Is there no longer a **p**
2Ki   5: 8  know that there is a **p** in Israel."
      6:12  "but Elisha, the **p** who is in Israel,
     20: 1  The **p** Isaiah son of Amoz went
     22:14  Asaiah went to speak to the **p** Huldah,
2Ch  35:18  since the days of the **p** Samuel;
     36:12  himself before Jeremiah the **p**,
Ezr   5: 1  Haggai the **p** and Zechariah the **p**,
      6:14  under the preaching of Haggai the **p**
Ne    6:14  remember also the **p** Noadiah
Ps   51: T  *When the **p** Nathan came to him*
Jer   1: 5  I appointed you as a **p**
     23:11  "Both **p** and priest are godless;
     28: 1  Judah, the **p** Hananiah son of Azzur,
Eze   2: 5  know that a **p** has been among them.
     33:33  that a **p** has been among them."
Da    9: 2  the LORD given to Jeremiah the **p**,
Hos   9: 7  so great, the **p** is considered a fool,
Am    7:14  neither a **p** nor the disciple of a **p**,
Hab   1: 1  that Habakkuk the **p** received.
Hag   1: 1  LORD came through the **p** Haggai
Zec   1: 1  came to the **p** Zechariah son
Mal   4: 5  "See, I will send the **p** Elijah to you
Mt   10:41  to be a **p** will receive a prophet's
     11: 9  Yes, I tell you, and more than a **p**.
     12:39  it except the sign of the **p** Jonah.
Lk    1:76  will be called a **p** of the Most High;
      2:36  There was also a **p**, Anna,
      7:16  "A great **p** has appeared among
     20: 6  are persuaded that John was a **p**."
     24:19  "He was a **p**, powerful in word
Jn    1:21  "Are you the **P**?"
      7:40  said, "Surely this man is the **P**."
Ac    7:37  'God will send you a **p** like me

Ac   13: 6  and false **p** named Bar-Jesus,
     21:10  a **p** named Agabus came down
Rev   2:20  woman Jezebel, who calls herself a **p**.
     16:13  and out of the mouth of the false **p**.
     19:20  him the false **p** who had performed
     20:10  and the false **p** had been thrown.

## PROPHET'S [PROPHESY]

2Pe   1:20  about by the **p** own interpretation

## PROPHETESS* [PROPHESY]

Isa   8: 3  Then I made love to the **p**, and she

## PROPHETIC [PROPHESY]

2Pe   1:19  **p** message as something completely

## PROPHETS [PROPHESY]

Nu   11:29  that all the LORD's people were **p**
     12: 6  there are **p** of the LORD among
1Sa  10:11  Is Saul also among the **p**?"
     19:24  say, "Is Saul also among the **p**?"
     28: 6  answer him by dreams or Urim or **p**.
1Ki  18: 4  was killing off the LORD's **p**,
     18:40  them, "Seize the **p** of Baal.
     19:10  put your **p** to death with the sword.
2Ki  17:23  through all his servants the **p**.
1Ch  16:22  do my **p** no harm."
2Ch  18:22  in the mouths of these **p** of yours.
Ne    9:30  you warned them through your **p**.
Ps  105:15  do my **p** no harm."
Isa  44:25  who foils the signs of false **p**
Jer   5:13  The **p** are but wind and the word is
     14:14  "The **p** are prophesying lies in my
     23: 9  Concerning the **p**: My heart is
     23:30  "I am against the **p** who steal
La    2: 9  her **p** no longer find visions
Eze  13: 2  prophesy against the **p** of Israel who
Hos   6: 5  I cut you in pieces with my **p**,
Mic   3: 6  The sun will set for the **p**,
Zep   3: 4  Her **p** are unprincipled;
Zec   1: 5  And the **p**, do they live forever?
     13: 4  that day the **p** will all be ashamed
Mt    5:17  come to abolish the Law or the **P**;
      7:12  for this sums up the Law and the **P**.
      7:15  "Watch out for false **p**.
     22:40  Law and the **P** hang on these two
     24:24  messiahs and false **p** will appear
Mk    6: 4  own homes are **p** without honor."
Lk    4:24  "**p** are not accepted in their
      6:23  is how their ancestors treated the **p**.
     10:24  For I tell you that many **p** and kings
     11:49  'I will send them **p** and apostles,
     16:29  'They have Moses and the **P**;
     24:25  believe all that the **p** have spoken!
     24:44  of Moses, the **P** and the Psalms."
Ac    3:24  all the **p** who have spoken have
     10:43  All the **p** testify about him
     13: 1  the church at Antioch there were **p**
     26:22  saying nothing beyond what the **p**
     28:23  and from the **P** he tried to persuade
Ro    1: 2  promised beforehand through his **p**
      3:21  to which the Law and the **P** testify.
     11: 3  they have killed your **p** and torn
1Co  12:28  apostles, second **p**, third teachers,
     12:29  Are all **p**? Are all teachers?

1Co 14:32 The spirits of **p** are subject to the control of **p**.
14:37 If any think they are **p** or otherwise
Eph 2:20 the foundation of the apostles and **p**,
3: 5 Spirit to God's holy apostles and **p**.
4:11 the apostles, the **p**, the evangelists,
1Th 2:15 killed the Lord Jesus and the **p**
Heb 1: 1 our ancestors through the **p** at many
1Pe 1:10 the **p**, who spoke of the grace
2Pe 2: 1 were also false **p** among the people,
3: 2 spoken in the past by the holy **p**
1Jn 4: 1 because many false **p** have gone
Rev 11:10 because these two **p** had tormented
16: 6 the blood of your people and your **p**,
18:20 Rejoice, apostles and **p**!
22: 6 the God who inspires the **p**, sent his

## FALSE PROPHET(S) See FALSE

## PROPORTION
Dt 16:10 giving a freewill offering in **p**
16:17 you must bring a gift in **p** to the way

## PROPOSE* [PROPOSED]
Dt 1:14 me, "What you **p** to do is good."
Isa 8:10 **p** your plan, but it will not stand,

## PROPOSED [PROPOSE]
Ezr 10:16 So the exiles did as was **p**.
Ac 1:23 So they **p** the names of two men:

## PROPRIETY*
1Ti 2: 9 with decency and **p**,
2:15 in faith, love and holiness with **p**.

## PROSELYTE (KJV) See CONVERT

## PROSPECT*
Pr 10:28 The **p** of the righteous is joy,

## PROSPER [PROSPERED, PROSPERITY, PROSPEROUS, PROSPERS]
Ge 32: 9 relatives, and I will make you **p**,'
Dt 5:33 you, so that you may live and **p**
28:63 pleased the LORD to make you **p**
29: 9 you may **p** in everything you do.
1Ki 2: 3 this so that you may **p** in all you do
Ezr 6:14 **p** under the preaching of Haggai
Ps 51:18 May it please you to **p** Zion,
Pr 11:10 When the righteous **p**, the city
11:25 A generous person will **p**;
16:20 who give heed to instruction **p**,
17:20 whose heart is corrupt does not **p**;
19: 8 cherish understanding will soon **p**.
28:13 who conceal their sins do not **p**,
28:25 who trust in the LORD will **p**.
Isa 53:10 of the LORD will **p** in his hand.
Jer 12: 1 Why does the way of the wicked **p**?
29:11 "plans to **p** you and not to harm

## PROSPERED* [PROSPER]
Ge 39: 2 was with Joseph so that he **p**, and he
1Ch 29:23 He **p** and all Israel obeyed him.
2Ch 14: 7 on every side." So they built and **p**.

2Ch 31:21 And so he **p**.
Da 6:28 So Daniel **p** during the reign
8:12 It **p** in everything it did, and truth
Hos 10: 1 as his land **p**, he adorned his sacred

## PROSPERITY [PROSPER]
Dt 28:11 LORD will grant you abundant **p**—
30:15 I set before you today life and **p**,
Job 21:16 their **p** is not in their own hands,
36:11 will spend the rest of their days in **p**
Ps 25:13 They will spend their days in **p**,
73: 3 when I saw the **p** of the wicked.
122: 9 LORD our God, I will seek your **p**.
128: 2 blessings and **p** will be yours.
Pr 3: 2 years and bring you peace and **p**.
8:18 and honor, enduring wealth and **p**.
21:21 and love finds life, **p** and honor.
Ecc 6: 6 twice over but fails to enjoy his **p**.
Isa 45: 7 I bring **p** and create disaster;
La 3:17 I have forgotten what **p** is.

## PROSPEROUS [PROSPER]
Dt 30: 9 your God will make you most **p**
30: 9 delight in you and make you **p**,
Jos 1: 8 Then you will be **p** and successful.
Ps 10: 5 Their ways are always **p**;

## PROSPERS [PROSPER]
Ps 1: 3 whatever they do **p**.

## PROSTITUTE [PROSTITUTED, PROSTITUTES, PROSTITUTION]
Ge 34:31 he have treated our sister like a **p**?"
38:15 he thought she was a **p**, for she had
Ex 34:15 for when they **p** themselves to their
Lev 19:29 your daughter by making her a **p**,
20: 6 and spiritists to **p** themselves
Nu 15:39 not **p** yourselves by chasing
Dt 23:17 or woman is to become a shrine **p**.
Jos 2: 1 the house of a **p** named Rahab
6:25 But Joshua spared Rahab the **p**,
Pr 6:26 For a **p** can be had for a loaf
7:10 him, dressed like a **p** and with crafty
Isa 1:21 the faithful city has become a **p**!
Jer 3: 3 Yet you have the brazen look of a **p**;
Eze 16:15 and used your fame to become a **p**.
23: 7 She gave herself as a **p** to all
Hos 3: 3 you must not be a **p** or be intimate
Na 3: 4 the wanton lust of a **p**,
1Co 6:15 of Christ and unite them with a **p**?
6:16 who unites himself with a **p** is one
Heb 11:31 By faith the **p** Rahab, because she
Jas 2:25 Rahab the **p** considered righteous
Rev 17: 1 you the punishment of the great **p**,
19: 2 the great **p** who corrupted the earth

## PROSTITUTED [PROSTITUTE]
Jdg 2:17 but **p** themselves to other gods
Ps 106:39 by their deeds they **p** themselves.

## PROSTITUTES [PROSTITUTE]
1Ki 3:16 Now two **p** came to the king
14:24 There were even male shrine **p**
15:12 He expelled the male shrine **p**
Pr 29: 3 of **p** squanders his wealth.

Isa  57: 3  you offspring of adulterers and **p**!
Joel  3: 3  my people and traded boys for **p**;
Mic  1: 7  her gifts from the wages of **p**,
Mt 21:31  the **p** are entering the kingdom
Lk 15:30  your property with **p** comes home,
1Co  6: 9  adulterers nor male **p** nor practicing
Rev 17: 5  THE MOTHER OF **P** AND OF THE

## PROSTITUTION [PROSTITUTE]

Lev 19:29  the land will turn to **p** and be filled
Jer  3: 2  have defiled the land with your **p**
Eze 16:16  places, where you carried on your **p**.
       23: 3  engaging in **p** from their youth.
Hos  4:10  they will engage in **p** but not
       4:12  A spirit of **p** leads them astray;
Na  3: 4  who enslaved nations by her **p**

## PROSTRATE [PROSTRATING]

Dt  9:18  again I fell **p** before the LORD
1Ki 18:39  saw this, they fell **p** and cried,
Da  2:46  King Nebuchadnezzar fell **p** before
       8:17  standing, I was terrified and fell **p**.

## PROSTRATING [PROSTRATE]

Ge 43:28  bowed down, **p** themselves before him.

## PROTECT [PROTECTED, PROTECTION, PROTECTS]

Dt 23:14  moves about in your camp to **p** you
Est  9:16  assembled to **p** themselves and get
Ps 12: 7  will **p** us forever from the wicked,
       20: 1  the name of the God of Jacob **p** you.
       25:21  May integrity and uprightness **p** me,
       32: 7  you will **p** me from trouble
       40:11  love and faithfulness always **p** me.
       61: 7  your love and faithfulness to **p** him.
       91:14  I will **p** them, for they acknowledge
      140: 1  **p** me from the violent,
Pr  2:11  Discretion will **p** you,
       4: 6  forsake wisdom, and she will **p** you;
       14: 3  but the lips of the wise **p** them.
       27:18  those who **p** their masters will be
                honored.
Jn 17:11  **p** them by the power of your name,
       17:15  that you **p** them from the evil one.
2Th  3: 3  you and **p** you from the evil one.

## PROTECTED* [PROTECT]

Jos 24:17  He **p** us on our entire journey
1Sa 30:23  He has **p** us and delivered into our
Ezr  8:31  on us, and he **p** us from enemies
Job  5:21  You will be **p** from the lash
Mk  6:20  Herod feared John and **p** him,
Jn 17:12  I **p** them and kept them safe
2Pe  2: 5  people, but **p** Noah, a preacher

## PROTECTION [PROTECT]

Ge 19: 8  they have come under the **p** of my
Jos 20: 3  find **p** from the avenger of blood.
Ezr  9: 9  he has given us a wall of **p** in Judah
Ps  5:11  Spread your **p** over them, that those

## PROTECTS* [PROTECT]

Ps 34:20  he **p** all their bones, not one of them
       41: 2  The LORD **p** and preserves them—

Ps 116: 6  The LORD **p** the unwary;
Pr  2: 8  and **p** the way of his faithful ones.
Da 12: 1  the great prince who **p** your people,
1Co 13: 7  It always **p**, always trusts,

## PROTEST

Ac 18: 6  he shook out his clothes in **p**

## PROUD [PRIDE]

Dt  8:14  your heart will become **p** and you
2Ch 32:25  Hezekiah's heart was **p** and he did
Ps 31:23  him, but the **p** he pays back in full.
       94: 2  pay back to the **p** what they deserve.
      101: 5  has haughty eyes and a **p** heart,
      131: 1  My heart is not **p**, LORD, my eyes
      138: 6  he takes notice of the **p** from afar.
Pr  3:34  He mocks **p** mockers but shows
       16: 5  The LORD detests all the **p**
       16:19  than to share plunder with the **p**.
       21: 4  Haughty eyes and a **p** heart—
Isa  2:12  has a day in store for all the **p**
Eze 28:17  Your heart became **p** on account
Hos 13: 6  they were satisfied, they became **p**;
Ro 12:16  Do not be **p**, but be willing
1Co 13: 4  envy, it does not boast, it is not **p**.
2Ti  3: 2  of money, boastful, **p**, abusive,
Jas  4: 6  "God opposes the **p** but shows
1Pe  5: 5  "God opposes the **p** but shows
Rev 13: 5  was given a mouth to utter **p** words

## PROVE [PROOF, PROOFS, PROVED, PROVING]

Ge 44:16  How can we **p** our innocence?
Pr 29:25  To fear anyone will **p** to be a snare,
Hab  2: 3  of the end and will not **p** false.
Jn  2:18  can you show us to **p** your authority
       8:46  Can any of you **p** me guilty of sin?
       16: 8  he will **p** the world to be in the wrong
1Co  4: 2  been given a trust must **p** faithful.

## PROVED [PROVE]

Dt 13:14  and it has been **p** that this detestable
       17: 4  and it has been **p** that this detestable
Job 32:12  But not one of you has **p** Job wrong;
Ps 105:19  the word of the LORD **p** him true.
Isa  5:16  God will be **p** holy by his righteous
Eze 28:25  I will be **p** holy through them
Mt 11:19  wisdom is **p** right by her actions."
Ro  3: 4  you may be **p** right when you speak
1Pe  1: 7  may be **p** genuine and may result

## PROVERB [PROVERBS]

Ps 49: 4  I will turn my ear to a **p**;
Pr 26: 7  one who is lame is a **p** in the mouth
       26: 9  in a drunkard's hand is a **p**
Eze 18: 3  you will no longer quote this **p**
Lk  4:23  "Surely you will quote this **p** to me:

## PROVERBS [PROVERB]

1Ki  4:32  He spoke three thousand **p** and his
Pr  1: 1  The **p** of Solomon son of David,
       10: 1  The **p** of Solomon:
       25: 1  These are more **p** of Solomon,
Ecc 12: 9  out and set in order many **p**.

## PROVIDE [PROVIDED, PROVIDES, PROVISION, PROVISIONS]

Ge 22: 8 "God himself will **p** the lamb
22:14 that place The LORD Will **P**.
1Ch 17: 9 I will **p** a place for my people Israel
22:14 "I have taken great pains to **p**
Isa 43:20 because I **p** water in the wilderness
61: 3 and **p** for those who grieve in Zion—
Ac 27: 3 to his friends so they might **p** for his
1Co 10:13 **p** a way out so that you can endure
1Ti 5: 8 Anyone who does not **p** for their
Tit 3:14 in order to **p** for urgent needs

## PROVIDED [PROVIDE]

Ge 22:14 of the LORD it will be **p**."
1Ki 8:21 I have **p** a place there for the ark,
1Ch 29: 2 all my resources I have **p**
Ps 68:10 bounty, God, you **p** for the poor.
111: 9 He **p** redemption for his people;
Jnh 1:17 Now the LORD **p** a huge fish
4: 6 the LORD God **p** a gourd
4: 7 at dawn the next day God **p** a worm,
4: 8 rose, God **p** a scorching east wind,
Ro 11:22 **p** that you continue in his kindness.
Gal 4:18 to be zealous, **p** the purpose is good,
Heb 1: 3 After he had **p** purification for sins,

## PROVIDES [PROVIDE]

Ps 111: 5 He **p** food for those who fear him;
147: 9 He **p** food for the cattle
Pr 31:15 she **p** food for her family
Eze 18: 7 hungry and **p** clothing for the naked.
1Ti 6:17 who richly **p** us with everything
1Pe 4:11 do so with the strength God **p**,

## PROVING* [PROVE]

Ac 9:22 in Damascus by **p** that Jesus is
17: 3 and **p** that the Messiah had to suffer
18:28 **p** from the Scriptures that Jesus was

## PROVISION [PROVIDE]

Ps 144:13 will be filled with every kind of **p**.
Ro 5:17 those who receive God's abundant **p**

## PROVISIONS [PROVIDE]

Ps 132:15 I will bless her with abundant **p**;
Pr 6: 8 yet it stores its **p** in summer

## PROVOCATION* [PROVOKE]

Pr 27: 3 but a fool's **p** is heavier than both.

## PROVOKE [PROVOCATION, PROVOKED, PROVOKES]

Dt 2: 5 Do not **p** them to war, for I will not

## PROVOKED* [PROVOKE]

1Sa 1: 7 her rival **p** her till she wept
Ecc 7: 9 Do not be quickly **p** in your spirit,
Jer 32:32 Judah have **p** me by all the evil they

## PROVOKES* [PROVOKE]

Pr 25:23 a sly tongue—which **p** a horrified look.
Eze 8: 3 where the idol that **p** to jealousy

## PROWLS

1Pe 5: 8 enemy the devil **p** around like

## PRUDENCE* [PRUDENT]

Pr 1: 4 giving **p** to those who are simple,
8: 5 You who are simple, gain **p**;
8:12 "I, wisdom, dwell together with **p**;
12: 8 People are praised according to their **p**,
15: 5 whoever heeds correction shows **p**.
16:22 **P** is a fountain of life
19:25 mocker, and the simple will learn **p**;
21:16 Whoever strays from the path of **p**

## PRUDENT [PRUDENCE]

Pr 1: 3 receiving instruction in **p** behavior,
10:19 but the **p** hold their tongues.
12:16 at once, but the **p** overlook an insult.
12:23 The **p** keep their knowledge
13:16 All who are **p** act with knowledge,
14: 8 The wisdom of the **p** is to give
14:15 but the **p** give thought to their steps.
14:18 the **p** are crowned with knowledge.
19:14 but a **p** wife is from the LORD.
22: 3 The **p** see danger and take refuge,
27:12 The **p** see danger and take refuge,
Jer 49: 7 Has counsel perished from the **p**?
Am 5:13 Therefore the **p** keep quiet in such

## PRUNES* [PRUNING]

Jn 15: 2 does bear fruit he **p** so that it will be

## PRUNING [PRUNES]

Isa 2: 4 and their spears into **p** hooks.
Joel 3:10 and your **p** hooks into spears.

## PSALM [PSALMS]

Ps 47: 7 sing to him a **p** of praise.
Ac 13:33 As it is written in the second **P**:

## PSALMS* [PSALM]

Lk 20:42 himself declares in the Book of **P**:"
24:44 of Moses, the Prophets and the **P**."
Ac 1:20 "it is written in the Book of **P**:
Eph 5:19 speaking to one another with **p**,
Col 3:16 another with all wisdom through **p**,

## PUBLIC [PUBLICLY]

Pr 1:20 she raises her voice in the **p** square;
Eze 16:24 a lofty shrine in every **p** square.
Mt 1:19 want to expose her to **p** disgrace,
Lk 20:26 him in what he had said there in **p**.
Col 2:15 he made a **p** spectacle of them,
1Ti 4:13 devote yourself to the **p** reading
Heb 6: 6 and subjecting him to **p** disgrace.

## PUBLICAN (KJV) See PAGANS, TAX COLLECTOR

## PUBLICLY [PUBLIC]

Lk 1:80 the wilderness until he appeared **p**
Jn 7:13 no one would say anything **p**
Ac 20:20 have taught you **p** and from house
Heb 10:33 Sometimes you were **p** exposed

## PUFF* [PUFFS, PUFFED]
Col   2:18  unspiritual minds **p** them up

## PUFFED* [PUFF]
1Co  4: 6  will not be **p** up in being a follower
Hab  2: 4  "See, he is **p** up; his desires are not

## PUFFS* [ PUFF]
1Co  8: 1  knowledge **p** up while love builds

## PUL [TIGLATH-PILESER]
2Ki 15:19  **P** king of Assyria invaded the land,

## PULL [PULLED, PULLING]
Ru   2:16  Even **p** out some stalks for her
Mk   2:21  the new piece will **p** away

## PULLED [PULL]
Ge  19:10  out and **p** Lot back into the house
     37:28  his brothers **p** Joseph
Ezr   9: 3  **p** hair from my head and beard
Ne  13:25  some of them and **p** out their hair.
Mt  15:13  Father has not planted will be **p**

## PULLING* [PULL]
Mt  13:29  'because while you are **p** the weeds,

## PUNISH [PUNISHED, PUNISHES, PUNISHING, PUNISHMENT]
Ge  15:14  But I will **p** the nation they serve as
Ex  32:34  I will **p** them for their sin."
Lev 26:18  me, I will **p** you for your sins seven
2Sa  7:14  I will **p** him with a rod wielded
Pr  23:13  if you **p** them with the rod, they will
Isa 13:11  I will **p** the world for its evil,
Jer  2:19  Your wickedness will **p** you;
    21:14  I will **p** you as your deeds deserve,
Hos 10:10  When I please, I will **p** them;
Zep  1:12  and **p** those who are complacent,
Ac   4:21  could not decide how to **p** them,
     7: 7  But I will **p** the nation they serve as
1Th  4: 6  The Lord will **p** all those who
2Th  1: 8  He will **p** those who do not know
1Pe  2:14  by him to **p** those who do wrong

## PUNISHED [PUNISH]
Ge  19:15  be swept away when the city is **p**."
Ezr   9:13  you have **p** us less than our sins
Ps  99: 8  God, though you **p** their misdeeds.
Isa 53: 8  transgression of my people he was **p**.
La   3:39  should the living complain when **p**
Mk 12:40  men will be **p** most severely."
Lk  23:41  We are **p** justly, for we are getting
2Th  1: 9  They will be **p** with everlasting
Heb 10:29  to be **p** who have trampled the Son

## PUNISHES [PUNISH]
Ex  34: 7  he **p** the children and their children
Nu  14:18  he **p** the children for the sin

## PUNISHING [PUNISH]
Ex  20: 5  God, **p** the children for the sin
Dt   5: 9  God, **p** the children for the sin

## PUNISHMENT [PUNISH]
Ge   4:13  "My **p** is more than I can bear.
Ps  91: 8  eyes and see the **p** of the wicked.
Pr  16:22  prudent, but folly brings **p** to fools.
Isa 53: 5  the **p** that brought us peace was
Jer  4:18  This is your **p**. How bitter it is!
La   4: 6  The **p** of my people is greater than
Eze 39:21  all the nations will see the **p** I inflict
Hos  9: 7  The days of **p** are coming, the days
Zep  3:15  The Lord has taken away your **p**,
Mt  25:46  they will go away to eternal **p**,
Lk  12:48  and does things deserving **p** will be
    21:22  this is the time of **p** in fulfillment
Ro  13: 4  wrath to bring **p** on the wrongdoer.
Heb  2: 2  and disobedience received its just **p**,
2Pe  2: 9  to hold the unrighteous for **p**
1Jn  4:18  fear, because fear has to do with **p**.
Jude  1: 7  of those who suffer the **p** of eternal
Rev 17: 1  I will show you the **p** of the great

## PUR [LOT, PURIM]
Est  3: 7  the month of Nisan, the *p* (that is,

## PURCHASED
Ps  74: 2  the people you **p** long ago, the tribe
Rev  5: 9  your blood you **p** for God members
    14: 4  They were **p** from among the human

## PURE [PURIFICATION, PURIFIED, PURIFIES, PURIFY, PURITY]
Ex  25:11  Overlay it with **p** gold, both inside
    25:31  "Make a lampstand of **p** gold.
    37: 6  the atonement cover of **p** gold—
2Sa 22:27  to the **p** you show yourself **p**,
1Ki  6:21  the inside of the temple with **p** gold,
2Ki  2:22  water has remained **p** to this day,
Job  4:17  beings be more **p** than their Maker?
    14: 4  Who can bring what is **p**
Ps  19: 9  The fear of the Lord is **p**,
    19:10  than gold, than much **p** gold;
    24: 4  who have clean hands and a **p** heart,
    51:10  Create in me a **p** heart, O God,
  119: 9  who are young keep their way **p**?
Pr  15:26  gracious words are **p** in his sight.
    16: 2  People may think all their ways are **p**,
    20: 9  can say, "I have kept my heart **p**;
    20:11  so is their conduct really **p**
Isa 52:11  Come out from it and be **p**, you who
Hab  1:13  Your eyes are too **p** to look on evil;
Mt   5: 8  Blessed are the **p** in heart, for they
2Co 11: 2  I might present you as a **p** virgin
Php  1:10  may be **p** and blameless for the day
    2:15  you may become blameless and **p**,
    4: 8  whatever is **p**, whatever is lovely,
1Ti  1: 5  which comes from a **p** heart
    5:22  the sins of others. Keep yourself **p**.
2Ti  2:22  call on the Lord out of a **p** heart.
Tit  1:15  To the **p**, all things are **p**,
    2: 5  to be self-controlled and **p**, to be
Heb  7:26  blameless, **p**, set apart from sinners,
    10:22  our bodies washed with **p** water.
    13: 4  all, and the marriage bed kept **p**,
Jas  1:27  that God our Father accepts as **p**
    3:17  comes from heaven is first of all **p**;
1Jn  3: 3  purify themselves, just as he is **p**.

Rev 21:18 and the city of **p** gold, as **p** as glass.

## PURGE

Dt  13: 5 You must **p** the evil from among
    19:19 You must **p** the evil from among
Pr  20:30 and beatings **p** the inmost being.

**MUST PURGE** See MUST

## PURIFICATION [PURE]

Lev 12: 6 the days of her **p** for a son
Lk   2:22 time came for the **p** rites required
Ac  21:24 join in their **p** rites and pay their
Heb  1: 3 After he had provided **p** for sins,

## PURIFIED [PURE]

Ezr  6:20 Levites had **p** themselves and were
Ne  12:30 ceremonially, they **p** the people,
Ps  12: 6 flawless, like silver **p** in a crucible,
Da  12:10 Many will be **p**, made spotless
Ac  15: 9 them, for he **p** their hearts by faith.
1Pe  1:22 you have **p** yourselves by obeying

## PURIFIES* [PURE]

1Jn  1: 7 of Jesus, his Son, **p** us from all sin.

## PURIFY [PURE]

Ex  29:36 **P** the altar by making atonement
Nu  19:12 They must **p** themselves
Zep  3: 9 I will **p** the lips of the peoples,
2Co  7: 1 let us **p** ourselves from everything
Tit  2:14 to **p** for himself a people that are his
Jas  4: 8 you sinners, and **p** your hearts,
1Jn  1: 9 and **p** us from all unrighteousness.
     3: 3 hope in him **p** themselves,

## PURIM [PUR]

Est  9:26 (Therefore these days were called **P**,

## PURITY* [PURE]

Hos  8: 5 long will they be incapable of **p**?
2Co  6: 6 in **p**, understanding,
1Ti  4:12 in conduct, in love, in faith and in **p**.
     5: 2 women as sisters, with absolute **p**.
1Pe  3: 2 when they see the **p** and reverence

## PURPLE

Ex  25: 4 **p** and scarlet yarn and fine linen;
Pr  31:22 she is clothed in fine linen and **p**.
Da   5:29 Daniel was clothed in **p**, a gold
Mk  15:17 They put a **p** robe on him,
Rev 17: 4 The woman was dressed in **p**
    18:16 dressed in fine linen, **p** and scarlet,

## PURPOSE [PURPOSED, PURPOSES]

Ex   9:16 I have raised you up for this very **p**,
Job 36: 5 he is mighty, and firm in his **p**.
    42: 2 no **p** of yours can be thwarted.
Pr  19:21 it is the LORD's **p** that prevails.
Isa 46:10 I say, 'My **p** will stand, and I will
    55:11 and achieve the **p** for which I sent it.
Jer 51:12 The LORD will carry out his **p**,
Ro   8:28 have been called according to his **p**.
     9:11 that God's **p** in election might stand:
     9:17 "I raised you up for this very **p**,

1Co  3: 8 and the one who waters have one **p**,
2Co  5: 5 fashioned us for this very **p** is God,
Gal  3:19 What, then, was the **p** of the law?
     4:18 be zealous, provided the **p** is good,
Eph  1:11 in conformity with the **p** of his will,
     2:15 His **p** was to create in himself one
     3:11 to his eternal **p** that he accomplished
Php  2:13 to act in order to fulfill his good **p**.
2Ti  1: 9 but because of his own **p** and grace.
Heb  6:17 nature of his **p** very clear
Rev 17:17 to accomplish his **p** by agreeing

## PURPOSED* [PURPOSE]

Isa 14:24 and as I have **p**, so it will happen.
    14:27 For the LORD Almighty has **p**,
Jer 49:20 what he has **p** against those who
    50:45 what he has **p** against the land
Eph  1: 9 good pleasure, which he **p** in Christ,

## PURPOSES [PURPOSE]

Ps  33:10 he thwarts the **p** of the peoples.
Pr  20: 5 The **p** of the human heart are deep
Jer 23:20 until he fully accomplishes the **p**
    32:19 great are your **p** and mighty are
Ro   9:21 of clay some pottery for noble **p**
2Ti  2:20 some are for noble **p** and some

## PURSE [PURSES]

Hag  1: 6 to put them in a **p** with holes in it."
Lk  10: 4 Do not take a **p** or bag or sandals;
    22:36 "But now if you have a **p**, take it,

## PURSES [PURSE]

Lk  12:33 Provide **p** for yourselves that will

## PURSUE [PURSUED, PURSUES, PURSUING]

Lev 26: 7 You will **p** your enemies, and they
Dt  19: 6 of blood might **p** him in a rage,
Ps  34:14 and do good; seek peace and **p** it.
Pr  11:19 those who **p** evil go to their death.
    15: 9 he loves those who **p** righteousness.
Isa 51: 1 you who **p** righteousness and who
Jer  9:16 I will **p** them with the sword until I
Eze  5: 2 For I will **p** them with drawn sword.
Ro   9:30 who did not **p** righteousness,
1Ti  6:11 this, and **p** righteousness, godliness,
2Ti  2:22 of youth and **p** righteousness, faith,
1Pe  3:11 and do good; seek peace and **p** it.

## PURSUED [PURSUE]

Ex  14:23 The Egyptians **p** them, and all
Ps  18:37 I **p** my enemies and overtook them;
Ro   9:32 Because they **p** it not by faith but as

## PURSUES [PURSUE]

Jos 20: 5 If the avenger of blood **p** them,
Pr  13:21 Trouble **p** the sinner,
    21:21 Whoever **p** righteousness and love
    28: 1 The wicked flee though no one **p**,

## PURSUING [PURSUE]

Lev 26:17 will flee even when no one is **p** you.
Hos  5:11 in judgment, intent on **p** idols.
1Ti  3: 8 wine, and not **p** dishonest gain.

Tit    1: 7  not violent, not **p** dishonest gain.
1Pe   5: 2  not **p** dishonest gain, but eager to serve;

## PUSH

Dt    15:17  and **p** it through his ear lobe

## PUT [PUTS, PUTTING]

Ge     2:15  and **p** him in the Garden of Eden
       3:12  "The woman you **p** here with me—
       3:15  And I will **p** enmity between you
       4:15  the LORD **p** a mark on Cain so
       6:13  Noah, "I am going to **p** an end to all
      24: 2  had, "**P** your hand under my thigh.
      47:29  **p** your hand under my thigh
Ex     4: 6  So Moses **p** his hand into his cloak,
      16:34  Aaron **p** the manna with the tablets
Nu    14:15  If you **p** these people to death all
      17:10  "**P** back Aaron's staff in front
      21: 8  a snake and **p** it up on a pole;
      22: 6  come and **p** a curse on these people,
Dt    32:39  I **p** to death and I bring to life,
1Sa    5: 3  Dagon and **p** him back in his place.
       7: 4  So the Israelites **p** away their Baals
1Ki   11:36  city where I chose to **p** my Name.
2Ch   10: 4  "Your father **p** a heavy yoke on us,
      33: 7  I will **p** my Name forever.
Job   40: 4  I **p** my hand over my mouth.
Ps    22: 4  In you our ancestors **p** their trust;
      25: 1  In you, LORD my God, I **p** my trust.
      25: 2  do not let me be **p** to shame, nor let
      33:22  even as we **p** our hope in you.
      40: 3  He **p** a new song in my mouth,
      42: 5  **P** your hope in God, for I will yet
      78:18  They willfully **p** God to the test
     119:43  for I have **p** my hope in your laws.
     143: 8  for I have **p** my trust in you.
Isa    8:17  I will **p** my trust in him.
      11: 8  young children will **p** their hands
      42: 1  I will **p** my Spirit on him, and he
      59:17  He **p** on righteousness as his
Jer    1: 9  "I have **p** my words in your mouth.
      32:14  **p** them in a clay jar so they will last
      38: 6  **p** him into the cistern of Malkijah,
Eze   36:27  And I will **p** my Spirit in you
      37:14  I will **p** my Spirit in you and you
Da     9:26  the Anointed One will be **p** to death
Mal    3:15  they **p** God to the test,
Mt     4: 7  'Do not **p** the Lord your God
      12:18  I will **p** my Spirit on him, and he
Mk    12:44  out of her poverty, **p** in everything—
Jn     8:30  he spoke, many **p** their faith in him.
      11:45  what Jesus did, **p** their faith in him.
      20:25  **p** my finger where the nails were,
Ro     7:11  through the commandment **p** me
       8:13  if by the Spirit you **p** to death
       9:33  in him will never be **p** to shame."
      10:11  in him will never be **p** to shame."
1Co    4: 9  to me that God has **p** us apostles
      12:24  God has **p** the body together,
      13:11  I **p** the ways of childhood behind
      15:25  reign until he has **p** all his enemies
2Co    1:22  us, and **p** his Spirit in our hearts as
Eph    4:24  and to **p** on the new self,
       6:11  **P** on the full armor of God,
Php    3: 3  who **p** no confidence in the flesh—
Col    2:11  Your sinful nature was **p** off

Col    3:14  And over all these virtues **p** on love,
1Th    5:19  Do not **p** out the Spirit's fire.
Heb    2: 8  and **p** everything under their feet."
Rev    7: 3  or the trees until we **p** a seal

## PUT ... TO DEATH Ge 26:11; 38:7, 10; 42:37;
Ex 19:12; 21:12, 14, 15, 16, 17, 29; 22:19; 31:14,
15; 35:2; Lev 19:20; 20:2, 4, 9, 10, 11, 12, 13,
15, 16, 27; 24:16, 16, 17, 21; 27:29; Nu 1:51;
3:10, 38; 14:15; 18:7; 25:5, 15; 35:16, 17, 18, 19,
19, 21, 21, 30, 30, 31; Dt 9:28; 13:5, 9; 17:6, 6,
12; 18:20; 21:22; 24:16, 16; 32:39; Jos 1:18;
10:26; 11:17; Jdg 6:31; 20:13; 21:5; 1Sa 2:25;
11:12, 13; 14:45; 15:3, 33; 19:6; 20:32; 2Sa 4:10;
8:2; 14:7, 32; 19:21, 22; 21:1, 4, 9; 1Ki 1:51; 2:8,
24, 26; 18:9; 19:10, 14, 17, 17; 2Ki 11:8, 15, 16;
14:6, 6; 16:9; 19:35; 1Ch 2:3; 10:14; 2Ch 15:13;
22:9; 23:7, 14, 15; 25:4, 4, 4; Est 4:11; 9:15; Ps
78:31; Isa 37:36; 65:15; Jer 18:21; 26:15, 19, 21,
24; 29:21; 38:4; Eze 18:13; Da 2:13, 13, 14;
5:19, 19; 9:26; Mt 10:21; 15:4; 24:9; 26:59; 27:1;
Mk 7:10; 13:12; 14:55; Lk 21:16; Ac 2:23; 5:33;
12:2; 26:10; Ro 7:11; 8:13; Eph 2:16; Col 3:5;
Heb 11:37; 1Pe 3:18; Rev 2:13

## PUT ... TO THE SWORD Nu 21:24; Dt
13:15; 20:13; Jos 8:24; 10:28, 30, 32, 35, 37, 39;
11:10, 11, 12, 14; 13:22; 19:47; Jdg 1:8, 25;
20:37, 48; 21:10; 1Sa 22:19; 2Sa 15:14; 1Ki
1:51; 2:8; 19:10, 14, 17, 17; 2Ki 11:15; 2Ch
21:4; 23:14; Job 1:15, 17; Ps 78:64; Jer 15:9;
20:4; 21:7; 25:31; Ac 12:2

## PUTS [PUT]

Nu    23:12  I not speak what the LORD **p**
Mt     7:24  **p** them into practice is like a wise
Lk     9:62  "No one who **p** a hand to the plow

## PUTTING [PUT]

1Ki    9: 3  built, by **p** my Name there forever.
Jn    12:11  to Jesus and **p** their faith in him.
1Th    5: 8  **p** on faith and love as a breastplate,
Heb    2: 8  In **p** everything under them,
2Pe    2: 4  **p** them in chains of darkness to be

# Q

## QUAIL*

Ex    16:13  That evening **q** came and covered
Nu    11:31  and drove **q** in from the sea.
      11:32  the people went out and gathered **q**.
Ps   105:40  They asked, and he brought them **q**;

## QUAKE [EARTHQUAKE, EARTHQUAKES, QUAKED]

Ps    46: 3  the mountains **q** with their surging.
      75: 3  When the earth and all its people **q**,
Na     1: 5  The mountains **q** before him
Rev   16:18  on earth, so tremendous was the **q**.

## QUAKED* [QUAKE]

Jdg  5: 5  The mountains q before
2Sa 22: 8  The earth trembled and q,
Ps  18: 7  The earth trembled and q,
    77:18  the earth trembled and q.

## QUALIFIED

Col  1:12  who has q you to share
2Ti  2: 2  who will also be q to teach others.

## QUALITIES* [QUALITY]

Da   6: 3  by his exceptional q that the king
Ro   1:20  of the world God's invisible q—
2Pe  1: 8  if you possess these q in increasing

## QUALITY [QUALITIES]

1Co  3:13  and the fire will test the q of each

## QUARREL [QUARRELED, QUARRELING, QUARRELS, QUARRELSOME]

Pr  15:18  but those who are patient calm a q.
    17:14  Starting a q is like breaching a dam;
    17:19  Whoever loves a q loves sin;
    20: 3  strife, but every fool is quick to q.
    26:17  who rushes into a q not their own.
    26:20  without a gossip a q dies down.
Isa 45: 9  "Woe to those who q with their Maker,
Mt  12:19  He will not q or cry out; no one will
Jas  4: 2  what you want, so you q and fight.

## QUARRELED [QUARREL]

Ex  17: 7  Meribah because the Israelites q
Nu  20: 3  They q with Moses and said,

## QUARRELING [QUARREL]

Ge  13: 7  q arose between Abram's herders
Ro  14: 1  without q over disputable matters.
1Co  3: 3  there is jealousy and q among you,
2Co 12:20  I fear that there may be q, jealousy,
2Ti  2:14  Warn them before God against q

## QUARRELS [QUARREL]

1Ti  6: 4  q about words that result in envy,
2Ti  2:23  because you know they produce q.
Tit  3: 9  and arguments and q about the law,
Jas  4: 1  causes fights and q among you?

## QUARRELSOME [QUARREL]

Pr  19:13  a q wife is like the constant dripping
    21: 9  than share a house with a q wife.
    21:19  to live in a desert than with a q
    26:21  so is a q person for kindling strife.
1Ti  3: 3  gentle, not q, not a lover of money.
2Ti  2:24  Lord's servant must not be q

## QUEEN

1Ki 10: 1  When the q of Sheba heard
2Ch  9: 1  When the q of Sheba heard
    15:16  from her position as q mother,
Est  1:12  Q Vashti refused to come.
    2:17  and made her q instead of Vashti.
Isa 47: 7  said, 'I am forever—the eternal q!'
Jer  7:18  cakes to offer to the Q of Heaven.

La   1: 1  She who was q among the provinces
Eze 16:13  very beautiful and rose to be a q.
Mt  12:42  The Q of the South will rise
Ac   8:27  means "q of the Ethiopians").
Rev 18: 7  she boasts, 'I sit enthroned as q.

## QUENCH [QUENCHED]

SS   8: 7  Many waters cannot q love;
Isa  1:31  together, with no one to q the fire."
Jer  4: 4  burn with no one to q it.

## QUENCHED [QUENCH]

2Ki 22:17  against this place and will not be q.'
Isa 66:24  nor will their fire be q, and they will
Jer  7:20  and it will burn and not be q.
Mk   9:48  does not die, and the fire is not q.'
Heb 11:34  q the fury of the flames,

## QUESTION [QUESTIONS]

Job 38: 3  I will q you, and you shall answer
    40: 7  I will q you, and you shall answer
Mt  22:35  in the law, tested him with this q:
Mk  11:29  Jesus replied, "I will ask you one q.
Jn   8: 6  *They were using this q as a trap,*

## QUESTIONS [QUESTION]

2Ch  9: 1  to Jerusalem to test him with hard q.
Mt  22:46  no one dared to ask him any more q.
1Co 10:25  the meat market without raising q

## QUICK [QUICK-TEMPERED, QUICKLY]

Pr   6:18  feet that are q to rush into evil,
    20: 3  strife, but every fool is q to quarrel.
Ecc  5: 2  Do not be q with your mouth,
Jas  1:19  Everyone should be q to listen,

## QUICK, QUICKEN (KJV) See also [GIVE] LIFE, LIVING

## QUICK-TEMPERED* [QUICK, TEMPER]

Pr  14:17  The q do foolish things, and those
    14:29  but the q display folly.
Tit  1: 7  not q, not given to drunkenness,

## QUICKLY [QUICK]

Dt   4:26  that you will q perish from the land
Jos 23:16  and you will q perish from the good
Jdg  2:17  they q turned from following
Ps  22:19  are my strength; come q to help me.
    69:17  answer me q, for I am in trouble.
    71:12  come q, God, to help me.
    90:10  for they q pass, and we fly away.
Ecc  4:12  of three strands is not q broken.
    7: 9  Do not be q provoked in your spirit,
    8:11  for a crime is not q carried out,
Jn  13:27  "What you are about to do, do q."
Gal  1: 6  you are so q deserting the one who

## QUIET [QUIETED, QUIETLY, QUIETNESS]

Ps  23: 2  he leads me beside q waters,
Pr  17: 1  and q than a house full of feasting,

Ecc 9:17 The **q** words of the wise are more
Isa 62: 1 sake I will not remain **q**, till her
Am 5:13 Therefore the prudent keep **q**
Mk 4:39 the wind and said to the waves, "**Q!**
6:31 with me by yourselves to a **q** place
Lk 19:40 "if they keep **q**, the stones will cry
1Th 4:11 it your ambition to lead a **q** life:
1Ti 2: 2 peaceful and **q** lives in all godliness
2:12 authority over a man; she must be **q**.
1Pe 3: 4 beauty of a gentle and **q** spirit,

## QUIETED [QUIET]
Ps 131: 2 calmed myself and **q** my ambitions.

## QUIETLY [QUIET]
La 3:26 it is good to wait **q** for the salvation
Mt 1:19 he had in mind to divorce her **q**.

## QUIETNESS* [QUIET]
Job 3:26 I have no peace, no **q**; I have no
Isa 30:15 in **q** and trust is your strength,
32:17 its effect will be **q** and confidence
1Ti 2:11 A woman should learn in **q** and full

## QUIRINIUS*
Lk 2: 2 took place while **Q** was governor

## QUIVER
Ps 127: 5 Blessed is the man whose **q** is full
Isa 49: 2 arrow and concealed me in his **q**.

## QUOTE
Eze 16:44 quotes proverbs will **q** this proverb
18: 3 you will no longer **q** this proverb
Lk 4:23 "Surely you will **q** this proverb

---

# R

---

## RABBI [RABBONI]
Mt 23: 8 "But you are not to be called '**R**,'
26:49 Jesus, Judas said, "Greetings, **R!**"
Jn 1:38 "**R**" (which means "Teacher"),

## RABBONI* [RABBI]
Jn 20:16 him and cried out in Aramaic, "**R!**"

## RACE
Ezr 9: 2 have mingled the holy **r**
Ecc 9:11 The **r** is not to the swift or the battle
Ac 20:24 my only aim is to finish the **r**
Ro 9: 3 of my people, those of my own **r**,
1Co 9:24 know that in a **r** all the runners run,
Gal 2: 2 had not been running my **r** in vain.
5: 7 You were running a good **r**.
2Ti 4: 7 I have finished the **r**, I have kept
Heb 12: 1 with perseverance the **r** marked

## RACHEL
Daughter of Laban (Ge 29:16); wife of Jacob (Ge 29:28); bore two sons (Ge 30:22–24; 35:16–24;

46:19). Stole Laban's gods (Ge 31:19, 32–35). Death (Ge 35:19–20).

## RADIANCE* [RADIANT]
Job 31:26 if I have regarded the sun in its **r**
Eze 1:28 rainy day, so was the **r** around him.
10: 4 court was full of the **r** of the glory
Heb 1: 3 The Son is the **r** of God's glory

## RADIANT [RADIANCE]
Ex 34:29 that his face was **r** because he had
Ps 19: 8 The commands of the LORD are **r**,
34: 5 Those who look to him are **r**;
SS 5:10 My beloved is **r** and ruddy,
Isa 60: 5 Then you will look and be **r**,
Eze 43: 2 and the land was **r** with his glory.
Eph 5:27 present her to himself as a **r** church,

## RAGE [RAGING]
Dt 19: 6 of blood might pursue him in a **r**,
Job 15:13 so that you vent your **r** against God
Pr 29:11 Fools give full vent to their **r**,
Isa 41:11 "All who **r** against you will surely
Ac 4:25 " 'Why do the nations **r**
Gal 5:20 jealousy, fits of **r**, selfish ambition,
Eph 4:31 Get rid of all bitterness, **r** and anger,
Col 3: 8 anger, **r**, malice, slander, and filthy

## RAGING [RAGE]
Jnh 1:15 overboard, and the **r** sea grew calm.
Lk 8:24 rebuked the wind and the **r** waters;

## RAGS
Isa 64: 6 our righteous acts are like filthy **r**;
Jer 38:12 "Put these old **r** and worn-out clothes

## RAHAB
Prostitute of Jericho who hid Israelite spies (Jos 2; 6:22–25; Heb 11:31; Jas 2:25). Mother of Boaz (Mt 1:5).

## RAIDERS
Jdg 2:14 the hands of **r** who plundered them.

## RAIN [RAINBOW, RAINED, RAINS]
Ge 2: 5 the LORD God had not sent **r**
7: 4 from now I will send **r** on the earth
Ex 16: 4 "I will **r** down bread from heaven
Lev 26: 4 I will send you **r** in its season,
Dt 11:14 then I will send **r** on your land in its
1Ki 17: 1 there will be neither dew nor **r**
18: 1 and I will send **r** on the land."
2Ch 6:26 there is no **r** because your people
Job 38:28 Does the **r** have a father?
Ps 147: 8 he supplies the earth with **r**
Isa 45: 8 above, **r** down my righteousness;
Jer 14:22 idols of the nations bring **r**?
Zec 14:17 Almighty, they will have no **r**.
Mt 5:45 and sends **r** on the righteous
7:25 The **r** came down, the streams rose,
Jas 5:17 prayed earnestly that it would not **r**,
Jude 1:12 They are clouds without **r**,
Rev 11: 6 it will not **r** during the time they are

## RAINBOW [RAIN]
Ge   9:13  I have set my **r** in the clouds, and it
Eze  1:28  the appearance of a **r** in the clouds
Rev  4: 3  A **r** that shone like an emerald
      10: 1  in a cloud, with a **r** above his head;

## RAINED* [RAIN]
Ge  19:24  the LORD **r** down burning sulfur
Ex   9:23  So the LORD **r** hail on the land
Ps  78:24  he **r** down manna for the people
     78:27  He **r** meat down on them like dust,
Eze 22:24  cleansed or **r** on in the day of wrath.'
Lk  17:29  fire and sulfur **r** down from heaven

## RAINS [RAIN]
Dt  11:14  both autumn and spring **r**,
Jer   5:24  autumn and spring **r** in season,
Joel  2:23  both autumn and spring **r**, as before.
Jas  5: 7  waiting for the autumn and spring **r**.

## RAISE [RISE]
Dt  18:15  The LORD your God will **r**
1Sa  2:35  I will **r** up for myself a faithful
Pr   8: 1  Does not understanding **r** her voice?
Isa  11:12  He will **r** a banner for the nations
    14:13  I will **r** my throne above the stars
Mt   3: 9  these stones God can **r** up children
Jn   2:19  and I will **r** it again in three days."
    6:39  me, but **r** them up at the last day.
Ac   3:22  'The Lord your God will **r**
1Co  6:14  from the dead, and he will **r** us also.
2Co  4:14  the dead will also **r** us with Jesus
Heb 11:19  that God could even **r** the dead,

## RAISED [RISE]
Ex   9:16  But I have **r** you up for this very
Jdg  2:18  Whenever the LORD **r** up a judge
Ps  89:19  I have **r** up a young man from among
Isa  40: 4  Every valley shall be **r** up,
    52:13  he will be **r** and lifted up and highly
Mt  17:23  the third day he will be **r** to life."
Lk   7:22  the dead are **r**, and the good news is
Ac   2:24  But God **r** him from the dead,
    10:40  but God **r** him from the dead
    13:30  But God **r** him from the dead,
    13:34  God **r** him from the dead
Ro   4:25  was **r** to life for our justification.
    6: 4  just as Christ was **r** from the dead
    8:11  he who **r** Christ from the dead will
    9:17  "I **r** you up for this very purpose,
    10: 9  your heart that God **r** him
1Co 15: 4  he was **r** on the third day according
   15:20  Christ has indeed been **r**
2Co  5:15  who died for them and was **r** again.
Eph  2: 6  And God **r** us up with Christ
Col  2:12  **r** with him through your faith

## RAISES [RISE]
1Sa  2: 8  He **r** the poor from the dust and lifts
Ps 113: 7  He **r** the poor from the dust and lifts
Jn   5:21  For just as the Father **r** the dead

## RAISINS
Nu  6: 3  drink grape juice or eat grapes or **r**.
SS  2: 5  Strengthen me with **r**, refresh me

## RALLY*
Isa  11:10  the nations will **r** to him, and his

## RAM [RAMS, RAMS']
Ge  22:13  in a thicket he saw a **r** caught by its
Ex  25: 5  **r** skins dyed red and another durable
    29:22  (This is the **r** for the ordination.)
Lev  8:22  He then presented the other **r**, the **r**
Da  8: 3  there before me was a **r** with two

## RAMAH
Jer 31:15  "A voice is heard in **R**,
Mt  2:18  "A voice is heard in **R**,

## RAMESES
Ex  1:11  and **R** as store cities for Pharaoh.

## RAMOTH GILEAD [GILEAD]
1Ki 22: 6  "Shall I go to war against **R**,

## RAMPART* [RAMPARTS]
Ps  91: 4  will be your shield and **r**.

## RAMPARTS [RAMPART]
Ps  48:13  consider well her **r**, view her
Hab  2: 1  watch and station myself on the **r**;

## RAMS [RAM]
1Sa 15:22  to heed is better than the fat of **r**.
Ps 114: 4  the mountains leaped like **r**, the hills
Mic  6: 7  be pleased with thousands of **r**,

## RAMS'* [RAM]
Jos  6: 4  priests carry trumpets of **r**' horns
1Ch 15:28  with the sounding of **r**' horns

## RAN [RUN]
Ge  39:12  in her hand and **r** out of the house.
1Ki 18:46  he **r** ahead of Ahab all the way
    19: 3  Elijah was afraid and **r** for his life.
Jnh  1: 3  But Jonah **r** away from the LORD

## RANGE
2Ch 16: 9  the LORD **r** throughout the earth
Zec  4:10  **r** throughout the earth will rejoice

## RANK [RANKS]
1Sa 18: 5  Saul gave him a high **r** in the army.
Est  10: 3  Mordecai the Jew was second in **r**

## RANKS [RANK]
Gal  2: 4  false believers had infiltrated our **r**

## RANSOM [RANSOMED]
Nu 35:31  " 'Do not accept a **r** for the life
Ps  49: 8  the **r** for a life is costly, no payment
Mt  20:28  to give his life as a **r** for many."
Mk 10:45  to give his life as a **r** for many."
1Ti  2: 6  who gave himself as a **r** for all
Heb  9:15  he has died as a **r** to set them free

## RANSOMED [RANSOM]
Lev 19:20  not been **r** or given her freedom,

## RARE
1Sa 3: 1  days the word of the LORD was **r**;
Pr 20:15  that speak knowledge are a **r** jewel.

## RASH [RASHLY]
Nu 30: 6  or after her lips utter a **r** promise
Ps 106:33  and **r** words came from Moses' lips.

## RASHLY* [RASH]
Pr 13: 3  those who speak **r** will come to ruin.
20:25  It is a trap to dedicate something **r**

## RATHER
Job 32: 2  for justifying himself **r** than God.
Mt 10: 6  Go **r** to the lost sheep of Israel.
Mk 7:15  **R**, it is what comes out of you
Ac 5:29  "We must obey God **r** than human
1Co 9:12  anything **r** than hinder the gospel
14: 5  but I would **r** have you prophesy.
14:19  in the church I would **r** speak five
1Pe 4: 2  desires, but **r** for the will of God.

## RAVEN [RAVENS]
Ge 8: 7  and sent out a **r**, and it kept flying
Job 38:41  food for the **r** when its young cry

## RAVENS [RAVEN]
1Ki 17: 6  The **r** brought him bread and meat
Ps 147: 9  and for the young **r** when they call.
Lk 12:24  Consider the **r**: They do not sow

## RAW
Ex 12: 9  Do not eat the meat **r** or boiled
1Sa 2:15  boiled meat from you, but only **r**."

## RAYS
Mal 4: 2  will rise with healing in its **r**.

## RAZOR
Nu 6: 5  no **r** may be used on their head.
Jdg 16:17  "No **r** has ever been used on my
1Sa 1:11  no **r** will ever be used on his head."

## REACH [REACHES]
Dt 30:11  difficult for you or beyond your **r**.
Job 37:23  The Almighty is beyond our **r**
Ps 144: 7  **R** down your hand from on high;
Isa 11:11  day the Lord will **r** out his hand
Mic 5: 4  his greatness will **r** to the ends
Rev 12:14  half a time, out of the serpent's **r**.

## REACHES [REACH]
Ge 11: 4  with a tower that **r** to the heavens,
Ps 57:10  your faithfulness **r** to the skies.
71:19  God, **r** to the skies, you who have
Da 12:12  for and **r** the end of the 1,335 days.

## READ [READER, READING, READS]
Ex 24: 7  the Covenant and **r** it to the people.
Dt 17:19  he is to **r** all the days of his life so
Jos 8:34  Joshua **r** all the words of the law—
2Ki 23: 2  He **r** in their hearing all the words
Ne 8: 8  They **r** from the Book of the Law
8: 8  understood what was being **r**.

Isa 34:16  in the scroll of the LORD and **r**:
Jer 36: 6  **r** to the people from the scroll
36:23  Whenever Jehudi had **r** three or four
Da 5:16  If you can **r** this writing and tell me
Mk 12:10  Haven't you **r** this passage
Lk 4:16  as was his custom. He stood up to **r**,
2Co 3: 2  hearts, known and **r** by everyone.
3:15  Even to this day when Moses is **r**,

## READER* [READ]
Mt 24:15  let the **r** understand—
Mk 13:14  let the **r** understand—then let those

## READINESS* [READY]
2Co 7:11  concern, what **r** to see justice done.
Eph 6:15  feet fitted with the **r** that comes

## READING [READ]
Ac 8:30  you understand what you are **r**?"
1Ti 4:13  yourself to the public **r** of Scripture,

## READS* [READ]
Da 5: 7  "Whoever **r** this writing and tells
Rev 1: 3  is the one who **r** aloud the words

## READY [ALREADY, READINESS]
Ps 119:173  May your hand be **r** to help me,
Mt 24:44  So you also must be **r**,
25:10  The virgins who were **r** went
Lk 1:17  to make **r** a people prepared
12:38  servants whose master finds them **r**,
1Pe 1: 5  the salvation that is **r** to be revealed
Rev 9:15  the four angels who had been kept **r**
19: 7  and his bride has made herself **r**.

## REAFFIRM
2Co 2: 8  therefore, to **r** your love for him.

## REAL* [REALITIES, REALITY, REALLY]
Jn 6:55  For my flesh is **r** food and my blood is
**r** drink.
1Jn 2:27  all things and as that anointing is **r**,

## REALITIES* [REAL]
1Co 2:13  spiritual **r** with Spirit-taught words.
Heb 10: 1  not the **r** themselves.

## REALITY* [REAL]
Col 2:17  the **r**, however, is found in Christ.

## REALIZE [REALIZED]
Hos 7: 2  but they do not **r** that I remember all
Jn 12:16  Jesus was glorified did they **r**
13: 7  "You do not **r** now what I am
20:14  but she did not **r** that it was Jesus.
21: 4  but the disciples did not **r** that it was

## REALIZED [REALIZE]
Ge 3: 7  opened, and they **r** they were naked;
Jdg 6:22  When Gideon **r** that it was the angel
13:21  Manoah **r** that it was the angel
1Sa 3: 8  Eli **r** that the LORD was calling
18:28  When Saul **r** that the LORD was
1Ki 3:15  and he **r** it had been a dream.

Mk   5:30   At once Jesus **r** that power had gone

## REALLY [REAL]
Ge    3: 1   "Did God **r** say, 'You must not eat
Jdg   6:31   If Baal **r** is a god, he can defend
1Ki   8:27   "But will God **r** dwell on earth?
Jn   13:38   "Will you **r** lay down your life
1Jn   2:19   us, but they did not **r** belong to us.

## REALM [REALMS]
Nu   16:30   they go down alive into the **r** of the
              dead,
Ps    9:17   wicked go down to the **r** of the dead,
     16:10   not abandon me to the **r** of the dead,
     49:15   God will redeem me from the **r** of the
              dead;
Isa  14:15   brought down to the **r** of the dead,
Ac    2:27   not abandon me to the **r** of the dead,

## REALMS* [REALM]
Eph   1: 3   the heavenly **r** with every spiritual
      1:20   at his right hand in the heavenly **r**,
      2: 6   in the heavenly **r** in Christ Jesus,
      3:10   and authorities in the heavenly **r**,
      6:12   forces of evil in the heavenly **r**.

## REAP [REAPER, REAPS]
Lev  19: 9   " 'When you **r** the harvest of your
Job   4: 8   evil and those who sow trouble **r** it.
Ps  126: 5   sow with tears will **r** with songs
Pr   11:18   who sow righteousness **r** a sure reward.
     22: 8   Those who sow injustice **r** calamity,
Hos   8: 7   sow the wind and **r** the whirlwind.
     10:12   **r** the fruit of unfailing love,
Lk   12:24   They do not sow or **r**, they have no
Jn    4:38   to **r** what you have not worked for.
Ro    6:22   the benefit you **r** leads to holiness,
1Co   9:11   too much if we **r** a material harvest
2Co   9: 6   sows sparingly will also **r** sparingly,
Gal   6: 7   People **r** what they sow.
      6: 8   from the Spirit will **r** eternal life.
Rev  14:15   "Take your sickle and **r**,

## REAPER [REAP]
Am    9:13   "when the **r** will be overtaken
Jn    4:36   and the **r** may be glad together.

## REAPS* [REAP]
Jn    4:37   'One sows and another **r**' is true.

## REAR
Nu   10:25   as the **r** guard for all the units,
Jos   6: 9   and the **r** guard followed the ark.
Isa  52:12   God of Israel will be your **r** guard.

## REASON [REASONED, UNREASONING]
Ge    2:24   For this **r** a man will leave his father
Ps   38:19   hate me without **r** are numerous.
Isa   1:18   let us **r** together," says the LORD.
Mt   19: 5   this **r** a man will leave his father
Lk    6: 7   were looking for a **r** to accuse Jesus,
Jn   12:27   it was for this very **r** I came to this
     15:25   'They hated me without **r**.'
     18:37   the **r** I was born and came

1Pe   3:15   asks you to give the **r** for the hope
2Pe   1: 5   For this very **r**, make every effort
1Jn   3: 8   The **r** the Son of God appeared was

## REASONED [REASON]
Ac   17:17   So he **r** in the synagogue with both
1Co  13:11   thought like a child, I **r** like a child.

## REASSURED
Ru    2:13   "You have **r** me and have spoken kindly

## REBEKAH
Sister of Laban, secured as bride for Isaac (Ge 24).
Mother of Esau and Jacob (Ge 25:19–26). Taken by
Abimelech as sister of Isaac; returned (Ge 26:1–11).
Encouraged Jacob to trick Isaac out of blessing (Ge
27:1–17).

## REBEL [REBELLED, REBELLING, REBELLION, REBELLIOUS, REBELS]
Ex   23:21   Do not **r** against him; he will not
Nu   14: 9   Only do not **r** against the LORD.
Jos  22:18   you **r** against the LORD today,
1Sa  12:14   and do not **r** against his commands,
Mk   13:12   Children will **r** against their parents

## REBELLED [REBEL]
Nu   20:24   both of you **r** against my command
Dt    1:26   you **r** against the command
Ne    9:26   were disobedient and **r** against you;
Ps   78:56   the test and **r** against the Most High;
    106:33   for they **r** against the Spirit of God,
Isa  63:10   Yet they **r** and grieved his Holy

## REBELLING [REBEL]
Ro   13: 2   the authority is **r** against what God

## REBELLION [REBEL]
Ex   23:21   he will not forgive your **r**, since my
     34: 7   and forgiving wickedness, **r** and sin.
Nu   14:18   in love and forgiving sin and **r**.
Jos  24:19   He will not forgive your **r** and your
1Sa  15:23   For **r** is the sin of divination,
Da    8:13   the **r** that causes desolation,
Mk   14:48   "Am I leading a **r**," said Jesus,
2Th   2: 3   day will not come] until the **r** occurs
Heb   3: 8   your hearts as you did in the **r**,

## REBELLIOUS [REBEL]
Dt   21:18   **r** son who does not obey his father
Ps   25: 7   the sins of my youth and my **r** ways;
Pr   24:21   son, and do not join with **r** officials,
Eze   2: 5   for they are a **r** house—

## REBELS [REBEL]
Jos   1:18   Whoever **r** against your word
Mk   15:27   They crucified two **r** with him,
Ro   13: 2   whoever **r** against the authority is
1Ti   1: 9   righteous but for lawbreakers and **r**,

## REBIRTH* [BEAR]
Tit   3: 5   saved us through the washing of **r**

## REBUILD [BUILD]

Jos    6:26  who undertakes to **r** this city,
Ezr    5: 2  set to work to **r** the house of God
Ne     2:17  let us **r** the wall of Jerusalem,
Ps  102:16  For the LORD will **r** Zion
Isa   58:12  Your people will **r** the ancient ruins
Ezr    5: 3  "Who authorized you to **r** this temple
Da     9:25  **r** Jerusalem until the Anointed One,
Am     9:14  "They will **r** the ruined cities
Hag    1: 2  yet come to **r** the LORD's house.' "
Mt   26:61  of God and **r** it in three days.' "
Ac   15:16  will return and **r** David's fallen tent.

## REBUILT [BUILD]

2Ch 24:13  They **r** the temple of God according
Ezr    6: 3  Let the temple be **r** as a place
Ne     7: 1  After the wall had been **r** and I had
Eze  36:36  that I the LORD have **r** what was
Zec    1:16  and there my house will be **r**.

## REBUKE [REBUKED, REBUKES, REBUKING]

Lev  19:17  **R** your neighbor frankly so you will
Ps     6: 1  do not **r** me in your anger
     119:21  You **r** the arrogant, who are
     141: 5  let him **r** me—that is oil on my
Pr     3:11  discipline, and do not resent his **r**,
       9: 8  Do not **r** mockers or they will hate
      17:10  A **r** impresses a discerning person
      19:25  **r** the discerning, and they will gain
      25:12  of fine gold is the **r** of a wise judge
      27: 5  Better is open **r** than hidden love.
      30: 6  he will **r** you and prove you a liar.
Ecc    7: 5  to heed the **r** of a wise person than
Isa   54: 9  with you, never to **r** you again.
Jer    2:19  your backsliding will **r** you.
Hos    2: 2  "**R** your mother, **r** her, for she is not
Zec    3: 2  Satan, "The LORD **r** you, Satan!
Zep    3:17  his love he will no longer **r** you,
Mk     8:32  took him aside and began to **r** him.
Lk    17: 3  or sister sins against you, **r** them;
1Ti    5: 1  Do not **r** an older man harshly,
2Ti    4: 2  correct, **r** and encourage—
Tit    1:13  Therefore **r** them sharply,
       2:15  Encourage and **r** with all authority.
Jude   1: 9  slander but said, "The Lord **r** you!"
Rev    3:19  Those whom I love I **r**

## REBUKED [REBUKE]

Ps  106: 9  He **r** the Red Sea, and it dried up;
Mt     8:26  he got up and **r** the winds
      17:18  Jesus **r** the demon, and it came
Lk     3:19  John **r** Herod the tetrarch because
       4:39  So he bent over her and **r** the fever,
2Pe    2:16  he was **r** for his wrongdoing

## REBUKES [REBUKE]

Job  22: 4  "Is it for your piety that he **r** you
Ps     2: 5  He **r** them in his anger and terrifies
Pr    28:23  Whoever **r** a person will in the end
      29: 1  many **r** will suddenly be destroyed—
Heb  12: 5  and do not lose heart when he **r** you,

## REBUKING [REBUKE]

2Ti    3:16  and is useful for teaching, **r**,

## RECALL* [RECALLED, RECALLING]

2Pe    3: 2  I want you to **r** the words spoken

## RECALLED* [RECALL]

Isa   63:11  Then his people **r** the days of old,
Eze  23:19  more promiscuous as she **r** the days
Jn     2:22  his disciples **r** what he had said.

## RECALLING [RECALL]

1Ti    1:18  **r** them you may fight the battle well,

## RECEDED

Ge     8: 3  The water **r** steadily from the earth.
Rev    6:14  The sky **r** like a scroll, rolling up,

## RECEIVE [RECEIVED, RECEIVES, RECEIVING]

Ge     4:11  its mouth to **r** your brother's blood
Nu    18:23  They will **r** no inheritance among
Dt     9: 9  on the mountain to **r** the tablets
Ps    24: 5  They will **r** blessing
      27:10  forsake me, the LORD will **r** me.
Pr    28:10  trap, but the blameless will **r** a good
Isa   61: 7  shame you will **r** a double portion,
Da    12:13  rise to **r** your allotted inheritance."
Hos  14: 2  all our sins and **r** us graciously,
Mt    10:41  to be righteous will **r** a righteous
Mk   10:15  anyone who will not **r** the kingdom
      10:30  fail to **r** a hundred times as much
Lk     7:22  The blind **r** sight, the lame walk,
Jn     1:11  his own, but his own did not **r** him.
       1:12  Yet to all who did **r** him,
      16:24  Ask and you will **r**, and your joy
      20:22  them and said, "**R** the Holy Spirit.
Ac     1: 8  But you will **r** power when the Holy
       2:38  you will **r** the gift of the Holy Spirit.
      19: 2  "Did you **r** the Holy Spirit
      20:35  more blessed to give than to **r**.' "
Ro    11:31  that they too may now **r** mercy as
1Co    4: 5  time each will **r** their praise
       9:14  the gospel should **r** their living
2Co    4: 4  comfort ourselves **r** from God.
       6:17  no unclean thing, and I will **r** you."
Gal    3:14  faith we might **r** the promise
1Ti    1:16  believe in him and **r** eternal life.
Heb    4:16  so that we may **r** mercy and find
      11:13  They did not **r** the things promised;
Jas    1: 7  not think they will **r** anything
       1:12  they will **r** the crown of life
1Pe    5: 4  you will **r** the crown of glory
2Pe    1:11  you will **r** a rich welcome
1Jn    3:22  and **r** from him anything we ask,
Rev    4:11  to **r** glory and honor and power,
       5:12  to **r** power and wealth and wisdom
      13:16  to **r** a mark on their right hands
      18: 4  you will not **r** any of her plagues;

## RECEIVED [RECEIVE]

Nu    23:20  I have **r** a command to bless;
Jos   14: 1  are the areas the Israelites **r** as
      14: 4  The Levites **r** no share of the land
Mt     6: 2  you, they have **r** their reward in full.
      10: 8  Freely you have **r**, freely give.
Mk   11:24  believe that you have **r** it, and it will
Jn     1:16  of his fullness we have all **r** grace

Ac 8:17 on them, and they r the Holy Spirit.
10:47 They have r the Holy Spirit just as
Ro 8:15 the Spirit you r brought about your
11:30 to God have now r mercy as a result
1Co 2:12 We have not r the spirit of the world
11:23 For I r from the Lord what I
Eph 4: 1 worthy of the calling you have r.
Col 2: 6 just as you r Christ Jesus as Lord,
4:17 you complete the work you have r
1Ti 4: 4 rejected if it is r with thanksgiving,
Heb 8: 6 ministry Jesus has r is as superior
1Pe 2:10 but now you have r mercy.
4:10 should use whatever gift you have r
2Pe 1: 1 Savior Jesus Christ have r a faith as
1:17 He r honor and glory from God
Rev 2:27 just as I have r authority from my
19:20 deluded those who had r the mark
20: 4 and had not r his mark on their

## RECEIVES [RECEIVE]
Pr 18:22 good and r favor from the LORD.
Lk 11:10 For everyone who asks r;
Ac 10:43 who believes in him r forgiveness
Rev 14:11 or for anyone who r the mark of its

## RECEIVING [RECEIVE]
Pr 1: 3 for r instruction in prudent behavior,
Ro 9: 4 the covenants, the r of the law,
1Pe 1: 9 for you are r the end result of your
3Jn 1: 7 went out, r no help from the pagans.

## RECENT*
1Ti 3: 6 He must not be a r convert, or he

## RECITE [RECITED, RECITING]
Dt 27:14 The Levites shall r to all the people
Ps 45: 1 a noble theme as I r my verses

## RECITED* [RECITE]
Dt 31:30 Moses r the words of this song

## RECITING* [RECITE]
Dt 32:45 Moses finished r all these words

## RECKLESS
Pr 12:18 words of the r pierce like swords,

## RECKONED [RECKONING]
Ge 21:12 Isaac that your offspring will be r.
Ro 9: 7 Isaac that your offspring will be r."
Heb 11:18 Isaac that your offspring will be r."

## RECKONING* [RECKONED]
Isa 10: 3 What will you do on the day of r,
Hos 5: 9 will be laid waste on the day of r.
9: 7 coming, the days of r are at hand.

## RECLAIM* [CLAIM]
Isa 11:11 time to r the surviving remnant

## RECLINED* [RECLINING]
Lk 7:36 Pharisee's house and r at the table.
11:37 so he went in and r at the table.
22:14 Jesus and his apostles r at the table.

## RECLINING [RECLINED]
Est 7: 8 on the couch where Esther was r.
Jn 13:23 Jesus loved, was r next to him.

## RECOGNITION* [RECOGNIZE]
Est 6: 3 r has Mordecai received for this?"
1Co 16:18 and yours also. Such men deserve r.
1Ti 5: 3 Give proper r to those widows who

## RECOGNIZE [RECOGNITION, RECOGNIZED, RECOGNIZING]
Ge 42: 8 his brothers, they did not r him.
Job 2:12 a distance, they could hardly r him;
Mt 7:16 By their fruit you will r them.
Lk 19:44 because you did not r the time
Jn 1:10 him, the world did not r him.
1Jn 4: 2 This is how you can r the Spirit
4: 6 This is how we r the Spirit of truth

## RECOGNIZED [RECOGNIZE]
Mt 12:33 be bad, for a tree is r by its fruit.
Lk 24:31 eyes were opened and they r him,
Ac 12:14 When she r Peter's voice, she was
Ro 7:13 in order that sin might be r as sin,

## RECOGNIZING* [RECOGNIZE]
Lk 24:16 but they were kept from r him.

## RECOMMENDATION*
2Co 3: 1 letters of r to you or from you?

## RECOMPENSE*
Isa 40:10 him, and his r accompanies him.
62:11 and his r accompanies him.' "

## RECONCILE* [RECONCILED, RECONCILIATION, RECONCILING]
Ac 7:26 He tried to r them by saying, 'Men,
Eph 2:16 and in one body to r both of them
Col 1:20 and through him to r to himself all

## RECONCILED* [RECONCILE]
Mt 5:24 First go and be r to that person;
Lk 12:58 try hard to be r on the way, or your
Ro 5:10 we were r to him through the death
5:10 having been r, shall we be saved
1Co 7:11 or else be r to her husband.
2Co 5:18 who r us to himself through Christ
5:20 you on Christ's behalf: Be r to God.
Col 1:22 But now he has r you by Christ's

## RECONCILIATION* [RECONCILE]
Ro 5:11 whom we have now received r
11:15 For if their rejection brought r
2Co 5:18 Christ and gave us the ministry of r:
5:19 committed to us the message of r.

## RECONCILING* [RECONCILE]
2Co 5:19 that God was r the world to himself

## RECORD [RECORDED, RECORDS]
Ps 56: 8 R my misery; list my tears on your
130: 3 you, LORD, kept a r of sins, Lord,

Hos 13:12  is stored up, his sins are kept on **r**.
1Co 13: 5  angered, it keeps no **r** of wrongs.

## RECORDED  [RECORD]

Nu  33: 2  command Moses **r** the stages
Jos 24:26  Joshua **r** these things in the Book
1Ch  9: 1  in the genealogies **r** in the book
Est  9:20  Mordecai **r** these events, and he sent
Job 19:23  that my words were **r**, that they
Jn  20:30  which are not **r** in this book.
Rev 20:12  to what they had done as **r**

## RECORDS  [RECORD]

1Ch  4:22  (These **r** are from ancient times.)
Ezr  2:62  These searched for their family **r**,
Ne  7:64  These searched for their family **r**,

## RECOUNT*

Ps 119:13  With my lips I **r** all the laws

## RECOVER  [RECOVERY]

Isa 38: 1  are going to die; you will not **r**."

## RECOVERY  [RECOVER]

Isa 38: 9  king of Judah after his illness and **r**:
Ro  11:11  they stumble so as to fall beyond **r**?

## RED

Ge  25:25  The first to come out was **r**, and his
Ex  15: 4  officers are drowned in the **R** Sea.
    25: 5  ram skins dyed **r** and another
Nu  19: 2  bring you a **r** heifer without defect
2Ki  3:22  across the way, the water looked **r**—
Ps 106: 9  He rebuked the **R** Sea, and it dried
Pr  23:31  Do not gaze at wine when it is **r**,
Isa  1:18  though they are **r** as crimson,
Zec  1: 8  was a man mounted on a **r** horse.
    6: 2  The first chariot had **r** horses,
Mt  16: 3  for the sky is **r** and overcast.'
Heb 11:29  people passed through the **R** Sca as
Rev  6: 4  horse came out, a fiery **r** one.
    6:12  the whole moon turned blood **r**,
    9:17  Their breastplates were fiery **r**,
    12: 3  an enormous **r** dragon with seven

## REDEDICATE*  [DEDICATE]

Nu  6:12  They must **r** themselves to the LORD

## REDEEM  [REDEEMED, REDEEMER, REDEEMS, REDEMPTION]

Ex  6: 6  and I will **r** you with an outstretched
    13:13  **R** every firstborn among your sons.
Lev 25:25  to come and **r** what they have sold.
Ru  4: 6  my own estate. You **r** it yourself.
2Sa  7:23  out to **r** as a people for himself,
Ps  31: 5  **r** me, LORD, my faithful God.
    44:26  **r** us because of your unfailing love.
    49: 7  No one can **r** the life of another
    49:15  God will **r** me from the realm
    130: 8  He himself will **r** Israel from all
Hos 13:14  I will **r** them from death.
Lk  24:21  the one who was going to **r** Israel.
Gal  4: 5  to **r** those under the law, that we
Tit  2:14  for us to **r** us from all wickedness

## REDEEMED  [REDEEM]

Ex  15:13  you will lead the people you have **r**.
Dt  15:15  and the LORD your God **r** you.
Ne  1:10  whom you **r** by your great strength
Ps  71:23  praise to you—I, whom you have **r**.
    107: 2  Let the **r** of the LORD tell their
Isa  35: 9  But only the **r** will walk there,
    44:22  Return to me, for I have **r** you."
    63: 9  In his love and mercy he **r** them;
Lk  1:68  has come to his people and **r** them.
Gal  3:13  Christ **r** us from the curse of the law
1Pe  1:18  that you were **r** from the empty way
Rev 14: 3  except the 144,000 who had been **r**

## REDEEMER  [REDEEM]

Job 19:25  I know that my **r** lives,
Ps  19:14  sight, LORD, my Rock and my **R**.
    78:35  that God Most High was their **R**.
Isa  44: 6  Israel's King and **R**, the LORD
    48:17  your **R**, the Holy One of Israel:
    59:20  "The **R** will come to Zion, to those

## REDEEMS*  [REDEEM]

Ps  34:22  The LORD **r** his servants;
    103: 4  who **r** your life from the pit

## REDEMPTION  [REDEEM]

Ru  4: 7  for the **r** and transfer of property
Ps 130: 7  unfailing love and with him is full **r**.
Lk  2:38  forward to the **r** of Jerusalem.
    21:28  because your **r** is drawing near."
Ro  3:24  by his grace through the **r** that came
    8:23  our adoption, the **r** of our bodies.
1Co  1:30  is, our righteousness, holiness and **r**.
Eph  1: 7  In him we have **r** through his blood,
    1:14  our inheritance until the **r** of those
    4:30  you were sealed for the day of **r**.
Col  1:14  in whom we have **r**, the forgiveness
Heb  9:12  own blood, thus obtaining eternal **r**.

## REDUCE  [REDUCED]

2Ki 10:32  days the LORD began to **r** the size
Jer  10:24  anger, or you will **r** me to nothing.

## REDUCED  [REDUCE]

Ps  79: 1  they have **r** Jerusalem to rubble.
Eze 16:27  against you and **r** your territory;

## REED  [REEDS]

2Ki 18:21  that splintered **r** of a staff,
Isa  42: 3  A bruised **r** he will not break,
Mt  12:20  A bruised **r** he will not break,
Lk  7:24  A **r** swayed by the wind?

## REEDS  [REED]

Ex  2: 3  put it among the **r** along the bank

## REEL  [REELED, REELING, REELS]

Isa  28: 7  stagger from wine and **r** from beer:

## REELED*  [REEL]

Ps 107:27  They **r** and staggered like

### REELING* [REEL]
Zec 12: 2 sends all the surrounding peoples r.

### REELS* [REEL]
Isa 24:20 The earth r like a drunkard, it sways

### REFINE* [REFINED, REFINER]
Jer 9: 7 "See, I will r and test them,
Zec 13: 9 I will r them like silver and test
Mal 3: 3 the Levites and r them like gold

### REFINED [REFINE]
Job 28: 1 silver and a place where gold is r.
Ps 12: 6 a crucible, like gold r seven times.
Isa 48:10 I have r you, though not as silver;
Da 12:10 made spotless and r, but the wicked
1Pe 1: 7 perishes even though r by fire—

### REFINER* [REFINE]
Mal 3: 3 He will sit as a r and purifier

### REFLECT [REFLECTION, REFLECTS]
Ecc 5:20 seldom r on the days of their lives,

### REFLECTION* [REFLECT]
1Co 13:12 now we see only a r as in a mirror;

### REFLECTS* [REFLECT]
Pr 27:19 As water r the face, so one's life r the
heart.

### REFORM
Jer 18:11 and r your ways and your actions.'

### REFRAIN
Ps 37: 8 R from anger and turn from wrath;
Ecc 3: 5 a time to embrace and a time to r,

### REFRESH [REFRESHED, REFRESHES,
REFRESHING]
Jer 31:25 I will r the weary and satisfy
Phm 1:20 in the Lord; r my heart in Christ.

### REFRESHED [REFRESH]
Ps 68: 9 you r your weary inheritance.
Pr 11:25 whoever refreshes others will be r.

### REFRESHES [REFRESH]
Ps 23: 3 he r my soul. He guides me

### REFRESHING* [REFRESH]
Ps 19: 7 the LORD is perfect, r the soul.
Ac 3:19 times of r may come from the Lord,

### REFUGE
Nu 35:11 some towns to be your cities of r,
Dt 33:27 The eternal God is your r,
Jos 20: 2 Israelites to designate the cities of r,
Ru 2:12 wings you have come to take r."
2Sa 22: 3 stronghold, my r and my savior—
22:31 He shields all who take r in him.
Ps 2:12 Blessed are all who take r in him.

Ps 5:11 let all who take r in you be glad;
9: 9 The LORD is a r
11: 1 In the LORD I take r.
16: 1 safe, my God, for in you I take r.
17: 7 your right hand those who take r
31: 2 be my rock of r, a strong fortress
34: 8 blessed are those who take r in him.
36: 7 People take r in the shadow of your
46: 1 God is our r and strength,
59:16 fortress, my r in times of trouble.
62: 8 your hearts to him, for God is our r.
71: 1 In you, LORD, I have taken r;
91: 2 "He is my r and my fortress,
118: 8 better to take r in the LORD than
144: 2 in whom I take r, who subdues
Pr 14:26 and for their children it will be a r.
14:32 in death the righteous seek r in God.
30: 5 a shield to those who take r in him.
Isa 25: 4 You have been a r for the poor, a r
Jer 16:19 my fortress, my r in time of distress,
Na 1: 7 is good, a r in times of trouble.

### REFUSE [REFUSED]
Ex 8: 2 If you r to let them go, I will send
Lev 26:21 toward me and r to listen to me,
Nu 14:11 How long will they r to believe
Eze 3:27 and whoever will r let them r;
Jn 5:40 yet you r to come to me to have life.
Heb 12:25 it that you do not r him who speaks.

### REFUSED [REFUSE]
Ex 13:15 Pharaoh stubbornly r to let us go,
Jdg 2:19 They r to give up their evil practices
Jer 5: 3 crushed them, but they r correction.
2Th 2:10 They perish because they r to love
Heb 12:25 when they r him who warned them
Rev 16: 9 but they r to repent and glorify him.

### REFUTE [REFUTED]
Job 32: 3 they had found no way to r Job,
Tit 1: 9 doctrine and r those who oppose it.

### REFUTED* [REFUTE]
Ac 18:28 For he vigorously r the Jews

### REGARD [REGARDED, REGARDS]
1Sa 2:12 they had no r for the LORD.
Ps 41: 1 Blessed are those who have r
74:20 Have r for your covenant,
Isa 8:13 is the one you are to r as holy, he is
Ro 14: 6 Those who r one day as special
1Co 14:20 In r to evil be infants, but in your
1Th 5:13 in the highest r in love because

### REGARDED [REGARD]
Ex 11: 3 and Moses himself was highly r
Isa 40:17 they are r by him as worthless
Ac 5:13 even though they were highly r
2Co 5:16 Though we once r Christ in this
Heb 11:26 He r disgrace for the sake of Christ

### REGARDS [REGARD]
Ro 14:14 if anyone r something as unclean,

## REGIONS

2Co 10:16  the gospel in the **r** beyond you.
Eph  4: 9  descended to the lower, earthly **r**?

## REGISTER

Lk   2: 5  He went there to **r** with Mary,

## REGRET [REGRETTED]

1Sa 15:11  "I **r** that I have made Saul king,
2Co  7:10  leads to salvation and leaves no **r**,

## REGRETTED* [REGRET]

Ge   6: 6  LORD **r** that he had made human beings
1Sa 15:35  the LORD **r** that he had made Saul king

## REGULAR

Nu  28: 3  as a **r** burnt offering each day.
2Ki 25:30  gave Jehoiachin a **r** allowance as

## REGULATION [REGULATIONS]

Heb  7:18  The former **r** is set aside because it

## REGULATIONS [REGULATION]

Ex  12:43  "These are the **r** for the Passover:
Lev 26:46  the **r** that the LORD established
Dt  12:28  to obey all these **r** I am giving you,
Col  2:23  Such **r** indeed have an appearance
Heb  9:10  external **r** applying until the time

## REHOBOAM

Son of Solomon (1Ki 11:43; 1Ch 3:10). Harsh treatment of subjects caused divided kingdom (1Ki 12:1–24; 14:21–31; 2Ch 10–12).

## REIGN [REIGNED, REIGNS]

Dt  17:20  his descendants will **r** a long time
1Sa  8:11  the king who will **r** over you will
Ps  68:16  mountain where God chooses to **r**,
Pr   8:15  By me kings **r** and rulers issue
Isa  9: 7  He will **r** on David's throne
    24:23  for the LORD Almighty will **r**
    32: 1  a king will **r** in righteousness
Jer 23: 5  a King who will **r** wisely and do
La   5:19  You, LORD, **r** forever;
Eze 20:33  I will **r** over you with a mighty hand
Lk   1:33  he will **r** over the house of Jacob
Ro   6:12  Therefore do not let sin **r** in your
1Co  4: 8  You have begun to **r**
    15:25  For he must **r** until he has put all his
2Ti  2:12  we endure, we will also **r** with him.
Rev  5:10  God, and they will **r** on the earth."
    11:15  and he will **r** for ever and ever."
    11:17  great power and have begun to **r**.
    20: 6  will **r** with him for a thousand years.
    22: 5  And they will **r** for ever and ever.

## REIGNED [REIGN]

Ro   5:21  so that, just as sin **r** in death,
Rev 20: 4  and **r** with Christ a thousand years.

## REIGNS [REIGN]

Ex  15:18  "The LORD **r** for ever and ever."
Ps   9: 7  The LORD **r** forever;
    47: 8  God **r** over the nations;

Ps  93: 1  The LORD **r**, he is robed
    96:10  the nations, "The LORD **r**."
    97: 1  The LORD **r**, let the earth be glad;
    99: 1  The LORD **r**, let the nations
   146:10  The LORD **r** forever, your God,
Isa 52: 7  who say to Zion, "Your God **r**!"
Lk  22:53  is your hour—when darkness **r**."
Rev 19: 6  For our Lord God Almighty **r**.

## REIN

Jas  1:26  and yet do not keep a tight **r** on their

## REJECT [REJECTED, REJECTION, REJECTS]

Lev 26:15  if you **r** my decrees and abhor my
1Sa 12:22  the LORD will not **r** his people,
2Ch  7:20  will **r** this temple I have consecrated
Ps  44:23  Rouse yourself! Do not **r** us forever.
    94:14  the LORD will not **r** his people;
Isa 31: 7  day every one of you will **r** the idols
Hos  4: 6  I also **r** you as my priests;
Jn  12:48  a judge for those who **r** me
Ro  11: 1  I ask then: Did God **r** his people?
1Th  4: 8  this instruction does not **r** a human
     5:22  **r** whatever is harmful.

## REJECTED [REJECT]

Nu  11:20  because you have **r** the LORD,
Dt  32:15  him and **r** the Rock his Savior.
1Sa  8: 7  not you they have **r**, but they have **r** me
            as their king.
    15:23  he has **r** you as king."
1Ki 12: 8  Rehoboam **r** the advice the elders
    19:10  The Israelites have **r** your covenant,
2Ki 17:15  They **r** his decrees and the covenant
    17:20  Therefore the LORD **r** all
Ps  60: 1  You have **r** us, God, and burst
    66:20  to God, who has not **r** my prayer
   118:22  stone the builders **r** has become
Isa  5:24  for they have **r** the law
    41: 9  chosen you and have not **r** you.
    53: 3  He was despised and **r** by others,
Jer  8: 9  Since they have **r** the word
    14:19  Have you **r** Judah completely?
Hos  8: 3  But Israel has **r** what is good;
Zec 10: 6  will be as though I had not **r** them,
Mt  21:42  stone the builders **r** has become
Mk   9:12  of Man must suffer much and be **r**?
Ac   4:11  is " 'the stone you builders **r**,
1Ti  4: 4  nothing is to be **r** if it is received
Heb 10:28  Anyone who **r** the law of Moses
1Pe  2: 4  **r** by human beings but chosen
     2: 7  stone the builders **r** has become

## REJECTION* [REJECT]

Ro  11:15  if their **r** brought reconciliation

## REJECTS [REJECT]

Lk  10:16  listens to me; whoever **r** you **r** me;
    10:16  whoever **r** me **r** him who sent me."
Jn   3:36  whoever **r** the Son will not see life,
1Th  4: 8  anyone who **r** this instruction does

## REJOICE [JOY]

Dt  12: 7  shall **r** in everything you have put

Dt 32:43 **R**, you nations, with his people,
1Ch 16:10 of those who seek the LORD **r**.
   16:31 Let the heavens **r**, let the earth be
2Ch 6:41 may your faithful people **r** in your
Ps 5:11 those who love your name may **r**
   9:14 Zion, and there **r** in your salvation.
  14: 7 let Jacob **r** and Israel be glad!
  31: 7 I will be glad and **r** in your love,
  34: 2 let the afflicted hear and **r**.
  51: 8 let the bones you have crushed **r**.
  63:11 But the king will **r** in God;
  64:10 The righteous will **r** in the LORD
  66: 6 come, let us **r** in him.
  68: 3 righteous be glad and **r** before God;
  89:16 They **r** in your name all day long;
  97: 1 let the distant shores **r**.
 104:31 may the LORD **r** in his works—
 105: 3 of those who seek the LORD **r**.
 118:24 let us **r** today and be glad.
 119:14 I **r** in following your statutes as one
 119:162 I **r** in your promise like one who
 149: 2 Let Israel **r** in their Maker;
Pr 5:18 may you **r** in the wife of your youth.
  23:25 May your father and mother **r**;
  24:17 stumble, do not let your heart **r**,
  29: 2 the righteous thrive, the people **r**;
Isa 9: 3 they **r** before you as people **r**
  29:19 the needy will **r** in the Holy One
  35: 1 the wilderness will **r** and blossom.
  61: 7 of disgrace you will **r** in your
  62: 5 bride, so will your God **r** over you.
Jer 31:12 they will **r** in the bounty
Hab 3:18 yet I will **r** in the LORD, I will be
Zep 3:17 but will **r** over you with singing."
Zec 9: 9 **R** greatly, Daughter Zion!
Lk 6:23 "**R** in that day and leap for joy,
  10:20 but **r** that your names are written
  15: 6 together and says, '**R** with me;
  15: 9 together and says, '**R** with me;
Ro 12:15 **R** with those who **r**;
  16:19 so I **r** because of you;
Php 2:17 I am glad and **r** with all of you.
  3: 1 brothers and sisters, **r** in the Lord!
  4: 4 **R** in the Lord always. I will say it
      again: **R**!
1Th 5:16 **R** always,
1Pe 4:13 **r** inasmuch as you participate
Rev 18:20 **R**, apostles and prophets!
  19: 7 Let us **r** and be glad and give him

## REJOICED [JOY]

1Ch 29: 9 The people **r** at the willing response
Job 31:25 if I have **r** over my great wealth,
Ps 122: 1 I **r** with those who said to me,
Jn 8:56 Your father Abraham **r**

## REJOICES [JOY]

1Sa 2: 1 "My heart **r** in the LORD;
Ps 13: 5 my heart **r** in your salvation.
  16: 9 my heart is glad and my tongue **r**;
Pr 11:10 the righteous prosper, the city **r**;
  23:24 fathers a wise son **r** in him.
Isa 61:10 my soul **r** in my God.
  62: 5 as a bridegroom **r** over his bride,
Lk 1:47 and my spirit **r** in God my Savior,
Ac 2:26 my heart is glad and my tongue **r**;

1Co 12:26 part is honored, every part **r** with it.
  13: 6 delight in evil but **r** with the truth.

## REJOICING [JOY]

2Sa 6:12 to the City of David with **r**.
Ne 12:43 The sound of **r** in Jerusalem could
Ps 30: 5 a night, but **r** comes in the morning.
Pr 8:30 after day, **r** always in his presence,
  14:13 and **r** may end in grief.
Lk 15: 7 the same way there will be more **r**
Ac 5:41 **r** because they had been counted
2Co 6:10 sorrowful, yet always **r**;

## REKAB

Jer 35: 6 Jehonadab son of **R** gave us this

## REKABITES

Jer 35: 3 the whole family of the **R**.

## RELATE*

Ps 71:15 though I know not how to **r** them all.

## RELATIONS

Ex 22:19 "Anyone who has sexual **r**
Lev 18: 6 any close relative to have sexual **r**.
  18:22 " 'Do not have sexual **r** with a man
  20:13 " 'If a man has sexual **r** with a man
Ro 1:26 women exchanged natural sexual **r**
1Co 7: 1 man not to have sexual **r** with a
      woman."

## RELATIONSHIP

Jn 1:18 closest **r** with the Father,

## RELATIVE [RELATIVES]

Lev 18: 6 approach any close **r** to have sexual
  25:25 their nearest **r** is to come
Ru 2:20 added, "That man is our close **r**;
  3: 2 is a **r** of ours.
Pr 7: 4 and to insight, "You are my **r**."
  27:10 better a neighbor nearby than a **r** far

## RELATIVES [RELATIVE]

Lev 25:48 One of their **r** may redeem them:
Pr 19: 7 The poor are shunned by all their **r**—
Mk 6: 4 among their **r** and in their own
Lk 21:16 sisters, **r** and friends, and they will
1Ti 5: 8 who does not provide for their **r**,

## RELEASE [RELEASED]

Isa 61: 1 **r** from darkness for the prisoners,
Mt 27:15 the festival to **r** a prisoner chosen

## RELEASED [RELEASE]

Lev 25:54 their children are to be **r** in the Year
  27:21 When the field is **r** in the Jubilee,
2Ki 25:27 he **r** Jehoiachin king of Judah
Mk 15:15 crowd, Pilate **r** Barabbas to them.
Ac 3:14 asked that a murderer be **r** to you.
Ro 7: 2 she is **r** from the law that binds her
  7: 6 we have been **r** from the law so
1Co 7:27 Do not seek to be **r**.
Rev 20: 7 over, Satan will be **r** from his prison

## RELENT [RELENTED, RELENTS]
Ex   32:12   **r** and do not bring disaster on your
Dt   32:36   LORD will vindicate his people and **r**
Ps  135:14   vindicate his people and **r** concerning
              his servants.
Jer  18: 8   then I will **r** and not inflict on it
     26: 3   I will **r** and not inflict on them
Joel  2:14   may turn and **r** and leave
Jnh   3: 9   God may yet **r** and with compassion

## RELENTED* [RELENT]
Ex   32:14   the LORD **r** and did not bring
Jdg   2:18   LORD **r** because of their groaning
2Sa  24:16   the LORD **r** concerning the disaster
1Ch  21:15   saw it and **r** concerning the disaster
Ps  106:45   and out of his great love he **r**.
Jer  42:10   I have **r** concerning the disaster
Am   7: 3   So the LORD **r**. "This will not
     7: 6   So the LORD **r**. "This will not
Jnh   3:10   turned from their evil ways, he **r**

## RELENTS* [RELENT]
Joel  2:13   and he **r** from sending calamity.
Jnh   4: 2   a God who **r** from sending calamity.

## RELIABLE [RELY]
2Ti   2: 2   entrust to **r** people who will also be
2Pe   1:19   message as something completely **r**,

## RELIANCE* [RELY]
Ps   26: 3   lived in **r** on your faithfulness.
Pr   25:19   a lame foot is **r** on the unfaithful

## RELIED [RELY]
2Ch  13:18   were victorious because they **r**
     16: 8   Yet when you **r** on the LORD,
Ps   71: 6   From birth I have **r** on you;

## RELIEF
1Sa   8:18   cry out for **r** from the king you have
Est   4:14   **r** and deliverance for the Jews will
      9:22   the Jews got **r** from their enemies,
Job  35: 9   they plead for **r** from the arm
Ps   94:13   you grant them **r** from days
    143: 1   and righteousness come to my **r**.
La    3:49   will flow unceasingly, without **r**,
      3:56   not close your ears to my cry for **r**."
2Th   1: 7   and give **r** to you who are troubled,

## RELIES* [RELY]
Isa  28:16   one who **r** on it will never be stricken

## RELIGION* [RELIGIOUS]
Ac   25:19   dispute with him about their own **r**
     26: 5   to the strictest sect of our **r**,
1Ti   5: 4   of all to put their **r** into practice
Jas   1:26   themselves, and their **r** is worthless.
      1:27   **R** that God our Father accepts as

## RELIGIOUS [RELIGION]
Am    5:21   "I hate, I despise your **r** festivals;
Col   2:16   or with regard to a **r** festival, a New
Jas   1:26   Those who consider themselves **r**

## RELY [RELIABLE, RELIANCE, RELIED, RELIES]
2Ch  14:11   for we **r** on you, and in your name
Ps   59:10   my God on whom I can **r**.
     59:17   my God on whom I can **r**.
Isa  50:10   of the LORD and **r** on their God.
Eze  33:26   You **r** on your sword, you do
Ro    2:17   if you **r** on the law and boast
2Co   1: 9   that we might not **r** on ourselves
Gal   3:10   All who **r** on observing the law are
1Jn   4:16   and **r** on the love God has for us.

## REMAIN [REMAINED, REMAINS]
Nu   33:55   you allow to **r** will become barbs
Jos  23: 7   with these nations that **r** among you;
Jdg   2:23   had allowed those nations to **r**
2Ch  33: 4   said, "My Name will **r** in Jerusalem
Ps  102:27   But you **r** the same, and your years
Jn    1:32   heaven as a dove and **r** on him.
     15: 4   **R** in me, as I also **r** in you.
     15: 4   can you bear fruit unless you **r**
     15: 5   If you **r** in me and I in you,
     15: 7   If you **r** in me and my words **r**
     15: 9   have I loved you. Now **r** in my love.
Ro   13: 8   Let no debt **r** outstanding,
1Co   7:20   of you should **r** in the situation you
     13:13   And now these three **r**:
Heb   1:11   They will perish, but you **r**;
1Jn   2:27   just as it has taught you, **r** in him.
Rev   2:13   Yet you **r** true to my name.
     14:12   commands and **r** faithful to Jesus.

## REMAINED [REMAIN]
2Sa  11: 1   But David **r** in Jerusalem.
Mk   14:61   But Jesus **r** silent and gave no
1Jn   2:19   to us, they would have **r** with us;
Rev  14: 4   for they **r** virgins.

## REMAINS [REMAIN]
Dt   24:20   Leave what **r** for the foreigner,
Jos  13: 2   "This is the land that **r**:
Ps  146: 6   he **r** faithful forever.
Hag   2: 5   And my Spirit **r** among you.
Jn    3:36   see life, for God's wrath **r** on them.
      6:56   flesh and drinks my blood **r** in me,
2Co   3:14   to this day the same veil **r**
2Ti   2:13   if we are faithless, he **r** faithful,
Heb   7: 3   Son of God, he **r** a priest forever.
1Jn   3: 9   sin, because God's seed **r** in them;

## REMARKABLE*
Mk    6: 2   these **r** miracles he is performing?
Lk    5:26   "We have seen **r** things today."
Jn    9:30   The man answered, "Now that is **r**!

## REMEDY*
2Ch  36:16   his people and there was no **r**.
Pr    6:15   suddenly be destroyed—without **r**.
     29: 1   suddenly be destroyed—without **r**.
Isa   3: 7   day he will cry out, "I have no **r**.
Jer  30:13   plead your cause, no **r** for your sore,
Mic   2:10   is defiled, it is ruined, beyond all **r**.

## REMEMBER [REMEMBERED, REMEMBERS, REMEMBRANCE]

Ge 9:15 I will r my covenant between me
Ex 20: 8 "R the Sabbath day by keeping it
33:13 R that this nation is your people."
Lev 26:42 I will r my covenant with Jacob
Dt 5:15 R that you were slaves in Egypt
8:18 But r the LORD your God, for it is
Jos 1:13 "R the command that Moses
1Ch 16:12 R the wonders he has done,
Ne 5:19 R me with favor, my God, for all I
13:31 R me with favor, my God.
Job 10: 9 R that you molded me like clay.
36:24 R to extol his work, which people
Ps 25: 6 R, LORD, your great mercy
63: 6 On my bed I r you; I think of you
74: 2 R the people you purchased long
77:11 I will r the deeds of the LORD;
Ecc 12: 1 R your Creator in the days of your
Isa 46: 8 "R this, keep it in mind, take it
64: 9 do not r our sins forever.
Jer 31:34 and will r their sins no more."
La 5: 1 R, LORD, what has happened
Eze 36:31 Then you will r your evil ways
Hos 7: 2 realize that I r all their evil deeds.
Hab 3: 2 in wrath r mercy.
Mk 8:18 but fail to hear? And don't you r?
Lk 1:72 and to r his holy covenant,
17:32 R Lot's wife!
23:42 r me when you come into your
Gal 2:10 we should continue to r the poor,
Php 1: 3 I thank my God every time I r you.
2Ti 2: 8 R Jesus Christ, raised from the dead,
Heb 8:12 and will r their sins no more."
Jas 5:20 r this: Whoever turns a sinner
Rev 3: 3 R, therefore, what you have

## REMEMBERED [REMEMBER]

Ge 8: 1 But God r Noah and all the wild
19:29 cities of the plain, he r Abraham,
30:22 Then God r Rachel; he listened
Ex 2:24 he r his covenant with Abraham,
6: 5 and I have r my covenant.
1Sa 1:19 wife Hannah, and the LORD r her.
Ps 78:35 They r that God was their Rock,
98: 3 He has r his love and his
106:45 for their sake he r his covenant
111: 4 He has caused his wonders to be r;
136:23 He r us in our low estate
Isa 17:10 you have not r the Rock,
65:17 The former things will not be r,
Eze 18:22 committed will be r against them.
33:13 things they have done will be r;
Mt 26:75 Peter r the word Jesus had spoken:
Jn 2:17 His disciples r that it is written:
Rev 16:19 God r Babylon the Great and gave
18: 5 heaven, and God has r her crimes.

## REMEMBERS [REMEMBER]

1Ch 16:15 He r his covenant forever,
Ps 103:14 are formed, he r that we are dust.
111: 5 he r his covenant forever.
Isa 43:25 own sake, and r your sins no more.

## REMEMBRANCE [REMEMBER]

Lk 22:19 given for you; do this in r of me."
1Co 11:24 is for you; do this in r of me."

## REMIND [REMINDER]

Jn 14:26 will r you of everything I have said
2Pe 1:12 So I will always r you of these

## REMINDER [REMIND]

Ex 13: 9 a r on your forehead that this law
Heb 10: 3 those sacrifices are an annual r

## REMISSION (KJV) See FORGIVENESS

## REMNANT

Ge 45: 7 you to preserve for you a r on earth
2Ki 19:31 For out of Jerusalem will come a r,
2Ch 36:20 carried into exile to Babylon the r,
Ezr 9: 8 has been gracious in leaving us a r
Ne 1: 2 the Jewish r that had survived
Isa 10:21 A r will return, a r of Jacob will
11:11 reclaim the surviving r of his people
Jer 23: 3 "I myself will gather the r of my
50:20 for I will forgive the r I spare.
Zec 8:12 inheritance to the r of this people.
Ro 9:27 by the sea, only the r will be saved.
11: 5 the present time there is a r chosen

## REMOTE

Lev 16:22 itself all their sins to a r place;

## REMOVAL* [REMOVE]

Isa 27: 9 be the full fruit of the r of his sin:
1Pe 3:21 not the r of dirt from the body

## REMOVE [REMOVAL, REMOVED]

Ex 12:15 the first day r the yeast from your
Job 9:34 someone to r God's rod from me,
Ps 39:10 R your scourge from me;
119:22 R from me their scorn
Isa 1:25 your dross and r all your impurities.
Eze 36:26 I will r from you your heart of stone
Zec 3: 9 'and I will r the sin of this land
Lk 6:42 you will see clearly to r the speck

## REMOVED [REMOVE]

2Ki 17:18 Israel and r them from his presence.
Ps 30:11 you r my sackcloth and clothed me
103:12 so far has he r our transgressions
Jn 20: 1 that the stone had been r
2Co 3:14 It has not been r, because only
Rev 6:14 and island was r from its place.

## REND*

Isa 64: 1 that you would r the heavens
Joel 2:13 R your heart and not your garments.

## RENEW [RENEWAL, RENEWED, RENEWING]

Ps 51:10 and r a steadfast spirit within me.
Isa 40:31 in the LORD will r their strength.
La 5:21 we may return; r our days as of old
Hab 3: 2 R them in our day, in our time make

## RENEWAL* [RENEW]
Job 14:14 service I will wait for my **r** to come.
Isa 57:10 You found **r** of your strength,
Mt 19:28 at the **r** of all things, when the Son
Tit  3: 5 of rebirth and **r** by the Holy Spirit,

## RENEWED [RENEW]
2Ch 34:31 **r** the covenant in the presence
Ps 103: 5 that your youth is **r** like the eagle's.
2Co  4:16 yet inwardly we are being **r** day
Col  3:10 which is being **r** in knowledge

## RENEWING* [RENEW]
Ro 12: 2 transformed by the **r** of your mind.

## RENOUNCE* [RENOUNCED]
Pr  28:13 confess and **r** them find mercy.
Eze 14: 6 and **r** all your detestable practices!
Da  4:27 **R** your sins by doing what is right,
Rev  2:13 You did not **r** your faith in me,

## RENOUNCED* [RENOUNCE]
Ps 89:39 You have **r** the covenant with your
Mt 19:12 others have **r** marriage because
2Co  4: 2 we have **r** secret and shameful

## RENOWN*
Ge  6: 4 were the heroes of old, men of **r**.
Ps 102:12 your **r** endures through all
   135:13 endures forever, your **r**, LORD,
Isa 26: 8 and **r** are the desire of our hearts.
   55:13 This will be for the LORD's **r**,
   63:12 to gain for himself everlasting **r**,
Jer 13:11 'to be my people for my **r**
   32:20 have gained the **r** that is still yours.
   33: 9 Then this city will bring me **r**, joy,
   49:25 the city of **r** not been abandoned,
Eze 26:17 city of **r**, peopled by men of the sea!

## REPAID [PAY]
Pr  14:14 The faithless will be fully **r** for their
Jer 18:20 Should good be **r** with evil?
Lk  6:34 to sinners, expecting to be **r** in full.
   14:14 you will be **r** at the resurrection
Col  3:25 Those who do wrong will be **r**

## REPAIR [REPAIRED, REPAIRER, REPAIRING]
2Ch 24: 5 Israel, to **r** the temple of your God.
Ezr  9: 9 the house of our God and **r** its ruins,
Am  9:11 I will **r** its broken walls and restore

## REPAIRED [REPAIR]
2Ch 15: 8 He **r** the altar of the LORD
   29: 3 temple of the LORD and **r** them.
Ne  3: 4 son of Hakkoz, **r** the next section.
Jer 19:11 jar is smashed and cannot be **r**.

## REPAIRER* [REPAIR]
Isa 58:12 you will be called **R** of Broken

## REPAIRING [REPAIR]
2Ki 12: 7 "Why aren't you **r** the damage done
Ezr  4:12 the walls and **r** the foundations.

## REPAY [PAY]
Dt  7:10 those who hate him he will **r** to their
   32: 6 Is this the way you **r** the LORD,
   32:35 It is mine to avenge; I will **r**.
Ru  2:12 May the LORD **r** you for what you
Ps 28: 4 **R** them for their deeds and for their
   35:12 They **r** me evil for good and leave
   103:10 or **r** us according to our iniquities.
Isa 59:18 so will he **r** wrath to his enemies
Jer 25:14 I will **r** them according to their
   51:56 God of retribution; he will **r** in full.
Eze  7: 3 and **r** you for all your detestable
Joel  2:25 "I will **r** you for the years
Ro 12:17 Do not **r** anyone evil for evil.
   12:19 I will **r**," says the Lord.
Heb 10:30 I will **r**," and again, "The Lord will
1Pe  3: 9 Do not **r** evil with evil or insult
Rev  2:23 and I will **r** each of you according

## REPAYING [PAY]
1Ti  5: 4 own family and so **r** their parents

## REPEALED
Est  1:19 which cannot be **r**, that Vashti is
Da  6: 8 and Persians, which cannot be **r**."

## REPEAT [REPEATS, REPEATED]
Pr  26:11 so fools **r** their folly.

## REPEATED [REPEAT]
Heb 10: 1 the same sacrifices **r** endlessly year

## REPEATS* [REPEAT]
Pr  17: 9 whoever **r** the matter separates close

## REPENT [PENITENT, REPENTANCE, REPENTED, REPENTS]
1Ki  8:47 and **r** and plead with you in the land
Job 36:10 commands them to **r** of their evil.
   42: 6 I despise myself and **r** in dust
Isa 59:20 those in Jacob who **r** of their sins,"
Jer  8: 6 None of them **r** of their wickedness,
   15:19 "If you **r**, I will restore you that you
Eze 18:32 the Sovereign LORD. **R** and live!
Mt  3: 2 and saying, "**R**, for the kingdom
   4:17 time on Jesus began to preach, "**R**,
Mk  6:12 and preached that people should **r**.
Lk 13: 3 But unless you **r**, you too will all
   17: 3 and if they **r**, forgive them.
Ac  2:38 Peter replied, "**R** and be baptized,
   3:19 **R**, then, and turn to God,
   17:30 all people everywhere to **r**.
   26:20 I preached that they should **r**
Rev  2: 5 **R** and do the things you did at first.
   2:21 I have given her time to **r** of her
   9:20 by these plagues still did not **r**
   16: 9 they refused to **r** and glorify him.

## REPENTANCE [REPENT]
Isa 30:15 "In **r** and rest is your salvation,
Mt  3: 8 Produce fruit in keeping with **r**.
Mk  1: 4 preaching a baptism of **r**
Lk  3: 8 Produce fruit in keeping with **r**.
   5:32 call the righteous, but sinners to **r**."

Lk 24:47 **r** for the forgiveness of sins will be
Ac 5:31 that he might bring Israel to **r**
11:18 to Gentiles God has granted **r**
20:21 that they must turn to God in **r**
26:20 demonstrate their **r** by their deeds.
Ro 2: 4 is intended to lead you to **r**?
2Co 7:10 Godly sorrow brings **r** that leads
2Ti 2:25 God will grant them **r** leading them
Heb 6: 1 not laying again the foundation of **r**
2Pe 3: 9 to perish, but everyone to come to **r**.

## REPENTED [REPENT]
2Ch 32:26 Hezekiah **r** of the pride of his heart,
Zec 1: 6 "Then they **r** and said,
Mt 11:21 they would have **r** long ago
Lk 11:32 for they **r** at the preaching of Jonah;

## REPENTS* [REPENT]
Eze 33:12 And if someone who is wicked **r**,
Jer 18: 8 if that nation I warned **r** of its evil,
Lk 15: 7 over one sinner who **r** than over
15:10 of God over one sinner who **r**."

## REPHAITES
Ge 15:20 Hittites, Perizzites, **R**,
Dt 2:11 they too were considered **R**,
1Ch 20: 4 one of the descendants of the **R**,

## REPLANTED* [PLANT]
Eze 36:36 and have **r** what was desolate.

## REPLY
Pr 15:23 person finds joy in giving an apt **r**—
Mt 27:14 But Jesus made no **r**, not even

## REPORT [REPORTS]
Ge 37: 2 he brought their father a bad **r**
Nu 13:32 spread among the Israelites a bad **r**
1Ki 10: 7 you have far exceeded the **r** I heard.
Lk 7:22 and **r** to John what you have seen

## REPORTS [REPORT]
Ex 23: 1 "Do not spread false **r**. Do not help
Mt 14: 1 time Herod the tetrarch heard the **r**
Ac 9:13 "I have heard many **r** about this

## REPOSES*
Pr 14:33 Wisdom **r** in the heart

## REPRESENT [REPRESENTATION]
Da 8:22 was broken off **r** four kingdoms
Gal 4:24 for the women **r** two covenants.
Heb 5: 1 is appointed to **r** them in matters

## REPRESENTATION* [REPRESENT]
Heb 1: 3 glory and the exact **r** of his being,

## REPRIMAND*
Ru 2:15 among the sheaves and don't **r** her.
Pr 29:15 A rod and a **r** impart wisdom,

## REPROACH
Jos 5: 9 "Today I have rolled away the **r**
Job 27: 6 my conscience will not **r** me as long

Isa 51: 7 Do not fear the **r** of mere mortals
Jer 20: 8 brought me insult and **r** all day long.
1Ti 3: 2 Now the overseer is to be above **r**,

## REPROVE*
1Ti 5:20 sinning you are to **r** before everyone,

## REPUTATION
1Ti 3: 7 also have a good **r** with outsiders,
Rev 3: 1 you have a **r** of being alive, but you

## REQUEST [REQUESTS]
Est 7: 3 And spare my people—this is my **r**.
Ps 21: 2 have not withheld the **r** of his lips.

## REQUESTS [REQUEST]
Ps 20: 5 May the LORD grant all your **r**.
Php 4: 6 thanksgiving, present your **r** to God.

## REQUIRE [REQUIRED,
## REQUIREMENT, REQUIREMENTS,
## REQUIRES]
Ps 40: 6 and sin offerings you did not **r**.
Mic 6: 8 what does the LORD **r** of you?

## REQUIRED [REQUIRE]
Ac 15: 5 and **r** to keep the law of Moses."
Ro 2:14 do by nature things **r** by the law,
1Co 4: 2 Now it is **r** that those who have

## REQUIREMENT [REQUIRE]
Ro 8: 4 righteous **r** of the law might be fully met

## REQUIREMENTS [REQUIRE]
Dt 11: 1 LORD your God and keep his **r**,
2Ki 23:24 did to fulfill the **r** of the law written
Jer 8: 7 my people do not know the **r**
Ro 2:15 that the **r** of the law are written

## REQUIRES [REQUIRE]
1Ki 2: 3 what the LORD your God **r**:
Jn 6:28 we do to do the works God **r**?"
Heb 9:22 the law **r** that nearly everything be

## RESCUE [RESCUED, RESCUES]
Ge 37:21 he tried to **r** him from their hands.
Ex 3: 8 So I have come down to **r** them
Dt 28:29 and robbed, with no one to **r** you.
1Sa 17:37 **r** me from the hand of this Philistine."
Job 5:19 From six calamities he will **r** you;
Ps 22: 8 they say, "let the LORD **r** him.
31: 2 ear to me, come quickly to my **r**;
35:10 You **r** the poor from those too
69:14 **R** me from the mire, do not let me
82: 4 **R** the weak and the needy;
91:14 says the LORD, "I will **r** them;
143: 9 **R** me from my enemies, LORD,
Isa 31: 5 he will 'pass over' it and will **r** it."
Jer 1: 8 for I am with you and will **r** you,"
Eze 34:10 I will **r** my flock from their mouths,
Da 6:20 been able to **r** you from the lions?"
Mt 27:43 Let God **r** him now if he wants him,
Ro 7:24 Who will **r** me from this body
Gal 1: 4 our sins to **r** us from the present evil

2Pe  2: 9  the Lord knows how to **r** the godly

## RESCUED [RESCUE]
Ex   18:10  who **r** the people from the hand
1Sa  11:13  this day the LORD has **r** Israel."
     17:37  who **r** me from the paw of the lion
Ps   18:17  He **r** me from my powerful enemy,
     81: 7  your distress you called and I **r** you,
Pr   11: 8  The righteous are **r** from trouble,
Isa  35:10  those the LORD has **r** will return.
     51:11  Those the LORD has **r** will return.
Da    3:28  sent his angel and **r** his servants!
      6:27  He has **r** Daniel from the power
Ac   12:11  and **r** me from Herod's clutches
Col   1:13  For he has **r** us from the dominion

## RESCUES* [RESCUE]
1Sa  14:39  as the LORD who **r** Israel lives,
Ps   55:18  He **r** me unharmed from the battle
Pr   12: 6  but the speech of the upright **r** them.
Jer  20:13  He **r** the life of the needy
Da    6:27  He **r** and he saves;
1Th   1:10  who **r** us from the coming wrath.

## RESEMBLED* [RESEMBLING]
Rev   9: 7  gold, and their faces **r** human faces.
      9:17  The heads of the horses **r** the heads
     13: 2  The beast I saw **r** a leopard, but had

## RESEMBLING* [RESEMBLED]
Heb   7: 3  **r** the Son of God, he remains a priest

## RESENT* [RESENTFUL, RESENTMENT]
Pr    3:11  discipline, and do not **r** his rebuke,
     15:12  Mockers **r** correction, so they avoid

## RESENTFUL* [RESENT]
2Ti   2:24  to everyone, able to teach, not **r**.

## RESENTMENT [RESENT]
Job   5: 2  **R** kills a fool, and envy slays
     36:13  "The godless in heart harbor **r**;

## RESERVE [RESERVED]
1Ki  19:18  Yet I **r** seven thousand in Israel—

## RESERVED [RESERVE]
Ge   27:36  "Haven't you **r** any blessing
Ro   11: 4  "I have **r** for myself seven thousand
2Pe   2:17  Blackest darkness is **r** for them.
      3: 7  heavens and earth are **r** for fire,

## RESETTLE* [SETTLE]
1Ch   9: 2  Now the first to **r** on their own
Eze  36:33  all your sins, I will **r** your towns,

## RESIDED
Ex    6: 4  where they **r** as foreigners.

## RESIST [RESISTED]
Jdg   2:14  whom they were no longer able to **r**.
Pr   28: 4  but those who heed it **r** them.

Da   11:32  know their God will firmly **r** him.
Mt    5:39  I tell you, do not **r** an evil person.
Lk   21:15  of your adversaries will be able to **r**
Ac    7:51  You always **r** the Holy Spirit!
Ro    9:19  who is able to **r** his will?"
Jas   4: 7  **R** the devil, and he will flee
1Pe   5: 9  **R** him, standing firm in the faith,

## RESISTED* [RESIST]
Job   9: 4  Who has **r** him and come
Da   10:13  Persian kingdom **r** me twenty-one
Heb  12: 4  you have not yet **r** to the point

## RESOLVE* [RESOLVED]
Mal   2: 2  if you do not **r** to honor my name,"

## RESOLVED* [RESOLVE]
2Ch  20: 3  Jehoshaphat **r** to inquire
Da    1: 8  Daniel **r** not to defile himself
Mal   2: 2  you have not **r** to honor me.
1Co   2: 2  For I **r** to know nothing while I was

## RESOUND [RESOUNDED, RESOUNDING]
Ps   98: 7  Let the sea **r**, and everything in it,
    118:15  joy and victory **r** in the tents

## RESOUNDED* [RESOUND]
2Sa  22:14  the voice of the Most High **r**.
Ps   18:13  the voice of the Most High **r**.
     77:17  water, the heavens **r** with thunder;

## RESOUNDING* [RESOUND]
2Ch  30:21  **r** instruments dedicated to the LORD.
Ps  150: 5  cymbals, praise him with **r** cymbals.
1Co  13: 1  I am only a **r** gong or a clanging

## RESPECT [RESPECTABLE, RESPECTED, RESPECTS]
Lev  19: 3  of you must **r** your mother
     19:32  show **r** for the elderly and revere
Mal   1: 6  a master, where is the **r** due me?"
Mk   12: 6  of all, saying, 'They will **r** my son.'
Ro   13: 7  if revenue, then revenue; if **r**, then **r**;
Eph   5:33  and the wife must **r** her husband.
      6: 5  obey your earthly masters with **r**
1Th   4:12  that your daily life may win the **r**
1Ti   3: 4  do so in a manner worthy of full **r**.
      3: 8  way, deacons are to be worthy of **r**,
      3:11  the women are to be worthy of **r**,
      6: 1  their masters worthy of full **r**,
Tit   2: 2  worthy of **r**, self-controlled,
1Pe   2:17  Show proper **r** to everyone,
      3: 7  them with **r** as the weaker partner

## RESPECTABLE* [RESPECT]
1Ti   3: 2  self-controlled, **r**, hospitable,

## RESPECTED [RESPECT]
Dt    1:13  and **r** men from each of your tribes,
Pr   31:23  Her husband is **r** at the city gate,
Heb  12: 9  disciplined us and we **r** them for it.

## RESPECTS [RESPECT]
Pr 13:13 whoever r a command is rewarded.

## RESPLENDENT*
Ps 76: 4 You are r with light, more majestic
132:18 will be adorned with a r crown."

## RESPOND [RESPONSE]
2Ch 32:25 he did not r to the kindness shown
Ps 102:17 He will r to the prayer
Pr 13: 1 mocker does not r to rebukes.
Isa 19:22 and he will r to their pleas and heal
Jer 2:30 they did not r to correction.
17:23 would not listen or r to discipline.
Hos 2:21 "In that day I will r,"
Ac 16:14 The Lord opened her heart to r

## RESPONSE [RESPOND]
1Ki 18:26 But there was no r;
1Ch 29: 9 at the willing r of their leaders,

## RESPONSIBILITIES [RESPONSIBLE]
Nu 8:26 are to assign the r of the Levites."

## RESPONSIBILITY [RESPONSIBLE]
Mt 27:24 blood," he said. "It is your r!"

## RESPONSIBLE [RESPONSIBILITIES, RESPONSIBILITY]
Nu 1:53 The Levites are to be r for the care
14:37 these men who were r for spreading
Jnh 1: 8 who is r for making all this trouble
Lk 11:50 this generation will be held r
1Co 7:24 all of you, as r to God,

## REST [RESTED, RESTING, RESTLESS, RESTS, SABBATH-REST]
Ge 8: 4 the seventh month the ark came to r
Ex 16:23 is to be a day of sabbath r, a holy
31:15 seventh day is a day of sabbath r,
33:14 go with you, and I will give you r."
Lev 23:24 you are to have a day of sabbath r,
25: 4 land is to have a year of sabbath r,
25: 5 The land is to have a year of r.
Nu 10:36 Whenever it came to r, he said,
Dt 12:10 and he will give you r from all your
Jos 1:13 LORD your God will give you r
11:23 Then the land had r from war.
14:15 Then the land had r from war.
21:44 The LORD gave them r on every
2Sa 7:11 give you r from all your enemies.
1Ki 5: 4 the LORD my God has given me r
1Ch 22: 9 who will be a man of peace and r,
28: 2 build a house as a place of r
Job 3:17 and there the weary are at r.
Ps 16: 9 my body also will r secure,
62: 1 Truly my soul finds r in God;
62: 5 Yes, my soul, find r in God;
90:17 favor of the Lord our God r on us;
91: 1 the Most High will r in the shadow
95:11 'They shall never enter my r.' "
Pr 6:10 a little folding of the hands to r—
Isa 11: 2 Spirit of the LORD will r on him—
30:15 repentance and r is your salvation,

Isa 32:18 homes, in undisturbed places of r.
44:17 From the r he makes a god, his idol;
57:20 which cannot r, whose waves cast
Jer 6:16 it, and you will find r for your souls.
47: 6 [you cry,] 'how long till you r?
Mt 11:28 and burdened, and I will give you r.
Mk 6:31 to a quiet place and get some r."
1Co 2: 5 your faith might not r on human
2Co 12: 9 so that Christ's power may r on me.
1Th 4:13 so that you do not grieve like the r,
Heb 3:11 'They shall never enter my r.' "
4: 3 we who have believed enter that r,
4:10 for those who enter God's r also r
Rev 14:11 There will be no r day or night
14:13 Spirit, "they will r from their labor,

## RESTED [REST]
Ge 2: 2 on the seventh day he r from all his
Ex 16:30 So the people r on the seventh day.
20:11 in them, but he r on the seventh day.
Nu 11:25 When the Spirit r on them,
2Ch 36:21 all the time of its desolation it r,
Heb 4: 4 the seventh day God r from all his

## RESTING [REST]
2Ki 2:15 spirit of Elijah is r on Elisha."
Ps 132: 8 and come to your r place,
Isa 11:10 and his r place will be glorious.
28:12 "This is the r place, let the weary

## RESTITUTION
Ex 22: 3 who steals must certainly make r,
Lev 6: 5 They must make r in full, add a fifth
Nu 5: 8 relative to whom r can be made

## RESTLESS [REST]
Ge 4:12 You will be a r wanderer
Jas 3: 8 It is a r evil, full of deadly poison.

## RESTORATION [RESTORE]
2Co 13:11 Strive for full r, encourage

## RESTORE [RESTORATION, RESTORED, RESTORES]
Dt 30: 3 your God will r your fortunes
2Ch 24: 4 later Joash decided to r the temple
Ne 4: 2 Will they r their wall?
Ps 51:12 R to me the joy of your salvation
80: 3 R us, O God; make your face shine
126: 4 R our fortunes, LORD,
Isa 49: 6 to be my servant to r the tribes
Jer 15:19 I will r you that you may serve me;
31:18 R me, and I will return, because you
La 5:21 R us to yourself, LORD, that we
Da 9:25 the time the word goes out to r
Hos 6: 2 on the third day he will r us, that we
Am 9:11 day I will r David's fallen shelter—
Na 2: 2 The LORD will r the splendor
Zec 9:12 announce that I will r twice as much
Mt 17:11 Elijah comes and will r all things.
Ac 1: 6 this time going to r the kingdom
15:16 ruins I will rebuild, and I will r it,
Gal 6: 1 by the Spirit should r that person
1Pe 5:10 will himself r you and make you

## RESTORED [RESTORE]
| | | |
|---|---|---|
| Ex | 4: 7 | it was **r**, like the rest of his flesh. |
| 2Ki | 5:10 | your flesh will be **r** and you will be |
| Job | 42:10 | the LORD **r** his fortunes |
| Ps | 85: 1 | you **r** the fortunes of Jacob. |
| Eze | 21:27 | The crown will not be **r** until he |
| Mk | 3: 5 | out, and his hand was completely **r**. |
| | 8:25 | opened, his sight was **r**, and he saw |
| 2Co | 13: 9 | is that you may be fully **r**. |

## RESTORES* [RESTORE]
| | | |
|---|---|---|
| Ps | 14: 7 | When the LORD **r** his people, |
| | 41: 3 | and **r** them from their bed of illness. |
| | 53: 6 | When God **r** his people, let Jacob |
| Mk | 9:12 | does come first, and **r** all things. |

## RESTRAIN [RESTRAINED, RESTRAINING, RESTRAINT]
| | | |
|---|---|---|
| Job | 9:13 | God does not **r** his anger; |

## RESTRAINED [RESTRAIN]
| | | |
|---|---|---|
| Ps | 78:38 | Time after time he **r** his anger |
| 2Pe | 2:16 | voice and **r** the prophet's madness. |

## RESTRAINING* [RESTRAIN]
| | | |
|---|---|---|
| Pr | 27:16 | **r** her is like **r** the wind |
| Col | 2:23 | any value in **r** sensual indulgence. |

## RESTRAINT [RESTRAIN]
| | | |
|---|---|---|
| Pr | 17:27 | have knowledge use words with **r**, |
| | 29:18 | is no revelation, people cast off **r**; |

## RESTS [REST]
| | | |
|---|---|---|
| Dt | 33:12 | one the LORD loves **r** between his |
| 2Ch | 28:11 | for the LORD's fierce anger **r** |
| | 36:21 | The land enjoyed its sabbath **r**; |
| Pr | 19:23 | then one **r** content, |
| Lk | 2:14 | to those on whom his favor **r**." |
| 1Pe | 4:14 | Spirit of glory and of God **r** on you. |

## RESULT [RESULTED]
| | | |
|---|---|---|
| Nu | 25:18 | when the plague came as a **r** |
| Ezr | 9:13 | to us is a **r** of our evil deeds and our |
| Ro | 6:22 | to holiness, and the **r** is eternal life. |
| | 11:31 | too may now receive mercy as a **r** |
| 2Co | 3: 3 | from Christ, the **r** of our ministry, |
| 2Th | 1: 5 | as a **r** you will be counted worthy |
| 1Pe | 1: 7 | proved genuine and may **r** in praise, |
| | 1: 9 | receiving the end **r** of your faith, |

## RESULTED* [RESULT]
| | | |
|---|---|---|
| Ro | 5:18 | just as one trespass **r** in condemnation |
| | 5:18 | one righteous act **r** in justification |

## RESURRECTION*
| | | |
|---|---|---|
| Mt | 22:23 | who say there is no **r**, came to him |
| | 22:28 | at the **r**, whose wife will she be |
| | 22:30 | the **r** people will neither marry nor |
| | 22:31 | But about the **r** of the dead— |
| | 27:53 | came out of the tombs after Jesus' **r** |
| Mk | 12:18 | who say there is no **r**, came to him |
| | 12:23 | At the **r**, whose wife will she be, |
| Lk | 14:14 | be repaid at the **r** of the righteous." |
| | 20:27 | who say there is no **r**, came to Jesus |

| | | |
|---|---|---|
| Lk | 20:33 | at the **r** whose wife will she be, |
| | 20:35 | in the **r** from the dead will neither |
| | 20:36 | since they are children of the **r**. |
| Jn | 11:24 | rise again in the **r** at the last day." |
| | 11:25 | said to her, "I am the **r** and the life. |
| Ac | 1:22 | become a witness with us of his **r**." |
| | 2:31 | he spoke of the **r** of the Messiah, |
| | 4: 2 | in Jesus the **r** of the dead. |
| | 4:33 | to testify to the **r** of the Lord Jesus. |
| | 17:18 | good news about Jesus and the **r**. |
| | 17:32 | they heard about the **r** of the dead, |
| | 23: 6 | of the hope of the **r** of the dead." |
| | 23: 8 | Sadducees say that there is no **r**, |
| | 24:15 | that there will be a **r** of both |
| | 24:21 | 'It is concerning the **r** of the dead |
| Ro | 1: 4 | in power by his **r** from the dead: |
| | 6: 5 | be united with him in a **r** like his. |
| 1Co | 15:12 | say that there is no **r** of the dead? |
| | 15:13 | If there is no **r** of the dead, then not |
| | 15:21 | the **r** of the dead comes also through |
| | 15:29 | Now if there is no **r**, what will those |
| | 15:42 | So will it be with the **r** of the dead. |
| Php | 3:10 | yes, to know the power of his **r** |
| | 3:11 | attaining to the **r** from the dead. |
| 2Ti | 2:18 | that the **r** has already taken place, |
| Heb | 6: 2 | on of hands, the **r** of the dead, |
| | 11:35 | they might gain an even better **r**. |
| 1Pe | 1: 3 | a living hope through the **r** of Jesus |
| | 3:21 | It saves you by the **r** of Jesus Christ, |
| Rev | 20: 5 | This is the first **r**. |
| | 20: 6 | those who have part in the first **r**. |

## RETAIN
| | | |
|---|---|---|
| Lk | 8:15 | who hear the word, **r** it, |

## RETALIATE*
| | | |
|---|---|---|
| 1Pe | 2:23 | their insults at him, he did not **r**; |

## RETIRE*
| | | |
|---|---|---|
| Nu | 8:25 | fifty, they must **r** from their regular |

## RETREAT
| | | |
|---|---|---|
| Ps | 44:10 | You made us **r** before the enemy, |
| | 74:21 | Do not let the oppressed **r** |

## RETRIBUTION*
| | | |
|---|---|---|
| Ps | 69:22 | may it become **r** and a trap. |
| Isa | 34: 8 | a year of **r**, to uphold Zion's cause. |
| | 35: 4 | with divine **r** he will come to save |
| | 59:18 | to his enemies and **r** to his foes; |
| Jer | 51:56 | For the LORD is a God of **r**; |
| Ro | 11: 9 | a stumbling block and a **r** for them. |

## RETURN [RETURNED, RETURNS]
| | | |
|---|---|---|
| Ge | 3:19 | you are and to dust you will **r**." |
| | 18:10 | "I will surely **r** to you about this |
| | 29:18 | for you seven years in **r** for your |
| Lev | 25:10 | you is to **r** to your family property |
| Nu | 10:36 | came to rest, he said, "**R**, LORD, |
| Dt | 30: 2 | your children **r** to the LORD your |
| 2Sa | 12:23 | go to him, but he will not **r** to me." |
| 2Ch | 30: 9 | If you **r** to the LORD, then your |
| Ne | 1: 9 | but if you **r** to me and obey my |
| Job | 10:21 | before I go to the place of no **r**, |
| | 16:22 | pass before I take the path of no **r**. |

Job 22:23 If you **r** to the Almighty, you will
Ps 80:14 **R** to us, God Almighty!
90: 3 saying, "**R** to dust, you mortals."
116:12 What shall I **r** to the LORD
126: 6 to sow, will **r** with songs of joy,
Pr 2:19 None who go to her **r** or attain
Ecc 3:20 all come from dust, and to dust all **r**.
Isa 10:21 A remnant will **r**, a remnant
35:10 the LORD has rescued will **r**.
44:22 **R** to me, for I have redeemed you."
55:11 It will not **r** to me empty, but will
Jer 3:12 " '**R**, faithless Israel,'
4: 1 you, Israel, will **r**, then **r** to me,"
24: 7 for they will **r** to me with all their
31: 8 a great throng will **r**.
31:22 woman will **r** to the man."
La 3:40 them, and let us **r** to the LORD.
Hos 5: 4 deeds do not permit them to **r**
6: 1 "Come, let us **r** to the LORD.
12: 6 But you must **r** to your God;
14: 1 **R**, Israel, to the LORD your God.
Joel 2:12 "**r** to me with all your heart,
Zec 1: 3 'and I will **r** to you,'
10: 9 will survive, and they will **r**.
Mal 3: 7 **R** to me, and I will **r** to you,"
Ro 9: 9 "At the appointed time I will **r**,

## RETURNED [RETURN]

Ge 8: 9 so it **r** to Noah in the ark.
Nu 13:25 forty days they **r** from exploring
1Ki 17:22 and the boy's life **r** to him, and he
Ezr 2: 1 to Babylon (they **r** to Jerusalem
Ps 35:13 my prayers **r** to me unanswered,
Am 4: 6 town, yet you have not **r** to me,"
Mt 27: 3 **r** the thirty pieces of silver
Ro 14: 9 **r** to life so that he might be the Lord
1Pe 2:25 but now you have **r** to the Shepherd

## RETURNS [RETURN]

Pr 3:14 silver and yields better **r** than gold.
26:11 As a dog **r** to its vomit, so fools
Ecc 12: 7 and the dust **r** to the ground it came
Isa 52: 8 When the LORD **r** to Zion,
Mt 24:46 finds him doing so when he **r**.
2Pe 2:22 "A dog **r** to its vomit," and,
2:22 sow that is washed **r** to her wallowing

## REUBEN [REUBENITES]

Firstborn of Jacob by Leah (Ge 29:32; 46:8; 1Ch 2:1). Attempted to rescue Joseph (Ge 37:21–30). Lost birthright for sleeping with Bilhah (Ge 35:22; 49:4). Tribe of blessed (Ge 49:3–4; Dt 33:6), numbered (Nu 1:21; 26:7), allotted land east of Jordan (Nu 32; 34:14; Jos 13:15), west (Eze 48:6), failed to help Deborah (Jdg 5:15–16), supported David (1Ch 12:37), 12,000 from (Rev 7:5).

## REUBENITES [REUBEN]

Nu 32: 1 The **R** and Gadites, who had very
Dt 29: 8 gave it as an inheritance to the **R**,
Jos 13: 8 the **R** and the Gadites had received

## REUEL See JETHRO

## REVEAL [REVEALED, REVEALS, REVELATION, REVELATIONS]

Nu 12: 6 you, I **r** myself to them in visions,
Da 2:11 No one can **r** it to the king except
Mt 11:27 to whom the Son chooses to **r** him.
Gal 1:16 to **r** his Son in me so that I might

## REVEALED [REVEAL]

Dt 29:29 but the things **r** belong to us
Est 2:10 Esther had not **r** her nationality
Isa 40: 5 the glory of the LORD will be **r**,
43:12 I have **r** and saved and proclaimed—
53: 1 has the arm of the LORD been **r**?
65: 1 "I **r** myself to those who did not ask
Da 2:19 During the night the mystery was **r**
Mt 11:25 and **r** them to little children.
16:17 for this was not **r** to you by flesh
Lk 17:30 this on the day the Son of Man is **r**.
Jn 2:11 signs through which he **r** his glory;
12:38 has the arm of the Lord been **r**?"
17: 6 "I have **r** you to those whom you
Ro 1:17 the righteousness of God is **r**—
8:18 with the glory that will be **r** in us.
10:20 I **r** myself to those who did not ask
16:26 now **r** and made known through
1Co 2:10 for God has **r** them to us by his
3:13 It will be **r** with fire, and the fire
2Co 4:11 may also be **r** in our mortal body.
Eph 3: 5 generations as it has now been **r**
2Th 1: 7 the Lord Jesus is **r** from heaven
2: 3 and the man of lawlessness is **r**,
1Pe 1: 7 and honor when Jesus Christ is **r**.
1:20 but was **r** in these last times for your
4:13 be overjoyed when his glory is **r**.
Rev 15: 4 your righteous acts have been **r**."

## REVEALS* [REVEAL]

Nu 23: 3 Whatever he **r** to me I will tell
Job 12:22 He **r** the deep things of darkness
Da 2:22 He **r** deep and hidden things;
2:28 is a God in heaven who **r** mysteries.
Am 4:13 and who **r** his thoughts to mortals,

## REVELATION* [REVEAL]

2Sa 7:17 David all the words of this entire **r**.
1Ch 17:15 David all the words of this entire **r**.
Pr 29:18 Where there is no **r**, people cast off
Da 10: 1 a **r** was given to Daniel (who was
Hab 2: 2 "Write down the **r** and make it
2: 3 For the **r** awaits an appointed time;
Lk 2:32 a light for **r** to the Gentiles,
Ro 16:25 with the **r** of the mystery hidden
1Co 14: 6 to you, unless I bring you some **r**
14:26 a **r**, a tongue or an interpretation.
14:30 And if a **r** comes to someone who is
Gal 1:12 I received it by **r** from Jesus Christ.
2: 2 I went in response to a **r** and,
Eph 1:17 give you the Spirit of wisdom and **r**,
3: 3 mystery made known to me by **r**,
Rev 1: 1 The **r** from Jesus Christ, which God

## REVELATIONS* [REVEAL]

2Co 12: 1 on to visions and **r** from the Lord.

2Co 12: 7 of these surpassingly great **r**.

## REVELED* [REVELRY]
Ne  9:25 they **r** in your great goodness.
Ac  7:41 and **r** in what their own hands had made.

## REVELING [REVELRY]
2Pe  2:13 **r** in their pleasures while they feast

## REVELRY [REVELED, REVELING]
Ex  32: 6 and drink and got up to indulge in **r**.
1Co 10: 7 drink and got up to indulge in **r**."
Zep  2:15 This is the city of **r** that lived in safety.

## REVENGE [VENGEANCE]
Lev 19:18 " 'Do not seek **r** or bear a grudge
Jdg 16:28 one blow get **r** on the Philistines
Ro  12:19 Do not take **r**, my dear friends,

## REVENUE
Ro  13: 7 owe taxes, pay taxes; if **r**, then **r**;

## REVERE* [REVERED, REVERENCE, REVERENT, REVERING]
Lev 19:32 for the elderly and **r** your God.
Dt   4:10 learn to **r** me as long as they live
    13: 4 must follow, and him you must **r**.
    14:23 to **r** the LORD your God always.
    17:19 may learn to **r** the LORD his God
    28:58 book, and do not **r** this glorious
Job 37:24 Therefore, people **r** him, for does he
Ps  22:23 **R** him, all you descendants
    33: 8 let all the people of the world **r** him.
    102:15 kings of the earth will **r** your glory.
Isa  25: 3 cities of ruthless nations will **r** you.
    59:19 of the sun, they will **r** his glory.
    63:17 our hearts so we do not **r** you?
Hos 10: 3 because we did not **r** the LORD.
Mal  4: 2 But for you who **r** my name, the sun
1Pe  3:15 in your hearts **r** Christ as Lord.
Rev 11:18 your people who **r** your name,

## REVERED [REVERE]
Mal  2: 5 called for reverence and he **r** me

## REVERENCE [REVERE]
Lev 19:30 and have **r** for my sanctuary.
Ne   5:15 of **r** for God I did not act like that.
Ps   5: 7 in **r** I bow down toward your holy
Jer 44:10 not humbled themselves or shown **r**,
Da   6:26 must fear and **r** the God of Daniel.
2Co  7: 1 perfecting holiness out of **r** for God.
Eph  5:21 to one another out of **r** for Christ.
Col  3:22 sincerity of heart and **r** for the Lord.
1Pe  3: 2 see the purity and **r** of your lives.

## REVERENT* [REVERE]
Ecc  8:12 fear God, who are **r** before him.
Tit  2: 3 women to be **r** in the way they live,
Heb  5: 7 heard because of his **r** submission.
1Pe  1:17 time as foreigners here in **r** fear.
    2:18 Slaves, in **r** fear of God submit

## REVERING* [REVERE]
Dt   8: 6 in obedience to him and **r** him.
Ne   1:11 who delight in **r** your name.

## REVERSE*
Isa 43:13 When I act, who can **r** it?"

## REVILE
Ps  10:13 Why do the wicked **r** God?
    74:10 Will the foe **r** your name forever?

## REVIVE*
Ps  80:18 **r** us, and we will call on your name.
    85: 6 Will you not **r** us again, that your
Isa 57:15 to **r** the spirit of the lowly and to **r** the heart of the contrite.
Hos  6: 2 After two days he will **r** us;

## REVOKE* [REVOKED, REVOKING]
Ps 132:11 David, a sure oath that he will not **r**:

## REVOKED* [REVOKE]
Est  8: 8 and sealed with his ring can be **r**."
Isa 45:23 integrity a word that will not be **r**:
Zec 11:11 It was **r** on that day, and so

## REVOKING* [REVOKE]
Zec 11:10 **r** the covenant I had made with all

## REWARD [REWARDED, REWARDING, REWARDS]
Ge  15: 1 am your shield, your very great **r**."
1Sa 24:19 May the LORD **r** you well
Ps  17:14 of this world whose **r** is in this life.
    19:11 in keeping them there is great **r**.
    62:12 "You **r** everyone according to what
    127: 3 the LORD, offspring a **r** from him.
Pr   9:12 are wise, your wisdom will **r** you;
    11:18 sow righteousness reap a sure **r**.
    12:14 work of their hands brings them **r**.
    19:17 he will **r** them for what they have
    25:22 head, and the LORD will **r** you.
Isa 40:10 See, his **r** is with him, and his
    49: 4 hand, and my **r** is with my God."
    61: 8 my faithfulness I will **r** my people
    62:11 See, his **r** is with him, and his
Jer 17:10 to **r** everyone according to their
    32:19 you **r** everyone according to their
Mt   5:12 because great is your **r** in heaven,
    6: 1 you will have no **r** from your Father
    6: 5 they have received their **r** in full.
    10:41 a prophet will receive a prophet's **r**,
    16:27 then he will **r** everyone according
Lk   6:23 because great is your **r** in heaven.
    6:35 Then your **r** will be great, and you
1Co  3:14 the builder will receive a **r**.
    9:17 If I preach voluntarily, I have a **r**;
Eph  6: 8 that the Lord will **r** each one of you
Col  3:24 an inheritance from the Lord as a **r**.
Heb 11:26 he was looking ahead to his **r**.
Rev 22:12 My **r** is with me, and I will give

## REWARDED [REWARD]
Ru   2:12 May you be richly **r** by the LORD,

2Sa 22:21 cleanness of my hands he has **r** me.
2Ch 15: 7 give up, for your work will be **r**."
Ps 18:24 The LORD has **r** me according
Pr 13:13 whoever respects a command is **r**.
13:21 the righteous are **r** with good things.
14:14 their ways, and the good **r** for theirs.
Jer 31:16 for your work will be **r**,"
1Co 3: 8 and they will each be **r** according
Heb 10:35 it will be richly **r**.
2Jn 1: 8 for, but that you may be **r** fully.

## REWARDING* [REWARD]
Rev 11:18 for **r** your servants the prophets

## REWARDS [REWARD]
1Sa 26:23 The LORD **r** every man for his
Heb 11: 6 he **r** those who earnestly seek him.

## REZIN
Isa 7: 1 King **R** of Aram and Pekah son

## RHODA*
Ac 12:13 a servant named **R** came to answer

## RIB* [RIBS]
Ge 2:22 a woman from the **r** he had taken

## RIBLAH
2Ki 25: 6 taken to the king of Babylon at **R**,

## RIBS* [RIB]
Ge 2:21 he took one of the man's **r**
Da 7: 5 it had three **r** in its mouth between

## RICH [ENRICH, ENRICHED, RICHES, RICHEST, RICHLY]
Ge 26:13 The man became **r**, and his wealth
2Sa 12: 1 town, one **r** and the other poor.
Job 34:19 does not favor the **r** over the poor,
Ps 21: 3 came to greet him with **r** blessings
49:16 be overawed when others grow **r**,
145: 8 slow to anger and **r** in love.
Pr 13: 7 One person pretends to be **r**, yet has
21:17 wine and olive oil will never be **r**.
22: 2 **R** and poor have this in common:
23: 4 Do not wear yourself out to get **r**;
28: 6 blameless than the **r** whose ways are
28:20 to get **r** will not go unpunished.
28:22 The stingy are eager to get **r** and are
Ecc 5:12 of the **r** permits them no sleep.
Isa 33: 6 a **r** store of salvation and wisdom
53: 9 and with the **r** in his death,
Jer 9:23 or the **r** boast of their riches,
Eze 34:14 there they will feed in a **r** pasture
Mt 19:23 hard for the **r** to enter the kingdom
Lk 1:53 but has sent the **r** away empty.
6:24 "But woe to you who are **r**, for you
12:21 but are not **r** toward God."
16: 1 "There was a **r** man whose manager
16:19 "There was a **r** man who was
21: 1 he saw the **r** putting their gifts
2Co 6:10 poor, yet making many **r**;
8: 2 poverty welled up in **r** generosity.
8: 9 his poverty might become **r**.
9:11 You will be made **r** in every way so

Eph 2: 4 love for us, God, who is **r** in mercy,
1Ti 6: 9 Those who want to get **r** fall
6:17 Command those who are **r** in this
6:18 to be **r** in good deeds, and to be
Jas 1:10 But the **r** should take pride in their
2: 5 the eyes of the world to be **r** in faith
5: 1 Now listen, you **r** people,
2Pe 1:11 you will receive a **r** welcome
Rev 2: 9 and your poverty—yet you are **r**!
3:17 You say, 'I am **r**; I have acquired
3:18 in the fire, so you can become **r**;

## RICHES [RICH]
1Ki 10:23 King Solomon was greater in **r**
Job 36:18 careful that no one entices you by **r**;
Ps 49: 6 wealth and boast of their great **r**?
62:10 though your **r** increase, do not set
119:14 statutes as one rejoices in great **r**.
Pr 3:16 in her left hand are **r** and honor.
11:28 Those who trust in their **r** will fall,
22: 1 name is more desirable than great **r**;
27:24 for **r** do not endure forever,
30: 8 give me neither poverty nor **r**,
Isa 10: 3 Where will you leave your **r**?
60: 5 you the **r** of the nations will come.
Jer 9:23 strength or the rich boast of their **r**,
Lk 8:14 by life's worries, **r** and pleasures,
Ro 9:23 to make the **r** of his glory known
11:12 their loss means **r** for the Gentiles,
11:33 the depth of the **r** of the wisdom
Eph 2: 7 he might show the incomparable **r**
3: 8 to the Gentiles the boundless **r**
Col 1:27 among the Gentiles the glorious **r**
2: 2 they may have the full **r** of complete

## RICHEST [RICH]
Isa 55: 2 and you will delight in the **r** of fare.

## RICHLY [RICH]
Pr 28:20 A faithful person will be **r** blessed,
Ro 10:12 and **r** blesses all who call on him,
Col 3:16 dwell among you **r** as you teach
1Ti 6:17 who **r** provides us with everything

## RID
Ge 21:10 "Get **r** of that slave woman and her
35: 2 "Get **r** of the foreign gods you have
Jdg 10:16 Then they got **r** of the foreign gods
1Sa 7: 3 **r** yourselves of the foreign gods
Lk 22: 2 for some way to get **r** of Jesus,
1Co 5: 7 Get **r** of the old yeast, so that you
Gal 4:30 "Get **r** of the slave woman and her
Eph 4:31 Get **r** of all bitterness,
Col 3: 8 **r** yourselves of all such things as
Jas 1:21 get **r** of all moral filth and the evil
1Pe 2: 1 **r** yourselves of all malice and all

## RIDDLE [RIDDLES]
Jdg 14:12 "Let me tell you a **r**," Samson said
Ps 49: 4 with the harp I will expound my **r**:

## RIDDLES* [RIDDLE]
Nu 12: 8 face to face, clearly and not in **r**;
Pr 1: 6 the sayings and **r** of the wise.
Da 5:12 dreams, explain **r** and solve difficult

## RIDE [RIDER, RIDERS, RIDES, RIDING, RODE]
Ps  45: 4  In your majesty r forth victoriously

## RIDER [RIDE]
Rev  6: 2  Its r held a bow, and he was given
     19:11  whose r is called Faithful and True.

## RIDERS [RIDE]
Rev  9:17  and r I saw in my vision looked like

## RIDES* [RIDE]
Dt  33:26  who r on the heavens to help you
Ps  68: 4  extol him who r on the clouds;
     68:33  him who r the ancient skies above,
    104: 3  and r on the wings of the wind.
Isa  19: 1  the LORD r on a swift cloud and is
Rev  17: 7  of the woman and of the beast she r,

## RIDICULE [RIDICULED]
2Ki  19: 4  has sent to r the living God,
Ps  123: 4  We have endured no end of r
Isa  37:17  to r the living God.

## RIDICULED [RIDICULE]
2Ki  19:22  Who is it you have r and blasphemed?
Jer  20: 7  I am r all day long;
Lk  23:11  and his soldiers r and mocked him.

## RIDING [RIDE]
Zec  9: 9  lowly and r on a donkey, on a colt,
Mt  21: 5  gentle and r on a donkey,
Rev  19:14  r on white horses and dressed

## RIGGING*
Pr  23:34  the high seas, lying on top of the r.
Isa  33:23  Your r hangs loose: The mast is not

## RIGHT [RIGHTFULLY, RIGHTS]
Ge   4: 7  If you do what is r,
     4: 7  But if you do not do what is r,
    13: 9  If you go to the left, I'll go to the r;
    18:19  of the LORD by doing what is r
    18:25  not the Judge of all the earth do r?"
    48:13  on his r toward Israel's left hand
Ex  14:22  with a wall of water on their r
    15: 6  Your r hand, LORD, was majestic
    15:26  God and do what is r in his eyes,
Dt   5:32  do not turn aside to the r
     6:18  Do what is r and good
    13:18  and doing what is r in his eyes.
    28:14  you today, to the r or to the left,
Jos  1: 7  do not turn from it to the r
1Sa 12:23  you the way that is good and r.
1Ki  3: 9  to distinguish between r and wrong.
     8:36  Teach them the r way to live,
    15: 5  David had done what was r
2Ki  7: 9  other, "What we're doing is not r.
Ne   9:13  and laws that are just and r,
Job 40:14  that your own r hand can save you.
    42: 7  have not spoken of me what is r,
Ps  16: 8  With him at my r hand, I will not be
    16:11  eternal pleasures at your r hand.
    17: 7  your r hand those who take refuge

Ps  18:35  shield, and your r hand sustains me;
    19: 8  The precepts of the LORD are r,
    23: 3  guides me along the r paths
    25: 9  He guides the humble in what is r
    33: 4  For the word of the LORD is r
    44: 3  it was your r hand, your arm,
    45: 4  let your r hand achieve awesome
    51: 4  so you are r in your verdict
    63: 8  your r hand upholds me.
    73:23  you hold me by my r hand.
    80:17  hand rest on the man at your r hand,
    89:13  hand is strong, your r hand exalted.
    91: 7  ten thousand at your r hand, but it
   106: 3  act justly, who always do what is r.
   110: 1  "Sit at my r hand until I make your
   110: 5  The Lord is at your r hand;
   118:15  "The LORD's r hand has done
   137: 5  may my r hand forget its skill.
   139:10  me, your r hand will hold me fast.
Pr   1: 3  doing what is r and just and fair;
     3:16  Long life is in her r hand; in her left
     4:27  Do not turn to the r or the left;
     8: 9  To the discerning all of them are r;
    12:15  The way of fools seems r to them,
    14:12  There is a way that appears to be r,
    16:13  value persons who speak what is r.
    16:25  There is a way that appears to be r,
    18:17  a lawsuit the first to speak seems r,
    21: 2  may think all their ways are r,
    28: 5  Evildoers do not understand what is r,
Ecc  7:20  no one who does what is r
SS   1: 4  How r they are to adore you!
Isa  1:17  learn to do r!
     7:15  to reject the wrong and choose the r,
    30:10  us no more visions of what is r!
    30:21  Whether you turn to the r
    41:10  you with my righteous r hand.
    41:13  God who takes hold of your r hand
    48:13  my r hand spread out the heavens;
    64: 5  to the help of those who gladly do r,
Jer  22: 3  Do what is just and r.
    23: 5  and do what is just and r in the land.
Eze  1:10  on the r side each had the face
    18: 5  man who does what is just and r.
    18:21  decrees and do what is just and r,
    33:14  their sins and do what is just and r—
Hos 14: 9  The ways of the LORD are r;
Am   3:10  "They do not know how to do r,"
Jnh  4:11  people who cannot tell their r hand
Zec  3: 1  and Satan standing at his r side
Mt   5:29  If your r eye causes you to stumble,
     6: 3  know what your r hand is doing,
    22:44  my r hand until I put your enemies
    25:33  He will put the sheep on his r
Mk   7:27  "for it is not r to take the children's
    14:62  of Man sitting at the r hand
Jn   1:12  he gave the r to become children
Ac   2:34  said to my Lord: "Sit at my r hand
     7:55  Jesus standing at the r hand of God.
Ro   3: 4  that you may be proved r when you
     8:34  is at the r hand of God and is
     9:21  Does not the potter have the r
    12:17  careful to do what is r in the eyes
1Co  6:12  "I have the r to do anything,"
     7:35  but that you may live in a r way
     9: 4  Don't we have the r to food
    10:23  "I have the r to do anything,"

| | | | | | |
|---|---|---|---|---|---|
| 2Co | 8:21 | we are taking pains to do what is r, | Ps | 145:17 | The LORD is r in all his ways |
| Eph | 1:20 | and seated him at his r hand | | 146: 8 | down, the LORD loves the r. |
| | 6: 1 | parents in the Lord, for this is r. | Pr | 3:33 | but he blesses the home of the r. |
| Php | 4: 8 | whatever is r, whatever is pure, | | 4:18 | path of the r is like the morning sun, |
| Col | 3: 1 | where Christ is seated at the r hand | | 10: 6 | Blessings crown the head of the r, |
| Heb | 1: 3 | he sat down at the r hand | | 10: 7 | The name of the r is used |
| | 1:13 | "Sit at my r hand until I make your | | 10:11 | The mouth of the r is a fountain |
| | 10:12 | he sat down at the r hand of God, | | 10:16 | The wages of the r is life, |
| Jas | 2: 8 | as yourself," you are doing r. | | 10:20 | The tongue of the r is choice silver, |
| 1Pe | 3:14 | if you should suffer for what is r, | | 10:24 | what the r desire will be granted. |
| | 3:22 | into heaven and is at God's r hand— | | 10:28 | The prospect of the r is joy, |
| 1Jn | 2:29 | who does what is r has been born | | 10:32 | lips of the r know what finds favor, |
| | 3: 7 | one who does what is r is righteous, | | 11: 9 | but through knowledge the r escape. |
| Rev | 1:16 | In his r hand he held seven stars, | | 11:23 | The desire of the r ends only |
| | 2: 7 | I will give the r to eat from the tree | | 11:30 | The fruit of the r is a tree of life, |
| | 3:21 | I will give the r to sit with me | | 12:10 | The r care for the needs of their |
| | 22:11 | let those who do r continue to do r; | | 12:21 | No harm overtakes the r, |
| | 22:14 | that they may have the r to the tree | | 13: 5 | The r hate what is false, |

## RIGHT HAND  See HAND

## RIGHT IN THE EYES OF THE †LORD
See EYES

# RIGHT-HANDED* [HAND]
1Ch 12: 2  or to sling stones r or left-handed;

# RIGHTEOUS [OVERRIGHTEOUS,
RIGHTEOUSLY, RIGHTEOUSNESS]

| | | |
|---|---|---|
| Ge | 6: 9 | Noah was a r man, |
| | 18:23 | "Will you sweep away the r |
| | 38:26 | said, "She is more r than I, since I |
| Nu | 23:10 | Let me die the death of the r, |
| Dt | 4: 8 | is so great as to have such r decrees |
| 1Sa | 24:17 | "You are more r than I," he said. |
| Ne | 9: 8 | your promise because you are r. |
| | 9:33 | you have remained r; |
| Job | 4:17 | 'Can a mortal be more r than God? |
| | 36: 7 | He does not take his eyes off the r; |
| Ps | 1: 5 | nor sinners in the assembly of the r. |
| | 4: 5 | sacrifices of the r and trust |
| | 5:12 | Surely, LORD, you bless the r; |
| | 7:11 | God is a r judge, a God who |
| | 9: 4 | sitting enthroned as the r judge. |
| | 11: 7 | For the LORD is r, he loves |
| | 15: 2 | who do what is r, who speak |
| | 34:15 | The eyes of the LORD are on the r |
| | 37: 6 | make your r reward shine |
| | 37:16 | little that the r have than the wealth |
| | 37:21 | not repay, but the r give generously; |
| | 37:25 | yet I have never seen the r forsaken |
| | 37:30 | The mouths of the r utter wisdom, |
| | 55:22 | he will never let the r be shaken. |
| | 64:10 | The r will rejoice in the LORD |
| | 65: 5 | with awesome and r deeds, |
| | 68: 3 | But may the r be glad and rejoice |
| | 71:15 | mouth will tell of your r deeds, |
| | 72: 7 | In his days may the r flourish |
| | 112: 4 | gracious and compassionate and r. |
| | 116: 5 | The LORD is gracious and r; |
| | 118:19 | Open for me the gates of the r; |
| | 118:20 | through which the r may enter. |
| | 119: 7 | upright heart as I learn your r laws. |
| | 119:137 | You are r, LORD, and your laws |
| | 119:144 | Your statutes are always r; |
| | 140:13 | Surely the r will praise your name, |
| | 143: 2 | for no one living is r before you. |

| | | |
|---|---|---|
| | 13: 9 | The light of the r shines brightly, |
| | 14:32 | even in death the r seek refuge |
| | 15:28 | heart of the r weighs its answers, |
| | 15:29 | but he hears the prayer of the r. |
| | 18:10 | the r run to it and are safe. |
| | 20: 7 | The r lead blameless lives; |
| | 21:15 | it brings joy to the r but terror |
| | 23:24 | The father of a r child has great joy; |
| | 24:16 | for though the r fall seven times, |
| | 28: 1 | but the r are as bold as a lion. |
| | 29: 2 | When the r thrive, the people |
| | 29: 6 | but the r shout for joy and are glad. |
| | 29: 7 | The r care about justice |
| | 29:27 | The r detest the dishonest; |
| Ecc | 7:15 | the r perishing in their |
| | 7:20 | there is no one on earth who is r, |
| | 8:14 | wicked who get what the r deserve. |
| Isa | 5:16 | will be proved holy by his r acts. |
| | 26: 7 | The path of the r is level; |
| | 41:10 | uphold you with my r right hand. |
| | 45:21 | from me, a r God and a Savior; |
| | 53:11 | by his knowledge my r servant will |
| | 64: 6 | and all our r acts are like filthy rags; |
| Jer | 12: 1 | You are always r, LORD, when I |
| | 23: 5 | I will raise up for David a r Branch, |
| | 23: 6 | called: The LORD Our R Savior. |
| | 33:15 | time I will make a r Branch sprout |
| | 33:16 | called: The LORD Our R Savior.' |
| La | 1:18 | "The LORD is r, yet I rebelled |
| Eze | 3:20 | "Again, when the r turn from their |
| | 18: 5 | "Suppose there is a r man who does |
| | 18:20 | of the r will be credited to them, |
| | 33:12 | The r, if they sin, |
| Da | 9:14 | us, for the LORD our God is r |
| Hab | 2: 4 | the r will live by their faithfulness— |
| Zep | 3: 5 | The LORD within her is r; |
| Zec | 9: 9 | to you, r and having salvation, |
| Mal | 3:18 | see the distinction between the r |
| Mt | 5:45 | and sends rain on the r |
| | 13:43 | the r will shine like the sun |
| | 13:49 | and separate the wicked from the r |
| | 25:37 | "Then the r will answer him, 'Lord, |
| | 25:46 | but the r to eternal life." |
| Mk | 2:17 | I have not come to call the r, |
| Lk | 23:47 | said, "Surely this was a r man." |
| Ac | 3:14 | You disowned the Holy and R One |
| | 24:15 | will be a resurrection of both the r |
| Ro | 1:17 | "The r will live by faith." |
| | 2: 5 | his r judgment will be revealed. |

| | | |
|---|---|---|
| Ro | 2:13 | those who hear the law who are **r** |
| | 3:10 | "There is no one **r**, not even one; |
| | 3:20 | Therefore no one will be declared **r** |
| | 5:18 | one **r** act resulted in justification |
| | 5:19 | one man the many will be made **r**. |
| | 7:12 | commandment is holy, **r** and good. |
| | 8: 4 | order that the **r** requirement |
| Gal | 3:11 | because "the **r** will live by faith." |
| 1Ti | 1: 9 | that the law is made not for the **r** |
| 2Ti | 4: 8 | which the Lord, the **r** Judge, |
| Tit | 3: 5 | because of **r** things we had done, |
| Heb | 10:38 | "But my **r** one will live by faith. |
| Jas | 2:21 | our father Abraham considered **r** |
| | 2:25 | Rahab the prostitute considered **r** |
| | 5:16 | The prayer of a **r** person is powerful |
| 1Pe | 3:12 | For the eyes of the Lord are on the **r** |
| | 3:18 | for sins, the **r** for the unrighteous, |
| | 4:18 | "If it is hard for the **r** to be saved, |
| 1Jn | 2: 1 | Jesus Christ, the **R** One. |
| | 3: 7 | what is right is **r**, just as he is **r**. |
| Rev | 15: 4 | for your **r** acts have been revealed." |
| | 19: 8 | (Fine linen stands for the **r** acts |

## RIGHTEOUSLY* [RIGHTEOUS]

| | | |
|---|---|---|
| Isa | 33:15 | Those who walk **r** and speak what is |
| Jer | 11:20 | who judge **r** and test the heart |

## RIGHTEOUSNESS [RIGHTEOUS]

| | | |
|---|---|---|
| Ge | 15: 6 | and he credited it to him as **r**. |
| Dt | 6:25 | commanded us, that will be our **r**." |
| | 9: 4 | of this land because of my **r**." |
| 1Sa | 26:23 | Lord rewards every man for his **r** |
| 1Ki | 10: 9 | you king to maintain justice and **r**." |
| Job | 37:23 | in his justice and great **r**, he does |
| Ps | 7:17 | to the Lord because of his **r**; |
| | 9: 8 | He rules the world in **r** and judges |
| | 18:20 | dealt with me according to my **r**; |
| | 22:31 | They will proclaim his **r**, |
| | 33: 5 | The Lord loves **r** and justice; |
| | 35:24 | Vindicate me in your **r**, Lord my |
| | 35:28 | My tongue will proclaim your **r**, |
| | 36: 6 | Your **r** is like the highest |
| | 45: 7 | You love **r** and hate wickedness; |
| | 48:10 | your right hand is filled with **r**. |
| | 50: 6 | And the heavens proclaim his **r**, |
| | 71: 2 | In your **r**, rescue me and deliver me; |
| | 71:19 | Your **r**, God, reaches to the skies, |
| | 72: 2 | May he judge your people in **r**, |
| | 85:10 | **r** and peace kiss each other. |
| | 89:14 | **R** and justice are the foundation |
| | 96:13 | He will judge the world in **r** |
| | 98: 2 | and revealed his **r** to the nations. |
| | 98: 9 | He will judge the world in **r** |
| | 103: 6 | The Lord works **r** and justice |
| | 103:17 | his **r** with their children's children— |
| | 106:31 | to him as **r** for endless generations |
| | 111: 3 | his deeds, and his **r** endures forever. |
| | 132: 9 | your priests be clothed with your **r**; |
| | 145: 7 | and joyfully sing of your **r**. |
| Pr | 8:20 | I walk in the way of **r**, |
| | 10: 2 | value, but **r** delivers from death. |
| | 11: 5 | The **r** of the blameless makes their |
| | 11: 6 | The **r** of the upright delivers them, |
| | 11:18 | those who sow **r** reap a sure reward. |
| | 12:28 | In the way of **r** there is life; |
| | 13: 6 | **R** guards the person of integrity, |

| | | |
|---|---|---|
| Pr | 14:34 | **R** exalts a nation, but sin condemns |
| | 15: 9 | but he loves those who pursue **r**. |
| | 16:12 | for a throne is established through **r**. |
| | 16:31 | attained in the way of **r**. |
| | 21:21 | Whoever pursues **r** and love finds |
| Ecc | 7:15 | the righteous perishing in their **r**, |
| Isa | 1:26 | you will be called the City of **R**, |
| | 9: 7 | with justice and **r** from that time |
| | 11: 4 | but with **r** he will judge the needy, |
| | 11: 5 | **R** will be his belt and faithfulness |
| | 16: 5 | justice and speeds the cause of **r**. |
| | 26: 9 | the people of the world learn **r**, |
| | 28:17 | measuring line and **r** the plumb line; |
| | 32: 1 | a king will reign in **r** and rulers will |
| | 32:17 | The fruit of that **r** will be peace; |
| | 33: 5 | will fill Zion with his justice and **r**. |
| | 42: 6 | the Lord, have called you in **r**; |
| | 42:21 | sake of his **r** to make his law great |
| | 45: 8 | heavens above, rain down my **r**; |
| | 46:13 | I am bringing my **r** near, it is not far |
| | 51: 5 | My **r** draws near speedily, |
| | 51: 6 | last forever, my **r** will never fail. |
| | 51: 8 | But my **r** will last forever, |
| | 56: 1 | and my **r** will soon be revealed. |
| | 58: 8 | then your **r** will go before you, |
| | 59:17 | He put on **r** as his breastplate, |
| | 61:10 | and arrayed me in a robe of his **r**, |
| | 63: 1 | is I, speaking in **r**, mighty to save." |
| Jer | 9:24 | justice and **r** on earth, for in these I |
| Eze | 3:20 | when the righteous turn from their **r** |
| | 14:20 | save only themselves by their **r**. |
| | 18:20 | The **r** of the righteous will be |
| | 33:12 | that person's former **r** will count |
| Da | 9:24 | to bring in everlasting **r**, to seal |
| | 12: 3 | and those who lead many to **r**, |
| Hos | 2:19 | I will betroth you in **r** and justice, |
| | 10:12 | Sow for yourselves, reap the fruit |
| | 10:12 | he comes and showers his **r** on you. |
| Am | 5:24 | a river, **r** like a never-failing stream! |
| Mic | 7: 9 | me out into the light; I will see his **r**. |
| Zep | 2: 3 | Seek **r**, seek humility; |
| Mal | 4: 2 | the sun of **r** will rise with healing |
| Mt | 3:15 | for us to do this to fulfill all **r**." |
| | 5: 6 | those who hunger and thirst for **r**, |
| | 5:10 | who are persecuted because of **r**, |
| | 5:20 | you that unless your **r** surpasses |
| | 6: 1 | not to do your 'acts of **r**' in front |
| | 6:33 | But seek first his kingdom and his **r**, |
| Jn | 16: 8 | to be in the wrong about sin and **r** |
| Ac | 24:25 | As Paul talked about **r**, |
| Ro | 1:17 | a **r** that is by faith from first to last, |
| | 3: 5 | brings out God's **r** more clearly, |
| | 3:22 | This **r** is given through faith |
| | 4: 3 | and it was credited to him as **r**." |
| | 4: 5 | ungodly, their faith is credited as **r**. |
| | 4: 6 | to whom God credits **r** apart |
| | 4: 9 | faith was credited to him as **r**. |
| | 4:13 | through the **r** that comes by faith. |
| | 4:22 | why "it was credited to him as **r**." |
| | 6:13 | to him as an instrument of **r**. |
| | 6:16 | or to obedience, which leads to **r**? |
| | 6:18 | sin and have become slaves to **r**. |
| | 6:19 | yourselves as slaves to **r** leading |
| | 8:10 | the Spirit gives life because of **r**. |
| | 9:30 | have obtained it, a **r** that is by faith; |
| | 10: 3 | they did not submit to God's **r**. |
| | 10: 4 | there may be **r** for everyone who |

Ro 14:17 but of **r**, peace and joy in the Holy
1Co 1:30 is, our **r**, holiness and redemption.
2Co 3: 9 is the ministry that brings **r**!
　　 5:21 him we might become the **r** of God.
　　 6: 7 with weapons of **r** in the right hand
　　 6:14 For what do **r** and wickedness have
　　 9: 9 their **r** endures forever."
　　 9:10 will enlarge the harvest of your **r**.
　　 11:15 also masquerade as servants of **r**.
Gal 2:21 if **r** could be gained through the law,
　　 3: 6 and it was credited to him as **r**."
　　 3:21 **r** would certainly have come
Eph 4:24 created to be like God in true **r**
　　 5: 9 consists in all goodness, **r** and truth)
　　 6:14 with the breastplate of **r** in place,
Php 1:11 the fruit of **r** that comes through
　　 3: 6 as for **r** based on the law, faultless.
　　 3: 9 not having a **r** of my own
1Ti 6:11 all this, and pursue **r**, godliness,
2Ti 2:22 evil desires of youth and pursue **r**,
　　 3:16 correcting and training in **r**,
　　 4: 8 is in store for me the crown of **r**,
Heb 5:13 with the teaching about **r**.
　　 7: 2 Melchizedek means "king of **r**";
　　 11: 7 and became heir of the **r** that is
　　 12:11 it produces a harvest of **r** and peace
Jas 2:23 and it was credited to him as **r**,"
　　 3:18 sow in peace reap a harvest of **r**.
1Pe 2:24 we might die to sins and live for **r**;
2Pe 2:21 not to have known the way of **r**,
　　 3:13 and a new earth, where **r** dwells.

## RIGHTFULLY* [RIGHT]
Eze 21:27 he to whom it **r** belongs shall come;

## RIGHTS [RIGHT]
Ex 21: 9 his son, he must grant her the **r**
　　 21:10 of her food, clothing and marital **r**.
Dt 21:16 sons, he must not give the **r**
Job 36: 6 alive but gives the afflicted their **r**.
Pr 31: 8 for the **r** of all who are destitute.
Isa 10: 2 to deprive the poor of their **r**
La 3:35 deny people their **r** before the Most
1Co 9:15 But I have not used any of these **r**.
Heb 12:16 sold his inheritance **r** as the oldest

## RING
Ge 41:42 Pharaoh took his signet **r** from his
Est 3:12 himself and sealed with his own **r**.
　　 8:10 dispatches with the king's signet **r**,
Pr 11:22 Like a gold **r** in a pig's snout is
Jer 22:24 were a signet **r** on my right hand,
Da 6:17 king sealed it with his own signet **r**
Hag 2:23 I will make you like my signet **r**,
Lk 15:22 Put a **r** on his finger and sandals

## RIOT [RIOTS]
Mk 14: 2 they said, "or the people may **r**."
Ac 17: 5 a mob and started a **r** in the city.

## RIOTS* [RIOT]
Ac 24: 5 **r** among the Jews all over the world.
2Co 6: 5 in beatings, imprisonments and **r**;

## RIPE
Joel 3:13 the sickle, for the harvest is **r**.
Am 8: 2 "The time is **r** for my people Israel;
Na 3:12 like fig trees with their first **r** fruit;
Mk 4:29 As soon as the grain is **r**, he puts
Jn 4:35 at the fields! They are **r** for harvest.
Rev 14:15 for the harvest of the earth is **r**."

## RISE [ARISE, RAISE, RAISED, RAISES, RISEN, RISES, RISING, ROSE]
Nu 10:35 out, Moses said, "**R** up, LORD!
　　 24:17 a scepter will **r** out of Israel.
Ps 7: 6 **r** up against the rage of my enemies.
　　 27:12 for false witnesses **r** up against me,
　　 74:22 **R** up, O God, and defend your
　　 94: 2 **R** up, Judge of the earth;
　　 139: 9 If I **r** on the wings of the dawn, if I
Isa 26:19 their bodies will **r**—let those who
　　 30:18 will **r** up to show you compassion.
Da 7:17 four kings that will **r** from the earth.
　　 12:13 the days you will **r** to receive your
Am 8:14 they will fall, never to **r** again."
Mal 4: 2 of righteousness will **r** with healing
Mt 5:45 He causes his sun to **r** on the evil
　　 27:63 'After three days I will **r** again.'
Mk 8:31 killed and after three days **r** again.
　　 13: 8 Nation will **r** against nation,
Lk 18:33 On the third day he will **r** again."
Jn 5:29 who have done what is good will **r**
　　 20: 9 that Jesus had to **r** from the dead.)
Ac 17: 3 had to suffer and **r** from the dead.
Eph 5:14 sleeper, **r** from the dead, and Christ
1Th 4:16 and the dead in Christ will **r** first.

## RISEN [RISE]
Dt 34:10 then, no prophet has **r** in Israel like
Mt 28: 6 is not here; he has **r**, just as he said.
Mk 16: 6 He has **r**! He is not here.
Lk 24:34 The Lord has **r** and has appeared

## RISES [RISE]
Ecc 1: 5 The sun **r** and the sun sets,
Isa 2:19 when he **r** to shake the earth.
　　 60: 1 the glory of the LORD **r** upon you.
Lk 16:31 if someone **r** from the dead.' "
2Pe 1:19 the morning star **r** in your hearts.

## RISING [RISE]
Ps 113: 3 From the **r** of the sun to the place
Mk 9:10 discussing what "**r** from the dead"
Lk 2:34 the falling and **r** of many in Israel,

## RITES
Heb 6: 2 instruction about cleansing **r**,

## RIVAL [RIVALRY]
1Sa 1: 7 her **r** provoked her till she wept

## RIVALRY* [RIVAL]
Php 1:15 preach Christ out of envy and **r**,

## RIVER [RIVERS]
Ge 2:10 A **r** watering the garden flowed
　　 15:18 the Wadi of Egypt to the great **r**,

Ge   41: 2  of the **r** there came up seven cows,
Dt    1: 7  as far as the great **r**, the Euphrates.
     11:24  and from the Euphrates **R**
Jos   1: 2  cross the Jordan **R** into the land I am
     24: 2  lived beyond the Euphrates **R**
Ps   46: 4  There is a **r** whose streams make
     78:44  He turned their **r** into blood;
Isa  48:18  peace would have been like a **r**,
     66:12  "I will extend peace to her like a **r**,
La    2:18  let your tears flow like a **r** day
Eze  47:12  will grow on both banks of the **r**.
Da    7:10  A **r** of fire was flowing,
Am    5:24  But let justice roll on like a **r**,
Mt    3: 6  baptized by him in the Jordan **R**.
Rev  12:15  the serpent spewed water like a **r**,
     22: 1  the angel showed me the **r**

## RIVERS  [RIVER]

Ps   78:16  and made water flow down like **r**.
    137: 1  By the **r** of Babylon we sat
Jn    7:38  **r** of living water will flow
Rev   8:10  fell from the sky on a third of the **r**
     16: 4  angel poured out his bowl on the **r**

## ROAD  [CROSSROADS, ROADS]

Nu   22:22  stood in the **r** to oppose him.
Mt    7:13  gate and broad is the **r** that leads
Mk   11: 8  people spread their cloaks on the **r**,

## ROADS  [ROAD]

Lk    3: 5  The crooked **r** shall become

## ROAR  [ROARING, ROARS]

Ps   46: 3  though its waters **r** and foam
Isa  17:13  Although the peoples **r** like the **r**
Jer  25:30  " 'The LORD will **r**
Hos  11:10  he will **r** like a lion.
Joel  3:16  The LORD will **r** from Zion
2Pe   3:10  The heavens will disappear with a **r**;
Rev  10: 3  he gave a loud shout like the **r**
     14: 2  heaven like the **r** of rushing waters
     19: 6  like the **r** of rushing waters and like

## ROARING  [ROAR]

Ps   65: 7  who stilled the **r** of the seas, the **r**
1Pe   5: 8  prowls around like a **r** lion looking

## ROARS  [ROAR]

Hos  11:10  When he **r**, his children will come
Am    1: 2  "The LORD **r** from Zion

## ROB  [ROBBER, ROBBERS, ROBBERY, ROBS]

Lev  19:13  defraud your neighbors or **r** them.
Mal   3: 8  "Will a mere mortal **r** God?

## ROBBER*  [ROB]

Jn   10: 1  some other way, is a thief and a **r**.

## ROBBERS  [ROB]

Jer   7:11  Name, become a den of **r** to you?
Mt   21:13  you are making it 'a den of **r**.' "
Lk   10:30  when he fell into the hands of **r**.
     19:46  you have made it 'a den of **r**.' "

Jn   10: 8  come before me are thieves and **r**,

## ROBBERY  [ROB]

Isa  61: 8  I hate **r** and wrongdoing.
Eze  22:29  practice extortion and commit **r**;

## ROBE  [ROBED, ROBES]

Ge   37: 3  he made a richly ornamented **r**
Ex   28: 4  an ephod, a **r**, a woven tunic,
Jos   7:21  in the plunder a beautiful **r**
1Sa   2:19  year his mother made him a little **r**
     15:27  caught hold of the hem of his **r**,
     24: 4  and cut off a corner of Saul's **r**.
2Sa  13:18  was wearing a richly ornamented **r**,
Isa   6: 1  the train of his **r** filled the temple.
     61:10  me in a **r** of his righteousness,
Zec   8:23  hold of one Jew by the hem of his **r**
Lk   15:22  Bring the best **r** and put it on him.
Jn   19: 5  crown of thorns and the purple **r**,
Heb   1:12  You will roll them up like a **r**;
Rev   1:13  dressed in a **r** reaching down to his
      6:11  each of them was given a white **r**,
     19:13  He is dressed in a **r** dipped in blood,

## ROBED*  [ROBE]

Est   6:11  He **r** Mordecai, and led him
Ps   93: 1  he is **r** in majesty; the LORD is **r** in
            majesty
Isa  63: 1  Who is this, **r** in splendor,
Rev  10: 1  He was **r** in a cloud, with a rainbow

## ROBES  [ROBE]

Ps   45: 8  All your **r** are fragrant with myrrh
Mk   12:38  like to walk around in flowing **r**
Rev   7:13  asked me, "These in white **r**—
     22:14  are those who wash their **r**, that they

## ROBS*  [ROB]

Pr   19:26  Whoever **r** their father and drives
     28:24  Whoever **r** their father or mother

## ROCK  [ROCKS, ROCKY]

Ge   49:24  of the Shepherd, the **R** of Israel,
Ex   17: 6  Strike the **r**, and water will come
     33:22  I will put you in a cleft in the **r**
Nu   20: 8  Speak to that **r** before their eyes
Dt   32: 4  He is the **R**, his works are perfect,
     32:13  him with honey from the **r**,
     32:15  him and rejected the **R** his Savior.
     32:31  For their **r** is not like our **R**, as even
1Sa   2: 2  there is no **R** like our God.
2Sa  22: 2  "The LORD is my **r**, my fortress
Ps   18: 2  The LORD is my **r**, my fortress
     19:14  LORD, my **R** and my Redeemer.
     27: 5  tabernacle and set me high upon a **r**.
     40: 2  he set my feet on a **r** and gave me
     61: 2  lead me to the **r** that is higher than I.
     62: 2  Truly he is my **r** and my salvation;
     92:15  he is my **R**, and there is no
Isa  26: 4  the LORD, is the **R** eternal.
     44: 8  No, there is no other **R**; I know not
     48:21  water flow for them from the **r**;
     51: 1  Look to the **r** from which you were
Da    2:34  you were watching, a **r** was cut out,
Zec  12: 3  make Jerusalem an immovable **r**

Mt   7:24   man who built his house on the **r**.
    16:18   and on this **r** I will build my church,
Mk  15:46   and placed it in a tomb cut out of **r**.
Ro   9:33   and a **r** that makes them fall,
1Co 10:  4   the spiritual **r** that accompanied
    10:  4   and that **r** was Christ.
1Pe  2:  8   and a **r** that makes them fall."

## ROCKS [ROCK]

Ps  78:15   He split the **r** in the wilderness
   137:  9   infants and dash them against the **r**.
Isa  2:19   People will flee to caves in the **r**
Ob   1:  3   you who live in the clefts of the **r**
Na   1:  6   the **r** are shattered before him.
Mt  27:51   The earth shook, the **r** split
Rev  6:15   and among the **r** of the mountains.

## ROCKY [ROCK]

Mk   4:  5   Some fell on **r** places, where it did

## ROD [RODS]

2Sa  7:14   I will punish him with a **r** wielded
Ps   2:  9   break them with a **r** of iron;
    23:  4   your **r** and your staff, they comfort
Pr  13:24   who spare the **r** hate their children,
    22:15   the **r** of discipline will drive it far
    23:13   if you punish them with the **r**,
    29:15   A **r** and a reprimand impart
Isa 11:  4   the earth with the **r** of his mouth;

## RODE [RIDE]

Hab  3:  8   the sea when you **r** your horses
Rev  6:  2   and he **r** out as a conqueror bent

## RODS [ROD]

2Co 11:25   Three times I was beaten with **r**,

## ROLL [ROLLED, ROLLING]

Am   5:24   But let justice **r** on like a river,
Mk  16:  3   "Who will **r** the stone away
Heb  1:12   You will **r** them up like a robe;

## ROLLED [ROLL]

Jos   5:  9   "Today I have **r** away the reproach
Lk   24:  2   They found the stone **r** away

## ROLLING [ROLL]

Rev  6:14   The sky receded like a scroll, **r** up,

## ROMAN [ROME]

Ac  16:37   even though we are **R** citizens,
    22:25   to flog a **R** citizen who hasn't even

## ROMANS [ROME]

Jn  11:48   then the **R** will come and take away

## ROME [ROMAN, ROMANS]

Ac  18:  2   had ordered all Jews to leave **R**.
    28:14   And so we came to **R**.
Ro   1:15   the gospel also to you who are in **R**.

## ROOF [ROOFS]

Ge  19:  8   under the protection of my **r**."
Jos   2:  6   she had taken them up to the **r**

2Sa 11:  2   the **r** he saw a woman bathing.
Ps  22:15   tongue sticks to the **r** of my mouth;
Pr  21:  9   a corner of the **r** than share a house
Mt   8:  8   to have you come under my **r**.
Mk   2:  4   an opening in the **r** above Jesus
Ac  10:  9   city, Peter went up on the **r** to pray.

## ROOFS [ROOF]

Mt  10:27   in your ear, proclaim from the **r**.

## ROOM [ROOMS, STOREROOM]

Mt   6:  6   go into your **r**, close the door
Mk  14:15   He will show you a large **r** upstairs,
Lk   2:  7   there was no guest **r** available
Jn   8:37   because you have no **r** for my word.
    14:  2   My Father's house has plenty of **r**;
    21:25   the whole world would not have **r**
Ro  12:19   but leave **r** for God's wrath, for it is
2Co  7:  2   Make **r** for us in your hearts.

## ROOMS [ROOM]

Mt  24:26   is, in the inner **r**,' do not believe it.
Lk  12:  3   ear in the inner **r** will be proclaimed

## ROOSTER

Mt  26:34   before the **r** crows, you will disown
    26:75   "Before the **r** crows, you will

## ROOT [ROOTED, ROOTS]

Pr  12:12   but the **r** of the righteous flourishes.
Isa 11:10   day the **R** of Jesse will stand as
    53:  2   and like a **r** out of dry ground.
Mt   3:10   ax is already at the **r** of the trees,
    13:21   But since they have no **r**, they last
Ro  11:16   if the **r** is holy, so are the branches.
    15:12   "The **R** of Jesse will spring up,
1Ti  6:10   the love of money is a **r** of all kinds
Rev  5:  5   the tribe of Judah, the **R** of David,
    22:16   I am the **R** and the Offspring

## ROOTED* [ROOT]

Eph  3:17   you, being **r** and established in love,
Col  2:  7   **r** and built up in him,

## ROOTS [ROOT]

Isa 11:  1   from his **r** a Branch will bear fruit.
Jer  17:  8   that sends out its **r** by the stream.
Eze  17:  9   many people to pull it up by the **r**.
Hos  14:  5   of Lebanon he will send down his **r**;
Mt  15:13   planted will be pulled up by the **r**.

## ROSE [RISE]

Ge   7:18   The waters **r** and increased greatly
1Ch 21:  1   Satan **r** up against Israel and incited
SS   2:  1   I am a **r** of Sharon, a lily
Eze  1:19   when the living creatures **r** from the
                ground,
Mt   2:  2   saw his star when it **r** and have come
    7:25   the streams **r**, and the winds blew
Ac  10:41   with him after he **r** from the dead.
1Th  4:14   believe that Jesus died and **r** again,

## ROT [ROTS, ROTTED]

Pr  10:  7   but the name of the wicked will **r**.
Hos  5:12   like **r** to the people of Judah.

Zec 14:12 Their flesh will r while they are still

## ROTS* [ROT]
Pr 14:30 to the body, but envy r the bones.

## ROTTED* [ROT]
Jas 5: 2 Your wealth has r, and moths have

## ROUGH* [ROUGHER]
Isa 40: 4 the r ground shall become level,
    42:16 them and make the r places smooth.
Lk 3: 5 become straight, the r ways smooth.
Jn 6:18 was blowing and the waters grew r.

## ROUGHER* [ROUGH]
Jnh 1:11 The sea was getting r and r.

## ROUND
Ecc 1: 6 r and r it goes, ever returning on its

## ROUSE [AROUSE, AROUSED]
Job 3: 8 those who are ready to r Leviathan.
Ps 59: 5 r yourself to punish all the nations;

## ROUTED [ROUTS]
Ps 18:14 great bolts of lightning he r them.
Heb 11:34 in battle and r foreign armies.

## ROUTS* [ROUTED]
Jos 23:10 One of you r a thousand,

## ROW
Jnh 1:13 the men did their best to r back

## ROYAL
Jos 11:12 Joshua took all these r cities
1Ki 9: 5 I will establish your r throne over
2Ch 22:10 to destroy the whole r family
Ps 45: 9 your right hand is the r bride in gold
Isa 62: 3 a r diadem in the hand of your God.
Da 1: 8 not to defile himself with the r food
Jas 2: 8 If you really keep the r law found
1Pe 2: 9 are a chosen people, a r priesthood,

## RUBBLE
Jer 26:18 Jerusalem will become a heap of r,
Mic 3:12 Jerusalem will become a heap of r,
2Ch 7:21 temple will become a heap of r.

## RUBIES [RUBY]
Job 28:18 the price of wisdom is beyond r.
Pr 3:15 She is more precious than r;
    8:11 for wisdom is more precious than r,
    31:10 She is worth far more than r.

## RUBY [RUBIES]
Rev 4: 3 had the appearance of jasper and r.

## RUDDER*
Jas 3: 4 by a very small r wherever the pilot

## RUDDY
SS 5:10 My beloved is radiant and r,

## RUGGED
Ps 68:16 why gaze in envy, you r mountain,
Isa 40: 4 become level, the r places a plain.

## RUIN [RUINED, RUINS]
Dt 28:20 and come to sudden r because
Job 22:19 The righteous see their r
Pr 10: 8 but a chattering fool comes to r.
    10:14 but the mouth of a fool invites r.
    10:29 but it is the r of those who do evil.
    11:17 the cruel bring r on themselves.
    11:29 Those who bring r on their families
    15:27 greedy bring r to their households,
    18:24 unreliable friends soon comes to r,
    19: 3 One's own folly leads to r,
    19:13 A foolish child is a father's r,
    26:28 and a flattering mouth works r.
Ecc 4: 5 Fools fold their hands and r themselves.
SS 2:15 the little foxes that r the vineyards,
Isa 25: 2 the fortified town a r, the foreigners'
Eze 21:27 A r! A r! I will make it a r!
Hos 4:14 understanding will come to r!
Mic 6:13 you, to r you because of your sins.
Zep 1:15 a day of trouble and r, a day
Hag 1: 4 while this house remains a r?"
1Ti 6: 9 desires that plunge people into r
Rev 18:19 one hour she has been brought to r!'

## RUINED [RUIN]
Ex 10: 7 you not yet realize that Egypt is r?'"
Isa 3:14 "It is you who have r my vineyard;
    6: 5 "I am r! For I am a man of unclean
Jer 4:27 "The whole land will be r, though I
Mt 12:25 divided against itself will be r,
Mk 2:22 wine and the wineskins will be r.

## RUINS [RUIN]
Ezr 9: 9 house of our God and repair its r,
Ne 2:17 Jerusalem lies in r, and its gates
Isa 51: 3 look with compassion on all her r;
Jer 9:11 "I will make Jerusalem a heap of r,
Am 9:11 its broken walls and restore its r—
Ac 15:16 Its r I will rebuild, and I will restore
2Ti 2:14 value, and only r those who listen.

## RULE [RULER, RULER'S, RULERS, RULES, RULING]
Ge 1:26 so that they may r over the fish
    3:16 husband, and he will r over you."
    4: 7 but you must r over it."
    37: 8 Will you actually r us?"
Dt 15: 6 You will r over many nations
Jdg 8:22 said to Gideon, "R over us—
1Sa 12:12 'No, we want a king to r over us'—
2Ch 6: 6 David to r my people Israel.'
Ps 67: 4 for you r the peoples with equity
    119:133 to your word; let no sin r over me.
Pr 12:24 Diligent hands will r, but laziness
    17: 2 A prudent servant will r over
Isa 28:10 this, do that, a r for this, a r for that;
    32: 1 and rulers will r with justice.
Mic 4: 7 The LORD will r over them
Zec 6:13 and will sit and r on his throne.
    9:10 His r will extend from sea to sea
Ro 15:12 who will arise to r over the nations;

1Co 7:17 This is the **r** I lay down in all
Gal 6:16 and mercy to all who follow this **r**—
Eph 1:21 far above all **r** and authority,
Col 3:15 the peace of Christ **r** in your hearts,
2Th 3:10 were with you, we gave you this **r**:
Rev 2:27 they 'will **r** them with an iron
12: 5 who "will **r** all the nations
17:17 to give the beast their power to **r**,
19:15 "He will **r** them with an iron

## RULER [RULE]

Ex 2:14 "Who made you **r** and judge over
1Sa 10: 1 LORD anointed you **r** over his
inheritance?
13:14 appointed him **r** of his people,
2Sa 7: 8 and appointed you **r** over my people
Ps 82: 7 you will fall like every other **r**."
Pr 19: 6 Many curry favor with a **r**,
23: 1 When you sit to dine with a **r**,
25:15 Through patience a **r** can be
29:12 If a **r** listens to lies, all his officials
29:26 Many seek an audience with a **r**,
Ecc 9:17 than the shouts of a **r** of fools.
Isa 60:17 governor and well-being your **r**.
Da 5:29 was proclaimed the third highest **r**
9:25 the Anointed One, the **r**, comes,
Mic 5: 2 me one who will be **r** over Israel,
Mt 2: 6 will come a **r** who will shepherd my
Ac 7:27 'Who made you **r** and judge over
Eph 2: 2 of the **r** of the kingdom of the air,
1Ti 6:15 the blessed and only **R**, the King
Rev 1: 5 and the **r** of the kings of the earth.
3:14 witness, the **r** of God's creation.

## RULER'S [RULE]

Ge 49:10 nor the **r** staff from between his

## RULERS [RULE]

Jdg 16: 5 The **r** of the Philistines went to her
Job 12:17 He leads **r** away stripped
Ps 2: 2 and the **r** band together against
8: 6 You made them **r** over the works
119:161 **R** persecute me without cause,
Pr 8:15 and **r** issue decrees that are just;
31: 4 drink wine, not for **r** to crave beer,
Isa 1:10 of the LORD, you **r** of Sodom;
32: 1 and **r** will rule with justice.
40:23 and reduces the **r** of this world
Da 7:27 and all **r** will worship and obey
Mt 2: 6 by no means least among the **r**
20:25 that the **r** of the Gentiles lord it over
Ac 4:26 the **r** band together against the Lord
13:27 and their **r** did not recognize Jesus,
Ro 13: 3 For **r** hold no terror for those who
1Co 2: 6 of this age or of the **r** of this age,
Eph 3:10 God should be made known to the **r**
6:12 blood, but against the **r**,
Col 1:16 or powers or **r** or authorities;

## RULES [RULE]

Nu 15:15 is to have the same **r** for you
2Sa 23: 3 when he **r** in the fear of God,
Ps 22:28 LORD and he **r** over the nations.
66: 7 He **r** forever by his power, his eyes
103:19 heaven, and his kingdom **r** over all.
Isa 29:13 on merely human **r** they have been

Isa 40:10 with power, and his arm **r** for him.
Mk 7: 7 their teachings are merely human **r**.'
Lk 22:26 and the one who **r** like the one who
Col 2:20 to the world, do you submit to its **r**:
2Ti 2: 5 by competing according to the **r**.
Rev 17:18 is the great city that **r** over the kings

## RULING [RULE]

Ex 15:25 the LORD issued a **r** and instruction
Pr 25:11 is a **r** rightly given.
Jn 3: 1 a member of the Jewish **r** council.

## RUMOR [RUMORS]

Eze 7:26 calamity will come, and **r** upon **r**.
Jn 21:23 the **r** spread among the believers

## RUMORS [RUMOR]

Jer 51:46 or be afraid when **r** are heard
Mt 24: 6 You will hear of wars and **r** of wars,

## RUN [RAN, RUNNERS, RUNNING, RUNS]

1Sa 31: 4 your sword and **r** me through,
Ps 19: 5 champion rejoicing to **r** his course.
119:32 I **r** in the path of your commands,
Pr 4:12 when you **r**, you will not stumble.
18:10 the righteous **r** to it and are safe.
Isa 10: 3 To whom will you **r** for help?
40:31 they will **r** and not grow weary,
Jer 51:45 **R** from the fierce anger
Joel 3:18 ravines of Judah will **r** with water.
Hab 2: 2 so that a herald may **r** with it.
Mt 6:32 the pagans **r** after all these things,
1Co 9:24 **R** in such a way as to get the prize.
Php 2:16 on the day of Christ that I did not **r**
Heb 12: 1 let us **r** with perseverance the race

## RUNNERS* [RUN]

1Co 9:24 not know that in a race all the **r** run,

## RUNNING [RUN]

Ps 133: 2 on the head, **r** down on the beard,
Pr 5:15 cistern, **r** water from your own well.
Jnh 1:10 (They knew he was **r** away
Lk 17:23 Do not go **r** off after them.
1Co 9:26 do not run like someone **r** aimlessly;
Gal 2: 2 I was not **r** and had not been **r** my race
in vain.
5: 7 You were **r** a good race. Who cut

## RUNS [RUN]

Jn 10:12 he abandons the sheep and **r** away.
2Jn 1: 9 Anyone who **r** ahead and does not

## RUSH [RUSHES, RUSHING]

Pr 1:16 for their feet **r** into evil, they are
6:18 feet that are quick to **r** into evil,
Isa 59: 7 Their feet **r** into sin; they are swift

## RUSHES [RUSH]

Pr 26:17 who **r** into a quarrel not their own.

## RUSHING [RUSH]

Pr 18: 4 fountain of wisdom is a **r** stream.

Eze  1:24  like the roar of **r** waters,
     43: 2  voice was like the roar of **r** waters,
Rev  1:15  was like the sound of **r** waters.
     14: 2  heaven like the roar of **r** waters
     19: 6  like the roar of **r** waters and like

## RUST

Mt   6:19  where moth and **r** destroy,

## RUTH

Moabitess; widow who went to Bethlehem with mother-in-law Naomi (Ru 1). Gleaned in field of Boaz; shown favor (Ru 2). Proposed marriage to Boaz (Ru 3). Married (Ru 4:1–12); bore Obed, ancestor of David (Ru 4:13–22), Jesus (Mt 1:5).

## RUTHLESS [RUTHLESSLY]

Ps  37:35  **r** flourishing like a luxuriant native
Pr  11:16  honor, but **r** men gain only wealth.
Isa  29:20  The **r** will vanish, the mockers will

## RUTHLESSLY [RUTHLESS]

Ex   1:14  labor the Egyptians used them **r**.
Lev 25:43  Do not rule over them **r**, but fear

---

# S

---

## SABACHTHANI*

Mt  27:46  voice, *"Eli, Eli, lema s?"*
Mk  15:34  voice, *"Eloi, Eloi, lema s?"*

## SABAOTH (KJV) See ALMIGHTY

## SABBATH [SABBATHS]

Ex  16:23  of **s** rest, a holy **s** to the LORD.
    20: 8  "Remember the **S** day by keeping it
    31:14  " 'Observe the **S**, because it is
Lev 23:16  up to the day after the seventh **S**,
    25: 2  the land itself must observe a **s**
Nu  15:32  found gathering wood on the **S** day.
Dt   5:12  "Observe the **S** day by keeping it
2Ch 36:21  The land enjoyed its **s** rests;
Ne  13:17  desecrating the **S** day?
Ps  92: T  *A song. For the **S** day.*
Isa  56: 2  who keep the **S** without desecrating
    58:13  if you call the **S** a delight
Jer  17:21  not to carry a load on the **S** day
Mt  12: 1  through the grainfields on the **S**.
Mk  2:28  Son of Man is Lord even of the **S**."
Lk   6: 9  ask you, which is lawful on the **S**:
    13:10  On a **S** Jesus was teaching in one
    14: 3  law, "Is it lawful to heal on the **S**
Col  2:16  a New Moon celebration or a **S** day.

## SABBATH-REST* [REST]

Heb  4: 9  then, a **S** for the people of God;

## SABBATHS [SABBATH]

Ex  31:13  Israelites, 'You must observe my **S**.
Lev 26:34  the land will rest and enjoy its **s**.
Eze 20:12  I gave them my **S** as a sign between

## SACKCLOTH

1Ch 21:16  elders, clothed in **s**, fell facedown.
Ps  30:11  you removed my **s** and clothed me
Da   9: 3  in fasting, and in **s** and ashes.
Joel  1:13  spend the night in **s**, you who
Jnh  3: 5  the greatest to the least, put on **s**.
Mt  11:21  would have repented long ago in **s**

## SACRED

Ex  12:16  On the first day hold a **s** assembly,
    23:24  and break their **s** stones to pieces.
    28: 2  Make **s** garments for your brother
    30:31  'This is to be my **s** anointing oil
Lev 23: 2  you are to proclaim as **s** assemblies.
Isa  1:29  be ashamed because of the **s** oaks
Hos  3: 4  prince, without sacrifice or **s** stones,
Joel  1:14  a holy fast; call a **s** assembly.
Mt  7: 6  "Do not give dogs what is **s**;
Ro  14: 5  one day more **s** than another;
1Co  3:17  for God's temple is **s**, and you
2Pe  1:18  were with him on the **s** mountain.
    2:21  turn their backs on the **s** command

## SACRIFICE [SACRIFICED, SACRIFICES]

Ge  22: 2  **S** him there as a burnt offering
Ex  5:17  'Let us go and **s** to the LORD.'
    12:27  'It is the Passover **s** to the LORD,
Jdg  11:31  and I will **s** it as a burnt offering."
1Sa  2:13  any of the people offered a **s**,
    15:22  To obey is better than **s**, and to heed
1Ki 18:38  the LORD fell and burned up the **s**,
1Ch 21:24  or **s** a burnt offering that costs me
Ps  40: 6  **S** and offering you did not desire—
    50:14  "**S** thank offerings to God,
    50:23  who **s** thank offerings honor me,
    51:16  You do not delight in **s**, or I would
    51:17  My **s**, O God, is a broken spirit;
    54: 6  I will **s** a freewill offering to you;
   107:22  Let them **s** thank offerings and tell
   141: 2  of my hands be like the evening **s**.
Pr  15: 8  The LORD detests the **s**
    21: 3  acceptable to the LORD than **s**.
    21:27  The **s** of the wicked is detestable—
Eze 20:26  the **s** of every firstborn—
Da  8:13  the vision concerning the daily **s**,
    9:27  of the 'seven' he will put an end to **s**
    12:11  the time that the daily **s** is abolished
Hos  6: 6  not **s**, and acknowledgment of God
Zep  1: 7  The LORD has prepared a **s**;
Mt  9:13  'I desire mercy, not **s**.'
Ro  3:25  God presented Christ as a **s**
    12: 1  offer your bodies as a living **s**,
Eph  5: 2  as a fragrant offering and **s** to God.
Php  2:17  out like a drink offering on the **s**
    4.18  an acceptable **s**, pleasing to God.
Heb  9:26  away with sin by the **s** of himself.
    10: 5  "**S** and offering you did not desire,
    10:10  have been made holy through the **s**
    10:14  one **s** he has made perfect forever
    10:18  **s** for sin is no longer necessary.
Heb 11:17  God tested him, offered Isaac as a **s**.
    13:15  offer to God a **s** of praise—
1Jn  2: 2  He is the atoning **s** for our sins,
    4:10  sent his Son as an atoning **s** for our

## SACRIFICED [SACRIFICE]

| | | |
|---|---|---|
| Ge | 8:20 | birds, he s burnt offerings on it. |
| | 22:13 | s it as a burnt offering instead of his |
| Lev | 18:21 | of your children to be s to Molek, |
| 2Ki | 17:17 | They s their sons and daughters |
| Lk | 22: 7 | the Passover lamb had to be s. |
| Ac | 15:29 | are to abstain from food s to idols, |
| 1Co | 5: 7 | our Passover lamb, has been s. |
| | 8: 1 | Now about food s to idols: |
| Heb | 7:27 | He s for their sins once for all |
| | 9:28 | so Christ was s once to take away |
| Rev | 2:14 | to sin so that they ate food s to idols |
| | 2:20 | and the eating of food s to idols. |

## SACRIFICES [SACRIFICE]

| | | |
|---|---|---|
| Ex | 3:18 | to offer s to the LORD our God.' |
| | 22:20 | "Whoever s to any god other than |
| Lev | 17: 7 | offer any of their s to the goat idols |
| Dt | 12:31 | in the fire as s to their gods. |
| Jos | 22:26 | but not for burnt offerings or s.' |
| 2Ch | 7: 1 | the burnt offering and the s, |
| | 7:12 | place for myself as a temple for s. |
| Ezr | 6: 3 | be rebuilt as a place to present s, |
| Ps | 4: 5 | Offer the s of the righteous and trust |
| | 50: 8 | against you concerning your s |
| Isa | 1:11 | "The multitude of your s— |
| | 56: 7 | and s will be accepted on my altar; |
| Jer | 6:20 | your s do not please me." |
| Am | 5:25 | "Did you bring me s and offerings |
| Mk | 12:33 | than all burnt offerings and s." |
| 1Co | 10:20 | but the s of pagans are offered |
| Heb | 7:27 | he does not need to offer s day |
| | 9:23 | themselves with better s than these. |
| | 13:16 | for with such s God is pleased. |
| 1Pe | 2: 5 | offering spiritual s acceptable |

## SAD [SADDENED]

| | | |
|---|---|---|
| Ne | 2: 1 | I had not been s in his presence |
| Ecc | 7: 3 | because a s face is good |
| Lk | 18:23 | he became very s, because he was |

## SADDENED* [SAD]

| | | |
|---|---|---|
| Mk | 14:19 | They were s, and one by one they |

## SADDUCEES

| | | |
|---|---|---|
| Mt | 16: 1 | The Pharisees and S came to Jesus |
| | 16: 6 | the yeast of the Pharisees and S." |
| | 22:34 | that Jesus had silenced the S, |
| Mk | 12:18 | Then the S, who say there is no |
| Ac | 23: 7 | out between the Pharisees and the S, |

## SAFE [SAVE]

| | | |
|---|---|---|
| 2Sa | 18:29 | asked, "Is the young man Absalom s?" |
| Ezr | 8:21 | and ask him for a s journey for us |
| Job | 21: 9 | Their homes are s and free from fear; |
| Ps | 12: 7 | will keep the needy s and will |
| | 16: 1 | Keep me s, my God, for in you I take |
| | 27: 5 | of trouble he will keep me s in his |
| | 37: 3 | in the land and enjoy s pasture. |
| Pr | 18:10 | the righteous run to it and are s. |
| | 28:18 | whose walk is blameless are kept s, |
| | 28:26 | who walk in wisdom are kept s. |
| | 29:25 | trusts in the LORD is kept s. |
| Jer | 12: 5 | If you stumble in s country, |
| Lk | 15:27 | because he has him back s and sound.' |

| | | |
|---|---|---|
| Jn | 17:12 | kept them s by that name you gave |
| 1Jn | 5:18 | who was born of God keeps them s, |

## SAFE-CONDUCT* [CONDUCT]

| | | |
|---|---|---|
| Ne | 2: 7 | they will provide me s until I arrive |

## SAFEGUARD* [GUARD]

| | | |
|---|---|---|
| Php | 3: 1 | to you again, and it is a s for you. |

## SAFELY [SAVE]

| | | |
|---|---|---|
| Ge | 19:16 | and led them s out of the city, |
| | 28:21 | I return s to my father's household, |
| Lev | 25:18 | laws, and you will live s in the land. |
| 1Ki | 22:28 | Micaiah declared, "If you ever return s, |

## SAFETY [SAVE]

| | | |
|---|---|---|
| Dt | 12:10 | you so that you will live in s. |
| Ps | 4: 8 | alone, LORD, make me dwell in s. |
| | 141:10 | into their own nets, while I pass by in s. |
| Pr | 3:23 | Then you will go on your way in s, |
| Isa | 14:30 | and the needy will lie down in s. |
| Jer | 33:16 | saved and Jerusalem will live in s. |
| Eze | 34:28 | They will live in s, and no one will |
| Hos | 2:18 | land, so that all may lie down in s. |
| 1Th | 5: 3 | "Peace and s," destruction will |

## SAIL [SAILED, SAILORS]

| | | |
|---|---|---|
| 2Ch | 20:37 | and were not able to set s to trade. |

## SAILED [SAIL]

| | | |
|---|---|---|
| Jnh | 1: 3 | and s for Tarshish to flee |
| Lk | 8:23 | As they s, he fell asleep. |

## SAILORS [SAIL]

| | | |
|---|---|---|
| Jnh | 1: 5 | All the s were afraid and each cried |

## SAINT(S)

Translated in the TNIV as "faithful," "faithful people," "faithful servants," "God's people," "godly," "his people," "holy people," "Lord's people," "his own people," "people of God," "your people."

Following are all NIV references to "saints": 1Sa 2:9; 2Ch 6:41; Ps 16:3; 30:4; 31:23; 34:9; 52:9; 79:2; 85:8; 116:15; 132:9, 16; 145:10; 148:14; 149:1, 5, 9; Da 7:18, 21, 22, 25, 25, 27; 8:12; Ac 9:13, 32; 26:10; Ro 1:7; 8:27; 15:25, 26, 31; 16:2, 15; 1Co 6:1, 2; 14:33; 16:15; 2Co 1:1; 8:4; 9:1; 13:13; Eph 1:1, 15, 18; 3:18; 6:18; Php 1:1; 4:21, 22; Col 1:4, 12, 26; 1Ti 5:10; Phm 1:5, 7; Jude 1:3; Rev 5:8; 8:3, 4; 11:18; 13:7, 10; 14:12; 16:6; 17:6; 18:20, 24; 19:8

## SAKE

| | | |
|---|---|---|
| Ge | 12:16 | He treated Abram well for her s, |
| | 18:24 | the s of the fifty righteous people |
| Lev | 26:45 | their s I will remember the covenant |
| Jos | 23: 3 | done to all these nations for your s, |
| 1Sa | 12:22 | the s of his great name the LORD |
| 1Ki | 11:12 | for the s of David your father, I will |
| Ps | 23: 3 | the right paths for his name's s. |
| | 25:11 | For the s of your name, LORD, |
| | 44:22 | your s we face death all day long; |
| | 69: 7 | For I endure scorn for your s, |
| | 106: 8 | Yet he saved them for his name's s, |
| | 109:21 | LORD, help me for your name's s; |
| | 132:10 | For the s of your servant David, |

| | | |
|---|---|---|
| Isa | 42:21 | for the s of his righteousness |
| | 43:25 | for my own s, and remembers your |
| | 48: 9 | my own name's s I delay my wrath; |
| | 48:11 | For my own s, for my own s, I do |
| | 62: 1 | For Zion's s I will not keep silent, |
| Jer | 14: 7 | LORD, for the s of your name. |
| | 14:21 | the s of your name do not despise |
| Eze | 20: 9 | But for the s of my name, I brought |
| | 20:14 | the s of my name I did what would |
| | 20:22 | the s of my name I did what would |
| | 36:32 | that I am not doing this for your s, |
| Da | 9:17 | For your s, Lord, look with favor |
| Mt | 10:39 | loses their life for my s will find it. |
| | 19:29 | my s will receive a hundred times as |
| Ro | 8:36 | your s we face death all day long; |
| | 9: 3 | from Christ for the s of my people, |
| | 14:20 | the work of God for the s of food. |
| 1Co | 9:23 | I do all this for the s of the gospel, |
| 2Co | 4:11 | given over to death for Jesus' s, |
| | 8: 9 | yet for your s he became poor, |
| | 12:10 | is why, for Christ's s, I delight |
| Php | 3: 7 | consider loss for the s of Christ. |
| Heb | 11:26 | disgrace for the s of Christ as |
| 1Pe | 2:13 | for the Lord's s to every human |
| 3Jn | 1: 7 | It was for the s of the Name |

## SALE [SELL]

| | | |
|---|---|---|
| Dt | 28:68 | you will offer yourselves for s |
| Ps | 44:12 | gaining nothing from their s. |

## SALEM

| | | |
|---|---|---|
| Ge | 14:18 | Melchizedek king of S brought |
| Heb | 7: 2 | also, "king of S" means "king |

## SALIVA*

| | | |
|---|---|---|
| 1Sa | 21:13 | and letting s run down his beard. |
| Jn | 9: 6 | made some mud with the s, and put |

## SALT [SALTED, SALTINESS, SALTY]

| | | |
|---|---|---|
| Ge | 19:26 | back, and she became a pillar of s. |
| Lev | 2:13 | all your grain offerings with s. |
| Nu | 18:19 | covenant of s before the LORD |
| 2Ki | 2:20 | bowl," he said, "and put s in it." |
| Mt | 5:13 | "You are the s of the earth. |
| Mk | 9:50 | "S is good, but if it loses its |
| Col | 4: 6 | seasoned with s, so that you may |
| Jas | 3:11 | s water flow from the same spring? |

## SALTED [SALT]

| | | |
|---|---|---|
| Mk | 9:49 | Everyone will be s with fire. |

## SALTINESS [SALT]

| | | |
|---|---|---|
| Lk | 14:34 | but if it loses its s, how can it be |

## SALTY [SALT]

| | | |
|---|---|---|
| Mt | 5:13 | how can it be made s again? It is no |

## SALVATION* [SAVE]

| | | |
|---|---|---|
| Ex | 15: 2 | he has become my s. |
| 2Sa | 22: 3 | my shield and the horn of my s. |
| | 23: 5 | he would not bring to fruition my s |
| 1Ch | 16:23 | proclaim his s day after day. |
| 2Ch | 6:41 | be clothed with s, may your faithful |
| Ps | 9:14 | Zion, and there rejoice in your s. |
| | 13: 5 | my heart rejoices in your s. |

| | | |
|---|---|---|
| Ps | 14: 7 | that s for Israel would come |
| | 18: 2 | my shield and the horn of my s, |
| | 27: 1 | The LORD is my light and my s— |
| | 28: 8 | a fortress of s for his anointed one. |
| | 35: 3 | Say to me, "I am your s." |
| | 35: 9 | in the LORD and delight in his s. |
| | 37:39 | The s of the righteous comes |
| | 50:23 | to the blameless I will show my s." |
| | 51:12 | Restore to me the joy of your s |
| | 53: 6 | that s for Israel would come |
| | 62: 1 | rest in God; my s comes from him. |
| | 62: 2 | Truly he is my rock and my s; |
| | 62: 6 | Truly he is my rock and my s; |
| | 62: 7 | My s and my honor depend on God; |
| | 67: 2 | on earth, your s among all nations. |
| | 69:13 | O God, answer me with your sure s. |
| | 69:27 | do not let them share in your s. |
| | 69:29 | may your s, God, protect me. |
| | 74:12 | he brings s on the earth. |
| | 85: 7 | love, LORD, and grant us your s. |
| | 85: 9 | Surely his s is near those who fear |
| | 91:16 | satisfy them and show them my s." |
| | 95: 1 | us shout aloud to the Rock of our s. |
| | 96: 2 | proclaim his s day after day. |
| | 98: 1 | his holy arm have worked s for him. |
| | 98: 2 | The LORD has made his s known |
| | 98: 3 | of the earth have seen the s of our |
| | 116:13 | I will lift up the cup of s and call |
| | 118:14 | he has become my s. |
| | 118:21 | you have become my s. |
| | 119:41 | your s, according to your promise; |
| | 119:81 | soul faints with longing for your s, |
| | 119:123 | looking for your s, looking for your |
| | 119:155 | S is far from the wicked, for they do |
| | 119:166 | I wait for your s, LORD, and I |
| | 119:174 | I long for your s, LORD, and your |
| | 132:16 | I will clothe her priests with s, |
| Isa | 12: 2 | Surely God is my s; I will trust |
| | 12: 2 | he has become my s." |
| | 12: 3 | will draw water from the wells of s. |
| | 25: 9 | let us rejoice and be glad in his s." |
| | 26: 1 | God makes s its walls and ramparts. |
| | 26:18 | We have not brought s to the earth, |
| | 30:15 | "In repentance and rest is your s, |
| | 33: 2 | morning, our s in time of distress. |
| | 33: 6 | a rich store of s and wisdom |
| | 45: 8 | the earth open wide, let s spring up, |
| | 45:17 | the LORD with an everlasting s; |
| | 46:13 | and my s will not be delayed. |
| | 46:13 | I will grant s to Zion, |
| | 49: 6 | that my s may reach to the ends |
| | 49: 8 | and in the day of s I will help you; |
| | 51: 5 | near speedily, my s is on the way, |
| | 51: 6 | But my s will last forever, |
| | 51: 8 | my s through all generations." |
| | 52: 7 | who proclaim s, who say to Zion, |
| | 52:10 | the earth will see the s of our God. |
| | 56: 1 | for my s is close at hand and my |
| | 59:16 | so his own arm achieved s for him, |
| | 59:17 | and the helmet of s on his head; |
| | 60:18 | you will call your walls S and your |
| | 61:10 | has clothed me with garments of s |
| | 62: 1 | the dawn, her s like a blazing torch. |
| | 63: 5 | so my own arm achieved s for me, |
| Jer | 3:23 | in the LORD our God is the s |
| La | 3:26 | wait quietly for the s of the LORD. |
| Jnh | 2: 9 | 'S comes from the LORD.' " |

Zec 9: 9 righteous and having s,
Lk 1:69 He has raised up a horn of s for us
1:71 s from our enemies
1:77 of s through the forgiveness of their
2:30 For my eyes have seen your s,
3: 6 all people will see God's s.' "
19: 9 "Today s has come to this house,
Jn 4:22 we do know, for s is from the Jews.
Ac 4:12 S is found in no one else, for there is
13:26 that this message of s has been sent.
13:47 that you may bring s to the ends
28:28 know that God's s has been sent
Ro 1:16 brings s to everyone who believes:
11:11 s has come to the Gentiles to make
13:11 because our s is nearer now than
2Co 1: 6 it is for your comfort and s;
6: 2 and in the day of s I helped you."
6: 2 of God's favor, now is the day of s.
7:10 brings repentance that leads to s
Eph 1:13 word of truth, the gospel of your s.
6:17 Take the helmet of s and the sword
Php 2:12 to work out your s with fear
1Th 5: 8 and the hope of s as a helmet.
5: 9 to receive s through our Lord Jesus
2Ti 2:10 that they too may obtain the s that is
3:15 make you wise for s through faith
Tit 2:11 appeared that offers s to all people.
Heb 1:14 to serve those who will inherit s?
2: 3 we escape if we ignore so great a s?
2: 3 This s, which was first announced
2:10 of their s perfect through what he
5: 9 of eternal s for all who obey him
6: 9 the things that have to do with s.
9:28 to bring s to those who are waiting
1Pe 1: 5 the coming of the s that is ready
1: 9 of your faith, the s of your souls.
1:10 Concerning this s, the prophets,
2: 2 by it you may grow up in your s,
2Pe 3:15 that our Lord's patience means s,
Jude 1: 3 to write to you about the s we share,
Rev 7:10 "S belongs to our God, who sits
12:10 "Now have come the s
19: 1 S and glory and power belong to our

## SAMARIA [SAMARITAN, SAMARITANS]

1Ki 16:24 the hill, calling it S, after Shemer,
16:32 the temple of Baal that he built in S.
20:43 of Israel went to his palace in S.
2Ki 17: 6 the king of Assyria captured S
Isa 7: 9 The head of Ephraim is S,
36:19 Have they rescued S from my hand?
Eze 23: 4 Oholah is S, and Oholibah is
Hos 8: 5 S, throw out your calf-idol!
Am 6: 1 to you who feel secure on Mount S,
Mic 1: 6 "Therefore I will make S a heap
Jn 4: 4 Now he had to go through S.
Ac 1: 8 and in all Judea and S,
8: 1 scattered throughout Judea and S.
8:14 heard that S had accepted the word

## SAMARITAN [SAMARIA]

Lk 10:33 But a S, as he traveled, came where
17:16 and thanked him—and he was a S.
Jn 4: 7 When a S woman came to draw
8:48 we right in saying that you are a S

Ac 8:25 the gospel in many S villages.

## SAMARITANS [SAMARIA]

Jn 4: 9 (For Jews do not associate with S.)

## SAME

Ge 11: 6 people speaking the s language they
Ex 5: 8 to make the s number of bricks as
7:11 did the s things by their secret arts:
7:22 Egyptian magicians did the s things
8: 7 the magicians did the s things
34:16 they will lead your sons to do the s.
Dt 7:19 The LORD your God will do the s
1Sa 2:34 they will both die on the s day.
Ps 102:27 But you remain the s, and your
Ecc 2:14 that the s fate overtakes them both.
9: 3 The s destiny overtakes all.
Mt 5:12 for in the s way they persecuted
7: 2 For in the s way you judge others,
Ac 1:11 in the s way you have seen him go
11:17 God gave them the s gift he gave us
Ro 2: 1 who pass judgment do the s things.
10:12 the s Lord is Lord of all and richly
12: 4 do not all have the s function,
15: 5 give you the s attitude of mind
1Co 10: 3 They all ate the s spiritual food
12: 4 but the s Spirit distributes them.
12: 5 kinds of service, but the s Lord.
Php 2: 5 have the s attitude of mind Christ
4: 2 to be of the s mind in the Lord.
1Ti 3: 6 and fall under the s judgment as
Heb 1:12 But you remain the s, and your
13: 8 Jesus Christ is the s yesterday

## SAMSON*

Danite judge. Birth promised (Jdg 13). Married to Philistine, but wife given away (Jdg 14). Ven-geance on the Philistines (Jdg 15). Betrayed by Delilah (Jdg 16:1–22). Death (Jdg 16). Feats of strength: killed lion (Jdg 14:6), 30 Philistines (Jdg 14:19), 1,000 Philistines with jawbone (Jdg 15:13–17), car-ried off gates of Gaza (Jdg 16:3), pushed down tem-ple of Dagon (Jdg 16:25–30; Heb 11:32).

## SAMUEL

Ephraimite judge and prophet (Heb 11:32). Birth prayed for (1Sa 1:10–18). Dedicated to temple by Hannah (1Sa 1:21–28). Raised by Eli (1Sa 2:11, 18–26). Called as prophet (1Sa 3). Led Israel to vic-tory over Philistines (1Sa 7). Asked by Israel for a king (1Sa 8). Anointed Saul as king (1Sa 9–10). Farewell speech (1Sa 12). Rebuked Saul for sacrifice (1Sa 13). Announced rejection of Saul (1Sa 15). Anointed David as king (1Sa 16). Protected David from Saul (1Sa 19:18–24). Death (1Sa 25:1). Re-turned from dead to condemn Saul (1Sa 28).

## SANBALLAT

Led opposition to Nehemiah's rebuilding of Jerusalem (Ne 2:10, 19; 4; 6).

## SANCTIFIED* [SANCTIFY]

Jn 17:19 myself, that they too may be truly s.
Ac 20:32 among all those who are s.
26:18 a place among those who are s

Ro 15:16 to God, **s** by the Holy Spirit.
1Co 1: 2 to those **s** in Christ Jesus and called
6:11 you were **s**, you were justified
7:14 husband has been **s** through his
7:14 wife has been **s** through her
1Th 4: 3 It is God's will that you should be **s**:
Heb 10:29 blood of the covenant that **s** them,

## SANCTIFY* [SANCTIFIED, SANCTIFYING]

Jn 17:17 **S** them by the truth; your word is
17:19 For them I **s** myself, that they too
1Th 5:23 peace, **s** you through and through.
Heb 9:13 are ceremonially unclean **s** them so

## SANCTIFYING* [SANCTIFY]

2Th 2:13 be saved through the **s** work
1Pe 1: 2 through the **s** work of the Spirit,

## SANCTUARIES [SANCTUARY]

Lev 26:31 into ruins and lay waste your **s**,

## SANCTUARY [SANCTUARIES]

Ex 15:17 made for your dwelling, the **s**, Lord,
25: 8 "Then have them make a **s** for me,
Lev 10:13 Eat it in the **s** area,
19:30 and have reverence for my **s**.
Nu 3:28 responsible for the care of the **s**.
18: 1 for offenses connected with the **s**,
1Ki 6:19 He prepared the inner **s** within
1Ch 22:19 to build the **s** of the LORD God,
Ezr 9: 8 and giving us a firm place in his **s**,
Ps 15: 1 LORD, who may dwell in your **s**?
20: 2 May he send you help from the **s**
60: 6 God has spoken from his **s**:
63: 2 I have seen you in the **s** and beheld
68:24 of my God and King into the **s**.
68:35 You, God, are awesome in your **s**;
73:17 till I entered the **s** of God;
74: 7 They burned your **s** to the ground;
102:19 looked down from his **s** on high,
114: 2 Judah became God's **s**, Israel his
134: 2 Lift up your hands in the **s**
150: 1 Praise God in his **s**; praise him
La 1:10 she saw pagan nations enter her **s**—
Eze 5:11 because you have defiled my **s**
37:26 I will put my **s** among them forever.
Da 8:11 and his **s** was thrown down.
9:26 come will destroy the city and the **s**.
Heb 6:19 enters the inner **s** behind the curtain,
8: 2 and who serves in the **s**, the true
8: 5 They serve at a **s** that is a copy
9:24 Christ did not enter a **s** made

## SAND

Ge 22:17 the sky and as the **s** on the seashore.
32:12 make your descendants like the **s**
41:49 of grain, like the **s** of the sea;
Ex 2:12 the Egyptian and hid him in the **s**.
1Ki 4:20 Israel were as numerous as the **s**
Jer 33:22 and as measureless as the **s**
Hos 1:10 "Yet the Israelites will be like the **s**
Mt 7:26 man who built his house on **s**.
Ro 9:27 of the Israelites be like the **s**
Heb 11:12 sky and as countless as the **s**

Rev 20: 8 In number they are like the **s**

## SANDAL [SANDALS]

Ge 14:23 not even a thread or the thong of a **s**,
Ru 4: 7 one party took off his **s** and gave it

## SANDALS [SANDAL]

Ex 3: 5 "Take off your **s**, for the place
12:11 your **s** on your feet and your staff
Dt 25: 9 take off one of his **s**, spit in his face
29: 5 wear out, nor did the **s** on your feet.
Jos 5:15 "Take off your **s**, for the place
Mt 3:11 I, whose **s** I am not worthy to carry.

## SANG [SING]

Ex 15: 1 and the Israelites **s** this song
15:21 Miriam **s** to them:
Nu 21:17 Then Israel **s** this song:
Jdg 5: 1 Barak son of Abinoam **s** this song:
1Sa 18: 7 As they danced, they **s**:
29: 5 Isn't this the David they **s**
2Sa 3:33 The king **s** this lament for Abner:
22: 1 David **s** to the LORD the words
2Ch 5:13 in praise to the LORD and **s**:
29:30 So they **s** praises with gladness
Ezr 3:11 thanksgiving they **s** to the LORD:
Ne 12:42 The choirs **s** under the direction
Job 38: 7 while the morning stars **s** together
Ps 106:12 his promises and **s** his praise.
Mt 11:17 we **s** a dirge, and you did not
Rev 5: 9 And they **s** a new song, saying:
14: 3 they **s** a new song before the throne
15: 3 **s** the song of God's servant Moses

## SANHEDRIN

Mt 26:59 the whole **S** were looking for false
Jn 11:47 Pharisees called a meeting of the **S**.
Ac 4:15 them to withdraw from the **S**
5:21 arrived, they called together the **S**—
6:12 and brought him before the **S**.

## SANK [SINK]

Ex 15: 5 they **s** to the depths like a stone.
1Sa 17:49 The stone **s** into his forehead,
Jer 38: 6 and Jeremiah **s** down into the mud.
Jnh 2: 6 the roots of the mountains I **s** down;

## SAP

Hos 7: 9 Foreigners **s** his strength, but he
Ro 11:17 the nourishing **s** from the olive root,

## SAPPHIRA*

Ac 5: 1 together with his wife **S**, also sold

## SAPPHIRE*

Rev 21:19 jasper, the second **s**, the third agate,

## SARAH [SARAI]

Wife of Abraham, originally named Sarai; barren (Ge 11:29–31; 1Pe 3:6). Taken by Pharaoh as Abraham's sister; returned (Ge 12:10–20). Gave Hagar to Abraham; sent her away in pregnancy (Ge 16). Name changed; Isaac promised (Ge 17:15–21; 18:10–15; Heb 11:11). Taken by Abimelech as Abraham's sister;

returned (Ge 20). Isaac born; Hagar and Ishmael sent away (Ge 21:1–21; Gal 4:21–31). Death (Ge 23).

## SARAI [SARAH]
Ge 17:15 you are no longer to call her S;

## SARDIS
Rev 3: 1 the angel of the church in S write:

## SASH [SASHES]
Ex 28: 4 a woven tunic, a turban and a s.
Isa 11: 5 faithfulness the s around his waist.
Rev 1:13 with a golden s around his chest.

## SASHES [SASH]
Rev 15: 6 wore golden s around their chests.

## SAT [SIT]
Ge 48: 2 his strength and s up on the bed.
Ex 2:15 Midian, where he s down by a well.
Jdg 19:15 They went and s in the city square,
Ru 4: 1 So he went over and s down.
1Ki 19: 4 s down under it and prayed that he
Ne 1: 4 these things, I s down and wept.
Ps 137: 1 By the rivers of Babylon we s
Mt 5: 1 up on a mountainside and s down.
13: 2 that he got into a boat and s in it,
28: 2 rolled back the stone and s on it.
Lk 7:15 The dead man s up and began
10:39 who s at the Lord's feet listening
Jn 4: 6 the journey, s down by the well.
12:14 found a young donkey and s on it,
Heb 1: 3 he s down at the right hand
8: 1 who s down at the right hand
10:12 he s down at the right hand of God,
12: 2 and s down at the right hand
Rev 3:21 and s down with my Father on his
4: 3 And the one who s there had
5: 1 of him who s on the throne a scroll

## SATAN
1Ch 21: 1 S rose up against Israel and incited
Job 1: 6 and S also came with them.
2: 1 and S also came with them
Zec 3: 2 "The LORD rebuke you, S!
Mt 4:10 said to him, "Away from me, S!
12:26 If S drives out S, he is divided
16:23 said to Peter, "Get behind me, S!
Mk 4:15 it, S comes and takes away the word
Lk 10:18 "I saw S fall like lightning
22: 3 Then S entered Judas,
Jn 13:27 took the bread, S entered into him.
Ac 5: 3 is it that S has so filled your heart
26:18 and from the power of S to God,
Ro 16:20 will soon crush S under your feet.
1Co 5: 5 hand this man over to S
7: 5 so that S will not tempt you because
2Co 2:11 in order that S might not outwit us.
11:14 S himself masquerades as an angel
12: 7 a messenger of S, to torment me.
2Th 2: 9 be in accordance with how S works.
1Ti 1:20 whom I have handed over to S to be
5:15 already turned away to follow S.
Rev 2: 9 are not, but are a synagogue of S.
2:13 where S has his throne.

Rev 3: 9 who are of the synagogue of S,
12: 9 or S, who leads the whole world
20: 2 or S, and bound him for a thousand
20: 7 S will be released from his prison

## SATISFACTION [SATISFY]
Ecc 2:24 eat and drink and find s in their toil.
3:13 drink, and find s in all their toil—

## SATISFIED [SATISFY]
Lev 26:26 You will eat, but you will not be s.
Dt 6:11 then when you eat and are s,
Ps 17:15 I will be s with seeing your likeness.
22:26 The poor will eat and be s;
63: 5 I will be fully s as with the richest
104:28 hand, they are s with good things.
Pr 13: 4 the desires of the diligent are fully s.
18:20 the harvest of their lips they are s.
27:20 Death and Destruction are never s,
30:15 are three things that are never s,
Ecc 5:10 those who love wealth are never s
Isa 53:11 he will see the light of life and be s;
Hos 13: 6 when they were s, they became
Mt 14:20 They all ate and were s,
15:37 They all ate and were s.
Lk 6:21 who hunger now, for you will be s.

## SATISFIES* [SATISFY]
Ps 103: 5 who s your desires with good things
107: 9 for he s the thirsty and fills
147:14 and s you with the finest of wheat.

## SATISFY [SATISFACTION, SATISFIED, SATISFIES]
Ps 90:14 S us in the morning with your
91:16 With long life I will s them
132:15 her poor I will s with food.
145:16 s the desires of every living thing.
Pr 5:19 may her breasts s you always,
6:30 he steals to s his hunger when he is
Isa 55: 2 and your labor on what does not s?
58:10 and s the needs of the oppressed,
Jer 31:25 refresh the weary and s the faint."
Joel 2:19 and olive oil, enough to s you fully;

## SAUL [PAUL]
1. Benjamite; anointed by Samuel as first king of Israel (1Sa 9–10). Defeated Ammonites (1Sa 11). Rebuked for offering sacrifice (1Sa 13:1–15). Defeated Philistines (1Sa 14). Rejected as king for failing to annihilate Amalekites (1Sa 15). Soothed from evil spirit by David (1Sa 16:14–23). Sent David against Goliath (1Sa 17). Jealousy and attempted murder of David (1Sa 18:1–11). Gave David Michal as wife (1Sa 18:12–30). Second attempt to kill David (1Sa 19). Anger at Jonathan (1Sa 20:26–34). Pursued David: killed priests at Nob (1Sa 22), went to Keilah and Ziph (1Sa 23), life spared by David at En Gedi (1Sa 24) and in his tent (1Sa 26). Rebuked by Samuel's spirit for consulting witch at Endor (1Sa 28). Wounded by Philistines; took his own life (1Sa 31; 1Ch 10). Lamented by David (2Sa 1:17–27). Children (1Sa 14:49–51; 1Ch 8).
2. See PAUL

## SAVAGE*

Eze 34:25  and rid the land of **s** beasts
Ac  20:29  **s** wolves will come in among you

## SAVE [SAFE, SAFELY, SAFETY, SALVATION, SAVED, SAVES, SAVING, SAVIOR]

Ge  45: 5  because it was to **s** lives that God
Dt   4:42  one of these cities and **s** their life.
2Sa 22:28  You **s** the humble, but your eyes are
1Ch 16:35  Cry out, "**S** us, God our Savior;
Job 40:14  that your own right hand can **s** you.
Ps   6: 4  **s** me because of your unfailing love.
    17: 7  you who **s** by your right hand those
    18:27  You **s** the humble but bring low
    28: 9  **S** your people and bless your
    31:16  **s** me in your unfailing love.
    69:35  for God will **s** Zion and rebuild
    71: 2  turn your ear to me and **s** me.
    72:13  needy and **s** the needy from death.
    86: 2  **s** your servant who trusts in you.
    91: 3  Surely he will **s** you
   109:31  to **s** their lives from those who
   146: 3  in human beings, who cannot **s**.
Pr   2:12  Wisdom will **s** you from the ways
     2:16  Wisdom will **s** you
Isa 33:22  is our king; it is he who will **s** us.
    35: 4  retribution he will come to **s** you."
    36:20  have been able to **s** their lands
    38:20  The LORD will **s** me, and we will
    45:20  who pray to gods that cannot **s**.
    46: 7  it cannot **s** them from their troubles.
    59: 1  of the LORD is not too short to **s**,
    63: 1  in righteousness, mighty to **s**."
Jer 15:20  I am with you to rescue and **s** you,"
    17:14  **s** me and I will be saved, for you are
La   4:17  for a nation that could not **s** us.
Eze  3:18  evil ways in order to **s** their lives,
    14:14  it, they could **s** only themselves
    34:22  I will **s** my flock, and they will no
Hos  1: 7  and I will **s** them—not by bow,
Zep  1:18  nor their gold will be able to **s** them
Zec  8: 7  "I will **s** my people
Mt   1:21  because he will **s** his people
    16:25  wants to **s** their life will lose it,
    27:42  they said, "but he can't **s** himself!
Lk   6: 9  to do evil, to **s** life or to destroy it?"
    19:10  to seek and to **s** what was lost."
    23:37  the king of the Jews, **s** yourself."
Jn   3:17  but to **s** the world through him.
    12:27  'Father, **s** me from this hour'?
    12:47  judge the world, but to **s** the world.
Ac   2:40  "**S** yourselves from this corrupt
Ro  11:14  people to envy and **s** some of them.
1Co  7:16  whether you will **s** your husband?
     7:16  whether you will **s** your wife?
     9:22  all possible means I might **s** some.
1Ti  1:15  came into the world to **s** sinners—
Heb  7:25  to **s** completely those who come
Jas  2:14  Can such faith **s** them?
     5:20  way of error will **s** them from death
Jude 1:23  **s** others by snatching them

## SAVED [SAVE]

Ex  14:30  day the LORD **s** Israel

Dt  33:29  like you, a people **s** by the LORD?
Jdg  2:16  who **s** them out of the hands
1Sa 14:23  that day the LORD **s** Israel,
2Ch 32:22  So the LORD **s** Hezekiah
Ps  18: 3  and I have been **s** from my enemies.
    22: 5  They cried to you and were **s**;
    33:16  No king is **s** by the size of his army;
    34: 6  he **s** him out of all his troubles.
   106: 8  Yet he **s** them for his name's sake,
   106:21  They forgot the God who **s** them,
   116: 6  when I was brought low, he **s** me.
Isa 25: 9  we trusted in him, and he **s** us.
    45:17  Israel will be **s** by the LORD
    45:22  "Turn to me and be **s**, all you ends
    64: 5  How then can we be **s**?
Jer  4:14  the evil from your heart and be **s**.
     8:20  has ended, and we are not **s**."
    17:14  save me and I will be **s**, for you are
Eze  3:19  but you will have **s** yourself.
    33: 5  they would have **s** themselves.
Joel 2:32  the name of the LORD will be **s**;
Mt  10:22  who stand firm to the end will be **s**.
    19:25  and asked, "Who then can be **s**?"
    24:13  stands firm to the end will be **s**.
Mk  15:31  "He **s** others," they said, "but he
Lk   7:50  the woman, "Your faith has **s** you;
    13:23  only a few people going to be **s**?"
Jn  10: 9  enters through me will be **s**.
Ac   2:21  on the name of the Lord will be **s**.'
     2:47  daily those who were being **s**.
     4:12  heaven by which we must be **s**."
    15:11  of our Lord Jesus that we are **s**,
    16:30  "Sirs, what must I do to be **s**?"
Ro   5: 9  how much more shall we be **s**
     8:24  For in this hope we were **s**.
     9:27  the sea, only the remnant will be **s**.
    10: 1  the Israelites is that they may be **s**.
    10: 9  him from the dead, you will be **s**.
    10:13  on the name of the Lord will be **s**."
    11:26  and in this way all Israel will be **s**.
1Co  1:18  to us who are being **s** it is the power
     3:15  will suffer loss but yet will be **s**—
     5: 5  so that his spirit may be **s** on the day
    10:33  of many, so that they may be **s**.
    15: 2  By this gospel you are **s**, if you hold
Eph  2: 5  it is by grace you have been **s**.
     2: 8  For it is by grace you have been **s**,
2Th  2:10  refused to love the truth and so be **s**.
     2:13  to be **s** through the sanctifying work
1Ti  2: 4  who wants all people to be **s**
     2:15  will be **s** through childbearing—
2Ti  1: 9  who has **s** us and called us to a holy
Tit  3: 5  he **s** us, not because of righteous
     3: 5  He **s** us through the washing
Heb 10:39  but of those who believe and are **s**.
1Pe  4:18  it is hard for the righteous to be **s**,

## SAVES [SAVE]

1Sa 17:47  sword or spear that the LORD **s**;
Ps   7:10  High, who **s** the upright in heart.
    34:18  **s** those who are crushed in spirit.
    55:16  I call to God, and the LORD **s** me.
    68:20  Our God is a God who **s**;
   145:19  he hears their cry and **s** them.
Pr  14:25  A truthful witness **s** lives, but a false
Zep  3:17  you, the Mighty Warrior who **s**.
1Pe  3:21  It **s** you by the resurrection of Jesus

## SAVING [SAVE]
Ge 50:20 being done, the **s** of many lives.
1Sa 14: 6 can hinder the LORD from **s**,
Ps 40: 9 I proclaim your **s** acts
40:10 your faithfulness and your **s** help.
40:16 may those who long for your **s** help
70: 4 who long for your **s** help always say,
71:15 of your **s** acts all day long—

## SAVIOR* [SAVE]
Dt 32:15 him and rejected the Rock his **S**.
2Sa 22: 3 stronghold, my refuge and my **s**—
22:47 be my God, the Rock, my **S**!
1Ch 16:35 Cry out, "Save us, God our **S**;
Ps 18:46 to my Rock! Exalted be God my **S**!
24: 5 and vindication from God their **S**.
25: 5 for you are God my **S**, and my hope
27: 9 reject me or forsake me, God my **S**.
38:22 to help me, my Lord and my **S**.
42: 5 yet praise him, my **S** and my God.
42:11 yet praise him, my **S** and my God.
43: 5 yet praise him, my **S** and my God.
51:14 O God, you who are God my **S**,
65: 5 God our **S**, the hope of all the ends
68:19 to God our **S**, who daily bears our
79: 9 us, God our **S**, for the glory of your
85: 4 God our **S**, and put away your
89:26 Father, my God, the Rock my **S**.'
Isa 17:10 You have forgotten God your **S**;
19:20 he will send them a **s** and defender,
43: 3 God, the Holy One of Israel, your **S**;
43:11 and apart from me there is no **s**.
45:15 himself, the God and **S** of Israel.
45:21 from me, a righteous God and a **S**;
49:26 am your **S**, your Redeemer,
60:16 am your **S**, your Redeemer,
62:11 Daughter Zion, 'See, your **S** comes!
63: 8 and so he became their **S**.
Jer 14: 8 of Israel, its **S** in times of distress,
23: 6 be called: The LORD Our Righteous **S**.
33:16 be called: The LORD Our Righteous **S**.'
Hos 13: 4 no God but me, no **S** except me.
Mic 7: 7 the LORD, I wait for God my **S**;
Hab 3:18 I will be joyful in God my **S**.
Lk 1:47 and my spirit rejoices in God my **S**,
2:11 the town of David a **S** has been born
Jn 4:42 that this man really is the **S**
Ac 5:31 and **S** that he might bring Israel
13:23 has brought to Israel the **S** Jesus,
Eph 5:23 his body, of which he is the **S**.
Php 3:20 we eagerly await a **S** from there,
1Ti 1: 1 Jesus by the command of God our **S**
2: 3 This is good, and pleases God our **S**,
4:10 God, who is the **S** of all people,
2Ti 1:10 through the appearing of our **S**,
Tit 1: 3 me by the command of God our **S**,
1: 4 the Father and Christ Jesus our **S**.
2:10 teaching about God our **S** attractive.
2:13 of the glory of our great God and **S**,
3: 4 and love of God our **S** appeared,
3: 6 through Jesus Christ our **S**,
2Pe 1: 1 **S** Jesus Christ have received a faith
1:11 of our Lord and **S** Jesus Christ.
2:20 our Lord and **S** Jesus Christ and are
3: 2 Lord and **S** through your apostles.
3:18 of our Lord and **S** Jesus Christ.

1Jn 4:14 his Son to be the **S** of the world.
Jude 1:25 to the only God our **S** be glory,

## SAW [SEE]
Ge 1: 4 God **s** that the light was good,
1:31 God **s** all that he had made, and it
3: 6 When the woman **s** that the fruit
6: 2 of God **s** that these daughters were
6:12 God **s** how corrupt the earth had
22:13 there in a thicket he **s** a ram caught
Ex 2: 2 When she **s** that he was a fine child,
2: 5 She **s** the basket among the reeds
2:11 He **s** an Egyptian beating a Hebrew,
3: 2 Moses **s** that though the bush was
24:10 and **s** the God of Israel.
34:35 they **s** that his face was radiant.
Nu 22:23 When the donkey **s** the angel
Dt 4:15 You **s** no form of any kind the day
32:19 The LORD **s** this and rejected
2Sa 11: 2 the roof he **s** a woman bathing.
Ps 31: 7 for you **s** my affliction and knew
73: 3 the arrogant when I **s** the prosperity
139:16 your eyes **s** my unformed body.
Ecc 2:13 I **s** that wisdom is better than folly,
8:17 then I **s** all that God has done.
Isa 6: 1 died, I **s** the Lord seated on a throne,
Eze 1: 1 were opened and I **s** visions of God.
Da 2:26 able to tell me what I **s** in my dream
4:10 These are the visions I **s** while lying
8: 2 my vision I **s** myself in the citadel
10: 7 was the only one who **s** the vision;
Am 9: 1 I **s** the Lord standing by the altar,
Mt 2: 2 We **s** his star when it rose and have
3:16 he **s** the Spirit of God descending
9: 2 When Jesus **s** their faith, he said
Mk 1:10 he **s** heaven being torn open
3:11 Whenever the evil spirits **s** him,
15:39 **s** how he died, he said,
Lk 9:32 they **s** his glory and the two men
Jn 1:29 The next day John **s** Jesus coming
19:35 The man who **s** it has given
20: 1 **s** that the stone had been removed
20: 8 also went inside. He **s** and believed.
Ac 2: 3 They **s** what seemed to be tongues
7:55 up to heaven and **s** the glory of God,
10:11 He **s** heaven opened and something
11:23 and **s** what the grace of God had done,
Heb 11:27 persevered because he **s** him who is
Rev 1: 2 who testifies to everything he **s**—
1:12 And when I turned I **s** seven golden
5: 6 Then I **s** a Lamb, looking as if it had
21: 1 Then I **s** "a new heaven and a new
22: 8 one who heard and **s** these things.

## SAY [SAYING, SAYINGS, SAYS]
Ge 3: 1 "Did God really **s**, 'You must not
12:19 Why did you **s**, 'She is my sister,'
18:13 "Why did Sarah laugh and **s**,
26: 9 Why did you **s**, 'She is my sister'?"
Ex 7: 2 are to **s** everything I command you,
Job 40: 5 twice, but I will **s** no more."
Ps 14: 1 Fools **s** in their hearts,
53: 1 **s** in their hearts, "There is no God."
Pr 4:10 accept what I **s**, and the years
5: 7 do not turn aside from what I **s**.
8: 6 for I have trustworthy things to **s**;

Mt   5:37   you need to s is simply 'Yes' or 'No';
    10:19   worry about what to s or how to s it.
    16:15   he asked. "Who do you s I am?"
Mk   2: 9   to s to this paralyzed man,
     8:27   them, "Who do people s I am?"
Lk  11:54   catch him in something he might s.
Jn   8:26   "I have much to s in judgment
     8:43   you are unable to hear what I s.
    12:49   who sent me commanded me to s all
    16:12   "I have much more to s to you,
    18:37   Jesus answered, "You s that I am a king.
1Co 15:12   of you s that there is no resurrection
Tit  2:12   It teaches us to s "No"
Jas  5:12   you need to s is a simple "Yes" or "No."
Rev 22:17   The Spirit and the bride s,

## SAYING [SAY]

1Ti  1:15   Here is a trustworthy s that deserves
     3: 1   Here is a trustworthy s:
     4: 9   This is a trustworthy s that deserves
2Ti  2:11   Here is a trustworthy s: If we died
Tit  3: 8   This is a trustworthy s. And I want
Rev  5:12   In a loud voice they were s:
     5:13   and all that is in them, s: "To him

## SAYINGS [SAY]

Pr   1: 6   the s and riddles of the wise.
    22:17   turn your ear to the s of the wise;
Ecc 12:11   goads, their collected s like firmly
Jn  10:21   "These are not the s of someone

## SAYS [SAY]

Ex  23:22   If you listen carefully to what he s
1Sa  9: 6   and everything he s comes true.
Ac  19:26   He s that gods made by human
Ro   3:19   we know that whatever the law s,
Jas  1:23   not do what it s are like people who

## WHAT THE SOVEREIGN †LORD SAYS
See †LORD

## WHAT THE †LORD SAYS See †LORD

## †LORD ALMIGHTY SAYS See †LORD

## SAYS THE †LORD See †LORD

## SCALE [SCALES]

1Sa 17: 5   wore a coat of s armor of bronze
Ps  18:29   with my God I can s a wall.

## SCALES [SCALE]

Lev 11: 9   may eat any that have fins and s.
    19:36   Use honest s and honest weights,
Pr  11: 1   The LORD detests dishonest s,
    16:11   Honest s and balances belong
Da   5:27   You have been weighed on the s
Ac   9:18   something like s fell from Saul's
Rev  6: 5   Its rider was holding a pair of s

## SCAPEGOAT [GOAT]

Lev 16:10   sending it into the wilderness as a s.

## SCARECROW*

Jer 10: 5   Like a s in a melon patch, their idols

## SCARLET

Ge  38:28   so the midwife took a s thread
Ex  25: 4   purple and s yarn and fine linen;
Lev 14: 4   s yarn and hyssop be brought
Nu  19: 6   hyssop and s wool and throw them
Jos  2:21   she tied the s cord in the window.
Isa  1:18   "Though your sins are like s,
Mt  27:28   him and put a s robe on him,
Heb  9:19   s wool and branches of hyssop,
Rev 17: 3   I saw a woman sitting on a s beast

## SCATTER [SCATTERED, SCATTERING, SCATTERS]

Lev 26:33   I will s you among the nations
Dt   4:27   The LORD will s you among
Ne   1: 8   I will s you among the nations,
Ecc  3: 5   a time to s stones and a time
Jer  9:16   I will s them among nations
    30:11   all the nations among which I s you,
Zec 10: 9   Though I s them among the peoples,

## SCATTERED [SCATTER]

Ge  11: 4   not be s over the face of the whole
Nu  10:35   May your enemies be s;
Dt  30: 3   from all the nations where he s you.
2Ch 18:16   "I saw all Israel s on the hills like
Ps  89:10   strong arm you s your enemies.
    112: 9   They have s abroad their gifts
Isa 11:12   he will assemble the s people
Jer 31:10   'He who s Israel will gather them
La   4:16   The LORD himself has s them;
Eze 34:12   shepherds look after their s flocks
Zec  1:19   "These are the horns that s Judah,
     2: 6   "for I have s you to the four winds
    13: 7   and the sheep will be s, and I will
Mt  26:31   and the sheep of the flock will be s.'
Jn  11:52   but also for the s children of God,
Ac   8: 1   apostles were s throughout Judea
     8: 4   who had been s preached the word
2Co  9: 9   "They have s abroad their gifts
Jas  1: 1   To the twelve tribes s among
1Pe  1: 1   exiles s throughout the provinces

## SCATTERING [SCATTER]

Jer 23: 1   and s the sheep of my pasture!"
Mk   4: 4   As he was s the seed, some fell

## SCATTERS [SCATTER]

Mt  12:30   whoever does not gather with me s.
Jn  10:12   the wolf attacks the flock and s it.

## SCEPTER

Ge  49:10   The s will not depart from Judah,
Nu  24:17   a s will rise out of Israel.
Est  4:11   unless the king extends the gold s
Ps  45: 6   a s of justice will be the s of your
    125: 3   The s of the wicked will not remain
Heb  1: 8   a s of justice will be the s of your
Rev  2:27   they 'will rule them with an iron s
    12: 5   rule all the nations with an iron s."
    19:15   "He will rule them with an iron s."

## SCHEME [SCHEMES, SCHEMING]

Est  9:25   that the evil s Haman had devised
Ecc  7:27   another to discover the s of things—

## SCHEMES [SCHEME]

Ex 21:14 But if anyone s and kills someone
Ps 21:11 against you and devise wicked s,
Pr 6:18 a heart that devises wicked s,
24: 9 The s of folly are sin, and people
2Co 2:11 For we are not unaware of his s.
Eph 6:11 take your stand against the devil's s.

## SCHEMING* [SCHEME]

Ne 6: 2 But they were s to harm me;
Eph 4:14 of people in their deceitful s.

## SCOFF [SCOFFED, SCOFFERS, SCOFFS]

Ps 59: 8 you s at all those nations.
La 2:15 they s and shake their heads

## SCOFFED* [SCOFF]

2Ch 36:16 s at his prophets until the wrath

## SCOFFERS [SCOFF]

Isa 28:14 you s who rule this people
2Pe 3: 3 that in the last days s will come,

## SCOFFS* [SCOFF]

Ps 2: 4 the Lord s at them.
Pr 29: 9 the fool rages and s, and there is no

## SCOOP*

Ps 7:15 s it out fall into the pit they have made.
Pr 6:27 Can a man s fire into his lap without

## SCORCH* [SCORCHED, SCORCHING]

Rev 16: 8 and the sun was allowed to s people

## SCORCHED [SCORCH]

Ge 41:27 heads of grain s by the east wind:
Pr 6:28 hot coals without his feet being s?
Da 3:27 their robes were not s, and there was
Mk 4: 6 the plants were s, and they withered

## SCORCHING [SCORCH]

Jnh 4: 8 God provided a s east wind,
Jas 1:11 For the sun rises with s heat

## SCORN [SCORNED, SCORNING, SCORNS]

Ps 39: 8 do not make me the s of fools.
69: 7 For I endure s for your sake,
69:20 S has broken my heart and has left
89:41 he has become the s of his
109:25 I am an object of s to my accusers;
119:22 Remove from me their s
Isa 43:28 Jacob to destruction and Israel to s.
Eze 36: 7 around you will also suffer s.
Mic 6:16 you will bear the s of the nations."

## SCORNED [SCORN]

Ps 22: 6 I am s by everyone,
SS 8: 7 house for love, it would be utterly s.

## SCORNING* [SCORN]

Heb 12: 2 he endured the cross, s its shame,

## SCORNS* [SCORN]

Pr 13:13 Whoever s instruction will pay
30:17 that s an aged mother, will be

## SCORPION [SCORPIONS]

Lk 11:12 asks for an egg, will give him a s?
Rev 9: 5 of the sting of a s when it strikes.

## SCORPIONS [SCORPION]

1Ki 12:11 I will scourge you with s.' "
Rev 9:10 like s, and in their tails they had

## SCOUNDREL [SCOUNDRELS]

Isa 32: 5 fool be called noble nor the s

## SCOUNDRELS [SCOUNDREL]

1Sa 2:12 Eli's sons were s;
1Ki 21:10 But seat two s opposite him
Pr 16:27 S plot evil, and on their lips it is like
Isa 32: 7 S use wicked methods,

## SCOURGE

Ps 39:10 Remove your s from me;
Isa 28:15 an overwhelming s sweeps by,
28:18 the overwhelming s sweeps by,

## SCREAM*

Ge 39:15 When he heard me s for help, he left
Dt 22:24 was in a town and did not s for help,

## SCRIBE [SCRIBE'S]

Jer 36:32 and gave it to the s Baruch son

## SCRIBE'S* [SCRIBE]

Jer 36:23 the king cut them off with a s knife

## SCRIPTURE [SCRIPTURES]

Mk 12:10 Haven't you read this passage of S:
Lk 4:21 "Today this s is fulfilled in your
Jn 2:22 they believed the s and the words
7:42 Does not S say that the Messiah will
10:35 and S cannot be broken—
Ac 1:16 the S had to be fulfilled
8:32 of S the eunuch was reading:
1Ti 4:13 yourself to the public reading of S,
2Ti 3:16 All S is God-breathed and is useful
2Pe 1:20 that no prophecy of S came

## SCRIPTURES [SCRIPTURE]

Da 9: 2 understood from the S,
Mt 22:29 error because you do not know the S
Mk 14:49 But the S must be fulfilled."
Lk 24:27 said in all the S concerning himself.
24:45 so they could understand the S.
Jn 5:39 You study the S diligently because
5:39 These are the very S that testify
Ac 17:11 examined the S every day to see
18:28 the S that Jesus was the Messiah.
1Co 15: 3 died for our sins according to the S,
15: 4 on the third day according to the S,
2Ti 3:15 infancy you have known the Holy S,

2Pe 3:16 as they do the other **S**, to their own

## SCROLL [SCROLLS]
Ex 17:14 "Write this on a **s** as something
Dt 17:18 for himself on a **s** a copy of this law,
1Sa 10:25 He wrote them down on a **s**
Ps 40: 7 it is written about me in the **s**.
Isa 8: 1 "Take a large **s** and write on it
29:11 is nothing but words sealed in a **s**.
34: 4 and the heavens rolled up like a **s**;
Jer 36: 4 to him, Baruch wrote them on the **s**.
45: 1 a **s** the words Jeremiah the prophet
Eze 3: 1 eat what is before you, eat this **s**;
Da 12: 4 seal the words of the **s** until the time
Zec 5: 1 and there before me was a flying **s**.
Mal 3:16 A **s** of remembrance was written
Lk 4:17 and the **s** of the prophet Isaiah was
Heb 10: 7 it is written about me in the **s**—
Rev 1:11 "Write on a **s** what you see
5: 2 to break the seals and open the **s**?"
6:14 The sky receded like a **s**, rolling up,
10: 8 take the **s** that lies open in the hand
22:18 plagues described in this **s**.

## SCROLLS [SCROLL]
Ac 19:19 sorcery brought their **s** together
2Ti 4:13 at Troas, and my **s**,

## SCUM*
La 3:45 You have made us **s** and refuse
1Co 4:13 We have become the **s** of the earth,

## SEA [SEAS, SEASHORE]
Ge 1:26 they may rule over the fish in the **s**
32:12 descendants like the sand of the **s**,
41:49 of grain, like the sand of the **s**;
Ex 14:16 the Israelites can go through the **s**
14:27 the LORD swept them into the **s**.
15: 1 and driver he has hurled into the **s**.
Nu 11:31 and drove quail in from the **s**.
34: 6 be the coast of the Mediterranean **S**.
Dt 11:24 River to the Mediterranean **S**.
30:13 Nor is it beyond the **s**,
1Ki 7:23 He made the **S** of cast metal,
2Ki 25:13 the bronze **S** that were at the temple
Ne 9:11 You divided the **s** before them,
Job 11: 9 than the earth and wider than the **s**.
Ps 46: 2 fall into the heart of the **s**,
74:13 It was you who split open the **s**
93: 4 mightier than the breakers of the **s**—
95: 5 The **s** is his, for he made it, and his
106: 7 they rebelled by the **s**, the Red **S**.
139: 9 if I settle on the far side of the **s**,
Ecc 1: 7 All streams flow into the **s**, yet the **s**
11: 1 Ship your grain across the **s**;
Isa 10:22 people be like the sand by the **s**,
48:18 well-being like the waves of the **s**.
57:20 the wicked are like the tossing **s**,
Da 7: 3 the others, came up out of the **s**.
Jnh 1: 4 LORD sent a great wind on the **s**,
Mic 7:19 iniquities into the depths of the **s**.
Hab 2:14 LORD as the waters cover the **s**.
Zec 9:10 His rule will extend from **s** to **s**
Mt 18: 6 were drowned in the depths of the **s**.
Mk 11:23 throw yourself into the **s**,' and do
1Co 10: 1 that they all passed through the **s**.

Heb 11:29 people passed through the Red **S** as
Jas 1: 6 who doubts is like a wave of the **s**,
Jude 1:13 They are wild waves of the **s**,
Rev 4: 6 there was what looked like a **s**
8: 8 A third of the **s** turned into blood,
10: 2 He planted his right foot on the **s**
13: 1 I saw a beast coming out of the **s**.
15: 2 I saw what looked like a **s** of glass
20:13 The **s** gave up the dead that were
21: 1 and there was no longer any **s**.

## SEAL [SEALED, SEALS]
Ex 28:21 each engraved like a **s**
Est 8: 8 and **s** it with the king's signet ring—
Ps 40: 9 I do not **s** my lips, LORD, as you
SS 8: 6 Place me like a **s** over your heart,
Isa 8:16 **s** up God's instruction among my
Eze 28:12 " 'You were the **s** of perfection,
Da 8:26 but **s** up the vision, for it concerns
9:24 to **s** up vision and prophecy
12: 4 **s** the words of the scroll until
Mt 27:66 secure by putting a **s** on the stone
Jn 6:27 him God the Father has placed his **s**
1Co 9: 2 For you are the **s** of my apostleship
2Co 1:22 set his **s** of ownership on us, and put
Eph 1:13 you were marked in him with a **s**,
Rev 6: 3 the Lamb opened the second **s**,
6: 5 When the Lamb opened the third **s**,
6: 7 the Lamb opened the fourth **s**,
6: 9 When he opened the fifth **s**, I saw
6:12 I watched as he opened the sixth **s**.
7: 2 east, having the **s** of the living God.
7: 3 or the trees until we put a **s**
8: 1 When he opened the seventh **s**,
9: 4 those people who did not have the **s**
10: 4 "S up what the seven thunders have
22:10 me, "Do not **s** up the words

## SEALED [SEAL]
Isa 29:11 nothing but words **s** in a scroll.
Da 6:17 the king **s** it with his own signet ring
12: 9 up and **s** until the time of the end.
Eph 4:30 with whom you were **s** for the day
2Ti 2:19 stands firm, **s** with this inscription:
Rev 5: 1 on both sides and **s** with seven seals.
7: 4 the number of those who were **s**:
20: 3 and locked and **s** it over him,

## SEALS [SEAL]
Rev 5: 2 "Who is worthy to break the **s**
6: 1 opened the first of the seven **s**.

## SEAMLESS*
Jn 19:23 This garment was **s**, woven in one

## SEARCH [SEARCHED, SEARCHES, SEARCHING]
Ezr 5:17 let a **s** be made in the royal archives
Est 2: 2 "Let a **s** be made for beautiful
Ps 4: 4 beds, **s** your hearts and be silent.
139:23 **S** me, God, and know my heart;
Pr 2: 4 and **s** for it as for hidden treasure,
11:27 evil comes to those who **s** for it.
25: 2 to **s** out a matter is the glory
25:27 nor is it honorable to **s** out matters

Ecc   3: 6  a time to s and a time to give up,
SS     3: 2  I will s for the one my heart loves.
Jer  17:10  "I the LORD s the heart
Eze  34:11  I myself will s for my sheep
     34:16  I will s for the lost and bring back
Mt    2: 8  and make a careful s for the child.
Lk   15: 8  and s carefully until she finds it?

## SEARCHED [SEARCH]
1Sa  23:14  Day after day Saul s for him,
Ps  139: 1  You have s me, LORD, and you
Ecc  12:10  The Teacher s to find just the right
1Pe   1:10  s intently and with the greatest care,

## SEARCHES [SEARCH]
1Ch  28: 9  for the LORD s every heart
Ro    8:27  he who s our hearts knows the mind
1Co   2:10  The Spirit s all things, even the deep
Rev   2:23  will know that I am he who s hearts

## SEARCHING [SEARCH]
Jdg   5:15  Reuben there was much s of heart.
Am   8:12  east, s for the word of the LORD,
Lk    2:49  "Why were you s for me?"

## SEARED*
1Ti    4: 2  whose consciences have been s as
Rev 16: 9  They were s by the intense heat

## SEAS [SEA]
Ge    1:10  the gathered waters he called "s."
Ps   65: 7  who stilled the roaring of the s,
     93: 3  The s have lifted up, LORD,
Jnh   2: 3  into the very heart of the s,

## SEASHORE [SEA]
Ge  22:17  in the sky and as the sand on the s.
Jos  11: 4  as numerous as the sand on the s.
1Ki  4:20  as numerous as the sand on the s;
     4:29  as measureless as the sand on the s.
Jer  33:22  as the sand on the s.' "
Hos   1:10  will be like the sand on the s,
Heb 11:12  as countless as the sand on the s.
Rev 20: 8  they are like the sand on the s.

## SEASON [SEASONED, SEASONS]
Lev  2:13  S all your grain offerings with salt.
   26: 4  I will send you rain in its s,
Dt  28:12  to send rain on your land in s
Ps    1: 3  which yields its fruit in s and whose
Pr  20: 4  Sluggards do not plow in s;
Ecc   3: 1  and a s for every activity under
2Ti   4: 2  be prepared in s and out of s;
Tit   1: 3  at his appointed s he has brought

## SEASONED* [SEASON]
Col   4: 6  be always full of grace, s with salt,

## SEASONS [SEASON]
Ge    1:14  let them serve as signs to mark s
Ps 104:19  He made the moon to mark the s,
Gal   4:10  days and months and s and years!

## SEAT [SEATED, SEATS]
Ex  18:13  The next day Moses took his s
2Ki 25:28  gave him a s of honor higher than
Pr  31:23  he takes his s among the elders
Da   7: 9  and the Ancient of Days took his s.
Mt  23: 2  and the Pharisees sit in Moses' s.
Lk  14: 9  to you, 'Give this person your s.'
Ro  14:10  all stand before God's judgment s.
2Co  5:10  all appear before the judgment s

## SEATED [SEAT]
Ps  47: 8  God is s on his holy throne.
Isa   6: 1  died, I saw the Lord s on a throne,
Lk  22:69  of Man will be s at the right hand
Jn  12:15  is coming, s on a donkey's colt."
  20:12  s where Jesus' body had been,
Eph  1:20  and s him at his right hand
   2: 6  and s us with him in the heavenly
Col   3: 1  where Christ is s at the right hand
Rev  4: 4  s on them were twenty-four elders.
  11:16  who were s on their thrones before
  14:14  s on the cloud was one like a son
  19: 4  God, who was s on the throne.
  20: 4  were s those who had been given
  20:11  throne and him who was s on it.
  21: 5  He who was s on the throne said,

## SEATS [SEAT]
1Sa   2: 8  he s them with princes and has them
Ps 113: 8  he s them with princes,
Lk  11:43  you love the most important s

## SECLUSION*
Lk   1:24  and for five months remained in s.

## SECOND [TWO]
Ge  22:15  to Abraham from heaven a s time
  41: 5  fell asleep again and had a s dream:
Ex   4: 8  first sign, they may believe the s.
Lev 19:10  not go over your vineyard a s time
Nu   9:11  the fourteenth day of the s month
Dt  24:20  not go over the branches a s time.
1Ki  9: 2  LORD appeared to him a s time,
Est  10: 3  Mordecai the Jew was s in rank
Eze 10:14  the s the face of a human being,
Da   7: 5  "And there before me was a s beast,
Jnh   3: 1  the LORD came to Jonah a s time:
Hag  2:20  came to Haggai a s time
Zec 11:14  I broke my s staff called Union,
Mt  22:39  And the s is like it:
Jn   3: 4  "Surely they cannot enter a s time
1Co 12:28  first of all apostles, s prophets,
  15:47  of the earth; the s man is of heaven.
Tit   3:10  once, and then warn them a s time.
Heb  9:28  and he will appear a s time,
Rev  2:11  will not be hurt at all by the s death.
   4: 7  was like a lion, the s was like an ox,
   6: 3  When the Lamb opened the s seal,
   8: 8  The s angel sounded his trumpet,
  11:14  The s woe has passed; the third woe
  16: 3  The s angel poured out his bowl
  20: 6  The s death has no power over
  20:14  The lake of fire is the s death.
  21: 8  This is the s death."

## SECRET [SECRETLY, SECRETS]

Ex 7:11 did the same things by their s arts:
7:22 did the same things by their s arts,
8: 7 did the same things by their s arts;
8:18 tried to produce gnats by their s arts,
Dt 29:29 The s things belong to the LORD
Jdg 16: 6 "Tell me the s of your great
Est 2:20 But Esther had kept s her family
Ps 51: 6 taught me wisdom in that s place.
90: 8 you, our s sins in the light of your
139:15 you when I was made in the s place.
Pr 9:17 food eaten in s is delicious!"
11:13 but the trustworthy keep a s.
21:14 A gift given in s soothes anger,
Jer 23:24 Who can hide in s places so that I
Mt 6: 4 so that your giving may be in s.
6: 4 who sees what is done in s,
6: 6 who sees what is done in s,
6:18 who sees what is done in s,
Mk 4:11 "The s of the kingdom of God has
2Co 4: 2 we have renounced s and shameful
Eph 5:12 what the disobedient do in s.
Php 4:12 I have learned the s of being content
2Th 2: 7 For the s power of lawlessness is

## SECRETLY [SECRET]

Dt 13: 6 or your closest friend s entices you,
2Ki 17: 9 The Israelites s did things against
Mt 2: 7 Herod called the Magi s and found
Jn 19:38 but s because he feared the Jewish
2Pe 2: 1 They will s introduce destructive
Jude 1: 4 long ago have s slipped in among

## SECRETS [SECRET]

Ps 44:21 it, since he knows the s of the heart?
Mt 13:11 knowledge of the s of the kingdom
Ro 2:16 judges everyone's s through Jesus
1Co 14:25 as the s of their hearts are laid bare.
Rev 2:24 not learned Satan's so-called deep s,

## SECT

Ac 24: 5 He is a ringleader of the Nazarene s
26: 5 to the strictest s of our religion,

## SECURE [SECURELY, SECURES, SECURITY]

Dt 33:12 beloved of the LORD rest s in him,
2Sa 22:33 strength and keeps my way s.
1Ki 2:45 throne will remain s before
Ps 16: 5 you have made my lot s.
16: 9 my body also will rest s,
18:32 strength and keeps my way s.
22: 9 you made me feel s
112: 8 Their hearts are s, they will have no
122: 6 "May those who love you be s.
Pr 14:16 fool is hotheaded and yet feels s.
14:26 fear the LORD have a s fortress,
Am 6: 1 you who feel s on Mount Samaria,
Zec 1:15 angry with the nations that feel s.
Mt 27:64 to be made s until the third day.
Heb 6:19 as an anchor for the soul, firm and s.
2Pe 3:17 and fall from your s position.

## SECURELY [SECURE]

Pr 10: 9 Whoever walks in integrity walks s,

## SECURES* [SECURE]

Ps 140:12 the LORD s justice for the poor

## SECURITY [SECURE]

Dt 24: 6 be taking a person's livelihood as s.
Job 31:24 or said to pure gold, 'You are my s,'
Ps 122: 7 walls and s within your citadels."
Pr 17:18 pledge and puts up s for a neighbor.
22:26 in pledge or puts up s for debts;
Jer 30:10 Jacob will again have peace and s,

## SEDUCE* [SEDUCED, SEDUCES, SEDUCTIVE]

2Pe 2:14 they s the unstable;

## SEDUCED* [SEDUCE]

Pr 7:21 she s him with her smooth talk.

## SEDUCES* [SEDUCE]

Ex 22:16 a man s a virgin who is not pledged

## SEDUCTIVE* [SEDUCE]

Pr 2:16 wayward woman with her s words,
7: 5 wayward woman with her s words.

## SEE [NEARSIGHTED, SAW, SEEING, SEEN, SEES, SIGHT]

Ge 2:19 man to s what he would name them;
8: 8 a dove to s if the water had receded
9:16 clouds, I will s it and remember
13:15 All the land that you s I will give
Ex 12:13 and when I s the blood, I will pass
14:13 and you will s the deliverance
16: 4 and s whether they will follow my
33:20 for no one may s me and live."
Nu 14:23 them will ever s the land I promised
Dt 12: 8 everyone doing as they s fit,
34: 4 I have let you s it with your eyes,
Jdg 2:22 s whether they will keep the way
Job 19:26 yet in my flesh I will s God;
Ps 11: 7 the upright will s his face.
16:10 you let your faithful one s decay.
34: 8 and s that the LORD is good;
115: 5 but cannot speak, eyes, but cannot s.
Isa 40: 5 and all people will s it together.
53:10 he will s his offspring and prolong
53:11 he will s the light of life and be
65:17 "S, I will create new heavens
Eze 8:12 say, 'The LORD does not s us;
Da 3:25 I s four men walking around
Joel 2:28 your young men will s visions.
Mic 7: 9 I will s his righteousness.
Mt 5: 8 pure in heart, for they will s God.
7: 5 you will s clearly to remove
13:16 are your eyes because they s,
Mk 8:18 Do you have eyes but fail to s,
14:62 you will s the Son of Man sitting
16: 6 S the place where they laid him.
Lk 3: 6 people will s God's salvation.' "
Jn 9:25 I was blind but now I s!"
14:19 the world will not s me anymore,
16:16 a little while you will s me no more,
Ac 2:17 your young men will s visions,
2:27 will not let your holy one s decay.

1Co 13:12 then we shall **s** face to face.
2Co 13: 5 yourselves to **s** whether you are
Heb 12:14 holiness no one will **s** the Lord.
1Jn 3: 2 like him, for we shall **s** him as he is.
5:16 **s** any brother or sister commit a sin
Rev 1: 7 and "every eye will **s** him,
22: 4 They will **s** his face, and his name

## SEED [SEED-BEARING, SEEDS, SEEDTIME]

Ge 1:11 the land that bear fruit with **s** in it,
Lev 19:19 plant your field with two kinds of **s**.
Ecc 11: 6 Sow your **s** in the morning,
Isa 6:13 so the holy **s** will be the stump
55:10 so that it yields **s** for the sower
Mt 13: 3 "A farmer went out to sow his **s**.
13:31 of heaven is like a mustard **s**,
17:20 have faith as small as a mustard **s**,
Mk 4:31 It is like a mustard **s**, which is
Lk 8:11 The **s** is the word of God.
Jn 12:24 and dies, it remains only a single **s**.
1Co 3: 6 I planted the **s**, Apollos watered it,
9:11 have sown spiritual **s** among you,
2Co 9:10 Now he who supplies **s** to the sower
Gal 3:16 spoken to Abraham and to his **s**.
3:29 then you are Abraham's **s**, and heirs
1Pe 1:23 again, not of perishable **s**,
1Jn 3: 9 because God's **s** remains in them;

## SEED-BEARING* [SEED]

Ge 1:11 **s** plants and trees on the land
1:29 "I give you every **s** plant

## SEEDS [SEED]

Jn 12:24 But if it dies, it produces many **s**.
Gal 3:16 Scripture does not say "and to **s**,"

## SEEDTIME* [SEED]

Ge 8:22 as the earth endures, **s** and harvest,

## SEEING [SEE]

Isa 6: 9 be ever **s**, but never perceiving.'
Mt 13:14 you will be ever **s** but never
15:31 the lame walking and the blind **s**.
Jn 8:56 rejoiced at the thought of **s** my day;
2Co 3:13 prevent the Israelites from **s** the end

## SEEK [SEEKING, SEEKS, SELF-SEEKING, SOUGHT]

Ex 18:15 people come to me to **s** God's will.
Lev 19:18 " 'Do not **s** revenge or bear
19:31 turn to mediums or **s** out spiritists,
Dt 4:29 there you **s** the LORD your God,
23: 6 Do not **s** a treaty of friendship
1Ki 22: 5 of Israel, "First **s** the counsel
1Ch 28: 9 If you **s** him, he will be found
2Ch 7:14 pray and **s** my face and turn
15: 2 If you **s** him, he will be found
Ezr 9:12 Do not **s** a treaty of friendship
Ps 4: 2 you love delusions and **s** false gods?
9:10 never forsaken those who **s** you.
24: 6 who **s** him, who **s** your face,
34:10 but those who **s** the LORD lack no
63: 1 God, are my God, earnestly I **s** you;
105: 3 of those who **s** the LORD rejoice.

Ps 105: 4 and his strength; **s** his face always.
119: 2 and **s** him with all their heart—
119:10 I **s** you with all my heart; do not let
119:176 **S** your servant, for I have not
Pr 8:17 me, and those who **s** me find me.
18:15 for the ears of the wise **s** it out.
28: 5 those who **s** the LORD understand
Isa 1:17 **S** justice, encourage the oppressed.
55: 6 **S** the LORD while he may be
65: 1 found by those who did not **s** me.
Jer 29:13 You will **s** me and find me when you **s** me with all
Hos 10:12 for it is time to **s** the LORD,
Am 5: 6 **S** the LORD and live, or he will
Zep 2: 3 **S** the LORD, all you humble
2: 3 **S** righteousness, **s** humility;
Mt 6:33 But **s** first his kingdom and his
7: 7 be given to you; **s** and you will find;
7: 8 asks receives; those who **s** find;
Lk 12:31 But **s** his kingdom, and these things
19:10 For the Son of Man came to **s**
Jn 5:30 for I **s** not to please myself but him
5:44 do not **s** the glory that comes
Ac 15:17 the rest of humanity may **s** the Lord,
Ro 10:20 found by those who did not **s** me;
1Co 7:27 Do not **s** to be released.
10:24 No one should **s** their own good,
Heb 11: 6 rewards those who earnestly **s** him.
1Pe 3:11 and do good; **s** peace and pursue it.

## SEEKING [SEEK]

1Ch 22:19 and soul to **s** the LORD your God.
2Ch 30:19 who sets their heart on **s** God—
Pr 20:18 Plans are established by **s** advice;
Mal 3: 1 the Lord you are **s** will come to his
Jn 8:50 I am not **s** glory for myself;
1Co 10:33 For I am not **s** my own good

## SEEKS [SEEK]

Pr 11:27 Whoever **s** good finds favor,
14: 6 The mocker **s** wisdom and finds
15:14 The discerning heart **s** knowledge,
Jn 4:23 the kind of worshipers the Father **s**.
Ro 3:11 there is no one who **s** God.

## SEEM [SEEMED, SEEMS]

Zec 8: 6 but will it **s** marvelous to me?"

## SEEMED [SEEM]

Ge 29:20 they **s** like only a few days to him
Nu 13:33 We **s** like grasshoppers in our own
Ac 2: 3 They saw what **s** to be tongues
Rev 13: 3 of the beast **s** to have had a fatal

## SEEMS [SEEM]

Jos 24:15 serving the LORD **s** undesirable
Pr 12:15 The way of fools **s** right to them,
Heb 12:11 No discipline **s** pleasant at the time,

## SEEN [SEE]

Ge 16:13 "I have now **s** the One who sees
Ex 3: 7 "I have indeed **s** the misery of my
33:23 but my face must not be **s**."
Nu 14:14 LORD, have been **s** face to face,
Dt 4: 9 forget the things your eyes have **s**

Jos  23: 3  yourselves have **s** everything
Jdg  6:22  I have **s** the angel of the LORD
     13:22  said to his wife. "We have **s** God!"
Ezr  3:12  heads, who had **s** the former temple,
Ps   37:25  old, yet I have never **s** the righteous
     37:35  I have **s** the wicked and ruthless
     98: 3  the earth have **s** the salvation of our
Ecc  1:14  I have **s** all the things that are done
Isa  6: 5  and my eyes have **s** the King,
     9: 2  in darkness have **s** a great light;
     64: 4  no eye has **s** any God besides you,
Mt   2: 9  the star they had **s** when it rose went
     4:16  in darkness have **s** a great light;
Lk   2:30  For my eyes have **s** your salvation,
Jn   1:14  We have **s** his glory, the glory
     1:18  No one has ever **s** God, but the one
     6:46  No one has **s** the Father except
     14: 9  Anyone who has **s** me has **s**
     20:25  told him, "We have **s** the Lord!"
     20:29  blessed are those who have not **s**
Ro   8:24  But hope that is **s** is no hope at all.
1Co  2: 9  "What no eye has **s**, what no ear
Php  4: 9  or heard from me, or **s** in me—
1Ti  3:16  by the Spirit, was **s** by angels,
1Pe  1: 8  Though you have not **s** him,
1Jn  1: 3  We proclaim to you what we have **s**
     4:12  No one has ever **s** God; but if we
3Jn  1: 11  does what is evil has not **s** God.
Rev  1:19  "Write, therefore, what you have **s**:

## SEER [SEERS]

1Sa  9: 9  prophet of today used to be called a **s**.)
     9:19  "I am the **s**," Samuel replied.
2Sa  24: 11  come to Gad the prophet, David's **s**:
1Ch  29:29  in the records of Samuel the **s**,
     29:29  and the records of Gad the **s**,
2Ch  9:29  Iddo the **s** concerning Jeroboam son
     29:30  words of David and of Asaph the **s**.
Am   7:12  said to Amos, "Get out, you **s**!

## SEERS [SEER]

2Ki  17:13  through all his prophets and **s**:
Mic  3: 7  The **s** will be ashamed

## SEES [SEE]

Ge   16:13  now seen the One who **s** me."
Nu   24: 3  of one whose eye **s** clearly,
     24:15  of one whose eye **s** clearly,
Ps   33:13  looks down and **s** all humankind;
Isa  11: 3  judge by what he **s** with his eyes,
     47:10  and have said, 'No one **s** me.'
Mt   6: 4  Father, who **s** what is done in secret,
     6: 6  Father, who **s** what is done in secret,
     6:18  Father, who **s** what is done in secret,
Jn   5:19  do only what he **s** his Father doing,
1Jn  3:17  material possessions and **s** a brother

## SEIR

Ge   32: 3  to his brother Esau in the land of **S**,
Dt   2: 4  descendants of Esau, who live in **S**.
Eze  35: 2  man, set your face against Mount **S**;

## SELAH

The Hebrew word for "*Selah*" is not translated in the TNIV, but is indicated in the notes to Psalms and Habakkuk.

Following is a list of all occurrences of "*Selah*" in the NIV: Ps 3:2, 4, 8; 4:2, 4; 7:5; 9:16, 20; 20:3; 21:2; 24:6, 10; 32:4, 5, 7; 39:5, 11; 44:8; 46:3, 7, 11; 47:4; 48:8; 49:13, 15; 50:6; 52:3, 5; 54:3; 55:7, 19; 57:3, 6; 59:5, 13; 60:4; 61:4; 62:4, 8; 66:4, 7, 15; 67:1, 4; 68:7, 19, 32; 75:3; 76:3, 9; 77:3, 9, 15; 81:7; 82:2; 83:8; 84:4, 8; 85:2; 87:3, 6; 88:7, 10; 89:4, 37, 45, 48; 140:3, 5, 8; 143:6; Hab 3:3, 9, 13

## SELECT [SELECTED]

Ex   12:21  and **s** the animals for your families
     18:21  **s** capable men from all the people—
Nu   35:11  **s** some towns to be your cities of refuge
Isa  66:21  I will **s** some of them also to be priests

## SELECTED [SELECT]

Nu   18: 6  I myself have **s** your fellow Levites

## SELF [SELFISH]

Lk   9:25  and yet lose or forfeit your very **s**?
Ro   6: 6  know that our old **s** was crucified
Eph  4:22  to put off your old **s**, which is being
Col  3:10  and have put on the new **s**, which is
1Pe  3: 4  it should be that of your inner **s**,

## SELF-CONDEMNED* [CONDEMN]

Tit  3: 11  are warped and sinful; they are **s**.

## SELF-CONTROL* [CONTROL]

Pr   16:32  with **s** than those who take a city.
     25:28  through is a person who lacks **s**.
Ac   24:25  **s** and the judgment to come,
1Co  7: 5  tempt you because of your lack of **s**.
Gal  5:23  gentleness and **s**.
2Ti  3: 3  slanderous, without **s**, brutal,
2Pe  1: 6  and to knowledge, **s**; and to **s**, perseverance;

## SELF-CONTROLLED* [CONTROL]

1Ti  3: 2  his wife, temperate, **s**, respectable,
Tit  1: 8  what is good, who is **s**, upright,
     2: 2  worthy of respect, **s**, and sound
     2: 5  to be **s** and pure, to be busy
     2: 6  encourage the young men to be **s**.
     2:12  and to live **s**, upright and godly lives

## SELF-DENIAL* [DENY]

Ps   132: 1  remember David and all his **s**.

## SELF-DISCIPLINE* [DISCIPLINE]

2Ti  1: 7  but gives us power, love and **s**.

## SELF-INDULGENCE* [INDULGE]

Mt   23:25  inside they are full of greed and **s**.
Jas  5: 5  have lived on earth in luxury and **s**.

## SELF-SEEKING* [SEEK]

Ro   2: 8  for those who are **s** and who reject
1Co  13: 5  it is not **s**, it is not easily angered,

## SELFISH* [SELF]

Ps   119:36  your statutes and not toward **s** gain.
Pr   18: 1  An unfriendly person pursues **s** ends
Gal  5:20  fits of rage, **s** ambition, dissensions,

Php 1:17 preach Christ out of s ambition,
2: 3 Do nothing out of s ambition
Jas 3:14 envy and s ambition in your hearts,
3:16 you have envy and s ambition,

## SELL [SALE, SELLING, SELLS, SOLD]
Ge 23: 9 so he will s me the cave
25:31 "First s me your birthright."
Lev 25:14 " 'If you s land to any of your
Pr 23:23 Buy the truth and do not s it—
Mk 10:21 s everything you have and give
Rev 13:17 buy or s unless they had the mark,

## SELLING [SELL]
Ge 25:33 to him, s his birthright to Jacob.
Mk 11:15 those who were buying and s there.
Lk 17:28 buying and s, planting and building.
Jn 2:14 courts he found people s cattle,

## SELLS [SELL]
Pr 31:24 makes linen garments and s them,

## SEND [SENDING, SENDS, SENT]
Ge 7: 4 from now I will s rain on the earth
Ex 23:27 "I will s my terror ahead of you
33: 2 I will s an angel before you
Lev 16:21 He shall s the goat away
Dt 11:14 then I will s rain on your land in its
28:20 The LORD will s on you curses,
1Sa 5:11 said, "S the ark of the god of Israel
Ps 43: 3 S me your light and your faithful
104:30 When you s your Spirit, they are
Isa 6: 8 the Lord saying, "Whom shall I s?
6: 8 And I said, "Here am I. S me!"
Mal 3: 1 "I will s my messenger, who will
4: 5 I will s the prophet Elijah to you
Mt 9:38 to s out workers into his harvest
11:10 " 'I will s my messenger ahead
24:31 And he will s his angels with a loud
Mk 1: 2 "I will s my messenger ahead
1:17 "and I will s you out to fish for people."
6: 7 he began to s them out two by two
10: 4 of divorce and s her away."
Lk 11:49 'I will s them prophets and apostles,
20:13 I will s my son, whom I love;
Jn 3:17 God did not s his Son into the world
14:26 whom the Father will s in my name,
15:26 whom I will s to you
16: 7 but if I go, I will s him to you.
Ac 3:20 and that he may s the Messiah,
1Co 1:17 For Christ did not s me to baptize,

## SENDING [SEND]
Ex 3:10 I am s you to Pharaoh to bring my
23:20 I am s an angel ahead of you
Joel 2:13 love, and he relents from s calamity.
Jnh 4: 2 a God who relents from s calamity.
Mt 10:16 "I am s you out like sheep among
Jn 20:21 the Father has sent me, I am s you."
Ro 8: 3 God did by s his own Son

## SENDS [SEND]
Ps 57: 3 He s from heaven and saves me,
Mt 5:45 and s rain on the righteous

## SENNACHERIB
Assyrian king whose siege of Jerusalem was overthrown by the LORD following prayer of Hezekiah and Isaiah (2Ki 18:13—19:37; 2Ch 32:1–21; Isa 36–37).

## SENSE [SENSES, SENSITIVE, SENSITIVITY]
Dt 32:28 They are a nation without s, there is
Pr 6:32 man who commits adultery has no s;
7: 7 a youth who had no s.
9: 4 To those who have no s she says,
10:21 but fools die for lack of s.
11:12 who have no s deride their neighbors,
12:11 those who chase fantasies have no s.
15:21 Folly brings joy to those who have no s,
17:18 One who has no s shakes hands in pledge
Ecc 10: 3 they lack s and show everyone how

## SENSES* [SENSE]
Lk 15:17 "When he came to his s, he said,
1Co 15:34 Come back to your s as you ought,
2Ti 2:26 that they will come to their s

## SENSITIVE [SENSE]
Dt 28:56 gentle and s woman among you—

## SENSITIVITY* [SENSE]
Eph 4:19 Having lost all s, they have given

## SENSUAL* [SENSUALITY]
Col 2:23 value in restraining s indulgence.
1Ti 5:11 when their s desires overcome their

## SENSUALITY* [SENSUAL]
Eph 4:19 given themselves over to s so as

## SENT [SEND]
Ge 2: 5 the LORD God had not s rain
8: 8 he s out a dove to see if the water
45: 5 to save lives that God s me ahead
Ex 3:14 'I AM has s me to you.' "
Nu 13:17 When Moses s them to explore
16:29 then the LORD has not s me.
21: 6 the LORD s venomous snakes
Jos 2: 1 son of Nun secretly s two spies
24:12 I s the hornet ahead of you,
1Sa 14:15 It was a panic s by God.
2Sa 24:15 So the LORD s a plague on Israel
2Ki 14: 9 "A thistle in Lebanon s a message
Ps 107:20 He s out his word and healed them;
Isa 55:11 achieve the purpose for which I s it.
61: 1 He has s me to bind
Jer 3: 8 and s her away because of all her
28: 9 will be recognized as one truly s
44: 4 again I s my servants the prophets,
Eze 39:28 though I s them into exile among
Da 5:24 who has s his angel and rescued his
6:22 My God s his angel, and he shut
Mt 10:40 me welcomes the one who s me.
Mk 1:12 At once the Spirit s him
Lk 1:26 God s the angel Gabriel
4:18 He has s me to proclaim freedom

| | | |
|---|---|---|
| Lk | 9: 2 | and he **s** them out to proclaim |
| | 10:16 | rejects me rejects him who **s** me." |
| | 13:34 | prophets and stone those **s** to you, |
| Jn | 1: 6 | There was a man **s** from God whose |
| | 3:28 | the Messiah but am **s** ahead of him.' |
| | 4:34 | "is to do the will of him who **s** me |
| | 5:24 | believes him who **s** me has eternal |
| | 8:16 | I stand with the Father, who **s** me. |
| | 9: 4 | must do the works of him who **s** me. |
| | 16: 5 | now I am going to him who **s** me. |
| | 17: 3 | and Jesus Christ, whom you have **s**. |
| | 17:18 | As you **s** me into the world, I have **s** |
| | 20:21 | As the Father has **s** me, I am |
| Ro | 10:15 | anyone preach unless they are **s**? |
| Gal | 4: 4 | time had fully come, God **s** his Son, |
| 1Jn | 4:10 | **s** his Son as an atoning sacrifice |
| Rev | 22:16 | have **s** my angel to give you this |

## SENTENCE [SENTENCED]

| | | |
|---|---|---|
| Ecc | 8:11 | the **s** for a crime is not quickly |
| Ac | 13:28 | no proper ground for a death **s**, |
| 2Co | 1: 9 | we felt we had received the **s** |

## SENTENCED [SENTENCE]

| | | |
|---|---|---|
| Jer | 26:16 | "This man should not be **s** to death! |
| Lk | 24:20 | handed him over to be **s** to death, |

## SEPARATE [SEPARATED, SEPARATES]

| | | |
|---|---|---|
| Ex | 26:33 | The curtain will **s** the Holy Place |
| Pr | 16:28 | and gossips **s** close friends. |
| Mt | 19: 6 | has joined together, let no one **s**." |
| Ro | 8:35 | Who shall **s** us from the love |
| 1Co | 7:10 | A wife must not **s** from her |
| 2Co | 6:17 | "Come out from them and be **s**, |
| Eph | 2:12 | at that time you were **s** from Christ, |

## SEPARATED [SEPARATE]

| | | |
|---|---|---|
| Ge | 1: 4 | and he **s** the light from the darkness. |
| | 1: 7 | **s** the water under the vault |
| Isa | 59: 2 | your iniquities have **s** you from your |
| Eph | 4:18 | **s** from the life of God because |

## SEPARATES [SEPARATE]

| | | |
|---|---|---|
| Pr | 17: 9 | repeats the matter **s** close friends. |
| Mt | 25:32 | another as a shepherd **s** the sheep |

## SEPULCHRE(S) (KJV) See GRAVE(S), TOMB(S)

## SERAPHS*

| | | |
|---|---|---|
| Isa | 6: 2 | Above him were **s**, each with six |
| | 6: 6 | one of the **s** flew to me with a live |

## SERIOUS [SERIOUSNESS]

| | | |
|---|---|---|
| Ex | 21:23 | But if there is **s** injury, you are |
| Jer | 6:14 | my people as though it were not **s**. |

## SERIOUSNESS* [SERIOUS]

| | | |
|---|---|---|
| Tit | 2: 7 | In your teaching show integrity, |

## SERPENT [SERPENT'S]

| | | |
|---|---|---|
| Ge | 3: 1 | Now the **s** was more crafty than any |
| | 3:13 | woman said, "The **s** deceived me, |
| Isa | 27: 1 | Leviathan the gliding **s**, |

| | | |
|---|---|---|
| Rev | 12: 9 | that ancient **s** called the devil, |
| | 20: 2 | that ancient **s**, who is the devil, |

## SERPENT'S [SERPENT]

| | | |
|---|---|---|
| Isa | 65:25 | the ox, but dust will be the **s** food. |
| 2Co | 11: 3 | Eve was deceived by the **s** cunning, |

## SERVANT [SERVE]

| | | |
|---|---|---|
| Ge | 16: 1 | had an Egyptian **s** named Hagar; |
| | 16: 5 | I put my **s** in your arms, and now |
| | 21:13 | the son of the **s** into a nation also, |
| | 35:25 | sons of Rachel's **s** Bilhah: |
| | 35:26 | sons of Leah's **s** Zilpah: |
| Ex | 14:31 | their trust in him and in Moses his **s**. |
| | 21: 2 | "If you buy a Hebrew **s**, he is |
| Nu | 12: 7 | But this is not true of my **s** Moses; |
| Dt | 5:14 | nor your male or female **s**, |
| 1Sa | 3:10 | "Speak, for your **s** is listening." |
| 2Sa | 7:19 | the future of the house of your **s**— |
| 1Ki | 3: 7 | you have made your **s** king in place |
| | 8:56 | he gave through his **s** Moses. |
| | 8:66 | LORD had done for his **s** David |
| | 20:40 | While your **s** was busy here |
| Job | 1: 8 | "Have you considered my **s** Job? |
| | 2: 3 | "Have you considered my **s** Job? |
| | 42: 8 | My **s** Job will pray for you, |
| Ps | 19:11 | By them your **s** is warned; |
| | 19:13 | Keep your **s** also from willful sins; |
| | 31:16 | Let your face shine on your **s**; |
| | 78:70 | He chose David his **s** and took him |
| | 89: 3 | one, I have sworn to David my **s**, |
| | 105:26 | He sent Moses his **s**, and Aaron, |
| Pr | 11:29 | and the fool will be **s** to the wise. |
| | 14:35 | but a shameful **s** arouses his fury. |
| | 17: 2 | A prudent **s** will rule over |
| Isa | 24: 2 | for mistress as for her **s**, |
| | 41: 8 | Israel, my **s**, Jacob, whom I have |
| | 42: 1 | "Here is my **s**, whom I uphold, |
| | 43:10 | "and my **s** whom I have chosen, |
| | 44: 1 | Jacob, my **s**, Israel, whom I have |
| | 45: 4 | For the sake of Jacob my **s**, of Israel |
| | 48:20 | LORD has redeemed his **s** Jacob." |
| | 49: 3 | said to me, "You are my **s**, Israel, |
| | 52:13 | See, my **s** will act wisely; he will be |
| | 53:11 | my righteous **s** will justify many, |
| Jer | 30:10 | do not be afraid, Jacob my **s**; |
| | 33:21 | my covenant with David my **s**— |
| Eze | 34:24 | my **s** David will be prince among |
| Zec | 3: 8 | I am going to bring my **s**, |
| Mt | 8:13 | his **s** was healed at that very hour. |
| | 20:26 | great among you must be your **s**, |
| | 24:45 | then is the faithful and wise **s**, |
| | 25:21 | 'Well done, good and faithful **s**! |
| Lk | 1:38 | "I am the Lord's **s**," |
| | 1:54 | He has helped his **s** Israel, |
| | 1:69 | for us in the house of his **s** David |
| Jn | 12:26 | and where I am, my **s** also will be. |
| Ac | 3:13 | our fathers, has glorified his **s** Jesus. |
| | 12:13 | a **s** named Rhoda came to answer |
| Ro | 1: 1 | Paul, a **s** of Christ Jesus, called to be |
| | 13: 4 | authority is God's **s** for your good. |
| | 14: 4 | are you to judge someone else's **s**? |
| Php | 2: 7 | by taking the very nature of a **s**, |
| Col | 1:23 | of which I, Paul, have become a **s**. |
| 2Ti | 2:24 | And the Lord's **s** must not be |
| Heb | 3: 5 | "Moses was faithful as a **s** in all |

Rev 15: 3 sang the song of God's s Moses
19:10 I am a fellow s with you

## SERVANT OF THE †LORD Dt 34:5; Jos
1:1, 13, 15; 8:31, 33; 11:12; 12:6, 6; 13:8; 14:7;
18:7; 22:2, 4, 5; 24:29; Jdg 2:8; 2Ki 18:12; 2Ch
24:6; Ps 18:T; 36:T; Isa 42:19

## SERVANT'S [SERVE]
1Sa 1:11 you will only look on your s misery
2Ki 6:17 Then the LORD opened the s eyes,
2Ch 6:19 give attention to your s prayer
Ps 119:122 Ensure your s well-being; do not let

## SERVANTS [SERVE]
Lev 25:55 for the Israelites belong to me as s.
Dt 32:36 relent concerning his s when he sees
1Sa 2: 9 guard the feet of his faithful s,
25:42 attended by her five female s,
2Ki 10:19 in order to destroy the s of Baal.
17:23 through all his s the prophets.
Ezr 5:11 "We are the s of the God of heaven
Job 4:18 If God places no trust in his s, if he
Ps 34:22 The LORD redeems his s;
90:13 Have compassion on your s.
103:21 hosts, you his s who do his will.
104: 4 his messengers, flames of fire his s.
113: 1 Praise the LORD, you his s;
Pr 31:15 and portions for her women s.
Isa 44:26 who carries out the words of his s
65: 8 in it,' so will I do in behalf of my s;
65:14 My s will sing out of the joy of their
Jer 7:25 again I sent you my s the prophets.
Da 9: 6 not listened to your s the prophets,
Lk 17:10 do, should say, 'We are unworthy s;
Jn 15:15 I no longer call you s, because s do
Ac 4:29 enable your s to speak your word
Ro 13: 6 for the authorities are God's s,
1Co 3: 5 Only s, through whom you came
2Co 11:15 then, if his s also masquerade as s
Heb 1: 7 spirits, and his s flames of fire."
Rev 7: 3 the foreheads of the s of our God."
19: 2 avenged on her the blood of his s."
22: 3 in the city, and his s will serve him.

## SERVE [SERVANT, SERVANT'S,
## SERVANTS, SERVED, SERVES,
## SERVICE, SERVING]
Ge 1:14 let them s as signs to mark seasons
15:14 punish the nation they s as slaves,
25:23 and the older will s the younger."
Ex 28: 1 so they may s me as priests.
Nu 1: 3 or more and able to s in the army.
Dt 6:13 s him only and take your oaths
10:12 to s the LORD your God with all
11:13 God and to s him with all your heart
13: 4 s him and hold fast to him.
28:47 you did not s the LORD your God
Jos 22: 5 him and to s him with all your heart
24:14 and s him with all faithfulness.
24:15 household, we will s the LORD."
24:18 We too will s the LORD,
1Sa 7: 3 to the LORD and s him only,
12:20 s the LORD with all your heart.
12:24 s him faithfully with all your heart;
2Ki 17:35 to them, s them or sacrifice to them.

2Ch 19: 9 "You must s faithfully
Ne 9:35 they did not s you or turn from their
Job 36:11 If they obey and s him, they will
Ps 2:11 S the LORD with fear
Isa 60:12 that will not s you will perish;
Jer 2:20 you said, 'I will not s you!'
25: 6 Do not follow other gods to s
Da 3:17 If the God we s is able to deliver us,
Mt 4:10 Lord your God, and s him only.' "
6:24 You cannot s both God and money.
Mk 10:45 but to s, and to give his life as
Lk 16:13 "No one can s two masters.
Ro 12: 7 if it is serving, then s; if it is
Gal 5:13 s one another humbly in love.
Eph 6: 7 S wholeheartedly, as if you were
1Th 1: 9 to God from idols to s the living
1Ti 6: 2 they should s them even better
Heb 9:14 so that we may s the living God!
1Pe 4:10 gift you have received to s others,
4:11 If you s, you should do so with the
strength
5: 2 dishonest gain, but eager to s;
Rev 1: 6 and priests to s his God and Father—
5:10 a kingdom and priests to s our God,
7:15 the throne of God and s him day

## SERVED [SERVE]
Ge 29:20 So Jacob s seven years to get
Jos 24:15 gods your ancestors s beyond
Jdg 2:13 they forsook him and s Baal
Jer 5:19 s foreign gods in your own land,
Mt 20:28 Son of Man did not come to be s,
Jn 12: 2 Martha s, while Lazarus was among
Ac 17:25 And he is not s by human hands,
Ro 1:25 and s created things rather than
1Ti 3:13 Those who have s well gain

## SERVES [SERVE]
Lk 22:26 one who rules like the one who s.
Jn 12:26 Whoever s me must follow me;
Ro 14:18 because anyone who s Christ in this

## SERVICE [SERVE]
Nu 8:25 they must retire from their regular s
18: 7 I am giving you the s
2Ch 5:14 could not perform their s because
Job 7: 1 "Do not mortals have hard s
Lk 9:62 and looks back is fit for s
12:35 "Be dressed ready for s and keep
Ro 15:17 in Christ Jesus in my s to God.
1Co 12: 5 There are different kinds of s,
16:15 to the s of the Lord's people.
2Co 9:12 This s that you perform is not only
10:13 sphere of s God himself has assigned
Eph 4:12 to equip his people for works of s,
Rev 2:19 and faith, your s and perseverance,

## SERVING [SERVE]
Jos 24:15 if s the LORD seems undesirable
Jdg 2:19 following other gods and s
2Ch 12: 8 between s me and s the kings
Pr 15:17 Better a small s of vegetables with love
Ro 12: 7 if it is s, then serve; if it is teaching,
12:11 your spiritual fervor, s the Lord.
16:18 people are not s our Lord Christ,
Eph 6: 7 as if you were s the Lord,

Col  3:24  It is the Lord Christ you are **s**.
2Ti  2: 4  No one **s** as a soldier gets involved
1Pe  1:12  that they were not **s** themselves

## SET [SETS, SETTING, SETTINGS]

Ge  9:13  I have **s** my rainbow in the clouds,
     28:18  under his head and **s** it up as a pillar
     31:45  took a stone and **s** it up as a pillar.
     35:14  Jacob **s** up a stone pillar at the place
Ex  24: 4  and **s** up twelve stone pillars
     26:30  "**S** up the tabernacle according
     40:18  When Moses **s** up the tabernacle,
Lev 20:26  I have **s** you apart from the nations
Nu  8:17  in Egypt, I **s** them apart for myself.
     9:23  the LORD's command they **s** out.
Dt  10:15  Yet the LORD **s** his affection
     16:21  Do not **s** up any wooden Asherah
     27: 2  you, **s** up some large stones and coat
     28: 1  LORD your God will **s** you high
     30:15  See, I **s** before you today life
Jos  4: 9  Joshua **s** up the twelve stones
1Sa  5: 2  temple and **s** it beside Dagon.
2Ki 25: 9  He **s** fire to the temple
Ps  4: 3  the LORD has **s** apart his faithful
     8: 1  You have **s** your glory
     142: 7  **S** me free from my prison, that I
Pr  8: 5  who are foolish, **s** your hearts on it.
     9: 1  she has **s** up its seven pillars.
Isa 50: 7  Therefore have I **s** my face like
Eze 14: 4  When any of the Israelites **s** up idols
Da  9:27  And at the temple he will **s**
     11:28  his heart will be **s** against the holy
Mk 15:17  a crown of thorns and **s** it on him.
Lk  4:18  the blind, to **s** the oppressed free,
     16:26  a great chasm has been **s** in place,
Jn  8:32  truth, and the truth will **s** you free."
Ac  1: 7  or dates the Father has **s** by his own
Ro  8: 2  Spirit who gives life has **s** you free
2Co  1:22  **s** his seal of ownership on us,
Gal  5: 1  for freedom that Christ has **s** us free.
Col  3: 1  **s** your hearts on things above,
Heb  4: 7  God again **s** a certain day, calling it

## SETH

Ge  4:25  birth to a son and named him **S**,

## SETS [SET]

2Ch 30:19  who **s** their heart on seeking God—
Job  5:11  The lowly he **s** on high, and those
Ps  68: 6  God **s** the lonely in families,
     146: 7  The LORD **s** prisoners free,
Ecc  1: 5  The sun rises and the sun **s**,
Mt  5:19  Anyone who **s** aside
2Th  2: 4  so that he **s** himself up in God's
Heb 10: 9  He **s** aside the first to establish

## SETTING [SET]

Dt  11:26  I am **s** before you today a blessing
Jer  21: 8  I am **s** before you the way of life
Mk  7: 9  a fine way of **s** aside the commands
Eph  2:15  by **s** aside in his flesh the law

## SETTINGS [SET]

Pr  25:11  gold in **s** of silver is a ruling rightly

## SETTLE [RESETTLE, SETTLED, SETTLES]

Ge  47: 4  So now, please let your servants **s**
Nu  33:53  possession of the land and **s** in it,
Isa  2: 4  will **s** disputes for many peoples.
Jer  29: 5  "Build houses and **s** down;
Eze 37:14  and I will **s** you in your own land.
Mt  5:25  "**S** matters quickly with your
2Th  3:12  in the Lord Jesus Christ to **s** down

## SETTLED [SETTLE]

Ex  24:16  of the LORD **s** on Mount Sinai.
     40:35  meeting because the cloud had **s**
Dt  19: 1  driven them out and **s** in their towns
2Ki 18:11  to Assyria and **s** them in Halah,

## SETTLES [SETTLE]

Ps  113: 9  He **s** the childless woman in her
Pr  18:18  Casting the lot **s** disputes and keeps

## SEVEN [SEVENS, SEVENTH]

Ge  4:15  will suffer vengeance **s** times over."
     7: 2  Take with you **s** pairs of every kind
     21:28  Abraham set apart **s** ewe lambs
     29:18  "I'll work for you **s** years in return
     41: 2  of the river there came up **s** cows,
     41: 5  **S** heads of grain, healthy and good,
Ex  2:16  a priest of Midian had **s** daughters,
     12:15  For **s** days you are to eat bread
     25:37  make its **s** lamps and set them
     29:35  you, taking **s** days to ordain them.
Lev  4: 6  of it **s** times before the LORD,
     12: 2  be ceremonially unclean for **s** days,
     15:19  her monthly period will last **s** days,
     15:24  him, he will be unclean for **s** days;
     23:15  offering, count off **s** full weeks.
     23:42  in temporary shelters for **s** days:
     25: 8  " 'Count off **s** sabbath years—
     26:18  you for your sins **s** times over.
Nu  23: 1  said, "Build me **s** altars here,
Dt  7: 1  **s** nations larger and stronger than
     15: 1  every **s** years you must cancel debts.
Jos  6: 4  march around the city **s** times,
Jdg 16:13  Delilah took the **s** braids of his
1Sa  2: 5  was barren has borne **s** children,
1Ki 19:18  Yet I reserve **s** thousand in Israel—
2Ki  5:10  wash yourself **s** times in the Jordan,
Ps  79:12  our neighbors **s** times the contempt
     119:164  **S** times a day I praise you for your
Pr  6:16  hates, **s** that are detestable to him:
     9: 1  she has set up its **s** pillars.
     24:16  for though the righteous fall **s** times,
     26:25  for **s** abominations fill their hearts.
Isa  4: 1  that day **s** women will take hold
Da  3:19  the furnace heated **s** times hotter
     4:16  animal, till **s** times pass by for him.
     9:25  comes, there will be **s** 'sevens,'
Zec  3: 9  There are **s** eyes on that one stone,
     4: 2  a bowl at the top and **s** lamps on it,
Mt  12:45  "I tell you, not **s** times, but **s** times.
Mk 12:20  Now there were **s** brothers.
     16: 9  *out of whom he had driven **s** demons.*
Lk  11:26  takes **s** other spirits more wicked
Ro  11: 4  for myself **s** thousand who have not
Rev  1: 4  To the **s** churches in the province

Rev 1: 4 from the s spirits before his throne,
1:12 I turned I saw s golden lampstands,
1:16 In his right hand he held s stars,
3: 1 him who holds the s spirits of God
4: 5 These are the s spirits of God.
5: 1 both sides and sealed with s seals.
6: 1 Lamb opened the first of the s seals.
8: 2 and s trumpets were given to them.
10: 4 And when the s thunders spoke,
12: 3 enormous red dragon with s heads
15: 1 s angels with the s last plagues—
15: 7 to the s angels s golden bowls filled
16: 1 pour out the s bowls of God's wrath
17: 9 The s heads are s hills

## SEVENS* [SEVEN]
Da 9:24 "Seventy 's' are decreed for your
9:25 will be seven 's,' and sixty-two 's.'
9:26 After the sixty-two 's,' the Anointed

## SEVENTH [SEVEN]
Ge 2: 2 the s day God had finished the work
Ex 16:30 So the people rested on the s day.
20:10 the s day is a sabbath to the LORD
23:11 but during the s year let the land lie
23:12 but on the s day do not work,
Lev 16:29 day of the s month you must deny
23:16 up to the day after the s Sabbath,
23:24 the first day of the s month you are
23:27 tenth day of this s month is the Day
23:34 the s month the LORD's Festival
25: 4 in the s year the land is to have
Jos 6:16 The s time around, when the priests
Heb 4: 4 "On the s day God rested from all
Rev 8: 1 When he opened the s seal,
11:15 The s angel sounded his trumpet,
16:17 The s angel poured out his bowl

## SEVENTY
Ge 46:27 which went to Egypt, were s in all.
Ex 24: 1 Abihu, and s of the elders of Israel.
Nu 11:25 on him and put it on the s elders.
2Ch 36:21 until the s years were completed
Ps 90:10 Our days may come to s years,
Jer 25:12 "But when the s years are fulfilled,
Da 9: 2 of Jerusalem would last s years.
9:24 "S 'sevens' are decreed for your

## SEVENTY-SEVEN
Ge 4:24 seven times, then Lamech s times."
Mt 18:22 you, not seven times, but s times.

## SEVENTY-TWO
Lk 10: 1 this the Lord appointed s others

## SEVERE
Ge 3:16 make your pains in childbearing very s;
12:10 a while because the famine was s.
41:57 the famine was s everywhere.
Nu 11:33 and he struck them with a s plague.
1Ki 18: 2 Now the famine was s in Samaria,
2Ki 25: 3 the city had become so s that there
Lk 4:25 there was a s famine throughout
15:14 there was a s famine in that whole
Ac 11:28 a s famine would spread over

2Co 8: 2 In the midst of a very s trial,
1Th 1: 6 the midst of s suffering with the joy

## SEWED [SEWS]
Ge 3: 7 so they s fig leaves together

## SEWS [SEWED]
Mt 9:16 "No one s a patch of unshrunk

## SEX* [SEXUAL, SEXUALLY]
Ge 19: 5 so that we can have s with them."
Jdg 19:22 to your house so we can have s

## SEXUAL [SEX]
Ex 22:19 "Anyone who has s relations
Lev 18: 6 close relative to have s relations.
20:15 " 'If a man has s relations
Nu 25: 1 to indulge in s immorality
Mt 5:32 except for s immorality,
15:19 adultery, s immorality, theft,
19: 9 divorces his wife, except for s immorality
Ac 15:20 from s immorality, from the meat
Ro 1:24 of their hearts to s impurity
13:13 not in s immorality and debauchery,
1Co 5: 1 there is s immorality among you,
6:13 is not meant for s immorality
6:18 Flee from s immorality.
10: 8 should not commit s immorality,
2Co 12:21 s sin and debauchery in which they
Gal 5:19 s immorality,
Eph 5: 3 not be even a hint of s immorality,
Col 3: 5 s immorality, impurity, lust,
1Th 4: 3 that you should avoid s immorality;
Jude 1: 7 gave themselves up to s immorality
Rev 2:14 idols and committed s immorality.
2:20 my servants into s immorality
9:21 their s immorality or their thefts.

## SEXUALLY* [SEX]
1Co 5: 9 to associate with s immoral people—
5:11 fellow believers but are s immoral
6: 9 Neither the s immoral nor idolaters
6:18 but those who sin s sin against their
1Ti 1:10 for the s immoral, for those practicing
Heb 12:16 See that no one is s immoral, or is
13: 4 the adulterer and all the s immoral.
Rev 21: 8 the murderers, the s immoral,
22:15 practice magic arts, the s immoral,

## SHACKLES
2Ch 33:11 bound him with bronze s and took
36: 6 him with bronze s to take him
Ps 2: 3 throw off their s."
Na 1:13 your neck and tear your s away."

## SHADE
Ps 121: 5 the LORD is your s at your right
SS 2: 3 I delight to sit in his s, and his fruit
Isa 25: 4 the storm and a s from the heat.
Eze 31: 6 all the great nations lived in its s.
Jnh 4: 6 over Jonah to give s for his head
Mk 4:32 that the birds can perch in its s."

## SHADOW [SHADOWS]
2Ki 20:11 the LORD made the s go back

1Ch 29:15  Our days on earth are like a **s**,
Ps   17:  8  hide me in the **s** of your wings
        36:  7  take refuge in the **s** of your wings.
        57:  1  the **s** of your wings until the disaster
        63:  7  help, I sing in the **s** of your wings.
        91:  1  will rest in the **s** of the Almighty.
Isa  49:  2  in the **s** of his hand he hid me;
        51:16  covered you with the **s** of my hand—
Mt    4:16  the **s** of death a light has dawned."
Lk    1:79  in darkness and in the **s** of death,
Ac    5:15  at least Peter's **s** might fall on some
Col   2:17  These are a **s** of the things that were
Heb  8:  5  is a copy and **s** of what is in heaven.
       10:  1  The law is only a **s** of the good

## SHADOWS [SHADOW]
Job  14:  2  like fleeting **s**, they do not endure.
Jas   1:17  who does not change like shifting **s**.

## SHADRACH [HANANIAH]
Hebrew exiled to Babylon; name changed from Hananiah (Da 1:6–7). Refused defilement by food (Da 1:8–20). Refused to worship idol (Da 3:1–18); saved from furnace (Da 3:19–30).

## SHAGGY*
Da    8:21  The **s** goat is the king of Greece,

## SHAKE [SHAKEN, SHAKES, SHAKING, SHOOK]
Ps   10:  6  "Nothing will ever **s** us."
        64:  8  all who see them will **s** their heads
        99:  1  the cherubim, let the earth **s**.
Isa   2:19  when he rises to **s** the earth.
Hag  2:  6  I will once more **s** the heavens
        2:21  that I am going to **s** the heavens
Mk    6:11  **s** the dust off your feet when you
Heb 12:26  "Once more I will **s** not only

## SHAKEN [SHAKE]
Ps   15:  5  does these things will never be **s**.
        16:  8  at my right hand, I will not be **s**.
        30:  6  secure, I said, "I will never be **s**."
        55:22  he will never let the righteous be **s**.
        62:  2  he is my fortress, I will never be **s**.
       112:  6  Surely the righteous will never be **s**;
Isa  54:10  Though the mountains be **s**
        54:10  you will not be **s** nor my covenant
Mt   24:29  and the heavenly bodies will be **s**.'
Lk    6:38  down, **s** together and running over,
Ac    2:25  is at my right hand, I will not be **s**.
Heb 12:28  a kingdom that cannot be **s**, let us be

## SHAKES [SHAKE]
Ps   29:  8  voice of the LORD **s** the desert;
Pr   22:26  not be one who **s** hands in pledge
Isa  30:28  He **s** the nations in the sieve

## SHAKING* [SHAKE]
Ps   22:  7  they hurl insults, **s** their heads.
Mt   27:39  hurled insults at him, **s** their heads
Mk   15:29  at him, **s** their heads and saying,

## SHALLOW
Mt   13:  5  up quickly, because the soil was **s**.

## SHALLUM
King of Israel (2Ki 15:10–16).

## SHALMANESER*
King of Assyria; conquered and deported Israel (2Ki 17:3–4; 18:9).

## SHAME [ASHAMED, SHAMED, SHAMEFUL]
Ge    2:25  were both naked, and they felt no **s**.
Ps    4:  2  will you men turn my glory into **s**?
        25:  3  hopes in you will ever be put to **s**,
        25:  3  but **s** will come on those who are
        34:  5  their faces are never covered with **s**.
        69:  6  seek you not be put to **s** because
        97:  7  who worship images are put to **s**,
Pr    3:35  inherit honor, but fools get only **s**.
        13:  5  a stench and are filled with **s**.
        13:18  discipline comes to poverty and **s**,
        18:13  that is folly and **s**.
Isa  30:  5  everyone will be put to **s** because
        45:17  you will never be put to **s**
        61:  7  of your **s** you will receive a double
Jer   8:  9  The wise will be put to **s**;
        8:12  No, they have no **s** at all;
Eze  39:26  They will forget their **s** and all
Da    9:  7  but this day we are covered with **s**—
        12:  2  life, others to and everlasting
Ro    5:  5  And hope does not put us to **s**,
        9:33  in him will never be put to **s**."
       10:11  in him will never be put to **s**."
1Co   1:27  things of the world to **s** the wise;
Php   3:19  and their glory is in their **s**.
Heb 12:  2  scorning its **s**, and sat down
1Pe   2:  6  trusts in him will never be put to **s**."

## SHAMED [SHAME]
Jer  10:14  all goldsmiths are **s** by their idols.
Joel  2:26  never again will my people be **s**.

## SHAMEFUL [SHAME]
Jer   3:24  our youth **s** gods have consumed
Ro    1:26  this, God gave them over to **s** lusts.
        1:27  committed **s** acts with other men,
2Co   4:  2  have renounced secret and **s** ways;
Eph   5:12  It is **s** even to mention what
Rev  21:27  nor will anyone who does what is **s**

## SHAMGAR*
Judge; killed 600 Philistines (Jdg 3:31; 5:6).

## SHAPE [SHAPED, SHAPES, SHAPING]
Ex   32:  4  it into an idol cast in the **s** of a calf,
2Ki  17:16  two idols cast in the **s** of calves,
Job  38:14  The earth takes **s** like clay under

## SHAPED [SHAPE]
Job  10:  8  "Your hands **s** me and made me.

## SHAPES [SHAPE]
Isa  44:10  Who **s** a god and casts an idol,
Jer  10:  3  a skilled worker **s** it with a chisel.

## SHAPHAN
2Ki 22: 8 high priest said to S the secretary,

## SHAPING* [SHAPE]
Jer 18: 4 pot he was s from the clay
18: 4 another pot, s it as seemed best

## SHARE [SHARED, SHARERS, SHARES, SHARING]
Ge 21:10 slave woman's son will never s
Lev 6:18 come it is his perpetual s of the food
6:22 It is the LORD's perpetual s and is
19:17 neighbor frankly so you will not s
Nu 18:20 any s among them; I am your s
Dt 10: 9 That is why the Levites have no s
Jos 14: 4 The Levites received no s
22:25 You have no s in the LORD.'
2Sa 20: 1 shouted, "We have no s in David,
2Ch 10:16 "What s do we have in David,
Ne 2:20 you have no s in Jerusalem or any
Ps 69:27 do not let them s in your salvation.
Pr 22: 9 for they s their food with the poor.
Ecc 9: 2 All s a common destiny—
Eze 18:20 The child will not s the guilt
Mt 25:21 and s your master's happiness!'
Lk 3:11 who has two shirts should s
15:12 'Father, give me my s of the estate.'
Ac 8:21 have no part or s in this ministry,
Ro 8:17 if indeed we s in his sufferings
8:17 that we may also s in his glory.
12:13 S with the Lord's people who are
15:27 it to the Jews to s with them their
2Co 1: 7 so also you s in our comfort.
Gal 4:30 the slave woman's son will never s
6: 6 in the word should s all good things
Eph 4:28 they may have something to s
Col 1:12 who has qualified you to s
2Th 2:14 that you might s in the glory of our
1Ti 5:22 and do not s in the sins of others.
6:18 and to be generous and willing to s.
2Ti 2: 6 the first to receive a s of the crops.
Phm 1: 6 good thing we s for the sake of Christ.
Heb 3:14 We have come to s in Christ,
12:10 good, that we may s in his holiness.
13:16 to do good and to s with others,
1Pe 5: 1 will s in the glory to be revealed:
Rev 18: 4 so that you will not s in her sins,
22:19 away from you your s in the tree

## SHARED [SHARE]
Ps 41: 9 I trusted, one who s my bread,
Jn 13:18 'He who s my bread has lifted up
Ac 1:17 our number and s in our ministry."
4:32 own, but they s everything they had.
Heb 2:14 he too s in their humanity so
6: 4 gift, who have s in the Holy Spirit,

## SHARERS* [SHARE]
Eph 3: 6 s together in the promise in Christ

## SHARES [SHARE]
2Jn 1:11 Anyone who welcomes them s

## SHARING [SHARE]
1Co 9:10 do so in the hope of s in the harvest.

2Co 9:13 for your generosity in s with them
Php 2: 1 if any common s in the Spirit,

## SHARON
SS 2: 1 I am a rose of S, a lily

## SHARP [SHARPENED, SHARPENS, SHARPER]
Pr 5: 4 as gall, s as a double-edged sword.
Isa 5:28 Their arrows are s, all their bows
Ac 15:39 They had such a s disagreement
Rev 1:16 coming out of his mouth was a s,
2:12 are the words of him who has the s,
14:14 his head and a s sickle in his hand.
19:15 out of his mouth is a s sword

## SHARPENED [SHARP]
Isa 49: 2 He made my mouth like a s sword,
Eze 21: 9 sword, a sword, s and polished—

## SHARPENS* [SHARP]
Pr 27:17 As iron s iron, so one person s another.

## SHARPER* [SHARP]
Heb 4:12 S than any double-edged sword,

## SHATTER [SHATTERED, SHATTERS]
Isa 30:31 voice of the LORD will s Assyria;
Jer 51:20 with you I s nations, with you I
Hag 2:22 and s the power of the foreign

## SHATTERED [SHATTER]
Ex 15: 6 right hand, LORD, s the enemy.
1Ki 19:11 and s the rocks before the LORD,
Job 16:12 All was well with me, but he s me;
17:11 days have passed, my plans are s.
Ecc 12: 6 before the pitcher is s at the spring,
Isa 7: 8 years Ephraim will be too s to be
Na 1: 6 the rocks are s before him.

## SHATTERS [SHATTER]
Ps 46: 9 He breaks the bow and s the spear;

## SHAVE [SHAVED]
Nu 6:18 the Nazirite must s off the hair
Dt 14: 1 or s the front of your heads
Jdg 16:19 someone to s off the seven braids

## SHAVED [SHAVE]
Nu 6:19 the Nazirite has s off the hair
Jdg 16:17 If my head were s, my strength
Ac 21:24 so that they can have their heads s.
1Co 11: 5 it is the same as having her head s.

## SHEAF [SHEAVES]
Ge 37: 7 the field when suddenly my s rose
Lev 23:11 wave the s before the LORD so it
Dt 24:19 in your field and you overlook a s,

## SHEAR [SHEARER, SHEARERS]
Dt 15:19 do not s the firstborn of your sheep.

## SHEARER* [SHEAR]
Ac    8:32   and as a lamb before its s is silent,

## SHEARERS [SHEAR]
Isa  53: 7   and as a sheep before its s is silent,

## SHEATH
Eze  21: 3   draw my sword from its s
Jer  47: 6   Return to your s; cease and be still.'

## SHEAVES [SHEAF]
Ge   37: 7   while your s gathered around mine
Ru    2:15   "Let her gather among the s
Ps  126: 6   songs of joy, carrying s with them.

## SHEBA
1. Benjamite; rebelled against David (2Sa 20).
2. Queen of Sheba (1Ki 10; 2Ch 9).

## SHECHEM
1. Raped Jacob's daughter Dinah; killed by Simeon and Levi (Ge 34).
2. City where Joshua renewed the covenant (Jos 24). Abimelech as king (Jdg 9).

## SHED [SHEDDING, SHEDS]
Ge    9: 6   human beings shall their blood be s;
Nu   35:33   by the blood of the one who s it.
Dt   19:10   innocent blood will not be s in your
2Ki  21:16   s so much innocent blood that he
Ps  106:38   They s innocent blood, the blood
Pr    6:17   tongue, hands that s innocent blood,
Isa  59: 7   they are swift to s innocent blood.
Eze  22:12   people who accept bribes to s blood;
Hab   2: 8   For you have s human blood;
      2:17   For you have s human blood;
Mt   23:35   blood that has been s on earth,
Ro    3:15   "Their feet are swift to s blood;
Col   1:20   through his blood, s on the cross.
Rev  16: 6   for they have s the blood of your

## SHEDDING [SHED]
Heb   9:22   without the s of blood there is no
     12: 4   resisted to the point of s your blood.

## SHEDS* [SHED]
Ge    9: 6   "Whoever s human blood,
Pr   20:27   lamp of the LORD that s light
Eze  18:10   who s blood or does any of these

## SHEEP [SHEEP'S, SHEEPSKINS]
Lev   1:10   flock, from either the s or the goats,
Nu   27:17   not be like s without a shepherd."
Dt   17: 1   God an ox or a s that has any defect
1Sa  15:14   then is this bleating of s in my ears?
     17:35   it and rescued the s from its mouth.
2Sa  12: 4   from taking one of his own s
1Ki  22:17   the hills like s without a shepherd,
Ps   44:22   we are considered as s to be
     74: 1   your anger smolder against the s
     78:52   he led them like s through
     78:70   and took him from the s pens;
    100: 3   are his people, the s of his pasture.
    119:176  I have strayed like a lost s.

SS    4: 2   teeth are like a flock of s just shorn,
Isa  13:14   gazelle, like s without a shepherd,
     53: 6   We all, like s, have gone astray,
     53: 7   as a s before its shearers is silent,
Jer  23: 1   and scattering the s of my pasture!"
     50: 6   "My people have been lost s;
Eze  34:15   I myself will tend my s and have
Zec  13: 7   and the s will be scattered, and I
Mt    9:36   helpless, like s without a shepherd.
     10: 6   Go rather to the lost s of Israel.
     10:16   you out like s among wolves.
     12:11   "If any of you has a s and it falls
     25:32   as a shepherd separates the s
Lk   15: 4   go after the lost s until he finds it?
Jn   10: 1   anyone who does not enter the s pen
     10: 3   He calls his own s by name
     10: 7   I tell you, I am the gate for the s.
     10:11   lays down his life for the s.
     10:15   and I lay down my life for the s.
     10:27   My s listen to my voice;
     21:17   Jesus said, "Feed my s.
Ac    8:32   "He was led like a s
Ro    8:36   we are considered as s to be
Heb  13:20   Jesus, that great Shepherd of the s,
1Pe   2:25   For "you were like s going astray,"

## SHEEP'S* [SHEEP]
Mt    7:15   They come to you in s clothing,

## SHEEPSKINS* [SHEEP]
Heb  11:37   They went about in s and goatskins,

## SHEET [SHEETS]
Isa  25: 7   the s that covers all nations;
Ac   10:11   like a large s being let down to earth

## SHEETS* [SHEET]
Ex   39: 3   They hammered out thin s of gold
Nu   16:38   Hammer the censers into s

## SHEKEL [SHEKELS]
Ex   30:13   This half s is an offering

## SHEKELS [SHEKEL]
Ge   37:28   sold him for twenty s of silver
Lev  27: 3   twenty and sixty at fifty s of silver,
     27: 4   a female, set her value at thirty s;
1Ch  21:25   David paid Araunah six hundred s
Hos   3: 2   I bought her for fifteen s of silver

## SHELAH
Ge   38:11   until my son S grows up."
     46:12   Onan, S, Perez and Zerah (but Er

## SHELTER [SHELTERED, SHELTERS]
Ps   27: 5   hide me in the s of his tabernacle
     31:20   In the s of your presence you hide
     55: 8   I would hurry to my place of s,
     61: 4   take refuge in the s of your wings.
     91: 1   in the s of the Most High will rest
Ecc   7:12   Wisdom is a s as money is a s,
Isa   1: 8   Daughter Zion is left like a s
      4: 6   It will be a s and shade
     25: 4   a s from the storm and a shade
     32: 2   Each one will be like a s

Isa 58: 7 provide the poor wanderer with **s**—
Am 9:11 I will restore David's fallen **s**—
Jnh 4: 5 There he made himself a **s**, sat in its

## SHELTERED* [SHELTER]
Zep 2: 3 perhaps you will be **s** on the day

## SHELTERS [SHELTER]
Lev 23:42 Live in temporary **s** for seven days:
Ne 8:14 live in temporary **s** during the festival
Mk 9: 5 Let us put up three **s**—one for you,

## SHEM
Son of Noah (Ge 5:32; 6:10). Blessed (Ge 9:26). Descendants (Ge 10:21–31; 11:10–32; Lk 3:36).

## SHEMAIAH
1Ki 12:22 of God came to **S** the man of God:
2Ch 12: 5 the prophet **S** came to Rehoboam
Jer 29:31 Because **S** has prophesied to you,

## SHEMER
1Ki 16:24 after **S**, the name of the former

## SHEPHERD [SHEPHERDED, SHEPHERDS]
Ge 48:15 God who has been my **s** all my life
 49:24 because of the **S**, the Rock of Israel,
Nu 27:17 will not be like sheep without a **s**."
1Sa 21: 7 Doeg the Edomite, Saul's chief **s**.
2Sa 7: 7 I commanded to **s** my people Israel,
1Ki 22:17 on the hills like sheep without a **s**,
1Ch 11: 2 you, 'You will **s** my people Israel,
Ps 23: 1 The LORD is my **s**, I lack nothing.
 28: 9 be their **s** and carry them forever.
 78:71 him to be the **s** of his people Jacob,
 80: 1 Hear us, **S** of Israel, you who lead
Ecc 12:11 given by one **s**.
Isa 40:11 He tends his flock like a **s**:
Jer 31:10 will watch over his flock like a **s**.'
Eze 34: 5 scattered because there was no **s**,
Mic 5: 4 and **s** his flock in the strength
Zec 10: 2 like sheep oppressed for lack of a **s**.
 11: 4 "**S** the flock marked for slaughter.
 11: 9 and said, "I will not be your **s**.
 11:17 "Woe to the worthless **s**,
 13: 7 "Strike the **s**, and the sheep will be
Mt 2: 6 come a ruler who will **s** my people
 25:32 another as a **s** separates the sheep
 26:31 " 'I will strike the **s**, and the sheep
Mk 6:34 they were like sheep without a **s**.
Jn 10:11 "I am the good **s**. The good **s** lays
 10:14 "I am the good **s**; I know my sheep
 10:16 there shall be one flock and one **s**.
Heb 13:20 Jesus, that great **S** of the sheep,
1Pe 2:25 now you have returned to the **S**
 5: 4 And when the Chief **S** appears,
Rev 7:17 before the throne will be their **s**;

## SHEPHERDED* [SHEPHERD]
Ps 78:72 David **s** them with integrity of heart;
Zec 11: 7 So I **s** the flock marked for slaughter,
 11: 7 the other Union, and I **s** the flock.

## SHEPHERDS [SHEPHERD]
Ge 46:34 for all **s** are detestable
Ex 2:19 Egyptian rescued us from the **s**.
Nu 14:33 Your children will be **s** here
Isa 13:20 there no **s** will rest their flocks.
 56:11 They are **s** who lack understanding;
Jer 3:15 I will give you **s** after my own heart,
 23: 1 "Woe to the **s** who are destroying
 50: 6 their **s** have led them astray
Eze 34: 2 prophesy against the **s** of Israel;
 34:12 As **s** look after their scattered flocks
Zec 10: 3 "My anger burns against the **s**,
Lk 2: 8 there were **s** living out in the fields
Ac 20:28 Be **s** of the church of God, which he
1Pe 5: 2 Be **s** of God's flock that is under
Jude 1:12 **s** who feed only themselves.

## SHESHBAZZAR
Ezr 1: 8 them out to **S** the prince of Judah.
 5:16 "So this **S** came and laid

## SHEWBREAD (KJV) See BREAD OF THE PRESENCE

## SHIBBOLETH* [SIBBOLETH]
Jdg 12: 6 they said, "All right, say '**S**.' "

## SHIELD [SHIELDED, SHIELDS]
Ge 15: 1 I am your **s**, your very great
Ex 40: 3 in it and **s** the ark with the curtain.
Dt 33:29 He is your **s** and helper and your
2Sa 22:36 You make your saving help my **s**;
Ps 3: 3 you, LORD, are a **s** around me,
 5:12 them with your favor as with a **s**.
 7:10 My **s** is God Most High, who saves
 18: 2 my **s** and the horn of my salvation,
 28: 7 LORD is my strength and my **s**;
 33:20 he is our help and our **s**.
 84:11 For the LORD God is a sun and **s**;
 91: 4 his faithfulness will be your **s**
 115: 9 he is their help and **s**.
 119:114 You are my refuge and my **s**;
 144: 2 my **s**, in whom I take refuge,
Pr 2: 7 he is a **s** to those whose walk is
 30: 5 he is a **s** to those who take refuge
Isa 31: 5 LORD Almighty will **s** Jerusalem;
Zec 9:15 the LORD Almighty will **s** them.
Eph 6:16 take up the **s** of faith,

## SHIELDED [SHIELD]
Dt 32:10 He **s** him and cared for him;
1Pe 1: 5 who through faith are **s** by God's

## SHIELDS [SHIELD]
Dt 33:12 for he **s** him all day long,

## SHIFTING*
Jas 1:17 does not change like **s** shadows.

## SHIFTLESS*
Pr 19:15 on deep sleep, and the **s** go hungry.

## SHILOH
Jos 18: 1 of the Israelites gathered at **S**

1Sa  1:24  to the house of the LORD at **S**.
Ps  78:60  He abandoned the tabernacle of **S**,

## SHIMEI

Cursed David (2Sa 16:5–14); spared (2Sa 19:16–23). Killed by Solomon (1Ki 2:8–9, 36–46).

## SHINAR

Ge  11: 2  they found a plain in **S** and settled

## SHINE  [SHINES, SHINING, SHONE]

Nu  6:25  the LORD make his face **s** on you
Job  33:30  that the light of life may **s** on them.
Ps  4: 6  Let the light of your face **s** on us.
     37: 6  your righteous reward **s** like
     67: 1  bless us and make his face **s** on us—
     80: 1  between the cherubim, **s** forth
     94: 1  O God who avenges, **s** forth.
     118:27  and he has made his light **s** on us.
Isa  60: 1  "Arise, **s**, for your light has come,
Da  12: 3  are wise will **s** like the brightness
Mt  5:16  let your light **s** before others,
     13:43  the righteous will **s** like the sun
Lk  1:79  to **s** on those living in darkness
2Co  4: 6  said, "Let light **s** out of darkness,"
Eph  5:14  the dead, and Christ will **s** on you."
Php  2:15  you will **s** among them like stars
Rev  21:23  need the sun or the moon to **s** on it,

## SHINES*  [SHINE]

Ps  50: 2  Zion, perfect in beauty, God **s** forth.
     97:11  Light **s** on the righteous and joy on
Pr  13: 9  The light of the righteous **s** brightly,
Isa  62: 1  till her vindication **s** out like
Lk  11:36  of light as when a lamp **s** its light
Jn  1: 5  The light **s** in the darkness,

## SHINING  [SHINE]

Pr  4:18  **s** ever brighter till the full light
Lk  23:45  for the sun stopped **s**.
2Pe  1:19  as to a light **s** in a dark place,
1Jn  2: 8  and the true light is already **s**.
Rev  1:16  His face was like the sun **s** in all its

## SHIP  [SHIPS, SHIPWRECK, SHIPWRECKED]

Ecc  11: 1  **S** your grain across the sea;
Jnh  1: 4  storm arose that the **s** threatened
Ac  27:22  only the **s** will be destroyed.

## SHIPS  [SHIP]

1Ki  9:26  also built **s** at Ezion Geber, which is
     22:48  built a fleet of trading **s** to go
Ps  107:23  Some went out on the sea in **s**;
Pr  31:14  She is like the merchant **s**,
Jas  3: 4  Or take **s** as an example.

## SHIPWRECK*  [SHIP]

Eze  27:27  the sea on the day of your **s**.
1Ti  1:19  so have suffered **s** with regard

## SHIPWRECKED*  [SHIP]

2Co  11:25  three times I was **s**, I spent a night

## SHIRT  [SHIRTS]

Lk  6:29  do not withhold your **s**.
     9: 3  no bread, no money, no extra **s**.

## SHIRTS*  [SHIRT]

Lk  3:11  "Anyone who has two **s** should share

## SHISHAK

2Ch  12: 2  **S** king of Egypt attacked Jerusalem

## SHOCKED*  [SHOCKING]

Ge  34: 7  They were **s** and furious, because
Eze  16:27  who were **s** by your lewd conduct.

## SHOCKING*  [SHOCKED]

Jer  5:30  **s** thing has happened in the land:

## SHOE(S)  (KJV) See SANDAL(S)

## SHONE  [SHINE]

Mt  17: 2  His face **s** like the sun, and his
Lk  2: 9  the glory of the Lord **s** around them,
Rev  21:11  It **s** with the glory of God, and its

## SHOOK  [SHAKE]

Ps  18: 7  the foundations of the mountains **s**;
Isa  6: 4  and thresholds **s** and the temple was
Mt  27:51  The earth **s**, the rocks split
Ac  13:51  So they **s** the dust off their feet as
     18: 6  he **s** out his clothes in protest

## SHOOT  [SHOOTS]

Isa  11: 1  A **s** will come up from the stump
     53: 2  grew up before him like a tender **s**,
     60:21  They are the **s** I have planted,
Ro  11:17  though a wild olive **s**, have been

## SHOOTS  [SHOOT]

Ps  128: 3  be like olive **s** around your table.
Hos  14: 6  his young **s** will grow.

## SHORE  [SHORES]

Ex  14:30  the Egyptians lying dead on the **s**.
Lk  5: 3  asked him to put out a little from **s**.
Rev  13: 1  dragon stood on the **s** of the sea.

## SHORES  [SHORE]

Ps  72:10  and of distant **s** bring tribute to him.
     97: 1  let the distant **s** rejoice.

## SHORT  [SHORTENED]

Nu  11:23  Moses, "Is the LORD's arm too **s**?
Isa  50: 2  Was my arm too **s** to deliver you?
     59: 1  of the LORD is not too **s** to save,
Mt  13:21  have no root, they last only a **s** time.
     24:22  "If those days had not been cut **s**,
Lk  19: 3  because he was **s** he could not see
Jn  7:33  "I am with you for only a **s** time,
Ac  26:28  such a **s** time you can persuade me
Ro  3:23  and fall **s** of the glory of God,
1Co  7:29  and sisters, is that the time is **s**.
Heb  4: 1  you be found to have fallen **s** of it.
Rev  12:12  he knows that his time is **s**."

Rev 20: 3 that, he must be set free for a **s** time.

## SHORTENED* [SHORT]
Mt 24:22 of the elect those days will be **s**.
Mk 13:20 whom he has chosen, he has **s** them.

## SHOULD
Mt 23:23 You **s** have practiced the latter,
Lk 18: 1 show them that they **s** always pray
Php 2:10 the name of Jesus every knee **s** bow,

## SHOULDER [SHOULDERS]
Isa 22:22 I will place on his **s** the key
Zep 3: 9 of the LORD and serve him **s** to **s**.

## SHOULDERS [SHOULDER]
Ex 28:12 on his **s** as a memorial before
Dt 33:12 LORD loves rests between his **s**."
Ps 81: 6 "I removed the burden from their **s**;
Isa 9: 4 the bar across their **s**, the rod
9: 6 and the government will be on his **s**.
Mt 23: 4 and put them on other people's **s**,
Lk 15: 5 finds it, he joyfully puts it on his **s**

## SHOUT [SHOUTED, SHOUTING, SHOUTS]
Nu 23:21 the **s** of the King is among them.
Jos 6:16 Joshua commanded the army, "**S**!
Ezr 3:11 And all the people gave a great **s**
Ps 20: 5 May we **s** for joy over your victory
35:27 delight in my vindication **s** for joy.
47: 1 **s** to God with cries of joy.
66: 1 **S** for joy to God, all the earth!
95: 1 let us **s** aloud to the Rock of our
98: 4 **S** for joy to the LORD,
100: 1 **S** for joy to the LORD,
Isa 12: 6 **S** aloud and sing for joy,
26:19 in the dust wake up and **s** for joy—
35: 6 deer, and the mute tongue **s** for joy.
40: 9 lift up your voice with a **s**, lift it up,
42: 2 He will not **s** or cry out, or raise his
44:23 **s** aloud, you earth beneath.
54: 1 burst into song, **s** for joy, you who
Jer 31:12 and **s** for joy on the heights of Zion;
Zec 9: 9 **S**, Daughter Jerusalem!
Rev 10: 3 he gave a loud **s** like the roar

## SHOUTED [SHOUT]
Lev 9:24 it, they **s** for joy and fell facedown.
1Sa 17: 8 stood and **s** to the ranks of Israel,
Job 38: 7 together and all the angels **s** for joy?
Mk 15:13 "Crucify him!" they **s**.
Rev 18: 2 With a mighty voice he **s**:
19: 3 And again they **s**: "Hallelujah!

## SHOUTING [SHOUT]
Mt 21:15 the children **s** in the temple courts,
Jn 12:13 and went out to meet him, **s**,

## SHOUTS [SHOUT]
2Sa 6:15 up the ark of the LORD with **s**
Ps 27: 6 his tabernacle I will sacrifice with **s**
47: 5 God has ascended amid **s** of joy,
Ecc 9:17 to be heeded than the **s** of a ruler

## SHOW [SHOWED, SHOWING, SHOWN, SHOWS]
Ge 12: 1 household to the land I will **s** you.
22: 2 offering on a mountain I will **s** you."
24:12 **s** kindness to my master Abraham.
Ex 9:16 that I might **s** you my power
18:20 and **s** them the way they are to live
25: 9 exactly like the pattern I will **s** you.
33:18 said, "Now **s** me your glory."
Dt 1:17 Do not **s** partiality in judging;
4: 6 for this will **s** your wisdom
7: 2 with them, and **s** them no mercy.
Jos 2:12 you will **s** kindness to my family,
Ru 1: 8 May the LORD **s** you kindness,
1Sa 20:14 But **s** me unfailing kindness like
2Sa 9: 1 Saul to whom I can **s** kindness
22:26 the faithful you **s** yourself faithful,
Ezr 2:59 they could not **s** that their families
Ps 17: 7 **S** me the wonders of your great
18:26 to the pure you **s** yourself pure,
25: 4 **S** me your ways, LORD, teach me
39: 4 "**S** me, LORD, my life's end
85: 7 **S** us your unfailing love, LORD,
102:13 Zion, for it is time to **s** favor to her;
143: 8 **S** me the way I should go, for to you
Ecc 10: 3 and **s** everyone how stupid they are.
SS 2:14 the mountainside, **s** me your face,
Isa 30:18 he will rise up to **s** you compassion.
Jer 32:18 You **s** love to thousands but bring
La 3:32 he will **s** compassion, so great is his
Hos 1: 6 I will no longer **s** love to the house
2:23 I will **s** my love to the one I called
Joel 2:30 I will **s** wonders in the heavens
Mic 7:20 and **s** love to Abraham, as you
Zec 7: 9 **s** mercy and compassion to one
Mt 22:19 **S** me the coin used for paying
Mk 12:40 and for a **s** make lengthy prayers.
Jn 2:18 "What sign can you **s** us to prove
14: 8 **s** us the Father and that will be
Ac 2:19 I will **s** wonders in the heaven
10:34 it is that God does not **s** favoritism
Ro 2:11 For God does not **s** favoritism.
1Co 12:31 yet I will **s** you the most excellent
2Co 11:30 of the things that **s** my weakness.
Gal 2: 6 God does not **s** favoritism
Eph 2: 7 ages he might **s** the incomparable
Tit 2: 7 In your teaching **s** integrity,
Jas 2:18 **S** me your faith without deeds,
1Pe 2:17 **S** proper respect to everyone,
Jude 1:23 to others **s** mercy, mixed with fear—
Rev 1: 1 **s** his servants what must soon take
4: 1 I will **s** you what must take place
17: 1 I will **s** you the punishment
21: 9 "Come, I will **s** you the bride,

## SHOWED [SHOW]
Ge 39:21 he **s** him kindness and granted him
Dt 34: 1 There the LORD **s** him the whole
1Ki 3: 3 Solomon **s** his love for the LORD
Mt 4: 8 **s** him all the kingdoms of the world
Lk 24:40 this, he **s** them his hands and feet.
Jn 20:20 this, he **s** them his hands and side.
1Jn 4: 9 This is how God **s** his love among
Rev 21:10 and **s** me the Holy City, Jerusalem,
22: 1 the angel **s** me the river of the water

## SHOWERS
Dt  32: 2  like dew, like **s** on new grass,
Ps  68: 9  You gave abundant **s**, O God;
Jer  3: 3  Therefore the **s** have been withheld,
Eze 34:26  there will be **s** of blessing.
Hos 10:12  and **s** his righteousness on you.

## SHOWING [SHOW]
Ex  20: 6  **s** love to a thousand generations
Dt  5:10  **s** love to a thousand generations
Jn  15: 8  **s** yourselves to be my disciples.

## SHOWN [SHOW]
Ex  25:40  the pattern **s** you on the mountain.
Dt  4:35  You were **s** these things so that you
1Ki  3: 6  "You have **s** great kindness to your
Ps  78:11  done, the wonders he had **s** them.
Mic  6: 8  He has **s** all you people what is good.
Mt  5: 7  merciful, for they will be **s** mercy.
Jn  10:32  "I have **s** you many good works
1Co  3:13  their work will be **s** for what it is,

## SHOWS [SHOW]
Dt  10:17  who **s** no partiality and accepts no
Ps 123: 2  our God, till he **s** us his mercy.
Pr  3:34  but **s** favor to the humble and
          oppressed.
    10:17  Whoever heeds discipline **s** the way
    15: 5  heeds correction **s** prudence.
1Pe  5: 5  opposes the proud but **s** favor

## SHREWD [SHREWDLY]
2Sa 22:27  to the devious you show yourself **s**.
Mt  10:16  Therefore be as **s** as snakes and as

## SHREWDLY* [SHREWD]
Ex  1:10  we must deal **s** with them or they
Lk  16: 8  manager because he had acted **s**.

## SHRINE [SHRINES]
Ge  38:21  "Where is the **s** prostitute who was
Dt  23:17  woman is to become a **s** prostitute.
1Ki 14:24  There were even male **s** prostitutes
Hos  4:14  and sacrifice with **s** prostitutes—

## SHRINES [SHRINE]
1Ki 12:31  Jeroboam built **s** on high places
Eze 16:25  street corner you built your lofty **s**

## SHRINK* [SHRINKS]
Heb 10:39  we are not of those who **s** back
Rev 12:11  not love their lives so much as to **s**

## SHRINKS* [SHRINK]
Heb 10:38  no pleasure in the one who **s** back."

## SHRIVEL [SHRIVELED]
Isa  64: 6  we all **s** up like a leaf, and like

## SHRIVELED [SHRIVEL]
1Ki 13: 4  stretched out toward the man **s** up,
Mk  3: 1  and a man with a **s** hand was there.

## SHUDDER
Eze 32:10  and their kings will **s** with horror
Jas  2:19  the demons believe that—and **s**.

## SHUHITE
Job  2:11  Bildad the **S** and Zophar

## SHULAMMITE
SS  6:13  Come back, come back, O **S**;

## SHUN* [SHUNNED, SHUNS]
Job 28:28  and to **s** evil is understanding."
Pr  3: 7  fear the LORD and **s** evil.
    14:16  wise fear the LORD and **s** evil,

## SHUNAMMITE
1Ki  1: 3  a **S**, and brought her to the king.
2Ki  4:12  to his servant Gehazi, "Call the **S**."

## SHUNNED* [SHUN]
Job  1: 1  he feared God and **s** evil.
Pr  14:20  The poor are **s** even by their
    19: 7  The poor are **s** by all their

## SHUNS* [SHUN]
Job  1: 8  a man who fears God and **s** evil."
    2: 3  a man who fears God and **s** evil.
Isa  59:15  and whoever **s** evil becomes a prey,

## SHUT [SHUTS]
Ge  7:16  Then the LORD **s** him in.
    19: 6  them and **s** the door behind him
Dt  11:17  he will **s** the heavens so that it will
2Ch 22:22  "When the heavens are **s**
Isa  22:22  what he opens no one can **s**,
    52:15  kings will **s** their mouths because
    60:11  they will never be **s**, day or night,
Da  6:22  and he **s** the mouths of the lions.
Mt  23:13  You **s** the door of the kingdom
Heb 11:33  who **s** the mouths of lions,
Rev  3: 7  What he opens no one can **s**,
    11: 6  They have power to **s** up the sky so
    21:25  On no day will its gates ever be **s**,

## SHUTS [SHUT]
Isa  22:22  and what he **s** no one can open.
Rev  3: 7  and what he **s** no one can open.

## SIBBOLETH* [SHIBBOLETH]
Jdg 12: 6  If he said, "**S**," because he could

## SICK [SICKBED, SICKNESS]
Pr  13:12  Hope deferred makes the heart **s**,
Eze 34: 4  healed the **s** or bound up the injured.
Mt  8:16  with a word and healed all the **s**.
    9:12  who need a doctor, but the **s**.
    10: 8  Heal the **s**, raise the dead,
    25:36  I was **s** and you looked after me,
Jn  11: 1  Now a man named Lazarus was **s**.
Ac  19:12  touched him were taken to the **s**,
1Co 11:30  many among you are weak and **s**,
2Ti  4:20  and I left Trophimus **s** in Miletus.
Jas  5:14  Is anyone among you **s**?

## SICKBED* [BED, SICK]
Ps  41: 3  LORD sustains them on their s

## SICKLE
Joel  3:13  Swing the s, for the harvest is ripe.
Rev 14:14  his head and a sharp s in his hand.

## SICKNESS [SICK]
Ex  23:25  I will take away s from among you,
Mt   4:23  disease and s among the people.
Jn  11: 4  said, "This s will not end in death.

## SIDE [SIDES]
1Ch 22: 9  rest from all his enemies on every s.
2Ch 15:15  LORD gave them rest on every s.
    20:30  God had given him rest on every s.
Ps  91: 7  A thousand may fall at your s,
    124: 1  the LORD had not been on our s—
Pr   3:26  for the LORD will be at your s
     8:30  Then I was constantly at his s.
Jer 20:10  whispering, "Terror on every s!
Eze  1:10  on the right s each had the face
     4: 4  number of days you lie on your s.
Joel  3:12  to judge all the nations on every s.
Zec  3: 1  standing at his right s to accuse him.
Jn  18:37  Everyone on the s of truth listens
    19:18  one on each s and Jesus
    19:34  the soldiers pierced Jesus' s
    20:20  he showed them his hands and s.
2Ti  4:17  the Lord stood at my s and gave me
Heb 10:33  at other times you stood s by s
Rev 22: 2  On each s of the river stood the tree

## SIDES [SIDE]
Ex  12: 7  and put it on the s and tops
    29:16  splash it against the s of the altar.
Nu  33:55  in your eyes and thorns in your s.
Job 11: 6  wisdom, for true wisdom has two s.
Eze  2:10  On both s of it were written words
Da   7: 5  It was raised up on one of its s,
Rev  5: 1  a scroll with writing on both s

## SIDON
Jdg  1:31  drive out those living in Akko or S
1Ki 17: 9  once to Zarephath in the region of S
Eze 28:21  of man, set your face against S;
Mt  11:21  had been performed in Tyre and S,
Mk   7:31  vicinity of Tyre and went through S,
Lk   4:26  in Zarephath in the region of S.

## SIEGE [BESIEGED]
Dt  28:52  They will lay s to all the cities
2Ki  6:25  the s lasted so long that a donkey's
    18: 9  against Samaria and laid s to it.
    24:10  on Jerusalem and laid s to it,
Ps  31:21  when I was in a city under s.

## SIEVE*
Isa 30:28  the nations in the s of destruction;
Am   9: 9  the nations as grain is shaken in a s,

## SIFT*
Jdg  7: 4  and I will s them for you there.
Lk  22:31  Satan has asked to s all of you as

## SIGH* [SIGHED, SIGHING]
Mk   7:34  and with a deep s said to him,

## SIGHED* [SIGH]
Mk   8:12  He s deeply and said, "Why does

## SIGHING [SIGH]
Isa 35:10  and sorrow and s will flee away.

## SIGHT [SEE]
Ge   6:11  the earth was corrupt in God's s
Ex   3: 3  will go over and see this strange s—
     4:11  Who gives them s or makes them
Nu  20:12  me as holy in the s of the Israelites,
Ps  19:14  of my heart be pleasing in your s,
    51: 4  and done what is evil in your s;
    72:14  for precious is their blood in his s.
    90: 4  years in your s are like a day
   116:15  in the s of the LORD is the death
Pr   3: 4  a good name in the s of God
Jer 18:10  if it does evil in my s and does not
Mt  11: 5  The blind receive s, the lame walk,
Ac   1: 9  and a cloud hid him from their s.
1Co  3:19  this world is foolishness in God's s.
2Co  5: 7  We live by faith, not by s.
Eph  1: 4  to be holy and blameless in his s.
1Pe  3: 4  which is of great worth in God's s.

## SIGN [SIGNS]
Ge   9:12  "This is the s of the covenant I am
    17:11  and it will be the s of the covenant
Ex   3:12  this will be the s to you that it is I
     4: 8  or pay attention to the first s,
    12:13  The blood will be a s for you
    13:16  And it will be like a s on your hand
Nu  16:38  Let them be a s to the Israelites."
    17:10  to be kept as a s to the rebellious.
Dt  13: 1  and announces to you a s or wonder,
Jdg  6:17  eyes, give me a s that it is really you
1Ki 13: 3  same day the man of God gave a s:
Isa  7:14  the Lord himself will give you a s:
    55:13  for an everlasting s, that will endure
Eze 20:12  my Sabbaths to be a s between us,
    24:24  Ezekiel will be a s to you;
Mt  12:38  we want to see a s from you."
    12:39  adulterous generation asks for a s!
    16: 1  him to show them a s from heaven.
    24: 3  what will be the s of your coming
    24:30  that time the s of the Son of Man
Mk   8:12  no s will be given to it."
Lk   2:12  This will be a s to you:
    11:29  will be given it except the s
    23: 8  he hoped to see him perform a s
Jn   2:18  "What s can you show us to prove
     6:14  the people saw the s Jesus performed,
    10:41  "Though John never performed a s,
Ac   4:16  they have performed a notable s,
Ro   4:11  he received circumcision as a s,
1Co 14:22  are a s, not for believers
Rev 12: 1  and wondrous s appeared in heaven:
    12: 3  Then another s appeared in heaven:
    15: 1  another great and marvelous s:

## SIGNAL
Mk 14:44  Now the betrayer had arranged a s

## SIGNET

Ge 41:42 Pharaoh took his **s** ring from his
Est 3:10 So the king took his **s** ring from his
8: 2 The king took off his **s** ring,
Jer 22:24 were a **s** ring on my right hand,
Da 6:17 king sealed it with his own **s** ring
Hag 2:23 'and I will make you like my **s** ring,

## SIGNS [SIGN]

Ge 1:14 let them serve as **s** to mark seasons
Ex 4: 9 if they do not believe these two **s**
7: 3 though I multiply my **s** and wonders
Nu 14:11 in spite of all the **s** I have performed
Dt 4:34 by testings, by **s** and wonders,
34:11 who did all those **s** and wonders
Ps 74: 9 We are given no **s** from God;
78:43 the day he displayed his **s** in Egypt,
105:27 They performed his **s** among them,
Isa 8:18 We are **s** and symbols in Israel
44:25 who foils the **s** of false prophets
Da 6:27 he performs **s** and wonders
Mt 16: 3 but you cannot interpret the **s**
24:24 and perform great **s** and wonders
Mk 13:22 perform **s** and wonders to deceive,
Jn 2:11 **s** through which he revealed his glory;
2:23 people saw the **s** he was performing
3: 2 could perform the **s** you are doing
4:48 "Unless you people see **s** and wonders,"
7:31 he perform more **s** than this man?"
9:16 can a sinner perform such **s**?"
12:37 Jesus had performed so many **s**
20:30 Jesus performed many other **s**
Ac 2:19 above and **s** on the earth below,
2:43 with awe at the many wonders and **s**
5:12 The apostles performed many **s**
14: 3 enabling them to perform **s** and wonders
Ro 15:19 by the power of **s** and wonders,
1Co 1:22 Jews demand **s** and Greeks look
2Co 12:12 including **s**, wonders and miracles.
2Th 2: 9 sorts of displays of power through **s**
Heb 2: 4 God also testified to it by **s**,
Rev 13:13 And it performed great **s**,
16:14 are demonic spirits that perform **s**,
19:20 these **s** he had deluded those who

## SIGNS AND WONDERS Ex 7:3; Dt 4:34;

6:22; 7:19; 26:8; 34:11; Ne 9:10; Ps 135:9; Jer
32:20, 21; Da 4:2; 6:27; Mt 24:24; Mk 13:22; Jn
4:48; Ac 4:30; 5:12; 14:3; 15:12; Ro 15:19; 2Th
2:9

## SIHON

Nu 21:21 to say to **S** king of the Amorites:
Dt 31: 4 will do to them what he did to **S**
Ps 136:19 **S** king of the Amorites

## SILAS*

Prophet (Ac 15:22–32); co-worker with Paul on
second missionary journey (Ac 16–18; 2Co 1:19).
Co-writer with Paul (1Th 1:1; 2Th 1:1); Peter (1Pe
5:12).

## SILENCE [SILENCED, SILENT]

Ps 8: 2 to **s** the foe and the avenger.
1Pe 2:15 good you should **s** the ignorant talk
Rev 8: 1 there was **s** in heaven for about half

## SILENCED [SILENCE]

Ps 63:11 while the mouths of liars will be **s**.
Pr 10:31 but a perverse tongue will be **s**.
Mt 22:34 that Jesus had **s** the Sadducees,
Ro 3:19 so that every mouth may be **s**
Tit 1:11 They must be **s**, because they are

## SILENT [SILENCE]

Est 4:14 For if you remain **s** at this time,
Ps 30:12 may sing your praises and not be **s**.
32: 3 When I kept **s**, my bones wasted
39: 2 So I remained utterly **s**, not even
50: 3 Our God comes and will not be **s**;
83: 1 God, do not remain **s**;
Pr 17:28 are thought wise if they keep **s**,
Ecc 3: 7 a time to be **s** and a time to speak,
Isa 53: 7 as a sheep before its shearers is **s**,
62: 1 For Zion's sake I will not keep **s**,
Jer 4:19 pounds within me, I cannot keep **s**.
Hab 2:20 let all the earth be **s** before him.
Zep 1: 7 Be **s** before the Sovereign LORD,
Mk 14:61 But Jesus remained **s** and gave no
Ac 8:32 and as a lamb before its shearer is **s**,
1Co 14:34 Women should remain **s**

## SILOAM

Jn 9: 7 of **S**" (this word means "Sent").

## SILVER

Ge 37:28 him for twenty shekels of **s**
Ex 11: 2 ask their neighbors for articles of **s**
20:23 not make for yourselves gods of **s**
25: 3 gold, **s** and bronze;
Dt 17:17 not accumulate large amounts of **s**
Jos 7:21 two hundred shekels of **s**
2Ch 1:15 The king made **s** and gold as
Ps 12: 6 like **s** purified in a crucible,
66:10 God, tested us; you refined us like **s**.
115: 4 But their idols are **s** and gold,
Pr 2: 4 if you look for it as for **s** and search
3:14 for she is more profitable than **s**
8:10 Choose my instruction instead of **s**,
22: 1 to be esteemed is better than **s**
25: 4 Remove the dross from the **s**,
25:11 of **s** is a ruling rightly given.
Isa 48:10 I have refined you, though not as **s**;
Eze 22:18 They are but the dross of **s**.
Da 2:32 its chest and arms of **s**, its belly
5: 4 they praised the gods of gold and **s**,
Hag 2: 8 'The **s** is mine and the gold is
Zec 11:12 So they paid me thirty pieces of **s**.
13: 9 I will refine them like **s** and test
Mal 3: 3 will sit as a refiner and purifier of **s**;
Mt 26:15 out for him thirty pieces of **s**.
Ac 3: 6 Peter said, "**S** or gold I do not have,
1Co 3:12 on this foundation using gold, **s**,
2Ti 2:20 are articles not only of gold and **s**,
1Pe 1:18 not with perishable things such as **s**

## SILVERSMITH

Ac 19:24 A **s** named Demetrius, who made

## SIMEON

Son of Jacob by Leah (Ge 29:33; 35:23; 1Ch 2:1).
With Levi killed Shechem for rape of Dinah (Ge

34:25–29). Held hostage by Joseph in Egypt (Ge 42:24—43:23). Tribe of blessed (Ge 49:5–7), numbered (Nu 1:23; 26:14), allotted land (Jos 19:1–9; Eze 48:24), 12,000 from (Rev 7:7).

## SIMON [PETER]
1. See PETER.
2. Apostle, called the Zealot (Mt 10:4; Mk 3:18; Lk 6:15; Ac 1:13).
3. Samaritan sorcerer (Ac 8:9–24).

## SIMPLE
| | | |
|---|---|---|
| Ex | 18:22 | the s cases they can decide |
| Ps | 19: 7 | are trustworthy, making wise the s. |
| | 119:130 | it gives understanding to the s. |
| Pr | 1:22 | long will you who are s love your s |
| | 8: 5 | You who are s, gain prudence; |
| | 14:15 | The s believe anything, |

## SIN [SIN'S, SINFUL, SINNED, SINNER, SINNER'S, SINNERS, SINNING, SINS]
| | | |
|---|---|---|
| Ge | 4: 7 | is right, s is crouching at your door; |
| Ex | 20: 5 | the children for the s of the parents |
| | 32:32 | But now, please forgive their s— |
| | 34: 7 | wickedness, rebellion and s. |
| Lev | 4: 3 | bull without defect as a s offering |
| | 5: 6 | goat from the flock as a s offering; |
| Nu | 5: 7 | and must confess the s they have |
| | 14:18 | love and forgiving s and rebellion. |
| | 32:23 | be sure that your s will find you out. |
| Dt | 24:16 | each of you will die for your own s. |
| 1Sa | 12:23 | that I should s against the LORD |
| | 15:23 | rebellion is like the s of divination, |
| 1Ki | 8:46 | for there is no one who does not s— |
| | 13:34 | This was the s of the house |
| 2Ki | 14: 6 | each of you will die for your own s." |
| 2Ch | 7:14 | I will forgive their s and will heal |
| Ne | 13:26 | even he was led into s by foreign |
| Job | 1:22 | Job did not s by charging God |
| | 2:10 | this, Job did not s in what he said. |
| Ps | 4: 4 | Tremble and do not s; when you are |
| | 32: 2 | are those whose s the LORD does |
| | 32: 5 | Then I acknowledged my s to you |
| | 32: 5 | And you forgave the guilt of my s. |
| | 36: 2 | too much to detect or hate their s. |
| | 38:18 | I am troubled by my s. |
| | 39: 1 | ways and keep my tongue from s; |
| | 51: 2 | iniquity and cleanse me from my s. |
| | 66:18 | If I had cherished s in my heart, |
| | 119:11 | heart that I might not s against you. |
| | 119:133 | to your word; let no s rule over me. |
| Pr | 10:19 | S is not ended by multiplying |
| | 14: 9 | Fools mock at making amends for s, |
| | 14:21 | It is a s to despise one's neighbor, |
| | 16: 6 | love and faithfulness s is atoned for; |
| | 17:19 | Whoever loves a quarrel loves s; |
| | 20: 9 | I am clean and without s"? |
| | 29: 6 | Evildoers are snared by their own s, |
| Ecc | 5: 6 | not let your mouth lead you into s. |
| Isa | 3: 9 | they parade their s like Sodom; |
| | 6: 7 | taken away and your s atoned for." |
| | 53:10 | his life an offering for s, |
| | 53:12 | For he bore the s of many, |
| | 64: 5 | we continued to s against them, |
| Jer | 16:18 | for their wickedness and their s, |

| | | |
|---|---|---|
| Jer | 31:30 | everyone will die for their own s; |
| Eze | 18:26 | their righteousness and commit s, |
| | 18:26 | the s they have committed they will |
| Da | 9:20 | confessing my s and the s of my |
| Hos | 13: 2 | Now they s more and more; |
| Mic | 6: 7 | of my body for the s of my soul? |
| | 7:18 | you, who pardons s and forgives |
| Zec | 3: 4 | I have taken away your s, and I will |
| Mt | 6:14 | others when they s against you, |
| Mk | 3:29 | but is guilty of an eternal s." |
| Jn | 1:29 | who takes away the s of the world! |
| | 8: 7 | who is without s be the first to throw |
| | 8:34 | everyone who sins is a slave to s. |
| | 8:46 | any of you prove me guilty of s? |
| | 16: 9 | about s, because people do not |
| Ac | 7:60 | do not hold this s against them." |
| Ro | 2:12 | All who s apart from the law will |
| | 4: 8 | are those whose s the Lord will |
| | 5:12 | just as s entered the world |
| | 5:20 | But where s increased, |
| | 6: 2 | We are those who have died to s; |
| | 6:11 | count yourselves dead to s but alive |
| | 6:14 | s shall no longer be your master, |
| | 6:23 | For the wages of s is death, |
| | 7: 7 | not have known what s was had it |
| | 7:25 | sinful nature a slave to the law of s. |
| | 8: 2 | has set you free from the law of s |
| | 14:23 | that does not come from faith is s. |
| 1Co | 8:12 | When you s against them |
| | 15:56 | The sting of death is s, |
| 2Co | 5:21 | God made him who had no s to be s |
| Gal | 2:17 | that mean that Christ promotes s? |
| | 6: 1 | if someone is caught in a s, you who |
| Eph | 4:26 | "In your anger do not s": |
| Heb | 4:15 | just as we are—yet he did not s. |
| | 9:26 | to do away with s by the sacrifice |
| | 10:18 | for s is no longer necessary. |
| | 11:25 | to enjoy the fleeting pleasures of s. |
| | 12: 1 | and the s that so easily entangles. |
| Jas | 1:15 | it gives birth to s; and s, |
| | 4:17 | do and don't do it, you s. |
| 1Pe | 2:22 | "He committed no s, and no deceit |
| 1Jn | 1: 7 | Jesus, his Son, purifies us from all s. |
| | 1: 8 | If we claim to be without s, |
| | 2: 1 | this to you so that you will not s. |
| | 2: 1 | But if anybody does s, we have |
| | 3: 4 | in fact, s is lawlessness. |
| | 3: 5 | away our sins. And in him is no s. |
| | 3: 6 | continues to s has either seen him |
| | 3: 9 | born of God will not continue to s, |
| | 5:16 | sister commit a s that does not lead |
| | 5:16 | There is a s that leads to death. |
| | 5:17 | All wrongdoing is s, and there is s |

## SIN OFFERING Ex 29:14, 36; 30:10; Lev 4:3, 8, 14, 20, 21, 24, 25, 29, 32, 33, 34; 5:6, 7, 8, 9, 9, 11, 11, 12; 6:17, 25, 25, 30; 7:7, 37; 8:2, 14; 9:2, 3, 7, 8, 10, 15, 15, 22; 10:16, 17, 19, 19; 12:6, 8; 14:13, 19, 22, 31; 15:15, 30; 16:3, 5, 6, 9, 11, 11, 15, 25; 23:19; Nu 6:11, 14, 16; 7:16, 22, 28, 34, 40, 46, 52, 58, 64, 70, 76, 82, 87; 8:8, 12; 15:24, 25, 27; 28:15, 22; 29:5, 11, 11, 16, 19, 22, 25, 28, 31, 34, 38; 2Ch 29:21, 23, 24, 24; Ezr 6:17; 8:35; Eze 43:19, 21, 22, 25; 44:27; 45:19, 22, 23; 46:20; Ro 8:3; Heb 13:11

## SIN OFFERINGS Lev 16:27; 2Ki 12:16; Ne
10:33; Ps 40:6; Eze 40:39; 42:13; 44:29; 45:17, 25; Hos 8:11; Heb 10:6, 8

## SIN'S* [SIN]
Heb   3:13   may be hardened by s deceitfulness.

## SINAI
Ex    19: 1   they came to the Desert of S.
      19:20   descended to the top of Mount S
      31:18   speaking to Moses on Mount S,
Lev  27:34   Moses on Mount S for the Israelites.
Nu    1:19   he counted them in the Desert of S:
Ps   68:17   the Lord has come from S into his
Gal   4:24   One covenant is from Mount S

## MOUNT SINAI See MOUNT

## SINCERE* [SINCERELY, SINCERITY]
Da   11:34   many who are not s will join them.
Lk   20:20   sent spies, who pretended to be s.
Ac    2:46   ate together with glad and s hearts,
Ro   12: 9   Love must be s. Hate what is evil;
2Co   6: 6   in the Holy Spirit and in s love;
     11: 3   somehow be led astray from your s
1Ti   1: 5   and a good conscience and a s faith.
      3: 8   are to be worthy of respect, s,
2Ti   1: 5   I am reminded of your s faith,
Heb  10:22   God with a s heart in full assurance
Jas   3:17   and good fruit, impartial and s.
1Pe   1:22   that you have s love for each other,

## SINCERELY [SINCERE]
Job  33: 3   my lips s speak what I know.

## SINCERITY* [SINCERE]
1Co   5: 8   with the unleavened bread of s
2Co   1:12   with you, with integrity and godly s.
      2:17   Christ we speak before God with s,
      8: 8   I want to test the s of your love
Eph   6: 5   fear, and with s of heart, just as you
Col   3:22   but with s of heart and reverence

## SINEWS
Col   2:19   held together by its ligaments and s,

## SINFUL [SIN]
Ps   51: 5   Surely I was s at birth,
Pr    1:10   My son, if s men entice you,
Isa   1: 4   Ah, s nation, a people whose guilt is
Eze  37:23   them from all their s backsliding,
Lk    5: 8   from me, Lord; I am a s man!"
      7:37   town who lived a s life learned
Ro    7: 5   we were controlled by our s nature,
      7:18   dwell in me, that is, in my s nature.
      7:25   in my s nature a slave to the law
      8: 3   in the likeness of s humanity to be
      8: 4   do not live according to the s nature
      8: 8   by the s nature cannot please God.
      8: 9   are not controlled by the s nature
      8:13   if you live according to the s nature,
     13:14   to gratify the desires of the s nature.
1Co   5: 5   for the destruction of the s nature so
Gal   5:13   freedom to indulge the s nature;
      5:16   gratify the desires of the s nature.

Gal   5:19   The acts of the s nature are obvious:
      5:24   Jesus have crucified the s nature
Eph   2: 3   the cravings of our s nature
Col   2:11   Your s nature was put off when you
      2:13   the uncircumcision of your s nature,
Heb   3:12   and sisters, that none of you has a s,
1Pe   2:11   to abstain from s desires, which war
1Jn   3: 8   The one who does what is s is

## SINFUL NATURE Ro 7:5, 18, 25; 8:3, 4, 5, 6,
8, 9, 12, 13; 13:14; 1Co 5:5; Gal 5:13, 16, 17, 17, 19, 24; 6:8; Eph 2:3; Col 2:11, 13; 2Pe 2:10

## SING [SANG, SINGERS, SINGING,
SINGS, SONG, SONGS, SUNG]
Ex    15: 1   "I will s to the LORD, for he is
Dt    31:19   to the Israelites and have them s it,
Jdg    5: 3   will s to the LORD;
1Sa   21:11   Isn't he the one they s about in their
Ps     5:11   you be glad; let them ever s for joy.
      13: 6   I will s the LORD's praise, for he
      30: 4   S the praises of the LORD, you his
      30:12   that my heart may s your praises
      33: 1   S joyfully to the LORD,
      33: 3   S to him a new song;
      47: 6   S praises to God, s praises; s praises to
             our King, s praises.
      57: 7   I will s and make music.
      59:16   in the morning I will s of your love;
      63: 7   I s in the shadow of your wings.
      66: 2   S the glory of his name;
      68: 4   S to God, s in praise of his name,
      89: 1   I will s of the LORD's great love
      95: 1   let us s for joy to the LORD;
      96: 1   S to the LORD a new song;
      98: 1   S to the LORD a new song, for he
     101: 1   I will s of your love and justice;
     108: 1   I will s and make music with all my
     119:172   May my tongue s of your word,
     137: 3   "S us one of the songs of Zion!"
     147: 1   How good it is to s praises to our
     149: 1   S to the LORD a new song,
Isa    5: 1   I will s for the one I love a song
      27: 2   "S about a fruitful vineyard:
      54: 1   "S, barren woman, you who never
Jer   31: 7   "S with joy for Jacob;
1Co   14:15   I will s with my spirit, but I will also
             s with my understanding.
Eph    5:19   S and make music from your heart
Jas    5:13   Let them s songs of praise.

## SING ... PRAISE See PRAISE

## SING ... PRAISES See PRAISES

## SINGED*
Da    3:27   nor was a hair of their heads s;

## SINGERS [SING]
Ps   68:25   In front are the s, after them

## SINGING [SING]
Ex   32:18   it is the sound of s that I hear."
Ps   63: 5   s lips my mouth will praise you.
      68: 6   he leads out the prisoners with s;
      98: 5   with the harp and the sound of s,
SS    2:12   the season of s has come, the cooing

Isa  35:10  They will enter Zion with s;
     51:11  They will enter Zion with s;
Zep   3:17  but will rejoice over you with s."
Ac   16:25  were praying and s hymns to God,
Col   3:16  s to God with gratitude in your

## SINGLE [SINGLED]
Ex   23:29  I will not drive them out in a s year,
Nu   13:23  cut off a branch bearing a s cluster
Zec   3: 9  the sin of this land in a s day.
Mt    6:27  worrying add a s hour to your life?
Jn   12:24  and dies, it remains only a s seed.
Heb  12:16  a s meal sold his inheritance rights
Rev  21:21  pearls, each gate made of a s pearl.

## SINGLED* [SINGLE]
1Ki   8:53  For you s them out from all

## SINGS [SING]
Eze  33:32  more than one who s love songs

## SINK [SANK]
Dt   28:43  but you will s lower and lower.
Ps   69: 2  I s in the miry depths, where there is
Jer  51:64  'So will Babylon s to rise no more

## SINNED [SIN]
Lev   5: 5  confess in what way they have s
Nu   14:40  Surely we have s!"
1Sa  15:24  Saul said to Samuel, "I have s.
2Sa  12:13  "I have s against the LORD."
     24:10  "I have s greatly in what I have
2Ch   6:37  'We have s, we have done wrong.
Job   1: 5  "Perhaps my children have s
     33:27  'We have s, we have perverted what
Ps   51: 4  have I s and done what is evil
Jer   2:35  you because you say, 'I have not s.'
     14:20  we have indeed s against you.
La    5: 7  Our parents s and are no more,
Da    9: 5  we have s and done wrong.
Mic   7: 9  Because I have s against him, I will
Mt   27: 4  "I have s," he said, "for I have
Lk   15:18  I have s against heaven and against
Jn    9: 2  who s, this man or his parents,
Ro    3:23  for all have s and fall short
      5:12  came to all people, because all s—
Jas   5:15  If they have s, they will be forgiven.
2Pe   2: 4  did not spare angels when they s,
1Jn   1:10  If we claim we have not s, we make

## SINNER [SIN]
Pr   13: 6  but wickedness overthrows the s.
Ecc   9:18  war, but one s destroys much good.
Lk   15: 7  heaven over one s who repents than
     18:13  said, 'God, have mercy on me, a s.'
Jn    9:16  "How can a s perform such signs?"
Jas   5:20  Whoever turns a s from the way
1Pe   4:18  become of the ungodly and the s?"

## SINNER'S* [SIN]
Pr   13:22  but a s wealth is stored

## SINNERS [SIN]
Ps    1: 1  stand in the way that s take or sit
     25: 8  therefore he instructs s in his ways.

Ps   37:38  But all s will be destroyed;
     51:13  ways, and s will turn back to you.
Pr   23:17  Do not let your heart envy s,
Isa   1:28  rebels and s will both be broken,
Mt    9:13  come to call the righteous, but s."
Mk   14:41  Man is delivered into the hands of s.
Lk   15: 2  "This man welcomes s and eats
     24: 7  must be delivered over to the hands of
             s,
Ro    5: 8  While we were still s, Christ died
Gal   2:17  find ourselves also among the s,
1Ti   1:15  came into the world to save s—
Heb   7:26  set apart from s,
     12: 3  endured such opposition from s,

## SINNING [SIN]
Ge   13:13  were s greatly against the LORD.
Ex   20:20  be with you to keep you from s."
Ps   78:32  In spite of all this, they kept on s;
Ro    6: 1  Shall we go on s so that grace may
1Co  15:34  senses as you ought, and stop s;
1Ti   5:20  elders who are s you are to reprove
Heb  10:26  If we deliberately keep on s after we
1Jn   3: 6  No one who lives in him keeps on s.
      3: 8  because the devil has been s

## SINS [SIN]
Lev   4: 2  'When anyone s unintentionally
      4: 3  " 'If the anointed priest s,
      5: 1  anyone s because they do not speak
     16:30  you will be clean from all your s.
     26:40  if they will confess their s and the s
Nu   15:30  " 'But anyone who s defiantly,
1Sa   2:25  but if anyone s against the LORD,
2Ki  17:22  persisted in all the s of Jeroboam
Ezr   9: 6  because our s are higher than our
      9:13  punished us less than our s deserved
Ne    9: 2  confessed their sins and the s
Ps   19:13  your servant also from willful s;
     32: 1  are forgiven, whose s are covered.
     51: 9  Hide your face from my s and blot
     79: 9  forgive our s for your name's sake.
     85: 2  your people and covered all their s.
    103: 3  who forgives all your s and heals all
    103:10  he does not treat us as our s deserve
    130: 3  LORD, kept a record of s, Lord,
Pr    5:22  the cords of their s hold them fast.
     28:13  who conceal their s do not prosper,
     29:22  person commits many s.
Ecc   7:20  who does what is right and never s.
Isa   1:18  "Though your s are like scarlet,
     38:17  have put all my s behind your back.
     40: 2  LORD's hand double for all her s.
     43:25  and remembers your s no more.
     59: 2  your s have hidden his face
     64: 6  like the wind our s sweep us away.
Jer  31:34  will remember their s no more."
La    3:39  complain when punished for their s?
Eze   3:18  wicked people will die for their s,
     18: 4  The one who s is the one who will
     33: 8  wicked people will die for their s,
     33:10  offenses and s weigh us down,
     36:33  day I cleanse you from all your s,
Hos  14: 1  Your s have been your downfall!
     14: 2  "Forgive all our s and receive us
Mic   7:19  you will tread our s underfoot

| | | |
|---|---|---|
| Mt | 1:21 | will save his people from their **s**." |
| | 6:15 | if you do not forgive others their **s**, your |
| | | Father will not forgive your **s**. |
| | 9: 6 | has authority on earth to forgive **s**." |
| | 18:15 | "If a brother or sister **s**, |
| | 26:28 | for many for the forgiveness of **s**. |
| Mk | 1: 5 | Confessing their **s**, they were |
| Lk | 5:24 | has authority on earth to forgive **s**." |
| | 11: 4 | Forgive us our **s**, for we also forgive |
| | | everyone who **s** against us. |
| | 17: 3 | "If a brother or sister **s** against you, |
| Jn | 8:24 | you will indeed die in your **s**." |
| | 20:23 | If you forgive the **s** of anyone, |
| Ac | 2:38 | Christ for the forgiveness of your **s**. |
| | 3:19 | so that your **s** may be wiped out, |
| | 10:43 | forgiveness of **s** through his name." |
| | 22:16 | be baptized and wash your **s** away, |
| | 26:18 | they may receive forgiveness of **s** |
| Ro | 4: 7 | are forgiven, whose **s** are covered. |
| | 4:25 | delivered over to death for our **s** |
| 1Co | 6:18 | All other **s** people commit are |
| | 15: 3 | Christ died for our **s** according |
| 2Co | 5:19 | counting people's **s** against them. |
| Gal | 1: 4 | gave himself for our **s** to rescue us |
| Eph | 1: 7 | the forgiveness of **s**, in accordance |
| | 2: 1 | dead in your transgressions and **s**, |
| Col | 2:13 | When you were dead in your **s** |
| | 2:13 | He forgave us all our **s**, |
| 1Ti | 5:22 | and do not share in the **s** of others. |
| Heb | 1: 3 | he had provided purification for **s**, |
| | 2:17 | atonement for the **s** of the people. |
| | 7:27 | He sacrificed for their **s** once for all |
| | 8:12 | will remember their **s** no more." |
| | 9:28 | once to take away the **s** of many; |
| | 10: 4 | of bulls and goats to take away **s**. |
| | 10:12 | for all time one sacrifice for **s**, |
| | 10:26 | of the truth, no sacrifice for **s** is left, |
| Jas | 5:16 | Therefore confess your **s** to each |
| | 5:20 | and cover over a multitude of **s**. |
| 1Pe | 2:24 | "He himself bore our **s**" in his |
| | 3:18 | For Christ also suffered once for **s**, |
| | 4: 8 | love covers over a multitude of **s**. |
| 1Jn | 1: 9 | will forgive us our **s** and purify us |
| | 2: 2 | He is the atoning sacrifice for our **s**, |
| | 3: 5 | so that he might take away our **s**. |
| | 4:10 | Son as an atoning sacrifice for our **s**, |
| Rev | 1: 5 | freed us from our **s** by his blood, |

## SION (KJV) See ZION

## SISERA

| | | |
|---|---|---|
| Jdg | 4: 2 | **S**, the commander of his army, |
| | 5:26 | She struck **S**, she crushed his head, |

## SISTER [SISTERS]

| | | |
|---|---|---|
| Ge | 12:13 | Say you are my **s**, so that I will be |
| | 20: 2 | of his wife Sarah, "She is my **s**." |
| | 26: 7 | "She is my **s**," because he was |
| Lev | 18: 9 | have sexual relations with your **s**, |
| Pr | 7: 4 | "You are my **s**," and to insight, |
| SS | 4: 9 | stolen my heart, my **s**, my bride; |
| Jer | 3: 7 | and her unfaithful **s** Judah saw it. |
| Eze | 16:46 | Your older **s** was Samaria, |
| Mk | 3:35 | does God's will is my brother and **s** |
| Lk | 10:40 | don't you care that my **s** has left me |
| Jn | 11: 5 | loved Martha and her **s** and Lazarus. |

| | | |
|---|---|---|
| Ro | 16: 1 | I commend to you our **s** Phoebe, |
| 1Co | 7:15 | The brother or **s** is not bound |
| 2Jn | 1:13 | The children of your **s**, who is |

## SISTERS [SISTER]

| | | |
|---|---|---|
| Mt | 19:29 | left houses or brothers or **s** or father |
| Mk | 6: 3 | Aren't his **s** here with us?" |
| 1Ti | 5: 2 | and younger women as **s**, |

## SIT [SAT, SITS, SITTING]

| | | |
|---|---|---|
| Ex | 18:14 | Why do you alone **s** as judge, |
| Dt | 6: 7 | about them when you **s** at home |
| | 11:19 | about them when you **s** at home |
| 1Ki | 8:25 | have a successor to **s** before me |
| Ps | 1: 1 | or **s** in the company of mockers, |
| | 26: 5 | and refuse to **s** with the wicked. |
| | 80: 1 | You who **s** enthroned between |
| | 110: 1 | "**S** at my right hand until I make |
| | 139: 2 | You know when I **s** and when I rise; |
| SS | 2: 3 | I delight to **s** in his shade, and his |
| Isa | 14:13 | I will **s** enthroned on the mount |
| | 16: 5 | in faithfulness a man will **s** on it— |
| | 28: 6 | justice to those who **s** in judgment, |
| Jer | 33:17 | fail to have a man to **s** on the throne |
| Eze | 28: 2 | I **s** on the throne of a god |
| Mic | 4: 4 | Everyone will **s** under their own |
| Mal | 3: 3 | He will **s** as a refiner and purifier |
| Mt | 20:23 | but to **s** at my right or left is not |
| | 22:44 | "**S** at my right hand until I put your |
| | 23: 2 | and the Pharisees **s** in Moses' seat. |
| Mk | 14:32 | his disciples, "**S** here while I pray." |
| Lk | 22:30 | in my kingdom and **s** on thrones, |
| Jn | 6:10 | said, "Have the people **s** down." |
| Ac | 2:34 | to my Lord: "**S** at my right hand |
| Heb | 1:13 | "**S** at my right hand until I make |
| Rev | 3:21 | I will give the right to **s** with me |
| | 18: 7 | she boasts, 'I **s** enthroned as queen. |

## SITS [SIT]

| | | |
|---|---|---|
| Ps | 29:10 | The Lord **s** enthroned over |
| | 99: 1 | he **s** enthroned between |
| | 113: 5 | the One who **s** enthroned on high, |
| Isa | 40:22 | He **s** enthroned above the circle |
| Mt | 19:28 | Son of Man **s** on his glorious throne, |
| Rev | 4: 9 | thanks to him who **s** on the throne |
| | 5:13 | "To him who **s** on the throne |
| | 6:16 | the face of him who **s** on the throne |
| | 17: 1 | prostitute, who **s** by many waters. |

## SITTING [SIT]

| | | |
|---|---|---|
| 2Ch | 18:18 | I saw the Lord **s** on his throne |
| Est | 2:19 | Mordecai was **s** at the king's gate. |
| Mt | 26:64 | the Son of Man **s** at the right hand |
| Lk | 8:35 | had gone out, **s** at Jesus' feet, |
| Rev | 4: 2 | in heaven with someone **s** on it. |
| | 17: 3 | There I saw a woman **s** on a scarlet |

## SITUATION [SITUATIONS]

| | | |
|---|---|---|
| 1Co | 7:24 | should remain in the **s** in which God |
| Php | 4:12 | of being content in any and every **s**, |

## SITUATIONS* [SITUATION]

| | | |
|---|---|---|
| 2Ti | 4: 5 | you, keep your head in all **s**, |

## SIX [SIXTH]

Ex  20: 9  **S** days you shall labor and do all
1Sa 17: 4  His height was **s** cubits and a span.
1Ch 20: 6  there was a huge man with **s** fingers
Pr    6:16  There are **s** things the LORD
Isa   6: 2  were seraphs, each with **s** wings:
Rev  4: 8  the four living creatures had **s** wings

## SIXTH [SIX]

Lev 25:21  you such a blessing in the **s** year
Rev  6:12  I watched as he opened the **s** seal.
      16:12  The **s** angel poured out his bowl

## SIXTY

Mt  13: 8  **s** or thirty times what was sown.

## SIZE

2Ki 10:32  began to reduce the **s** of Israel.
Ps  33:16  king is saved by the **s** of his army;

## SKIES [SKY]

Ps  19: 1  the **s** proclaim the work of his
      36: 5  heavens, your faithfulness to the **s**.
      68:33  him who rides the ancient **s** above,
      71:19  reaches to the **s**, you who have done
      89: 6  For who in the **s** above can compare
    108: 4  your faithfulness reaches to the **s**.
Jer  51: 9  for her judgment reaches to the **s**;
Mt  11:23  will you be lifted up to the **s**?

## SKILL [SKILLED, SKILLFUL, SKILLFULLY, SKILLS]

Ps 137: 5  may my right hand forget its **s**.
Ecc 10:10  is needed, but **s** will bring success.

## SKILLED [SKILL]

Ex  35:10  "All who are **s** among you are
1Ch 28:21  every willing person **s** in any craft
Pr  22:29  Do you see those who are **s** in their
Jer   4:22  They are **s** in doing evil;
Mic   7: 3  Both hands are **s** in doing evil;

## SKILLFUL [SKILL]

Ps  45: 1  my tongue is the pen of a **s** writer.
      78:72  with **s** hands he led them.

## SKILLFULLY [SKILL]

Ps  33: 3  play **s**, and shout for joy.

## SKILLS [SKILL]

Ex  31: 3  and with all kinds of **s**
      35:31  knowledge and with all kinds of **s**—

## SKIN [SKINS]

Ge    3:21  LORD God made garments of **s**
Job   2: 4  "**S** for **s**!" Satan replied.
      19:20  I am nothing but **s** and bones;
      19:26  And after my **s** has been destroyed,
Jer  13:23  Can an Ethiopian change his **s**

## SKINS [SKIN]

Ex  25: 5  ram **s** dyed red and another durable
      26:14  covering of ram **s** dyed red,

Lk    5:37  do, the new wine will burst the **s**;

## SKIRTS

Isa  47: 2  Lift up your **s**, bare your legs,
La    1: 9  Her filthiness clung to her **s**;

## SKULL

2Ki  9:35  they found nothing except her **s**,
Mt  27:33  (which means "the place of the **s**").

## SKY [SKIES]

Ge    1: 8  God called the vault "**s**."
      22:17  as numerous as the stars in the **s**
      26: 4  as numerous as the stars in the **s**
Ex  24:10  lapis lazuli, as bright blue as the **s**.
Lev 26:19  and make the **s** above you like iron
Dt    1:10  you are as many as the stars in the **s**.
Ps  89:37  moon, the faithful witness in the **s**."
Pr  30:19  the way of an eagle in the **s**, the way
Isa  34: 4  the stars in the **s** will be dissolved
Jer  33:22  me as countless as the stars in the **s**
Mt  16: 3  to interpret the appearance of the **s**,
      24:30  the Son of Man will appear in the **s**,
Mk  13:25  the stars will fall from the **s**,
Ac    1:10  up into the **s** as he was going,
Php   2:15  will shine among them like stars in the **s**
Rev   6:13  and the stars in the **s** fell to earth,
      6:14  The **s** receded like a scroll,
      12: 4  swept a third of the stars out of the **s**

## SLACK*

Pr  18: 9  One who is **s** in his work is a close

## SLAIN [SLAY]

1Sa 18: 7  "Saul has **s** his thousands,
      21:11  " 'Saul has **s** his thousands,
      29: 5  " 'Saul has **s** his thousands,
Pr    7:26  her **s** are a mighty throng.
Eze 37: 9  four winds and breathe into these **s**,
Da    7:11  I kept looking until the beast was **s**
Rev   5: 6  looking as if it had been **s**,
      5:12  who was **s**, to receive power
      6: 9  those who had been **s** because
      13: 8  life, the Lamb who was **s**

## SLANDER [SLANDERED, SLANDERER, SLANDERERS, SLANDEROUS, SLANDEROUSLY, SLANDERS]

Lev 19:16  spreading **s** among your people.
Ps  15: 3  who have no **s** on their tongues,
      54: 5  Let evil recoil on those who **s** me;
Pr  10:18  lying lips and spreads **s** is a fool.
Mt  15:19  immorality, theft, false testimony, **s**.
2Co 12:20  of anger, factions, **s**, gossip,
Eph  4:31  brawling and **s**, along with every
Col   3: 8  malice, **s**, and filthy language
1Ti   5:14  give the enemy no opportunity for **s**.
Tit   3: 2  to **s** no one, to be peaceable
Jas   4:11  and sisters, do not **s** one another.
1Pe   2: 1  envy, and **s** of every kind.
      3:16  in Christ may be ashamed of their **s**.
Jude  1: 9  dare to condemn him for **s** but said,
Rev 13: 6  to **s** his name and his dwelling place

## SLANDERED [SLANDER]
1Co  4:13  when we are s, we answer kindly.
1Ti   6: 1  and our teaching may not be s.

## SLANDERER* [SLANDER]
Jer   9: 4  is a deceiver, and every friend a s.

## SLANDERERS* [SLANDER]
Ps 140:11  May s not be established
Eze 22: 9  s who are bent on shedding blood;
Ro   1:30  s, God-haters, insolent,
1Co  5:11  greedy, idolaters or s,
     6:10  nor drunkards nor s nor swindlers
Tit   2: 3  live, not to be s or addicted to much

## SLANDEROUS* [SLANDER]
2Ti  3: 3  unforgiving, s, without self-control,

## SLANDEROUSLY* [SLANDER]
Ro   3: 8  as we are being s reported as saying

## SLANDERS* [SLANDER]
Dt  22:14  and s her and gives her a bad name,
Ps 101: 5  Whoever s their neighbor in secret,

## SLAP* [SLAPPED, SLAPS]
2Co 11:20  forward or s you in the face.

## SLAPPED [SLAP]
2Ch 18:23  went up and s Micaiah in the face.
Mt  26:67  him with their fists. Others s him

## SLAPS* [SLAP]
Mt   5:39  If anyone s you on the right cheek,
Lk   6:29  If someone s you on one cheek, turn

## SLAUGHTER [SLAUGHTERED]
Ex  12: 6  of Israel must s them at twilight.
    29:11  S it in the LORD's presence
Lev  1: 5  s the young bull before the LORD,
     3: 2  and s it at the entrance to the tent
Dt  12:15  you may s your animals in any
Pr   7:22  her like an ox going to the s,
Isa  53: 7  he was led like a lamb to the s,
Jer 11:19  been like a gentle lamb led to the s;
Zec 11: 4  "Shepherd the flock marked for s.
Ac   8:32  "He was led like a sheep to the s,

## SLAUGHTERED [SLAUGHTER]
Nu  11:22  if flocks and herds were s for them?
    14:16  so he s them in the wilderness.'
Ps  44:22  we are considered as sheep to be s.
Ro   8:36  we are considered as sheep to be s."

## SLAVE [ENSLAVE, ENSLAVED, ENSLAVING, SLAVERY, SLAVES]
Ge  9:26  May Canaan be the s of Shem.
   21:10  "Get rid of that s woman and her
   39:19  "This is how your s treated me,"
Ex   1:11  So they put s masters over them
     3: 7  crying out because of their s drivers,
   21:26  who hits a male or female s in the eye
Ps 123: 2  the eyes of a female s look to the hand

Pr  22: 7  the borrower is s to the lender.
Mk 10:44  wants to be first must be s of all.
Jn   8:34  you, everyone who sins is a s to sin.
Ac   7: 9  they sold him as a s into Egypt.
Ro   7:14  I am unspiritual, sold as a s to sin.
1Co  7:21  Were you a s when you were
     9:19  I have made myself a s to everyone,
   12:13  whether Jews or Gentiles, s or free—
Gal  3:28  Jew nor Gentile, neither s nor free,
     4:30  "Get rid of the s woman and her
Eph  6: 8  you do, whether you are s or free.
Col  3:11  Scythian, s or free, but Christ is all,
1Ti  1:10  for s traders and liars and perjurers.
Phm 1:16  no longer as a s, but better than a s,
Rev 13:16  free and s, to receive a mark

## SLAVERY [SLAVE]
Ex  2:23  The Israelites groaned in their s
   20: 2  out of Egypt, out of the land of s.
Dt   7: 8  redeemed you from the land of s,
Ne  5: 5  subject our sons and daughters to s.
Gal  4: 3  in s under the elemental spiritual
1Ti  6: 1  of s should consider their masters

## SLAVES [SLAVE]
Ge  9:25  The lowest of s will he be to his
   15:14  punish the nation they serve as s,
Ex   6: 6  I will free you from being s to them,
Dt   5:15  Remember that you were s in Egypt
   16:12  that you were s in Egypt, and follow
1Ki  9:22  Solomon did not make s of any
Ps 123: 2  As the eyes of s look to the hand
Ecc 10: 7  while princes go on foot like s.
Jer 34: 9  was to free their Hebrew s,
Mal  1: 6  his father, and s honor their master.
Jn   8:33  and have never been s of anyone.
Ro   6: 6  we should no longer be s to sin—
     6:16  someone as obedient s, you are s
     6:19  used to offer yourselves as s to impurity
     6:22  from sin and have become s of God,
     8:15  you received does not make you s,
1Co  7:23  do not become s of human beings.
Gal  2: 4  in Christ Jesus and to make us s.
     4: 7  So you are no longer s, but God's
     4: 8  you were s to those who by nature
Eph  6: 5  S, obey your earthly masters
Col  3:22  S, obey your earthly masters
     4: 1  provide your s with what is right
Tit   2: 9  Teach s to be subject to their
2Pe  2:19  while they themselves are s
     2:19  for "people are s to whatever has

## SLAY [SLAIN, SLAYS]
Ge  22:10  hand and took the knife to s his son.
Job 13:15  Though he s me, yet will I hope
Ps  34:21  Evil will s the wicked; the foes
Isa  11: 4  of his lips he will s the wicked.
Rev  6: 4  and to make people s each other.

## SLAYS* [SLAY]
Job  5: 2  kills a fool, and envy s the simple.

## SLEEK
Ge 41: 4  ugly and gaunt ate up the seven s,
Dt  32:15  with food, he became heavy and s.

## SLEEP [ASLEEP, SLEEPER, SLEEPING, SLEEPLESS, SLEEPS, SLEPT]

Ge 2:21 caused the man to fall into a deep s;
15:12 Abram fell into a deep s, and a thick
28:11 it under his head and lay down to s.
Ex 22:27 What else can your neighbor s in?
Dt 24:13 so that your neighbor may s in it.
1Sa 26:12 LORD had put them into a deep s.
Ps 4: 8 In peace I will lie down and s,
13: 3 light to my eyes, or I will s in death,
76: 5 lie plundered, they s their last s;
78:65 Then the Lord awoke as from s,
121: 4 Israel will neither slumber nor s.
127: 2 for he grants s to those he loves.
132: 4 I will allow no s to my eyes
Pr 6: 9 When will you get up from your s?
6:10 A little s, a little slumber, a little
Ecc 5:12 The s of laborers is sweet,
Isa 29:10 has brought over you a deep s:
Da 8:18 I was in a deep s, with my face
10: 9 I fell into a deep s, my face
12: 2 Multitudes who s in the dust
Jnh 1: 5 he lay down and fell into a deep s.
Ac 20: 9 sinking into a deep s as Paul talked
1Co 15:51 We will not all s, but we will all be
1Th 4:13 those who s in death,
5: 7 For those who s, s at night,

## SLEEPER* [SLEEP]

Eph 5:14 "Wake up, s, rise from the dead,

## SLEEPING [SLEEP]

1Ki 18:27 Maybe he is s and must be
Mt 26:40 to his disciples and found them s.
Mk 13:36 suddenly, do not let him find you s.

## SLEEPLESS* [SLEEP]

2Co 6: 5 in hard work, s nights and hunger;

## SLEEPS [SLEEP]

Dt 27:20 "Cursed is anyone who s with his
Pr 6:29 So is he who s with another man's
10: 5 son, but he who s during harvest is

## SLEPT [SLEEP]

SS 5: 2 I s but my heart was awake. Listen!

## SLIMY*

Ps 40: 2 He lifted me out of the s pit,

## SLING

Jdg 20:16 each of whom could s a stone
1Sa 17:50 over the Philistine with a s
1Ch 12: 2 or to s stones right-handed
Pr 26: 8 tying a stone in a s is the giving

## SLIP [SLIPPED, SLIPPERY, SLIPPING]

Dt 4: 9 let them s from your heart as long as
32:35 In due time their foot will s;
Ps 37:31 is in their hearts; their feet do not s.
121: 3 He will not let your foot s—

## SLIPPED [SLIP]

Ps 73: 2 But as for me, my feet had almost s;

Jn 5:13 for Jesus had s away into the crowd
2Co 11:33 in the wall and s through his hands.

## SLIPPERY* [SLIP]

Ps 35: 6 may their path be dark and s,
73:18 Surely you place them on s ground;
Jer 23:12 their path will become s;

## SLIPPING [SLIP]

Ps 66: 9 our lives and kept our feet from s.
94:18 "My foot is s," your unfailing love,

## SLOW

Ex 4:10 I am s of speech and tongue."
34: 6 and gracious God, s to anger,
Nu 14:18 'The LORD is s to anger,
Dt 7:10 he will not be s to repay to their
Ne 9:17 s to anger and abounding in love.
Ps 86:15 and gracious God, s to anger,
103: 8 and gracious, s to anger,
145: 8 s to anger and rich in love.
Joel 2:13 s to anger and abounding in love,
Jnh 4: 2 s to anger and abounding in love,
Na 1: 3 The LORD is s to anger but great
Lk 24:25 are, and how s to believe all
Jas 1:19 s to speak and s to become angry,
2Pe 3: 9 The Lord is not s in keeping his

## SLUGGARD [SLUGGARD'S, SLUGGARDS]

Pr 6: 6 Go to the ant, you s;
6: 9 How long will you lie there, you s?
26:14 its hinges, so a s turns on the bed.

## SLUGGARD'S* [SLUGGARD]

Pr 13: 4 A s appetite is never filled,

## SLUGGARDS [SLUGGARD]

Pr 20: 4 S do not plow in season;
21:25 craving of s will be the death of them,
26:15 S bury their hands in the dish

## SLUMBER

Ps 121: 3 he who watches over you will not s;
121: 4 over Israel will neither s nor sleep.
Pr 6:10 a little s, a little folding of the hands
Ro 13:11 for you to wake up from your s,

## SLUR*

Ps 15: 3 no wrong, who cast no s on others;

## SLY*

Pr 25:23 unexpected rain is a s tongue—
Mt 26: 4 plotted to arrest Jesus in some s way
Mk 14: 1 law were looking for some s way

## SMALL [SMALLEST]

1Ki 18:44 "A cloud as s as a man's hand is
Isa 49: 6 "It is too s a thing for you to be my
Mic 5: 2 though you are s among the clans
Mt 7:14 But s is the gate and narrow
7:20 if you have faith as s as a mustard
Mk 12:42 and put in two very s copper coins,
Lk 19:17 been trustworthy in a very s matter,

Jas   3: 5  the tongue is a **s** part of the body,

## SMALLEST [SMALL]

Mt   5:18  not the **s** letter, not the least stroke
Mk   4:31  which is the **s** of all seeds on earth.

## SMASH [SMASHED]

Ex  34:13  **s** their sacred stones and cut down
Dt  12: 3  **s** their sacred stones and burn their

## SMASHED [SMASH]

2Ki 11.18  They **s** the altars and idols to pieces
    18: 4  **s** the sacred stones and cut down
Jer 19:11  this city just as this potter's jar is **s**
Da   2:34  its feet of iron and clay and **s** them.

## SMELL

Dt   4:28  which cannot see or hear or eat or **s**.
Ps 115: 6  but cannot hear, noses, but cannot **s**.
Ecc 10: 1  As dead flies give perfume a bad **s**,
Da   3:27  and there was no **s** of fire on them.

## SMOKE [SMOKING]

Ex  19:18  Mount Sinai was covered with **s**,
Ps  68: 2  May you blow them away like **s**—
   104:32  touches the mountains, and they **s**.
Isa  6: 4  and the temple was filled with **s**.
Joel 2:30  blood and fire and billows of **s**.
Ac   2:19  blood and fire and billows of **s**.
Rev  8: 4  The **s** of the incense,
     9: 2  darkened by the **s** from the Abyss.
    15: 8  the temple was filled with **s**

## SMOKING* [SMOKE]

Ge  15:17  a **s** firepot with a blazing torch

## SMOLDER* [SMOLDERING]

Ps  74: 1  does your anger **s** against the sheep
    80: 4  will your anger **s** against the prayers

## SMOLDERING [SMOLDER]

Isa 42: 3  and a **s** wick he will not snuff out.
Mt  12:20  and a **s** wick he will not snuff out,

## SMOOTH

1Sa 17:40  chose five **s** stones from the stream,
Ps  55:21  His talk is **s** as butter, yet war is
Pr   6:24  wife, from the **s** talk of a wayward
     7:21  she seduced him with her **s** talk.
Isa 42:16  them and make the rough places **s**.
Lk   3: 5  become straight, the rough ways **s**.

## SMYRNA

Rev  2: 8  the angel of the church in **S** write:

## SNAKE [SNAKES]

Ex   4: 3  it on the ground and it became a **s**,
     7:10  and his officials, and it became a **s**.
Nu  21: 8  "Make a **s** and put it up on a pole;
2Ki 18: 4  into pieces the bronze **s** Moses had
Pr  23:32  In the end it bites like a **s**
Mic  7:17  They will lick dust like a **s**,
Mt   7:10  he asks for a fish, will give him a **s**?
Jn   3:14  lifted up the **s** in the wilderness,

Ac  28: 5  But Paul shook the **s** off into the fire

## SNAKES [SNAKE]

Nu  21: 6  sent venomous **s** among them;
Mt  10:16  Therefore be as shrewd as **s** and as
Lk  10:19  given you authority to trample on **s**
1Co 10: 9  of them did—and were killed by **s**.
Rev  9:19  for their tails were like **s**,

## SNARE [ENSNARE, ENSNARED, SNARED, SNARES]

Ex  23:33  of their gods will certainly be a **s**
Dt   7:16  gods, for that will be a **s** to you.
Ps  69:22  table set before them become a **s**;
    91: 3  he will save you from the fowler's **s**
   142: 3  where I walk people have hidden a **s**
Pr   6: 5  like a bird from the **s** of the fowler.
    29:25  To fear anyone will prove to be a **s**,
Ro  11: 9  "May their table become a **s**

## SNARED [SNARE]

Pr   3:26  will keep your foot from being **s**.
    29: 6  Evildoers are **s** by their own sin,

## SNARES [SNARE]

Jos 23:13  they will become **s** and traps
Jdg  2: 3  you, and their gods will become **s**
Ps  18: 5  the **s** of death confronted me.
Pr  13:14  turning a person from the **s** of death.

## SNATCH [SNATCHED, SNATCHES, SNATCHING]

Jn  10:28  no one will **s** them out of my hand.

## SNATCHED [SNATCH]

Am   4:11  You were like a burning stick **s**
Zec  3: 2  Is not this man a burning stick **s**

## SNATCHES [SNATCH]

Mt  13:19  and **s** away what was sown in their

## SNATCHING* [SNATCH]

Jude 1:23  save others by **s** them from the fire;

## SNEER

Ps  35:21  They **s** at me and say, "Aha!

## SNEEZED*

2Ki  4:35  The boy **s** seven times and opened

## SNIFF*

Mal  1:13  and you **s** at it contemptuously,"

## SNOUT*

Pr  11:22  a pig's **s** is a beautiful woman who

## SNOW [SNOW-COOLED, SNOWS]

Ex   4: 6  it had become as white as **s**.
Nu  12:10  it became as white as **s**.
2Ki  5:27  it had become as white as **s**.
Ps  51: 7  me, and I will be whiter than **s**.
Isa  1:18  scarlet, they shall be as white as **s**;
Da   7: 9  His clothing was as white as **s**;

Mt  28: 3  and his clothes were white as s.
Rev  1:14  as white as s, and his eyes were like

### SNOW-COOLED* [SNOW]
Pr  25:13  Like a s drink at harvest time

### SNOWS* [SNOW]
Pr  31:21  When it s, she has no fear for her

### SNUFF [SNUFFED]
Isa  42: 3  a smoldering wick he will not s out.
Mt  12:20  a smoldering wick he will not s out,

### SNUFFED [SNUFF]
Job  21:17  is the lamp of the wicked s out?
Pr  13: 9  but the lamp of the wicked is s out.

### SO-CALLED* [CALL]
1Co  8: 5  For even if there are s gods,
Rev  2:24  not learned Satan's s deep secrets,

### SOAKED
Jn  19:29  was there, so they s a sponge in it,

### SOAP*
Job  9:30  Even if I washed myself with s
Jer  2:22  Although you wash yourself with s
Mal  3: 2  a refiner's fire or a launderer's s.

### SOAR [SOARED]
Isa  40:31  They will s on wings like eagles;
Jer  49:22  An eagle will s and swoop down,
Ob  1: 4  Though you s like the eagle

### SOARED* [SOAR]
2Sa  22:11  he s on the wings of the wind.
Ps  18:10  he s on the wings of the wind.

### SOBER
Ro  12: 3  think of yourself with s judgment,
1Th  5: 6  but let us be awake and s.
      5: 8  we belong to the day, let us be s,
1Pe  1:13  with minds that are alert and fully s,
      4: 7  Therefore be alert and of s mind.
      5: 8  Be alert and of s mind.

### SOCKET
Ge  32:25  he touched the s of Jacob's hip so

### SODOM
Ge  13:12  plain and pitched his tents near S.
      13:13  Now the people of S were wicked
      18:20  said, "The outcry against S
      19:24  rained down burning sulfur on S
Isa  1: 9  we would have become like S,
Eze  16:49  this was the sin of your sister S:
Lk  10:12  on that day for S than for that town.
Ro  9:29  we would have become like S,
Jude  1: 7  way, S and Gomorrah
Rev  11: 8  which is figuratively called S

### SODOMITE(S) (KJV) See SHRINE [PROSTITUTE(S)]

### SOIL
Ge  4: 2  kept flocks, and Cain worked the s.
      9:20  a man of the s, proceeded to plant
Ex  23:19  the firstfruits of your s to the house
Mt  13:23  the seed falling on good s refers

### SOLD [SELL]
Ge  37:28  s him for twenty shekels of silver
Ex  22: 3  they must be s to pay for their theft.
Lev  25:23  land must not be s permanently,
Dt  32:30  unless their Rock had s them,
Jdg  4: 2  So the LORD s them
      10: 7  He s them into the hands
1Ki  21:25  who s himself to do evil in the eyes
Mt  10:29  Are not two sparrows s for a penny?
      13:44  in his joy went and s all he had
      13:46  went away and s everything he had
Ac  5: 1  Sapphira, also s a piece of property.
Ro  7:14  I am unspiritual, s as a slave to sin.
1Co  10:25  Eat anything s in the meat market
Heb  12:16  a single meal s his inheritance rights

### SOLDIER [SOLDIERS]
1Co  9: 7  Who serves as a s at his own
2Ti  2: 3  like a good s of Christ Jesus.

### SOLDIERS [SOLDIER]
Mt  27:27  the governor's s took Jesus
      28:12  plan, they gave the s a large sum
Jn  19:23  When the s crucified Jesus,
      19:34  one of the s pierced Jesus' side

### SOLE
Dt  28:65  resting place for the s of your foot.
Isa  1: 6  From the s of your foot to the top

### SOLEMN
Jos  6:26  time Joshua pronounced this s oath:
Eze  16: 8  I gave you my s oath and entered

### SOLID
1Co  3: 2  I gave you milk, not s food, for you
2Ti  2:19  God's s foundation stands firm,
Heb  5:14  But s food is for the mature,

### SOLITARY
Mk  1:35  the house and went off to a s place,
      6:32  by themselves in a boat to a s place.

### SOLOMON [JEDIDIAH]
Son of David by Bathsheba; king of Judah (2Sa 12:24; 1Ch 3:5, 10). Appointed king by David (1Ki 1); adversaries Adonijah, Joab, Shimei killed by Benaiah (1Ki 2). Asked for wisdom (1Ki 3; 2Ch 1). Judged between two prostitutes (1Ki 3:16–28). Built temple (1Ki 5–7; 2Ch 2–5); prayer of dedication (1Ki 8; 2Ch 6). Visited by Queen of Sheba (1Ki 10; 2Ch 9). Wives turned his heart from God (1Ki 11:1–13). Jeroboam rebelled against (1Ki 11:26–40). Death (1Ki 11:41–43; 2Ch 9:29–31).

Proverbs of (1Ki 4:32; Pr 1:1; 10:1; 25:1); psalms of (Ps 72; 127); song of (SS 1:1).

## SOMBER*

Mt   6:16   do not look s as the hypocrites do,

## SOME [SOMEHOW, SOMEONE, SOMETHING]

Ge    3: 6   She also gave s to her husband,
Mk    4:15   S people are like seed along
      8:28   replied, "S say John the Baptist;
1Co   9:22   all possible means I might save s.
1Ti   4: 1   later times s will abandon the faith
2Pe   3:16   His letters contain s things that are

## SOMEHOW [HOW, SOME]

Ro   11:14   that I may s arouse my own people
Gal   4:11   that s I have wasted my efforts
Php   3:11   and so, s,

## SOMEONE [ONE, SOME]

Ex    4:13   Please send s else."
     12:30   was not a house without s dead.
Nu   35:11   who has killed s accidentally may
Job  14:14   If s dies, will they live again?
Pr   26:17   s who rushes into a quarrel
Eze  22:30   looked for s among them who would
              build
Lk    7:19   come, or should we expect s else?"
     16:31   will not be convinced even if s rises
Ro   10:14   can they hear without s preaching

## SOMETHING [SOME, THING]

Ex   24:10   his feet was s like a pavement made
Nu   16:30   LORD brings about s totally new,
Dt    8:16   s your ancestors had never known,
Mt   25:35   hungry and you gave me s to eat,
Ac    3: 5   expecting to get s from them.
      9:18   s like scales fell from Saul's eyes,
Php   2: 6   equality with God s to be used to his
Rev   8: 8   and s like a huge mountain,
      9: 7   their heads they wore s like crowns

## SON [SONS, SONS', SONSHIP; see also CHILD]

Ge    5: 3   he had a s in his own likeness, in his
     15: 4   but a s coming from your own body
     17:19   your wife Sarah will bear you a s,
     21: 2   bore a s to Abraham in his old age,
     21:10   rid of that slave woman and her s,
     22: 2   said, "Take your s, your only s,
     22:12   have not withheld from me your s,
     25:11   God blessed his s Isaac,
Ex    4:23   so I will kill your firstborn s.' "
     11: 5   Every firstborn s in Egypt will die,
Nu   18:15   you must redeem every firstborn s
Dt    1:31   as a father carries his s, all the way
      8: 5   heart that as a man disciplines his s,
     18:10   among you who sacrifices their s
     21:18   rebellious s who does not obey his
2Sa   7:14   be his father, and he will be my s.
1Ki   3:23   'My s is alive and your s is dead,'
      8:19   but your s, who is your own flesh
2Ki   6:29   So we cooked my s and ate him.
1Ch  22:10   He will be my s, and I will be his

Ps    2: 7   He said to me, "You are my s;
      2:12   Kiss his s, or he will be angry
     80:15   planted, the s you have raised
Pr    3: 1   My s, do not forget my teaching,
      3:12   as a father the s he delights in.
      4: 3   For I too was a s to my father,
      6:20   My s, keep your father's command
Isa   7:14   will conceive and give birth to a s,
      8: 3   she conceived and gave birth to a s.
      9: 6   is born, to us a s is given,
Jer  31:20   Is not Ephraim my dear s, the child
Da    3:25   and the fourth looks like a s
      7:13   there before me was one like a s
Hos  11: 1   him, and out of Egypt I called my s.
Mal   1: 6   "A s honors his father, and slaves
Mt    1: 1   of Jesus the Messiah the s of David, the
              s of Abraham:
      1:23   will conceive and give birth to a s,
      2:15   "Out of Egypt I called my s."
      3:17   said, "This is my S, whom I love;
      4: 3   "If you are the S of God, tell these
      8:20   the S of Man has no place to lay his
     11:27   one knows the S except the Father,
     12: 8   For the S of Man is Lord
     12:32   who speaks a word against the S
     12:40   so the S of Man will be three days
     13:55   "Isn't this the carpenter's s?
     14:33   "Truly you are the S of God."
     16:16   Messiah, the S of the living God."
     16:27   For the S of Man is going to come
     17: 5   said, "This is my S, whom I love;
     19:28   when the S of Man sits on his
     20:18   the S of Man will be delivered over
     20:28   just as the S of Man did not come
     21: 9   "Hosanna to the S of David!"
     22:42   the Messiah? Whose s is he?"
     24:27   will be the coming of the S of Man.
     24:30   the sign of the S of Man will appear
     24:44   because the S of Man will come
     25:31   "When the S of Man comes in his
     26:63   you are the Messiah, the S of God."
     27:54   "Surely he was the S of God!"
     28:19   and of the S and of the Holy Spirit,
Mk    1:11   "You are my S, whom I love;
      2:28   So the S of Man is Lord even
      8:38   the S of Man will be ashamed
      9: 7   "This is my S, whom I love.
     10:45   For even the S of Man did not come
     13:32   nor the S, but only the Father.
     14:62   you will see the S of Man sitting
     15:39   said, "Surely this man was the S
Lk    1:32   and will be called the S of the Most
      1:35   be born will be called the S of God.
      2: 7   she gave birth to her firstborn, a s.
      3:22   "You are my S, whom I love;
      9:35   saying, "This is my S, whom I have
      9:58   the S of Man has no place to lay his
     12: 8   the S of Man will also acknowledge
     15:21   longer worthy to be called your s.'
     18: 8   when the S of Man comes, will he
     18:31   about the S of Man will be fulfilled.
     19:10   For the S of Man came to seek
     20:44   How then can he be his s?"
Jn    1:49   "Rabbi, you are the S of God;
      3:14   so the S of Man must be lifted up,
      3:16   that he gave his one and only S,
      3:36   believes in the S has eternal life,

Jn   5:19  the S can do nothing by himself;
     6:40  is that everyone who looks to the S
    11: 4  God's S may be glorified through
    12:34  'The S of Man must be lifted up'?
    13:31  "Now is the S of Man glorified
    17: 1  Glorify your S, that your S may
Ac   7:56  the S of Man standing at the right
    13:33  " 'You are my s; today I have
Ro   1: 4  holiness was appointed the S of God
     5:10  to him through the death of his S,
     8: 3  by sending his own S in the likeness
     8:29  be conformed to the image of his S,
     8:32  He who did not spare his own S,
1Co 15:28  the S himself will be made subject
Gal  2:20  I live by faith in the S of God,
     4: 4  God sent his S, born of a woman,
     4:30  rid of the slave woman and her s,
Col  1:13  into the kingdom of the S he loves,
1Th  1:10  and to wait for his S from heaven,
Heb  1: 2  days he has spoken to us by his S,
     1: 5  God ever say, "You are my S;
     4:14  into heaven, Jesus the S of God,
     5: 5  God said to him, "You are my S;
     7:28  appointed the S, who has been made
    10:29  punished who have trampled the S
Jas  2:21  he offered his s Isaac on the altar?
2Pe  1:17  saying, "This is my S, whom I love;
1Jn  1: 3  is with the Father and with his S,
     1: 7  Jesus, his S, purifies us from all sin.
     2:23  acknowledges the S has the Father
     3: 8  The reason the S of God appeared
     4: 9  only S into the world that we might
     4:14  the Father has sent his S to be
     5: 5  believes that Jesus is the S of God.
     5:11  eternal life, and this life is in his S.
Rev  1:13  lampstands was someone like a s
     2:18  are the words of the S of God,
    12: 5  She gave birth to a s, a male child,
    14:14  on the cloud was one like a s of man

## MY SON Ge 21:10; 22:7, 8; 24:3, 4, 6, 7, 8, 37,
38, 40; 27:1, 8, 13, 18, 20, 21, 21, 24, 25, 26, 27,
37, 43; 34:8; 37:35; 38:11, 26; 42:38; 43:29;
45:28; 48:19; 49:9; Ex 4:23; Jos 7:19; Jdg 8:23;
17:2, 3; 1Sa 3:6, 16; 4:16; 10:2; 14:39, 40, 41,
42; 22:8, 8; 24:16; 26:17, 21, 25; 2Sa 7:14;
13:25; 14:11, 16; 16:11; 18:22, 33, 33, 33, 33,
33; 19:4, 4, 4; 1Ki 1:21, 33; 3:20, 21, 22, 23;
17:12, 18; 2Ki 6:28, 29; 14:9; 1Ch 17:13; 22:5,
7, 10, 11; 28:5, 6, 9; 29:1, 19; 2Ch 25:18; Ps 2:7;
Pr 1:8, 10, 15; 2:1; 3:1, 11, 21; 4:10, 20; 5:1, 20;
6:1, 3, 20; 7:1; 23:15, 19, 26; 24:13, 21; 31:2, 2;
Ecc 12:12; Hos 11:1; Mt 2:15; 3:17; 17:5, 15;
21:37; Mk 1:11; 9:7, 17; 12:6; Lk 3:22; 9:35, 38;
15:31; 20:13; Ac 13:33; 1Co 4:17; 1Ti 1:18; 2Ti
2:1; Phm 1:10, 10; Heb 1:5, 5; 5:5; 12:5; 1Pe
5:13; 2Pe 1:17

## SON OF AARON Ex 6:25; 38:21; Lev 7:33;
Nu 3:32; 4:16, 28, 33; 7:8; 16:37; 25:7, 11; 26:1;
Jos 24:33; Jdg 20:28; Ezr 7:5

## SON OF DAVID 2Sa 13:1, 1; 1Ch 29:22; 2Ch
1:1; 13:6; 30:26; 35:3; Pr 1:1; Ecc 1:1; Mt 1:1,
20; 9:27; 12:23; 15:22; 20:30, 31; 21:9, 15;
22:42; Mk 10:47, 48; 12:35; Lk 3:31; 18:38, 39;
20:41

## SON OF GOD Mt 4:3, 6; 8:29; 14:33; 26:63;
27:40, 43, 54; Mk 3:11; 15:39; Lk 1:35; 3:38;
4:3, 9, 41; 22:70; Jn 1:49; 5:25; 11:27; 19:7;
20:31; Ac 9:20; Ro 1:4; 2Co 1:19; Gal 2:20; Eph
4:13; Heb 4:14; 6:6; 7:3; 10:29; 1Jn 3:8; 4:15;
5:5, 10, 12, 13, 20; Rev 2:18

## SON OF JESSE 1Sa 16:18; 20:27, 30, 31; 22:7,
8, 9, 13; 25:10; 2Sa 23:1; 1Ch 10:14; 12:18;
29:26; Ps 72:20; Lk 3:32; Ac 13:22

## SON OF MAN Ps 80:17; Eze 2:1, 3, 6, 8; 3:1,
3, 4, 10, 17, 25; 4:1, 16; 5:1; 6:2; 7:2; 8:5, 6, 8,
12, 15, 17; 11:2, 4, 15; 12:2, 3, 9, 18, 22, 27;
13:2, 17; 14:3, 13; 15:2; 16:2; 17:2; 20:3, 4, 27,
46; 21:2, 6, 9, 12, 14, 19, 28; 22:2, 18, 24; 23:2,
36; 24:2, 16, 25; 25:2; 26:2; 27:2; 28:2, 12, 21;
29:2, 18; 30:2, 21; 31:2; 32:2, 18; 33:2, 7, 10, 12,
24, 30; 34:2; 35:2; 36:1, 17; 37:3, 9, 11, 16; 38:2,
14; 39:1, 17; 40:4; 43:7, 10, 18; 44:5; 47:6; Da
7:13; 8:17; Mt 8:20; 9:6; 10:23; 11:19; 12:8, 32,
40; 13:37, 41; 16:13, 27, 28; 17:9, 12, 22; 19:28;
20:18, 28; 24:27, 30, 30, 37, 39, 44; 25:31; 26:2,
24, 24, 45, 64; Mk 2:10, 28; 8:31, 38; 9:9, 12,
31; 10:33, 45; 13:26; 14:21, 21, 41, 62; Lk 5:24;
6:5, 22; 7:34; 9:22, 26, 44, 58; 11:30; 12:8, 10,
40; 17:22, 24, 26, 30; 18:8, 31; 19:10; 21:27, 36;
22:22, 48, 69; 24:7; Jn 1:51; 3:13, 14; 5:27; 6:27,
53, 62; 8:28; 9:35; 12:23, 34, 34; 13:31; Ac 7:56;
Rev 1:13; 14:14

## SONG [SING]
Dt  31:21  this s will testify against them,
    32:44  all the words of this s in the hearing
Jdg  5: 1  Barak son of Abinoam sang this s:
Ps  33: 3  Sing to him a new s;
    40: 3  He put a new s in my mouth,
    69:30  I will praise God's name in s
    96: 1  Sing to the LORD a new s;
    98: 4  burst into jubilant s with music;
   119:54  the theme of my s wherever I lodge.
   149: 1  Sing to the LORD a new s;
Isa  5: 1  sing for the one I love a s about his
    49:13  burst into s, you mountains!
    54: 1  burst into s, shout for joy, you who
    55:12  hills will burst into s before you,
Rev  5: 9  And they sang a new s, saying:
    14: 3  could learn the s except the 144,000
    15: 3  sang the s of God's servant Moses

## SONGS [SING]
2Sa 23: 1  God of Jacob, the hero of Israel's s:
1Ki  4:32  and his s numbered a thousand
Ne  12:46  for the s of praise and thanksgiving
Job 35:10  my Maker, who gives s in the night,
Ps  77: 6  I remembered my s in the night.
   100: 2  come before him with joyful s.
   126: 6  to sow, will return with s of joy,
   137: 3  for there our captors asked us for s,
Eph  5:19  hymns and s from the Spirit.
Col  3:16  hymns and s from the Spirit.
Jas  5:13  Let them sing s of praise.

## SONS [SON; see also CHILDREN]
Ge   6: 2  the s of God saw that these
     9: 1  Then God blessed Noah and his s,

Ge 10:32 These are the clans of Noah's **s**,
   35:22 heard of it. Jacob had twelve **s**:
Ex 13:15 and redeem each of my firstborn **s**.'
   28: 9 on them the names of the **s** of Israel
Nu 18: 7 and your **s** may serve as priests
Dt  7: 3 not give your daughters to their **s**
Ru  4:15 who is better to you than seven **s**,
Ps 82: 6 you are all **s** of the Most High.'
  89:30 "If his **s** forsake my law and do not
 132:12 If your **s** keep my covenant
Joel  2:28 Your **s** and daughters will prophesy,
Ac  2.17 Your **s** and daughters will prophesy,
2Co  6:18 and you will be my **s** and daughters,
Heb  2:10 In bringing many **s** and daughters

**AARON AND HIS SONS** Ex 27:21; 28:4,
  41, 43; 29:4, 9, 9, 10, 15, 19, 20, 24, 27, 28, 32,
  35, 44; 30:19, 30; 39:27; 40:12, 31; Lev 2:3, 10;
  6:9, 16, 20, 25; 7:31, 35; 8:2, 6, 14, 18, 22, 27,
  31, 31, 36; 9:1; 10:6; 17:2; 21:24; 22:2, 18; 24:9;
  Nu 3:9, 10, 38, 48, 51; 4:5, 15, 19, 27; 6:23;
  8:13, 19, 22

**AARON'S SONS** Ex 28:40; Lev 1:5, 8, 11;
  2:2; 3:2, 5, 8, 13; 6:14; 8:13, 24; 10:1; Nu 3:3

**SONS OF AARON** Lev 1:7; 7:10; 16:1; 21:1;
  Nu 3:2; 10:8; 1Ch 6:3; 24:1; 2Ch 13:9, 10

**SONS OF KORAH** Ex 6:24; Ps 42:T; 44:T;
  45:T; 46:T, 47:T; 48:T, 49.T; 84·T; 85:T; 87·T;
  88:T

**SONS'** [SON]
Ge  6:18 wife and your **s**' wives with you.
Lev 10:13 your **s**' share of the food offerings

**SONSHIP**\* [SON]
Ro  8:15 brought about your adoption to **s**.
Gal  4: 5 we might receive adoption to **s**.
Eph  1: 5 for adoption to **s** through Jesus Christ,

**SOON**
Ps 37: 2 for like the grass they will **s** wither,
 106:13 But they **s** forgot what he had done
Pr  5:14 And I was **s** in serious trouble
Isa 56: 1 my righteousness will **s** be revealed.
Da  9:23 As **s** as you began to pray, a word
Ro 16:20 peace will **s** crush Satan under your
Rev  1: 1 his servants what must **s** take place.
  3:11 I am coming **s**. Hold on to what you
 22: 7 "Look, I am coming **s**!
 22:12 "Look, I am coming **s**!
 22:20 things says, "Yes, I am coming **s**."

**SOOTHING**
Pr 15: 4 The **s** tongue is a tree of life,

**SORCERER** [SORCERY]
Ac 13: 6 There they met a Jewish **s** and false

**SORCERERS** [SORCERY]
Ex  7:11 then summoned wise men and **s**,
Jer 27: 9 mediums or your **s** who tell you,
Da  2: 2 **s** and astrologers to tell him what he

**SORCERESS** [SORCERY]
Ex 22:18 "Do not allow a **s** to live.

**SORCERIES** [SORCERY]
Isa 47: 9 in spite of your many **s** and all your
Na  3: 4 the mistress of **s**, who enslaved

**SORCERY** [SORCERER, SORCERERS,
  SORCERESS, SORCERIES]
Dt 18:10 fire, who practices divination or **s**,
Ac  8: 9 a man named Simon had practiced **s**
  8:11 amazed them for a long time with his **s**.
 19:19 who had practiced **s** brought their

**SORE** [SORES]
Jer 30:13 no remedy for your **s**, no healing

**SOREK**\*
Jdg 16: 4 of **S** whose name was Delilah.

**SORES** [SORE]
Job  2: 7 Job with painful **s** from the soles
Hos  5:13 not able to heal your **s**.
Rev 16: 2 festering **s** broke out on the people

**SORROW** [SORROWFUL]
Ps  6: 7 My eyes grow weak with **s**;
 90:10 best of them are but trouble and **s**,
 116. 3 I was overcome by distress and **s**
Pr 23:29 Who has **s**? Who has strife?
Ecc  1:18 with much wisdom comes much **s**;
Isa 35:10 and **s** and sighing will flee away.
 51:11 and **s** and sighing will flee away.
 60:20 light, and your days of **s** will end.
Jer 31:12 garden, and they will **s** no more.
Mk 14:34 "My soul is overwhelmed with **s**
Ro  9: 2 I have great **s** and unceasing
2Co  7:10 Godly **s** brings repentance that leads

**SORROWFUL** [SORROW]
2Co  6:10 **s**, yet always rejoicing;

**SORT** [SORTS]
Lk 23: 8 to see him perform a sign of some **s**.

**SORTS** [SORT]
1Co 14:10 there are all **s** of languages in the world,
2Th  2: 9 all **s** of displays of power through signs

**SOUGHT** [SEEK]
Ex 32:11 Moses **s** the favor of the Lᴏʀᴅ his
1Sa 13:14 the Lᴏʀᴅ has **s** out a man after his
2Ch 26: 5 As long as he **s** the Lᴏʀᴅ,
 31:21 he **s** his God and worked
Ps 34: 4 I **s** the Lᴏʀᴅ, and he answered
 119:45 for I have **s** out your precepts.
 119:58 I have **s** your face with all my heart;
Isa  9:13 them, nor have they **s** the Lᴏʀᴅ
Ro 11: 7 of Israel **s** so earnestly they did not

**SOUL** [SOULS]
Dt  6: 5 and with all your **s** and with all your
 10:12 all your heart and with all your **s**,

Dt 30: 6 all your heart and with all your s,
Jos 22: 5 all your heart and with all your s."
2Ki 23:25 and with all his s and with all his
Ps 19: 7 LORD is perfect, refreshing the s.
23: 3 he refreshes my s. He guides me
42: 1 of water, so my s pants for you,
42:11 Why, my s, are you downcast?
62: 5 Yes, my s, find rest in God;
103: 1 Praise the LORD, my s;
108: 1 sing and make music with all my s.
116: 7 my s, for the LORD has been good
Pr 13:19 A longing fulfilled is sweet to the s,
16:24 sweet to the s and healing
La 3:20 and my s is downcast within me.
Mic 6: 7 fruit of my body for the sin of my s?
Mt 10:28 of the One who can destroy both s
16:26 you give in exchange for your s?
22:37 and with all your s and with all your
Mk 8:36 the whole world, yet forfeit your s?
Lk 1:46 "My s glorifies the Lord
2:35 sword will pierce your own s too."
Jn 12:27 "Now my s is troubled,
1Th 5:23 s and body be kept blameless
Heb 4:12 it penetrates even to dividing s
6:19 this hope as an anchor for the s,
1Pe 2:11 desires, which war against your s.
3Jn 1: 2 even as your s is getting along well.

## SOULS [SOUL]
Pr 11:30 life, and those who win s are wise.
Jer 6:16 it, and you will find rest for your s.
Mt 11:29 and you will find rest for your s.
1Pe 2:25 Shepherd and Overseer of your s.
Rev 6: 9 I saw under the altar the s of those
20: 4 I saw the s of those who had been

## SOUND [FINE-SOUNDING, SOUNDED, SOUNDING]
Ge 3: 8 his wife heard the s of the LORD
Ex 32:18 "It is not the s of victory, it is not the
s of defeat; it is the s of singing
Dt 4:12 You heard the s of words but saw
Ps 66: 8 let the s of his praise be heard;
115: 7 nor can they utter a s with their
Pr 3:21 preserve s judgment and discretion;
8:14 Counsel and s judgment are mine;
Isa 6: 4 the s of their voices the doorposts
Eze 3:12 me a loud rumbling s as the glory
Joel 2: 1 s the alarm on my holy hill.
Jn 3: 8 You hear its s, but you cannot tell
Ac 2: 2 Suddenly a s like the blowing
1Co 14: 8 if the trumpet does not s a clear call,
15:52 For the trumpet will s, the dead will
1Ti 1:10 else is contrary to the s doctrine
6: 3 does not agree to the s instruction
2Ti 1:13 keep as the pattern of s teaching,
4: 3 will not put up with s doctrine.
Tit 1: 9 can encourage others by s doctrine
2: 1 what is appropriate to s doctrine.
Rev 1:15 his voice was like the s of rushing

## SOUNDED [SOUND]
Rev 6: 6 I heard what s like a voice among
19: 6 Then I heard what s like a great

## SOUNDING [SOUND]
Ps 47: 5 the LORD amid the s of trumpets.
150: 3 Praise him with the s of the trumpet,

## SOUR
Jer 31:29 'The parents have eaten s grapes,
Eze 18: 2 " 'The parents eat s grapes,
Rev 10: 9 It will turn your stomach s,

## SOURCE
Heb 5: 9 he became the s of eternal salvation

## SOUTH
Ge 13:14 to the north and s, to the east
Ps 89:12 You created the north and the s;
Da 11: 5 king of the S will become strong,
Zec 14: 4 moving north and half moving s.
Mt 12:42 The Queen of the S will rise

## SOVEREIGN [SOVEREIGNTY]
Ge 15: 2 But Abram said, "S LORD,
Ex 23:17 are to appear before the S LORD.
2Sa 7:18 "Who am I, S LORD, and what is
7:22 "How great you are, S LORD!
Ps 71: 5 you have been my hope, S LORD,
71:16 your mighty acts, S LORD;
140: 7 S LORD, my strong deliverer,
Isa 25: 8 The S LORD will wipe away
40:10 the S LORD comes with power,
50: 4 The S LORD has given me
61: 1 The Spirit of the S LORD is
61:10 to grow, so the S LORD will make
Jer 32:17 "Ah, S LORD, you have made
Da 4:25 Most High is s over the kingdoms
Hab 3:19 The S LORD is my strength;
Zep 1: 7 Be silent before the S LORD.
2Pe 2: 1 even denying the s Lord who
Jude 1: 4 deny Jesus Christ our only S
Rev 6:10 "How long, S Lord, holy and true,

## WHAT THE SOVEREIGN †LORD SAYS
See †LORD

## SOVEREIGN †LORD See †LORD

## DECLARES THE SOVEREIGN †LORD
See †LORD

## SOVEREIGNTY [SOVEREIGN]
Da 7:27 Then the s, power and greatness

## SOW [SOWED, SOWER, SOWN, SOWS]
Ex 23:10 six years you are to s your fields
Dt 28:38 You will s much seed in the field
Job 4: 8 evil and those who s trouble reap it.
Ps 126: 5 Those who s with tears will reap
Pr 11:18 s righteousness reap a sure
22: 8 who s injustice reap calamity,
Ecc 11: 6 S your seed in the morning,
Hos 8: 7 "They s the wind and reap
10:12 S for yourselves righteousness,
Mt 6:26 they do not s or reap or store away
13: 3 "A farmer went out to s his seed.
1Co 15:36 What you s does not come to life
Gal 6: 7 People reap what they s.

Jas    3:18   Peacemakers who s in peace reap
2Pe    2:22   "A s that is washed returns to her

## SOWED [SOW]
Mt    13:24   is like a man who s good seed in his

## SOWER* [SOW]
Isa   55:10   so that it yields seed for the s
Mt    13:18   to what the parable of the s means:
Jn     4:36   so that the s and the reaper may be
2Co    9:10   Now he who supplies seed to the s

## SOWN [SOW]
Mt    13: 8   sixty or thirty times what was s.
Mk     4:15   away the word that was s in them.
1Co    9:11   we have s spiritual seed among you,
      15:42   The body that is s is perishable, it is

## SOWS [SOW]
Mt    13:39   the enemy who s them is the devil.
Mk     4:14   The farmer s the word.
2Co    9: 6   Whoever s sparingly will also reap

## SPACIOUS
Ex     3: 8   of that land into a good and s land,
Ps    18:19   He brought me out into a s place;

## SPAN
Ex    23:26   I will give you a full life s.

## SPARE [SPARED, SPARES, SPARING]
Ge    18:24   not s the place for the sake
Est    7: 3   And s my people—this is my
Pr    13:24   Those who s the rod hate their children,
Jer   50:20   for I will forgive the remnant I s.
Eze    6: 8   " 'But I will s some, for some
Zec   11: 5   Their own shepherds do not s them.
Ro     8:32   He who did not s his own Son,
      11:21   God did not s the natural branches,
2Pe    2: 4   if God did not s angels when they
       2: 5   if he did not s the ancient world

## SPARED [SPARE]
Ge    12:13   my life will be s because of you."
      19:20   Then my life will be s."
Jos    6:25   But Joshua s Rahab the prostitute,
Ps    30: 3   you s me from going down

## SPARES* [SPARE]
Est    4:11   scepter to them and s their lives.
Mal    3:17   and s his son who serves him.

## SPARING [SPARE]
Pr    21:26   but the righteous give without s.

## SPARKLE*
Zec    9:16   They will s in his land like jewels

## SPARROW [SPARROWS]
Ps    84: 3   Even the s has found a home,

## SPARROWS [SPARROW]
Mt    10:29   Are not two s sold for a penny?

Lk    12: 7   you are worth more than many s.

## SPEAK [SPEAKER, SPEAKING, SPEAKS, SPOKE, SPOKEN]
Ge    18:27   I have been so bold as to s
      37: 4   and could not s a kind word to him.
Ex     4:12   I will help you s and will teach you
       6:30   "Since I s with faltering lips,
      33:11   The LORD would s to Moses face
Nu    12: 8   With him I s face to face,
      20: 8   S to that rock before their eyes
      22:35   the men, but s only what I tell you."
Dt    18:20   a prophet who presumes to s in my
1Sa    3: 9   and if he calls you, say, 'S, LORD,
2Ki   18:26   Don't s to us in Hebrew
Job   13: 3   But I desire to s to the Almighty
Ps    15: 2   who s the truth from their hearts;
      49: 3   My mouth will s words of wisdom;
     135:16   have mouths, but cannot s, eyes,
Pr    18:17   In a lawsuit the first to s seems right,
      20:15   that s knowledge are a rare jewel.
      23: 9   Do not s to fools, for they will scorn
      31: 8   S up for those who cannot s
Ecc    3: 7   a time to be silent and a time to s,
Isa   28:11   strange tongues God will s to this
      40: 2   S tenderly to Jerusalem,
Jer   10: 5   a melon patch, their idols cannot s;
Eze    3:18   or s out to dissuade them from their
Da     7:25   He will s against the Most High
Zec   10: 2   The idols s deceitfully, diviners see
Mt    13:13   This is why I s to them in parables:
Mk     7:37   the deaf hear and the mute s."
Jn    12:49   For I did not s on my own,
Ac     2: 4   began to s in other tongues as
       4:18   commanded them not to s or teach
1Co   12:30   Do all s in tongues?
      14: 2   For those who s in a tongue do not s
      14: 3   But those who prophesy s to people
      14: 5   greater than those who s in tongues,
      14:19   I would rather s five intelligible
Jas    1:19   slow to s and slow to become angry,

## SPEAKER [SPEAK]
1Co   14:11   I am a foreigner to the s, and the s is

## SPEAKING [SPEAK]
Dt     5:26   the voice of the living God s
Mt    10:20   Spirit of your Father s through you.
Mk    12:36   David himself, s by the Holy Spirit,
Ac    10:46   For they heard them s in tongues
1Co   12:10   to another s in different kinds
Eph    4:15   Instead, s the truth in love, we will
       5:19   s to one another with psalms,

## SPEAKS [SPEAK]
Ex    33:11   face to face, as one s to a friend.
Dt     5:24   can live even if God s with them.
      18:19   that the prophet s in my name.
Pr     8: 7   My mouth s what is true, for my
      22:11   and who s with grace will have
      31:26   She s with wisdom, and faithful
Mt    12:32   but anyone who s against the Holy
Lk     6:45   overflow of the heart the mouth s.
Heb   11: 4   And by faith Abel still s,
      12:25   it that you do not refuse him who s.

## SPEAR [SPEARS]
1Sa 17: 7 His **s** shaft was like a weaver's rod,
    19:10 eluded him as Saul drove the **s**
    20:33 Saul hurled his **s** at him to kill him.
Ps  46: 9 breaks the bow and shatters the **s**;
Jn  19:34 soldiers pierced Jesus' side with a **s**,

## SPEARS [SPEAR]
Isa  2: 4 and their **s** into pruning hooks.
Joel  3:10 and your pruning hooks into **s**.
Mic  4: 3 and their **s** into pruning hooks.

## SPECIAL
Nu  6: 2 or woman wants to make a **s** vow,
Dt  12: 6 your tithes and **s** gifts, what you
Ro  14: 6 who regard one day as **s** do so
Gal  4:10 You are observing **s** days
Jas  2: 3 If you show **s** attention to the one

## SPECK
Mt  7: 4 'Let me take the **s** out of your eye,'

## SPECTACLE
1Co  4: 9 We have been made a **s** to the whole
Col  2:15 he made a public **s** of them,

## SPEECH
Ge  11: 1 had one language and a common **s**.
Ex  4:10 I am slow of **s** and tongue."
Ps  19: 2 Day after day they pour forth **s**;
    19: 3 They have no **s**, they use no words;
Jn  10: 6 Jesus used this figure of **s**,
2Co  8: 7 in faith, in **s**, in knowledge,
1Ti  4:12 set an example for the believers in **s**,

## SPEED* [SPEEDILY]
Ro  9:28 out his sentence on earth with **s**
2Pe  3:12 to the day of God and **s** its coming.

## SPEEDILY [SPEED]
Isa  51: 5 My righteousness draws near **s**,

## SPELL* [SPELLS]
Rev  18:23 your magic **s** all the nations were

## SPELLS [SPELL]
Dt  18:11 or casts **s**, or who is a medium
Mic  5:12 and you will no longer cast **s**.

## SPEND [SPENT]
Ge  19: 2 "we will **s** the night in the square."
Jdg  19:20 Only don't **s** the night
Pr  31: 3 Do not **s** your strength on women,
Isa  55: 2 Why **s** money on what is not bread,
2Co  12:15 So I will very gladly **s** for you

## SPENT [SPEND]
Pr  5:11 when your flesh and body are **s**.
Mk  5:26 many doctors and had **s** all she had,
Lk  6:12 and **s** the night praying to God.
    15:14 After he had **s** everything, there was

## SPICES
Ex  25: 6 **s** for the anointing oil
1Ki  10:10 large quantities of **s**,
Mt  23:23 You give a tenth of your **s**—
Jn  19:40 it, with the **s**, in strips of linen.

## SPIED [SPY]
Jos  6:22 the two men who had **s** out the land,

## SPIES [SPY]
Ge  42: 9 them and said to them, "You are **s**!
Jos  6:17 because she hid the **s** we sent.
Heb  11:31 because she welcomed the **s**,
Jas  2:25 did when she gave lodging to the **s**

## SPIN
Mt  6:28 They do not labor or **s**.

## SPIRIT [SPIRIT'S, SPIRITIST, SPIRITISTS, SPIRITS, SPIRITUAL]
Ge  1: 2 the **S** of God was hovering over
    6: 3 "My **S** will not contend with human
Ex  31: 3 I have filled him with the **S** of God,
Nu  11:25 the power of the **S** that was on him
    11:25 When the **S** rested on them,
    16:22 "O God, God of every human **s**,
    24: 2 by tribe, the **S** of God came on him
    27:16 the God of every human **s**,
Dt  34: 9 the **s** of wisdom because Moses had
Jdg  6:34 Then the **S** of the LORD came
    11:29 Then the **S** of the LORD came
    13:25 the **S** of the LORD began to stir
    14: 6 The **S** of the LORD came on him
    15:14 The **S** of the LORD came on him
1Sa  10: 6 The **S** of the LORD will come
    16:13 day on the **S** of the LORD came
    16:14 Now the **S** of the LORD had
    16:15 an evil **s** from God is tormenting
    28: 8 "Consult a **s** for me," he said,
2Sa  23: 2 "The **S** of the LORD spoke
2Ki  2: 9 inherit a double portion of your **s**,"
    2:15 said, "The **s** of Elijah is resting
2Ch  18:21 be a lying **s** in the mouths of all his
Ne  9:20 You gave your good **S** to instruct
Job  33: 4 The **S** of God has made me;
Ps  31: 5 Into your hands I commit my **s**;
    34:18 saves those who are crushed in **s**.
    51:10 and renew a steadfast **s** within me.
    51:11 or take your Holy **S** from me.
    51:17 My sacrifice, O God, is a broken **s**;
    106:33 they rebelled against the **S** of God,
    139: 7 Where can I go from your **S**?
    143:10 may your good **S** lead me on level
Pr  16:18 a haughty **s** before a fall.
    20:27 The human **s** is the lamp
    29:23 low, but the lowly in **s** gain honor.
Ecc  12: 7 the **s** returns to God who gave it.
Isa  11: 2 The **S** of the LORD will rest
    30: 1 but not by my **S**, heaping sin
    32:15 till the **S** is poured on us
    40:13 fathom the **S** of the LORD,
    42: 1 I will put my **S** on him, and he will
    44: 3 pour out my **S** on your offspring,
    48:16 has sent me, endowed with his **S**.
    57:15 who are contrite and lowly in **s**,

Isa 59:21 "My **S**, who is on you, and my
61: 1 The **S** of the Sovereign LORD is
63:10 rebelled and grieved his Holy **S**.
Eze 3:12 Then the **S** lifted me up, and I heard
11:19 heart and put a new **s** in them;
13: 3 prophets who follow their own **s**
36:26 a new heart and put a new **s** in you;
Da 4: 8 and the **s** of the holy gods is in him.)
Joel 2:28 I will pour out my **S** on all people.
Zec 4: 6 but by my **S**,' says the LORD
Mt 1:18 to be pregnant through the Holy **S**.
3:11 IIe will baptize you with the Holy **S**
3:16 he saw the **S** of God descending like
4: 1 was led by the **S** into the wilderness
5: 3 "Blessed are the poor in **s**, for theirs
10:20 but the **S** of your Father speaking
12:31 blasphemy against the **S** will not be
26:41 The **s** is willing, but the flesh is
28:19 and of the Son and of the Holy **S**,
Mk 1: 8 will baptize you with the Holy **S**."
Lk 1:15 the Holy **S** even before he is born.
1:35 "The Holy **S** will come on you,
1:80 child grew and became strong in **s**;
3:16 He will baptize you with the Holy **S**
4: 1 full of the Holy **S**, left the Jordan
4:18 "The **S** of the Lord is on me,
11:13 in heaven give the Holy **S** to those
23:46 into your hands I commit my **s**."
Jn 1:33 on whom you see the **S** come down
1·33 who will baptize with the Holy **S**.'
3: 5 being born of water and the **S**.
3: 6 to flesh, but the **S** gives birth to **s**.
3:34 for God gives the **S** without limit.
4:24 God is **s**, and his worshipers must
4:24 worshipers must worship in the **S**
6:63 The **S** gives life;
7:39 By this he meant the **S**,
14:17 the **S** of truth. The world cannot
14:26 the Holy **S**, whom the Father will
15:26 the **S** of truth who goes
16:13 But when he, the **S** of truth, comes,
20:22 and said, "Receive the Holy **S**.
Ac 1: 5 will be baptized with the Holy **S**."
1: 8 when the Holy **S** comes on you;
2: 4 of them were filled with the Holy **S**
2:17 I will pour out my **S** on all people.
2:38 will receive the gift of the Holy **S**.
4:31 they were all filled with the Holy **S**
5: 3 that you have lied to the Holy **S**
6: 3 who are known to be full of the **S**
7:51 You always resist the Holy **S**!
8:15 that they might receive the Holy **S**,
9:17 and be filled with the Holy **S**."
11:16 will be baptized with the Holy **S**.'
13: 2 the Holy **S** said, "Set apart for me
19: 2 "Did you receive the Holy **S**
19: 2 even heard that there is a Holy **S**."
Ro 1: 9 I serve in my **s** in preaching the gospel
7: 6 we serve in the new way of the **S**,
8: 4 sinful nature but according to the **S**.
8: 5 minds set on what the **S** desires.
8: 9 if anyone does not have the **S**
8:13 but if by the **S** you put to death
8:15 the **S** you received brought
8:16 The **S** himself testifies with our **s**
8:23 who have the firstfruits of the **S**,
8:26 the **S** helps us in our weakness.

1Co 2:10 The **S** searches all things,
2:14 person without the **S** does not accept
2:14 things that come from the **S** of God
5: 3 present, I am with you in **s**.
6:17 with the Lord is one with him in **s**.
6:19 bodies are temples of the Holy **S**,
12: 1 Now about the gifts of the **S**,
12: 4 but the same **S** distributes them.
12:13 we were all baptized by one **S**
14:37 or otherwise gifted by the **S**,
2Co 1:22 put his **S** in our hearts as a deposit,
3: 3 ink but with the **S** of the living God,
3: 6 but the **S** gives life.
3:17 Now the Lord is the **S**,
5: 5 who has given us the **S** as a deposit,
7: 1 that contaminates body and **s**,
Gal 3: 2 Did you receive the **S** by observing
3:14 might receive the promise of the **S**.
5:16 say, walk by the **S**, and you will not
5:22 But the fruit of the **S** is love, joy,
5:25 let us keep in step with the **S**.
6: 1 who live by the **S** should restore
6: 8 those who sow to please the **S**,
Eph 1:13 with a seal, the promised Holy **S**,
2:18 have access to the Father by one **S**.
2:22 in which God lives by his **S**.
4: 3 the unity of the **S** through the bond
4: 4 There is one body and one **S**, just as
4:30 do not grieve the Holy **S** of God,
5·18 Instead, be filled with the **S**,
5:19 hymns and songs from the **S**.
6:17 of salvation and the sword of the **S**,
Php 2: 2 being one in **s** and of one mind.
Col 1: 9 and understanding that the **S** gives,
2: 5 body, I am present with you in **s**
3:16 psalms, hymns and songs from the **S**,
1Th 5:23 May your whole **s**, soul and body be
2Th 2:13 the sanctifying work of the **S**
1Ti 3:16 was vindicated by the **S**, was seen
2Ti 1: 7 the **S** God gave us does not make us
4:22 The Lord be with your **s**.
Heb 2: 4 of the Holy **S** distributed according
4:12 even to dividing soul and **s**,
6: 4 gift, who have shared in the Holy **S**,
10:29 who have insulted the **S** of grace?
1Pe 1: 2 the sanctifying work of the **S**, to be
3: 4 beauty of a gentle and quiet **s**,
2Pe 1:21 were carried along by the Holy **S**.
1Jn 3:24 We know it by the **S** he gave us.
4: 1 do not believe every **s**, but test
4:13 he in us: He has given us of his **S**.
Jude 1:20 holy faith and praying in the Holy **S**,
Rev 1:10 On the Lord's Day I was in the **S**,
2: 7 let them hear what the **S** says
4: 2 At once I was in the **S**, and there

## EVIL SPIRIT See EVIL

## HOLY SPIRIT See HOLY

## MY SPIRIT Ge 6:3; 2Ki 5:26; Job 6:4; 7:11;
10:12; 17:1; Ps 31:5; 73:21; 77:3, 6; 142:3;
143:4, 7; Isa 26:9; 30:1; 38:16; 42:1; 44:3; 59:21;
La 1:16; Eze 3:14; 36:27; 37:14; 39:29; Joel
2:28, 29; Hag 2:5; Zec 4:6; 6:8; Mt 12:18; Lk
1:47; 23:46; Ac 2:17, 18; 7:59; Ro 1:9; 1Co
14:14, 15, 15; 16:18

## SPIRIT OF GOD Ge 1:2; 41:38; Ex 31:3;
35:31; Nu 24:2; 1Sa 10:10; 11:6; 19:20, 23; 2Ch
15:1; 24:20; Job 33:4; Ps 106:33; Eze 11:24; Mt
3:16; 12:28; Ro 8:9, 14; 15:19; 1Co 2:11, 14;
7:40; 12:3; Eph 4:30; 1Jn 4:2

## SPIRIT OF THE †LORD Jdg 3:10; 6:34;
11:29; 13:25; 14:6, 19; 15:14; 1Sa 10:6; 16:13,
14; 2Sa 23:2; 1Ki 18:12; 2Ki 2:16; 2Ch 20:14;
Isa 11:2; 40:13; 63:14; Eze 11:5; 37:1; Mic 3:8

## SPIRIT'S* [SPIRIT]
1Co  2: 4  a demonstration of the S power,
1Th  5:19  Do not put out the S fire.

## SPIRITIST* [SPIRIT]
Lev 20:27  s among you must be put to death.
Dt  18:11  or who is a medium or s or who

## SPIRITISTS [SPIRIT]
Lev 19:31  not turn to mediums or seek out s,
1Sa 28: 3  the mediums and s from the land.
2Ki 23:24  Josiah got rid of the mediums and s,

## SPIRITS [SPIRIT]
Ru   3: 7  and drinking and was in good s,
Ps  78: 8  whose s were not faithful to him.
Mt  12:45  it seven other s more wicked than
Lk   4:36  power he gives orders to evil s
Ac   8: 7  shrieks, evil s came out of many,
1Co 12:10  to another distinguishing between s,
    14:32  The s of prophets are subject
Heb  1: 7  "He makes his angels s,
    12: 9  should we submit to the Father of s
1Pe  3:19  proclamation to the imprisoned s—
1Jn  4: 1  but test the s to see whether they are
Rev  1: 4  from the seven s before his throne,
    16:13  I saw three evil s that looked like

## EVIL SPIRITS See EVIL

## SPIRITUAL [SPIRIT]
Ro   1:11  to you some s gift to make you
     7:14  We know that the law is s; but I am
    12:11  but keep your s fervor,
    15:27  have shared in the Jews' blessings,
1Co  2:13  the Spirit, explaining s realities
     3: 1  I could not address you as s but as
     9:11  If we have sown s seed among you,
    10: 3  They all ate the same s food
    14: 1  of love and eagerly desire s gifts,
    15:44  it is raised a s body.
Eph  1: 3  realms with every s blessing
     6:12  against the s forces of evil
1Pe  2: 2  crave pure s milk, so that by it you
     2: 5  are being built into a s house to be
     2: 5  offering s sacrifices acceptable

## SPIT
Dt  25: 9  of his sandals, s in his face and say,
Mt  27:30  They s on him, and took the staff
Mk  14:65  Then some began to s at him;
Lk  18:32  mock him, insult him and s on him;
Rev  3:16  I am about to s you out of my

## SPLASH
Ex  29:16  blood and s it against the sides

## SPLENDOR
1Ch 16:29  the LORD in the s of his holiness.
    29:11  the glory and the majesty and the s,
Job 37:22  of the north he comes in golden s;
Ps  21: 5  you have bestowed on him s
    29: 2  the LORD in the s of his holiness.
    45: 3  clothe yourself with s and majesty.
    96: 6  S and majesty are before him;
    96: 9  the LORD in the s of his holiness;
   104: 1  you are clothed with s and majesty.
   110: 3  Arrayed in holy s,
   145: 5  of the glorious s of your majesty—
   145:12  and the glorious s of your kingdom.
   148:13  his s is above the earth
Pr  16:31  Gray hair is a crown of s;
    20:29  strength, gray hair the s of the old.
Isa  2:10  LORD and the s of his majesty!
    49: 3  in whom I will display my s."
    55: 5  for he has endowed you with s."
    60:21  my hands, for the display of my s.
    61: 3  the LORD for the display of his s.
    62: 3  You will be a crown of s
    63: 1  robed in s, striding forward
Hos 14: 6  His s will be like an olive tree,
Hab  3: 4  His s was like the sunrise;
Mt   6:29  in all his s was dressed like one
Lk   9:31  appeared in glorious s,
2Th  2: 8  and destroy by the s of his coming.
Rev 21:24  of the earth will bring their s into it.

## SPLINTERED
2Ki 18:21  on Egypt, that s reed of a staff,

## SPLIT
Nu  16:31  this, the ground under them s apart
1Ki 13: 3  The altar will be s apart
    16:21  of Israel were s into two factions;
Ps  74:13  It was you who s open the sea
Zec 14: 4  the Mount of Olives will be s in two
Mt  27:51  The earth shook, the rocks s
Rev 16:19  The great city s into three parts,

## SPOIL [SPOILS]
Ps 119:162  promise like one who finds great s.
1Pe  1: 4  that can never perish, s or fade.

## SPOILS [SPOIL]
Ex  15: 9  I will divide the s; I will gorge
Nu  31:27  Divide the s equally between
Isa 53:12  he will divide the s with the strong,
Jn   6:27  Do not work for food that s,

## SPOKE [SPEAK]
Ge  16:13  name to the LORD who s to her:
    39:10  though she s to Joseph day
Ex  20: 1  And God s all these words:
Nu   3: 1  the LORD s to Moses on Mount Sinai.
    23: 7  Then Balaam s his message:
Dt   4:12  the LORD s to you out of the fire.
     5: 4  The LORD s to you face to face
1Ki  4:32  He s three thousand proverbs
     4:33  He also s about animals and birds,

Job 42: 3 Surely I s of things I did not
Ps   99: 7 He s to them from the pillar
Jer 35:17 I s to them, but they did not listen;
Mt   9:33 out, the man who had been mute s.
Mk   4:33 similar parables Jesus s the word
Jn   8:30 Even as he s, many put their faith
Heb  1: 1 In the past God s to our ancestors
     13: 7 who s the word of God to you.
2Pe  1:21 s from God as they were carried

## SPOKEN [SPEAK]
Ex  34:29 face was radiant because he had s
Nu  12: 2 "Has the LORD s only through
Dt  18:22 is a message the LORD has not s.
Ezr  1: 1 word of the LORD s by Jeremiah,
Job 42: 7 because you have not s of me what
Ps  60: 6 God has s from his sanctuary:
Isa 45:19 I have not s in secret,
Lk  20:19 knew he had s this parable against
Jn   2:21 the temple he had s of was his body.
Ac   2: 6 their own language being s.
Heb  1: 2 in these last days he has s to us

## SPONGE
Mk  15:36 ran, filled a s with wine vinegar,
Jn  19:29 put the s on a stalk of the hyssop

## SPOT [SPOTLESS, SPOTS, SPOTTED]
Isa 28: 8 and there is not a s without filth.
    46: 7 From that s it cannot move.
1Ti  6:14 to keep this command without s

## SPOTLESS* [SPOT]
Da  11:35 and made s until the time of the end,
    12:10 will be purified, made s and refined,
2Pe  3:14 make every effort to be found s,

## SPOTS [SPOT]
Jer 13:23 change his skin or a leopard its s?

## SPOTTED [SPOT]
Ge  30:32 them every speckled or s sheep,

## SPRANG* [SPRING]
Jnh  4:10 It s up overnight and died overnight.
Mt  13: 5 It s up quickly, because the soil was
Mk   4: 5 It s up quickly, because the soil was
Ro   7: 9 came, sin s to life and I died.

## SPREAD [SPREADING, SPREADS]
Ge  10:32 these the nations s out over the earth
Ex  23: 1 "Do not s false reports. Do not help
    37: 9 cherubim had their wings s upward,
1Ch 14:17 So David's fame s throughout every
Ps   5:11 S your protection over them,
    78:19 "Can God really s a table
   143: 6 I s out my hands to you; I thirst
Pr  15: 7 The lips of the wise s knowledge,
Isa 48:13 my right hand s out the heavens;
Lk  19:36 people s their cloaks on the road.
Jn  21:23 the rumor s among the believers
Ac   6: 7 So the word of God s.
    12:24 of God continued to increase and s.
    13:49 of the Lord s through the whole
    19:20 way the word of the Lord s widely

2Co  2:14 s the aroma of the knowledge of him
2Th  3: 1 message of the Lord may s rapidly
2Ti  2:17 Their teaching will s like gangrene.

## SPREADING [SPREAD]
1Sa  2:24 report I hear s among the LORD's
1Ki  8:38 and s out their hands toward this
Pr  29: 5 who flatter their neighbors are s nets
Jer  2:20 under every s tree you lay down as
    17: 2 Asherah poles beside the s trees
Eze  1:11 They each had two wings s
1Th  3: 2 in God's service in s the gospel

## SPREADS [SPREAD]
Job 36:29 Who can understand how he s
Pr  10:18 lying lips and s slander is a fool.

## SPRING [SPRANG, SPRINGS, SPRINGTIME]
Ge  16: 7 the LORD found Hagar near a s
Dt  11:14 both autumn and s rains, so that you
Ecc  4: 4 all achievement s from one person's
Isa 45: 8 let salvation s up, let righteousness
    58:11 like a s whose waters never fail.
Jer  2:13 forsaken me, the s of living water,
     9: 1 that my head were a s of water
    17:13 the LORD, the s of living water.
Jn   4:14 become in them a s of water welling
Ro  15:12 "The Root of Jesse will s up,
Jas  3:12 can a salt s produce fresh water
Rev 21: 6 without cost from the s of the water

## SPRINGS [SPRING]
Ge   7:11 day all the s of the great deep burst
Ps  114: 8 a pool, the hard rock into s of water.
Pr   5:16 Should your s overflow
Isa 49:10 and lead them beside s of water.
2Pe  2:17 These people are s without water
Rev  7:17 'he will lead them to s of living

## SPRINGTIME* [SPRING]
Zec 10: 1 Ask the LORD for rain in the s;

## SPRINKLE [SPRINKLED]
Lev 16:14 with his finger s it on the front
Nu   8: 7 S the water of cleansing on them;
Isa 52:15 so he will s many nations, and kings
Eze 36:25 I will s clean water on you, and you

## SPRINKLED [SPRINKLE]
Heb 10:22 having our hearts s to cleanse us
1Pe  1: 2 Jesus Christ and s with his blood:

## SPROUT
Nu  17: 5 to the man I choose will s, and I will
Pr  23: 5 for they will surely s wings and fly
Jer 33:15 I will make a righteous Branch s

## SPUR*
Heb 10:24 consider how we may s one another

## SPURNED [SPURNS]
Pr   1:30 accept my advice and s my rebuke,
Isa  1: 4 they have s the Holy One of Israel

La    2: 6  his fierce anger he has **s** both king

## SPURNS* [SPURNED]
Pr   15: 5  A fool **s** a parent's discipline,

## SPY [SPIED, SPIES, SPYING]
Dt    1:22  "Let us send men ahead to **s**
Jos   2: 2  have come here tonight to **s**
Gal   2: 4  had infiltrated our ranks to **s**

## SPYING [SPY]
Ge   42:30  treated us as though we were **s**

## SQUANDERED [SQUANDERS]
Lk   15:13  and there **s** his wealth in wild living.

## SQUANDERS* [SQUANDERED]
Pr   29: 3  of prostitutes **s** his wealth.

## SQUARE [SQUARES]
Ge   19: 2  "we will spend the night in the **s**."
Ex   27: 1  it is to be **s**, five cubits long and five
     28:16  It is to be **s**—a span long and a span
     30: 2  It is to be **s**, a cubit long and a cubit
Jdg  19:20  don't spend the night in the **s**."
Ne    8: 1  in the **s** before the Water Gate.
Pr    1:20  raises her voice in the public **s**;
Rev  21:16  The city was laid out like a **s**,

## SQUARES [SQUARE]
Pr    7:12  now in the street, now in the **s**,

## STABILITY*
Pr   29: 4  By justice a king gives a country **s**,

## STAFF [STAFFS]
Ge   38:25  seal and cord and **s** these are."
     49:10  nor the ruler's **s** from between his
Ex    4: 4  it turned back into a **s** in his hand.
      7:12  Aaron's **s** swallowed up their staffs.
     14:16  Raise your **s** and stretch out your
Nu   17: 6  and Aaron's **s** was among them.
     20:11  and struck the rock twice with his **s**.
Ps   23: 4  your rod and your **s**, they comfort
Mic   7:14  Shepherd your people with your **s**,
Zec  11:10  I took my **s** called Favor and broke
Mt   27:48  wine vinegar, put it on a **s**,
Mk   15:19  they struck him on the head with a **s**
Heb   9: 4  manna, Aaron's **s** that had budded,

## STAFFS [STAFF]
Ex    7:12  Aaron's staff swallowed up their **s**.
Nu   17: 7  Moses placed the **s** before

## STAGES
Nu   33: 1  Here are the **s** in the journey

## STAGGER [STAGGERED, STAGGERS]
Ps   60: 3  have given us wine that makes us **s**.
Isa  28: 7  these also **s** from wine and reel
     29: 9  but not from wine, **s**, but not
Jer  25:16  they will **s** and go mad because
Am    8:12  People will **s** from sea to sea

## STAGGERED [STAGGER]
Ps  107:27  They reeled and **s** like drunkards;

## STAGGERS* [STAGGER]
Isa   3: 8  Jerusalem **s**, Judah is falling;

## STAIN* [STAINED]
Jer   2:22  the **s** of your guilt is still before
Eph   5:27  without **s** or wrinkle or any other

## STAINED [STAIN]
Isa  63: 1  with his garments **s** crimson?
Jude  1:23  hating even the clothing **s**

## STAIRWAY
Ge   28:12  he saw a **s** resting on the earth,
2Ki  20:11  it had gone down on the **s** of Ahaz.

## STAKES
Isa  54: 2  your cords, strengthen your **s**.

## STALK [STALKS]
Ge   41: 5  good, were growing on a single **s**.
Jn   19:29  sponge on a **s** of the hyssop plant,

## STALKS* [STALK]
Jos   2: 6  hidden them under the **s** of flax she
Ru    2:16  Even pull out some **s** for her
Ps   91: 6  nor the pestilence that **s**

## STALL [STALLS]
Ps   50: 9  I have no need of a bull from your **s**

## STALLS [STALL]
1Ki   4:26  Solomon had four thousand **s**
Hab   3:17  in the pen and no cattle in the **s**,

## STAND [STANDING, STANDS, STOOD]
Ex    9:11  magicians could not **s** before Moses
     14:13  **S** firm and you will see
Lev  19:32  " '**S** up in the presence of the aged,
     26:37  be able to **s** before your enemies.
Nu   30: 4  which she obligated herself will **s**.
Dt   10: 8  to **s** before the LORD to minister
     11:25  No one will be able to **s** against you.
Jos   3: 8  waters, go and **s** in the river.' "
     10:12  "Sun, **s** still over Gibeon, and you,
2Ch  20:17  **s** firm and see the deliverance
Job  19:25  that in the end he will **s** on the earth.
Ps    1: 1  or **s** in the way that sinners take
      1: 5  Therefore the wicked will not **s**
     10: 1  Why, LORD, do you **s** far off?
     24: 3  Who may **s** in his holy place?
     33:11  plans of the LORD **s** firm forever,
     40: 2  rock and gave me a firm place to **s**.
     76: 7  Who can **s** before you when you are
     78:13  made the water **s** up like a wall.
     93: 5  Your statutes, LORD, **s** firm;
    119:120  fear of you; I **s** in awe of your laws.
    130: 3  a record of sins, Lord, who could **s**?
Pr   10:25  but the righteous **s** firm forever.
Isa   7: 9  If you do not **s** firm in your faith,
     11:10  the Root of Jesse will **s** as a banner

Isa  29:23  will **s** in awe of the God of Israel.
Jer  15: 1  and Samuel were to **s** before me,
Eze  22:30  **s** before me in the gap on behalf
Mic   5: 4  He will **s** and shepherd his flock
Hab   3: 2  I **s** in awe of your deeds, LORD.
Zec  14: 4  that day his feet will **s** on the Mount
Mal   3: 2  Who can **s** when he appears?
Mt   10:22  who **s** firm to the end will be saved.
     12:25  divided against itself will not **s**.
Lk    4: 9  had him **s** on the highest point
     21:19  S firm, and you will win life.
Ac   11.17  to think that I could **s** in God's way?"
Ro    5: 2  into this grace in which we now **s**.
     14: 4  for the Lord is able to make them **s**.
     14:10  we will all **s** before God's judgment
1Co  15:58  my dear brothers and sisters, **s** firm.
     16:13  on your guard; **s** firm in the faith;
2Co   1:24  joy, because it is by faith you **s** firm.
Gal   5: 1  S firm, then, and do not let
Eph   6:11  can take your **s** against the devil's
Col   4:12  that you may **s** firm in all the will
2Th   2:15  **s** firm and hold fast to the teachings
Jas   5: 8  be patient and **s** firm,
Rev   3:20  I **s** at the door and knock.

## STANDARD  [STANDARDS]
Nu    1:52  in their own camp under their **s**.

## STANDARDS  [STANDARD]
Lev  19:35  " 'Do not use dishonest **s**
Nu    2:34  way they encamped under their **s**,
Eze   7:27  by their own **s** I will judge them.

## STANDING  [STAND]
Ge   18:22  but Abraham remained **s** before
Ex    3: 5  where you are **s** is holy ground."
Nu   22:23  angel of the LORD **s** in the road
Jos   4:10  who carried the ark remained **s**
      5:15  the place where you are **s** is holy."
Ru    2: 1  side, a man of **s** from the clan
      4:11  May you have **s** in Ephrathah
2Ch  18:18  all the host of heaven **s** on his right
Eze   3:23  the glory of the LORD was **s** there,
Am    7: 7  The Lord was **s** by a wall that had
      9: 1  I saw the Lord **s** by the altar, and he
Zec   1: 8  He was **s** among the myrtle trees
      3: 1  Satan **s** at his right side to accuse
Mt    6: 5  love to pray **s** in the synagogues
Lk    9:32  glory and the two men **s** with him.
Ac    7:55  and Jesus **s** at the right hand of God.
1Co  10:12  So, if you think you are **s** firm,
1Ti   3:13  have served well gain an excellent **s**
Jas   5: 9  The Judge is **s** at the door!
1Pe   5: 9  Resist him, **s** firm in the faith,
Rev   7: 9  **s** before the throne and in front
     20:12  great and small, **s** before the throne,

## STANDS  [STAND]
1Ki   7:27  also made ten movable **s** of bronze;
2Ki  25:13  the movable **s** and the bronze Sea
Ps   89: 2  that your love **s** firm forever,
    119:89  it **s** firm in the heavens.
Pr   12: 7  the house of the righteous **s** firm.
Jn    1:26  among you **s** one you do not know.
     16:11  of this world now **s** condemned.
2Ti   2:19  God's solid foundation **s** firm,

Heb   4: 1  promise of entering his rest still **s**,

## STAR  [STARGAZERS, STARRY, STARS]
Nu   24:17  A **s** will come out of Jacob;
Isa  14:12  heaven, morning **s**, son of the dawn!
Mt    2: 2  We saw his **s** when it rose and have
2Pe   1:19  the morning **s** rises in your hearts.
Rev   2:28  I will also give them the morning **s**.
      8:11  the name of the **s** is Wormwood.
      9: 1  The **s** was given the key to the shaft
     22:16  David, and the bright Morning S."

## STARGAZERS*  [STAR]
Isa  47:13  those **s** who make predictions

## STARRY  [STAR]
2Ki  17:16  They bowed down to all the **s** hosts,
Isa  40:26  He who brings out the **s** host one
Da    8:10  it threw some of the **s** host down

## STARS  [STAR]
Ge    1:16  He also made the **s**.
     15: 5  up at the heavens and count the **s**—
     37: 9  eleven **s** were bowing down to me."
Dt    1:10  today you are as many as the **s**
Job  38: 7  while the morning **s** sang together
Ps  148: 3  praise him, all you shining **s**.
Isa  14:13  raise my throne above the **s** of God;
Da   12: 3  like the **s** for ever and ever.
Joel  2:10  darkened, and the **s** no longer shine.
Mk   13:25  the **s** will fall from the sky,
Php   2:15  you will shine among them like **s**
Rev   1:16  In his right hand he held seven **s**,
      6:13  and the **s** in the sky fell to earth,
      8:12  and a third of the **s**, so that a third
     12: 1  a crown of twelve **s** on her head.
     12: 4  Its tail swept a third of the **s**

## START
Ne    2:18  They replied, "Let us **s** rebuilding."
Pr   22: 6  S children off on the way they should go

## STARVE  [STARVING]
Ex   16: 3  this desert to **s** this entire assembly

## STARVING  [STARVE]
Pr    6:30  to satisfy his hunger when he is **s**.
Lk   15:17  to spare, and here I am **s** to death!

## STATE  [STATEMENTS]
Job  23: 4  I would **s** my case before him
Isa  43:26  **s** the case for your innocence.
Lk    1:48  of the humble **s** of his servant.

## STATEMENTS*  [STATE]
Mk   14:56  him, but their **s** did not agree.

## STATUE
Da    2:31  there before you stood a large **s**—

## STATURE*
1Sa   2:26  boy Samuel continued to grow in **s**
SS    7: 7  Your **s** is like that of the palm,

## STATUTES

| | | |
|---|---|---|
| Ps | 19: 7 | The s of the LORD are |
| | 93: 5 | Your s, LORD, stand firm; |
| | 119: 2 | Blessed are those who keep his s |
| | 119:14 | in following your s as one rejoices |
| | 119:24 | Your s are my delight; they are my |
| | 119:36 | Turn my heart toward your s |
| | 119:99 | teachers, for I meditate on your s. |
| | 119:111 | Your s are my heritage forever; |
| | 119:125 | that I may understand your s. |
| | 119:129 | Your s are wonderful; |
| | 119:138 | The s you have laid down are |
| | 119:152 | your s that you established them |
| | 119:167 | I obey your s, for I love them |
| Isa | 24: 5 | laws, violated the s and broken |

## STAY [STAYED]

| | | |
|---|---|---|
| Ge | 13: 6 | that they were not able to s together. |
| Ex | 16:29 | Everyone is to s where they are |
| Pr | 7:11 | defiant, her feet never s at home; |
| | 14: 7 | S away from the foolish, for you |
| Mic | 7:18 | You do not s angry forever |
| Mk | 14:34 | "S here and keep watch." |

## STAYED [STAY]

| | | |
|---|---|---|
| Ex | 24:18 | And he s on the mountain forty days |
| Nu | 9:18 | as the cloud s over the tabernacle, |
| Lk | 2:43 | the boy Jesus s behind in Jerusalem, |

## STEADFAST* [STEADFASTLY]

| | | |
|---|---|---|
| Ps | 51:10 | God, and renew a s spirit within me. |
| | 57: 7 | My heart, O God, is s, my heart is s; |
| | 108: 1 | My heart, O God, is s; I will sing |
| | 112: 7 | their hearts are s, |
| | 119: 5 | my ways were s in obeying your |
| Pr | 4:26 | and be s in all your ways. |
| Isa | 26: 3 | peace those whose minds are s, |
| 1Pe | 5:10 | and make you strong, firm and s. |

## STEADFASTLY* [STEADFAST]

| | | |
|---|---|---|
| 2Ch | 27: 6 | because he walked s before |

## STEADY

| | | |
|---|---|---|
| Ex | 17:12 | that his hands remained s till sunset. |
| 1Ch | 13: 9 | reached out his hand to s the ark, |
| Isa | 35: 3 | hands, s the knees that give way; |

## STEAL [STEALING, STEALS, STOLE, STOLEN]

| | | |
|---|---|---|
| Ex | 20:15 | "You shall not s. |
| Lev | 19:11 | " 'Do not s. " 'Do not lie. |
| Dt | 5:19 | "You shall not s. |
| Jer | 23:30 | "I am against the prophets who s |
| Mt | 6:19 | and where thieves break in and s. |
| | 19:18 | you shall not s, you shall not give |
| Jn | 10:10 | The thief comes only to s and kill |
| Ro | 13: 9 | "You shall not s," "You shall not |
| Eph | 4:28 | have been stealing must s no longer, |

## STEALING [STEAL]

| | | |
|---|---|---|
| Ro | 2:21 | You who preach against s, do you |

## STEALS [STEAL]

| | | |
|---|---|---|
| Ex | 22: 3 | "Anyone who s must certainly |

## STEEL (KJV) See BRONZE

| | | |
|---|---|---|
| Pr | 6:30 | a thief if he s to satisfy his hunger |

## STEERED*

| | | |
|---|---|---|
| Jas | 3: 4 | they are s by a very small rudder |

## STEP [FOOTSTEPS, STEPS]

| | | |
|---|---|---|
| Ps | 1: 1 | those who do not walk in s with the wicked |
| Job | 34:21 | he sees their every s. |
| Gal | 5:25 | let us keep in s with the Spirit. |

## STEPHEN*

Deacon (Ac 6:5). Arrested (Ac 6:8–15). Speech to Sanhedrin (Ac 7). Stoned (Ac 7:54–60; 8:2; 11:19; 22:20).

## STEPS [STEP]

| | | |
|---|---|---|
| Ex | 20:26 | And do not go up to my altar on s, |
| 2Ki | 20: 9 | Shall the shadow go forward ten s, |
| Ps | 37:23 | The LORD makes firm the s |
| Pr | 5: 5 | her s lead straight to the grave. |
| | 14:15 | the prudent give thought to their s. |
| | 16: 9 | but the LORD establishes their s. |
| | 20:24 | A person's s are directed |
| Jer | 10:23 | it is not for them to direct their s. |
| 1Pe | 2:21 | that you should follow in his s. |

## STERN [STERNNESS]

| | | |
|---|---|---|
| Pr | 15:10 | S discipline awaits those who leave |

## STERNNESS* [STERN]

| | | |
|---|---|---|
| Ro | 11:22 | Consider therefore the kindness and s of God: s to those who fell, |

## STEW

| | | |
|---|---|---|
| Ge | 25:29 | when Jacob was cooking some s, |
| 2Ki | 4:39 | he cut them up into the pot of s, |

## STEWARDS

| | | |
|---|---|---|
| 1Pe | 4:10 | as faithful s of God's grace |

## STICK [STICKS]

| | | |
|---|---|---|
| 2Ki | 6: 6 | Elisha cut a s and threw it there, |
| Eze | 37:16 | take a s of wood and write on it, |
| Hos | 4:12 | and are answered by a s of wood. |
| Am | 4:11 | You were like a burning s snatched |
| Zec | 3: 2 | Is not this man a burning s snatched |

## STICKS [STICK]

| | | |
|---|---|---|
| Pr | 18:24 | there is a friend who s closer than |

## STIFF-NECKED [NECK]

| | | |
|---|---|---|
| Ex | 32: 9 | to Moses, "and they are a s people. |
| | 34: 9 | Although this is a s people, |
| 2Ki | 17:14 | and were as s as their ancestors, |
| Pr | 29: 1 | Whoever remains s after many |
| Ac | 7:51 | "You s people! Your hearts |

## STILL [STILLED]

| | | |
|---|---|---|
| Ge | 9: 4 | eat meat that has its lifeblood s in it. |
| Ex | 14:14 | you need only to be s." |

Lev 19:26 eat any meat with the blood s in it.
Jos 10:13 So the sun stood s, and the moon
Ps  37: 7 Be s before the LORD and wait
    46:10 "Be s, and know that I am God;
    89: 9 its waves mount up, you s them.
Da  11:35 it will s come at the appointed time.
Hab  3:11 moon stood s in the heavens
Zec  2:13 Be s before the LORD, all people,
Mk   4:39 Be s!" Then the wind died down
     8:17 Do you s not see or understand?
Jn  12:37 they s would not believe in him.
Ro   5: 8 While we were s sinners,
Heb 11: 4 And by faith Abel s speaks,

## STILLED [STILL]

Ps  65: 7 who s the roaring of the seas,

## STIMULATE*

2Pe  3: 1 of them as reminders to s you

## STING

1Co 15:55 Where, O death, is your s?"
Rev  9: 5 that of the s of a scorpion when it

## STINGY*

Pr  28:22 The s are eager to get rich and are

## STIPULATIONS

Dt   6:20 you, "What is the meaning of the s,
Jer 44:23 his law or his decrees or his s,

## STIR [STIRRED, STIRRING, STIRS]

Pr  15:18 The hot-tempered s up dissension,
    16:28 The perverse s up dissension,
    28:25 The greedy s up dissension,

## STIRRED [STIR]

1Ki 14:22 the sins they committed they s
Ps  45: 1 My heart is s by a noble theme as I
Hag  1:14 So the LORD s up the spirit
Ac  13:50 They s up persecution against Paul

## STIRRING [STIR]

Pr  30:33 so s up anger produces strife."
Ac  17:13 agitating the crowds and s them up.

## STIRS [STIR]

Pr   6:19 a person who s up dissension
    10:12 Hatred s up dissension, but love
    15: 1 wrath, but a harsh word s up anger.
    29:22 An angry person s up dissension,
Lk  23: 5 "He s up the people all over Judea

## STOIC*

Ac  17:18 S philosophers began to debate

## STOLE [STEAL]

Ge  31:19 Rachel s her father's household
2Sa 15: 6 so he s the hearts of the people
Mt  28:13 s him away while we were asleep.'

## STOLEN [STEAL]

Ex  22: 4 If the s animal is found alive in their
Lev  6: 4 they must return what they have s

Ps  62:10 or put vain hope in s goods;
Pr   9:17 "S water is sweet; food eaten
SS   4: 9 You have s my heart, my sister,
Eze 33:15 return what they have s,

## STOMACH

Eze  3: 3 giving you and fill your s with it."
Mk   7:19 go into your heart but into your s,
1Co  6:13 "Food for the s and the s for food,
Php  3:19 their god is their s, and their glory is
1Ti  5:23 use a little wine because of your s
Rev 10: 9 It will turn your s sour, but 'in your

## STONE [CAPSTONE, CORNERSTONE, MILLSTONE, MILLSTONES, STONED, STONES, STONING]

Ge  28:18 Jacob took the s he had placed
    31:45 So Jacob took a s and set it up as
    35:14 Jacob set up a s pillar at the place
Ex  17: 4 They are almost ready to s me."
    24: 4 up twelve s pillars representing
    28:10 six names on one s
    31:18 law, the tablets of s inscribed
    34: 1 out two s tablets like the first ones,
Lev 26: 1 image or a sacred s for yourselves,
Dt   4:13 then wrote them on two s tablets.
    16:22 and do not erect a sacred s, for these
    19:14 your neighbor's boundary s set
    28:36 other gods, gods of wood and s.
1Sa  7:12 Then Samuel took a s and set it
    17:50 the Philistine with a sling and a s;
2Ki 10:27 They demolished the sacred s
Ps  91:12 will not strike your foot against a s.
   118:22 The s the builders rejected has
Isa  8:14 of Israel he will be a s that causes
    28:16 "See, I lay a s in Zion, a tested s,
Jer  3: 9 and committed adultery with s
Eze 11:19 remove from them their heart of s
    36:26 remove from you your heart of s
Zec  3: 9 There are seven eyes on that one s,
Mt   4: 6 not strike your foot against a s.' "
     7: 9 asks for bread, will give him a s?
    23:37 the prophets and s those sent to you,
    24: 2 you, not one s here will be left
Mk  12:10 " 'The s the builders rejected has
    16: 3 "Who will roll the s away
Lk   4: 3 God, tell this s to become bread."
    20:18 on that s will be broken to pieces,
Jn   8: 7 be the first to throw a s at her."
     8:59 they picked up stones to s him,
    10:32 For which of these do you s me?"
    19:13 at a place known as the S Pavement
Ac   4:11 Jesus is " 'the s you builders
Ro   9:32 They stumbled over the stumbling s.
2Co  3: 3 not on tablets of s but on tablets
1Pe  2: 4 As you come to him, the living S—
     2: 6 "See, I lay a s in Zion, a chosen
Rev  2:17 of them a white s with a new name
    21:19 with every kind of precious s.

## STONED [STONE]

Lev 24:23 outside the camp and s him.
Nu  15:36 outside the camp and s him to death,
Jos  7:25 Then all Israel s him,

1Ki 21:13 outside the city and **s** him to death.
2Ch 24:21 order of the king they **s** him to death
Ac 14:19 They **s** Paul and dragged him

## STONES [STONE]

Ex 23:24 and break their sacred **s** to pieces.
28: 9 "Take two onyx **s** and engrave
28:21 There are to be twelve **s**,
Dt 27: 2 set up some large **s** and coat them
Jos 4: 3 take up twelve **s** from the middle
1Sa 17:40 hand, chose five smooth **s**
1Ki 18:31 Elijah took twelve **s**, one for each
2Ki 17:10 They set up sacred **s** and Asherah
18: 4 smashed the sacred **s** and cut down
Ps 102:14 For her **s** are dear to your servants;
Ecc 3: 5 a time to scatter **s** and a time
Mt 3: 9 of these **s** God can raise up children
4: 3 God, tell these **s** to become bread."
Mk 13: 1 What massive **s**!
Lk 19:40 they keep quiet, the **s** will cry out."
1Co 3:12 silver, costly **s**, wood, hay or straw,
1Pe 2: 5 like living **s**, are being built

## STONING* [STONE]

Nu 14:10 assembly talked about **s** them.
1Sa 30: 6 the men were talking of **s** him;
Jn 10:33 "We are not **s** you for any good
Ac 7:59 While they were **s** him,
Heb 11:37 They were put to death by **s**;

## STOOD [STAND]

Ge 28:13 There above it **s** the LORD, and he
Ex 15: 8 The surging waters **s** up like a wall;
Dt 5: 5 that time I **s** between the LORD
Jos 3:17 of the Jordan and **s** on dry ground,
10:13 So the sun **s** still, and the moon
Zec 3: 5 while the angel of the LORD **s** by.
Lk 10:25 occasion an expert in the law **s**
18:11 The Pharisee **s** by himself
22:28 You are those who have **s** by me
Jn 19:25 Near the cross of Jesus **s** his mother,
20:19 Jesus came and **s** among them
Ro 16:10 whose fidelity to Christ has **s** the test.
2Ti 4:17 But the Lord **s** at my side and gave
Jas 1:12 because when they have **s** the test,
Rev 22: 2 each side of the river **s** the tree

## STOOP [STOOPS]

Mk 1: 7 sandals I am not worthy to **s** down

## STOOPS [STOOP]

Ps 113: 6 who **s** down to look on the heavens

## STOP [STOPPED]

Job 37:14 **s** and consider God's wonders.
Isa 1:13 **S** bringing meaningless offerings!
1:16 out of my sight! **S** doing wrong,
2:22 **S** trusting in human beings,
Jer 32:40 I will never **s** doing good to them,
Mk 9:39 "Do not **s** him," Jesus said.
Jn 2:16 **S** turning my Father's house into a
5:14 **S** sinning or something worse may
6:43 "**S** grumbling among yourselves,"
7:24 **S** judging by mere appearances,
20:27 **S** doubting and believe."

Ac 5:39 you will not be able to **s** these men;
Ro 14:13 Therefore let us **s** passing judgment
1Co 14:20 and sisters, **s** thinking like children.
Rev 4: 8 Day and night they never **s** saying:

## STOPPED [STOP]

Nu 16:48 and the dead, and the plague **s**.
Jos 3:16 the water from upstream **s** flowing.
10:13 The sun **s** in the middle of the sky
2Sa 24:25 land, and the plague on Israel was **s**.
2Ki 4: 6 a jar left." Then the oil **s** flowing.
Mk 5:29 Immediately her bleeding **s** and she
Lk 23:45 for the sun **s** shining.

## STORE [STORED, STORES, STORING]

Pr 2: 1 and **s** up my commands within you,
2: 7 He holds success in **s**
7: 1 and **s** up my commands within you.
10:14 The wise **s** up knowledge,
21:20 The wise **s** up choice food
Isa 2:12 LORD Almighty has a day in **s**
33: 6 a rich **s** of salvation and wisdom
Mt 6:19 "Do not **s** up for yourselves
6:26 not sow or reap or **s** away in barns,
Lk 12:21 those who **s** up things for themselves
2Ti 4: 8 Now there is in **s** for me the crown

## STORED [STORE]

Pr 13:22 but a sinner's wealth is **s**
Lk 6:45 out of the good **s** up in their heart,
Col 1: 5 spring from the hope **s** up for you

## STOREHOUSE [HOUSE]

Dt 28:12 the heavens, the **s** of his bounty,
Mal 3:10 Bring the whole tithe into the **s**,

## STOREHOUSES [HOUSE]

Job 38:22 "Have you entered the **s**
38:22 of the snow or seen the **s** of the hail,
Ps 33: 7 sea into jars; he puts the deep into **s**.
135: 7 and brings out the wind from his **s**.
Isa 39: 2 showed them what was in his **s**—

## STOREROOM* [ROOM]

Mt 13:52 his **s** new treasures as well as old."
Lk 12:24 sow or reap, they have no **s** or barn;

## STORES [STORE]

Pr 6: 8 yet it **s** its provisions in summer

## STORIES*

2Pe 1:16 we did not follow cleverly devised **s**
2: 3 will exploit you with fabricated **s**.

## STORING* [STORE]

Ecc 2:26 **s** up wealth to hand it over
Ro 2: 5 you are **s** up wrath against yourself

## STORM

Ex 9:24 It was the worst **s** in all the land
Job 38: 1 LORD spoke to Job out of the **s**.
40: 6 LORD spoke to Job out of the **s**:
Ps 107:29 He stilled the **s** to a whisper;
Isa 25: 4 a shelter from the **s** and a shade

Jer 30:23 the **s** of the LORD will burst
Jnh 1:12 is my fault that this great **s** has come
Na 1: 3 way is in the whirlwind and the **s**,
Lk 8:24 the **s** subsided, and all was calm.

## STRAIGHT [STRAIGHTEN, STRAIGHTENED]

Ps 27:11 lead me in a **s** path because of my
   107: 7 He led them by a **s** way to a city
Pr 2:13 who have left the **s** paths to walk
   3: 6 him, and he will make your paths **s**.
   4:11 wisdom and lead you along **s** paths.
   4:25 Let your eyes look **s** ahead;
   5: 5 her steps lead **s** to the grave.
   11: 5 the blameless makes their paths **s**,
   15:21 have understanding keep a **s** course.
Isa 40: 3 make **s** in the desert a highway
Mt 3: 3 the Lord, make **s** paths for him.' "
Lk 3: 5 The crooked roads shall become **s**,
Jn 1:23 'Make **s** the way for the Lord.' "
2Pe 2:15 They have left the **s** way

## STRAIGHTEN [STRAIGHT]

Ecc 7:13 Who can **s** what he has made

## STRAIGHTENED [STRAIGHT]

Ecc 1:15 What is crooked cannot be **s**;
Lk 13:13 her, and immediately she **s**

## STRAIN* [STRAINING]

Ex 18:23 you will be able to stand the **s**,
Mt 23:24 You **s** out a gnat but swallow

## STRAINING [STRAIN]

Php 3:13 behind and **s** toward what is ahead,

## STRANGE [STRANGER, STRANGER'S, STRANGERS]

Ex 3: 3 "I will go over and see this **s** sight—
Isa 28:11 and **s** tongues God will speak to this
Eze 3: 5 of obscure speech and **s** language,
Heb 13: 9 away by all kinds of **s** teachings.

## STRANGER [STRANGE]

Ge 23: 4 "I am a foreigner and **s** among you.
Ps 119:19 I am a **s** on earth; do not hide your
Mt 25:35 I was a **s** and you invited me in,
Jn 10: 5 But they will never follow a **s**;
Heb 11: 9 in the promised land like a **s**

## STRANGER'S* [STRANGE]

Jn 10: 5 they do not recognize a **s** voice."

## STRANGERS [STRANGE]

Ge 15:13 years your descendants will be **s**
Lev 25:23 my land as foreigners and **s**.
1Ch 16:19 in number, few indeed, and **s** in it,
Pr 5:17 alone, never to be shared with **s**.
Heb 11:13 they were foreigners and **s** on earth.
   13: 2 not forget to show hospitality to **s**,
3Jn 1: 5 even though they are **s** to you.

## STRAW

Ex 5:10 'I will not give you any more **s**.

Isa 11: 7 and the lion will eat **s** like the ox.
1Co 3:12 silver, costly stones, wood, hay or **s**,

## STRAY [ASTRAY, STRAYED, STRAYS]

Ps 119:10 do not let me **s** from your
Pr 7:25 turn to her ways or **s** into her paths.
Eze 14:11 of Israel will no longer **s** from me,

## STRAYED [STRAY]

Ps 44:18 our feet had not **s** from your path.
   119:176 I have **s** like a lost sheep.
Jer 31·19 After I **s**, I repented; after I came

## STRAYS [STRAY]

Pr 21:16 Whoever **s** from the path
Eze 34:16 for the lost and bring back the **s**.

## STREAM [STREAMS]

1Sa 17:40 chose five smooth stones from the **s**,
Isa 2: 2 the hills, and all nations will **s** to it.
Am 5:24 righteousness like a never-failing **s**!
Mic 4: 1 the hills, and peoples will **s** to it.

## STREAMS [STREAM]

Ge 2: 6 but **s** came up from the earth
Dt 10: 7 to Jotbathah, a land with **s** of water.
Job 6:15 as undependable as intermittent **s**,
Ps 1: 3 They are like a tree planted by **s**
   42: 1 As the deer pants for **s** of water,
   46: 4 is a river whose **s** make glad the city
   126: 4 LORD, like **s** in the Negev.
Ecc 1: 7 All **s** flow into the sea,
Isa 35: 6 in the wilderness and **s** in the desert.
   44: 4 like poplar trees by flowing **s**.
La 3:48 **S** of tears flow from my eyes
Mt 7:27 The rain came down, the **s** rose,

## STREET [STREETS]

Mt 6: 5 and on the **s** corners to be seen
   22: 9 Go to the **s** corners and invite
Rev 21:21 The great **s** of the city was of gold,
   22: 2 the middle of the great **s** of the city.

## STREETS [STREET]

Ps 144:14 captivity, no cry of distress in our **s**.
Zec 8: 5 The city **s** will be filled with boys
Mt 12:19 no one will hear his voice in the **s**.

## STRENGTH [STRONG]

Ex 15: 2 "The LORD is my **s** and my
Nu 14:17 may the Lord's **s** be displayed,
Dt 4:37 by his Presence and his great **s**,
   6: 5 all your soul and with all your **s**.
   33:25 and your **s** will equal your days.
Jdg 7: 2 me, 'My own **s** has saved me.'
   16:15 told me the secret of your great **s**."
1Sa 2: 9 "It is not by **s** that one prevails;
2Sa 22:33 It is God who arms me with **s**
2Ki 23:25 with all his soul and with all his **s**,
1Ch 16:11 Look to the LORD and his **s**;
   16:28 ascribe to the LORD glory and **s**.
   29:12 In your hands are **s** and power
Ne 8:10 the joy of the LORD is your **s**."
Ps 18: 1 I love you, LORD, my **s**.
   21:13 Be exalted in your **s**, LORD;

Ps 28: 7 The LORD is my **s** and my shield;
29:11 The LORD gives **s** to his people;
33:17 despite all its great **s** it cannot save.
46: 1 God is our refuge and **s**,
59: 9 You are my **s**, I watch for you;
59:17 You are my **s**, I sing praise to you;
65: 6 having armed yourself with **s**,
73:26 but God is the **s** of my heart and my
84: 5 Blessed are those whose **s** is in you,
84: 7 They go from **s** to **s**, till each
96: 7 ascribe to the LORD glory and **s**.
105: 4 Look to the LORD and his **s**;
118:14 The LORD is my **s** and my
147:10 pleasure is not in the **s** of the horse,
Pr 24: 5 who have knowledge muster their **s**.
30:25 Ants are creatures of little **s**,
31:25 She is clothed with **s** and dignity;
Ecc 9:16 I said, "Wisdom is better than **s**."
Isa 12: 2 LORD, is my **s** and my defense;
31: 1 and in the great **s** of their horsemen,
40:26 of his great power and mighty **s**,
40:31 in the LORD will renew their **s**.
63: 1 forward in the greatness of his **s**?
Jer 9:23 the strong boast of their **s** or the rich
Mic 5: 4 his flock in the **s** of the LORD,
Hab 3:19 The Sovereign LORD is my **s**;
Mk 12:30 all your mind and with all your **s**.'
1Co 1:25 of God is stronger than human **s**.
Eph 1:19 power is the same as the mighty **s**
Php 4:13 all this through him who gives me **s**.
2Ti 4:17 stood at my side and gave me **s**,
Heb 11:34 whose weakness was turned to **s**;
1Pe 4:11 do so with the **s** God provides,
Rev 3: 8 I know that you have little **s**,
5:12 wealth and wisdom and **s** and honor
7:12 power and **s** be to our God for ever

## STRENGTHEN [STRONG]

Jdg 16:28 God, **s** me just once more, and let
2Ch 16: 9 to **s** those whose hearts are fully
Ps 89:21 surely my arm will **s** him.
119:28 **s** me according to your word.
Isa 35: 3 S the feeble hands, steady the knees
41:10 I will **s** you and help you;
Eze 34:16 bind up the injured and **s** the weak,
Zec 10:12 I will **s** them in the LORD
Lk 22:32 have turned back, **s** your brothers."
Ac 15:32 to encourage and **s** the believers.
Eph 3:16 of his glorious riches he may **s** you
1Th 3:13 May he **s** your hearts so that you
2Th 2:17 hearts and **s** you in every good deed
Heb 12:12 **s** your feeble arms and weak knees.

## STRENGTHENED [STRONG]

Job 4: 3 many, how you have **s** feeble hands.
Eze 34: 4 You have not **s** the weak or healed
Lk 22:43 heaven appeared to him and **s** him.
Ac 16: 5 So the churches were **s** in the faith
Col 1:11 being **s** with all power according
2: 7 **s** in the faith as you were taught,
Heb 13: 9 good for our hearts to be **s** by grace,

## STRENGTHENING [STRONG]

1Co 14: 3 prophesy speak to people for their **s**,

## STRENUOUSLY*

Col 1:29 To this end I **s** contend

## STRETCH [OUTSTRETCHED, STRETCHED, STRETCHES]

Ex 3:20 So I will **s** out my hand and strike
14:16 and **s** out your hand over the sea
Ps 138: 7 You **s** out your hand against
Zep 1: 4 "I will **s** out my hand against Judah
Mk 3: 5 said to the man, "S out your hand."
Ac 4:30 S out your hand to heal and perform

## STRETCHED [STRETCH]

Ex 14:21 Moses **s** out his hand over the sea,
2Sa 24:16 When the angel **s** out his hand
1Ki 13: 4 the hand he **s** out toward the man
Isa 45:12 My own hands **s** out the heavens;
Jer 10:12 and **s** out the heavens by his

## STRETCHES [STRETCH]

Ps 104: 2 he **s** out the heavens like a tent
Zec 12: 1 The LORD, who **s** out the heavens,

## STRICKEN [STRIKE]

Isa 53: 4 him punished by God, **s** by him,

## STRICT [STRICTEST, STRICTLY]

Mk 3:12 But he gave them **s** orders not to tell
Ac 5:28 "We gave you **s** orders not to teach
1Co 9:25 in the games goes into **s** training.

## STRICTEST* [STRICT]

Ac 26: 5 that I conformed to the **s** sect of our

## STRICTLY* [STRICT]

Lk 9:21 Jesus **s** warned them not to tell this
Jas 3: 1 who teach will be judged more **s**.

## STRIFE [STRIVE]

Pr 13:10 Where there is **s**, there is pride,
17: 1 than a house full of feasting, with **s**.
18: 6 The lips of fools bring them **s**,
20: 3 It is to one's honor to avoid **s**,
22:10 out the mocker, and out goes **s**;
23:29 Who has **s**? Who has complaints?
30:33 so stirring up anger produces **s**."
Ro 1:29 envy, murder, **s**, deceit and malice.
1Ti 6: 4 about words that result in envy, **s**,

## STRIKE [STRICKEN, STRIKES, STROKE, STRUCK]

Ge 3:15 your head, and you will **s** his heel."
Ex 3:20 **s** the Egyptians with all the wonders
12:12 and **s** down every firstborn of both
17: 6 S the rock, and water will come
Ps 91:12 you will not **s** your foot against
Isa 11: 4 He will **s** the earth with the rod
Zec 13: 7 "S the shepherd, and the sheep will
Mal 4: 6 **s** the land with total destruction."
Mt 4: 6 you will not **s** your foot against
Mk 14:27 " 'I will **s** the shepherd,
1Co 9:27 No, I **s** a blow to my body
Rev 11: 6 and to **s** the earth with every kind
19:15 with which to **s** down the nations.

## STRIKES [STRIKE]
Ex   21:12  "Anyone who s someone a fatal

## STRINGED
Ge    4:21  father of all who play s instruments

## STRIPPED [STRIPS]
Ge   37:23  his brothers, they s him of his robe—
Ex   33: 6  So the Israelites s off their
Isa  20: 3  as my servant Isaiah has gone s
Mt   27:28  They s him and put a scarlet robe
Ac   16:22  the magistrates ordered them to be s

## STRIPS [STRIPPED]
Jn   11:44  and feet wrapped with s of linen,
     20: 5  in at the s of linen lying there

## STRIVE* [STRIFE, STRIVING]
Ac   24:16  So I s always to keep my
2Co  13:11  S for full restoration,
1Ti   4:10  That is why we labor and s,
1Th   5:15  but always s to do what is good

## STRIVING [STRIVE]
Php   1:27  s together with one accord for the faith

## STROKE [STRIKE]
Mt    5:18  letter, not the least s of a pen,
Lk   16:17  than for the least s of a pen to drop

## STRONG [STRENGTH,
    STRENGTHEN, STRENGTHENED,
    STRENGTHENING, STRONGER]
Nu   24:18  be conquered, but Israel will grow s.
Dt    3:24  your greatness and your s hand.
     31: 6  Be s and courageous. Do not be
Jos   1: 6  Be s and courageous, because you
     10:25  Be s and courageous.
     23: 6  "Be very s; be careful to obey all
Jdg   5:21  March on, my soul; be s!
2Sa  10:12  Be s, and let us fight bravely for our
1Ki   2: 2  "So be s, act like a man,
1Ch  22:13  Be s and courageous.
     28:20  his son, "Be s and courageous,
2Ch  32: 7  "Be s and courageous. Do not be
Ps   24: 8  The LORD s and mighty,
     31: 2  of refuge, a s fortress to save me.
     35:10  the poor from those too s for them,
    140: 7  Sovereign LORD, my s deliverer,
Pr   31:17  her arms are s for her tasks.
Ecc   9:11  not to the swift or the battle to the s,
SS    8: 6  for love is as s as death, its jealousy
Isa  35: 4  fearful hearts, "Be s, do not fear;
     53:12  he will divide the spoils with the s,
Jer   9:23  or the s boast of their strength
     50:34  Yet their Redeemer is s;
Eze   3:14  with the s hand of the LORD
Da    2:40  will be a fourth kingdom, s as iron—
Joel  3:10  Let the weakling say, "I am s!"
Hag   2: 4  But now be s, Zerubbabel,'
Zec   8: 9  'Let your hands be s so
Mt   12:29  can anyone enter a s man's house
Lk    1:80  child grew and became s in spirit;
      2:40  And the child grew and became s;

Ro   15: 1  We who are s ought to bear
1Co   1:27  things of the world to shame the s.
     16:13  in the faith; be courageous; be s.
2Co  12:10  For when I am weak, then I am s.
Eph   6:10  be s in the Lord and in his mighty
2Ti   2: 1  be s in the grace that is in Christ
1Pe   5:10  himself restore you and make you s,

## STRONGER [STRONG]
Nu   14:12  a nation greater and s than they."
Dt    7: 1  nations larger and s than you—
2Sa   3: 1  David grew s and s, while the house
1Co   1:25  of God is s than human strength.

## STRONGHOLD [STRONGHOLDS]
1Sa  22: 4  him as long as David was in the s.
Ps    9: 9  oppressed, a s in times of trouble.
     18: 2  and the horn of my salvation, my s.
     27: 1  The LORD is the s of my life—
     52: 7  the one who did not make God his s
    144: 2  my fortress, my s and my deliverer,

## STRONGHOLDS [STRONGHOLD]
Zep   3: 6  their s are demolished.
2Co  10: 4  have divine power to demolish s.

## STRUCK [STRIKE]
Ex   12:29  midnight the LORD s down all
Nu   20:11  and s the rock twice with his staff.
1Sa  17:49  and s the Philistine on the forehead.
Ps   78:20  True, he s the rock, and water
Da    2:34  It s the statue on its feet of iron
Zec  13: 8  "two-thirds will be s down
Mk   14:65  him, s him with their fists, and said,
Ac   23: 3  law by commanding that I be s!"

## STRUCTURE
1Ch  29: 1  because this palatial s is not

## STRUGGLE [STRUGGLED]
Ro   15:30  join me in my s by praying to God
Eph   6:12  For our s is not against flesh
Heb  12: 4  In your s against sin, you have not

## STRUGGLED [STRUGGLE]
Ge   32:28  because you have s with God
Hos  12: 3  as a man he s with God.

## STUBBLE
Ob    1:18  the house of Esau will be s,
Na    1:10  they will be consumed like dry s.
Mal   4: 1  and every evildoer will be s,

## STUBBORN [STUBBORNLY,
    STUBBORNNESS]
Lev  26:19  I will break down your s pride
Ps   78: 8  a s and rebellious generation,
Mk    3: 5  deeply distressed at their s hearts,

## STUBBORNLY [STUBBORN]
Ex   13:15  When Pharaoh s refused to let us

## STUBBORNNESS [STUBBORN]
Dt    9:27  Overlook the s of this people,

Jer 3:17 No longer will they follow the s
Ro 2: 5 But because of your s and your

## STUDENT* [STUDY]

1Ch 25: 8 old alike, teacher as well as s,

## STUDENTS* [STUDY]

Mt 10:24 "S are not above their teacher,
10:25 It is enough for s to be like their teacher
Lk 6:40 S are not above their teacher,

## STUDIED* [STUDY]

Ac 22: 3 I s under Gamaliel and was thoroughly

## STUDY* [STUDENT, STUDENTS, STUDIED]

Ezr 7:10 Ezra had devoted himself to the s
Ecc 1:13 I applied my mind to s
12:12 end, and much s wearies the body.
Jn 5:39 You s the Scriptures diligently

## STUMBLE [STUMBLED, STUMBLES, STUMBLING]

Ps 37:24 though they s, they will not fall,
119:165 law, and nothing can make them s.
Pr 3:23 in safety, and your foot will not s.
24:17 enemies fall; when they s,
Isa 8:14 be a stone that causes people to s
Jer 13:16 before your feet s on the darkening
31: 9 a level path where they will not s,
Eze 7:19 for it has caused them to s into sin.
Da 11:35 Some of the wise will s, so that they
Hos 14: 9 them, but the rebellious s in them.
Mal 2: 8 teaching have caused many to s;
Mt 5:29 If your right eye causes you to s,
11: 6 does not s on account of me."
18: 6 those who believe in me—to s,
Mk 9:43 If your hand causes you to s,
Lk 17: 1 cause people to s are bound to come,
Jn 11: 9 who walk in the daytime will not s,
11:10 people walk at night that they s,
Ro 9:33 Zion a stone that causes people to s
11:11 Did they s so as to fall beyond
14:20 that causes someone else to s.
1Co 10:32 Do not cause anyone to s,
Jas 3: 2 We all s in many ways.
1Pe 2: 8 "A stone that causes people to s
2: 8 They s because they disobey
2Pe 1:10 do these things, you will never s,
1Jn 2:10 is nothing in them to make them s.

## STUMBLED [STUMBLE]

Ps 17: 5 my feet have not s.
Ro 9:32 They s over the stumbling stone.

## STUMBLES [STUMBLE]

Jas 2:10 yet s at just one point is guilty

## STUMBLING [STUMBLE]

Lev 19:14 or put a s block in front of the blind,
Ps 56:13 me from death and my feet from s,
Eze 14: 3 and put wicked s blocks before their
Mt 16:23 You are a s block to me; you do not
Ro 9:32 They stumbled over the s stone.

Ro 11: 9 a s block and a retribution for them.
14:13 up your mind not to put any s block
1Co 1:23 a s block to Jews and foolishness
8: 9 rights does not become a a s block
2Co 6: 3 We put no s block in anyone's path,
Jude 1:24 keep you from s and to present you

## STUMP

Isa 6:13 so the holy seed will be the s
11: 1 will come up from the s of Jesse;

## STUPID [STUPIDITY]

Pr 12: 1 but whoever hates correction is s.
Ecc 10: 3 and show everyone how s they are.
2Ti 2:23 to do with foolish and s arguments,

## STUPIDITY* [STUPID]

Ecc 7:25 to understand the s of wickedness

## STUPOR

Ro 11: 8 "God gave them a spirit of s,

## SUBDUE [SUBDUED, SUBDUES]

Ge 1:28 fill the earth and s it.
1Ch 17:10 I will also s all your enemies.

## SUBDUED [SUBDUE]

Jos 10:40 So Joshua s the whole region,
Ps 47: 3 He s nations under us,

## SUBDUES [SUBDUE]

Ps 18:47 me, who s nations under me,

## SUBJECT [SUBJECTED]

Dt 20:11 people in it shall be s to forced labor
Jdg 1:30 Zebulun did s them to forced labor.
Mt 5:22 or sister will be s to judgment.
9:20 then a woman who had been s
1Co 14:32 of prophets are s to the control
15:28 the Son himself will be made s
Tit 2: 5 and to be s to their husbands,
2: 9 Teach slaves to be s to their masters
3: 1 Remind the people to be s to rulers
Heb 2: 8 left nothing that is not s to them.

## SUBJECTED [SUBJECT]

Ro 8:20 For the creation was s to frustration,
Heb 2: 5 to angels that he has s the world

## SUBMISSION [SUBMIT]

1Co 14:34 but must be in s, as the law says.
1Ti 2:11 should learn in quietness and full s.
Heb 5: 7 was heard because of his reverent s.

## SUBMISSIVE* [SUBMIT]

Jas 3:17 considerate, s, full of mercy

## SUBMIT [SUBMISSION, SUBMISSIVE, SUBMITS, SUBMITTED]

2Ch 30: 8 your parents were; s to the LORD.
Ps 81:11 Israel would not s to me.
Pr 3: 6 in all your ways s to him,

Lk   10:17  even the demons **s** to us in your
Ro    8: 7  it does not **s** to God's law, nor can it
     13: 5  it is necessary to **s** to the authorities,
1Co 16:16  to **s** to such as these and to everyone
Eph  5:21  **S** to one another out of reverence
Col   3:18  **s** yourselves to your husbands, as is
Heb 12: 9  How much more should we **s**
     13:17  your leaders and **s** to their authority,
Jas   4: 7  **S** yourselves, then, to God.
1Pe   2:13  **S** yourselves for the Lord's sake
      3: 1  Wives, in the same way **s** yourselves
      5: 5  younger, **s** yourselves to your elders.

## SUBMITS* [SUBMIT]
Eph   5:24  Now as the church **s** to Christ,

## SUBMITTED [SUBMIT]
1Pe   3: 5  **s** themselves to their own husbands,

## SUBTRACT*
Dt    4: 2  command you and do not **s** from it,

## SUCCEED [SUCCESS, SUCCESSFUL, SUCCESSOR]
2Sa   7:12  will raise up your offspring to **s** you,
1Ki 22:22  " 'You will **s** in enticing him,'
Ps   20: 4  heart and make all your plans **s**.
Pr   15:22  but with many advisers they **s**.
     21:30  plan that can **s** against the LORD.
Ecc  11: 6  for you do not know which will **s**,

## SUCCESS [SUCCEED]
Ge   39:23  and gave him **s** in whatever he did.
1Sa 18:14  In everything he did he had great **s**,
1Ch 12:18  **S**, **s** to you, and **s** to those who help
     22:13  you will have **s** if you are careful
2Ch 26: 5  the LORD, God gave him **s**.
Ne    2:20  The God of heaven will give us **s**.
Ps  118:25  LORD, grant us **s**!
Pr    2: 7  holds **s** in store for the upright,
Ecc  10:10  is needed, but skill will bring **s**.

## SUCCESSFUL [SUCCEED]
Ge   24:12  make me **s** today, and show kindness
Jos   1: 7  that you may be **s** wherever you go.
2Ki  18: 7  he was **s** in whatever he undertook.
2Ch 20:20  in his prophets and you will be **s**."

## SUCCESSOR [SUCCEED]
1Ki   2: 4  never fail to have a **s** on the throne
      8:25  never fail to have a **s** to sit before me
      9: 5  never fail to have a **s** on the throne

## SUCH
Ex   32:21  that you led them into **s** great sin?"
Lev  25:21  I will send you **s** a blessing
Ps  139: 6  **S** knowledge is too wonderful
Jer   5: 9  avenge myself on **s** a nation as this?
Mt    8:10  anyone in Israel with **s** great faith.
Mk   13: 7  **S** things must happen, but the end is
Lk   12:30  pagan world runs after all **s** things,
Jn    9:16  can a sinner perform **s** signs?"
1Co   9:24  Run in **s** a way as to get the prize.
2Co   3: 4  **S** confidence we have through
Heb   7:26  **S** a high priest truly meets our

Heb  12: 3  him who endured **s** opposition
1Jn   2:22  **S** a person is the antichrist—
2Jn   1: 7  Any **s** person is the deceiver
3Jn   1: 8  show hospitality to **s** people so

## SUDDEN [SUDDENLY]
Lev  26:16  I will bring on you **s** terror,
Dt   28:20  come to **s** ruin because of the evil
Pr    3:25  Have no fear of **s** disaster

## SUDDENLY [SUDDEN]
Ps   73:19  How **s** are they destroyed,
Mal   3: 1  **s** the Lord you are seeking will
Mt   28: 9  **S** Jesus met them.
Mk   13:36  If he comes **s**, do not let him find
Ac    9: 3  **s** a light from heaven flashed around
1Th   5: 3  destruction will come on them **s**,

## SUE*
Mt    5:40  if anyone wants to **s** you and take

## SUFFER [LONG-SUFFERING, SUFFERED, SUFFERING, SUFFERINGS, SUFFERS]
Job  15:20  All their days the wicked **s** torment,
     36:15  But those who **s** he delivers in their
Ps   16: 4  run after other gods will **s** more
Pr    9:12  you are a mocker, you alone will **s**.
Isa  53:10  to crush him and cause him to **s**,
Mk    8:31  the Son of Man must **s** many things
Lk   22:15  this Passover until you before I **s**.
     24:26  the Messiah have to **s** these things
     24:46  The Messiah will **s** and rise
Ac    3:18  saying that his Messiah would **s**.
1Co   3:15  the builder will **s** loss but yet will be
2Co   1: 6  of the same sufferings we **s**.
Php   1:29  on him, but also to **s** for him,
Heb   9:26  to **s** many times since the creation
1Pe   3:17  to **s** for doing good than for doing
      4:16  if you **s** as a Christian, do not be
Rev   2:10  be afraid of what you are about to **s**.

## SUFFERED [SUFFER]
Isa  53:11  After he has **s**, he will see the light
Mk    5:26  She had **s** a great deal under the care
Heb   2: 9  glory and honor because he **s** death,
      2:10  salvation perfect through what he **s**.
      2:18  Because he himself **s** when he was
      5: 8  learned obedience from what he **s**
1Pe   2:21  called, because Christ **s** for you,
      4: 1  since Christ **s** in his body,

## SUFFERING [SUFFER]
Ex    3: 7  and I am concerned about their **s**.
Job   2:13  they saw how great his **s** was.
Ps   22:24  or scorned the **s** of the afflicted one;
    119:50  My comfort in my **s** is this:
Isa  53: 3  a man of **s**, and familiar with pain.
La    1:12  Is any **s** like my **s** that was inflicted
Mt    4:24  diseases, those **s** severe pain,
      8: 6  lies at home paralyzed, **s** terribly."
     15:22  is demon-possessed and **s** terribly."
     17:15  "He has seizures and is **s** greatly.
Ac    5:41  been counted worthy of **s** disgrace
Ro    5: 3  know that **s** produces perseverance;

2Ti 1: 8 But join with me in **s** for the gospel,
2: 3 Join with me in **s**,
Heb 13: 3 as if you yourselves were **s**.
Jas 5:10 example of patience in the face of **s**,

## SUFFERINGS [SUFFER]

Ro 5: 3 but we also glory in our **s**,
8:18 that our present **s** are not worth
2Co 1: 5 share abundantly in the **s** of Christ,
1: 7 know that just as you share in our **s**,
Php 3:10 and participation in his **s**,
1Pe 1:11 when he predicted the **s** of Christ
4:13 as you participate in the **s** of Christ,
5: 9 are undergoing the same kind of **s**.

## SUFFERS* [SUFFER]

Pr 13:20 for a companion of fools **s** harm.
1Co 12:26 If one part **s**, every part **s** with it;

## SUFFICIENT

2Co 12: 9 said to me, "My grace is **s** for you,

## SUITABLE

Ge 2:18 I will make a helper **s** for him."

## SUKKOTH

Ge 33:17 why the place is called **S**.
Jdg 8:16 taught the men of **S** a lesson

## SULFUR

Ge 19:24 the Lord rained down burning **s**
Ps 11: 6 will rain fiery coals and burning **s**;
Lk 17:29 fire and **s** rained down from heaven
Rev 9:17 mouths came fire, smoke and **s**.
14:10 with burning **s** in the presence
19:20 alive into the fiery lake of burning **s**.
20:10 thrown into the lake of burning **s**,
21: 8 to the fiery lake of burning **s**.

## SUMMED* [SUMS]

Ro 13: 9 be, are **s** up in this one command:

## SUMMER

Pr 6: 8 yet it stores its provisions in **s**
Mk 13:28 come out, you know that **s** is near.

## SUMMON [SUMMONS]

Ps 68:28 **S** your power, God; show us your
Isa 45: 4 I **s** you by name and bestow on you

## SUMMONS [SUMMON]

Ps 50: 1 **s** the earth from the rising of the sun
Isa 45: 3 God of Israel, who **s** you by name.

## SUMS* [SUMMED]

Mt 7:12 to you, for this **s** up the Law

## SUN [SUNLIGHT, SUNRISE, SUNSET]

Jos 10:13 So the **s** stood still,
Jdg 5:31 may all who love you be like the **s**
Ps 72: 5 May he endure as long as the **s**,
84:11 For the Lord God is a **s**
113: 3 of the **s** to the place where it sets,
121: 6 the **s** will not harm you by day,

Ps 136: 8 the **s** to govern the day,
148: 3 Praise him, **s** and moon;
Pr 4:18 of the righteous is like the morning **s**,
Ecc 1: 9 there is nothing new under the **s**.
SS 6:10 bright as the **s**, majestic as the stars
Isa 60:19 The **s** will no more be your light
Joel 2:31 The **s** will be turned to darkness
3:15 The **s** and moon will be darkened,
Mic 3: 6 The **s** will set for the prophets,
Mal 4: 2 the **s** of righteousness will rise
Mt 5:45 He causes his **s** to rise on the evil
13:43 the righteous will shine like the **s**
17: 2 His face shone like the **s**, and his
Mk 13:24 distress, " 'the **s** will be darkened,
Lk 1:78 the rising **s** will come to us from heaven
23:45 for the **s** stopped shining.
Ac 2:20 The **s** will be turned to darkness
7:42 to the worship of the **s**, moon and stars.
Eph 4:26 Do not let the **s** go down while you
Rev 1:16 His face was like the **s** shining in all
8:12 and a third of the **s** was struck,
9: 2 The **s** and sky were darkened
10: 1 his face was like the **s**, and his legs
12: 1 a woman clothed with the **s**,
21:23 The city does not need the **s**
22: 5 light of a lamp or the light of the **s**,

## UNDER THE SUN Ecc 1:3, 9, 14; 2:11, 17,

18, 19, 20, 22; 3:16; 4:1, 3, 7, 15; 5:13, 18; 6:1,
12; 8:9, 15, 15, 17; 9:3, 6, 9, 9, 11, 13; 10:5

## SUNG [SING]

Mt 26:30 When they had **s** a hymn, they went

## SUNLIGHT [SUN]

Zec 14: 6 On that day there will be no **s**,

## SUNRISE [SUN]

2Sa 23: 4 light of morning at **s** on a cloudless
Hab 3: 4 His splendor was like the **s**;

## SUNSET [SUN]

Ex 17:12 that his hands remained steady till **s**.
22:26 cloak as a pledge, return it by **s**,
Dt 24:15 them their wages each day before **s**,

## SUPER-APOSTLES* [APOSTLE]

2Co 11: 5 in the least inferior to those "**s**."
12:11 not in the least inferior to the "**s**,"

## SUPERIOR

Ro 2:18 what is **s** because you are instructed
11:18 to be **s** to those other branches.
11:25 so that you may not think you are **s**:
12:16 Do not think you are **s**.
Heb 1: 4 So he became as much **s**
1: 4 as the name he has inherited is **s**
8: 6 ministry Jesus has received is as **s**
8: 6 he is mediator is **s** to the old one,

## SUPERSTITIONS*

Isa 2: 6 They are full of **s** from the East;

## SUPERVISION

Gal 3:25 we are no longer under the **s**

## SUPPER

Lk   22:20  after the **s** he took the cup, saying,
1Co  11:25  way, after **s** he took the cup, saying,
Rev  19: 9  to the wedding **s** of the Lamb!' "

## SUPPLICATION [SUPPLICATIONS]

1Ki   8:30  Hear the **s** of your servant
2Ch   6:24  making **s** before you in this temple,
Zec  12:10  of Jerusalem a spirit of grace and **s**.

## SUPPLICATIONS* [SUPPLICATION]

1Ki   8:54  these prayers and **s** to the Lord,
2Ch   6:21  Hear the **s** of your servant

## SUPPLIED [SUPPLY]

Ac   20:34  hands of mine have **s** my own needs
Php   4:18  I am amply **s**, now that I have

## SUPPLIES [SUPPLY]

Ps   147: 8  he **s** the earth with rain and makes
2Co   9:10  Now he who **s** seed to the sower

## SUPPLY [SUPPLIED, SUPPLIES, SUPPLYING]

Lev  26:26  When I cut off your **s** of bread,
Ps   78:20  Can he **s** meat for his people?"
2Co   8:14  your plenty will **s** what they need,
1Th   3:10  and **s** what is lacking in your faith.

## SUPPLYING* [SUPPLY]

2Co   9:12  you perform is not only **s** the needs

## SUPPORT [SUPPORTED, SUPPORTING, SUPPORTS]

Jdg  16:26  can feel the pillars that **s** the temple,
Ps   18:18  disaster, but the Lord was my **s**.
Ro   11:18  You do not **s** the root, but the root
1Co   9:12  others have this right of **s** from you,

## SUPPORTED [SUPPORT]

Ps   94:18  your unfailing love, Lord, **s** me.
Col   2:19  **s** and held together by its ligaments

## SUPPORTING [SUPPORT]

Ezr   5: 2  prophets of God were with them, **s**
Eph   4:16  held together by every **s** ligament,

## SUPPORTS [SUPPORT]

Ro   11:18  support the root, but the root **s** you.

## SUPPRESS*

Ro   1:18  of human beings who **s** the truth

## SUPREMACY* [SUPREME]

Col   1:18  in everything he might have the **s**.

## SUPREME [SUPREMACY]

Isa  20: 1  In the year that the **s** commander,

## SURE [SURELY]

Nu   28:31  Be **s** the animals are without defect.
     32:23  you may be **s** that your sin will find

Dt    6:17  Be **s** to keep the commands
     14:22  Be **s** to set aside a tenth of all
     23:23  your lips utter you must be **s** to do,
     29:18  make **s** there is no root among you
Jos  23:13  you may be **s** that the Lord your
1Sa  12:24  But be **s** to fear the Lord
Ps   19: 9  The ordinances of the Lord are **s**,
     69:13  answer me with your **s** salvation.
    132:11  a **s** oath that he will not revoke:
Pr   27:23  Be **s** you know the condition
Isa  28:16  cornerstone for a **s** foundation;
Eph   5: 5  For of this you can be **s**:
Heb  11: 1  Now faith is being **s** of what we

## SURELY [SURE]

Ge    6:13  I am **s** going to destroy both them
     18:18  Abraham will **s** become a great
     22:17  I will **s** bless you and make your
     28:16  "S the Lord is in this place,
     50:24  But God will **s** come to your aid
Ex   13:19  said, "God will **s** come to your aid,
Nu   26:65  told those Israelites they would **s** die
Jos  10:14  S the Lord was fighting
Job   1:11  he will **s** curse you to your face."
      2: 5  he will **s** curse you to your face."
Ps    5:12  S, Lord, you bless the righteous;
     23: 6  S your goodness and love will
     54: 4  S God is my help; the Lord is
     73: 1  S God is good to Israel, to those
     85: 9  S his salvation is near those who
Pr   23:18  There is **s** a future hope for you,
Isa  12: 2  S God is my salvation; I will trust
     53: 4  S he took up our pain and bore our
Eze  33:15  life, and do no evil, they will **s** live;
Mt   28:20  And **s** I am with you always,
Mk   14:19  by one they said to him, "S not I?"
     15:39  "S this man was the Son of God!"
Lk   23:47  said, "S this was a righteous man."
2Co   1:18  But as **s** as God is faithful,

## SURFACE

Ge    1: 2  darkness was over the **s** of the deep,
      7:18  the ark floated on the **s** of the water.

## SURGING

Ex   15: 8  The **s** waters stood up like a wall;
Ps   89: 9  You rule over the **s** sea;
Zec  10:11  the **s** sea will be subdued and all

## SURPASS* [SURPASSED, SURPASSES, SURPASSING]

Pr   31:29  noble things, but you **s** them all."

## SURPASSED* [SURPASS]

Jn    1:15  me has **s** me because he was before
      1:30  me has **s** me because he was before

## SURPASSES* [SURPASS]

Ps  138: 2  solemn decree that it **s** your fame.
Pr    8:19  what I yield **s** choice silver.
Mt    5:20  that unless your righteousness **s**
Eph   3:19  to know this love that **s** knowledge—

## SURPASSING* [SURPASS]

Ps  150: 2  praise him for his **s** greatness.

2Co 3:10 now in comparison with the s glory.
9:14 of the s grace God has given you.
Php 3: 8 a loss because of the s worth

## SURPRISE [SURPRISED]
Ps 35: 8 may ruin overtake them by s—
1Th 5: 4 this day should s you like a thief.

## SURPRISED [SURPRISE]
Jn 3: 7 You should not be s at my saying,
1Pe 4: 4 They are s that you do not
4:12 do not be s at the fiery ordeal
1Jn 3:13 Do not be s, my brothers and sisters,

## SURRENDER [SURRENDERED]
Jer 38:21 if you refuse to s, this is what

## SURRENDERED [SURRENDER]
Lk 23:25 asked for, and s Jesus to their will.

## SURROUND [SURROUNDED, SURROUNDING, SURROUNDS]
Ps 5:12 you s them with your favor as
22:12 Many bulls s me; strong bulls
22:16 Dogs s me, a pack of villains
32: 7 and s me with songs of deliverance.
89: 7 more awesome than all who s him.
97: 2 Clouds and thick darkness s him;
125: 2 As the mountains s Jerusalem,

## SURROUNDED [SURROUND]
Ge 19: 4 both young and old—s the house.
Jdg 19:22 wicked men of the city s the house.
Eze 1:27 and brilliant light s him.
Lk 21:20 you see Jerusalem being s
Heb 12: 1 since we are s by such a great cloud
Rev 20: 9 and s the camp of God's people,

## SURROUNDING [SURROUND]
Rev 4: 4 S the throne were twenty-four other

## SURROUNDS* [SURROUND]
Ps 32:10 unfailing love s those who trust
89: 8 mighty, and your faithfulness s you.
125: 2 so the LORD s his people both

## SURVEYED*
Ecc 2:11 Yet when I s all that my hands had

## SURVIVE [SURVIVED, SURVIVES, SURVIVORS]
Dt 4:27 few of you will s among the nations
Am 7: 2 How can Jacob s? He is so small!"
7: 5 How can Jacob s? He is so small!"
Mk 13:20 short those days, no one would s.

## SURVIVED [SURVIVE]
Ex 14:28 into the sea. Not one of them s.
Nu 14:38 Nun and Caleb son of Jephunneh s.
Ne 1: 2 Jewish remnant that had s the exile,

## SURVIVES [SURVIVE]
Isa 37: 4 pray for the remnant that still s."

1Co 3:14 If what has been built s, the builder

## SURVIVORS [SURVIVE]
Isa 1: 9 Almighty had left us some s,
Eze 14:22 Yet there will be some s—

## SUSA
Ezr 4: 9 and Babylon, the Elamites of S,
Ne 1: 1 year, while I was in the citadel of S,
Est 1: 2 his royal throne in the citadel of S,

## SUSPECTS [SUSPICIONS]
Nu 5:14 and s her even though she is not

## SUSPENDS*
Job 26: 7 he s the earth over nothing.

## SUSPENSE
Jn 10:24 "How long will you keep us in s?

## SUSPICIONS* [SUSPECTS]
1Ti 6: 4 in envy, strife, malicious talk, evil s

## SUSTAIN [SUSTAINED, SUSTAINING, SUSTAINS]
Ru 4:15 your life and s you in your old age.
Ps 51:12 grant me a willing spirit, to s me.
55:22 on the LORD and he will s you;
Isa 46: 4 I am he, I am he who will s you.
46: 4 I will s you and I will rescue you.

## SUSTAINED [SUSTAIN]
Ne 9:21 For forty years you s them

## SUSTAINING* [SUSTAIN]
Heb 1: 3 s all things by his powerful word.

## SUSTAINS [SUSTAIN]
Ps 18:35 shield, and your right hand s me;
146: 9 the foreigner and s the fatherless
147: 6 The LORD s the humble but casts
Isa 50: 4 to know the word that s the weary.

## SWADDLED, SWADDLING, SWADDLINGBAND (KJV) See [WRAPPED IN] CLOTHS

## SWALLOW [SWALLOWED]
Nu 16:34 "The earth is going to s us too!"
Ps 21: 9 The LORD will s them up in his
84: 3 and the s a nest for herself,
Isa 25: 8 he will s up death forever.
Jnh 1:17 provided a huge fish to s Jonah,
Mt 23:24 You strain out a gnat but s a camel.

## SWALLOWED [SWALLOW]
Ge 41: 7 of grain s up the seven healthy,
Nu 16:32 earth opened its mouth and s them
Ps 106:17 The earth opened up and s Dathan;
1Co 15:54 "Death has been s up in victory."
2Co 5: 4 so that what is mortal may be s

## SWARM
Dt   14:19  All flying insects that s are unclean

## SWAYED
Mt   11:  7  A reed s by the wind?
     22:16  You aren't s by others, because you
2Ti   3:  6  and are s by all kinds of evil desires,

## SWEAR  [SWEARING, SWEARS, SWORE, SWORN]
Ge   22:16  and said, "I s by myself,
Lev  19:12  " 'Do not s falsely by my name
Jos   2:12  please s to me by the LORD
     23:  7  names of their gods or s by them.
Ps   24:  4  trust in an idol or s by a false god.
Isa  45:23  by me every tongue will s.
Mt    5:34  I tell you, do not s an oath at all:
Heb   6:13  was no one greater for him to s by,
Jas   5:12  my brothers and sisters, do not s—

## SWEARING*  [SWEAR]
Jer   5:  2  lives,' still they are s falsely."

## SWEARS  [SWEAR]
Zec   5:  3  everyone who s falsely will be
Mt   23:16  'If anyone s by the temple, it means

## SWEAT*
Ge    3:19  the s of your brow you will eat your
Lk   22:44  his s was like drops of blood falling

## SWEEP  [SWEEPS, SWEPT]
Ge   18:23  "Will you s away the righteous
Ps   90:  5  Yet you s people away in the sleep
SS    8:  7  rivers cannot s it away.
Lk   15:  8  s the house and search carefully

## SWEEPS  [SWEEP]
Pr    1:27  disaster s over you like a whirlwind,
Isa  40:24  a whirlwind s them away like chaff.

## SWEET  [SWEETER, SWEETNESS]
Ex   15:25  the water, and the water became s.
Job  20:12  "Though evil is s in his mouth
Ps 119:103  How s are your words to my taste,
Pr    9:17  "Stolen water is s; food eaten
     13:19  A longing fulfilled is s to the soul,
     16:24  s to the soul and healing
     20:17  Food gained by fraud tastes s,
Ecc   5:12  The sleep of laborers is s,
Isa   5:20  who put bitter for s and s for bitter.
Eze   3:  3  it tasted as s as honey in my mouth.
Rev  10:10  It tasted as s as honey in my mouth,

## SWEETER*  [SWEET]
Jdg  14:18  said to him, "What is s than honey?
Ps   19:10  they are s than honey, than honey
    119:103  my taste, s than honey to my mouth!

## SWEETNESS*  [SWEET]
SS    4:11  Your lips drop s as the honeycomb,
      5:16  His mouth is s itself;

## SWELL
Dt    8:  4  feet did not s during these forty

## SWEPT  [SWEEP]
Ge   19:15  you will be s away when the city is
Ex   14:27  and the LORD s them into the sea.
Ps   58:  9  the wicked will be s away.
Mt   12:44  s·clean and put in order.
Hos  10:  7  king will be destroyed, s away
Rev  12:  4  Its tail is a third of the stars

## SWIFT  [SWIFTLY]
Pr    1:16  into evil, they are s to shed blood.
Ecc   9:11  The race is not to the s or the battle
Isa  59:  7  they are s to shed innocent blood.
Jer  46:  6  "The s cannot flee nor the strong
Ro    3:15  "Their feet are s to shed blood;
2Pe   2:  1  bringing s destruction

## SWIFTLY  [SWIFT]
Ps  147:15  to the earth; his word runs s.
Isa  60:22  in its time I will do this s."

## SWINDLERS*
1Co   5:10  or the greedy and s, or idolaters.
      5:11  or slanderers, drunkards or s.
      6:10  nor slanderers nor s will inherit

## SWINE  (KJV) See PIG

## SWING
Joel  3:13  S the sickle, for the harvest is ripe.

## SWIRLED*
2Sa  22:  5  The waves of death s about me;
Jnh   2:  3  seas, and the currents s about me;

## SWORD  [SWORDS]
Ge    3:24  and a flaming s flashing back
Ex   18:  4  saved me from the s of Pharaoh."
Lev  26:  7  they will fall by the s before you.
Nu   14:  3  this land only to let us fall by the s?
Dt   32:41  when I sharpen my flashing s
Jos   5:13  of him with a drawn s in his hand.
1Sa  17:45  "You come against me with s
     17:47  here will know that it is not by s
     31:  4  so Saul took his own s and fell on it.
2Sa  12:10  the s will never depart from your
1Ch  21:30  he was afraid of the s of the angel
Ne    4:18  the builders wore his s at his side as
Ps   22:20  Deliver me from the s, my precious
     44:  3  by their s that they won the land,
     44:  6  my s does not bring me victory;
     45:  3  Gird your s on your side,
    149:  6  and a double-edged s in their hands,
Pr    5:  4  as gall, sharp as a double-edged s.
Isa   2:  4  will not take up s against nation,
     49:  2  made my mouth like a sharpened s,
Jer  15:  2  those for the s, to the s;
La    1:20  Outside, the s bereaves;
Eze   5:  2  For I will pursue them with drawn s.
Hos   2:18  Bow and s and battle I will abolish
Mic   4:  3  will not take up s against nation,
Mt   10:34  did not come to bring peace, but a s.

Mt 26:52 all who draw the s will die by the s.
Lk 2:35 a s will pierce your own soul too."
Ac 12: 2 of John, put to death with the s.
Ro 13: 4 for rulers do not bear the s for no
Eph 6:17 of salvation and the s of the Spirit,
Heb 4:12 Sharper than any double-edged s,
11:34 and escaped the edge of the s;
11:37 they were killed by the s.
Rev 1:16 mouth was a sharp, double-edged s.
6: 4 To him was given a large s.
13:14 the beast who was wounded by the s
19:15 of his mouth is a sharp s

## PUT ... TO THE SWORD See PUT

## SWORDS [SWORD]
Pr 12:18 words of the reckless pierce like s,
Ps 37:15 their s will pierce their own hearts,
57: 4 arrows, whose tongues are sharp s.
64: 3 They sharpen their tongues like s
Isa 2: 4 They will beat their s
Joel 3:10 Beat your plowshares into s
Mk 14:48 "that you have come out with s

## SWORE [SWEAR]
Ge 26: 3 and will confirm the oath I s to your
Ex 6: 8 to the land I s with uplifted hand
32:13 to whom you s by your own self:
Nu 14:30 of you will enter the land I s
Dt 6:10 into the land he s to your fathers,
Ps 89:49 in your faithfulness you s to David?
132:11 The LORD s an oath to David,
Lk 1:73 the oath he s to our father Abraham:
Heb 6:13 him to swear by, he s by himself,
Rev 10: 6 And he s by him who lives for ever

## SWORN [SWEAR]
Jos 21:43 gave Israel all the land he had s
Ps 89:35 for all, I have s by my holiness—
110: 4 The LORD has s and will not
Jer 32:22 You gave them this land you had s
Eze 20:42 the land I had s with uplifted hand
Heb 7:21 "The Lord has s and will not

## SYCAMORE-FIG [FIG]
Am 7:14 and I also took care of s trees.
Lk 19: 4 and climbed a s tree to see him,

## SYCHAR*
Jn 4: 5 came to a town in Samaria called S,

## SYMBOL* [SYMBOLIC, SYMBOLIZES, SYMBOLS]
Ex 13:16 and a s on your forehead
Nu 6: 7 because the s of their dedication

## SYMBOLIC* [SYMBOL]
Zec 3: 8 you who are s of things to come:

## SYMBOLIZES* [SYMBOL]
Nu 6: 9 the hair that s their dedication,
6:18 the hair that s their dedication.
6:19 the hair that s their dedication,
1Pe 3:21 this water s baptism that now saves

## SYMBOLS* [SYMBOL]
Dt 6: 8 Tie them as s on your hands
11:18 tie them as s on your hands and bind
Isa 8:18 and s in Israel from the LORD
57: 8 you have put your pagan s.

## SYMPATHETIC* [SYMPATHY]
1Pe 3: 8 like-minded, be s, love one another,

## SYMPATHIZE* [SYMPATHY]
Job 2:11 by agreement to go and s with him

## SYMPATHY [SYMPATHETIC, SYMPATHIZE]
Ps 69:20 I looked for s, but there was none,

## SYNAGOGUE [SYNAGOGUES]
Mt 13:54 began teaching the people in their s,
Lk 4:16 the Sabbath day he went into the s,
8:41 a man named Jairus, a s leader,
Jn 16: 2 They will put you out of the s;
Ac 13:14 On the Sabbath they entered the s
14: 1 went as usual into the Jewish s.
17: 2 Paul went into the s, and on three
18: 4 Every Sabbath he reasoned in the s,
18:26 He began to speak boldly in the s.
Rev 2: 9 and are not, but are a s of Satan.
3: 9 those who are of the s of Satan,

## SYNAGOGUES [SYNAGOGUE]
Mt 4:23 teaching in their s,
6: 2 as the hypocrites do in the s
10:17 councils and be flogged in the s.
Lk 12:11 "When you are brought before s,
Jn 18:20 "I always taught in s
Ac 13: 5 the word of God in the Jewish s.

## SYNTYCHE*
Php 4: 2 and I plead with S to be of the same

## SYRIA [SYRIAN]
Mt 4:24 News about him spread all over S,
Gal 1:21 Then I went to S and Cilicia.

## SYRIAN* [SYRIA]
Mk 7:26 a Greek, born in S Phoenicia.
Lk 4:27 only Naaman the S."

## SWORE [SWEAR]
Ge 26: 3 and will confirm the oath I s to your
Ex 6: 8 to the land I s with uplifted hand
32:13 to whom you s by your own self:
Nu 14:30 of you will enter the land I s
Dt 6:10 into the land he s to your fathers,
Ps 89:49 in your faithfulness you s to David?
132:11 The LORD s an oath to David,
Lk 1:73 the oath he s to our father Abraham:
Heb 6:13 him to swear by, he s by himself,
Rev 10: 6 And he s by him who lives for ever

## SWORN [SWEAR]
Jos 21:43 gave Israel all the land he had s
Ps 89:35 for all, I have s by my holiness—
110: 4 The LORD has s and will not

Jer 32:22 You gave them this land you had s
Eze 20:42 the land I had s with uplifted hand
Heb 7:21 "The Lord has s and will not

## SYCAMORE-FIG [FIG]
Am 7:14 and I also took care of s trees.
Lk 19: 4 and climbed a s tree to see him,

## SYCHAR*
Jn 4: 5 came to a town in Samaria called S,

## SYMBOL* [SYMBOLIC, SYMBOLIZES, SYMBOLS]
Ex 13:16 and a s on your forehead
Nu 6: 7 because the s of their dedication

## SYMBOLIC* [SYMBOL]
Zec 3: 8 you who are s of things to come:

## SYMBOLIZES* [SYMBOL]
Nu 6: 9 the hair that s their dedication,
6:18 the hair that s their dedication.
6:19 the hair that s their dedication,
1Pe 3:21 this water s baptism that now saves

## SYMBOLS* [SYMBOL]
Dt 6: 8 Tie them as s on your hands
11:18 tie them as s on your hands and bind
Isa 8:18 and s in Israel from the LORD
57: 8 you have put your pagan s.

## SYMPATHETIC* [SYMPATHY]
1Pe 3: 8 like-minded, be s, love one another,

## SYMPATHIZE* [SYMPATHY]
Job 2:11 by agreement to go and s with him

## SYMPATHY [SYMPATHETIC, SYMPATHIZE]
Ps 69:20 I looked for s, but there was none,

## SYNAGOGUE [SYNAGOGUES]
Mt 13:54 began teaching the people in their s,
Lk 4:16 the Sabbath day he went into the s,
8:41 a man named Jairus, a s leader,
Jn 16: 2 They will put you out of the s;
Ac 13:14 On the Sabbath they entered the s
14: 1 went as usual into the Jewish s.
17: 2 Paul went into the s, and on three
18: 4 Every Sabbath he reasoned in the s,
18:26 He began to speak boldly in the s.
Rev 2: 9 and are not, but are a s of Satan,
3: 9 those who are of the s of Satan,

## SYNAGOGUES [SYNAGOGUE]
Mt 4:23 teaching in their s,
6: 2 as the hypocrites do in the s
10:17 councils and be flogged in the s.
Lk 12:11 "When you are brought before s,
Jn 18:20 "I always taught in s
Ac 13: 5 the word of God in the Jewish s.

## SYNTYCHE*
Php 4: 2 and I plead with S to be of the same

## SYRIA [SYRIAN]
Mt 4:24 News about him spread all over S,
Gal 1:21 Then I went to S and Cilicia.

## SYRIAN* [SYRIA]
Mk 7:26 a Greek, born in S Phoenicia.
Lk 4:27 only Naaman the S."

---

# T

---

## TABERNACLE [TABERNACLES]
Ex 25: 9 Make this t and all its furnishings
38:21 of the materials used for the t, the t
40:18 When Moses set up the t, he put
40:34 the glory of the LORD filled the t.
Nu 1:50 charge of the t of the covenant law—
Heb 8: 2 the true t set up by the Lord,
9:11 more perfect t that is not made
Rev 15: 5 that is, the t of the covenant law—

## TABERNACLES [TABERNACLE]
Lev 23:34 the LORD's Festival of T begins,
Dt 16:16 of Weeks and the Festival of T
Zec 14:16 and to celebrate the Festival of T.
Jn 7: 2 the Jewish Festival of T was near,

## TABITHA* [DORCAS]
Disciple, also known as Dorcas, whom Peter raised from the dead (Ac 9:36–42).

## TABLE [TABLES]
Ex 25:23 "Make a t of acacia wood—
Nu 3:31 care of the ark, the t, the lampstand,
Ps 23: 5 You prepare a t before me
78:19 "Can God really spread a t
1Co 10:21 the Lord's t and the t of demons.

## TABLES [TABLE]
Mk 11:15 He overturned the t of the money
Jn 2:15 changers and overturned their t.
Ac 6: 2 word of God in order to wait on t.

## TABLET* [TABLETS]
Pr 3: 3 write them on the t of your heart.
7: 3 write them on the t of your heart.
Isa 30: 8 write it on a t for them, inscribe it
Lk 1:63 He asked for a writing t,

## TABLETS [TABLET]
Ex 31:18 the t of stone inscribed by the finger
32:19 and he threw the t out of his hands,
Dt 10: 5 and put the t in the ark I had made,
2Co 3: 3 not on t of stone but on t of human

## TAIL [TAILS]
Dt 28:13 will make you the head, not the t.
Jdg 15: 4 foxes and tied them t to t in pairs.

Rev 12: 4 Its **t** swept a third of the stars

## TAILS [TAIL]

Rev 9:10 They had **t** with stingers,
9:10 in their **t** they had power to torment
9:19 was in their mouths and in their **t**;
9:19 for their **t** were like snakes,

## TAKE [TAKEN, TAKES, TAKING, TOOK]

Ge 15: 7 give you this land to **t** possession
22: 2 Then God said, "**T** your son,
22:17 Your descendants will **t** possession
Ex 3: 5 "**T** off your sandals, for the place
6: 7 I will **t** you as my own people, and I
21:23 injury, you are to **t** life for life,
22:22 "Do not **t** advantage of a widow
34: 9 sin, and **t** us as your inheritance."
Lev 10:17 to you to **t** away the guilt
25:14 do not **t** advantage of each other.
Nu 1: 2 "**T** a census of the whole Israelite
13:30 go up and **t** possession of the land,
Dt 1: 8 **t** possession of the land the LORD
12:32 do not add to it or **t** away from it.
31:26 "**T** this Book of the Law and place
1Sa 8:11 He will **t** your sons and make them
1Ki 11:34 I will not **t** the whole kingdom
19: 4 "**T** my life; I am no better than my
1Ch 17:13 I will never **t** my love away
Job 23:10 But he knows the way that I **t**;
Ps 2:12 Blessed are all who **t** refuge in him.
25:18 my distress and **t** away all my sins.
27:14 be strong and **t** heart and wait
31:24 Be strong and **t** heart, all you who
34: 8 blessed are those who **t** refuge
36: 7 **t** refuge in the shadow of your wings.
49:17 for they will **t** nothing with them
51:11 or **t** your Holy Spirit from me.
73:24 afterward you will **t** me into glory.
89:33 but I will not **t** my love from him,
118: 8 It is better to **t** refuge in the LORD
119:43 Never **t** your word of truth from my
Pr 4: 4 "**T** hold of my words with all your heart
22:23 for the LORD will **t** up their case
Isa 62: 4 for the LORD will **t** delight in you,
Jer 51:11 The LORD will **t** vengeance,
Eze 3:10 **t** to heart all the words I speak
33:11 I **t** no pleasure in the death
Da 8:13 "How long will it **t** for the vision
11:36 has been determined must **t** place.
Hos 14: 2 **T** words with you and return
Mic 4: 3 Nation will not **t** up sword against
Mt 1:20 afraid to **t** Mary home as your wife,
2:13 "**t** the child and his mother
2:20 **t** the child and his mother and go
7: 5 first **t** the plank out of your own
11:29 **T** my yoke upon you and learn
16:24 deny themselves and **t** up their cross
17:27 **T** the first fish you catch;
26:26 to his disciples, saying, "**T** and eat;
Mk 2: 9 say, 'Get up, **t** your mat and walk'?
8:34 deny themselves and **t** up their cross
14:36 **T** this cup from me.
Lk 21: 7 sign that they are about to **t** place?"
Ac 1:20 and, " 'May another **t** his place
Ro 12:19 Do not **t** revenge, my dear friends,

2Co 12: 8 with the Lord to **t** it away from me.
Eph 6:11 that you can **t** your stand against
1Ti 3: 5 how can he **t** care of God's church?)
6:12 **T** hold of the eternal life
Heb 9:28 sacrificed once to **t** away the sins
Rev 1: 1 his servants what must soon **t** place.
4: 1 I will show you what must **t** place
5: 9 "You are worthy to **t** the scroll
22:17 let all who wish **t** the free gift

## TAKEN [TAKE]

Ge 2:23 for she was **t** out of man."
27:36 and now he's **t** my blessing!"
Lev 6: 4 they have stolen or **t** by extortion,
Nu 8:16 I have **t** them as my own in place
19: 3 it is to be **t** outside the camp
Jos 7:11 They have **t** some of the devoted
1Sa 10:21 Finally Saul son of Kish was **t**.
2Sa 7:15 my love will never be **t** away
12:13 "The LORD has **t** away your sin.
Ps 31: 1 In you, LORD, I have **t** refuge;
Ecc 3:14 be added to it and nothing **t** from it.
Isa 6: 7 your guilt is **t** away and your sin
Jer 13:17 LORD's flock will be **t** captive.
38:28 This is how Jerusalem was **t**:
Da 5: 2 Nebuchadnezzar his father had **t**
Zec 3: 4 "See, I have **t** away your sin, and I
Mt 13:12 even what they have will be **t**
24:40 one will be **t** and the other left.
26:39 possible, may this cup be **t** from me.
Lk 24:51 left them and was **t** up into heaven.
Jn 20:13 "They have **t** my Lord away,"
Ac 1: 9 he was **t** up before their very eyes,
Php 3:13 consider myself yet to have **t** hold
1Ti 3:16 on in the world, was **t** up in glory.
Heb 11: 5 By faith Enoch was **t** from this life,

## TAKES [TAKE]

Lev 24:17 " 'Anyone who **t** the life
1Ki 20:11 not boast like one who **t** it off.' "
Ps 149: 4 the LORD **t** delight in his people;
Isa 57: 1 and no one **t** it to heart;
Na 1: 2 The LORD **t** vengeance on his foes
Mk 4:15 **t** away the word that was sown
Lk 6:30 and if anyone **t** what belongs to you,
Jn 1:29 who **t** away the sin of the world!
10:18 No one **t** it from me, but I lay it
Rev 22:19 if any one of you **t** words away

## TAKING [TAKE]

Php 2: 7 himself nothing by **t** the very nature

## TALEBEARER (KJV) See GOSSIP, [SPREADING] SLANDER

## TALENT [TALENTS]

Ex 25:39 A **t** of pure gold is to be used

## TALENTS [TALENT]

Est 3: 9 give ten thousand **t** of silver

## TALES*

1Ti 4: 7 with godless myths and old wives' **t**;

**TALK** [TALKED, TALKING, TALKS]
Dt      6: 7   **T** about them when you sit at home
Pr    12:13   are trapped by their sinful **t**, and so
Ro     9:20   human being, to **t** back to God?

**TALKED** [TALK]
Ge   35:14   the place where God had **t** with him,
1Co 13:11   When I was a child, I **t** like a child,

**TALKING** [TALK]
Mt    17: 3   them Moses and Elijah, **t** with Jesus.
Jn      4:27   to find him **t** with a woman.

**TALKS**\* [TALK]
Pr    20:19   so avoid anyone who **t** too much.

**TALL** [TALLER]
1Ch 11:23   an Egyptian who was five cubits **t**.

**TALLER** [TALL]
1Sa     9: 2   he was a head **t** than anyone else.

**TAMAR**
    1. Wife of Judah's sons Er and Onan (Ge 38:1–10).
Tricked Judah into fathering children when he refused
her his third son (Ge 38:11–30; Mt 1:3).
    2. Daughter of David, raped by Amnon (2Sa 13).

**TAMARISK**
Ge   21:33   Abraham planted a **t** tree

**TAME**\*
Jas      3: 8   but no one can **t** the tongue. It is

**TANNER**
Ac     9:43   some time with a **t** named Simon.

**TAR**
Ge   14:10   Valley of Siddim was full of **t** pits,

**TARES** (KJV) See WEEDS

**TARGET**
Job   16:12   He has made me his **t**;
La      3:12   and made me the **t** for his arrows.

**TARSHISH**
Ps    48: 7   them like ships of **T** shattered
Isa   60: 9   in the lead are the ships of **T**,
Jnh     1: 3   from the Lord and headed for **T**.

**TARSUS**
Ac     9:11   ask for a man from **T** named Saul,
       11:25   Barnabas went to **T** to look for Saul,

**TASK** [TASKS]
1Ch 29: 1   The **t** is great, because this palatial
Mk   13:34   each with an assigned **t**, and tells
Ac   20:24   the **t** of testifying to the good news
1Co   3: 5   the Lord has assigned to each his **t**.
2Co   2:16   And who is equal to such a **t**?
1Ti     3: 1   to be an overseer desires a noble **t**.

**TASKS** [TASK]
Pr    31:17   her arms are strong for her **t**.

**TASSELS**
Dt    22:12   Make **t** on the four corners
Mt    23: 5   and the **t** on their garments long;

**TASTE** [TASTED, TASTY]
Ps    34: 8   **T** and see that the Lord is good;
      119:103   How sweet are your words to my **t**,
Pr    24:13   from the comb is sweet to your **t**.
SS      2: 3   shade, and his fruit is sweet to my **t**.
Mt    16:28   here will not **t** death before they see
Col     2:21   Do not **t**! Do not touch!'"?
Heb    2: 9   God he might **t** death for everyone.

**TASTED** [TASTE]
Eze     3: 3   it **t** as sweet as honey in my mouth.
Heb    6: 4   who have **t** the heavenly gift,
1Pe     2: 3   you have **t** that the Lord is good.
Rev   10:10   It **t** as sweet as honey in my mouth,

**TASTY** [TASTE]
Ge   27: 4   Prepare me the kind of **t** food I like

**TATTOO**\*
Lev   19:28   dead or put **t** marks on yourselves.

**TAUGHT** [TEACH]
Dt      4: 5   I have **t** you decrees and laws as
      31:22   that day and **t** it to the Israelites.
2Ki  17:28   **t** them how to worship the Lord.
2Ch  17:9   They **t** throughout Judah,
Ps 119:102   laws, for you yourself have **t** me.
Pr      4: 4   Then he **t** me, and he said to me,
      31: 1   inspired utterance his mother **t** him.
Isa   29:13   human rules they have been **t**.
      40:14   and who **t** him the right way?
      50: 4   my ear to listen like one being **t**.
      54:13   All your children will be **t**
Hos  11: 3   It was I who **t** Ephraim to walk,
Mt     7:29   because he **t** as one who had
Mk     4: 2   He **t** them many things by parables,
Jn      6:45   'They will all be **t** by God.'
      7:15   learning without having been **t**?"
Ac   20:20   to you but have **t** you publicly
1Co   2:13   not in words **t** us by human wisdom
Gal     1:12   any human source, nor was I **t** it;
1Ti     1:20   to Satan to be **t** not to blaspheme.
      4: 1   spirits and things **t** by demons.
1Jn     2:27   just as it has **t** you, remain in him.

**TAUNT** [TAUNTS]
1Ki  18:27   At noon Elijah began to **t** them.
Ps   102: 8   All day long my enemies **t** me;

**TAUNTS** [TAUNT]
Ps 119:42   then I can answer anyone who **t** me,
Eze   36:15   No longer will I make you hear the **t**

**TAX** [TAXES]
2Ch  24: 6   Jerusalem the **t** imposed by Moses
Mt      5:46   not even the **t** collectors doing that?
      11:19   a friend of **t** collectors and sinners.'

Mt  17:24  your teacher pay the temple t?"
    22:17  right to pay the imperial t to Caesar
Lk  18:10  Pharisee and the other a t collector.

## TAX COLLECTOR Da 11:20; Mt 10:3; 18:17;
Lk 5:27; 18:10, 11, 13; 19:2

## TAX COLLECTORS Mt 5:46; 9:10, 11; 11:19;
21:31, 32; Mk 2:15, 16, 16; Lk 3:12; 5:29, 30;
7:29, 34; 15:1

## TAXES [TAX]
Ro  13: 7  what you owe: If you owe t, pay t;

## TEACH [TAUGHT, TEACHER, TEACHERS, TEACHES, TEACHING, TEACHINGS]
Ex   4:12  speak and will t you what to say."
    18:20  T them his decrees and instructions,
    33:13  t me your ways so I may know you
Lev 10:11  and so you can t the Israelites all
Dt   4: 9  T them to your children and to their
     6: 1  your God directed me to t you
     8: 3  to t you that people do not live
    11:19  T them to your children,
1Sa 12:23  I will t you the way that is good
1Ki  8:36  T them the right way to live,
Job  6:24  "T me, and I will be quiet;
    21:22  "Can anyone t knowledge to God,
Ps  25: 4  ways, LORD, t me your paths.
    32: 8  and t you in the way you should go;
    34:11  I will t you the fear of the LORD.
    51:13  I will t transgressors your ways,
    78: 2  I will t you lessons from the past—
    78: 5  our ancestors to t their children,
    90:12  T us to number our days, that we
   143:10  T me to do your will, for you are my
Pr   9: 9  t the righteous and they will add
    22:17  apply your heart to what I t,
Jer 31:34  longer will they t their neighbors,
Mic  4: 2  He will t us his ways, so that we
Mt   5: 2  and he began to t them. He said:
Lk  11: 1  "Lord, t us to pray, just as John
    12:12  for the Holy Spirit will t you
Jn  14:26  will t you all things and will remind
Ac   5:28  "We gave you strict orders not to t
Ro   2:21  you, then, who t others, do you not t
    12: 7  if it is teaching, then t;
    15: 4  in the past was written to t us,
Col  3:16  dwell among you richly as you t
1Ti  1: 3  not to t false doctrines any longer
     2:12  I do not permit a woman to t
     3: 2  respectable, hospitable, able to t,
2Ti  2: 2  will also be qualified to t others.
     2:24  to everyone, able to t, not resentful.
Tit  2: 1  must t what is appropriate to sound
     2:15  then, are the things you should t.
Heb  5:12  to t you the elementary truths
     8:11  longer will they t their neighbors,
Jas  3: 1  that we who t will be judged more
1Jn  2:27  you do not need anyone to t you.

## TEACHER [TEACH]
Ezr  7: 6  He was a t well versed in the Law
Ne   8: 1  told Ezra the t of the Law
    12:36  Ezra the t of the Law led the procession

Ecc  1: 1  The words of the T, son of David,
    12: 9  Not only was the T wise, but he
Mt  10:24  "Students are not above their t,
    13:52  "Therefore every t of the law who
    22:36  "T, which is the greatest
    23:10  for you have one T, the Messiah.
Lk   6:40  are fully trained will be like their t.
Jn   1:38  said, "Rabbi" (which means "T"),
     3: 2  know that you are a t who has come
    13:14  your Lord and T, have washed your
1Co  1:20  Where is the t of the law?

## TEACHER OF THE LAW See LAW

## TEACHERS [TEACH]
Ps 119:99  I have more insight than all my t,
Pr   5:13  I would not obey my t or turn my
Mt   7:29  and not as their t of the law.
Mk  12:38  "Watch out for the t of the law.
Lk  20:46  "Beware of the t of the law.
1Co 12:28  prophets, third t, then miracles,
Eph  4:11  the evangelists, the pastors and t,
2Ti  4: 3  around them a great number of t
Heb  5:12  by this time you ought to be t,
Jas  3: 1  many of you should presume to be t,
2Pe  2: 1  as there will be false t among you.
     2: 3  their greed these t will exploit you

## TEACHERS OF THE LAW See LAW

## TEACHES [TEACH]
Ps  25: 9  in what is right and t them his way.
    94:10  Does he who t human beings lack
Isa 48:17  God, who t you what is best for you,
Hab  2:18  Or an image that t lies?
Mt   5:19  t others accordingly will be called
1Ti  6: 3  If anyone t otherwise and does not
Tit  2:12  It t us to say "No" to ungodliness
1Jn  2:27  But as his anointing t you about all

## TEACHING [TEACH]
Ezr  7:10  to t its decrees and laws in Israel.
Ps  78: 1  My people, hear my t;
Pr   1: 8  and do not forsake your mother's t.
     3: 1  son, do not forget my t, but keep my
     6:23  command is a lamp, this t is a light,
    13:14  The t of the wise is a fountain
Mt  28:20  t them to obey everything I have
Mk   1:27  A new t—and with authority!
    11:18  whole crowd was amazed at his t.
Lk   4:15  He was t in their synagogues,
    19:47  Every day he was t at the temple.
Jn   7:17  out whether my t comes from God
     8:31  "If you hold to my t, you are really
    14:23  who loves me will obey my t.
Ac   2:42  devoted themselves to the apostles' t
     5:42  to house, they never stopped t
Ro  12: 7  if it is t, then teach;
Eph  4:14  there by every wind of t
Col  1:28  and t everyone with all wisdom,
2Th  3: 6  live according to the t you received
1Ti  4:13  of Scripture, to preaching and to t.
     5:17  whose work is preaching and t.
     6: 3  our Lord Jesus Christ and to godly t,
2Ti  2:17  Their t will spread like gangrene.
     3:16  is God-breathed and is useful for t,
Tit  1:11  by t things they ought not to teach—

Tit   2: 7   In your **t** show integrity,
Heb  5:13   with the **t** about righteousness.
2Jn   1: 9   in the **t** of Christ does not have God;
       1:10   to you and does not bring this **t**,
Rev   2:20   By her **t** she misleads my servants

## TEACHINGS [TEACH]

Pr    7: 2   guard my **t** as the apple of your eye.
Mt   15: 9   their **t** are merely human rules.' "
Col   2:22   on merely human commands and **t**.
2Th   2:15   hold fast to the **t** we passed
Heb   6: 1   let us move beyond the elementary **t**
      13: 9   away by all kinds of strange **t**.

## TEAR [TEARING, TEARS, TORE, TORN]

1Ki  11:13   Yet I will not **t** the whole kingdom
Ecc   3: 3   a time to **t** down and a time to build,
Mt    7: 6   and then turn and **t** you to pieces.
Mk    2:21   from the old, making the **t** worse.
Rev   7:17   God will wipe away every **t**
      21: 4   'He will wipe every **t** from their

## TEARING [TEAR]

2Co  10: 8   rather than **t** you down,

## TEARS [TEAR]

Job  12:14   What he **t** down cannot be rebuilt;
Ps   42: 3   My **t** have been my food day
     126: 5   Those who sow with **t** will reap
Pr   15:25   The LORD **t** down the house
Isa  25: 8   LORD will wipe away the **t**
Jer   9: 1   water and my eyes are a fountain of **t**!
     31:16   from weeping and your eyes from **t**,
     50: 4   of Judah together will go in **t** to seek
La    1:16   I weep and my eyes overflow with **t**.
Lk    7:38   she began to wet his feet with her **t**.
2Co   2: 4   anguish of heart and with many **t**,
Php   3:18   and now tell you again even with **t**,
Heb   5: 7   and **t** to the one who could save him

## TEETH [TOOTH]

Nu   11:33   the meat was still between their **t**
Job  19:20   escaped only by the skin of my **t**.
Ps    3: 7   break the **t** of the wicked.
     35:16   they gnashed their **t** at me.
Jer  31:29   and the children's **t** are set on edge.'
Da    7: 7   It had large iron **t**; it crushed
Mt    8:12   will be weeping and gnashing of **t**."
Ac    7:54   furious and gnashed their **t** at him.
Rev   9: 8   hair, and their **t** were like lions' **t**.

## TEKEL*

Da    5:25   MENE, MENE, T, PARSIN
      5:27   **T**: You have been weighed

## TEKOA

2Sa  14: 4   the woman from **T** went to the king,
Am    1: 1   Amos, one of the shepherds of **T**—

## TELL [TELLING, TELLS, TOLD]

Ex    6:11   **t** Pharaoh king of Egypt to let
Nu   22:35   men, but speak only what I **t** you."
Dt   18:18   He will **t** them everything I
Jdg  14:12   "Let me **t** you a riddle,"

Ru    3: 4   He will **t** you what to do."
1Sa   3:15   He was afraid to **t** Eli the vision,
2Ch  18:15   I make you swear to **t** me nothing
Ps    5: 6   you destroy those who **t** lies.
     50:12   If I were hungry I would not **t** you,
     66:16   let me **t** you what he has done
     78: 4   we will **t** the next generation
    105: 2   **t** of all his wonderful acts.
Isa  41:23   **t** us what the future holds, so we
Eze  40: 4   **T** the house of Israel everything you
Da    2: 4   **T** your servants the dream, and we
Jnh   4:11   people who cannot **t** their right hand
Mt    4: 3   **t** these stones to become bread."
     12:16   He warned them not to **t** others
Jn   20:15   away, **t** me where you have put him,
Ac   13:32   "We **t** you the good news:
1Co  15:51   Listen, I **t** you a mystery:

## TRULY I TELL YOU See TRULY

## TELLING [TELL]

Jn   13:19   "I am **t** you now before it happens,

## TELLS [TELL]

Pr   12:17   but a false witness **t** lies.
Mt   24:26   "So if anyone **t** you, 'There he is,
Jn   19:35   He knows that he **t** the truth, and he

## TEMANITE

Job   2:11   Eliphaz the **T**, Bildad the Shuhite

## TEMPER* [EVEN-TEMPERED, HOT-TEMPERED, QUICK-TEMPERED]

1Sa  20: 7   **t**, you can be sure that he is determined

## TEMPERANCE (KJV) See SELF-CONTROL

## TEMPERATE*

1Ti   3: 2   reproach, faithful to his wife, **t**,
      3:11   not malicious talkers but **t**
Tit   2: 2   Teach the older men to be **t**,

## TEMPEST

Ps   50: 3   him, and around him a **t** rages.
     55: 8   shelter, far from the **t** and storm."

## TEMPLE [TEMPLES]

Jdg   4:21   She drove the peg through his **t**
     16:30   and down came the **t** on the rulers
1Sa   5: 2   they carried the ark into Dagon's **t**
1Ki   6: 1   began to build the **t** of the LORD.
      6:38   the **t** was finished in all its details
      8:11   the glory of the LORD filled his **t**.
      8:27   How much less this **t** I have built!
2Ki  25: 9   He set fire to the **t** of the LORD,
2Ch  24: 4   to restore the **t** of the LORD.
     36:23   appointed me to build a **t** for him
Ezr   3:12   the foundation of this **t** being laid,
      5: 3   authorized you to rebuild this **t**
      6:15   The **t** was completed on the third
Ps   27: 4   the LORD and to seek him in his **t**.
     30: T   *For the dedication of the* **t**.
Isa   6: 1   and the train of his robe filled the **t**.
Jer   7:14   bears my Name, the **t** you trust in,

Eze 10: 4 The cloud filled the t, and the court
43: 4 Lord entered the t through
Da 5: 2 had taken from the t in Jerusalem,
9:27 And at the t he will set up
Mic 4: 1 the Lord's t will be established
Hab 2:20 The Lord is in his holy t;
Zec 4: 9 have laid the foundation of this t;
Mt 4: 5 stand on the highest point of the t.
12: 6 that one greater than the t is here.
23:35 whom you murdered between the t
26:61 'I am able to destroy the t of God
27:51 moment the curtain of the t was torn
Mk 15:38 The curtain of the t was torn in two
Lk 21: 5 about how the t was adorned
Jn 2:14 the t courts he found people selling
2:21 the t he had spoken of was his body.
Ac 2:46 to meet together in the t courts.
5:42 in the t courts and from house
1Co 3:16 that you yourselves are God's t
2Co 6:16 For we are the t of the living God.
Eph 2:21 rises to become a holy t in the Lord.
2Th 2: 4 so that he sets himself up in God's t,
Rev 3:12 will make pillars in the t of my God.
11:19 Then God's t in heaven was opened,
21:22 Almighty and the Lamb are its t.

## TEMPLE OF ... GOD Jdg 9:27; 2Ki 19:37;
1Ch 28:12, 21; 29:2, 3, 3, 7; 2Ch 3:3; 4:11; 5:14;
7:5; 15:18; 22:12; 23:3, 9; 24:5, 7, 13, 27; 25:24;
28:24; 31:13; 32:21; 33:7; 34:9; 36:18; Ezr 1:4,
7; 6:3, 7; 7:16, 17, 19, 20, 23; Isa 37:38; Da 1:2,
2; 5:3; Mt 26:61; 2Co 6:16; Rev 3:12; 11:1

## TEMPLE OF THE †LORD 1Ki 3:1; 6:1, 37;
7:12, 40, 45, 51; 8:10, 63, 64; 9:1, 10; 10:5, 12;
12:27; 14:26; 15:15; 2Ki 11:3, 4, 4, 10, 13, 15,
18, 19; 12:4, 9, 9, 10, 11, 12, 13, 16, 18; 14:14;
15:35; 16:8, 14, 18; 18:15, 16; 19:1, 14; 20:5, 8;
21:4, 5; 22:3, 4, 5, 8, 9; 23:2, 2, 4, 6, 7, 11, 12,
24; 24:13, 13; 25:9, 13, 16; 1Ch 6:32; 22:14;
23:4, 24, 28, 32; 24:19; 25:6; 26:12, 22, 27;
28:12, 13, 20; 29:8; 2Ch 3:1; 4:16; 5:1, 13; 7:2,
7, 11, 11; 8:1, 16, 16; 9:4, 11; 12:9; 20:5, 28;
23:5, 6, 12, 14, 18, 20; 24:4, 8, 12, 14, 18; 26:16,
21; 27:2, 3; 28:21; 29:3, 5, 15, 16, 17, 18, 20, 25,
31, 35; 30:1, 15; 31:10, 11, 16; 33:4, 5, 15; 34:8,
14, 15, 17, 30, 30; 36:7, 10, 14; Ezr 1:3, 7; 3:10;
Isa 37:1, 14; 38:20, 22; 66:20; Jer 7:4, 4, 4; 20:1;
24:1; 38:14; 52:13, 17, 20; Eze 8:16; 44:4, 5;
Hos 9:4; Zec 6:12, 13, 14, 15

## TEMPLES [TEMPLE]
Ac 17:24 and does not live in t built by hands.
1Co 6:19 your bodies are t of the Holy Spirit,

## TEMPORARY
2Co 4:18 since what is seen is t, but what is

## TEMPT* [TEMPTATION, TEMPTED,
TEMPTER, TEMPTING]
1Co 7: 5 Satan will not t you because of your
Jas 1:13 by evil, nor does he t anyone;

## TEMPTATION* [TEMPT]
Mt 6:13 And lead us not into t, but deliver us

Mt 26:41 pray so that you will not fall into t.
Mk 14:38 pray so that you will not fall into t.
Lk 11: 4 And lead us not into t.' "
22:40 "Pray that you will not fall into t."
22:46 pray so that you will not fall into t."
1Co 10:13 No t has overtaken you except what
1Ti 6: 9 who want to get rich fall into t

## TEMPTED* [TEMPT]
Mt 4: 1 the wilderness to be t by the devil.
Mk 1:13 forty days, being t by Satan.
Lk 4: 2 for forty days he was t by the devil.
1Co 10:13 not let you be t beyond what you
10:13 But when you are t,
Gal 6: 1 yourselves, or you also may be t.
1Th 3: 5 in some way the tempter had t you
Heb 2:18 he himself suffered when he was t,
2:18 able to help those who are being t.
4:15 but we have one who has been t
Jas 1:13 When t, no one should say,
1:13 For God cannot be t by evil,
1:14 you is t when you are dragged away

## TEMPTER* [TEMPT]
Mt 4: 3 The t came to him and said, "If you
1Th 3: 5 in some way the t had tempted you

## TEMPTING* [TEMPT]
Lk 4:13 the devil had finished all this t,
Jas 1:13 no one should say, "God is t me."

## TEN [TENS, TENTH, TITHE, TITHES]
Ge 18:32 What if only t can be found there?"
Ex 34:28 the T Commandments.
Lev 26: 8 of you will chase t thousand,
Dt 4:13 his covenant, the T Commandments,
10: 4 the T Commandments he had
1Sa 1: 8 I mean more to you than t sons?"
2Ki 20: 9 Shall the shadow go forward t steps,
Ps 91: 7 side, t thousand at your right hand,
Da 1:12 test your servants for t days:
7:24 The t horns are t kings who will
Mt 25: 1 will be like t virgins who took their
25:28 give it to the one who has t bags.
Lk 15: 8 suppose a woman has t silver coins
Rev 5:11 and t thousand times t thousand.
12: 3 dragon with seven heads and t horns
17:12 "The t horns you saw are t kings

## TENANTS
Mt 21:34 servants to the t to collect his fruit.

## TEND [TENDING, TENDS]
Jer 23: 2 to the shepherds who t my people:
Eze 34:14 I will t them in a good pasture,

## TENDER [TENDERLY, TENDERNESS]
Isa 53: 2 grew up before him like a t shoot,
Lk 1:78 because of the t mercy of our God,

## TENDERLY* [TENDER]
Ge 34: 3 young woman and spoke t to her.
Isa 40: 2 Speak t to Jerusalem, and proclaim
Hos 2:14 the wilderness and speak t to her.

## TENDERNESS* [TENDER]
Isa  63:15  Your **t** and compassion are withheld
Php   2: 1  the Spirit, if any **t** and compassion,

## TENDING [TEND]
Ex    3: 1  Now Moses was **t** the flock
1Sa  16:11  "He is **t** the sheep."

## TENDS [TEND]
Isa  40:11  He **t** his flock like a shepherd:

## TENS [TEN]
1Sa  18: 7  and David his **t** of thousands."
Ps    3: 6  I will not fear though **t** of thousands

## TENT [TENTMAKER, TENTS]
Ex   27:21  In the **t** of meeting,
     33: 7  calling it the "**t** of meeting."
     40: 2  up the tabernacle, the **t** of meeting,
2Sa   7: 2  the ark of God remains in a **t**."
Ps   61: 4  I long to dwell in your **t** forever
Isa  33:20  abode, a **t** that will not be moved;
     54: 2  "Enlarge the place of your **t**,
Ac   15:16  return and rebuild David's fallen **t**.
2Co   5: 1  that if the earthly **t** we live in is
2Pe   1:13  as long as I live in the **t** of this body,
Rev   7:15  throne will spread his **t** over them.

## TENT OF MEETING Ex 27:21; 28:43; 29:4,
     10, 11, 30, 32, 42, 44; 30:16, 18, 20, 26, 36;
     31:7; 33:7, 7; 35:21; 38:8, 30; 39:32, 40; 40:2, 6,
     7, 12, 22, 24, 26, 29, 30, 32, 34, 35; Lev 1:1, 3,
     5; 3:2, 8, 13; 4:4, 5, 7, 7, 14, 16, 18, 18; 6:16, 26,
     30; 8:3, 4, 31, 33, 35; 9:5, 23; 10:7, 9; 12:6;
     14:11, 23; 15:14, 29; 16:7, 16, 17, 20, 23, 33;
     17:4, 5, 6, 9; 19:21; 24:3; Nu 1:1; 2:2, 17; 3:7, 8,
     25, 25, 38; 4:3, 4, 15, 23, 25, 25, 28, 30, 33, 35,
     37, 39, 41, 43, 47; 6:10, 13, 18; 7:5, 89; 8:9, 15,
     19, 22, 24, 26; 10:3; 11:16; 12:4; 14:10; 16:18,
     19, 42, 43, 50; 17:4; 18:4, 6, 21, 22, 23, 31; 19:4;
     20:6; 25:6; 27:2; 31:54; Dt 31:14, 14; Jos 18:1;
     19:51; 1Sa 2:22; 1Ki 8:4; 1Ch 6:32; 9:21, 23;
     23:32; 2Ch 1:3, 6, 13; 5:5

## TENTH [TEN]
Ge   14:20  Abram gave him a **t** of everything.
Nu   18:26  you must present a **t** of that tithe as
Dt   14:22  Be sure to set aside a **t** of all
1Sa   8:15  He will take a **t** of your grain
Isa   6:13  And though a **t** remains in the land,
Lk   11:42  because you give God a **t** of your
     18:12  a week and give a **t** of all I get.'
Heb   7: 4  the patriarch Abraham gave him a **t**

## TENTMAKER* [TENT]
Ac   18: 3  and because he was a **t** as they were,

## TENTS [TENT]
Ge   13:12  plain and pitched his **t** near Sodom.
Nu    1:52  are to set up their **t** by divisions,
2Sa  20: 1  Everyone to your **t**, Israel!"
Ps   84:10  than dwell in the **t** of the wicked.

## TERAH
Ge   11:27  **T** became the father of Abram,

## TEREBINTH
Isa   6:13  as the **t** and oak leave stumps

## TERMS
Dt   29: 1  These are the **t** of the covenant
Jer  11: 3  is everyone who does not obey the **t**

## TERRIBLE [TERROR]
2Ti   3: 1  There will be **t** times in the last

## TERRIFIED [TERROR]
Dt    7:21  Do not be **t** by them, for the LORD
     20: 3  do not be **t** or give way to panic
Est   7: 6  Then Haman was **t** before the king
Ps   90: 7  anger and **t** by your indignation.
Jer   1:17  Do not be **t** by them, or I will terrify
Eze   2: 6  of what they say or be **t** by them,
Mt   14:26  walking on the lake, they were **t**.
     17: 6  they fell facedown to the ground, **t**.
     27:54  they were **t**, and exclaimed,
Mk    4:41  They were **t** and asked each other,

## TERRIFYING [TERROR]
Heb  12:21  The sight was so **t** that Moses said,

## TERRITORY
Ex   34:24  before you and enlarge your **t**,
Jos   1: 4  Your **t** will extend from the desert
1Ch   4:10  would bless me and enlarge my **t**!
2Co  10:16  already done in someone else's **t**.

## TERROR [TERRIBLE, TERRIFIED,
     TERRIFYING, TERRORS]
Ex   23:27  "I will send my **t** ahead of you
Dt    2:25  very day I will begin to put the **t**
     28:67  of the **t** that will fill your hearts
Job   9:34  his **t** would frighten me no more.
Ps   31:13  whispering, "**T** on every side!"
     91: 5  You will not fear the **t** of night,
Pr   21:15  to the righteous but **t** to evildoers.
Isa  13: 8  **T** will seize them, pain and anguish
     24:17  **T** and pit and snare await you,
     51:13  live in constant **t** every day because
     54:14  **T** will be far removed; it will not
Jer  20:10  many whispering, "**T** on every side!
Lk   21:26  People will faint from **t**,
Ro   13: 3  rulers hold no **t** for those who do

## TERRORS [TERROR]
Ps   55: 4  the **t** of death have fallen on me.
La    2:22  so you summoned against me **t**

## TERTIUS*
Ro   16:22  I, **T**, who wrote down this letter,

## TEST [TESTED, TESTER, TESTING,
     TESTINGS, TESTS]
Ex   16: 4  In this way I will **t** them and see
Dt    6:16  your God to the **t** as you did
      8: 2  **t** you in order to know what was

Jdg 3: 4 They were left to t the Israelites
6:39 Allow me one more t
1Ki 10: 1 she came to t Solomon with hard
1Ch 29:17 that you t the heart and are pleased
Ps 26: 2 T me, LORD, and try me,
78:18 to the t by demanding the food they
106:14 the wilderness they put God to the t.
139:23 t me and know my anxious
Jer 9: 7 I will refine and t them, for what
11:20 judge righteously and t the heart
Mal 3:10 T me in this," says the LORD
Lk 4:12 put the Lord your God to the t.' "
10:25 expert in the law stood up to t Jesus.
Ac 5: 9 could you conspire to t the Spirit
Ro 12: 2 you will be able to t and approve
16:10 fidelity to Christ has stood the t.
1Co 3:13 and the fire will t the quality of each
10: 9 We should not t Christ, as some
2Co 13: 5 you are in the faith; t yourselves.
Gal 6: 4 of you should t your own actions.
1Th 5:21 but t them all; hold on to what is
Jas 1:12 because when they have stood the t,
1Jn 4: 1 t the spirits to see whether they are
Rev 2:10 put some of you in prison to t you,
3:10 the whole world to t those who live

## TESTED [TEST]

Ge 22: 1 Some time later God t Abraham.
Ex 17: 7 because they t the LORD saying,
Nu 14:22 disobeyed me and t me ten times—
Job 23:10 when he has t me, I will come forth
34:36 that Job might be t to the utmost
Ps 66:10 For you, God, t us; you refined us
Pr 27:21 but people are t by their praise.
Ecc 7:23 All this I t by wisdom and I said,
Isa 28:16 I lay a stone in Zion, a t stone,
48:10 I have t you in the furnace
Da 1:14 to this and t them for ten days.
Lk 11:16 Others t him by asking for a sign
1Ti 3:10 They must first be t;
Heb 11:17 when God t him, offered Isaac as

## TESTER* [TEST]

Jer 6:27 "I have made you a t of metals

## TESTIFIED [TESTIFY]

Mk 14:56 Many t falsely against him, but their
Jn 5:37 me has himself t concerning me.
Heb 2: 4 God also t to it by signs,

## TESTIFIES [TESTIFY]

Jn 5:32 There is another who t in my favor,
19:35 truth, and he t so that you also may
21:24 This is the disciple who t to these
Ro 8:16 The Spirit himself t with our spirit
Rev 1: 2 who t to everything he saw—
22:20 He who t to these things says,

## TESTIFY [TESTIFIED, TESTIFIES, TESTIMONY]

Dt 31:21 them, this song will t against them,
Pr 24:28 Do not t against your neighbor
Isa 59:12 your sight, and our sins t against us.
Jer 14: 7 Although our sins t against us,
Jn 1: 7 came as a witness to t concerning

Jn 1:34 I t that this is God's Chosen One."
5:39 These are the very Scriptures that t
7: 7 it hates me because I t that its works
15:26 from the Father—he will t about me.
Ac 4:33 power the apostles continued to t
10:43 All the prophets t about him
Ro 3:21 which the Law and the Prophets t.
1Jn 4:14 t that the Father has sent his Son
5: 7 For there are three that t:

## TESTIMONY [TESTIFY]

Ex 20:16 shall not give false t against your
Nu 35:30 murderer only on the t of witnesses.
Dt 19:18 proves to be a liar, giving false t,
Isa 8:20 instruction and the t of warning.
Mt 15:19 immorality, theft, false t, slander.
24:14 the whole world as a t to all nations,
Mk 14:59 Yet even then their t did not agree.
Lk 21:13 you will bear t to me.
22:71 said, "Why do we need any more t?
Jn 2:25 He did not need human t
8:17 that the t of two witnesses is true.
21:24 We know that his t is true.
2Ti 1: 8 So do not be ashamed of the t
1Jn 5: 9 We accept human t, but God's t is
greater because it is the t of God,
Rev 1: 9 the word of God and the t of Jesus.
12:11 the Lamb and by the word of their t;
19:10 For the t of Jesus is the Spirit

## ARK OF THE TESTIMONY See ARK [OF THE COVENANT]

## TESTING* [TEST]

Dt 13: 3 The LORD your God is t you
Eze 21:13 " 'T will surely come.
Lk 8:13 but in the time of t they fall away.
Ac 20:19 in the midst of severe t by the plots
Heb 3: 8 rebellion, during the time of t
Jas 1: 3 that the t of your faith produces

## TESTINGS* [TEST]

Dt 4:34 nation, by t, by signs and wonders,

## TESTS [TEST]

Pr 17: 3 for gold, but the LORD t the heart.
1Th 2: 4 people but God, who t our hearts.

## TETRARCH

Mt 14: 1 time Herod the t heard the reports
Lk 3:19 John rebuked Herod the t because

## THADDAEUS

Apostle (Mt 10:3; Mk 3:18); probably also known as Judas son of James (Lk 6:16; Ac 1:13).

## THANK [THANKFUL, THANKFULNESS, THANKING, THANKS, THANKSGIVING]

Lev 22:29 you sacrifice a t offering
2Ch 29:31 brought sacrifices and t offerings,
Ps 50:14 "Sacrifice t offerings to God,
116:17 I will sacrifice a t offering to you
Da 2:23 I t and praise you, God of my
Lk 18:11 'God, I t you that I am not like other

Jn    11:41  I t you that you have heard me.
1Co   10:30  because of something I t God for?
Php    1: 3  I t my God every time I remember
1Th    3: 9  How can we t God enough for you

## THANKFUL [THANK]
Col    4: 2  to prayer, being watchful and t.
Heb  12:28  let us be t, and so worship God

## THANKFULNESS* [THANK]
Lev    7:12  they offer it as an expression of t,
1Co   10:30  If I take part in the meal with t,
Col    2: 7  were taught, and overflowing with t.

## THANKING* [THANK]
1Ch   25: 3  using the harp in t and praising

## THANKS [THANK]
Ne    12:31  assigned two large choirs to give t.
Ps     7:17  I will give t to the LORD because
      35:18  I will give you t in the great
     107: 1  Give t to the LORD, for he is
     136: 2  Give t to the God of gods.
Mt    14:19  he gave t and broke the loaves.
Ro     1:21  glorified him as God nor gave t
1Co   11:24  and when he had given t, he broke it
      15:57  But t be to God! He gives us
2Co    2:14  But t be to God, who always leads
       9:15  T be to God for his indescribable
1Th    5:18  give t in all circumstances;
Rev    4: 9  and t to him who sits on the throne
       7:12  glory and wisdom and t and honor
      11:17  "We give t to you, Lord God

**GAVE THANKS** 2Ch 7:3, 6; Ne 12:40; Mt
     14:19; Mk 6:41; 8:7; Lk 2:38; 9:16; 22:17, 19;
     24:30; Jn 6:11; Ac 27:35; Ro 1:21

**GIVE ... THANKS** 1Ch 16:34, 35, 41; 29:13;
     2Ch 5:13; 20:21; 31:2; Ne 12:31; Ps 7:17; 35:18;
     100:4; 106:1, 47; 107:1, 8, 15, 21, 31; 118:1, 19,
     21, 29; 119:62; 136:1, 2, 3, 26; Jer 33:11; Ro
     14:6, 6; 1Co 10:16; 2Co 1:11; 1Th 5:18; Rev 4:9;
     11:17

## THANKSGIVING [THANK]
Ezr    3:11  and t they sang to the LORD:
Ne    12:27  the dedication with songs of t
Ps    95: 2  Let us come before him with t
     100: 4  Enter his gates with t and his courts
1Co   10:16  Is not the cup of t for which we give
2Co    9:11  us your generosity will result in t
Php    4: 6  with t, present your requests to God.
1Ti    4: 3  to be received with t by those who

## THEFT* [THIEF]
Ex    22: 3  they must be sold to pay for their t.
Mt    15:19  adultery, sexual immorality, t,
Mk     7:21  sexual immorality, t, murder,

## THEFTS* [THIEF]
Rev    9:21  their sexual immorality or their t.

## THEME*
Ps    22:25  From you comes the t of my praise

Ps    45: 1  by a noble t as I recite my verses
     119:54  Your decrees are the t of my song

## THEOPHILUS*
Lk     1: 3  account for you, most excellent T,
Ac     1: 1  In my former book, T, I wrote

## THESSALONIANS*
[THESSALONICA]
1Th    1: 1  Paul, Silas and Timothy, To the church
             of the T
2Th    1: 1  the church of the T in God our

## THESSALONICA
[THESSALONIANS]
Ac    17: 1  they came to T, where there was
      17:11  noble character than those in T,
Php    4:16  for even when I was in T, you sent

## THICK
Ge    15:12  a t and dreadful darkness came over
Ex    19:16  with a t cloud over the mountain,
Ps    97: 2  and t darkness surround him;

## THIEF [THEFT, THEFTS, THIEVES]
Pr     6:11  poverty will come on you like a t
       6:30  People do not despise a t if he steals
Lk    12:39  at what hour the t was coming,
Jn    10:10  The t comes only to steal and kill
1Th    5: 2  of the Lord will come like a t
1Pe    4:15  it should not be as a murderer or t
Rev   16:15  "Look, I come like a t!

## THIEVES [THIEF]
Mt     6:19  and where t break in and steal.
Jn    10: 8  All who have come before me are t
1Co    6:10  nor t nor the greedy nor drunkards

## THIGH [THIGHS]
Ge    24: 2  he had, "Put your hand under my t.
      47:29  eyes, put your hand under my t
Rev   19:16  on his t he has this name written:

## THIGHS [THIGH]
Da     2:32  of silver, its belly and t of bronze,

## THIN
Ge    41: 7  The t heads of grain swallowed
Ex    16:14  t flakes like frost on the ground

## THING [EVERYTHING, NOTHING, SOMETHING, THINGS]
Ge     1:21  and moving t with which the water
       7:21  Every living t that moved
      19: 7  Don't do this wicked t.
Jdg   19:24  don't do such an outrageous t."
2Sa   13:12  Don't do this wicked t.
2Ki    5:18  This is an easy t in the eyes
Ps    27: 4  One t I ask from the LORD,
      84:11  no good t does he withhold
Isa   43:19  See, I am doing a new t!
Jer   31:22  The LORD will create a new t
Mt    19:16  what good t must I do to get eternal

Mk 10:21 "One t you lack," he said.
Jn 9:25 not, I don't know. One t I do know.
Php 3:13 But one t I do: Forgetting what is

## THINGS [THING]

Nu 10:29 the LORD has promised good t
2Sa 7:28 you have promised these good t
Ps 15: 5 Whoever does these t will never be
71:19 skies, you who have done great t.
118:15 right hand has done mighty t!
Pr 6:16 There are six t the LORD hates,
31:29 "Many women do noble t, but you
Isa 66: 2 Has not my hand made all these t,
Jer 10:16 these, for he is the Maker of all t,
Joel 2:21 Surely the LORD has done great t!
Mt 19:26 but with God all t are possible."
Mk 11:33 what authority I am doing these t."
Lk 6:45 Good people bring good t
9:22 Son of Man must suffer many t
10:42 but few t are needed—
Jn 1: 3 Through him all t were made;
1:50 You will see greater t than that."
14:12 will do even greater t than these,
21:25 Jesus did many other t as well.
1Co 2:10 The Spirit searches all t,
Eph 1:22 And God placed all t under his feet
Col 1:17 He is before all t, and in him all t
1Pe 4: 7 The end of all t is near.
Rev 4:11 for you created all t, and by your
21: 4 the old order of t has passed away."
22: 6 to show his servants the t that must

## THINK [THINKING, THINKS, THOUGHT, THOUGHTS]

Ps 40:17 may the Lord t of me.
63: 6 I t of you through the watches
144: 3 mere mortals that you t of them?
Isa 44:19 No one stops to t, no one has
Eze 28: 2 though you t you are as wise as
Mt 22:42 "What do you t about the Messiah?
Jn 5:39 Scriptures diligently because you t
Ro 12: 3 Do not t of yourself more highly
1Co 8: 2 Those who t they know something
10:12 if you t you are standing firm,
14:37 If any t they are prophets
Php 4: 8 t about such things.

## THINKING [THINK]

Pr 23: 7 of person who is always t
Lk 5:22 Jesus knew what they were t
1Co 14:20 but in your t be adults.
2Pe 3: 1 to stimulate you to wholesome t.

## THINKS [THINK]

Job 24:15 watches for dusk; he t, 'No eye will see

## THIRD [THREE]

Eze 5:12 and a t I will scatter to the winds
10:14 being, the t the face of a lion,
Da 5: 7 he will be made the t highest ruler
Hos 6: 2 on the t day he will restore us,
Mk 14:41 Returning the t time, he said
Lk 18:33 On the t day he will rise again."
Jn 21:17 because Jesus asked him the t time,
Ac 20: 9 he fell to the ground from the t story

2Co 12: 2 ago was caught up to the t heaven.
Rev 4: 7 an ox, the t had a face like a man,
6: 5 When the Lamb opened the t seal,
8:10 The t angel sounded his trumpet,
12: 4 Its tail swept a t of the stars

## THIRD DAY See DAY

## THIRST [THIRSTS, THIRSTY]

Ps 69:21 food and gave me vinegar for my t.
Mt 5: 6 who hunger and t for righteousness,
Jn 4:14 the water I give them will never t.
2Co 11:27 I have known hunger and t and have
Rev 7:16 never again will they t.

## THIRSTS* [THIRST]

Ps 42: 2 My soul t for God, for the living

## THIRSTY [THIRST]

Ex 17: 3 the people were t for water there,
Ps 107: 9 for he satisfies the t and fills
Pr 25:21 if he is t, give him water to drink.
Isa 55: 1 all you who are t,
Mt 25:35 I was t and you gave me something
Jn 6:35 believes in me will never be t.
7:37 "Let anyone who is t come to me
19:28 be fulfilled, Jesus said, "I am t."
Ro 12:20 if he is t, give him something
Rev 21: 6 the t I will give water without cost
22:17 Let those who are t come; and let all

## THIRTY

Ge 41:46 Joseph was t years old when he
Lev 27: 4 a female, set her value at t shekels;
2Sa 23:24 Among the T were:
Pr 22:20 Have I not written t sayings for you,
Mt 13: 8 sixty or t times what was sown.
Lk 3:23 Jesus himself was about t years old

## THISTLE [THISTLES]

2Ki 14: 9 "A t in Lebanon sent a message

## THISTLES [THISTLE]

Ge 3:18 It will produce thorns and t for you,
Heb 6: 8 produces thorns and t is worthless

## THOMAS* [DIDYMUS]

Apostle, also called Didymus (Mt 10:3; Mk 3:18; Lk 6:15; Jn 11:16; 14:5; 21:2; Ac 1:13). Doubted resurrection (Jn 20:24–28).

## THONGS

Mk 1: 7 I, the t of whose sandals I am not

## THORN* [THORNBUSH, THORNBUSHES, THORNS]

Mic 7: 4 most upright worse than a t hedge.
2Co 12: 7 I was given a t in my flesh,

## THORNBUSH [THORN]

Jdg 9:14 "Finally all the trees said to the t,
Isa 55:13 of the t will grow the juniper,

## THORNBUSHES [THORN]
Lk  6:44  People do not pick figs from t,

## THORNS [THORN]
Ge  3:18  It will produce t and thistles for you,
Nu 33:55  in your eyes and t in your sides.
Jer 12:13  They will sow wheat but reap t;
Mt 13: 7  Other seed fell among t, which grew
Jn 19: 2  twisted together a crown of t
Heb 6: 8  land that produces t and thistles is

## THOROUGH [THOROUGHLY]
Ac 18:24  man, with a t knowledge

## THOROUGHLY [THOROUGH]
Ps 119:140  Your promises have been t tested,
Ac 22: 3  and was t trained in the law of our
2Ti 3:17  all God's people may be t equipped

## THOUGH
Job 13:15  T he slay me, yet will I hope in him;
Ps 17: 3  T you probe my heart, t you
  27:10  T my father and mother forsake me,
  37:24  t they stumble, they will not fall,
Isa  1:18  "T your sins are like scarlet,
Hab 2: 3  T it linger, wait for it;
  3:17  T the fig tree does not bud
Lk  8:10  so that, " 't seeing, they may not
Jn 11:25  in me will live, even t they die;
Ro  8:10  even t your body is subject to death
  9: 6  It is not as t God's word had failed.

## THOUGHT [THINK]
1Sa  1:13  was not heard. Eli t she was drunk
1Ch 28: 9  understands every desire and every t.
Ps 106: 7  they gave no t to your miracles;
Pr 14:15  but the prudent give t to their steps.
  21:29  but the upright give t to their ways.
1Co 13:11  I talked like a child, I t like a child,
2Co 10: 5  we take captive every t to make it

## THOUGHTS [THINK]
Ge  6: 5  of the t of the human heart was only
Ps 92: 5  LORD, how profound your t!
 139:23  test me and know my anxious t.
Pr 15:26  The LORD detests the t
Isa 55: 8  "For my t are not your t, neither are
Mt  9: 4  Knowing their t, Jesus said,
  15:19  For out of the heart come evil t,
Ro  2:15  and their t now accusing, now even
1Co 2:11  who knows a person's t except
Heb 3: 1  calling, fix your t on Jesus,
  4:12  it judges the t and attitudes

## THOUSAND [THOUSANDS]
Dt  7: 9  love to a t generations of those who
  32:30  How could one man chase a t,
Jos 23:10  One of you routs a t,
Jdg 15:16  jawbone I have killed a t men."
Ps  50:10  is mine, and the cattle on a t hills.
  84:10  in your courts than a t elsewhere;
  90: 4  A t years in your sight are like a day
  91: 7  A t may fall at your side, ten t
 105: 8  he made, for a t generations,
SS  5:10  and ruddy, outstanding among ten t.

Mt 14:21  those who ate was about five t men,
  15:38  of those who ate was four t men,
Mk  8: 9  About four t were present.
2Pe  3: 8  With the Lord a day is like a t years,
Rev  5:11  thousands, and ten t times ten t.
  20: 4  and reigned with Christ a t years.

## THOUSANDS [THOUSAND]
Ex 34: 7  maintaining love to t, and forgiving
1Sa 18: 7  "Saul has slain his t, and David his tens
      of t."
Ps 68:17  The chariots of God are tens of t and
      t of t;
Da  7:10  T upon t attended him;
Heb 12:22  You have come to t upon t of angels
Jude 1:14  the Lord is coming with t upon t
Rev  5:11  of many angels, numbering t upon t,

## THREAT [THREATENED, THREATS]
Isa 30:17  A thousand will flee at the t of one;

## THREATENED [THREAT]
Ex 32:14  on his people the disaster he had t.
Isa 38:14  I am being t; Lord, come
Jnh  3:10  on them the destruction he had t.

## THREATS [THREAT]
Ac  4:21  After further t they let them go.
  9: 1  out murderous t against the Lord's

## THREE [THIRD]
Ge  6:10  Noah had t sons: Shem,
  18: 2  up and saw t men standing nearby.
Ex 23:14  "T times a year you are to celebrate
Dt 14:28  At the end of every t years, bring all
  19:15  the testimony of two or t witnesses.
1Sa 31: 8  his t sons fallen on Mount Gilboa.
2Sa 23: 9  As one of the t mighty warriors,
Job  2:11  When Job's t friends,
Pr 30:15  "There are t things that are never
  30:18  "There are t things that are too
  30:21  "Under t things the earth trembles,
  30:29  "There are t things that are stately
Ecc  4:12  of t strands is not quickly broken.
Da  3:24  "Weren't there t men that we tied
  7: 5  it had t ribs in its mouth between its
Am  1: 3  "For t sins of Damascus,
Jnh  1:17  belly of the fish t days and t nights.
Mt 12:40  For as Jonah was t days and t nights
  12:40  so the Son of Man will be t days
  17: 4  If you wish, I will put up t shelters—
  18:20  two or t come together in my name,
  26:34  you will disown me t times."
  26:75  you will disown me t times.
  27:46  About t in the afternoon Jesus cried out
  27:63  said, 'After t days I will rise again.'
Mk  8:31  be killed and after t days rise again.
  14:30  yourself will disown me t times."
Jn  2:19  and I will raise it again in t days."
1Co 13:13  And now these t remain:
  14:27  or at the most t—should speak,
2Co 12: 8  T times I pleaded with the Lord
  13: 1  testimony of two or t witnesses."
1Jn  5: 7  For there are t that testify:

## THRESH [THRESHED, THRESHING]
Mic 4:13 "Rise and t, Daughter Zion, for I
1Co 9:10 when farmers plow and t,

## THRESHED [THRESH]
Ru 2:17 she t the barley she had gathered,

## THRESHING [THRESH]
Ru 3: 3 Then go down to the t floor,
2Sa 24:18 altar to the LORD on the t floor
Hos 9: 1 of a prostitute at every t floor.
Lk 3:17 fork is in his hand to clear his t floor

## THRESHOLD
1Sa 5: 4 broken off and were lying on the t;
Eze 10:18 from over the t of the temple
47: 1 under the t of the temple toward
Zep 1: 9 all who avoid stepping on the t,

## THREW [THROW]
Ex 7:10 Aaron t his staff down in front
15:25 He t it into the water, and the water
32:19 and he t the tablets out of his hands,
2Ki 6: 6 Elisha cut a stick and t it there,
Da 3:24 that we tied up and t into the fire?"
6:16 Daniel and t him into the lions' den.
Jnh 1:15 took Jonah and t him overboard,
Mt 27: 5 So Judas t the money
Rev 20: 3 He t him into the Abyss, and locked

## THRIVE
Pr 11:28 the righteous will t like a green leaf.
29: 2 When the righteous t, the people
29:16 When the wicked t, so does sin,

## THROAT [THROATS]
Ps 5: 9 Their t is an open grave;
Pr 23: 2 put a knife to your t if you are given

## THROATS [THROAT]
Ro 3:13 "Their t are open graves;

## THROB*
Isa 60: 5 your heart will t and swell with joy;

## THRONE [ENTHRONED,
ENTHRONES, THRONES]
Ex 17:16 up against the t of the LORD,
2Sa 7:13 I will establish the t of his kingdom
1Ch 17:12 and I will establish his t forever.
Ps 11: 4 the LORD is on his heavenly t.
45: 6 Your t, O God, will last for ever
47: 8 God is seated on his holy t.
89:14 justice are the foundation of your t;
Pr 20:28 through love his t is made secure.
Isa 6: 1 I saw the Lord seated on a t,
66: 1 "Heaven is my t, and the earth is
Jer 33:21 have a descendant to reign on his t.
Eze 1:26 their heads was what looked like a t
28: 2 I sit on the t of a god in the heart
Da 7: 9 His t was flaming with fire, and its
Mt 5:34 either by heaven, for it is God's t;
19:28 Son of Man sits on his glorious t,
Lk 1:32 The Lord God will give him the t

Ac 7:49 " 'Heaven is my t, and the earth is
Heb 1: 8 the Son he says, "Your t, O God,
4:16 then approach God's t of grace
12: 2 at the right hand of the t of God.
Rev 2:13 where Satan has his t.
3:21 give the right to sit with me on my t,
4: 2 there before me was a t in heaven
4:10 They lay their crowns before the t
5:13 "To him who sits on the t
20:11 I saw a great white t and him who
22: 3 The t of God and of the Lamb will

## THRONES [THRONE]
Mt 19:28 me will also sit on twelve t,
Col 1:16 whether t or powers or rulers
Rev 4: 4 the throne were twenty-four other t,
20: 4 I saw t on which were seated those

## THRONG
Ps 42: 4 joy and praise among the festive t.
Jer 31: 8 a great t will return.

## THROUGH
Ge 12: 3 on earth will be blessed t you."
21:12 you, because it is t Isaac that your
22:18 t your offspring all nations on earth
Ex 14:22 the Israelites went t the sea on dry
Ps 72:17 all nations will be blessed t him,
Pr 16: 6 T love and faithfulness sin is atoned
Isa 43: 2 When you walk t the fire,
Mt 1:18 to be pregnant t the Holy Spirit.
Jn 10: 9 whoever enters t me will be saved.
14: 6 comes to the Father except t me.
Ro 5: 1 since we have been justified t faith,
1Co 8: 6 t whom all things came and t whom
Eph 2: 8 grace you have been saved, t faith—

## THROW [THREW, THROWN]
Ex 1:22 that is born you must t into the Nile,
4: 3 LORD said, "T it on the ground."
Jos 24:23 "t away the foreign gods that are
Zec 11:13 said to me, "T it to the potter"—
Mt 5:30 to stumble, cut it off and t it away.
7: 6 do not t your pearls to pigs.
Jn 8: 7 *the first to t a stone at her."*
Heb 10:35 So do not t away your confidence;
12: 1 let us t off everything that hinders

## THROWN [THROW]
Da 3:21 and t into the blazing furnace.
6:12 would be t into the lions' den?"
Rev 19:20 them were t alive into the fiery lake
20:10 was t into the lake of burning sulfur,
20:14 Hades were t into the lake of fire.

## THRUST
2Ki 17:20 until he t them from his presence.
Isa 8:22 they will be t into utter darkness.

## THUMMIM
Ex 28:30 Urim and the T in the breastpiece,
Ezr 2:63 ministering with the Urim and T.

## THUNDER [THUNDERED, THUNDERS]

Ex    9:23  the sky, the LORD sent t and hail,
      20:18 When the people saw the t
Job  40: 9  and can your voice t like his?
Ps   93: 4  Mightier than the t of the great
Joel  3:16  from Zion and t from Jerusalem;
Mk    3:17  which means "sons of t"),
Rev   4: 5  lightning, rumblings and peals of t.
      6: 1  living creatures say in a voice like t,
      16:18 peals of t and a severe earthquake.

## THUNDERCLOUD* [CLOUD]

Ps   81: 7  you, I answered you out of a t;

## THUNDERED [THUNDER]

Ps   18:13  The LORD t from heaven;
Jn   12:29  was there and heard it said it had t;

## THUNDERS [THUNDER]

Job  37: 5  God's voice t in marvelous ways;
Ps   29: 3  the God of glory t, the LORD t
Jer  10:13  When he t, the waters
Rev  10: 3  the voices of the seven t spoke.

## THWART* [THWARTED, THWARTS]

Isa  14:27  has purposed, and who can t him?

## THWARTED* [THWART]

Job  42: 2  no purpose of yours can be t.
Isa   8:10  your strategy, but it will be t;

## THWARTS [THWART]

Ps   33:10  he t the purposes of the peoples.

## THYATIRA

Ac   16:14  from the city of T named Lydia,
Rev   2:18  the angel of the church in T write:

## TIBERIAS [GALILEE]

Jn    6: 1  Sea of Galilee (that is, the Sea of T),

## TIBERIUS*

Lk    3: 1  year of the reign of T Caesar—

## TIBNI*

      King of Israel (1Ki 16:21–22).

## TIDINGS*

Isa  52: 7  who bring good t, who proclaim

## TIE [TIED, TIES, TYING]

Dt    6: 8  T them as symbols on your hands
      11:18 t them as symbols on your hands
Mt   23: 4  They t up heavy, cumbersome loads

## TIED [TIE]

Ge   38:28  a scarlet thread and t it on his wrist
Jos   2:21  she t the scarlet cord in the window.
Lk   19:30  you will find a colt t there, which no

## TIES [TIE]

Hos  11: 4  of human kindness, with t of love.

## TIGHT* [TIGHTFISTED]

Jas   1:26  and yet do not keep a t rein on their

## TIGHTFISTED* [TIGHT]

Dt   15: 7  not be hardhearted or t toward them.

## TIGLATH-PILESER [PUL]

2Ki  16: 7  to say to T king of Assyria, "I am
1Ch   5: 6  whom T king of Assyria took

## TIGRIS*

Ge    2:14  The name of the third river is the T;
Da   10: 4  on the bank of the great river, the T,

## TILES*

Lk    5:19  his mat through the t into the middle

## TIMBREL [TIMBRELS]

Ex   15:20  Aaron's sister, took a t in her hand,
Ps   150: 4  praise him with t and dancing,

## TIMBRELS [TIMBREL]

Jdg  11:34  dancing to the sound of t!
Isa  24: 8  The gaiety of the t is stilled,
Jer  31: 4  Again you will take up your t

## TIME [TIMES]

Ge    4:26  At that t people began to call
      6: 5  human heart was only evil all the t.
Dt   32:35  In due t their foot will slip;
Ne    9:28  you delivered them t after t.
Est   4:14  royal position for such a t as this?"
Ps  119:126 It is t for you to act, LORD;
Ecc   3: 1  There is a t for everything,
      3:11  made everything beautiful in its t.
      8: 5  wise heart will know the proper t
Da    7:25  his hands for a t, times and half a t.
      12: 1  There will be a t of distress such as
      12: 7  "It will be for a t, times and half a t.
Hos  10:12  for it is t to seek the LORD,
Lk   21: 8  'I am he,' and, 'The t is near.'
Ro    5: 6  at just the right t, when we were still
      9: 9  "At the appointed t I will return,
1Co   4: 5  that t each will receive their praise
      7:29  and sisters, is that the t is short.
2Co   6: 2  now is the t of God's favor,
Gal   4: 4  But when the set t had fully come,
2Ti   1: 9  Jesus before the beginning of t,
Tit   1: 2  promised before the beginning of t,
Heb   9:28  and he will appear a second t,
      10:12 had offered for all t one sacrifice
1Pe   4:17  For it is t for judgment to begin
Rev   1: 3  is written in it, because the t is near.
      2:21  I have given her t to repent of her
      3: 3  will not know at what t I will come
      12:14 for a t, times and half a t,
      22:10 of this scroll, because the t is near.

**APPOINTED TIME** See APPOINTED

## TIMES [TIME]

| | | |
|---|---|---|
| Ge | 4:15 | will suffer vengeance seven t over." |
| Ex | 23:14 | "Three t a year you are to celebrate |
| Jos | 6: 4 | march around the city seven t, |
| Ps | 9: 9 | a stronghold in t of trouble. |
| | 31:15 | My t are in your hands; |
| | 62: 8 | Trust in him at all t, you people; |
| Pr | 17:17 | A friend loves at all t, and a brother |
| | 24:16 | for though the righteous fall seven t, |
| Isa | 46:10 | from ancient t, what is still to come. |
| Da | 7:25 | hands for a time, t and half a time. |
| Am | 5:13 | quiet in such t, for the t are evil. |
| Mt | 16: 3 | cannot interpret the signs of the t. |
| | 18:22 | not seven t, but seventy-seven t. |
| Mk | 4: 8 | some sixty, some a hundred t." |
| | 14:30 | yourself will disown me three t." |
| Lk | 17: 4 | they sin against you seven t in a day |
| Ac | 1: 7 | "It is not for you to know the t |
| 1Ti | 4: 1 | later t some will abandon the faith |
| 2Ti | 3: 1 | There will be terrible t in the last |
| Rev | 5:11 | and ten thousand t ten thousand. |
| | 12:14 | care of for a time, t and half a time, |

## TIMID*

| | | |
|---|---|---|
| 2Co | 10: 1 | who am "t" when face to face |
| 2Ti | 1: 7 | gave us does not make us t, |

## TIMOTHY

Believer from Lystra (Ac 16:1). Joined Paul on second missionary journey (Ac 16–20). Sent to settle problems at Corinth (1Co 4:17; 16:10). Led church at Ephesus (1Ti 1:3). Co-writer with Paul (1Th 1:1; 2Th 1:1; Phm 1).

## TIP

Job 33: 2 my words are on the t of my tongue.

## TIRE [TIRED]

2Th 3:13 never t of doing what is good.

## TIRED [TIRE]

| | | |
|---|---|---|
| Ex | 17:12 | When Moses' hands grew t, |
| Isa | 40:28 | He will not grow t or weary, and his |
| Jn | 4: 6 | Jesus, t as he was from the journey, |

## TIRZAH

1Ki 15:33 became king of all Israel in T,

## TISHBITE

| | | |
|---|---|---|
| 1Ki | 17: 1 | Now Elijah the T, from Tishbe |
| 2Ki | 1: 8 | king said, "That was Elijah the T." |

## TITHE [TEN]

| | | |
|---|---|---|
| Lev | 27:30 | " 'A t of everything |
| Nu | 18:26 | of that t as the LORD's offering. |
| Dt | 12:17 | your own towns the t of your grain |
| Ne | 10:37 | we will bring a t of our crops |
| Mal | 3:10 | Bring the whole t |

## TITHES [TEN]

| | | |
|---|---|---|
| Nu | 18:21 | the Levites all the t in Israel as their |
| Ne | 10:37 | it is the Levites who collect the t |
| Mal | 3: 8 | "In t and offerings. |

## TITLE*

| | | |
|---|---|---|
| Isa | 45: 4 | and bestow on you a t of honor, |
| Rev | 17: 5 | This t was written on her forehead: |

## TITUS*

Gentile co-worker of Paul (Gal 2:1–3; 2Ti 4:10); sent to Corinth (2Co 2:13; 7–8; 12:18), Crete (Tit 1:4–5).

## TOBIAH

Enemy of Nehemiah and the exiles (Ne 2:10–19; 4; 6; 13:4–9).

## TOBIJAH

Zec 6:14 crown will be given to Heldai, T,

## TODAY

| | | |
|---|---|---|
| Ex | 14:13 | the LORD will bring you t. |
| | 34:11 | Obey what I command you t. |
| Dt | 5: 3 | with all of us who are alive here t. |
| | 30:15 | I set before you t life and prosperity, |
| Ps | 2: 7 | t I have become your father. |
| | 95: 7 | T, if only you would hear his voice, |
| Mt | 6:11 | Give us t our daily bread. |
| Lk | 2:11 | T in the town of David a Savior has |
| | 4:21 | "T this scripture is fulfilled in your |
| | 19: 9 | him, "T salvation has come to this |
| | 23:43 | t you will be with me in paradise." |
| Ac | 13:33 | t I have become your father.' |
| Heb | 1: 5 | t I have become your Father"? |
| | 3: 7 | "T, if you hear his voice, |
| | 3:13 | as long as it is called "T," |
| | 4: 7 | set a certain day, calling it "T." |
| | 13: 8 | Christ is the same yesterday and t |

## TOES

Da 2:42 As the t were partly iron and partly

## TOGETHER

| | | |
|---|---|---|
| Ge | 3: 7 | so they sewed fig leaves t and made |
| Dt | 22:10 | with an ox and a donkey yoked t. |
| Ps | 2: 2 | the rulers band t against the LORD |
| | 85:10 | Love and faithfulness meet t; |
| | 133: 1 | when God's people live t in unity! |
| | 139:13 | you knit me t in my mother's |
| Isa | 1:18 | let us reason t," says the LORD. |
| | 11: 6 | calf and the lion and the yearling t; |
| | 65:25 | The wolf and the lamb will feed t, |
| Eze | 37: 7 | and the bones came t, bone to bone. |
| Mt | 19: 6 | Therefore what God has joined t, |
| Ac | 2:44 | All the believers were t and had |
| | 4:26 | the rulers band t against the Lord |
| | 5:12 | to meet t in Solomon's Colonnade. |
| 2Co | 6:14 | Do not be yoked t with unbelievers. |
| Eph | 3: 6 | the gospel the Gentiles are heirs t |
| Rev | 16:16 | they gathered the kings t |

## TOIL [TOILED, TOILING]

| | | |
|---|---|---|
| Ge | 3:17 | through painful t you will eat of it |
| | 5:29 | painful t of our hands caused |
| Ecc | 2:24 | and find satisfaction in their t. |
| | 3:13 | and find satisfaction in all their t— |
| | 4: 4 | I saw that all t and all achievement |
| | 5:19 | accept their lot and be happy in their t |
| | 6: 7 | Everyone's t is for the mouth, |

## TOILED [TOIL]
2Co 11:27  I have labored and t and have often

## TOILING [TOIL]
2Th  3: 8  t so that we would not be a burden

## TOLA
A judge of Israel (Jdg 10:1–2).

## TOLD [TELL]
Ge   3:11  "Who t you that you were naked?
    22: 9  the place God had t him about,
Dt   1:18  time I t you everything you were
Jdg 16:17  So he t her everything.
1Ki 10: 7  Indeed, not even half was t me;
Ps  44: 1  our ancestors have t us what you did
Isa 48: 5  Therefore I t you these things long
Lk   2:20  which were just as they had been t.
Jn  14:29  I have t you now before it happens,
Ac  11: 4  Peter t them the whole story:

## TOLERATE
Hab  1:13  you cannot t wrongdoing.
Rev  2: 2  that you cannot t wicked people,

## TOMB [TOMBS]
Mt  27:65  make the t as secure as you know
Mk  15:46  and placed it in a t cut out of rock.
Lk  24: 2  the stone rolled away from the t,

## TOMBS [TOMB]
Mt  23:29  You build t for the prophets
    27:52  and the t broke open. The bodies

## TOMORROW
Pr  27: 1  Do not boast about t, for you do not
Isa 22:13  drink," you say, "for t we die!"
Mt   6:34  Therefore do not worry about t, for t
1Co 15:32  "Let us eat and drink, for t we die."
Jas  4:14  not even know what will happen t.

## TONGUE [TONGUES]
Ex   4:10  I am slow of speech and t."
Job 33: 2  my words are on the tip of my t.
Ps  34:13  keep your t from evil and your lips
    39: 1  my ways and keep my t from sin;
    51:14  Savior, and my t will sing of your
    52: 4  every harmful word, you deceitful t!
    71:24  My t will tell of your righteous acts
   119:172  May my t sing of your word, for all
   137: 6  May my t cling to the roof of my
   139: 4  Before a word is on my t you,
Pr   6:17  a lying t, hands that shed innocent
    12:18  but the t of the wise brings healing.
    15: 4  The soothing t is a tree of life,
    18:21  The t has the power of life
    25:15  and a gentle t can break a bone.
    26:28  A lying t hates those it hurts,
    28:23  than one who has a flattering t.
SS   4:11  milk and honey are under your t.
Isa 32: 4  and the stammering t will be fluent
    45:23  by me every t will swear.
    50: 4  has given me an instructed t,

Isa 59: 3  and your t mutters wicked things.
Mk   7:33  he spit and touched the man's t.
Lk  16:24  of his finger in water and cool my t,
Ro  14:11  every t will confess to God.' "
1Co 14: 2  those who speak in a t do not speak
    14: 4  who speak in a t edify themselves,
    14: 9  speak intelligible words with your t,
    14:13  those who speak in a t should pray
    14:19  than ten thousand words in a t.
    14:26  a revelation, a t or an interpretation.
    14:27  If anyone speaks in a t, two—
Php  2:11  and every t acknowledge that Jesus
Jas  3: 5  the t is a small part of the body,
     3: 8  but no one can tame the t. It is
1Jn  3:18  let us not love with words or t

## TONGUES [TONGUE]
Jdg  7: 5  lap the water with their t like a dog
Ps   5: 9  with their t they tell lies.
    12: 4  who say, "By our t we will prevail;
    37:30  and their t speak what is just.
   126: 2  laughter, our t with songs of joy.
Pr  10:19  words, but the prudent hold their t.
    11:12  have understanding hold their t.
    17:28  and discerning if they hold their t.
Isa 28:11  and strange t God will speak to this
Jer 23:31  the prophets who wag their own t
Ac   2: 3  saw what seemed to be t of fire
     2: 4  in other t as the Spirit enabled them.
    10:46  For they heard them speaking in t
    19: 6  and they spoke in t and prophesied.
Ro   3:13  their t practice deceit."
1Co 12:10  speaking in different kinds of t,
    12:10  still another the interpretation of t.
    12:28  guidance, and of different kinds of t.
    12:30  Do all speak in t? Do all interpret?
    13: 1  If I speak in human or angelic t,
    13: 8  where there are t, they will be
    14: 5  like every one of you to speak in t,
    14: 5  greater than those who speak in t,
    14:18  I speak in t more than all of you.
    14:21  "With other t and through the lips
    14:39  and do not forbid speaking in t.
Jas  1:26  rein on their t deceive themselves,

## TOOK [TAKE]
Ge   2:21  he t one of the man's ribs
     3: 6  wisdom, she t some and ate it.
     5:24  no more, because God t him away.
Jos 11:16  So Joshua t this entire land:
Ps  68:18  you t many captives;
    78:70  and t him from the sheep pens;
Isa 53: 4  Surely he t up our pain and bore our
Da   7: 9  and the Ancient of Days t his seat.
Mt   4: 5  Then the devil t him to the holy city
     4: 8  Again, the devil t him to a very high
     8:17  "He t up our infirmities and bore
    26:26  they were eating, Jesus t bread,
    26:27  Then he t the cup, and when he had
1Co 11:23  the night he was betrayed, t bread,
    11:25  after supper he t the cup, saying,
Eph  4: 8  he t many captives and gave gifts
Php  3:12  for which Christ Jesus t hold of me.

## TOOTH [TEETH]
Ex  21:24  eye for eye, t for t, hand for hand,

Lev 24:20 for fracture, eye for eye, t for t.
Mt   5:38 was said, 'Eye for eye, and t for t.'

## TOP [TOPS]
Ge  28:12 earth, with its t reaching to heaven,
Ex  19:20 Moses to the t of the mountain.
Dt  28:13 you will always be at the t,
Isa   1: 6 foot to the t of your head there is no
Mt  27:51 was torn in two from t to bottom.
Jn  19:23 in one piece from t to bottom.

## TOPHETH
2Ki 23:10 He desecrated T, which was
Jer  19:12 I will make this city like T.

## TOPPLE
Isa 40:20 to set up an idol that will not t.

## TOPS [TOP]
Ex  12: 7 t of the doorframes of the houses

## TORCH [TORCHES]
Ge  15:17 firepot with a blazing t appeared
Isa  62: 1 dawn, her salvation like a blazing t.
Rev   8:10 blazing like a t, fell from the sky

## TORCHES [TORCH]
Eze   1:13 like burning coals of fire or like t.
Da  10: 6 his eyes like flaming t, his arms

## TORE [TEAR]
Ge  37:34 Then Jacob t his clothes,
Jos   7: 6 Then Joshua t his clothes and fell
1Ki 14: 8 I t the kingdom away
Mt  26:65 the high priest t his clothes and said,

## TORMENT [TORMENTED, TORMENTORS]
Job 15:20 All their days the wicked suffer t,
Lk  16:28 not also come to this place of t.'
2Co 12: 7 flesh, a messenger of Satan, to t me.
Rev 18: 7 Give her as much t and grief

## TORMENTED [TORMENT]
1Sa 16:14 evil spirit from the LORD t him.
Rev 11:10 two prophets had t those who live
    20:10 They will be t day and night

## TORMENTORS* [TORMENT]
Ps 137: 3 songs, our t demanded songs of joy;
Isa  51:23 I will put it into the hands of your t,

## TORN [TEAR]
Ge  37:33 Joseph has surely been t to pieces."
Lev 22: 8 found dead or t by wild animals,
1Sa 28:17 The LORD has t the kingdom
Mk   1:10 he saw heaven being t open
Lk  23:45 curtain of the temple was t in two.
Gal  4:15 you would have t out your eyes
Php  1:23 I am t between the two: I desire

## TORTURE [TORTURED]
Mt   8:29 to t us before the appointed time?"

## TORTURED* [TORTURE]
Mt  18:34 him over to the jailers to be t,
Heb 11:35 There were others who were t,

## TOSS [TOSSED, TOSSING]
Mt  15:26 bread and t it to the dogs."

## TOSSED [TOSS]
Eph  4:14 t back and forth by the waves,
Jas   1: 6 of the sea, blown and t by the wind.

## TOSSING [TOSS]
Isa 57:20 But the wicked are like the t sea,

## TOTAL [TOTALLY]
Ex  38:26 old or more, a t of 603,550 men.
Nu  26:51 The t number of the men of Israel

## TOTALLY [TOTAL]
Nu  16:30 brings about something t new,
Dt   7: 2 them, then you must destroy them t.
Am   9: 8 Yet I will not t destroy the house

## TOUCH [TOUCHED, TOUCHES]
Ge   3: 3 and you must not t it, or you will
Ex  19:12 the mountain or t the foot of it.
Nu   4:15 But they must not t the holy things
Job  5:19 in seven no harm will t you.
Ps 105:15 "Do not t my anointed ones;
Isa 52:11 out from there! T no unclean thing!
Eze  9: 6 do not t anyone who has the mark.
Mt   9:21 "If I only t his cloak, I will be
Lk  24:39 T me and see; a ghost does not have
2Co  6:17 T no unclean thing, and I will
Col  2:21 Do not taste! Do not t!'"?
Heb 11:28 firstborn would not t the firstborn

## TOUCHED [TOUCH]
Ge  32:25 he t the socket of Jacob's hip so
1Sa 10:26 valiant men whose hearts God had t.
Isa  6: 7 With it he t my mouth and said,
Jer  1: 9 out his hand and t my mouth
Da  10:16 who looked like a man t my lips,
Mt   8: 3 reached out his hand and t the man.
    14:36 and all who t him were healed.
Mk   5:30 and asked, "Who t my clothes?"
Ac  19:12 aprons that had t him were taken
1Jn  1: 1 looked at and our hands have t—

## TOUCHES [TOUCH]
Ex  19:12 Whoever t the mountain is to be put
Ps 104:32 it trembles, who t the mountains,
Am   9: 5 he t the earth and it melts, and all
Zec  2: 8 for whoever t you t the apple of his

## TOWER [WATCHTOWER]
Ge  11: 4 with a t that reaches to the heavens,
Ps  61: 3 refuge, a strong t against the foe.
Pr  18:10 name of the LORD is a fortified t;
Lk  14:28 one of you wants to build a t.

## TOWN [HOMETOWN, HOMETOWNS, TOWNS]
Ne   7: 6 and Judah, each to his own t,

Mt    2:23  and lived in a **t** called Nazareth.
Lk    2: 3  went to their own **t** to register.
       2:11  in the **t** of David a Savior has been

## TOWNS [TOWN]

Nu   35: 2  Israelites to give the Levites **t** to live
       35:15  These six **t** will be a place of refuge
Jos   14: 4  of the land but only **t** to live in,
Ezr   2: 1  and Judah, all to their own **t**,
Jer   11:13  have as many gods as you have **t**;
Mt    9:35  Jesus went through all the **t**
       10:23  finish going through the **t** of Israel
       13:57  in their own **t** and in their own homes
Mk    6: 4  "Only in their own **t**,

## TRACE [TRACED, TRACING]

Heb   7: 6  did not **t** his descent from Levi,

## TRACED* [TRACE]

Ro    9: 5  from them is **t** the human ancestry

## TRACING* [TRACE]

Ro    11:33  and his paths beyond **t** out!

## TRACK

Job   14:16  my steps but not keep **t** of my sin.

## TRADE [TRADED, TRADERS, TRADING]

Ge    42:34  you, and you can **t** in the land.' "
Isa   23:17  will ply her **t** with all the kingdoms
Rev   18:22  worker of any **t** will ever be found

## TRADED [TRADE]

Joel   3: 3  people and **t** boys for prostitutes;

## TRADERS [TRADE]

1Ti   1:10  for slave **t** and liars and perjurers.

## TRADING [TRADE]

1Ki   10:22  The king had a fleet of **t** ships at sea
Pr    31:18  She sees that her **t** is profitable,

## TRADITION [TRADITIONS]

Mt    15: 2  "Why do your disciples break the **t**
Mk    7:13  your **t** that you have handed down.
Col   2: 8  which depends on human **t**

## TRADITIONS [TRADITION]

Mk    7: 8  and are holding on to human **t**."
Gal   1:14  zealous for the **t** of my fathers.

## TRAIL

1Ti   5:24  the sins of others **t** behind them.

## TRAIN* [TRAINED, TRAINING, TRAINS, UNTRAINED]

Isa   2: 4  nor will they **t** for war anymore.
       6: 1  the **t** of his robe filled the temple.
Mic   4: 3  nor will they **t** for war anymore.
1Ti   4: 7  rather, **t** yourself to be godly.

## TRAINED [TRAIN]

Lk    6:40  all who are fully **t** will be like their
Ac    22: 3  was thoroughly **t** in the law of our
Heb   5:14  by constant use have **t** themselves
       12:11  for those who have been **t** by it.

## TRAINING* [TRAIN]

1Co   9:25  in the games goes into strict **t**.
Eph   6: 4  instead, bring them up in the **t**
1Ti   4: 8  For physical **t** is of some value,
2Ti   3:16  correcting and **t** in righteousness,

## TRAINS* [TRAIN]

2Sa   22:35  He **t** my hands for battle;
Ps    18:34  He **t** my hands for battle;
       144: 1  my Rock, who **t** my hands for war,

## TRAITOR [TREASON]

Lk    6:16  and Judas Iscariot, who became a **t**.
Jn    18: 5  Judas the **t** was standing there

## TRAITORS [TREASON]

Ps    59: 5  show no mercy to wicked **t**.

## TRAMPLE [TRAMPLED]

Ps    44: 5  through your name we **t** our foes.
Joel   3:13  Come, **t** the grapes,
Am    2: 7  They **t** on the heads of the poor as
       8: 4  you who **t** the needy and do away
Mt    7: 6  do, they may **t** them under their feet,
Lk    10:19  I have given you authority to **t**
Rev   11: 2  They will **t** on the holy city for 42

## TRAMPLED [TRAMPLE]

2Ki   9:33  the horses as they **t** her underfoot.
Isa   63: 6  I **t** the nations in my anger;
Da    7: 7  and **t** underfoot whatever was left.
       8: 7  knocked it to the ground and **t** on it,
       8:10  down to the earth and **t** on them.
Mt    5:13  to be thrown out and **t** underfoot.
Lk    21:24  Jerusalem will be **t**
Heb   10:29  be punished who have **t** the Son
Rev   14:20  They were **t** in the winepress

## TRANCE*

Ac    10:10  was being prepared, he fell into a **t**.
       11: 5  praying, and in a **t** I saw a vision.
       22:17  praying at the temple, I fell into a **t**

## TRANQUILLITY*

Ecc   4: 6  handful with **t** than two handfuls

## TRANSACTION* [TRANSACTIONS]

Jer   32:25  silver and have the **t** witnessed.' "

## TRANSACTIONS* [TRANSACTION]

Ru    4: 7  the method of legalizing **t** in Israel.)

## TRANSCENDS*

Php   4: 7  God, which **t** all understanding,

## TRANSFER*

Ru    4: 7  and **t** of property to become final,

2Sa 3:10 and t the kingdom from the house

## TRANSFIGURED*
Mt 17: 2 There he was t before them.
Mk 9: 2 There he was t before them.

## TRANSFORM* [TRANSFORMED]
Php 3:21 will t our lowly bodies so that they

## TRANSFORMED [TRANSFORM]
Ro 12: 2 be t by the renewing of your mind.
2Co 3:18 are being t into his image

## TRANSGRESSED*
[TRANSGRESSION]
Ps 17: 3 my mouth has not t.
Da 9:11 All Israel has t your law and turned

## TRANSGRESSION*
[TRANSGRESSED,
TRANSGRESSIONS,
TRANSGRESSORS]
Ps 19:13 be blameless, innocent of great t.
Isa 53: 8 the t of my people he was punished.
Da 9:24 people and your holy city to finish t,
Mic 1: 5 All this is because of Jacob's t,
1: 5 What is Jacob's t? Is it not Samaria?
3: 8 to declare to Jacob his t, to Israel his
6: 7 Shall I offer my firstborn for my t,
7:18 forgives the t of the remnant of his
Ro 4:15 where there is no law there is no t.
11:11 because of their t, salvation has
11:12 if their t means riches for the world,

## TRANSGRESSIONS*
[TRANSGRESSION]
Ps 32: 1 are those whose t are forgiven,
32: 5 I said, "I will confess my t
39: 8 Save me from all my t; do not make
51: 1 great compassion blot out my t.
51: 3 For I know my t, and my sin is
65: 3 by sins, you forgave our t.
103:12 so far has he removed our t from us.
Isa 43:25 am he who blots out your t, for my
50: 1 your t your mother was sent away.
53: 5 But he was pierced for our t, he was
Mic 1:13 for the t of Israel were found in you.
Ro 4: 7 are those whose t are forgiven,
Gal 3:19 added because of t until the Seed
Eph 2: 1 you were dead in your t and sins,
2: 5 even when we were dead in t—

## TRANSGRESSORS*
[TRANSGRESSION]
Ps 51:13 Then I will teach t your ways,
Isa 53:12 death, and was numbered with the t.
53:12 and made intercession for the t.
Lk 22:37 'And he was numbered with the t';

## TRANSITORY*
2Co 3: 7 because of its glory, t though it was,
3:11 And if what was t came with glory,

## TRANSPARENT*
Rev 21:21 city was of gold, as pure as t glass.

## TRAP [TRAPPED, TRAPS]
Ps 31: 4 Keep me free from the t that is set
69:22 may it become retribution and a t.
Pr 20:25 It is a t to dedicate something rashly
28:10 evil path will fall into their own t,
Isa 8:14 people of Jerusalem he will be a t
Mt 22:15 and laid plans to t him in his words.
Lk 21:34 will close on you suddenly like a t.
Ro 11: 9 their table become a snare and a t,
1Ti 3: 7 into disgrace and into the devil's t.
6: 9 and a t and into many foolish
2Ti 2:26 and escape from the t of the devil,

## TRAPPED [TRAP]
Pr 6: 2 you have been t by what you said,
11: 6 the unfaithful are t by evil desires.
12:13 Evildoers are t by their sinful talk,

## TRAPS [TRAP]
Jos 23:13 will become snares and t for you,
Jdg 2: 3 become t for you, and their gods
La 4:20 life breath, was caught in their t.

## TRAVEL [TRAVELED, TRAVELER]
Ex 13:21 so that they could t by day or night.
Pr 4:15 Avoid it, do not t on it; turn from it
Mt 23:15 You t over land and sea to win

## TRAVELED [TRAVEL]
Ge 12: 6 Abram t through the land as far as
Ex 15:22 For three days they t in the desert
1Ki 19: 8 he t forty days and forty nights until

## TRAVELER [TRAVEL]
Job 31:32 my door was always open to the t—
Jer 14: 8 like a t who stays only a night?

## TREACHEROUS [TREASON]
Ps 25: 3 on those who are t without cause.
Isa 24:16 With treachery the t betray!"
Hab 1:13 Why then do you tolerate the t?
2Ti 3: 4 t, rash, conceited, lovers of pleasure

## TREACHERY [TREASON]
Isa 59:13 rebellion and t against the LORD,

## TREAD [TREADING, TREADS]
Dt 33:29 and you will t on their heights."
Ps 91:13 You will t on the lion and the cobra;
Mic 7:19 you will t our sins underfoot
Hab 3:19 he enables me to t on the heights.

## TREADING [TREAD]
Dt 25: 4 Do not muzzle an ox while it is t
1Co 9: 9 "Do not muzzle an ox while it is t
1Ti 5:18 "Do not muzzle an ox while it is t

## TREADS [TREAD]
Am 4:13 and t on the heights of the earth—
Rev 19:15 He t the winepress of the fury

## TREASON [TRAITOR, TRAITORS, TREACHEROUS, TREACHERY]
2Ki 11:14 tore her robes and called out, "T! T!"

## TREASURE [TREASURED, TREASURES, TREASURIES, TREASURY]
Pr    2: 4 and search for it as for hidden t,
Isa 33: 6 of the LORD is the key to this t.
Eze  7:22 robbers will desecrate the place I t.
Mt   6:21 For where your t is, there your heart
     13:44 of heaven is like t hidden in a field.
     19:21 poor, and you will have t in heaven.
Lk  12:33 a t in heaven that will never fail,
2Co  4: 7 But we have this t in jars of clay
1Ti  6:19 In this way they will lay up t

## TREASURED* [TREASURE]
Ex  19: 5 nations you will be my t possession.
Dt   7: 6 to be his people, his t possession.
     14: 2 chosen you to be his t possession.
     26:18 his t possession as he promised,
Job 23:12 I have t the words of his mouth
Ps 135: 4 own, Israel to be his t possession.
Isa 64:11 fire, and all that we t lies in ruins.
Mal  3:17 "they will be my t possession.
Lk   2:19 But Mary t up all these things
     2:51 his mother t all these things in her

## TREASURES [TREASURE]
Dt  33:19 seas, on the t hidden in the sand."
2Ki 20:13 and everything found among his t.
    24:13 Nebuchadnezzar removed the t
1Ch 29: 3 my God I now give my personal t
Pr  10: 2 Ill-gotten t have no lasting value,
Isa 45: 3 I will give you the t of darkness,
Mt   2:11 they opened their t and presented
     6:19 store up for yourselves t on earth,
    13:52 his storeroom new t as well as old."
Col  2: 3 in whom are hidden all the t
Heb 11:26 of greater value than the t of Egypt,

## TREASURIES [TREASURE]
2Ch 16: 2 out of the t of the LORD's temple
Pr   8:21 who love me and making their t full.

## TREASURY [TREASURE]
Ezr  2:69 to the t for this work 61,000 darics
Mt  27: 6 against the law to put this into the t,
Mk  12:43 more into the t than all the others.

## TREAT [TREATED, TREATING, TREATMENT]
Lev 22: 2 his sons to t with respect the sacred
Nu  14:11 "How long will these people t me
Ps 103:10 he does not t us as our sins deserve
Mt  18:17 t them as you would a pagan
    18:35 how my heavenly Father will t each
Jn  15:21 They will t you this way because
Ro  14:10 t your brother or sister with contempt?
Eph  6: 9 t your slaves in the same way.
1Th  5:20 Do not t prophecies with contempt
1Ti  5: 1 T younger men as brothers,
1Pe  3: 7 t them with respect as the weaker

## TREATED [TREAT]
Ge  12:16 He t Abram well for her sake,
Ex  18:11 those who had t Israel arrogantly."
Lev 19:34 you must be t as your native-born.
    25:40 They are to be t as hired workers
1Sa 24:17 "You have t me well, but I have t
Lk   6:23 how their ancestors t the prophets.
Heb 10:29 who have t as an unholy thing

## TREATING [TREAT]
Ge  18:25 t the righteous and the wicked alike.
Heb 12: 7 God is t you as his children.

## TREATMENT [TREAT]
Col  2:23 and their harsh t of the body,

## TREATY
Ex  34:12 not to make a t with those who live
Dt   7: 2 Make no t with them, and show
    23: 6 Do not seek a t of friendship
Jos  9: 6 make a t with us."
Am   1: 9 disregarding a t of brotherhood,

## TREE [TREES]
Ge   1:29 every t that has fruit with seed in it.
     2: 9 of the garden were the t of life and the
           t of the knowledge of good
     3: 1 not eat from any t in the garden'?"
     3:24 to guard the way to the t of life.
2Sa 18: 9 Absalom's hair got caught in the t.
1Ki 14:23 hill and under every spreading t.
Ps   1: 3 They are like a t planted by streams
    52: 8 I am like an olive t flourishing
    92:12 righteous will flourish like a palm t,
Pr   3:18 She is a t of life to those who take
    11:30 fruit of the righteous is a t of life,
    27:18 who guard a fig t will eat its fruit,
Isa 65:22 For as the days of a t, so will be
Jer 17: 8 They will be like a t planted
Eze 17:24 I the LORD bring down the tall t
Da   4:10 and there before me stood a t
Hos  9:10 seeing the early fruit on the fig t.
    14: 6 His splendor will be like an olive t,
Mic  4: 4 own vine and under their own fig t,
Hab  3:17 Though the fig t does not bud
Zec  3:10 to sit under your vine and fig t,'
Mt   3:10 every t that does not produce good
    12:33 for a t is recognized by its fruit.
Mk  11:13 Seeing in the distance a fig t in leaf,
Lk  19: 4 climbed a sycamore-fig t to see him,
Ro  11:24 grafted into a cultivated olive t,
Jas  3:12 sisters, can a fig t bear olives,
Rev  2: 7 the right to eat from the t of life,
    22: 2 side of the river stood the t of life,
    22:14 may have the right to the t of life
    22:19 from you your share in the t of life

## TREES [TREE]
Ge   1:11 and t on the land that bear fruit
     3: 2 eat fruit from the t in the garden,
Dt  20:19 do not destroy its t by putting an ax
Jdg  9: 8 One day the t went out to anoint
1Ch 14:15 marching in the tops of the poplar t,
Ps  96:12 let all the t of the forest sing for joy.
Isa 55:12 all the t of the field will clap their

Eze 47:12 Fruit **t** of all kinds will grow on both
Zec 4:11 "What are these two olive **t**
Mt 3:10 The ax is already at the root of the **t**,
Mk 8:24 they look like **t** walking around."
Jude 1:12 autumn **t**, without fruit
Rev 8: 7 a third of the **t** were burned up,
11: 4 They are "the two olive **t**"

## TREMBLE [TREMBLED, TREMBLES, TREMBLING]

Ex 15:14 The nations will hear and **t**;
1Ch 16:30 **T** before him, all the earth!
Ps 4: 4 **T** and do not sin;
99: 1 LORD reigns, let the nations **t**;
114: 7 **T**, earth, at the presence of the Lord,
Isa 66: 2 and who **t** at my word.
Jer 5:22 "Should you not **t** in my presence?
Eze 38:20 of the earth will **t** at my presence.
Joel 2: 1 Let all who live in the land **t**,
Hab 3: 6 he looked, and made the nations **t**.
Ro 11:20 Do not be arrogant, but **t**.

## TREMBLED [TREMBLE]

Ex 19:16 Everyone in the camp **t**.
20:18 mountain in smoke, they **t** with fear.
2Sa 22: 8 The earth **t** and quaked,
Ac 7:32 Moses **t** with fear and did not dare

## TREMBLES [TREMBLE]

Ps 97: 4 up the world; the earth sees and **t**.
104:32 and it **t**, who touches the mountains,
119:161 cause, but my heart **t** at your word.
Jer 10:10 When he is angry, the earth **t**;
Na 1: 5 The earth **t** at his presence,

## TREMBLING [TREMBLE]

Ps 2:11 fear and celebrate his rule with **t**.
Da 10:10 me and set me **t** on my hands
Mk 16: 8 **T** and bewildered, the women went
Php 2:12 out your salvation with fear and **t**,
Heb 12:21 that Moses said, "I am **t** with fear."

## TRENCH

1Ki 18:38 and also licked up the water in the **t**.
Da 9:25 It will be rebuilt with streets and a **t**,

## TRESPASS* [TRESPASSES]

Ro 5:15 But the gift is not like the **t**.
5:15 many died by the **t** of the one man,
5:17 if, by the **t** of the one man,
5:18 just as one **t** resulted
5:20 in so that the **t** might increase.

## TRESPASSES* [TRESPASS]

Ro 5:16 but the gift followed many **t**

## TRIAL [TRIALS]

Nu 35:12 not die before standing **t** before
Ps 37:33 be condemned when brought to **t**.
Mal 3: 5 "So I will come to put you on **t**.
Mk 13:11 you are arrested and brought to **t**,
2Co 8: 2 In the midst of a very severe **t**,
Jas 1:12 are those who persevere under **t**,
Rev 3:10 you from the hour of **t** that is going

## TRIALS* [TRIAL]

Dt 7:19 saw with your own eyes the great **t**,
29: 3 own eyes you saw those great **t**,
Lk 22:28 who have stood by me in my **t**.
1Th 3: 3 one would be unsettled by these **t**.
2Th 1: 4 persecutions and **t** you are enduring.
Jas 1: 2 whenever you face **t** of many kinds,
1Pe 1: 6 had to suffer grief in all kinds of **t**.
2Pe 2: 9 how to rescue the godly from **t**

## TRIBAL [TRIBE]

Jos 11:23 Israel according to their **t** divisions.

## TRIBE [HALF-TRIBE, TRIBAL, TRIBES]

Nu 1: 4 One man from each **t**, each of them
17: 3 staff for the head of each ancestral **t**.
36: 9 may pass from one **t** to another,
Jos 13:14 the **t** of Levi he gave no inheritance,
Jdg 21: 6 "Today one **t** is cut off
1Ki 11:13 will give him one **t** for the sake
Ps 78:68 but he chose the **t** of Judah,
Heb 7:13 that **t** has ever served at the altar.
Rev 5: 5 the Lion of the **t** of Judah, the Root
5: 9 for God members of every **t**
11: 9 days many from every people, **t**,
14: 6 to every nation, **t**,

## TRIBE OF JUDAH See JUDAH

## TRIBES [TRIBE]

Ge 49:28 All these are the twelve **t** of Israel,
Ex 24: 4 pillars representing the twelve **t**
39:14 the name of one of the twelve **t**.
1Ki 11:31 Solomon's hand and give you ten **t**.
18:31 each of the **t** descended from Jacob,
Ps 122: 4 That is where the **t** go up—the **t**
Isa 49: 6 my servant to restore the **t** of Jacob
Mt 19:28 judging the twelve **t** of Israel.
Jas 1: 1 To the twelve **t** scattered among
Rev 21:12 the names of the twelve **t** of Israel.

## TRIBES OF ISRAEL See ISRAEL

## TRIBULATION*

Rev 7:14 who have come out of the great **t**;

## TRIBUTE

Nu 31:28 set apart as **t** for the LORD one
1Ki 4:21 These countries brought **t** and were

## TRICK* [TRICKERY]

1Th 2: 3 motives, nor are we trying to **t** you.

## TRICKERY* [TRICK]

Ac 13:10 are full of all kinds of deceit and **t**.
2Co 12:16 fellow that I am, I caught you by **t**!

## TRIED [TRY]

Ge 37:21 he **t** to rescue him from their hands.
Ex 2:15 heard of this, he **t** to kill Moses,
8:18 the magicians **t** to produce gnats
Dt 4:34 Has any god ever **t** to take
Ps 73:16 When I **t** to understand all this,
95: 9 they **t** me, though they had seen
Jn 5:18 For this reason they **t** all the more

Jn    19:12  then on, Pilate **t** to set Jesus free,
Gal    1:23  is now preaching the faith he once **t**
Heb    3: 9  your ancestors tested and **t** me,

## TRIES [TRY]
Lk    17:33  Whoever **t** to keep their life will

## TRIMMED
Mt    25: 7  virgins woke up and **t** their lamps.

## TRIUMPH [TRIUMPHAL, TRIUMPHANT, TRIUMPHED, TRIUMPHING, TRIUMPHS]
Ps     9:19  Arise, LORD, do not let mortals **t**;
      25: 2  nor let my enemies **t** over me.
      54: 7  and my eyes have looked in **t** on my
     112: 8  the end they will look in **t** on their
     118: 7  I look in **t** on my enemies.
Pr    28:12  When the righteous **t**, there is great
Isa   42:13  cry and will **t** over his enemies.
Rev   17:14  the Lamb will **t** over them

## TRIUMPHAL* [TRIUMPH]
Isa   60:11  their kings led in **t** procession.
2Co    2:14  as captives in Christ's **t** procession

## TRIUMPHANT* [TRIUMPH]
Da    11:12  thousands, yet he will not remain **t**.

## TRIUMPHED [TRIUMPH]
Dt    32:27  and say, 'Our hand has **t**;
Rev    5: 5  of Judah, the Root of David, has **t**.
      12:11  They **t** over him by the blood

## TRIUMPHING* [TRIUMPH]
Col    2:15  of them, **t** over them by the cross.

## TRIUMPHS* [TRIUMPH]
Jas    2:13  Mercy **t** over judgment.

## TRIVIAL*
1Ki   16:31  He not only considered it **t**
Eze    8:17  Is it a **t** matter for the house
1Co    6: 2  you not competent to judge **t** cases?

## TROOPS
Ex    14: 9  and chariots, horsemen and **t**—
Ps   110: 3  Your **t** will be willing on your day
Rev    9:16  of the mounted **t** was two hundred

## TROPHIMUS
2Ti    4:20  Corinth, and I left **T** sick in Miletus.

## TROUBLE [TROUBLED, TROUBLEMAKERS, TROUBLER, TROUBLES]
Ge    41:51  God has made me forget all my **t**
Nu    11:11  "Why have you brought this **t**
Jos    7:25  "Why have you brought this **t**
1Ki   18:18  "I have not made **t** for Israel,"
Job    2:10  accept good from God, and not **t**?"
       5: 7  to **t** as surely as sparks fly upward.
      14: 1  are of few days and full of **t**.

Job   42:11  him over all the **t** the LORD had
Ps     7:14  are pregnant with evil conceive **t**
       7:16  The **t** they cause recoils on them;
       9: 9  a stronghold in times of **t**.
      10:14  you, God, see the **t** of the afflicted;
      22:11  for **t** is near and there is no one
      27: 5  the day of **t** he will keep me safe
      32: 7  you will protect me from **t**
      37:39  he is their stronghold in time of **t**.
      41: 1  LORD delivers them in times of **t**.
      46· 1  strength, an ever-present help in **t**.
      50:15  and call on me in the day of **t**;
      59:16  my fortress, my refuge in times of **t**.
      66:14  my mouth spoke when I was in **t**.
      90:10  yet the best of them are but **t**
      91:15  I will be with them in **t**, I will
     107: 6  cried out to the LORD in their **t**,
     119:143  **T** and distress have come upon me,
     138: 7  Though I walk in the midst of **t**,
     143:11  righteousness, bring me out of **t**.
Pr    11: 8  The righteous are rescued from **t**,
      12:13  talk, and so the innocent escape **t**.
      12:21  but the wicked have their fill of **t**.
      13:21  **T** pursues the sinner, but the righteous
      19:23  one rests content, untouched by **t**.
      24:10  If you falter in a time of **t**,
      25:19  on the unfaithful in a time of **t**.
      28:14  who harden their hearts fall into **t**.
Ecc   12: 1  before the days of **t** come
Jer   30: 7  It will be a time of **t** for Jacob,
Da     9:25  and a trench, but in times of **t**.
Jnh    1: 8  for making all this **t** for us?
Na     1: 7  is good, a refuge in times of **t**.
Zep    1:15  and anguish, a day of **t** and ruin,
Mt     6:34  Each day has enough **t** of its own.
      13:21  When **t** or persecution comes
Jn    16:33  In this world you will have **t**.
Ro     8:35  Shall **t** or hardship or persecution
2Co    1: 4  any **t** with the comfort we ourselves
2Th    1: 6  He will pay back **t** to those who **t**
Jas    5:13  Is anyone among you in **t**?

## TROUBLED [TROUBLE]
Ge     6: 6  and his heart was deeply **t**.
Ps    38:18  I am **t** by my sin.
Mk    14:33  began to be deeply distressed and **t**.
Lk     1:29  Mary was greatly **t** at his words
Jn    14: 1  "Do not let your hearts be **t**.
      14:27  Do not let your hearts be **t** and do
2Th    1: 7  and give relief to you who are **t**,

## TROUBLEMAKERS* [TROUBLE]
1Sa   30:22  But all the evil men and **t** among
Pr     6:12  **T** and villains, who go about

## TROUBLER* [TROUBLE]
1Ki   18:17  him, "Is that you, you **t** of Israel?"

## TROUBLES [TROUBLE]
Ps    34: 6  he saved him out of all his **t**.
      34:17  he delivers them from all their **t**.
      34:19  The righteous may have many **t**,
      40:12  For **t** without number surround me;
      54: 7  have delivered me from all my **t**,
Isa   46: 7  it cannot save them from their **t**.
1Co    7:28  those who marry will face many **t**

2Co 1: 4 who comforts us in all our t,
4:17 momentary t are achieving for us
6: 4 in t, hardships and distresses;
7: 4 all our t my joy knows no bounds.
Php 4:14 it was good of you to share in my t.

## TRUE [TRULY, TRUTH]

Nu 11:23 not what I say will come t for you."
12: 7 this is not t of my servant Moses;
Dt 18:22 does not take place or come t, that is
1Sa 9: 6 and everything he says comes t.
1Ki 10: 6 achievements and your wisdom is t.
2Ch 6:17 your servant David come t.
15: 3 time Israel was without the t God,
Job 11: 6 wisdom, for t wisdom has two sides.
Ps 33: 4 word of the LORD is right and t;
119:142 is everlasting and your law is t.
119:151 and all your commands are t.
119:160 All your words are t;
144:15 is the people of whom this is t;
Pr 8: 7 My mouth speaks what is t, for my
Ecc 12:10 what he wrote was upright and t.
Isa 65:16 swear by the one t God.
Jer 10:10 But the LORD is the t God;
28: 9 only if his prediction comes t."
Eze 33:33 "When all this comes t—
Lk 1:20 which will come t at their appointed
16:11 who will trust you with t riches?
Jn 1: 9 The t light that gives light
4:23 the t worshipers will worship
5:32 his testimony about me is t.
6:32 Father who gives you the t bread
7:28 authority, but he who sent me is t.
8:16 if I do judge, my decisions are t,
15: 1 "I am the t vine, and my Father is
17: 3 the only t God, and Jesus Christ,
19:35 testimony, and his testimony is t.
21:24 We know that his testimony is t.
Ac 10:34 "I now realize how t it is that God
11:23 them all to remain t to the Lord
14:22 them to remain t to the faith.
17:11 day to see if what Paul said was t.
Ro 3: 4 Let God be t, and every human
12: 1 this is t worship.
Eph 4:24 to be like God in t righteousness
Php 4: 8 whatever is t, whatever is noble,
Col 1: 5 heard in the t word of the gospel
1Th 1: 9 idols to serve the living and t God,
1Jn 2: 8 and the t light is already shining.
5:20 so that we may know him who is t.
5:20 we are in him who is t by being
5:20 He is the t God and eternal life.
3Jn 1:12 you know that our testimony is t.
Rev 2:13 Yet you remain t to my name.
3: 7 the words of him who is holy and t,
3:14 the faithful and t witness, the ruler
6:10 Lord, holy and t, until you judge
15: 3 Just and t are your ways,
16: 7 t and just are your judgments."
19: 2 for t and just are his judgments.
19: 9 "These are the t words of God."
19:11 whose rider is called Faithful and T.
21: 5 these words are trustworthy and t."
22: 6 "These words are trustworthy and t.

## TRULY [TRUE]

Col 1: 6 and t understood God's grace.

## TRULY I TELL YOU Mt 5:18, 26; 6:2, 5, 16;
8:10; 10:15, 23, 42; 11:11; 13:17; 16:28; 17:20;
18:3, 13, 18, 19; 19:23, 28; 21:21, 31; 23:36;
24:2, 34, 47; 25:12, 40, 45; 26:13, 21, 34; Mk
3:28; 8:12; 9:1, 41; 10:15, 29; 11:23; 12:43;
13:30; 14:9, 18, 25, 30; Lk 4:24; 9:27; 12:37, 44;
18:17, 29; 21:3, 32; 23:43; Jn 1:51; 3:3, 5, 11;
5:19, 24, 25; 6:26, 32, 47, 53; 8:34, 51, 58; 10:1,
7; 12:24; 13:16, 20, 21, 38; 14:12; 16:7, 20, 23;
21:18

## TRUMPET [TRUMPETERS, TRUMPETS]

Ex 19:16 mountain, and a very loud t blast.
Lev 23:24 commemorated with t blasts.
25: 9 sound the t throughout your land.
Nu 10: 5 When a t blast is sounded, the tribes
Isa 27:13 And in that day a great t will sound.
Eze 33: 5 Since they heard the sound of the t
Joel 2:15 Blow the t in Zion, declare a holy
Zec 9:14 Sovereign LORD will sound the t;
Mt 24:31 send his angels with a loud t call,
1Co 14: 8 if the t does not sound a clear call,
15:52 For the t will sound, the dead will
1Th 4:16 archangel and with the t call of God,
Rev 1:10 behind me a loud voice like a t,
8: 7 The first angel sounded his t,

## TRUMPETERS [TRUMPET]

2Ch 5:13 The t and musicians joined

## TRUMPETS [TRUMPET]

Nu 10: 2 "Make two t of hammered silver,
29: 1 It is a day for you to sound the t.
Jos 6: 8 carrying the seven t before
Jdg 7:19 They blew their t and broke the jars
Ps 47: 5 the LORD amid the sounding of t.
Mt 6: 2 do not announce it with t,
Rev 8: 2 and seven t were given to them.

## TRUST* [ENTRUST, ENTRUSTED, TRUSTED, TRUSTFULLY, TRUSTING, TRUSTS, TRUSTWORTHY]

Ex 14:31 the LORD and put their t in him
19: 9 and will always put their t in you."
Nu 20:12 "Because you did not t in me
Dt 1:32 you did not t in the LORD your
9:23 You did not t him or obey him.
28:52 walls in which you t fall down.
Jdg 11:20 did not t Israel to pass through his
2Ki 17:14 who did not t in the LORD their
18:30 not let Hezekiah persuade you to t
1Ch 9:22 to their positions of t by David
Job 4:18 If God places no t in his servants,
8:14 What they t in is fragile;
15:15 If God places no t in his holy ones,
31:24 "If I have put my t in gold or said
39:12 Can you t it to haul in your grain
Ps 4: 5 the righteous and t in the LORD.
9:10 Those who know your name t
13: 5 But I t in your unfailing love;
20: 7 Some t in chariots and some

Ps  20: 7  we t in the name of the LORD
    22: 4  In you our ancestors put their t;
    24: 4  who do not put their t in an idol
    25: 1  my God, I put my t.
    25: 2  I t in you; do not let me be put
    31: 6  as for me, I t in the LORD.
    31:14  But I t in you, LORD; I say,
    32:10  love surrounds those who t in him.
    33:21  rejoice, for we t in his holy name.
    37: 3  T in the LORD and do good;
    37: 5  t in him and he will do this:
    40: 3  the LORD and put their t in him.
    40: 4  those who make the LORD their t,
    44: 6  I put no t in my bow, my sword
    49: 6  those who t in their wealth
    49:13  fate of those who t in themselves,
    52: 8  I t in God's unfailing love for ever
    55:23  But as for me, I t in you.
    56: 3  When I am afraid, I put my t in you.
    56: 4  in God I t and am not afraid.
    56:11  in God I t and am not afraid.
    62: 8  T in him at all times, you people;
    62:10  Do not t in extortion or put vain
    78: 7  Then they would put their t in God
    78:22  in God or t in his deliverance.
    84:12  blessed are those who t in you.
    86: 4  Lord, for I put my t in you.
    91: 2  my fortress, my God, in whom I t."
    115: 8  them, and so will all who t in them,
    115: 9  House of Israel, t in the LORD—
    115:10  House of Aaron, t in the LORD—
    115:11  who fear him, t in the LORD—
    118: 8  in the LORD than to t in human
    118: 9  in the LORD than to t in princes.
    119:42  who taunts me, for I t in your word.
    119:66  for I t your commands.
    125: 1  Those who t in the LORD are like
    135:18  them, and so will all who t in them.
    143: 8  love, for I have put my t in you.
    146: 3  Do not put your t in princes,
Pr   3: 5  T in the LORD with all your heart
    11:28  Those who t in their riches will fall,
    16:20  blessed are those who t in the LORD.
    21:22  the stronghold in which they t.
    22:19  So that your t may be
    23: 4  do not t your own cleverness.
    28:25  those who t in the LORD will prosper.
    28:26  Those who t in themselves are fools,
Isa  8:17  I will put my t in him.
    12: 2  I will t and not be afraid.
    26: 3  because they t in you.
    26: 4  T in the LORD forever,
    30:15  in quietness and t is your strength,
    31: 1  who t in the multitude of their
    36.15  not let Hezekiah persuade you to t
    42:17  But those who t in idols, who say
    50:10  t in the name of the LORD
Jer  2:37  the LORD has rejected those you t;
     5:11  the fortified cities in which you t.
     7: 4  Do not t in deceptive words and say,
     7:14  the temple you t in, the place I gave
     9: 4  do not t any of your people.
    12: 6  Do not t them, though they speak
    17: 5  "Cursed are those who t in mortals,
    17: 7  blessed are those who t in the LORD,
    28:15  you have persuaded this nation to t
    29:31  and has persuaded you to t in lies,

Jer  39:18  with your life, because you t in me,
    48: 7  Since you t in your deeds
    49: 4  you t in your riches and say,
Eze  33:13  but then they t in their righteousness
Mic  7: 5  Do not t a neighbor;
Na   1: 7  He cares for those who t in him,
Hab  2:18  make them t in their own creations;
Zep  3: 2  She does not t in the LORD,
     3:12  remnant of Israel will t in the name
Lk  16:11  who will t you with true riches?
Jn  12:36  Put your t in the light while you
    14: 1  T in God; t also in me.
Ac  14:23  Lord, in whom they had put their t.
Ro  15:13  all joy and peace as you t in him,
1Co  4: 2  been given a t must prove faithful.
     9:17  simply discharging the t committed
2Co 13: 6  I t that you will discover that we
Heb  2:13  again, "I will put my t in him."

## TRUSTED* [TRUST]

1Sa 27:12  Achish t David and said to himself,
2Ki 18: 5  Hezekiah t in the LORD, the God
1Ch  5:20  their prayers, because they t in him.
Job 12:20  He silences the lips of t advisers
Ps   5: 9  a word from their mouth can be t;
    22: 4  they t and you delivered them.
    22: 5  in you they t and were not
    26: 1  I have t in the LORD and have not
    41: 9  someone I t, one who shared my
    52. 7  stronghold but t in his great wealth
    116:10  I t in the LORD when I said,
Pr  27: 6  Wounds from a friend can be t,
Isa  20: 5  Those who t in Cush and boasted
    25: 9  we t in him, and he saved us.
    25: 9  This is the LORD, we t in him;
    47:10  You have t in your wickedness
Jer  13:25  forgotten me and t in false gods.
    38:22  those t friends of yours.
    48:13  was ashamed when they t in Bethel.
Eze 16:15  " 'But you t in your beauty
Da   3:28  They t in him and defied the king's
     6:23  on him, because he had t in his God.
Zep  3: 4  are unprincipled; they cannot be t.
Lk  11:22  away the armor in which the man t
    16:10  "Whoever can be t with very little can
           also be t with much,
Ac  12:20  a t personal servant of the king,
Tit  2:10  but to show that they can be fully t,
     3: 8  those who have t in God may be

## TRUSTFULLY* [TRUST]

Pr   3:29  your neighbor, who lives t near you.

## TRUSTING* [TRUST]

Job 15:31  themselves by t what is worthless,
Ps  112: 7  hearts are steadfast, t in the LORD.
Isa  2:22  Stop t in human beings, who have
Jer  7: 8  you are t in deceptive words that are

## TRUSTS* [TRUST]

Ps  21: 7  For the king t in the LORD;
    22: 8  "He t in the LORD," they say,
    28: 7  my heart t in him, and he helps me.
    86: 2  save your servant who t in you.
Pr  29:25  but whoever t in the LORD is kept
Mt  27:43  He t in God. Let God rescue him

Ro    4: 5  but **t** God who justifies the ungodly,
1Co 13: 7  protects, always **t**, always hopes,
1Pe  2: 6  the one who **t** in him will never be

## TRUSTWORTHY* [TRUST]

Ex 18:21  **t** men who hate dishonest gain—
2Sa  7:28  Your covenant is **t**, and you have
Ne   7: 2  he was **t** and feared God
    13:13  because they were considered **t**.
Ps  19: 7  The statutes of the LORD are **t**,
   111: 7  all his precepts are **t**.
  119:86  All your commands are **t**;
 119:138  down are righteous; they are fully **t**.
 145:13  The LORD is **t** in all he promises
Pr   8: 6  for I have **t** things to say;
  11:13  a confidence, but the **t** keep a secret.
  12:22  delights in people who are **t**.
  13:17  but a **t** envoy brings healing.
  25:13  harvest time is a **t** messenger
Da  2:45  is true and its interpretation is **t**."
   6: 4  because he was **t** and neither corrupt
Lk 16:11  if you have not been **t** in handling
  16:12  if you have not been **t** with someone
  19:17  'Because you have been **t** in a very
Jn  8:26  he who sent me is **t**,
1Co 7:25  as one who by the Lord's mercy is **t**.
1Ti  1:12  that he considered me **t**,
  1:15  Here is a **t** saying that deserves full
  3: 1  Here is a **t** saying:
  3:11  but temperate and **t** in everything.
  4: 9  This is a **t** saying that deserves full
2Ti  2:11  Here is a **t** saying: If we died
Tit  1: 9  the **t** message as it has been taught,
  3: 8  This is a **t** saying. And I want you
Rev 21: 5  for these words are **t** and true."
  22: 6  to me, "These words are **t** and true.

## TRUTH* [TRUE, TRUTHFUL, TRUTHFULLY, TRUTHFULNESS, TRUTHS]

Ge 42:16  tested to see if you are telling the **t**.
1Ki 17:24  LORD from your mouth is the **t**."
  22:16  the **t** in the name of the LORD?"
2Ch 18:15  the **t** in the name of the LORD?"
Ps 15: 2  who speak the **t** from their hearts;
  25: 5  Guide me in your **t** and teach me,
  45: 4  forth victoriously in the cause of **t**,
  52: 3  falsehood rather than speaking the **t**.
 119:43  Never take your word of **t** from my
 145:18  on him, to all who call on him in **t**.
Pr 12:17  An honest witness tells the **t**,
  22:21  honest and to speak the **t**,
  23:23  Buy the **t** and do not sell it—
Isa 45:19  I, the LORD, speak the **t**;
  48: 1  but not in **t** or righteousness—
  59:14  **t** has stumbled in the streets,
  59:15  **T** is nowhere to be found,
Jer  5: 1  who deals honestly and seeks the **t**,
  5: 3  do not your eyes look for **t**?
  7:28  **T** has perished; it has vanished
  9: 3  it is not by **t** that they triumph
  9: 5  friend, and no one speaks the **t**.
  26:15  in **t** the LORD has sent me to you
Da  8:12  did, and **t** was thrown to the ground.
  9:13  sins and giving attention to your **t**.
  10:21  what is written in the Book of **T**.

Da 11: 2  I tell you the **t**: Three more kings
Am  5:10  and detest the one who tells the **t**.
Zec  8: 3  will be called the City of **T**,
  8:16  Speak the **t** to each other, and render
  8:19  Therefore love **t** and peace."
Mt 22:16  of God in accordance with the **t**.
Mk  5:33  with fear, told him the whole **t**.
  12:14  of God in accordance with the **t**.
Lk 20:21  of God in accordance with the **t**.
Jn  1:14  from the Father, full of grace and **t**.
  1:17  and **t** came through Jesus Christ.
  3:21  those who live by the **t** come
  4:23  the Father in the Spirit and in **t**,
  4:24  must worship in the Spirit and in **t**."
  5:33  to John and he has testified to the **t**.
  7:18  the one who sent him is a man of **t**;
  8:32  Then you will know the **t**, and the **t** will set you free."
  8:40  a man who has told you the **t** that I
  8:44  not holding to the **t**, for there is no **t** in him.
  8:45  Yet because I tell the **t**, you do not
  8:46  If I am telling the **t**, why don't you
  9:24  glory to God and tell the **t**,"
  14: 6  "I am the way and the **t** and the life.
  14:17  the Spirit of **t**. The world cannot
  15:26  the Spirit of **t** who goes
  16:13  But when he, the Spirit of **t**, comes,
  16:13  he will guide you into all the **t**.
  17:17  Sanctify them by the **t**; your word is **t**.
  18:23  But if I spoke the **t**, why did you
  18:37  into the world is to testify to the **t**.
  18:37  on the side of **t** listens to me."
  18:38  "What is **t**?" retorted Pilate.
  19:35  He knows that he tells the **t**, and he
Ac 20:30  distort the **t** in order to draw away
  21:24  everyone will know there is no **t**
  21:34  could not get at the **t** because
  24: 8  to learn the **t** about all these charges
  28:25  "The Holy Spirit spoke the **t**
Ro  1:18  human beings who suppress the **t**
  1:25  They exchanged the **t** about God
  2: 2  who do such things is based on **t**.
  2: 8  and who reject the **t** and follow evil,
  2:20  embodiment of knowledge and **t**—
  9: 1  I speak the **t** in Christ—I am not
  15: 8  of the Jews on behalf of God's **t**,
1Co 5: 8  unleavened bread of sincerity and **t**.
  13: 6  in evil but rejoices with the **t**.
2Co 4: 2  by setting forth the **t** plainly we
  11:10  As surely as the **t** of Christ is in me,
  12: 6  because I would be speaking the **t**.
  13: 8  we cannot do anything against the **t**, but only for the **t**.
Gal  2: 5  that the **t** of the gospel might remain
  2:14  in line with the **t** of the gospel,
  4:16  your enemy by telling you the **t**?
  5: 7  you to keep you from obeying the **t**?
Eph 1:13  when you heard the word of **t**,
  4:15  Instead, speaking the **t** in love,
  4:21  in accordance with the **t** that is
  5: 9  in all goodness, righteousness and **t**)
  6:14  belt of **t** buckled around your waist,
2Th 2:10  because they refused to love the **t**
  2:12  who have not believed the **t**
  2:13  the Spirit and through belief in the **t**.
1Ti  2: 4  and to come to a knowledge of the **t**.

1Ti    2: 7  I am telling the **t**, I am not lying—
       3:15  the pillar and foundation of the **t**.
       4: 3  who believe and who know the **t**.
       6: 5  who have been robbed of the **t**
2Ti    2:15  who correctly handles the word of **t**.
       2:18  who have departed from the **t**.
       2:25  them to a knowledge of the **t**,
       3. 7  to come to a knowledge of the **t**.
       3: 8  so also these teachers oppose the **t**.
       4: 4  will turn their ears away from the **t**
Tit    1: 1  their knowledge of the **t** that leads
       1:13  He has surely told the **t**!
       1:14  commands of those who reject the **t**.
Heb  10:26  received the knowledge of the **t**,
Jas    1:18  give us birth through the word of **t**,
       3:14  do not boast about it or deny the **t**.
       5:19  one of you should wander from the **t**
1Pe    1:22  by obeying the **t** so that you have
2Pe    1:12  established in the **t** you now have.
       2: 2  and will bring the way of **t**
1Jn    1: 6  we lie and do not live out the **t**.
       1: 8  ourselves and the **t** is not in us.
       2: 4  are liars, and the **t** is not in them.
       2: 8  its **t** is seen in him and in you,
       2:20  One, and all of you know the **t**.
       2:21  you because you do not know the **t**,
       2:21  and because no lie comes from the **t**.
       3:18  or tongue but with actions and in **t**.
       3:19  we know that we belong to the **t**
       4: 6  is how we recognize the Spirit of **t**
       5: 6  testifies, because the Spirit is the **t**.
2Jn    1: 1  whom I love in the **t**—
       1: 1  but also all who know the **t**—
       1: 2  because of the **t**, which lives in us
       1: 3  Son, will be with us in **t** and love.
       1: 4  of your children walking in the **t**,
3Jn    1: 1  friend Gaius, whom I love in the **t**.
       1: 3  testify to your faithfulness to the **t**,
       1: 4  my children are walking in the **t**.
       1: 8  that we may work together for the **t**.
       1:12  and even by the **t** itself.

### TRUTHFUL* [TRUTH]
Pr    12:19  **T** lips endure forever, but a lying
      14:25  A **t** witness saves lives, but a false
      22:21  so that you bring back **t** reports to those
Jer    4: 2  and if in a **t**, just and righteous way
Jn     3:33  it has certified that God is **t**.
2Co    6: 7  in **t** speech and in the power of God;

### TRUTHFULLY* [TRUTH]
Eph    4:25  and speak **t** to your neighbor, for we

### TRUTHFULNESS* [TRUTH]
Ro     3: 7  "If my falsehood enhances God's **t**

### TRUTHS* [TRUTH]
1Ti    3: 9  keep hold of the deep **t** of the faith
       4: 6  nourished on the **t** of the faith
Heb    5:12  teach you the elementary **t** of God's

### TRY [TRIED, TRIES, TRYING]
Ps    26: 2  and **t** me, examine my heart and my
Isa    7:13  Will you **t** the patience of my God
Lk    12:58  **t** hard to be reconciled on the way,
      13:24  will **t** to enter and will not be able

Ac    15:10  why do you **t** to test God by putting
1Co   10:33  even as I **t** to please everyone
      14:12  **t** to excel in those that build
2Co    5:11  the Lord, we **t** to persuade people.
Tit    2: 9  in everything, to **t** to please them,

### TRYING [TRY]
Nu    16:10  now you are **t** to get the priesthood
Da     8:15  the vision and **t** to understand it,
Mt     2:20  those who were **t** to take the child's
2Co    5:12  We are not **t** to commend ourselves
Gal    1:10  Am I now **t** to win human approval,
       3: 3  are you now **t** to finish by human
1Th    2: 4  We are not **t** to please people
1Pe    1:11  **t** to find out the time
1Jn    2:26  those who are **t** to lead you astray.

### TUCK [TUCKED, TUCKING]
2Ki    4:29  "**T** your cloak into your belt,
       9: 1  him, "**T** your cloak into your belt,

### TUCKED* [TUCK]
Ex    12:11  with your cloak **t** into your belt,

### TUCKING* [TUCK]
1Ki   18:46  Elijah and, **t** his cloak into his belt,

### TUMORS
1Sa    5: 6  on them and afflicted them with **t**.
       6: 4  "Five gold **t** and five gold rats,

### TUNE [TUNED]
1Co   14: 7  anyone know what **t** is being played

### TUNED* [TUNE]
Job   30:31  My lyre is **t** to mourning, and my

### TUNIC [TUNICS]
Ex    28: 4  robe, a woven **t**, a turban and a sash.

### TUNICS [TUNIC]
Ex    29: 8  Bring his sons and dress them in **t**

### TUNNEL*
2Ki   20:20  the **t** by which he brought water
Job   28:10  They **t** through the rock; their eyes

### TURBAN
Ex    28: 4  robe, a woven tunic, a **t** and a sash.
Zec    3: 5  So they put a clean **t** on his head

### TURMOIL
Ps    65: 7  their waves, and the **t** of the nations.
Pr    15:16  LORD than great wealth with **t**.

### TURN [TURNED, TURNING, TURNS]
Ex    23:27  make all your enemies **t** their backs
      32:12  **T** from your fierce anger;
Lev   19: 4  " 'Do not **t** to idols or make metal
Nu    32:15  If you **t** away from following him,
Dt     5:32  do not **t** aside to the right
      28:14  Do not **t** aside from any
      30:10  **t** to the LORD your God with all

Jos 1: 7 do not **t** from it to the right
1Ki 8:58 May he **t** our hearts to him, to walk
2Ch 7:14 face and **t** from their wicked ways,
30: 9 He will not **t** his face from you
Ne 9:29 in order to **t** them back to your law,
Job 33:30 to **t** them back from the pit,
Ps 4: 2 How long will you men **t** my glory
6: 4 **T**, LORD, and deliver me;
25:16 **T** to me and be gracious to me, for I
28: 1 my Rock, do not **t** a deaf ear to me.
34:14 **T** from evil and do good;
51:13 ways, and sinners will **t** back to you.
78: 6 they in **t** would tell their children.
119:36 **T** my heart toward your statutes
119:132 **T** to me and have mercy on me,
Pr 4: 5 my words or **t** away from them.
4:27 Do not **t** to the right or the left;
7:25 Do not let your heart **t** to her ways
22: 6 they are old they will not **t** from it.
Isa 6:10 their hearts, and **t** and be healed."
17: 7 and **t** their eyes to the Holy One
28: 6 to those who **t** back the battle
29:16 You **t** things upside down,
30:21 Whether you **t** to the right
41:18 I will **t** the desert into pools
45:22 "**T** to me and be saved, all you ends
55: 7 Let them **t** to the LORD, and he
56:11 they all **t** to their own way,
Jer 18:11 So **t** from your evil ways, each one
31:13 I will **t** their mourning
Eze 18:21 if the wicked **t** away from all the sins
33: 9 if you do warn the wicked to **t**
33:11 they **t** from their ways and live. **T**!
33:18 the righteous **t** from their righteousness
Joel 2:14 He may **t** and relent and leave
Am 1:11 I will not **t** back [my wrath].
Jnh 3: 9 compassion **t** from his fierce anger
Mal 4: 6 He will **t** the hearts of the parents
Mt 5:39 **t** to them the other cheek also.
10:35 to **t** " 'a man against his father,
Lk 1:17 to **t** the hearts of the parents to their
Jn 12:40 understand with their hearts, nor **t**—
16:20 grieve, but your grief will **t** to joy.
Ac 3:19 and **t** to God, so that your sins may
26:18 and **t** them from darkness to light,
1Co 14:31 For you can all prophesy in **t** so
1Ti 6:20 **T** away from godless chatter
2Ti 4: 4 They will **t** their ears away from the
truth and **t** aside to myths.
Heb 12:25 if we **t** away from him who warns
1Pe 3:11 **T** from evil and do good;
Rev 10: 9 It will **t** your stomach sour,

## TURNED [TURN]
Ex 4: 4 and it **t** back into a staff in his hand.
Dt 23: 5 **t** the curse into a blessing for you,
1Sa 7: 2 people of Israel **t** back to the LORD.
1Ki 11: 4 old, his wives **t** his heart after other
2Ch 15: 4 their distress they **t** to the LORD,
Est 9: 1 now the tables were **t** and the Jews
9:22 when their sorrow was **t** into joy
Ps 14: 3 All have **t** away, all have become
30:11 You **t** my wailing into dancing;
40: 1 he **t** to me and heard my cry.
66: 6 He **t** the sea into dry land,
114: 3 looked and fled, the Jordan **t** back;
Ecc 2:12 I **t** my thoughts to consider wisdom,

Isa 9:12 his anger is not **t** away, his hand is
53: 6 each of us has **t** to our own way;
Hos 7: 8 Ephraim is a flat loaf not **t** over.
Joel 2:31 The sun will be **t** to darkness
Jnh 3:10 and how they **t** from their evil ways,
Zec 7:11 stubbornly they **t** their backs
Lk 22:32 And when you have **t** back,
Jn 2: 9 the water that had been **t** into wine.
Ro 3:12 All have **t** away, they have together
Rev 6:12 the whole moon **t** blood red,
10:10 I had eaten it, my stomach **t** sour.

## TURNING [TURN]
2Ki 21:13 dish, wiping it and **t** it upside down.
Pr 2: 2 **t** your ear to wisdom and applying
14:27 **t** a person from the snares of death.
Gal 4: 9 it that you are **t** back to those weak

## TURNS [TURN]
Dt 30:17 if your heart **t** away and you are not
2Sa 22:29 the LORD **t** my darkness
Pr 15: 1 A gentle answer **t** away wrath,
Ecc 7: 7 Extortion **t** the wise into fools,
Isa 44:25 of the wise and **t** it into nonsense,
2Co 3:16 But whenever anyone **t** to the Lord,
Jas 5:20 Whoever **t** a sinner from the way

## TURTLE(S), TURTLEDOVE (KJV)
See DOVE(S)

## TWELVE [12,000, 144,000]
Ge 35:22 Israel heard of it. Jacob had **t** sons:
49:28 All these are the **t** tribes of Israel,
Ex 24: 4 up **t** stone pillars representing the **t**
28:21 There are to be **t** stones,
Jos 4: 3 to take up **t** stones from the middle
1Ki 11:30 wearing and tore it into **t** pieces.
18:31 Elijah took **t** stones, one for each
Mt 10: 1 Jesus called his **t** disciples to him
Mk 3:14 appointed **t** that they might be with him
Lk 9:17 the disciples picked up **t** basketfuls
Jas 1: 1 To the **t** tribes scattered among
Rev 12: 1 and a crown of **t** stars on her head.
21:12 high wall with **t** gates, and with **t**
21:12 written the names of the **t** tribes
21:14 wall of the city had **t** foundations,
21:14 were the names of the **t** apostles
21:21 The **t** gates were **t** pearls, each gate
22: 2 tree of life, bearing **t** crops of fruit,

## TWENTY
Nu 1: 3 the men in Israel who are **t** years old

## TWICE [TWO]
Ex 16: 5 is to be **t** as much as they gather
Nu 20:11 and struck the rock **t** with his staff.
1Ki 11: 9 Israel, who had appeared to him **t**.
Mk 14:30 the rooster crows **t** you yourself will

## TWILIGHT [LIGHT]
Ex 12: 6 of Israel must slaughter them at **t**.
16:12 'At **t** you will eat meat,
Lev 23: 5 The LORD's Passover begins at **t**

## TWIN* [TWINS]
Ge  25:24  there were **t** boys in her womb.
SS    4: 2  Each has its **t**; not one of them is

## TWINKLING*
1Co 15:52  a flash, in the **t** of an eye, at the last

## TWINS* [TWIN]
Ro    9:11  before the **t** were born or had done

## TWIST* [TWISTED, TWISTING, TWISTS]
Ps  56: 5  All day long they **t** my words;

## TWISTED [TWIST]
Ex  26: 1  with ten curtains of finely **t** linen
Mt  27:29  then **t** together a crown of thorns

## TWISTING* [TWIST]
Pr  30:33  and as **t** the nose produces blood,

## TWISTS [TWIST]
Ex  23: 8  see and **t** the words of the righteous.

## TWO [SECOND, TWICE]
Ge   1:16  God made **t** great lights—
      4:19  Lamech married **t** women,
      6:19  into the ark **t** of all living creatures,
Ex  31:18  he gave him the **t** tablets
     34: 1  out **t** stone tablets like the first ones,
Lev 16: 8  He is to cast lots for the **t** goats—
Dt    4:13  then wrote them on **t** stone tablets.
    17: 6  On the testimony of **t** or three
    22: 9  Do not plant **t** kinds of seed in your
    25:13  Do not have **t** differing weights
1Ki  3:16  Now **t** prostitutes came to the king
Ps  62:11  has spoken, **t** things I have heard:
Pr  30: 7  "**T** things I ask of you, Lord;
   30:15  "The leech has **t** daughters. 'Give!
Ecc  4: 9  **T** are better than one, because they
Isa  6: 2  **t** wings they covered their faces,
Eze  1:11  They each had **t** wings spreading
Da   8: 3  before me was a ram with **t** horns,
Zec  4:11  "What are these **t** olive trees
   14: 4  of Olives will be split in **t** from east
Mt   6:24  "No one can serve **t** masters.
  18:16  be established by the testimony of **t**
  19: 5  and the **t** will become one flesh'?
Mk  6: 7  he began to send them out **t** by **t**
  12:42  and put in **t** very small copper coins,
  15:27  They crucified **t** rebels with him,
Lk  9:30  **T** men, Moses and Elijah,
  17:35  **T** women will be grinding grain
  18:10  "**T** men went up to the temple
1Co  6:16  "The **t** will become one flesh."
Gal  4:24  the women represent **t** covenants.
Eph  2:14  who has made the **t** one and has
Rev 11: 3  And I will appoint my **t** witnesses,
  19:20  The **t** of them were thrown alive

## TWO-EDGED (KJV) See
DOUBLE-EDGED

## TYCHICUS*
Companion of Paul (Ac 20:4; Eph 6:21; Col 4:7; 2Ti 4:12; Tit 3:12).

## TYING [TIE]
Mt  12:29  without first **t** up the strong man?

## TYRANNICAL*
Pr  28:16  A **t** ruler practices extortion, but one

## TYRANNUS*
Ac  19: 9  daily in the lecture hall of **T**.

## TYRE
1Ki  5: 1  Hiram king of **T** heard that Solomon
Ps  45:12  The city of **T** will come with a gift,
Isa  23: 1  A prophecy concerning **T**:
Eze 27: 2  man, take up a lament concerning **T**.
  28:12  a lament concerning the king of **T**
Mt  11:22  it will be more bearable for **T**

# U

## UGLY
Ge  41: 3  seven other cows, **u** and gaunt,

## UNAPPROACHABLE*
1Ti  6:16  is immortal and who lives in **u** light,

## UNASHAMED*
1Jn  2:28  and **u** before him at his coming.

## UNAUTHORIZED
Lev 10: 1  and they offered **u** fire before

## UNAWARE
Lev  4:13  even though the community is **u**
   5: 2  they are **u** that they have become
2Co  2:11  For we are not **u** of his schemes.

## UNBELIEF* [UNBELIEVER, UNBELIEVERS, UNBELIEVING]
Mk  9:24  help me overcome my **u**!"
Ro  4:20  not waver through **u** regarding
  11:20  they were broken off because of **u**,
  11:23  And if they do not persist in **u**,
1Ti  1:13  because I acted in ignorance and **u**.
Heb  3:19  not able to enter, because of their **u**.

## UNBELIEVER* [UNBELIEF]
1Co  7:15  But if the **u** leaves, let it be so.
  10:27  If an **u** invites you to a meal
  14:24  if an **u** or an inquirer comes in while
2Co  6:15  believer have in common with an **u**?
1Ti  5: 8  the faith and is worse than an **u**.

## UNBELIEVERS* [UNBELIEF]
Lk  12:46  and assign him a place with the **u**.
Ro  15:31  be kept safe from the **u** in Judea
1Co  6: 6  and this in front of **u**!
    14:22  a sign, not for believers but for **u**;
    14:22  is not for **u** but for believers.
    14:23  and inquirers or **u** come in, will they
2Co  4: 4  this age has blinded the minds of **u**,
    6:14  Do not be yoked together with **u**.

## UNBELIEVING* [UNBELIEF]
Mt  17:17  "You **u** and perverse generation,"
Mk  9:19  "You **u** generation," Jesus replied,
Lk  9:41  "You **u** and perverse generation,"
1Co  7:14  the **u** husband has been sanctified
    7:14  and the **u** wife has been sanctified
Heb  3:12  **u** heart that turns away
Rev  21: 8  But the cowardly, the **u**, the vile,

## UNBLEMISHED*
Heb  9:14  the eternal Spirit offered himself **u**

## UNCEASING [UNCEASINGLY]
Ro  9: 2  sorrow and **u** anguish in my heart.

## UNCEASINGLY* [UNCEASING]
La  3:49  My eyes will flow **u**, without relief,

## UNCERTAIN*
1Ti  6:17  which is so **u**, but to put their hope

## UNCHANGEABLE*
[UNCHANGING]
Heb  6:18  that, by two **u** things in which it is

## UNCHANGING*
[UNCHANGABLE]
Heb  6:17  to make the **u** nature of his purpose

## UNCIRCUMCISED
[UNCIRCUMCISION]
Ex  12:48  in the land. No **u** male may eat of it.
Lev  26:41  when their **u** hearts are humbled
1Sa  17:26  Who is this **u** Philistine that he
Jer  9:26  whole house of Israel is **u** in heart."
Ac  7:51  Your hearts and ears are still **u**.
Ro  3:30  and the **u** through that same faith.
    4:11  he had by faith while he was still **u**.
1Co  7:18  Was a man **u** when he was called?
Col  3:11  or Jew, circumcised or **u**, barbarian,

## UNCIRCUMCISION*
[UNCIRCUMCISED]
1Co  7:19  is nothing and **u** is nothing.
Gal  5: 6  neither circumcision nor **u** has any
    6:15  circumcision nor **u** means anything;
Col  2:13  and in the **u** of your sinful nature,

## UNCLEAN [UNCLEANNESS]
Ge  7: 2  one pair of every kind of **u** animal,
Lev  10:10  between the **u** and the clean,
    11:11  since you are to regard them as **u**,
    17:15  will be ceremonially **u** till evening;

Lev  20:25  between clean and **u** animals
Ezr  6:21  themselves from the **u** practices
Isa  6: 5  For I am a man of **u** lips,
    52:11  Touch no **u** thing! Come out from it
La  1:17  has become an **u** thing among them.
Ac  10:14  never eaten anything impure or **u**."
Ro  14:14  that nothing is **u** in itself.
2Co  6:17  Touch no **u** thing, and I will receive

## UNCLEANNESS [UNCLEAN]
Eze  36:29  I will save you from all your **u**.
Jn  18:28  to avoid ceremonial **u** they did not

## UNCLOTHED*
2Co  5: 4  because we do not wish to be **u**

## UNCONCERNED*
Eze  16:49  were arrogant, overfed and **u**;

## UNCOVER [UNCOVERED]
Ru  3: 4  Then go and **u** his feet and lie down.

## UNCOVERED [UNCOVER]
Ge  9:21  drunk and lay **u** inside his tent.
Ru  3: 7  quietly, **u** his feet and lay down.
1Co  11: 5  her head **u** dishonors her head—
    11:13  to pray to God with her head **u**?
Heb  4:13  Everything is **u** and laid bare before

## UNDER
Ge  4:11  Now you are **u** a curse and driven
    24: 2  he had, "Put your hand **u** my thigh.
    47:29  eyes, put your hand **u** my thigh
Ex  6: 7  from **u** the yoke of the Egyptians.
1Ki  4:25  everyone **u** their own vine and fig
Ps  8: 6  you put everything **u** their feet:
    91: 4  **u** his wings you will find refuge;
    95: 7  of his pasture, the flock **u** his care.
Jer  3:13  foreign gods **u** every spreading tree,
Mic  4: 4  Everyone will sit **u** their own vine
Mt  5:15  light a lamp and put it **u** a bowl.
    22:44  I put your enemies **u** your feet." '
Lk  13:34  hen gathers her chicks **u** her wings,
Jn  13: 3  had put all things **u** his power,
Ac  4:12  is no other name given **u** heaven
Ro  6:14  because you are not **u** the law, but **u**
1Co  9:21  God's law but am **u** Christ's law),
    15:27  he "has put everything **u** his feet."
Gal  1: 8  that person be **u** God's curse!
    1: 9  that person be **u** God's curse!
    4: 5  to redeem those **u** the law, that we
Rev  6: 9  I saw **u** the altar the souls of those

## UNDER THE SUN  See SUN

## UNDERFOOT [FOOT]
Heb  10:29  trampled the Son of God **u**,

## UNDERGOES* [UNDERGOING]
Heb  12: 8  and everyone **u** discipline—

## UNDERGOING* [UNDERGOES]
1Pe  5: 9  the world are **u** the same kind

## UNDERNEATH

Dt   33:27  and **u** are the everlasting arms.

## UNDERSTAND

[UNDERSTANDING,
UNDERSTANDS, UNDERSTOOD]

Ge   11: 7  so they will not **u** each other."
Job  38: 4  Tell me, if you **u**.
     42: 3  Surely I spoke of things I did not **u**,
Ps   14: 2  race to see if there are any who **u**,
     73:16  When I tried to **u** all this, it troubled
     119:27  Cause me to **u** the way of your
     119:125  that I may **u** your statutes.
Pr    2: 5  you will **u** the fear of the LORD
      2: 9  Then you will **u** what is right
     30:18  amazing for me, four that I do not **u**:
Ecc   7:25  and to **u** the stupidity of wickedness
     11: 5  so you cannot **u** the work of God,
Isa   1: 3  not know, my people do not **u**."
      6:10  with their ears, **u** with their hearts,
     44:18  They know nothing, they **u** nothing;
     52:15  they have not heard, they will **u**.
Jer   9:24  that they **u** and know me,
     17: 9  and beyond cure. Who can **u** it?
     31:19  after I came to **u**, I beat my breast.
Da    1:17  Daniel could **u** visions and dreams
      9:25  "Know and **u** this: From the time
Hos  14: 9  Let them **u**. The ways
Mt   13:15  ears, **u** with their hearts and turn,
     13:23  people who hear the word and **u** it.
     24:15  let the reader **u**—
Mk    4:13  "Don't you **u** this parable?
Lk   24:45  so they could **u** the Scriptures.
Jn   13: 7  I am doing, but later you will **u**."
Ac    8:30  "Do you **u** what you are reading?"
Ro    7:15  I do not **u** what I do. For what I
     15:21  those who have not heard will **u**."
1Co   2:12  that we may **u** what God has freely
      2:14  and cannot **u** them because they are
Eph   5:17  but **u** what the Lord's will is.
Heb   5:11  because you no longer try to **u**.
     11: 3  By faith we **u** that the universe was
1Ti   6: 4  they are conceited and **u** nothing.
2Pe   1:20  all, you must **u** that no prophecy
      3: 3  all, you must **u** that in the last days
      3:16  some things that are hard to **u**,

## UNDERSTANDING

[UNDERSTAND]

Dt    4: 6  your wisdom and **u** to the nations,
1Ki   4:29  of **u** as measureless as the sand
Job  12:12  Does not long life bring **u**?
     28:12  Where does **u** dwell?
     28:28  is wisdom, and to shun evil is **u**."
     32: 8  of the Almighty, that gives them **u**.
     36:26  How great is God—beyond our **u**!
     37: 5  he does great things beyond our **u**.
Ps   49:20  lack **u** are like the beasts that perish.
     111:10  follow his precepts have good **u**.
     119:34  Give me **u**, so that I may keep your
     119:100  I have more **u** than the elders, for I
     119:104  I gain **u** from your precepts;
     119:130  it gives **u** to the simple.
     136: 5  who by his **u** made the heavens,
     147: 5  mighty in power; his **u** has no limit.

Pr    1: 6  for **u** proverbs and parables,
      2: 2  and applying your heart to **u**—
      2: 6  his mouth come knowledge and **u**.
      3: 5  heart and lean not on your own **u**;
      3:13  who find wisdom, those who gain **u**,
      4: 5  Get wisdom, get **u**; do not forget my
      4: 7  Though it cost all you have, get **u**.
      9:10  knowledge of the Holy One is **u**.
     10:23  but those who have **u** delight
     11:12  but those who have **u** hold their
     14:29  Those who are patient have great **u**,
     15:21  but those who have **u** keep a straight
     15:32  those who heed correction gain **u**.
     17:27  who have **u** are even-tempered.
     18: 2  Fools find no pleasure in **u**
     19: 8  those who cherish **u** will soon
Ecc   1:17  I applied myself to the **u** of wisdom,
Isa   6: 9  " 'Be ever hearing, but never **u**;
     11: 2  the Spirit of wisdom and of **u**,
     40:14  or showed him the path of **u**?
     40:28  weary, and his **u** no one can fathom.
     56:11  They are shepherds who lack **u**;
Jer   3:15  will lead you with knowledge and **u**.
     10:12  stretched out the heavens by his **u**.
Da    1:17  and **u** of all kinds of literature
      5:12  a keen mind and knowledge and **u**,
     10:12  day that you set your mind to gain **u**
Hos   4:11  and new wine take away their **u**.
Mk    4:12  and ever hearing but never **u**;
     12:33  with all your **u** and with all your
Lk    2:47  who heard him was amazed at his **u**
Ac   28:26  will be ever hearing but never **u**;
Ro   10:19  angry by a nation that has no **u**."
2Co   6: 6  in purity, **u**, patience and kindness;
Eph   1: 8  With all wisdom and **u**,
Php   4: 7  which transcends all **u**, will guard
Col   1: 9  wisdom and **u** that the Spirit gives,
      2: 2  have the full riches of complete **u**,
Jas   3:13  Who is wise and **u** among you?
1Jn   5:20  God has come and has given us **u**,

## UNDERSTANDS* [UNDERSTAND]

Dt   29: 4  has not given you a mind that **u**
1Ch  28: 9  every heart and **u** every desire
Job  28:23  God **u** the way to it and he alone
Isa  57: 1  no one **u** that the righteous are taken
                  away
Ro    3:11  there is no one who **u**; there is no
1Co  14: 2  Indeed, no one **u** them; they utter
                  mysteries

## UNDERSTOOD [UNDERSTAND]

Ne    8: 8  people **u** what was being read.
      8:12  because they now **u** the words
Ps   73:17  then I **u** their final destiny.
Isa  40:21  Have you not **u** since the earth was
Da    9: 2  I, Daniel, **u** from the Scriptures,
Ro    1:20  being **u** from what has been made,

## UNDERTAKEN

Lk    1: 1  Many have **u** to draw up an account

## UNDESIRABLE*

Jos  24:15  serving the LORD seems **u** to you,

## UNDIVIDED*
1Ch 12:33 to help David with **u** loyalty—
Ps 86:11 give me an **u** heart, that I may fear
Eze 11:19 I will give them an **u** heart and put
1Co 7:35 in a right way in **u** devotion

## UNDOING [UNDONE]
Pr 18: 7 The mouths of fools are their **u**,

## UNDONE [UNDOING]
Lk 11:42 latter without leaving the former **u**.

## UNDYING*
Eph 6:24 Lord Jesus Christ with an **u** love.

## UNENDING* [END]
Ps 21: 6 you have granted him **u** blessings
Jer 15:18 Why is my pain **u** and my wound

## UNEQUALED*
Mt 24:21 **u** from the beginning of the world
Mk 13:19 of distress **u** from the beginning,

## UNFADING*
1Pe 3: 4 the **u** beauty of a gentle and quiet

## UNFAILING*
Ex 15:13 your **u** love you will lead the people
1Sa 20:14 But show me **u** kindness like
2Sa 22:51 he shows **u** kindness to his anointed,
Ps 6: 4 save me because of your **u** love.
13: 5 But I trust in your **u** love;
18:50 he shows **u** love to his anointed,
21: 7 through the **u** love of the Most High
26: 3 been mindful of your **u** love
31:16 save me in your **u** love.
32:10 but the LORD's **u** love surrounds
33: 5 the earth is full of his **u** love.
33:18 those whose hope is in his **u** love,
33:22 May your **u** love be with us,
36: 7 How priceless is your **u** love,
44:26 redeem us because of your **u** love.
48: 9 O God, we meditate on your **u** love.
51: 1 O God, according to your **u** love;
52: 8 I trust in God's **u** love for ever
62:12 and with you, Lord, is **u** love";
77: 8 Has his **u** love vanished forever?
85: 7 Show us your **u** love, LORD,
90:14 us in the morning with your **u** love,
94:18 your **u** love, LORD, supported me.
107: 8 thanks to the LORD for his **u** love
107:15 thanks to the LORD for his **u** love
107:21 thanks to the LORD for his **u** love
107:31 thanks to the LORD for his **u** love
109:26 save me according to your **u** love.
119:41 May your **u** love come to me,
119:76 May your **u** love be my comfort,
119:88 In your **u** love preserve my life,
130: 7 for with the LORD is **u** love
138: 2 your **u** love and your faithfulness,
143: 8 bring me word of your **u** love, for I
143:12 In your **u** love, silence my enemies;
147:11 who put their hope in his **u** love.
Pr 19:22 What a person desires is **u** love;
20: 6 Many claim to have **u** love,

Isa 54:10 yet my **u** love for you will not be
Jer 31: 3 I have drawn you with **u** kindness.
La 3:32 compassion, so great is his **u** love.
Hos 10:12 reap the fruit of **u** love, and break

## UNFAILING LOVE See LOVE

## UNFAITHFUL [UNFAITHFULNESS]
Lev 6: 2 is **u** to the LORD by deceiving
Nu 5: 6 and so is **u** to the LORD is guilty
5:12 wife goes astray and is **u** to him
1Ch 10:13 Saul died because he was **u**
Ezr 10: 2 "We have been **u** to our God
Pr 11: 6 but the **u** are trapped by evil desires.
13: 2 the **u** have an appetite for violence.
13:15 but the way of the **u** leads to their
22:12 but he frustrates the words of the **u**.
23:28 and multiplies the **u** among men.
25:19 foot is reliance on the **u** in a time
Jer 3:20 have been **u** to me,"
Eze 20:27 blasphemed me by being **u** to me:
Hos 5: 7 They are **u** to the LORD;
Mal 2:10 by being **u** to one another?
2:11 Judah has been **u**.
2:14 You have been **u** to her,
2:15 do not be **u** to the wife
2:16 and do not be **u**.

## UNFAITHFULNESS [UNFAITHFUL]
Nu 14:33 suffering for your **u**, until the last
1Ch 9: 1 to Babylon because of their **u**.
Eze 18:24 Because of the **u** they are guilty
Hos 1: 2 land is guilty of **u** to the LORD."
Ro 3: 3 Will their **u** nullify God's faithfulness?

## UNFINISHED* [FINISH]
Tit 1: 5 left **u** and appoint elders in every town,
Rev 3: 2 your deeds **u** in the sight of my God.

## UNFIT*
Tit 1:16 and **u** for doing anything good.

## UNFOLDING*
Ps 119:130 The **u** of your words gives light;

## UNFORGIVING*
2Ti 3: 3 without love, **u**, slanderous,

## UNFORMED*
Ps 139:16 your eyes saw my **u** body.

## UNFRIENDLY*
Pr 18: 1 An **u** person pursues selfish ends

## UNFRUITFUL
Mk 4:19 in and choke the word, making it **u**.
1Co 14:14 my spirit prays, but my mind is **u**.

## UNGODLINESS* [UNGODLY]
Isa 32: 6 They practice **u** and spread error
Jer 23:15 Jerusalem **u** has spread throughout
Tit 2:12 It teaches us to say "No" to **u**

## UNGODLY [UNGODLINESS]
Pr   11:31  earth, how much more the **u**
Ro    4: 5  trusts God who justifies the **u**,
       5: 6  still powerless, Christ died for the **u**.
1Ti   1: 9  and rebels, the **u** and sinful,
2Ti   2:16  in it will become more and more **u**.
2Pe   2: 6  of what is going to happen to the **u**;
Jude  1:15  to convict all the **u** of all the **u** acts they
            have done in an **u** way,

## UNGRATEFUL*
Lk    6:35  because he is kind to the **u**
2Ti   3: 2  disobedient to their parents, **u**,

## UNHARMED
Da    3:25  unbound and **u**, and the fourth looks

## UNHEARD-OF*
Eze   7: 5  " 'Disaster! **U** disaster!
Da  11:36  will say **u** things against the God

## UNHOLY*
1Ti   1: 9  and sinful, the **u** and irreligious,
2Ti   3: 2  to their parents, ungrateful, **u**,
Heb 10:29  have treated as an **u** thing the blood

## UNINFORMED
1Th   4:13  to be **u** about those who sleep in death,

## UNINTENTIONALLY
Lev   4: 2  'When anyone sins **u** and does what
Nu  15:22  if you as a community **u** fail to keep
Dt    4:42  they had **u** killed a neighbor without

## UNION [UNITE]
Zec 11:14  I broke my second staff called **U**,
Mt    1:25  he had no **u** with her until she gave

## UNIT
Ex  36:18  clasps to fasten the tent together as a **u**.

## UNITE [UNION, UNITED, UNITES, UNITY]
1Co  6:15  Christ and **u** them with a prostitute?

## UNITED [UNITE]
Ge   2:24  and mother and be **u** to his wife,
Mt  19: 5  and mother and be **u** to his wife,
Ro    6: 5  If we have been **u** with him
1Co  1:10  that you be perfectly **u** in mind
      6:17  But whoever is **u** with the Lord
Eph  5:31  and mother and be **u** to his wife,
Php   2: 1  from being **u** with Christ, if any
Col   2: 2  encouraged in heart and **u** in love,

## UNITES* [UNITE]
1Co  6:16  he who **u** himself with a prostitute is

## UNITY* [UNITE]
2Ch 30:12  the people to give them **u** of mind
Ps  133: 1  God's people live together in **u**!
Jn   17:23  they may be brought to complete **u**.
Eph   1:10  to bring **u** to all things in heaven

Eph   4: 3  keep the **u** of the Spirit through
      4:13  until we all reach **u** in the faith
Col   3:14  binds them all together in perfect **u**.

## UNIVERSE*
1Co  4: 9  made a spectacle to the whole **u**,
Eph  4:10  in order to fill the whole **u**.)
Heb  1: 2  through whom also he made the **u**.
     11: 3  understand that the **u** was formed

## UNJUST
Eze 18:25  Hear, house of Israel: Is my way **u**?
Lk   18: 6  "Listen to what the **u** judge says.
Ro    3: 5  That God is **u** in bringing his wrath
      9:14  shall we say? Is God **u**? Not at all!
Heb  6:10  God is not **u**; he will not forget your
1Pe  2:19  pain of **u** suffering because you are

## UNKNOWN
Ps   81: 5  I heard an **u** voice say:
Ac  17:23  with this inscription: TO AN **U** GOD.

## UNLAWFUL
Mt   12: 2  Your disciples are doing what is **u**
Ac  16:21  by advocating customs **u** for us

## UNLEAVENED
Ex  12:17  "Celebrate the Festival of **U** Bread,
Dt  16:16  at the Festival of **U** Bread,
Mt  26:17  first day of the Festival of **U** Bread,

## THE FESTIVAL OF UNLEAVENED
   **BREAD** See FESTIVAL

## UNLESS
Ps   94:17  **U** the LORD had given me help,
   127: 1  **U** the LORD builds the house,
La    5:22  **u** you have utterly rejected us
Lk   13: 3  But **u** you repent, you too will all
Jn    4:48  "**U** you people see signs
    12:24  you, **u** a kernel of wheat falls
Ac    8:31  "**u** someone explains it to me?"
Rev 13:17  not buy or sell **u** they had the mark,

## UNLIKE
2Co  2:17  **U** so many, we do not peddle
Heb  7:27  **U** the other high priests, he does not

## UNLOVED*
Dt  21:17  the son of his **u** wife as the firstborn

## UNMARRIED
1Co  7: 8  Now to the **u** and the widows I say: It is
           good for them to stay **u**, as I do.
     7:32  An **u** man is concerned

## UNNATURAL*
Ro    1:26  natural sexual relations for **u** ones.

## UNPLOWED
Ex  23:11  the seventh year let the land lie **u**
Jer   4: 3  "Break up your **u** ground and do
Hos 10:12  love, and break up your **u** ground;

## UNPRINCIPLED*
Zep  3: 4  Her prophets are **u**;

## UNPRODUCTIVE
Tit  3:14  for urgent needs and not live **u** lives.
2Pe  1: 8  **u** in your knowledge of our Lord

## UNPROFITABLE*
Isa  30: 6  humps of camels, to that **u** nation,
Tit  3: 9  because these are **u** and useless.

## UNPUNISHED
Ex  34: 7  Yet he does not leave the guilty **u**;
Nu  14:18  Yet he does not leave the guilty **u**;
Pr  6:29  no one who touches her will go **u**.
   11:21  The wicked will not go **u**, but those
   19: 5  A false witness will not go **u**,
   28:20  one eager to get rich will not go **u**.
Joel  3:21  leave their innocent blood **u**?
Na  1: 3  LORD will not leave the guilty **u**.
Ro  3:25  the sins committed beforehand **u**—

## UNQUENCHABLE
Lk  3:17  will burn up the chaff with **u** fire."

## UNREASONING* [REASON]
2Pe  2:12  They are like **u** animals,
Jude  1:10  understand by instinct, like **u** animals

## UNREPENTANT*
Ro  2: 5  your stubbornness and your **u** heart,

## UNRIGHTEOUS*
  [UNRIGHTEOUSNESS]
Isa  55: 7  and the **u** their thoughts.
Zep  3: 5  not fail, yet the **u** know no shame.
Mt  5:45  rain on the righteous and the **u**.
1Pe  3:18  the righteous for the **u**, to bring you
2Pe  2: 9  to hold the **u** for punishment

## UNRIGHTEOUSNESS
  [UNRIGHTEOUS]
1Jn  1: 9  us our sins and purify us from all **u**.

## UNRULY
Pr  9:13  Folly is an **u** woman;

## UNSCHOOLED*
Ac  4:13  John and realized that they were **u**,

## UNSEARCHABLE
Ro  11:33  How **u** his judgments, and his paths

## UNSEEN*
Mt  6: 6  and pray to your Father, who is **u**.
   6:18  but only to your Father, who is **u**;
2Co  4:18  but on what is **u**,
   4:18  but what is **u** is eternal.

## UNSETTLED*
1Th  3: 3  no one would be **u** by these trials.
2Th  2: 2  not to become easily **u** or alarmed

## UNSHRUNK
Mt  9:16  "No one sews a patch of **u** cloth

## UNSPIRITUAL*
Ro  7:14  but I am **u**, sold as a slave to sin.
Col  2:18  their **u** minds puff them up with idle
Jas  3:15  down from heaven but is earthly, **u**,

## UNSTABLE*
Jas  1: 8  double-minded and **u** in all they do.
2Pe  2:14  they seduce the **u**; they are experts
   3:16  which ignorant and **u** people distort,

## UNSWERVINGLY*
Heb  10:23  Let us hold **u** to the hope we

## UNTHINKABLE*
Job  34:12  It is **u** that God would do wrong,

## UNTIE
Mk  1: 7  am not worthy to stoop down and **u**.
Lk  13:15  of you on the Sabbath **u** your ox

## UNTRAINED* [TRAIN]
2Co  11: 6  I may indeed be **u** as a speaker,

## UNVEILED*
2Co  3:18  with **u** faces contemplate the Lord's

## UNWARY*
Ps  116: 6  The LORD protects the **u**;

## UNWASHED*
Mt  15:20  with **u** hands does not defile you."
Mk  7: 2  hands that were defiled, that is, **u**.

## UNWHOLESOME*
Eph  4:29  Do not let any **u** talk come

## UNWISE*
Dt  32: 6  LORD, you foolish and **u** people?
Eph  5:15  how you live—not as **u** but as wise,

## UNWORTHY*
Ge  32:10  I am **u** of all the kindness
Job  40: 4  "I am **u**—how can I reply to you?
Lk  17:10  do, should say, 'We are **u** servants;
1Co  11:27  Lord in an **u** manner will be guilty

## UNYIELDING
Ex  7:14  to Moses, "Pharaoh's heart is **u**;
Pr  18:19  wronged is more **u** than a fortified

## UPHELD [UPHOLD]
Ps  9: 4  For you have **u** my right and my

## UPHOLD [UPHELD, UPHOLDING, UPHOLDS]
Ps  41:12  In my integrity you **u** me and set me
   82: 3  **u** the cause of the poor
Isa  41:10  I will **u** you with my righteous right
   42: 1  whom I **u**, my chosen one in whom

Ro   3:31  Not at all! Rather, we **u** the law.

## UPHOLDING* [UPHOLD]

Isa   9: 7  establishing and **u** it with justice

## UPHOLDS* [UPHOLD]

Ps   37:17  but the LORD **u** the righteous.
     37:24  the LORD **u** them with his hand.
     63: 8  I cling to you; your right hand **u** me.
     140:12  poor and **u** the cause of the needy.
     145:14  The LORD **u** all who fall and lifts
     146: 7  He **u** the cause of the oppressed

## UPLIFTED [LIFT]

Ex   6: 8  the land I swore with **u** hand to give
Ps  106:26  to them with **u** hand that he would

## UPPER

Eze  42: 5  Now the **u** rooms were narrower,

## UPRIGHT [UPRIGHTLY, UPRIGHTNESS]

Ge   37: 7  suddenly my sheaf rose and stood **u**,
Dt   32: 4  who does no wrong, **u** and just is he.
Job   1: 1  This man was blameless and **u**;
      1: 8  he is blameless and **u**, a man who
      2: 3  he is blameless and **u**, a man who
     33: 3  My words come from an **u** heart;
Ps    7:10  High, who saves the **u** in heart.
     11: 7  the **u** will see his face.
     25: 8  Good and **u** is the LORD;
     33: 1  it is fitting for the **u** to praise him.
     64:10  all the **u** in heart will glory in him!
     92:15  proclaiming, "The LORD is **u**;
     97:11  righteous and joy on the **u** in heart.
     112: 4  in darkness light dawns for the **u**,
     119: 7  an **u** heart as I learn your righteous
Pr    2: 7  He holds success in store for the **u**,
      2:21  For the **u** will live in the land,
      3:32  but takes the **u** into his confidence.
     11: 3  The integrity of the **u** guides them,
     15: 8  but the prayer of the **u** pleases him.
     21:29  but the **u** give thought to their ways.
Isa  26: 7  you, the **U** One, make the path
Mic   2: 7  do good to those whose ways are **u**?
Tit   1: 8  who is self-controlled, **u**,
      2:12  **u** and godly lives in this present age,

## UPRIGHTLY [UPRIGHT]

Pr   14: 2  fears the LORD walks **u**,

## UPRIGHTNESS [UPRIGHT]

Ps   25:21  May integrity and **u** protect me,
     111: 8  ever, enacted in faithfulness and **u**.

## UPRISINGS*

Lk   21: 9  When you hear of wars and **u**,

## UPROOT [UPROOTED]

2Ch   7:20  then I will **u** Israel from my land,
Ecc   3: 2  die, a time to plant and a time to **u**,
Jer   1:10  and kingdoms to **u** and tear down,

## UPROOTED [UPROOT]

Dt   28:63  You will be **u** from the land you are
Pr   10:30  The righteous will never be **u**,
Jer  18: 7  that a nation or kingdom is to be **u**,
     31:40  The city will never again be **u**
Lk   17: 6  tree, 'Be **u** and planted in the sea,'
Jude  1:12  autumn trees, without fruit and **u**—

## UPSET

Lk   10:41  worried and **u** about many things,

## UPWARD

Ex   37: 9  cherubim had their wings spread **u**,
Eze   1:11  each had two wings spreading out **u**,

## UR

Ge   15: 7  you out of **U** of the Chaldeans
Ne    9: 7  him out of **U** of the Chaldeans

## URGE [URGED, URGENTLY, URGING]

Ru    1:16  "Don't **u** me to leave you or to turn
Ro   12: 1  Therefore, I **u** you,
1Co   4:16  Therefore I **u** you to imitate me.
Tit   2: 4  Then they can **u** the younger women
Jude  1: 3  **u** you to contend for the faith

## URGED [URGE]

Ge   19:15  of dawn, the angels **u** Lot, saying,
Ex   12:33  The Egyptians **u** the people to hurry

## URGENTLY [URGE]

Jnh   3: 8  Let everyone call **u** on God.

## URGING [URGE]

Ru    1:18  to go with her, she stopped **u** her.
1Th   2:12  **u** you to live lives worthy of God,

## URIAH

Hittite husband of Bathsheba, killed by David's order (2Sa 11).

## URIM

Ex   28:30  put the **U** and the Thummim
1Sa  28: 6  did not answer him by dreams or **U**
Ezr   2:63  was a priest ministering with the **U**

## USE [USED, USEFUL, USELESS, USES]

Lev  19:35  " 'Do not **u** dishonest standards
Jdg   2:22  I will **u** them to test Israel and see
Mt    7: 2  and with the measure you **u**, it will
Gal   5:13  do not **u** your freedom to indulge
1Ti   5:23  and **u** a little wine because of your
1Pe   4:10  you should **u** whatever gift you have

## USED [USE]

Mt   22:19  Show me the coin **u** for paying
Jn   10: 6  Jesus **u** this figure of speech,
Php   2: 6  something to be **u** to his own advantage;
1Co   9:15  But I have not **u** any of these rights.

## USEFUL [USE]

Eph   4:28  doing something **u** with their own

2Ti  2:21  **u** to the Master and prepared to do
      3:16  God-breathed and is **u** for teaching,
Phm  1:11  now he has become **u** both to you

## USELESS [USE]
1Sa 12:21  Do not turn away after **u** idols.
1Co 15:14  our preaching is **u** and so is your
Tit   3: 9  these are unprofitable and **u**.
Phm  1:11  Formerly he was **u** to you, but now
Heb  7:18  set aside because it was weak and **u**
Jas   2:20  that faith without deeds is **u**?

## USES [USE]
1Ti   1: 8  the law is good if one **u** it properly.

## UTMOST
Job 34:36  to the **u** for answering like a wicked

## UTTER [UTTERANCE, UTTERED, UTTERLY]
Dt  23:23  Whatever your lips **u** you must be
Ps  37:30  mouths of the righteous **u** wisdom,
     115: 7  nor can they **u** a sound with their
Mt  13:35  I will **u** things hidden since
1Co 14: 2  they **u** mysteries by the Spirit.
Rev 13: 5  was given a mouth to **u** proud words

## UTTERANCE [UTTER]
2Sa 23: 1  inspired **u** of David son of Jesse,

## UTTERED [UTTER]
Ps  89:34  or alter what my lips have **u**.
Jer  29:23  and in my name they have **u** lies—

## UTTERLY [UTTER]
Ps  119: 8  do not **u** forsake me.
Ecc   1: 2  says the Teacher. "**U** meaningless!
SS    8: 7  for love, it would be **u** scorned.
Ro    7:13  sin might become **u** sinful.

## UZ
Job   1: 1  of **U** there lived a man whose name

## UZZAH
2Sa   6: 6  **U** reached out and took hold
1Ch 13: 9  **U** reached out his hand to steady

## UZZIAH [AZARIAH]
Son of Amaziah; king of Judah also known as Azariah (2Ki 15:1–7; 1Ch 6:24; 2Ch 26). Struck with leprosy because of pride (2Ch 26:16–23).

---

# V

---

## VAIN
Lev 26:20  Your strength will be spent in **v**,
Ps    2: 1  conspire and the peoples plot in **v**?
     33:17  A horse is a **v** hope for deliverance;
     73:13  in **v** I have kept my heart pure
     127: 1  the builders labor in **v**.

Isa  65:23  They will not labor in **v**, nor will
La    4:17  eyes failed, looking in **v** for help;
Eze   6:10  I did not threaten in **v** to bring this
Mt   15: 9  They worship me in **v**;
Ac    4:25  rage and the peoples plot in **v**?
1Co 15: 2  Otherwise, you have believed in **v**.
     15:58  your labor in the Lord is not in **v**.
2Co   6: 1  you not to receive God's grace in **v**.
Gal   2: 2  had not been running my race in **v**.
      3: 4  if it really was in **v**?
Php   2: 3  out of selfish ambition or **v** conceit.

## VALIANT
1Sa 10:26  by **v** men whose hearts God had
     31:12  all their **v** men marched through

## VALID
Jn    8:14  my testimony is **v**, for I know where

## VALLEY [VALLEYS]
Jos   7:26  that place has been called the **V**
     10:12  you, moon, over the **V** of Aijalon."
Jdg  16: 4  in the **V** of Sorek whose name was
1Sa 17: 3  another, with the **v** between them.
2Ki 23:10  which was in the **V** of Ben Hinnom,
2Ch 33: 6  in the fire in the **V** of Ben Hinnom,
Ps  23: 4  though I walk through the darkest **v**,
Isa  22: 1  A prophecy concerning the **V**
     40: 4  Every **v** shall be raised up,
Eze  37: 2  many bones on the floor of the **v**,
Hos   2:15  will make the **V** of Achor a door
Joel  3:14  multitudes in the **v** of decision!
Lk    3: 5  Every **v** shall be filled in,

## VALLEYS [VALLEY]
Dt    8: 7  with springs flowing in the **v**
SS    2: 1  I am a rose of Sharon, a lily of the **v**.

## VALUABLE [VALUE]
Lk   12:24  And how much more **v** you are than

## VALUE [VALUABLE, VALUED]
Lev  27: 3  set the **v** of a male between the ages
1Ki 10:21  of little **v** in Solomon's days.
Pr   10: 2  treasures have no lasting **v**,
     16:13  they **v** persons who speak what is
     31:11  in her and lacks nothing of **v**.
Mt   13:46  When he found one of great **v**,
Lk   16:15  What people **v** highly is detestable
Ro    3: 1  or what **v** is there in circumcision?
Php   2: 3  in humility **v** others above yourselves,
1Ti   4: 8  For physical training is of some **v**, but
               godliness has **v** for all things,
Heb   4: 2  they heard was of no **v** to them,
     11:26  as of greater **v** than the treasures

## VALUED [VALUE]
Lk    7: 2  whom his master **v** highly,

## VANISH [VANISHED, VANISHES]
Ps  104:35  But may sinners **v** from the earth

## VANISHED [VANISH]
Ps   12: 1  those who are loyal have **v**
     77: 8  Has his unfailing love **v** forever?

## VANISHES [VANISH]
Jas 4:14 appears for a little while and then **v**.

## VANITIES, VANITY (KJV) See
BREATH, DECEIT, DELUSIONS,
DESTRUCTION, DISHONEST,
EMPTY, EVIL, FALSE, FALSEHOOD,
FLEETING, FRUSTRATION, FUTILE,
FUTILITY, LIES, MEANINGLESS,
WORTHLESS [IDOLS]

## VARIOUS
Ge 1:11 in it, according to their **v** kinds."
Jdg 2:12 and worshiped **v** gods of the peoples
Mk 1:34 healed many who had **v** diseases.
Heb 1: 1 at many times and in **v** ways,
1Pe 4:10 of God's grace in its **v** forms.

## VASHTI*
Queen of Persia replaced by Esther (Est 1–2).

## VAST
Ge 2: 1 were completed in all their **v** array.
Dt 1:19 of the Amorites through all that **v**
8:15 He led you through the **v**
Ps 139:17 How **v** is the sum of them!

## VATS
Pr 3:10 and your **v** will brim over with new
Joel 2:24 the **v** will overflow with new wine

## VAULT
Ge 1: 6 "Let there be a **v** between the waters
1: 8 God called the **v** "sky." And there was
1:14 "Let there be lights in the **v** of the sky
Eze 1:22 what looked something like a **v**,
10: 1 the **v** that was over the heads of the

## VEGETABLES
Pr 15:17 Better a small serving of **v** with love
Da 1:12 Give us nothing but **v** to eat
Ro 14: 2 whose faith is weak, eats only **v**.

## VEGETATION
Ge 1:11 God said, "Let the land produce **v**:

## VEIL [VEILED]
Ex 34:33 to them, he put a **v** over his face.
La 3:65 Put a **v** over their hearts, and may
2Co 3:13 who would put a **v** over his face
3:15 is read, a **v** covers their hearts.

## VEILED [VEIL]
2Co 4: 3 And even if our gospel is **v**, it is **v**

## VENGEANCE [AVENGE, AVENGED,
AVENGER, AVENGES, AVENGING,
REVENGE]
Ge 4:15 kills Cain will suffer **v** seven times
Nu 31: 3 carry out the LORD's **v** on them.
Isa 34: 8 For the LORD has a day of **v**,
61: 2 favor and the day of **v** of our God,

Jer 50:15 Since this is the **v** of the LORD,
Na 1: 2 The LORD takes **v** on his foes

## VENOM [VENOMOUS]
Dt 32:33 Their wine is the **v** of serpents,
Ps 58: 4 Their **v** is like the **v** of a snake,

## VENOMOUS [VENOM]
Nu 21: 6 the LORD sent **v** snakes among
Jer 8:17 I will send **v** snakes among you,

## VENT
Pr 29:11 Fools give full **v** to their rage,
La 4:11 The LORD has given full **v** to his
Da 11:30 **v** his fury against the holy covenant.

## VERDANT
Jer 50: 7 their **v** pasture, the LORD,

## VERDICT
1Ki 3:28 all Israel heard the **v** the king had
Jn 3:19 This is the **v**: Light has come

## VERSED*
Ezr 7: 6 He was a teacher well **v** in the Law

## VERY
Ge 1·31 that he had made, and it was **v** good.
15: 1 your shield, your **v** great reward."
17: 6 I will make you **v** fruitful,
Dt 30:14 No, the word is **v** near you; it is
Jos 23:11 So be **v** careful to love the LORD
1Ki 19:10 "I have been **v** zealous
Ps 104: 1 LORD my God, you are **v** great;
Mt 4: 8 devil took him to a **v** high mountain

## VICTIM [VICTIMS]
Ps 10:10 they collapse; they fall **v**

## VICTIMS [VICTIM]
Ps 10:14 The **v** commit themselves to you;
Pr 7:26 Many are the **v** she has brought
Na 3: 1 full of plunder, never without **v**!

## VICTOR'S* [VICTORY]
2Ti 2: 5 does not receive the **v** crown except
Rev 2:10 I will give you life as your **v** crown.

## VICTORIES* [VICTORY]
Jdg 5:11 They recite the **v** of the LORD, the **v** of
his villagers
2Sa 22:51 "He gives his king great **v**;
Ps 18:50 He gives his king great **v**;
21: 1 great is his joy in the **v** you give!
21: 5 Through the **v** you gave, his glory is
44: 4 my God, who decrees **v** for Jacob.

## VICTORIOUS [VICTORY]
Rev 2: 7 To those who are **v**,
2:11 who are **v** will not be hurt
2:17 To those who are **v**,
2:26 To those who are **v** and do my will
3: 5 Those who are **v** will,
3:12 who are **v** I will make pillars

Rev 3:21 To those who are v,
15: 2 those who had been v over the beast
21: 7 who are v will inherit all this,

## VICTORIOUSLY* [VICTORY]
Ps 45: 4 In your majesty ride forth v

## VICTORY [VICTOR'S, VICTORIES, VICTORIOUS, VICTORIOUSLY]
Ex 32:18 "It is not the sound of v, it is not
2Sa 8: 6 LORD gave David v wherever he
Ps 20: 5 May we shout for joy over your v
44: 6 bow, my sword does not bring me v;
60:12 With God we will gain the v, and he
129: 2 they have not gained the v over me.
149: 4 crowns the humble with v.
Pr 11:14 but v is won through many advisers.
21:31 battle, but v rests with the LORD.
24: 6 v is won through many advisers.
1Co 15:54 has been swallowed up in v."
15:57 He gives us the v through our Lord
1Jn 5: 4 This is the v that has overcome

## VIEW
Pr 5:21 ways are in full v of the LORD,
17:24 person keeps wisdom in v,
2Ti 4: 1 and in v of his appearing and his

## VILE [VILEST]
2Ki 23:13 for Ashtoreth the v goddess
23:13 for Chemosh the v god of Moab,
Ps 15: 4 who despise those whose ways are v
101: 3 with approval on anything that is v.
Eze 5:11 my sanctuary with all your v images
Rev 21: 8 unbelieving, the v, the murderers,

## VILEST* [VILE]
1Ki 21:26 He behaved in the v manner

## VILLAGE
Mt 10:11 Whatever town or v you enter,
Mk 6: 6 went around teaching from v to v.

## VINDICATE [VINDICATED, VINDICATES, VINDICATION]
Dt 32:36 The LORD will v his people
Ps 26: 1 V me, LORD, for I have led
35:24 V me in your righteousness,
54: 1 by your name; v me by your might.
135:14 For the LORD will v his people
138: 8 The LORD will v me;

## VINDICATED [VINDICATE]
Job 13:18 my case, I know I will be v.
Ps 17:15 I will be v and will see your face;
Jer 51:10 " 'The LORD has v us;
1Ti 3:16 in a body, was v by the Spirit,

## VINDICATES* [VINDICATE]
Ps 57: 2 to God, who v me.
Isa 50: 8 He who v me is near.

## VINDICATION [VINDICATE]
Ps 24: 5 and v from God their Savior.

Ps 37: 6 your v like the noonday sun.
Isa 54:17 and this is their v from me,"
62: 1 till her v shines out like the dawn,

## VINE [VINES, VINEYARD, VINEYARDS]
Ge 49:22 "Joseph is a fruitful v, a fruitful v
Dt 32:32 Their v comes from the v of Sodom
1Ki 4:25 everyone under their own v and fig
Ps 80: 8 You transplanted a v from Egypt;
128: 3 like a fruitful v within your house;
Isa 36:16 one of you will eat from your own v
Jer 2:21 I had planted you like a choice v
Eze 17: 6 and became a low, spreading v.
Hos 10: 1 Israel was a spreading v;
Mk 14:25 of the fruit of the v until that day
Jn 15: 1 "I am the true v, and my Father is
Rev 14:18 clusters of grapes from the earth's v,

## VINEGAR
Nu 6: 3 must not drink v made from wine
Pr 10:26 As v to the teeth and smoke
Mk 15:36 filled a sponge with wine v, put it

## VINES [VINE]
Dt 24:21 do not go over the v again.
Hab 3:17 and there are no grapes on the v,

## VINEYARD [VINE]
Ge 9:20 of the soil, proceeded to plant a v.
Dt 22: 9 plant two kinds of seed in your v;
1Ki 21: 1 an incident involving a v belonging
Pr 31:16 out of her earnings she plants a v.
SS 1: 6 my own v I had to neglect.
Isa 5: 1 for the one I love a song about his v:
27: 2 "Sing about a fruitful v:
Mt 21:33 was a landowner who planted a v.
1Co 9: 7 Who plants a v and does not eat

## VINEYARDS [VINE]
Lev 25: 3 and for six years prune your v
SS 2:15 the little foxes that ruin the v, our v

## VIOLATE [VIOLATED, VIOLATION]
Lev 26:15 commands and so v my covenant,
Ps 89:31 if they v my decrees and fail to keep

## VIOLATED [VIOLATE]
Jos 7:11 they have v my covenant, which I
Jdg 2:20 this nation has v the covenant I
Da 11:32 those who have v the covenant,

## VIOLATION [VIOLATE]
Heb 2: 2 every v and disobedience received

## VIOLENCE [VIOLENT]
Ge 6:11 in God's sight and was full of v.
Ps 7:16 their v comes down on their own
Isa 53: 9 though he had done no v, nor was
60:18 No longer will v be heard in your
Eze 22:26 Her priests do v to my law
45: 9 Give up your v and oppression
Joel 3:19 because of v done to the people
Ob 1:10 of the v against your brother Jacob,

Jnh   3: 8  give up their evil ways and their **v**.
Hab   2:17  The **v** you have done to Lebanon
Zep   3: 4  the sanctuary and do **v** to the law.
Mt   11:12  of heaven has been subjected to **v**,

## VIOLENT [VIOLENCE]

2Sa  22: 3  from **v** people you save me.
Pr    3:31  Do not envy the **v** or choose any
Eze  18:10  "Suppose he has a **v** son, who sheds
Mt   11:12  and **v** people have been raiding it.
      28: 2  There was a **v** earthquake,
1Ti   1:13  and a persecutor and a **v** man, I was
       3: 3  to drunkenness, not **v** but gentle,
Tit   1: 7  not **v**, not pursuing dishonest gain.

## VIPER [VIPER'S, VIPERS]

Pr   23:32  like a snake and poisons like a **v**.
Ac   28: 3  the fire, a **v**, driven out by the heat,

## VIPER'S* [VIPER]

Isa  11: 8  will put their hands into the **v** nest.

## VIPERS [VIPER]

Ps  140: 3  the poison of **v** is on their lips.
Lk    3: 7  baptized by him, "You brood of **v**!
Ro    3:13  "The poison of **v** is on their lips."

## VIRGIN [VIRGINS]

Dt   22:15  at the gate proof that she was a **v**.
1Ki   1: 2  look for a young **v** to serve the king
Job  31: 1  not to look lustfully at a **v**.
Isa   7:14  The **v** will conceive and give birth
Jer  31:21  Return, V Israel, return to your
Mt    1:23  "The **v** will conceive and give birth
Lk    1: 34  asked the angel, "since I am a **v**?"
1Co   7:28  and if a **v** marries, she has not
2Co  11: 2  I might present you as a pure **v**

## VIRGINS [VIRGIN]

Mt   25: 1  will be like ten **v** who took their
1Co   7:25  Now about **v**: I have no command
Rev  14: 4  with women, for they remained **v**.

## VIRTUES*

Col   3:14  And over all these **v** put on love,

## VISIBLE

Eph   5:13  exposed by the light becomes **v**—
Col   1:16  heaven and on earth, **v** and invisible,
Heb  11: 3  was not made out of what was **v**.

## VISION [VISIONS]

Ge   15: 1  the LORD came to Abram in a **v**:
      46: 2  God spoke to Israel in a **v** at night
Nu   24: 4  who sees a **v** from the Almighty,
1Sa   3:15  He was afraid to tell Eli the **v**,
Ps   89:19  Once you spoke in a **v**, to your
Isa  22: 1  concerning the Valley of V:
Da    2:45  the meaning of the **v** of the rock cut
       7: 2  "In my **v** at night I looked,
       8: 1  I had a **v**, after the one that had
      8:26  but seal up the **v**,
      9:24  to seal up **v** and prophecy
      10: 7  was the only one who saw the **v**;
Zec   1: 8  During the night I had a **v**, and there

Lk    1:22  They realized he had seen a **v**
Ac    9:10  The Lord called to him in a **v**,
      10:17  about the meaning of the **v**, the men
      16: 9  During the night Paul had a **v**
      26:19  disobedient to the **v** from heaven.
Rev   9:17  riders I saw in my **v** looked like this:

## VISIONS [VISION]

Nu   12: 6  I reveal myself to them in **v**, I speak
1Sa   3: 1  there were not many **v**.
Isa  30.10  "Give us no more **v** of what is
Jer  23:16  They speak **v** from their own minds,
Eze   1: 1  were opened and I saw **v** of God.
Da    1:17  And Daniel could understand **v**
Joel  2:28  dreams, your young men will see **v**.
Ac    2:17  your young men will see **v**, your old

## VISIT [VISITS]

Mt   25:36  in prison and you came to **v** me.'

## VISITS* [VISIT]

Mic   7: 4  has come, the day God **v** you.
1Pe   2:12  and glorify God on the day he **v** us.

## VOICE [VOICES]

Ex   19:19  and the **v** of God answered him.
Dt    4:33  Has any other people heard the **v**
      30.20  listen to his **v**, and hold fast to him.
Job  40: 9  and can your **v** thunder like his?
Ps   19: 4  Yet their **v** goes out into all
      27: 7  Hear my **v** when I call, LORD;
      29: 3  The **v** of the LORD is over
      95: 7  Today, if only you would hear his **v**,
Pr    1:20  she raises her **v** in the public square;
       8: 1  Does not understanding raise her **v**?
Isa  30:21  your ears will hear a **v** behind you,
      40: 3  A **v** of one calling:
Jer  31:15  "A **v** is heard in Ramah,
Eze   1:24  waters, like the **v** of the Almighty,
Mt    2:18  "A **v** is heard in Ramah,
       3:17  And a **v** from heaven said, "This is
Mk    1: 3  "a **v** of one calling
Jn    1:23  "I am the **v** of one calling
       5:25  the dead will hear the **v** of the Son
      10: 3  him, and the sheep listen to his **v**.
      12:28  Then a **v** came from heaven,
Ro   10:18  "Their **v** has gone out into all
      15: 6  one mind and one **v** you may glorify
1Th   4:16  with the **v** of the archangel
Heb   3: 7  "Today, if you hear his **v**,
2Pe   1:17  God the Father when the **v** came
Rev   3:20  If anyone hears my **v** and opens

## VOICE OF THE †LORD  Dt 5:25; 18:16; Ps
29:3, 4, 4, 5, 7, 8, 9; Isa 30:31; Hag 1:12

## VOICES [VOICE]

Nu   14: 1  of the community raised their **v**
Rev  10: 3  the **v** of the seven thunders spoke.
      11:15  and there were loud **v** in heaven,

## VOLUNTARILY [VOLUNTARY]

1Co   9:17  If I preach **v**, I have a reward;

## VOLUNTARY* [VOLUNTARILY, VOLUNTEERED]
Phm 1:14 not seem forced but would be **v**.

## VOLUNTEERED [VOLUNTARY]
1Ch 12:38 All these were fighting men who **v**
Ne 11: 2 The people commended all who **v**

## VOMIT [VOMITED]
Lev 18:28 it will **v** you out as it vomited
Pr 26:11 As a dog returns to its **v**, so fools
Isa 28: 8 All the tables are covered with **v**
2Pe 2:22 "A dog returns to its **v**," and,

## VOMITED [VOMIT]
Lev 18:25 and the land **v** out its inhabitants.
Jnh 2:10 fish, and it **v** Jonah onto dry land.

## VOW [VOWED, VOWS]
Ge 28:20 Then Jacob made a **v**, saying,
Nu 6: 2 a **v** of dedication to the LORD as
21: 2 Israel made this **v** to the LORD:
30: 2 a man makes a **v** to the LORD
Dt 23:21 If you make a **v** to the LORD your
Jdg 11:30 Jephthah made a **v** to the LORD:
1Sa 1:11 And she made a **v**, saying,
Ecc 5: 4 When you make a **v** to God, do not
5: 5 not to make a **v** than to make one
Ac 18:18 because of a **v** he had taken.

## VOWED [VOW]
Dt 12: 6 what you have **v** to give and your
Jdg 11:39 father, and he did to her as he had **v**.
Jnh 2: 9 What I have **v** I will make good.

## VOWS [VOW]
Nu 6:21 the Nazirite who **v** offerings
30: 4 all her **v** and every pledge
30: 5 it, none of her **v** or the pledges
Ps 22:25 who fear you I will fulfill my **v**.
50:14 God, fulfill your **v** to the Most High,
116:14 I will fulfill my **v** to the LORD
Pr 20:25 and only later to consider one's **v**.
Jnh 1:16 to the LORD and made **v** to him.
Mt 5:33 fulfill to the Lord the **v** you have made.'

## VULTURE [VULTURES]
Hab 1: 8 They fly like a **v** swooping

## VULTURES [VULTURE]
Mt 24:28 is a carcass, there the **v** will gather.

---

# W

---

## WADI
Nu 34: 5 join the **W** of Egypt and end
2Ki 24: 7 territory, from the **W** of Egypt

## WAGE [WAGED, WAGES, WAGING]
Mic 3: 5 they prepare to **w** war against you.

2Co 10: 3 we do not **w** war as the world does.

## WAGED [WAGE]
Jos 11:18 Joshua **w** war against all these kings

## WAGES [WAGE]
Lev 19:13 " 'Do not hold back the **w**
Pr 10:16 The **w** of the righteous is life,
Mic 1: 7 her gifts from the **w** of prostitutes,
Mal 3: 5 who defraud laborers of their **w**,
Lk 10: 7 you, for workers deserve their **w**.
Jn 6: 7 "It would take almost a year's **w**
12: 5 It was worth a year's **w**."
Ro 4: 4 their **w** are not credited to them as
6:23 For the **w** of sin is death, but the gift
1Ti 5:18 and "Workers deserve their **w**."
2Pe 2:15 who loved the **w** of wickedness.

## WAGING [WAGE]
Da 7:21 this horn was **w** war against the holy
Ro 7:23 **w** war against the law of my mind

## WAIL [WAILED, WAILING]
Isa 13: 6 **W**, for the day of the LORD is
Mic 1: 8 Because of this I will weep and **w**;

## WAILED [WAIL]
Nu 11:18 The LORD heard you when you **w**,

## WAILING [WAIL]
Ex 12:30 and there was loud **w** in Egypt,
Nu 11: 4 again the Israelites started **w**
Ps 30:11 You turned my **w** into dancing;

## WAIST
2Ki 1: 8 had a leather belt around his **w**."
2Ch 10:10 finger is thicker than my father's **w**.
Isa 11: 5 faithfulness the sash around his **w**.
Jer 13: 1 linen belt and put it around your **w**,
Mt 3: 4 he had a leather belt around his **w**.
Jn 13: 4 and wrapped a towel around his **w**.
Eph 6:14 belt of truth buckled around your **w**,

## WAIT [AWAIT, AWAITS, WAITED, WAITING, WAITS]
Ps 27:14 **W** for the LORD;
33:20 We **w** in hope for the LORD;
119:166 I **w** for your salvation, LORD,
130: 5 I **w** for the LORD, my whole being
130: 6 I **w** for the Lord more than watchmen
Pr 1:18 These men lie in **w** for their own
Isa 30:18 Blessed are all who **w** for him!
La 3:26 it is good to **w** quietly
Hab 2: 3 Though it linger, **w** for it;
3:16 Yet I will **w** patiently for the day
Ac 1: 4 **w** for the gift my Father promised,
Ro 8:23 groan inwardly as we **w** eagerly
1Th 1:10 and to **w** for his Son from heaven,
Tit 2:13 while we **w** for the blessed hope—

## WAITED [WAIT]
Ps 40: 1 I **w** patiently for the LORD;
Jnh 4: 5 **w** to see what would happen

## WAITING [WAIT]

Heb 9:28 to those who are **w** for him.

## WAITS [WAIT]

Da 12:12 Blessed is the one who **w**
Ro 8:19 The creation **w** in eager expectation

## WAKE [AWAKE, AWAKEN, AWOKE, WAKENS, WOKE]

Isa 26:19 let those who dwell in the dust **w**
Ro 13:11 has already come for you to **w**
Eph 5:14 "**W** up, sleeper, rise from the dead,
Rev 3: 2 **W** up! Strengthen what remains

## WAKENS* [WAKE]

Isa 50: 4 He **w** me morning by morning, **w** my
ear to listen

## WALK [WALKED, WALKING, WALKS]

Ge 17: 1 **w** before me faithfully and be
Lev 26:12 I will **w** among you and be your
Dt 5:33 **W** in obedience to all
 6: 7 and when you **w** along the road,
 10:12 your God, to **w** in obedience to him,
 11:19 and when you **w** along the road,
 11:22 to **w** in obedience to him and to hold
 26:17 that you will **w** in obedience to him,
 28: 9 God and **w** in obedience to him.
Jos 22: 5 your God, to **w** in obedience to him,
1Ki 2: 3 **W** in obedience to him, and keep his
Ps 1: 1 Blessed are those who do not **w**
 15: 2 Those whose **w** is blameless,
 23: 4 Even though I **w** through the darkest
 84:11 from those whose **w** is blameless.
 89:15 who **w** in the light of your presence,
 115: 7 but cannot **w**, nor can they utter
 119:45 I will **w** about in freedom, for I have
Pr 4:12 When you **w**, your steps will not be
 6:22 When you **w**, they will guide you;
 9: 6 **w** in the way of insight."
 13:20 **W** with the wise and become wise,
 28:26 those who **w** in wisdom are kept safe.
Ecc 2:14 while fools **w** in the darkness;
Isa 2: 3 so that we may **w** in his paths."
 2: 5 let us **w** in the light of the LORD.
 30:21 saying, "This is the way; **w** in it."
 33:15 Those who **w** righteously and speak
 40:31 weary, they will **w** and not be faint.
 43: 2 When you **w** through the fire,
 57: 2 Those who **w** uprightly enter
Jer 6:16 But you said, 'We will not **w** in it.'
Da 4:37 those who **w** in pride he is able
Am 3: 3 Do two **w** together unless they have
Mic 4: 5 All the nations may **w** in the name
 6: 8 and to **w** humbly with your God.
Mk 2: 9 say, 'Get up, take your mat and **w**'?
Jn 8:12 Whoever follows me will never **w**
 11: 9 who **w** in the daytime will not stumble,
Ac 3: 8 jumped to his feet and began to **w**.
Gal 5:16 So I say, **w** by the Spirit,
1Jn 1: 6 with him and yet **w** in the darkness,
 1: 7 But if we **w** in the light, as he is
2Jn 1: 6 his command is that you **w** in love.
3Jn 1: 3 telling how you continue to **w** in it.
Rev 9:20 idols that cannot see or hear or **w**.

Rev 21:24 The nations will **w** by its light,

## WALKED [WALK]

Ge 5:24 Enoch **w** faithfully with God;
 24:40 before whom I have **w** faithfully,
Jos 14: 9 which your feet have **w** will be your
Mt 14:29 **w** on the water and came toward

## WALKING [WALK]

Dt 8: 6 **w** in obedience to him and revering
1Ki 3: 3 the LORD by **w** according
Da 3:25 I see four men **w** around in the fire,
Mt 14:26 the disciples saw him **w** on the lake,
Ac 3: 8 the temple courts, **w** and jumping,
2Jn 1: 4 some of your children **w** in the truth,
3Jn 1: 4 that my children are **w** in the truth.

## WALKS [WALK]

Pr 10: 9 Whoever **w** in integrity **w** securely,

## WALL [WALLS]

Ex 14:22 with a **w** of water on their right
Jos 2:15 she lived in was part of the city **w**.
 6:20 gave a loud shout, the **w** collapsed;
2Ki 25: 4 the city **w** was broken through,
Ne 1: 3 The **w** of Jerusalem is broken down,
 2:17 let us rebuild the **w** of Jerusalem,
 12:27 dedication of the **w** of Jerusalem,
Da 5: 5 and wrote on the plaster of the **w**,
Zec 2: 5 I myself will be a **w** of fire around
Ac 9:25 basket through an opening in the **w**.
2Co 11:33 in a basket from a window in the **w**
Eph 2:14 barrier, the dividing **w** of hostility,
Rev 21:12 a great, high **w** with twelve gates,

## WALLOWING

2Pe 2:22 returns to her **w** in the mud."

## WALLS [WALL]

Dt 1:28 are large, with **w** up to the sky.
Ne 2:13 Gate, examining the **w** of Jerusalem,
Ps 51:18 to build up the **w** of Jerusalem.
 122: 7 May there be peace within your **w**
Pr 25:28 a city whose **w** are broken through
Isa 26: 1 God makes salvation its **w**
 54:12 and all your **w** of precious stones.
 58:12 be called Repairer of Broken **W**,
 60:18 you will call your **w** Salvation
Jer 52:14 down all the **w** around Jerusalem.
Heb 11:30 By faith the **w** of Jericho fell,

## WANDER [WANDERED, WANDERER, WANDERING]

Nu 32:13 he made them **w** in the wilderness
Pr 5: 6 her paths **w** aimlessly,
Jas 5:19 one of you should **w** from the truth

## WANDERED [WANDER]

1Ch 16:20 they **w** from nation to nation,
Ps 107: 4 Some **w** in desert wastelands,
Eze 34: 6 My sheep **w** over all the mountains
Mt 18:12 go to look for the one that **w** off?
1Ti 6:10 have **w** from the faith and pierced

## WANDERER [WANDER]
Ge    4:12  You will be a restless **w**

## WANDERING [WANDER]
Dt   26: 5  "My father was a **w** Aramean,

## WANT [WANTED, WANTING, WANTS]
Lev  26: 5  you will eat all the food you **w**
1Sa   8:19  they said. "We **w** a king over us.
1Ki   3: 5  whatever you **w** me to give you."
Mt    8:29  "What do you **w** with us,
     19:21  "If you **w** to be perfect, go,
Lk   18:41  "Lord, I **w** to see," he replied.
     19:14  say, 'We don't **w** this man to be our
Ro    7:15  For what I **w** to do I do not do,
     13: 3  Do you **w** to be free from fear
2Co  12:14  to you, because what I **w** is not your
Gal   4:21  me, you who **w** to be under the law,
Php   3:10  I **w** to know Christ—yes, to know
      4:12  whether living in plenty or in **w**.

## WANTED [WANT]
Ex    4:19  for all those who **w** to kill you are
Jnh   4: 8  He **w** to die, and said, "It would be
Mt   14: 5  Herod **w** to kill John, but he was
     21:31  of the two did what his father **w**?"
1Co  12:18  of them, just as he **w** them to be.
Heb   6:17  Because God **w** to make

## WANTING [WANT]
Da    5:27  weighed on the scales and found **w**.
2Pe   3: 9  with you, not **w** anyone to perish,

## WANTS [WANT]
Mt    5:42  away from the one who **w** to borrow
     20:26  whoever **w** to become great among
Mk    8:35  For whoever **w** to save their life will
     10:43  whoever **w** to become great among
Ro    9:18  on whom he **w** to have mercy,
1Ti   2: 4  who **w** all people to be saved
2Ti   3:12  everyone who **w** to live a godly life
1Pe   5: 2  you are willing, as God **w** you to be;

## WAR [WARRIOR, WARS]
Ex   17:16  will be at **w** against the Amalekites
     32:17  "There is the sound of **w**
Jos  11:23  Then the land had rest from **w**.
1Sa  15:18  make **w** on them until you have
2Sa  11: 1  at the time when kings go off to **w**,
Ps   68:30  Scatter the nations who delight in **w**.
    120: 7  but when I speak, they are for **w**.
    144: 1  who trains my hands for **w**,
Ecc   3: 8  a time for **w** and a time for peace.
      9:18  is better than weapons of **w**, but one
Isa   2: 4  nor will they train for **w** anymore.
Da    7:21  horn was waging **w** against the holy
      9:26  **W** will continue until the end,
Ro    7:23  me, waging **w** against the law of my
2Co  10: 3  we do not wage **w** as the world
1Pe   2:11  desires, which **w** against your soul.
Rev  12: 7  And there was **w** in heaven.
     17:14  They will make **w** against the Lamb,
     19:11  With justice he judges and makes **w**.

## WARM [LUKEWARM, WARMS, WARMTH]
Ecc   4:11  But how can one keep **w** alone?
Hag   1: 6  You put on clothes, but are not **w**.
Jas   2:16  keep **w** and well fed," but does

## WARMS [WARM]
Isa  44:15  some of it he takes and **w** himself,

## WARMTH* [WARM]
Ps   19: 6  nothing is deprived of its **w**.

## WARN* [WARNED, WARNING, WARNINGS, WARNS]
Ex   19:21  **w** the people so they do not force
Nu   24:14  let me **w** you of what this people
1Sa   8: 9  but **w** them solemnly and let them
1Ki   2:42  swear by the LORD and **w** you,
2Ch  19:10  you are to **w** them not to sin against
Ps   81: 8  me, my people, and I will **w** you—
Jer  42:19  Be sure of this: I **w** you today
Eze   3:18  you do not **w** them or speak
      3:19  if you do **w** the wicked and they do
      3:20  Since you did not **w** them, they will
      3:21  if you do **w** the righteous not to sin
     33: 3  blows the trumpet to **w** the people,
     33: 6  blow the trumpet to **w** the people
     33: 9  if you do **w** the wicked to turn
Lk   16:28  Let him **w** them, so that they will
Ac    4:17  we must **w** them to speak no longer
1Co   4:14  but to **w** you as my dear children.
Gal   5:21  I **w** you, as I did before, that those
1Th   5:14  **w** those who are idle and disruptive,
2Th   3:15  but **w** them as fellow believers.
2Ti   2:14  **W** them before God against
Tit   3:10  **W** divisive people once, and then
            **w** them a second time.
Rev  22:18  I **w** everyone who hears the words

## WARNED [WARN]
2Ki  17:13  The LORD **w** Israel and Judah
Ne    9:29  "You **w** them in order to turn them
      9:30  you **w** them through your prophets.
      9:34  or the statutes you **w** them to keep.
Ps    2:10  be **w**, you rulers of the earth.
     19:11  By them your servant is **w**;
Jer  18: 8  if that nation I **w** repents of its evil,
     22:21  I **w** you when you felt secure,
Mt    2:12  having been **w** in a dream not to go
      2:22  Having been **w** in a dream,
      3: 7  Who **w** you to flee from the coming
1Th   4: 6  as we told you and **w** you before.
Heb  11: 7  when **w** about things not yet seen,
     12:25  they refused him who **w** them

## WARNING [WARN]
Jer   6: 8  Take **w**, Jerusalem, or I will turn
Eze  33: 5  the trumpet but did not heed the **w**,
Ac   13:51  shook the dust off their feet as a **w**
1Ti   5:20  so that the others may take **w**.

## WARNINGS [WARN]
1Co  10:11  and were written down as **w** for us,

## WARNS [WARN]
Heb 12:25　from him who **w** us from heaven?

## WARPED
Dt　32: 5　they are a **w** and crooked generation.

## WARRIOR [WAR]
Ex　15: 3　The LORD is a **w**; the LORD is
1Ch 28. 3　because you are a **w** and have shed
Pr　16:32　Better a patient person than a **w**,
Jer　20:11　LORD is with me like a mighty **w**;

## WARS [WAR]
Nu　21:14　Book of the **W** of the LORD says:
Ps　46: 9　He makes **w** cease to the ends
Mt　24: 6　You will hear of **w** and rumors of **w**,

## WASH [WASHED, WASHING, WHITEWASH, WHITEWASHED]
Ex　40:31　his sons used it to **w** their hands
2Ki　5:10　"Go, **w** yourself seven times
Ps　51: 7　**w** me, and I will be whiter than
Jer　4:14　**w** the evil from your heart and be
Lk　11:38　did not first **w** before the meal.
Jn　9: 7　"**w** in the Pool of Siloam" (this
13: 5　and began to **w** his disciples' feet,
Ac　22:16　be baptized and **w** your sins away,
Jas　4: 8　**W** your hands, you sinners,
Rev 22:14　are those who **w** their robes,

**MUST WASH** See MUST

## WASHED [WASH]
Ps　73:13　and have **w** my hands in innocence.
Jn　9:11　So I went and **w**, and then I could
1Co　6:11　But you were **w**, you were
Heb 10:22　and having our bodies **w** with pure
2Pe　2:22　and, "A sow that is **w** returns to her
Rev　7:14　they have **w** their robes and made

## WASHING [WASH]
Ex　30:18　basin, with its bronze stand, for **w**.
2Ch　4: 6　was to be used by the priests for **w**.
Jn　2: 6　used by the Jews for ceremonial **w**,
Eph　5:26　the **w** with water through the word,
1Ti　5:10　**w** the feet of the Lord's people,
Tit　3: 5　He saved us through the **w** of rebirth

## WASTE [WASTED, WASTING]
Isa　24:16　But I said, "I **w** away, I **w** away!
Jer　2:15　They have laid **w** his land;
Eze　4:17　will **w** away because of their sin.
Mk　14: 4　another, "Why this **w** of perfume?

## WASTED [WASTE]
Jn　6:12　are left over. Let nothing be **w**."

## WASTELAND [LAND]
Isa　43:19　the wilderness and streams in the **w**.

## WASTELANDS [LAND]
Ps 107: 4　Some wandered in desert **w**,

## WASTING [WASTE]
2Co　4:16　Though outwardly we are **w** away,

## WATCH [WATCHED, WATCHES, WATCHFUL, WATCHING, WATCHMAN, WATCHMEN]
Ge　31:49　the LORD keep **w** between you
Dt　4:15　Therefore **w** yourselves very
Job　7:20　you who **w** over us all?
Ps　39: 1　"I will **w** my ways and keep my
59: 9　You are my strength, I **w** for you;
90: 4　gone by, or like a **w** in the night.
141: 3　keep **w** over the door of my lips.
Pr　4: 6　love her, and she will **w** over you.
6:22　you sleep, they will **w** over you;
Jer　31:10　them and will **w** over his flock like
Mic　7: 7　for me, I **w** in hope for the LORD,
Mt　7:15　"**W** out for false prophets.
24:42　"Therefore keep **w**, because you do
26:41　"**W** and pray so that you will not
Mk　13:35　"Therefore keep **w** because you do
Lk　2: 8　keeping **w** over their flocks at night.
Php　3: 2　**W** out for those dogs,
1Ti　4:16　**W** your life and doctrine closely.
Heb 13:17　because they keep **w** over you as
2Jn　1: 8　**W** out that you do not lose what we

## WATCHED [WATCH]
Mt　26:16　on Judas **w** for an opportunity

## WATCHES* [WATCH]
Nu　19: 5　While he **w**, the heifer is to be
Job 24:15　The eye of the adulterer **w** for dusk;
Ps　1: 6　For the LORD **w** over the way
33:14　his dwelling place he **w** all who live
63: 6　of you through the **w** of the night.
119:148　My eyes stay open through the **w**
121: 3　he who **w** over you will not
121: 4　he who **w** over Israel will neither
121: 5　The LORD **w** over you—
127: 1　Unless the LORD **w** over the city,
145:20　The LORD **w** over all who love
146: 9　The LORD **w** over the foreigner
Pr　31:27　She **w** over the affairs of her
Ecc 11: 4　Whoever **w** the wind will not plant;
La　2:19　night, as the **w** of the night begin;
4:16　he no longer **w** over them.

## WATCHFUL [WATCH]
Col　4: 2　to prayer, being **w** and thankful.

## WATCHING [WATCH]
Jer　1:12　for I am **w** to see that my word is
44:27　For I am **w** over them for harm,
Mk　15:40　Some women were **w**
Lk　12:37　servants whose master finds them **w**
1Pe　5: 2　under your care, **w** over them—

## WATCHMAN [WATCH]
Eze　3:17　I have made you a **w** for the house
33: 6　but I will hold the **w** accountable

## WATCHMEN [WATCH]
Ps 130: 6　the Lord more than **w** wait

Isa 56:10  Israel's **w** are blind, they all lack
Mic  7: 4  The day of your **w** has come,

## WATCHTOWER [TOWER]

Isa 21: 8  after day, my lord, I stand on the **w**;

## WATER [WATERED, WATERING, WATERS, WELL-WATERED]

Ge   1: 6  the waters to separate **w** from **w**."
     1:20  said, "Let the **w** teem with living
     7:18  ark floated on the surface of the **w**.
Ex   7:20  all the **w** was changed into blood.
    15:25  He threw it into the **w**, and the **w**
    17: 1  but there was no **w** for the people
Nu   5:19  may this bitter **w** that brings a curse
    20: 2  Now there was no **w**
    21: 5  There is no **w**! And we detest this
2Ki  2: 8  rolled it up and struck the **w** with it.
     6: 5  tree, the iron axhead fell into the **w**.
Ps   1: 3  like a tree planted by streams of **w**,
    22:14  I am poured out like **w**, and all my
    42: 1  As the deer pants for streams of **w**,
Pr   5:15  Drink **w** from your own cistern,
     9:17  "Stolen **w** is sweet; food eaten
    25:21  if he is thirsty, give him **w** to drink.
Isa 12: 3  joy you will draw **w** from the wells
    30:20  of adversity and the **w** of affliction,
    32: 2  like streams of **w** in the desert
    49:10  and lead them beside springs of **w**.
Jer  2:13  the spring of living **w**,
    17: 8  a tree planted by the **w** that sends
    31: 9  I will lead them beside streams of **w**
Eze 36:25  I will sprinkle clean **w** on you,
Zec 14: 8  On that day living **w** will flow
Mt  14:29  walked on the **w** and came toward
Mk   1: 8  I baptize you with **w**, but he will
     9:41  anyone who gives you a cup of **w**
Lk   5: 4  "Put out into deep **w**, and let down
Jn   2: 9  of the banquet tasted the **w** that had
     3: 5  of God without being born of **w**
     4:10  he would have given you living **w**."
     7:38  rivers of living **w** will flow
    19:34  a sudden flow of blood and **w**.
Eph  5:26  washing with **w** through the word,
Heb 10:22  our bodies washed with pure **w**.
Jas  3:11  Can both fresh **w** and salt **w** flow
1Pe  3:21  this **w** symbolizes baptism that now
2Pe  2:17  These people are springs without **w**
1Jn  5: 6  by **w** only, but by **w** and blood.
Rev  7:17  lead them to springs of living **w**.'
    21: 6  To the thirsty I will give **w** without cost
    21: 6  cost from the spring of the **w** of life.
    22: 1  showed me the river of the **w** of life,
    22:17  take the free gift of the **w** of life.

## WATERED [WATER]

Ps 104:16  The trees of the LORD are well **w**,
1Co  3: 6  I planted the seed, Apollos **w** it,

## WATERING [WATER]

Ge   2:10  A river **w** the garden flowed
Isa 55:10  not return to it without **w** the earth

## WATERS [WATER]

Ge   1: 2  of God was hovering over the **w**.

Ge   1:10  the gathered **w** he called "seas."
     7: 7  the ark to escape the **w** of the flood.
Ex  14:21  it into dry land. The **w** were divided,
Jos  4: 7  the **w** of the Jordan were cut off.
Ps  18:16  he drew me out of deep **w**.
    23: 2  he leads me beside quiet **w**,
   106:32  the **w** of Meribah they angered
SS   8: 7  Many **w** cannot quench love;
Isa 11: 9  the LORD as the **w** cover the sea.
    43: 2  When you pass through the **w**, I will
    55: 1  you who are thirsty, come to the **w**;
    58:11  like a spring whose **w** never fail.
Hab  2:14  the LORD as the **w** cover the sea.
1Co  3: 7  nor the one who **w** is anything,
Rev  8:11  A third of the **w** turned bitter,

## WAVE [WAVES]

Ex  29:24  have them **w** them before the LORD as a
                **w** offering.
Lev 23:11  **w** the sheaf before the LORD so it
Jas  1: 6  the one who doubts is like a **w**

## WAVE OFFERING Ex 29:24, 26; 35:22; 38:24, 29; Lev 7:30; 8:27, 29; 9:21; 10:15; 14:12, 24; 23:15, 17, 20; Nu 6:20; 8:11, 13, 15, 21; 18:18

## WAVER*

1Ki 18:21  "How long will you **w** between two
Ro   4:20  Yet he did not **w** through unbelief

## WAVES [WAVE]

2Sa 22: 5  The **w** of death swirled about me;
Ps  89: 9  when its **w** mount up, you still them
Isa 57:20  rest, whose **w** cast up mire and mud.
Mt   8:27  the winds and the **w** obey him!"
Eph  4:14  tossed back and forth by the **w**,
Jude 1:13  They are wild **w** of the sea,

## WAX

Ps  22:14  My heart has turned to **w**;
    97: 5  mountains melt like **w** before

## WAY DOORWAY, GATEWAY, WAYS]

Ge   3:24  forth to guard the **w** to the tree
Ex  13:21  of cloud to guide them on their **w**
    18:20  show them the **w** they are to live
Dt   1:33  to show you the **w** you should go.
    32: 6  Is this the **w** you repay the LORD,
1Sa 12:23  I will teach you the **w** that is good
2Sa 22:31  "As for God, his **w** is perfect;
1Ki  8:23  continue wholeheartedly in your **w**.
     8:36  Teach them the right **w** to live,
2Ch  6:27  Teach them the right **w** to live,
Job 23:10  But he knows the **w** that I take;
Ps   1: 1  stand in the **w** that sinners take or sit
     1: 6  the LORD watches over the **w**
    18:30  As for God, his **w** is perfect:
    32: 8  teach you in the **w** you should go;
    37: 5  Commit your **w** to the LORD;
    86:11  Teach me your **w**, LORD, that I
   119: 9  who are young keep their **w** pure?
   139:24  if there is any offensive **w** in me,
   139:24  and lead me in the **w** everlasting.
Pr   4:11  I instruct you in the **w** of wisdom
    12:15  The **w** of fools seems right to them,

Pr  14:12  There is a **w** that appears to be right,
    16: 7  LORD takes pleasure in anyone's **w**,
    19: 2  more will hasty feet miss the **w**!
    22: 6  off on the **w** they should go,
    30:19  and the **w** of a man with a young
Isa 30:21  behind you, saying, "This is the **w**;
    35: 8  it will be called the **W** of Holiness;
    40: 3  the wilderness prepare the **w**
    48:17  directs you in the **w** you should go.
    53: 6  each of us has turned to our own **w**;
Jer  5:31  and my people love it this **w**.
    21: 8  I am setting before you the **w** of life and
           the **w** of death.
Mal  3: 1  who will prepare the **w** before me.
Mt   3: 3  'Prepare the **w** for the Lord,
     5:12  in the same **w** they persecuted
Lk   7:27  will prepare your **w** before you.'
Jn  14: 6  "I am the **w** and the truth
Ac   1:11  in the same **w** you have seen him go
     9: 2  any there who belonged to the **W**,
    19: 9  and publicly maligned the **W**.
    22: 4  followers of this **W** to their death,
    24:14  our ancestors as a follower of the **W**,
1Co  9:24  Run in such a **w** as to get the prize.
    10:13  also provide a **w** out so that you can
    12:31  will show you the most excellent **w**.
    14: 1  Follow the **w** of love and eagerly
Col  1:10  the Lord and please him in every **w**:
Tit  2:10  every **w** they will make the teaching
Heb  2:17  his brothers and sisters in every **w**,
     4:15  who has been tempted in every **w**,
     9: 8  the **w** into the Most Holy Place had
    10:20  living **w** opened for us through
    13:18  desire to live honorably in every **w**.
Jas  5:20  from the **w** of error will save them
2Pe  2:21  have known the **w** of righteousness,

## WAYS [WAY]

Ge   6:12  on earth had corrupted their **w**.
Ex  33:13  teach me your **w** so I may know you
Dt  32: 4  are perfect, and all his **w** are just.
2Ki 17:13  "Turn from your evil **w**.
2Ch 11:17  years, following the **w** of David
Job 34:21  "His eyes are on the **w** of mortals;
Ps  25: 4  Show me your **w**, LORD, teach me
    25:10  All the **w** of the LORD are loving
    37: 7  fret when people succeed in their **w**,
    51:13  I will teach transgressors your **w**,
    77:13  Your **w**, God, are holy. What god is
   119:59  I have considered my **w** and have
   139: 3  you are familiar with all my **w**.
   145:17  The LORD is righteous in all his **w**
Pr   2:12  save you from the **w** of wicked men,
     3: 6  in all your **w** submit to him, and he
     3:17  Her **w** are pleasant **w**, and all her
     4:26  feet and be steadfast in all your **w**.
     5:21  For your **w** are in full view
     6: 6  consider its **w** and be wise!
     7:25  Do not let your heart turn to her **w**
    16: 2  may think all their **w** are pure,
    16:17  who guard their **w** preserve their
    21: 2  may think all their **w** are right,
Isa  2: 3  He will teach us his **w**, so that we
    42:24  For they would not follow his **w**;
    55: 7  Let the wicked forsake their **w**
    55: 8  neither are your **w** my **w**,"
Jer 10: 2  "Do not learn the **w** of the nations

Jer 18:11  So turn from your evil **w**, each one
Eze 16:47  You not only followed their **w**
    28:15  in your **w** from the day you were
    33: 8  out to dissuade them from their **w**,
Da   4:37  does is right and all his **w** are just.
Hos 14: 9  The **w** of the LORD are right;
Jnh  3:10  how they turned from their evil **w**,
Hag  1: 5  "Give careful thought to your **w**.
Lk   3: 5  straight, the rough **w** smooth.
Ro   1:30  they invent **w** of doing evil;
1Co 13:11  I put the **w** of childhood behind me.
Col  3: 7  You used to walk in these **w**,
Jas  3: 2  We all stumble in many **w**.
Rev 15: 3  Just and true are your **w**,

## WAYWARD [WAYWARDNESS]

Pr   2:16  woman, from the **w** woman with her
     6:24  the smooth talk of a **w** woman.
    23:27  pit and a **w** wife is a narrow well.

## WAYWARDNESS* [WAYWARD]

Pr   1:32  the **w** of the simple will kill them,
Hos 14: 4  "I will heal their **w** and love them

## WEAK [WEAKENED, WEAKER, WEAKLING, WEAKNESS, WEAKNESSES]

Jdg 16: 7  I'll become as **w** as any other man."
Ps  41: 1  are those who have regard for the **w**;
    72:13  He will take pity on the **w**
    82: 3  Defend the **w** and the fatherless;
    82: 4  Rescue the **w** and the needy;
Eze 34: 4  You have not strengthened the **w**
Mt  26:41  spirit is willing, but the flesh is **w**."
Ac  20:35  of hard work we must help the **w**,
Ro  14: 1  Accept those whose faith is **w**,
    15: 1  to bear with the failings of the **w**
1Co  1:27  God chose the **w** things of the world
     8: 9  become a stumbling block to the **w**.
     9:22  To the **w** I became **w**, to win the **w**.
    11:30  That is why many among you are **w**
2Co 12:10  For when I am **w**, then I am strong.
Gal  4: 9  that you are turning back to those **w**
1Th  5:14  help the **w**, be patient
Heb  7:18  is set aside because it was **w**
    12:12  your feeble arms and **w** knees.

## WEAKENED [WEAK]

Ro   8: 3  to do because it was **w** by the sinful

## WEAKER* [WEAK]

2Sa  3: 1  the house of Saul grew **w** and **w**.
1Co 12:22  that seem to be **w** are indispensable,
1Pe  3: 7  them with respect as the **w** partner

## WEAKLING* [WEAK]

Joel 3:10  Let the **w** say, "I am strong!"

## WEAKNESS* [WEAK]

La   1: 6  **w** they have fled before the pursuer.
Ro   8:26  way, the Spirit helps us in our **w**.
1Co  1:25  the **w** of God is stronger than human
     2: 3  I came to you in **w** with great fear
    15:43  it is sown in **w**, it is raised in power;
2Co 11:30  boast of the things that show my **w**.

2Co 12: 9 my power is made perfect in **w**."
   13: 4 he was crucified in **w**, yet he lives
Heb 5: 2 since he himself is subject to **w**.
   7:28 as high priests men in all their **w**;
   11:34 whose **w** was turned to strength;

## WEAKNESSES* [WEAK]
2Co 12: 5 about myself, except about my **w**.
   12: 9 all the more gladly about my **w**,
   12:10 sake, I delight in **w**, in insults,
Heb 4:15 is unable to empathize with our **w**,

## WEALTH [WEALTHY]
Dt 8:18 gives you the ability to produce **w**,
1Sa 2: 7 The LORD sends poverty and **w**;
1Ki 3:13 —both **w** and honor—
2Ch 1:11 desire and you have not asked for **w**,
Ps 37:16 that the righteous have than the **w**
   39: 6 up **w** without knowing whose it will
   49: 6 those who trust in their **w** and boast
   49:10 perish, leaving their **w** to others.
   49:12 Human beings, despite their **w**,
Pr 3: 9 Honor the LORD with your **w**,
   10: 4 poverty, but diligent hands bring **w**.
   10:22 blessing of the LORD brings **w**,
   11: 4 **W** is worthless in the day of wrath,
   13: 7 pretends to be poor, yet has great **w**.
   13:22 but a sinner's **w** is stored
   15:16 of the LORD than great **w**
Ecc 5:10 those who love **w** are never satisfied
   5:13 **w** hoarded to the harm of its owners,
SS 8: 7 to give all the **w** of one's house
Ob 1:13 nor seize their **w** in the day of their
Mt 13:22 deceitfulness of **w** choke the word,
Mk 10:22 away sad, because he had great **w**.
   12:44 They all gave out of their **w**;
Lk 15:13 and there squandered his **w** in wild
   16:11 trustworthy in handling worldly **w**,
1Ti 6:17 arrogant nor to put their hope in **w**,
Jas 5: 2 Your **w** has rotted, and moths have
   5: 3 You have hoarded **w** in the last
Rev 3:17 I have acquired **w** and do not need
   5:12 to receive power and **w** and wisdom

## WEALTHY [WEALTH]
Ge 13: 2 Abram had become very **w**
Lk 19: 2 was a chief tax collector and was **w**.

## WEANED
Ps 131: 2 I am like a **w** child with its mother;

## WEAPON [WEAPONS]
Ne 4:17 one hand and held a **w** in the other,
Isa 54:17 no **w** forged against you will

## WEAPONS [WEAPON]
Ecc 9:18 Wisdom is better than **w** of war,
Isa 13: 5 the LORD and the **w** of his wrath—
Jn 18: 3 carrying torches, lanterns and **w**.
2Co 6: 7 with **w** of righteousness in the right
   10: 4 The **w** we fight with are not the **w**

## WEAR [WEARING, WORE, WORN]
Lev 19:19 " 'Do not **w** clothing woven
Dt 8: 4 Your clothes did not **w** out and your

Dt 22: 5 woman must not **w** men's clothing, nor
   a man **w** women's clothing,
   29: 5 your clothes did not **w** out, nor did
Ps 102:26 they will all **w** out like a garment.
Pr 23: 4 Do not **w** yourself out to get rich;
Isa 51: 6 the earth will **w** out like a garment
Mt 6:31 or 'What shall we **w**?'
Heb 1:11 they will all **w** out like a garment.
Rev 3:18 and white clothes to **w**, so you can
   19: 8 and clean, was given her to **w**."

## WEARIED [WEARY]
Isa 43:22 you have not **w** yourselves for me,
   43:24 sins and **w** me with your offenses.
Mal 2:17 You have **w** the LORD

## WEARIES* [WEARY]
Ecc 10:15 The toil of fools **w** them;
   12:12 no end, and much study **w** the body.

## WEARING [WEAR]
Ge 37:23 richly ornamented robe he was **w**—
1Sa 18: 4 Jonathan took off the robe he was **w**
2Sa 13:18 She was **w** a richly ornamented
1Ki 11:30 took hold of the new cloak he was **w**
Jn 19: 5 Jesus came out **w** the crown
Jas 2: 3 attention to the one **w** fine clothes
1Pe 3: 3 hairstyles and the **w** of gold jewelry
Rev 7: 9 They were **w** white robes and were

## WEARY [WEARIED, WEARIES]
Ps 68: 9 you refreshed your **w** inheritance.
Isa 1:14 I am **w** of bearing them.
   40:28 He will not grow tired or **w**, and his
   40:31 they will run and not grow **w**,
   50: 4 know the word that sustains the **w**.
Jer 9: 5 they **w** themselves with sinning.
Mt 11:28 all you who are **w** and burdened,
Gal 6: 9 Let us not become **w** in doing good,
Heb 12: 3 so that you will not grow **w** and lose
Rev 2: 3 my name, and have not grown **w**.

## WEDDING
Ps 45: T *A maskil. A **w** song.*
Mt 22: 2 a king who prepared a **w** banquet
   22:11 who was not wearing **w** clothes.
Rev 19: 7 For the **w** of the Lamb has come,

## WEED* [WEEDS]
Mt 13:41 and they will **w** out of his kingdom

## WEEDS [WEED]
Mt 13:25 and sowed **w** among the wheat,

## WEEK [WEEKS]
Mt 28: 1 at dawn on the first day of the **w**,
Lk 18:12 I fast twice a **w** and give a tenth
1Co 16: 2 On the first day of every **w**,

## WEEKS [WEEK]
Ex 34:22 "Celebrate the Festival of **W**
Lev 23:15 offering, count off seven full **w**.

## WEEP [WEEPING, WEPT]

Ps   69:10 When I **w** and fast, I must endure
Ecc   3: 4 a time to **w** and a time to laugh,
La    1:16 "This is why I **w** and my eyes
Lk    6:21 Blessed are you who **w** now, for you
      23:28 of Jerusalem, do not **w** for me;

## WEEPING [WEEP]

Ne    8: 9 people had been **w** as they listened
Ps    6: 8 for the LORD has heard my **w**.
      30: 5 **w** may remain for a night,
      126: 6 Those who go out **w**, carrying seed
Jer   31:15 mourning and great **w**, Rachel **w**
Mt    2:18 Rachel **w** for her children
      8:12 where there will be **w** and gnashing
      13:42 where there will be **w** and gnashing
      22:13 where there will be **w** and gnashing
      24:51 where there will be **w** and gnashing
      25:30 where there will be **w** and gnashing

## WEIGH [OUTWEIGHS, WEIGHED, WEIGHS, WEIGHTIER, WEIGHTS]

1Co 14:29 the others should **w** carefully what

## WEIGHED [WEIGH]

1Sa   2. 3 knows, and by him deeds are **w**.
Job  28:15 nor can its price be **w** out in silver.
Ecc   8: 6 a person may be **w** down by misery.
Da    5:27 You have been **w** on the scales
Lk   21:34 or your hearts will be **w** down

## WEIGHS [WEIGH]

Pr   12:25 Anxiety **w** down the heart,
     15:28 heart of the righteous **w** its answers,
     21: 2 right, but the LORD **w** the heart.
     24:12 not he who **w** the heart perceive it?

## WEIGHTIER* [WEIGH]

Jn    5:36 "I have testimony **w** than

## WEIGHTS [WEIGH]

Lev  19:36 Use honest scales and honest **w**,
Dt   25:13 Do not have two differing **w** in your
Pr   11: 1 but accurate **w** find favor with him.
     20:23 The LORD detests differing **w**,

## WELCOME [WELCOMED, WELCOMES]

Mt   10:14 If anyone will not **w** you or listen
Mk    9:37 welcomes me does not **w** me
2Pe   1:11 you will receive a rich **w**
2Jn   1:10 them into your house or **w** them.
3Jn   1:10 that, he refuses to **w** other believers.

## WELCOMED [WELCOME]

Lk   10: 8 "When you enter a town and are **w**,

## WELCOMES [WELCOME]

Mt   10:40 "Anyone who **w** you **w** me, and anyone
          who **w** me **w** the one who sent me.
     18: 5 **w** one such child in my name **w** me.
2Jn   1:11 Anyone who **w** them shares in their

## WELL [WELLED, WELLING, WELLS]

Ge   12:16 He treated Abram **w** for her sake,
Dt    5:16 and that it may go **w** with you
      6: 3 to obey so that it may go **w** with you
      12:28 so that it may always go **w** with you
2Ch   6: 8 'You did **w** to have it in your heart
Ps  105:40 he fed them **w** with the bread
Pr    5:15 running water from your own **w**.
      23:27 and a wayward wife is a narrow **w**.
Isa   3:10 Tell the righteous it will be **w**
Jer  32:39 all will then go **w** for them
Mt    3:17 with him I am **w** pleased."
      15:31 the crippled made **w**, the lame
      17: 5 with him I am **w** pleased."
      25:21 "His master replied, 'W done,
Lk   14: 5 falls into a **w** on the Sabbath day,
     17:19 your faith has made you **w**."
Jn    4: 6 Jacob's **w** was there, and Jesus,
Ac   15:29 You will do **w** to avoid these things.
Eph   6: 3 "so that it may go **w** with you
1Ti   1:18 you may fight the battle **w**,
Jas   5:15 offered in faith will make them **w**;
2Pe   1:17 with him I am **w** pleased."
3Jn   1: 2 and that all may go **w** with you,

## WELL-BEING

Ezr   6:10 pray for the **w** of the king and his
Ps   35:27 delights in the **w** of his servant."

## WELL-FED* [FED]

Jer   5: 8 They are **w**, lusty stallions,
Mal   4: 2 and frolic like **w** calves.

## WELL-KNOWN* [KNOW]

Nu   16: 2 With them were 250 Israelite men, **w**
Mt   27:16 At that time they had a **w** prisoner

## WELL-MIXED* [MIXED]

Lev   6:21 oil on a griddle; bring it **w**

## WELL-WATERED [WATER]

Isa  58:11 You will be like a **w** garden,
Jer  31:12 They will be like a **w** garden,

## WELLED* [WELL]

2Co   8: 2 their extreme poverty **w** up in rich

## WELLING* [WELL]

Jn    4:14 in them a spring of water **w**

## WELLS [WELL]

Dt    6:11 did not provide, **w** you did not dig,
Ne    9:25 kinds of good things, **w** already dug,
Isa  12: 3 draw water from the **w** of salvation.

## WENT

Hos  11: 2 the more they **w** away from me.

## WEPT [WEEP]

Nu   14: 1 raised their voices and **w** aloud.
Ezr   3:12 temple, **w** aloud when they saw
Ps  137: 1 and **w** when we remembered Zion.
Isa  38: 3 And Hezekiah **w** bitterly.
Lk   19:41 and saw the city, he **w** over it

| Lk | 22:62 | And he went outside and **w** bitterly. |
| Jn | 11:35 | Jesus **w**. |
| Rev | 5: 4 | I **w** and **w** because no one was found |

## WEST [WESTERN]

| Ge | 13:14 | north and south, to the east and **w**. |
| Ps | 103:12 | as far as the east is from the **w**, |
| | 107: 3 | from east and **w**, from north |
| Isa | 43: 5 | the east and gather you from the **w**. |
| Zec | 14: 4 | will be split in two from east to **w**, |
| | 14: 8 | half of it **w** to the Mediterranean Sea, |

## WESTERN [WEST]

| Nu | 34: 6 | " 'Your **w** boundary will be |

## WET

| Lk | 7:38 | she began to **w** his feet with her |

## WHALE(S) (KJV) See CREATURES, [HUGE] FISH, MONSTER

## WHAT [WHATEVER]

| Ex | 3:13 | and they ask me, '**W** is his name?' |
| Dt | 10:12 | **w** does the LORD your God ask |
| | 30:11 | Now **w** I am commanding you today |
| Eze | 24: 6 | piece by piece in **w** order it comes. |
| Mic | 6: 8 | has shown all you people **w** is good. |
| | 6: 8 | **w** does the LORD require of you? |

## WHATEVER [WHAT]

| 2Ch | 1: 7 | "Ask for **w** you want me to give |
| Ps | 1: 3 | **w** they do prospers. |
| | 135: 6 | The LORD does **w** pleases him, |
| Eze | 24: 6 | piece by piece in **w** order it comes. |
| Mt | 16:19 | **w** you loose on earth will be loosed |
| | 18:18 | **w** you bind on earth will be bound |
| Mk | 11:24 | I tell you, **w** you ask for in prayer, |
| Jn | 14:13 | I will do **w** you ask in my name, |
| | 15:16 | so that **w** you ask in my name |
| | 16:23 | my Father will give you **w** you ask |
| Php | 4: 8 | **w** is noble, **w** is right, **w** is pure, |
| 1Th | 5:22 | reject **w** is harmful. |
| 1Jn | 5:15 | know that he hears us—**w** we ask— |

## WHEAT

| Ex | 34:22 | with the firstfruits of the **w** harvest, |
| Mt | 3:12 | gathering his **w** into the barn |
| | 13:25 | and sowed weeds among the **w**, |
| Lk | 22:31 | has asked to sift all of you as **w**. |
| Jn | 12:24 | you, unless a kernel of **w** falls |

## WHEEL [WHEELS]

| Eze | 1:16 | to be made like a **w** intersecting a **w**. |

## WHEELS [WHEEL]

| Ex | 14:25 | He jammed the **w** of their chariots |
| Eze | 1:16 | appearance and structure of the **w**: |
| Da | 7: 9 | with fire, and its **w** were all ablaze. |

## WHENEVER

| Dt | 4: 7 | our God is near us **w** we pray |
| 1Co | 11:26 | For **w** you eat this bread and drink |
| 2Co | 3:16 | But **w** anyone turns to the Lord, |
| Jas | 1: 2 | **w** you face trials of many kinds, |

## WHERE [EVERYWHERE, WHEREVER]

| Ex | 3: 5 | the place **w** you are standing is holy |
| Dt | 11:24 | Every place **w** you set your foot will |
| | 32:37 | "Now **w** are their gods, the rock |
| Job | 28:12 | But **w** can wisdom be found? |
| | 28:23 | to it and he alone knows **w** it dwells, |
| Ps | 26: 8 | I love the house **w** you live, |
| | 42: 3 | me all day long, "**W** is your God?" |
| | 121: 1 | **w** does my help come from? |
| | 139: 7 | **W** can I go from your Spirit? **W** can |
| Hos | 13:14 | **W**, O death, are your plagues? **W**, |
| Mal | 1: 6 | **w** is the honor due me? |
| Mt | 6:21 | For **w** your treasure is, there your |
| | 28: 6 | Come and see the place **w** he lay. |
| 1Co | 15:55 | "**W**, O death, is your victory? **W**, |
| Col | 3: 1 | **w** Christ is seated at the right hand |
| 2Pe | 3: 4 | "**W** is this 'coming' he promised? |

## WHEREVER [WHERE]

| Jos | 1: 7 | you may be successful **w** you go. |
| 1Ch | 18: 6 | LORD gave David victory **w** he went. |
| Mk | 14: 9 | **w** the gospel is preached throughout |
| Lk | 9:57 | him, "I will follow you **w** you go." |
| Rev | 14: 4 | They follow the Lamb **w** he goes. |

## WHETHER

| Ro | 14: 8 | So, **w** we live or die, we belong |
| 1Co | 12:13 | **w** Jews or Gentiles, slave or free— |
| Php | 4:12 | situation, **w** well fed or hungry, |
| Col | 3:17 | you do, **w** in word or deed, do it all |
| 1Jn | 4: 1 | but test the spirits to see **w** they are |

## WHILE

| Ps | 32: 6 | pray to you **w** you may be found; |
| Isa | 55: 6 | Seek the LORD **w** he may be |
| | 65:24 | **w** they are still speaking I will hear. |
| Da | 9:21 | **w** I was still in prayer, Gabriel, |
| Jn | 12:35 | Walk **w** you have the light, |
| | 16:16 | a little **w** you will see me no more, |
| Ro | 5: 8 | **W** we were still sinners, Christ died |
| 2Co | 5: 4 | For **w** we are in this tent, we groan |
| Tit | 2:13 | **w** we wait for the blessed hope— |
| 1Pe | 5:10 | after you have suffered a little **w**, |

## WHIP [WHIPS]

| Jn | 2:15 | So he made a **w** out of cords, |

## WHIPS [WHIP]

| Jos | 23:13 | **w** on your backs and thorns in your |

## WHIRLWIND [WIND]

| 2Ki | 2:11 | and Elijah went up to heaven in a **w**. |
| Ps | 77:18 | Your thunder was heard in the **w**, |
| Hos | 8: 7 | "They sow the wind and reap the **w**. |
| Na | 1: 3 | His way is in the **w** and the storm, |

## WHISPER [WHISPERED]

| 1Ki | 19:12 | And after the fire came a gentle **w**. |
| Job | 26:14 | how faint the **w** we hear of him! |
| Ps | 107:29 | He stilled the storm to a **w**; |

## WHISPERED [WHISPER]

| Mt | 10:27 | what is **w** in your ear, |

## WHITE [WHITER]

| | | |
|---|---|---|
| Isa | 1:18 | scarlet, they shall be as **w** as snow; |
| Da | 7: 9 | hair of his head was **w** like wool. |
| Zec | 1: 8 | him were red, brown and **w** horses. |
| | 6: 3 | the third **w**, and the fourth dappled— |
| Mt | 5:36 | you cannot make even one hair **w** |
| | 28: 3 | and his clothes were **w** as snow. |
| Ac | 1:10 | dressed in **w** stood beside them. |
| Rev | 1:14 | hair on his head was **w** like wool, |
| | 2:17 | of them a **w** stone with a new name |
| | 3: 4 | dressed in **w**, for they are worthy. |
| | 6: 2 | and there before me was a **w** horse! |
| | 7:13 | asked me, "These in **w** robes— |
| | 14:14 | and there before me was a **w** cloud, |
| | 19:11 | and there before me was a **w** horse, |
| | 20:11 | I saw a great **w** throne and him who |

## WHITER [WHITE]

| | | |
|---|---|---|
| Ps | 51: 7 | wash me, and I will be **w** than snow. |
| Mk | 9: 3 | **w** than anyone in the world could |

## WHITEWASH [WASH]

| | | |
|---|---|---|
| Eze | 13:10 | wall is built, they cover it with **w**, |
| | 22:28 | Her prophets **w** these deeds for them |

## WHITEWASHED [WASH]

| | | |
|---|---|---|
| Mt | 23:27 | You are like **w** tombs, which look |
| Ac | 23. 3 | "God will strike you, you **w** wall! |

## WHOEVER

| | | |
|---|---|---|
| Lev | 18: 5 | for **w** obeys them will live by them. |
| Pr | 10: 9 | **W** walks in integrity walks securely, |
| Mt | 10:32 | "**W** publicly acknowledges me I |
| | 12:50 | For **w** does the will of my Father |
| Mk | 3:29 | But **w** blasphemes against the Holy |
| | 8:35 | For **w** wants to save their life will |
| | 9:40 | for **w** is not against us is for us. |
| Jn | 3:36 | **W** believes in the Son has eternal |
| Ro | 10: 5 | "**W** does these things will live by them." |
| 1Jn | 4:16 | **W** lives in love lives in God, |

## WHOLE [WHOLEHEARTED, WHOLEHEARTEDLY, WHOLLY]

| | | |
|---|---|---|
| Ge | 11: 1 | Now the **w** world had one language |
| | 18:28 | Will you destroy the **w** city for lack |
| Ex | 12:47 | The **w** community of Israel must |
| | 19: 5 | Although the **w** earth is mine, |
| Lev | 16:17 | and the **w** community of Israel. |
| Nu | 14:21 | of the LORD fills the **w** earth, |
| | 32:13 | until the **w** generation of those who |
| Dt | 13:16 | all its plunder as a **w** burnt offering |
| | 19: 8 | gives you the **w** land he promised |
| Jos | 2: 3 | have come to spy out the **w** land." |
| 1Sa | 1:28 | For his **w** life he will be given over |
| | 17:46 | the **w** world will know that there is |
| 1Ki | 10:24 | The **w** world sought audience |
| 2Ki | 21: 8 | will keep the **w** Law that my servant |
| Ps | 48: 2 | the joy of the **w** earth, |
| | 72:19 | may the **w** earth be filled with his |
| Pr | 4:22 | them and health to one's **w** body. |
| | 8:31 | rejoicing in his **w** world |
| Isa | 1: 5 | Your **w** head is injured, your **w** heart |
| | 6: 3 | the **w** earth is full of his glory." |
| | 14:26 | the plan determined for the **w** world; |

| | | |
|---|---|---|
| La | 2:15 | of beauty, the joy of the **w** earth?" |
| Eze | 34: 6 | were scattered over the **w** earth, |
| | 37:11 | man, these bones are the **w** house |
| Da | 2:35 | mountain and filled the **w** earth. |
| Zep | 1:18 | of his jealousy the **w** earth will be |
| Zec | 14: 9 | will be king over the **w** earth. |
| Mal | 3:10 | Bring the **w** tithe |
| Mt | 5:29 | your body than for your **w** body |
| | 6:22 | your **w** body will be full of light. |
| | 16:26 | it be for you to gain the **w** world, |
| | 24:14 | in the **w** world as a testimony to all |
| Mk | 15:33 | came over the **w** land until three |
| Lk | 21:35 | who live on the face of the **w** earth. |
| Jn | 12:19 | Look how the **w** world has gone |
| | 13:10 | their **w** body is clean. |
| | 21:25 | even the **w** world would not have |
| Ac | 17:26 | that they should inhabit the **w** earth; |
| | 20:27 | proclaim to you the **w** will of God. |
| Ro | 3:19 | and the **w** world held accountable |
| | 8:22 | the **w** creation has been groaning as |
| 1Co | 4: 9 | made a spectacle to the **w** universe, |
| | 5: 6 | a little yeast leavens the **w** batch |
| | 12:17 | If the **w** body were an eye, |
| Gal | 5: 3 | he is obligated to obey the **w** law. |
| Eph | 2:21 | In him the **w** building is joined |
| | 4:10 | in order to fill the **w** universe.) |
| | 4:13 | attaining to the **w** measure |
| 1Th | 5:23 | May your **w** spirit, soul and body be |
| Tit | 1:11 | they are disrupting **w** households |
| Jas | 2:10 | For whoever keeps the **w** law |
| 1Jn | 2: 2 | but also for the sins of the **w** world. |
| | 5:19 | that the **w** world is under the control |
| Rev | 3:10 | to come on the **w** world to test those |
| | 6:12 | hair, the **w** moon turned blood red, |
| | 12: 9 | Satan, who leads the **w** world astray. |
| | 13: 3 | The **w** world was filled with wonder |

## WHOLEHEARTED* [HEART, WHOLE]

| | | |
|---|---|---|
| 2Ki | 20: 3 | and with **w** devotion and have done |
| 1Ch | 28: 9 | serve him with **w** devotion |
| | 29:19 | my son Solomon the **w** devotion |
| Isa | 38: 3 | and with **w** devotion and have done |

## WHOLEHEARTEDLY* [HEART, WHOLE]

| | | |
|---|---|---|
| Nu | 14:24 | a different spirit and follows me **w**, |
| | 32:11 | they have not followed me **w**, |
| | 32:12 | for they followed the LORD **w**.' |
| Dt | 1:36 | he followed the LORD **w**." |
| Jos | 14: 8 | followed the LORD my God **w**. |
| | 14: 9 | followed the LORD my God **w**.' |
| | 14:14 | the LORD, the God of Israel, **w**. |
| 1Ki | 8:23 | your servants who continue **w** |
| 1Ch | 29: 9 | given freely and **w** to the LORD. |
| 2Ch | 6:14 | your servants who continue **w** |
| | 15:15 | oath because they had sworn it **w**. |
| | 19: 9 | and **w** in the fear of the LORD. |
| | 25: 2 | the eyes of the LORD, but not **w**. |
| | 31:21 | he sought his God and worked **w**. |
| Eph | 6: 7 | Serve **w**, as if you were serving |

## WHOLESOME*

| | | |
|---|---|---|
| 2Pe | 3: 1 | to stimulate you to **w** thinking. |

## WHOLLY* [WHOLE]

Nu   3: 9   who are to be given **w** to him.
     8:16   who are to be given **w** to me.
1Ti  4:15   give yourself **w** to them,

## WHORE(S) (KJV) See
PROMISCUOUS, PROSTITUTE(S),
PROSTITUTION, UNFAITHFUL

## WHOREDOM (KJV) See ADULTERY,
PROSTITUTION, UNFAITHFULNESS

## WHY

Ge   4: 6   said to Cain, "**W** are you angry?
    12:19   **W** did you say, 'She is my sister,'
    32:29   replied, "**W** do you ask my name?"
Jdg 13:18   replied, "**W** do you ask my name?
Job 24: 1   "**W** does the Almighty not set times
Ps   2: 1   **W** do the nations conspire
    10: 1   **W**, LORD, do you stand far off?
    22: 1   my God, **w** have you forsaken me?
    42: 5   **W**, my soul, are you downcast?
    79:10   **W** should the nations say,
Isa  1: 5   **W** do you persist in rebellion?
    40:27   **W** do you complain, Jacob? **W** do
La   5:20   **W** do you always forget us? **W** do
Am   5:18   **W** do you long for the day
Mt   9:11   "**W** does your teacher eat with tax
    17:19   "**W** couldn't we drive it out?"
    27:46   God, **w** have you forsaken me?").
Mk  10:18   "**W** do you call me good?"
Ac   9: 4   Saul, **w** do you persecute me?"

## WICK

Isa 42: 3   a smoldering **w** he will not snuff
Mt  12:20   a smoldering **w** he will not snuff

## WICKED [OVERWICKED, WICKEDLY,
WICKEDNESS]

Ge  13:13   Now the people of Sodom were **w**
    18:23   away the righteous with the **w**?
    39: 9   could I do such a **w** thing and sin
Nu  14:35   things to this whole **w** community,
Dt  15: 9   careful not to harbor this **w** thought:
Jdg 19:22   some of the **w** men of the city
1Sa 15:18   completely destroy those **w** people,
    25:17   He is such a **w** man that no one can
2Sa 13:12   Don't do this **w** thing.
2Ki 17:11   They did **w** things that aroused
2Ch  7:14   my face and turn from their **w** ways,
    19: 2   "Should you help the **w** and love
Ne  13:17   them, "What is this **w** thing you are
Job 15:20   All their days the **w** suffer torment,
    20:29   Such is the fate God allots the **w**,
    27: 4   my lips will not say anything **w**,
    27:13   is the fate God allots to the **w**,
Ps   1: 1   who do not walk in step with the **w**
     1: 5   Therefore the **w** will not stand
     7: 9   to an end the violence of the **w**
    10:13   Why do the **w** revile God?
    11: 6   On the **w** he will rain fiery coals
    26: 5   and refuse to sit with the **w**.
    32:10   Many are the woes of the **w**,
    36: 1   concerning the sinfulness of the **w**:

Ps  37:13   but the Lord laughs at the **w**, for he
    37:40   he delivers them from the **w**
    49: 5   when **w** deceivers surround me—
    50:16   But to the **w**, God says:
    58: 3   Even from birth the **w** go astray;
    73: 3   when I saw the prosperity of the **w**.
    82: 2   unjust and show partiality to the **w**?
   112:10   The **w** will see and be vexed,
   119:61   Though the **w** bind me with ropes,
  119:155   Salvation is far from the **w**, for they
   140: 8   Do not grant the **w** their desires,
   141:10   Let the **w** fall into their own nets,
   146: 9   but he frustrates the ways of the **w**.
Pr   2:12   save you from the ways of **w** men,
     4:14   Do not set foot on the path of the **w**
     5:22   evil deeds of the **w** ensnare them;
     6:18   a heart that devises **w** schemes,
     9: 7   rebukes the **w** incurs abuse.
    10:20   the heart of the **w** is of little value.
    10:28   the hopes of the **w** come to nothing.
    11: 5   but the **w** are brought down by their
    11:10   when the **w** perish, there are shouts
    11:21   The **w** will not go unpunished,
    12: 5   but the advice of the **w** is deceitful.
    12:10   the kindest acts of the **w** are cruel.
    10:23   Fools find pleasure in **w** schemes,
    14:19   the **w** at the gates of the righteous.
    15: 3   keeping watch on the **w**
    15:26   detests the thoughts of the **w**,
    21:10   The **w** crave evil;
    21:29   The **w** put up a bold front,
    24: 1   Do not envy the **w**, do not desire
    28: 1   The **w** flee though no one pursues,
    28: 4   forsake instruction praise the **w**,
    29: 7   but the **w** have no such concern.
    29:16   When the **w** thrive, so does sin,
    29:27   the **w** detest the upright.
Ecc  7:15   and the **w** living long in their
     8:14   who get what the **w** deserve,
Isa 11: 4   breath of his lips he will slay the **w**.
    13:11   for its evil, the **w** for their sins.
    26:10   But when grace is shown to the **w**,
    48:22   says the LORD, "for the **w**."
    53: 9   He was assigned a grave with the **w**,
    55: 7   Let the **w** forsake their ways
    57:20   But the **w** are like the tossing sea,
Jer 12: 1   Why does the way of the **w** prosper?
    35:15   of you must turn from your **w** ways
Eze  3:18   those **w** people will die for their
    13:22   because you encouraged the **w** not
    14: 7   put a **w** stumbling block before their
    18:21   if the **w** turn away from all the sins
    18:23   any pleasure in the death of the **w**?
    21:25   profane and **w** prince of Israel,
    33: 8   those **w** people will die for their
    33:11   no pleasure in the death of the **w**,
    33:19   And if the **w** turn away from their
Da  12:10   but the **w** will continue to be **w**.
Na   1:15   No more will the **w** invade you;
Mt  12:39   "A **w** and adulterous generation
    12:45   other spirits more **w** than itself,
Lk   6:35   he is kind to the ungrateful and **w**.
Ac   2:23   with the help of **w** men, put him
1Co  5:13   "Expel the **w** person from among
2Jn  1:11   them shares in their **w** work.
Rev  2: 2   that you cannot tolerate **w** people,

## WICKEDLY [WICKED]

2Ch  6:37  we have done wrong and acted **w**';
Ne   1: 7  We have acted very **w** toward you.

## WICKEDNESS [WICKED]

Ge   6: 5  The LORD saw how great the **w**
Ex  34: 7  and forgiving **w**, rebellion and sin.
Lev 16:21  and confess over it all the **w**
    19:29  to prostitution and be filled with **w**.
Dt   9: 4  on account of the **w** of these nations
Ps  45: 7  You love righteousness and hate **w**;
    92:15  Rock, and there is no **w** in him."
Pr  11: 5  are brought down by their own **w**.
    13: 6  but **w** overthrows the sinner.
Ecc  3:16  in the place of justice—**w** was there.
Jer  3: 2  land with your prostitution and **w**,
     8: 6  None of them repent of their **w**,
    14:20  We acknowledge our **w**, LORD,
    31:34  "For I will forgive their **w** and will
Eze 18:20  the **w** of the wicked will be charged
    28:15  you were created till **w** was found
    33:19  the wicked turn away from their **w**
Da   4:27  and your **w** by being kind
     9:24  end to sin, to atone for **w**, to bring
Hos  9: 9  God will remember their **w**
Jnh  1: 2  it, because its **w** has come up before
Mt  24:12  Because of the increase of **w**,
Lk  11:39  inside you are full of greed and **w**.
Ac   1:18  (With the reward he got for his **w**,
Ro   1:18  **w** of human beings who suppress the
            truth by their **w**,
1Co  5: 8  bread leavened with malice and **w**,
2Co  6:14  and **w** have in common?
2Ti  2:19  the Lord must turn away from **w**."
Tit  2:14  for us to redeem us from all **w**
Heb  1: 9  loved righteousness and hated **w**;
     8:12  For I will forgive their **w** and will
2Pe  2:15  of Bezer, who loved the wages of **w**.

## WIDE

Ps  81:10  Open **w** your mouth and I will fill it.
Isa 54: 2  stretch your tent curtains **w**, do not
Mt   7:13  For **w** is the gate and broad is
    23: 5  They make their phylacteries **w**
2Co  6:13  open **w** your hearts also.
Eph  3:18  to grasp how **w** and long and high

## WIDOW [WIDOW'S, WIDOWHOOD, WIDOWS, WIDOWS']

Ex  22:22  "Do not take advantage of a **w**
Dt  10:18  cause of the fatherless and the **w**,
    25: 9  his brother's **w** shall go up to him
Ru   4: 5  the dead man's **w**, in order
Ps 146: 9  sustains the fatherless and the **w**,
Isa  1:17  fatherless, plead the case of the **w**.
La   1: 1  How like a **w** is she, who once was
Mk  12:19  the man must marry the **w** and raise
Lk   2:37  had been a **w** for eighty-four years.
    18: 3  there was a **w** in that town who kept
    21: 3  "this poor **w** has put in more than
1Ti  5: 4  if a **w** has children or grandchildren,
Rev 18: 7  I am not a **w**; I will never mourn.'

## WIDOW'S [WIDOW]

Ge  38:14  she took off her **w** clothes,
Job 29:13  I made the **w** heart sing.
Pr  15:25  but he sets the **w** boundary stones

## WIDOWHOOD [WIDOW]

Isa 54: 4  no more the reproach of your **w**.

## WIDOWS [WIDOW]

Dt  14:29  the **w** who live in your towns may
Ps  68: 5  a defender of **w**, is God in his holy
Mal  3: 5  wages, who oppress the **w**
Lk   4:25  you that there were many **w** in Israel
Ac   6: 1  Jews because their **w** were being
1Co  7: 8  to the unmarried and the **w** I say:
1Ti  5: 3  to those **w** who are really in need.
Jas  1:27  after orphans and **w** in their distress

## WIDOWS' [WIDOW]

Mk  12:40  They devour **w**' houses

## WIFE [WIVES, WIVES']

Ge   2:24  and mother and be united to his **w**,
     3:20  Adam named his **w** Eve,
    12:18  didn't you tell me she was your **w**?
    19:26  But Lot's **w** looked back, and she
    20:11  they will kill me because of my **w**.'
    24:67  So she became his **w**, and he loved
Ex  20:17  shall not covet your neighbor's **w**,
Lev 18: 8  relations with your father's **w**;
    20:10  adultery with another man's **w**—
Nu   5:12  'If a man's **w** goes astray and is
Dt   5:21  shall not covet your neighbor's **w**.
    21:15  is the son of the **w** he does not love,
    24: 5  happiness to the **w** he has married.
Ru   4:13  took Ruth and she became his **w**.
2Sa 12:10  took the **w** of Uriah the Hittite to be
Ps 128: 3  Your **w** will be like a fruitful vine
Pr   5:18  you rejoice in the **w** of your youth.
     6:24  you from your neighbor's **w**,
     6:26  another man's **w** preys on your very life
    12: 4  A **w** of noble character is her
    18:22  He who finds a **w** finds what is good
    19:13  a quarrelsome **w** is like the constant
    19:14  but a prudent **w** is from the LORD.
    31:10  A **w** of noble character who can
Ecc  9: 9  Enjoy life with your **w**, whom you
Hos  1: 2  for like an adulterous **w** this land is
Mal  2:14  you and the **w** of your youth.
Mt   1:20  afraid to take Mary home as your **w**,
     5:32  you that anyone who divorces his **w**,
    19: 3  for a man to divorce his **w** for any
Mk   6:18  for you to have your brother's **w**."
    10: 2  lawful for a man to divorce his **w**?"
    12:23  At the resurrection whose **w** will she
Lk  17:32  Remember Lot's **w**!
    18:29  "no one who has left home or **w**
1Co  7: 2  sexual relations with his own **w**,
     7:11  a husband must not divorce his **w**.
     7:33  how he can please his **w**—
Eph  5:23  head of the **w** as Christ is the head
     5:28  He who loves his **w** loves himself.
     5:33  must love his **w** as he loves himself,
     5:33  and the **w** must respect her husband.
1Ti  3: 2  faithful to his **w**, temperate,

1Ti 3:12 A deacon must be faithful to his **w**
Tit 1: 6 faithful to his **w**, a man whose
Rev 21: 9 you the bride, the **w** of the Lamb."

## WILD [WILDERNESS]

Ge 1:25 God made the **w** animals according
8: 1 all the **w** animals and the livestock
Ex 32:25 saw that the people were running **w**
Lev 26:22 I will send **w** animals against you,
Mk 1: 6 and he ate locusts and **w** honey.
1:13 He was with the **w** animals,
Lk 15:13 squandered his wealth in **w** living.
Ro 11:17 and you, though a **w** olive shoot,
1Co 15:32 If I fought **w** beasts in Ephesus
Tit 1: 6 not open to the charge of being **w**
1Pe 4: 4 them in their reckless, **w** living,
Jude 1:13 They are **w** waves of the sea,

## WILDERNESS [WILD]

Ex 3: 1 far side of the **w** and came to Horeb,
4:27 "Go into the **w** to meet Moses."
16:32 the **w** when I brought you out of Egypt.'
Nu 14:29 In this **w** your bodies will fall—
32:13 wander in the **w** forty years,
Dt 8:16 He gave you manna to eat in the **w**,
29: 5 that I led you through the **w**,
Ne 9:21 forty years you sustained them in the **w**;
Ps 68: 7 you marched through the **w**,
78:15 He split the rocks in the **w**
78:19 Can God really spread a table in the **w**?
78:52 led them like sheep through the **w**.
106:14 in the **w** they put God to the test.
Isa 40: 3 "In the **w** prepare the way
Eze 20:13 Israel rebelled against me in the **w**.
Hos 2:14 I will lead her into the **w** and speak
13: 5 I cared for you in the **w**,
Am 2:10 led you forty years in the **w**
Mk 1: 3 "a voice of one calling in the **w**,
1:13 and he was in the **w** forty days,
Jn 6:31 ate the manna in the **w**;'
Heb 3: 8 the time of testing in the **w**,
Rev 12: 6 woman fled into the **w** to a place
17: 3 carried me away in the Spirit into a **w**.

## WILL [FREEWILL, WILLFUL, WILLFULLY, WILLING, WILLINGLY, WILLINGNESS]

Ex 18:15 people come to me to seek God's **w**.
Dt 10:10 It was not his **w** to destroy you.
33:21 out the LORD's righteous **w**,
1Sa 2:25 it was the LORD's **w** to put them
2Sa 7:21 your word and according to your **w**,
1Ch 13: 2 if it is the **w** of the LORD our God,
Ezr 7:18 accordance with the **w** of your God.
10:11 of your ancestors, and do his **w**.
Ps 40: 8 I desire to do your **w**, my God;
103:21 you his servants who do his **w**.
143:10 Teach me to do your **w**, for you are
Isa 53:10 Yet it was the LORD's **w** to crush
Eze 12:25 But I the LORD **w** speak what I **w**,
Mt 6:10 kingdom come, your **w** be done,
7:21 but only those who do the **w** of my
10:29 Yet not one of them **w** fall
26:39 Yet not as I **w**, but as you **w**."
Mk 3:35 Whoever does God's **w** is my
14:36 Yet not what I **w**, but what you **w**."

Lk 22:42 yet not my **w**, but yours be done."
23:25 and surrendered Jesus to their **w**.
Jn 1:13 human decision or a husband's **w**,
4:34 "is to do the **w** of him who sent me
6:38 but to do the **w** of him who sent me.
7:17 chooses to do the **w** of God **w** find
9:31 to the godly person who does his **w**.
10:28 no one **w** snatch them out of my hand.
Ac 4:28 **w** had decided beforehand should
20:27 to you the whole **w** of God.
21:14 and said, "The Lord's **w** be done."
Ro 2:18 if you know his **w** and approve
9:19 For who is able to resist his **w**?"
12: 2 Then you **w** be able to test and approve
what God's **w** is—
1Co 7:37 but has control over his own **w**,
Eph 1: 5 with his pleasure and **w**—
1: 9 us the mystery of his **w** according
1:11 with the purpose of his **w**,
5:17 but understand what the Lord's **w** is.
6: 6 doing the **w** of God from your heart.
Php 2:13 for it is God who works in you to **w**
Col 1: 9 of his **w** through all the wisdom
4:12 may stand firm in all the **w** of God,
1Th 4: 3 It is God's **w** that you should be
5: 8 for this is God's **w** for you in Christ
2Ti 2:26 has taken them captive to do his **w**.
Heb 2: 4 Spirit distributed according to his **w**.
10: 7 I have come to do your **w**,
13:21 everything good for doing his **w**,
Jas 4:15 "If it is the Lord's **w**, we **w** live
1Pe 2:15 For it is God's **w** that by doing good
3:17 if it is God's **w**, to suffer for doing
4: 2 desires, but rather for the **w** of God.
4:19 God's **w** should commit themselves
2Pe 1:21 never had its origin in the human **w**,
1Jn 2:17 whoever does the **w** of God lives
5:14 we ask anything according to his **w**,
Rev 2:26 victorious and do my **w** to the end,

## WILLFUL [WILL]

Ps 19:13 Keep your servant also from **w** sins;

## WILLFULLY* [WILL]

Ps 78:18 They **w** put God to the test

## WILLING [WILL]

Ex 10:27 and he was not **w** to let them go.
35: 5 Everyone who is **w** is to bring
2Ki 8:19 the LORD was not **w** to destroy
24: 4 the LORD was not **w** to forgive.
1Ch 28: 9 devotion and with a **w** mind,
29: 5 who among you is **w** to consecrate
Ps 51:12 salvation and grant me a **w** spirit,
Da 3:28 were **w** to give up their lives rather
Mt 8: 3 "I am **w**," he said.
18:14 Father in heaven is not **w** that any
23: 4 they themselves are not **w** to lift
23:37 her wings, and you were not **w**.
26:41 The spirit is **w**, but the flesh is
Lk 22:42 if you are **w**, take this cup from me;
Ro 12:16 be **w** to associate with people of low
1Ti 6:18 and to be generous and **w** to share.
1Pe 5: 2 must, but because you are **w**, as God

## WILLINGLY [WILL]

Jdg   5: 2  the people **w** offer themselves—
1Ch 29:17  joy how **w** your people who are here
La    3:33  For he does not **w** bring affliction

## WILLINGNESS* [WILL]

2Co   8:11  so that your eager **w** to do it may be
      8:12  For if the **w** is there, the gift is

## WIN [WINNING, WINS, WON]

Pr    3: 4  you will **w** favor and a good name
     11:30  those who **w** souls are wise.
Mt   23:15  land and sea to **w** a single convert,
Lk   21:19  Stand firm, and you will **w** life.
1Co   9:19  everyone, to **w** as many as possible.
Gal   1:10  I now trying to **w** human approval,
Php   3:14  on toward the goal to **w** the prize
1Th   4:12  your daily life may **w** the respect

## WIND [WHIRLWIND, WINDS]

1Ki  19:11  but the LORD was not in the **w**.
Ps    1: 4  like chaff that the **w** blows away.
     18:10  he soared on the wings of the **w**.
    104: 3  and rides on the wings of the **w**.
Pr   11:29  on their families will inherit only **w**,
     30: 4  hands have gathered up the **w**?
Ecc   1:14  meaningless, a chasing after the **w**.
      8: 8  As no one has power over the **w**
Eze   5: 2  And scatter a third to the **w**.
Hos   8: 7  "They sow the **w** and reap
Jnh   1: 4  the LORD sent a great **w**
      4: 8  God provided a scorching east **w**,
Mk    4:41  Even the **w** and the waves obey
Jn    3: 8  The **w** blows wherever it pleases.
Ac    2: 2  of a violent **w** came from heaven
Eph   4:14  there by every **w** of teaching
Jas   1: 6  the sea, blown and tossed by the **w**.

## WINDOW

Jos   2:21  she tied the scarlet cord in the **w**.
1Sa  19:12  Michal let David down through a **w**,
Ac   20: 9  in a **w** was a young man named
2Co  11:33  in a basket from a **w** in the wall

## WINDS [WIND]

Ps   104: 4  He makes **w** his messengers,
Mt    7:25  and the **w** blew and beat against
      8:27  Even the **w** and the waves obey
     24:31  will gather his elect from the four **w**,

## WINE

Ge    9:21  When he drank some of its **w**,
     19:32  Let's get our father to drink **w**
Nu    6: 3  they must abstain from **w** and other
Dt    7:13  your grain, new **w** and olive oil—
Jdg  13: 4  Now see to it that you drink no **w**
1Sa   1:15  I have not been drinking **w** or beer;
Ne   13:12  grain, new **w** and olive oil
Ps    4: 7  when their grain and new **w** abound.
     75: 8  is a cup full of foaming **w** mixed
    104:15  **w** that gladdens human hearts,
Pr    3:10  vats will brim over with new **w**.
      9: 2  prepared her meat and mixed her **w**;
     20: 1  **W** is a mocker and beer a brawler;
     23:20  join those who drink too much **w**

Pr   23:31  Do not gaze at **w** when it is red,
     31: 4  it is not for kings to drink **w**,
     31: 6  **w** for those who are in anguish!
Ecc   2: 3  I tried cheering myself with **w**,
      9: 7  drink your **w** with a joyful heart,
     10:19  for laughter, **w** makes life merry,
SS    1: 2  your love is more delightful than **w**.
      7: 9  May the **w** go straight to my
Isa   5:22  those who are heroes at drinking **w**
     28: 7  stagger from **w** and reel from beer:
     51:21  one, made drunk, but not with **w**.
     55: 1  buy **w** and milk without money
Da    1: 8  himself with the royal food and **w**,
Joel  2:24  the vats will overflow with new **w**
      3:18  day the mountains will drip new **w**,
Am    2:12  you made the Nazirites drink **w**
Mic   2:11  will prophesy for you plenty of **w**
Mt    9:17  No, they pour new **w** into new
     27:34  There they offered Jesus **w** to drink,
Lk   23:36  They offered him **w** vinegar
Jn    2: 3  When the **w** was gone,
      2: 9  water that had been turned into **w**.
Ac    2:13  said, "They have had too much **w**."
Ro   14:21  drink **w** or to do anything else
Eph   5:18  Do not get drunk on **w**, which leads
1Ti   3: 8  not indulging in much **w**, and not
      5:23  and use a little **w** because of your
Rev  14: 8  the nations drink the maddening **w**
     14:10  will drink of the **w** of God's fury,
     16:19  the cup filled with the **w** of the fury
     18: 3  have drunk the maddening **w** of her

## WINEPRESS

Dt   15:14  your threshing floor and your **w**.
Isa  63: 2  like those of one treading the **w**?
La    1:15  his **w** the Lord has trampled Virgin
Rev  14:19  into the great **w** of God's wrath.
     19:15  He treads the **w** of the fury

## WINESKINS

Job  32:19  wine, like new **w** ready to burst.
Mt    9:17  do people pour new wine into old **w**.

## WING [WINGED, WINGS]

2Ch   3:11  touched the **w** of the other cherub.

## WINGED [WING]

Ge    1:21  every **w** bird according to its kind.

## WINGS [WING]

Ex   19: 4  how I carried you on eagles' **w**
     37: 9  had their **w** spread upward,
Ru    2:12  under whose **w** you have come
1Ki   8: 7  cherubim spread their **w** over
Ps   17: 8  hide me in the shadow of your **w**
     91: 4  under his **w** you will find refuge;
Isa   2: 6  each with six **w**
     40:31  They will soar on **w** like eagles;
Eze   1: 6  of them had four faces and four **w**.
     10:21  Each had four faces and four **w**,
Zec   5: 9  **w**! They had **w** like those of a stork,
Lk   13:34  hen gathers her chicks under her **w**,
Rev   4: 8  the four living creatures had six **w**

## WINNING [WIN]
Ex   17:11  the Israelites were **w**,

## WINNOW [WINNOWING, WINNOWS]
Isa  41:16  You will **w** them, the wind will pick
Jer  15: 7  I will **w** them with a winnowing

## WINNOWING [WINNOW]
Mt   3:12  His **w** fork is in his hand, and he

## WINNOWS* [WINNOW]
Pr   20: 8  he **w** out all evil with his eyes.
     20:26  A wise king **w** out the wicked;

## WINS* [WIN]
Pr   13:15  Good judgment **w** favor,

## WINTER
Ge   8:22  summer and **w**, day and night will
Ps   74:17  you made both summer and **w**.
Mk   13:18  that this will not take place in **w**,

## WIPE [WIPED]
Ge   7: 4  I will **w** from the face of the earth
Ex   32:12  to **w** them off the face of the earth'?
1Ki  21:21  I will **w** out your descendants and cut
Isa  14:22  "I will **w** out Babylon's name and
     25: 8  Sovereign LORD will **w** away
Rev  7:17  God will **w** away every tear
     21: 4  'He will **w** every tear from their

## WIPED [WIPE]
Ge   7:23  on the face of the earth was **w** out;
Ps   119:87  They almost **w** me from the earth,
Lk   7:38  Then she **w** them with her hair,
Ac   3:19  so that your sins may be **w** out,

## WISDOM [WISE]
Ge   3: 6  and also desirable for gaining **w**,
Ex   28: 3  to whom I have given **w** in such
Dt   4: 6  for this will show your **w**
1Ki  4:29  God gave Solomon **w** and very great
     10: 6  achievements and your **w** is true.
2Ch  1:10  Give me **w** and knowledge, that I
Job  9: 4  His **w** is profound, his power is vast.
     11: 6  of **w**, for true **w** has two sides.
     12:13  "To God belong **w** and power;
     28:12  But where can **w** be found?
     28:28  that is **w**, and to shun evil is
Ps   37:30  The mouths of the righteous utter **w**,
     51: 6  you taught me **w** in that secret place.
     111:10  the LORD is the beginning of **w**;
Pr   1: 7  but fools despise **w** and instruction.
     1:20  Out in the open **w** calls aloud,
     2: 6  For the LORD gives **w**;
     3:13  Blessed are those who find **w**,
     4: 5  Get **w**, get understanding;
     4: 7  The beginning of **w** is this: Get **w**.
     8:11  for **w** is more precious than rubies,
     9: 1  **W** has built her house; she has set
     9:10  the LORD is the beginning of **w**,
     11: 2  but with humility comes **w**.
     13:10  **w** is found in those who take advice.

Pr   19: 8  Those who get **w** love their own
     23:23  **w**, instruction and insight as well.
     29: 3  A man who loves **w** brings joy
     29:15  A rod and a reprimand impart **w**,
     31:26  She speaks with **w**, and faithful
Ecc  1:13  explore by **w** all that is done under
     2: 3  my mind still guiding me with **w**.
     2:13  I saw that **w** is better than folly,
     7:12  **W** is a shelter as money is a shelter,
     9:18  **W** is better than weapons of war,
     10: 1  so a little folly outweighs **w**
Isa  11: 2  rest on him—the Spirit of **w**
     28:29  wonderful, whose **w** is magnificent.
Jer  9:23  "Let not the wise boast of their **w**
     10:12  he founded the world by his **w**
Eze  28:12  full of **w** and perfect in beauty.
Da   2:14  Daniel spoke to him with **w**
     5:14  intelligence and outstanding **w**.
Mic  6: 9  and to fear your name is **w**—
Mt   11:19  **w** is proved right by her actions."
     12:42  the earth to listen to Solomon's **w**,
     13:54  "Where did this man get this **w**
Lk   2:40  he was filled with **w**, and the grace
     2:52  he increased in **w** and in favor
Ac   6: 3  known to be full of the Spirit and **w**.
Ro   11:33  the depth of the riches of the **w**
1Co  1:17  not with **w** and eloquence,
     1:19  "I will destroy the **w** of the wise;
     1:20  Has not God made foolish the **w**
     1:30  has become for us **w** from God—
     2: 7  we declare God's **w**, a mystery
     3:19  the **w** of this world is foolishness
     12: 8  through the Spirit a message of **w**,
Eph  1:17  may give you the Spirit of **w**
Col  1: 9  of his will through all the **w**
     1:28  and teaching everyone with all **w**,
     2: 3  are hidden all the treasures of **w**
     2:23  indeed have an appearance of **w**,
Jas  1: 5  If any of you lacks **w**, you should
     3:13  in the humility that comes from **w**.
     3:17  But the **w** that comes from heaven is
Rev  5:12  and wealth and **w** and strength
     7:12  Praise and glory and **w** and thanks
     13:18  This calls for **w**. Let those who have
     17: 9  "This calls for a mind with **w**.

## WISDOM'S [WISE]
Pr   15:33  **W** instruction is to fear the LORD,

## WISE [OVERWISE, WISDOM, WISDOM'S, WISELY, WISER]
Ge   41:39  no one so discerning and **w** as you.
Ex   7:11  Pharaoh then summoned his men
Dt   4: 6  "Surely this great nation is a **w**
     16:19  for a bribe blinds the eyes of the **w**
1Ki  3:12  I will give you a **w** and discerning
Job  5:13  He catches the **w** in their craftiness,
     32: 9  It is not only the old who are **w**,
Ps   2:10  Therefore, you kings, be **w**;
     19: 7  trustworthy, making **w** the simple.
     94: 8  fools, when will you become **w**?
     107:43  Let all who are **w** heed these things
Pr   3: 7  Do not be **w** in your own eyes;
     6: 6  consider its ways and be **w**!
     9: 9  Instruct the **w** and they will be wiser
     10: 1  **W** children bring joy to their father,

Pr  10:14  The **w** store up knowledge,
    11:30  life, and those who win souls are **w**.
    13: 1  A **w** child heeds a parent's
    13:20  Walk with the **w** and become **w**,
    14:16  The **w** fear the LORD
    16:23  of the **w** make their mouths prudent,
    17:28  Even fools are thought **w** if they
    23:15  if your heart is **w**, then my heart will
    24: 5  The **w** prevail through great power,
    26: 5  or they will be **w** in their own eyes.
    29.11  but the **w** bring calm in the end.
Ecc  2:14  The **w** have eyes in their heads,
     7:19  Wisdom makes one **w** person more
     9:17  The quiet words of the **w** are more
    12:11  The words of the **w** are like goads,
Isa  29:14  the wisdom of the **w** will perish,
Jer   8: 9  The **w** will be put to shame;
      9:23  "Let not the **w** boast of their
Eze  28: 6  " 'Because you think you are **w**,
Da    2:21  He gives wisdom to the **w**
     11:35  Some of the **w** will stumble,
     12: 3  Those who are **w** will shine like
Mt   11:25  have hidden these things from the **w**
     25: 2  them were foolish and five were **w**.
Lk   12:42  then is the faithful and **w** manager,
Ro    1:22  Although they claimed to be **w**,
     16:27  to the only **w** God be glory forever
1Co   1:19  will destroy the wisdom of the **w**;
      1:26  of you were **w** by human standards;
      3:10  I laid a foundation as a **w** builder,
      3:18  "fools" so that you may become **w**.
      3:19  "He catches the **w** in their
Eph   5:15  not as unwise but as **w**,
Col   4: 5  Be **w** in the way you act toward
2Ti   3:15  to make you **w** for salvation through
Jas   3:13  Who is **w** and understanding among

## WISELY [WISE]

Isa  52:13  See, my servant will act **w**;
Jer  23: 5  a King who will reign **w** and do

## WISER [WISE]

1Ki   4:31  He was **w** than anyone else,
Pr    9: 9  the wise and they will be **w** still;
     26:16  Sluggards are **w** in their own eyes
1Co   1:25  of God is **w** than human wisdom,

## WISH [WISHED, WISHES]

Job  11: 5  Oh, how I **w** that God would speak,
Jn   15: 7  ask whatever you **w**, and it will be
Ro    9: 3  I could **w** that I myself were cursed
Gal   4: 9  Do you **w** to be enslaved by them all
Rev   3:15  I **w** you were either one or the other!
     22:17  all who **w** take the free gift

## WISHED [WISH]

Mt   17:12  have done to him everything they **w**.

## WISHES [WISH]

Da    4:25  earth and gives them to anyone he **w**.

## WITCH  (KJV) See SORCERESS, SORCERY

## WITCHCRAFT* [BEWITCHED]

Dt   18:10  interprets omens, engages in **w**,
2Ki   9:22  **w** of your mother Jezebel abound?"
2Ch  33: 6  practiced divination and **w**,
Mic   5:12  I will destroy your **w** and you will
Na    3: 4  prostitution and peoples by her **w**.
Gal   5:20  idolatry and **w**;

## WITH

### I AM WITH YOU  Ge 26:24; 28:15; Jos 3:7;
    1Sa 14:7; 2Ki 10:15; Isa 41:10; 43:5; Jer 1:8, 19;
    15:20; 30:11; 42:11; 46:28; Hag 1:13; 2:4; Mt
    28:20; Jn 7:33; Ac 18:10; 1Co 5:3, 4; Gal 4:18

### I WILL BE WITH YOU  Ge 26:3; 31:3; Ex
    3:12; Jos 1:5; Jdg 6:16; 1Ki 11:38; Isa 43:2; Jn
    13:33

## WITHER [WITHERED, WITHERS]

Ps    1: 3  season and whose leaf does not **w**—
     37:19  In times of disaster they will not **w**;

## WITHERED [WITHER]

Ge   41:23  **w** and thin and scorched by the east
Zec  11:17  May his arm be completely **w**,
Mt   13: 6  they **w** because they had no root.
     21:19  Immediately the tree **w**.

## WITHERS [WITHER]

Ps   129: 6  roof, which **w** before it can grow;
Isa   40: 7  The grass **w** and the flowers fall,
Jn    15: 6  a branch that is thrown away and **w**;
1Pe    1:24  the grass **w** and the flowers fall,

## WITHHELD [WITHHOLD]

Ge   22:12  because you have not **w** from me
Ps   66:20  my prayer or **w** his love from me!
     77: 9  he in anger **w** his compassion?"
Hag   1:10  of you the heavens have **w** their dew

## WITHHOLD [WITHHELD, WITHHOLDS]

Ne    9:20  You did not **w** your manna
Ps   40:11  Do not **w** your mercy from me,
     84:11  no good thing does he **w** from those
Pr   23:13  Do not **w** discipline from children;

## WITHHOLDS [WITHHOLD]

Dt   27:19  "Cursed is anyone who **w** justice
Eze  18:17  He **w** his hand from mistreating

## WITHIN

Ex    3: 2  him in flames of fire from **w** a bush.
Ps   40: 8  your law is **w** my heart."
     42: 5  Why so disturbed **w** me?
     46: 5  God is **w** her, she will not fall;
     51:10  and renew a steadfast spirit **w** me.
    122: 7  May there be peace **w** your walls
    142: 3  When my spirit grows faint **w** me,
Pr    2: 1  and store up my commands **w** you,

Pr 4:21 your sight, keep them **w** your heart;
Zep 3: 5 The LORD **w** her is righteous;
   3:12 But I will leave **w** you the meek
Zec 2: 5 LORD, 'and I will be its glory **w**.'
Mt 6:23 If then the light **w** you is darkness,
Mk 7:21 For from **w**, out of your hearts,
Jn 7:38 water will flow from **w** them."
1Co 2:11 except that person's own spirit **w**?
Rev 11:19 **w** his temple was seen the ark of his

## WITHOUT

Ex 12:15 you are to eat bread made **w** yeast.
  34:28 days and forty nights **w** eating bread
Lev 1: 3 you are to offer a male **w** defect.
Nu 27:17 not be like sheep **w** a shepherd."
2Ch 15: 3 long time Israel was **w** the true God,
  18:16 on the hills like sheep **w** a shepherd,
Ps 69: 4 who hate me **w** reason outnumber
Pr 6:27 his lap **w** his clothes being burned?
  19: 2 Desire **w** knowledge is not good—
Isa 13:14 gazelle, like sheep **w** a shepherd,
  52: 3 **w** money you will be redeemed."
  55: 1 buy wine and milk **w** money and **w**
Mt 9:36 helpless, like sheep **w** a shepherd.
  23:23 the latter, **w** neglecting the former.
Jn 3: 3 kingdom of God **w** being born again."
  3:34 for God gives the Spirit **w** limit.
  8: 7 *who is **w** sin be the first to throw*
Eph 2:12 **w** hope and **w** God in the world.
Php 2:14 Do everything **w** grumbling
Col 1:22 his sight, **w** blemish and free
1Th 2: 1 our visit to you was not **w** results.
Heb 9:22 **w** the shedding of blood there is no
Jas 2:18 Show me your faith **w** deeds, and I
1Pe 1:19 Christ, a lamb **w** blemish or defect.
Rev 21: 6 the thirsty I will give water **w** cost

## WITHSTAND

Jos 10: 8 one of them will be able to **w** you."
  23: 9 day no one has been able to **w** you.
Na 1: 6 Who can **w** his indignation?

## WITNESS [EYEWITNESSES, WITNESSES]

Ge 31:44 and let it serve as a **w** between us."
Nu 35:30 on the testimony of only one **w**.
Dt 19:15 One **w** is not enough to convict
Jos 22:27 it is to be a **w** between us and you
Jdg 11:10 replied, "The LORD is our **w**;
1Sa 12: 5 "The LORD is **w** against you,
  20:42 'The LORD is **w** between you
Job 16:19 Even now my **w** is in heaven;
Pr 12:17 An honest **w** tells the truth, but a false
    **w** tells lies.
  14:25 A truthful **w** saves lives,
  19: 9 A false **w** will not go unpunished,
  21:28 Those who give false **w** will perish,
Jn 1: 8 he came only as a **w** to the light.
Ro 2:15 their consciences also bearing **w**,
1Pe 5: 1 and a **w** of Christ's sufferings who
Rev 1: 5 who is the faithful **w**, the firstborn
  2:13 my faithful **w**, who was put to death
  3:14 the faithful and true **w**, the ruler

## WITNESSES [WITNESS]

Dt 17: 6 or three **w** a person is to be put

Dt 19:15 by the testimony of two or three **w**.
  30:19 and the earth as **w** against you that I
Jos 24:22 "You are **w** against yourselves
Ru 4:10 Today you are **w**!'"
Ps 27:12 foes, for false **w** rise up against me,
Isa 43:10 "You are my **w**,"
Mt 18:16 by the testimony of two or three **w**.'
  26:60 though many false **w** came forward.
Mk 14:63 "Why do we need any more **w**?"
Ac 1: 8 and you will be my **w** in Jerusalem,
  2:32 to life, and we are all **w** of the fact.
  6:13 They produced false **w**,
Heb 12: 1 by such a great cloud of **w**, let us
Rev 11: 3 And I will appoint my two **w**,

## WIVES [WIFE]

Ge 6:18 wife and your sons' **w** with you.
Dt 17:17 He must not take many **w**, or his
  21:15 If someone has two **w**, and he loves
1Ki 11: 3 and his **w** led him astray.
1Ch 14: 3 In Jerusalem David took more **w**
Ezr 10:11 you and from your foreign **w**."
Mt 8:14 divorce your **w** because your hearts
Eph 5:22 **W**, submit yourselves to your own
  5:25 love your **w**, just as Christ loved
Col 3:18 **W**, submit yourselves to your
1Pe 3: 1 **W**, in the same way submit
  3: 1 words by the behavior of their **w**,
  3: 7 considerate as you live with your **w**,

## WIVES'* [WIFE]

1Ti 4: 7 with godless myths and old **w**' tales;

## WIZARD (KJV) See SPIRITIST

## WOE [WOES]

Job 10:15 If I am guilty—**w** to me! Even if I
Pr 23:29 Who has **w**? Who has sorrow?
Isa 3:11 **W** to the wicked! Disaster is
  5: 8 **W** to you who add house to house
  5:20 **W** to those who call evil good
  6: 5 "**W** to me!" I cried. "I am ruined!
    in the fields.
Jer 13:27 in the fields. **W** to you, Jerusalem!
  23: 1 "**W** to the shepherds who are
La 5:16 **W** to us, for we have sinned!
Hos 9:12 **W** to them when I turn away
Am 5:18 **W** to you who long for the day
Na 3: 1 **W** to the city of blood, full of lies,
Hab 2:19 **W** to him who says to wood,
Zec 11:17 "**W** to the worthless shepherd,
Mt 18: 7 **W** to the world because of the things
  18: 7 **w** to the person through whom they
  23:13 "**W** to you, teachers of the law
  23:16 "**W** to you, blind guides!
Mk 14:21 **w** to that man who betrays the Son
Lk 6:24 "But **w** to you who are rich, for you
  11:42 "**W** to you Pharisees, because you
  11:52 "**W** to you experts in the law,
1Co 9:16 **W** to me if I do not preach
Jude 1:11 **W** to them! They have taken
Rev 8:13 call out in a loud voice: "**W**! **W**!
  18:10 will stand far off and cry: " '**W**!

## WOES* [WOE]

Ps 32:10 Many are the **w** of the wicked,
Rev 9:12 two other **w** are yet to come.

## WOKE [WAKE]
Ge   41: 7  Then Pharaoh **w** up; it had been
Mt    1:24  When Joseph **w** up, he did what
      25: 7  "Then all the virgins **w**

## WOLF [WOLVES]
Isa  11: 6  The **w** will live with the lamb,
     65:25  The **w** and the lamb will feed
Jn   10:12  So when he sees the **w** coming,

## WOLVES [WOLF]
Eze  22:27  her are like **w** tearing their prey,
Zep   3: 3  her rulers are evening **w**, who leave
Mt    7:15  but inwardly they are ferocious **w**.
     10:16  you out like sheep among **w**.
Ac   20:29  savage **w** will come in among you

## WOMAN [WOMEN, WOMEN'S]
Ge    2:22  the LORD God made a **w**
      2:23  she shall be called '**w**,' for she was
      3: 6  When the **w** saw that the fruit
      3:12  "The **w** you put here with me—
      3:15  put enmity between you and the **w**,
      3:16  To the **w** he said, "I will make your
     12:11  "I know what a beautiful **w** you are.
     20: 3  she is a married **w**."
     21:10  "Get rid of that slave **w** and her
     24:43  If a young **w** comes out to draw water
Ex    3:22  Every **w** is to ask her neighbor
     21:10  If he marries another **w**, he must not
     21:22  are fighting and a pregnant **w** is hit
Lev  12: 2  'A **w** who becomes pregnant
     15:19  " 'When a **w** has her regular flow
     18:17  have sexual relations with both a **w**
     18:22  with a man as one does with a **w**;
     20:13  with a man as one does with a **w**,
Nu    5:29  of jealousy when a **w** goes astray
     30: 3  "When a young **w** still living in her
     30:10  "If a **w** living with her husband
Dt    4:16  whether formed like a man or a **w**,
     20: 7  Has anyone become pledged to a **w**
     21:11  among the captives a beautiful **w**
     22: 5  A **w** must not wear men's clothing,
     24: 1  If a man marries a **w** who becomes
Jdg   4: 9  Sisera into the hands of a **w**."
      9:54  they can't say, 'A **w** killed him.' "
     14: 2  "I have seen a Philistine **w**
     16: 4  love with a **w** in the Valley of Sorek
Ru    3:11  that you are a **w** of noble character.
1Sa   1:15  "I am a **w** who is deeply troubled.
     25: 3  was an intelligent and beautiful **w**,
     28: 7  "Find me a **w** who is a medium,
2Sa  11: 2  From the roof he saw a **w** bathing.
     13:17  "Get this **w** out of my sight and bolt
     14: 2  had a wise **w** brought from there.
     20:16  a wise **w** called from the city,
1Ki   3:18  was born, this **w** also had a baby.
     17:24  Then the **w** said to Elijah, "Now I
2Ki   4: 8  And a well-to-do **w** was there,
      8: 1  to the **w** whose son he had restored
      9:34  "Take care of that cursed **w**,"
Ezr  10:14  who has married a foreign **w** come
Job   2:10  "You are talking like a foolish **w**.
     14: 1  born of **w**, are of few days and full
Ps  113: 9  He settles the childless **w** in her
Pr    6:24  the smooth talk of a wayward **w**.

Pr    9:13  Folly is an unruly **w**; she is simple
     11:16  A kindhearted **w** gains honor,
     11:22  snout is a beautiful **w** who shows no
     14: 1  The wise **w** builds her house,
     30:19  way of a man with a young **w**.
     30:23  a contemptible **w** who gets married,
     31:30  a **w** who fears the LORD is to be
Isa  54: 1  barren **w**, you who never bore
     62: 5  As a young man marries a young **w**,
Jer   2:32  Does a young **w** forget her jewelry,
     51:22  shatter young man and young **w**,
Mt    5:28  a **w** lustfully has already committed
      9:20  then a **w** who had been subject
     15:22  A Canaanite **w** from that vicinity
     19: 9  and marries another **w** commits
     26: 7  a **w** came to him with an alabaster
Mk    7:25  him, a **w** whose little daughter was
Lk    7:37  A **w** in that town who lived a sinful
     10:38  a village where a **w** named Martha
     13:12  her forward and said to her, "**W**,
     15: 8  suppose a **w** has ten silver coins
Jn    2: 4  "**W**, why do you involve me?"
      4: 7  a Samaritan **w** came to draw water,
      8: 4  *this w was caught in the act*
     19:26  he said to her, "**W**, here is your
     20:15  He asked her, "**W**, why are you
Ac    9:40  Turning toward the dead **w**, he said,
     16:14  of those listening was a **w**
     17:34  also a **w** named Damaris,
Ro    7: 2  by law a married **w** is bound to her
     16:12  another **w** who has worked very
1Co   7: 2  and each **w** with her own husband.
      7:34  An unmarried **w** or virgin is
      7:39  A **w** is bound to her husband as long
     11: 3  and the head of the **w** is man,
     11: 6  For if a **w** does not cover her head,
     11: 7  but **w** is the glory of man.
Gal   4: 4  born of a **w**, born under the law,
      4:27  barren **w**, you who never bore
      4:30  "Get rid of the slave **w** and her son,
      4:31  we are not children of the slave **w**,
1Ti   2:11  A **w** should learn in quietness
      5:16  any **w** who is a believer has widows
Rev   2:20  You tolerate that **w** Jezebel,
     12: 1  a **w** clothed with the sun,
     12: 4  in front of the **w** who was
     12:13  he pursued the **w** who had given
     17: 3  There I saw a **w** sitting on a scarlet
     17:18  The **w** you saw is the great city

## WOMB
Ge   25:23  "Two nations are in your **w**,
Ex   13: 2  of every **w** among the Israelites
Dt    7:13  He will bless the fruit of your **w**,
Jdg  13: 5  dedicated to God from the **w**.
1Sa   1: 5  and the LORD had closed her **w**.
Job   1:21  I came from my mother's **w**,
Ps   22: 9  Yet you brought me out of the **w**;
    139:13  knit me together in my mother's **w**.
Pr   31: 2  Listen, son of my **w**!
Ecc  11: 5  the body is formed in a mother's **w**,
Jer   1: 5  I formed you in the **w** I knew you,
Lk    1:44  the baby in my **w** leaped for joy.
Jn    3: 4  into their mother's **w** to be born!"
Ro    4:19  and that Sarah's **w** was also dead.

## WOMEN [WOMAN]

| | | |
|---|---|---|
| Ge | 4:19 | Lamech married two **w**, one named |
| Nu | 25: 1 | sexual immorality with Moabite **w**, |
| Jdg | 5:24 | "Most blessed of **w** be Jael, |
| | 21:21 | seize a wife from the young **w** of Shiloh |
| Ru | 2: 8 | Stay here with the **w** who work for me. |
| Ezr | 10: 2 | God by marrying foreign **w** |
| Ne | 13:26 | he was led into sin by foreign **w**. |
| Ps | 68:25 | are the young **w** playing the timbrels. |
| | 78:63 | their young **w** had no wedding songs; |
| SS | 1: 3 | No wonder the young **w** love you! |
| | 1: 8 | most beautiful of **w**, |
| | 2: 2 | my darling among the young **w**. |
| Isa | 3:12 | my people, **w** rule over them. |
| La | 2:21 | and young **w** have fallen by the sword. |
| Zec | 5: 9 | and there before me were two **w**, |
| Mal | 2:11 | marrying **w** who worship a foreign god. |
| Mt | 11:11 | **w** there has not risen anyone greater |
| | 24:41 | Two **w** will be grinding with a hand |
| | 28: 5 | The angel said to the **w**, "Do not be |
| Mk | 15:41 | In Galilee these **w** had followed him |
| Lk | 1:42 | "Blessed are you among **w**, |
| | 8: 2 | some **w** who had been cured of evil |
| | 23:27 | him, including **w** who mourned |
| | 23:55 | The **w** who had come with Jesus |
| | 24:11 | But they did not believe the **w**, |
| Ac | 1:14 | along with the **w** and Mary |
| | 2:18 | both men and **w**, I will pour out my |
| | 8:12 | were baptized, both men and **w**. |
| | 16:13 | to the **w** who had gathered there. |
| | 17: 4 | Greeks and not a few prominent **w**. |
| Ro | 1:26 | Even their **w** exchanged natural |
| | 16:12 | those **w** who work hard in the Lord. |
| 1Co | 14:34 | **W** should remain silent |
| Gal | 4:24 | for the **w** represent two covenants. |
| Php | 4: 3 | help these **w** since they have |
| 1Ti | 2: 9 | I also want the **w** to dress modestly, |
| | 2:15 | But **w** will be saved through |
| | 3:11 | the **w** are to be worthy of respect, |
| | 5: 2 | older **w** as mothers, and younger **w** |
| 2Ti | 3: 6 | and gain control over gullible **w**, |
| Tit | 2: 3 | teach the older **w** to be reverent |
| | 2: 4 | they can urge the younger **w** to love |
| Heb | 11:35 | **W** received back their dead, |
| 1Pe | 3: 5 | this is the way the holy **w** of the past |

## WOMEN'S* [WOMAN]

| | | |
|---|---|---|
| Dt | 22: 5 | nor a man wear **w** clothing, |
| Rev | 9: 8 | Their hair was like **w** hair, and their |

## WON [WIN]

| | | |
|---|---|---|
| 1Sa | 19: 5 | The LORD **w** a great victory |
| Est | 2:15 | Esther **w** the favor of everyone who |
| Ps | 44: 3 | by their sword that they **w** the land, |
| Pr | 11:14 | victory is **w** through many advisers. |
| Mt | 18:15 | listen to you, you have **w** them over. |
| 1Pe | 3: 1 | they may be **w** over without words |

## WONDER [WONDERED, WONDERFUL, WONDERFULLY, WONDERING, WONDERS]

| | | |
|---|---|---|
| Dt | 13: 1 | and announces to you a sign or **w**, |
| SS | 1: 3 | No **w** the young women love you! |
| Isa | 29:14 | these people with **w** upon **w**; |
| Rev | 13: 3 | whole world was filled with **w** |

## WONDERED* [WONDER]

| | | |
|---|---|---|
| Lk | 1:29 | **w** what kind of greeting this might |
| | 1:66 | Everyone who heard this **w** about it, |

## WONDERFUL* [WONDER]

| | | |
|---|---|---|
| 2Sa | 1:26 | Your love for me was **w**, more **w** than that of women. |
| 1Ch | 16: 9 | praise to him; tell of all his **w** acts. |
| Job | 42: 3 | things too **w** for me to know. |
| Ps | 9: 1 | I will tell of all your **w** deeds. |
| | 26: 7 | and telling of all your **w** deeds. |
| | 75: 1 | people tell of your **w** deeds. |
| | 105: 2 | tell of all his **w** acts. |
| | 107: 8 | and his **w** deeds for humankind, |
| | 107:15 | and his **w** deeds for humankind, |
| | 107:21 | and his **w** deeds for humankind. |
| | 107:24 | LORD, his **w** deeds in the deep. |
| | 107:31 | and his **w** deeds for humankind. |
| | 119:18 | that I may see **w** things in your law. |
| | 119:27 | I may meditate on your **w** deeds. |
| | 119:129 | Your statutes are **w**; therefore I obey |
| | 131: 1 | great matters or things too **w** for me. |
| | 139: 6 | Such knowledge is too **w** for me, |
| | 139:14 | your works are **w**, I know that full |
| | 145: 5 | I will meditate on your **w** works. |
| Isa | 9: 6 | And he will be called **W** Counselor, |
| | 25: 1 | you have done **w** things, |
| | 28:29 | whose plan is **w**, whose wisdom is |
| Mt | 21:15 | of the law saw the **w** things he did |
| Lk | 13:17 | with all the **w** things he was doing. |
| 1Pe | 2: 9 | you out of darkness into his **w** light. |

## WONDERFULLY* [WONDER]

| | | |
|---|---|---|
| Ps | 139:14 | because I am fearfully and **w** made; |

## WONDERING [WONDER]

| | | |
|---|---|---|
| Ac | 10:17 | While Peter was **w** |

## WONDERS [WONDER]

| | | |
|---|---|---|
| Ex | 3:20 | all the **w** that I will perform among |
| | 11:10 | all these **w** before Pharaoh, |
| | 15:11 | awesome in glory, working **w**? |
| Dt | 10:21 | awesome **w** you saw with your own |
| 2Sa | 7:23 | awesome **w** by driving out nations |
| 1Ch | 16:12 | Remember the **w** he has done, |
| Job | 37:14 | stop and consider God's **w**. |
| Ps | 17: 7 | Show me the **w** of your great love, |
| | 31:21 | he showed me the **w** of his love |
| | 65: 8 | earth is filled with awe at your **w**; |
| | 78:32 | in spite of his **w**, they did not |
| | 89: 5 | The heavens praise your **w**, |
| | 136: 4 | to him who alone does great **w**, |
| Da | 4: 3 | are his signs, how mighty his **w**! |
| Joel | 2:30 | I will show **w** in the heavens |
| Mt | 24:24 | perform great signs and **w** to deceive, |
| Jn | 4:48 | you people see signs and **w**," |
| Ac | 2:11 | we hear them declaring the **w** |
| | 2:19 | I will show **w** in the heaven |
| 2Co | 12:12 | including signs, **w** and miracles. |
| 2Th | 2: 9 | signs and **w** that serve the lie, |
| Heb | 2: 4 | it by signs, **w** and various miracles, |

## WOOD [WOODEN, WOODS]

| | | |
|---|---|---|
| Ge | 6:14 | make yourself an ark of cypress **w**; |
| | 22: 9 | altar there and arranged the **w** on it. |

Ex  15:25  LORD showed him a piece of **w**.
    25:10  them make an ark of acacia **w**—
    25:13  make poles of acacia **w** and overlay
    25:23  "Make a table of acacia **w**—
    26:15  of acacia **w** for the tabernacle.
    27: 1  "Build an altar of acacia **w**,
Lev 14: 4  live clean birds and some cedar **w**,
Dt  28:64  gods of **w** and stone, which neither
1Ki 18:23  put it on the **w** but not set fire to it.
Isa 44:19  Shall I bow down to a block of **w**?"
    60:17  Instead of **w** I will bring you bronze,
Eze 20:32  the world, who serve **w** and stone."
    37:16  take a stick of **w** and write on it,
Hos  4:12  and are answered by a stick of **w**.
Hab  2:19  Woe to him who says to **w**,
1Co  3:12  costly stones, **w**, hay or straw,

## WOODEN [WOOD]

Dt  16:21  any **w** Asherah pole beside the altar
Ne   8: 4  stood on a high **w** platform built
Isa 48: 5  my **w** image and metal god ordained

## WOODS [WOOD]

2Ki  2:24  two bears came out of the **w**

## WOOL

Nu  19: 6  scarlet **w** and throw them onto
Dt  18: 4  the first **w** from the shearing of your
    22:11  Do not wear clothes of **w** and linen
Pr  31:13  She selects **w** and flax and works
Isa  1:18  red as crimson, they shall be like **w**.
Da   7: 9  hair of his head was white like **w**.
Rev  1:14  hair on his head was white like **w**,

## WORD [BYWORD, WORDLESS, WORDS]

Ge  15: 1  the **w** of the LORD came to Abram
    37: 4  could not speak a kind **w** to him.
Nu  23: 5  back to Balak and give him this **w**."
    23:16  with Balaam and put a **w** in his mouth
    30: 2  he must not break his **w** but must do
Dt   8: 3  but on every **w** that comes
    30:14  No, the **w** is very near you; it is
Jos  1:18  Whoever rebels against your **w**
1Sa  3: 1  those days the **w** of the LORD was
2Sa 22:31  the LORD's **w** is flawless.
1Ki  8:56  Not one **w** has failed of all the good
    17: 2  the **w** of the LORD came to Elijah:
1Ch 17: 3  But that night the **w** of God came
2Ch 36:22  fulfill the **w** of the LORD spoken
Ps  33: 4  For the **w** of the LORD is right
    56: 4  In God, whose **w** I praise—in God I
    56:10  in the LORD, whose **w** I praise—
    107:20  He sent out his **w** and healed them;
    119: 9  By living according to your **w**.
    119:11  I have hidden your **w** in my heart
    119:42  who taunts me, for I trust in your **w**.
    119:74  for I have put my hope in your **w**.
    119:89  Your **w**, LORD, is eternal;
    119:105 Your **w** is a lamp to my feet
    119:172 May my tongue sing of your **w**,
    139: 4  Before a **w** is on my tongue you,
Pr  12:25  the heart, but a kind **w** cheers it up.
    15: 1  wrath, but a harsh **w** stirs up anger.
    15:23  and how good is a timely **w**!
    30: 5  "Every **w** of God is flawless; he is

Isa  1:10  Hear the **w** of the LORD,
    40: 8  the **w** of our God endures forever."
    55:11  so is my **w** that goes out from my
Jer  5:13  but wind and the **w** is not in them;
    23:29  "Is not my **w** like fire,"
Da   9: 2  to the **w** of the LORD given
    9:23  consider the **w** and understand
Mt   4: 4  but on every **w** that comes
    12:36  every empty **w** they have spoken.
    15: 6  Thus you nullify the **w** of God
Mk   4:14  The farmer sows the **w**.
Lk   1: 2  eyewitnesses and servants of the **w**.
Jn   1: 1  In the beginning was the **W**, and the
             **W** was with God, and the **W**
    1:14  The **W** became flesh and made his
    8:37  you have no room for my **w**.
    17:17  them by the truth; your **w** is truth.
Ac   4:31  and spoke the **w** of God boldly.
    6: 4  prayer and the ministry of the **w**."
Ro   9: 6  is not as though God's **w** had failed.
    10: 8  "The **w** is near you; it is in your
2Co  2:17  we do not peddle the **w** of God
    4: 2  nor do we distort the **w** of God.
Eph  6:17  of the Spirit, which is the **w** of God.
Php  2:16  as you hold firmly to the **w** of life.
2Ti  2:15  and who correctly handles the **w**
Heb  1: 3  all things by his powerful **w**.
    4:12  For the **w** of God is alive and active.
    6: 5  tasted the goodness of the **w** of God
Jas  1:21  humbly accept the **w** planted in you,
    1:22  Do not merely listen to the **w**,
1Pe  1:23  the living and enduring **w** of God.
2Pe  3: 5  ago by God's **w** the heavens came
1Jn  2: 5  But if anyone obeys his **w**,
Rev  3: 8  yet you have kept my **w** and have
    12:11  and by the **w** of their testimony;
    19:13  and his name is the **W** of God.
    20: 4  Jesus and because of the **w** of God.

## WORD OF GOD  1Ki 12:22; 1Ch 17:3; Pr

30:5; Mt 15:6; Mk 7:13; Lk 3:2; 5:1; 8:11; 11:28;
Jn 10:35; Ac 4:31; 6:2, 7; 8:14; 11:1; 12:24; 13:5,
7, 46; 17:13; 18:11; 1Co 14:36; 2Co 2:17; 4:2;
Eph 6:17; Col 1:25; 1Th 2:13, 13; 1Ti 4:5; Tit
2:5; Heb 4:12; 6:5; 13:7; 1Pe 1:23; 1Jn 2:14; Rev
1:2, 9; 6:9; 19:13; 20:4

## WORD OF THE †LORD  Ge 15:1, 4; Ex

9:20, 21; Nu 3:16, 51; Dt 5:5; 1Sa 3:1, 7; 15:10,
23, 26; 2Sa 7:4; 12:9; 24:11; 1Ki 6:11; 12:24;
13:1, 2, 5, 9, 17, 18, 20, 21, 26, 26, 32; 15:29;
16:1, 7, 12, 34; 17:2, 8, 16, 24; 18:1, 31; 19:9;
20:35; 21:17, 28; 22:19, 38; 2Ki 1:17; 3:12; 4:44;
7:1; 9:26, 36; 10:17; 14:25; 15:12; 20:4, 16, 19;
23:16; 24:2; 1Ch 10:13; 15:15; 22:8; 2Ch 11:2;
12:7; 18:18; 29:15; 30:12; 34:21; 36:12, 21, 22;
Ezr 1:1; Ps 33:4, 6; 105:19; Isa 1:10; 2:3; 28:13,
14; 38:4; 39:5, 8; 66:5; Jer 1:2, 4, 11, 13; 2:1, 4,
31; 6:10; 7:2; 8:9; 9:20; 13:3, 8; 14:1; 16:1;
17:15, 20; 18:5; 19:3; 20:8; 21:11; 22:2, 29; 24:4;
25:3; 27:18; 28:12; 29:20, 30; 31:10; 32:6, 8, 26;
33:1, 19, 23; 34:12; 35:12, 36:27; 37:6; 39:15;
42:7, 15; 43:8; 44:24, 26; 46:1; 47:1; 49:34; Eze
1:3; 3:16; 6:1; 7:1; 11:14; 12:1, 8, 17, 21, 26;
13:1, 2; 14:2, 12; 15:1; 16:1, 35; 17:1, 11; 18:1;
20:2, 45, 47; 21:1, 8, 18; 22:1, 17, 23; 23:1; 24:1,
15, 20; 25:1; 26:1; 27:1; 28:1, 11, 20; 29:1, 17;

30:1, 20; 31:1; 32:1, 17; 33:1, 23; 34:1, 7, 9;
35:1; 36:1, 16; 37:4, 15; 38:1; Da 9:2; Hos 1:1;
4:1; Joel 1:1; Am 7:16; 8:12; Jnh 1:1; 3:1, 3; Mic
1:1; 4:2; Zep 1:1; 2:5; Hag 1:1, 3; 2:1, 10, 20;
Zec 1:1, 7; 4:6, 8; 6:9; 7:1, 4, 8; 8:1, 18; 9:1;
11:11; 12:1; Mal 1:1

## WORD OF THE †LORD CAME Ge 15:1,
4; 1Sa 15:10; 2Sa 7:4; 1Ki 6:11; 13:20; 16:1, 7;
17:2, 8; 18:1; 19:9; 21:17, 28; 2Ki 20:4; 1Ch
22:8; 2Ch 11:2; 12:7; Isa 38:4; Jer 1:2, 4, 11, 13;
2:1; 13:3, 8; 14:1; 16:1; 18:5; 24:4; 28:12; 29:30;
32:6, 26; 33:1, 19, 23; 34:12; 35:12; 36:27; 37:6;
39:15; 42:7; 43:8; 46:1; 47:1; 49:34; Eze 1:3;
3:16; 6:1; 7:1; 11:14; 12:1, 8, 17, 21, 26; 13:1;
14:2, 12; 15:1; 16:1; 17:1, 11; 18:1; 20:2, 45;
21:1, 8, 18; 22:1, 17, 23; 23:1; 24:1, 15, 20; 25:1;
26:1; 27:1; 28:1, 11, 20; 29:1, 17; 30:1, 20; 31:1;
32:1, 17; 33:1, 23; 34:1; 35:1; 36:16; 37:15; 38:1;
Hos 1:1; Joel 1:1; Jnh 1:1; 3:1; Mic 1:1; Zep 1:1;
Hag 1:1, 3; 2:1, 10, 20; Zec 1:1, 7; 4:8; 6:9; 7:1,
8

## WORDLESS* [WORD]
Ro     8:26   intercedes for us through **w** groans.

## WORDS [WORD]
| | | |
|---|---|---|
| Ex | 20: 1 | And God spoke all these **w**: |
| | 24: 3 | told the people all the LORD's **w** |
| | 34:28 | the tablets the **w** of the covenant— |
| Dt | 11:18 | Fix these **w** of mine in your hearts |
| | 13: 3 | you must not listen to the **w** |
| | 18:19 | to my **w** that the prophet speaks |
| | 31:24 | writing in a book the **w** of this law |
| | 32:45 | Moses finished reciting all these **w** |
| | 32:47 | They are not just idle **w** for you— |
| Jos | 8:34 | Joshua read all the **w** of the law— |
| 2Sa | 23: 1 | These are the last **w** of David: |
| Ps | 5: 1 | Listen to my **w**, LORD, |
| | 12: 6 | the **w** of the LORD are flawless, |
| | 19: 3 | use no **w**; no sound is heard |
| | 19: 4 | their **w** to the ends of the world. |
| | 19:14 | May these **w** of my mouth and this |
| | 49: 3 | My mouth will speak **w** of wisdom; |
| | 64: 3 | and aim cruel **w** like deadly arrows. |
| | 119:103 | How sweet are your **w** to my taste, |
| | 119:130 | The unfolding of your **w** gives light; |
| | 119:160 | All your **w** are true; |
| Pr | 2: 1 | if you accept my **w** and store up my |
| | 2:16 | woman with her seductive **w**, |
| | 7:21 | persuasive **w** she led him astray; |
| | 10:19 | Sin is not ended by multiplying **w**, |
| | 12:18 | The **w** of the reckless pierce like |
| | 16:24 | Gracious **w** are a honeycomb, |
| | 26:22 | The **w** of a gossip are like choice |
| | 30: 6 | Do not add to his **w**, or he will |
| Ecc | 5: 2 | are on earth, so let your **w** be few. |
| | 10:14 | and fools multiply **w**. No one knows |
| | 12:11 | The **w** of the wise are like goads, |
| Jer | 15:16 | When your **w** came, I ate them; |
| Da | 9:12 | have fulfilled the **w** spoken against |
| Hos | 6: 5 | killed you with the **w** of my mouth— |
| Zec | 1: 6 | But did not my **w** and my decrees, |
| Mt | 7:24 | everyone who hears these **w** of mine |
| | 12:37 | by your **w** you will be condemned." |
| | 24:35 | but my **w** will never pass away. |

| | | |
|---|---|---|
| Mk | 12:13 | to Jesus to catch him in his **w**. |
| Lk | 4:32 | because his **w** had authority. |
| | 6:47 | me and hear my **w** and put them |
| Jn | 6:68 | You have the **w** of eternal life. |
| | 15: 7 | in me and my **w** remain in you, |
| Ac | 2:40 | With many other **w** he warned them; |
| 1Co | 2:13 | but in **w** taught by the Spirit, |
| | 14:19 | rather speak five intelligible **w** |
| 1Pe | 3: 1 | they may be won over without **w** |
| 1Jn | 3:18 | let us not love with **w** or tongue |
| Rev | 1: 3 | is the one who reads aloud the **w** |
| | 19: 9 | "These are the true **w** of God." |
| | 22: 6 | "These **w** are trustworthy and true. |
| | 22:19 | of you takes **w** away from this scroll |

## WORE [WEAR]
| | | |
|---|---|---|
| Mk | 1: 6 | John **w** clothing made of camel's |
| Rev | 9: 7 | their heads they **w** something like |
| | 15: 6 | **w** golden sashes around their chests. |

## WORK [CO-WORKERS, HANDIWORK, HARDWORKING, METALWORKER, WORKED, WORKER, WORKERS, WORKING, WORKS]
| | | |
|---|---|---|
| Ge | 2: 2 | seventh day he rested from all his **w**. |
| | 2:15 | him in the Garden of Eden to **w** it |
| | 4:12 | When you **w** the ground, it will no |
| Ex | 20:10 | On it you shall not do any **w**, |
| | 23:12 | "Six days do your **w**, but on the seventh day do not **w**, |
| | 32:16 | The tablets were the **w** of God; |
| | 40:33 | And so Moses finished the **w**. |
| Lev | 25:40 | they are to **w** for you until the Year |
| Nu | 8:11 | be ready to do the **w** of the LORD. |
| Dt | 5:14 | On it you shall not do any **w**, |
| | 27:15 | the LORD, the **w** of skilled hands— |
| 1Ch | 22:16 | Now begin the **w**, and the LORD |
| 2Ch | 2: 7 | a man skilled to **w** in gold |
| | 8:16 | All Solomon's **w** was carried out, |
| Ezr | 4: 5 | bribed officials to **w** against them |
| | 4:24 | Thus the **w** on the house of God |
| | 6: 7 | interfere with the **w** on this temple |
| Ne | 2:18 | So they began this good **w**. |
| Job | 1:10 | You have blessed the **w** of his |
| Ps | 8: 3 | your heavens, the **w** of your fingers, |
| | 19: 1 | the skies proclaim the **w** of his |
| | 90:17 | establish the **w** of our hands for us— |
| Pr | 14:23 | All hard **w** brings a profit, but mere |
| | 21:25 | because their hands refuse to **w**. |
| | 31:17 | She sets about her **w** vigorously; |
| Ecc | 11: 5 | so you cannot understand the **w** |
| Isa | 2: 8 | bow down to the **w** of their hands, |
| | 64: 8 | we are all the **w** of your hand. |
| Jer | 48:10 | are lax in doing the LORD's **w**! |
| Lk | 13:14 | people, "There are six days for **w**. |
| Jn | 5:17 | is always at his **w** to this very day, |
| | 6:27 | Do not **w** for food that spoils, |
| | 6:29 | answered, "The **w** of God is this: |
| | 9: 4 | is coming, when no one can **w**. |
| | 17: 4 | by finishing the **w** you gave me |
| Ac | 13: 2 | and Saul for the **w** to which I have |
| Ro | 4: 5 | to anyone who does not **w** but trusts |
| | 14:20 | Do not destroy the **w** of God |
| | 16:12 | those women who **w** hard |

1Co 3:13 their **w** will be shown for what it is,
    4:12 We **w** hard with our own hands.
   12:11 All these are the **w** of one
Gal 2: 8 at **w** in Peter as an apostle to the Jews,
    2: 8 at **w** in me as an apostle to the Gentiles.
Eph 3:20 to his power that is at **w** within us,
    4:16 up in love, as each part does its **w**.
Php 1: 6 he who began a good **w** in you will
    2:12 continue to **w** out your salvation
Col 3:23 you do, **w** at it with all your heart,
1Th 4:11 business and **w** with your hands,
    5:12 those who **w** hard among you,
2Th 2: 7 of lawlessness is already at **w**;
    3:10 is unwilling to **w** shall not eat."
1Ti 5:17 those whose **w** is preaching
2Ti 2:21 and prepared to do any good **w**.
    3:17 equipped for every good **w**.
Heb 4: 4 day God rested from all his **w**."
    6:10 he will not forget your **w**
   13:17 Do this so that their **w** will be a joy,
1Pe 1:17 judges each person's **w** impartially,
1Jn 3: 8 was to destroy the devil's **w**.
2Jn 1:11 them shares in their wicked **w**.
3Jn 1: 8 that we may **w** together for the truth.
Rev 2: 2 your hard **w** and your perseverance.
    9:20 not repent of the **w** of their hands;

## WORKED [WORK]

Ge 4: 2 kept flocks, and Cain **w** the soil.
   29:30 he **w** for Laban another seven years
Ex 1:13 and **w** them ruthlessly.
Ps 98: 1 his holy arm have **w** salvation
Jn 4:38 to reap what you have not **w** for.
1Co 15:10 No, I **w** harder than all of them—
2Th 3: 8 the contrary, we **w** night and day,
2Jn 1: 8 you do not lose what we have **w** for,

## WORKER [WORK]

1Ki 7:14 and a skilled **w** in bronze.
Isa 40:19 As for an idol, a metal **w** casts it,
Jer 10: 3 a skilled **w** shapes it with a chisel.
2Ti 2:15 **w** who does not need to be ashamed
Rev 18:22 No **w** of any trade will ever be found

## WORKERS [WORK]

Ex 31: 6 ability to all the skilled **w** to make
   36: 8 the **w** made the tabernacle
1Ki 5:18 The skilled **w** of Solomon and Hiram
2Ki 12:14 it was paid to the **w**,
Ne 4:22 guards by night and as **w** by day."
Ecc 3: 9 What do **w** gain from their toil?
Mt 9:37 is plentiful but the **w** are few.
   20: 1 to hire **w** for his vineyard.
Lk 10: 2 to send out **w** into his harvest field.
Lk 10: 7 give you, for **w** deserve their wages.
Ac 19:24 no little business for the skilled **w** there.
2Co 11:13 false apostles, deceitful **w**,
1Ti 5:18 and "**W** deserve their wages."

## WORKING [WORK]

Ex 15:11 awesome in glory, **w** wonders?
Jn 5:17 to this very day, and I too am **w**."
1Co 12: 6 There are different kinds of **w**,
Col 3:23 all your heart, as **w** for the Lord,
Jas 2:22 and his actions were **w** together,

## WORKS [WORK]

Dt 3:24 do the deeds and mighty **w** you do?
   32: 4 He is the Rock, his **w** are perfect,
Ps 8: 6 You made them rulers over the **w**
   92: 5 How great are your **w**, LORD,
  103: 6 The LORD **w** righteousness
  138: 8 do not abandon the **w** of your hands.
  145: 6 of the power of your awesome **w**—
Pr 8:22 me forth as the first of his **w**,
  31:31 let her **w** bring her praise at the city
Jn 7: 3 disciples there may see the **w** you do.
  10:25 **w** I do in my Father's name testify
  10:32 many good **w** from the Father.
  10:38 believe the **w**, that you may know
  14:11 at least believe on the evidence of the **w**
  15:24 among them the **w** no one else did,
Ro 3:27 The law that requires **w**?
  4: 6 credits righteousness apart from **w**:
  8:28 in all things God **w** for the good
Eph 1:11 plan of him who **w** out everything
  2: 9 not by **w**, so that no one can boast.
  2:10 in Christ Jesus to do good **w**,
  4:12 to equip his people for **w** of service,
Php 2:13 for it is God who **w** in you to will
Col 1:29 the energy Christ so powerfully **w**
2Th 2: 9 be in accordance with how Satan **w**.

## WORLD [WORLDLY]

Ge 11: 1 Now the whole **w** had one language
  11: 9 the language of the whole **w**.
  41:57 all the **w** came to Egypt to buy grain
2Ki 5:15 no God in all the **w** except in Israel.
1Ch 16:30 The **w** is firmly established;
Ps 9: 8 He rules the **w** in righteousness
  19: 4 their words to the ends of the **w**.
  50:12 for the **w** is mine, and all that is
  90: 2 you brought forth the whole **w**,
  96:13 He will judge the **w** in righteousness
Pr 8:23 beginning, when the **w** came to be.
Isa 13:11 I will punish the **w** for its evil,
Mt 4: 8 him all the kingdoms of the **w**
  5:14 "You are the light of the **w**.
  16:26 it be for you to gain the whole **w**,
Jn 1:10 the **w** did not recognize him.
  1:29 who takes away the sin of the **w**!
  3:16 God so loved the **w** that he gave his
  3:17 but to save the **w** through him.
  8:12 he said, "I am the light of the **w**.
  9: 5 in the **w**, I am the light of the **w**."
  15:19 but I have chosen you out of the **w**.
  16:33 In this **w** you will have trouble.
  16:33 I have overcome the **w**."
  17: 5 I had with you before the **w** began.
  17:18 I have sent them into the **w**.
  18:36 said, "My kingdom is not of this **w**.
Ac 17:31 he will judge the **w** with justice
Ro 3:19 and the whole **w** held accountable
  5:12 sin entered the **w** through one man,
  10:18 their words to the ends of the **w**."
1Co 1:27 things of the **w** to shame the wise;
  3:19 the wisdom of this **w** is foolishness
  6: 2 the Lord's people will judge the **w**?
2Co 5:19 that God was reconciling the **w**
  10: 3 we do not wage war as the **w** does.
1Ti 1:15 came into the **w** to save sinners—
  6: 7 For we brought nothing into the **w**,

Heb 1: 6 God brings his firstborn into the **w**,
11: 7 By his faith he condemned the **w**
11:38 the **w** was not worthy of them.
Jas 1:27 from being polluted by the **w**.
4: 4 a friend of the **w** becomes an enemy
1Pe 1:20 chosen before the creation of the **w**,
1Jn 2: 2 but also for the sins of the whole **w**.
2:15 not love the **w** or anything in the **w**.
5: 4 the victory that has overcome the **w**,
Rev 11:15 of the **w** has become the kingdom
13: 8 was slain from the creation of the **w**.

## WORLDLY [WORLD]

Lk 16:11 trustworthy in handling **w** wealth,
1Co 3: 1 address you as spiritual but as **w**—
Tit 2:12 to ungodliness and **w** passions,

## WORM [WORMS]

Ps 22: 6 But I am a **w**, not a human being;
Isa 41:14 Do not be afraid, you **w** Jacob,
Mk 9:48 where " 'their **w** does not die,

## WORMS [WORM]

Ac 12:23 and he was eaten by **w** and died.

## WORMWOOD*

Rev 8:11 the name of the star is **W**. A third

## WORN [WEAR]

Ge 18:12 "After I am **w** out and my lord is

## WORRIED [WORRY]

Lk 10:41 "you are **w** and upset about many

## WORRIES [WORRY]

Lk 8:14 way they are choked by life's **w**,

## WORRY [WORRIED, WORRIES, WORRYING]

Mt 6:25 I tell you, do not **w** about your life,
6:34 Therefore do not **w** about tomorrow,
10:19 do not **w** about what to say or how

## WORRYING [WORRY]

Mt 6:27 you by **w** add a single hour to your

## WORSE [WORST]

Mt 12:45 of that person is **w** than the first.
Jn 5:14 something **w** may happen to you."
1Ti 5: 8 faith and is **w** than an unbeliever.
2Pe 2:20 they are **w** off at the end than they

## WORSHIP [WORSHIPED, WORSHIPERS, WORSHIPING, WORSHIPS]

Ex 4:23 "Let my son go, so he may **w** me."
20: 5 not bow down to them or **w** them;
34:14 Do not **w** any other god,
Dt 12: 4 You must not **w** the LORD your
Jos 22:27 that we will **w** the LORD at his
2Ki 17:37 wrote for you. Do not **w** other gods.
1Ch 16:29 **W** the LORD in the splendor of his
Ps 95: 6 let us bow down in **w**, let us kneel

Ps 97: 7 All who **w** images are put to shame,
100: 2 **W** the LORD with gladness;
Jer 23:27 forgot my name through Baal **w**.
Da 3:28 or **w** any god except their own God.
Jnh 1: 9 am a Hebrew and I **w** the LORD,
Zec 14:17 go up to Jerusalem to **w** the King,
Mt 2: 2 it rose and have come to **w** him."
4: 9 "if you will bow down and **w** me."
Lk 4: 8 'W the Lord your God and serve
Jn 4:24 his worshipers must **w** in the Spirit
Ro 12: 1 and pleasing to God—this is true **w**.
Heb 10: 1 perfect those who draw near to **w**.
Rev 4:10 throne and **w** him who lives for ever
13:12 and its inhabitants **w** the first beast,
14: 7 **W** him who made the heavens,

## WORSHIPED [WORSHIP]

Ex 12:27 the people bowed down and **w**.
Dt 29:26 They went off and **w** other gods
Jos 24: 2 Euphrates River and **w** other gods.
2Ch 24:18 and **w** Asherah poles and idols.
29:30 gladness and bowed down and **w**.
Mt 28: 9 to him, clasped his feet and **w** him.
Rev 5:14 and the elders fell down and **w**.
13: 4 People **w** the dragon because he had
20: 4 They had not **w** the beast or his

## WORSHIPERS [WORSHIP]

Jn 4:24 and his **w** must worship in the Spirit

## WORSHIPING [WORSHIP]

Jdg 2:19 other gods and serving and **w** them.
Ac 13: 2 While they were **w** the Lord
Rev 9:20 they did not stop **w** demons,

## WORSHIPS [WORSHIP]

Isa 44:15 But he also fashions a god and **w** it;

## WORST [WORSE]

1Ti 1:16 so that in me, the **w** of sinners,

## WORTH [WORTHLESS, WORTHY]

Job 28:13 No mortal comprehends its **w**;
Pr 31:10 She is **w** far more than rubies.
Mt 10:31 you are **w** more than many
Jn 12: 5 It was **w** a year's wages."
Ro 8:18 sufferings are not **w** comparing
Php 3: 8 of the surpassing **w** of knowing Christ
1Pe 1: 7 of greater **w** than gold,
3: 4 which is of great **w** in God's sight.

## WORTHLESS [WORTH]

Ge 41:27 so are the seven **w** heads of grain
Dt 32:21 and angered me with their **w** idols.
Ps 31: 6 I hate those who cling to **w** idols;
60:11 the enemy, for human help is **w**.
Pr 11: 4 Wealth is **w** in the day of wrath,
Jer 2: 5 They followed **w** idols and became
**w** themselves.
Zec 11:17 "Woe to the **w** shepherd,
Mt 25:30 And throw that **w** servant outside,
Heb 6: 8 and thistles is **w** and is in danger
Jas 1:26 themselves, and their religion is **w**.

## WORTHY [WORTH]

| | | |
|---|---|---|
| 1Ch | 16:25 | is the LORD and most **w** of praise; |
| Ps | 18: 3 | to the LORD, who is **w** of praise, |
| | 145: 3 | is the LORD and most **w** of praise; |
| Mt | 3:11 | whose sandals I am not **w** to carry. |
| | 10:37 | or mother more than me is not **w** |
| | 10:38 | cross and follow me is not **w** of me. |
| Lk | 3:16 | whose sandals I am not **w** to untie. |
| | 15:19 | I am no longer **w** to be called your |
| Ro | 16: 2 | in the Lord in a way **w** of his people |
| Eph | 4: 1 | live a life **w** of the calling you have |
| Php | 1:27 | live in a manner **w** of the gospel |
| Col | 1:10 | you may live a life **w** of the Lord |
| 1Ti | 3: 8 | way, deacons are to be **w** of respect, |
| | 3:11 | the women are to be **w** of respect, |
| Tit | 2: 2 | men to be temperate, **w** of respect, |
| Heb | 3: 3 | Jesus has been found **w** of greater |
| | 11:38 | the world was not **w** of them. |
| 3Jn | 1: 6 | on their way in a manner **w** of God. |
| Rev | 3: 4 | me, dressed in white, for they are **w**. |
| | 4:11 | "You are **w**, our Lord and God, |
| | 5: 2 | "Who is **w** to break the seals |
| | 5:12 | "**W** is the Lamb, who was slain, |

## WOUND [WOUNDS]

| | | |
|---|---|---|
| Ex | 21:25 | burn for burn, **w** for **w**, |
| Pr | 25:20 | or like vinegar poured on a **w**, |
| Jer | 10:19 | of my injury! My **w** is incurable! |
| La | 2:13 | Your **w** is as deep as the sea. |
| Na | 3:19 | can heal you; your **w** is fatal. |
| 1Co | 8:12 | way and **w** their weak conscience, |
| Rev | 13: 3 | beast seemed to have had a fatal **w**, |

## WOUNDS [WOUND]

| | | |
|---|---|---|
| Job | 5:18 | For he **w**, but he also binds up; |
| Ps | 147: 3 | brokenhearted and binds up their **w**. |
| Pr | 27: 6 | **W** from a friend can be trusted, |
| Isa | 53: 5 | on him, and by his **w** we are healed. |
| Zec | 13: 6 | 'The **w** I was given at the house |
| 1Pe | 2:24 | "by his **w** you have been healed." |

## WOVEN

| | | |
|---|---|---|
| Ex | 28: 4 | a robe, a **w** tunic, a turban |
| Jn | 19:23 | **w** in one piece from top to bottom. |

## WRAPPED [WRAPS]

| | | |
|---|---|---|
| Mk | 15:46 | down the body, **w** it in the linen, |
| Lk | 2: 7 | She **w** him in cloths and placed him |
| Jn | 13: 4 | and **w** a towel around his waist. |
| | 20: 7 | that had been **w** around Jesus' head. |

## WRAPS [WRAPPED]

| | | |
|---|---|---|
| Ps | 104: 2 | The LORD **w** himself in light as |

## WRATH

| | | |
|---|---|---|
| Nu | 16:46 | **W** has come out from the LORD; |
| Dt | 32:22 | For a fire will be kindled by my **w**, |
| 2Sa | 6: 8 | because the LORD's **w** had broken |
| 1Ch | 27:24 | God's **w** came on Israel on account |
| 2Ch | 36:16 | at his prophets until the **w** |
| Ps | 2: 5 | his anger and terrifies them in his **w**, |
| | 6: 1 | anger or discipline me in your **w**. |
| | 37: 8 | Refrain from anger and turn from **w**; |
| | 76:10 | Surely your **w** against human beings |
| Pr | 15: 1 | A gentle answer turns away **w**, |

| | | |
|---|---|---|
| Isa | 13:13 | at the **w** of the LORD Almighty, |
| | 51:17 | of the LORD the cup of his **w**, |
| Jer | 6:11 | I am full of the **w** of the LORD, |
| | 25:15 | cup filled with the wine of my **w** |
| La | 4:11 | LORD has given full vent to his **w**; |
| Eze | 5:13 | when I have spent my **w** on them, |
| | 20: 8 | said I would pour out my **w** on them |
| Na | 1: 2 | vengeance and is filled with **w**. |
| Zep | 1:15 | That day will be a day of **w**— |
| Mt | 3: 7 | you to flee from the coming **w**? |
| Jn | 3:36 | life, for God's **w** remains on them. |
| Ro | 1:18 | The **w** of God is being revealed |
| | 2: 5 | are storing up **w** against yourself for the day of God's **w**, |
| | 5: 9 | saved from God's **w** through him! |
| | 9:22 | although choosing to show his **w** |
| | 9:22 | great patience the objects of his **w**— |
| Eph | 2: 3 | we were by nature deserving of **w**. |
| 1Th | 1:10 | who rescues us from the coming **w**. |
| | 5: 9 | God did not appoint us to suffer **w** |
| Rev | 6:17 | the great day of their **w** has come, |
| | 15: 1 | with them God's **w** is completed. |
| | 19:15 | the fury of the **w** of God Almighty. |

## WRESTLED [WRESTLING]

| | | |
|---|---|---|
| Ge | 32:24 | and a man **w** with him till daybreak. |

## WRESTLING* [WRESTLED]

| | | |
|---|---|---|
| Col | 4:12 | He is always **w** in prayer for you, |

## WRETCHED

| | | |
|---|---|---|
| Ro | 7:24 | What a **w** man I am! |
| Rev | 3:17 | you do not realize that you are **w**, |

## WRINKLE*

| | | |
|---|---|---|
| Eph | 5:27 | without stain or **w** or any other |

## WRIST [WRISTS]

| | | |
|---|---|---|
| Ge | 38:28 | thread and tied it on his **w** and said, |

## WRISTS [WRIST]

| | | |
|---|---|---|
| Ac | 12: 7 | and the chains fell off Peter's **w**. |

## WRITE [WRITER, WRITES, WRITING, WRITTEN, WROTE]

| | | |
|---|---|---|
| Ex | 17:14 | "**W** this on a scroll as something |
| | 34:27 | to Moses, "**W** down these words, |
| Nu | 17: 2 | **W** the name of each man on his |
| Dt | 6: 9 | **W** them on the doorframes of your |
| | 10: 2 | I will **w** on the tablets the words |
| | 17:18 | he is to **w** for himself on a scroll |
| | 27: 8 | And you shall **w** very clearly all |
| Pr | 3: 3 | **w** them on the tablet of your heart. |
| | 7: 3 | **w** them on the tablet of your heart. |
| Jer | 31:33 | their minds and **w** it on their hearts. |
| Lk | 1: 3 | too decided to **w** an orderly account |
| Jn | 8: 6 | *to **w** on the ground with his finger.* |
| Heb | 8:10 | minds and **w** them on their hearts. |
| 1Jn | 2: 1 | I **w** this to you so that you will not |
| Rev | 1:19 | "**W**, therefore, what you have seen: |
| | 3:12 | I will **w** on them the name of my |
| | 21: 5 | Then he said, "**W** this down, |

## WRITER* [WRITE]

| | | |
|---|---|---|
| Ps | 45: 1 | my tongue is the pen of a skillful **w**. |

## WRITES [WRITE]
Dt 24: 1 and he **w** her a certificate of divorce,

## WRITING [WRITE]
Ex 32:16 the **w** was the **w** of God,
Dt 31:24 Moses finished **w** in a book
Da 5: 7 "Whoever reads this **w** and tells me
1Co 14:37 what I am **w** to you is the Lord's
1Jn 2: 7 I am not **w** you a new command
2Jn 1: 5 I am not **w** you a new command
Rev 5: 1 the throne a scroll with **w** on both

## WRITTEN [WRITE]
Ex 32:32 me out of the book you have **w**."
Dt 28:58 which are **w** in this book, and do not
Jos 1: 8 be careful to do everything **w** in it.
23: 6 obey all that is **w** in the Book
1Ki 2: 3 as **w** in the Law of Moses.
2Ki 23:21 God, as it is **w** in this Book
Ne 8:14 They found **w** in the Law,
Ps 40: 7 it is **w** about me in the scroll.
Pr 22:20 Have I not **w** thirty sayings for you,
Da 12: 1 everyone whose name is found **w**
Mal 3:16 remembrance was **w** in his presence
Mt 26:24 of Man will go just as it is **w**
27:37 they placed the **w** charge against
Lk 10:20 that your names are **w** in heaven."
24:44 must be fulfilled that is **w** about me
Jn 20:31 these are **w** that you may believe
21:25 If every one of them were **w** down,
Ro 2:15 of the law are **w** on their hearts,
15: 4 that was **w** in the past was **w**
1Co 4: 6 "Do not go beyond what is **w**."
10:11 were **w** down as warnings for us,
2Co 3: 3 **w** not with ink but with the Spirit
Heb 10: 7 it is **w** about me in the scroll—
12:23 whose names are **w** in heaven.
Rev 2:17 stone with a new name **w** on it,
13: 8 all whose names have not been **w**
14: 1 and his Father's name **w** on their
17: 5 This title was **w** on her forehead:
19:12 He has a name **w** on him that no one
20:15 All whose names were not found **w**
21:12 the gates were **w** the names
21:27 only those whose names are **w**

## IT IS ... WRITTEN Jos 8:34; 10:13; 2Sa 1:18;
2Ki 23:21; 2Ch 35:12; Ne 8:15; 10:34, 36; Ps
40:7; Da 9:13; Mt 4:4, 6, 7, 10; 11:10; 21:13;
26:24, 31; Mk 1:2; 7:6; 9:13; 14:21, 27; Lk 2:23;
3:4; 4:4, 8, 10, 17; 7:27; 19:46; 22:37; Jn 2:17;
6:31, 45; 8:17; 12:14; Ac 1:20; 13:33; 15:15;
23:5; Ro 1:17; 2:24; 3:4, 10; 4:17; 8:36; 9:13, 33;
10:15; 11:8, 26; 12:19; 14:11; 15:3, 9, 21; 1Co
1:19, 31; 2:9; 3:19; 9:9; 10:7; 14:21; 15:45; 2Co
4:13; 8:15; 9:9; Gal 3:10, 13; 4:22, 27; Heb 10:7;
1Pe 1:16

## WRITTEN IN THE ... BOOK Jos 8:31; 34;
10:13; 23:6; 2Sa 1:18; 1Ki 11:41; 14:19, 29;
15:7, 23, 31; 16:5, 14, 20, 27; 22:39, 45; 2Ki
1:18; 8:23; 10:34; 12:19; 13:8, 12; 14:6, 15, 18,
28; 15:6, 11, 15, 21, 26, 31, 36; 16:19; 20:20;
21:17, 25; 22:16; 23:24, 28; 24:5; 2Ch 16:11;
25:26; 27:7; 28:26; 34:24; 35:12, 27; 36:8; Ezr

6:18; Est 10:2; Da 10:21; 12:1; Lk 3:4; Ac 1:20;
7:42; Gal 3:10; Rev 13:8; 17:8; 20:15; 21:27

## WRONG [WRONGDOER,
## WRONGDOERS, WRONGDOING,
## WRONGED, WRONGS]
Ex 23: 2 not follow the crowd in doing **w**.
Nu 5: 7 restitution for the **w** they have done,
Dt 32: 4 A faithful God who does no **w**,
1Sa 26:21 and have been terribly **w**."
1Ki 8:47 we have done **w**, we have acted
Job 34:12 is unthinkable that God would do **w**,
Ps 5: 5 You hate all who do **w**;
119:128 precepts right, I hate every **w** path.
Isa 7:15 he knows enough to reject the **w**
Da 9: 5 we have sinned and done **w**.
Zep 3: 5 her is righteous; he does no **w**.
3:13 They will do no **w**; they will tell no
Lk 23:41 But this man has done nothing **w**."
Jn 16: 8 world to be in the **w** about sin
Ac 23: 9 "We find nothing **w** with this
Ro 13: 4 But if you do **w**, be afraid, for rulers
Col 3:25 Those who do **w** will be repaid
1Th 5:15 sure that nobody pays back **w** for **w**,
Rev 22:11 those who do **w** continue to do **w**;

## WRONGDOER* [WRONG]
Nu 5: 8 which atonement is made for the **w**.
Ro 13: 4 wrath to bring punishment on the **w**.

## WRONGDOERS [WRONG]
1Co 6: 9 **w** will not inherit the kingdom of God?

## WRONGDOING [WRONG]
Job 1:22 did not sin by charging God with **w**.
Hab 1:13 you cannot tolerate **w**.
1Jn 5:17 All **w** is sin, and there is sin

## WRONGED [WRONG]
Nu 5: 7 give it all to the person they have **w**.
Pr 18:19 A brother **w** is more unyielding
1Co 6: 7 Why not rather be **w**?

## WRONGS [WRONG]
Ge 50:15 pays us back for all the **w** we did
Pr 10:12 but love covers over all **w**.
1Co 13: 5 angered, it keeps no record of **w**.

## WROTE [WRITE]
Ex 24: 4 **w** down everything the LORD had
34:28 he **w** on the tablets the words
Dt 10: 4 The LORD **w** on these tablets what
2Ch 32:17 also **w** letters ridiculing the LORD,
Da 5: 5 The king watched the hand as it **w**.
Jn 1:45 about whom the prophets also **w**—
5:46 believe me, for he **w** about me.
8: 8 *he stooped down and **w** on the ground.*
Ac 1: 1 I **w** about all that Jesus began to do

# X

## XERXES*

1. The father of Darius the Mede (Da 9:1).
2. King of Persia (Ezr 4:6; Est 1–3; 6–10); husband of Esther (Est 2:16; 7:5; 8:1, 7). Deposed Vashti; replaced her with Esther (Est 1–2). Sealed Haman's edict to annihilate the Jews (Est 3). Received Esther without having called her (Est 5:1–8). Honored Mordecai (Est 6). Hanged Haman (Est 7). Issued edict allowing Jews to defend themselves (Est 8). Exalted Mordecai (Est 8:1–2, 15; 9:4; 10:1–3).

# Y

## YAHWEH  See †LORD

## YARN

Ex 25: 4 purple and scarlet **y** and fine linen;
2Ch 2: 7 crimson and blue **y**, and experienced

## YEAR [YEAR'S, YEARS]

Ge 17:21 bear to you by this time next **y**."
Ex 23:14 "Three times a **y** you are
    34:23 Three times a **y** all your men are
Lev 16:34 to be made once a **y** for all the sins
    25: 4 in the seventh **y** the land is to have
    25:11 The fiftieth **y** shall be a jubilee
Nu 14:34 one **y** for each of the forty days you
Dt 1: 3 In the fortieth **y**, on the first day
1Sa 1: 3 **Y** after **y** this man went up from his
    7:16 From **y** to **y** he went on a circuit
1Ki 10:25 **Y** after **y**, everyone who came
2Ki 4:16 "About this time next **y**,"
Ne 10:31 Every seventh **y** we will forgo
Isa 6: 1 In the **y** that King Uzziah died,
    34: 8 day of vengeance, a **y** of retribution,
    61: 2 to proclaim the **y** of the LORD's
    63: 4 the **y** for me to redeem had come.
Zec 14:16 go up **y** after **y** to worship the King,
Lk 2:41 Every **y** Jesus' parents went
    13: 8 'leave it alone for one more **y**,
Jn 11:49 who was high priest that **y**,
    18:13 of Caiaphas, the high priest that **y**.
Heb 9: 7 and that only once a **y**, and never
    10: 1 repeated endlessly **y** after **y**,

## YEAR'S [YEAR]

Mk 6:37 "That would take almost a **y** wages!
Jn 6: 7 almost a **y** wages to buy enough bread

## YEARNS*

Job 19:27 How my heart **y** within me!
Ps 84: 2 My soul **y**, even faints,
Isa 26: 9 My soul **y** for you in the night;
Jer 31:20 Therefore my heart **y** for him;

## YEARS [YEAR]

Ge 1:14 to mark seasons and days and **y**,
    25: 8 old age, an old man and full of **y**;
    35:29 to his people, old and full of **y**.
    41:26 The seven good cows are seven **y**,
    41:30 seven **y** of famine will follow them.
    47: 9 My **y** have been few and difficult,
Ex 12:40 people lived in Egypt was 430 **y**.
    16:35 The Israelites ate manna forty **y**,
Lev 25: 8 " 'Count off seven sabbath **y**—
Nu 1: 3 men in Israel who are twenty **y** old
    14:34 For forty **y**—one year for each
Dt 2: 7 These forty **y** the LORD your God
    8: 4 did not swell during these forty **y**.
2Sa 21: 1 was a famine for three successive **y**;
2Ch 36:21 until the seventy **y** were completed
Ezr 5:11 temple that was built many **y** ago,
Ne 9:21 For forty **y** you sustained them
Job 36:26 number of his **y** is past finding out.
Ps 90: 4 A thousand **y** in your sight are like
    90:10 Our days may come to seventy **y**,
    95:10 For forty **y** I was angry
Pr 3: 2 they will prolong your life many **y**
    9:11 and **y** will be added to your life.
    10:27 but the **y** of the wicked are cut short.
Ecc 6: 6 if he lives a thousand **y** twice over
Jer 25:12 when the seventy **y** are fulfilled,
Da 9: 2 of Jerusalem would last seventy **y**.
Joel 2:25 for the **y** the locusts have eaten—
Mt 2:16 its vicinity who were two **y** old
    9:20 to bleeding for twelve **y** came
Lk 3:23 Jesus himself was about thirty **y** old
    13:16 has kept bound for eighteen long **y**,
Jn 2:20 "It has taken forty-six **y** to build
2Pe 3: 8 the Lord a day is like a thousand **y**,
    3: 8 and a thousand **y** are like a day.
Rev 20: 2 and bound him for a thousand **y**.

## YEAST

Ex 12:15 you are to eat bread made without **y**.
    12:20 Eat nothing made with **y**.
Lev 2:11 for you are not to burn any **y**
Mt 16: 6 on your guard against the **y**
1Co 5: 6 a little **y** leavens the whole batch
Gal 5: 9 "A little **y** works through the whole

## YES

Mt 5:37 All you need to say is simply '**Y**'
2Co 1:17 in the same breath I say both "**Y**,
    1:20 has made, they are "**Y**" in Christ.
Jas 5:12 All you need to say is a simple "**Y**"

## YESTERDAY

Heb 13: 8 Jesus Christ is the same **y** and today

## YET

Job 13:15 he slay me, **y** will I hope in him;
    19:26 **y** in my flesh I will see God;
Ps 42: 5 for I will **y** praise him, my Savior
Pr 30:24 small, **y** they are extremely wise:
    30:25 **y** they store up their food
Ecc 1: 7 into the sea, **y** the sea is never full.
Am 4: 6 **y** you have not returned to me,"
Hab 3:16 **Y** I will wait patiently for the day
Mal 1: 2 "**Y** I have loved Jacob,

Mt 6:26 y your heavenly Father feeds them.
Mk 8:36 whole world, y forfeit your soul?
Jn 2: 4 "My hour has not y come."
6:70 Y one of you is a devil!"
7: 6 told them, "My time is not y here;
7: 8 my time has not y fully come."
7:39 since Jesus had not y been glorified.
8:20 because his hour had not y come.
20:29 have not seen and y have believed."
Ro 8:25 we hope for what we do not y have,
Heb 12: 4 you have not y resisted to the point
Rev 9:12 two other woes are y to come.
17:10 one is, the other has not y come;

## YIELD [YIELDED, YIELDING]
Ge 4:12 it will no longer y its crops for you.
Lev 25:19 Then the land will y its fruit,
Pr 8:19 what I y surpasses choice silver.
Isa 42: 8 I will not y my glory to another

## YIELDED* [YIELD]
Ps 107:37 vineyards that y a fruitful harvest;
Isa 5: 2 good grapes, but it y only bad fruit.
Lk 8: 8 It came up and y a crop, a hundred

## YIELDING [YIELD]
Rev 22: 2 of fruit, y its fruit every month.

## YOKE [YOKED]
Ex 6: 6 from under the y of the Egyptians.
Dt 28:48 He will put an iron y on your neck
1Ki 12: 4 "Your father put a heavy y on us,
Mt 11:29 Take my y upon you and learn
11:30 For my y is easy and my burden is
Gal 5: 1 be burdened again by a y of slavery.

## YOKED [YOKE]
Dt 22:10 with an ox and a donkey y together.
Ps 106:28 They y themselves to the Baal
2Co 6:14 Do not be y together

## YOUNG [YOUNGER, YOUNGEST,
YOUTH, YOUTHS]
Ex 23:19 "Do not cook a y goat in its
Lev 1:14 are to offer a dove or a y pigeon.
5: 7 or two y pigeons to the LORD as
14:22 and two doves or two y pigeons,
Nu 30: 3 "When a y woman still living in her
Dt 22: 6 do not take the mother with the y.
32:25 The y men and y women will perish,
Ru 2: 5 does that y woman belong to?"
1Sa 2:17 This sin of the y men was very great
2Ch 10:14 he followed the advice of the y men
36:17 spared neither y man nor y woman,
Ps 37:25 I was y and now I am old, yet I have
78:63 Fire consumed their y men,
119: 9 can those who are y keep their way
Pr 7: 7 I noticed among the y men, a youth
20:29 The glory of y men is their strength,
Isa 11: 8 y children will put their hands
40:11 he gently leads those that have y.
Jer 1: 6 I am too y."
La 1:18 My y men and y women have gone
Da 1: 4 y men without any physical defect,
1:17 To these four y men God gave

Joel 2:28 dreams, your y men will see visions.
Mk 14:51 A y man, wearing nothing
16: 5 they saw a y man dressed in a white
Lk 2:24 "a pair of doves or two y pigeons."
Ac 2:17 your y men will see visions,
7:58 at the feet of a y man named Saul.
20: 9 in a window was a y man named
1Ti 4:12 down on you because you are y,
Tit 2: 6 encourage the y men to be
1Jn 2:13 I am writing to you, y people,

## YOUNGER [YOUNG]
Ge 19:35 and the y daughter went in and slept
25:23 and the older will serve the y."
29:27 we will give you the y one also,
Ro 9:12 told, "The older will serve the y."
1Ti 5: 1 Treat y men as brothers,
5:14 So I counsel y widows to marry,
Tit 2: 4 they can urge the y women to love
1Pe 5: 5 you who are y, submit yourselves

## YOUNGEST [YOUNG]
Ge 9:24 found out what his y son had done
42:20 you must bring your y brother
Jos 6:26 at the cost of his y he will set up its
1Sa 17:14 David was the y. The three oldest
1Ki 16:34 gates at the cost of his y son Segub,
Lk 22:26 among you should be like the y,

## YOUTH [YOUNG]
Nu 11:28 who had been Moses' aide since y,
1Sa 17:33 he has been a warrior from his y."
Ps 71: 5 LORD, my confidence since my y.
103: 5 your y is renewed like the eagle's.
144:12 in their y will be like well-nurtured
Pr 2:17 who has left the partner of her y
5:18 you rejoice in the wife of your y.
7: 7 young men, a y who had no sense.
Ecc 4:13 Better a poor but wise y than an old
11:10 for y and vigor are meaningless.
12: 1 your Creator in the days of your y,
Eze 16:60 with you in the days of your y, and I
Mal 2:14 between you and the wife of your y.
2Ti 2:22 Flee the evil desires of y and pursue

## YOUTHS [YOUNG]
Isa 40:30 Even y grow tired and weary,
65:20 at a hundred will be thought mere y;

---

# Z

---

## ZACCHAEUS
Lk 19: 2 A man was there by the name of Z;

## ZADOK [ZADOKITES]
2Sa 15:27 The king also said to Z the priest,
1Ki 1:26 and Z the priest, and Benaiah son
Ne 13:13 Shelemiah the priest, Z the scribe,

## ZADOKITES* [ZADOK]
Eze 48:11 the Z, who were faithful in serving

## ZALMON

Jdg  9:48  and all his men went up Mount Z.
Ps  68:14  it was like snow fallen on Mount Z.

## ZALMUNNA

Jdg  8: 5  and I am still pursuing Zebah and Z,
Ps  83:11  all their princes like Zebah and Z,

## ZAPHON

Jos  13:27  Z with the rest of the realm of Sihon
Ps  48: 2  like the heights of Z is Mount Zion,

## ZAREPHATH

1Ki  17: 9  "Go at once to Z in the region
Lk   4:26  but to a widow in Z in the region

## ZEAL  [ZEALOUS, ZEALOUSLY]

Nu  25:11  I did not put an end to them in my z.
Dt  29:20  wrath and z will burn against them.
2Ki 10:16  me and see my z for the LORD."
    19:31  "The z of the LORD Almighty
Ps  69: 9  for z for your house consumes me,
   119:139 My z wears me out, for my enemies
Isa 37:32  The z of the LORD Almighty will
    59:17  wrapped himself in z as in a cloak.
Eze  5:13  I the LORD have spoken in my z.
Jn   2:17  "Z for your house will consume
Ro  10: 2  their z is not based on knowledge.
    12:11  Never be lacking in z, but keep your

## ZEALOUS  [ZEAL]

Nu  25:13  because he was z for the honor
1Ki 19:10  "I have been very z for the LORD
    19:14  "I have been very z for the LORD
Pr  23:17  but always be z for the fear
Eze 39:25  and I will be z for my holy name.
Ac  21:20  and all of them are z for the law.
Ro  10: 2  about them that they are z for God,
Gal  1:14  was extremely z for the traditions
     4:17  Those people are z to win you over,
     4:18  It is fine to be z,

## ZEALOUSLY*  [ZEAL]

Ne   3:20  of Zabbai z repaired another section,

## ZEBAH

Jdg  8: 5  I am still pursuing Z and Zalmunna,
Ps  83:11  Zeeb, all their princes like Z

## ZEBEDEE  [ZEBEDEE'S]

Mt   4:21  James son of Z and his brother John.
    26:37  the two sons of Z along with him,
Mk   1:20  they left their father Z in the boat
    10:35  John, the sons of Z, came to him.
Lk   5:10  the sons of Z, Simon's partners.

## ZEBEDEE'S*  [ZEBEDEE]

Mt  20:20  the mother of Z sons came to Jesus
    27:56  Joseph, and the mother of Z sons.

## ZEBOYIM

Dt  29:23  Sodom and Gomorrah, Admah and Z,
Hos 11: 8  can I make you like Z?

## ZEBUL

Jdg  9:30  When Z the governor of the city

## ZEBULUN

Son of Jacob by Leah (Ge 30:20; 35:23; 1Ch 2:1).
Tribe of blessed (Ge 49:13; Dt 33:18–19), numbered
(Nu 1:31; 26:27), allotted land (Jos 19:10–16; Eze
48:26), failed to fully possess (Jdg 1:30), supported
Deborah (Jdg 4:6–10; 5:14, 18), David (1Ch 12:33),
12,000 from (Rev 7:8).

## ZECHARIAH

1. Son of Jeroboam II; king of Israel (2Ki
15:8–12).
2. Post-exilic prophet who encouraged rebuilding
of temple (Ezr 5:1; 6:14; Zec 1:1).

## ZEDEKIAH  [MATTANIAH]

1. False prophet (1Ki 22:11–24; 2Ch 18:10–23).
2. Mattaniah, son of Josiah (1Ch 3:15), made king
of Judah by Nebuchadnezzar (2Ki 24:17—25:7; 2Ch
36:10–14; Jer 37–39; 52:1–11).

## ZEEB

Jdg  7:25  the Midianite leaders, Oreb and Z.
Ps  83:11  Make their nobles like Oreb and Z,

## ZELOPHEHAD  [ZELOPHEHAD'S]

Nu  26:33  (Z son of Hepher had no sons;
Jos 17: 3  Now Z son of Hepher, the son

## ZELOPHEHAD'S  [ZELOPHEHAD]

Nu  36: 6  LORD commands for Z daughters:

## ZEPHANIAH

Prophet; descendant of Hezekiah (Zep 1:1).

## ZERUBBABEL

Descendant of David (1Ch 3:19; Mt 1:3). Led return from exile (Ezr 2:2; Ne 7:7). Governor of Israel;
helped rebuild altar and temple (Ezr 3; Hag 1–2;
Zec 4).

## ZERUIAH  [ZERUIAH'S]

2Sa  2:18  The three sons of Z were there:

## ZERUIAH'S*  [ZERUIAH]

1Ch  2:16  Z three sons were Abishai,

## ZEUS

Ac  14:12  Barnabas they called Z, and Paul

## ZIBA

2Sa  9: 2  of Saul's household named Z.
    16: 1  summit, there was Z, the steward
    19:26  But Z my servant betrayed me.

## ZIKLAG

1Sa 27: 6  So on that day Achish gave him Z,
    30: 1  They had attacked Z and burned it,
    30:26  When David reached Z, he sent

## ZILPAH
Servant of Leah, mother of Jacob's sons Gad and Asher (Ge 30:9–12; 35:26, 46:16–18).

## ZIMRI
King of Israel (1Ki 16:9–20).

## ZIN
Nu  13:21  the Desert of **Z** as far as Rehob,

## ZION
2Sa    5: 7  David captured the fortress of **Z**—
2Ki  19:31  out of Mount **Z** a band of survivors.
Ps      2: 6  "I have installed my king on **Z**,
        9:11  of the LORD, enthroned in **Z**;
       14: 7  for Israel would come out of **Z**!
       48: 2  the heights of Zaphon is Mount **Z**,
       50: 2  From **Z**, perfect in beauty,
       65: 1  Praise awaits you, our God, in **Z**;
       74: 2  Mount **Z**, where you dwelt.
     78:68  of Judah, Mount **Z**, which he loved.
       87: 2  **Z** more than all the other dwellings
       87: 6  "This one was born in **Z**."
     102:13  arise and have compassion on **Z**,
     137: 3  "Sing us one of the songs of **Z**!"
SS      3:11  out, and look, you daughters of **Z**.
Isa      1:27  **Z** will be delivered with justice,
        2: 3  The law will go out from **Z**,
     14:32  "The LORD has established **Z**,
     28:16  I lay a stone in **Z**, a tested stone,
       40: 9  You who bring good news to **Z**,
       51: 3  The LORD will surely comfort **Z**
       51:11  They will enter **Z** with singing;
       52: 1  awake, **Z**, clothe yourself
       52: 8  When the LORD returns to **Z**,
Jer    50: 5  They will ask the way to **Z** and turn
La      2:13  comfort you, Virgin Daughter **Z**?
Joel    2: 1  Blow the trumpet in **Z**;
        3:21  The LORD dwells in **Z**!
Am      1: 2  "The LORD roars from **Z**
        6: 1  to you who are complacent in **Z**,
Mic    3:12  of you, **Z** will be plowed like a field,
        4: 2  The law will go out from **Z**,
Zec     1:17  the LORD will again comfort **Z**
        9: 9  Rejoice greatly, Daughter **Z**!
Mt     21: 5  "Say to Daughter **Z**, 'See, your king
Ro      9:33  I lay in **Z** a stone that causes people
     11:26  "The deliverer will come from **Z**;
Heb  12:22  But you have come to Mount **Z**,
1Pe     2: 6  I lay a stone in **Z**, a chosen
Rev   14: 1  standing on Mount **Z**, and with him

## DAUGHTER ZION  See DAUGHTER

## MOUNT ZION  See MOUNT

## ZIPH  [ZIPHITES]
1Sa  23:14  and in the hills of the Desert of **Z**.

## ZIPHITES*  [ZIPH]
1Sa  23:19  The **Z** went up to Saul at Gibeah
       26: 1  The **Z** went to Saul at Gibeah
Ps     54: T  *When the **Z** had gone to Saul and said,*

## ZIPPOR
Nu  22: 4  So Balak son of **Z**, who was king

## ZIPPORAH
Daughter of Reuel; wife of Moses (Ex 2:21–22; 4:20–26; 18:1–6).

## ZITHER
Da    3: 7  the sound of the horn, flute, **z**, lyre,

## ZIV
1Ki  6: 1  Israel, in the month of **Z**, the second

## ZOAN
Ps  78:43  his wonders in the region of **Z**.

## ZOAR
Ge  19:22  (That is why the town was called **Z**.)
     19:30  his two daughters left **Z** and settled

## ZOBAH
1Sa  14:47  the kings of **Z**, and the Philistines.
1Ch  18: 3  defeated Hadadezer king of **Z**,

## ZOPHAR*
One of Job's friends (Job 2:11; 11; 20; 42:9).

## ZORAH
Jdg  13: 2  A certain man of **Z**, named Manoah,

---

# NUMERALS

---

## 40*  [FORTY]
Eze  4: 6  I have assigned you **40** days,

## 42
Rev  11: 2  trample on the holy city for **42** months.

## 153*
Jn  21:11  It was full of large fish, **153**,

## 666*
1Ki  10:14  received yearly was **666** talents,
2Ch   9:13  received yearly was **666** talents,
Ezr    2:13  of Adonikam **666**
Rev  13:18  number of a man. That number is **666**.

## 1,260*
Rev  11: 3  they will prophesy for **1,260** days,
       12: 6  she might be taken care of for **1,260**

## 1,290*
Da  12:11  set up, there will be **1,290** days.

## 1,335*
Da  12:12  reaches the end of the **1,335** days.

## 12,000*
Rev  7: 5  From the tribe of Judah **12,000**
      7: 5  from the tribe of Reuben **12,000**,

Rev  7: 5  from the tribe of Gad **12,000,**
    7: 6  the tribe of Asher **12,000,**
    7: 6  from the tribe of Naphtali **12,000,**
    7: 6  from the tribe of Manasseh **12,000,**
    7: 7  from the tribe of Simeon **12,000,**
    7: 7  from the tribe of Levi **12,000,**
    7: 7  from the tribe of Issachar **12,000,**
    7: 8  from the tribe of Zebulun **12,000,**
    7: 8  from the tribe of Joseph **12,000,**
    7: 8  from the tribe of Benjamin **12,000,**
  21:16  found it to be **12,000** stadia in length,

## 144,000*

Rev  7: 4  of those who were sealed: **144,000**
  14: 1  with him **144,000** who had his name
  14: 3  learn the song except the **144,000**

## 601,730*

Nu   26:51  of the men of Israel was **601,730.**

## 603,550*

Ex   38:26  a total of **603,550** men.
Nu    1:46  The total number was **603,550.**
   2:32  by their divisions, number **603,550.**

We want to hear from you. Please send your comments about this book to us in care of zreview@zondervan.com. Thank you.

**ZONDERVAN.com/**
**AUTHORTRACKER**
*follow your favorite authors*